This Book is a Gift

in Memory of

Rev. John Keane

Kenrick-Glennon Library

The
New Dictionary
of
Sacramental Worship

The
New Dictionary
of
Sacramental Worship

Editor: Peter E. Fink, S.J.

A Michael Glazier Book
THE LITURGICAL PRESS
Collegeville, Minnesota

A Michael Glazier Book
published by
THE LITURGICAL PRESS

Special Thanks to Sudabeh Balakhani for her work on the design and production of this volume.

Cover design by Plucid Stuckenschneider, O.S.B. Typography by Brenda Belizzone, Mary Brown, and Phyllis Boyd LeVane

1   2   3   4   5   6   7   8   9

Library of Congress Cataloging-in-Publication Data

The New dictionary of sacramental worship / editor, Peter E. Fink.
    p.   cm.
   "A Michael Glazier book."
   Includes bibliographical references and index.
   ISBN 0-8146-5788-5
   1. Catholic Church—Liturgy—Dictionaries. 2. Liturgics-
-Dictionaries.   I. Fink, Peter E.
BV173.N485 1990
264'.02'003—dc20
                               90-33911
                                 CIP

Editorial Preface

One of the major achievements of the Second Vatican Council was to set the liturgy of the church firmly at the center of Christian life and mission. "The liturgy is the summit toward which the activity of the Church is directed; it is also the fount from which all her power flows" (S.C., 10). The liturgical reform which the council set in motion, as well as the refreshingly new way in which it spoke of the liturgy in its *Constitution on the Sacred Liturgy*, both reflect and are guided by this seminal vision of the church at prayer. The aim of the reform, as indeed the aim of the council as a whole, was clearly stated: "to impart an ever-increasing vigor to the Christian life of the faithful; to adapt more closely to the needs of our age those institutions which are subject to change; to foster whatever can promote union among all who believe in Christ; to strengthen whatever can help to call all mankind into the Church's fold" (S.C., 1). The council called for both the reform and the promotion of the liturgy to help achieve these goals.

A little more than twenty-five years after the council, the effects of this promotion and reform already far exceed the hopes and dreams which led up to, and were captured in, the *Constitution on the Sacred Liturgy*. And these effects reach far beyond the Latin rite of the Roman Catholic church which was the constitution's primary concern. The Anglican, Lutheran and Reformed churches of the West, and many churches of the East as well, have been inspired to their own liturgical reform and renewal by the council's vision and call. Where once the church was divided over issues of sacrament and worship, a new convergence, indeed a new *koinonia*, of worship is gradually and graciously coming about.

This dictionary of sacramental worship arises both to celebrate and to serve the ongoing task of liturgical reform and renewal. Represented in its pages is the vision which was framed by Vatican II now enfleshed in its many faces at the hands of dedicated men and women who have given their professional lives to the service of the worshipping church. While most of the contributors come from the Latin rite of the Roman Catholic church, the voices of almost all the sacramental churches are present here speaking from the ecumenical church to the ecumenical church.

The dictionary was guided in its aim and its purpose by *The New Dictionary of Theology* (eds. Komonchak, Collins, Lane [Glazier, 1987]). This present work likewise emerges from the conviction that theology must be carried out locally. Contributors have therefore been invited from all over the English-speaking world, and it is to the concerns of the English-speaking churches that these essays are primarily addressed. In addition, because it emerges in the wake of Vatican II and seeks to assess the impact of the *Constitution on the Sacred Liturgy*, its primary focus is on the revised Roman

Catholic liturgical texts and questions which implementation of those texts involves. Even within this strong Roman Catholic perspective, however, the range of concerns can be no less than the range of influence which the *Constitution on the Sacred Liturgy* enjoys. Thus the churches of the East and the various churches of the West rightly belong in its pages.

The dictionary is structured as a theological and pastoral resource, covering a wide range of activities that are constitutive of a sacramental church. The entries include the strictly theological, the practical liturgical, the pastoral and the social. There are thus many "genres" of writing here. This reflects an additional conviction, that the worship of God in the church embraces these many dimensions, and that these ought to be housed, as it were, under the same roof.

Authors were invited to address an issue from their own sense of what the issue is. Though in many cases some editorial guidance was given, the bottom line request was simply this: "if you were to go to a theological and pastoral resource to get some input on the issue, what would you want to find there?" The tone of a particular piece, whether doctrinal, catechetical, liturgical or pastoral, as well as its ecumenical scope, is determined both by the topic and by the sense of the author. The dictionary thus represents as well the collective vision of theologians, liturgists and pastors alive and serving well in the church of the late-20th century.

In order to facilitate use of this volume, three editorial devices are offered. At the end of most entries there are the usual cross references, offered to guide the reader to entries obviously linked to the one at hand. In addition there is a simple alphabetical index that lists all the entries, with the corresponding page references, as they appear in the volume. Finally, there is a topical index which arranges all the substantial entries under seven (a fitting number for a sacramental dictionary) major headings: the worshipping church; the heritage of the church; the sacramental life of the church; the praying church; the church and the arts; the reflecting church; and, the pastoral mission of the church. It is hoped that one or all of these devices will make the dictionary more useful to its readers, be they pastors, theological and divinity students, lay men and women engaged in ministry in the church.

Credit for the idea of this dictionary, as well as much gratitude and a special dedication, is given to Michael Glazier, to whom the world of religious scholarship is deeply indebted. His imagination, his boldness and above all his kindness have become in the eyes of many his second trademark. In addition, the gratitude of the editor must also be given to Eileen Daney Carzo, Elizabeth McLaughlin, Joseph Quinn and Diane Barrett. Their varied labors are too numerous to list, yet much too valued to let pass unsung.

Peter E. Fink, S.J.
Editor

Contents

10

A

ABSOLUTION

Absolution is the ritual action which completes the sacrament of penance. Through the words and gestures of the priest who has the faculty to absolve sins (and censures), "God grants pardon to sinners who in sacramental confession manifest their change of heart" (Rite of Penance, 6d). In traditional sacramental terminology, absolution is the "form" of the sacrament of penance.

It consists of three elements on the part of the priest: imposition of hands over the penitent (or at least the extension of the right hand) in an epicletic gesture invoking the Holy Spirit; proclamation of the formulary of absolution; and tracing the sign of the cross over the penitent. The essential words of the formulary are: "I absolve you from your sins in the name of the Father and of the Son and of the Holy Spirit."

The complete formulary which must be used in its entirety, except in the case of imminent danger of death, contains both the deprecatory and declarative prayer forms. The deprecatory form is much older in the tradition of the Church. It prays to God for forgiveness very much like the response to the Confiteor and the penitential rite of the Mass: "May almighty God have mercy on us. . . ." The declarative form dates only from the 13th century and states authoritatively: "I absolve you. . . ." Although the ritual of penance emphasizes the pastoral, paternal, Good Shepherd image of the minister, it does not deny the need for prudence, wisdom and discernment of spirits guided by the teaching authority of the church and fervent prayer. To balance between judge and healer, between justice and mercy, is the challenge of the minister (C.I.C., 978). The formulary reflects this balance: "God, the Father of mercies, through the death and resurrection of his Son has reconciled the world to himself and sent the Holy Spirit among us for the forgiveness of sins; through the ministry of the Church may God give you pardon and peace and I absolve you from your sins in the name of the Father and of the Son and of the Holy Spirit."

Though somewhat long, the formulary expresses the ecclesial sense of forgiveness: coming from the mercy of the Father; connected with the paschal mystery of Christ; stressing the role of the Holy Spirit; showing the ecclesial aspect of forgiveness since reconciliation with God is given through the ministry of the church (Rite of Penance, 19).

Absolution takes place in different ways in the different celebrations of reconciliation. In his post-synodal Apostolic Exhortation "On Reconciliation and Penance" Pope John Paul II states: "The first form—*reconciliation of individual penitents*—is the only normal and ordinary way of celebrating the sacrament, and it cannot and must not be allowed to fall into disuse or be neglected."

11

The second form—*reconciliation of a number of penitents with individual confession and absolution*—even though in the preparatory acts it helps to give greater emphasis to the community aspects of the sacrament, is the same as the first form in the culminating sacramental act, namely individual confession and individual absolution of sins. It can thus be regarded as equal to the first form as regards the normality of the rite. The third form however—*reconciliation of a number of penitents with general absolution*—is exceptional in character. It is therefore not left to free choice but is regulated by a special discipline (32).

A priest who has the faculty may also absolve from canonical censures (excommunication, interdict, and suspension of an ordained minister). When this takes place in connection with the absolution of sin, no change is to be made in the formulary but the confessor should intend to absolve the properly disposed penitent (Order of Penance, Appendix I, 1). Absolution of a common censure outside sacramental penance has the following formulary: "By the power granted to me, I absolve you from the bond of excommunication (or suspension or interdict). In the name of the Father, and of the Son, and of the Holy Spirit. Amen."

Ralph Keifer, Frederick R. McManus, *The Rite of Penance: Commentaries-Understanding the Document* (Washington, D.C.: The Liturgical Conference 1975). Frederick R. McManus, *The Code of Canon Law: A Text and Commentary*, "The Sacrament of Penance (CC 959-997)," (New York: Paulist Press, 1983).

JOSEPH L. CUNNINGHAM

ABSOLUTION, GENERAL

Absolution, or the effective proclamation of the forgiveness of sin, is considered "general" when it is pronounced over a number of penitents simultaneously. It may follow a general confession of sins, as in the Rite for Reconciliation of Several Penitents with General Confession and Absolution (Sacramental Form III of the revised Rite of Penance of the Roman Ritual, 1973) where the request for absolution is made by some kind of sign, such as kneeling, bowing the head or standing. Or it may follow individual confessions made separately to confessors and be pronounced as a communal act of forgiveness in response to confessions made privately (though no approved Roman Catholic ritual offers this possibility). It may be employed positively, to celebrate the communal nature of the sacrament, or negatively, due to the scarcity of priest-confessors or in an emergency situation. It's primary characteristic is its address to several persons together.

The revised Rite of Penance offers this possible form of the sacrament together with two other forms: the Rite of Reconciliation of Individual Penitents (Form I) and the Rite for Reconciliation of Several Penitents with Individual Confession and Absolution (Form II). It is presented in the Rite of Penance as one of three sacramental options, and appears to be, along with the other two forms, an ordinary mode of celebrating the sacrament.

In fact, however, the current discipline of the Roman Catholic church severely restricts the use of general absolution, and clearly promotes the private mode of celebration, with individual confession and absolution (as in Forms I and II), as "the only ordinary way by which the faithful person who is aware of serious sin is reconciled with God and with the Church..." (C.I.C., 960). Three canons devoted to general absolution (961-963) delineate the restrictions which apply to it.

Can. 961 establishes the conditions under which general absolution may be imparted: (a) in danger of death where time does not allow for individual confession; (b) serious necessity, where the number of penitents is too large for the available priests to provide individual confession *and* where such inability would force people to be deprived of the eucharist for a long time. Numbers alone do not warrant the use of general absolution. It is up to the diocesan bishop to determine whether these conditions apply.

Can. 962 requires of the penitent both a proper disposition to celebrate the sacrament and the intent "to confess individually the serious sins which at present cannot be so confessed." An act of contrition is to precede general absolution, if there is time, even in emergency circumstances.

Finally, can. 963 advises individual confession after general absolution (a) as soon as there is opportunity to do so and (b) before receiving general absolution again, provided no just cause dictates otherwise.

On the restrictions imposed on this form of absolution, F. McManus notes Rome's constant concern lest private, auricular confession, already fallen into disuse among Catholics, be even further diminished in the life of the church (see *The Code of Canon Law: a Text and Commentary*, p. 675). If this assessment is correct, one can understand why, though nonetheless lament that, a factor extrinsic to the liturgy itself is here brought in to determine a liturgical decision.

On the other hand, it must be acknowledged that a difficulty presents itself within the Rite of Penance itself, and especially in the introduction that explains the sacramental rite. There are two different theological visions within this introduction which lead to two different assessments of this form of absolution and sacramental celebration. The one announces the celebration of this sacrament as "an act in which the Church proclaims its faith, gives thanks to God for the freedom with which Christ has made us free, and offers its life as a spiritual sacrifice in praise of God's glory, as it hastens to meet the Lord Jesus"(7b). This view focuses on the sacrament as a liturgical act of the church in assembly. The other sees the sacrament in more remedial terms: "God grants pardon to the sinner who in sacramental confession manifests his change of heart to the Church's minister"(6d). This view focuses on the individual penitent, his or her personal conversion and repentance, and the presentation of one's sins to the ordained minister of the church. The two are in fact complementary; they yield, however, a conflict on the value of general absolution.

Those who stress the sacrament as a liturgical act will cite the *Constitution on the Sacred Liturgy*: "Whenever rites, according to their specific nature, make provision for communal celebration involving the presence and active participation of the faithful, it is to be stressed that this way of celebrating them is to be preferred, as far as possible, to a celebration that is individual and, so to speak, private" (S.C., 27). Accordingly, priority of place should be given to Form III as the fullest celebration of sacramental reconciliation, with more private forms, dictated as they may be by personal need, to be understood and evaluated in relation to the communal form. On the other hand, those who stress the personal nature of the sacrament will consider as essential the individual presentation of one's sins to the confessor and an appropriate individual response on the part of the confessor to what is thus presented. They will give priority of place to Form I, with the more communal forms of value only to the extent that they serve the private. Form III, in this view, will remain reserved for emergency situations. Clearly the bias of the Catholic church's current discipline is toward the former.

Nonethelesss, pressure continues to mount to shift this disciplinary bias towards the communal. For some the

14

pressure is for practical reasons. Except for large urban areas where a large number of priests from neighboring parishes may be readily available for the celebration of Forms I or II, Form III presents the only realistic option for celebrating the sacrament in many parish communities. The non-availability of priests presents a more serious situation than the Code seems to acknowledge. For some it is rather an issue of pastoral recognition and pastoral concern: people seem to enjoy more communal forms of the sacrament and partake of them in large numbers, even while continuing to shun the individual form. The private form simply is not attracting the faithful to its doors. For others, finally, the issue is theological. The recovery of the communal, liturgical dimension of all our sacraments is seen as too important to be compromised in the case of this one sacrament alone.

In many ways, the current situation is not unlike an earlier moment in the history of this sacrament when the process of evolution was the opposite, i.e., when the personal form was resisted as an abuse and the communal form considered the only way of enacting the sacrament. When the canonical form of penance fell into disuse, the private, Celtic form arose to fill in the gap and eventually to take its place.

The guiding norm for future development and discipline remains that given in the liturgy constitution: "Finally, there must be no innovations unless the good of the Church genuinely and certainly requires them; care must be taken that any new forms adopted should in some way grow organically from forms already existing" (S.C., 23). The Rite for Reconciliation of Several Penitents with General Confession and Absolution certainly fulfills the latter condition; whether or not it fulfills the former, only time will tell.

See **Reconciliation, sacrament of; Reconciliation, liturgies of; Reconciliation, ministers of**

J. Coriden, T. Green and D. Heintschel, eds., *The Code of Canon Law ... Commentary* (New York: Paulist, 1985), 673-680. P. Fink, ed., *Alternative Futures for Worship: Reconciliation*, Vol. 4 (Collegeville: Liturgical Press, 1984), 109-126.

ABSTINENCE

The practice of refraining from an otherwise wholesome activity for reasons of penitence or anticipation. This may be part of a process of repentance for sin or of purification in anticipation of a festal celebration or joyful event. The practice of abstinence from certain foods has traditionally found its way into the various liturgical calendars of the churches, especially during seasons devoted to repentance (e.g., Lent) or expectation (e.g., Advent).

See **Penitential days; Penitential practices**

ADAPTATION, LITURGICAL

As the expression implies, "liturgical adaptation" refers to the process by which the liturgy is modified in such a way as to render it "more suitable," "more appropriate," "more meaningful" to a given group of worshippers in a given context. While the term "adaptation" has been criticized as connoting an overly timid and even paternalistic attitude toward this process, the documents of the Second Vatican Council and the revised liturgical books use this word in a variety of contexts to express a range of nuanced ideas: from the most superficial kinds of rubrical changes to the creation of new liturgical forms springing from the genius of a particular culture. A careful reading of these documents, especially S.C. 37-40, will reveal that the term "adaptation" when applied to the liturgy variously refers to concepts borrowed from the social sciences such as "localization," "acculturation," "contextualization," "indigenization," and "inculturation," as well as the more theological expression "incarnation."

Examples from the History of the Liturgy

Liturgical adaptation, however, while a relatively new expression in the liturgical lexicon, is not a new phenomenon in the history of the liturgy. As the *Constitution on the Sacred Liturgy* itself points out, the liturgy "is made up of immutable elements, divinely instituted, and of elements subject to change" (S.C., 21). Even a cursory review of the history of Christian worship illustrates that the church both consciously and unconsciously adapted these "elements subject to change" not only from one generation to the next but also from one culture to another in order to express and celebrate the mystery of Christ in a meaningful way.

Given the Jewish background of the first generation of believers, it is not surprising that the earliest forms of Christian liturgy were profoundly rooted in the ritual patterns of first century Judaism. The most obvious case in point is the reinterpretation (one could say "adaptation") of the Passover meal from a domestic memorial of the exodus of Israel from slavery and oppression to the Christian eucharist: the memorial of the "passover" of Christ celebrated in homes by small groups of believers. Just as the Hebrew scriptures were reinterpreted by the early church in a christological light, so basic Jewish ritual actions such as the laying-on of hands, baptismal washing, and anointings were given new meanings in the context of the Christ event. Both the New Testament and extra-biblical witnesses to early Christian worship patterns such as the *Didache* (9, 10) and the *First Letter of Clement* (59-61) betray a marked indebtedness to Jewish forms of prayer and blessing rooted in the Hebrew scriptures, though now refocused on Jesus, the servant of God. This characteristic influence of the Hebrew scriptures and the cultural world-view expressed by them would never be totally lost by the church as it moved from one culture to another down through the centuries.

As the new church attracted more and more converts from paganism, it also entered into a dialogue with the dominant Greco-Roman culture which affected its worship. While this dialogue was often polemical, characterized by a total rejection of cultural expressions based on polytheism, practices which were not intrinsically linked to pagan worship were incorporated into the Christian liturgy and usually interpreted typologically in light of the Hebrew Scriptures. Thus we find in the *Apostolic Tradition* of Hippolytus that after the newly baptized received the eucharist for the first time, they were given a drink of milk and honey. Hippolytus explains the significance of this action as "the fulfillment of the promise God made to the patriarchs, that he would give them a land flowing with milk and honey" (*Apost. Trad.,* 21). Yet, this type of drink would not have been unfamiliar to a Christian neophyte since it was ancient Roman custom to give a similar drink to newborns as a sign of welcome into the family and to ward-off evil spirits (Chupungco, *Cultural Adaptation,* p. 16). Clearly, what is at work here is an adaptation of a "welcoming" rite practiced in the surrounding culture to illustrate the significance of full initiation into the church imaged as the "family of God."

Once Christianity was made a legal religion in 313 by Constantine and then the official religion of the Empire during the reign of Theodosius (379-395), the church's dialogue with Greco-Roman culture became progressively more positive. This was a period of great creativity and the era which saw the gradual birth of the liturgical families of rites in East and West. Each one of these developing rites was marked not only by the theological controversies and political instability of the age, but also by the pastoral concern to adapt the church's worship to the needs of the huge influx of new converts through the assimilation and reinterpretation of cultural symbols drawn from the religious and political usages with which the new Christians were already familiar.

One aspect of this adaptation can be seen in the worship space of the Christian assembly. The simple house-church or "house of the assembly" (*domus ecclesiae*) which was able to accommodate only a small number of worshippers was transformed into an imperial basilica, capable of holding vast throngs of the faithful. While maintaining the image of the church as the "household of God," this image became progressively more stylized in the appointments of the new Christian basilicas: the apse where the emperor or magistrate was enthroned to hold court became the place where the bishop presided from his *cathedra* or chair surrounded by his council of elders or *presbyterium*. Not surprisingly, the liturgy itself became more stylized and formal. It began to reflect the new position of the church vis-à-vis the political and social order, borrowing elements of imperial court ceremonial from the now Christian emperor whose functionaries the bishops partially became. Liturgical vesture in East and West, which has undergone numerous changes down through the centuries, still reflects the formal dress of imperial officials of the late empire. It is also important to note that while the liturgy is still very deeply rooted in the scriptures, the patristic authors of this period began to legitimate the now more formal liturgical practices through recourse to the cultus of the Jerusalem Temple as described in the Hebrew Scriptures and the NT, especially the

letter to the Hebrews. A "sacralization" of both the persons ministering to the community and the place where it gathers to pray, gradually took place which paralleled religious attitudes toward the sacred found in both Judaism and paganism.

Significantly, it was during the 4th century that the very language of worship of the Roman church was adapted to a changed cultural situation. It must be remembered that the Roman church, until the 3rd century, was predominantly Greek-speaking. It was just before the reign of Pope Damasus in the middle of the 4th century that Latin, now the language of the majority of the Christians of Rome, definitively found its way into the liturgy of the City. While this change was essentially a pastoral one, to enable the faithful to understand what was being prayed, the form of the Latin adopted for Christian worship was in many ways stylistically similar to that employed in the pre-Christian, Roman cultus. The litanic responses *Libera nos, Domine* and *Te rogamus, audi nos* both derive from the pagan Roman practice of invoking the gods with a series of intercessory acclamations. The typical Roman concern for juridical precision through the piling up of synonyms in sacrificial formulas also became a feature of the liturgical prayer of Christians. A recent Roman convert from paganism would have been very familiar indeed with the stylized expression specifying the gifts presented at the eucharist such as *haec dona, haec munera, haec sacrificia illibata* appearing in the *Te igitur* section of the Roman Canon and which reflects the hieratic language of the pagan Roman cultus.

This adaptation extended beyond just the verbal. A gesture of reverence still prescribed today in the Roman liturgy, kissing the altar and book of the gospels, also finds its origin in the pagan Roman custom of venerating the sacred with a kiss. Moreover, the development of some aspects of the liturgical year would be incomprehensible without a knowledge of previous pagan celebrations such as the Mithraic celebration of the *dies natalis solis invicti* celebrated at the winter solstice and reinterpreted by the Christian church into the annual celebration of the birth of Christ, the "sun of righteousness" spoken of by the prophet Malachi. These and many other examples illustrate the church's constant (and sometimes unconscious) attempt to adapt its worship to its changed cultural context through the reinterpretation of religious, social, and political customs already extant in the world in which it lived.

This era of the "classic Roman liturgy" which extended from the 4th to the 7th centuries is a crucial one from the point of view of liturgical adaptation since the reforms of the liturgy which took place after Vatican II, being very much influenced by the liturgical movement of the this period as a kind of blueprint which was to guide the liturgical renewal of the Roman rite throughout the world. The great English liturgical historian Edmund Bishop, writing at the beginning of the century, lists the characteristics of the classic Roman rite which, in effect, describe the cultural values or "genius" of Roman culture as: "simplicity, practicality, a great sobriety and self-control, gravity and dignity" ("The Genius of the Roman Rite," *Liturgica Historica*, Oxford, 1918, p. 12). These values have served in subsequent periods of liturgical reform as a kind of yardstick by which such reforms were measured. These values played a key role in the liturgical renewal of Vatican II: "The rites should be marked by a noble simplicity; they should be short, clear, unencumbered by useless repetitions; they should be within the peoples' power of comprehension and as a rule not require much explanation" S.C., 34).

As Frankish and Germanic peoples entering the areas of what was the old Roman Empire were evangelized, it was only natural that their worship, too, was influenced by their particular culture. In the period prior to the 9th century when the Roman rite was imposed on the Frankish Kingdom by Pepin and Charlemagne, Western liturgical rites developed quite independently from the Roman, and reveal very different approaches to Christian worship. One can easily see in the style of the prayers found in the various non-Roman sacramentaries of this period a reflection of the challenges which beset these local churches expressed in styles proper to the particular national "genius" of these people. In Ireland, where the harp of the wandering troubadour still functions as a national symbol, the prayers of the Celtic rite excelled in lyrical compositions and hymnody. In the face of serious Arian opposition to orthodoxy, the former thoroughly Romanized province of Spain produced the so-called Mozarabic or Visigothic rite centered around the cities of Toledo and Braga which combined a refined Latin erudition with a special concern for orthodoxy of expression. The more "barbarian" province of Gaul produced prayers which tended to be prolix, moralizing, and emotional, but which liberally incorporated quotations from the scriptures.Though all of these rites employed Latin in worship, their style is unmistakably different from the more restrained and abstract Roman "genius."

The See of Rome, however, commanded enormous respect in the West, being the center of pilgrimage to the shrines of the apostles Peter and Paul and the only Patriarchate in the West. Many of these pilgrims returned home to incorporate liturgical practices that they had witnessed at Rome into their own worship. It was also to Rome that Charlemagne turned in an astute political move to unify his kingdom by means of imposing uniform liturgical observances on his dominions. While the liturgical unification he promoted used the liturgy of the city of Rome as its base, his borrowing of Roman liturgical forms was not wholesale. Under Charlemagne's auspices a supplement to the Roman sacramentary he had received from the pope was composed which included the blessing of the Easter candle (our present *Exsultet*) as well as ordination prayers, blessings, formulas for consecration of churches and exorcisms—all of which reflect the characteristic Franco-Germanic verbosity coupled with a love of scripture. This "supplement" was eventually incorporated into the Roman section of the sacramentary and was brought back to Rome and became, with a few alterations down through the centuries, the "Roman" missal used by the Roman rite until the reforms of Vatican II.

It was also about the same time, during the reforms of the papacy undertaken by the Ottonian emperors in the 9th and 10th centuries, that we see the influence of the early medieval culture on liturgical practice. The Roman-Germanic Pontifical of the 10th Century, a fusion of the ancient *Roman Ordines* (guides to liturgical celebrations) with material from the north of Europe, contains dramatic evidence of the influence of feudalism; for example, six sections of the book are dedicated to the *Iudicia Dei* or "trials by ordeal." While these "barbaric" ceremonies were dropped by subsequent pontificals, feudalism continues to influence the liturgy. The gesture of fealty used by a knight to his liege was introduced into the ordination rite for presbyters by the end of 13th century in Rome. When the ordinand places his hands between the hands of the bishop to promise obedience, he is imitating that feudal gesture of "hommage" given by a vassal to his lord.

Although there was an attempt under Gregory VII (1073-1085) and Innocent III (1198-1216) to return to what was perceived to be the traditions and practices of the ancient Roman "fathers," these reforms were impeded by a lack of documentation and historical sophistication. The Roman liturgy therefore evinced not only the sobriety and gravity of ancient Rome, but also the allegorism, moralization, verbosity and flair for the dramatic which characterized the peoples of northern Europe. It was this essentially hybrid liturgy, purified of abuses by the Council of Trent, which is contained in the Missal of Pius V promulgated in 1570.

The Reformers of the 16th century approached the problem of adaptation from another point of view. Instead of adapting the liturgy in light of what was perceived to be the ancient practices of the Roman church, they made a conscious attempt to look at worship as presented in the scriptures. One of the problems they perceived in medieval worship was that it was monopolized by the clergy and was unintelligible to the people because it was celebrated in Latin. It therefore needed to be translated into the vernacular, purged of what they regarded to be Roman error and supersitition, and firmly based on the word of God. Luther, Zwingli, Bucer, Calvin and later Cranmer all produced new vernacular liturgies which attempted to return to the worship of the early church. While these revisions were successful insofar as they once again made the words of worship comprehensible to the people, they were unable to "turn the clock back" to the 1st century because the NT contains no formal worship services and hence no pattern to emulate. As with the attempted reform of Gregory VII in the 11th century, historical study and theological reflection was not sufficiently developed in the 16th century to do anything more than to create worship services shorn of direct references to Catholic doctrines problematic to the reformers such as eucharistic sacrifice.

While they were assiduous at translating both the scriptures and prayers used in church, the reformers produced liturgies which very much reflected the cultural ethos of Northern Europe during the late Middle Ages. Although their services emphasized the primacy of the word of God interpreted by every Christian, a word which was now accessible to a much broader section of the population through the invention of the printing press, their liturgies also reflect the strong penitential emphasis and interest in subjectivity already present in the late Middle Ages in such spiritual movements as the *devotio moderna*.

The apparent rejection of centuries of liturgical tradition by the reformers, as well as what was perceived to be their deviations from doctrinal orthodoxy, led the participants in the Council of Trent to reaffirm what it regarded as ancient tradition. The rite of the Mass inspired by this council was protected from any change or modification by canonical regulations which legislated absolute compliance to the most minute rubrical detail under pain of sin. The four hundred years between the promulgation of the Missal of Pius V in 1570 and that of Paul VI in 1970 is a history of rigid liturgical centralization and uniformity in the Roman Catholic church, largely immune to any attempts at adaptation. It was during this period that, having no outlet to modify the liturgy as such, that both popular devotions and a manifest theatricality increasingly began to "frame" the eucharistic liturgy and other rites of the church. Medieval practices such as processions and expositions of the Blessed Sacrament, novenas to the saints, the rosary, and the dramatizations of biblical stories performed both inside and outside the church were maintained, especially in the Spanish part of the Catholic world. While the rite of the Mass itself could not be changed, its celebration was peripherally embellished by full orchestras and choirs performing complex musical compositions. The churches built during this period resemble theaters where the faithful, like an audience, "attended" the various ceremonies of the church "performed" in a dramatic setting designed to inspire feelings of devotion and awe. During this age of "divine right monarchs" it is also not by chance that many churches resembled throne rooms where the great king of heaven present in the Blessed Sacrament held court, enthroned in an ornate tabernacle on the main altar, surrounded by candles, flowers and incense.

Ironically, these four hundred years also corresponded to a period of great missionary outreach by the church to peoples of different cultures in the Americas, Africa, Asia and Oceania. One notable exception to this Roman insistence on uniformity was an experiment promoted by Matteo Ricci, a Jesuit missionary in China, which became the object of controversy from 1610-1742. Ricci obtained important indults from the Holy See to adapt the Mass, liturgical vestments, and language of the liturgy to Chinese culture. Moreover, he also urged that the practice of the Chinese, derived from Confucianism, to honor their ancestors by bowing before "ancestor" tablets not be interpreted as idolatry or superstition, but be permitted to Chinese converts by the church as a cultural expression which was an integral part of Chinese identity. These attempts at rooting the gospel and the worship of Chinese Catholics in their own culture were met by serious opposition from other missionaries, notably the Dominicans, who accused Ricci and the Jesuits of promoting idolatry. In a very interesting instruction to the Vicars Apostolic of the Far East, issued by *Propaganda Fide* in 1659, the idea of transplanting Europe to China as necessary for evangelization was labelled as absurd. The instruction clearly draws a distinction between the faith and its European cultural expression, and states that the faith does not demand that rites and customs of non-Europeans be repudiated or destroyed in order for them to become Christian; that indeed, the faith wills that these rites and customs be preserved intact in order to serve as vehicles for evangelization, provided they are not "depraved" ("Instructio Vicariorum Apostolicorum ad Regna Synarum Tonchini et Cocinnae Profisiscentium," in *Collectanea Sacrae Congregationis Propaganda Fide*, I, Rome, 1907). This instruction, therefore, lays down the principle of liturgical adaptation which would be echoed in Pius XII's encyclical *Summi Pontificatus* of 1939, (*Acta Apostolica Sedis* 31 (1939):429) and in the *Constitution on the Sacred Liturgy* of Vatican II, 37.

Unfortunately, the insights of both Matteo Ricci and *Propaganda Fide* were lost in the intervening years. Chinese performance of ancestral rites was condemned by the bull *Ex quo singulari* in 1742 which "spelled the loss of China and Indochina to the Church" (Chupungco, *Cultural Adaptation*, p. 38). It became clear to many potential converts outside of western Europe that to become Christian meant to become European.

Vatican II and Liturgical Adaptation

The fifty years prior to Vatican II witnessed a renewed interest in matters liturgical and in making the liturgy truly the prayer of the church. Prompted by both the liturgical movement and the liturgical reforms of Pius X, Pius XII, and John XXIII, the liturgy once again became the object of serious study by theologians, historians, and missionaries. Since it was also during this period that the church was wrestling with the modernist controversy which discouraged the open questioning of any aspect of church life which was considered traditional, it is not surprising that these studies most often revolved around a return to the sources of the Roman rite as it was practiced in the city of Rome from the 4thto the 7th centuries. The effort was to recapture the valued "Roman genius" of the liturgy and clearly distinguish the classical forms from the medieval and baroque accretions which, in the mind of many in the liturgical movement, tended to blur the true nature of liturgical celebrations.

Thus, it was on the basis of historical precedent that a call went out to adapt the liturgy to the needs of the day. Like the liturgical reform attempted by Gregory VII in the 11th century, one could characterize both the papal reforms of the liturgy and the approach of liturgists during this period as a "repristinization" of the Roman rite; a return to the simplicity, sobriety, and clarity of expression characteristic of the classic Roman genius in order to render the worship of the church more accessible to the faithful, especially to those in mission lands. It was on the basis of historical precedent, then, that the restoration of the Easter vigil (1951) and Holy Week (1955) by Pius XII was undertaken and the participation of the assembly in the liturgical action through "dialogue" Masses was promoted by some in the liturgical *avant-garde* both in Europe and the United States. It was also on the basis of historical research into the liturgy that the period just prior to Vatican II began to hear more and more calls for the use of the vernacular in worship.

Because of the ground-work done by liturgists and historians in the years prior to Vatican II, the Preparatory Commission on the Liturgy established by the pope in 1959 was in a position to quickly draft a *schema* of the document on the liturgy. It reflects the advanced state of the research on the liturgy prior to the council that this *schema* became the first order of business of Vatican II.

The norms for liturgical adaptation to

the customs and traditions of peoples are outlined by Vatican II (S.C., 37-40). These articles clearly move beyond what many critics had labeled an "archaeological" approach which characterized much of the pre-conciliar research on the liturgy and open the way for real adaptation of the liturgy based on a reformed Roman rite characterized by a "noble simplicity, brevity and clarity" (S.C., 34) and which is now seen as the starting point, not the goal of liturgical renewal. While the council proposes the Roman rite as a "universal" rite, it does so fully aware that there will have to be important differences in the way in which it is celebrated in cultures as diverse as those found in Africa and Asia.

Article 37 of *S.C.* announces the general principle governing liturgical adaptation and is based on Pius XII's encyclical *Summi Pontificatus*. This article opens the door to true liturgical pluralism within the Roman rite by stating that "the Church has no wish to impose a rigid uniformity in matters which do not affect the faith or the good of the whole community; rather the church respects and fosters the genius and talents of various races and peoples." Clearly, the principle enunciated in this article reflects the historical reality lived by the church down through the ages, except for the anomalous period after the Council of Trent; that it is the faith itself which constitutes ecclesial unity and not a rigid uniformity in the cultural expression of that faith in the liturgy. The article further establishes two general criteria for admitting elements of a particular people's way of life in the worship of the local church. One is negative: "that anything not indissolubly bound up with superstition and error" may be admitted into the liturgy. The other is positive: that these elements be "in harmony with the true and authentic spirit of the liturgy." Both of these criteria require interpretation that is not exhaustively provided

by *S.C.* and will become the object of subsequent debate after the council.

Having stated these general principles of adaptation, S.C. 38-39 then moves to more concrete proposals regarding their implementation and to what could be termed the first level of adaptation of the Roman rite. It provides for "legitimate variations and adaptations to different groups, regions, and peoples" in the revision of the liturgical books. These revisions and adaptations are to be done "especially in mission lands" although the sense of the word "especially" (*praesertim*) as explained by the conciliar commission, while emphasizing the need for adaptation in mission lands, does not mean to exclude the possibility of adaptation in countries where Christianity and the Roman rite have known a long history.

S.C. 37 sets a limit to these adaptations with the expression, "provided the substantial unity of the Roman rite is preserved." The expression "substantial unity of the Roman rite" is nowhere defined by *S.C.*, but is most probably referring to article 39 which speaks of adaptation within the limits set by the *editio typica* of the liturgical books. This means to say that the unity of the Roman rite is safeguarded when the norms for adaptation, written into the official liturgical books issued by Rome are observed; norms which give some limited freedom to the "competent territorial authority," i.e., a national conference of bishops, to adapt the liturgy to local needs. It should be noted that if the liturgical books provide for it, the bishops' conferences may institute modifications in the liturgy which go beyond simple cosmetic changes, and which even restructure the rite itself. Article 39 further states that this kind of adaptation is to be applied "especially in the case of the administration of the sacraments, the sacramentals, processions, liturgical language, sacred music and the arts." This mandate is reiterated in article 63 which calls on the bishops' conferences to prepare new rituals adapted "to the needs of the different regions."

Thus, the approach to adaptation taken by these articles (S.C. 38-39) could be described by the term "acculturation" defined as an initial encounter between the Roman rite and the local culture. While maintaining the nucleus of the Roman rite, a translation of those elements which are contingent on western culture would be re-coded or re-interpreted into the particular forms and expressions of the "receiving" culture in order to make them more expressive of the faith.

Article 40 deals with a more radical form of adaptation which can be rightly called "inculturation." While the norms proposed for acculturating the liturgy as found in the revised liturgical books might be sufficient for renewing the liturgy in a European country like Italy, for example, the council wisely foresaw that in areas of the world that are not heirs to an exclusively western European cultural tradition the need for adapting the liturgy would require not only more profound modifications of the Roman rite, but a real inculturation of the liturgy which can be defined as an ongoing process of a reciprocal, critical interaction and assimilation between the Roman rite and the local culture. Although the initial draft of the first part of this article specifically mentioned the missions, this reference was dropped in the final redaction of the document in order to allow the application of this article to other "places and circumstances" not considered "missionary" (*Schema Constitutionis de Sacra Liturgia*, Typis Polyglottis Vaticanis 1962, 27).

S.C. 40 spells out the nature of these adaptations and the procedure that is to govern their implementation in three paragraphs. The first paragraph stipulates that the "competent territorial ecclesi-astical authority" is "to carefully and prudently weigh what elements from the traditions and culture of individual peoples may be appropriately admitted into divine worship." The adaptations judged opportune should then be submitted to the Holy See for approval. The second paragraph deals with the Holy See's granting the bishops' conferences the authority to direct "preliminary experiments" for a specified length of time and within certain groups so that "the adaptations are made with all the circumspection they demand." Finally, the third paragraph speaks of the technical assistance of experts, "particularly in mission lands," where the problems associated with this kind of adaptation would presumably be more complex.

While articles 37-40 of S.C. mark a revolutionary departure from the centuries-old Roman resistance to any kind of liturgical adaptation, they should also be read in the context of other articles which speak of more general principles of liturgical reform such as article 24 which emphasizes the importance of the liturgy being thoroughly grounded in Sacred Scripture. Also, article 23 reflects a more cautious attitude toward both liturgical adaptation and the unity of the Roman rite. It states that even after careful "theological, historical and pastoral investigation" as well as a "study of the experience derived from recent liturgical reforms" that "... there must be no innovations unless the good of the Church genuinely and certainly requires them; care should be taken that any new forms adopted should in some way grow organically from forms already existing." The same article warns against "marked differences between rites used in neighboring areas." While these caveats might seem today to be overly cautious, they reflect the "compromising nature" of a conciliar document drafted to assuage the anxieties of some of the more traditional conciliar participants who feared not only ill-considered innovation but the wholesale destruction of the Roman rite.

Articles other than 37-40 of the same document, however, speak in very specific terms of the possible need for the radical adaptation or inculturation of the liturgy in "mission lands"; especially in the celebration of the sacraments of initiation and marriage. Article 65 proposes that "besides what is part of Christian tradition, those initiation elements in use among individual peoples, to the extent that such rites are compatible with the Christian rite of initiation" be allowed. In much the the same spirit, article 77 which speaks of the revision of the marriage rite states that "the competent, territorial ecclesiastical authority . . . is free to draw up . . . its own rite suited to the usages of place and people."

This call for adaptation expressed by the *Constitution on the Sacred Liturgy* becomes even more insistent and sophisticated in subsequent conciliar documents which treat of the relationship between the church and culture, especially the *Decree on the Missionary Activity of the Church* (A.G., 9, 10, 11, 21, 22) and the *Pastoral Constitution on the Church in the Modern World* (G.S., 44, 58). These documents, along with the *Dogmatic Constitution on the Church* (L.G., 13, 17, 23) and the *Declaration on the Relation of the Church to Non-Christian Religions* (N.A., 2), being the product of a more mature degree of conciliar thought on the question of adaptation, help to describe in more detail the relationship of the church to culture and hence clarify some of the ambiguity noted in the liturgy document relative to liturgical adaptation.

One of the most important theological constructs proposed by the council to describe the relation of church to culture is found in the *Decree on the Missionary Activity of the Church* (A.G., 10). This article proposes the incarnation of Christ as the paradigmatic way in which the universal church relates to local cultures. The *Pastoral Constitution on the Church in the Modern World* defines this relationship as reciprocal; it is not simply a question of the church "translating" into another cultural idiom the datum of the faith whose western European expression is considered somehow normative. Rather, citing the historical relationship between the church and culture, it belongs to the church itself to again profit from the "riches hidden in different cultures" and "to learn to express the Christian message in the concepts and language of different peoples" through fostering a "vital contact and exchange between the Church and different cultures" (G.S., 44). Moreover, "the Church has been sent to all ages and nations and, therefore, is not tied exclusively and indissolubly to any race or nation, to any one particular way of life, or to any customary practices, ancient or modern" (G.S., 58).

These teachings of the council clearly have implications for the more radical adaptation or inculturation of the liturgy as described in S.C. 40 in groups and nations which are not heirs to the western European cultural tradition.

Post-conciliar Developments

The period just after the council saw intense activity on the part of the various commissions established to revise and translate the new liturgical books into modern languages. It should be pointed out that the very translation of the official Latin *editio typica* versions of the liturgical books constitutes an adaptation. The Instruction *Comme le prévoit* of 1969, on the translation of liturgical texts for celebration with a congregation (D.O.L., 838-880), clearly enunciates principles and norms which emphasize that the text "as a ritual sign, is a medium of spoken communication" (D.O.L., 842) and discourages a literal fidelity to the Latin text, opting for the principle of "dynamic equivalence" whereby the concepts expressed in the Latin text are rendered in a modern language by proposing an equivalent concept drawn from the culture where the language is used. Realizing the complex nature of this enterprise, the Consilium also wisely notes that "after sufficient experiment and passage of time, all translations will need review" (D.O.L., 838). Finally, the document takes into account the limitation of translations by noting that the mere translation of texts is "not sufficient for a fully renewed liturgy. The creation of new texts will be necessary" (D.O.L., 880).

Looking at the introductions and ritual directions in the revised and translated liturgical books, the word "adaptation" is applied to the liturgy in two distinct ways. The first kind of adaptation concerns the alternatives provided by the liturgical books themselves to be selected by those who prepare the liturgy so that the celebration might "correspond as fully as possible to the needs, spiritual preparation, and mentality of the participants" (*General Introduction to the Rite of Mass*, 313). The Instruction *Actio Pastoralis*, on Masses for special groups and the *Directory for Masses with Children* issued by the Congregation for Divine Worship makes further provision for this kind of adaptation of the eucharistic celebration based on the number, age, and spiritual needs of those who make up the assembly. The revised rites of initiation, for example, also contain articles which provide guidelines for the presider's adaptation of the celebration (R.C.I.A., 67, Rite of Baptism for Children 27-31, Rite of Confirmation 18).

A second kind of adaptation proposed by the post-conciliar documents already enunciated in S.C. 38 and 39 falls within the purview of national bishops conferences deputed by S.C. 63 to compose their own rituals "adapted to the needs of their specific regions" and which were to be confirmed by the Holy See. Elements from the local culture can be incorporated into the liturgy which substitute or illustrate the Roman Ritual. This "acculturation" of the liturgy parallels to some degree the principle of "dynamic equivalence" at work in the translation of verbal texts. Much of the post-conciliar work on adaptation, especially in Africa and Asia has used this method. The recent "Roman Missal for the Dioceses of Zaïre" approved by the Congregation for Divine Worship in 1988 ("Le Missel Romain pour diocèses du Zaïre," *Notitiae* 24 (1988):454-472), is a good example of the use of this approach. This missal "interprets" the Roman Missal in the cultural idiom of this region of Africa, restructuring the rite, adding local gestures, and proposing alternate prayers that reflect deeply held values in Africa such as respect for ancestors.

The third and most radical form of adaptation, inculturation, is not provided for by the liturgical books except in the case of marriage. The *Introduction to the Rite of Marriage* speaks not only of assuming elements from the local culture to illustrate what is contained in the Roman Ritual (O.C.M., 13-16), but for the creation of a whole new rite based on the culture of the place, as long as the presence of the minister who witnesses the vows is safeguarded and the nuptial blessing is given. In this case, the Rite of Marriage seems to be asking for a genuine dialogue with the local culture; a dialogue that presupposes a real reciprocity by encouraging the use of marriage customs and traditions originating in the pre-Christian culture. However, in general, there seems to be a marked hesitance on the part of the Roman authorities to implement fully the possibilities inherent in article 40 of the *Constitution on the Sacred Liturgy*.

On the one hand, there seems to be a fear that inculturation would lead to a total disintegration of the Roman rite whose theological and formal characteristics are deemed worthy of retention, even in very different cultural contexts. On the other hand, not very much time has elapsed for true inculturation to take place. As we know from history, it took several centuries for the "Christianization" of the Roman Empire to get to the point where the church felt comfortable in adopting formerly pagan customs into Christian worship. Although conciliar documents like *Nostra Aetate* (2) spoke of a real openness and respect for non-Christian religions, it seems that a similar process needs to take place in non-European areas before the liturgy can truly be described as having inculturated elements from non-Christian religions which are an integral part of the cultural identity of these countries.

Conclusion

As the previous pages have demonstrated, liturgical adaptation is not a new phenomenon. Since the liturgy is the self-expression of the church, it has and must continue to adapt itself to the different and changing cultural environments in which it finds itself or risk becoming irrelevant. Much more is at stake than simply making people feel more "at ease" in worship; the very mission of the church to preach the Gospel to all nations is compromised when adaptation does not take place. As Anscar Chupungco notes, "the refusal to adapt amounts to a denial of the universality of salvation" (Chupungco, *Cultural Adaptation*, p. 87). The challenge that faces all local churches at present, especially those in non-European settings, is essentially one of evangelization: to proclaim and celebrate the message of the gospel and the mystery of Christ in a way that is meaningful to the many cultures of the human race. This can only be done if local churches are allowed to continue on the road to true liturgical inculturation indicated by the Vatican II. As Paul VI pointed out, "Evangelization loses much of its force and effectiveness if it does not take into consideration the actual people to whom it is addressed, if it does not use their language, their signs and symbols, if it does not answer the questions they ask, and if it does not have an impact on their concrete life" (*Evangelii Nuntiandi*, 63).

G.A. Arbuckle, "Inculturation not Adaptation: Time to Change Terminology," *Worship* 60 (1986): 511-520. Anscar J. Chupungco, *Cultural Adaptation of the Liturgy* (New York: Paulist Press, 1982). Anscar J. Chupungco, "A Definition of Liturgical Inculturation," *Ecclesia Orans* 5 (1988): 11-23. A. Roest Crollius, "What is so New About Inculturation? A Concept and Its Implication," *Gregorianum* 59 (1978): 721-738. Joseph Jungmann, *The Early Liturgy to the Time of Gregory the Great.* Trans. by F.A. Brunner (Notre Dame: University of Notre Dame Press, 1959). Frank Senn, *Christian Worship and its Cultural Setting* (Philadelphia: Fortress, 1983).

MARK R. FRANCIS, C.S.V.

ADORATION, THEOLOGY OF

The theology of adoration is really a part of a broader question: communion and worship of the eucharist outside its celebration. The purpose of this article is to give a brief historical sketch of communion practice and the origins of eucharistic devotions outside the celebration of the eucharist. From these we hope to draw the theological roots of eucharistic adoration and the challenges it presents today.

To start with, the early Christians had celebrated their eucharist in the context of an ordinary meal. The emphasis was on the action of eating and drinking, of sharing a meal with the risen Christ and with one another. They were especially concerned with the purpose of all this, namely, nourishing the Christ life already within them through baptism, unity with each other in Christ and eternal life through a share in Christ's resurrection (cf. Jn 6:51-58; 1 Cor 10: 16-18; Acts 2:42-47).

As time went on, the eucharist was separated from the ordinary meal, probably because of abuses (cf. 1 Cor 11: 17-34). This was the case by the time of Justin Martyr (d. 165) who describes the eucharist in terms of a "stylized" meal, i.e., one in which the bread and wine alone serve as food and drink. Justin makes the point that " . . . the gifts over which the thanksgiving has been spoken are distributed, and everyone shares in them, while they are also sent via the deacons to the absent brethren" (Deiss, L., *Springtime of the Liturgy*, trans. by M.J. O'Connell, Collegeville, MN: The Liturgical Press, 1979, p. 93-94). All who are present receive and communion is brought to the sick so that they also can share the Sunday celebration. Thus the first evidence of communion outside of Mass links it intimately with the celebration itself and this holds true until the end of the 4th century (cf. Mitchell, 11, 28).

The stress also continued to be on the receiving of communion and its purpose. Augustine (d. 430) put it so well: "If you receive well, you are what you have received.... Since you are the body of Christ and his members, it is your mystery that is placed on the Lord's table; it is your mystery that you receive.... Be what you see, and receive what you are" (Megivern, 68). This same point was made by Pope St. Leo the Great (d. 461): "The partaking of the body and blood of Christ has no other effect than to make us pass over into what we receive"(Ibid. 72).

Up to the 4th century, the rule was that all the faithful partook in communion. But then with unexpected rapidity, at least in some countries, the number dropped off sharply. The reasons are numerous and complex and were to give rise to a shift in attitudes which would provide the setting for eucharistic devotions outside the Mass. First, there were the christological controversies. Arianism's attempt to play down Christ's divinity led to an overemphasis of that divinity almost to the exclusion of his humanity, despite Chalcedon's effort in 451 to strike a balance. The risen Jesus became a distant God. This eventually led to the liturgy and clergy becoming distant as well. Second, the eucharistic action and eucharistic food were disengaged from communal acts of dining. This in turn led to a new interpretation in which " . . . the ancient human symbols of dining together were reinterpreted as *ritual drama*, vivid symbolic reenactments of Jesus' life, death and resurrection" (Mitchell, 5). From there it was a short step to dramatic allegorizations like those of Amalar of Metz which emphasized recalling the past rather than present participation through communion as Augustine and those before him had stressed. Third, the gradual limiting of the knowledge of the language of the liturgy (in this case Latin) to a select few widened the gap between the people and the celebration. The inability of the ordinary people to understand the language of the liturgy and thus to participate in it led them to seek an alternate language. Eating and drinking the eucharist would gradually give way to "occular communion," the desire to see the host. Finally, the growing distance and awesomeness of Christ and the liturgy was eventually to lead to a demand (9th century on) for sacramental confession before each communion and for longer fasts in preparation for communion (Jungmann, 56-70, 498-502; Mitchell, 4-5, 116-119; Megivern, 63-66, 73-74, 81).

These factors probably account, at least in part, for the widespread use in the 9th century of unleavened bread, a tube or straw to drink from the chalice, communion on the tongue instead of the hand and communion *in church* outside the celebration of eucharist. The same factors plus controversies in the 9th, 11th and 12th centuries over Christ's presence in the eucharist and the "moment of consecration," focused more attention on the elements of bread and wine and miracles in their regard, e.g., bleeding hosts. An ever decreasing number of communicants followed. No longer able to participate actively in the language of the liturgy and out of extreme reverence or fear hesitating to partake in communion, the faithful were ripe for other forms of expressing their belief in Christ's presence in the eucharist. The attitude that the eucharist was something to be looked at and adored rather than eaten was to become characteristic of medieval eucharistic piety (Jungmann, 89-92; 502-512; Megivern, 29-33, 43, 78-84; Mitchell, 5-6).

Reservation of the sacrament had obviously been a practice from the start so that communion could be brought to the sick and dying. In addition, in earlier times people were allowed to bring communion home for use during the week. The origin of prayer before the sacrament seems to be the priest's prayer before communion (11th century). This evolved into the people's praying after the elevation (late 12th century) and visits to the Blessed Sacrament (early 13th century). Reservation near or on the altar in the 13th century tended to focus the devotion in that area (cf. Jungmann, 522-23; Mitchell, 164-70).

Eucharistic processions appear as early as the 11th century, at least in England. As devotion to looking upon the host grew, these became a way to honor Christ in the Blessed Sacrament and to gaze at the host even longer. On the continent, the bishop of Liège approved the feast of Corpus Christi for his diocese in 1276. It soon spread and included a procession of the Blessed Sacrament (cf. Mitchell, 170-76).

The earliest form of exposing the eucharistic species was just before communion with an expression like, "Holy things for the holy." Until the beginning of the 13th century this was the only place that the people were invited to gaze upon the sacred species and reverence them.

With the introduction of the elevation, which in the 14th century came to be regarded as the supreme moment of the celebration, the people were invited to adore our Lord immediately after the words of "consecration." Earlier it had been an invitation to partake of communion. Now, however, the invitation was to contemplation or "ocular communion." So far exposition had been from within the liturgy itself—at communion, at viaticum or communion to the dying, or Corpus Christi. In 1380 a popular custom arose in some parts of Germany to expose the sacrament in a monstrance. This eventually led to exposition in a monstrance apart from the liturgy (cf. Mitchell, 176-81).

The origin of Benediction of the Blessed Sacrament was also from within the liturgy of the hours and of Corpus Christi. In the early 13th century it became popular to sing Marian hymns at the end of evening or night prayer. In the 14th century the trend was to do so in the presence of the Blessed Sacrament to enhance this devotion rather than to increase honor to the sacrament. On Corpus Christi as early as 1301, there were stations or pauses where the priest would bless the people with the sacrament and at the end of the procession they would be blessed by a monstrance or similar vessel (cf. Mitchell, 181-84).

All these devotions to the eucharist outside of Mass had their origins, then, in the liturgy. In addition, many of them seem to have appeared first in communities of religious.

As is often the case, the main theological lines of these attitudes and devotions emerge from history. Their roots lie in the belief that the risen Christ is really present in the eucharistic celebration and in the desire to extend that celebration to those who were sick or dying, in danger of persecution or absent for some other good reason. This is anthropologically as well as theologically sound and leads to what Piet Fransen describes as the "law of extension." Symbolic realities, when they have central importance in our lives, tend to extend themselves in similar, if only analogical, expressions. A married couple, for instance, find many ways of expressing their love in addition to the marital act, e.g., kisses, touches, gazes. It is important not to disparage these extensions simply because they are not the central act or were not there from the very beginning, e.g., eucharistic processions. It is equally important, however, to recall their original source and background and to relate them to that central celebration (cf. P. Fransen, *Intelligent Theology*, Vol. I, Chicago: Franciscan Herald Press, 1969).

The origin of all eucharistic devotions outside Mass lies, as history tells us, in the liturgy itself. To lose sight of this is to lose sight of their purpose. Underlying all of them is belief in Christ's presence, first in the sharing of the meal and then, by extension, in the remaining bread and wine. If Christ is present in the bread and wine, it seems legitimate and beneficial to adore him there. The difficulty, historically and theologically, is that this worship outside the celebration of the eucharist sometimes seemed to be loosed from its moorings. That is its weakness. Its strength rests in its ability to give people time and quiet to reflect on what it means to receive the body of Christ—the whole body, as Augustine would say, head and members—into one's heart. There were good elements in the "elevation" or "tabernacle" piety, namely, personal devotion to Jesus, an awareness of the sacrificial character of the eucharist and an awareness of the power of the eucharist to draw one to imitate Christ's self-sacrifice. Perhaps more attention to these elements today would help us appropriate more deeply the paschal mystery of Christ which we celebrate in the eucharist (Jungmann, 90-91; cf. also E. Diederich, "Notes on Liturgy" and

"The Eucharistic Mystery in All Its Fullness," *Review for Religious 42* (May-June and Nov-Dec, 1983) 363-380, 914-927).

Pastorally, the future is challenging. Is it possible to return to the center without losing the values of eucharistic devotions outside of Mass? "The celebration of the Eucharist in the sacrifice of the Mass is truly the origin and goal of the worship which is shown to the Eucharist outside of Mass" (*Instruction on Eucharistic Worship*, May 25, 1967, Washington, D.C.: 1967, art. 3e). Is it possible to rediscover the value of eucharistic devotions outside of Mass without letting them again slip loose from their moorings? Mitchell's quote from T.S. Eliot's "Little Gidding" is on target: We shall not cease from exploration. And the end of all our exploring will be to arrive where we started and know the place for the first time (Mitchell, 8).

All the eucharistic devotions, even the most elaborate, have as their purpose or end to bring us back to the beginning—to Jesus Christ, crucified and risen, sharing this meal and his paschal mystery with his people.

Joseph Jungmann, *The Mass of the Roman Rite*, Trans. by F. Brunner and rev. by C. Riepe (New York: Benziger Bros., 1961). James J. Megivern, *Concomitance and Communion: A Study in Eucharistic Doctrine and Practice*, Studia Friburgensia, New Series #33 (New York: Herder, 1963). Nathan Mitchell, *Cult and Controversy: The Worship of the Eucharist Outside Mass* (New York: Pueblo, 1982).

JOHN H. McKENNA, C.M.

ADULT COMMITMENT, RITUAL FOR

A ritual for adult commitment is a ceremony in which adults express their assent to the beliefs of their church. It is appropriate for those who joined the church when they were too young to make their personal assent, or those who have long adhered to their church's teachings but find themselves at a stage of life's journey when they feel moved to recommit themselves to that faith.

Rituals of this nature have grown in popularity in the last part of the 20th century due to advances in psychology, anthropology, and sacramental theology. Since human life expectancy has grown longer, psychologists have identified several "stages" through which human beings pass from childhood throughout their adult life. With the guidance of anthropology, theologians have argued for marking those stages of development with appropriate rituals. Since people seem to go through stages of faith as well as psychological development, rituals have followed to help the faithful express their new level of commitment to the church.

An example may be found in the *Lutheran Book of Worship*. There is found the ritual for "Affirmation of Baptism," a service which may take place in three different forms: confirmation, reception into membership, and restoration to membership. Each service marks a time in the life of the member who is ready to restate his or her commitment to the local church. In the first instance, after careful study, one comes before the bishop for prayer. In the second, one transfers membership from one congregation to another. In the third, one who has been away from membership is restored.

Another example is in the Anglican *Book of Common Prayer*. Here, too, the rite of confirmation is expanded to include two similar services, reception for those joining from another baptized communion and reaffirmation for those making a personal recommitment to the church.

A difficulty has arisen in the Roman Catholic church since it has no ritual for adult commitment in the same way as other Christian denominations have. The Catholic liturgy approaches adult commitment from other sources.

The example *par excellence* in the Catholic liturgy is the Rite of Christian Initiation of Adults. Here one finds a complex of liturgical rites to accompany change of heart. Whether the adults in question have never been baptized or are joining the Catholic church from another communion, they make a ritual commitment to the Catholic church with the assistance of these rites.

Another example is the sacrament of reconciliation. A believer who has sinned may seek to heal the separation from the church through a ritual of reconciliation with the church's minister. The act of reconciliation to the church is especially evident when the rite is celebrated in common. Although not properly a rite of "commitment," reconciliation implies a recommitment of one's life to the gospel and to the church community.

Still another example of adult commitment in the Catholic liturgy is the celebration of Easter Sunday. Both in the vigil Mass and the Masses of Easter day, Catholics renew their baptismal promises in place of reciting the creed. Each year the celebrant asks the congregation to renounce Satan and express its belief in Christ, and each year the assembly recommits to its baptismal creed.

In recent years the pastoral practice in many dioceses around the world has been to use the rite of confirmation as a ritual of adult commitment. In this case, Catholics who were baptized as infants delay their celebration of confirmation till young adulthood. Catechesis surrounding the confirmation of young adults has encouraged them to make personally the commitment others made for them when they were young.

This practice has its problems. The difficulty is reconciling how one rite which is initiatory for adults and children of catechetical age becomes a rite of commitment for those baptized in infancy. In any event, confirmation has been made to fill the gap in a church which has no ritual for adult commitment as other denominations have developed.

A ritual for adult commitment may be simply devised: The faithful who have expressed a desire to recommit to their faith may present themselves to the assembly. The liturgy of the word may be celebrated with texts drawn from the rite of baptism. Then those who wish to recommit themselves could do so through the renewal of their baptismal promises and the prayer of the celebrant and assembly. Blessings and dismissal may conclude the celebration. Such a ritual would be repeatable, and faithful could be encouraged to celebrate it as they felt so moved at different stages of life's journey.

Gerald Austin, *The Rite of Confirmation: A-nointing with the Spirit* (New York: Pueblo Publishing Company, 1985). *The Book of Common Prayer* (New York: Church Hymnal Corporation, 1979). Aidan Kavanagh, *Confirmation: Origins and Reform* (New York: Pueblo Publishing Company, 1988). *Lutheran Book of Worship* (Minneapolis: Augsburg Publishing House, 1978). Daniel B. Stevick, *Baptismal Moments; Baptismal Meanings* (New York: The Church Hymnal Corporation, 1987). Paul Turner, *The Meaning and Practice of Confirmation: Perspectives from a Sixteenth-Century Controversy* (Bern: Peter Lang, 1987).

PAUL TURNER

ADVENT

The season of preparation for Christmas, known also in some Eastern churches as the season of Announcement. The Prayer of this season "looks forward" in relation to the triple coming of the Lord: in history, in grace, at the end of time. Its tone is of anticipation, expectation, yearning.

See **Christmas season**

AESTHETICS, LITURGICAL

The term "aesthetics" derives from a Greek root meaning "of or pertaining to things perceptible by the senses, things material (as opposed to things thinkable or immaterial)" (O.E.D.). Since the 18th century the term has come to designate the theory and interpretation of the beautiful in art and in nature. Liturgical aesthetics comprehends both the modern and classical ranges of meaning of the term. Thus the scope of this article includes the concept of beauty in relation to prayer and ritual as well as reflection on the sensible signs and various "languages" of worship such as time, space, sound and silence, movement and gesture, sacramental sign-acts, and the artistic environment.

Relations between beauty, the human senses and the worship of God are both obvious and difficult to trace in their complexity. Liturgical worship requires corporately shared forms into which a community of faith enters, and through which it is formed in and gives expression to adoration, praise, thanksgiving, and petition. Because liturgy is more than texts and rubrics governing the correct performance of ritual acts, the "poetics of liturgical celebration" is of primary importance. The study of literary qualities of texts is only one strand in such a poetics. Since the mystery of God's self-communication in word and sacrament is always in and through specific forms, the poetics of liturgical celebration constitute a simultaneously theological and anthropological inquiry. Poetics as the study of how living discourse utilizes the powers of language is here applied to the broad range of liturgical utterance and to the arts of ritual enactment.

Liturgy possesses great formative and expressive power over human imagination, thought, emotion and will. Speaking theologically, we may say that, over time, Christian liturgy forms persons in the paschal mystery which it signifies, and at the same time brings to communal expression the lived experience of the gospel. From a phenomenological or anthropological point of view, liturgy may be said to form human persons (and communities) in specific symbol systems and fundamental ways of being in the world. At the same time, liturgical rites become the means of expressing primary identity and passional self-understanding. Both the formative and expressive dimensions of liturgy require structure and particular elements—words, actions, symbols, music and related art forms. But what gives such elements and the structure of the rites life is style—a particular way of celebrating the rites. As Aidan Kavanagh has observed, " . . . the artful symbolism which is the liturgy is never secured in the abstract or in general. It is accomplished in specific acts done by people in certain places at given times" ("The Politics of Symbol and Art in Liturgical Expression," in Maldonado and Power, 39). Liturgical aesthetics investigates what is signified and experienced and how it is so signified and experienced in actual worshipping assemblies.

If Christian liturgy is understood as a complex of communal sign-actions and texts brought together in symbolic patterns about the scriptures, the font and the table, then liturgical aesthetics studies the perceptual elements and the art of ritual enactment which render these human activities alive with significant form. If Christian liturgy is understood as an epiphany of the mystery of the divine self-communication, then liturgical aesthetics must address the question of how the style of celebration opens access to understanding and participation in that which theology cannot explain but can only comprehend in wonder and adoration. Both conceptions of liturgy and both methodologies are necessary.

Liturgy and Aesthetics: Historical Ambiguities

The matrix of artistic creativity for pre-Reformation cultural life in the West was the Christian liturgy. Liturgical art was, to a great extent, the fountainhead of popular art, and the cultural imagination was permeated with biblical stories and liturgical images. Such an historical period furnishes ample evidence of the power of liturgy to shape and to receive cultural modes of perception. By contrast, the prophetic side of Christianity has from the beginning been suspicious of human imagination, voicing objection to the disassociation of the aesthetic from the ethical or the holy. The words of Amos echo in other historical periods: "Take away from me the noise of your song; to the melody of your harps I will not listen. But let justice roll down like waters, and righteousness like an ever-flowing stream" (Amos 5:23-24). Furthermore, the iconoclastic impulse to resist the uses of art emerges in the name of holiness to guard against idolatrous confusion of images with the divine reality they are to represent or express.

At the outset Christianity had considerable reservations about the arts and a relatively unadorned liturgy. The immoralities of songs in the context of pagan rites provided good reason for such suspicion. The pattern of life which was associated with music and the other arts of the theatre was cause of great concern to the church. There was an asceticism in the earliest monastic movements which regarded the ease and even the sensuality of the post-persecution church as apostate. While the prophetic biblical traditions feared idolatry, the use of music, for example, seemed at home in the chanting of psalms. But the traditions springing from the philosophy of Plato also influenced the early church. Aware of the enormous emotional power of music, poetry and dance upon the human psyche, such traditions regarded artistic endeavor as traffic with the ambiguities of sensuality. The strictures against flute-playing in Plato's *Republic* emerged in the Christian assembly's initial resistance to the use of instruments in worship. The mistrust of matter and images itself led to a chaste role of iconography in the early buildings. Gradually, especially in the East, the idea of the icon as an image which mediates but does not contain the sacred, emerged.

The theological and philosophical suspicions of art and of the aesthetic power of liturgy surfaced virulently again with some of the Reformers of the 16th century. The systematic destruction of images and religious art in places such as Zürich in 1524 at the hands of the Zwinglian town council testify to the fear of external rites, material form and visible symbols. The suppression of all music in the liturgy seems even more extreme, especially at the hands of such an accomplished musician as Ulrich Zwingli. Yet such a reduction of the aesthetic dimension of Christian worship among the Reformers resulted from an enormous drive to purify and to spiritualize worship forms in a period when the aesthetic and symbolic profusion of the Roman rites seemingly overwhelmed the central mystery of God's gracious acts and the primary symbols of faith. The 16th century simplifications were partly a result of a new stress on scripture as a primary source for liturgical norms arising in that period; but they also depended upon an opposition between reason and emotion, alongside a dualism of spirit and the physically sensate. Luther was not such a liturgical purist. In fact, as the liturgical iconoclasm of the Reformation grew more extreme, he spoke, even while defending simplification of the rites, of his eagerness to "see all the arts, especially music, in the service of him who gave and created them." The liturgical aesthetics of the three magisterial Reformers—Luther, Calvin and Zwingli—show a remarkable range of differences among themselves respecting the material forms which worship employs. None of them refers substantially to the earlier traditions which struggled with these same tensions, namely those of the early patristic figures, most especially St. Augustine.

It was St. Augustine who asserted that, despite human sin and limitation, divine providence could yet work through the human experience of beautiful things to illuminate the ground of all human perception and understanding in God. For Augustine the recognition of truth and beauty in and through the created order (the physical and the sensual) revealed a divine lure turning human beings away from desires linked with sensuality and mortality to love of God. Before him, Basil, in his treatise *On the Holy Spirit* had argued that honor given an image would move on to its origination in God. In contrast to the early theological suspicion of the arts and to the more extreme Reformation, there has been an alternative tradition from Augustine to Aquinas, rediscovered in later historical and cultural periods—as with the 19th century Oxford Movement and neo-Thomist revivals associated with J. Maritain and E. Gilson—which regarded aesthetic activity and its liturgical bearing as defined in light of the relation of God to all human perception and to the goodness of the created order itself.

The history of styles of celebration and the "ceremonial" employed in liturgical rites has shown wide extremes in the history of the church, especially in the West. This fact shows that the aesthetic dimensions of Christian worship are ingredient in any change, whether of complex elaboration over time, or of dramatic reform and simplification. The last third of the 20th century is witnessing one of the most extraordinarily complex periods of reform and renewal in the history of the Western churches. The emergence of liturgical aesthetics as a discipline is partly a necessary outcome of these developments.

Liturgy as Art: Symbolic Form and Mystery

Any consideration of liturgical aesthetics must begin with the acknowledgement of this ambiguity in the long history of Christian faith and artistic expression. Still there remains the fact that liturgy itself employs cultural forms in imaginatively powerful ways. Liturgical action does not simply use art, it IS art—dialogue with God in symbolic form. To speak of liturgical aesthetics, then, is to refer to that which is ingredient in the enactment of the rites, both sacramental and non-sacramental. There is an intrinsically aesthetic character to all liturgical celebration and environment. This fact is at the heart of what liturgy is, according to the *Constitution on the Sacred Liturgy* of the Second Vatican Council. The liturgical assembly is the articulation and expression of the saving mystery of God in Christ, and of the nature of the church. The symbolic action of the liturgy is also an experience and manifestation of the church and a participation in the mystery of the triune life of God which animates the world. Such manifestation and participation is always in and through specific cultural forms: language, symbol, ritual sign-acts, music, gesture, visual and tactile environments.

Explorations in the domain of liturgical aesthetics, therefore, seek to interpret and to understand the various relations between beauty and holiness in particular liturgical contexts. Bearing in mind the ambiguities of the human imagination per se and the possibilities of mistaking the symbol for the reality symbolized, liturgical aesthetics proceeds on the assumption that there is an ultimate connection between beauty and the reality of God. Liturgical aesthetics is based on the fact that liturgy is a complex art form and that right praise and thanksgiving to God require the engagement of the full range of human emotion, intellect and will. Liturgical worship employs corporately shared forms which invite and engender a fully human participation, neither exclusively cognitive (mental) nor exclusively emotive or volitional.

The symbolic value and the beauty of the various elements of the liturgy derive from the material and form of each, while the sacredness or holiness derives from the mystery of the events celebrated "in, with, and through" Jesus Christ. These principles are based on the claim that God has created all things and called them good and has become incarnate in Jesus Christ, gathering an historical human community—always culturally embedded and embodied—for worship and service in the world. Liturgical aesthetics is thus rooted and grounded in the doctrines of creation and incarnation. All things are rendered holy by virtue of creation and the redemptive action of God, and are to be so regarded and brought to expression in communal worship of God. Liturgical worship respects the difference between creature and Creator, employing the things of earth to signify the glory and mercy and justice of God. This calls for a fundamental religious sensibility oriented to splendor and to appropriate sobriety and awe in the use of language, symbol, gesture, and the various languages of the rites.

Yet there is also a permanent tension involved in the use of material objects, the domain of the senses, and the imaginative powers of human art. This is because human beings are not in full harmony with the created order, nor is any human community or culture congruent with a fully transformed world. Our liturgies remain "east of Eden" and captive to the limits of human cultural perception as well. In short, Christian communities remain sinful and culturally bound. This means that whatever significant form is realized in liturgical celebration conveying the self-giving of God, we still "see through a glass darkly."

Hence liturgical aesthetics must always point to an eschatological self-critique of the use of forms. This permanent tension in liturgy as art is but a reflection of the situation of faith—we live in a good but fallen creation, between the initiation of redemptive history and its consummation. Any given liturgical aesthetic belonging to a particular time and culture requires a counterpoint in a religious sensibility oriented to that which transcends culture, to that "which eye has not seen, nor ear heard," which God has prepared for the children of earth.

The eschatological reservation concerning the cultural embeddedness of all aesthetic dimensions of Christian liturgy will be made more explicit at the end of this essay. To a discussion of various languages and the aesthetic dimension of all liturgical rites enacted we now turn.

Time and Space

From the beginning, Christian liturgical celebrations involved the use of cultural modes of communication, language itself being a primary instance. The words and texts employed in the liturgy operate within a complex of non-verbal phenomena. The sense and force of the words employed in worship depend radically for their range and depth upon the non-verbal features of the rites and how they are enacted. The meaning of a sung text, for example, has a greater aesthetic range than the same text recited. The same text or ritual gesture—or their combination—has a different connotative range in different seasons or feasts during the church year.

Among the primary non-verbal languages which constitute the poetics of liturgical celebration is time. Because liturgical rites are temporal, unfolding the juxtaposition of text, symbols, and ritual acts over time, participation is itself a temporal art. Within the duration of a single liturgical rite, for example, a eucharistic celebration, the meaning of the texts and the symbols are cumulative

and dramatic rather than self-contained. Each text or gesture or liturgical sub-unit may possess its own determinate sense, but the significance and the broader radiations of meaning can only be discerned in light of the whole pattern. Worship may be impoverished, of course, by lack of coherence or structural dislocation, illustrated by the proliferation of sequences in the Renaissance period. Thus the poetry of an entrance hymn or a festival Gloria may be fully grasped only after its connection with the praise and thanksgiving of the eucharistic prayer is sounded. The remarkable complexity and aesthetic power of images in the Exsultet at the Easter vigil does not fully unfold until the temporal process of reading and hearing the whole sequence of readings is completed and the baptismal covenant is sounded. Liturgy is a temporal art and is, in this sense, properly analogous to music, to drama and to dance. This is why liturgical participation requires a sense of the "dance" and the "drama" of the rites, even when these art forms do not appear explicitly. The temporal art of liturgical celebration is in this respect intrinsically musical and dramatic.

The language of time also works in the accumulative associative power of specific elements within a rite. Thus, the aesthetic range and significance of eating and drinking together takes time. In everyday life we come to understand the multiple levels of meaning of such acts only after we have had meals together on birthdays, after funerals, on anniversaries and through the changing seasons of human lives in a wide range of ordinary circumstances. Symbols deepen as human beings mature with them. The source of the inexhaustibility of primary symbols is located here. At the level of texts the same is true. The same antiphon or full responsorial psalm, when used in different seasons of the year, yields a different range of potential value and force in texts (hymns, psalms, prayers and lections).

The language of time also involves discipline in the cycles of the week, the day and the year. The aesthetic depth of liturgical participation is related to the experience of feasts and seasons. The liturgical year is a treasury of the church's memories of who God is and what God has done. The temporal cycles of day, week and year intersect with the sanctoral cycle of holy men and women to form a powerful hermeneutical pattern.

A second non-verbal language is that of space. Because the liturgical assembly occupies a place and arranges the furnishings in that space, a pattern of acoustic, visual and kinetic perception is set up. The places form environments which house the action of the liturgy. Each space and its interior arrangement may be said to possess specific aesthetic properties, encouraging specific kinds of actions and discouraging others. Some spaces invite a static and sedentary approach to God, in fixed auditoria for example. Others invite freedom of encounter and movement, or uncluttered contemplation. The visual focus of the room has a profound effect upon the poetics of textual images and the function of vestments, vessels, gestures and the uses of light within the liturgy.

There is also the history of the use of the building and the interior spaces which influences the tone and style of the liturgical celebration. So in a space where families have gathered for generations, where weddings, funerals and rites of passage have taken place, where the very sound of sung prayer has given association to the action itself, the aesthetic values of the space may dominate or even conflict with the actual style of celebration. At the same time, how we arrange furnishings—altar, ambo, font, musical instruments, presider's chair, the paschal candle—bears strongly upon what can potentially be brought to expression within the assembly.

Sound and Sight

Within the temporal-spatial setting the acoustic and the visual domains come into play. The art forms of music, whether congregrational, choral or instrumental, depend in larger measure on the properties of the building and the arrangements of the space. The relationship of sound and silence is crucial to music; but it is also part of the intrinsic music of the rites themselves. So all liturgical utterance has pitch, rhythm, intensity and pacing. The silences between words spoken and sung are as important as the sounds themselves, for together they create the primary acoustical images of praise and prayer. Analogously, the pace, intensity, rhythm and tone of ritual actions are part of the hidden music of the rites enacted.

The aesthetics of sound and sight are not ornamental to liturgy, but are intrinsic to the very nature of liturgical celebration. Thus music is not to be conceived primarily as something "inserted" into the rites. Rather, the explicit music should seek to bring to expression the implicit music of the rites. The implicit music is at one and the same time related to the juxtaposition of texts, ritual acts and symbols, and to the specific rites in their context. The actual acoustical experience of prayer or of preaching may carry more force than the semantic context of the actual words. Thus fully articulate musical liturgy is more festive and generates a greater range in levels of participation. At the same time, the style and quality of music must be judged appropriate to the nature of the rites and the nature of the assembly.

Following the Vatican II, the United States Bishops' Committee on the Liturgy published documents pertaining to the aesthetic dimensions of Christian liturgy. *Music in Catholic Worship* (1972, 1983) and *Liturgical Music Today* (1982) present complementary sets of guidelines concerning music in the liturgy and provide a theological groundwork for integrity in liturgical music. The earlier document deals with the role of music, both instrumental and choral/vocal in various rites, while the latter proposes criteria for planning and conducting liturgical celebrations.

The whole liturgical environment is to be served by the arts—this is the primary concern of a third document, *Environment and Art in Catholic Worship* (1978; English/Spanish edition, 1986). Particular emphasis is placed upon the liturgical assembly as a servant to God's created world, and its calling to be "sign, witness, and instrument of the reign of God" (par. 38). Precisely because the assembly seeks to remember and to cultivate the redemptive power of God, it must nurture a climate of wonder, awe, reverence, thanksgiving and praise. Therefore liturgy must seek what is beautiful in its total ethos as well as in the specific objects, gestures, sign-actions, music and related art forms employed.

In these documents the acoustic, visual and kinetic dimensions of liturgical celebration are integral to one another. The confluence of these arts in liturgy enables the assembly to discern the presence of God in the whole of the symbolic action. The materials and the form are to reflect the beauty and dignity of the rites they intend to serve. Special focus is devoted to the climate of hospitality, the experience of mystery, the reality and the efficacy of the range of symbols through word, gesture, and movement. A paragraph in E.A.C.W. concerning the concept of the beautiful in Christian liturgy is especially noteworthy: "Because the assembly gathers in the presence of God to celebrate his saving deeds, liturgy's climate is one of awe, mystery, wonder, reverence, thanksgiving and praise. So it cannot be satisfied with anything less than the beautiful in its environment and all its artifacts, movements, and appeals to the senses ... the beautiful is related to the sense of the numinous, the holy. Where there is evidently no care for this, there is an environment basically un-friendly to mystery and awe, an environment too casual, if not careless, for the liturgical action. In a world dominated by science and technology, liturgy's quest for the beautiful is a particularly necessary contribution to full and balanced human life" (par. 34).

Liturgical Aesthetics and Human Emotion

The relation between liturgy and human emotion is complex, but it is evident that Christian worship forms and expresses particular patterns of emotional dispositions in human beings. Music, poetry, dance, symbolic action—all these have to do with the affective capacities in human life. Liturgy may be regarded as a time and place where the language, sign-action and symbols concerning the divine shape and express human persons in such deep emotions as gratitude to God, hope, repentance, grief, compassion, aversion to injustice and delight in the created order. The Christian life itself is characterized by the having of such emotions and their having become wellsprings of attitude and action in life. The language of scripture, prayer and the sacraments has to do with elemental features of human existence: emotions linked to birth and death, suffering, sin, and oppression as well as with desire, joy, hope and happiness. These deep emotions are not simply named or described in the language of liturgy, they are evoked, portrayed, sustained and refined in the rites.

Coming to have and to exercise gratitude to God, holy fear, repentance and amendment of life depend upon sharing deeply in the mystery of prayer and ritual action as in the shared meal of the eucharist. The language of the liturgy in descriptive, ascriptive and performative force shapes us in particular affectional ways of being by addressing God and being open to God. So eucharistic participation points toward a life of gratitude and self-giving. The very four-fold action of taking the bread and cup, blessing God over them, breaking the bread, and giving the gifts presents the pattern which the eucharistic community is to live out in daily life.

To learn gratitude to God or awe or love of God and neighbor one must learn to pray with the church. The graciousness, the holiness and the love of God create the possibility of authentic worship. But the experiential power and range of liturgy is required in turn for the deepening of such dispositions. The integrity of the art of common prayer and ritual action requires that such gratitude, awe and love is not confined to the liturgical event itself. That is, these religious affections are not simply aesthetically held states of feeling. Yet without the aesthetic dimension of participation in and through the forms, no sacramental self-understanding in life can emerge. As *Environment and Art* rightly observes: "In view of our culture's emphasis on reason, it is critically important for the Church to reemphasize a more total approach to the human person by opening up and developing the non-rational elements of liturgical celebration: the concerns for feelings of conversion, support, joy, repentance, trust, love, memory, movement, gesture, wonder" (par. 35).

Christian liturgy which seeks emotional and symbolic authenticity and depth must always pay attention to the material and the forms employed. Language which is only clear or cognitively precise with no overplus of poetic meaning will diminish the power of the symbols to hold together multiple levels of meaning. If the ritual actions are perfunctory or merely efficient, the texts and symbols will be diminished. If the music is always immediately accessible and without surprise or tension or durability, the texts wedded to such music suffer reduction in imaginative power and metaphoric range. The quality of texts, gestures, movements,

and the form of the symbols is critical to levels of participation. Attention to each element and to their interrelation in the whole pattern of the liturgy is necessary to the power of liturgy to draw us, as church, into the gospel proclaimed and the saving mystery enacted. This is what leads Joseph Gelineau to say, "Only if we come to the liturgy without hopes or fears, without longings or hunger, will the rite symbolize nothing and remain an indifferent or curious 'object.' Moreover, people who are not accustomed to poetic, artistic, or musical language or symbolic acts among their means of expression and communication find the liturgy like a foreign country whose customs and language are strange to them" (98-99).

Liturgical Style and Culture

The question of style is not a matter of mere technique. If it were so we could produce awe-inspiring liturgical rites by manipulating lighting and symbols. But the aesthetic dynamism of authentic liturgical celebration is the opposite of manipulation and magic; it is the opening of the mystery of the realities signified, proclaimed, and ritually participated in. This "opening" is a matter of faithfulness and attentiveness to the whole environment of worship. Each unit or element of the liturgical assembly, and each "subrite," invites a particular quality of disposition which is appropriate to the nature of the rite and its context. This goes together with honesty and integrity of materials and the aesthetic adequacy of the forms. Both the leaders and the assembly as a whole share mutual responsibilities for the art of the liturgy. The presider and other specific ministers become focal points and representations of the prayerful participation of the assembly. Activities of gathering, singing, praying, reading, listening, bowing, touching, eating and drinking all require a heightened sense of receptivity and active participation as a community of mutuality. The cultural variables here are many, since different cultures exhibit differences in behavior in the course of such activities.

The church's teaching and catechetical approach to preparing the worshippers—both long term and immediately in the room of celebration—cannot neglect the aesthetic dimensions of specific cultures. The study of liturgical forms and teaching the primary symbols of faith must create a hospitable environment. Assisting the worshippers to participate fully in the musical forms, for example, requires sensitivity to the range of musical styles available to the people. Giving the assembly a model of good "performance practice" in responsorial psalmody, the hymns or sung responses can open up new dimensions of the cultural heritage. The problems of musical participation raise all the issues of liturgical participation. Creating appropriate spaces of silence for reflection on the readings and in relation to the sign-acts and symbols is part of the non-manipulative art of the liturgy.

The poetics of celebration requires examination of the specific cultural context of the assembly. In our post-conciliar period, new emphasis is being placed on the modes of expression indigenous to the social/cultural history of the people. If the liturgy is to signify the divine/human interaction, then modes of appropriating and sharing the basic symbols must be mediated in and through the language, music, visual, and bodily style of the people. The aesthetics of liturgy thus demands that we know the differences between, for example, patterns proper to a North-American cultural tradition formed principally in Northern Europe and patterns that are Afro-American or Hispanic.

At the same time, the symbolic action points to realities which are in tension with all inherited cultural assumptions and patterns of behavior. The permanent tension in the poetics of liturgy is between the necessity of local cultural modes of perception (expression and interpretation) and the common culture of Christian faith and life. Only by maintaining this tension can we also assert specifically Christian faith and life over against the assumptions of much post-modern and technological culture. Though each sub-culture has its own integrity, there is a manner of celebration which is Christian, stemming from the particular claims of the paschal mystery. There is a way of enacting the rites which is ultimately the human reception of what God has done in creation and in Jesus Christ. This has been referred to by Gelineau and others as the "paschal human in Christ"—a manner enacted in particular cultural languages which evidences "both reserve and openness, respect and simplicity, confident joy ... and true spontaneity...." (113).

Afterword

Liturgy belongs to the created world and thus is an art, for the created order belongs to God. The aesthetics of authentic liturgy concerns the intrinsic means, not simply the external decoration, or the rites themselves. Without such aesthetic considerations such as honesty of materials, quality of craft and performance, appropriateness, proportionality and integrity within the liturgy of the art forms and the people, the whole of the liturgy is diminished in its symbolic power.

Yet, lest we take delight only in the beautiful forms we have managed, and not discern the enabling grace of God in and through the forms, the final word must be eschatological. All artistic effort is itself proleptic as well as participatory in God's creativity. The mystery celebrated is never exhausted nor fully contained in the liturgy. Liturgical rites authentically celebrated point beyond themselves to the eschatological vision and the "heavenly liturgy" of Christ of which all earthly celebrations are but hints and guesses. This way all attention to the aesthetics of Christian liturgy is but a servant of the vision of a created order transformed and reconciled to the life of God. There all that is creaturely will be permeated with light, dance and song. Insofar as we experience the prefigurement of that reality in particular times and places, the aesthetics of liturgical celebration become congruent with the holiness and the beauty of the triune life of God, at once incarnate in the world and yet transcendent in glory beyond all created things.

See **Art, liturgical; Architecture, liturgical; Music, liturgical; Imagination and worship; Doxology; Holy Spirit in Christian worship; Liturgical time, theology of; Gesture and movement in the liturgy; Dance, liturgical; Vestments, liturgical; Vessels, sacred**

Art and Environment in Catholic Worship, English/Spanish edition (Washington, D.C.: United States Catholic Conference, 1986). Hans Urs Von Balthasar, *The Glory of the Lord: A Theological Aesthetics, Vol. I: Seeing the Form*, trans. by Erasmo Leiva-Merikakis—ed. by Joseph Fessio, S.J., and John Riches (New York: Crossroad Publications and San Francisco: Ignatius Press, 1982). Balthasar Fischer, *Signs, Words and Gestures*, trans. by Matthew J. O'Connell (New York: Pueblo Publishing Co., 1981). Joseph Gelineau, *The Liturgy Today and Tomorrow* (New York: Paulist Press, 1978). Lawrence A. Hoffman, *The Art of Public Prayer* (Washington, D.C.: The Pastoral Press, 1988). Robert Hovda, *Strong, Loving and Wise* (Washington, D.C.: The Liturgical Conference, 1977). *Liturgical Music Today* (Washington, D.C.: United States Catholic Conference, 1982). Luis Maldonado, and David Power, eds. *Symbol and Art in Worship*, Concilium: Religion in the Eighties, No. 132 (New York: The Seabury Press, 1980). *Music in Catholic Worship*. Rev. ed. (Washington, D.C.: United States Catholic Conference, 1983). David N. Power, *Unsearchable Riches: The Symbolic Nature of Liturgy* (New York: Pueblo Press, 1984). Don E. Saliers, *The Soul in Paraphrase: Prayer and the Religious Affections* (New York: Seabury Press, 1980). Geoffrey Wainwright, *Doxology: The Praise of God in Worship, Doctrine and Life* (London: Epworth, and New York: Oxford University Press, 1980). Gerardus Van der Leeuw, *Sacred and Profane Beauty: The Holy in Art*. trans. David E. Green (New York: Holt, Rinehart and Winston, 1963).

DON E. SALIERS

AGAPE

The love feast was shared by the early Christians as a common fellowship meal. Sacred meals were common features of pagan and Jewish cults in antiquity. Regulations for a communal meal are found in the *Manual of Discipline* of the Qumran community by the Dead Sea. Gregory Dix argued that the meals shared by Jesus and his disciples were typical of the *chaburoth*, the formal fellowship meals shared by pious Jews. This need not stand in opposition to the last supper also being a Passover meal. Such a *chaburah* could also share the Passover meal.

The early Christians continued to have meal fellowship. A distinction between the *agape* and the Lord's Supper is not easy to make because the Lord's Supper was also celebrated in the context of a communal meal (see 1 Cor 11:17-34). J.-P. Audet has contended that *Didache* 9-10 describes an agape meal while ch. 14 refers to the eucharist. This view must contend against the fact that the text in ch. 9 is headed with the description, "Now concerning the Eucharist," and that if the prayers in chs. 9-10 are not for the eucharist, there is no detailed description of this central Christian rite in a manual which otherwise includes all areas of church life. It is possible that a distinction between the *agape* and the sacrament cannot be made, and that ch. 14 concerns church discipline more than the eucharist.

Acts mentions "the breaking of bread" as a distinctive Christian activity. Jude makes the only clear use of the term *agape* with reference to a meal in the NT (v. 12).

With the loss of the Jewish *chaburoth* background, communal meals in the predominantly Gentile churches took on the less restrained characteristics of pagan banquets. Paul's admonitions in 1 Corinthians indicate that such abuses were already taking place, and that the table fellowship was marred by drunkenness and gluttony as well as the class distinctions which undermined the Lord's Supper as a sacrament of unity. Nevertheless, it is not likely that this kind of situation alone caused the separation of the Lord's Supper from the communal meal. An imperial ban on evening meetings of clubs and associations might have caused Christians to meet in the morning for the eucharist. Later, when evening meetings could be resumed the sacrament continued to be celebrated in the morning and a community meal was held in the evening. This might be indicated in the letter of the Roman governor Pliny the Younger to the Emperor Trajan (A.D. 111-12), although Pliny's scanty comments are subject to various interpretations. Nevertheless, Justin Martyr, in *Apology* I, 67 (ca. A.D. 150), reports a unified service of the word and eucharistic meal on Sunday mornings. This meal makes use only of the eucharistized bread and wine mixed with water.

The *Apostolic Tradition* of Hippolytus (ca. A.D. 215) makes a clear distinction between the eucharist and the agape meal, or love feast, although the unbaptized are excluded from both. The agape was celebrated in private homes with the clergy invited. The guests could eat their full, but leftovers were given by the host to other members of the church. It is possible that the agape was merged with the funeral meal, which was also an occasion for feeding the poor. The possibility of abuse, combined with a more formal approach to church life, led to conciliar decrees from the 4th century on discouraging these meals. The agape died out in the West first and lingered on in the East, but by the 8th century it was virtually defunct. One example of survival of the agape was among the Mar-Thomas Christians in southern India.

In the 16th century there were efforts among radical groups such as the Mennonites, Dunkers, and Moravian Brethren, to revive the NT agape, along with the kiss of peace and the washing of feet. It flourished in the 18th century in Germany and The Netherlands and was brought to North America by more zealous members of these groups. John Wesley encountered the agape among the Moravians in Georgia and at Herrnhut, and in 1738 brought it to Britain. It was celebrated as the climax of the Methodist band (later class) meetings. These agapes were held monthly at first, later quarterly, and finally annually. Methodists brought the agape to America, where it became a substitute for the Lord's Supper since it could be led by deacons in the absence of ordained elders. The ordination of additional preachers in the early 19th century did nothing to reverse this practice because the agape had become popular and the unchurched could be included in it. The love feast died throughout world Methodism in the latter 19th century as the Methodist societies became more conscious of themselves as a church.

There has been something of a revival of the agape meal in the 20th century in the form of parish fellowship meals. A more intentional revival has occurred in ecumenical circles as a way of providing table fellowship along Christians who cannot celebrate the eucharist together. It has been included as the last meal of courses at the Ecumenical Institute at the Château de Bossey, Switzerland, and as a way of expressing unity between Roman Catholics and Protestants in The Netherlands.

J.-P. Audet, *La Didachè. Instruction des Apôtres* (Paris: Cerf, 1958). Frank Baker, *Methodism and the Love-Feast* (London: Epworth, 1957). Gregory Dix, *The Shape of the Liturgy* (Westminster: Dacre Press, 1945). Arthur Vööbus, *Liturgical Material in the Didache* (Stockholm: Estonian Theological Society in Exile, 1968).

FRANK C. SENN

ALL SAINTS, FEAST OF

The Solemnity of All Saints, a celebration of the unity of the church across time, is celebrated on Nov. 1.

History

This feast, originally a celebration of all the nameless martyrs of the persecutions, arose first in the East, where it was celebrated on May 13, or on the Sunday after Pentecost (Antioch), or the Friday after Easter (East Syria), or in the fall (Armenia and among the Copts).

In Rome, the day was first celebrated under Boniface IV in 609 on May 13, when the Pantheon became a Christian church honoring Mary and all martyrs.

Under Gregory III (731-741), a chapel in honor of the Savior, Mary, the apostles, martyrs and confessors was opened in St. Peter's Basilica. It seems that the chapel may have been dedicated on Nov. 1. This late and feast spread throughout the West, at first particularly in England, and then the northern countries. The east had a vigil from the beginning, and in the Middle Ages an octave was added. Both were abolished in the 1955 simplification of the rubrics.

Theology of the Celebration

The eucharistic liturgy for the feast is a celebration of sanctity and holiness in the church. This manifests itself in a variety of ways.

It is *joy-filled* (entrance antiphon, preface, prayer after communion). The people who live the lives of saints are *happy, blessed*, bearing the characteristics of the Beatitudes (gospel, Mt 5:1-2).

Holiness entails *forgiveness and love* (opening prayer, prayer over the gifts).

This holiness is rooted in the fact that each person is *created* by God and thus becomes *a manifestation of God's love and saving plan*. We are *God's children*, and will one day live in the light (alternative opening prayer, prayer after communion, second reading: 1 Jn 3:1-3).

To arrive at this life of holiness is a *journey of pilgrimage*. We are nourished by the eucharistic bread and sustained by those who have gone before us and even now accompany us on our journey (preface, prayer after communion [the pilgrimage motif does not get translated into English]).

The goal of this journey is the new and eternal *Jerusalem*. Jerusalem is the site of God's throne and where the hosts of God's court sing songs of endless praise. It is the place where all God's people are in communion with one another (preface, prayer after communion).

The liturgy of the hours presents three themes. The first is the idea, found also in the eucharist, of the *fundamental unity of heaven and earth*, of those in heaven and those yearning for heaven while still on earth. The basis of that unity is Jesus Christ, the Lamb that was slain (Office of Readings: Rev 5:1-4; Bernard of Clairvaux). The second is that the heavenly *Jerusalem* is our goal. It is the place where God's children are gathered in praise and rejoicing (Evening Prayer I: Heb 12:22-24; Daytime Prayer: Isa 65:18-19; Rev 21:10-11a; 22, 3b-4). The third is that the church, God's *temple* made up of his faithful ones, is a holy place, and building towards holiness: towards likeness to God in Jesus Christ (Morning Prayer Eph 1:17-18; Daytime Prayer: 1 Pet 1:15-16; Evening Prayer II 2 Cor 6: 16b;7:1).

The solemnity of All Saints is both a look back at those who have gone before, as well as a commitment to what we must become: a holy people united together by a common life in God. It is a hope of our future glory in the new and eternal Jerusalem.

See **Calendar, liturgical**

A. Adam, *The Liturgical Year* (New York, 1981), pp. 228-230. A. Nocent, *The Liturgical Year* (Collegeville, 1977), Vol. 4:403f. A.G. Martimort, et al., *The Liturgy and Time*, The Church at Prayer IV (Collegeville, 1986), esp. pp. 114-117.

MICHAEL WITCZAK

ALL SOULS, FEAST OF

All Souls Day, the commemoration of the faithful departed, is celebrated on Nov. 2, and intimately connected with the Nov. 1 celebration of All Saints. It has the rank of a solemnity, but is not officially listed as such in the Roman Calendar. When it falls on Sunday, the Mass texts are from All Souls, and the texts for morning and evening prayer are taken from the Office for the Dead. The rest of the liturgy of the hours is taken from Sunday.

History

While the idea of remembering all the faithful departed seems to have arisen from the ordinary Christian customs surrounding death and burial, the first evidence for this celebration comes from Isidore of Seville (d. 636) whose monastic rule includes a liturgy for all the dead on the day after Pentecost. Various dates in various places were common till Odilo of Cluny in 998 prescribed a celebration on Nov. 2 for all Cluniac houses. The custom spread rapidly throughout northern Europe, but was only accepted in Rome in the 13th century.

The custom of celebrating three Masses began with the Dominicans of Valencia before 1500. The custom was extended to the whole of Spain, Portugal and Latin America in 1748 by Benedict XIV. The universal church was granted the privilege of three Masses on this day by Benedict XV in 1915, during the carnage of World War I.

Theology of the Celebration

The readings for the celebration of the eucharist can be chosen from among those for the Masses for the Dead (Lectionary nos. 789-793). For a fine commentary on each of these readings, see Fuller (cited below): "Since death holds us in bondage, we are in need of redemption, and this is what the gospel offers us in Jesus Christ. He, the new Adam, has broken through the gate of death and opened up the way to eternal life.... Only in Christ, the second Adam, will all not merely survive but be 'made alive'" (p. 594).

The prayers offer a variety of themes for reflection and praise. The primary datum of faith, the basis for all Christian prayer and reflection about death, is that through the death and resurrection of Jesus Christ, the hope is given to us that all who die in faith will share that life (virtually every prayer and preface in the set). The underlying basis for this understanding of Jesus and ourselves is God's creation of and ongoing care for his people (opening prayer III, solemn blessing, preface IV).

The prayers affirm the reality, power and sadness of death (prayer over the gifts and prayer after communion III, prefaces I, IV). That reality is a reminder that we are all in need of forgiveness and purification (prayer over the gifts and prayer after communion II, solemn blessing, prefaces III, IV). There is a conviction that death is not an end, but a moment of transition: "Lord, for your faithful people life is changed, not ended" (preface I). They entered this transition already at baptism (prayer over the gifts II, prayer after communion III).

The final goal is new life, eternal life, a life that is lived to God alone (most prayers). This life is characterized as a place of light and peace (prayer after communion I, prayer over the gifts II, prayer after communion III, solemn blessing), joy (opening prayer II, prayer after communion III, solemn blessing), glory in the presence of God (prayer over the gifts I, opening prayer II, prayer over the gifts II, opening prayer III).

For us who remain, these statements of faith are an expression of hope and a source of consolation (opening prayer I, solemn blessing).

The celebration of the liturgy of the hours is taken from the Office for the Dead. While not a common celebration in most parishes, its presence in the revised version of the *Rite of Christian Funerals* indicates that it may become more frequent. It too is a profound expression of the Christian hope in the resurrection.

The celebration of All Souls day is an opportunity to reflect on our own future and to celebrate those who have preceded us in death. It is a great profession of faith in the resurrection, not just as a reality for Jesus Christ, but as the promise of our own future glory.

See **Calendar, liturgical**

A.Adam, *The Liturgical Year* (New York, 1981), pp. 237-240. R. Fuller, *Preaching the Lectionary*, rev. ed. (Collegeville, 1984), pp. 593-617. D.K. Tripp, "The Spirituality of the Little Office of the B.V.M. and the Office for the Dead," *Worship* 63 (1989) 210-232, esp. 218-221.

MICHAEL WITCZAK

ALTAR

As usually understood in Christian liturgy, the altar is a table whereon the church ritually re-enacts the Last Supper (a paschal meal which pre-figured the crucifixion) as well as the post-Resurrection meals of Jesus with his disciples (e.g., on the shore of the Sea of Galilee or on the way to Emmaus). According to Josef Jungmann in *Pastoral Liturgy* the altar was in its origins a place to set the bread and wine, a merely necessary piece of functional furniture. It has been, however, given many archetypal significances over the centuries. Early in Christianity the altar's predecessors were, for instance, both the four-cornered ("horned") stone in the Temple in Jerusalem and the altar of symbolic sacrifice in the Greco-Roman theater. The altars for incense, immolation, and sacrifice all had Levitical prescriptions which played a part, often times, in later design decisions.

In the latter centuries of early Christendom the relationship of the members of the universal church suffering, militant, and triumphant, was symbolized by the presence of pieces of relics of dead Christians. After Helena of Constantinople, small pieces of the "true cross" were also incorporated. Eventually, the relics were made more aesthetically palatable; they were imbedded into the altar itself, in more recent centuries, in a small square "altar stone," whose blessed presence would "consecrate" the altar. The altar's shape began to reflect its reliquary function by appearing more sepulchral.

There are two seemingly contrary concepts about the symbolic meaning of the altar. On the one hand, it is a table for the ritual meal—a re-enactment of the paschal meal shared by Jesus and his disciples in the upper room of Holy Thursday. On the other hand, it is a stone of sacrifice whereon the "unbloody sacrifice" of the eucharist re-enacts the "bloody sacrifice" of Calvary. During the periods of imperial accoutrements, (e.g., under Constantine, Charlemagne, Otto) the altar also served as a symbolic throne for the imperial deity. The Carolingian intellectuals developed a special "showing" place for the host and the altar became a base for the monstrance.

Since Vatican II the reclamation, almost exclusively, of the meal imagery of the eucharistic liturgy has resulted in what is tantamount to a universal preference for the table archetype in the altar. This is timely, of course. But it is vital to remember with historical retrospect that the aberrations of the past are often countered by aberrations of equal vigor in the present. Although there is no need for an altar to make liturgy on some enlightened plane of objective reality, the need for a church building itself arises from more subtle human needs. Gerardus van der Leeuw, in *Sacred and Profane Beauty: the Holy in Art* tellingly judges that God needs no house, but humankind needs God to need a house—like our own. The archetype of altar, like the church building itself as its wide back-drop, represents for us the Christ re-presenting himself, making himself present among us, for us, with us, over and over again, whenever we are gathered in his name in this way. Mircea Eliade's *Illud Tempus* or Rudolph Otto's *mysterium tremendum* is here-and-now "present" after the fashion of Odo Casel.

It is because of all the different presences that he can have that we must not allow the altar to be reduced to the service of absolute dicta which are unfortunately bound up in one particular time. Christ eternal, Christ born and needy, Christ dead, buried, Christ suf-fering, Christ resurrected; the many faces of Christ must be allowed at the altar.

That having been said, we can look at the present understanding of what an altar is, what it represents, what its universal requirements are.

The altar is the focus of the sacramental presence of Christ. This piece of furniture is the place where the worshipping com-munity calls for the promised presence of Christ, high-priest of the mystical body, who offers himself to the Father for the total community united for this ritual meal by the Holy Spirit alive in the Bride. So many things are going on at this table, all focused in the ritual gifts. The bread and wine representing the people-gath-ered are brought *to* the altar. God is praised for the very gifts-which-we-are at the very moment that the gifts represen-ting us are placed *on* the altar. The prayers asking the grace of the Holy Spirit are said *over* those gifts and the narrative of consecration is told while the liturgical drama is fixed on a separate consecration, symbolizing, for those with eyes for it, in the separation of body and blood, the death of Christ, into which we all must step. Finally, the body and blood are raised to the Father, together, symbolizing further that the communion is in the rejoined species, the resurrected Christ is present within the mystical body. The gifts are then shared *among* the members.

Where is the altar for all of this oblation-immolation? It is merely the place-where. What does it represent? Naturally, it represents all of this drama of the eucharist. It is a very special place-where. The conflict about how to treat this holy object is easily polarized. At the height of the Middle Ages Bernard of Citeaux and the Abbot Suger of Abbey St. Denis couched the argument in terms of response to the immensity. Suger's approach to church furnishing was to realize that in our giftedness we must give the very best we have in thank-offering; his authority for such an opinion rests in the OT offering of the unblemished lamb, and the descriptions of the Davidic/ Solomonic temple. Bernard, on the other hand, suggests, for us priestly people a response of complete austerity, simple beauty, no extravagance, no extra windows, no decoration. This is an ages-old conflict, found even in the "J" and "P" traditions, interwoven, woof and warp, into the tapestry of the Temple-building descriptions, contrary motiva-tions blended to amicably describe the actualities of Hebrew history.

These conflicts are, of course, resolved in practice by the community. The fact is, however, that the altar has an important place in the church and its dignity must be accorded in such a way that it does not play second-fiddle to any other symbolic piece of furniture. The Vatican Council has emphasized, even more than did Trent, the significance of the single altar. [Before Trent, it will be remembered, there was an almost superstitious rever-ence for the altar which resulted in a multiplication of altars within the con-fines of one church building.] The single altar represents the place where Christ himself steps into time and space among us. It thus represents him, himself, and deserves utmost reverence even outside the liturgy.

For particular communities, the varieties of climate, wealth, pictorial sensitivity, national heritage, etc. all impinge on the kind of church that exists, breathes, lives. But the altar as the symbol of Christ's presence must be a focal point of worship. Should it be decorated, or stone, or moveable? These are appropriate questions for particular communities according to their particular needs.

However, should the altar seem anything less than the ambo or the presider's seat, or the tabernacle, or baptismal fountain? Here is the central variable: in what context must the central importance of this congregation's altar find itself? The answers found in various national bishops' conferences are essentially to accord the single altar in a church the esteem befitting God's presence in *this* place, at *this* time, according it material and placement and decoration appropriate to the specific worshipping community, in aesthetic relationship to the ambo, presidential seat, ecclesial accommodations, and the *domus*, house, itself.

See **Architecture, liturgical**

DENNIS McNALLY, S.J.

AMEN

A Hebrew word meaning "so be it" which, when appended to prayers or proclamations (e.g., "the body of Christ") marks the giving over of the person or the assembly to the truth of what is prayed or proclaimed. It is not simply "agreement," nor even simply a statement of belief. It is a word of personal and communal commitment and surrender.

See **Doxology; Prayer, types of, in the liturgy**

ANAMNESIS

This Greek word is practically untranslatable in English. "Memorial," "commemoration," "remembrance" all suggest a recollection of the past, whereas *anamnesis* means making present an object or person from the past. Sometimes the term "reactualization" has been used to indicate the force of anamnesis.

In Semitic thought memorial is a "recalling to God" of a past person or promise. J. Jeremias suggests that the words of Jesus, "Do this in remembrance of me" (1 Cor 11:26), mean that his disciples should pray " ... that God may remember me." The point of re-calling to God the sacrifice of Christ is that its benefits may be made present to the faithful here and now. In the eucharistic tradition the formal remembering before God of the sacrifical life and death of Christ is therefore connected with the offering of the bread and wine, through which the benefits of Christ's sacrifice will be received in holy communion.

A formal anamnesis came into the eucharistic prayer in connection with the institution narrative. In the Anaphora of Hippolytus the institution narrative is the climax of the thanksgiving for the wonders of God in salvation history. The words "Do this in remembrance of me" serve to introduce the anamnesis: "Remembering, therefore, his death and resurrection ..."; and the anamnesis, in turn, introduces the oblation. Eucharistic traditions which lack an institution text, such as the *Didache*, the *Acts of Thomas*, and the Mar Esaya text of the Anaphora of Addai and Mari, also lack a formal anamnesis. In the West Syrian anaphoras the anamnesis serves as a reprise of the thanksgiving in remembrance of God's saving work in Christ and introduces the supplicatory part of the prayer, including the oblation, epiclesis, and intercessions. Cesare Giraudo points to the transition in the Jewish *todah* tradition from remembrance to supplication by way of a succinct recall of what has been commemorated. He calls this a move from *memores* to *memento*, or from the faithfulness of the people in keeping the memorial that has been commanded by God to the prayer that God will remember his covenantal promises. While caution must be maintained in drawing comparisons between the Christian *eucharistia* and the Jewish *berakoth*, we may at least observe a similar pattern in this connection.

The Roman tradition places the institution narrative and anamnesis in the supplicatory section of the prayer (the post-Sanctus "Canon") rather than at the end of the thanksgiving in remembrance of Christ. In this tradition the institution text and anamnesis serve more as a warrant for the church's oblation than as a recapitulation of salvation history. It is noteworthy that the sacrificial aspect of the eucharist is more prominent in the Alexandrian and Roman traditions than in traditions which lack a formal anamnesis, such as the *Didache* and *Addai and Mari*. Because the words of institution acquired consecratory force in the Western church, associated with the transubstantiation of the elements, medieval theologians misunderstood the anamnesis-oblation to be an offering of the body and blood of Christ. While the text of the Roman Canon speaks only of the "holy and spotless" oblation in reference to the bread and wine, although they are called the "bread of life" and the "cup of salvation," Roman eucharistic prayer IV in the current Roman Sacramentary has, for the first time in the history of the eucharistic prayer, referred to the oblation as the body and blood of Christ. This can only exacerbate the controversy over the eucharistic sacrifice which has plagued Western Christianity since the 16th-century Reformation. A study of the ancient anamnesis formularies would show the polysemous nature of offering-language in the eucharistic prayers and bring to light images of redemption other than that of sacrifice.

See **Anaphora; Eucharistic prayers; Sacrifice**

Louis Bouyer, *Eucharist*, trans. by Charles U. Quinn (Notre Dame: University of Notre Dame Press, 1968). Cesare Giraudo, *La Struttura Letteraria della Preghiera Eucharistica* (Rome: Biblical Institute Press, 1981). Joachim Jeremias, *The Eucharistic Words of Jesus*, trans. by Norman Perrin (New York: Charles Scribner's Sons, 1966). Louis Ligier, "The Origins of the Eucharistic Prayer," *Studia Liturgica* 9 (1973), 161-85. David N. Power, "The Anamnesis: Remembering, We Offer," in Frank C. Senn, ed., *New Eucharistic Prayers* (New York and Mahwah: Paulist Press, 1987), pp. 146-68.

FRANK C. SENN

ANAPHORA

From the Greek *anaphero*, "I offer up." This is the standard Greek name for the eucharistic prayer; hence the Anaphora of Addai and Mari, the Anaphora of St. James, the Anaphora of St. Basil, the Anaphora of St. John Chrysostom, the Anaphora of St. Mark, etc. The name anaphora suggests the connection between the eucharist and sacrifice.

Didache 14 compares the Christian eucharist to the OT prophecy of the pure offering of the Gentiles in the messianic age (Mal 1: 11, 14). This OT allusion associates the eucharist with the concept of sacrifice, but also provides the safeguard against possible misunderstanding. The eucharistic sacrifice is not just an outward ritual performance, but an interior disposition, which is why a purifying act of confession precedes the celebration of the eucharist. The "pure offering" concept of the eucharist is expressed in the invitatory verse, *Sursum corda* ("Life up your hearts"); or alternately, "Lift up your mind" (*Apostolic Constitutions*, Book VIII) and "Lift up our minds and our hearts" (Anaphora of St. James).

The early Christian apologists were at pains to point out that they had no temples, no altars, no sacrifices. Minucius Felix wrote in the 2nd century, "How should I offer as sacrifice to God what he has given for my use, and return to him his own gifts? That would be ungrateful.

A genuine sacrifice, on the contrary, is a good soul, a pure mind ..." (*Letter to Octavius* 32). Where Christians employed the vocabulary of sacrifice it was applied to prayer and the grateful life. The martyred Apollonius declared before his judge at the end of the 2nd century, "A sacrifice bloodless and pure, I too and all the Christians bring to almighty God ..." (*Acta Apollonii* 8). The Letter of Barnabas 2:6 also points out that material gifts are not offered to God because sacrifice is spiritual and pertains to prayer. The Christian sacrifice is the prayer of thanksgiving (*eucharistia*).

It was not until the end of the 2nd century that the material gifts of bread and wine were also "offered." Irenaeus of Lyons gave prominence to the material gift-offerings in reaction to the exaggerated spiritualism of the Hellenistic gnosis. It is at the beginning of the 3rd century that we have the earliest evidence of the offertory procession of the faithful. The gift-offerings or oblations became the focus of the eucharistic prayer in the Anaphora of St. Hippolytus (*Apostolic Tradition*). The offering of the bread and cup occurs in conjunction with the remembrance (*anamnesis*) of the redemptive sacrifice of Christ. "Remembering therefore his death and resurrection, we offer to you the bread and the cup, giving you thanks because you have held us worthy to stand before you and minister to you." In this earliest anaphoral text (ca. A.D. 215) the polysemous character of the eucharistic sacrifice is articulated: it is the self-offering of Christians, the material offerings of the church, and the memorial of the redemptive sacrifice of Christ.

See **Anamnesis; Eucharistic prayers; Sacrifice**

Louis Bouyer, *Eucharist*, trans. by Charles U. Quinn (Notre Dame: University of Notre Dame Press, 1968). Walter H. Frere, *The Anaphora of Great Eucharistic Prayer* (London: S.P.C.K., 1938). Josef A. Jungmann, *The Mass: An Historical, Theological, and Pastoral Survey*, trans. by Julian Fernandes, ed. by Mary Ellen Evans (Collegeville: The Liturgical Press, 1976).

FRANK C. SENN

ANGELS, FEASTS OF

Certain apocryphal books, and the literature of some heterodox sects, reveal an exaggerated fascination with angelology. Orthodox Christianity, on the other hand, has always sought to keep the subject in perspective (Col 2:18). The Nicene Creed affirms that angels ("all that is ... unseen") were created by the one God, and are not themselves divine beings. The Roman Canon (Eucharistic Prayer I) affirms the belief that angels somehow assist our prayers and offerings to God (Rev 8:3-4), while the Prefaces, in introducing the Sanctus (Isa 6:3), explicitly join our earthly worship to the eternal praise rendered by the heavenly hosts: "May our voices blend with theirs as we join in their unending hymn...." This is because "In the earthly liturgy we take part in a foretaste of that heavenly liturgy which is celebrated in the Holy City of Jerusalem toward which we journey as pilgrims, where Christ is sitting at the right hand of God" (S.C., 8). The early 6th-century writings of Pseudo-Dionysius the Areopagite, the first Christian author to present a fully-developed angelology, describe all of Christian liturgy and sacraments as an imitation of the eternal worship that the angels render to God. "We imitate as much as we can their abiding, unwavering, and sacred constancy, and we thereby come to look up to the blessed and ultimately divine ray of Jesus himself" (*Ecclesiastical Hierarchy* 1:1).

The Bible repeatedly shows God communicating with humans by means of angels—indeed the Greek word (*ággelos*) and its Hebrew counterpart (*mal'ākh*) both mean "messenger." Thus the angel with the most important role in salvation history is Gabriel, who brought the message of the Annunciation to the Virgin Mary (Lk 1:26-38). In the East his feast is traditionally observed on March 26, the day after the Feast of the Annunciation. A feast of Gabriel on March 24, the day before, was introduced into the Roman rite in 1921. In the same year an October 24 feast was established for Raphael, a miraculous healer in the deutero-canonical book Tobit, who is venerated as a promoter of health and a patron of medicine. The Coptic and Ethiopian churches have long celebrated Raphael's feast on 3 Nesy, the Egyptian equivalent of August 26.

In general, however, Christians have had the greatest devotion to Michael, captain of the heavenly armies, who protects the true Israel against the forces of evil (Dan 10:21, Jude 9, Rev 12:7). A good example is the prayer "St. Michael the Archangel, defend us in battle," which was normally recited after low Mass from 1884 to 1965. Some feasts of Michael commemorate miracles or apparitions, such as September 6 in the Byzantine rite (the Miracles at Colossae) and May 8 in the Roman rite (the Apparition at Monte Gargano). The great French abbey Mont-St. Michel marks the site of another apparition. Other feasts are the anniversaries of the days particular churches were dedicated to him, including the Roman feast on September 29 (the Dedication of the Basilica of St. Michael on the Salarian Way) and perhaps also the Byzantine feast on November 8. In the Coptic and Ethiopian churches the same day is 12 Hatur in the Egyptian calendar. Because the devotion to Michael is so intense, his feast is also commemorated on the twelfth day of every Egyptian month (Christmas and certain feasts of Mary and other saints are also commemorated monthly).

The feasts of Michael have tended to become occasions for honoring the angels more generally. Thus the Byzantine feast on November 8 now honors "The Arch-angels Michael and Gabriel and All the Heavenly Powers." The day after 12 Hatur (November 9) is celebrated by the Copts and Ethiopians as the Feast of "Myriads of Angels." The Roman feast of the Guardian Angels (cf. Mt 18:10) was introduced in 1670 on October 2, the first free day after September 29. In the Anglican *Book of Common Prayer*, September 29 is traditionally the Feast of St. Michael and All Angels. The new Roman Calendar of 1969 took this same approach by making this day the combined Feast of Sts. Michael, Raphael, and Gabriel, Archangels.

The Coptic and Ethiopian churches also have feast days for other heavenly spiritual beings, located close to Michael's feast. The Four Bodiless Creatures of the Apocalypse (Rev 4:6-8) are honored on 8 Hatur (November 4) and the 24 Elders (Rev 4:4, 9-11) on 24 Hatur (November 20). Because the Greek word for elder (*presbyteros*) is translated as "priest," the latter feast has come to focus on the mystery of the priesthood, by which earthly and heavenly worship are united.

Karl Rahner, "Angel," *Sacramentum Mundi* 1 (New York: Herder and Herder, 1968) 27-35. *S. Th.* Pars 1a, q. 50-64, 106-14. Jean Danielou, *The Angels and their Mission according to the Fathers of the Church*, translated by David Heimann (Westminster, Md.: Christian Classics, 1957, 1976). Pseudo-Dionysius, *The Complete Works*, translated by Colm Luibheid, The Classics of Western Spirituality (New York: Paulist Press, 1987).

PETER JEFFERY

ANNULMENT

A juridical process employed in the Latin Catholic church to establish the freedom to marry for those whose previous marriage is found to have lacked the proper conditions for validity. It is not required of those churches which recognize divorce outright, or, as in some Eastern churches, which see the dissolution of marriage as a penitential, rather than juridical, procedure.

See **Marriage, sacrament of; Marriage, canonical issues concerning; Marriage tribunal**

ANOINTING

To anoint is to touch someone or something with a substance to bring about some effect, either within the person or thing or in the way others perceive that person or thing. While oil has been the substance frequently used in anointings, other materials such as water, blood, mud, fat, and saliva have also been used. Oil, which was used as soap, was employed most widely whether in athletic events, religious rites, or civil ceremonies.

The practice of anointing, whether in the context of ritual or not, is an ancient one. It did not originate with Judaism or Christianity. Anointing with oil, especially olive oil, can be traced back to certain customs in the Near East. Sometimes the anointing took place in the context of a ritual and sometimes not. When anointing had a liturgical context, it often was the way in which a culture dealt with such life crises as suffering, sickness, and death. Religious anointing in many of these older societies was one of the many ways in which they attempted to give meaning to situations of human fragmentation. Often the anointing was connected with something that seemed to be out of harmony with the universe, a liminal situation. Because ancient peoples had difficulty explaining the origins of sickness, they often created myths to explain what appeared to be unnatural or even evil. Since ritual is a combination of mythic content and external activity, a rite of anointing would easily be used to express a belief in an order which transcends the limitations of sickness and death.

It would be impossible to distinguish which of these ancient rituals were directed to physical healing and which were concerned with spiritual effects. Because these cultures took a more holistic view of the person, anointings were both occasions of providing meaning in situations of human brokenness, and a form of medicine to restore a person to physical health. Such anointings very easily possessed a sacramental character in that they were symbolic actions by means of which one reality existed in another. There was no clear dichotomy between material and spiritual dimensions of the rites. Although there has been considerable ambiguity regarding the proper effects of the anointings, it can be said that they at least inserted the persons anointed within the larger system of meaning in their particular communities. This more holistic perspective was as characteristic of ancient Israel as of its pagan neighbors. It is an approach which should not be considered naive. Today anointing is again seen as a way of engaging the whole person, a way of healing the body/mind split.

Anointing in the Bible has both a religious and a secular purpose. In a land characterized by dry weather it was only natural that anointing with oil would have a cosmetic and therapeutic intention. The secular use of oil is clear from Ezek 16:9 where it is the completion of the bathing process. Isa 61:3 speaks of the "oil of gladness instead of mourning," which indicates a more symbolic experience of anointing. 2 Sam 14:2 makes it clear that the absence of anointing is the sign of grief. There are many other instances of anointing in the Bible which operate in a religious context: anointing the heads of guests as a sign of respect (Mt 26:7), anointing the feet of visitors (Lk 7:46), anointing those freed from captivity (2 Chr 28:15), the wounded (Isa 1:6), and the dead as part of the preparation for burial (Mk 16:1).

There are many biblical examples of anointing in a religious context, especially in the Hebrew Scriptures. To anoint a person or an object was to bless that person or thing and set them apart for religious purposes. For instance, Moses anointed the ark, the altar, and lamp stand as well as Aaron and his sons. Exod 30:22-29 records the anointing of sacred furniture and vessels. For the most part only priests and kings were anointed in the Bible. Exod 28:40-42 describes the consecration of priests, although the anointing may have been usually restricted to the high priest. Prophets were also anointed, but this practice may have been connected with the anointing of kings (1 Kgs 19:16). Clearly, kings were anointed. It was an anointing done both by prophets and priests and it had the special meaning of designating the king as anointed of Yahweh (1 Sam 10:1; 16:13; 24:6). The anointing of the king is a good example of how often the civil and religious meanings of anointing blended together. The ceremony may have been civil, but the meaning was religious. Even the secular meaning of kingly anointing is being consecrated to God's service. Through anointing the king was removed from ordinary life and was made directly responsible to God.

While the NT is rich in the healing ministry of Christ and his followers and in the designation of Christ as the Anointed One, there is little about the practice of anointing with oil beyond those found in the Hebrew scriptures. Because healings took place in the name of Christ, often no specific symbolic action was involved, although there is evidence of human gesture connected with healing situations. Anointings are recorded in the NT as in Mt 26:7 which tells of Jesus being anointed in Bethany shortly before his death. Here anointing was a sign of honor. Anointings were also employed in conjunction with exorcisms such as indicated by Mk 6:13, "And they cast out many demons and anointed with oil many that were sick and healed them." And, of course, there is the celebrated text of Jas 5:13-16 which includes "Is any among you sick? Let him call for the elders of the church, and let them pray over him, anointing him with oil in the name of the Lord."

The title of Jesus is the Anointed One. He comes in the line of Hebrew prophets who were sometimes recognized as charismatic persons through anointing. This signaled that their mission was under the power of the Spirit of God. Christ inserts himself in that tradition when he quotes Isa 61:1, "The Spirit of the Lord God is upon me, because the Lord has anointed me." The Christian church has interpreted Mk 1:9-11, which depicts the baptism of Jesus by John and the descending of the Spirit on Jesus, as the "Messianic anointing of Jesus" by the Holy Spirit. It was only logical that the therapeutic use of oil by the Jews and the theologizing of the early church on the baptism of Jesus would lead to anointing becoming part of the sacramental activity of the church, especially in the rites of initiation, ordination, and healing.

The biblical practice of anointing, which may have originated from an Egyptian and Canaanite context, continued on into post-biblical times. It was especially significant in the Middle Ages in connection with the enthronement ceremonies of kings, popes, and emperors. There seems to be little distinction on the general level between liturgical anointings and these civil anointings. The anointings located in the initiation rites, such as the anointing of catechumens and those to be confirmed, as well as the anointing of kings were perceived as removing the person from the profane dimension of life. The anointing of kings survived until modern times, into the 19th century when, for instance, Charles X of France was anointed in 1825. The religious mystique that these anointings added to the crowning of a king was a way of strengthening the prestige of any particular dynasty. The anointing would rarely be only political or spiritual, but usually was a combination. During the High Middle Ages the anointing of a king had a quasi-sacramental character, although eventually that understanding changed. The anointing of the king differed from that of bishop in that the king was anointed between the shoulders and not on the head. He was anointed without the use of chrism. It was in the best interest of civil authorities not to make their power dependent on the anointing as such, for that would have rendered their position subordinate to the church.

Popes were anointed also but not in order to be designated as pope. The anointing was connected with the ordination of the person as a bishop. And when in the 11th century the popes were chosen from the ranks of bishops, anointing ceased to be part of the papal enthronement.

The use of oil in Christian initiation is very old, dating from the 2nd and 3rd centuries. Its meaning and role has differed greatly. In some localities anointing was considered more preeminent than in others where it would have played a supporting role in bringing out the meaning of initiation as a whole. Because oil is such a polyvalent symbol, it has and can trigger the many associations that speak of the inner transformation of new life in Christ that initiation signals. Historically, two kinds of oil have been associated with the baptismal part of the initiation: the plain kind, which today is used before the water baptism, and the chrism, perfumed oil, which is used after the water ceremony. Each has its distinct meanings and clustering of images.

The oil used before baptism has had other names such as "oil of exorcism," but its name today is the ancient one of "oil of catechumens," since its origin is in the anointing of those who were preparing for baptism. Thus, this oil has been in close association with the prayer of exorcism both in the ancient rite and in the present Roman rite. It expresses the care of the church for the adults who have just renounced the devil and the forces of evil. The church prays that they will be strong in professing their faith and will persevere in the same. The prayer of blessing of the oil of the catechumens asks of God: "Grant them your wisdom to understand the gospel more deeply and your strength to accept the challenge of Christian life. Enable them to rejoice in the baptism and to partake of a new life in the church as true children of your family" (102). In infant baptism, the pre-baptismal anointing follows the exorcism prayer because it expresses the liberation of the child from the power of sin.

The method of anointing has changed through the centuries. In the early church period in some of the major liturgical centers the oil was poured over the naked candidates and then smeared over the entire body. St. Ambrose compares the candidates to wrestlers who grease themselves completely to make it more difficult for their opponent to get a hold on them. In 5th-century Rome the anointing was restricted to the ears, nostrils, and chest. These three bodily places were chosen for symbolic reasons: the ears so that the candidate could hear the gospel, the nostrils so that their service to God lasted as long as they drew in the breath of life, and the chest because it is the seat of the heart where Christ now dwells. In the Middle Ages a two-fold anointing took place, on the chest and on the back, both in the form of a cross. This form lasted until the most recent revisions, and now the presider anoints children on the breast only. In the U.S., this pre-baptismal anointing is optional and since the children are not really catechumens, it may be pastorally advisable to omit it. There are those, however, who maintain that it still can be significant if it is properly done. When a generous amount of oil is used and rubbed in, it can be recognized as the manifestation of the care of Christ for the infant. Just as an infant moves from the world of the womb to the outside world and so needs the loving touch of parents lest it feel abandoned, so the person in baptism needs loving care and support as it moves into a different world. Oil is a protective ointment and so can easily symbolize the church's protection for its progeny. The pre-baptismal anointing concludes and sums up the celebration of the word and now the church is prepared to celebrate the sacrament proper.

The ancient Roman rite has two anointings with chrism which completed the ritual of baptism. First, the newly baptized were anointed by the presbyter and then second by the bishop. It is difficult to say what the origin of this double anointing was. When the initiation rites broke apart, the second chrismatic anointing became identified as the separate sacrament of confirmation. There were other practices in the early church in which there was only one post-baptismal anointing and that one became identified with confirmation. Today, in the Roman rite the anointing by the presbyter is omitted if there is confirmation in the same ceremony. There was a third pattern in initiation in which there was no post-baptismal anointing.

This oil of chrismation is clearly distinct from the oil of catechumens. The latter is the oil of exorcism, the gesture of protection administered on the chest, the medicine of strengthening, while the former is the oil of gladness poured upon the head, the oil of thanksgiving, the perfumed oil. This oil of gladness is to be given lavishly. The anointing prayer in infant baptism in the Roman rite says that God has freed the child from sin, given it new birth by water and the Holy Spirit, welcomed it into the People of God and then continues: "He now anoints you with the chrism of salvation. As Christ was anointed Priest, Prophet, and King, so may you live always as members of his body, sharing everlasting life" (62). Through the power of the Holy Spirit and the sacramental action of anointing the child is now identified with Christ, the "one who has been anointed." It seems that this anointing in Christian initiation was suggested by the anointing Jesus received from God during his baptism in the Jordan where the Spirit descended upon him. What needs to be noted is that this anointing is an event of joy, recognizing the oneness in Christ with which the newly baptized now lives. Being anointed with this oil of thanksgiving means that this person is now a member of the chosen race, the royal priesthood, God's own people and is commissioned to bring light to the darkness, to proclaim the works of God in the assembly of the people, and to bear witness to the name of Christ in the world.

Both the American *Book of Common Prayer* and the *Lutheran Book of Worship* make provisions for a post-baptismal anointing. Both indicate that the person baptized is now sealed by the Holy Spirit and marked as Christ's own. The Episcopal blessing of chrism adds the notion of sharing in the priesthood of Christ.

Anointing in Confirmation

At its origin confirmation is the sacramental link between baptism and eucharist. There are theological differences about the meaning of confirmation today. However, it is best understood as part of the initiation process, a confirming of baptism. The use of chrismatic anointing is appropriate to this rite. In the Roman Catholic church the bishop is the ordinary minister of the sacrament, although presbyters can be delegated to confirm. As the minister traces the sign of the cross with chrism on the forehead of the person being confirmed he says: "N., be sealed with the Gift of the Holy Spirit."

In the American Episcopal church, baptism is considered full initiation by water and the Holy Spirit. There is only one anointing which is done immediately after water baptism. The rite of confirmation is administered by the imposition of hands. The latter is also the practice of the *Lutheran Book of Worship.*

For the first five hundred years plain oil was generally used, as was the case for the pre-baptismal anointing. According to Hippolytus (3rd. c.) the pre-baptismal oil was exorcised, while the oil of confirmation was blessed. Ritually, this makes sense because before baptism the prayer is to free the person from the forces and structures of evil while the prayer after baptism is in thanksgiving for the gifts of God, especially baptism itself. The anointing or sealing here has the basic NT meaning that the Spirit has now been fully given to the person to be anointed. It would seem that the use of oil as concluding the bathing process in the ancient world rendered this sealing open to this theological interpretation.

After the 6th century, perfumed oil was the common practice and chrism takes on further overtones of joy, embodiment, and sensuality. Some of the ancient prayers connect the smell of the oil to the sweet odor of Christ. Two themes emerge from these prayers: the bonding between the baptized and Christ, and the gift of the knowledge of Christ. The West interprets the bonding along more feudalistic lines of defending and strengthening, and the East sees the aroma of chrism as a metaphor for the presence of God. Those anointed with this aromatic presence will be able to sense the hidden life of God in prayer, liturgy, and all creation. This Eastern emphasis on confirmation as the sacrament of interior growth, with its sensitivity to the spiritual dimension of life and the authority which flows from contemplative prayer, is not in contradiction to the extroverted and active approach to confirmation in the West. But the Western theology of confirmation with its stress on public witness and institutional identification could profit from the tempering which would take place if there were a better wedding of the two theological perspectives.

As with all anointings, the oil needs to be applied generously. A stingy sign of the cross on the forehead does not express well that the person is marked with Christ, that the anointed one now lives out of the gift of the Spirit, that the confirmed belongs to a new covenant established in the death and resurrection of Christ. It is fitting that the anointing be done with the sign of the cross since so much of the imagery surrounding confirmation moves to the central metaphor that the person is "signed and sealed" by God in Christ. But this is no excuse for a meager use of oil. This chrismation is still done with the oil of thanksgiving, confirming Christians in their initiation into the community. Anointing in confirmation should not be so construed as to give the impression that there are two separate sacraments of initiation. Initiation is one process with two stages. Both baptism and confirmation initiate one into the single mystery of Christ and anointings in both sacraments sign one with the same sign of death and resurrection.

Anointing in Ordinations

The Christian rites of ordination did not have anointings from the beginning. The liturgical expression of this sacrament had developed for several centuries before anointings became part of the ritual. In the Franco-Germanic churches of the 7th and 8th centuries there is evidence of rites of anointing in the ordination liturgies. At the ordination of a bishop, besides the giving of the crozier and ring and the bishop's enthronement, there was an anointing of the head with chrism. Likewise, for the priest there was anointing of the hands in addition to the giving of the bread and wine and a second laying on of hands indicating the power to forgive sins. The first laying on of hands is already recorded by Hippolytus (c. 230). All these additional rites reflect the Germanic influence on the Roman liturgy. This northern spirit placed a great deal of emphasis on the handing over of the instruments of power, princely power in the case of the bishop, and cultic power in the case of the priest. By the 10th century there is a clear merging of these Germanic elements with the Roman rite.

The reformed Roman ordination of a bishop differs from the previous Franco-Germanic rite in the anointing in that the action takes place after the consecratory prayer and there is no anointing of the bishop's hands. In the old rite the anointing of the bishop's head took place in the midst of the prayer. Anointing of the head in the reformed rite is accompanied by a prayer which prays that as God has brought this person into a share of the priesthood of Christ, so may this person receive the "oil of mystical anointing" and be filled with spiritual blessings.

The Roman ordination of the presbyter manifests the same desire for simplification. The bishop anoints the palms of the hands of the newly ordained and prays that Jesus may preserve him to sanctify the Christian people and offer sacrifice to God. The anointing, as do the other elements in the ordination rites, represents an attempt to return to an early understanding of ministry. The bishop is seen as the shepherd and leader of the people. The presbyter is seen as one with Christ in building up the people of God as the body of Christ and temple of the Holy Spirit. The image of the presbyter is one who preaches the gospel and celebrates the worship of God. There is no anointing in the ordination rites of the Anglican and Protestant churches.

Anointing of the Sick

The anointing with oil is the central symbol of the sacrament of the anointing of the sick. It has the same basic meaning as the laying on of hands which is found in most of the sacraments. The imposition of hands is the most fundamental sacramental gesture and so anointing with oil is a form of laying on of hands. But there are other meanings of anointing with oil as it is used in this rite for the sick, elderly, and dying. To anoint is one way to acknowledge the blessings that God gives to God's people. Healing is a blessing of God which is especially asked for and for which thanksgiving is rendered in this rite. And the way that healing comes to those anointed is in the context of the Holy Spirit. Thus, there is the aspect of mission and commissioning since here the Holy Spirit is given for more than individual salvation. This Spirit-filled blessing of healing does not primarily refer to physical healing. It does refer to health, but in the sense of contributing to the building of the Kingdom of God in some way, whether it be through the witnessing of the person anointed, or the mutual contribution to community of the anointed and those doing the anointing.

The Christian community has consistently made use of anointing in regard to the ministerial sacraments of baptism, confirmation, and orders. The anointing with oil in the case of the sick and elderly is related to these other sacramental anointings in that anointing the sick and elderly is delegating them for ministry in the church. The sick and elderly as ill and old in the church may not belong to the permanent structures of the church in the same way they do as baptized, but they can and are called upon to fulfill a ministerial function. In baptism and confirmation the person was anointed with oil ritually so as to conform to Christ, the Anointed One. By entering more deeply into the paschal mystery through the suffering of sickness and the marginality of old age, this person now is further conformed to Christ, and so anointing in this sacrament recapitulates that of baptism and confirmation.

The oil used in the sacrament of the sick is specially blessed for this purpose by the bishop at the Chrism Mass on or near Holy Thursday. It is usually olive oil but other oil may be blessed, especially at situations such as communal anointings. In the reformed Roman Ritual the number of anointings has been reduced from five to two and the formula which accompanies the anointing has moved away from a penitential understanding which implied an association of sinfulness with the senses. The new formula has a fuller theology which stresses help for the person through the power of the Holy Spirit, and the healing power of God's grace extended to the person already freed from sin.

In the service for the Ministration to the Sick in the American *Book of Common Prayer* the central action is the laying on of hands. The anointing with oil is optional. The prayer accompanying the anointing asks for the forgiveness of sins, release from suffering, restoration to wholeness and strength, and deliverance from evil.

Anointing of Objects

In the liturgy of the dedication of a church there is an anointing of the altar and the walls. Anointing of these inanimate objects and the other rites such as incensation express in a visible way aspects of the invisible work which God accomplishes through the church. Anointing the altar with chrism signifies that the altar is a symbol of Christ, the Anointed One. Christ is the High Priest who on the altar of his body offers his life in sacrifice for the salvation of the world. In anointing the altar the bishop pours oil on the middle of the altar and on the four corners. He should anoint the entire altar. Anointing the walls of the building indicates that the purpose of the church

building is that it be given over to Christian worship. Either twelve or four anointings are prescribed to show that the church is an image of the holy city of Jerusalem. As the altar representing Christ stands for the head, so the walls of the church represent the people, the body. The people are the church and the dedication of the church is the dedication of the People of God and so the anointing of the walls represents the anointing of the people. The dedication of the church is a concelebrated liturgy with bishop, clergy, and all the people taking part. The rite brings out how all clergy and laity share in the one priesthood of Christ.

The Blessing of Oils and Consecration of Chrism

The blessing of the oil of the sick and the oil of catechumens as well as the consecration of the oil of holy chrism (oil mixed with balsam) take place during the Chrism Mass prior to the beginning of the Easter Triduum. The blessing prayers give some understanding of the meaning of the various liturgical anointings in which these oils are used.

In the Roman rite the blessing of the oil of the sick takes place at the end of the eucharistic prayer immediately before the final doxology. The bishop's prayer addresses God, who brings healing to the sick through Jesus Christ. He asks that God send the Holy Spirit to serve our needs. He prays that all who are anointed with this oil may receive God's blessing, be freed from pain and illness, and be made well in body, mind, and soul.

The blessing of the oil of catechumens takes place after communion. The bishop, surrounded by the concelebrating priests, prays that those who are anointed with this oil may have wisdom and strength as they prepare for baptism. He asks that through anointing they may have a deeper understanding of the gospel, that they may meet the challenge of Christian living, and be led to the joy of new birth in the family of the church.

56

The consecration of the chrism is more elaborate. After praying that God will bless the oil so that those who are anointed with it will be inwardly transformed, the bishop sings a consecratory prayer in *berakah* (Jewish blessing prayer) style giving thanks for how the earth brings forth fruit-bearing trees from which comes the oil for this chrism. He recounts how the prophet David sang of the life and joy that oil brings and how after the flood the dove brought to Noah an olive branch as a sign of peace. He recalls that now the waters of baptism wash away our sins and the anointing with oil makes us radiant with joy. The prayer continues with the image of Aaron washed in water and anointed priest by Moses, all this foreshadowing Christ's baptism in the Jordan by John. This fulfilled the prophecy of David that Christ would be anointed with the oil of gladness beyond his fellow men and women. The bishop asks God to bless the oil with the power of the Spirit of Christ, the Anointed One, from whom the oil takes its name. He asks that it become a sign of life and salvation for those to be baptized, that they be washed of the evil inherited from Adam, that they become temples of glory, that they have royal, priestly, and prophetic honor, that they be clothed with incorruption, and that it be, indeed, the chrism of salvation.

James L. Empereur, *Prophetic Anointing: God's Call to the Sick, the Elderly, and the Dying* (Wilmington: Michael Glazier, Inc., 1982). Mark Searle, *Christening: The Making of Christians* (Collegeville: The Liturgical Press, 1980). Mark Searle, *The Rites of the Catholic Church*: Vol. 2 (New York: Pueblo Publishing Co., 1980).

JAMES L. EMPEREUR, S.J.

ANOINTING OF THE SICK

See Sick, pastoral care of the; also Sick, anointing of, frequency of

ANOINTING, POST-BAPTISMAL

Found early in the development of Christian baptismal rites, an anointing with chrism (oil to which a fragrance, most often balsam, has been added) follows the water bath of baptism. Though originally lavish, it eventually became a simple anointing in the form of a cross on the forehead of the person baptized. Both christological and pneumatological in its import, it signifies the bestowal of the Holy Spirit and the sealing, a contractual branding, of the baptized person with the cross of Christ.

Biblical precedents for anointing hearken back to the OT. There we find its root symbolic meaning in the anointing of kings and priests and the associated empowerment by the Holy Spirit. In Lev 8:12 we find Moses anointing Aaron to consecrate him as priest. In 1 Sam 10:1 Saul is anointed to be prince over God's people, Israel. In 1 Sam 16:12, 13, Samuel anoints David: ". . . and the Spirit of the Lord came mightily upon David from that day forward" (v. 13).

Anointing with chrism at baptism takes its primary meaning from Jesus' anointing as our great High Priest (the Christ, the Anointed One) and consequently, of our anointing into Christ and into his priesthood in which all believers share. The words surrounding this anointing, all derived from the Greek *chriein*, to anoint, point to connection with Christ: Christ, chrism, Christian, chrismation, chrisom.

Anointing with chrism proclaims Christ; it also symbolizes the gift of the Holy Spirit. Paul links together anointing, sealing, and the giving of the Holy Spirit: "But it is God who has established us with you in Christ, and has anointed us (kai chrísas hemas); he has put his seal upon us and given us his Spirit in our hearts as a guarantee (2 Cor 1:21, 22). While it is not possible to determine decisively whether or not oil was actually used in the NT as here, where anointing is mentioned in connection with the Holy Spirit, clear evidence of early post-baptismal anointings comes to us from the 3rd century in the works of Hippolytus and Tertullian. In the 4th century Cyril of Jerusalem called chrism "the gift of Christ; and by the presence of his Godhead, it causes in us the Holy Ghost" (Mitchell, p. 44). Ancient expressions from the Church Fathers further illuminate this act of anointing, "chrism of salvation"; "chrism of incorruption"; "shield of righteousness"; "tunic of immortality." Recognizing the value of this tangible sign to convey a spiritual reality, Ephraem in the 4th century states: "Christ and chrism are conjoined, the secret with the visible is mingled: the chrism anoints visibly—Christ seals secretly" (Mitchell, p. 34).

The Orthodox church, and some other Eastern churches, held to the pattern found in early baptismal liturgies where baptism, anointing and signation (chrismation), and eucharist formed a unified whole. In the West this anointing became at first separated from baptism's water bath, and eventually, when a post-baptismal anointing did return to the baptismal liturgy, became two anointings. Anointing with chrism as a sealing in the Holy Spirit occurred separately as the sacrament of confirmation. The anointing within the baptismal liturgy retained only its Christic significance.

Today in Roman Catholicism when adults are baptized, confirmation again immediately follows baptism, to be followed in turn by the eucharist, thus restoring the original unity of initiation into the church. In such instances, the so-called "post-baptismal" anointing is omitted. However, when children are baptized, confirmation continues to be delayed and the anointing with chrism in the baptismal service declares baptism's gifts of forgiveness, new life in Christ, and membership in Christ's body.

The Reformers discarded altogether this anointing with chrism. However, as the study of early baptismal liturgies has sharpened, the most recent liturgies of some Protestant denominations (e.g., Presbyterian and Lutheran), now make a provision for this anointing and signing with chrism within the sacrament of holy baptism. The words used remain (with small alterations) remarkably consistent through the ages, noting the sealing of the Holy Spirit and the grafting into Christ forever. Once again the words of sealing and incorporation into Christ are clothed in tangible form, that flesh and blood people might better sense God's invisible acts of baptism. This cross of chrism glistening briefly on the forehead of the newly baptized visibly proclaims our eternal identity. Together we are the Spirit-anointed ones of the Anointed One!

See **Anointing; Confirmation**

Gerard Austin, O.P., *Anointing with the Spirit. The Rite of Confirmation: The Use of Oil and Chrism* (New York: Pueblo Publishing Co., 1985). Leonel L. Mitchell, Th.D., *Baptismal Anointing* (London: S.P.C.K. 1966).

JEAN C. ZEIDLER

APOSTLES, FEASTS OF

The apostles are particularly honored by the church because of their intimate relationship to Jesus Christ the Lord. They were called by him and were his first witnesses. The celebrations in the Roman calendar are: Solemnity of Ss. Peter and Paul (June 29); the Feast of the Conversion of St. Paul (Jan 25); the Chair of St. Peter (Feb 22); Ss. Philip and James (May 3; formerly May 1, the date of the dedication of the basilica of the apostles in Rome in 570, and moved to May 11 in 1955 when the feast of St. Joseph the Worker was introduced); St. Matthias (May 14; transferred from Feb 24 to remove it from Lent and put it closer to Ascension); St. Thomas (July 3; transferred from Dec 21 to remove it from

58

Advent); St. James (July 25); St.
Bartholomew (Aug 24); St. Matthew,
apostle and evangelist (Sept 21); Ss.
Simon and Jude (Oct 28); St. Andrew
(Nov 30); St. John, apostle and evangelist
(Dec 27); and the obligatory memorial of
St. Barnabas (June 11). There is also the
optional memorial of the dedication of
the basilicas of Ss. Peter and Paul
(Nov 18).

History
Celebrations of the apostles are found
in the earliest Western sources. The
Chronographus of 354, which contains
information dating from 336, includes a
Feast of St. Peter on Feb 22. The
Veronese (Leonine) Sacramentary
(ca. 550; actually a collection of prayers
from various sources rather than a sacramentary) contains 29 sets of Mass
formularies for the Feast of Ss. Peter and
Paul on June 29. It was a three-liturgy
day: one each at the basilicas of St. Peter
and St. Paul, and at the catacomb of St.
Sebastian where their relics were temporarily housed at the time of the Valerian
persecution (258). The Veronese also
contains texts for feasts of St. Andrew
(Nov 30; four sets); and St. John (Dec 27)
placed after the Holy Innocents).
A feast of all the apostles was celebrated
within the octave of Ss. Peter and Paul by
the time of the Old Gelasian Sacramentary (ca. 650).
Feasts of individual apostles gradually
entered the Roman calendar, taken from
other churches or celebrating the translation of relics to Rome from time to
time. The Old Gelasian adds a feast of Ss.
Philip and James (May 1). The double
commemoration (since 1558) of the Chair
of St. Peter at Rome (Jan 18) and at
Antioch (Feb 22) was combined in 1960.
The feast of the Conversion of St. Paul
seems to have been the octave day of the
Gallican (Jan 18) celebration of Peter.
Several other celebrations were eliminated in 1960: St. John at the Latin Gate

(May 6); the Commemoration of St.
Paul (June 30; probably the transfer of
one of the Masses of the previous day);
St. Peter in Chains (Aug 1).

Theology of the Celebrations
In the texts for the celebration of the
eucharist, the scripture readings are
generally chosen because they contain
reference to the apostles who are being
honored that day.
The prayers reveal many of the apostles'
characteristics and give us the church's
understanding of who the apostles are
and what they do. They are first and
foremost witnesses and preachers of the
word, a living gospel (Simon and Jude,
Andrew, John, preface of apostles II), the
ones who believe in Jesus as Lord
(Thomas). They call us to be witnesses as
well (Matthias, John, Barnabas). Because
of their fidelity to the gospel (Chair of
Peter, Peter and Paul), they are the
foundation and guardians of the church
(Conversion of Paul, Dedication of the
basilicas, preface of apostles I) and the
signs of unity and peace (Chair of Peter,
Bartholomew). Their sufferings transform them into even more apt witnesses
of Christ (Philip and James, James).
They are our intercessors in heaven (Peter
and Paul).
The celebration of the liturgy of the
hours holds up two items for our prayer
and reflection. 1) The apostles had an
intimate bond with the Lord Jesus. The
antiphons especially delight to use the
words of the Lord from John 15: you are
my friends, love one another. This closeness to the Lord is also ours through the
apostles, as we hear St. Paul: imitate me
as I imitate Christ (Office of Readings, 1
Cor 4, 1-16). 2) The apostles build up the
church into the body of Christ by their
preaching, the witness of sharing goods
in common, their suffering and their
intercession.
The celebrations of the apostles
throughout the course of the year are a

continual reminder of our link to the original message and community of Christ Jesus the Lord.

See **Calendar, liturgical**

A. Adam, *The Liturgical Year* (Collegeville, 1981), pp. 141-142, 235-237, 240-247. P. Rado, *Enchiridion Liturgicum* (Rome, 1961), Vol 2:1369-77.

MICHAEL WITCZAK

ARCHITECTURE, LITURGICAL

A worthy architecture for the celebration of liturgy must be in continuing dialogue with 1. the self-understanding of Christians; 2. history of the tradition; 3. new orientations; 4. needs of contemporary liturgy; and 5. a theology of visibility.

1. The Self-Understanding of Christians

Biblical architectural vocabulary functions 1) to designate actual buildings; and 2) metaphorically. The portable tabernacle or "tent of meeting" used by nomads during the exodus served as a worship center. Here God abided. Of the Israelite shrines, the temple built by Solomon in Jerusalem as "House for the name of Yahweh" was greatest (2 Chr 24; JBC 76:39ff). As places where God dwells, these structures are relativized in the NT; "tent" serves as figure of the mortal body (1 Cor 5:1); the human person is God's "temple" (1 Cor 3:16) or "shrine" (2 Cor 6:16); and Jesus declares that worship in the Jerusalem temple is superseded (Jn 4:21). No temple building is needed in heaven, since the city is completely permeated by the glory of God and the Lamb (Rev 21:22).

The term "church" is derived from the OT Hebrew *qāhāl*, translated in the LXX as *ekklēsia* = assembly of the Israelites a) wandering in the desert; b) at liturgical gatherings (JBC 79:149-156). Paul applies the metaphor of the building process ("edification") on numerous occasions to the community of those who believe in Christ and to what supports their growth. They form the eschatological temple, with Jesus Christ as its foundation. Paul compares himself to a "skilled master builder" (1 Cor 3:10) whom God has commissioned for the building project. Eph 2:19-22 describes the faith-community as part of a building of which apostles and prophets are the foundations and Christ is the main cornerstone. In the Spirit, God lives in this house under construction. The sense of the term church is personal and dynamic.

In Paul "church" refers to the local community (Rom 16:1, 4, 5, 16, 23) or to the "church of God" in Judea linked to the Israelite "congregation" of old. The phrase "the church in the house of..." 1 Cor 11:18, 16:19; Rom 16:5; Phil 2; Col 4:15) refers to such local assemblies gathered in a tenement apartment of an eastern city of the Roman empire, its largest room, that for dining, on the top floor (Acts 20:7-9); or to the town and village house with rooms arranged around a central courtyard. The community, "breaking bread from house to house" (Acts 2:46), would be hosted by a wealthier householder.

2. History of the Tradition
(a) House of the Church

The gradual acquisition of properties by Christian communities specifically for their corporate use led to the transferred meaning "house-church" or "house of the church": a community center or meeting house. The oldest of these is the renovated (A.D. 231) community house at Dura-Europos, Syria, with assembly hall, adjacent room (for the catechumens?) and separate baptistery. The Syrian *Didascalia apostolorum* (ca. 250) describes the disposition of a congregation: presbyters in the eastern end of the assembly room around the bishop's seat; laymen in the remainder of the eastern section; then the women; boys and girls seated apart. A mosaic (Paris, Louvre) depicts a middle-eastern church-house of the 4th century. Since persecutions were sporadic, properties were acquired during the age of the martyrs. But these belong to the genus of domestic architecture. A handful of depictions in the catacombs suggests as well the domestic character of liturgical furnishings. The 3rd-century Roman convert Minucius Felix declared, "We have neither temple nor altars." At best, new construction consisted of a barnlike hall. Churches or *tituli* in Rome which rose over or were renovated from pre-Constantinian buildings and named from their original owner may have replaced earlier house-churches; proof is lacking.

(b) *The Basilica* - "Audience Hall of the King"

With Constantine's triumph over Maxentius at the battle of the Milvian Bridge (312), Christianity had a patron and its bishops access to imperial architects and building stores. The great Roman Christian *basilicas* were adaptations of a design secular at base: clerestoried nave flanked by lower aisles and terminated by an apse, with or without transverse wings flanking a chancel area little distinguished from the nave. Here was a structurally simple building type which was not linked to pagan rites and was suitable for rich interior decor of marble, fresco and mosaic. Most important, with its longitudinal emphasis it could accommodate large crowds and splendid processions in a manner appropriate for a faith newly under imperial patronage. Their size discouraged preaching. St. John Lateran (begun 312/313) with its baptistery, was the seat of the bishop of Rome; outside the walls rose the covered cemeteries of St. Sebastian, St. Lawrence and St. Peter (319/22-329), the last focused on the 2nd-century memorial of the apostle.

In Jerusalem the five-aisled martyrium at Golgotha (ca. 335) rose to the east of the cube-shaped Mount of Calvary and tomb, situated in an open courtyard. Egeria's pilgrim diary (ca. 385) allows the imaginative reader to reconstruct the shape of the Jerusalem liturgy in its classical period. By the time of Egeria's visit, a huge rotunda rose over the tomb as architectural symbol of Christ's resurrection. (This meaning, together with the baptismal connotation of dying to self, governed the scale, design and location of the Pisa baptistery (1153ff) outside the west facade of that central Italian cathedral.) Bethlehem, too, had its Constantinian basilica. None of these basilicas seems to have had a fixed altar.

Eusebius, expounding on the beauty of the church at Tyre (*Hist. eccl.*, X. 4), indicates something of the hierarchical ranking of clergy which was assimilated into the church from the empire: "After completing the great building, he furnished it with thrones high up, to accord with the dignity of the prelates, and also with benches arranged conveniently throughout. . . . He placed in the middle the Holy of Holies—the altar—excluding the general public from this part too by surrounding it with wooden trellis-work." The imperial origin of these basilicas is seen in the fact that their facades faced east, as with Greek and Roman temple architecture.

In imperial Milan Ambrose copied Constantine's Church of the Holy Apostles, Constantinople, in his Basilica Apostolorum (382); here is the first indication in the West that the Latin cross-shaped plan was intended to bear an explicit symbolism. Ambrose observed, "The temple is in the form of the cross . . . a triumphal image (which) marks the place with the sacred victory of Christ.' When the bones of the martyrs Gervase and Protase were translated to S. Ambrogio in 387, Ambrose explained the appropriateness of placing them under the altar (Rev 6:9), where Christ is the victim. By reserving a grave for himself as celebrating priest next to them, Ambrose underlined the developing notion of the altar area as a place of sacred cult connected especially to priesthood.

North African church design corresponded better to the old Roman ecclesial sensibility: the altar should be accessible since the gathered people are offering subject of the liturgy. "If you are the body of Christ," Augustine taught, "your mystery is laid on the table, your mystery you receive." In North Africa the altar was placed in the middle of the nave; the apsidal area was utilized for the liturgy of the Word.

The period 380-480 saw the building of many parish churches in Rome (e.g., the exquisite Sta. Sabina on the Aventine hill). The city formed the unique subject of the liturgy when the whole church met here for solemn stational service on Ash Wednesday. Much smaller than the Constantinian foundations, these basilicas with eastern apse, nave flanked by two aisles, without transept but with a *solea* (area enclosed by barriers projecting into the nave in front of the sanctuary) were eminently suited to the Roman liturgy. The solea harbored procession, cantors and choir. The people's gifts of bread and wine were collected, probably at the head of the aisles reserved for men and women, after the liturgy of the Word; here also the people approached for communion. A mural in the lower church of S. Clemente (11th century) shows the Roman practice of Mass facing the people.

From the time of Gregory the Great (590-604) dates the reconstruction of the west end of Old St. Peter's. The floor was raised to form a platform; a semicircular passageway beneath it allowed access to the memorial of Peter from the rear. A stone altar and *ciborium* (canopy) were placed directly over the *confessio* for the relic. The bishop's *cathedra* (throne) was on the major axis facing altar and people.

Without disturbing Mass, pilgrims could venerate the shrine. This gave architectural expression to the West's emphasis on the sacrificial nature of the eucharist and its commemoration of the cross and also to the growing cult of relics. The linkage of these two levels of veneration had a profound impact on medieval church design.

Pilgrims flooded Rome, and took home with them the bones of martyrs (and other Christians as well) interred in the catacombs. Carolingian monasteries met the challenge: they adapted the stational liturgy of Rome to a single church by multiplying altars and monk-priests. Cf. the ideal plan of the monastery of St. Gall, where cubicles containing altars took over the nave space. The rule ran: a relic needs an altar, an altar demands a Mass, only one Mass per day can be celebrated at an altar. In the enormous Romanesque church at Cluny the radiating choir chapels of the developed Cluniac plan ordered a monastic layout which provided space for lay pilgrims as well. After the Carolingians, in architecture as in liturgy, Rome was destined to receive more than it would give.

(c) Architecture of the Eastern Churches

In the Middle East, Nestorian churches in northern Syria were designed with a U-shaped *bema* (here designating the platform for reading and preaching) large enough to seat clergy in the midst of the nave. Remains of the altar have been found in some instances at the top of high steps against the east end. The eucharist was celebrated facing east, back to the congregation, by the priest chosen for that day. The plan, bema, doors and disposition of worshippers (women behind the bema at the west) was conservative, paralleling synagogue design.

The Byzantine Divine Liturgy took shape in the basilica, often with galleries, endemic to the late Roman-Christian empire. Under the influence of shrines at the biblical Holy Places, preeminent among them the Anastasis Rotunda at the Holy Sepulchre, the centralized church crowned by one or several domes and semi-domes became the normative design. For the liturgy celebrated at the Holy Places commemorated the person or event not only once annually, but every Sunday. Martyrs also merited the centralized mausoleum type. Another category of church: the palace-church, drew on imperial architectural precedent. Hagia Sophia in Constantinople (532-537) is the most breathtaking. Here the emperor in the company of the patriarch worshipped that Ruler whom he represented under the great golden dome of heaven, suspended giddyingly overhead. Light flowing in from the windows immediately under the dome gives the impression that the latter is suspended from heaven. Of this Church of the Holy Wisdom Procopius exclaimed, "Radiance is generated within."

Ritual flourished in such an ambience. Entrance was gained, nearly simultaneously by the processing clergy and people, through nine doors in the western portal. An ambo protected by a *solea* extended outward on the main axis into the nave from the chancel or *bema*, where the altar was situated behind an open column-screen. The Riha Paten (Washington, D.C.: Dumbarton Oaks) depicts such an altar and screen, at which Christ presides to communicate the apostles with his body and blood. The sense of Christ's active presence secures the resurrection motif which dominates Byzantine liturgy. Behind the altar in the apse rose staged seating for the clergy, with the patriarchal throne at the top. No wonder that Germanus, patriarch of Constantinople (8th century) commented, "The bema is the stepped place and throne where Christ the ruler of all presides with his apostles ... and it also shows the second parousia, when he will come, sitting in the seat of majesty to judge the world."

After such exertions, the architects of the middle Byzantine period had energy to construct only relatively small buildings, cubical in form topped by domes (Daphni, outside Athens; Phocis, Hosios Loukas, 1020). Lavish interior mosaics depicted Christ and his life, Mary and the saints; through the image the worshipper encountered its prototype. Episodes from the paschal mystery, however, are not often met under the central dome; the Divine Liturgy itself was the chief image of the saving death, descent into Hades and Resurrection. The *iconostasis* or solid screen bearing icons and separating chancel from nave appeared late (Russia, 16th century). Otherwise the unrevised Divine Liturgy has not called for new architectural solutions.

(d) Romanesque and Gothic in the West

Monastic architecture, some of it rural, proved to be the seedbed for the urban Gothic cathedral. The abbey church at Cluny (10th-12th cents.), an "epitome of medieval mathematical and musical theory," was built to accommodate the *opus Dei* carried on untiringly within its walls. It spawned smaller versions of its basilican plan with *transepts* (transverse arms) along the pilgrim routes of France. The pointed barrel vault of Cluny's third church was perfectly suited to plainsong. Its high altar was a stone table. Chapels radiating from the choir fittingly housed the abbey's relics. Its Benedictine monks, with room in the choir for orderly grouping according to rank, imagined themselves in "the walk of the angels." Suger's abbey church of Saint-Denis (1137-44, 13th cent.) capitalized on the light-refracting glories of gold and gems while it inaugurated seemingly weightless masonry, an innovative vaulting system, and new programs in stained glass. Suger's excuse was that such material loveliness as accompaniment to rich liturgy transports the worshipper from the inferior to the higher immaterial world.

The abbey church of Fontenay (1139-47) still stands with much of the original monastery at the head of a secluded valley, as witness to the ascetic Cistercian formula. Its architectural rigor underlines visually Bernard of Clairvaux's condemnation of Cluniac architecture: the immense height of these Benedictine churches, their immoderate length, excessive width, sumptuous decoration and finely executed pictures diverted "the attention of those who are praying and impede devotion." With square east end, pointed barrel vault and masonry walls built by lay brothers, Fontenay was a reduced version without towers of that which he lamented. It lacked color and sculpture but was acoustically remarkable.

Both Suger's Saint-Denis and early Cistercian were needed for the dialectic which produced the classical Gothic of Chartres Cathedral (1194-1220). Chartres' basilican plan with transept was completely unified in both plan and elevation; it could support visually western towers of unequal height and differing design. Elaborate sculptural programs on the exterior related the building, microcosm of the Christian cosmos, to the urban lay world. The cathedral's solid walls were turned outwards at right angles to form buttresses and allow for the insertion of walls of stained glass. The interior was transubstantiated into a mystical world: harmony of proportion and intensification of light provided a similitude of the heavenly Jerusalem, whose earthly counterpart even then the crusaders were fighting to regain. The Gothic cathedral was at once a distinctly corporate symbol of an age of faith and a building for worship in which personal devotion and "the gaze which saves" substituted for active liturgical participation; the clergy "offered" on behalf of the people.

(e) Renaissance/Reformation; Counter-Reformation, Baroque
The early Renaissance humanist Alberti (*De re aedificatoria*, Bk. VII) had a passion for the centralized geometric plan, for the classical world, and for church reform. The Reformers were of their time; their principles for church architecture were based both on the NT and on theory of the period. They called for "temples" where God's "Word is heard and scrupulously observed"; believers were themselves temples of the Holy Spirit. There must be preaching (Calvin), and not separation of ministers from people. Simplicity was in order: the only things necessary were bell, pulpit, baptismal basin, and tables for the Lord's Supper (Church of Scotland, 1560). Lutherans preferred to group together the simple furnishings required for the liturgy.

Although Luther took exception to this course of action, the Reformation ushered in a period of iconoclasm not unlike that which convulsed the Byzantine Empire in the 8th and 9th centuries. Contrarily, the Counter-Reformation made the most of the arts as propaganda for the faith. Preaching was possible even in such a large single-naved building as the Gesù (1568ff).

The Reformation was precipitated in part by the building program for the new St. Peter's (15th-17th centuries). Requiring the destruction of the Constantinian basilica, Renaissance architects were unable to bring the revolutionary architectural project, in plan a Greek cross, to completion. Self-imposed demands for perfection and completeness were incompatible with the scope of their dreams. Baroque architects, however, were able to shape space so as to create a symbol of a church whose self-image was universality. No human scale was built into either facade or interior of this grandiloquent statement in stone. Liturgy must therefore be drama and spectacle. Bernini, who designed the altar with ciborium and cathedra and the monumental piazza, spoke of the latter's encircling colonnade as the arms of Christ embracing humankind. Baroque architecture becomes ecclesiological assertion.

The Catholic Baroque paradigm of the theatre and specifically the opera had a reduced Protestant manifestation. "Concert stage" designs of the 1860s and after put the choir on display behind the pulpit on a high platform, militating against the people's direct participation in worship.

Whether Catholic or Protestant, 17th-century churches were frequently centralized in plan. Style collaborated with theory and function. After the London fire of 1666 Sir Christopher Wren built over fifty churches: one-roomed buildings of a size and design so "that all who are present can both hear and see." Wren's steeples were memorable, and much copied. The Minutes of the Methodist Conference (1770) read, "Build all preaching-houses, if the ground will admit, in the octagon form. It is the best for the voice, and on many accounts more commodious than any other." Galleries allowed excellent visibility as well as audibility. Congregational meeting houses (a New World innovation) favored first a square, then a rectangular plan of domestic origin, with the entrance on the long side and a high, perhaps three-decker pulpit opposite. The small altar-table was placed at the pulpit base. Eighteenth-century Georgian churches with classical details were longitudinal in plan with galleries above the side aisles and across the back, and a raised platform at the front for the preacher.

Modern Anglicans inherited numerous Gothic cathedrals and churches which continue to shape their worship. The "two-room" plan: divided chancel containing facing choir stalls, with altar at its head and choir screen intervening in front of the nave, the high pulpit located at one side of the entrance, has been a strong influence on some Protestant church design.

(f) The Romantic Revivals

The 19-century Victorian revivals affected church as well as domestic building. A vernacular Greek Revival with Gothic details marked much of rural North America; among others, Baptist "preaching sheds" still punctuate that landscape. In larger churches of most denominations Gothic had a mighty impact. The Oxford Movement, devoted to liturgy, was echoed by the Cambridge Movement with its archeologism in church building.

(g) The Modern Period

"Form follows function," axiom of modern architecture, gave visual expression to liturgical movement goals. New building materials assisted a return to centralized designs preferred in the 16th and 17th centuries. Reinforced concrete (Auguste Perret in Notre Dame, Le Raincy, 1925) opened up the single-naved longitudinal hall to new unity and enabled the greater liturgical participation enjoined for Roman Catholics by Pius X. (Concrete would be given plastic shape by Le Corbusier in Notre Dame, Ronchamp, 1955.) Rudolf Schwarz's theories emphasized symbol and simplicity, leading to designs related to the 18th century meeting-house: nave wider than deep for the organic body of the assembly gathered about Christ its head. The 1930s in Europe saw new ideas and materials applied also in Reformed churches. Honest use of natural materials: stone, brick, wood and clear glass, recalled the pre-Constantinian house-church. Liturgical centers, relieved of clutter and "symbols," regained their symbolic value.

3. New Orientations

Vatican II's liturgical directives made possible collaboration and "reception" of liturgical, architectural and artistic values among a broad spectrum of churches. The Constitution on the Liturgy called for "noble simplicity" in the revised rites. Buildings and renovations were to facilitate active participation (S.C., 124). The primacy of the assembly together with the president's role in animating gifts and ministries was recognized. *S.C.* gave prominence to the word and preaching: its communication model demanded that sight-lines and acoustics be addressed. As eucharist regained its meal-character alongside the theme of sacrifice, mobility and accessibility to the altar-table became values. Assisted by artists, liturgy was to be adapted to times and cultures. Planning was to be carried out by competent local persons.

Other values reclaimed in the post-conciliar period include the communicative power of the non-verbal and non-figurative and the human social character of sacrament. The enunciation of the liturgical principles above coincided with new directions in the arts: form following function; simplicity in design and authenticity of materials; recognition of color and abstract form as analogy for spiritual experience.

4. *Needs of Contemporary Liturgy*

The variety of liturgical functions, initial and replacement costs, and population mobility call for multi-purpose buildings with accessibility for the differently abled and flexibility of interior arrangement. A communal discernment process undertaken by clients and architect, and collaboration between building committees, pastoral team, artists and liturgical consultant, is the model which, when used, is producing a new generation of buildings. The following points need to be kept in view:

The place of worship is a meeting place for the local church (function). It has a gathering place or foyer, which functions much like the courtyard of the early Christian basilica. Through immersion in abundant, living water the community grows (initiation). The font or pool may be located near the entrance to the assembly hall and allow for descent and ascent by an adult baptizand. Because the assembly actualizes in that place the great church and represents persons called together to form God's people from many places and times, it has referents beyond itself. The building should remind the gathered people of where they have come from: their origins and history (tradition). There they enter into dialogue with God through the Incarnate Word, in whom they have an acceptable response (word). Utilizing the goodness and inherent beauty of created things expresses relation to all God's creation (sacrament). The gathering nourishes for humanity's destiny: sitting down together at God's table in the kingdom (eucharist; eschatology). To this end the assembly witnesses, serves, celebrates. The past which roots it, the future which it enjoys proleptically, is celebrated now, in a structure which not only allows communication but leads to the experience of communion both with other human beings and with the triune God (communion ecclesiology). Needs of individual persons must also be met: of reconciliation and healing, of devotion, care (of children, the aged), education, vocation, death.

The various aims of this architecture range over the practical (including responsible stewardship) to the symbolic and aesthetic orders. Building, interior design and furnishings collaborate to manifest certain "absolute" or ultimate qualities: beauty, which calls the beholder to self-transcendence; centrality of the assembly, which challenges its clients to new and purer ways of being, seeing, and acting as a body; simplicity or poverty before God which rejects consumerism, the merely decorative, and comfortable pieties, and is therefore open to receive God's gifts.

5. *A Theology of Visibility*

Liturgy can be defined as the shape of God's grace in the form of the expression of the faith of the church, of which Christ in the Spirit is living source (E.J. Kilmartin). The building which houses the church under one roof is sacrament of that faith-community: sign and credo of the community's corporate faith, concrete hope and common commitment. It provides a home where persons embody their faith in common worship and other endeavors of the Christian life. It uses created things in its sign-acts. Thus a certain visibility is attained for the ultimate values which engage the assembly's prayer.

Architecture for this ecclesial understanding seeks to express God's transcendence-in-immanence. Since the Spirit is present and active in daily life, it does not separate sacred and secular but acknowledges that the sacred achieves visibility when life is lived faithfully. In other words, life has the potential for transfiguration. The house of the church is a kind of sacrament of God's offer of self-communication. Therefore it is hospitable rather than overbearing. Its beauty lies in simplicity rather than decoration. Because the assembly is active subject of liturgy and is a primary mode of Christ's presence, and because the church is built up by actions of the faithful, clarity or transparency governs the design of its assembly hall. It looks incomplete without people and their leaders, for liturgical centers, not works of art, serve as foci. Its spaciousness is analogue of God's mercy. Ancillary areas express the presence in mystery of the Holy One.

Its acoustic design is concerned with audibility of spoken word as well as song. Flexible seating allows proximity to chair, ambo and sacramental actions. Modular platforms can be given varying configurations without demarcating space beyond the functional. Given the global village with its ethical demands for sharing of goods, inclusiveness and justice, the church's house is "ordinary" architecture treated with extraordinary reverence. It does not ape ecclesiastical or "sacred" style.

The building can be called the *domus Dei* (house of God) because it is *domus ecclesiae*, meeting-house of the church. It houses a holy people who encounter Christ, priest of their worship, through the symbolic words and actions which they undertake together, and who, with renewed commitment to God's action, go out to meet the ethical demands of daily life.

H.W. Turner, *From Temple to Meeting House* (The Hague: Mouton, 1979). R. Krautheimer, *Early Christian and Byzantine Architecture* (New York: Penguin, 1979). T.F. Mathews, *The Early Churches of Constantinople: Architecture and Liturgy* (University Park, PA: Pennsylvania State University Press, 1971). K. Conant, *Carolingian and Romanesque Architecture* (Baltimore: Penguin, 1959). W. Swaan, *The Gothic Cathedral* (London: Elek, 1969). J.F. White, *Protestant Worship and Church Architecture* (New York: Oxford University Press, 1964). A. Christ-Janer and M.M. Foley, *Modern Church Architecture* (New York: McGraw-Hill, [n.d.]). *Liturgy*, Vol. 5, no. 4 (1986). Bishops' Committee on the Liturgy, *Environment and Art in Catholic Worship* (Washington: NCCB, 1978). W.S. Huffman and S.A. Stauffer, *Where We Worship*. 2 vols. (Minneapolis: Augsburg, 1987). *Reformed Liturgy & Music*, Vol. 22, no. 2 (1988). S. Scales, *Church Site and Building: New Development; Evaluating Your Church Site and Building for Redevelopment* (Episcopal Church Building Fund, [n.d.]).

MARY M. SCHAEFER

ART, LITURGICAL

To look at the long tradition in the West of the use of imagery for worship is to discover that at its best, the purpose of liturgical art has always been disclosure and revelation. Early Christian catacomb art of the 2nd and 3rd centuries was anamnetic; that is, its function was to remind the viewers of God's faithfulness to a chosen people through many generations. The attention was on images that would jog the memory, such as the three youths in the fiery furnace, or Noah in the ark, or Moses striking the rock.

The idea was to reveal the ongoing fidelity of God, to remind early Christians of who God is. To reveal something about who God is, is a quite different enterprise from describing what God looks like! There are very few images of Christ at all, and, of the few images that do appear, no two are the same. That there was no real concern about what a portrait of God might have looked like is revealed by the diversity of facial types. Twentieth-century viewers, conditioned by a later Byzantine image of a rather gaunt, elongated, dark-haired Semitic Christ, or worse, by a 19th-century sentimental portrait, might not even recognize them as representations of Christ at all. Those diverse images of the early centuries tell us something *about* Christ, that he is the attentive shepherd looking after his flock, and that his domain is both of this world and of heaven. Subsequent representations show Christ as teacher, a role among the apostles which in turn is intended as model for the bishop, as teacher among his priests. With the advent of the Emperor Constantine the parallel image of Christ as King appears. Only in the 4th century and later do we find Christ clad in the imperial gold garments of heavenly majesty.

In the first few centuries of Christian experience artists had as their focus the revelation of truths about how God acts among a beloved people. What Christ personally might have looked like had no relevance at all. This was not art of description, but of disclosure. Artists looked to their experience and the experience of their ancestors for the definition of what God was like. Their imagery was rooted in human experience and memory.

Within Eastern Christian worship there is another ancient tradition of sacred imagery, that of painted icons. Leonid Ouspensky writes that "the icon is not merely the expression of an autonomous sphere of human creative activity that the church happens to use in an accessory way. Rather, the icon belongs to the *esse* or essential being of the church; it is a vital part of that general order of human activity within the church that serves to express Christian revelation." [Leonid Ouspensky, "Icon and Art," in *Christian Spirituality*, ed. by Bernard McGinn *et al* (New York, 1987), p. 282.]

Icons have such an extraordinary role because their very existence lies in the christological controversies of early centuries. Icons of Christ and the Virgin witness to the dogma of the incarnation in affirming that God became fully human and that human beings will become divine. That is the economy of God's salvation. The human images (as opposed to symbolic images such as the lamb for Christ) represent a new view of the world: the Christian stance that matter is a vehicle of salvation. In the 7th century John of Damascus wrote: "I do not worship matter. I worship the Creator of matter who became matter for my sake, who willed to take his abode in matter, and who through matter wrought my salvation" (Ouspensky, p. 384). An important aspect of the content of icons is that they affirm the reality of the revelation of God in human circumstances.

The form in which that reality finds expression surprises us, for it is not the realism of classical antiquity. In these Christian icons, the depiction of realistic space, naturalistic descriptions of human bodies, the three-dimensional modelling of forms all disappear in favor of a rather flat, quite abstract design of non-naturalistic elongated proportions. The images are far more than illustrations. They invite the viewer to transcend the material image and to venerate the prototype, to honor the person to whom the image refers, and to enter into the reality of what is represented, a reality far greater and more complex than could ever be illustrated in a descriptive or merely narrative way. The image provides access to the larger and greater truth. The image becomes a way to communicate with God.

The early Christian expectation that imagery be rooted in human experience and memory, and the Eastern Christian presumption that icons lead the viewer beyond the image to the reality to which it refers, a reality of a graced humanity and a creation revelatory of redemption, represent principles equally appropriate for contemporary liturgical art. The goal is not to "decorate" churches, but to respond to human spirits which cry out to be lifted up, consoled, joyously encountered by the divine, the holy.

Imagery for public worship, whether permanent such as statues, other sculptures, paintings, mosaics, stained glass, or temporary objects such as seasonal hangings, plants and flowers, thematic arrangements or gestures of hospitality, requires authenticity and artistic merit to insure that it be worthy of the dignity of the activity of which it is a part. The American Bishops' document *Environment and Art in Catholic Worship* reminds us that the liturgy demands of all the arts quality and appropriateness. This means that every object should reflect honesty of materials, beauty, and care in the craftsmanship. The work of art 1) "must be capable of bearing the weight of mystery, awe, reverence, and wonder which the liturgical action expresses"; and 2) "it must clearly *serve* (and not interrupt) ritual action which has its own structure, rhythm and movement" (E.A.C.W., 19-20). The plea is made in the document for a transparency, "so that we see and experience both the work of art and something beyond it" (E.A.C.W., 21). The "transparency" spoken of here certainly resonates with our understanding of icons, leading the viewer from the apparent image to a larger and deeper meaning which finds its beginning point in the here and now.

What are the expectations of a work of art for worship? Guiding questions might inquire whether an image is evocative and provocative: Does it disclose intimations of ultimate concerns and holiness by virtue of being rooted in human and therefore accessible experience? Criteria for art for worship include: 1) that the work of art demand participation by resonating with human experience; 2) that works of art shape the imagination and lead to encounter with ultimate meaning; and 3) that works of art serve as occasions for revelation rather than as definitions of revelation.

How do such criteria help in making choices about particular works of art for worship? Among the many forms of art for worship, there is implied a priority of images utilized in the worship of the whole assembly. The primary honor of place belongs to those items which affect the communal worship, not the personal devotion of individuals. The importance and symbolic meaning of the works of art should be apparent in their forms. The focal points are the font, table, pulpit, and presider's chair. Nothing should challenge these priorities. Thus statues or other images of the saints, stations of the cross, or other images of popular devotion should not demand attention in the main worship space.

In the midst of the assembly, the altar stands as the primary object around which the assembly gathers. Its meaning encompasses Christ who is altar, priest, and victim. It encompasses both sacrifice and banquet. Clearly no ordinary table can disclose the richness and profundity of all these realities. The altar must be a piece of furniture of such beauty that it stirs reverence, of such dignity that it honors the holiness of what occurs there, of such stature that it is worthy of the mystery celebrated there, of such eloquent simplicity that it invites the placement of ordinary bread and wine as the appropriate offering of a people whose very lives are surrendered with those gifts in the eucharistic prayer.

The baptismal font requires special consideration so that it might bear the weight of the mystery of going down into the waters of death with Christ in order to rise from those waters into new life with Christ and new life in the community of believers. This means that the water, the major symbol of baptism, must be abundant and living and should be permanently located within the assembly for all the water rites and blessings that nurture the assembly's ritual life together. The font should be large enough to accommodate the baptism of adults as well as the immersion of infants, and accomplish this in a way that inspires awe and wonder at the life-giving properties of that water. The font should be a major image within the assembly, linked in scale and unity of form, as well as visual axis, with the altar so that the journey from font to altar becomes image of the Christian journey. The font is a place for memorable rituals marking births and deaths and blessings and spiritual journeys. The vessel for the water essential for Christian life deserves significance, permanence, dignity, beauty.

The ambo embodies far more than a lectern or podium. It is a table of the word, a reading table. The proclamation of the word of God is the activity it supports. The ambo itself should not overwhelm the lector in its scale or its grandiosity. It is not a podium for academic discourse and thus should not look like a classroom lecture stand. On the ambo rests the lectionary, exemplifying Christ present in his word, as the lector proclaims the sacred text. The ambo honors the proclamation of the word. It is not a shrine. Its form and appearance should reflect its role and evoke reverence

and attentiveness when it becomes the objective center of attention.

The presider represents Christ present in the assembly in the person of the ordained minister who calls the assembly to prayer and leads the worship. The presider's chair symbolizes the ordering of the assembly and anchors the place from which the designated leader conducts the ritual activity. The chair is not an immobile throne signifying rank and authority in the assembly, but rather the dignity and leadership focus of the present celebration. Care must be taken that the image the presider's chair projects is one that implies an appropriate role for the leader of prayer, for the presider's literal relationship to the gathered assembly visually expresses the ecclesiology prevailing in the community.

Today the assembly is understood in a new way, as a powerful symbol of the presence of Christ, along with the word, the eucharist, and the presider. The holiness of the assembly is honored when surrounded with plants and flowers, special lighting, or color (not signboards exhorting to action or acclamation, but color in hangings and shapes that speak to the season, the mood, the event). When the assembly, rather than just furniture pieces such as the altar and ambo, or the wall behind the altar, is embraced by color and image, so then is the total activity of the assembly, all its holy actions, enveloped in honor.

The choice and placement of any object in the worship space depends upon answering the primary question of what the item has to do with worship. The function of the work of art in question needs to be fairly clear. For example, to include stained glass in a new church building simply because stained glass is beautiful, because it is "churchy," and because it is low risk—everybody likes stained glass—can subvert the whole purpose of gathering the people of God at the Lord's banquet table.

A stained glass wall behind the altar, or even flanking the altar often constitutes a visual distraction and can even obliterate visibility of the altar area. Lest stained glass demand attention for itself within the assembly, its role should have some focus. The transformation of light quality in the baptistry, eucharistic reservation chapel, reconciliation room, clerestory, or foyer/gathering area allows the art form to be affective. The glory of stained glass' transparency and translucency lies in its capacity to interpret and express complex ideas and feelings in ways that vary according to the exterior light quality, weather, and seasons of the year, thus changing how one experiences that space. The mere illustration of figures of saints or emblems limits the artist as well as the material. Stained glass is a medium of transformation and of disclosure. When used with discretion it is a prime means for serving ritual.

In the recent past religious images for devotional purposes in places of worship tended to be limited to pious representations of saints and scriptural subject matter. One should keep in mind that powerful visual evocations of the contemporary human search for God need not be limited to those traditionally thought of as "religious." Those aspects of human life that provide poignant, not to mention dramatic revelations of the presence of God, offer possibilities for imagery that discloses and reveals life as God-touched. Gestures of compassion and tenderness, such as a parent for a child, remind us of God's compassion and mercy in our own day and place. An image of bone-weary age reminds us of the need to rest in the Lord. An abstract evocation of pure joy and exuberance at the entry might just recall the Lord's delight in the people he has formed and nurtured and convened.

To think of images as the occasion for but not the definition of revelation opens up possibilities for art to transform our perceptions in order to recreate and renew us. To think of images in this way also challenges us to carefully consider the expressive content of subject matter that deals with theological and scriptural content. A major barrier is a historicism concerning salvation history, a historicism which denotes a particular moment in the past without the openness and ambiguity in which revelation and mystery unfold. For example, what do those large wall-mounted representations of the resurrected Christ really say? Do they bear the weight of the paschal mystery as image for the Christian community? Would not the cross represent the fuller sign of a life lived in Christ Jesus, a life which is anticipating by virtue of the cross, but which has not yet experienced the resurrection of the last day?

The ubiquitous statues of saints, each standing quietly with his or her identifying attribute, invite reconsideration. Could the representations of those significant personages who have gone before us in the faith effectively provide encounter with the cantankerousness of those with the gift of prophetic vision, the anguish experienced by a mother like Monica over the chaotic and undisciplined life of her son, the subdued resignation of those oppressed by the church's own injustice, or the Lord's mercy in a gentle touch, a gesture of forgiveness? Such images would transcend the limits of historical narrative, breaking open the realization that in all times and places believers share in both the suffering and the triumph of Christ.

Liturgical vesture deserves artistic consideration as well. Ministerial vesture designates the presider and other ministers, but also serves to express the movement and gesture of ritual. Thought should be given to the shape of the presidential gestures so that fabrics can move expressively, and so that designs and color patterns respond to the expressive needs. Such reflection might guide designers away from symmetrical arrangements of symbols that "decorate" vestments to stronger visual emphasis in pattern and color for legibility throughout the assembly of movement such as arms lifted high in the invitation to prayer. In this way vesture serves the ritual activity.

The vessels used for eucharist, the containers for the oils, braziers for incense, and any other items used for worship require attentiveness to their function, their purpose, their meaning. Raising such questions calls for designs enabling those objects to support and enhance the ritual activity of which they are a part. Then they will not draw attention to themselves as objects, but function as sources of disclosure when they are used.

Liturgical art serves the life of the assembly when it supports and enhances ritual, when it discloses God's faithful presence in the times and places and lives of ordinary people, when it invites people to celebrate the beauty and honesty and integrity of creation, when it bears the weight of the mystery of faith and redemption.

See Aesthetics, liturgical; Architecture, liturgical

MARCHITA B. MAUCK

ASCENSION THURSDAY

Celebrated during the sixth week of Easter, this feast brings specific focus to the *exaltation* of Jesus in his risen life. It also marks a shift in post-Easter mystagogy to the missionary dimension of Christian discipleship: "Go into all the world and preach the gospel to all creation" (Mk 16:15; Mt 28:18-20).

See Easter season

ASH WEDNESDAY

The first part of the Easter season, i.e.,

Lent, begins with a solemn call to repentance (Joel 2:12-18). This period of 40 days is traditionally both a time of final preparation for those to be initiated at the Easter vigil, and a time of repentance for those to be reconciled during the Easter triduum. The custom of imposing ashes, a symbol of ancient penitential practice, is a symbolic act signifying human mortality ("Remember that you are dust and into dust you shall return") and total human dependence on the graciousness and mercy of God. It is a fitting act to begin the prayer and purification that is proper to Lent.

See Lent; Penitential practices

ASSEMBLY

The term "assembly" translates the Septuagint *ekklesia*, itself the Greek rendering of the Hebrew *qahal* which signifies the divine call that summons to a gathering as well as those who respond and come together in a community event. The *qahal* is the event of assembly (Deuteronomy 5). The emphasis is clearly upon the divine initiative of the call as constitutive of the assembly and the source of unity in its gathering. The OT *qahal* is an assembly of those who are gathered together by the Lord for life in the presence of the Lord.

The NT choice of *ekklesia* to name the assembly which is the church was influenced not only by its OT background but also by secular Greek usage which applied the term to political city states in Greece. *Sunagoge* (Hebrew *edah*), on the other hand, was the term applied to Jewish religious assemblies. Thus the Christian community attempted to distinguish itself more precisely from the Jewish *qahal* while at the same time reaping the benefits of the word's heritage in its Greek translation. The term *ekklesia* is used first in reference to the local community of Jerusalem, considered to be the mother church (Acts 8:1). The sense of the word quickly developed to signify not only the members of local communities at Jerusalem or Antioch or "throughout Judea, Galilee and Samaria" (Acts 9:31), but also the universal church (Acts 15), that is, all the faithful who are believers in Jesus Christ. The Synoptics use *ekklesia* twice (Mt 16:18; 18:18) in reference to the community of disciples formed by Jesus. Paul, who is first to employ the term in the NT, makes use of *ekklesia* 65 times, mostly applying it to local churches which are regarded as equals in view of his use of the plural form of the word. In Colossians Christ is head of his body which is the church and Ephesians proclaims church as the fullness (*pleroma*) and body of Christ. Because church is the body of Christ, all belong together in a shared life of profound union and cooperation (1 Colossians 12; Romans 12) which is given symbolic expression by the one eucharistic bread (1 Col 10:17). John says that Jesus is the vine and the disciples in shared life with him are the branches (John 15) meant for the same kind of unity enjoyed by Jesus and his Father (John 17). John himself does not use the term *ekklesia* in the gospel passages, though it is found several times in 3 John. Thus a central NT understanding of church is that it is an assembly, called by God through Christ, for which the word *ekklesia* is used. Assembly is church.

In a liturgical context, assembly is the technical word in general usage to describe the gathered liturgical community. This represents the church's understanding of the liturgical event as the preeminent place in which the basic reality of the church is manifestly actualized. The Second Vatican Council's *Sacrosanctum Concilium* put clear emphasis on this point: "The liturgy is thus the outstanding means by which the faithful can express in their lives, and manifest to others, the mystery of Christ and the real nature of the true church" (S.C., 2). Because the church is a mystical communion of shared life with the risen Christ and each other in Christ, the classical liturgical focus on celebration of the paschal mystery as the very source of the community's life is the basis of *S.C.'s* teaching that "Christ is always present in his church, especially in her liturgical celebrations" (S.C., 7), for "it was from the side of Christ as he slept upon the cross that there issued forth the sublime sacrament of the whole church" (S.C., 5). Thus, while Vatican II affirms in *Lumen Gentium* that "the church, in Christ, is in the nature of sacrament" (L.G., 1) and is "the universal sacrament of salvation" (L.G., 48), S.C. further affirms that the sacramental church is most completely expressed in the liturgical assembly. Similarly Pope John Paul II teaches in his Apostolic Letter on the Twenty-fifth Anniversary of the liturgy Constitution (December 4, 1988) that "the council saw in the liturgy an epiphany of the church: it is the church at prayer" (9). *S.C.* had proclaimed that "the principal manifestation of the church consists in the full, active participation of all God's holy people in the same liturgical celebrations, especially in the same eucharist, in one prayer, at one altar, at which the bishop presides, surrounded by his college of priests and by his ministers" (S.C., 41).

In a related sense, the traditional axiom *lex orandi, lex credendi* ("law of prayer, law of belief") expresses the connection between the entire range of the church's life of faith and the liturgical celebration by the assembly in whose prayer that ecclesial faith is resident. Linking faith, church, and liturgical assembly, the bishops of the United States conclude: "Among the symbols with which liturgy deals, none is more important than this assembly of believers" (*Environment and Art in Catholic Worship*, 28). The liturgical assembly is a community of faith and its gathering in the event of prayer is the self-realization of the faith of the church.

The christological character of the assembly is assured by the presence of Christ in the gathered community, a point taught clearly by Pius XII's encyclicals *Mystici Corporis* (1943) and *Mediator Dei* (1947) which may be regarded as modern statements that prepare the way for the clarity of *S.C.*: "Christ, indeed, always associates the church with himself in this great work in which God is perfectly glorified and people are sanctified" (S.C., 7). Twentieth-century magisterial witness to the church's tradition affirms Christ's active presence in the assembly and his specific role of presiding at the community's prayer. This venerable tradition, rooted in Mt 18:20, "where two or three are gathered in my name, there am I in the midst of them," has enjoyed immemorial respect in the church's life and piety and has flourished with renewed vigor in this century when so much attention has been given to ecclesiological and christological questions. So *S.C.*: "The liturgy, then, is rightly seen as an exercise of the priestly office of Jesus Christ. It involves the presentation of people's sanctification under the guise of signs perceptible by the senses and its accomplishment in ways appropriate to each of these signs. In it full public worship is performed by the Mystical Body of Jesus Christ, that is, by the Head and his members" (S.C., 7).

The ecclesiological character of the liturgical assembly which manifests "the real nature of the true church" (S.C., 2) is rooted in the mystical union of Christians with Christ. So *S.C.*: "From this it follows that every liturgical celebration, because it is an action of Christ the Priest and of his body, which is the church, is a sacred action surpassing all others. No other action of the church can equal its efficacy by the same title and to the same degree" (S.C., 7).

Liturgical assembly, the community gathering of Head and members of the mystical body of Christ, accomplishes the action of liturgy by the "full, conscious, and active participation in liturgical celebrations which is demanded by the very nature of liturgy, and to which the Christian people, 'a chosen race, a royal priesthood, a holy nation, a redeemed people' (1 Pet 2:9, 4-5) have a right and obligation by reason of their baptism" (S.C., 14). Liturgical action, in fact, is defined as what the members of the assembly do in their graced mystical unity with Christ and each other in the celebration of the paschal mystery. By their mutual presence to each other, the grace of Christ's real presence is sacramentalized and delivered by and in the community members in a variety of specific liturgical events each of which is shaped in a particular symbolic expression ranging from eucharist and the other sacraments to the liturgy of the hours and the sacramentals. "Thus, for well-disposed members of the faithful the liturgy of the sacraments and sacramentals sanctifies almost every event of their lives with the divine grace which flows from the paschal mystery of the passion, death and resurrection of Christ. From this source all sacraments and sacramentals draw their power"(S.C.,61). Members of the assembly employ in their liturgical symbol-making elements of human experience, like meal-sharing and washing with water, as well as materials of God's creation in the world, to manifest the invisible presence of the Christ who is present and powerfully at work in his church in the actions, gestures, words, and very presence of the members of the assembly. Indeed, "There is scarcely any proper use of material things which cannot thus be directed toward the sanctification of people and the praise of God" (S.C., 61). When human actions and material things are gathered into and become what the assembly does and shapes in the celebration of liturgy, the event is the visible manifestation of the invisible reality of divine grace and so is the very reality of church as the sacrament of Christ risen. The saving and transformative grace of divine initiative has the priority in constituting the ecclesial assembly and the liturgy which it celebrates "in the unity of the Holy Spirit." While all Christian life and activity is accomplished by the gift of the Holy Spirit, "Nevertheless the liturgy is the summit toward which the activity of the church is directed; it is also the fount from which all her power flows" (S.C., 10). Without underestimating the importance and richness of each individual's personal freedom and journey of faith but, on the contrary, depending on the gift of faith of all the believers who gather in assembly for liturgy, the assembly nonetheless transcends in the communal and ecclesial dimensions all individual faith. So S.C.: "Liturgical services are not private functions but are celebrations of the church.... Therefore, liturgical services pertain to the whole body of the church" (S.C., 26).

An immediate implication of the ecclesial nature of the assembly's liturgy is "that rites which are meant to be celebrated in common, with the faithful present and actively participating, should as far as possible be celebrated in that way rather than by an individual and quasi-privately" (S.C., 27). The fullest rationale for this principle may be found in the very nature of the assembly itself whose self-realization in its liturgy calls for the active participation of its members by their graced mutual presence and action. To the extent that the members of the assembly respond to and cooperate with divine grace and thus empowered fulfill their roles in the community event of shared prayer, the church's liturgy is accomplished as the paschal mystery is celebrated.

Just as there is a diversity of gifts, roles, and ministries in the church's life at large,

a similar diversity of gifts and roles finds its expression in a rich and wide range of liturgical ministries that serve the assembly at prayer. The assembly's liturgies "touch individual members of the church in different ways, depending on their orders, their role in the liturgical services, and their actual participation in them" (S.C., 26). The most fundamental liturgical ministry belongs to the assembly itself in its communal wholeness as it participates in the dual function of rendering praise and thanksgiving to the Lord and offering the gift of sanctification to the people of God. The bishops of the United States write: "The most powerful experience of the sacred is found in the celebration and the persons celebrating, that is, it is found in the action of the assembly: the living words, the living gestures, the living sacrifice, the living meal.

This was at the heart of the earliest liturgies. Evidence of this is found in their architectural floor plans which were designed as general gathering spaces, spaces which allowed the whole assembly to be part of the action" (E.A.C.W., 29). This basic ministry of the assembly as such serves as point of departure for the diversification of services that are offered in the community for building up the body of Christ and thus giving glory to God. S.C.: "In liturgical celebrations each person, minister, or layperson who has an office to perform, should carry out all and only those parts which pertain to his office by the nature of the rite and the norms of the liturgy" (S.C., 28). The text continues: "Servers, readers, commentators, and members of the choir also exercise a genuine liturgical function. They ought, therefore, to discharge their offices with the sincere piety and decorum demanded by so exalted a ministry and rightly expected of them by God's people" (S.C., 29). The General Instruction of the Roman Missal develops the same point: "Everyone in the eucharistic assembly has the right and duty to take his own part according to the diversity of orders and functions. In exercising his function, everyone, whether minister or layperson, should do that and only that which belongs to him, so that in the liturgy the church may be seen in its variety of orders and ministries" (G.I.R.M., 58).

It is clear from the teaching of the Second Vatican Council and from the Missal of Paul VI (1969) in these texts that in the assembly the genuine diversity of ministries, clearly acknowledged as true ministries, is rooted in the rights and duties of the members themselves as they serve the assembly and that, furthermore, one person's ministry ought not be co-opted by another person. The leadership ministry in the assembly's prayer belongs to the priest "who, in the person of Christ, presides over the assembly ..." (G.I.R.M., 60). The venerable phrase of the tradition, "in the person of Christ," used to describe the ministry of the priest, does not mean to suggest that the other members of the assembly do not live and act in Christ by the power of the Holy Spirit but refers to Christ's specific role of leadership which is sacramentalized by the priest's ministry.

In an even fuller sense, the life of the assembly may be intensified when the bishop presides at community prayer: "In the person of the bishop, with his priests around him, Jesus Christ, the Lord, who became High Priest for ever, is present among you. Through the ministry of the bishop, Christ himself continues to proclaim the gospel and to confer the mysteries of faith on those who believe" (*Rite of Ordination*, 18). The bishop's ministry of presiding sacramentalizes Christ's service of leadership and in this way assists in the building up of the body of Christ which is the assembly.

The years following the Second Vatican Council have witnessed the gradual identification of specific ministries in the assembly, a process given considerable

impetus by the Apostolic Letter *Ministeria Quaedam* of Paul VI in 1972. Of particular significance has been the continuing discussion about who might exercise individual ministries in the assembly and especially what ministerial roles women might rightfully exercise. Historical studies which indicate the unnecessary narrowing of the assembly's ministries to sacramental orders as well as the widespread modern recognition of the unfortunate exclusion of women from secular and ecclesial roles has cast much light on the question of ministries in the assembly.

At the same time, theological reflection on the relationship of celibacy to ecclesial ministry has become a significant part of the discussion about the diversity of roles and ministries in the assembly. A half-century ago, candidates for church ministry were limited to the single choice of sacramental orders to which the spiritual discipline of celibacy was attached. Today the assembly welcomes a wide range of non-celibate ministries, even within the sacramental order of diaconate. It is not surprising that there are fewer candidates for celibate ordination in these circumstances in which more possibilities for ministry have been identified for which celibacy is not a condition.

The 1983 Code of Canon Law, recognizing this legitimate development of the assembly's ministries, states that, in addition to the work of sanctification expressed in the exercise of ordained liturgical ministries, "The other members of Christ's faithful have their own part in this sanctifying office, each in his or her own way actively sharing in liturgical celebrations, particularly in the eucharist. Parents have a special share in this office when they live their married lives in a christian spirit and provide for the christian education of their children" (can. 835, §4). The assembly rejoices in the richness of diversity in its ministerial roles.

An especially important theme in contemporary ecclesiology as well as in pastoral life in the latter part of the 20th century has been the recognizing of the local church, especially as manifest in the liturgical assembly, as the incarnational realization in history of the very reality of church. Attention to this theme of the local church, called by L.G. 26 an "altar community" (26) in explicit reference to its liturgical assembling, is in fact a return to the vision of the earliest church which included both local and universal senses of *ekklesia* in its understanding of assembly. So *L.G.*: "This church of Christ is really present in all legitimately organized local groups of the faithful, which, in so far as they are united to their pastors, are also quite appropriately called churches in the NT. For these are in fact, in their own localities, the new people called by God, in the power of the Holy Spirit and as the result of full conviction (1 Thess 1:5). In them the faithful are gathered together through the preaching of the gospel of Christ, and the mystery of the Lord's Supper is celebrated 'so that, by means of the flesh and blood of the Lord the whole brotherhood of the body may be welded together.' In each altar community, under the sacred ministry of the bishop, a manifest symbol is to be seen of that charity and 'unity of the mystical body, without which there can be no salvation.' In these communities, though they may often be small and poor, or existing in the diaspora, Christ is present through whose power and influence the One, Holy, Catholic and Apostolic church is constituted" (L.G., 26).

In order to foster the life and appropriate development of the local assembly within the cultural ethos where it lives and finds its particular incarnational shape, *S.C.* states a fundamental principle: "Even in the liturgy the church does not wish to impose a rigid uniformity in matters which do not involve the faith or the good of the whole community. Rather does she respect and foster the qualities and talents of the various races and nations" (S.C., 39). This principle, which offers a distinction between the substance or core of faith-life and the diversity of ways it may be expressed, serves as point of departure for the establishing of norms to be observed in the practice of the inculturation of the liturgy of the assembly (S.C., 38-40). The council's rediscovered respect for the pluralism which characterizes the life of the church, far from representing a novel breakthrough into uncharted territories, is rather a recovered loyalty to authentic tradition. So *S.C.*: "Provided that the substantial unity of the Roman rite is preserved, provision shall be made, when revising the liturgical books, for legitimate variations and adaptations to different groups, regions, and peoples, especially in mission countries" (S.C., 38).

It is expected that it would be entirely normal for the assembly's liturgy to find itself deeply affected and creatively energized by the cultural life of the members who gather for prayer, and that, on a regular basis. The necessary inculturation of liturgy, however, is a process which demands full attention to the varied aspects of the liturgy as well as the elements and parts which may be subject to development and change. *S.C.* listed the requirements: "In order that sound tradition be retained, and yet the way remain open to legitimate progress, a careful investigation—theological, historical, and pastoral—should always be made into each part of the liturgy which is to be revised. Furthermore the general laws governing the structure and meaning of the liturgy must be studied in conjunction with the experience derived from recent liturgical reforms and from the indults granted to various places. Finally, there must be no innovations unless the good of the church genuinely and certainly requires them, and care must be taken that any new forms adopted should in some way grow organically from forms already existing" (S.C., 23). Thus the assembly is responsible both for the preservation of the authentic tradition and for its legitimate development.

In addition to the regularly experienced need for the normal and organic development of the assembly's liturgy, S.C. envisions that the cultural impact could sometimes be even more intense and insistent: "In some places and circumstances, however, an even more radical adaptation of the liturgy is needed, and this entails greater difficulties" (S.C., 40). The difficulties to which S.C. alludes arise from the challenges presented both by a careful analysis of the cultural elements which are to be incorporated by the assembly into the liturgy as well as the necessarily painstaking study and evaluation of the liturgical elements themselves, especially as bathed in the light of the authentic tradition, as S.C. 23 has already noted. Success for the inculturation of the assembly's liturgy requires that the whole complexity of liturgical and cultural elements be addressed so that fidelity to the genuine tradition is maintained while at the same time the necessary and appropriate development of the tradition in cultural terms is assured.

This process of inculturation will be continued as long as local churches continue to develop their life in their cultural ethos in succeeding ages of history. As the inculturation process unfolds it must be guided by remembering that the Second Vatican Council's emphasis on the local assembly as the self-realization of the church suggests that there does not exist somewhere a cultural prototype which holds the primacy as model for all cultures and ages. It is precisely that mistake of implicitly suggesting the existence of a cultural prototype which the council, and particularly S.C. sought to correct and to avoid in the future by making the distinction between authentic tradition and the pluralism of its diverse cultural expressions. In particular, a eurocentric predisposition to the arrangement of liturgical prayer in the assembly may be expected to decline to the extent that L.G.'s teaching (26) on "each altar community," described as "church" in the NT, is more fully realized.

The local assembly is the church of Christ. Yet, the tensions experienced by the ancient church as she began the attempt to live and express the gospel message in the language, elements, myth, and ritual of the Greco-Roman culture will always be repeated in new moments of history and in new ways as the diversity of human experience intersects with the power of the gospel message which is encountered in new situations and circumstances. The "Rite of Christian Initiation of Adults" states that each territorial conference of bishops has the responsibility "carefully and prudently to weigh what elements of a people's distinctive traditions and culture may suitably be admitted into divine worship" and "to retain distinctive elements of any existing local rituals, as long as they conform to the Constitution on the Liturgy and correspond to contemporary needs" and "to prepare translations of the texts that genuinely reflect the characteristics of various languages and cultures and to add, whenever helpful, music suitable for singing ..." (Introduction 30). The gospel becomes incarnate in the local assembly which is purified and transformed by the presence of the risen Christ in its members who embody in their cultural milieu this divine presence.

The preeminent example of assembly is found in the eucharistic community which is the fullest manifestation of church. As the "General Instruction of the Roman Missal" indicates, "The worshipping community is the people of God, won by Christ with his blood, called together by the Lord, and nourished by his word" (Introduction 5). The Roman

Missal used in the eucharistic liturgy states clearly that "The celebration of Mass is the action of Christ and the people of God hierarchically assembled. For both the universal and the local church, and for each person, it is the center of the whole Christian life" (G.I.R.M., I, 1). This understanding of the assembly, united with Christ, as the subject of the liturgical action strongly contributes to the sense of assembly as church for it is the church which celebrates liturgy. Pius XII, speaking of the mystical body as subject of the liturgical action, put emphasis on the union of Christ with the community in this act, "the entirety of its Head and members," and so liturgy is the worship which the "community of the faithful renders" (*Mediator Dei*, 20).

Following the same logic of development as *L.G.* in its first two chapters, furthermore, the missal first establishes the fundamental reality of assembly as church as the point of departure for a discussion of the roles and ministries to be exercised by the church's members so that everyone in the eucharistic celebration "may take their own proper part in it and thus gain its fruit more fully" (G.I.R.M., 2). The fundamental principle at work is that the gathered assembly, physically present and exercising its proper diversity of ministries, is truly the manifestation of the church at prayer: "The presence and active participation of the people show plainly the ecclesial nature of the celebration" (G.I.R.M., 4).

Liturgy belongs to the church, the people of God, given self-realization in the local assembly. For the church truly to become the full manifestation of the church at prayer, all the members of each particular assembly, in whatever culture it may live, are called to exercise their liturgical ministries. As the "General Instruction" states: "The purpose will be accomplished if the celebration takes into account the nature and circumstances

of each assembly and is planned to bring about conscious, active, and full participation of the people, motivated by faith, hope, and charity" (G.I.R.M., 3). This participation, accomplished in prayer by the mutual presence of Christians to each other, is the exercise of baptismal priesthood. Again, as the "General Instruction" indicates: "Such participation of mind and body is desired by the church, is demanded by the nature of the celebration, and is the right and duty of Christians by reason of their baptism" (G.I.R.M., 3). The physical characteristics of symbol-making by assemblies in every culture point to the need "to select and arrange the forms and elements proposed by the church, which, taking into account individual and local circumstances, will best foster active and full participation and promote the spiritual welfare of the faithful" (G.I.R.M., 5). The very environment of the liturgical action of eucharist and other community prayers critically affects the possibilities of liturgy for the assembly since "The general plan of the building should suggest in some way the image of the congregation. It should also allow the most advantageous arrangement of everything necessary for the celebration and help the carrying out of each function" (G.I.R.M., 257). The goal for the eucharistic environment is to enable the assembly to be itself most fully: "While these elements must express a hierarchical arrangement and the difference of offices, they should at the same time form a complex and organic whole which clearly expresses the unity of the people of God" (G.I.R.M., 257). If the environment presents obstacles to the self-realization of the assembly in its liturgy, to that extent are the possibilities of the assembly's being true church negatively affected.

The "celebration of Mass is a communal action," the G.I.R.M. states (14), and therefore the entirety of the event seeks to enable and promote the mutual presence and shared actions of the assembly members gathered for eucharist. Even the physical arrangement of persons' bodies and their interactive deportment is at issue for the eucharistic assembly: "A common posture, observed by all, is a sign of the unity of the assembly and its sense of community" (G.I.R.M., 20). The structure of the assembly's eucharist is so arranged that the table of God's word (G.I.R.M., 8) is an event in which the word of God is both proclaimed in faith and listened to with faith (G.I.R.M., 9). At the same time, the table of Christ's body (G.I.R.M., 8) is the assembly's gathering for the paschal meal (G.I.R.M., 56) at which "the whole congregation joins Christ in acknowledging the works of God and in offering the sacrifice" (G.I.R.M., 54) in the eucharistic prayer, petitions for daily, including eucharistic, bread and for forgiveness from sin. In the rite of peace, "Christians express their love for one another and beg for peace and unity in the church and for all," and share the bread and the cup (G.I.R.M., 56).

The eucharistic memorial of Christ's death and resurrection is "a sacrament of love, a sign of unity, a bond of charity" (S.C., 47) in the assembly, entrusted to the church which is "his beloved spouse" (*Ibid.*). So the members of the assembly are not present in the eucharistic gathering "as strangers or silent spectators" but on the contrary take part "in the sacred action, conscious of what they are doing, with devotion and full collaboration" (S.C., 48). The stated focus of the assembly's eucharist is so entirely communal that every part of the Mass expects and requires the mutual sharing of the participants because the word and the meal are not meant simply for individuals but for the community and all its individual members who are united in love and peace. Especially in the Sunday assembly for eucharist, the Vatican II liturgical renewal has provoked a dramatic, if not entirely finished, process of change in vision and practice that has transformed the Mass from an exercise in individual piety to an event of shared prayerful experience.

With eucharist as model for assembly prayer, the other sacraments and liturgies which build up the body of Christ and offer worship to God (S.C., 59) have more easily become gifted celebrations of Christ's shared presence, with the result that earlier forms of familiar language which were used to describe liturgical events, like "receiving" the sacraments, have been found less and less appropriate as they yield to the community's appreciation of the assembly's "celebrating the sacraments" together.

A secure index that serves to describe renewed appreciation for the meaning and role of the assembly in liturgical prayer is a simple comparison between the Missal of Pius V (1570) and the Missal of Paul VI (1969). While G.I.R.M. very carefully and very vigorously explains that both missals are excellent and faithful witnesses to the faith of the church and especially to her eucharistic piety and teaching, nonetheless the efforts of the Second Vatican Council have allowed us to see in these two missals that the church is not only guardian of what is "'old' in the deposit of tradition" but, at the same time, "it fulfills another responsibility, that of examining and prudently introducing the 'new' (see Mt 13:52)" (G.I.R.M., Introduction 15). Further, the instruction claims that "the liturgical norms of the Council of Trent have been completed and perfected in many ways by those of the Second Vatican Council" (*Ibid.*).

In particular, with regard to a sense of the meaning of the liturgical assembly, the Missal of Paul VI represents a considerable advance beyond the Missal of Pius V in the sense that, while the latter shows great respect for the piety of the faithful who attend the Mass, the Missal of 1570 nonetheless gives almost exclusive attention to the prayers of the ordained priest who is celebrating. But the Missal of Paul VI locates the presider's ministry within the overarching reality of the entire assembly and, in that context, seeks to actualize the long-dormant ministry of the assembly at large as well as the whole range of diverse ministries constituted by the gifts of each and all of its members. What is true of the Roman Missal is also the case of all the official liturgical books that have been produced by the reform of the Second Vatican Council, most especially in the instance of the R.C.I.A. which may stand as model for the liturgical assembly and its ministry.

E. Schillebeeckx, *The Church with a Human Face: A New and Expanded Theology of Ministry* (New York: Crossroad, 1987). Schmidt, ed. New Concilium *Liturgy: Self Expression of the Church,* (New York: Herder and Herder, 1972). P. Fink, "The Challenge of God's Koinonia," *Worship* 59, 5 (September 85): 386-403.

JOHN GALLEN, S.J.

B

BAPTISM

Commissioned by Christ (Mt 28:19), and enacted in the name of the Trinity by all major Christian churches, this first sacrament of Christian initiation incorporates new members into the church and into the mystery of Jesus Christ. It accomplishes what it signifies: new birth, new life, new creation. It arises in response to evangelization, the proclamation of God's word, to repentance and conversion to faith, and to a desire to be one with Christ in his church. This ritual act which combines a water bath and an anointing with oil confers grace, the priesthood of the baptized, and the gift of the Holy Spirit. In addition to the entries on baptism that follow, see also: Initiation, Christian; Anointing; Conversion to faith; Catechumenate; Evangelization; Mystagogy; Anointing, post-baptismal; Exorcism in baptismal rite; Sacraments in the Eastern churches; Sacraments in the Reformation churches

BAPTISM AND ORIGINAL SIN

I. Original Sin

The traditional teaching on original sin describes the state from which humanity is saved by Christ. The teaching is based on an interpretation of Rom 5:12. The interpretation that all have sinned in Adam appears to have been based on the practice of infant baptism, which influenced the development of the doctrine.

Original sin received its early formulation among the Church Fathers, most notably St. Augustine in his controversies against the Pelagians. The Council of Trent formulated the authoritative distinction that baptism removes the guilt of original sin, although concupiscence (the tendency toward evil) remains.

The contemporary church has witnessed a rethinking of the doctrine of original sin in the light of biblical criticism and the sciences. There are many schools of interpretation, but they generally agree that humanity has its dark side which cries out for redemption in Christ.

II. Baptism

Baptism incorporates individuals into Christ and forms them into God's people. In so doing, according to the traditional formulation, it removes the original power of evil. To say, "Baptism takes away original sin" is to express one aspect of "Baptism incorporates into Christ."

The liturgy of baptism has two expressions in the Roman Catholic church: the *Rite of Christian Initiation of Adults* and the *Rite of Baptism for Children*. Although baptism is the same reality in each rite, only in the latter is there an explicit reference to the doctrine of original sin.

In the *Rite of Baptism for Children* is found this formula in the prayer of exorcism and anointing before baptism: "We pray for these children: set them free from original sin, make them temples of your glory, and send your Holy Spirit to dwell within them" (49). An alternate formula for the same prayer reads, "By (Jesus') victory over sin and death, bring these children out of the power of darkness" (221). This alternate formula is a literal translation of *a potestate tenebrarum* from the 1969 *Editio Typica*, rather than of *ab originalis culpae labe* which is found in the 1973 *Editio Typica Altera*. This prayer is omitted in the shorter rite of baptism designed for the use of catechists (20).

In addition to this explicit reference to original sin is an implied one in the prayer accompanying the anointing with chrism following baptism: "God the Father of our Lord Jesus Christ has freed you from sin...." This is an ancient formula most likely composed with adults in mind, but it has been used, together with many other texts for adult initiation, for infant baptism. The implication is that since the children have not committed personal sin, it is original sin from which Christ has freed them.

The Sacred Congregation for Divine Worship first promulgated the *Rite of Baptism for Children* in 1969 (*Editio Typica*). At the insistence of Pope Paul VI (who personally observed the omission of references to original sin) and the Sacred Congregation for the Doctrine of the Faith, several changes were introduced in the second edition (*Editio Typica Altera*), promulgated in 1973. Among these were some which strengthened the influence of the doctrine of original sin.

For example, the General Introduction formerly spoke of the "natural human condition"; now it speaks of "the power of darkness" (2). The same introduction proclaims that baptism "washes away every stain of sin"; now it specifies that this applies to both "original and personal" sin (5). Also, the prayer of exorcism and anointing before baptism formerly asked freedom from "the power of dark-

ness"; now it prays for freedom "from original sin."

The Rite of Christian Initiation of Adults, however, makes no such explicit references to original sin. Its prayers and exorcisms beg freedom from the power of darkness and from personal sin. With adults, the obvious emphasis is on conversion of heart and entrance into the body of Christ. These prayers do not deny the doctrine of original sin; they simply concern matters which seem more appropriate to the nature of conversion.

By comparison, the baptism of a child has less to do with conversion of heart than with incorporation into the body of Christ. Hence, when the rite does speak of the sin from which the child is saved, it speaks of original, not personal, sin.

In the past a sense of urgency has surrounded the baptism of an infant. This was partly because of a fear of what would happen to the child if it died before baptism. This fear arose from a combination of factors: the infant mortality rate, the theory of limbo (a place for children who died before baptism), and the doctrine of original sin.

The *Rite of Baptism for Children* strives to lessen this fear. It urges that children be baptized within the first weeks after birth at a time when the child and its mother are well enough to attend the ceremony, and the family has had opportunity to make adequate pastoral preparation for the celebration. The rite actually encourages a further delay if the parents are unprepared to bring up their children as Christians (8). By shifting the focus of baptism from "freedom from original sin" to "incorporation into the body of Christ" the sharp sense of urgency has been modified.

The *Rite of Funerals* contains a set of texts which may be used for the burial of a child who dies before baptism. These texts differ from the other prayers for a deceased child in that they do not refer to the benefit of the sacraments the child enjoyed in life. However, by including these texts in the funeral rites of the church, the liturgy implies that a child of a Christian family who dies before its intended baptism still enjoys the eternal benefits of a Christian. The power of original sin in such cases may be presumed broken.

Annibale Bugnini, *La riforma liturgica* (1948-1975), Rome: CLV—Edizioni Liturgiche, 1983, pp. 582-595. Gabriel Daly, OSA, "Original Sin," *The New Dictionary of Theology*, Joseph A. Komonchak, Mary Collins, and Dermot A. Lane, eds., (Wilmington: Michael Glazier, Inc., 1987). Balthasar Fischer, "De Ordine Baptismi parvulorum," *Notitiae* 41 (1968): 235-245. Sacred Congregation for Divine Worship, "De Editione Typica Altera Ordinis Baptismi parvulorum," *Notitiae* 85 (1973): 268-272. Daniel Stevick, *Baptismal Moments; Baptismal Meanings* (New York: The Church Hymnal Corporation, 1987), pp. 11-12.

PAUL TURNER

BAPTISM IN SCRIPTURE

The English word "baptism" derives from the Greek verbs *baptō* and *baptizō*. In Greek *baptō* means "dip," "dye" by dipping something into dye, and "draw" (water). The intensive form *baptizō* means "dip," or "cause to perish" by drowning or sinking (a ship). The nouns derived from these verbs are *baptismos* ("dipping, washing") and *baptisma* ("baptism"). The usual Hebrew equivalent for *baptō* and its cognates is *tābal*; both terms imply an immersion and often carry the sense of destruction by drowning. In the context of religious purifications the Greek verbs *louō* ("wash"), *niptō* ("wash, rinse"), and *rainō* ("sprinkle") are more common than *baptō* or *baptizō*.

The ambivalence expressed in the words *baptō* and *baptizō* is based on the natural symbolism of water, which holds an important place in all religious traditions. Water can refer to both the life-giving blessings of God and the evil forces opposing God's authority.

Since all forms of biological life need water to exist, water is a natural symbol of life. Water quenches thirst and renews the human body. We use water to cleanse our bodies, and to purify our food and all objects related to human life. An abundant supply of water—either through rain or from springs and rivers—brings growth, fertility, and prosperity. For those who live in dry climates water is a special sign of happiness and divine favor.

Yet water can be destructive as well as life-giving. Floods destroy homes, crops, and persons. Polluted water carries infectious diseases. The formlessness and force of water in a storm at sea or at a raging river make it a fitting symbol of chaos. In a religious setting water can symbolize powers in opposition to the creator God who imposes form and stability upon creation. The ambivalence of the terminology for baptism and of water as a symbol finds expression in what the NT writers say about baptism.

Origin

The remote antecedents of Christian baptism are to be found in OT texts concerning ritual purification. Before carrying out rites in the Tent of Meeting (and later in the Jerusalem temple) priests washed themselves with water (Exod 40:12, 30-32). On the Day of Atonement the high priest bathed his body before putting on the priestly garments and performing sacrifices (Leviticus 16). The Pentateuch also prescribed washings as part of rites intended to end ritual uncleanness brought about through contact with unclean objects (Lev 11:24-40; 14:1-8; 15:1-13; Num 19:1-24). Ritual washings were so familiar to OT writers that they used them in metaphors, thus endowing them with moral and spiritual dimensions (Pss 24:4; 51:7) and in some cases eschatological overtones (Ezek 36:25; Zech 13:1).

Closer in time to early Christian baptism were Jewish practices that arose from or adapted the biblical rules about

84

ritual purity. Part of the Pharisees' program for a "priestly" Israel was the observance even by non-priests of the biblical rules for ritual purity. Ritual immersion baths from Second Temple times have been discovered by archaeologists at several sites in the land of Israel (Masada, Herodium, Jericho, Jerusalem, Qumran), a sign that ritual immersions were widely practiced.

The elaborate system of water channels found at Qumran indicates that ritual purification was a regular feature of life within the Essene community. The *Community Rule* (cols. 2—3, 5—6) suggests that initiation into the Qumran community was accompanied by a special rite of washing that symbolized the initiate's interior life: "And when his flesh is sprinkled with purifying water and sanctified by cleansing water, it shall be made clean by the humble submission of his soul to all the precepts of God" (3:8-9). The community lived in expectation of the coming visitation of the Lord. From the beginning of their association with the sect, the members had a strong eschatological consciousness.

Two other possible antecedents for baptism are more controversial. The "proselyte baptism" in rabbinic literature (see *b. Yebamot* 46a—47b) is sometimes proposed as a model. A female convert to Judaism was required to undergo a ritual immersion, and a male convert underwent both circumcision and ritual immersion before undertaking Jewish life in its fullness. But doubts about how early this ritual was used and whether it should be called a "baptism" analogous to Christian baptism render it a questionable influence.

Likewise, the rites associated with initiation into Greco-Roman mystery religions are uncertain antecedents for baptism. That Jews of Jesus' time knew about such rituals is entirely possible. But it is unlikely that such rites exercised more than a passing influence on the vocabulary and practice of baptism among the followers of John the Baptist and Jesus.

The Jewish rite most influential on early Christian baptism was the baptism of John the Baptist. John's activity was centered in the Judean wilderness, by the river Jordan. Not far from Qumran, this area seems to have attracted several "baptist" sects in the first century. The Mandaean movement probably originated in this milieu, though their claims to a direct tie to John the Baptist arose late, in response to Islam. Though part of a larger "baptist" movement, John was so striking a figure as to merit the title "the Baptist/Baptizer" from both Josephus (*Antiquities* 18:116-119) and the Evangelists (Mk 1:2-11 parr.).

Whereas most of the Jewish ritual washings were self-administered, John's baptism was administered by another. Whereas most Jewish ritual washings were repeated, John's baptism seems to have been a once-for-all-time affair. John's baptism demanded a turning around of one's life in the face of the coming kingdom of God. Several important characteristics of early Christian baptism derive from John's baptism: a water ritual, once-for-all-time, administered by another, involving conversion, and oriented toward the coming kingdom.

Two features distinguish Christian baptism from John's baptism: Christian baptism is "in Jesus' name" and involves the gift of the Spirit.

The point of contact between John's baptism and Jesus' baptism was Jesus' membership in John's movement (Mk 1:9) and the attraction of some of John's disciples to Jesus when he went off on his own (Jn 1:35-42). That Jesus accepted baptism from John is one of the best attested facts of his life. Yet the accounts of his baptism (Mk 1:9-11; Mt 3:13-17; Lk 3:21-22; Jn 1:31-34) are more concerned with presenting that event as the manifestation of God's Son and Servant han as a model for Christian baptism. Despite the silence of the synoptic gospels, it is possible that Jesus himself baptized (Jn 3:22, 26; 4:1), though this would not qualify as "Christian" baptism. The "great commission" of Mt 28:19 reflects the liturgical language of the late-first century church. Neither Jesus' own baptism by John, nor his activity as a baptizer, nor the great commission provides the one definitive link between John's baptism and Jesus' baptism. But given the common membership in the two movements, it seems that Jesus' followers would have understood baptism "in Jesus' name" and with the Holy Spirit (Mk 1:8 parr.) as the continuation and fulfillment of John's baptism.

Meaning

Christian baptism takes place "in Jesus' name," a formula which represents an earlier stage than the trinitarian formula of Mt 28:19. This christological formula is taken for granted by Paul (Rom 6:3; 1 Cor 1:13, 15; Gal 3:27) and expressed in various ways in Acts (2:38; 8:16; 10:48; 19:5). The Semitic expression underlying "in the name of" (lesēm in Hebrew, lesum in Aramaic) admits of several interpretations: with respect to, for the sake of, and with thought for. The basic point is that the baptized person now belongs to God through the saving-event associated with Jesus. In baptism one belongs to Jesus (1 Cor 1:10-17) and confesses him as Lord (1 Cor 12:3; Rom 10:9), thus putting aside all other masters. Perhaps with a deliberate allusion to slavery, Paul refers to baptism as the "seal" (2 Cor 1:22). In baptism one is delivered from the dominion of darkness and transferred to the kingdom of God's beloved Son (Col 1:13).

Christian baptism also differs from John's baptism by its association with the gift of the Holy Spirit (Mk 1:8; Acts 1:5; 11:16). Although the fullness of the Spirit is reserved for the eschaton, baptism brings the "first fruits of the Spirit" (Rom 8:23). The present experience of the Spirit is also described as the "down payment" or "first installment" (arrabōn) of what will be in the future (2 Cor 1:22; 5:5; Eph 1:14).

The precise relation between water baptism and the gift of the Spirit seems to have been a problem for some early Christians. That the two belong together is affirmed by many NT texts (Jn 3:5; 1 Cor 12:13; 2 Cor 1:22; Tit 3:5). How they fit together becomes problematic mainly because of some strange texts in Acts. At Pentecost the gift of the Spirit is a consequence of water baptism (Acts 2:38). Whereas some Samaritans had been baptized in Jesus' name but had not yet received the Spirit (8:14-17), in the Cornelius episode Gentiles first receive the Spirit and then undergo water baptism (10:44-48). Those at Ephesus who had received John's baptism need to receive the Spirit through the agency of Paul (19:1-7). Nevertheless, despite the variety in order, Luke's basic point in all these texts is that water baptism and the gift of the Spirit belong together.

The most extensive and profound reflection on the meaning of baptism appears in Romans 6. There Paul joins the baptismal themes of belonging to Jesus as Lord and the first installment of the gift of the Spirit to his theology of the cross: "Do you not know that all of us who have been baptized into Christ Jesus were baptized into his death? We were buried therefore with him by baptism into death, so that as Christ was raised from the dead by the glory of the Father, we too might walk in newness of life" (Rom 6:3-4). The connection between baptism and Jesus' death may have been suggested by the ambivalence of water as a symbol—both life-giving and death-dealing. Paul finds in baptism a death to the world ruled by the evil powers (sin, death, the Law) and the possibility of living a new life under the guidance of the Spirit (Romans 8). Yet the new life is not yet fully realized; it demands conduct appropriate to one who is led by the Spirit (Rom 12:1-8) and rejects the idea that "all things are lawful" (1 Cor 6:12; 12:23). Thus in Romans 6 Paul specifies the point of identity between Christ and the baptized person as Jesus' death and resurrection, underlines the preliminary nature of the gift of the Spirit, and challenges his readers to "walk" appropriately as they await the fullness of God's kingdom.

The notion of baptism as passing from the dominion of sin, death, and the Law to the dominion of Jesus and the Spirit is Paul's way of talking about a motif that runs from John's baptism to Christian baptism: the forgiveness of sins (Mk 1:4; Lk 3:3; Acts 2:38; 10:43; 26:18). This motif is also the starting point for reflection on the problem of repentence after apostasy (Heb 6:1-6; 10:26). Other NT baptismal motifs associated with the forgiveness of sins include baptism as "an appeal to God for a clear conscience" (1 Pet 3:21), as a means of rebirth (Jn 3:3, 5; 1 Pet 1:3; 23; Tit 3:5-7), and as a washing (1 Cor 6:11; Eph 5:26; Tit 3:5; Heb 10:22).

The communal dimension of baptism and its power to incorporate even non-Jews into the people of God emerges from Paul's reflection on people of faith as the true children of Abraham: "For as many of you were baptized into Christ have put on Christ.... And if you are Christ's, then you are Abraham's offspring, heirs according to promise" (Gal 3:27, 29). In the midst of that conclusion Paul quotes an early Christian baptismal slogan: "There is neither Jew nor Greek, neither slave nor free, neither male nor female, for you are all one in Christ Jesus" (3:28). Though Paul showed interest in only the first of the three pairs, the content of the slogan corresponds to his themes of nonpartiality before God (Rom 2:11) and the equality of access to God's grace in Christ (1 Cor 10:1-6; Eph 2:1-16).

Baptismal motifs are so prominent in 1 Peter that it has been interpreted as a baptismal instruction or catechesis Whatever the validity of this interpretation, it is fair to describe the spirituality of 1 Peter as thoroughly baptismal. A consequence of the author's reflection on baptism is his bold address to a largely Gentile community in terms applied in Exod 19:5-6 to Israel at Sinai: "a chosen race, a royal priesthood, a holy nation God's own people" (1 Pet 2:9). What makes possible such assertions is the incorporation of non-Jews into God's people through baptism "in Jesus name."

Order

There is no explicit description of the rite of baptism in the NT. What can be said about that rite must be inferred from passing comments. This is a dangerous procedure, since one can imagine all kinds of rituals on the basis of metaphors and other figures of speech.

With that caution in mind, it is possible to say the following about the rite of baptism in NT times. The person to be baptized received a form of catechesis (1 Cor 15:1-8; Heb 6:1-2). As with John's baptism, Christian baptism was administered by another (1 Cor 1:14-17) The word *baptizō*, the imagery of baptism as a drowning (Rom 6:1-11), and the practices associated with Jewish ritual ablutions and baths (*miqwā'ōt*) all indicate that immersion was the usual method of baptizing. Women may have been baptized by other women (Rom 16:2) though this is never made explicit. Where there was not sufficient water available for immersion, it was allowable to "pour water three times on the head" (*Did.* 7:3) The person was baptized "in the name of"—at first that of Jesus, and later that of the Father, Son, and Holy Spirit (Mt 28:19; *Didache* 7:3). There may also have been questions directed to the congregation about the candidate's fitness (Acts 8:37; Mk 10:14), hymns (Col 1:12-

20; Eph 5:14) confessions of faith (Rom 10:9; 1 Cor 12:13; Heb 4:14; 1 Jn 4:15; 5:5), and the imposition of hands (Acts 8:16-17; 19:6).

The premise behind most NT baptismal texts is that candidates were normally adults. It cannot be proved (or disproved) that young children or infants were also baptized in NT times. The arguments brought forward in support of infant baptism in the NT are weak. It is not certain that texts about the baptisms of entire households (1 Cor 1:16; Acts 2:38-39; 11:14; 16:15; 33-34; 18:8) really include infants. Peter's promise "to you and to your children" in Acts 2:39 refers to the succeeding generation(s), not to infant baptism. Jesus' rebuke of his disciples, "let the children come to me, do not hinder them" (Mk 10:14), had nothing to do with baptism in NT times. Whether young children or infants should be baptized raises the question about the nature of baptism. Is the essence of baptism the candidate's confession of faith, or is it the reception and appropriation of the salvation offered "in Jesus' name?"

Perhaps the strangest element in the NT teaching about baptism is the practice of baptism for the dead: "Otherwise, what do people mean by being baptized on behalf of the dead? If the dead are not raised at all, why are people baptized on their behalf?" (1 Cor 15:29). It seems that people in Corinth had themselves baptized vicariously for dead people. Instead of criticizing this custom directly, Paul uses it to bolster his argument about the reality of resurrection. The practice was continued by the Marcionites and other heretical groups but condemned by the church at large. Paul's point was that this practice was a sign of belief in resurrection at Corinth. The magical assumptions behind it ran counter to Paul's insistence on "walking in newness of life" (Rom 6:4), as his reflection on the wilderness generation shows: "all were baptized into

Moses in the cloud and in the sea ... with most of them God was not pleased" (1 Cor 10:2, 5).

Kurt Aland, *Did the Early Church Baptize Infants?* (Philadelphia: Fortress, 1963). George R. Beasley-Murray, *Baptism in the New Testament* (New York: St. Martin's Press, 1962). Oscar Cullmann, *Baptism in the New Testament* (Philadelphia: Westminster, 1978). James D.G. Dunn, *Baptism in the Holy Spirit* (Naperville, IL: Allenson, 1970). Joachim Jeremias, *The Origins of Infant Baptism* (Naperville, IL: Allenson, 1963). Rudolf Schnackenburg, *Baptism in the Thought of St. Paul* (New York: Herder & Herder, 1964). Surveys: Gerhard Barth, "Taufe auf den Namen Jesu," *Ser Evangelische Erzieher* 40 (1988): 124-36. Werner G. Kümmel, "Das Urchristentum, II. Arbeiten zu Spezialproblemen, c. Taufe and Gottesdienst," *Theologische Rundschau* 51 (1986): 239-68.

DANIEL J. HARRINGTON, S.J.

BAPTISM, ECCLESIAL NATURE OF

The rite of acceptance into the Order of Catechumens is the first major ritual step of the *Rite of Christian Initiation of Adults*. One of the questions usually asked of the candidates at the beginning of the rite is "What do you ask of God's Church?" (51) The *Rite of Baptism for Children* begins with the reception of the child. After asking the parents what name they have given their child, the celebrant asks, "What do you ask of God's Church for N.?" (37) From the outset, both of these rites make it clear that baptism is an ecclesial event.

This conviction has its roots in the NT where one of the meanings associated with baptism is that all who are baptized into Christ have become one in Christ Jesus (Gal 3:27-28). Paul uses the image of the body in order to express this union. In 1 Cor 12:13 he reminds the Corinthians that all who were baptized were made one body, in the one Spirit, and in Rom 6:3-5 he describes baptism into union with Christ Jesus as a matter of being incorporated into his death and risen life. In Acts 2:41 those who were baptized in response to Peter's preaching are said to be added to the community that day and the verses that follow (42-47) present a summary of the characteristics of life in the Christian community. In an exhortation on the meaning of baptism which appears in 1 Peter, members of the community are told that they have become "a chosen race, a royal priesthood, a holy nation, God's own people" (2:9).

The word used in Paul, Acts, and 1 John to express the union into which those baptized into Christ are brought is *koinōnia* which suggests a sharing or participation in something with others. The foundation of Christian *koinōnia* is God's call to share in the life of Jesus Christ (1 Cor 1:9) and the gift in which all participate is the gift of Christ's Spirit (Phil 2:1). Sharing a common life is the outcome of the gift (Acts 2:42) and this communion is expressed and deepened when members of the community participate in the Body and Blood of the Lord (1 Cor 10:16-17). Those who share the one Spirit are also expected to share their material goods with one another when there is need (Rom 15:22-27; Acts 2:44-45). Those who have received the Spirit and share the message of the gospel are called to proclaim it to others so that all may have *koinōnia* with the Father and with Jesus Christ (1 Jn 1:3).

The ecclesial nature of baptism is evident in the descriptions we have of the sacrament from the early centuries of the church's life. From the mid-2nd century we have the *First Apology* of Justin Martyr. In his description of the preparation for baptism he mentions that those preparing were expected to pray and ask God, while fasting, for the forgiveness of sin, but he goes on to say that "we pray and fast with them" (61). After the baptismal washing took place the newly baptized were led to the assembly where they were able to engage in common prayer and then celebrate the eucharist as members of the community (65). This link between baptism and the

assembly that celebrates eucharist is also obvious in the *Apostolic Tradition* which comes to us from the early 3rd century. Baptism took place after a time of preparation which could last three years and, by this time, the annual vigil celebration of Pascha had become recognized as the most appropriate context. Those to be baptized were brought to the water where they removed their clothes, renounced Satan, were anointed with oil of exorcism, went down into the water, professed their faith and were baptized, came out of the water and were anointed with oil of thanksgiving, got dressed and were brought to the assembly. There, in the midst of the assembly the bishop imposed hands on them with prayer, anointed them and sealed them on the forehead, and gave each the kiss of peace. When all this had transpired the newly baptized were allowed to pray with the assembly, give the kiss of peace, and celebrate the eucharist, the climax of the process. The right to engage in common prayer, give the kiss of peace, and participate in the eucharist were all symbols of full membership in the church.

Over the course of time the ecclesial nature of baptism lost its dominant place in Christian consciousness. Most of those being baptized were infants and baptism was no longer the climax of a process of initiation into the community. The dominant meaning associated with baptism came to be cleansing from original sin and gradually Easter, the Christian community's major feast, was abandoned as the most appropriate time for baptism.

The documents of Vatican Council II disclose a rediscovery of baptism as an ecclesial event. Members are incorporated into the church through baptism and deputed by their baptismal character to Christian worship (L.G., 11). Baptism is identified as the source of the Christian people's right and obligation to have full, conscious and active participation in liturgical celebrations (S.C., 14). Baptism is said to form persons into the likeness of Christ because they are baptized into one body in one Spirit (L.G., 7). In a discussion of the restoration of the catechumenate, Christian initiation is said to be the concern of the whole community of believers "so that from the outset the catechumens will have a sense of being part of the people of God" (A.G., 14). Finally, baptism is also recognized as the source of a bond between those who are fully incorporated in the church and those who are Christian but not in communion with the Roman Catholic church (L.G., 15).

The conviction that Christian initiation is a communal concern permeates the *Rite of Christian Initiation of Adults.* The initiation of catechumens is described as "a gradual process that takes place within the community of the faithful," one which will allow the faithful to renew their own conversion and thereby provide an example for the catechumens (4). The initiation of adults is said to be the responsibility of all the baptized and the entire community is called upon to help those preparing by their hospitality, their presence and active participation in the various rituals that make up the rite, their example of penance, faith and charity (9). Special roles within the community are designated for sponsors, godparents, the bishop, priests, deacons and catechists (10-16).

The rite of acceptance into the Order of Catechumens is described as being of the utmost importance because here, in a public assembly, individuals declare their intention to the church which accepts them as persons who intend to become its members (41). During that rite, the cate-chumens are invited to "come into the church, to share with us at the table of God's word" (60). The goal of the cate-chumenate is identified as that of training the candidates in the Christian life (75) and the rites of that period have the intention of leading persons "into the life of faith, worship, and charity belonging to the people of God" (76).

It is the church who judges the readiness of the catechumens and elects them, in God's name, for the sacraments of initiation (119-122). The bishop or his delegate carries out the election and has the responsibility for showing its ecclesial significance (121,125). During the rite the catechumens are asked if they wish "to enter fully into the life of the Church through the sacraments of baptism, confirmation, and the eucharist" (132). The Lenten season which follows election is described as a time of preparation for the celebration of the paschal mystery for both the elect and the local community (138).

In the celebration of the sacraments of initiation which is the final step in the R.C.I.A., the elect receive pardon for their sins and are admitted into the People of God (206). The faith they personally profess during the celebration is the faith which has been handed down by the church and the candidates are baptized in that faith (211). This faith is also professed by the rest of the assembly during the service. Participation in the eucharist is the culmination of initiation and the newly baptized do so as part of the royal priesthood (217). Finally, the Sunday Masses of the Easter season are identified as the main setting for postbaptismal catechesis, a time "for the community and the neophytes together to grow in deepening their grasp of the paschal mystery and in making it part of their lives through meditation on the Gospel, sharing in the eucharist, and doing the works of charity" (244,247).

The introduction to the *Rite of Baptism for Children* states that "children should not be deprived of baptism, because they are baptized in the faith of the Church, a faith proclaimed for them by their parents and godparents...." (2). The various ways in which the local community participates in the baptism as well as the love and help its members give the child before and after baptism are said to be ways of making it clear that "the faith in which the children are baptized is not the private possession of the individual family, but the common treasure of the whole Church of Christ" (4). Baptism is normally to be celebrated in the parish church so that it "may clearly appear as the sacrament of the Church's faith and of incorporation into the people of God" (10).

During the rite itself there are a number of expressions of this corporate dimension. The symbolic action by which the child is received at the beginning is the signing on the forehead with the sign of the cross. The celebrant introduces the action by announcing that the Christian community welcomes the child with great joy and that he is acting in its name, claiming the child for Christ our savior by the sign of the cross. The parents and godparents are then invited to do the same (41). Later, as he asks the parents and godparents to renew their own baptismal vows by rejecting sin and professing their faith in Christ Jesus, the celebrant tells them that the faith in which the child is to be baptized is the faith of the church (56). Following the triple profession of faith, the celebrant says "This is our faith. This is the faith of the Church. We are proud to profess it, in Christ Jesus our Lord" (59). All are expected to respond with "Amen." Preceding the actual baptism the celebrant asks the parents and godparents if it is their will that the child be baptized in the faith of the church (60), and the post-baptismal anointing of the child with chrism is described as a sign of the royal priesthood of the baptized and of their enrollment into the company of the People of God (18).

Another important source for exploring the ecclesial nature of baptism is *Baptism, Eucharist, and Ministry*, the 1982 document from the Faith and Order Commission of the World Council of Churches. There is much to be studied in its pages and the limitations of space do not allow a treatment of it here. However, the following quote may serve as a stimulus for further reflection on the topic: "Through baptism, Christians are brought into union with Christ, with each other and with the Church of every time and place. Our common baptism, which unites us to Christ in faith, is thus a basic bond of unity. We are one people and are called to confess and serve one Lord in each place and in all the world" (6).

Kenan B. Osborne, O.F.M., *The Christian Sacraments of Initiation: Baptism, Confirmation, Eucharist* (Mahwah: Paulist, 1987). Mark Searle, *Christening: The Making of Christians* (Collegeville: The Liturgical Press, 1980). E.C. Whitaker, ed. *Documents of the Baptismal Liturgy* (London: S.P.C.K., 1970).

MARGARET MARY KELLEHER, O.S.U.

BAPTISM, HISTORY OF

Baptism is the initiatory action which brings a believing person into the redemptive life whose sign community is the church. Such Christian theological meaning employs common materials and actions: virtually universally water has a capacity to symbolize life and death and washing. Ritual actions which use water to signify cleansing or rebirth, can be found in most world religions.

The Christian rite clearly derived from earlier material. The priestly washings of Judaism may have provided a partial model, even though such lustrations were often repeated. The washings, especially the initiatory bath, of the Qumran community (witnessed to by the pools and cisterns of the monastic ruins as well as by the scrolls) were significant antecedents. The Jewish practice of proselyte baptism, which cannot be shown to antedate the Christian era, but which Judaism was unlikely to have copied from the Christians, anticipated Christian baptism in ceremonial custom and in some interpretive meanings.

The principal source for NT baptism undoubtedly was the ministry of John the Baptist, who administered a decisive rite of baptism as a sign of inward repentance and expectancy. Jewish ethnic identity was not in itself sufficient in view of the urgency of the time (Mt 3:1-12; Lk 3:2-17).

Jesus' own baptism by John (see Mt 3:13-17; Mk 1:9-11; Lk 3:21f; and Jn 1:29-34), which does not actually recount a baptism) was the inaugural act of his public career and his identification with the sinful, but repenting and expectant people drawn by John. The accounts of Jesus's baptism, with the appearance of the Spirit as a dove and the voice from heaven attesting Jesus' divine sonship (Mt 3:16bf; Mk 1:10f; Lk 3:22), influenced the development of early baptism rites and symbolism.

The synoptic gospels do not say that Jesus or his disciples baptized, but the fourth gospel (in a single early passage) depicts Jesus as leading a baptizing movement which first paralleled and then surpassed John the Baptist's (Jn 4:1f, cf. 3:26f). No one is spoken of in the NT as having been baptized by Jesus—tending to support the synoptics. But none of the critics, who drew contrasts between Jesus and John, remarked on Jesus' failure to follow John's use of baptism as a sign of repentance, suggesting that he did baptize. His not baptizing would draw more comment than would his doing so.

The book of Acts depicts the church from the beginning as a preaching, baptizing movement (Acts 2:38). When a convert evidenced signs of faith, baptism took place at once (2:41; 8:35-38; 9:17-19; 16:14f,33). Often the term "baptize" suggests a unified, simple rite. But on several occasions a more complex action is indicated. At Samaria, converts who had been baptized under Philip's mission did not receive the gift of the Spirit until apostles came from Jerusalem and laid hands on them (8:14-17). The sequence was: preaching and faith, followed by baptism, and only later by the Spirit. The action was not intended to model a two-stage sacramental rite such as developed in the West, but to unite the Samaritan Christians with the parent community at Jerusalem. Another pattern is shown when, at the house of Cornelius, as Peter preached, the Holy Spirit came upon the household, and then the converts were baptized (10:44-48, cf. 15:8). The sequence in this instance was: preaching and faith, followed by the unmistakable access of the Spirit, to which baptism was an appropriate response. Here the event, marking the passage of the gospel to Gentile believers, is regarded as a New Pentecost (10:47, 15:8), and as at Pentecost, baptism follows from the initiative of the Spirit.

Acts gives no circumstantial description of how baptism was carried out. In one instance a convenient outdoor body of water was used (8:36). At other times baptism evidently took place in a domestic dwelling (9:18, 10:47; 16:15, 33), where, in the Roman world, water would be accessible. Acts speaks of the baptism of households, which would include parents, children, and probably servants (16:15,33). Although the conclusion of Matthew includes the risen Jesus' direction to the disciples to baptize in the triadic name (Mt 28:19), there is no indication that this passage was taken to be a "formula" for baptizing, for the baptisms in Acts are in the name of Jesus (2:38; 8:16; 10:48; 19:5; 22:16, and cf. 1 Cor 1:13ff).

The NT supplies baptismal meanings. Baptism is for the forgiveness of sins (Acts 2:38). Through baptism one is identified with the death and resurrection of Christ (Rom 6:3-11; Col 2:12). It brings a believer into the one body (1 Cor 12:13), a unity in which the deepest human divisions are transcended (Gal 3:26-28). It provides a new birth (Jn 3:5). It is a "washing of regeneration" (Tit 3:5), an illumination (Eph 5:8-14; Heb 6:4), and a seal (2 Cor 1:22; Eph 1:13; 4:30). 1 Peter, which may be a baptismal homily, contains imagery of being born anew (1:23), tasting and feeding (2:2f), being called out of darkness into light, and made a new people (2:9f), and of persons summoned to live quietly and without reproach. The NT terms are performative; baptism not only signifies salvation, it conveys and enacts what it signifies (1 Pet 3:21).

In the generations following the NT period, the church's initiatory rite developed into a quietly dramatic form. The catechumenate, a stage of probation and instruction, came before baptism (*Did.*, 7.1 is the earliest evidence; see too Justin Martyr, Apol. 61 and Hippolytus, *Apost. Trad*, 15-17). Before being accepted as a catechumen, a person's way of life was inquired into. Idolatry was so pervasive in the Hellenistic world that occupations which involved compromise with the worship of false gods or of the emperor had to be left. Although it was preliminary, this was a serious step. In many respects the catechumens, even though not yet baptized, were bonded into the community of faith. This pre-baptismal period was of indeterminate length, but could last up to three years. During this time, the catechumens would receive instruction, take part in the congregation's works of charity, and have a real, but limited part in the church's Sunday liturgy (they would be dismissed following the readings and the homily and before the eucharist meal).

Baptism, in the early centuries, was administered only at Easter (or, if necessary, at Pentecost, the end of the days of Easter) and under the general presidency of the bishop. In the weeks prior to Easter, those who were to be baptized received special instruction and were assigned special austerities. (This period of intensified preparation of the catechumens for baptism was the origin of Lent.) The event took place before dawn, so that the baptism itself would coincide with sunrise on Easter day. The actual baptism became somewhat complex. There was a preference for using running ("living") water. At first, the persons to be baptized and the ministers and attendants went to the water, which might be a stream. When they arrived, prayer was said over the water. In time, as it could, the church built baptistries— buildings, often octagonal, located at the bishop's church, which contained a pool, with water perhaps two feet in depth, often with three steps going into the water and three more leading out. These baptistries were separate from, but not far from the eucharistic room. The water would be audibly flowing, and the room and the pool were decorated with mosaics of baptismal symbols. It was the rule in the early church that persons be baptized in the nude. All clothing was set aside, and all jewelry removed so that the water could touch the entire body. Modesty dictated that changing cubicles be provided in the baptistries, and women attendants be present; and, of course, the rite was performed in a largely dark room.

In the water there was, in some places, an anointing with the oil of exorcism. The candidates, in some places, turned to the West, the direction of the dying light, and renounced Satan and all his pomp and works—referring to previous affiliation with pagan religions, the products of the great Deceiver. Then they would turn to the East, where the sun of Easter day was rising, and be asked three questions, corresponding to the three sections of the Apostles' Creed: "Do you believe in God, the Father almighty. . . . In Jesus Christ his only Son, ... The Holy

Spirit, the church, and the life ever-lasting?" At each question, the candidate replied "I do," and was baptized. The creed thus grew up as the Christian baptismal confession.

The water rite became associated with other actions, of which anointing with oil was the most common. In the Syrian church, there was an anointing before the water baptism, and none following it. In other parts of the early church, West as well as East, the baptism would have been followed by an anointing, with prayer for the Holy Spirit, performed by the minister of baptism. In Rome only (assuming that Hippolytus reports Roman customs), there were two post-baptismal anointings—one at the water, by a presbyter, and probably of the entire body; the other in the eucharistic room, by the bishop, only of the head (*Apost. Trad.*, 21). Other parts of the church used additional post-baptismal ceremonies, including foot-washing and the sign of the cross. The newly baptized were garbed in special white tunics; they then joined the "faithful" who had been keeping vigil in the eucharistic room under the presidency of the bishop. There, for the first time, the new Christians took part in the shared sign of peace and in the prayers of the faithful; they made their offering of bread and wine, and partook of the body and blood of Christ. The Easter communion, at least in some places, included a chalice of water (probably signifying inner cleansing) and a chalice of milk and honey (signifying the food of the newborn or the pledge of the promised land).

In the days following Easter, the newly baptized attended instructions ("mystagogic catecheses") by the bishop. These lessons explained what had been said and done at the baptism and the first communion. The compact actions and words of the rite, the darkness, and the secrecy of the text, made explanation desirable—explanation which would not have been fully clear before the hearers had under-gone the experience itself. Our knowledge of the liturgy and theology of this period is significantly carried by four great sets of catecheses: by Cyril of Jerusalem, Theodore of Mopsuestia, John Chrysostom, and Ambrose of Milan. Although they describe a common Christian pattern, each teacher represents his own location and tradition, and each set of lectures shows individual genius.

Analysis by anthropologists (especially Arnold Van Gennep, in his classic *Rites of Passage*, 1909, *Editio Typica*, 1960) has found that changes in states of life move by three stages: *separation* from one condition and social solidarity, *transition* when one is no longer in the old but not yet fully in the new, and *incorporation* when one has taken one's place in a new status and internalized a new order of reality. Without benefit of modern social studies, the early Christians developed a succession of actions which effectively carried a new believer from an old way of faith and life into a new. These initiatory actions would have given form to interior experience; they would have been a ritualization of conversion.

Although baptism itself was a universal sign of Christian belonging, it figured in some complex doctrinal and disciplinary controversies. One was the question of return after lapse. Was it possible for persons who had, perhaps under great pressure, renounced their baptism to return to the church? Some rigorists, as early as the NT book of Hebrews, thought not. In time (see *The Shepherd of Hermas, Mand.* 4.3.1) the possibility of a second repentance gained strength. Eventually penance and restoration after sin became more routinely accessible. A second was schismatic baptism. When persons who had been baptized in a schismatic group, whose baptism followed the correct words and actions sought to unite with the Catholic church, should they be baptized again? (Cyprian of Carthage held that they should.) Or did the validity of baptism belong to the name so that baptism given in schism should stand? (Stephen of Rome thought so, but he regarded the bishop's laying on of hands as a gesture of reconciliation.) A third was the question of original sin. If, as some theologians thought, baptism is an essentially retroactive absolution, a Christian should seek forgiveness for sins after baptism through the developing penitential system. Tertullian, in *On Baptism* (c. 215 C.E., the earliest treatise devoted to one of the sacraments), pioneered this line of argument. Such ideas reduced the urgency of infant baptism, and supported the postponing of baptism until late in life, a practice prevalent for several centuries. Other theologians (principally Augustine) argued (in part from an interpretation of Paul, and in part from the church's use of baptism, including its renunciations and exorcisms, for infants) that guilt is inherited from the primal parents. This thesis made baptism of infants imperative.

In time, the entry into the catechumenate became a formalized ceremony at which salt was given and a summary history of redemption was narrated. The creed, which had originally been secret until the actual baptism, became publicly known, and it was "delivered" to the catechumens at a point in their preparation. The brief formula of baptism had originally been used in the churches of the East, but in the passive form: "*N.* is baptized in the name. . . . " It was adopted in the West, where it took the place once occupied by the interrogatory use of the creed. The Western formula was active: "*N.*, I baptize you in the name. . . . "

The pattern of initiation which the early church devised gave form to the experience of adult converts. From early times, when parents became Christians, their children were baptized with them. (Presumably children born to Christian parents after their baptism were baptized rather than kept unbaptized until some

later life stage. But the documents from the earliest generations are not concerned with the matter.) When most of the population of an area had become Christian, adult baptisms became rare; the catechumenate disappeared; and baptism became a rite for the children of believers.

These developments occurred (at locally different times) throughout the East and the West. In the East, baptism came to be performed a few days after the birth of a child, breaking the link of initiation with Easter. The local priest was and is the usual minister of the entire rite. The water baptism is followed at once by chrismation, using chrism blessed by the bishop (or patriarch). The rite leads to the child's first communion. These ritual events are regarded as comprising a sacramental unity.

In the West too baptism was ordinarily administered to infants soon after birth. The rite commonly began at the church door where some initial questions and ceremonies that had originally admitted adults to the catechumenate took place. Then the liturgy moved to the font (now a furnishing located within the church itself) with sponsors making the renunciations and promises in the name of the child. In most regions of the West (Spain, Gaul, North Italy, and perhaps others) baptism was followed, as in the East, by an anointing, given by the minister of baptism. Until late in the Middle Ages, newly baptized children were given communion. Functionally baptism changed from being a long process, bringing an adult into the church, to being a brief action centering on a child a few days old. Instead of identifying a community of instructed, convinced believers, it became a sign of the continuity of a Christian society. But through this functional shift, few adaptations were made in the rite itself or in the theological account of its meaning.

In Rome, and only there, baptism was

followed by two anointings, one by the priest at the baptism, the second by the bishop, either at the baptism or as soon as possible thereafter. The churches in Gaul had followed the prevailing custom of a single anointing at the time of baptism. But when under Charlemagne there was an effort to bring consistency to the fragmented church, the Roman model was introduced widely in Europe—a model requiring a second post-baptismal anointing by the bishop, without which the baptism was incomplete. The medieval church in the West sought to make these regulations effective. In the vicinity of Rome, where dioceses were small, and most baptisms continued to be at Easter, and bishops were never far away, the two anointings were workable. But in northern Europe, where dioceses were large, the Roman pattern was impracticable. Bishops were remote, and travel was difficult. A time opened between baptism and the bishop's post-baptismal anointing. Legislation required that a child be brought to the bishop within a few years—five, seven?—of baptism and that no one receive communion before being "bishopped." But the bishop's anointing often did not take place. When it did occur, it was commonly some time after the water baptism. Since it came in later childhood, this bishop's anointing was associated with some minimal instruction. Eventually this medieval development was made the basis of a novel rationale of the rite. The two stages of initiation ritualized life stages: baptism was to birth as confirmation (the medieval Western term) was to coming of age.

This late medieval two-stage initiatory pattern was accepted both by the principal 16th century Reformers and by the Counter-Reformation church. The Reformers reworked the baptismal rites so that they suited the baptism of infants, which was then the universal practice. Luther understood baptism as a pledge of God's grace and faithfulness—a pledge that would stand whatever else failed. Calvin stressed baptism as admission to the redeemed society. Confirmation, the second stage of initiation, was a time of coming of age in the church, of owning for oneself the pledges of baptism. Throughout the 16th and 17th centuries, in Catholic and in Protestant communities, catechisms were written and strenuous educational efforts were put forward to secure an informed level of Christian life. (The Protestant pietists thought of confirmation as an occasion for conversion—the conversion of the already baptized.)

The Anabaptist strain of the Reformation, however, broke with this inherited pattern. Baptism should be of intelligent, confessing believers. Children of Christian parents were not baptized, but were held, under instruction and prayerful guidance, until, at an "age of discretion," they could declare their own faith. Infant baptism could not be regarded as true baptism at all, thus calling in question the practice which had brought into being large Christian populations. The issues were (and remain) ecclesial as well as sacramental; and the ecumenical divisions over them have not been resolved.

Beginning in the medieval period and continuing until the mid-20th century, it was taken for granted that baptism was a private, not a congregational or ecclesial rite, to be attended by family and friends. It was cut off from confirmation and from any obvious association with the eucharist.

In the 19th century, beginning in Europe, but soon spreading more widely, the practice of a ceremonially important "first communion," a few years prior to confirmation came to be common in the Roman communion. Baptism and holy communion were thus brought into closer association, but at the cost of flawing the sequence of the sacramental signs.

In the world-wide missionary expansion of the 16th-19th centuries, or in the rapidly growing "third church" of the mid-20th century, baptism has often recovered its power as a ritual enactment of conversion. But in the older centers of Christian population, Catholic and Protestant, a high proportion of the society is baptized, but only a small proportion seems to give evidence of adult Christian commitment or membership. Baptism has become a rite of reduced significance.

Various movements of "baptismal reform" have sought to raise standards of pastoral diligence. Quite rapidly in the final third of the 20th century significant changes in initiatory rites and practices have been introduced in many churches. The link between baptism and Easter (or the festal occasions of the year) is being reestablished. Baptism is coming to involve congregations, permitting baptized Christians to be reminded of their own baptism and its commitments. The level of pre-baptismal instruction for parents and sponsors, and of course for adults preparing for baptism, is being raised. In the Roman communion, the post-council *Rite of Christian Initiation of Adults* ("R.C.I.A.," *Editio Typica*, 1974) has had a marked influence. The rite (like new rites in several other communions) restores much of the shape of the baptismal process of the early church—catechesis, leading to baptism at Easter, followed at once by confirmation and first communion, and mystagogia. Such initiatory rites hold before the church what can properly be expected from its members.

DANIEL B. STEVICK

BAPTISM, INFANT

Early History

Baptism has from initial days of Christianity been the ritual center of the initiatory process. It is clear in scripture that adult persons professing faith, becoming part of the community of believers, and accepting the person of Jesus, celebrated a rite of baptism. The initial years of church experience provided a growing awareness of the many implications of baptism. And with this growth came changes in praxis.

Thus, for example, the timing moved from immediately after conversion, to a Sunday eucharistic gathering, to the annual Easter event. And the process of preparation expanded to what became the catechumenate. And at some time by the end of the 2nd century children were among the candidates for baptism. Yet even in the 4th century adult baptism was quite common.

Mixed reasons would be given for the baptism of children. There was an increasing fundamentalist understanding of the necessity of baptism, taking the Johannine gospel phrasing in a literal manner (see, Jn 3:3). There was also a high infant mortality rate. To all of this was added the theological explanation of Cyprian that it was the sin of Adam that was forgiven in baptism; with Augustine it was "original sin."

By the 5th century, the practice of infant baptism was universal in the West and by the end of the 8th century, when efforts were made to provide a universal common ritual for the Holy Roman Empire, it was presumed that the subject of baptism was the infant. While phrases and remnants of the adult baptism (the catechumenate, and the annual Easter celebration were retained, the practical reality that came to be standard was that all children were baptized in infancy.

In the process there was a shift in the understanding of the meaning of baptism. The baptism which the Fathers of the church had written about was an experiential reality of conversion in adult life, a statement of faith confirmed and a way of life accepted. By the time the

Scholastics wrote of baptism (*de facto*, infant baptism), society and church were practically co-terminous. The candidate was not saved from a pagan world into an ecclesial world or from a life of sin to forgiveness. The candidate was taken from a sinful state (i.e, original sin) to the state of grace.

Later History

With the reformers the practice of infant baptism varied. This was due to a shifting understanding of the church and the place of grace and faith in Christian life. Anabaptists directly rejected the concept of infant baptism. Luther, on the other hand, did not. Calvin's view of predestination made the question of infant baptism moot. For him children might be baptized but this was not, of itself, efficacious.

The Catholic response at Trent spoke directly to several of the underlying issues but did not address the question of infant baptism as such. It was deemed sufficient simply to condemn as heretical some of the Reformers' positions on the question. In the point/counterpoint manner of the "dialogue" of the day, the real dilemma was never faced: namely, that the praxis of infant baptism failed to engage people in the conversion to Christ. But while the bishops came forth strong on the issue of baptizing infants, they were sufficiently aware of the problem to call for catechesis, albeit in the years that would follow the sacrament.

Immediate History Leading to Vatican II

The pastoral liturgical movement of the 20th century encouraged a triple renewal in the whole process of Christian initiation: in the manner of celebration; in the level of catechesis; and indeed by changes in the very rituals themselves. Even before the Second Vatican Council, the Easter vigil was restored and the focus of the people was directed to the baptismal implications of the vigil. And in the *Constitution on the Sacred Liturgy*

there was issued a call for a renewal of the entire process of Christian initiation, a restoration of the catechumenate and the revision of the rite of infant baptism along with the composition of a new rite of adult baptism (S.C., 64ff).

Vatican II

The liturgy constitution was strong in its call for the catechumenate and its attention to adult initiation. But it was equally strong in its attention to infant baptism. "The rite for the baptism of infants is to be revised and it should be suited to the fact that those to be baptized are infants. The roles as well as the obligations of parents and godparents should be brought out more clearly in the rite itself" (S.C., 67). Three documents capture the fruit of this reform: the *Roman Rite of Baptism for Children* (1969); the *Rite of Christian Initiation of Adults* (1972); and the revised *Code of Canon Law* (1983). Before addressing these documents and noting the present praxis of the Catholic celebration of infant baptism a brief word on the dialogue that followed Vatican II is in order.

Post Vatican II Debate

While initial reception of the revised infant baptismal ritual was enthusiastic in most American parishes there was nonetheless more than a little concern raised by academics and pastors concerning elements of the new initiatory praxis being introduced, especially later in the light of the *Rite of Christian Initiation of Adults*. In western Europe first, and later in the United States, many articles appeared searching for the theological rationale of infant baptism, questioning what the new rites for adult initiation said about the baptism of infants, etc.

The concern of both pastors and theologians surfaced in the area of faith. In infant baptism clearly it is the faith of the believing community that gives title to the celebration. In adult initiation the catechumen professes faith directly. This difference was less noticed in a culture where church and society were as one. In the secularized society of the later 20th century, questions and concerns surface more readily. When parents, showing little evidence of faith commitment, surface in local churches in a time when the mobility of people provides pastors with little awareness of the parents' roots and no clear picture of their future, serious questions arise.

While many of the articles concluded with the legitimacy of infant baptism, most were not enthusiastic. Sufficient questions were raised for the Congregation for the Doctrine of the Faith to issue an instruction (1980) affirming the Roman practice of baptizing infants. The instruction cites the traditional doctrine and then addresses several of the difficulties raised in the literature of the seventies: the order and sequence of "preaching, faith, sacrament"; that grace intended for a person "should be accepted and appropriated by the person who receives it"; restriction of the freedom of the infant; the pluralistic society in which the child will be reared; the begging of the question of adult evangelization in the baptizing of infants.

Arguing against each of these difficulties, the document then offers pastoral directives. The suggestion of "definitive abandonment" of infant baptism is not accepted. Two principles are offered. First, the value of infant baptism clearly suggests a gift for infants which must not be delayed. Secondly, assurances that the gift can grow by way of education and the Christian life must be given. If these assurances are not present there are grounds for delay; if the assurances are certainly non-existent, there are grounds for refusing the sacrament.

The instruction not-withstanding, there remains less than a clear, enthusiastic statement supporting infant baptism in current literature. Thus, e.g., Bernard Cooke in *Sacraments and Sacramentality*, page 116 *et passim* (Mystic CT: Twenty Third Publications, 1983).

Ecumenical Reflection

The academic and pastoral activity that led to the present situation was not limited to the Catholic community. More than a few churches have produced renewed rites in recent years emphasizing initiation and the Easter event. Ecumenical perspective on this can be seen in the January 1982 Faith and Order statement, *Baptism, Eucharist and Ministry*, promulgated at Lima, Peru. For a summary of the infant baptism question implicit in this statement, cf. Michael Amaladoss S.J., "Baptism in the Ecumenical Context," *Month*, 18:328-333 and Edward Kilmartin S.J., "Faith and Baptism: Sacramental Theology in the Lima Document" in *Catholic Perspectives on Baptism, Eucharist and Ministry*, Michael Fahey, editor (Lanham MD, University Press, 1986).

The Lima document, cautioning against indiscriminate baptism, recognized the practice of infant baptism while respecting the discipline of churches that celebrated only believer's baptism. This having been said, however, the document does not touch many of the related questions; e.g., the manner of the continuation of the initiation process following the infant baptism or the manner in which churches which practice believer's baptism accept or reject the baptism of those already baptized as infants.

Having noted some ecumenical elements of the discussion, the following will focus on the Roman Catholic situation where the greatest pastoral development concerning infant baptism has occurred.

1969 Rite of Baptism for Children

The council called for a rite that would be adapted to the actual condition of children recognizing and expressing clearly the role and responsibilities of parents and godparents. Adaptations were to be provided for the baptism of a large number of persons. Adaptations were also to be allowed for baptism by catechists in mission lands where the ordinary minister of baptism was unavailable.

The seven chapters of the rite are preceded by a general introduction and specific introduction. The order of the rite includes reception of the child(ren), celebration of God's word, celebration of the sacrament, and conclusion of the rite. In the specific introduction the manner of arranging the rite within the Mass is detailed (paragraphs 29—30).

In the rite of reception, the name of the child is identified, the purpose of the gathering is noted, the responsibilities of the parents and godparents are attested and the child(ren) signed with the cross.

Chapter seven provides a number of pericopes for the celebration of God's word. Intercessions, prayer of exorcism and anointing with the oil of catechumens follow the homily. In the celebration of the sacrament, reminder is given of the symbol of water and the water of the font, if not already blessed, is blessed. Sin is renounced and faith is professed. This renunciation and profession is done by the parents and godparents themselves— not in the person of the infant. The child is immersed—or water is poured—with the trinitarian formula "I baptize you in the name of the Father and of the Son and of the Holy Spirit."

Three elements of the celebration of the sacrament follow: anointing with chrism, clothing with the white garment and receiving the "light of Christ" from the lighted candle. The conclusion of the rite includes the Lord's Prayer and blessing.

Preparation for the Rite

Perhaps the most significant change in pastoral practice concerning the baptism of infants in the post-Vatican II era is in the area of preparation. Typical pre-of infants in the post-Vatican II era is in the area of preparation. Typical pre-Vatican II procedure presumed sufficient at designated hours, usually with parents arriving unscheduled and priest and parents and godparents meeting one another just as the celebration would begin.

Without detailing a format for the catechesis, the new rite clearly identified a need for such, and a variety of styles emerged. Many of the catechetical publishers have produced programs, structures, printed materials and audio-visuals supporting such catechesis. Typically this is directed by volunteer laity and includes pastoral visit or presence by the professional pastoral staff. The preparation period generally includes instructional elements on the theology of sacraments and initiation, spiritual reflection on the immediate and future tasks of parenting and ritual comments preparing for the actual celebration of the rite.

While sometimes programmed during the days of pregnancy, the preparation process has more often than not delayed the actual baptism to several weeks or months following birth in contrast to an earlier custom of baptism within the first week of birth. Can. 867 of the 1983 *Code of Canon Law* directs parents to see to it "within a few weeks."

Infant

The candidate for the rite is an infant. The rationale for baptizing infants is briefly noted in par. 2 of the introduction, citing John 3 ("unless one is reborn of water and the spirit") as the foundation for why children should not be deprived of baptism; adding that children are baptized in the faith of the church. Augustine is quoted.

Infants are children up to the age of reason, that is "those who have not reached the age of discernment and therefore cannot have or profess personal faith" (par. 1). In the *Rite of Christian*

Initiation of Adults there is specific provision for older children, that is, children of catechetical age, children of age to understand. These are to be catechized and then receive the three sacraments of initiation in the one liturgical celebration. Older children who are *non sui compos*, however, are considered infants.

Parents

The place of parents is accented strongly. It is they who present the infant. As a rule, it is they, or at least one of them, who profess faith, they who will rear the child in the faith.

Typically in parishes today parents register for the baptism of their child early, in the days of pregnancy. A preparation process follows as noted above. In the rite itself they publicly ask for baptism; they sign the child with the sign of the cross; they renounce Satan; they profess faith; they carry the child to the font; they receive a blessing.

As the role of parents is accented, a question surfaces when parents fall short of the mark. First to be noted is a presumption of faith. When hostility is evident, it is for the pastor to delay the decision of baptism until things are worked out. When one or both of the parents is not Christian and yet a sincere request is made with assurance of Christian upbringing, the baptism proceeds and the pastor notes the additional demand this places on the sponsor. Following the 1980 instruction, when parental assurance of Christian upbringing is non-existent, baptism is refused.

Sponsors

Each child may have a godfather and a godmother. Godparents should be present to be added spiritually to the immediate family of the one to be baptized and "to represent Mother Church" (General Introduction, par. 8ff.). As occasion offers, the godparent will be ready to help the parents bring up their child to profess the faith and to show this by living it.

Together with the parent, they profess the church's faith, in which the child is being baptized. Thus godparents should be mature enough to undertake this responsibility, should have received the three sacraments of initiation: baptism, confirmation, and the eucharist, and should be a member of the Catholic church and canonically free to carry out this office. Par. 10 of the general introduction noted that "A baptized and believing Christian from a separated church or community may act as a godparent or Christian witness along with a Catholic godparent, at the request of the parents and in accordance with the norms for various ecumenical cases." The 1983 Code, however, would have such a person "only as witness" (can. 874).

Community of Faith

The child has a right to the love and help of the community. The People of God, that is the church, made present in the local community, has an important part to play in the baptism of children. This is expressed especially in the assent after the profession of faith by parents and godparents.

Time and Place

Par. 8 of the introduction spells out principles concerning the time for the baptism. If the child is in danger of death, the baptism is to be done without delay. In other cases, as soon as possible and even before the child is born, the parents should be in touch with the parish priest that proper preparation may be made. An infant should be baptized within the first weeks after birth; a longer interval may be determined by the conference of bishops. When parents are not yet prepared to profess the faith or to undertake the duty of bringing up their children as Christians, it is for the parish priest, subject to directives of the conference of bishops, if any, to determine the time for the baptism of infants.

It is recommended that baptism be celebrated during the Easter vigil or on Sunday. It should not be celebrated more than once on any given Sunday. It may be celebrated during Sunday Mass so that the entire community may be present and that the relationship to eucharist be clearly seen. But baptism at Sunday Mass should not be done too often; thus typically parishes schedule baptism for the Sunday Mass at designated intervals.

The place for the baptism of infants is the baptistry of the parish church. Provision is allowed for a temporary font elsewhere in the church for pastoral reasons or, with the permission of the bishop and consultation of the local parish priest, at a font established at another church or public oratory within the parish boundaries (Introduction, par. 10 ff.). Except in danger of death, baptism is not to be celebrated in private houses and except in emergency, not in hospitals. The 1983 Code reinforces this strong statement for the place of baptism in the parish church (cf. can. 857).

Danger of Death

As noted, provision is made for baptism in danger of death when no priest or deacon is available. Chap. 5 of the *Rite of Baptism for Children* provides a ritual for any suitable member of the church to minister. Prayer, profession of faith, baptism, clothing with the white garment and the Lord's Prayer are detailed. In the absence of one able to lead the prayer, it is sufficient for any one to profess the creed and to baptize, with water, "N., I baptize you in the name of the Father, and of the Son, and of the Holy Spirit." The parish priest is to be notified and if the infant survives, the ritual of chap. 6 is to be observed.

Mystagogia and Continuation of Initiation

The baptism of children presumes continued attention to the sharing of faith experiences and religious education as the child matures. The process of continuing the initiation begun in infant baptism has been the subject of much debate. The rite clearly keeps the order and sequence of baptism, confirmation and eucharist in perspective. The practice, since the call of Pope St. Pius X for the age of first eucharist to be lowered, developed, at least in most areas of United States, for confirmation to be delayed until after first eucharist. The sequence of initiation has been further complicated with the celebration of the rite of reconciliation prior to confirmation and/or eucharist. While the 1983 Code continues the tradition of the sequence of baptism, confirmation, and eucharist, pastoral practice for many continues to follow a different sequence.

Congregation for the Doctrine of the Faith, "Instruction on Infant Baptism" *Acta Apostolica Sedis*, 72:1137-56,29 November 1980; *Origins*, 10:474-480,8 January 1981. Paul Covino, "The Postconciliar Infant Baptism Debate in the American Catholic Church," *Worship*, 56:240-260, May 1982. Julia Ann Upton, "A Solution to the Infant Baptism Problem," *Living Light*, 16:484-496 Winter 1979.

RICHARD J. BUTLER

BAPTISM, INFANT, PARENTS IN

The involvement of parents in the baptism of their children is documented in the earliest accounts of infant baptism. Referring to little children who are to be baptized and who cannot "answer for themselves," Hippolytus said "let their parents answer or someone from their family" (*Apost. Trad.* XXI, 4). As the emphasis on immediate or *quam primum* baptism developed, mothers were commonly absent from the baptism, and the godparents or sponsors gradually took over the role of answering for the children and even holding the infants during the baptism. In the *Roman Ritual* prior to the reforms mandated by Vatican II, the father, and the mother when she was present, had no formal role in the baptismal rite (*Ordo Baptismi parvuli*).

The *Constitution on the Sacred Liturgy* called for the revision of the rite of infant baptism and decreed that "the roles of parents and godparents, and also their duties, should be brought out more clearly in the rite itself" (S.C., 67). In the *Rite of Baptism for Children* (R.B.C.), parents once again exercise a "more important ministry and role in the baptism of infants than the godparents" (7). An *Instruction on Infant Baptism* (Instr.) from the Sacred Congregation for the Doctrine of the Faith in 1980 and the 1983 *Code of Canon Law* (C.I.C.) both reaffirm the parents' role and responsibilities, which fall into three categories:

(1) Prior to the baptism, at least one of the parents must give consent for the baptism to take place and "provide a founded hope that the infant will be brought up in the Catholic religion" (C.I.C., 868). If the parents are not able to provide such an assurance, pastors may delay the baptism (R.B.C., 8-4, 25; Instr., 30). Even before the child is born, parents are expected to prepare for the baptism through instruction, prayer and religious rites under the direction of the pastor or catechists (R.B.C., 5-1, 7-1, 8-2, 27; C.I.C., 851). Parents also designate the sponsors in infant baptism (C.I.C., 874).

(2) At the baptismal liturgy, the presence of both parents is of such importance that the baptism may be delayed if the mother is not healthy enough to participate (R.B.C., 8). The parents make the responses, not answering for their child, but speaking of their own faith and their commitment to form the child in the faith. They ask that the child be baptized, they sign their child with the cross, they renounce Satan and profess the faith, they carry the child to the font, they hold the lighted candle, and they are blessed with special prayers. A parent who cannot make the profession of faith may keep silent during the rite. All that is asked is that such a parent permit the child to be instructed in the faith (R.B.C., 5-4).

(3) After the baptism, it is the parents' responsibility to bring the child up in the faith, enabling the child "to know God ... to receive confirmation, and to participate in the holy eucharist" (R.B.C., 5-5). This formation in the faith fulfills "the true meaning of the sacrament" (R.B.C., 3). The godparents' role, described in the questions at the beginning of the baptismal liturgy, is to help the parents in this duty (R.B.C., 40).

This emphasis on the parents' role and responsibility before, during and after the baptism is supported by other church documents. The *Dogmatic Constitution on the Church*, for example, speaks of the family as the domestic church in which "parents, by word and example, are the first heralds of the faith with regard to their children" (L.G., 11). Pastoral practice in the years since Vatican II has correspondingly expanded from immediate preparation of the parents for baptism to include pastoral care of potential parents (i.e., engaged and recently married couples) and ongoing support for parents throughout the years in which they are raising children.

"Baptizing Children," *National Bulletin on Liturgy*, vol. 13 (March-April 1980) no. 73 (Canadian Conference of Catholic Bishops, Publications Service, 90 Parent Avenue, Ottawa, Ontario KIN 7B1). Gabe Huck, *Infant Baptism in the Parish: Understanding the Rite* (Chicago IL: Liturgy Training Publications, 1980). Mark Searle, *Christening. The Making of Christians* (Collegeville MN: The Liturgical Press, 1980).

PAUL F. X. COVINO

BAPTISM, MINISTERS OF

Ministers of baptism are ministers of an initiation process. Initiation into any organization presumes some relationship between the members of that body and the individual seeking incorporation. Anthropologists and sociologists have studied rituals of incorporation present in diverse societies. An individual becomes a member of any society through some form of ritual process no matter how formal or informal this process might be.

The full development of the human person in any cultural setting is significantly affected by the ritual process of incorporation. Erik Erikson has pointed out the role which ritual plays in the incorporation of the infant/child into a particular culture. Parents, extended family and the society in general all play a role in the process. Through a ritual process, the individual becomes one with a particular people, community, society.

Incorporation into the Christian community is no exception. Historical evidence points to the presence of an initiation process whereby adults desiring membership in the church spent months and even years in preparation for full membership. The process involved the entire Christian community. While some members had specific, detailed responsibilities toward the one to be initiated, the entire community was involved particularly through prayer and fasting for those to become members.

A more detailed account of the initiation process is given in the 3rd century text, the *Apostolic Tradition*. Here we see the relationship that exists between the one to be initiated and the individual who first brings this person to the community. "...those who have brought them shall bear witness about them, whether they are capable of hearing the word. They shall be questioned about their state of life...." The "sponsor" obviously takes some responsiblity for the individual who is brought before the community for the first time.

"Teachers" are responsible ministers in this 3rd century church. They are to question the individuals as to their "reason for coming to the faith." "After their prayer, when the teacher has laid hands on the catechumens, he shall pray and dismiss them. Whether the teacher is a cleric or a layman, let him act thus."

Not only do the teachers give instruction in the faith, but they do so within the context of prayer and are called upon to lay hands on those under instruction. Note also, that the role of teacher was not restricted to clerics.

Primarily, ministry associated with initiation in the early church was twofold. In regard to the individual to be initiated, the minister was to proclaim the Word, thus enabling a conversion of heart and change of life style in the one to be initiated. On the other hand, the minister was responsible to the community, determining the suitability of the particular individual seeking membership in the faith community.

The historical shift in ministry in the church eventually places sole emphasis on the priest as minister of baptism. With the disappearance of the catechumenate, and the growth in infant baptism as the normal mode of initiation, the priest alone ministers to the individual to be initiated. Ordinarily, this ministry is limited to the celebration of the sacrament of baptism. When an adult desired to become a member of the church, the priest alone conducted "convert" sessions with the individual. Often, the baptism itself was a private affair, with priest and two godparents (representing the community) gathering in the baptistry at a time that did not interfere with the parish Mass schedule.

Diversity of ministries in baptism, particularly as evident in the historical development of the rites indicates how important the involvement of the entire Christian community is in the process. With the implementation of the R.C.I.A., the "convert" no longer seeks from the local priest alone. Instead, a process of collaborative ministry is employed as the individual moves through the various stages of formation in the faith. The adult wishing to become a member of the Christian community plays a vital role in the process of formation. One must undergo a radical transformation of life style as one prepares to live life in Christ. Yet, due to the very nature of this commitment, it must be made in communion with other Christians. To live life in Christ is to be a member of his body, the church.

Due to the reforms in ecclesiology and soteriology set forth in the decrees of Vatican II, it is now possible to base one's understanding of ministry on the presence of a believing, faith community. It is into this vibrant body of believers who live their lives in union with Christ and in communion with one another that the new member is incorporated.

The many charisms or gifts present in the local church are surfaced and employed during the stages of the catechumenate. Based on the premise that the faith is "caught" not "taught," it is in the context of various faith-sharing sessions with a diversity of individuals that the catechumen is able to begin to accept the faith. This concept of diversity of ministries becomes the model for all ministry in the church.

The *Decree on the Church's Missionary Activity* (A.G.,14) points to the responsibility of all the baptized to make known the message of Christ to the world. This is a major shift from the encyclical *Mystici Corporis* (article 17) in which Pius XII claims that it is the church's chief members, that is, the clergy, who are responsible for carrying out the mission of Christ in the world. The *baptized* are called upon to be the body of Christ; therefore, they are to welcome newcomers into their midst giving clear evidence of the spirit of Christ which binds them one to the other.

Whenever possible, all the faithful should gather with the catechumens to support them in prayer. This is particularly true at the transitional periods in the life of the catechumen (scrutinies, exorcisms, etc.) particularly during the Lenten season.

In the ancient church it was essential that some member of the community *sponsor* the individual seeking membership. Some knowledge of the interested party's moral character, intention for seeking membership and some sign of faith were important in order to assure that no harm would be done to the fabric of life of the Christian community. Today, a *sponsor* is called upon to do likewise, that is, to bring the individual to the church and to attest to the credibility of the person's request for membership in the catechumenate. This presumes a relationship between the sponsor and the one to be baptized. Often, it is the sponsor who has inspired the inquirer to begin the process of initiation.

The *Rite of Christian Initiation of Adults* calls for both a sponsor and a godparent. While on occasion the same person might fulfill both, the roles are nevertheless distinct. While the sponsor is responsible for attesting to the life stance of the individual, the godparent forms a unique relationship with the catechumen. The catechumen, priest and local community all have roles to play in the choice of godparent. A godparent is chosen from among the assembly as one who leads an exemplary Christian life possible of being emulated by the catechumen. Note, emphasis is placed on the ability of the godparent to witness to and share the faith with the catechumen. Choice of godparent is not based on degree of friendship nor familial relationship.

Godparents are responsible "to show the candidates how to practice the gospel in personal and social life, to sustain the candidates in moments of hesitancy and anxiety, to bear witness, and to guide the candidates' progress in the baptismal life" (R.C.I.A., 11). The godparent participates in faith-sharing sessions with the catechumens and is present as witness for the community at the various rituals of incorporation. Therefore, the godparent is an active member of the community; an individual recognized as one who lives the Christian life daily and participates fully in the activities of the local church.

At the *Rite of Election*, the godparents exercise their roles for the first time as they come forward when called by name and testify before the assembly as to the readiness of the catechumen to become one of the elect. They, together with the catechumen, write their names in the book of the elect.

In the ancient rite of initiation found in the *Apostolic Tradition*, the bishop, priest and deacons all had roles in the process. In addition, the text indicates that the individual who engaged the catechumens in the actual instruction process was either a "cleric or a layman" (*Apost. Trad.*, 19). In time, the priest alone filled all roles. With the revision of the rites, various roles are now assigned to bishop and priest with deacons being called upon to assist when necessary in the process. The role of teacher or catechist is given to a member of the assembly possessing the charism.

The *bishop,* as chief teacher of the diocese, is responsible for the formation in the faith of all catechumens. It is his role to implement the spirit of the R.C.I.A. in his diocese and to see that all who wish to participate in this process of initial formation might be able to so. Ideally, it is the bishop who presides over the election ritual and the Easter vigil. Where this is not possible, the local parish priest presides.

The *priest,* as pastor of the local church, is responsible for the formation of the candidates. It is the priest, along with catechists and other ministers, who establishes the catechumenate in the local church. Where possible, the priest, along with catechists and godparents, establishes a personal relationship with each catechumen providing pastoral care and instruction in the faith. He also selects, along with catechists and catechumens, appropriate godparents for each candidate.

Generally, it is the priest who presides over the various transitional rites of the catechumenate. He also presides over the baptism of an adult (or child of catechetical age) and in the absence of the bishop, confirms the candidate.

Deacons may, where pastoral necessity requires, take the place of the priest in the various stages of the initiation process including presiding at the celebration of the sacrament.

The reforms subsequent to Vatican II contain two unique expressions of initiation: one set of rituals for the initiation of adults, the R.C.I.A., and one for the initiation of children (those who have not yet reached the age of discernment). Due to the very different nature of initiation of children, the church's ministry responds accordingly.

While the community, priest, deacon and godparents continue to play a role in the process, it is the parents who take the primary ministerial role in the baptism of children.

It is the parents who take the role of sponsor, bringing their child to the church for initiation. They publicly ask that the child be baptized, an act which calls for a commitment in faith on their part. Both mother and father have roles to play in the actual ritual of baptism. They make a public profession of faith on the part of the child and declare that they will continue to assist the child on the journey of faith.

The parents continue their ministry in the initiation process as they share the life of faith with their growing child. They are the first teachers of the child in the faith. As their child prepares to complete the initiation process with the reception of first eucharist and confirmation, the parents continue to play an active role in the process.

In the R.C.I.A., the bishop and his local representative, the parish priest, have the responsibility of providing adequate formation for the candidates. In the initiation of young children, the necessary formation is given to the parents. Some process, similar to that of the catechumenate is designed for parents or children to be baptized providing them with the opportunity to share faith with other members of the community as they prepare to bring their child for baptism.

Godparents play a special role in the life of the young Christian. Often, they are chosen because they are the "significant others" in the life of the child. They will witness to the faith as the child matures and they will be present in times of need. Because of their particular ministry, godparents are often included in the faith sharing sessions provided for parents prior to the baptism of their child. They are also given a special place in the actual celebration of the sacrament of baptism.

While the local priest is ultimately responsible for the formation of the parents prior to baptism, other members of the community are called upon to share their gifts in the process. The catechist, in conjunction with other members of the community, shares faith with the parents in an informal setting. At times, a more formal classroom setting will also be appropriate for some aspects of preparation.

See **Initiation, Christian; Sponsors for initiation; Baptism, infant, parents in; Easter season**

Aidan Kavanagh, *The Shape of Baptism* (Pueblo Press, 1978). Bishops' Committee on the Liturgy, *Christian Initiation of Adults: A Commentary.* Study Text 10 (United States Catholic Conference, 1985).

MARY ALICE PIIL, C.S.J.

BAPTISM, MODES OF ADMINISTERING

Christian baptism is rooted in the NT, but the biblical writings neither describe the rite nor direct how it should be carried out. The verb *bapto* means "dip" or "immerse" or "bathe" or "wash" or even "drown"—actions which would require varying amounts of water. In the NT this word, which is infrequent, is used of washing one's hands (Lk 11:38), of dipping (Jn 13:26), and in Rev 19:13 it may mean "dye." The Christian rite is always designated by the related term *baptizo* (v.), *baptisma* (n.), which had come into use in Judaism prior to the Christian era to speak of ceremonial lustrations and of proselyte baptism. *Baptisma* is also used figuratively of Jesus' passion (Mk 10:38; Lk 12:50). The word "sprinkle," *rantizo*, which is used for ceremonial purification in LXX, in Mk 7:4, and in Heb 9:13,19,21;10:22, is never used in connection with the Christian initiatory rite.

At the portion of the Jordan where John is presumed to have baptized, the river is shallow and marshy. Reaching deep water would be difficult. But it is usually assumed that John's baptism brought penitents under the water. In Jewish proselyte baptism, candidates entered the water in the nude and immersed themselves.

No baptism is described circumstantially in the book of Acts or in the epistles. The term "baptize" was so widely understood that it could stand without explanation. Several of the early baptisms seem to have been performed in domestic dwellings and with little preparation (Acts 10:47; 16:15,33). Roman houses would have a supply of water; although persons could step into the impluvium, a pool in the atrium of most well-to-do homes, it would be rather shallow. The account in Acts 8:36-39 indicates that Philip and the eunuch stepped into and out of a convenient outdoor body of water. The Pauline imagery of baptism as burial and resurrection with Christ (Rom 6:3-5, which is not the only NT baptismal imagery) need not imply baptism by immersion, for in the ancient world bodies were often buried by placing them in a cave or a wall, and as Sophocles' *Antigone* indicates, ceremonial burial could be performed by casting earth on the body.

The earliest documentary evidence subsequent to the NT, the *Didache* (early 2nd century?), gives flexible directions: "Baptize in running water.... And if you do not have running water, baptize in some other. If you cannot in cold, then in warm. If you have neither, then pour water on the head three times" (7.1-3). Immersion in cold, running water was preferred; but if this could not be done, other actions and other kinds of water were acceptable. Some of the adaptability and good sense of this and later church orders has marked the tradition: when you cannot do what you would prefer, do what you must. The rite can be true to itself while varying in execution.

Early baptismal pools are extant from before and after the Peace of the church (such as in the well-known house church at Dura-Europos, c. 250 C.E.; and the many later baptisteries, such as that at St. John Lateran in Rome, c. 500 C.E.) which show a conspicuous, decorated pool, often octagonal in shape, with steps leading down into it and out on the opposite side, located outside the eucharistic room (indeed usually in a separate building). The pool holds a large amount of water, flowing in and out (where that is possible), the water being anywhere from a few inches to two feet in depth.

These pools, located only at the bishop's churches, were used once a year. The baptismal water was to reach the entire body, but the pools themselves were relatively shallow. Paintings indicate that often the candidates stood in the water, in the nude, at the baptism, they bent down while water was dashed over them using a large bowl.

In time the persons baptized were almost exclusively infants; the church moved to colder regions; and Roman virtuosity with water was lost. Baptism came to be performed over a bowl which stood on a pedestal in or near the eucharistic room. Baptism was performed, essentially privately, when the child was a few days old. In the Eastern churches infants continue to be baptized in the nude and are dipped into the water. In the West, baptism in the nude lapsed; the child was held by the minister of baptism, who poured water over the child's head, usually three times. Medieval fonts became highly decorated, and when the baptismal water became a source of abuses, large covers were built for the fonts—at times requiring hoists to raise them when the font was to be used. The quantity and centrality of the water was reduced, while the water-holder became an object of interest in its own right.

These furnishings and customs continued in the medieval and modern Catholic tradition as well as in the major changes of the Reformation. Several Protestant traditions sought to have baptisms take place when the congregation was present, but until recent years, such efforts largely failed. Some modern Protestant bodies (through delicate sensibility, rather than through theologically informed conviction) began to baptize by "sprinkling," using only a few drops of water. This practice is the extreme of the reduction of the water itself as constitutive of the sacramental sign.

From the early 16th century, certain Protestant groups held, on NT grounds, that true baptism is a declarative act made by a believer; hence the baptism of an infant, who can give no sign of faith, is no baptism at all. This conviction meant that most of the Christians in Europe had to be regarded as not truly baptized. The ecclesiastical disruptions were violent, and the ecumenical divisions that were raised remain generally unresolved. Usually this emphasis on "believer's baptism" was associated with the practice of

108

total immersion—the Pauline imagery of baptism as death, burial and resurrection with Christ (Rom 6:3-5) was taken to give the normative meaning. Churches were built in which a large baptismal pool is located in full sight of the congregation. Baptism is administered, always by total immersion, only to persons competent to give an account of their faith. Baptist churches differ in the recognition they grant to baptisms made by modes other than immersion.

The Roman service books allowed for baptism by immersion, and the rubrics of Anglican and some Lutheran churches expressly offered it, sometimes as the first option. (The minister "shall dip the child in the Water discreetly, or shall pour Water upon him," *Anglican Prayer Book*.) The Eastern tradition has always maintained it. In missionary areas where adult converts are common, it has often been used. Modern times have seen an emphasis on baptism as a sign of a life-changing divine redemption. The Roman Catholic R.C.I.A. (Editio Typica, 1974) holds the baptism of converted, prepared adults before the congregations as a significant, constitutive function of the Christian community. In many communions, baptism is now administered at a Sunday eucharist, at Easter or at one of the major feasts of the church's year, and in full view of the congregation, with participatory roles for many. The use of immersion for the baptism of children and of adults expresses the life-and-death power of the act, and this mode is growing in use, particularly in the U.S. But change in the mode of baptism requires appropriate furnishings. Fonts are being brought into greater visibility, with water made a richer sign. And they are often designed as pools, with baptism of adults by immersion in mind, while other ways of carrying out the initiatory action remain possible as well.

DANIEL B. STEVICK

BAPTISM, SYMBOLS IN

This article will consider the role of symbols in baptism by focusing on the symbolic dimension of the baptismal rite for adults (R.C.I.A.). It is divided into four sections: 1) role of symbols in Christian initiation; 2) symbolic dimension of the catechumenate; 3) symbolic dimensions of baptism at the Easter vigil; 4) catechesis of baptismal symbols.

Role of Symbols in Christian Initiation

The symbols which are part of the sacramental celebration of baptism today evolved in the context of the initiation of adult converts during the first four centuries. For these converts, coming to believe in God revealed in Jesus Christ, deciding to accept the salvation offered in Christ's life, death, resurrection and outpouring of the Holy Spirit, and learning how to live a life faithful to the risen Lord above all else as members of the Spirit-filled community could be a disorienting experience. Those undergoing conversion had to learn to perceive, think, speak, and behave in a way often radically different from that to which they were accustomed. Both the early communities' need to help the converts through the process of conversion, and their ever-deepening theological reflection on the meaning of baptism in water and the Spirit as they experienced it being lived out in common, contributed to the progressive ritualization of Christian initiation, rich in symbolic expression. In addition to the water-rite itself, symbolic gestures such as imposition of hands, anointings, casting off old garments and being clothed in new, etc., became part of the baptismal rite. These symbolic rites both gave expression to the converts' inner experience of God's work in their lives, and, simultaneously, by representing this spiritual reality in a tangible way, provided initiates with a palpable means of making contact with the paschal mystery in order to be drawn more fully into it.

The central symbols of the baptismal rite: water, oil, and touching, are natural symbols which are found in initiatory rites in other religions. The way they are understood in Christian baptism, however, while including their natural and cultural meaning, is more immediately derived from their role in salvation history and scriptural imagery. Thus, while water as natural symbol can signify birth, or destruction, or sustenance of life, the waters of baptism are understood through the experience of salvation history as symbolizing the waters of creation, or of the flood, or the living waters Jesus promises to those who believe in him so that they will never thirst. Similarly, patristic understanding of baptism in terms of contemporary cultural symbolism of, e.g., the nuptial bath, is rooted in Eph 5:26, where Christ washes his bride, the church, with water and the word.

Symbols have a number of characteristics which help explain their role in the rite of initiation: symbols are multivalent, that is, they have more than one level of meaning; reflection on a given level of meaning (e.g., water as birth) can lead to discovery of another meaning (e.g., water as death), and to reflection on the relationship of the meanings (how can something be simultaneously birth and death?), and to the relationship of the various meanings to what is being symbolized (how is baptism into Jesus who is anointed with the Holy Spirit both birth and death?). Since the work of the Holy Spirit in Christian conversion has many dimensions, and ultimately defies any single verbal formula, scripturally derived ritual symbols which are also many-dimensioned are a privileged means both to express that work and to help draw converts more deeply into it. Similarly, because symbols are multivalent, they are also ambiguous, and this is another reason why symbolic expression is particularly appropriate in the ritualization of conversion. While the theological reality of being plunged into the paschal mystery is the same for all baptized Christians, the perceived experience of living out Christian conversion is not. The rich ambiguity of symbolic ritual allows a given rite to be perceived by all converts as a genuine articulation of their own unique experience of the work of the Holy Spirit in their lives, and as a vehicle through which they can surrender themselves to that work. Further, part of the ambiguous quality of symbols is that they conceal as well as reveal what they signify. Immersion in the waters of baptism and rising up from them in one sense makes present the initiate's burial and resurrection with Christ, and yet in another sense the symbolic action points beyond itself to a deeper reality. This capacity of symbols both to reveal and yet point beyond themselves allows them to express what is beyond words.

The symbolic expressions which are part of the rite of baptism today evolved as early Christian communities reflected on the many dimensions of the salvation in Christ they had experienced in light of the witness of scripture, and sought ways to enable converts to enter into the fullness of that salvation through the rituals of Christian initiation. The natural symbols used in baptism are understood in terms of their role in salvation history; as all symbols, they are multivalent, ambiguous, and lead those experiencing them beyond themselves.

The Symbolic Dimension of the Catechumenate (R.C.I.A.)

In the *Rite of Christian Initiation of Adults* (1972), which is based on the experience of the early church, the catechumens' process of conversion is given rich ritual symbolic expression. While the symbolic dimension of initiation is most readily apparent in the culminating rites of the Easter vigil, it is not confined to those rites. In fact, part of what enables converts to experience the paschal rites as effective symbols of salvation in Christ is the symbolic dimension of the entire initiatory process which has prepared them for those rites, beginning with the rite of acceptance (or enrollment) into the order of catechumens. Throughout the catechumenate and final period of purification and enlightenment the converts are progressively initiated into the symbolic world of scripture and ritual action.

The specific ritual gestures which are part of Christian initiation function symbolically to draw catechumens into salvation in Christ, and thus, into the ongoing story of salvation history. The proclamation of the scriptural account of God's actions to save at the rites of the catechumenate provides the context which gives these gestures meaning. The process of conversion to Christ is full of experience for which converts have no names or categories, and thus is disorienting. The scripture lessons proclaimed at the rites of the catechumenate provide the converts with the framework within which they can organize the unfamiliar experiences of growing in the Christian faith and begin to understand them; the scripture lessons enable the catechumens to begin to perceive themselves and what is happening to them in scriptural terms, and provide them with scriptural language to articulate it. In order to know how to grow in relationship to God, the converts must know what God is like; by proclaiming how God has acted in relationship to others in various situations in the past, the scripture lessons in the R.C.I.A. set forth positive and negative models to guide the converts in learning to be faithful (cf. 1 Cor 10:11).

In addition to introducing the figures of salvation history, whose experience of God will help the catechumens understand their own, the lessons and prayers of the catechumenate provide the converts with the landscape of scriptural imagery and metaphor for conversion within which they can begin to perceive their own experience. The dominant metaphor of the catechumenate is that of a journey between opposite extremes: darkness and light, slavery and freedom, falsehood and truth, death and life; at the end of this journey is a new birth into a kingdom of love celebrated with a feast in a new age. The scripture lessons not only offer the converts this picture of where they are going from and where they are going to, but also abundant imagery depicting them, the church, and Christ, who is the Way on the journey to salvation. Thus, when the catechumens find themselves searching for names and concepts to express the new experience of conversion to Christ, the scripture lessons give them a vocabulary of imagery and metaphor with which they can reflect on it coherently.

rites of the catechumenate, however, goes beyond pointing out moral examples or offering imagery to function on an even deeper symbolic level. In the lessons the church community is proclaiming to the catechumens its memory of its forebears' encounters with God; as the catechumens absorb the church's memory, they come to share its identity. As they are encouraged by preaching to identify with those before them who encountered God, they themselves are drawn into that encounter.

This symbolic dimension of the proclamation of scripture to graft the catechumens into the story of salvation history provides the context for the specific ritual gestures of the rites of the catechumenate, which will now be discussed in sequence. In the rite of acceptance into the order of catechumens, after the catechumens formally ask to enter the church's way of faith in Christ, their foreheads are signed with the cross, marking them as now belonging to Christ and under his protection. Following this, their senses and others parts of their body are also signed, that every means of perception and response may be claimed for Christ and begin to function as it was created and redeemed to function, in a way fitting for those who are to be members of Christ's body, the church. Thus, the candidates' ears are signed that they may be attentive to the word of God and begin to be able to recognize the voice of the Lord in their lives, guiding them into greater faithfulness. Their eyes are signed that they may begin to perceive as Christ perceives (and thus be able to respond as he would respond), that awareness of the all-surprising glory of God may begin to be the central motivation of their lives. Their lips are signed that they may begin to learn to speak as Christ speaks, responding faithfully to the Father's loving call and proclaiming his goodness. They are signed over their hearts "that Christ may dwell there by faith," enabling them to experience the situations of their daily lives as Christ would; their shoulders are signed that they may "bear the gentle yoke of Christ." (In the United States, there is also signing of the hands and feet, that the catechumens may make known the presence of Christ in the world through the work that they do, and that they may walk, conduct their lives, as Christ would.) These signings of the senses are normally performed by the catechumens' sponsors, thus expressing from the beginning that the faith the catechumens are seeking to enter into is not only doctrinal assent but is a way of living as part of a community of Christ's faithful. When the sponsors have completed the signing, the celebrant alone makes the sign of the cross over the catechumens, sealing their entrusting of their entire selves to Christ with the trinitarian blessing. Then, as the catechumens are now taking their first steps toward entering the church, they physically enter the church building; since the church is most fully itself at worship of the triune God, the catechumens are led into the church by being escorted into a liturgy of the word. During the proclamation of the word and the homily, the scriptures which previously have been a closed book to them, are opened to the catechumens and begin to become their story; after the homily, a book of the gospels may be given to them. Thus from the very first rite of the catechumenate, the church community addresses the converts through symbols which are both expressive and evocative of their experience of conversion to Christ.

The symbolic ritual gestures of the other rites of the catechumenate continue to draw the catechumens into the symbiotic relationship between faith-experience and ritual action. The anointings with the oil of catechumens and exorcisms symbolize the converts' need for strength as they struggle to let go of their old way of life and begin to live a life of faith, and the community's care for them. At the rite of election, the catechumens' desire to commit themselves to accepting God's call to them is expressed in the enrollment of their names among those the church has elected for Easter baptism. The three scrutinies, through their scripture lessons, prayers, and exorcisms, both express the catechumens' deep need for purification and enlightenment, and begin to effect it through the power of the proclamation of Christ as living water, as light, and as life. The formal presentation of the creed ritualizes the church community's entrusting the candidates with the infinitely precious gift of faith which they first asked for when they became catechumens; the presentation of the Lord's Prayer (if it is not anticipated, but celebrated after the third scrutiny) symbolizes the comunity's beginning to share with the elect soon to be joined to it the familiar language used by those adopted as God's children when they come before him as a family. In the preparation rites on the Holy Saturday, the *ephphetha* rite gives ritual expression to the converts' need for grace in order to hear God's call to them and respond to it to enter into salvation; the recitation of the creed allows them to make this response by professing the faith that saves as their own. Throughout the catechumenate one of the most powerful symbolic gestures is the formal dismissal of the catechumens before the liturgy of the eucharist. Through this dismissal, the church community affirms that it is the celebration of the eucharist which constitutes it as the church; those in whom the gift of faith has not sufficiently matured for them to be considered "faithful" are not yet capable of being part of such a celebration.

Symbolic Dimension of Baptism at the Easter Vigil

By the time the elect arrive at the Easter vigil they have had sufficient experience of the church's use of symbolic expression (including physical posture) to understand the symbolic language of paschal baptism. The service of light sets the scene for the celebration of the sacraments of initiation by proclaiming Christ as light who comes to dispel the darkness of sin as the paschal candle is carried through the darkened church. The *Exsultet* announces that the entire church community is assembled to celebrate its Passover from slavery to sin to new creation in Christ, the wedding of heaven and earth.

In the scripture lessons of the vigil, the church is proclaiming the many ways God has acted to save, re-presenting them as a point of contact through which all in the assembly can grasp and be grasped by God's saving power in their own lives. All of the scripture lessons of the vigil speak symbolically of baptism. The church's use of the scripture lessons in the rites of the catechumenate, to share its story of its relationship to God with the catechumens in order to draw them into it and make them part of it, thus reaches its climax. The principle that God acts in correspondences, that God's saving actions in the past help explain his saving action now in Christ, seen already in the NT (1 Cor 10:1-13; 1 Pet 3:18-22) and learned in the catechumenate, enables the elect to receive from the readings their final catechesis for baptism.

In hearing the reading from the beginning of Genesis, the elect know that the Spirit of God will soon move over the waters of the font, and they will be a new creation; they recognize Christ as light shining out of darkness. In the Abraham and Isaac reading they ponder God's providing a lamb for sacrifice. The Exodus reading draws their attention back to the paschal candle, reminding them that as the Lord in a pillar of fire led his people through the dark waters of their Exodus, so Christ the light will lead them safely to freedom from the bondage of sin through the waters of baptism. In Isaiah 54 the elect are assured that the flood of baptism will not kill them, that God in fact wants to marry them, make a covenant with them. Isaiah 55 urges the elect to forsake their sin and call on the Lord while he is near, to come to the waters and drink, because his word of forgiveness accomplishes its purpose. The reading from Baruch warns them not to forsake the fountain of wisdom, but to turn to God's commandments of life. Finally, the reading from Ezekiel proclaims God's promise to gather the unfaithful, to sprinkle them with clean water and free them from false worship, to give them a new heart and his own Spirit which will enable them to obey, in a land he has chosen for them. The psalms which respond to these OT lessons resound with rejoicing in God as the one who saves, and are full of such symbolic images as thirsting for the Lord and drinking from the waters of salvation. After the singing of the *Gloria*, in celebration of God's fidelity to his promise to save so abundantly proclaimed, the reading of Romans 6 depicts baptism as death to sin, burial into Christ's death and resurrection into life with God; Matthew 28 evokes the source of that life, Christ's own resurrection. After the homily the liturgy of baptism takes place.

By beginning the blessing of the water with the litany of the saints, the local church bears witness that it is only part of a much broader community, and that they are helped by the prayers of those who have gone before in bringing the elect to new birth in Christ; the elect are reminded that they are being baptized into Jesus Christ, risen and living in his people, not into an abstract opinion. The blessing of the water itself draws on the imagery and accounts of God's saving through water already proclaimed at the vigil or in the rites of the catechumenate; the elect thus approach the waters of the font seeing them as the waters of creation over which the Spirit breathed, the flood waters which washed away sin, the Exodus waters through which freedom came, the Jordan waters where Christ was anointed by the Spirit, the waters flowing from the side of Christ on the cross. During the blessing the paschal candle is plunged into the font, symbolizing Christ the light giving life to the church, which is brought to birth in baptism.

The elect are then asked to make explicit their desire to reject Satan and sin, to make faith in Christ the determining principle of their lives, and to give their assent to that faith as proclaimed by the church; the candidates are then immersed (or have water poured over their heads) three times with the invocation of the Trinity. While the candidates are baptized their godparents touch them, symbolizing the church community's responsibility and support. (If baptism is not followed by confirmation, an anointing with chrism follows, symbolizing the baptized's new union with Christ who is priest, prophet and king.) The clothing with a baptismal garment which follows gives tangible form to the neophytes' new identity as a new creation, and to the ethical responsibility which that entails: the baptized have been clothed in Christ and must keep themselves from the stains of sin. Similarly, in the presentation of a lighted candle, the godparents light a candle from the paschal candle which has symbolized Christ throughout the vigil and give it to the newly baptized; the neophytes are exhorted to walk always by the Christ-light the church has shared with them, and keep the flame of faith burning in their hearts. The clothing and presentation of the candle understood together evoke the parable of the wedding feast (Mt 22:1-14) and of the wise and foolish virgins (Mt 25:1-13), and thus the heavenly marriage into which the neophytes have been drawn.

Then, as the waters of baptism made palpable for the baptized the drowning of their sin, their washing and rebirth, their anointing at confirmation concretizes for them the seal of the Spirit with which the Anointed One anoints his people. The expectation of the R.C.I.A. that the sacraments of initiation normally will be celebrated together at the Easter vigil is itself a powerful symbol of the unity of the paschal mystery and of the unity of baptism, confirmation, and eucharist: eucharist is the way baptism and confirmation are lived out in time. The symbolic use of scripture and ritual action at the Easter vigil evokes and effectively articulates the experience of salvation through water, anointing with the Spirit, feasting at the eschatological banquet. The cumulative effect is to make clear that what is happening to the candidates is more than changing opinions on matters of doctrine or deciding to be better behaved; it is about joining a new world.

Cathechesis of Baptismal Symbols

The symbols in baptism developed in the context of the initiation of adults, where they helped give expression to the miltifaceted work of grace in conversion: converts were hearing God's word of grace and making a free response of commitment, being united with Christ, dying and rising with him and so receiving salvation, being cleansed and forgiven from sin, being reborn as a new creation, becoming members of his body, the church. The symbols in the baptismal rite functioned both to provide means through which converts could experience a tangible connection to workings of grace which were ultimately beyond words, and to provide a variety of ritual actions to articulate the many facets of that grace. In the 4th century (Cyril of Jerusalem and Ambrose of Milan) formal instruction on the paschal rites of initiation was given only after the neophytes had experienced them during the week after Easter. Although today sacramental instruction normally precedes baptism, there remains a need for catechesis to ensure that converts appreciate the symbolic richness of the sacramental rites of initiation and can experience them as effective signs. A study of 4th century explanations of the rites of initiation can provide useful principles for contemporary catechesis. In composing these explanations, Cyril and Ambrose combined the use of scripture with natural and cultural symbols in the way they considered most helpful to the particular group of persons they were addressing at that time. These explanations enabled the converts to organize the complex of sensual, emotional and spiritual experiences of the rites of initiation and to appropriate the grace given through these rites; by associating specific ritual actions with specific aspects of the working of grace, they helped converts to remember the many different facets of God's gift of salvation to them, and thus to be able to continue to respond to them.

In developing contemporary catechesis on the symbols in the rites of initiation, several things should be kept in mind. First, part of what the rites of initiation initiate converts into is learning to perceive reality through the lens of the scriptural symbolic world and to relate to God through ritual symbols. Since the Christian life into which converts are initiated is in fact a life of ongoing conversion which is appropriated through the same symbolic language of conversion learned in the catechumenate, it is essential that catechumens become fluent and unselfconscious in ritual symbolic expression. Similarly, it is crucial to provide converts with the vocabulary of scriptural imagery and type which gives the rites their richness of meaning. The clothing with the baptismal garment and presentation of a lighted candle, for example, which 4th century preachers used powerfully as basis for reflection on baptism as marriage to God or eucharist as anticipation of the eschatological wedding feast, lose their nuptial resonance if neophytes do not recognize the parables on which the accompanying prayers are based. Because the prayers of the rites are so redolent of such scriptural symbolism, especially the prayers of the scrutinies and the vigil, it could be helpful to encourage the candidates to meditate on these prayers and to reflect on what they are actually petitioning God for through them. Finally, in preparing catechesis on the symbols in baptism for those participating in the celebration of the rite of infant baptism, it should be remembered that these symbols evolved in the context of adult conversion and initiation. While the grace given in the sacrament is the same, the infant's profession of faith in the saving word of the gospel and desire for a life of conversion to Christ lie ahead, and those who bring the child for baptism thus take on a responsibility that the child hear that word and be raised to desire that life; the explanation of the symbolism of the rites should take this into account.

In sum, since the experience of conversion to Christ entails becoming a new creation, joining a new world unlike anything converts can imagine, there is a need for a means to organize and articulate this experience which goes beyond ordinary language. The biblical and ritual symbols of baptism express the richness and complexity of Christian conversion and provide a means through which converts can enter into it more deeply.

See **Easter season; Holy week, liturgies of**

Jean Danielou, *The Bible and the Liturgy* (Notre Dame: University of Notre Dame Press, 1956). Aidan Kavanagh, *The Shape of Baptism: The Rite of Christian Initiation* (New York: Pueblo, 1978). Louis Ligier, "The Biblical Symbolism of Baptism in the Fathers of the Church and the Liturgy," in *Adult Baptism and the Catechumenate* (*Concilium* 22) (New York: Paulist, 1967). Hugh Riley, *Christian Initiation: A Comparative Study of the Baptismal Liturgy in the Mystagogical Writings of Cyril of Jerusalem, John Chrysostom, Theodore of Mopsuestia and Ambrose of Milan* (Washington: Catholic University of America Press, 1974).

PAMELA JACKSON

BAPTISM, THEOLOGY OF

1. Initiation into the Church

The most obvious, and the most fundamental, thing to say about baptism is that it is a rite by which we become members of the church (L.G., 11). Since Vatican II it has become usual to speak of baptism in this sense as a sacrament of initiation. Baptism, however, is not the only rite of initiation: the R.C.I.A. classes baptism with confirmation and first communion as the three "sacraments of Christian initiation" (General Introduction, 1; cf. S.C., 71, P.O., 5, A.G., 36). These three sacraments are so closely linked that it is difficult to distinguish precisely between the effects of each; indeed, when they are celebrated at the same time at the baptism of adults, they form a single action, so that it is pointless to attempt exact distinctions. Consequently at least some of the effects of baptism which we examine in this article could be attributed in part to the other two sacraments of initiation.

The sacraments of initiation are not the only sacraments which have an ecclesial dimension. The Vatican II understanding of the church as itself a sacrament (L.G., 1, 9) implies that each of the sacraments is a particular realization of the church's general sacramental reality (L.G., 11). Moreover each of the seven sacraments in its particular way relates the recipient to the church in a new or more profound manner. Thus ordination and marriage establish the Christian in a new position in the church with new responsibilities as an ordained minister or as husband or wife; reconciliation brings back into full fellowship sinners who have estranged themselves from the church. This ecclesial effect which each sacrament brings about is commonly known as the *res et sacramentum*: as the effect of the sacrament it is a "reality" (*res*), but in its turn it is the sign and cause (*sacramentum*) of a further effect, namely the grace of the Holy Spirit working in the individual Christian within the church. Baptism, as the first of the sacraments by which we are initiated into the church, and the gate which gives access to the church's spiritual resources, clearly exemplifies this ecclesial understanding of the sacraments.

Another way of expressing this truth is to speak of the *character* conferred by baptism. Baptism, like confirmation and holy orders, is traditionally said to imprint a character, or "spiritual mark" on the soul. St. Thomas explained the character as a participation in the high priesthood of Christ (S. Th., 3.63.3). Some modern theologians (e.g. E. Schillebeeckx, O.P., *Christ the Sacrament*, Sheed and Ward, London, Melbourne and New York, 1963, p. 197) identify the character conferred by each of these three sacraments with their ecclesial effect or *res et sacra-*

mentum: the character is the permanent ecclesial effect of those sacraments which are unrepeatable. Thus the character imparted by baptism is membership in the church. We cannot become a member of the church more than once. "It is impossible to restore again to repentance those who have once been enlightened [i.e. baptized]" (Heb 6:4). Even the baptized sinner who has cut himself off from the fellowship of the church by his sins, and extinguished in himself the life of grace, does not lose the baptismal character so that he ceases to be a member of the church; he needs, not rebaptism for re-entry into membership, but the sacrament of reconciliation. The weeds remain among the good crops until the definitive separation at the final harvest (Mt 13:24-30).

St. Thomas' understanding of the sacramental character as a participation in Christ's priesthood fits in with the NT representation of the church as a 'royal priesthood' (1 Pet 2:9; cf. 2:5; Rev 1:6; Exod 19:6). Baptism is therefore the sacrament by which each Christian enters into this sacerdotal state. This priestly language used to describe the Christian calling can be interpreted at one level in liturgical terms, as a right and duty to participate actively in the church's public worship (S.C., 14). But this liturgical worship should be the expression of a deeper reality. The 'spiritual sacrifices' which are mentioned in this context (1 Pet 2:5) seem to consist of the glory which is offered to God by the witness of lives dedicated to the performance of his will and the service of one's neighbor (L.G., 10; Heb 13:15-16; Rom 12:1-2). 1 Peter's words on the royal priesthood are written in the context of baptism, and are probably intended to indicate the responsibility for Christian living undertaken by the baptized.

There are occasional indications in the NT and the Fathers that baptism was seen as the rite by which a person contracts into the New Covenant. St. Paul in one passage compares baptism to the OT sign of the Covenant, circumcision (Col 2:11-12). The word "seal" (*sphragis*) which the Fathers often apply to baptism, sometimes at least implies a reference to circumcision (e.g., Cyril of Jerusalem, *Myst. Cat.*, 5.6).

Since baptism is a rite of entry into the church, it is appropriate that the modern R.C.I.A. should stress the role of the community in the process of initiation (nn. 4, 9, etc.; Vatican II, A.G., 14), and in particular the duties of catechists, sponsors and godparents (R.C.I.A., nn. 10, 11, 16, etc.). Before the candidate's name is accepted for baptism, the whole community is required to "arrive at a judgment about the catechumens' state of formation and progress" (n. 121). It is a pity that the modern rite does not make so much as the Fathers did of the greeting of the newly baptized by the congregation (e.g., Chrysostom, *Baptismal Homily*, Wenger 2.27, Harkins p. 53).

This understanding of baptism as a process of entry into the Christian community accords well with modern anthropoligical investigations of the "rites of passage" by which members of a society acquire a new status within the group (e.g., A. Van Gennep).

2. *Incorporation into Christ*

The church into which we enter through baptism is not merely a society of human beings but the body of Christ. "By one Spirit we were all baptized into one body" (1 Cor 12:13). Being "baptized into Christ" we "put on Christ" (Gal 3:27). Specifically the baptized are incorporated into the risen Christ: we are baptized "into his death . . . so that as Christ was raised from the dead by the glory of the Father, we too might walk in newness of life" (Rom 6:3-4). Elsewhere St. Paul suggests that the risen life of the baptized begins here below: "you were buried with him in baptism, in which you were also raised with him through faith in the working of God" (Col 2:12-13). But in Romans the author indicates that the resurrection of the baptized includes future resurrection after death: "if we have died with Christ, we believe that we shall also live with him" (Rom 6:8).

From NT times the Christian's baptism has sometimes been seen not only as incorporation into the crucified and risen Christ, but as a participation in his baptism at the hands of John the Baptist. St. Luke seems to be making this point when he structures his second book, Acts, as an echo of his gospel: the baptism of Jesus, at which the Father proclaims him as his Son, the anointed Messiah-king (Lk 3:21-22), is matched in Acts by the Pentecostal descent of the Spirit and the baptism of the first converts. As Jesus' mission in the power of the Spirit begins with his baptism, so the life in Christ of the whole church and of each Christian begins with their baptism: 'Repent, and be baptized ... and you shall receive the Holy Spirit" (Acts 2:38). The baptismal font is linked in the liturgy with the Jordan (R.C.I.A., 222; Cyril of Jerusalem, *Myst. Cat.* 3.1). The Christian's entry into the royal priesthood, of which we have written above, is thus a participation in Jesus' messianic anointing; that the baptized become "Christs," i.e., anointed ones, is perhaps the earliest interpretation of the anointing which regularly accompanies baptism (cf. Cyril of Jerusalem, *Myst. Cat.* 3.1; *Didascalia*, chap. 16). As Jesus' baptism laid upon him the duty to bear his cross (Lk 12:50; cf. Mk 10:38), so the baptism of Christians entails the obligation to follow Jesus in bearing their cross after him.

Again, just as Jesus, being baptized, heard the Father's voice proclaiming him to be Son, while the Holy Spirit descended on him, so the Christian's incorporation into Christ at baptism implies adoption into the life of the Trinity. The one baptism creating one body is inextricably linked with the one Spirit, one Lord, and one Father (Eph 4:4-6). We are baptized "into" the name of the Father, Son and Holy Spirit (Mt 28:19). To become one with the Son is to receive the Spirit of adoption and to become sons and daughters of the heavenly Father. Consequently the doctrine that confirmation is a sacrament which confers the Holy Spirit must not be interpreted in such a way as to minimize the fact that the Holy Spirit is already conferred on the baptized.

This new life of the Spirit which the baptized enter implies such a radical break with the past that it can be called a new birth, "the washing of regeneration and renewal in the Holy Spirit" (Tit 3:5; cf. Jn 3:5). Rebirth is a recurrent theme in 1 Peter, which is, as we have seen, a writing which focuses on baptism (1:3, 23; 2:2). In the early church the newly baptized, with reference to their second birth, were described as "infants," whatever their age; in some places they were given at the baptismal Mass, besides the normal eucharistic chalice, a cup containing the baby-food of milk and honey (*Apost. Trad.*, Botte n. 21). The life-giving properties of water, especially the flowing water that was originally prescribed (*Did.* 7), was a fitting symbol for the new life conferred at baptism (cf. Ezekiel 47; Rev 22:1-2). In the first book of the Bible the history of the world begins with God's creative Spirit or wind moving over the waters (Gen 1:2). Jesus is the source of "living water" (Jn 4:10; cf. 7:37). Favorite motifs in early sacred art are the deer drinking from a pool (cf. Ps 42:1: "As a hart longs for flowing streams ... "), and birds drinking from a basin.

3. Conversion and Forgiveness

However, before the water of baptism can be life-giving it needs to be purifying. Before "sanctifying" his bride the church, the Bridegroom "cleansed her by the washing of water with the word" (Eph 5:26). "You were washed, you were sanctified, you were justified in the name of the Lord Jesus Christ and in the Spirit of our God" (1 Cor 6:11). The Council of Florence in 1439 taught that the effect of baptism is "the remission of all original and actual fault, and also of all punishment which is owing in proportion to that fault" (D.S., 1316; cf. the Council of Trent, D.S., 1672; R.C.I.A., General Introduction, 5).

Baptism is not only the means by which past sins are *forgiven*: it also involves *conversion*, which is a determination to live a new, sinless life in the future. The first converts at Pentecost are told to "repent and be baptized" (Acts 2:38). We are crucified with Christ in baptism so that "we might no longer be enslaved to sin" (Rom 6:6; cf. 6:11-14). Consequently the catechumenate leading up to baptism is regarded as a process of conversion: before candidates are admitted to the catechumenate they are expected to have experienced an "initial conversion" (R.C.I.A., 6, 42); before they are allowed to enroll for baptism they "are expected to have undergone a conversion in mind and in action" (R.C.I.A., 120). The three scrutinies celebrated during the "Period of Enlightenment" are intended as 'rites for self-searching and repentance" which "complete the conversion of the elect" (R.C.I.A., 141). The succession of exorcisms which punctuates the process of initiation contributes to the deepening of conversion. Finally shortly before baptism the candidates express their new resolve in the rite of the renunciation of sin and of its personification in Satan. In the early church this ceremony formed part of a dramatic declaration of a change of allegiance: the renunciation (*apotaxis*) was followed by an act of adhesion (*suntaxis*) to Christ, during which in renouncing the devil the candidates faced west, the seat of darkness, and then turned eastward towards the sunrise to express their new loyalty to Christ (e.g. Cyril of Jerusalem, *Myst.*

Cat. 1.8-9). The modern rite, though pairing a profession of faith with the renunciation, does not bring out the change of allegiance so clearly (R.C.I.A., 224-5).

4. *The Sacrament of Faith*

From the NT to the modern R.C.I.A., baptism is so closely linked with faith that the two seem sometimes almost synonymous. St. Paul couples the statement, "In Jesus Christ you are all sons of God, through faith," with a second statement, "For as many of you as were baptized into Christ have put on Christ" (Gal 3:27). In a passage much quoted in church documents, the long ending of Mark makes belief and baptism the joint conditions for salvation (Mk 16:16). The connection which baptism has with faith was expressed by its name 'enlightenment' (Heb 6:4; Justin, *1 Apol. 64*); for the same reason the baptized have been known as the "faithful". St. Augustine called baptism "the sacrament of faith" and derived from this definition the conclusion that babies obtain faith from baptism, since a sacrament resembles the reality of which it is a sign (Ep. 98.9, C.S.E.L., 34.531; the passage is cited in the Council of Trent's Decree on Justification, D.S., 1529). The R.C.I.A., (General Introduction, 3) echoes St. Augustine's phrase.

Faith is both a prerequisite and an effect of baptism. In the NT baptism follows after faith in the proclaimed word (e.g., Acts 2). But though faith is a prerequisite for baptism, the process of initiation is also a means by which the candidate comes to faith. According to Vatican II, faith is "received in baptism" (G.E., 3). The second question asked of the candidates seeking admission into the catechumenate is: "What do you ask of God's Church?" to which the answer is: "Faith" (R.C.I.A., 50); but before the request can be granted they must show evidence of a "first faith" conceived during the pre-catechumenate (R.C.I.A., 42); to be enrolled for baptism they must have "progressed in faith" (R.C.I.A., 6). The catechumenate is therefore the means by which the candidates grow in faith; but it is also true that faith is one of the supernatural gifts infused into the soul through the instrumentality of baptism at the moment of justification (Trent, Decree on Justification, D.S., 1529-30). The resolution of this apparent paradox is that the faith infused at that moment is an aspect of the habitual or sanctifying grace that becomes a permanent disposition given by God when a convert is justified; the faith that is conceived before justification, though a supernatural gift, is a preliminary disposition which becomes a permanent principle of knowledge and choice only when the believer is baptized.

The close association between baptism and faith is shown by the prominence of credal professions in the rite of initiation. In many baptismal rites in the early church the formula was not "I baptize you in the name of the Father....," but a trinitarian profession of faith in question and answer form. At an earlier stage in the rites the candidates was taught the words and the meaning of the creed in two ceremonies called the "Presentation" and the "Recitation of the Creed"; they have been reintroduced in the modern R.C.I.A.

Two problems emerge from this understanding of baptism as the sacrament of faith. The first concerns the sense in which faith can be said to be a precondition for baptism in the case of babies, or alternatively how baptism can be the cause of justification for babies if they are incapable of faith. This question is investigated in another article. Briefly, as the revised rite of infant baptism makes clear, it is the faith of the church, professed and offered, that provides the primary warrant for baptism of the child.

The second question concerns the salvation of those who have not been baptized. As we have seen, the NT regards baptism as a requisite for salvation, a doctrine reaffirmed by the Council of Trent (D.S., 1524, 1618, 1672). Does this mean that all the unbaptized are excluded from salvation? Trent's answer is that those who do not actually receive the sacrament can be saved by the "desire" (*votum*) of baptism (D.S., 1524). Since early times there has also existed the belief that an unbaptized martyr is saved by "baptism of blood". K. Rahner has developed the doctrine of baptism of desire into the theory of "anonymous Christians", who are saved by an implicit faith in Christ which is unrecognized to themselves. This theory can claim support from the Vatican II decree on the church's mission, which speaks of truth and grace being found among the unbaptized "as a sort of secret presence of God" (A.G.,9).

5. *The Missionary Duty of the Baptized*

We have seen how the baptized are pledged to exercise their royal priesthood by living lives that give glory to God. One aspect of such Christian lives is the witness they give to Christ. "All Christians are bound to show forth, by the example of their lives and by the witness of their speech, that new man which they put on at baptism, and that power of the Holy Spirit by whom they were strengthened at confirmation" (A.G., 11; cf. 36; L.G., 3; A.A.,3). The Faith and Order document (*Baptism, Eucharist and Ministry*) speaks in this connection of baptism as the "sign of the kingdom" (Baptism 7). This is true not only in the sense of Christ's statement that only the baptized can enter the Kingdom of God, conceived apparently as a synonym for eternal life (Jn 3:5), but also in the sense that the baptized have the responsibility of working for the establishment of God's Kingdom on earth.

However, this duty incumbent on all the baptized to promote the Kingdom is not only to be fulfilled in the exercise of apostolate in the strict sense of making Christ known. It includes the call to perfect "the work of justice under the inspiration of charity" (G.S., 72). Vatican II's teaching on the lay vocation derives from this understanding of the responsibilities which follow upon baptism: "The laity, by their very vocation, seek the Kingdom of God by engaging in temporal affairs and by ordering them according to the plan of God" (L.G., 31).

6. *Instituted by Christ*

The NT clearly attributes the institution of the sacrament to Jesus Christ himself. Even though the fourth gospel gives an inconsistent answer to the question whether Jesus himself baptized during his ministry (Jn 3:22; 4:2), it shows him teaching the necessity of baptism in his dialogue with Nicodemus (Jn 3:5), while Matthew attributes a command to "make disciples of all nations, baptizing them" to the risen Lord (Mt 28:19; cf. Mk 16:16). Even though many modern critics question whether these passages give grounds for certainty that Jesus explicitly instituted the sacrament in the course of his life and resurrection appearances, there seems to be no doubt that the early church believed that its practice of baptism was due to the authority of the Lord himself (see W.F. Flemington, *The New Testament Doctrine of Baptism*, S.P.C.K., London, 1948, pp. 115-119).

There were perhaps two decisive considerations which lay behind the adoption of baptism as a Christian rite of initiation. The first was Jesus' own baptism, with its many layers of meaning. His baptism showed his will to be identified with the sinful people he came to serve; it was the moment when he was named Son of God and received his mission as Messiah, for which he was strengthened by the power of the Holy Spirit. Christians not only accepted baptism in order to follow the Lord's example by acknowledging their need of purification from their sins; their baptism *into* Christ (Gal 3:27) was some-

times seen as linked specifically with his baptism (*Didascalia*, chap. 9). The need to express in ritual form this sharing by the baptized in Jesus' messianic "anointing" may explain why anointing came to be attached to Christian baptism (Winkler). A second factor perhaps was the belief that the New Covenant required a rite of entry which would correspond to circumcision and its accompaniment of proselyte baptism (Flemington, pp. 3-11; S. Brock, "The Transition to a Post-baptismal Anointing in the Antiochene Rite", in *The Sacrifice of Praise*, C.L.V. Edizioni Liturgiche, Rome, 1981, pp. 215-225).

7. *Baptism and Confirmation*

There is no need for us to deal explicitly with the sacrament of confirmation, for it forms the subject of several other articles. What is necessary for us here is to discuss briefly the relationship between that sacrament and baptism, since it is a question which has emerged at several points in the present article.

The revised rite of confirmation promulgated in 1971 states that the effect of the sacrament is the gift of the Holy Spirit which "conforms believers more fully to Christ and strengthens them so that they may bear witness to Christ for the building up of his Body in faith and love" (2). Yet, as we have seen, baptism already confers the Holy Spirit, and calls the new Christian to be a witness to Christ. This apparent duplication poses no problem if, as happens when adults are baptized, confirmation is conferred immediately after baptism, as then the two sacraments can be seen as two representations of different aspects of a single sacramental effect. The problem arises when confirmation is separated from baptism, and seems to confer nothing which the earlier sacrament has not already conferred.

The solution of Vatican II is that confirmation imparts *in a special way* what has already been imparted in baptism. "Bound *more intimately* to the church by the sacrament of confirmation, they are endowed by the Holy Spirit with *special strength*. Hence they are *more strictly* obliged to spread and defend the faith ... " (L.G., 11, my emphasis). However, the precise nature of this "special" effect which confirmation adds to baptism the Vatican II documents do not explain.

The ecclesial effect of the sacraments (*res et sacramentum*) discussed above indicates a possible solution to the problem. Confirmation establishes the Christian in a new calling within the church: whereas all have a duty to be witnesses to Christ, the confirmed reaffirm their acceptance of this duty on behalf of the whole church, as a result of which the Holy Spirit, who already dwells within them since baptism as a principle of their Christian lives, empowers them for their new responsibilities. A parallel is provided by some of the other sacraments, in which an obligation already incumbent on the baptized is now confirmed in a new way for the sake of the whole church. Thus all Christians have the obligation to worship; but the sacrament of holy orders confers on the ordained a special responsibility for the worship of the whole community, together with the grace which is required for the fulfilment of this duty. Again, all Christians have the duty to bear sickness in a Christlike way; but the sacrament of anointing conveys a special obligation to bear the limitations of sickness in union with the crucified Christ on behalf of the church, and confers the strength of the Holy Spirit which this vocation requires.

3. *Ecumenical Consequences*

The Catholic church recognizes the validity of baptism celebrated in other churches, provided it is "properly" administered, i.e., with cleansing with water and invocation of the trinitarian name (Council of Florence, D.S., 1314; R.C.I.A., General Introduction, 5). This, together with the faith in Christ of which baptism is the sacrament, is the basis of the deep, though imperfect, communion which exists between the Catholic and other churches. (As even a lay person can be an extraordinary minister of the sacrament, acceptance of the validity of a church's baptism does not necessarily imply recognition of its orders.) Consequently the churches which celebrate these baptisms are said to possess "elements of sanctification and truth" (L.G., 8), and to be in "a certain, though imperfect, communion with the Catholic Church" (U.R., 3).

However, baptism, which together with faith is the basis of the imperfect communion which exists between separated Christian churches, is also sadly a source and sign of their divisions. Baptism is traditionally seen as incorporation, not only into the body of Christ, but also into a particular Christian church, to the exclusion of membership of other churches. Ecumenists, however, sometimes question this principle, and seek a theological justification for allowing the children of an "inter-church" marriage (i.e., one in which the parents are committed members of different churches) to be enrolled at baptism into both of their parents' churches. Baptism, it is said, is basically not incorporation into a particular Christian denomination, but into Christ's own church, although one cannot enter Christ's church in the abstract, but always as it exists in the form of a particular ecclesial body. It is accordingly suggested that the children of an inter-church family can be baptized into Christ's one church as it exists in each of the churches to which the parents belong. Church membership need not, in this view, be restricted to one particular ecclesial body. This is, however, a field of speculation which urgently requires deeper exploration.

9. *The Church's Affirmation of Faith*

It is not until Vatican II that the church's affirmations of faith concerning baptism represent the full richness of the subject. In the early centuries they deal with such contested issues as the rebaptism of heretics (Pope Stephen I, A.D. 254, D.S., 110) and the baptism of babies for the remission of original sin (Council of Carthage, A.D. 418, D.S., 223). In the Middle Ages the conciliar statements concerning baptism were mostly concerned with its right administration and with the remission of sins it confers (Lateran IV, D.S., 802; Florence, D.S., 1314-6), though the latter council also contains the essential teaching that baptism is the "gateway of the spiritual life," by which we become "members of Christ and of the body of the Church" (D.S., 1314). The Council of Trent, facing the challenge of the Reformation, affirms the role of baptism in the process of justification (D.S., 1526, 1529), and condemns a number of errors (D.S., 1614-27). The new insights on baptism are to be found throughout the Vatican II documents, especially the decrees on the church, the liturgy, ecumenism, and the church's mission; and its fullest form in the reformed liturgical texts for the initiation of adults and the baptism of children, especially in their introductory sections.

B. Neunheuser, O.S.B., *Baptism and Confirmation*, (Freiburg: Herder and London: Burns and Oates, 1964). K. Rahner, S.J., "Christianity and the Non-Christian Religions," in *Theological Investigations*, Vol. 5, (Baltimore: Helicon Press, and London: Darton Longman and Todd, 1966): 115-134. B. Neunheuser and G. Baum, "Baptism," in *Sacramentum Mundi*, Vol. 1, (New York Herder and Herder and London: Burns and Oates, 1968), 136-146. G. Winkler, "The Original Meaning of the Prebaptismal Anointing and its Implications," in *Worship* 52 (January 1978): 24-45. E.J. Yarnold, S.J., "Initiation: Sacrament and Experience", in *Liturgy Reshaped*, ed. K. Stevenson, (London: S.P.C.K., 1982), 17-31. *Baptism, Eucharist and Ministry*, Faith and Order Paper No. 111, World Council of Churches, (Geneva, 1982). R.D. Duggan (ed.), *Conversion and Catechumenate* (Ramsey, NJ: Press, 1984).

EDWARD J. YARNOLD, S.J.

BAPTISM, TIMES FOR

Particular times for baptism emerged as early as the late 2nd or early 3rd centuries. The writings of Tertullian express a preference for Easter or the Easter season, but go on to say that "every day is the Lord's; every moment is apt for baptism" (*De Baptismo*, c. 19). The classic outline of initiation found in Hippolytus assumes that baptism is at Easter (*Apost. Trad.*, XX-XXI). In Rome, Easter remained the usual occasion for baptism until the 12th century, but in other places baptism began to be celebrated more frequently by the 6th century. The high infant mortality rate together with the doctrine of original sin encouraged baptism shortly after birth rather than waiting for an annual celebration of initiation. As the catechumenate fell into disuse, the connection between Easter and baptism was also broken in the case of adults.

The current revised rites of initiation reestablish the ancient emphasis on particular times for baptism. In several places, the *Rite of Christian Initiation of Adults* speaks of the Easter vigil as "the proper time for the sacraments of initiation" (R.C.I.A., 8, 17, 23, 26, 207). Only for serious pastoral needs may a day other than Easter be chosen, and then the preference is given to days within the Easter octave or the Easter season (R.C.I.A., 23, 26). The emphasis on Easter is explained by the paschal character of baptism "since the initiation of Christians is the first sacramental sharing in Christ's dying and rising" (R.C.I.A., 8).

The *Rite of Baptism for Children* (R.B.C.) presents several factors to determine the time for baptism. The first requires baptism within the first weeks after birth so that the child "may not be deprived of the benefit of the sacrament" (R.B.C., 8). A longer interval between birth and baptism may be allowed when the mother is not healthy enough to be present at the baptism, or when the parents are not prepared to profess the faith or to undertake the Christian formation of their children. In danger of death, a child is baptized immediately.

The second factor concerns the sacrament's paschal character. Although the urgency to baptize infants does not permit the postponement of baptism beyond a few weeks to an annual celebration at Easter, there is a preference for celebrating the sacrament "during the Easter vigil or on Sunday, when the church commemorates the Lord's resurrection" (R.B.C.,9). Third, since the children are baptized in the faith of the church, preference is given to communal celebrations "for all the recently born children, and in the presence of the faithful" (R.B.C., 32). Baptism may be celebrated during Mass on Sunday to permit community participation and to manifest the relationship between baptism and eucharist. Finally, baptism "should not be celebrated more than once on the same day in the same church" (*Christian Initiation: General Introduction*, 27).

Pastoral practice in the years since the promulgation of R.C.I.A. has moved closer and closer to the rite's clear emphasis on Easter vigil as the normative time for adult baptism. The implicit tension among the variety of factors to determine the time for the baptism of children has, on the other hand, produced a wide array of pastoral practice. A developing practice of celebrating the baptism of children several times a year on occasions of paschal significance (e.g., Easter, Pentecost, Baptism of the Lord, the parish's patronal feast) offers an opportunity to respect the paschal and ecclesial character without unduly delaying baptism.

Gabe Huck, *Infant Baptism in the Parish: Understanding the Rite* (Chicago, IL: Liturgy Training Publications, 1980). Aidan Kavanagh, *The Shape of Baptism: The Rite of Christian Initiation* (New York: Pueblo Publishing Co., 1978). Mark Searle, *Christening: The Making of Christians* (Collegeville, MN: The Liturgical Press, 1980).

PAUL F.X. COVINO

BAPTISMAL FORMULAE IN EAST AND WEST

Baptismal *formulae* are the words which characteristically accompany the administration of water during Christian baptism. These words give definition to the symbolic act of administering the water and call on the power of God as named in the formula. They name the God with whom the baptizing community is in relationship and summarize the Christian faith as understood by that community.

Theology and Practice

Most Western churches use the formula, "*Name*, I baptize you in the name of the Father and of the Son and of the Holy Spirit," whereas most Eastern churches use the formula, "The Servant of God, *Name*, is baptized in the name of the Father and of the Son and of the Holy Spirit." These two *formulae* are called "trinitarian baptismal *formulae*" because they symbolize and summarize Christian belief in the Trinity. The 1982 *Baptism, Eucharist, Ministry* document of the World Council of Churches (which has over three hundred member churches) states that "baptism is administered with water in the name of the Father, the Son and the Holy Spirit" (section on baptism, par. 17). Most of the 143 churches responding to the document either did not question this statement or explicitly affirmed that it represents their practice.

The words "The Servant of God, *Name*, is baptized" (used by the Orthodox churches) are theologically significant because they point to the triune God, and not priest or minister, as the main actor in baptism. "I baptize you," on the other hand, points to the human agency of the officiant. It does not explicitly state that the sacrament is effective through God's power; this explicit statement is important to Orthodox believers. The Eastern formula is called "passive" and the Western "active" because of the verb used.

At the beginning of these *formulae*, the name of the person being baptized is spoken. Not the family name, but only the Christian or given name of the person being baptized, is used, since this name represents a new identity in Christ beyond a person's identity given by natural birth and cultural context.

Another baptismal formula which has been used occasionally up to the present is "I baptize you in the name of Jesus" or "I baptize you in the name of Christ." This alternative was accepted by the Scholastics and by other Roman Catholic theologians and church leaders up until the Council of Trent, so long as the administrant was not intending to deny trinitarian theology.

Sometimes groups augment the trinitarian baptismal formula with a statement which more specifically defines their baptismal faith and practice. Thus, U.S. Presbyterians add "child of the covenant," to emphasize their belief that baptized children are part of the covenant community of faith. Those who baptize only those who confess Christian faith for themselves may indicate as part of the formula that the person being baptized has professed Christian faith. Riverside Church in New York City has added "one God, Mother of us all" at the end of the formula to avoid naming God only in masculine terms.

History

There may have been considerable variation of the words spoken during the administration of water in baptism in the East until the 4th century and the West until the 8th century.

In the NT are found three groups of phrases associated with baptism which may or may not have been spoken during baptismal liturgies. In one group of passages, baptism is said to be done in the name of Jesus Christ or the Lord Jesus. In Acts, baptisms are administered "in the name of Jesus Christ" (2:38; 10:48) or "into the name of the Lord Jesus" (8:16; 19:5). In 1 Cor 6:11, Paul says that his readers were baptized ("washed ... sanctified ... justified") "in the name of the Lord Jesus Christ and in the Spirit of our God." The Pauline and deutero-Pauline literature includes a second group of passages in which persons are said to be baptized "in Christ" or "into Christ," without including the words "in the name of" (Gal 3:27 and Rom 6:3; 1 Cor 12:13 and Col 3:10, 11 are related passages). The third phrase is found in Mt 28:19, in which Jesus says, "Go therefore and make disciples of all nations, baptizing them in the name of the Father and of the Son and of the Holy Spirit." According to Edward Schweizer and a number of other biblical scholars, it is unlikely that the baptismal formula from Mt 28:19 represents the exact words of Jesus (Schweizer, 530). Without scholarly consensus on the dating of Matthew or Acts, and without certainty that the phrases used by Paul were actually spoken in baptismal liturgies, it would be risky to claim that any of these phrasings was the first to be used in Christian baptisms.

Church documents of the 2nd through the 4th centuries also vary as to the baptismal words which they quote or to which they allude. The *Didache* speaks both of baptizing "in the name of the Father and of the Son and of the Holy Spirit" and of baptizing "in the name of the Lord" (Whitaker, *Documents*, 1). Justin Martyr speaks of baptizing "in the name of the Father and Lord God of all things, and of our Savior Jesus Christ, and of the Holy Spirit" (Whitaker, *Documents*, 2). However, authors as late as Ambrose could report that baptism was done "in the name of the Father and of the Son and of the Holy Spirit," while not reporting use of those words during the administration of water in baptism. Instead, candidates were asked three questions about their belief in God, and after responding in the affirmative each time, they were immersed in the water.

The earliest extant full model for a baptismal liturgy is found in *Apostolic Tradition*, usually dated around A.D. 215 The questions in this document are:

Dost thou believe in God the Father almighty?

Dost thou believe in Christ Jesus, the Son of God,

Who was born of Holy Spirit and the Virgin Mary,

Who was crucified in the days of Pontius Pilate,

And died,

And rose the third day living from the dead

And ascended into the heavens,

And sat down at the right hand of the Father,

And will come to judge the living and the dead?

Dost thou believe in the Holy Spirit in the Holy Church,

And the resurrection of the flesh? (Whitaker, *Documents*, 5-6, rubrics and responses omitted)

As candidates answered, "I believe," to each question, they were immersed in the water.

Baptismal liturgies from the 2nd through the 8th centuries often followed this pattern of asking three questions, one about each person of the Trinity, rather than using a declarative formula baptizing persons "in the name of the Father and of the Son and of the Holy Spirit." The exact phrasing of the questions varied considerably.

The Eastern churches apparently preceded churches of the West in arriving at characteristic use of the declarative trinitarian baptismal formula. A Syrian document, *The Acts of Xanthippe and Polyxena*, dated around A.D. 250, tell a story of Paul baptizing and speaking the declarative trinitarian formula (Whitaker, *Documents*, 20); but some later Syrian documents, including Cyril's *Mystagogical Catecheses*, report a questioning rather than a declarative formula. In the 4th-century baptismal catecheses of Chrysostom and Theodore of Mopsuestia, it is specified that the words "[Name] is baptized in the name of the Father and of the Son and of the Holy Spirit" are spoken during the administration of water in baptism. These writings provide the earliest documentation of the "passive" baptismal formula. Chrysostom says that this shows the priest "is only the minister of grace and merely offers his hand because he has been ordained to this end by the Spirit. The one fulfilling all things is the Father and the Son and the Holy Spirit, the undivided Trinity" (Whitaker, *Documents*, 41). The declarative formula became standard in churches of Asia Minor and Palestine and later of Orthodoxy, without much variation after the 4th century.

Evidence for use of the declarative trinitarian formula is first found in northern Egypt in the 5th century, in Spain in the 5th or 6th century, in Gaul about A.D. 700, and in Rome in the 8th century; documents before that time either report a threefold questioning or are not specific (Whitaker, "History," 1-12). Several reasons have been suggested for the change in usage from asking three questions about candidates' faith in the Trinity to using a declarative trinitarian formula. First, the transition to infant baptism made the interrogatory form less appropriate. Second, the Donatist controversy may have led to greater emphasis on uniform administration of baptism. Third, trinitarian controversies often led to increasing use of the trinitarian formula ("in the name of the Father and of the Son and of the Holy Spirit") in worship (Jungmann, 15-32).

By the 9th century, use of the formula "I baptize you in the name of the Father and of the Son and of the Holy Spirit" was characteristic in the Western church in baptismal liturgies. By the 16th century, other forms were virtually excluded from liturgical practice. Baptism "in the name of Jesus [Christ]" or "the Lord Jesus" re-emerged around the beginning of the 20th century in groups such as Pentecostal Holiness churches who found it appropriate to base their baptismal practice on the accounts in Acts.

Baptismal Formulae and Ecumenical Discussion

Mutual recognition of baptism is a key issue in ecumenical discussions, because anything less implies failure to affirm the Christian identity of other groups. Mutual acceptability of the words spoken during administration of water is important to mutual recognition. Since these words summarize Christian faith as understood by those baptizing, to accept another group's formula is in essence to accept their basic understanding of faith.

Three barriers exist to agreement on baptismal formulae: the difference between the "active" and "passive" forms of the formula; the continued practice by some churches of baptizing "in the name of Jesus"; and the emerging concern in some liberal Protestant groups which affirm trinitarian faith but question the predominantly masculine language of the formula. Some of these questions may be very difficult to resolve, but they are also important, since they involve understandings of Christian unity and faith and of justice among humanity.

J.D.C. Fisher, *Christian Initiation: Baptism in the Medieval West* (London: S.P.C.K., 1965). David R. Holeton, "Changing the Baptismal Formula: Feminist Proposals and Liturgical Implications," *Ecumenical Trends* 17 (May 1988): 69-72. Josef Jungmann, *Pastoral Liturgy* (New York: Herder and Herder, 1962). Eduard Schweizer, *The Good News According to Matthew* (Richmond, Va.: John Knox Press, 1975). E.C. Whitaker, *Documents of the Baptismal Liturgy* (London: S.P.C.K., 1960, 1970). E.C. Whitaker, 1965a. "The History of the Baptismal Formula," JEH 16 (April 1965): 1-12. World Council of Churches, Faith and Order Commission, *Baptism, Eucharist, & Ministry*, Faith and Order Paper 111 (Geneva: World Council of Churches, 1982).

RUTH C. DUCK

BAPTISMAL RECORDS

See **Records, sacramental**

BAPTISMAL VOWS, RENEWAL OF

One of the most pressing needs for the church today is to rediscover a spirituality of baptism. This need is all the more imperative in view of the fact that most Christians are baptized in infancy and have no conscious memory of this gateway sacrament to the Christian life. Opportunities need to be provided for Christians to renew their baptismal promises from time to time and to claim for themselves the commitment undertaken for them by their parents and godparents on the day of their baptism.

Communal forms of baptismal renewal are built into the liturgical year, especially during the season of Lent with the restored scrutiny Sundays of the Samaritan woman, the man born blind, and the raising of Lazarus: readings from John's gospel steeped in baptismal imagery which figure so prominently in the *Rite of Christian Initiation of Adults*. At the Easter vigil, the privileged time for the initiation of adult converts, and on Easter Sunday itself, the entire congregation is invited to renew its baptismal commitment, the fruit of the annual Lenten retreat which began on Ash Wednesday. Sundays, the weekly Easter in the liturgical year and preferred time for the baptism of children, also present an occasion for the renewal of baptism with the rite of blessing and sprinkling with holy water, especially during the Easter season so strongly marked by a baptismal mystagogy.

Communal forms of baptismal renewal which have fallen into disuse are the earlier Sunday vespers on the octave day of Easter with a procession to the baptismal font, a description of which is found in the ancient Ordo XXVIII, and the *pascha annotinum*, in which during the first thousand years of the church parents and sponsors would bring to church the children baptized the year before to celebrate with gratitude the anniversary of their baptism.

The celebration of other sacraments is also an opportunity for the renewal of baptismal vows. This renewal is part of the rite of confirmation and may be inserted into the ceremony of first communion. For that matter, every eucharist, the one initiation sacrament that may be repeated, is a renewal of baptism. The sacrament of penance may also be seen as a recovery of the grace of baptism and a reintegration into the eucharistic community of the church. Finally, funerals— with the introductory rites involving the Easter candle, sprinkling with holy water, and white pall symbolic of the baptismal garment—celebrate death as a final stage of growth into the paschal mystery of Jesus Christ which began at baptism.

Baptismal reminders preserved in the family are the baptismal garment and baptismal candle, which may be incorporated into a celebration of faith on the anniversary of baptism and at other important occasions. (See, *Catholic Household Blessings and Prayers*). A praiseworthy custom being rediscovered today is a letter written by the sponsors or the parish community for the child to open later and treasure for a lifetime. Individual forms of recalling baptism in the devotional life of a Christian are the Lord's Prayer and Apostles' Creed, recited at the beginning and end of the day in the tradition of the Eastern and Western churches, and the sign of the cross, particularly when conjoined with holy water.

The ancient format for making and renewing baptismal vows consists of a three-fold renunciation of evil and a three-fold affirmation of the creed framed in a trinitarian perspective. The Episcopal *Book of Common Prayer* contains an interesting adaptation which expands this credal faith into a commitment to participate in the church's life and mission. The Episcopal, Lutheran, Methodist and Presbyterian churches also include liturgical forms for renewing one's baptismal commitment from time to time as prompted by pastoral need or personal faith.

Balthasar Fischer, "Formes de las commemoration du bapteme en Occident," *La Maison Dieu* 58 (1959): 111-134. John Rotelle, "The Commemoration of Baptism in the Life of a Christian," *Ephemerides Liturgicae* LXXXVI (1972): 475-485.

CHARLES W. GUSMER

BAPTISTRY

The baptistry (also baptistery) was a most important building on the cityscape of the provincial capitals of the old Roman Empire. Both eastern and western cities of paleo-Christianity had initiation rites centered in buildings for baptism.

These early ritual buildings, had of course, antecedents in the pagan cultures wherein they developed. But there is a root in the Bible, too. John baptized in the River Jordan; a summary ritual cleansing of the people of the Old Covenant is what this washing became in the context of what the evangelists tell us Jesus' baptism was about. Jesus' baptism was a bathing in the new life of the Holy Spirit.

There are, thus, within the early Christian community, two strands woven into the fabric of baptismal "sacramentology." The one a cleansing, the other new life in the Holy Spirit. Paul develops, in

Romans, a clear sacramental theology which both joins and scrambles these two strands. He correlates this new life in the Spirit with Christian initiation into the salvific blood-letting of Christ when he says that we enter, through baptism, into his death in order that we might rise with him in his resurrection.

The Johannine theology in Revelation further correlates the washing and dying into new life. John says that the elect wear white because they are washed in the blood of the Lamb. The fascinating image of white robes, so frequently used in sacramental rituals, here, in John, takes on a lovely meaning because the color is totally *reflective*. The ones in white reflect the light of the Lamb in whose presence they are gathered. The baptized in white reflect the Easter light of faith in Christ, crucified and risen, symbolized in the paschal candle, a flickering, fragile faith, dependent on the wiles of the wind.

It is necessary when considering the function of the baptistry to look at all of the legitimate reverberations of rich symbolism which inhabit the rite, whether housed in a separate building or in the sanctuary itself, or in some space between the sacred and profane precincts. Let us consider the symbolisms that exist in the Western church at present because the functions have been divided and separated and the sense of their interrelationship lost in the profusion of disparate symbols represented in multiple holy water fonts, discrete baptistry buildings, and the separation of baptism from the ongoing liturgical worship of the adult community. The compartmentalization of ritual was unfortunately coupled with a scholastic insistence on the purgative nature of baptism. Post-Thomistic philosophy resulted in a rather widespread fear about the need for infant baptism before "limbo" be unleashed as the theoretical place of all joy except the Beatific Vision, a place "invented" for those poor innocents released from life without benefit of the sacramental cleansing from original sin. In Ravenna, Italy, are two baptistries dating from the 6th century. Both the Orthodox and the Arian baptistries are domed octagons with central, walled pools the entering of which initiates the believer into a particular sect of Christianity. Other sacraments took place in other places. The insider/outsider focus, so clear in Ravenna's two baptistries, untouched by the second millennium, is a prototype for many centuries of baptistry building.

The credal repetitions in the rite, in the form of serious questions, historically linked to 3rd-century formulae reiterate the faith of the community into which the initiate is being baptized. There are rights and duties for the new member symbolized in the flickering candle and the white robe, and, by faith, actualized in the pouring of or the entering into the water.

The current state of sacramental theology associates gift in sacrament with ministry to the body. Entering the water blessed by the Holy Spirit fills the neophyte with the intangible, necessary grace which makes it possible to believe the creed, a faith in Christ signified in water, symbolized in the paschal candle. (The little light is easily extinguished and easily relighted by another member of the community. The symbol of the paschal candle thus reinforces the connection of faith and ministry, the white robe reflecting this light of Christ more fully than any other color, symbolizes how the new Christian must reflect Christ's Light to the community.) The blessing with oil asks for all the natural helps that God can give the baptized to fulfill this covenant within the community. So, the baptistry, with water-font symbolizing the primordial water of life, needs to be at the entry to the church but, because it is most appropriately used in the eucharist, especially at Easter, it needs to be accessible to the community at the eucharistic liturgy.

The constantly appropriate symbols of paschal candle and holy oils, find an appropriate home in the vicinity of the water of life, because they can remind all Christians of their rights and duties as they enter the holy place, the church building, which symbolizes the aspirations of the whole church, aspirations to become the Kingdom, the body of Christ, the bride of the Lamb.

See Architecture, liturgical

DENNIS McNALLY, S.J.

BAUMSTARK, ANTON (1872-1948)

A pioneer liturgical scholar whose primary work was in the study of comparative liturgy and the historical development of Christian liturgy. Began and edited *Oriens Christianus*, dedicated to the study of liturgy in the Christian East, and with Odo Casel, co-founded the *Jahrbuch fur Liturgiewissenschaft*. Principal work in English: *Comparative Liturgy* (London, 1958).

See Liturgical movement; Historical research and liturgical renewal

BEAUDUIN, LAMBERT (1873-1960)

Benedictine of the Abbey of Mont-César in Louvain, and student of Dom Columba Marmion. He pioneered the liturgical movement in Europe, and is considered by many as the movement's principal founder.At the Malines Catholic Congress in 1909 he set forth what is surely the movement's *Manifesto*, a call for active participation of the faithful in the liturgy and a greater understanding of liturgical texts and rites. At Mont-César he orchestrated a series of *Liturgical Weeks*, principally for clergy. Later became professor of liturgy at St. Anselmo in Rome, where he was editor

of *Irenikon*. Principal work in English: *Liturgy, the Life of the Church* (Collegeville, 1926).

See Liturgical movement; Benedictines and liturgical renewal

Bernard Botte, *From Silence to Participation: An Insider's View of Liturgical Renewal*, tr. J. Sullivan (Washington, DC: Pastoral Press, 1988).

BENEDICTINES AND LITURGICAL RENEWAL

Dom Prosper Guéranger (1805-1875) first used the expression "liturgical movement" to describe the revival of liturgical studies and the growing interest in understanding and improving liturgical practice. As a young priest, Guéranger lamented the disunity within and among French dioceses due to the multiplicity of local usages dating from the Enlightenment era. While serving as chaplain to religious from Rome, Guéranger came to know and appreciate what he considered to be the surpassing treasures of the Roman missal and breviary.

Guéranger set out to make his love for the Roman liturgy visible, audible and tangible in a particular setting: the restored St. Peter's Abbey at Solesmes. In 1833, he and several associates began to live a communal life there based on the *Rule* of St. Benedict. Guéranger explained that he chose the Benedictine way of life precisely because of the importance it placed on the celebration of the divine office in choir, and because of the possibility of undertaking serious study of the liturgy with an eye to its renewal. Guéranger's monastery at Solesmes served as a kind of showcase for the proper celebration of the Mass and divine office, and as a workshop for the pursuit of liturgical scholarship. Monastics and lay persons could "come and see" what revived communal life and communal prayer looked like in a country where they had all but disappeared.

Guéranger's goals regarding the liturgical life may be summarized as: 1) forming monks and other Christians through the liturgy and 2) recovering and authenticating such historical documents as patristic texts, and later, collecting and editing Gregorian chant (an effort that won Pope Pius X's approval). These goals lay behind two of Guéranger's more significant writings, *Institutions liturgiques* (1840, 1841, 1851) a three-volume history of liturgical tradition from ancient Israel to his own time, and *L'Année liturgique* (1841-1866) a nine-volume meditative commentary on the texts and prayers of the Mass and divine office for each day of the year. Guéranger's purpose in these volumes was to deepen comprehension of liturgical texts, especially the scriptures, which he saw as the chief requirement for renewed participation. "His teaching upon the Church as the Mystical Body, the centrality of the paschal mystery, the doctrinal character of the liturgy, and his insistence upon the need to study the texts of the liturgy, all these ideas were absolutely original in the 19th century" (Johnson, p. 350). Guéranger can justly be called the herald of the liturgical movement.

Monastic Centers of Renewal

The influence of Guéranger's liturgical theology, scholarship and practice extended far beyond the walls of Solesmes to German abbeys like Beuron, its Belgian foundation of Maredsous, and to French parish churches. Guéranger's legacy of monasteries and parishes transformed into vibrant centers of liturgical energy has been well chronicled by R.W. Franklin in *Worship* magazine (see the bibliography). Clearly the chief means to renewal of community life, then as now, was liturgical formation and active participation in the Mass and divine office on the part of all. While monks became the premier promoters of the 19th-century liturgical movement, they understood that the liturgy needed the whole people of God to celebrate it, not just clerics and religious. This understanding led Dom Gérard van Caloen of Maredsous to publish his *Missel des fidèles*(1882), the first complete Latin-French missal to receive episcopal endorsement. The inexpensive review which accompanied it from 1884, *Le Messager des fidèles*, would serve as the model for popular liturgical pamphlets of subsequent decades.

The Abbey of Beuron, refounded by Maurus and Placidus Wolter in 1863, was to be in many ways a mirror of Solesmes. Maurus, its first abbot, had studied with Guéranger and had become imbued with his love of the liturgy. Beuron's dedication to Solesmes' principles was reflected in its *Messbuch der heiligen Kirche* (1884)and vesperale (1893), in which the phrase "liturgical movement" was first used in Germany. This so-called Schott missal, which provided translations and explanations of all the Mass prayers, was immensely popular; seven million copies in fifty-six editions had been sold by the eve of the Second Vatican Council. Around the turn of the century, artist Desiderius Lenz founded a school and studio at Beuron that made his abbey renowned for a distinctive style of religious art.

"The nature of the monastery as an institution which is both a center of learning and of daily life shaped the liturgical movement along a creative "middle way" which was at once conservative, in that it looked to the past for models, and progressive, in that it sought to create a revived community life appropriate for modern conditions" (Franklin, "The Nineteenth-Century Liturgical Movement," p. 38). "Modern conditions" clearly were before the participants in the National Congress of

Catholic Works at Malines, Belgium, in September 1909, which is generally recognized to have launched the liturgical movement as an organized endeavor. Here, Dom Lambert Beauduin (1873-1960), a monk of Mont-César in Louvain, encouraged industrial workers to make the parish Mass the great weekly gathering of the Christian people for "the true prayer of the Church." To help shape personal and family prayer in accord with the liturgy, Beauduin published translations of the texts for Sunday Mass and Vespers in the periodical *La Vie Liturgique* (1909-1913). Under Beauduin's leadership, the movement radiated from the Belgian abbeys of Maredsous and its foundation, Mont-César.

World War I halted the movement, but the post-war interest in liturgy found a two-fold expression: the ever increasing research into liturgical history, and the growing desire for better instruction in liturgical matters. The focus of leadership in the liturgical movement shifted from Belgium to Germany.

At the Rhineland Abbey of Maria Laach, Abbot Ildefons Herwegen (1913-1946, abbacy) and his monks insisted that liturgical celebration must recapture the spirit of worship of the patristic era, not the Middle Ages, and they propagated that spirit in publications and conferences. The series *Ecclesia Orans*, begun by Herwegen in 1918, was directed toward a popular audience. The volumes of *Liturgiegeschichtliche Quellen und Forschungen* (begun in 1918 and superseded by the *Archiv für Liturgiewissenschaft* in 1950), and the annual *Jahrbuch für Liturgiewissenschaft* were important means of disseminating results of research to intellectuals and priests. Herwegen set Dom Odo Casel (1886-1948), one of his monks, on the path that led to Casel's development of his "mystery doctrine" (*Mysterienlehre*), by which he attempted to explain how Christ is present and active in the sacramental mysteries of the church.

At Maria Laach, art and architecture, as well as chant and publications, became a significant part of liturgical renewal. Courses on liturgy and "Liturgical Weeks" served as a means of spiritual revitalization for their often well-educated participants. In 1921, Prior Albert Hammenstede began celebrating Mass facing these visitors in the crypt of the old Romanesque abbey church. There, lay brothers and novices took a full and active part in their morning Mass by reciting the *Gloria* and *Credo* with the celebrant, making the responses in unison, and bringing their own bread to the altar rail in an offertory procession. The appropriateness and beauty of these old-but-new practices made a lasting impression on the visiting Fr. Godfrey Diekmann of St. John's Abbey in Collegeville, Minnesota, who later helped draft Vatican II's *Constitution on the Sacred Liturgy*.

New Initiatives in the New World

During 1924 and 1925, another monk of St. John's had visited all the major European centers of liturgical renewal. At Maria Laach, Dom Virgil Michel studied liturgy, at Beuron art, at Solesmes chant, at Maredsous publishing. But it was from Dom Lambert Beauduin at Mont-César that Fr. Virgil received the clearest inspiration and enduring interests that made him the pioneer of the American liturgical movement.

In 1926, Dom Virgil founded the journal *Orate Fratres* (renamed *Worship* in 1951) which was addressed especially to parish clergy and lay persons. Its first issue announced itself as "a review devoted to the liturgical apostolate," and it became one of the most important means of promoting liturgical renewal in America. The Liturgical Press, also founded by Dom Virgil, published his translation of Beauduin's *La Piété de* l'Église (*Liturgy the Life of the Church*, 1926) as the first volume in its "Popular Liturgical Library" series, as well as numerous pamphlets and worship leaflets.

Fr. Virgil had three main and related goals: the revival of Catholic worship in America, the rediscovery of the social mission of the Roman Catholic church, and the renewal of Catholic education on all levels in the United States. His extensive leadership in these efforts was anchored in his teaching on the mystical body of Christ: all the members of that body, both clergy and lay persons, are called to share in the worship and work of the church. Dom Virgil believed that society, so disordered by the individualism and ruthless competition that had led to economic collapse in the Great Depression, had to be reformed by means of the spiritual vision glimpsed in the liturgy. Worship in which all participate actively and consciously would witness to a new Christian humanism and personalism, and thus the experience and spirit of the liturgy would flow into a "reconstruction of the social order." Fr. Virgil sought to illustrate and implement the connection between participation in the liturgy and involvement in the pursuit of peace and justice in the world. Lambert Beauduin said of Fr. Virgil that liturgy was for him "above all a powerful means of doing apostolic work, by increasing the faith and devotion of the faithful." The eucharist, Dom Virgil believed, continually challenges the Christian community to become the body of Christ in the body politic of American culture.

One early 20th-century critic of the liturgical revival labeled it a "Benedictine innovation." Fr. Virgil's collaborators in the United States, many of whom were diocesan clergy and lay persons, helped to insure that the American liturgical movement would develop as more than a solely monastic and academic enterprise. They did not minimize the need for scholarship in scripture, patristics and the history of the rites if the practice of the liturgy was to be revised and reformed; but while many European promoters envisioned liturgical renewal as an end in itself, their American counterparts were one with Dom Virgil in situating the movement in a wider reform of American political and economic life. For the latter, the church's worship and social mission were bound together. They believed the Christian's participation in the Mass to be "a sublime school of social service," as Dom Virgil declared. "The Christian will find it necessary to live out in his daily life what he enacts in his worship at the altar of God."

Toward Vatican II

In the decades preceding the Second Vatican Council, Benedictines contributed their expertise to pastoral gatherings and in turn were enriched by such experiences. In 1929, the monks of St. John's Abbey sponsored the first "Liturgical Day" held in the United States, thereby imitating those begun by Dom Lambert Beauduin two decades earlier. In October 1940, the first U.S. National Liturgical Week was held in Chicago under the auspices of the Benedictine Liturgical Conference. Subsequent liturgical weeks at St. Paul (1941), St. Meinrad Archabbey (1942) and again at Chicago (1943) were also sponsored by the Benedictine Conference. At the 1943 meeting, the monks handed the leadership for these gatherings to the Liturgical Conference.

Benedictines also joined other scholars in probing liturgical questions that were to shape the Council's reforms. In the field of history, Doms Fernand Cabrol and Henri Leclercq edited *Dictionnaire d'archéologie chrétienne et de liturgie* (1903-1953). Doms Marius Férotin, Germain Morin, André Wilmart, Bernard Capelle, Cunibert Mohlberg and Ildefonso Schuster contributed important historical and textual studies of liturgical books. *The Shape of the Liturgy* (1945) by Dom Gregory Dix, an Anglican Benedictine of Nashdom Abbey, did much to revive and popularize liturgical studies in the Church of England and was favorably received by Roman Catholic scholars. The Latin-French missal prepared by Dom Gaspar Lefebvre of Saint-André was translated into many languages and published in numerous editions. Benedictine women also were no strangers to liturgical renewal, as evidenced in publications and artistic works such as finely crafted vestments. Pastoral liturgy became the subject of periodicals like Saint-André's *Bulletin paroissial et liturgique* (renamed *Paroisse et liturgie* in 1944) and Mont-César's *Questions liturgiques et paroissiales.*

The experience of one outstanding Benedictine liturgiologist over almost seven decades is recounted by Dom Bernard Botte of Mont-César (1893-1980) in his memoir, *From Silence to Participation.* He and Dom Bernard Capelle, also of Mont-César, played a significant role in various subcommittees which drafted the *Constitution on the Sacred Liturgy.* Later, as consultors to the Commission for the Implementation of the Constitution on the Sacred Liturgy (*Consilium*), Dom Botte and Dom Cyprian Vagaggini of Saint-André helped prepare the reformed sacramental rites mandated by the council.

Today and Tomorrow

The spirit of the liturgical renewal, cultivated for over a century in monastic settings in Europe and the United States, worked its welcome effects in the accomplishments of the Second Vatican Council and their implementation in parishes and religious communities. Dom Vagaggini correctly observes that "there could be nothing more gratifying to those Benedictines who have truly penetrated this spirit" (*Theological Dimensions of the Liturgy* trans. Leonard J. Doyle and

W.A. Jurgens [Collegeville, Minnesota: The Liturgical Press, 1976], p. 683). But since World War II, leadership of the liturgical movement has been in the hands of those who are not Benedictines: episcopal conferences, national organizations and diocesan offices of worship. This has served to underscore the fact that liturgical spirituality is for all Christians, not just monks.

Throughout their long history, Benedictines have developed their own liturgical customs (but not their own eucharistic rite) and what might be called a "monastic choreography." They "have regularly evaluated liturgical laws in the light of theological criteria and have interpreted them in terms of theological and specifically monastic sources. As a result a rich liturgical tradition has developed among Benedictines for which they are highly esteemed by the Church" (R. Kevin Seasoltz, O.S.B., in a presentation to the monks of St. John's Abbey, Collegeville, Minnesota, December 1, 1987). Pope Paul VI, for example, hoped that Benedictines would be conservators of the pre-Vatican II liturgy by maintaining the Latin version of the Divine Office and Gregorian chant. Benedictine communities do respect their heritage, but in accord with the post-conciliar permission to prepare their own forms of the liturgy of the hours (within certain limits), they continue to produce versions that blend old and new ingredients into nourishing fare.

Benedictines have begun to address questions about the frequency of the eucharistic celebration, the practice of concelebration, and appropriate God-language in liturgical prayer. "These are difficulties which do not concern the Benedictines only, but they tend to become more apparent because the pace of liturgical renewal seems to progress faster here than in the Church at large" (Terrence Kardong, O.S.B., *The Benedictines* [Wilmington, Delaware: Michael

Glazier, Inc., 1988] p. 175). As they seek to revitalize their celebrations of the eucharist and the liturgy of the hours, Benedictines can help the church to understand that unity need not require uniformity.

For Benedictines today, the challenge of liturgical renewal is changed, not ended. According to monastic historian Dom Jean Leclercq, they retain a significant role in "animating" the movement they pioneered, especially through their present scholarship and efforts to produce a religious culture based on biblical, patristic and liturgical sources (Leclercq, p. 252). It is not surprising that Benedictines, who have relished and cherished the riches of the liturgy for over fourteen centuries, should continue to share them through writing and publishing, teaching, leading retreats, and giving careful attention to the aesthetics of worship, both among themselves and with others. The biennial meetings of the Benedictine Musicians of the Americas and Caribbean, begun in 1966, provide opportunities for members to share their own compositions and to address questions pertaining to the work of directing music and liturgy in their communities. The Monastic Liturgy Forum, an organization formed in 1988 of Benedictine women and men who serve their monasteries as liturgists, seeks to enhance worship and deepen liturgical spirituality in monastic communities.

The monastic liturgical spirit, nurtured in silence and contemplation, has often flowered in an abundance of artistic compositions, especially music and prayer texts. The monks of St. John's Abbey in Collegeville, Minnesota, concretized (literally) their liturgical ideals in the new abbey church (1961) designed by Marcel Breuer of the *Bauhaus* tradition, a worship space which anticipated many requirements of the post-Vatican II liturgy.

Today monasteries are, or are called to become once again, places where a contemplative religious culture will favor a synthesis of the arts around the worship of the church. The monastic style of celebration will be one that "gives people a way out of verbal thickets, that provides space to hear the silence that exposes real human needs and feelings" (Mitchell, p. 16). Benedictine communities should find it easy to understand that physical hospitality to guests, which is a hallmark of monastic life, is closely linked to liturgical hospitality: the divine hospitality shown to God's people in the beloved Son is to be mirrored in our hospitality to each other, and never more so than in the liturgy. Through their continuing attention to the outward forms and inner spirit of worship, which Dom Guéranger promoted in the 19th century, monasteries can be oases where those "who are to be welcomed as Christ" (*Rule* of Benedict 53:1) can join their hosts in drinking with delight from the wellsprings of communal prayer and be refreshed for their journey of service in the world.

See **Liturgical movement, the (1830-1969); Mystery theology**

Bernard Botte, *From Silence to Participation: An Insider's View of Liturgical Renewal.* Trans. from the French *Le mouvement liturgique: Témoignage et souvenirs* by John Sullivan, O.C.D. (Washington, D.C.: The Pastoral Press, 1988). R.W. Franklin, Articles in order of publication in *Worship* magazine: "Guéranger: A View on the Centenary of His Death," 49 (June-July 1975): 318-328; "Guéranger and Pastoral Liturgy: A Nineteenth-Century View," 50 (March 1976): 146-162; "Guéranger and Variety in Unity," 51 (September 1977): 378-399; "The Nineteenth-Century Liturgical Movement," 53 (January 1979): 12-39. R.W. Franklin, and Robert L. Spaeth, *Virgil Michel: American Catholic* (Collegeville, Minnesota: The Liturgical Press, 1988). Cuthbert Johnson, O.S.B., *Analecta Liturgica 9: Prosper Guéranger (1805-1875): A Liturgical Theologian: An Introduction to his Liturgical Writings and Work,* Studia Anselmiana 89. (Rome: Pontificio Ateneo S. Anselmo, 1984). Jean Leclercq, "Le rôle des moines dans le mouvement liturgique," *Paroisse et liturgie,* 50 (1968): 248-255. Nathan Mitchell, "Monks and the Future of Worship," *Worship,* 50 (January 1976): 2-18. Sonya A. Quitslund, *Beauduin: A*

Prophet Vindicated (New York: Newman Press, 1973).

MICHAEL KWATERA, O.S.B.

BISHOP

In Roman Catholic church order (L.G., 20), as well as the orders of many other Christian churches, the office of bishop is the primary pastoral office of the local church. The bishop is the sign and minister of unity both within the local church and of the local church with the church universal. It is said that the fullness of ministerial priesthood resides in the office of bishop, a statement which has more to do with the office as an ecclesial office, the bishop ordained to be *sacramentum ecclesiae*, than to any sense of ranking or parcelling out the ministerial priesthood of Christ. The Roman Catholic ritual for ordination of bishops reminds the ordinand that "the title of bishop is not one of honor but of function, and therefore a bishop should strive to serve rather than to rule" (Homily-Instruction). It names the bishop as steward of the mysteries of Christ, as father and brother to all in his care, guardian of the faith, builder of the church, and servant of the gospel. The ministry of the bishop is a trinitarian ministry: a personification of the Father in the church; a fulfillment of Christ's role as teacher, priest and shepherd; an agent of the Spirit who gives life to the church. Bishops serve the church as a body, a college of bishops in which the apostolic college is continued (C.D., 4).

See **Church order; Priesthood; Ordination rites; Orders, sacrament of; Orders, symbols of**

BODY OF CHRIST

Language plays a central role in the life of any community as it expresses and shapes its identity. From the 1st century to the present the phrase "body of Christ" has been part of the Christian community's vocabulary for communicating something of its self-understanding and its understanding of the eucharist. Anyone engaged in a study of ecclesiology or the theology and spirituality of the eucharist will have to explore this notion.

The Pauline literature provides us with our earliest evidence for the use of this image in the Christian scriptures. In addressing himself to the divisions and conflicts experienced by the church of Corinth, Paul described the interdependence that exists among the parts of a human body and informed the Corinthians that they were one body, Christ's body, as a result of their baptism (1 Cor 12:12-27). At that time it was not uncommon to use the image of a body when referring to a social organization. We get a sense of the depth of the bond uniting Christians from Paul's statement that their union is grounded in the sharing of the one Spirit (1 Cor 12:13). Sharing in the one Spirit, Christ's Spirit, is the result of being incorporated into his death and resurrection through baptism (Rom 6:3-8).

Those who have been incorporated into Christ through baptism are engaged with other members of the body in an ongoing process of transformation into the likeness of Christ (2 Cor 3:18). Their corporate identity as the body of Christ is renewed every time they celebrate the Lord's Supper and share in the body and blood of Christ (1 Cor 10:16-17). *Koinōnia* is the word used by Paul in these verses and elsewhere to express the relationship which is at the heart of the Christian community's identity. The word suggests having a common share or participation in something greater than oneself. Paul uses it to speak of sharing in the life of Jesus Christ (1 Cor 1:9). Persons are brought into this relationship of communion with Christ and one another through baptism when they receive the one Spirit. This is a dynamic relationship in which the gift must be continuously realized in various forms of expression. There are consequences for those who have been brought into the body of Christ.

Those who have received the same gospel and who have come to share in the one Spirit are also called to participate in one another's sufferings. Paul makes this clear when he refers to the collection taken up by the Gentile Christians for the Jewish Christians who were suffering from famine (Rom 15:22-27). Furthermore, those who come together to share in the body and blood of Christ are called to be attentive to all those, rich and poor, who constitute the body of Christ, lest they be guilty of desecrating that body (1 Cor 11:17-34). The gifts of each member are to be used for the building up of the community (1 Cor 12-14; Rom 12:4-8). Finally, for those who are baptized into union with Christ there are no more distinctions between Jew and Greek, slave and free, male and female, for all are one person in Christ Jesus (Gal 3:27-28).

The notion of the body undergoes significant development in the letters to the Colossians and Ephesians, letters whose Pauline authorship is questioned by many scholars. In these letters the church is explicitly identified as the body of Christ and Christ is designated as head of the body (Col 1:18;1:24; Eph 1:22;4:15). This distinction between Christ as head and the church as body was not present in the earlier letters. In Ephesians, the relationship between Christ and the church is likened to the love between a husband and wife and the image of the bride comes to be associated with the church which is Christ's body (Eph 5:21-33). In these letters, the holiness of the church and the love that exists between Christ and the church are two important themes.

Patristic literature provides many examples of the church and the eucharist depicted as the body of Christ. Limits of space allow for the presentation of only a few. In the middle of the 2nd century, Justin, while explaining Christian worship to the emperor, wrote that the bread and wine of the eucharist is not received as common bread or common drink but as the flesh and blood of the incarnate Jesus (*First Apology,* 66). In a homily on 1 Cor 10:16-18, John Chrysostom (d. 407) emphasized Paul's teaching that the bread is the body of Christ and that all who partake of this bread become the body of Christ. In a homily on 1 Cor 11: 23-28 he tells his congregation that those who neglect or overlook the hungry and do not give liberally to the poor eat the bread and drink the cup of the Lord unworthily and will be guilty of the body and blood of the Lord. Augustine is well known for his strong sense of the ecclesial dimensions of the eucharist. In one of his homilies to the newly baptized he reminds them of Paul's words, "You are the body of Christ, and His members" and goes on to say the following: "If, therefore, you are the body of Christ and His members, your mystery has been placed on the Lord's table, you receive your mystery. You reply 'Amen' to that which you are, and by replying you consent. For you hear 'The Body of Christ' and you reply 'Amen'. Be a member of the body of Christ so that your 'Amen' may be true. . . Be what you see, and receive what you are" (*Sermon* 272).

In the early centuries of the church's life the intimate relationship between the church as body of Christ and the eucharist as body of Christ was expressed in praxis and theology. When an assembly gathered to celebrate the eucharist its members provided the bread and wine, were understood to be active subjects in the celebration because of their union with Christ, shared in the body and blood of the Lord as the climax of the service. Communion in the bread and wine of the eucharist was an expression of membership in the ecclesial body of Christ. Guests who were recognized as legitimate members of the church were welcomed to the table as a sign of hospitality. Members who had cut themselves off from the body by grievous sin were excluded from the table. In the course of time the church's eucharistic praxis underwent significant change and new questions emerged in eucharistic theology. There were corresponding shifts in the meaning of the body of Christ.

During the 9th century theologians began to question the relationship between the eucharistic body of Christ and the historical body of Jesus, the manner in which Christ is present in the eucharist and the kind of change that occurs in the bread and wine during the eucharist. The eucharistic praxis within which such questions were explored was quite different from that of the early tradition. It was not uncommon for people to be present at the eucharist but to refrain from communicating in the body and blood of the Lord. Many did not understand the Latin language and this contributed to the emerging sense that the clergy rather than the whole assembly were the active subjects of the liturgy. It was during the 9th century that other changes in the relationship between the laity and the bread of the eucharist became apparent. Whereas, for centuries the people had made the bread, presented it at the service, and received it into their own hands at the time of communion, legislation now appeared requiring that the bread be unleavened, made by clergy or monks, and received by lay persons in the mouth. In addition, lay persons were no longer allowed to bring the eucharist to the sick. Such a context did not support a strong sense of a local assembly expressing and deepening its identity as the body of Christ in its celebrations of the eucharist.

Paschasius Radbertus, one of the 9th century theologians, identified the body of Christ present in the eucharist with that which was born of Mary and is now glorified. This position attained a certain dominance but was challenged by Berengar in the 11th century. A controversy erupted and Berengar's teachings were eventually condemned by Pope Leo IX in 1050. Berengar reluctantly signed a confession in 1059 which contained a very strong statement about the physical presence of the Lord in the eucharist, then rejected it and returned to his earlier views. Eventually he accepted a more refined version of the oath at the Synod of Rome in 1079.

As theologians were discussing the real presence of Christ in the eucharist and asking questions about the exact moment at which this presence is realized, new ways of recognizing and responding to that presence were appearing in the church's eucharistic praxis. The practice of elevating the host during the institution narrative had begun in some places by the end of the 12th century. In the early 13th century a synod held in Paris decreed that the elevation was not to occur until after the words: "This is my body," thereby settling a controversy regarding the moment of consecration. Reception of the body and blood of the Lord was rare at this time but there was a great desire to see the host and adore Christ present in the eucharist. The notion of spiritual communion also became popular.

The Feast of Corpus Christi was established for the entire church in 1264. The idea for such a feast had been promoted in the first part of the century by Juliana of Liège as a way of honoring Christ present in the eucharist. Devotional practices such as visits to the Blessed Sacrament, processions with the Blessed Sacrament, eucharistic exposition and benediction also made their appearance at this time. These practices which eventually became part of a eucharistic cult outside of Mass have their roots in the liturgy itself. Their emergence cannot be adequately understood apart from the social, cultural, political, economic, and religious context of the time.

Since there was little in the liturgy that supported the notion of the assembly expressing and renewing its identity as the body of Christ, the link between the eucharistic body and the ecclesial body was severely weakened in eucharistic praxis. It is interesting to note, however, that the social dimension of the eucharist did not disappear. On those rare occasions during the year when it was customary for everyone in a parish to receive, doing so signified that one was a member of the church in good standing. The idea of the church as the body of Christ was also present in the writings of some 12th and 13th century theologians. Thomas Aquinas was not alone in identifying Christ's mystical body as the ultimate reality signified by the eucharist (S.Th., III,73:1). In his book *Corpus Mysticum* Henri de Lubac has shown how this term, originally used of the eucharist, came to be used of the church during the theological discussions of the medieval period.

The manner in which the eucharist is the body of Christ and the identity of the church as the body of Christ were both issues in the theological controversies of the 16th century. Trent strongly reaffirmed the real presence of the body and blood of Jesus in the eucharist in response to those who denied it. The notion of the church as the body of Christ became intertwined with a distinction between the visible and invisible church that was used by some of the Reformers. Some of them identified the mystical body of Christ with the elect but not with the whole of the visible church. This was a way of rejecting the Roman tendency to equate the visible hierarchical church centered upon the papacy with the true church. The ecclesiology of the post-Tridentine Roman Catholic church, strongly influenced by Robert Bellarmine (1542-1621) emphasized the visibility of

the church and the position that the pope represents Christ as head of the body which is the church. A notion of the church as a perfect society held sway far into the 20th century. Such an ecclesiology emphasizes structural and institutional components, those elements which give the church its visibility. Biblical imagery was not in the forefront of the church's self-consciousness.

The documents of Vatican II bear witness to a recovery of a variety of biblical images for the church including that of the body of Christ. There are also many statements which point to the significance of the eucharist in the life of the church. In speaking of the church as the mystical body of Christ, the *Dogmatic Constitution on the Church* states that the visible society with its structure and the spiritual community or mystical body are to be understood as one complex reality rather than two (L.G.,8). However, it does not identify the mystical body with the Roman Catholic church as Pius XII had done in his encyclical *Mystici Corporis*. Instead it says that this church, which is given life by the Spirit of Christ, subsists in the Catholic church and goes on to recognize that there are elements of sanctification and truth to be found elsewhere. In a similar fashion *Lumen Gentium*, 14 and 15, identify a variety of ways of being incorporated into Christ's body which is the church.

L.G. 7 gathers together a number of NT ideas about the body of Christ: the Spirit of Christ as source of life in the body, baptism as the sacrament of entry into the body, the fact that all members are called to be formed in the likeness of Christ, and the realization that sharing in the body of the Lord in the eucharist continually effects communion with him and with one another.

The principle that liturgy is ecclesial action permeates *Sacrosanctum Concilium* and the church is often presented under the image of a body. For example, S.C. 7 states that "in the liturgy the whole public worship is performed by the mystical body of Jesus Christ, that is, by the Head and his members." S.C. 26 indicates that liturgical services manifest and have effects upon the whole body of the church. The sacraments are said to have as one of their purposes the building up of the body of Christ (S.C., 59) and the divine office is set out as the prayer which Christ together with his body address to the Father. (S.C., 84) The faithful are said to offer the sacrifice of the eucharist with the priest (S.C., 48) and full, active participation by all the people is identified as the primary aim that should be operative in revising the liturgy (S.C.,14). Finally, while maintaining the familiar notion of Christ being present in the person of his minister and especially in the eucharistic species, the constitution refreshes the church's memory that Christ is present in the sacraments, in his word as it is proclaimed, and in the church when it gathers to pray and sing (S.C.,7).

The liturgical rites revised in the years following the council are faithful to these ideas. *The General Instruction of the Roman Missal* presents the reception of the Lord's body and blood as the normal completion of the eucharistic celebration for all who are properly disposed and several of the symbolic actions which are part of the communion rite are explained within a communal context (56). The sign of peace is described as a plea for peace and unity for the church and the whole human family as well as a sign of mutual love. The breaking of bread is identified as "a sign that in sharing in the one bread of life which is Christ we who are many are one body." The desirability of having the people receive the Lord's body from hosts consecrated at the same Mass and, when permissible, to share in the chalice is encouraged as an expression of their sharing in the sacrifice which is actually being celebrated. Finally, the communion song is supposed to be an expression of the communicants' union in spirit and a way of making the procession to receive Christ's body more fully an act of community.

The Rite for Holy Communion and Worship of the Eucharist Outside Mass maintains the validity of such practices as eucharistic reservation, exposition and benediction of the Blessed Sacrament but clearly states that these need to be understood in relation to the celebration of the eucharist which takes place in Mass and culminates in the reception of communion (2-4;82). People are reminded that the primary and original reason for reservation of the eucharist outside Mass is the administration of viaticum (5). The unique presence of Christ in the eucharistic elements is presented within the context of his presence in the assembly gathered in his name, in his word when the scriptures are read and proclaimed, and in the person of the minister (6). Exposition of the eucharist is said to be both an acknowledgment of Christ's marvelous presence in the sacrament and an invitation to the spiritual union with him that culminates in sacramental communion (82). Prayer before Christ sacramentally present is described as something which extends the union with Christ which the faithful have reached in communion and as an action which should lead persons to become witnesses of Christ (81). *The Rite of Pastoral Care of the Sick* emphasizes the link between the community's eucharistic celebration, especially on the Lord's Day, and the communion of the sick and suggests that communion be taken to them from the community's celebration (73).

One of the changes made in the liturgy of the eucharist was the restoration of the ancient formula, "the body of Christ," with its response of "Amen." In 1977 the U.S. Bishops' Committee on the Liturgy published a booklet entitled *The Body of Christ* which was intended to serve as part of the catechesis associated with restoring the practice of receiving communion in the hand. An explanation of the meaning of the formula is included. By saying "Amen" to the words "the body of Christ" "we profess our belief in the presence of Christ in the eucharistic bread and wine as well as in his body the Church" (p.21). The use of the phrase "the body of Christ" "seeks to highlight the important concept of the community as the body of Christ. . . brings into focus the assent of the individual in the worshipping community. . . and demonstrates the importance of Christ's presence in liturgical celebrations" as set out in S.C. 7 (p. 22).

This strong emphasis on the ecclesial dimension of the body of Christ is absent from the explanation of the meaning of the formula given in *This Holy and Living Sacrifice*, the directory for the celebration and reception of communion under both kinds issued by the U.S. National Conference of Catholic Bishops in 1985. This document is a summary of the church's liturgical laws concerning communion under both kinds. The significance of the eucharist in the life of the church is made clear in a number of places but when the act of communion is described, the communicant's "Amen" to "The body of Christ" and "the blood of Christ" is presented as an act of faith, "a profession in the presence of the saving Christ, body, soul and divinity, who now gives life to the believer." (16) The document is concerned with emphasizing that the communicant makes an act of faith in the total presence of the Lord Jesus Christ whether in communion under one or both forms and this concern seems to have eclipsed the earlier concern to call the community to a recognition of its identity as the body of Christ.

Although the formula familiar to Augustine and the church of his time has been restored, many in the church have yet to explore and appropriate the depth of its meaning. As people do realize that

in saying "Amen" they are also assenting to their identity as members of the body of Christ, more attention may be given to the social and ethical implications that accompany such an identity.

See **Eucharist; Assembly; Ecclesiology and liturgy**

Raymond E. Brown, *The Churches the Apostle Left Behind* (N.Y.: Paulist, 1984). Gary Macy, *The Theologies of the Eucharist in the Early Scholastic Period* (Oxford: Clarendon Press, 1984). Nathan Mitchell, *Cult and Controversy: The Worship of the Eucharist Outside Mass* (N.Y.: Pueblo, 1982). George Panikulam, *Koinonia in the New Testament: A Dynamic Expression of Christian Life* (Rome: Biblical Institute Press, 1979). John A.T. Robinson, *The Body: A Study in Pauline Theology* (London: SCM Press LTD, 1963).

MARGARET MARY KELLEHER, O.S.U

BURIAL, CHRISTIAN

A. *Tradition*

The roots of the tradition of Christian burial are found in Judaism. In the Jewish community, burial has long been regarded as both an obligation and a work of mercy, and what scattered references we have to their ancient burial rites reflect both realism and simplicity.

Jesus, was buried according to Jewish custom. Although the nearness of the Sabbath, coupled with fear of the authorities, prevented his friends from anointing the body in the usual way, both the synoptic and the Johannine gospels, while differing in specific details, record that his body was wrapped in linen, with myrrh and aloes between the bands (Mt 27:59; Mk 15:46; Lk 23:53, 56; 24:1; Jn 14:39-40), and laid to rest in the tomb.

The Jews viewed dead bodies as unclean and therefore disposed of them before going back to prayers or going on with business as usual. Mourners were forbidden to work, bathe or have sexual intercourse for up to as long as 30 days. Male mourners were served a "meal of comfort" (*labra'ah*) after the funeral, consisting of eggs and lentils, prepared by friends and neighbors and served with wine.

Jewish practices were not without a hint of superstition, however. It was their custom, for example, to dispose of all water in the house after someone died. Explanations for this custom vary. Some believed that before leaving earth the soul might have cleansed itself in the water, while others feared that the soul might live in the water if there were no room in the House of the Dead. Another explanation was the belief that the Angel of Death washed the blood of the dead off its sword in the waters, or might even be lurking there, waiting for the next victim.

It is the Kaddish—the sanctification—however, that gives us a synthesis of Jewish theology with regard to death. This prayer was originally the concluding prayer of the synagogue liturgy. It is an eschatological prayer, similar to the Lord's Prayer. Traditionally, the Kaddish must be recited every day for eleven months following the death of a parent, blood relative or spouse.

In the developing funeral liturgies of the Christian community in its early days, Roman influence was strongest. Roman customs reveal an attraction to the mystery cults of the East as well as the practices of Egypt. Initially, Christians and pagans were buried side by side in cemeteries, with only decorations or inspirations to distinguish one grave from the other. Early Christian symbolism depicted Jesus as tending sheep, fishing, or presiding over the heavenly banquet. In time, however, as the theology of death became more paschal in character, symbols of deliverance began to predominate. Jesus' miracles, particularly the raising of Lazarus and the curing of the blind man, were popular representations.

We find records of "funeral meals" as customary in early Christianity. These funeral meals probably had their origin in the Roman custom of graveside feasts,

rather than in the Jewish "meals of comfort" held in the homes of the mourners. Roman funeral meals were connected with either the belief that the dead needed nourishment or the idea that the "tedium" of the dead would be relieved by such feasts. Often they became occasions of such raucous behavior that most of our knowledge of them is derived from various bishops condemning them. These condemnations addressed the scandal that such excesses caused, and encouraged prayer vigils, fasting and gifts to the needy as more appropriate customs to develop.

The weeping and wailing associated with mourning, as well as black mourning garments, were also considered to be "unchristian," because despair rather than hope was seen to be their motivation. Consequently, devout Christians developed more suitable means of expressing their grief, replacing weeping and wailing with singing psalms and hymns.

From the writings of the Fathers we learn of other "unchristian" behavior that was gradually adapted to reflect more accurately the theology of the Christian community. One example of this was the custom of placing eucharistic bread in the corpse's mouth. This custom probably traced its origin to the mystery cults where a coin was placed in the mouth of the deceased so that he or she would be able to pay the fare to Charon on the ferry across the river Styx. Various councils [Hippo (393), Carthage (419 and 525), Auxerre (578), and Trullo (692)] condemned this practice of giving eucharist to the dead, who could neither "take" nor "eat," but supported the practice of giving eucharist to the dying as "food for the journey" (*viaticum*). In the 2nd century Ignatius of Antioch referred to eucharist as "medicine of immortality and the antidote which wards off death but yields continuous life in union with Jesus Christ" (Ign. *Eph* 20:2).

The oldest Roman ritual for death and

burial is Ordo 49, which dates from the 7th century. Rather than a highly structured ritual, the Ordo presents an outline for the service. The ritual consisted of two parts: the first, which ritualized death, took place in the home of the deceased; the other, a burial ritual, took place in the church and cemetery.

When death appeared to be imminent, the Christian was given the eucharist, as a token of the resurrection he or she was about to experience. From that time until the moment of death, family and friends would read the passion narrative to the one dying. When they thought the soul was about to leave the body, those gathered in prayer would respond, "Come, saints of God: advance angels of the Lord. . . ." Then, after reciting Psalm 113 they would pray, "May the choir of angels receive you."

After death, the body was placed on a litter and carried in procession to the church. There the community recited an "office," consisting of psalms, using the poignant antiphon: "May the angels lead you into paradise, may the martyrs welcome you and guide you into the holy city Jerusalem." While reciting Psalm 117, the procession continued on its way, escorting the body to the cemetery, and responding, "Open the gates for me, and once I am within I shall praise the Lord." Psalms 113 and 117 formed part of the structure of the Jewish Passover meal. The intention in using these psalms in the funeral liturgy as well might have been to demonstrate that Christian death completes the paschal "exodus."

There is a dramatic shift in focus when we move into the medieval period. Gradually the peaceful, paschal vision of the Christian's final journey was replaced by harsh scenes of the final judgment. God and the company of angels were no longer waiting to welcome Christians at the moment of death, but instead stood guard, waiting to scrutinize them before the heavenly court. Christian death ceased to be recognized as an accomplishment of the paschal exodus, and was seen instead as yet another ordeal.

The Ordo of 1614 included funeral rites along with rites for sacraments and blessings. The official book attempted to bring order to the collection of monastic rituals that had been developing. The funeral rite reflects two strands of belief: death as triumph or reward and death as ordeal. We see both these strands weaving in and out of the ritual.

The service began at the door of the church, where the priest met the body of the deceased and the company of mourners. He sprinkled the coffin with holy water, symbolizing purification from sin. Although trust in God's mercy underlies the prayers, they beg God repeatedly to spare the sinner from the pains of hell.

The liturgy's attitude toward death is particularly evident in the sequence, *Dies Irae*. Its apocalyptic character seems to be more reflective of the superstitions of pagan mythology than of a people formed in the resurrection of Christ.

The eucharistic prayer sounds a note of genuine hope in the liturgy. "For those who have been faithful, Lord, life is not ended, but merely changed; and when this earthly abode dissolves, an eternal dwelling place awaits them in heaven." This image is more compatible to Christian faith than one of being swallowed by the pit.

B. *Order of Christian Funerals*

The *Order of Christian Funerals* (O.C.F.) is a 1989 revision, reorganization and English translation of the *Ordo Exsequiarium* (August 15, 1969) which actualized the reform initiated at Vatican II (S.C., 81). The rites have been rearranged and developed so that they represent a cohesive theology of death and Christian burial, and can be of greater use to ministers, both in preaching and in presiding. The general introduction is an expansion of the introduction given in the Latin edition, and also contains pastoral notes before each of the rites. In addition, there are newly composed prayers to provide for situations not addressed in the Latin edition.

The *Order of Christian Funerals* provides the Roman Catholic community with a coherent means of ministering to both the social and spiritual needs of members of the community who face the searing pain of death. The progression of rites brings hope and consolation to the living by immersing the faithful again and again in the wonder of the paschal mystery.

The *Praenotanda* for the revised rites establishes the appropriate focus for the funeral rites, immediately making the connection between the paschal mystery and baptism. Since baptism has already united the Christian to that great mystery of faith, it is at the eucharist that this mystery is most completely celebrated. Therefore, the funeral Mass is the principal celebration surrounding Christian burial.

The *Order of Christian Funerals* emphasizes the fact that all members of the church share in the ministry of consolation: caring for the dying, praying for the dead, and comforting those who mourn. Although this ministry primarily involves active participation in the funeral rites, the order suggests other possibilities for members of the community.

Those members of the community who hold special office are called upon to exercise their ministry in keeping with their office in the ministries of reader, musician, pallbearer, usher, etc.

Where conditions permit, the priest is the most appropriate presider at the funeral rites. When this is not possible, however, a deacon or lay person may preside (O.C.F., 14). Other ministries in the funeral rites invite the participation of lay persons as readers, musicians, ushers, pallbearers, and as special ministers of the eucharist where existing norms permit (O.C.F., 15).

The church's ministry to the deceased extends beyond the Roman Catholic community. Not only may the church's funeral rites be celebrated for the child whose parents intend to have their child baptized, but under certain circumstances, the local ordinary may permit use of the church's funeral rites for the baptized member of another church, when the church's minister is unavailable (O.C.F., 18).

C. *Funeral Liturgies*

The funeral liturgy, which might be celebrated within or outside Mass, is the community's principal celebration for the deceased. Ideally, funerals are celebrated at a time which permits as many members of the community to be present as possible. Generally this is early in the day. In some places, however, evening funerals are feasible and occur regularly. In other situations, particularly where there are few ordained ministers, it has become more practical to celebrate funerals in conjunction with the daily eucharist.

Because the eucharist is "a sacrament of love, a sign of unity, a bond of charity, a paschal banquet in which Christ is eaten, the mind is filled with grace, and a pledge of future glory is given to us" (S.C., 47), it is most appropriate that the community gather to celebrate eucharist together when one of its members dies. Full and active participation of the assembly is encouraged and members of the larger parish assume their ususal roles in the parish's celebration of funerals as they would in the Sunday celebration.

Funeral Masses may not be celebrated during the Sacred Triduum, on solemnities of obligation, or on the Sundays of Advent, Lent or Easter (G.I.R.M., 336). Therefore, when it is not possible to have a funeral Mass, the funeral liturgy takes place outside Mass before the rite of committal. A Mass for the deceased would then be scheduled at another time. In such a case, a deacon or designated lay person may preside at the funeral liturgy (O.C.F., 151).

The funeral Mass, while ordinarily celebrated in the parish church, may be celebrated in the home of the deceased or some other appropriate place, at the discretion of the local ordinary. The liturgy includes reception of the body, the liturgy of the word, the liturgy of the eucharist, and the final commendation and farewell.

Standing at the door of the church, the members of the community welcome the deceased as their own. In the name of the community the priest greets the company of mourners. National flags and/or insignia of other associations are removed before the body of the deceased is brought into the church. The priest sprinkles the body with holy water, recalling the waters of baptism, and covers the coffin with a pall, again recalling the garment with which the deceased had been clothed in baptism.

The procession, led by the priest and assisting ministers, enters the church, and the coffin is placed near the sanctuary. The paschal candle, recalling the foundational mystery of the community's faith and its source of hope, while not carried in the procession, may be placed near the coffin.

The order regards the liturgy of the word as a central element of the church's ministry in the funeral liturgy for "the readings proclaim the paschal mystery, teach remembrance of the dead, convey the hope of being gathered together again in God's kingdom, and encourage the witness of Christian life ... tell of God's design for a world in which suffering and death will relinquish their hold on all whom God has called his own" (O.C.F., 137).

A homily based on the scripture texts is an essential part of the funeral liturgy. Rather than dwelling on the life of the deceased as is customary in a eulogy, the homilist tries to focus on God's compassionate love and the community's faith in the paschal mystery, and through these

words, the community receives strength and consolation.

In the liturgy of the eucharist which follows, "all are given a foretaste of eternal life in Christ and are united with Christ, with each other, and with all the faithful, living and dead" (O.C.F., 143).

The funeral liturgy usually concludes with the final commendation. However, this may be celebrated instead at the place of committal.

Before the final commendation begins, it is sometimes customary for someone to speak in remembrance of the deceased. This may be a friend or a member of the family, and may meet the needs the community has for eulogizing the deceased. These words are spoken before the members of the community entrust the deceased "to the tender and merciful embrace of God" (O.C.F., 146). Without denying the reality and pain of separation, this farewell underscores once again the common bonds of faith that unite the gathered assembly.

The presider invokes God, aware of the sadness present in this last farewell, but taking comfort in the hope that one day we shall once again enjoy the friendship of the desceased. "Although this congregation will disperse in sorrow, the mercy of God will gather us together again in the joy of his kingdom. Therefore let us console one another in the faith of Jesus Christ " (O.C.F., 171B).

A brief period of silence gives the individual members of the community an opportunity for private prayer and remembrance before the customary signs of farewell. Then the body is sprinkled with holy water either before or during the community's song of farewell, traditionally the "*In Paradisum.*" Other hymns are sung as well when the community processes together to the place of committal.

The procession to the place of committal, mirroring the journey of human life and the pilgrimage to the new and eternal Jerusalem, is led by the priest and assisting ministers, who precede the coffin. The company of mourners follows when possible.

When it is not possible for a funeral Mass to be celebrated, the community still gathers to be strengthened by the word of God and to commend the deceased to God (O.C.F., 177).

D. *Committal*

For the community of mourners, the rite of committal marks the final separation from the deceased in this life. The rite's stark simplicity underscores the radical separation between life and death, while its prayers continue to look forward to the day when the entire community will be reunited for all eternity.

The funeral rites conclude with the rite of committal, which may take place at the grave, tomb, or crematorium. This rite may also be used for burial at sea (O.C.F., 204). In this rite, the community performs its final act in caring for the body of its deceased member, and for this reason it is most appropriate for the rite to be celebrated at the actual place of committal—the open grave or other place of interment.

Following upon the funeral liturgy, the order provides two forms of the rite of committal, one of which includes the final commendation. This second form of this rite is intended for use either when the final commendation does not take place during the funeral liturgy, or when no funeral liturgy is celebrated.

When the funeral procession arrives at the place of committal, the presiding minister, who may be a parish minister, a friend, or a member of the family, invites the community gathered to pray for the deceased and for themselves, that they may one day be reunited with the deceased.

A brief scripture verse is read to focus the community's attention on Jesus' promise that heaven is our true home (Phil 3:20).

The minister then prays over the place of committal, and then says the words of committal. Several selections are provided in the O.C.F., suited to the particular method of interment, whether the body is to be buried in the earth, at sea, or entombed, or the cremated remains are to be buried, entombed, or scattered. According to the movement of the rites, committal more appropriately takes place at this time, although it may take place at the conclusion of the rite instead.

The intercessions follow, which may be read by another minister. These petitions pray for comfort, consolation, strength, an increase of faith, etc., for those who mourn, as well as mercy for the deceased. The intercessions conclude with the invitation to join in praying the Lord's Prayer.

Several concluding prayers are provided (O.C.F., 222, 408), after which the minister asks those gathered to bow their heads and pray for God's blessing. All pray silently, and then the minister, with outstretched hands, prays over the people.

The traditional petitions for eternal rest follow. The minister who is a priest or deacon invokes God's blessing on the community, while the rite provides an alternative blessing for a lay minister to use.

The minister concludes the celebration by urging the community to "Go in the peace of Christ," to which they give the familiar reply, "Thanks be to God." A song may then follow or some sign or gesture of leave-taking, such as placing flowers or soil on the coffin.

The rite of committal with the final commendation has essentially the same structure, with a few exceptions.

1) The invitation to prayer includes reference to the fact that the community has gathered not only to commit the deceased's body to the earth/elements, but also to commend their brother or sister to God.

2) The final commendation follows

the reading from scripture. Its form is identical to that in the funeral liturgy.

3) Committal follows or takes place at the conclusion of the rite.

4) The rite concludes with the prayer over the people described previously, a song, and/or some sign or gesture of leave-taking.

For a variety of reasons, the final disposition of the body might not follow directly upon the rite of committal. Weather, labor disputes, or other unpredictable causes, might delay opening the grave. (Cremated remains might be interred (or scattered) at another time. It would be possible, in such cases, to repeat the rite of committal when the actual interment takes place (O.C.F., 212).

When a body has been donated to science, the rite of committal is celebrated whenever interment takes place.

E. *Wake Services*

The *Order of Christian Funerals* provides ministers with a variety of rites that may be celebrated between the time of death and the funeral liturgy, or before the rite of committal in the event that there is no funeral liturgy. Sensitive to the fact that the death of a loved one brings about emotional extremes, e.g., bewilderment, anger, grief, relief, the church's ministry at this time takes the form of companionship.

Two forms of the wake service, or "Vigil for the Deceased," are provided in the order: one for use when the vigil is celebrated in the church; the other when the vigil is celebrated in the home of the deceased, a funeral home, or some other suitable place.

Vigil for Deceased at the Funeral Home

This is the principal rite celebrated by the church between the time of the person's death and the funeral liturgy. "At the vigil the Christian community keeps watch with the family in prayer to the God of mercy and finds strength in Christ's presence" (O.C.F., 56).

Structurally, the vigil takes the form of the liturgy of the word, with introductory rites, readings from scripture, intercessory prayer, and a conclusion.

The liturgy of the word consists of a reading from the OT or NT, proclaimed by a member of the family or parish community. In response, the community sings (or recites) an appropriate psalm. The gospel is then proclaimed, followed by a brief homily that draws out the message of the readings and situates it in the experience of grief through which the community is passing.

The prayer of intercession follows, consisting of a litany, the Lord's Prayer and a concluding prayer. Various prayers for the dead, which might be used as the concluding prayer, are provided in O.C.F. 398-399. This is another time when a friend or member of the family might speak in remembrance of the deceased.

The vigil concludes with a blessing. After saying, "Blessed are those who have died in the Lord; let them rest from their labors for their good deeds go with them," the minister may sign the forehead of the deceased while praying the family petitions for peace with the community. Recalling the signing that begins our celebration of the sacraments of initiation, this is a very powerful gesture for the community. It not only ties together Christian initiation and Christian death theologically, but experientially as well.

The community is also blessed by the presiding minister, whether a priest or deacon. The lay person who presides may also invoke God's blessing, signing himself or herself with the sign of the cross, saying: "May the love of God and the peace of the Lord Jesus Christ bless and console us and gently wipe every tear from our eyes: in the name of the Father, and of the Son, and of the Holy Spirit" (O.C.F., 81).

Vigil for the Deceased with Reception at the Church

The *Order of Christian Funerals* also

provides a vigil for the deceased that is celebrated in the church. Funeral customs vary from place to place, so while this option might strike some as unusual, for others it is the expected ritual.

The introductory rites begin with a greeting at the door of the church that orients that community to the consoling presence of God. The coffin is then sprinkled with holy water, recalling the waters of baptism that already united the deceased to Christ's death and resurrection. The pall, a further reminder of baptism, can then be placed on the coffin if such is the local custom. The procession then enters the church, while the community sings a psalm, song or responsory. The Easter candle may be placed near the coffin. The invitation to prayer and opening prayer then follow, as previously described.

F. *Other Prayer Services*

In the first section of the *Order of Christian Funerals* one finds "related rites and prayers," consisting of three brief services: "Prayers after Death," "Gathering in the Presence of the Body," and "Transfer of the Body to the Church or to the Place of Committal." These provide the minister with a way to meet the varying needs of mourners, especially when the priest has been called to administer the anointing of the sick, only to discover that death has already occurred.

The "Prayers after Death" (O.C.F., 101-108) give a model for the minister to use when he or she first meets the family. Consisting of a reading, response, prayer and blessing, it gives the family a simple way to begin their ritual of mourning.

The "Gathering in the Presence of the Body" (O.C.F., 109-118) provides a model service which can be used when the family gathers around the body of the deceased soon after death, or when they gather in the funeral home after the body has been prepared for burial. This service begins with the sign of the cross and a brief reading from scripture. Recalling the living water into which the Christian has been baptized, the body is sprinkled with holy water. A psalm follows, and the rite concludes with a prayer and blessing.

The "Transfer of the Body..." (O.C.F., 119-127) gives a third model for possible intermediary rites. This rite is intended to precede the transferral of the body to either the church or the place of committal. It begins with an invitation to prayer and a brief scripture verse. This is followed by a litany, the Lord's Prayer and a concluding prayer before everyone is invited to join in the procession.

Office of the Dead

Part IV of the *Order of Christian Funerals* (348-395) contains the Office of the Dead, providing a setting of morning prayer and evening prayer that may be used or adapted. In the case of 2- or 3-day wakes, evening prayer might be celebrated one night, and the vigil another night. If the funeral liturgy is celebrated at night and the rite of committal is not to take place until the following morning, the community might gather for morning prayer before processing to the place of committal. When the community cannot participate in any of the funeral rites for one of its members—if it takes place in a far-distant city, for example—they may choose to pray the Office of the Dead. This could also provide a meaningful expression of support for a member of the community whose family member died in another locality. When he or she returns from the funeral rites, the community might gather to celebrate the Office of the Dead, which unites us with the universal church and "acknowledges that spiritual bond that links the church on earth with the church in heaven" (O.C.F., 349).

G. *Symbols*

Since the liturgical celebrations bring together family and friends who are experiencing deep grief, the *ritual* itself becomes a minister. Therefore, the ritual is attentive to all the senses; marked by beauty and reverence, and with simplicity, the ritual invites the participation of the community.

The word of God ministers to the grieving as it proclaims the paschal mystery and comforts the sorrowful. Although non-biblical readings should not replace scripture, they can be used in addition to biblical readings at the non-eucharistic services (O.C.F., 24). The psalms are particularly responsive to the needs and moods of the community, expressing the depths of grief as well as the heights of praise. These ancient songs cut through time and culture to touch the core of human longing, which is why their use is encouraged in many sections of the funeral rites (O.C.F., 25, 26).

The O.C.F. provides a variety of prayers that "capture the unspoken prayers and hopes of the assembly and also respond to the needs of the mourners" (O.C.F., 28). The prayers of intercession even more directly address the needs of the deceased, those who mourn, and the entire assembly. Models are provided, which can be adapted to the particular circumstances as needed (O.C.F., 29).

Because of its power to evoke strong feelings, music has an important place in all of the funeral rites. Songs can console and uplift the mourners by their references to the paschal character of Christian death, and the community's share in Christ's victory. Full participation of the assembly is encouraged at celebrations of the funeral rites (O.C.F., 30-33).

There is also a place for reverent *silence* in the funeral rites, which can evoke awe as the community stands in the face of the mystery of death.

Local custom dictates the degree to which each of the following Christian symbols "speaks" in the funeral rites.

The *paschal candle* serves as a continuous reminder to the community of Christ's victory along with our share in that victory. This symbol recalls both the Easter celebration and the sacrament of baptism during which the newly baptized receive the light of faith symbolized by the baptismal candle.

Holy water, sprinkled on the coffin at the beginning of the funeral liturgy, likewise recalls our incorporation into Christ's death and resurrection through the waters of baptism.

Incense is used in the funeral rites to lend greater dignity to the celebration. After the bread and wine have been prepared, they are incensed, together with the altar and the paschal candle. This gives visual expression to our prayers as they rise to God.

The *pall*, recalling that the deceased "put on" Christ in baptism, may be placed over the coffin as it is received at the door of the church.

A *Bible* or *Book of the Gospels* may be placed on the coffin to symbolize the deceased's fidelity to God's word.

The *cross*, with which the Christian is first marked in baptism, may also be placed on the coffin.

Flowers, subtle reminders that life and beauty transcend present suffering also enhance celebration.

Liturgical color should reflect Christian hope, without negating human grief.

Processions, with pallbearers carrying the coffin, have a significance as we go from one ritual to the next. They recall not only early Christian funerals, but also "the journey of human life, the Christian pilgrimage to the heavenly Jerusalem" (O.C.F., 41, 42).

H. *Funeral Homes and Directors*

Either with the support of the pastoral team or without it, funeral directors play a leading role in the immediate care of the bereaved family. Perhaps more than anyone else, they are able to see the larger picture, by virtue of their vast experience and the fact that they must attend to so many minute and hidden details of which the rest of the team is often unaware. They complement and complete the parish's ministry. The "Code of Ethics" and the "Code of Professional Practices for Funeral Directors" of the National Funeral Directors Association of the United States explains the contribution funeral directors make to furthering the mission of the church through ministry to the bereaved.

Philippe Aries, *Western Attitudes Toward Death: From the Middle Ages to the Present*, trans. Patricia M. Ranum (Baltimore: The Johns Hopkins University Press, 1974). Philippe Aries, ed. *Death in America* (Philadelphia: University of Pennsylvania Press, 1975). Robert A. Krieg, "The Funeral Homily: A Theological View," *Worship* 58 (1984): 222-239. Michael Marchel, *Parish Funerals* (Chicago: Liturgy Training Publications, 1987). Jean Masamba and Richard A. Kalish, "Death and Bereavement" The Role of the Black Church," *Omega* 7 (1976): 23-34. Frederick R. McManus, "Liturgy of Final Commendation," *American Ecclesiastical Review* 162 (1970): 405-408. Frederick R. McManus, "The Reformed Funeral Rite," *American Ecclesiastical Review* 116 (1972): 45-59; 124-139. John P. Meier, "Catholic Funerals in the Light of Scripture," *Worship* 48 (1974): 206-216. Geoffrey Rowell, *The Liturgy of Christian Burial: An Introductory Survey of the Historical Development of Christian Burial Rites* (London: S.P.C.K., 1977). Richard Rutherford, *The Death of a Christian: The Rite of Funerals.* Studies in the Reformed Rites of the Catholic Church, 7 (New York: Pueblo, 1980). Bishops' Committee on the Liturgy, *Study Text No. 13* (Washington, DC: United States Catholic Conference, 1989). [Publication pending release of the O.C.F.]

JULIA UPTON, R.S.M.

C

CALENDAR, LITURGICAL

I. Description

The term *liturgical calendar* can be used in two ways. In its more narrow sense it refers to a schematic presentation of the months of the year, bearing alongside of the numeral indicating each day, the designation of any festival or memorial of fixed date assigned to that day. Such a calendar, if found at the beginning of a liturgical book, will sometimes present for each date a letter of the alphabet running from *a* to *g* and then repeating. This "dominical letter," as it is called, makes it possible to identify the days of the week in any year, once the day of the week for any one date is known. If, e.g., in a given year a Sunday falls on a calendar date with the dominical letter *b*, then every day marked with a *b* will be a Sunday in that year. The provision of this dominical letter points to the primary importance the church has always assigned to the celebration of the resurrection of Christ on the first day of the week.

Beyond that, many Christian feasts and seasons are ordered toward specific days of the week, and therefore cannot be assigned to fixed dates. For this reason, liturgical calendars are also prepared for a particular year; and such a calendar, commonly called an *ordo* (order), can show on the appropriate days of the week all feasts of fixed date as well as those moveable feasts or fasts whose dates will vary from year to year. Such calendars help to resolve questions that arise when a festival of fixed date conflicts with the date of a moveable observance, as, e.g., when Good Friday falls on March 25, normally the Feast of the Annunciation.

In its broader sense, *liturgical calendar* refers to the whole shaping of the week and the year by religious observances, a tradition of liturgical articulation of time that has its roots in the OT and that has continued in Christianity from the first century forward. Over the centuries variable texts appropriate to each day of the liturgical calendar (scripture readings, hymns, anthems, prayers) have been organized in books intended for the conduct of worship. The number of such books and their organization has differed widely from one moment of the tradition to another, but three general categories of observances can be recognized as common to most of the tradition: a seasonal cycle; a sanctoral cycle; and, occasional texts or *votive* texts.

A. The Seasonal Cycle, Proprium de tempore. Sometimes called "the Christian Year," this cycle of feasts and seasons is predicated upon the life of Christ and organized about two major poles. The first of these is the Feast of the Nativity of Christ, observed on December 25 (except by the Armenians, who continue to celebrate that event on January 6, the date once generally observed in the East). The other pole is Easter, the Feast of the Resurrection of Christ, a moveable feast whose date in the West is computed as the first Sunday after the full moon that follows the vernal equinox. (A number of factors frequently and regrettably result in different dates for Easter in Eastern and Western churches. It is always, however, a Sunday.) A number of other observances depend on the date of Easter: the preceding Holy Week, the forty days of the fast before Easter that we know as Lent, and (at times) the preceding three Sundays of pre-Lent; Pentecost (the period of fifty days following Easter and also the festival on the fiftieth day), the Feast of the Ascension on the fortieth day (therefore always a Thursday), and a series of festivals in the weeks following Pentecost. The Feast of the Nativity of Christ on December 25, Christmas, is preceded by a preparatory period, the four Sundays of Advent, and is followed by the Feast of the Epiphany on January 6 (or the Sunday following) and the Feast of the Baptism of Our Lord on the Sunday after Epiphany.

All these are tied closely to the fixed dates of December 25 and January 6, while the observances dependent on the date of Easter shift more widely from year to year, yielding a varying number of Sundays after Epiphany and a varying number of Sundays after Pentecost. These are frequently spoken of as "neutral zones," and their treatment has varied and varies still in particular traditions. In the present Latin rite, they are treated as a continuous series of thirty-three or thirty-four weeks *anni circuli*, a traditional Latin expression that has proved difficult to render in English. The common English translation is "ordinary time." The liturgical texts provided are used for the Sundays between the Epiphany and Lent as needed, and then the series is resumed after Pentecost. The last of the Sundays after Pentecost is now the Feast of Christ the King, on the Sunday before the seasonal cycle begins again with Advent.

Ember Days. Early Roman liturgical books included in the seasonal cycle four fasts at the four natural seasons, the *quattuor tempora*, and the careful attention given to these in early documents suggests that they were regarded as of great importance in the Roman liturgical year. Assigned eventually to the first, fourth, seventh and tenth months, these were a peculiar characteristic of the liturgy of Rome, and antedate the Sundays of Advent and many other important observances in the Roman calendar. In the time of Leo I (440-461), to whose preaching we owe our earliest clear picture of

these observances, these seasonal fasts fell in the first week of Lent, the week following Pentecost, in September and in December. The observance consisted in a solemnization of the regular weekly fasts on Wednesday and Friday, an extension of the Friday fast through Saturday, and a vigil through the night from Saturday to Sunday, concluding with the eucharist early Sunday morning.

The once popular attempt of Germain Morin to trace these to three Roman *feriae conceptivae* has proved groundless, and the ultimate origin of these "Ember Days," as they are known in English (from the German contraction of the Latin designation, *quattuor tempora*, to *Quatember*), remains unknown. They seem to have been regularized, at least, in the 4th century, and the pontificates of Damasus (d. 384) or his successor, Siricius, are most frequently suggested. From the time of Gelasius I at the end of the 5th century, they were among the days designated as especially appropriate for the ordination of deacons and presbyters. The association with ordination had a deep influence on the later spirituality of the Ember Days, although their liturgy, antedating their use as ordination days, did not reflect that use.

Gregory VII assigned the precise times for them that remained in force until the reforms under Paul VI in this century: the Wednesday, Friday and Saturday of the first week of Lent, of the octave of Pentecost, and following September 14 and December 13. Their times and frequency are now expected to be established in each place by the appropriate episcopal conference, as are the Rogation Days (see below), but their once prominent role in the Roman liturgical year is now greatly diminished, if not forgotten.

B. The Sanctoral Cycle, Proprium de sanctis. This is a series of festivals of fixed date on which are commemorated the lives of martyrs and other saints who have been examples to the church, or particular events in the life of Christ or the Blessed Virgin Mary. In the case of the saints, the commemoration is assigned most commonly to the date of their death, and this is spoken of as their *dies natalis*, their birthday into the Kingdom of Heaven. Derivatively, that term, *natale*, comes to mean simply an anniversary and can be applied to the annual commemoration of the dedication of a church. Many commemorations in the sanctoral cycle are rooted in such anniversaries of dedications (e.g., Holy Cross Day on September 14, or St. Michael and All Angels on September 29). The tradition has also celebrated the conceptions and nativities of St. John the Baptist and the Blessed Virgin, as well as those of Christ.

C. Occasional Masses. The liturgical books have also provided proper texts for other occasions that arise in the lives of the faithful but are not related to particular liturgical times, though often controlled by them. These include themes that may be dictated by particular historical circumstances (such as a time of famine) or by the devotion of the community or its leaders. In general, these are known as *missae votivae*, "votive masses," and their celebration is variously regulated by the liturgical calendar, to which they do not strictly belong.

These three categories were represented in the three books into which one of our earlier liturgical manuscripts was divided, the *Liber Sacramentorum Romanae Aecclesiae Ordinis Anni Circuli*, more commonly known as the Gelasian Sacramentary (*Vat. reg. lat.* 316). Here Liber I is devoted to the seasonal cycle, Liber II to the sanctoral cycle, and Liber III to votive masses (although it is here as well that we find a series of proper texts for Sundays not covered in Liber I, those that are now designated as "ordinary time").

It is perhaps worthy of note that the Byzantine *typikon* divides liturgical observances slightly differently, distinguishing only between festivals of fixed date and those of moveable date (although, as with the *ordo*, these are united for each particular year in an annual publication, also known as the *typikon*).

II. Historical Development

Although it was once commonplace to assign the origins of the liturgical year to the time following the conversion of Constantine and the so-called "Peace of the Church," more recent studies have shown that regular annual religious observances, in addition to the weekly observance of Sunday, are much more ancient. Such primitive annual patterns constitute the primary stratum of the liturgical calendar, and the oldest of them can be said to be coeval (though not coextensive) with the observance of the liturgical week. It is, nonetheless, with the week that any consideration of the historical roots of the calendar must begin.

A. The Liturgical Week. The cycle of seven days observed in the OT is of such antiquity that some scholars, at least, believe it to antedate the settlement of the people in Canaan. The commandment to observe the Sabbath is found in all recensions of the Law, and the priestly writers even ground the seven-day week in creation itself. The term "Sabbath" means that which stops, and points to the seventh day as the determinant of the weekly cycle. Only "Sabbath" names a day of the week in the Bible, and the other days are simply numbered from the Sabbath.

Biblical and non-biblical sources suggest the possibility that a very primitive West Asiatic calendar was built upon multiples of seven, the next larger unit being a week of weeks to which was added a festival day for a total of fifty days. Seven of these periods would yield 350 days, to which two festival weeks (in the spring and autumn) were added, for a total of 364 days. While such a calendar may lie behind the Jewish week, it would have some days (the fiftieth days) that belonged to no week and to that extent would differ from the biblical week. The insistence on the unvarying observance of every seventh day as a day of rest is characteristically biblical and must be seen as Judaism's contribution to our culture.

The first Christians continued to observe Sabbath and took the seven-day cycle determined by it to be fundamental. The gospels put the resurrection of Christ on the first day of the week (*hê mia tôn sabbatôn*), and record his appearance to his disciples both on that day and on the first day of the following week. The Acts of the Apostles (20:7) suggests that this was the day on which the church gathered for the breaking of bread (the eucharist), but various interpretations of the relation of this day to the Sabbath are encountered. It has been suggested that the church gathered in the evening of the first day, the hour of the Lord's post-resurrection appearance, as an assertion of distinction from Judaism, recognizing Christ as "Lord of the Sabbath." More frequently it is suggested that the Christian assemblies gathered immediately upon the closing of the Sabbath at sundown, and therefore in the beginning hours of what we would call Saturday evening, already the beginning of Sunday when the day was reckoned in the Jewish manner from sundown to sundown. In later centuries we find the church continuing (with a few exceptions) the Jewish prohibition of fasting on Sabbath, which suggests a sense of continuity with Sabbath rather than a repudiation of it.

From as early as Revelation 1:10, the Christian day for eucharistic assembly was known as "the Day of the Lord" (*kyriakê hêmera*). Although some assign a different meaning to that phrase in Rev 1:10, a very similar expression is used for the weekly day of eucharistic assembly in *Didache* 14, and recent opinion has tended to assign to that Church Order a date very near that of Revelation. Unlike the Sabbath, the Day of the Lord (Sunday in the planetary calendar) was not a publicly supported day of rest, and we may be sure that the gathering of the community for worship fell outside normal working hours.

In addition to the Sunday assembly for eucharist, *Didache* 8 orders fasting on two days in the week, Wednesday and Friday, distinguishing these from the Mondays and Thursdays which were observed as fasts by those called "the hypocrites." While that derogatory expression surely indicates the Pharisees (at least), it has often been noted that it could reflect a repudiation of that party by Jewish sectaries in addition to Christians. The calendar of the Essenes at Qumran was structured in such a way as to assign all religious observances of fixed month dates to Wednesdays, Fridays, or Sundays.

In the course of the 2nd century the two weekly fast days came to be called "stations," a term roughly equivalent to *m'amadoth*, used of assemblies of Jews outside Jerusalem for prayer at the times of the temple sacrifices. Tertullian, writing in North Africa at the end of the century, relates the term *statio* to the military vocabulary. Sunday, during the 2nd century, came to be called also "the Eighth Day," pointing to the eschatological character of the resurrection on the first day of the week as being, in fact, the beginning of a new era, the day that follows the Sabbath, not merely the first of a series of days leading toward the Sabbath. Sunday, as the first day of a new creation, superseded the Sabbath, even as the church bound herself closely to the week defined originally by the Sabbath. Latin Christianity in the 2nd or 3rd century began to use the term *feria* (festival) as equivalent to Sabbath, and continued the

Hebrew and NT custom of numbering weekdays in order from that day, although the first day was now never *feria prima*, but *dies dominica*, the Day of the Lord. The seventh day itself continued to be called *Sabbatum*.

There is every reason to believe that such a Christian shaping of the week was adopted in all parts of the church by the end of the 1st century, and some Christians of Jewish background continued a measure of Sabbath observance as well. At the very least, apart from Rome and perhaps a few other western regions, Sabbath continued to be a day on which fasting was forbidden by Christians. One Sabbath in the year was an exception to that rule, and that requires us to turn from the liturgical week to the liturgical year.

B. The Liturgical Year. The OT ordered three festivals in the year as binding upon all males, and from the time of Josiah (7th century B.C.), these were to be celebrated only in Jerusalem. Distinguished from other festivals by the term *chag*, these represented the oldest stratum of Jewish festivals, combining the nomadic Passover (*pesach*), the spring sacrifice of a lamb commemorating the exodus, with three agricultural festivals adopted in Canaan: Unleavened Bread in the spring, the Feast of Weeks (seven weeks after Unleavened Bread), and *Sukkoth*, Booths or Tabernacles, which marked the ingathering of the harvest in the autumn. The reform of Josiah united Passover and Unleavened Bread into a single festival kept at the full moon in the spring. At different times either the spring or autumn festival, both celebrated for a week, had marked the turning of the year. By contrast to these, the Feast of Weeks, celebrated on a single day, seems to conclude an extension of the week of Unleavened Bread to a week of weeks, although it came to be recognized as a distinct festival on the fiftieth day, called Pentecost ("fiftieth") in the Septuagint and the NT.

The gospel of John puts the crucifixion of Jesus on the Preparation of the Passover, 14 Nisan, at the time of the slaying of lambs for the feast that would begin at nightfall. This same chronological tradition may lie behind Paul's assertion, ca. A.D. 55, that "Christ, our Passover lamb, has been sacrificed for us" (1 Cor 5:7). The synoptic gospels identify Jesus' Last Supper with his disciples as the Passover, eaten at the beginning of 15 Nisan, but it is the Johannine tradition of his death on 14 Nisan that has been most significant in shaping the liturgical year.

By the 2nd century, sources from Asia Minor show the Christian observance of a fast on that day, followed by a vigil from sundown to cockcrow and concluded with the eucharist. This total observance is called *pascha*, the Aramaic equivalent of *pesach* ("passover" in the English OT), and Asian Christians kept it on the same day as the Jewish Passover, albeit now with emphasis on the fast and extended vigil as memorial of the death of Jesus and a watch for his coming again. The observance of that date according to the Jewish lunar calendar was difficult since the calendar was corrected on an empirical basis by Palestinian authorities, and Asian Christians eventually adopted the local solar calendar, keeping pascha on the 14th day of the first spring month, Artemisios. The adoption of the Roman calendar after the founding of Constantinople made that date April 6. A more historical concern to establish the precise date of the crucifixion determined the year to have been A.D. 29, and 14 Nisan in that year to have been March 25. Both dates, April 6 and March 25, are found as fixed dates for the paschal obervance. The content of the festival was the entire mystery of Christ: his incarnation, passion, death, resurrection and glorification, and the outpouring of the Spirit on the church.

This annual observance on a fixed date was in contrast to the observance of the first day of every week, with its eucharist as celebration of Christ's resurrection. Probably at Jerusalem, the two traditions were first elided, so that the fast was concluded with the eucharist only in the early hours of Sunday. This had the effect of making the one day of the fast fall on Sabbath, the exception to the rule against Sabbath fasting mentioned above. This also put that one day fast adjacent to the older weekly fast on Friday, and many began to fast for two days. With the concluding Sunday celebration, this constituted the original meaning of *triduum sacrum*, the paschal observance of Friday, Saturday and Sunday. While some churches, such as Rome, continued to observe only this *triduum*, in the 3rd century in Syria and Egypt the two-day fast was extended to six days, giving us the week-long observance of pascha that we now know as Holy Week.

Already in the 2nd century the celebration of the resurrection was continued for fifty days, and the earliest references to the Christian Pentecost are to this period of unbroken rejoicing. In the course of the 4th century the fiftieth day took on the character of a distinct celebration of Christ's ascension and the sending of the Spirit upon the church, and in the last two decades of the century we encounter the separation of that dual theme, and the celebration of the ascension on the fortieth day. By the final decade of the 4th century in northern Italy, at least, the tradition of unbroken rejoicing had been dismantled by a fast before the Feast of the Ascension, as Filastrius of Brescia testifies (CCL IX, p. 312).

In the next century the three days before Ascension Day were marked in Gaul by rogations (with processional litanies) that became a regular interruption of the paschal rejoicing by fasting and supplication for the state of the crops. With the introduction of these "Rogation Days" by Mammertus, Bishop of Vienne, the original meaning of the Pentecost was vitiated, but these fast days achieved great popularity in the Middle Ages. When they were adopted at Rome, they were known as the "lesser litanies," by contrast to the "major litany," a 7th-century Christian adaptation of the pre-Christian *Robigalia* on the day that would later become as well the feast of St. Mark (April 25). The Rogation Days are no longer assigned to paschaltide in the Latin rite, but are now to be established on whatever days seem appropriate to local episcopal conferences. This accords with the restoration of the integrity of the fifty days of unbroken rejoicing, which has been a major concern of recent liturgical reform.

For Christianity as for the OT, Pentecost refers to the fifty days of rejoicing as well as to the final festival of the single, fiftieth day. Pascha (Easter) is observed, as was Passover, for a total of eight days, but Pentecost no longer has an octave. In England, this final Sunday of the paschal season was known as "Whitsunday." Although this is commonly taken by lexicographers to mean, "white Sunday," it was suggested by Hamon L'Estrange in the 17th century (*The Alliance of Divine Offices*, Annotation V upon chap. V) that it derives from the French *huit* or *huitième dimanche*, the eighth Sunday of Easter.

The paschal season, from the six days of the paschal fast to the final day of Pentecost, can be understood to be in more or less direct continuity with the OT festivals of Passover-Unleavened Bread and *Shabbuoth* (Weeks). Evidence for a Christian continuance of the autumnal festival of Tabernacles, on the other hand, is lacking. In spite of that, patristic writers regularly appealed to OT texts regarding the three pilgrim festivals as authority for the Christian observance of Pascha, Pentecost, and the feast of the Epiphany (January 6).

There is a possible (but highly hypothetical) connection between Tabernacles and Epiphany. M. D. Goulder has suggested that the evangelists arranged their materials to correspond to the pentateuch readings that began on *Simchat Torah*, at the conclusion of the Tabernacles celebration, and we shall suggest below that the Epiphany marked the beginning of a gospel course reading.

The oriental nativity festival of Epiphany, with its occidental parallel of December 25, constitutes one of the more thorny questions in the history of the liturgical year. Both festivals have celebrated the nativity of Christ, but other themes have also attached to the Epiphany: the baptism of Jesus, the miracle at the Cana wedding-feast, the visit of the Magi, and even (in one source) the Transfiguration.

Two lines of interpretation are encountered for the origin of these festivals of the nativity. The "History of Religions" school sees both as derived from pre-Christian festivals, December 25 from the "birthday of the Invincible Sun" (*dies natalis solis invicti*) at Rome, and January 6 from the "birth of Aion" at Alexandria. Eduard Norden sought to relate both dates to the winter solstice, but his explanation would require the use of the Julian calendar in the 20th century B.C., while in fact it was devised only in the 1st century B.C. The Roman festival of the Invincible Sun on December 25, the traditional date of the winter solstice, was instituted by the Emperor Aurelian in A.D. 274, and seems to represent his attempt to offer a syncretistic monotheism that could unify the many cults practiced in the empire.

Those who argue for the derivation of Christmas from this festival lay great emphasis on the role of Constantine, who is known to have been a devotee of the Sun prior to his protection of Christianity. On the other hand, there is no indication of Christmas at Constantinople during his lifetime, and it was there rather than at Rome that his influence was focussed

from 324 forward. During that time he visited Rome only once, from July 18 through September of 326.

The first clear documentary evidence for Christmas comes from 336. A list of martyrs' burials in the *Chronograph of 354* begins with December 25 and indicates beside that day, *natus Christus in Betleem Iudeae.* That list and a parallel list for bishops have been shown to have been drawn up originally in 336. On the basis of North African evidence, especially Augustine's Sermon 202, some have argued that Christmas antedates the Donatist schism (ca. 311) and therefore the accession of Constantine, but others reject that conclusion as an *argumentum ex silentio.* The same complaint, however, has been made of the derivation of Christmas from the pagan festival, since the first assertion of such a connection appears in a Syriac gloss on a manuscript of Dionysius bar Salibi late in the 12th century. Quite apart from this festival on the traditional date of the winter solstice, Christ was frequently associated with the sun in early Christianity and many texts point to him as the "sun of righteousness" of Mal 4:2.

The association of the oriental nativity feast on January 6 with the "birth of Aion" festival at Alexandria rests on the testimony of Epiphanius (*Pan. haer.* 51.22), who describes a ceremony through the night from January 5 to 6. Messala, a Roman writer of the 1st century B.C., said that the feast of Aion was kept at Alexandria on January 5. The same date is given by Pliny (*Nat. Hist.* II. 106) for a miraculous flow of wine at the temple of *Pater Liber* on Andros, and Pausanius confirms that this was a festival of Dionysus. Some have taken this to be related to the celebration of the Cana wedding feast on Epiphany. The discrepancy between January 5 given for these pagan festivals and the Epiphany date of January 6 has not been satisfactorily explained, and the claim of a pagan background for the Epiphany, although frequently encountered, has never been made with such precision as has the appeal to the Roman festival of December 25.

An alternative to this "history of religions" approach was offered by Mgr. Louis Duchesne at the end of the last century, and his suggestion is spoken of today as "the computation hypothesis." Observing that symbolic number systems are intolerant of fractions, he suggested that the date of Christ's death was taken to be also the date of the beginning of his life at his conception, and therefore his nativity was set nine months after that date. Where, as at Rome in the early 3rd century, March 25 was regarded as the date of the passion, assignment of the conception to the same date would yield a nativity date of December 25. In the East, the association of the passion (and conception) with April 6 would give a nativity date of January 6.

As contrived as such a computation may seem to modern minds, it resembles a rabbinic tradition that identified the dates of the births and deaths of the patriarchs, and evidence that theologians in the 4th and following centuries did think in such terms is afforded by Augustine (P.L., 42.849), Chrysostom (P.G., 49.358), and others. January 6, it seems, was known already to Clement of Alexandria at the end of the 2nd century as date of the nativity and as celebration of the baptism of Jesus.

While the influence of Aurelian's festival of *sol invictus* on the origin of Christmas remains in contention, the computation hypothesis should not be taken to exclude influence from solar symbolism, as Duchesne himself acknowledged. Important elements of both lines of explanation are found in the 4th-century tractate ascribed to Pontius Maximus, *De solstitia et aequinoctia conceptionis et nativitatis domini nostri iesu christi et iohannis baptistae* (P.L.,

222.557-568). If the date of Christmas was arrived at independently, we may be sure that the festival atmosphere of Rome around the end of the year contributed greatly to the popularity of the Christian feast.

During the later 4th century, the Western nativity festival spread to Constantinople, Cappadocia and Antioch, and to Alexandria in the following century, leaving the baptism of Jesus the sole content of the Epiphany. At Jerusalem, this separation of the taking of humanity at Bethlehem from the acknowledgement of divine Sonship at the Jordan was strongly resisted by Monophysite elements, and it was only in the 6th century that Christmas was finally adopted in the Holy City. Armenians continued to resist the festival and still do not observe it, celebrating both the nativity and the baptism on Epiphany.

A similar content for the Epiphany was found in Gaul, and its observance there by the emperor Julian in 361, evidently as the sole celebration of the nativity, is recorded by a contemporary historian. In northern Italy a bit later the Epiphany celebrates the baptism of Jesus, or sometimes the first miracle at Cana. its focus on Bethlehem, and the nativity narrative was divided so that the visit of the Magi provided the content of Epiphany, leading to the common but regrettable narrowing of the meaning of the feast to "the manifestation of Christ to the Gentiles." In Gaul, after the adoption of Christmas there, Epiphany celebrated the *tria miracula*, the visit of the Magi, the baptism in Jordan, and the first miracle at Cana.

The rich content of the festival of the manifestation of God in Christ is more understandable if we see the themes in relation to the beginnings of the gospels. If we may hypothesize that Epiphany was already regarded as the beginning of the liturgical year when we first encounter it in the 2nd century, then we may suppose that it marked the beginning of the reading of a gospel especially associated with a local church. Where, as at Ephesus, that gospel was John, then the festival would celebrate both the incarnation and baptism, followed quickly by the wedding at Cana. At Jerusalem we encounter a fundamental reliance on Matthew, and that would accord with the strong emphasis on the nativity, including the visit of the Magi, there. At Alexandria the favored gospel was Mark, and there the feast celebrates the baptism of Jesus. As communication between churches increased, there was an exchange of influences, and a much more complex picture emerges in the 4th century. Still, behind that complexity may lie simply the reading of one gospel, beginning from the Epiphany, and reaching to the passion narrative at pascha.

Later Egyptian sources, supported by texts as early as the 3rd century, report that the primitive celebration of Christ's baptism there on the Epiphany was followed at once by a fast of forty days, commemorative of Christ's temptation in the wilderness. This was concluded in the sixth and final week with the conferral of baptism and the feast of Palms, celebrating the entry into Jerusalem. All this was distinct from the paschal fast, begun some weeks later, at which the passion narrative must have been read. The conferral of baptism prior to Palm Sunday, retained by the Coptic church today, was in contrast to the custom elsewhere of conferring baptism at Easter, first mentioned by Tertullian in Africa and Hippolytus at Rome, but extended to other churches in the course of the 3rd century. Paschal baptism, also, was preceded by a period of fasting, exorcism, and catechesis. Such prebaptismal fasting was ordered already in *Didache*, chap. 7, but the one or two days called for there were extended to several weeks when the baptism came to be performed at Easter. After the Council of Nicea (325), we encounter a general designation of this fast before paschal baptism as "the fast of forty days," and this seems to represent a continuity with the much earlier Alexandrian custom, albeit transferred to the time before the paschal fast. At Rome, those forty days ran from the sixth Sunday before Easter (*Quadragesima*) to the Thursday before Easter (on which day penitents were reconciled), and the two-day paschal fast of Friday and Saturday followed. At Antioch and Constantinople, the forty days were reckoned from Monday of the seventh week before Easter to Friday of the week preceding Great (Holy) Week, and that fast was broken for two days before the paschal fast of six days was begun on the following Monday. At Constantinople, as in early Alexandria, the Sunday following the close of the forty days was the Feast of Palms.

In the post-Nicene arrangement of the fast, this Feast of Palms was now the Sunday at the head of Holy Week, and in Jerusalem it was marked with a procession with palms down the Mount of Olives. Pilgrims carried that custom back to their homelands, and Palm Sunday came to be recognized as the first day of Holy Week. Although the forty days had first been reckoned as a continuous period, including days not actually fasted, by the 7th century there was a general tendency to extend the fast so that the total number of fast days in the paschal fast and the preceding "Lent" would total forty. At Rome, where Sundays were not fasted, the six weeks yielded but 36 fast days, and four more days were added from the preceding week. This Wednesday, called *caput ieiunii*, was the occasion for the enrollment of penitents. In Gaul and Germany this ceremony included sprinkling the penitents with ashes, a custom extended to all the people in the 11th century. Since then, the first day of Lent in the Western church has been known as "Ash Wednesday."

Although Lent (a term rooted in Teutonic expressions for spring) refers specifically to the fast before Easter, other fasts of forty days have been observed, and such a fast before Christmas, beginning on November 11, was often referred to as "St. Martin's Lent." This period of six weeks is represented in the Comes of Würzburg (a Roman epistle list dating from 602) by five Sundays, to which was added the Sunday that concluded the older December Embertide. Already in the preaching of Leo in the 5th century, that Embertide drew its themes from the expectation of the second coming of the Lord. In the epistle list, that theme is woven together with expectation of the first coming. Abbreviated at first to five weeks, and then to four, the season of Advent still moves between these two meanings of *parousia*, Christ's coming at the end of time and his coming in the flesh at the incarnation.

As we have seen, the Feast of the Nativity marked the beginning of the liturgical calendar in the *Chronograph of 354*. Later liturgical books would precede that with a vigil. Still later, the Advent season was set before the vigil, and the *proprium de tempore* now moves from the first Sunday of Advent to the Feast of Christ the King on the final Sunday after Pentecost.

C. The Sanctoral Cycle of the Liturgical Calendar. Martyrdom had been a significant concept in all OT spirituality, and the primitive church continued to remember those witnesses "of whom the world was not worthy" (Heb 11:38). Christ's sufferings could be seen within this tradition of martyrdom, but his passion and resurrection marked the beginning of a new age in which his disciples were called, quite literally, to take up the Cross and follow him. Already in the account of the death of the first martyr, Stephen (Acts 7:58-60), Christian martyrdom can be seen as reflecting the death and triumph of Christ himself.

The oldest of the passions of the martyrs preserved to us, *The Martyrdom of Polycarp*, is in the form of a letter of the Church of Smyrna to the Christian community of Philomelium, written A.D. 156. Here we see explicitly the Christian understanding of martyrdom as imitation of the passion of Christ, and this same document shows already the central elements in the cult of the martyrs: the careful collection and deposition of Polycarp's remains, and regular assemblies at the tomb, "to celebrate the day of his martyrdom as a birthday, in memory of those athletes who have gone before, and to train and make ready those who are to come hereafter" (18:3).

The same connection of the celebration of martyrs with the places of their burial is found in the *Chronograph of 354*, where the list of martyrs' memorials designates not only the day of the observance, but also the cemetery where it is held. By 336 when that list was prepared, however, the movement of peoples was beginning to qualify that primitive local connection, and there are two commemorations in Rome of African martyrs. No cemetery is assigned for the celebration of Perpetua and Felicity, but the notice of Cyprian adds *Romae celebratur in Callisti*, assigning the commemoration of the great Bishop of Carthage to the cemetery of Callistus, the preferred burial place of the Bishops of Rome.

A martyrology from somewhat later in the 4th century, preserved today only in a Syriac version dated 411 (London, BM add. 12150) but originally in Greek, reports martyrs' commemorations for the entire church, listing for each day both the martyr venerated and the city where the memorial is made. Here, too, we find one of the earlier mentions of a commemoration of all the martyrs, at Nisibis on the Friday after Easter. Chrysostom in Antioch celebrated such a feast (made necessary by the vast numbers who died under Diocletian) on the Sunday after Pentecost, and this had the effect of prolonging the paschal celebration so that normal fasting was resumed only after this celebration "of all the saints who have suffered martyrdom throughout the world" (P.G., 50.705).

Both of those dates for a feast of all the martyrs may have been known briefly at Rome, but it was the dedication of the old Pantheon by Boniface IV to the Blessed Virgin Mary and all the martyrs on May 13, 609, that provided the major celebration of all the martyrs until the adoption of the alternative western European date, November 1, by Gregory IV in 835.

The linking of the veneration of the martyrs with the Blessed Virgin in that dedication points to the role of Marian devotion in the development of the sanctoral calendar. The Jerusalem lectionaries of the early 5th century (preserved in Armenian) reveal a feast of the Theotokos on August 15, kept at a place three miles from Bethlehem, a place associated with the birth of Christ in the *Protoevangelium of James* (17:2). This was a celebration of her role as the mother of the Savior (the gospel is Lk 2:1-7), and seems to have had no reference to her death (dormition or assumption). The reason for the choice of this date remains obscure, but this is, nonetheless, the oldest feast of the Blessed Virgin known to us.

In the preceding century, the fortieth day after Epiphany was celebrated at Jerusalem as a commemoration of the meeting with Simeon and the prophetess Anna recorded by Luke (2:22-40), but that festival— now on February 2— has not been considered a feast of Mary consistently. It was only in the 6th century that Justinian promulgated the feast of the Annunciation on March 25, although that date had been associated with the conception of the Lord since at least the 4th century. Here, as in the Presentation or Purification, we are dealing at once with a feast of Christ and of Mary.

In the 7th century, Rome observed on January 1 its first festival of the Blessed Virgin. Eclipsed by other Marian festivals later, that original feast has now been restored to the calendar of the Latin rite.

It is clear that in the 4th century the martyrs were accorded a special place in the economy of salvation, and it could well seem that the sanctoral calendar observed them alone. Whether the list of *Depositiones Episcoporum Romanorum* in the *Chronograph of 354* indicates liturgical commemorations have been disputed, but the dates of the burials of bishops, not martyrs, from 255 to 352 are arranged in calendrical rather than historical order (apart from Marcus and Julius, added later) and the places of burial are indicated. A Carthaginian martyrology of the 6th century bears a title that is explicit: "Here are contained the birthdays of the martyrs and the burials of bishops whose anniversaries the Church of Carthage celebrates." The annual remembrance of the burial of every local bishop, of course, would rather quickly become impracticable, but this does show that the understanding of the liturgical celebration of Christian witness was extending beyond those who gave their lives in the persecutions.

The Carthaginian list also includes the nativity of St. John the Baptist (June 24, the traditional summer solstice date). In 732, Gregory III dedicated (at St. Peter's) a chapel to "the Redeemer, His holy Mother, all the Apostles, Martyrs, Confessors, and all the just and perfect who are at rest throughout the whole world," and that broad understanding of the veneration of saints was reflected in individual feasts in the Gregorian sacramentaries of the 9th century.

III. Festival and Doctrine

The interaction of liturgy and theology is too complex a matter to be treated here, but brief notice must be taken of the ways in which these have related to the liturgical calendar. The very oldest festivals celebrated critical moments in the history of salvation, events of such depth that they included several strata of meaning. The primitive pascha, e.g., made the memorial of Christ's death by celebrating not only his suffering, but the triumph revealed in the resurrection and the glorification completed in the sending of the Spirit upon the church. Later liturgical development sought to reveal that theological richness by assigning the several strata of the complex to separate observances, from Good Friday to Pentecost. Similarly, the Epiphany celebration of the manifestation of God in human history has been a rich theological complex whose several strata were later distinguished in a series of observances from Advent through the Epiphany season.

By contrast to this articulation of the rich theological content of a liturgical mystery, the second millennium saw the introduction of new festivals celebrating a single theological or devotional theme, often a theme inherent in every celebration of the liturgy. The Feast of the Most Holy Trinity, finally acknowledged and made a universal observance in the West by John XXII in 1334 in spite of the protests of predecessors in the 11th and 12th centuries, represents a slow evolution occasioned by incomplete liturgical prescription for the time after Pentecost and fed by preoccupation with theology as an abstract science. From its appearance in the 11th century, the festival grew in importance to the point that in a great many nations of northern Europe it was from Trinity Sunday, rather than Pentecost, that the remaining Sundays of the year were numbered, a convention retained in *The Book of Common Prayer* of the Church of England, but relinquished in modern Anglican liturgical reforms. Adrian Nocent (Vol. 3, p. 278) has good reason to say, "a celebration of this type could become popular only at a time when the liturgical life and the

proper understanding of the Bible were on the wane."

In the 13th century we encounter the first instance of direct papal promulgation of a new festival for the whole church in the Bull *Transiturus* of Urban IV in 1264, ordering a solemnity in honor of the Blessed Sacrament to be observed on the Thursday after the octave of Pentecost. This institution of the feast of Corpus Christi can hardly be understood apart from the scholastic theological ferment of the day regarding eucharistic consecration, as is shown by the reported miracle at Bolsena that moved the pope to act (a priest tortured by doubts of the Real Presence saw a host turn to bloody flesh).

Much less precise is the object of the Feast of the Sacred Heart, but this, too, represents the establishment of a festival as a promotional or instructional instrument. First kept on August 30 as a very local celebration by John Eudes in the 17th century, the popularity of the devotion was fed by the visionary experience of Margaret Mary Alacoque, and the feast was made universal for the Latin rite by Pius IX in 1856, set on the Friday after the octave of Corpus Christi.

In 1925, Pius XI established the Feast of Christ the King, in the hope that it might be a vehicle for spiritual teaching in the face of growing secularization, as he said in the encyclical of promulgation, *Quas primas*. Set then on the Sunday before All Saints' Day, it has been moved in recent reform to the final Sunday after Pentecost, where, as the Sunday before Advent, it better reinforces the older liturgical structures of the Christian Year.

IV. Deformation and Reformation of the Liturgical Calendar

We have already observed how certain of the calendrical concerns of the early church were vitiated even in the latter years of the 4th century (e.g., the introduction of a preparatory fast before the

Ascension). The wider interpretation accorded the veneration of saints, when martyrdom became more rare after the major persecutions, led to ever greater concentrations of sanctoral commemorations. Further, the celebration of more and more festivals over a period of eight days, an octave, led to increasing complication of the calendar, as did the observance of vigils preceding them. The resulting conflicts between observances competing for available time in the calendar required a system of rankings and rules of precedence of dizzying complexity.

At the same time, the past hundred years have seen the historical study of the liturgy illuminate afresh the broad lines of the tradition as it emerged from the OT into the NT to give shape to the proclamation of the gospel. Those studies have given rise to extensive reformation of particular observances and of the liturgical calendar itself in most Western churches, with the Roman Catholic church taking the lead. As with the original development of the cycle of annual observances, this reform began with the restoration of the Paschal Vigil in 1951, followed four years later by the restoration of all the rites of Holy Week.

The first document of the Second Vatican Council, the justly renowned .Constitution on the Sacred Liturgy, devoted its fifth chapter to "The Liturgical Year." There it was decreed that the weekly Lord's Day is the original feast day of the paschal mystery on which the church hears the word of God and participates in the eucharist, and it is to be given preference over any other observance unless one of the greatest importance (S.C., 106). Revision was called for to allow the keeping of traditional customs and discipline of the seasons in accordance with modern times, so that they truly nourish the piety of the faithful (S.C., 107). The proper of seasons is to be given preference over feasts of saints, "so that the entire cycle of the mysteries of

salvation may be suitably recalled" (S.C., 108). The two-fold character of Lent, as preparation for baptism and as time of penitence, is to be brought into greater prominence in teaching and liturgical observance, with restoration of such disused baptismal features as may seem desirable (S.C., 109). The penitential observance of Lent should be not just individual, but social and external, in ways that are appropriate to our times and places; the paschal fast, however, is to be kept sacred, observed on Good Friday and, where feasible, extended throughout Holy Saturday (S.C., 110). Finally the feasts of saints should not take precedence over the feasts which commemorate the mysteries of salvation, and to that end only those of truly universal importance are to be extended to the whole church; others can be observed by a particular church or nation or family of religious (S.C., 111).

That program of reform eloquently invokes the authentic tradition, and its main lines have been adopted by virtually all Western churches with strong liturgical traditions. The centrality of the paschal mystery on every Sunday is firmly established, although traditions will differ slightly as to what other festivals may be observed on Sunday. The annual celebration of pascha with the paschal fast and vigil has been restored to a prominence and solemnity that were absent in the first half of this century, and the baptismal reference of Lent has been reasserted, especially where there is an active catechumenate. The integrity of the fifty days of rejoicing has been carefully implemented, and the latter weeks of the time after Pentecost admirably build on eschatological themes leading to the celebration of Christ's reign, which leads again into expectation for his adventus. The veneration of the saints reflects the richness and the variety of the many cultures and traditions that make up the church, while those that belong to the common deposit of scripture and tradition are celebrated more widely. While not all anomalies have been resolved, such differences as still distinguish the local liturgical calendars of churches and nations are, for the most part, such differences as the tradition has always known.

That recovery of authentic tradition, however, only casts a stronger light upon the most glaring scandal in the Christian liturgical articulation of time, i.e., our continuing division regarding the date of Easter, a problem that in one way or another has plagued Christianity since the 2nd century. This division brings us face to face with the profoundly demanding problems of truly ecumenical convergence, but in 1969 a gracious initiative of the Ecumenical Patriarch proposed a universal determination of the date as the second Sunday of April, and the welcome reception accorded his proposal in the West suggests that here, too, the Spirit is moving in the church.

Adolf Adam, *The Liturgical Year: Its History and Its Meaning After the Reform of the Liturgy*, Trans. by Matthew J. O'Connell (New York: Pueblo Publishing Co., 1981). Peter Brown, *The Cult of the Saints: Its Rise and Function in Latin Christianity*, (Chicago: University of Chicago Press, 1981). Louis Duchesne, *Christian Worship, Its Origins and Evolution*, Rev. by Bernard Botte, Trans. by M.L. McClure (London: S.P.C.K., 1949). M.D. Goulder, *The Evangelists' Calendar: A Lectionary Explanation of the Development of Scripture* (London: S.P.C.K., 1978). A.G. Martimort, gen. ed., *The Church at Prayer*, 4 vols. Vol. IV: *The Liturgy and Time*, by Irénée Henri Dalmais, Pierre Jounel, and Aimé Georges Martimort. Trans. by Matthew J. O'Connell (Collegeville, Minn.: The Liturgical Press, 1986). Adrian Nocent, *The Liturgical Year*. 4 vols. Trans. by Matthew J. O'Connell (Collegeville, Minn.: The Liturgical Press, 1977). Thomas J. Talley, *The Origins of the Liturgical Year*, (New York: Pueblo Publishing Co., 1986). Robert Taft, S.J., *Beyond East and West: Problems in Liturgical Understanding*, (Washington, D.C.: The Pastoral Press, 1984). Cyrille Vogel, *Medieval Liturgy: An Introduction to the Sources*. Trans. and rev. by William Storey and Niels Rasmussen (Washington, D.C.: The Pastoral Press, 1986). Wiebe Vos and Geoffrey Wainwright, eds., *Liturgical Time: Papers Read at the 1981 Congress of Societas*

Liturgica, (Rotterdam: Liturgical Ecumenical Center Trust, 1982).

THOMAS J. TALLEY

CASEL, ODO (1886-1948)

See **Mystery theology; Theologians, modern, and liturgical renewal; Benedictines and liturgical renewal**

CATECHESIS, LITURGICAL

Introduction

The word *catechesis* literally means a "sounding down," a "re-echoing down to another" (from the Greek *katēchein; kata* = down, and *ēchein* = to sound). Early Christians adopted the word in their follow-up work of teaching the gospel and used it to mean "instruction given by word of mouth" (e.g., Lk 1:4; Acts 18:25; 1 Cor 14:19; Gal 6:6). The word *liturgy* literally means "work of/for the people" (from the Greek *lēitourgia; laitos/lēitos* = of the people, the *laos*, and *ergon* = work). In general usage, the word stood for "an act of public service." Early Christians adopted the word to mean acts of service to others, donations, etc. on behalf of the gospel (e.g., Phil 2:30; Rom 15:27; 2 Cor 9:12), the offering of Christian life as a sacrifice (e.g., Rom 15:16;), and acts of public worship (e.g., Acts 13:2; Heb 8:2, 6). For the early community there was an obvious continuity and flow from preaching the gospel to catechesis, from catechesis to liturgy, from liturgy to further catechesis and to gospel service. The common goal of this combined pastoral ministry was to nurture the disciples on their journey of conversion, faith, Christian living, and witness.

By the 19th century, the relationship between catechesis and liturgy had been severed for the most part; they occupied separate pastoral niches. Catechesis had been narrowed down to a question-and-answer instruction in the truths of the faith which were set down in a catechism and presented, primarily to children, for intellectual assent and understanding. Liturgy had been narrowed both in pastoral practice and in theory. Pastorally, liturgy was understood as the "ceremony" performed publicly by the priest before a passive congregation for the honor and glory of God; theologically, liturgy was reduced to the essential minimum (matter and form) required to "confect" a sacrament.

In the past century, both catechesis and liturgy have gone through an extended process of renewal, and new questions now arise about how they are related and what shape liturgical catechesis might take. This article will survey the parallel renewal movements, suggest a vision of a holistic pastoral ministry which draws catechesis and liturgy into close relationship, and reflect on the nature and key qualities of liturgical catechesis.

Two Renewal Movements

The liturgical and catechetical movements have common roots in the mid and late 19th century. In church life, as in society in general, a movement of "return to the origins" was underway. The past was to be retrieved, however, not in a static form, but in an organic process. The unfolding character of human history was increasingly accepted. The same sense of historicity and process was at work in the study of human life, with attention to human growth and development. During this period, historical research in the writings of the Fathers and in the Bible spawned the patristic and biblical movements. A new ecclesiology elaborated a more active and organic sense of community and community life and action. It was in this context that the liturgical and catechetical movements took shape.

Liturgical Movement

The liturgical movement unfolded in a series of four phases. The first phase, in the latter part of the 19th century and through the turn of this century, has been called the monastic phase. At the Abbey of Solesmes in France, Dom Guéranger spearheaded a study of the liturgy and particularly a revival of Gregorian chant. In this phase the liturgical movement was more intent on restoring a liturgy to be celebrated in a monastic setting than on adapting it to the pastoral needs of the church at large.

The second phase, the pastoral phase, was inaugurated by Pius X's *motu proprio* on church music, *Tra le Sollecitudini* (1903), and by Dom Beauduin, under whose leadership a conference held in Malines, Belgium, in 1909 called for an extension and a more pastoral orientation of the liturgical movement. In this period the liturgy came to be seen as the center of Christian life and spirituality, and priority was given to the "active participation" of the people, a phrase first used officially by Pius X. Early and frequent communion was promoted, community singing was restored, the Roman missal was translated to provide a devotional manual for the people, and the liturgy's power to instruct people in Christian faith and life was rediscovered. These pastoral concerns, fostered first in Belgium and Austria (esp. by Josef Jungmann and Pius Parsch) and later in America (esp. by Dom Virgil Michel, who was equally devoted to issues of justice), found support in a renewal of liturgical and sacramental theology. In Germany, Dom Odo Casel inspired a theological discussion on the active presence of Christ in the liturgical assembly which was to influence the teachings of both Pius XII and Vatican II and contribute to the "encounter model" of sacrament later developed by Schillebeeckx and others.

The third phase began with Pius XII's encyclical on the liturgy, *Mediator Dei* (1947), and continued through the *Consti-*

tution on the Sacred Liturgy (S.C.) promulgated in 1963 by Vatican II. During this period the central agenda of the pastoral phase of the liturgical movement received full ecclesiastical approval. In his encyclical, Pius XII officially set aside the purely ceremonial understanding of liturgy and spoke of it as the public worship of the entire mystical body, head and members. The Easter Vigil was restored (1951) and Holy Week was reformed (1955), returning the paschal mystery to its central liturgical position. Guidelines were given for increased participation (*De Musica Sacra*, 1955), and the ceremonies of the liturgy were simplified (1955). During the 1950s there was also a series of national and international conferences on liturgy which brought together pastoral and theological concerns and prepared the way for the discussions of Vatican II. S.C., 7 contains the heart of the council's teaching on the liturgy, that Christ is present in the liturgy in many ways and that the liturgy is the action not just of the priest, but of Christ and his body, the church. Several things follow: full, conscious, and active participation is the baptismal right and duty of every Christian (S.C., 14); appropriate liturgical instruction is to be provided for the faithful so that they can participate both internally and externally (S.C., 14, 19); and the rites are to be celebrated with assembly present and actively participating (S.C., 27).

The fourth phase, the time since the council, has been one of implementation and renewal. The Roman rites have been revised under the direction of the *Consilium* established to oversee implementation of the liturgical reforms of Vatican II, and they have been translated into English by the International Commission on English in the Liturgy (I.C.E.L.). Extensive programs of instruction and catechesis have been an integral part of the liturgical renewal project. Throughout the post-conciliar work of reform and renewal, the full, conscious, and active participation of the faithful has remained the most fundamental pastoral goal and principle.

Catechetical Movement

The 19th-century themes of return to the origins, historicity and process, and human growth and development which influenced the liturgical movement helped to shape the catechetical movement as well. Dissatisfied with the catechism approach, forged as it was in counter-Reformation polemic and speculative theology, religious educators turned to human psychology, particularly to theories of learning, and later to developmental psychology for help in renewing catechesis. This led to the concern for effective catechetical methods which characterized the first phase of the catechetical movement early in this century. The "Munich method," devised in Germany in the early 1900s and imported into the U.S. in the 1920s, later inspired parallel attempts in Italy, France, and Spain. Attention to how humans learn and to the value of action and of learning by doing are common motifs that have lasted beyond the "methods" phase into present catechesis.

In the 1930s the catechetical movement entered a second phase, usually designated the "kerygmatic" phase. Josef Jungmann's *The Good News and Our Own Preaching of the Faith*, published in 1936, triggered a shift of attention from method to content. The message handed on in catechesis is the "kerygma," the history of salvation centered in the person of Jesus of Nazareth. The goal of catechesis is a living faith which responds to God's call to us in Jesus. Subsequent catechetical theory and documents have retained both the Christo-centrism and the centrality of the word espoused in the "kerygmatic" phase. Another leader during this phase, Johannes Hofinger, stressed that catechesis is a form of pastoral ministry, specifically a form of ministry of the word. This theme was to become a staple of the catechetical movement as well, and it was incorporated into the Vatican II decrees on missionary activity (A.G.) and the pastoral office of bishops (C.D.). Method is not neglected, however; it is refocused on the "four languages"—biblical, liturgical, existential, and doctrinal—in which the "kerygma" is addressed to us. This "pedagogy of signs" was developed in the 1940s and 1950s, particularly at the Lumen Vitae center in Brussels, and has left its mark on the *National Catechetical Directory* (N.C.D.) of the U.S. National Conference of Catholic Bishops (NCCB). During these decades there was a convergence between the catechetical and liturgical movements not only thematically, but also in major figures involved in both movements, e.g., Josef Jungmann and Virgil Michel.

The third phase of the catechetical movement, still underway, is often characterized as the "missionary" or "political" phase. Earlier stress on saving history during the kergymatic quickly led to a complementary concern for contemporary human experience. A series of international study weeks, especially those from Eichstätt (1960) through Medellin (1968), provided a natural transition from the emerging anthropological concerns into missionary and political concerns. These study weeks, all held in third world countries except for Eichstätt, set the theme of catechesis in the context of mission. The understanding that catechesis is a form of ministry of the word, elaborated in the second phase and sanctioned at Vatican II, was expanded and nuanced in these study weeks. Catechesis is seen as the continuation of the proclamation of the "kerygma" first accomplished in evangelization, just as evangelization is the continuation of pre-evangelization. For this total ministry of the word to be effective, it must address people in their own context. As the third

world experience readily illustrates, that context is a complex web of political, cultural, socio-economic, and environmental factors. Themes of justice and liberation become part and parcel of the catechetical message. And the experiential catechesis that had long been a part of the catechetical movement and an area of significant U.S. contribution can no longer be content to focus on isolated individual experience; it must attend to the larger issues woven into human interdependence on local, national, and global scales.

Convergence and Divergence

There are many points of convergence in the two renewal movements. Common themes and motifs run through both: the centrality of Christ, the preeminence of the word, the need for actively engaging the people not only as recipients but also as primary agents of catechesis and liturgy, the dynamics of process and address-response common to both activities, and the need for a more symbolic, holistic approach to the process of learning and celebrating.

The seeds of a potential divergence of interests and energy are also latent in the rhythms of the two movements. As noted, in its third phase the maturing liturgical movement won ecclesiastical approval which culminated in the *Constitution on the Sacred Liturgy* of Vatican II. The current phase has been one of consolidation and implementation. The signals being given in liturgical documents on the relation between catechesis and liturgy are somewhat mixed. In the constitution itself (S.C., 14, 19), as in much subsequent documentation implementing the liturgical reform, the vision of liturgical catechesis seems to be limited to an immediate program of "liturgical instruction" on the revised rites and their meaning. Nevertheless, the restoration of the catechumenate has laid the foundations for a much broader vision of a pre-baptismal and post-baptismal catechesis integrated into a process of pastoral care and ritual celebrations (R.C.I.A., 75, 244-247).

By contrast, in the current "political" or "missionary" phase, the maturation and ecclesiastical approval of the catechetical movement have taken place in obvious interdependence, and the vision of catechesis is generally much larger. The themes of Christo-centrism and the placing of catechesis within an unfolding ministry of the word so prominent in the second and third phases of the movement had a strong impact on various conciliar decrees, especially those on the pastoral office of the bishops (1965), which affirmed the primacy of ministry of the word (C.D., 12-13, 44), and on missionary activity (1965), which set the catechumenate within the pastoral task of evangelization (A.G., 13-15).

Three particular lines of mutual influence between the catechetical movement and official documents can be traced. First, the decree on the pastoral office of the bishops mandated the preparation of the *General Catechetical Directory* for the instruction of the Christian people (C.D., 44).

That *General Catechetical Directory* (G.C.D.) appeared in 1971 and influenced both the First International Catechetical Congress in Rome (1971) and the preparation of national statements and directories such as the NCCB's *Basic Teachings for Catholic Religious Education* (1973) and *Sharing the Light of Faith: National Catechetical Directory* (1977; N.C.D.). Second, the decree on missionary activity helped set the agenda and theological vision for subsequent international catechetical study weeks which explored the relationship between missionary activity and catechesis in the third world context. That linking of themes extended through the First International Catechetical Congress held in Rome (1971) to the General Synod on evangelization in the modern world (1974) and the General Synod on catechesis in the modern world (1977).

These synods led to the apostolic exhortations of Paul VI, *Evangelii Nuntiandi* (E.N.) in 1975, and John Paul II's, *Catechesi Tradendae* (C.T.) in 1979. In these two strands of mutual influence there is a consistent stress on seeing catechesis as a form of ministry of the word within the pastoral office of the church. The third line of influence reaches from the conciliar decree on Christian education (1965) to the NCCB's pastoral message on Catholic education, *To Teach As Jesus Did* (1972). In these documents, as in the NCCB's *Basic Teachings*, concern for the integral content of catechesis becomes prominent.

Catechesis and Liturgy

The above survey suggests that there is a close relation between catechesis and liturgy (C.T., 23; N.C.D., 36, 113) and that there should be collaboration between them (N.C.D., 139). In both pastoral practice and theological discussion, however, catechesis and liturgy sometimes seem to co-exist or even go off in different directions, making the link between them tenuous at best. Closer reflection on the relationship is needed.

The first and most important task may be to recover a vision of a more integral pastoral care which embraces both catechesis and liturgy. Three memories preserved in our tradition offer such a vision.

Emmaus. The first is the story of the two disciples on the way to Emmaus, the story of the "first eucharist" in the Christian community. In that story we find two disciples journeying *away from* the band in Jerusalem, their world in disarray, their inchoate faith in Jesus as the Messiah shattered. Their words to the stranger, "we were hoping that he would be the one ..." (Lk 24:21), reveal the depth of their disillusionment. The stranger, with the care of a host, draws out their experience in all its hurt and bewilderment. And when their story is finished, he retells it from another point of view, that of its victory. "Did not the Messiah have to undergo all this so as to enter into his glory?" (24:27). Their hearts captivated by his recasting of their experience, they invite him to stay with them. In return, he once again hosts them, this time in the breaking of the bread. "With that their eyes were opened and they recognized him" (24:31). Now they are able to name the burning in their hearts, and newly born in the Easter faith of disciples, they immediately rise to return to those from whom they had fled, with a mission to tell them "what had happened on the road and how they had come to know him in the breaking of the bread" (24:35).

Several comments are in order. The journey of the two is a journey from a shattered first faith to full Easter faith. To use contemporary terms, it is a journey from pastoral encounter to catechesis, from catechesis to liturgy, and from liturgy to mystagogy and mission. The catechesis was effective only because the stranger first listened to their story and only then retold it in familiar biblical words. Its effect was to set their hearts burning and to prepare them for the ritual moment that followed. It was only because the catechesis had thus readied them, that they were able to recognize him in the breaking of the bread, to know him as the Risen Lord and themselves as believing disciples. And it was only because that moment of recognition was so powerful that they were compelled into a mission of witness and service to the others. The connection between catechesis and liturgy is unbroken, and the stranger is the model host-catechist-liturgist.

Pentecost. The second memory is enshrined in the story of the "first initiation" in the early community, the sequel to the Pentecost story. In that story, two questions, two moments, and two thresholds frame the experience of the first converts to the new way. After witnessing the Pentecostal event, they are filled with amazement and even a little cynicism about new wine. Their initial question is one of idle curiosity: "What does this mean?" (Acts 2:12). This question triggers a kerygmatic moment in which Peter cites prophet and psalm to cast a different light on what they have experienced. Their question now becomes deeply personal: "What are we to do, brothers?" (2:37). In asking this new question they have crossed a threshold, from a curiosity of the mind to the searching of a heart now open to conversion and faith. Their question invites a catechetical moment in which Peter instructs them and urges them to "save yourselves from this generation" (2:40). "Those who accepted his message" (2:41) have crossed a second threshold on their journey to faith. And so they were baptized and "added (to the community) that day" (2:41). The account ends with an idealized description of their life in common (2:42-47).

Again, a few words are in order. The account reveals a nuanced connection between evangelization and catechesis staged to address the developing quest of the converts. As in the Emmaus story, their human experience provides the starting point, and their questions mark new stages along the way. And as in the Emmaus story, catechesis leads to a profession of faith set in a context of ritual action, and this moment is prolonged into mystagogy, liturgical celebration, and mutual service.

The Catechumenate. The third illustration is not only a memory, for the ancient catechumenate has now been restored in the *Rite of Christian Initiation of Adults* (R.C.I.A.). In the R.C.I.A., catechesis and ritual celebration are brought back together, especially in the periods of the catechumenate proper (R.C.I.A., 75) and of mystagogy (R.C.I.A., 244-247). Together catechesis and liturgy are set into an unfolding process, a spiritual journey (R.C.I.A., 4-5). Christ in his paschal mystery stands at the center of the process (R.C.I.A., 8), and the entire community is charged with active responsibility for the initiation of new members (R.C.I.A., 9). The R.C.I.A. brings to realization what both the catechetical and the liturgical movements have sought to recover.

Catechesis and Liturgy. Gathering some motifs from the longer tradition's vision, it can be said that catechesis and liturgy are linked intrinsically to each other; liturgy without catechesis can easily become an impoverished, hollow ritualism, and catechesis which does not issue into liturgy can become too intellectualized (C.T., 23). Both are rooted in faith; in its own way each expresses, nurtures, and strengthens that faith as it enables people to reflect on its meaning in their lives. The goals of both are the same: to enable people to live the gospel, to be a prophetic voice in their world, and to share their faith and way of life with the next generation.

There is also a certain overlapping of the two that resists too radical a separation. Liturgy itself has a formative power (N.C.D., 36), exercised through proclamation of the word and symbolic ritual gesture. As a ministry of the word, catechesis also has a formative power to shape faith through reflection on what the word proclaimed and celebrated means for daily Christian life; in a sense catechesis itself is celebrative.

Catechesis and liturgy are not identical, however. In the larger sweep of pastoral care, catechesis first prepares people for full, conscious, and active participation in the liturgy and then helps them reflect back on the worship experience to relate it to daily life (N.C.D., 113), so that catechesis and liturgy are caught up in a recurring cycle in which each reinforces the other.

To clarify the relationship between catechesis and liturgy further, catechesis can be described as a systematic, sustained effort to reflect on God's word made known to us in scriptures, in liturgical proclamation and sacramental celebration, and in our experience on Christian life and service in the world, so that we may respond to God more fully. This understanding, central to kerygmatic catechesis and the pedagogy of signs, points to an important aspect of the relation between catechesis and liturgy. In catechesis the immediacy of God's call experienced in proclamation, celebration, and living service gives way to reflective appropriation of that experience. The classical theological dictum that liturgy is "first theology" and that what theologians do is "second theology" offers us a parallel. Liturgy with its formative power is a "first catechesis," while the systematic reflection on that experience done under the guidance of a catechist is "second catechesis."

Liturgical Catechesis

What, then, is liturgical catechesis and what qualities are to be sought in shaping an effective liturgical catechesis?

Scope and Range. One functional description of catechesis reads: "Within the scope of pastoral activity, catechesis is the term to be used for that form of ecclesial action which leads both communities and individual members of the faithful to maturity of faith" (G.C.D., 21). In this view, the task of catechesis is "to foster mature faith" (N.C.D., 33), to "put people not only in touch, but in communion, in intimacy with Jesus Christ" (C.T., 5). Similarly, the function of liturgical catechesis is to enable people to participate actively, both internally and externally (S.C., 19), in the liturgy which celebrates that faith.

As the name itself suggests, liturgical catechesis is only one part of that larger catechetical ministry. Naming it *liturgical* catechesis implies a narrowing of the catechetical focus in some way. One such focus is to make liturgy the object, the content of the catechesis. If this is the only focus, liturgical catechesis risks making people self-conscious worshippers and turning their symbols into didactic signs. Another way to narrow the focus is to give the catechetical process a liturgical framework and orientation. Various forms of prayer and celebration are incorporated into the catechetical process, so that participants experience a movement from prayer to reflection to celebration. For example, catechumens gather not only for instruction, but also around the word and for blessings, anointings, and scrutinies. A third way to focus on the liturgy is to use liturgical experience as a source for catechetical reflection, not just on the liturgy itself, but on the relationship between God and God's people celebrated in the liturgy. Though it is the most difficult of the three, this way of focusing liturgical catechesis is most central to its task.

In keeping with the model established for initiation, two kinds of liturgical catechesis should be distinguished. The R.C.I.A. calls for pre-baptismal catechesis and post-baptismal catechesis (mystagogia). The norm for every sacrament would then be both pre-sacramental and post-sacramental catechesis. The first prepares recipients for a sacramental rite, takes place in a specific period, and is of a more general, elementary kind; the second is life-long and leads people to reflect on their sacramental experience and its meaning for their lives (N.C.D., 6). In pre-sacramental catechesis, rehearsal of the rites and detailed interpretation of the symbols are far less important than a spiritual readying of the recipients to live into the liturgical moment when their growing relationship with the Lord is marked with a distinctive sacramental sign. Invitation into that relationship and formation in the symbolic ways, both human and religious, in which it is expressed take pastoral priority for this catechesis. In post-sacramental catechesis, the liturgical experience of God's presence and action provides the starting point

and focus for the catechetical reflection. In broad strokes, this mystagogy might simply be described as the reflective continuation of the "opening up of symbols" begun in the liturgy itself (N.C.C.B., *Environment and Art in Catholic Worship*, 15).

Desired Qualities. Liturgical catechesis should be Christ-centered, formative-transformative, communal, and experientially-based.

Christ-centered. The first concern of liturgical catechesis is to help people develop the individual and communal relationship to the crucified and risen Christ first nurtured and sacramentalized in the experience of Christian initiation (R.C.I.A., 8). Christ is the center of Christian life, liturgy, and catechesis, and his paschal mystery is the focal point for all Christian spirituality. The ultimate concern of liturgical catechesis is not liturgical history, the rites, symbolic objects, or the truths "taught" by the liturgy, but the person of Jesus and how the assembled people meet God in him. The key sources for liturgical catechesis are to be found where that Jesus is revealed to his disciples: in the proclaimed word, in sacramental gesture, and in the living witness of those who live as his disciples.

Formative-transformative. Liturgical catechesis, like all catechesis and like the liturgy itself, is a formative experience. Formation in faith and conversion would thus seem to be the appropriate goal for both. But entering into and growing in a relationship with Christ is ultimately a transformative experience accomplished only through the work of the Spirit. The appropriate goal of both liturgy and catechesis is to form people in a way that invites them into transformation; neither can be so programmed as to transform people automatically. The same holds true of liturgical catechesis; it forms for the sake of transformation. And since transformation is a journey of faith and conversion that takes a lifetime, liturgical catechesis is needed by disciples of every age according to their level of development (S.C., 19; N.C.D., 177-189), with a certain primacy accorded to adult catechesis as the "chief form of catechesis" (N.C.D., 188).

Communal. By its very nature liturgy is a communal action. The assembly itself is the most important of the liturgical signs (N.C.C.B., *Environment and Art in Catholic Worship, 28*). The very act of gathering, the constant use of the first person plural in public prayer, the common hearing of the word of God, and the one sacramental action in which all participate shape the liturgical experience as a communal one in which the people meet Christ together. Liturgical catechesis needs a setting and a format in which the reflection on the meaning of the liturgical experience can be done in common, since the meaning is a public, shared meaning. Liturgical catechesis should also be communal in the sense that it is the common work of all in the community. All are to accept the formative role their witness has for others (R.C.I.A., 9) and adults in particular are to play a central role in their own catechesis (N.C.D., 185).

Experientially-based. If catechesis in general should be concerned with making people attentive to their more significant experiences (G.C.D., 74), this holds especially true for liturgical catechesis. And if it is crucial for any learning method to take account, not only of goals and the learners, but also of the subject to be studied, liturgical catechesis needs to devise methodologies that are attentive to what is most characteristic of the liturgical experience. Four such characteristics stand out.

First, liturgical celebration is *repetitious*. General structural patterns of gathering and sending, word and action, prescribed ritual dialogue, and patterned action repeat themselves in almost every rite. Within a given liturgical rite most words are prescribed, even prescripted,

and the ritual interactions are stylized and predictable. Like all ritual, liturgy is a "known language" in which people dwell and which they use, not to create a totally new story, but to tell of and mark a journey of discipleship already underway.

Second, liturgical celebration is *symbolic* in expression. This is true not only of ritual actions, but to a great extent of the words as well. Liturgy conveys its meaning not in an explanatory, didactic fashion, but in a metaphoric, evocative way. Symbols speak to the whole persons in whole ways, not just to the mind for the sake of information-sharing. Space, time, action, and speech form a highly non-verbal array of interlocking liturgical languages. In addition, the symbols used in the liturgy have roots not only in religious tradition, but also in human usage. For example, bathing and anointing someone, or sharing food together, serve as both human and religious symbols. Religious symbolism typically incorporates and builds on human symbolism.

Third, liturgical celebration is at its core symbolic *ritual action*. Ritual is its own way of valuing and knowing, prior to and often without words. Liturgical rites enact meaning rather than talk about it. In liturgy, God and people literally keep covenant in Christ, in the remembrance of his dying and rising. Liturgy is a saying-doing of the complete God-human *Amen* uttered in Christ (2 Cor 1:20).

Fourth, liturgical celebration is repeated symbolic ritual action *which the people do together*. Though each one in the assembly can find personal meaning in the rites, the meaning symbolically enacted is a shared, public meaning which goes beyond personal meanings. In the moment of ritual, individual stories and journeys are transposed and become part of the larger story told and enacted in memory of what God has done in Christ.

172

These four characteristics together urge that liturgical catechesis follow a procedure which does several things. From the perspective of human experience, liturgical catechesis first evokes the experience beneath liturgical symbols such as bathing with water and anointing with oil, and not just in its individual expression but also in its cultural, political, and socio-economic context. It attends to the dark side of the symbols as well as the bright side, e.g., that we both bond and fight with food. Second, it enables people to interpret that experience in its fullness and in the light of God's word revealed in Jesus and handed on to us in the community, such as the memory of the breaking of the bread. Third, it entrusts to people the task of living out that human experience in the world in full consonance with the faith, so they may spread the story of how they came to know him. What this means from the religous point of view, first, is that liturgical catechesis will start with the people's experience of the liturgy itself and pay careful attention to the ways in which symbol and ritual help them to see and mark the place of God's presence and action in their lives and to hear the call to further conversion. Second, the larger liturgical tradition will be presented as a living history of a people at prayer to the God who walks as a companion on the journey, so that we can more easily relate to that story. Third, the meaning liturgy is to have for people today and tomorrow will not be imposed but called forth in the creative meeting of contemporary human experience and the received tradition.

Conclusion

The twin renewal movements in liturgy and catechesis have opened the way to a closer collaboration between these two ministries. A more holistic vision of pastoral ministry in which liturgy and catechesis support and complement each other can now be recovered. Out of that

vision, a liturgical catechesis that is Christ-centered, formative-transformative, communal, and experientially-based can take shape.

See **Liturgical movement, the (1830-1969); Initiation, Christian; Catechumenate; Mystagogy; Imagination and worship; Ritual; Symbol**

Robert L. Browning, Roy A. Reed, *The Sacraments in Religious Education and Liturgy: An Ecumenical Model* (Birmingham, AL: Religious Education Press, 1985). Sr. Mary Charles Bryce, "The Interrelationship of Liturgy and Catechesis," *American Benedictine Review* 28 #1 (March 1977): 1-29. National Conference of Catholic Bishops, *Sharing the Light of Faith: National Catechetical Directory* (Washington, D.C.: USCC, 1979). Gwen Kennedy Neville-John H. Westerhoff, *Learning through Liturgy* (New York: Seabury Press, 1978). Gilbert Ostdiek, *Catechesis for Liturgy. A Program for Parish Involvement* (Washington, D.C.: The Pastoral Press, 1986). Mark Searle, "The Pedagogical Function of the Liturgy," *Worship* 55 (1981): 332-359. John H. Westerhoff-William H. Willimon, *Liturgy and Learning through the Life Cycle* (New York: Seabury Press, 1980).

GILBERT OSTDIEK, O.F.M.

CATECHUMENATE

The catechumentate is a period of formation of undetermined length during which an individual desiring incorporation into the Christian community prays, studies and discerns in conjunction both with others who seek the faith and with members of the faith community who are chosen to assist these individuals.

Incorporation into the Christian community demands a conversion of life, a transformation of the individual in Christ. Erik Erikson demonstrates the significance of stages in development of the human person within the human community. Ritual plays a significant role in Erikson's process of becoming an adult member of a given society.

Generally, initiation into any society places a balance between the needs of the individual and those of the community. The individual needs to be accepted, to experience a sense of belonging, to accept as one's own the philosophy of the group. The community on the other hand needs assurance that the new member will be one who will live the life professed by the group and will support the members of the group in their pursuit of life within the community.

The Christian community lives the life of Christ. Conversion to this life in Christ implies acceptance of the challenge offered by Christ to his followers to bring about the kingdom through the proclamation of the gospel. Thus one who desires incorporation into this body, the church, evidences a passion for this mission of Christ. Membership in the church is not limited to an adherence to rules and teachings. It is a way of life: a life lived in relationship with Christ, particularly through prayer; a life lived in relationship with the Christian community, particularly through the proclamation of the gospel as evidenced in an approach to life and in the expression of the unity which exists within the church in the liturgy.

Historical evidence points to the presence of a catechumenate in the ante-Nicene communities. During the period of the catechumenate (which lasted from several months to years), the individual experienced a growth in the acceptance of the Christian way of life. Members of the community worked with the individual to enter into a change of life style. During the period of the catechumenate, the candidates led a life of prayer and fasting. Various rituals were used to mark transition moments during the course of these years of discernment on the part of the individual and of the community.

Included among the decrees of the Second Vatican Council is the call for the restoration of the catechumenate: "The catechumenate for adults, comprising several distinct steps, is to be restored and brought into use at the discretion of the local ordinary. By this means the time of the catechumenate, which is intended as

a period of suitable instruction, may be sanctified by sacred rites to be celebrated at successive intervals of time" (S.C., 64).

The challenge set forth in the Liturgy Constitution was met with the promulgation of the *Rite for the Christian Initiation of Adults* in January of 1972. Included in the decree from the Congregation for Divine Worship is the reception of the council's call for the restoration of the catechumenate.

The catechumenate is preceded by a period of evangelization often referred to as the pre-catechumenate. During this period, the Good News of salvation is heard for the first time by the individual who begins to inquire into the faith. Those who are not yet members of the Christian community are introduced to gospel values as they meet informally with Christians and begin to hear of the love of God for them.

The catechumenate is a period of formation in the Christian way of life; it is a time for discernment and prayer. While the various dogmas and precepts of the church are introduced by priest or catechist, primary emphasis is placed on hearing the word of God within the context of the assembled faithful and then discussing how that word might transform the lives of all, in particular, the lives of the catechumens. The catechumens are formed by their participation in the communal life of the assembly including its apostolic works, by instruction and through participation in the various liturgical rites.

The individual seeking incorporation into the Christian community generally participates in the order of catechumens, a group of individuals who participate in the formation process together, sharing faith with members of the community and participating in the various apostolic works of the community. While responsibility for the formation of the catechumens is given to the entire community, some members are chosen to minister directly to the process. It is with these individuals that the catechumens meet to listen to the word and share faith within the context of a liturgy of the word.

Catechists and other ministers encourage the catechumens to enter into reflections on the word in dialogue with their life experiences. This lectionary-based catechesis is based on readings from the Bible which yield the church's self-identity. Rather than being didactic, this liturgical catechesis breaks open the word of God for the catechumen. Catechesis is not simply education but conversion, and conversion takes time.

Catechesis takes place within the context of prayer. Liturgical rites during this period are designed to assist in the formation of the catechumens. The public nature of these rites underscores the fact that not only the catechumen but the entire Christian community is in the process of entering into a new relationship.

The first of the rituals of the catechumenate is the "Rite of Acceptance into the Order of Catechumens." In the presence of the assembly, the priest or deacon greets the catechumens and their sponsors. During the liturgy, the catechumens are marked with the sign of the cross and are given the book of gospels during the liturgy of the word. The names of the catechumens are written in the registry and, after the community prays over them, they are dismissed. They will not participate in the liturgy of the eucharist until the Easter vigil.

While these are the general signs of acceptance suggested by the ritual, other optional rites are permitted where a particular culture might have a distinct ritual act associated with such an acceptance.

Once accepted into the order of catechumens, the individual now enjoys a particular relationship with the Christian community. Each catechumen will hear the word proclaimed within the context of the assembled body weekly. In the event of death during this period, the catechumen will be buried as a member of the community.

The length of time spent by any individual in the catechumenate will depend on the particular needs of that person and of the community. While catechumens enter into the conversion process with others seeking incorporation, the group is not a class but rather individuals sharing faith as they hear the word in common. Therefore, some members of the group might be ready to enter the next period of formation before others.

In addition to participation in the weekly gatherings for the celebration of the word, various liturgical rituals are suggested during the period of the catechumenate. Great flexibility is suggested in the use of the various minor exorcisms, blessings and rites of anointing offered for use during this time in the life of the individual undergoing conversion. Catechists, priests, deacons or other ministers lead the catechumens in prayer and offer the various rituals when deemed appropriate.

Of great significance to the entire catechumenate is the season of Lent often called the great retreat of preparation for the celebration of the sacraments at the Easter vigil. On the first Sunday of Lent catechumens appear before the assembled community where testimony is given of those involved in their formation. The church then accepts this testimony and chooses the catechumens for entry into the church. Generally, the election on the part of the church is presided over by the bishop. The ritual of election is followed by the enrollment of names of the catechumens in the book of those seeking initiation.

Now, the "elect" participate in the Lenten celebrations as the final stage of their preparation. During this period of purification and enlightenment their spiritual formation is more intense. Godparents play a more direct role in the process as they assist the catechumen to achieve an ever deeper awareness of the presence of Christ working in their lives.

Particular ritual components assist the process. Within the liturgy, during the Sundays of Lent, scrutinies with their accompanying exorcisms are included in the liturgy of the word to assist the catechumen in the conversion process. During the final days of Lent, after the completion of scrutinies, the Creed and the Lord's Prayer are formally presented to the candidates.

See **Initiation, Christian; Easter season**

Aidan Kavanagh, *The Shape of Baptism* (Pueblo Press, 1978). Committee on the Liturgy, *Christian Initiation of Adults: A Commentary.* Study Text 10 (United States Catholic Conference, 1985).

MARY ALICE PIIL, C.S.J.

CHALICE, MODES OF DISTRIBUTION OF

When communion under both species of bread and wine was partially restored in the Roman rite in 1965, the Apostolic See permitted four different modes of distributing the consecrated wine: (1) direct administration of the cup, (2) intinction, (3) the rite with a tube, and (4) the rite with a spoon. The directives to be observed for these four modes of administration are found in the General Instruction of the Roman Missal, nn. 244-252.

Among the four modes, the Holy See has judged that the direct administration of the cup to the communicant is preferable, that it "ranks first" (D.O.L., 2115). The National Conference of Catholic Bishops (N.C.C.B.) has made this the policy for the United States: "Because of its ancient sign value '*ex institutione Christi*,' Communion from the cup or chalice is always to be preferred to any other form of ministering the precious

blood"(N.C.C.B., n. 44). The gospels record Jesus' command to eat the bread and drink from the cup of wine given to his disciples at the Last Supper, and to continue doing this in his memory. Direct reception from the cup most effectively signifies fidelity to this dominical command.

The cup is administered by a deacon, assisting priest, acolyte, or special minister of the eucharist. When presenting the cup, the minister says, "The blood of Christ," and the communicant responds, "Amen." If there are no other ministers present, the presiding priest himself separately administers the bread and wine, or he can request from the assembly the assistance of one or more persons, observing the "Rite of Commissioning a Special Minister to Distribute Holy Communion on a Single Occasion" in the Roman Pontifical. There must always be a minister of the cup; the minister is part of the sign of communion, signifying Christ's giving himself through the ministry of the church. Church discipline prohibits communicants from taking the cup directly from the altar, or passing it from one to another.

By intinction is meant communion in the form of bread which the minister dips in the wine and places on the communicant's tongue. Church discipline prohibits recipients from taking the host and dipping it in the cup on their own because the sign value of the minister is neglected. Historically certain Roman popes and councils had forbidden intinction because Christ gave the bread and wine separately, and only Judas dipped his bread in the cup. Today the N.C.C.B. disapproves of intinction because everyone in the assembly may not be able or may not wish to receive the precious blood, and because intinction eliminates the option of receiving communion in the hand (N.C.C.B., nn. 51, 52).

For the distribution of the precious blood through a tube, the communicant goes to the minister of the cup, receives the tube from the minister, places it in the cup, and drinks a little. The communicant then removes the tube, places it in a container of water held by the minister, sips a little water to purify the tube, then puts it on a paten or in another container presented by the minister.

For the rite using a spoon, the minister of the cup pours a small spoonful of the consecrated wine on the tongue of the recipient, taking care that the spoon does not touch the lips or tongue. The rites using a tube or spoon, although they are lawful options, are by and large mere historical curiosities; neither is customary in the Latin church today.

_____

National Conference of Catholic Bishops, *This Holy and Living Sacrifice: Directory for the Celebration and Reception of Communion under Both Kinds* (Washington: United States Catholic Conference, 1985). Archdale King, *Reception of the Chalice: Its Revival* (Carlow, Ireland: Liturgy Centre, 1972).

JOHN M. HUELS, O.S.M.

CHARACTER, SACRAMENTAL

In its narrowest and most straightforward meaning, the phrase *sacramental character* refers to the Roman Catholic teaching that for three sacraments, viz., baptism, confirmation and orders "there is ... imprinted on the soul a character, that is, a certain spiritual and indelible mark, by reason of which they cannot be repeated" (Council of Trent: Session 7, can. 9).

More broadly, and in an historical context, this is a rich and complex notion. While the term *character* gained popularity from its use by St. Augustine, it does have scriptural precedent in the concept of *seal, sphragis* (Eph 1:13; 4:30; 2 Cor 1:22) whereby the Spirit of God's ownership of the soul is expressed. Cognately, the idea of sealing, stamping, or tattooing was used by the Greek Fathers

to indicate the "marking for God" that occurs in our reception of baptism.

St. Augustine used the word *character* when arguing against the Donatist practice of rebaptizing heretics who returned to the church. For Augustine, and for subsequent Catholic theology, baptism effects in us an irreversible and permanent reorientation of our lives towards Christ (2 Cor 5:17ff; Gal 3:27). Whether our baptism bears greater or less fruit, or even if we deny or repudiate it, once baptized, we are baptized for ever and that action is not to be repeated (cf. *De Bapt. contr Donat.* 5, 24, 34 *et al.*).

As confirmation became separated from baptism it, too, was considered to be a once-and-for-all action. In Aquinas, e.g., the character of confirmation is a power to confess the faith publicly by words (S.Th. III q. 63 art. 3).

Likewise, the sacrament of orders was regarded as bringing with it a radical and permanent commission to act in the name of Christ.

Apart from the observable rite, *sacramentum*, of a sacrament, the fact of a sacramental character, *sacramentum et res*, was generally accepted for several centuries prior to the Reformation. The Council of Trent's Canon 9 (see above) is a response to Luther's denial in his *Babylonian Captivity* of the existence of a sacramental character. Calvin and Zwingli followed Luther's thinking. All of them saw such dynamism in the word of God that it could not be managed or controlled by any human person or "priestly" character.

We can find also, in Augustine's writings, the foundation for the later development of a theory that not only do baptism, confirmation and orders have the character of non-repeatability but that, in a looser sense of the word, each of the Catholic sacraments has a "character" of its own. Obviously this usage of the phrase *sacramental character* refers rather to the particular dimension under which

ach of the other sacraments presents us
with the opportunity of encounter with
Christ.

Today perhaps the most commonly
accepted view of the sacramental character of baptism, confirmation and orders
is that these sacraments begin and then
particularize or deepen within their recip-
ents an irreversible consecration to worship God (L.G., 11) to grow into Christ
and to witness to him (*ibid.*), and to act in
the name and person of Christ (P.O., 2).
The ritual celebrations of the beginning
of this process and also of its key moments
of realization are of such significance
both to the individual recipient and to the
community as not to bear repetition (see
also, C.I.C., 845.1).

Bernard Cooke, *Ministry to Word & Sacrament*
Philadelphia, Fortress, 1976). Jean Galot, *La
Nature du charactère sacramentel: étude théolo-
gique médiévale* (Paris, 1958). Bernard Leeming,
Principles of Sacramental Theology (London,
1960).

PATRICK BISHOP, S.J.

CHILDREN AND DEATH

Research in child development has
helped us to know a little more about
how the minds and thinking of children
develop, but we still have scant knowledge
about how they think about death. It is
perfectly understandable, in a society
that has often been described as death-
defying and death-denying, that the topic
of death is rarely discussed among children. With significant decreases in the
incidence of childhood mortality, fewer
children die. A relatively small percentage
of children during their childhood years
experience the death of a sibling or a
parent. Since personal encounter and
experience with death is exceptional
among children, questions remain: how
do children think about death, the death
of others, or their own personal death?

An understanding and appreciation of
the processes of life and death, growth,
maturation, and development are the
products of learning and experience.
Since a child's experience with death is
limited during the childhood years, many
adults have assumed that children have
little awareness of death and little fear of
it.

Until the 1940s, there was no systematic
study of children's understanding and
attitudes toward death. Maria Nagy, a
Hungarian psychiatrist and a follower of
the renowned child developmentalist,
Jean Piaget, researched the application
of developmental stages to children's
understanding of death. In her work, she
concluded that children under the age of
five relate to death in egocentric ways,
considering death to be reversible and
subject to the same magical powers which
they think govern many other physical
phenomena.

In the middle years of childhood,
between the ages of five and nine years,
Nagy observed that children tended to
give death a personality, acknowledging
it as permanent, and conceptualizing
death in concrete terms, yet as something
external to the self. She concluded that
children after the age of nine have a
realistic knowledge about death as an
inevitable and irreversible human experience that has its genesis within the
body. Children at this age grasp the
finality of death and, with this understanding in place, display more affective
responses to death than younger children
characteristically exhibit.

Nagy's early research has been criticized for its methodological inadequacies.
Common to critiques of her theory is the
claim that it does not sufficiently take
into account the roles of environment,
culture, and experience as contributing
factors to a child's understanding of
death.

For example, one would have to conclude that, until approximately age ten,

children are not generally aware of the nature and the implications of death. However, we all know that a child's close, personal experience of death concretizes for that child what death is all about, even though his or her thoughts may exhibit some ambiguity about what happens on the philosophical or the biological level. In certain cultures and environments, and especially where there is personal experience of death, children are in fact more aware of death at far earlier ages than many cognitive developmentalists would have considered possible.

Unawakened by immediate personal experience, children's awareness of death appears to be tied to the normal processes of cognitive maturation. However, any significant and personal exposure to death may impress upon a child a sophisticated awareness of death at an earlier age than normal development would anticipate. For children, even very young ones, who live in an environment in which either they themselves, a parent, a grandparent, or a sibling is diagnosed with a life-threatening illness, one can expect that the child's awareness of death will be keener than might have been considered possible.

Coping with the Reality of Death

As adults, we rely on a wide repertory of coping skills. These skills begin to take shape in childhood. An essential skill is the ability to cope with loss. Death represents a primary loss. For a child, death in a family context can threaten the base of security within the family itself. Children are not protected from feelings of sadness and loneliness, fears of abandonment and betrayal, anger at the deceased, and worry about themselves and about others within the family who survive.

Because the experience of death for a young child accelerates the child's understanding of death, it is reasonable to expect that children, likewise, need to grieve just as adults. Although the manifestations of grieving among children are comparable to adults, they are distinct in their characteristics and intensity. Children will sob and cry and express sadness and longing. They will remember the deceased and will tell stories of shared experiences, will imitate actions performed by the deceased, and will talk to pictures of the deceased. As grieving adults do, children will also deny the fact of death and will avoid the subject of death, particularly during the early stages of bereavement.

In clinical studies of children's grief reactions, certain findings are common. Children's grief is not simply a set of symptoms that begin after a loss and gradually fade away. Rather, children's grief is more accurately a succession of responses that blend into and replace one another. It should be anticipated that any child who experiences the death of a significant member of the family to whom he or she was attached in important ways will react to that death with an emotional response involving pain and grief. Children between the ages of two and ten will cry, will display moodiness, and will display a variety of expressions of longing. It is not unusual to expect that children are prone to speak about the deceased as if they continue to live. In very real ways, this is an attempt on a child's part to deny the reality of death, and, in a way, to buy emotional time for their grieving.

As children progress in their grief, they come to a certain understanding and acceptance of the loss, together with a decrease of the primary defensive measures that they drew upon in the early stages of their grieving. It is not uncommon to see these primary defenses replaced by a broad repertory of fears. Principal among these fears is the expressed concern about being abandoned or left alone. If the death experience involved a parent, children often are quite worried about the surviving parent's possible death. This apprehension is often verbalized. These fears can easily translate into anxiety, since death has a way of shattering the securities of a child's world and introducing dangerous and threatening possibilities. In these situations, it is not unusual that children will exaggerate their dependence upon other members of the family and find it more difficult to achieve even temporary separations from care providers. Children can become overly aggressive and hyperactive in their behaviors, creating behavioral disturbances within the family and school contexts. These somewhat dramatic changes in temperament and behavior are related to their experiences of loss.

The literature on children's understanding of death supports the conclusion that youngsters entertain basic concerns about losses, endings, and separation. It is axiomatic that the more a person understands phenomena, the more he or she is able to deal with the consequences of such realities. In the case of children, immaturity in age, understanding, experience, and ego defenses can leave a child more vulnerable than an adult to the threats and realities of death.

It is easy for significant adults to deny a child's understanding of death. In these cases, the child will suffer alone the inner experiences and fears of death and will often seek solace in defensive fantasies. The evolution of these fantasies is tied to cognitive development. It is not surprising that many of the fantasies that support children's play involve the attribute of omnipotence. Children picture themselves able to fight off monsters and beasts of gigantic proportions much in the vein of the biblical David in combat with the mighty Goliath. This dependence upon fantasized power and strength is a primitive defense that children frequently use to cope with the subjective threat of death.

Pastoral Intervention and Support
As with adults, when a child encounters an event that upsets his or her characteristic patterns of thought and behavior, children resort to primitive problem solving strategies until equilibrium is restored. A crisis is a situation where habitual emotional and behavioral responses prove insufficient. Crisis leads to a state of upset that is ordinarily accompanied by heightened fear, anger, or guilt. Because a child cannot remain long in a state of disequilibrium, crisis is frequently self-limited.

The new balance that is achieved by resolving or facing a crisis, such as the experience of a death represents in the life of a child, may be either an adaptive behavior that promotes either personal growth or a maladaptive response that may indicate psychological problems. A crisis, therefore, is a transition or turning point that significantly impacts on a child's adaptation and ability to meet future crises.

In general, we have suggested that a child's understanding of death seems to follow rather closely a cognitive developmental model. However, we have also asserted that a child's view of death seems to be shaped heavily by life experiences. When death enters into a child's experience, he/she experiences crisis. Although death is a stressful life event, it may also enrich a child's beliefs and values, forcing the child to assimilate these new experiences and to integrate those experiences into his/her understanding. In this sense, a life crisis, such as dying, can accelerate development in the child of new, cognitive, and personal skills because such skills are needed for effective adaptation.

In pastoral practice, there are several issues that need to be identified in working with children who are dealing with the crisis of death. The first task involves helping a child to understand the meaning of the situation. This, of course, is a principal task of parents and significant other family members. However, in some instances, pastoral care persons will become part of this conversation. Parents may look to pastoral workers for assistance in mediating discussion of death with children. Whenever a death occurs, the loss must be accepted intellectually and be explained appropriately. These explanations need to be communicated in language that children can understand, and at a level of explanation that is age-appropriate.

A second set of tasks involves dealing with the reality and responding to the requirements of the external situation. If death occurs within the family system, this has immediate and direct impact on the life of the child. Certain supplies, both material and emotional, may be interrupted by the death. A child will need help in readjusting his or her needs that have been disrupted by the situation of death.

A third set of tasks is to sustain as much as possible the other relationships that exist with family members and significant others who can be of continued help as the child works to resolve the crisis. Because adults within a family are often engaged in managing their own concerns during the crisis triggered by the death of one of its members, children are often neglected and are not as able to supply for their own needs during this period. Particular attention needs to be paid to helping the family system to be supportive to itself, and for others to supply whatever additional support may be necessary on a temporary basis during the period of the crisis.

Likewise, it is important to help maintain emotional equilibrium in the entire family during a crisis. Crises have a way of catalyzing many powerful emotions, including a sense of failure and self-blame, anger and grief, tension and fear. These powerful emotional states within a family can be perceived as significant threats to a child's security, and a child needs to be reassured in the face of these powerful emotions that they are, in fact,

temporary and that things will be better.

Finally, a child needs to realize that he or she will have the ability to survive this significant loss and continue effectively with his or her own life. Although many of these concepts are adult, they need not only to figure into the pastoral intervention and support for adult members of a family system, but also to be a particular concern of those who provide assistance to children in crisis.

There are many excellent books about death that have been written for young readers. These stories, based on human experiences of death, can be enormously helpful in supporting children who face loss related to death, or who themselves are raising important questions, seeking understanding about this human experience.

Summary

Death is a reality for children as it is for their adult counterparts. Children are capable of understanding what death involves and what it means. Children, likewise, mourn and grieve at the death of a loved one. Although the dynamics of a child's grief are different in certain aspects from that of adults, there are many characteristics that they share in common. A child's grief is frequently short-lived, but one will see many aspects of grieving in a child's play, in other behaviors, and in verbal and non-verbal communications.

If adults are aware and sensitive, they can be of significant help to a child's integration of his or her understanding of death, and this integration can be of great importance to the ongoing development of the child. Adults need to be sensitive to the understandings and the fantasies that dominate a child's thoughts about death if we are to be able to talk effectively with children about death and to assist them in the grief that attends such loss. Adults need to enter the world of the child with respect and sensitivity. Children do understand death and are affected by it.

In pastoral and liturgical ministries, these realities need to be in the consciousness of those who minister to children who are attempting to understand and assimilate the experience of death.

J.E. Schowalter, P. Buschman, P.R. Patterson, A.H. Kutscher, M. Tallmer, R.G. Stevenson, *Children and death: Perspectives from birth through adolescence* (New York: Praeger Publishers, 1987). W.J. Smith, *Dying in the human life cycle: Psychological, biomedical and social perspectives* (New York: Holt, Rinehart, and Winston, 1985). W.J. Smith, *Books to help children cope with separation and loss* (New York: R.R. Bonker, 1983).

WALTER J. SMITH, S.J.

CHILDREN, DEATH OF

Research supports the assertion that among the most stressful human life crises is the death of a child. For a parent, the death of one's own child is among the most painful losses one can experience. The death of a child, however, also impacts upon the couple, upon the family unit, and upon society as a whole. It is important to comment on each of these human experiences of loss, since each of them suggests distinct approaches in ministry and pastoral care.

Grief of an Individual Parent

Parenting is a unique expression of human bonding, on the physiological, psychological, and social levels. It is one of the most powerful relationships that human life can generate. Relative to the meaning, strength, and duration of this bond with a child, an individual parent's grief response can be measured.

There are some common characteristics observed in the grief reaction of many parents who have lost children. The individual experience of grief is often reported as severe. This means that the sense of loss is profound. Secondary effects of the loss, including depression,

eating and sleep disruptions, emotional outbursts of sobbing and crying, are also intense. In comparison with other losses of friends or adult family members, the symptoms associated with normal grieving of a deceased child tend to be longer lasting and more complex.

Each child commands a special meaning for a parent. This specific meaning includes the hopes, dreams, fantasies, and wishes that a parent treasures for the child and for his or her life. A parent normally tends to be invested significantly in a child. This investment is not always apparent to a spouse or to another member of the family. When the death of a child interrupts the unique relationship that exists between parent and child, all aspects of the lost relationship bear on the individual parent's grief responses.

Each child, even a very young child, has a unique personality, differing traits and characteristics, differing abilities and talents. All of these variables contribute to the distinctive role that a child exercises in relationship to each of his or her parents and to the family unit. When a child dies, all of those qualities of relationship are lost to the parent who survives, as well as to the family unit.

Parents whose children have died speak a common language; they frequently say that they have a lost a part of themselves. Because this expression is common in the experience of so many bereaved parents, it signals a particular characteristic of parental grief. By this expression of personal loss, they indicate not only a loss of an important part of their physical and emotional relationship with the deceased child, but they disclose a perception that they have lost a part of each other, their family, and indeed, their future.

While the focus of this discussion has centered on children and adolescents, it is important to note that parents at later stages of the life-cycle experience comparable feelings when they survive the death of their adult children. One cannot minimize a parent's pain associated with the death of a child, no matter when it occurs in the life course. An eighty-year old parent can report intense feelings of loss when confronted with the death of a sixty-year old son or daughter. The timing and circumstances of the death, however, do contextualize and interpret the specific grief reactions that one observes in surviving parents.

Impact of a Child's Death on the Couple Relationship

While it is important to consider the individual parent and the particular experience of loss that he or she sustains, it is also necessary to consider the couple relationship. In an intact couple relationship, both parents face the experience of grief simultaneously. This is particularly the case when the child's death is sudden, as in Sudden Infant Death Syndrome (SIDS), or in an accidental child death, as in a drowning.

In these contexts of child loss, parents display a particular vulnerability to a wide range of feelings. It is not uncommon that parents experience guilt, helplessness, or blame when confronted with a child's death, and it is not uncommon that parents have a tendency to project their feelings onto the other spouse.

Just as an individual parent's relationship to a deceased child is unique so, too, will the grief reaction be particular. Not only will parents grieve different aspects of the lost relationship with the child, but the grieving process itself will be varied. This creates obvious difficulties for a couple relationship. One parent's style of grieving may be more open and emotive, while the other's style may be more interior and non-expressive.

These differing styles can create misunderstandings, alienation, and open conflict within the couple relationship. One spouse, for example, may be desirous of speaking about the loss at a time when the other spouse wishes to avoid discussion and turns attention to other things. This lack of synchronicity between spousal needs and desires creates an environment of tension. Spouses do not always understand the dynamics discussed above and may be helped in a context of pastoral care where these issues are appropriately identified and discussed.

The birth of a child inaugurates a new identity for the couple as parents. These roles develop continually throughout the course of a parent's lifetime relationship with the son or daughter. The role of parent changes and modifies through the adult years. However, the parental role becomes an important part of the identity of the individual. When death of a child occurs, changes in the parental identity also take place.

A couple who had consciously encouraged in each other the appropriation of parental identity and roles during the pregnancy and early childhood of their offspring confessed that, when their first and only child died at fifteen months of age, they experienced a significant conflict in their understanding of their identity. While they felt that they were still parents, they also felt awkward in talking about themselves any longer as parents since they no longer had a child who was alive. In a bereavement group of parents, they were able to articulate this perception of their loss, which other parents of a single child immediately understood. This tends to be less problematic for parents who have other children. The situation of being parents of a single child dramatizes the ways in which identity as parent is significantly affected by the death of the child.

Effects of Death on the Family

The death of a child also has an impact on the family system itself. Regardless of the age of the deceased child, each child exercises certain roles within the family context. The death of a child introduces changes into the dynamics of the interrelationships within the family. The death of a child also interrupts the assumed "pecking order" of death within a family. Unconsciously, at least, we expect that older members of the family will predecease the younger members. When a child dies, this introduces dissonance into the comforting assumption about the "pecking order" of dying. Not only does this confront individual members with their own mortality, but it challenges the fundamental assumptions about control and predictability.

It is not uncommon that survivors tend to idealize the memory of the deceased. This is also true about the ways in which children are idealized by their parents, grandparents, and other members of the family. This can create a certain tension within the family for surviving members who may feel neglected and underappreciated, almost as if they would be of more value to the family were they also to die. Parents, in working through their own grief for a deceased child, can fail to see how their memories of the deceased child and preoccupation with the idealized aspects of that child create new problems for their surviving children.

Finally, it is not uncommon to observe compensatory behaviors in parents toward their surviving children. They oftentimes become more vigilant and overprotective with respect to their other children, almost as if defensively attempting to prevent a possible repetition of the death event in their surviving children.

A Child's Death and Reactions Outside the Family

A final concern touches on the ways in which the wider social network deals with the death of children and with the family members in which a child's death has occurred. Death, in all of its aspects, touches a sensitive nerve in many adults. The death of a child has a particular poignancy in focusing the issue of mortality. A child's death will often precipitate anxieties and fears in other adults. These persons will attempt to manage their anxieties and fears by denial and avoidance. This defensive posture presents difficulties for bereaved family members. At the very time in which they need the presence and support of other friends, these persons may not be available emotionally to them. This phenomenon occurs in other contexts, such as in widowhood, but the death of a child has a particular way of focusing those anxieties.

Adults may empathize with the sadness and loss experienced by a parent and family, but be unable or inadequate to respond to their perceptions of these feelings. The lack of positive responsiveness and availability of friends to bereaved parents and families is an additional source of burden for the grieving individuals. Not only are they faced with coping with the loss of a child, but also in managing the negative feelings of anger and resentment they feel for those friends and relatives whom they judge to have abandoned them.

Pastoral Initiatives

If one considers the death of children from within these various perspectives, the pastoral worker will be better equipped not only to understand the particular needs of bereaved individuals, but be more creative in planning ways to assist individual family members in coping with the loss of a child. There are some issues which a pastoral worker should keep in mind in assisting family members in this experience of loss.

It is very important that parents and other significant members of the family actualize their loss. This means concretely that opportunities be given to them to speak about the child, to express their feelings, both negative and positive.

Because the work of grief involves a certain emotional withdrawal from the deceased child, pastoral care needs to help to facilitate this process. In some significant ways, pastoral care can provide the environment, time, and space for a family to appropriately grieve the lost child. It is important to communicate the appropriateness of taking this time and doing the work of grieving. A pastor can be helpful in interpreting the "normal" behaviors that are associated with grief. Some parents experience grief for the first time in the death of a child. This may be, for some, the first significant death they have had to grieve. It is important that their experiences of grief be legitimated. This means helping them to know that their reactions to their child's death are normal and appropriate.

Also, it is important to assist them to see that there are different ways in which members of the family deal with this loss, and that each individual bereaved member of the family has a right to grieve in his or her own manner. A pastoral care provider can be a dependable source of continuing support for a bereaved family, particularly when other members or other friends or relatives may not be able to be the kind of support that the family needs.

Finally, a pastoral care worker can be a useful source of referral for professional treatment of those individual members of the family whose grief responses indicate pathology. In those exceptional situations, a pastoral care worker who has been of ongoing support to the family during its crisis can be a useful point of connection to appropriate professional care.

Because other parents' experiences of loss are important sources of connection, self-help groups of bereaved parents can be of assistance to a family in crisis. Local chapters of *Compassionate Friends* offer immediate and personal support for parents who have lost a child. These groups tend not only to be supportive to parents during the period of early bereavement, but are effective bridges to a future in a world forever impoverished because of the death of a child.

D. Klass, *Parental grief: solace and resolution* (New York: Springer Publishing Company, 1988). T.A. Rando, ed. *Parental loss of a child* (Champaign, IL.: Research Press Company, 1986). W.J. Smith, *Dying in the human life cycle: psychological, biomedical, and social perspectives* (New York: Holt, Rinehart, and Winston, 1985).

WALTER J. SMITH, S.J.

CHILDREN, EUCHARIST AND

We are historically far enough removed from a mentality that children are merely adults in miniature. Studies in the social sciences, especially child psychology, educational theory and method, and the sociology of the family and childhood, enable us to minister to children as Jesus did. "And he took them in his arms and blessed them laying his hands upon them" (Mk 10:16). The gospel heritage also indicates that all who come to the table must learn a sense of childhood. "Truly, I say to you, whoever does not receive the kingdom of God like a child shall not enter it" (Mk 10:15). Three items are important in dealing with children and eucharist. We ask: what children are we talking about and what is the context of their lives? Secondly, we address the eucharist celebrated by children. This includes an assembly of children alone or with adults present. Finally we draw out one pastoral consequence.

1. What Children and What Context

Each local church is entrusted with the pastoral care of its children. We want to be specific about what children we are dealing with. First, they are pre-adolescent. Secondly, their situations may vary widely. Some children are baptized as infants and their faith is nurtured by a dedicated parent or parents. These children will be confirmed later and then will come to the table to complete their initiation. "The sacraments of baptism, confirmation, and the most holy eucharist are so interrelated that they are required for full Christian initiation" (C.I.C., can. 842, 2). (It is important to note that the legal and educational praxis continue to be in conflict. The former reaffirms the classical shape of baptism, confirmation and eucharist. The latter continues to place communion before confirmation.)

Other children are baptized without family catechesis. These children need the involvement of baptismal sponsors, parish members, pastors, catechists and other children in order to assist these uncatechized children in their faith development and to assure readiness for communion. Still other children, neither baptized in their infancy nor nurtured in faith, become catechumens and await communion as the climax of their initiation (See R.C.I.A., 252-330). This may sometimes involve adolescent and adult family members in the same conversion process or it may not. Thus there is need to clarify what children we are talking about in each instance.

In addition, children's home environments are also a factor in their readiness to celebrate the eucharist. This includes the cultural context rooted in their ethnic and racial heritage, the kinds of bonding children have experienced, and where these children are on the economic spectrum running from affluence to poverty. Their ability to celebrate the eucharist can be influenced by their ability to be attentive, how well they have developed their imagination, whether they are nutritionally healthy or malnourished, and whether they are cared for in safety or are the victims of abuse.

A final, crucial factor is the assembly of adults in the midst of whom children learn and live out their Christian lives. Is this assembly open to children, receptive to them and their needs? Is it willing to take responsibility for them? Is this assembly able and willing to be involved with children from the time of their baptism until such time as they are communicated? Certainly no assembly is, or will be, perfect or ideal. Yet each assembly carries responsibility for witnessing its faith, holding out a sense of hope and expressing its love for its children.

2. Children and Eucharist

Pre-adolescent children, including those physically, mentally and environmentally disabled, are the concern of each assembly. The *Directory for Masses with Children* recognizes that children live in circumstances that do not favor their spiritual progress (Directory, 1). But it acknowledges that children are capable of celebrating eucharist. This is especially true when the words and signs of the liturgy are adapted. This does not mean that liturgy is trivialized or childish in its celebration. What it does mean is that pastoral care and liturgical action draw out children in their openness to mystery, the numinous and the mystical as well as the incarnational stories and images of God found in the Bible (Directory, 2-6). Readiness and formation for eucharistic celebration are helped by how children grow and come to know Christ, each other and by other humanizing experiences. "All who have a part in the formation of children should consult and work together toward one objective: that even if children already have some feeling for God and the things of God, they may also experience, in proportion to their age and personal development, the human values that we present in the eucharistic celebration" (Directory, 9).

This is spelled out further. Children become able to celebrate eucharist by learning community activity. They learn by doing, i.e., by exchanging greetings, by listening to one another, by seeking and granting pardon, by giving thanks, by sharing meals of friendship, by celebrating festive events and by acting out symbolic actions. These kinds of operational values are taught in family circles. Often parents are the first teachers of prayer. In addition, assembly members are a school which teaches by its sense of welcome, its exercise of charity and its manner of celebrating eucharist. A kind of reciprocity exists where the witness of adult belief influences children and where adults benefit by experiencing the part children have within the Christian community (Directory, 16).

When children celebrate eucharist with adults, there are a number of ways in which the children can be enriched. Children, like adults, need to be acknowledged as celebrating members of the assembly. This can be done in the introductory rite immediately after the sign of the cross, in the homily and in the prayer of the faithful. Children can be dismissed in order that they may share the word among themselves while the adults remain to hear the entire number of readings assigned to a particular Sunday. Both the dismissal and the reunion become noticeable to children and adults. Children can also involve themselves in tasks such as presenting the gifts of bread and wine and in song (Directory, 17-18).

When children celebrate eucharist alone or with only a few adults present, there are a number of ways in which they can be actively engaged. Children can ready the liturgical space, decorate it, attend to its visual elements (seating, lighting, art and placement of cross, candles, etc.), and assist in making the space one of ease and hospitality (Directory, 25, 29, 35, 36). There are also a number of ways to involve them in the actual liturgical action. This includes their participation in specific ministries such as reader, cantor, musician, choir member, respondent during the homily, leader of intercession and presenter of the gifts of bread and wine. Adults who join children do not act as monitors, but as co-celebrating members of the assembly (Directory, 20-23). Children, whose attention levels vary among themselves and differ from those of adults, are able to remain engaged in eucharistic action when musical acclamations are used and are suited to their capabilities, when processions at the beginning, at the gospel and at communion are done, when gesturing is developed, and when visual elements are integrated into the principal liturgical actions (Directory, 29-36).

Three adaptations hold the most promise for children celebrating eucharist. The first is the development of lectionaries for children. This allows for a single reading rather than multiple readings. It includes a desire for quality over quantity (Directory, 43-44). The second is the option that an adult, other than the presider, may speak after the gospel in instances when the presider has a hard time adapting to the mentality of children. This means that the preacher, whether the presider or another adult, needs to fashion the homiletic message in such a way that the word shapes the spirit of children. This can include the use of dialogue in the homily (Directory, 24, 48). The third adaptation is the composition of three eucharistic prayers for children. These try to adapt to children without being childish. They recognize the limits of children's attentiveness by including ample spoken or sung acclamations. These responses help foster a sense that the eucharistic prayer is the assembly's prayer of offering and that the nature of the prayer is both dialogical and doxological (Directory, 51). These excellent adaptations for children may eventually teach the entire assembly how to pray well.

The Directory (27, 54) also encourages that eucharist be complemented by meditation, spontaneity and celebrations of the word as well as expanded forms of blessing so that children be helped to encounter Christ readily and joyfully and to stand with him in the presence of his Father. In short, children at eucharist are nurtured in liturgical action and are deepened in other forms of prayer.

3. Pastoral Consequence

No celebration of the eucharist is without its pastoral, missionary consequence. If we develop children's eucharist well, we also want to involve the children in the mission of Christ in the world. Children who celebrate the eucharist, if they learn to use symbols well, will include the full range of God's creation in their celebrations. This calls for assemblies to teach their children to be responsible for the well-being of the earth, its eco-system and its future survival as icon of the holy. Children who celebrate the eucharist in the U.S. and other affluent countries will learn that there are children, in both their own and other countries, who are victims of famine, malnutrition, war and poverty. This calls for assemblies to involve children in justice and peace for other children. Children who celebrate the eucharist in an environment of care and belonging will learn to encounter the paschal mystery in children who are homeless, alone, neglected and abused. This calls for assemblies to engage in advocacy for children and in outreach to the victims of violence. Finally, children who come to the eucharist as people made up of many races, colors, languages and ways of life will learn the true universality of the church and the sacredness of humankind. This calls for assemblies to cherish the many fabric pieces that weave together to become the quilt called church and to work for the ending of racial, language, ethnic and gender prejudice.

Congregation for Divine Worship, *Directory for Masses with Children* (1 November 1973) in *The Sacramentary* (New York: Catholic Book Publishing Company, 1985). Maria Harris, *Teaching and Religious Imagination* (San Francisco: Harper and Row Publishers, 1987).

JOHN J. O'BRIEN, C.P.

CHILDREN, FIRST PENANCE AND

The issue of admitting children to first penance before first eucharist or delaying it until after first eucharist has generated debate on theological, pastoral, catechetical and canonical levels since Vatican II. Two schools of thought formed during the post-conciliar decades: one encouraged the practice of children receiving first communion while allowing some years to elapse before first confession; the other maintained the more familiar practice of first penance before first eucharist.

The conviction of sacramental theologians, the experience of pastors and the research of developmental psychologists as well as insights of confessors, catechists, parents and children led to the practice in the United States and other countries of delaying first penance for two or three years after first eucharist. Since the 1917 Code of Canon Law which was operative through the 1970s did not prescribe the sequence of these sacraments, pastors freely accepted the claim of theologians, religious educators and psychologists that a later admittance than seven years of age to the sacrament of penance would be more beneficial. When children confessed sins in kind and number but failed to perceive the motives of their actions they would inevitably develop a mechanical and formalistic attitude toward both sin and repentance at an early age. Proponents of this position claimed that tendency was avoided in the new practice.

By the early 1970s more than half the parishes in the United States adopted this new practice. Religious educators testified that clearer and more meaningful catechesis for each sacrament was possible when first penance was separated from first communion by two or three years. The delay also had the benefit of avoiding a potentially distressing experience; the child may already be aware of the difference between right and wrong though not yet developed in a sense of either personal sin or the communal dimension of sin. An older child with a more developed notion of a relationship with

God and the beginnings of a sense of responsibility to a social group and interpendence within it showed less fear of individual confession and more understanding, freedom and faith. Thus the proper disposition for the sacrament was more readily demonstrated.

Proponents of the opposite position supporting the reception of first communion after first confession grounded their stance on the principle of protecting the child's right to receive the sacrament of penance. Complaints came to the Holy See from parents who claimed catechists and pastors blocked their children from first penance. Those who wished to retain confession before communion argued that children with the use of reason are denied a right to which the law entitles them when they are refused the sacrament of penance. They are also deprived of an opportunity for development in the Christian sense of penance and conversion as well as the efficaciousness of the sacrament itself. Furthermore, since first penance before first communion had been considered a safeguard and protection for worthy participation in eucharist at least since the beginning of this century, it seemed the pastor's responsibility to judge the child's proper disposition to receive first eucharist without prior sacramental confession was further complicated.

Widespread experimentation with delaying first confession until after first communion provided the context in which the Sacred Congregation for the Clergy issued the General Catechetical Directory and its addendum on "The First Reception of the Sacraments of Penance and Eucharist" (1971). The addendum addressed the "experiments" of permitting children to receive first eucharist without first penance while allowing two or three years between them: "The suitable age for the first reception of [penance and eucharist] is deemed to be that which in the documents of the Church is called the age of discretion." The authority cited for imposing a return to this practice was Pius X's *Quam singulari* (1910) and its principle on the age of admission to first communion which the Sacred Congregation on the Sacraments had used in the decree's conclusion: "The age of discretion, both for first confession and first communion, is the time when a child begins to reason, that is approximately the age of seven years. From that time on the obligation of satisfying the precept of both confession and communion begins." The citing of this principle in the addendum significantly changed the meaning of the original decree. *Quam singulari* never condemned delaying confession until after first communion nor did it make a statement that the age of seven was suitable for first confession. Its intention was that children have access to confession from that appropriate age. The decree only ensured the possibility of confession from the age of discretion; it did not take a position on the suitability, value or propriety of confessing at that age. Pius X was not primarily concerned with children's *obligations* but more with their basic *rights* as baptized Christians. He was convinced that children must not be kept from receiving communion. He assumed the existing discipline of confession before communion but did not make a judgment about the propriety of such a practice. Therefore, to build an argument for retaining the more familiar practice on a cloudy interpretation of the 1910 decree was to base conclusions on a weak foundation which was sure to cause continuing confusion and conflict. And so it happened.

At the International Catechetical Congress held in Rome in September 1971, Cardinal John Wright, prefect for the Congregation of the Clergy, was questioned regarding the status of the addendum. He assured catechists that it did not have the force of law but aimed to offer guidance to national hierarchies. Despite repeated remarks reassuring that stance, the addendum's binding force remained uncertain.

The following year the bishops of the United States surveyed patterns in pastoral practice. Their findings showed that eighty-five percent of the ordinaries agreed that the delay of first penance was more pastorally effective. After the results were presented at the November 1972 meeting of the National Conference of Catholic Bishops, Cardinal John Krol, president of the conference, sent a letter to Wright requesting a two-year extension of the experiment to admit children to first communion before first confession. This request in a sense confused the issue; the desire was not to administer communion before confession but to delay confession until children were better equipped to understand and celebrate the sacrament in faith.

While the American bishops waited for a response to Krol's letter, the Congregation for the Discipline of the Sacraments and the Congregation for the Clergy jointly issued the declaration *Sanctus pontifex* in May 1973. It reaffirmed the addendum's position and mandated the end of all experimentation by the close of that 1972-73 school year. *Quam singulari* was "to be obeyed everywhere and by all." Once again, citing that decree to support the 1973 declaration was an attempt to secure an argument on foundations that simply were not there. Although this document appeared to raise the binding force of the addendum to a new legislative status, pastors and catechists received it as an unreasonable request within the given time frame; they also remained unconvinced by its argumentation. As a result several dioceses soon asserted their pastoral prerogatives and issued their own guidelines.

At their November 1973 meeting the American bishops called for a broad pastoral interpretation so that no impression of obligation to confess before first communion would be given. Around the same time a committee of the Canadian Catholic Conference met in Rome with the two congregations and requested a clarification of *Sanctus pontifex*. The Canadians were assured that the declaration did not impose the obligation of confession before first communion since it was not a decree. Nor did it seek to foster conditions that would keep children from first penance before first communion. Apparently the Roman authorities' desire was to safeguard the child's rights to penance and to ensure adequate catechesis in order to exercise that right.

At this juncture it seemed the controversy was finally approaching a resolution. However, a March 1977 letter from Cardinals John Wright and James Knox further confused the issue. While catechists had been assured that neither the addendum nor the declaration implied legal obligation of penance before first communion, the letter treated both documents as carrying the force of law despite that distinction already made between a declaration and a decree. The letter also referred to *Quam singulari* as assigning the same age for first confession and first communion. Then it concluded that the child had the obligation to receive both sacraments at the appropriate age of seven and in the designated sequence, that is, confession before communion. In point of fact *Quam singulari* made no claim about an obligation to receive the two sacraments in any particular order. Simply listing one sacrament before the other hardly sets up an obligation to receive them in that order. Another erroneous claim on the content of canon 854 was made in the 1977 letter. It claimed the pastor's judgment on proper disposition for first communion could not be made without the child's confession before communion. However, the canon actually stated that the judgment on proper disposition for first communion remained the responsibility of a confessor and the parents. Therefore, the code did not imply that the priest arrives at a judgment only in the confessional.

The confusion generated by this 1977 letter is typical of the tension which characterized this debate since the 1971 publication of the General Catechetical Directory and its addendum. The source of the conflict can be located in the varying interpretations of *Quam singulari*. Then it is no surprise that the bishops of the United States decided to leave the question open in the National Catechetical Directory, *Sharing the Light of Faith* (1979). They did not want to offend the Roman congregations by explicitly stating that children were under no obligation to confess before communion. Nor did the bishops want to imply any sense of obligation whatsoever. So they discreetly steered a middle course. In a similar way, since the Roman authorities wanted neither to acquiesce nor close off exchange, they recommended the insertion of a sentence: "Reception of the sacrament of reconciliation should normally precede first communion." The American bishops incorporated a reworked version: "The Sacrament of Reconciliation normally should be celebrated prior to the reception of first communion." The word "normally" was included to describe the priority of first penance and to respect the fact that it is not always mandated before first eucharist. The recrafting of that final formulation is significant. Its precision preserved continuity with the Roman suggestion while it reduced the practical legal requirements. The short though carefully constructed sentence states that penance should be celebrated before first communion; it does not state that any or all children must receive the sacrament of penance before first communion.

Once more, when an agreeable resolution seemed to be reached, an unexpected intrusion stirred up the issue anew. Two canons in the revised Code of Canon Law (1983) deal directly with preparation of children for first eucharist. Canon 913 secures adequate catechetical and spiritual formation for children before first eucharist. An oblique reference to the sacrament of penance appears in canon 914 which deals with the responsibilities of parents, those who take their place, as well as pastors to provide preparation for children of the appropriate age to receive eucharist "preceded by sacramental confession." The insertion of this phrase may appear problematic only if it is not interpreted in its text and context (c. 17).

A way into these canons is to pose the pastoral question: can a child who does not wish to approach first penance be denied first communion? The law yields a negative response. Canon 913 deals with the minimal prerequisites for a child's admittance to first eucharist ("sufficient knowledge and careful preparation so as to understand the mystery of Christ according to their capacity" and an ability to "receive the Body of the Lord with faith and devotion") but there is no indication that "careful preparation" includes sacramental confession. Such an addition would be expected if it were the code's intent to establish confession as one among the minimal requirements for licit admission to first eucharist.

Canon 914 ensures provisions for catechesis before first eucharist and advises pastors to limit admittance to those sufficiently prepared. Since these requirements are not directed to children but to parents and pastors, the children themselves are not explicitly the subject of an obligation to confess before making first communion. Children then are similarly bound by canon 916 as adult Catholics are: confession before communion is normally required in the case of anyone conscious of grave sin unless serious reason dictates otherwise. Therefore, this applies only to children who are aware of grave sin and thus helps to clarify canon 913. Furthermore, the confessing of venial sins was never a legal requirement but a recommendation; no mention is made of it in the context of first communion (can. 988.2). Freedom and a reverent disposition are required for the proper reception of a sacrament; then no one should be forced to receive a sacrament. Therefore, if a child does not wish to receive the sacrament of penance, especially when the parents also feel the child needs some time, a pastor cannot asssume on this basis alone that the child is not ready for first communion. The right to receive first communion cannot be denied to children solely because they do not choose to approach the sacrament of penance.

The law then suggests that the requirement of penance before first communion is not absolute. As many exceptions as there might be, it would be problematic to set up the experiment of the post-conciliar years as a general policy. That practice of penance after first eucharist would effectively deny or restrict the child's access to the sacrament of penance. Although parents and pastors are obligated by law to provide catechesis on penance before the child's first communion, the choice of actually going to the sacrament must always be primarily that of the individual child with respect to the views of the parents (can. 226.2).

The controversy generated from the debate of admitting children to first penance before first eucharist or delaying it until afterwards continues to influence not only the practice of the reception of the sacrament of penance but also the theological and catechetical understanding of the sacraments of initiation. The promulgation and implementation of the Rite of Christian Initiation of Adults (R.C.I.A.) has restored the integral unity and proper sequence of the sacraments of initiation. If the underlying significance of these sacraments is to realize an initial union with Christ, the practice of first penance prior to first eucharist is to claim the reactualization of a union with Christ for a small child who has not yet realized the fullness of the initial union in baptism, confirmation and eucharist. The entry of first penance prior to the completion of that sequence ruptures that unity and alters the processive flow of the sacraments of initiation. This theological and pastoral dilemma calls for a re-examination of the current pastoral practice of admitting young children to first penance before first eucharist.

Linda Gaupin, "'Let Those Who Have Faith Not Be Hasty:' Penance and Children," in *Reconciliation: The Continuing Agenda*, ed. Robert J. Kennedy (Collegeville, Minn.: Liturgical Press, 1987): 219-238. John M. Huels, *Disputed Questions in the Liturgy Today* (Chicago: Liturgy Training Publications, 1988), 67-74. *Liturgy Documentary Series 7: Penance and Reconciliation in the Church* (Washington, D.C.: U.S.C.C., 1986). Norbert Mette, "Children's Confession—A Plea for a Child-centered practice of Penance and Reconciliation," trans. Graham Harrison, *The Rate of Confession, Concilium* 190, eds. Mary Collins and David Power (Edinburgh: T. & T. Clark, 1987), 64-73. James M. Provost, "The Reception of First Penance," *Jurist* 47 (1987): 294-340. Thomas F. Sullivan, "The Directory and First Confession," *Living Light* 16 (1979): 192-208.

DANIEL P. GRIGASSY, O.F.M.

CHILDREN, LITURGIES FOR

A child's first sacramental experience-the first experience of God even before birth—is in the loving passion and tenderness, the security and care, the prayer and respect, the playing and joking voices of a man and a woman devoted to each other and to their offspring in Christian marriage. The climate of trust in the marital covenant spills over into a welcoming, faith-nurturing, peace-and-justicebuilding, parent-child bond: the household church (*oikos tou Xristou* [see 1 Cor 1:16; Heb 3:6], *ecclesia domestica*).

The life-bearing and life-sustaining bond between mother and child—the privileged, totally giving, totally receiving symbiosis that leads to successful individuation—flows from the sacrament of marriage.

When the marital covenant is weak or absent or when the parent-child bond is weak or absent, God still breaks through with healing love, strength, joy, peace, and community. Sin and death impede human action but not God's sacramental action.

Introduction

Why Liturgies for Children? Jesus said, "Let the children come to me, do not stop them; the reign of God belongs to such as these" (Mk 10:14). For this reason, the universal church (ecumenical: "household of the world"[see Rom 10:18; Ps 19:4]), diocesan church ("local household"), and parish church presume with care and confidence to celebrate the love of God mirrored in individual household churches—and to pray for God's healing and to reach out with help when households are broken—in liturgies for and with children.

When the church on any scale decides to welcome children into sacramental worship, we say to God, "We are open to your Holy Spirit in these children, we are willing to receive your truth through them, and we take responsibility for nurturing them in the faith of your son, our Lord, Jesus Christ." In every liturgy, as the source and summit of life—whether for children or adults—God invites the church to celebrate the love of God that we receive in creation and redemption through Jesus Christ, to participate in the healing and comforting work of the Spirit, and to reach out as instruments in building communities of peace and justice that mark the coming of God's reign (S.C., 5-13).

General Requirements of Liturgies for Children. The first and most important requirement of liturgy for children is that it be good liturgy, that it fulfill the requirements of all liturgy, which are outlined in S.C., *General Instruction of the Roman Missal* (G.I.R.M.), fourth

edition of 1975, *Music in Catholic Worship* (M.C.W.), promulgated in 1972 and revised in 1983, *Liturgical Music Today* (L.M.T.), 1982, *Environment and Art in Catholic Worship*(E.A.C.W.), 1978, and in such fine studies as *Elements of Rite: A Handbook of Liturgical Style* by Aidan Kavanagh (New York: Pueblo Publishing Company, 1982), *Strong, Loving and Wise: Presiding in Liturgy* by Robert W. Hovda (Washington: The Liturgical Conference, 1976), *Liturgy with Style and Grace* by Gabe Huck, second edition (Chicago: Liturgy Training Publications, 1984), and *Liturgy Made Simple* by Mark Searle (Collegeville: The Liturgical Press, 1981). "The church earnestly desires that all the faithful be led to that full, conscious, and active participation in liturgical celebrations-.... Such participation by the Christian people as 'a chosen race, a royal priesthood, a holy nation, God's own people' (1 Pet 2:9) is their right and duty by reason of their baptism" (S.C., 14). These requirements for all good liturgy apply with double force for children.

But Jesus also "put his arms around the children and blessed them" (Mk 10:16). Adaptation to the needs, interests and capacities of children is also important. "With zeal and patience pastors must promote the liturgical instruction of the faithful and also their active participation in the liturgy both internally and externally, taking into account their age and condition, their way of life, and their stage of religious development" (S.C., 19).

The *Directory of Masses with Children* (D.M.C.) of 1973 is a deliberate effort by the Vatican to follow the adaptive example of Jesus and the mandate of the Second Vatican Council. Edward Matthews, in *Celebrating Mass with Children: A Commentary on the Directory of Masses with Children*, discusses the elements of adaptation and education proposed by the D.M.C.. Before any other catechetical or educational consideration, however, the D.M.C. must be understood clearly: "Even in the case of children, the liturgy itself always exerts its own inherent power to instruct" (D.M.C., 13). There are additional ways to introduce children into full participation in sacramental worship. The sections on sacraments and liturgy in the *General Catechetical Directory* of 1971 and *Sharing the Light of Faith: National Catechetical Directory for Catholics of the United States* of 1979 shed helpful light on cognitive, informational topics. In *To Dance with God: Family Ritual and Community Celebration* (New York: Paulist Press, 1986), Gertrud Mueller Nelson discusses how sacramental formation in the household church and in the parish church interconnect, especially around the liturgical calendar. And in *Teaching and Religious Imagination: An Essay in the Theology of Teaching* (San Francisco: Harper and Row, 1987), Maria Harris offers rich pedagogical insight into the dreams, hopes, visions and awe that lie at the core of the sacramental life of children and adults.

Sunday Eucharist

For Children. Masses for children—or what in the United States used to be called "Family Masses"—are not appropriate for the Sunday or weekend celebration but belong during the week (D.M.C., 20). Rather, the weekend eucharistic liturgy is for the whole diocese, the entire parish, the full assembly (S.C., 26, 42). It is public and inclusive, a dynamic coordination of orders: catechumens, servers, penitents, deacons, the newly baptized, veteran members, presbyters and bishops. And it addresses itself primarily to the assembly's complete ministry, the world (Kavanagh, *Elements*, 45-46).

The tradition of the Lord's Day functions as the ongoing and deepening plunge of *all* baptized persons "into the paschal mystery of Christ: they died with him, are buried with him, and rise with him; they receive the spirit of adoption as children 'in which we cry: Abba, Father' (Rom 8:15), and thus become true adorers whom the Father seeks. In like manner, as often as they eat the supper of the Lord they proclaim the death of the Lord until he comes" (S.C., 6).

Sunday eucharist is not just for God's chronological children. It is for all God's children: the child in everyone.

With Children. Usually both adults and children benefit from each other's presence in the Sunday assembly. Children learn from the example of adults who are committed to the faith, and adults are reminded by the presence of children of the attitude needed to be a true follower of Jesus Christ. Infants and children who have not yet received full initiation into the church through baptism, confirmation and eucharist, however, may best have their own separate places for child care or for catechumenal celebrations of the word according to the capacity and age of the individual. The catechetical aid, *Sunday*, by Christiane Brusselmans, Paule Freeburg, Edward Matthews, Monique Piret, and Christopher Walker, published in several countries in several languages, is useful for this need. These infants and children may be brought in to join the rest of the assembly for the final blessing and dismissal (D.M.C., 16).

Whenever children are present in a Sunday assembly that includes a majority of adults, even though the celebration is directed primarily to those adults, great care must be taken that the children do not feel neglected. There are several things that can help them feel welcome; if they can participate in the action of the assembly, they will feel more at home. Can they see the action of the sacred celebration? (D.M.C., 35) Can they sense simple dignity, grace, a certain self-discipline, some order and a lot of respect? (D.M.C., 33) Can they pray with the assembly? Can they participate in special dialogues? Can they sing acclamations, hymns, responses and psalms? (D.M.C., 30). Can they hear and understand the proclamation of the word? Can they follow the gestures of the sign of the cross, invitation, greeting, blessings, epiclesis, sign of peace and observe the movement of processions, communion, and dismissal? (D.M.C., 34). Can they smell the incense, Easter lilies, Christmas trees, aromatic chrism, wine, burning beeswax, or even the distinctive scent of a familiar room? Can they hear sounds that convey sacred celebration: melodies, instrumental music, bells, tones of voice, censer chains, water, applause or special familiar words? (D.M.C., 30-32). Can they use silences constructively? (D.M.C., 37, 46). Can they be comfortable in the furniture? Can they feel the touch of blessings and greetings?

Can the presider address respectful, caring words of welcome to children at the beginning of a Sunday Mass at which they are present, confirming their dignity and calling their attention to things for which they should listen or watch? Can the homilist spend a minute summarizing the message of God's word in language directed specifically to the children present? Before the final blessing and dismissal, can the presider in a sentence or two invite the children to go forth to the ministry of evangelizing the world in their own special way?

On the occasion of the gospel reading from Lk 17:11-19, the story of the healing of the ten lepers, one homilist included ten children in the entrance procession. During the proclamation of the gospel, one by one the children turned away from the lectern and silently walked out of the assembly. After the proclamation was completed, one boy turned back again toward the lectern and shouted at the top of his voice from the back of the church, "My God, I forgot. Thanks." Neither children nor adults missed the point of the story. And it added only three seconds to the length of the cele-

bration. This—along with bringing forward wine, water and bread for the preparation of gifts, passing out palms, music, bulletins, and candles, or singing a song for the Mass—is the kind of task children can perform for the benefit of all (D.M.C., 18).

Unless the homilist addresses children directly in the homily, if only for a sentence or two, it is appropriate—even if the children are fully initiated into the church through baptism, confirmation, and eucharist—to celebrate the word "in a separate but not too distant room. Then, before the eucharistic liturgy begins, the children are led back to the place where the adults have meanwhile celebrated their own liturgy of the word" (D.M.C., 17: see also 24).

The "separate but not too distant room" can be made into a place for sacred celebration with inviting furniture, a candle, lectionary, freedom from distractions, flowers, or appropriate works of art. The celebration may include dismissal from the larger assembly after the opening prayer, a somewhat orderly walk to the room, regrouping prayer, sung acclamation, proclamation of one or two (always the gospel) readings, drama or mime, a homily of story sharing in which the form and content suit both the word proclaimed and the capacity of the children, a profession of faith, and general intercessions. Some parishes divide age levels for these celebrations. Some age levels find a carpeted floor serves best for sitting. Some parishes have timekeepers; others have intercom systems to get fully initiated children back with the larger community in time for the eucharistic prayer. In some parishes, catechetical aids are handed out for the celebration of the word, while in others, the minister of the word may hand them out to the child or guardian after Mass for use in the home or classroom later.

Adaptations of lectionary texts for

proclamation with children should be faithful to original biblical languages, consistent with central doctrinal traditions, respectful of the vocabulary and cognitive ability of the age group, and sensitive to the emotional needs of children for self-esteem.

"Avoiding any childish style of speech" (D.M.C., 23) is one reason that for proclamation with children, some highly respected sacramental catechists like Mary Perkins Ryan and Mary Reed Newland favor the use of a good, standard lectionary for adults rather than adaptations for children. They are concerned lest a dilution of the important biblical images and church traditions result not only in a loss of verbal challenge for the children but also in a waste of liturgical and biblical catechetical opportunity. "How sad," they might say, "to miss a chance with four-year-olds to homilize about the simple, powerful transformations in nature, for example, if you must use the phrase 'come to life' rather than the word 'resurrection,' because the latter has too many syllables."

Weekday Eucharist

"Weekday Mass in which children participate can certainly be celebrated with greater effect and less danger of boredom if it does not take place every day (for example, in boarding schools). Moreover, preparation can be more careful if there is a longer interval between diverse celebrations" (D.M.C., 27). Weekday eucharistic celebrations with children in which only a few adults participate (D.M.C., 20-54) should not detract from the Sunday parish celebration. Lectionary readings for a subsequent Sunday are not to be anticipated on a weekday. Weekday Masses can undermine a child's or teenager's motivation for the parish Sunday liturgy. The reason is that now more emphasis is placed on careful preparation for the celebration (D.M.C., 29) and on full participation in the celebration (D.M.C., 22-24). "Sometimes it will be preferable to have common prayer, to which the children may contribute spontaneously, or else a common meditation, or a celebration of the word of God. These are ways of continuing the eucharistic celebrations already held and of leading to a deeper participation in subsequent celebrations" (D.M.C., 27).

Singing and Music. "Singing must be given great importance in all celebrations, but it is to be especially encouraged in every way for Masses celebrated with children, in view of their special affinity for music. The culture of various peoples and the capabilities of the children present should be taken into account" (D.M.C., 30).

Despite immense strides in liturgical music for children over the past 30 years, there is still far to go. Latin plainsong gave way to the vernacular first in the form of 19th-century romantic, subjective, sentimental hymns. Children of the late 20th century seldom found themselves at home here. Then, in response to M.C.W. and L.M.T. of the United States Catholic Conference, came some liturgically stronger works (in antiphonal, responsorial, acclamatory, and litanic forms) but musically uninspired, this time in a general Broadway or "pop" style. "Pop" is the widest-spread trend in the liturgical music industry in the United States today. Spiritually hungry children are still asked to sing weak words to poor melodies.

Liturgical music in folk idioms (like jazz, ballad, American spiritual, dance and other forms) rendered authentically with evocative, rhythmic, improvisational and narrative forms sometimes breathes fresh air into children's liturgies. Occasionally children are heard to sing even the old sacred classics: the Renaissance masterpieces of Palestrina, Praetorius, or Byrd; the baroque works of Rome's Vivaldi, Saxony and London's Handel, and Germany's Bach; the classical marvels of Mozart; romanticism's later Beethoven with his Ninth Symphony's choral finale and its setting for Schiller's "Ode to Joy"—have you heard children sing that?—or a Schubert with his "Ave Maria."

In 20th-century music, although the "classicism" of Stravinsky differs from that of Mozart, for example, the rational approach remains. It is this *rationality and purity in good taste* of the classical traditions, along with the commitment of many composers like Bartok, Britten, Copland, Hovhaness, Ives, Kodaly, Orff, Rutter, Gelineau and those at Taize to the *bodily element, passion, feeling*—as opposed to sentimentality—that is lacking in much contemporary liturgical music. Some rock has helped free children for this important bodily aspect of music.

The great choral settings of the Jewish, Anglican, Lutheran, Methodist, Orthodox, Roman and Shaker traditions, the great vocal and instrumental works of the classical and folk traditions yesterday and today—this great music might well replace much of what is currently used in liturgies for children.

Within limits, perhaps because they have less to unlearn, children can sing harmonically and rhythmically "more difficult" music than most adults can. There is a fine line between great music for adults and great music for children but a giant chasm between great music and poor music.

Point: there are three qualities needed in liturgical music for children. First, liturgies for children need fine music with roots in the classical and folk traditions of the past and present. Second, liturgies for children need liturgical music—acclamations, litanies, psalms, responses, *Gloria, Alleluia, Credo, Sanctus, Amen, Agnus Dei* (D.M.C., 31), and Lord's Prayer—rendered in a manner appropriate to the liturgy. Third, a strong, developmental musical repertoire is needed—a pedagogical sequence with inner coherence that helps children build lasting interest, skill, and reward.

Teachers and directors of liturgical music for children who are better trained in all three of these areas are much needed. Even harder to find is the great contemporary composer with skills in these three areas. Noteworthy exceptions include composers in the style of Jerome Coller, Bernadette Farrell, the early Bernard Huijbers, Augusta Thomas, and David Wilcox.

Children Need an Expanded Narthex. Even more than adults, children need an intermediate space to gather en route to the work and play of sacramental worship and, after the dismissal, en route to the work and play of the evangelization of the world. The direct transition from assembly to world is too abrupt. A chance to meet, greet, inquire, share, and become the body of Christ informally enhances the sense of assembly at liturgy. A chance for peers to reinforce each other in the evangelizing task for which members of the body are sent forth gives the liturgical experience a stronger link with daily life.

Initiation

Of Infants. With a few brief, local exceptions, Christians always have and always will baptize infants. It is unlikely that John the Baptist imposed age restrictions in his ministry, that Jesus did not welcome children or place them at the center of the reign of God (Mk 9:33-37; 10:13-16; Mt 18:1-6; Lk 9:46-48; 18:15-17), that the apostles ignored the infants when they baptized entire households (Acts 2:37-39).

Christians hold up children as models of faith for all people approaching baptism: "Rid yourselves of all malice and all deceit, insincerity, envy, and all slander; like newborn infants, long for pure spiritual milk so that through it you may grow into salvation, for you have tasted that the Lord is good" (1 Pet 2:1-3).

Vatican II called for the revision of the rite of confirmation "in order that the intimate connection of this sacrament with the whole of Christian initiation may stand out more clearly" (S.C., 71). According to the revised rite of confirmation, 11, promulgated in 1971, the confirmation of those baptized as infants is to be *postponed* until the age of reason. The word "postponed" recalls the original practice in the Roman church of confirming immediately after baptism. In the 1983 *Code of Canon Law,* canon 891 likewise prescribes "the age of discretion," that is, about seven years of age, as the age of confirmation. Canon 889 does not require that a confirmand have the use of reason. Rather, "if they have the use of reason, they must be suitably instructed, properly disposed, and able to renew their baptismal promises." The rite of confirmation, 13, states that Christian initiation "reaches its culmination in the communion of the body and blood of Christ. The newly confirmed should therefore participate in the eucharist which completes their Christian initiation." The modal verb in the last sentence is "should," not "must." This means that confirmation is optimally conferred on children at about the age of seven during the eucharist at which they also receive first communion.

Since 1910, the practice in most dioceses and parishes of the United States has been to change confirmation from a sacrament of initiation to a sacrament of transition into adulthood, conferring it on teenagers outside its traditional order several years *after* first communion. Restoring the traditional order of the sacraments of initiation—baptism, confirmation, eucharist—accords with scripture, the patristic writings, Vatican II, the rite of confirmation itself, canon law, the clear witness of the "Rite of Christian Initiation of Adults" (R.C.I.A.), liturgical and sacramental theology and pastoral practice in Roman Catholic churches in many other countries and in all Orthodox churches. Restoring this order is discussed with pastoral examples at the diocesan

and parish level in *When Should We Confirm? The Order of Initiation*, edited by James A. Wilde (Chicago: Liturgy Training Publications, 1989).

Of Children of Catechetical Age. The section of R.C.I.A. entitled "Christian Initiation of Children Who Have Reached Catechetical Age" (252-330) adapts the order for adults to the needs and capacities of children between the ages of about seven and fifteen. The steps include: acceptance into the order of catechumens, election or enrollment of names (optional), penitential rites (scrutinies), and sacraments of initiation.

Baptism, confirmation, and eucharist are to be conferred in that order at one, single celebration of the eucharist, "preferably at the Easter vigil or on a Sunday, the day that the church devotes to the remembrance of Christ's resurrection" (see *Rite of Baptism for Children*, Introduction, 9; R.C.I.A., 304).

The North American Forum on the Catechumenate (Forum) sponsors consultations and institutes on the order of Christian initiation of children, having discovered that the need is far greater than formerly thought. The sacramental, catechetical, spiritual, ritual, and pastoral observations of Forum are available in *Catechumenate: A Journal of Christian Initiation*, 11 (March 1989). See also the broad discussion in *Issues in the Christian Initiation of Children*, edited by Kathy Brown and Frank C. Sokol (Chicago: Liturgy Training Publications, 1989).

Reconciliation

The experience of reconciliation begins early in the life of a child. The acknowledgment and celebration of reconciliation early within the household church can strongly and positively affect the deep experience of self-respect and respect for others throughout a person's life. The experience of God's forgiveness, a function of God's mercy, can subtly, powerfully, and permanently change the life of a child or adult. The parable of the prodigal son and the even more prodigal father (Lk 15:3-32) needs to be acted out by children in the domestic and parish church. Growth in appreciating reconciliation—intimately linked with esteem—is gradual. This growth reaches several high points in life, one of which is usually during the teen years. In fact, it may be that the fuller implications of the sacrament of reconciliation are best drawn in those years—seldom earlier.

Canon 914 makes some good pastoral points: "It is the responsibility, in the first place, of parents and those who take the place of parents as well as of the pastor to see that children who have reached the use of reason are correctly prepared and are nourished by the divine food as early as possible, preceded by sacramental confession; it is also for the pastor to be vigilant lest any children come to the Holy Banquet who have not reached the use of reason or whom he judges are not sufficiently disposed."

With canons 213, 226, 843, 913, and 914 (above), we can conclude that obligations are imposed on parents, guardians and pastors to prepare a child according to her or his capacity. If a child does not wish to approach the sacrament of reconciliation, that does not by itself constitute grounds to deny her or him the right to receive first communion. "The requirement of reconciliation before first communion is not absolute; it can admit of exceptions" (John M. Huels, "First Confession," *Disputed Questions in the Liturgy Today*, Chicago: Liturgy Training Publications, 1988). The right and obligation of parents and pastors to catechize children about God's love and willingness to forgive is always the first and last word.

Liturgies of Morning and Evening Prayer for Children

Adaptations of the liturgy of the hours for children are greatly needed in the domestic churches, parish churches, and church schools. Frequently it may be better for both children and adults to celebrate these liturgies of the word rather than liturgies of the eucharist during the week (D.M.C., 27). The same creative principles of art, environment and music apply to morning and evening prayer. Devotion to the real presence of Christ in the word, in the assembly, and in the ministers is there. The treasures of the lectionary, the patristic and other writings, and the church calendar with its feasts, fasts, seasons, cycles, saints and Sundays are opened amply. Simplicity and progressive solemnity remain options (D.M.C., 14).

Vatican II envisioned the liturgies of morning and evening prayer as celebrations for the whole church (S.C., 83-101). With hymns, psalms, readings, canticles, prayers, and blessings, these celebrations can open children to a rich tradition of liturgical prayer. They complement and enhance the Sunday eucharist. And they allow the heroes and heroines of the sanctoral cycle to be powerful sources of encouragement in the faith for children, if presented in an emotionally healthy way. The faith of martyrs, the dedication of Mother Cabrini, the generosity of Vincent de Paul, the consuming love in John Bosco, or the missionary zeal of Francis Xavier can challenge children to begin creating the work of art that is their own life.

Morning and evening prayer can ring out the spirit of high seasons like Lent/Triduum/Eastertime or Advent/Christmas/Epiphany just as effectively as liturgies of the eucharist can. All these liturgies point joyfully to the central paschal mystery of Christ. The liturgies of eucharist, morning prayer and evening prayer can constructively and powerfully link children in the domestic church, school, parish church, cathedral church, or universal church together through the liturgical calendar.

Pastoral Liturgical Possibilities for Children in the Future

A few of the many areas of emerging practice under current discussion and that may point toward the future are:

Adaptation of the Catechumenate for Infants. In household churches strong in Christian faith, parents may opt for their infant's acceptance into the order of catechumens rather than immediate baptism. Whether for a period of weeks or years, the status of a catechumen as a member of the household of Christ allows for blessings, other suffrages, marriage or burial in the church (National Statutes for the Catechumenate, 8-10).

If and when the faithful and actively practicing Christian parent(s) of an infant or child catechumen request full initiation for her or him, after a suitable time of election and catechesis, the sacraments of baptism-confirmation-eucharist are conferred at a single eucharistic celebration. The triadic unity of the sacraments of initiation is acknowledged, therefore, for infants also. Baptism-confirmation-eucharist constitute a coherent whole according to the most ancient and pervasive Christian traditions. Just as the Father, Son, and Holy Spirit are one, so are baptism-confirmation-eucharist one, and they are celebrated as one, any time between birth and death. (Communion by intinction works well for infants and toddlers.)

Sacrament of Reconciliation for Teenagers. Catechesis and celebration of reconciliation begins in the household church already for infants. When household members esteem one another, forgive one another, acknowledging weakness and sin in everyone but giving intensely to help heal that brokenness, the stage is set for happy experiences of wholeness and reconciliation. These directly prepare for experiences of sacramental reconciliation.

Such preparation has not worked effectively when first confession before first communion at about age seven meant that the quality and intensity of catechesis for that sacrament relaxed afterward. People in mid-life were catechetically arrested at age seven regarding reconciliation, and their attitudes and words showed it. Adults confessed sins the way they were taught in the second grade, their social consciousness was stunted, or they stopped availing themselves of the sacrament entirely. The path leading to adult sacramental reconciliation could well be lengthened—a lengthening accompanied by household-church, peer-church, and parish-church catechesis, awareness raising, and experience. Delay without suitable catechesis, social consciousness expansion, and experience serves no one. But if there is a sacrament that marks the adult assumption of responsibility for oneself and others, it is reconciliation, which may best occur first in the late teens.

Point: Jesus Christ and the church are for sinners who want to be one with God, themselves, and their neighbor. All Christians are children growing in love and union fractions becoming integers. The child in us all cries out to experience, acknowledge, and celebrate this wholeness, this communion.

Mary Ann Simcoe, ed. *The Liturgy Documents: A Parish Resource,* rev. ed. (Chicago: Liturgy Training Publications, 1985), esp. *Directory for Masses with Children.* National Conference of Catholic Bishops, *Sharing the Light of Faith: National Catechetical Directory for Catholics of the United States* (Washington: United States Catholic Conference, 1979). Elizabeth McMahon Jeep, *The Welcome Table: Planning Masses with Children* (Chicago: Liturgy Training Publications, 1982). Aidan Kavanagh, *Elements of Rite: A Handbook of Liturgical Style* (New York: Pueblo Publishing Company, 1982). Edward Matthews, *Celebrating Mass with Children: A Commentary on the Directory of Masses with Children* (Glasgow: Wm. Collins Sons and Co. Ltd., 1975). Gertrude Mueller Nelson, *To Dance with God: Family Ritual and Community Celebration* (New York: Paulist Press, 1986).

JAMES A. WILDE

CHRIST, FEASTS OF

Vatican II reminds us that the Lord's Day, the "eighth day of the week" which commemorates Christ's Resurrection as the beginning of the New Creation, is "the original feast day" of Christ (S.C., 106).

The reforms of that same council directed the church's focus of attention to those feasts of Christ in which the Christian community celebrates the central mysteries of salvation (S.C., 108). Thus feasts of "idea" (J. Jungmann), such as *Corpus Christi*, are clearly subordinated to celebrations of the principal saving "events."

The primary feast of Christ is Easter, celebrated in a cycle which moves from Palm Sunday to Pentecost Sunday. Next to Easter in importance is the celebration of Christmas, commemorated in a cycle which goes from Christmas Eve to the Feast of the Baptism of Our Lord.

The Easter Cycle

Palm Sunday. Christ's entrance into Jerusalem amidst acclamation expresses his own determination to bring his message to the center of Jewish faith and authority for a final confrontation. The entrance is thus a provocative one, but, more deeply, it is the expression of Christ's passionate longing that Jerusalem open itself to his message. His journey up to Jerusalem now becomes the way to the cross where acclamation gives way to desertion and jeers. In this liturgy the Church community carries the palm branches as a sign of its readiness to accompany Christ as he enters upon his Pasch.

Holy Thursday. The Pasch of the Lord begins with the Last Supper and the institution of the Holy Eucharist. On the night he was betrayed Christ affirmed the relation between his imminent death and the blessings of the Kingdom (Christ's primary symbol for salvation) which during his ministry had been mediated in a principal way to his disciples and others through table-fellowship with him. He thus showed his trust that God's promised salvation would occur not simply despite but rather by means of his self-giving on the cross into the hands of sinners and into the hands of his Father. On Holy Thursday the complete freedom of Christ's self-offering comes to expression, as well as its character as service (expressed in the washing of the feet). Israel's primal themes of exodus and covenant, blessing and commemoration provide the interpretive framework for Christ's words and actions at his Last Supper. In the light of Christ's Pasch the liturgy views the great saving events of Israel's history as "types" which receive their definitive fulfillment in Christ's passover. Indeed, while differing in their chronology, both the Synoptics and John indicate that Christ's last meal possessed characteristics of the Jewish Passover. Christ's command, "do this in memory of me," establishes the eucharistic action as the church's unbloody sacrifice of praise which sacramentally re-presents Christ's self-offer as the means of continued participation in the blessings of the Kingdom and in the New Covenant wrought by the Lord's life, death and resurrection.

Good Friday. The liturgy of Good Friday in its overall simplicity of word and gesture draws the Christian community into reverent and grateful relationship to the mystery of the cross. While the last words of Christ differ according to the different evangelists and reflect each one's religious and theological concerns, they also express the various dimensions of the cross as saving-event. Christ dies stripped of his habitual experience of God yet calls out to that same God (Mark). He dies with forgiveness in his heart for those crucifying him (Luke), so different from some OT voices which cried out for the vindication of the just at the expense of their persecutors. Finally, his death is the consummation of his life because both were pure *diakonia* in full commitment to God's saving will (John). On the cross Christ reconciles sinners to God as in his body he represents three things: the destructiveness of sin, his own faithful and forgiving love for sinners as the historical expression of the Father's love, and the meeting of both, in which sin is no match for that love when they meet head on (2 Cor 5:21). Christ is compassionate priest, free victim and gracious offering: he offers himself to God fully and to sinners fully and, as the very incarnation of God's love for sinners *in extremis*, absorbs in himself the destructiveness of their sin.

Easter Vigil and Easter Sunday. Easter and Good Friday may not be exaggeratedly contrasted as if on the cross God abandons Christ who supposedly bears the full brunt of God's wrath in the place of sinners, while at Easter God becomes reconciled to Christ and sinners. More faithfully to the NT it can be said that on the cross Christ died into the resurrection (K. Rahner). Christ's death and resurrection are distinct events but, for all that, inseparable. The unity of life and intention bonding Christ and his Father, which became hidden from Christ on the cross, brought him through his suffering and death into the depths of God's life, filling him with God's glory. That glorification, in turn, rendered him, in the Spirit, present in a wholly new way to the world. In and through the church, the visible continuation of his presence, the Risen Lord is redemptively involved in all the joys and the numberless crucifixions of ongoing human history.

In the Easter event a double movement occurs: Christ's going to the Father in the Spirit and a coming to his own in a new way in that same Spirit. Accordingly, his resurrection is bodily in a two-fold way: first, God's Spirit transforms and glorifies all of Christ's personal being and, secondly, that same Spirit, in the raising of Christ, creates a community of witnesses

to that saving event, a community which provides the historical sacramental sign of Christ's victorious presence, viz., the church as the body of Christ. The church has needed many expressions to give witness to the import of Christ's resurrection. Easter, as the definitive arrival of God's reign, is the divine vindication of Christ's message and person in the face of his rejection and death. Inseparably united to the cross, it spells God's victory over the law of sin and death and God's triumph over the Evil One. Through the cross and resurrection sinners are justified and their guilt expiated. Finally, Easter is the most profound sign of God's creative fidelity to the covenantal promises made to creation and to Israel, which all along were groaning for redemption.

Ascension Thursday. Drawing on the Lucan periodicization of the season of Easter the church celebrates Christ's *ascensus* to the Father as a chronologically separate event, while in John it is related more closely to Christ's glorification. This feast reminds the faithful that the risen Christ is present in the church and to the world in mystery and not as a reality "at hand." The experienced absence of the Lord on one level invites the church to deeper experience of him as one present in the living faith of the community and recognizable, not by looking up to heaven, but in the "breaking of bread" together and in deeds of loving service for the least of the brothers and sisters.

Pentecost Sunday. Again the Lucan schematization holds center stage as yet another primary dimension of the total Easter event is commemorated: the prophetically promised outpouring of the Holy Spirit "in the last days." Through Christ's Pasch, the Father bestowed the life-giving Spirit on chosen witnesses, creating the church and its ministry of reconciliation. This Spirit manifests itself in prophecy, in *parrhesia* (bold speech in confession of God's saving deed in Christ), and in multiple charisms of service. The church lives out of the power of that Spirit who continually calls it to renewal of life and service and into a future when there will be a new heaven and a new earth. As the creation of the Spirit and as spatio-temporal institution, the church is the earthen vessel of election, combining free grace and stable structures, where structures are meant to give grace a body and grace is the raison d'etre of the structures. The church is the fundamental sacrament of the ongoing presence of Christ in history, Christ who is himself the primary sacrament of God.

The Christmas Cycle

The feast of *Christmas* is the celebration of the incarnation of the divine Word and the birth of Our Lord for our salvation. Its celebration on December 25 was intended to replace the pagan observance of the birthday of the sun, *Natalis Solis Invicti*, which itself was timed to fall on the winter solstice. The most tangible and human of feasts, it has claimed the Christian imagination more powerfully than the events of the Resurrection, and thus has traditionally been the more popular festival. Modern scholarship shows that we really know very little historiographically about the circumstances of Christ's birth. Both Matthew and Luke, in the light of their resurrection-faith, feel free to narrate the story of Christ's birth as the fulfillment of OT prophecy and the recapitulation of Israel's and Moses' history (Matthew), as the revelation, in all poverty, of the Good News to the poor and marginalized members of Israel's society (Luke), and as the time when he receives his primary names as Christ, Lord, Son of David, Emmanuel, Son of God and Savior.

The Incarnation is classically understood as the creative assumption by the divine Word, in the power of the Holy Spirit, of the integral human nature of Christ from the first moment of conception. Christmas expresses this truth of faith more narratively and evocatively as the birth of a baby whose vulnerability is the disarming foreshadowing of the vulnerability, thoroughly adult and freely chosen, which will mark his ministry of action and of suffering. The shepherds' responsive action upon hearing the divine ("angelic") revelation (Lk 2:8-14) and the contemplative silence of Mary (Lk 2:19) presage the two dimensions of authentic discipleship (Lk 10:29-42).

The *Logos* of John's Prologue, the pre-existent Wisdom and creative Word of God, comes to dwell among God's people, thus revealing that God has all the room in the world—for the world: for its joys and pains, its anxieties and tyrannies, its longings and its addictions. Pure hospitality and transforming grace are the ways of the Word in the Spirit, revealed as such in the gracious ways of Christ as babe and, later, as itinerant preacher and charismatic healer in the service of God's Good News.

At the adult feast of Christmas, the one for whom there was no room at the inn offers room to our own "bloody births" as we suffer losses, relinquish parts of ourselves and identify with the oppressed in their struggle for freedom, as we seek under grace to accompany Christ on his way.

The Christmas cycle continues with explicitation of further dimensions of the revelation of God through Christ in the Spirit.

The Solemnity of the Epiphany of Our Lord celebrates, in the Western churches, the adoration of the Magi from the East as the story of the revelation of the mystery of God's saving will (Eph 1:9) as embracing Gentiles as well as Jews. In the Eastern churches Christmas (January 6, an ancient date for the winter solstice and formerly the pagan feast of Dionysus) commemorates the birth of Christ and the homage of the Magi, while Epiphany marks Christ's baptism. The mystery of Christ as one sent by the Father in the Spirit to all nations and races and the essentially missionary character of the church both find memorial in this feast. Moreover, the Magi's following of the star to the crib has always expressed the longing of philosophers and sages for the fullness of truth, which only is found in full surrender to God in Christ, the Wisdom of God. For Western Christians the feast can be a reminder as well of the profound riches of worship, theology and spirituality which the Eastern churches bring to the *catholica.*

The Christmas cycle ends with the *Baptism of Our Lord.* This is at once an event of revelation, naming and anointing on God's part and, on Christ's part, an event of prophetic gesture of self-emptying solidarity with sinners as he identifies with their longing for redemption and desire to be part of the "saved remnant." The story of the washing in the Jordan and (in an anticipation of Easter) the descent of the Spirit upon Christ in its various synoptic versions brings the mystery of incarnation forward to the adult stage of Christ's life as he stands poised for public ministry. As at the baptism so too in his ministry he will be empowered by God's continual naming of him in the Spirit, and thus will be able to pour out himself in compassionate service of sinners and those oppressed in body and spirit. For present-day Christians, the feast is a celebration as well of the discipleship-way which began with their own baptism into Christ and into his life of service. Furthermore, it is a reminder that they can learn, over a lifetime, to draw strength from the sacrament's washing and anointing in the name of the Trinity.

Secondary Solemnities and Feasts of Christ's Saving Events

Feast of the Presentation of the Lord. The customary Jewish ritual of the consecration of the first-born son to God as an event of Christ's life becomes, in this feast, the celebration of his being "born of a woman, born under the Law" and living a life of total dedication to his Father's will in and through the gifts and limitations of his own humanity and of his religious, social and cultural milieu, whose deepest aspirations he will fulfill as the crucified and risen one.

Solemnity of the Annunciation of the Lord. The divine election of Mary and her gracious "yes" to God's initiative in the incarnation comes to focus in this feast, which highlights the freely chosen dependence of Almighty God on a human freedom exercised in co-operative grace. In the incarnation of the divine Word all happens totally of grace and all happens totally in human freedom (St. Bernard).

The Feast of the Transfiguration. On the mountain of revelation, Christ is shown as the fulfillment of the law (Moses) and the prophets (Elijah), and as the beloved Son who shares God's glory. For a moment this glory fills him and becomes evident to the three chosen disciples who will later be asked to enter the Garden of Gethsemane with their Master. That same glory will permanently suffuse him only after and because (Phil 2:9) he has suffered "many things" in fidelity to God and sinners.

Solemnities and Feasts of Christ Which Do Not Focus on a Saving Event

Feast of the Holy Family (December 30). Celebrated within the Christmas cycle, this feast commemorates the saving truth that Christ grew up nourished by human love and subject to human authority, yet was destined, in the Spirit, to be oriented to God the Father's will and word in a way which relativized all fleshly ties (Mk 3:34-35).

Solemnity of the Most Holy Body and Blood of Christ (second Sunday after Pentecost). This feast, which traditionally involves a solemn procession with the eucharistic bread, developed in the 13th century when the visual experience of the eucharistic host as such was accorded greater value than in the post-Vatican II church. *Corpus Christi* retains its theological significance as a celebration of God's gift of Christ in the Spirit to the church and world as its food and drink of everlasting life. Moreover, in the celebration of this feast the church as the body of Christ experiences itself called to let the Spirit fashion it more and more into bread and drink for the world.

Solemnity of the Most Sacred Heart of Jesus (Friday after the Solemnity of the Most Holy Body and Blood of Christ). The theological significance of this feast consists, fundamentally, in the worshipful celebration of the divine and human mystery of love revealed in Christ. The specific focus on the heart of Christ amounts to a focus on his freely chosen love for sinful humanity, taking the physical heart as the real symbol of his (relatively autonomous) human center of freedom and choice. In the Son, the free "victim" of sin's violence, both God's constant love and sin's destructive power are revealed in an encounter that is full of grace and death. The feast can best avoid false sentiment and bad theology when the praying community remembers the victims of oppression, abuse, warfare and addiction as those with whom the glorified Christ (who can die no more) chooses to identify. The call to offer reparation, traditionally associated with this feast and devotion, then becomes an invitation to enter into the graced struggle, motivated by love of the whole Christ, for a more just, peaceful and loving world.

Feast of the Triumph of the Holy Cross (September 14). Associated historically with the conversion of Emperor Constantine and Helena's "finding" of the true Cross, the feast has its theological significance in the paradox which the feast's name itself contains. On the cross Christ resisted evil in the sense that he refused to conspire with its dark power. But, even more fundamentally, in the power of the Spirit he absorbed the destructive force of sin, by relating to sinners not as the holy one, apart from and superior to them, but as one who chose to be in total solidarity with them, without sinning. Thus God in Christ triumphed over sinners by absorbingly conquering sin and offering nothing but mercy to the sinners. This weakness of God, this "foolish" love on the cross, showed itself more powerful than the violent power of sinful human beings (1 Cor 1:25).

Solemnity of Our Lord Jesus Christ, Universal King (last Sunday in ordinary time). The feast was established by Pope Pius XI in 1925 in the consciousness of the increasing secularization of the West. The meaning of kingship, when said of Christ, must be derived from an understanding in faith of the ministry, death and resurrection of Christ. In this feast Christians offer to Christ all their concerns expressed in naming him "king"— concern for order, for respect for the church, for the final triumph of the Good News of christianity, for the conversion of atheists and agnostics, etc. Christ in turn accepts these concerns and does them justice, while freeing the Christians who express them from all anxious ecclesiastical self-concern and self-justification and invites them to loving service of, and prophetic challenge to, the world in the manner of Christ himself.

See **Liturgical calendar; Christmas season; Easter season; Holy Week, liturgies of**

F.J. van Beeck, *Christ Proclaimed: Christology As Rhetoric* (New York/Ramsey/Toronto: Paulist Press, 1979).

BRIAN O. McDERMOTT, S.J.

CHRISTMAS SEASON

The Christmas season officially encompasses that part of the liturgical year from evening prayer I of Christmas (Christmas Eve) through the Sunday after the actual celebration of Epiphany or after January 6 according to the *General Norms for the Liturgical Year and the Calendar*. Theologically and culturally however, the Christmas season includes extensions both before and after the feasts of Christmas and Epiphany. These are specifically the season of Advent, "which begins with evening prayer I of the Sunday falling on or closest to 30 November and ends before evening prayer I of Christmas" (GNLYC v, 40); the Feast of the Baptism of the Lord which is celebrated on the Sunday following January 6; and two feasts intimately related to Christmas but separated in time, namely the Presentation of the Lord on February 2, and the Solemnity of the Annunciation on March 25. In addition to these extensions of the Christmas season proper, Christmas itself has an octave day, celebrated on January 1 as the Solemnity of Mary, Mother of God. Within the octave week are several other feasts: that of the Holy Family on the Sunday within the octave; Saint Stephen, First Martyr on December 26; Saint John, Apostle and Evangelist on December 27; and the Holy Innocents on December 28. The three remaining days within the octave (December 29, 30, and 31) are marked by their own Mass propers as part of the Christmas octave. Lastly, if there is a Sunday between January 2 and January 5 it is celebrated as the Second Sunday after Christmas.

Historical Development

The center of the liturgical year in the early church was the Pascha, the annual celebration of the passover of Christ who was the "firstborn" from the dead, and consequently of all those baptized in his name. This, in turn, may have been a development of, or at least a coincident occurrence with the weekly celebration of the Resurrection each Sunday. Subse-quent to the beginnings of the annual Pascha was the development of an annual commemoration of the Nativity, a commemoration which took different forms in the Eastern and Western parts of the church. In the East it centered on January 6 and had multiple emphases, in the West it centered on December 25 and was focused on the actual nativity of Jesus.

Christmas. The origins of the Western Christmas feast are elusive; our first evidence from Rome comes from the Chronograph of 354, a list of important dates and personages for the city of Rome which includes, at the top of its list of burial dates for martyrs, the entry on December 25 for the birth of Christ in Bethlehem of Judaea. By taking into account some discrepancies in the chronological order, the chronograph reveals a celebration of Christmas dating back to 336. This dating and evidence provides the basis for one of two main theories on the origins of Christmas in contemporary scholarship.

The first theory uses the history of religions, specifically the deliberate replacement or countering of a pagan festival with one of Christian content. In 274, the emperor Aurelian re-established a specifically Roman version of the sun festival related to the winter solstice, called *natalis solis invicti*. Both the popularity of this festival and the long history of sun worship in Rome provided fertile ground for the development of a Christian feast of the unconquered sun, building on the already existing symbolism which described Jesus as the "Sun of Righteousness." Nature also contributed to the Christian feast with the rebirth of light following the solstice, adding a symbolism of renewal to the birth of Jesus in Bethlehem of Judaea.

The second theory in contemporary scholarship on the origins of Christmas relies on calendrical computation, specifically the relation of December 25 to March 25, the death date of Jesus. In the

West by the time of Hippolytus (early 3rd century) March 25 was already believed to have been the historical date of the passion. The significance of the death date to the establishment of a nativity date lies in a theological belief inherited from Judaism and prevalent in the early church, namely that the death and birth dates of the religiously significant are the same. Not only are the patriarchs' birth and death dates the same, but also the creation and parousia will align, a belief that contributes to the eschatological dimension of the origins of Christmas. The specifically Christian twist to this dating is the establishment of March 25 as the death date and the *conception* date, thereby establishing the birth date nine months later on December 25. Also connected to this computation theory is the birth of John the Baptist six months prior to Jesus, based on the story of the annunciation to Mary in Lk 1:36 where Gabriel announces that Elizabeth was in her sixth month of pregnancy. John's birth would fall at the summer solstice with his conception at the autumn equinox, while Jesus' birth would fall at the winter solstice with his conception at the spring equinox. This dating not only lends itself to rich theological symbolism but exemplifies the double-dating (or balancing) evident in the establishment of liturgical feasts in the early church. Contributing to this theory of the origin of Christmas are some supportive documents from North Africa. Augustine of Hippo, in an Epiphany sermon (Sermon 202) relates that the Donatists do not celebrate the Feast of Epiphany, celebrated by Augustine's Catholic church, but makes no mention of their not celebrating Christmas, a feast established prior to Epiphany in the West. If the Donatists were celebrating Christmas it would have been established prior to the Donatist schism in 311 as they would not have adopted a Catholic feast after the schism. This earlier dating of Christmas in North Africa is supported by two anonymous writings, *De pascha computus* (c. 243), and *De solstitiis et aequinoctiis* (4th century) which both reveal the birth/death dating and the theme of "sun of righteousness" (Mal 4:2). Both of these works may be from North Africa, giving rise to the speculation that the Feast of Christmas may have originated in North Africa, independent of Aurelian's festival of *natalis solis invicti*. Although this theory may prove to be more sound for the origins of Christmas, the influence of the pagan Roman festival certainly contributes to the development of the Feast of Christmas.

The development of Christmas in Rome during the 5th and 6th centuries is easier to trace than its origins. Most notable is the triple celebration of Christmas within the city of Rome, each celebration with its own station. The earliest liturgy is the celebration at St. Peter's on Christmas Day with its gospel reading of the prologue of John. Following the building of the church of St. Mary Major in the 5th century, a creche in imitation of Bethlehem was added in an adjacent oratory and a nocturnal liturgy (vigil) was added there, eventually becoming another eucharistic celebration. The third station was a Mass at dawn of Christmas day, celebrated at the Church of St. Anastasia, the center of the imperial Byzantine presence in Rome. Originally celebrated by the bishop of Rome as a recognition of the significance of St. Anastasia to the Eastern Christians, the liturgy gradually acquired Christmas themes. This papal stational pattern of Christmas liturgies for the city of Rome was adopted by Charlemagne in the 9th century and standardized throughout his domain.

Christmas Octave. The octave day of Christmas was established in the 7th century as the first Marian feast in the Roman calendar, *Natale S. Mariae*

(Anniversary of St. Mary). Prior to this, the pagan New Year's celebration was countered in the church by fasting and penance as exemplified by the Second Council of Tours in 567, ascetical practices which were observed primarily in Gaul and Spain. After the establishment of a liturgical celebration of Mary and the recognition of an octave day for Christmas, another Gallican feature, the Circumcision of Jesus, was added to the January 1st celebration. The Gallican observance of the circumcision was added to the Roman calendar in the 13/14th centuries, creating a multifaceted celebration which was unified only in 1969 as the Solemnity of Mary, Mother of God.

Of the three days following Christmas the first two, Feast of Stephen, first martyr, and John, apostle and evangelist, were originally eastern feasts. Both date from the 4th century Syriac tradition and were adopted in the West a century later. The third feast, that of the Holy Innocents on December 28, appears first in North Africa in 505. In the Middle Ages the three celebrations were given the name *Comites Christi* (Companions of Christ) and epitomized as representing the three types of martyrdom. The Sunday within the octave of Christmas, the Feast of the Holy Family, has no early origins; it was established as an idea-feast in 1921.

Epiphany. The Western feast of Christmas, celebrated on December 25, was adopted in the East in Cappadocia and Antioch in the 4th century, in Egypt in the 5th century, and in Jerusalem as late as the 6th century (the Armenian church has never adopted December 25 as a nativity feast). These adoptions by the Eastern church were only half of the exchange. The West in turn also adopted the celebration of the Eastern Feast of the Epiphany by the second half of the 4th century in Rome and earlier in Gaul and Spain. But while the adoption of the Western Christmas in the East was uniformly that of a nativity celebration, the transferral of the Eastern Epiphany to the West was part of a complex evolution and disintegration of the original feast.

Our first written traces of an Epiphany celebration are from the hand of Clement of Alexandria at the end of the 2nd century, writing in his first book of the *Stromateis* about the Basilidian Gnostic celebration of the baptism of Jesus on January 6, which was also the date of Jesus' birth according to Clement (*Strom.* I, 21, 146, 1-2). Other Eastern writers confirm the identification of January 6 as the birth date of Jesus like Clement. As with the Western Christmas, there are theories from both the history of religions and calendrical computation as to the origins of Epiphany. It has affinities in place and date with the Egyptian celebration of the birth of Aion, the god of time and eternity. Also related was the festival of the drawing of water from the Nile, the source of life in Egypt. The Coptic tradition of bathing in living water (i.e., running water as in a stream) and later in special pools built into the church floor may be a reflection of the pagan festival and the Christian emphasis on the baptism of Jesus at Epiphany. The argument from computation is based on the quartodeciman pascha of April 6, a date perhaps derived from the Eastern Christian adaptation of the Jewish 14 Nisan (Passover date) based on a recension of the Julian solar calendar. The use of April 6 as the death and conception date would yield January 6 as the birth date.

Although the January 6 date was widely accepted in the East, the meaning of the feast varied widely. The literal meaning of Epiphany is *manifestation*, but the manifestations of God were many, and different aspects of the feast were celebrated together as complementary theophanies. In Egypt, the original stress was apparently on the baptism of Jesus, which may reflect the fact that their gospel of choice, Mark, began with the baptism story. Even in Egypt, however, the tradition was also familiar with the nativity of Jesus on that date, and eventually added to that the changing of water into wine as another expression of the manifestation of God. The celebration of the baptism of Jesus on Epiphany is widespread in the East, especially in the East Syrian and Armenian traditions. The dual emphasis on birth and baptism may have found its clearest liturgical expression in their baptismal theology, where the baptisms of all Christians were modelled on the baptism of Jesus and proclaimed as a birth into the family of God, rather than stressing the Pauline assimilation to Jesus' death found elsewhere. There is not much evidence to establish Epiphany as the common date for the celebration of baptisms in spite of the theological connection. After the adoption of the Western Christmas on December 25, however, the unity of the birth/baptism of Jesus on Epiphany is split, leaving Epiphany as a baptism-only celebration in places such as Constantinople. Although the Byzantine tradition continues with preferred times for baptism (including Epiphany and Easter) the traditional times of the year begin to break down in the centuries following, as fewer adults present themselves for baptism and infants become the norm throughout the year. The centrality of Epiphany is still seen in the Armenian church which commemorates the birth and baptism of Jesus on January 6; in the Greek church the nativity is celebrated on December 25 and the baptism on January 6, a pattern far more common among other Orthodox churches. The central rite on the Feast of Epiphany is the blessing of water, a practice recalling the importance of Jesus' baptism and the hallowing of all waters by that act.

The adoption of Epiphany in the West resulted in a very different celebration. The West's aversion to focusing solely on the baptism of Jesus may have been a reaction to the christological controversies of the time, and perhaps as a result, the secondary themes of Eastern Epiphany became primary in the West. The first Western account of Epiphany is from Gaul, where the emphasis was on the nativity. By the 5th century, however, there developed many dimensions: in Gaul the three miracles of the Magi, the baptism, and the wedding at Cana were stressed; in Northern Italy the transfiguration was added to these. Rome adopted the feast after 354 (perhaps during the pontificate of Damasus, 366-384) where the stress is a repetition of December 25 and the nativity. As a result, the proclamation to the shepherds remained on December 25, and the manifestation to the Magi moved to January 6. By the time of Augustine and Leo, the feast was narrowed to the manifestation of Christ to the Gentiles, whom the Magi represent. This theme which focuses on the Magi in the West led to the identification of the Magi as three kings by the 6th century, and the popular naming of the kings in the 9th century. The Gallic extension of Epiphany by the addition of an octave in the eighth century led to a further disintegration of unified celebration by moving the baptism of Jesus to the octave of Epiphany, a feast which did not officially become part of the Roman calendar until 1960. Since 1969, the Sunday after January 6, or the Monday following Epiphany if it falls on the 7th or 8th of January, is celebrated as the Baptism of Christ. (In the United States, Epiphany is a Sunday celebration, regardless of the actual calendar date).

Advent. The development of a liturgical season preparatory to Christmas is Western in its origins and celebration. The dual origins of Advent are still visible in the double focus of the contemporary season which reflects both the end time, the second coming of Christ, and prepares for the celebration of Christmas, the commemoration of the first coming of Christ.

Our first accounts of Advent come from Spain and Gaul. In the canons of the Synod of Saragossa (380), the laity are reminded of their obligation to be in church on a daily basis from December 17 through January 6. In 5th century Gaul we hear of an ascetical fast of three days a week beginning on or near St. Martin's Day (November 11) and extending to Christmas. While fasting on Wednesdays and Fridays was an ancient Christian tradition (*Didache*, 1st century), the addition of Monday appears to mark off the season. Neither of these pre-Christmas or pre-Epiphany accounts defends the earlier theory that Advent began as a catechumenate prior to Epiphany baptism. Baptism, while celebrated in Spain on Epiphany, was also celebrated on Christmas in the 380s (to the dismay of the Roman bishop). The designation of December 17-January 6 would coincide with the pagan celebration of Saturnalia, an event of much concern in later Christian synodical writings. The beginning of Advent's core (December 17-December 24) could be in this case a Christian ascetical practice to counter the ribald pagan celebration. The Gallican fast, on the other hand, may have found its origins in the Celtic monastic practice of triannual forty-day fasts, a practice which soon became mandatory for laity also. These ascetical practices of Gaul seem to provide the criteria for the later liturgical season. In Gaul, the season of Advent (varying from four to six weeks) took on a penitential dimension paralleling the early medieval Lent, with the use of the color purple, the dropping of the *Gloria* and the *Alleluia* from eucharistic liturgies, and the dropping of the *Te Deum* from the liturgy of the hours. The adoption of Celtic penitential practices and the rising emphasis on judgment at the parousia color the Gallican season of Advent, exemplified by the sequence *Dies Irae*, a

hymn composed for the beginning of Advent.

In Rome, the origins of Advent seem to be a combination of Gallican influence and indigenous tradition. There is already evidence of a pre-Christmas fast at the end of the 4th century in Rome, a fast that may not have any relation to Christmas. Also related to the time of year but perhaps originally independent of Christmas are the Ember days, quarterly fast times of recollection. Gregory the Great (late 6th century) witnesses to a liturgical tradition of four Sunday Masses and three Ember day Masses in preparation for Christmas, which stresses the coming commemoration rather than the judgment themes seen in the Gallican tradition. In the 7th century, the composition of the poetic "O Antiphons" exemplifies this preparation for the solemnity of the nativity, and by the 8th and 9th centuries, the sacramentaries reveal the position of Advent at the beginning of the church year, replacing Christmas as the the head of liturgical new year. The liturgical traditionalism of Rome made itself felt in the widespread adoption of the Roman four week Advent (replacing the longer Gallican and Spanish Advents) but by the 12th century Rome was influenced by the penitential aspects of the Gallican Advent and dropped the *Gloria* from the Mass, retaining the *Alleluia* as a vestige of an earlier non-penitential approach to Advent.

Feasts of Christmas Outside the Season. The Feast of the Presentation begins its official greeting with "Forty days ago we celebrated the joyful feast of the birth of our Lord Jesus Christ..." (*Sacramentary*, February 2), but its direct liturgical focus back to Christmas and forward to the redemption of all Christians is obscured by its very placement in the *Proper of Saints*, far removed from the Christmas season. This Christmas feast is first attested to by Egeria (c. 383) in her diary of 4th-century Jerusalem

liturgies. It was known as *Hypapante* or
meeting (the meeting between Simeon
and Jesus). By the 5th century, the liturgy
had been augmented by a procession
with candles, a procession that becomes
widespread and a central aspect of the
feast. The feast was accepted in Rome in
the second half of the 7th century, where
under Pope Sergius I the procession took
on a penitential character, following a
common stational route from the forum
to St. Mary Major. By the mid-8th
century, its adoption in the Frankish
empire found it being renamed the Purification of Mary, a designation which
existed simultaneously for two centuries
before the Marian aspects overwhelmed
the christological origins. The accompanying blessing of candles dates from a
10th century Germanic custom, finding
its way to Rome by the 12th century.
The Roman calendar re-adopted the
feast as the Presentation of the Lord in
1969, and the sacramentary still includes
a candle blessing and procession echoing
the light imagery of the feast's Christmas
origins: "May we who carry these candles
in your church come with joy to the light
of glory."

The Feast of the Annunciation is also a
feast of the Lord which was restored as
such in 1969, before which it was known
under the title of the Annunciation of the
Blessed Virgin Mary. This feast is intimately linked with the whole process of
calendrical computation discussed above.
It forms, very probably, the basis of
Christmas as determined from the date of
the conception of Jesus. The distinct
celebration of this feast, however, has
often been obscured since the expansion
of the penitential aspects of Lent, the
season during which March 25 most
often occurs. Solutions to this problem
historically saw the Annunciation moved
to a different date, such as December 18
in Spain and to the Sunday before Christmas in Milan. Today its celebration is
restored to March 25, but again often

overlooked for the same reason of conflict
with Lent.

See **Calendar, liturgical; Christ, feasts of**

Bernard Botte, *Les origines de la Noel et de
l'épiphanie. Textes et études liturgiques* I (Louvain,
1932). Adrien Nocent, *The Liturgical Year* I
(Collegeville, 1977). Thomas Talley, *The Origins of
the Liturgical Year* (New York, 1986).

LIZETTE LARSON-MILLER

CHRISTOLOGY AND LITURGY

In its public worship the church both
continues the priestly office of Jesus
Christ and gives full public expression to
its faith (*Mediator Dei*; Neuner-Dupuis,
p. 346). Thus it is not surprising that the
traditional principle of *lex orandi, lex
credendi* ("the law of praying is the law of
believing") obtains in a classic way for the
emergence of christological dogma in the
early church.

Amid the struggles to formulate an
orthodox view of Christ's relation to God
at the time of the Arian controversies,
Athanasius made appeal to the centuries-
old church practice of worshipping Jesus
Christ as one equal with God the Father
to justify, and provide the ultimate context of signification for, the affirmation
that the divine Word or Son was *homoousios* ("consubstantial") with the Father.
To be sure, the fact that the church
regularly addressed its prayer *to* the
Father *through* Jesus Christ became for
the Arians an argument in favor of the
subordination of the Son to the Father.
Yet the Fathers argued that Christ's role
as the definitive mediator between God
and humankind demanded, rather than
called into question, his full oneness in
being with the Father. Furthermore, they
could point to the devotional life of the
church in which, from earliest times,
prayer was addressed directly to Christ.
Thus the church's prayer was a primary
source for the dogma of the First General
Council of Nicaea (325) regarding Christ's

full divinity. Once the church came to a firm consensus about the meaning of *homoousios*, the dogma became in its turn a firm support for the liturgical practice of the church wherein Christians were invited to surrender all to Christ in discipleship to the glory of God.

The church's practice of worshipping Jesus Christ raised the further question of the basis for worshipping Christ's humanity. The Council of Ephesus (431), in condemning and deposing Nestorius, Patriarch of Constantinople, anathematized a view attributed (mistakenly) to him at the time that Jesus Christ is two sons, son of God and son of Mary. Making Cyril of Alexandria's second letter to Nestorius its own, the council affirmed that the divinity and humanity in Christ are united "according to *hypostasis*" and thus there is one Christ and Lord who is worshipped. In affirming against Nestorius that the already traditional name *Theotokos* (Mother of God) was a proper title for Mary which implied a true statement about Christ, the council re-affirmed the traditional understanding and practice of the *communicatio idiomatum* according to which divine attributes and human attributes could be predicated not only of the respective natures in Christ, but also of the one subject, the eternal Word or Son of God, Jesus Christ. The council thus affirmed that the church worships Christ's humanity with the worship reserved for God alone (*latria*) insofar as the humanity is united to the divine Word or Son. Once again the rule of prayer led to a rule of belief which, in turn, became a clarifying support for the church's life of worship.

The traditional and very modern question of the authentic humanity of Jesus Christ provides another dimension of Christology which relates profoundly to the church's worship. The liturgy of the word, which the reforms of Vatican II restored to its proper role in sacramental worship, involves the proclaimed narrative of the saving deeds of God in the OT and NT, with special honor accorded to the gospel accounts which witness to Christ as the subject of a life and destiny which can and must be *narrated*.

The narrative character of Jesus' life expressed in the church's central public act of proclamation of the gospel has not always received support from Christology as it has been elaborated by theologians and has taken hold on Christian imaginations. The affirmation of the divine Word or Son as the sole subject of the human life of Christ with the human nature conceived as an "instrument" of the divine person has often hampered the recognition that the human experiences andorical Jesus were intrinsically significant for himself in his own human development. Beginning with certain motifs in John's gospel, some Church Fathers taught, for example, that Jesus' ignorance was feigned, and that all he humanly did and said was meant to be exemplary and instructive for others but not part of the process of his own growth as a human "someone" before the Father and other people and in relation to himself. Following the General Council of Chalcedon's (451) affirmation of Jesus Christ as one *prosopon* and *hypostasis* in two complete natures, divine and human, the Third General Council of Constantinople (681) affirmed, against certain forms of Monophysitism, that Jesus Christ possesses two wills and two activities, human and divine.

This further explicitation of Chalcedon's commitment to Christ's integral human nature has encouraged modern theologians to attribute to Christ a human center of consciousness and freedom in dialogical relation with his Father, while seeking to preserve the divine Word as the ultimate "uniting unity" of the total reality of Christ. Indeed, Pope Pius XII's encyclical *Sempiternus Rex* (1951) on the 15th centenary of the Council of Chalcedon did not rule out christological theory which would affirm a relatively autonomous human center.

In any case, the interpretation of Christ's "hypostatic union" cannot be such that it undermines the humanity of Jesus as the immediate source of an authentically human and narratable life while it affirms that that humanity is rooted totally in the divine Word, and thus the source of a narrative which discloses in human terms the very nature of God. In other words, the rule of prayer, i.e., the church's delight in narrating the events of Jesus' life as real experiences constitutive to various degrees of his human life as well as occurring "for our sakes," encourages the development of theological interpretations of Christ's personal unity which are "narrative-friendly."

The church's liturgy expresses the identity of Christ as not only a personal but a corporate or social identity as well. For the action of the worshipping community as animated and united to its Head in the Holy Spirit is ultimately the action of Christ himself, for Christ is present in the word, in the sacramental signs, in the priest and in the praying community (S.C., 7). Thus in the liturgy one recognizes the most explicit action of Christ in our world.

Finally, recent theology has drawn attention to the context in which theological statements most fully convey their point. Church dogmas make their point finally and fully not as a result of an examination of the technical terms involved or their mutual relations, but when they are reinserted into the performative language-context which is the church's worship and service of others in Christ's name. For in the church's liturgy and in its service of the world, Christ's full consubstantiality with God and with ourselves becomes persuasive Good News when it translates, again and again, into the worshipping church's continuing self-surrender to God in Christ as an offering which extends hospitality to all that is human, graced and broken about us (Incarnation). That hospitality then becomes an invitation for all that is human to submit itself to the Lordship of Christ in the Spirit (Cross) who transforms it and draws it into the future which God has prepared for it and all that is destined to be part of God's reign (Resurrection).

See **Liturgy and doctrine**

J. Neuner and J. Dupuis, (eds.), *The Christian Faith in the Doctrinal Documents of the Catholic Church*, rev. ed. (London: Collins, 1983). F.J. van Beeck, *Christ Proclaimed: Christology as Rhetoric* (New York/Ramsey/Toronto: Paulist Press, 1979). J.D. Crichton, "A Theology of Worship" in C. Jones, G. Wainwright and E. Yarnold (eds.), *The Study of Liturgy* (London: S.P.C.K., 1978), pp. 1-29.

BRIAN O. McDERMOTT, S.J.

CHURCH ORDER

The concept of church order is not strictly univocal. Sometimes discussion of church order is paramount to the discussion of ordained ministry and ecclesiastical office. At other times, it has to do with states of life and distinct ways of participating in the life and service of the church among all its members. In still other contexts, what is intended is the ritual and regulatory ordering that offers a pattern to follow through the cycle of the day and of the year in living the common life of the church and in celebrating its worship. These diverse understandings are interconnected.

To address the topic in as clear a way as possible, this article will first look at the concept of church order that comes from early canonico-liturgical documents. This serves as a constant point of reference. Second, it will look at the vocabulary of order in its more ecclesiastical usage and in its vocational usage. How these two usages interconnect or separate has much to do with the development of ecclesiology and of the ordering of church life. Third, the article will give more detailed and specific attention to the issue of ordering mission and ministry. Finally, it will offer a contemporary approach to an understanding of church order that is inspired by the early canonico-liturgical material but is organic rather than hierarchical. It is divided as follows: The Canon of Church Order; Order as Ecclesiastical Group; Order as Vocational Group; Order, Office and Ministry; An Ecclesiology of Organic Order.

The Canon of Church Order
A number of documents dating back to early Christian centuries are referred to as church orders. Principal among these are the Didache, the *Apostolic Tradition* of Hippolytus, the *Testament of the Lord*, the *Didascalia* and the *Apostolic Constitutions*. They are collections of practical directives for the following of Christ, intended to regulate the common life of particular churches and subsequently adopted in part or in whole by others. They include instructions about the right way of celebrating the church's worship and some texts to be used in it. They give directives about such things as fast days, common and private prayer, the use of charisms of healing, how to receive guests and the care of the poor of the community. In the course of these directives mention is made of different groups in the church, such as the *kleros*, widows, virgins, charismatics, confessors, deaconesses, readers, porters and cantors, specifying the duties of each or what is expected of them. Many of these church orders follow the convention of claiming apostolic authority so that they might carry greater weight, but in fact the exact origins and even the textual history of most of them are clouded in obscurity.

Nonetheless, they were clearly important in early centuries as canonico-liturgical documents helping to order the life of churches and subsequently appealed to as authoritative sources. They might be a nightmare to persons trying to codify law for the contemporary church, and yet it is their comprehensive quality that constitutes their particular appeal. From them one sees how the ordering of worship, private prayer, the moral life, ecclesiastical discipline, and credal formulation all belong together as one organic unity. Later centuries make clearer distinctions between liturgical books, codes of law, credal pronouncements, moral treatises and methods of prayer, but sometimes at the cost of obscuring the connection between them. It belongs however to theology to reflect on the relationships and to maintain the comprehensive vision of church life mirrored in these ancient church orders and encompassing questions of ministry, vocation, mission, church law and sacrament.

To explain the relation between the different groups, especially in the assembly, some of these treatises resort to nautical imagery. Thus we have this passage in the *Apostolic Constitutions* 2, 57. 2-10: "When thou (O bishop) callest an assembly of the Church as the one that is commander of a great ship, appoint the assemblies to be made with all possible skill, charging the deacons as mariners to prepare places for the brethren as for passengers with all due care and decency.... In the middle let the bishop's throne be placed and on each side of him let the presbytery sit down; and let the deacons stand near at hand.... In the middle let the reader stand upon some high place; let him read ... let some other sing the hymns of David.... Let the porters stand at the entries of the men and observe them. Let the deaconesses also stand at those of the women, like shipmen." (English translation by James Donaldson, *The Ante-Nicene Fathers* 7, 421).

There is already a concept of ordering in the sense of ranking in this passage as

214

elsewhere in these documents, springing from the distinction between the clergy and the people. This was, however, to be accentuated later with the enlargement of the ranks of the clergy to include others besides bishops, presbytery and deacons and by the adoption of a paradigm of hierarchy.

Order As Ecclesiastical Group

It seems to have been Tertullian, followed closely in this by Cyprian, who introduced the word and notion of *ordo* and *ordinatio* into ecclesiastical Latin and into church life. In classical Latin, *ordo* was used to designate particular groups of persons who had roles to play in the ordering of public life or who had a particular public profile. Thus, there were the *ordo senatorius*, the *ordo equester*, the *ordo iudicum*, the *ordo scribarum*, the *ordo decurionum*, the *ordo matronarum* and the *ordo canentium*. The verb *ordinare* and its substantive *ordinatio* meant such things as determining public ordinances, putting order into the life of a group, or naming somebody to public office, as, for example, to the order of magistrates. Tertullian used *ordo* and *ordines* in this rather generic sense to refer to such groups as bishops, designated ministers of different kinds, virgins and widows. At the same time, we find him distinguishing between the *ordo sacerdotalis* and the *plebs*, or faithful in general (*De Exhortatione Castitatis* VII, 2-3:CCL II, 1024f).

It is in this connection that *ordinare* and *ordinatio* began to take on a more precise meaning in Cyprian's Latin usage: *Epistolae*

55,24:	*C.S.E.L., III*	642;
59,5:	*ibid.,*	672;
66,9:	*ibid.,*	733;
67,5:	*ibid.,*	739.

These references pertain to the appointment to church office, to investiture in it by whatever process or ritual was followed, and even more specifically to the laying-on of hands for the induction of bishops.

Beginning with these two writers, through late antiquity and through the early Middle Ages, one finds this parallel usage of the Latin terminology. On the one hand, any group that is given a distinctive place in the church's public gathering, especially in its worship, is an order. Thus there is mention of the order of bishops, the order of presbyters, the order of deacons, the order of readers, the order of virgins, the order of widows, the order of catechumens and even the order of penitents. In passing it may be noted that in the East the concept of *taxis* or economy allows for such groupings of church members. On the other hand, in church Latin there is the distinction that becomes more markedly noted between the order of the clergy and the people, paralleled in Greek by *kleros/laikos*. Fostered by local councils and most of all by the Roman church, the binomy clergy/laity prevailed and led to the ordering into ranks of the *ordo clericalis* itself, as well as to its absorption of offices and liturgical ministries that would otherwise have belonged within the body of the faithful. Such are the liturgical ministries of reader, acolyte, subdeacon, cantor and psalmist, and the offices of porter, notary, defensor, gravedigger and body-servant or chamberlain to the bishop. Designations for these clerical groups or their offices that serve as alternatives to *ordo* are *gradus, officium, honor, munus* and *dignitas*.

The history of the clericalization of church life is complex. It appears to have had much to do with preoccupation over what ought to be expected of those designated to the service of the altar. The canonico-liturgical church orders mentioned earlier make a clear distinction between installation into office by *cheirotonia* or the laying-on of hands and other forms of appointment, such as simple naming to office, giving of instruments or praying over. Only bishops, presbyters and deacons received the laying-on of hands because they alone were to minister at the altar. At first, it is they who constitute the *ordo sacerdotalis* or the *kleros*. Demands of sanctity were quickly placed on them, for otherwise it was not seen how they could exercise so holy a service.

The development of a greater order of clergy, ranked within itself and markedly distinct from the body of the faithful, is well-exemplified in the *cursus honorum* of the Roman church. It begins with the sacralization of the offices of bishop, presbyter and deacon and with the moral demands made of them. In papal decretals of the 4th and 5th centuries there is an increasing parallelism between the ordained ministry of the church and the levitical priesthood of the OT, centered around the offering of sacrifice. The parallelism grounded the expectation that bishops and their attendant clergy practice continence, poverty and a life of constant prayer. Introduction into the ranks of the lower clergy at an early age provided a school of spiritual learning and discipline for those who would later receive the laying-on of hands and greater ecclesiastical responsibility. By reason of association, lesser offices, whether liturgical or otherwise, assumed the sacred aura of the higher. All official service in the church thus came to appear as a sacred duty and dignity that separated the clergy from the *plebs* and imposed on them a distinctive way of life.

Disciplinary though it was in part, the distinction was given theological legitimation through a broader concept of order or hierarchy that represented the very nature of creation. In such an influential writer as St. Augustine, the idea of ecclesiastical order was already allied with a broader conception, one connected with the universe as it comes from God's hands and with the whole progress of history. Since it is of the very nature of the human that there be leaders and that the lesser be guided by the higher, the church too has to have its leadership. This leadership is marked by the intensity of the following of Christ and is one through which Christ himself may be said to act as leader of his people.

That Augustine should have expected the clergy of Hippo to follow a common rule of life under the bishop is not at all surprising, given this theological vision. It is, however, by no means confined to Augustine and can be found in the ordination prayers for bishop, presbyter and deacon of the *Sacramentarium Veronense* which praise the providence of God for its serried ordering of the world, as well as of the OT people and the church of the NT.

In the Middle Ages, however, the concept of hierarchy and its application to the church received its strongest and lasting support from the writings of the Pseudo-Dionysius, who distinguished both ecclesiastical and spiritual hierarchies in the church, comparable to the hierarchies of the heavenly hosts. Of the visible ordering of groups, only the clerical orders seemed to hold their place. Virgins, widows, catechumens and penitents might still be mentioned in the liturgical litanies and intercessions, but little sign of this was retained in the actual ordering of the assembly. So marked off were the clergy from all the other parts of the church by the second millennium that an acute commentator like St. Thomas Aquinas could ask whether the lesser orders actually represented some modicum of participation in the sacrament of priesthood (*S. Th., Suppl.*, Q. 37, art. 1 ad 2).

Medieval treatises with titles such as *De Ordinibus* or *De Ecclesiasticis Officiis* continued to establish the ranks within the clergy and the offices included within ecclesiastical order. The Gallican canonical collection *Statuta Ecclesiae Antiqua* (ed. Ch. Munier, Paris 1964) and the

Pseudo-Hieronomian work *De Septem Ordinibus Ecclesiae* (ed. A.W. Kalff, Ettal, 1938) appear to have been the principal ancient sources for these treatises. The former had the sequence: doorkeeper, lector, exorcist, acolyte, subdeacon, presbyter, and bishop. The latter listed: gravedigger, doorkeeper, lector, subdeacon, deacon, presbyter and bishop. In the Roman church, the eventual listing included bishop, presbyter, deacon and subdeacon in the higher orders, and acolyte, exorcist, lector and porter in the lower, with tonsuring as the entry into the clergy.

One of the ways in which the clerical orders were given special dignity was to relate them to the life and works of Christ, so that each order could be said to be in some measure representative of Christ. One of the principal instruments in establishing this connection was the development of the treatise on the Ordinals of Christ. This probably had its origins in Egypt in the 4th century. It showed up extensively in different forms throughout the Latin West, from Ireland to Italy, so that there are over seventy versions of it in all. One important example of its use in the 11th century is that of Yves of Chartres. For Yves, Christ acted as doorkeeper when he used the whip in the temple, as reader in the synagogue of Nazareth at the beginning of his ministry, as exorcist in casting out demons, as acolyte when he declared himself the light, as subdeacon when he washed the feet of his disciples, as deacon when he gave the chalice of his blood to the twelve at the supper, as priest when he changed bread and wine into his body and blood, and as bishop when he blessed the disciples on his ascent into heaven (*Sermo de Excellentia*: P.L. 162, 514-519). This reflects both the respective liturgical ministries of the orders and the christological concept of the clerical state. It is an even more concrete way than that of Thomas Aquinas of relating all the clerical orders to the sacrament of order.

The 16th-century Reformers took exception to the clergy/laity distinction, especially when it was bolstered by the theory of an ontological distinction of sacramental character. While they retained the idea of a divinely instituted ministry of word and sacrament, and of a divine call to minister, they rejected the ideas of a sacrificing priesthood and of a sacred hierarchy. In their own church orders, some of them found place for pastors, deacons and elders as well as for ministers of word and sacrament, and they subjected appointment to office to variant measures of lay control, whether exercised by public officials or by local congregations. All of this was a conscious attempt to adopt patterns that reflected NT usage.

From time to time in the course of history, there have been attempts to regain some greater sense of church order and to lessen the gap between clergy and laity. Within the latter part of the 20th century there has been a more concentrated and universal trend in this direction. For one thing, the liturgical movement and then the liturgical directives of the Vatican II recognized that public worship is the prayer and concern of all and that it allows for a diversity of ministries not all associated with the clerical state but rooted in baptismal membership of God's people. Similarly, Catholic Action, the teachings of the same council and recent movements in church life have fostered the participation of the baptized in the mission and ministry of the church in quite a comprehensive way.

Greater participation does require ordering and cannot be left to personal whim or regulated purely on the basis of competency, even when this is a necessary criterion for selection. The canonical and liturgical regulation of this broader activity offers a chequered history and shows that basic notions about the church, its liturgy and its mission are not yet securely developed nor commonly shared. In a *motu proprio* of 1972, (*Ministeria Quaedam,* A.A.S., 64 [1972] 529-534), Pope Paul VI attempted to reinstate the ministries of reader and acolyte as baptismal rather than clerical acts, but the directives included compromises with clericalism that made them ineffective so that even now installation into them is more common in seminaries than elsewhere. There is much dissension at different levels about the ministries that can be exercised by women in the liturgy and about whether lay ministers may do what is proper to them when there are ordained ministers or clerics present in the assembly to do it. There are even odd quarrels here and there about whose feet are to be washed by whom on Maundy Thursday. In non-liturgical matters the provisions of the 1983 Code of Canon Law have by no means settled all questions of the laity's rights and ministries in the church, or about their participation in decision-making at parish, diocesan and universal levels.

In his 1989 post-Synodal document on the laity (*Christifideles Laici,* A.A.S. LXXXXI [1989]), Pope John Paul II repeated the importance of the liturgical ministry of the baptized, of their part in the teaching and caring ministry of the church, and especially of their apostolic role in serving God's reign in human society. Many practical questions however remain for further clarification, as do the gender questions that have so deeply affected the development of church order throughout the centuries. How some of the theoretical and practical questions are to be addressed cannot be seen without taking account of the notion of order as vocation that has always mingled with the notion of ecclesiastical order.

Order as Vocational Group

St. Paul clearly thought that an apostle could not be genuinely such without evident personal configuration to the mystery of Christ, and Ignatius of Antioch was anxious to see his own apostolic ministry crowned by martyrdom. Neither of these, however, was under the illusion that all who served the church in a public way were necessarily more holy than others, however much they wanted to see service sanctioned by sanctity.

From the time of Origen, it has been customary to distinguish between a ministerial hierarchy and a spiritual hierarchy in the church and this was given, as indicated, firm comprobation by the Pseudo-Dionysius. The works that go under that pseudonym enumerate the ministerial hierarchy of bishop, presbyter and deacon and the spiritual hierarchy of monk, baptized faithful and catechumen. The modes of living the inner life of the Spirit were incorporated into the understanding of the church and brought to influence the very concept of church office by way of a particular application of the universal notion of order.

This idea of order as a particular vocational group is much associated with St. Augustine but it is already found in Origen. In referring to Ezek 14:14, both Origen (*In Ezech,* hom. 4: G.C.S., 33, 358-370) and Augustine (*Quaestiones Evangeliorum* 1, 12 and II, 44: P.L. 35, 1326 and 1357; *Epistola* III, 4: C.S.E.L., 34, 8: *De Excidio Urbis Romae Sermo* I, 1: C.C.L., XLVI, 249; *De Peccatorum Meritis et Remissione* II, 10, 12: C.S.E.L., 60, 83-90; *Enarratio in ps. 132,* 4, 5: C.C.L., XL, 1929) took Noah, Daniel and Job as representatives of three kinds of people: churchleaders, contemplatives, and those who followed Christ in the midst of the affairs of the world. Thed in such writers as Cyril of Alexandria (*In Ezech hom:* P.G., 70, 1457-1459) and Gregory the Great (*Moralia* I, 14-20: B.L., 75, 535; *In Ezech hom.* lib. II, hom. 4, 5: P.L., 76, 976) and it became commonplace in Latin medieval literature.

In medieval Latin writings the constant reference is to *tria genera hominum* or to *tres ordines fidelium.* Alternative terms to *ordo* are *gradus, conditio, status* and *professio.* The three groupings however do not always exactly correspond to those given by Augustine. Thus for Gregory the Great the distinction was between preachers, the continent and spouses. However it was used and whatever the penchant for the number three, the idea of order allowed for different ways in which people could follow the Christian vocation. It also made it possible to relate the spiritual life to ways of participating in church ministry, in the life of prayer and in the affairs of the world.

In the High Middle Ages, the recognition of different categories of Christian vocation was of considerable importance. Though the number three kept cropping up, and Noah, Daniel and Job still served their purpose as exemplars, the actual categories mentioned far exceeded this number. It included prelates, doctors, the married, virgins, monks, mendicants, contemplatives and preachers. As for those who followed Christ in pursuing the social enterprise, the orders included kings, lords, peasants, knights and even burghers. Numberings mixed the vocations and one categorization mentioned those who governed, those who prayed and those who took arms to defend Christendom or the defenseless of society. What is of particular interest here is how much attention was given not only to monks, clergy, mendicants and other obviously churchly groups, but also to the secular walks of life such as those of farmer, merchant and knight.

The analogy sometimes used was that of the body of Christ and its diverse members. One side of this body was said to be made up of those following spiritual pursuits and the other of those following temporal. Speaking of the organs by which the body was compacted, Honorius

Augustodunensis listed these orders: *praelati, ecclesiàm* subditi, doctores, religiosi, magistri, milites armis defendentes, coniugati, agricolae, virgines and lastly, *continentes orantes (In Cant.* tr. II, c. 5: P.L., 172, 444).

There was some tension in the ordering of walks of life between a hierarchical conception of the church and an organic one. As long as authors had participation in the life of Christ in mind, they seem to have used organic imagery whereby in one body all contribute diversely to the growth and health of the whole. In turning to structure and the exercise of power in diffusing the life of Christ, however, they mostly adopted hierarchical patterns. Discussion of the states of life allowed for an influence of person upon person or of persons on the health of the whole body. This was however obscured in discussions about church office and ordained ministry. As a result, there was no clear perception of how personal charism and official ministry converged nor of how ministry was exercised by those not holding office.

To see this ordering of walks of life in proper perspective, two things need to be kept in mind. First, church and society were coterminous and the law of Christ was to keep it so. The ideal was that of a Christian order, maintained by spiritual and temporal power alike. The enemies of one, whether heretics or Islam, were considered the enemies of the other. Second, the issues of church order in larger or narrower sense were solved in terms of a universal church and its organization rather than primarily in terms of a particular or local church. What was at stake was what had to be done if a Christian order were to govern the totality of life and of civilization.

It was this concern with the universal that was one of the primary factors in allowing vocation to diverse forms of religious life and ecclesiastical ministry to intersect. Disputes between monks, mendicants and regular clergy over pastoral ministry and privilege were tempestuous and rancorous. They were often resolved in favour of the mendicants by appeal to the sovereign and universal jurisdiction of the Roman pontiff.

St. Bonaventure's treatment of the role of the papacy is noteworthy in that regard. He shows the hierarchy of jurisdiction in any part of the church to flow from pope to metropolitan to diocesan ordinary to parish priest, each of these authorities having the right to intervene in the jurisdiction of the lower should the greater need require it (cf. *Commentarium in Sententias* Dist. XIX, III, I, 4; Dist. XXIV, II, II, 4). Through such argumentation the religous orders who claimed the authority of the pope in their favour could claim exemption from the jurisdiction of the closer prelate, both in regulating their own lives and in many aspects of their pastoral work. If they had a sovereign mandate to preach or to confess penitents, or to minister a place of public worship, who could impede them? Such exemption was bolstered by the ideals of a higher calling that ranked mendicants above regular clergy in their state of life.

In earlier times, pastoral ministry had been confided to monasteries in the interests of the faithful when localme an ideal of the good pastor. With the appearance of the mendicant friars, more mobile in their ministry and at first unpropertied, regular clergy and religious functioned alongside each other, claiming different jurisdictions and often quarrelling over the right of access to the people. Not only jurisdiction but virtue could give the edge to the religious.

While St. Thomas Aquinas saw the episcopacy as a state of perfection because of its high calling (II-II, 184, 5), he also believed in the ideal of combining the contemplation of divine things with their transmission through teaching (II-II, 181, 3). A religious order of universal expansion could be seen to offer a distinctive ministry and to serve an order of communion beyond the particular church. It could also be seen as following a higher call. On both counts, the change had its effect on diocese and on regular clergy, whose scope and image began to take on some of the properties of the universal religious order. Earlier called upon to imitate the monk in the following of Christ, the diocesan priest was now expected to model himself on the friar. Clearly here was an issue of church order that served the option for an ecclesiology of universal institution and of higher states of life as principle of organization.

On the side of the laity, the relation of Christian life to concerns of the world became more complex and varied. It escaped the categorizations where it was enough to list ascetics, widows, virgins and the married. It was not even enough in due course to list the ruler, the ruled and the knight defender. The social and economic life of Europe underwent great upheaval during the High Middle Ages and beyond. Merchant classes found their place on the scene and looked to theologians, often among the friars, for an ethic suited to their class and trade. The whole social order passed beyond the feudal to the life of the commune and the city state. Within what is more narrowly called ecclesiastical life there were the popular evangelical movements, the aspirants to the devout life who pursued their own rule of life without joining a monastery or convent, and in time the sodalities and confraternities of rich diversity. Having attempted to embrace this state of affairs through use of the concept of order, theology's eventual response was to develop the treatise on the states of life and to give more attention to the life of the individual person in tracts on grace and on the virtues.

In conjunction with this kind of treatment of the human person, there emerged a canon law and a theological vision that depended greatly on the distinction between clergy, religious and laity. This was less an organic vision than an organizational and societal one. It bolstered that view of the church which in the post-Reformation era saw it as a society of hierarchical order, designed to meet the spiritual needs of persons and be a presence in society pursuing the interests of God's rule and kingdom. Women religious and some branches of the laity might be very necessary to this plan, but they took their place in a society completely ordered by hierarchy and clergy. They were offered a spirituality that exploited the distinction between priest, religious and laity, itself a kind of spiritual hierarchy providing different rules of life and leading to different degrees of perfection.

It is of note that even within the newly developing and more organic ecclesiology of the Vatican II, there is a reliance on this threefold distinction. Paragraph 33 of the *Constitution on the Church* differentiates between the ordained, religious and laity by placing them in relation to the church and to the world respectively. The ordained are said to be responsible for the sacred ministry, the religious to be witnesses to the beatitudes of God's reign, and the laity to have a call which has a clearly secular character immersing them in the affairs of society. It has been much argued whether this is a constitutive or descriptive definition, but in any case it continues to be pursued in the teachings of the magisterium as a key to church order and the fulfillment of its mission. The sense of a spiritual hierarchy has been toned down. However, a clear canonical and theological distinction between the three appears to be thought necessary, in order to work out their respective roles in the church.

Since what is said of the ordained and of the laity has a clear functional perspective and what is said of religious has a more abstractly spiritual focus, the part of these last in the life and mission of the church tends to remain obscure, as though belonging in neither sanctuary nor market-place they had no clear profile. This affects women religious more than men, who in great part belong to clerical orders and congregations and so have recourse to their priestly ministry when the contours of the religious side of their vocation become blurred.

Despite the apparent conceptual clarity of the distinction between ordained, religious and baptized, hierarchical, vocational and spiritual concepts of order have merged. This provides an inadequate foundation for the church order to guide the future.

Order, Office and the Ordained Ministry

Essential to a discussion of church order is the issue of the ordained ministry, its origins, its forms and its nature. In the aftermath of the Vatican II, the question has taken on new tonality because of ecumenical dialogue and because of the efforts to relate the ordained ministry's participation in Christ's mission to the participation of all the baptized. The treatment is internal to an ecclesiology that is less centralized and more attentive to the reality of local churches, their specific concerns and their specific cultural forms.

The challenge which the 16th-century Reformation put to the Catholic church was that its ministry was unevangelical and that it had betrayed its apostolic origins. The only ministry which the Reformers found in the NT was that of word and sacrament and though most of them admitted to elements of church order therein they found no warrant for the distinction between clergy and laity. The Council of Trent responded by anathematizing those who denied that sacrificing priesthood and hierarchy had their foundations in the will and prescription of Christ himself. The conciliar participants were aware of the obscurity surrounding the exact historical origins of the tripartite ministry of bishop, presbyter and deacon, but did not think that this affected the divine origins of hierarchy and priesthood. In the present period of ecumenical dialogue and convergence, there is greater sensitivity on all sides to the historical and cultural influences found in the development of order and ministry and a much more circumspect approach to NT foundations.

In reading the NT on ministry, it is necessary to distinguish between kinds and prototypes of ministry, the ordering of local churches within themselves and in their relation to other churches, and the rite or service of ordination. Apart from the fact that Jesus Christ in his exercise of *exousia* and *diakonia* is the exemplar of all ministry, the most authoritative figure in the NT church is that of the apostle. In itself, the image of the apostle owes more to Paul than to the twelve, but it is used of them in a specific way by Luke to show continuity of the preaching of the gospel with the group of disciples who received their mandate from Jesus himself and witnessed his death and resurrection.

Broadly speaking, to be an apostle meant to be a witness to the resurrection of the Crucified One, to have received a commission from the Risen Christ, to be filled with his Spirit and to proclaim the gospel by word and faithful witness. The root of all ministry throughout the ages is in this apostolic witness and all proclamation of the gospel must be seen to be in continuity with it. The exact historical part which those named as the twelve took in the spread of the gospel and in the foundation of churches is obscure, and the inclusion of others in the original apostolic ministry is all but certain. Nonetheless, the image of the twelve apostles as found in the NT is a constant and important point of reference in all further development of church ministry and church order. Alongside them, the figure of the apostle Paul is a powerful paradigm for the power and exercise of apostolic preaching.

In the description of NT churches, ministry is aroused and guided by the outflow of the charismatic Spirit. The variety of ministries is almost without number. The one criterion for the discernment of charisms is that they be truly of service to the building up of the body in unity and charity, its praise of the Lord and its proclamation of the good news. It is this very profusion of gifts that makes it difficult to decipher the nature and structure of church order and the locus of authority or leadership. There is certainly no identification between charism, ministry and office, and ministry whether of mutual care, of word or of worship is not confined to church leaders. The concern with order and authoritative leadership, however, is clearly not absent from the NT books, even though it appears in them in varying degrees.

The basic order is that unity in the Spirit and in the one apostolic witness be kept. Life in the church is non-discriminatory and is guided by promptness to serve. This is reflected in the words of Jesus about service recorded in Luke's account of the Last Supper (Lk 22:24-27), in John's account of the washing of the feet and the love commandment (Jn 13:1-20), and in the credal formula of Gal 3:25-29. As for organization, it is now customary to distinguish between the kinds of order found in the Jerusalem church, in the Pauline churches, in the Johannine churches and in the churches mirrored in the Pastoral Letters, though it is hard to be very specific about any of them. The extent of borrowing from the social and cultural milieu to identify fitting organizational structures has to be acknowledged and consequently the diversity of structure and leadership. Thus there arose the house-churches of the Pauline letters, the rule of elders at

Jerusalem and the overseer/elders of Antioch and Ephesus.

One of the difficulties in detailing such structures is that the meaning of particular words such as *episkopos, presbyteros* and *diakonos* is unclear. It would certainly be erroneous to confuse them with the same titles used in later centuries. Another problem is the relative unconcern with order in some writings. This is particularly true in the Johannine writings, where it is the gift of the Spirit to each and all that animates and congregates the church rather than any authoritative figure. There are however two constants as far as authority is concerned: fidelity to the apostolic word and the power of the Spirit brought to evidence in deeds of service. No authority can be claimed that does not meet these criteria.

It is in the Pastoral Letters that one comes across the concern with the continuity of a later generation with the apostolic, and with it the attempt to determine more uniform structures of transmission of office, as well as the possible beginnings of an ordination rite (1 Tim 4:14; 5:22), though the interpretation of these texts is in question. In similar vein there is the submission of a local church to the greater and more wide-ranging apostolic authority, represented in the figure of Paul introduced into these letters. Whether or not one finds these writings excessively conservative, patriarchal and institution-minded, the issues that emerge are clearly necessary.

While the Catholic and Orthodox churches have always in principle upheld the tripartite ministry of bishop, presbyter and deacon, and while the World Council of Churches in its BEM document appeals for its restoration in Protestant churches, historically it is only with Ignatius of Antioch that one finds clear evidence of churches structured in this way. In particular, it is only in his writings that a strong episcopal figure emerges. This is all the more interesting given the evidence that in his time other churches, such as those of Rome and Alexandria, were probably governed collegially by the presbyterium. However, even while noting the influence of Ignatius, Irenaeus, Cyprian and Hippolytus in presenting the ideal figure of the bishop for subsequent generations, one has to note that elements of collegiate government were kept in the churches which they represent through the body of the presbyterium. One also notes the organic quality of ministry and church life which allowed for the varied services of such persons as deacons, readers, cantors, acolytes, widows and virgins, as well as the continuing presence of charismatics. Whatever the authority of the bishop, his was not a sole and isolated ministry. It was exercised in the heart of the church united at the one eucharistic table and bonded in the Spirit through a variety of gifts and ministries.

As for the authority and leadership that is attributed to the bishop by the above-mentioned writers, it first seems to have emerged as a practical necessity and was then given its theology, in much the way that we now see practice and theory to interact in the development of a tradition. The episcopacy served the self-definition of the church, the setting of its doctrinal and disciplinary boundaries, and became a focal point of the church's apostolic continuity. The arguments often appear to be circulatory but this does not make them invalid, especially since episcopal appointment and leadership is subject to reception and to the bond of communion with other churches. In Ignatius, Cyprian and Hippolytus we find the pressing urgency to have one eucharistic table for the local church, since without this true unity cannot be conceived. Given this urgency, there is the question of admission to the table and of the faith that is professed in its celebration. The argument is circular because the bishop's authority comes from the apostolic tradition and succession, and yet it is he who decides what constitutes it.

There is a check on his authority in that the bishop has to be in one way or another chosen and approved by the people and installed with the participation of neighboring churches and their bishops. Furthermore, in the exercise of his leadership he is bound by the synodal forms of presbyteral participation in the local church and conciliar convocation or exchange in the communion of churches. All of this constitutes a testing of the Spirit, one that is greatly enhanced if the bishop leads an exemplary evangelical and apostolic life. Ignatius and Cyprian were not insensitive to the authority conferred on their ministry by their own martyrdom, and the former positively desired it as though it were truly necessary.

In later times, there is the same concern to find the bishop's ministry confirmed by the witness of an apostolic life. This led to efforts to assure the choice of the right candidate. In the East the ideal bishop was the monk-bishop, as we find in Basil of Caeserea, and in the West a peculiar combination of qualitiesmade Martin of Tours the exemplary type of episcopacy. He was known for his ascetic life, he had founded a monastic community, he took the position under duress and the choice was confirmed by a process of discernment and by the people's acclamation. Martin was moreover an ardent apostle throughout his term of office, travelling far and wide to preach the gospel and to supplant pagan cults with Christian worship.

In effect, this concern with the ideal candidate whose life would confirm his works had much to do with merging the two types of order mentioned above, the ecclesiastical and the vocational. Cyprian and Augustine focussed on the relation of the bishop to Christ, a relationship to be found both in his life and in the power

accredited to his ministry. Ambrose in his treatise *De Officiis Ministrorum* (P.L. 16, 25-194) simply perceived the call to episcopacy as a call to a higher sanctity, one for which a person had to strive on appointment or on receiving the call, whether he had previously attained such holiness or not. An exalted notion of the relationship to Christ, the need to reinforce episcopal authority in leadership and teaching, and the desire to foster candidates trained in the spiritual life had much to do with the clericalization of church order that gained momentum throughout the Middle Ages.

This was not without its ironic consequences, for it meant that bad choices were often upheld, despite the less than exemplary lives of the ordained. In the endeavor to maintain authority and good order even under such circumstances, the holiness of apostolic witness was gradually attached to the office itself rather than to the person ordained to it in the Spirit. The sacralization of sacramental power and of magisterial teaching meant that the action of Christ in the sacraments and the authentication of rule and teaching were guaranteed by the office itself, independently of the life of the minister. What was difficult to maintain was the evidence that even in the case of unworthy ministers, the sacramental power and the apostolic tradition were grounded in the reality of an ecclesial life lived in the power and unity of the Spirit, on local and universal level. The statement that the minister acted as minister of the church (understood as a large institution) or in the faith of the church was something of a safeguard, but it was not enough to prevent an increasingly sacral and authoritarian view of ecclesiastical office that formed an ever-thickening wedge between the ordained and the laity.

One can follow two distinct paths in tracing the ongoing development of the sacrament of order and the ministry of the ordained. One is to have an eye principally on the institutional aspects and so to trace functionally and theologically what became of the offices of bishop, presbyter and deacon. The other is to look for the less easily determined but vastly important cultural configurations given to the ideals and the forms of ministerial and pastoral action.

Institutionally and theologically, the development of the presbyterate/priesthood is the heart of the matter. With the multiplication of communities and places of worship, in trying to keep some form of local (or as we would now say, diocesan) unity, the role of the presbyter was transformed from that of a member of the presbytery to that of pastor of a smaller community in city, town or village. Presbyters were ordained by and remained under the supervision of the bishop, who in turn was increasingly isolated from a pastorate in a eucharistic community. Hence the presbyter became the priest whose principal function was the offering of the eucharistic sacrifice and whose other functions were related to this. Even with this emergence of the presbyter, however, the same order did not prevail in every church. In part this had to do with the difference between a city church and a rural church. In a city church such as Rome or Hippo, bishop and presbyters served the places of worship from one center and lived variant measures of a common life. In rural churches the presbyters resided in the village communities, sometimes augmented in service by the presence of deacons or lesser orders. In this case, the cathedral church was the center of a network of communities and the pastoral visitation of the bishop kept them united and provided with ministers as needed. It is this context that is reflected in the model of bishop provided by Martin of Tours and in the Gallican ordination rites of the *Missale Francorum*. In either situation, rural or metropolitan, the bishop was surrounded by clerics, not always presbyters, who provided a measure of collegiate responsibility in church government, especially in the administration of church property or in the making of appointments to office. This is the origin of what came to be known as the cathedral chapter, vestiges of which are still found in European countries in the persons of diocesan canons and archdeacons.

From quite early on, the good ordering of a church by the bishop could be subverted by the ordination of presbyters to serve the interests and the households of lords and landowners. Some attempt was made to keep that order through which bishops presided over communities of worship through the ordination of chorbishops, who would serve in rural areas. While ordained to the episcopacy, they did not have a full part in the exercise of episcopal collegiality but were deemed lesser in rank to those whoe enjoyed the rank of bishop without prefix. Their position was too indefinite to last, so that in effect presbyters did take over as local pastors in areas not directly under the care of bishops.

In the 8th century, Agobardus of Lyons fulminated against the ordination of *homiunculi* who were little better than ignorant vassals to some rude lord (*De Privilegio et Jure Sacerdotii* XI: P.L., 104, 138-139). This had to do with the establishment of proprietary churches in the Frankish realm. These were churches on the property of large landowners which by and large escaped the jurisdiction of bishops, even the presbyter being usually ordained at the behest of the local lord rather than nominated by the bishop.

The incidence of concubinage and financial corruption among the medieval clergy is but evidence of the difficulty experienced in coordinating structures of ministry with ideals of holiness. It had much to do with the increasing control of churchs and nominations to ministry by secular princes and lords. However, whatever the difficulties encountered, the role of presbyter as local pastor and sacramental minister was firmly established through the Middle Ages and remained even after the Gregorian reform.

Since this was indeed the role assumed by presbyters, in scholastic theology the sacrament of orders was defined as the power to consecrate the body and blood of Christ and to offer the sacrifice. The diaconate, to the extent that it still mattered, was but preparatory to this and the episcopacy was more readily defined as a jurisdiction than as a sacrament. This did indeed reflect the life of the church. The people were dependent on the priest for sacraments and for whatever doctrinal instruction he could give. From the days when he was charged with the care of the poor and the administration of church property, as well as with whatever pastoral functions the bishop would commit to him, the deacon lost all practical importance and the conferral of the order became a preparation for priesthood. The bishop looked to the overall unity of the diocese, appointed and ordained priests, performed such liturgies as seemed to fall under this supervisory care such as the consecration of churches, the consecration of virgins and the blessing of knights, and protected the interests of the church against the temporal lords. He also exercised his doctrinal responsibility of keeping the deposit of faith in conjunction with brother bishops, often through attendance at provincial councils.

Thus matters had emerged by the end of the first millennium of the common era and thus they were confirmed, with some reforming zeal, at the Council of Trent. If they were confirmed, it was of course because they had been challenged. The Reformers wanted the ministry of word and sacrament to prevail and they wanted nothing of sacrificing priesthood. They could find no warrant in the NT for a special sacrament of ordination, even though they did want to keep some form of ritual installation in ministry. They did not countenance the hierarchy and distinct offices of bishop and priest as defined in Catholicism but held to the one ministry of word and sacrament, even in those churches where as a matter of order and discipline they kept the office of bishop without special ordination to it.

Beyond the notion of the one NT and divinely instituted ministry, they had differing ideas of the order required by discipline. Though they effaced the radical distinction between clergy and laity they were usually loath to put ministry on too charismatic and egalitarian a basis. Since they saw a strong link between church and state in the service of God's kingdom, whether in dukedom or in city-state as at Geneva and Zurich, they tended to give some authority in the appointment of ministers to temporal officers and to the community to be served. It is of course a canard to say that they saw the minister as a delegate of the people, for all their emphasis on the common and royal priesthood. For local purposes of order and discipline, Calvin kept what he thought to be the NT church offices of pastor, deacon and elder, alongside the ministry of word and sacrament. The pertinence of these offices has remained a constant, if at times ill-defined, part of the history of churches in the Reformed tradition.

In the current evolution of this three-fold ministry, developments are taking place both within the Catholic church and in churches that have membership in the World Council of Churches. The Second Vatican Council gave new if not untroubled attention to the relation between the mission and office of all the baptized and that of the ordained ministry. One of its earliest acts was to define the episcopacy as a sacrament and to describe all ordination as appointment to the threefold office of governing, teaching and worship. It also espoused the restoration of the diaconate as a permanent rather than a transitory office. In its definition of this order it combined mention in a rather unintegrated way of the ministry of word and worship with the ministry of works of charity and administration. It thus rendered dues both to the origins of the diaconate and to the functional service which it could now render as auxiliary to the priesthood, and allowed the married into the ranks of the clergy.

In the meantime, through a succession of dialogues, the Faith and Order document BEM has asked for the recognition of the tripartite ministry as an ancient and respected tradition and as a point around which further communion between churches might be fostered. Of the *episkope* it says that it "is necessary to express and safeguard the unity of the body" and that it is best kept where the threefold pattern is observed. "The orderly transmission of the ordained ministry" it dubs "a powerful expression of the continuity of the Church throughout history." At the same time, the document is careful to describe ordination as an act of the whole church and to set down the conditions whereby its grounding in the life and unity of the church may best be served.

All churches, including the Catholic, now see that even with the threefold pattern it is impossible to see a uniform order throughout the centuries, just as it is impossible to exact strict uniformity across the globe today. In fact the plea for a common pattern of ministry and order is accompanied by an increasing attention to the cultural diversity of local churches. There is a move away from an ecclesiology that accentuated the universal structure and organization of the one church in many places, to an ecclesiology that gives primacy to the local church and that envisages the universal as the communion of many churches

rather than as one monolithic structure and government. What this, along with the multiple exercise of the charisms of the baptized, bodes for church order is as much a matter of future projection as it is one of present realization.

When ministry is seen in the light of culture and history rather than simply as an office and an institution, the differences in pattern are even greater. Configurations of space are keen indicators of the concept and ordering of the church that prevailed in each cultural epoch. Roughly, it is possible to distinguish between periods marked by the house-church, the city-church, the monastery, the order of the High Middle Ages, the Reformation and Counter-Reformation, the siege upon religion of the Enlightenment, and the cultural pluralism of the latter half of the 20th century.

In the centuries before Constantine, the church was in point of fact and not only in theory a eucharistic community; its boundaries were set by this weekly gathering. Its works were centered in it and its ministries defined in service of it. Seen from outside, the house-church was home to a community bonded by its very difference from the rest of society, yet not anxious to have too strong a profile nor wanting to have a heavy impact on public order. Seen from within, what is done to internal space reveals a history internal to the community. It is often remarked that churches of the NT epoch gathered in the homes spacious and charitable enough to accommodate them and that social household-codes influenced institutional development. This had rather ambivalent results. On the one hand, it meant that women could play a larger role in ministry and order than has ever been recognized since then. On the other hand, it meant that the patriarchy of the home influenced the ordering of the church. Simplicity and domesticity in any case marked celebration and relations, despite the threat that social distinctions presented to agapic communion. It is in such a setting that Ignatius of Antioch strove for the one eucharist and for an orthodoxy that kept the community intact, and that he praised the harmony sounded by presbyters and deacons in unison with their bishop. From the little information that comes from architectural diggings, it seems that internal spatial setting gave distinctive place to these ministers and officers within the epoch still marked by the house-church, an epoch that lasted longer in East Syria or Mesopotamia than elsewhere. The raised beam in the middle of the room gave prominence to those who read or taught the word and the addition of an apse to what was otherwise a large room gave an aura of holiness to the eucharistic table and a sacred character to those who ministered at it.

The church of the post-Constantinian era is marked by its basilicas and its courtly ritual, and by its city-wide liturgy. The church was a public institution, a power in society, which by its ritual mapped out the space of the city itself. The stational liturgies of Rome and Constantinople ordered space and time for the populace. While the influence of church may have been most obvious in these centers, it can be remarked also in places like Milan, Carthage, Antioch and Hippo. Even the rural hamlets fell under the power of the city church, and Leo the Great could not countenance the indignity of having a brother bishop in some of the obscure castelli of the Alban hills (*Epist* XII, 10: P.L., 54, 654). Such is the setting for the clericalization of ministry and church order already outlined. It suited a public cultural need more than it responded to any intrinsic evangelical necessity, but since then the church has never been totally free of the paradigmatic quality that clerical order assumed in this age of the expansion of Christianity.

Still using space as an indicator, one cannot ignore the period of history during which monasticism made its mark on ministry. It has already been remarked that the desire for a bishop who gave witness as well as teaching led Basil of Caesarea to look for the ideal candidate in the monastic brotherhood and Augustine of Hippo to impose a rule of common life on his clergy. In later centuries the corruption of mores in city and countryside, the poor economy of farming and the lack of Christian education were countered by the growing influence of monasteries, owning large tracts of land and organizing the economic and religious life of the populace around the monastic center. Under such influence, asceticism, contemplation and the ordering of time through the hours and the cycles of public worship, became common Christian ideals. Not only were large numbers of monks ordained to ministry and given pastoral charges, but the monk became the ideal for all priests and the monastic rhythm of prayer and liturgy the ideal for the parish church and the good Christian. Given their power and potential, monasteries did not escape being used by princes for their purposes, nor were they free of Roman influence. In the Carolingian era, it seems some effort was made to plan monastic liturgy and to map monastic churches on the pattern of the Roman stational liturgy.

The concept of ministry as hierarchy is the culmination of these clerical and monastic configurations of ministry and church order. If it has its spatial metaphor, it is that of the Gothic or Romanesque cathedrals with their steeples and their towers dominating the landscape and stretching heavenward. The concept of hierarchy, brought to fine articulation by the Pseudo-Dionysius, could be used to order both the ideals of the spiritual life and the ministerial functioning of the church as public institution, serving at the same time to forge a conjunction between the two. This was the period during which the church was developing as a spiritual power that had influence over the whole temporal order and as a universal organization with one center rather than as a local community of believers. The concept of hierarchy served to link the different parts of this Catholic church and to promote the image of the priest as public minister of an ecclesiastical institution without confine, acting in the power of Christ its head and founder. It could thus even legitimate acts of worship, especially the offering of the sacrifice of the Mass, that were not linked to any particular community or place.

The development was not without challenge from within. Popular evangelical movements and mendicant friars sought a simpler way of life in imitation of the poverty of Christ and wanted a church free of clerical privilege and control. The evangelical movement had its popular appeal, but it also had its Francis and its Dominic who combined a deep reverence for priesthood with the desire for evangelical simplicity, universal brotherhood and the preaching of the gospel. Innocent III was astute enough to harness this movement to what he saw as the more legitimate and spiritual aims of hierarchy. The unwillingness to be attached to any place and to serve the spread of the gospel wherever needed that he found in Francis and his followers in the long run served to strengthen the papacy and the centralization of the church as one universal organization. Hierarchy and evangelical itinerancy combined in fostering a more centralized church and in spreading Roman influence, even in such a matter as the widespread adoption of a form of the *Breviarium* of the Roman Curia for all clergy. The cathedral reaching out to the skies and the wanderings of the friar who settled in no fixed place are the spatial contours of the hierarchy of ministry. So are the praying of the same office in all parts of the church, the exposition of the Blessed Sacrament for public veneration, the retention of the Roman see even in the exile of Avignon, and the offering of the Mass by a priest in a secluded place for the obtainment of fruits that could redound to the whole church and even burst the boundaries between heaven and earth to the comfort of the departed.

With such a notion, even the saints and the angels could be expected to gather around the worshipping church, whether this was in a secluded chapel or in a fine sanctuary. They could also be expected to compete with each other in giving patronage to their favoured cities and villages. The pope could attempt to have his say in the running of the University of Paris and could collect monies in Germany for the building of a basilica in Rome, just as any friar with a reputation as a confessor could absolve sins in the name of Christ and the church in the royal chapel or in the village church. Though not much might be heard of the word of the gospel, the saints and the sacrament and the power of the priest assured the closeness of God and redemption through Christ's blood.

Calvin's Geneva, with its godly order, its absence of frivolity, its charity among citizens, and its denuded minister, in which pulpit and table alone caught the eye, may well represent the reaction against hierarchy and the evangelical concept of ministry espoused by the Reformation. The Reformers sought a ministry that gave pride of place to God's word, to justification by faith rather than by priestly ministrations, to the royal priesthood of all believers rather than to hierarchy, and to the freedom of the secular from the constraints of the sacred, believing that godly order was better served that way.

The Catholic Reformation countered the Protestant by an intensified centralization. It brought the concept and realities of hierarchy even more to the fore.

While it invented the seminary in the interests of a holier and better educated priesthood, it reinforced the image of a higher calling and increased dependency on the priest's sacramental ministry. It found its instrument in the Jesuits who completed the friars' independence from place with a more formidable centralized organization and who fostered a spirituality that allowed the individual access to divine mysteries in ways quite free of the need for community and community prayer. It was an ideal model for the clergy, applicable in any place or circumstance. The spatial metaphors for such ministry are the Baroque church with its gaudy world of grace, counterblast to Puritan severity, and the lonely hut providing the missionary a place to say Mass in pagan territory.

The cultural images of ministry can be completed by the neo-Gothic church, filled with the sounds of neo-Gregorian chant, or by the parish plant in Europe, the Americas, Asia or Africa alike, with its church, its rectory, its convent, its school and its hospital. Nostalgia for Rome and the need to fortify the faithful against the dominance of the secular combined in developing even further the Catholic Reformation's ideals of order and ministry. This type of ministry served its purpose well enough, for it preserved the heritage of doctrine, kept faith alive and fostered great piety in the ranks of clergy, religious and laity alike. One might see it in God's providence as a cultural necessity in a given era, though it endured beyond its time. It was left to Pope John XXIII and Vatican II to ask whether a more highly educated Christian people, more deliberately conscious of the workings of the Spirit, more open to ecumenical collaboration among all the followers of Christ, and respectful of cultural and religious diversity, might not serve God's reign better than a church entrenched. This of course puts difficult questions to both the institutional and the cultural forms of church order, questions that fortunately Christian churches are beginning to address together rather than in opposition to one another.

An Ecclesiology of Organic Order

To meet 20th-century developments in church life and ministry, an order of organic rather than hierarchical unity is postulated. This has six qualities. First, its foundation is an ecclesiology of communion, focussed on the local church and allowing for a universal ordering which is that of a communion of churches. Second, it is evangelical in the sense that it learns from evangelical movements in the church of past and present times. Third, it is sacramental in the sense that it is unified by its eucharistic gathering and sacramental liturgies and is thereby enlivened in the Spirit by the memory of Christ's Pasch. Fourth, it is diaconal in that it incorporates a variety of charisms and ministries into the life of the local church with whatever ritual recognition is appropriate and non-discriminatory in language and symbol. Fifth, it is non-patriarchal and ready to overcome a long history of gender discrimination. Sixth, in providing the forms of social and institutional order and identity that are needed it allows for synodal types of government in both local and universal church.

Communion. It is said that the ecclesiology of the Second Vatican Council is an ecclesiology of communion, but this can be ambiguous. On the one hand, such an ecclesiology denotes a shared meaning, value and vision, so that unity in the body prevails over special interests. The theological foundation of this is that all share in the communion of the one Trinity of divine life, as it is communicated through Christ and the Spirit. On the other hand, the diversity in unity, or the communion of the diverse, needs to be equally appreciated. Consequently some theologians are developing a theology of the universal or catholic as the communion of local churches, diverse in their cultural, historical and organizational physiognomies, yet united together in the service of God's reign. This recognition of diversity is important for a church that is as readily African or Asian as it is European or American, and that is open to communion in diversity between historically divided communities.

Evangelical. During Vatican II there was a group of bishops from different countries who used to meet regularly, calling themselves the Church of the Poor. They had a double concern. One was to address the needs of peoples whose lives are impaired by harsh poverty, taking the preaching of the gospel to the poor as the church's major orientation. Second, and in conjunction with this, they wanted a church that in its style of life and in its organization would show greater simplicity and evangelical poverty. It was not the first time in church history that groups asked for church reform in head and members on the basis of this twofold exigency. Though none of the specific recommendations of this episcopal group found their way directly into conciliar documents, their concerns did have an influence. A church ordered by this evangelism would give primacy to the mission to serve God's reign in society and would spell this out in terms of service to the poor and oppressed and a struggle for a just society. Its common life would be marked by simplicity, poverty and non-discrimination. Its service would derive from charism, spiritual authority and competency, and it would make use of the criterion of the discernment of spirits in the ritual and official ordering of its ministries. The paradigm of order would be organic, not hierarchical. Institutional needs are not ignored in this paradigm but ministry is not confined to office-holders. Neither is there an attempt to reduce all ministries to strict categories or to rank charisms.

Sacramental. The realization of this quality starts from praxis. It comes from the pragmatic and symbolic role that ritual plays in a body in ordering relations, in expressing values and corporate identity, in serving the corporate memory, in fixing perceptions of time and space, and in providing a vision of the future. No body of people will exist as such without its focal symbols and its rituals, constantly renewed through the invocation of the corporate memory, relating it to the community's life and practice. The church, people of God, body of Christ, new creation in the Spirit, comes to be and moves towards the future through its sacramental action. It is in the living reality of its communion in Christ and of Christ's oneness with it through the Spirit that it finds sacramental expression. The narratives, prayers, symbols and rituals of sacrament are such that they embrace human existence in its most fundamental needs and desires, in its oneness with all of creation, and in that hope which orients its pathways through history. When in common parlance it is said that the church itself is the primary sacrament of Christ, this does not signify a reality that, already existing, then performs sacramental acts. What is meant is that it exists as a reality in and through a sacramental remembrance and worship that is allied to practice.

A Christian community ought to be unified through its eucharistic gathering and through the ritual celebrations that in a variety of ways relate to this. The eucharist is centered on the common table, in obedience to the gospel command to take, eat and drink the body and blood of Christ and to keep memory of him. At this table there is no discrimination or distinction and the elements of bread and wine blessed in the power of Christ's Spirit relate the participants not only to each other but to creation and to society's ordering of the resources of the earth, whether in justice or in exploitation. Grace is channelled through the human and the earthly and the presence of Christ is his presence through these gifts in the community. The power of that presence is the power of the dangerous memory of his suffering and of the hopeful memory of his Resurrection. The prevailing image of a church's memory reflects its perception of salvation, whether this image be that of sacrifice, covenant, the struggle with unholy powers or the *abba* experience of the suffering servant. The sacramental practice of a community is discerned not only in its relation to tradition but just as importantly in relation to its ethical practice of justice, charity and service to humanity.

Diaconal. Church order needs to be an order of service. This is a particular aspect of being evangelical. Its model is the washing of the feet of the disciples by Jesus, a testamental memory that ought to be kept alive in the course of the worship of the communion table. The aspect of service being brought to the fore in the grass-roots ordering of ministries in many churches is the relation of the temporal or material to the spiritual, or the unity between life in the body and life in the spirit. The ancient order of deacons serves in some measure as a paradigm for this service. With all due allowance for historical criticism, the fact remains that ecclesial tradition has long taken Acts 6 as the root text for the order of deacons. According to that text, Stephen and his companions were appointed for the service of tables when the poor of the Gentile communities were being neglected. Stephen at least combined the preaching of the gospel and the witness of his death with that service. In the church order of the *Apostolic Tradition* and the *Didascalia*, and in other early church documents, it is apparent that the deacon's eucharistic service in taking and presenting the gifts to the bishop is one with the administration of the church's patrimony to the poor. Litur-

gical ministry and social ministry are perfectly blended. This historical model helps to give orientation to the contemporary efforts to restore the permanent order of deacons to service. It indicates that the attention directed to corporal needs and to the gospel of justice belongs to the very nature of the church as a sacramental communion and that provision for this has to be made in the ordering of ministries. While this is partly realized through the restoration of the permanent diaconate, it postulates a larger inclusion of diverse ministries of service in the ordering of the church.

Non-patriarchal. Another way of saying that church order needs to become non-patriarchal is to say that it has to give evidence of repentance for centuries of sexism and gender discrimination. There is a very obvious difference between the credal formula of Gal 3:24-29 and the place of women in the apostolic and house ministry of NT times on the one hand, and the discriminatory attitudes towards them meshed with the church orderings of later centuries. What the practical consequences of corporate penance would be is not clear but there will be none if there is not penance. Even in defending the tradition of ordaining only men to ecclesial and sacramental leadership in 1977 (*Inter Insigniores*, A.A.S., 69 [1977] 98-116), the Congregation for the Doctrine of the Faith dissociated itself from most of the arguments that had been used in the past by such personages as John Chrysostom and Thomas Aquinas, since they supposed a natural superiority of man over woman. The two arguments which remain are the longevity of the practice and the representation of Jesus Christ by the minister, a representation which is said to require that this be a male. Both arguments however need close scrutiny for the possible residue of sexual bias. The NT foundations for the exclusion of women from office are certainly shaky.

The argument from representation may overlook aspects of the doctrine of the Incarnation and most of all the transforming power of the Resurrection which overcomes in Christ all differences between Jew and Gentile, slave and free, male and female. At any rate, from now on it is necessary that church order take account of the diverse ways in which women minister as much as it takes account of the diverse ways of men. Family ministry is not only the woman's responsibility just as it is not exclusively her duty. The active apostolate of women cannot be provided for purely under canon law and rules for religious congregations, but has to become an integral part of all church law and order.

Aspects of this non-patriarchal turn in ordering ministry and church life occur under the four previous headings. The evangelical community is in its essence non-discriminatory. The ritual of sacrament has to follow rites and language usage that are purged of sexism and hierarchy. The communion of church and churches has to give voice and power to both sexes. The renewed interest in the diaconal may bring us to the perception that in practice this has been kept alive through the centuries by women more than by men and that it is time to give canonical recognition to a historical fact.

Synodal. The word synodal is used to indicate that decision-making in doctrine and practice is a shared responsibility. Synodal structures attempt to give value and orientation to this truth. The old juridical distinctions between the *ecclesia discens* and the *ecclesia docens*, the universal and the particular, or the authoritative and the consultative, are inadequate to the present time. The very diversity between local churches requires structures of communion that foster dialogue and shared responsibility so that the central role of the Roman church can assume a new form. In diocese and parish a start has been made with pastoral and parish councils, but their effectiveness is hindered by laws and attitudes that belong in a hierarchial vision of world and church. One danger to be avoided is that the juridical be separated from the sacramental in another form of the medieval distinction between order and jurisdiction. It makes little ecclesial or social sense to provide for the laity's participation in decision-making and ministerial ordering if the ritual of their liturgical participation retains symbols of sacred distinction. Access to the table as a communion table is as vital as a seat on the parish council or an office in the chancery. The symbolic is actually at the core of church law and in forging a common identity and vision bad ritual derogates from the best of laws.

Conclusion

The interpretive quality of this entry is obvious. It is not enough to recount facts, to the extent that these are obtainable. The meaning expressed in church order in its relation to history, place, social order and culture is all important, as is the capacity for taking a critical look at it. Without this, the retrieval of gospel roots and the needs of the present time will not be served. That is why from the complex history of order in the church the move was made in the last section to some prognostication for the future.

Antonio Acerbi, *Due Ecclesiologia, Ecclesiologia Giuridica ed Ecclesiologia di Communione nella 'Lumen Gentium '*(Bologna: ed. Dehoniane, 1975). Pierre Van Beneden, *Aux Origines d'une Terminologie Sacramentelle, Ordo, Ordinare, Ordinatio dans la Littérature Chrétienne avant 313* (Leuven: Spicilegium Sacrum Lovaniense, 1974). Hans von Campenhausen, *Kirchliches Amt und geistliches Vollmacht in den ersten drei Jahrhunderten* (Tübingen: Mohr, 1953). Yves Congar, *Etudes d'Ecclésiologie Médiévale* (London: Variorum Reprints, 1983). Georges Duby, *Les Trois Ordres ou l'Imaginaire du Feudalisme* (Paris: Gallimard, 1978); Alexandre Faivre, *Naissance d'une Hiérarchie Les Prémières Etapes du Cursus Clérical* (Paris: Beauchesne, 1977). Alexandre Faivre, *Les Laïcs* aux Origines de l'Eglise (Paris: Centurion, 1983). Vinzen Fuchs, *Der Ordinationstitel von seiner Entstehung bis auf Innocenz III:eine Untersuchung zur kirchlichen Rechtsgeschichte, mit besondere Berucksichtung der Anschauungen Rudolph Sohms* (Amsterdam: P. Schippers, 1963). Vincenzo Monachino, *La Cura Pastorale a Milano, Carthagine e Roma nel secolo IV* (Roma: Analecta Gregoriana, 1947). Heribert Mühlen, *Entsakralisierung, Ein epochales Schlagwort in seiner Bedeutung für die Zukunft der christlichen Kirchen* (Paderborn: Schoningh, 1971). Thomas F. O'Meara, *Theology of Ministry* (New York: Paulist, 1983). Roger E. Reynolds, *The Ordinals of Christ from their Origins to the Twelfth Century* (Berlin/New York: Walter De Gruyter, 1978). René Roques, *L'Univers Dionysien: Structure Hiérarchique du Monde selon le Pseudo-Denys* (Paris: Aubier, 1954).

DAVID N. POWER, O.M.I.

COLLEGE CAMPUS, LITURGY ON

Worshipping communities on college or university campuses are different enough from regular parish communities to merit special attention. While the promotion of good liturgy anywhere calls for knowledge, piety and much hard work, campus ministers face some special obstacles that others do not face. At the same time, however, they also enjoy some special advantages. We will look at some of these obstacles and advantages and discuss specific strategies to meet the worship needs of students.

Obstacles

One obstacle is the way young people in general feel toward the church today. Recent studies have shown that while Catholic adolescents in the United States have a keen interest in God, they generally do not find this need met by their local parish. Most teens' experience of Sunday Mass is negative; they do not fully understand it; it is perceived by them to be directed to adults and the action itself is perceived as lacking meaning. Only 44% of Catholic teenagers attend Mass every Sunday and only 24% would go to Mass if their parents did not force them. These attitudes are typical of young adolescents, but they are also shared by students when they first come to college.

Another obstacle campus ministers face is a regular disruption of continuity in the congregation on campus. Relative stability of a liturgical assembly is taken for granted in the average parish. It is a quality that has to be carefully nurtured on campuses. Campus ministers know that for the purpose of building a faith community they have students present for only six months out of the year. No activities designed for student involvement can be held during the weeks preceding semester exams, nor, of course, during vacation times. What usable time remains consists in two discontinuous three-month periods: September through November and February through April. Moreover, every autumn brings a new obstacle to building a faith community: one quarter of the student population has disappeared through graduation and has been replaced by as many newcomers in need of incorporation into the assembly. They need to be invited, lured, seduced into the assembly and socialized at a rapid pace. The departure of the seniors has also meant the loss of the best-trained liturgical ministers and the most experienced student leadership.

Another drawback to effective liturgical life on campus is the fact that in most cases the students will not be present at school to celebrate the great feasts of Easter, Christmas or even Pentecost. They are usually present for the preparatory seasons of Advent and Lent but cannot celebrate the feasts together. This can be very disheartening to members of the assembly, but especially to those students and staff who might be involved in the adult catechumenate or who have worked to enhance the integral celebration of the liturgical seasons.

Commuter campuses present special difficulties in the area of worship. Aside from liturgical services which mark special events such as the beginning or end of term, or celebrations focused on critical world, national or campus issues and events, the worship life of the average commuter student takes place off campus.

This pattern of life makes it very difficult to establish patterns of worship on campus and inhibits the building of one vital part of a faith community: regular Sunday eucharistic assembly.

Ministerial Strategy

To counter these obstacles requires energy, imagination, commitment and good organization. It is a tribute to campus ministers that so many have been very successful in drawing students into the worshipping communities on campus. What helps to bring this about?

First of all, regular invitations to students to participate in programs, a hospitable atmosphere in campus ministry offices and liturgical celebrations, and a community of peers who can set good example by being actively involved in ministry and worship themselves, seem to be essential. Scheduling services at times when the students are available and disposed to worship is also important. The large number of late Sunday evening Masses in college chapels is an unusual but sensitive pastoral practice introduced in response to students' lifestyles.

Liturgists should be mindful of the sensibilities of the academic world and should make use of all the legitimate liturgical options in our rites. Where possible they should implement the R.C.I.A. and encourage the celebration of the liturgy of the hours. There must also be regular invitations to students to exercise liturgical ministries; yearly training programs on introductory and advanced levels must be offered.

Adults affiliated with the school can sometimes help to strengthen the continuity of campus congregations. But it is rare that a sufficient number of college faculty or staff attend liturgies on campus to provide a strong core assembly that remains through the seasons and the years. Most faculty and staff people find the center of gravity of their worship life to be off campus in local parishes. But there is often a reliable group providing this sense of continuity. It is that unusual group of people found on many campuses these days which is composed of "refugees" from local parishes who have found a nourishing faith community on campus and have chosen to worship there in season and out of season. These adults are to be cherished by campus ministers because, in addition to continuity, they provide much needed adult role models of religious commitment for students.

Campus ministers sometimes respond to student needs and lifestyle by fostering numerous small group liturgies, even on Sundays. These relatively intimate celebrations can foster excellent participation in the liturgy. They are a wise pastoral practice, but every campus ought also to have a central place of worship of some size where Sunday celebrations of greater beauty and of greater majesty may be held. These larger celebrations provide an experience of the church at prayer impossible to achieve in smaller celebrations. They also help the students feel at home in larger congregations and, indeed, in the larger, worldwide church.

Advantages

Besides the obstacles the college campus situation offers to building effective worshipping communities, it does offer some unique advantages. The first is the relative homogeneity of the assembly. It is far easier to plan liturgies for, and to preach to, a homogeneous group of students than a typical heterogeneous parish community. Students have many things in common: they live in the same buildings, attend the same classes, recreate together, study together, have the same daily order of time and confront many of the same personal problems and challenges. Having common interests and common problems can foster a sense of shared identity, and the liturgical celebration can address that shared life and build upon that shared identity as the community remembers and reflects on the loving action of God.

A second advantage the college liturgical assembly has is precisely its youthfulness. In this post-Vatican II age of ecclesial and liturgical renewal new ideas and new ways of doing things are inescapably being developed and are breaking through to our assemblies. New ideas are more easily introduced to the young, especially in a campus situation where new thinking and different behavior patterns are traditionally given at least some respectful consideration.

Special Needs of Students

The stage of human development that persons in college traverse frequently demands that they focus an immense amount of energy on themselves. They must often deal with issues of their own inner development, with areas of fear and tension that can cause great difficulty. Young people in this time of life have a great need for personal understanding and personal acceptance by others. One religious aspect of college-age people's intrapersonal orientation is the fact that many students have a keen interest in the way the Spirit may be guiding them in their development. Campus homilies should address such intrapersonal issues regularly.

While college years are a prime time for the development of individual friendships, students also have a strong need to feel they belong to identifiable groups. This is especially true of the early years of college. Liturgical celebrations can provide a supportive faith-filled atmosphere to take account of these interpersonal needs as well as the intrapersonal dimensions of students' lives mentioned above. Celebrations which provide lively, interpersonal time for gathering at the start, as well as significantly long, well-prepared periods of silent prayer during the course of the service are not only appropriate to a student assembly but are simply good liturgy for almost all assemblies.

Not all students come to a liturgical celebration to celebrate their faith. Many come, sometimes encouraged by their friends, to seek meaning for their lives.

The liturgical act itself has strong evangelical force, but the periods of time surrounding the liturgy are also prime opportunities for evangelization. The gathering time before and the fellowship time after liturgy provide opportunities for human interaction on a deeper than ordinary level; they offer an occasion for the gift of God in Christ to be discussed and even lovingly confessed.

Finally, students need to be challenged by the gospel. Typical contemporary American failings such as excessive individualism, materialism and consumerism are in special need of attention. And campus preachers should not forget that idealism still lives in the hearts of the young. They desire to hear, again and again, the confident, hope-filled call of Christ to dedicate themselves to selfless service of the world.

During the 1960s and early 1970s campus ministers who were not quite young themselves frequently found it difficult to minister to the young. Happily that does not seem to be the case today. What is needed in the minister today is a sense of critical loyalty to the church, excitement and passion about the Christian mission, an ecumenical spirit, and a sense of confidence.

See **Young adults, liturgy for**

U.S. Bishops, "Empowered by the Spirit: Campus Ministry Faces the Future" *Options*, 15 (Feb. 13, 1986): 569ff. "Youth Ministry in the United States," A Survey on youth pastoral work in the U.S. conducted by the Secretariat on the Laity and Family Life of the N.C.C.B., *Origins* 18 (Jan 19, 1989): 518-28. Campus Ministry in the Church of Today and Tomorrow," An address by Joseph Cardinal Bernardin *Origins*, 18 (Feb. 2, 1989): 553-56.

LAWRENCE J. MADDEN, S.J.

COMMUNICATION, RITUAL AS

"Ritual is a symbolic transformation

of experience that no other medium can adequately express." So writes the philosopher Suzanne Langer when she reflects upon the meaning-making activity of human beings and on ritual as the language of religion (Langer, 49). Meaning-making is the activity of composing and being composed by the connections among things. To have meaning in one's life is to recognize pattern in the disparate elements of existence, to seek order, significance, and wholeness. Meaning is anchored in trust and is the ground of hope. Without it, human beings cannot survive. In its most comprehensive dimensions, this meaning-making activity is the activity of faith, carried out in a dialectic between fear and trust, hope and hopelessness, power and powerlessness, alienation and belonging. At the level of faith, meaning must embrace both the seen and the unseen, and is, therefore, necessarily composed by means of images or metaphors which become symbols when used as keys to whole patterns of connections. Words are our most efficient symbols, but when we want to communicate "more than words can say," we turn to ritual.

We are personally engaged in this meaning-making, symbolizing, faith activity, yet ultimately we cannot do it alone; it is a profoundly relational activity. And thus it is that a participant in the central ritual of Christian faith—the eucharist—is identified as a "communicant," a participant in a web of communication by which the fabric of human life is composed and re-composed.

To communicate is to make common to many; to share, exchange, convey, impart, confer, converse, transmit, bestow, receive, participate, use, enjoy, to put oneself into familiar relations with, to hold intercourse. To communicate is to confer, transmit, or receive something intangible or abstract such as light, heat, motion, a quality, feeling, spirit—or Spirit. Therefore, religion, which at its

best is a distillation of shared, fitting images powerful enough to make meaning of the disparate elements of our experience, necessarily depends upon ritual to grasp, reveal, name, and initiate us— invite us—into the immanent, transcendent truth of the sacred, interdependent reality that we are and that is "more than words can say."

Every culture has a ritual to hold the awkward absence of words upon the occasion of a first meeting—be it the handshake of western Europeans, the bow of the Japanese, or the namaste of India. Likewise, in every culture weddings and funerals are the most complex of ritualized occasions because the social fabric is being so profoundly re-woven. Primary relationships, integral to the patterns of connection among us, are being transformed at depths beyond words. These ritual occasions reverberate throughout the whole of life and are thus ultimately religious. For finally the function of religion is to relate us, to connect us, and thus its hallmark is communion-communication. Religion is the working out of the divine-human relation, the human-human relation, the intra-human relation, the relations of the whole earth community with the angels and archangels, things past, things present, and things to come.

The Oxford dictionary suggests that communication between "vessels, spaces, and rooms" means "to open into each other by a common channel or aperture whereby the whole becomes one space." This is a fitting metaphor for religious ritual by which persons are enabled to share in common, actions, objects, place and time such that the whole is composed into a unity which holds the particularity and integrity of every person, act, object, and moment. This formation of a fitting communion occurs only as there is a recognition of "a common channel or aperture"—Spirit—manifest in the shared creation of a common story and vision

237

(See, Groome). It might be noted that in much of secular western culture watching the TV evening news has become a pervasive, common ritual. Tele-communication media serve as a common "channel" by which people seek to be connected to, in touch with, a larger whole—presided over by the revered high priests of network news, anchormen who determine the shape of our story and vision.

The creation of a shared story and vision that is to function in an adequate religious sense must be approached not as a performance for a passive audience, but rather with an expectation of motion, an interchange, a flow of giving and receiving, of speaking and being addressed, of offering gesture and observing act, of affecting and being affected. It is only as one's story—including the telling of both deep suffering and greatest joy—shares in and contributes to the community's story and as one's vision threatens, inspires and is informed by the community's vision that religious ritual as communication functions to weave a meaningful whole which can nourish and sustain truthful, ongoing, lived, communal experience. Thus the most powerful ritual, and certainly religious ritual, is necessarily public—belonging to the whole people, shaped by the whole people, and vitalizing/inspiriting the whole people.

Further, a faithful communication-communion among "the whole people" must manifest a recognition of the living and the dead, the born and the yet unborn. Ritual as communication makes present the story and vision of the forebears of the community as created by tradition, the present in its unprecedented reality, and the future as best anticipated. Ritual that communicates faithfully is an art which composes the fitting relation between continuity and discontinuity, the familiar and the novel. These dimensions of reality, woven in time through ritual, forge the ever-changing words and

acts which symbolize and communicate the "evidence of things unseen" by which faith—meaning-making in the dimensions that are most ultimate and intimate—is composed and recomposed. Thus as Edward Fischer has rightly observed, if ritual is "not allowed to unfold through the easy stages of evolution, it . . . finds itself [inevitably] in the throes of revolution" (*Roots of Ritual*, 162). For the human heart and the human mind will fiercely seek meaning and demand faith, yet must do so with nothing else but ritual to communicate—create a communion—that is "more than words can say."

See **Ritual**

Suzanne Langer, *Philosophy in a New Key: A Study in the Symbolism of Reason, Rite, and Art*, 3rd ed. (Cambridge, MA: Harvard University Press, 1976). Thomas H. Groome, *Christian Religious Education: Sharing Our Story and Vision* (San Francisco: Harper & Row, 1981). Edward Fischer, "Ritual as Communication," *The Roots of Ritual*, ed. J. Shaughnessy (Grand Rapids: Eerdmans, 1973), 161-184.

SHARON DALOZ PARKS

COMMUNION SERVICE

The service of Holy Communion is the name given by several Protestant traditions to that order of worship in word and sacrament which in the Eastern Orthodox tradition is called "The Divine Liturgy," and in the Roman Catholic tradition is called "the Mass." Among Eastern Orthodox and Roman Catholics, "Communion Service" refers to an order of worship in which holy communion is administered, but the eucharist is not celebrated. It is in this second sense that this article deals with the topic.

The origin of this kind of Communion Service is found in the Liturgy of the Pre-sanctified Gifts, celebrated in the Byzantine tradition, and named after St. Gregory the Great, or St. Gregory the

Theologian. This liturgy developed to satisfy the desire for communion on fast days when the eucharist would not be celebrated. There is evidence in the 2nd and 3rd centuries that the faithful could take the consecrated elements to their homes and commune themselves at the end of a period of fasting; or the elements were carried to the absent by the deacons from the Sunday eucharist. During the 4th century, self-communion was discouraged and the practice waned. But some form of administration of communion in the church had to be developed to meet popular need. This was the Liturgy of the Pre-sanctified, in which the consecrated elements from the Sunday eucharist would be distributed.

The Typicon of the Great Church in Constantinople (10th century) gives us a system of the eucharist being celebrated every Saturday and Sunday of the year, every day from Pascha through Pentecost, and on festivals of our Lord and our Lady and on some saints' days. But no eucharist is to be celebrated on the ferial days of Lent, on Monday through Wednesday of Holy Week, or on Wednesdays and Fridays throughout the non-paschal time of the year (the traditional fast days). The Liturgy of the Pre-sanctified could be celebrated on these days. This became the pattern of all the Eastern churches except the Coptic, which joined the Roman practice in allowing the eucharist to be celebrated on fast days.

The present Liturgy of the Pre-sanctified is the office of vespers followed by communion from the reserved sacrament. The gospel reading is included as a reading in vespers, followed by the ecumenic prayer and the dismissal of the catechumens. There is an entrance with the sacrament, although not the usual offertory prayers since these are the consecrated gifts. Byzantine teachers, such as Nicholas Cabasilas, had to instruct the faithful on the difference between the Great Entrance with the gifts

at the eucharist (which gifts should not be venerated) and the entrance with the gifts at the Pre-sanctified (which could be venerated). The priest says the usual pre-communion devotional prayers and the people are invited to receive communion: "Come in fear of God with faith and love." After communion there is a thanksgiving, the dismissal, a prayer for the keeping of a holy Lent during that season, and concluding psalmody.

This kind of communion service never became a tradition in the West, except on Good Friday. In the liturgy of Good Friday there is a Mass of the Pre-sanctified in which holy communion is administered after the liturgy of the word and the special devotions for this day comprising the veneration of the Cross. The Pre-sanctified in the Roman rite has the same structure as in the Byzantine tradition from which it was received: entrance with the sacrament, typical communion devotions, reception of communion, post-communion prayer, and dismissal. The Holy Week reforms of 1955 restored the Mass of the Pre-sanctified to the more simple form it had at the time of its introduction in Rome in the 7th century when preparation for communion consisted simply in the recitation of the Our Father by all those present. It should be noted that the older practice was to refrain from holy communion entirely on Good Friday. But the Western Christian piety which dwelt on the passion of Christ made Good Friday a principal communion day in the church year. This was also the case in German Protestantism.

The form of the Liturgy of the Pre-Sanctified influenced the order for the extended distribution of the sacrament to the sick and dying. In the medieval *Ordo ad visitandum infirmum* three sacraments were linked together: penance (auricular confession), unction (anointing the body), and administration of holy communion. The eucharistic elements were carried from the place of reservation to the house of the sick or dying in a pyx, which was preceded by a bell and lantern. The light brought honor to the sacrament and the bell, first prescribed by the Council of Reading (1279), was to arouse people along the way to reverence.

A revised order for the distribution of holy communion outside Mass after the Council of Trent is found in the *Rituale Romanum* of 1614. It is extremely terse: *Confiteor*, said by the server; *Misereatur vestri*, said by the priest; *Ecce Agnus Dei*, said by the priest holding up the host, with the response: *Domine, non sum dignus*...; distribution of communion; antiphon: *O sacrum convivium*, said by the priest; verse and response; concluding collect.

The reformed rite of Distributing Holy Communion outside Mass after the Vatican II was promulgated in 1973. It is even simpler than the 1614 rite, with the addition of a celebration of the word of God which could include readings from Votive Masses of the Holy Eucharist or the Precious Blood or from the lectionary. The order is: greeting, penitential rite, celebration of the word of God, Our Father, sign of peace, "This is the Lamb of God...," distribution of holy communion, post-communion prayer, and benediction. There is an alternate form of Administration of Communion and Viaticum by an Extraordinary Minister (i.e. a designated lay person). Viaticum includes a profession of baptismal faith and prayer for the sick person after the reading of the word.

There are instances of communion of the sick from the reserved sacrament in some Reformation church orders: the Manual of Olavus Petri in Sweden (1529) and the Mark Brandenburg Church Order (1540). There was a provision for communion from the reserved sacrament in the 1549 *Book of Common Prayer*, but this was eliminated in the 1552 Prayer Book. Lutherans and Anglicans contin-

ued the practice of communing the sick and dying, but the rite took the form of the Communion Service itself, with confession and absolution, collect, reading of the word, consecration, Our Father, ministration, post-communion prayer, and benediction. There was an aversion to reserving the sacrament in the Reformation tradition because of concern for emphasizing the "true use" of the sacrament as a meal to be shared, and not as objects to be venerated in and of themselves. A liturgical characteristic of Reformation Communion Services, both in the assembly and in the house of the sick or dying, is exhortations to repentance and desire for the sacrament of holy communion.

While the 1979 Episcopal *Book of Common Prayer* and the 1982 *Occasion Services* of the *Lutheran Book of Worship* make provision for the Celebration of Holy Communion in Special Circumstances, there is also provision for the Distribution of Communion to those in Special Circumstances, which could make use of designated lay communion ministers. These Episcopal and Lutheran orders are similar in structure to the reformed Roman Catholic rite. They include: greeting; optional confession and greeting of peace (in different locations between the two orders); reading of the word; Our Father; verse (Episcopal: "The gifts of God for the people of God"; Lutheran: "As often as we eat this bread and drink this cup, we proclaim the Lord's death until he comes"); ministration; prayer; blessing or dismissal. These orders of extended distribution of the sacrament have the advantage of keeping the absent united in the sacramental elements with those who gathered in the eucharistic assembly. On the other hand, prolonged exposure only to this kind of Communion Service cuts off the communicant from the liturgical actions of praise and thanksgiving.

The Rites of the Catholic Church, English trans. prepared by The International Commission on English in the Liturgy (New York: Pueblo Publishing Co., 1976), pp. 449-512. The Book of Common Prayer (The Church Hymnal Corporation and the Seabury Press, 1977), pp. 453ff. Occasion Services: A Companion to Lutheran Book of Worship (Minneapolis: Augsburg Publishing House, 1982), pp. 76-88. Philip H. Pfatteicher, Commentary on the Occasional Services (Philadelphia: Fortress Press, 1983), pp. 113-38. Robert Taft, "The Frequency of the Eucharist Throughout History," in Beyond East and West: Problems in Liturgical Understanding (Washington, D.C.: The Pastoral Press, 1984), pp. 61-80. Eric E. Yelverton, The Manual of Olavus Petri 1529 (London: S.P.C.K., 1953).

FRANK C. SENN

COMMUNION UNDER BOTH KINDS

In the Latin rite of the Roman Catholic church, holy communion can be given to the faithful in the form of bread alone or, when permitted, under both kinds, the bread and the wine; in a case of necessity when a person is unable to consume bread, it can be given under the form of wine alone (can. 925).

Communion under both kinds was the normative practive in the Western church for about the first twelve centuries. Communion in the form of wine was given to infants, and in the form of bread to those who could not be present for the eucharistic celebration. Beginning in the 12th century and continuing in the 13th, Western churches gradually abandoned communion in the form of wine for all except the presiding priest. Various factors led to this change. The eucharistic piety of the period centered on the adoration of the host, not on the reception of communion. In an age of intense sacramental realism, the fear of spillage was widespread. Developments in theology also contributed to the demise of the lay chalice, especially the doctrine of concomitance, which holds that the whole Christ is received under either species of bread or wine.

By the 14th century the custom of giving communion sub una (in the form of bread alone) had become universal in the West, and those Christians who returned to the original practice were considered schismatics or heretics. In response to Bohemian utraquists who insisted on the right of the laity to receive the chalice, the Council of Constance in 1415 declared communion sub una to be the law of the church. The Council of Trent in the 16th century attempted to respond to Protestant Reformers who had reintroduced the lay chalice. However it failed to achieve consensus, and referred the issue to the pope. To placate various civil rulers, especially Emperor Ferdinand I, Pope Pius IV in 1564 granted indults permitting communion under both kinds in a number of states and dioceses in central Europe. However, all of these indults were withdrawn by subsequent popes, and from 1621 until 1965 communion under both kinds was restricted to the presiding priest everywhere in the Latin rite. No such development took place in Eastern Christianity which remained faithful to the practice of the Lord's Supper and the early church.

The restoration of communion under both kinds was an important objective of the 20th century liturgical movement. The issue sparked lively and prolonged debate at Vatican II, resulting in a text of the liturgy constitution conceding communion under both kinds, in the judgment of the bishops, to clerics, religious, and laity in cases to be defined by the Apostolic See (S.C., 55). The 1965 Rite for Distributing Communion Under Both Kinds listed several occasions when it could be given, and these were expanded in subsequent church documents until the list of cases for the universal church was finalized in the 1970 Roman Missal (G.I.R.M., 242).

In 1970 the Apostolic See authorized episcopal conferences and ordinaries to concede the faculty for communion under both kinds in cases not determined by universal law. In that same year the National Conference of Catholic Bishops of the United States approved the practice, in the judgment of the ordinary, at all Masses except on Sundays and holy days of obligation. In 1978 the N.C.C.B. extended the permission to Sundays and holy days, in the judgment of the ordinary who is to determine whether communion can be distributed in an orderly and reverent manner.

Although a complete restoration of communion under both kinds is not yet a reality in the universal church, it is recognized by the Holy See as the ideal practice because of its symbolic value (G.I.R.M. 56h, 240, 241, and 14 of the Introduction). The National Conference of Catholic Bishops of the United States commends the practice more forcefully, saying that it "is to be desired in all celebrations of the Mass" so that "fuller light may fall upon the import of Christ's words at the Last Supper and in the eucharistic prayer, and for the sake of the faithful's greater participation in the mystery" (N.C.C.B., n.19).

John Huels, *The Interpretation of the Law on Communion under Both Kinds*, The Catholic University of America Canon Law Studies, 505 (Washington, D.C., 1982). John Huels, "The Cup of Blessing," In *One Table, Many Laws: Essays on Catholic Eucharistic Practice* (Collegeville: Liturgical Press, 1986),37-53. National Conference of Catholic Bishops, *This Holy and Living Sacrifice: Directory for the Celebration and Reception of Communion under Both Kinds* (Washington: United States Catholic Conference, 1985).

JOHN M. HUELS, O.S.M.

COMMUNION, FREQUENCY OF RECEPTION OF

In the early centuries of Christianity the faithful received communion as often as the eucharist was celebrated, and sometimes even more often because of the practice of taking the consecrated elements home. After the 4th century the frequency of receiving holy communion dropped drastically throughout the church, East and West. In the Reformation there was an effort to increase the frequency of reception, sometimes by reducing the frequency of celebration of the eucharist under the rule that there should be no Masses without communicants. In various Protestant traditions different frequencies of celebration became customary. In post-Tridentine Roman Catholicism the people were exhorted to receive the sacrament more frequently, but this reception often occurred after or outside of the Mass. Only in the 20th century, under the impact of the liturgical movement, has there been any real progress toward restoring the ancient practice of receiving communion as a climax of the eucharistic celebration.

In the Ancient and Medieval Church

The earliest eucharistic text and commentary, I Corinthians 11, assumes that as often as Christians celebrate the Lord's Supper they will eat and drink from the bread and the cup. The sacrament takes place in the context of a real meal and should not begin until all are present. Nor does it end until "the cup of blessing" is produced after supper and the thanksgiving is said before all drink of it. There is no evidence in the early literature that Christians did not receive communion at every celebration, which usually meant every Lord's Day. Only the catechumens and penitents were excluded from the celebration and reception of holy communion. Justin Martyr testifies to the concern to include even the absent in the communion by dispatching the deacons to them with the consecrated elements after the service (*Apology*, I, 67). Tertullian (*De Oratione*, 19) and Cyprian (*De Lapsis*, 26) testify that during times of fasting or persecution, Christians took the consecrated elements home and communed themselves at the conclusion of their fast or when it was not feasible to gather with the assembly. This practice continued longer in Egypt than elsewhere (Basil, *Ep.* 93), and hermits and monks in the desert would also take the consecrated elements back to their habitats from the Saturday and Sunday celebrations for self-communion. This practice generally waned during the 4th century as a result of superstitious abuse: e.g., people carrying the consecrated bread with them on journeys to ward off evil. The sacrament had to be consumed before people left the church.

In the West the practice of a daily eucharist also developed during the 4th century. This practice appealed to the spiritually stalwart who could partake of "the daily physic of the body of Christ" (Augustine, *Ep.* 54:3-4). But many did not commune. This contributed to the development whereby the faithful did not receive communion every time the eucharist was celebrated. From the end of the 4th century the frequency of receiving communion declined rapidly in both the East and the West. John Chrysostom complained that, particularly among the Greeks, there was no one to partake of the sacrament (*In Eph. hom.*, 3, 4). The Synod of Agde in Gaul (506) found it necessary to require communion three times a year as a minimum, at Christmas, Easter, and Pentecost (Mansi, VII, 327). Rome must have been an exception in this development, because the rubrics in *Ordo Romanus* I as late as the 7th century anticipate a large number of communicants at papal station Masses. There were efforts during the Carolingian reform to restore weekly communion, at least during Lent, but these efforts had no lasting effect. By the Fourth Lateran Council (1215) the faithful had to be admonished to receive communion once a year at Easter. Only the monasteries were exceptions, and even there the lay brothers sometimes received no more than four times a year.

There are several reasons for this development. The heightened awesomeness of the celebration of the eucharist during the 4th and 5th centuries contributed to a sense of unworthiness in the holy presence among ordinary Christians. Perhaps more effective in discouraging the communion of the laity was the practice of abstinence, especially from sexual relations between spouses, before receiving. Since the early Middle Ages, access to the sacrament was also made more restrictive than it had been in the ancient church by the penitential discipline of requiring sacramental confession before reception of communion. The eucharistic movement of the 12th century magnified the cult of the sacrament, but did not encourage more frequent reception of communion. Indeed, the idea of spiritual communion developed whereby desire for the sacrament was deemed a substitute for receiving. Other results of this heightened eucharistic devotion made the sacrament less accessible. Infants who could not swallow the bread were communed in the species of the wine only. But the removal of the cup from lay communicants effectively ended the practice of communing all the baptized at the time of their baptism. Finally, by the end of the Middle Ages the idea emerged that the priest received communion as a representative of the whole community.

The Reformation

One of the most positive contributions of the Reformation was bringing together the celebration and reception of holy communion. All of the Protestant reformers were agreed that there should be no Masses without communicants. Martin Luther especially extolled the benefits of the sacrament and exhorted the faithful to receive communion frequently (see *Admonition concerning the Sacrament*, 1530). At the same time Philip Melanchthon testified that "The sacrament is offered to those who wish for it after they have been examined and absolved" (*Apology*, XXIV, 1). Catechetical examination of communicants and private confession remained gateways to the altar. As a result, in Lutheranism the whole congregation seldom communed. Luther himself recommended that communicants be grouped together in the chancel so that they could be seen by all (*Formula Missae, de communio populi*, 1523). The church orders prepared by Johannes Bugenhagen provided that if there were no communicants the Mass would be terminated after the liturgy of the word with the litany and Lord's Prayer. Nevertheless, the historical record reveals that in many Lutheran churches during the 16th, 17th, and 18th centuries, holy communion was celebrated every Sunday, festival, and day of devotion in the church year. This situation lasted until the time of the Enlightenment when Rationalism discouraged frequent communion.

Ulrich Zwingli's approach in Zurich was different from Luther's. His rationalistic understanding of God left no room for a sacramental union of the believer and Christ. The very lack of the sense of the mystery of the real presence may have contributed to Zwingli's sense of the fellowship aspect of holy communion. It was important that the whole congregation participate in the Lord's Supper, and time was taken to accomplish this. Hence he recommended that holy communion be celebrated four times a year: at Easter, Pentecost, Christmas, and once in the autumn (*Action oder Bruch des Nachtmals*, 1525). The practice of quarterly communion solidified very quickly in the Reformed tradition. While John Calvin urged weekly communion, he was never able to change the quarterly communion practice in Geneva. John Knox carried this practice from Geneva to Scotland. An exception to this rule was the German Reformed church centered in Strasbourg. Under the leadership of Martin Bucer, Holy Communion was celebrated every Sunday with full congregational participation.

Bucer was a respected consultant in England during the Reformation under Edward VI (1548-53). In an extended critique of the Edwardian Prayer Book known as the *Censura*, Bucer criticized the lack of emphasis on weekly communion. Indeed, the 1549 *Book of Common Prayer* retained the medieval requirement of one communion per year, although parishes were urged to celebrate as frequently as there were communicants. Unlike Lutheranism, Morning Prayer (Matins) was used when there was no communion. The great Anglican divines of the 17th century, beginning with Lancelot Andrewes, cultivated a warm sacramental piety. More frequent eucharistic celebration was retarded, however, as a result of the attempt of the Church of England to comprehend the views of the Puritan party. In the Restoration, after the Puritan Commonwealth, there could no longer be any illusion that the Church of England could comprehend all of English Christianity. The Caroline divines made an effort to maintain a daily eucharist with communion in some cathedral and London churches. But this proved the exception rather than the rule. In most parishes holy communion was celebrated only three or four times a year.

Post-Tridentine Catholicism

The Reformation had some positive impact on the Council of Trent. The bishops assembled at Trent showed a clear desire for the people to commune at Mass. In the decree on "The Doctrine of the Sacrifice of the Mass," chap 6 (Sept 17, 1562), they asserted: "This holy synod strongly desires that at each Mass, the faithful who are present should communicate not only spiritually but sacramentally through reception of the eucharist" (D.S., 1747). Most Catholics, however, received communion after Mass or in viaticum. The *Rituale Romanum* of Pope Paul V (1614) provided for communion outside of Mass, even while continuing to stress that "The communion of the people ought to occur within Mass..." (p. 50). It emphasized the pastor's responsibility to provide regular catechesis about the sacrament and to exhort the faithful to receive often.

More frequent reception of communion was fostered by the devotion to the Sacred Heart in the 17th century. This included reception on the first Friday of the month, with the holy hour of adoration on each Thursday as a "eucharistic reparation." Despite theological reservations about this popular devotion, it became very entrenched in the piety of the people.

American Protestantism

Two frequencies of celebration of holy communion dominated Protestant churches in North America: quarterly among the Presbyterians and monthly among the Congregationalists. Lutherans and Methodists, who might have weekly communion, were hampered in this by the conditions of church life on the frontier and the shortage of ordained ministers.

In New England Congregationalism the Lord's Supper was celebrated once a month. This was sometimes reduced in the winter months, but communion opportunities were then increased the rest of the year. The date of the monthly celebration was staggered in cities like Boston so that it was possible for church members to receive more often than once a month by attending different meeting houses. Some of these congregations dismissed the unregenerate before the celebration; others allowed them to attend in the hope that they would have a regenerate experience. The influence of Presbyterian ministers, especially in the ill-fated Plan of Union in 1801, and the impact of the Second Great Awakening, lessened the importance of holy communion in the Congregationalist churches. The influence of Revivalism on worship heightened the preaching of the word and decreased the emphasis on holy communion throughout the 19th century in most American Protestant churches.

The Methodists had been urged by John Wesley to celebrate holy communion every Lord's Day, but this proved impossible in America because of the shortage of ordained elders to reach backwoods settlements. The love feast was substituted for the Lord's Supper since a deacon could preside at it. Once more ordained ministers were available in the early 19th century, desire for the Lord's Supper had diminished.

Communion was not common in the black Methodist and Baptist Churches because freedom of movement was denied their ministers and they were dependent on white ministers to administer the sacrament. The African Methodist Episcopal church was first organized in 1816, at a time when holy communion was not being emphasized in American Protestant churches.

The one exception to this rule was the Disciples of Christ. The Disciples separated from the Methodists and Presbyterians in the early 19th century over the question of more frequent celebration of holy communion. The Disciples promoted lay presidency at the eucharist as a matter of principle to ensure the celebration of the Lord's Supper every Lord's Day.

The Modern Liturgical Movement

The "return to the sources" which characterizes the early stage of the modern liturgical movement led to the desire in many churches to return to the ancient pattern of celebrating the eucharist every Sunday and festival. In many Episcopal churches in the early 20th century, holy communion was celebrated as the early service on Sundays while Morning Prayer continued to be the principal morning service. Anglo-Catholic parishes were sometimes able to offer daily spoken eucharistic services as well.

In Protestant churches the concern has been to increase the frequency of celebration since there are potential communicants. This has been done by appealing to historical authorities (e.g. Luther, Calvin, Wesley) and by extolling the benefits of the sacrament. Very often the experience of weekly eucharist has been its most compelling advocate.

In the Roman Catholic church the concern has been to increase the number of communicants since the Mass is celebrated often, but also to urge the faithful to receive at Mass rather than apart from Mass. One approach toward more frequent reception has been to relax the requirements for preparation. The eucharistic fast has been relaxed in three stages in the 20th century. In 1953 Pope Pius XII decreed, in *Christus Dominus,* that ordinary water does not break the eucharistic fast, although the requirement of abstaining from food from the previous midnight remained in effect. Special exemptions were given to the ill, to travelers, and to laborers whose work was fatiguing. In 1957 Pius XII modified the eucharistic fast even further, in *Sacram Communionem*, by establishing the rule of a 3-hour fast from food and alcoholic beverages before receiving communion. In 1964 Pope Paul VI reduced the period of fasting from food and drink to one hour before receiving communion; and even this minimum can be dispensed with in the case of the ill and infirm. These modifications made it easier for Catholics to commune at whatever Mass they were attending.

Accompanying these changes has been a persistent catechesis that has also been emphasized in non-Roman churches: Sunday as the day of celebration of the resurrection of Christ, the manifold modes of Christ's presence, and the unity of word and sacrament. New worship books have made the holy communion, i.e. the liturgy of the word and eucharistic meal, the chief service for Sundays and festivals. Throughout Western Christianity there is a discernable move to recover the ancient church's pattern of celebrating the Lord's Supper on the Lord's Day among the Lord's people.

The Byzantine Tradition

Frequent communion was dying out in the East already during the 4th century, and it declined precipitously after that. The stress on the holy character of the consecrated elements, first stressed by Cyril of Jerusalem, combined with abstinence from sexual intercourse in marriage before reception and the penitential discipline, all discouraged most communicants. In the East as well as the West, infrequent communion of the laity means that devotion had to be focused elsewhere rather than in the act of communion. The Eastern churches, unlike the Western, experienced no Reformation, and the liturgical movement has yet to make inroads in these churches (although the theology and practice of the Byzantine churches would surely make liturgical renewal easier in the Orthodox churches than in the Western churches with their more individualistic pieties). In a few places there is evidence of renewal and more frequent communion, especially in North America.

Doug Adams, *Meeting House to Camp Meeting: Toward a History of American Free Church Worship from 1620 to 1835* (Austin: The Sharing Co., 1981). Yngve Brilioth, *Eucharistic Faith and Practice, Evangelical and Catholic,* trans. by A.G. Hebert. Joseph A. Jungmann, *The Mass of the Roman Rite,* II, trans. by Francis A. Brunner (New York: Benziger Brothers, 1955), 359-67. Nathan Mitchell, *Cult and Controversy: The Worship of the Eucharist Outside Mass* (New York: Pueblo Publishing Co., 1982).

FRANK C. SENN

CONFESSION OF SINS

"Confession" until recently was the popular name for the sacrament of penance, although it is only one aspect of the entire rite. Confession of sins is an integral part of penance, whether it be generic confession or individual confession. Both emanate from a true knowledge of self before God and from contrition for the sins committed. In generic or general confession one prays and states only that one has sinned using, for example, the Act of Contrition or the Confiteor. Such generic confessions are required before general absolution and are often made by Christians in community worship. Individual confession is a specific statement of one's sins to a confessor in a one-on-one situation.

Canon 988 states: "A member of the Christian faithful is obliged to confess in kind and in number all serious sins committed after baptism and not yet directly remitted through the keys of the Church nor acknowledged in individual confession, of which one is conscious after diligent examination of conscience."

Any sin committed before baptism, for which one is sorry at the time of baptism, is forgiven. It need never be confessed. However, serious sins incurred subsequent to baptism must be confessed to a priest in the sacrament of penance. The type of sin and the number of times one has fallen must be acknowledged in individual confession after a search of conscience. By such a confession, the penitent is opening up to the minister in an unique way; one's heart is laid bare to seek forgiveness of God through the minister of God and the church. Acting in the person of Christ, the minister makes a spiritual judgement and forgives or retains the sin (Rite of Penance, 6b).

Anyone capable of committing a serious sin, and who in fact has done so, is obliged to confess at least once a year. This is an obligation dating to the Fourth Lateran Council of 1215 but it is clear that only those who have in fact committed serious sin are so obliged (C.I.C., 989). There is no specified time during the year when this confession of sin must take place.

Persons who have made a general confession of sin either in the celebration of general absolution or because of some extraordinary circumstance, e.g., emergency or lack of privacy, should resolve to confess in due time each of the serious sins which they could not confess (Rite of Penance, 33).

From earliest times the church has included a confession of sin in the celebration of the sacrament of penance. In times of public penance and in the Celtic practice of the sacrament dating to the 6th century, confession was an integral aspect of the rite. The tariff penances were determined by the seriousness of the sin confessed. So today, penance should be related to sin, and this depends upon the confessor's prudent judgment after knowing the sin. The role of judge and the role of healer are the responsibility of the priest who is the mediator of the church in the sacrament. Pope John Paul II states: "The confession of sins cannot be reduced to a mere attempt at psychological self-liberation, even though it corresponds to that legitimate and natural need inherent in the human heart to open oneself to another. It is a liturgical act, solemn in its dramatic nature, yet humble and sober in the grandeur of its meaning. It is the act of the Prodigal Son who returns to his Father and is welcomed by him with the kiss of peace. It is an act of honesty and courage. It is an act of entrusting oneself, beyond sin, to the mercy that forgives" (*Post-Synodal Apostolic Exhortation on Reconciliation and Penance*, 31).

The church has also held that the sacramental seal is *inviolable*. Canon 983 states that "it is a crime for a confessor in any way to betray a penitent by word or in any other manner or for any reason." Direct violations of the seal result in the immediate excommunication of the confessor and forgiveness of this penalty is reserved to the Apostolic See (C.I.C., 1388,1).

Penitents are free to confess their sins to any approved confessor of their choice, even one from another rite (C.I.C., 991). This freedom cannot be denied and no one may be coerced in any way. Also confession of sin may be done through an interpreter who is bound by the seal of confession as well.

Anyone conscious of grave sin cannot celebrate Mass or receive communion without prior sacramental confession. However, in circumstances when there is a grave reason to celebrate or receive the eucharist and there is no possibility of confessing, the person should make a perfect act of contrition and include the intention of confessing as soon as possible (C.I.C., 916).

Venial sins are not required to be confessed but it is recommended that they be. Confession of sins is an opportunity within the total rite of penance to dialogue with the confessor about the root causes of sin in one's life. Thus frequent and careful celebrations of the sacrament are a means of perfection. One should seek out a confessor who is holy and insightful and with whom one is comfortable. The opportunity of confessing in a penitential room, face to face with a confessor, can enable candid dialogue. The purpose is to get at the root causes of sin, change one's life and strive to perfect the grace of baptism within each Christian person.

See **Confidentiality**

Frederick R. McManus, *The Code of Canon Law: A Text and Commentary*, "The Sacrament of Penance (CC 959-997)," (New York: Paulist Press, 1983).

JOSEPH L. CUNNINGHAM

CONFESSIONAL

See **Reconciliation room**

CONFIDENTIALITY

Confidentiality is a restriction on communication, requiring that we not convey to others something that has been revealed to us. Confiders confide (etymology: entrust) in a confidant under assurance that matters will not be shared with others. These matters may include not only problems or sins, but anything that a person wants, would want, or should want to keep private. While everyone must at times keep confidences, professionals acknowledge a special duty to do so in their work.

Persons in ministry should respect the revelations of those who confide in them, particularly during counselling and the rite of reconciliation, but also in everyday contexts where personal problems and ethical or religious issues are often disclosed. There is near universal agreement on the importance of confidentiality. There is, however, some debate over the reasons for it, and considerable uncertainty arises over when and how strictly it should apply.

New Problems and Old Paradoxes

Usually, the extent of confidentiality is only informally established. People gradually learn which matters should be kept confidential and which should not. A large grey area remains in ordinary life. In professional relationships the limits are normally explicit, though with the advent of team ministry, supervision, computerized records, etc., the boundaries of confidentiality are undergoing revision. For example, hospital chaplains have to decide judiciously what to divulge to other members of a health care team. Similarly new questions arise in practices such as lengthy face-to-face celebrations of penance, in-depth sacramental preparations, and group counselling, as well as in the use of verbatims, case studies, and collective problem solving.

Because of finitude and sin, paradoxes abound: free communication depends on first restricting communication. Confidentiality simultaneously liberates and limits the human desire to know and be known. Useful things are learned which cannot be used. Confidentiality encourages appropriate but also inappropriate disclosures. Further, communal life is enhanced by fostering privacy. Penitents are reconciled to the community through a rite that proscribes informing the community. Confidentiality enables some to serve, but keeps others uninformed and therefore unable to help. Confidences unite people in a relationship which then excludes other persons. In brief, limits can free persons, and secrecy promotes openness.

Basis in Tradition

For Christians, confidentiality is not an intrinsic good. We are encouraged to live in the light, and to confess our sins to one another (Eph 5:12-13; Lk 12:2-3; Jas 5:16). Our community forms the body of Christ, and includes mutual sharing (1 Cor 11-12). Concealing matters and lying to the community bring death (Acts 5:1-11). In the eschaton, we shall have perfect knowledge and see face to face (1 Cor 13:12). God wills to reveal as completely as possible God's own self. Thus, it is a Christian ideal to live in an atmosphere of complete openness.

In history, however, God's self-revelation takes place gradually and not equally to all. In imitation of Christ, we properly strive to be unreservedly open to God, but not with all human beings (Mt 10:26-27, 13:10-17). At times we should let others see our good deeds, and at other times we should not let our right hand know what our left hand is doing (Mt 5:14-16, 6:1-6). Thus, theologically speaking, confidentiality functions within the pattern of disclosure and concealment that characterizes all historical life.

Reasons for Confidentiality

Contemporary philosophers, focusing on professional confidentiality, usually ground the practice in autonomy, privacy or human need. They begin with the duty not to disclose, and then inquire about

exceptions. A different approach is taken here. Openness is the ideal, but there are at least four basic reasons for restricting communication: reverence for individuals; need for relationships; fulfilling promises; and encouraging persons to seek help. After discussing these, we shall take up confidentiality's limits.

Reverence. We human beings are each mysteries living within God's mystery. Public scrutiny can damage the unique and often delicate ways that God works with us; it can deform the frail identity we are fashioning for ourselves. When reverence for our dignity is lacking, we become for others mere objects, susceptible to unlimited inquiry and discussion. While God's complete knowledge of us fosters our true self, other persons' knowledge of us is not so consistently upbuilding.

According to psychologists, as children we take a major developmental step when we develop secrets, since to have a secret is to have a separate self. The correlative desire to share our self then arises. We usually want those we trust to know us, but we fear that others may use knowledge of us for their purposes, not ours. To act without regard to what others may think or do is hardly a Christian ideal; still, we need safe harbors where the winds of social expectation do not easily throw us off our course. The integrity of our identity depends on acting according to a pattern that makes coherent sense to us. Where we would be deflected by others from realizing that integrity, we properly keep them at a safe distance. Not everyone will treat us with reverence, so we use discretion as to whom we will reveal ourselves, and under what conditions. Under conditions of confidentiality, we retain some control over what we have revealed.

Relationships. Our relationships often fall into typical patterns or roles, e.g., friend or bishop; each pattern has its own implied set of general rules or expectations. We may have more than one type of relation with the same person, and thus we may have to be clear about which kinds of disclosures are appropriate to each. Our self is like a series of concentric circles, from an inmost core known only by God to a public self known by any sentient being that cares to notice. Thus our social interactions vary in depth and extension. Without confidentiality, our alliances in this world would tend to be superficial or rife with alienation.

Relationships are created by self-disclosure, and the type of the relation both depends on and determines the quality and depth of what we share. Some conversations are restricted not because the issues are sensitive, but because third parties are "outsiders." For example, a woman personally might want to tell each of her friends that she is pregnant, and she would properly resent it if others usurped her role. Each human relation creates its own shared world. (There is of course considerable overlap in these worlds because everyone has multiple relationships.) Within a shared world, each person corrects misunderstandings and molds meanings. Outsiders cannot know the personal context of any self-revelation nor will they feel bound by the loyalties a revelation creates. God alone is able to share in relationships without being an outsider, because God is not one person among other persons, but rather the personal ground of all relations.

Promises. Confidentiality often rests upon an implicit or explicit promise not to reveal. Through the promise, one alienates some freedom of action: here, to tell what one knows. A promise presupposes and further establishes trust, which is a central virtue, especially for Christians who remember the story of Judas. Trust belongs to a unity of important human values such as intimacy, privacy, security, respect, reliance, and self-discovery. Any breach of confidentiality threatens these. When a professional breaks trust, the whole profession is defamed; if a minister breaks trust, the church is wounded, and the individual's relation to God may be strained.

Assistance. Without confidentiality, those most vulnerable or at risk might not ask for the help they need. Confidentiality makes possible the uninhibited self-examination that is often crucial to growth. The fear of public repercussions, and more fundamentally a prideful self-image, keep people from acknowledging problems even to themselves, and hence from remedying them. We learn by speaking, particularly if the listener and the conditions are right. In contrast, unprotected self-revelation and the vulnerability that ensues could be foolish or even sinful. In this world there is always someone ready to exploit exposed weaknesses. Hence confidential roles, e.g., spouse or priest, are socially established so that we may find reconciliation and healing. As John Calvin noted, confidentiality is necessary, "lest sinners be hindered from coming to repentance, and from making a free confession of their faults."

Dangers of Confidentiality

We have indicated four broad reasons for confidentiality. It is not, however, without significant dangers, and to a few of these we now turn.

Power and Status. A confidential interchange involves power, and power can be abused. A professional wields, even if unintentionally, enormous power to define what is good or bad, orthodox or deviant. Psychological studies show that when persons reveal themselves to someone who is not reciprocally self-revealing, the status of the confidant increases over the one who confides. Ministers should be wary of welcoming confidences as a way to enhance their importance in their own eyes and in the eyes of others. The point is not that ministers must be mutually self-revealing; rather they ought to keep in mind that, for Christians, status and power are for the sake of service, especially to protect or enable the vulnerable. Those who confide, particularly if the matters are sensitive, become vulnerable.

Confidentiality can also be used as a shield to hide problems or to avoid responsibility. Not rarely have bad judgments or decisions of those in authority, whether in the church or out, been protected from scrutiny by a claim of confidentiality. To be sure, public institutions need secrets. But such arrangements notoriously can be used to promote the interests either of those in power or of the institution itself more than the people they serve. We properly ask of public institutions a higher degree of accountability and openness than individuals.

Mutual Responsibilities. Confidentiality includes *mutual* rights to self-determination, self-possession, and free association. Usually authors focus on the duties of the confidant. The confider also has obligations, even in professional relationships. Each person has a right to enter or end a relation. Within a relation confiders have some duty appropriately to reveal themselves. Not everything should be told to everyone, but some self-revelation is required.

On the other hand, some people overuse confidentiality, e.g., expecting secrecy for matters that should be disclosed, asking for anonymity as a way of avoiding responsibility, or evoking secrecy as a license to pass on matters that should not be disclosed. Confiders should recognize that what they reveal about a third party may alter the relation between the confidant and that third party, without the participation or consent of the third party.

The confidant also deserves some of the protections of confidentiality. In a pastoral setting advice is often relative to the confider, and it ought not be indiscriminately broadcast. Because of the mutuality of the conversation and because of an obligation to foster a practice of confidentiality, confidants ordinarily should not be compelled to discuss conversations even when the confider waives confidentiality.

Mean between Extremes. Excessive confidentiality reflects and reinforces individualism and privatism, thereby devaluing relationships and open communication. Community life is fostered when there is relatively free exchange of information. A weak sense of community results if members are reluctant to pass on anything of what they learn in ordinary conversations. Communal decisions often depend on having adequate input. Strict confidentiality tends to restrict a professional's awareness and concern to individual confiders, thereby ignoring others who might be affected.

On the other hand, communal life is impeded through unwarranted disclosure of confidences. Excessive openness erodes trust and a proper sense of privacy, e.g., today's secret is featured in tomorrow's homily. Totalitarian societies prohibit confidentiality by claiming that everything has significance for society. The church, which needs pluralism and whose structures can be used in totalitarian ways, should champion confidentiality.

Conflicts

Confidentiality is experienced as a duty because it counteracts internal and external pressures to talk about matters which may be interesting, bizarre, or even highly relevant. Apart from the "seal of confession," however, it is only a *prima facie* duty, i.e., one that can be overridden by other, more compelling duties. There is an inconsistency when a minister offers confidentiality to facilitate full disclosure, and then breaks confidentiality because of what full disclosure reveals. This inconsistency should rarely be embraced, though under the tragic conditions of human finitude, at times it may have to be. Even legitimate exceptions, however, tend to erode the practice of confidentiality. When confidentiality is expected, one should be very wary of breaking that trust.

Prudence. No simple rules, however, can set down in advance what in non-confessional conversations may be revealed. For professionals, a relatively rigid stance is appropriate. For all, discretion plus common sense are needed: some matters are strictly confidential, some may be shared—perhaps in disguised form—with certain others, and some may be freely discussed. The setting alone is not decisive. People reveal very personal matters in the midst of casual conversation. Conversely, in counselling and even in the sacrament of penance, trivial things may be mentioned. Not everything is equally worthy of strict confidentiality. (Still, care must be taken since what is ordinary to one party may be sensitive to another.)

Permission to discuss confidential matters with others should be explicitly sought. Consultation is best pursued with strangers or only after making the case anonymous; and anyone consulted should be bound to confidentiality. In cases where confidential matters become public knowledge, the confidential relation still deserves some protection. This can be accomplished by indicating that what is known has been learned through public sources, not through private discussion.

Seal of Confession. The theory and practice of confidentiality has evolved partly through reflection on the priest-penitent relation. Early forms of the sacrament of penance were public, not really confidential. Over time, a requirement of silence arose; this was expressly formulated by at least the 5th or 6th century, and canonically formalized six centuries later. Penalties included excommunication and perpetual pilgrimage or life-time imprisonment in a monastery.

There is unanimous agreement that the "seal of confession" should not be broken, though the grounds for that position are seldom defended. The ancient maxim that "about confessional matters the priest knows even less than what he knows nothing about" bears repeating. A priest may not directly reveal or even modify his external behavior in accord with what he learns in penance, though he is encouraged to pray for his penitents. What counts as indirect use—and is therefore either less sinful or permissible—varies somewhat throughout the tradition. Only after 1682 were priests forbidden all use of confessional material. As a general rule, anything that might lead to distrust towards either a penitent or the sacrament itself is proscribed.

Legal Protection. In the United States, statutory law in 49 states protects the "seal" as privileged communication, a legal term pertaining to exemption from giving evidence in the judicial system. The protection is not absolute: several states presently require persons to report even suspicions, not to mention confessions, of child abuse. As in the past, priests might have to go to jail to protect the "seal." Civil law offers less "privilege" to pastoral or psychological counselors. However, the more the ministerial role or activity is officially recognized by the church, the more likely it is protected by the First Amendment. Whatever the law, it would be tragic if, out of worry over legal liabilities, necessary ministries were neglected.

For legal purposes, confidentiality is privileged if it meets four criteria. The confider must believe the communication will not be disclosed; confidentiality must be essential to the purpose of the relation; the harm in disclosing must be greater than the benefits to justice in testifying; and society must foster the confidential relation for the common good. Thus, in ministry, the communication usually must occur in the course of a discipline sanc-

252

tioned by the church. But case law varies greatly: thus, in some states, a third person's presence, e.g., a spouse, invalidates privilege. Some authors do not advocate malpractice insurance because insurance companies can require disclosure of confidences in a defense against a legal suit.

Exceptions. When strict confidentiality is the rule, two kinds of exceptions are commonly discussed. The first concerns minors or mentally incapacitated persons; the usual norms on making decisions for others, or paternalism, arise here. The second concerns harm either to the confider, e.g., a threat of suicide, or to others. Prospective harms may permit or require disclosure more than past harms, since the evil to be done may still be avoided. Also, the greater the potential harm and the more likely it will occur, the more reason there is to break the confidence. There is a duty to warn and an obligation to prevent some evils. Still, as a general rule, confidentiality should prevail.

When confidences must be revealed, the cooperation of confiders should be sought. Respect for their autonomy diminishes, however, when they are clearly set on a course that is destructive to themselves or others. Similarly, a prior promise of confidentiality is not absolute, since silence may amount to "material cooperation." Nevertheless, regular breaking of confidences should not occur; and, in professional relations, clients should be forewarned that disclosure of certain matters may be ethically and legally required. Whenever possible, role-expectations and social settings should explicitly indicate the extent of confidentiality.

In individual cases, the four grounds for confidentiality should be considered. Will disclosure violate reverence for the confider, especially if vulnerable? Will it weaken or destroy a trust-relationship? Will it break a promise? And will it cause more harm (to the practice of confiden-

tiality, to society, to the confider or confidant, to others) than it prevents? In this historical order, confidentiality is often necessary, even as full self-communication is a Christian goal.

William Harold Tieman, and John C. Bush, *The Right to Silence: Privileged Clergy Communication and the Law* (Nashville: Abingdon, 1983). Karen Lebacqz, *Professional Ethics* (Nashville: Abingdon, 1985). Sissela Bok, *Secrets* (New York: Pantheon, 1982).

EDWARD COLLINS VACEK, S.J.

CONFIRMATION

This second sacrament of Christian initiation, employing an anointing with oil and the laying on of hands, complements baptism, even as the two are complemented and completed by the eucharist. The term is proper to Western usage. In the East it is more properly known as *chrismation*. In addition to the entries on confirmation that follow, see also: Initiation, Christian, Anointing; Anointing, post-baptismal; Holy Spirit, gifts of the; Holy Spirit, baptism in the; Sacraments in the Eastern churches.

CONFIRMATION IN SCRIPTURE

The Council of Trent in its seventh session (1547) declared that the rite of confirmation was "a true and proper sacrament," one of the seven "sacraments of the New Law." This definition was directed against the position of the Reformers which recognized only two "sacraments of the Gospel," baptism and the eucharist, and saw the other rites as historical developments of greater or lesser value. This contrasting evaluation of the rites of the church involved confirmation in the theological polemics which largely characterized theology after

Trent. It was common ground among both parties that the gift of the Holy Spirit was an effect of Christian initiation. Following their dogmatic position, Protestant scholars maintained that the NT asserted that this gift was exclusively an effect of baptism. Accordingly, they denied that those texts which seemed to attribute this gift to a post-baptismal rite of imposition of hands did, when rightly interpreted, mean this. Catholic scholarship could afford to be more flexible here, since Catholic sacramental theology had, following an older tradition, come to assert a twofold gift of the Spirit in Christian initiation, one in baptism and a further in confirmation. Catholic scholars could therefore agree that the NT did teach that baptism conferred the Holy Spirit and yet maintain that a further gift was conferred by the post-baptismal or confirmational rite (whether imposition of hands, anointing or a combination of both).

In this century, which has witnessed a more independent and objective approach by biblical scholarship, one might expect that these rather dogmatically determined positions would have been transcended, as has been the case in so many other areas of theology, and that at least a broad consensus concerning the NT's teaching on the gift of the Spirit and Christian initiation would have emerged. Surprisingly, this has not proved to be the case. Instead, a rather bewildering variety of viewpoints has been put forward by the different writers who attempt to discuss this issue. These views might be grouped together, in a rather summary and schematic manner, as follows. (1) The gift of the Spirit is exclusively an effect of baptism. (2) The Spirit, or a further gift thereof, is conferred through the post-baptismal rite of imposition of hands. (It is universally recognized today that NT references to anointing in this context are purely figurative.) (3) In the early church the Spirit

was a free gift of God to a baptized person unmediated by any external sign or rite but usually manifesting itself in some charismatic manner which enabled the church to recognize and acknowledge that the Spirit had been given. But many variations, combinations and modifications of these basic positions have also been advocated.

This surprising variety of contradictory viewpoints on a single issue in NT studies today calls for comment. At least as regards basic positions, scholarship does not seem to have advanced far beyond the polemical days of post-Tridentine theology. It is clear that dogmatic, confessional positions are still influential and that the question is too often not approached with that objective detachment which discussion of NT texts requires and which in nearly all other areas is usual today in biblical scholarship. But a blurring of confessional lines is also noticeable. Thus, one finds Protestant and Anglican scholars, not all of whom might be regarded as of a liberal tendency, maintaining the confirmational significance of those passages which refer to a post-baptismal rite. Some Catholic writers, on the other hand, deny that the NT provides any explicit evidence for confirmation.

It has to be admitted, I think, that discussion of this issue by biblical scholarship has not been satisfactory. A feature of this study which may be significant is the fact that there have been very few studies devoted specifically to the question or prepared to discuss it with the thoroughness it requires. Most of this discussion occurs in general commentaries or as a question arising incidentally in a study devoted to another topic and treated in a separate short scholion or appendix. Discussion of the question too often occurs en passant and is too often characterized by sweeping, general statements which a more thorough study would have to modify.

What this situation seems to indicate is the lack of any agreed methodology for serious study of this issue. This seems to be the greatest need at the moment.

The Question of Methodology

An appropriate methodology for study of the topic in hand can only be determined on the basis of answers to the following questions: What precisely is the question at issue? What strata of NT material throw light on this question? How are these strata related to one another?

In general terms the question at issue may be described as the place of the gift of the Spirit of God in the practice of Christian initiation in the early church. But the matter requires closer definition.

The gift and presence of God's Spirit in the church is a prominent assertion and theme of the NT. This gift is presented as a fruit of the redemptive victory of Christ and as a foundational event which brings into existence and thereafter maintains the Christian community or church. It is a *community* endowment establishing *this* community with its specific identity. Apart from the original individuals who, precisely as forming the *original* community, received the Spirit directly (Jn 20, Acts 2), all others receive this gift only by becoming members of this community and thereby sharing in the Spirit with which it has been endowed *ab origine*. To receive the gift of the Holy Spirit is simply to become a member of this Spirit-filled community. The precise question to be faced is this: how in the actual practice and understanding of the early church was this gift received—as an effect of baptism or of a post-baptismal rite or as somehow a free gift of God later acknowledged by the community?

The NT material bearing on this issue has to be situated within the particular stratum of NT literature to which it belongs. Following this principle one may group the relevant material as follows. (1) The evidence in the Acts of the Apostles on the practice of Christian initiation in the early church. (2) The references in the genuine Pauline letters on baptism and the gift of the Spirit. (3) Material in the synoptic gospels which reflects the early church's practice and understanding of initiation. (Of special significance here is the way in which Jesus' baptism by John is reported.) (4) References to initiation in the other documents of the NT.

The important question which arises concerning these different blocks of material is how to assess their relative value. It can be said immediately that the group which contains the least valuable material is the fourth group. Though these documents do contain significant references to initiation, these are usually too generic in character as regards the precise question under discussion here (but note the reference to the rite of imposition of hands in Heb 6:2), and in any case, since most of these writings come from the later period of the NT canon, they can only be understood in the light of the information provided by the earlier strata. (The much discussed text of Jn 3:5 is a particular case in point.)

As regards the other groups, Acts and the synoptic gospels clearly belong together here. Both reflect, directly or indirectly, the faith and practice of the church over the early decades of its existence. The evidence of the synoptics, however, on our question is very indirect. This material is directly concerned with the life of Jesus and any information provided here on the initiation practice of the early church is by way of implication and inferred interpretation. Acts, on the other hand, is specifically concerned with giving a picture of the life of the church in the early period. Its narrative thus bears directly on the issue under discussion and for this reason is the most hopeful document we possess for information on the early practice of Christian initiation. The more indirect synoptic material will therefore have to be interpreted in the light of the assessment of the material in Acts.

The remaining but crucial question now is the relation between Acts and the Pauline material on this question. There is general agreement today that there is no explicit reference to a post-baptismal rite in Paul. On the contrary, according to many scholars, the Spirit here seems to be associated exclusively with baptism. Since the genuine Pauline letters are the earliest written documents of the NT and since Paul, together with the fourth gospel, presents the most advanced and significant theology of the NT, this silence has led many commentators to the conclusion that no such rite existed in the early church and therefore that the apparent contrary references in Acts have to be explained in some other manner—a question on which there is no consensus. The result is that, on this issue, Paul, as so interpreted, is given a controlling priority over the face-value evidence of Acts.

For many reasons, which cannot be discussed in any detail here, this widely-held conclusion has to be rejected as unsatisfactory.

As long as a very skeptical attitude towards the historical value of the Acts of the Apostles as presenting a picture of the life of the early church prevailed, an attitude initiated by the Tübingen School of the 19th century and culminating perhaps in Haenchen's great commentary (1961), this position could be plausibly argued. This skeptical attitude, however, now no longer prevails. The historical value of Acts for a portrayal of the general life and thought of the early church, if not for specific details, has in more recent times been strongly asserted and vindicated by many scholars. This more recent evaluation effectively removes one of the major bases of the argument for the controlling priority of Paul on this question. Once a respectable historical value is acknowledged for Acts, then the existence of a post-baptismal rite (imposition of hands) for the gift of the Spirit, as described in chaps. 8 and 19, can scarcely be denied. But if one accepts this argument for the existence of this rite, then clearly it was a known and accepted practice to Paul, as in fact Acts 19:1-6 explicitly asserts. The question mark has now to be transferred to the interpretation of the Pauline material.

Apart from the evaluation of the historicity of Acts, the argument for Pauline priority largely reduces itself to an argument from silence, the most difficult of all arguments in historiography. The argument in this instance does not pass the required test. Another and better explanation for this alleged silence can be provided. But further comment on this question will have to be postponed until Paul's understanding of Christian intitiation and the gift of the Spirit is discussed. But it can be confidently stated that the main interest of Paul does not lie in giving any description of the initiation practice with which he and the addressees of his letters are familiar, but rather with developing a much deeper understanding of what this now past event means in the present and the future for Christian faith and life. This is essentially and totally a *theological* enterprise and *not* an exercise in description of current ritual practice.

What emerges from this brief analysis of the NT material on the gift of the Spirit in Christian initiation may be summarized as follows. For information on the initiation *practice* of the early church, Acts of the Apostles is the primary and controlling source; for developed theological insight, Paul is the significant writer.

The Initiation Practice of the Early Church

The understanding of the gift of the Spirit in the Acts of the Apostles has its determining source in the event of Pentecost. This event signifies the endowment of the community of Jesus' disciples with the promised eschatological gift of God's Spirit. Together with the resurrection and exaltation of Jesus, this event signifies the effective dawn of the Messianic Age and establishes the community of Jesus' disciples as the Messianic Community, the group which has received and now possesses the promised Messianic blessings. Pentecost is thus the second foundation event which brings the Christian church into existence and gives it its identity. The first and prior of these events is the life, death and resurrection of Jesus Christ which brings into existence the community of the disciples of Christ. The second is the coming of the Spirit which establishes this already existing community as the *Spirit-filled* community of the disciples of Christ.

It is important to note that the coming of the Spirit is a *community* gift and endowment. The question which arises, and which arose immediately, was how others could come to share in the blessings which the community now possesses, including the gift of the Spirit. This is the question of the initiation practice of the early church, the system whereby new converts were admitted to membership in the community. The question arose immediately on Pentecost Sunday, according to Acts chap. 2, in the reaction to Peter's sermon. In reply to his audience's question, "what shall we do?" (2:37), Peter answers; "Repent, and be baptized, everyone of you, in the name of Jesus Christ for the forgiveness of your sins; and you shall [N.E.B., more accurately, "will"] receive the gift of the Holy Spirit" (2:38). The text goes on to state that on that day three thousand "were added" to the number of the community (2:41).

This passage describes, however summarily, the earliest practice of Christian initiation. A number of points arising from the text deserve notice. The words "were added" show that it is a question of new members joining an already existing group and coming to share in their specific status and privileges. The issue which arises is what process or system of initiation the passage envisages. This process is described very summarily in Acts 2:38. The text mentions explicitly the rite of immersion, baptism, which is directly associated with "the name of Jesus Christ," that is, personal adherence to or discipleship of Christ, and its effect is described as "the forgiveness of sins." There then follows the reference to the gift of the Holy Spirit: "and you shall/will receive the gift of the Holy Spirit." The double reference to Christ and the Spirit clearly refers to and reproduces the two events which brought the community into existence and have given it its identity. This double reference, the christological and the pneumatological, will continue to characterize mention of Christian initiation not only throughout the NT but throughout Christian history.

The question is how Acts 2:38 envisages the relation between the water rite of baptism and the gift of the Spirit. At first reading three interpretations seem possible: the gift of the Spirit is an effect of baptism itself; the coming of the Spirit is a subsequent event in the life of the baptized person unmediated by any rite; the Spirit is conferred by means of a subsequent rite which the author here feels no obligation to mention explicitly. While most commentators tend to rush to judgment here and assume the first interpretation as correct, with little attempt at critical examination, it needs to be stressed that, taken in itself, the text has to be left open in its meaning and can only be finally exegeted in the light of how Christian initiation is presented throughout the rest of Acts of the Apostles. For it is evident that the author here refers to and presupposes what he regards as the regular practice of Christian initiation in the early church. But it should be noted that the particular Greek grammatical structure here, an imperative followed by a future indicative, already strongly suggests that the first interpretation can scarcely be the correct one.

It is not possible to undertake here any detailed examination of the material throughout Acts referring to Christian initiation. It must suffice to mention summarily some basic factors which enable one to determine the meaning implicit in Acts 2:38 concerning the gift of the Spirit.

A number of studies have made clear that consistently throughout Acts the gift of the Spirit is *not* presented or envisaged as an effect of baptism. (J.N.G. Dunn, *Baptism in the Holy Spirit*, has effectively established this point at least). Commentators have generally paid too little attention to the precise concept of the Holy Spirit which Acts presents. This is the classical biblical and Jewish concept of the prophetic Spirit. But this concept in itself is not intrinsically connected either with ritual washing or forgiveness of sins, the stated effect of baptism in Acts. It would be very extraordinary indeed if such an intrinsic connection now suddenly appeared in early Christianity which, for its own thought and practice, was so heavily indebted to biblical and Jewish concepts.

Further, Acts 2:38 clearly presupposes a particular system of Christian initiation which is here alluded to in a summary manner. When the author later in the work comes to describe more fully the initiation practice he has in mind, and which he clearly regards as regular in the church from the beginning down to his own day and situation (Acts was probably written in the decade A.D. 80-90), we find that this practice consists of baptism *and* the rite of imposition of hands for the gift of the Spirit (Acts 8:12-17; 19:1-7). Apart from Luke's obvious familiarity with this initiation ritual, it is also clear that whatever sources he was relying on (probably oral, not documentary) confirmed him in his view.

Various other data which can be gleaned from Acts concerning Christian initiation cohere with and strengthen this assessment. Moreover, material from the synoptic gospels now also falls easily into line. This applies in particular to the narrative of Jesus' baptism by John in the Jordan. As described by the synoptics (Mt 3:16-17; Mk 1:9-11; Lk 3:21-22), this event is undoubtedly presented as a paradigmatic model of the initiation of the Christian convert and reflects the church's early initiation practice. It is therefore highly significant that this event also consists of immersion in water followed by the descent of the Spirit upon Jesus. "In those days Jesus came from Nazareth in Galilee and was baptized (i.e., immersed) by John in the Jordan. And when he came up out of the water, immediately he saw the heavens opened and the Spirit descending on him like a dove..." (Mk 1:9-10). Here also the coming of the Spirit is a post-baptismal event. Given the literary form within which Mark is writing, those scholars who would wish to see the gift of the Spirit as an effect intrinsic to the baptismal rite of immersion would logically have to maintain that here the dove alighted on Jesus while he was immersed *under* the water, a picture the absurdity of which requires no comment. The text of Heb 6:2 adds its further confirming weight to the argument advocated here concerning the practice of initiation in the early church. This text can only be understood as implying a reference to Christian initiation as consisting of two rites, baptism and imposition of hands.

The conclusion to this summary investigation of the NT sources concerning the initiation practice of the early church is that this consisted of *two* rites, baptism followed by imposition of hands for the gift of the Spirit (or, in later terminology, confirmation). It may seem surprising to us today that formal entry into the Christian community was thought to require two distinct rites. In any normal circumstances one would have thought one was quite sufficient. This however is to impose a very modern, rationalistic approach upon the much more imaginative and symbolic mind of former ages. One has to remember the seed bed from which early Christianity, as regards both thought and practice, derived, namely, late Judaism, with the biblical history which lay behind it and the actual experience of the members of the foundational Christian church.

The original community recognized and identified itself as the community of the New Age, the promised Messianic Community inheriting and possessing the Messianic Blessings. In typical biblical manner, this community and its privileges are presented as coming into existence in accordance with the model or pattern of salvation history, that is, a series of separate events following one another and building on one another until eventually a climax is achieved. The foundational community experienced the culmination of this history in the events of Christ and the Spirit, the two climactic events which have brought the community into existence and gave it its identity as the Spirit-filled community of the disciples of Jesus. In opening itself to new converts, the community reproduces and expresses in effective symbol or sacrament the salvation history it has experienced. Hence the double reference in its initiation ritual, the christological and pneumatological, expressed by means of the two distinct rites.

This initiation ritual, however, based as it is on the model of salvation history and the actual experience of the original community, poses a challenge to the Christian mind to discern the unity which lies behind its discrete references. This challenge, which is an invitation to a strictly *theological* enterprise, was soon recognized and addressed. Herein lies the significance of Paul on the gift of the Holy Spirit and Christian initiation.

Deepening Insight: Paul

The Holy Spirit is a prominent theme in the thought and writings of Paul. The Spirit is an endowment of and a vital presence in the Christian community and its members. It is clear that the gift of the Spirit is an effect of the past, once-for-all event of Christian initiation. But it represents an abiding presence and Paul's main interest lies not in the particular moment of the past, or any description thereof, but rather in illuminating the significance of this presence *now* for the life of the church and the Christian. This is the reason why he shows little or no interest in any factual description of the actual event of initiation and why so little information can be gleaned from his scattered references concerning it. He is not what we today would call liturgically minded. His interest lies elsewhere, in developing a deeper understanding of what Christian faith and life mean. This is a theological enterprise in the proper sense, an effort of faith seeking understanding. It is an effort which searches earnestly for the unity underlying the discrete references of Christian faith and practice and in pursuing its tasks often finds itself embarrassed by these references and the salvation history model which has determined them.

Paul's silence concerning a post-baptismal rite is largely explained by this context. For it has to be assumed that he was familiar with what we have seen was the regular practice of the early church. His references re-echo much of the same general understanding of initiation found in the early church as presented by Acts. The characteristic double reference, the christological and pneumatological, occur again and again in the Pauline texts. But Paul's effort to develop a deeper understanding of the mystery of Christian initiation leads him to develop new emphases and to bring the separate references together into a deeper unity. This is his significance and his achievement and it is in this enterprise that the key to his thought and texts lies. His references are concerned with illuminating the existing, regular practice of the church and they thus constitute, in the fine words of Schnackenburg, "a marriage of the existing rite with the weighty thought of his theology" (*Baptism in the Thought of St. Paul*, p. 30).

Central to this bold effort of Paul is the new concept of the Spirit of God which he introduces and which is to have such a profound influence in Christian theology. The understanding of the Spirit in early Christianity was the Spirit of Prophecy who inspired forceful preaching of the gospel and accompanied that preaching with confirming signs. But Paul now retrieves the other biblical concept of the Spirit, the *life-giving* Spirit (prominent in the prophets, see esp. Ezek, chaps. 36, 37). This provides him with one of the foundation ideas he is seeking to develop, a more unified understanding of Christian faith. It enables him to connect together the separate references and bring them into an harmonious unity. In particular, he is now able to unite the christological and pneumatological references of initiation. To be united to Christ means also to share in the Spirit of Christ, the Spirit of God; to receive the Holy Spirit implies union with Christ. This explains why the typical Pauline expressions, to be "in Christ," "in the Spirit," in their deepest significance shade into one another and become almost synonymous.

This achievement of theological insight now enables Paul to see the power of the Spirit at work also in the process of baptism itself, both in the genesis of faith and conversion preceding the sacrament, and in the union with Christ therein accomplished (see de la Potterie "L'Onction du Chrétien par la foi"). He is thus able to present Christian initiation

as the unity which it is and this is the main thrust and direction of his thought. But this does not at all mean that on his own initiative he would have interfered with the established and inherited practice of Christian initiation and bent it at his will to his way of thinking. Nothing in his writings suggest he was that kind of radical innovator. Nor did he need to be. His theological enterprise simply transcended the salvation history model he was commenting on. Consciously or unconsciously, this was his purpose and his achievement.

But it is worth noting that in his most extensive and significant reference to baptism, Romans 6, 3-11, Paul makes no mention whatever of the Holy Spirit. This latter theme, so prominent in his thought, is not introduced here until chap. 8. It is very difficult to see how, if in the initiation practice of the church, the gift of the Spirit was seen as an effect of baptism, he could have avoided some reference to the Spirit in this passage. No doubt the structure of Romans is important here. Nevertheless, if there is an argument from silence in the Pauline writings on this issue, it surely lies here.

Conclusion

The remaining documents of the NT throw little further light on our question. But something of the influence of Paul is discernible in the close linking in some texts of the work of Spirit with baptism (e.g., Jn 3:5; Tit 3:5). Though such references are often interpreted as implying that the Spirit is given in baptism, this judgment is overhasty (see de la Potterie "Naître de l'eau et naître de l'Esprit—le texte baptismal de Jean 3,5"). We meet here again the Pauline understanding of the Holy Spirit and the Spirit's role in the whole process of initiation. No more than in Paul himself, therefore, this close association of the christological and pneumatological references does not imply any denial of the existence of a special post-baptismal rite of the Spirit.

Viewing the evidence of the NT as a whole, therefore, one finds that Christian initiation in the early church consisted of two rites, baptism followed by imposition of hands for the gift of the Spirit. This complex ritual was derived from and determined by the perspective of biblical salvation history and the personal experience of the original disciples. Paul, introducing a new and more profound understanding of the Spirit, was able to envisage and indicate the unity which underlay this complex ritual with its discrete references. We meet here for the first time the tension between these two approaches to understanding Christian faith and practice, the theological and the salvation history approach. Both methods will continue in the church, the salvation history model more congenial to catechetical and homiletic commentary, the theological to the effort to achieve a more unified understanding. But both approaches are necessary. Neither can be reduced to the other. When one approach tends to over-dominate, false questions arise and inevitably receive false solutions. Much of the later oft-referred-to "confusion" concerning the sacrament of confirmation has its source here. The legitimacy and necessity of both approaches have to be recognized and a balanced tension maintained. This is the way towards progress and understanding in this important area of Christian faith and practice. It is also the way which offers the best hope for ecumenical discussion. This is perhaps the most important and valuable lesson which the NT teaches us today concerning the gift of the Holy Spirit in Christian initiation.

G.R. Beasley-Murray, *Baptism in the NT* (London, 1962). J.D.G. Dunn, *Baptism in the Holy Spirit* (London, 1970). W.F. Flemington, *The NT Doctrine of Baptism* (London, 1948/1957). A. George, *et. al.*, *Baptism in the NT* (London, 1964). I. de la Potterie and S. Lyonnet, *La Vie Selon L'Esprit* (Paris, 1965): "Naître de l'eau et naître de l'Esprit'-le texte baptismal de Jean 3, 5", 31-63 (de la Potterie); "L'Onction du Chrétien par la foi," 107-167 (de la Potterie). T.A. Marsh, *Gift of Community: Baptism and Confirmation* (Delaware, 1984). T.A. Marsh, "The Holy Spirit in Early Christian Teaching," *ITQ* 45 (1978): 101-116. G.T. Montague, *The Holy Spirit: Growth of a Biblical Tradition* (New York, 1976). R. Schnackenburg, *Baptism in the Thought of St. Paul* (Oxford, 1964). J. Ysebaert, *Greek Baptismal Terminology, Its Origins and Early Development* (Nijmegen, 1962).

THOMAS A. MARSH

CONFIRMATION, HISTORY OF

Most people would probably assume that the history of the sacrament of confirmation is a simple, straightforward story. It is, on the contrary, one of the most difficult and complex questions in the history of the church. There are many reasons for this. The rite varied in its practice from place to place and period to period. In many cases, documentary evidence concerning it is either entirely lacking, tantalizingly insufficient or the meaning of extant evidence is disputed. However, despite these problems the body of evidence which does exist enables the general history of the practice and understanding of the sacrament to be reconstructed. The story, however, can only be presented here in brief outline.

Any account of the history of confirmation must pay attention to the different significant periods in the practice of the sacrament and the distinct development of the rite in the East and the West. Bearing this in mind, this presentation will proceed as follows: 1) the history of the rite of confirmation; 2) the history of the theology of the sacrament; 3) the history of the age for confirmation.

History of the Rite

Subsequent to the NT period, one may discern in broad outline three main periods in the history of the rite of confirmation: (a) the early centuries (2nd to 4th centuries); (b) the early medieval period (5th to 11th centuries); (c) the central medieval period to modern times and recent developments. Discussion here will follow this order. It will be presupposed that the rite of confirmation, i.e., post-baptismal imposition of hands for the gift of the Holy Spirit, was a regular practice of the apostolic church in the NT period.

(a) The Early Centuries. The 3rd and 4th centuries represent the classic period in the ancient church of the catechumenate which culminated in the solemn initiation ceremony of the Easter vigil. This practice was obviously the flowering of a system already developing in the 2nd century. Unfortunately, however, this period is really one of silence concerning the sacrament of confirmation. The most significant reference to Christian intiation occurs in Justin Martyr (d.c. 165), *Apologia* 1, 65, but even this is too summary and inexplicit to be really useful. Though some scholars have maintained that this silence is significant, showing that confirmation was not a regular practice in the church at this time, this argument cannot be sustained. The Christian writings of the period are not of such a character that one would expect to find in them a description of the rites of Christian intiation. Their silence on this issue is therefore rather to be expected. But from early in the 3rd century this veil of silence is lifted, at least as regards the Western church. Both Tertullian from N. Africa and Hippolytus of Rome in his *Apostolic Tradition* (c. 215) give us a good description of how Christian initiation was performed in the West at the time. The initiation rites described by both writers reveal the same basic structure: baptism; post-baptismal anointing; prayer and imposition of hand for the gift of the Spirit, i.e., confirmation. The Roman rite, however, shows one variation which will be significant for the future. The anointing of the forehead, which would have been part of the post-baptismal anointing in Tertullian, is here reserved to the bishop and performed by

him *after* the general imposition of hand. As so performed it represents here the individual application of the general prayer and imposition of hand for the gift of the Spirit. In other words, the individual application was now performed not by simply touching the head but by anointing the forehead. This is the origin of the rite of chrismation which today constitutes the essential rite of confirmation.

It is worth noting that the basic shape of the initiation rite as evidenced for Carthage and Rome at this period displays the same structure as that described in Acts, chaps. 8 and 19, though the baptismal anointing is a post NT development. There can be no doubt, therefore, that the evidence attests a strong continuity in the church's initiation practice from the NT period into the 3rd century, at least as regards the West.

Over the next two centuries, that is, to the beginning of the 5th century and the time of St. Augustine, Rome and the western provinces continued this initiation practice. Evidence for this period varies from place to place, more plentiful for Rome, Italy and N. Africa, scanty for Spain and Gaul. But the general pattern remains the same. The Roman rite of final chrismation, however, was not adopted in the provinces which continued to follow their own obviously more primitive practice. It is clear that no great doctrinal significance was attached to the peculiar Roman rite, which very probably had a purely practical origin.

The question of confirmation in the East over this period presents a different story. Documentation here is not as plentiful or as straightforward as in the West. The question presents many difficulties and the whole area requires much further patient study. The earliest document throwing any definite light on initiation practice in the East is the Syriac document, *Didascalia Apostolorum* (c. 235). The ritual which this document briefly describes contains no post-baptismal rite; baptism is here followed immediately by participation in the eucharist. Later documents show that this practice was widespread in the East. Most of the evidence points to the region of the Syriac-speaking church. But the discovery in the 1950s of the lost baptismal instructions of St. John Chrysostom, delivered when he was the catechist in the great city of Antioch (c. 388-89), describe the same ritual as standard in this great center of Eastern Greek-speaking Christianity. It is therefore clear that in the 3rd and 4th centuries over large parts at least of the Eastern church no special confirmation rite existed in Christian initiation.

How to assess this evidence and this situation is a difficult task. Too many aspects remain obscure and sufficient clear evidence to resolve all the issues involved simply is not available. All efforts at a total explanation have, for the moment at least, to remain tentative and speculative. But there is also evidence that this practice was not universal in the East and that it does not represent an inherited primitive tradition. There are indications that a change may have occurred at some early stage in the Eastern practice, at least in some areas, which involved the suppression of the distinct post-baptismal rite of the Spirit and the incorporation of the special pneumatological reference of Christian initiation either with the significance of the baptismal rite itself or, though less likely, the rite of pre-baptismal anointing. Such a development might have had its origin in the church's conflict with Gnostic sects, such as the Valentinians, and a consequent desire to radically distinguish its initiation practice from theirs. Involved here would have been a different understanding of the Spirit of God and the relation between the Spirit and the church. Involved also would have been a different and more Semitic concept of time, especially as relating to sacraments, from that which prevailed in Greco-Roman culture generally. But all efforts at historical reconstruction as of now must remain speculative.

What is certain is that from about the middle of the 4th century onwards a post-baptismal anointing appears in the Eastern initiation rite and gradually spreads. The earliest evidence comes from the mystagogical catecheses of St. Cyril of Jerusalem (bp c. 349-86) where this anointing is expressly presented as signifying reception of the Holy Spirit. This rite gradually became regular practice in the initiation ceremony of the Eastern or Byzantine church and remains so today. In sharp contrast, however, to the different development already under way in the Latin West, the Eastern church allowed priests to administer this confirmation rite [a chrismation] immediately after baptism, though always with chrism blessed by the bishop. The formula which accompanied the anointing was and is: "The seal of the gift of the Spirit." Eventually most of the other Eastern churches adopted this practice of the Byzantine church. This Eastern rite of confirmation (chrismation) has since remained unchanged and is still the regular practice today.

(b) *Early Medieval Period.* Just when the Eastern rite was becoming regular practice, a very different development was under way in the West. Here, from around the beginning of the 5th century, the conferring of confirmation gradually became separated from that of baptism and its attendant ceremonies. In its origins this development was purely practical and in no way involved any doctrinal or theological position. The situation which determined this development was the significant increase in the Christian population over the 4th century following the Peace of Constantine (313) and the consequent spread of organized Christian communities in the smaller towns and even into the countryside. In these circumstances it proved simply impossible to maintain the traditional practice of the one annual ceremony of initiation in the episcopal church at the Easter vigil presided over by the bishop who would himself have administered the confirmation rites. Instead, priests were now permitted to administer baptism and its ancillary rites in the outlying churches and later those baptized were expected to receive confirmation from the bishop either in the episcopal church or when the bishop was visiting the churches of his jurisdiction.

Two observations must be made concerning this development. First, in origin it was an attempt to maintain the *unity* of Christian initiation, and the role of the bishop in it is a very new situation which had caught the church somewhat by surprise. But, second, the development soon proved a rather theoretical solution. It did not work. In the context of the very disturbed situation throughout the Western empire from the 5th century on, the possibility of people from outlying districts visiting the episcopal church to receive confirmation or receiving a visit from their bishop in their own locale for that purpose proved very problematic. Though it was the intention of the church, declared again and again, that those requiring confirmation should receive it as soon as possible after baptism, the interval between baptism and the problematic confirmation varied immensely, with the tendency over the years for the time gap to increase. Meanwhile, however, it should be noted that Rome itself maintained the traditional unified ceremony of Christian initiation.

In many parts of the West from the 6th to the 8th century, especially in Gaul, the extant evidence suggests that episcopal confirmation disappeared altogether, the pneumatological reference of initiation, instead, being associated with the post-baptismal anointing performed by the priest at baptism. This practice, understandable in the circumstances, appears too similar to the Greek practice to be mere coincidence. The influence of Greek Christianity in many parts of the West at this period is well documented. But whatever may have been the practice in these areas at this period, the situation changed when Charlemagne came to power. Liturgical reform was a significant part of Charlemagne's program and he had a powerful ally here in the guiding hand of Alcuin. The reform consisted in restoring Roman practice in ritual matters. This led to the introduction of the Roman episcopal rite of confirmation throughout the West. The sacrament, however, was again administered in separation from baptism, and the old story of the lengthening interval began all over again.

(c) Central Medieval Period to Modern Times. From the 13th century onwards very little change occurs in the rite of confirmation. The traditional Roman rite prevails universally. Some minor regulations concerning details issue from Rome but nothing of any significance. The most discussed question concerns the *essential* rite of the sacrament: is it the general imposition of hand *or* the chrismation? It was the canonists especially who were forced to address this question. Basically, the question is a false one, introducing an "either/ or" into something which really is a "both/ and." But it had a practical application which concerned a candidate who, arriving late for the ceremony, missed the opening prayer and imposition but was able to proceed and receive the frontal chrismation. Official Roman observations on this question stated that the essential rite consisted of an imposition of hand by way of anointing. Though historically correct, this reply was in the circumstances something of a Delphic oracle which left the practical problem largely

untouched. General episcopal practice, when a particular case arose, tended to repeat the whole ceremony privately *sub conditione.*

The Second Vatican Council, in its *Constitution on the Sacred Liturgy,* called for a revision of the church's sacramental rites. This task was taken in hand over the years after the council and revised rites for all the sacraments were eventually issued. The rite for confirmation appeared in 1971. The rite, however, contained little new. It was basically the historical Roman rite of confirmation again. The most significant change was in the formula accompanying the chrismation. This was changed from its unexpressive medieval form to: "Be sealed with the Gift of the Holy Spirit." This closely approached the corresponding formula in the Greek Orthodox church. The major innovations affecting the sacrament occurred not in the rite itself but rather in the accompanying directions of the *Apostolic Constitution* and the *Introduction (Praenotanda).* The following are the most important.

These documents declared that the essential rite of confirmation *now* is the chrismation. The initiation rite of imposition of hand, according to the *Introduction* (no. 9), "does not belong to the essence of the sacramental rite," though it hastens to add that it "contributes to the integral perfection of that rite and to a clearer understanding of the sacraments." This declaration settles, for the moment at least, the practical problem referred to earlier. But it achieves this only by interfering with the integrity of the historical Roman rite. This rite, as even a casual reading reveals, is one whole, a unity. It consists of a prayer for the gift of the (sevenfold) Spirit pronounced during the gesture of the bishop's upheld hands (imposition) over the general body of candidates followed by an individual application of this prayer and gesture which at Rome, at least from the time of

Hippolytus, was performed by way of the frontal chrismation (Acts 8:14-17). By opting for the chrismation as the *essential* rite over against the opening prayer and gesture, the unity and integrity of the historical rite is interfered with. Some day, perhaps, it may be restored.

Another innovation concerns the age for confirmation, a topic which will be discussed later. The occasions on which priests are permitted to administer the sacrament are extended. But the most significant and influential development regarding confirmation in the new rites was the issuing of the R.C.I.A.. This document reintroduced the unified ceremony of Christian initiation, baptism, confirmation and eucharist, for adult converts and children of catechetical age. It thus restored to the church the concept and experience of the unity of baptism and confirmation as sacraments of initiation bringing about full membership in the church and leading to full participation in the eucharist where that membership is expressed and celebrated.

Theology of Confirmation

Theological understanding of the sacrament of confirmation over the centuries has been much influenced by the history and vicissitudes of the practice of the rite. Theological reflection on a sacrament usually reflects the form of its celebration at the particular time and place. This means that theological understanding of confirmation tends to follow and be determined by the complex history of the rite. The sacramental status of the rite, when and wherever it existed, was never in question. When the term *sacrament* began to be reserved for the seven special rites of the church (Peter Lombard, 12th century), confirmation was always one of the number, always named in second place after baptism. Eventually, the Council of Trent canonized this status by formal definition (1547).

In the early centuries the most significant theological comment on confirmation occurs in the catechetical and mystagogical instructions on Christian initiation. These instructions envisage the solemn unified rite of initiation at the Easter vigil. Here the significance of the rite is simply the pneumatological reference of Christian initiation, the gift of the Spirit of God. What this gift means is presented and illustrated biblically, especially from the gospel and NT story: the descent of the Spirit upon Jesus at the Jordan; the power of the Spirit in the ministry of Jesus and his promise of the Spirit to his followers; the fulfilment of this promise at Pentecost and the work of the Spirit in the early church. This is the perspective of biblical salvation history. The presentation is very Lucan, relying heavily for its references on the 3rd gospel and Acts. Given this background, the concept of the Spirit here is very much that of the prophetic Spirit.

Later, as theological thought came to associate the work of the Spirit also with baptism (e.g., the blessing of the baptismal water) and as the two sacraments came to be separated in practice, a theory developed of *two* gifts of the Spirit in Christian initiation, one in baptism and a further in confirmation. St. Augustine, who was the first to express this view, had a particular influence here on later Latin theology. The notion of the two gifts provided the medieval commentators with a convenient theological framework for relating the Holy Spirit to both baptism and confirmation. But as confirmation was now separated from baptism by an interval of some years, it lost much of its initiation character and the particular gift of the Spirit which it confers was associated rather with a later state of life, especially as a strengthening (*robur*) for public profession of the faith.

Today, theological understanding of confirmation seeks to restore it again as an *initiation* sacrament intimately related to baptism. The R.C.I.A. has had a particular influence here. It also sees the "two gifts" framework as rather too convenient. The NT does not speak of two gifts of the Spirit but of one, however many aspects it may recognize in that one gift. Further, the NT emphasizes that the recipient of the Spirit is primarily and essentially the church itself. New converts receive the Spirit not as isolated individuals but by becoming members of the Spirit-filled community which the church is. It is clear that the theme of the Spirit in the church is a basic key to a true and developed theology of confirmation. But the emergence of such a theology must probably await the retrieval of an effective and vital pneumatology, which for so long has been conspicuous by its absence in Latin theology.

The Age for Confirmation

The *Introduction* to the new rite of 1971 (no. 11) reaffirmed the canonical position, as stated in the 1917 C.I.C., 788, that in the Latin church (Greek Uniate churches follow Greek practice) children are confirmed "about the seventh year." But it went on to state that "for pastoral reasons, episcopal conferences may choose an age which seems more appropriate, so that the sacrament is given at a more mature age after appropriate formation."

The revised C.I.C. (1983) summarizing this recent position, states it as follows: "The sacrament of Confirmation is to be conferred on the faithful at about the age of discretion unless the conference of bishops determines another age..." (891). In allowing this elasticity in the age for reception of confirmation, in the context of infant baptism, the document was but canonizing a practice which, though strictly uncanonical, had become general in the Western church in more recent times, where children were usually confirmed around the age of 12, some years after their first communion. Since then many countries and places have availed themselves of this permission and have postponed confirmation still further, into early and mid-teenage years. Many have remained undisturbed by this issue and have continued in the practice of confirming around twelve. Some have begun experimenting with a system of combining confirmation with first communion at the age of seven. Here once again then, confirmation has led to variety in practice. But the emergence of this issue has ensured that the question of the appropriate age for confirmation, in the context of infant baptism, is today a much discussed question. The issue does not concern unbaptized adults or children of catechetical age who, if seeking Christian initiation, are to be initiated according to the R.C.I.A..

The history of confirmation throws little light on this question concerning age. In the early centuries, when the unified rite of initiation prevailed, the question simply did not arise. Infants, children of all ages and adults were equally proper subjects for full Christian initiation. But even then exceptional circumstances could arise. A catechumen who fell seriously ill and was considered to be in danger of death (a frequent enough occurrence, one must presume, in ancient times), would have been baptized by a presbyter on his/her sick bed (hence the term "clinical" baptism), but later, if they recovered, they were expected to "complete" their baptism, i.e., to receive the other sacraments of initiation, confirmation and the eucharist, from the bishop. The later separation of baptism and confirmation in the Western church was, in many ways, but an extension of this practice to a new situation.

As confirmation came to be separated from baptism by a lengthening interval of years, the age of the sacrament was accordingly postponed. At first, this was a purely factual situation, with the church insisting officially and theoretically that confirmation be received as soon after baptism as possible. But, at least from the beginning of the 13th century on, a virtue was made of this fact by the introduction of the notion of "age of discretion" for confirmation and first communion. Though variously interpreted over the centuries, the age of twelve years was common in practice. The mind of the church had always been that confirmation should precede first communion. But here again practice varied greatly until the classic sequence was officially made normative by the Catechism of Trent (1566). From the middle of the 18th century, however, a practice developed and gradually spread in France whereby confirmation was postponed until *after* first communion. In the latter part of the 19th century this practice began to infiltrate other countries also. Then in 1910 St. Pius X decreed that children should receive first communion at the age of seven years, a practice which quickly became universal. The declaration, however, made no reference to confirmation, and the age for this sacrament remained unaltered at around twelve. So came about the sequence: baptism (infancy); first communion (c. 7 years); confirmation (c. 12 years). Meanwhile, paradoxically, this practice was strictly uncanonical, as the 1917 C.I.C. (788) made plain, a position reinforced later by a number of Roman replies. The practice, however, had by now become entrenched in most parts of the Latin church and could appeal to some form of contrary custom. The wider option allowed by the new rite has now reopened this whole question. In doing so it has led to its own variety in practice and to animated discussion.

The facts of history provide little assistance for deciding the question of the appropriate age for confirmation today. Practically every option can claim some support, at least, from the complex history of the sacrament. A decision on this question depends on many factors. The concrete, actual situation and local cultural conditions have to be given due weight. It may well be that different solutions may be advisable in different areas. But this question also remains fundamentally a theological question. It must basically be decided in the light of the *meaning* of confirmation as a sacrament of Christian initiation intimately linked to baptism. Whatever age is advocated for the reception of the sacrament in whatever particular situation or circumstances, the decision will always have to justify itself before this criterion.

See **Confirmation in scripture; Initiation, Christian; Anointing; Anointing, post-baptismal**

J.D.C. Fisher, *Christian Initiation: Baptism in the Medieval West* (London, 1965). L. Ligier, *Confirmation: Sen set Conjuncture Oecumenique Hier et Aujourd'hui* (Paris, 1973). A.G. Martimort, ed., *The Church's Prayer, Vol. 3, The Sacraments* (London, 1988). T.A. Marsh, *Gift of Community; Baptism and Confirmation* (Delaware, 1984). B. Neunheuser, *Baptism and Confirmation* (London, 1964). E.C. Whitaker, *Documents of the Baptismal Liturgy* (London, 1970). E. Yarnold, *The Awe-Inspiring Rites of Initiation: Baptismal Homilies of the 4th Century* (London, 1971). E. Yarnold, *Instructions on the Revised Roman Rites* (London, 1979).

THOMAS A. MARSH

CONFIRMATION, MINISTERS OF

According to the 1971 *Rite of Confirmation* (R.C.), it is the responsibility of the people of God to prepare the baptized for confirmation, and the pastor's obligation "to see that all the baptized come to the fullness of Christian initiation and are carefully prepared for confirmation" (R.C. 3). R.C. further delineates the roles and duties of those charged to prepare and support candidates for the sacrament, recognizes the different pastoral and catechetical needs of adults and children, and designates ministers for administering the sacrament in various pastoral situations. Laudably, R.C. and subsequent legislation extend the scope of ministerial roles beyond defensive Tridentine declarations on the ordinary minister of the sacrament. Similar to ongoing debates about the age of confirmands, suitable preparation, the proper sequence of confirmation and first communion, etc., discussions on the nature and duties of the expanded roles, including the proper minister of confirmation, reflect various perspectives on the ecclesial and pastoral dimensions of sacramental initiation.

As one of the "highest responsibilities of the people of God," it is incumbent upon the local church to welcome and encourage those seeking membership. The Spirit which moves individuals toward the sacraments, incorporating them into Christ and forming them into Christ's people, does not operate apart from the community. The *Rite of Christian Initiation of Adults* (R.C.I.A.) has demonstrated vividly that the heart of religious formation is the liturgy, from which the church's mission and ministries find their source and move into the larger arena of ecclesial life. While every believer may not undertake a specific catechetical or ministerial role, the worshipping assembly witnesses, prays and pledges support to candidates for initiation. In the actual celebration, members of the local church join parents, sponsors, friends and relatives, to share their common faith and elation (*General Introduction to Christian Initiation*, 7).

When preparing children and adolescents, parents exercise a pivotal role, for their influence and example precede any program. Parents minister to their children by their own growth in faith, participation in the Sunday eucharist, and supporting the catechetical efforts of the local parish. During the celebration of confirmation, parents may present their children to the presiding minister. More and more catechetical programs require parent participation (*National Catechetical Directory*, 119); professionals avoid pedantic approaches and attitudes. While parents can benefit from instruction on the sacraments, those responsible for catechesis solicit and include parents' hopes and concerns into the process of religious formation. Parents appreciate opportunities to learn from their peers how to share their faith with children. With the passing of many devotions, religious leaders can aid parents with finding ways to pray and observe the liturgical year within the home. The recently released *Catholic Household Blessings and Prayers* from the United States Catholic Conference equips families with a rich resource for mutual discovery.

Each candidate should have a sponsor who encourages the confirmand to witness the Christian life and fulfill one's Christian duties. A qualified sponsor is a confirmed Catholic, a worthy role model, neither under canonical penalty nor parent of the confirmand, and if possible, is the candidate's godparent (canons 874, 892, 893). R.C. acknowledges that the sponsor's role is conditioned by the age and situation of the confirmand. Parents have the most influence over small children, whereas adult candidates may require assistance from beyond the immediate family. Likewise, local customs and family traditions shape how the sponsor fulfills the role. In either case, the sponsor's role requires a commitment to the confirmed beyond an honorific or ceremonial function.

The catechist helps a person's faith to become "living, conscious, and active, through the light of instruction" (*Christus Dominus*, 14), a task greater than imparting information. Catechists assist in efforts to foster community spirit, and promote active, genuine participation in the worship of the church where the faithful are formed by and for prayer,

and learn the creeds (*General Catechetical Directory*, 25). In cooperation with other ministers the catechists, themselves imbued with the word, assist candidates in the ongoing appropriation and conformation to that word.

The parish clergy exercise a unique role through their liturgical ministry, providing support and direction as required for the catechetical program, and through their participation in the discernment of each candidate's readiness for the sacraments. In consultation with catechists, sponsors, and parents, the pastor establishes parochial guidelines in accordance with church law and diocesan policy. Ultimately, the pastor determines which individuals are admitted to the sacraments, and which are delayed for want of adequate preparation or desire. Whenever possible, the clergy provide encouragement and pastoral care for the discouraged and hesitant (R.C.I.A. 13).

R.C. and the *Code of Canon Law* (C.I.C.) of 1983, in accord with their predecessors and pastoral practice in the western church, state that a bishop is the ordinary minister of confirmation (canon 882) "so there will be a clearer reference to the first pouring forth of the Holy Spirit on Pentecost" (R.C., 7). As the "chief stewards of the mysteries of God," bishops are responsible for the entire liturgical life of the churches committed to them (*Christus Dominus*, 15). It is most appropriate, therefore, that bishops preside at confirmation.

In large dioceses where the ordinary cannot preside at every celebration, he may designate fellow bishops, usually auxiliaries, to confirm (canon 884), a practice criticized for creating a "confirmation engine" out of auxiliary bishops whose primary task is substituting for the chief shepherd of the diocese. Parishioners tend to identify their pastor with the local bishop. The link between the parish and the ordinary becomes more opaque when administered by a bishop from outside the diocese. Others maintain that while the ordinary is the preferred minister, any bishop can adequately represent the episcopal office. Some have suggested that more dioceses be created, freeing the ordinary to preside, or that faculties be extended more liberally to presbyters, citing the example of the Eastern churches where the bishop is present vicariously through the blessed chrism. The law allows presbyteral confirmations, with restrictions extenuated by circumstance.

Pastors or any priest, of course, can confirm those in danger of death (canon 883,3°), and the law automatically gives faculties to presbyters in particular situations. Generally, the manner and sequence in which the church incorporates candidates prior to confirmation, i.e., infant baptism or adult initiation, determine the minister of the sacrament. When children are baptized as infants and brought through a conventional catechetical course, with reception of first communion preceding confirmation by several years, the bishop presides at confirmation. He may associate priests with himself to administer the sacrament for serious reason, e.g., large number of candidates, and priests should have a visible ecclesial connection, such as vicars, pastors, or priests involved in the catechetical preparation of the candidates (R.C., 8). While canon 884 allows the bishop to give the faculty to specified presbyters, frequency and scope of permission vary from place to place. In some frontier dioceses, the parochial pastor regularly confirms by local policy. Likewise, the faculty is extended within some dioceses and parishes where confirmation is not delayed beyond the age of discretion and immediately precedes first communion.

The Rite of Christian Initiation of Adults, which also applies to children of catechetical age and persons seeking membership from other ecclesial communities, preserves initiatory sequence and integrity. Ideally, the bishop would preside at the Easter vigil, baptize confirm, and welcome initiates to the eucharist. R.C.I.A. recognizes that on the vigil, episcopal presidency is limited to the cathedral, and thereby extends to presbyters the faculties to confirm in the following circumstances:

(1) When a priest baptizes an adult or child of catechetical age, he confirms the same unless serious reasons require postponement (R.C.I.A., 14, 24).

(2) Priests confirm when receiving a member of another Christian church (R.C.I.A., 481), except in the case of Orthodox Christians entering the Catholic church, when the rite of reception is discretionary and a simple profession of faith can suffice (R.C.I.A., 474, *Orientalium Ecclesiarum*, 25).

(3) An adult, baptized as an infant in the Catholic church and having received no further catechetical instruction or sacramental participation, completes initiation into the church through the R.C.I.A., and is confirmed by the presiding priest, preferably at the Easter vigil (R.C.I.A., 409).

(4) When a baptized, though not confirmed Catholic, has formally abandoned the Catholic church by joining another ecclesial community, that person is regarded as a baptized non-Catholic, and returns to the Catholic church through the Rite of Reception of Baptized Christians into full communion with the Catholic church. Hence, the priest who receives can confirm.

Pastors may request the faculty to confirm baptized adults who have been catechized and admitted to the eucharist at an earlier time. The law leaves this to the discretion of the ordinary (can. 884). Many parishes prefer to confirm these adults with candidates from the R.C.I.A. at the Easter vigil, rather than placing them in line with children and adolescents when the bishop makes the rounds. In some dioceses, the faculty is freely given, while others are quite restrictive.

The laws stipulating who confirms, with their interpretations and exceptions, are akin to discussions on the substance and functions of the other ministries associated with initiation. At the heart of each canon is an ecclesiology. Recognition and sanction of expanded ministries do not in themselves define the nature of the church. Rather, ministries evolve out of the church's apostolic mission. Questions about who does what, and how ministry is enacted, become more lucid as the church heeds the dominical mandate. In so doing, the church discloses its very nature and its head.

See **Sponsors for initiation; Baptism, ministers of**

Gerard Austin, *Anointed with the Spirit* (NY: Pueblo Publishing Co., 1985).

A. BRANDT HENDERSON

CONFIRMATION, PREPARATION FOR

Prior to and following the promulgation of the reformed *Rite of Confirmation* (R.C.) in 1971, religious educators, clergy, and theologians have struggled with the theology of the sacrament and means of effective catechesis. The apostolic constitution, *Divinae Consortium Naturae,* presupposes that confirmation, even when conferred apart from baptism, follows the ancient initiatory sequence and precedes the reception of first communion. R.C. provides, for pastoral reasons, an option to confirm at a time later than the age of discretion to impart "appropriate formation at a more mature age." While not linking delay to maturity, canon 891 permits episcopal conferences to determine the age of confirmation for those baptized as infants, and authorizes confirmation at any age for those in danger of death. To date, the National Conference of Catholic Bishops has not stipulated an age, allowing local ordinaries to do so in their dioceses. In addition, many religious educators have urged that confirmation be delayed until the high school years. Consequently, the vast majority of candidates for the sacrament are adolescents who were baptized as infants and received first communion in early childhood.

One pastoral-catechetical rationale for delaying confirmation maintains that youth, not small children, are capable of making a more informed, mature, and personal commitment to Christ and the church. Preparation programs may incorporate a service requirement to witness to one's faith, and candidates' progress may be marked by liturgical celebrations with roots in other rites, e.g., a declaration of candidacy similar to students preparing for holy orders, an election ceremony modeled on the milestone for catechumens in the Rite of Christian Initiation of Adults (R.C.I.A.). Those charged with preparation perceive their roles as facilitators and companions; the environment for catechesis frequently includes dialogue within small groups of candidates. The sacramental theology behind delay stresses the anthropological nature of sacraments and their identity with rites of passage, as well as the candidate's personal expression of faith.

Another approach accentuates the teaching of doctrine; the longer the period between reception of first communion and confirmation, the greater the opportunity for intensive, if not remedial education. The pedagogy is more magisterial, the setting a classroom. Various parties who argue for delay differ on the content and delivery of catechesis, but all perceive adolescence as a critical time for religious formation.

Delay, however, generates a dilemma for the theology of confirmation celebrated years after first communion, and the appropriate catechesis for youth who typically question authority and pedagogical structures. Confirmation often is depicted as a rite a passage, a maturity sacrament, the "completion" of initiation; each explanation lacks compelling justification in tradition, and inadvertently suggests that infant baptism is deficient, and/or confirmation is somehow more significant than eucharist. Rather than ritualizing entrance into Christian corporate life, the sacrament becomes a recognition or reward for individual achievement. Likewise, while confirmation may be delayed to prolong programs of religious education, postponement does not effectively retain the majority in active church membership for the duration of their youth.

The same pastoral concern which spurs the delay of confirmation has motivated others to reinstate confirmation prior to first communion. A handful of dioceses and parishes in the United States and abroad have established guidelines for catechetical programs preparing any baptized Catholic of the age of discretion, and with appropriate formation, for confirmation prior to first communion. Typi-cally, the candidates range from seven to nine years old. In most instances, the bishop or his designate confirms the candidates within the context of the Mass. Following the seal of confirmation, the *confirmati* are admitted to the eucharist. Like the sequence in the R.C.I.A., subsequent formation concentrates on the effects of sacramental initiation and responsibilities of full stature within the church, i.e., it is *mystagogical*, an extended period of post-initiation catechesis through childhood, adolescence and beyond, to further embrace the mystery into which one has been incorporated. Proponents of this order cite the experience of the R.C.I.A., in which all three sacraments are conferred in the traditional order of baptism, confirmation, eucharist, and the initiatory process which identifies these sacraments with

entrance into ecclesial life, not completion of a curriculum.

Bestowing confirmation before first communion relieves some of the theological and catechetical difficulties resulting from delay. When confirmation is restored as the link between font and table, pastors, parents, and religious educators need not manufacture theologies apart from confirmation's liturgical and ecclesial significance. What baptism begins and eucharist sustains is bridged by a sealing of sacred chrism in the assembly. Rather than being associated with rewards for personal achievement or graduation exercises from religious education, confirmation's ecclesial dimension comes to fore, i.e., disclosing a gift of God for the edification of the church. In addition, confirmation is freed from a nexus with rites of passage found in some civil and religious ceremonies, and the frequent commercialism accompanying the same.

Proponents of this sequence relinquish a degree of control over the religious education process. After initiation, students are not compelled to attend classes by want of a sacrament. When confirmation is no longer the culmination of religious education, parents, pastors, and catechists must formulate new strategies in their pastoral and catechetical response to the needs of youth. Preliminary evidence indicates that attrition is minimal-to-nil in American parishes which have adopted the confirmation-prior-to-first communion progression. Success is attributed to involving parents throughout the process and redirecting energies toward comprehensive youth ministry, additional opportunities for spiritual and doctrinal formation, and liturgical celebrations marking rites of passage, such as baccalaureate Masses, and spiritual growth or awakening, e.g., solemn communions, penance services, induction into liturgical and social ministries. In short, successful formation employs many of the worthy components found in some confirmation programs for adolescents, minus associations which, it is argued, confound the significance of the sacrament.

Catechesis for Confirmation

Whenever candidates are prepared for confirmation, the catechesis includes common ingredients, adapted for the age and abilities of the candidates. The guidelines for the Archdiocese of St. Paul and Minneapolis provide an exemplary model for catechetical content.

The Rite:
The ritual
Laying on of hands
Anointing
Sign of the Cross
Baptismal vows

Prayer:
Prayer
The Lord's Prayer
The creed
Litany

Christian Acts:
Prayer
Fasting
Service
Welcoming
Study of Scripture
Contact with
   community of
   believers
Discipline

Symbols:
Sign of the
   Cross on forehead
Anointing with oil
Water
Oil
Candle

These elements constitute a worship-based catechesis and extend to the theology and responsibilities which follow entrance into the church. In accord with the principle of *lex orandi, lex credendi*,

doctrine and discipline arise out of participation in worship, the cycle of the liturgical year, devotions, and personal prayer. Preparation for first communion, or the study of baptism and other sacraments, would include a similar list, teaching from those elements proper to the specific sacrament. While this schema does not simulate some of the more conventional content of catechetical curricula, each element can introduce the church's systematic reflection and doctrine. Ritual and lectionary become the primary texts for catechesis. Also, young people who do not frequent the liturgy develop an interest in and see the relationship between catechesis and worship.

Like the catechumenate, the method of catechesis begins with study of the lections proclaimed in the Sunday assembly. Whether child or adult, the candidate can deliberate on one's personal experience, and begin to objectify and verbalize that experience in encounter with the divine presence disclosed through word, sacrament, and assembly. Clearly this method requires directed discussion in a setting which promotes sharing one's experience without fear of judgment.

In articulating the faith tradition, the catechist invites the candidates to weigh that tradition with their own history, encourages them to appropriate for themselves the vision and faith of the church, and assists them in finding ways to express and act upon their faith. Service projects can be the vehicle for witness, and become an integral component of formation prior to any preparation dedicated to confirmation.

Catechesis which begins with the rite of confirmation and all its elements can bypass some of the *adiaphora* which sap energies and obscure the meaning of the sacrament, e.g., wearing stoles and taking a new name. Confirmation is not ordination, and one's baptismal name has sufficient dignity to last a lifetime.

The state of flux regarding the age and

order of sacraments, and appropriate formation, reflects various theologies of the sacrament and how these theologies address the pastoral and catechetical responsibilities of the church for its children and adolescents. Whether our understanding of confirmation will converge remains unknown. If the R.C.I.A. becomes, as mandated, the normative means of adult initiation, its sequence and methods of catechesis will impact the praxis of confirmation for those baptized prior to the age of discretion.

Gerard Austin, *Anointed with the Spirit* (NY: Pueblo Publishing Co., 1985). Aidan Kavanagh, *Confirmation: Origins and Reform* (NY: Pueblo Publishing Co., 1988). James A. Wilde, ed., *When Should We Confirm?* (Chicago: Liturgy Training Publications, 1989).

A. BRANDT HENDERSON

CONFIRMATION, SPONSORS FOR

See Sponsors for initiation

CONFIRMATION, THEOLOGY OF

It has been said, and quite correctly, that confirmation is a rite in search of a theology. It might be more correctly stated that there are several forms of confirmation, each in search of a theology (Quinn, p. 325).

1. The first is the post-baptismal conclusion to baptism, historically associated with the bishop, especially in Roman practice, and leading to eucharistic fellowship. If not originally, then by the late 4th or early 5th century in the West the episcopal rite was associated with a specific giving of the Holy Spirit by the bishop through handlaying and/or chrismation. In the contemporary R.C.I.A. the former exclusively episcopal conclusion to baptism is called confirmation and consists of a twofold action, the imposition of hands with prayer for the Holy Spirit and a consignation with chrism on the forehead with a formula indicating reception of that Spirit and identified in the Apostolic Constitution of Paul VI as being a "laying on of hand" (O.C., Apost. Const.).

2. A later rite, rooted in (a) the 5th century Gallican practice of having the bishop ratify baptisms over which he had not presided and in the (b) peculiar Roman practice of adding an episcopal chrismation to the prayer with handlaying. The separation of the episcopal rite from the baptismal rites created the need to explain and to justify "confirmation." The theology of this rite, which became the medieval sacrament of confirmation, reached its fullest development in the *Summa Theologiae* of Thomas Aquinas. This same theology, with a more emphatic focus on the Holy Spirit's role, is that of the contemporary rite of confirmation (O.C., *Apost. Const.*).

3. The 16th century Reformers, in repudiating the medieval sacrament of confirmation, created their own version, a rite which concluded catechism study with the personal affirmation of the baptismal covenant and admitted the candidate to eucharistic fellowship. Today the Reformation rite has been transformed by American Lutherans and Episcopalians into a series of affirmation rites, one of which is still called confirmation, which allow candidates to affirm their faith at different points in their post-baptismal journey.

In the following pages the sources of confirmation theology will be presented and the received theology examined. Since scholastic theologians would use such sources uncritically and out of context it should be noted that we are not intending to present a development of the theology of confirmation as if it were entirely consistent with and completely applicable to contemporary praxis.

The Post-baptismal Conclusion to Baptism

Scripture. The NT is a witness to the importance of baptismal initiation but demonstrates neither a clear nor a consistent picture of the rite or rites which make it up. Instead, the scriptures focus on faith and baptism as the means whereby we share in the salvation won for us by Jesus Christ (Mk 16:15-16; cf. Mt 28:19). The baptism of Jesus in the Jordan seems to provide the paradigm for Christian baptism. Since the special features of that baptism, the overshadowing of Jesus and the voice of God testifying to his divine Sonship, along with the descent of the Spirit in the form of a dove, appear to be separate from the Johannine baptism itself (Mk 1:9-11; cf. Mt 3:13-17, Lk 3:21-22, Jn 1:29-34), some find here the origin of a twofold baptismal pattern. They find corroboration in the Acts of the Apostles where there is evidence of a separation between water baptism and the giving of the (ecstatic) Spirit, generally through a post-baptismal, apostolic laying on of hands. In fact, Acts 8:14-17, in which the apostles Peter and John complete the baptism of the Samaritans, who were earlier converted and baptized by Philip with the granting of the Spirit through an imposition of hands, will early on be used as a proof text, identifying the post-baptismal episcopal action with that of the apostles in Acts. If these scriptural citations do testify to a complex baptismal ritual in the synoptics and Acts, the same cannot be said for Paul or John where all is complete in the baptism itself. Such differences have been explained in terms of a difference in the theologies of the Spirit in the NT, that of Luke being a more primitive view of the Holy Spirit as an external, prophetic force, not connected in any way to baptism with its forgiveness of sins, and those of Paul and John being more advanced views of the Spirit as personal and as the very agent of baptism as well as, especially in John, a permanent possession of the baptized. Contrary to Acts, for example, one is born of water *and* Spirit in John 3:5 (Marsh, pp. 43-101).

The Acts of the Apostles, according to scholars such as Marsh, foreshadows the complex Western baptismal rites of the late 2nd century, witnessed to by Tertullian and the *Apostolic Tradition.* The model for these later rites is the twofold baptismal pattern discovered in Acts. This pattern is rooted in the Lucan belief that baptism in water is for the forgiveness of sins, while the post-baptismal handlaying signifies the bestowal of that prophetic Spirit which returns to Israel first in Jesus' baptism in the Jordan, where the overshadowing is called an anointing (Lk 4:18; Acts 10:38), comes to the church, the new Israel, at Pentecost (Acts 2:1-4), and is given to each individual Christian in baptism (Acts 2:17, 38). Although at a later period the more profound Pauline and Johannine theology of the Holy Spirit would govern Christian teaching, the pattern for baptism would already have been set in place.

It may be questioned, however, whether the evangelists' recording of Jesus' baptism in the Jordan testifies so much to a twofold ritual action as it does to the need to make clear the difference between John's baptism and Christian baptism, the latter being related to the Holy Spirit. Thus, there would be a distancing from the actual baptism of John to indicate that his followers of Christ would receive a baptism of divine adoption, accomplished through the work of the Holy Spirit. Furthermore, in Acts one can certainly question whether the need to promote the apostles' authority in matters baptismal is testimony to a common ritual practice in Luke's church. Nevertheless, Acts 8 did become a "proof text" for the medieval sacrament of confirmation.

Other NT passages concerning anointing and sealing will also be applied to confirmation (e.g., 2 Cor 1:21; Eph 1:13). What is overlooked is that these passages refer more directly to baptism itself as the seal of the Spirit and to the work of the Holy Spirit in baptism itself as an anointing. Actual post-baptismal anointing will become a ritual reality in the second century, but in its first appearance the anointing will be messianic in character, both in East and West (Winkler, pp. 24-25; Kavanagh, p. 41).

The Early Church: Tertullian and Apostolic Tradition. Tertullian (c. 160-c. 225) dedicated an entire treatise to baptismal initiation (*De Baptismo*). He was the first to speak of a post-baptismal anointing, founded on Aaron's anointing by Moses and a symbol of Christ's messianic anointing by God (De Bap. 7). Thus, the first evidence of anointing is that which testifies to the neophytes' participation in Christ's royal priesthood and which is clearly connected with the baptism itself. As noted above this anointing is found in both East and West though not necessarily always at the same place in the baptismal ritual.

Tertullian also witnesses to a handlaying which, with its blessing, is a prayer for the Spirit. The author relates this handlaying to the overshadowing of Christ at the Jordan as well as to the blessing Jacob gave to his grandsons, Ephraim and Manasseh (De Bap. 8). Elsewhere, Tertullian describes the handlaying as an illumination of the soul by the Holy Spirit ("The flesh is overshadowed by the imposition of hand so that the soul might be illuminated by the Spirit" (De carnis res. 8). It should also be noted that this North African writer is a clear witness to the fact that eucharist concludes baptismal initiation.

Some have assumed that Tertullian's description of post-baptismal handlaying is equivalent to the post-baptismal episcopal rites found in *Apostolic Tradition* 21. In this document, however, there is an important addition: a second post-baptismal anointing following the episcopal handlaying prayer. Why such an addition? It would seem to arise from the fact that baptism with its messianic anointing was performed by presbyters and deacons out of view of the assembly since the candidates for baptism were naked; the bishop remained with the assembly. The bishop completed the baptisms by adding to the presbyteral anointing of the body an anointing of the head, at the time he received the newly baptized with handlaying and prayer. This double anointing, found here for the first time, will become a standard part of baptismal praxis in the Roman church, and each of the anointings will acquire a different meaning. In other words, two independent rites of anointing or consignation will evolve from this more primitive 3rd century rite, the first a presbyteral anointing related to the water bath, the second an episcopal anointing related to the imposition of hand with prayer. The second anointing will affect Western, non-Roman baptismal practice beginning in the 5th century (C. of Orange, 8 Nov. 441, c. 2); at least by the 9th century the Roman pattern will become the ordinary baptismal pattern in much of western Europe.

Apostolic Tradition 21 provides the prayer to be used with the bishop's handlaying. Is this particular rite the same as that in Tertullian, which has an explicitly pneumatic character? Does this baptism along with handlaying and its prayer correspond to the twofold ritual supposedly encountered in Acts? This is clearly the opinion of one author who finds in Tertullian and *Apost. Trad.* 21 the connecting link between the Spirit rite in Acts and future confirmation (Marsh, pp. 124-127). Others insist that to come to such a conclusion is to read too much into the sparse evidence at hand. Furthermore, from the point of view of ritual structure, one author believes that the episcopal rites of *Apos. Trad.* 21 are nothing more than a particularly solemn form of liturgical dismissal rites, in which the worshippers come under the bishop's hand for a blessing dismissing them from the service. As the conclusion to baptism the dismissal is more complicated, since it combines both the bishop's anointing, a ratification of the baptisms done at his behest by deacons and presbyters, with a conclusion to the entire initiation process which in effect is a dismissal of the newly baptized to their first eucharistic assembly (Kavanagh, pp. 41-52).

Corroborating evidence that the episcopal rites are simply a primitive *missa* might possibly be found in the prayer accompanying the handlaying. The Verona Latin text of this prayer reads: "Lord God you have made them worthy to receive remission of sins through the laver of regeneration of the Holy Spirit; send upon them your grace, that they may serve you according to your will, for to you is glory, etc." Writers have assumed that the scribe dropped a line from this prayer. Basing themselves on the later versions of the prayer they have added an explicit invocation begging God to send the Holy Spirit upon the baptized (e.g., the editor of the "reconstituted" text of *Apostolic Tradition*, Bernard Botte). But is this the case? Is not the prayer perfectly intelligible in itself and entirely consistent with the episcopal rite if the latter is a dismissal rite rather than a new element in baptismal initiation? Thus, while the ritual genesis of what would become confirmation is found in *Apost. Trad.* 21, with its prayer and handlaying and unique second post-baptismal anointing, the interpretation of those episcopal actions continues to be in contention.

Innocent I, the Holy Spirit, and the Episcopal Post-baptismal Rite. However *Apostolic Tradition's* episcopal rites are currently interpreted, there seems to be no doubt that the ritual pattern found there evolved into the more complex rites of the later Roman sacramentaries. Even before this a letter of Innocent I to Decentius of Gubbio (416) already witnesses to the double post-baptismal anointing of *Apost. Trad.* becoming two entirely independent ritual actions and to the post-baptismal episcopal action receiving a clearly pneumatic interpretation. Moreover, the actions of the bishops are identified with the apostolic handlaying in Acts 8. From now on, according to Innocent, the presbyteral, messianic anointing is only to be given on the crown of the head while the episcopal anointing is to be given on the forehead (Ep. ad Decentium, P.L., 20:554B). In either case the oil to be used is perfumed oil, chrism, which becomes an important liturgical symbol of the Holy Spirit in the late 4th century.

Question has been raised to which rite Innocent specifically refers as giving the Holy Spirit, handlaying or episcopal consignation with chrism. Some prefer the latter and so translate phrases of Innocent's letter as follows: "The right of bishops alone to seal and to deliver the Paraclete . . . and even then they (presbyters) are not to sign the brow with that oil, for this is reserved to bishops alone when they deliver the Paraclete" (Whitaker, pp. 229-230). Or is the pneumatic rite that of handlaying, which would better correspond to the association of the bishops' actions with those of the apostles in Acts 8? In this case the same phrases have been translated as follows: "This pontifical rank belongs to bishops only, so that, when they seal or when they give (*ut vel consignent, vel tradant*) the Paraclete Spirit . . . and even then they are not to sign the forehead with that same oil, for this is reserved to bishops alone, at the time (*solis debetur episcopis, cum tradunt*) that they deliver the Paraclete Spirit" (Ligier, pp. 40-41).

Even if this latter interpretation is correct, there is no doubt that the episcopal consignation is closely bound up with handlaying because of the peculiar character of the Roman rite, that is, the double post-baptismal chrismation. The reservation of the signing of the forehead to the bishop gave sacramental force to chrismation because it *was* associated with episcopal handlaying. Future theology would focus on anointing and, in fact, Roman liturgical books, such as the Gelasian Sacramentary, would designate the entire episcopal rite of handlaying with prayer and anointing with chrism as a rite of consignation, *Ad consignandum* (Reg. 316, no. 450).

The need to give a pneumatic focus to some element in the baptismal complex, both East and West, could be because of the 4th and 5th century battles over the divinity of the Holy Spirit. In the East in particular the chrism was identified with the Holy Spirit (Ligier, pp. 157-161) and the messianic anointing rite received a strong pneumatic emphasis. In the West it may well have been that a rite associated with the bishop—and his handlaying—received the same emphasis. Also, it is clear from Innocent's letter that he is establishing a particular episcopal practice, one not to be shared with presbyters; he may well be upholding the rights of bishops with regard to the post-baptismal rites by giving them a close connection to the apostles' handlaying in Acts 8 (Kavanagh, pp. 61-64). One could ask, however, whether such an identification with the apostles' handlaying might not argue more for Innocent's thinking of episcopal handlaying as delivering the Spirit rather than simply the episcopal anointing.

Oddly enough, in the later Gelasian and Gregorian sacramentaries, as well as in all Roman Pontificals down to the period of Vatican II, it is only the prayer accompanying the handlaying which gives expression to the pneumatic character of the rite described by Innocent I; the now thoroughly pneumatized prayer includes both the Johannine language of rebirth (Jn 3:5) and the Johannine title of Paraclete, as well as the Isaian sevenfold gifts of the Holy Spirit (Reg. 316, par. 451). By contrast the chrismation formula in the West never specified the role of the Holy Spirit. It is only in the epicletic prayer during handlaying that we have a clear idea of the pneumatic character of the rite. The episcopal consignation in the Gelasian Sacramentary is christic, that in later sacramentaries and pontificals is trinitarian. Perhaps it is only because of the classic prayer for the sevenfold Spirit that one can determine what individual chrismation is about. Both handlaying with its prayer for the sevenfold, prophetic Spirit, and the signing of the forehead with chrism, should have been necessary for a theology of "confirmation." Instead, later theologians tended to focus only on the anointing.

Confirmation

The First Appearance of "Confirmation" in Southeast Gaul. Confirmation as a word for the post-baptismal episcopal intervention comes from the region of southeast Gaul, not Rome. At first it does not have the particular theological connotation of "strengthening," as it later will. Rather, its immediate reference is to a bishop's personal involvement in a baptism over which he has not presided. In other words, the baptism preceded his "confirming" the neophytes by a longer or shorter period and was done by others. This use of the term confirmation is first encountered in the mid-fifth century (Council of Riez, 18 November 439, canon 3, *confirmare neophytos*; Council of Orange, 8 November 441, canon 2, *in confirmatione*).

The non-availability of bishops to those desiring baptism was a problem, especially in the rural areas of southeast Gaul where there was an increase of Christians

278

in the 5th century. Later, the same non-availability seems to have spread to the cities. "Confirmation" does not at first so much refer to a specific rite as to the personal involvement of the bishop himself with those being "confirmed." It might be said then that the genesis of the later sacrament of confirmation is found in the separation of the bishop from the baptisms over which he would normally exercise oversight. He, in effect, approves the baptisms celebrated by those other than himself. Whether this also meant that several of the post-baptismal rites which he was normally associated with in Rome, such as imposition of hand and prayer, would have been dropped from baptism, or were even originally part of Gallican baptism, is controverted. Some claim that the rites the bishop performed "in confirmatione" had not been part of ordinary baptismal practice in Gaul, since they are not found in any of the later Gallican sacramentaries (Winkler, 12-13, Kavanagh, 66). Others feel that Gaul had rites similar to those found in Tertullian in North Africa, where there was a post-baptismal handlaying and prayer for the Holy Spirit.

With the separation of the bishop from baptism and the subsequent insistence that those not baptized by their bishop needed to come to him to have themselves "confirmed," there was the need to explain why such an action was necessary. Clear indication of this is found in a homily of a bishop from the same region, Faustus of Riez, who, between about 450 and 470, preached on a Pentecost Sunday in answer to the peoples' question: "After the mystery of baptism what good can the ministry of the one confirming do me?" (*Homilia de Pentecosten*). Faustus' efforts to convince his people to come to the bishop to have their baptisms completed or "confirmed" would not be particularly important except for the fact that portions of his sermon became the sources for the medieval theology of the

sacrament of confirmation, being passed on by way of the Ps. Isidorean *Decretals* and later canonical collections as the words of two popes, Urban and Melchiades. As the statements of important Roman figures rather than those of the minor, and semi-Pelagian, bishop of Riez, the sermon of Faustus acquired a theological and doctrinal import which, in reality, it never had. To Faustus we owe that medieval theology of the sacrament of confirmation which centers on the concept of the strengthening of the baptized. Faustus preached that confirmation was necessary for those who survived infancy and, consequently, had to live in a world filled with trouble and strife. Confirmation equipped them with arms for battle. The Holy Spirit given in confirmation protected those regenerated in Christ by providing them with a growth in grace (*augmentum ad gratiam*). Parenthetically, we might note that, even with the connection of the Spirit to the action of confirming by the bishop, Faustus speaks of a twofold descent of that Spirit, one at baptism, in the blessing of the water, and the other with the bishop's handlaying and prayer for the sevenfold Spirit. Even before Faustus, of course, in the writing of Tertullian, we find this same need to try to make explicit the time(s) when the Spirit descends upon the water or the candidate (*De bap.* 6-8).

By confirmation, then, the baptized are strengthened and "confirmed for battle." Faustus gave a twist to the meaning of confirmation which determined the future direction of confirmation theology: confirmation equals strengthening (*robur*). The rite which accomplished this strengthening was the imposition of hand with prayer for the Spirit; there is no mention of a second anointing, although it would seem that the Roman practice was known, and disapproved of, in this region (cf. C. of Orange, c. 2). Thus, the medieval theology of confirmation was influenced by, and dependent upon, the efforts of a bishop to encourage his people to be confirmed; such an explanation was necessitated by reason of the separation, for whatever reason, of the bishop from baptismal initiation. Also, the giving of the Holy Spirit was clearly identified with the action of the bishop, even as it was in the letter of Innocent I. In Faustus' sermon, of course, the Holy Spirit is given for a specific purpose, i.e., for strength and fortitude to live in an unfriendly world.

Later Gallican contributions to the future theology of the medieval sacrament of confirmation appear in the writings of Alcuin (Letter to Oduin, Ep. 134, [A.D. 798]) and Rabanus Maurus (*De Clericorum Institutione* 30, [ca. A.D.819]). Alcuin bases part of his description on the Roman author John the Deacon's "Letter to Senarius" (6th C.). But part of his description reports Gallican practice. For example, baptism is concluded by "confirmation with bread and cup." Only at a later date is there the imposition of the bishop's hand through which the baptized receive the "Spirit of sevenfold grace in order to be strengthened by the Holy Spirit to preach to others." It might be noted that with the military conquests and the baptismal policy of Charlemagne the late 8th century was faced, for a brief moment, with a new phenomenon—a number of adult baptisms.

Rabanus Maurus quotes directly from Alcuin and adds something new, an explanation of what might be a recent addition to the bishop's rite, a second post-baptismal anointing, modelled on Roman practice. Could it be the Roman episcopal practice is just entering into Gallican initiation rites? The pattern would already have been known in that region because of the Roman books which had earlier been imported into France and copied, such as the Gelasian Sacramentary. At any rate, basing himself on Augustine (Sermon 265.7) Rabanus claims that there are two gifts of the Holy Spirit represented by the two anointings, one a resurrection gift, the other a Pentecost gift. The second anointing on the forehead, performed by the bishop as Innocent I had insisted several centuries before, is related to the imposition of the bishop's hand by an explanation which clearly is in accord with Alcuin's concept of the meaning of handlaying: "By grace thus comforted the [anointed] bear themselves intrepidly and audaciously before the rulers of this world and preach the name of Christ with free voice." It should be noted that neither Alcuin nor Rabanus speak of the post-baptismal episcopal actions as confirmation. But it would not take a genius to connect the idea of *strengthening* to preach with the Faustian notion of *strengthening* for life's battles.

The only use of the word confirmation in authentic Roman documents is the "confirmation" of the bread with the cup of consecrated wine (e.g., cf. Ordo Romanus I). When used of the postbaptismal episcopal practice in supposedly Roman texts, it is a good guess that this might be due to the re-editing of the documents outside of the city of Rome. For example, in *Ordo Romanus XI* the word confirmation appears twice with regard to the final rites of baptism, once for the bishop's prayer for the Holy Spirit and once as a warning that such rites are necessary to "confirm" baptism with the name of Christianity (O.R. XI, 96-104).

Scholastic Theology and the Sacrament of Confirmation. By the end of the first millennium the episcopal conclusion to baptism was so elaborated in liturgical books such as the mid-tenth century Romano-Germanic Pontifical that it seemed quite independent of baptism. This independence was further enhanced by the addition of a prayer identifying the activity of the bishops with the apostles in Acts 8 (R.G.P., 99:388).

Along with this greater independence

there were, as we have seen, witnesses to confirmation's meaning sufficient enough to provide the bricks and mortar for the medieval and scholastic theology of the sacrament of confirmation. Such witnesses found their way into the mainstream of medieval European theology through inclusion in a number of canonical collections. Thus, parts of Faustus' sermon were provided with the names of two popes, Urban and Melchiades. Alcuin's explanation of the bishop's action, filtered through Rabanus and with his additional comments about the second post-baptismal anointing, became part of the common heritage of Western theology, and testified to a connection between confirmation and preaching as well as to a double bestowal of the Spirit, one paschal and one pentecostal. Demands for fasting and penance before confirmation as well as warnings against its reiteration were also included in the canonical collections. One canon, attributed to Ps. Melchiades, though from the hand of an author other than Faustus, claimed the superiority of imposition of hand to baptism because of the individual granting it, i.e., the bishop.

With independent rite and authoritative witnesses, medieval theologians were able to declare confirmation one of the seven sacraments. What these scholastics experienced was an episcopal action, performed but once, sufficiently distinct from baptism, and interpreted as a giving of the Holy Spirit for strengthening, especially for strengthening to preach. The rite had its own name, confirmation, found both in the statements of pseudonymous popes (= Faustus) as well as in Gallicanized Roman liturgical texts.

Despite some attention to handlaying and prayer, the most important element in the sacrament was clearly consignation with chrism, with its quite unremarkable and certainly non-pneumatic formula of administration. This rite formed the *sacramentum tantum.* One reason the ancient prayer for the sevenfold Spirit had such little impact on the medievals may well have been because of the growing concentration on strengthening as fortitude rather than as gift of the Spirit. An important witness to this change in direction is William of Auvergne (1180-1249), who claimed that the Holy Spirit was not given in confirmation, since it had already been given in baptism. The prayer was simply for the praise and glory of the Holy Spirit. Confirmation, both in form and name, implied the gift or virtue of fortitude, a strengthening against the irascible appetites for the purpose of fearlessly professing Christ's name (Tractate on the Sacraments). Thus, the determined grace effect (the *res* or reality signified), distinct from baptism and earlier identified with the reception of the fullness of the Holy Spirit, was based on the key concept of Faustus, that confirmation is a strengthening, a *robur.* As this idea dominated theological thought, the bestowal of the Spirit receded into the background and a growth model of sacramental grace claimed attention, baptism being related to first birth and the grace of regeneration, confirmation to growth and an increase of grace. It should also be added that since grace was so christologically conceived the role of the Holy Spirit would also tend to be diminished.

Like baptism, confirmation was not repeated. Consequently, it was thought to have its own character (*res et sacramentum*). There was disagreement, however, over how it differed from that of baptism. Concerning the institution of the sacrament there were a number of opinions: confirmation was either directly instituted by Christ, or by the apostles (Acts 8), or, later, by the church at the Council of Meaux (9th century)! One problem with institution was the emphasis in the scriptures on the handlaying of the apostles and the emphasis in medieval theology on chrismation. The need to harmonize these two different practices (assuming, of course, that the sacrament of confirmation *is* in any authentic sense related to apostles' actions) continues until this day (cf. the *Apost. Const.* in the O.C.).

Thomas Aquinas (1225-1274) provided the definitive medieval theology of the sacrament of confirmation, especially in his last work, the *Summa Theologiae* (3.72). The concepts of spiritual strength and maturity dominate his thinking: as baptism relates to birth, confirmation pertains to growth, and eucharist to spiritual nourishment. Thus, the Faustian concept of confirmation as strengthening is fundamental to Thomas' ideas about sacraments and spiritual growth (S.Th.3.72.1c). Such comparisons between the physical and spiritual realms are, of course, analogical. In other words, spiritual maturity is *somewhat like* physical maturity. As Thomas notes, if they were the same then children and women would not need the sacrament since in real life they do not need to be strengthened for combat (S.Th.8)!

Christ instituted the sacrament (S.Th. 72.1.ad 1), although, since the Spirit could not be granted until after Jesus' resurrection and ascension, he did so by way of promising the Spirit rather then clearly manifesting it (Jn 7:39; 16:7). Ignoring handlaying with its prayer, Thomas focused on chrism as the matter of the sacrament, using Ps. Dionysius (72.2 & 3) as his authority. Chrism, always consecrated by the bishop, symbolized the fullness of the Holy Spirit, a strengthening necessary for (spiritual) maturity. Oil signified the grace of the Spirit and the perfume the good odor of Christ diffused to others.

The form of the sacrament was that which was in existence in his day: "I sign you with the sign of the cross and confirm you with the chrism of salvation in the name of the Father, and of the Son, and of the Holy Spirit" (72.4). As with other scholastics, in this non-pneumatic formula Thomas discerned the cause of the sacrament (the Trinity), the spiritual effect (strength = "confirm"), and the sign which was given to the spiritual soldier of Christ (cross). Form and matter, the actual signing of the forehead with chrism using the prescribed words, made up the sacrament of confirmation (IV Sent. 4.7.1.2.3 ad 2).

Confirmation conferred a character separate from that of baptism. For Thomas character was a deputation, a certain spiritual power ordered to sacred actions, that is, a consecration for worship. Whereas the character of baptism was related to personal salvation, that of confirmation pertained to the spiritual battle against enemies of the faith. While baptism gave one the power to confess Christ by receiving the other sacraments, confirmation provided a *quasi ex officio* power to profess one's faith in words. Here we see a combination of Faustus and Alcuin/Rabanus. The idea of a kind of *ex officio* deputation to confess Christ would lead, in the 20th century, to such aberrant interpretations of confirmation as a sacrament of catholic action or as a sacrament for the ordination of the laity.

The specific grace of confirmation was an increase of grace for strength (an *augmentum gratiae* rather than, as Faustus phrased it, an *augmentum ad gratiam*). Since this strengthening perfected baptism by making each of the baptized into a temple of the Holy Spirit, it was only fitting that the bishop alone be the minister of confirmation (3.11).

In sum, it can be said that Thomas' writing on confirmation is filled with images of growth and strengthening and public confession of the faith. The Angelic Doctor is radically indebted to a writer we now know as a minor 5th century, semi-Pelagian bishop, Faustus of Riez, as well as to a few other churchmen, such as Alcuin/Rabanus. With the emphasis on an increase of grace for growth, of strengthening for battle, and of audaciously preaching the faith, the Holy Spirit's role, though not absent in Thomas, is considerably downplayed. And except for the fact that the traditional order of the sacraments of initiation is maintained—baptism, confirmation, eucharist—confirmation plays no real role in what we today speak of as Christian initiation.

Despite the internal consistency of Thomas' arguments, since the very foundations of this theology are so problematic, the theology itself has been called into question as not being rooted in reality. There is no doubt, however, that this theology corresponded well with the way the rite was being developed and practiced. The emphasis on strengthening is particularly evident in the rite organized by Thomas' contemporary, William Durand, bishop of Mende (1285-1295). It is in this bishop's pontifical that we find the first evidence of the slap on the face (the *alapa*) which reminded candidates of their need to be soldiers of Christ and which remained standard in the rite until its contemporary revision. It will be remembered that it was this bishop's pontifical which became the ancestor of the Roman Pontifical.

From the time of Thomas until Vatican II little changed in the received theology of confirmation. The Council of Florence resurrected Thomas' *De articulis fidei et sacramenti ecclesiae* as the basis for the Western church's view of the sacraments in the Decree for the Armenians (22 November 1439), only softening Thomas' strictures against presbyteral confirmation, since it was assumed that the Eastern messianic sealing corresponded to the Western sacrament of confirmation. Confirmation was defined as one of the seven sacraments by the Council of Trent. Ritually the only change, outside of the stabilization of the rite by the Roman Pontifical of 1595(6), was a new rubric in

later Roman Pontificals calling for a handlaying during the chrismation of the forehead (Austin, 22-23). Modern theology simply reiterated the teaching of Aquinas and defended the Catholic notion of confirmation's sacramentality against the Reformers' denial.

Confirmation as Conclusion to Catechetical Study: Reformation Confirmation

Sixteenth century reformers generally repudiated all sacraments, save baptism and eucharist, although other rituals were kept as ordinances, such as marriage and ordination. In particular, they firmly rejected the Catholic sacrament of confirmation, since all was complete in baptism. Instead they developed rites suited to the completion of catechetical study which, at the same time, admitted the candidates to the eucharistic table. These rites were also called confirmation and were even related to the apostles' activities in Acts. The difference between such rites and the Catholic sacrament was that, in the case of the former, nothing new, i.e., "sacramental," happened to the candidate. Instead, by such rites candidates ratified the baptismal vows made for them by their godparents. In the Reformation period then the third type of confirmation appears, created both out of reaction to Roman Catholics and from a need to provide a fitting conclusion to the post-baptismal study of those baptized as infants. Ironically, in contrast to the Catholic sacrament of confirmation, the Reformation catechetical rites were much more susceptible to the medieval theology of strengthening and soldiering and preaching the faith fearlessly than was a rite which originated as the episcopal conclusion to baptism.

Contemporary Practice and Theology

The three different systems of confirmation which we have described are part of contemporary praxis, even though somewhat changed. The first has been restored as the conclusion to baptism in the new R.C.I.A. rites (1972), or where the candidates have already been baptized, the conclusion to their formation process. The second, the medieval sacrament of confirmation, is the basis for the new *Order of Confirmation* (1971) and is generally intended for those baptized in infancy. Finally, Reformation confirmation has been transformed into a series of contemporary American Episcopal and Lutheran affirmation rites which can be celebrated in the presence of the community at significant moments in life. Along with the repeatable rites, however, the two church bodies insisted that one of them remain a "non-repeatable" confirmation, and that it function as did the original Reformation confirmation, that is, as a conclusion to initial formation. Given this restriction it is still true to say that the Reformation rite has finally been understood in a non-polemical fashion. It is not analogous to Catholic confirmation in that it does not complete or conclude baptism. We might also note hat both churches have relocated in their baptismal rites (optional) anointing and handlaying rites, adding to baptism those elements which were first reported centuries ago by Tertullian and which are found once more, *mutatis mutandis*, in Catholic adult baptism.

Three such distinct ritual systems call for different theological interpretations. Despite the fact that Roman Catholic confirmation, even when it is part of baptismal initiation, is still interpreted in the same way as a confirmation long separated from baptism and, most likely, eucharist, this is poor mystagogic theology; in fact it is simply poor theology. As part of baptism, confirmation functions as the pneumatic conclusion to washing in water and entrance into the priestly body of Jesus Christ. It is the transition rite to the celebration of the actual confirmation of baptism, the eucharist. Special focus on the Holy Spirit at this point does not derogate from the role of

the Spirit in the whole of Christian initiation, especially since the prayer for the prophetic Spirit makes memorial of what has just occurred in baptism itself through "water and the Holy Spirit" (R.C.I.A., 228).

Separate confirmation, which since the early part of this century ordinarily occurs after eucharistic fellowship has been inaugurated, no longer concludes baptism and admits to eucharist. True, the separate rite calls for a renewal of baptismal vows and reminds assembly and candidates that the context for confirmation's celebration is the eucharist. But quite clearly it is impossible to "make believe" that what has happened has not happened. Furthermore, unlike that post-baptismal rite concluding baptism and making explicit baptism's pneumatic character and leading to the eucharist, *the* celebration of the enspirited community, separate confirmation tends to impress the candidates with a realization that they are receiving the Holy Spirit for the first time. This perception is heightened by the prepared homily given in the revised rite: "You have already been baptized and now you will receive the power of the Spirit .... So now, before you receive the Spirit, I ask you...," and by the addition to the credal questions of a special question on the Holy Spirit: "Do you believe in the Holy Spirit, the Lord, the giver of life, who came upon the apostles at Pentecost and today is given you sacramentally in confirmation?" (O.C., 22-23). Even though we explain that this is not a first pouring forth of the Spirit upon the candidates, and even though it is insisted that this rite is part of Christian initiation and completes baptism, such assurances ring hollow. History, in this case the homily of Faustus, tells a different tale: separation occurred at the time of Faustus' homily. In the mid-5th century a rite not part of baptism called for a theological explanation which provided a justification for

284

the separate rite and at the same time supported its necessity and desirability in the lives of the baptized.

Although the *Apostolic Constitution* of Paul VI and the *Pastoral Introduction* to the 1971 *Order of Confirmation* insist on the proper order of the sacraments, at whatever age conferred, the need to provide a separate confirmation with a more pneumatic theology leads the author of the *Apostolic Constitution* to graft the scholastic and especially Thomistic theology of confirmation as strengthening onto a renewed appreciation for the role of the Holy Spirit. It also leads him to emphasize the ancient pneumatic prayer for the Holy Spirit by the restoration of a general handlaying to it, and to associate the gesture of consignation with chrism with a formula drawn from the Byzantine post-baptismal sealing rite—"Be sealed with the Gift of the Holy Spirit"(O.C., 9).

The new charismation formula is somewhat ambiguous. First of all, as part of the messianic sealing rite in Byzantine baptismal practice, it is related, not to the Western confirmation anointing, but to the traditional post-baptismal presbyteral, messianic anointing. Unlike the West, where this anointing has remained more messianic than pneumatic, the Byzantine anointing rite became predominantly pneumatic. Secondly, the original Greek formula lacks a verb, since it is simply a repetition of a phrase from a prayer immediately preceding the sealing. The Eastern formula, along with the chrismation, would seem, then, to apply to each individual what has been prayed for all more generally (Ligier, 202-206). Finally, Byzantine practice never separates sealing from baptism itself and is thus much more closely related to the post-baptismal messianic anointing as found in the *Order of Baptism for Infants* than it is to the Western sacrament of confirmation.

Questions can be raised, then, whether the Eastern churches have confirmation

(Quinn, 325-326). Despite the constant emphasis in the *Apostolic Constitution* on chrismation as the essential ritual gesture of confirmation and on its being equivalent to apostolic and later handlaying, as well as to Eastern sealing, one remains somewhat unconvinced (*Apost. Const.*). This leaves the theologian with the classic prayer for the Holy Spirit, with its restored handlaying, as a way of contextualizing and "explaining" the chrismation. The prayer invokes God, through whom the baptized have been regenerated by water and Spirit, to send that same Holy Spirit, the Paraclete, with the gifts of Isaiah 61:2, upon those about to be chrismated. Such a prayer asks, and here is where some of the thoughts of an Alcuin/Rabanus could be *a propos*, that the candidates live out their baptisms in ways pleasing to God and in service of humanity. This sentiment correlates with the description of confirmation found in such documents as the Constitution on the Church (L.G., 10) and the Decree on Priests (P.O., 2), as well as to the General Introduction to Christian Initiation. It would seem that this would make for a better source of "confirmation" theology than the sermon of a 5th-century semi-pelagian bishop. Moreover, any theology of spiritual strengthening and Christian maturity pertains more to the catechumenate and to baptism than to confirmation.

It would also seem best to focus on confirmation as the pneumatic conclusion to baptism, a modest rite which is part of the great sacrament of baptism and which leads to the climactic sacrament of the eucharist. Such a rite focuses attention on one aspect of the Spirit's operation within us and within the church, impelling us to live out in this world the gift we have received in baptism. In other words we are not to bury our talents but to use them, lest we lose them. Baptized into Christ through the action of the Spirit, and made his priestly people, we are gifted with the Spirit of Christ to preach to others what we have received and to be ever proud of our being born again in Christ Jesus. All of this is sealed in eucharistic fellowship.

In the separate rite of confirmation, especially when eucharist has preceded it, it is much more difficult to develop this same modest theology. The rite takes on a life of its own, as we have already seen. It tends to be identified with that third form of confirmation, repeatable affirmation, especially in terms of the renewal of baptismal vows. Although theologians can abstract from such ritual infelicities, preachers cannot. And so a mystagogic theology of confirmation, in the case of the separated rite, calls for great sensitivity, to avoid giving the impression that the Spirit is now being conferred for the first time, or that this is the way Catholics ratify their baptismal vows, or that this is the sacrament of adolescent strengthening or of Catholic action or of the "ordination of the laity!" None of these pious explanations parading as theology has advanced our knowledge or practice of confirmation or been, for that matter, a healthy development.

Confirmation is the pneumatic conclusion to baptism; it precedes the eucharist. Its core rite consists of handlaying with prayer for God to send the (prophetic) Spirit upon the one whose sins have been forgiven and who has entered into new life in Christ and in his church through water and Spirit, along with the individual application of the benefits of this prayer to each candidate through a signing with perfumed oil on the forehead using the words "N., be sealed with the Gift of the Holy Spirit." As part of Christian initiation confirmation allows us to contemplate the role of the Spirit in our lives. As separated from Christian initiation, confirmation has been prey to those explanations which seemed useful or necessary at the time but which ultimately did no service

to the sacrament. It began with Faustus and it is not yet over.

Letter to Oduin Alcuin, *Epistolae Karolini Aevi*, ed., Ernest Duemmler, Vol. 2, *Monumenta germaniae historica; Epistolarum*, Vol. 4 (Berlin: Weidmann, 1895. Gerard Austin, *The Rite of Confirmation: Anointing with the Spirit*, Studies in the Reformed Rites of the Catholic Church, 3 (New York: Pueblo Publishing Co., 1985). Faustus of Riez, *Homilia de Pentecosten*, In: L.A. van Buchem, *L'Homelie pseudo-Eusebienne de Pentecote* (Nijmegen: Drukkerif Gebr. Janssen N.V., 1967), 38-44. John the Deacon, *Epistola ad Senarium*, *Epistola ad Senarium*, In: Andre Wilmart *Analecta Regi nensia*, pp 170-79, Studie Testi 59 (Vatican City: Biblioteca apostolica vaticana, 1933). Aidan (New York: Pueblo Publishing Co., 1988). Louis Ligier, *La Confirmation: Sens et Conjoncture Ecumenique Hier et Aujourd'hui*, Theologie historique 23 (Paris: Beauchesne, 1973). Thomas Marsh, *Gift of Community: Baptism and Confirmation* Wilmington: Michael Glazier, 1984). Frank C. Quinn, "Confirmation, Does It Make Sense?", *Ecclesia Orans* 5 (1988): 321-340. E.C. Whitaker, *Documents of the Baptismal Liturgy*. rev. ed. (London: S.P.C.K., 1970). Gelasian Sacramentary = Leo Cunibert Mohlberg, ed., *Liber sacramentorum Romanae aeclesiae ordinia anni circuli*. Rerum ecclesiasticarum documenta. Series major. Fontes 4. (Rome: Casa editrice Herder, 1968). O.C. = Pontificale Romanum ex decreto sacrosancti oecumenici concillii Vatican II instauratum auctoritate Pauli PP. VI promulgatum, *Ordo confirmationis*, Editio typica (Vatican City: Typis polyglottis, 1971). Translation: *Rite of Confirmation*, I.C.E.L., 1973.

FRANK C. QUINN, O.P.

CONSCIENCE, PRIORITY OF HUMAN

The courageous witness of martyrs who remain faithful to their religious convictions even in the face of death, the insistence in moral theology on one's duty to follow a well-formed conscience even if erroneous, and Cardinal Newman's famous toast to "conscience first," all highlight the Roman Catholic esteem for the priority that must be given to one's personal conscience.

Priority of conscience becomes controversial, and even threatened, when a religious culture or community is dominated by concerns about order, conformity, and adherence to established standards. It is directly challenged whenever those in authority insist that specific moral principles are "absolute," "unchangeable," and the unquestionable manifestations of God's will.

"Priority" refers to the rightful decision to act which one is obliged to make in favor of one's own judgment and personal evaluation of a particular situation or conflict. Since such a decision may be perceived by many, perhaps initially including the subject as well, to be in direct violation of a known and widely recognized ethical directive, it may be widely judged to be immoral. Questions of suspicion will abound. Has the subject here succumbed to sheer, if unrecognized, subjectivism? Will the subject henceforth find it necessary to formulate self-serving rationalizations in order to legitimate this apparently arbitrary and anti-authoritarian decision?

Yet the opposite may be true as well. Might not this same human subject, in this apparently unpopular and unconventional choice, be exhibiting conscientious discernment and brave, mature action? Could this subject be embodying the most careful and responsible procedures which actualize one's God-given human intelligence?

Many today are given to justifying their most controversial and personally difficult decisions allegedly on the basis of such subjectively faithful determinations, for example, in aborting an apparently defective foetus, or in assisting a long-suffering and alert, elderly parent to commit suicide. Are these correct decisions or not? Decisions of conscience are seldom unambiguous.

The issues to be weighed in decisions of conscience are three: first, one's personal level of moral maturity (does one regularly act in conformity with the "crowd", or more consistently in favor of received norms and vision, or is one becoming appreciative as well of one's own tested insights, standards and per-

spectives?); second, one's prevailing ethical stance (is one a relativist, even a blatant pragmatist or opportunist, or does one espouse some objective standards and some sense of ethical obligation and accountability?); and third, one's habitual, learned procedure for practical decision-making (does one act impulsively, intuitively, directly out of respectful adherence to authoritative directives, or only after attentive, intelligent inquiry and critical reflection regarding the situation, its context, the known directives, and one's own assessment of the converging values, all the while maintaining consistency with one's overall, established sense of personal purpose?).

The manner and degree to which one's religious, and specifically Roman Catholic, sense of value and meaning has been subjectively appropriated is of paramount importance. The church directs the formation of conscience in at least three areas.

First, in fostering the subject's personal maturation, the church explicitly promotes legitimate, relative independence of the individual Christian. "Children and young people ... should be trained to acquire gradually a more perfect sense of responsibility in the proper development of their own lives..." (G.E., 1).

Secondly, in assisting the subject to assume a specific moral stance the church champions moral principles and virtuous dispositions. It also calls for ongoing personal conversion and an overall commitment to God, the Transcendent Truth and Good, who has revealed God's abiding presence in and saving purpose for human history. "Children and young people have the right to be stimulated to make sound moral judgments based on a well-formed conscience and to put them into practice with a sense of personal commitment, and to know and love God more perfectly" (G.E., 1). And in *Gaudium et spes*: "One must aim at encouraging the human spirit to develop its faculties of wonder, of understanding, of contemplation, of forming personal judgments and cultivating a religious, moral and social sense" (G.S., 59).

Thirdly, to provide continuous guidance within the decision-making process the church presents specific directives of the magisterium, the proclamation and interpretation of the gospel, the witness of the Catholic tradition and examples in the lives of the saints. Moreover, by its counsel and sustenance, the local church community promotes both the process of discerning and realizing one's own calling, and of conducting regular self-criticism of the individual, and indeed the church itself in the face of the gospel. The latter is to be accomplished in particular through the examination of conscience in the various rites of reconciliation.

It is essential to take seriously and investigate the apparent controversy between the priority of conscience and conformity to objective moral standards, i.e., between subjectivity (which some regard as subjectivism) and objectivity. One may be assisted here by reflecting on the differing accents in the understanding of conscience as found in some pre- and post-Vatican II official statements and in the writings of prominent theologians.

Perspectives of Modern and Post-Modern Philosophies

A brief tour into the shifting field of philosophy seems appropriate as a preliminary step, since cultural attitudes of a given period and locale are so strongly influenced, whether consciously or not, by the prevailing philosophical system or worldview.

Fascination with the human subject and the human power of reasoning which the Enlightenment espoused (along with the endorsement of the empirical method) was accompanied by a suspicion, if not outright rejection, of both tradition and constituted human authority, the long-standing definers of the true and the good.

The human subject engaging in self-realization and self-transcendence became the central feature of an optimistic approach of 20th century personalism. Meanwhile personal experience and human freedom, and the search for their meaning, were emphasized by the existentialists, who had little positive regard for "objectivity" from any other source.

The stage was set for the exaltation of the autonomous human subject, and the championing of unfettered human freedom and self-determination. Eventually this led to the emergence, particularly in the United States, of an extreme form of individualism, which has been called "ontological individualism," i.e., "a belief that the individual has a primary reality, whereas society is a second-order, derived or artificial construct..." (*Habits of the Heart*, Robert Bellah et.al. Berkeley: Univ. of California Press, 1985, p.334).

Only with the appearance of what Gregory Baum calls "the second phase of enlightenment" (Doherty, p. 82) did a critical and necessarily self-critical movement begin in earnest. Recognizing the ambiguity of consciousness and the historical and cultural conditioning of human reason, proponents of this phase sought to identify critical principles and to examine truth claims, both to society and its structures, human consciousness and its potential for transformation.

In the midst of these cultural, philosophical developments, the church, for the most part, retained a posture of resistance. It remained relatively unchanged in its teaching about human conscience and personal accountability to God and God's revelation, and to the legitimate authority of the church, about human sinfulness, intellectual pride and moral weakness, about the necessity of self-accusation and the grace of reconciliation. These traditional teachings were defended with but limited success, especially among the influential, liberal, intellectual elite. Only gradually, and not without considerable controversy, still unresolved, did the insights of modern psychology, cognitive theory, and sociology become incorporated into theological studies of conscience and authority.

Conscience Redefined

At the Second Vatican Council, the explanation of conscience included two passages of special importance. The first emphasizes the distinctive, personal experience of God's will: "Conscience is a person's most secret core and sanctuary, in which one is alone with God, whose voice resonates in one's depths" (G.S., 16). Rather than designating primarily a rational procedure whereby one conforms one's behavior to carefully articulated religious and natural laws, stress is given to the human person, the human subject, in some perhaps pre-rational consciousness of God's loving presence and purpose. God is understood to be the interior foundation of one's own inherent yearning for the true and the good. That personal orientation, one may conclude, is not to be rejected out of hand, even were it to differ with a particular official position on occasion, but would require careful discernment. Some appreciation of the priority of conscience is intimated here. The second instruction of the council states: "Through fidelity to conscience Christians are joined with other persons in the search for truth and for the truthful solution to so many moral problems which arise both in the lives of individuals and in social relationships" (G.S., 16). While the context here emphasizes explicitly the divine law, as inwardly experienced, and objective norms of morality, the text nonetheless recognizes the necessity of some process of consultation and cooperation in the search for appropriate resolutions to the complex and ambiguous situations of our day. In other words, traditionally accepted answers may not always fit contemporary questions and may require some respectful

but critical re-examination of earlier precedents as well as of the present situation.

Moreover, persons who have participated in such a process of scrutiny may, on occasion, arrive at conclusions which either oppose or anticipate official moral teaching in a given area. Their position is understood as *dissent*, a term never officially invoked in the conciliar documents, but one which became commonplace with the responses to the 1968 papal encyclical *Humanae Vitae*. It should be noted here that after further reflection on this difficult topic, the National Conference of Catholic Bishops, in its 1968 pastoral *Human Life in Our Day*," specified three conditions for dissent to be legitimate: (1) the reasons must be serious and well-founded; (2) the manner of the dissent must not question or impugn the teaching authority of the church; and (3) the dissent must not be such as to give scandal (USCC ed., p. 19). The conciliar statement three years earlier does not rule out the possibility that one might reach a dissenting conclusion through such a critical and self-critical inquiry. Hence, again, in the conciliar statement and in the 1968 pastoral some appreciation of the priority of conscience is intimated.

Differences Among Contemporary Scholars

The post-conciliar period has been laced with frequent controversy and followed up by definitive disciplinary procedures against individual theologians. The central issue, in bold strokes, continues to be one's ethical stance: does one advocate full adherence to the official moral teaching of the church, or the following of one's well-formed conscience, in matters which are not formally defined? Significantly divergent theological positions have been formulated.

Representative of a more conservative posture is Germain Grisez. In his recent foundational work he defines conscience as: "one's last and best judgment concerning what one should choose. Genuine judgments of conscience are derived from sound moral principles. One's knowledge of these principles and of their application develops. This development is the formation of conscience. It is based on natural law and assisted by the teaching of the Church" (Grisez, p. vi). Grisez, while critical of the classical natural law tradition, nonetheless focuses heavily upon principles and their application in what resembles a deductive process, bolstered by official church teaching. There is little here to award legitimacy to any subjective determination that deviates from the received principles and teaching. And there is little which acknowledges the possibility of an interior orientation and original responsiveness of the human subject to value.

In a considerably different vein, Walter Conn comments on and advances the approach which Bernard Lonergan has articulated. Conn explains conscience from a developmental perspective as "the radical drive for self-transcendence realized in creative understanding, critical judging, responsible deciding and generous loving" (Conn, p. 1). Here we find far more attention given to the interiority of the human subject as dynamic, with distinctive and cumulative levels of consciousness. This subject arrives at responsible decisions not simply by applying received norms to particular cases. Instead, the journey to decide and love is appropriately preceded first by careful attention to all the relevant data available both to the senses and to one's consciousness. There follows the effort to pursue intelligent inquiry and critical reflection regarding this data. A reasoned investigation is next to be conducted of whatever controverted truth claims, whether of the received traditional norms and values, or of the understanding and interpretation peculiar to one's own group or oneself. Further, one must engage in continual criticism of one's own moral stance and adhere consistently to that stance. The attitude toward authority, the constant heeding of the word of God, and a respectful but critical attitude toward authoritative statements all must be a part of this more subject-oriented approach. Here the challenge is not exclusively to apply moral principles to individual situations and problems. Particularly in conflict situations, it is to attend to all the morally relevant data, and creatively to interpret the norms and identify the values which they espouse within a given situation. After responsible deliberation regarding various options, one may decide to act. In this approach, the priority of a responsibly resolved conscience is explicitly espoused.

See **Internal forum**

Walter Conn, *Christian Conversion* (Mahwah, N.J.: Paulist Press, 1986). Dennis Doherty, ed., *Dimensions of Human Sexuality* (Garden City, N.Y.: Doubleday and Company, Inc., 1979). Germain Grisez, *The Way of the Lord Jesus* (Chicago, IL.: Franciscan Herald Press, 1983).

ANDREW L. NELSON

CONTRITION

Contrition is "heartfelt sorrow and aversion for the sin committed along with the intention of sinning of more" (Denz-Schon, 1676). This definition of contrition formulated at the Council of Trent is repeated in the Rite of Penance (6a) and is seen as the most important act of the penitent.

Historically, contrition has been seen to be of two kinds: perfect, sorrow for sins committed based on the love of God; and imperfect or attrition, sorrow for sins committed based on a lesser reason, for example, fear of punishment. Before and after the Council of Trent theologians debated the sufficiency of imperfect contrition for the effective reception of the sacrament of penance to forgive serious sins. The Rite of Penance approaches *metanoia* (change of heart) from a scriptural point of view rather than a scholastic viewpoint, thus side-stepping the long debate. "We can only approach the Kingdom of Christ by *metanoia*. This is a profound change of the whole person by which one begins to consider, judge, and arrange one's life according to the holiness and love of God, made manifest in his Son in the last days and given to us in abundance (Paul VI's Apostolic Constitution, "Paenitemini," Feb. 17, 1966: A.A.S. 58 [1966] 179).

Conversion of the sinner affects the person from within. It is the turning away from evil and turning to choose the right—it is the personally decisive moment of *metanoia*, remorse, contrition. "It is distinctive of contrition to add pure and more valid motives to the conscious regret of personal failure. These are the motives of seeing sin as an offense against God and as a sundering of ecclesial communion . . . (Pope Paul VI's address on new rite of penance Apr. 3, 1974) (Notitiae 10 (1974) 225-227).

It is by restoring the word of God to the sacramental celebration of penance that the church hopes to facilitate conversion and contrition. It is the word of the scripture proclaimed in individual and communal celebrations that motivates contrition. Both the homily and the examination of conscience awaken true contrition for sin.

Prayers of contrition or prayers of general confession are formulas for stating *metanoia*, conversion and contrition. No longer are these prayers statements of both attrition and contrition but rather bold statements of love of God based on the scriptures.

See **Conversion from sin; Reformation of life**

James Dallen, *The Reconciling Community, The Rite of Penance* (New York: Pueblo Publishing Co., Inc., 1986). Joseph Martos, *Doors to the Sacred* (Garden City: Image Books, 1982). Bernard Poschmann, *Penance and the Anointing of the Sick* (New York, Herder and Herder, 1968).

JOSEPH L. CUNNINGHAM

CONVERSION FROM SIN

The opening words of Jesus' public ministry, "The time is fulfilled, and the kingdom of God is at hand; repent (*metanoiete*), and believe. . .". (Mk 1:15), constitute an urgent and dramatic call to radical conversion. Catholic tradition has long explained that this central theme of Jesus' teaching incorporates both a positive aspect (*conversio ad Deum*, or conversion to God, and hence to a life of loving service in and for the reign of God which Jesus inaugurated and embodied) and a negative aspect (*aversio a peccatis*, or renunciation of sin and the reign of sin in all its dimensions, in association with the victory of the Risen Lord).

Contemporary biblical scholars recognized the prominence, power and comprehensiveness of this biblical theme, conversion (*metanoia*). Their insights contribute substantively to the shifting of the principal focus of moral theology. This has come to be the historical human person, a living, dynamic subject called to transform/change/convert both self and world.

It is worth noting that this refocusing process in moral theology, emphasizing the human subject engaged in a graced transition from sinfulness and toward God, began in the 1950s on the European continent. It gained broad endorsement during the era of the Second Vatican Council, and is now arriving at some consolidation in theological literature.

This article will offer a brief consideration of the conciliar teaching, one example of post-conciliar papal teaching, and one recent theoretical reflection. This last, the work of Walter Conn, carried on in dialogue with developmental psychologists such as Erik Erikson and

Lawrence Kohlberg, may provide a broader framework for understanding and expanding the official teaching regarding this provocative theme: "conversion", in its negative aspect, "from sin".

The Second Vatican Council

A number of the documents of the Second Vatican Council address the theme "conversion from sin" either explicitly or by implication. The following brief summary of this composite teaching may clarify its principal features. It was explained, first, as a central focus of the mission of the church: "the Church announces the good tidings of salvation to those who do not believe, so that all ... may know the one true God and Jesus Christ whom he has sent and may be converted from their ways, doing penance" (S.C., 9). Secondly, as a persistent confrontation with all evil: "Let them (the laity) ... express (their hope) ... in continual conversion and in wrestling against the world rulers of this darkness, against the spiritual forces of iniquity' (Eph 6:12)" (L.G., 35). Thirdly, as initiated by God's invitation, and as entailing a radical and comprehensive interior transformation of the sinner: "This conversion (of those who turn to God through preaching and the power of the Spirit) is, indeed, only initial; sufficient however to make (them) realize that (they) have been snatched from sin .... This transition, which involves a progressive change of outlook and morals, should be manifested in its social implications and effected gradually..." (A.G.D., 13). Fourth, as ecclesial, both in the effects of the perpetration of evil, and as the sacramental and communal context for the Christian disciple to engage in the process of conversion: "Those who approach the sacrament of Penance ... are reconciled with the Church, which they have wounded by their sins and which by charity, by example and by prayer labors for their conversion" (L.G., 11). Fifth, as

incorporating a specifically social dimensions, viz., a renunciation of the world's injustice and animosity: (To correct the imbalances in today's world) "much reform in economic and social life is required along with a change of mentality and of attitude by all" (G.S., 63); and, "But it (humankind) will not succeed in accomplishing the task awaiting it, that is, the establishment of a truly human world for all men over the entire earth, unless everyone devotes himself to the cause of true peace with renewed vigor" (G.S., 77).

In a precise manner, the Council examined, described and explained "sin" (from which all are called to conversion): "Man (sic), enticed by the evil one, abused his freedom at the very start of history. He lifted himself up against God, and sought to attain his goal apart from him .... They served the creature rather than the creator .... Often refusing to acknowledge God as his source, man has also upset the relationship which should link him to his last end; and at the same time he has broken the right order that should reign within himself as well as between himself and other men and all creatures" (G.S., 13). Here both the idolatrous and alienating features of human sin are identified, including the vertical and horizontal, personal, social and historical dimensions of its willful devastation, dimensions which are further developed in 25 and 37.

The full text of 13 offers both a biblical and an experientially convalidated presentation of this mysterious, culpable participation in evil. Sin is depicted as a negative dynamic operating within human life which continually places in jeopardy the dignity and calling of every human person. Yet mention is made here as well of God's liberating intervention: God "inwardly renews the sinner", casting off the sinner's slavery to sin. A developed presentation of the process of conversion, however, is not provided.

Pope John Paul II's 1984 Apostolic Exhortation, *Reconciliation and Penance*, is a response of the pope and the Synod of 1983 to the wounds, tensions, conflicts and divisions which these bishops identify in the present world. The approach embodies traditional perspectives especially social responsibility, in continuity with the conciliar teaching. The church's central mission is described here as the task of reconciling people, i.e., "changing an historical condition of hatred and violence into a civilization of love," and of being the sacrament of reconciliation in the world (4; also cf. 11).

The notion of conversion from sin is prominent throughout the discussion, and particularly in close association with the dominant themes of the document. For John Paul II, conversion from sin seems to be employed at times as synonymous with penance and reconciliation, and at other times, as the general category which subsumes both.

Penance, according to the papal teaching, is "a conversion that passes from the heart to deeds, and then to the Christian's whole life" (4). Here the pope emphasizes the *depth* of the personal transformation: "one's whole existence ... becomes penitential," espousing in one's concrete daily life an asceticism which entails losing one's own life for Christ, putting off the old person, overcoming what is of the flesh, rising from the things of here below. John Paul insists that participation in the church's traditional penitential discipline "cannot be abandoned without grave harm" for the individual and the church (26).

The extent of the *effects* of this conversion are likewise featured in his treatment of penance. The pope speaks of changing one's life, striving for what is better in one's deeds, and acts of penance in one's concrete daily effort. This comprehensive change is to accord with one's change of heart (4).

John Paul also relates conversion to reconciliation, a term which indicates the comprehensive *goal* of this conversion of heart. Reconciliation is explained as the overcoming of a radical break or alienation in fundamental relationships, i.e., with God, oneself, and others, including especially one's family, church, professional and social environment (13), and the whole of creation (9). In fact, the pope explains sin, or the kingdom of sin, primarily in terms of these central realities of alienation. The essential first step in returning to God is "to acknowledge one's sin," so that one can detach oneself "consciously and with determination from the sin into which one has fallen" (13).

A key concern here for both pope and synod is what they identify as the contemporary loss of a proper sense of sin. The pope attributes this prinicpally to a grave spiritual crisis today brought on largely by a pervasive secularism and psychologism, and fortified by ethical relativism or by a shallow legalism. A proper and ever more highly acute sense of sin must be achieved. This is integral to the process of authentic conversion which is aided by the pastoral ministry of sound catechetics, respect for the magisterium, and participation in the sacrament of penance and reconciliation (18, 23).

When he speaks of sin, the pope insists that, in the proper sense, it is always a personal act, the product of a person's freedom. Its first and most important consequence is in the individual sinner, in that person's spirit, whose will is weakened and whose intellect is clouded (16). Individual sin negatively affects others, the church and the human community as well. It consists of either the direct attack on one's neighbor, that person's dignity, rights and freedom, or by extension, the violation of the common good. An individual can act unjustly against a community. Furthermore, an entire community can perpetrate an injustice against an individual, or against another community (16).

In such instances, every individual member of the sinning community bears some responsibility for participating in this "communion of sin." What today many may call "social sin" or "sinful situations" are "the result of the accumulation and concentration of many personal sins" (16). The pope further specifies this type of sinfulness in a passage he later inserted in his encyclical *On Social Concern*: "It is the case of the very personal sins of those who cause or support evil or who exploit it; of those who are in a position to avoid, eliminate or at least limit certain social evils but who fail to do so out of laziness, fear of the conspiracy of silence, through secret complicity or indifference; of those who take refuge in the supposed impossibility of changing the world, and of those who sidestep the effort and sacrifice required, producing specious reasons of a higher order. The real responsibility, then, lies with individuals" (16).

Even if structural and institutional aspects of sinful situations are changed, such change will be incomplete, or even counterproductive "if the people directly or indirectly responsible for that situation are not converted" (16). Thus does the pope identify specific requirements for conversion, viz., the renunciation of carefully honed habits of clever, subtle rationalization and self-serving complicity in the evildoing of others.

The radical evil of freely rejecting God, God's law, and the covenant of love which God offers is paralleled with "turning in on oneself, or to some created and finite reality" (17). This insidious process of aversion from God and conversion to creatures (as ultimate goods) is precisely what is to be reversed in authentic conversion from sin.

The pope contrasts the "mystery of sin" with the great "mystery of God's infinite loving kindness towards us," i.e., the mystery of the incarnation and redemption: "(This mystery) is capable of penetrating to the hidden roots of our iniquity, in order to evoke in the soul a movement of conversion, in order to redeem it and set it on the course towards reconciliation" (20).

Here again, the effective divine initiative, the radicalness of the evil to be overcome, and the ongoing, deeply interior process of overcoming one's alienation are identified as central to conversion from sin. Once more John Paul insists that conversion is not a lofty abstraction but "a concrete Christian value to be achieved in our lives" (22).

A Contemporary Reflection

Walter Conn espouses Bernard Lonergan's understanding of specific conversions as central to the human subject's process of achieving authentic, self-transcending subjectivity. In the case of moral conversion, one shifts to a radically new horizon, i.e., "from a radically egocentric orientation in which the criterion for decision is self-interested satisfaction to a social orientation in which the criterion for decision is value (in various conventionally defined forms)" (Conn, p. 28).

The human subject who has reached "the existential moment," has come to understand that one truly creates oneself "in every deed, decision and discovery" of one's life, for good or ill (p. 114). In other words, one gains a deeper grasp not just of the sins one has committed, but of the sinfulness in which one participates, and the sinner one is: "moral conversion provides a programmatic base for the conscious, deliberate development of sustained moral self-transcendence" (p. 113).

To explain more precisely how one can sustain this "new personal agenda," Conn advances Lonergan's thinking on affective conversion. He describes this associated notion as "a wholesome, self-transcending commitment to love another person or persons" (pp. 149-150). For any conversion from sin to be truly effective, then, it must be linked with a personal commitment to good. Moreover, it must seek to uncover and reject any personal symbol-system which conceals or condones an emotional attachment to sin.

Conn suggests a further refinement of this conversion from sin, the "critical" moral conversion, in which "one can critically recognize and accept the responsibility of discovering and establishing one's own values (in dialogue with one's community)" (p. 116). Conventional norms and values, whether cultural, ecclesial or civil, may incorporate some unjust or misleading aspects, promoting to that extent evil rather than good. The critically morally converted will move to renounce any individual or social judgments and actions which accord with these evil aspects. Hence, the morally converted subject, by consistent, courageous judgments and decisions marked by realism and objectivity, establishes a post-conventional morality grounded in "self-chosen universal ethical principles of justice" and love (p. 127).

The following conclusions are drawn in light of Conn's reflections. The person who has engaged in a critical moral conversion has come to face squarely one's own evil, one's biases, one's own "demon." This person, in community, is endeavoring to unmask and eradicate as well the deeper strongholds of sin and evil, in their subtler incorporations in (uncritically) accepted widsom and commonsense. Such a one is struggling to be converted from sin of every sort: from pre-personal dispositions, personal sinfulness in act, habit and way of life, in one's presuppositions and symbol system, from social and structural sin, in fact, from all that the mysterious reign of sin encompasses.

Walter Conn, *Christian Conversion* (Mahwah, N.J.: Paulist Press, 1986). Pope John Paul II. Apostolic Exhortation *Reconciliation and Penance*

(Hales Corners, WI: Priests of the Sacred Heart, 1984).

ANDREW L. NELSON

CONVERSION TO FAITH

Recent years have seen an increasing number of thorough studies of Christian conversion considered from the perspective of moral theology, philosophy, developmental psychology, and scriptural interpretation. Since such studies are readily available (see bibliography), this article will focus instead on conversion to Christian faith from an ecclesial and sacramental perspective, i.e., the experience of converts coming to faith ritually enacted in the church community. A community's understanding of its identity and what must happen in order for a non-member to come to share that identity are ritually enacted in its initiatory rites. This article will thus reflect on the understanding of conversion to faith which emerges from the rite through which those who were not Christian believers become Catholic Christians, the *Rite of Christian Initiation of Adults* (1972).

The faith to which the R.C.I.A. is intended to enable adults to convert is a life lived as part of a Spirit-filled community celebrating the memorial of Christ's death and resurrection in the eucharist. This faith thus goes beyond doctrinal assent to include real transformation of mind, emotional life and behavior, and arises in response to grace. In the R.C.I.A., the process of conversion to a faith which is mature enough for membership in the church is seen as having four dimensions: doctrinal formation, learning to live the life of Christian faith among those who are already living it, participation in public worship, and learning to share in the church's apostolic mission (75).

First, conversion to faith in the gospel

of Jesus Christ requires knowledge of what that gospel is. The knowledge needed for conversion includes not only intellectual acquaintance with Christian revelation, which even a non-believer may have, but a growing awareness that this revelation is true and an appreciation of what its truth means for oneself and all humanity, i.e., "a profound sense of the mystery of salvation in which they (the converts) desire to participate" (75, 1).

Second, since conversion to faith is conversion to a graced life of living in common in the community of faith, it grows and deepens by practicing the Christian faith under the guidance of those who are already living it. Above all, even as "conversion in the NT requires the acknowledgment that Jesus is the obedient and chosen Messiah of God, and that acknowledgement in turn requires a life of obedience" (Gaventa, p. 150), the community of the faithful helps those converting to learn "to obey the Holy Spirit more generously" (4), "to follow supernatural inspiration in their deeds" (75, 2). The R.C.I.A. specifies various aspects of this obedience of faith in which converts grow as their faith matures.

Those coming to faith are helped by the community to learn how to pray (75, 2), so that they can come to know Christ as Savior (153), as Resurrection and Life (174), and have the personal, living faith and mature desire for a new covenant with Christ necessary for baptism (211).

Further, in order to live the life of faith, converts must undergo a transformation of their perception and patterns of thinking. They must learn to see by God's light, to make the mind of Christ their own (52). This involves counting all as loss compared to knowing Christ (94), and thus being freed from false values that blind them (168). They must allow their desires to change, that they may seek after what is holy and just, prefer the folly of the cross to the wisdom of the world, and long for baptism in water and the Spirit that will bring them eternal life (167, 153). They must learn to trust the truth and wisdom of Christ so that they can know freedom of mind and heart and be able to follow Christ (52, 153, 167); they must allow the Spirit to free them from fear and give them confidence, to fill them with a sure hope set on Christ, as well as with faith and charity (167, 174, 161, 175). The converts must develop genuine self-knowledge, a sense of sin and horror of it, and true repentance (152, 153, 174, 142).

Finally, the converts learn in the community how to practice the gospel in their personal and social life (11). They learn to pattern their lives on the teaching of the gospel, so that love of God and neighbor is their central motivation, that in all their actions they seek to follow the example of Christ (52). They renounce error, reject everything in their lives displeasing to Christ and learn to keep the commandments (211, 153, 57, 97); they learn how to listen to God's will for them with receptive minds and generously undertake whatever he asks, and to practice self-denial (97, 65, 118, 90). From the community the converts learn to "practice love of neighbor, even at the cost of self-renunciation" (75), to have hearts more responsive to the needs of others, to grow in freedom from selfishness, putting others first (65, 113, 134). Thus they learn to be true worshippers of God, constantly thinking of the One who called them to salvation and responding to his love (153, 154, 174, 161, 182).

In this gradual transformation of behavior which demonstrates that a candidate is indeed converting to faith, the R.C.I.A. emphasizes both the role of the Holy Spirit and the role of the community of faith. It is the Spirit who enables people to believe and be converted to the Lord and commit their lives to him (36), who teaches them who God is and how to please him, and gives them power to overcome weakness (153). Yet the Spirit works through the church community, who are responsible for the converts' formation in faith and who decide when that faith is mature enough that they are ready to be baptized (122); one of the criteria of election for baptism is that converts have "shared the company of their Christian brothers and sisters and joined with them in prayer" (131). When the converts are baptized they are understood to "embrace the faith that through divine help the church has handed down and (be) baptized in that faith" (211).

Third, the heart of the church community's enabling the candidates' conversion to faith is the worshipping assembly. Conversion to Christianity involves learning to experience reality as the Christian community does; converts learn to share the community's experience by learning the language through which they perceive, and the Christian community's language is the language of scripture and ritual symbol. Further, the R.C.I.A. is clear that the liturgical rites mediate the grace which enables conversion: "by means of the sacred rites celebrated at successive times they are led into the life of faith, worship and charity belonging to the people of God" (76). It is at the beginning of the first rite of the catechumenate that the converts ask the church community for the faith that will give them eternal life; the community then signs the candidates' senses petitioning God to change the way they (the candidates) perceive the world and act in it (56). The celebrations of the word and prayers of exorcism and blessing assist in the nurturing and growth of the catechumens' faith and conversion to God and purify and strengthen them (35, 75). The power of the word proclaimed in the worshipping assembly renews the catechumens (66), and enables them to know God and love their neighbor (52); the celebrations of the word implant in their hearts the "morality characteristic of the NT, the forgiveness of injuries and insults,

a sense of sin and repentance, the duties Christians must carry out in the world," as well as provide instruction and experience in the different ways of prayer, explain the liturgy, and prepare "them gradually to enter the worship assembly of the entire community" (82). In the minor exorcisms, which "draw the attention of the catechumens to the real nature of the Christian life, the struggle between flesh and spirit" (90), the worshipping assembly petitions God to remove specific sins from the converts' lives, such as love of money and lawless passions, and quarreling (94).

After the converts are accepted as candidates for baptism, the community's assistance in helping their faith to mature through liturgical rites intensifies. The liturgies of the three scrutinies, intended to reveal whatever is weak or sinful in the elect, inspire a deeper desire for redemption, and manifest and strengthen what is good; the elect are expected to progress in their awareness of sin and desire for salvation from the first to the final scrutiny (141, 143). Because the scrutinies deliver the elect from the power and effects of sin and the influence of Satan, protect them from temptation and give them new strength, filling their spirit with Christ the Redeemer, these rites "should complete the conversion of the elect and deepen their resolve to hold fast to Christ and carry out their decision to love God above all" (141, 144, 143). The presentations of the Creed and Lord's Prayer are intended to refine and deepen the faith of the elect (147); the rite at which the creed is presented is preferably to be celebrated at a eucharist of the faithful and makes it clear that it is through the worshipping community that the elect receive the faith they are learning to profess (157, 160). The importance of the liturgical dimension of enabling converts to grow into the faith of the community is seen in the influence it has on the doctrinal dimension; doctrinal catechesis is to be "accommodated to the liturgical year, and solidly supported by celebrations of the word" (75, 1). The liturgy of the church is a privileged locus for the word of the Spirit in bringing about conversion to faith; its rich language of biblical narrative and imagery and ritual symbols expresses and mediates the coming to know God in faith which is ultimately beyond words.

The fourth dimension which the R.C.I.A. describes as part of the process of conversion to faith is the converts' coming to share in the church community's apostolic mission (75, 4). As converts bear witness to the faith they are beginning to have both through evangelization and through works of mercy, they become more aware of how God has acted in their lives already, and of their responsibility to grow in living by and sharing the faith of the community.

The R.C.I.A. sees these four dimensions of conversion to faith as taking place simultaneously over time in the church community, within a structure which enables this conversion to grow and mature. In order to be accepted as catechumens (those whom the community is instructing in living the life of faith), converts must have a beginning of faith and conversion and "the intention to change their lives and enter into a relationship with God in Christ" in the church (42). Converts remain catechumens until the church community judges their conversion and faith to be strong; this may take several years. Such a lengthy process makes it clear to the candidates that conversion to faith is a lifelong process; when they have sufficiently progressed in learning about how to convert that they will be able to sustain a life of ongoing conversion, they are ready to be accepted as members in the Christian community which seeks to live that life. The community decides they are capable of membership (and thus accepts them for paschal baptism) on the basis of how they have progressed in the four dimensions of conversion: whether they have reached a conversion in mind and action seen in the example of their lives, and have sufficient knowledge of Christian teaching "as well as a spirit of faith and charity" (120, 112). After the rite of election those chosen for baptism enter into a final period (normally during Lent) which is intensely centered on conversion, seeking "an intimate knowledge of Christ and his church" (142) through purification of mind and heart by searching of conscience and doing penance, and a deeper awareness of Christ as Savior (35, 139).

When converts are baptized they are expected to have a personal faith which they will keep a "living faith" (211). The process of converting to this faith, surrendering to the gift of an obedient relationship to God in Christ lived as part of the Spirit-filled community, involves transformation of mind, emotional life, and action; this transformation takes place by grace in the community of faith and is mediated in a special way by participation in the community's acts of worship.

The Rite of Christian Initiation of Adults, (I.C.E.L.) in *The Rites of the Catholic Church, Vol. IA, Initiation* (New York: Pueblo, 1988). Walter Conn, *Christian Conversion: A Developmental Interpretation of Autonomy and Surrender* (New York: Paulist, 1986). Beverly Roberts Gaventa, *From Darkness to Light: Aspects of Conversion in the New Testament* (Philadelphia: Fortress, 1986). Lewis Rambo, "Current Research on Religious Conversion." *Religious Studies Review* 8 (1982): 145-159.

PAMELA JACKSON

COVENANT

Definition and Linguistic Usage

The OT Hebrew term traditionally translated "covenant" (*bᵉrît*) describes a contract of treaty between individuals (1 Sam 18:3), between heads of state (1 Kgs 5:12), between God and a favored human being (Abraham in Gen 15:18; 17; David in 1 Sam 7), and between God and Israel (Exod 19-24). The term can also suggest obligation and the imposition of a sovereign will, as shown by such phrases as "to command the covenant" (Ps 111:9; cf. Judg 2:20) and by association with the terms law and commandment (Deut 4:13; 33:9; Isa 24:5; Pss 50:16; 103:18). The wide range of the Hebrew term has tempted interpreters unduly to narrow *b^erît* toward either mutuality or imposition of divine will. The OT, however, is generally unconcerned about apportioning precisely divine and human agency and holds both tendencies together. The old English legal term "covenant," defined as a mutual agreement between two or more persons to do or refrain from doing certain acts, has translated the OT term since at least the 14th century; it emphasizes mutality and freedom. The Greek translators of the 3rd and 2nd century B.C. did not catch the range of *b^erît* and emphasized divine initiative at the expense of mutuality. They avoided the ordinary Greek legal term for convenant (*synthē kē*) in favor of the hellenistic word for last will and testament (*diathē kē*). The NT simply took over the Septuagint interpretation of *diathē kē* (33 instances: 9 in Paul; 17 in Hebrews; 4 in Synoptics; 2 in Acts; 1 in Revelations; 7 of these are OT citations.)

Covenant in the OT

Covenant was part of the legal world of the ancient Near East, which has been well described as "a society of gentlemen." Virtually all important agreements were sworn in oaths calling the gods to witness the swearing. A typical covenantal formula would be: "May the gods do such and such to me if I do not do to you as I have sworn today in their presence!" In an honor-shame society one must be as good as one's word. Covenants were ordinarily oral; only those affecting many people or future generations were written.

There are two major covenant types in the OT: the conditional covenant between Yahweh and Israel mediated by Moses at Mount Sinai, and the "unconditional" (or promissory) covenant between Yahweh and Abraham or David. The Sinai covenant is chiefly described in Exodus 19-24 (now incorporated into the "Sinai pericope" of Exod 19:1-Num 10:11). The accompanying narrative is the best commentary. The Lord frees the Hebrews from serving Pharaoh in Egypt and leads them to serve him in Canaan (Exodus 1-15). On the journey they encounter the Lord at Sinai and, after freely assenting to be his people (Exodus 19), accept the "ten words" (Exodus 20) and the additional legislation of Exodus, Leviticus, and Numbers. The covenant is ratified by the blood of an animal sprinkled on an altar representing God and on the people (Exodus 24).

An extra-biblical parallel to the Sinai covenant is, by scholarly consensus since the 1960s, suzerainty treaties like those the Hittite Old Kingdom (1450-1200 B.C.) made with its vassal states. The suzerainty or vassal treaty genre is attested from this mid-second to the late first millennium. The following outline is typical.

Titulary.

History of the relationship between the two kings, usually in precise detail, and in personal terms.

Statement of the relationship.

Stipulations.

List of divine witnesses.

Curses and blessings.

It has been recently suggested that the treaty genre influenced not the Sinai covenant described in Exodus but the book of Deuteronomy. Exodus describes a true covenant of course but not one modeled on a suzerainty treaty. Only Deuteronomy reflects self-consciously about covenant and follows the exact outline of the treaty genre: historical prologue with exhortation in chaps. 5-11; stipulations in 12:1-26:15; invocation and oath in 26:16-19; blessings and curses in chap. 28. The model for Deuteronomy would then have been the treaty genre as used by the Neo-Assyrian Empire (935-612 B.C.) to rule its western vassals. Israel would have adopted the genre to express its relationship to its suzerain.

The second major OT covenant type is Yahweh's unconditional covenant with Abraham (reaffirmed to the other patriarchs) and with David. Genesis 15 and 17 explicitly call God's promise of land and progeny to Abraham a covenant. Circumcision is the sign of the covenant; the "obligation" is to worship the God of the Father under his various titles. Emphasis is on God who promises.

The Bible itself underlines the connection between the Abrahamic and Davidic covenants (Gen 14:17-24; Gen 22:2 and 1 Chron 3:1). The unconditional covenant with David is most clearly set forth in 2 Sam 7 (and Psalm 89): "I will be his father and he shall be my son. When he commits iniquity, I will chasten him with the rod of men ... but I will not take my steadfast love from him...." The Royal Psalms develop that promise (Pss 2, 18, 20, 21, 45, 72, 101, 110, 132, and 144). M. Weinfeld has suggested that this type of covenant is modeled on the covenant of grant attested in the Hittite and Syro-Palestinian areas; the god grants to the king or servant land and progeny for their loyal service.

Covenant is so central in OT thought that the future can be imagined as a new covenant (Jer 31:31-35). Unlike the Mosaic covenant, which the people broke, "I will put my law within them, and I will write it upon their hearts. I will be their God, and they shall be my people."

New Testament

The NT accepts Septuagint usage: covenant means testament, dispensation. For Paul, covenant is a code for the entire old era and is the antithesis to the new age of Christ. 2 Cor 3:6 contrasts the old written and death-dealing covenant with the new covenant, which is of the Spirit and life-giving, a reference to Jer 31:31-34. Gal 4:21-31 is the strongest Pauline contrast between the two covenants: Hagar, a slave woman bearing children according to the flesh for slavery, and Sarah, a free woman bearing children according to the spirit for freedom. Hebrews contains the same contrast between old and new covenant but adds its heaven-earth typology and connects covenant to sacrificial worship.

The most important synoptic passage is Mk 14:24 (also, Mt 26:28; Lk 22:20): "This is my blood of the covenant, which is poured out for many." Lk 22:20 reflects the tradition found also in 1 Cor 11:25: "this cup which is poured out for you is the new covenant in my blood." Luke's reinterpreted Passover meal with its soteriological and "sacrificial" overtones (cf. v. 19c) alludes to the new covenant of Jer 31:31-35 and to Exod 24:3-8, where the Sinai covenant was ratified by the sprinkling of an animal's blood. Jesus' own body replaces the Passover lamb.

Covenant in the NT is a more restricted term than in the OT and has also been caught up in Pauline polemics. The relational aspect of the OT covenant is conveyed in the NT by other terms, e.g., church, faith, and discipleship.

J. Behm, "*Diatheke*," *TDNT*, II. 106-134. D. J. McCarthy, *Treaty and Covenant* (Analecta Biblica 21a; Rome: Biblical Institute Press, 1978). M. Weinfeld, "B'rith," *Theological Dictionary of the Old Testament* (Grand Rapids: Eerdmans, 1975) II.253-279.

RICHARD J. CLIFFORD, S.J.

CREATION THEOLOGY AND WORSHIP

The ecological crisis has heightened interest in the relation of worship to the natural world. Apart from some of the Psalms, the created order has not been a conscious and consistent point of reference in worship and liturgical practice. Worship has concentrated on the divine-human relation and the salvation of humanity. The natural world, by contrast, has not been an issue. But now the world of nature, the matrix within which human life is set, can no longer be taken for granted, and the salvation of this world has suddenly become a priority. Therefore it is not surprising that worship, which celebrates life, should reach out consciously to incorporate the natural order.

What are the underlying reasons for this neglect of creation in the past? (1) It may be traceable to the fact that the Judaism from whence Christianity sprang was in fierce competition with middle-eastern fertility cults that viewed the forces of nature as gods and "worshipped and served the creature rather than the Creator." In their idolatry "they exchanged the truth about God for a lie" (Rom 1:25). An emphasis upon nature in worship may for this reason seem problematic. (2) Gnostic influences on Christianity led to an interpretation of the world as "fallen" and a source of temptation because of its materiality. It was thus to be avoided as contradictory to the "spiritual," which is the real object of God's concern and saving activity. (3) Enlightenment rationalism and scientific empiricism have sought to do away with all superstition and mystery by turning the world into an object, the truth of which is known only by reductionistic methods. This has led to the assertion that the natural world occupies a quite different dimension of reality than religion, and religious attitudes toward it are at best anthropomorphic and poetic, and at worst superstitious.

There are resources in the tradition, however, which encourage more positive approaches. (1) The Psalmist, who has provided Christians much of their hymnic material for worship, sees the natural world as displaying the glory and providential care of the Creator. Without

deifying the world, Jewish piety viewed it as expressing God's faithfulness and blessing. The "land" was always an essential part of Israel's relationship to Yahweh. And Judaism never felt called upon to interpret the Fall as turning the material world into a curse. (2) In the Eastern church Fathers an important theme was salvation as a cosmic process restoring both humanity and nature to their original purposes in the intention of the Creator by way of *recapitulation* in Christ and *theosis* in humanity. (3) In the Western church there have also been those whom Matthew Fox terms "creation mystics"—Hildegard of Bingen, Mechtild of Magdeburg, Meister Eckhart, Julian of Norwich, and even Thomas Aquinas. None surpasses St. Francis of Assisi, whose "Canticle of Brother Sun" celebrates the interrelatedness of humanity and nature and unites all creatures in the praise

The forms and emphases of worship respond to the felt needs of every age. Therefore we can anticipate that cosmic themes will come into their own more and more as the consciousness increases that the rescue of the natural world is intimately tied to our own salvation. The world may be viewed as the original sacramental gift through which God gives Godself to humankind. Because of our forfeiture of our responsibility as the image of God to care for the earth, what was a blessing is fast become a curse, a threat to our lives and those of future generations. Christ, in his mission of redemption, identifies with this world gone awry and its inhabitants. In eucharistic worship he invites us to participate in himself, in his body and his kingdom of justice and peace, enabling us to see the world once again as the Creator's sacramental blessing and to transform our praxis in accordance with that fact. Thus the salvation in Christ celebrated in worship includes the restoration of the cosmos as integral to salvation, and ends the bifurcation of the material and the spiritual that has had such deleterious effects in the West.

Sources for this reinterpretation of the relation of worship to the world are emerging from several places, as the following examples indicate: (1) *Process theology*, with its origins in a Whiteheadian metaphysic, has a keen interest in the relation of the physical world to God. The *panentheism* favored by process theologians is distinguished from pantheism in that the world is not itself divine but is *in* God and God is at work in and through it. Thus God transcends the world, yet interpenetrates every part of its interrelatedness and its process of becoming. (2) Jürgen Moltmann employs trinitarian doctrine to overcome the dichotomy between God and the world often found in Protestant thought. Divine love creates the world as covenant partner and the object of love, granting the world independent existence while maintaining a continuing participation and stake in it through the Spirit, and leading the world, when it becomes estranged, toward a new future through the Son, the Messiah of the age to come. Thus, according to Moltmann, the world cannot be viewed without being aware of the *Shekinah*, the aura of God's love, care and glory, which surrounds and indwells it. (3) Pierre Teilhard de Chardin pioneered the re-union of cosmology and theology which had been severed from each other by the scientific positivism of the last century and theology's response to this positivism by limiting itself to the personal, interpersonal and subjective. Giving the evolutionary process a Christian interpretation, Teilhard posited a spiritual power working *within* the evolutionary process, *radial* energy, which is powered by the attraction of the goal, the *omega point* of the reunification of all things in God. The principle at the heart of Christianity, the incarnation, requires that this *telos* cannot be realized apart from the participation of the whole material world. The eucharistic transformation celebrated on the church's altars is the paradigm of cosmic transformation. "Step by step it irresistibly invades the universe" in the one great Mass and Communion by which both humanity and the cosmos are changed (*The Divine Milieu*, 123-26). (4) Matthew Fox has popularized "creation spirituality," attacking the preoccupation of traditional Western Christianity with the individual self and its sin, and the separation of soul from body. Drawing upon scripture, upon those Christian mystics who have incorporated the world into their vision of the redemptive processes of God, and upon his own visions of the plight of the planet and the necessity for new spiritual paradigms, Fox seeks to re-form worship as a paean of praise to the Creator and to inspire a new praxis that will defend and restore Mother Earth. "What ritual essentially does is to awaken the human to his or her cosmic identity" (*The Coming of the Cosmic Christ*, 214). (5) Although Vatican II predated the more intense awareness of the ecological crisis, the call for justice which it issued implies justice for the earth as well. The Council decried economic systems whose only object is exploitation and "prodigious material growth" (P.C., 18ff), and sought obedience to the vision of "a new earth in which righteousness dwells" (L.G., 39). These themes were taken up by the Medellin Conference of Latin American bishops, which condemned the "internal colonialism" and "external neocolonialism" which exploit both the impoverished masses and the natural resources of third-world nations. Recognizing the legitimacy of these demands for justice, John Paul II has called for "solidarity" with exploited peoples and has pointed to the "evangelical duty" of the church "to take her stand beside the poor" (*Sollicitudo Rei Socialis*, 39f). Such concerns are readily transferable to solidarity with God's creation and the church's need to take her stand in behalf of the endangered planet. Genuine participation in worship contributes to the formation of Christians in this spirituality.

John B. Cobb, *God and the World* (Philadelphia: Westminster Press, 1969). Matthew Fox, *Original Blessing* (Santa Fe: Bear & Co., 1983). *The Coming of the Cosmic Christ* (San Francisco: Harper & Row, 1988). Jürgen Moltmann, *God in Creation* (San Francisco: Harper & Row, 1985). Theodore Runyon, "The World as the Original Sacrament," *Worship*, Vol. 54, No. 6 (Nov 1980), 495-511. Pierre Teilhard de Chardin, *The Divine Milieu* (London: Collins/Fontana Books, 1964).

THEODORE RUNYON

CREATIVITY, LITURGICAL

Liturgical creativity is the process by which succeeding generations make traditions of Christian worship their own, through exercise of the gifts of the Spirit in the church. Creativity in worship means calling forth the gifts of leaders and all participants. Among these gifts are the ability to write and speak prayers which express the faith and praise of the community; the ability to use space, the visual arts, and movement for fitting praise of God; and musical gifts. Liturgical creativity is not the same as liturgical innovation—for the goal is not to entertain through the novel, but to call forth authentic contemporary praise of God, whether in local, denominational, or ecumenical settings. Learning what is done in other worshipping communities can feed liturgical creativity, but creativity is not imitation, since it depends on the specific gifts and abilities in each worshipping community.

The process of evoking creative gifts for worship is not uniform, since it involves the working of the Spirit. However, some strategies can assist the process. First, leaders of denominations and congregations must find ways to honor and nurture gifts which can contribute to worship. Second, the work of planning and leading worship must be surrounded by prayer. Third, liturgical creativity requires a commitment of time as worship leaders and committees seek ways to speak to and from the heights and depths of Christian experience rather than seizing upon the first suggestion or resource that comes their way.

A particular challenge which calls on the creativity of planners and leaders of worship is to work with past traditions so that they continue to be intelligible and consistent with a community's theological understandings. For example, the early church drew on Jewish worship traditions while expressing distinctive Christian insights; thus the passover *seder* became the paschal liturgy. Sometimes the transition is linguistic, for example the movement from Latin to the vernacular or from King James to contemporary English. Sometimes the transition is theological, for example the revision of baptismal rites in the last three decades in accordance with a renewed theology of baptism and Christian mission. At times, transitions involve a radical change, when church leaders seek to bring out basic meanings and actions in rites which have lost their focus over time. In all cases, liturgical creativity calls for awareness of the piety and sensitivities of worshipping communities. It is important to understand what worship traditions mean to a community before revising or eliminating them.

In recent years, the Roman lectionary and other lectionaries based upon it have become a major source of liturgical creativity, as many Christian churches seek to give scripture a more central place in their worship. Hymns, anthems, and prayers composed in response to lectionary texts can enrich and unify Christian worship.

See Adaptation, liturgical; Imagination and worship

RUTH C. DUCK

CREED, PRAYING THE

A creed is a concise, accepted, and approved statement of the central beliefs held by an individual or community, the classical instances in the Christian tradition being the Apostles' Creed and the Ecumenical Creed of Nicea-Constantinople. The Athanasian Creed, which found a minor place in the liturgy of the hours, is of a very different sort.

The Christian creed is at once a doxology that acclaims the glory of God, and a confession of praise and thanksgiving for what God has done in Christ Jesus. Through its public recitation in the eucharistic liturgy and its use in the rites of baptism, the creed expresses identity with the Christian community and a willingness to live a way of life motivated by the Lordship of Jesus Christ and the power of the Spirit. The repetition of the creed week by week in the Sunday eucharist narrates the saving events that are the basis of Christian faith: God's activity in creation, redemption in Jesus Christ, and presence in and through the Spirit who enlivens, enlightens, guides and heals the human and Christian communities.

The term "creed" derives from the Latin *credo* which means to put one's heart into something or to give oneself to someone or something. It thus implies commitment.

The Christian creeds have their origins in the baptismal ritual, though there are affirmations of a quasi-credal nature in some of the early NT writings. To assure the integrity of their faith, candidates for baptism were asked to affirm a short formula of Christian belief. These "interrogatory" creeds of the 2nd and 3rd centuries differed from place to place but were consistent in their trinitarian structure. In answer to three questions pertaining to belief in the Father, Son, and Spirit, the candidate would respond: "I believe" (*credo*).

The move from interrogatory to "declaratory" creeds was a consequence of the church's catechetical ministry. Declaratory creeds began to appear in the 3rd century as part of the catechetical instruction to baptism. These first-person affirmations were not simply assertions of belief in the triune God. This trinitarian belief is affirmed by making the Father, Son, and Holy Spirit the basic structure of the creed. By the 4th century, baptismal confessions of faith had become strikingly similar, and were nearly uniformly tripartite in structure, following Matthew 28:19.

Using baptismal creeds as a rule of faith and standard of orthodoxy spread rapidly during the 4th century with the Council of Nicea (325) and, especially, the Council of Constantinople (381). What has come to be popularly called the Nicene Creed is not that of the Council of Nicea, but the creed approved by the Council of Constantinople of 381. In the Middle Ages, the *filioque* (statement that the Spirit proceeds from the Father *and* the Son) was added to it in the West.

The creed is recited publicly during the eucharist on Sundays and great feasts. Its recitation in the eucharistic liturgy is an act of praise and testimony, by which Christians confess before God and one another what God has done and is doing in and through Jesus Christ by the power of the Holy Spirit. The present practice of standing and reciting the creed of Nicea-Constantinople after the gospel and homily has its roots in local custom in Antioch in the 5th century, gradually spreading through East and West.

The recitation of the creed after the proclamation of the word in the gospel and the homily expresses the assembly's verbal response to the story of salvation proclaimed in the scriptures and celebrated most fully at the eucharistic table. When viewed as the assembly's active, verbal response to the story of salvation proclaimed in the scriptures, the dialogical nature of the creed, more apparent in the interrogatory credal formulas of the ancient church, may be more fully appreciated.

With the reform of the rites following the Second Vatican Council, the interrogatory form of the creed replaced the declaratory form in the baptismal liturgy, a practice more in keeping with the ancient rite of baptism as it was known in Rome at the beginning of the 3rd century. The *Rite of Christian Initiation of Adults* restores the handing over or presentation of the creed, *traditio symboli* and the recitation or giving back of the creed, *redditio symboli* to the prominence they once enjoyed in the baptismal rites of the early church. In the final stages of preparation for initiation, a declaratory form of the creed is "handed over" to the catechumens, and "given back" or recited by them, while in the rite of baptism itself an interrogatory form of either the Apostles' Creed or the Ecumenical Creed of Nicea-Constantinople is used.

The Apostles' Creed and the creed of Nicea-Constantinople continue to be generally accepted by the Christian churches in the West. The creed has thus been promoted as a basis for Christian unity. It has also been proposed as a means for overcoming the gap brought about by the great schism between East and West. But this cannot finally be accomplished until the issue of the inclusion of the *filioque* is resolved.

J.N.D. Kelly, *Early Christian Creeds*, 3rd ed. (London: Longmans, 1972). Berard L. Marthaler, *The Creed* (Mystic, CT: Twenty-Third Publications, 1987). Geoffrey Wainwright, "Creeds and Hymns," in *Doxology. The Praise of God in Worship, Doctrine, and Life*. (NY: Oxford University Press, 1980, 182-217).

MICHAEL DOWNEY

CROSS

The cross is one of the oldest symbols known in the world. It is found in primitive as well as advanced cultures. From the earliest records of humanity, the cross is found carved in stone, in metals, on shells, in pottery and in other materials. It would be a grave mistake to suppose the cross to be of exclusively Christian origin or even explicitly religious origin. For example, from existing records it is probable that the figures of crosses and circles were used as a game in antiquity. The meanings of these pre-Christian crosses are often obscure and sometimes interrelated. For example among Egyptian hieroglyphs, a cross with a loop at the top was known as the Cross of Horus, an Egyptian god. Bearing some reference to life, this symbol was adapted by the Phoenicians to represent their goddess Astarte, the one who offers life. The Greeks transfigured the Egyptian cross in displaying an image of their goddess of life. The Swastika cross is of Sanskrit origin. It appears in early emblems of the Buddhists and is still used by some Hindu sects to represent meanings such as good fortune.

The cross in the Christian era is a symbol rooted in the meaning of Jesus. The terminology associated with the cross in Christian worship, the representation of the cross in various forms of art, and the development of legends about the cross over the last two millennia have Jesus as their foundational reference.

Finding of the Cross

According to early Christian tradition, the mother of Constantine (St. Helena) found the three buried crosses on Golgotha in the 4th century. There are several reports concerning the verification of the "true cross" of Jesus. Some say it was verifiable due to a miracle which confirmed its identity; others say it was identified by a still legible title inscribed upon the cross. St. Ambrose in his *Oratio de Obitu Theodos* (395) offers the first written reference to the connection of the cross with Helena. Other early church fathers speak of the connection with variations on the theme, though curiously, St. Jerome never mentions the subject, even though he lived near the place where the discovery apparently took place.

Veneration of the Cross

The diary of a 4th century Spanish nun, St. Egeria (Etheria), describes in vivid detail the Holy Week services in Jerusalem, including a rite for veneration of the cross. This devotion seems to have spread to Rome in the church of Santa Croce in Gerusalemme where a piece of the true cross was taken and revered in a reliquary. Eventually the devotion spread to other churches which did not have the relic of Jesus' cross. It seems that it was not until Carolingian times that specific presidential prayers were required in association with this ceremony of veneration of the cross.

In the Latin rite of the Christian church today, a ritual veneration of the cross occurs on Good Friday. Ceremonies similar to this veneration occur in the Eastern churches on September 14, the feast of the Holy Cross/ Exaltation of the Cross. This feast originally celebrated the recovery of the true cross from the Persians by Emperor Heraclius in 629. The first clear record of this feast is by Pope Sergius (687-701).

Meanings of the Cross

True to the nature of a symbol, the significance of the cross is multivalent in its meanings. Jesus' cross communicates a contradiction: how could an instrument of death be a sign of life? It is a paradox of Christian faith that such a sign of ignominious death (cf. Dt 21:23) could reveal the divinity of a human person. Jesus' cross reminds the believer that God *saves* through the cross (1 Cor 1:17; Eph 2:16, Col 1:20, Gal 6:14). Belief in this fact allows a Christian to face the cross with a certain equanimity and trust in the power of God. Another significance of the cross is that it reveals the extent to which God has gone to manifest God's

love for all people. The cross means freedom from slavery to selfishness (Rom 6:6). The cross means reconciling with God and neighbor, being willing and able to return to one another, face to face (Eph 2:16, Col 1:20, 2:14). The cross means renewing life in this world and finding life in the next (Gal 3:1, 6:14). The cross is the means of modeling Jesus (Gal 5:24). To be a true disciple and follower of Jesus, one must choose to take up the cross, even daily (Lk 9:23, 14:27; Mk 8:34;Mt 16:24).

Forms of the Cross

There is some evidence in the *Church History* by Socrates that St. John Chrysostom encouraged orthodox believers to carry a silver cross in procession to counter the hymn-singing Arians who processed at night at the end of the 4th century. At least by the end of the 6th century in the hymn *Vexilla Regis Prodeunt* composed by Fortunatus we find testimony to the existence of a processional cross. Numerous examples of different kinds of processional crosses remain since the Middle Ages. Also common during the Middle Ages was the placement of a cross as a central feature of the rood screen which separated the nave from the presbytery.

The form of the cross varies depending upon the rite, tradition, culture and particularities associated with a given saint or event which is being ritualized. Throughout Christian history, the cross has been depicted in scores of shapes, and there are countless varieties of decoration and embellishment surrounding the cross. The Western crosses tend to be more three-dimensional, while Eastern crosses tend to be more in the form of the icon. One design of the cross with a corpus of Jesus' beaten and bloody body attached to it is called a crucifix. There is some evidence that the crucifix dates to at least the 5th century. The early church emphasized the risen Christ, so only a lamb or another biblical symbol or the risen body of Jesus would adorn the cross. In 692 the Council of Constantinople ordered the presence of Jesus' human body on the cross and not, e.g., a lamb. The Carolingian period encouraged a more realistic portrayal of the extent of Jesus' suffering. This increasing emphasis upon stark, graphic realism about Jesus' wounded and bloody body reached its apex between the 12th and 14th centuries. By this point the crucifix replaced the cross as the object of veneration.

Placement of the Cross

Christian churches throughout the world today present the cross as one of their distinguishing symbols. A cross is frequently positioned in a prominent place, for example, atop a steeple or a bell tower of a Christian church. Perhaps a cornerstone, the side of a building, a doorway, a window, a wall, a ceiling, a floor, a tombstone will bear the mark of a cross. The list is far from exhaustive.

During the celebration of Christian worship, the presence of some form of the cross is not only desirable, but often required by Christian traditions. As early as the 5th century in Syria a cross was to be placed on the altar during Mass. Though required use of the cross on the altar was not widespread until the 13th century, soon afterwards the crucifix replaced the cross as a required piece of ceremonial. Yet it was not until the 1570 edition of the Roman Missal that the obligation of a crucifix upon the altar appeared. Prior to 1969 the Roman Catholic church required the crucifix as a central symbol on the altar. Since the recent post-conciliar liturgical reform, the guideline of the American Catholic bishops is to position a cross in a prominent place near the altar, but not on it.

Sign of the Cross

The gesture of signing someone or some thing or some place with the form of a cross is a way of designating a Christian relationship with God and praying for the growing significance of this relationship. This gesture is often used at sacramental celebrations and other Christian rituals.

From some evidence as early as the 2nd century, marking one's body with the sign of the cross was a form of Christian devotion. Sometimes a Christian signed the forehead (St. Basil mentions this); other times a Christian signed the breast or the eyes (and sometimes with the eucharistic bread), and later the entire upper body (5th century). One response to the monophysite heresy was the 6th century custom of signing the body using two fingers (expressing and cultivating the belief in the two natures of Christ) or three fingers (Trinity). In the West it was not until the directive of Innocent III (13th century) that the prescription of signing the body with three fingers and touching the right and then the left shoulder emerged. Later the directive was changed to open the entire hand and move from the left to the right shoulder.

The sign of the cross was customary in some forms of Christian liturgy by at least the 3rd century, for example, the bishop signed the newly initiated with a cross on the forehead (cf. Hippolytus c. 215). It was not until a 9th century decree of an episcopal synod that we find the rubric for the priest to make the sign of the cross over the offerings at Mass with the thumb and two fingers extended. It is unclear when a formula prayer associated with the gesture of the sign of the cross first entered the Christian tradition. The oldest formula seems to have been the trinitarian one, though the Eastern churches use other formula prayers as well.

The marking of the forehead, lips and heart with small signs of the cross by the thumb was a medieval development expressing a desire to open the mind to the word of God, to speak the Good News and to hold it carefully in the heart. The

Reformation pruned from Christian liturgy the frequent repetition of signs of the cross within one service. With the advent of the Second Vatican Council, the Roman Catholic church also desired to remove accretions and embellishments which tended to obscure the central actions of Christian worship.

Way of the Cross

The Way of the Cross or the Stations of the Cross, as it is sometimes called, is a Christian devotion which arose as a pious practice to honor the sufferings and death of Jesus. It developed in imitation of the custom of visiting places in the Holy Land where the events of Jesus' passion and death are believed to have occurred. The Franciscans especially encouraged this devotion and it became popular in the 15th century. The number of stations and what scene is recalled before each station have varied over the centuries, though in modern times fourteen stations have been customary. Essentially this devotion includes the positioning of a cross in different locations and meditating before each station with prescribed prayers. Often these crosses are accompanied by an artistic rendering associated with the specific event connected with Jesus' suffering and death.

Throughout the history of Christianity many saints became associated with symbols which characterize them in Christian art. Traditionally many of these symbols include a cross; for example, the representations for the apostles Peter, Andrew, Philip and Simon the Zealot. Other saints whose symbolic representations characteristically include a cross are St. Lawrence and St. Ansanus and St. Margaret of Antioch (3rd century), St. Anthony the Great and St. Helena and St. Jerome (4th century), St. Ursula (5th century), St. Scholastica (6th century), St. Bernard (12th century), St. Bonaventura and St. Louis and St. Anthony of Padua (13th century), and St. Catherine of Siena (14th century).

G.W. Benson, *The Cross: Its History and Symbolism* (New York: Hacker Art Books, 1976). G. Ferguson, *Signs and Symbols in Christian Art* (Oxford: University Press, 1980). F.E. Hulme, *Symbolism in Christian Art* (Dorset: Blanford Press, 1976). C.E. Pocknee, *Cross and Crucifix in Christian Worship and Devotion* (London: Mowbray, 1962). P. Regan, "Veneration of the Cross," in *Worship* 52 (Jan 78): 2-12.

T. JEROME OVERBECK, S.J.

CULTURE, LITURGY AND

Sustained and intensive concern for the cultural roots and contexts of Roman Catholic liturgy is one of the principal results of the Second Vatican Council. This concern received additional impetus with the completion of the process of textual and ritual revision in the mid-seventies and the recognition that the adaptation of the revised liturgy to various cultures would constitute a principal task of ongoing liturgical renewal.

This essay will examine the history of liturgical adaptation to culture, as well as the insights of Vatican II and the postconciliar era on the cultural elements of liturgical reform. It will set forth the principal theological paradigms operative in post-conciliar thinking on the relationship between liturgy and culture and indicate some methodological aspects of critical study in this area.

The History of Cultural Adaptation

The emergence of the liturgical and ecclesial forms of early Christianity involved an intrinsic process of cultural creativity. The Christian eucharist is a study in the manner in which traditional Jewish prayer forms were infused with Christian meaning and incorporated into a new ritual synthesis. This process was accompanied by theological controversies about the appropriate relationship that should exist between the Christian and Jewish orders. A process of profound cultural creativity can be identified in diverse ways in the early history of other Christian rites and symbols.

In general, three elements of adaptation were operative in the formation of early Christian liturgy. The first was the movement to imbue the Jewish liturgy with Christian faith and to retain elements and institutional links with the religion of Israel. The second was the extension of the gospel into non-Jewish environments and the adjustment of the requirements made upon pagan converts to Christianity. The third was the advance of Christianity into non-Jewish environments and the recognition that Christian faith must engage the religious convictions and aspirations of pagan religions (Chupungco, 9). However, while Christian liturgy in the early period sought consciously to maintain its roots in the Jewish tradition, the growing alienation of Christians from the Jewish community led to the emergence of a Christian liturgical order independent of the Jewish background. At this time, Christian liturgy began to be marked by the influence of Greco-Roman culture, although this was accompanied by considerable conceptual caution about the dangers and corruptions of paganism.

With the recognition of Christianity as the state religion of the empire in the early 4th century, Christian rites took on a notably public and splendid character and began to be shaped by their celebration in the imperial basilicas. There is ample evidence of the influence of imperial court ceremonial on clerical and episcopal theology, ritual and vesture. The rites of initiation began to incorporate some elements from pagan usage and Christian prayer and teaching began to be influenced by pre-Christian formularies and conventions. The new cultural situation of the church led to a considerable loss of hostility toward pagan cult, although there began to emerge at the same time a certain caution about secular or "mundane contamination" (Chupungco, 20).

The Roman liturgy, fixed in its basic shape and character by the 7th century, incorporated a new set of cultural influences as it moved northward into Franco-Germanic territory. The relatively sober Roman liturgical ethos began to take on a more notably dramatic and expressive character. Notable influences of Franco-Germanic elaboration which became thereafter enduring elements of the Roman liturgy are found in the liturgy of Holy Week and especially the Easter vigil. The more elaborate liturgical life generated in the Franco-Germanic regions was eventually received back in Rome in the 10th century.

Toward the end of the medieval period, the development of the liturgy became more extensive than intensive as the liturgy gave rise to passion plays, dramatic representation of gospel events and extra-liturgical pageants of various kinds. The development of liturgical life in this direction was not surprising given the state of affairs by which the liturgy had become inaccessible to the people and no longer expressed in their language.

The reforms following the Council of Trent gave way to the Baroque "flare for festivity, external manifestations of grandeur and triumphalism" and to an excessively sensuous and ornate liturgical style (Chupungco, 34). In this period, the Roman liturgy began to be celebrated in a notably theatrical, even operatic, manner in keeping with contemporary cultural sensibility.

Perhaps the most celebrated attempt to adapt the Roman liturgy to a non-Western culture was that associated with Mateo Ricci and the missionaries to China in the early 17th century. The Jesuit missionaries proposed the incorporation into Catholic usage of Chinese terminology and sought a Christian adaptation of the traditional ancestral rites which were a profoundly constitutive element of Chinese piety. The controversies which erupted on this matter gave rise to the Roman Instruction of 1659 which distinguished between Christian faith and its European expression. The instruction recognized that Christian faith can make use of non-Christian rites and symbols and that these can serve as suitable instruments in the spread of the gospel. However, the outcome of the Chinese Rites Controversy, as it is called, was not a positive one and the experiment was finally grounded under a pall of official suspicion.

In general, the history of cultural adaptation in liturgical matters can be seen as the interaction of four elements, each operating to a greater or lesser degree at particular moments. The first is a desire to remain faithful to NT origins, themselves organically connected to the religious forms of Israel. The second is represented in the process by which the Christian liturgical order incorporates ritual forms and customs from non-Christian environments. The third is a periodic reassertion of a normative Roman liturgy, especially in moments of perceived ritual corruption or compromise. The fourth is the conscious attempt to conceptualize the relationship between the liturgical tradition and non-Christian cultures so that non-Christian elements may be used as vehicles of the gospel without compromising the gospel and the Christian tradition.

The Constitution on the Sacred Liturgy

The intentions of the Second Vatican Council on liturgical matters are set forth in Article 21 of the *Constitution on the Sacred Liturgy* which declares: "In order that the Christian people may more certainly derive an abundance of graces from the sacred liturgy, Holy Mother Church seeks to undertake with great care a general restoration of the liturgy itself" (S.C., 21). The article then goes on to assert that, "the liturgy is made up of unchangeable elements divinely instituted, and of elements subject to change. These latter not only may be changed, but ought to be changed with the passage of time if they have suffered from the intrusion of anything out of harmony with the inner nature of the liturgy and have become less suitable" (ibid.).

The conciliar commitment to reform the liturgy by means of a recovery of the historic core of the Roman rite was complemented by a desire to adapt the liturgy to new cultural environments. The constitution declares: "The Church does not wish to impose a rigid uniformity in matters which do not involve the faith or the good of the whole community. Rather does she respect and foster the qualities and talents of the various races and nations" (S.C., 37). Accordingly, "anything in these peoples' way of life which is not indissolubly bound up with superstition and error she studies with sympathy, and, if possible, preserves intact. She sometimes even admits such things into the liturgy itself, providing they harmonize with its true and authentic spirit" (ibid.).

Provided that the substantial unity of the Roman liturgy is safeguarded, "provision should be made, when revising the liturgical books, for legitimate variations and adaptations to different groups, regions and peoples, especially in mission countries" (S.C., 38). The constitution recognizes the competence of local ecclesiastical authority to specify adaptations regarding the sacraments, sacramentals, processions, language, music and the arts. Article 40 allows for even more radical adaptation of the rites and prescribes that local ecclesiastical authority must "carefully and prudently consider which elements from the traditions and cultures of individual peoples might appropriately be admitted into divine worship." It prescribes that this process be carried out through a process of approved experimentation and involve the input of experts in cultural adaptation.

In accordance with these principles, the reforms of the liturgical books after

Vatican II provided for *accommodationes* by which individual ministers may adapt some ritual and textual elements to particular congregations and pastoral needs. They also provided for more formal adaptation of rites (*adaptiones*) by episcopal conferences which must be submitted for approval and confirmation by the Roman See.

Among the more significant examples of post-conciliar adaptation has been the program of the church in Zaïre to modify its liturgy according to the local cultural environment. The stated principles undergirding the new rite are "fidelity to the values of the gospel; fidelity to the essential nature of the Catholic liturgy; and fidelity to the religious and culture heritage of Zaïre" (Tovey, 35). Underlying the rite is a search for "authenticity that is truly Christian and truly African" (ibid.). The rite incorporates the vesture of tribal chiefs, dance, and the invocation of ancestors.

In North American Catholicism, liturgies adapted to various ethnic communities have been widely proposed. In particular, some attempts have been made to incorporate into the liturgy the musical traditions and festive elements of Hispanic and Black communities.

The practical difficulties of carrying out appropriate adaptation of rites, both in Western and non-Western countries, have proved to be considerable. Theoretical agreement on principles does not translate easily into practical consensus.

Liturgy and Culture: Four Paradigms

Modern discussions about the cultural adaptation of the liturgy are related to fundamental theological convictions about the relationship between the Christian tradition and human culture. In general, four paradigms to the faith/culture relationship appear to be operative in modern American Catholicism. These are the conservative, liberal, radical and neo-conservative.

The conservative paradigm maintains an absolute commitment to the inherited shape of Catholicism and has very little openness to modern culture. While conservatism often manifests strong commitment to traditional cultures in which religion and social life were integrated, it generally regards modern culture as inimical to authentic religious life and practice. Among the more notable examples of the conservative paradigm is the integralist movement in French Catholicism in the earlier part of this century. Archbishop Marcel Lefebvre, founder of the Society of St. Pius X, remains the most notable representative of the conservative position today.

The conservative paradigm places strong emphasis on the cultural integrity and autonomy of Catholicism. The church, accordingly, is viewed as a perfect society and conceptions of doctrine and ecclesiastical practice generally have a classicist character which fails to account for change and development within the tradition.

In liturgical matters, this paradigm generates strong opposition to liturgical change or adaptation. It precludes the possibility of significant use of non-Christian ritual elements and symbols in the liturgy. Indeed, it takes a generally hostile attitude towards non-Christian religions, regarding them as defective vehicles for the gospel.

The conservative position is represented by those who reject or merely tolerate the liturgical revisions initiated by the Second Vatican Council. Adherents of this view generally opt for the normative character of the so-called Tridentine Mass and deny that the liturgy should be adapted or changed for cultural or pastoral reasons.

Cultural adaptation of the liturgy in this mode tends to be superficial and incidental. The project here is appropriately characterized as *accommodation*, whereby some local or native artistic elements or customs are allowed a minor role in liturgical celebrations. The principal concern, however, remains the integrity of the Latin rite in all its elements and expressions.

The liberal paradigm in modern Roman Catholicism is characterized by a commitment to intensive dialogue between the gospel and human culture. It has a strong openness to the religious significance of modern culture and the revelatory character of ongoing human experience. It seeks to overcome the rupture between Christian tradition and the modern world and tends to be optimistic about the congruence between the gospel and culture. It is enthusiastic about cultural pluralism, interreligious dialogue and the emergence of a world church incarnated in diverse cultures.

In liturgical matters, the liberal attitude is strongly committed to cultural adaptation. It is confident that Catholic liturgy can be extricated from its Roman and European forms and expressions. The project here is appropriately described as *inculturation*, whereby local ritual and symbolic forms are invested with Christian meaning. The goal is to create styles of worship that are authentically Christian, yet structured around the ritual and symbol systems of the particular culture. The project typically involves attempts to "baptize" some non-Christian rites, particularly those associated with passage and transition.

Liturgical inculturation is not, however, free from considerable ambiguity. The attempts to identify and adapt non-Christian ritual and symbolic forms as vehicles for Christian expression can easily be compromised by the internal dynamics and semantic tenaciousness of the forms themselves. Accordingly, the liberal project to wed Christian meanings and cultural forms has a tendency to underestimate the complexity of the project involved.

The radical paradigm is distinguished from the liberal by its commitment to a substantial reformulation of Christian faith. In general, radicalism has a limited and selective commitment to the inherited tradition and generally allows a hermeneutic of suspicion a central role in the appropriation of that tradition. The interest is not so much in opening the gospel or the Christian tradition to cultures as it is in generating a critique of both the gospel and human culture and establishing a new religious/cultural order. Accordingly, the radical project is often apocalyptic and millenarian. Radicalism favors a pluralistic view of religion, allowing other religions equal or similar status to Christianity and asserting the possibility of a number of Christ-figures or saviors. For these reasons, it is not committed to upholding the uniqueness of Christ or of Christian faith.

The radical dialogue between Christianity and other religions is appropriately described as *inreligionisation*, whereby Christianity undertakes a self-emptying into non-Christian religion so that a new religious order will emerge. What Christianity has to offer other religions in this paradigm is not particular forms or doctrines or an institutional order but a liberating dynamic for self-expression and freedom.

The radical approach is operative in some strands of Christian feminist thought and practice which seek a reconstruction of Christian tradition in order to overcome perceived structures of patriarchy, sexism and oppression. Some feminists, critical of both Christian tradition and patriarchical culture, promote a process similar to inreligionisation whereby Christianity enters into dialogue with non-Christian feminist and utopian traditions and generates new ritual and symbolic expressions.

In the radical paradigm, adaptation brings about a profound reconfiguration of inherited liturgical forms. It favors local religious elements and symbols and rejects those imported from other cultures. It accords scriptural status to non-biblical readings and gives narrative and mythic expression to minority or "suppressed" voices.

The neo-conservative paradigm shares with the conservative an absolute commitment to the priority of the Christian tradition, but is distinguished from it by a more sophisticated appreciation of change and development within the tradition. This paradigm shares with the liberal an appropriation of the positive values of human culture and the need for the church to have a credible presence in diverse cultural environments. However, it incorporates a fundamentally critical and cautious attitude toward modern liberal culture and is aware of the danger to Christian faith in a wholesale embrace of liberal values and philosophical schemes. Accordingly, neo-conservative scholarship is acutely attentive to social-scientific analysis of the anti-institutional, atomistic and individualistic character of modern culture.

Neo-conservatism allows that the church can accept from cultural encounter those elements that will enrich, but not compromise, the ritual and doctrinal integrity of the historic tradition. The point of synthesis is located within the church's historical tradition in such a way that cultural elements may be incorporated into the Church's life when that is deemed fitting, but not allowed to act as significant modifiers of the tradition. The neo-conservative paradigm generates a strong conviction of the creative power of Christian institutions and is skeptical about any project that allows American cultural experience a determinative role in modern Catholic renewal.

The neo-conservative paradigm also generates skepticism about the project to create a liturgical order adapted to modern secular culture. In the advancement of Catholic life in non-Western cultural environments, it promotes a process of *acculturation* rather than inculturation. By this is meant a process by which ritual and symbolic elements compatible with the Roman liturgical tradition are incorporated in a significant way. The process is one of purification and reorientation of cultural elements, of careful and critical assimilation of cultural forms to the Christian tradition. The neo-conservative approach rejects any discontinuity with the past and is opposed to substantial modifications of the given liturgical tradition. In the incorporation of new cultural elements, it is careful to ensure that developments in the church's liturgy are in continuity with the pre-existing tradition. It has, on the one hand, a strong conviction about the ability of the inherited forms of Catholic life to speak across cultures and, on the other, an appreciation of the inevitable distance that must mark the relationship of the gospel to all cultures.

These four paradigms of the faith/culture relationship are not, of course, rigidly self-contained or mutually exclusive. Considerable overlap is evident in theory and practice and, depending on the issue, there is considerable movement back and forth.

Developing Methodologies

The study of the relationship between liturgy and culture is carried on today in a variety of ways and incorporates methodologies developed in a number of different fields. The philosophical and scientific study of religion provides a general background to the cultural study of liturgical rites. The insights of the phenomenology of religion (Otto, Eliade, Van der Leeuw), philosophy (Ricoeur, Langer), psychology (Freud, Erikson, Jung), and sociology (Berger, Palmer, Bellah) have been usefully appropriated in the study of Christian rites. Of particular importance are the methodologies and findings of ritual studies, the study of popular religion, and the literature of cultural criticism.

Ritual studies is a relatively new field unifying the study of ritual traditionally carried out in the fields of anthropology, sociology, psychology and art criticism. Though the methodologies employed in ritual studies remain quite diverse, they share a common appreciation of the highly dynamic role of ritual and symbol in cultural and religious communities. Much of the work in the field is carried on through minute study of the internal dynamics of ritual elements and systems. An increasing number of liturgists have begun to attend to the operations of Christian liturgy through the insights that are gained from the field of ritual studies. Among the theorists whose work is relevant to liturgical studies are Victor Turner, Mary Douglas, Clifford Geertz and Ronald Grimes. Liturgical scholars are as yet, however, only at the beginning of the process of developing an adequate methodology for the application of ritual studies to the study of Christian liturgy.

An area of study that provides significant insight into the culture/liturgy relationship is that of folk or popular religion. Here attention is not so much upon non-Christian religious communities but upon traditional Catholic societies where a fusion of Catholic ritual and pre-Christian rites and customs has long been effected. While study in this area has traditionally embodied the conviction that folk religion represents a corruption of Christian practice and an unhealthy syncretism, more recent study has come to regard popular or folk religion as expressive of a positive and pastorally appropriate concretization of the gospel in particular cultures.

Impetus for a more positive appreciation of popular religion in Latin America was provided by the meetings of CELAM at Medellin in 1968 and at Puebla in 1978. The study of Hispanic folk religion has since then become an important feature of church life in both Latin America and North America. Considerable attention has also been devoted to the insights for liturgical adaptation that may be gained for the study of Filipino Catholicism, Black Christianity in North America and analyses of Polish, Spanish and Italian Catholicism.

The literature of cultural criticism also provides important elements of reflection for liturgical scholars concerned about cultural adaptation in modern secular societies. American culture critics (Lasch, Sennett, Meyerowitz, Bloom) have analyzed the individualistic, subjectivist and atomistic character of American culture and generated caution among some theologians and liturgists about the prospect of an indigenized American Catholicism. The compatibility of American culture with Roman Catholicism has been the source of debate among neo-conservatives, with some (Schindler, Olsen) arguing for fundamental incompatibility and others (Weigel, Novak, Neuhaus) arguing for a fundamental compatibility, despite the present disorder of American culture.

See **Adaptation, liturgical**

Anscar J. Chupungco, *Cultural Adaptation of the Liturgy* (New York/Ramsey: Paulist Press, 1982). Norbert Greimacher and Norbert Mette, eds. *Popular Religion*, Concilium 186, (Edinburgh: T. and T. Clark, Ltd., 1986). Ronald L. Grimes, *Research in Ritual Studies: A Programmatic Essay and Bibliography* (Metuchen, N.J., ed. London: The Scarecrow Press, Inc., 1985). David N. Power, "Unripe Grapes: The Critical Function of Liturgical Theology " *Worship* 52 (1978): 386-399. Herman Schmidt and David Power, eds. *Liturgy and Cultural Religious Traditions*, Concilium 102, (New York: The Seabury Press, 1977). Philip Tovey, *Inculturation: The Eucharist in Africa* Alcuin/Grow. Liturgical Study 7, Grow Liturgical Study 55, (Bramcote: Grove Books, Ltd., 1988). Geoffrey Wainwright, "Christian Worship and Western Culture," in *Studia Liturgica* 12 (1977): 20-33.

M. FRANCIS MANNION

D

DANCE, LITURGICAL

The term *liturgical dance* refers to dance that is an integral part of a religious service. It may be practiced by a soloist, a group of dancers or the entire assembly of worshippers. Through its art form and communal involvement it can serve to deepen the prayer life of the congregation and enrich the celebration. Liturgical dance is formed by its function and purpose within the liturgy, with the reference point being how it serves the worship of the congregation. This entry will focus on history, theology and contemporary developments.

History

The roots of liturgical dance reach far back in time and connect with the wider field of sacred dance. Sacred dance is found in all primitive rituals, and together with drum and chant gave expression to the fundamental religious impulses of humankind. Among both western and eastern civilizations, and on every continent, including the great cultures of India, Tibet, Egypt, Greece and Africa, there is a tradition of sacred dance. In the Americas, from pre-Colombian South America to the native American cultures in the north, we find dance to be an indigenous expression of religion. Dance is a primary, universal mode of religious expression, testifying to a primeval sense of the union of body and soul.

Dance is also a rich part of Jewish tradition, and this heritage is often referred to by religious leaders and dancers as they seek historical roots in Judeo-Christianity. W. Gunther Plaut, and Bernard J. Bamberger (*The Torah: A Modern Commentary*, Union of American Hebrew Congregations, 1981) state that there are at least eleven Hebrew words denoting dance, and suggest that ritual choreography was extensive and well-developed. There is "a time to mourn and a time to dance" (Eccl 3:4). There were victory dances, dances connected to courtship and wedding, dances to celebrate the harvest. On Sukkoth, a religious festival of thanksgiving and gathering, there were ritual dance processions around the altar, followed by torch dances and the waving of festive palm branches. And the psalms tell us of dances in praise of God: "Let them praise his name with dancing, making melody to him with timbrel and lyre!" (Ps 149).

The Hasidic Jews to this day sway in prayer, dance alone or in a circle, holding one another's shoulders or waists. On the feast of Simhat Torah the rabbi dances, holding the Torah (the book of the Law) close to his heart. Dance was such an ingrained aspect of Jewish religious expression that it was not seen as implying assimilation of practices of the surrounding cultures. When Israelites danced around the golden calf, it was their lapse into idol worship that was deplored, and not that they danced.

While dance remained a part of the

314

Jewish community, various factors seem to have contributed to the gradual decline of dance in the early Christian church. The church was in the process of forming its own identity, and therefore separating itself from the customs of the Jewish community, including dance. It was rejecting at the same time the Roman culture and the "degraded" forms of dance within pagan worship. Finally, the church was being influenced by Greek platonic philosophy that separated the soul from the body. In the Hebrew tradition there has been no such separation, but rather the understanding that we are by nature unified beings.

We must also consider the great cultural change that arose with the official acceptance of Christianity by Constantine, which resulted in major changes in the style of Christian worship. Small, private gatherings of Christians were replaced by a more grandiose and formal style of worship in huge basilicas. The priest no longer sat among the people. The seat of the bishop was removed from the center where the congregation was, to the apse, and later the altar was placed there as well. The ultimate and spontaneous relationship among people was altered, and this change in spirit inevitably affected the practice of dance (Gagne, Kane, VerEecke, pp. 42, 43).

Throughout the early church and during the Middle Ages the struggle continued between approving of dance as a scriptural symbol and metaphor for heavenly bliss, and the actual dance as practiced by the people. The Fathers of the Church viewed dance as a pastoral issue and their sermons and writings colorfully reflect the above dichotomy. St. Ambrose, Bishop of Milan (340-397), referred to King David's dance (2 Sam 6:14) as a model for the performance of sacred dance. After admonishing against indecent dances, he goes on to say: "No, the dance should be conducted as did David when he danced before the ark of the Lord, for everything is right which springs from the fear of God. Let us not be ashamed of a show of reverence which will enrich the cult and deepen the adoration of Christ.... But thou, when thou comest to the font, do thou lift up thy hands. Thou art exhorted to show swifter feet in order that thou mayest thereby ascend to the everlasting life. This dance is an ally of faith and an honoring of grace." [*On Repentance 11. 6:42* (See, M.F. Taylor, *A Time to Dance*, Philadelphia United Church Press, 1967, p. 77)].

On the other hand, John Chrysostom (345-407) stated, "For where dancing is, there is the evil one. For neither did God give us feet for this end, but that we may walk orderly ... that we may join the choirs of angels" (Gagne, Kane, VerEecke, p. 50).

During the Middle Ages the best known expressions of dance were associated with the Feast of Fools, the Children's Festival, and the Dance of Death, as well as dances that took place in churchyards to celebrate the victory of martyrs and dance processions for healing in which relics of saints were carried.

In Spain there is an unbroken tradition of liturgical dance known as *los seïses*, six or twelve boys in two sets dance before the altar in a minuet style with castanets. *Los seïses* continues to be performed for the feasts of Corpus Christi and the Immaculate Conception, in Seville and Toledo as part of the Mozarabic rite.

In our times, renewed interest in religious dance has its beginning in the liturgical movement and the liturgical reforms of Vatican II which reaffirmed the importance of the body and the active participation of the faithful in the liturgy. "To promote active participation, the people should be encouraged to take part by means of acclamations, responses, psalmody, antiphons, and songs, as well as by actions, gestures, and bodily attitudes... "(*Sacrosanctum concilium*, 30).

The division in our culture of all aspects of life into either sacred or secular categories makes it difficult for persons not familiar with the potency of dance for religious expression to conceive of its place in the liturgy. Pope Paul VI, desiring to heal the split between the church and her artists, addressed the artists of Rome with these heartfelt words: "We need you. Our ministry has need of your collaboration because, as you know, our ministry is that of preaching and rendering accessible, comprehensible, even soul-stirring, the world of the spirit, the world of the invisible, of the ineffable, of God ... " (Rome, Sistine Chapel, 1964).

Theology

The following brief discussion of a supportive theology of dance is derived from the work of J.G. Davies and is founded on an understanding of human nature based on the biblical view of the person as a unified being. One does not possess a body and soul. Each person is a body-soul unity. St. Paul wrote, "Do you not know that your bodies are members of Christ?"(1 Cor 6:15), and " ... you are the body of Christ ... " (1 Cor 12:27). Our very selves are the body of Christ, the living sacrifice to God. To be created in the image of God affirms our material spiritual unity. The body cannot be dismissed as separate and irrelevant to human spiritual life. Just as sacraments are material channels of divine grace applied to the human body, dance is not only a physical activity. It illuminates and inspires because it enhances material-spiritual unity. We are exhorted to glorify God in our bodies (1 Cor 6:19-20). We are present to one another and to God in our bodies.

God has created the cosmos, God has created matter. Matter cannot be anti-spiritual, but instead is a vehicle of blessing. All the sacraments of the Christian church are channels of divine grace through matter, and their administration involves movement and gesture which are necessarily minimal "dances." We pour the water of baptism; we break the bread of the eucharist; we lift our arms in prayer. With these movements we are already dancing and expressing through our unified body-soul the divine presence and action.

The sacred movements of the sacraments are signs of the advent of the Kingdom of God in our midst. In the Hebrew Scripture, dance in particular was a sign of God's favor and grace. There is no reason why it should be anything less for Christians.

Contemporary Developments

By their nature great gatherings and festivities call for music and dance, and dance has indeed been a part of the celebrations of the universal church. Dance was part of the 38th International Congress in Bombay, 1973, the 40th International Congress in Melbourne and Nairobi, 1975, and the 41st Eucharistic Congress in Philadelphia, 1976. Dance has also been included in the ceremonies surrounding papal visits to various countries, notably in Montreal, 1984, under the direction of Fr. Jacques Dubuc. Fr. Dubuc recently stated in the Montreal newspaper, *LeDevoir*, March 1989, that reintegrating the body at the heart of eucharistic liturgies renders more accessible and credible the mystery of the "Verbe incarné." Perhaps of greatest significance as a model for future official inclusion of dance in liturgical rites is the recent approval of the Roman Rite for the Diocese of Zaïre, fall 1987. In this rite dance plays as integral a role as does music throughout the liturgy.

The essay on dance in the churches, published in *Notitiae*, II, in 1975, has had a negative effect on liturgical dance in the United States. It affirms the use of dance in cultures where dance is still a reflection of religious values, such as the Syriac, Ethiopian and Byzantine traditions, but looks dubiously on dance in western culture, stating that dance is considered to be primarily connected with diversion and profaneness. This document is considered a reference point for study and offers a challenge for contemporary Christian dancers and religious teachers to affirm the inherent spiritual value of dance that is rooted in the cultural and religious expression of the people.

In the United States today the styles of dance are multiform, ranging from folk to classical ballet and modern dance. Led by Mexican, native and African American traditions, folk dances from all the cultures that have settled America are available to us. Many of these dance traditions find expression in paraliturgical celebrations, such as wedding parties, and can be adapted to liturgical celebrations as a natural, sacred expression of culture. At the conclusion of their Easter liturgy, the Benedictine monks of Weston Priory in Vermont annually perform international folk dances. The folk dance, among its other merits, can serve to bridge the distance between clergy and lay people.

The beautifully disciplined dance styles of ballet, modern and jazz, along with the dance/movement meditations of Yoga, T'ai Chi and similar traditions, are increasingly part of the American consciousness. America has produced some of the outstanding leaders of the dance world, including Ruth St. Denis and Isadora Duncan, who may be considered one day "founding mothers" of sacred dance in this country. Martha Graham, José Limon, Erik Hawkins, Alvin Ailey, to name but a few more contemporary figures, are a rich heritage for dancers seeking movement inspiration for sacred works. The writings and performances of these great artists attest to the depth of their spiritual search. It is precisely because we do not have a handed-down tradition of sacred dance, as in India for example, that these diverse schools are so important. With discernment and adaptation, they have much to offer to the development of a rich vocabulary of sacred dance movements for inclusion within the church.

Liturgical dance has been slowly and quietly developing in the United States. Workshops on sacred dance held throughout the country have been major opportunities for sharing and growth. Requests for both workshops and trained dancers come from retreat centers, high schools and colleges, religious orders, including monasteries and convents, as well as individual churches. The Sacred Dance Guild, founded in 1958, is an inter-faith organization that holds annual conferences on all aspects of sacred dance.

Dance expresses the whole range of human emotions, and therefore is ideally suited for the major feast days and seasons of the church calendar. During Advent dances are part of the procession with the wreath, and prayer gestures may accompany the lighting of the candles. Christmas is a time that has been favorable to the inclusion of dances for children along with adults in celebration of the Nativity. Dancing extends into Epiphany with processions, often to carols, depicting the coming of the Magi. During Lent there are dances choreographed to express both the penitential side of the season and the mystery of Jesus' suffering on the cross. Palm Sunday dances often incorporate the use of palms; dances at Easter seem to spring forth like the flowers, joyous and exuberant. Pentecost has inspired dances that are intense, vibrant and sweeping in nature, like the wind and the tongues of flame.

Dance should be conceived with the overall flow of the liturgy in mind, and be included in such a way as to be an integral part of the worship. It should never be regarded as a spectacle or merely as ornament. The length and appropriateness of the dance is determined by its function in the liturgy and follows generally the same guidelines used for choosing the music. The style of dancing, including use of costumes, will vary from church to church and season to season, should reflect the solemnity or festivity of the day, and bear in mind the congregation it serves.

Dance lends itself to processions, including the gospel procession and the presentation of gifts. The psalm, which customarily follows the first reading, may be both sung and danced. A solo dancer or small dance choir may perform the verses while the congregation joins with appropriate gestures to the antiphon. Simple dance gestures and movements for the entire congregation can easily be taught in a few minutes before the service begins. Dance can stylistically enact the gospel, or guide a meditation on it or other readings of the day. Dance can accompany the acclamation of faith, or the Great Amen. Dance can include the entire congregation in line and circle dances at the conclusion of the liturgy (Gagne, Kane, VerEecke, pp. 95-115).

The contribution of dance to the liturgy is inseparable from its quality of inspired movement and the aesthetic, religious and spiritual values that underline its expression. In the document *Environment and Art in Catholic Worship.* (National Conference of Catholic Bishops, 1978, 4) we read, "God does not need liturgy; people do, and people have only their own arts and styles of expression with which to celebrate." Concerned with establishing guidelines for art in liturgy, they discuss the experience of mystery: "...a simple and attractive beauty in everything that is used or done in liturgy is the most effective invitation to this kind of experience. One should be able to sense something special (and nothing trivial) in everything that is seen and heard, touched and smelled, and tasted in liturgy" (*ibid.*, 12). The art has to be of high quality, and "be capable of bearing the weight of mystery, awe, reverence and wonder which the liturgical action expresses" (*ibid.*, 20).

The ministry of liturgical dance serves the community with the uniqueness of its gifts. By perceiving, gathering, shaping and celebrating in dance the religious hopes, struggles and joys of the people, it offers an enriched experience of the fullness of life. Keeping focused on the spiritual meaning of dance, we do not become overly preoccupied with preconditioned habits of mind regarding "propriety." As Thomas Merton reminds us, "... we are invited to forget ourselves on purpose, cast our awful solemnity to the winds, and join in the general dance" (*New Seeds of Contemplation*, New York: New Directions, 1961).

Liturgical dance has a healing and prophetic role to play in the church and for the world. It is not "icing on the cake." It epitomizes our relation to our bodies and by extension our relation to the earth. Redeeming the body and redeeming the earth are connected. In today's world, our earth is in trouble. The earth is dancing a passion. The vibrations of the earth's dance resound in everyone of our cells and the liturgical dance calls us to respond to the anguish around us with a reaffirmation of the spirit. The dance and the dancer may shake us from our lethargy to a positive re-engagement to help restore the earth's harmony.

Hugo Rahner, quoting Lucian of Samosata (*Man at Play*, NY: Herder & Herder, 1972) states: "Those who most accurately describe the genealogy of the dancer's art declare that its origin is the same as the world itself, and that it appeared together with that primal eros that is the beginning of all things...."

J.G. Davies, *Liturgical Dance, An Historical, Theological and Practical Handbook* (London: SCM Press, Ltd., 1984). Ronald Gagne, Thomas Kane, Robert VerEecke, *Introducing Dance in Christian,*

Worship (Washington, D.C.: The Pastoral Press, 1984). Carla De Sola, *The Spirit Moves: A Handbook of Dance and Prayer* (Washington, D.C.: The Liturgical Conference, 1977; Austin, TX: The Sharing Company, 1986).

CARLA DE SOLA

DE LA TAILLE, MAURICE (1872-1933)

Jesuit theologian, professor of theology at Angers and later at the Gregorian University in Rome, de la Taille was a major early figure in the 20th century attempt to rescue sacramental theology, and especially eucharistic theology, from the lifeless abstractions of post-Tridentine manual theology. With specific interest in the eucharist, he sought to unify two dimensions of eucharistic faith that had been kept apart, both in the decrees of Trent and afterwards: eucharist as sacrifice and eucharist as sacrament. Under the title *Mysterium fidei*, The Mystery of Faith (1940), he sought to hold together the Lord's Supper and the cross, a unity now taken for granted, but quite controverted in his day. He stands in the tradition of Odo Casel (1886-1948), seeking to recapture for Christian worship the category *mystery*, a category officially captured in *Mystici corporis* (1943) and *Mediator Dei* (1947) of Pius XII, claimed in abundance in the documents of Vatican II (esp. S.C. and L.G.), and continued as now common parlance for Christian worship in, e.g., *Eucharisticum mysterium* (1967) and Paul VI's *Mysterium fidei* (1965).

See Mystery theology; Theologians, modern, and liturgical renewal

DEACON

In the history of the church, the role and ministry of the deacon has varied. Always it has been a *diakonia*, a service, at times to the word, at times to the praying assembly, at times to the bishop.

In current Roman Catholic church order, the deacon is ordained and assigned to assist the bishop and the presbyter in the ministry of word and sacrament. In other church orders, and specifically in the Eastern churches, the deacon is always an auxiliary liturgical minister. Deacons assist; they do not preside. In current Roman Catholic church order, deacons both preach and preside: at the liturgies of baptism, matrimony, and at times Christian burial. Their ordained ministry is therefore far more linked to the ministerial priesthood than it has been to date. In the ministry of preaching and proclaiming the gospel they make present Christ in his word (S.C., 7), and in the ministry of presiding they present and represent both the *episcope* (the pastoral office of the bishop) and Christ (prophet, priest, and ruler). In the Roman Catholic ordination rite for deacons, the deacon is presented with the gospel as the primary instrument and sign of the diaconal office: "Receive the gospel of Christ whose herald you are; believe what you read, preach what you believe, and put into practice what you preach" (rite of commissioning). Deacons are recipients of the sacrament of orders; the term "lay deacon" as applied to deacons in the sacramental churches who do in fact ordain deacons is inaccurate.

See Church order; Priesthood; Ordination rites; Orders, sacrament of; Orders, symbols of

DEATH, MINISTRY AT THE TIME OF

Pastoral care for the dying and their families involves a special type of compassionate presence. This section will concentrate on a variety of approaches to this presence, emphasizing both the initial stages of ministry and the more immediate companionship during the final days and hours of life. How can a pastoral minister develop a strong relationship with the seriously ill and their families before the last days and what is involved in quality pastoral care as death approaches?

Initial Stages of Pastoral Care

The most effective way of assuring valuable pastoral presence at the time of death is for the minister to establish strong pastoral relationships with the seriously ill and their families as far in advance of the last days as possible. This is especially important because most of the crises in a person's faith occur over a period of time when emotional and physical health is stable enough to concentrate on their relationship with God. Ministers, therefore, need to be available during this grappling with faith in order to assist those facing death to come to an eventual peace with themselves and with God before the final days of life. Often people encountering terminal illness experience a battle with God concerning the reason for their sickness and God's role in it. They also review their lives in an attempt to find meaning and purpose. Mourning and grieving the major losses of their lives can be a painful and lonely process. Gradually most dying persons reach a point where they find an abiding sense of hope and trust and where they can leave the past and the future to God and live as fully as possible in the present.

In struggling with all of these aspects of preparing for death, the seriously ill benefit greatly from pastoral companions who have the time, the patience, the expertise and the trust to be present to them over the weeks and even months prior to the end of life. When the final vigil before death does begin, it becomes a deep consolation for the ill person and for the family and friends to have with them a pastoral minister who has accompanied them along the road from the very beginning.

Frequently a pastoral companion is called upon during both the initial and later phases of a terminal illness to act as a mediator between the seriously ill person and health care personnel, especially the physicians and nurses responsible for primary care. Although great sensitivity may be shown by medical personnel toward the patient, sometimes individuals and their loved ones become bewildered and anxious about what treatment is being pursued, about what medical care decisions need to be made, and about what comfort measures can be assured. Chaplains who are familiar with these concerns can encourage them to ask questions directly of the care-givers and can at the same time urge physicians and nurses to explain their answers and approaches in understandable and compassionate ways. When there are decisions about medical procedures which must be made, with input from both the dying person and the family, pastoral ministers as counselors and as members of a religious tradition can help them reach conclusions which respect life while not prolonging suffering unnecessarily. Their own experience in ministering with and to the dying will teach chaplains how important it is for families, both at the bedside of their dying relative and after death, to have made responsible and caring decisions about treatment. Without being intrusive, pastoral companions can offer their guidance to families in making these determinations so that later on they will live peacefully with the quality of care they provided their loved one.

Another one of the most valuable services which a chaplain can offer persons with serious illness and their families is to facilitate communication among themselves. Sometimes it is very painful to observe members of a family expending a great deal of energy shielding one another from their real feelings and reactions. Each individual may express emotions to some "outsider," fearing that it would be too difficult to be that direct with loved ones. Pastoral ministers often notice the emotional isolation which this approach produces, an isolation that keeps at odds with one another the very people who could potentially offer the best mutual support. By listening individually or in groups to family members who want to express their fears, worries, regrets, confusion, and hope, chaplains can affirm their feelings and then begin to encourage them to let the ill person know how they are reacting. If they are able to identify what makes them hesitate being honest before each other, then their anxieties have less control over them and they might take the risk of being more open. Because pastoral companions with the dying frequently notice that this directness brings tremendous relief and comfort, they can work skillfully and patiently to facilitate this communication, realizing that it will offer much consolation for everyone during the last days of life and in their mourning afterwards.

The celebration of the sacraments, especially reconciliation, communion and the anointing of the sick, represents another aspect of this initial ministry that helps prepare critically ill persons and their families to let go with trust in God. Clearly these sacramental celebrations are appreciated most readily by those who have been regularly involved over the years in the practice of their faith. When Roman Catholics who have participated in a local parish community and have valued the explicit support of their Christian faith are confronted with the trauma of serious illness, they often spontaneously seek the comfort of the sacraments. They bring to them a deeply nourished faith in the Lord. Others who face critical illness may not have been as involved in church communities, but may still appreciate the celebration of the sacraments, particularly after preparatory conversations with ministers who can expand their notions of reconciliation, communion and anointing. However, whether there is a history of participation in the sacraments or not, there is an indispensable need to plan these liturgical celebrations in the context of the pastoral relationships.

Over a period of time, chaplains become acquainted with the ill persons and with their families. They come to know their histories, attitudes, patterns of interactions, faith struggles, shared successes and tragedies, and their apprehensions as they approach death. In offering to celebrate the sacraments with them, pastoral ministers provide occasions for communal prayer which highlight and at the same time enhance the compassion of God as it may be experienced in the context of the ongoing love and concern among all who are involved with the dying person.

When the reality of their dying has had time to penetrate and they have begun to come to terms with their life and their death, seriously ill persons may approach their pastoral minister for help in preparing their funeral liturgy. By responding positively to this request, chaplains participate in a process that can contribute to an integration for the dying person and can be a source of peace for the family. In choosing scripture readings and hymns, in reflecting on the funeral homily and in naming specific loved ones to take part in the liturgy, the critically ill will often talk aloud about the meaning which their life has had and what brings them satisfaction and gratitude as they come to the end. They might articulate how God has been with them throughout life and especially now during their illness and dying. They may wonder about life after death and seek help from the chaplain in deepening their trust in God to take care of them after they die.

With families also there can be many opportunities during this time of preparing a funeral liturgy for reviewing the life they have shared with their dying loved one and with one another. Sometimes pastoral companions find themselves standing with family members who reevaluate their own faith and practices of faith as they are confronted with death and the meaning of their own lives. Whenever this funeral planning occurs together with the dying, their family and their pastoral minister, it helps everyone get in touch with the sources of their hope which will sustain them in the days ahead.

Pastoral Care at the Time of Death

As serious illness gradually depletes the sick person, leaving him or her weaker and weaker, and as death becomes more imminent, pastoral ministers are called upon to offer a unique type of presence. Since the seriously ill person is no longer struggling with looking back on life to discover meaning and purpose and has for the most part laid the past to rest, living one day at a time, chaplains discover that there is more silence in their visits, both with the dying person and with family members. Quite frequently relatives and friends become disturbed by this silence, particularly when they interpret it as rejection on the part of their dying loved one. They need reassurance from ministers that this lack of verbal communication is normal as a person approaches death and lets go of life. Although families may have been prepared for a death through weeks or months or even years of illness, they can become overwhelmed during the final days, experiencing a sense of anxiety or shock or confusion. A chaplain who has become a trusted friend during the time prior to the final vigil can offer a listening ear and heart to them, encouraging their expression of feelings. As the end draws near, a pastoral companion shows much compassion in gently urging the relatives to let their loved one die, to allow themselves and the dying person to let go.

During the last days or hours of a person's life a pastoral minister can offer valuable companionship. It is not a question of many words, but rather a quiet presence which supports all those around the bed of the dying person. By suggesting to the family that they hold the hand of their loved one or moisten parched lips or wipe a perspiring forehead, or by saying a short, simple prayer for God's loving presence, by making a sign of the cross on the dying person's forehead, by staying at the bedside while family members take a break, by all of these common-sense, straightforward gestures, they will speak more loudly of real care than do multiplied prayers and repeated rituals.

If the minister is present at the moment of death, there are some other practical approaches which can bring solace to the survivors. Suggesting that they touch the body and that they talk to it, assuring each of them some privacy if they wish to say good-bye individually, holding the hand of a family member or putting an arm around their shoulders, and letting one's own tears flow, if they are there, will support the family profoundly at a time which is deeply emotionally charged. After relatives and friends have had the chance to say good-bye, a brief prayer by the chaplain often brings closure to the vigil at the bedside and gives permission to the family to leave.

During the days and weeks which follow death, pastoral companionship continues for the family, sometimes by participating in or leading the funeral and afterwards by maintaining periodic contact with the survivors. It can happen frequently that the impact of a death really doesn't hit home for a family until after the funeral, even when they have anticipated the loss for some time. When they do begin to experience the strong feelings and memories relatives will benefit from a chaplain's compassionate listening. The chaplain and pastoral ministers can help them readjust their relationships with one another as part of their grieving, and can offer comfort by assuring them that they will eventually reach a peaceful equilibrium.

There can also be a second-guessing about medical decisions by the family, as they rethink and judge in retrospect their care of their loved one. With gentle firmness a minister may need to remind them that they made the best decisions possible in the circumstances and that, even if there are regrets, they need to move on and be understanding with themselves. Noticing that certain members of a family may be having a more difficult time in their mourning, chaplains might recommend some assistance from a grief counselor or from a support group. Encouraging this kind of help during the first few weeks of grieving invariably prevents serious readjustment difficulties later on. Because friends and relatives often scatter right after a funeral, those closest to the deceased may feel abandoned and disoriented. A sensitive pastoral companion who has known the family through an illness and a death can offer invaluable attention and care to help people experience peace and then move on with living.

After the death of a seriously ill person there is usually a need for care-givers, those who looked after the individual and the family, to mourn their loss and to become comfortable with the way they helped the person to die. Pastoral companions can help in this process by sharing their grief and by structuring a simple memorial service where the care-givers can remember and pray together. Because the end of a person's life can be quite abrupt for medical and other staff and since they are expected to carry on with their care of others, the sadness, the tenderness and sometimes the anger within them doesn't receive enough attention. In order to put the deceased person to rest and to continue to be engaged with other seriously ill women and men, care-givers require the opportunity to pay attention to their own and

to one another's feelings. Chaplains who spend time with them and urge them to express their reactions contribute to their experiencing a sense of enrichment from their relationships of care and enable them to let themselves be involved again and again with others who face the trauma of critical illness and dying.

How the Chaplain Grieves

Anyone who chooses to be pastorally present with the dying and their families is forced to learn how to handle personal grief in healthy ways. When true pastoral care is based on compassion by which ministers allow their hearts to be touched by the suffering of their sisters and brothers, they will inevitably experience their own pain of loss after the death has occurred. Sadness, loneliness, emptiness, frustration, regrets and other emotions can leave a chaplain depleted. Learning how to share some of these feelings, at least with one other individual, and reviewing the pastoral relationship with the family, can console the minister and provide some awareness of the meaning of his or her pastoral care. In their prayer, chaplains often are able to discover the gratitude of Christ which heals them and energizes them to reinvest in the lives of other dying persons and their families. Relaxing and enjoying life, creatively using leisure time and nourishing good friendships are also essential in helping pastoral companions to find new life amid the encounters with death.

Conclusion

Christian ministry at the time of death is a gift of the Spirit given to some of God's people. Those who accept it and enter into it will continually find their hearts expanded and their lives enriched, but they come to this only through feeling some of the fears and pain of individuals and families who struggle with the mystery of dying and death. When chaplains approach each person and each family as unique, not trying to categorize or capture the varied ways of dying, they learn over and over a deep respect for the human spirit, sustained by God that refuses to be broken even by the powerlessness and helplessness of death. For pastoral ministers the greatest satisfaction in accompanying the dying is not so much their growing in understanding what serious illness and death are all about, but rather that their encountering the loving face of Christ in the fragility of their brothers and sisters.

Gerald J. Calhoun, *Pastoral Companionship: Ministry with Seriously Ill Persons and Their Families* (New Jersey: Paulist Press, 1986). Elizabeth Kubler-Ross, *Questions and Answers on Death and Dying* (New York: Macmillan Publishing Co., Inc., 1974). Kenneth R. Mitchell and Herbert Anderson, *All Our Losses/All Our Griefs* (Philadelphia: Westminster Press. 1983).

GERALD J. CALHOUN, S.J.

DEATH, THEOLOGY OF

Death seldom stands in the center of Christian theology, yet it is an ultimate in human existence. It forces upon us the most serious questions about the meaning and goal of human life, about the very existence of meaning and goal. Faced with the inevitability of death, we feel threatened by forces outside and within ourselves. Faced with the bewildering complexity of our life threatened by death, the ability to remain centered is an ever-present challenge. Every epoch has its own answer to the question of death, but the inadequacy of each answer inevitably leads every new generation to pursue the search. Whatever answer may be given to the question of death, it cannot be given in terms of ideas and concepts, or in abstract generalities.

Death is the one basic reality that makes most manifest that the human participates in the biological and the cultural. As human beings, we live at the edge of a paradox. We belong both to nature and to culture and are consistently affected by the ambivalence of such a situation. Death as an inevitable fact of human existence can be perceived only from within the interplay of biology and culture. Death is as much a social event as a biological one; it is overlayed with symbolic and ritualistic meaning. We can secure our sense of death only from images, from symbols and rituals. In symbols the truth about life and about death is disclosed to us. Symbols light up our experience and give coherence to our existence, enabling us to be human. Far from being unsymbolizable, the language of death is the symbol.

These symbols are not creatures of fancy; they have their roots in the polarities and binarity of human existence, in the ongoing interplay of the negative and the positive. Christianity's answer to the questions of life and death is a complex of symbols: the paschal mystery. The decisive images are of Jesus Christ, of his life, death and resurrection. The images are those of birth, death and rebirth: their emphasis is on life graciously given, graciously sustained—death no longer stands as the ultimate fact, but as the penultimate.

Death in the Old Testament

For both Hebrew and Christian scriptures, the central issue in death is a theological one: the character of God. The OT, reflecting Israel's experience, has no single view of death. Life and death are not simply presented as logical opposites, for both belong to human existence as it issues from God. In the Rabbinic tradition, death is usually seen as a normal part of created existence; Adam, created out of dust, returns to dust. Death is a natural limitation to existence. Death is one thing when it comes to an elderly person, and another when it comes to a young person. In light of the creation story, death can be viewed as the consequences of sin.

Yet the basic concern in the Hebrew scriptures is for life. The God of Israel is the Living One (Deut 5:26; 2 Kgs 19:4; Ps 42:3). God is the source of and giver of life (Ps 36:9). Coming so fully from God, life must be considered as the highest of God's gifts; life is God's original blessing. Life is *shalom* or well-being; it is the good life in the here and now.

Since life issues from God, and from God alone, it is not an autonomous and inherent power of human existence, but is it totally dependent on God. It is God who gives life; it is God who withdraws life; God has authority over both life and death. "Good and evil, life and death, poverty and riches are from the Lord" (Sir 11:14). An essential dimension of life is the right relationship to God, for life is not understood simply as *bios* but as life-with-God. Death can therefore be understood as opposed to life in all of its manifestations. Death is all the non-life experienced in the course of one's existence: adversity, suffering, oppression, sickness. Death itself, though, is irreversible for once one is in Sheol, there is no deliverance. "For there is hope for a tree if it be cut down, that it will sprout again and that its shoots will not cease.... But man dies and is laid low; man breathes his last, and where is he?" (Job 14:7-10).

The influence of divine power seems to come to an end at the threshold of Sheol. Death is an event that comes between God and the individual, for death sets the seal for separation from God. Death is relationlessness, for Sheol is a realm of God's absence. "I am like one forsaken among the dead ... like those whom thou dost remember no more. For they are cut off from thy hand" (Ps 88:5).

In the OT there is a certain ambivalence concerning death. On the one hand, death is a limitation of human existence wanted by God, yet as a situation of unrelatedness to God, of disconnectedness, it can also be understood as a punishment on the part of God, as something unnatural, even as a curse (Gen 2:17; 3:19). And here lies the ambiguity of the OT concept of death. How can God be source of life, as shalom, and of death, as relationlessness. Since death has no power of its own and dualism plays no role in the OT, death becomes a question about God. Israel was essentially agnostic when it came to questions concerning the afterlife. Immortality was conceived in light of Israel's ideas of corporate personality: Israel as the basic unit of existence will remain. Yet the destiny and eternal salvation of the individual was bound to arise. Such questioning begins in the post-exilic period (Dan 12:2; 2 Macc 7). The breakthrough is clearly the result of Israel's on-going faith in God as the living God whose life-giving presence must overcome death itself. Relationship to God must survive death itself.

Death in the New Testament

For Christianity from its beginning death became redefined by the death and resurrection of Jesus. In life and in death we are under the lordship of Jesus Christ. By taking death upon himself, God has set us free both to live and to die. "If we live, we live to the Lord, and if we die, we die to the Lord; so then, whether we live or whether we die we are the Lord's" (Rom 14:8). In the NT, the question of death takes on a moral and theological dimension. "The last enemy to be destroyed is death" (1 Cor 15:26). Finitude and mortality are essential components of the finite embodied human condition. As such they are not sinful; they become an occasion for sin when they become the ultimate concern of human existence, when life is all that is sought for. When that happens mortality becomes "death" in the Pauline sense. And death enters into the theological realm.

Paul says that to be in sin is to be under the domination of death. Death in this sense is the ongoing attempt to hold on to life as one's own possession. The terror of death is the fear of losing ourselves. The wages of sin is death, for the roots of sin is domination and possessiveness. Death becomes an enemy apart from relation to God the giver and sustainer of life.

In the NT, death as a question about God's character is answered in terms of the paschal mystery. God is not only a God of the living but also a God of the dead. In Christ's death, God bears the relationlessness of death and in so doing reveals Godself as love.

Jesus' resurrection is a promise that ultimately we will not be abandoned, but not a promise that God will remove our suffering, pain and death. Jesus offers no palliatives for death in his cry from the cross. Even in the context of hope in the resurrection, death is recognized to be death. Death is a negative reality and this includes Jesus' death. Jesus, through his death and resurrection, turns death into a sacrament, into the expression of God's effective presence in human existence; God does make good with the life originally called into existence.

Death in the Christian Tradition

As we move into the Christian tradition, the theology of death becomes a theology of the afterlife, with its focus on the immortality of the soul. Within that perspective, death is described as the separation of the body from the soul. The emphasis in the patristic period is on salvation from death and the attainment of eternal life. This doctrine of salvation as the overcoming of death is present in liturgies and in the patristic writings. Without such a doctrine, no substantial happiness would be possible since death itself is inevitable. According to Justin, Christians are no longer afraid of death; indeed, they can even rejoice in death because of the promise of immortality, for salvation expresses itself in incorruption.

Salvation from death is intrinsically connected to salvation from sin. In fact, remission of sins in baptism is related to deliverance from death: with deliverance from death came a new life and regeneration. Death as the fundamental expression of human vulnerability and corruptibility stands in the way of man/woman's divinization. Salvation is a restoration of incorruptibility, and therefore a destruction of death. The emphasis is on death as a consequence of sin. That death is a consequence of sin is affirmed at the Council of Trent (D.S., 223).

Specific church teachings on death are rare. Several important statements have been made in our contemporary period. Vatican II, in its pastoral constitution *Gaudium et spes*, deals with the reality of death in a unique way. It does so in the context of a christological humanism where Christ is presented as the full revelation of what it means to be human. The text presents a coherent and existential understanding of death, reaffirming the anxiety produced by the inevitability of death. "It is in regard to death that man's [sic] condition is most shrouded in doubt" (G.S., 18). Yet there is a basic desire for eternal life. "A deep instinct leads him [sic] rightly to shrink from and to reject the utter ruin and total loss of his personality. Because he bears in himself the seed of eternity ... he rebels against death" (*ibid.*). While the human person cannot avoid death, yet his/her destiny is for eternal life.

Death is clearly mysterious; Christianity's answer to this mystery is another mystery, the paschal mystery. Humanity is destined to pass from death to life through Christ. The mystery of Christ and the mystery of man/woman are the same mystery. "Such is the nature and the greatness of the mystery of man [sic] as enlightened for the faithful by the Christian revelation. It is therefore through Christ, and in Christ, that light is thrown on the mystery [riddle] of suffering and death which, apart from his Gospel, overwhelms us" (22).

In 1979 the Congregration for the Doctrine of the Faith in its "Instruction on Certain Questions Concerning Eschatology" emphasized the need to acknowledge the existence of a fundamental continuity as well as a radical discontinuity between present and future lives. To ignore this radical discontinuity would be to ignore the finality of death and the uniqueness of historical existence. A creative tension must be maintained between the two spheres.

Death in Contemporary Theology

Theologians today approach death not primarily in terms of the afterlife, and not simply as a point at the end of life, but rather as a pervasive dimension of one's total existence. Death is not excluded from the experience of life, and no theological anthropology is possible without asking about the significance of death. The theology of death is clearly indebted to contemporary philosophical and psychological approaches.

For Martin Heidegger, death does not merely represent the last moment in man/woman's life, but even casts its shadow on the totality of life. Dying is a mode of being, which concerns man/woman existentially so that human existence must be regarded as being-to-death and therefore to be defined only in light of death. It is precisely death that allows human life to have meaning. To live in a realistic anticipation of death is to accept boundaries and to live with some purpose. Meaning is to be found within human life, not by ignoring mortality and finitude, but by taking the inevitability of death fully and frankly into account.

Jean-Paul Sartre made Heidegger's analysis the starting point of his own approach. Like Heidegger, Sartre sees life's mortality as an essential element of human existence. Unlike Heidegger, death is not opportunity for life, but purely a brutal, fortuitous fact, beyond our understanding. As such it leads to the removal of possibilities and the fragmentation of existence; death is the reverse side of freedom. Death deprives life of all meaning; the end of human existence in death is absolute meaninglessness—it is absurdity itself.

The more death is seen as a boundary that robs life of much—if not all—of its meaning, the more the individual and even society is forced to choose between capitulation or affirmation, despair or trust. Contemporary approaches to death make evident why denial and repression are deeply operative in our approaches to death. The pervasiveness of death leads Ernest Becker to affirm that the effort to repress the terror of death is the very foundation of all human culture. Humans cannot live without limiting their perception of reality; in the face of death there is a need to build an armor to protect ourselves. The basic fact of human reality is the realization that one has no control over death or over the meaning of one's life.

Becker's anthropology is centered on the conviction that the consciousness of one's mortality provides the key to understanding the human condition. Failure to cope with personal mortality leads to mental illness, and the denial of death is the core of most neuroses.

Contemporary approaches to death have forced Christian theology to concentrate on death not simply in the abstract, but as a concrete process, as dying. Death can no longer be considered as the instant when life finally ends, but as a recurrent experience where life itself is failing, such as in illness, as in losses and separations. Every illness, every loss is a dying, so that death is going on within us at all times.

Death as a Personal Act

The most important theological development concerning death is its emphasis on the personal nature of death.

According to Karl Rahner, because man / woman is a union of nature and person, death has two dimensions, a personal and a natural one. Because men and women always appear within a spatio-temporal world, over which they have no absolute control, their death will always have a natural aspect. Death is something which happens to them. Biologically, the human organism wears out. It weakens and collapses, or it is destroyed. In its personal aspect, though, death is something active and performed, not simply passive and suffered. Because human persons are free, they have the ability to dispose of themselves. In its personal aspect, then, death can be the culmination of personal history of freedom. As a person, one can assume a stance at the end of one's journey, a stance of acceptance or of rejection. "The end of man [sic] as a spiritual person is an active consummation from within, a bringing of himself to completion. A growth that preserves the issue of his life; it is total entry into possession of himself, the fullness of the being he has become by all his free acts" (K. Rahner, H. Vorgrimler, 117). Dying is an active personal consummation and maturation of what is already present in a person's life. Death is the ultimate act of human freedom which gathers up and in some way gives meaning to all the individual events that go into making up one's life. It is in the personal nature of death that the reality of sin plays a role. Biological death cannot be seen as a consequence of sin for death belongs to human finitude rather than to human sin. Yet in a sinful world, death as the dissolution of human personhood assumes terrors and anxieties of its own. Death is the dissolution of the person and of the personal realm.

Contemporary insights into the nature of persons are helpful in discerning all the implications of death as personal. According to many contemporary authors, the personal is essentially interpersonal. There is a for-otherness that is constitutive of the person as person. I am the person I am precisely because of my relationship to this history, this family, these friends. The personal is constituted by personal relatedness, by its relation to the other self. As a person, I begin to exist as one pole in the complex "you and I." The personal is constituted by personal relatedness.

From birth to death, the human environment, the human ecological context, is an interpersonal one. Life begins as a process of attachment, of separation and of bonding, of interconnectedness, and interdependence. The interpersonal context, the "holding environment," provides for a variety of needs such as security and place, social integration and friendship nurturing, reassurance of worth leading to self-esteem. Meaning never develops in a vacuum; it is always embedded in a specific context, in a web of relationships. The interpersonal context leads to structures of meaning. These are organized structures of understanding and emotional attachments by which individuals interpret and assimilate their environment. Personal meaning includes, therefore, a sense of attachment as well as of understanding, as when we say that something means a great deal. Clearly then, one of the most important products of relationships is the emergence of structures of meaning that are essential to our existence. Meanings are learned in the context of specific relationships and circumstances. Meanings and purposes are learned and consolidated through a lifetime's experience, are embodied in the relationships which sustain them.

With the emphasis on personhood as relational, and meaningfulness as interpersonal, the death of a person is the dissolution not only of an individual but of meaningfulness and of personal environment. Death strikes directly at the human person by threatening the person with radical relationlessness. Since communication, the ability to communicate and to receive communication, is a constitutional element of the person, death manifests itself in the absence of communication. Life consists in active participation in a set of relationships. Death for its part means the destruction of what has been slowly built up and has come to form the very fabric of a personal existence. The problem of death does not arise primarily because of our biological reality, but because of the unconditional and the uniqueness that is personhood. Death becomes a problem because it ends something unique and therefore is something more and other than a natural process. So human dying transcends medical and biological definition.

Because of the interpersonal nature of personhood, every threat to human solidarity and interdependence is perceived as personal threat. But whenever communication is fostered, community nurtured, relationships encouraged, death becomes more acceptable. This implies that there is a personal ecology to death and dying: at the core of this ecology is care. There is a responsibility to uphold the human dignity of the other person in their process of dying, and therefore the ecological system of human family and community may not be replaced by any other institution, medical or otherwise. In a personal world there can be no abdication of the care role to any institutions.

The personal nature of death and dying also implies the upholding of truthfulness, for the ultimate betrayal of personhood is to deceive another about his or her death. While there are many reasons to conceal the truth about death, such as the therapeutic and existential value of hope, yet awareness of death is also a fundamental element of the truth of life. We uphold each other not by concealing the truth about death, but by bringing this truth within the reality of personal existence.

Emphasis on human death as death of a person must also have an influence on the criteria used to certify death. The death of a human being cannot simply be conceived as the death of an organism . In determining what constitutes the death of a human being, we must consider the conditions of existence and non-existence of persons. The bare continuation of organismic function cannot be justified, for the concept of death is not simply the concept of the cessation of life.

The loss of temporality of embodiment, of holding environment, is a radical deprivation of essential elements of personal existence. It is death seen in its personal aspect that can also lead to a renewed understanding of immortality. The bond of personal relationship transcends distance and time, and can in a similar way bridge the gap of death. There is something about belonging at the personal level of existence that can prevail over the physical separation of death. Communion with the living and the dead is based on memory, on remembrance. Remembering is a fundamental element of personal belonging and of the interpersonal world. Within the Christian perspective the interpersonal world extends beyond this time and space.

The communion of saints means that we form a society with those who have lived and died in fellowship with Christ. Since personal existence is communal and interdependent, death within the Christian framework can be perceived as a transition from one form of personal existence to another, in continuity and discontinuity with this present life. What cannot be brought to an end with one's death is one's community. Within the paschal mystery, God remembers the dead for God is a God of the living and the dead. "Nothing can separate us from the love of God as manifested in Christ...." Solidarity with God and God's community remains; meaning is permanently attached to a community of love that death cannot in any way destroy. Within the Christian context, the death of a person does not mean entry into another world that is alien and inaccessible to the living. Within our human and temporal/spatial context, death is a loss of the I-Thou relationship and therefore a reduction to being an "It." Yet at another level, death itself cannot destroy a personal relation to God. The I-Thou relationship with God can be severed only by sin. Solidarity with God in Jesus means salvation from death.

Death and the Christian Sacraments

Within the framework of the paschal mystery, the binary opposition of life and death is resolved in a positive and meaningful way without denying the negativity of death: the mystery of Christian faith is that through dying, Christ conquers death and is life-giving. Both baptism and the eucharist are the two sacraments that ritualize most fully the paschal mystery. Baptism celebrates participation in the paschal mystery and the eucharist re-enacts it. Baptism is imaged as a participation in the death of Christ so that life in Christ might be secured. In baptism, one is immersed into water to die so that one might rise to new life in Christ as a member of his body, the church. In the eucharist this new life is nurtured, sustained and ritualized.

In its "Rite of Christian Death and Burial," the church emphasizes the interpersonal dimension of life and death. The church ritualizes the passage from life to death. Death is a liminal experience for the bereaved. The ritual of funeral and burial are rites of memory and change of status. The deceased is introduced into the realm of the dead as well as into the community of living with a new status. This new status must bring about a new relationship for the bereaved and the community of the living. After an individual's death, the focus is the family, the friends and the community of the deceased. Not only is the deceased person commended to God, but also the community and its hope. The ritual recalls the sacramental life of the deceased and identifies his/her future as being-with-Christ. The celebration of the eucharist at a funeral is an affirmation of the community that the deceased sought meaning in life and discovered such meaning in the person of Jesus Christ. In the celebration of the eucharist not only is the deceased commended to God but also the community. While the ritual identifies the future of the deceased as that of being-with-Christ, it promises this same future for the bereaving community. In celebrating the eucharist the community manifests and expresses its understanding of life and death and affirms that the deceased shared in this same meaningfulness. The worshipping community, as it proclaims the victory of Christ over death, intensifies its faith in the paschal mystery. In the sacramental life of the church and its worship, death is personalized.

To personalize death is not to privatize it, but it is to emphasize its social context. Without the Christian community death might well be meaningless. Without a community the solitariness of life would be the final victor in death. Loneliness in life is only a faint image of the isolation incurred when death happens without community. If meaning is found by incorporation into Christ, then the meaning itself is in and through the community of the body of Christ, the church.

Emphasizing the social nature of death should lead to a greater engagement with the concerns of this world. According to Leander Keck, "the starting point for a theology of death and of resurrection is moral outrage against the world in which there appears to be no justice on which the weak can count ..." (Keck, 97). The struggle for justice and the transformation of this world cannot be sustained when the fear of death leads to debilitating bondage. The paschal mystery is a symbol of the ultimate triumph of justice. The power of death pervades many economic and political structures. Moral outrage against such deaths is expressed in the sacramental life of the church. For the sacraments are anticipatory and mediating signs of ultimate justice and solidarity with God. They are symbols of protest, subversive acts, serving to unmask the injustice of an existence that perceives this time, this space, as all there is. The paschal mystery, sacramentalized in all of the Christian sacraments summons us to resistance to all personal and communal death and to liberating action in our world. The sacraments mediate, nourish, and keep alive fundamental hope in the liberating love of God. At the same time, the sacramental liturgy is the place where men and women can be made aware of the reality of their situation, of the "not yet" and pilgrim nature of their situation, of their creaturehood.

In an existence marked by conflict, the sacraments are signs of contradiction and of the possibility of an alternative vision. In their signifying role, they function prophetically in announcing universal salvation, universal peace, the overcoming of death in all of its modalities. As proclaimed in the last words of the Christian scriptures, "he will wipe away every tear from their eyes, and death shall be no more, neither shall there be mourning nor crying nor pain any more, for the former things have passed away" (Rev 21:4).

See **Burial, Christian; Funerals, preaching at**

Ladislaus Boros, *The Mystery of Death* (New York: The Seabury Press, 1965). Andre Godin, *Death and Presence: The Psychology of Death and the Afterlife* (Brussels: Lumen Vitae Press, 1972). Monika Hellwig, *What are they Saying About Death and Christian Hope?* (New York: Paulist Press, 1978). Robert J. Hoeffner, "A Pastoral Evaluation of the Rite of Funerals," *Worship* 55 (November 1981): 482-499. Eberhard Jungel, *Death: The Riddle and the Mystery*. Trans. by Ian and Ute Nicol (Philadelphia: Westminster Press, 1974).

Leander Keck, "New Testament Views of Death," in Liston Mills, ed., *Perspectives on Death* (Nashville: Abingdon, 1966), 33-98. Arthur C. McGill, *Death and Life. An American Theology* (Philadelphia: Fortress Press, 1987). Karl Rahner, *On the Theology of Death* (New York: Herder and Herder, 1965). Lawrence O. Richards and Paul Johnson, *Death and the Caring Community* (Portland: Multnomah Press, 1980). Michael Simpson, *The Facts of Death* (Englewood Cliffs, NJ: Prentice-Hall, 1979). Walter Smith, S.J., *Dying in the Human Cycle: Psychological, Biomedical and Social Perspectives* (New York: Holt, Rinehart and Winston, 1985). Helmut Thielicke, *Living With Death*, Trans. by Geoffrey W. Bromiley (Grand Rapids: Eerdmans, 1983).

LUCIEN J. RICHARD, O.M.I.

DEVOTIONS, POPULAR

Different approaches to the task of defining and describing popular devotions yield complementary understandings of the devotions themselves, and thus a deeper appreciation of them.

Legal Definition

Definition in legal terms is the clearest and most precise. In the strictest legal sense, popular devotions are peculiar to Roman Catholic worship. They are religious exercises—prayers, methods of meditation, orders of service, rituals, gestures—whose texts and rubrics are not contained in the official liturgical books of the Roman rite. Examples of popular devotions that were almost universally observed in the years just preceding Vatican II are: the rosary of the Blessed Virgin Mary, the Way of the Cross, eucharistic communion in honor of the Sacred Heart of Jesus on the first Fridays of nine consecutive months, and novenas (nine consecutive days of prayer) for various occasions or in honor of various heavenly patrons. Themes characteristic of these devotional exercises are also called devotions. Thus, devotion to the mercy of God or to our Lady of Lourdes.

Popular devotions have been and continue to be an important part of the Roman Catholic religious experience. Though some devotions are by their nature either for public and communal use or for private and individual use most of them may be observed either by individuals or groups. The devotions are clearly recognized by church authorities at every level as authentic and for the most part praiseworthy forms of Catholic worship, and they are frequently mentioned in church documents. Nonetheless, their status is somehow inferior or at least other than official: they are Catholic worship but not Catholic liturgy in the strict sense.

The twinned character of Roman Catholic worship, composed of the official liturgy and popular devotions yoked together in tandem, is a consequence of the reform of Catholic worship that occurred in the wake of the Council of Trent. In the third quarter of the 16th century, the content and extent of the official liturgy were determined in a new way by the issuance of authoritative liturgical books intended for the first time for uniform use in almost all the churches of the Latin rite. Whatever did not find a place in the books of the new worldwide Roman rite—no matter how widely practiced in other parts of the Latin West and no matter what its propriety and utility—was considered in a legal sense non-liturgical. Explicit authorization by the central Roman authority in time came to be considered an essential characteristic of the authentic Roman liturgy. And so rites that became universally popular after the appearance of the official books were practically incapable of attaining official status. Thus, for example, the Forty Hours devotion in honor of the reserved sacrament, though imposed by authority and usually celebrated in parishes and religious communities as one of the greatest solemnities of the church year, remained still just a devotion. It was, paradoxically, a devotion composed principally of a chain of strictly liturgical services. On the other hand, some themes that arose in popular devotions have found a place in the official church calendar and are observed in the official liturgy of the church with Masses and offices, for example, on feastdays dedicated to Jesus and Mary under different titles, as the Sacred Heart of Jesus, or Our Lady of Sorrows.

Though the distinction between popular devotions and the official liturgy dates from the period following the Council of Trent, many of the Western ways of worship later to be identified as popular devotions had flourished since the Middle Ages.

Some Western popular devotions have been imported into some of the Catholic Eastern churches, with different degrees of sensitivity about and adaptation to the different ecclesial settings. Phenomena analogous to Roman Catholic popular devotions are also found in some non-Catholic Eastern and Reformation churches.

Devotions and the Religious Emotions
If a legal approach to understanding popular devotions focuses on their popular, that is, non-official character, a second way of understanding considers them precisely as causes and effects of religious devotion. All forms of Christian worship, and especially those which are frequently and communally celebrated, express and form the consciousness of Christian believers. The emotional component of the Christian consciousness, which is set in resonance and is tuned by the experience of Christian worship, is called devotion. This complex of emotions and habits of feeling includes admiration at the wonderful works of God, security in God's loving providential care, familiarity with Jesus and the saints, the habit of praying frequently and specifically about concrete events, and joy in companionship with other believers.

Popular devotions express and foster devotion—the religious feelings of worshippers. Precisely for that reason the popular devotions reached such prominence in the worship life of the Roman Catholic church. The devotions compensated for a deficit in the ability of the official Roman liturgy to engage the emotions of believers. Roman prayer texts, in comparison with those of other ancient classical liturgies, are concise, elegant, rational—just as the Roman style in ritual too is restrained and utilitarian. Classical Roman prayers do speak about religious emotions, but in a distant and abstract way, as theological concepts rather than as actual experiences. They are prayers of the head and not of the heart. They do not express and cannot well engender emotion.

More importantly, for most of its history the Roman liturgy was celebrated in a language not directly intelligible to most of the worshippers. Both during liturgical services and in supplementary exercises, something had to be done "to occupy the people." These "somethings" were popular devotions.

The non-professional worshipper at the Tridentine liturgy—whether the eucharist or the divine office—was something like an intelligent and interested visitor to an important national archive. The visitor knows that significant treasures are safeguarded there, a few of the more spectacular of which are elegantly displayed. And the visitor realizes that the treasures are available as needed through the mediation of trusted, well-trained experts. But for all practical purposes, the visitor's experience of the archive is contained in and controlled by the guidebook in the visitor's hand. The actual Tridentine liturgy was in many ways an acted-out archive, and the trusty guidebook was some form of popular devotion.

A Principle of Liturgical Evolution

The special cultural and linguistic situation of the Roman rite has proved to have been a particularly favorable medium in which popular devotions could root and flourish. But there is a third way of understanding popular devotions which is founded upon a consideration of factors and tendencies common in the evolution of all Christian liturgies. Phenomena like popular devotions are generated whenever Christian liturgies grow.

There is about all Christian liturgy a givenness: the liturgy is always in the first instance something "handed on"—from one church to another and from one culture to another. Adjustments, accommodations, exploitations of the given in its new situation always take place. The adjustment may be as obvious as translation into a new language or a change of movements to fit a new physical space. Or the elaborations may over time respond to differences in the sense of cultural and religious propriety. Thus the classical liturgical families have developed different ways of ritualizing the so-called soft spots of the eucharistic liturgy. Such soft spots include all that precedes the readings; the space between the liturgy of the word and the eucharistic prayer itself, in which items like the transfer of the bread and wine and the approach of the ministers to the altar may be ceremonialized; and again the space between the end of the eucharistic prayer and communion. These elaborations, which introduce and link the more primitive "givens" of the Christian eucharist, have much of the character of popular devotions.

Elaborate processional and stational arrangements preceded the solemn papal and patriarchal liturgies of Rome and Constantinople, and have had lasting influence on the classical forms of the Roman and Orthodox eucharistic liturgies. Had these preliminary rites been invented a thousand years later, they would have fallen into the category of popular devotions. The church of Jerusalem in the 4th century created the weekly Sunday morning commemoration of the resurrection and the veneration of the cross for Good Friday. Both have become part of the liturgical heritage of many of the ancient churches. Had these rites become widespread in the 18th century, they would be popular devotions. The Way of the Cross, a Counter-Reformation import from Jerusalem in many respects analogous to the earlier veneration of the cross, is proving to be one of the most resilient of the devotions. If it were twelve hundred years older, it would be liturgy.

The impulse or genius that enables all Christian churches to make the originally received liturgy at home in new physical, linguistic, and cultural settings is the impulse or genius that creates popular devotions. The spirit that makes devotions is not optional but intrinsic. The devotional bent is not a somehow baleful tendency to the periphery, but a principle central to the evolution and transmission of the Christian liturgy.

A Form of Cathedral Worship

A fourth way of understanding popular devotions employs the distinction between the cathedral and monastic forms of liturgy. The cathedral-monastic distinction applies originally to styles of the liturgy of the hours, but it has implications important for the understanding of all kinds of communal worship.

Monastic worship developed initially to serve the needs of monks and nuns. It also tends to arise among religious professionals of any kind, when they pray with their own kind or design liturgies to cater to their own needs and tastes. Religious professionals are people with extreme familiarity with the religious sector of life, in whom a state of preparedness for worship (something like a state of recollection) can be assumed. Monastic worshippers in this sense would include in addition to monks and nuns: clergy; directors of liturgy, church music,

and religious education; campus ministers and their devotees. Monastic worship is long and long on text. It is thematically diffuse, relatively non-melodic, straightline in structure, unritualized, unconcerned with specific, transient situations (times of the day, natural seasons of the year, concrete needs), and full of variety. Monastic worship is characterized by intensity, motionlessness, closed eyes, postures of repose.

Cathedral worship is designed to be used by groups of ordinary Christians—laypersons led in prayer by the clergy. Though the word *cathedral* today implies grandeur, formality, hierarchical sensitivity, and rubrical precision, these connotations are misleading in this case. *Cathedral* here means parochial or popular. Specifically religious categories occupy only a relatively small part of the attention of ordinary believers. Cathedral worship is therefore fashioned to help the worshipper to cross the threshold between life "out there," with its legitimate concerns and beguilements, and life within the fields of force of the Christian community at prayer. Cathedral worship is relatively brief and has relatively little text. It is obvious, christocentric and staurocentric (i.e., cross-centered) in theme, melodic, spiral in structure, highly ritualized, concerned with concrete and specific persons and situations, and very repetitive. Cathedral worship is intrinsically initiatory: it comes in a series of similar small parcels which do not demand an extended attention span for their effectiveness.

Popular devotions, compared to the corresponding official liturgy, fall squarely within the category of cathedral worship. They represent the continuance of that strain in the prayer life of the Latin West in a hidden way, after the almost total monasticization of the liturgy of the hours removed the divine office from the comprehension of the ordinary faithful.

Medieval Beginnings

Though the dynamic which creates popular devotions is common to Christian worship in all its embodiments, the first forms of worship later to be identified as popular devotions can be traced to Western monastic reforms of the 8th century. The received monastic form of the liturgy of the hours, as laid out in the Rule of Saint Benedict, was supplemented with other prayers and offices. Among these were the gradual psalms, the penitential psalms, the Office of the Dead, and the Office of All Saints, soon supplanted by the Office of the Blessed Virgin Mary.

These prayers and services were in time universally celebrated intermingled with the older canonical hours of the original Benedictine monastic office. These new forms of worship are often given the name "accretions," and they are conventionally cited as examples of the lush overgrowth of the medieval Western liturgy that was to choke off the blooming spirit of authentic worship. In fact, the origins and subsequent history of these devotions make it just as reasonable to suppose that they originated precisely when the received monastic office was becoming inadequate as a vehicle for the real worship of the monks, and that most of the real communal praying of medieval monasteries took place during the devotional offices rather than during the adjacent canonical hours.

However that may be, the devotional offices were soon separated from their original setting and gathered together to form the nucleus of a collection of prayers called in English the Primer. This book of hours, first in Latin and then in the various vernaculars, and enriched over the centuries with other items, remained the prayer book of choice for the literate laity up through the 18th century. Nonclerical religious communities commonly used the Office of the Blessed Virgin as their form of hour prayer until the reforms following Vatican II.

The devotional offices were in structure and content exactly like their canonical counterparts. The elements (psalms, antiphons, readings, hymns, responsories, collects) were all arranged in the traditional way. But the selection was attractive: favorite psalms, often those already familiar from the Sunday canonical office; antiphons sometimes stunningly beautiful in language; central, obvious, evangelical themes. And there was only one office of each kind, to be used almost without variation each day of the year. Other office devotions, called little offices, were modeled on the commemorations that concluded the principal hours of the canonical liturgy of the hours. They were thematically unified; when possible, events chronicled in the scriptures were commemorated at the appropriate hour of the day, as in the hours of the Passion or of the Holy Spirit. Sometimes these offices were keyed to and associated with specific days of the week.

If one begins by assuming that the rangy, opaque, and diffuse canonical hour prayers of the medieval Western church are essential and the norm, then obviously the devotional offices will seem unessential and excessive. If the old office is the meal, then the new offices have to be the dessert. But if one compares the canonical office and the adjacent devotional offices as vessels of Christian prayer, then the devotional offices may well seem essential and appropriate, and the monastic canonical office more like an accumulation of accretions. The meat and drink of Christian prayer is certainly contained in the devotional offices; their canonical counterparts, certainly not dessert, are more like roughage. In any case, it seems clear that the devotional offices are nothing but the old cathedral hour prayer, forced by the conditions of medieval religious culture to appear in monastic garb.

Counter-Reformation Developments

Another kind of popular devotion had its origins not in a reformulation of the liturgy of the hours, but as an elaboration of specific observances in the calendars of some of the northern European churches. These services had long been intrinsic to and important in the life of these churches, but they fell into the category of popular devotions because they had not been observed at Rome and thus did not appear in the books of the purified Roman liturgy. Such devotions were thus free to continue to evolve during the Counter-Reformation period. In time the role played by the reserved sacrament in these devotions was enhanced, and the Blessed Sacrament became the popular focus of the re-enactment in worship of the death, burial, and resurrection of Jesus. These rites were frequented by crowds of enthusiastic worshippers in centuries when some of the strictly liturgical rites had become the province of the very devout few. While the clergy were picking their way through the rubrical thicket of the prescribed Easter vigil, anticipated early in the morning of Holy Saturday in the chancels of nearly empty churches, the popular paschal worship of the northern churches focused on the absolutely obvious public vigil before the hidden reserved eucharist in remembrance of the Lord's burial, and on the evidently triumphal eucharistic procession at dawn on Easter Sunday in commemoration of his rising from the dead.

Other devotions arose during the Counter-Reformation as means of mediating the official liturgy to worshippers. Medieval Mass-goers were taught to worship by looking: to follow and interpret the movements of the liturgical ministers, to study and to take to heart the great crucifix on the screen between the chancel and the nave, and to gaze with adoration at the sacred host when it was elevated during Mass.

Counter-Reformation Mass devotions are more verbal. In Catholic countries in which the vernacular tongue was not a romance language, programs of metrical hymns were composed to accompany the Mass. The congregation sang these songs in their own language to popular melodies while the priest and his assistants recited the official liturgy quietly in Latin. These early folk Masses paraphrase parts of the ordinary of the Mass (singing direct translations was forbidden). Or they are catechetical interpretations of the soft spots in the Mass liturgy.

In places where and on occasions when Mass hymns were not used, the laity not literate in Latin were expected to participate in the eucharist through some form of popular devotion. It might be the recitation of the rosary, sometimes communally but more frequently privately; or reflecting upon a sequence of written suggestions for meditation during Mass; or silently reading a series of prayers that paraphrased the official text of the Mass. In the generation immediately before Vatican II, the use of vernacular hand missals with close translations of the Latin text had become relatively common in some places. The translated text of the liturgy itself had become a Mass devotion, and the layperson became as adept as the priest at setting ribbon markers and flipping pages.

During the centuries between Trent and Vatican II, vernacular Mass devotions functioned as a kind of verbal icon screen. In one way they shielded the literal content of the official liturgy from ordinary worshippers; in another and more important way they revealed the meaning of the liturgy to laypersons in words they could understand and feel.

The liturgy of the hours was also given the devotional treatment. In some places a vernacular reduction of canonical vespers, shortened and simplified, was provided for use in parishes on Sundays and feastdays. More frequently, vernacular prayer services were composed in an entirely new style, reminiscent of the formal meditations that were being proposed for the private use of individuals. These prayer services exploited popular devotional themes but were also correlated with the principal seasons of the church year. They were intended for public worship on Sunday and feastday afternoons, usually in connection with canonical vespers and benediction of the Blessed Sacrament.

Exposition and Benediction

The centerpiece of Counter-Reformation popular piety was exposition of and benediction of the Blessed Sacrament. On special occasions it became the custom of some churches to expose the Blessed Sacrament in the monstrance to add solemnity to canonical vespers. Additional prayers and songs were appended to the service, and the people were blessed with the sacrament before it was replaced in the tabernacle. In time the eucharistic benediction became a separable unit that might be celebrated by itself or, more usually, in connection with some other service.

During the Counter-Reformation heyday of popular devotions, English-speaking Roman Catholics were restricted in their public church life both by minority status and penal statute. They had to be satisfied with unobtrusive observance of the minimum essential liturgical rites, and a distinctively English pattern of public popular devotions did not develop. By the mid-19th century, however, a more elaborate devotional life became possible. Its focus was the reserved sacrament. In England itself and in English-speaking lands overseas, the presence of the Blessed Sacrament rendered the sometimes poor and provisional and almost always recently constructed houses of Roman Catholic worship instantly sacred places. Prayers to the Mother of God and other heavenly patrons and Sunday vespers, an office still prescribed by local statutes to be celebrated with the people, inevitably concluded with eucharistic benediction.

The rite of benediction was highly ceremonious and easy to understand, in contrast to the inaudible low mass which was the ordinary Sunday eucharistic celebration of the same period. Eucharistic benediction unmistakably portrayed the benevolent and effective presence of the Lord in the midst of the church, and at the same time enabled worshippers to adore him clearly, directly, and graciously. It is probable that until the reforms mandated by Vatican II, the popular Roman Catholic sense of the meaning of the eucharist and the church was primarily formed by the experience of popular devotions to the Blessed Sacrament rather than by participation in Mass and the reception of holy communion.

Official and Professional Evaluations

Since the beginnings of widespread liturgical renewal in the years immediately preceding Vatican II, the attitude of church authority towards the popular devotions may be described as balanced and reserved. The Vatican II *Constitution on the Sacred Liturgy* maintains the distinction between devotions and the official liturgy. Devotions that conform to church laws and norms are recommended; they form part of the actual, though extra-liturgical, spiritual life of the church. Devotions which have long been part of the distinctive worship life of local churches deserve special esteem. The devotions should be oriented towards the official liturgy, which by its very nature is superior to them. Devotions should harmonize with the seasons of the church year. Devotions should lead people to the official liturgy. Church leaders, both by exhortation and example, have continued to foster a few central and almost universally observed devotions, like the Angelus, the rosary, and the Way of the Cross.

Popular liturgical reformers at first tended to view the devotions as obstacles to successful liturgical renewal. The devotions were, to superficial analysis anyway, patently "unliturgical." They did not seem to follow the supposed principles of authentic liturgy with regard to structure, content, and style. They were criticized as being practically bereft of the formal proclamation of scripture, tending to inculcate an individualistic and subjective piety. They were said to be unresponsive to the rhythms of the liturgical calendar, repetitious, and sentimental.

It is reasonable to assume that the real problem with the devotions was precisely that they were popular—frequented by many worshippers who seemed to be enjoying themselves—while the "liturgical" concoctions sometimes proposed to supplant them were not. Attempts to reform existing devotions or to create new ones have generally not been successful. Substitutes for the devotional services, often called "paraliturgies," mimicked liturgical forms, with much Bible reading and self-conscious use of symbolic gestures. The didactic element was strong and sometimes not straightforwardly advertised: worshippers expecting to be enabled to sympathize with the Lord in his sufferings might find themselves subjected to a lesson on the human suffering engendered by worldwide socio-economic injustice.

If the devotions have not fared well of late as means of worship, they have recently attracted the attention of thinkers and pastors for other reasons. For the years between Trent and Vatican II especially, the devotions provide privileged access to the religious experience and understanding of different generations, social classes, ethnic and political groupings and local churches. Scholars in women's studies note that some of the most prominent and successful devotions were initiated by women, and certainly most of the devotions were practiced mainly by women. If the official Roman liturgy can be fairly characterized as stereotypically masculine, then surely the popular devotions are stereotypically feminine. Reflection on the cathedral character of the devotions yields precious insights into the dynamic of all Christian prayer, both individual and communal. Some observers have suggested that movements for church renewal in Latin America would be strengthened by incorporating rather than ignoring the already existing devotional religion of the people. Some devotions, long associated with particular ethnic groups and until now practiced almost exclusively by them, are being appreciated both because they embody an experience of the gospel distinctive of their parent group and are potentially enriching for the larger church.

Present Status

Former appraisals of the relative value and propriety of the official liturgy and the devotions are no longer of interest. The changes in worship mandated by Vatican II have blurred the distinction between liturgy and devotions, and for many reasons the devotions are no longer so widely practiced. The many different novena forms common in the United States were usually couched in an idiom and style, both in language and music, that have become quaint and unsatisfying. The devotional occasion *par excellence*— afternoon or evening services in church— has been occupied by the afternoon celebration of the eucharistic liturgy, formerly possible only in the morning. Much of the appeal of the devotions lies in the use of the vernacular language, familiar expression, and light music; but now all of these find a place in the official liturgy itself. Warmth, directness, and informality in Roman Catholic worship had formerly been associated almost exclusively with the devotions, but can now be found sometimes in the official liturgy and always in the piety and styles of the Catholic charismatic movement. Explicit and detailed intercessory prayer, once a specialty of the devotions, is now a beloved moment— "the prayer of the faithful"—in most celebrations of the eucharist. And, though the typical American Catholic worshipper probably has more time to dispose of than ever before, less time is actually available for worship.

Some few great devotions are still commonly practiced, though with some diminishment. The Way of the Cross usually retains its place in the Lenten schedule of parishes. The rosary, formerly the all-purpose devotion adaptable to almost any group or religious occasion, is now only infrequently recited as a communal exercise; but there are indications that it is making a comeback as a form of individual prayer. Private devotion to the Blessed Sacrament reserved in the tabernacle still flourishes, and the recommended provision of a special chapel of reservation apart from the principal public worship area in parish churches is thought to encourage individual adoration. But the formerly common and highly prized ceremonious exposition and benediction of the Blessed Sacrament now seems somehow incongruous and overblown. Catholic worshippers have become accustomed to a more domestic approach to eucharistic reverence: they usually receive the host in their own hands and not infrequently themselves handle the consecrated bread and wine as extraordinary ministers of communion.

Enduring Values

The great days of popular devotions are over, and no one expects to see them return. Most of the conditions which generated the devotions have been banished in the reforms of Roman Catholic worship following Vatican II.

The principle that liturgical forms inherited from the distant past are somehow immutable and obligatory is no longer assumed, and the more recent ideal of liturgical uniformity has been dismantled. Instead, the currently reigning liturgical principle is carefully guided evolution of the liturgy, and local adaptation and variation of rites have become the ideal. The authentic liturgical books of the post-Tridentine Roman rite can be carried in a single attaché case with room for the morning paper and a sandwich besides; the Roman rite of today is comprised in a library of volumes printed in scores of different languages with a bewildering variety of textual and ritual variants. Even so it makes sense to ask which characteristics of the devotions one would like to see perennially enshrined in a new system of worship for the Roman Catholic church and, indeed, for the ecumenical church as well.

First, the devotions are a reminder that it is a worthy function of Christian worship to cultivate Christian affectivity. It is fair to say that the creators of the devotions had the knack of catering to the devotion—the religious feelings—of worshippers and that liturgical planners of our time do not. A clue to understanding our insufficiency in this regard may be found in the relative absence of rubrics in the devotions; in practice they were controlled by few rules outside the comprehension and experience of the worshippers. But contemporary reformers are still very dependent on the rubric—the law from outside—for their warrant and their sense of success. Of course it is seldom any more the rubric in the book that rules, or directions from a distant central authority that control. Rather today it is members of the professional liturgical establishment—communicators about liturgy, those who work in diocesan liturgy offices, parochial directors of liturgy—who dictate and are experienced as dictating to believers—

laypersons and clergy—what their experience of worship ought to be. Yet it is possible for a liturgy to be absolutely legal both according to the rubrics in the books and the rubrics in the air, i.e., to be exact in performance, fashionable in music, contemporary in expression, up-to-date in theology, current in social awareness, and inclusive in language, and still be perceived by worshippers more as a political statement or an educational moment than a way of knowing and feeling their relationship with God. Becoming conscious of and sophisticated about the experience of actual worshippers is an important task for those responsible for the management of continuing liturgical renewal. Their questions should precede their answers.

Secondly, devotions remind us that the educative function of Christian worship operates subtly and respectfully. Instruction, in the crude sense of the transmission of data, and motivation, in the sense of an efficient goad to some particular behavior, are not prominent features of the devotions. The devotional service is conceived of as enabling the worshipper to do something rather than doing something to the worshipper. The great devotions tirelessly recount the central mysteries of the Christian faith: the incarnation, the saving passion and resurrection of the Lord, the enduring presence of Jesus in the church, the continuing intervention of the God in the course of human life. The constant repetition of the same themes is not boring precisely because its purpose is not to inform the mind but to nourish the spirit of the believer. In the devotions the worshipper is not so much one to be instructed or motivated as a privileged person, a chosen and choosing one, a powerful intercessor who shares the friendship of the saints. Briefly, the worshipper is subject, not object. And the project is formation, not information. In the work of enfranchising worshippers,

we can learn from the devotions. Though they would hardly have used the words, practitioners of the devotions were constantly treated as, and thus came to know themselves to be, members of a royal priesthood.

Finally, the devotions are a reminder that Christian worship is a kind of prayer. The devotional structure is circular or spiral. Connections are by association rather than according to logic. The devotions are shaped more like musing than like formal discourse; they are more like a conversation than a lecture. Devotions typically consist of a number of small, similar units frequently repeated. They are almost unvarying in form. The devotional predilection for sameness and repetition is an indication that prayer has expectations and satisfactions of its own, which are not easily comprehended by those who do not pray. We can learn from the devotions that the rhythms of communal and individual prayer are similar; and that variety, whatever its attractiveness in other contexts, is not the spice of liturgical prayer.

Joseph P. Chinnici, ed., *Devotion to the Holy Spirit in American Catholicism* (Mahwah NJ: Paulist, 1985). Carl Dehne, "Devotion and Devotions," *The New Dictionary of Theology*, ed., Joseph A. Komonchak and others (Wilmington, DE: Michael Glazier, Inc, 1987), 283-288. Carl Dehne, "Roman Catholic Popular Devotions," *Worship* 49 (1975): 446-460. George Guiver, *Company of Voices* (New York: Pueblo, 1988). Robert Taft, *The Liturgy of the Hours in East and West* (Collegeville MN: Liturgical Press, 1986). Ann Taves, *The Household of Faith* (Notre Dame IN: University of Notre Dame Press, 1986). J.B.L. Tolhurst, ed., *The Monastic Breviary to the English Monastic Breviaries, HBS* Vol 80 (London: Harrison and Sons, 1942).

CARL DEHNE, S.J.

DISABILITIES, LITURGY AND PERSONS WITH

Jesus proclaimed the special places marginalized people have in the life of the Christian community: when you give a feast, invite the poor, the maimed, the lame, the blind..." (Lk 14:13). He reminds us that disabilities are not, of themselves, cause for excusing and thus excluding the persons who have them from feasting at the Lord's table. Nor is the Christian community whole if any of its members are missing or thought unnecessary for its life. "The eye cannot say to the hand, 'I have no need of you', nor again the head to the feet, 'I have no need of you'. On the contrary, the parts of the body which seem to be weaker are indispensable..." (1 Cor 12:21-22). However, enabling those who "seem weaker" to take their rightful place in the community of the baptized very often requires breaking down structural barriers and barriers of the heart and mind as well. Society tends to devalue persons with disabilities, perceiving them to be among its "weaker" members. Therefore, some awareness of the nature of disabilities, viewed in relationship to the persons who have them, is important for the Christian community's understanding of itself as the mystical body of Christ which it brings to public expression in its worship.

Disability, Personhood and the Christian Life

A disability is caused by an anatomical, physiological, mental or emotional impairment which restricts or prevents a person from meeting certain life activities in the manner or range considered normal. To walk, to see, to hear, to speak, to know and understand, to behave according to societal norms—these, in varying degrees, are among the areas in which disabling conditions occur. Disabilities are present in persons of all ages; they may be permanent or temporary, visible or invisible to the eye; they affect an estimated one out of ten persons.

More importantly, these disabilities do not define the people who have them, nor diminish their value or dignity, nor express their unique strengths, potential and gifts. Joining its voice to that of the United Nations' General Assembly, the Holy See, in its statement on *The International Year of Disabled Persons* (4 March 1981), underscored the principle: "...that the disabled person (whether the disability be the result of a congenital handicap, chronic illness or accident, or from mental and physical deficiency, and whatever the severity of the disability, is a fully human subject with the corresponding innate, sacred and inviolable rights" (chap. 1, 1). In its sweeping concerns for the integration of persons with disabilities in society, the statement urged Christian parishes and youth groups to a loving care, suitable catechesis and inclusion of these persons in cultural and religious activities "so as to ensure that they will be full members of their Christian community, in accordance with their clear right to appropriate spiritual and moral education" (chap. 2, 16).

That all the baptized should come together to actively participate in the church's liturgy, "the summit towards which the activity of the Church is directed," is made abundantly clear in the *Constitution on the Sacred Liturgy* (S.C. 10, 14). The challenge confronting the Christian community includes a transformation of fears, prejudices, ignorance and apathy towards its sisters and brothers who are disabled so that the community will truly become one heart, one mind, one body.

The Whole Body of Christ at Worship

Among the pastoral statements issued by episcopal conferences addressing worship and persons with disabilities is the *Pastoral Statement of U.S. Catholic Bishops on Handicapped People* (U.S.C.C., 16 November 1978). Stressing that the local parish community is the place where, for most Catholics, the community of believers is embodied, the bishops issued the challenge of making sure that the parish "door" is always open for participation of persons with disabilities in all forms of the community's liturgical celebrations (18-24). This open door, however, includes much more than just accessible buildings. In responding, the parish must first ask itself: "Who are our disabled sisters and brothers?"

Awareness

Persons with disabilities are often the invisible members of the local Christian community, some physically absent because of structural barriers, others because of denigrating attitudes or lack of awareness and sensitivity to their needs. Many of these persons and their families have been wounded not only by society but by the human frailties of the church. If their "invisibility" or absence is presumed to mean the non-existence of any persons, young or old, with any form or degree of disability, that would simply belie the realities of life and demographic information. But it is imperative to know who and where the disabled are if we will meet their needs for presence and participation.

Many need to hear again the proclamation that Jesus healed the blind, made the lame to walk, the deaf to hear, cleansed the lepers, raised the dead, and preached the good news to the poor (Mt 11: 4-5; Lk 7:22). Census and survey taking, awareness raising, networking within the parish community and with human service agencies—all these are among the avenues for reaching-out and extending the community's invitation. Seek out those isolated in their own homes and in community residences for persons mentally and emotionally disabled. It is then that persons with disabilities and, for those unable to speak for themselves, family members and advocates can make their needs known and thereby become the primary consultants in the community's ministry with them. The "with" is essential for negating any predisposition towards condescending patronization which fails to recognize that these persons know best what they

need, and have strengths, potential and gifts to bring to the discipleship of equals which identifies the Christian community as one of interdependent relationships.

Accessibility

For persons whose mobility is in any way impaired, distant parking spaces, curbs, church stairs and hard to manage doors fail to convey a message of welcome; rather, they suggest one of "enter if you can." Such structural barriers, including the absence of outdoor and indoor tactile clues for persons visually impaired (e.g., textured floor markers), impose handicapping conditions for accessing the community's life of prayer and other shared experiences. The interior space can likewise promote either inclusiveness or isolation, depending on how accommodating it is to a person's special needs. A greeting, an offer of assistance, consideration of the extra bit of time some need to take their place—these suggest "welcome." Those who use wheelchairs or other mobility assisting devices such as a walker will appreciate a choice of where to sit within the gathered assembly provided some pews have been modified. Similarly, locations for more optimal hearing and seeing by persons in whom those faculties are impaired should be identified or provided. For some, accessible, adapted toileting facilities are critical. However, while guidelines and other resource information for removing structural barriers are readily available, the transformation of the inaccessible to the accessible ultimately depends upon the commitment of the community's heart and finances.

Additional Resources

Different disabilities, uniquely experienced by each person, inform the need for other adaptations and resources. For example, a hearing impaired person may need nothing more than to be seated closer to a well-lit sanctuary for lipreading or an amplification system for an acoustically poor environment; conversely, an assistive hearing device may be required. Some persons who are deaf "hear" through the interpreting hands of another "speaking" in sign language. A person who uses a wheelchair may well be able to put his/her gifts of proclaiming the word at the community's service if the sanctuary is accessible and a portable microphone available. Blind or visually impaired persons can likewise serve as lectors using Braille or large print lectionaries respectively. The words of the eucharistic minister can be spoken by some who are deaf. Many persons who are developmentally delayed (e.g., mentally retarded), contrary to common misconceptions, are capable of serving in many ministerial roles (e.g., eucharistic ministers, ministers of hospitality, cross bearers, altar servers) if invited and provided with preparation adapted to their mode of learning. As a final example, there is also the gift of ministry of profoundly disabled persons who, by their presence alone, serve to call the Christian community deeper into the mystery of life and the paradox of the cross.

Liturgical Celebrations: Considerations

The elements of good liturgy are at the service of enabling persons with varied disabilities actively to participate. Concrete, recurring, sumptuous symbols of our faith; color; full but simple gestures for all to share; hymns that are singable and, for the voiceless, capable of evoking the body's own response; sensitive touching and being touched in warm, accepting gestures of welcome, reconciliation, love and peace; word proclaimed; silence—all provide a range of receptive and expressive communication available to the assembly of people drawn into relationship through baptism. What an individual person with mental retardation may not be able to know and understand through abstract language may become known at the intuitive level through symbol, gesture and human interaction. Adapting some of the community's liturgies, for example, through simplified texts and more prominent use of visual elements, can serve to accommodate not only the attention span and learning modes of children and some persons with mental and emotional disabilities, but the limited physical endurance of others. This can also provide some diversity for the larger community. The *Directory on Children's Masses* (S.C.D.W., 1 November 1973) offers suggestions and guidance in this regard.

Separate liturgies, held at times other than the community's regularly scheduled liturgical celebrations, may serve certain needs for smaller groups of the community, such as persons living with disabilities, to share and reflect on their common experience. They can also be an important part of the catechesis on Christian sacramental worship for persons with mental retardation. These separate liturgies, however, should not replace a coming together with the whole community. Any inclination towards excluding oneself or those with disabilities for reasons of impaired mobility, appearance, altered speech, mannerisms and other behaviors that may be considered disruptive or socially unacceptable fosters denigration and isolation. Conversely, the heart of the community may be best known by the hospitality, support and guiding presence it gives to those in need as all take their rightful place in the worshipping assembly. There, it gives public witness to the loving, inclusive wholeness of the mystical body of Christ, a light to the world.

Henri Bissonnier, *The Pedagogy of Resurrection,* trans. by Carolyn Frederick, O.S.F. (New York: Paulist Press, 1979). Walter Kern, *Pastoral Ministry with Disabled Persons* (New York: Alba House, 1985). *Opening Doors: Ministry with Persons with Disabilities* (2 Vols.) (Washington, D.C.: National Catholic Office For Persons With Disabilities, 1987).

MADELEINE B. PROVOST

DIVORCED, MINISTRY TO THE

This article contains elements of pastoral ministry suitable for any divorced people. Because of the special situation of Roman Catholics, however, it is directed primarily to them.

The Experience of Divorcing Catholics

Divorce affects people differently depending on their particular situations and personalities. A woman in her late sixties who has several adult children and is divorced after forty years of marriage, faces concerns unlike those which confront a younger woman whose marriage of two years ends. The problems which precede a separation and the turmoil which follows vary from one divorce to another; but in each case divorce alters every aspect of a person's life. ·

Socially, divorcing people often feel isolated. Friends avoid them or stop inviting them to social gatherings and dinners. Family members may live far away, and even those who are nearby often do not know how to offer support. Less frequently now than in the past when divorce was a rarer occurrence, some families ostracize those who are divorced or relate to them with an ill-concealed superiority. At times the well-meaning sympathy of others—such as a parent's assurance that the former spouse "never was good enough for you"—adds to their own ambivalence and pain. Even when families and friends reach out to them sympathetically, divorcing people may isolate themselves, feeling inadequate or unworthy.

Economically, divorce often has a disastrous affect, especially on women. The no-fault divorce laws which prevail in most states disregard the economic inequalities which existed during the marriage and which hamper single women's efforts to support themselves and their children. Child support, often inadequate, frequently goes unpaid and can be collected only with difficulty and with additional attorney's fees. Mothers of dependent children and older women who counted on the support of their husbands' pensions and health programs, often find themselves economically devastated. Men, too, find themselves financially burdened by the cost of the divorce proceedings and by supporting a former family while trying to begin a new one.

Divorcing people speak of the emotional roller-coaster they unwittingly boarded when their marriages ended. After the initial shock lifts, they are overwhelmed by feelings of rejection, anger (at the former spouses, families and friends, themselves, God and the church), and depression. They frequently enter long periods of anxiety about the future, about their financial situations, and about a host of other practical concerns the other person used to attend to. Loneliness becomes intense. Often their spouses were their best friends as well as their most constant companions, and now they have no one to share their lives with, no one to tell their problems to, no one to ask for advice. They miss the sexual intimacy they once had; they may become promiscuous or they may avoid any physical expression of affection. They liken the dissolution of their marriages to the death of a loved one, and they resonate with Elizabeth Kubler-Ross's outline of five stages of death and dying (denial, bargaining, anger, depression, acceptance). In many cases, one person takes the initiative in acknowledging the demise of the marriage by moving out or filing for divorce. That person may begin the mourning process before the actual break-up of the marriage and feel relieved by the time the divorce proceedings begin. The other person may be completely surprised by the other's actions and begin grieving only as the other finishes. The different timetables of grief often cause bitterness ("I'm depressed and my former spouse seems satisfied, even at peace; I thought our marriage meant more than that"). It takes years for most people to recover emotionally from a divorce, and all of them report that the feelings continue to resurface during the holidays or special occasions such as anniversaries and birthdays.

Divorcing Catholics turn to the church with ambivalence, in need of comfort but fearing judgment. They think they have failed not only themselves but God, and any hint of disapproval from clergy or others connected with the local church intensifies their guilt and makes them feel isolated and unwanted. They feel out-of-place in a church which so consistently promotes marital fidelity and family life and which condemns divorce. They imagine that all other parishioners know of their situations as if they are branded with a large "D" (for divorce) on their foreheads. Some parishes ask them to refrain from lectoring, serving as extraordinary ministers of the eucharist, teaching, or sitting on the parish council. Divorcing Catholics most frequently complain about feeling invisible in their parishes: no one acknowledges their presence, except perhaps on special occasions such as the Feast of the Holy Family and Mother's Day, and then only negatively. Confused about their ability to approach the sacraments, many stop receiving communion under the false impression that they are excommunicated. Some parishes, on the other hand, go out of their way to make them feel welcome, and their hospitality speeds their recovery.

Divorcing Catholics frequently find their previous understanding of their faith inadequate. They grew up believing that God loved them because they kept the commandments and more or less obeyed the rules, but their experience of separation and divorce makes them question these former assumptions. Wondering whether God still loves them, they are surprised by the moments of

grace which surface in the midst of their struggles. Many find themselves feeling closer to God than ever before and report hearing the gospel with new ears, identifying for the first time with the lost sheep Jesus sought while leaving the ninety-nine behind.

The Pastoral Needs of Divorcing Catholics

When divorcing Catholics turn to the church in their need, they automatically turn to their local churches, to particular parishes and pastors. Their experience of a parish and of one or two priests colors, for the most part, their perception of the church's concern for them. Homilies given by understanding pastors and expressions of support from parishioners mean more to them than hierarchical pronouncements. When they do learn of some official statements—usually through the news media—the divorced are often distressed; general condemnations of divorce seem to blame them for what they themselves most wish they could have avoided. When they speak—either favorably or with bitterness—about the church's concern (or lack of it) for them during their crisis, they most frequently describe how a specific local community and its pastoral leadership related to them.

The first thing divorcing Catholics seek from the church is acceptance. They do not expect or ask for the church's approval of the collapse of their marriage, since they themselves may be mourning the loss of a love they had counted on. They do, however, seek acceptance of themselves both as Catholics and as divorcing people.

Homilists need to recognize that a sizeable proportion of every congregation is touched by divorce in one way or another. To ignore the prevalence or complexity of divorce in contemporary life or to blame those who suffer from its pain for undermining the stability of the family, disregards the good faith, the sorrows, and the wisdom of Catholics who grieve the ending of a love they once cherished. Divorcing Catholics understand probably better than anyone else the "evils of divorce"—after all they know first hand the emotional and social turmoil it causes—but they cannot hear a homily on the subject without feeling personally judged and branded as evil. They ask for homilies which acknowledge their pain and difficulties without condemning them as failures, and most especially they long for assurances from the pulpit that God does indeed continue to love them and to offer them forgiveness and compassion.

Simple gestures during the liturgy communicate the acceptance divorcing Catholics seek: a single parent with children bringing the gifts forward at the presentation, a homily that acknowledges their faith commitment as well as their difficulties, an announcement in the bulletin about a diocesan retreat or a parish support group for divorcing Catholics.

Divorcing Catholics need support. They need to share their concerns, feelings, and problems with others who will understand them. Since they frequently cannot afford professional help, they often turn to self-help groups. Beginning in the early 1970s, support groups for separated and divorcing Catholics have developed throughout the United States and Canada. (The North American Conference of Separated and Divorced Catholics is a network of such groups and offers help in establishing and promoting groups.) Although groups vary in size, composition (some include widows and widowers), frequency of meetings (weekly, biweekly, or monthly), and format (open discussion, formal presentations, small group sharing), most groups present themselves as an informal gathering of people who care for each other's welfare, and all exist to offer mutual support to those in need. Whatever their structure, the most effective groups are directed by peers (i.e. divorcing Catholics helping divorcing Catholics) and meet consistently (at a regular time and in a set place). Just the presence of such a group in a parish lends support to many divorcing Catholics who may never turn to such a group themselves.

With their many questions about their standing in the church, divorcing Catholics need guidance and accurate information. In 1884 the American bishops meeting in Baltimore asked Rome to impose the penalty of excommunication on those Catholics in the United States who dared to contradict the church's authority and teaching that a sacramental marriage is indissoluble and who remarried invalidly after divorce. In 1977 the United State bishops voted to lift the penalty of excommunication imposed on divorced Catholics who have remarried. Some divorcing Catholics still think they are excommunicated (whether or not they are remarried), and they refrain from receiving the eucharist at the very time they are most in need of its grace. It is the responsibility of priests and pastoral ministers to inform them of the church's current teaching. Nothing in Canon Law or in the teaching of the church prevents them from approaching the sacraments simply because they are separated or divorced; indeed much in our tradition encourages believers who are in crises and in need of forgiveness and consolation to avail themselves of the sacraments. The case of Catholics who are divorced and remarried without the church's recognition is a different matter; they need the pastoral guidance of compassionate ministers to discern the extent of their participation in the sacramental life of the church. Priests and pastoral ministers can best serve divorcing Catholics—remarried or single—by clearly and consistently assuring them that they are not excommunicated and that nothing they have done excludes them from the church or God's love.

When divorcing Catholics find in the church a welcoming acceptance, open support, and guidance, they then are able to seek the church's aid in experiencing reconciliation. Burdened by anger, guilt, resentment, self-doubt, and feelings of failure, they look for something more meaningful and efficacious than words of absolution. They must face their own failing, accept responsiblity for their lives, assign guilt where it rightly belongs, seek forgiveness for their sins and comfort for their pain, let go of paralyzing memories, and begin risking again. Reconciliation takes time, and those who are involved in the process need encouragement and support. The sacrament of penance may be helpful in this process, although divorcing Catholics frequently are not prepared to celebrate it until later in their healing. Initially, the sacrament is linked in their minds too much with sin, guilt, and failure and "going to confession" only adds to their sense of inadequacy. Later, as they come to accept themselves as both good and flawed, both loved and sinning, and as they come to a more adequate understanding of the sacrament of penance, they find it a fitting conclusion to the forgiveness they have already begun to experience. With all of the ambivalence they feel about their ability to receive the eucharist, separated and divorcing Catholics instinctively feel drawn toward the eucharist as the source of reconciliation. They speak of it as medicine for those who are ailing and food for the journey, and they recall how Jesus met opposition for "welcoming sinners and eating with them" (Lk 15:2).

Support groups help divorcing Catholics in their efforts to forgive and be forgiven, and numerous retreat programs have been developed over the years to facilitate the process. "Beginning Experience" is a nationwide program which sponsors weekend retreats for those who suffer the loss of a loved one through death or divorce.

Divorcing Catholics speak more of recovery (a term borrowed from recent studies of dysfunctional families) than of reconciliation, although the two processes are familiar. Both result in an increase of confidence, a new-found self-identity, and the ability to face the future without being crippled by terror or distress. It is difficult to overestimate the impact of the trauma suffered by divorcing people. Creating a new sense of self, restructuring relationships with family and friends, establishing financial stability, and coming to peace with the church and God, take time and energy, and divorcing Catholics need all the help others can offer.

Critical Issues in Ministry with the Divorcing

Three major issues facing those who minister with divorced Catholics revolve around remarriage: (1) annulments; (2) internal forum; and (3) remarriage preparation. Possibly the most significant concern today is the effect of divorce on children.

(1) An annulment (a popularized term describing both a process and the decree of nullity issued by the tribunal) is the Roman Catholic church's way of determining whether a person is free to marry in the church after a previous marriage has ended in divorce. While an annulment allows some people to find a sense of reconciliation with themselves and their church and while it offers hope to those who desire to remarry in the church, it also produces resentment among those who do not understand the process or what it entails. Many find the procedure alienating and painful, offended by the cavalier way their pain and private lives are dealt with. Non-Catholics find the process totally incomprehensible and alienating; it reinforces their impression that the church is simply a bureaucracy and they object to having human beings judge their worthiness before God. Many

people worry that their children will become illegitimate if their marriage is declared null and void. Paradoxically, as the annulment process becomes more accessible, many divorced Catholics are beginning to see it as little more than an expensive and time-consuming exercise in administrative red-tape. Most people are disturbed, sometimes outraged, by the tribunal's judgment that what appeared to be a marriage was, in fact, not a marriage as the church describes it. Still mourning the ending of a relationship which once gave them joy, they are offended by the inference that they really were not married in the first place. Priests and pastoral ministers can help divorced Catholics by acknowledging the love, good intentions, hope and happiness that their previous marriages represent and by presenting the annulment process as the community's involvement in their healing and reconciliation.

(2) Priests and pastoral ministers need a better understanding of internal forum so that they can assist divorced Catholics who remarry without receiving an annulment to discern their ability to approach the sacraments. The issue of internal forum is a highly disputed one in the church, and it demands study and pastoral sensitivity. When the church's ministers fail to address the issue or to provide the necessary leadership, invalidly remarried Catholics who were unable to receive an annulment are left to their own resources. Often they leave the church (since they feel it first abandoned them) or turn to others for advice (and are told to do "what their consciences tell them to do").

(3) Programs for those who are considering remarriage must be developed to help them deal with their unique problems and concerns. People should be counselled to take sufficient time following a divorce to assess their part in the breakup of the previous marriage and to make sure they do not repeat former patterns of relating. They need special attention if children are involved. Some parishes and dioceses have the policy of excluding divorced people from marriage preparation programs unless they have already received an annulment. Such policies are meant to reinforce the church's teaching about the permanence of marriage, but they frequently alienate people who already feel condemned by the church. Even if they plan to be married in a ceremony not recognized by the church, divorced Catholics can profit from the preparation offered by such programs; they may have a positive experience of the church and its approach to marriage which will then lead them to explore the possibilites of having their union recognized by the church.

A major problem of confronting those who minister with divorcing Catholics is the effect of separation on children. Their grief is as real as that of their parents for they mourn the loss of a loved one or of a particular relationship, and they have fewer resources available to help them confront their anger and fears. They often feel responsible in some way for the break-up of their parent's marriage. They also feel abandoned, since frequently the non-custodial parent starts over with a new family and ignores or denies former ties. Divorcing couples often use their children, consciously or unconsciously, as weapons against each other, and the legal maneuverings about custody often leave children confused and hurt. Custodial parents, dealing with their own grief, have little or no emotional energy left over to give to their children. As the number of children living with a single parent or in a step-family increases, more energy and attention should be directed to their welfare and recovery.

See **Marriage, canonical issues concerning; Internal forum; Conscience, priority of human**

James J. Young, C.S.P. ed. *Ministering to the Divorced Catholic* (New York: Paulist Press, 1979).

Paula Ripple, *The Pain and the Possibility* (Notre Dame: Ave Maria Press). James J. Young, C.S.P. *Divorcing, Believing, Belonging* (Mahwah, NJ: Paulist Press, 1984).

CHRISTOPHER P. WITT, C.S.P.

DIX, GREGORY (1901-1952)

Anglican Benedictine of Nashdom Abbey of which he was elected prior in 1948, Dix is best known for his *Shape of the Liturgy* (Westminster: Dacre Press, 1945), a work which continues to be a liturgical classic. Presenting a rich picture of the eucharist in the early church, and indeed throughout its historical development, Dix formulated the action "shape" of the eucharist: "Our Lord (1) took bread; (2) 'gave thanks' over it; (3 broke it; (4) distributed it .... he (5) took a cup; (6) 'gave thanks' over that; (7) handed it to his disciples" (Shape, 48). He asserted that "with absolute unanimity the liturgical tradition reproduces these seven actions as four": the offertory, the prayer, the fraction and the communion. All rites for the eucharist, both East and West, share this common "shape."

See **Benedictines and liturgical renewal**

DOCTRINE, LITURGY AND

I. Substantial Consistency

"Our doctrine agrees with the eucharist, and the eucharist confirms the doctrine," wrote St. Irenaeus towards the end of the 2nd century (*Adv. Haer.* IV. 18, 5). The bishop of Lyons was establishing the internal coherence of Catholic faith and practice against the Gnostics. When, two or three generations earlier, the christological Docetists had given up the eucharist, they were at least, as Ignatius of Antioch informs us, being consistent: "They abstain from eucharist ... because they do not confess that the eucharist is the flesh of our Savior Jesus Christ which suffered for our sins and which the Father raised" (*Letter to the Smyrneans* 7:1). But the Gnostics of St. Irenaeus' time proved self-contradictory when they made sacramental use of elements from a material creation they despised. Catholic liturgy and doctrine, on the other hand, harmonized in their recognition that the creator and the redeemer were the same God, active throughout in the creative Word who had become flesh and given to humankind the sacraments and promise of salvation. The orthodox apologist argues aggressively: "How will they [the Gnostics] allow that the bread over which thanksgiving has been said is the body of their Lord, and that the chalice is the chalice of his blood, if they do not say that he is the Son of the creator of the world; that is to say, his Word through whom the tree bears fruit and the fountains flow and the earth yields first the blade, then the ear, then the full corn in the ear?" (*Adv. Haer.* IV. 18, 4).

And again: "Since, then, the cup which is mixed and the bread which is made receive the Word of God and become the eucharist of the body and blood of Christ, and of them the substance of our flesh grows and subsists: how can they [the Gnostics] deny that the flesh is capable of the gift of God which is eternal life, that flesh which is fed by the body and blood of the Lamb and is a member of him? ... And as the wood of the vine planted into the ground bears fruit in its season, and the grain of wheat falls into the ground and molders and is raised manifold by the Spirit of God; and afterwards through the wisdom of God they come to be used by human beings, and having received the Word of God become the eucharist which is the body and blood of Christ: so also our bodies, nourished by the eucharist, and put into the ground, and dissolved therein, will rise in their season, the Word of God giving them resurrection to the glory of the Father" (*Adv. Haer.* V. 2, 3).

Around the same time as Irenaeus,

Tertullian made with fierce irony a similar point against Marcion, who had not dared to drop the eucharistic institution from his bowdlerized gospel, nor his followers the sacraments from their practice: "[Your 'superior God'] has not up to now rejected the Creator's water, for in it he washes his own people; nor the oil with which he anoints them; nor the mixture of milk and honey on which he feeds his children; nor the bread by which he represents his own body. Even in his own 'sacraments' he needs things begged from the Creator" (*Adversus Marcionem* 1, 14).

And, in defending Catholic teaching on the resurrection of the body, Tertullian again points to the sacraments, for in them the body is already the means by which the soul receives grace: "The flesh (*caro*) is the hinge (*cardo*) of salvation. . . . The flesh is washed, that the soul may be made clean; the flesh is anointed, that the soul may be consecrated; the flesh is signed, that the soul may be strengthened; the flesh is shadowed by the imposition of the hand, that the soul may be enlightened by the Spirit; the flesh feeds on the body and blood of Christ, that the soul may feast on God. Therefore the things that are joined together in labor [i.e. body and soul] cannot be separated when it comes to the reward" (*De resurrectione carnis*, 8).

After the defeat, in principle, of Gnosticism, the next major test of the substantial consistency between liturgy and doctrine came with the Arian controversy, which lasted through most of the 4th century. In their desire to uphold the inferiority of the Son to the Father, Arians cited Catholic liturgical texts in an attempt to show that the Catholics themselves, while their doctrinal writings defended Nicea on the consubstantiality of the divine persons, in fact belied their own teaching in their worship: "They themselves [the Catholics] in the creed put the Father before the Son when they say 'Do you believe in God the Father almighty, maker of heaven and earth? Do you also believe in Christ Jesus his Son?'. . . They themselves in their oblations put the Father before the Son by saying 'It is right and fitting that we should give thanks to you here and everywhere, holy Lord, almighty God; and there is no one through whom we can have access to you, pray to you, offer a sacrifice to you, except the one whom you sent to us' and 'It is right proper and fitting that we should give thanks to you above all things, holy Lord, almighty Father, eternal God . . . asking you in your great and merciful kindness to accept this sacrifice which we offer you before the face of your divine goodness through Jesus Christ, our Lord and God, through whom we pray and ask. . .'" (from the so-called "Mai Fragments," published in G. Mercato, *Antiche reliquie liturgiche*, Rome 1902, pp. 45-71).

In meeting Arian arguments from the liturgy, the method adopted by St. Ambrose of Milan was not to "correct" or change the Catholic custom but rather to explain and defend such a practice as praying to the Father through the Son. Thus he writes to the emperor Gratian, with echoes of John 14:13f and 16:23: "The Father wishes to be asked through the Son, the Son wishes the Father to be asked. . . . Whatever the Father does, the Son does the same and likewise. The Son does it likewise and the same, but he wishes the Father to be asked for what he himself will do, not that one may see therein a sign of his incapacity but rather a sign of their unity in power" (*To Gratian, On the Faith* I.2, 12f).

It was, in fact, the Arian controversy which provoked the church to some of its most profound reflection on the coinherence of liturgy and doctrine, in the light particularly of soteriology. As already with Ignatius, Irenaeus and Tertullian in the confrontation with Docetists and Gnostics, it was again a matter of the nature of the saving God and of the salvation bestowed by this God on humankind. St. Athanasius and the Cappadocians recognized that the stakes were high. If Christ was, as the Arians taught, a creature, and if the divine epithets predicated upon him were mere "courtesy titles," then the Catholic worship of him would be idolatry (Athanasius, *Letter to Adelphius*, 3f; cf. Gregory Nazianzus, *Oration XL on Holy Baptism*, 42; Gregory of Nyssa, *On the Holy Spirit against Macedonius*). But ritual practice and a theological axiom are jointly advanced to show that the God who saves us, whom Christians worship, and in communion with whom human salvation consists, is in fact Trinity: the name confessed and invoked in the saving mystery of baptism is threefold, Father, Son and Holy Spirit; and only God can reveal, redeem, and sanctify, or give participation in God (Athanasius, *Letter to Serapion* I. 29f; Gregory of Nyssa, *Sermon on the Baptism of Christ;* Basil, *On the Holy Spirit,* 24-26; cf. Ambrose, *On the Mysteries* V. 28; Theodore of Mopsuestia, *Catechetical Homilies* XIV, 14-21).

St. Basil's treatise *On the Holy Spirit*, written around 373 against the Pneumatomachians who denied the deity of the Holy Spirit, is a sustained treatment of the relations between trinitarian worship and doctrine. In face of the accusation that he himself was innovating by introducing a "coordinated" form of doxology, Basil gives examples to show that the church has always used not only the "mediatorial" formulation of "Glory to the Father through (*dia*) the Son in (*en*) the Holy Spirit," but also such forms as "Glory to the Father with (*meta*) the Son with (*sun*) the Holy Spirit" and "Glory to the Father and the Son and the Holy Spirit," in which the three divine persons are "ranked" together. The mediatorial type is appropriate to thanksgiving, which is returned to God by the

same route as God's blessings first reached us: the Father's gifts come to humankind through the Son in the Spirit, and our prayers of thanks in the Spirit are directed through the Son to the Father. But the indivisibility of God's work in God's dealings with the world (the "economy") is grounded in the mutual coinherence of the three persons in the inner life of God; and so, when God is regarded *in se*, it is entirely fitting that the coordinated doxology be used. Just a few years after Basil, the Ecumenical Council of Constantinople (381) would declare its credal faith in "the Holy Spirit, ... who with the Father and the Son together is worshipped and glorified," thus completing the trinitarian teaching begun at the Council of Nicea (325) with the "consubstantiality" of the Son to the Father. Soteriologically, it is the engagement of God's very self with the world that allows the reconciled into communion with God.

It is again a matter of salvation in the next great occasion during the formative patristic period for the mutual consistency of liturgy and doctrine to be tested and established. Against Julian of Eclanum, who maintained that children are born without original sin, St. Augustine points to the practice of pre-baptismal exorcism as implying that, on the contrary, infants are until then in the power of the devil (*Against Julian* VI. 4-5). He further appeals to the fact that baptism itself, which is administered for the remission of sins, is given also to infants, and that infants also receive communion "in order that they may have eternal life": "Why have recourse to the remedy if the ailment is absent?" (*Sermon* 174). And against the semi-Pelagian monks of Marseilles Augustine defends his doctrine of grace-its necessity in both conversion and perseverance—by reference to the "prayers of the church" both that unbelievers may be brought by God to the faith and that believers may continue in the faith of

Christ (*On the Gift of Perseverance* 23, 63-65; cf. *Epistle* 217).

The argument with semi-Pelagianism provides the source for a formula which, as an abbreviated tag, has been twisted many ways in later discussions of the relations between liturgy and doctrine, namely *lex orandi, lex credendi*. To a letter of Pope Celestine I (422-432) there became attached certain "chapters" which are now thought to be the work of Prosper of Aquitaine, a lay monk and literary disciple and defender of Augustine. The phrase "ut legem credendi lex statuat supplicandi" there has the very precise meaning that the apostolic *command to pray* for the whole human race (1 Tim 2:1-4)—which every Catholic church obeys in its intercessions—*establishes* the *obligation to believe* that all faith, even the beginnings of good will as well as growth and perseverance, is from start to finish a work of grace (cf. also Prosper's treatise *On the Calling of All Nations*). It may incidentally be noted that the many collects in ancient Western sacramentaries which in turn appear to have been composed with a deliberate anti-Pelagian intent nevertheless recognize the place of works in the salvation of believers. In ways that leave open a variety of theological interpretations concerning the interplay between grace, faith and works, such prayers correspond to the deepest structures of worship, which show Christians ascribing salvation to God's grace alone yet themselves engaged in the active response of faith.

A final example concerning the consistency between worship and doctrine may be given, this time from the East again, from the close of the patristic period. In the iconoclastic controversy of the 8th and 9th centuries, the battles were fought theologically in the technical terms of Christ's person and natures. The soteriological heart of the matter was expressed, from the icondule side, by St. John of Damascus thus: "I do not worship matter, I worship the Creator of matter, who for my sake became matter, and accepted to dwell in matter, and through matter wrought my salvation. I will not cease reverencing matter, for it was through matter that my salvation was effected" (*On Icons* I. 16).

The judgments of the Second Council of Nicea (787) in favor of the use of icons were a reprise, at another level of liturgical practice, of the decision of the Council of Ephesus (431), against Nestorius, that Mary was properly called Theotokos, God-bearer: it was the understanding and reach of the incarnation, as it came to expression in the worship of the church, that was at stake in both cases.

So far, examples have been taken from the most formative period of church history to show, in a general way, the recognized need for consistency between "liturgy" and "doctrine," with an indication of which way the Catholic and Orthodox decision went in controversial cases. It is now time for a more systematic reflection on the meaning of "liturgy" and "doctrine" and the relations between them.

II. Rhetorical Relations

According to the gospels, the first declaration of the Christian faith can be either a second-person address to its object ("Thou art the Christ," Mk 8:29) or a first-person proclamation to others concerning him ("We have found the Christ," Jn 1:41). Transferred to the third-person, the confession "Jesus is Lord" (Rom 10:9; 1 Cor 12:3) is at once an acclamation, an announcement, and an assertion. In the most elemental cases of Christian speech, "liturgy" and "doctrine" thus coincide.

However, a diversification of purposes and contexts soon brings a differentiation of linguistic usage. As soon as functions and circumstances change, Christian language develops in a variety of ways, and there is a perpetual need to correlate what is said in the several modes in order to ensure that the reference and meaning remain the same.

A. Worship is the "sacrifice of praise," the "tribute of lips that acknowledge God's name" (Heb 13:15). In its loving address to God, worship tends towards exuberance and abandon. Here spontaneity is of the essence, though habituated hearts will easily find themselves drawing upon the familiar language of the scriptures and the phrases hallowed by previous intercourse with God. In the very act of self-surrender, Christian worshippers will not find it necessary to "justify" what is taking place. But they will quickly want to sing the praises of their divine lover before the world.

B. In *evangelization* Christian preachers have to accommodate to the culture which is hearing the gospel for the first time. Other languages will be corrected and filled, converted and brought captive to Christ, as their speakers are challenged and changed by the gospel. This process, when successful, will also enrich the linguistic repertoire of the whole Christian tradition.

C. In *apologetics* the defenders of the faith engage with those who resist, oppose and even attack it. Here language acquires a sharp point, takes on a combative edge. Yet the aim must remain to persuade opponents and win them for God's church and kingdom. Linguistic swords and spears are destined to become plowshares and pruning-hooks.

D. In its *internal controversies* the church is seeking by argument to clarify the gospel and the faith. Fine distinctions are drawn. When, after examination and debate, a position is deemed heretical, a doctrinal definition is made that will exclude it. In a combination of positive statement and explicit or implicit exclusion, the definition declares the faith. It thereby also, as George Lindbeck empha-

sized in *The Nature of Doctrine* (Philadelphia: Westminster Press, 1984), sets the rules for other Christian speech on the topic. In turn, the definition itself may get taken up into direct doxological usage. Most notably, the "Nicene-Constantinopolitan Creed" originated from baptismal professions of faith, was filled out by the conciliar definitions affirming the full deity of the Son and the Spirit, and eventually found a place in the eucharistic liturgies of both the Catholic East and West.

Signalled by the shifts and variety of linguistic use, an element of *theological reflection* thus belongs to debate within the church, to the defense and proclamation of the gospel, and even to the Christian worship of God. In the nature of the case, such reflection is in a sense secondary, but it is not essentially alien to the faith. In Anselm's famous phrase, theology is "faith seeking understanding." It may be even more accurate to say that reflective theology is faith seeking a *greater* or *deeper* understanding of itself and of its object. For faith involves the intelligence from the very start; the initial gift and act of faith already contain a moment of understanding, the *intellectus fidei*, whereby God enlightens the heart and mind and enables it to accept the truth of God's own being and history as these are testified in the gospel. Certainly theological reflection has played its part in the establishment and formulation of doctrine, which tells what is properly to be believed, how the gospel is to be purely preached, and how God is to be rightly worshipped—all the while seeking to maintain substantive consistency amid the various forms of speech appropriate to statements of belief, proclamation, and liturgy.

Christian doctrine is literally "the teaching." The teaching is characteristically kept close to the liturgy, both drawing on it as a resource, proof or illustration, and also, in the return direction, seeking to guide, purify and enrich the worship of Christians. In the early church, the decisive teaching was attached to baptism. After a more or less lengthy catechumenate in which they were instructed in the scriptures and in morals, the "elect" shortly before their baptism underwent the *traditio* and *redditio* of the creed and the Lord's prayer: these crucial texts were "handed over" to them and had to be "returned." If you were not ready to affirm the faith and to practice the prayer, you would not be baptized. Thereafter continuance in membership of the church meant sticking to the faith of your baptism and participating in the liturgical life to which you had been admitted. From extant "mystagogical catecheses" of the 4th and 5th centuries (see Edward J. Yarnold, *The Awe-Inspiring Rites of Initiation: Baptismal Homilies of the Fourth Century*, Slough, England: St. Paul's Publications, 1972) we know that Christians were taught the meaning of baptism, chrismation and the eucharist either just before their initiation (as in some series by St. John Chrysostom) or else in the immediately succeeding days (as in the lectures by Cyril, or John of Jerusalem, Ambrose of Milan, Theodore of Mopsuestia, and Narsai of Edessa and Nisibis). St Augustine's sermons show the bishop of Hippo, in teaching and exhorting his congregants, making frequent appeal to his hearers' baptism and to their experience of the eucharist.

In the centuries of Christendom, it was above all by their assistance at the liturgy that Christians learned the faith, whatever the degree or mode of formal catechesis undergone retroactively by those who had been baptized as infants. This persisting insight of Eastern Orthodoxy needed to be rediscovered in the modern liturgical movement among the Western churches in the midst of a society turning secular. Herein lies one of the great contributions of Dom Lambert Beauduin,

for example, which eventually bore fruit in the liturgical revisions following Vatican II. By encouraging active participation in rites whose symbolic lines are sharper through having their excrescences docked, the postconciliar services become the means for a continuing and deeper penetration into the faith. In Protestantism, the liturgical movement has meant, above all, the rediscovery of the principal sacraments and the enrichment of the repertory of communicative signs.

A number of prominent theologians in the Western churches have returned to the ancient baptismal creed as a structure for teaching the faith in a comprehensive yet concise form. Thus the Apostles' Creed is followed by the Swiss Reformed Karl Barth in his *Dogmatics in Outline* (German 1947; English trans. New York: Philosophical Library, 1949; Harper and Row, 1959), by the Roman Catholic Joseph Ratzinger in his *Introduction to the Christian Faith* (German 1968; English trans. London: Search Press, 1969), and by Jan Milic Lochman of the Czech Brethren in his *The Faith We Confess: An Ecumenical Dogmatics* (German 1982; English trans. Philadelphia: Fortress Press 1984), while the German Lutheran Wolfhart Pannenberg presented *The Apostles' Creed in the Light of Today's Questions* (German 1972; English trans. Philadelphia: Westminster Press, 1972). The French Catholic bishops have issued a catechism based on Eucharistic Prayer IV of the Missal of Paul VI, where the whole sweep of salvation history is rehearsed in doxological style: Il est grand le mystère de la foi (1978).

The Eastern tradition of a teaching commentary on the liturgy, with famous examples from Maximus the Confessor in the 7th century and Nicholas Cabasilas in the 14th, has been resumed by Alexander Schmemann of the Orthodox Church in America. In a basic description of "sacraments and orthodoxy" dating from 1963, Schmemann expounds worship as God's gift "for the life of the world" and as the exercise of the human vocation to a royal priesthood on behalf of all creation (*For the Life of the World*, Crestwood, NY: St. Vladimir's Seminary Press, rev. ed., 1973). Then Schmemann's *Of Water and the Spirit* (Crestwood, NY: St. Vladimir's Seminary Press, 1974) is a detailed interpretation of the rites of the catechumenate, baptism, chrismation and communion as entry into Christian existence. The posthumously published *The Eucharist* (Russian 1984; English trans. Crestwood, NY: St. Vladimir's Seminary Press, 1987) adopts the sequence of the rite itself to show it as "the sacrament of the assembly, of the kingdom, of entrance, of the word, of the faithful, of offering, of unity, of anaphora, of thanksgiving, of remembrance, of the Holy Spirit, of communion."

III. Dogmatic Authority

We have shown that liturgy and doctrine in principle coincide in substantive content and may even, at their most elemental, share a common expressive form. In Cardinal Ratzinger's felicitous phrase, the liturgy is *The Feast of Faith* (German 1981; English trans. San Francisco: Ignatius Press, 1986). Yet a differentiation of purposes and contexts, of functions and circumstances, may drive liturgy and doctrine apart. While the differentiation is natural and necessary, it may induce a certain "rivalry" between them. Which is to have the upper hand, the *lex orandi* or the *lex credendi*? How far are these "laws" descriptive, how far prescriptive? Where resides the authority to moderate them?

It was doubtless the experience of redemption at his hand that led the first Christians to worship Jesus Christ as Lord. If he is Lord, then it is a reasonable theological deduction that he has played a divine role from the beginning of things. Hence he will have always been the Father's agent in creation. That is

how the hymns embedded in the NT already describe him (1 Cor 8:6; Col 1:16; Jn 1:1-3), and it is Christian teaching that Christ is thus the mediator of creation from the side of God ("through whom all things were made," says Nicea of the Son). Again, it was the direct address of praise and prayers to Christ—for which we have rudimentary examples in the NT and then some other instances in popular literature and hymns in the first three centuries—which helped to establish the Nicene teaching of the Son as "homoousios" with the Father. With the defeat of Arianism, however, there also occurred a proliferation of strictly liturgical prayers to Christ alone, which veered in a dangerously monophysite direction and tended to eclipse the role of "Jesus Christ our Lord" as our mediator from the human side before God the Father (see J.A. Jungmann, *The Place of Christ in Liturgical Prayer*, German 1925, rev. 1962, English trans. London: Geoffrey Chapman 1965). Or yet again: the popular devotion to Mary as "spotless" and "Queen of heaven," celebrated in feasts that the Roman magisterium came to sanction and encourage, eventually led to the Immaculate Conception of Mary and her Assumption being solemnly proclaimed to be *de fide* by Popes Pius IX and Pius XII respectively. In all those cases, there is a sense in which worship has been "leading" doctrine, and theological—and ecclesiastical—judgments will vary as to how unmixed the blessings have been.

On the other hand, reflective theology may lead to critical action being taken upon particular manifestations of worship. The Protestant Reformers intended to correct developed liturgical and paraliturgical practices—"the sacrifices of Masses," indulgences, relics—that were in their eyes the outcrop of distorted teaching and belief concerning God, humankind and salvation. The Reformers acted in the name of the scriptures which, though they themselves were to a great extent liturgically composed, defined and transmitted, nevertheless possess a special doctrinal authority in view of their canonical status as word of God. In turn, the leading Reformers, with the help of sympathetic institutional powers in church and state, issued their own orders for public worship. Understandably in the circumstances, these had a somewhat aggressive doctrinal thrust. As a result, Protestant services have tended to an undue stress on the didactic over the latreutic, whereby (in, say, Dutch Calvinism) the eucharistic prayer is almost entirely displaced by exhortations to the communicants. This failing is not, however, these days limited to Protestants: Catholics with a "cause" have also taken to "using" the opportunity of the liturgy for "indoctrination."

At issue in the relations between liturgy and doctrine is pastoral authority and the place of dogma. There is everything to be said for the exercise of the extraordinary magisterium only in matters of genuinely fundamental and central importance where the gospel, the faith and the church are at stake. Absolutely decisive doctrinal deliverances are then carried forward in the fixed structures and parts of the liturgy. The job of the ordinary magisterium is to give particular teaching for the circumstances of everyday belief, witness and living. It is most appropriately exercised through the sermon. Coming after the biblical readings, the sermon is naturally grounded in the scriptures as the permanent norm of Christian faith and conduct. The stable liturgical structures provide a continuing tradition and an expectant context in which the hermeneutical "fusion of horizons" can be attempted. The setting of worship and sacrament reminds the preacher that all Christian teaching is directed toward "man's chief end," namely "to glorify God and enjoy Him for ever" (as the Westminster Catechism of 1648 puts it).

The precise nature, exercise and location of pastoral and dogmatic authority is, of course, controversial between the churches. But there are today some signs of ecumenical convergence in liturgy and doctrine, and the relations between them, that may make those problems more tractable.

IV. Ecumenical Opportunities

Drawing on and contributing to the complementary movements of biblical theology, patristic scholarship and ecclesiological renewal, the modern liturgical movement has brought the separated churches into many convergences among themselves where liturgy and doctrine are closely joined. The main rites of the church are now celebrated in similar ways by the different communities, with matching orders of service, formularies that are substantially identical, and indeed many texts in common. The most comprehensive documentation of these convergences in matters of sacramental belief and practice is found in "the Lima process," where some 200 churches, each at its "highest appropriate level of authority," have responded to the statement itself on *Baptism, Eucharist and Ministry* that issued from the WCC Commission on Faith and Order meeting at Lima, Peru, in 1982 after 55 years of remote and 15 years of proximate preparation.

The way in which the very significant response of the Roman Catholic church expresses its general appreciation of the sections on baptism and eucharist in particular deserves quotation, not only for its positive judgment but also because it captures very well the character, method and content of the original. First, baptism: "We find the text on baptism to be grounded in the apostolic faith received and professed by the Catholic Church. It draws in a balanced way from the major NT areas of teaching about baptism; it gives an important place to the witness of the early church. While it does not discuss all major doctrinal issues that have arisen about baptism, it is sensitive to the effect they have had on the development of the understanding of this sacrament and to the positive value of differing solutions that emerged; it appreciates the normative force that some forms of liturgical celebration may have and the significance of pastoral practice; within the ecumenical scope it sets for itself, it articulates the development of the Christian understanding of baptism with a coherent theological method. It has many affinities, both of style and of content, with the way the faith of the Church about baptism is stated in the Second Vatican Council and in the *Liturgy of Christian Initiation* promulgated by Pope Paul VI" (Max Thurian, ed., *Churches Respond to BEM* volume VI, Geneva: WCC Publications, 1988, p. 9f).

And with regard to the eucharist (ibid., p. 16f): "Catholics can recognize in the statement on the eucharist much that corresponds to the understanding and practice of the apostolic faith, or, as it is said in the document, the faith of the church through the ages. We especially appreciate the following:

a)   The sources employed for the interpretation of the meaning of the eucharist and the form of celebration are scripture and tradition. The classical liturgies of the first millennium and patristic theology are important points of reference in this text.

b)   The eucharist is described as pertaining to the content of faith. It presents a strong christological dimension, identifying the mystery of the eucharist in various ways with the real presence of the risen Lord and his sacrifice on the cross.

c)   The structure and ordering of the basic aspects of the document, as well as their relation to one another, conforms with Catholic teaching, specifically:

●The presentation of the mystery of the eucharist follows the flow of classical eucharist liturgies, with the eucharistic theology drawing heavily on the content of the traditional prayer and symbolic actions of these liturgies. The text draws on patristic sources for additional explication of the mystery of the eucharist.

●There is strong emphasis on the Trinitarian dimension. The source and goal of the eucharist is identified as the Trinity.

●The explanation of the content of the act of the church in the eucharistic prayer includes basic elements required by Catholic teaching as well: thanksgiving to the Father; memorial of the institution of the eucharist and the sacrifice of the cross; intercession made in union with Christ for the world; petition for the Spirit's coming on the bread and wine and on the community, in order that the bread and wine become the body and blood of Christ, and that the community be sanctified; the meal of the New Covenant.

d)   There is a strong eschatological dimension. The eucharist is viewed as a foretaste of Christ's parousia and of the final kingdom, given through the Spirit. It opens up the vision of the kingdom and the renewal of the world.

e)   The eucharist is presented as the central act of the church's worship. Because of this, the text recommends frequent celebration.

f)   The text has important ecclesiological dimensions and implications for mission."

It is important to notice that the Lima text not only contains such substantial agreement on the sacraments of baptism and the Lord's Supper, on which it focuses, but also, in an incidental and therefore rudimentary way, implies some common teaching on other topics of dogma, such as the Trinity, the person and work of Christ, the Holy Spirit, sin and redemption, grace and faith, the church and the kingdom. The Catholic theologian Hans-Joachim Schulz was prepared to argue on the basis of their eucharistic liturgies that there already exists among Roman Catholics, the Orthodox, and some Protestant churches sufficient "unity of faith" (*Ökumenische Glaubenseinheit aus eucharistischer Überlieferung*, Paderborn: Verlag Bonifacius-Druckerei, 1976). Certainly the Lima process suggests that the liturgical way towards unity in faith, doctrine and life holds great promise. Pursuance of that route will require further attention to doctrinal detail in the sacraments themselves (and perhaps a little consequent liturgical revision), the location of the sacraments in the broader dogmatic context (hence the importance of the current WCC Faith and Order study, "Towards the Common Expression of the Apostolic Faith Today"), and settlement of the thorny problem of the recognition of ministries.

The longing among many Christians for the possibility of a common celebration of a common faith is shown by the popular welcome given to the so-called "Lima Liturgy." Although this text was formulated for a particular occasion and is too strongly thematized towards "baptism, eucharist and ministry" to be suitable for general use, its widespread employment on ecumenical occasions testifies to a goal of unity in liturgy, doctrine and life.

J.J. von Allmen, *Worship: Its Theology and Practice*, trans. from the French by Harold Knight and W. Fletcher Fleet (New York: Oxford University Press, 1965). Constantin Andronikof, *Le sens de la liturgie*, (Paris: Editions du Cerf, 1988). Peter Brunner, *Worship in the Name of Jesus*, trans. from the German by M.H. Bertram, (St. Louis: Concordia Publishing House, 1968). Aidan Kavanagh, *On Liturgical Theology* (New York: Pueblo Publishing Company, 1984). Edward J. Kilmartin, *Christian Liturgy: Theology and Practice*, vol. I, *Theology*, (Kansas City: Sheed and Ward, 1988). Richard Schaeffler, *Das Gebet und das Argument: Zwei Weisen des Sprechens von Gott* (Düsseldorf: Patmos: Verlag, 1989). Alexander Schmemann, *Introduction to Liturgical Theology*. trans. from the Russian by Ashleigh E. Moorhouse (Portland, Maine: American Orthodox Press, 1966). Cipriano Vagaggini, *Theological Dimensions of the Liturgy*. trans. from the Italian by Leonard J. Doyle and W.A. Jurgens (Collegeville: The Liturgical Press, 1976). Vasileios of Stavronikita, *Hymn of Entry: Liturgy and Life in the Orthodox Church*, trans. from the Greek by Elizabeth Briere (Crestwood, NY: St. Vladimir's Seminary Press, 1984). Geoffrey Wainwright, *Doxology: The Praise of God in Worship, Doctrine and Life* (New York: Oxford University Press, 1980).

GEOFFREY WAINWRIGHT

DOCUMENTS, ROMAN LITURGICAL, SINCE VATICAN II

Nature and Provenance of the Documents

This article is concerned with the documents which form part of the postconciliar implementation of Vatican II's Constitution on the Sacred Liturgy, *Sacrosanctum concilium* (S.C.). Not all of them are postconciliar in the chronological sense, since the process had begun before council had finished. Since they number more than 550, merely to list their full titles and provenance would take more than the space allotted to this article. One has, of necessity therefore, to be selective. The 1496-page *Documents on the Liturgy 1963-1979, Conciliar, Papal, and Curial Texts*, published by the International Commission on English in the Liturgy, contains 554 documents, including 14 conciliar texts. When referring to that collection this article uses the letters D.O.L., followed by the number of the document in question.

The documents were published by the popes, by the Consilium for the Implementation of the Constitution on the Sacred Liturgy (see below) and by various Vatican congregations, more especially the ancient (est. 1588) Sacred Congregation for Rites (S.C.R.) until 8 May 1969, when by the Apostolic Constitution, *Sacra Rituum Congregatio* (D.O.L., 94), it was divided into the Sacred Congregation for Divine Worship (S.C.D.W.) and the Sacred Congregation for the Causes of the Saints (S.C.C.S). From then the S.C.D.W. published most non-papal documents on the liturgy until 11 July 1975, when, by the Apostolic Constitution, *Constans Nobis* (D.O.L., 101), it was merged with the Sacred Congregation for the Discipline of the Sacraments (S.C.D.S.) to form the Sacred Congregation for the Sacraments and Divine Worship (S.C.S.D.W.). However, the two congregations were again separated, from 1984 to 1988, by a hand-written document, a chirograph, of Pope John Paul II, *Quoniam in celeri*, 5 April 1984 (*Notitiae*, 1984, p. 237), only to be joined together again as the Congregation for Divine Worship and the Discipline of the Sacraments (S.C.D.W.D.S.), with the publication of Pope John Paul II's Apostolic Constitution, *Pastor bonus*, 28 June 1988 (*A.A.S.* 80 (1988) 841-923). A smaller number of non-papal documents on the liturgy have been published by other Roman Congregations, including the S.C.D.S., the Sacred Congregation for the Doctrine of the Faith (S.C.D.F.), which had been known as the Supreme Sacred Congregation of the Holy Office (S.S.C.H.O.) until 1965, the Secretariate for the Promotion of the Unity of Christians (S.P.U.C.), the Sacred Congregation for the Clergy (S.C.C.) and the Sacred Congregation for Bishops (S.C.B.).

The Consilium was disbanded in 1970, but the S.C.D.W. was allowed to retain the services of its experts and members until the completion of the liturgical reform. The Consilium thus had a considerable input into the postconciliar liturgical documents. Much is owed to the sizeable group of experts in liturgy, theology, the Bible, liturgical law, sociology and language who formed the Consilium's study-groups. It was they who did the necessary research and who prepared the drafts for the revision of the liturgical books. In this they were joined by some forty to fifty bishops, drawn from all five continents. All of them, bishops and experts, were pastorally movitated and many of them were people of outstanding competence in their own fields. They were drawn, in the main, from the pre-conciliar international grouping of people who had been in the forefront of the liturgical movement. It is they, by and large, who must be given the credit for the high quality of the postconciliar documents, for their pastoral sensitivity and excellent exposition of the nature of the liturgy.

The reform of the liturgy involved a thorough revision of the liturgical rites themselves, their translation and publication in the vernacular languages and, while this was under way, the interim adaptation of the existing rites. It also involved a massive pastoral-liturgical and theological education of pastors and people, plus occasional correction of abuses and responses to criticisms. There were thus over-lapping stages in the implementation of the reform and all of this is reflected in the documents.

Getting the Reform Under Way

Of mainly, but by no means exclusively, historical interest are documents which belong to the preliminary stage of the liturgical reform. These are the documents which launched and guided the process by which the liturgy was reformed, some of them prescribing the interim adaptations of the existing rites.

The five more important documents in this stage of the liturgical reform, two of them followed by implementing Decrees, are: (a) Pope Paul VI, motu proprio, *Sacram Liturgiam*, 25 January 1964 (D.O.L., 20), on how the reform of the liturgy was to be phased, on the instruction of the people and on the setting up of diocesan commissions. It ordered that certain prescriptions of the Constitution be put in effect immediately and announced the establishment of the Consilium for the Implementation of the Constitution on the Liturgy; (b) S.C.R. Instruction, *Inter Oecumenici*, On the Correct Implementation of the Constitution on the Sacred Liturgy, 26 September 1964 (D.O.L., 23), gave directives on the implementation of S.C., made changes in the celebration of Mass, issued directives on the use of the vernacular and on the competence of bishops; *Inter Oecumenici* was followed by a Decree of the S.C.R., *Nuper edita Instructione*, 27 January 1965 (D.O.L., 196), promulgating the changes it had made in the Mass; (c) S.C.R. Second Instruction, *Tres abhinc annos*, on the Correct Implementation of the Liturgy, 4 May 1967 (D.O.L., 39), introduced still further changes "to the end that the reform of the liturgy may, progressively, be brought to a satisfactory conclusion"; *Tres abhinc annos* was likewise followed by a S.C.R. Decree, *Per Instructionem alteram*, 18 May 1967 (D.O.L., 201), promulgating the further changes in the Mass; (d) S.C.D.W. Instruction, *Constitutione Apostolica*, on bringing the Roman Missal into use gradually, 3 April 1969 (D.O.L., 209); (e) S.C.D.W. Third Instruction, *Liturgiae instaurationes*, On the Correct Implementation of the Constitution on the Sacred Liturgy, 5 September 1970, (D.O.L., 52), on using to full pastoral advantage the Roman Missal and the Order of Scripture Readings for the Mass, on the responsibility of bishops and on unwarranted improvisations. This phase of the reform which, as far as guidance of the reform is concerned, still continues, is marked by a large number of addresses and documents by Pope Paul VI and Pope John Paul II. The more important of the papal documents will be dealt with later.

The earlier years of the reform saw several other statements on its progress, on the preparation of translations of the liturgical rites and on their publication. Statements issued by the Consilium between June 1965 and January 1969 include three on the reform in general: *Le renouveau liturgique*, 30 June 1965 (D.O.L., 31); *L'heureux développment*, 25 January 1966 (D.O.L., 32); *Dans sa récente allocution*, 21 June 1967 (D.O.L., 41); and four which were on specific topics: liturgical experiments, *Expériences litur-*

giques, December 1966 (D.O.L., 36); the use of mechanical and electronic devices in church, *Mécanique et Liturgie*, January 1967 (D.O.L., 38), gesture in worship, *Des gestes qui révèlent*, January 1968 (D.O.L., 42); and the translation of liturgical texts for celebrations with the people, the Consilium's main contribution on the subject, *Comme le prévoit*, 25 January 1969 (D.O.L., 123).

S.C.R. issued a Decree, *Cum nostra aetate*, 27 January 1966 (D.O.L., 134), on the publication of liturgical books and a Declaration, *Da qualche tempo*, on arbitrary liturgical innovations, 29 December 1966 (D.O.L., 35), and S.C.D.W. issued a Declaration, *Plures liturgiae*, that translations of liturgical texts may not omit anything of the original, 15 September 1969 (D.O.L., 125).

Ecumenical Dimensions

The validity of baptism administered in other Christian churches was acknowledged by Vatican II and is re-affirmed in S.P.U.C. Ecumenical Directory, Part 1, *Ad totam ecclesiam*, 9-20 (D.O.L., 147). Shared worship, or *communicatio in sacris*, is seen to present certain difficulties and the same document deals with it (38-63), as do three other documents issued by S.P.U.C. Declaration, *Dans ces derniers temps*, 7 January 1970 (D.O.L., 150); Instruction, *In quibus rerum circumstantiis*, on admitting other Christians to Eucharistic Communion in the Catholic Church, 1 June 1972; and Note, *Dopo la pubblicazione*, interpreting that Instruction, 17 October 1973 (D.O.L., 157). On the ordination of women the views of the Catholic church are at variance with those of the Anglican Communion. Pope Paul VI wrote two letters to the Archbishop of Canterbury on the subject in 1975 and 1976 (D.O.L., 161, 162) and more recently, 8 December 1988, Pope John Paul II in a letter to the Archbishop of Canterbury said that the Catholic church viewed it as a break with tradition of a kind we have no competence to authorize (*Origins*, 19, 4, p.64). See also S.C.D.F. document under "The Other Sacraments" below.

Directives on the liturgical celebration of marriages between Catholics and other Christians form part of three longer documents: S.C.D.F. Instruction, *Matrimonii sacramentum*, 18 March 1966 (D.O.L., 351), Decree, *Crescens matrimoniorum*, of the Sacred Congregation for the Eastern Churches, 22 February 1967 (D.O.L., 352) and Pope Paul VI Motu Proprio, *Matrimonia mixta*, 31 March 1970 (D.O.L., 354).

The Praenotanda to the Liturgical Books

The documents of most enduring importance are those which form the prefatory material, the *Praenotanda*, to the new liturgical rites. They are, especially, the Instructions on the liturgical rites and Introductions to them, plus the Apostolic Constitutions, Apostolic Letters and Decrees which promulgated the rites.

They contain a rich pastoral and sacramental theology and thus have had a crucial role in effecting the change of emphasis in sacramental administration introduced by Vatican II: "Since Trent the Church has been concerned to uphold the truth that the sacraments really effect what they signify. Now she is as strenuously concerned to ensure that they really signify what they effect" (Christopher Walsh, *Instructions on the Revised Roman Rites*, p. 9). The *Praenotanda* are designed to help celebrants ensure that, to quote some of the remarkable phrases in S.C., the faithful take part in liturgical celebrations with "their minds attuned to their voices . . . fully aware of what they are doing . . . and enriched by [the rites]:" (11) "[that the sacraments] nourish, strengthen and express [faith] . . . [and] that the faithful should easily understand the sacramental signs. . ." (59). To this end, the *Praenotanda* to each rite explain its meaning, structure, parts and mini-

sters, how it may be celebrated to maximum effect, inculcating concern not just with validity but with the clarity, effectiveness and wholeness of the sign, and how to secure maximum participation by the faithful.

The obligatory inclusion of the *Praenotanda* in the Latin originals and vernacular language editions of liturgical books (S.C., 63b) ensures their universal distribution and enduring availability.

After the publication of D.O.L. changes necessitated by the publication of the new Code of Canon Law were made in a number of the *Praenotanda*, as directed by S.C.D.W. Decree, *Promulgato Codice*, 12 September 1983 (*Notitiae* 1983, p. 539). They are listed in an article, *Variationes in Novas Editiones Librorum Liturgicorum*, hereafter referred to as *Var, (Notitiae* 1983, pp. 540 ff).

The Eucharist:Doctrinal and Pastoral Documents

Several important pastoral and doctrinal documents on the eucharist have been issued by Paul VI and John Paul II and by Roman congregations. We here list the more important.

On the eucharist in general: Paul VI's encyclical, *Mysterium Fidei*, On the Doctrine and Worship of the Eucharist, 3 September 1965 (D.O.L., 176), deals with "opinions that upset the faithful," about Masses said in private, transubstantiation and eucharistic devotion; S.C.R.; Instruction, *Eucharisticum mysterium*, On the Worship of the Eucharist, 25 May 1967 (D.O.L., 179), on catechesis on the eucharist, its proper celebration and worship of the reserved eucharist; John Paul II Apostolic Letter, *Dominicae cenae*, On the Mystery and Worship of the Eucharist, 24 February 1980 (*Origins*, 9, 41, pp. 653-665), addressed to bishops, priests and deacons about eucharistic worship and its relation to their life and ministry; S.C.S.D.W. Instruction, *Inaestimabile donum*, on Certain Norms Concerning the Worship of the Eucharistic Mystery,

3 March 1980 (*Vatican Collection*, Vol. 2, edited by Austin Flannery, O.P., hereafter referred to as F2, pp. 93-102); John Paul II Apostolic Letter, *Vicesimus quintus annus*, On the 25th Anniversary of the Promulgation of the Conciliar Constitution *Sacrosanctum concilium* on the Liturgy, 4 December 1988, (*Origins*, 19, 2, pp. 17-25), on the principles which guided the reform of the Mass, the need to accept it wholeheartedly and implement it loyally.

On special eucharistic celebrations: S.C.D.W. Instruction, *Actio pastoralis*, on Masses with special groups, 15 May 1969 (D.O.L., 275); S.C.D.W. *Pueros baptizatos*, Directory for Masses with Children, 1 November 1973 (D.O.L., 276); S.C.S.D.W. Circular Letter, *Officium mihi est*, extending indefinitely permission to use eucharistic prayers for children and for reconciliation, 13 December 1980 (F2, 118).

On the eucharist prayers and Prayers of the Faithful: S.C.R. Norms on the use of the Eucharistic Prayers I-IV, 23 May 1968 (D.O.L., 242); Consilium Letter, *La publication*, on the eucharistic prayers and how to use them, 2 June 1968 (D.O.L., 243); S.C.D.W. Circular Letter, *Eucharistiae participationem*, on the eucharistic prayers, 27 April 1973 (D.O.L., 248); S.C.D.F. Declaration on the Eucharistic Prayers and Liturgical Experiments, 21 March 1988 (*Notitiae*, 1988, pp. 234-236); Consilium, *The Universal Prayer or Prayer of the Faithful*, 13 January 1965, second edition, 17 April 1966 (D.O.L., 239).

On communion: Paul VI *Concession*, announced at public session of Vatican II, reducing eucharistic fast to one hour, 21 November 1964 (D.O.L., 272); S.C.D.W. Instruction, *Memoriale Domini*, report on a survey of hierarchies' views on communion in the hand, 29 May 1969 (D.O.L., 260); S.C.D.W. Letter, *En Réponse àla Demande*, to bishops' conferences who had requested permission for communion in the hand, 29 May 1969 (D.O.L., 261); S.C.D.W. Instruction, *Sacramentali Communione*, extending practice of communion under both kinds, 29 June 1970 (D.O.L., 270); S.C.D.S. Instruction, *Immensae caritatis*, on facilitating the reception of communion, 29 January 1973 (D.O.L., 264); S.C.S.D.W. Letter, *Instructione 'Memoriale Domini'* on communion in the hand, 17 March 1976 (D.O.L., 267); S.C.D.W. Notification on communion in the hand, 3 March 1985 (*Notitiae*, 1985 pp. 259-265).

On Ministers of the Eucharist: S.C.D.S. Instruction, *Fidei custos*, on special eucharistic ministers, 30 April 1969 (D.O.L., 259); S.C.D.F. Letter on Some Questions on the Minister of the Eucharist, 6 August 1983 (A.A.S. 75 (1983) 1001-1009, *Origins* 13, 14, pp. 229-233): only ordained priests can celebrate the eucharist.

The Eucharist: Praenotanda

The Mass: Apostolic Constitution on the Roman Missal, *Missale Romanum*, 3 April 1969, promulgating first edition of the Roman Missal (D.O.L., 202); S.C.D.W. Decree, *Cum Missale Romanum*, 27 March 1975, promulgating second edition of the Roman Missal (D.O.L., 207); S.C.D.W. General Instruction of the Roman Missal, 27 March 1975. This second edition incorporated changes made in 1970 and 1972 in the 1969 edition (D.O.L., 208). Further changes listed in *Var.*, 540-543; S.C.D.W. Decree, *Ordo lectionum*, promulgating, the Lectionary for Mass (D.O.L., 231) and Introduction to the Lectionary for Mass, 25 May 1969 (D.O.L., 232). A second edition published 21 January 1981 (F2, pp. 119-152). One change listed in *Var.*, p. 543.

Concelebration and communion: S.C.R. Rite of Communion under Both Kinds, 7 March 1965 (D.O.L., 268); S.C.R. Decree, *Ecclesiae semper*, promulgating the publication of the rite of concelebration and of communion under both kinds, 7 March 1965 (D.O.L., 222); S.C.R. Introduction,

Rite of Concelebration, 7 March 1965 (D.O.L., 223).

S.C.D.W. Decree, *Eucharistiae Sacramentum* and Introduction to Holy Communion and Worship of the Eucharist outside Mass, 21 June 1973 (D.O.L., 266 and 279). Changes in *Var.*, pp. 543-545.

Eucharistic Prayers: S.C.D.W. Decree, *Postquam de Precibus*, (D.O.L., 249) and Introduction, Eucharistic Prayers for Masses with Children and for Masses of Reconciliation, 1 November 1974 (D.O.L., 250).

Christian Initiation

S.C.D.W. Decree, *Ordinem Baptismi parvulorum*, promulgating Rite of Baptism of Children, 15 May 1969 (D.O.L., 292); S.C.D.W. Christian Initiation, General Introduction, second edition, 1973 (D.O.L., 294). Changes in *Var.*, pp. 545-546. S.C.D.W. Rite of Baptism of Children, Introduction, second edition, 1973 (D.O.L., 295). Changes in *Var.*, pp. 546-547; S.C.D.W. Decree, *Ordinis Baptismi* (D.O.L., 300) and Introduction, Rite of Christian Initiation of Adults, 6 January 1972 (D.O.L., 301). Changes in *Var.*, p. 547. S.C.D.W. Reflections on the Rite of Christian Initiation of Adults, chap. 4, 8 March 1973 (D.O.L., 302); S.C.D.F. Instruction, *Pastoralis actio*, 20 October 1980, on infant baptism (F2 pp. 103-117); Paul VI Apostolic Constitution, *Divinae consors naturae*, approving new rite of confirmation, 15 August 1971 (D.O.L., 303); S.C.D.W. Rite of Confirmation, Introduction, 22 August 1971 (D.O.L., 305). Changes in *Var.*, pp. 547-549. S.C.D.W. Decree, *Ritibus Hebdomadae sanctae* (D.O.L., 458) and Introduction, Rite of the Blessing of Oils and Rite of Consecrating the Chrism, 3 December 1970 (D.O.L., 459). Changes in *Var.*, p. 454.

The Other Sacraments

Paul VI's Motu Proprio, *Sacrum Diaconatus Ordinem*, restoring permanent diaconate in Latin Church, 18 June 1967 (D.O.L., 309); S.C.D.F. Declaration, *Inter insigniores*, on admitting women to the ministerial priesthood, 15 October 1976 (D.O.L., 321); Paul VI Apostolic Constitution, *Pontificalis Romani recognitio*, approving rites for ordination of deacons, priests and bishops, 18 June 1968 (D.O.L., 324); S.C.R. Decree, *Per Constitutionem Apostolicam*, promulgating rites of ordination of deacons, priests and bishops (D.O.L., 325) 15 August 1968; S.C.D.W. Decree, *Ministeriorum disciplina* (D.O.L., 341) and Introductions to rites of Institution of Readers, Institution of Acolytes, Admission to Candidacy for Ordination as Deacons and Priests, Commitment to Celibacy, 3 December 1972 (D.O.L., 342); S.C.D.W. Rite of Commissioning Special Ministers of Holy Communion, Introduction, 29 January 1973 (D.O.L., 343).

S.C.R. Decree, *Ordo celebrandi Matrimonium* (D.O.L., 348) and Introduction to Rite of Marriage, 19 March 1969 (D.O.L., 349).

Paul VI Apostolic Constitution, *Paenitemini*, on Christian penance, (excerpts), 17 February 1966 (D.O.L., 358); S.C.D.F. Pastoral Norms, *Sacramentum Paenitentiae*, on general absolution, 16 June 1972 (D.O.L., 361); S.C.D.W. Decree, *Reconciliationem inter Deum et homines* (D.O.L., 367) and Introduction to Rite of Penance, 2 December 1973 (D.O.L., 368). Changes in *Var.*, pp. 549-551. Three documents on confessions of children before first communion: S.C.D.S. Declaration, *Sanctus Pontifex*, 24 May 1973 (D.O.L., 379); S.C.S.D.W. and S.C.C. Letter, *Le Saint-Siége*, 30 April 1976 (D.O.L., 380); S.C.S.D.W. and S.C.C. Letter, *In Quibusdam Ecclesiae partibus*, 31 March 1977 (D.O.L., 381); Paul VI Apostolic Constitution, *Indulgentiarum doctrina*, on indulgences, 1 January 1967 (D.O.L., 386); Apostolic Penitentiary Decree, *In Constitutione Apostolica* (D.O.L., 389) and Norms for *Enchiridion indulgentiarum*, 29 June 1968 (D.O.L., 390).

Paul VI Apostolic Constitution, *Sacram Unctionem infirmorum*, on the sacrament of anointing the sick, 30 November 1972 (D.O.L., 408); S.C.D.W. Decree, *Infirmis in Ecclesia* (D.O.L., 409) and Introduction to Pastoral Care of the Sick; Rite of Anointing and Viaticum, 7 December 1972 (D.O.L., 410). Changes in *Var.*, pp. 551-553.

Formation and Ministries

S.C.C. General Directory, *Peregrinans in terra*, on pastoral ministry in tourism, 30 April 1969 (D.O.L., 326); Paul VI's Motu Proprio, *Pastoralis migratorum cura*, on pastoral care of migrants, 15 August 1969 (D.O.L., 327); S.C.B. *Ecclesiae imago*, Directory on the Pastoral Ministry of Bishops, 22 February 1973 (D.O.L., 329); S.C.B. Decree, *Apostolatus maris*, on pastoral care of seamen and ships' passengers, 24 September 1977 (D.O.L., 330); Sacred Congregation for Seminaries and Universities Instruction, *Doctrina et exemplo*, on liturgical formation of future priests, 25 December 1965 (D.O.L., 332); Sacred Congregation for Catholic Education, *In ecclesiasticam futurorum sacerdotum*, on liturgical formation in seminaries, 3 June 1979 (D.O.L., 335); Paul VI's motu proprio, *Ministeria quaedam*, on first tonsure, minor orders and subdiaconate, 15 August 1972 (D.O.L., 340); S.C.D.W. Directory for Sunday Celebrations in the Absence of a Priest, 21 May 1988 (*Notitiae* 1988 pp. 366-378; *Origins* 18, 19, pp. 301-307).

Religious Life

S.C.D.W. Decree, *Professionis ritus* (D.O.L., 391) and Introduction to Rite of Religious Profession, 2 February 1970, reprinted 1975 (D.O.L., 392). Changes in *Var.*, p. 554. S.C.D.W. Decree, *Consecrationis virginum* (D.O.L., 394) and Introduction to Rite of Consecration to a Life of Virginity, 31 May 1970; S.C.D.W. Guidelines, *Les principales indications*, on adapting the Rite of Religious Profession, 15 July 1970 (D.O.L., 397); S.C.D.W.

Decree, *Abbatem et Abbatissam* (D.O.L., 398) and Introduction to Rite of Blessing of an Abbot and an Abbess, 9 November 1970 (D.O.L., 399).

Funerals

S.C.H.O. Instruction, *Piam et constantem*, on cremation, 8 May 1963; S.C.D.W. Decree, *Ritibus exsequiarum* (D.O.L., 415) and Introduction to Rite of Funerals, 15 August 1969 (D.O.L., 416). Changes in *Var.*, pp. 554-555).

The Divine Office, The Liturgical Year, Our Lady, Saints

Paul VI's Apostolic Constitution, *Laudis canticum*, promulgating revised book of the liturgy of the hours, 1 November 1970 (D.O.L., 424); S.C.D.W. General Instruction on the Liturgy of the Hours, 2 February 1971 (D.O.L., 426). Changes in *Var.*, p. 555. S.C.D.W. Notification, *Universi qui Officium*, on the liturgy of the hours for contemplative religious communities, 6 August 1972 (D.O.L., 432).

Paul VI Motu Proprio, *Mysterii paschalis*, approving norms for liturgical year and the General Roman Calendar, 14 February 1969 (D.O.L., 440); S.C.R. Decree, *Anni liturgici ordinatione* (D.O.L., 441) and General Norms for the Liturgical Year and the Calendar, 21 March 1969; S.C.D.W. Circular Letter on Preparing and Celebrating the Paschal Feasts, 16 January 1988 (*Notitiae* 1988 pp. 81-107, *Origins* 17, 40, pp. 677-687).

S.C.D.W. Norms, *Pluries decursu temporis*, on crowning statues of Our Lady, 25 March 1973 (D.O.L., 466); Paul VI's, Apostolic Exhortation, *Marialis cultus*, on proper devotion to Mary, 2 February 1974 (D.O.L., 467); S.C.D.W. Introduction, Rite for Crowning Statues of the Blessed Virgin Mary, 15 March 1981 (*Notitiae* 1981, pp. 246ff); S.C.D.W. Decree, Introduction, Introduction to Lectionary, for Masses in Honour of the Blessed Virgin Mary, 5 August 1986 (*Notitiae* 1986 pp. 902-903, 907-921, 922-925).

S.C.R. Instruction, *Ad solemnia*, on celebrations in honor of saints and blesseds within a year of their canonization or beatification, 12 September 1968 (D.O.L., 472); S.C.D.W. Norms, *Patronus liturgica acceptione* on patron saints, 19 March 1973 (D.O.L., 477); S.C.D.W. Instruction, *Calendaria particularia*, on revision of particular calendars of dioceses and religious orders, 24 June 1970 (D.O.L., 481).

Music, Places of Worship, Vestments
S.C.R. Instruction, *Musicam sacram*, directives on singing and musical instruments in the liturgy, 5 March 1967 (D.O.L., 508). S.C.D.W. Preface to *Jubilate Deo*, a collection of Gregorian chants, 11 April 1974 (D.O.L., 524); S.C.D.W. Letter, *Voluntati obsequiens*, accompanying *Jubilate Deo*, 14 April 1974 (D.O.L., 523); S.C.R. Decree, *Cantus faciliores* (D.O.L., 536) and Introduction to second edition to The Simple Gradual, 22 November, 1974 (D.O.L., 537 with 533); S.C.D.W. Decree, *Thesaurum cantus gregoriani* (D.O.L., 534) and Introduction to *Ordo cantus Missae*, Gregorian chants for Mass, 24 June 1974 (D.O.L., 535); S.C.D.W. Note, *Passim quaeritur*, on music in vernacular editions of the Roman Missal, May 1975 (D.O.L., 538); S.C.D.W. Introduction, *Ordo cantus officii (Notitiae* 1983 pp. 244-245); S.C.D.W. Directory on Concerts in Churches, 5 December 1987 (*Notitiae* 1987 pp. 3-10). Paul VI's Address to the Pontifical Commission on Sacred Art in Italy, 17 December 1969 (D.O.L., 540); S.C.C. Circular Letter, *Opera artis*, on care of the historical and artistic heritage of the church, 11 April 1971 (D.O.L., 541); S.C.S.D.W. Decree, *Dedicationi ecclesiae* (D.O.L., 546) and Introductions to Rite of Dedication of a Church and an Altar, 29 May 1977 (D.O.L., 447). Changes in *Var.*, p. 553.
S.C.R. Instruction, *Pontificalis ritus*, on simplifying pontifical rites and insignia,

21 June 1968 (D.O.L., 550); Secretariate of State Instruction, *Ut sive sollicite*, on vestments, titles and insignia of cardinals, bishops and other prelates, 31 March 1969 (D.O.L., 551).

Blessings and Ceremonial for Bishops
S.C.D.W. Decree, *De Benedictionibus*, Promulgating The Book of Blessings, 31 May 1984 (Notitiae 1984, pp. 927-928); General Introduction (*Notitiae* 1982, pp. 928-939); S.C.D.W. Decree, promulgating *Caeremoniale Episcoporum*, Ceremonial for Bishops and Preface, 14 September 1984 (*Notitiae*, 1984 pp. 940-941, 941-944).

The International Commission on English in the Liturgy, *Documents on the Liturgy 1963-1979: Conciliar, Papal and Curial Texts* (Collegeville: The Liturgical Press). *The Rites of the Catholic Church as Revised by Decree of the Second Vatican Ecumenical Council and Published by Authority of Pope Paul VI*, Vols. 1 and 2 (New York: Pueblo Publishing Co). *Instructions on the Revised Roman Rites*, intro. by Christopher Walsh, (London: Collins). Austin Flannery, O.P., Vatican Collection, Vol. I, *Vatican II: Conciliar and Post-conciliar Documents*, Vol. 2, *Vatican II: More Postconciliar Documents* (New York: Costello Publishing). Reiner Kaczynski, ed., *Enchiridion Documentarum Instaurationis Liturgicae*, 1 (1963-1973), Marietti Turin, II (1973-1983) C.L.V. (Rome: Edizioni Liturgiche).

AUSTIN FLANNERY, O.P.

DOXOLOGY

Doxology (Gk. *doxologia*; from *doxa*, glory, and *logos*, word or utterance) is an utterance which expresses praise to God. Such utterances occur from the earliest strata of scripture (Gen 24:27, Exod 18:10), and are highly developed by the end of the scriptural era (Rev 19:1-18, Jn 17:1-5). They are a constant and necessary part of the worship of the Christian church.

Definition. The word *doxa* is almost invariably translated "glory" in English versions of scripture, and is most frequently used by the LXX to translate the Hebrew word *kabod*, though more than twenty other Hebrew words are also translated as *doxa. Kabod* comes from the root *kbd,* "to be heavy," and stands as a metaphor for that which is weighty, honorable, important, of high esteem. Thus, the scripture referent for the Advent "O Antiphon," Isa 22:22-24, speaks of the weight or glory which will hang on the one who bears the Key of David. *Kabod* designates the sum total of one's possessions, indeed of all that one is, as one's glory (Ps 49:16-17).

Though the root meaning of *kabod* is based on external objective criteria, it also refers to inner qualities and becomes a metaphor for the essence or essential quality of an individual or a people. *Kabod* is used to designate honor, renown and importance (Gen 45:13, Ps 8:6, 1 Kgs 3:13). It refers to the central identity of Israel (1 Sam 4:21). To ascribe glory to some one or some thing is to acknowledge power and authority and by implication, the respect and perhaps fealty of the one who ascribes (Esth 1:4). Thus, *kabod* referred to the qualities of power and holiness in God, reflecting the esteem which worshippers brought (Exod 16:4-7, Josh 7:19, Isa 42:12, 48:11, Jer 13:16, Mal 2:2).

Glory Breaking Through to Visibility. It is of the nature of God to "show forth" or to manifest glory. Throughout scripture there is an emphasis on the visibility of God's glory, and God's self-revelation, God's epiphany, is spoken of as a phenomenon of light. "To behold God's glory" is to reflect God's glory and to give glory to God, as with Moses (Exod 3:2-6, 19:16-21, 24:17, 34:29-35), who beheld God in light and whose face shone with the reflected glory of God's presence. God, in kenotic act, shares glory which shines forth as a cloud, and in the *shekeinah* which is known in the theophanies of tent and temple (Exod 29:43, Lev 9:22-24, Num 16:19, 1 Kgs 8:11, Isa 6, Ezek 9:3). The human response to God's glory is doxology.

The storm image of theophany is a dominant scriptural theme. Psalm 29, with its flashing flames and thundering glory, causes everyone and everything in the temple to respond "*Doxa!*" They respond with doxology (Ps 29:9). Ezekiel in his initiating vision saw fire flashing forth continually, and Ezekiel 1 is itself a doxology of praise, a reflection of the prophet's vision, though the prophet confesses at the end that it is but a poor reflection or representation. It is only a picture of a picture of a picture: ". . . such was the appearance of the likeness of the glory of the Lord" (Ezek 1:28). In this life, the doxology can never do justice to the infinite power and holiness, beauty and radiance, awesomeness and splendor, love and grace which God reveals.

Doxology In and Through Jesus Christ. Christ is the perfect doxology, the perfect reflection of the glory of God (Heb 1:3). So great was the awesomeness of God that the brightness of God's face was beyond human seeing (Exod 33:18-34:8). Yet, Christians have affirmed that God's glory is seen in the face of Jesus Christ (2 Cor 4:6) and that to see and receive this glory is salvation and empowerment. This is a glory that belonged to Jesus before creation (Jn 17:5) and to which he will return (17:22,24). Indeed, God doxologizes the Son as the Son doxologizes the Father (Jn 13:31-32, 17:1-5), the doctrine of *perichoresis.* While the transfiguration is a primary epiphany of the visible glory of Christ (Mt 17:1-8, Mk 9:2-8, Lk 9:28-36), the glorification *par excellence* is the paschal mystery of Jesus' death and resurrection, foreseen by Isaiah (Jn 12:41) and made complete when Jesus' hour had come (Jn 17:1, Heb 2:9, Lk 24:26). It was in Jesus' death-resurrection that the self-giving love of God, God's power and might, God's judgment on sin and injustice and God's will for humanity and society were most perfectly reflected. For this the church gives glory to God in endless doxology.

We ascribe glory to God through Christ. As Christ has entered into glory, so we draw near to God through Christ (Heb 7:25, 13:15) and ascribe glory to Christ as God (Heb 13:21). As early as the *Didache* we find, "For thine is the glory and the power through Jesus Christ for ever." The eucharistic prayer in the *Apostolic Tradition* of Hippolytus concludes with a prayer for the Holy Spirit and a doxology: "In order that we may praise and glorify you through your Child Jesus Christ, through whom be glory and honor to you, with the Holy Spirit in the holy church, now and unto ages of ages." A trinitarian doxology, differing slightly from rite to rite, has continued to mark the conclusion of eucharistic prayers down to the present time.

The Holy Spirit and Doxology. Through Christ, in the Holy Spirit, we have access to the Father, and when we behold Jesus Christ aright it is by the Holy Spirit that we are changed from glory into glory (2 Cor 3:12-18, esp. v. 18). Doxology is implicit epiclesis, voicing the prayer and desire that the Spirit will bring forth the fruit of glorification with Christ (Rom 8:16-23). It is the desire of the Christian to reflect and render glory to God, in service and obedience, so that God might be all in all (see Wainwright, *Eucharist and Eschatology*, chap. IV).

Doxologies in worship seek to give expression to the inexpressible. They seek to break the boundaries of the limitations of words. They are the work of the Holy Spirit seeking to bring the glory of God to word, song and adoration. Often they are summaries, and they bear the implication that everything which precedes them is insufficient to give expression to what God is and what God has done. Nonetheless, our words and song seek to express what the Spirit and indeed the whole creation seek to proclaim (Rom 8:16-23). Charismatic worship is replete with doxologies.

Doxologies in the Old Testament. The psalms are doxological. Psalm 29 is a very early ascription of glory. Representative are Psalms 19 (esp. v. 1) and 96 (esp. vv. 3 and 7). Each of the books of the psalter concludes with a doxology (41:13, 72: 18-19 and Ps 150). OT doxologies are often uttered as blessings (1 Kgs 8:56-61, Ezra 7:27). Frequently the doxology ends in an act of penitence (Job 42:1-6, Neh 9:6ff).

Isa 6:2ff is of primary interest because of the prominent place it has in the eucharistic prayers of the church: "Holy, holy holy is the Lord of hosts; the whole earth is full of his glory." Though taking place in the temple, the vision of glory is cosmic: *the whole earth.* When God's glory is revealed, *all flesh* will see it together (Isa 40:5). The celestial creatures of the Apocalypse join the song (Rev 4:8,11) and in the liturgy the church joins this all-encompassing doxology.

Doxologies in the New Testament. Doxologies break out spontaneously and very frequently in the NT. The angelic hosts sing, "Glory to God in the highest and peace to God's people on earth" (Lk 2:14); Simeon ascribes glory (2:32); Mary's song itself is a doxology (Lk 1:46-56). Jesus says that the one leper turned back "to give glory to God" (Lk 17:18). Paul's letters are punctuated with doxologies: each of the three main structural parts of the letter to the Romans ends with a doxology (Rom 8:38-39, 11:33-36, 16:25-27; see also Eph 3:20-21, Phil 2:5-11, 3:20-21, 4:19-20, 1 Tm 1:17, 2 Tm 4:18, 2 Pet 1:3, 17, 3:18, Jude 24-25 and the several hymns in the book of Revelation). It is noteworthy that many of these passages are considered to be hymns which were used in the worship of the apostolic church and thus figure prominently in early Christian worship.

The Lesser Doxology. The doxologies of the NT were early adapted to liturgical usage with the ascription of glory to God, and ended with "...forever. Amen" (Gal

1:15, Eph 3:21). In the period of the trinitarian controversies, the "through Jesus Christ" (Rom 16:27, I Pet 4:11) and the "in the Holy Spirit" (Prayers of Serapion) were changed in order to counter Arianism. The two verses of the resulting doxology avoid the supposed implicit subordinationism of the prepositions "through" and "in": "Glory to the Father and to the Son and to the Holy Spirit as it was in the beginning, is now and will be forever. Amen." This doxology came to be used almost universally in churches of both the East and the West as the summary conclusion to psalms and canticles, both in the Mass and in the daily office.

Metrical doxologies are the result of setting the Psalms to meter and the related transference to hymns. Within the Protestant churches, "The doxology" is almost univerally recognized to be the metrical translation of the *Gloria Patri* by Bishop Ken, set to the tune Old Hundredth: "Praise God from whom all blessings flow, Praise God all creatures here below, Praise God above, ye heavenly host, Praise Father, Son and Holy Ghost. Amen."

Similiar metrical doxologies are found in Roman breviaries.

The Greater Doxology (Gloria in Excelsis). The simple form of this doxology is found in Lk 2:14, "Glory to God in the highest and peace to God's people on earth." It is found in this form in the Liturgy of St. James. However, the form soon expanded and was elaborated in a number of variations (e.g., *Apostolic Constitutions*). An extensive 5th-century text is titled "Morning Hymn" and is found at the end of the Psalms and Canticles in the Codex Alexandrinus. A form of the Greater Doxology, sung as the climax of the *orthros* (morning prayer) in the Byzantine rite, is an early and consistent usage.

The use of the Greater Doxology, as a part of the eucharistic service of the church, is peculiar to the West. Though not yet in its final form, it had an established place in the eucharistic service in Rome by the beginning of the 6th century, though only when a bishop presided.

The final Latin form of the text is found in an 8th century manuscript in the British Museum (Reg. 2A. xx). It retains only the single biblical verse from Luke's gospel, but continues with three strophes of theological acclamation. By the 11th century, this version was commonly used in the Western Mass, though it was omitted during Advent, pre-Lent and Lent.

In the Roman rite as well as in the Lutheran liturgies, the *Gloria* is sung as a part of the entrance rite and before the collect of the day. In the 1552 *Book of Common Prayer* of the Church of England, the *Gloria* was moved to the conclusion of the euharist, after the postcommunion prayer. This utilized the Greater Doxology as a summarizing ascription to the entire eucharistic action. However, with the 1979 *Book of Common Prayer*, the *Gloria in Excelsis* is again within the entrance rite of the eucharistic liturgy. The "free churches" suggest the use of the Greater Doxology as an option following the penitential portion of the entrance rite (e.g., United Methodist and Presbyterian).

Doxologies and Prayers. It became customary to conclude a collect or other prayer with a trinitarian doxology after the 5th century. The wording of such conclusions was varied, though several formulae became common.

The eucharistic prayer came to have an almost invariably trinitarian acclamation of glory from an early date. This, which has come to be identified as "the great doxology of the eucharist," has taken various forms in various traditions. That of the Roman rite, "Jesus Christ, by whom and with whom and in whom, in the unity of the Holy Spirit, all honor and glory be to you, Father almighty, world without end," has continued as the paradigm for all Western rites, though in Cranmer's *Book of Common Prayer* the omission of "in whom" continued until it was restored in the 1979 *Book of Common Prayer*.

A similar development has taken place with reference to the baptismal prayer, though convergence to a concluding trinitarian doxology within the churches of the West is an achievement only of the latter half of the 20th century.

The Lord's Prayer (Mt 6:9-13, Lk 11:1-4) was given a closing doxology very early in Christian history. As early as the 2nd century the custom arose in the Eastern church of adding "for the kingdom, the power and the glory are yours, now and forever. Amen." at the end of the "Our Father." This became common when the Lord's Prayer was recited in public worship (see *Didache* 8:2-3, 9:4, 10:2). This doxology was inserted into some translations of the Matthean account, but this is a contribution of the church and not a part of earliest texts of scripture.

Amen As Doxology. 2 Cor 1:20 affirms that "we utter Amen through Christ to the glory of God." The word *Amen* (so be it) is repeated responsively by the Jewish congregation after doxologies and prayers and following each verse of the priestly benediction. People were encouraged to say "Amen" following blessings, e.g., those spoken before and after meals. The *Amen* was understood as the ratification of any blessing.

Christians continued this practice from the biblical period (1 Cor 14-16), though it was not at first repeated after liturgical formulae or creeds. It was, however, spoken vigorously at the conclusion of the eucharistic prayer and was spoken when communion was received and at the conclusion of other prayers. It signified the appropriation of the intent which had been expressed, and thus, functioned as an affirming doxology for worshippers.

Doxology and Ethics. The Christian who has caught a glimpse of the divine glory and who reflects, ascribes and renders glory to God comes to resemble that glory. Indeed, to sin is to deny the glory and to be cut off from the glory. To reflect the glory is to become an instrument of the glory. Thus, the whole creation, the miracle of human life and relationships, as well as the bread, wine and water, are transformed by doxology. In worship, both we and the material world, and most particularly the bread and the wine of Christ's glorification, render the divine glory and become doxology, the oblation by which God's glory fills the universe. Thus, we "glorify God in our human bodies" (1 Cor 6:19). We become doxology.

See **Holy Spirit in Christian worship**

ARLO D. DUBA

DRAMA, LITURGICAL

Throughout most of the history of civilization, the contemporary western distinction between drama and religious ritual has not existed. The earliest evidence of rituals and drama is found in Paleolithic times. Persons related to the sacred through symbols, myths, song, dance, and mimetic activity. In the Christian tradition, ritual drama has a theological base in the concepts of creation and incarnation. Matter, word, and embodiment express more than themselves; they point to the divine. Scripture has examples of God's messages being dramatized: Jeremiah broke a pot to give visual force to God's threat (Jeremiah 19); Ezekiel lay on the ground to illustrate the devastation of Jerusalem (Ezekiel 4). At the Last Supper, Jesus acted out, rather than merely tell his disciples, how they were to relate to others (John 13). He washed their feet. Then, as often through the ages, the dramatic message was so strong that some were distressed.

Jesus' action challenged hierarchical power relationships and this upset Peter. Drama empowers both those who share it and those who witness it because it evokes empathy and emotional involvement.

Religious ritual had developed into theater for entertainment among the classical Greeks and then the Romans. By the 4th century of the Christian era, violence and spectacle dominated entertainment. Tertullian called the theater the devil's church. Some have said the Christians' attitudes destroyed the theater, but actually the period of social upheaval, including the Lombard invasion in 568, brought the end of theater.

Drama seemed to have been lost, except for the wandering mimes, minstrels, or jugglers who might share a poem or story, and for folk celebrations which were associated with primitive rituals to invoke the fertility of the earth. Greek and Roman dramas were not performed and practically forgotten. An exception to this was the reading of Terence's plays in textbooks. These inspired the 10th century German nun, Hrotsvitha of Gandersheim, to write six plays for the moral edification of her readers, but the plays seem never to have been performed and have been neglected for centuries.

Liturgy As Drama

To understand the development of dramas used in liturgy from about 900 until 1700 and in the 20th century, it is important to consider how Christian ritual itself is dramatic. Drama can be defined as dialogue, movement, and impersonation. The liturgy, as drama, often has dialogical form with an utterance and then a response with parts for individuals, choruses, and congregations. Liturgy includes movement. Medieval persons thought of the liturgy as involving a type of impersonation.

Amalarius of Metz in the 9th century developed an extensive reflection on the Mass in which the introit to the gospel was said to represent Christ's life until the entry into Jerusalem, the offertory through the *Pater Noster* represented the passion and burial, and the rest of the liturgy represented the resurrection and the ascension. The outstretched arms of the priest were like those of Jesus on the cross and the deacons and subdeacons represented the prophets, the disciples, or the women at the cross. Honorius of Autun wrote that the celebrant impersonates Christ as the actor does the character in a tragedy. Though this and other allegorical interpretations can be criticized as unsound, they were extremely popular, substantially influenced piety, and gave a conceptual framework for the development of drama.

The liturgical year involves dramatic aspects such as the procession with palms on Palm Sunday, the washing of the feet on Holy Thursday, and the plunging of the catechumens into the "tomb" of water to be resurrected in baptism at the Easter vigil. During the 10th century, the practice of the "Depositio" began between Mass and Vespers on Good Friday. A consecrated host, a cross, or both were buried in a receptacle called the "sepulchrum," some type of chest or enclosure. The "Elevatio" would be a ceremony taking the host or cross from the sepulchre before matins Easter morning and displaying the empty grave linens. A ritual of Gallican origin for the dedication of a church had one of the clergy on the inside representing the evil spirit. The bishop and his procession came to the front door and began a dialogue saying "Lift up your heads, O ye gates; and be ye lifted up, ye everlasting doors; and the King of glory shall come in."

Drama in Liturgy

Charlemagne, as part of his political program of unification, spread the Roman rite with some Gallican elaboration. This period, the Carolingian Renaissance, brought both aspects of uniformity to liturgical texts and a great outpouring of artistic creativity including the development of tropes. A trope is an amplification (introduction, interpolation, and conclusion) of a part of the authorized liturgy to reinforce its meaning and enlarge its emotional appeal. Specific liturgical plays began in the tropes used in services.

The introit of Easter morning Mass was elaborated in a trope called *Quem Quaeritis* which is usually considered the first liturgical drama. The first version of this seems to be by the monk Tutilo of St. Gall written about 900. Nine texts of this drama survive from that century and almost fifty from the next century, and thirty-five from the 12th. In rules written by Bishop Ethelwold of Winchester between 959-979 can be found the directions for the Easter service. Three priests were to represent the three Marys and another dressed in white was to be the angel who said, "Whom to you seek in the sepulchre?" Dialogue, singing, movement, and bells were used.

In the countries of western Europe, more than four hundred texts of *Visitatio Sepulchri* were preserved in both manuscripts and printed books and the dramas were used for both Mass and the office. During the 10th, 11th, and 12th centuries the drama often became more elaborate with additions such as Mary Magdalene's encounter with Christ from Jn 20:11-18, Peter and John racing each other to the tomb, the women or men displaying the empty grave linens, and a non-biblical incident of negotiating with a spice merchant.

The drama called *Peregrinus* on the Emmaus story was used at different times, but especially for vespers on Easter Monday or during the Easter season. Antiphons, other liturgical texts, and hymns such as the *Victimae paschali* were woven into the drama. In some versions a structure for the pilgrims' shelter was constructed within the church.

Sometimes the altar itself was used for the table and rubrics described using wine and bread either in loaf or in water form. The story of Thomas was occasionally added to the pilgrim's drama.

About twenty Christmas plays, both visits of the shepherds (*Officium Pastorum*) and of the Magi (*Officium Stellae*) come from the 11th century. The Shepherds' plays were usually a part of matins. The crib was placed near the altar. Boys representing angels sang the "good tidings" and the "Gloria." Three or more shepherds came to the crib and were met by two priests representing the midwives who delivered the Christ child and they told the shepherds about it. Over two hundred and twenty manuscripts with variations of these two liturgical plays are extant.

Other liturgical plays associated with the Advent and Christmas season were *Prophetae* (prophets, Virgil, and the Sibyls testifying to Christ), *Lamentatio Rachel* for the feast of the Holy Innocents, and *Tres Reges* for Epiphany. Besides these there were Latin drama, *Conversio Beati Pauli Apostoli*, *Suscitatio Lazari*, *Daniel*, and dramas on Isaac and Rebecca, the Antichrist, St. Nicholas and St. Catherine of Alexandria who were the patrons of scholars, and other subjects.

While most of the dramas are by anonymous authors, Hilarius, a traveling scholar, who was a pupil of Abelard about 1125, is known by name. He wrote three Latin plays with a few French lines. The 12th century also produced the French dramas on Adam and on the resurrection which showed marked independence from the liturgical tradition.

By the 12th and 13th centuries many records throughout western Europe spoke of the popularity of religious dramas within liturgies, outside the church buildings, and in other places such as city squares. Objections that religious drama belonged only in the churches and should be done only by clerics and nuns (within their convents) arose, but guilds and townspeople also wanted to participate in the drama. On the other hand, as the dramas began using more human characterizations, some persons said the dramas belonged outside the churches and not within. Every country of western Europe has some records of the Feast of the Holy Innocents in which the choir boys would lead festivities and there would be a "Boy Bishop" who would go and jest with the real bishop. During the Mass, after the epistle, the reader threw a spear towards the congregation beginning a dramatization of the flight into Egypt. A cleric played Mary riding on an ass and the animal was led around the church. In some places the flight into Egypt was dramatized on the Feast of Fools. Eventually the feast became bawdy and was suppressed.

Few dramatizations of the crucifixion exist in relation to the very large number of those of the resurrection. In the 13th century, the composition form called the *planctus* or lament, expressing the emotions of one of the persons present at the crucifixion, was elaborated. Early forms were merely poems, but eventually some began to give directions for the dress and movement of Mary and John and the women. This was sometimes performed between the adoration of the cross and the communion of the Mass of the Presanctified on Good Friday.

Early theologians frequently described the atonement as a dramatic victory of Christ over Satan and used much heroic imagery. This seems to be the background of the popularity of the apocryphal legend of the Harrowing of Hell in the liturgy and in art. Katherine of Sutton, abbess of Barking from 1363 to 1376, developed a dramatic ceremony on the idea of the popular "Elevatio" service. The story of the Harrowing of Hell described Christ knocking at the gates of hell and then entering to free Adam, Eve, and others.

All the members of the religious community, who represented the patriarchs in hell awaiting the coming of Christ, were imprisoned in the chapel. The priest stood outside the door and said three times the passage beginning "Tollite portas." The doors were opened and the sisters processed out singing and waving palms of victory. The abbess wanted this to be a powerful drama to "dispel completely the sluggish indifference of the faithful."

In celebrations of the ascension clerics climbed constructed platforms or elevated pulpits to suggest Christ's movement. In some places a singer moved out of sight and sang alone the antiphon beginning "*Non vos relinquam orphanos.*" A record of a 15th century description of a dramatic trope mentions payment for the service of painting scars on Christ's hands. In 14th century Moosburg, the celebration was quite elaborate with a ring of silk cloths representing clouds into which the image of Christ was raised. Rings of flowers enclosing images of a dove and of an angel were slowly lowered at the appropriate times. Down below were choristers representing that twelve apostles, with names written on their crowns, Mary, and two angels. The closing rubric recommended dropping wafers and flowers at the end, but forbade the horseplay of dropping the effigy of the devil which seems to have been popular.

On Pentecost in many places, including St. Paul's in London, while the *Veni Creator* was sung, a variety of things were let down through a hole in the roof. These includes: a globe of fire, a dove, bits of burning towel to represent tongues of fire, flowers, pieces of flaky pastry, or a censor. For the annunciation or the day in Advent when the annunciation gospel was read, two clerics would dress as Mary and the angel for the gospel reading. A dove descended from the roof when the words "*Spiritus Sanctus supervenit in te*" were read.

Spanish, Italian, French, English, German, and Latin American nuns wrote of and sometimes recorded dramatizations of services, music, dance, theater, devotional exercises, and spiritual colloquies accompanied by music that contributed to their celebrations of the liturgical year and of religious professions.

Rebirth of Drama in the Western World

Not only is liturgical drama important in itself, but it brought about the rebirth of drama in the western world. These main types of plays developed: mystery plays, morality plays, and miracle plays. The mystery plays were based on biblical stories and began to develop in the vernacular languages, but had occasional Latin passages to add solemnity. The plays conveyed the grandeur of God's plan, but also had very human characters. Humor was frequently used and contemporary dress and characteristics brought the biblical characters very close to people's life experience. For instance, Annas and Caiaphas were in the garb of bishops.

Individual mystery plays were joined together in cycles. Some cycles went from creation to the day of judgment. In England cycles from York, Chester, Towneley, Wakefield, and Coventry survive; Beverley and Dublin cycles are spoken of in registers. Cornwall had a group of pageants. Corpus Christi was one of the most popular times for the cycles. For that feast, around 1400 in the York cycle, there were forty-eight plays which lasted from dawn to dusk. Scenes took place on carts that moved to twelve stations in different parts of the city and a large part of the population was involved in one way or another with this event. Corpus Christi meant the consecrated host and it also meant the mystical body of Christ, i.e., all the faithful throughout time. In the Corpus Christi procession the host was carried through the community and in the Corpus Christi plays the history of the faithful throughout time was presented.

Spanish missionaries brought religious dramas to the Americas and used them entensively in evangelization. The medieval mystery plays have survived as living traditions in *Los Pastores*, which are Christmas plays done in Latin America and in areas of the United States settled by the Spanish (esp. New Mexico, Texas, Arizona and Colorado).

The morality plays were allegories in which persons represented virtues and vices. The earlies recorded morality play was the *Paternoster* from 1387. The seven deadly sins had come to be connected with the seven petitions of this prayer. The play described a contest between personified sins and virtues for a person's soul. *Everyman* is the most popular example of a morality play and this piece, which originated among the Dutch, has been continuously performed. The morality play was different from the cycles in that it was not based on historical sources. The plays were associated with moral doctrine and related to a sacramental psychology. Miracle plays were a late development and were based on the lives of saints. After religious drama became popular, secular drama began to develop.

Liturgical drama and religious dramas outside of the churches did not die out spontaneously, but were often suppressed by the Reformation. There was a shift in world view from the older sacramental psychology to ethical, political and protopsychological doctrine. Though liturgical dramas can be found in 17th century Catholic service books, the Counter-reformation fear and defensiveness severely curtailed the variety and vitality of European liturgy after the Council of Trent.

The Modern Period

In the 20th century several aspects of renewal in worship have called forth a revival of liturgical drama. These aspects are summarized in ideas in the Constitution on the Sacred Liturgy: (1) the

374

desire for the full, conscious, and active participation of people (S.C., 14); (2) the desire for scripture to be proclaimed and explained more effectively (S.C., 24); (3) the desire to affirm the cultural expressions of people throughout the world (S.C., 37). Quality liturgical drama contributes to fulfilling these goals.

Drama has been used within celebrations of the eucharist, of other sacraments, of the liturgy of the hours, in many types of prayer and evangelization experiences, and in religious education. Drama may function as a means of proclamation, of homiletic reflection, to embody part of the prayers, or as a means of emphasizing and reflecting on symbolic actions which are already parts of the Christian ritual.

"Michael Moynahan (see, Mossi, *Modern Liturgy Handbook*, pp. 153-164) has written that there are at least seven types of liturgical drama: (1) interpretive proclamation of biblical and extra-biblical readings; (2) group interpretive proclamation (as multiple readers for the passion); (3) mime or pantomime (with silence, music, or narrative); (4) improvisation on a theme (which has been developed before the liturgy); (5) an adapted form of psycho-drama; (6) scenario or story dramatization of biblical text or a contemporary story interpreting the text; (7) the total dramatic liturgical experience (e.g., Holy Week liturgies). To Moynahan's list could be added the dramatic monologue which can portray biblical persons, saints, or other historical figures.

By the middle of the 20th century many denominations within the United States had committees, organizations, or elements of existing organizations for the promotion of drama. Though a number of denominational groups have waxed and waned, during the 1960s, 1970s and 1980s, there has been a general movement towards ecumenical groups. These groups seem to give artists more financial and moral support and creative stimulation.

Significant among these has been the Ecumenical Council for Drama and the Arts; the Inter-faith Forum on Religion, Art, Architecture, and the Environment; the Christians for the Fine Arts; and the sub-groups of the National Council of Churches of Christ, such as the Commission on Drama in the Department of Worship and the Arts and the Drama Committee of the Division of Christian Education; the National Clown, Mime, Drama, Puppet, Dance Ministry Conference; and Phoenix Rising.

The publication of the U.S. bishops' document, *Environment and Art in Catholic Worship*, in 1978 called for the encouragement and support of artists including those in drama, dance, mime, and audio-visual media. The document also encouraged the education of congregations on the artistic tradition of the church. Some dioceses, such as that of Oakland, Calif., through its use of quality drama, mime, storytelling, and dance in St. Francis de Sales Cathedral, have given models of how the arts can attract persons to the church, strengthen congregational unity and participation, and encourage social action. *Modern Liturgy* magazine, founded in 1973, and persons such as Judith Royer, Doug Adams, and Michael Sparough, S.J., have encouraged the development of religious drama.

E.K. Chambers, *The Mediaeval Stage*, vols. 1 and 2 (London: Oxford University Press, 1903). Harold Ehrensperger, *Religious Drama, Ends and Means* (New York: Abington Press, 1962). O.B. Hardison, Jr., *Christian Rite and Christian Drama in the Middle Ages* (Baltimore: Johns Hopkins Press, 1965). John Mossi, S.J., *Modern Liturgy Handbook* (New York: Paulist Press, 1976). Karl Young, *The Drama of the Medieval Church*, vols. 1 and 2 (London: Oxford University Press, 1933).

MARTHA ANN KIRK, C.C.V.I.

DYING, MINISTRY TO THE

See Sick, pastoral care of; Viaticum; Death, ministry at the time of; Presence, pastoral

E

EASTER SEASON, THE

The Easter season is a fifty day liturgical period, beginning with Easter Sunday. The season concludes on a Sunday, the fiftieth day, which has been called Pentecost Sunday since the late 4th century. The fifty days of the Easter season celebrate the mystery of the Christian passover, the new life of the Spirit, inaugurated in the passion, death and resurrection of Christ. Thus, the Easter season is intrinsically connected with the meaning and celebration of the paschal triduum. The Easter season is celebrated as one festival extending for a week of weeks, and has sometimes been called "the great Sunday." With the renewal of the catechumenate, the Easter season is also called the period of *mystagogia*, the fourth catechetical period of the Rite of Christian Initiation of Adults.

History

The earliest written evidence for the existence and importance of the fifty-day festival of Easter is provided in the writings of Tertullian at the beginning of the 3rd century. In his treatise *On Prayer* (23.2) he identifies the season as the *spatium pentecostes*, the space of pentecost. Thus, the word "Pentecost" is used to identify the fifty-day period of the Easter season, and not a single day, as it was later to be used. In his treatise *On Baptism* (19.2), Tertullian identifies the season as a *laetissimum spatium*, a most

joyful space of exultation. The joy of this "space," for Tertullian, is discovered in the eschatological hope given in the resurrection of Christ and poured forth in the Spirit upon the church, the promise of regenerated humanity gathered into God. During the days of Pentecost, there was to be no fasting or kneeling. Legislation to this effect is found in Canon 20 of the First Council of Nicea in 325. "Rejoicing in the presence of the bridegroom" was a common theme among the early writers to describe the motivation for the festivity of the Easter season. In the presence of the bridegroom the community could not fast or be sad.

Scholars have connected the origin of celebrating the Easter season for fifty days, or as a week of weeks, to the 1st century understanding of the Jewish Feast of Weeks. This feast of Israel is described in Exod 23:16 as the "feast of the harvest." It is also mentioned in Tob 2:1 and 2 Macc 12:32 as the Pentecost, or the fiftieth day of the festival. The more common name of the feast is *Shabuoth*, which means "Weeks." This harvest festival of Israel extended for seven weeks, beginning with the day after the "sabbath" of Passover and concluding with the Pentecost itself on the fiftieth day. These weeks, beginning with the feast of Unleavened Bread, brought the harvest season to a close. The Pentecost, or the fiftieth day was kept as a sacred feast with pilgrimage to Jerusalem as is attested in

Acts 2:9-11. The Pentecost was celebrated as the solemn conclusion of the period of weeks that had begun at Passover.

By the 1st century of the Common Era, Pentecost was celebrated more than simply the conclusion of the harvest festival of the week of weeks. For Israel, it also celebrated the renewal of the covenant and the giving of the Law. Traces of this meaning can be found in the *Book of Jubilees* (ca. 140-100 B.C.). In later Christian lectionaries, this celebration of law and the covenant renewal on the Pentecost was taken over in the choice of readings for the Pentecost vigil. The historicization of the festival of Pentecost as a time of the renewal of the covenant became part of the celebration in the Qumran community of the 1st century and it included the commemoration of the giving of the Law on Sinai. on Sinai.

Thus, the harvest festival of Israel with the Pentecost, or fiftieth day, that celebrated the renewal of the covenant is claimed by some scholars to be the origin of the fifty-day celebration of the Easter season. In the Christian celebration, each day was envisioned as having the same importance and value. Originally, the fiftieth day had no greater significance than any other day of the season. Early on, however, it was associated with both the ascension of the Lord and the giving of the Holy Spirit.

Many church writers attest to the importance of the fifty-day festival. Athanasius claims that the joy of the fifty days is really Christ's own joy, as the one slain who now lives. For Athanasius, the fifty days is a symbol of the eschatological time of the world to come. Basil reflects on the theological importance of the fifty days by commenting on the multiplication of the number seven. The number seven multiplied seven times is the eternal multiplication of the first day of the resurrection and symbolizes the fullness of life in the risen Christ. The fifty days

become the symbol of the life that is to be consummated in heaven.

Augustine mentions the importance of the singing of the alleluia during this season. This song echoes the song of the multitude portrayed in the eschatological victory of the book of Revelation 19. It is a song sung to the Lamb who was slain and in it the Christian community joins in eschatological hope of the risen promise.

By the 4th century, the unity of the fifty days began to be divided. Three divisions emerged: the Easter octave, the fiftieth day, as the closing feast of the period, and the fortieth day, commemorating the ascension of the Lord.

The Easter Octave. The Easter octave, or the week *in albis*, as it was called in Rome, originated from the concern of pastors for the post-baptismal catechesis of the newly baptized. Sometimes known as Easter week, the origin of celebrating the eight first days of the season may have its roots in the Passover and the seven days of the Unleavened Bread. Some scholars suggest that the Christian community may have taken the inspiration for the octave days from the testimony of the gospel of John which places the appearances of the risen Christ on the evening of Easter and again eight days later. By the 4th century, there is evidence that this week was used for the gathering of the neophytes by the bishop for the post-baptismal, or mystagogical catechesis.

The texts of the mystagogical catechesis still exist. The noted mystagogues are Cyril of Jerusalem, Ambrose of Milan, Augustine of Hippo, John Chrysostom and Theodore of Mopsuestia. Unfortunately, there are no traces of any Roman baptismal catechesis, although a set of homilies for the Easter octave are recorded, without mention made of the newly baptized. In Milan, in Spain and in Gaul there is evidence that two Masses were celebrated during the octave of

Easter, one for the newly baptized, with post-baptismal catechesis, and another for the octave day, attended by the faithful. Participation in the Masses of the octave of Easter was facilitated in Milan by a civil law enacted in 389 which made the entire week of the octave a holiday. The custom of a civil holiday being observed on Easter Monday, as well as the Monday after Pentecost, still remains in some parts of the world.

As the practice of the Easter octave continued, there emerged various ways of explaining the eight days following the Sunday of the resurrection. Special focus was given to the eighth day of the octave. This Sunday is often called the "Sunday to lay aside the white garments." This name originated from the neophytes' gesture of putting aside the white garments that were received at baptism. The mystagogues spoke of the eighth day of the octave as a symbol of the mystery of eternal life and its anticipation. Because this was the concluding day of the post-baptismal catechesis, the pastor took the occasion to offer the final words of exhortation to the new Christians to live faithfully in the midst of the world.

The Gregorian sacramentary entitles the closing day of the octave "the Sunday post albas." Some scholars interpret this to mean that in Rome the white garments were put aside on the Saturday of the Easter octave. Nevertheless, the Sunday following Easter was still celebrated as the final day of the octave of post-baptismal catechesis as is attested to in the Gelasian sacramentary and the evangelary of the mid-7th century.

The Fiftieth Day: Pentecost Sunday. Until the beginning of the 4th century, the festival of the fifty days was considered as a unitive feast in which each day, commemorating the richness of the paschal mystery, was celebrated with equal festivity. With the celebration of the Easter octave, which began to weaken the notion of the unitive festival, came

the celebration of the fiftieth day as a significant ending to the season. The first evidence of the celebration of the fiftieth day is found in a decree from the Council of Elvira which, in 300, prescribed that all were to celebrate the day of Pentecost. This decree was a corrective of the custom that was emerging of celebrating the end of the Easter season on the fortieth day. Regardless of the intent, this decree can be seen as contributing to the tendency to shift the meaning of the term Pentecost from signifying the fifty days of the Easter season to designating the last day of the festival. The fiftieth day, was seen as the commemoration of the descent of the Spirit upon the church.

In 332, Eusebius of Caesarea included the commemoration of the Lord's ascension with the fiftieth day, thus giving a dual nature to the closing day of the season. This dual nature of the fifty days is attested to in the journal of Egeria who wrote of the liturgical practices of Jerusalem in 383. Egeria reports that the morning services on the fiftieth day celebrated the outpouring of the Spirit on the church, while the afternoon celebration on the Mount of Olives recalls the ascension of the Lord.

The dual meaning of the celebration of the fiftieth day was not long-lived. In examining the Armenian lectionary (c.415-439), scholars have observed that the commemoration of the ascension had already been removed from the afternoon service of the Jerusalem liturgy, and the celebration of the bestowal of the Spirit was given prominence. Some have speculated that this move was made in the interest of promoting the importance given to the Spirit in the life of the Church. This importance was the direct result of the declaration of the divinity of the Holy Spirit at the First Council of Constantinople in 381.

By the close of the 4th century, there is ample testimony that the fiftieth day of the Easter season had gained its own focus and was given the name Pentecost. It was a day designated to celebrate the coming of the Spirit. Taking on its own importance, Pentecost began to parallel the celebration of Easter. Baptisms began to be celebrated at Pentecost and, in the course of a few centuries, a vigil Mass and the practice of fasting on the day before the feast were in place. The practice of fasting would have been unheard of in the Easter observance of the first centuries of the church.

By the beginning of the 7th century, the parallel with Easter Sunday was completed with the creation of a Pentecost octave for post-baptismal catechesis. By the 7th century, the celebration of a separate feast of Pentecost which imitated Easter by a preceding fast day, the celebration of baptisms and an octave for post-baptismal catechesis, disrupted the original sense of the Pentecost as a fifty-day unitive festival.

The Fortieth Day: The Commemoration of the Ascension. The celebration of the fortieth day of the Easter season as a commemoration of the ascension of the Lord further weakened the unitive sense of a fifty-day festival. The development of this commemoration corresponded to the growth of the fiftieth day as the Feast of Pentecost.

Besides the mention of the celebration of the fortieth day in the canon of the Council of Elvira in A.D. 300, a sermon on the ascension delivered by Gregory of Nyssa in 388 seems to be the first evidence of the celebration of the day. After this date, the testimony for the existence of the feast exists in both the East and the West in such authors as John Chrysostom and Augustine. The *Apostolic Constitutions*, the dating of which is not certain (c. 375-380), gives the most explicit mention of the time and content of the festivity. The homilies of Leo the Great for the Feast of the Ascension offer significant evidence for its meaning and celebration. The 5th century Armenian lectionary from Jerusalem lists the readings for the day and offers a clear sketch of the meaning of the festival.

The Effects on the Fifty Days. Three effects on the unitive experience of the fifty days resulted from the development of the fiftieth and fortieth day. First, as the fiftieth day was dedicated to the celebration of the outpouring of the Holy Spirit, the Great Fifty days were deprived of their traditional name, Pentecost. Second, the development of the fiftieth and fortieth days was closely associated with the development of orthodox beliefs of the late 4th and 5th centuries. The Feast of the Ascension, according to Leo the Great (Sermon 74, 3-4), was the proof of Christ's divinity. The fiftieth day, now Pentecost Sunday, supported the doctrine of the divinity of the Holy Spirit. Third, and most important of all, the introduction of the commemoration of the Ascension and Pentecost undermined the integrity of the Easter season by dividing it into two parts: one lasting forty days and extending from Easter to Ascension; the other lasting ten days and extending from Ascension to Pentecost.

By the time of the Tridentine reform, and up until the Second Vatican Council, this dual division of the original fifty days was the liturgical practice. The Easter season was seen to last for forty days. The extinguishing and removal of the paschal candle following the gospel proclamation during the Mass on the Feast of the Ascension demonstrated this division. The intervening days between Ascension and Pentecost were seen as days of preparation for Pentecost. The vigil of Pentecost began to be regularly celebrated in the morning, not unlike the Easter vigil of later practice. Pentecost Sunday continued to have its own octave, and was celebrated as the birthday of the church. The octave of Pentecost was similar to the Easter octave. An interesting twist that emerged through the centuries was the addition of three fast days, called

Ember days, associated with the changing of the seasons, and celebrated on the Wednesday, Friday and Saturday of the octave of Pentecost. These days were also seen as the occasion for the preparation for the celebration of ordination to the diaconate and the presbyterate, which was often the practice on the Saturday after Pentecost. The Rogation days, also days of fasting and prayer, were celebrated before the Feast of Ascension.

The 1969 Revision of the Roman Calendar

In the "General Norms for the Liturgical Year and the Calendar" (G.N.L.Y.), approved and promulgated by Pope Paul VI on 14 February 1969, the reforms of the Second Vatican Council dealt with the revision of the liturgical feasts and seasons. This document instituted measures to restore the unity of the fifty-day period of the Easter celebration that held prominent place in the church until the end of the 4th century. While maintaining the long standing tradition of celebrating the feasts of the Ascension and Pentecost, and preserving the Easter octave as days of solemnity, the unity of the fifty days of the Easter season was stressed. Par. 22 of G.N.L.Y. states that "the fifty days from Easter Sunday to Pentecost are celebrated as one feast day, sometimes called 'the great Sunday.'" In harmony with the ancient church practice, as mentioned by Augustine, the document states that the "singing of the alleluia is a characteristic of these days."

Several important changes will be noted. First, in order to keep the integrity of the fifty days as a *laetissimum spatium*, the Rogation days preceding the Feast of the Ascension have been suppressed. Ember days and Rogation days are to be arranged at other times of the liturgical year by the competent authorities to meet the different needs of the people. The removal of these fast days attempts to restore the integrity of the fifty days and the ancient custom of not fasting during the Easter season. The second change is the suppression of the octave of Pentecost. The octave originally extended the Easter festivity in order to provide a period of post-baptismal catechesis for the neophytes baptized at the Pentecost vigil.

A final change marks the attempt to unite the fifty days. Par. 23 of G.N.L.Y. adopts the Byzantine custom of calling the Sundays of the fifty days "the Sundays of Easter." In the pre-Vatican II calendar they were called "the Sundays after Easter," implying that Easter was a one day celebration, the Sunday of the Resurrection. The paschal candle, as the symbol of the risen Christ, is not to be extinguished at the Ascension, but is to remain in the sanctuary throughout the fifty days of Easter, to be removed only on Pentecost Sunday.

One inconsistency can, however, be noted. Par. 26 of G.N.L.Y. continues to put forward the notion that the days following the Ascension are a time of preparation for Pentecost. This orientation is expressed in the Mass orations for these days and in the recommendation that the vesper hymn during these days be *Veni Creator Spiritus*. There seems to be a contradiction here with par. 22 that sees the fifty days as a unitive festival.

The revision of the lectionary, sacramentary and the liturgy of the hours also makes of the fifty days a unitive celebration of the paschal mystery. Two books of the bible hold the privileged place in the lectionary of the Easter season: the gospel according to John and the Acts of the Apostles. The Acts of the Apostles is read as the first reading every Sunday and weekday of the season, and the gospel of John every weekday and every Sunday except the third in years A and B of the lectionary cycle, when the gospel of Luke is proclaimed. The second reading is taken from the first letter of Peter in year

A, the first letter of John in year B, and the book of Revelation in year C. The lectionary readings for the three Sunday cycles and weekdays have the unified message of proclaiming the resurrection of Christ and the meaning of Christian and ecclesial existence in the Spirit.

The sacramentary contains Mass formularies for each of the fifty days. These formularies are an addition to the former Roman Missal which had special Easter formularies only for the Sundays and for the octaves of Easter and Pentecost. The orientation of these formularies is specifically paschal in nature, attempting to maintain the theological focus of the season.

Among the significant additions in the Sacramentary are the five prefaces for the Easter season, each of which highlights a certain aspect of the mystery of Christ's resurrection. Preface I praises Christ as the true passover lamb whose death has destroyed death. Preface II proclaims that Christ is the new life in whose death we have become children of light. The third preface of Easter acknowledges the risen Christ as the great priest who makes intercession for us before the face of God. A cosmic image is hinted at in Preface IV. In it, Christ is portrayed as the founder of a new age in whom the world is renewed and humanity restored. Preface V declares Christ the priest, the altar and the lamb of sacrifice.

The sacramentary also includes two prefaces for the Ascension and one for Pentecost. Preface I for Ascension attempts to maintain the connection between the fifty days by concluding "The joy of the resurrection and ascension renews the whole world...." Preface II for the Ascension does not include this connection. The preface for Pentecost does two things. First, it commemorates the outpouring of the Holy Spirit and the beginning of the church. Second, it seeks to unite the feast with the celebration of the resurrection by concluding: "The joy of the resurrection renews the whole world...." This formula, used on Pentecost Sunday, is the conclusion of the five Easter prefaces. No mention of the Ascension is made.

The liturgy of the hours seeks to be consistent in maintaining the integrity of the fifty days. The hymns, responses and prayers of praise and intercession follow the orientation of a unitive feast. The readings chosen for the fifty days also maintain the integrity of the season. Of special note are the readings from the early church writings that are read at the office of readings. These forty-nine patristic texts focus on the meaning of the paschal mystery and its celebration during the Easter season. They include readings from fifteen authors who wrote in Greek or Syriac and eleven who wrote in Latin. Except for one text from the documents of Vatican II, and one that dates from the 12th century, the readings are from writings and sermons of the first nine centuries.

Although attempts have been made in the liturgical reforms to integrate the fifty days of Easter into a cohesive season, liturgists are quite aware of the inconsistencies that still remain in both the liturgical books and pastoral practice. It is not an uncommon observation of pastoral ministers that the celebration of the Easter season, in spite of the liturgical reforms, is a difficult season to keep alive for fifty days. Further studies need to be made as to the reasons, perhaps both cultural and theological, for the apparent difficulty in keeping the celebration of the fifty days as an extended Sunday festival.

R.C.I.A.: The Time of Mystagogy

The Rite of Christian Initiation of Adults (R.C.I.A.), promulgated in 1972, was revised and expanded in an edition approved for use in the United States in 1988. (All references will be to the United States edition). The R.C.I.A. has given renewed meaning to the celebration of Lent and Easter, as well as renewed importance to the paschal triduum, especially the Easter vigil, for the life of the church. The rite perceives the Easter season as the fifty-day period of post-baptismal catechesis. Unlike the ancient practice of focusing *mystagogia* in the first week after Easter, which was the origin of the Easter octave and the initial breakup of the fifty-day cele-bration, the *R.C.I.A.* calls for a fifty-day period of catechesis, called mystagogy. The *R.C.I.A.* brings to a clearer focus the intention of the liturgical reform to maintain and deepen the appreciation of Easter as a fifty-day festival. The rite suggests that the Easter season is a time for the entire Christian community to join with the neophytes "to grow in deepening their grasp of the paschal mystery and in making it part of their lives through meditation on the gospel, sharing in the eucharist, and doing the works of charity"(R.C.I.A., 24). According to the *R.C.I.A.*, the Easter season is the final phase of Christian initiation in which the neophytes are given a compre-hensive appreciation of the sacramental life of the community. Mystagogical catechesis, not unlike the ancient sermons of earlier centuries, is brought forward "from the new, personal experience of the sacraments and of the community" (R.C.I.A., 247). In the revised ritual, the primary place of the *mystagogia* is considered to be the Sunday eucharistic celebrations of the Easter season. The period of post-baptismal catechesis is thus extended beyond the week of the Easter octave to the entire fifty days, punctuated by the Sunday gatherings.

The *R.C.I.A.* suggests that the main features of the catechesis are the gathering with the community, the symbolic activity of the eucharistic table, and the lectionary readings. The A cycle readings may be used for the post-baptismal gatherings of the neophytes, even when Christian initiation has been celebrated outside of the paschal triduum.

Within the Sunday celebration, the rite prescribes that the neophytes and their godparents are to be given special places within the assembly throughout the fifty days. The homilies should take into account their needs and the general inter-cessions should reflect the community's support in prayer for them (R.C.I.A., 248). The conclusion can be drawn that the neophytes themselves serve as a signif-icant Easter symbol of the paschal mystery and become for the community a source of inspiration and hope. Their presence in the assembly during the Easter season is itself a sign of the unity of the Easter season.

In addition to the celebration of the Sunday eucharist, the rite suggests three other occasions of post-baptismal cate-chesis. First, in accord with the practice of keeping the fiftieth day as a noted festivity, par. 249 suggests that some sort of celebration should be held at the end of the Easter season near Pentecost Sunday. No further directive is given except to note that festivities that are in harmony with local custom may be inte-grated into the celebration.

Second, the rite asks that on the occasion of their baptismal anniversary, the neophytes "should be brought to-gether in order to give thanks to God, to share with one another their spiritual experiences, and to renew their com-mitment"(R.C.I.A., 250). This directive has been expanded by the bishops of the United States. In par. 24 of the *National Statutes for the Catechumenate*, ap-proved by the National Conference of Catholic Bishops on 11 November 1986 and confirmed by the Congregation for Divine Worship on 26 June 1988, it is stated that while the period of immediate post-baptismal catechesis is the mysta-gogy of the Easter season, for pastoral reasons, the program of mystagogy "should extend until the anniversary of Christian initiation, with at least monthly assemblies of the neophytes for their deeper Christian formation and incorporation into the full life of the Christian community."

The role of the diocesan bishop in the process of mystagogy is the third feature of post-baptismal catechesis. The rite suggests that the bishop, if unable to preside at the sacraments of initiation, should meet with the neophytes for the celebration of the eucharist at least once within the year after baptism (R.C.I.A., 251). This gathering, done to express the bishop's pastoral role, would be an opportunity for the bishop to share insights into the sacramental life of the Christian as well as to be inspired by the faith and enthusiasm of the newly initiated.

The *R.C.I.A.* supports the unitive celebration of the Easter season in several ways. First, the *R.C.I.A.* gives focus to the Easter season by uniting the fifty days in a common orientation of the catechetical formation, support and encouragement of the newly baptized. In turn, this mystagogical process deepens the faith of the entire community during the Easter season. Second, the presence of the neophytes within the Sunday assemblies of the Easter season gives witness to the continuity of the season and to the baptismal meaning of Easter. The *R.C.I.A.*, notes that homilists are to draw attention to the unfolding meaning of the paschal mystery by directing the homilies of the Easter season to include the neophytes. Third, the *R.C.I.A.*, sees each of the Sundays of the Easter season as the significant gatherings of the assembly. It gives no special importance to the Easter octave or the fortieth day. The mention of a special celebration at the end of the season does focus somewhat on Pentecost. This focus, however, does not intend to make Pentecost a separate feast. It considers this celebration as a closing of the formal period of mystagogy.

What remains to be accomplished is the conversion of the Catholic imagination towards the understanding and celebration of the Easter season as a unitive festival of fifty days. The ground work has been put into place by both the reform of the liturgical calendar and the revised rites of the catechumenate. Pastoral planning and liturgical creativity are necessary for their implementation. The cultural and psychological difficulties of sustaining a *laetissimum spatium*, that is, of sustaining a period of celebration for seven weeks, remains to be explored. Such a study may also offer insights into the original cause of the dissolution of the fifty-day celebration of the Easter season in the first centuries of the church.

See **Initiation, Christian; Mystagogy**

Robert Cabie, *La Pentecote: L'evolution de la Cinquantaine pascale au cours des cinq premiers siecles* (Tournai: Desclee, 1965). Patrick Regan, "The Fifty Days and the Fiftieth Day," *Worship* 55 (1981)194-218. A. G. Martimort, I. H. Dalmais, P. Jounel, *The Church at Prayer. Volume IV: The Liturgy and Time* (Collegeville: The Liturgical Press, 1986) 56-65. Thomas J. Talley, *The Origins of the Liturgical Year* (New York: Pueblo, 1986) 54-77. Enrico Mazza, *Mystagogy: A Theology of Liturgy in the Patristic Age* (New York: Pueblo, 1989). *The Roman Calendar: Text and Commentary* (Washington: United States Catholic Conference, 1976). Anthony Cernera, "The Celebration of Our Paschal Liberation," *The Way* (24) (1984) 224-238. *Liturgy: Easter's Fifty Days*. Vol. 3, no. 1 of *Liturgy, The Journal of the Liturgical Conference*, Winter 1982.

RICHARD N. FRAGOMENI

EASTERN CHURCHES

See **Traditions, liturgical in the East; Sacraments in Eastern churches; Eucharist, history of, in the East; Reform, liturgical, in Eastern churches**

ECCLESIOLOGY AND LITURGY

"For the liturgy, 'making the work of our redemption a present actuality', most of all in the divine sacrifice of the eucharist, is the outstanding means whereby the faithful may express in their lives and manifest to others the mystery of Christ and the real nature of the true Church" (S.C., 2). This statement, placed at the very beginning of the *Constitution on the Sacred Liturgy*, is an affirmation of the intimate relationship that exists between liturgy and the church. The principle appears throughout the document in a variety of contexts. Liturgical celebrations are identified as ecclesial actions which manifest and have effects on the church (26). Liturgy is described as "the summit toward which the activity of the Church is directed" as well as "the fount from which all the Church's power flows" (10). The *Dogmatic Constitution on the Church* echoes these ideas when it indicates that the sacraments "give actual expression to the sacred, organically structured nature of the priestly community" (11), and states that "in the sacrament of the eucharistic bread, the unity of all believers who form one Body in Christ (1 Cor 10:17) is both expressed and brought about" (3).

The conviction that the liturgy is a significant event in which the identity and unity of the church is expressed and brought about is one which goes back to the church's origins. Paul criticized the church of Corinth for the conflicts, misuse of gifts, and lack of attention to the poor that characterized its assemblies, because such behavior contradicted the church's remembrance of the tradition regarding the Lord's Supper and its identity as the body of Christ (1 Cor 11-14). One of the words used by early Christians to describe themselves was *ekklēsia*, or assembly. Gathering regularly to hear the apostles teach, to share the common life, to break bread and to pray was central to the identity of early Christian communities (Acts 2:42). A prayer from the *Didache* (A.D. 110) compares the gathering of the church into God's Kingdom to the bread of the eucharist made by gathering many grains into one (9:4).

Liturgy, a form of ecclesial ritual action, discloses a church's way of ordering itself. Hervé Legrand has noted that the NT prescribes nothing about a sacerdotal office for the presidency of the eucharist, and he suggests that it is probable that those who presided over the church (apostles, prophets, and teachers) presided at the eucharist (415-416). He recognizes that this hypothesis cannot be generalized for the church as a whole in NT times. However, he finds plenty of evidence in the literature of the pre-Nicene church to support the claim that "those who preside over the life of the Church preside at the Eucharist" (427). The letters of St. Ignatius of Antioch from the beginning of the 2nd century provide one one example. These letters, with the exception of the one to Rome, show that the churches he knew were presided over by a bishop who was assisted by presbyters and deacons. The bishop's authority over the liturgy is clear. In his letter to the church at Smyrna Ignatius advises them that they are not to baptize without authorization from the bishop and that the only eucharist which should be considered valid is one that is celebrated by the bishop himself or someone authorized by him (8).

The relationship between liturgy and the church's belief has also been recognized since the patristic period in the formula *legem credendi lex statuat supplicandi*, the principle that the law of worship establishes the law of belief. This often appears in the shortened form *lex orandi, lex credendi*. The formula is attributed to Prosper of Aquitaine in the mid-5th century but it was operative before that. For example, Augustine used the fact that the church practiced infant baptism as one of his arguments for original sin. Also, he and other bishops such as Cyril of Jerusalem, Ambrose of Milan, John Chrysostom, and Theodore of Mopsuestia regularly used the experience of the sacraments as a source for teaching Christian doctrine.

The relationship between the church's prayer and its belief has been a complex one. Although liturgy has often been used as a source for verifying or defending a particular belief, the church's beliefs have also influenced liturgical practice. For example, reaction to the Arian heresy made its appearance in the language and action of the church's baptismal and eucharistic liturgy. Also, at various points in history particular feasts have been introduced into the liturgy as a way of supporting certain beliefs. Numerous examples could be given to illustrate the fact that the church's beliefs are revealed and shaped in the liturgy. It is important to realize that any attempt to understand the relationship between the church's prayer and its belief should include questions about the ecclesiology operative at the time. What is the church's understanding of itself as a praying and believing assembly?

When the documents of Vatican II speak of the liturgy as the place where the church is manifested what do they mean by "the church"? The *Constitution on the Sacred Liturgy* tells us that the pre-eminent manifestation of the church is to be found in the full, active participation of all God's holy people in liturgical celebrations, especially the eucharist, which are presided over by the bishop surrounded by his priests and ministers (S.C., 41). However, it goes on to recognize that the bishop has to establish other groups such as parishes where the pastor takes the place of the bishop. These are described as representing, in some manner, the visible church established throughout the world (42). The *Dogmatic Constitution on the Church* presents an even clearer affirmation that the church realizes itself in local churches. "This Church of Christ is really present in all legitimately organized local groups of the faithful, which, in so far as they are united with their pastors, are also quite appropriately called Churches in the NT .... In them the faithful are gathered together through the preaching of the gospel of Christ, and the mystery of the Lord's Supper is celebrated 'so that, by means of the flesh and blood of the Lord the whole brotherhood of the Body may be welded together.' In each altar community, under the sacred ministry of the bishop, a manifest symbol is to be seen of that charity and 'unity of the mystical body, without which there can be no salvation'. In these communities, though they may often be small and poor, or existing in the diaspora, Christ is present through whose power and influence the One, Holy, Catholic and Apostolic Church is constituted" (L.G., 26).

Underlying statements such as these is the ancient principle that the assembly, because of its union with Christ, is the subject of liturgical action. The church manifests and realizes itself in assemblies all over the world, in their liturgical prayer and action, through language, symbol, roles, relationships, art, music, and use of space. Supporting this realization are those statements in the *Constitution on the Sacred Liturgy* that allow for the possibility of adapting the liturgy to various local contexts (S.C., 37-40). This recognition of the need for adaptation is tempered by the insistence that regulation of the liturgy "depends solely on the authority of the Church, that is, on the Apostolic See and, accordingly as the law determines, on the bishop" (22:1). Some power to regulate the liturgy within certain defined limits is recognized for various territorial bodies of bishops (22:2).

Those who study ecclesiology, who engage in reflection on the church, have a wealth of sources from which to gather data. Although it is often neglected, liturgy should have a significant place among them because of the role it plays in the ongoing constitution of the church.

Liturgy, as a form of ecclesial ritual action, is one of the activities in which the church manifests and creates itself. By studying the liturgy scholars may uncover some of the beliefs, memories, hopes and commitments that make the church what it is.

Liturgical history provides a rich source of information but so does present liturgical practice, for the church is continually in the process of realizing itself. Much data disclosing the intimate relationship between liturgical praxis and ecclesial identity can be found by studying efforts which have been made since Vatican II in liturgical adaptation and inculturation. Other important sources are rituals associated with popular religion and with groups such as Women-Church. Such rituals may offer a critique of that which is manifested in the official liturgy. They disclose beliefs, memories, hopes and commitments that are present in the life of the church but are not visible in its official prayer. Sometimes this kind of information may also be available in the actual performance of approved liturgical rites since what is actually done in liturgy does not always correspond with what is set out in the liturgical books.

The point is that the church's prayer and its identity are woven together. Ecclesiology which does not use liturgy as a source misses an essential part of the picture. Likewise, any study of liturgy which does not include attention to the ecclesiological context is inadequate.

See **Doctrine, liturgy and; Assembly**

James M. Gustafson, *Treasure In Earthen Vessels: The Church as a Human Community* (Chicago: University of Chicago Press, 1961). Hervé-Marie Legrand, "The Presidency of the Eucharist According to the Ancient Tradition," *Worship* 53 (1979): 413-438. Geoffrey Wainwright, *Doxology: The Praise of God in Worship, Doctrine, and Life* (New York: Oxford University Press, 1980). Herman Wegman, *Christian Worship in East and West: A Study Guide to Liturgical History*, trans. Gordon Lathrop (New York: Pueblo Publishing Co, 1985).

MARGARET MARY KELLEHER, O.S.U.

ECUMENISM AND THE LITURGY

"In worship we meet the problem, nay rather the sin of the disunion of the Church in its sharpest form." This sentence from the ecumenical report *Ways of Worship* (1951) summarizes one of the early encounters between the ecumenical and the liturgical movements. Just over a decade later, the Second Vatican Council would characterize both the liturgical and the ecumenical movements as movements of the Holy Spirit through the church (S.C., 43; U.R., 1, 4). The assessments of *Ways of Worship* and of the Second Vatican Council still stand. Each points to important aspects of the relationship between ecumenism and the liturgy: worship is both a locus of unity between the churches *and* a focus of their disunity. The theological roots for this doublefacedness of worship lie in the ecclesiological realm: if worship is truly the center of the church's life and an 'epiphany' of the very essence of the church, then worship does not only signify and effect the unity of the church, it will also be the place where the sinful divisions between the churches are most clearly and painfully manifested. The concurrently growing liturgical and ecumenical movements have brought this realization to the forefront.

The Liturgical Movement and the Ecumenical Movement

Historically, there are remarkable parallels between the growth of the two movements in the 20th century: the dates traditionally claimed as starting points (Mecheln 1909 for the Liturgical Movement, Edinburgh 1910 for the Ecumenical Movement) are very close; both movements draw on important, sometimes parallel, precursors in the 19th century; both profit, in the 20th century, from the same concurrent renewal movements (amongst others the Biblical Movement); both show a near parallel development of gaining ground in the churches in the 20th century; and both received unprecedented attention at the Second Vatican Council.

In light of these interconnections, it will not be surprising that the Ecumenical Movement already fairly early on devoted attention to the question of *Ways of Worship*—so the title of a 1951 report of the "Theological Commission on Worship" which had been appointed in 1937. The report was devoted to the study of patterns of worship characteristic of different churches; its methodology was primarily descriptive and comparative. This and other early documents of the Ecumenical Movement still see worship to a large extent as the focal point of existing divisions: "It is at this point that disunity becomes explicit and the sense of separation most acute." Not until the fourth World Conference on Faith and Order held at Montreal in 1963 was a report produced with the title *Worship and the Oneness of Christ's Church* which clearly indicated the ecumenical potential of the liturgy.

In the same year, the Second Vatican Council promulgated its *Constitution on the Sacred Liturgy* which, although not intended as a primarily ecumenical document, had far-reaching ecumenical ramifications.

Sacrosanctum Concilium and Unitatis Redintegratio

Sacrosanctum concilium's first paragraph already signals the ecumenical vision of the council, if not that of the constitution itself: "The sacred Council has set out ... to foster whatever can promote union among all who believe in Christ" (S.C., 1). The constitution itself of course focuses on the intra-Catholic reality of the worship of the Latin church. (The practical norms only apply to the Roman rite, not the Eastern Catholic churches.) This does not mean, however, that there are not many statements of fundamental ecumenical importance to be found in the text. To name but the

most important: the constitution acknowledges the need for and indeed lays the foundations for far-ranging liturgical reforms, thereby overcoming the "unchangeable" uniformity, rubricism and centralization which had characterized Roman Catholic worship after the liturgical reforms of the Council of Trent and set it apart from many other ecclesial communities' worship patterns.

Another important ecumenical signal was the new theological emphasis on worship as a dialogue between God and God's people, rather than as primarily a religious duty to be fulfilled by the faithful. This new emphasis proved especially encouraging in the ecumenical encounter with Protestant churches. These churches also found the christocentric emphasis of the constitution's theology of worship helpful while the Orthodox churches were painfully aware of the lack of an equally strong pneumatological emphasis. Furthermore, there were a number of ecclesiological shifts which encouraged ecumenical convergence: the newly emerging emphasis on the local church, the recognized need to decentralize liturgical responsibilities, the stress on the *actuosa participatio* of the whole people of God, and the move from liturgical uniformity to a legitimate diversity.

The points mentioned here are not "by chance" ecumenically relevant and fruitful. Many of the new emphases are a result of a return to earlier and common patterns of worship. Other points of ecumenical significance in *Sacrosanctum concilium's* reform program need to be mentioned here: the more prominent place given to the "table of the word," the change of liturgical language from Latin to the vernacular, the clearer structure of the liturgical rites, the emphasis on an active participation of the laity, the *celebratio versus populum*, provisions for communion under both species, the clear preference for communal celebrations of the liturgy rather than private ones, the reintroduction of "prayers of the people," the suggestion of the creation of a liturgy for eucharistic concelebration (largely modelled on the praxis of the Eastern churches), and the willingness to consider an ecumenically viable reform of the liturgical calendar. The last point contains the only explicit reference in the constitution to the "brethren who are not in communion with the Apostolic See." The separated brothers and sisters are, however, the clear focus of the *Decree on Ecumenism*, a document which also broadens the liturgical perspective beyond that of *Sacrosanctum concilium* with its concentration on an intra-Roman Catholic liturgical reform.

The *Decree on Ecumenism* stresses the ecumenical importance and potential of our common baptism into the body of Christ as one of the foundations of the ecumenical vision: "all who have been justified by faith in baptism are incorporated into Christ; they therefore have a right to be called Christians, and with good reasons are accepted as brothers (and sisters) by the children of the Catholic Church" (U.R., 3). But *Unitatis redintegratio* goes well beyond the acknowledgement of a common baptism by characterizing the liturgical life of non-Roman Catholic churches as a Spirit-filled reality: "In ways that vary according to the condition of each Church or community, these liturgical actions most certainly can truly engender a life of grace and, one must say, can aptly give access to the communion of salvation" (U.R., 3). This does not distract from, but in a sense intensifies, the problems of a *communicatio in sacris* (particularly a eucharistic one). *Unitatis redintegratio* adopts a two-fold position in regard to this problem. Since worship signifies the unity of the community of faith, worship amongst divided churches is generally not to be recommended. Since, however, worship is also a sharing in the means of grace, a common sharing even of divided Christians can sometimes be a necessity. Indeed, as far as the Orthodox churches are concerned, the *Decree on Ecumenism* unilaterally encouraged "some worship in common" (U.R., 15), an ecumenical advance generally not welcomed by the Orthodox.

Ecumenical Convergence in Worship

To a certain extent, the ecumenical reflections on worship since the Second Vatican Council have been overtaken by a growing ecumenical convergence in worship patterns—a phenomenon which is doubtlessly one of the key features of the churches' struggle towards unity in our time. This ecumenical convergence in worship has largely taken place as a result of thoroughgoing liturgical reforms in almost all the divided churches. These liturgical reforms have brought about a much greater affinity between the worship patterns of the divided churches than previously existed. The Roman Catholic liturgical reforms, initiated by the *Constitution on the Sacred Liturgy*, have played a key role here. Churches in the process of liturgical reform have increasingly taken into account the work done in other ecclesial communities, sometimes modelling their own work consciously on that of sister churches.

A number of examples for this ecumenical convergence in worship deserve particular mention. Over the last decades many churches have acknowledged the need for a weekly celebration of the holy eucharist as the central act of the church's worship. There is also a strong consensus on the fact that the eucharist is to be celebrated around the two foci of the "table of the word" and the "table of the bread." There is, moreover, growing agreement about the nature and the structure of the eucharistic prayer itself. Indeed, one particular eucharistic prayer from the new Roman Missal has, at least in North America, found entrance into a number of eucharistic rites of other churches. Since the prayer itself (Eucharistic Prayer IV) is modelled on Eastern sources, its reception history through the Roman Missal into the eucharistic liturgies of Protestant churches (for example the Episcopal church and the United Methodist church) is particularly remarkable. Another important ecumenical feature of liturgical life in North America is the creation of the *Common Lectionary* which has led to many churches sharing the same scripture passages every Sunday. The *Common Lectionary*, which is based largely on the *Ordo Lectionum Missae*, has found acceptance in Presbyterian, Episcopal, Lutheran, and United Methodist churches as well as with the Disciples of Christ and the United Church of Christ. In this way, the lectionary too has contributed to a greater convergence in worship patterns. It is remarkable that while fundamental theological problems remain, particularly as far as the eucharistic table-fellowship between the churches is concerned, the actual patterns of eucharistic celebration are becoming more and more close. The admonition of the instruction *Eucharisticum Mysterium* of 1967 nevertheless still stands: "It is above all in the celebration of the mystery of unity that all Christians should be filled with sorrow at the divisions which separate them" (8).

The growing ecumenical convergence in worship, of course, also affects parts of liturgical life other than the celebration of the eucharist. There is a growing consensus between the churches on the main features of the liturgical year (the Easter date still being an unresolved issue). With the Roman Catholic liturgical calendar regaining the primacy of the *temporale*, and substantially reducing the *sanctorale*, and with many Protestant churches regaining a sense of the importance of both the *temporale* and the *sanctorale*, there is an increasing convergence in the way the liturgical year is observed by the divided churches. Similar developments have taken place as far as the celebration of baptism, or the liturgy of the hours, or the observance of the Easter vigil are concerned, to name but three examples.

Ecumenical Liturgical Initiatives

Since prayer is "the soul of the whole ecumenical movement" (U.R., 8), ecumenical initiatives proper in the area of worship have not been lacking either.

Hymn-books have been an especially fruitful place for ecumenical convergence (and that by no means only in this century; already shortly after the Reformation, one can detect a "secret ecumenism" of borrowing from other ecclesial traditions' hymnody). The beginning ecumenical movement itself produced a hymn-book early on (*Cantate Domino*, 1924, revised by the World Council of Churches in 1980). Equally, if not more significant for an ecumenical convergence, have been the revisions of denominational hymn-books which are consciously enlarging the traditions they draw upon now to include hymns from throughout the churches, ages and places.

Important also for the worship of the divided churches has been the publication of an ecumenical calendar of intercessions (*With all God's people*) by the World Council of Churches. It encouraged the divided churches to pray for each other around the world on a weekly basis.

Ecumenical liturgical work on a more local level has also not been missing. To name but one example: The Consultation on Common Texts (which includes many of the major North American churches) has produced a number of common worship resources such as *Prayers We Have in Common, A Liturgical Psalter for the Christian Year, Ecumenical Services of Prayer, the Common Lectionary,* and *A Christian Celebration of Marriage.*

The divided churches have also come together for ecumenical worship services proper in an increasing way. Usually, these services follow one of two possible patterns: either one community invites others to come and join in its particular liturgical tradition, or the churches worshipping together create a worship service out of elements from the different ecclesial traditions represented. Favorite times for such services are the weeks of Lent, Thanksgiving Day, the Week of Prayer for Christian Unity, and, as the earliest form of modern ecumenical worship, the (Women's) World Day of Prayer.

Of course, the Ecumenical Movement itself has not stood still either while all these liturgical reforms and initiatives have been creating an important convergence in worship patterns. Ecumenical theological progress has been made, particularly in relation to the sacraments, which in itself is stimulating a re-thinking of liturgical life in the divided churches. To name but two examples: On a world level, the convergence document of the Faith and Order Commission of the World Council of Churches, *Baptism, Eucharist, Ministry*, contains not only important ecumenical advances in theological reflection, it also makes very concrete proposals about the liturgical celebrations of baptism, eucharist, and ordination. The so-called *Lima Liturgy* written on the basis of this convergence document has meanwhile become the ecumenical eucharistic liturgy par excellence. The celebration of the *Lima Liturgy* was a high point of the Sixth General Assembly of the World Council of Churches in Vancouver in 1983.

On the more local level, ecumenical doctrinal work has also resulted in creative liturgical work. The Consultation on Church Union, for example, in 1985 produced "Liturgies for Covenanting" together with a theological consensus statement. The liturgies are designed for declaring covenant, reconciling ministries and celebrating the eucharist as the beginning of a "Church Uniting."

Liturgy, Unity, and Diversity

Liturgy has to be an expression of the unity of the church *and* an expression of its legitimate diversity; it has to be both at the same time. This raises the theological question of how to translate "unity and diversity" liturgically. This question has by no means received a satisfactory answer yet, but one basic conviction has gained ground: liturgical unity-in-diversity will not be based on the integration of every separate ecclesial tradition into a common whole. There are individual liturgical traditions which are clearly non-integratable (for example non-eucharistic Sundays, or worship without the proclamation of the word). The liturgical life of the one-church-to-be will therefore not simply be a mixture of all that is there in the churches now. However, while the churches still struggle to discern how to worship authentically as the one people of God, new problems are emerging, threatening once again the growing ecumenical convergence. (An example of this would be the fact that some communities are beginning to baptize with alternative trinitarian formulas.) It is by now obvious that striving for a liturgical life which is at the same time an authentic reflection of the unity of the church *and* of the legitimate diversity in a communion of churches will never be a task fully accomplished. But whatever the worship of the one-church-to-be will look like, one characteristic is unquestionable: it will be a liturgical reality symbolized most effectively in the eucharistic table-fellowship of all God's children.

Baptism and Eucharist: Ecumenical Convergence in Celebration, ed. by Max Thurian/Geoffrey Wainwright (Faith and Order Paper 117), Geneva: World Council of Churches, 1983. Teresa Berger, "Unity in and through Doxology? Reflections on

Worship Studies in the World Council of
Churches," *Studia Liturgica* 16 (1986/87): 1-12.
Kilian McDonnell, "The Constitution on the
Liturgy as an Ecumenical Document," in: *Worship*
41 (1967): 486-497.

DR. D. TERESA BERGER

EPICLESIS

This Greek term meaning "invocation"
has been associated with the invocation
of the Holy Spirit on the eucharistic
bread and wine in the anaphora to
petition the fruits of communion. Already
in the anaphora of Hippolytus (ca. A.D.
215) the Holy Spirit is invoked on the
bread and wine in a petition for the unity
of those who partake. The 3rd century
anaphora of Addai and Mari asks the
Holy Spirit to "bless and sanctify" the
offering, "that it may be to us for the
remission of debts, forgiveness of sins,
and the great hope of resurrection from
the dead, and new life in the kingdom of
heaven, with all who have been pleasing
in your sight." The epiclesis developed in
the Syro-Byzantine anaphoras to the
point of asking the Holy Spirit to "make"
the bread and wine the body and blood of
Christ, "changing them by your Holy
Spirit" (anaphora of St. John Chrysostom). Cyril of Jerusalem and Theodore
of Mopsuestia looked to the epiclesis as
the "moment of consecration," although
John Chrysostom held to a more subtle
relationship between the words of Christ
and the invocation of the Holy Spirit.
The Holy Spirit in the eucharist is
associated with such benefits as unity,
forgiveness, eternal life, and the fullness
of the kingdom of heaven.

The Holy Spirit is not always invoked.
The *Didache* has no epiclesis, just as it
lacks an institution narrative. It has been
suggested that the invocation of the
divine name constitutes an epiclesis (10:2).
Odo Casel popularized the view that the
whole eucharistic prayer is consecratory,
and that the formal epiclesis within the
prayer plays a complementary role by
indicating the purpose of the invocation.
The anaphora of Serapion in 4th century
Egypt petitions the descent of the Logos
or Word, rather than the Holy Spirit, on
the bread and cup. Some Hispanic-
Gallican anaphoras have invocations of
the Holy Spirit; some do not. The Roman
canon has no invocation at all: it prays
for the acceptance of the gifts by the
Father in heaven (*Supra quae*) and asks
that they be taken to the heavenly altar
(*Supplices te*). These two portions of the
canon, located before and after the words
of institution, have prompted liturgists to
speak of a split-epiclesis, which is also
characteristic of the Alexandrian anaphoras.

The issue of the epiclesis has been
confused in the West by the development
of the view that the words of institution
constitute the moment of consecration.
This view can be traced to Ambrose of
Milan, Augustine of Hippo, and Thomas
Aquinas. This consecration theology has
bedeviled the composition of new eucharistic prayers for the Roman rite to be
used alongside the revised Roman canon.
It has been held that the *ingenium
Romanum* calls for a double epiclesis,
one on the gifts before the words of
institution and one on the people after
the *Verba,* petitioning the fruits of communion. This approach can only reinforce
a "magical" notion of the *Verba Christi*
and hinder the perception that the
eucharistic prayer is an economic whole.

New Lutheran, Episcopal, Methodist,
and Presbyterian eucharistic prayers have
opted for the West Syrian pattern of
placing a Spirit-epiclesis after the words
of institution. These epicleses typically
do not ask the Holy Spirit to change the
bread and wine, but they do connect the
Spirit working through the gifts of communion to effect unity, forgiveness, life
and salvation along the lines of the most
primitive anaphoras.

E.G.C.F. Atchley, *On the Epiclesis of the Eucharistic Liturgy and in the Consecration of the*

Font (London: Oxford University Press, 1935). Odo Casel, "Neue Beiträge zur Epiklesenfrage," JLW 4 (1924): 37-44. John H. McKenna, *Eucharist and Holy Spirit*, Alcuin Club Collections No. 57 (Great Wakering: Mayhew-McCrimmon, 1975). John H. McKenna, "The Epiclesis Revisited," in Frank C. Senn, ed., *New Eucharistic Prayers* (New York, Mahwah: Paulist Press, 1987): 169-94.

FRANK C. SENN

EPIPHANY, FEAST OF THE

In the East this feast celebrates the "manifestation" of the Lord to the world; it is called by those in the West the "Eastern Christmas." In the West it is an integral feast of the Christmas season, advancing the movement of the Lord's birth from its primary announcement to the Jews to its announcement to the Gentiles. In the East the Lord's birth, baptism and eschatological rule over the nations is captured in this celebration; the West separates these as the Nativity, the Epiphany and the Feast of the Lord's Presentation.

See **Calendar, liturgical; Christmas season**

EUCHARIST

Completing baptism and confirmation, this third sacrament of initiation is the centerpiece of the sacramental system and the primary act by which Christians worship God. Called variously the Mass, the Lord' Supper, the Service of the Mysteries, the Divine Liturgy, among other names, this act of the church is both the sacramental enactment of Christ's own sacrifice and the promise of its eschatological fulfillment. It is also the primary locus of Christ's sacramental presence in and to the church. In addition to the entries on eucharist that follow, see also: Body of Christ; Agape; Anaphora; Covenant; Sacrifice; Anamnesis; Epiclesis; Communion service; Traditions, liturgical, ...

EUCHARIST AND RECONCILIATION

God's unitive purpose for humankind is ritualized at the table of the Lord when the eucharist is celebrated. It is then that the community gathers to bless God for the salvific event of reconciliation effected centuries ago through the suffering, death and resurrection of Jesus and to participate again in the power of that event which holds the promise and even urgent necessity of reconciliation with our brothers and sisters in our world. "We who are many are one body, for we all partake of the one bread" (1 Cor 10:17).

Each eucharist is simultaneously a study in contrasts and a study in unity. A fragile, dismembered community comes together and is strengthened and reconstituted by the word and presence of God. Unfree people taste freedom. Strangers become friends. Sinners drink the cup of salvation.

That this should take place at a table seems particularly fitting since the table as a piece of furniture provides the opportunity for persons to look at each other, eye to eye, and to disclose themselves to one another. This happens most often in the context of a meal when food and drink provide the fuel for revelation and intimacy uncommon in other settings. At least temporarily, a bonding takes place among guests, nurtured by the host/ hostess who planned, prepared and served the meal. No ordinary bonding, the eucharist effects a *koinonia* among persons flawed by sin, divided not only against each other but conflicted even within themselves (Rom 7:15-23).

Such was the setting of the Last Supper which is recalled at every subsequent eucharistic celebration. Prescinding from the discussion concerning whether the Last Supper coincided with the timing of the Jewish Passover, it was at table with his disciples that Jesus reinforced the unifying and reconciling themes at the heart of his ministry. Jesus took bread, blessed it and did the same for the wine, investing the elements with his presence and the promise of transformative efficacy (Lk 22:19-21; 1 Cor 11:25). Clearly, the surprise factor of the Last Supper was that Jesus was not only host and servant but the food as well. Bread broken and eaten; blood poured out and consumed; in the paschal act of total self-giving, the reconciliation between God and humankind was effected.

The story of God's profligate love was disclosed at the table of the Last Supper and is remembered at all sacramental celebrations since then. God's story reveals a passionate yearning to end our exile and loneliness. The commitment of Jesus to effect this reconciliation led to his death, his victory over sin, his glorification, and a new beginning for each of us as reconciled sinners. "If any one is in Christ, that person is a new creation" (2 Cor 5:17).

Each eucharist remembers those once-and-for-all paschal events and invites believers to participate in their power (1 Cor 10:16-17). The sign-act of the eucharist is vivid and dramatic. By eating the body of Christ and drinking of the cup, believers share in the dynamism of Jesus' self-gift and are nourished through that communion to extend reconciliation to their brothers and sisters. The eucharist also has an eschatological referrant as it points to the fullness of the messianic banquet where a just order will reign as the community of all women and men gather.

Yet participation in the power of the sacramental memorial is not automatic. It is possible initially because our appetites for community and wholeness were whetted at baptism. In fact, baptismal reconciliation is itself oriented to eucharistic reconciliation and is a foretaste of its fullness.

Participation is also possible because the eucharist effects the forgiveness of sins and releases us from the tyranny of guilt. Gathered at the table of the Lord, God takes the initiative in this regard and offers us unconditional pardon and restoration. Our response to this utterly gratuitous gift takes many forms—including rejection—but the eucharist compels us to consider conversion by confronting our culpability with a contrite heart, urging us to repair the damage we caused, and to accept out incompleteness and dependency on God.

The grace of the eucharist pierces, revivifies, and cleanses the old self. It calls for transformation so that we might put on Christ and become new persons. Only then can the reconciliation within our own dividedness take place. Only then can the eucharist effect the healing of our own hearts that prepares us for reconciliations in our relationships with others. Accepting God's forgiveness is the first step in the process that enables us to enflesh the spirit of reconciliation that seeks, as a rule of life, to unite rather than to divide, to create bridges rather than chasms, to choose peace over the sword.

From this perspective, the eucharist emerges as the sacrament of reconciliation par excellence. The transparency of the eucharist to the signs it represents is uniquely profound. Yet it is also true that history has dimmed the original sign-value of the eucharist. And while a number of factors contributed to the obfuscation, the most notable include the development of a theology of the eucharist that shifted its concern from the transformation of a people to the transformation of food, a legalistic preoccupation with sin, a separation between those sins remitted through the eucharist and those requiring the separate forum of sacramental penance, and a concentration on extrinsic ritual rather than personal conversion.

But the history of reconciliation and the eucharist is not closed. The emerging awareness of the many reconciliations necessary in an individual's life (with one's psyche, body, parents, past, self, as well as with God and neighbor); the need for signs of depth to commemorate restored relationships; the yearning for peace in a culture familiar with close-range violence; the search for ways to be unburdened from the despair of one's separation from the earth; and the desire for *koinonia* all point to the need for eucharist. The eucharist points to the possibility of bonding in the middle of rubble; it promises presence and power in the middle of devastation and feebleness; and in the middle of this century's persistent hunger for meaning, it offers signs of connectedness that link people to other people and to all the living things in the universe.

Edmond Barbotin, *The Humanity of Man*, trans. by Matthew O'Connell (New York: Orbis Books, 1975); see, esp. Chap. 7, "The Meal," 319-338. Peter Fink, "History of the Sacrament of Reconciliation," in *Alternative Futures for Worship*, Vol. 4: Reconciliation (Collegeville, MN: The Liturgical Press, 1987): 73-89. Jean-Marie Tillard, "The Bread and the Cup of Reconciliation," in *Sacramental Reconciliation, Concilium 61* (New York: Herder & Herder, 1971): 38-54.

DORIS DONNELLY

EUCHARIST IN SCRIPTURE
Preliminary Remarks

Eucharist, from the Greek *eucharistia*, from the verb "to give thanks," is properly a NT term. For, though it finds a material equivalent in "songs of thanksgiving" (Jer 30:19) and "sacrifice of thanksgiving" (Ps 116:17) in the OT, *eucharistia* has no formal equivalent in Hebrew (see Conzelmann, *T.D.N.T.* 9.409). Its intelligibility, nevertheless, remains contingent upon an understanding of such OT and contemporary Jewish institutions as the Passover, the prayer of thanksgiving (*tôdâ*) and sacrifice. Its ultimate intelligibility, however, whether in the OT or the NT, depends on grasping the essential fact that all gratitude is the child of memory, that *eucharistia* is inseparable from *anamnēsis* (remembrance),

whether of the saving events of the Exodus or of the redemptive death of Christ on the cross "for us and for our sins."

The Pauline Data

From the middle of the 1st century we have from Paul, not only the earliest record of the institution of the Lord's Supper, but also its first interpretation. To commence the examination of the NT evidence with Paul is, therefore, to witness the interpretation of a tradition in the very act of its transmission. For, though less influential in shaping subsequent doctrinal developments than either John or the Synoptics, Paul's account in 1 Corinthians does set the pattern for all future interpretations of the tradition. Indeed, his approach to this tradition, to what he "received" and "delivered" (1 Cor 11:23), should spare both exegetes and theologians the *culs de sac* of interpreting beyond the sufferance of the text both the Johannine and the synoptic accounts.

Thus, the first statement in 1 Cor 11:23 that "I received from the Lord what I also delivered to you," not only puts the risen Lord at the source of the tradition as its author and the abiding guarantor of its authenticity, but also obviates the endless debates on the "historicity" of the institution accounts themselves. To create a dichotomy between the Jesus of Nazareth and the risen Lord would be to introduce an element alien to Paul's thought and inimical to Christian faith (cf. 1 Cor 7:10 with Mk 10:11 and par.). Therefore, to the catechetical question, "Who instituted the eucharist?" the response has to be unequivocally "the Lord Jesus" (1 Cor 11:23); and no "quest of the historical Jesus," old or new, can alter this fundamental datum.

Similarly, the "on the night when he was betrayed" (11:23b) is not a reference to the Passover but a linking of the institution to the Passion. Paul, of course, regards the Passover as one key to understanding the Passion ("Christ our paschal lamb has been sacrificed"—1 Cor 5:7); but nowhere does he link the feast itself to the Lord's Supper. This fact ought to alert us not to assume the existence of such a link elsewhere in the NT unless explicitly stated.

It is in Paul's account that Jesus' taking of the bread is followed by "when he had given thanks (*eucharistēsas*)." Of course, this is the verb whence, as early as the *Didache* (9:1; 10:7) and Ignatius of Antioch (*Philadelphians* 4), the substantive *eucharistia* came to designate what had hitherto been referred to as "the Lord's Supper" (1 Cor 11:20).

"This is my body which is for you" refers to the redemptive death of Christ for us, as is evident from the "for you." This fact is made explicit in v. 26: "For as often as you eat this bread and drink the cup, you proclaim the Lord's death until he comes." Futhermore, the reference to the eating and drinking applies the formulae themselves, not to the bread and wine, but to their consumption, i.e., not to the elements as such, but to the action of eating and drinking (see v. 27).

The injunction "Do this in remembrance of me" (vv. 24 and 25) is—as has often been remarked (Benoit, "Récit," p. 195)—a rubric rather than a report. But what has not sufficiently been remarked is that the reference to the whole person of Christ, the "me," is in parallel to "my body." In the common biblical acceptance of the term, "body (*sōma*) here refers to the whole person seen as the subject of relationships (see, e.g., "absent in body"—1 Cor 5:3). Thus "body" underlines further the "for us" aspect of the passion, even as the words over the "cup" stress the covenantal aspect of the new relationship that is now in force.

Paul, unlike Mark and Matthew, identifies the cup as "the new covenant in my blood" (v. 25). The fact that, here at least, the reference is not directly to "my blood of the covenant" (as it is in Mk 14:24 and

Mt 26:28) should alert us to the multiplicity of possible interpretations of the Lord's Supper even within the NT itself.

The transmission of any truly living tradition is, of course, an act of interpretation, as for instance the words over the cup, or the injunction to "do this . . . in remembrance (*anamnēsis*) of me" (vv. 24, 25), which is far more than an exhortation to perpetuate the pious memory of a departing hero. It is rather the essential element in the believer's response to the proclamation of the good news of salvation in Christ Jesus, whether in baptism (see the "baptized into his death" in Rom 6:3) or in the eucharist.

The *anamnēsis* is what put the believer in contact with the abiding redemptive effect of the death of Christ. Thus, when Paul interprets the whole action, he describes, as it were, a full circle: the *anamnēsis* puts the believer in contact with the efficacy of the gospel proclaimed, even as the eating and drinking proclaim the saving event announced by the gospel. Paul, therefore, provides an interpretation, not just of the Lord's Supper itself, but also of the celebration of the rite within the community of believers down the ages.

In his interpretation of the Lord's Supper, Paul also provides the fundamental clue to this and to every other sacrament: "For as often as you eat this bread and drink the cup, you proclaim the Lord's death until he comes" (1 Cor 11:26). Every sacrament is essentially the proclamation of the redemptive work of Christ; and the eucharist in particular is this proclamation par excellence. All sacraments derive their meaning and significance from the word they proclaim, even as each in its own way proclaims that same word. The sacraments are thus another mode of this proclamation, in their words no less than in their gestures and actions.

Elsewhere in the same letter to the Corinthians we find, not so much another version of the institution, as another interpretation of its content. In this instance, it is the interpretation that dictates the sequence in 1 Corinthians 10 of "the cup of blessing which we bless" preceding the "bread which we break" (10:16). Here "participation/communion" (*koinōnia* has both senses) is the key to the significance of the action. That the "cup of blessing which we bless" is a "*koinōnia* in the blood of Christ" makes explicit the function of the "remembrance" in "Do this in remembrance of me" (1 Cor 11:24, 25). It makes explicit, that is, the function of the celebration in putting the believer in contact with the redemptive death. But it stresses an aspect of this contact precisely as "*koinōnia* in the blood of Christ," i.e., in the death of Christ on the cross.

Moreover, in the following statement on the bread, it elaborates the notion further ("Because there is one bread, we who are many are one body, for we partake of the one bread"—10:17). It was this logical order of argument, and not some echo of a different tradition such as we find for instance in the *Didache*, that dictated the cup-bread order we have in 1 Cor 10:16-17.

By introducing the reference to the "body of Christ" in the sense of the community of the redeemed (Rom 12:5; 1 Cor 12:27), the interpretation of the "bread we break" as a *koinōnia* in "the body of Christ" underscores two aspects of the eucharist: it, like baptism (1 Cor 12:12-13; Rom 6:3-11), makes the believers beneficiaries of the redemptive act of Christ, at the same time that it incorporates them into this one body. The eucharist is the sacrament of the church in that it brings the church into being as the body of Christ; but it can take place only as an act of the church *as* the body of Christ. These two aspects are so inextricably linked that their converse is equally true. The absence of one makes the other impossible: "When you meet together, it is not the Lord's Supper that you eat" (1 Cor 11:20). Precisely as, and only in so far as, the community of believers assembles "as a church" (11:18) can it celebrate the eucharist and, celebrating it, become the body of Christ (1 Cor 10:17). "The Lord's Supper sets us in the Body of Christ, in the presence of the Exalted One who, having passed through death, now reigns: it therefore places us under the lordship of the *Kyrios*" (Käsemann, 132).

The *Didache* echoes this mode of understanding the eucharistic celebrations: "As this broken bread was scattered upon the mountains, but was brought together and became one, so let thy Church be gathered together from the ends of the earth into thy kingdom ... " (*Didache* 9.4).

Mark and Matthew

Both in their similarity to one another and in their concordant divergence from the accounts in Luke and in Paul, these two narratives of the institution can be treated simultaneously. The setting of the event in them is unmistakably the eating of the Passover (*to pascha*) (Mk 14:12-16; Mt 26:17-20). Therefore, whether or not the Last Supper itself was a Passover meal (see Jeremias, pp. 15-88; Taylor, pp. 664-667), there is reason for trying to interpret that action and the blessing pronounced (*eulogēsas*) in Passover categories. But this is not true of the altogether remarkable "this is my body ... ; this is my blood." For "important though the Passover motif may otherwise be in the christological ideas of early Christianity, for the words of institution it contributes nothing" (Bornkamm, 134; and see Léon-Dufour, 189-194).

Jesus "took bread, and blessed, and broke it and gave it *to them*" in Mk 14:22 is made explicit in Mt 26:26 as "to the disciples." Mark's "take; this is my body" becomes "take, eat" in Matthew. This latter modification would have been a negligible redactional retouch, did it not affect the meaning of the formula. In general, commentators are content to regard the addition as merely stylistic, setting the bread formula in parallel with that of the cup. Nevertheless, a case can be made for taking the neuter *touto* (this) in "this is my body" as referring, in what is called an *ad sensum* construction, to the taking and eating rather than to "body"(*sōma*), which is masculine. Thus, while in Mark the reference is clearly the bread, in Matthew a case can be made for taking it to be the "take, eat." If this be so, then we have even here, not one, but two interpretations of the formula, where Mark's would lead itself more readily to later disputations on the "substance" than would Matthew's. While the formula over the bread itself, either in Mark or in Matthew, does not in any way link the "body" to the death of Jesus (Benoit-Boismard II.384), the meaning of "body" in Mark is, and remains, more of a crux for interpreters than in Matthew.

The cup formula, however, evinces a marked difference between the two evangelists. In Mark it is pronounced by Jesus *after* "they all drank of it" (Mk 14:23). Thus here the question of the referent can and does arise: "this is my blood of the covenant" refers to the cup, since there is no mention of "wine" as there is of "bread" in v. 22. But it refers especially to the drinking, "And he took a cup ... gave it to them ... and they all drank of it" (Mk 14:23; see I Cor 11:26, where the reference to the eating and the drinking is unequivocal). In Matthew, however, the situation is slightly adjusted by the addition of the imperative "drink of it, all of you, for this is my blood ... " (Mt 26:27b-28).

Any understanding of the eucharist inevitably hinges on determining what precisely the "this" (*touto*) refers to. In Mark and Matthew it is the cup formula which really interprets the action as a

reference to the redemptive death: "which is poured out for many"(Mk 14:24) and, in Matthew, by "for the forgiveness of sins" (Mt 26:38). Thus in these two gospels, as in the other accounts of the institution in the NT, the narrative and its content are already theologically interpreted, and no amount of exegetical ingenuity can wholly separate the "fact" from that interpretation. Therefore, each account of the Last Supper in the NT is a distinct eucharistic theology.

Luke

Of all the accounts of institution, the one in the gospel of Luke is the most textually vexing. But, whether one adopts the shorter version (Lk 22:15-19a) or the longer (vv. 15-20), the order of cup-bread in the former or cup-bread-cup in the latter requires explanation. Descriptions of the Passover seder, of Jewish celebratory practices, and of their background in the OT, are all alike called upon to provide an explanation (see recent commentaries on Luke such as J.A. Fitzmyer, pp. 1385-1406; and I.H. Marshall, pp. 799-807). Nevertheless, the mere fact of the cup preceding the bread, if surprising, need not be inexplicable. As indicated above, in 1 Cor 10:16-17, the order of cup first is dictated by Paul's interpretation of the Lord's Supper in terms of the bread rather than of the cup. Though both "the cup of blessings which we bless" and "the bread which we break" are interpreted as *koinōnia* in the blood and the body of Christ respectively, it is the bread/body that provides Paul with the image he needs in order to proceed, "Because there is *one bread*, we who are many are *one body*, for we all partake of the *one bread*" (1 Cor 10:17). Moreover, since the reference to "blood" is clearly to the redemptive death, as it is elsewhere in Paul (e.g., Rom 3:25; 5:9), the cup-bread order in 1 Corinthians 10 is dictated by the logic of expository exigence as it is not in, for example, an almost equally ancient, extra-canonical work, the *Didache*: "And concerning the Eucharist [this is one of the earliest instances of the usage of this term], hold Eucharist thus: First, concerning the Cup, 'We give thanks to thee, our Father, for the Holy Vine of David thy child; to thee be glory for ever.' And concerning the broken Bread: 'We give thee thanks, our Father, for the life and knowledge which thou didst make known to us through Jesus thy child. To thee be glory forever'" (*Didache* 9.1-3).

Luke's text is usually regarded as closer to that of 1 Cor 11 than to Mark and Matthew. For, in addition to the "Do this is remembrance of me" (Lk 22:19b; cf. 1 Cor 11:24-25), it is prefaced by an explicit reference to the coming of the kingdom of God (22:16; cf. 1 Cor 11:26). Whether it be taken as integral to the account of the institution or regarded as prefatory to it, the reference indelibly marks the account and its understanding as eschatological, that is, as belonging to the "last times" inaugurated by the coming of the Lord. The eucharist is an act that proclaims the presence of the last times in our midst. No understanding of "the new covenant in my blood," in Luke or elsewhere, is possible without the realization that the covenant is both final and definitive (see Heb 7:27). Thus it is that the church in celebrating the eucharist has, with unfailing insight, coupled the Lord's Prayer and the words of the institution: "Thy kingdom come ... give us our bread" find their true meaning in the "for you" of the bread formula and in "the covenant" of the cup formula.

The Fourth Gospel

It is not an unremarked fact that the fourth gospel has no narrative of the eucharistic institution. If at first baffling, such omission is not the least logical of the gospel's qualities. What the Prologue climax affirms, "The Word became flesh" (Jn 1:14), is elaborated throughout both the "Book of Signs" (Jn 1-12) and the "Book of Glory" (chaps. 13-21). To have inserted an institution account in the closing chapters would have been redundant. What the fourth gospel does, however, is more illuminating. It explains, in the discourse on the bread of life in chap. 6, the meaning of the eucharist in terms of the Prologue. This is why the "sacramental realism" of Jn 6:53-58 can best be understood in terms of the Word which "became flesh" for the "life of the world." Here alone do we have the properly biblical coupling of "flesh and blood" and not, as elsewhere in the institution accounts, "body and blood."

It is at this point that one can best understand how the eucharist is, above all else, the "mystery of faith," faith in the flesh which the Word became. If a proper understanding of Jn 6:52-59 is to be sought, then it is to be sought, not in the abstract theological terminology of later eucharistic debates, but in its collocation in the same chapter with two major themes: the banquet of wisdom and the meaning of discipleship. The proper significance of the mystery is given final expression in the Petrine confession, "Lord, to whom shall we go? You have the words of eternal life; and we have believed, and have come to know, that you are the Holy One of God" (Jn 6:69).

J. Betz, "Eucharist: I. Theological," *Sacramentum Mundi*, in K. Rahner, ed., Vol. 2 (N.Y.: Herder & Herder, 1986): 257-267. P. Benoit, "Le récit de la Cène dans Lc. XXII, 15-20. Etude de critique textuelle et littéraire, in *Exégèse et Théologie*, Vol. 1 (Paris: Cerf, 1961). P. Benoit, M.-E. Boismard, *Synopse des quatre Evangiles*, tome II (Paris: Cerf, 1972). P. Benoit, R.E. Murphy, B. van Iersel, eds. *The Breaking of Bread*, Concilium 40; (N.Y.: Paulist Press, 1969). G. Bornkamm, "Lord's Supper and Church in Paul," in *Early Christian Experience* (London: SCM, 1969): 123-160. H. Conzelmann, "*eucharisteo, eucharistia, eucharistos*," in *Theological Dictionary of N.T.* 9.407-415. J. Delorme et al., *The Eucharist in the N.T.* (Baltimore: Helicon Press, 1964). J. Jeremias, *The Eucharistic Words of Jesus* (N.Y.: Scribner's, 1966). E. Käsemann, "The Pauline Doctrine of the Lord's Supper," in *Essays on NT Themes* Studies in Biblical Theology 41; (London: SCM, 1964): 108-

135. J. Kodell, *The Eucharist in the N.T.* (Wilmington, DE: Michael Glazier, 1988). X. Léon-Dufour, *Sharing the Eucharistic Bread* (N.Y.: Paulist Press, 1987). I.H. Marshall, *Last Supper and Lord's Supper* (Grand Rapids, MI: Eerdmans, 1980). J. Reumann, ed., *The Supper of the Lord: The N.T., Ecumenical Dialogues, and Faith and Order on Eucharist* (Philadelphia: Fortress, 1985). E. Schweizer, *The Lord's Supper According to the N.T.* (Facet Books; Philadelphia: Fortress, 1967). V. Taylor, *The Gospel According to Mark* 2nd ed. (N.Y.: St. Martin's Press. 1966).

STANLEY B. MARROW, S.J.

EUCHARIST, HISTORY OF, IN EARLY CHURCH

The history of the eucharist is inseparable from the history of the church. Our earliest evidence of Christianity is of communities (*ekklesiai*) whose life was centered in gatherings of the baptized for communal meals, normally held on the day after the Sabbath, the first day of the week, or "Lord's Day." Their writings, many but not all of which were later included in the NT, are replete with allusions to the receiving of the bread and wine over which blessings were offered as communion in the body and blood of Christ. While these allusions tell us less than we would now like to know about the eucharistic practices assumed by their readers, they provide us with the beginnings of the history of eucharistic celebration of the early church.

Background

Nothing has proved so important for the study of this evidence as recognition of Christian indebtedness to Jewish practices regarding the blessings offered over foods, and in particular the bread and wine at the family meals on the Sabbath and at the Passover (cf. *Mishnah*, Ber.). For Israel, these meals, together with the synagogue meetings, proclaimed and enacted the identity of Israel as the people of God. In them lie the roots of the Christian assumption that the eucharistic bread and wine are the sustenance of the new people called together through the death and resurrection of Christ. The Greek *eucharistia* (thanksgiving), the term destined to supplant "Lord's Supper" or "breaking of bread" as the common designation of the Christian meals as early as Ignatius of Antioch (see below), translates the Hebrew *berakah*, the term which denotes the blessing form of all Jewish prayers, including the prayers offered at meals.

Paul and the Gospels

The earliest evidence of eucharistic practice is found in Paul's instructions on the Lord's Supper in 1 Cor 11:17-34, his response to reports that groups of Corinthian Christians ate without waiting for all to gather for the blessings over the bread and wine. Here Paul appeals to the "tradition" he has already delivered (11:23ff) recounting the words and actions of Jesus at the Last Supper ("that the Lord Jesus, the night he was betrayed...") and the command that they be repeated as a "memorial," that is, done by the church to celebrate the redemptive work of Christ. This is, he says, a "showing forth of the Lord's death until he comes again" (11:26). The disunity evident in its neglect "profanes the body and blood of the Lord" and involves failure to "discern the body" (11:27-8). It is clear that Paul recognizes the Last Supper "tradition" as already implying that the death of Jesus is a new Passover sacrifice (cf. 5:7-8), and also that he, Paul, sees the "Lord's Supper" as he does baptism, as effecting the formation of the body of Christ through the Spirit. This is the subject of the extended discussion of the body and its members which follows (12:12-27).

The eucharistic practice which Paul enjoins plainly assumes the practice of Jewish meal blessings, but is specifically governed by the account of the blessings contained in the Last Supper "tradition." It is not clear, however, that these later so-called "words of institution" were for him liturgical formulas, and more likely that they simply constituted an explanation of the significance of the church's "memorial" of Christ's death. Nor is it clear that he assumes that the Lord's Supper is to be held on every Lord's Day (most probably on what we should call Saturday night, given Jewish reckoning of days from sunset), though this is the general deduction from his reference to a weekly gathering on the first day of the week (1 Cor 16:2).

The synoptic gospels incorporate the Last Supper "tradition" in a form or forms independent of Paul, both in their accounts of the miraculous feedings (Mk 6:41-2, 8:6-8; Mt 14:19-20, 15:36-7; Lk 9:16-17), which employ the technical terminology of "taking, blessing, breaking, and giving," and in the passion narrative. In the latter case, their locating of the last meal on the night of the slaughter of the passover lambs reflects the "tradition" in identifying the death of Jesus as a new passover sacrifice of which Christians partake. But Mk 14:22-5 and Mt 26:26-9 are less concerned with the actual relation of the blessings to the course of the meal than is Paul, while Lk 22:15-20, which seems to conflate Mark and 1 Corinthians, seems to some to suggest that the blessings over both bread and wine were conflated together at the end of the meal in the practice the author knew (cf. the eucharistic description of the resurrection appearance at Emmaus in Lk 24:30).

The gospel of John, exercises its "reserve" with respect to Christian practices by omitting reference to the Last Supper "tradition" from the passion narrative, substituting for it the account of the washing of the disciples' feet and the command that *it* be continued (Jn 13:1-11). However, the Johannine account of the miraculous feeding is the occasion for an extended eucharistic commentary (6:25-60), which counters the theme of the eucharistic bread as foreshadowed by the manna in the wilderness (cf. 1 Cor 10:1-4; Rev 2:17)

with emphasis on Jesus' body itself as the true "bread from heaven." The theme of the vine and the branches, developed in the discourse at the last meal (Jn 15:1-8), also has eucharistic overtones. As is well known, John differs from the Synoptics in setting the last meal, rightly or wrongly, "before the feast of Passover" (15:1), so that the last meal is not a Passover seder and Jesus' death itself takes place on the day of the slaughter of the Passover lambs.

Critical efforts to recover the historical basis of the Last Supper "tradition" will continue. For us, it is important to see that 1 Corinthians and the gospels, even including John, reflect prior use of the "tradition" as an explanation of the eucharistic meals of the earliest communities.

Wider NT and Related Evidence

There are few actual references to eucharistic meals in the other writings later included in the NT. Mention of the primitive Jerusalem community as "day by day attending the temple and breaking bread in their homes" (Acts 2:46), if indeed it is eucharistic, is unusual. The account in Acts 20:7-12 of Paul's healing of Eutychus at Troas during an evening meeting on the "first day of the week . . . to break bread" probably provides evidence of the celebration of the eucharist on Saturday night, but is essentially a miracle story rather than evidence to that point.

But these writings contain recurrent allusions which, if less frequent than those to baptism, witness to the central place of the eucharist in the life of the communities for which they were written. In Heb 6:4-5, for instance, it is hard to miss the eucharistic, no less than the baptismal, reference to Christians as those who have been "enlightened, and tasted the heavenly gift, and have become partakers of the Holy Spirit, and have tasted the goodness of the Word of God

and the powers of the age to come."
Moreover, it is in Heb 7:15-28 that we
first encounter the motif of Jesus' sacrifice
as foreshadowed in the account of the
Melchizedek priest (Gen 14:18), a motif
which elsewhere forms part of the
interpretation of the eucharist as the pure
sacrifice of bread and wine prophesied to
be offered in the last days (cf. Justin,
Dial. 41, 70, 117). In I Pet 2:5, the
description of Christians as "a royal
priesthood" called to make "spiritual
sacrifices" may well refer to the church as
eucharistic community. In Revelation,
eucharistic and baptismal references are
combined in the promise that the martyrs
will be given "to eat of the heavenly
manna ... and ... a new name" (2:17),
and the final consummation is
described as "the marriage feast of the
Lamb" (19:7-9). But it has also been
suggested that this apocalyptic vision,
described as occurring on the Lord's Day
(1:10), is more generally framed on the
outline of a gathering to hear the
scriptures and celebrate the eucharist.
Indeed, all of these writings should be
read, with due caution to be sure, as
coming from communities whose life was
focused in the eucharist.

The same is true of the contemporary
writings not included in the NT. Among
these, I Clement, a formal letter from the
Roman church to the church of Corinth
commonly dated after the Domitian
persecution of A.D. 96, offers support to
the authority of the Corinthian
leadership by comparing the members of
the Christian body (cf. 1 Cor 12:12-27) to
the high priests, Levites, and people of
Israel in their responsibilities for the
offering of sacrifices (1 Clement 40-41),
with obvious eucharistic implications so
far as the functions of those appointed by
the apostles for this work (42-4). Moreover,
the lyric blessing prayer or set of prayers
for the unity of the church, with which
the letter draws to an end (59.2-64.1),
while not specifically eucharistic, follows

the outline of Jewish blessing prayers
which we may suppose had become
habitual for the author from their eucharistic use.

Independent of Clement are the letters
of Ignatius, Bishop of Antioch, written to
churches he would visit on his way to
Rome for martyrdom sometime prior to
the death of the Emperor Trajan in A.D.
117. Concerned with the menace of
"docetic" or Gnostic teachers who deny
the incarnation of Christ, and either gather
disciples apart from the general body of
the baptized or absent themselves from
the eucharist, Ignatius recurrently stresses
the importance of the one eucharistic
community, gathered around the bishop,
presbyters, and deacons, as expressing
the faith that "there is only one flesh of
our Lord Jesus Christ and one cup to
unite us in his blood" (*Philad* 4, cf. *Eph*
13.1, *Smyrn* 7.1, etc.). In contrast to the
claims of his opponents, the eucharist is
"the medicine of immortality, the antidote
to death, giving life in Jesus Christ
forever" (*Eph* 20:1-2).

Nor can we omit mention of the
Martyrdom of Polycarp, Bishop of
Smyrna and one of Ignatius' correspon-
dents (d. 256), which contains a prayer
said to have been offered by Polycarp at
the point of death. Cast in the form of a
blessing of God that he has been "deemed
worthy" to drink "the cup of Christ" and
asking that he be received as an "acceptable sacrifice," this prayer may well be
framed on Polycarp's habitual eucharistic
blessing prayer. At the least it reflects, as
does the prayer of 1 Clement, the Gentile
Christian appropriation of the Jewish
berakah form.

Didache

In a category by itself is the recently
recovered *Didache* ("The Teaching of the
Twelve Apostles"), a 2nd-century Greek
compilation and edition of Aramaic
liturgical materials probably of rural
Syrian-Palestinian provenance from the

later decades of the 1st century. In its 2nd century form, this work brings together material to form a pre-baptismal catechesis (the "Two Ways" document of I-VI), a description of paschal baptism and eucharist (VII-X), and an exhortation to observe the Sunday eucharist (XIV) set amidst directions for the treatment of visiting prophets and the necessity of establishing a regular ministry of bishops and deacons (XI-XV). As such, it follows a 2nd-century pattern of liturgical description found in Justin Martyr and the *Apostolic Tradition* (see below).

Attention here must focus on the eucharistic materials of IX-X. These include blessings to be said before the meal over an initial cup of wine for "the vine of David, your child (*pais*, the servant of Isaiah in LXX = *Septuagint* version of OT"), and over the broken bread (*klasma*) for "the life and knowledge revealed through Jesus, your child," with the prayer that, as grain scattered on the hillside is made into the loaf of bread, so the church may be gathered into the kingdom. After the meal, there follows a connected series of blessings for the name of God and the knowledge and faith revealed in the servant Jesus, for food and drink and for spiritual food and drink given through Jesus, for the gathering of the church, and for the coming of the Kingdom.

Since these blessings do not include reference to the Last Supper "tradition," and since reference is later made to the necessity of the Sunday eucharist, the suspicion continues that these are not eucharistic blessings. Attention to the pattern of liturgical description mentioned above, however, suggests that these are eucharistic blessings, which certainly have in view the saving death of Christ, and which are set out as part of the description of paschal baptism and eucharist. But as this may be, they are easily recognized as Christian adaptations of Jewish sabbath and festival meal blessings, the final series following the order of the *Birkat ha-mazon* offered over the "cup of blessing" at the end of such formal Jewish meals.

Whatever else may be said of it, the *Didache* has given us actual blessing forms of the sort we may assume were adapted from Jewish practice. It may also offer some support for the contention (cf. Lk 22:15-20; 24:30) that such extended blessings for food and drink connected with the "cup of blessing" at the end of the meal eventually provided the context for the unified blessing over the bread and wine of which we have evidence from the 2nd century onward when the observance of the eucharist at an actual meal ceased to be the norm.

Toward the 2nd Century

The evidence thus far tells us much, but also omits much that we should like to know in the light of later practice. For instance, it is not clear what forms of instruction accompanied the eucharistic meals, especially where attendance at the synagogue ceased to be possible. Paul speaks only generally of hymns, scripture readings, revelations, and speaking in tongues at the meals at Corinth (I Cor 14:26-33), and the report of his speaking at length before the "blessing of bread" at Troas (Acts 20:7) need not refer to common practice. The Lucan account of Jesus interpreting the scriptures referring to himself on the way to the supper at Emmaus (Lk 24:27) may suggest that the author is familiar with such interpretations of the Jewish scriptures before the eucharistic meal. But there is no evidence as yet of any Christian adaptation of the structures of scripture reading, instruction, and prayer, common to the synagogue.

Again, it is not clear how wide-spread was any Christian observance of the Jewish Passover. While Paul presumably continued such observance as a Jew, his reference to Christians observing the feast "in spirit and truth" (I Cor 5:5-7) is notoriously obscure. Our evidence of Christian ("Quartodeciman") observance of 14 Nisan, and of its eventual abandonment (as it is now commonly described) in favor of a Christian Passover on a succeeding Lord's Day, comes from accounts of the 2nd-century "Paschal controversy" (Eusebius, HE. IV. 14, no. 22-23).

And again, it is unclear when and in what circumstances it became customary to detach the eucharistic blessings from an actual meal, or to gather for the eucharist on the morning of the Lord's Day. It is perhaps not wrongly assumed that the Gentile custom of reckoning days from sunrise rather than sunset, and the onset of opposition which rendered regular gatherings for meals difficult, contributed to this result, as well as to the consequent conflation of the blessings over the bread and wine for which the *Birkat ha-mazon* may have provided the context. The evidence of Pliny the Younger, governor of Bithynia ca. 112 (*Epp.* X. 96), that Christians met early on a specified day to "bind themselves with an oath," and later held an inoffensive meal, has been taken to be evidence of this development, but is open to a variety of interpretations.

Finally, it is not clear who might have been expected to offer the eucharistic blessings, since Jewish customs regarding the host at family meals could hardly have provided a general rule. By the time of 1 Clement and Ignatius, the responsibility is assumed to be that of the elders or bishops, and this may also be the import of the direction of *Did.* that, while visiting prophets may give thanks, bishops and deacons should be chosen by the congregation. But little else can be said on the subject.

In fact, however, there is at least enough clarity with respect to the eucharistic practice of the earliest communities to allow these points of obscurity to be recognized.

The First Prescriptions: Justin Martyr and the Apostolic Tradition

From the mid 2nd and early 3rd century come two works which, for different reasons, provide descriptions of liturgical practices, including the eucharist. These are Justin Martyr, *I Apology*, and the *Apostolic Tradition* commonly attributed to Hippolytus of Rome. Both emanate from the Greek-speaking Roman community; each has peculiar problems of interpretation, and each sheds light on liturgical developments in the Gentile churches at large.

Justin's work, datable ca. 155, is a general explanation and defense of Christianity for pagan readership, and concludes with a description of Christian meetings for baptism and eucharist (chaps. 61-67), that is designed at least in part to allay suspicions of their orgiastic character. By turns very general and quite technical, for reasons only occasionally clear to us now, this description follows the outline already noticed in present *Did.* where paschal baptism and eucharist ("How we dedicate ourselves to God when we are made new through Christ" 61ff.) precedes a description of the weekly eucharist ("On the day called of the sun, there is a meeting in one place ... " 67ff.). This outline, plainly not of Justin's making, reflects the liturgical practices of the Roman church, anchored on the annual paschal celebration, as they were defined by Bishop Anicetus on the occasion of the visit of the "Quartodeciman" Polycarp in 155 (Eusebius, *HE.* IV. 14). It may also be that it suggests the specific reason for the reorganization of earlier materials in our present *Did.*

Of the two descriptions of the eucharist required by this outline, the first commences where the newly baptized "join the brethren" for common prayers and the exchange of the kiss of peace (65). After this, bread and wine mixed with water (a detail several times repeated, presumably to show the sobriety of the occasion) are brought to "the one who presides" (doubtless a circumlocution for the bishop), who takes them, and then "sends up praise and glory to the Father of the universe through the name of the Son and of the Holy Spirit, and offers thanks at some length that we have been deemed worthy to receive these things ..., " after which the people "assent, saying Amen" (a word translated both here and in the second description). Deacons then give bread and wine and water to those present and absent.

Plainly, this eucharist takes place at an early morning hour following the vigil and baptism, and the action of "taking, blessing over, breaking (actually omitted in both descriptions) and giving" are done without an actual meal. Moreover, Justin says enough about the unified blessing prayer to suggest something of its form and contents, and here and elsewhere says that "the food eucharistized (his unusual term) by the word of prayer, by which our flesh and blood is nourished, is the body and blood of the incarnate Jesus," and explains the action as fulfilling the command of Jesus (apparent allusion to the 1 Corinthians form of the "tradition"), as a "memorial" of the incarnation, and as the prophesied pure sacrifice of the people of God (I *Apol.* 66, *Dial.* 41, 70, 117).

The subsequent description of the weekly eucharist on the first or Lord's Day, "on which God ... made the universe, and Jesus Christ ... rose from the dead" (I *Apol.* 67), merely refers to the action as taking place "as said before" and to the "one who presides" as praying "to the best of his ability." A single pattern of paschal and Sunday eucharist is here in view. New, however, is reference to readings from the Jewish scriptures and "the memoirs of the apostles" (obviously the gospels), followed by instruction from "the one who presides" before the common prayers and kiss of peace. Brief as it is, perhaps because unexceptionable,

it is our first evidence of the regular use of these preliminaries, shaped on the synagogue meetings, which Tertullian would call the "administration of the word of God" (*De cultu fem.* II. 11; cf. *Apol.* XX).

In Justin, then, we have evidence of a pattern of eucharistic practice already established, shaped from earlier customs in the circumstances of the 2nd century, and scarcely unique in general outline to the Roman church.

Apostolic Tradition

The second description from this period is contained in the work now commonly regarded as the *Apostolic Tradition* mentioned among the writings of Hippolytus (d. 235), theologian, presbyter of the Roman church, critic of several episcopal contemporaries, and finally schismatic bishop. Now pieced together from various sources replete with inconsistencies, it nevertheless, if rightly identified, purports to describe proper practice for the Roman church at the turn of the 3rd century. It is thus intended for a different readership from Justin's, is narrow in scope and far greater in specific detail, as well as half a century later.

Apost. Trad. follows the now familiar outline of paschal and weekly observances only in part. In this case, a prefatory description of ordinations (2-14) contains an extensive account of the eucharist of a newly consecrated bishop (4), so that the paschal eucharist (21) is virtually an appendix to the account of the initiatory rites which precede it (15-22). Only brief reference is made, and only in some versions, to the eucharist celebrated on Saturdays and Sundays (23, 27), though a more widely attested concluding section on various matters includes references to the survival of communal meals (25-6) which the author cautions against regarding as eucharistic.

Apost. Trad.'s several accounts of the eucharist follow the form already seen in Justin. In that of the newly consecrated bishop (4), which follows the kiss of peace, the deacons bring the bread and wine to the bishop, who lays his hand upon them. The episcopal eucharistic prayer which follows begins with the *sursum corda* (habitual hereafter, but likely much earlier). Its opening account of the works of God stresses the separate existence of the Word incarnate from the Virgin and gives as his purpose to assemble a holy people by his suffering and death. The prayer explicitly but freely rehearses the Last Supper "tradition," and combines the offering of the "memorial" with prayer for the Spirit to come upon "the offering of your holy church" that it may be united in faith and gathered into the kingdom. It concludes with a doxology and the assenting "Amen."

In the brief account of the paschal eucharist (22), the bishop now breaks the bread, and distributes the bread and wine with the somewhat confused help of presbyters and deacons, these using specified words to which the people again assent "Amen." Here cups of water, milk and honey, appropriately baptismal and eschatological, are administered to the newly baptized.

Attention naturally centers on the unusual features of the eucharistic prayer of *Apost. Trad.*, variously enjoined and offered as a model in different sources. Its stress on the independent existence of the Word suggests the influence of Hippolytus' differences with his Roman contemporaries on this subject. Its unified construction differs from the loosely constructed set of blessings found in the later Roman canon. And the prayer for the sending of the Spirit, while it does not ask for the transformation of the bread and wine in the manner of the later Eastern *epiclesis*, is in the position that such prayers occupy in such Eastern prayers as that of the later 4th-century *Apostolic Constitutions* (see below), which incorporates ordination materials from *Apost. Trad.*

But these peculiarities need not shake confidence in the Roman provenance of *Apost. Trad.* as a whole, or even of its eucharistic prayer. We know little of the limits of improvisation possible in the period, and much about the innovative theology of Hippolytus. If he left his own impress upon the eucharistic prayer, it has similarities with I Clement and the *Martyrdom of Polycarp* (see above) as well as with *Apost. Const.* In any case, it would be surprising if *Apost. Trad.* did not reflect traditions which its author thought consistent with Roman practice. As that may be, the work stands with Justin's as witness to the eucharistic developments in the formative period before the end of the persecutions and the "peace of the church."

Toward the "Peace of the Church"

Other evidence of the 2nd and 3rd centuries can be gleaned from the theological writings of the period, and from the recently recovered sources of the roots of the later rites of the churches of Egypt and Syria shortly to be discussed. Particularly important, however, is the increasing evidence of the physical settings in which Christians met for the eucharist in this period, since the eucharist is a physical as well as a verbal phenomenon. To be sure, even the Pauline letters contain references to Christian meetings in houses (Rom 16:5, Col 4:15, Phlm 2), presumably those of substantial members of congregations, and of the sort common to the domestic architecture of the ancient world, hidden from the street and constructed around one or more social rooms. From at least the 3rd century, however, we have evidence of such houses being made available for remodeling for liturgical use with space provided for baptism and eucharist, as in the small "house of Christians" discovered at Dura Europos on the Euphrates. Such a document as the early 3rd century north Syrian

Didascalia, with its directions for the behavior of the various people gathered for the eucharist (chap. 12) may be read with such a physical setting in view.

Equally important is the physical evidence of the catacombs at Rome and elsewhere. Here the recurrence of pictures showing figures lying or seated at tables displaying bread or fish embodies the Last Supper "tradition," rather than what we may imagine to be the later practice of standing at a small table-altar of the sort shown in mosaics from the 4th century onward. Of this latter custom, however, the innumerable "praying figures" (*orantes*), which show those interred standing with arms extended in the attitude of prayer, is a visible witness.

The importance of this physical evidence extends well into the period of the peace of the church. Not only do such Christian "houses" multiply in this period, but the great building complexes now erected retain something of their "domestic" character. These baptistries and eucharistic halls, constructed so as to be hidden from the streets and approached through secluded atriums, were strikingly different from the public religious buildings with which the ancient world was familiar. While their erection in itself reflected the changed relation of the church to the Roman Empire, they stood, as did the rites celebrated in them, as witnesses to the life of the new people of God which participation in the eucharist proclaimed and enacted.

The 4th Century and Beyond: the East

Beginning with the 4th century "peace of the church," evidence of eucharistic practice becomes increasingly extensive. It includes evidence not only of the rites of the great episcopal sees which took shape in the period but also of such earlier rites as were preserved either because they contributed to or had been superseded by them. In the main, this evidence is clearer with respect to the eucharistic practices of the Eastern sees of Alexandria, Antioch and Jerusalem, and the new capital of Constantinople, than with respect to the Western churches and the Roman see. Whether Eastern or Western, however, this is evidence of the emergence of the eucharist as what now comes to be called the public liturgy (*leitourgia*) of the Christian Roman Empire.

Egypt

Among the pieces of Egyptian evidence lying in the background of the Alexandrian rite of St. Mark, the most extensive is the "prayer book" (*euchologion*) associated with Serapion, Bishop of Thmuis and correspondent of Athanasius, and doubtless reflecting the liturgical practices of his church. Not seen in documents encountered by us before this, but characteristic of the elaborations of the period, are prayers to be used at the reading of the scriptures, the homily, the dismissal of the catechumens, and the prayers of the people, as well as at the breaking of the bread and the receiving of communion. But the *Serap.* eucharistic prayer or *anaphora* seems to belong to an Egyptian type of which earlier fragmentary examples survive (cf. the Der Balizeh and Strasbourg frags.), in which prefatory material leads to the Sanctus borrowed from the synagogue, and a loosely connected series of blessings includes invocations over the bread and wine before and after the Last Supper "tradition," as well as prayers for the living and dead before the final doxology. Peculiar to *Serap.*, is the invocation of the Word (*Logos*) rather than the Spirit upon the oblation, and the interruption of words of Jesus with a prayer not unlike that over the bread in *Did.* But the *anaphora* in general links the 4th-century Egyptian churches with earlier local forms otherwise largely lost to us.

Syria-Palestine

In contrast to that from Egypt, the

eucharistic evidence from Syria and Palestine is far more extensive and diverse. From East Syria, on the border of the Roman Empire, come various forms of the *Anaphora of Mari and Addai*, names associated with the foundation of the church of Edessa, a eucharistic *anaphora* which preserves blessing prayers similar to those which underlie our present *Did.* By stages on which there is no general agreement, this prayer has acquired a Sanctus, a narrative of the institution, and a form of memorial and invocation of the sort common to the 4th century. But its retention of the ancient blessing prayers is of interest as showing their continued use in a eucharistic tradition independent of the later influence of Constantinople within the Empire.

Far more comprehensive, however, is the West Syrian eucharistic evidence contained in the *Apost. Const.*, a compilation of liturgical materials from Antioch in the last decades of the 4th century. Perhaps intended as an editing of the diversity of practices in the region of the Syrian capital, this work includes (VII. 25-6) a reworking of the blessing prayers of *Did.* into a eucharistic *anaphora* before the communion, which installs the order of bread and wine, though without an institution narrative, and leaves what is left as a set of blessing prayers after the communion. A comparison with *Mari and Addai* suggests that this is another, rather different, effort to accommodate earlier Christian adaptations of Jewish blessings to the now conventional structure of a eucharistic *anaphora*.

Interest in *Apost. Const.*, however, centers chiefly on the large body of material (VIII. 1-15) which follows the general outline of Hippolytus', *Apost. Trad.*,, in its section on ordinations, and incorporates its blessing prayer for an episcopal ordination before passing to its description of the eucharist on such an occasion. In the place of the latter, *Apost. Const.* embarks on its own elaborate description of a eucharistic celebration (5-15) commonly taken to be that of the church of Antioch itself. Here brief reference is even made to scripture readings from the law, prophets, apostle, and gospels, to a homily, and to the dismissal of the unbaptized by a deacon. There follow litanic prayers for the catechumens, for the baptized, and for the church and the world, led by a deacon to Kyrial responses ("Lord have mercy") and concluded by appropriate blessings by the bishop before the kiss of peace. Pictured here is a public assembly, attended by the unbaptized as well as catechumens, and large enough to require overseeing by the deacons.

Similarly elaborate is the eucharist itself. Here the oblation is brought to the altar by the deacons; the bishop is assisted at the *anaphora* by deacons and surrounded at the altar by the presbyters; the bread is broken and communion distributed by the bishop and the deacons; and a prayer of thanksgiving and an episcopal blessing is added before a diaconal dismissal. The *anaphora* itself is of great length and richness, with an underlying structure not unlike that noticed in *Apost. Trad.* (see above). Here Preface and Sanctus lead to a rehearsal of the works of God, the institution narrative, an oblation of the memorial and an invocation of the Spirit to make the bread and wine the body and blood of Christ. Litanic prayers for the living and the dead, led by a deacon and concluded with a blessing by the bishop, intervene before the final doxology and the assent "Amen."

Constantinople

Certain features of the *anaphora* and other prayers of *Apost. Const.*, particularly their stress on the Father as the sole "uncreated" God and the Son as created "before the ages by his will and power," suggest that the compiler had Arian sympathies. But the wider significance of these sections of the work lies in its witness to a style of eucharistic celebration common in the region at this time. Moreover, it is now fairly widely agreed that the Antiochene eucharist, of which *Apost. Const.*, is our principal source, eventually provided the basis for the rite of the church of Constantinople, which in turn exercised a profound influence on the rites of the Eastern churches in communion with that of the new imperial capital.

Later Constantinopolitan elements grafted on this rite are easily noted. These include the common use of the *anaphora* attributed to John Chrysostom, as well as the occasional use of those of Basil the Great and of the Jerusalem Liturgy of St. James, all of which exhibit orthodox trinitarian features which give equal significance to the persons of the Godhead, and elevate the invocation of the Spirit on the bread and wine to a new prominence. They include also the eventual addition of the Lord's Prayer before the breaking of the bread, as well as of the Nicene creed of A.D. 381 at the bringing in of the oblation. And they include the preparation of the oblation and the solemn entrance of the bishop and people before the beginning of the rite. But these additions, of which we have evidence at various stages in Maximus the Confessor, (*Mystagogia*), and in the 9th century *euchologion* (Barberini MS), would not be intelligible for the additions they are without *Apost. Const.*

Nor would we grasp the rationale for the space provided for the celebration of the rite, as that would issue classically in Justinian's 6th-century basilica of the Holy Wisdom, without clues provided by *Apost. Const.*. Such space, with its centralized *bema* for the reading of scriptures, and its altar set on the chord of the apse, separated from the nave by an open screen and backed by tiers of seats for the presbyters and the throne of the bishop, is also of Syrian provenance.

The Calendar: Christmas and Epiphany

The period we are discussing saw elaborations in the calendar of Christian observances which had a material effect on the occasions of eucharistic celebration, anchored heretofore on the paschal and Sunday cycles, except for the observance of the anniversaries of the deaths of local martyrs. One elaboration of this pattern, attributable to the church of Jerusalem, now beset by pilgrims eager to visit the holy sites, was the extension backwards of the paschal baptismal fast into a week of observances at the sites recorded in the synoptic tradition from Palm Sunday until Good Friday, and the extension forward of the paschal celebration until Pentecost. The *Diary* of Egeria bears witness to the popularity of these observances, and to the impulse which led to their being copied elsewhere for people who could not themselves visit Jerusalem.

A different sort of elaboration is the observance of two festivals of the birth of Christ, Christmas on December 25 and Epiphany of January 6. We cannot here discuss the complicated question of the origin of these observances in earlier calculations of Jesus' death and birth or the pagan festivals of the Sol Invictus at Rome and of the birth of Dionysius at Alexandria. Suffice it to say that these observances, appropriated in different ways in both the Eastern and Western churches, came to constitute, especially in the later West, a countervailing cycle to the basic paschal and Sunday structure of eucharistic celebration.

The Latin West

The scattered eucharistic evidence of the Latin-speaking churches of the West, whether of Latin Africa, Spain, Gaul, or even Italy and Rome itself, provides us with no such clear picture as does the evidence of the East. Certainly no such steps as marked the formation of the Constantinopolitan rite can be traced there. The eventual promotion of the Roman rite in the ecclesiastical unity of the new Frankish Empire of Pepin IV and Charlemagne, followed a period of political decentralization, social dislocation, and population shifts. In the intervening period, the earlier rites, of which we have relatively little evidence in any case, gave way to or resisted that of the Roman church in degrees that are hard to measure.

Latin Africa

With respect to Latin Africa, the situation is peculiarly surprising. Despite the wealth of liturgical allusion in the writings of Tertullian and Cyprian, details of the Latin eucharistic rites of the 2nd and 3rd centuries, presumably open to influence from both Asia Minor and Rome, are generally lacking. Nor do we know much about the rites of the 4th and 5th centuries, despite the catechetical and homiletic works of Augustine and other African writers. From Augustine, we can deduce a plain introductory rite of scripture reading and psalmody, homily, dismissal of the catechumens, and prayers of the faithful. But of the eucharist itself little is said. Augustine's reference to the opening dialogue of the eucharistic prayer and to the Lord's Prayer "after the sacrifice" (*Serm.* 227) leaves much unsaid. His incidental reference to the operation of the Spirit in the consecration of the bread (*De trin.* III.4) may suggest an invocation of the Spirit, when read together with clearer references in Optatus *De schismat. Donat.* VI.I) and Fulgentius of Ruspe (*Ad Monitum.* II.6,10). But the reconquest of Latin Africa from the Vandals by Justinian in the 6th century, and the imposition of the rites of Constantinople, followed in turn by the Islamic invasion of the area, has left little more to go on.

Gallican Rites

By contrast with Latin Africa, a disconcerting profusion of evidence survives from the Gallo-Hispanic (Gallican) family of Latin eucharistic rites, in a schematic report of the elements of a eucharistic prayer from Isidore of Seville (*De eccl. off.* I.15), in such later sacramentaries as *Missale Gothicum*, the *Bobbio Missal* and the *Stowe Missal*, and in a wealth of prayers later preserved as collects, secrets, and other supplements to the Roman books produced in the Frankish Empire.

Interest in this evidence, which is itself difficult to reduce to any simple order, has been sustained partly from fascination with the differences between these rites and the Roman rite which supplanted them. Here attention is paid to the variability of elements of the eucharistic prayers, and to various similarities with contemporary Eastern rites, such as the litanic prayers led by deacons, the kiss of peace after the prayers of the faithful, and the initial preparation and subsequent procession of the oblation. But the search for direct Eastern influence can be overdone. These rites, the work of new peoples recently converted from Arian to Catholic Christianity, were indigenous to an area in constant contact with liturgically cosmopolitan north Italy but with no sense of separation from the contemporary Roman church.

North Italy and Rome

With regard to north Italy, and to Rome, the evidence is extensive, scattered, and difficult. The 4th-century replacement of Greek with Latin as the liturgical language of the area did not, as sometimes seems to be assumed, curtail Eastern influence. In the Roman eucharistic rite, it is attested by use of Kyrial litanies, later reduced to the use of the *Kyries* at the beginning of the rite, and the use of the Eastern office hymn, *Gloria in excelsis*, following them, at the solemn episcopal

Sunday eucharist celebrated week by week in the stational basilicas of the city. At the same time, however, such Roman borrowings are marked by a certain independence and restraint, while the introduction of brief collects before the scripture readings, classically associated with the name of Pope Leo I (d. A.D. 461) is a uniquely Roman phenomenon. In the eucharist itself, the same independence and restraint is seen in the lack of a solemn preparation and procession of the oblation, and the relative absence of prayers before and after the communion. Peculiar features of the eucharist, amounting to something of a reform, were later attributed to Pope Gregory I (d. A.D. 604), but are attested to by the earlier *Gelasian sacramentary*, wrongly attributed to Pope Gelasius I (d. A.D. 496). These include the placing of the kiss of peace before the communion, and the incorporation of the prayers of the faithful within the eucharistic prayer or canon. While the latter is not without Eastern precedent (cf. *Serap.*; *Apost. Const.*), the limitation of such prayers to this place in the rite must be counted a Roman peculiarity.

The provenance of the central prayers of the Roman canon continues to be a matter of debate. These prayers are plainly different from the prayer of *Apost. Trad.* with its unified structure, its peculiar stress on the independence of the Word before the institution narrative, and its subsequent pattern of oblation, memorial and invocation of the Spirit. By contrast, these prayers are a connected order of distinct prayers, invariable except for the preface before the Sanctus, and contain what may be a vestigial invocation before the institution narrative, but which is certainly a series of oblations of the memorial both before and after it. Indeed, it has been noticed that this canon has as many similarities with the Egyptian *Serap.* as does *Apost. Trad.* with the Antiochene *Apost. Const.* It has

also been suggested that its distinctive style bespeaks a particular point of composition, perhaps connected with the introduction of Latin as the Roman liturgical language.

It is possible to become overly preoccupied with such largely conjectural matters. We have seen reasons for thinking that the *anaphora* of *Apost. Trad.* is very much Hippolytus' own, and may not need to seek further than Italy for parallels with the later Roman canon. For instance, Ambrose, in his *De sacramentis* gives an explanation of the eucharist to the newly baptized which contains similar turns of phrase which need not be thought simply to reflect Roman influence on the rite of Milan. In the end, we simply do not know what we would like to know about the Roman canon in view of its eventual use throughout the Western churches under Frankish auspices. The Roman rite, for all its special local features, is of absorbing interest because of its promotion and acceptance as a point of continuity with the Christian Roman past at a time when political and social upheavals necessitated it. Like the long-aisled basilicas of the Frankish period, their transepts and interior arrangements, frequently drawn from the Roman shrine basilicas of Peter and Paul, provided an identity for the Christian society of the West.

Conclusion

The history of the eucharist in this period reflects, to a remarkable degree, the persistence of very early forms and structures. The transformation of the church from a Jewish sect to a largely Gentile movement is marked by the continuation of the traditions of the meal blessings over bread and wine and the synogogue meetings which gave the movement its identity. Similarly, the eucharistic practices of the period of persecution continued to underlie the elaborate public rites which evolved in the changing circumstances in which Christianity ceased to be a *religio illicita* and became the official cultus of the newly Christian Roman Empire. At the point to which we have arrived, in both East and West, the eucharistic rite has become, in a new way, the identifying activity of the Christian society which has emerged from the breakdown of the ancient imperial unity, both in its pagan and Christian forms. It is at this point that consideration of the consequences of the formation of this society on eucharistic practice and thought must begin.

See Sources, early liturgical; Traditions, liturgical in the East; Traditions, liturgical in the West: pre-Reformation

L. Bouyer, *Eucharist* (Notre Dame and London: University of Notre Dame Press, 1968). G.J. Cumings, *Hippolytus: A Text for Students*, Grove Liturgical Study, No. 8 (Bramcote, Notts: Grove Books, 1976). G.J. Cumings, *Essays on Hippolytus*, Grove Liturgical Study, No. 15 (Bramcote, Notts: Grove Books, 1978). J. Fenwick, ed., *Fourth Century Anaphoral Construction Techniques*, Grove Liturgical Study, No. 45 (Bramcote, Notts: Grove Books, 1986). W.H. Frere, *Anaphora* (London: S.P.C.K., 1938). C. Jones, "The New Testament," Jones, Wainwright, and Yarnold, eds., *The Study of Liturgy* (New York: Oxford University Press, 1978). J. Jungmann, *Mass of the Roman Rite,* 2 vols., tr. F.A. Brunner (New York: Benziger, 1950). T.E. Matthews, *The Early Churches of Constantinople* (University Park and London: Pennsylvania State University Press, 1977). W. Rordorf et al., *The Eucharist of the Early Christians* (New York: Pueblo, 1978). T.J. Talley, *The Origins of the Liturgical year* (New York: Pueblo, 1986). B.D. Spinks, ed., *Addai and Mari—The Anaphora of the Apostles,* Grove Liturgical Study, no. 24 (Bramcote, Notts: Grove Books, 1980). F. Van der Meer, *Early Christian Art* (Chicago: University of Chicago Press, 1959).

LLOYD G. PATTERSON

EUCHARIST, HISTORY OF, IN THE EAST

In the post-Constantinian period, the eucharistic liturgy in the East underwent a process of standardization, the result of a complex dynamic of cultural, theological and political factors. With the consolidation of ecclesiastical power

under the major urban centers of Antioch, Alexandria, Jerusalem, and Constantinople came the consolidation and further assimilation of local liturgical uses to those of the urban centers. As the various local uses either survived or died out, the major liturgical traditions were formed. These traditions in their turn then influenced the liturgical practices of other areas.

As regards the eucharistic liturgy, the developments of this period consisted of the filling-in of what have been termed the "soft points" of the eucharistic *ordo*: the places where in the early liturgies there was only unaccompanied action, e.g., the entrance of the clergy into the church, the kiss of peace and the transfer of the eucharistic gifts, and the fraction, communion, and dismissal rites. These points of unaccompanied action in the pre-Constantinian eucharistic rites were in this period covered over with liturgical chant and prayer. These liturgical units of action covered with chant and prayer eventually disintegrated, leaving behind the liturgical flotsam and jetsam found in today's Eastern eucharistic liturgies. In this process of growth of liturgical units, those elements of greatest antiquity often were eliminated in favor of more recent elements: for example, while the act of communion in the Byzantine rite seems at one time to have been covered by an antiphonal psalm, today only the antiphon of that psalm remains (the *koinônikon*).

Unfortunately, much of the history of the eucharistic liturgies of each Eastern liturgical tradition remains unknown. Paucity of texts and, where texts are available, lack of reliable critical editions, make any satisfactory reconstruction of a general "history of the eucharist in the East" impossible. This article has more modest aims: 1. to outline the liturgical traditions of the East and some of the circumstances of their evolution; 2. to outline briefly some of the major factors in the development of the eucharist in the East; and 3. to give a thumbnail sketch of the major sources for and points in the history of the eucharistic liturgies of each Eastern liturgical tradition, as far as these factors are known.

I. The Liturgical Traditions

In 395 the Roman Empire was divided into Eastern and Western halves, the consolidation of a process begun in 293 with the partition of the empire into four prefectures. The Eastern half of the empire contained four cities which were to become the centers of the Eastern patriarchates: Antioch, center of the civil diocese of Orient; Alexandria, center of the civil diocese of Egypt; Constantinople and Jerusalem, raised to the level of patriarchal seat in 381 and 451, respectively. During the 4th and 5th centuries, the liturgical usages of the cities, towns and villages surrounding these ecclesiastical centers unified more and more around the usages of the patriarchates.

Some liturgical traditions, however, developed partially or entirely outside the jurisdiction of the Roman Empire. The Chaldean, or East Syrian eucharistic rite developed primarily within the Persian Empire, and the Armenian rite grew up against the backdrop of constant power struggles between the two "superpowers" of late antiquity, the Roman and Persian Empires.

The result of this process of liturgical unification is the group of four basic Eastern liturgical traditions known today: 1. Syrian (East Syrian, West Syrian, and Maronite); 2. Byzantine; 3. Armenian; and 4. Alexandrian (Coptic and Ethiopian).

The eucharistic liturgies of the East are today celebrated by both Orthodox and Catholic churches (with the sole exception of the Maronite rite, which is celebrated only by Eastern rite Catholics). These liturgies are celebrated in a wide variety of languages, both classical and modern: from Greek, Syriac, Coptic, Slavonic, and Armenian to Arabic, various modern European languages, Chinese, Japanese, Malayalam, various Siberian and North American Indian languages, and English. While originally these rites were restricted to specific geographical locales, they are now found worldwide, the result both of missionary activity and of the Eastern Christian diaspora.

II. Influences Upon Development of the Traditions

One could list many influences upon the development of the liturgical traditions of the East and, hence, their eucharistic liturgies. We list six here. 1. The great dogmatic controversies of the early church, particularly the councils of Chalcedon (451) and Ephesus (431), the acceptance or rejection of whose decisions eventually determined the ecclesiastical divisions and practices of the various Eastern churches. 2. Monasticism in its many forms existing in Late Antiquity; liturgical practices often travelled via monks, who were always on the go, travelling the length and breadth of the inhabited world. 3. Pilgrimage to the holy city of Jerusalem; pilgrims often brought back to their native lands hagiopolite practices. 4. Geography, which either facilitated or hindered the spread of missionary activity and lines of commerce and communication. 5. The Roman and Persian empires, either against or for which many different churches acted and reacted. In addition, the influence of the Byzantine Empire eventually caused the abandonment of native eucharistic rites in favor of the Byzantine rite. 6. Individuals, whose work often helped along the evolution or establishment of liturgical practices: e.g., a Basil the Great, Išo'yabh III, or Gregory the Illuminator, to name three.

III. The Eucharistic Liturgies

We shall now turn to the individual rites themselves, in the following order:

A. Syrian: 1. East Syrian, 2. West Syrian, 3. Maronite; B. Byzantine; C. Armenian; D. Alexandrian: 1. Coptic, 2. Ethiopian. The treatment of the Syrian and Alexandrian traditions is preceded by a brief introduction.

A. The Syrian Tradition

Introduction. On the basis of investigations into the East Syrian (or Chaldean), West Syrian, and Maronite eucharistic and baptismal liturgies, the Jesuit liturgist William Macomber has posited the existence of three, possibly four, liturgical traditions in Greater Syria and Persia at the beginning of the 5th century, centered upon Antioch, Jerusalem, and Edessa, with a possible fourth tradition existing in the Persian church. Reaction to the councils of Ephesus in 431 and Chalcedon in 451 set in motion the process of liturgical isolation and fusion which led to the eucharistic liturgies of the East Syrian, West Syrian, and Maronite rites, as we shall see below.

1. *East Syrian:* The Chaldean rite of today, used by members of the church of the East (often erroneously called "Nestorians") and by Eastern rite Catholics in India, Iraq and the United States, is one development of the ancient rite of Edessa, a city located on the eastern frontier between the Roman and Persian empires. Edessa was the center of Syriac-speaking Christian culture and had been evangelized by the end of the 2nd century at the latest. The form of Christianity which developed in Edessa was of a truly Semitic idiom, and the eucharistic liturgy which emerged from Edessa likewise bore the marks of its Judeo-Christian ancestry.

The Chaldean eucharistic rite was the first to be standardized, a process which began in the 5th century and ended in the 7th or 8th century. The Council of Ephesus in 431 condemned the teaching of Patriarch Nestorius of Constantinople, and began the process of the Persian church's ecclesiastical separation, formalized at the Synod of Beth Lapat in 484. Thus, the eucharistic liturgy of the church of the East developed without substantial influence from outside liturgical practices.

The Chaldean tradition is rich in liturgical commentaries. The model for all Chaldean commentators is the liturgical commentary of Theodore of Mopsuestia. Although he did not comment upon the Chaldean eucharistic service, per se, his method of interpreting each liturgical action in terms of the events of Christ's life was to be paradigmatic for later Chaldean liturgical commentary. Some important figures are: 1. Narsai, 2. Gabriel bar Liphah Qatraya (615-616), and an anonymous commentator of the mid-to late-9th century. Later commentaries on the eucharistic service do not add anything new to these earlier works.

The first reference to the rite occurs in the canons of the first general synod of the church in Persia, held at Seleucia-Ctesiphon in 410. There, the bishops call for a standardization of the eucharistic rite to the "Western rite" used by bishops Marutha (of Martyropolis in the Roman Empire) and Isaac (of Seleucia). It is a strong possibility that this "Western rite" is that of Edessa.

In the 6th century, Catholicos Mar Aba I (540-552) added the anaphoras of Theodore of Mopsuestia and Nestorius to the eucharistic liturgy, translating them from the Greek. Catholicos Išo'yabh III (650-659) was largely responsible for the final standardization of the Chaldean rite through his editions of the *Taksa* (the euchology for priests), the *Hudra* (the antiphonary for Sundays), and his commentary on the ceremonies of the office, eucharistic liturgy, and other liturgical rites. Išo'yabh may have eliminated the institution narrative from the anaphora of Addai and Mari, which he is said to have shortened. He may also have eliminated other eucharistic prayers from the *Taksa.*

Missionaries of the church of the East spread through Central Asia to India and China by the 7th century. When the Portuguese arrived in South India in the 16th century, they found the Christians there using the Chaldean rite. The remainder of the 16th and 17th centuries saw the unification of these Malabar Christians with the see of Rome, their splintering into a variety of churches, some using the liturgical forms provided by the Portuguese, others placing themselves under the jurisdiction of the Jacobite Patriarch of Antioch (and, hence, using the Liturgy of St. James, now known as the Malankara rite), and yet others returning to the Catholicos of the church of the East. Today, the majority of Malabar Christians are Eastern-rite Catholics, and their eucharistic liturgy has been "restored" following the Second Vatican Council. Chaldean-rite Catholics in Iraq and the United States have also had their rite revised, but more conservatively than the Malabar rite. Finally the Liturgy of Addai and Mari continues to be used by a very small remnant of the church of the East in Iraq, Iran, and the United States.

2. *West Syrian*. Reaction to the Council of Chalcedon cut across all three liturgical traditions of 5th-century Syria. For at least a century after the council, both Chalcedonians and non-Chalcedonians continued to celebrate the eucharist according to the rite of their region. Chalcedonians were found in the cities of southern Syria and maritime Syria, as well as Palestine. Eventually, these primarily Greek-speaking groups gave up the Liturgy of St. James for the Byzantine rite. These groups are termed "Melkites," from the Syriac *malkā* or Arabic *malek*, "king," for of course the Byzantine emperor adhered to the christological definition of Chalcedon, and attempted to require adherence to Chalcedon in all areas under Byzantine control or influence.

The non-Chalcedonians, or Monophysites, were found in the Aramaic-speaking population, from northern Syria to Mesopotamia. The liturgy celebrated by these non-Chalcedonian groups became what is today known as the "West Syrian" or Jacobite liturgy (from the name of the organizer of the Monophysite church, the Syrian monk Jacob Baradai, who died in 578). The West Syrian tradition has a very large number of anaphoras (scholars count anywhere from seventy to one hundred), not all of which are in use today. The eucharistic liturgy is not entirely of West Syrian origin; it is a mixture of Greek elements from the eucharistic rites of Jerusalem (its anaphoral structure) and Antioch (the basic framework of the liturgy), soon translated into Syriac, and Edessa (metrical hymns). The Jacobites continued to borrow from Maronite and Byzantine sources in subsequent centuries.

The principal commentators upon the Jacobite eucharistic rite are: 1. Jacob of Edessa (640-708), in his letter to Thomas the Presbyter; 2. Moses bar Kepha (813-903); 3. George of the Arabs (724); and 4. Dionysius bar Salibi (d. 1171).

3. *Maronite*. It was once thought that the Maronite eucharistic rite was simply a branch of the West Syrian rite, because it shares much in common with the Liturgy of St. James. However, it is now believed that Aramaic-speaking Chalcedonians in Syria, especially in Lebanon and the Orontes Valley, were able to preserve a form of the ancient eucharistic rite of Edessa, as the features of the Maronite eucharistic liturgy which are most characteristically Maronite are not held in common with St. James, but rather with the Chaldean eucharistic rite. This ancient Edessene rite, however, has been overlaid through the centuries with borrowings from the Jacobite and Latin eucharistic rites. For example, the Maronite rite today includes anaphoras ascribed to some of the champions of the

Monophysite cause, such as Philoxenus of Mabboug and Dionysius bar Salibi, to name two. Other Jacobite borrowings seem to be the *sedro*-form of prayer, and a preparatory part of the rite which seems to have been borrowed in the late 15th century or early 16th century, when a Maronite was elected Monophysite Patriarch of Antioch. Contact with the Crusaders produced union with the see of Rome in 1182, although firm union was not established until the 16th century. From the 12th century, Latinisms began to be introduced into the Maronite Mass, culminating in the Latinization under Patriarch Rizzi in the 17th century. Subsequent centuries have seen the restoration of the old form of the Maronite rite.

B. The Byzantine Tradition

The eucharistic liturgy of the Great Church of Constantinople is the most widespread Eastern rite in existence today. It is impossible to give any more than a cursory glance over the rich history of the eucharistic liturgies of this tradition: St. Basil, St. John Chrysostom and the Liturgy of the Presanctified. Thanks to the work of the Jesuit liturgists Juan Mateos and Robert Taft, the history of this rite is one of the most well known.

The first mention of a rite of Constantinople is during the period of Chrysostom's episcopate (397-404). It seems that the eucharistic liturgy at that time basically followed the liturgy of Antioch. It seems that the earliest liturgical influences upon the eucharistic rite of Constantinople were Antiochene and Cappadocian, since many of the city's early bishops came from those two areas.

The first commentary on the Byzantine eucharistic service is the *Mystagogia* of St. Maximus the Confessor, written ca. 628-630. The next two witnesses to the eucharistic liturgy are the *Historia ecclesiastica* of Patriarch St. Germanus of Constantinople (d. ca. 730), and the

Barberini Codex gr 336, which dates from ca. 800. What these three sources show is that during the 7th to the 9th centuries the Byzantine eucharistic liturgy underwent considerable growth and evolution, precisely at the so-called "soft points" of the rite: the preparation of the gifts was removed from a point just before the "great entrance" to completely before the entire liturgy, and a service of three antiphons, derived from the stational liturgy of the city, grew up immediately before the liturgy of the word. During that time, more ancient elements in the service were either eliminated or moved in favor of the newer elements: the OT reading vanished, as did the prayers over the penitents, and the psalmodic elements of the service.

The Byzantine eucharistic rite reached its definitive synthesis in the 10th century, as witnessed by the 10th-century *Typicon of the Great Church*. The service underwent subsequent monastic influence, most notably in the form of a beginning and end to the service, taken from the Palestinian monastic office in force in Constantinople from the fall of the city in 1204. By the 14th century, the eucharistic rite had received the form it has today.

C. The Armenian Tradition

Armenia was evangelized simultaneously from Caesarea in Cappadocia in the West, and Edessa in the South. While the East Syrian influence perdured primarily in the calendar, the Cappadocian eucharistic liturgy formed the basis for the nascent Armenian eucharistic liturgy.

At the beginning of the 5th century the anaphora of St. Basil the Great was translated into Armenian; this anaphora was later erroneously ascribed to Gregory the Illuminator, the apostle to Armenia, who had received his training in Cappadocia. Toward the end of the 5th century, four other Caesarean anaphoras were translated from Greek into Armenian: 1. Catholicos Sahak, 2.

Gregory of Nazianzus, 3. Cyril, and 4. Athanasius.

Further byzantinization of the Armenian eucharistic rite took place from the 7th century, in spite of Armenian attempts to prevent the encroachment of Byzantine influence. The reason for this continuing byzantinization can perhaps be attributed to the presence of strong groups within the Armenian hierarchy and monastic ranks whose theological views approximated those of the Byzantines.

Sometime after the 10th century, the Liturgy of St. Basil was translated again into Armenian. But with the 10th-century ascendancy of the Liturgy of St. John Chrysostom over the Liturgy of St. Basil in Constantinople, the Liturgy of St. John Chrysostom was adopted by the Armenians, as well as the Liturgy of the Presanctified. The time of the Crusades saw contact between Armenians and Latins, whom the Armenians welcomed. From the 12th to the 14th centuries some Latin features entered the Armenian service.

Both Chosroes the Great (ca. 950) and St. Nerses of Lambron (d. 1198) wrote commentaries on the Armenian eucharistic liturgy. The eucharistic service in use today is that of St. Athanasius.

D. The Alexandrian Tradition

Introduction. Two Egypts existed side by side in late antiquity: Lower Egypt, whose center was the great city of Alexandria, the center of Hellenic, philosophical Christianity; and Upper Egypt, the cradle of monasticism and the Coptic-speaking populace of the country-side, the center of a popular Christianity based upon wisdom sayings, asceticism and ritual. After the Council of Chalcedon (451), the city of Alexandria remained in Chalcedonian hands, while the center of non-Chalcedonian power shifted to the monasteries. One monastery in particular became a powerful center of Monophysite Coptic Christianity: the Monastery of St. Macarius in Wadi al-Natrun in Scetis near the Nile Delta in Lower Egypt. The patriarchal seat in Alexandria was occupied by both Chalcedonian and non-Chalcedonian patriarchs after Chalcedon.

1. *Coptic.* The Greek Liturgy of St. Mark appears to have been used by Melkites in Egypt until the 12th century when, under Byzantine influence, they adopted the Byzantine eucharistic service (as did Melkites in Syria and Palestine).

However, among Monophysites the Liturgy of St. Mark was translated into Coptic and underwent further influence from Coptic monastic practice and Syrian liturgical practice, which came via the Syrian Jacobite monks who made their homes in Egypt, as well as the general ecclesiastical intercourse between Syrian and Egyptian Jacobites.

The first Coptic dialect used by the Egyptian Christians was Sahidic, which attained its classical form at the White Monastery in Upper Egypt, during the reign of Abbot Shenoute (ca. 383-451). However, as the Monastery of St. Macarius gained more prominence as a fortress of non-Chalcedonian Christianity following Chalcedon, the Bohairic Coptic dialect used there began slowly to supplant the earlier Sahidic texts. Eventually, Bohairic became the only Coptic dialect used in worship.

Today's eucharistic rite is essentially that of Scetis. In the 12th century, Patriarch Gabriel II Ibn Turayk (1131-1145) decreed that all local versions of the eucharistic prayer be suppressed, and that only three anaphoras be used throughout the entire Coptic church: St. Mark (also known as St. Cyril), St. Basil, and St. Gregory. In the 15th century, Patriarch Gabriel V composed his *Liturgical Order* (1411), still in use today. This work, along with *The Lamp of Darkness* of Abu al-Barakat (14th century), are two of the most important commentaries on the Coptic eucharistic liturgy.

2. *Ethiopian*. The historic date of the Christianization of Ethiopia is 340. It appears that Coptic and Syrian missionaries penetrated into the country, and that by the 5th century monasticism had been established in Ethiopia. At the time of Chalcedon, the Ethiopians sided with the Monophysites. About the same time, the famous Nine Saints are said to have arrived in Ethiopia, beginning the work of translating Coptic, Greek, and Syriac literature into Ge'ez, the classical form of the Ethiopian tongue. The head of the Ethiopian church, the *abuna*, was a Coptic monk chosen and sent from Egypt. In 1948, this relationship with the Coptic church was changed when the Ethiopian church was allowed a native *abuna*, consecrated in 1959.

The history of the Ethiopian eucharistic service is almost completely unknown, as it is perhaps the least-studied eucharistic liturgy of any in the East. Scholars have identified at least twenty different Ethiopian anaphoras of Syrian, Alexandrian and Ethiopian origin, one of the most intriguing being the Anaphora of Our Lady.

Given the strong ties between the Coptic church and the Ethiopian church, one can posit a strong Coptic influence upon the structure and content of the Ethiopian eucharistic service. Observers have also noted in the practices of this church the presence of elements seeming to originate in Judaism. However, given the great gaps in our knowledge of Ethiopian history (especially from 650 to 1270), reconstruction of the history of any of the Ethiopian eucharistic liturgy will be difficult at best. Clearly, the Ethiopian eucharistic liturgy presents a fascinating field of study for future scholars of liturgy.

See **Traditions, liturgical in the East; Reform, liturgical, in Eastern churches; Sacraments in the Eastern churches**

F.E. Brightman, *Liturgies Eastern and Western*, Vol. I: Eastern Liturgies (Oxford: Clarendon Press, 1896. Repr. 1965). I.H. Dalmais, *Eastern Liturgies*, trans. Donald Attwater (New York: Hawthorn Books, 1960). R.F. Taft, *Beyond East and West. Problems in Liturgical Understanding* (Washington, D.C.: The Pastoral Press, 1984).

GRANT SPERRY-WHITE

EUCHARIST, HISTORY OF, IN THE WEST

While the origins of a specifically "Western" or Latin liturgical tradition are difficult to trace, it seems clear that at least from the 3rd century those trends which are later clearly identified with Western practice are beginning to be found. Both Tertullian (c. 160—c.220) and Cyprian of Carthage (d.258) seem to be speaking of a Latin liturgy when writing about the eucharist. But these early rites and practices display a great deal of diversity, even though the *Apostolic Tradition* of Hippolytus (c. 215), for example, argues for the primacy of Roman eucharistic traditions. For a long time it was supposed that all Western rites had a common source in Rome, and spread from there to outlying areas in a systematic way as pagan peoples were converted to Christianity. More recently, however, scholars have come to see that the lines of liturgical influence are more complex, and it is now clear that important ritual developments took place in other Christian centers and were subsequently returned to Rome to influence eucharistic practice there. In any case, neat distinctions between "West" and "East," "Roman and non-Roman," are difficult to make in this early period of liturgical development.

Eucharistic Documents

We can be slightly more certain about Western eucharistic practice in the 6th to 7th centuries, since some documentary sources for this period exist (see, liturgical sources). Early evidence for the beginnings of Western eucharistic practice is found in liturgical books containing the various prayers used by presiders. Several of these collections, known as "sacramentaries," survive, and generally their contents follow the course of the church year, providing texts for each celebration in the calendar. Although the earliest such manuscript (the so-called "Leonine Sacramentary") dates from the 7th century, at least some of its liturgical material may be of a much earlier date. Analysis of these collections reveals the existence of a number of different euchological traditions, with Roman, Milanese, Spanish, Celtic, and Gallican books each expressing their own eucharistic personality.

Still later, but sometime before the 8th century, a group of liturgical documents called *Ordines* begins to appear, providing us with fuller information about how the eucharist was actually celebrated in Rome in the Early Middle Ages. The *Ordines* provide the practical, ceremonial details for all participants in the liturgy. When added to the prayers of the sacramentaries, the directions in the *Ordines* give us a picture of both eucharistic words and actions for various occasions. Often these books also contain important historical and political addenda.

Eucharistic Theology and Practice in the Early Middle Ages

Throughout this early period, despite the vigor of local varieties in celebration, there was a growing tendency toward standardization of the liturgy as authority came to be centered at Rome. At the same time, eucharistic theology emphasized the sacrificial aspects of the Mass, the localized presence of Christ in the bread and wine, and allegorical interpretations of the action at the altar. Because of these trends, a sense of awe and reverence surrounding the eucharist grew to dominate popular piety. The idea that ordinary communicants were unworthy to handle the body and blood of Christ in the form of bread and wine was fueled by an emphasis on penitence, resulting in the gradual decline of frequent communion of the laity. Gazing upon the eucharist at the moment of consecration was seen to be sufficient to produce a salvific effect. At the same time, the belief was strong that the eucharist was a representation of the propitiatory sacrifice of Christ, and this in turn led to the expectation that it might be practically employed to bring about desired objectives.

The theological poles of medieval eucharistic debate can be clearly seen in the controversy between the 9th-century monks. In the first systematic treatise devoted solely to the eucharist, Pascasius Radbertus (c. 785-c. 860) describes the ways in which Christ is present in the elements of bread and wine in extremely realistic and physical terms. Ratramnus of Corbie (d.c. 868) was provoked to respond, and attacked the carnal view of the real presence in favor of a more symbolic and spiritualized interpretation. In the end, Ratramnus' view was condemned as failing adequately to safeguard the doctrine of the real presence. The next three centuries saw an increasing identification of the bread and wine with the physical body and blood of Christ, and abuses of eucharistic practice were not uncommon.

By the 11th century, the structure of the eucharistic rite had reached a certain stability in the West, and Roman control had asserted itself over provincial control of ecclesiastical matters. Because of this, the eucharist as it was celebrated in Rome (and particularly as it was celebrated by the bishop of Rome), came to be normative for the rest of the Christian West. But while in Rome large numbers of liturgical personnel were available, in outlying areas a single priest might be called upon to conduct the eucharistic rites alone and the variety of books for each participant caused certain difficulties. The dissemination of Roman

Missals, which brought together the prayers, ceremonial directions, the sung parts of the Mass, and readings collected from a variety of liturgical books, not only made the celebration by a single person easier, but also further encouraged the uniformity of eucharistic rites and ceremonies according to Roman patterns.

Eucharistic Theology in the Late Middle Ages

Popular distortions of eucharistic theology, and particularly the grossly carnal interpretation of the elements of bread and wine, caused the 13th-century Scholastics to give it special consideration. In 1215, the Fourth Lateran Council used the term "transubstantiation" to describe the change of bread and wine into the body and blood of Christ, but it was not until Thomas Aquinas (1225-1274) applied Aristotelian philosophical categories to the eucharist that any systematic treatment of this change took place. Aquinas proposed that while what is perceptible (the "accidents" of bread and wine) remains unchanged, the essential reality (the "substance") is transformed into the body and blood of Jesus Christ. But even though transubstantiation was originally put forward to combat an overly realistic view of eucharistic presence, its philosophical nuances were difficult to translate into common terms, and in the centuries which followed it came to be itself increasingly associated with the carnal presence of Christ in the elements of bread and wine.

By the time of the 16th-century Reformation, several trends in eucharistic theology and practice had crystallized. Because of the fear of defiling the body and blood of Christ, laypersons received communion infrequently, and since the 13th century the chalice had been withheld from them. But eucharistic piety was high, and such popular devotions as benediction and exposition of the Blessed Sacrament, perpetual adoration, and the Feast of Corpus Christi can trace their roots to the Late Middle Ages. Because the Mass was thought to make present the propitiatory sacrifice of Christ, the number of Masses multiplied to ensure an abundance of saving grace. Many religious houses, as well as parish clergy, made their living from the "Mass stipends" paid by groups and individuals who wished the eucharist offered to bring about desired consequences, and especially the early release of souls from purgatory. Although Roman eucharistic practice tended to dominate, some local variety in rites, texts and lectionaries remained.

The Eucharist and the 16th-century Reformers

This combination of eucharistic piety and abuse set the stage for the radical re-evaluation of the eucharist by those in the 16th century who sought a reformation of the church. The Reformers' concern with the centrality of the word of God and their insistence on justification through faith alone and the priesthood of all the baptized put the eucharist at the center of Reformation debate. In *An Open Letter to the Christian Nobility of the German Nation* (1520), Martin Luther (1483-1546) argued that "the status of a priest among Christians is merely that of an office-holder." This redefinition of priesthood undercut the current theology of the sacraments, and particularly the sacrifice of the Mass, and laid the foundations for the eucharistic theology and practice of all of the Reformation churches.

In the *Babylonian Captivity of the Church* (1520), Luther continued his attack on current eucharistic piety and practice by criticizing transubstantiation and the denial of the cup to the laity. The presence of Christ in the eucharist, according to Luther, was like the presence of fire in a heated bar of iron, in which "every part is both iron and fire": in the same way, Christ's body and blood are wholly present in the eucharistic bread and wine. With regard to communion under both kinds, Luther argued that since Christ gave both bread and cup to his original disciples at the Last Supper, his present-day disciples deserve nothing less. Luther's *Formula Missae* (1523) and *Deutsche Messe* (1525-6), although both quite conservative rites, shaped the eucharist according to his reformed principles.

But others of the period desired a more thoroughgoing reformation of the church, and thus of the Lord's Supper. Swiss Reformers Ulrich Zwingli (1484-1531), Martin Bucer (1401-1551) and John Oecolampadius (1482-1531) found that Luther's retention of the carnal presence of Christ in the elements of bread and wine left too much opportunity for theological and practical abuse, and moved in the direction of a more symbolic and memorialistic view of the eucharist. At the Marburg Colloquy (1529), Luther, arguing the conservative side, and the more radical Swiss Reformers were unable to come to agreement on the matter of eucharistic presence, marking the fracture of the reformation into distinct theological camps. John Calvin (1509-1564), the reformer of the church at Geneva, attempted to moderate the Swiss and Lutheran views of eucharistic presence, arguing that Christ is truly, albeit spiritually, received by those who faithfully partake of the bread and wine.

The various Reformers could agree, however, on a number of practical matters regarding the Lord's Supper, and especially on the necessity of communion under both kinds, the reading and preaching of scripture at each celebration of the Lord's Supper, and that no eucharist be held without communicants present. Reformation eucharistic rites simplified greatly their medieval predecessors, and increased participation of the laity was facilitated by a vernacular liturgy and the addition of responses. Although the intention was to return to the practices of the primitive church, certain elements of pre-Reformation piety remained, such as the heavily penitential emphasis. The Reformers had hoped that a weekly service of the Lord's Supper might be instituted. But since most people were used to receiving communion infrequently (once a year was common), the celebration of the eucharist quarterly was all that generally could be achieved.

The Catholic Reformation and the Eucharist

At the same time, the Catholic Reformation (often called the Counter-Reformation) left its own mark on eucharistic practice and piety. An ecumenical council convened at Trent (1545-1563) sought to curb abuses and to settle matters which the success of Protestantism in Europe had thrown into question, and several of the council's sessions dealt directly with the eucharist. At the second meeting of the council (1551) the theology of the eucharist was more precisely defined, and both Lutheran and Zwinglian positions were specifically rejected. Later sessions reaffirmed the sacrificial character of the Mass. The issue of communion under both kinds was addressed at the third meeting of the council (1562), and it was determined that the cup was properly denied to the laity, with the understanding that the whole Christ was present in both bread and wine.

One important result of the council deliberations was the establishment of the Congregation of Sacred Rites. Aiming at the standardization of public worship according to the council's decrees, and with a uniform liturgy for all of Roman Catholicism as the ultimate goal, the congregation immediately undertook the reform of liturgical books, including the missal. In the end, the rites of the Tridentine Missal (1570) embodied what was current eucharistic practice in the city of Rome, and essentially ignored the diverse, local liturgical heritage of the church. Although some of these local rites (and especially those in France) continued to be used after Trent, the rites of the Tridentine Missal formed the official eucharistic liturgy of the Roman Catholic church until the Second Vatican Council undertook revision nearly four centuries later.

The Second Generation of Reformers

At the same time, a second generation of Reformers had established Protestant eucharistic practice in the British Isles and Scandinavia. Drawing from a variety of theological sources, Thomas Cranmer (1489-1556) embodied a reformed theology of the Lord's Supper in two successive editions of the *Book of Common Prayer* (1549 and 1552) for the Church of England. Symbolic of the thoroughness of English reform was the insertion at the end of the 1552 communion service of the famous "Black Rubric," which declared that kneeling at communion should not be interpreted as adoration of the eucharistic elements. Cranmer's counterpart in Scotland, John Knox (c.1505-1572), framed his own eucharistic rites according to strictly Calvinist principles, and these in turn had a significant impact on the communion service in English-speaking Presbyterianism.

During the 17th century, those desiring a more complete reformation of the church believed that the eucharist was still the occasion for much misunderstanding and abuse, and sought to remove those things which might lead to superstition. Any suggestion that the communion table was an altar, kneeling or adoration of the bread and wine, and the use of vestments, the sign of the cross, and the term "priest" were all points upon which these Puritans stood fast. The Society of Friends (Quakers) can be seen as the most extreme example of this puritanizing effort and, in their effort to make the sacraments wholly spiritual experiences, abolished the elements of bread and wine altogether. The Puritan view of the Lord's Supper was carried to the New World with the early settlers and came to shape much of American sacramental piety.

Enlightenment Influence on Eucharistic Piety and Practice

The Enlightenment of the 18th century made a profound impact on the eucharistic practice and piety of Protestants, but was also felt among Roman Catholics as well. The Enlightenment exaltation of reason led to the re-evaluation of eucharistic practice among Roman Catholics, and at the Synod of Pistoia (1786) several decrees were aimed at curbing abuses of the Mass. The synod encouraged local practices, forbade the placement of more than one altar in each church and the multiplication of Masses, and condemned the use of Latin. Although these decrees aroused both popular and official opposition, they stand as testimony to the impact of the Enlightenment on Roman Catholic eucharistic theology.

The suspicion of the supernatural, for which the Enlightenment is particularly noted, affected Protestant eucharistic theology as well. Preaching and informed study of scripture, as activities of the enlightened mind, came to dominate Protestant services of worship, and the sacraments were given a subordinate role. The Lord's Supper was viewed as a way of calling to mind the virtues of Christ, and was considered a duty for those who took seriously the Lord's command, "Do this for the remembrance of me." This practical and theological marginalization of the eucharist continues to this day in much of American Protestantism.

The Eucharist in the 19th Century

Nineteenth-century reaction to Enlightenment rationalism took two forms, and both of these had significant impact on eucharistic piety and practice. The first of these is generally termed "Romanticism," and sought to restore the more cohesive religious experience of an earlier day. Many figures in the Protestant Romantic Movement looked to the medieval period as the Golden Age of Christianity, and hoped to restore medieval eucharistic piety, even among those such as Lutherans and Anglicans who had so decisively rejected it in the 16th century. Frequency of communion increased dramatically among those groups touched by Romanticism, but concomitant with this was a tendency toward the privatization of religious experience and excessive sentimentality in eucharistic devotion. Roman Catholic romanticists sought a revival of the monasteries, whose numbers had seriously declined since the 18th century. But despite its emphasis on nostalgia, the search for the historic roots of Christian worship set the stage for modern liturgical scholarship, which would come to maturity as the Liturgical Movement of the 20th century.

The second major influence on Protestant eucharistic theology and practice in the 19th century was American revivalism. All across the frontier, camp-meetings were organized as a practical response to the religious needs of a largely unchurched, rural population, and established a pattern of worship which has persisted in many segments of American Protestantism. After several days of fervent prayer, preaching for conversion, and sentimental hymns, converts were baptized and the eucharist was celebrated. Although for most groups affected by revivalism the tendency toward infrequent communion prevailed, at least one revivalist group, the Christian church (Disciples of Christ), believed that scripture commanded a weekly celebration of the Lord's Supper presided over by a lay person. This practice continues to this day among Disciples.

At the same time, the Temperance Movement was also taking hold of the American religious imagination, and the imbibing of any form of fermented drink was seen as dangerously immoral. Increasing concern over eucharistic wine ensued, and by 1870 the scientific principles of Louis Pasteur had been applied to the pasturization of grape juice, which was then introduced as the normal eucharistic element among many American Protestants. On the other hand, the Church of Jesus Christ of Latter-Day Saints (Mormons) found that the growing of grapes was impractical in Utah where they had settled, and instituted the use of water in place of eucharistic wine.

In the 20th century, a renewal of attention to the eucharist has taken place among many western Christians. In Roman Catholicism, historical studies uncovered the earlier variety in eucharistic practice and documented the accumulation of devotional adjuncts. The stripping away of extraneous liturgical material in the eucharistic rites, the simplification of rubrics, the recovery of ancient signs and symbols, the attempts at indigenization of eucharistic practice, and what the Second Vatican Council referred to as "full, conscious, active participation" of the faithful were all aimed at restoring the eucharist to the center of the Christian life. At the same time, eucharistic theology underwent a similar renewal, with such classic works as Edward Schillebeeckx' *Christ the Sacrament of the Encounter with God* (1960) providing a systematic reflection on the Christocentric nature of sacramental grace. It is this more relational understanding of the eucharist which underlines the Second Vatican Council's *Constitution on the Sacred Liturgy* (December 4, 1963), as well as the new eucharistic prayers which began to appear in 1967.

In some of the Protestant churches

too, the eucharist has been the subject of renewed interest in the late-20th century. Beginning in the 1960s, the Roman Catholic liturgical agenda began to affect the revisions of Protestant services of the Lord's Supper, and historical studies and ecumenical contacts have made for some interdenominational convergence in eucharistic theology and practice. Most American Lutherans and Episcopalians have sought to reintroduce the eucharist as the main Sunday service, and some Methodists and Presbyterians also view this as a desirable goal. But many American Protestants, especially those with strong ties to revivalist worship patterns and Enlightenment sacramental theology, have remained relatively untouched by these trends, and non-eucharistic worship remains the norm. Most of the ecclesiastical descendants of the Reformers, however, have begun to search for their eucharistic roots in the early church and in the Continental and English Reformations, and have found a balance between ecumenical convergence and authentic Protestant diversity.

See **Liturgical movement; Liturgical sources**

Yngve Brilioth, *Eucharistic Faith and Practice* (London: S.P.C.K., 1953). Johannes H. Emminghaus, *The Eucharist* (Collegeville: Liturgical Press, 1978). Theodor Klauser, *A Short History of the Western Liturgy* (London: Oxford Univ. Press, 1969). Cyril Vogel, *Medieval Liturgy: An Introduction to the Sources*, rev. and trans. by N.K. Rasmussen and W.G. Storey (Washington, D.C.,: The Pastoral Press, 1981). James F. White, *Protestant Worship* (Louisville: Westminster/John Knox Press, 1989).

SUSAN J. WHITE

EUCHARIST, MINISTERS OF

The term "ministers of the eucharist" can have many meanings. In the categories of classical sacramental theology, where one prime concern was the proper or ordinary minister of the sacraments, the term refers to bishop and presbyter who alone, by virtue of ordination, are authorized and empowered to offer the eucharistic sacrifice and to consecrate the bread and wine into the body and blood of Christ. In the categories preferred by Vatican II, where the eucharist is clearly named a liturgical act in which there are many ministers and many ministries, the term expands to include readers, acolytes, musicians, ministers of hospitality, deacons, concelebrating bishops or presbyters, and in a real sense the liturgical assembly itself; in other words, all those who are liturgically active when the liturgy of the eucharist is enacted by a local church assembly. In this wider sense, the guiding norm is that "each one, minister or layperson, who has an office to perform, should do all of, but only, those parts which pertain to that office by the nature of the rite and the principles of the liturgy" (S.C., 28; G.I.R.M., 58). A second guiding norm is that the liturgy in its ordered ministries and varied actions display and enact the mystery of Christ and the true nature of the church (S.C., 2; G.I.R.M., 74). A third meaning of the term "ministers of the eucharist" points to the ministry of those who distribute the eucharistic bread and wine either during the eucharist itself or outside of the eucharistic celebration to those who have been unable to attend. This would include ministers to the sick, those who take viaticum to the dying and those who preside at services of communion in the absence of a bishop or presbyter. It may also include those who lead various eucharistic devotions, even where distribution of the eucharistic food is not part of such devotional acts (e.g., benediction). This article will offer some brief reflections on each use of the term.

Bishop and Presbyter

While it remains uncertain whether or not there was any strict regulation of eucharistic presidency in the earliest domestic churches, e.g., as in Acts 2:42, it is clear that by the time of Ignatius of

Antioch (c. 110) the role of the bishop was considered central: "Let that be considered a valid Eucharist which is celebrated by the bishop, or by one whom he appoints" (*Ad Smyrn.*, 8,2). By the 4th century, appointment of presbyters to the task had become normal practice. Since that time the priestly office, according to which one is authorized and empowered to offer the eucharistic sacrifice, has been seen to reside, by virtue of ordination, in both bishop and presbyter. As the ecclesial nature of both eucharist and ordination began to fade, the presidency of the eucharist lost its relationship to the eucharistic assembly; priest and bishop offered Mass "on behalf of" rather than "with" the assembly gathered.

Vatican II restored the ecclesial nature of the eucharist and thereby the sacramental role of the bishop/presbyter in relation to the eucharistic assembly. The eucharist, as indeed every liturgical celebration, is "an action of Christ the Priest and of his Body which is the Church" (S.C., 7). According to the ecclesial model endorsed by the council whereby the church is the people of God hierarchically gathered (L.G., 18), the distinctive iconic role of the bishop, and of the presbyters who are his helpers, is to represent the *hiereus*, i.e., Christ the priest, as the one who gathers the people of God into the unity of Christ's own body. This iconic role is the ministry of the eucharistic presider. It properly belongs in liturgical act to the one who fulfills it in ecclesial life.

Vatican II thus restored the bishop as the primary one to fulfill the ministry of eucharistic presidency: "In the local Church, first place should be given, because of its meaning, to the Mass at which the bishop presides surrounded by the college of presbyters and the ministers and in which the people take full and active part. For this Mass is the preeminent expression of the Church" (G.I.R.M., 74). The presbyter "is another who possesses the power of orders to offer sacrifice in the person of Christ" (G.I.R.M., 60), but does so as the bishop's "helper" and "coworker" (see, rite of ordination for presbyters, instruction); presbyters are joined with the episcopal order, and share in the function of the apostles in their own degree (P.O., 2).

As minister of the eucharist, bishop and presbyter fill the presidential role, and thereby serve as *sacramentum* or icon of Christ (*in persona Christi*). The ministry is threefold: to gather the assembly into Christ's own prayer to Abba; to enact for the assembly by way of invocation and consecration Christ's own promise ("I will pray to the Father, and he will give you another Counselor, to be with you forever" [Jn 14:16]); and to speak to the assembly Christ's own gathering words ("No longer do I call you servants...; but I have called you friends" [Jn 15:15]).

Ministers of Eucharist to the Assembly

The primary enactor of the eucharist is the full assembly itself. Eucharistic presidency is a specific ministry within the eucharistic assembly; it is not, however, the only ministry that is required. The other ministries can be divided into two categories: those that contribute to the quality of the celebration and those that contribute to the *sacramentality* of the celebration. The former, which include liturgical planners, music ministers, ministers of hospitality and, possibly, liturgical dancers find their warrant and commission when the *Constitution on the Sacred Liturgy* speaks of the relation between good celebration and sacramental effectiveness: "they (the sacraments) do indeed impart grace, but, in addition, the very act of celebrating them disposes the faithful most effectively to receive this grace in a fruitful manner" (S.C., 59). The latter, which include the readers, the deacon, those who present the gifts, those who distribute the gifts, and indeed the gathered assembly itself, find their warrant and commission in the four-fold presence of Christ in the eucharist: word, presiding minister, eucharistic food, assembly (S.C., 7). It is in the word proclaimed that Christ speaks. It is the assembly gathered that makes Christ present. It is in the person of those who present the gifts that the church presents itself; in the person who receives the gifts that Christ receives and welcomes the church; in the person who prays over the gifts that Christ consecrates both gifts and church; and, in the person who distributes the gifts that Christ personally presents himself.

Word and food are objects, impersonal, and in themselves incapable of communicating the personal presence of Christ. Those persons who proclaim the word and who handle the gifts serve as *sacramentum* or icon of the personal Christ whom word and food make present. In both the proclamation of the word and the handling of the food they add the human affections that are essential for both to become a personal symbol to present a personal Christ to the church.

Ministers of the Eucharistic Food

Ministers of the eucharist who distribute the eucharistic food include the presider, deacon, any priest concelebrants who may be present, those installed in the ministry of acolyte, those appointed as "auxiliary" ministers of the eucharist, and those assigned as *ad hoc* "extraordinary" ministers of the eucharist. In most cases the one who prays the eucharistic prayer should rightly return to the assembly the gifts he received from them. The deacon, who is traditionally the minister of the cup, and who usually assists the presider in receiving the gifts from the people and prepares the gifts for the presiding priest, likewise should assist in distributing the eucharistic food to the assembly. Beyond that, it is assumed that

auxiliary and extraordinary ministers will be drawn from the assembly only when there are not enough priests or deacons to distribute the food. The only thing that would seem to be precluded is employment of ministers who are not part of the eucharistic assembly, but who "show up," as it were, only at the time of communion. This is nowhere explicitly stated, but it would seem to follow from the integrity of the eucharistic action, from the fact that the language concerning the distribution of ministries assumes that those ministers are active participants in the liturgical act, and requires, moreover, that they carry out *all* and *only* what belongs to their office [i.e., priests should concelebrate, deacons should distribute among themselves the diaconal ministries, etc.] (S.C., 28), and by analogy from the principle which urges that "the faithful receive the Lord's body from hosts consecrated at the same Mass" (G.I.R.M., 56).

Whoever actually carries out this ministry of distribution, the ministry itself must be seen as more than a functional ministry. What the minister offers to Christ in that very act by which Christ gives of himself to his sisters and brothers, is *persona*, human embodiment, a personal presence. The ritual instruction at the installation of acolytes captures the fullness of this ministry and the proper faith and human affection that should attend it. "In performing your ministry, bear in mind that, as you share the one bread with your brothers and sisters, so you form one body with them. Show a sincere love for Christ's Mystical Body, God's holy people, and especially for the weak and the sick. Be obedient to the commandment which the Lord gave to his apostles at the Last Supper: 'Love one another as I also have loved you.'"

Ministers of Eucharist Beyond the Assembly

From its earliest days the church has

been concerned to extend the eucharist beyond the assembly, to those who are sick, those who are dying, and those who might gather in partial assembly (e.g., to partake of communion) and thus continue in another time and place the church's eucharistic action. Such extension is *communio* in the full sense of the word: union with Christ and union with the *ecclesia* of Christ. It is an extension of presence, of prayer and of care. In addition, there has grown up in the church's liturgical life an appreciation of the eucharistic food as the enduring presence of Christ to the church, an appreciation which has engendered reverence, devotion, adoration. Ministers of eucharist beyond the eucharistic assembly are those who take communion to the sick and the dying, those who conduct and preside at communion services, and those who lead acts of reverence, devotion and adoration to the Christ who is permanently present in the eucharistic food. All such extensions beyond the assembly have their root in the eucharistic assembly itself, and all such extensions are directed toward the eucharistic assembly as well.

Ministers of the eucharist beyond the assembly need to be commissioned publicly within the assembly itself. This is particularly important for those who take the eucharist to the sick and the dying, so that those who are ministered to may know that they are supported by an "enfleshed" Christ, i.e., a whole community of the church at prayer. Those who conduct services of communion should do so in such a way that the connection between this communion service and the church's full eucharistic assembly is made clear. Communion services do not stand on their own; they are extensions of, not substitutes for, the eucharistic act of the church. Finally, those who conduct forms of eucharistic worship outside of Mass must also know the relation between these acts of worship and the eucharistic act of the church. These too do not substitute for the Mass. Their purpose is to deepen eucharistic faith, faith in Christ's presence and faith in Christ's sacrifice, in order to lead those who participate in them to a fuller and more active participation in the church's eucharist itself.

See **Eucharistic worship outside Mass; Presiding, ministry of; Lay ministries, liturgical; Communion service; Presidential style; Sick, communion to the; Viaticum**

Robert Hovda, *Strong, Loving and Wise: Presiding in Liturgy* (Washington: The Liturgical Conference, 1976). David Power, *Gifts that Differ* (New York: Pueblo, 1980). N.C.C.B. *Eucharistic Worship and Devotion Outside Mass*, Study Text 11 (Washington: U.S.C.C., 1987).

PETER E. FINK, S.J.

EUCHARIST, REFORMATION CONTROVERSIES ON

Among Protestants, from the beginning of the Reformation to the close of the Council of Trent, eucharistic doctrine was a matter of vigorous controversy and rich development.

The fundamental document for the Protestant position is Luther's *Babylonian Captivity of the Church* (1520). The work as a whole calls for a new approach to Christian worship. While treating all seven sacraments of the medieval system, it is the eucharist which is Luther's chief concern. As Luther sees it, the eucharist should not be understood as a sacrifice offered to God, but rather as God's gracious gift of communion. It is *beneficium* rather than *sacrificium*. Luther was concerned that the theology of his day had lost sight of the Augustinian concept of grace. Late medieval Nominalism, as exemplified in the Mass commentary of Gabriel Biel, had moved quite far in the direction of Pelagianism, as Luther saw it, and it was to this that the central Protestant objection was aimed. In Luther's *A Treatise on the New Testament that is the Mass* (1520) he proposed that the Lord's Supper should be understood in biblical forms of covenant rather than in Scholastic terms of form and matter, substance and accidents. If the first objection was to the Pelagianism of the eucharistic theology of his day, the second objection was to its formulation in terms of Scholasticism.

In 1522 Andreas Carlstadt, reacting to Luther's call for a new approach to worship, put forward a spiritualist interpretation of the Lord's Supper developed from themes typical of late medieval Nominalism. Luther was not favorably impressed. Recognizing the incongruity of a spiritualist interpretation with the doctrine of the incarnation, Luther began to realize the importance of developing his own eucharistic doctrine more fully. While Luther was working to this end, there were others who tried their hand at the project.

By 1517 Christian Humanism had already challenged the Scholastic theological monopoly with some success. While Luther was primarily the product of Scholasticism, there were in South Germany a number of other theologians profoundly influenced by Christian Humanism and the new philological studies promoted by the Renaissance. Among these were Ulrich Zwingli, Martin Bucer, Wolfgang Capito, and John Oecolampadius. Having nothing to do with philosophical humanism, Christian Humanism advocated that theology return to the biblical and patristic sources of Christian thought. This concern for biblical philology made these Reformers more sensitive to the original meaning of scripture. While they were in complete agreement with Luther's objections to the doctrine of the eucharistic sacrifice, they had some objections of their own. Originally their objections to the Scholastic eucharistic doctrines were philological rather than philosophical. As Zwingli understood it, when the text of 1 Cor 10-11 is studied in the light of biblical grammar and rhetoric, one is led to interpret the words "This is my body" and "This is my blood" tropologically, and therefore the biblical text simply does not support the doctrine of the real presence as it had been developed during the Middle Ages. Oecolampadius had much the same objection. Being one of the leading patristic scholars of his generation, Oecolampadius looked into the origins of such terms as *mysterion* and *sacramentum* in both scripture and the usage of the ancient church, suggesting that a proper understanding of them would lead to a better sacramental theology. Both Johannes Bugenhagen, Luther's associate in Wittenberg, and Andreas Osiander, the Reformer of Nuremberg, wrote works objecting strongly to Zwingli's approach. Then Johann Brenz, a particularly capable supporter of Luther in South Germany, wrote his *Syngramma Suevicum* to refute Oecolampadius. Obviously the Sacramentarians, as Zwingli and Oecolampadius were popularly called, had not provided the new eucharistic doctrine Luther had envisioned, but they had gained some important insights.

Luther was horrified at Zwingli's attack on the doctrine of the real presence. Over the next few years Luther's position developed considerably. For him the basic concern was the meaning of the words of institution. Luther was just as concerned with the meaning of scripture as Zwingli, but for Luther it seemed quite impossible to take the eucharistic words tropologically. As he saw it, the words of institution are a summary of the gospel assuring the forgiveness of sin to those who believe. Luther insisted on a literal interpretation of "This is my body; this my blood," because only in such a way can the covenantal fellowship be actually established. The sacramental realism here is quite intentional and quite conscious. Luther's position, called *consubstantiation*, teaches not that the bread and wine are changed into the body and blood of Christ but rather that the communicant received the body and blood of Christ with the bread and wine. The emphasis is on what the communicant receives from Christ rather than on any miraculous transformation performed by the priest.

In 1529 the Marburg Colloquy was called by Philip of Hesse to try to bring the South German and North German Reformers into agreement. No agreement came about. Luther was very blunt; the words of Christ were, "This is my body," and no amount of philological analysis or reasoning about what God could or could not do was going to change his mind. For Zwingli the biblical evidence was clear; the ascension of Christ precluded a bodily presence, and Luther's doctrine of ubiquity compromised the true humanity of Christ. Unfortunately, Luther saw Zwingli as a rationalist. He completely missed the strong christological dimension of Zwingli's argument. While Luther and Zwingli parted with the conviction that their two positions were irreconcilable, Bucer suspected there was a way to affirm the real presence without ignoring the biblical exegesis of Zwingli. At the Diet of Augsburg in 1530, the great majority of German Protestants united together in the *Augsburg Confession* agreeing with Luther that Christ's body and blood are present in, with, and under the bread and wine. On the other hand, four cities of South Germany, led by Strasbourg's Reformer, Bucer, wanting to come up with a conciliatory statement of the South German position, adopted the *Tetrapolitan Confession*. In 1531 Zwingli and Oecolampadius died before coming up with a fully developed doctrine of the Lord's Supper. More and more Bucer gained support for his attempt at finding a middle ground and in 1536 a significant group of South Germans led by Bucer and Capito went to Wittenberg to assure Luther of their belief that, although the bread and wine

were signs of Christ's presence, they were not empty signs. The *Wittenburg Concord* was thereby achieved.

It was only with the younger generation of Reformers that the Reformed doctrine of the eucharist came to full expression in the work of Henry Bullinger, Peter Martyr Vermigli, and John Calvin. Bullinger, Zwingli's successor in Zurich, developed an understanding of the sacraments based on covenantal theology. As Bullinger saw it, the sacraments should be understood as signs of the covenant. Bullinger was picking up on ideas, expressed, but not developed by Luther, Zwingli, and Oecolampadius. By a thorough study of the biblical concepts behind such basic terms as sign, covenant, and memorial, Bullinger deepened considerably the position of his predecessor. The approach which Bullinger championed was essentially philological.

Vermigli, a Florentine by birth, educated in Italian *via antiqua* Scholasticism, came to know the discussion of eucharistic doctrine which was going on north of the Alps during his days as prior of the Augustinian community in Naples. As Luther, Vermigli was concerned to recover an Augustinian emphasis on grace in eucharistic doctrine. He was thoroughly opposed to the doctrine of the eucharistic sacrifice and was fascinated by the possibility of finding a way of affirming Christ's presence in worship without recourse to the doctrine of transubstantiation. Vermigli made great use of OT types, the covenantal meals of the patriarchs, the Passover feast, and the story of feeding on the manna. Like Bullinger he was concerned to use biblical imagery in trying to understand the sacrament. He put an emphasis on the sacrament as eucharist, that is, as thanksgiving, and liked to explain sacramental doctrine by its analogy to Chalcedonian Christology. In 1548 Cranmer had Vermigli appointed regius

428

professor of divinity at Oxford, and in 1549 he participated in the important Oxford Disputation which led to a wide dissemination of his ideas in England, where his influence was perpetuated by John Jewel, bishop of Salisbury.

Calvin, following Bucer, developed a strong doctrine of the work of the Holy Spirit in bringing about that which the sacrament signified. Christ is truly present, as Calvin understands it, through the Holy Spirit. The Holy Spirit works within the hearts of believers restoring the faithful in the image of Christ and uniting them in his body. For Calvin, not only is Christ present with us at the Lord's table, but we are present with him at the wedding feast of the Lamb. It is not a local presence which is at issue but rather a personal presence. Christ is present at the Supper that the faithful might enter into covenantal fellowship with him and be fed by him on the Word of Life. While this dimension of Calvin's eucharistic theology has often been called dynamistic, it is more properly understood as sapiential. It is the wisdom theology of the gospel of John, Calvin's interpretation of Augustine's *verbum visibile*.

Calvin, whose respect for Luther was enormous, did not want to part company with Luther, and being well read in the writings of the early Fathers he wanted to affirm Christ's presence at the Supper, even if he could not accept the standard Scholastic explanations of that presence. His *Short Treatise on the Lord's Supper* is an irenic statement of his position. At first Calvin's ideas were received in northern Germany, particularly by Melanchthon, but apparently also by Luther. On the other hand, Calvin was in obvious agreement with Bullinger's attempt to explain the sacraments in terms of covenant theology, and in 1549 Calvin and Bullinger were able to reach the *Consensus Tigurinus*.

When the *Consensus Tigurinus* became

known in northern Germany, it once more awakened fears of a spiritualist interpretation. Luther had died in 1546 and Joachim Westphal of Hamburg became the chief proponent of Lutheran orthodoxy in regard to eucharistic doctrine. The conversation was as brilliant as it was heated. Contrary to Calvin, Westphal believed, as Luther had before him, that the ubiquity of Christ's body allowed for the real presence of the ascended Christ in the eucharist. For Calvin this was inconsistent with Chalcedonian Christology. It confused the human nature of Christ with the divine nature of Christ. While Calvin wanted to affirm Christ's presence, he could not agree with Westphal to the point of saying that even the faithless received the body of Christ.

In England the discussion of eucharistic doctrine was late in developing. Although Henry VIII was one of the first to defend Catholic sacramental doctrine from Luther's *Babylonian Captivity*, he soon found it to his advantage to appoint Thomas Cranmer as his archbishop. Cranmer had gotten to know the eucharistic controversies firsthand while in Germany in 1532. Although he married the niece of Andreas Osiander, his ideas began to develop in the direction of the Reformed theologians of South Germany. With the death of Henry VIII in 1547, Cranmer was free to lead the Church of England in a clearly Protestant direction. He called Bucer to Cambridge and Vermigli to Oxford. Their teaching was received enthusiastically in many circles and when the *Prayer Book* of 1552 appeared it showed the clear influence of Reformed eucharistic theology. The new approach to the eucharist was above all championed by Hugh Latimer and Nicholas Ridley. With the accession of Elizabeth I in 1558, the theological climate changed. The new queen, motivated by political concerns, favored ambiguity in eucharistic doctrine. The *Thirty-nine*

Articles (1563), simply understood, supported the position of the younger Reformed theologians, but was capable of other interpretations. Elizabeth recognized the prevailingly Protestant sentiments of her subjects but wanted to offend no one who would recognize her authority over the church.

With the close of the Council of Trent in 1563 Protestant eucharistic theology entered a new phase.

Salvatore Corde, *Veritas Sacramenti, A Study in Vermigli's Doctrine of the Lord's Supper* (Zurich, 1975). B.A. Gerrish, "Sign and Reality: The Lord's Supper in the Reformed Confessions," *The Old Protestantism and the New* (Chicago, 1982). Hans Grass, *Die Abendmahleslehre bei Luther und Calvin*, 2nd edition (Gütersloh, 1954). Walter Köhler, *Zwingli und Luther, Ihr Streit über das Abendmahl nach seinen politischen* und *religiosen Beziehungen*, 2 vols. (Leipzig, 1924 and Gütersloh, 1953). Kilian McDonnell, *John Calvin: The Church and the Eucharist* (Princeton, 1967). Paul Rorem, "Calvin and Bullinger on the Lord's Supper," *The Lutheran Quarterly* 2 (1988): 155-184, 357-389. Hermann Sasse, *This Is My Body: Luther's Contention for the Real Presence in the Sacrament of the Altar* (Minneapolis, 1959). Joseph N. Tylenda, "The Calvin-Westphal Exchange," *Calvin Theological Journal* 9 (1974): 182-209. Carl Wisloff, *The Gift of Communion, Luther's Controversy with Rome on Eucharistic Sacrifice* (Minneapolis, 1964).

HUGHES OLIPHANT OLD

EUCHARIST, RESERVATION OF THE

The food of eucharist is reserved after the eucharistic celebration primarily to extend the nourishment and the grace of Christ's table to those unable to participate in the liturgy itself, particularly the sick and the dying. This is clearly stated in the 1967 instruction *Eucharisticum mysterium*: "the primary and original purpose of the reserving of the sacred species in church outside Mass is the administration of the Viaticum" (E.M., III, I, A). Other reasons for its reservation are distribution of communion to the faithful at times other than Mass, and the adoration of Christ in this sacramental form which represents and presents his continued presence to the church. In some churches of the West the eucharist is also reserved from the liturgy of Holy Thursday for the reception of communion during the liturgy of Good Friday; in some churches of the East eucharistic reservation for a liturgy of the "pre-sanctified" occurs frequently, especially during Lent. The eucharistic food is usually reserved in the form of bread alone, though provision is made for the reservation of consecrated wine as well where it may be necessary to provide communion for the sick who are unable to receive the eucharistic bread (E.M., II, III, K).

Apart from the liturgical reservation of the sacrament on Holy Thursday, where the directives in the Roman sacramentary name the place of reservation or reposition as "a chapel suitably decorated for the occasion," the documents offer a variety of suggestions as to the place where the sacrament is to be reserved. They also reveal a shift in the understanding of eucharistic reservation that has grown with an evolved understanding of the eucharistic celebration itself. While the 1967 document does suggest a chapel distinct from the middle or central part of the church as a place suitable for private prayer and devotion, its main concern is to separate the place of reservation from a liturgical space where marriages and funerals are frequent, or where churches may receive a large number of tourist visitors. Otherwise E.M. suggests that "the Blessed Sacrament should be reserved in a solid, inviolable tabernacle in the middle of the main altar or on a side altar, but in a truly prominent place" (III, II, C). It also allows that "Mass may be celebrated facing the people even though there is a tabernacle on the altar, provided this is small yet adequate" (*ibid.*). In contrast, the U.S. bishops' document *Environment and Art in Christian Worship* (1978) gives priority of place to a special eucharistic chapel because the major space of a church should be designed for the eucharistic *action*, whereas the space for eucharistic reservation should be designed for *individual devotion*. "A room or chapel specifically designed and separate from the major space is important so that no confusion can take place between the celebration of the eucharist and reservation. Active and static aspects of the same reality cannot claim the same human attention at the same time" (E.A.W., 78). The document is clear to insist that this does not lower the importance of eucharistic reservation; rather, "a space carefully designed and appointed can give proper attention to the reserved sacrament" (*ibid.*).

There has thus been a growing recognition that the use and design of space that is appropriate to the eucharistic celebration cannot be at the same time appropriate to the private devotion that should attend eucharistic reservation. This recognition is missed in places where a eucharistic chapel is constructed as a miniature version of the main church, and used as well for the eucharistic celebration on weekdays, or when the assembly is small. It would seem to follow that if the main church space which is designed for the eucharistic action is inappropriate for the private devotion proper to eucharistic reservation, the converse would also be true: a proper eucharistic chapel, suitable for private devotion, would be equally inappropriate for the eucharistic celebration.

Separation of the place of reservation from the main space of eucharistic assembly does pose a symbolic problem which may require some form of ritual address. In the Catholic imagination, tabernacle and sanctuary lamp have traditionally spoken the presence of Christ in the reserved eucharistic food. Extinguish the lamp and leave the tabernacle door open, as in the time between Good Friday and the Easter vigil, and a powerful statement of Christ's nonpresence was also made and recognized. As the connection between eucharistic reservation and the full eucharistic assembly grows in importance, the imagination will have to be trained in this connection as well.

It has become important, for example, that the eucharistic food sent to the sick be publicly sent from the eucharistic assembly precisely so that those in the assembly, should they become sick and recipients of the eucharist from the assembly, will know with some symbolic richness whence that eucharist has come. Public ritual is required to make the connection clear. In like manner, if communion is to be properly distributed outside Mass for whatever reason, and if the connection between that distribution and the full eucharistic assembly is to be properly maintained, some ritual of placement of the eucharistic food from the eucharistic assembly into the chapel of reservation will be required. A clue to this may be found in the procession that accompanies the eucharistic food to the place of repose on Holy Thursday. Only those gathered on Good Friday who were participants in the Holy Thursday liturgy will really know the source of the food for Friday's communion, and the full symbolic richness which the link between Thursday and Friday (Supper and Cross) involves. For those who were not present on Thursday, the food may appear to come from nowhere. The symbolic link will be diminished or lost.

A final point to be made concerns the piety that should attend eucharistic reservation. Since the two major purposes of eucharistic reservation focus on Christ for the absent and Christ present to the church, these two points of focus identify the kind of prayer that is proper to eucharistic devotion. Christ is present *to* the church *for* the church, as the constant sign of God's constant fidelity to the human race. *Eucharistia*, thanksgiving, ought to dominate the prayer. Christ is not present in need of the church to comfort him; he is present because the church needs to be comforted by him; comforted and assured that the covenant of God, sealed by his death and resurrection, still holds. Humble reception of God's fidelity and trust in that fidelity ought also to shape prayer in the presence of the reserved sacrament. And finally, Christ is present for those who are absent, and for those not yet touched by his saving word and work. Prayer before Christ in the eucharist, far from drawing us in and away from the world of everyday life, should draw our attention outward in concern both for those with whom Christ has already set us in communion, and for those with whom Christ yearns to set us in communion. In that way, devotion to Christ outside of Mass will deepen faith, trust and the love that is communion, and enable those who pray outside of Mass to achieve a deeper and fuller level of participation when they gather again in assembly for the eucharistic celebration itself.

See **Adoration, theology of; Eucharistic worship outside Mass; Eucharistic chapel; Body of Christ; Communion service; Sick, communion to the; Viaticum**

PETER E. FINK, S.J.

EUCHARIST, THEOLOGY OF

The eucharist (Gk. *eucharistia*, thanksgiving) is the central act of Christian worship and indeed of the whole Christian life (*Eucharisticum mysterium*, 1967; G.I.R.M., chap. 1, 1). Composed of two essential parts, liturgy of the word and liturgy of the eucharist, it is nonetheless, because of the intimate union between the two, a single act of worship (G.I.R.M., chap. 1, 8). Vatican II gives a concise statement of the meaning of this act of the church: "At the Last Supper, on the night when he was betrayed, our Savior instituted the eucharistic sacrifice of his body and blood. He did this in order to perpetuate the sacrifice of the Cross throughout the centuries until he should come again, and so to entrust to his beloved spouse, the church, a memorial of his death and resurrection: a sacrament of love, a sign of unity, a bond of charity, a paschal banquet in which Christ is eaten, the mind is filled with grace, and a pledge of future glory is given to us" (S.C., 47).

More narrowly, eucharist refers to the bread and wine consecrated during the eucharistic liturgy (e.g., holy eucharist), received in communion and kept in reserve both for the sick and as a sign of Christ's enduring presence in and to the church. While it is still proper to use the term in this restricted sense, Vatican II restored its primary use for the whole liturgical action.

Eucharist is but one of many names for this liturgical act. In the NT it is also called "the breaking of the bread" (Lk 24:35; Acts 2:46); "the Lord's supper" (1 Cor 11:20); "the new paschal feast" (1 Cor 5:8); and "*koinonia* (participation, communion) in the body and blood of Christ" (1 Cor 10:16). Among the various churches it has been called, in addition to some of these NT terms, "Mass" (Latin Roman Catholic), the "Divine Liturgy" (Byzantine Orthodox and Catholic), the "Holy Communion" (Anglican), the "Mysteries" (West Syrian), and the "Sanctification or Oblation" (Coptic). Among the churches it is enacted according to a variety of complex ritual forms which differ among themselves in secondary structure and nuance (see, traditions, liturgical . . .). In all churches, however, the essential structure is the same: readings from scripture, prayers of intercession, and the meal of the bread and wine which are presented, blessed and distributed. All this is done in *anamnesis* (remembrance) of God's deeds made manifest in Jesus Christ (1 Cor 11:24-25; Lk 22:19).

Origins

Christian eucharist had its beginnings in the Jewish customs of faith and prayer which Jesus himself carried out with his disciples. The liturgy of the word derives from the synagogue where the scriptures were read and discussed, and where prayers of intercession were raised to God. The meal derives from the customs of the home where every meal was accompanied by *berakoth* (blessing prayers) that named the deeds of God and asked God's continued blessing and action. After the experience of Christ's resurrection, and while they still considered themselves and were considered to be Jews, the disciples continued their familiar practices, altering them where needed to bring into primary focus God's "new deed" who is Jesus, once dead and now risen. In the synagogue they continued to read and discuss the (Hebrew) scriptures, now seeking to understand Jesus in their light. In their homes they continued to bless God at their common meals, a blessing now surely made in terms of the risen Christ.

Two factors, however, urged evolution beyond these familiar Jewish patterns: the destruction of the Jerusalem temple (A.D. 70) and the expansion of Christianity to the Gentiles. The language of "newness" gained ascendancy: Christ the "new" temple, his sacrifice the "new" Passover, God's deed the "new" covenant. And the once familiar patterns of faith and prayer had to be translated for those Gentiles who did not know or understand their ways (as witnessed in 1 Cor 11: 17-34). In time, elements of synagogue and meal came together. In time, the full meal was replaced by a symbolic meal comprised of those elements over which the *berakoth* were prayed: bread and the cup

(of thanksgiving). Multiple blessing prayers (as in the *Didache*, c. A.D. 110) were joined into a single prayer (as in *Apost. Trad. of Hippolytus*, c. A.D. 215), and the essential structure of all later eucharistic prayers and rites was established. After the peace of Constantine (c. A.D. 312), more fixed formularies for its enactment began to take hold (see Bouley).

Understandings

From the beginning Christians tried to understand this "new deed" of God, the death and resurrection of Jesus Christ, and at the same time the meal of eucharist which is its *anamnesis*. The theology of eucharist embraces all forms of such attempts. Four forms of theological interpretation are considered here: (a) the biblical witness, (b) eucharistic anaphoras, (c) instructional writings of the early church, and (d) systematic reflection through the Middle Ages and beyond.

(a) Biblical Witness

The first, and foundational, form of eucharistic understanding is the biblical witness of the NT, where understanding is drawn primarily from OT imagery. Paul interprets Jesus and his remembrance in light of Passover: "Christ, our paschal lamb, has been sacrificed. Let us therefore celebrate the festival..." (1 Cor 5:8). John does the same in his passion narrative by having Jesus die at the same time the Passover lambs are slain (Jn 19:31). Paul also interprets eucharist in light of the exodus (1 Cor 10:1-5), and in his *traditio* of the "institution" twice identifies eucharist explicitly as *anamnesis* (remembrance) (1 Cor 11: 24-25). As remembrance, eucharist is the source of *koinonia* (participation, fellowship) with Christ (1 Cor 10: 16). John uses water rather than food to identify this participation in Christ, "If I do not wash you, you have no part in me" (Jn 13:8), and, though this is usually spoken of as baptismal rather than eucharistic imagery, John's gospel is probably too early to allow such a distinction. The synoptic accounts name eucharist in terms of Passover (Mk 14:12-16; Mt 26:19-20; Lk 22:15). Matthew adds the note of sacrifice (26:28) and both Luke and Paul the note of eschatological promise (Lk 22:16; 1 Cor 11:26). Finally, John 6 (esp. vv. 35-51) interprets the eucharistic food in terms of the desert manna of Exod 16, and identifies the "new" manna with Christ himself. In the NT the full scope of eucharistic faith is already firmly established.

(b) Eucharistic Anaphoras

The second form of eucharistic understanding is found in the tradition (evolution) of the *anaphora* or eucharistic prayer. These prayers were as much shaped by the christological and trinitarian controversies among the churches as by a growing understanding of the eucharist itself. Though both the structure and the content of these prayers give witness to a variety of understandings (e.g.: the thanksgiving narrative being christological or trinitarian; focused on redemption alone or on creation, redemption and the on-going work of the Spirit; the invocation of Word or of Spirit, or in the Roman canon, the angels; and the placement of intercessions as part of the narrative, the *anamnesis* [memorial], or the *epiclesis* [invocation of Spirit]), the prime indicator of eucharistic understanding is found in the "request formularies" that are most usually the *epiclesis*. There one finds three stages of evolution: the first request (e.g., in *Didache*, A.D. 110., and *Apost. Trad. of Hippolytus*, 3rd cent.) gives primary emphasis to the union of all in Christ; the second (e.g., in the *Anaphora of Addai and Mari*, early 4th cent.) gives primary emphasis to strengthening the faith of Christians, with a secondary focus on sanctifying the bread and wine; the third (e.g., in the *Euchology of Serapion of Thmuis*, 4th

cent., and the anaphoras of *St. John Chrysostom* and *Basil of Caesarea*, both 4th cent.) gives primacy to the conversion of the food, with secondary focus on the food as a source of strength. The prayer for unity in this third stage becomes tertiary (*St. Basil*), incidental (*Der Balyzeh* fragment, c. 5th cent.) or simply absent (*Chrysostom, St. Mark, Roman canon*). These request formularies are a prime theological source because they reveal the purpose of the eucharist intended by the church and the hopes of those who enact it.

These eucharistic prayers likewise reveal, at the third stage, a diversity of views as to who is the agent in the conversion of food and in the effectiveness of the eucharistic prayer. In the Roman canon, where the influence of Ambrose (*De myst.*, 43-54) is felt and where the *Verba Jesu* (institution narrative) are at the center, the agent is Christ's own words. In the prayer attributed to John Chrysostom (*epiclesis*: "...having changed them by the Holy Spirit"), the agent is clearly the Spirit, though this position is more securely that of Cyril of Jerusalem (*Catechetical lectures*, xix, 7; xxi, 3) since Chrysostom himself inclined towards the agency of Christ's words (*De prod. Jud* i. 6). In the *Euchology of Serapion*, where the Logos (Word) is invoked rather than the Spirit, it is again Christ who is agent, though the bread and wine are offered as *figura* (image) of the body and blood, and the Logos is invoked that the bread become the body of the Logos and the wine the blood of truth (see Bouyer, 204). Finally, the Syrian or Cilician *Testamentum Domini* (4th cent.) invokes the full Trinity for consecration.

(c) Instructional Writings

The third form of eucharistic understanding is contained in the various pre- and post-Nicene writings: apologetic (e.g., Justin Martyr, fl. c. 150), instructional (e.g., Origen, d. 253), homiletic (e.g., Chrysostom, d. 407) and mystagogical catecheses (e.g., Ambrose, d. 397, Cyril of Jerusalem, fl. 347), where two eucharistic questions began to take shape, viz., the presence of Christ in the eucharistic food and the sacrificial nature of the eucharistic act. Both questions are constant concerns, though they are not yet developed in any systematic way.

The earliest concerns for articulating and reflecting on the presence of Christ in the eucharistic food were primarily christological. The *fact* of Christ's presence was taken for granted. It was used by Justin to prove the incarnation and by Irenaeus (c. 180) to prove the resurrection. Only later is the *fact*, or at least the nature of the fact, called into question.

D. Stone (*A History of the Doctrine of the Holy Eucharist*, chaps. 2, 3) traces the gradual evolution of insight into the question of Christ's presence. In the pre-Nicene era, three different ways of speaking arose: (a) what is given in eucharist is a spiritual gift, the exact nature of which is not defined [e.g., "life and knowledge" (*Didache*), "medicine of immortality" (Ignatius of Antioch)]; (b) what is given in eucharist is a symbol [Gk. *symbolon*] (Clement of Alexandria) or figure [Lat. *figura*] (Tertullian) of the body and blood of Christ; (c) what is given in eucharist is the body and blood of Christ (Justin, Irenaeus). After Nicea these three views continue, with others as well: (a) there are general references to eucharist as a means of receiving the body and blood of Christ (e.g., "But now we, eating of the Word of the Father, and having the lintels of our hearts sealed with the blood of the new covenant, acknowledge the grace given us from the Savior" [Athanasius, *Festal letters*, v. 5]); (b) the elements are spoken of as figure, symbol, likeness and image of the body and blood of Christ (e.g., "the symbols of his body and his saving blood" [Eusebius of Caesarea, *Demonstratio Evangelica*,

I, x, 28]); (c) the elements are spoken of as having heightened efficacy (e.g., "As the bread of the Eucharist after the invocation of the Holy Ghost is no longer simple bread but the body of Christ, so also after the invocation this holy chrism is no longer ... common but becomes Christ's gift of grace" [Cyril of Jerusalem, *Catechetical lectures*, xxi. 3]); (d) the elements are spoken of as the body and blood of Christ (e.g., "Since then He declared and spake of the bread, 'This is My body,' who will dare to doubt any longer? And since he affirmed and said, 'This is My blood,' who will ever hesitate so as to say it is not His blood?" [Cyril of Jerusalem, *Catechetical letters*, xxii. 1]). In addition, Christ's presence is said to be of a spiritual character, and the eucharist is connected with the church as body of Christ (esp. Augustine). There was little or no attempt to explain the intrinsic relationship between the presence of Christ and the elements. Two apparently opposed views vied for attention: one that drew the connection between incarnation and eucharist, emphasizing the abiding reality of the elements even after consecration (Nestorius, Theodoret, Pope Gelasius), and the other affirming a definite change in the elements themselves (Cyril of Jerusalem, Gregory of Nyssa).

The language of eucharistic sacrifice, while constant, is less developed. Stone traces this as well. In the pre-Nicene era, two convictions take hold: (a) the repudiation of all carnal sacrifices; (b) their place taken by Christian life, belief and worship which are spiritual sacrifices. Where the language of sacrifice is connected to the eucharist, it is drawn via the prophecy of Malachi (Mal 1:11, "From the rising of the sun ... "). There is no explanation of the sense in which sacrifice is applied to eucharist. After Nicea the general sacrificial terminology continues, with the memorial connected at times with the passion and death of Christ, and at times not only his death but also his resurrection, ascension and heavenly life. The Christian's act in offering the sacrifice culminates in communion which brings union with Christ. True sacrifice (Augustine) is dedication of self to God.

(d) Systematic Reflection

The fourth form of eucharistic understanding is the mode of systematic reflection. Key figures in the East are Maximus the Confessor (7th cent.), John of Damascus (8th cent.), Nicholas Cabasilas (14th cent.) and Symeon of Thessalonica (15th cent.), with a key event being the iconoclast controversy (8th cent.) and its resolution at the Seventh Ecumenical Council (II Nicea, A.D. 787). Key figures in the West, prior to the Reformation, are Augustine, who formulated an early systematic theology of sacraments, Amalarius of Metz (9th cent.), who offered allegorical interpretations of the Mass, Radbertus and Ratramnus (9th cent.), who debated *real* vs. *symbolic* presence of Christ in the eucharistic food, Berengarius of Tours (11th cent.), Hugh of St. Victor (12th cent.) and the great scholastic theologians (13th cent.), Aquinas, Bonaventure, Scotus, et al. Key voices after the Reformation are Luther, Calvin, Zwingli, and the Catholic decrees of the Council of Trent.

The East began to secure for faith the transformation of the bread and wine into the body and blood of Christ at the invocation of the Holy Spirit (*epiclesis*). The impact of the iconoclast controversy was to distinguish the bread and wine *before* the invocation (as an *image* of Christ) from the same *after* the invocation (as the *actual body and blood* of Christ). The eucharist was also secured as true sacrifice offered to God, with the entire trinitarian Godhead recipient of the sacrifice offered by Christ. The ecclesial nature of the eucharist was stressed, along with the relationship between the earthly offering (liturgy) and the heavenly liturgy. The eucharistic action was pre-sented and developed allegorically as the unfolding of the mysteries of Christ's life, death and resurrection (esp. Maximus the Confessor and Nicholas Cabasilas).

In the West a sharp distinction occurred between eucharistic piety and eucharistic reflection. The action of the eucharist became the action of the priest alone, a sacred drama which the people attended. The key moment became the consecration (the words of Jesus at the Supper), which was regarded as an epiphany of the great King, royally enthroned upon the altar, and greeted with astonished eyes and adoring hearts. Mystagogy (the catechetics of doers) was replaced by allegory (the catechetics of watchers) and from Amalarius onward the parts of the Mass were exposed as symbolic re-enactments, first of all salvation history, and eventually (12th cent.) of the passion of Christ only. The Mass was offered by the priest (offertory prayer: " . . . which I your unworthy servant offer to you on behalf of . . . ") to win benefits for the living and the dead. At the heart of this shift in eucharistic piety was a christological image shift: Christ no longer in the midst of the assembly, but at the right hand of the Father in heaven (Jungmann, *The Place of Christ in Liturgical Prayer*, 1965).

Reflective attention was focussed first on the *fact* of Christ's presence, and later (13th cent. onward) on the *mode* or *manner* of Christ's presence. Controversies in the 9th cent. (Radbertus and Ratramnus) and the 11th cent. (Berengarius) examined the eucharistic elements as either symbolic pointers to Christ who was elsewhere (i.e., heaven) or transformed elements which presented the historical flesh and blood of Jesus. In spite of the fact that reason urged the former, while being repelled by the latter, the church opted for real over symbolic presence, leaving for a later time a systematic understanding of how this was so. That time came (13th cent.) with the rediscovery of Aristotelian categories which allowed a distinction that the earlier Platonic categories did not. At stake was the accessibility of Christ (real presence) and at the same time the divinity of Christ (irreducible to created matter). The substance-accident distinction of Aristotle, two principles of being contained within created matter, with one (accident) representing what the senses perceived (hence: size, shape, texture, place) and the other (substance) a universal principle not limited to any one of its manifestations, provided a way out of the intellectual stalemate. With these categories in hand, and though it in fact involved a theological twist of Aristotle's own use of the terms, it was possible to name a universal element *within* the bread and wine that was changed into Christ (substance) while allowing the senses their proper due (accidents unchanged). The term "transubstantiation" was brought forward from Tertullian to name this ontological change. With great subtlety they insisted that this change be such as (a) not to violate creation, and (b) to insure that creation itself is redeemed. For a time at least reason served faith and was not offended by it.

The subtlety of the scholastic solution, however, did not endure. It did not endure for Luther who, though the term "consubstantiation" is often attributed to him as counter-point to Catholic "transubstantiation," preferred to side with the biblical witness (thus real presence: "This *is* my body") and shun philosophical attempts at explanation. It did not endure for Calvin whose bias toward the exalted Christ (as opposed to the incarnate or crucified Christ) would allow that Christ only be really present now through his Advocate, the Paraclete, the Holy Spirit. Nor did it endure for Zwingli who alone among the Reformers opted for a symbolic rather than real presence (elements point to and remind one of Christ who is elsewhere). Whether or not

its subtlety endured at Rome, the scholastic solution was claimed by the Council of Trent as "most apt" (*aptissime*) to secure its own faith confession that the words of Jesus bring about "the conversion of the whole substance of bread into the body and of the whole substance of the wine into the blood, while the appearances of bread and wine nonetheless remain" (D.S., 1652).

In regard to the question of eucharistic sacrifice, there is little development in systematic reflection in the West between the end of the patristic era and the Reformation. The essential pieces had long been in place: the eucharist is the sacrifice which Christ offers to God together with his church; it is Christ who offers and Christ who is offered. The fruit of the sacrifice is the union of Christians with Christ as well as spiritual benefits that come from such union.

What did happen to pave the way for the Reformation controversies on eucharistic sacrifice was an increasing reification of the benefits of the sacrifice in categories of merit and satisfaction for sin. This, coupled with the loss of an ecclesiological dimension of the sacrifice (Christ *and* his church offered and offering) and the increased sacerdotalizing of the sacrifice (priest offers on behalf of the people), led in both praxis and popular piety to an "economic" model for understanding the sacrificial nature of the eucharist: *quid pro quo*. This inadequate framework for articulating the fruit of Christ's sacrifice as it is received by the living and the dead distorted faith and led to the abusive behavior ("Mass" priests; multiplicity of Masses without congregations) which triggered the Reformation.

The Reformers generally rejected the then current notion of eucharistic sacrifice as a human work capable of influencing God: Christ's sacrifice was once for all; people are saved by faith, not works; eucharist is praise and thanksgiving (and in that sense sacrifice); it is not propitiatory for the living and the dead. The Catholic response at Trent, while trying to clear up the abuses which the Reformers decried, held two seemingly contradictory confessions in tandem: Christ's sacrifice was indeed once for all; nonetheless, the eucharist is true sacrifice offered for the living and the dead (D.S., 1751). The church of the West splintered.

Subsequent reflection on the side of the Reformers developed word and fellowship, and continued to fend off any note of the eucharist as a propitiatory sacrifice with the *sola fide* cry. Subsequent reflection on the Catholic side continued to foster transubstantiation and eucharistic sacrifice. Unfortunately, Catholic teaching on real presence was jeopardized as the term substance moved, in the 17th cent., from being a metaphysical category to being a physical category (as in physical science); teaching on sacrifice remained jeopardized by the "economic model" which was somewhat modified to clear up abuses, but which nonetheless remained the framework for sacrifice discourse. Only in the 20th cent., with its recovery of biblical and patristic language, with the writings of Odo Casel, Pius XII, Bernard Leeming, Edward Schillebeeckx, et al., and, of course, with Vatican II, was this double jeopardy finally lifted.

These four forms of eucharistic understanding, biblical witness, eucharistic anaphora, early church writings and subsequent systematic reflection, represent the full *traditio* of the eucharist, and all are called into play by Vatican II as it not only instituted liturgical reforms for the eucharist and other liturgical acts of the church but also spoke its eucharistic and sacramental faith in fresh new ways.

Fundamental Concepts

Before turning to a consideration of eucharistic faith in the light of Vatican II, four key concepts at the heart of eucha-

ristic theology need to be identified: (a) eucharist as *sacrament*; (b) eucharist as *anamnesis* (an act of remembrance); (c) eucharist as *worship*; and (d) eucharist as *koinonia* (communion or fellowship).

(a) Sacrament

The term sacrament (Gk. *mysterion*, Lat. *sacramentum*) has long been defined for English speaking Catholics as "an outward sign instituted by Christ to give grace." This terse definition was designed to carry the faith articulated at Trent that Christ, not the early church, instituted sacraments, and that sacraments both contained the grace they conferred and conferred the grace they contained. The model was of a "holy thing" given by the church and received by the faithful. In Catholic theology there were seven, no more, no less. This classic definition has been radically revitalized in the latter half of the 20th century.

E. Schillebeeckx (*Christ the Sacrament of the Encounter with God*, 1960) began to speak of Christ as sacrament, meaning by this that Christ is the visible and tangible presence, the human embodiment, of the mystery of God. K. Rahner (*The Church and the Sacraments*, 1963) spoke in much the same way of the church as sacrament of Christ, a usage formally adopted at Vatican II (L.G., 1; S.C., 5). It is in the context of this double usage of the term for Christ and for the church that the eucharist as sacrament of the church must be understood. The church comes together (*ec-clesia*) to enact the eucharistic liturgy. In both its assembling (church as sacrament) and its eucharistic action (eucharist as sacrament) it becomes the visible and tangible and active presence, the human embodiment, of the mystery of Jesus Christ (S.C., 2). Eucharist is no longer to be seen in the first instance as a "holy thing" given and received. It is first and foremost a holy action of a holy people gathered by Christ, joined to Christ, enacting with

Christ his worship of God and his salvation of humanity (S.C., 7).

(b) Remembrance

When the church gathers to enact the eucharist it does so in remembrance (Heb. *zikkaron*, Gk. *anamnesis*, Lat. *memoria*) of Jesus Christ. The word itself has had many meanings. When translated into Latin it became an act of imitation (what Jesus did at the Last Supper) and obedience (his command, "Do this in remembrance of me"). In Greek it had more the meaning of "participation," the *koinonia* which Paul describes in 1 Cor 10:16. The Hebrew, from which both the Greek and the Latin are derived, is much richer in meaning (see Childs). Gen 9: 8-17 gives its full scope: God makes a covenant; God establishes a sign of the covenant; the sign is presented to God *so that God will remember* and act once again according to the covenant.

The exact nature of the injunction, "Do this in remembrance of me," is disputed among biblical scholars. What is not disputed is that in the Pauline text at least the eucharistic gathering is named remembrance. Western theology in general, and Catholic theology in particular, has read this phrase as *memoria*, a command to imitate Jesus' own actions at the Supper. Eastern theology has not held exactly the same ties to the Supper, and has given more stress to *anamnesis* (= *koinonia*, participation) than to obedience and imitation. The recovery of the Hebrew understanding as more primitive and far richer than either *anamnesis* or *memoria* invites both East and West to recover the fullness of remembrance which the eucharist in fact is.

In Jesus Christ, especially in his resurrection from the dead and the sending of the Spirit, God makes covenant with all men and women (" ... the new covenant in my blood" 1 Cor 11:25). Jesus himself is raised up to be the "sign" of the covenant. To do *zikkaron*-remembrance of Jesus is to raise to God the covenant sign, Jesus himself, that God will see, remember and act once again. Israel makes remembrance by reciting the deeds of God which constitute God's covenant in the concrete. Christians make remembrance in exactly the same way, by telling the story of Jesus, God's new deed, in a variety of ways. It is an act of memory (recalling what God has done) and hope (expecting God to act once again). It involves faith-filled proclamation and humble receptivity. In more classic terms, it involves Word and consecration.

(c) Worship

Most generally worship is an act of reverence and honor shown to God. God is acknowledged to be God and given what is due to God alone. Worship may be expressed in public ritual action, or it may simply manifest itself in ordinary human deeds that flow from this inner attitude of reverence and respect. Public worship that does not spring from and express this inner attitude is empty and vain.

Throughout the OT God claims worship from Israel. "I am the Lord your God, who brought you out of the land of Egypt, out of the house of bondage. You shall have no other gods before me" (Deut 5:6-7). God's claim is not for ritual deeds, but for love: "Hear, O Israel: the Lord our God is one Lord; and you shall love the Lord your God with all your heart, and with all your soul, and with all your might" (Deut 6:5-5). The prophets decried religious ritual that lacked this inner love (e.g., Isa 1:12-17) and reminded Israel again and again that God's desire was to claim the human heart. "If you are willing and obedient, you shall eat the good of the land; but if you refuse and rebel, you shall be devoured" (Isa 1:19-20).

The NT names Jesus' stance before God as obedience (Phil 2:8; Heb 10:7), the giving over of his whole life to Abba's lead. It was obedience fulfilled in his death on the cross. This giving over of oneself to God, which Paul calls spiritual sacrifice (Rom 12:1-2), is likewise enjoined upon all Christians. Worship, sacrifice and obedience all signify the same human act, generous giving of oneself to the claims of God.

The eucharist is enacted in worship of God. "It is the culminating action whereby God sanctifies the world in Christ and men (sic) worship the Father as they adore him through Christ the Son of God" (G.I.R.M., chap. 1, 1). Eucharist is an action of the assembled church bringing to expression Christ's own stance before *Abba* (S.C., 2). It is a ritual act that is true worship only when those who enact it express in ritual form an inner movement of the heart. Christians make their own Christ's obedient offering of himself and bring this to expression in a variety of ways (creed, intercession and especially the presentation of gifts). This inner attitude of reverence, honor, willingness and obedient giving over of one's life to God is the true meaning of the classic term offering or offertory.

(d) Communion

Communion is relationship, a unity and harmony among people. Paul uses the word *koinonia* for the Lord's supper to signify a double relationship: "The cup of blessing which we bless, is it not a participation in the blood of Christ? The bread which we break, is it not a participation in the body of Christ?" (1 Cor 10:16). The cup is the covenant; *koinonia* is harmony and relationship with the God who makes covenant. The bread is the body; *koinonia* is harmony and relationship with the body, i.e., with Christ who is head and with all who are members. The meal establishes relationship among those who eat and with him whose body is eaten. The meal *berakoth* establishes relationship with the God who is blessed and praised.

The communion of eucharist is established and brought about by God. It is God's rules that govern relationships in

the body of Christ. In Christ "there is neither Jew nor Greek, there is neither slave nor free, there is neither male nor female; for you are all one in Christ Jesus" (Gal 3:28). It is thus essential in the doing of eucharist that God's agenda first be proclaimed (word, memory) and that the human heart be given over to him who is proclaimed (offering, offertory). God will act upon that which is given over to transform it "according to the working of his great might which he accomplished in Christ when he raised him from the dead" (Eph 1:20) (consecration, hope), and when the heart is transformed love (*koinonia*, communion) is established. The classic movement of word, offertory, consecration and communion which is rooted in remembrance, worship and *koinonia* thus spells out the inner dynamic of the eucharistic action and allows a people to join with Christ in that act by which "God is perfectly glorified and men (sic) are sanctified" (S.C., 7).

Eucharistic Faith

We turn now to consider the major ingredients of eucharistic faith. We consider here five elements of this faith: (a) the ecclesial nature of the eucharist; (b) the institution of eucharist by Christ; (c) the presence of Christ in the eucharist; (d) the sacrificial nature of the eucharist; and (e) the eucharist as eschatological pledge.

(a) Ecclesial Nature of the Eucharist

Vatican II reversed the medieval shift that sacerdotalized the eucharist and made the priest its only human agent. As a liturgical act it is carried out by Christ the priest and his body which is the church (S.C., 7); it is an action of Christ and the people of God hierarchically ordered (G.I.R.M., chap. 1,1). In this as in all liturgical acts the faithful express the mystery of Christ which is at the same time the true nature of the church (S.C., 2). Because the whole church assembled is its primary human agent, eucharist is able to build up the church and transform the people into a temple of the Lord (S.C., 2). People are affected by what they do. It is for this reason that the constitution enjoins that, in renewing the liturgy, "the full and active participation by all the people is the aim to be considered above all else" (S.C., 14).

This restoration of the eucharist as an act of the whole church is most noticeable in the prayers that accompany the preparation of gifts. Where once the priest said, "Accept . . . this spotless host which I . . . offer unto you," he now says, "Blessed are you . . . we have these gifts to offer." There is a corresponding shift in the ordination rite for presbyters. Where once the bishop said to the new priest, "Receive the power to offer sacrifice for the living and the dead," he now says, "Receive the gifts from the people to be offered to God." The presiding priest acts together with the people; he does not act in their stead.

(b) Institution of Eucharist by Christ

Vatican II affirmed again the age-old confession of faith that "at the Last Supper, on the night when he was betrayed, our Savior instituted the eucharistic sacrifice of his body and blood" (S.C., 47). For centuries this statement has been taken to be both a theological statement, naming Jesus himself as the source and origin of every Christian eucharist, and a historical statement, identifying the Supper itself as the originating moment when Jesus altered the familiar Passover meal ("This is my body; this is my blood") and commanded his disciples to imitate this in the future in remembrance of him. This is remembrance-*memoria* as described above.

The statement still stands as a theological statement. It can no longer stand, however, as a strictly historical statement for two reasons: (a) the challenge of biblical scholarship which has identified the Supper narratives as liturgical formularies and not historical chronologies, with some doubt cast whether the "command formularies" are original words of Jesus; and, (b) the challenge of liturgical scholarship which has recognized the gradual evolution of Christian eucharist from Jewish patterns of faith and prayer. The radical newness of the eucharist remains, as does its origin in Jesus Christ. But the origin cannot be explained by a literal historical reading of the Last Supper narratives. Since the eucharist is enacted in remembrance of Jesus, and not specifically of the Last Supper, what is needed is to draw first the connection between Jesus and the eucharist and only then the connection between eucharist and the Last Supper event.

The original sense of remembrance, whether or not the "command formularies" are traceable to Jesus, is *zikkaron*, not *memoria*. Eucharist as remembrance has to do with the covenant of God, with Jesus as sign of that covenant, and with the expectation that God will remember his covenant and include those who do eucharist in its saving grasp. To understand the link between Jesus and the eucharist it is necessary to understand the link between event and remembrance of the event.

The relationship between the exodus (event) and passover (remembrance) provides the needed insight. It is not in the first instance a relationship of ritual to ritual. It is rather a relationship based on an inner dynamic which the ritual expresses. The exodus story tells of the initiative of God (God's agenda) calling forth obedient response from the people (sacrifice, expressed in the slaughter of the lamb). It tells further of God's deliverance (blood on the doorposts, the "sign" of covenant) and the formation of a covenant people (eating of the lamb). Passover does not follow the ritual detail of the exodus event. It does, however, bring forward the same fourfold inner dynamic. The story is told (God's agenda), the lamb is slain (obedience of the people), the blood is poured out (sign of the covenant) and the people are included in the covenant (the Passover meal).

The death of Jesus was understood in terms of exodus-passover. Jesus is named the pasch, the lamb whose life, sealed by his death, is obedient sacrifice to God. For this God exalts him (deliverance) and makes him "first born," the head of a new people, the church. A new covenant is established; a new sign of covenant given; a new people of covenant formed. Jesus' life, death and resurrection becomes the new event which summons forth remembrance.

Eucharist is not designed to mimic Jesus' life, nor indeed any particular part of it. It is designed to express (within a range of proper expressions) the mystery of Christ (S.C., 2): his life, death, resurrection and exaltation. It is designed to express his role as the "first born," the head and founder of the new covenant people. It is designed to be *zikkaron* of the mystery of Christ. As in his life, so in eucharist, God's agenda is primary (proclamation of the word). As in his life, so in eucharist, the human heart is raised in obedient surrender (offertory). As in his life, so in eucharist, God remembers and acts to transform all that is placed with Christ (consecration). And as from his life, so from the eucharist, the new people who become Christ's body (communion) are formed. The full mystery of Christ, lived first in his own life and given expression again and again in the eucharist, is the event which eucharist remembers, the event which brings the eucharist into being.

The originating event of the first eucharist, and of every eucharist, is the paschal mystery itself. Jesus institutes the eucharist by passing through it, and by himself becoming the event that generates remembrance. One could say he instituted it at the Supper, for there he joined his life and impending death to the mystery of God's covenant which Passover proclaimed. One could also say he instituted it on the cross, or in the resurrection, or with the sending of the Spirit. All are equally true, for all are key moments in the one paschal mystery which Jesus himself became, the one paschal mystery which eucharist remembers. No single event provides the whole of it, and certainly no single event provides ritual detail for enacting the eucharist. Only the mystery as a whole, with its inner dynamic of obedient surrender (offertory) to God (Word) in a death that is transformed (consecration) into a life destined for and shared with all (communion), can provide the fullness of the eucharist, the fullness of remembrance.

(c)The Presence of Christ

Through most of its history, the question of Christ's presence in the eucharist has been focussed on the consecrated bread and wine. Vatican II broadened the focus to be first on the whole eucharistic action, and then within it, to include four distinct modes of Christ's presence: word, presiding priest, bread and wine, and assembly. It did not by this diminish attention to be given to the bread and wine as Christ's body and blood. Rather it provided the proper context for this particular mode of Christ's presence to be properly understood.

Vatican II advanced the question in one very significant way. It named the *purpose* of Christ's presence among us. His primary reason is not that he be adored or attended to. He is present *pro nobis*, on our behalf. His primary purpose is to associate the people of the church with himself "in this great work in which God is perfectly glorified and men are sanctified" (S.C.,7). His presence is an active presence, to gather us into his worship of *Abba* and to be for us the agent of our salvation. To carry out his purpose more than one mode of presence is required.

In each of the modes of Christ's presence his presence is *real*. The special notice that continues to be given to his presence under the form of bread and wine is not meant to imply otherwise. "This presence of Christ under the species is called (real) not in an exclusive sense, as if the other kinds of presence were not real, but par excellence" (*Eucharisticum mysterium*, chap. 1, E). There is only one Christ who is present in the eucharist. His presence is real. Each mode of his presence is ordered to serve his presence and his purpose in its own particular way.

The four modes of Christ's presence are related within the total dynamic of the eucharistic action, and in fact are related to the four inner movements that constitute the eucharist as *zikkaron*-remembrance. His presence in the word corresponds to the liturgy of the word: he is present in this form to speak to our hearts ("it is he himself who speaks when the holy scriptures are read"). His presence in the presiding minister is to be the primary agent in the sacramental act ("when anybody baptizes it is really Christ who baptizes"). His presence in the assembly ("where two or three are gathered together in my name there am I in the midst of them") is to constitute this assembly as his body ("the head and his members"). And his presence in the eucharistic food is to be and do what food does: to nourish and to unite.

Each mode of Christ's presence involves a different human dynamic. Word involves listening; it is only by listening that Christ's presence will be recognized. The presider embodies the Christ who bids welcome, gathers together, and invites into his own prayer. It is only by following that lead, by being welcomed, by being gathered and by entering into Christ's prayer that Christ's presence will

be recognized. The food most tangibly presents Christ as the agent of human transformation and as the source of Christian unity. It is only by reverencing this bit of creation transformed, by allowing it to announce the destiny of all human life and creation, and by eating and drinking in a common meal that Christ's presence in food will be recognized. And the assembly represents the continued incarnation of Christ whose mission remains to enter and transform human life, not to stand apart from it. Only as life is in fact transformed, and reverenced by each in each other, will Christ's presence be recognized. These four modes of Christ's presence cannot be reduced to or conflated into one; neither can the four modes of interaction with Christ be reduced, conflated or confused.

The term transubstantiation was called upon in Catholic theology to affirm an ontological change in the bread and wine, and not merely a change in its noetic structure. In the years immediately preceding Vatican II attempts were made to translate the term itself into categories of contemporary phenomenology. Words such as transignification (new meaning) and transfinalization (new purpose) were explored (see, Powers, chap. 4; Schillebeeckx, chap. II), though finally recognized as inadequate (Paul VI, *Mysterium fidei*, 1965). Both meaning and purpose would be vitiated if the reality itself were not radically transformed. As the focus of Christ's presence broadens to include word, priest and assembly, the ontological insight into the consecrated bread and wine needs to be directed to these as well. In fact, however, the theological tradition has long spoken of ontological transformation in regard to these others. With word it has spoken of "inspiration." With both baptism and orders it has employed the elusive term "character." These need to be woven into a eucharistic theology that proclaims word, priest and assembly as modes of Christ's real presence.

Reflection on the presence of Christ in the eucharist needs to go forward in three directions. The first will recognize that the presence of Christ is a personal presence, and that his primary appeal is to the human heart. The transformation he desires is conversion of heart. Reflection on Christ's presence must include the process of conversion as the primary noetic structure of this confession of faith. The second recognizes that each of the modes of Christ's real presence is nonetheless a symbol that mediates Christ. Christ is never experienced *immediately*. Reflection on Christ's presence must move beyond the opposition between "symbolic" and "real" and formulate a symbolic ontology where "symbolic depth," which constitutes a symbol to be symbol, is in some way transformed into Christ. The final direction, related to this second, concerns not so much the question, "how is Christ present," as "how do *we know* Christ present?" How do we engage the symbols that mediate him in order to meet him? This recognizes that the confession of Christ's presence in the eucharist is, finally, not a statement of a "fact" to be proven, but the announcement of a "person" who is to be met.

(d) Sacrificial Nature of the Eucharist

The major significance of Vatican II in regard to eucharistic sacrifice has been not so much to advance the question with new insight as to speak of it once again in biblical and patristic imagery. By so doing the council has reversed most if not all of the medieval shifts that severely restricted, and at times distorted, the meaning of this confession of faith. Gone is the view of eucharistic sacrifice as an objective "thing" whose effects can be measured in mechanistic terms of merit and satisfaction for sin. Gone too is the consignment of sacrificial offering to the priest alone acting as surrogate agent for

the faithful. The primary image of the eucharistic sacrifice set forth in *Sacrosanctum concilium* is of Christ the priest associating the church with himself both in his worship of the Father and in his saving act for the world (S.C., 7). And the primary language of eucharistic effectiveness is focused on the signs and symbols of the eucharist itself. "The liturgy, then, is rightly seen as an exercise of the priestly office of Jesus Christ. It involves the presentation of man's sanctification under the guise of signs perceptible by the senses and its accomplishment in ways appropriate to each of these signs" (*ibid.*).

The eucharistic sacrifice is an action of Jesus Christ. The once for all sacrifice of the cross is neither repeated nor augmented, as if it were insufficient in itself. The proper language is the language of *zikkaron*-remembrance: the action of Christ on the cross is *remembered*. By words, symbols, actions and interactions each new eucharistic assembly narrates the deed of God of which the cross is an essential constitutive element. The once-for-all gift of Christ to *Abba* for the salvation of the world is, by narrative, made present to God, that God will remember, and to the assembly, that men and women be drawn into it. The language of a "reified" sacrifice employed in the past inevitably gave rise to the Reformation dilemma where it seemed at least that multiple sacrifices (the cross of Christ *plus* the sacrifices of the church) were being offered. The language of the council avoids this. It speaks rather of the once-for-all sacrifice of the cross being continuously brought to expression in order that all may be included directly in its saving power.

Eucharistic sacrifice is first and foremost a function of Christ's presence. He is present in *zikkaron*-remembrance as God's deed, and therefore always actively related both to God in worship and to women and men as their source of salvation. The language of sacrifice gives specific nuance to his presence, with the purpose of his presence, as Vatican II names it, providing the link. As a specific nuance of the entire paschal mystery of Christ which names the process of human salvation and sanctification, the sacrifice of the eucharist presents Christ and his cross "under the guise of signs perceptible by the senses and its accomplishment in ways appropriate to each of these signs" (S.C., 7).

Vatican II sheds fresh light on the often misunderstood Catholic position that sacraments achieve their effect *ex opere operato* (by the action being carried out). In a more mechanistic framework, and in a liturgical environment where only the priest was agent and all else were passive recipients of grace, eucharistic sacrifice too easily appeared as a human work that put controls upon grace and "worked its salvation" automatically, almost magically. In fact, however, there is nothing automatic or magical about this. This classic position says little more than that people are affected by what they do, and when people faithfully enact the saving actions of Christ the effect it has on them is to bring about their salvation. The classic position required two things: that the priest do what the church intends (as guided and controlled by the Christ-mystery itself) and that people put no obstacle in the way (positively, that they be open to what is done). With the eucharist restored as an action of the entire assembly which brings Christ's full saving action to expression through word, offertory, consecration and communion, actions with their own dynamic and their own appropriate effect on those who carry them out, the automatic and the magical give way once again to the appeal of grace. The dynamic of the eucharistic signs, symbols, actions and interactions makes an appeal to freedom, and in freedom summons the believer to surrender to God's action in his/her life. Word calls forth the surrender of one's life to the deed of God that is proclaimed. Meal calls forth commitment to one's fellow that is reconciliation, the healing of division, the victory over sin. Word and meal together provide the dynamic by which eucharist is true sacrifice, the one sacrifice of Christ into which the assembly is called and to which the assembly is united.

An irony presents itself at this point. Though the language of Catholic teaching on eucharistic sacrifice, at least since the Council of Trent, insisted that the sacrifice was propitiatory for the living and the dead, popular piety and liturgical praxis both seemed to direct its effectiveness primarily to those who were not assembled rather than to those who were. Masses were offered for "intentions," most frequently for the dead. People requested that the Mass be offered, and accompanied their request with a financial offering (stipend), but since the people did not otherwise participate in the eucharistic act, the language was scarce as to how they themselves were saved by the sacrifice. The language restored by Vatican II reverses this. It is easier to name how those who do eucharist, the actual enacting assembly, are saved by the doing than to explain the effectiveness of the sacrifice for those not present.

What was lost in the Middle Ages, and needs to be re-captured in the contemporary church, is a strong sense of the prayer of intercession. The medieval shift in christological imagery removed Christ from the midst of the assembly and located him "at the right hand of the Father." In place of Christ, the church's primary intercessor before God, the saints in heaven and the priest on earth were given a mediatorial role, to intercede with God *and* Christ. Ordinary Christians, it came to be believed, had little or no power directly to approach God. They could do so only by asking the priest or by asking the saints to do so for them. Vatican II restored the christo-logical image whereby Christ, in the midst of the assembly and associating the church with his own prayer, is once again primary intercessor. Yet it is the ecclesial Christ, the head with his members, that is envisioned. A strong sense of intercession does not involve Christians asking anyone to intercede for them, not priest, not saints, not even Christ himself. A strong sense of intercession implies that Christians need only name those for whom they pray in the midst of the eucharistic action, and their prayer, by the very fact that it is made within the eucharist, becomes Christ's own prayer to *Abba*. The effectiveness of the eucharist as propitiatory for both the living and the dead depends on this strong sense of intercession. To name someone in prayer in the eucharistic assembly is the highest priestly act of the church. When someone is thus named, even if they be physically absent from the assembly, they are nonetheless brought into its power as the sacrifice of Jesus Christ.

(e) Eucharist as Eschatological Pledge

The eschatological dimension of the eucharist is, for the Western churches at least, the most obscure and least under-stood dimension of eucharistic faith. Some of the Eastern churches (e.g., Chaldean, Maronite) have preserved it more forcefully. In the West it appears in the liturgies of Christian burial, in the time immediately before Advent and in Advent itself. It has been passed on in the religious imagination by way of the hymn attributed to Thomas Aquinas, *O Sacrum Convivium*, where eucharist is called a "pledge of future glory." Beyond that the eschatological dimension of the eucharist lingers in the popular imagination as a banquet somewhere in the distant future which will be the reward of all who have lived faithful Christian lives.

Vatican II brought this eschatolo-gial dimension into fresh focus both theo-logically and liturgically. Theologically it restored the understanding of the church on earth as a "pilgrim people" totally ordered to the Kingdom of God which will be fully established at the eschaton (L.G., 14). And it restored the eucharist as a sacrament of "journey," by recapturing it as the sacrament of ongoing Christian initiation (R.C.I.A.). Liturgically the conciliar reform restored the invo-cation for unity as a major and explicit hope (*epiclesis*), a hope that expresses as well yearning and longing for all to be gathered into one. The reform also restored the sense of "waiting" which is at the heart of eschatological prayer: "We wait in joyful hope for the coming of our savior Jesus Christ" (embolism of Lord's prayer). It offered explicit images of "looking forward": "Then, in your kingdom set free from the corruption of sin and death, we shall sing your glory with every creature" (E.P., III). And it gave sharp notice to the Holy Spirit as the agent of God's unfinished work by naming the Spirit as the one sent "to complete his work on earth and bring us the fullness of grace" (E.P., IV).

It is important to understand how eschatological imagery operates in Christian faith and prayer. These images do in fact invite a "forward look," but it is a forward look for the sake of the present. They do not present a future that will come about of its own accord pro-vided we simply wait long enough. Rather they name the "incompleteness" of things in order to generate yearning and longing for completeness. These images properly serve Christian prayer by offering an image of the future toward which people may freely choose. The yearning and desire that emerges when the vision of completeness meets the experience of incompleteness provides the motive for the choice.

Properly understood the eucharist is an eschatological event. It contains within itself both a vision of completeness and an experience of incompleteness which ought to evoke restless yearning as well as simple thanksgiving. The meal itself celebrates and enacts a union of Christians with Christ and with each other already achieved. This is and must be the experiential base for both thanksgiving and hope. Yet this same union is likewise announced as the proper destiny desired by God of all humanity: "And I, when I am lifted up from the earth, will draw all men to myself"(Jn 12:32). The union that is already achieved exposes as well the union not yet achieved, and invites and challenges all in the assembly to choose beyond what is into the "not yet," toward a greater and greater realization of that future which the eucharist holds out to them.

Something similar can be said about "transubstantiation" which is finally an eschatological term. The context for its intelligibility for faith is the transformation of all creation into Christ (Rom 8:18-25). The reason that the Scholastics were so intent on insuring, however else the term be understood, that creation not be violated in the consecration of bread and wine is that bread and wine, as bits of creation converted into Christ, announce the destiny of all creation, and serve as sacrament (*sacramentum*, seal) of that full transformation yet to be realized. Part of the reverence due to the eucharistic food must include yearning for the day, and choosing towards the day, when this transformation of all creation into Christ will be brought about.

Eschatological imagery, whether eucharistic or not, cannot be seen as prediction of the future. As creation cannot be violated by God's act, neither can human freedom. Images provide "vision" and vision obviates the need for hope. "Now hope that is seen is not hope ... we hope for what we do not see" (Rom 8:24-25). The images do not provide a vision of the outcome, some "thing" that we might hope in. They carry instead the promise or pledge of God spoken in covenant when God raised Jesus from the dead. They provide some "one" in whom we hope. To speak of the eucharist as eschatological pledge finally has little or nothing to do with a banquet somewhere off in the distant future. It names the covenant of God and draws us to the God of covenant in whom alone with Christ we place our trust.

The eschatological dimension of eucharistic faith in not unrelated to the presence of Christ. In fact it is a function of Christ's presence. While the theology of presence insists that Christ's presence is *real*, eschatology reminds us that what is real is only *partially realized* in human life and human history. It sets the fullness of the mystery of Christ, all men and women united to him and all creation transformed into him, as *the eschatological project*. It invites and challenges people to choose toward its realization in history, provides yearning and desire to motivate the choice, and holds up the covenant of God and the God of covenant as the one who is both the source and the object of all Christian hope. The Christ who is present, and present with a purpose, himself yearns for the fulfillment in God's kingdom of his life, death and resurrection, of which eucharist is both remembrance and pledge. He is present in the eucharist to bring this about.

See **Adoration, theology of; Eucharist, reservation of the; Eucharistic devotions; Ecumenism and the liturgy; Traditions, liturgical . . .**

A. Bouley, *From Freedom to Formula* (Washington, D.C.: Catholic University of America Press, 1981). L. Bouyer, *Eucharist* (Notre Dame: University of Notre Dame Press, 1966). B. Childs, *Memory and Tradition in Israel* (Chatham: W.&J. Mackay & Co., 1962). J. Emminghaus, *The Eucharist: Essence, Form, Celebration*, trans. M. O'Connell (Collegeville: Liturgical Press, 1978). T. Guzie, *Jesus and the Eucharist* (New York: Paulist, 1974). E. Kilmartin, *Christian Liturgy* (Kansas City: Sheed and Ward, 1988). J. Powers, *Eucharistic Theology* (New York: Herder and Herder, 1967). E. Schillebeeckx, *The Eucharist* (New York: Sheed and Ward, 1968). K. Seasoltz, ed., *Living Bread, Saving Cup* (Collegeville: Liturgical Press, 1982). D. Stone, *A History of the Doctrine of the Holy*

Eucharist (London: Longmans, Green, and Co., 1909). M. Thurian, *The Mystery of the Eucharist* (Grand Rapids: Eerdmans, 1983). P. Fink, "Perceiving the Presence of Christ," in *Worship* 58 (Jan 84): 17-28; "Living the sacrifice of Christ," in *Worship* 59 (Mar 85): 133-147; "The Challenge of God's *Koinonia*" in *Worship* 59 (Sept 85): 386-403.

PETER E. FINK, S.J.

EUCHARISTIC CHAPEL

The term *eucharistic chapel* is used by the Roman Catholic tradition to designate a place for Christian worship which reserves some of the eucharistic bread in a place of honor.

In the Christian tradition, chapels originated as special rooms or buildings set aside for prayer. Christian ecclesial and political leaders built these chapels. With the increasing reverence for the exemplary lives of the Christian martyrs, shrines/chapels were erected, and placed under the auspices of the local bishop by the 5th century councils. Yet it was not until the increasing popularity of devotion to Christ in the reserved sacrament, especially in the 12th and 13th centuries, that the eucharist was kept in special chapels for adoration.

While reserving some of the eucharistic bread dates back to the patristic period, the purpose for the reservation was broadened in the later centuries. Originally the purpose for reservation was to bring communion (viaticum) to dying Christians and to those who could not worship with the community. Another purpose for the reserved sacrament entered the Christian tradition at a time when the regular reception of communion declined for the laity. One of the distinctive characteristics of late medieval piety was a devotion to the reserved sacrament which expressed itself in adoration of the Blessed Sacrament both in private and in public worship.

By the 16th century, it became customary to place the tabernacle on the altar where the eucharistic action took place. The 1614 Roman Missal prescribed this practice. The Reformers disassociated themselves with the custom, finding this development a medieval accretion which was justified neither in the Bible nor patristic tradition.

In the contemporary liturgical reform stemming from the Second Vatican Council, the Catholic church chose to clarify the primary and original purpose of the reserved eucharist and reemphasize the intimate connection between the action of the eucharistic assembly and the reserved sacrament. Since an altar is a place for action and not reservation, the bishops of the United States have stated that the reserved eucharist be placed in a wall niche, on a pillar or a eucharistic tower rather than on an altar. When possible, the eucharistic chapel should be adjacent to the space for regular Sunday worship. It is hoped that only one altar would be visible to worshippers in order to signify the unity present in Jesus in the church, especially during the one eucharist.

The significance of adoration of the reserved sacrament was reaffirmed and promoted by the Second Vatican Council, though clearly distinguished as secondary and derivative of the primary action of the eucharistic assembly.

The design of the eucharistic chapel should be conducive for quiet prayer. The chapel should provide a contemplative atmosphere which focuses upon the tabernacle. If religious art is used in the eucharistic chapel, care should be exercised so as not to compete with the primary focus upon the tabernacle.

See **Eucharist, reservation of the; Eucharistic worship outside Mass**

International Commission on English in the Liturgy, *Documents on the Liturgy 1963-1979: Conciliar, Papal, and Curial Texts* (Collegeville: The Liturgical Press, 1982). National Conference of Catholic Bishops, *Environment and Art in Catholic Worship* (Washington: United States Catholic Conference Publications, 1978). National Conference of Catholic Bishops, *Bishops' Committee on the Liturgy Newsletter*, XXV (May 1989): 19. H.J. Schroeder. *The Canons and Decrees of the Council of Trent* (Rockford: Tan Books and Publishers, 1978).

T. JEROME OVERBECK, S.J.

EUCHARISTIC LITURGY, NAMES FOR THE

The eucharist has had a number of different names reflecting different theological emphases. Some of these names have been used concurrently in Christian history, so our approach here is to take them in alphabetical rather than chronological order. The names to be discussed are: breaking of bread, communion, eucharist, Lord's Supper, Mass, oblation, and sacrament of the altar.

Breaking of Bread. The "breaking of bread" (*fractio panis*) was the technical name for the eucharist in Acts 2:42, 46; 20:7, 11.

In Judaism the breaking of bread was the ritual tearing of the bread at the beginning of the meal. J. Jeremias argued that the fact that "breaking of bread" refers to the whole eucharistic rite indicates that the eucharist has already become a ritual meal separated from the actual meal (sometimes referred to as the agape). In the Lucan tradition the emphasis in the meal was on the bread. A controverted text in Lk 22:19-20 introduces a second cup in the institution narrative "after supper." The manuscript evidence suggests that this could have been an addition to Luke to bring this institution text into conformity with the other institution texts in the NT. If so, then the sequence of the Last Supper in Lk 22:17-18 is cup-bread, and the interpretative words of Jesus are spoken only over the bread. While this is not the normal eucharistic pattern that emerged in liturgical history, the same sequence can be found in 1 Cor 10:16-17, *Didache*, 9, and *Acts of Thomas*, 27. It would have been a standard practice in Jewish meals to use a cup of wine before the bread was broken. There is no reason why such a practice could not have prevailed in Semitic Christianity. This made the breaking and sharing of the bread a stabler and theologically more important part of the meal. As A. Vööbus suggested, the bread became the vehicle of the presence of Christ—"This is my body." After the resurrection, Jesus was recognized by the two disciples at Emmaus "in the breaking of bread" (Lk 24: 28-35).

This action has never been merely utilitarian. Already in 1 Cor 10:16 the action of breaking the bread received a symbolic interpretation: those who share in the broken bread become one body in Christ. Again, *Didache* 9:4 regarded the broken loaf as a sign of the gathering into one of the children of God. The breaking of bread (fraction) came to have a place in the actions of the developing eucharistic rite. In the Syro-Byzantine and Roman rites the fraction occurred after the Lord's Prayer and before the ministration of holy communion. However, it became the subject of allegorical interpretation during the Middle Ages. A favorite interpretation of the fraction was that it is symbolic of the death of Christ, and the pieces of bread were sometimes arranged in the form of a cross. The theme of the Passion is frequent in the prayers and songs which accompany the fraction in Eastern liturgies.

Because of these allegorical interpretations, the fraction received no place in the Lutheran Mass in the 16th century. In the Reformed celebration of the Lord's Supper, however, the fraction was included in imitation of the actions of Jesus at the Last Supper. A rubric in the 1662 *Book of Common Prayer* required the fraction to take place during the words of institution in the consecration prayer at the words, "he brake." It was perhaps in reaction to this that Gregory Dix emphasized the fraction as one of the four-fold actions of the eucharist: offertory, thanksgiving, fraction, communion. The popularity of Dix's scheme helped to achieve a place for the fraction in reformed contemporary liturgies.

Communion. The eucharist has been from the beginning a fellowship (*koinonia, communio*) among Christians and between Christians and their Lord. So important is this aspect of the eucharist that the name "holy communion" has been applied not only to the reception of the sacrament but also to the eucharistic service itself.

Paul develops the idea of communion/fellowship in 1 Cor 10:17: "we being many are one bread, one body; for we all partake of the one bread." There is a connection between the sacramental body and the ecclesial body. In Acts 2:42 the term *koinonia* occurs in connection with "the breaking of bread." J. Jeremias attempts to distinguish between the *koinonia* (communion) as the Lord's Supper and "the breaking of bread" as the agape meal, but in the 1st century a distinction between the ritual meal and the actual meal is not easy to maintain. The fellowship idea is also prominent in the *Didache* and in Justin Martyr. In Justin the eucharist not only includes and unites all the baptized, but those who are not able to be present at the celebration share in the eucharistic elements through the ministry of the deacons (*Apology* I, 67). The act of receiving communion was from the beginning the chief expression of Christian fellowship. Churches which could practice eucharistic hospitality with one another were in fellowship with one another.

Yngve Brilioth asserted that the idea of the eucharist as the expression of fellowship was weakened during the Middle Ages in the West, when the frequency of reception of holy communion also declined. The recovery of the fellowship aspect of the eucharist, and the emphasis on the frequent reception of holy communion, was one of the most positive and constructive aspects of the Reformation eucharist. The name "holy communion" was applied to the eucharistic liturgy especially in the Anglican and Lutheran traditions. The Council of Trent also urged a more frequent reception of communion, but in post-Tridentine Catholicism this often occurred after Mass. The reforms of the Second Vatican Council again emphasized the reception of communion as a high point of the Mass and underscored the fellowship aspect of the eucharistic celebration.

Eucharist. From about the beginning of the 2nd century the preferred name for the celebration of the Lord's Supper in the Greek writers was *eucharistia,* or thanksgiving.

The term "eucharist" was applied to the meal liturgy of Christians in the letters of Ignatius of Antioch (*Ephesians* 3; *Philadelphians* 4; *Smyrnaeans* 7, 8); in the *Didache* 9, 10; and by Justin Martyr (*Apology* I,66). From the 3rd century on it was applied more to the eucharistic prayer than to the eucharistic liturgy. Tertullian, Cyprian, and Augustine applied the term "eucharist" to the consecrated elements. After Augustine this name dropped out of use in this sense until it was revived by the medieval theologians. In the 20th century the name "eucharist" has again been used to designate the eucharistic liturgy as a whole.

Lord's Supper. In the NT and early Christian literature the term "Lord's Supper" is associated with the eschatological dimension of the eucharistic meal.

Throughout most of Christian history there has been a connection between eucharist and Sunday, between Lord's Supper and Lord's Day. It is the risen Christ who is present at the supper. Paul connects this eucharistic presence with the judgment of Christ (1 Cor 11:17-34). Only those should eat and drink the meal who can withstand eschatological judgment. The selfish behavior of the Corinthians at the supper is turning the Lord's Supper into their own supper; to eat and drink the sacramental elements without discerning the body (i.e. the church) is to become guilty of the body and blood of the Lord. There is a relationship between the ecclesial body and the sacramental body.

As the eschatological dimension of the meal receded, the Lord's Supper became more narrowly identified with the historical Last Supper of Jesus. From the 4th century on, this identification was emphasized by the commemoration of the institution of the Lord's Supper on Maundy Thursday.

The 16th-century Reformers favored the term "Lord's Supper" (*Herrenmahl*) because of its Pauline association. It became the common name for the eucharist in the Reformed tradition.

Mass. "Mass" became the name of the eucharistic liturgy in the Western church. In the Middle Ages the terms "Mass" and "Lord's Supper" were interchangeable. Thus the eucharistic liturgy in the 1549 *Book of Common Prayer* is entitled, "The Supper of the Lord and Holy Communion, commonly called the Mass." The name "Mass" was retained in German and Scandinavian Lutheranism as well as in Roman Catholic use.

The name *missa* derives from the words of dismissal in the Roman rite: *Ite missa est.* This almost untranslatable phrase is probably as old as the Latin rite itself. It was used to conclude every eucharistic liturgy and finally gave its name to the liturgy as a whole. The name "Mass" can serve to remind us of the mission dimension of the eucharist. The eucharist strengthens Christians for service in the world. Revised contemporary eucharistic liturgies have tended to move as directly as possible from the ministration of communion to the dismissal in order to underscore the relationship between the eucharistic celebration and the mission of God in the world.

Oblation. From the Latin *oblatio*, a synonym for "offering." This name focuses on the material elements of the bread and wine.

In the first two centuries there was little emphasis on the material gifts. They received greater emphasis in reaction to Gnostic spiritualism. From the 3rd century on, the bread and wine were actually offered in the offertory procession of the faithful. The oblation was expressed in connection with the anamnesis (*memores ... offerimus*, "remembering ... we offer") already in the *Anaphora of Hippolytus* (ca. A.D. 215). If "eucharist" was the preferred name for the celebration of the meal in the first two centuries, the terms *oblatio* or *sacrificium* were preferred beginning in the 3rd century. This name became more important in the West with the development of the concept of the votive Mass, the eucharist offered for special intentions.

Luther attacked the concept of oblation as a blasphemous reversal of the purpose of the sacrament in *The Babylonian Captivity*: it changes the direction of the sacrament from God to his people to from the people to God, and thereby obscures the gift of communion. Zwingli more than Luther objected that the oblationary character of the Mass denigrated the uniqueness of Christ's sacrifice. Some Reformers, however, were willing to apply the concept of offering to the disposition of the worshippers. No other issue has divided Western Christianity since the 16th century as much as the concept of eucharistic oblation. This affects the language of eucharistic prayer. The recent translation of the *Anaphora of Hippolytus* in the *Lutheran Book of Worship* had to render "we offer to you the bread and the cup" as "we lift this bread and cup before you."

Sacrament of the Altar. This name of the eucharist was used in the Middle Ages and in Luther's catechisms. It draws attention to the meal-character of the eucharist by focusing on the table.

The Latin *altare* means the place where the sacrifice is offered. This need not imply a stone structure. Indeed, the early Christians used wooden tables. The custom of having stone altars is associated with the celebration of the eucharist on the tombs of the saints, thus linking the concepts of altar and tomb. From the 4th century on, altars were built over the tombs of martyrs or confessors, or else relics of the saints were encapsulated in a cavity in the altar mensa.

At the time of the Reformation many stone altars were destroyed and replaced by wooden tables, especially in the Reformed churches. Lutherans, on the other hand, retained altars and referred to the "sacrament of the altar" to emphasize its meal character. Comparative religious studies in the 20th century have rediscovered the origins of sacrifice in the sacred meal. Sacrifice is an act of thanksgiving, and not just an act of propitiation.

Gregory Dix, *The Shape of the Liturgy* (Westminster: Dacre Press, 1945). Joachim Jeremias, *The Eucharistic Words of Jesus*, trans. by Norman Perrin (New York: Charles Scribner's Sons, 1966). Joseph A. Jungmann, *The Mass of the Roman Rite*, II trans. by Francis A. Brunner (New York: Benziger Brothers, 1955). Arthur Vööbus, *The Prelude to the Lukan Passion Narrative* (Stockholm: Estonian Theological Soceity in Exile, 1968). Yngve Brilioth, *Eucharistic Faith and Practice: Evangelical and Catholic*, trans. by A.G. Hebert (London: S.P.C.K., 1965). Werner Elert, *Eucharist and Church Fellowship in the First Four Centuries*, trans. by N.E. Nagel (St. Louis: Concordia, 1966). Willy Rordorf, *Sunday*, trans. by A.A.K. Graham (Philadelphia: Westminster, 1968). Geoffrey Wainwright, *Eucharist and Eschatology* (New York: Oxford University Press, 1981). J.D. Davies, *Worship and Mission* (London: S.P.C.K., 1966). W. Jardine Grisbrooke, "Oblation at the Eucharist," *Studia Liturgica* 3 (1964): 227-39; 4 (1965): 37-55. Josef A. Jungmann, *The Early Liturgy to the Time of Gregory the Great*, trans. by Francis A. Brunner (Notre Dame: University of Notre Dame Press, 1959). Carl F. Wisloff, *The Gift of Communion*, trans. by Joseph M. Shaw (Minneapolis: Augsburg, 1964).

FRANK C. SENN

EUCHARISTIC PRAYERS

The eucharistic prayer is the Christian assembly's Great Thanksgiving over the bread and the cup at the eucharistic liturgy. As such, it is, together with the holy communion, the high point of the Christian sacramental act *par excellence*, the eucharistic celebration. In its more developed forms, God is praised and thanked, the accomplishments of Jesus Christ are remembered, and God is asked to send the Holy Spirit upon the gifts of bread and wine and upon those who will share them. It is both a table prayer in view of consuming the bread and the wine in community and a liturgical action that expresses and nourishes Christian faith and discipleship.

Theology of the Eucharistic Prayer

Liturgical theological reflection since the early 1970s has attempted to uncover the significance of this prayer as it functions in the Christian assembly. Thus, as a prayer of thanksgiving, the eucharistic prayer underlines God's graciousness toward creation. God is "philanthropos," lover of the human race, who has acted in creation and in history on behalf of people. Most of all in Jesus Christ God has brought salvation to humankind. The assembly therefore acknowledges in praise and thanksgiving what God has accomplished for it.

At the same time, the eucharistic prayer is a prayer of remembrance, of *anamnesis*. In it God's work in Jesus Christ is recalled. Theologically this recall is understood to manifest the continuing present efficacy of the past acts of Jesus Christ. Thus when the assembly, in obedience to Jesus' command to do the supper in remembrance of him, recalls his death, resurrection, ascension and coming again, the effects of the past acts are made present in the assembly in a context of eschatological anticipation.

As its Greek designation indicates, the eucharistic prayer is also a prayer of offering, an *anaphora*. In it the assembly recalls the once-for-all offering of Jesus Christ and joins to it in acknowledgment an offering of praise and thanksgiving over the bread and the wine. Like all nourishment, these are gifts from God's creation; yet in this act they become for the assembly the body and blood of Jesus Christ, whose own words at the Last Supper are recalled in the prayer. It is in this way that the community often explicitly expresses its own awareness of being joined to the once-for-all offering of Jesus Christ.

Besides being a prayer of thanksgiving the eucharistic prayer is also a prayer of supplication, in particular that the Holy Spirit might come upon the gifts and upon those who will share in them. From this perspective the thanksgiving and the supplication are intimately joined to one another in view of the eating and drinking of this bread and this wine. Thus, like a home meal grace, the prayer acknowledges that God is the source of all life and holiness, but it also prays that these particular gifts of bread and wine be linked to the bread and the wine over which Jesus spoke his own interpretative words the night before he died. Thus, the supplication is placed in the context of the memorial thanksgiving and the two become complementary components of the eucharistic prayer.

Recalling as it does the reconciliation willed by God and won by Jesus Christ, the prayer has an underlying theme of reconciliation because the assembly is the gathering of those who have been baptized "for the forgiveness of sins." This reconciliation reaches its highest expression in the holy communion, to which the table prayer is intimately bound. The assembly's sharing of the bread and the cup, the signs of Jesus Christ's body broken and his blood poured out for the forgiveness of sins, manifests that the church is a community of reconciliation because it has accepted the reconciliation won for it in Jesus Christ.

Finally, while the acts of thanksgiving and praise, remembrance and offering, and supplication, flow from the trinitarian structure of the prayer, and reconciliation is a consequence of the prayer, the whole prayer is seen to function as a prayer of sanctification or consecration. By it the priestly people finds itself renewed in its baptismal commitment, and the gifts of bread and wine become for the assembly the body and blood of Jesus Christ, whose consumption unites the communicants more deeply in the body of Christ, the church. This consecration is intensely manifested in the recitation of the Lord's words and in the petition that God send the Holy Spirit upon the gifts and upon those who receive them.

In the various eucharistic prayers, one theme may receive more emphasis than another. Thus, before the reform of the Second Vatican Council, the particular eucharistic prayer called "the Roman canon" was experienced by Roman Catholics especially as a prayer in which the consecration took place and the sacrifice was made. It is no exaggeration to say that, in the churches of the West, the perception of the richness of the eucharistic prayer was severely restricted. In general there was only the Roman canon, vernacular eucharistic prayers in some Protestant churches that had "corrected" the canon, but themselves needing correction, or the reading from the NT of the account of the institution with or without surrounding prayers. For collections of eucharistic prayers in English, see Jasper and Cuming for early and reformed eucharistic prayers, and Thurian and Wainwright for contemporary eucharistic prayer texts in addition to a selection of ancient ones.

Reform of the Eucharistic Prayer

Although the *Constitution on the Sacred Liturgy* had not spoken of the reform of the eucharistic prayer, members of Coetus X of the Consilium (the Congregation of Rites) met to discuss the possibility of reworking the Roman canon. This quickly led to a discussion and proposals for creating new eucharistic prayers by returning to the sources. On May 23, 1968, the Consilium announced Paul VI's approval of three new eucharistic prayers together with eight new prefaces for the Roman rite. On November 1, 1974, the Congregation for Worship presented on an experimental basis two prayers for Masses of reconciliation and three prayers for Masses with children. Meanwhile the corpus of prefaces in the Roman Missal had increased to more than eighty. Thus the Roman church enriched its eucharistic euchology by adopting the practice of the Eastern churches of having a number of eucharistic prayers rather than a single one and by adding considerably to its own practice of having variable prefaces for the Roman canon and for Eucharistic Prayers II and III. On all this, see Bugnini for the Consilium background and Mazza for the history and theology of the prayers.

The creation of the new Roman eucharistic prayers was greatly influenced by the anaphoras found in the liturgies of the Eastern churches. In the Byzantine rite since the 6th century, the eucharistic prayer was called simply the anaphora. The anaphoras in the Eastern churches are divided into three large families: the Antiochene or Greek West Syrian, the Alexandrian or Egyptian, and the Syriac East Syrian or Chaldean. The division into families results from the placement of the component parts in the anaphora.

In the collection of Hängii and Pahl, the place assigned to the intercessions in the anaphora is the distinguishing criterion in this system. In the Antiochene family, the intercessions are found after the single epiclesis toward the end of the prayer; in the Alexandrian family they occur at the beginning of the prayer before the sanctus; and in the East Syrian family they come before the epiclesis at the end of the prayer. Thus the arrangement of the component parts of the classically developed anaphoras for the Antiochene family are: dialogue, praise and thanksgiving, introduction to the sanctus, sanctus, post-sanctus prayer, institution narrative, anamnesis, epiclesis, intercessions and doxology. In the Alexandrian family, they run: dialogue, praise and thanksgiving, intercessions, introduction to the sanctus, sanctus, post-sanctus epicletic prayer, institution narrative, anamnesis, a second epiclesis and doxology. In the East Syrian family, the arrangement is: dialogue, praise and thanksgiving, introduction to the sanctus, sanctus, post-sanctus prayer, institution narrative (may be lacking in the Anaphora of Addai and Mari), anamnesis, intercessions, epiclesis and doxology.

The Roman canon, *sui generis*, shows affinities with the Alexandrian structure. The new eucharistic prayers of the Roman rite, however, follow the Antiochene structure, since they group the intercessions just before the doxology. At the same time they retain an Alexandrian structure by the presence of two epicleses, one before and one after the institution narrative. The principal model for the new Roman prayers was the Egyptian anaphora of Basil or Alexandrian Basil, which follows the Antiochene structure. An adaptation of the spirit and structure of this prayer became Roman Eucharistic Prayer IV. It is meant to illustrate a fully developed eucharistic prayer and is recommended for use on especially solemn occasions. It is particularly noteworthy for its preface which praises God for creation and for its long post-sanctus prayer that relates the history of salvation. For a discussion of the principal Byzantine anaphoras of Basil and John Chrysostom, see Schulz.

For its Eucharistic Prayer II, the

Roman rite adapted the eucharistic prayer of Hippolytus from the *Apostolic Tradition* (c. 215) to its modified Antiochene structure. This meant that to Hippolytus' original prayer was added a sanctus, a post-sanctus transition to an epiclesis on the gifts, and intercessions. At the same time some of the original wording of Hippolytus was also changed. Coetus X thought that simply to adopt the prayer of Hippolytus would be an act of archaism; however, in 1983, *I.C.E.L.'s* subcommittee on eucharistic prayers, noting the prayer's inclusion in the revised service books of several churches, prepared a translation of it for possible eventual adoption by its members.

Eucharistic Prayer III appears to be modelled on the Roman canon, insofar as it has no preface of its own, but it is also adapted to the Antiochene structure with explicit epicleses in the Alexandrian places. At the same time, its creators were conscious of operating with the freedom of Gallican and Mozarabic models, from which certain ideas and phrases were woven into the new prayer. This extraordinary explanation of the origins of Eucharistic Prayer III is perhaps an extreme case of adaptation, but it is illustrative of much contemporary adaptation of eucharistic prayers, and even that of the early church, in a period of renewal, creativity and liturgical borrowing.

This recovery of the eucharistic prayer was part of the liturgical agenda of many of the Western churches. The phenomenon of intense liturgical creativity outside parish settings, in small groups, in homes or in colleges and universities led to an explosion of unofficial eucharistic prayers that were filling the gap while waiting for official eucharistic prayers, and even rivaling them when they finally appeared. Thus in the 1960s there was a whole climate of creativity and renewal, some of whose results have been studied by the present author.

In the non-Roman Western churches, liturgical committees were assembled to create eucharistic prayers. Many of these churches were heirs to the 16th century abolition of the Roman canon in favor of a communion service marked by exhortations, admonitions, and doctrinal explanation. In those cases where there was a eucharistic prayer in place, revision committees expressed some dissatisfaction with it either in terms of its language, its theological stresses or omissions, or its structure.

In the United States, the reforms of the Episcopal, Lutheran, Methodist, and Presbyterian churches each have their own story to tell. But it is a story that is repeated in Canada, in the worldwide Anglican communion, and in the Reformed churches on the European continent. While many options taken by these churches are similar to the Roman ones, others are quite different. For example, many favor the pure Antiochene structure over the Alexandrian modified structure of the Roman rite, or they have prayers with various structures. The Episcopal church's eucharistic prayers, Forms 1 and 2 for use on certain occasions, allow for some freedom of improvisation unusual in churches that favor fixed texts. In many Protestant churches, alongside new eucharistic prayers are options that permit the communion service structure of the Reformation liturgies. In some churches this remains the preferred form. But where eucharistic prayers have been revised or introduced, traditional prayers are found alongside those that attempt to achieve a more contemporary idiom with emphasis on contemporary theological themes expressed in inclusive language. In the official committees, battles have been fought over the inclusions of an offering or offering language in the prayer, of an epiclesis and intercessions, of certain traditional formulas and even of single words. For the texts of the eucharistic prayers of the worldwide Anglican communion, see Buchanan. For a study of the composition of American eucharistic prayers, see Senn.

Parts of the Eucharistic Prayer

In his Apostolic Constitution introducing the Roman missal, Paul VI had called the addition of new eucharistic prayers to the Roman rite the chief innovation of its reform and urged their explanation to the faithful. On June 7, 1968, the Consilium issued statements on the structure and elements that make up the eucharistic prayer, and section 55 of the General Instruction to the Roman Missal listed the constitutive parts of the prayer. These parts, taken in the Antiochene order, may be briefly described.

The eucharistic prayer begins with an opening dialogue that serves to unite presider and assembly in offering its Great Thanksgiving with their hearts lifted up. Thus at the outset the prayer is seen as the assembly's prayer and not simply that of the presider, who proclaims it in the assembly's name. The acclamations throughout the prayer, here in the dialogue, at the sanctus, at the anamnesis, either before or after it, and at the "Amen" at the end of the prayer, all show that the prayer belongs to the entire assembly. In fact, a characteristic of many new eucharistic prayers is to increase the congregational participation by means of acclamations. This development is seen in some of the new eucharistic prayers of nearly all churches. In the Roman rite it is found particularly in children's Eucharistic Prayer II.

In continuation of the assembly's response to the presider's invitation to give thanks, the preface follows with motives for giving thanks. In the invariable prefaces of the anaphoras, the focus is principally on God and what God has accomplished on behalf of humankind in creation and redemption. In the variable prefaces of the Roman rites and those of other Western churches, some aspect of the mystery of faith is generally singled out. Its content is influenced by the liturgical season, feast day, or particular ritual celebration. When the children's eucharistic prayers are used, motives for thanksgiving may be invited from the children before beginning the dialogue.

It has become traditional in the eucharistic prayer to link the praise of God by the assembly to that of the heavenly liturgy so that with one voice all creation praises God. The Sanctus, adapted from Isaiah 6, and its introduction, which in some ancient prayers was heavily influenced by Ezek 10, Dan 7:10. and Rev 4:8-10, form a liturgical unit. To the Sanctus was added an acclamation from Mt 21:9, a psalmic adaptation to Jesus Christ, "Blessed is he who comes in the name of the Lord."

After this Sanctus/Benedictus, the prayer traditionally develops, however briefly, some image from it such as the holiness of God or the idea of fullness. In many contemporary prayers this leads into a remembrance of the role of God and Jesus Christ in the history of salvation. In Eucharistic Prayers II and III, it serves principally as a transition to the first epiclesis upon the gifts of bread and wine that they might become the body and blood of Christ.

The institution narrative follows and is thereby made part of the prayer. In the liturgical tradition this narrative is often worded differently from any one of its forms in the NT. By its very structure, length and content, which recalls not only what Jesus did at the Last Supper but what the assembly is doing right now, it draws attention to itself and is often accompanied by ritual gestures and, as in some of the anaphoras, with acclamations of Amen.

In many liturgies a memorial acclamation follows the institution narrative, but it also takes place after the anamnesis, where it may make a transition to the intercessions. The acclamation in the Roman prayers is addressed to Christ, whereas in the tradition, with some exceptions, the entire eucharistic prayer is addressed to the Father.

The anamnesis or memorial prayer recapitulates what Jesus has accomplished for us. It is made as a response to the command of Jesus that the meal be done in remembrance of him. The assembly makes explicit this remembrance by referring, among other events, to Jesus' life, death, resurrection, ascension and promise to come again. In addition to the heightened eschatological sense that may be developed at this point, many eucharistic prayers join an offering to the remembrance. This makes explicit the assembly's sense of being united to the redemptive act of Christ. Thus, the assembly in this context of dynamic relationships offers its gifts of bread and wine, the symbols of the body and blood of Jesus Christ, to God.

In typical Antiochene anaphoras this leads to the petition that the Holy Spirit come upon the gifts and upon those who will communicate in them. Since the Roman prayers have already petitioned the descent of the Spirit upon the gifts earlier in the prayer, they limit themselves here to a petition for unity among the worshippers who will participate in the gifts.

For most churches the intercessions follow. In certain anaphoras these are quite developed, whereas in some contemporary Protestant eucharistic prayers they are omitted since they are seen as duplicating the prayer of the faithful. In the new Roman prayers, as in the Roman canon, there are not only intercessions for the living and the dead but expressions of ecclesial communion across time and space. The Roman canon had intercessions both before and after the institution narrative.

The eucharistic prayer closes with a doxology, a brief prayer of praise, which in the Roman prayers is worded so as to emphasize the mediatorial role of Jesus Christ within the trinitarian framework, whereas in other anaphoras it is worded to present Father, Son and Holy Spirit in the traditional order. The whole prayer thus returns to the praise of God and brings into focus its very trinitarian structure. The congregation ratifies the prayer with its Amen, often called the "Great Amen" since it follows the Great Thanksgiving.

This Antiochene outline has been fleshed out by the creators of contemporary eucharistic prayers, who by their theological choices modify the language of the component parts to give expression to their faith. At present, however, it is this structure and its component parts that have led to a remarkable convergence in the reform of eucharistic prayers throughout the world.

Scholarly Research

Research into the history and variety of eucharistic prayers has played and continues to play a remarkable role in the recovery of the eucharistic prayer in the contemporary period. In recent times researchers have studied the Jewish blessing or *berakah* as the ancestor of the Christian eucharistic prayer while others have concentrated on Jewish verb forms related to thanksgiving. The Jewish table grace or *birkat ha-mazon* has been proposed as the probable place of origin of the Christian table prayer. The structure of this Jewish prayer, of which we have no extant fixed form before the destruction of the temple, has been reconstructed into a blessing of God, followed by a thanksgiving and a supplication. Scholars have compared this reconstructed prayer with later Christian prayers, most notably those of the *Didache* (c. 100, but may be earlier). This has led to a consideration of bi-partite and tri-partite structures of table prayers, the former divided into thanksgiving and supplication and the latter into praise, thanksgiving and supplication. For all this see, Heinemann, Ledogar, and Talley. Since the earliest prayers were improvised, that is, were not written fixed prayers, but enjoyed variation according to circumstances and the oratorical gifts of the speaker, while no doubt following a known outline and a certain traditional vocabulary, there is very little evidence on which to base firm conclusions about the form and content of the early eucharistic prayers. Bouley has studied extensively the movement from oral improvisation to written texts.

Other research has attempted to discover how the institution narrative entered the prayer. In the prayer of Hippolytus it is in the thanksgiving part, whereas in the Roman canon it is in the supplicatory part. In other cases it is suggested it may have stood outside the prayer or it may not have been present at all except by some reference to the Last Supper. It may have entered alone or together with the anamnesis. In any event, when and where it entered a particular prayer, it generally had effects on the theological emphasis of the prayer and could reshape some of the elements preceding it.

Other lines of research have explored the possibility that the Christian eucharistic prayer was influenced by the Jewish thanksgiving offering called the *todah*. They trace the development of some very early eucharistic prayers out of the bread blessing at the beginning of the Jewish meal, and illustrate certain resemblances among the prayers that may constitute a supposed genealogy of the eucharistic prayer.

All these hypotheses have attempted to deal (1) with the relationship of Christian eucharistic prayers to Jewish prayer forms, both domestic and synagogal, (2) with the variety of structures exhibited by the eucharistic prayer within the great tradition and outside it, (3) with the variety of emphases found in the eucharistic prayer itself, and (4) with when and with what effect various component parts entered into an original dominant pattern. They do this without understanding this to be some sort of ur-anaphora or even an ur-pattern.

Most recently attention has been drawn to a suggestion that has attempted to move back beyond the Jewish *berakoth* into the OT for the distant roots of the Christian anaphora. The thesis of Giraudo points to a literary genre called the *todah*, exemplified in Neh 9:6-37. This *todah* would be a confession, in the sense of a creed, an admission of failure or a complaint, composed of a celebratory commemorative part (an anamnesis) and a petitionary part (an epiclesis). God's great acts on behalf of God's people are recalled, and this people now asks that God accomplish for them a specific request. Inserted into one of the two parts is a pertinent scriptural passage, an embolism, that has to do with God's promise. In the Christian anaphora, this embolism would be the institution narrative and depending on whether it is inserted into the anamnetic part or the supplicatory part gives a principle of classification for the anaphora. The Jewish *berakah* would also have its roots in this *todah* genre.

What is interesting about this thesis is how it takes up so much of the previous research already mentioned and attempts to put it in a larger, coherent framework. Other scholars have objected, however, that the thesis' literary genre, the *todah*, is not sufficiently grounded, and that when it is applied to later Christian anaphoras it forces them in their variety into a procrustean bed. However, serious study of all the implications of this thesis has hardly been done in English, and it is only on the verge of being incorporated into the research.

Final Assessment

The recovery of the eucharistic prayer

within the Western churches has played its part in an ecumenical convergence that has been massive. Many Catholic, Episcopal, and Protestant congregations are praying at the eucharistic assembly in prayer forms that are very similar. Not too long ago this was hardly conceivable. The very theology of the eucharistic prayer as one addressed to the Father, having a trinitarian structure, in which God is praised for creation, Jesus Christ's entire paschal mystery is remembered, and the Holy Spirit is invoked in an eschatological context, means that Christians separated into confessional churches are beginning more and more to worship like one another and are being formed liturgically in a similar way. They come to regard the eucharistic prayer as the Great Thanksgiving and as their prayer precisely as an assembly.

With the publication and use by the World Council of Churches of the eucharistic prayer of the Lima liturgy, a stage in the development of the worldwide recovery of the eucharistic prayer was reached. Recently with the approval by Roman authorities in 1988 of the liturgy of the Mass for the dioceses of Zaire, which have adapted for native African congregations the Roman eucharistic rite, a new impetus has been given toward the inculturation of the eucharistic prayer in the Catholic church. This joins the efforts of other churches as we enter more and more into the phase of inculturation of liturgical prayer.

At the same time, the continuing study of early eucharistic prayers is leading to suggestions of various models of eucharistic prayers for different occasions. Musicians are increasingly turning their efforts to sung eucharistic prayers and exploring various settings so that the impression given of a eucharistic prayer with some sung parts yields to the idea of a sung eucharistic prayer capable of uniting presider and congregation ever more closely.

For the English speaking Catholic church in North America and abroad I.C.E.L. has shown leadership in the development of new eucharistic prayers. Not only has it prepared a study edition of the eucharistic prayer of Hippolytus in 1983 and one of the anaphora of Basil in 1985, but, after many years of consultation, it also issued in 1984 and revised in 1986 Eucharistic Prayer A, which has been approved by several bishops' conferences and now awaits Roman approval. This indicates some of the movement in the Roman Catholic church, but there is also creative movement in the Protestant churches, and it would appear that the reforms referred to throughout this article may be only a preparation for another stage of the ongoing liturgical reform even while interiorization of the spirituality of the eucharistic prayer and its catechesis remain a present concern.

See **Traditions, liturgical. . .**

Allen Bouley, *From Freedom to Formula* (Washington, D.C.: Catholic University of America Press, 1981). Colin O. Buchanan, ed., *Latest Anglican Liturgies 1976-1984* (London: SPCK, 1985). Annibale Bugnini, *La Riforma Liturgica (1948-1975)* (Rome: Edizioni Liturgiche, 1983). Cesare Giraudo, *La Struttura Letteraria della Preghiera Eucharistica* (Rome: Biblical Institute Press, 1981). Anton Hängii and Irmgard Pahl, *Prex Eucharistica* (Fribourg, Switzerland: Editions Universitaires, 1968). Joseph Heinemann, *Prayer in the Talmud: Forms and Patterns* (Berlin, New York: Walter de Gruyter, 1977). R.C.D. Jasper and G.J. Cuming, *Prayers of the Eucharist: Early and Reformed*, 3rd ed. rev. and enlarged (New York: Pueblo Publishing Co., 1987). Robert J. Ledogar, *Acknowledgment: Praise Verbs in the Early Greek Anaphora* (Rome: Herder, 1968). Enrico Mazza, *The Eucharistic Prayers of the Roman Rite*, trans. Matthew J. O'Connell (New York: Pueblo Publishing Co., 1986). Irmgard Pahl, *Coena Domini I* (Fribourg, Switzerland: Editions Universitaires, 1983). John Barry Ryan, *The Eucharistic Prayer: A Study in Contemporary Liturgy* (New York: Paulist Press, 1974). Hans-Joachim Schulz, *The Byzantine Liturgy: Symbolic Structure and Faith Expression*, trans. Matthew J. O'Connell (New York: Pueblo Publishing Co., 1986). Frank Senn, ed., *New Eucharistic Prayers* (New York: Paulist Press, 1987). Kenneth Stevenson, *Eucharist and Offering* (New York: Pueblo Publishing Co., 1986). Thomas J. Talley, "The Literary Structure of the Eucharistic

Prayer," *Worship* 58 (1984): 404-420. Max Thurian and Geoffrey Wainwright, eds., *Baptism and Eucharist: Ecumenical Convergence in Celebration* (Geneva: World Council of Churches and Grand Rapids: Wm. B. Eerdmans, 1983).

JOHN BARRY RYAN

EUCHARISTIC WORSHIP OUTSIDE MASS

Thirty years ago an article on eucharistic devotion and worship outside of Mass would have begun something like this: "Popular eucharistic devotions such as we know them today began in the late Middle Ages." Such a statement would have expressed the continuous popularity and substantial uniformity of eucharistic worship outside Mass from the 13th to the mid-20th century. With the implementation of the post-conciliar eucharistic reforms there has been a shift in the expression of eucharistic devotion and piety. The present article describes briefly the long period of continuity and its relationship to the eucharistic practice of the church of the first millennium, explains the shifts in post-conciliar eucharistic worship outside Mass, identifies doctrinal themes proposed in post-conciliar teaching concerning the eucharist which help us understand the shift, and finally, considers the relevance of eucharistic worship outside Mass for ongoing liturgical renewal.

Eucharistic Worship Outside Mass Before Vatican II

Public forms of eucharistic devotions outside Mass before Vatican Council II consisted in the annual celebration of Forty Hours Devotion, regular celebrations of benediction either with or without other popular devotions, holy hours of adoration, and perpetual adoration carried on by pious groups or by religious communities. The most common private form of eucharistic devotions were visits to churches and chapels to pray before the reserved sacrament.

Even the frequent reception of holy communion during Mass had much in common with the devotional spirit of eucharistic worship outside Mass. Those who received holy communion daily or frequently were quite conscious that the practice expressed their concern for their personal holiness and their individual moral reform. Frequent communion was a kind of index of the intensity of this concern and of devotional fervor.

It is obvious that holy communion and worship of the eucharist outside Mass is based on the church's faith in Christ's enduring presence in the eucharistic species. In the sacrifice of the Mass Christ the Lord *begins* to be sacramentally present under the appearance of bread and wine and *remains* present as long as the eucharist is reserved in our churches and oratories. "Day and night he is in our midst; full of grace and truth, he dwells among us" (see S.C.R. Decr. EuchSacr, n.2).

This faith that Christ remains under the appearance of bread and wine in the reserved eucharist is implicit in the eucharistic practice of the 2nd century. Justin Martyr, describing a Sunday celebration of the eucharist about 150, reports that the deacons carried the food over which thanks had been offered to those not present (see *First Apology*, nos. 66, 67).

St. Augustine witnesses to the early church's faith in the real presence of Christ in the eucharistic species when he speaks of the adoration which is expressed in the inclinations before receiving the sacrament: "No one eats this flesh unless he has first adored . . . not only do we not sin by adoring, but we would sin by not adoring" (*Ennar. in ps.* 98, 9, P.L. 37, 1264c).

The first significant evidence of worship of the reserved sacrament outside the liturgical functions is linked to the eucharistic controversies of the 9th century. These controversies along with those of the 11th century focused both theology and devotion more and more upon the real presence of Christ in the eucharistic species. This enriched eucharistic devotion by showing the fittingness of adoring and worshipping Christ in the eucharist outside Mass. However this development had the negative effect of isolating this worship from the celebration of Mass itself.

The great development however in eucharistic worship and devotion outside Mass came in the 13th century. During that century worship of the reserved sacrament became an object of universal concern in the Latin rite church of the West. The establishment of the Feast of Corpus Christi as a great feast of the liturgical year in the 14th century gave this popular devotion official approval.

Because of the controversies concerning the real presence of Christ in the eucharist at the time of the Council of Trent, the doctrine of the real presence was proclaimed with new clarity and insistence. We have architectural evidence of the enthusiasm with which devotion to the Blessed Sacrament was promoted during the 17th and early 18th centuries. Numerous baroque and rococo high altars are designed as shrines for enthroning the elaborately designed monstrances. Impressive too were the elaborately designed settings for the reservations of the Blessed Sacrament from Holy Thursday until Holy Saturday.

In the European religious revival of the 19th century, devotion to the Blessed Sacrament played an important part. Many of the religious congregations begun during that period gave an important place to the devotion in their religious practice. One might say that much of the contemplative spirit of that period was focused upon worship of the reserved eucharist. Devotion to the eucharist was also closely linked to devotion to the Sacred Heart in this century.

The 19th century and the beginning decades of the 20th brought with them the beginnings of the Liturgical Movement. Pope Pius XII made clear in his encyclical on the liturgy, *Mediator Dei* (1947), that the progress of the Liturgical Movement was not to allow the adoration of the reserved sacrament and visits to the Lord in the tabernacle to be neglected. In his allocution to the participants of the International Congress on Pastoral Liturgy (September 22, 1956), the pope in his own way prepared for the post-conciliar emphasis upon the unity of the celebration of Mass and the worship or the eucharist outside Mass. He said that awareness of the unity of the worship or adoration of the eucharist and the act of sacrifice was more important than a realization of their differences: "It is one and the same Lord who is immolated on the altar and honored in the tabernacle" (see *Papal Teachings*, n. 816).

Shift in Eucharistic Devotion and Piety

During the first decade of post-conciliar liturgical reform, attention was focused on implementing the changes in the celebration of Mass. Communities learned how to participate in the celebration actively and fully. As a consequence, attention was more upon the eucharistic mystery as actualized in the celebration of Mass and less upon the worship of the eucharist outside Mass. During this same period the annual celebration of Forty Hours Devotion and regular celebrations of benedictions, which were once popular expressions of worship of the eucharist outside Mass, all but disappeared in an impressive number of churches and chapels. Their disappearance is an external sign of a shift in eucharistic devotion and piety.

A second external sign of a shift is that the number of those receiving holy communion has increased dramatically since the implementation of the liturgical reforms. Almost everyone present in a church or chapel for the celebration of Mass participates sacramentally in the eucharistic banquet.

We need to reflect upon the interiority underlying these changes. It is simpler to begin with the increased number of those receiving holy communion. Frequent communion, as promoted and experienced in the first four decades of this century, was motivated by a concern for one's personal spiritual growth and union with Christ. That almost all those who come to church for Sunday Mass at the present time receive holy communion is an index of the success of the efforts to achieve full and active participation. Receiving holy communion is the normal, expected way of participating fully and actively in the eucharistic celebration. One would call attention to oneself by not coming to the table of Christ's body and blood.

When we reflect upon the decline in popularity of Forty Hours Devotion and benediction, we sense a discontinuity in faith awareness between participation in the celebration of Mass and worship of the eucharist outside Mass in the post-conciliar church. The difference is experienced in the dynamic of prayer of praise and adoration. The celebration of the eucharist is the culmination of our worship of God, of our prayer of praise, thanksgiving and adoration. In the doxology of the eucharistic prayer we lift up the eucharistic elements, not to praise Christ present in them, but rather through him, with him, in him, in the unity of the Holy Spirit to offer the Father all glory and honor. In a word we are alive in faith to the dynamic of Christ's presence among us, which is to lift us up with himself to the Father in praise.

Up to this point at least we have yet to find a prayer of adoration of the eucharist outside Mass which deepens the same dynamic which we find in the celebration itself. We have yet to find a unity of the two movements of eucharistic worship which will help us enter into the fullness of the eucharistic mystery.

Doctrinal Themes Emphasized in Post-conciliar Teaching on the Eucharist

An important source of the church's official post-conciliar teaching on worship of the eucharist outside Mass is the ritual book, *Holy Communion and the Worship of the Eucharist Outside Mass*, promulgated by the Sacred Congregation for Divine Worship with the decree, *Eucharistiae sacramentum* (21 June 1973). This ritual book in turn draws heavily upon an earlier instruction of the Congregation of Rites, *Eucharisticum mysterium* (1967), on worship of the eucharist.

The first doctrinal theme explaining the shift in eucharistic devotion since Vatican II is that of the centrality of the celebration of Mass in the church's life. The opening sentence of the ritual book referred to above states this centrality for both the universal church and its local congregations. The actual celebration of Mass is " ... truly the origin and the purpose of the worship that is shown to the eucharist outside Mass" (see S.C.R. Instr. EuchSacr, no. 2). The primary concern of this new ritual is to promote eucharistic devotion and worship outside Mass by integrating it both doctrinally and liturgically with the celebration of the eucharist. As is clear from the previous section, we seem sufficiently focused upon the celebration of Mass. It remains to attend to and promote the worship of the eucharist outside Mass in order to consider the eucharistic mystery in all its fullness (see S.C.R. EuchSacr, no. 5).

A second doctrinal theme emphasized in post-conciliar documents is the multiple presence of Christ gradually unfolded in the eucharistic celebration. Christ's real presence in the eucharistic elements is considered the culmination of this unfolding. Faith awareness of this multiple presence of Christ unfolded in the eucharistic celebration is surely one of the strongest supports for prayerful interiority at each moment in the celebration of Mass. It is significant that it finds one of its most compelling formulations in the ritual book on worship of the eucharist outside Mass. The truth of the multiple presence of Christ unfolded in the celebration of Mass is an important doctrinal theme for promoting worship of the eucharist outside Mass.

Significance of Worship of the Eucharist Outside Mass for the Ongoing Liturgical Renewal

The eucharist is *mysterium fidei*, the mystery of the death and resurrection of the Lord made present to be his church's sacrifice and the spiritual food and drink for her pilgrimage. Only the Spirit can open our eyes to recognize the Lord in our midst. The most likely time for this to transpire is in a prayer-filled breaking of the bread.

It is the purpose of the worship of the eucharist outside Mass to rehearse for such a prayer-filled breaking of the bread. A most stimulating support for such a prayerful rehearsal is found in the paragraphs of the ritual book, *Holy Communion and the Worship of the Eucharist Outside Mass*, describing prayer before the reserved sacrament (see S.C.R., EuchSacr, nos. 8-81). Such prayer before Christ the Lord sacramentally present in the reserved eucharist cannot but deepen the interiority of active participation in the celebration of Mass.

A sign that such prayer is considered important is the architectural efforts being made to provide more intimate prayer space in churches before the tabernacle. Satisfying one's individual longing for personal union with Christ was an important motive in the past for attracting individuals to pray before the Blessed Sacrament. Such longing exists today. It needs direction.

The private prayer of individuals itself needs direction. It needs to be formed and practiced in the forms of ritual worship of the eucharist outside Mass. We have been given a ritual book with these forms. These forms provide the Lord with opportunities for more leisurely walks with his pilgrim disciples whose minds and hearts are filled with meaningless events. His spirit will give them light and warmth, and they will want to stay on with him. From well-celebrated rites of exposition and benediction their hunger and their thirst for him will grow. There will be a deeper recognition of him in the next breaking of the bread. The pilgrim church will be satisfied with the bread of life in communion and find deeper union with him and through him with the Father and each other. He will send his refreshed and renewed ecclesial body forth to feed a spiritually hungry world.

See **Eucharist, theology of; Adoration, theology of; Body of Christ; Eucharist, reservation of; Eucharistic chapel**

Emile Bertaud, Robert Fortin, Eugenio G. Nuñez, Giuseppe Vassali, "Devotion eucharistique," *Dictionnaire de Spiritualité*, t. IV, premiere partie (Paris: Beauchesne, 1960), cols. 1621-1647. Nathan Mitchell, *Cult and Controversy: The Worship of the Eucharist Outside Mass* (New York: Catholic Book Publishing Company, 1976). NCCB, *Eucharistic Worship and Devotion Outside Mass*, Study Text 11 (Washington: U.S.C.C., 1987).

EVERETT A. DIEDERICH, S.J.

EUCHOLOGY

Refers to a collection of prayers or a prayer book, from the Greek *Euchologion*, as in the *Euchology of Serapion of Thmuis*, which is sometimes called a prayer book or a sacramentary. The term appears more frequently in French, *Eucologe*, less frequently in English.

FRANK C. SENN

EVANGELISTS, FEASTS OF

Evangelists, those who recorded the

good new of Jesus Christ for the good of the Christian community and the whole world, are honored by four feasts: St. Mark (Apr. 25); St. Matthew (Sept. 21); St. Luke (Oct. 18); and St. John (Dec. 27).

History

Commemoration of John, the Beloved Disciple and the revealer of the mystery of the Word, is a most ancient celebration, found already in the Veronese (Leonine) sacramentary (ca. 550; actually a compendium of texts rather than a true sacramentary) for the days after Christmas, though no exact date is given. This saint has been particularly associated with the mystery of the incarnation at Christmas: the prologue of his gospel has been read on Christmas day since the 5th century (see the sermons of Leo the Great [d. 461]). He became the object of great popular piety in the Middle Ages, including the story of his emerging unscathed from a cauldron of boiling oil at Rome's Latin Gate; hence the Feast of St. John at the Latin Gate (May 6; abolished in 1960).

Mark was the associate of Peter and Paul and was venerated early on in Alexandria, where he was said to have been bishop. His relics were transferred to Venice in the 6th century. His feast entered the Roman calendar in the 10th and 11th centuries.

According to tradition, the tax collector Matthew preached in Ethiopia. It was from there that his relics supposedly were transferred to Salerno in the 10th century, and a basilica in his honor erected there and dedicated by Gregory VII in 1084.

Luke the physician (Col 4:4) accompanied Paul on his missionary journeys and is said to have preached in Greece and was subsequently buried in Thebes. His relics were brought to Constantinople in 357 and placed in the Church of the Apostles. He has been in the Roman calendar since the 9th century.

Theology of the Celebrations

For the celebration of the eucharist, the readings attempt to capture the character and the fundamental message of each evangelist. Mark is characterized by steadfastness, his association with Peter and the call to proclaim the gospel to the whole world (1 Pet 5:5-14; Mk 16:15-20, ironically, part of the much controverted longer conclusion). Matthew's call and the need of apostles and evangelists to build up the church are the foci of the Matthean readings (Eph 4:1-7, 11-13; Mt 9:9-13). Steadfastness and the spread of the gospel are the concerns of the readings for Luke (2 Tim 4:9-17; Lk 10:1-9). The readings for John are interesting in the light of the Christmas context; the word of life and the light of the world are contrasted with the disciple who sees the empty tomb and believes (1 Jn 1:1-4; Jn 20:2-8).

The prayers give ample food for thought about the role and purpose of the evangelists: the variety of the evangelists proclaims the breadth of the gospel message. First and foremost they are servants of the mystery of the word (John, Mark), a living gospel (preface of apostles II, used for the feasts of evangelists). This word is spoken on behalf of our salvation (John) and we too are called to go out and preach it (Mark). This gospel demands our fidelity and calls us to live the life of Christ (Mark, Matthew). The gospel reveals that we can welcome Christ with joy into our lives, even though we are sinners (Matthew). The gospel is for all peoples, especially the poor and sick (Luke).

The celebration of the liturgy of the hours is a more extended exploration of these same themes. Matthew is the one who particularly stresses that the gospel is even for sinners, that God is a God of mercy. The offices for John reveal the great devotion to this saint, particularly his reverance for the word, his virginity and care for the Virgin Mary, and his great profession of faith at the tomb. Mark and Luke share many of the same texts and focus on the spread of the gospel to the nations.

Celebrating the evangelists is a way of specifying the celebration of the apostles: they have a particular mission of preaching and witnessing to the incarnate and risen Lord and call each one to share that mission.

See **Calendar, liturgical**

A. Adam, *The Liturgical Year* (Collegeville, 1981), pp. 141-142, 242, 245-246. P. Rado, *Enchiridion Liturgicum* (Rome, 1961), Vol. 2:1128-29, 1372-73.

MICHAEL WITCZAK

EVANGELIZATION

Evangelization is the process of proclaiming the good news (gospel, Greek: *euangelion*; Latin: *evangelium*) and enabling the good news to be accepted more readily by those people disposed by grace to receive it.

The term *evangelization* has only recently been used in the Roman Catholic church. Appearing in the late 1950s, the term was incorporated into several of the documents of the Second Vatican Council in the 1960s; since then, the term has been widely used.

Most references to the term in Roman Catholic circles rely on the encyclical of Pope Paul VI, *Evangelii Nuntiandi* (Evangelization in the Modern World), promulgated in December 1975, as a way of reporting and furthering the discussion and conclusions of the Fourth Synod of Bishops which met in Rome from September 27 to October 26, 1974. That encyclical specified evangelization as a process of conversion of people individually and of society culturally (E.M.W., 18).

While the term is borrowed from Protestant and Evangelical usage, it does not connote for Roman Catholics the implicit theology that it sometimes connotes in Protestant and Evangelical circles,

namely, the confession of Jesus as personal savior (to the exclusion of "good works" or sacraments). Rather to the contrary, evangelization, as understood by Roman Catholics, extends through all Christian life, from the earliest "pre-evangelization" contact between believer and non-believer to the ongoing growth of the whole church as it realizes the impact of the good news of Jesus in its life and in the world. In this way, Pope Paul VI named as "beneficiaries" of evangelization all the baptized, their children, those who have ceased practicing their faith, peoples of non-Christian religions and atheists (E.M.W., chap. 5).

In its programmatic sense, evangelization covers all those activities that seek the renewal of the Christian community and its connection with those who are not members or are not active members. Its methods could include preaching as well as mass publicity.

Evangelization, then, cannot simply be equivalent to "mission" which is the "outward" movement of believers toward non-believers; it also has an "inward" dimension of renewal and re-conversion for the believers themselves. Evangelization must then be viewed in both its outward and inward dimensions.

(a) Outward dimension

In its strictest sense, evangelization takes place prior to any liturgical setting. In as much as the first liturgical act is enrollment in the catechumenate, as indicated in the Rite of Christian Initiation of Adults, evangelization takes place prior to the celebration of that rite (R.C.I.A., Intro., 9).

It begins with contact between believers and non-believers in the pre-evangelization or evangelization phase. The initial contact leads to a period of inquiry. While no rites have been composed by the universal church to mark either the beginning or end of this period, various episcopal conferences are free to develop instruments to help people inquire about the church and to welcome them (R.C.I.A., Intro., 12).

The Rite of Christian Initiation of Adults is the liturgical and sacramental process of incorporation into the church after conversion. Incorporation and membership begins with the celebration of the Rite of Catechumens (R.C.I.A., Intro., 14); it reaches its climax with the reception of baptism, confirmation and eucharist, the sacraments toward which the Rite of Initiation of Adults is ordered, preferably celebrated at the Easter vigil (R.C.I.A., Intro., 8). It concludes with the post-initiation period of "mystagogia."

It is appropriate here to note that the term "conversion" pertains only to those unbaptized who, upon evangelization, experience conversion and incorporation into the church. It does not pertain to people properly baptized in another Christian tradition who subsequently seek membership in the Roman Catholic church.

The responsibility for evangelization belongs to everyone in the church; in a special way, however, lay people who, through their daily secular lives come in contact with those who do not have belief, share in that responsibility through the many opportunities they have for such contact.

(b) Inward dimension

As an "inward" dimension of the church, the purpose of evangelization is not simply conversion in the strict sense, but continued renewal and re-conversion through the Holy Spirit. In this dimension, the liturgy both effects continued evangelization in believers and is itself an act of evangelization for all.

Effecting Evangelization. The sacrament of baptism, as the first sacrament of initiation, celebrates membership in the Christian community, the reception of grace and mercy, the Christian identity with the Lord, and the outpouring of the Holy Spirit. This sacrament, which celebrates the good news of salvation both in the individual and the community, is completed with the sacrament of confirmation whose anointing in the Holy Spirit empowers the individual and the community to bear witness to the grace of God both in the church and in the world.

The sacrament of the eucharist, in which the faithful gather to be fed by the word of God and the Lord's Supper, reaffirms the bond between God and the faithful, as well as the bonds among the faithful themselves. Sustained and refreshed, believers find strength in their own faith and strength to reach out to others.

The sacrament of reconciliation likewise effects continued evangelization in the faithful, reaffirming the grace of baptismal conversion in the celebration of renewal and mercy. When celebrated along with the sacrament of the sick, it calls in a special way for people in crisis to recognize and acknowledge God's mercy and renewing power.

The sacrament of marriage celebrates that bond through which God's love is manifested and a family unit created. Through the family unit the world is touched on a daily basis and new members are born into the family of faith.

The sacrament of holy orders charges each ordained person to proclaim the word of God and to live in accord with that word in service to the church and the world.

Evangelizing Acts. In addition to effecting evangelization in the members of the church, the sacraments themselves serve as instruments of evangelization.

The eucharistic assembly, in all its communal and liturgical roles, invites people to be part of the community of Jesus. Ushers and greeters welcome all into the assembly; commentators provide the context of the worship; lectors proclaim the word of God; the homilist exposes the power of that word for the assembly; acolytes, deacons and the presider model the diversity of ministry which the assembly upholds.

The sacraments of reconciliation and healing are, in themselves, movements of outreach toward the spiritually and physically afflicted. As the mercy and healing of Jesus were, in his day, signs of the presence of God's Kingdom, so these sacraments announce the presence of the Kingdom in our day. This good news is proclaimed, in the first instance, to those who recognize their need for mercy and healing.

The communal expressions of the rite of reconciliation can be dramatic invitations to personal renewal and reconversion (*Rite of Penance*, Intro., 36). Many programs that seek to reach the formerly active believer are, in reality, extensions of the spirit of the sacrament of reconciliation; some of these programs are actively modeled on the process of the Rite of Christian Initiation of Adults.

The sacrament of marriage, gathering as it does many of the associates of the marrying couple, proclaims the love and grace of God to people who often have no exposure to such proclamation.

The sacrament of holy orders invites all the faithful to consider the common ministry that each baptized person has as well as the responsibility of each person for the sanctification of the world. Although the ministry of the ordained differs from that of the non-ordained, it is a ministry of the universal church and it underscores the fact that each baptized person has received a calling to serve.

Likewise those who have been initiated, especially those recently converted, because of the freshness of their experience and the enthusiasm of their conversion, have a particularly powerful role in attracting others to become catechumens and to continue with the process of initiation in the Rite of Initiation of Adults. The rite, through its recognition of sponsors and godparents, specifically charges people to support the process of evangelization and conversion. The Easter vigil, at which catechumens complete their initiation, can be viewed as a powerful liturgical call for the conversion of the friends and families of the initiated and for the re-conversion of all believers.

Although evangelization, as a term, is recent, the dynamics of mission and conversion have always been part of the church's life. The word, however, serves the added purpose of calling the faithful to reveal the force of their faith in their daily lives, especially to non-believers and to those who have abandoned the practice of the faith. Likewise, it underscores the importance of continued conversion and re-awakening for the baptized believer.

Evangelization integrates the good news with every aspect of Christian life and with every person, whether believer or not, whether active or not, through liturgical celebration and spiritual growth, as a call to realize the good news of the Lord in its fullness. It gathers people, through their diverse relationships and ministries, around the table of the Lord, that the world may be served and all people united. As a process, it anticipates the Kingdom which it proclaims.

See **Initiation, Christian; Mystagogy**

Paul VI, *Evangelii Nuntiandi (Evangelization in the Modern World)*, *Acta Apostolicae Sedis* LXVII, 1, pp. 5-76. Maruasusai Dhavamony, S.J., ed. *Evangelisation*, Documenta Missionalia 9 (Università Gregoriana, Rome, 1975). René Laurentin, *L'Evangélisation aprés le Quatriène Synode*, (Editions du Seuil, Paris, 1975). Kenneth Boyack, C.S.P., ed., *Catholic Evangelization Today* (Mahwah: Paulist Press, 1987).

FRANK DeSIANO, C.S.P.

EXORCISM IN BAPTISMAL RITE

Exorcism is prayer for deliverance from the power of evil. Because of over-dramatization in the popular culture it conjures up bizarre images of demonic possession. However, in the baptismal rites it takes the form of ritual prayer for the unbaptized.

A prayer of exorcism accompanies the Rite of Baptism for Children and occurs several times in the more extended Rite of Christian Initiation of Adults.

When a child is baptized the prayer of exorcism accompanies the pre-baptismal anointing. Since the Rite of Baptism for Children is a radically condensed and adapted version of the rites for adults, the child is anointed at this time with the oil of catechumens.

There are two versions of the prayer. They acknowledge the power of Jesus, sent to the world "to cast out the power of Satan" and "to rescue us from the slavery of sin." The intention of the prayer is that God will set the children "free from original sin" and to bring them "out of the power of darkness." In short, the anamnetic formulae acknowledge the power of Christ over the power of evil, and the petitionary formulae seek freedom from the power of evil.

In the abbrieviated version of the rite celebrated by a catechist, the exorcism and anointing with the oil of catechumens is omitted.

In the Rite of Christian Initiation of Adults exorcisms are celebrated several times: in the rite of acceptance into the Order of Catechumens, the minor exorcisms during the period of the catechumenate, the anointing of the catechumens, and the scrutinies.

In the rite of acceptance the exorcism is optional. In regions where false worship is widespread this first exorcism may accompany the renunciation of false worship.

During the period of the catechumenate, minor exorcisms may be part of the celebration of the word of God. The exorcisms are prayers addressed to God to help the catechumens in their struggle to be faithful to the Christian way of life. The presider may be a priest, deacon, or qualified catechist appointed by the bishop. These prayers may be used throughout the period of the catechumenate.

During similar celebrations the catechumens may also be anointed with the oil of catechumens. In these cases, when the oil has already been blessed by the bishop, the celebrating priest or deacon offers a prayer of exorcism before making the anointing. When oil has not been blessed, he says a prayer to bless the oil, a prayer in which the exorcism is inchoate.

Finally, exorcism forms the heart of the three scrutinies immediately preceding baptism. The formula is more elaborate. After intercessory prayer the celebrant begs God's deliverance and imposes hands on the elect; finally, he prays for the coming of the Holy Spirit to replace the spirit of evil.

In baptismal rites, then, exorcisms are prayers that God will free the unbaptized from that power of evil which formerly governed their lives, and fill them with the power of the Holy Spirit who will incorporate them into the people of God.

National Conference of Catholic Bishops, *Rite of Christian Initiation of Adults*, 1988; and *Rite of Baptism for Children*, 1970.

PAUL TURNER

F

FASTING

Fasting is a physical process of restricting one's level of use of such things as food, drink, play, etc., ordinarily for some religious rationale. It may be to acknowledge that the things one ordinarily uses come from God, and one "fasts" to praise God for the gifts. It may be a penitential act, fasting in atonement for sins. It may be a ritual act, in preparation for a festivity; one fasts to heighten the enjoyment of the feast. It may be an act of communion, fasting in solidarity with those who live in want.

The liturgical cycle frequently employs "days of fast" and even "seasons of fast." Lent is the church's major season of fast, where fasting is primarily in preparation for the Easter feast, and secondarily, where a reconciliation process is observed, a penitential act. Traditional days of fast are vigils before feasts and days of harvest (rogation days) to mark God's providence over the crops and the seasons. Contemporary times of fasting include days of solidarity with the poor such as the Oxfam fast or fasts to raise funds for victims of war. In the tradition of fasting, the contemporary phenomenon of the "march" or the "walk" may serve the same religious purpose: e.g., the "walk" for hunger, the "march" for life, the "walk" against AIDS, etc.

As with all restrictive activities, the religious danger is to focus on the negative, "giving up" rather than "giving for."

Such focus on the negative distorts the value of fasting as a religious act. The paradigm for Christians of any embrace of the negative is, of course, Christ on the cross. His endurance of suffering and death, however, was an act of love *pro nobis* and an act of worship, surrender, to God. Fasting gains its true Christian meaning from Christ, and from Christ's command that we love one another as he himself loved us.

See **Calendar, liturgical; Penitential days; Penitential practices; Sacrifices**

FEMINISM AND THE LITURGY

Liturgy, although defined through its etymology as the "work of the people," has been confined for most of Christian and Jewish liturgical history to the "work of men," and further restricted in most situations to the work of male clergy. Women's leadership and the expression of women's experiences have been excluded from its symbols and rituals. Thus in this corporate activity where God and human beings encounter one another, a narrow authorship has denied both women and men aspects of divine and human revelation. Feminism, a movement based on a vision of equality between women and men of all cultures and races, critiques this male domination and suggests as a counterbalancing factor transformative contributions from women's experiences. Feminism addresses the form, content and meaning of liturgical practice.

Rationale

The study of feminism from the perspective of many disciplines, especially feminist theology and feminist social theory, has provided systematic understandings of the androcentric and mysogynist bias that plagues human history. It is no surprise that in societies in which "the male" has been considered the norm and the "female," a sub-species whose primary value is to serve the norm, appraisals of human worth have been seriously distorted. Both women and men are affected. Women are demeaned and rendered invisible. Men are inappropriately inflated with the result that men perceive power as their right and domain. The developing public awareness of pervasive domestic violence, in which women and children are the primary victims, is a vivid example of the violent implications of this power imbalance. Feminism, through a system of thought and action, addresses the long-distorted relationships between women and men.

Though scholars can trace some small fragmentary evidence of the integration of women and women's experiences within liturgical celebrations throughout religious history, in general the liturgies of church and synagogue reflect a similar androcentric bias. In the last twenty years the consciousness-raising brought about by the women's and civil rights' movements has introduced important concerns that affect liturgical practice. Women from a variety of cultural and religious backgrounds, among them feminists, womanists (feminists of color), mujeristas (Hispanic feminists) as well as lesbian feminists have identified the particularities of sexist-prejudice within worship traditions. The male bias, as normative for everyone, pervades every aspect of liturgy: graphic images, metaphors, choices and interpretations of texts, music, leadership and forms.

Images and Metaphors

Christian and Jewish teaching assures us that God cannot be fully known or named and that any attempt to describe God simply encompasses a mere part of the mystery. No word, color, gesture, or sound can convey the entirety of God's nature. Liturgical communities depend on symbols, both representational images and metaphors, to express qualities of divine/human encounters.

The sources of our description emerge from human experience, conveyed through tradition, both written and oral, past and present. Scripture, doctrinal formulations and liturgical usage are our basic resources.

Since the writing of scripture occurred during a patriarchal time (as has most of the rest of history), it is no surprise to discover that the predominant divine images within it (verbal and visual) are male, primarily, Father, King, Lord, Prince. Feminist biblical scholars respond to this situation in two ways. First, they acknowledge the limitations of the patriarchal-historical context. Images are historically-rooted. As such they cannot be considered "objectively" true or appropriate for all time. They require constant scrutiny for continuing suitability. This examination leads feminists not only to identify the problem but also to suggest some solutions. One correction consists in alternative words for exclusively male images. Examples include Sovereign for Lord, Ruler for King, Mother and Father or Parent for Father, The Human One for Son of Man (Inclusive Language Lectionary). Another is to uncover new metaphors that express contemporary experiences of God such as Spinner, Weaver, Liberator, Sustainer and Lover.

Second, feminist scholars point to female images from the biblical tradition that break into this dominant androcentric pattern (womb of God, God writhing in labor pains, God as a mother nursing her young, woman in search of a lost coin), that have been all but lost in the patriarchal emphasis of the Christian tradition. Honest liturgical practice requires a rediscovery and appropriation of existing female images as metaphors for the activity of God among us.

Similarly, theologians understand the influence of historical contexts on the study of doctrine. This analysis, along with the reflections of those who participate regularly in liturgy, offers a critical contribution for liturgical change. Feminists point to the predominant use of gender-specific terms to express the nature of God in prayers, hymns, and visual representations. God is known primarily as Father, referred to by the pronoun "he," and understood "most perfectly" in the trinitarian formula (Father, Son and Holy Ghost). Feminists suggest that these historically rooted metaphors are some, but not all, (and not necessarily the best) of many imaginable expressions of God, each one with its own limitations and assets. The insistence that any one is essential and irreplaceable in the celebration of the sacraments is idolatrous because it claims to exhaust the mystery suggesting that God can be contained in one formula. Varied images for God rather than a few are more consistent with honest liturgical practice. Other metaphors which include distinctly female experiences (Sister, Mother, Nurturer, Life-sustainer) as well as gender-indefinite terms (Giver, Gift, Holy Spirit: see Richard Norris) are equally valuable in expressing relationships about and within God.

In addition to words and images for God there is the problem of the male-identified Christ. Clearly glorification of the male and a license for domination has resulted from a distorted Christology which highlights Christ's maleness rather than Christ's humanity. The feminist challenge is to open up the christological reality beyond its maleness to testify more fully to the redemptive suffering and the resurrected expression of all peoples. Christian communities will discover new dimensions of embodied divinity through a crucifix with a female corpus. It will press identification with and acknowledgment of the women throughout history who have been and continue to be undeniable witnesses to the tradition of suffering servants.

Names for God express only half of the equation in liturgical assemblies. Human experience shapes an important aspect as well, that is, how we name or refer to ourselves. This area demands careful attention. To call Israel a whore and ourselves children of Israel connects primary sinfulness with women's sexuality, an all too common feature of religious tradition. Similarly, to describe women saints as virgins, wives and mothers relegates their importance to their sexual functioning and relationship or non-relationship to men. Women live and contribute much beyond these categories.

Biblical Narratives

Not only do individual images and metaphors discredit and disregard the worth of women but also the choice and interpretation of biblical narratives in Christian worship reinforce the same message. Too often they depict women as perpetrators of sin (Eve), as whores (Mary Magdalen), as passive, asexual, innocent recipients of God's activity (Mary). Feminists offer reinterpretations of these texts (Eve as mother of all humanity, Mary Magdalen as first witness to the resurrection, Mary as liberator of the poor and suffering). They demand also that biblical texts which portray women as brutalized for the sake of men, such as in the story of the unnamed concubine and the rape of Tamar, be read and understood as witnessing to the contemporary experience of many women. As to appropriate texts for liturgy, feminists raise questions about the sole use of canonical texts written in patri-archal eras. They suggest adding other equally challenging literature that conveys God's continuing activity among all of humankind.

Not unrelated to the primacy of scripture is a similar preference in current liturgical practice for verbal rather than embodied or visual texts. If we take seriously the well-taught doctrine that all human creatures are embodied images of God, and the importance of bodily gestures and positions which have become an integral part of our liturgies, then limiting our experience to verbal texts again denies access to aspects of both divine and human revelation. Feminists are particularly concerned about embodi-ment because women, whose bodies are essential for the perpetuation of human life, nevertheless have born the scourge of ridicule, disparagement, even the accusation of being temptations to sin, because of their bodies. Feminists claim the body as good, as a testimony to the realities of compassion, life, honesty, struggle. Acknowledging the importance of the revelation about God and about others that emerges concretely and di-rectly from our bodies, feminists insist on correcting the tradition which undergirds the evil of women's bodies, and on adding the use of our bodies as an important contribution to contemporary liturgical practice. Such determination runs the gamut: from resistance to such unexamined practices as bowing our head for a blessing often prayed by men (a gesture with inherent dominance, men over women, clergy over laity, incon-sistent with the feminist principle of mutuality) to experimenting with dif-ferent forms of movement and touch. Sensuality, sexuality and spirituality are closely interlinked for feminists.

Leadership

Since the primary medium for our understanding of God is through other human beings, both male and female, male-centered liturgical leadership poses theological inconsistencies and serious liturgical problems. First, it makes too easy the consequent connection between male humanity and God, a connection both inaccurate and idolatrous, as dis-cussed above. Second, it affects the participation of the assembly. The pre-sumption that only men have a special charism given by God for the most important liturgical tasks, i.e., to preside over the celebration of moments of divine/ human encounters and to interpret scripture, reinforces a demeaning image of women. In hearing that the sacraments are not valid without male clerical presence, women and men conclude that women are not as significant as men for the "work of the people." No attempt to salvage the situation by claiming that women and men have different roles is adequate when the roles themselves are so suggestive of the ordering of "God's preference." Some women respond by accepting their inferior role as part of God's plan; others accept the situation as inevitable, not knowing anything could be different. Some insist that it is enough to be part of the secondary leadership roles, when possible. Others (both women and men) are justifiably angry, making it impossible to be fully engaged in the experience. In each situation, the ex-clusiveness of male leadership limits the full and active engagement of many members of any worshipping community.

Form

Feminist critiques of liturgical forms encompass a variety of perspectives. They include an institutional persistence to reform the aspects of the liturgy as mentioned above by adding women's names and stories from the tradition. Primarily, this attempt addresses the content of the form. However, another viewpoint maintains that all liturgical forms shaped by a patriarchal history are inherently sexist and cannot meet women's emerging needs. Some women turn to the Wicca movement with its emphasis on connectedness to nature, the equality of all human beings and its goddess-centered images. Others, determined to redeem and use the most valuable assets of the tradition while remaining highly critical of form as well as content, gather outside the church's official structures, often in homes. Moved by the recognition that the inherited forms themselves are too hierarchical to reflect feminist principles of mutuality and also by the immediate need to survive in a sexist church, these intentional communities shape new forms for themselves. Though the actual format may vary from time to time, some characteristics remain constant: they replace hierarchy with mutuality (no domination by a single person); minimalism with graced excess (more water, more ashes, more beauty rather than only what is required); soberness with compassion and enjoyment (seriousness includes play and laughter); isolation with bonding; passivity with active listening, spontaneity, and articulated responses to the performances of the liturgy. The form supports new content, not only references to distinctive experiences of women, such as menstruation and menopause, battering, rape, breast or vaginal cancer, friendship and bonding, but also real connections to the oppression women have felt with support for transformative liberation. Consistent with the focus of liturgy, feminists design contexts where the encounter with divine reality can support change that emphasizes women's worth rather than women's limitations.

The partriarchal tradition of liturgy has hobbled Christian and Jewish communities for centuries, denying women's existence, determining how they should express their beliefs in an articulation based on male insights. The study and experience of feminism offers a new challenge to church and synagogue inviting congregations to probe their practices carefully and honestly. They begin by asking such questions as: When have I experienced moments of transformation? What characterized the time? What name or quality expressed my need for a transcendent reality? When is my human experience most sacred and most unjust? What motivates change in me? How does my religious experience connect with the challenges of the neighboring and world community? What do I treasure most about the liturgical experience I have known and why? The contribution of feminism to liturgy is to ask probing, profound, disturbing questions, to experiment in response to them and constantly to evaluate the entire process. Such a procedure is not new in the history of church and synagogue. What is different is the emphasis on the value of all the participants' experience, specifically, though not exclusively, womens' experience. Feminism acknowledges particularity with regard to culture, race, gender, human capability. Feminism searches for ways to include these differences rather than project a preference or a "norm." Liturgy as a paradigmatic moment along a journey is an experience of transformation and liberation when it takes seriously the value of each person's contribution to its structure and its content. Feminism offers an opportunity to reexamine the integration of form, content and meaning in liturgy. Beginning at the heart of liturgy, feminism challenges the ways humans, primarily men, have limited God's revelation among us and have restricted our witness of that revelation to each other. Feminism offers corrections and recommendations, integral components of the promise inherent in the liturgical renewal of church and synagogue in this century.

See **Inclusive language**

Elisabeth Schüssler Fiorenza, *In Memory of Her:*

A Feminist Theological Reconstruction of Christian Origins (New York: Crossroad, 1983). Marjorie Procter-Smith, *In Her Own Rite: Constructing Feminist Liturgical Tradition* (Nashville: Abingdon, 1990). Rosemary Ruether, *Women-Church: Theology and Practice* (New York: Harper and Row, 1985). Phyllis Trible, *God and the Rhetoric of Sexuality* (Philadelphia: Fortress, 1978).

JANET WALTON

FORGIVENESS, THEOLOGY OF

Forgiveness is an intentional process in which the forgiver freely chooses not to return injury for injury but rather to respond in a loving way to the person or situation that has inflicted some harm. The process of forgiveness is not only between an individual and God or between individuals, but includes the forgiveness of self, pardon between groups and the forgiveness of social and political structures. The capacity for forgiveness generally arises out of the experience of being forgiven and leads to reconciliation or mutual acceptance. Forgiveness is a difficult process because it is unconditional. It is offered even though it may not be accepted. It requires an ability to deal with one's own pain, pride, emotions and desire to retaliate. Basically forgiveness recognizes human weakness but also the possibilities of the human spirit. Forgiveness creates new possibilities for growth and relationship because it affirms the genuine worth of the other person and it enables the forgiver to be free and independent of a destructive force in his or her own life.

Forgiveness in Scripture

The human experience of forgiveness finds its source and its inspiration in the reality of God's forgiveness. A Christian theology of forgiveness is rooted in the gratuitous mercy of God. The English word "mercy" is an inadequate translation of the biblical concept of *hesed*, which is linked to and expressed in many images. In the OT, the God of mercy is the God of the covenant. Yahweh's love fashions a people who enter into a covenant relationship that is characterized by mutual love and faithfulness. The God of mercy is the God of forgiveness. Israel was often unfaithful but Yahweh's love endures (Isa 54:10). The infinite mercy of God again and again called Israel back to faithfulness. Only by experiencing God's mercy did the Israelites recognize and name their sinfulness. In experiencing God's mercy, Israel is empowered to manifest God's forgiveness and love to others. The God of mercy is the God of compassion. Yahweh hears the cry of the poor and the helpless. Yahweh shows them favor because of Yahweh's mercy and great kindness. The psalmist appeals to these qualities of compassion and mercy when asking for forgiveness (Ps 25:6; 40:12; 51:3). The God of mercy is the God who saves. Mercy is the fundamental motive underlying all of Yahweh's mighty deeds and the motive which gives unity and meaning to all Yahweh's actions in the lives of the covenant people.

The mercy of God is revealed in Jesus. Jesus manifests God's mercy in human words, actions and relationships. Jesus tells the disciples stories of mercy, generosity and redemption in order to help them gain insight into the gratuitous, gracious love of God and to help them make the experiences of forgiveness and reconciliation a reality in their lives. The parables stress the initiative of God in forgiveness. The appropriate response to God's love is love for one another. God's forgiveness is not a gift simply bestowed or received; it is always empowerment. It opens up possibilities of greater discipleship. The experience of the forgiveness of God intensifies and increases the human person's capacity to love and forgive. It is "God who has first loved us." Forgiveness calls for an acceptance and a response by humankind, but ultimately forgiveness is always God's free gift. Forgiveness goes beyond conditions, recompense or requirements. The parables and the sayings make it clear that there are no limits to forgiveness, that God's mercy extends to all humankind and to the whole cosmos.

The actions of Jesus, often a scandal to society, taught the disciples that forgiveness meant reaching out to the marginalized, to the "lost," and to those despised by society. Forgiveness is not merely an attitude, it is an action. Many passages of the gospels show the compassion and the forgiveness with which Jesus welcomed those who were considered as outcasts by the authorities (Lk 15:2). He was even ridiculed for being a friend of tax collectors and sinners (Mt 11:19; Lk 7:34). Jesus defended this relationship with sinners by stating that those who are well have no need of a physician and that he had come to call not the righteous but sinners (Mk 2:17; Lk 5:32). No one is excluded from God's mercy and compassion.

Not only does Jesus welcome sinners; the gospels provide a number of examples in which Jesus mediates the forgiveness of sins (Mk 2:5; Lk 7:48; 19:9, 23:43; Jn 5:14; 8:11). God's mercy is reflected in and experienced through Jesus. Jesus' declaration that sin was forgiven was blasphemy to the scribes because forgiveness was the prerogative of God alone (Exod 34: 6-7; Isa 43:25) and in Judaism the forgiveness of sin did not take place in the present, but only as a future event. The early kerygma affirmed Jesus' power to forgive sins on earth and justified the church's claim to declare the forgiveness of sins in the name of Jesus. Forgiveness of sin was integral to the very nature of the church.

Even worship and prayer are to give way to forgiveness and reconciliation: "If you know that someone has something against you, leave your gift at the altar and go first to be reconciled (Mt 5:23). Mt 7:1-5 warns against judging others and reminds the listeners that their relationship to God brings about a new relationship to each other. Those who have received mercy are to show mercy. The promise to forgive others in the Lord's Prayer (Lk 11:1-4; Mt 6:9-15) identifies forgiveness as an intrinsic quality of the disciple.

How often is the disciple required to forgive? The sum of "seventy times seven" (Mt 18:21-35) is a number beyond count because the follower of Jesus is to forgive as often as it is necessary. Everyone must be given the opportunity to change. As often as one promises repentance, one must be offered forgiveness.

The centrality of reconciliation in the life and teaching of Jesus culminates in his liberating death: "This is my blood of the covenant which is poured out for many *for the forgiveness of sins* (Mt 26:28). "My blood of the covenant" is the new and everlasting covenant founded on Christ's own life, death and resurrection.

"For the forgiveness of sins" summarizes what Matthew's gospel has already affirmed about God's mercy manifest in Jesus. He is the saviour who saves people from their sin (1:21); he is the servant of Yahweh who took upon himself the infirmities and sufferings of those who were afflicted (8:17; 12:18) and who gives his life in the service of many (20:38). The death of Jesus is freely offered for the life of the world (27:51-54). Thus, many of the OT themes of mercy—God's will to save, God's covenant of love and faithfulness, God's intervention in human history, God's fulfillment of eschatological promises—become visible in the life, death and resurrection of Jesus

Forgiveness in the Early Church

The gospels identify forgiveness as an essential characteristic of the reign of God and a fundamental quality of a disciple. Christians reconciled to God through Christ are entrusted with the message of forgiveness and reconciliation (2 Cor 5:18). Through baptism for the forgiveness of sins, the Christian is incorporated into the community of believers and its mission. The early Christians had a deep sense of awareness that they were the body of Christ and that therefore sin committed after baptism negated the very nature of the church. They also understood that God's mercy was manifested and mediated through the community of believers because Christ is present in the church. The church is the sacrament of God's mercy through Christ in the Spirit. Reconciliation with the community was the sign of forgiveness and reconciliation with God.

Gradually, community structures of forgiveness evolved that were both preventive and corrective for the sinner. Throughout the centuries these ecclesial forms of forgiveness changed in order to meet the concrete needs of people within a particular historical context. When medieval theologians attempted to define the meaning of sacrament and to determine the number of the central liturgical rites, penance was identified as the sacrament of forgiveness. From then on the sacrament of penance became the primary if not the sole means of forgiveness for Catholic Christians. An overview of the major historical and theological developments in the sacrament of penance indicates that shifts in sacramental practice brought about corresponding shifts in understanding the ways forgiveness was effected.

In the NT churches, baptism was for the forgiveness of sin. In the Pentecost account, Peter preached repentance in order that the people "be baptized in the name of Jesus for the forgiveness of sins and you shall receive the Holy Spirit" (Acts 2:38). When the disciples gathered for "the breaking of the bread" they remembered that this action of Christ in the Spirit was also for the "forgiveness of sin" (Mt 26:28). Baptism was the initial action for forgiveness of sin, and eucharist was the memorial that both called the community to forgiveness of one another and expressed the forgiving nature of the community.

It is possible that the early church never envisioned any public sign of forgiveness other than baptism. However, the reality of the sinfulness of its members after baptism forced it to struggle with the meaning of the eucharist and with the understanding of forgiveness presented by Jesus. Paul describes the community as the body of Christ (1 Cor 12:27). The believers are Christ; it is through them that Christ's mission of proclaiming God's love in word and deed is continued and made manifest. The mark of this community is unity, an organic unity that points up the interdependence of its members (1 Cor 10:17). This unity, integral to the body, is expressed and deepened by the eucharist. The very nature of the body is contradicted by selfishness and division and they who eat and drink without recognizing the body eat and drink a judgment on themselves (1 Cor 11:29).

Penitential practices developed in the apostolic communities that began to shape the church's ministry of forgiveness. Means of pardon and reconciliation were fraternal correction (Mt 8:15-20; Gal 6:1-2), prayer (1 Jn 5:16; Jas 5:16), confession to one another (Mt 5:23-24), and especially the sharing of the eucharistic meal. Other forms of forgiveness were fasting, almsgiving and works of mercy.

A special process was set in motion with regard to serious and public sins (1 Cor 5:1-5; 2 Cor 2:5-11). It involved excluding the member for a time from the eucharistic meal and from the life of the community because such sin was not only an offense against God but also a contradiction to membership in the church and, in fact, a denial of the very nature of the church. The judgment to exclude the sinner was the prerogative of the community (Mt 18:17; 1 Cor 5:3-5) and was intended to be remedial in nature. It afforded the sinner a concrete way of manifesting conversion and enabled the community to support the sinner through prayer and charity. Paul tells the Corinthian church that the ministry and message of reconciliation is given to the whole community (2 Cor 5:14-19) and that the members must take responsibility for one another.

In its origins, the act of reconciliation with the church was a renewal of baptismal commitment that found expression and strengthening in eucharistic communion. In the restoration of the baptismal bonding the sinner found once again God's forgiveness in Christ. Reconciliation with the church was reconciliation with God.

Rituals of Forgiveness

The 3rd century was marked by a number of controversies concerning the forgiveness and reconciliation of sinners. Tertullian (d. 225), as a Montanist, supported the permanent exclusion of those guilty of capital sins and attempted to distinguish between remissible and irremissible sins. St. Cyprian (d. 258), Bishop of Carthage, dealt with many of the practical problems of the penitential discipline arising from the Decian persecutions. Cyprian maintained that the subjective, personal element of doing penance effected the forgiveness of sins but the objective ecclesial aspect of reconciliation presupposes the divine pardon. Hippolytus of Rome (d. 235), in opposition to Pope Callistus, denied the church's right to forgive serious sins and Novatian (d. 258) refused forgiveness and reconciliation to apostates. These controversies contributed to the development of a more formal, ritualized means of reconciliation than was present in the NT church. Tertullian describes the process as having three stages. First, the penitent confessed his or her sinfulness by appearing before the community in penitential garb and begging the intercession of the community. Second, the penitent was assigned specific works of penance in order to foster conversion. Third, when the period of expiation was finished, the penitent was readmitted to the community and to the eucharistic table. This form of penance, a restoration of one's baptismal grace, had to be performed in the midst of the community to work to salvation. The forgiveness of sin is effected by the intercession of the church.

Gradually this penitential process developed into the institutional form of canonical penance. It paralleled the Christian initiation of its members in that it was a lengthy process and took place in and through the community. The primary purpose of canonical penance was to enlist the prayers and concern of the community on behalf of the penitents. At the eucharist, the bishop blessed the penitents and prayed for their perseverance. In participating in the conversion of the penitents the community itself was called to conversion, deeper faith and commitment of life. When the penance was completed the penitents were publicly received back into full communion with the church through the bishop's prayer and imposition of hands.

The reconciliation of the penitent was considered the work of the whole church. The penitential works of the sinner, encouraged and supported by the community, and the bishop's prayer and imposition of hands, were considered essential elements in the reconciliation of the penitent to the church, which was the sign of forgiveness. The early church understood the Holy Spirit to be the source of reconciliation and the church to be the embodiment of the Spirit. Reconciliation with the church is the means by which the Spirit is communicated to the penitent.

Canonical penance was directed to only a small number of people and to serious, scandalous sin. Baptism continued to be the preeminent means of forgiveness with "daily penance"—good works, almsgiving, charity to the poor and infirm, prayer, particularly the Lord's prayer—as the ordinary form of forgiveness for sinfulness (St. Augustine, *Serm.* 351 and 352).

Canonical penance declined around the 5th century, due primarily to the rigidity and severity of the penances and the rule that penance was non-repeatable. It was replaced by "tariff" penance which permitted penance more than once in a lifetime, was available to every individual and required a detailed confession of sin in order that the confessor could assign a penance (tariff) corresponding to the gravity of the fault. The tariffs determined for each sin were listed in the penitential books used by the confessors. The satisfaction or fulfillment of the penitential works effected the forgiveness of sin. When the satisfaction was completed the penitents were readmitted to the eucharist, which was the sign of forgiveness.

Even in tariff penance, confession of sin was considered only one form of forgiveness of sin. *The Penitential of Cummean*, which was widely circulated on the Continent during the 8th and 9th centuries, offered twelve means of remission of sin. Baptism was the premier means of forgiveness. Others were: charity, almsgiving, tears, confession of sin, acceptance and endurance of suffering, continuing conversion, prayers for one another, mercy, conversion of others, forgiveness of others, and martyrdom. The ecclesial form of reconciliation was always placed within the context of the whole Christian life.

Gradually, the custom arose of reconciling the penitent before the completion of the penance. The reconciliation of the sinner before satisfaction was explained by equating the humiliation and embarrassment inherent in confession with the satisfaction. Confession per se began to constitute the most important part of the penitential discipline in the 11th and 12th centuries and theologians taught that confession was absolutely necessary for the remission of sin.

Theological Disputes

Twelfth-century theologians struggled with the question of how the sinner was forgiven. The context of the dispute was the change in liturgical practice in which satisfaction, which had been the outward sign of contrition and the pre-requisite for forgiveness, now followed absolution. Theologians agreed that confession was necessary for forgiveness. The disagreement centered on whether it was contrition (which included the intention of confessing), the actual act of confessing or the absolution of the priest that effected forgiveness. Peter Abelard (d. 1130) taught that contrition effects forgiveness. Confession and the imposition of a penance by the priest are the outward signs of a repentant heart. The role of the priest is to pray for the sinner and to impose a penance in order to expiate the temporal punishment due to sin. Peter Lombard (d. 1160), the most influential of the 12th-century theologians, supported Abelard and maintained that sinners were forgiven before they confessed, that is, from the moment that they turned to God in sorrow and repentance (IV, d. 17 c. 2). The function of the priest is to declare that the sins are forgiven. In opposition, Hugh of St. Victor (d. 1142) argued that forgiveness is dependent upon the absolution of the priest.

The dispute about how the sacrament of penance effects forgiveness continued in the 13th century, resulting in a distinction between contrition (sorrow for sin motivated by the love of God) and attrition (sorrow prompted by other motives).

St. Thomas Aquinas (d. 1274) took up these same distinctions teaching that contrition, and not merely attrition, is required for God's forgiveness. Aquinas applied Aristotelian terms of matter and form to the sacraments in a systematic way and achieved a valuable synthesis. With regard to penance, he speaks of a quasi-matter, that is, the penitent's three-fold action of contrition, confession and satisfaction and a form that is the indicative words of absolution. Both matter and form were necessary for the efficacy of the sacrament and therefore there was an intrinsic relationship between contrition and absolution.

Duns Scotus, in opposition to Thomas, considered attrition sufficient for pardon; once the penitents have been forgiven through the sacrament, the grace of the sacrament changes their disposition of attrition to contrition. The position of Duns Scotus on attrition, and also his teaching on absolution as the essence of the sacrament, came to be the generally accepted opinions. The acts of the penitent were not causes of forgiveness but conditions for the effectiveness of absolution. By the end of the 13th century, absolution was seen as the means of forgiveness.

The Council of Trent (1545-1563), in refutation of the Reformers, did not settle the controversy between attritionists and contritionists. With regard to forgiveness, the council affirmed that faith alone was not sufficient for the forgiveness of sins, but that the acts of the penitent and the words of the minister are required. The interpretation of the Council of Trent in succeeding centuries led to an almost exclusive identification of forgiveness with the sacrament of penance. Forgiveness was seen almost entirely in terms of absolution.

From the Council of Trent until the Second Vatican Council the theology of forgiveness remained almost unchanged.

Vatican II

Vatican II called for a revision of the rite of penance to more clearly express both the nature and effect of the sacrament (S.C., 72) by restoring the baptismal and communal context of reconciliation: "by baptism priests introduce women and men into the People of God; by the sacrament of penance they reconcile sinners with God and with the church" (O.P., 5). The praenotanda of the *Rite of Penance* (1974) incorporated and extended these fundamental understandings. The major theme of the rite is the mercy of God and, in the context of mercy, the sacrament is once again understood as an act of worship. The rite presents the sacrament as an aspect of the mercy of God who reconciled the world in Christ. Christ's ministry of forgiveness and reconciliation is continued in the church whose very nature is expressed whenever it manifests itself as the sacrament of God's mercy. It is only by the "grace of a merciful God" that the sinner comes back to "that Father who first loved us" (1 Jn 4:19). In the sacrament, the faithful "obtain from the mercy of God" pardon for their sins and reconciliation with the church (n. 4). In the sacrament, faithful Christians experience and proclaim the mercy of God in their lives as they celebrate with the priest the liturgy by which the church continually renews itself (n. 11). The whole church as a priestly people, is to "help the sinner to obtain the mercy of God who alone can forgive sins" (n. 8).

The focus of the sacrament is clearly on the mercy of God; the confession of sins is secondary to this mystery. Confession is first a confession of faith and confession of praise. The sacrament is the celebration of faith in a God who loves men and women freely and forgives them out of mercy for the glory of God's name, through Jesus Christ in the Spirit. It is the celebration of the gratuitousness of God's forgiveness, mercy, grace and love. Forgiveness and reconciliation are the church's gift and task and continue the very activity of God revealed as mercy.

God's action is closely linked with the activity of God's church, and penance always involves reconciliation with others who are harmed by our sins (n. 5). In the communal forms provided by the new rite, the church as a forgiving community is more clearly discernible. The priest has a privileged ministry in the absolution and reconciliation of the penitent, but the whole community has a varied and active role in the mystery of God's mercy and forgiveness. Forgiveness is more than words; it is action. The ecclesial nature of penance impels the Christian community to work closely with others for "justice and peace in the world" (n. 5).

In the introduction to the ritual, the sacrament is situated within the framework of God's will to save and to reconcile humankind. The sacrament is placed within salvation history as another concrete instance of God's intervention and care for God's people. The relationship of penance to baptism and eucharist is once again restored. Penance is presented as the renewal of baptism, and the completion of forgiveness is participation in the eucharist. Through the sign of absolution God grants pardon to the sinner and this is expressed in a renewed and more fervent sharing of the Lord's Table (n. 6).

Summary

A theology of forgiveness is bound closely to the history of the development of the sacrament of penance. Within that history certain values emerge and recur that are valid for a current understanding of forgiveness.

Forgiveness is God's action in the Christian's life. It is an event that gives rise to a sense of awe and wonder because the Christian is confronted with the depth and the mystery of God's saving love. In the experience of forgiveness, the Christian is called to respond to God's covenant love by struggling against sin in oneself, the church and the world.

Baptism is the fundamental sacrament of forgiveness and eucharist is the sign and source of unity in Christ. The sacrament of reconciliation is a renewal of the baptismal covenant and the manifestation of the nature of the church as a reconciled and reconciling community.

Reconciliation is the ministry of the whole community because of the baptismal bonding in Christ, and Christians must continue to search for ways of making this ministry viable and visible.

Forgiveness, reconciliation and conversion are not restricted to the sacramental moment. Traditional forms of forgiveness—prayer, works of charity, mutual forgiveness, fasting, almsgiving—as well as contemporary forms are a part of God's saving action and as such must be integrated into the sacramental rituals of reconciliation.

Forgiveness is not merely an individual action or attitude but is inseparably connected with the communal and ecclesial experience of repentance and pardon. The church is the fundamental sacrament of mercy and compassion and the individual experience of this gift must still find sacramental expression because all saving action ultimately has a sacramental character.

The social aspect of grace and sin, by which the actions of individuals in some degree affect the whole body of the church, is a basis for the development of a spirituality of forgiveness that not only addresses personal sin but the sinfulness of structures in society.

Forgiveness as a quality of the Christian life is a gift. "God is rich in mercy; because of God's great love for us, God brought us to life with Christ when we were dead in sin . . . this is not your own doing, it is God's gift" (Eph 2:4-5,8). Forgiveness as a quality of the Christian life is a commitment to making the richness of God's mercy a reality wherever there is alienation or division in today's world.

See **Reconciliation, sacrament of; Reconciliation, liturgies of; Reconcilation, ministers of**

Pope John Paul II, "Rich in Mercy," (*Dives in misericordia) The Pope Speaks* 26 (1981): 20-58. Casiano Floristan and Christian Duquoc, eds., *Forgiveness.* Vol. 184/2 *Concilium* (Edinburgh: T. & T. Clark, 1986). Jerome Murphy-O'Connor, "Sin and Community in the New Testament," *Sin and Repentance*, ed. by Denis O'Callaghan (Dublin: Gill, 1967): 18-50.Clement Tierney, *The Sacrament of Repentance and Reconciliation* (New York: Costello Publishing, 1983).

CATHERINE DOOLEY, O.P.

FORMATION, LITURGICAL

When Vatican II initiated the renewal of the church's rituals, it was also aware that ritual reform must be accompanied by liturgical formation at every level of the praying church. With the realization that the liturgy is the summit of the activity of the church and fount of all her powers (S.C., 10), the council called for a formation which leads to "full, conscious, and active participation" (S.C., 14) in the prayer life of the church. Vatican II identified liturgical formation in very broad terms as proper preparation of those responsible for the teaching and celebration of the liturgy: namely, professors of liturgy (S.C., 15); and seminarians for whom major and mandatory course work was to be coupled with liturgical formation in their spiritual lives (S.C., 16-17). At the pastoral level, the council instructed priests to understand better what they are doing, and urged the promotion of liturgical instruction of the faithful (S.C., 18-19). In the period following Vatican II, pastoral experience has demonstrated that liturgical formation includes, in addition to good instruction: good experience of liturgical prayer for congregational formation, good planning of the ongoing liturgical life of the diocese and each parish, particular skills for those exercising the different ministries at each liturgical celebration, and overall attention to the use and function of symbol and ritual.

Addressing these concerns the American bishops, through the Bishops' Committee on the liturgy, have produced, among others, the following documents reflecting both an awareness of the spirit of liturgical reform and the needs of the American church for liturgical formation: 1) *Art and Environment in Catholic Worship*, 1986; 2) *Music in Catholic Worship*, rev. ed., 1983; 3) *Promoting Liturgical Renewal: Guidelines for Diocesan Liturgical Commissions and Offices of Worship*, 1988; 4) *Directory on the Pastoral Ministry of Bishops*, 1973; 5) *Liturgical Formation in Seminaries: A Commentary*, 1984.

Formation Through Liturgical Experience

Liturgical formation is the process which enables each individual to take his or her rightful place within the church (the local *domus ecclesiae*) when it engages in its most characteristic acts of sacramental worship. This means that the most natural setting for liturgical formation is the worshipping community. "The most powerful experience of the sacred is found in the celebration and the persons celebrating, that is, it is found in the action of the assembly: the living words, the living gestures, the living sacrifice, the living meal" (*Environment and Art*, 29). Thus, liturgical life, which never operates in isolation, has a very specific context: a *faith* context which reflects the gospel; a *spatial* context in which the worshipping community sacramentalizes that faith; and a *ritual* context in which that faith is vitalized. To be formed liturgically means that every worshipping Christian must become conversant in the context of faith; at home in the spatial context of the church, and articulate in the language of ritual activity. Thus, liturgical formation can never be limited to some members of the church, but is incumbent on all the faithful, because involvement in the liturgical life of the church is the right and duty of every Christian by reason of baptism (S.C., 14). Further, any attempt to identify liturgical formation solely as a pedagogical process which takes place outside the act of worship fails to understand that the best master of the praying church is liturgical prayer itself. Attention must be placed first on the act of worship before turning to the study and organizational aspects of the sacramental prayer life of the church.

The Spatial Context

Congregations as well as individuals are formed by the space in which they gather, and for this reason good liturgical space is a prime factor in proper liturgical formation. The environment of worship needs to be authentic and appropriate. Good architecture, art and furnishing create the proper setting for good liturgical celebrations. "The environment is appropriate when it is beautiful, when it is hospitable, when it clearly invites and needs an assembly of people to complete it. Furthermore, it is appropriate when it brings people close together so that they can see and hear the entire liturgical action, when it helps people feel involved and become involved" (*Environment and Art*, 24). This does not mean that the liturgical space must be elaborate or expensive, but that careful attention must be given to the main focal points demanded by the liturgical celebrations. In even the most humble building, attention should be paid to the quality of the space; liturgical space has to be prayerful, calling both the congregation and each individual to ritual and devotional prayer. Lack of resources can never be an excuse for either poor artistic design or poor worship, since prayerful space will be achieved by demanding quality and appropriateness from architecture, music and the other arts. "Whatever the style or type,

no art has a right to a place in liturgical celebration if it is not of high quality and if it is not appropriate" (*Environment and Art*, 19). To meet the demands of the liturgical assembly any work of art must also be appropriate in two ways: "it must be capable of bearing the weight of mystery, awe, reverence and wonder which the liturgical action expresses"; and, " it must clearly serve (and not interrupt) ritual action which has its own structure, rhythm and movement" (*Environment and Art*, 21).

In each diocese the model of good liturgical space should be the cathedral, the mother church of the diocese. It is the bishop's task to make the "cathedral church outstanding in its beauty, observance of regulations, and popular Christian fervor, so that this church may indeed appear as the mother and teacher of the other churches of the diocese" (*Promoting*, 5). Since local artistic and liturgical talent are frequently found in each parish, every diocese should have a quality liturgy and art committee to offer advice and direction.

The Ritual Context

The ritual context of Christian worship calls for formation into a community whose symbolic activity functions with memorial and celebration. This is a challenge to the American church which operates in a social context that is uncomfortable with symbolic activity, focuses on the contemporary and frequently transitory, and considers religious convictions as a private matter. By contrast, good liturgical celebrations affirm a different set of values: community, symbol, memorial, celebration.

Community. First of all, liturgical worship is communal. The activity of the assembled congregation can never be private or impersonal. Western society in general, and Americans in particular, need specific orientation and formation into the communal nature of Christian worship. "A culture which is oriented to efficiency and production has made us insensitive to the symbolic function of persons and things. . . . As a consequence, we tend to identify anything private and individual as 'personal'. But, by inference, anything communal and social is considered impersonal. For the sake of good liturgy, this misconception must be changed" (*Environment and Art*, 16).

Any conscious community building at the parish level is of its very nature liturgical formation. The ecclesiology of Vatican II provides the theological basis for the local community, describing the church as the body of Christ constituted by all of the people of God. This community of faith, even though it is hierarchically structured, functions with shared ministries when it gathers for worship. It is by virtue of baptism that each Christian becomes a member of the worshipping community, assuming the right to participate to the fullest when gathered around font, pulpit, and altar. Further, baptism is the basis for any liturgical ministry which the individual exercises. Christians are first formed into the liturgical community when they assume their rightful position in communal prayer.

Symbol. Since the gathered assembly worships in sign, symbol and ritual, all of its members must become comfortable and conversant in the language of sacramental symbols. A conscious awareness of the symbolic nature of worship can best be achieved through careful attention to an authentic use of symbols in every liturgical celebration. "Renewal requires the opening up of our symbols, especially the fundamental ones of bread and wine, water, oil, the laying on of hands, until we can experience all of them as authentic and appreciate their symbolic value" (*Environment and Art*, 15). Whenever the worship service becomes heavily verbal, rational, and catechetical, the symbolic dimension of sacramental prayer suffers.

Liturgical prayer has a healthy and human balance between word and rite, the rational and the symbolic. By letting the symbols speak their own language they communicate a truth proper to sacramental reality. This truth is realized not only in word, but also in gesture, i.e., walking, assembling, bathing, eating, anointing, reconciling, singing, and all of the other visible forms of sacramental prayer. In short, liturgical worship calls for a commitment to truth in word and ritual. Put negatively, anything which hinders or diminishes such symbolic activity in worship can only be understood as a denial of the baptismal rights of the faithful to the fount and source of the true Christian spirit (S.C., 10).

The bishops have described liturgical formation into the symbolic nature of worship as follows: "To gather intentionally in God's presence is to gather our total selves, our complete persons—a living 'sacrifice'. . . . Liturgy is total, and therefore must be much more than a merely rational or intellectual exercise. . . . In view of our culture's emphasis on reason, it is critically important for the church to reemphasize a more total approach to the human person by opening up and developing the non-rational elements of liturgical celebration: the concerns for feelings of conversion, support, joy, repentance, trust, love, memory, movement, gesture, wonder" (*Environment and Art*, 35).

Memorial. The mystery of God's presence celebrated in Christian worship is a mystery tied to the history of salvation. God's loving redemption unfolds within human history. The contemporary experience of God has its spiritual roots in a pattern of divine activity which becomes normative for the present relationship between God and his people, or more exactly in the historical and redemptive ministry of Christ. In the biblical notion of memorial (*anamnesis*), the faithful call to mind this pattern of divine activity as a way of renewing and reliving that same divine pattern in their lives. This creative recall is at the heart of Christian worship. Each Christian must both understand and know how to make memorial. In a society deeply committed to the contemporary and the transitory, it is important that worship be rooted in solid biblical patterns. Liturgical formation into Christian worship involves learning how creatively to recall the deeds of salvation history, as well as one's own personal history of God's activity in one's own life. Failure to understand Christian memorial severely limits one's understanding of Christian worship.

Celebration. Christian worship is a joyful celebration of the mystery of God in the midst of his people. The praise of God done by the congregation is a response of awe and wonder to God's love. Memorial and celebration come together through a realization that the pattern of the divine relationship was established when God broke into human history. The common past is salvation history recorded in scripture, and individual past is the personal history of each Christian. As inheritors of that past the Christian can celebrate with praise and thanksgiving God's saving presence. The call to worship is answered by those who know how to celebrate the great deeds of the history of salvation.

Liturgical Ministries and Formation

While it is true that Christian worship is congregation worship, it is also true that the liturgical assemblies are hierarchically structured. Each type of liturgical celebration has its special ministers, whose essential functions are largely responsible for the success of good liturgies. A successful liturgical celebration depends for the most part on ministers who both understand their function, and properly carry it out while not overstepping or interfering with other ministerial functions.

The Presiding Minister. Each liturgical celebration has a presiding minister who gathers the community together, leads in prayer, prays in the name of the community, and performs the tasks which are proper to the presiding minister, such as the eucharistic prayer. Most frequently the presiding minister is the local parish priest, but there are occasions when others can preside: deacons at baptism; religious not in orders at the Divine Office, appropriate ministers at communion services when no priest is available and at paraliturgical services such as wakes. Such tasks presume an individual who has a prayerful presence and a clear and distinct voice trained in public speaking, and who is at least capable of handling some minimal musical tasks. The presider must be at home with ritual prayer, i.e., both familiar and comfortable with the symbolic words and actions of each celebration. Since liturgical prayer is first and foremost a prayer of *this* assembled community, the presider should also be aware of the specific needs of *this* congregation and the way in which God is present to *this* community in their daily lives. Each presiding minister must be trained in the basic skills needed to serve as leader of the praying community, and also have a deep familiarity with the inner structure of the rite, the rhythm by which the rite unfolds, and the relationship of the various parts of that rite. A properly trained presider will not assume functions which properly belong to another minister. The presider performs with authority and dignity only those functions which belong properly to the president of the assembly.

Other Ministers. In addition to the presiding minister, each liturgical celebration calls for a variety of different ministers: lectors, cantors, ministers at the altar, communion ministers, musicians and the choir, to mention a few. Each ministry serves a specific liturgical function which is properly its own. That function operates as an integral part of the complete liturgical act, and should not be performed by any other than the proper minister. Liturgical ministers do not act in their own names, but as servants of the community and facilitators of the overall act of worship. These ministers must have the physical, spiritual, technical and communal qualities necessary for their ministry. They must also understand the overall structure of the liturgical act, and their precise function therein.

Lectors should have a clear voice for proclaiming the word of God, and an understanding of the scriptures. Ministers at the altar should know the nature of the eucharistic action, have a sense of presence and service at the altar, not distract from the principal action in progress, facilitate not distract from the offertory, the eucharistic prayer, the breaking of the bread and the communion action. Music ministers, in addition to having musical talent, need preparation in the structure of the different rituals, the role of liturgical music in worship, the proper moments for, and distinctions between, singing by the congregation, the choir, and the cantor. Guidelines for music ministers and the role of music in the liturgical action are provided in the statement of the Bishops' Committee on the Liturgy, *Music in Catholic Worship*, rev. ed., 1983.

Role of the Bishop in Liturgical Formation

As head of the local church the bishop has a special responsibility and exercises a unique function in the area of liturgical formation. Two documents deal specifically with this role of the bishop: *Ecclesiae Imago (The Directory)*, from the Congregation on Divine Worship; and *Promoting of Liturgical Renewal*, from the American Bishops' Committee on the Liturgy. The bishop is the principal presiding minister as well as the moderator-promoter-custodian of the liturgical life of the diocese. "To lead those assembled for prayer is the first and primary liturgical role of the bishop" (*Directory*, 78). He is expected to maintain high standards of liturgical presidency. "The bishop presiding at worship, both in the cathedral and in the parishes of the dioceses, is the model of all liturgical gatherings of the local Church" (*Promoting*, 5). Worship in the cathedral church should both in fact and in perception be understood as the center of divine worship in the diocesan community. The bishop himself should frequently preside over the divine mysteries and the liturgy of the hours, especially on Sundays and other solemn feasts of the year. He should also try to make the liturgical life of the cathedral church outstanding in its beauty, observance of regulations, and popular Christian fervor, so that his church may indeed appear as the mother and teacher of the other churches of the diocese (*Directory*, 81a).

A second aspect of the bishop's liturgical role is to be a moderator, promoter, and custodian of the liturgical life within the diocese he serves. Since a liturgical spirituality is the most available way in which the majority of the faithful of a diocese come to an integrating experience of God's presence in their lives, the bishop is encouraged to use the liturgy as one of the main instruments of exercising his pastoral ministry (*Promoting*, 7). "The bishop should take care that in his diocese the liturgy, which is the common and public worship of the people of God, should be celebrated with as much dignity as possible and with an active, devout and fruitful participation of all, with the sacred minister presiding, in accordance with the prescribed norms" (*Directory*, 80). A sacramental catechesis should be provided for all of the faithful. It is the task of the bishop as high priest and chief moderator of divine worship in the particular church to "... promote the liturgical training of the faithful through appropriate commissions (e.g., liturgical, music, and sacred art commissions, etc.) and officials, through pastors and other priests, through religious and through lay people prepared for this work and dedicated to the apostolate of the liturgy" (*Directory*, 82). The document even calls for the bishop to consider under the proper norms "new liturgical experiments whereby the impulse and warmth of authentic faith may show its vigor by evolving new and meaningful ways to fulfill the expectations and more clearly interpret the spirit of the religious life of the community" (*Directory*, 84).

In the exercise of his pastoral role as "moderator, promoter, and custodian," the bishop does not work alone. As a member of the college of bishops his task is carried out consistent with the norms established by the American bishops, and by the universal church. In every case the bishop is advised to employ the assistance of those who have special preparation in the area of liturgical studies, theology, pastoral practice. The *Directory* advises the local bishop to employ suitable, chosen collaborators— clerics, religious, or lay people—with whom he shares the pastoral mission of liturgical formation (*Directory*, 198; 211).

Liturgical Formation in Seminaries

Since one of the principal tasks of priests is to preside at worship in such a manner that the other members of the assembly are led to pray, particular attention has been given to the liturgical formation of those preparing for the priestly and diaconal ministries. In 1979 the Sacred Congregation for Catholic Education issued the *Instruction on Liturgical Formation in Seminaries*, and in 1984 the American Bishops' Committee on the Liturgy and the Bishops' Committee on Priestly Formation issued a commentary under the title, *Liturgical Formation in Seminaries: A Commen-*

tary. These documents call for a spiritual formation of the candidates for orders which is liturgically based.

The liturgical life of the seminary should be of the highest quality where there is the full range of liturgical prayer including the communal praying of the liturgy of the hours. The teaching of the sacred liturgy in seminaries has the highest priority as a major course of study. Professors of liturgy are to be experts specially trained in the discipline of liturgical studies which includes the history, theology, and pastoral practice of the sacramental prayer life of the church (*Instruction*, 51). The professor of liturgy "should well understand that his work is not simply scientific and technical but rather 'mystagogical,' so that he may introduce the students into the liturgical life and into its spiritual character." Further, "the strict connection between the liturgy and the doctrine of the faith has a special importance for the correct liturgical formation of future priests. . . . Scholars working in the field of sacred liturgy are to investigate carefully the tradition of divine worship, particularly when they study the nature of the Church and the doctrine and discipline of the sacraments" (*Instruction*, 44). And "above everything else liturgical acts, both as regard their texts and their ceremonies, must be explained to the students. The prayers and orations offered by the sacred liturgy are to be explained in a way that sheds light upon the doctrinal treasures and the spiritual values they contain" (*Instruction*, 46). There is to be special emphasis on the history of the rites as well as introduction into the traditions of the Oriental churches so that there is, as much as possible, a wide grasp of the whole liturgical tradition of prayer. "Given the importance of sacred music in liturgical celebrations, the students should be trained in music by experts, including a practical training, in those things necessary for them in their future roles as presidents and moderators of liturgical celebrations" (*Instruction*, 56). "Finally, it is extremely necessary that the students be taught the art of speaking and of using symbols, as well as how to use communications media. Indeed, in liturgical celebrations it is of the highest importance that the faithful be able to understand the priest, not only in what he says, whether in the homily or in the prayers and orations, but also in what he does by way of gestures and actions. Formation for this purpose is of such high importance in the renewed liturgy that it deserves very special consideration" (*Instruction*, 58). These principles of liturgical formation spelled out in detail for those training for the priesthood apply equally to anyone involved in liturgical ministries.

Formation Through Education

Good liturgies will result from careful planning. Each parish should have a parish liturgical committee whose task is to be concerned with the proper function of the liturgical life of the parish. Its overall concern is for a healthy prayer life of the parish. Members of such a committee should have an intimate and commanding knowledge of the various types of liturgical prayer of the church, understand how ritual and communal praying operates and provides a physical, social, and spiritual context in which liturgical prayer can take place. In cooperation with the presiding ministers the committee serves a valuable formative function for the local worshipping church through planning and facilitating every dimension of the liturgical life of the parish. In addition to planning the Sunday liturgy, the committee should be concerned with baptism, marriages, penance services, anointing of the sick, daily prayer services, and the devotional life of the parish. Many parishes have secured the services of a trained liturgist to function as liturgical coordinator, edu-

cator, and chairperson of the liturgical committee.

At the diocese and national level, liturgical commissions and offices of worship serve as policy-setting and educational arms of the church. Through these groups implementation of liturgical changes and educational programs are effectively carried out. Each diocese is to have a liturgical commission whose concern is to advise and aid the bishop in setting policy for the total prayer life of the whole diocese. In addition to a diocesan liturgical commission many dioceses also have an office of worship which can give its full attention to providing resources and conducting workshops in liturgical formation (*Promoting*, 14). The office of worship is to function as a major diocesan resource for the purpose of liturgical formation. These commissions are to be staffed with people who have special competence and training in the area of liturgical studies. Experts in the field are necessary to provide insight, training, leadership, and a critical evaluation of the overall celebration of the liturgy. "When a bishop relies on a volunteer diocesan liturgical commission as the only diocesan worship structure, he should realize that its effectiveness may be limited. Often the nature and scope of the tasks facing the commission's members will put a heavy burden on their time and resources. Competing responsibilities of the members may often prevent long-term projects and future planning" (*Promoting*, 15). The American bishops have issued their guidelines in *Promoting Liturgical Renewal: Guidelines for Diocesan Liturgical Commissions and Offices of Worship*, Bishops' Committee on the Liturgy: National Conference of Bishops, 1988.

At the national level there are two organizations for the promotion of liturgical formation: The Federation of Diocesan Liturgical Commissions (F.D.L.C.) and the Bishops' Committee on the Liturgy (B.C.L.). The F.D.L.C., first convened in 1969 by the secretariat of the Bishops' Committee on the Liturgy, is a national organization of diocesan liturgical commissions, or their equivalent structures, in the United States and its territories. The B.C.L. is a standing committee of the National Conference of Catholic Bishops (N.C.C.B.) with a history dating back to November 1958. The committee, assisted by a Secretariat in Washington, D.C., is composed of seven member bishops, various consultant bishops, and ten advisors (lay, religious, and priests). The functions of the B.C.L. are: to contribute to the preparation of appropriate liturgical rites, texts, and books; to assist bishops individually and collegially in implementing the official norms and directives of the Holy See and of the N.C.C.B.; and to assist the bishops in the development of liturgical catechesis and the continued liturgical renewal of priests, deacons, religious men and women, and the laity of the church (*Promoting*, 17).

At the international level there is the International Commission on English in the Liturgy (I.C.E.L.), and the Congregation of Divine Worship and the Discipline of the Sacraments. I.C.E.L. was established in 1963, during the Second Vatican Council, by the principal conferences of bishops from English--speaking countries. The primary program of I.C.E.L. is the translation into English of the official Latin texts of the Roman liturgy. In May 1969, Pope Paul VI divided the Sacred Congregation of Rites into two distinct congregations, the Congregation for Divine Worship and the Congregation for the Causes of Saints. In 1975, Pope Paul VI established a new congregation, the Sacred Congregation for the Sacraments and Divine Worship, to take the place of the Congregation of the Sacraments (created by Pope Pius X in 1908) and the Congregation for Divine Worship. In 1984, Pope John Paul II

divided the former congregation into the Congregation for the Sacraments and the Congregation for Divine Worship, and in 1988, he reunited these two congregations under the title of Congregation for Divine Worship and the Discipline of the Sacraments. The Congregation for Divine Worship and the Discipline of the Sacraments is responsible for the pastoral, spiritual, canonical, and disciplinary dimensions of the sacraments and other liturgical rites of the church. This congregation also publishes *Notitiae*, a monthly journal containing short articles on liturgical renewal, and reports on the liturgical activities of episcopal conferences and national liturgical commissions.

See **Catechesis, liturgical; Liturgical committee**

Art and Environment in Catholic Worship, (Washington, D.C.: National Conference of Catholic Bishops, 1986). *Directory on the Pastoral Ministry of Bishops* (Washington, D.C.: National Conference of Catholic Bishops, 1973). *Liturgical Conference of Catholic Bishops, 1984. Music in Catholic Worship*, rev. ed., (Washington, D.C.: National Conference of Catholic Bishops, 1983). *Promoting Liturgical Renewal: Guidelines for Diocesan Liturgical Commissions and Offices of Worship* (Washington, D.C.: National Conference of Catholic Bishops, 1988).

EMMANUEL CUTRONE

FUNERALS

See **Burial, Christian**

FUNERALS, PREACHING AT

The preaching event at a funeral should always be a clear proclamation of the gospel of Jesus Christ, with special emphasis on his death and resurrection. It may also include a grateful reference to the life of the deceased, mentioning specific gifts, characteristics, and achievements of the deceased. The central thrust of the sermon, as of the entire funeral service, should be a witness to the resurrection.

The funeral sermon should avoid the extremes of being morbid, or death denying. It should avoid the extremes of being completely impersonal, or being a eulogy which gives a romantic and hence false description of the life of the deceased. *God*, not the deceased, should be the focus of the funeral message. This can be enhanced by closing the coffin *before* the funeral service and keeping it closed. The funeral sermon may be more effective in a setting of worship *following* the interment of the body.

The three inescapable aspects of the funeral setting and sermon are: God, the reality of death, and the congregation. The funeral sermon should interweave the three stories of God, the dead person, and the listeners. The listeners include not only the mourners but members of the community of faith who may or may not have known the deceased well, plus non-church people who are related in some way to the deceased.

The funeral sermon should face the reality of the death of the deceased, acknowledging that the loss is real and final. The preacher should use the name of the dead person, mentioning significant events, activities and characteristics of the deceased. Recalling the life of the deceased encourages the grieving process. It also can help the mourners move from relating to the deceased in life to relating through memory and in the communion of saints.

The funeral message should proclaim the majesty, power, steadfast love and wisdom of God. Since the ultimate comfort of the bereaved is found in the mercy of God, the funeral sermon should point to God, and God's gift of eternal life through Christ, rather than focus on the feelings of the bereaved.

The funeral message is God's word to the living and therefore should enable those present to relate their own living and dying to the good news of Christ's death and resurrection. The sermon should motivate all hearers, Christian and non-Christian, to reflect on their own death and to remember that the act of dying is but a dramatic symbol of what has been happening all along as we journey through death to life. The funeral message should call hearers to die to self and sin daily and to accept the free gift of eternal life through Christ.

The sermon at the time of death should deal with feelings—both negative and positive. The preacher should avoid euphemisms for death such as 'passing' or 'passed away' and should use death, died, and dead as ways of emphasizing the reality of what has happened. This will enable mourners to deal more effectively with their feelings of loneliness, anger, anxiety, as well as affection, hope and joy. The sermon should be sensitive to feelings mourners may have of anger toward God, frustration, and even a sense of the absence of God in their grief. Laments from the scriptures can help voice such feelings which are normal human reactions to loss.

The funeral sermon is part of the whole funeral process which serves as a "rite of passage" enabling mourners and the community to deal with the loss, and celebrating the moving of the deceased from the land of the living to the life beyond the grave. This rite of passage involves separation, transition and incorporation, and the funeral sermon may pick up and deal with these movements, showing how death separates the deceased from the living, celebrates the transition to the life hereafter and affirms the incorporation of deceased Christians in the communion of the saints.

The funeral message should celebrate Christ's victory over death which embraces all believers. In baptism believers die and rise with Christ. But this "end time" reality does not deny the reality of biological death: "For as in Adam all die, so also in Christ shall all be made alive" (1 Cor 15:22). The resurrection of the

Christian's body always remains future. Death, the last enemy, will eventually be destroyed.

There are two ways of viewing life after death: focus on the immortality of the soul, or focus on resurrection of the body. The first is rooted in Greek philosophy and Gnosticism. It says that the soul is immortal (does not die). Plato was one who claimed that human beings are a union of body and soul, a union that is dissolved at death. The soul is freed from the body as a person might be freed from a prison. While the body is destroyed, the soul, pre-existent and post-existent, continues. This became a generally accepted belief of the church and was formally defined as church doctrine by the Fifth Lateran Council (1512-1517). According to this view the soul as the unchanging kernel of life at the center of each individual continues untouched by death. According to medieval theology the souls of the dead were already enjoying bliss with God, waiting only for reunion with their glorified bodies on the last day.

A strong case can be built for a biblical view of eternal life, of course. This life grounded in God through faith is not destroyed or separated from God by death. But this life with God now and beyond the grave is a gift of God, not a natural aspect of all human life.

There can also be made a strong case for the resurrection of the body, as we affirm in the Apostles' Creed. In more recent years Christian theology has shifted more toward an emphasis on the resurrection of the body rather than on the immortality of the soul. According to the view of the resurrection of the body, death is a devastating reality because the entire person dies. For this reason anxiety is a very normal and understandable response to death. The terror which death holds for humans lies not so much in fear of hell as in the fact that humans are a totality of body/soul and therefore in death one is totally dead.

The funeral sermon should face squarely the mystery and absurdity of death. Because we are dealing with matters of faith and mystery we must use metaphors. While the metaphor of the language of immortality of the soul was chosen by many church Fathers to stress the continuing of the individual self beyond death, it seems to deny the reality and discontinuity of death. But the metaphor of resurrection is grounded in Hebrew thought and biblical faith. It takes death seriously, with all its mystery and absurdity. The sermon links individual human deaths with Jesus' death which is stressed in the Apostles' Creed: "crucified, dead, and buried; he descended into hell." But on the third day God raised him from the dead. And we believe that God will "also raise us by his power" (1 Cor 6:14). Paul, writing to the Philippians, indicates that a believer's total life and being will be transformed by the risen Christ "to be like his glorious body" (Phil 3:21).

In order to communicate metaphors found in resurrection language, the preacher should look for contemporary images as well as draw on biblical ones. The image of the butterfly, of the dying of the grain of wheat, and of reconciliation with God all may be helpful in making the funeral sermon effective in conveying Christian hope. The image of reconciliation takes seriously the break in relationship with God which death causes. But through God's saving act in Christ we are reconciled to God, leading to a joyful human experience. This image of reconciliation can link the present to the future as we anticipate being restored to God in the life beyond the grave. There are weaknesses in every metaphor. But we are forced to use them to convey religious truth, in spite of the fact the best metaphors conceal as well as reveal.

The funeral sermon should enable mourners to affirm once again the hope of new life in Christ. And it should confront the non-believer with the Christian teaching of the resurrection and life with God beyond the grave. This can best be achieved through stories, images and metaphors. The apostle Paul uses images of different kinds of "bodies" and of the seed dying in order to receive a new body, radically different from the body of the seed that was sown.

The funeral message, by necessity, is developed under the pressure of time, usually two or three days at most. While visiting with the family of the deceased, when this is possible, the preacher should listen for clues to the significance of the life of the deceased in order to help weave the fabric of the funeral sermon. Each funeral sermon is unique for it deals with God's grace and the life of a unique human being whose death is unlike that of any other death.

There are a great variety of approaches to developing the funeral sermon using standard structures as the following: biographical, drawing on the life of a biblical character who faced death, such as David who mourned the death of his little son; doctrinal, which focuses on a Christian doctrine such as the providence of God, the grace of God, or the future life. The expository sermon is based on the exegesis of a biblical passage especially relevant to that particular occasion. With the life situation sermon the preacher begins with the congregation as it mourns the death of a particular individual and then relates God's comforting love to those who grieve. In an occasional sermon the message would take into account the unique occasion of the death: after a long illness, as a result of an accident, crime or suicide, or if it occurred on Christmas, Easter or the deceased's birthday or anniversary. A textual sermon takes a text from scripture and relates the thrust of the text to the funeral occasion. With the help of a concordance the preacher can discover the text especially fitting for the particular funeral.

The narrative form of sermon is especially fitting for a funeral sermon as it allows the preacher to weave the sermon with the threads of the life of the deceased, the grace of God, and the grief of the mourners. The sermon might be thought of as a series of episodes, with various images and metaphors which enable hearers to relate to God and one another in love. The funeral sermon should focus on one particular key aspect of the funeral occasion. By shaping the sermon around a single issue the minds of mourners are given a sense of clarity and reality. Two of the pitfalls of funeral sermons are generality and abstraction. The sermon should acknowledge that there are no simple answers to the mystery surrounding death. Final answers are not expected. The funeral message can provide mourners a frame of reference and a sense of the presence of God to help them work through their grief and to try to make sense of death's dilemma.

See **Death, theology of**

Perry H. Biddle, Jr., *Abingdon Funeral Manual: Revised* (Nashville: Abingdon Press, 1976). Paul Irion, *The Funeral and the Mourners: Pastoral Care of the Bereaved* (Nashville: Abingdon Press, 1954). Robert G. Hughes, *A Trumpet in Darkness* (Philadelphia: Fortress Press, 1985).

PERRY H. BIDDLE, JR.

G

GATHERING RITES

The term "gathering rites" refers to the ritual beginning of official rites as well as to the liturgical opening of other non-sacramental convocations. The more structural language better indicates the function of the ritual element than the various designations given in specific rites (e.g., "greeting" in penance, "entrance rite" in matrimony, or "introductory rites" in eucharist). Whatever the context, the intent is "that the faithful coming together take on the form of a community and prepare themselves" properly to enter into the celebration (G.I.R.M., 4th ed., 24). The pattern generally includes song, gesture (e.g., procession), greeting and (presidential) prayer or *collect*.

In the first place, it should be noted that the most fundamental and theologically significant factor is the act of assembling itself. This ancient emphasis cannot be missed in the liturgical theology of *Sacrosanctum concilium* and *Lumen gentium* which insist on the significance of the liturgical assembly. However elaborate or simple the accompanying adornment, the gathering of the Christian people in assembly for worship constitutes an ecclesial event.

Gathering for worship expresses itself ritually in a movement from other occupations, places and concerns to a unity in worship which is based in common Christian identity. Thus, gathering enacts a transition and an integration. It is possible to distinguish three phases in this movement: arrival/welcome, establishment of identity, beginning/opening. Clearly the three phases are closely related, but each has its own primary agenda; mixing the agendas can often lead to confusion.

For the first several centuries beginning the celebration could be accomplished very simply. The eucharist, for example, began directly with the bishop's greeting ("Peace to you," or "The Lord be with you," completed by "And with your spirit.") and the readings. But the entrance into the church is one of the moments which attract elaborations, and over time it became much more complex. The missal of Paul VI represents an effort to shape the ritual without benefit of a single model from which to work. We will illustrate the agenda of gathering by examining the "introductory rites" as they presently stand in that missal.

Welcome

It would seem natural that welcoming members, visitors and strangers belongs at the point of arrival. This might not have been necessary in the ancient town church, but it is increasingly significant in communities in which such natural patterns of relating and mutual recognition cannot be presumed. An authentic welcome eases the transition into a different experience of community, helps to create a sense of belonging and prepares for communal action. As sensitivity to this moment has increased, more and more importance has been given to what are called ministries of hospitality. The welcome and greeting which people receive upon their arrival situate them as members of the community which is gathering and as participants in that community's common act of worship. Thus *liturgically apt* hospitality goes beyond the merely warm reception and seeks to express reverence for the person and for the event. Cultural sensitivity and custom surely condition the experience of welcome and belonging; at this point such considerations can be given free expression adapted to different persons.

Establishment of Identity

This movement may include procession, song and ritual greeting. While the style and degree of elaborateness of articulation will vary according to season, feast or occasion, the central purpose is to recognize and give expression to the fact that this is a gathering of the Christian people specifically as church.

As ritual, the procession is a choreographed gesture which signals the beginning of the celebration and expresses the identity of the congregation and its ministers as participants in the mystery being celebrated. The act of moving through the community sweeps the participants along to the precincts of altar, ambo and chair. Ministers and congregation are not, therefore, identified over against one another, but reciprocally.

From about the 4th century there is evidence of a processional entrance of the celebrant which came to include the book of the gospels and other ministers as well as candles and incense. Naturally this procession came to be accompanied by song, in the first place by an antiphon and as many verses of an appropriate psalm as were needed. The early collections of antiphons and chants reflect the effort to set the tone of the celebration by announcing the feast or the mystery being celebrated. The missal of Paul VI continues this tradition and allows the use either of the antiphon provided or another song which will fulfill the same function. The *General Instruction of the Roman Missal* goes beyond the simply functional use of song as accompaniment; its purpose here is first to "intensify the unity of the gathered people, lead their thoughts to the mystery of the season or feast ... "(25). Given this appropriate attention to song as part of the entrance, it is difficult to justify the direction in the following paragraph that, if there is no singing, the antiphon "is recited either by the faithful ... [or] by the priest after the greeting." The veneration of the altar by the ministers is part of the entrance and may be enhanced by the use of incense. The older Roman tradition (and most Eastern traditions to this day) also include reverence to the book of the gospels. The entrance concludes with the (seemingly misplaced) sign of the cross and the greeting.

As we have noted above, the *greeting* was originally very simple, and the ancient forms are preserved in the missal of Paul VI along with two other substantially biblical greetings, also in the form of a ritual dialogue. The exchange depends for its vitality upon the awareness of being the Christian people; in turn, it enhances that common identity by expressing it ritually. The practice of appending or substituting more colloquial greetings or casual remarks would seem to miss this ritual point and to blur the integrity of the exchange as a typically Christian sign of mutual recognition and respect. Any additional spoken overture at this moment should be clearly in the form of an invitation or orientation to prayer and not a didactic "introduction" or exhortation.

Rite of Blessing and Sprinkling Holy Water

This memorial of baptism is provided

for use on Sundays. It is especially appropriate during the Easter season, and may be indicated for other Sundays as well when Christian baptismal identity is a special focus of the celebration. Since the gesture of sprinkling the people would seem to call for a kind of procession through the community, use of this rite would suggest a simple entrance procession. When this rite is used, it replaces the penitential rite.

Penitential Rite

An innovation of the missal of Paul VI, the communal penitential rite presents particular problems. It would seem to be in continuity with the prayers at the foot of the altar of the previous missal, especially when the *Confiteor* is used, but that perception is mistaken since the previous practice was a private gesture. Indeed, the use of the *Confiteor* would seem almost always to be the least desirable option because of its heavily individualistic orientation. Such a redirection obviously confuses the professedly communal nature of the gathering itself and would seem to require a kind of retrieval of the community's attention. The second form provided is a kind of brief responsory which confesses sinfulness and calls for God's mercy. Its brevity, communal expression and confidence in God's mercy would recommend this option for simpler celebrations where a penitential emphasis is warranted. The third form for the penitential rite presents a series of litanic acclamations incorporating the *Kyrie* as a response. The models provided contain acclamations of praise and pleas for mercy in a way that suggests their aptness for Lent and at other more solemn gatherings with a penitential orientation. This form of the penitential rite has unfortunately come to be used as a kind of communal "examination of conscience" in some places. Surely this is a disruption and misdirection of the liturgy and a confusing reversion to a privatized spirituality,

however covertly expressed. Finally, a word should be said of the invitations which open the penitential rite. While the first two options provided serve as useful models, the third, " ... to prepare ourselves to celebrate ... let us call to mind our sins," is a most unfortunate translation of an infelicitous (Latin) original. This language expressly reverses the communal orientation of the gathering and brings the sense of confidence and joy in God's loving, merciful presence to full stop.

Gloria

The *Gloria* expresses in anthem form essentially the same sentiments as the litanic (third) form of the penitential rite in an expanded and more jubilant way. By tradition the singing of this anthem marks more festive and joyful occasions. It is difficult to understand how recitation (cf. G.I.R.M., 31) of the text could possibly realize a desirable result.

Prayer

The presider's opening prayer or *collect* concludes the act of gathering, formally opens the celebration and serves as a transition to the liturgy of the word. In its function as an opening, the prayer thematically introduces the mystery being celebrated. As a *collect* the prayer gathers into one the silent sentiments of the community and gives them collective expression, often in the form of a petition that the community might realize the fruits of the celebration. Clearly, the pause for silent prayer by all and the acclamation, "Amen", are integral elements of the prayer and contribute to its ritual function.

Gathering rites cannot succeed when they are trivialized by dull routine or when they are overblown into an "event" in themselves. They fulfill their purpose when they help people to grasp their Christian identity at worship and orient the assembly to the event which brings the community together. It would seem that this is only possible in the case of the Mass when care is taken to select from among the many disparate elements which are collected in the missal of Paul VI. Only such a careful selection will shape a coherent and unifying act of gathering for worship which leads naturally to the service which follows.

See **Assembly; Hospitality**

Ralph A. Keifer, *To Give Thanks and Praise* (Washington, D.C.: National Association of Pastoral Musicians, 1980). John F. Baldovin, S.J., "Kyrie Eleison and the Entrance Rite of the Roman Eucharist," *Worship* 60 (July 1986): 334-347. Joseph A. Jungmann, S.J., *The Mass of the Roman Rite*, Trans. by Francis A Brunner (New York: Benziger, 1951).

KENNETH HANNON, O.M.I.

GESTURE AND MOVEMENT IN THE LITURGY

By *gesture* is meant all non-verbal action by the subject of the liturgy, ministers and assembly, involving the use of the human body as an instrument of meaningful communication. This rather broad category of gesture includes all movement (e.g., procession, dance) that involves the use of the body in meaningful non-verbal communication activity on the part of an individual or group. Such movement—individual or collective—involves spatial mobility.

The liturgical reform initiated by the Second Vatican Council both underscored the principle of active participation by the entire liturgical assembly and emphasized the place of gesture and movement in the liturgical action. The *Constitution on the Sacred Liturgy* states that "to promote active participation, the people should be encouraged to take part by means of acclamations, responses, psalmody, antiphons, and song, as well as by actions, gestures and bearing" (S.C., 30). Furthermore, the introduction of the vernacular and the presence of ministers who preside facing the assembly has brought about a new awareness of the need and importance of good and meaningful gesture and movement within the liturgy.

The use of gesture and movement within the liturgy rests solidly upon basic principles derived from anthropology, theology and liturgy.

Anthropological Principles

Because liturgy is an action of a community of persons bound together by a common faith that is given visible expression in precise ritual forms, it is also influenced by the basic principles of cultural anthropology.

The human body is both a source of individuation and of personal identity. But as a unity of spirit and matter, a person utilizes the bodily to give expression to the non-material. The body, therefore, becomes not only the primary symbol of the individual composite but also the instrument of communication by that individualized and unique unity that constitutes each human person.

When inserted into a given society, a person will make use of both verbal (e.g., language) and non-verbal (e.g., gesture) forms for the purpose of self-expression and interpersonal communication. The greater part of such processes, however, takes place on the level of the non-verbal. Within the context of a specific society, the individual through the process of socialization learns the acceptable and meaningful communication patterns of the culture on the verbal and non-verbal levels so that both forms can be used with meaning and profit. Because the verbal and non-verbal forms of expression are in fact culture-bound and therefore arbitrary, the meaning of the individual elements of communication and expression is not to be found in the elements themselves (e.g., a particular sound or gesture). Rather, the meaning of any element is an acquired or an attributed one, but at the same time one that has been agreed upon and accepted within a common cultural frame of reference. To use these elements in an idiosyncratic manner is to render meaningful human communication more difficult. Indeed, the very purpose of the elements is frustrated since they no longer bear or relate to the agreed upon meaning they have been given or have acquired within a specific cultural framework.

Finally, within a culture, the acceptable forms of verbal and non-verbal expression and communication remain open to possible mutation, addition or subtraction. Furthermore, even an existing form, while remaining the same, can actually be given or gradually assume a new meaning within a given cultural context. Such changes may be introduced by agents of change from within or from without the existing cultural system, attesting to both the dynamic character of culture and to the arbitrary nature of the various forms of its verbal and non-verbal expression.

As one can readily see, the general anthropological principles enunciated above are applicable, *mutatis mutandis*, to the specific area of the non-verbal elements (gestures and movement) employed in worship. The body is used in prayer. It is a means of expressing and communicating one's faith stance in worship. Since no language is inborn, the meaning of most gestures needs to be learned. Because of the dynamic elements of expression, gestures are open to change in both meaning and form.

Theological Principles

Moving now beyond the underlying principles offered by the behavioral and social sciences, we consider a second set of principles on the use of movement and gesture in the liturgy as found in Judaeo-Christian theology.

Creation Theology. Theological reflection on creation gives rise to two principles in our consideration of gesture and movement in the liturgy. The works of divine creation are good; the works of creation manifest the very nature of God.

The Christian believes that the works of creation are intrinsically good by the design of the Creator (see Gen 1:4, 10, 12, 18, 21, 25, 31). Any other belief would be a denial of the goodness of the Creator and the intrinsic value of the creative work of God. Furthermore, it is beyond the Christian belief to make a dichotomy between the material and spiritual realms of creation as if one were good and the other evil. Thus, when considering the human person, Christian theology does not repudiate the body because it is material and, therefore, of less value. Rather creation theology recognizes how the material and spiritual realms are integrally related in the plan of God, and that together they give glory to the Creator and work toward that final transformation of all creation. This is not to reject the presence of sin by the human person who by free will can mar the creative work of God.

If all creation is good, it is also revelatory, since in creation God is also engaged in self-manifestation. Therefore, all of creation is an expression of the wisdom and the love of the Creator who freely manifests his own nature in moving beyond himself in absolute freedom to create works completely distinct from his being. Such divine creative self-communication underscores the value of all our attempts to express ourselves in worship by the use of specific communicative and revelatory actions, including human gestures and movements.

Christology. It is in the person of Christ, the Incarnate Word, that we find manifested the full plan of creation and redemption. In creation Christ is the mediator. In the incarnation Christ is the sacrament of encounter with God. In the paschal mystery of death and resurrection he is revealed as the saving Redeemer. In the words, gestures, and movements of Christ, the Christian finds manifest Christ's own person and indeed, the three persons of the Trinity. Therefore, it is no wonder that the church, the body of Christ, employs in its worship the human language of verbal and non-verbal signs and symbols, gestures and movements.

Ecclesiology. The worshipping community offers worship in union with Christ. As a faith community that is both universal and local in nature, the church employs an array of signs, symbols, gestures and movements that might be either universal or local in meaning and expression. Incarnate in time and in space, the local church has no other option if it is to be and remain true to its very nature.

Legitimate diversity in ecclesial expression will follow when room is made for those variations and adaptations to different groups, regions and peoples that the *Constitution on the Sacred Liturgy* permits and calls for (S.C., 38). This principle is as applicable to gesture and movement (non-verbal language) as it is to verbal communicative forms (e.g., vernacular usages, music, etc.).

Sacramental Theology. The sacraments as systems of verbal and non-verbal communication make present and effective the mystery symbolized. To refer to the sacraments as symbols is, at the same time, to recognize that they are the medium through which the mystery-reality is expressed, made present and effective. As a ritual process, human and tangible symbols are used, surrounded by select verbal and non-verbal cultural elements (such as gesture and movement) to both disclose the meaning of the sacrament and to convey the deepest expressions of the worshipping community.

Liturgical Theology. In the broad category of theology one can isolate several basic liturgical principles for the use of gestures and movement within the liturgy. The liturgy is an action by the faith community that involves the entire person. The deepest levels of faith and belief are expressed in both verbal and non-verbal forms. In this way active participation by the individual and community in the mystery celebrated is facilitated and externalized through such means as individual or collective gestures and movements.

This setting side by side of a series of repetitive verbal and non-verbal forms in the liturgy makes for ritual structures. Just as in ordinary human ritual patterns, liturgical rituals reinforce belief systems, bond the community, and disclose meaning. In the liturgical act, ritual elements such as gesture and movement contribute to both the expression and the understanding of the sacramental moment as well as to its particular efficacy.

The entire assembly and its various ministers have their particular roles within the liturgical act. Some gestures and movements might be common to all; others may be unique to individual ministries. Such role distinctions need to be respected also in the use of gestures and movements.

The type of gesture or movement used within the liturgy depends on its purpose. Furthermore, if it is to convey meaning, it must be executed in a way that is truly understandable and appropriate for the space and occasion. Unnecessary or repetitive use of gestures or movements can hinder both the communicative process and the transmission of meaning. Gestures and movements should be clear and marked by noble simplicity.

Thought should be given to using gestures and movements that come from and are expressive of the local worshipping community. Such is the present challenge in terms of the inculturation of the liturgy.

Liturgical Gestures

History. Since gestures and movements are intrinsically tied up with the communication process, it is no wonder that from the beginning, they have been employed in Christian worship. The NT and a study of the liturgical documents from the early church evidences their gradual development. With regard to the situation in the church of Rome as described in the *Apostolic Tradition* of Hippolytus, it has been noted that "apart from the rite of total immersion, the laying-on of hands for confirmation, the laying-on of hands over the offerings by the concelebrants during the Eucharistic prayer and the laying of hands on bishops and priests during their ordination, and the laying-on of hands on the deacon by the bishop, there is no insistence of gesture symbols" (Nocent, 21). Even during the period after 313, the Peace of Constantine, when liturgical creativity spread, more attention was given to the development of texts (euchology) than to gestures and movements. The reason for this remains conjectural, although it could have come from the desire to distinguish Christianity from pagan religions by emphasizing the spiritual character of Christian worship. That the development of gestures was more significant in the East is attested to by Egeria in her late 4th century account of the liturgy in Jerusalem. Influenced by the Church in the East and the North (Franco-Germanic practices) the Roman church began to adopt additional symbols, gestures and movements in its liturgy while at the same time introducing some that were then unique to Rome (e.g., the *fermentum*). Roman ritual austerity prevailed until the end of the 13th century when an appreciable French influence was asserted on the Roman liturgy (i.e., the pontifical of William Durandus). For the greater part such practices remained inflexible until the reform initiated by the Second Vatican Council.

The operative principles in the Vatican reform of the Roman rite are found in the S.C. 21-40. The reform, based on sound theological, historical and pastoral principles, was introduced "in order that the Christian people may more surely derive an abundance of graces from the liturgy" (S.C., 21). More precisely, with reference to their ritual expression and content, the Vatican constitution directed that "the rites should be marked by a noble simplicity; they should be short, clear, and unencumbered by useless repetitions; they should be within the people's power of comprehension and as a rule not require much explanation" (S.C., 34). In the light of such directives the post-conciliar liturgical reform was undertaken. The results of the reform are evident in the revised liturgy of the Roman rite and reflected in the type, place and use of gestures.

Types of Gestures. The variety of liturgical gestures almost defies categorization. The function of the various gestures, however, suggests the form of classification presented here. It should be noted that a particular gesture may in fact be placed into more than one category depending upon its function and/or meaning. Whereas some liturgical gestures are biblical in origin, others are the result of cultural influences (e.g., Jewish, Roman, Byzantine, etc.).

1. *Epicletic*: The gesture of imposing hands while calling upon the Holy Spirit, invoking the power of God. As one of the oldest and most significant liturgical gestures, it is used in the eucharist, confirmation, ordination, etc.

2. *Demonstrative*: A movement of the hand intended to simply indicate or point out the attitude of the person (e.g., striking one's breast to show sorrow, humble repentance; kiss of peace to express reciprocal Christian love).

3. *Unitive*: A positioning of the hand intended to express moral unity with another (e.g., the optional gesture of priest concelebrants during the eucharistic institution narrative).

4. *Salutatory*: The gesture that accompanies a greeting as, for example,

with the opening salutation of a liturgical service.

5. *Signing*: The gesture that accompanies the making of the sign of the cross, blessing, marking, etc.

6. *Reverential*: A gesture intended to express reverence or respect as in a bow, genuflection, incensation, a kiss, or as in the gesture of reverencing the altar, incensing a person, etc.

7. *Utilitarian*: A gesture that is employed for practical reasons as, for example, the breaking of the consecrated bread (*fractio*), the elevation of the consecrated bread for all to see, the washing of the hands after the distribution of ashes, etc. In some cases, the original purely functional gestures have been given a theological or spiritualized interpretation. The washing of hands after the reception of the gifts was originally a practical matter but was later interpreted as a gesture of seeking interior cleanliness. The mixing of water with wine was a common meal practice at the time of Christ in Palestine, Rome, and elsewhere, but in other cultures was given an allegorical interpretation in the liturgy (i.e., representing Christ's humanity and divinity or the blood and water that flowed from his side).

8. *Postural*: The gesture that is used in the very bearing of one's body in a particular position for a longer period, e.g., standing (expressing resurrection), orant posture (standing with hands extended in prayer), kneeling (expressing a penitential attitude), sitting (indicating authority or attentive listening), prostration (supplication), extended period of bowing (readiness to receive blessing, as in the solemn blessing of the eucharist), etc.

The Place of Gestures. In the celebration of the liturgy gestures are part of the entire communication genre of the ritual action. The rites themselves indicate not only what gestures are to be used but also their precise place within the structural flow. It was for this reason that in the recent revision of the various liturgical rites, attention was given not only to the written liturgical texts but also to the directives for the employment of gestural language on the part of both the ministers and the assembly.

A careful study of each rite reveals the place of non-verbal language within it. By way of illustration, the gestures that are used in the Rite for Reconciliation of Individual Penitents are spelled out here. In this particular rite of penance the non-verbal gestures, although limited, are part of the acceptable and required ritual language. An initial salutatory gesture is involved in the welcoming of the penitent: "The priest should welcome the penitents with fraternal charity" (D.O.L., 368, no. 16). The sign of the cross (signing gesture) is added to the introductory rites. The primary gesture accompanies the absolution. The priest extends his hands over the head of the penitent (or at least extends his right hand) as he begins the form of absolution (epicletic gesture) and concludes the words of absolution with the sign of the cross. The postural gesture of the penitent (sitting, kneeling) reflects the inner attitude of the person.

Use of Gestures. Although the precise place and nature of each non-verbal gesture is noted in the individual rites, the manner in which the ministers employ the prescribed gestures is significant. A poorly articulated language (verbal or non-verbal) is counterproductive in terms of communication and the transmission of the intended meaning. Liturgical gestures must be done with deliberate intent, care and reverence so that they serve as authentic bearers of the deeper levels of meaning. Commenting on gestures, the Consilium established for the implementation of the Constitution on the Liturgy stated that "they will be effective as such only to the degree that they are motivated directly by an inner vision, the contemplation of mystery.

Careful observance of the rubrics, necessary though it is, is not enough here" (D.O.L., 42, no. 487).

In the use of gestures one must be aware of the difficulties that can arise. 1) The repetition of the same gestures on the part of ministers or assembly (e.g., the sign of the cross) can lead to a mechanical or perfunctory usage. In 1968 the Consilium raised the relevant question: "How can gestures that have become mechanical from habit, sloppy from routine, half-hearted from apathy still function as signs of the work of salvation?" (D.O.L. 42, no. 487). 2) There is the danger of reducing gestures to their bare minimum. In the process, however, their communicative value is proportionally lessened as is seen, for example, in the gesture of the minister who washes his finger tips rather than his hands, uses a few drops of water for the baptismal washing rather than flowing water or immersion, dabs the sick with oil rather than anointing them with generous and visible portions of oil, and reduces the sign of the cross at the final blessing of the assembled Sunday community to postage stamp proportions. 3) In some societies there is the danger of thinking that unless the gestures have utilitarian value, they have little or no significance and can be set aside easily. Such might be the case with the celebrant who refuses to proclaim the eucharistic prayer with hands in the outstretched, orant posture. 4) There is the danger of expanding gestures out of proportion and so disrupting the intended ritual flow of the liturgical act, thus blowing the one ritual element out of proportion in relation to the entire rite. As an example one might suggest the practice where the presider at the eucharist feels he must extend the sign of peace to each and every person in the community and in the process clericalizes the gesture and expands the ritual moment dis-proportionately.

Minister of Gestures. In the process of human communication the use of the body is natural to everyone. Liturgical body language as found in ritual gestures is not limited to one or the other person. Since all in the assembly are to become active participants in worship, all are invited to incorporate significant ritual gestures into their prayer. The time, place and manner in which one does so is, however, structured by the particular rite. The principle enunciated in the General Instruction of the Roman Missal is applicable to the use of gestures by the members of the liturgical assembly: "...all, whether ministers or laypersons, should do all and only those parts that belong to them, so that the very arrangement of the celebration itself makes the Church stand out as being formed in a structure of different orders and ministries" (D.O.L. 208, no. 58).

Meaning of Gestures. Like all gestures, liturgical gestures are open to various meanings. Simply stated, such gestures can have four levels of meaning: the ordinary, the contextual, the theological, and the symbolic-sacramental.

The first level of meaning is the ordinary, i.e., that which is given to gestures by one's culture—by the common understanding outside of the liturgical action and which is recognized even by the non-initiated (e.g., the use of water for cleansing). When placed in worship setting such gestures take on a second level of meaning (contextual) drawn from the understanding of the religious tradition. Thus a ritual washing in a specific liturgical context is recognized as Christian baptism. The theological meaning of gestures is that which is a result of theological reflection on scripture and ecclesial tradition. Thus, in the baptismal gesture one understands, in a doctrinal manner, the Christian teaching about new birth, cleansing from sin, etc. On the fourth and highest level of meaning, gestures reveal a sacramental meaning which involves both symbolic presence and efficacy. The celebrant's gestures in the celebration of Christian baptism, for example, reveal Christ's presence as the Constitution on the Liturgy clearly states: "By his power he [Christ] is present in the sacraments, so that when a man baptizes it is really Christ himself who baptizes" (S.C., 7). Moreover, the celebrant's gesture of pouring the baptismal water also speaks to the believer of the efficacy of the sacred symbol. This symbolic-sacramental level of meaning can best be illustrated in the general introduction to the Rite of Christian Initiation when it speaks about the effects of baptism: "Through baptism men and women are incorporated into Christ. They are formed into God's people and they obtain forgiveness of all their sins. They are rescued from the power of darkness and brought to the dignity of adopted children, a new creation through water and the Holy Spirit. Hence they are called and are indeed the children of God" (D.O.L. 720, no. 2251). This fourth level of meaning is comprehensible only with the eyes of faith.

Liturgical Movement

By liturgical movement is understood the purposeful transfer from one place to another of the human body by an individual or group for religious reasons within a liturgical action. Like gestures in general such planned movements are based on principles grounded in anthropology, theology, and liturgy. Recognition is given to the value of the human body in prayer, the ability of bodily movement to express and communicate inner sentiments of faith, and the need for personal active participation in worship. Rather than some sort of religious spectacle, rhythmic movements (including dance) are expressions of a person or persons engaged in communal prayer.

Types of Movements. In the liturgy of the West, movements from one place to another have been traditionally limited to various types of processions. More recently, however, in some cultures, Christian worship has begun to incorporate rhythmic movements and dance as expressive forms of prayer.

Processional Movements

Processions can be divided into three categories: functional, ordinary and extraordinary.

Functional Processions. Functional processions are those which are established elements of a given ritual structure. For this reason they are also called ritual or ceremonial processions. A liturgical rite may have its own proper functional processions. In the Order of the Mass, for example, there are functional processions in the introductory rites (opening procession), in the liturgy of the word (the procession with the book of the gospels), in the liturgy of the eucharist (at the presentation of the gifts), in the communion rite (the communion procession) and in the concluding rite (the closing procession). In the Order of Christian Funerals there are functional processions which involve the transfer of the body to the church and place of committal. The functional dimension of a procession does not exclude the possibility of other reasons for the movement. For example, the utilitarian purpose of moving the book of the gospels from the altar to the ambo is also a gesture of profound respect and reverence for the word of God.

Ordinary Processions. Those liturgical processions which are established in the liturgical books or by church custom for use during the course of the liturgical year are called ordinary processions. Among these are those held on: The Presentation of the Lord (blessing of candles and procession); Passion Sunday (Palm Sunday); the Easter vigil (Easter candle procession); the Body and Blood of Christ (Sunday after Trinity Sunday) with its blessed sacrament procession. In these ordinary processional movements the assembly commemorates with profound religious sentiments the various mysteries of the Lord. They are normally accompanied by other ritual elements, e.g., song, symbols, etc.

Extraordinary Processional Movements. Processions which are incorporated into the liturgical calendar by an episcopal conference or a local bishop are extraordinary processions. These are introduced because of the particular needs of peoples (e.g., the traditional Rogation Day procession in the fields on the feast day of St. Mark, April 25, to ward off pestilence) or to praise God through the honor and respect shown to certain saints (e.g., the traditional May procession honoring the Blessed Virgin), processions with specific relics, sacred images, etc. Such extraordinary processions are means of witnessing to the faith by public expressions of praise, petition, penance, etc.

With reference to processions in which the eucharist is carried in public, the 1973 Roman ritual entitled *Holy Communion and Worship of the Eucharist Outside Mass* leaves the advisability and the scheduling to the bishops. "It is for the local Ordinary to decide on both the advisability of such processions in today's conditions and on the time, place and plan for them that will ensure their being carried out with decorum and without any loss of reverence toward this sacrament" (D.O.L. 279, no. 2221).

History of Processional Movement. The use of parades for civic occasions and of processions for religious motives is common to all peoples. The OT and the NT provide biblical bases for the Judaeo-Christian practice. The processional prototype is the OT Exodus theme (Exod 12) reflected in other passages such as the procession at the destruction of Jericho (Josh 6: 1-16), the procession at the dedication of the wall of Jerusalem (Neh 12: 27-43), etc. OT processional psalms

indicate the presence of such movement among the chosen people (e.g., Psalms 24, 68, 118, 132). The NT recounts the procession that accompanied the triumphal entrance of Jesus into Jerusalem (Lk 19: 28-40). The development and use of processions in Western liturgy is witnessed to in the liturgical books developed after the Peace of Constantine (4th century) and the experience of Christian religious in the West. The development from simple and exceptional events to the elaborate and frequent ones is characteristic of the Middle Ages. In the Vatican II reform the position of processions was treated in the 1984 *Ceremoniale Episcoporum* (Chap. XXI).

Rhythmic Movement
In view of recent developments in the style of Christian worship in the West, rhythmic movement and dance have been recognized as acceptable forms of liturgical movement. The term "rhythmic liturgical movement" is used to describe a procession which is accompanied by a limited pattern of rhythmic bodily movement (e.g., two steps forward and one back) on the part of one or many persons, usually accompanied by vocal or instrumental music. The rhythm is a unifying element; it binds together the various elements of ritual expression: body, spirit, music and gesture. Rhythmic movement has been introduced locally with several ritual elements: the entrance procession, responses to the proclamation of the word, presentation of gifts, acclamations, the Lord's Prayer, post-communion praise, and recessional.

Liturgical dance may be defined as the series of rhythmical motions and steps set to purposeful dance forms and patterns to express authentic sentiments of prayer in public worship.

History of Rhythmic Liturgical Movement. In the Roman rite rhythmic liturgical movement is of recent development. After Vatican II local communities (e.g.,

African, Indian and North American black communities) began to incorporate rhythmic movement as culturally valid expressions of faith. Such dance patterns at times reflect practices used in non-Catholic communities.

In 1988 the Congregation for Divine Worship confirmed the use of *The Missal for the Dioceses of Zaire* in which the incorporation of rhythmic movements during a eucharistic celebration within the Roman rite was officially approved. The general instruction to the Zaire eucharistic liturgy, as presented in *Notitiae* (Vol. 24, 1988) states that: "Rhythmic movements which express the participation of the body in prayer are done by the assembly as it remains in place during the entrance procession, during the acclamation chant after the assembly has placed itself in the presence of God, during the presentation of the gifts and the recessional" (no. 28). Furthermore, the same general introduction to the Zairian liturgy states that "the dance around the altar, done by the ministers during the Gloria or its equivalent, during the incensation of the altar, shows the desire to communicate with the force of life which radiates from the altar, the sacrifice of Christ" (no. 29).

Style of Liturgical Movement. The style of processions and rhythmic movement within the liturgy is determined by a number of factors. Among these are: 1) the specific liturgy being celebrated; 2) the size of the assembly; 3) the cultural context; 4) the environment where the movement is to occur; 5) and existing liturgical norms.

In every case the movement is to be carried out in a becoming manner with the avoidance of that which speaks of the pompous, spectacular, theatrical and entertaining. It is to be authentic expression of communal prayer.

General Conclusion

Word, gesture and movement to one degree or another have always been used to communicate and express religious belief and sentiments. The audio and the visual go together; word and gesture are mutually supporting. At a time when Western liturgical expression tends toward the wordy, the use of the nonverbal, when done in an appropriate and careful manner, is especially welcome.

Good liturgy engages and expresses the entire human person. It is humanly holistic. Gestures and movement add a necessary dimension to religious expressions that can too easily remain on the abstract, intellectual and cerebral plane. The entire person must be encouraged to participate fully in the liturgical action. In this regard catechesis might be needed to assist individuals to understand the higher levels of meaning associated with both gesture and movement.

Gesture and movement have a ministerial role within the liturgy. Like other accepted and encouraged artistic forms, they serve as vehicles for a fuller and richer expression of the prayer of the assembly. Their incorporation in the liturgy "must flow from the community itself as it seeks an authentic, visible, cultural expression of its inner faith stance before the ineffable mystery of God" (Krosnicki, 352).

The competent authorities need to adapt gestures and movements to the felt psychological, cultural and religious needs of the community. This is the case, for example, in eucharistic liturgies with children. The 1973 *Directory for Masses with Children* observes that "if, in accord with the norm of the *General Instruction of the Roman Missal*, a conference of bishops adapts the congregation's actions at Mass to the mentality of a people, it should take the special condition of children into account or should decide on adaptations that are for children only" (D.O.L. 276, no. 2166). All of the revised Roman rites indicate areas where adaptations by conferences of bishops, local bishops and individual ministers can be made. Little has been done in this area; it remains the agenda for the future.

Joseph Gelineau, et al., *Nelle Vostre Assemblee: Teologia pastorale delle celebrazioni liturgiche* (Brescia: Queriniana, 1970). Thomas A. Krosnicki, "Dance Within the Liturgical Act," *Worship* 61, 5 (July 1987), 349-357. Louis Luzbetak, *The Church and Culture: New Perspectives in Missiological Anthropology* (Maryknoll: Orbis, 1988). A.G. Mortimort, *The Church at Prayer: An Introduction to the Liturgy, Vol. 1: Principles of the Liturgy* (Collegeville: Liturgical Press, 1987). Adrian Nocent, "Gestures, Symbols and Words in Present-day Western Liturgy," in *Symbol and Art in Worship*, L. Maldonado Arenas and D. Power, eds., *Concilium* 132 (New York: Crossroad, 1980): 19-27. Mario Righetti, *Manuale di Storia Liturgica: Introduzione Generale*, Vol. 1 (Milano: Ancora, 1950). Domenico Sartore, Achille M. Triacca, et al., *Nuovo Dizionario di Liturgia* (Roma: Paoline, 1984). George S. Worgul, *From Magic to Metaphor: A Validation of Christian Sacraments* (New York: Paulist, 1980).

THOMAS A. KROSNICKI, S.V.D.

GESTURES, LITURGICAL

In the *Constitution on the Sacred Liturgy*, the church acknowledged the necessary participation of the whole person in liturgical worship: "To promote active participation, the people should be encouraged to take part by means of acclamations, responses, psalmody, antiphons and songs, as well as by actions, gestures and bearing" (S.C.,30). This engagement of the person is accomplished not only by means of verbal communication but by non-verbal as well.

Human communication consists of complex systems of interaction. One can speak of verbal language systems which convey ideas through words and sentences, and emotions through pitch and intensity. A non-verbal language system can complement a verbal with gestures that interpret the verbal (e.g., sign language) or with gestures and actions that emphasize the verbal (e.g., striking the breast in the confiteor). A non-verbal language system is not dependent on the verbal, however. Gestures and actions can express the intensity of an emotion without any verbal component. Postures can express relationships between persons without need for verbal articulation.

Religious rituals are no different from ordinary human rituals in their use of verbal and non-verbal languages. In religious rituals, however, the communication happens not only between persons but also is directed toward God. Religious ritual is therefore specially suited to a non-verbal communication that is evocative and symbolic. The history and praxis of Judeo-Christian prayer reveals the significant role that bodily movements, actions and gestures play in liturgical worship.

In this article, under the heading "liturgical gestures," we include all those postures, gestures and bodily actions used by presider, other ministers and people in the liturgical assembly. Liturgical gesture can be categorized by those actions of the body which: a) express or embody an interior attitude (e.g., folding or opening and lifting hands); b) serve a symbolic purpose (e.g., the imposition of hands as a symbol of empowerment); c) express the relationship between persons in the assembly (e.g., joining hands for the Our Father) or between the assembly and the transcendent (e.g., genuflection and kneeling); and, d) serve a functional purpose (e.g., movement of a person from one place to another in order to perform an action).

Certain of these postures, gestures and actions can fall into multiple categories. An entrance procession, e.g., (a) expresses a particular attitude of celebration; (b) can symbolize a journey of the people; (c) expresses the relationship of the people who are gathering; and, (d) is functional in that it moves people and ministers to the place where the liturgical action will be).

Definitions

Posture. A posture is a position of the whole body that is set by a preliminary action and sustained for a period of time.

Ordinary postures in liturgical worship include standing, sitting, kneeling and prostration. Postures can be expressive of different attitudes (e.g., respect, reverence, awe, adoration, supplication, contrition, attentiveness). They can be symbolic (the standing posture as symbolic of the dignity of the human person). Postures express the different relationships within the assembly because of the variation of spatial levels (the assembly kneels while the presider stands for the eucharistic prayer). They can also be functional (sitting is the most comfortable posture for listening). Postures are often complemented by specific gestures or positions of the arms and hands (e.g., standing with arms raised in the "*orans*" position, sitting with hands in open or folded position, kneeling with head bowed, lying prostrate with arms extended in cross position).

Uniformity of posture is demanded by the communal nature of liturgical worship: "The uniformity in standing, kneeling, or sitting to be observed by all taking part is a sign of the community and unity of the assembly; it both fosters and expresses the spiritual attitude of those taking part " (G.I.R.M., 20).

Actions. Bodily actions are ordinarily movements of the whole body that change the position of the body in space or through space. Ordinary liturgical actions are genuflection, turning (orientation), bowing, and procession. There is as well a special class of liturgical actions that have a privileged role as primary sacramental actions: immersion, anointing, imposition of hands, breaking bread and pouring wine. Certain of these do not involve the whole body but are categorized as *actions* because of their special significance. Actions, like postures, can be many things. They may express interior attitudes (e.g., genuflection expresses reverence and respect). They can be symbolic (e.g., turning to the east as symbol of resurrection). They are some-times relational (e.g., bowing before altar, book or sacred elements). And they may be functional (e.g., processions move persons from one place to another).

Gestures. Gestures are movements of some part of the body, usually the hands or arms, which have an expressive or symbolic purpose. Ordinary gestures include signing of the cross, kissing of sacred objects, kissing or greeting of persons (sign of peace), elevation of arms or hands, eyes or object, extension of hands (reception of communion), blessing of objects or persons.

Liturgical gestures therefore, include a wide range of physical movement which combine functional, expressive, symbolic, and relational elements. The following study of each of the postures, gestures and actions will further illustrate the purpose of each in the liturgical assembly.

Postures

Standing. In general this posture expresses an attitude of respect between persons (one usually stands when someone enters a room). It also defines the relationship between persons (one stands in the presence of an authority or one of greater rank). Standing is the posture that symbolizes human readiness (one is able to move easily from this posture). It has also come to symbolize human dignity.

Because of its primary meaning as an expression of respect, standing has been the principal posture of Judaeo-Christian prayer. This tradition is rooted in the scriptures. The description of the reading of the Law from the prophet Nehemiah gives an instance of the standing posture in the liturgical assembly: "And Ezra opened the book in the sight of all the people, for he was above all the people; and when he opened it all the people stood. And Ezra blessed the Lord, the great God and all the people answered, 'Amen, Amen,' lifting up their hands;

and they bowed their heads and worshipped the Lord with their faces to the ground" (Neh 8:5-7). Other texts which illustrate the standing posture for prayer and receiving the word of God include: Exod 20:21; 33:10; Neh 9:5; and Dan 10:11. As a symbol of "readiness" standing is the posture for the celebration of the Passover meal (Exod 12:11).

Standing for prayer continues to be the model in the gospels. In Mk 11:25, Jesus says, "When you stand to pray...." Both the Pharisee and the publican stand in prayer even though there is a difference in attitude (Lk 18:11-13).

This traditional posture of prayer derived from the Jewish tradition finds a new symbolism in light of the experience of the resurrection and the expectation of Christ's second coming. Paul uses the standing posture as a symbol of a slavery that has ended (Gal 5:1; Eph 6:14). The book of Revelation adds the dimension of "worthiness" to stand in the presence of God, and the "readiness" in waiting for Christ's coming again in glory (Rev 7:9).

This posture of standing for prayer with hands uplifted continues to be the ordinary posture of Christian prayer in the earliest centuries. It is evidenced in paintings in the catacombs and in a number of writings in the early period. These writers reinforce the liturgical custom of standing for prayer, but specifically interpret its meaning in the light of the resurrection.

According to Tertullian (*De Oratione*, 23, C.C.L..1:271-2) Christians stand on Sundays and during Easter time as a symbol of the joy of the resurrection. They are forbidden to fast and to kneel during these times (*De Corona Militis* 3, C.C.L..2:1043). This is echoed by Jerome when he says, "it is a time of joy and of victory when we do not kneel or bow to the earth, but risen with Christ, we are raised to the heavens" (*Epist. ad Ephes.* pro. P.L. 26:472). Justin, in his *Questions to the Orthodox* (115 P.G. 6:1363) says

"we do not kneel on Sundays as a sign of the resurrection through which we are freed from our sin by the grace of Christ."

An explicitly eschatological dimension is given in the interpretation of Basil (Treatise on the Holy Spirit, 27): "we stand to pray not only because, risen with Christ and seeking the things that are above, we recall to our memory the day consecrated to the Resurrection but because this day is an image of the time to come" (P.G. 32:190-191).

These patristic writers give clear testimony to the symbolic and relational dynamic of the standing posture for the early Christians. As a paschal people made worthy to stand in the presence of God through their share in the resurrection of Christ, Christians stand ready to greet him when he comes again. In the contemporary liturgical context, standing is once again the principal posture of Christian prayer: "At every Mass the people should stand from the beginning of the entrance song or when the priest enters until the end of the opening prayer or collect; for the singing of the Alleluia before the gospel; while the gospel is proclaimed; during the profession of faith and the general intercessions; from the prayer over the gifts to the end of the Mass except at the places indicated later in this paragraph" (G.I.R.M., 21).

Kneeling. This posture can signify supplication and adoration. It can have as well a penitential meaning or it can be a posture for private prayer. The power of this posture as supplication comes from the obvious difference of levels between the one who is entreating and the one being entreated, as in Mt 18:26: "So the servant fell on his knees, imploring him, 'Lord, have patience with me, and I will pay you everything.'" Its power as a posture of adoration is evidenced in Psalm 95: "Come, let us worship and bow down, let us kneel before the Lord, Our Maker," and in Paul's letter to the Ephesians (3:14): "For this reason, I bow my knees before the Father."

The sense of "awe" before the Creator moves the person "to the knees." This same sense of "awe" is coupled with a sense of unworthiness in the example of Peter falling to his knees in Lk 5:8: "When Simon Peter saw it, he fell down at Jesus' knees saying, 'Depart from me for I am a sinful man.'" Jesus himself uses this posture of private prayer as he prays in the garden before his passion in Lk 22:41: "And he withdrew from them about a stone's throw and knelt down and prayed." Stephen kneels to pray before his martyrdom (Acts 7:60).

In the earliest centuries kneeling was seen to be inappropriate for celebration of the Sunday eucharist and during the Easter season because of its penitential and private association. It was forbidden during the Easter season by Canon 20 of the Council of Nicea. St. Irenaeus gives the reasoning behind the prohibition: "the practice of not kneeling on the Lord's Day is a symbol of the resurrection by which, thanks to Christ, we have been delivered from sin and from the death which he put to death (Fragment 7 of a treatise on Easter; P.G. 7:1234).

Although the patristic witnesses acknowledge the appropriate use of standing for prayer on Sundays and during the Easter season they also affirm the use of kneeling for prayer as an expression of penitence and humility. For example, Tertullian: "As for other times, who would hesitate to bow before God, at least for the first prayer by which we begin the day. And on the days of fasting, all the prayers are made kneeling" (De oratione, 23; C.C.L. 1:272).

Origen echoes this sentiment in his treatise "On Prayer" when he says that "one ought to kneel when one accuses oneself before God of his own sins and supplicating God to be healed and pardoned" (Peri Euxus 31; P.G. 11:552).

An example of the the use of kneeling for prayer in the first centuries is given in the Apostolic Constitutions which details the liturgical practice for pentitents and catechumens during the ordination of a bishop. They are invited to kneel as the deacon leads the community in prayer for them. They then rise for the presider's prayer and bow their heads for his blessing. The whole community kneels for the "universal prayer" and then stands for the presider's prayer and blessing. (Apost. Const. 8:6.8-12.2).

During the Middle Ages there is a significant change in this ancient practice of kneeling before the oration. Jungmann describes it as such: "A new thing had appeared, or rather a substitution: kneeling not before but during the oration. This change concurred with the gradual contraction of the pause which the "Flectamus genua" implied. The Ordo Romanus antiquus (about 950) offers a transitional aspect ... 'Let us pray. Let us kneel. Almighty and eternal God ... Let us stand.' Thus the pause during which the congregation was to pray was filled with the priest's oration" (pp. 245-246).

The increasing popularity and use of kneeling throughout the liturgical service is evidenced in Canon 37 of the Synod of Tours (813) which insists on kneeling as the ordinary posture of prayer, except for Sundays and solemnities. The emphasis in the 13th cent. on eucharistic adoration (i.e., the "real presence") intensifies the need not only for kneeling during the pentitential and confessional moments of prayer but also for adoration during the canon. In the Ordo of John Burchard (1502) the people kneel throughout except for the gospel. For sung Masses, Sundays, or feasts or ferias in the Easter season, the people kneel for the confession and stand until the "adoration" in the canon during which they kneel. They then stand until the dismissal. This is also the first evidence of the priest's genuflection after the words of consecration.

It is clear that during the Middle Ages there was a dramatic change in understanding of the identity and role of the assembly. Their identity as *circumstantes*, made worthy to stand around the table through Christ's resurrection, had changed to *penitentes*, unworthy even to behold the sacred elements. Their role as active participants in worship was gradually delegated to the choir in the sung Mass and to acolytes in the low Mass. Private prayer, penance and distant adoration became the dominant mode of eucharistic worship which continued to the 20th century. Even reception of communion, when it took place, happened kneeling at the altar rail. Kneeling, therefore, was the most appropriate posture given this role and identity of the assembly.

Although the *Constitution on the Sacred Liturgy* has returned to the assembly its rightful role as full participants, there has been a reluctance to restore the original identity of the assembly as equals to the priest/presider, specifically at the time of the consecration of the elements. This moment continues to be interpreted as one which demands the adoration of the assembly although the *General Instruction on the Roman Missal* does allow for variation if the people are "prevented by the lack of space, the number of people present, or some other good reason" (21).

There is presently a wide variety of practice in this use of the standing and kneeling postures during the eucharistic prayer. Some communities stand throughout despite the official legislation. Some kneel immediately after the *Sanctus* and rise after the *Great Amen*. Some kneel only throughout the Institution Narrative. In some communities one can find some who kneel and some who stand. There is also variation in the posture at the acclamation, "Lamb of God": some

churches opt for kneeling as an expression of adoration and others for standing in readiness to receive the Lord.

Excluding the use of kneeling for the consecration, contemporary practice has reserved this ancient posture for private prayer and devotion and occasional liturgical use. There are a number of special uses of the kneeling posture in the Holy Week services, especially at the transference and exposition of the Sacrament at the conclusion of the Holy Thursday eucharist as a sign of adoration and also at the beginning of the Good Friday service when the presider prostrates himself as a sign of penance and total submission.

Sitting. This posture signifies presence and repose and as such is used by the one who presides with authority over a group as well as by those who receive instruction. The person with power and authority sits on a special seat or throne to judge, rule or preside. "You will see the Son of man seated at the right hand of Power" (Mk 14:62). Jesus often teaches his disciples from a seated position, as in the sermon on the mount (Mt 5:1), or, after he has read from the scripture, he sits before he begins to interpret them (Lk 4:20). The person who listens with attention also adopts the seated position: "Mary sat at the Lord's feet and listened to his teaching" (Lk 10:39).

In contemporary liturgical practice, the seated posture is used during times of reflection, meditation, and reception of instruction: "The people should sit during the readings before the gospel and during the responsorial psalm, for the homily and the presentation of the gifts, and, if this seems helpful, during the period of silence after communion" (G.I.R.M., 21). Although the seated posture was ordinarily reserved for the presider/bishop in the early centuries and was not available for the assembly because of the lack of seats in church, this posture has become an integral part of the church's worship in the liturgical renewal.

Prostration. This dramatic posture signifies complete submission to a greater power and a sense of unworthiness. Its use in scripture is in circumstances that reveal intensity of feeling before God, e.g., the call of Abraham (Gen 17:2). Jesus falls prostrate on the ground in the intensity of his prayer in the garden (Mt 26:39). This posture can be seen as a more dramatic supplication than kneeling and has been used in this way in liturgical worship, especially for penitents and catechumens in the first centuries (Jungmann, p.302).

The present use includes the beginning of the Good Friday service, although kneeling is optional. It is prescribed as well during ordination and consecration rites as a posture of intense prayer while the litany of the saints is being sung.

There are two kinds of prostrations: on both knees with the face to the ground and the full prostration with the whole body extended lengthwise. One probable reason for the substitution of the simple kneeling position with head bowed for the prostration is the obvious lack of space to execute this posture properly in a crowded church space. The present environment in most worship spaces with pews or seating arrangements mitigates against this ancient posture although it continues to be used in monastic communities and in some churches that provide open spaces for prayer.

Actions

Bowing. This action of inclining the head or torso expresses the interior attitude of respect and reverence toward a person or object. The action of bowing reveals one's relationship to the other person through the lowering of the head or torso which changes the focus and level of encounter. Bowing is an abbreviated form of prostration.

In the OT, bowing is symbolic of a people's recognition of the power of a deity: "You shall not bow down to their gods" (Exod 23:24). In the Psalms it signifies the adoration due to the sovereign God: "There is none like thee among the gods, O Lord, nor are there any works like thine. All the nations thou hast made shall come and bow down before thee, O Lord, and shall glorify thy name" (Ps. 86).

Bowing is traditionally the action associated with receiving a blessing. Numerous evidences of the deacon's call, "Bow your heads to receive God's blessing," are found in the *Apostolic Constitutions*. Cesaire of Arles (A.D. 532) says in his *Sermon 77*, "Each time the deacon invites you with a loud voice to pray, bow faithfully not only your heart but also your body." He continues to chastise those who are not willing to make this sign of humble adoration. "Those who neglect kneeling for prayer and lowering the head for benediction are those who choose to chat rather than sing." Even the sick are expected to curve the back and lower the head (C.C.L. 103:316-7).

A more profound bow from the waist is called for at moments which demand a momentary expression of adoration, i.e., the doxology. This action of respect and adoration has always played an important role in the liturgy of the Eastern churches. It has unfortunately been replaced by the genuflection in the Western liturgy which is mistakenly understood as a fuller expression of adoration. Genuflection is in fact a more awkward action for the human body to execute and in practice does not express the reverence and grace of a profound bow. In popular practice, however, the profound bow is beginning to replace the genuflection, even when the genuflection is prescribed.

Bows of the head at the mention of the divine names, the name of Jesus and Mary, as well as the name of the saint whose feast is celebrated are prescribed in contemporary liturgy. Bows of the body are reserved for the presider as he reverences the altar and for the whole assembly at the words of the creed "and he became flesh of the virgin Mary" (G.I.R.M., 234).

Genuflection. This action which is a "bow or bend of the knee" is an abbreviated version of the posture of kneeling and as such it expresses respect or veneration. In the early church it was rejected because of its association with adoration of the emperor and in some places with the mockery of Jesus in his passion (Mt 27:29; Mk 15:19).

With the popularity of kneeling becoming more in evidence, however, it is understandable that this abbreviated form of the posture of kneeling would take the place of the bow in those places in the liturgy that called for a momentary action of adoration. In fact, there is a gradual development in which genuflection is less associated with moments of prayer and more with salutation of authorities and veneration of sacred objects. By the 4th cent., genuflection became the sign of veneration of the cross during the liturgy of Good Friday in Jerusalem, as is evidenced by *Egeria the Pilgrim* (C.C.L. 175:81). The Council of Nicea (787) approved genuflection before images. And in the first *Roman Ordo* (A.D. 950), the deacon kneels for a moment to kiss the feet of the bishop of Rome as a sign of adoration. In the *Ordo of John Burchard* (1502), the priest genuflects after the words of consecration while the assembly is kneeling throughout the prayer. The *Roman Missal of Pius V* (1572) establishes genuflection and kneeling as the primary action and posture of adoration.

Genuflection had become the preferred action of reverence and adoration for the ministers who were unable to lead the prayer in the kneeling position yet who were expected to adore and venerate the consecrated species or other sacred objects or persons.

In today's liturgy, genuflection is prescribed as an act of adoration for the presider after the elevation of the host and chalice and before communion. It is as well the action of adoration before the tabernacle (G.I.R.M., 233). In the creed, on the feasts of Annunciation and Christmas, genuflection replaces the bow at the words, "he became flesh" (G.I.R.M., 98).

Turning (Orientation). Early Christians found an obvious symbolism in turning toward the east for prayer because of the rising of the sun and its association with the resurrection of Jesus. Origen says, "We pray to the east, the origin of light" (*Peri Euxus*, 32; P.G.11:557-8).

Christians were thought to be worshippers of the sun because of this eastward orientation (Tertullian, Apol.16, 9-10; C.C.L. 1:116). Or as Basil explains, "We look to the east, but there are only a few who know that we are searching for an ancient homeland, paradise, which God planted in Eden, in the east"(On the Holy Spirit, 27; P.G. 32:190-191).

This priority given toward turning to the east for prayer created the habit of building churches with an eastward orientation as well as the presider's leading the prayer facing the east with the assembly and only turning toward them for the blessing.

Other churches built in the westward or basilican position allowed the presider to face the assembly throughout the entire service. It is this orientation of presider facing the assembly which is in use in contemporary worship because of the primary need to be seen and heard in leading the community in prayer.

Processions. This action which involves a number of people moving forward with a definite purpose can be expressive of different interior attitudes depending on the liturgical context. A funeral procession is dramatically different from a wedding procession because of the human context. The procession on Good Friday to venerate the cross has a different emotional content than the procession with palms on Passion Sunday. In other words, there are different attitudes expressed in these processions, i.e., adoration, festive celebration, supplication. Processions are usually accompanied by litany or song which are indicative of their mood and intent.

Within a liturgical context there are those processions which involve the whole assembly moving from a gathering place outside the church into the nave and sanctuary. The procession with candles and light on the Feast of the Presentation, that of carrying palms on Passion Sunday, and the Easter vigil procession led by the paschal candle are examples of this kind of gathering. Other processions that involve the whole assembly within the liturgical service include the procession to the table for communion and the veneration of the cross on Good Friday. There are also those processions which involve a limited number of persons, usually the ministers, with the assembly joining in song or in silence, regarding the procession as one beholds a parade. These include the entrance procession in the Roman rite and the small and great entrances in the Oriental rites, the gospel procession, that of the newly baptized, the procession with the holy oils at the Mass of Chrism and the transfer of the eucharist at the conclusion of the Holy Thursday liturgy.

Processions are not only expressive of interior attitudes but serve a strong symbolic purpose as well. Central to the symbolic experience of Jews and Christians is the "Exodus," the journey of God's people toward the "promised land." Processions are evocative of this experience as well as others that evoke the sense of a people moving together purposefully.

Processions with rhythmic movement are becoming more popular in African liturgy, especially in the approved "Roman rite for the diocese of Zaire." These kinds of processions wed music and rhythm together with the movement of the body and are not simply "walking processions." Even in western cultures attempts are being made to introduce rhythmic movement as an important component of processional form.

There is as well a rich tradition of procession outside the liturgical celebration as an expression of faith or solemn supplication, i.e., Marian processions, penitential processions in the Middle Ages, processions with the blessed sacrament, especially on the feast of Corpus Christi.

Sacramental Actions. There is a special class of liturgical actions that have a privileged place in the repertoire of liturgical gestures because of their essential use in the sacramental life of the church. They are *imposition of hands, immersion* and *pouring water, anointing, breaking of bread* and *pouring wine.* Each is grounded in scripture and has always played a primary role in the celebration of sacraments and as such are symbolic actions.

Gestures

Liturgical gestures use some part of the body to express an interior attitude, i.e., the elevation of hands and eyes, folding the hands together, striking the breast. They are used as well to express a specific relationship to a person or sacred object, i.e., kissing the altar, gospel book or kiss of peace. Other liturgical gestures have a primarily symbolic purpose, i.e., the sign of the cross, extension of the hands in blessing.

Elevation of Eyes and Hands. The classic posture of prayer, the *orans* position for early Christians, includes the raising of eyes and hands. In Jesus' prayer he often would "raise his eyes toward heaven" (Jn 6:5; 11:41). Paul urges the community to pray "lifting holy hands" (1 Tim 2:8). Origen says, "as there are many dispositions of the body, it is uncontestable that those which consist in raising hands and eyes should be preferred above all, for the body brings to prayer the image of the qualities of the soul" (*Peri Euxus*, 31; *P.G.* 11:552). Tertullian sees the image of the crucified Christ in this position. "Not only do we raise our hands, but we raise them in a cross like our Lord in his passion, and by this attitude we confess Christ" (*De Oratione* 14; C.C.L. 1:265).

Although this gesture was clearly the preferred way of praying for early Christians, subsequent developments which emphasized the kneeling position for the assembly diminished its use. It was replaced by the *folding of the hands together*, a gesture which was more suitable to private prayer and the kneeling position and whose derivation seems to come from the Frankish feudal custom of a vassal presenting himself to his lord. The *orans* position was left to the presider alone.

In the contemporary life of the church, the charismatic renewal has "recovered" this way of prayer for the whole assembly during the eucharistic prayer. There is also evidence that communities are beginning to pray the "Our Father" with open and extended hands. In general use, however, this classic position of prayer has not yet recovered its rightful place.

Striking the Breast. This dramatic gesture expresses an interior attitude of repentance, humility and extreme sorrow. In the gospel of Luke, it is used by the tax collector, who "standing far off, would not even lift up his eyes to heaven, but beat his breast, saying, 'God, be merciful to me, a sinner!'"(Lk 18:13). It is likewise the gesture used by the witnesses of the crucifixion (Lk 23:48) St. Augustine cautions against the overuse of this gesture for those who strike their breast every time they hear the word "Confiteor" (Serm. 67,1; P.L. 38:443).

Its use in contemporary worship is limited to the confession of faults and by some as an accompanying gesture with the "Lamb of God."

Kissing the Altar, Gospel Book and Cross. This gesture expresses a reverence and respect for sacred objects, especially those which symbolize Christ. The kiss as a gesture of honor and respect was taken over from the ancient custom of kissing the threshold of the temple as well as the images of the gods. As early as the 4th century the saluting of the altar with a kiss made its appearance as a popular practice. In the Middle Ages, the rubrics called for the priest's kissing the altar frequently throughout the ritual, and the gospel book before the proclamation (Jungmann pp. 210-211, 287).

This practice has continued in contemporary worship, although the altar is reverenced only at the beginning and end of the liturgy. This same attitude of reverence expressed through a kiss is found in the veneration of the cross on Good Friday.

Kiss of Peace. This gesture, which expresses an attitude of interior peace, was used by early Christians as a seal of the prayer which had preceded it. As Tertullian says, "What prayer is complete without the holy kiss?" (*De Oratione*, 18; C.C.L. 1:267).

Jungmann details the development of this "seal and pledge" of prayer in this way: "The original place of the kiss of peace was, in reality, at the end of the service of readings and prayers rather than at the start of the Sacrifice-Mass. According to the ancient Christian conception, it formed the seal and pledge of the prayers that preceded it. But after the service of readings and prayers had been joined to the celebration of the Eucharist, regard for our Lord's admonition (Mt 5:23 f.) about the proper dispositions in one who wishes to make an offering would probably have led to placing the kiss of peace (as guarantee of fraternal sentiment) closer to the moment when one is 'bringing his gift before the altar'" (p.480).

At a very early date (5th century), the peace was proclaimed after the canon as a pledge of the assent of the people to the eucharistic prayer that had preceded it. With the insertion of the "Our Father" after the canon at the time of Gregory the Great, the kiss of peace became an illustration of the words: "as we forgive those who trespass against us."

Although the kiss of peace has retained this place in contemporary eucharistic liturgy, there is a tendency on the part of many presiders to move it to its original place at the completion of the liturgy of the word, before the gifts are presented. There is as well a tendency on the part of the assembly to see it not so much as a formal, ritual gesture but rather as an opportunity to exchange greetings. There are some who object to this transformation of a reverent, ritual gesture into an opportunity for "socializing." It is perhaps the absence of any moment of greeting each other at the beginning of the ritual that has brought about this social exchange at the time of the peace.

Sign of the Cross. This distinctively Christian gesture symbolizes a person's unity with Christ, confessing the cross as central to the mystery of salvation and confirming one's identity as a Christian. In the early centuries it was common to sign the forehead with great frequency as Tertullian attests: "at every forward step and movement ... in all the ordinary actions of daily life" (*De Corona Militis*, chap.3; C.C.L. 1:1043). Making the sign of the cross on the forehead was thus seen as a way of strengthening oneself in one's Christian identity.

It is clear that this tangible sign of the cross was associated with the administration of the sacraments, especially those of initiation, as Augustine relates: "Only when the sign of the cross is made on the foreheads of the faithful, as on the water itself with which they are regenerated, or on the oil with which they are anointed with chrism, or on the sacrifice with which they are nourished, are any of these things duly performed" (*Tract. in Joan.* 118; P.L.35 p.1950).

The custom of signing on the forehead, lips and breast before the reading of the gospel as well as signing the book comes from the 11th century and remains as a ritual gesture for the assembly. The multiple signings throughout the canon in the Tridentine liturgy have been reduced in the present ritual to one sign of the cross during the *epiclesis.*

Although the sign of the cross was traced on the forehead, or other parts of the body in the early centuries, by the 8th century there is evidence of the sign being made with the first three fingers of the right hand, tracing the sign from the forehead, to the chest, to the right shoulder and then the left. This custom has continued in the Greek church. In the Latin church, a change was made in the 13th century and one adopted the modern usage which consists of holding the hand open and moving from left to right (H. Leclercq, pp.1343-44).

The sign of the cross which begins so much of Roman Catholic prayer with its accompanying words, "In the name of the Father, and of the Son and of the Holy Spirit," is meant to have a clear baptismal reference. The efficacy of this sign as a blessing, confession of faith and identification with the mystery of Christ continues to make it a primary symbolic gesture for many Christians.

Extension of the Hands in Blessing. This gesture symbolizes the transmission of power from one person to another or to the assembly. In the OT, there are many references to the extension of one's hands as an expression of power. Moses "stretches out his hand over the sea ... and the waters were divided" (Exod 14:21). When his hands grow weary in the Israelites' battle with the Amalekites, Aaron and Hur hold his hands up until the victory is accomplished (Exod 17:11-12). The Lord God "with a mighty hand and outstretched arm" brings back his people (Ezek 20:33).

This gesture of outstretched arms and

hands is the primary one associated with blessing at the end of the eucharistic and other liturgies. The *imposition of hands* in the rites of initiation, ordination, reconciliation and healing derives its meaning from this gesture. In these cases, however, there is the added dimension of human touch as it communicates power and grace to another person.

Extension of the Hands for Communion. The practice of receiving communion in the hand in the early centuries was given a symbolic meaning as is evidenced in the *Mystagogic Catechesis* of the 4th century: "When you approach, do not go stretching out your open hands or having your fingers spread out, but make the left hand into a throne for the right will receive the King, and then cup your open hand and take the body of Christ, reciting the Amen. Then sanctify with all care your eyes by touching the Sacred Body and receive it" (Jungmann, p. 508). The present discipline of the church encourages the return to this ancient practice of communion received in the hands.

Other Gestures. It is a natural human tendency to express oneself through bodily gestures and actions. Despite an official reticence to allow spontaneous expression in the church's liturgy, there has been a desire on the part of many to include a fuller range of gestural expression. It is now common for the assembly to join hands during the "Our Father" if it is spoken, or to use gestures if it is sung. Moments of acclamation, i.e., gospel Alleluia, eucharistic acclamations, are often accompanied by some gestures. The influence of contemporary liturgical music has led to the inclusion of simple, prayerful gestures throughout the service. Leaders of song or animators of the assembly use a variety of gestures to engage the community in song.

Although these gestures are not legislated, they contribute to the active participation called for by the *Constitution on the Sacred Liturgy.* It is especially important in liturgies for children that they be engaged by means of gestures and postures as is indicated in the *Directory for Masses with Children* (33,34).

Conclusion

Liturgical gestures offer the assembly of the faithful a wealth of expressive and symbolic movements, postures and actions which not only enhance communal prayer but are in themselves a non-verbal language of prayer. The continuing challenge to the reform of the liturgy is to encourage the fullest use of these liturgical gestures in a way which reveals their significance as well as their beauty.

J.A. Jungmann, *The Mass of the Roman Rite* (New York: Benziger, 1951). A.G. Martimort, *The Church at Prayer* Vol.1 (Collegeville: The Liturgical Press, 1987). *Dictionnaire d'archeologie Chretienne et de liturgie*, ed. by F.Cabrol, H. Leclerq (Paris: Letouzey et Ane, 1907-53). *Gestes et paroles dans les diverses familles liturgique*, Conferences Sainte-Serge, xxiv Semaine d'etudes liturgiques ... 1977 (Bibliotecha El, Subsidia 14; Rome: Edizioni liturgiche, 1978).

ROBERT VEREECKE, S.J.

GLORY TO GOD

See **Doxology; Holy Spirit in Christian worship**

GOD, IMAGES OF, IN LITURGY

Images of God in liturgy are mediated in so many ways that any system of categories is imperfect. I will use the general categories of physical or sensory setting, language, and social setting, even though there is some overlap and interaction of categories. The sensory category covers art, architecture, lighting, incense, flavors tasted, instrumental and vocal music (but not words), amplification, acoustics, etc. The language category covers language which is read, heard, spoken, or sung, whether printed or not. The social setting category illustrates the saying that actions speak louder than words, and covers how people are treated, the cultural and sub-cultural context, the community situation, and the liturgy leaders, with attention to inclusion and diversity. Images of God in liturgy are expressed in and formed by elements in each of these categories. Images of God will be analyzed along with images of each *Persona* of the Trinity.

A number of aspects or principles which are true for liturgy in general are applicable when considering images of God in liturgy. For instance, some features of liturgy, including divine imagery, are explicit, while other features are implicit. Similarly, the general principle that neither the explicit nor the implicit aspects of the liturgy should counteract, contradict, or distract from the gospel message is certainly applicable to the images of God communicated through the liturgy.

The implicit material can be hard to identify. For example, the choice of certain sermon topics will convey that God is interested in those topics but not others. A related idea is that some things are unspeakable. Also, some things which are seemingly irrelevant to divine imagery influence it nevertheless. For instance, to take an example from the social setting category, whether children always or never contribute to liturgical leadership will suggest to many people (including children) that God is either accepting of children or is tolerant of their exclusion. The decision might have been made for a particular reason, or the matter might not ever have been deliberately addressed. Yet regardless of the *purpose*, the results may *function* in unintended ways.

It is frustrating for liturgists to know that despite their care in planning, people are getting unintended messages, some of which are a result of human carelessness and sin rather than accurate reflections or deliberate proclamations of the nature and values of God.

This is related to what has been called the "halo effect," which means that what the church does or tolerates is understood as either what God wants, or at least what is acceptable to God, and this is more pronounced or emphatic for children, who do not have the intellectual understanding of alternate explanations. The "halo effect" can charge anything connected with the church with an aura of divine meaning and power, and it applies to language, arts, and actions, where it influences images of God, among other things. It enhances some inadequate or sinful aspects of liturgy, as well as enhancing many good things which are routine.

Vulnerability is another common and related aspect of liturgy. Many people are especially sensitive to hurts and affirmations when they approach the liturgy and God. This natural sensitivity deserves respect.

Liturgists can expect different people to be responsive to different elements of the liturgy. For one person, any sung text has a double weight, while another person gets absorbed in the music and does not notice the words. For one person, anything the clergy say is authoritative, while for another anything sung or said in unison is most impressive and powerful. One person trusts and focuses on the printed texts while another gives great weight to anything seemingly from the heart, such as sermons or extemporaneous prayer. Repetition will add weight for some people, and maybe something sung, heard, and read will be most emphatic. Because people respond individually, and because in the liturgy they are interacting with God, it is impossible for liturgists to control the experience. Nevertheless they have substantial responsibility.

Two other principles: people are selective in their focus of attention, and a caption or explanation offers an interpretation and meaning to what might otherwise be misunderstood or mystifying.

Images of God in liturgy are deeply affected and formed by the whole liturgical context, and not just by the visual images on the walls or the explicit words spoken aloud. Thoughtful liturgical planning can arrange many elements of liturgy so that what is communicated is a consistent, deliberate, and faithful proclamation of the gospel.

The Physical or Sensory

Perhaps the most obvious images of God in liturgy are the literal visual ones, such as a crucifix, a nativity scene, a dove on a banner, the hand of God in an icon or stained-glass window, a statue or icon of Mary and the Christ child, etc. Such two and three dimensional images found in the room where the liturgy takes place, or printed in bulletins or books, are considered in this section, along with other physical or sensory aspects of the liturgical space which can form or affect images of God.

Many of the visual images are representatives of Jesus, God incarnate, while other images are symbols of God, sometimes abstract and sometimes representational. For instance, the triangle symbol of the Trinity is obviously abstract, and the two most common symbols of the Holy Spirit, the dove and the flames, are sometimes more abstract than representational.

While a crucifix is clearly an image of God incarnate, the empty cross has more than one set of meanings. When it is understood as a reminder of how Jesus got the death penalty, or as a symbol of the Christian faith, then it is not likely to be regarded as an image of God. But when it represents Christ's sacrifice and God's power to overcome sin and death, then it is more likely to be considered an image of God, of who God is and how God acts.

Because of its widespread use in church decoration, the plain cross may be the most common visual symbol in liturgy. But it so common in some buildings, appearing on every pew and light fixture and at every other opportunity, that it is more apt to convey "religiousness" than any vivid or direct or powerful imagery of God.

Some visual images of God are missed by many viewers because they lack interpretive captions and nobody has explained the symbolism. For example, the mother pelican "vulning" herself to feed her young with her blood is perhaps the most widespread female image of God in liturgical art, yet because the symbolism is no longer commonly known it is often not recognized as representing Christ's sacrifice on the cross, the atonement, and the blessed sacrament of holy communion (See Mollenkott, pages 44-48).

Most of the visual images of God in church art are images of Jesus, and thus are male images. There are a few female images of God, like the pelican, in traditional liturgical art, and a few more in contemporary liturgical art. The remaining divine images, such as the Pentecost flames, are not sex-specific.

If preachers can familiarize themselves with local decorations, and point them out when they are relevant to the Bible readings or sermon themes, then many of the decorations will retain associations of meaning in the minds of those present.

Selectivity and individuality of response and interpretation are illustrated by the person who, seeing a stained-glass window of St. Mary Magdalene, thinks, "Christ called her, a woman, on Easter morning, as an apostle to the other apostles, and the church should ordain women—that's God's will," thus confirming a particular image of God. Another person would just give a passing glance to an anonymous image of a saint. The first might choose to dwell on the saint, while the second might look around and focus on a crucifix, or upon something that was not an image of God.

Language

Linguistic analysis of divine imagery in liturgy must include all texts used routinely, texts just used occasionally (for funerals or special services), propers and commons, and words spoken only once (sermons, announcements, pastoral prayer, etc.). It will also include bulletins or other papers or books placed in the hands of the congregation, words projected for reading or singing, inscriptions on the walls, writing on banners and what the choir sings.

There are two major ways to find images of God in liturgical language—in words addressed to God or describing God (such as Almighty, Lord, Jesus, Father, Everliving, Holy, Merciful, sweet heavenly dove, Christ, Blessed Trinity, Holy Spirit, slow to anger, etc.), and the stories of how God acts, which implicitly describe God by their content (God frees Israel from slavery, keeps commitments, demands justice, etc.). Imagery in the first category is usually explicit, but in both categories there are aspects which subtly affect imagery without many people being aware of them.

The rest of this section will focus on male and female images of God because this is an area of controversy and it can illustrate principles applicable in other cases.

A distinction is made in this article between male and female images of God on the one hand, and masculine and feminine images of God on the other hand, although not all writers are careful in their use of terminology. The use of the masculine and feminine imagery helps to promote and maintain sex role stereotypes, especially when masculinity is equated with maleness and femininity with femaleness. Such stereotypes are inherently sexist. Male and female divine imagery can also be used in sexist ways, as when a certain selection of images is used to encourage complementarity of women and men (as distinct from co-operation with equality). But female and male images of God do not have to be used that way, and, indeed, should not be. Sex role stereotypes in each culture are so familiar that liturgists, especially song writers and preachers, have to plan attentively to avoid them.

There is a growing body of literature about female images of God in the Christian tradition, yet many basic facts are not well-known. For example:

—Male images of God are not inherently sexist.

—The Bible has both male and female images of God.

—Female images of God do not conflict with sound trinitarian theology. Female imagery has been used for each *Persona* of the Trinity, and for the One God.

—Christian writers have used female images of God in every century.

—These writers include men and women, Protestants and Eastern Orthodox and Roman Catholics and others, native writers on every inhabited continent, and writers of various literary genres.

—Female images of God occur in Christian art as well as literature.

—Good liturgy can use a balance of both female and male imagery of God. Many believe it should do this.

The father image of God is God-given, and along with some other male images of God it should be used liturgically just as carefully as the novel female images of God are introduced and used. Male images of God in liturgy will be stronger and more meaningful if they are not used carelessly or haphazardly or automatically, but instead are used deliberately, thoughtfully, and with attention to the rest of the liturgy (Piccard, pp. 1-2).

Even when liturgists do not *feel* uncomfortable with sexism in liturgy, and even if they do feel comfortable with female images, they are still responsible for how these matters are dealt with in public worship; their private devotions are another matter.

A congregation's over-all long-term pattern of worship should be balanced in ways in which particular services can be imbalanced. Thus a parish might have a non-sexist service focusing on the fatherhood of God if it had another service sometime focusing on the motherhood of God. So long as no sex role stereotypes were used, a balanced non-sexist pattern would be maintained.

Worship services for special occasions when a unique congregation will be gathered should be planned with attention to its time together. Thus if a conference has three services, there should be a balance of elements (such as male and female images of God) among the three services. Or if there is a special occasion when many visitors will be present, it is usually wise for the service to be internally balanced in isolation from the parish's other services. Balancing can be done either by having an equal weight and number of female and male images of God, or by eliminating all sex-specific divine images. A subtle stereotype to avoid would be using 5 or 10 different male images of God but only using one or two female images, especially maternal ones!

Some people are so sensitive on certain issues that these matters affect their very ability to participate in liturgy—or even to remain in the building. Thus funerals, the sacraments, baccalaureate services, etc., are certainly times for sensitive and careful planning.

If people think of God as male (or as more male-like than female-like), or think of the word "God" as a male word, then the very word "God" which is not inherently sex-specific will be fundamentally sex-specific for them. Similarly, words associated with sex role stereotyped traits and jobs and behavior (nurturing, almighty) will be interpreted as sex-specific by some people. There is disagreement about whether or not the word "Goddess" is suitable liturgically. It does communicate powerfully and it has remedial effects, but because of its feminine ending it is inherently sexist.

Knowing about all the centuries of Christian literature using female images of God some liturgists are hesitant to develop their own. But whenever an image can be accurately described as *an image of the God revealed in the Bible* then there is ample authority for its use.

The liturgical use of racist and sexist language and content (that is, what is said as well as how it is said), can convey the idea that racism and sexism are acceptable to God. The old hymn text "strong men and maidens meek" is an illustration because, although it is inclusive (in that both sexes are included), it is also a blatant example of sexist content by the use of sex role stereotypes. Other hymn texts like "keep them white and clear" are more obviously racist than the routine mistranslation of Cant 1:5 as "I am very dark , but comely."

The church is a long way from perfection on these matters, and setting goals and timetables for education and change, and writing local guidelines, can be very helpful. Guidelines for avoiding sexism and racism in sermons and hymns need to go to all preachers and hymn selectors, not just white men.

God uses different images to reach different people. The liturgy should be rich enough to serve the whole community.

Social Setting

How people are treated in the liturgy and in the rest of the world, and how the liturgy recognizes the social settings of their lives, will deeply affect their understanding of God's interest in them individually and God's interest in the conditions of their lives. For this reason it is especially important for the clergy and lay leadership to be aware of social dynamics and trends, and to be sensitive and mature in dealing with people.

Preachers and ushers or greeters must be chosen with care, and training will be needed from time to time because good intentions alone are not enough. How visitors or unusual people are treated (or mentioned) will say a lot to them and to others about God. Justice, dignity, acceptance, and respect ought to be automatic, but even people of goodwill are not always sure how to show it best. Misunderstandings can occur, and may be serious problems.

A number of people remark on how someone *represents* God's care to them, or represents or symbolizes God to them in varied life situations. As God's obvious representatives, the clergy especially *do* influence the imagery for God for many people in their congregations. Their behavior in the liturgy and elsewhere, the content of their sermons, and the particularities of their individuality can each be significant in this way for some people. Individual features (race, sex, abilities and disabilities, degree and style of conformity to expectations, quirks, etc.) are all potentially influential.

A person does not have to be "holier than thou" to be a lector or singer, but the diversity of the congregation should be represented around the altar. (Perhaps only the diversity of grave and notorious sin should be excepted from the diversity represented.)

Liturgy is not just what happens during the scheduled services, but also includes the preparation and cleanup. Who gets consulted and how they are treated, who has decision-making power and responsibility, and who does which work are all significant.

For example, if a category of people is included and treated with respect in liturgy planning and leadership, then many people will receive the message that *God* accepts and affirms that category of people. Thus images of God are shaped. Race, sex, and age are not the only factors to consider, but also such groupings as the homeless and renters and homeowners, ethnic majorities and minorities, able-bodied and disabled people, clergy and lay, people with varying sexual preferences, dropouts and well-schooled people, workers and students and unemployed and retired people, people of varying intelligence, immigrants and natives, etc.

Of course, if a low status or oppressed group is included but is routinely given cleanup responsibility, or secondary and overly simple tasks, the church (if not also God) will be seen as accepting the unjust *status quo.*

How much rehearsal time is needed so everyone can contribute appropriately with confidence? Although sarcasm in the sacristy may not cause the obvious liturgical changes, it obviously affects the meaning of the liturgy for those involved, and can affect their understanding of God. Is the liturgy a place where people are safe to make a contribution without being attacked? Is it a place where people are held acceptable for keeping commitments about preparation? How these routine matters are dealt with will affect self-esteem and divine imagery.

Liturgy often treats some difficult topics as unspeakable, like incest and domestic violence, which are acutely relevant to images of God as Father. And sometimes sin is denounced as if the church were blameless. An example, like the Wareham Guild, established so needleworkers on vestments would get a living wage, is a fine illustration of the *church's* corporate amendment of life for corporate sin.

Actions do speak louder than words, but some words are needed. The sermon content has a major role in the shaping of images of God in connection with the social setting. The social strengths and health and maturity, as well as the corporate (social) sins, which are important in the community life need to be addressed in the light of the gospel. In addition to being addressed in sermon content these matters can be addressed explicitly in prayer and prayer invitations.

To fail to recognize and address strengths and weaknesses, grace and sin, conveys the idea that God is uninterested. But what kind of God would be uninterested in these things which so influence peoples' lives?

Ideally a variety of images of God will be integrated in liturgy, demonstrating how all life flows from the divine and is related to the divine.

Linda Clark, Marian Ronan and Eleanor Walker, *Image-Breaking/Image-Building: A Handbook of Creative Worship with Women of Christian Tradition* (New York: Pilgrim Press, 1981). Margaret R. Miles, *Image As Insight: Visual Understanding in Western Christianity and Secular Culture* (Boston: Beacon Press, 1985). Virginia Ramey Mollenkott, *The Divine Feminine: The Biblical Imagery of God As Female* (New York: Crossroad, 1983). Sharon Neufer Emswiler and Thomas Neufer Emswiler, *Women and Worship: A Guide to Non-Sexist Hymns, Prayers, and Liturgies,* rev. ed. (San Francisco: Harper and Row, 1974, 1984). Kathryn Ann Piccard, *Non-Sexist Hymn Concert Handbook* (West Newton, MA: Episcopal Women's Action, 1982). Sandra M. Schneiders, *Woman and the Word: the Gender of God in the NT and the Spirituality of Women* (New York: Paulist Press, 1986).

KATHRYN ANN PICCARD

GUÉRANGER, PROSPER (1805-1875)

Benedictine of the Abbey of Solesmes, which he revived in 1833, and which was re-established as an abbey, with Guéranger himself as first abbott, in 1837. His own work, and indeed the work of the monastic community at Solesmes, was devoted to the careful and prayerful celebration of the Mass and the liturgy of the hours. Solesmes itself is known for its revival of Gregorian chant. Guéranger's best known works are: (a) his *Institutions Liturgiques,* in which he set forth his plea for a liturgy that was simple, pure and uniform, and (b) his *L'annee liturgique,* meditations on the liturgical texts, feasts, and the scriptures for the church's liturgical year. This second served as inspiration for later works in the same tradition, esp., *The Church's Year of Grace* (Pius Parsch) and *The Liturgical Year* (Adrian Nocent).

See Liturgical movement, the (1830-1969); Benedictines and liturgical renewal

H

HEALING

Healing is no stranger to the Judaeo-Christian tradition. In the Hebrew scripture God affirms "I am the Lord your physician" (Exod 15:22). A central description for God's work in the creation is that of healing. Healing is one expression of God's special care for people: "I am the Lord, your healer"(Exod 15:26b). God orders people with power and destroys enemies and deceivers. God's will for the people, a will that is not without condition, is imaged through that of God as healer. Both disease and health originate with God: "I kill and I make alive; I wound and I heal; and there is none that can deliver out of my hand"(Deut 32:39).

God relates to people both positively and negatively. In Hosea, God is represented as being in despair over Israel's seeming incurableness. In Jeremiah, Yahweh affirms: "Your hurt is incurable, and your wound is grievous. There is no one to uphold your cause, no medicine for your wound, no healing for you"(Jer 30:12-13). Yet God's compassion is infinite; God simply cannot abandon Israel. Both the discipline and the healing of Israel is from God: "Yet it was I who taught Ephraim to walk, I took them up in my arms; but they did not know that I healed them" (Hos 11:3).

Yahweh heals the diseases which have their origin in God and are the consequences of human infidelity and sinfulness. Often the situation of Israel is compared to someone who is left without medical help: "Is there no balm in Gilead? Is their no physician there? Why then has the daughter of my people not been restored?" (Jer 8:22). While many texts refer to the healing and the sickness of individuals, the healing from Yahweh is primarily for the reconstitution of Israel. The importance of these various texts lies in the fact that Yahweh is represented as the restorer and orderer of human life.

In the NT, Jesus' miraculous healings are presented as the signs that the Messiah has arrived and the Kingdom of God is in our midst. Among the powers of the Messiah is the power to heal the sick (Lk 7:21; also Mt 11:4-6). Jesus' healings are presented in the gospel as the product of his charismatic power.

From a historical point of view, Jesus stood in the tradition of Jewish charismatic healers. Touching is a very important aspect of Jesus' ministry of healing. In fact, in the Hebrew Scripture the language of the senses is used to express God's compassion. God is the one who sees our afflictions, who hears our cries and feels our pain. The ministry of Jesus represents God as salvific God, a God of life.

Jesus' ministry of healing is in line with his constant emphasis upon compassion. The root meaning of compassion is "being moved by" another's situation at the very core of one's being. Not only does compassion characterize Jesus' ministry and is the basic ground for his deeds of healing, but for Jesus, God is also the compassionate one. Jesus invites his disciples to be imitators of God's compassion: "Be compassionate, even as your Father is compassionate" (Lk 6:36). Jesus' movement must be characterized by compassion. In fact Jesus sent his disciples out to continue his ministry of healing (Mk 6:7-13; Mt 10:5-10; Lk 9:1-6). In the letter of James we find the classic NT text on the implementation of this ministry (5:14-16).

Jesus performed healings on the sabbath in defiance of the law (Mk 3:1-6). He healed individuals who were considered on the margin of society such as a tax-collector (Lk 19:1-10). He healed individuals outside the land of Israel (Mk 7:31-7). In his healing he rebuked the forces that seem to make people sick (Lk 13:16). Illness is viewed by Jesus as a destructive and deteriorating force. Any attitude that would glorify sickness is alien to Jesus' attitude. Jesus as the Savior is the great physician (H. Beyer, T.D.N.T., 130).

Toward a Theology of Healing

While healing is an important element of Jesus' ministry and redemptive work, it has never been a major concern of theology. A theology of healing is quite absent from the Christian tradition. Developments in many areas of theological concern, and the re-discovery of the importance of the healing ministry in the charismatic movement, demand a theology of healing.

Such a theology presupposes first of all a definition of health. Health is often understood as merely the absence of disease or infirmity. Yet the preamble of the charter of the World Health Organization attempts to convey a holistic view of health: "Health is a state of complete physical, mental and social well being and not merely the absence of disease or infirmity." To this definition one should add a spiritual element. The root of the word implies completeness, wholeness. Yet unlike disease which is frequently recognizable, tangible, and rather easily defined, health is a more nebulous reality, difficult to define and never in a state of perfection.

A theology of healing must emphasize the centrality of the concept of personhood and the principle of totality. Health must be defined in such as way as to encompass the total good of the person. Christianity insists that we see healing and disease with the eyes of faith. It offers the triadic framework of creation, fall and redemption as its basic worldview. The framework can be expressed in the following way: *Creation*: original blessing, light, freedom, integrity, peace, health; *Fall*: deprived human condition, blindness, bondage, brokenness, estrangement, disease; *Redemption*: restored human potential, enlightenment, liberation, reintegration, reconciliation, health.

A theology of healing must be anchored within this framework; the major operative elements have to be a theological anthropology and an anthropological soteriology.

From an anthropological perspective all forms of dualism have to be avoided. The body-soul unity is a necessary implication of the doctrines of creation and resurrection. The human spirit lives in and through expressive embodiment, because the human person is a psychophysical unity. Within this anthropology, woman and man should not be considered as a composite of several levels such as body, soul, spirit, but as a multidimensional unity. Different dimensions of human reality do not lie one alongside the other. In every stage of life all dimensions are potentially or actually present.

Salvation itself can be described as the act of healing. In many languages the root of the word "salvation" indicates this. The Greek word *soteria*, comes from *saos*, and the German *heiland* from *heil*. All of these different roots mean whole, not yet split, not disrupted. Healing is the re-establishment of a whole that was broken, disrupted, disintegrated. Ultimately healing in the sense of salvation implies victory over death itself.

In the NT the concept of salvation implies the deliverance of human beings from all forms of evil, from sickness, from mental illness, demonic powers, and ultimately from death. The concept of reconciliation emphasizes the restoration of broken relationship. Redemption connotes freedom from various forms of bondage; the term salvation is a rich and complex one and cannot be restricted simply to the restoration of broken relation with God. It encompasses the total good of the person and in that sense it connotes the process of healing.

There can be no total dichotomy between eschatological salvation and salvation in this world, between "secular" history and salvation history, between healing for eternal life and healing for this life. For salvation to be truly human, salvation must have some experimental dimensions. It must reflect at least partially what women and men experience as saving. Ultimately we do not know what salvation implies. To indicate this mystery the Greek fathers spoke of the divinization of woman and man.

No human techniques of healing can ever remove fully the various forms of suffering that afflict humanity. Victory over suffering is essentially partial and limited. It would be false to understand salvation uniquely as meaning perfect wholeness, for such wholeness means ultimately liberation from finitude and basically from mortality. Ultimate salvation does not in any way imply that salvation comes to humanity simply from outside. Salvation is from within, from what occurs here within our human context. The NT gives us an expression of

this: one is judged ultimately according to one's compassion (Mt 25:34-40).

According to the NT, salvation involves two movements that are not to be separated: a movement beyond this world, eschatological in nature, and a movement within this world, towards wholeness in life through the gifts of this world such as medicine, rest, friendship. While within the Christian perspective there are values higher than life, life in all of its dimensions is of real value.

Jesus' ministry of healing continues in the church and takes place in charitable, charismatic and sacramental ways. The charitable expresses itself in the ongoing tradition in the church of caring for the sick in hospitals and other institutions. The charismatic ministry of healing is very much present in the contemporary church. The sacramental ministry of healing, while expressed in the eucharist and penance, is most fully operative in the sacrament of the anointing of the sick. The evolution of this sacrament is indicative of the many problems involved in developing a theology of healing. In the early church the sacrament was understood primarily as an unction for healing. But step by step this was transformed into unction as preparation for death and had more to do with forgiveness of sins than with bodily healing. It was eventually perceived as the final sacrament for the dying. The healing intended is a spiritual healing (T. Aquinas, III, Supp. 29.1).

In the *Constitution on the Sacred Liturgy* (S.C., 73ff), and in *Pastoral Care of the Sick: Rites of Anointing and Viaticum* (1983), the original purpose of the unction is restored as a sign and prayer for the return to physical health. The new rite is intended to help us understand human sickness in the context of the whole mystery of salvation. Here the gift of bodily health is looked upon as ancillary to the good of the soul. Yet the restoration of physical health remains uncertain. It must be admitted that the ultimate triumph over sickness and evil is achieved eschatologically (Rom 8:18-20). Sickness and suffering are not unqualifiedly contrary to the will of God. The mystery of God's will for life remains paschal in nature; the suffering of Christ, in light of the resurrection, was not a defeat of God's will. Yet the church's ministry of healing is an affirmation of the primacy of life and its ultimate victory over death, a victory proleptically achieved in the resurrection of Jesus. All healing then must be understood as originating in God as the giver of life. No healing can be effective in separation from the structures of life itself.

Finally, a contemporary theology of healing must address the basic question of addiction as a pervasive situation. Any addiction is a limitation of the freedom of human desire. It involves the severe loss of willpower and brings about a radical distortion of reality.

Now the basic metaphor used in the scriptures for sinfulness is that of bondage or slavery from which one must be delivered into freedom. Addiction is related to sin. It is the bodily and psychological dimension of sinfulness. Deliverance and healing from addictive is a freeing of the will in its journey to God. Our addictions hinder our seeing the truth. Healing of addictive behavior is freeing, an experience of God's salvific presence. It is the re-lived experience of the Exodus, the experience of spiritual deliverance.

See **Sick, pastoral care of the**

Rene Jules Dubos, *Health and Disease* (NY: Time Inc., 1965). James N. Lapsley, *Salvation and Health: The Interlocking Processes of Life* (Philadelphia: Westminster Press, 1972). Morton T. Kelsey, *Healing and Christianity: In Ancient Thought and Modern Times* (New York: Harper & Row, 1973). John A. Sanford, *Healing and Wholeness* (New York: Paulist Press, 1977). Kenneth L. Vaux, *This Mortal Coil: The Meaning of Health and Disease* (New York: Harper & Row, 1978).

John Wilkinson, *Health and Healing: Studies in New Testament Principles and Practice* (Edinburgh: Handsel Press 1980): 4. Thomas E. Clarke, S.J, "Touching in Power: Our Health System," in *Above Every Name: The Lordship of Christ and Social Systems* (Ramsey, New Jersey: Paulist, 1980): 253. Martin Marty and Kenneth L. Vaux, *Health, Medicine and the Faith Traditions: An Inquiry Into Religion and Medicine* (New York: Crossroad, 1982). Richard A. McCormick, *Health and Medicine in the Catholic Tradition* (New York: Crossroad, 1984). William L. Nute, Jr., "Health and Salvation: Definitions and Implications," *Study Encounter* 2:3 (1966): 137-141. Thomas Talley, "Healing: Sacrament or Charism," *Worship* 46:9 (November 1972): 518ff. "The Concept of Health", *Hasting Center Studies*, 1:3 (1973): 2-88. U.S. Bishops', "Pastoral Letter on Health and Health Care, *Origins* 11:25 (Dec. 8, 1981): 396-402.

LUCIEN J. RICHARD, O.M.I.

HERMENEUTICS AND WORSHIP

The public worship of God, whether in a tradition of canonically defined texts and sign-acts, or in a more oral, spontaneous tradition, is intrinsically hermeneutical. Texts, both written and spontaneous, are necessary if worship is based in Christian scriptures and the biblical tradition. The interpretation and understanding of such texts and of the words used in worship is determined by the performative or "event" character of liturgy. Scripture and liturgical texts occur in a highly interactive context of communal actions and symbols and thus are activated by the performative character of liturgy. In other words, a human community celebrating the liturgy constitutes an essential matrix for interpreting and understanding the texts which are read, sung, prayed and proclaimed.

The term "hermeneutics" is commonly used to designate the theory of interpretation of texts, most especially of biblical texts. The hermeneutics of worship recognizes that historical/critical and literary intepretation of the scriptural texts cannot finally be separated from the actual worship context in which they are employed. H.-G. Gadamer observes, "Understanding is not to be thought of so much as the action of one's subjectivity, but as the placing of oneself within a process of tradition, in which past and present are constantly fused. This is what must be expressed in hermeneutical theory" (*Truth and Method*, p. 258).

The liturgy is principally constituted by biblical texts and sign-actions of the gathered assembly, woven together in symbolic rites which manifest and proclaim the mystery of God's self-giving. Thus interpretation and understanding of texts must be integrated into the hermeneutics of the whole liturgical celebration. The cycles of readings require biblical interpretation in preparation of the homily as well as in catechetical instruction of the faithful. The lectionary orders scripture over cycles of time, both temporal and sanctoral, thus creating a pattern of selectivity and juxtaposition with symbol and sign-action which generate a complex set of reciprocal relationships between biblical texts, sacramental sign-acts, prayer and proclamation.

Liturgical hermeneutics moves beyond traditional biblical hermeneutics in two primary ways: it shares with recent biblical interpretation a stress upon text/reader/context interaction; and it places texts of several kinds in the situation of actual ritual and prayer. Traditionally "hermeneutics" involved the formulation of rules for the interpretation and understanding of ancient texts. The focus was particularly upon grammar, vocabulary and literary style. Traditional hermeneutics recognized that literary texts were conditioned by specific historical and cultural factors. Twentieth century developments have come to emphasize that the contemporary interpreter's standpoint and range of interests brought to the texts must also be taken into account. No longer can it be assumed that understanding ancient texts is achieved by making appropriate references from a system of objectively stated rules. Just as

the modern reader's standpoint and social/cultural "situatedness" is crucial to biblical hermeneutics today, so the contemporary worshipping assembly's social/cultural character, interests and perceptions are central to the interpretation of liturgy and liturgical experiences.

Interpretation must examine the constantly shifting interaction of texts, sacramental actions, symbols and the whole environment in which worship takes place. The "poetics" of liturgical action cause the texts themselves to yield different layers and levels of meaning as they appear and reappear in worship over time. Thus a given lection or psalm, occuring in two different seasons or worship environments, may have a distinctively different force and point in each context. Biblical texts and central symbols as well as ritual acts also have a previous history. Thus they carry layers of juxtaposed meaning with them into the liturgy, so to speak. Both the texts and the symbols signify and speak to the assembly. This means that the symbols and sign-actions can never be treated as mere illustrations of the meaning of the biblical texts. Neither can we regard the biblical texts as simply giving warrant for the employment of the symbols. Hermeneutics with respect to the liturgy examines the ever-changing interanimation of text, sign-act and symbol.

In light of the foregoing sketch, the work of Paul Ricoeur on symbolism advances the discussion. He identifies three dimensions of symbolism: the cosmic, the oneiric and the poetic. The liturgical assembly activates these three dimensions. Celebrating the liturgy together gives rise to the reflective dimension of symbol—to theological and devotional thought. The cosmic dimension of symbol concerns symbols as concrete features of the world—food, elements, persons, events and the like. Symbols are oneiric in that they appear in our dreams and collectively shared stories about the world which bear deep emotional and intellectual power. Living symbols are poetic in that they condense wide ranges of meaning, presenting imaginative fusions and transfigurations of human experience, often allowing us to grasp the mystery of a veiled reality in terms of a visible and palpable reality. Symbols are polysemantic and participatory, taking us beyond the literal and the obvious.

So in liturgy we encounter texts, sign-actions and symbols which interpret one another. Consider the paradigm, water. Water has been associated with the manifestation of the sacred in human experience from time immemorial. It is life-giving and death-dealing in the world of everyday. The oceans are deep and seemingly unfathomable, suggesting danger and life. Water is for drinking and bathing and cleansing. At the same time, human beings can drown in water. It is a primary element of the world in common human social experience. At the same time, water appears in our dreams and imagination. The fear and awe and wonder or delight associated with water surfaces in our unconscious and in all human literatures. Waters of chaos and womb-water rise before us in dreaming and imagining. Poetry has found in water images an enormous range: "Spins to the widow-making unchilding unfathering deeps," sings Gerard Manley Hopkins of the sea-storm in "The Wreck of the Deutschland" (line 104).

In primary symbols such as water we find the confluence of textual depth with the cosmic, oneiric and poetic dimensions. The power of the symbol is activated in the liturgical enactment of the rites of baptism or of sprinkling. When the liturgy of the Easter vigil is celebrated, the water is surrounded by biblical and prayer texts which speak insistently of water, from Genesis through Isaiah through Romans. The psalms which are sung or recited are themselves permeated with the multivalency of water. Thus texts which speak the many-layered meanings of the biblical witnesses come to interact with the signification of actual baptismal water in the midst of a people gathered about fire, the stories, water and the feast. The symbols thus give rise to reflection on the word of God and the divine mystery of the paschal feast. In the lections, prayers, psalms and homily, we find discursive reference to those cosmic, oneiric and poetic fields of force which constitute living symbolism.

In less dramatic ways, every liturgical assembly is a hermeneutical event, giving focus to a range of meanings out of the whole range available in the texts. The eucharistic rite itself is given participatory depth by careful attention to the liturgy of the word. A powerful reading, a thoughtful homily, a well-sung psalm, or a pastorally sensitive, biblically based set of intercessions can lead the worshippers into a more intense sharing in the communion rite. The eucharistic prayer itself, with its thankful remembrance of who God is and all that God has done, recapitulated in Jesus Christ, is a receiving point of all that has preceded it in the liturgy. This is why equal care must be given to all the details of the whole service in liturgical planning and in the celebration. How each unit—readings, responsorial psalmody, prayers, acclamations—is related to the whole musical, visual and choreographical ethos of the rite in its context affects the assembly's depth of participation and experience.

Christian worship both forms the community in and gives expression to the church's self-understanding before God. Being drawn into the triune life of God is to come to understand and to interpret the world as created, sustained and redeemed. In this way liturgical hermeneutics takes us beyond the interpretation of actual texts to interpretation and understanding of the world and our baptismal vocation as God's people therein. The development of an adequate liturgical hermeneutics requires knowledge of and sensitivity to plurality in cultural expression as well as to the anthropological dimensions of sign, symbol and language. The pastoral implications already alluded to are far-ranging. The study of how antiphons function to provide the assembly a way of hearing and praying the psalms, for example, can bring musicians and congregation into deeper mutuality. The study of the eucharistic prayer and its surrounding action, or the baptismal prayers surrounding the font, contributes to a more vital celebration and a deeper living hermeneutic in the assembly. The recovery of the Bible as the church's living memory made active in the ritual context is at the heart of the pastoral work just begun by the recent 20th century liturgical reforms.

Participation in all the dimensions of liturgy brings understanding. The assembly gathered about the book, the font and the table is at one and the same time an event of interpretation (texts, symbols, persons and the world) and an event in which the assembly is interpreted by the living tradition. Both together constitute the larger horizon of worship and hermeneutics.

See **Aesthetics, liturgical; Symbol; Imagination and worship; Preaching the scriptures**

Hans-Georg Gadamer, *Truth and Method* (London: Sheed and Ward, 1975). David N. Power, *Unsearchable Riches: The Symbolic Nature of Liturgy* (New York: Pueblo, 1984). Paul Ricoeur, *Interpretation Theory: Discourse and the Surplus of Meaning* (Fort Worth: Texas Christian University Press, 1976). Paul Ricoeur, *The Symbolism of Evil* (Boston: Beacon Press, 1967). Anthony C. Thiselton, *Language, Liturgy and Meaning*, Grove Liturgical Studies No. 2 (Nottingham: Grove Books, 1975).

DON E. SALIERS

HISTORICAL RESEARCH AND LITURGICAL RENEWAL

Although some may disagree about the extent to which historical research has caused, accelerated and shaped the contemporary renewal of Roman Catholic liturgy, few scholars would deny that the causal relationship is anything less than massive.

Lest the question be begged, however, it must first be observed that contemporary liturgical renewal is neither complete nor wholly successul. As a movement driven more by the pen of scholars than by felt needs in the communities of worship, its implementation has relied heavily on administrative fiat. Frequently, there was little in the religious life of the local churches to make them receptive to liturgical renewal. And when the renewal itself, as often happened, was carried out awkwardly or less than satisfactorily, it was no longer the perceived tyranny of the rubricist but that of the historicist which tended to be given the blame.

Second, the recent flowering of historical research in liturgy is but a relatively small part of a much larger development: the discovery of historical consciousness in modern Roman Catholic thought. Within the past fifty years, the historical-critical method has moved from being regarded as dangerous, even heretical, to a position of quasi-normativity in the work of Catholic scripture scholars. Historical contextualization has, in significant ways, historically relativized the definition of the great councils. The development of doctrine is no longer seen as a formula for heresy but as a foundational concept for every serious student of theology. In other words, the ossification which characterized the liturgy from the post-Tridentine reforms up to the renewal of the Easter vigil in the 1950s and the post-Vatican II liturgical reforms was only a small part of this general ossification of Roman Catholic intellectual life. Thus, the way contemporary liturgical renewal is moved forward by historical research is only part of a much larger picture in which the whole theological life of the church is being moved forward by historically conscious research. E.g., Richard P. McBrien's *Catholicism* (1980) and Bernard J.F. Lonergan's *Method in Theology* (1972) amply illustrate how pervasive historical consciousness now is at all levels of critical Catholic theological thought. Let us examine, then, within this larger context, the role which historical research has played in liturgical renewal.

Renaissance Scholarship. Although it had no effect on the liturgy controlled by the post-Tridentine reforms, the work of the renaissance scholars, in which we can find the early traces of modern historical-critical scholarship, actually laid the first foundations for a liturgical renewal that was to take effect only centuries later. The late 15th century invention of printing made the broad dissemination of texts possible. The polemical situation of the Protestant and Catholic Reformations motivated Christian scholars to recover the testimony of history contained in the theological writings of the past. Prominent among these were liturgical writings. Producing liturgical collections from the earlier medieval writings seems to have been the main achievement of the Catholic liturgical scholars of the 16th century. The work of Melchior Hittorp, *De catholicae ecclesiae divinis officiis ac ministeriis* (1568), stands out. However, there was still very little by way of critical editing of texts, and the great patristic sources remained largely unknown and untapped.

17th and 18th Centuries. It is to this period that liturgiology as a true science can trace its origins. The era of specialization was beginning. What church historians, patrologists and positive theologians were doing in their respective disciplines, liturgical scholars were also beginning to do in theirs. In particular, the Benedictine Maurists distinguished themselves by their critical editions and studies of the Western liturgies. In addition, learned treatises on the liturgy itself began to appear in impressive numbers. The work of the Oratorian, P. Lebrun (d. 1729), *Explication littéale, historique et dogmatique des prières et des cérémonies de la Messe*, is one outstanding example among many. Some texts and studies of the Eastern liturgies also began to appear. In all this, however, the assumptions of a "positive theology" dominated, i.e., one did not study the past in order to learn from it how one might reform or renew the present, but primarily in order to find in the past historical legitimation for the achieved doctrines and practices of one's own particular church. Only later, in the 19th century, does one begin to find the historical consciousness that enables historical research to become a catalyst for liturgical renewal.

19th and 20th Centuries. The key figure here is unquestionably Prosper Guéranger, O.S.B., Abbot of Solesmes from 1837 to his death in 1875. Practically the whole modern liturgical movement can trace its lines to him. The most noted among his voluminous works are his *Institutions liturgiques* (3 vols. 1840-51) and *L'Année liturgique* (9 vols., 1841-66). Of tremendous importance was also the Oxford Movement. Its interest in the Fathers and Christian antiquity included, of course, attention to the ancient liturgies. In particular, the reflections of J.H. Newman on the development of doctrine made that question something from which no subsequent Roman Catholic theologian could legitimately prescind. From this time, and in ever increasing numbers, scores and eventually hundreds of scholars became engaged in publishing liturgical texts, recovering and studying the liturgies of the ancient church, both East and West, reflecting on the significance of these studies for contemporary sacramentary theology and liturgical practice, and disseminating these ideas in popular writings. Centers for liturgical study sprang up all over the Western world, including, eventually, North America (Collegeville and Notre Dame).

For a long time, however, all this had little effect on the public worship of the church as a whole. Apart from the restoration of frequent access to the eucharistic table under Pius X, the eucharistic liturgy of the mid-20th century was hardly distinguishable from that of the late 16th century: a highly stylized Latin ritual which, while indeed inculcating a reverent sense of the sacred and a deep awe of the *tremendum*, relegated most of the faithful to roles of mere passive participation. An in-principle corrective and invitation to genuine renewal was issued in Pius XII's encyclical *Mediator Dei* (1947). As his earlier encyclical *Divino afflante Spiritu* (1943) was for biblical studies, so too this can be seen as the *Magna Charta* for modern liturgical scholarship and the movement of liturgical renewal.

However, it was not as if this encyclical initiated the great modern flowering of liturgical studies. That was already well under way. Most of the scholarly and historical periodicals and serials and the popular journals which carried the movement had already been published or had been publishing for decades: in England, *Liturgy* (earlier *Music and Liturgy*) since 1929; in France, *Monumenta Ecclesiae Liturgica* (1900-12), *Dictionnaire d'Archéologie Chrétienne et de Liturgie* (1907-57), *La Maison-Dieu* since 1945, *L'Art sacré* since 1935; in the Low Countries, *Les Questions Liturguiques et Paroissiales* since 1910, *Paroisse et Liturgie* since 1919, *Tijdschrift voor Liturgie* since 1919; in Germany and Austria, *Antike und Christentum* (1929-50) continued by the *Jahrbuch für Antike und Christentum* since 1958, *Oriens Christianus* since 1901, *Liturgiegeschichtliche Quellen und Forschungen* since 1918, *Jahrbuch für Liturgiewissenschaft* (1921-41) later the *Archiv für Liturgiewissenschaft* since 1950, *Ecclesia Orans*

since 1920, the *Handbuch der Liturgik* (2 vols., 1932-33; abbreviated Engl. trans as *The Liturgy of the Roman Rite*, New York, 1961), *Texte und Arbeiten* since 1919; in Italy, *Ambrosius* (serving the Milanese rite) since 1925, *Ephemerides Liturgicae* since 1881, *Rivista Liturgica* since 1914; in Spain and Portugal, *Liturgia* since 1945; in United States, *Orate Fratres* since 1926 (*Worship* since 1951), *Liturgical Arts* since 1928.

This by no means exhaustive list, which does not even begin to list the works of the great scholars of the modern liturgical revival such as Dix, Jungmann, Michel, and a host of others, suggests the extent to which Pius XII was not initiating but just giving his blessing to an already extensive research movement which was poised to take off as a movement of concrete renewal across the whole church. And take off it did. Within five years of *Mediator Dei*, the new rite of the restored Easter vigil had been promulgated *ad experimentum*, and within another five years it had been extended to the whole church. This one development functioned like a match set to tinder. Within another ten years Vatican II had come and gone; its constitution on the sacred liturgy, *Sacrosanctum concilium* of Dec. 4, 1963, had already been followed by a series of post-conciliar decrees and instructions instituting the practice of concelebration and of communion under both species, returning the liturgy to the vernacular, etc. Other developments followed in quick succession: the reform of the lectionary and the liturgical calendar; the new sacramentary with multiple prefaces and eucharistic prayers; the restoration of the offices of deacon and lector; new rituals for the burial of the dead, for baptism, marriage, and the other sacraments; the reform of the breviary; the restoration of the catechumenate in the Rite of Christian Initiation of Adults, etc.

This veritable explosion of renewal, not all of it, admittedly, implemented with the same success, was caused and, in many instances, directly shaped by historical research. In many cases it consisted of a reappropriation of the forgotten wealth of the early church. Among these retrieved treasures, the "mystery theology" associated with the name of Odo Casel stands out. The fundamental insight of mystery theology, the mystery-presence (*Vergegenwärtigung*) of the paschal mystery of Christ in the eucharist, and the insight that the central reality of every sacrament is an entrance into the paschal mystery and a personal encounter with the risen Christ, has become the foundational insight of contemporary liturgical theology, contemporary theology of church and sacrament, and contemporary ecumenical theology among those churches which have maintained a strong sacramental identity. Casel drew this fundamental insight directly from the Fathers of the church. The great (Vatican II) conciliar and post-conciliar theologians such as O. Semmelroth, E. Schillebeeckx and K. Rahner have used it to set the fundamental agenda on the theology of worship, sacraments and church on which we are still working.

In summary, the reason why the extensive historical research into the liturgy which preceded our own day failed to have a direct effect in liturgical renewal lies, it seems, less in the nature and quality of that research than in the attitudes towards history which pervaded Roman Catholic life and thought until recent decades. As soon, however, as historical consciousness found itself welcome in Roman Catholic thought, as gradually took place in the two decades following the Second World War, the historical research that liturgiologists, historians, patristic scholars and theologians had been doing for centuries was liberated from its monastic walls and dusty bookshelves and set free to work as an explosive catalyst in the life and worship of the church. But explosive

catalysts make for unevenness in renewal. The church's struggle to make up for centuries of dormant or suppressed renewal makes, at times, for a messy church. That is our present situation. The future should be, one may hope, not a new stasis in which no further development can take place—for that would only make another explosion inevitable—but a new equilibrium in which the findings of historical research can act as a gentle, natural leaven in the liturgical life of the people of God.

See **Liturgical movement the (1830-1969); Mystery theology; Theologians, modern, and lit. renewal; Benedictines and liturgical renewal; Papacy, modern, and liturgical renewal**

ROBERT J. DALY, S.J.

HOLY SPIRIT IN CHRISTIAN WORSHIP

This article will reflect upon the specific nature and function of Christian worship as seen from a theology of the Holy Spirit. Christian worship is not something in which the Spirit occasionally has a function, but rather something which from beginning to end is the proper work of the Holy Spirit. It is the specific "personal" characteristic of the third person of the Trinity to fulfill the divine work of glorification accomplished in Christ. Christians give God glory, or worship God, by acknowledging God's supreme act of self-glorification which is the creation and salvation of the world.

The experience and concept of God which lie at the heart of Christian worship make it something quite distinctive, from the point of view of its nature, goal and necessity. In order to appreciate this, it seems worthwhile to begin first with a few introductory remarks about religion and worship in general. Then we shall investigate the nature and function of worship, first in the OT and then in the

NT, where the connection between worship and the Spirit becomes explicit. Finally, we shall consider how this all finds expression in the eucharist, the church's central act of worship.

I. Worship and the Religious Dimension of Humanity

Persons who study religion and the human act of worship which is its heart find themselves investigating something which is as central and universal in its significance as it is difficult to define. We all know what we mean when we refer to the different religions. Most of us could make a list of quite a number of them. We are accustomed to refer to the "world religions" as if they shared a common essence or at least exhibited an obvious similarity in nature or in function. Closer inspection reveals that it is not so simple. Each certainly seems to involve both a view of life and a corresponding way of life. But perhaps that is where the common similarity ends and an extraordinary variety begins. Each bears witness to the strikingly different ways in which human beings have experienced both the depth and the ambiguity of reality and have tried to respond to it. The religions exhibit the perennial and typically human concern with ultimacy, with the ultimate questions raised especially by what some call "limit-experiences." What, if anything, is the ultimate truth and meaning of reality? What does that have to say about who I am, where I came from, where I am going, how I shall get there? These are the basic questions which touch on the *religious* dimension of our existence. We cannot avoid them. The fact that we raise them so seriously reveals both our distinctive nature as transcendent beings and our search for the Transcendent. In this sense we can and must speak of the religious dimension as *constitutive* of human life.

But religions do not arise merely from questions. As Rudolph Otto suggests, it is experience of the Wholly Other, the *mysterium tremendum et fascinans*, that we properly call *religious*. This is the sort of experience which gives birth to religion and worship, whatever other factors might be involved in the historical genesis of a particular religion. Religion begins where there is some manifestation of the power and presence of the transcendent which is able to throw new light on the meaning of reality as a whole and thereby offer some kind of answers to the basic religious questions already mentioned. This is expressed in its customs, discipline, rituals and doctrines.

Although the etymology of "religion" remains somewhat obscure, and is limited by its western provenance as a general descriptive term, the word suggests several important points. Religion is what "binds" (Lat. *re-ligio*) human beings with the realm of the divine and with one another as a particular worshipping (and often socio-political) community. Cult and culture are inseparable. Properly speaking, of course, there is no such thing as a one-person religion. Religion is not a purely private matter of a solitary individual in relationship to God(s); nor on that account is it merely a generally public collection of such individuals. It is precisely *communal*. In the proper sense of the word, religion is something which only makes sense in community: it literally makes the community, binds it together in its devotion to God(s). In its ritual, the believers "re-bind" themselves to the divine as a community. Thus religion, especially in its ritual, is fundamentally concerned with the acknowledgment of and participation in the divine reality which alone has the power to hold everything together: to make the community and the cosmos whole.

Bearing in mind that no adequate definition for such a diverse phenomenon can be given, we might first understand *worship* most broadly as creaturely response to the divine. As such it concerns a reality which is perceived as numinous, awesome, mysterious and radically Other, a reality which transcends any of its particular manifestations or symbolic representations. It concerns that reality upon which all else depends. In other words, worship is proper to God alone, however God might be conceived. We may praise others, but we do not worship them. It is expressed in bodily gestures, and in some languages, the word for worship indicates bowing down, prostration or kissing.

Even in such gestures, worship is seen to be a form of direct address. The heart and purpose of worship is not to talk about God but to talk to God, to enter into relationship with God. Worshippers often address God in praise and petition. Both the gestures and the words which are at the heart of worship are forms of direct address, implying the personal character of the one worshipped and the personal relationship with God which worship articulates.

Worship is not merely a response subsequent to an experience of divine revelation; it continues to be a special time and place of presence. Almost universally in the history of religions, cult is something in which the action of the divine upon humanity takes place as well as the human worship of the divine. Indeed, it is an on-going arena of manifestation and participation. We often find the conviction that the believers are called, summoned, even commanded to come together in worship by their God and may expect God to manifest himself or herself. Particularly good examples of this are the ancient *mystery religions* which highlight the dramatic reality of revelation and the roots of religious ritual in drama. Though it is unlikely that they form the proximate historical source of Christian worship, the similarity is obvious and was captured quite early in liturgical terminology (*mysterion, sacramentum*).

The way a people worship is an expression of its conviction about who God is and who it is for God and how God is related to the world. In worship, therefore, we may speak of a *transcendent* dimension, a *communal* dimension and a *cosmic* dimension.

II. Old Testament

The concrete history of Israel's religious institutions, the development and shifting significance of the different cultic practices, liturgical forms and places of worship is long and complex. But in all of its forms, and whatever its particular focus, worship for Israel means the acknowledgment of the divine glory which God himself has revealed. It is God who glorifies himself by revealing himself in the world.

1. God's Glory. God's glory (*kabod*, "weightiness," "worthiness," "majesty," "brilliance") is seen in the majesty, beauty and order of creation. "The heavens declare the glory of God" (Ps 19:2). Wisdom is seen as a personification of God herself precisely as "an aura of the might of God and a pure effusion of the glory of the Almighty" (Wis 7:25). But Israel's God is not simply a Creator who was active *in illo tempore*, nor merely a transcendent presence felt in the majesty or powers of nature. Israel experienced God as present and personally active in the events of its own history. Thus, the countless texts in the OT which express praise and glory to God nearly always include a recounting of the significant events through which God has shaped Israel's history. In order to speak of God's glory, Israel tells it own story.

"In the beginning, God created...": the central revelation of God's glory and the living heart of Israel's history is found, not in the cosmologies of Genesis, but in the Exodus from Egypt culminating in the Sinai covenant. The glory of YHWH is revealed in his mighty deed, which is the liberation of Israel from slavery and the creation of them into a people. Thus God's self-revelation is precisely as the redeemer/creator of the people. In Israel's experience of God and in her memory, God's power and glory will be forever connected with its very beginning, life and future.

This is the event in which Israel comes to personal knowledge of the God of their ancestors. It speaks of God's utter sovereignty and intimate presence with and for them for all generations and it shows in mighty deeds that he is indeed the One who is with them in their suffering and who has come to save them. Israel comes to believe in YHWH because of his triumph over Egypt and its idols and breaks into song, praising God for his glorious deeds (Exodus 15).

With the revelation of the divine name YHWH and with the decisive events of the Exodus, a whole new level of commitment and relationship is established. On Sinai, we have the formal proclamation of this fact by God and recognition of this fact by Israel. YHWH solemnly identifies himself: "I, the Lord, am your God, who brought you out of the land of Egypt, that place of slavery" (Exod 20:2; = cf. Deut 5:6). This is where YHWH has revealed that he is the only true God (Deut 6:4) and that Israel is his people. It is the reason why Israel must worship YHWH and him alone (Exod 20:3f; Deut 5:7f) and why Israel must love YHWH with all its heart, soul and strength. It is the basis of the great commandment and the heart of the whole Mosaic Law; it is the one thing that Israel must forever remember and take to heart (Deut 6:4f).

2. Israel's Worship as Memorial: Zik-karon. In all of its various forms (including rituals for purification, sacrificial offerings of atonement, prayers of petition and intercession, harvest offerings of thanksgiving, and so on), Israel's worship remained centered in the YHWH cult surrounding the Exodus and Sinai covenant. To worship God means to praise and thank YHWH, the God of the covenant. It means to remember that event in order to enter into it personally, acknowledging its demands and living in its promise.

Of course, this process of redemption/creation is one that was really only just begun in the Exodus event. The entire story chronicled in the OT is really the concrete history of a single process of redemption/creation; a single process of God's revealing or accomplishing his glory as the God and life-giver of his covenant people. It is also a remarkably candid admission of failure by Israel. Through bitter experience, Israel learns the truth of Moses' warning on the banks of the Jordan: "If, however, you turn away your hearts and will not listen, but are led astray and adore and serve others gods . . . you will certainly perish" (Deut 30:17f). In light of its own experience of infidelity, Israel's confession and praise of God's glory precisely in his covenant fidelity takes on special significance and forms the basis upon which Israel can approach the Lord again and again seeking life through mercy and forgiveness. Thus even those cultic actions which focus on purification, repentance and atonement have their basis in the praised-filled remembrance of God's saving deeds and constant fidelity. The community finds courage and confidence to seek forgiveness as it remembers (and reminds God!) what God has already done and promised.

This becomes especially evident in the prophetic tradition. The prophets plead with Israel to come to its senses, to understand itself, its present condition and its future by remembering its origins. Memory is what leads Israel back to God and "back" to its future. In God and God's gracious action, Israel finds its true identity, learns to interpret its present condition and renews its hope in a promised future.

In its remembering, the wholeness and

meaning of its life appear. Precisely because Israel's worship is a remembrance of God's saving deeds, it is the place where the wholeness and meaning of its life are manifested, celebrated and renewed. This is especially evident in Israel's major feasts: Unleavened Bread, Weeks, Booths and Passover. Passover, later combined with the Feast of Unleavened Bread, is of central significance. The celebration of Passover is not simply an anniversary of what happened to the ancestors. Through God's initiative, it is an effective re-presentation of the saving events of the past as a present reality. The faithful of each generation are enabled to journey out of Egypt themselves and enter into the life of the covenant promise.

Thus, what we have here is not simply the quite understandable necessity of memory for the people to know who they are, where they came from, what their promise and future is. The remembering is established as memorial by God himself. Israel is commanded by God to remember. Thus the remembering of the people is something which happens within the totality of the single saving act of God. It is taken up and included so to speak in the saving/creating action. The significance of the command to remember is precisely one of historical mediation of the saving events. God's command is at once a divine pledge making Israel's worship a means to perpetuate his saving action.

The dynamic of memorial (*zikkaron*) is thoroughly sacramental: both praise for God's saving deeds and participation in the salvation they effect. Doxology and soteriology are intrinsically united. In and through the worship of the community, God continues the act of redemption and creation begun in the Exodus.

3. *Spirit and Sacrifice.* Throughout Israel's history and in many different forms, sacrifice was the central act of worship. It must be understood as an acknowledgment of God's deeds and promises. Both the covenant with Abraham and the covenant on Sinai are solemnized and symbolized in blood sacrifices. In Israel's later history, the different gifts offered in sacrifice are signs of and responses to the gracious gifts of the Lord. In offering them, the community expresses its desire to enter more deeply into the covenant union with God. Thus sacrificial worship is not a means to placate or persuade God. It is a sign of the community's remembrance of God's fidelity and of its own repentance and renewed desire for union with God. It expresses the surrender of one's spirit (whole self) to God in order to be filled and renewed with God's own Spirit.

This is the notion which underlies the strong criticism of temple worship and sacrifice which is evident especially in the prophetic literature and the emphasis on spiritual sacrifice in the Psalms. True worship, precisely as the acknowledgement of YHWH's mighty deeds, really consists in the spiritual (personal) surrender of love (Ps 40:6-10; 50:8-13; 51:16-19). This is the only appropriate response to the loving deeds of God who creates and renews the people by filling them with his spirit (compare Ps 51:10f; Ezek 11:19f; 36:26f; 37:14; 39:29). The externals of worship have true meaning only as expressions of interior devotion and love. Such love will express itself not only in cultic acts, but even more so in the life of the community. God is glorified when covenant love and justice inform the community's life (Amos 5:21-25; Mic 6:6-8). Without this, external cult is worthless. Of what use is a temple and its cult to YHWH, whose glory fills the heavens and the earth? Of what value the holocausts and grain offerings to the One who created the universe and all its creatures (Isa 66:3)? Where justice and mercy are done, there shines the glory of the Lord (Isaiah 58). What God desires is love not sacrifice (Hos 6:6). In an extraordinary image expressing her future consolation, Jerusalem, wrapped in the cloak of justice, crowned with the glory of the eternal name, is called "the peace of justice, the glory of God's worship" (Bar 5:4). Thus worship has a fundamental ethical orientation to the life of the community precisely because of its orientation to God. The people, here symbolized by Jerusalem, will itself be the revelation of God's glory when it manifests God's justice and peace.

This last image is a good example of another important development in Israel's worship. The post-exilic writings of the OT evidence a growing awareness of the universal cosmological and eschatological scope of the promise rooted in the Exodus and covenant. This influences Israel's worship notably. The glory of God's presence (*shekinah*) is not limited to fire, cloud and tent, but is seen more and more in the eschatological perspective of the new heavens and the new earth which YHWH will make, when God's wisdom and Spirit will fill the earth (compare Sirach 24; Ezek 36:26f; Joel 3:1f). On that day, the Lord himself will come to gather people from every nation to see and proclaim his glory. They shall all be brought to Jerusalem as an offering to the Lord. And all men and women will worship before him (Isa 66:18ff).

4. Worship as Sacrifice of Praise and Thanksgiving. The true nature of sacrifice is especially seen in two forms of worship which take place in the context of a meal. They are of particular significance for understanding the origins and development of the Christian eucharistic liturgy. The first is the table-fellowship meal which was quite common in the time of Jesus and probably the sort of meal which Jesus celebrated with his disciples just before his death. Bread is broken, and several cups of wine, including the "cup of blessing" are shared. There are prayers of petition and a final prayer of praise. Its heart is a series of three solemn

berakoth, joyful, memorial prayers of praise, thanksgiving and acknowledgement of God's saving deeds. The first praises God as the creator of all life. The second recalls the Exodus, covenant and the fruits they have yielded for the people. The third is dominated by the petition that the creating, redeeming action of God be renewed today and that it may be fulfilled in the coming of the Messiah, who will restore Jerusalem and universally establish the kingdom where God will be glorified eternally for his saving deeds.

The second is the *toda*, a sacrificial meal offering of thanks made by someone who has been saved from death or some other life-threatening situation. Many of the psalms (22, 30-31, 40, 41, 66, 107, 116, to name a few) have this ritual meal as their *sitz im leben*. The story is recounted and the saving action of God is confessed, often in the context of Israel's salvation history as a whole, from its founding events to its promised future. Even more than the holocaust offering or the unleavened bread and wine which were a part of such rituals, the act of thanksgiving and praise itself (*toda*) was the heart of worship, the true sacrifice which glorifies YHWH (compare Ps 50:14,23; 116:17). It was an expression of the offering of self, the sacrifice God truly desires (compare Ps 51:17-19; 40:7-11). It looked forward to the end-time when God's saving deeds would attain their final and universal dimension (Ps 22:28f). According to an old rabbinic tradition, while all other rituals would cease in the messianic age, the *toda* would be sung throughout eternity. Some scholars argue that the eucharistic celebration of the early church should be understood not only in terms of the last *berakoth* meal of Jesus with the disciples, but as the *toda* of the risen Lord.

III. New Testament

Whatever may be said of the different influences upon Christian worship throughout its history and its similarities to the cultic practices of other religions, its roots are to be found in the Jewish experience and worship of God we have just described. Turning to the NT, we find the same basic characteristics: the elements of thanksgiving, praise and adoration as the people remember and proclaim the mighty acts in which God has revealed himself, especially in Jesus Christ, who is confessed, only in the Spirit, to be Lord (1 Cor 12:3). The so-called "High Priestly Prayer" of Jesus in John 17 and the opening sections of many of the letters of the NT, especially the Pauline epistles, are good examples of "Christian" *berakah* and *tefillah*.

But Christian worship is not only spontaneous human expression of joy and celebration. The NT anchors worship in the command of Jesus and in the power of the Holy Spirit. In the OT, the presence and action of God were already spoken of in terms of God's word and Spirit, which, as the figure of wisdom shows, were not sharply distinguished from each other. In the NT, especially in terms of the community's liturgical practice, we see the beginnings of the distinctions which would form the basis of later trinitarian theology. The close relationship between the Son (Word) and the Spirit is increasingly spoken of in terms of personal distinction, based no doubt on the community's new experience of God, not just in Jesus (who gone, would return again), but now present and active within it. As the personal identity and role of the Spirit come to be recognized more clearly, we observe the particular association of the Spirit with the identity and mission of the church in general, and with the nature and purpose of the church's worship in particular. A few remarks on the former will help to illuminate the latter.

1. God's Glory. Before the resurrection, the person and ministry of Jesus may have raised many hopes and even elicited a kind of faith (Lk 24:21). But even when compared to the unfortunate destinies of the other prophets, Jesus' life and death on a cross could hardly be seen in any traditional sense as the glorification of God. It is only when Jesus is raised by God in the power of the Spirit that his own life and death may be seen as the glorification of God in his complete offering of self, rather than the just punishment of a blasphemer.

Still, what is new, what is "good news," is not the fact that a pious man has glorified God, but that God has glorified Jesus and given those "who had been hoping" a share in his Spirit. In the light of the resurrection, the Christ event is seen as the act of God himself. Only in this way is the cross the revelation of the glory of the divine, self-surrendering love. Jesus is the fulfillment of all God's promises and previous actions (2 Cor 1:20); the outpouring of his Spirit is the inauguration of the eschatological and therefore universal fulfillment of all the world (Acts 2:17ff) and as such, the completion of God's creating/redeeming action in Word/Spirit. This is revealed in the raising of Jesus from the dead by the "glory of the Father" (Rom 6:4), and indwelling of this same Spirit in the believers (Rom 8:11).

The divine glory (*doxa*), the OT *kabod* revealed in God's actions, is shown to be the divine nature or life itself as it has appeared (*ōphthē*) in Jesus (Eph 1:17; 2 Cor 4:6; Heb 1:3) and as it is communicated in the Spirit to the world (Eph 3:14-21; 1 Pet 4:14). Thus, we may say that for the NT, God glorifies himself by communicating the divine life itself to the world. The glory of God is the salvation of the world. Doxology and soteriology are one theologically.

The Spirit carries out the divine work of God's saving glory, established in Christ, to its completion. That is why glory is particularly associated with the Spirit's ministry (2 Cor 3:8), which will be to bear witness to Christ (Jn 15:26), and to lead men and women into the fullness of the truth revealed in Christ (Jn 16:13).

The Spirit glorifies Jesus by enabling believers to see his life, death and resurrection as the revelation of the glory of the divine love and by transforming them in the power of this love, making of them living witnesses of its glory (2 Cor 3:8, 17f).

The resurrection of Jesus is the revelation of the Spirit and it is with the sending of the Spirit that the church comes into existence and is constituted as the Spirit's own witness to the truth of God's self-revelation in Christ. The glory which believers have heard, seen and touched in Christ is now to become visible in their own lives, especially in their love for one another. In this way, the Spirit gives witness through the church in every age to the revelation of God's enduring love for the whole world in Jesus Christ, making the glory of this past event shine forth in power as a present, transforming reality. The power of the Spirit active in the church is the real "proof" that Jesus has been raised.

It is the loving union (koinōnia, communio) of believers in Christ which seeks out the least of the brethren and excludes no one, that most fundamentally reveals the glory of God in Christ and the presence of the risen Lord as Spirit in the church. Only as a community reconciled in Christ can they be effective in the Spirit's ministry of reconciliation (compare 2 Cor 5:16-21). This loving union is proper to the person of the Spirit and is the Spirit's final goal and greatest work (1 Corinthians 12; 2 Cor 13:13; compare Phil 2:1ff).

2. Authentic Worship. It has been claimed by some scholars who recognize the primary significance of the *communio* (one often suspects views of the OT and its relationship to the NT bordering on Manichaeism, and reactions to a triumphalistic, almost magical sacra-

mentalism which has been evident in the church's history), that in the gospel of the kingdom, Jesus announced an end to the law and the abolishment of religious cult as prescribed therein. "Community, Yes; Cult, No!"? In view of the fact that some of the oldest traditions represented in the NT deal with liturgical matter, quite specifically with the memorial commanded by the Lord (in the Synoptics and Paul), such a view seems untenable. What is new is neither the abolishment of cult, nor the invention of an absolutely new one; Jesus *reinterprets* the existing liturgical form of the *berakoth* meal when he says "Do this in remembrance of me." And the very form of celebration as meal highlights its intrinsic connection with the *communio*.

It is true that Jesus, like the prophets before him, was critical of the degeneration of the temple cult. Like them, he urged that the sacrifice desired by God was the heart, not a burnt offering. It is what is called worship "in the Spirit" by Paul, who was attacked for "influencing people to worship God in ways that are against the law" (Acts 18:13). John speaks of worship "in spirit and truth" (4:23f), James of "pure worship" (Jas 1:27). This has three senses. (1) Christian worship, completely in the prophetic traditions of the OT, is *spiritual* (i.e., personal) in nature. It means the surrender of one's whole self to God who has graciously acted on the world's behalf (Rom 12:1; 1 Pet 2:5). (2) Such worship has as its ground and goal the life of the community as a whole (2 Cor 1:20; Jas 1:26f). (3) Such worship is inspired and directed by the Spirit (Phil 3:3) in whom the believing community remains in Jesus and his word, and therefore in communion with each other (Jn 4:23).

Once this is seen, the significance of the criticism of the temple cult can be appreciated. The community itself is designated the temple of the living God (2 Cor 6:16), built of living stones, an edifice of spirit (1 Pet 2:5) and dwelling place of the Spirit of God (1 Cor 3:16). This people is created in the new covenant (Jer 31:31ff) as a priestly people claimed by God to proclaim the glory of God's works (1 Pet 2:9-10). Its worship is the offering of "spiritual sacrifices acceptable to God through Jesus Christ" (1 Pet 2:5). The spiritual worship acceptable to God is the offering of oneself as a living sacrifice (Rom 12:1).

The people is at once spiritual temple, holy priesthood and living sacrifice, all by the action of the Holy Spirit who forms it into the body of Christ, himself temple (Jn 2:21; compare Heb 10:20), high priest (Heb 5:1f) and perfect offering (Heb 9:12, 14; 10:10).

In other words, through the Spirit, the church's worship of God is its communal "Yes" to what God has done in Christ (2 Cor 1:20) and, therefore, a participation in the worship of Christ the High Priest. This worship consists in a participation in the sacrifice of Christ, which is the surrender of one's whole self to Christ's mission for the salvation of the world as it is announced and effected in the kingdom.

IV. Spirit and Eucharist

The Spirit builds up the church in communion with Christ and empowers it to carry out its mission in a variety of ways and through a variety of gifts, but especially in the church's worship, through word and sacrament. In its memorial sacrifice of praise and thanksgiving, the Spirit enables the church to remember the saving action of God in Jesus Christ, makes it a present reality in which believers are called to acknowledge and participate, and fashions them ever more fully into a communion of divine love as the body of Christ. "One body, one Spirit in Christ," they share both in his life and in his mission: that universal community of love in the Spirit which is the Kingdom. Only because of the presence and action of the Spirit is the community able to obey (and understand the full implications of) the Lord's command: "Do this in remembrance of me." Thus, as we already saw in the OT, "memorial" is not merely a subjective act of remembering a past event, but an action of God, an institution established by God and given to God's people in order to perpetuate (make present) God's saving action.

The unity of the church, and its mission of reconciling unification, is meant to come to particular expression as it celebrates the memorial of the paschal mystery of Christ, which is the heart of its worship (1 Cor 10:16f; 11:17ff). This is especially evident when one considers the structure of the eucharistic liturgy. Like the Jewish table-fellowship meals from which it arose, the eucharist is primarily a communal act of thanksgiving (*berakah/toda, eucharistia/eulogia, gratias agere*) and praise in which the community remembers and proclaims (*zikkaron, anamnesis, memoria*) the saving deeds of God and brings gifts (*anaphora*) of bread and wine, elements which come to symbolize both the supper and sacrifice of the Lord, and the offering of self which is the goal of true worship "in the Spirit." Within a few centuries (West Syrian rite, later forms of Addai and Mari, later versions of Hippolytus) we find the role of the Spirit explicitly stated in the form of what came to be called the *epiclesis*, more or less a conclusion of the *anamnesis*. Through the power of the Spirit, those who partake in the holy mysteries are to be filled with the Spirit, being gathered together into the body of Christ to the glorification of God the Father.

In its primitive forms, before the introduction of an invocation of the Spirit to transform the elements themselves, or to consecrate them as sacrificial offerings, the *epiclesis* highlights the fundamental purpose of the eucharistic celebration (and, it may be said, the fundamental role of the Spirit in Christian worship): the fulfillment of the church in unity in order to glorify the Father through the Son. This is expressed in the most ancient form of the great doxology: "Glory be *to* the Father *through* the Son *in* the Holy Spirit" (before developments in trinitarian theology in the 4th century led to a focus on the divinity of the Spirit and corresponding changes in liturgical formulae to stress this (e.g., Basil's doxology, which lives today in popular form: "Glory be to the Father and to the Son and to the Holy Spirit...").

The current form of the great doxology in the Roman church is quite similar: "Through him, with him, in him, in the unity of the Holy Spirit, all glory and honor is yours, Almighty Father, forever and ever." It may serve as a summary and conclusion of this article. It reminds us of the connection between the community act of worship and its life: both are "in the unity of the Holy Spirit." This formula may express the glory which the church gives to the triune God, but it also expresses the deeper truth that the glory which is truly God's is to be found in the living communion of love which the Holy Spirit establishes through, with and in Christ. In other words, the Father's glory *is* the unity of the believers *in the Holy Spirit*, through, with and in Christ. Thus the Spirit is called "Lord and Giver of Life" by the ancient creeds precisely because it is the Spirit who is and who bestows life as the life of persons in communion. All of the "marks" of the church as it is built up by the Spirit, one, holy, catholic, and apostolic, are essentially ways of expressing the union which the Spirit effects between believers with Christ and in him with one another.

The community gives God glory chiefly by living in loving union. This is precisely what the example of Christ teaches (Phil 2:1-11). It is not the liturgy per se, but the transformation of life, the reconciliation of human beings with God and with one another, which is the ultimate aim of glorifying God "in the Spirit." This is what the liturgy is meant to express and effect. As Matthew 25 reminds us, the only public works (liturgy) which are absolutely necessary for salvation are what used to be called the corporal works of mercy (see the warning of L.G., 14, the assurance of L.G., 16). Sacramental worship of God should lead us with God to the world, which after all is God's creative, redemptive work (liturgy!). As Rahner points out, it is important not because in it something happens which does not happen at all elsewhere but because it makes visible the "divine depth" of our real, everyday lives as they are created, redeemed and sustained by God's Spirit. Indeed, it is necessary both as a symbolization of the hidden reality of this "liturgy of the world" and as the ongoing renewal of the *communio* God has made to be a witness thereof. Whether or not the world comes to the eucharistic worship of the church (S.C., 10) seems quite secondary.

Where worship fails to illumine the sacred depth of the "secular," where it no longer prepares people and enables them to encounter God in everyday life, where worship becomes removed from God's desire to establish the kingdom, or from our mission as church to be a real and effective mediation of God's love in action, we make of God's saving *opus operatum* in Christ an esoteric ritual, "something to be done" and done correctly, but robbed of its life-giving, transforming power. Ritual*ism* is a "sin against the Holy Spirit."

Through "right worship" (*orthodoxia*), the Holy Spirit leads the community in owning, celebrating and renewing its identity and mission. Made one through Christ, the church is a visible sign or sacrament of salvation. As sacrament of the Spirit (Kasper), it symbolizes in a real and effective way the kingdom which God's Spirit is finally bringing about, not solely "within" the visible church, but in the whole of human history: intimate union with God and the unity of all humankind (L.G.,1). This is how the Spirit glorifies the Son and so brings the process of God's self-glorification to its completion.

See **Eucharist, theology of; Doxology; Reverence; Worship; Jewish worship; Jewish roots of Christian worship**

L. Bouyer, *Eucharist* (Notre Dame: University of Notre Dame Press, 1968). O. Casel, *The Mystery of Christian Worship* (Westminster, MD: Newman Press, 1962). Y. Congar, *I Believe in the Holy Spirit,* 3 vols. (New York: Harper and Row, 1983). O. Cullmann, *Early Christian Worship* (London: SCM Press, 1953). F. Hahn, *The Worship of the Early Church* (Philadelphia: Fortress Press, 1973). W. Kasper, "Einheit und Vielfalt der Aspekte der Eucharistie. Zur neuerlichen Diskussion um Grundgestalt und Grundsinn der Eucharistie", *IKZ* 14 (1985), pp. 196-215. W. Kasper (ed.), *Gegenwart des Geistes. Aspekte der Pneumatologie* (Freiburg: Herder, 1979). F. Porsch, *Pneuma und Wort. Ein exegetischer Beitrag zur Pneumatologie des Johannesevangeliums* (Frankfurt: Knecht, 1974). K. Rahner, "On the Theology of Worship", TI 19, pp. 141-149. N. Smart, *The Concept of Worship* (London: The Macmillan Press, 1972). M. Thurian, *The Eucharistic Memorial,* 2 vols. (London: Lutterworth, 1960-1). E. Underhill, *Worship* (London: Nisbet, 1936). H. U. von Balthasar, *Spiritus Creator,* Einsiedeln: Johannes Verlag, 1967), especially "Die Messe, ein Opfer der Kirche?", pp. 166-217). G. Wainwright, *Doxology. The Praise of God in Worship, Doctrine, and Life* (New York: Oxford University Press, 1980).

JOHN R. SACHS, S.J.

HOLY SPIRIT, BAPTISM IN THE

The exact meaning of "baptism in the Spirit" is disputed among Christians. No one denies that intensified experiences of the Spirit (often accompanied by the gift of glossalalia) have occurred in the lives of believers since the earliest days of the Christian era, but there is considerable difference of opinion about the significance of these events.

Classical Pentecostalism maintains that the experience of being baptized in the Spirit is the decisive moment in personal salvation. Water baptism is understood as a kind of rebirth that signals an individual's conversion, but Spirit baptism ("the second blessing") is recognized as the definitive experience of being filled with the Spirit of Jesus and empowered to witness to the gospel. Pentecostals also maintain that the charism of speaking in tongues (glossalalia) is the inevitable evidence of this experience of being sanctified. According to these Christians, therefore, there is no salvation without baptism in the Spirit and there is no baptism in the Spirit that is not accompanied by the gift of tongues.

This distinguishing characteristic of Classical Pentecostalism finds its source in the NT witness, primarily that provided by the author of Luke-Acts (Acts 2:37-39). In the letters of Paul there are several texts which affirm that Christian life is a gift of the Spirit of Jesus (Rom 8:9, 14ff; Gal 4:6; 1 Cor 12:13); that life in Christ is an incorporation into his dying and rising (Rom 6:3ff; 8:11; Col 2:12); and that the experience of being washed in the baptismal waters by the community of believers is an occasion for receiving the gift of the Spirit from the God of Jesus (1 Cor 6:11; 12:13; 2 Cor 1:21-22). Paul links incorporation into Christ through water baptism to the experience of being immersed in the Spirit. Water baptism and Spirit baptism are therefore understood as interrelated without being identified. The Christian community (with the exception of the Pentecostal churches) has generally understood the gift of the Spirit as the effect of the ritual of (water) baptism in the name of Jesus. "Baptism in the Spirit" is therefore not always understood as an event subsequent to water baptism; it is also thought of as an aspect of Christian initiation itself. All who are baptized into Christ are filled with the Spirit of Christ.

The Pentecostal churches understand water baptism in the name of Jesus as a rebirth that ratifies one's repentance or conversion, but that remains ineffective without the outpouring of the gift of the Spirit. The Catholic and mainline Protestant churches, on the other hand, understand Christian (water) baptism as the sacramental cause of the gift of the Spirit. The two are distinct, but not separate.

A third way of interpreting baptism in the Spirit is associated with the charismatic renewal in both Catholic and Protestant communities. Although there are various attempts to explain the phenomenon whereby members of the renewal experience the fullness of the Spirit, the most helpful is probably that which explains this event as a reaffirmation and renewal of a person's baptismal identity. Members of such communities claim that they have experienced a kind of "second baptism" in which the gift of the Spirit of Jesus was made manifest in their lives in a new and transforming way. These "baptisms in the Spirit" are oftentimes marked by the reception of one or other of the charisms (1 Corinthians 12 and 14). A person who wishes to be baptized in the Spirit asks others to pray that this extraordinary gift may be bestowed. The experience usually occurs after intercessory prayer and the laying on of hands by members of the prayer community who have previously been baptized in the Spirit. For members of the renewal, therefore, "baptism in the Spirit" is more often thought of as an experience of the presence and power of the Spirit, than an event marking the initial reception of the Spirit. It is a gift of awareness and empowerment rather than the definitive sign of salvation. A person who has been baptized in the Spirit tends to be undeniably convinced that God's love has been poured out upon him or her (Rom 5:5).

These various interpretations of "baptism in the Spirit" raise deeper issues about the manner in which God is experienced. How is God both other than yet intimately one with me? How can I believe in one who lies utterly beyond the realm of my being? How are God's call, my response, and God's gift of Self related?

Pentecostals, for example, understand salvation in Christ as a three-part process which begins with repentance (in response to the hearing of the gospel) and is followed first by baptism in the name of Jesus and finally by the gift of the Spirit. For Pentecostalism faith and water baptism are preparatory—faith as our movement away from sin toward God and the ritual of water baptism as the church's ratification of our conversion. But it is the experience of being baptized in the Spirit that is God's definitive act of claiming us as his son or daughter. The latter may (and usually does) occur sometime after a person's incorporation into the church through the ritual of baptism.

Such an understanding separates faith and the act of Christ in and through his church from the gift of the Spirit. For Catholic theology, however, this separation is impossible. There is no incorporation into the body of Christ that is not effected by the presence and power of the Spirit. Furthermore, there is no act of faith that is not empowered by the prior (although admittedly usually implicitly experienced) presence of the Spirit. "No one can say 'Jesus is Lord' except in the Holy Spirit" (1 Cor 12:3). There is a distinction between the rite of baptism and the experience of the Spirit, but that distinction is never a separation. Whether or not one interprets the water rite as the sacramental cause of the experience of being filled with the Spirit of Jesus is another question.

Yves Congar, *I Believe in the Holy Spirit*, 3 vols. Trans. by David Smith (New York: Seabury Press, 1983), see 2:189-201. James J.D. Dunn, *Baptism in the Holy Spirit* (Philadelphia: The Westminster Press, 1970).

BARBARA FINAN

HOLY SPIRIT, GIFTS OF THE

The gifts of the Holy Spirit are usually thought of in terms of the seven-fold gift of the Spirit prayed for in the Sequence of Pentecost. Those gifts—wisdom, understanding, counsel, knowledge, might, piety, and fear of the Lord—are derived from the list of messianic "spirits" delineated by the author of Isaiah (11:2-3). In Isaiah only six of the traditional seven are explicitly mentioned. Piety is used in the Septuagint (and Vulgate) to translate the first occurrence of fear of the Lord. Although it was probably simply a mistranslation, piety nonetheless extends the list to the symbolic number of fullness and thus reminds us of the unlimited character of the Spirit's power to graciously sensitize us to live under the sway of the love of God.

The gifts of the Holy Spirit need to be understood within the context of a theology of grace. A theology which explains grace as the gift by means of which the soul is readied for the indwelling of the Trinity will tend to treat the gifts differently from a theology which understands grace and holiness as the effect of the presence of the Holy Spirit. In the former approach the gifts tend to be thought of as discrete realities which perfect the exercise of the virtues so that we may respond with the power of God (and not simply with unaided reason) to divine inspirations. In the latter, however, they are more aptly understood as one of the many facets of the mysterious and gracious bonding with God that the Spirit enables. They are the names we give to the experience of being led by the Spirit from within our spirit into the ambience of the triune God. The gifts are a kind of divinely bestowed possibility to live under the direct influence of God; they give us an habitual instinct to freely respond under, with and within the stirrings of grace.

The history of theology reveals that the gifts were not thought of as distinct from the theological and moral virtues until the 13th century. Philip the Chancellor is the first to have made this distinction, but it was Thomas Aquinas who developed the most complete synthesis of the interdependence of the gifts not only with the virtues, but also with the beatitudes and the fruits. Thomas' understanding of the gifts as divine dispositions for acting under the influence of the Spirit has predominated in all subsequent theological reflection.

Central to the presentation in Thomas' theology is his conviction that only those who are led by the Spirit can be sons and daughters of God (Rom 8:14). The gifts of the Spirit make it possible for us to act under the direct influence of God so that God (and not simply human reason) becomes the principle of our good acts. The Spirit of God is the condition without which the infinity of God's grace and the finitude of human freedom could never be one. God is thus not only the distant goal, but also the intimate presence by means of which we move toward God. The gifts are thus a kind of interior divine prompting enabling us to respond to God's beckoning from beyond. When we pray for the fullness of the experience of the gifts of the Spirit, therefore, we beseech God to live in us as the infinitely intimate presence with which we can be more and more deeply available to God's influence.

Because of the gifts, our virtuous response toward God, self or others is lifted beyond the realm of the merely human. Because of the gifts, our relationship with God (through faith, hope and charity) and our bondedness with self and others (through prudence, justice, fortitude and temperance) are borne on the power of God's own infinite act of self-consciousness. The gifts perfect the virtues by making it possible to live the Christian life in a manner which transcends the limits of reason. Human reason and freedom become divinized so that our good acts are elevated beyond the realm of the merely finite. God enables us to act divinely. The gifts of the Spirit empower us to be one with God (in our knowledge and love of self and others) without ceasing to be other than God. They prepare our spirit for the inspirations of grace so that our response to infinity is without limit. We are, therefore, able to live as persons possessed by God. The one act of faith, the one movement of hope, love, justice or prudence is both ours and God's. The infinite transcendence who is God becomes one with our finite transcendence. It is not just the Spirit loving in us; we do the loving. Yet the love of our hearts is inseparable from the love of God's Spirit. God's spirit of wisdom and understanding, of counsel and might, of knowledge, piety and holy fear is one with (without ceasing to be other than) ours.

Thomas understood the theological and cardinal virtues as well as the beatitudes and the gifts (and fruits) of the Spirit in terms of an organic synthesis. He thus devoted separate questions to each of the seven gifts and took great care to describe the particular functions of each as well as the way in which these various aspects of the life of grace were interrelated (S.Th., IIa IIae). Although the parallels which Thomas draws may be somewhat artificial, they nonetheless serve to remind us of the unifying function of God's Spirit.

Since the charismatic renewal, reference to the gifts of the Spirit evokes not only awareness of the traditional seven from Isaiah, but also the gifts or charisms delineated in the letters of Paul (1 Corinthians 12 and 14). The latter are those gifts (for example, tongues, healing, teaching, prophecy) described in scholastic theology as the *gratiae gratis datae*. Traditionally these graces have been understood as extraordinary manifestations of the power of the Spirit in the lives of individual Christians for the edification and encouragement of the community of believers. They are necessary for the good of the community, but are not required for individual salvation. One or more of the charisms or *gratiae gratis datae* are usually associated with "baptism in the Spirit" which some Christians experience, whereas the seven gifts are received by all Christians in the sacraments of initiation.

Either set of gifts serves to remind us that the ultimate gift of God is the Spirit of the risen Lord. The diversity of the experiences of God's transcendent presence within believers (as individuals and as a community) is the symbol of the fundamental gift of unity that is the Spirit of the Father of Jesus. It is the presence of the Spirit that makes our lives one with each other and God in the person of Jesus. The gifts of the Spirit manifest the utter gratuity and universality of God's transforming presence within us.

Yves Congar, *I Believe in the Holy Spirit*, 3 vols. Trans. by David Smith (New York: Seabury Press, 1983), see 2:134-141. Anthony J. Kelly, "The Gifts of the Spirit: Aquinas and the Modern Context," *The Thomist* 38 (1974):193-231.

BARBARA FINAN

HOLY WEEK, LITURGIES OF

Holy Week, also called Great Week in the Eastern Christian churches, contains the most solemn liturgies of the liturgical year. It begins with the procession with palms on Palm (Passion) Sunday and lasts until the end of the great vigil of Easter the following Saturday night. In a sense Holy Week is not an official unit of the liturgical year since it comprises both Lent, which ends with the beginning of the Mass of the Lord's Supper on Holy Thursday, and most of the Easter triduum, which begins with the Mass of the Lord's Supper and ends with Easter Sunday vespers. Holy Week derives its name from the fact that this period contains the annual celebration of the most solemn mysteries of the Christian faith—the passion, death and resurrection of Jesus Christ.

The liturgies that make up the observance of Holy Week developed at different times in the history of the church. The earliest is the Paschal vigil, most probably the earliest of all annual Christian liturgical celebrations. While this vigil and feast may be of apostolic origin in some places, there are others (for example, Rome) where the vigil may not have been celebrated until the middle of the 2nd century. In the latter places, every Sunday had been the sole celebration of the passion, death and resurrection of Christ.

Holy Week came into existence as an intense period of preparation (prayer and fasting) for initiation at the Easter vigil. We know (from the *Didache* and Irenaeus of Lyons) that this fast lasted from one to several days in the first two Christian centuries. By the 3rd century, in the Syrian *Didascalia Apostolorum*, we have evidence for a week-long fast preceding the vigil. A 4th-century source describing the liturgies of Jerusalem, the *Pilgrimage Diary* of Egeria, speaks specifically of Great Week. This information is confirmed by subsequent lectionaries which treat Holy (Great) Week as a distinct unit from Lent. Thus from the 4th century on what we know as Holy Week is firmly in place. Today it has become customary to emphasize the distinction between Lent, which ends on Holy Thursday, from the Paschal triduum (see, e.g., *General Norms for the Liturgical Year and the Calendar*, 18-21). Here we shall deal with the liturgies of Holy Week, not in their order of importance (working back from the Paschal vigil), but in the order in which they appear in the calendar.

Passion (Palm) Sunday

The 1969 Roman Calendar significantly changed the title of the first day of Holy Week from Palm to Passion Sunday. Hitherto the previous Sunday (the Fifth Sunday of Lent) had been called Passion Sunday and the two weeks preceding Easter, Passiontide. With the restoration of the liturgies for the last stage of the catechumenate in Lent it was decided to restore the older Roman name to Palm Sunday. The eucharistic liturgy of the day falls into two parts: the commemoration of the Lord's entry into Jerusalem and the Mass, whose readings all concentrate on the Lord's Passion.

The Commemoration of the Lord's Entry into Jerusalem. The commemoration of Jesus' entry into the city of his passion may take one of three forms: a procession, a solemn entrance, or a simple entrance. The procession is to be used only once, at the principal Mass of the day in any church. The people gather at a subsidiary chapel or other place at which an antiphon is sung ("Hosanna to the Son of David..." Mt 21:9), all are invited to the observance of Holy Week, palm branches are blessed, the gospel of Jesus' entry is proclaimed (Matthew in Year A, Mark or John in Year B, and Luke in Year C), and all process to the church singing some or all of the following: Psalm 24, Psalm 47 (with appropriate antiphons) and Theodulph of Orleans' 8th-century hymn "All Glory, Laud, and Honor." The Mass then begins with the opening prayer.

The remote origins of the procession with palms can be found in Jerusalem in the 4th-century practice of processing with song and carrying palms down the Mount of Olives to the Church of the Holy Sepulchre on the afternoon of Palm Sunday. Although the origins of the observance of Palm Sunday may have been connected with pre-4th-century Jerusalem liturgy, namely the liturgy of Alexandria (see, Thomas J. Talley, *The Origins of the Liturgical Year*, New York: Pueblo, 1986, 39-40), it is in Jerusalem that we find the first evidence of the procession of palms. This particular day was chosen on the basis of John's gospel: "Six days before the Passover Jesus came to Bethany" (Jn 12:1). In 4th-century Jerusalem Jesus was represented in the procession by the bishop. The medieval imagination represented him in a number of ways: the bishop, a donkey (at times wooden), or even the blessed sacrament. The procession with palms did not enter the papal form of the Roman rite until the 12th century, when palms were blessed at the chapel of St. Sylvester at the Lateran Palace and the eucharistic liturgy took place at the Lateran Basilica (for the medieval Roman liturgies of Holy Week, see Schuster, *The Sacramentary*, Vol. II, 171-312).

The solemn entrance may take place at all other Masses or, when no provisions for a procession can be made, even for the principal Mass. In this form only the procession from a place other than the church is omitted. A simple form of entrance is provided which contains only an antiphon. The sacramentary suggests in this case that a separate Bible service on the theme of the Lord's entry be held on the preceding Saturday evening or at another time on Sunday.

The Mass. From the opening prayer on it is clear that the focus of the liturgy is the cross and passion of Christ. The third Servant Song of Isaiah (50:4-7) is the first reading; it is followed by Psalm 22. The second reading is the well-known christological hymn in Paul's Letter to the Philippians (2:6-11). The verse before the gospel (Phil 2:8-9), employed during the whole of this week, is taken from the christological hymn. The proclamation of the passion of our Lord Jesus Christ follows. The version read depends on the year in the liturgical cycle (A—Matthew, B—Mark, C—Luke) and may be done in either a longer or shorter form. The Lectionary of the Roman Missal makes no provision for a choral reading of the passion. The earlier Roman tradition

had been to read Matthew's passion narrative on Palm Sunday, relegating Mark to Tuesday and Luke to Wednesday of Holy Week. A brief homily is recommended on this day.

No mention of the candidates for sacramental initiation at the upcoming Paschal vigil is made in the rites for Passion Sunday, but one might assume that the candidates might be dismissed before the prayer of the faithful in a particularly poignant way on this day, since it is the last time they will be dismissed prior to their baptism. In medieval Spain and Gaul, Palm Sunday marked the handing over of the creed to the candidates for initiation.

In the sacramentary of 1969 a new Preface has been provided for this Sunday. As with all the new Prefaces it contains in a nutshell the theology of the particular feast: "Though he was sinless, he suffered willingly for sinners. Though innocent, he accepted to save the guilty. By his dying he has destroyed our sins. By his rising he has raised us up to holiness of life..." Thus the eucharistic prayer for Passion (Palm) Sunday sets the passion of the Lord within the context of the entire mystery of his death and resurrection.

Monday, Tuesday, Wednesday

The liturgies for the first three weekdays of Holy Week do not have a special character nor do they contain special ceremonies. They do, however, represent a significant change from the traditional Roman rite. The passion narratives of Mark and Luke had been read on Tuesday and Wednesday respectively. They have been replaced by gospel readings that portray the betrayal of Jesus.

The readings for Monday in the missal of Paul VI are the first Servant Song of Isaiah (Isa 42:1-7) and Jn 12:1-12. In the Tridentine Missal they had been Isa 50:5-10 and Jn 12:1-9. On Tuesday the missal of Paul VI replaces the Markan passion narrative with Jn 13:21-33, 36-38, and Jer 11:18-20 with Isa 49:1-6 (the second Servant Song). The 4th/5th century liturgy of Jerusalem had observed a long vigil on Tuesday evening at the Basilica of the Eleona atop the Mount of Olives at which Jesus' eschatological discourse (Mt 24:1-26:2) was read.

Wednesday continues the reading of the Isaian Servant Songs, this time the third: Isa 50:4-9. The gospel reading is taken from Matthew's account of the betrayal of Jesus (Mt 26:14-25). The medieval Roman liturgy for Wednesday of Holy Week reveals a somewhat different pattern. In the morning a service of prayer was held at the Lateran. This service, consisting of the Solemn Prayers of the Roman rite, repeated at the Good Friday liturgy, was probably linked to the community's desire to pray for the candidates for initiation. The afternoon liturgy (Lenten eucharistic liturgies were celebrated in the afternoon because of the observance of the fast) contained two readings before the gospel (Isa 62:11;63:1-7 and Isa 53:1-12). The retention of the solemn prayers as well as two readings before the gospel is an example of Anton Baumstark's "law" that the most solemn days of the liturgical year retain the oldest ceremonies. This law of retention is exhibited several times throughout the liturgies of the triduum.

Holy Thursday

Holy Thursday, sometimes called "Maundy Thursday" (after the Latin "mandatum" or command of Jn 13:34), has a rich and complex liturgical history. It has been associated with three liturgical rites: the consecration of the chrism, the Mass of the Lord's Supper, and the solemn reconciliation of public penitents.

The Consecration of the Chrism. Around the 4th century when presbyters began to be deputed to preside at solemn initiation during the paschal vigil it be-

came necessary to consecrate the chrism apart from the vigil service itself. This was (and is) the case because the bishop alone traditionally had the right to bless this particular holy oil used both at baptism and confirmation. The consecration of the chrism was moved to the last eucharist before the vigil, i.e., the Mass of the Lord's Supper, so that the oil might be distributed to presbyters for use in their own churches. In the Roman rite this blessing was performed after communion at the Mass of the Lord's Supper (up to the reforms of 1955). The oil of catechumens and the oil of the sick had separate blessing formulas in the early Roman sacramentary. When the Roman rite was brought to northern European churches in the 7th and 8th centuries, the blessing of chrism was added to the other two blessings of oil and performed at a distinct Mass on Holy Thursday.

In the Missal of Paul VI the Chrism Mass takes place on the morning of Holy Thursday or some weekday preceding if this is more convenient. The clear aim of this liturgy is the manifestation of the unity of the presbyterate around the diocesan bishop. Two aspects of this liturgy manifest this unity: first, it must be a concelebrated Mass with priests attending from at least all of the significant areas of the diocese; and second, an innovation under Paul VI, priests are invited to renew their priestly commitment at this celebration. In this sense Paul VI clearly viewed Holy Thursday as the "Feast of Priests."

The renewal of priestly commitment takes place after the homily. The blessing of the oil of the sick takes place before the doxology of the eucharistic prayer. The blessing of the oil of catechumens and the consecration of the chrism take place immediately after the post-communion prayer. The missal provides the option of the blessing of all three oils after the liturgy of the word. Two different forms are provided for the consecration of the chrism; both follow the pattern of Roman consecratory prayers and are similar to the consecration of the font at the paschal vigil, the nuptial blessing and the consecratory prayers for ordinations.

Although the focus of the celebration is on the unity of the presbyterate, in many American dioceses this focus has been somewhat mitigated by the expectation that lay representatives of the parishes be expected to participate in the liturgy, especially by presenting the oils at the preparation of the gifts and by being given the blessed oils to take back to their parishes. The readings for the liturgy are as follows: Isa 61:1-3, 6, 8-9 (anointing); Rev 1:5-8 (priesthood—of all Christians); and Lk 4:16-21 (Christ as the Anointed One). This liturgy also has its own proper preface (P20—Priesthood—Chrism Mass) which sets the priesthood of the ordained within the context of the priesthood of Christ and the royal priesthood of his people.

The Mass of the Lord's Supper. The major liturgy of Holy Thursday and the solemn opening of the paschal triduum is the Mass of the Lord's Supper. It is to be celebrated in the evening with the participation of as many of the faithful as possible. In fact, Masses without a congregation are prohibited on this day and the local parish church is urged to have only one celebration of the eucharist.

This celebration has a somewhat mixed character. Understanding its nature correctly is crucial to the understanding and celebration of the triduum as a whole. On the one hand the Mass of the Lord's Supper is the festal opening of the triduum, signalled by the use of white vestments and the singing of the Gloria. On the other hand it maintains a somewhat lower key than the paschal vigil itself. Theologians and liturgical scholars have made a good deal of the unity of the triduum, i.e., the three days all celebrate the passion, death and resurrection of the Lord. The various celebrations are not discrete imitations of the historical events that occurred two thousand years ago. Therefore, it would be incorrect to focus on the institution of the eucharist or the ordination of priests at this celebration. Rather, as the second reading, the institution narrative contained in Paul's First Letter to the Corinthians (1 Cor 11:23-26), and the gospel, the washing of the feet (Jn 13:1-15), make clear, the Mass of the Lord's Supper centers on two acted parables which express the meaning of the death and resurrection of Jesus. Both acts, the eucharist and the foot-washing, ritually and symbolically express the fact that true life is to be found in the sacrifice of service. In this vein one might have wished that the framers of the lectionary had put Paul's version of the institution narrative within the context of the unjust meal practice of the Corinthians. Thus, the direction in the sacramentary that the homily should explain the institution of the eucharist, the institution of the priesthood and Christ's commandment of love needs to be understood within the framework of the triduum as a whole. The selection of music for the triduum should be governed by the unitive nature of the three major celebrations and not by an attempt to recreate historical circumstances.

The first reading (the narrative of the passover meal—Exod 12:1-8, 11-14) places the celebration of the triduum within the context of the Jewish feast of liberation from slavery.

A ritual washing of the feet takes place after the homily "depending on pastoral circumstances." In this act the president of the assembly imitates the action of the Servant Christ. The sacramentary does not indicate the number of people to be chosen for this ritual. Although the sacramentary does use the Latin term "vir" = "male" of those whose feet are to be washed, it is an overly literal understanding of the action of the historical Jesus to exclude women from this ritual.

There are several positive reasons for including women at this point. First, an overly literal desire to imitate the actions of Jesus robs the ritual of its evocative and symbolic power. Second, and more important, the exclusion of women might give the erroneous impression that the identity of the baptized in representing Christ is limited to males alone. The sacramentary provides several recommended antiphons (all taken from John 13) as song to accompany the ritual action.

It should be noted that this is the only occasion in the course of the liturgical year that the sacramentary states that gifts for the poor be presented along with the gifts of bread and wine. Although bringing up monetary gifts with the gifts for the celebration itself is praiseworthy in any eucharistic celebration (see *General Instruction on the Roman Missal*, 49), it is especially appropriate that the connection between the paschal triduum and the self-sacrifice of the church be stressed at this celebration. Once again the sacramentary provides a recommended antiphon ("Where charity and love are found, there is God") to accompany the procession, but another appropriate song might be used.

The Preface to be used at this liturgy is "Holy Eucharist I." In light of what has been said above about the unitive nature of the triduum, one might have hoped for a formula that stressed the nature of the Mass of the Lord's Supper as an introduction to the celebration of the whole paschal mystery rather than focusing exclusively on the eucharist. When the first eucharistic prayer of the Roman missal is used, there are several embolisms added to it.

It should go without saying that Holy Thursday is a most appropriate occasion for the distribution of communion under both the bread and the wine, even if this unfortunately might not be the usual custom of the local church.

The Mass of the Lord's Supper concludes with a procession of the eucharistic bread to be reserved for communion on Good Friday. This reservation is to take place in "a chapel suitably decorated for the occasion," i.e., not in the main section of the church building. Care should be taken to involve the people themselves in the procession and not to forget that they themselves have just participated in the body and blood of Christ. A procession that involved the ministers alone might give the impression that immediately after communion one needed to look exclusively to the eucharistic species to find the presence of Christ. St. Thomas Aquinas' hymn "Pange lingua" is employed during the procession. The last two verses ("Tantum ergo . . . ") are sung after the procession has reached the chapel of reservation. People are invited to pray before the reserved sacrament until midnight.

After the celebration has concluded the altar is stripped and crosses are removed from the church or covered, but no ritual has been provided as had been the case with the reformed Order for Holy Week of 1955.

Reconciliation of Penitents. A third factor in the traditional celebration of Holy Thursday which has no parallel in the liturgical rites today is the formal reconciliation of penitents. A service of reconciliation took place in the medieval Roman church on the morning of Holy Thursday. It enabled those who had undergone formal or canonical penance during Lent to participate fully in the eucharist during the triduum.

A formal reconciliation of those who, for one reason or another, have been alienated from the Roman Catholic church is currently being ritualized in some dioceses on Holy Thursday, often in connection with the Mass of the Lord's Supper. It remains to be seen whether this will become a regular feature of the Roman rite, but it certainly parallels the church's concern with initiation at the paschal vigil.

Good Friday

The solemn celebration of the Lord's passion takes place on the afternoon of Good Friday around three o'clock or at some other time during the day which is convenient for the people. Although the focus of this day's liturgy is clearly on the passion and death of Christ, the tone of the celebration is set by the proclamation of the passion narrative from the gospel of John, which combines the suffering of the Lord with his exaltation. Thus, Good Friday is not a day for "pretending" that the Lord is dead but rather for the joyful (if low-key) remembrance of this death which is life-giving.

The liturgy of Good Friday falls into three parts: Liturgy of the Word, Veneration of the Cross, and Holy Communion. The eucharist is not celebrated on this day. In fact, with the exception of penance and the anointing of the sick, nor are the other sacraments celebrated on Good Friday or Holy Saturday. Good arguments can be made for not scheduling the celebration of penance during the triduum in order to distinguish this solemn period from Lent, which ends with the beginning of the Mass of the Lord's Supper. The more appropriate season for the expression of penance is Lent.

Liturgy of the Word. One of the keys to the liturgy of the word is the silent entrance of the ministers and their prostration before the altar. Contrary to a recent Roman document ("Circular Letter Concerning the Preparation and Celebration of the Easter Feasts," Congregation for Divine Worship, January 1988, no. 65) the reason for this somber entrance is not the grief and sorrow of the church so much as the retention of the earliest form of the Roman eucharistic entrance rite. Hence it is another example, along with not using musical instruments, of retaining the most ancient practices on the most solemn days. The liturgy then begins not with a greeting or invitation but simply with the opening prayer.

The first reading is the fourth Servant Song of the prophet Isaiah (Isa 52:13-53:12). It is the most beautiful and powerful of these poems and culminates the reading of the previous songs during the earlier weekday liturgies. The second reading is taken from the Letter to the Hebrews (Heb 4:14-16; 5:7-9); it deals with Christ the High Priest, who because of his sacrifice has gained us salvation. As we have already mentioned, St. John's triumphant passion narrative follows. A brief homily is recommended.

The liturgy of the word culminates with the common prayers of the church. On this day the text of the ancient solemn prayers of the Roman rite, parts of which go back to the 4th century, is provided in the sacramentary. The prayer takes the form: invitation by the priest, silence, and concluding oration. The diaconal invitations to kneel and rise may be employed. The sacramentary, however, allows considerable latitude both in the form that the prayers take (e.g., adding a sung response by the people) and the posture to be adopted during the prayer. The content of these prayers serves as a model for the comprehensiveness of the general intercessions of the Roman rite: the church, the pope, the clergy and laity, candidates for initiation, unity of Christians, the Jewish people, non-Christians, unbelievers, civil authorities, and all those in need.

Veneration of the Cross. The veneration of the cross follows the solemn prayers. It may be performed in one of two ways: either by gradually uncovering it in the course of a procession from the church door or by carrying the uncovered cross in procession. The chant, "This is the wood of the cross . . . ," with its response, is sung three times as the procession stops. Then all venerate the cross either in common or individually.

Several comments are in order. First,

the sacramentary is quite explicit that only one cross ought to be used. Second, it consistently uses the term "cross" and not "crucifix." Third, if because the crowds are so huge that individual veneration cannot take place in the course of the service itself, then individual veneration ought to be postponed for all, including the ministers, until after the liturgy is concluded. A number of chants, including the traditional *Reproaches* and ("Popule meus") and Venantius Fortunatus' 6th-century hymn "Pange lingua, gloriosi," are provided in the sacramentary. In a number of places the *Reproaches* are no longer used since they run the risk of being misunderstood as anti-semitic. The *Trisagion* ("Holy is God, Holy and Strong ... "), has however been adapted in many places for the procession at the veneration. It is a venerable antiphon from the Eastern Christian tradition, probably inserted into the Roman rite in the 6th century when Byzantine influence was strong at Rome. Moreover, in this solemn liturgy it serves as a good sign of the breadth of the Catholic tradition.

Holy Communion. A very simple service of holy communion concludes the solemn liturgy of Good Friday. The reserved sacrament is brought to the altar at the end of the veneration of the cross, the Lord's Prayer with its embolism is said, and the people are invited to communion with the usual invitation. The Roman missal makes no provision for communion under both kinds on this day; this is reasonable since communion under both kinds might give the erroneous impression that the service is a eucharist rather than a kind of "Liturgy of the Presanctified." In fact, participation in communion on Good Friday seems almost an afterthought. Traditionally most Eastern Christians, and for a long time the pope as well, do not receive holy communion on this day. The concluding prayer, and prayer over the people are

done with great simplicity. There is no blessing, nor is there a dismissal—perhaps an indication that the liturgies of the triduum form a whole. Begun on Holy Thursday evening they are not concluded until the joyful dismissal of the paschal vigil.

The Paschal Vigil

The great vigil of Easter is by far the most complex and significant liturgy of the liturgical year. One of the oldest of Christian celebrations (from at least the mid-2nd century if not earlier) this vigil is both a solemn celebration of the Lord's resurrection and an expression of the joyful expectation of the final coming of Christ. It is also the most solemn moment for Christian initiation in the liturgical cycle. Although we do not know of any connection between the vigil and initiation in the 1st and 2nd centuries, it is clear that in many Christian churches the paschal vigil was *the* occasion for initiation in the 3rd century and especially in the 4th from which we possess the great mystagogical sermons of Cyril of Jerusalem, Ambrose of Milan, John Chrysostom and Theodore of Mopsuestia. At the paschal vigil the newly baptized became as it were walking, breathing icons of the risen Christ, a means for the assembly to focus on the contemporaneity of the Lord's resurrection. Needless to say, churches which do not celebrate solemn initiation at the vigil lose much of the impact of the celebration.

A vigil is by definition a nocturnal celebration. The directions of the Roman missal are quite clear that it should begin after nightfall and end before dawn. Everything possible should be done to emphasize its uniqueness; i.e., not to make it seem like another Saturday evening Mass. Only one vigil is to be celebrated in each liturgical community. In some communities which employ multiple languages the people separate for the liturgy of the word in their own language and then join together for initiation and the eucharist.

The Easter vigil is divided into four parts: the service of light, the service of readings, solemn baptism and confirmation, and the eucharist. We shall consider these aspects of the vigil in order.

Service of Light. The service of light begins in complete darkness preferably at a designated place outside of the church building. In imitation of the ancient frequent practice of the *Lucernarium* (lamp-lighting) at nightfall, the paschal candle is lit from a new fire. The missal of Paul VI allows considerable latitude with regard to this ritual and explicitly encourages adaptation to the culture of the people and local circumstances.

In any case, the deacon (or in his absence, a priest) leads a procession of the people into the church with the lit paschal candle, stopping three times to intone the formula "Light of Christ," to which is responded "Thanks be to God." The candle is then placed on a stand in the midst of the sanctuary or near the ambo and is honored with incense. The deacon or priest (or, in the absence of either who can sing, a cantor) then, with the people holding their lit candles, intones the Easter Proclamation, a venerable text which has come down from the 7th century at the latest. Now known from its opening as the "Exsultet," it is only one of the beautiful sung Easter proclamations that we possess from the Western liturgical tradition. The current missal offers both long and short forms of this richly symbolic hymn in honor of Christ, the Light of the World. This proclamation in itself contains an elaborate and powerful theology of our redemption in Christ and is worthy of study and meditation.

Liturgy of the Word. A rich feast of seven readings from the Hebrew Scriptures constitutes the second part of the paschal vigil. Each reading is followed by a (sung) responsorial psalm and a prayer. The missal of Paul VI directs that the number of readings may be reduced for pastoral reasons, but at least two readings (one of which must be Exodus 14) are to be read. The paschal vigil, however, is no time for minimalism in the liturgy. True, when poorly done, the readings can be tedious, but the proclamation of God's word to the people of Israel and to the church, its spiritual heir, can be done with reverence and power. The long vigil of readings underlines our expectation of the coming of the Lord and the immediate and reverential preparation of the candidates for their sacramental initiation. It takes place, both literally and metaphorically in the light of Christ.

The readings are as follows: 1. Genesis 1-2 (Creation); 2. Genesis 22 (The sacrifice of Abraham); 3. Exodus 14 (The passage through the Red Sea); 4. Isaiah 54 (A vision of the New Jerusalem); 5. Isaiah 55 (The free offer of salvation); 6. Baruch 3 (Wisdom and the commandments of life); 7. Ezekiel 36 (New heart and new spirit).

The choice and number of readings from the Hebrew Scriptures have varied throughout the centuries. The earliest list we possess, from Jerusalem in the 5th century, contains twelve readings always ending with the Canticle of the Three Children. There, as Talley has shown (*Origins of the Liturgical Year*, 47-54), the selection of readings may well have been structured on the pattern of the Jewish "Poem of the Four Nights": the night of Creation, the night of Abraham's sacrifice (the *Akedah*), the night of liberation from bondage, and the night of final redemption. In some churches, for example, Constantinople which had a series of fifteen readings, the readings coincided with the baptisms which were taking place privately (of necessity because of the nudity of the candidates) in the baptistery nearby.

The joyful singing of the Gloria follows

the last of the readings from Hebrew Scripture and the liturgy of the word proceeds, as at a normal eucharist, with the proclamation of Paul's baptismal theology in Romans 6 and one of the synoptic resurrection narratives, according to the liturgical cycle. The traditional solemn three-fold Alleluia sung by the presider serves as the gospel acclamation. A homily concludes the liturgy of the word.

The missal of Paul VI has transformed the structure of the paschal vigil as it was revived under Pius XII in 1952. In the earlier revision, the vigil service as a whole, including baptism, preceded the liturgy of the eucharist. The former structure had the advantage of emphasizing the vigil aspect of the first part of this liturgy. The current rite has been somewhat smoothed-out or "rationalized" such that it is possible to get the impression of a eucharist with a somewhat longer liturgy of the word. All the more reason, then, for the readings from the Hebrew scripture to be done in full and with great care.

Liturgy of Baptism. At the paschal vigil the liturgy of baptism consists of an invitation, litany of the saints, blessing of the baptismal water (which now may be performed even when there are no candidates for baptism as long as the church is one in which baptisms normally occur), renunciation and profession of faith, baptism proper, clothing with a white garment, giving of the light of Christ, and confirmation. Then all of the people are invited to renew their baptismal promises in solidarity with the newly baptized.

In some churches the peace is exchanged both with the newly baptized and throughout the assembly at the end of the sprinkling rite which follows the renewal of baptismal promises. This seems a fitting time for the congregation to greet its new members as well as serving as a kind of breather in the long liturgy of this night. Many churches also make provisions for baptism by immersion at the vigil, even when they do not have permanent fonts for baptism by immersion. As we have noted above, the paschal vigil is no time for sacramental minimalism.

Liturgy of the Eucharist. The liturgy of the eucharist proceeds as usual with the following notes: it is appropriate for the newly baptized to bring the gifts forward at the preparation rite; two formulas specifically referring to the newly baptized are added to Eucharistic Prayer I; and the liturgy is concluded with a special dismissal. In addition, it is appropriate to highlight the first communion of the newly baptized since, after all, participation in communion is the high point and culmination of their sacramental initiation.

Conclusion

The most notable feature of the liturgies of Holy Week is its processional character. At no other time in the liturgical year do we note so much movement within the liturgical rites. In part this is due to the retention of so many traditional features in these solemn liturgies, features which hearken back to a time when the Roman liturgy with its stational character contained so much movement from place to place and within the church building itself. Understanding the various processional movements at each of the four major Holy Week celebrations is the key to choreographing an experience of worship that corresponds to the most genuine liturgical piety and serves as a reminder of the dynamic character of Christian faith.

See **Calendar, liturgical; Lent; Easter season**

A.G. Martimort, ed., *The Church at Prayer: Vol. 4—The Liturgy and Time,* 2nd ed. (Collegeville: Liturgical Press, 1986). United States Catholic Conference, *Study Text 9: The Liturgical Year: Celebrating the Mystery of Christ and His Saints,* (Washington, DC, 1985). Thomas J. Talley, *The Origins of the Liturgical Year* (New York: Pueblo, 1986). Kenneth Stevenson, *Jerusalem Revisited:*

The Liturgy of Holy Week (Washington, DC: Pastoral Press, 1988). Gabe Huck, *The Three Days* (Chicago: Liturgy Training Publications, 1981). Gabe Huck and Mary Ann Simcoe, eds., *A Triduum Sourcebook* (Chicago: Liturgy Training Publications, 1983). Adrian Nocent, *The Liturgical Year: Vol. 2—Lent and Holy Week* (Collegeville: Liturgical Press, 1977). Ildephonse Schuster, *The Sacramentary: Historical and Liturgical Notes on the Roman Missal*, Vol. 2 (London: Burns, Oates and Washbourne, 1925).

JOHN F. BALDOVIN, S.J.

HOMILETICS

See **Preaching** ...

HOMILY

Popular dictionaries give a wide range of definitions for the word "homily." For some it is a biblical sermon; for others, a doctrinal talk. Some say its aim is to edify a congregation; others give as its purpose moral instruction. Even among the Christian churches there is diversity of use. Many Protestant homileticians still prefer the word "sermon," even when they refer to preaching that occurs within the liturgy. When they do use the word "homily," they describe it as a "walking through the text, step by step." Roman Catholics, on the other hand, now widely use "homily" for the renewed form of preaching ushered in by the liturgical reforms of Vatican II; it is that form of preaching which flows from and immediately follows the scriptural readings of the liturgy and which leads to the celebration of the sacraments. In current Roman Catholic parlance, "homily" is distinguished from "sermon" where the latter names a form of preaching that is not necessarily connected to the biblical readings and is heard outside the context of the liturgy.

The *Constitution on the Sacred Liturgy* restored the biblical form of preaching which had been an integral part of the liturgy of the primitive church (see Justin's *Apology*, 67). While conciliar documents acknowledged the importance of other forms of preaching, e.g., pastoral preaching, catechetics and other forms of Christian instruction, the council gave the liturgical homily "pride of place" (D.V., 24). The homily was defined by distinction, i.e., by distinguishing it from other forms of preaching.

It was Origen (185-253) who first distinguished between *logos* or *sermo* and *homilia* or *tractatus*. *Logos* followed the shape of classical rhetoric, while the form of *homilia* was direct and free. *Homilia* was a popular exposition and application of scripture.

Just as Origen made a distinction between *logos* and *homilia*, the reformers of Vatican II wanted to distinguish the homily from the popular form of preaching of the day, the sermon. While the sermon often relied on biblical texts, especially to prove a doctrinal point, it was not rooted in the scriptural readings of the day. Before the council, church documents and liturgical authors sometimes described the sermon as an "enhancement" or a "secondary interruption" of the liturgy. This is in marked contrast with the post-conciliar church where the homily is seen to flow from "the sacred text" and is "highly esteemed as part of the liturgy itself" (S.C., 52).

While the homily was given "pride of place," no single definition located in conciliar and post-conciliar documents adequately describes the emerging meaning of this form of preaching for our times. Just as there is a wide range of meaning of "homily" in the popular dictionaries, so there is a wide range of meaning in church documents and liturgical literature. Since no definition of a word is final, we must look at the way in which words are used in spite of their limitations. What follows is an exploration of the rich landscape of the use of the word "homily" and the contemporary developments of that exploration.

The Distinctive Characteristics

Four characteristics of preaching were restored from the ancient tradition by Vatican II in order to distinguish this renewed form of preaching, the homily, from other forms. Homiletic preaching is (a) biblical, (b) liturgical, (c) kerygmatic, and (d) familiar.

A. Biblical

The tradition of an exposition of biblical readings is found in the synagogue practice (Lk 4:16 ff; Acts 13:14 ff). It was a tradition of interpreting and applying the scriptural message to the contemporary situation. This hermeneutical practice included *midrash halakah* which interpreted the fundamental principles of the *Torah*, and *midrash haggadah* which commented on the rest of scripture through imaginative instruction and exhortation. Jesus' homily on the book of Isaiah in the synagogue of Nazareth signals the prophetic nature of the scriptural exposition: "Today this Scripture passage is fulfilled in your hearing" (Lk 4:21).

This prophetic exposition of scripture was continued in the liturgical preaching of the early Christian churches. Justin's description of a 2nd-century liturgy includes preaching that is more than an exegesis of the sacred texts: "... and the memoirs of the apostles or the writings of the prophets are read, as long as there is time. Then, when the reader has finished, the president of the assembly verbally admonishes and invites all to imitate such examples of virtue" (*I Apology*, 67). The first and foremost of all Christian homilists was Origen who strove through allegorical exegesis to adapt the scripture to all levels of his congregation through "spiritual understandings" (*Hom. Lev.*, 1.4).

The Peace of Constantine (313) brought a new set of circumstances to the church which affected the character of preaching: the increased number of catechumens; the theological debates of the day; the birth of new liturgical seasons and feast days of saints and martyrs; the appointment of bishops like Augustine who were schooled in the art of rhetoric. These circumstances gave rise to catechetical, mystagogical, thematic, and rhetorical features which affected the popular exposition of biblical texts. For example, scripture readings were chosen to fit the feast and, therefore, the preacher had the new task of opening up the readings in light of the feast. Nevertheless, from Origen to St. Bernard (12th century), the homily remained a popular exposition of scripture read or sung in the liturgical assembly.

In medieval times, the homily became a speech independent of the liturgy and thus of the sacred text read or sung in the liturgy. The pulpit became a platform for theological debate, denunciations of heresies, and devotional, moralistic tales from the lives of the saints. Medieval preachers often employed biblical citations but, for the most part, the tradition of applying the biblical readings to the liturgical assembly was lost.

The ancient tradition of preaching from scripture was not revived by the Council of Trent. *The Catechism of the Council of Trent* provided preachers with a guide for doctrinal instruction. The preaching that prevailed during the time immediately before Vatican II was often based on outlines of doctrinal topics with little or no reference to the biblical texts of the liturgy.

The influence of "the biblical movement," however, is clearly found throughout the documents of Vatican II. The council insisted that "all the preaching of the Church must be nourished and ruled by Sacred Scripture" (D.V., 21). Preaching was to "draw its content mainly from scriptural and liturgical sources" (S.C., 35) and the homily was described as flowing "from the sacred text" (S.C., 52). In an instruction which implemented the council's liturgical reforms, a definition of the "sacred text" was given: "an explanation either of certain aspects of the readings from the Sacred Scriptures or of some other text from the ordinary or proper of the day taking into account, however, peculiar needs of the congregation" (I.O., 54). Thus, the reformers of Vatican II returned to the ancient tradition of preaching which flowed directly from the biblical readings proclaimed in the liturgy and led to the celebration of the sacraments.

B. Liturgical

Justin's description of a mid-2nd-century liturgy reveals how the homily acted as a unifying force. It expounded the scriptures and led to an active participation in the eucharist. Ancient Christian homilies contained what some authors name the mystagogical feature of preaching. The homily invited the congregation to the mysteries of Christ celebrated at the eucharist. For Origen, preaching made the Word flesh again in the liturgical assembly.

The homily eventually became cut off from the liturgical action which it once developed and explained. Preaching became an independent and autonomous event which had no relation to worship. The celebration of Masses without a congregation encouraged the elimination of the homily from the rite. The medieval revivals of preaching, such as the ones brought about by the friars, were concerned with sermons delivered outside of the liturgy. The independence of preaching from the celebration of the eucharist is reflected in church architecture where the pulpit came into prominence outside the sanctuary.

In the early 1960s, some liturgists were still referring to preaching as a "secondary interruption" of the Mass. Ordination of bishops, religious professions, the blessing of spouses at marriage that took place within the Mass, were called "primary interruptions." Some authors declared that the sermon was accidental to the Mass. Moralists stressed that one's obligation to "attend Mass" began after the liturgy of the word. Such terminology revealed a loss of appreciation of the liturgical dimensions of preaching.

The sacramental theology of revelation proposed by K. Rahner, O. Semmelroth, Y. Congar, E. Schillebeeckx, et al., provided Vatican II with a renewed understanding of the relation between the liturgy of the word and the eucharist. For these theologians, the sacraments were inconceivable without preaching. They stressed preaching as a proclamation of the saving events celebrated at the table of the Lord. The council, therefore, sought to restore "the intimate connection between rites and words" in the liturgy and declared that the homily was "to be highly esteemed as part of the liturgy itself" (S.C., 35, 52).

C. Kerygmatic

The word most frequently used for preaching in the NT is keryssein, "to proclaim." The preacher is like the herald (keryx) who returns from the battle to proclaim a glorious message (kerygma) to a people waiting in anticipation. The herald proclaims, in the name of the king, the good news that, "We have won! The victory is ours!" The herald metaphor connotes preaching that is beyond the words of a mere human messenger. These are the saving words of God spoken through the herald. It is not the preacher but Christ the Lord who is preached (2 Cor 4:5). Proclamation is not about a teaching but an event. Proclamation is not about doctrines defended but saving acts boldly announced. The primary focus of proclamation is not the future but the present reality. This kind of preaching does not depend upon the persuasive words of rhetoric but upon the demonstration of spirit and power (1 Cor 2:4). Kerygmatic preaching compels those who hear it with the necessity of a response. Such preaching is found in the apostolic preaching of Acts (e.g., 2:14-40; 3:12-26; 10:28-43).

Vatican II insisted that a kergymatic character permeate the homily. It emphasized "the proclamation of God's wonderful works in the history of salvation, which is the mystery of Christ ever made present and active in us, especially in the celebration of the liturgy" (S.C., 35). Kergymatic preaching received its original impetus from liturgical scholars such as Joseph A. Jungmann in the late 1930s. Kergymatic preaching captured the spirit of the preaching of the apostles who proclaimed the good new of Jesus, through whom God has acted and continues to act in our lives. Once again, the council distinguished this form of preaching, which proclaims the wonderful things God has done and is doing for people, from preaching that is a list of do's and don'ts that we must follow in order to win God's favor.

D. Familiar Conversation

The word "homily" is derived from the Greek *homou* (together) and *homilos* (a crowd). The word connotes a familiar conversation with a group of people or a pastor conversing with a flock in words and images that they recognize. The crowd is not some haphazard mob of strangers but a gathering of friends, people familiar to the preacher. It is not a conversation of imposition nor of persuasion but, rather *cor ad cor loquitur* (Newman's motto adopted from Augustine for his coat of arms as Cardinal).

The word is used to describe the conversation that the two disciples engaged in as they were on their way to Emmaus "discussing (*homiloun*) as they went all that had happened" (Lk 24:14). In the present form, the story of Emmaus reflects the pattern of early Christian worship. Before the risen Lord proclaims the good news, he listens and enters into their story of distress and lost hope. His interpretation of the things that went on in Jerusalem "these past days" is different from their own. The preacher sheds light on their story and makes their hearts burn. The preacher does not force his preaching upon his listeners. He awaits their invitation to "stay with us." The story is literally framed by the theme of recognition which happens in the preaching and at the table. Here word and sacrament are recognized as integral parts of a single coming of Christ to people. The familiar conversation on the road to Emmaus reminds us that preaching is more than information, it is interpretation that leads to recognition of the good. news. The purpose of preaching is faith (1 Cor 2:4).

Origen used the word "homily" to describe the familiar style in which he preached. His style was direct and free, in sharp contrast to the Second Sophistic of his day. Origen's homilies manifest a structure of exordium, mystical exegesis of scripture, practical application, and final exhortation, but the tone set is one of familiar conversation rather than the rhetorical elaboration of his contemporaries.

The art of rhetoric came into the pulpit with Augustine who was a former *rhetor*. Augustine presented a new homiletic style by borrowing from the rhetorical canons of *to teach, to please*, and *to persuade*. He deplored poorly fashioned homilies and encouraged preachers to learn from the persuasive rhetoric of his day (*De Doctrina Christiana*, 4).

While there are traces of familiar conversation throughout the history of Christian preaching, there also exists a firm tradition of a preaching style that more closely resembles a lawyer's brief. It is a style that is deductive and sets out to prove or persuade by arguments and points. Scripture is not opened up for meaning but used as proofs for the preacher's teachings.

The documents of Vatican II offered no models for a new preaching style but hinted that the homily was to be preached as a familiar conversation. *The Decree On the Ministry And Life Of Priests* (4) states that if today's preaching is to be effective, it "must expound the Word of God not merely in a general and abstract way but by an application of the eternal truth of the Gospel to the concrete circumstances of life." The earliest instruction (1964) on the implementation of *S.C.* speaks of the homily as attending to "the peculiar needs of the congregation" (I.O., 54).

Developing Trends

The word "homily" continues to develop in meaning. The four characteristics given above: biblical, liturgical, kergymatic, and familiar, still help to define the word, but must be further nuanced in light of liturgical praxis and cultural shifts.

A. Biblical

Coinciding with the renewal of biblical preaching at the time of Vatican II, was the publication of new biblical commentaries that seemed a blessing to those preachers who were now supposed to base their homilies on the sacred texts. The dominant method of biblical interpretation in the new commentaries was the historical-critical. Indeed, the council officially blessed this method when it insisted that the interpreter of scripture "should carefully search out the meaning which the sacred writers really had in mind" (D.V., 12). A popular homiletic method that followed the council concentrated on applying the insights of a historical-criticial study of the sacred texts "to the concrete circumstances of life" (P.O., 4).

The historical-criticial method still provides necessary and helpful parameters in which the preacher can move and construct a convincing homiletic. However, preachers are discovering other biblical methods of interpretation, e.g., literary, feminist, sociological, canonical, and liberation criticism, which offer new possibilities for homiletic method.

Recent literature on the homily emphasizes not so much an interpretation of scripture, followed by an application to life, but an interpretation of life *in light of* the sacred texts. The N.C.C.B.'s 1982 document, *Fulfilled in Your Hearing: The Homily in the Sunday Assembly*, speaks of "a scriptural interpretation of human existence which enables a community to recognize God's active presence" (F.I.Y.H., 29). In the homily, "the preacher does not so much attempt to explain the scriptures as to interpret the human situation through the Scriptures" (F.I.Y.H., 20). This document advances the definitions of homily found in *S.C.* It incorporates the "reading of the signs of the times" motif from the *Pastoral Constitution on the Church in the Modern World*. This new shift, from an interpretation of scripture with an application to life, to an interpretation of the human situation through scripture, echoes contemporary Christology with the mystery of the word "from below" rather than "from above." The new shift also helps us to name grace not only in the liturgy, but in our world of limitations.

B. Liturgical

Vatican II insisted that since the homily was "highly esteemed as part of the liturgy itself ... at those Masses which are celebrated on Sundays and holidays of obligation, with the people assisting, it should not be omitted except for a serious reason" (S.C., 52). That rule now seems strange in light of current liturgical praxis where the homily has become an expected part of the liturgy, and not just for those specific times mentioned in the rule. The liturgical homily has achieved its esteemed place in all liturgies. "The homily has a place and must not be neglected in the celebration of all the sacraments, at paraliturgies, and in assemblies of the faithful. It will in every case be a privileged moment for preaching the word of the Lord" (E.N., 43).

Despite the return of the homily to its central place in the liturgy, however, there are still relics of pre-Vatican II liturgical practices. Making the sign of the cross before and after the homily is a remnant from times past when the sermon was an "interruption" in the liturgy and, therefore, needed pious parentheses. Lengthy "meditations" after the homily obscure the homily's function as preaching on the sacred texts which leads to the celebration of eucharist. In paying attention to the fact that the homily should lead to thanksgiving and praise, some preachers tack on a "let us, as we go to the eucharist" ending. Such conclusions are predictable at best. They do not substitute for a homily whose entire tone leads the assembly to celebrate the liturgy "more deeply and more fully—more faithfully— and thus be formed for Christian witness in the world" (F.I.Y.H., 18).

C. Kerygmatic

Although the term "kerygmatic" is not as fashionable as it was during the time of Vatican II, it nevertheless offers a significant bench mark for defining the character that should permeate a homily. The herald image reminds us that the preacher is a minister of the church who preaches from the Bible as the church's book. The herald image challenges the preacher who is narcissistic and ignorant of the church's tradition.

Besides the image of the herald, there exists the image of the witness in early Christian preaching (Acts 20:24). Homiletic literature since Vatican II speaks of the homilist as a witness whose own story of a "wounded healer" might appropriately serve to convey the good news. In a social analysis of contemporary communication style, Paul VI declared, "Modern man (sic) listens more willing to witnesses than to teachers, and if he does listen to preachers, it is because they are witnesses" (A.A.S., 66, 1974, 568).

In the NT, "proclamation" is sometimes joined with "teaching" (Mt 4:23; 9:35; 11:1; Acts 28:31). Teaching is the preaching that naturally follows the proclamation of the gospel. There was lively debate during the writing of *The Constitution on the Sacred Liturgy* concerning the kerygmatic and catechetical nature of the homily. Some were concerned that in emphasizing the kerygmatic nature of the homily, the teaching element of preaching would be sacrificed. Hence, there exists an ambivalence even within the document. In par. 35, the word "sermon" is used, but it is defined more like our contemporary use of the word "homily" since it names it as a "proclamation." In par. 52, the word "homily" is used, but it is defined more like our contemporary use of the word "sermon" since it is defined as the preaching where "the mysteries of faith and the guiding principles of Christian life are expounded from the sacred text during the course of the liturgical year." *The Code of Canon Law* (1983) locates homily in the "Book on the Teaching Office of the Church" and draws upon par. 52 to supply a definition.

In recent years, there has been a call, in some corners, to highlight the catechetical nature of the liturgical homily. Some have argued for a return to outlines, based on the lectionary readings, which would ensure a systematic presentation of the teachings of the church. But the homily does not "primarily concern itself with a systematic theological understanding of the faith. The liturgical gathering is not primarily an educational assembly (F.I.Y.H., 17-18). While the homily is not primarily a catechetical instruction, Paul VI declared that it can certainly be a means of catechesis for Christian communities, (E.N., 43, 44). There is need for educational opportunities in and through which people can reflect more deeply on the meaning of their faith and the teaching of the church. In the early church this systematic presentation of the mysteries of the faith was given to the newly baptized in the post-baptismal preaching know as mystagogy.

D. Familiar Conversation

The homilist today is defined as a "mediator of meaning" (F.I.Y.H., 7). This phrase is in concert with the familiar manner of preaching that marks the homily. "The preacher represents this community voicing its concerns, by naming its demons, and thus enabling it to gain some understanding and control of the evil which afflicts it. He represents the Lord by offering the community another word, a word of healing and pardon, of acceptance and love" (F.I.Y.H., 7). The primary task of the homilist, therefore, is not to explain but to interpret. As "mediator of meaning," the homilist seeks to attend to the present moment as revelatory of God. Past events and future possibilities are seen in light of present theophanies.

Although Vatican II hinted at the homily as familiar conversation, it offered no new models for the shape of the homily. Post-conciliar documents in generic ways stress that the homily should be preached "in a way that is suited to the community's capacity and way of life and that is relevant to the circumstances of the celebration" (E.P., April 27, 1973, 15); "it (the homily) should be neither too long nor too short" (C.T., October 16, 1979, 48).

Current homileticians stress the importance of creating homilies in word and images that the assembly will recognize. In the present homiletic literature, one traditional form, the deductive (introduction, three "points" and an exhortation) is challenged as not appropriate to a familiar mode of preaching and not effective in a media-bombarded society. Other forms, such as inductive and narrative, are suggested as effective alternatives to a didactic style. These forms, rather than other forms of rhetorical discourse, seem more appropriate to serving the function of the homily as enabling God's people to recognize a living word of meaning in the eucharist and in the "concrete circumstances of their lives."

See **Preaching . . . ; Mystagogy; Word, theology of the**

———

Bishops' Committee on Priestly Life and Ministry: N.C.C.B., *Fulfilled in Your Hearing: The Homily in the Sunday Assembly* (Washington, D.C.: United States Catholic Conference, 1982). Yngve Brilioth, *A Brief History of Preaching* (Philadelphia: Fortress, 1965). Gregory Dix, *The Shape of the Liturgy* (London: Dacre Press, 1945). Thomas K. Carroll, *Preaching the Word* (Wilmington, Glazier, 1984). Paulinus Milner, *The Ministry of the Word* (Collegeville: Liturgical Press, 1967). Karl Rahner, ed., *The Renewal of Preaching: Theory and Practice* (New York: Paulist, 1968). William Skudlarek, *The Word in Worship: Preaching in a Liturgical Context* (Nashville: Abingdon, 1981). Robert P. Waznak, *Sunday After Sunday: Preaching the Homily As Story* (New York: Paulist, 1983).

ROBERT P. WAZNAK, S.S.

HOSPITALITY

Hospitality is defined as "the art or practice of being hospitable; the reception and entertainment of guests, visitors or strangers with liberality and good will" (*Oxford English Dictionary*). It is related to hospital, host, hostel, hotel, and, finally, hot.

The term has gained liturgical currency in the reforms of Vatican II, particularly in the council's stress on "full and active participation of all the faithful" (S.C., 14). It is not, however, without biblical warrant. Paul writes to the Christians at Rome: "Contribute to the needs of the saints, practice hospitality. . . . Rejoice with those who rejoice, weep with those who weep. Live in harmony with one another. . . . 'If your enemy is hungry, feed him; if he is thirsty, give him drink; for by doing so you will heap burning coals upon his head'" (Rom 12:13-21).

Hospitality, which is a dominant element contributing to the climate of group experience, influences architectural and environmental form. An intangible ingredient affecting how people act in groups, hospitality calls from deep within an individual a sense of identity and a feeling of being "at home." Although hospitality may take many forms, that which Paul recommends to the Christians at Rome is one of gracious, almost embarrassing, generosity.

To convey the importance of hospitality, one might call upon Raymond Panikkar's definition of freedom: "not simply the power of option, but the power of creating possbilities" (*Myth, Faith and Hermeneutics*, p. 209). In worship, hospitality allows the participants to be at one in freedom with what is expected of them.

Although it originates in attitudes of people, hospitality is also projected by the design of a place. Church architecture might have developed simply in function of geographical climate. In fact, however, the "climate of life" shared by Christians at various times and places is far more determinative of church architectural style. The strongest architectural statements emerge when the communal climate is assumed or well understood. This communal climate, as it affects and influences liturgical worship, is largely a function of the sacramental theology that is in vogue. As culture, theology, scriptural focus and the interpretation of history change, the ritual form and its required environment likewise change.

We consider here four forms of hospitality: (a) domestic, (b) monarchical, (c) hierarchical, and (d) relational or circular. We conclude with some focus on hospitality in light of Vatican II.

Domestic Hospitality

The earliest known architectural environment designated for Christian communal ritual is the Roman house church found at Dura-Europos. This was used during the first half of the 3rd century.

The only fixed architectural space for sacrament in this environment was the area for the baptismal bath. Richly decorated, this was located deep within the interior rooms. The font is scaled for adult baptism, for the room is small and private. Its location within the floor plan indicates that the ritual it served was not conducted in the midst of the gathering. Its spatial proportions imply that only a few could have attended the actual baptism. The available evidence suggests a climate of privacy, secrecy and protectiveness, qualities for which a domestic hospitality associated with a house would have been appropriate.

Except for the baptistry, the rooms of the house church do not contain fixed furnishings such as altar, seats or stone benches. Therefore their use in regard to the word and the eucharist can only be speculated.

The family-oriented architectural form of this early Christian ritual site contrasts with that of temple buildings which offered a more public kind of hospitality. Public, however, does not mean simply "a public building." Andre Grabar (*Early Christian Art*) observes a similarity between the decoration in the house church and that in the synagogue in the same community and suggests from this that the Christians and Jews were in close communication with each other. The fact that the synagogue at Dura was a public building indicates that its ritual use was acceptable to civil authority. The users of the Christian space apparently felt that their worship would not be welcomed in a public structure. Environmentally, however, both were shaped by the domestic form.

Monarchical Hospitality

The climate and style of Christian ritual hospitality changed when Christian beliefs were adopted by Constantine and successive monarchs. Architecturally, this shift was reflected in the use of the basilica form. Apparently, the monarchs recognized that architecture would strengthen their endorsement of Christianity. According to Grabar, the specifications for the basilica form were neither derived from previous Christian experience nor prescribed by Constantine. Rather, the form was accepted by architects to serve the need for a structure whose importance was befitting monarchical patrons.

Although the basilica is a monumental structure, its emphasis on interior space distinguished it from classical temples with their stress on external form. The basilica's fixed presbytery seating in the apse presents a strong, authoritative statement that serves monarchical hospitality and clerical authority.

Constantine called the early church councils to define doctrinal orthodoxy. In this climate of monarchical control, the role of the ritual leader included assuring the faithful that they could depend on and trust authority.

Spiro Kostof (*A History of Architecture*) cites a description of an early ritual as it took place in a setting designed to serve a climate of monarchical hospitality. In such a building, the appropriate iconography for the major wall was the image of Christ enthroned in a seat of judgment. Great domed spaces, designed to inspire awe, are organic to this style of hospitality.

Hierarchical Hospitality

Prior to Vatican II, Roman Catholic ritual environments served a specific sacramental theology which was coded by rubrics and a climate of what might be called parochial or hierarchical hospitality. The interior spaces in churches, as well as the furniture and liturgical objects conformed to well-defined standards. For example, the communion rail separated the ordained from the non-ordained. The aula seating pattern, with parallel rows of pews screwed down to the floor, kept the laity lined up like a platoon. This is a pattern that discouraged communication among the laity themselves. In such spaces the meaning of the term *hierarchical* is clear. One is obliged to be in the presence of the ordained who prays for and on behalf of those who are present.

Hierarchical refers to a body of priests or ecclesiastical leaders. It can itself vary in specific tonality. It is clear that the post-Vatican II church continues a focus on the liturgical assembly as hierarchical: "The celebration of the Mass (is) an action of Christ and the people of God hierarchically ordered … " (*General Instruction of the Roman Missal*, chap. 1, 1). The role of the priest in the assembly is to represent this gathering Christ. The proper sense of the term *hierarchical*, however, as it is used in contemporary sacramental theology, needs to be clearly understood not only to ritualize it, but also to give it proper architectural form. It could revert to the monarchical (Christ the King). It could also, however, refer to quite different understandings of the gathering Christ, such as host (Christ of the eucharistic table) or servant (Christ washing feet). In the post-Vatican II church, even where the term *hierarchical* continues to be used, more welcoming images of the Christ who gathers begin to surface.

Relational or Circular Hospitality

Susanne Langer (*Feeling and Form*) proposed that the "magic circular dance," in which participants faced each other, was the beginning of defined architectural space. The circular pattern reflects a form of hospitality in which all present are of equal importance. The format is that of the dining room table, which supports family rituals. It is the format for entrepreneurial decision-making groups in which everyone's input is valued. The circular pattern matches the context of the invitation to sacrament in the documents of Vatican II, where the "full and active participation by all the people is the aim to be considered before all else" (S.C., 14). The ordained are to draw those present into the prayer of the church, and thus appear to be praying *with* the people, and not only *on their behalf.*

Interestingly enough, the council hall itself arranged the bishops in a relational, if not quite circular, form. Photographs of the Vatican II meetings showed two seas of white mitres facing each other in grandstands. This pattern of seating serves to support communal presence, in this case, of the hierarchy to each other.

This shift toward the relational and the inclusive does mark a definite shift from earlier architectural environments, whether Romanesque, Gothic or Renaissance, where the liturgical action of the ordained was clearly separated from that of the laity. In these earlier forms, ritual involvement occurred on two distinct levels, that of the enactor and that of the spectator. The latter was drawn into the former, though frequently only indirectly. In the Gothic form, for example, with its enclosed divided choir, the sound of chant, flowing in one-note-at-a-time mathematical rhythms, flowed beyond the screens to touch those outside with an awesome sense of the sacred. These outsiders, however, were not directly involved in the chanting. In the post-Vatican II liturgy there are no "outsiders," and all are invited to enter the liturgical action *on the same level.*

Hospitality in Light of Vatican II

In their document, *Environment and Art in Catholic Worship*, the American bishops gave strong notice to the importance of hospitality in worship. "As common prayer and ecclesial experience, liturgy flourishes in a climate of hospitality: a situation in which people are comfortable with one another, either knowing or being introduced to one another; a space in which people are seated together, with mobility, in view of one another as well as the focal points of the rite, involved as participants and *not* as spectators" (11). Later, in the same document, they speak of "the gathering of the faith community in a participatory and hospitable atmosphere for word and eucharist, for initiation and reconciliation, for prayer and praise and song" (40).

This open style of hospitality was emphasized by inclusion of the sense of touch in ritual, e.g., in approved practices of lay distribution of the eucharist, communion in the hand, receiving from a common cup and offering the sign of peace. It also shows itself in a much greater openness to such things as reception of the eucharist at ecumenical weddings, absolution in communal reconciliation, and the inclusion of both women and men in a variety of liturgical functions. In this regard, the note on hospitality offered by Levi-Strauss (*The Origin of Table Manners*) is most descriptive: hospitality determines how table manners will be acted out in ritual.

It must be said, however, that since the publication of *Environment and Art in Catholic Worship*, some of the openness and invitational generosity has been edited out, whether because of the comfort of old habit or reversal by authority.

What is clear is that in the contemporary church, those forms of hospitality which welcome all into the ritual space are those most appreciated and responded to. In a world where there is an abundance of loneliness, alienation and broken relationships, as well as a general distrust of authority, environments that are monarchical or separatist fail to touch the human spirit effectively. In a culture where people prefer having things done *with* them, rather than *for* them, there is need for ritual and ritual space that exudes this inclusive and welcoming hospitality. Such hospitality need not exclude a hierarchical perspective. People can be moved by generosity and inspired by dedicated spiritual leaders. It must, however, be an open hospitality where all, strangers included, are welcome.

To envision such a form of public hospitality in relation to present day needs is for ritual and ritual space to respond to Jungman's prophetic plea (*The Good News Yesterday and Today*, p. 178), for "not so much a better method as a better understanding and a more relevant presentation of the very core and substance of the Christian message."

See Art, liturgical; Architecture, liturgical

Ernest Kitzinger, *Byzantine Art in the Making: Main Lines of Stylic Development in Mediterranean Art, 3rd-7th Centuries* (Cambridge: Harvard University Press, 1977). Andre Grabar, *Early Christian Art, (Vol. 9), The Arts of Mankind*, eds. Andre Malraux and George Salles (New York: Odyssey Press, 1968). Raymond Panikkar, *Myth, Faith and Hermeneutics* (New York: Paulist, 1979). Claude Levi-Strauss, *The Origin of Table Manners* (New York: Harper Colophon Books, 1978). Joseph Jungmann, *The Good News Yesterday and Today* (New York: Sadlier, 1962). Spiro Kostof, *A History of Architecture, Settings and Rituals* (New York: Oxford University Press, 1985). Bishops' Committee on the Liturgy, *Environment and Art in Catholic Worship*, 1978.

WILLY MALARCHER

HOURS, LITURGY OF THE

History

Communal prayer was a chief activity of the church in its earliest days (Acts 1:14; 2:42; 4:24; 12:5, 12). This prayer developed structured forms for daily celebration throughout the universal church in both parochial and monastic settings by the 4th century, and gradually, especially in the West, became a monastic and clerical preserve for which laity largely substituted popular devotions. The liturgical reform following the Second Vatican Council included a reform in the Roman rite of the Divine Office (a term by which liturgy of the hours was more frequently designated before the

council). The intention of the reformers was to restore at least the chief hours, morning prayer and evening prayer, to popular participation. This restoration remains generally unrealized, but a thorough examination of salient aspects of the long and complex history of the hours would reveal not only the tenaciousness of prayer in common within the church (and thus the possibility for renewal of and popular participation in forms of liturgy of the hours) but also shifts in ecclesial consciousness, sacramental practice, and societal perspectives which today militate against ecclesial prayer (and thus the great difficulty of restoration and renewal of the liturgy of the hours on the popular level). No more than a cursory glance at that history is possible here.

Jewish Precedents. Claims have been made for direct continuity between primitive Christian communal prayer and Jewish synagogal and temple practice, but the evidence for such is not universally definitive. Several systems of daily prayer were prevalent in Palestinian and Egyptian Judaism at the time of the NT. Not only was the *Shema* (Deut 6:4-9; 11:13-21: Num 15:37-41) recited twice daily, morning and evening, with accompanying benedictions or prayers of thanksgiving, but *tefillah* or benedictions were prayed three times daily. The *tefillah* for the morning and for the evening were eventually combined with the recitations of the *Shema* both in private and in synagogue services. Perhaps the morning and evening *tefillah* were meant to correspond to the morning and evening sacrifices in the temple, but it can be said at least that the morning and evening hours both in and outside of Jerusalem became the principal times in a day for communal and for private prayer.

The Prayer of Jesus. Not only was Jesus given to praying privately (e.g., Mk 7:34; Lk 3:21-22; 6:12; 9:28-29), but, "as was his custom," he engaged regularly in the communal prayer of the synagogue (Lk 4:16). He prayed the customary blessings over food and drink (Mt 14:19; 15:36; 26:26; Lk 24:30) and publicly uttered praise, thanks, and petition to God, his *abba*, at significant moments in his life (e.g., Mt 19:13; 26:26; Mk 14:36; Lk 10:21-22; Jn 17:1-26). To his disciples he commanded prayer (e.g., Mt 5:44; Mk 13:33; Lk 6:28), but did not leave them without a model for fulfilling that command (Mt 6:9-13; Lk 11:2-4). The author of the Letter to the Hebrews understood prayer as a central component of the life of Jesus (Heb 5:7) and of the existence of the glorified Christ (Heb 7:25).

The Prayer of the Early Church. According to the NT constant and daily prayer was characteristic of the earliest Christians (Acts 2:46; 1 Thess 1:2) whether they were alone (Acts 20:36-38; 21:5) or gathered together at home (Acts 2:46), in the synagogue (Acts 13:14-15), or in the temple (Acts 3:1). Like the Jews, at least some Christians prayed at set times of the day (*Didache* 8:2-3; *1 Clem* 40:1-4) although the structure and form of their prayer differed more or less from that of their Jewish neighbors. Exhortations, however, to "pray without ceasing" (1 Thess 5:16-18; Eph 6:18; Lk 18:1) provided not only the basis for some caution regarding prayer at fixed times (Clement of Alexandria, *Stromata* VII, 7, 40:3) but also for the development of such prayer in what became the liturgy of the hours precisely in order to foster ceaseless prayer. Some sources of the 3rd century (Origen, *On Prayer* 12:2; 32 and Clement of Alexandria, *Stromata* VII, 7, 40:3; 49:3-4; *Pedagogue* 2:9-10) suggest that a pattern of prayer at morning, noon, evening, and night may have prevailed in Egypt. North African sources of the same century (Tertullian, *On Prayer* 25 and Cyprian, *On the Lord's Prayer* 34-36) as well as *The Apostolic Tradition*, presumably of Roman provenance (ca. 215), all witness to a pattern which will

become the standard cursus in the 4th century; prayer on rising; at the third, sixth, and ninth hours; at the time of retiring; during the night. Tertullian regarded prayer in the morning and in the evening as *orationes legitimae*, thus suggesting their major importance, and Cyprian indicated that morning prayer commemorated the Lord's resurrection while evening prayer looked to his eschatological coming. Scattered references to the content of the prayers of this period reveal that biblical psalms and canticles as well as some non-scriptural hymns were used. Both Tertullian (*Apology* 39:18) and the author of *The Apostolic Tradition* (41) knew a ritual surrounding the lighting of the evening lamps (precursor of the later *lucernarium*) symbolizing Christ, the Light of the World. The practice of orientation in prayer, to which Clement of Alexandria, Origen, and Tertullian witness, suggests that the rising sun, too, symbolized the risen Christ expected to come again. Both morning and evening prayer times for at least some Christian communities, then, evoked the mystery of Jesus' passover from death to life. To the other hours of prayer were given various significations. The third, sixth, and ninth hours recalled events of the passion according to Mark (*The Apostolic Tradition*) or events in the apostolic church recounted in Acts (Tertullian and Cyprian). Prayer at night fostered vigilance for the coming of Christ (Clement of Alexandria and *The Apostolic Tradition*).

The Cathedral Office. The Peace of Constantine in the 4th century allowed for the development of structured communal prayer in local churches throughout the Mediterranean area. Eusebius, Bishop of Caesarea in Palestine in the early part of that century, noted that throughout the Christian world, morning and evening prayer were celebrated publicly and daily (*Commentary on Ps*

64). He alluded to the widespread use of Psalm 62 (63) at morning prayer and of Psalm 140 (141) at evening prayer (*Commentary on Ps 64* and *Commentary on Ps 142*). Later 4th and 5th-century sources (e.g., Gregory of Nyssa, *Life of St. Macrina* 22; John Chrysostom, *Homily on Ps 140*; *The Apostolic Constitutions* II, 59; VII, 47-48; VIII, 34-39; Egeria's diary, chap 24, and Theodoret of Cyr, *Questions on Exodus* 28) confirm Eusebius' claims and provide evidence of additional elements: a *lucernarium* (light service) to begin evening prayer; the ceremonial offering of incense within it; and intercessions together with blessing to conclude both morning and evening prayer. Western sources from the 4th through the 8th centuries, especially in Gaul and in Spain (e.g., 6th and 7th-century synodal canons of Agde, Tours, Barcelona, and Toledo and the homilies of Caesarius of Aries) indicate the use of additional psalms and biblical canticles at both morning and evening prayer. Psalm 50 (51) enjoyed widespread use as the initial morning psalm, and Psalms 148-150 (the *laudes*) formed the climax of the morning psalmody. On Sundays and feasts, morning prayer usually included the Canticle of the Three Young Men from Daniel 3. Thus, a typical morning prayer (matins) would consist of selected morning psalms and canticles usually including Psalm 62 (63), *Gloria in excelsis*, Psalms 148-150, intercessions, blessing, and dismissal. Evening prayer (vespers) would include the *lucernarium* or light service with evening hymn; evening psalmody including Psalm 140 (141), incensation, intercessions, blessing, and dismissal.

In addition to daily morning and evening prayer, a weekly nighttime vigil marked the celebration of the Lord's Day in many of the local churches throughout the Mediterranean world (cf. *Apostolic Constitutions* II, 59; Egeria's diary, chap 24). The weekly nighttime or resurrection vigil would typically include three responsorial psalms or canticles (commemorating the three-day entombment of Jesus' body), intercessions, incensation (recalling the myrrh-bearing women), proclamation of a gospel account of the Lord's resurrection, blessing, and dismissal. In time other occasional vigils consisting of psalmody, readings, prayers, and preaching developed within this "cathedral office."

The ecclesial prayer of a local church was termed "cathedral office" by the liturgiologist Anton Baumstark (1872-1948; see *Comparative Liturgy*, chap 7) because it was common prayer celebrated in the physical edifice housing a local church and presided over by its bishop and clergy. The term also served to contrast this type of ecclesial prayer with that designated "monastic office" utilized by the early monks. The cathedral office, in contrast to the monastic, was almost entirely invariable in structure and in content; selective in its use and christological in its interpretation of psalmody; related to the time of day at which it was prayed; inclusive of non-verbal symbols (incense, darkness, light); usually without readings, and consisting predominantly of praise, thanksgiving, adoration, and petition.

The Egyptian Monastic Office. Within primitive Egyptian monasticism there originated types of communal prayer designed to express and to foster the ceaseless prayer which the early monks strove to cultivate. In marked contrast to the communal prayer of the urban churches, "pure" monastic prayer of the second half of the 4th century generally had no relation to the time of day at which it was prayed; employed the integral psalter over a determined period of time, and incorporated *lectio continua* (the continuous reading of the scriptures). Thus, while maintaining a fixed structure for prayer, this monastic office allowed for variety in psalmody and readings. One type of this prayer to which John Cassian gives witness in Books II and III of his *Institutes* was that of the monks of Scetis in Lower Egypt. Cassian's description of the prayer of the semi-anchorites of this region, while somewhat idealized and probably incorporating elements from other monastic traditions, gives at least roughly the form and the content of the two meetings or *synaxes* which these monks had for prayer, one in the early morning (cockcrow) and the other in the evening of at least every Saturday and Sunday. While they may not have met daily in full assembly for these offices as Cassian thought they did (*Institutes* III, 2), the monks undoubtedly prayed them alone or with a few others on weekdays. The two hours had the same structure: twelve psalms, *currente psalterio*, i.e., as they occur in the psalter, recited by a soloist; silent prayer by all standing and with arms extended; brief prostration and silent prayer; prayer again standing and with arms extended; collect recited by the one presiding; responsorial psalmody (with *Gloria Patri* concluding it as it concluded all the psalms); two scriptural readings, one from the Hebrew scriptures, the other from the NT on weekdays. On Saturday, Sunday, and during the Easter season, both readings were from the NT, one from the epistles or Acts, the other from one of the gospel accounts. Cassian had been accused of combining elements (e.g., readings) from another monastic tradition, the Pachomian, with that of the tradition of Scetis in his description of Egyptian monastic prayer, but it seems probable that he gives a substantially accurate description of the monastic prayer of Lower Egypt.

Pachomius' monks in Upper Egypt, however, seem to have used a somewhat different format for their customary morning and evening prayer. At each office a monk read a scriptural passage (on Sundays, a psalm). At a signal all of the monks then made the sign of the cross on their foreheads. Standing, they said the Our Father with arms extended and again signed themselves. Prostrated, they prayed in silence and, standing again, once more signed themselves and prayed in silence until a signal was given to be seated. They then listened to another scriptural passage read by a monk, and the cycle began again. Perhaps six such cycles occurred at each meeting for prayer. The entire monastery of Pachomian monks seems to have prayed together at dawn (rather than at cockcrow as in Lower Egypt), but in the evening each house (division of a monastery) prayed by itself the evening prayer.

In some contrast, then, to the cathedral offices, the primitive Egyptian monastic offices, designed to foster that ceaseless prayer so characteristic of the early monks, displayed a stimulative rather than a worshipful emphasis. It may even be possible that Cassian's structure of twelve psalms for each daily office was a later development from an early practice which encouraged ceaseless prayer by having monks pray twelve times during the day and twelve times during the night.

The Urban Monastic Office. Fourth-century monks not only populated the Egyptian deserts but dwelt near and within the urban centers of Palestine, Syria, Cappadocia, and Mesopotamia. Spreading throughout the East and the West in succeeding centuries, they exerted sometimes powerful influences on the liturgical practices of local churches. Urban monasteries knew both the traditions of Egyptian monks and the tradition of the cathedral office in their respective areas. Through various combinations of elements from the cathedral and monastic traditions, these monks created what has conveniently been termed the urban monastic office. It is this hybrid tradition which has shaped the structure and content of the liturgy of the hours in virtually all Christian rites. The urban monks added to the twice-daily common prayer of the Egyptian monks (Cassian, *Institutes* II and III) both a communal prayer at the ancient times for Christian private prayer, viz., the third, sixth, and ninth hours (terce, sect, and none) and a communal prayer before retiring at night (compline). The hour later known as prime may also owe its origin to a morning prayer (*novella sollemnitas*) established, according to Cassian (*Institutes* III, 4), in a monastery at Bethlehem. Three psalms were characteristic of each of the minor hours of terce, sext, and none; Psalm 90 enjoyed widespread use at compline, and prime contained elements borrowed from cathedral morning prayer. The urban monks combined the monastic and cathedral elements at morning prayer (matins) and evening prayer (vespers) in various ways.

In Palestine and Syria the tendency seems to have been to add the *laudes* (Psalms 148-150) of cathedral matins to the nocturnal monastic psalmody to form morning prayer. In Cappadocia, on the other hand, cathedral matins remained intact, and the monastic continuous psalmody constituted a separate office (nocturns or vigils) at midnight. It is more difficult to discern the shape of vespers in the initial stages of the urban monastic tradition, but given later developments, especially in the East, it would seem that the cathedral elements of *lucernarium*, Psalm 140 (141) with incense, and intercessions were appended to the continuous monastic psalmody.

Eastern Offices. The many rites of the Christian East have variously developed their inheritance of the liturgy of the hours from antiquity. The Armenian and East-Syrian rites have preserved much of the cathedral tradition in their morning and evening offices. West-Syrian and Maronite rites have juxtaposed cathedral and monastic elements within some hours, whereas the Coptic rite and, to some extent, the Ethiopian rite have maintained the monastic elements of the hours separate from the cathedral elements. The residue of the latter can be found in services outside the monastic cursus. The most widely known of the Eastern rites, the Byzantine, has interwoven monastic and cathedral elements extensively.

The Armenian office developed seven hours: night, morning, sunrise, midday, evening hours, the hour of peace, and the hour of rest. The only hour which has continuous monastic psalmody is the night hour. Matins and vespers, still celebrated (often together in the morning) by many parishes, contain the elements of ancient cathedral morning and evening prayers with additional material.

Chaldean and Malabar Christians, who worship in the East-Syrian or Assyro-Chaldean rites, can today still experience the full cycle of the cathedral office in their parish worship; matins (*Sapra*), vespers (*Ramša*), and the early Sunday morning vigil (*Qale d šahra*) which is appended to the monastic night office. The monastic nocturnal office (*Lelya*) contains continuous psalmody divided so that the entire psalter is used in the course of six weeknights. The other hours are today celebrated only occasionally or united in abridged form to other offices. Terce and sext are said only on Lenten weekdays; compline occurs only on some feasts; some remnants of terce appear in the opening of the eucharistic liturgy, and a residue of none is attached to the beginning of vespers. To the ancient elements of these hours have been added in the course of the centuries what has characterized East-Syrian liturgy—hymns and prayers of praise without petition.

The liturgy of the hours in the West-Syrian (Syro-Antiochene) rite and related Maronite rite contains all the usual hours; nocturns, matins, terce, sext, none, vespers, and compline. Matins (*Safro*) in both Syrian and Maronite rites is essentially a cathedral office which has absorbed some elements of the cathedral vigil. Poetic chants have in the course of time replaced some of the original elements of matins and especially the psalmody in nocturns (*Lilyo*), terce, sext, and none. The offering of incense is highlighted in vespers (*Ramšo*) which, in the Maronite rite at least, clearly juxtaposes monastic and cathedral elements. Compline (*Sutoro*) still contains psalmody in which are included Psalms 4 and 90 (91). The common practice today, where the liturgy of the hours is celebrated outside monastic communities, groups the hours in two synaxes. The first, in the morning, includes nocturns (*Lilyo*), matins (*Safro*), terce, and sext; the second, in the evening, includes none, vespers (*Ramšo*), and compline (*Sutoro*). Among the Syro-Malankarese Catholics in Kerala, India, and among Maronite Catholics in the United States a vigorous liturgical renewal shows great promise of a revitalized celebration of the hours.

In the Coptic rite with its heavy monastic influence, the hours in the *horologion* (office book) have, not surprisingly, a monastic cast. Six hours (matins, terce, sext, none, eleventh hour [vespers], and compline) have essentially the same structure: initial prayers, psalmody (twelve psalms, ideally, from the psalter distributed throughout the six hours), gospel reading, *troparia* (poetic refrains), *Kyrie eleison* (repeated at length), *Trisagion*, Our Father, prayer of absolution, and final prayer. Two hours, "Prayer of the Veil" (a second, monastic compline) and a midnight office of three nocturns do not conform to the usual structure and repeat psalmody already found in the other hours. These are undoubtedly late additions to the cursus. Remnants of the cathedral office can be found in additional services: Offering of Incense for morning and for evening and Psalmodia for the night, for the morning, and for the evening.

The complexity of material for the hours in the Ethiopian rite has yet to be thoroughly subjected to scholarly analysis. The cathedral office consisting of vespers (*Wāzēmā*), Sunday nocturns (*Mawaddes*), and matins (*Sebehāta nagh*) is still celebrated in large churches on especially solemn days by professional cantors in the intricate chant of this rite. Other services, including the third, sixth, and ninth hours, are added at certain times. Elements from both monastic and cathedral traditions are interwoven in most of these offices. The monastic traditions of the hours is perhaps more prominently represented in four distinct *horologia* or *sa'ātāta* which contain offices other than the cathedral services, but even here cathedral elements are interspersed with monastic. Of the four *horologia*, that known as the *Sa'ātāt* of Abba Giyorgis Saglawi is the common cursus for the Ethiopian Orthodox church. Only in monasteries of this church is the complete office celebrated.

The Byzantine rite, as a liturgical tradition which has combined cathedral usages of Antioch and Jerusalem synthesized in the practice of Hagia Sophia, the Great Church of Constantinople, with monastic usages of the Laura of St. Sabas in Palestine and the monasteries in Constantinople influenced by St. Theodore Studites (d. 826), offers a rich complexity of traditions in its liturgy of the hours. The cathedral office of Hagia Sophia yielded almost entirely to the monastic "Sabaitic" and "Studite" practices after the fall of Constantinople to the Latin crusaders in 1204. Today the Byzantine office combines elements of nocturns, cathedral matins, and (on Sundays) the cathedral vigil in *orthros*. Poetic odes of monastic origin called the "canon" have virtually replaced the biblical canticles once part of *orthros*. Vespers (*hesperinos*) retains most of the elements of evening prayer in the cathedral office, but opens with a derivative of monastic vespers. Parish worship still includes *orthros* and *hesperinos*, generally with some adaptation. On Saturday nights in parishes of Russian tradition the "all-night vigil" (*pannychis* or *vsenoshchnoe bdenie*) occurs. Though lengthy, this office does not ordinarily last the whole night long. It combines vespers and *orthros* usually without the additional psalmody of the monasteries. To the monasteries belong the additional hours of prime, terce, sext, none, and compline.

Characteristic, certainly, of the liturgy of the hours, especially of vespers, in the Eastern churches is the preservation of elements and distinct units of the cathedral office. Even when monasticized, vespers and matins remained viable and popular forms of common prayer in parishes.

Western Offices. The history of the liturgy of the hours in the West is primarily its history in the Roman rite. It is well to recall, however, that other pre-Reformation rites existed in the West and, within them, diverse forms of the hours. Evidence of the monastic office from the 4th through the 11th centuries is certainly more abundant than evidence of the cathedral office due in great measure to the significant role monasteries played in the destabilized society of that period. Throughout the West monastic practice overwhelmed cathedral practice and left fewer traces of the cathedral office than can be found in the Eastern rites. The Spanish rites as a notable exception, however, preserved both diversity and popular participation in forms of the cathedral office until Pope Gregory VII (1073-1085) suppressed them and imposed the Roman office. In the 16th century some churches of the Reformation attempted to reform the massive, monasticized, and clericalized Roman office and to restore it as parochial worship. In the case of Archbishop Cranmer and the Church of England, the reforming effort was ingenious and the restorative effort, eminently successful. Despite periodic attempts at reform in the Roman rite before the Second Vatican Council, the Roman office remained largely a privatized and clericalized activity. The reform of the office after the council, while in many respects thorough and offering hope of its restoration as parochial liturgy, remains still generally an achievement of new books, not of renewed practice.

Western Monastic Offices. The 4th-century *Ordo monasterii*, which influenced both St. Augustine's and St. Caesarius' rules, prescribed six hours—matins, terce, sext, none, lucernarium, and nocturns—in which were employed responsorial and antiphonal psalmody as well as scriptural readings. From Cassian's *Institutes* II and III can be gleaned some characteristics of the monastic office in southern Gaul in the 5th century. Generally similar to the Palestinian monastic office, the Provencal office seems not to have concluded nocturns with the *laudes* (Psalms 148-150) but to have used them at the conclusion of a separate morning office or matins. Cassian's system was modified in the 6th century as witnessed by the rules of Sts. Caesarius and Aurelian of Arles. Here cathedral hours of matins and *lucernarium* exist together with their respective monastic equivalents, nocturns and *duodecima*. The little hours and, with Aurelian, prime and compline round out the cursus. On feasts the cathedral hours were celebrated by the monks for the people in a public oratory. In the same century, with St. Columban's *Rule of Monks*, one encounters an Irish monastic office in which the amount of psalmody, especially in the night office, is staggering—almost a hundred psalms on a weekend night in winter! Sts. Isidore of Seville (d. 633) and Fructuosus of Braga (d. ca. 665) provide in their respective monastic rules descriptions of Spanish monastic offices similar to those in southern Gaul. The most important pre-Benedictine rule by far to supply information on the monastic office in Italy is the *Rule of the Master.* Here the hours—nocturns, matins, the little hours, vespers, and compline—have each basically the same structure—psalmody (antiphonal and responsorial), reading from St. Paul, gospel reading (at matins and vespers probably gospel canticle), and intercessions (*rogus dei*). Psalms used antiphonally, except at matins and compline, were taken as they occur in the psalter, and each psalm was prayed in a unit (*inpositio*) comprising psalm, *Gloria Patri*, prostration, and silent prayer.

The prescriptions for the office in *The Rule of the Master* and some form of the basilican (monastic) office of the church of Rome were the two major sources for the content and structure of the office in the *Rule of St. Benedict.* Little is known directly of the old Roman basilican office, ancestor of the modern Roman office, but through Benedict's rule, the *Rule of the Master* (itself a derivative of a form of the basilican office), and 8th-century *ordines Romani* something of its nature can be reconstructed. The monastic predilection for the use of the integral psalter over a given period of time found expression in this office in the weekly distribution of Psalms 1-107 (108) continuously at vigils (nocturns) and Psalms 108 (109)-150 at vespers. The continuous reading of the scriptures at nocturns (vigils), another monastic predilection, was undoubtedly part of the basilican office, for the 8th-century *Ordo XIV*, giving the order of readings for the office in St. Peter's basilica in the late 6th or early 7th century, indicates that all of scripture was read from the beginning of a year to its end. Matins, the minor hours (including prime), and compline had fixed psalms. There were twelve psalms (twenty-four on Sundays) at nocturns, six (including

the *laudes*) at matins, six at vespers, and three at each of the little hours and compline. St. Benedict is credited with modifying this arrangement by distributing the variable psalms of vigils and vespers throughout all the hours of a day except compline; by reducing to twelve the number of psalms at Sunday vigils; by removing psalms used at other hours from the cursus of vigils and vespers; by placing the readings after the first six psalms of vigils rather than at the end of the twelve, and by introducing hymnody into each of the hours. This office supplanted almost all other monastic offices in the West by the 11th century.

Some years after the Second Vatican Council the Benedictine Confederation under the leadership of its Abbot Primate, Rembert Weakland, O.S.B., provided a rich source in *Thesaurus Liturgiae Horarum Monasticae* (Rome, 1976) for Benedictine monasteries to shape the monastic office according to their local needs and circumstances. The introduction to this work is available in English translation and is entitled "The Directory for the Celebration of the Work of God." It remains an outstanding statement of the rationale for and the principles of not only the monastic office but also, in great measure, of the liturgy of the hours for any local church or group of Christians.

Western Cathedral Offices. Evidence for the cathedral office in the West is scattered and late. St. Ambrose (339-397) witnesses to the existence of cathedral matins, vespers, and vigils in Milan as does St. Augustine (354-430) for North Africa. In addition to the Gallic synods already mentioned, St. Gregory of Tours (538-594) in his *History of the Franks* and *Lives of the Fathers* attests to a cathedral office in Gaul of which matins undoubtedly consisted of Psalm 50 [51], the canticle from Daniel 3, Psalms 148-150, and *capitella*, intercessions composed from verses of psalms. In his homilies and *Vita*, St. Caesarius of Arles provides scattered information on the rather full cathedral office in Arles. Matins, which seems to have had basically the same structure attested to by St. Gregory at Tours and at which Caesarius preached, was preceded by a vigil in which scripture readings were interspersed with psalms each followed by prayer in silence and an oration (collect) by the presider. Caesarius himself introduced the minor hours into the cathedral cursus and sometimes preached also at *lucernarium* which with the monastic *duodecima* constituted cathedral vespers.

The cathedral office in Visigothic Spain is known, as previously indicated, principally through the canons of numerous Iberian councils. Of particular significance in Iberian vespers was the opening light ritual, *oblatio luminis*, in which a lighted candle was elevated with the proclamation, "In the name of Our Lord Jesus Christ, light and peace!" To this the congregation answered, "Thanks be to God!" In addition to the customary Psalm 140 [141] other vesperal psalms having the theme of light (e.g., Psalms 17 [18], 35 [36], 111 [112]) found place. Otherwise, vespers and matins were apparently similar to the respective hours in southern Gaul.

Evidence of a distinct cathedral office in Rome is sparse. Some would see in units of the 5th-century basilican nocturns, matins, and vespers as reflected in Benedict's *Rule* remnants of ancient Roman cathedral hours. For example, the third nocturn of Sunday vigils in the *Rule* consists of three biblical canticles with "alleluia" refrain and a proclamation of a passage from the gospel—a striking parallel to the weekly cathedral vigil. Such units may indeed be cathedral remnants, but the monastic influence in the Roman basilicas was early and heavy. It marked their offices with a stamp that has survived in the one Roman office eventually issuing from them even

through the reform of that office following the Second Vatican Council.

As in the East, the monastic office of the West was integrated with the cathedral office in various ways. Unlike the office in the East, however, the distinction between monastic and cathedral elements in the Western parochial offices did not remain as clear, nor did the hybrid forms long survive as vibrant worship among the faithful.

The Roman Office. The first clear statement of what constituted the structure and content of the Roman office comes from Amalarius of Metz (ca. 780-850) in his *Liber Officialis*, IV, 1-2 and *Liber de ordine antiphonarii*, 1-7. By the time these works were written, of course, some form of the Roman basilican office had been transmitted to the British Isles in the Romanization of the Celtic church and thence to German and Frankish lands in the missionary effort of the Anglo-Irish monks. What Amalarius describes, then, is a Romano-Frankish office which in the process of transmission and use has undergone some modification. From Amalarius' works and from a Roman *ordo* (Ordo XII) of his time can be outlined the form of the Roman office which remained essentially the same into the 20th century. Nocturns (vigils, much later termed matins) began with an invitatory which included Psalm 94 (95) with antiphon. A first nocturn of twelve psalms without antiphons on Sundays, but with antiphons on weekdays, and only three psalms on feasts followed. Three readings with responsories concluded the nocturn. Two other nocturns arranged similarly followed, each having three psalms (with antiphons). The hymn *Te Deum* replaced the final responsory in the third nocturn. Matins (later termed lauds) consisted of seven psalms (Psalms 50 [51] on weekdays and 92 [93] on Sundays, 62 [63], 65 [66], a variable psalm, and 148-150), a biblical canticle, *capitulum* (short reading), the gospel canticle *Benedictus*, and intercessions. Prime included Psalm 53 (54), two sections of Psalm 118 (119), versicle, *Kyrie, Pater*, Apostles' Creed, Psalm 50 (51), versicle, and collect. The minor hours of terce, sext, and none comprised three octonaries from Psalm 118 (119) without antiphons, a short reading, response, and *preces* (intercessions). The core of vespers consisted of five variable psalms (drawn from Psalms 109 [110]-147), *capitulum*, responsory, versicle (Ps 140 [141]:2 with incense offering in Amalarius' time), the gospel canticle *Magnificat*, intercessions (on weekdays only for Amalarius), and collect. Compline used Psalms 4, 30 (31):1-6, 90 (91), and 133 (134) without antiphons daily and the gospel canticle *Nunc dimittis*.

Local celebration of the Roman office before the 8th century did not necessarily mean the performance of all hours in a given church. Often enough the office was parceled out among the various churches of an area. But beginning shortly before and continuing throughout the Carolingian reform of the 8th and 9th centuries, the obligation for all clergy to celebrate all the hours in each church gradually became the norm. Between the 11th and 15th centuries both the doubling of offices (ferial and festal) on feasts and various additions to the office, including hymns at all the hours, a considerable extension of prime, offices of the dead and of the Blessed Virgin Mary, gradual psalms, penitential psalms, suffrages, and lengthened *preces*, made the performance of the office burdensome to the clergy who gradually became, along with monks, almost the only celebrants of the hours. Lay people, also finding the office burdensome as well as incomprehensible, abandoned the hours to focus on popular devotions such as the rosary or on the recent and apparently more palatable accretions to the hours as these were collected in primers, books of hours, and, somewhat later, in manuals of piety.

Relief for some clergy was found in the frequent use of festal or sanctoral offices which were shorter than the ferial offices but limited in their use of the psalms. Relief was also discovered in the adoption of the 13th-century office of the Roman Curia, itself an abridgement of the Roman office as used by the pope and his household. The propagation of this office by the Franciscans, however, did not displace the Roman office which continued to suffer both the expansion of legendary hagiographical readings and the contraction and elimination of scriptural and patristic readings at nocturns. Dispensations from choral celebration with consequent obligation to private recitation of the hours increased, as education and other activities took clergy away from their local churches. From its original purpose as a kind of *ordo* to find one's way among the books utilized for the hours, viz., psalter, antiphonary, lectionary, and collectary, the breviary gradually became a compendium of the entire office for those reciting it privately and gave further impetus to an already existing practice of bunching hours together.

Feeble efforts to reform the office came to naught until Francisco Cardinal Quiñonez (1485-1540) and his associates at the direction of Pope Clement VII (1523-1534) produced what came to be known as *The Breviary of the Holy Cross*. Designed for private recitation and spiritual edification, this breviary featured three psalms at each hour and scriptural readings arranged at matins (nocturns) in semi-continuous fashion such that most of the Bible would be read in the course of a year. Psalms were placed according to their suitability for each hour, the whole psalter being distributed over the course of a week. Two editions and over 100 printings testify to the popularity of this breviary, but the objection of theologians that this office vitiated the very nature of the hours as communal worship won the day. The

Council of Trent (1545-1563) decreed a correction of the old Roman office, and Pope Pius V in publishing it in 1568 banned further use of Quiñonez's breviary.

French reforms of the office in the 17th and 18th centuries were the most notable between Quiñonez' and that of Pope Pius X (1903-1914). The so called neo-Gallican breviaries were the products of diocesan reforms founded on some of the principles Quiñonez had used. Most utilized scripture more extensively, redistributed the psalms to allow for relatively equal length at most hours, abbreviated nocturns (matins), permitted only one of the *laudes* (Psalms 148-150) at matins (lauds), and used ferial psalms on all but major feasts to encourage recitation of the whole psalter weekly. All was directed primarily to the private recitation and edification of the clergy even though choral celebration of the office still existed in cathedrals and parishes, and laity continued to attend at least vespers on Sundays.

Despite other minor reforming efforts, the structure and content of the Roman office remained essentially the same until the reform of Pope Pius X in 1911. Beyond the celebration of the full office in monasteries and of Sunday vespers in many parishes, the office had become the private affair of clergy and some religious who were considered deputed or mandated to pray the hours in the name of the church. Pius X's bull, *Divino afflatu* (November 1, 1911) decreed what was intended to be the first stage of a comprehensive reform of the office. The psalms were redistributed, divided where necessary, and the number for each day reduced. Entailed in this redistribution and reduction was the loss of Psalms 148-150 as a daily component of lauds (matins)—a rupture with a centuries-old, universal tradition. Weekly recitation of the psalter was restored by suppressing supplementary offices as daily obligations

and restoring priority of the temporal cycle over the sanctoral. The number of psalms at matins (nocturns) was reduced to nine and at lauds (matins), four. Too brief scriptural readings and unhistorical hagiographic readings at matins (nocturns) were, however, left unrevised. Something of Pius X's reform was continued in the work of the historical section of the Sacred Congregation of Rites, established within the Congregation by Pope Pius XI (1922-1939) in 1930, and by the Pontifical Commission for the Reform of the Liturgy formed under Pope Pius XII (1939-1958) with the aid of the historical section of the Congregation. A major project of the Pian Commission was reform of the Roman office. Study of needed reforms was prolonged and thorough, but actual reforms were few. The major result could be considered the reduction of matins (nocturns) to one nocturn on most days of the year, and this change was promulgated in the *Codex rubricarum* of 1960. The Preparatory Liturgical Commission for the Second Vatican Council, established by Pope John XXIII (1958-1963), prepared in its *schema* for reform of the liturgy a chapter on the office and advocated restoration of the traditional sequence of the hours prayed at their appropriate times (*veritas horarum*), recognition of lauds and vespers as the chief hours of the day, reform of matins (nocturns) for use at any hour and of the minor hours for use at the appropriate times. The commission also rejected a plea by some for a double office, one for private recitation, the other for communal celebration. A distribution of the psalms over a period of time longer than one week was recommended. All of these proposals, together with one which abolished the hour of prime, found expression in Chapter IV of the definitive conciliar constitution, *Sacrosanctum concilium*, promulgated by Pope Paul VI (1963-1978) on December 4, 1963.

The post-conciliar commission for the reform of the liturgy, while scrupulously faithful to the text of Chapter IV of the constitution, moved beyond its concern to provide primarily a better office for private recitation of the clergy, and clearly summoned all in the church to the communal celebration especially of the chief hours of lauds and vespers (*General Instruction on the Liturgy of the Hours*, nn. 20-27). The psalms were distributed over a four-week cycle, divided where appropriate, and placed more fittingly at the various hours. Matins (nocturns) became the office of readings, suitable for use at any time, its readings fully revised. A hymn now began each hour, and the minor hours, still obligatory for those bound to communal celebration, could be reduced to one midday hour by those not so bound. The number of biblical canticles was increased, the invitatory at matins (nocturns) recommended for lauds (matins) if the latter were the first hour in the day, and the structure of all the hours simplified and rendered similar. Morning prayer and evening prayer begin with opening verse (or invitatory in morning prayer) and are followed by psalmody (morning psalm, OT canticle, psalm of praise in the morning; two psalms and NT canticle in the evening), scriptural reading, short response, gospel canticle (*Benedictus* in the morning, *Magnificat* in the evening), prayers (offering and praise in the morning, intercessions in the evening), Lord's prayer, concluding prayer, and blessing. The minor hours or midday prayer consist essentially of a hymn, three psalms (or sections of psalms), short reading and response, concluding prayer, and blessing. Compline, on a one week cycle, has a hymn, usually one psalm, short reading, response, gospel canticle (*Nunc dimittis*), prayer, and blessing. The office of readings, expandable on Saturday nights to a lengthier vigil office, has (after the invitatory), three psalms (or sections of psalms), versicle, biblical and patristic or hagiographical readings each with responsory, *Te Deum*, prayer, and blessing.

Although the possibility for radical revision was available to the reformers of the Roman office and was urged by some among them, they chose to compromise and thus retain the essentially monastic structure of this office. The reform, nevertheless, was substantial and laboriously achieved. Its imaginative implementation and indigenization will undoubtedly make apparent its possibilities as contemporary yet traditional communal prayer.

The Office in Reformation Churches. There have been many attempts to restore liturgy of the hours in churches of the Reformation. Among the more notable are those in the Lutheran tradition, in the Church of England, and in the community of Taizé.

Martin Luther's attempt to reform matins (morning prayer) and vespers by making them services for all was a commendable attempt to restore these hours to the people, but his emphasis on scripture reading and preaching in these cathedral hours was an unavoidable misunderstanding of them. Twentieth-century Lutherans in the United States have recovered better the components of a traditional cathedral office in their *Lutheran Book of Worship*. Matins contains, among other elements, selected psalmody, hymn, optional gospel canticle, and Lord's Prayer. A light service can begin vespers, and other elements include the vesperal Psalm 140 (141), selected psalmody (including NT canticle), *Magnificat*, litany, and Lord's Prayer.

Relying on Quiñonez' reforming principles, Archbishop Cranmer produced two daily offices for the Church of England which restored communal celebration of liturgy of the hours to both clergy and people. Both the morning and evening hours, inserted in *The Book of Common Prayer*, had essentially identical structures of which the core was psalmody, scriptural reading, canticle, scriptural reading, canticle. While matins was a combination of elements from the Sarum usage of Roman nocturns, lauds, and prime, Cranmer's evensong brought together portions of vespers and compline. These hours, like Luther's, emphasized the orderly reading of scripture. Within the Anglican communion there have been a number of recent refinements of the daily offices as these appear in new service books such as *The Alternative Service Book* (1980) in England and *The Book of Common Prayer* (1979) in the United States.

Perhaps the most notable modern restoration of the liturgy of the hours is the Taizé office. Published in 1963 for the ecumenical religious community in Taizé, France, it has undergone revision throughout the years and has been experienced by thousands of people from all walks of life who visit the community each year. While this office has a simplified form of the little hours and compline, the principal hours are morning prayer and evening prayer. The latter is expanded on Saturday evening and eves of feasts to form a vigil office. Morning and evening prayers now have the basic structure of introduction, psalmody, reading, response, silence, hymn, intercessions, collect for the week, free prayer, general collect, and blessing.

Offices in *The Book of Common Prayer, L'Office de Taizé*, and other Protestant offices, especially *L'Office Divin de chaque jour* edited by R. Paquier and A. Bardet for Swiss Calvinists, were utilized in the preparation of the Roman *Liturgia horarum* after the Second Vatican Council. Although the influence of these offices on the structure and content of the new Roman liturgy of the hours is negligible, those engaged in the reform of that office gained a better understanding and appreciation of the Protestant offices themselves and through them, of what should be retained or modified in the Roman hours.

Theology and Practice

The various hours which constitute the office in all traditions have a basic structure which has been termed dialogical. Some elements of the structure demand attentive listening to the word of God through which God calls or teaches us. Other elements are responsive in nature. Through them we respond to God's call in praise, thanksgiving, or petition. The readings and even the psalmody, from one point of view, manifest the call or address of God to us. Hymns, prayers, intercessory elements, and psalmody manifest our response to that call. While such a view certainly represents something of the theological meaning of the liturgy of the hours, it is inadequate. All Christian liturgy is fundamentally a celebration of the paschal mystery of Christ, of his dying and rising not simply as action inaugurating salvation, but as present event actualized here and now in the lives of his faithful people who constitute his body, the church. The hours, as liturgy, are truly that, and in being that, are dialogical, for the paschal mystery is itself a dialogue, personalized in Christ who is both the Word of God to humankind and the ultimate and absolutely faithful human response of praise, thanksgiving, self-offering, and petition to God.

Both the ancient cathedral and monastic forms of liturgy of the hours were ritualized actualizations of the paschal mystery and of its dialogical dimension. But each form can be said to have had a different emphasis. Whereas the cathedral hours emphasized the human response to the salvific approach of God in Christ, i.e., put the accent on worship, the monastic office tended to focus on the divine offer of salvation and human receptivity to it in Christ. Both forms were ritualized expressions of a mystery that must be lived first in order for those expressions to be authentic and to be means of further deepening the living of the mystery. Of course, both forms coalesced in the urban monastic office and its derivatives so that the emphasis distinctive of each was diminished. The diminishment in emphasis, however, did not lessen the significance of the liturgy of the hours as a ritual celebration of the paschal mystery of Christ even if that significance, especially in the West, became unclear due to the clericalization and privatization of the office and to a concern with fulfillment of obligation and of mandate.

One of the purposes of the liturgy of the hours is sometimes stated as the "sanctification of time" (*General Instruction on the Liturgy of the Hours*, nn. 10-11). This phrase, often unexamined, can lend itself to misinterpretation. It should not mean that the liturgy of the hours somehow renders secular time sacred, but that this liturgy suggests at certain times of a day what the quality of all times should be, i.e., an experience of time which is sacramental or revelatory of the mystery of Christ and a means of union with God in him. Matins and vespers, for example, in the cathedral tradition were intended for the "sanctification of time" in the sense that their rites and texts illuminated critical moments of the day, evening and morning, as revealing certain aspects of the paschal mystery of Christ (viz., his dying and rising), which grounds and suffuses all of Christian life. They thus encouraged the seeing of all moments of a day as sacramental expressions of that mystery.

The hours as sanctification of time have been misunderstood in another way. Dom Gregory Dix suggested in his *Shape of the Liturgy* that the early church celebrated the eucharist as an eschatalogical cult, but eventually, when private devotional prayer assumed a communal form as the offering of human endeavor to God, a kind of liturgy very different from the eschatological eucharist was introduced into Christian worship. Thus the hours, as a liturgy sanctifying time, were opposed to the eucharist, a liturgy wholly focused on the eschatological. Such a dichotomy does not exist. Both eucharist and hours have eschatological and temporal dimensions since they both celebrate, albeit in different modes, the one mystery of Christ which is both temporal and eschatological.

Similarity in the content of what is celebrated in eucharist and hours, however, has led some to posit a close relationship between them. The widespread notion of an intimate link is even expressed in *The General Instruction on the Liturgy of the Hours*, n. 12. There it is said that the praise, thanksgiving, memorial of the mysteries of salvation, petitions, and foretaste of heaven present in the eucharist are extended throughout the day by the liturgy of the hours as if the hours could not be of themselves sacramental celebrations of the mystery of Christ. History, however, shows "that for centuries eucharist and hours were not regarded as related ritual actions such that eucharist was, so to speak, the culmination of the hours or their source in sanctifying time. Rather, the hours have stood independent of the eucharist and have focused their celebration on the mystery as present in every moment of time, modelling and encouraging that ceaseless prayer which must be the concomitant of lives caught up in that mystery.

The linking of hours to eucharist, however, may not be as major a problem for their proper understanding and use as the seeing inability or lack of opportunity of many within the Roman rite to experience liturgy of the hours as prayer. The remarkable, contemporary revival of and interest in personal prayer has hardly contributed to an appreciation or use of the hours as prayer. Perhaps centuries-long abuse of the office as a clerical and monastic preserve, an obligatory ceremonial more often than not performed in private and, until recently, in a foreign language, has rendered the prayerful possibilities of the office obscure. The unfortunate distinction, too, between liturgy as public, communal activity and prayer as a personal and private undertaking seems to have kept many from experiencing the hours as communal prayer which is also personal. Authentic Christian life has both personal and communal or social dimensions which need to be present in all forms of prayer, would cease to express and to nourish a community's life of faith if it were not also a personal form of prayer for each one engaged in it.

That the liturgy of the hours can be a kind of "school of prayer" wherein one can learn how to pray well is attributable, among other things, to its objectivity and its metaphoric quality. Its objectivity lies in its universality with respect to the mystery it ritually symbolizes, its unfetteredness to particular subjective needs and concerns. Its metaphoric quality is that of any sacramental activity of the church, an activity which does not merely denote the mystery it symbolizes but connotes its rich complexity, inviting participants to ever deeper immersion in it. The liturgy of the hours, then, can be a framework in which the authentic dimensions of Christian prayer are apprehended, practiced, and made one's own. Schooled in the common prayer of the hours, one can enter more deeply into "private" prayer and, thus enriched, bring ever greater intensity and sensitivity to the liturgy of the hours.

See **Time, liturgical**

Paul F. Bradshaw, *Daily Prayer in the Early Church* (London: Alcuin/S.P.C.K., 1981). Anne Field, ed., *Directory for the Celebration of the Work of God. Guidelines for the Monastic Liturgy of the Hours Approved for the Benedictine Confederation* (Riverdale, MD: Exordium Books, 1981). Peter Fink, "Public and Private Moments in Christian Prayer," *Worship* 58 (1984): 482-499. John Gallen, ed., *Christians at Prayer* (Notre Dame: Univ. of Notre Dame Press, 1977). W.J. Grisbrooke, "A Contemporary Liturgical Problem: The Divine Office and Public Worship," *Studia Liturgica* 8 (1971-72): 129-168: 9 (1973):3-18, 81-106. George Guiver, *Company of Voices: Daily Prayer and the People of God* (New York: Pueblo Pub. Co., 1988). Cheslyn Jones, Geoffrey Wainwright, Edward Yarnold, eds., *The Study of Liturgy*, Chap V: "The Divine Office" (New York: Oxford Univ. Press, 1978). Joseph A. Jungmann, *Christian Prayer through the Centuries*, trans. by John Coyne (New York: Paulist Press, 1978). *The Liturgy of the Hours. The General Instruction on the Liturgy of the Hours with a Commentary by A.-M. Roguet*, trans. by Peter Coughlan and Peter Purdue (Collegeville: Liturgical Press, 1971). A.G. Martimort, "The Liturgy of the Hours" in *The Church at Prayer*, New edition, Vol. 4; *The Liturgy and Time*, ed. by A.G. Martimort, trans. by Matthew J. O'Connell (Collegeville: Liturgical Press, 1986) 153-275. J. Mateos, "The Morning and Evening Office," *Worship* 42 (1968): 31-47; "The Origins of the Divine Office," *Worship* 41 (1967): 477-485. Pierre Salmon, *The Breviary through the Centuries*, trans. by Sr. David Mary (Collegeville: Liturgical Press, 1962). Robert Taft, *The Liturgy of the Hours in East and West. The Origins of the Divine Office and Its Meaning for Today* (Collegeville: Liturgical Press, 1986).

STANISLAUS CAMPBELL, F.S.C.

HUMAN SCIENCES, SACRAMENTS AND THE

Before the Second Vatican Council it was common to find the sacraments treated in manuals of theology together with various moral and disciplinary directives for the clergy. The principal focus of this treatment was the proper performance of the rites and the effects they had on those who participated in them. As such it fell largely within the province of Canon Law.

The canons of proper performance specified the appropriate minister of the sacrament (e.g., bishop, priest, lay person), the matter of the sacrament (e.g., bread and wine, chrism, water, laying on of hands) and the form of the sacrament (the words to be used, e.g., "I baptize you in the name of the Father and the Son and the Holy Spirit"). If the canons were duly observed, the sacrament was said to be licit (i.e., lawfully performed) and valid (i.e., juridically and ontologically effective). If minor infractions of the canons occurred, the sacrament was said to be illicit but still valid. If a major infraction occurred (e.g., totally inappropriate minister, matter or form), the sacrament was said to be invalid, that is, it was regarded as being completely ineffective.

In its outlook, this approach to the church's sacraments was individualistic and essentialistic. It directed attention toward the individual performers in the rituals and toward the essential effects bestowed on the recipients. Theological speculation as to the types of effects was limited by the essentialist and non-empirical method of classical philosophy. Although the manuals acknowledged communal and existential dimensions of the sacraments, these further dimensions were for the most part unexplored or left to the province of pastoral and spiritual theology.

The liturgical movement which gained momentum during the decades prior to Vatican II broadened the Catholic perspective on the sacraments so that they could be seen as having greater significance for the lives of all Christians as well as for the corporate life of the church itself. In addition, the ecumenical movement expanded the Catholic awareness of sacraments so that they could be seen as having parallels in other Christian churches and even in non-Christian religions. Viewed under these lights, the sacraments fell under the scrutiny of a wider variety of the human sciences than classical philosophy.

It should be noted that in this context the *sacraments* are the rites themselves, not the metaphysical concomitants of the rites spoken of in scholastic theology (e.g., as in the phrase, "receiving the sacraments") nor the speculative dimensions of the rites proposed by other theological systems (e.g., that sacraments are encounters with Christ). Only the observable and recordable aspects of the sacraments are open to empirical investigation, although the reportable experiences of the participants in the rites also need to be included under this rubric. In this article the *human sciences* shall be taken to encompass all studies of human behavior and experience which claim to have a methodology which yields conclusions that can be verified through similar methodological investigation.

Philosophy

The most ancient of the human sciences is *philosophy*, which goes back to the ancient Greeks, and which in the Middle Ages was called the handmaiden of theology. The Fathers of the church used Platonic and neo-Platonic philosophy to understand the workings of the sacraments, and their effort was superseded by the Scholastics who used the Aristotelian categories of matter and form, substance and accidents cause and effect to analyze and explain the sacraments. As can be seen from the discussion above, a number of these terms were incorporated into the church's Canon Law, which still regulates the proper performance of the sacraments.

Shunning the apparently antagonistic philosophies of the Enlightenment, Catholic theologians through the Modern Era continued to follow the Aristotelian method of investigation. Contemporary sacramental theology, however, has returned to the practice of utilizing categories and systems of thought borrowed from non-Catholic and even non-Christian philosophies to understand the sacraments, much as the Church Fathers used Plato and the Scholastics used Aristotle.

Edward Schillebeeckx (*Christ the Sacrament of the Encounter with God*, 1963), Karl Rahner (*The Church and the Sacraments*, 1963) and others in the neo-Thomistic movement were the first to

578

break out of the strictly scholastic mold by drawing on phenomenology and existentialism to amplify the personal and interpersonal dimensions of sacramental worship. Juan Luis Segundo (*The Sacraments Today*, 1974) and other liberation theologians have incorporated Marxist elements into their examination of how the sacraments operate in Christian society. Bernard Lee (*The Becoming of the Church*, 1974) has developed a theology of the church and sacraments within the framework of Whitehead's process philosophy. Even linguistic analysis has been put to use by theologians to interpret the various functions of language within sacramental rituals.

A consequence of this return to the practice of adapting philosophies to the needs of theology has been an increase in the number of ways that the sacraments can be understood. When all theologians used the Aristotelian system exclusively, there was basically a single sacramental theology within the church. Variations within this framework divided theologians into different schools of thought over minor issues, but all discussion took place within the single framework of scholastic philosophy. The adoption of multiple frameworks or systems of thought has bred a multiplicity of systematic theologies in all areas including systematic reflection on the sacraments. Rather than there being a single Catholic sacramental theology, therefore, there now exists a plurality of sacramental theologies, such as those referred to above.

Today the unity of the philosophical endeavor to understand the sacraments is located on the underlying level of methodology rather than on the surface level of results. Even though different theologians may say widely diverse things about the sacraments, they are united in a common effort to understand the sacraments from a philosophical perspective that sheds light on one or more of the many dimensions of sacramental worship.

History

Although *history* as a study of human behavior also dates from ancient Greece, the historical investigation of the sacraments dates only from the 19th century. Before the inquiry of Prosper Gueranger and the monks of Solesmes into the origins of the liturgy and Gregorian chant, it had been largely assumed that the sacraments had remained virtually unchanged since the time of Christ and the apostles.

Even the earliest investigations, however, showed that the church's sacramental history had been marked by diversity as well as continuity. By the turn of the century, researchers were discovering, collecting and cataloguing ancient and medieval liturgical texts that had remained hidden for centuries in the libraries of the Vatican and numerous monasteries. During the first half of the 20th century, scholars built on this foundational research and constructed detailed histories of the sacramental rites of both Eastern and Western Christianity, culminating in such works as J. Jungmann's *The Mass of the Roman Rite* and a number of the volumes of Herder's *Handbuch der Dogmengeschichte* and Edition du Cerf's *Lex Orandi*. By the Second Vatican Council in the 1960s, the acknowledgement of liturgical change in the past made it possible for the church's bishops to decide that the Latin rites, which had been stabilized since the Counter-Reformation in the 16th century, should be allowed to change again.

Among the discoveries of the historians regarding the development of the sacraments, the following can be cited as some of the more notable.

Baptism and confirmation were originally not separate rites but two moments in a lengthy ceremony which completed the initiation of adult catechumens into the church. This discovery has led to a restoration of adult catechesis and baptism as the primary analogue for understanding the sacrament and to the development of the Rite of Christian Initiation of Adults as a catechetical process for unbaptized persons seeking to become Catholics. At the same time that confirmation has received new meaning as an integral part of the initiation process, however, confirmation as a separate sacrament for Catholics baptized in infancy has suffered a loss of meaning. The medieval explanation, introduced to justify the practice of the separate sacrament, namely, that it bestows an increase of the Holy Spirit to prepare souls for the spiritual battles of adulthood, no longer seems tenable, and a completely satisfactory alternative has yet to be developed.

Penance or the sacrament of reconciliation in the form of private and repeatable confession to a priest evolved from an extra-canonical practice of Celtic monks who introduced it to the European mainland in the 5th and 6th centuries, after which it received approval by the hierarchy and became standard in the church. An earlier form of penance, the public repentance of notorious sinners, had emerged in the 2nd century out of the necessity of reconciling apostates and others who had left the Christian community, without resorting to a second baptism. This practice, presided over by the bishop and limited to once in a penitent's lifetime, was never extended to more than a small fraction of the Christian population, and by the 6th century it had practically disappeared. The adaptability of reconciliation in the church to cultural change accounts on the one hand for the development of three new rites since Vatican II, and on the other hand for the tendency of Catholics today to frequent the sacrament less than they had in the recent past.

Anointing of the sick was an extra-canonical practice with many regional variations until it was entered into the Gregorian Sacramentary in the 9th century and promulgated throughout the Holy Roman Empire. Originally intended for the sick, conditions in the Middle Ages led to the sacrament being performed mainly for the dying, as a result of which its name was changed to extreme unction, meaning "last anointing." The original name and intention of the sacrament have been restored in recent decades, although the revised rite makes provision for its use both in the case of serious illness and in the case of proximate death.

Even though the sacredness of Christian marriage had been recognized since the time of the apostles and the sacramentality of marriage had been discussed by Augustine, matrimony as an ecclesiastical ritual was not officially introduced in the Latin church until the 12th century. After some initial hesitance to call marriage a sacrament because of negative attitudes towards sexuality, the church's deep involvement in the ceremony and its consequences led to its being designated as a sacrament similar to the other six. The major developments since that time have occurred quite recently, both in the rite itself and in the theology of marriage, as a consequence of Vatican II.

Ordination in the sense of passing on ministerial office through the laying on of hands has been practiced since NT times, but the designation of some of the ordained as priests (*hiereis, sacerdotes*) emerged only gradually, first being applied to local church supervisors or bishops and later to community elders or presbyters. Many early ministers were married and they supported themselves by work apart from their ministry, but by the 4th century they constituted a separate class with diverse duties and ranks, whence the name holy orders. Beginning in the 6th century celibate monks were ordained for missionary work and Christian Europe became accustomed to an unmarried clergy, which custom became church law in the 12th century. Clerical training and ordination took place through a series of seven steps (minor and major orders), but since Vatican II this number has been reduced to three (diaconate, presbyterate and episcopate), and married men are again ordained to the diaconate. During the Middle Ages and afterwards the theology of the sacrament emphasized priestly power (e.g., to consecrate the eucharist and to administer absolution), but the revised rite focuses attention on the ministry of priestly service.

The weekly celebration of eucharist originated as a communal supper with a ritual sharing of bread and wine, but rather early the full meal was replaced by preparatory prayers and readings from the Sacred Scriptures. During the patristic era this simple liturgy was greatly expanded and embellished in the manner still observable in the Eastern churches. At the same time, the development of a high Christology and emphasis on the bread and wine as the body and blood of Christ led many to refrain from communion out of a sense of unworthiness. During the Middle Ages the laity were further excluded from participation in the liturgy by its being said in Latin and, for the most part, in silence. Devotional and theological attention was directed toward the consecration of the bread and wine, which the Scholastics explained by the theory of transubstantiation, while the Mass itself was interpreted as a participation in Christ's sacrifice. To counteract liberties which were taken with the sacrament, strict rubrics were enforced after the Council of Trent, and the Mass remained virtually unchanged for four centuries. More frequent reception of communion was encouraged, but preparation by first going to confession was regarded as the norm. After Vatican II the liturgy was revised with a more patristic model in mind, translated into modern languages, and allowed to be adapted to different cultures. Eucharistic theology returned to an emphasis on the sacred meal, and in that light the reception of communion has greatly increased.

Perhaps the greatest insight to be gleaned from the historical study of the sacraments is that the church has exercised tremendous liturgical creativity in response to pastoral need and cultural change. This creativity has been initiated sometimes within and sometimes outside the limits of Canon Law, but changes which were perceived as beneficial were eventually endorsed by the hierarchy.

Contemporary Human Sciences

The human sciences which have emerged in the modern era have shed additional light on the individual and social dimensions of ritual worship. Researchers and theorists in these fields study the outer and inner behavior of participants in religious rituals (or the records of such behavior) in order to arrive at general conclusions which describe and in some measure explain the human experience of such practices. To the extent that the sacraments are similar to practices in other religions, the conclusions of these investigators can be used to understand the Catholic experience of worship.

The *history of religions* and *comparative religions* reveal similarities between types of rituals and the symbolism they employ to refer to sacred mysteries and unseen realities. Almost all religions make use of initiation rites to mark a person's entry into a religious group or into a special class within that group. The initiate's new status is often signified by distinctive clothing and other appropriate symbols, such as the white garment which is received in baptism and the vestments which are worn in ordination. Transition rites, which are similar but broader in scope, designate passage from one condition to another within the larger religious community. Confirmation, when separate from baptism, can be perceived as such a ritual, as can matrimony, although marriage also brings with it duties and privileges which could qualify it as an initiation rite. Healing rites can be employed to effect either spiritual or physical well-being or both, especially in cultures which do not distinguish sharply between the two. Anointing of the sick, in its original and present forms, can be seen as being for both physical and spiritual healing, but in the later Middle Ages it was primarily for spiritual healing. Penance has always been a sacrament of spiritual healing, but as its new designation as the sacrament of reconciliation implies, the rite has also been an instrument of social healing. Ritual meals and sacrifices are also common in the world's religions, and it is understood better today than in the past why the two are usually found together. The essence of sacrifice is not killing or destruction but self-giving, symbolized by the sharing of food (that necessarily has to be prepared in some way), which results in an experience of communion. In the eucharistic liturgy all of these aspects are found: the self-giving of Christ to the Father and to the church, and the self-giving of the assembly to their Lord and to one another, recalled and symbolized in thankful offering and communion.

Although the above topologies are mainly for the purpose of classification, understanding the different types of rites provides helpful insights into the Catholic sacraments. An anthropologically more accurate understanding of sacrifice, for example, helps correct misunderstandings which were prevalent in medieval interpretations of the Mass, and a deeper appreciation of the nature of religious meals can help in the preparation of liturgies to highlight the dynamics of self-giving and communion. Similarly, spec-

ifying confirmation as a transition ritual raises questions about the nature of the transition which is celebrated in that sacrament, and leads to an examination of how Christians are or should be different after they are confirmed.

The *sociology of religion* and *religious anthropology* study the social aspects of religion present and past, including the social aspects of religious ritual. Arnold van Gennep (*The Rites of Passage*, 1960) in a now classical work on "rites of passage" has shown how initiation and transition rites contain the same basic three-fold structure. At the beginning of the rite, the subject or subjects of the ritual are in one condition, at the end of it they are in a different condition, and during their participation in the ritual they are strictly speaking in neither condition but in a state of passage from one to the other. The bride and groom at a wedding, for example, are neither single nor married while the ceremony is being performed but in transition from the single to the married state. Similar descriptions could be given for ordination, baptism and confirmation. The same analysis could be analogously extended even to healing rites, which effect a passage from a condition of illness to one of well-being. The traditional Catholic insistence that the sacraments are effective rituals (that they "effect what they signify") is thus supported by the findings of the human sciences.

In contrast to rites of passage are rites of intensification, which celebrate a condition already achieved and intensify the awareness of it. The ceremonies of religious feasts (such as Christmas and Easter) and of secular holidays (such as Thanksgiving and Independence Day) celebrate not something new but something already real and present in the life of the community. Participation in the rituals intensifies the awareness of the realities being celebrated. Of the seven sacraments, eucharist alone is primarily a rite of intensification, celebrating the reality of unity with and in Christ, although all rituals can intensify the awareness of the sacred realities symbolized. Important to point out in this context is the necessity of the actual presence of the reality being celebrated. To the extent, for example, that a parish lacks real unity as a cohesive body of Christ, there is less to celebrate than could otherwise be the case.

It is possible, however, for ritual to create as well as to reflect human realities. As a result of initiation and transition rites, for instance, human beings actually become something that they were not prior to the performance of the rite, e.g., members of the church, priests, married persons. Because they embody and communicate the ideas and values of a religious group, rituals also invite participants to believe more firmly in those ideas and to live according to those values. Nevertheless, rituals are not automatically effective in this way, but only to the extent that the rites vividly convey a convincing sense of the reality that they symbolize, and to the extent that participants actually perceive the ritual as revelatory of a sacred reality.

From the perspective of the *sociology of knowledge*, religious rites such as the sacraments perform a number of cognitive functions, some of which have already been alluded to. They have a unifying function since they gather a group in common performance around common symbols, thus enabling the members to perceive themselves as united in faith. They have a legitimating function since they publicly express values, beliefs and hopes, and thus give these ideas and ideals an objective standing in the social world. They have a communicating function since they pass knowledge of the religion from one generation to the next and from the more to the less initiated members of the community, and provide a social space in which to internalize that

knowledge. They also have what may be termed a prophetic function inasmuch as they symbolically speak out the deepest beliefs and highest values of the group, calling the members to live out in their everyday lives what they say about themselves in ritual.

On the one hand, generalizations such as these may be taken as descriptions of what occurs in sacramental rituals, but on the other hand they can also serve as prescriptions of what ought to be happening during these celebrations. That is, they provide heuristic clues as to what is often occurring during the ceremonies, but they also provide general norms as to what ought to be occurring in and for the religious community. To the extent that a particular celebration fails to fulfill these functions, liturgists and congregations have reason to examine their performance and participation in the sacrament in order to discover and correct the shortcomings in the next celebration.

This attitude of critical self-examination can help overcome the complacency which is endemic to all rituals inasmuch as the language of ritual is commonly declarative. That is, the words of the rite overtly declare what is happening in and through the ritual and only covertly disclose what ought to be happening but might in fact not be happening in any particular instance or series of instances. For example, in the baptism of an infant the words declare that the child is beginning a new life of faith in Christ, yet in a particular instance it might actually be the case that the parents have no intention of raising the child as an active member of the church. The same sort of analysis could also be extended to couples who want a church wedding but who do not fully appreciate the implications of Christian marriage, to young people who allow themselves to be confirmed but who are not in a position to live out their commitment, and to congregations that attend Mass every Sunday but are hardly a community who know one another and give themselves in service to one another.

Turning attention from the participants in the ritual to the celebration itself, one can search for shortcomings in the ritual that might be surmounted by more careful liturgical planning or more deliberate liturgical performance. Sacraments which do not unite participants but allow individuals to look on as scattered spectators, or which do not communicate but speak their message weakly and obscurely, are not living up to their full potential as symbolic acts of a religious community. An analysis of the sacraments from a variety of sociological perspectives can intensify the awareness of what they are and what they ought to be, not only generically as rituals but also specifically as celebrations of the particular realities they purport to symbolize. Such a study can help to perfect the congruence between the symbolic act and the living out of what the symbols refer to in the church.

Language, Symbol and Religious Psychology

The relation between symbols and what they symbolize has been an object of investigation in a number of human sciences ranging from philosophy to linguistics and from sociology to psychology. On the one hand, all language is conceded to be symbolic to a greater or lesser extent, and on the other, any symbol system has many of the properties of a language. Just as a language has a grammar and syntax which govern the proper use of words, a symbol system is governed by rules which determine the proper use of symbols.

In Christianity these rules are supplied by nature, tradition and doctrine. Natural symbols such as water, fire, light and darkness have a spontaneous propensity to convey meanings analogous to their symbolic forms, for example, refreshment, warmth, goodness and evil. Tra-

ditional symbols such as oil and the laying on of hands can convey meanings such as healing and empowerment, but only to those who are familiar with their traditional significance, since their use in ritual is somewhat removed from their occurrence in everyday life. Doctrine also governs the use of symbols, sometimes restricting the range of appropriate symbols as in the case of bread and wine for the eucharistic meal, but always designating the specifically Christian meaning of the symbols.

One reason for the doctrinal regulation of symbols is that in themselves symbols can have a variety of disparate meanings, not all of which are intended in any given symbolic act. At the same time, however, this richness of potential meaning is what gives symbols their power in ritual. Unlike ordinary words that have commonly accepted and well understood meanings, and unlike simple signs that have a one-to-one correspondence to what they signify, symbols can convey many meanings simultaneously. Water, for example, can mean not only refreshment and cleansing but also destruction and drowning. Touching can convey meanings of healing, forgiveness and empowerment. Eating can symbolize nourishment, sharing and communion. Even when some one meaning is intended in the symbolic act, other meanings may be evoked consciously or unconsciously.

This depth and richness of symbolism is one reason why *psychology* has been brought to bear on the understanding of symbolic ritual. The *depth psychology* of Carl Jung (*Psychology and Religion*, 1960) suggests not only that all symbols connect with hidden meanings in the personal unconscious of individuals but that some symbols point to universal meanings in the collective unconscious of all human beings. Many of these so-called archetypal symbols are natural symbols in the sense discussed above, but some of them have more to do with human nature than with the world of nature, referring to birth and death, strength and weakness, masculinity and femininity, age and youth, wisdom and folly. When symbolic rituals connect with these universal human meanings, they arouse feelings for what is most fundamental in life and a sense of solidarity with all who share the experience of being human.

If religion is taken in its etymological sense of binding back or reconnecting, religious ritual can be understood as providing opportunities in the life of the individual or community wherein they can feel reconnected with divine and transcendent mysteries. Such religious experiences have been termed hierophanies or manifestations of the sacred by Mircea Eliade (*The Sacred and the Profane*, 1959) in his work on the history of religions. Those who enter affectively and intentionally into a religious ritual find themselves psychologically transported from the world of ordinary space and time to a realm of sacred space and time in which the most meaningful realities become manifest to them. In this altered state of consciousness the participants encounter the divine and respond to its presence, acknowledge its truth and importance in their lives, and perceive its relevance to the human situation which is the occasion for the ritual.

This state of being in felt relationship with the transcendent has been variously described in the *psychology of religion*. William James (*The Varieties of Religious Experience*, 1932) called it a feeling of objective presence and a sense of the palpably real. Rudolph Otto (*The Idea of the Holy*, 1950) referred to it as the experience of the holy, something at once both awesome and fascinating, utterly different and profoundly entrancing. Victor Turner (*Forests of Symbols*, 1967) termed it a state of liminality, a condition on the edge of the ordinary but not entirely divorced from it, in which the sense of unity with the divine and community with others is heightened.

This type of human experience, found not just in Christianity but in all religions, suggests an experiential basis for some of the basic terminology in Catholicism's understanding of its sacraments. The most obvious is the doctrine of the real presence with regard to the eucharist, but to this must be added the belief that the presence and action of God are found in all the sacraments. The theology of sacramental grace, which at times seems very abstract and theoretical, is arguably rooted in experiences of God's graciousness encountered in sacramental worship. The new life which is begun through baptism, the strengthening which is attributed to confirmation, the forgiveness which is received in confession, and the healing which is bestowed through the anointing of the sick are all concepts which can be correlated to religious experiences. Likewise, the bond of marital love and the empowerment of priestly ministry can be understood as sacred realities which are perceived as initiating in their fullness from an assent to their disclosure in a sacramental moment.

Just as the sociological analysis of sacramental worship can reveal both what is and what ought to be occurring in the life of a religious community, so also a psychological analysis can reveal what is and ought to be happening for participants in symbolic rituals. To the extent that the symbols are actually functioning as symbols connecting or reconnecting participants with transcendent realities, religious persons encounter sacred meaning in the realm sacred time and space. To the extent that the symbols fall short of their purpose, however, participants fail to encounter the sacred and their experience is little different from their ordinary awareness of themselves and the world around them.

As suggested earlier, this shortfall may be traceable to inadequacies in the performance of liturgical rites which fail to evoke an experience of the sacred in the participants. In this case the performance itself has to be examined to determine what improvements could be made in order to elicit the appropriate response. But the shortfall may on the other hand be traceable to inabilities in the participants themselves to enter the realm of the sacred, in which case the participants' psychological capacity for ritual needs to be examined.

This psychological inability to fully engage in symbolic ritual or to fully appreciate its effects may be due to a number of factors both individual and cultural. *Developmental psychology*, especially the work of Erik Erikson (*Toys and Reasons*, 1977), suggests that individuals acquire the ability to engage in ritual through a series of stages, each of which builds upon and complements the preceding ones as the individual matures. Inadequate mastery of the earlier stages has a negative effect on the individual's ability to complete the later stages, and in the case of religious ritual such incompleteness could well result in an individual's going through the outward motions without having the inner experiences to which the rite symbolically refers.

The remedies for such incomplete development would seem to lie in religious education and catechesis, especially in preparation for the sacraments, through which individuals could be helped to understand the nature of religious ritual, appreciate its symbolism, and perceive its relevance to their lives. Moreover, since individuals develop not only during childhood but also through various phases of adult maturing, such efforts need to extend through the entire life cycle. This is true not only for sacraments which mark passages into different stages of the Christian life, but also for those which, like eucharist and reconciliation, are celebrated regularly.

Ritual and Culture

More difficult to remedy is an incapacity for ritual that may arise not on an individual but on a cultural level. Anthropologist Mary Douglas (*Natural Symbols*, 1973) has observed that in stable and socially stratified cultures, people enter more easily into ritual and are willing to be governed by its symbolized values and ideals, whereas in changing and socially mobile cultures people do not find ritual as meaningful. Along the same lines, Robert Bellah (*Habits of the Heart*, 1986) and others have argued that the individualism and pragmatism of contemporary culture make it difficult for people to affirm common beliefs such as those embodied in traditional religious ritual apart from those which have practical or personal significance.

One solution to this modern cultural trend would be to exercise tight canonical controls on the performance of the sacraments and strict doctrinal controls on their allowable meanings. This approach would have some sociological benefits for the institutional church inasmuch as the public celebration and interpretation of the sacraments would be clearly defined for those within and outside the church. On the other hand, given the diversity of global cultures in which Catholicism finds itself and the general fluidity of post-industrial culture, this approach would seem to be of questionable utility in meeting the diverse psychological needs of individuals and groups in those cultures. A more complex but potentially more satisfactory solution would seem to lie in the direction of permitting responsible experimentation in catechesis and celebration under broad canonical guidelines in order to discover ways to make the sacraments as meaningful and effective as possible.

Conclusion

The full range of human sciences could

be enlisted in such an endeavor to revitalize the sacraments in a variety of cultures and local situations. Psychology could help to understand the cognitive and affective impact of different ritual styles on different ethnic and age groups. Sociology could help to uncover the group dynamics which work best catechetically and liturgically. History could at once provide both examples from the past and instruction in pastoral sensitivity for creatively meeting the needs of the church both local and universal. And philosophy could supply a number of intellectual frameworks for interpreting the sacraments in ways that are theologically in keeping with the fundamental doctrines of Christianity.

See **Aesthetics, liturgical; Culture, liturgy and; Hermeneutics and worship; Historical research and liturgical renewal; Ritual; Symbol**

T. Fawcett, *The Symbolic Language of Religion* (Minneapolis: Augsburg, 1971). B. Lee, ed., *Alternative Futures for Worship* (7 vols.) (Collegeville: Liturgical Press, 1987). J. Martos, *The Catholic Sacraments* (Wilmington: Michael Glazier, 1983). J. Martos, *Doors to the Sacred* (New York: Doubleday, 1981). E. Nottingham, *Religion: A Sociological View* (New York: Random House, 1971). D. Power and L. Maldonado, *Liturgy and Human Passage (New York: Seabury Press, 1979).* G. Spinks, *Psychology and Religion* (Boston: Beacon Press, 1967). A. Wallace, *Religion: An Anthropological View* (New York: Random House, 1966). G. Worgul, *From Magic to Metaphor* (New York: Paulist Press, 1980).

JOSEPH MARTOS

I

IMAGINATION AND WORSHIP

Imagination is itself an "imaginative" word. In contrast to words like analysis, reflection, or explanation, which tend to narrow the focus of attention towards ordering, clarification and understanding, the term *imagination*, along with its verbal ally *creativity*, is evocative, opens out, points to the world of the new, the untried, the possible. Imagination plays many roles in its relation to Christian worship. Four will be examined here: (a) imagination in its popular sense as "creative" of worlds, i.e., worlds of fantasy, of fiction, of "make believe"; (b) imagination as a practical tool for planning and serving liturgical acts; (c) imagination as a personal appeal to human affections; and (d) imagination as a theological resource and an agent in human conversion. The overall aim is to uncover the service which imagination renders to the church in the worship of God and to God in the salvation and redemption of the world.

Imagination and the Creation of Worlds

In its popular sense *imagination* is a power to create new worlds. It produces Oz, Middle Earth, the Enterprise, Gotham City, the First and Second Foundations. It peoples these worlds with creatures of great variety: hobbits and Vulcans, witches and wizards, animals that talk and trees that walk. It sets people on great adventures and gives them bold undertakings. The worlds of imagination parallel our own, follow their own rules, offer their own terrors and delights. At first glance, imagination in this popular sense would seem to have little or nothing to do with Christian worship. A second glance, however, yields just the opposite.

The imaginative creation of worlds has a very definite role to play in Christian worship. Worship brings us into the reign of God, and the reign of God, as scripture portrays it, is not unlike some of the magical worlds of fiction and fantasy. The reign of God is inhabited by angels with six wings (two to cover their face, two to cover their feet, and two with which to fly), who touch coals to the prophet's tongue and give new boldness to the prophet's heart (Is 6:1-10); by dry bones that take on new flesh and new life (Ezek 37-6); by a woman who brings forth a child and a dragon who waits to devour it (Rev 12:1-6). It is peopled by children who die for the Prince of Peace, by a rider on a white horse, by a Lamb who opens scrolls. It is a land where milk and honey freely flow; a field where creatures cast themselves before a throne and cry "Worthy" (Rev 5:1—6:4). It is a world where a young boy sold into slavery rises to save both his family and his nation; where seas are parted and shepherds become kings, where devils are cast out and lame beggars walk. It is a mustard seed, a pearl of great price, a new city descending from on high. And it has its own rules. In the reign of God the poor are rich, the lowly are raised up, the dead are brought back to life. In the reign of God a carpenter turns his gaze to a city that welcomes, rejects, and then stands humbly and silent before him.

The worlds of fantasy delight those who enter them. They create new affinities among people; they fire up vision; they inspire great and noble deeds. They produce laughter and wonder, romance and bravado, and they awaken, as they say, the "little child" that resides in all of us. The reign of God is likewise a world that delights: lambs and lions play together and people rejoice as at a wedding feast. It summons forth hermits who dwell in its wonder, missionaries who travel far to tell its tale, martyrs who embrace even death in the serenity of its hope and its promise. And its cardinal rule? Unless you become as a little child, you cannot enter the reign of God.

In the action of Christian worship, men and women encounter God and enter into God's reign. There they meet all the creatures who inhabit God's reign, and form with them a voice that cries: "Holy," "Worthy," "Hosanna," "Amen." In Christian worship new relationships are forged, a wonderful vision is set out, and noble deeds are inspired and set in motion. Imagination is a powerful force to signify the holy deeds of God and to draw men and women mightily into those deeds. While it may seem at first glance that this popular sense of the imagination can have little or nothing to do with Christian worship, on second glance it is very much at worship's core.

Imagination and the Liturgical Act

Beyond the popular level, however, imagination means more than the creation of worlds. It is also a practical tool that serves both in planning and in bringing to life the liturgical actions of the church at prayer. Liturgical ritual is presented to the church in the most meager form of written text interspersed with even more meager rubrics or directives for its enactment. It falls to imagination to help transform those written texts into living actions by which people may "express in their lives and manifest to others the mystery of Christ and the nature of the true church" (S.C., 2). Imagination fulfills this task in three primary ways: translation, adaptation and creation.

Translation immediately suggests linguistic translation, e.g., from Latin text into English text. This is the narrowest sense of translation, and but the first undertaking of the practical imagination. Where linguistic translation needs to be made, four norms laid down for translation in the *Foreward* to the English edition of the Roman *Sacramentary* offer a helpful guide. (a)Translation should aim to preserve the intent and substance of the original; it should not be a literal transmission of each individual word. (b) The unit of meaning is the whole passage, not the individual word. (c) Translation should not exaggerate the importance of individual phrases to the extent that it weakens the meaning of the whole. (d) Some expressions may need to be paraphrased in order to concretize them for the celebration and needs of today.

In its larger sense, translation is from written text to liturgical act. This is not simply a piece by piece enactment, much less a mere recital, of the written text. There is substance and intent to every ritual act, and to each part of the ritual act, and this substance and intent need to be preserved and served.

The four norms given above for linguistic translation can serve this larger translation task as well. The ritual act is analogous to the linguistic sentence; it has its own proper order, logic, structure, and patterns of meaning. As with the sentence, so with the ritual act, it is the whole more than the individual pieces that is to be served. The unit of meaning is the sections of the ritual rather than the individual prayers or gestures that comprise it. Individual elements ought not be exaggerated in importance to the extent that the ritual section or the ritual as a whole is weakened or distorted. Some prayers already translated and possibly paraphrased may need to be paraphrased even further, and some ritual actions may need the non-verbal analogue of paraphrasing, to concretize them for the celebration and needs of today.

The liturgical documents recognize that even this larger sense of translation may not be sufficient in the transit from liturgical text to liturgical act. *Adaptation* may be required as well. "Even in the liturgy the Church has no wish to impose a rigid uniformity in matters that to not affect the faith or the good of the whole community" (S.C., 37). Two levels of adaptation are envisioned. "Provisions shall also be made, even in the revision of liturgical books, for legitimate variations and adaptations to different groups, regions and people..." (S.C., 38). "In some places and circumstances, however, an even more radical adaptation of the liturgy is needed" (S.C., 40).

A careful use of imagination is required in the process of adaptation. Two dangers in particular present themselves. The first is superficiality, the transfer from one symbolic form to another without sufficiently grasping the intent, the purpose, or the symbolic context of either. The suggestion to use pizza and coke for eucharist with teenagers on the grounds that this is their "common food" is an example of such superficial transfer. The second is a form of rationalism, the

transfer to a new symbolic form based on an idea drawn from the old form. Reduction of the flowing waters of the baptismal fount to a sarcophagus-shaped pool to represent the death into which one is baptized is an example of rationalistic transfer. Imagination needs to grasp the emotional content or affect of a symbol as well as its suggestive possibilities, and not simply its "meaning," before it can successfully bring forth true symbolic adaptation.

Finally, there is *creation*. At times new symbolic forms need to be forged. The danger here is to think that symbols can be created *ex nihilo*, and to forget that it belongs to God alone, and not to humans, to create from nothing. The "bottom line" norm set down in the *Constitution on the Sacred Liturgy* for liturgical creativity is not only liturgically sound, it is symbolically sound as well: "Finally, there must be no innovations unless the good of the Church genuinely and certainly requires them; care must be taken that any new forms adopted should in some way grow organically from forms already existing" (S.C., 23).

Symbols arise to express a depth of experience that cannot be expressed in any other way (Paul Ricoeur). Creation of symbols requires newness of experience. Yet experience itself is guided by existing symbols. New symbols are required, not when the old symbols fail, but when they succeed in taking one to a new experiential depth which they themselves can no longer express. New ideas are born by holding together elements of thought that previously were not held together. New symbols are born by holding together symbolic pieces that previously were not held together. It is in this "bringing together" of what was previously held apart that true creativity lies. A triumphant hymn during the Good Friday adoration of the cross, a menorah candle lit between the new fire and the paschal candle of the Easter vigil, photographs of war victims, hunger victims, victims of those who threaten human life as a modern day "stations of the cross" are but some few examples of such creativity.

This practical task of the liturgical imagination, involving translation, adaptation and creation, can be aided by a simple, five-stage process. These stages constitute the passage from liturgical text to liturgical act; they can serve as a process of liturgical planning as well. The five stages are: (1) preparing the text; (2) dwelling with the text; (3) locating the text; (4) enlivening the text; and, (5) enacting the text. Each of these involves the imagination in a variety of ways.

(1) Preparing the Text

By "text" is meant here the entire collection of prayers, readings, introductions and responses that serve as the basic sub-structure of the liturgy. When the liturgy in question does not have a text given (e.g., a prayer service during a retreat), the first task is to draw on liturgical resources and / or creative talent to construct the text. When the liturgy in question does have a text given, the task involves selection, evaluation, and assessment of intent, purpose and aptness for a particular assembly or occasion. "There must be the utmost care to choose and to make wise use of those forms and elements provided by the Church that, in view of the circumstances of the people and the place, will best foster active and full participation and serve the well-being of the faithful" (G.I.R.M., chap. 1, 5).

Things to note in the text: (a) theme or themes that flow through the text, especially those proper to season or occasion; (b) flow of the ritual (preserving the rhythm, giving major stress to major parts, minor stress to minor parts): (c) language and imagery (being sensitive to employ inclusive language and images that invite participation); (d) appropriate-

ness of various options (e.g., penitential rite may not be proper for some celebrations). The liturgical sources contain a rich mine of materials upon which the liturgical imagination can train itself; it is rarely necessary, and seldom possible, to create texts *ab ovo*.

(2) Dwelling with the Text

The aim here is to come in touch with the inner spirit of the text. This can serve the imagination in coming to a deeper sense of the sub-structure of the text (its inner "feel" or affect). A helpful process: read the liturgical text aloud; identify what stands out; try to name why it stands out; identify clusters of sentiment and mood; put the scripture readings and the inner spirit together in some context of prayer. This second phase is *not* concerned with concrete details of planning, and should not turn to that too soon. Its aim is to bring the imagination into the inner spirit of the particular liturgical text which it seeks to translate into prayer.

(3) Enlivening the Text

Drawing on the mood surfaced in (b), and with respect for the dynamics of the individual parts of the text, the attempt here is to discover the proper medium of expression for the text and its various parts. Concern is for music (what parts are best expressed in musical mode), movement (are there gestures or movements that need to be incorporated), ritual action (what actions suggest themselves or are integral to the text, and how best to enact them). One has imagined at this point an already highly translated liturgical text: the "enlivened" text. It is with this text the imagination should continue to work.

(4) Locating the Text

Two things are involved here: the proper use of space to allow the liturgy to begin and the proper use of space that allows the liturgy to unfold. Under the first, it should be remembered that the assembly encounters the space *before* the action of liturgy begins, and for them at least the liturgy begins in this space. The atmosphere and mood of the space need to be appropriate and integral to the liturgical act that will take place in it. Under the second, it should be noted that different parts of the liturgy call for different space configurations. Attention should be paid to those configurations; they should be such as to allow the intended action properly to take place within them. At the same time, they should not be intrusive on other parts of the liturgy where they are inappropriate.

Questions of space involve more than configurations. The document produced by the U.S. Bishops' Committee on the Liturgy, *Environment and Art in Catholic Worship* (1978), is indispensable for "locating the text." To name just some of the elements which the document sets forth: liturgical space should be hospitable (11), convey a sense of mystery (12), and, quite simply, be beautiful (34). The demands which liturgy places on liturgical space and all that fills it are two: quality (20) and appropriateness (21).

(5) Enacting the Text

Text is not liturgy until the people assemble and begin to act. As the liturgy unfolds, proper ministries should be observed and the ministers should be competent to fulfill the assigned ministries. People should be appointed in advance, trained (in walking, reading, speaking, moving, etc.), and urged to carry out their ministry prayerfully. The rhythm and flow of the liturgical action need to be respected, and anything abrupt, haphazard or simply sloppy needs studiously to be avoided. It is important that as many ministers as possible engage in the planning. This way they will grasp both the inner spirit and the outward flow of the liturgical action which they are responsible to enact.

Imagination and Human Affections

As the liturgical act begins to unfold, imagination takes on yet another liturgical task. It serves the action of grace by appealing to and shaping human affections. Imagination here takes on a more profound meaning than either the creation of worlds or the practical transit from liturgical text to liturgical act. It becomes, as William Lynch names it, "all the resources of man, all his faculties, his whole history, his whole life, and his whole heritage, all brought to bear upon the concrete world inside and outside of himself, to form images of the world, and thus to find it, cope with it, shape it, even make it" (*Christ and Prometheus*, p. 23). Within the liturgical act imagination becomes a power of the human person to reconstruct reality: to liberate from bondage, to transform one's image of oneself, to reshape the way the world sees itself. Within the liturgical act imagination brings new life to the human spirit, and in so doing, can change persons, relationships, indeed the course of human history itself.

To understand the importance and scope of this task, four points of contrast between the pre- and post-conciliar church need to be noted. First, in the 1917 Code of Canon Law sacraments were treated under the heading "*de rebus*, on things"; they are treated in the revised Code (1983) under the heading "The Office of Sanctifying in the Church." Second, before the council sacraments were seen as vehicles of grace to be conferred by the proper minister and in the proper form upon the recipients; in the *Constitution on the Sacred Liturgy* they are liturgical acts of the church in assembly, actions "of Christ the Priest and of his Body which is the Church" (S.C.,7). Third, prior to the council the sign value of sacraments was not given primary treatment in the question of sacramental efficacy; Christ was the agent, and his agency was governed by the minimal observance of matter and form. In the *Constitution on the Sacred Liturgy*, the sign value of sacraments is strongly linked to sacramental efficacy: "In the liturgy, by means of signs perceptible to the senses, human sanctification is signified and brought about in ways proper to each of these signs" (*ibid.*). Finally, the conception of grace as conferred by sacraments was somewhat reified in pre-conciliar sacramental theology: grace as *thing*. Post-conciliar sacramental theology embraces the conception of grace formulated by E. Schillebeeckx (grace as *encounter*) and by K. Rahner (grace as a *free offer* of God's own self).

In the post-conciliar church, therefore, sacraments are envisioned as liturgical events in which God graciously offers God's own self to men and women and seeks to call out from them a free and generous surrender to God's action within them. Since this is done through the medium of signs and symbols, imagination is very much involved in the process. And since the offer is made to the human heart, the desires and the affections of those who enact sacraments are likewise very much involved in the process.

Within the liturgical act, the primary task of imagination is to make God's offer powerful and commanding, and to effect receptivity and response on the part of those to whom it is offered. Imagination can do this only by making *appeal* to human affections. The action of God cannot be forced or imposed. God's offer is a free gift of love, and must wait upon a free response of love in return. The images set forth in Christian liturgy are not the only images that claim and operate in human life. The resistance to grace, which theology names sin, is also the operation of imagination and affection. The affections of sin are powerful. Christian faith does not diminish, much less erase them. It simply proclaims that the affections of grace are stronger, and more humanly true, and sets forth its own images of faith in the hope that their appeal will be stronger, and that in freedom people will be drawn to embrace them. It sets forth in images the action and desires of God. Imagination serves these by awakening desires in and appealing to the affections of those whose *Amen*, i.e., free surrender, God desires.

D. Saliers identifies the importance of affections in the human relationship with God: "The concept of affection designates a basic attunement which lies at the heart of a person's way of being and acting. In quite specific ways, our affections qualify our perceptions, our fundamental attitudes, and our behavior" (*The Soul in Paraphrase*, p. 7). He reminds us that the activities of Christian prayer, and in particular of Christian liturgy, are not just activities. They carry within themselves their own proper affections toward God, toward ourselves and toward each other, affections that are the affections of Jesus Christ himself.

These affections can be powerful in us because Christ himself, as the revelation of God, is likewise the revelation of our own deepest human truth. His affections are not extrinsic or foreign to us; they are our own proper affections, and known to be such, when we touch and are in tune with our own deepest truth. The appeal made by imagination in service of grace is not to graft something alien upon the human heart, but rather to awaken in the human heart what is most properly its own. Christian liturgy exposes human life to itself, and at the same time fashions human life to its own deepest truth.

Imagination in worship, therefore, has a constructive as well as an instructive role to play. The affections are appealed to so that a free response may be given to God. They are at the same time shaped and fashioned in such wise that the more they become the affections of Christ the more they become the true affections of the human heart which the human heart was designed by God to express and follow. Recognition of this identify between what appears to come as imposed from without and what is in fact awakened from within is itself the point of free human response to God's gracious self-offer. Surrender to this identity is salvation and sanctification.

In service of human affections and desires, there are several things both practical and theological that the liturgical imagination must attend to. (a) Both texts and rites should express clearly the holy things they signify (S.C., 21). (b) The symbolic purpose of the rites and symbols is to dispose the faithful to receive the gracious action of God upon them fruitfully and effectively (S.C., 59). (c) Symbols should be employed generously, not sparingly. (d) Symbols gain in power when they are associated with other symbols in a rich "symbolic world" (Ricoeur). (e) Rites and symbols are not designed to communicate information; they convey the personal presence and approach of God; they present God's free offer of love (Rahner). (f) Rites and symbols seek to awaken the response of surrender, *Amen*, to the approach and action of God. (g) Rites and symbols thus aim to appeal to human freedom and to human affections that humans may choose the way of God over the way of sin. (h) The task of imagination within the liturgical act is to make the ways of God desirable, and to bring one's human affections into such harmony with the affections of Christ that the human affections find there and recognize there their own proper shape and truth.

Imagination and Human Behavior
The final role of imagination which we consider here follows closely upon this last. Imagination serves to transform human behavior and thus serves the process of human conversion.

Ricoeur speaks of the proper response to symbols as "consent wrested from refusal." It is toward that end that imagination needs to make its powerful appeal. Along the path to consent, one must ask, and be guided to ask, "what does this mean to me?" Liturgically this is the deeper sense of participation which S.C. had in mind when it declared: "The Church earnestly desires that all the faithful be led to that full, conscious, and active participation in liturgical celebrations called for by the very nature of the liturgy. Such participation by the Christian people as 'a chosen race, a royal priesthood, a holy nation, God's own people' (1 Pet 2:9) is their right and duty by reason of their baptism. In the reform and promotion of the liturgy this full and active participation by all the people is the aim to be considered before all else. For it is the primary and indispensable source from which the faithful are to derive the true Christian spirit..." (S.C., 14). Participation in the liturgical act is not simply a question of standing, singing, moving, responding; it is finally a question of prayer and conversion.

The existential question includes both meaning and implication for action. As it brings the liturgical rites and symbols to focus on one's concrete human life, it brings both judgment (what does it mean) and possibility for choice (what might it mean). Appeal to the affections contains within itself appeal to behavior as well. Consent, if freely given, internalizes within oneself that which was presented: God's own presence and action. In such internalization one finds that one both *wants* to do what God's offer of love suggests and that one *can* do what God's offer of love suggests. It is both conversion of heart and empowerment for action.

William Lynch presents this under the rubric of hope, itself the affection of desire and yearning. Lynch equates hope with imagination (*Images of Hope, p. 23*), and offers several characteristics of the way hope "imagines" which must be observed if hope is to liberate one from hopelessness and bondage. Hope imagines the *real* (it transforms one's actual life; it does not provide escape from it). Hope is not *unlimited* (not everything can be hoped for; to think so is to fall prey to disillusionment). Hope imagines *with* (hopelessness emerges at the limits of one's own resources; hope requires the imagination of another). Hope is related to *wishing and desire* (it arises from deep within the person's affections).

Christian liturgy presents its participants with a real option for human life, the way first *lived* by Jesus Christ. It addresses the participants, not at a superficial level of their life, but at its core, where their own deepest desires as human persons emerge. It presents the imagination of the *Other* who is capable of seeing into human life far beyond our own limited view, and who therefore can lead us deeper into its mystery. And it does this, not simply by cognitive instruction, but rather by actively engaging us in the behavior that is proper to life in God. In Christian liturgy we *do* heal, we *do* forgive, we *do* greet each other in peace. The way of Christ is presented not as something we might possibly some day be able to live ourselves; for a brief moment in Christian liturgy we do in fact live it. At this point imagination is more than appeal to affection. It is itself the conversion of life, the restructuring of reality according to the ways of Christ. It is not only the actual (as lived by Christ) made possible; it is the possible made actual in our lives. Imagination is the human encounter with God who graciously offers himself in love and even more graciously gives human life its own proper shape.

Conclusion

We have ranged in this article from the playful to the profound in tracking the role of imagination in Christian worship. We have equally ranged from its service to ritual, as a practical tool to shape those special moments of worship which are named sacraments, to its service to grace, as a power to awaken in the lives of men and women that full and true worship of God which Paul proclaimed at Rome (Rom 12:1-2). Through it all imagination emerges as indispensable to the act of worship. It is clear that without imagination one cannot worship God at all. But more becomes clear as well. As a power to transform all creation toward God, human imagination is itself the worship of God, and the power of God made flesh.

See **Adaptation, liturgical; Creativity, liturgical; Symbol; Reverence; Liturgy and Christian life; Conversion from sin; Conversion to faith**

John Coulson, *Religion and Imagination: "in aid of a grammar of assent"* (New York: Oxford; London: Clarendon, 1981). Ray L. Hart, *Unfinished Man and the Imagination* (New York: Herder and Herder, 1968). Urban T. Holmes, III, *Ministry and Imagination* (New York: Seabury, 1976). Philip S. Keane, *Christian Ethics and Imagination* (New York: Paulist, 1984). William Lynch, *Christ and Prometheus* (Notre Dame: University Press, 1970); *Images of Hope* (Notre Dame: University Press, 1974, orig. 1965). John Macmurray, *Reason and Emotion* (London: Faber and Faber, 1935). Karl Rahner, *Foundations of Christian Faith*, trans. W. Dych (New York: Seabury, 1978). Paul Ricoeur, *Symbolism of Evil*, trans. E. Buchanan (New York: Harper & Row, 1967). Philip J. Rossi, *Together Toward Hope* (Notre Dame: University Press, 1983). Don E. Saliers, *The Soul in Paraphrase: Prayer and the Religious Affections* (New York: Seabury, 1980). Peter E. Fink, S.J., "Three Languages of Christian Sacraments," in *Worship* 52, 6 (Nov 78): 561-575; "Liturgy and Pluriformity," in *The Way* (April 1980): 97-107. Madeleine Simon, "Space for Worship," in *The Way* (April 1980): 108-118.

PETER E. FINK, S.J.

INCENSE, USES OF

The word incense comes from the

Latin *incendere*, which means to burn or to kindle. Most of the substances used as incense come from trees and plants. These substances include aloe, camphor, cloves, sandalwood, cinnamon or cassia, myrrh, frankincense, cedar, juniper, and balsam. The most used among these has been frankincense or *olibanum*. Frankincense is gum or resin yielded from trees of the *boswellia* species.

The use of incense was a significant part of religious rites in various cultures of the ancient world. In the pre-Christian world, six uses of incense can be identified: 1) as a sacrifice to the deity; 2) as an exorcism to drive away evil spirits; it was also associated with healing and purification; 3) as a sacrifice to the shades of a deceased human being; 4) to give veneration to a living person; 5) as an accompaniment to processions, offering a touch of flair, festivity and rejoicing; 6) as a refreshing perfume at banquets and other occasions.

Underneath these religious and cultic uses for incense is the practical use that it had in attempting to do away with unpleasant odors such as sweat and putrefaction. Early evidence for the use of incense is found in countries and cultures situated in warm climates, where incense would be necessary in attempting to do away with these unpleasant smells. To offer something pleasant to the nostrils seems to be an important motivation for the use of incense in religious rites and in daily life.

The use of incense was a widespread practice in Jewish religious cult, as is attested to in the Hebrew Scriptures, especially the books of Exodus, Leviticus and Numbers. The meaning of incense is proffered in the psalms. Psalm 141, for example, likens the use of incense to an oblation offered to obtain the protection and the blessing of God.

During the early centuries of the Common Era, Christianity was most reluctant to include the use of incense in its worship. In fact, early Christian writers of the first four centuries denounced the use of incense. No doubt, this reluctance was prompted by the association of incense with emperor worship, the ceremonies of the pagan world and the test of loyalty to the emperor which Christians were forced to endure.

The earliest instance of a Christian use of incense is in the funeral procession of St. Peter of Alexandria in 311. The use of incense at funeral processions portrayed the difference between the Christian and the pagan attitudes to death. The pagan attitude understood death as practically an end, without future prospects. The Christian attitude was one of hope in a world where death had lost its sting. Christian funeral processions, therefore, copied triumphal processions in which incense had an important part.

Christian writers of the 4th century slowly began to change their views on the use of incense. The honorific use of incense to venerate the relics of saints, altars, holy places and persons was initially the most common reason for its usage. The introduction of incense into the offices of matins, lauds and vespers signalled a sacrificial use of incense. In his *Commentary on Ps 140*, John Chrysostom claimed that the vesper service was basically a penitential rite. The use of incense during vespers was thus given a propitiatory meaning. It expressed the human self-offering of repentance.

By the Middle Ages, complex rubrics associated with the many uses of incense were a part of the Western liturgy. From these usages, three principle meanings of incense came to be identified in the medieval world. First, incense was considered an honorific, by which persons, places and things were given veneration and honor. Second, it was regarded as a propitiatory oblation for forgiveness and repentance. Third, the use of incense was understood as a form of exorcism. This third meaning is attested to in the texts of

596

the blessing of the censer which prayed that the incense would dispel demons and protect persons and places from evil.

The liturgical reforms of the Second Vatican Council have modified the uses of incense. In the Roman rite incense continues to be used in various liturgical ceremonies at the choice and discretion of the ministers. In the celebration of the eucharist, incense, if it is used, is used in the entrance procession, at the proclamation of the gospel and at the preparation of the gifts to incense the offerings, the ministers and the assembly. For the celebration of the liturgy of the hours, the people and the altar may be incensed during the gospel canticle of morning and evening prayer. Incense is used around the paschal candle before the singing of the Easter *Praeconium*. During the celebration of the dedication of a church building, incense is used to consecrate the eucharistic table. This usage originated in the practice of accompanying the procession of the relics of saints with incense. Relics of saints continue to be imbedded in the altar table during its consecration. Incense is used at the celebration of eucharistic devotions and at the rites of Christian burial. The new rubrics stipulate *when* incense is to be used, but refrain from attributing a *meaning* to this usage.

Incense continues to be a constitutive part of the celebration of the liturgy in the Eastern churches; its use in the Roman liturgy, since the reforms of the council, is changing. Pastorally, in some parts of the church, there is a tendency to use incense rarely, or not at all. This seems to be because its usage is seen to be connected with attitudes of triumphalism of a former liturgical order. In future developments, other cultural considerations will influence the frequency and the manner of the use of incense.

E.G. Cuthbert, F. Atchley, *A History of the Use of Incense* (London: Longmans, Green and Co., 1909).

Kjeld Nielsen, *Incense in Ancient Israel* (Leiden: E.J. Brill, 1986).

RICHARD N. FRAGOMENI

INCLUSIVE LANGUAGE

The term "inclusive language" refers to words intentionally selected to redress the bias inherent in centuries-long use of language employed by the dominant culture. It refers to words, therefore, which remove women from the invisibility and inferiority imposed upon them by such phrases as "mankind," "brotherhood of man," "the weaker sex," etc. It refers to the conscious substitutions of positive phrases in referring to people of color, instead of vilifying expressions like "blackmail," "blackball," "blackguard," etc. And it refers to deliberately chosen words which refer to those who suffer patently observable impairments, calling them "mute," for instance, instead of "dumb," or "differently abled" instead of "disabled" or "handicapped."

Inclusive language emphasizes clarity and honesty. It proceeds from an overriding value-judgment that one race or gender is not superior to another, or that one is not less human for being sense-impaired. Inclusive language identifies the positive and equally important contributions of many different peoples and experiences. Inclusive language pertains to verbal and nonverbal images that describe both humankind and God.

Human or "Horizontal" Language

Discriminatory descriptions of women provide the most common illustrations of the need for inclusive language. Women are categorized as inferior to men. Such sexist or exclusive language evolved from the socio-cultural bias against women, where the nouns "man," "men" and "brothers" and the pronoun "he" refer to both women and men. This androcentric language clearly conveys that male is the norm and female is a subspecies of male. Inclusive language corrects this misconception through both gender-specific language and "emancipatory" language, i.e., words and images that acknowledge the distinctive contribution women make to the fullness of human experience (Procter-Smith). In addition to concerns about gender, inclusive language is sensitive to all examples of implicit bias in our language: race superiority (white is purer than black); physical ability ("rectitude" as a word describing right and "sinister" the left; sheep on the right, goats on the left); and a host of others.

History

A cursory glance at significant moments in linguistic history makes clear that the choice of male pronouns and nouns used generically was based on the patriarchical view of the ordering of society. As early as 1560 there is evidence that grammar was determined by the "natural" order, i.e., man precedes woman. By 1850 an Act of Parliament in England eliminated the use of "he or she" when referring to human beings, substituting "he" alone.

Since the beginning of the 20th century, questions have been raised about androcentric words used generically for all humankind. The most serious challenges have occurred since 1960 in conjunction with the civil rights and women's movements. Linguistic scholars suggest that "true generics" implies equal application. This mutuality does not exist with words such as "man," "brothers," and "men" because no one understands woman to imply man, sisters to include brothers, nor women, men. Instead, the use of such language renders women invisible and implies inferiority. Inclusive language offers one of many necessary correctives for this situation.

Theological or "Vertical" Language

The patriarchal context that influenced "horizontal" language impacted the development of theological language as well. The primacy of male language for God also was fully acceptable. Recent linguistic and theological thinking raises serious questions about the "normative" character of male imagery for God. It offers fresh interpretations of biblical texts and theological positions long used to undergird traditional arguments for the sole use of male metaphors for God, predominantly Father, though also King, Lord, Master, and Prince. Male language limits the revelation of God and promotes idolatry (the worship of any image of God as though it were God).

Theologians throughout history understand their task as one of relating the nature of God to contemporary experience. Christological doctrines and trinitarian formulas have emerged from such study and debate. In the ongoing explanation of these aspects of human/divine relationship questions appear. One such critique concerns the use of exclusively male metaphors for God. They inherently communicate that God is like a man (especially *father*) and that men are like God. Such implications undermine the power of women to be images of God as well as to mediate God's grace.

Implications for Sacramental Practice

Invitations of God embodied in the process of preparation for and performance of the sacraments involve an offer of freedom, of access to inexhaustible divine mystery and of a relationship of unimaginable love. This articulation requires utmost sensitivity and honesty. Language restrictions that suggest some human participants in this sacramental encounter are more significant than others, or that God's image is more concretely known through male metaphors rather than female ones, limit the fullness of the encounter. Examples span a spectrum from hymns, prayers, gestures, and models of leadership, which do not express an integrated human community, to "essential" theological formulas which use only male metaphors such as Father, Son and Holy Spirit. (Though some suggest that the Holy Spirit has female referents, pronouns do not ordinarily confirm any such tradition.)

Concerns about inclusive language provide a serious critique of sacramental practice. They challenge the post-conciliar church to examine the theology and ecclesiology embodied in the celebration of sacramental liturgies so that the significance of these moments reflects more honestly the fullness of divine/human relationships.

See **Language, liturgical; Language and human experience**

Marjorie Procter-Smith, *In Her Own Rite: Constructing Feminist Liturgical Tradition* (Nashville: Abingdon, 1990). *An Inclusive Language Lectionary*, National Council of the Churches of Christ in the U.S.A., 1983. Mary Collins, "Inclusive Language: A Cultural and Theological Question," in *Worship: Renewal to Practice* (Washington, D.C.: Pastoral Press, 1987).

JANET WALTON

INCULTURATION OF THE LITURGY

As the title of this essay indicates, our concern is not with inculturation *and* the liturgy, but inculturation *of* the liturgy. The focus will be on the process, methods, attitudes, and persons involved in assuring that the liturgy truly reflect the culture of those who celebrate it. While many aspects of the church's liturgy deserve attention, we will reflect for the most part on the eucharistic liturgy.

The larger *context*, however, for a discussion of the inculturation of the liturgy must be the question of authentic living, giving witness to, and celebrating the Christian faith. The liturgy is surely a privileged area of inculturation, one most tangible. But liturgy is the public celebration of the faith of a particular people, and unless that lived faith is inculturated into the customs and culture of that people, the liturgy will remain foreign or even imposed, rather than flowing from the lives of the people.

The *goal* desired in inculturation of the liturgy is a eucharistic celebration that is vital, challenging, and liberating. The worshipping community is confronted and comforted by the word of God which is explored in a homily that relates the word to their particular context. Then they are sacramentally linked with the paschal mystery of Jesus Christ and strengthened to go forth and live that mystery in their situation. The eucharist, if truly inculturated, is indeed the source and summit of Christian life, and impels those who actively participate to go forward to witness to that life in the marketplace.

The *problem* of inculturation of the liturgy arises precisely because, in at least the most recent history of the liturgy, there has been in the Latin Catholic church an emphasis preserving the unity of the church's liturgy, often at the expense of her catholicity. The Tridentine rite had been the predominant form of worship in Latin Roman Catholicism from Trent until the breakthrough of the Second Vatican Council. This meant that even as the church expanded from Europe to North and South America, to India and the Far East, and more recently to Africa, it was this same Roman rite that was uniformly celebrated.

In the movement towards full inculturation, authors speak of *degrees* or *stages* of inculturation. A first stage, which is really the absence of inculturation is *imposition*, where the theology and liturgy of Europe, for example, is exported to the Americas or to Africa, with no input from the receiving culture. A second stage or degree is *translation*, where at least the local languages are employed in catechesis and liturgy. A third stage would be *adaptation*, or *accommodation*. Here minor changes are allowed, and at least some attention and respect is given to the local culture. This is explored in Vatican II in S.C. 37-39. Finally, true *inculturation* can occur where the local culture is seriously studied and supplies new creative impetus and input for liturgical celebrations. S.C. 40 speaks of this deeper or more radical adaptation. Yet in reality, one must admit that there are only a few examples of such true inculturation, e.g., in the liturgy of Zaire and in certain Indian churches.

Vatican II was clearly part of the recent trend to appreciate cultural diversity and richness. The *Constitution on the Sacred Liturgy*, with its fostering of the vernacular language in the liturgy, is simply one small beginning in the more difficult and unexplored moves to inculturation of the liturgy. The *Pastoral Constitution on the Church in the Modern World* presents a new appreciation of culture and impels the church to dialogue with the modern world rather than withdraw from it. So too, the *Decree on the Missionary Activity of the Church* sees mission as flowing from the incarnation of the Word, and states that the same pattern of incarnation must take place in every culture on this earth. The seeds of the Word (*semina Verbi*) are present in all cultures, and thus the missionary treads on holy ground when he or she encounters another culture. All of these provide a foundation and impetus for inculturation in all areas of Christian life, including in a special way the liturgy.

How does this inculturation take place? What are the attitudes that must be present in church leadership and in the people of God for it to occur? Who actually carries out the challenging task of inculturation of the liturgy? We will attempt to address these key questions through the employment of the pastoral circle. Imagine a circle with three points

on its circumference, and with arrows pointing back and forth between the points on the circumference. The first point of the circle represents the rich liturgical traditions of the church going back to the NT. This would also include contemporary official church teaching on the liturgy as in Vatican II as well as the rich diversity of liturgical expression found throughout the Catholic church today. The second point of the circle represents the local community in its particular cultural situation or context. This might be in New York or Nairobi or a small village in India or in Africa. The third point refers to the pastoral or liturgical leadership of that local community—those in charge of planning and celebrating the liturgy.

To assure that a liturgy be truly local and hence inculturated, and yet to assure that it be truly Christian and Catholic, the liturgical leaders need familiarity with the various possibilities of liturgical expression and symbolism offered by the Christian tradition (the first point of the circle). They also need to be immersed in their local culture, so that they know how that particular community gathers, prays, sings, expresses its faith most in accord with their cultural heritage (the second point on the circle). The leadership must of course not act on its own, but always in dialogue with the larger church, and with the authorities of the church. And the leadership (the third point on the circle) must realize that it will succeed only to the extend that it calls forth and involves the gifts, talents, and sensibilities of the community for which it is responsible. Liturgy is indeed the public prayer of the people, of the local community, and it must be an expression of their faith and their struggle for a life of justice, their living the Kingdom vision. Thus in the moving to a truly inculturated liturgy, it is the entire community that must eventually take responsibility for the liturgy, even if in its formative stages this will depend heavily upon the liturgical leaders and their collaborators.

Inculturation of the liturgy thus must occur in every local church, and not simply be thought of as applying to Africa or Asia. As a matter of fact, the need for inculturation can be seen most clearly in non-Western cultures. But the need for it can also be seen in a black or Hispanic parish in the U.S. So too, a liturgy for children or you should have a different tone than one for adults, and a liturgy in the heart of New York City must be somewhat different from one in a rural area of Montana. Thus every Christian community has the challenging task of celebrating the liturgy in a manner that is faithful to the Christian tradition (represented by the first point on the circle) and appropriate to its particular context (the second point on the circle).

There are several areas of inculturation of the liturgy, just as there are degrees of inculturation. One might begin with the language of the celebration or with liturgical vestments that better reflect local culture and clothing. The music might be adapted to employ local instruments. Yet these are only small beginnings. Every aspect of liturgy must be creatively examined, including the time and space for the celebration, the gestures and postures (sitting rather than kneeling), the forms of prayer (more use of litany/responses), art and architecture (local or imported stations of the cross), images and symbols that grow from the religious and cultural sensibilities of the people, the mode of leadership (individual or communal, male and/or female). Even the basic elements of the celebration, food and drink, become part of the search of the local community for ways in which to live and celebrate liturgically its Christian faith. If this community, led by the Spirit, with the help of liturgical expertise, and in union with the universal church, creatively and faithfully expresses its faith, then it will in turn be contributing to the growth of the catholicity of the church. We see this already occurring through the church in Zaire, and through the possibilities it offers both to African Catholics and to the universal church.

How did this creative new liturgical expression originate? One must first recall that the Roman rite even at the time of Vatican II was only one, even if very important, rite of the church. One must see that the form of the liturgy as brought to Africa by the missionaries is indeed one form, and one that can be developed in accord with liturgical principles and guidelines from church authorities. And even within the present rite there is space for and a call for adaptation and limited flexibility. Celebrants should take advantage of the various options now possible for the entrance rite, and for the introduction to the Lord's Prayer, to cite two examples. Then through catechesis and discussion, one begins to encourage the local community to explore its own religious heritage and move to an authentic inculturation of the liturgy for that local community. The local community must keep in dialogue with the larger church. The fact that progress can be made is attested to in the evolution and approval of the Zairean liturgy for certain parts of Zaire. But we must immediately admit that the liturgy of Zaire is the exception rather than the rule, and that for 99 percent of Africa, the process of inculturation of the liturgy has scarcely begun.

Inculturation of the liturgy must be seen therefore as a key part of the ongoing process of any local Christian community in its attempts to truly live and witness to its Christian faith. It is universal and ongoing, that is, called for in every local church, and in every time. Cultures are changing. The forces of technology and modernization are offering new possibilities and challenges to Christian communities. Unless the Christian remains in dialogue with these new developments, his or her faith life and subsequent liturgical life will be out of touch and will have no creative impact on these developing cultures. The mission of the church will suffer.

Finally, and this flows from all we have said, inculturation should become something natural, not added on. It simply is the creative living and celebrating of Christian faith in particular contexts. The fact that at present we must single out and focus on inculturation is an indication that we have failed to be engaged in the ongoing inculturation of the liturgy. Our efforts now are corrective. One looks for the time when these corrective efforts are no longer necessary, when every local Christian community takes seriously its charge and challenge to be truly Christian and be truly local, faithful to and yet not uncritical of its particular culture.

See **Culture, liturgy and**

Michael Amaladoss, *Do Sacraments Change?* (Bangalore, India: Theological Publications in India, 1979). Anscar J. Chupungco, *Cultural Adaptation of the Liturgy* (New York: Paulist Press, 1982). *Liturgies of the Future: the Process and Methods of Inculturation* (New York: Paulist Press, 1989). Frank Senn, *Liturgy in Its Cultural Setting* (Philadelphia: Fortress Press, 1983). Canadian Conference of Catholic Bishops, *National Bulletin on Liturgy*, Vol. 17, 95 (September-October 1984) *Culture and Liturgy*, Vol. 19, Number 105 (September-October 1986) *Culture and Liturgy*.

PETER SCHINELLER, S.J.

INITIATION, CHRISTIAN

Origins

The source of the Christian ritual of baptism is unclear. The custom appears to have been derived from John the Baptist, but the roots of his practice are in turn uncertain. Some scholars have argued that it was based on the ablutions of the Essene community at Qumran, but these were repeated washings related to the need for ritual purity and do not seem to have included an initiatory baptism. Other scholars have suggested that John was influenced by the baptism of new converts to Judaism, but there is some doubt whether this was being done in his time or whether it was only adopted at a later date. A third possibility is that John's baptism arose out of the tradition of prophetic symbolism in the OT, where mention had already been made of God's people being cleansed with pure water in preparation for the advent of the Messianic Age (see, e.g., Ezek 36:25-28).

Whether the Christian adoption of baptism began with Jesus himself or only within the church after his resurrection cannot easily be resolved. All three synoptic gospels record Jesus' own baptism by John but say nothing of him baptizing his followers. The gospel of John, on the other hand, does not mention Jesus being baptized but does speak of him baptizing others (Jn 3:22, 26; 4:1; but cf., 4.2). Mt 28:16-20 contains the command to baptize all nations, but there are difficulties in accepting this as an authentic saying of the risen Lord.

Whatever its origins, however, from early times it seems to have become the usual custom to initiate new converts into the church through a process which included baptism, performed perhaps in a river, a pool, or a domestic bath-house. What else besides the immersion might have been involved in the initiatory process is not made explicit in the NT. There may possibly have been a preliminary period of instruction, and it is likely that the ritual included a confession of faith in Jesus in one form or another. Some scholars would see the references to a post-baptismal imposition of hands in Acts 8:17f, and 19:5f. as indicating that this too was a regular part of all initiation rites at the time (cf. also Heb 6:2). Others would argue that these descriptions are of exceptional situations and tell us nothing about normal baptismal practice, and would point to the fact that a post-baptismal imposition of hands was by no means a universal feature of the initiation rites of the early centuries, a surprising omission if it were of apostolic origin. Similarly, it is sometimes suggested that behind NT expressions such as "anointed with the Holy Spirit" (e.g., 1 Jn 2:20, 27) lies a liturgical practice of a literal anointing with oil, whereas others would see such references simply as vivid metaphors.

Whatever the ritual practices of early Christianity, what is clear from the NT is that the experience of "becoming a Christian" was interpreted and expressed in a variety of different ways. While Paul's principal image is that of union with Christ in his death and resurrection (Rom 6:3f), in the fourth gospel the focus is on rebirth (Jn 3:3f). The early speeches in the Acts of the Apostles speak of receiving forgiveness of sins and the gift of the Holy Spirit (2:38), and these themes recur in other NT books. The experience is also described as being "enlightened" (Heb 6:4; 10:32; 1 Pet 2:9), as having "put off the old nature" and "put on the new" (Col 3:9-10), and as being marked or "sealed" as God's people (2 Cor 1:22; Eph 1:13; 4:30; Rev 7:3). All these images and metaphors are not intended to constitute a systematic explanation of different things which happen when a person becomes a Christian, but are diverse ways of attempting to describe and understand one and the same reality.

Initiation As Process

The evidence for the practice of Christian initiation becomes more solid in the centuries which followed. Here it is clear that "becoming a Christian" was seen as involving not just a liturgical rite, or even a series of such rites, but rather a process which might take a considerable period of time.

According to the *Apostolic Tradition* attributed to Hippolytus of Rome (*c.* A.D. 215), the only extensive description of initiation practice which is extant prior to the 4th century, those who desired to become Christians had to undergo a catechumenate which might last up to three years. In order to enter upon this, they were required to have sponsors who could attest to their capacity to "hear the word" and also to their way of life, because certain occupations were held to be incompatible with Christianity. During this preparatory period the catechumens received regular instruction in the faith, but were not permitted to attend the celebration of the eucharist, nor even to pray together with those who were already baptized or to exchange the kiss of peace with them, since they were regarded as not yet holy. At the end of this time their lives were again examined in order to determine whether they were ready to be baptized, and their sponsors had to bear witness to the fact that they had displayed good conduct while catechumens, especially with regard to works of charity.

Only if this evidence of the genuineness of their conversion was forthcoming were the catechumens permitted to proceed to the next stage of the process, the period of final preparation, which was probably only of a few weeks' duration. During this time those who had been chosen (later called *electi* at Rome) received a daily exorcism to complete their purification from the evil of the world around them, and fasted for the last two days before the baptismal rite took place which seems to have been at the Easter vigil, though the author does not make this entirely clear. The rites began at cockcrow with the blessing by the bishop of the two oils to be used, the oil of exorcism and the oil of thanksgiving (later termed *chrism*). When the candidates had removed all their clothing, they made a final renunciation of Satan and were anointed with the oil of exorcism, seemingly intended to ward off evil spirits.

Then they went down into the water and were asked to affirm their belief in God the Father, in Jesus Christ, and in the Holy Spirit. As the candidates made their response to each one of these three credal interrogations, they were immediately immersed in the water, thus expressing the intimate connection between faith and baptism. After coming up out of the water their bodies were anointed with the oil of thanksgiving, and they dried themselves and put on their clothes.

Up to this point everything had taken place where water was available and away from the assembly of the faithful, no doubt as much for the sake of propriety as for reasons of convenience. Now, however, the newly baptized joined the congregation for the remaining post-baptismal ceremonies, which were performed by the bishop himself. He laid his hands on them and said a prayer, and then apparently performed a second anointing with the oil of thanksgiving, this time pouring it on the head alone. Finally, he made the sign of the cross on the forehead of each person and greeted them with a kiss, signifying their acceptance into the community of faith. After this the newly baptized immediately joined in the activities which had been denied to them while catechumens, participation in the prayers the faithful, the exchange of the kiss of peace, and the celebration of the eucharist. When they made their communion for the first time, they received not only bread and wine but also water, to symbolize the inner cleansing of their initiation, and milk and honey, to symbolize their rebirth as children and their entry into the promised land.

Evidence from later centuries confirms that the main outlines of the procedure here described continued to be followed at Rome, even if some of the details varied. The most notable development was an increasing stress upon the association of the bestowal of the Holy Spirit with the post-baptismal prayer and anointing performed by the bishop.

In Syria, on the other hand, evidence from the period before the 4th century reveals a somewhat different pattern of Christian initiation. While some preparation was undoubtedly necessary, there does not seem to have been a formalized catechumenate, nor any exorcism of the candidates. Even evidence for a formal renunciation of evil or an expression of adherence to Christ is lacking prior to the 4th century, although it is probable that something like the latter was normally included. This more meager provision seems to reflect a continuation of the earliest practice in Jewish Christianity, when faith in Christ was viewed as the fulfillment of Judaism and hence converts did not need to reject their old religion, reform their way of life, or receive extensive instruction in order to enter the church.

The initiatory rite itself seems to have consisted simply of an anointing with oil followed by an immersion in water. The anointing appears to have been understood not as exorcistic but rather as an identification with Jesus in his messianic anointing with the Holy Spirit at his baptism in the Jordan. The immersion was accompanied by the minister's recitation of an indicative formula that the person was being baptized "in the name of the Father, and of the Son, and of the Holy Spirit." It is uncertain at this early date whether the immersion formula was spoken in the active voice, "I baptize you," as is typical of later tradition in the West, or in its passive form, "N. is baptized," as is typical of later tradition in the East.

There were no post-baptismal ceremonies at all, but the eucharist followed directly. Unlike the West, the focus in this tradition was not upon the paschal mystery with its principal motif of participation in the death and resurrection of Christ, but upon such images as adoption, rebirth, and divinization, and its practice does not seem to have been especially associated with Easter.

Later Developments

It was not until the 4th century, when Christianity became the established religion of the Roman Empire, that an increasing measure of standardization of the theology and practice of Christian initiation began to emerge. Thus, the East incorporated both a pre-baptismal exorcism and a post-baptismal anointing which was associated with the giving of the Holy Spirit; and Easter, though not necessarily the paschal vigil itself, became the preferred time for the celebration of baptism and was preceded by a formal period of final preparation of the candidates. Similarly, the West eventually moved the triple profession of faith to a preliminary position and adopted the indicative formula from the East to accompany the immersion.

However, much more significant changes than the arrangement of the details of the rites were beginning to take place. First, the catechumenate itself was declining. After the conversion of the emperor Constantine in the 4th century, large numbers of people wanted to join the church, and not always for entirely laudable reasons. In its enthusiasm to win members, the church tended to welcome them as catechumens without as rigorous an examination of the genuineness of their conversion and of their lifestyle as had earlier been customary. Moreover, those who became catechumens did not always want to proceed quickly to baptism. Since it was thought that the remission of sins which baptism was believed to convey could only be obtained once, there was a widespread tendency to delay baptism itself as long as possible in order to be more sure of winning ultimate salvation. As a result the length of the nominal catechumenate tended to grow, while the "real" cate-chumenate shrank to what had previously been the period of final preparation, now tending to be of six to eight weeks' duration as the season of Lent developed.

The second major change in baptismal practice in the post-Constantinian period came about because it could no longer be assumed that those who came to baptism had already undergone a profound conversion experience either before or during their catechumenate. In response to this difficulty, the style of the initiatory rites began to change and to incorporate elements from pagan mystery religions, especially highly theatrical features designed to produce an intense and lasting psychological impression on the candidates and to bring about a change in their lives. The element of secrecy, which in earlier times had sometimes been a practical necessity because of sporadic persecution, was now regularly employed to add dramatic tension to the occasion, the candidates not being told in advance what was going to happen to them and only having the meaning of various striking pre- and post-baptismal ceremonies explained to them after they had undergone them. Thus, the emphasis of the rites shifted from their being a ritualization of a prior experience to their being a means of effecting that experience.

The candidate was also becoming less an active collaborator in the process and more a passive recipient of it. Early Christian theologians emphasized that the reformation of the candidate's way of life was an essential part of becoming a Christian. Thus, for example, Tertullian could say, "we are not washed in order that we may cease sinning but because we have ceased" (*De Penitentia* 6), and Origen affirmed that "if someone who is still sinning comes to the bath, he does not receive the forgiveness of sins" (*Hom. in Luc.* 21). However, as time went by, there was a tendency to stress the reality of the invisible, metaphysical baptismal seal bestowed by God through the performance of the rites, at the expense of the necessity of the visible, external transformation of character evidenced in the catechumenate.

Even more striking changes came about when infants began to replace adults as the normal candidates for initiation. Children had begun to be baptized along with adults at least as early as the end of the 2nd century, and the practice may even go back as far as NT times, though the evidence is uncertain. Nevertheless, the majority of baptismal candidates continued to be adults, and no adaptations were made to the rites when infants were included, except that parents or sponsors had to make the responses on their behalf. Even in the 4th century many children of Christian parents were not baptized until they reached maturity. From the 5th century onwards, however, the initiation of infants began to be much more common, and consequently the baptism of adults declined. This development largely resulted from the same fear of failing to obtain salvation which had in the 4th century caused many to delay baptism as long as possible. The high infant mortality rate of the period, coupled with St. Augustine's teaching on original sin, led to a desire to baptize babies as quickly as possible so that they should not risk dying unbaptized.

It was this transition from adult to infant baptism which finally brought about the disappearance of the catechumenate. Because many baptisms could not be delayed until the Easter season but had to be performed soon after the child's birth, this part of the process was in most places either abandoned altogether or highly compressed so as to form the first few minutes of the baptismal rite itself. In conservative Rome, however, for several centuries babies were still solemnly enrolled in the catechumenate at the beginning of Lent and brought to church on the following Sundays to hear instruction and receive exorcism before their baptism at Easter.

The widespread need for such "emergency" or "clinical" baptisms led to another major development, initiation in the absence of the bishop. The normal practice adopted throughout most of Christendom was for a presbyter to take over the bishop's role in the rites, just as had already happened in the case of the eucharist. Although the bishop continued to consecrate the oils which were to be used, the presbyter performed the rest of the rite, including the blessing of the baptismal water and the post-baptismal anointing. Only at Rome was this procedure not followed. Here the stress upon the bishop's exclusive rite to bestow the Holy Spirit resulted in the whole rite, including the first post-baptismal anointing, being delegated to a presbyter in cases of necessity, but the second anointing, which was unique to Rome, being reserved to the bishop and performed by him at a later time. Because of the small size of dioceses in central Italy, the delay between the two parts of the rite was usually very short.

When in the course of time the Roman usage was imposed upon the whole Western church, however, it did not work nearly as well, not least because of the larger size of dioceses and the greater difficulty in travel. Consequently the delay between baptism and what came to be called confirmation grew longer owing to the rarity of episcopal visits. This problem was compounded by the negligence of parents in bringing their children back to church, on occasions when a bishop was there, for a brief ceremony which did not seem to add anything vital—the child having already been admitted as a communicant member of the church and assured of eternal salvation at baptism. In order to try to remedy this unsatisfactory situation, many provincial councils attempted to fix age limits by which children must have been presented for confirmation and to threaten parents with penalties if this were not done. Although some of these set ages as low as three or even one, higher limits were more common. Gradually, however, these *maximum* upper age limits began to be thought of as the normal *minimum* ages for confirmation, and so by the end of the medieval period seven years of age or ever later was generally thought appropriate for this.

This lengthy separation of confirmation from baptism in the West was encouraged by the emergence of a theological interpretation of the rite which regarded confirmation as bestowing an additional gift of grace to strengthen, arm, and equip Christians for the struggles and battles of life; clearly such a gift was better received not immediately after baptism but when most needed as the child grew up. This doctrine of confirmation was derived from a sermon included in the collection known as the *False Decretals,* published about A.D. 850. Since it was wrongly attributed to a 4th century pope, Melchiades (instead of to its real author, Faustus of Riez, a 5th century bishop of no particular importance), it gained wide currency in the centuries which followed and was cited by a number of leading medieval theologians.

Although in this way confirmation became detached from the rest of the initiation process, children still continued to be admitted to communion at their baptism, just as they were in the East where chrismation remained part of a unified rite. In the 12th century in the West, however, with the growth in the doctrine of "realism" with regard to Christ's presence in the eucharistic elements, doubts began to be expressed about the propriety of giving bread to infants, because they would be unable to consume it with sufficient reverence. The obvious solution seemed to be to give communion to them with wine alone. Unfortunately, however, it was not long afterwards that communion from the

chalice was withdrawn from all the laity, thus effectively—though unintentionally—excommunicating children. It then became the general rule that they should not be admitted to communion until they reached "years of discretion" (but there was some diversity of interpretation as to what age this was), although in a few places infant communion lingered on until it was finally abolished by the Council of Trent in 1552.

Thus, Christian initiation had ceased to be a process and became instead a series of three separate rites in the West—baptism, confirmation, and admission to communion—widely separated in time from one another and associated now with stages of biological development rather than with spiritual growth. It had also largely become privatized and ceased to take place within the context of the community of faith, and its symbolism had been minimized—the dramatic descent into the baptismal waters, for example, had been replaced by the pouring of a few drops on the candidate's head. Moreover, by the end of the Middle Ages much of its meaning had ceased to be understood by ordinary people and superstitious notions about the significance of the baptismal ceremonies were widespread. Unfortunately, the Council of Trent did nothing to remedy the situation, and the *Rituale Romanum* (1614) and the *Pontificale Romanum* (1595) effected no reforms: they merely imposed uniformity of practice in baptism and confirmation respectively and brought to an end local variations. The only change of any significance in the centuries which followed was made by Pius X in 1910, who lowered the age for the reception of communion but not that for confirmation. Thus, with penance also being required before communion, the sequence of initiation now became: baptism—penance—communion—confirmation.

The Reforms of the Second Vatican Council

The results of the revision of the rites of Christian initiation were published in three stages—the rite for the baptism of children of 1969, the rite of confirmation in 1971, and the rite of Christian initiation of adults (R.C.I.A.) in 1972, although the interim English translation of the latter did not appear until 1974 and the final version until 1985, being made mandatory in the U.S. from 1988. The R.C.I.A. is also to be used, with appropriate adaptations, for children who have reached "catechetical age."

The general introduction to the rites implies that it is the R.C.I.A. which is to be considered normative and the other two rites are to be understood in relation to it. It describes baptism, confirmation, and eucharist as "the three sacraments of initiation" which "closely combine to bring us, the faithful of Christ, to his full stature" (2). With regard to baptism, two images prevail. The first is that of the paschal mystery: "we are freed from the power of darkness and joined to Christ's death, burial, and resurrection" (1); "we pass from the death of sin into life" (6). The second is that of adoption: "we are called and are indeed the children of God" (2); "baptism ... makes us sharers in God's own life and his adopted children.... Baptism is a cleansing water of rebirth" (5). The ecclesiological dimension of baptism is also stressed: its recipients "are incorporated into the Church and are built up together in the Spirit into a house where God lives, into a holy nation and a royal priesthood" (4).

While it is affirmed that the Holy Spirit is indeed active in baptism, confirmation is regarded as completing baptism and bringing a special gift of the Spirit. In the general introduction this gift is described exclusively in terms of participation in the mission of Christ, "so that we may bear witness to him before all the world and work to bring the body of Christ to its fullness as soon as possible" (2). Only in the introduction to the separate rite of confirmation and in the Apostolic Constitution *Divinae consortium naturae* which accompanied it, is the medieval concept of "strengthening" explicitly mentioned.

The unity of the three sacraments is further emphasized in the references to the eucharist in the general introduction, where the ecclesiological and missiological themes are repeated: we participate in communion "so that we may have eternal life and show forth the unity of God's people ... and we pray for a greater outpouring of the Holy Spirit, so that the whole human race may be brought into the unity of God's family" (2).

The R.C.I.A.: Its Contents

The R.C.I.A. is not so much a rite but a process, divided into four periods of time which are linked to one another by three liturgical "steps." It begins with a period of evangelization and precatechumenate of no fixed duration or structure, during which there is a dialogue between the local church and the inquirer. Only when it is judged that the candidates have attained a basic grounding in Christian teaching, the beginnings of faith and a commitment to a changed way of life is it intended that they should be accepted into the catechumenate itself, and a liturgical rite is provided for this step.

This second period may last for several years (a minimum of one year is prescribed in the U.S.) and consists of formation and maturation, through teaching, through the support of others in the Christian life, through regular participation in the church's worship, and through active involvement in the church's mission. Several liturgical rites are provided for use during this time. Of particular note is the expectation that the catechumens will generally be dismissed during worship before the eucharistic celebration itself begins—a dramatic, public sign of their status. For while they are rightly regarded, on the one hand, as "joined to the Church ... part of the household of Christ" [R.C.I.A., 47], they are not yet fully initiated into its eucharistic fellowship.

When those responsible for the catechumens' formation (clergy, catechists, godparents, and other representatives of the local church) have determined that they are ready, they may proceed to the next stage, known as the period of purification and enlightenment. This will usually coincide with Lent and is intended as a time of spiritual recollection. The whole local church is involved in the rite of election or enrollment of names which constitutes the "step" to this period. This rite usually takes place on the first Sunday of Lent and is presided over by the bishop. Further rites follow during the season: the elect are publicly scrutinized about their intentions and exorcized on the third, fourth, and fifth Sundays; and they are formally presented with the Creed and the Lord's Prayer at a convenient public celebration and expected to recite them back on a subsequent occasion. All this closely adheres to ancient Roman custom.

The third step, the sacraments of initiation themselves—baptism, confirmation, and the eucharist—will then normally take place within the Easter vigil, though some preparatory rites may be done at an earlier assembly of the elect on Holy Saturday. This transfer of the subordinate parts of the rite gives the central elements a bold simplicity. After the homily at the vigil Mass, the ministers, the elect and their sponsors go to the font for the blessing of the baptismal water. The elect then make their renunuciation of evil and the profession of faith and are immediately baptized. In order to give fuller symbolic expression to the meaning of the baptism, the use of immersion is encouraged, and the baptism is followed by

further "explanatory rites"—the anointing of the head with chrism; a sign of incorporation into the priestly, prophetic, and kingly body of Christ; the clothing in a white robe, a sign of entry into the new creation; and the presentation of a lighted candle, a sign of the enlightenment of Christ. Unfortunately, the effect of these post-baptismal rites is somewhat diminished by the fact that the second is optional, and the first, though an ancient part of the Roman tradition, is only to be used in the rare situation where confirmation is for some reason deferred.

In normal circumstances, however, confirmation follows immediately. This is made possible by the provision that it may be administered by presbyters and not only by the bishop, to whom it had traditionally been restricted in the Roman rite. The intention is not to deprive the bishop of a part in the initiatory process but to signify more clearly its unified nature and to suggest that the bishop's true role is to preside, where possible, over the whole sequence, including the rite of election and the other Lenten catechumenal liturgies. The confirmation prayer asks for the traditional sevenfold gifts of the Spirit, and the formula accompanying the anointing is modeled on that used for chrismation in the East and speaks of sealing with the Holy Spirit. The presiding minister greets the newly confirmed and the eucharist continues with the preparation of the gifts, in which some of the newly baptized take part.

There is yet one more stage to the process, and that is the period of post-baptismal catechesis or *mystagogia*, for initiation does not end with the celebration of the paschal sacraments, but is a continuing reality as the newly baptized are absorbed into the body of the church and strengthened on their way. It is suggested that this be a feature of the Sunday Masses of the Easter season and involve some form of final celebration on

Pentecost Sunday. In the U.S. this mystagogy is to be extended until the following Easter with assemblies at least once a month to avoid the problem of the newly baptized being simply cast adrift instead of being fully incorporated into the life and mission of the local community.

The R.C.I.A.: Its Vision

It has been said that the importance of the R.C.I.A. lies "less in its ceremonial details than in its strategic vision of the church local and universal" (Aidan Kavanagh, *The Shape of Baptism*, p. 127). The image of the church depicted here is of a people brought together by a common experience of conversion and faith in Jesus Christ and endowed with new life in the Spirit through baptism. This is something which has an effect not only on the catechumens themselves but on all the faithful, who are thereby called to reflect on the quality of their own spiritual life and to seek the renewal of their faith. The church is also portrayed as committed to the mission of its Lord through evangelization, conversion, catechesis, and sacramental celebration. Moreover, this task is understood as belonging not merely to clergy alone but to all the baptized; the whole community of faith is involved, not just by witnessing it taking place in their midst, but by actively participating in the variety of ministries which are required (R.C.I.A., 9-16).

The R.C.I.A.'s return to the patristic heritage of the church is not simply a piece of antiquarianism but reflects a renewed understanding. Christian initiation is not a single sacramental moment or event but a gradual process, the duration of which cannot be definitively prescribed. Nor is it just something which is done to the catechumen. It requires active participation in a spiritual journey of response to God's grace. Because its later stages are closely related to the dynamic of the liturgical year, this journey is understood as culminating in entry into the paschal mystery. Thus, catechesis is here understood not primarily as doctrinal instruction but as conversion, that is, allowing one's whole life to be transformed according to the gospel of Jesus Christ. Furthermore, this is not something undertaken by individuals in isolation but within the context of the community of faith into which they are steadily being drawn.

The implementation of the vision, however, is more problematic: process can so easily become nothing but a highly structured program, and enthusiasm for the celebration of rites can mask the absence of the reality which they are meant to ritualize. Nor are the details of the rites themselves entirely without fault: the slavish reconstruction of some ancient features may eventually need to be reconsidered in the light of pastoral experience, the continued adherence to archaic terminology being a case in point. On the other hand, some very ancient elements which failed to find their way into the rites may also deserve a reevaluation: for example, the use of only one post-baptismal unction is a welcome simplification, but it is to be regretted that the Christic and Messianic themes of the first anointing did not find their way into the confirmation anointing, and that the greeting of the newly baptized did not include the traditional kiss of peace. Nevertheless, minor weaknesses such as these should not divert attention from the power of the promise contained in this revision.

Adapting the R.C.I.A. for Baptized Christians

In many places the vast majority of those seeking to grow in the Christian faith and to be incorporated more fully into the life of the church will not be the unbaptized, who are the primary subjects of the R.C.I.A.'s vision. Three categories of people present special problems.

First, there are those who have been fully initiated in a sacramental sense but have never experienced genuine spiritual renewal in their lives. Although they may in many ways be in a similar position to those who have never received any of the sacraments, to allow their association with those entering the catechumenate is to confuse the initial experience of conversion with the ongoing renewal which should be a part of the experience of all Christians. There are other ways in which their needs may be met, not least by a revitalized liturgy of penance which could once again center around the process of recognition, reformation, and reconciliation which characterized it in primitive times.

Second, there are those who have already been baptized but not confirmed or communicated. They may legitimately be included in the appropriate parts of the process and rites of the R.C.I.A., since their original initiation was incomplete, and in the U.S. additional (optional) rites are provided for such groups. Care needs to be taken, however, that their numerical strength does not distort the character of the R.C.I.A. as centered around baptism, and a clear distinction should be made by the manner in which the rites are celebrated with these candidates and with the catechumens who are being baptized.

Finally, there are those who have already been members of another Christian denomination and who are now seeking admission to the Roman Catholic church. No rules can be laid down for their treatment, but each case will have to be examined in order to discern how much of the initiatory process is requisite or appropriate for the individual.

The Rites of Baptism for Children and Confirmation

Several unresolved points of tension between the treatment of those baptized in infancy and those entering the church through the R.C.I.A. as older children or adults still remain. The most obvious difference between the two is the continuing deferral for several years of confirmation and admission to communion in the case of those baptized in infancy, which sharply contrasts with the unitive character of the R.C.I.A.. The latter affirms that the conjunction of baptism and confirmation "signifies the unity of the paschal mystery, the close link between the mission of the Son and the outpouring of the Holy Spirit" (215). What then is signified by their separation?

On the other hand, while the temporal delay still exists, efforts have nevertheless been made in the rite of confirmation to bring out its connection to baptism, especially by the inclusion of a renewal of baptismal promises by the candidates. Moreover, the rite insists that "Christian initiation reaches its culmination in the communion of the body and blood of Christ. The newly confirmed therefore participate in the eucharist, which completes their Christian initiation" (13). Thus, both here and in other official documents, there is a clear expectation that the normal sequence will be baptism—confirmation—first communion.

Unfortunately, while confirmation at about seven years of age is affirmed as the general practice of the Latin church, the possibility of deferring the rite until "the recipients are more mature" is still admitted (11). This not only destroys the initiatory sequence and makes its theological unity more obscure; it effectively changes the emphasis of confirmation from the perfection of baptism through the reception of the Holy Spirit to a personal ratification of the candidates' baptismal faith. While it may well be argued that the creation of such a rite is pastorally desirable, confirmation should not be asked to play that role.

The second major difference is the fact that the catechumenate is not as integral a part of the rites as it is in the R.C.I.A. Catechesis after baptism is certainly implied, not least by the stress which the rite lays upon the responsibility of the parents to bring the child up in the practice of the faith, and by the renewal of baptismal promises in the rite of confirmation. But there is less of a sense of a continuing process of spiritual growth with appropriate points of ritualization and more of an impression of a series of disparate rites linked to certain stages of biological development. A further problem is caused by the interpretation of canon 914 in the 1983 Code of Canon Law as continuing to require first penance before the reception of first communion in the case of those baptized in infancy. This not only adds yet another rite to the sequence but creates the theologically anomalous situation of ritually reconciling the child to a community into which he/she has not yet been fully initiated!

In general, the rite of baptism for children is modelled on the baptismal rite of the R.C.I.A.. Preference is expressed for its celebration on a Sunday and in the presence of the faithful, which represents an important step towards the restoration of its communal character, although this is not insisted upon and the force of the statement is considerably reduced by the permitted alternative, "or at least of relatives, friends and neighbors" (32). Moreover, the parents are given a more central role in the rite than the godparents (5), and they are no longer required to make the profession of faith on behalf of the infant. Instead they profess their own adherence to the faith of the church into which it is said that the child is being baptized. While these developments express the importance of the nurturing of faith which is required of the community and of the family, they leave unresolved the question of the relationship of the communal faith of the church to that of the candidate, which is seen as a prerequisite for baptism in the R.C.I.A.

Developments in Other Churches

Most of the other Western churches have also recently undertaken revisions of their rites of initiation, and these display a number of similarities to the Roman Catholic reforms. In many cases adult baptism has now been set forth as the archetypal rite, with the baptism of infants an adaptation of it. They generally presuppose a communal celebration of the sacrament both for adults and for infants and include a more extensive use of symbolism, especially in the introduction of appropriate post-baptismal ceremonies. In the case of infant baptism, they tend to display a similar ambivalence to the Roman rite over the faith which is required: some emphasize strongly the faith of the community, most stress the importance of the parents' own faith, but some still insist that the profession of faith is also made on behalf of the child in some way.

On the other hand, those churches which include a separate rite of confirmation tend to see it as chiefly concerned with the personal ratification of the candidate's faith. The Holy Spirit is regarded as having been bestowed in baptism, and the baptismal rite generally includes a post-baptismal imposition of hands and/or anointing especially associated with the Spirit. In some churches confirmation constitutes the gateway to the eucharist, but in others young children who have not yet been confirmed are admitted to communion. The most significant difference from the Roman Catholic reforms, however, is that these churches have been concerned chiefly to produce new rites: they have not taken the major step of setting these explicitly within an ongoing, unitive process of conversion.

Gerard Austin, *Anointing with the Spirit* (New York: Pueblo, 1985). Michel Dujarier, *A History of the Catechumenate: The First Six Centuries* (New York: Sadlier, 1979). David Holeton, *Infant Communion—Then and Now* (Nottingham, England: Grove Books, 1981). Aidan Kavanagh, *The Shape of Baptism* (New York: Pueblo, 1978). Aidan Kavanagh, *Confirmation: Origins and Reform* (New York: Pueblo, 1988). Murphy Center for Liturgical Research (ed.), *Made, Not Born: New Perspectives on Christian Initiation and the Catechumenate* (Notre Dame: University of Notre Dame Press, 1976). *The Rites of the Catholic Church* (New York: Pueblo, 1976, revised ed. 1988). Mark Searle (ed.), *Alternative Futures for Worship 2: Baptism and Confirmation* (Collegeville: Liturgical Press, 1987). E.C. Whitaker, *Documents of the Baptismal Liturgy* (London: S.P.C.K., 2nd ed. 1970). Edward Yarnold, *The Awe-Inspiring Rites of Initiation: Baptismal homilies of the fourth century* (Slough, England: St. Paul Publications, 1971).

PAUL F. BRADSHAW

INSTALLATION OF MINISTERS

The term *installation* refers to actions and rites other than ordination which in general have to do with the beginning of a specific ministry or with a community's initial or renewed recognition of individual ministers or groups of ministers. Other terms that are sometimes used include affirmation, commissioning, deputation, induction, institution, reception, and recognition. These terms may or may not be used as synonyms, and their precise meaning in each particular circumstance needs to be discerned. Both ordained ministers and lay ministers may be installed.

Ordained ministers. The only official Roman Catholic liturgy of installation is the "Reception of the Bishop in the Cathedral Church," printed as an appendix to *The Roman Pontifical* (Eng. tr. 1978). This rite itself uses installation as a synonym for reception. In addition, an unofficial rite for the installation of a pastor has been published in the *National Bulletin on Liturgy* (September-October 1987).

Other churches celebrate installations more frequently. *The Book of Common Prayer* (1979) of the Episcopal church contains a "Celebration of New Ministry" which may be used, with appropriate adaptations, for rectors of parishes, assistant presbyters, vicars of missions, deans and canons of cathedrals, chaplains of institutions, non-stipendiary clergy, as well as for deacons and lay persons with pastoral responsibilities. *The Book of Occasional Services* (1979) of the same church includes rites of "Recognition and Investiture of a Diocesan Bishop" and of "Welcoming and Seating of a Bishop in the Cathedral."

The Lutheran liturgical book, *Occasional Services* (1982), includes rites for the "Installation of a Bishop," "Installation of a Pastor," and "Installation to a Regional or Churchwide Office." To give another example, the *Book of Worship* (1986) of the United Church of Christ contains an "Order for Installation of a Pastor."

Lay Persons. As indicated above, the rite of "Celebration of a New Ministry" of *The Book of Common Prayer* (1979) may be used for lay persons who have pastoral responsibilities. In addition, *The Book of Occasional Services* (1979) of the Episcopal church includes a liturgy of "Commissioning for Lay Ministries in the Church." This may be used for 15 specific categories of persons, e.g., wardens and members of the vestry, servers at the altar, singers, parish visitors. The list concludes with "other lay ministers." The rite begins by stating that "lay persons are commissioned for their ministry by the Sacrament of Holy Baptism, and no form of commissioning for special functions is necessary." It explains further that the rite "is intended for use when a public recognition of a special function is desired."

The Lutheran *Occasional Services* (1982) includes rites for the "Installation of Elected Parish Officers," both the "Installation of a Lay Professional Leader" and the "Commissioning of a Lay Professional Leader," the "Induction of a Christian Day School Teacher," and the "Commissioning of Missionaries" (who may be ordained as well as lay). In addition, there is a rite of "Recognition of Ministries in the Congregation," which "brings to the attention of the congregation the ministry which is part of the life of all the baptized, and specifically recognizes those who are or will be offering themselves in a particular ministry of the congregation." Areas of ministry that may be recognized include worship, education, witness, service, and stewardship. Finally, *Occasional Services* contains a rite of "Affirmation of the Vocation of Christians in the World," as lay persons "serve through family, occupation, voluntary organizations, the community and nation."

The *Book of Worship* (1986) of the United Church of Christ contains both an "Order for Commissioning" and an "Order for Affirmation of Ministry" (Installation of Lay Leaders). In the first, "the people of God celebrate Christ's gift of diverse ministries to the church." The rite explains that "Commissioning . . . recognizes and authorizes that member whom God has called to a specific church-related ministry which is recognized by [the church] but not requiring ordination or licensing." The second Order is "a service of recognition and installation for those who consent to serve in an elected or appointed office in the church. Equally, it is a service of recognition and affirmation for those actively engaged in a variety of ministries in the world. . . . It is used when people want to be recognized and supported and to be called to accountability by the local church of which they are members."

The modern history of installing lay ministers in the Roman Catholic church begins in 1972 with the publication by Pope Paul VI of the motu proprio *Ministeria quaedam*. This abolished the traditional minor orders and established two "ministries," those of reader and of acolyte; both are restricted to males. They have a dual character in that they are required of candidates for ordination to the diaconate and presbyterate, but are open to other lay men as well. (As

entrance into the clerical state is now joined to the diaconate, seminarians are still lay men.)

These two instituted ministries are distinct from the much more common uninstituted ministries of reader and acolyte, which are exercised by women as well as men. For various reasons, including the sexual distinction made, many local churches have not made use of the instituted ministries.

The conferring of these ministries is known as "institution," whereas formerly young men were ordained to the minor orders. Institution is carried out by the bishop or the major superior of a clerical religious institute, and the designated liturgical rites are included in the *Roman Pontifical* (Eng. tr. 1978).

In 1973 the instruction *Immensae caritatis* was issued to make provision "lest reception of Communion become impossible or difficult because of insufficient [ordained] ministers." It allowed for communion to be distributed by lay persons in a variety of circumstances. However, this role is not officially viewed ar lay ministry, but as a "special," "auxiliary," or "extraordinary" ministry that is carried out in the physical or moral absence of a deacon or presbyter. Two rites of installation are provided. The "Rite of Commissioning Special Ministers of Holy Communion" is for those who will carry out this ministry on a regular basis. The second is the "Rite of Commissioning a Special Minister to Distribute Holy Communion on a Single Occasion."

Finally, the Roman *Book of Blessing* (Eng. tr. 1987) contains both an "Order for the Blessing of Missionaries Sent to Proclaim the Gospel" and an "Order for the Blessing of Those Appointed as Catechists." The first order may be used for clerics as well as laity. It is to be noted that the title "catechist" is used for those who exercise a ministry of catechesis properly so called as well as for those who exercise a more general pastoral and liturgical leadership role in the absence of a resident presbyter.

These official liturgies are complemented by a widespread practice of installing many other lay ministers and by the use of a wide variety of installation rites prepared by various national, diocesan and parochial bodies. In Canada, for example, *A Book of Blessings* (1981) and the September-October 1987 issue of the *National Bulletin on Liturgy* propose installation rites for a large number of lay church ministries as well as for those who minister in the broader community.

Several issues arise in relation to the installation of lay ministers. First, the term "ministry" is used in various ways. Some use it in a very broad way to include the whole of Christian life and hence all baptized persons. Others go in the opposite direction to include only ordained persons. A middle ground is taken by those who use it to include liturgical ministers and other church ministries, or to include these plus certain types of work outside the church community. Finally, some try to use the term in all of these ways, but distinguish among the different meanings.

Use of "ministry" to include all the baptized may lead to rites of installation that recognize everyone in a congregation or parish. In other cases such an understanding leads to an unwillingness to install lay persons in any specific ministries, as such an action is seen to exclude others who are also considered ministers. The question is asked, "Why install some lay ministers but not others? And who is to choose?" This whole question continues to be discussed.

Ministries that are proper to lay persons need to be distinguished from those exercised by laity as temporary replacements for ordained ministers. Special ministers of communion are officially considered to be in the latter category, though parochial practice and

popular understanding may view them differently. Real lay ministries have their roots in baptism and not in deputation, establishment or the bestowal of new gifts on laity by ordained ministers.

Installation of lay ministers can have a variety of meanings, including the following: (a) prayer and intercession for ministers, whether at the beginning of a ministry or regularly or occasionally in the midst of it; (b) support for or affirmation of a ministry already undertaken; (c) recognition of satisfactory completion of some educational training or formation program or experience that has prepared one for a new ministry or that enables one to carry out his or her present ministry better; (d) public commitment and dedication on the part of individuals to their ministries; (e) the commissioning of a minister by the community as its representatives; (f) the indication of a new relationship between the community and someone who is singled out or designated for a particular ministry; (g) confirmation of the authority that goes with certain ministries; (h) an indication that one has certain competencies required in one or another ministry; (i) the incorporation into one or another body or association of ministers; (j) a farewell and assurance of support for those being sent out from their communities for particular ministries; (k) the authentication of an individual's claim to be gifted in a certain ministry.

Particular acts of explicit recognition or installation may have more than one meaning and purpose, and, to the extent that it is possible to do so, these should be identified, stated, and distinguished. In the case of lay ministers it is best to place an emphasis on the recognition of baptismal gifts, on prayers of thanksgiving for these gifts and on prayers of support, rather than on commissioning and empowering by the clergy.

J. Frank Henderson, *Ministries of the Laity*, rev.

ed. (Canadian Studies in Liturgy no. 2) (Ottawa: Canadian Conference of Catholic Bishops, 1986). David N. Power, *Gifts That Differ: Lay Ministries Established and Unestablished* (New York: Pueblo Publishing, 1980).

J. FRANK HENDERSON

INTERNAL FORUM

The expression, a symbolic one, signifies the internal world of the human spirit and describes it as a "place," *forum*, where laws are operating and judgments are made. It is distinct from the "external forum" where human laws are enacted and enforced, and where justice is dispensed by courts on the basis of visible and tangible evidence.

"Internal forum" is a broad expression that allows for several interpretations, overlapping but not identical. While each construction can claim legitimacy *in its context*, none of them should be regarded as exclusive of the others.

In a Christian context and at the deepest theological level, the internal forum is where a human person meets the Spirit of God, takes cognizance of his demands, and decides to accept or reject a divine call. There too he or she is judged through the voice of conscience.

In a humanistic context and at a purely philosophical level, the internal forum is where the human spirit operates, forms rational judgments and makes responsible decisions, following an internal light which acts as guide and judge.

In a merely juridical context internal forum may mean that aspect of the conscience which can be reached and bound by external laws, be they ecclesiastical or civil. Thus some canon lawyers speak of the one and undivided power of the church that can bind and loose the faithful in both the external and internal forum. Similar arguments can be presented in favor of a secular authority and its laws and decrees: they too can impose not only external performance but also an internal obligation.

The theological and philosophical explanations have in common that they fully identify the internal forum with the conscience of a human person. For them, the source of any further explanation is then in the doctrine of conscience, as it has developed historically and as it is interpreted systematically.

The juridical explanations of internal forum speak of the conscience in a restricted way only: insofar as it can be subject to external laws and decrees. They are undoubtedly correct in asserting that there are external laws which can generate an internal obligation. But if they went further and claimed that the whole internal world of a human person is always under external laws, they would subvert a sacred hierarchy.

Catholic theology acknowledges the absolute priority of conscience, hence of the internal forum over the external one in matters of religious or moral duties. Vatican II both implies and explains this in its *Declaration on Religious Freedom*: "It is through his conscience that man sees and recognizes the demands of the divine law. He is bound to follow this conscience faithfully in all his activity so that he may come to God, who is his last end. Therefore he must not be forced to act contrary to his conscience. Nor must he be prevented from acting according to his conscience, especially in religious matters" (D.H., 3). Such an absolute priority, however, can be operative only if the process leading up to a decision of conscience is at least subjectively impeccable, which means that the person took pains to gather all necessary information and formulated a critically well-grounded judgment about the action to be taken.

Catholic Canon Law distinguishes carefully between the external and internal forum: "The power of governance is normally exercised in the external forum, but sometimes it is exercised in the internal forum only, but in such a way that the effects which its exercise normally has in the external forum are not acknowledged in this forum except as is established by law in certain instances" (can. 130, *Code of Canon Law*, trans. by CLSA). This means that the church vindicates the use of the "power of the keys" or "the power of binding and loosing" not only in external matters which can be brought before its courts, but also in internal matters which are manifest to God alone. This exercise of power in the internal forum can be sacramental, as when sins are forgiven in the sacrament of penance, or non-sacramental as when a dispensation is given from a marriage impediment which is occult and cannot be proved before any court.

In an ideal universe, there should be full harmony between the external and internal forums. In our less than perfect world we should strive for this harmony but with the awareness that it can never be achieved, not even in the church. All laws and decrees made by human beings are marked by their limited knowledge; they are also impersonal and abstract. The source of the dictates of conscience is ultimately in divine grace; the internal promptings always refer to a concrete and personal action. Thus conflicts may develop: the demands of external laws and decrees may appear incompatible with those of the conscience, or they may attempt to withdraw liberties which the conscience grants. Should such an event occur, the clue for the resolution of the conflict is in determining the correct hierarchy among the values that the person must pursue. Before God the highest value is in a fidelity to that internal light by which a person is guided and judged.

In sacramental worship such conflicts may arise especially concerning the reception of the sacraments: there could be cases where a person is under a legal sanction but is innocent before God; or vice-versa: someone is legally pure but corrupt in heart. Such cases are usually complex and they require both the learning and the wisdom of an expert in moral theology and Canon Law to unravel them.

A great deal of relevant material can be found in Vatican II's *Declaration on Religious Freedom* and its commentaries. The *Code of Canon Law* contains numerous references to the external and internal forum and their mutual relationship in matters of dispensations, marriage cases, remission of penalities, etc. (see Coriden).

See **Conscience, priority of human**

Philippe Delhaye, *The Christian Conscience*, trans. from the French (New York: Desclée, 1968). James A. Coriden, et al. (eds.), *The Code of Canon Law: A Text and Commentary* (New York: Paulist, 1985).

LADISLAS ÖRSY, S.J.

J

JEWISH ROOTS OF CHRISTIAN WORSHIP

Introduction

Hardly a year goes by that students of Christian origins are not made more aware of the Jewish roots of those origins. NT studies increasingly show that Christianity began not as an already fully reformed and monolithic movement but as a variety of "schools" which reacted differently to the ministry and death of Jesus, known as the *Christos*, Anointed One, or Messiah foretold in rich ambiguity by Jewish tradition. Among these schools of thought and practical living was the pre-dispersion Palestinian one centered in the pentecostal Mother Church of Jerusalem (Acts 1-11). With the dispersion of Jew and Christian from the City in the Roman destruction of 70 C.E., other schools appeared: one centered in Antioch, perhaps around the author or editor of Matthew; another grew around Paul's peripatetic ministry; still another around the Johannine corpus; and others which produced the canonical books of 1 and 2 Peter, James, Jude, Hebrews (?) and the post-canonical writings of 1 Clement, the Letter of Barnabas and those of Ignatius. In all these schools Jewish influence is felt in greater or lesser degree, the OT remaining for early Christians the Holy Scriptures they still shared, even in tension of interpretation, with Jews "of the circumcision." But recent research makes clear that scriptural sharing between Jews and Christians had its practical base in liturgical worship throughout the year, and early Christians had their precedents and paradigms for the most part from Jewish patterns of worship, or *seders*, found in temple, synagogue, and home. However much evolving Christian schools of thought and practice might differ, one thing that held them together was their adaptation of this pattern of worship, which remains, along with the Hebrew Bible, Judaism's most lasting contribution to historic Christianity.

Jewish Liturgical Sources

These fall into four main categories. First are the Jewish canonical scriptures, "The Law and Prophets," in which one gets historic notice of how such liturgical foci as Passover (*pesach*), Sabbath, feasts, sacrifices, and prayer were understood. Second are later codifications, made well into the Christian era, of traditional lore assembled by various schools of rabbis. Among these are the great Babylonian and lesser Palestinian Talmuds, which are collections of rabbinical studies of scripture and oral tradition, and the *Mishna* (ed. H. Danby 1933). The *Mishna* embodies three types of teaching: 1) *midrash*, which interprets or comments on scripture, especially the Law (Torah); 2) *halaka*, which are categorical laws deriving from Torah and developed in traditional observance; 3) *haggada*, which are expositions of scripture by way of narrative accounts and parables. The three types of teaching, which are roughly equivalent to theory (*midrash*), law (*halaka*), and history (*haggada*), are woven together into six sections which touch matters of prayer, feasts and liturgical order. Third are actual orders of worship (*seder*) with commentary, such as *Seder R. Amram Gaon* (ed. D. Hedegard, 1951), one of the two earliest texts of the full synagogue service (8th century C.E.). Fourth are Jewish authorized daily prayer books used in modern synagogues and homes. Although none of these sources dates from the time of Jesus (in fact not from much before the 4th century C.E.) they all contain elements that certainly date from much earlier times—particularly liturgical elements, which tend to be most conservative and resistive to change.

The Liturgical Year

The Christian liturgical year owes its origins to the Jewish liturgical year, and many of the concepts basic to such a year-of-worship are common to the two. The Jewish notion of time was neither rectilinear (modern) nor cyclical (pagan), but what might be called structured linearity. That is, time moved from a beginning toward an end, being structured throughout by God's gracious will in a series of "due seasons" based in the annual order of nature observed in agriculture and animal husbandry as well as in the much larger order of God's will for Israel. Judaism's responses to these "due seasons," whether in field or synagogue, temple or home, constituted its fidelity (or infidelity) to God.

The Jewish festal system rested on four major such seasons: *Passover (pesach)*, which seems to have predated the Exodus (Exod 5:1; 10:9), and the three agricultural feasts which were adopted in Canaan, i.e., *Unleavened Bread*, which became associated with the domestic and sacrificial *pesach* to constitute the developed Passover; the *Feast of Weeks* or Harvest, observed for a "week of weeks" or fifty days (and hence Pentecost); and *Tabernacles* or Tents or Ingathering. With the exception of Tabernacles (given some prominence in John), all these survive in the Christian year along with the seven-day week, in which the day of religious emphasis was shifted from Sabbath (Saturday) to Sunday (the "Lord's Day" of resurrection), a shift which also appears to have pulled the weekly fast days with it from Monday and Thursday to Wednesday and Friday (*Didache*, 8). Passover becomes the Christian *Pascha* (from the Aramaic form of *pesach*), the day commemorating Christ's death; Pentecost becomes the Christian fifty days of jubilation following the Sunday of Pascha culminating in the great octave of octaves on the fiftieth day, which concludes the Easter season. Unleavened Bread remains merged with *pesach* as it had done already in Judaism.

Determining the crucial date of Pascha required reckoning what was the 14th day of the first month, Nisan, according to lunar rather than solar calculations (Exodus 12). The feast, being movable, could fall on any day of the week, but there were different calendars for this computation in the Judaism of Jesus' time. Thus the synoptic gospels have Jesus eating the Passover meal on 14 Nisan and dying on the 15th, while in John he dies on the 14th as the lambs were being slain in the temple, a chronology Paul also seems to follow (1 Cor 5:7). The discrepancy may be explained (Jaubert) by the Synoptics using the official calendar, John, a Qumran calendar in which Passover that year occurred on Tuesday-Wednesday (the day ran from sundown to sundown) rather than on Thursday-Friday. Jesus could thus have eaten the Passover meal on Tuesday evening, been tried and judged on Wednesday and Thursday, and then been crucified on the Friday, 14 Nisan according to the official calendar. This hypothesis not only reconciles divergent chronologies between two groups of early Christian writings, but it also provides a more ample chronology for the passion events and diminishes the likelihood that Jesus' last meal with his closest disciples was anything less than a Passover meal—the origin of subsequent Christian reflection on the eucharist.

Early Christian attempts at reconciling the lunar 14 Nisan with Gentile solar calendars yielded different dates for Jesus' actual death. Yet this computation was embedded still in rabbinical tendencies to set the birth and death of patriarchs on the same day, either at Passover or Tabernacles in the autumn month of Tishri. The anonymous Christian *De solstitiis et aequinoctiis* computes Christ's conception, birth, and death similarly, beginning with the conception of the Baptist six months prior to Jesus' conception (Lk 1:36) since Zechariah, while performing his priestly duties during Tishri at the autumn equinox, was informed by an angel that Elizabeth his wife had conceived. John would then be born nine months later, at the summer solstice, and Jesus six months after that, at the winter solstice. Counting back nine months from that date, Jesus would have been conceived on 25 March or 6 April, the spring equinox depending on which solar calendar, Eastern or Western, was used. Jesus' conception date was *a priori* his death date, his nativity nine months later falling either on 25 December or on 6 January (Epiphany).

The method of these determinations, curious to us today, is nonetheless resolutely scriptural and rabbinical, giving us not only the date of the Lord's death but the feasts of the Annunciation to Mary (his conception), Christmas, Epiphany, Lent, and the paschal fast of Holy Week. The paschal fast seems to have originated in the Jewish custom of fasting during the afternoon of 14 Nisan while the Passover lambs were being slaughtered. Lent originated in Christian Egypt, where the beginning of the year on 6 January, Epiphany, began a course reading of Mark with the account of Jesus's baptism and temptation during his forty days in the desert (Mk 1:1-12). The Egyptian church thus fasted for forty days after Epiphany, ending with baptisms and Palm Sunday (Mk 11:1-11)—a fixed sequence not yet coordinated with the moveable Pascha and its preceding week of fast (Talley, 203-214). Only later would this Epiphany fast be moved to just before Holy Week and Easter. All these determinations helped anchor the reality of Jesus' life and ministry in real time and place against Gnostic attempts to mythologize him. They also provided a starting point for lectionary systems to begin course reading the gospels at the beginning of each year, the winter solstice, when the incarnate Word of God was manifested in the world by his nativity and baptism.

Orders of Service

There are three orders of worship service, or seders, of particular concern to Christian liturgical tradition: temple, synagogue, and domestic.

The temple seder involved a complex round of prayer, psalm, and sacrifice (Leviticus), certain elements of which influence later Christian usage. Two of these elements were the communion sacrifice, *zebach todah* (Greek *thusia eucharistein*) or "sacrifice of thanksgiving" which Philo commented on (Laporte), and the liturgy of the Day of Atonement (*yom kippur*), which forms a core image in the epistle to the Hebrews concerning the nature and work of Christ. Further, the times of temple sacrifice (morning, evening and, later, midday) determined the times of synagogue worship, and through this medium the times of early Christian prayer as well, the basis of the later liturgy of the hours or divine office. Yet the temple seder as such was regarded by Christians as having been rendered obsolete by the sacrificial death of the true Lamb of God. This attitude, combined with the destruction of the temple and its cult by the Romans in 70 C.E., meant that the temple seder would not have the same liturgical influence on Christian procedures as would synagogue and domestic seders.

For it is in the synagogue seder, full texts of which emerge by the Gaonic period in the 8th-9th centuries C.E., that the prayer structures of Jewish worship may be seen in their deployed liturgical forms (Hedegard, Hoffman). The service may be schematically outlined as follows:

1. "Passages of Song"—hallel psalms recited quietly before the service proper begins.

2. *Shema* (Deut 6:4-9; 11:13-21; Num 15:37-41)— at dawn with prayers of blessing (*berakoth*) and *Kaddosh* (Isaiah 6).

3. *Tefilla*—eighteen public petitionary *berakoth*, also known as *sh'mone esre* ("the eighteen") and *amida* ("standing," since they were said standing).

4. *Tachanunim*—quasi-private supplications.

5. Readings from Torah and Prophets, done on Monday, Thursday, and especially Sabbath according to three or seven year cycles, between Tachanunim and the evening service.

Less a single service, this is an order of distinct and self-sufficient "offices" which might be spread out from dawn through an entire morning. The seder is strictly one of prayer, and may originally have terminated with the priestly blessing from the temple liturgy (Num 7:24-26) which concludes the *Tefilla* section. Of all its parts *Shema* and *Tefilla* are the oldest, going back to the time of Jesus and beyond. *Tachanunim* and the Readings seem less formal, and the latter may have

undergirded commentary by rabbis (teachers) on the texts read, whence may have been generated the wealth of rabbinical teachings gradually codified by the academies in the Persian and Palestinian Talmuds and Mishna. Both morning and evening services are consciously related to the temple sacrifices being accomplished at the same times, a fact which cautions against too facile views on opposing the "carnal" temple and the "spiritual" synagogue cults; the two were a single complementary worship system.

It is however, especially in the prayer forms (Heinemann) that insight into later Christian evolutions are to be found. Three of these deserve comment.

1. *Berakah (euologia)*. Created things are never blessed, only their creator, and this blessing both opens and closes the form: "Blessed are you ... for you nourish us and the whole universe. Blessed are you...." The statement of motive, "you nourish us...," is expandable even to great length (e.g., Gen 24:27; 1 Chr 29:10-19; 2 Chr 6:1-11; Neh 9:5—10:40; etc.). Sometimes, especially when another *berakah* follows, the concluding blessing (*hatima*, seal) is omitted. In the synagogue service *Shema* is surrounded by lengthy *berakoth* which lead up to recitation of *kaddosh. Berakah* is for creation.

2. *Yadah (eucharistia)*. God is thanked for revelation. "We will give you thanks ... for you have given us ... the covenant and the law.... For all these things we will give you thanks..." (cf. Mt 11:25-30; Jn 11:41-44). Often the statement of motive includes *haggada* (narrative) expansion on salvation history as revelation of God. God is *thanked* for revelation.

3. *Tefilla (proseuche)*. God is petitioned or begged for redemption both now and in the future. "Have mercy ... on us your people Israel and on your city Jerusalem .... Blessed are you who build Jerusalem." The statement of motive here is

also often greatly expanded. God is *petitioned* for Jerusalem.

The forms, simple and often short, are capable of being expanded and linked together so that they undergird a vast reservoir not only of prayer but of proclamation and confession in all circumstances of Jewish life whether informal or formal. This euchology is the source of all subsequent Christian liturgical prayer, which centers on and revolves around *eucharistia* and *proseuche*, thanksgiving and petition, to this day.

The third category of seder, the domestic, includes procedural orders for meals, especially the weekly Sabbath *kiddush* meal hallowing the day on Friday evenings, and the once-yearly Passover meal, which follows the same order with some additions. The meal seder is simple:

1. Short opening *berakah* over an unmixed cup of wine.

2. *Berakah* over broken bread.

3. The meal itself.

4. Concluding "table blessing" (*birkat ha mazon*) over a cup of wine and water mixed:

a. *Berakah* of God who nourishes creation).

b. *Yadah* to God for the land, covenant, law (revelation).

c. *Tefilla* of God for Jerusalem (redemption).

The same order is observed on Passover, except that: 1) between breaking the unleavened "bread of affliction our fathers ate in the desert" and its *berakah*, the *haggadah* of Exodus and *midrashes* of it are given; 2) a second cup of wine, the "Cup of Redemption," is blessed and drunk before the meal begins with bread and bitter herbs; and 3) the *tefillah* for Jerusalem is expanded with an eschatological "remembrance" of the Messiah to come.

Last Supper and Eucharist

The temple seder gives imagery for Christ's work of atonement in the Christian "sacrifice of thanksgiving" of the eucharist; the synagogue seder deploys statutory prayer forms used in the eucharist; and the domestic meal seders of Sabbath and Passover suggest how the Last Supper may well have gone, particularly if that supper was, as seems likely (*pace* Dix), a Passover seder.

Concerning that Supper there are two NT traditions, one represented in Mk 14:17-26 and Mt 26:26-30, another in Lk 22:14-20 and 1 Cor 11:23-29. Neither tradition gives a full description of the Supper, being more concerned to report what Jesus said (his own *midrashes* of the Supper) than what he did in so familiar a meal. The two traditions describe the Supper thus:

Mk-Mt	*Lk-1 Cor*
1. As they were eating...	1. He sat at table.... He took a cup.... He gave thanks and gave it, saying: "Take this and divide it ... I shall not drink the fruit of the vine until the kingdom of God comes."
2. He took bread, Blessed, Broke, Gave, Said: "Take, eat, this is my body."	2. He took bread, Gave thanks Broke, Gave, Said: "This is my body [given] for you. Do this as my commemoration."
3.	3. (The meal follows)
4. He took a cup.... Gave thanks, Gave, they drank. He said: "This is my blood of the covenant, poured out for many. I shall not drink it again	4. Likewise the cup after Supper... Saying: "This is the new covenant in my blood [poured out for you]. Do this as often

| outside the king-
dom." | as you drink
it, as my com-
memoration." |
| 5. They sang a hymn
and went out.... | 5. And he came out ...
(Lk 22:39). |

The differences between the two traditions are striking. In Mk-Mt there is no "first" cup; the bread is "blessed" rather than given thanks over as in Lk-1 Cor; no meal section is mentioned; and Jesus' words about the first cup in Lk-1 Cor are transposed to the (final?) cup. In Lk-1 Cor there is no "blessing" (*berakah*) terminology, only "thanksgiving" (*yadah*) terminology; there are two cups mentioned; a meal is clearly implied; and the command to repeat the act as "my commemoration" is reiterated twice.

The structural contrasts between the two reports suggest that Lk-1 Cor is recounting the Last Supper historically as a Passover seder beginning with that seder's *second* cup, the "Cup of Redemption," which would have been hallowed and drunk at the conclusion of the Exodus midrashes *before* the bread was hallowed and eaten. It is not impossible that those great midrashes, unreported in Lk-1 Cor, may be found summarized in Jn 13-18:1, midrashes in this unique event on Jesus' own "exodus" consummating his earthly life and ministry. Such a context helps clarify his "I shall not drink the fruit of the vine until the kingdom of God comes": when he then drinks the final mixed cup after the meal at the *birkat ha mazon* of the paschal seder, his hearers would have understood the kingdom to be indeed revealed and present among them. This final cup Paul, the rabbi, calls by its Jewish name, "the cup of blessing" (1 Cor 10:16), drunk now always in the Kingdom into which Christ's death has ushered us.

Mk-Mt on the other hand seems to report the Last Supper in terms of one primitive form of eucharistic usage in which there is no preliminary cup and the bread and "cup of blessing" are no longer separated by a meal. Such a eucharist may have taken place either within a meal ("As they were eating...") or after it, as 1 Cor 11 suggests. The retention of "bless" to describe the bread prayer suggests the primitiveness of this usage: in Lk-1 Cor and *Didache* 9-10 the prayers are all "thanksgiving," a change that implies a Christian move toward making Christ the Revealer the major motive for Christian address to God, and perhaps Christian regard of the eucharist as the definitive sacrifice—of thanksgiving (*zebach todah*)—thus continuing the highest form of temple sacrifice consummated and transformed in the Messiah or Christ himself to have become the "pure offering" of all nations (Mal 1:11). The whole remains anchored for Mk-Mt in the holy food—the seder's "bread of affliction" become the body of Christ, the "cup of blessing" the poured out blood of the true paschal Lamb of God drunk now in the Kingdom of God revealed by that same Lamb during his last meal with all those whom he loves, and *for* them. The whole is nothing less than an entire new covenant.

In addition to the eucharistic order apparent in Mk-Mt, an order (unlike Lk-1 Cor) unprecedented in the seder service, there is another perhaps equally primitive order in *Didache* 9-10 (Jasper and Cuming, 23-24). This document, dated prior to 100 C.E., and possibly as early as 40-60, comes from Syria and is replete with Jewish influence. Chapters 1-6 detail how one teaches those coming to baptism (chap. 7) the "way of life" and the "way of death," themes in rabbinical teaching and in OT wisdom literature (Kavanagh, 1-12). Chaps. 8-10 describe baptized life as one of prayer and fasting on days different from those of the Jews (chap. 8), and of "thanksgiving" (chaps. 9-10). The eucharist does not follow the complex Passover seder but the simpler seder of the Sabbath *kiddush* meal. It opens with a brief thanksgiving over a cup of wine and then a thanksgiving over broken bread. The meal follows. After this there is a Christian *birkat ha mazon* over an implied mixed cup involving 1) *thanksgiving* for revelation, 2) *thanksgiving* for creation and food and non-carnal gifts, and 3) *petition* for redemption represented in the new Israel, the church. The relationship of this three-fold structure to the Jewish form is clear, but the sequence of creation-revelation-redemption has been altered and only thanks is given in 1) and 2). What we may have here is a Christianization of the kiddush meal moved from Friday to Saturday evening or Sunday morning. The short "eucharistic" prayers and the *proseuche* for redemption clearly betray Jewish euchology, and the meal is kept, separating the bread and (second) cup, unlike Mk-Mt whose order of service is consequently somewhat less Jewish than this one. It is plausible that *Didache* represents a eucharist in conservative Judaeo-Christian churches, the Mk-Mt order a eucharist-within-a-meal among churches of the Gentile missions, whose sensitivity to Jewish forms would have been weak or nonexistent.

Conclusions

Christians generally, and the origins of their worship forms in particular, have never been easy to explain, but apart from Judaism they are inexplicable. Their year, basic methods of teaching and living, fundamental worship events, prayer forms, and indeed their very Bible for some generations are all Jewish in origin because there were no other precedents available at the time. Nowhere is this more clear than in the earliest forms of Christian worship, where God is thanked for a Revealer and Redeemer who was himself Jewish to the core and, precisely because of this, entirely universal in his care and love for all nations.

Gregory Dix, *The Shape of the Liturgy* (London: Dacre Press, 1945). J. van Goudoever, *Biblical Calendars* (Leiden: E.J. Brill, 1959; rev. ed. 1961). Joseph Heinemann, *Prayer in the Talmud: Forms and Patterns* (New York: de Gruyter, 1977). Lawrence Hoffman, *The Canonization of the Synagogue Service* (Notre Dame: University Press, 1979). Annie Jaubert, *The Date of the Last Supper* (Staten Island: Alba House, 1965). R. Jasper and G. Cuming, *Prayers of the Eucharist: Early and Reformed* (New York: Pueblo, 1987). Jean Laporte, *Eucharist in Philo* (New York: E. Mellen Press, 1983). Aidan Kavanagh, *The Shape of Baptism: The Rite of Christian Initiation* (New York: Pueblo, 1978). Jakob Petuchowski, ed., *Contributions to the Scientific Study of Jewish Liturgy* (New York: Ktav Pub. House, 1970). Judah Benzion Segal, *The Hebrew Passover* (London: Oxford University Press, 1963). Thomas Talley, *The Origins of the Liturgical Year* (New York: Pueblo, 1986); "The Literary Structure of the Eucharistic Prayer," *Worship* 58 (1984): 404-420.

AIDAN KAVANAGH, O.S.B.

JEWISH WORSHIP

Institutional Origins

Jewish worship is simultaneously rabbinic worship, that is, worship as defined by the generations of authorities known loosely as "the rabbis," namely: the Pharisees (circa, 2nd century B.C.E.-70 C.E.); the tannaim (sing. tanna, 70-200 C.E.); the amoraim (sing. amora, 200-circa 6th/7th centuries); and the geonim (sing. gaon, 757-1038). Rabbinic myths of origins date some rabbinic customs as far back as Moses and even the patriarchs, but in fact, it is difficult to establish even elementary rabbinic worship prior to the 2nd century B.C.E., and only in the 1st century C.E. does it come clearly into focus. The tannaim, particularly, are responsible for the *structure* of rabbinic worship, and the geonim are responsible for canonizing a particular set of prayers as the liturgy of preference for later generations.

It was once believed that the tannaim established rabbinic worship by well-defined general proclamations reached by central bodies able to enforce a monolithic rabbinic will on a willing population. Philologically oriented scholars thus sought out putative "original texts" of prayer out of which current variations had grown, along with the exact dates and circumstances that gave rise to the latter. We now know that the tannaim were a diverse group with often ineffective centralized authority; that despite general agreement on certain principles, variation of interpretation was the rule; and that, consequently, there are no single authoritative "original" prayers to be found. Instead, tannaitic (and even amoraic) worship is characterized by relatively freewheeling expressions of specific worship themes, and an abundance of equally old prayer texts, most of which have been lost to history.

Three institutions, especially, contributed to the earliest rabbinic worship: the Temple, the *chavurah* and the synagogue. The Temple is pre-rabbinic, but lasted until the tannaim who knew its worship forms—which they respected as scripturally ordained. Even after the Temple's fall in 70 C.E., the rabbis accepted its sacrificial system as paradigmatic for ideal worship and predicted a rebuilt Temple with a restored cult at the end of time. Until then, they consciously modeled their own worship after real or imaginary cultic blueprints, characterizing prayer itself, for example, as "an offering of the lips," likening the householder's table around which prayers were said to an altar, and announcing that the primary rabbinic prayer, the *Tefillah*, was in lieu of the defunct *Tamid* or daily sacrifice.

Nonetheless, two alternative loci for worship, the *chavurah*, and the synagogue, both of which had predated the Temple's fall, now rose to prominence. The *chavurah* (pl. *chavurot*) appears in our records by Pharisaic times. *Chavurot* are tableship groups emphasizing worship around meals, and featuring purity rules that liken average Israelites to priests, and tables to Temple altars. They were either *ad hoc* gatherings, or ongoing associations, where men (but not women) went to celebrate such things as feast days and the birth of children. Out of this milieu grew the Passover *seder*, benedictions over food, and the Grace after meals (*Birkat hamazon*).

The synagogue too predates the Temple's fall, but not by the many centuries often imagined. Evident in the gospels, and known both to Paul and to Josephus, the synagogue must have been well established by the first century C.E. But neither written nor archeological data indicate origins much prior to that, certainly not before the 2nd century B.C.E. Sources prior to the Hasmonean revolt (167 B.C.E.)—including Daniel, written on its very eve—are alike in knowing nothing of synagogues, which, therefore, can certainly *not* be dated to the Babylonian exile, as is often claimed.

Texts reflecting conditions in the 2nd-1st century B.C.E. portray public worship in village squares under the institutional aegis of a *ma'amad*. The *ma'amad* was originally an extension of the cult in that it was a local gathering for worship at the time that the sacrifices were being offered in Jerusalem; but we hear also of extensive worship there, complete with a *Tefillah* (the rabbinic prayer par excellence), by assemblies seeking relief from drought. It is thus probable that the synagogue developed out of the *ma'amad*.

We know little about the relationship of the rabbis to the early synagogue. They seem to have preferred other institutions, especially the study academy, for their prayers. The *ma'amad* ritual had been led by Elders (*zekenim*), and early synagogue worship was probably conducted by a new functionary, the *chazzan* (pl. *chazzanim*). Nonetheless, the ritual followed there was increasingly that of the rabbis, who emerged as the dominant force behind synagogue worship, whether they actually attended prayers there or not.

The *ma'amad*/synagogue and the

chavurah/home thus became twin foci for Jewish worship, following the Temple's fall. Though Jews can and do worship elsewhere, worship to this day is normally enacted at set times in either or both of these locales, three times daily (see below) and even more extensively on holy days.

The Liturgical Text
a. The Primacy of the Blessing

Rabbinic prayers hark back to biblical prototypes, but they are unique in that they feature a standardized prose style known as a *berakhah* (a blessing or benediction). Stylistic rules for benedictions evolved through the centuries but were largely in place by the 3rd century C.E. Blessings are either short or long. Short blessings are one-line formulas of the following sort: "Blessed art Thou, Lord our God, Ruler of the Universe, who...." Long Blessings may or may not feature an introduction ("Blessed art Thou..."), but they always conclude with a *chatimah* (lit.: "seal") which sums up the blessing's theme ("Blessed art Thou who..."); they are "long" in that they contain thematic development in the body of the benediction, so that each one is in essence a small essay on some aspect of rabbinic thought. Worship services are constituted by a variety of verbal material, but primarily by clusters of blessings strung one after the other. Of these, the following two stand out: the blessings that surround the *Shema* and the *Tefillah* (see below).

These "blessing/essays" however are not the product of single authors; they are composite works reflecting centuries of oral transmission and editorial redaction. They thus betray the fact that the rabbinic tradition is far from monolithic. One major strand, for example, is Jewish gnosticism (known generally as the praxis of *Yordei Merkavah*, the "Chariot" or "Throne" mystics) which, from as early as the 2nd or 3rd centuries C.E., empha-sized mantra-like formulas, word strings of synonyms that produced rhythmic regularity without any necessary cognitive enrichment; sometimes accompanied by fasting and body movement, this worship was trance-inducing, the goal being to join the heavenly angels seen by Isaiah (chap. 6), there to praise God.

At the same time, other rabbinic strands stressed the cognitive pole of meaning, by mandating regular worship organized according to set themes. Indeed, for centuries, it was this unvarying thematic progression that identified worship as properly rabbinic despite its many verbal manifestations in different synagogues. Generally speaking, each theme was allotted its own blessing, the style of which allowed for great variation, in that even after the basic rules for beginning and ending it were in place, there still remained the blessing's body where the theme could be elaborated freely. Thus expression of a theme varied widely from place to place, and even from time to time in the same place, as prayer leaders exercised considerable imagination in their renditions. Regardless of the vast differences in wording that resulted, however, the same *order* of blessings, and thus, the same progression of themes, was the rule, so that even a highly unusual version of a worship service would be recognizable as just one more interesting delivery of the appropriate thematic element.

b. From Unfixed Text to Prayer Book

Somewhere between the 3rd and the 8th centuries the various strands of prayer coalesced into fixed liturgies. Lengthy poetic versions of benedictions known as *piyyutim*, originally, perhaps, every-day alternatives, were eventually reserved for fast or feast days. The mystical mantra-like strata were combined with information-rich theological expressions of the themes, to produce final formulations of composite texts betraying both the mystical affective side of worship and the theological cognitive pole as well. More than one such amalgam persisted for centuries, with two recognizable clusters of them taking shape: the Palestinian rite in Palestine and Egypt, and the Babylonian rite in the Tigris-Euphrates basin. The former remained particularly rich in poetry, preferring to continue the age-old tradition of encouraging novel expressions of the mandated blessings at the expense of a single "canonized" prayer text. The latter, however, chose fixity as its goal: it limited poetry to a bare minimum and established set texts to be recited from beginning to end of the standard worship services.

In the middle of the 9th century, Amram Gaon, the titular leader of Babylonian Jewry, established his own particular set of texts as incumbent on all Jews. His decree, our first known comprehensive prayer book, is known as *Seder Rav Amram* ("The *Seder* [or order of prayers according to] Rav Amram"). Accepted as normative by the young Jewish communities in western Europe especially, it eventually became the basis for all subsequent rites, particularly in the wake of Palestinian Jewry's destruction at the hands of the Crusaders, and the parallel success of the Babylonian legal tradition in establishing its cultural hegemony over its Palestinian parallel.

Seder Rav Amram contained all required prayer texts for home and synagogue devotion, along with the *halakhic* regulations for saying them. To be sure, it omitted much more than it included, in that Palestinian alternatives especially were overlooked. But in principle, Jewish worship was henceforth associated with the act of reading one's way through relevant paragraphs of a book, following the requisite *halakhic* guidelines regarding such things as bodily position, congregation/prayer-leader antiphony, and musical rendition. In the centuries that followed, the book expanded with new

poetry expressive of this or that community's identity. But before turning to these expansions, we should look briefly at the contents of *Seder Rav Amram*'s basic service, since it was to remain the essential outline of Jewish worship in all branches of Judaism to this day.

c. Outline of Services—Structure and Theology

In apt continuity with rabbinic tradition generally, *Seder Rav Amram* does *not* feature the Bible among its prayers. True, three biblical citations (Deut 6:4-9; 11:13-21; Num 15:37-41) constitute the well-known *Shema Yisra'el*, which is recited morning and evening; and psalms too appear here and there in their totality, especially in psalm collections known as *Hallel*. But the *Shema* has been recast as only a centerpiece bracketed by introductory and concluding blessings; and psalmody is decidedly insignificant here, relative to the blessing structure that predominates. The theology of rabbinic worship thus reflects the rabbinic doctrine that the written Bible requires interpretation according to the insights of the oral tradition.

The most important worship units are 1) the *Shema* and its benedictions, and 2) the *Tefillah*, or "The Prayer" *par excellence*, which singly or together had constituted the bulk of every synagogue service since the 1st century at least.

The *Shema* resembles a Jewish creed, in which the assertion of God's unity is elaborated through the accompanying blessings which acknowledge God as 1) *Creator* of light and darkness, 2) *Revealer* of Torah = *Covenant-maker* with Israel, and 3) *Redeemer* of Israel from Egyptian bondage. God is thus the sole deity, who, moreover, is responsible for creation, revelation, and redemption. Historical recollection is anamnetically linked to eschatological expectation in that God's redeeming act at the Red Sea is merely the archetype for a future act whereby

Israel will receive final deliverance at the end of created time, when the covenant's promise comes ultimately to its fruition.

Eschatological hope figures even more prominently in the *Tefillah*, a series of 19 (originally 18) benedictions, largely petitionary, organized at the end of the 1st century. God is asked to grant the necessary insight that leads to repentance, and thus to divine pardon and salvation. The blessings that follow define the paradigmatic rabbinic doctrine of salvation: God will heal the sick, restore fertility to the Land of Israel, return the exiles to their land, reestablish the Jewish justice system, punish heretics, reward the righteous, rebuild Jerusalem, and bring the messiah son of David to rule in perfect peace.

Along with the *Shema* and the *Tefillah*, early worship featured the reading of Torah (the first five books of the Bible), on Mondays, Thursdays and Sabbaths. More than one lectionary seems to have been in effect: Palestinians favored the so-called triennial cycle (actually, a 3 ½-4 year cycle, despite its title), while Babylonian Jewry developed an annual cycle, which prevails today, as a consequence of the Babylonian cultural victory described above. Saturday mornings saw an additional reading (called *Haftarah*), drawn from the prophets (and the narrative books—known also as "prophets" in Jewish tradition) and linked in some way to the primary Torah text. But scripture was customarily followed by an interpretive homily (or *midrash*), which ended with a *nechemta* (a word of hope) and then with the *Kaddish*, a prayer calling for the coming of the reign of God. By the 8th century, the *Kaddish* was associated with mourning and assumed to be of benefit to the dead, but its earliest appearance is as a concluding prayer to the study of Torah.

The rabbis favored private spirituality as well, and thus introduced benedictions (usually the short ones) as a means of injecting religious significance into everyday events, as disparate as eating an apple to seeing a rainbow, or even to going to the bathroom (at which time, one was to marvel at the system of ducts and tubes that constitute the human body). Similarly, benedictions preceded the performance of commandments (or *mitzvot*. sing. *mitzvah*) affirming that the act about to be performed—kindling Chanukkah lights, perhaps, or performing a circumcision—was of covenantal magnitude. Perhaps the most significant *mitzvah* was the study of Torah, understood generically as the ongoing revelation of God's word and including both written scripture and oral tradition. Rabbinic spirituality favored such study every morning upon awakening, especially with texts describing the defunct Temple cult, as if reading about sacrifice was the next best thing to doing it. In his *Seder*, Amram included a particular collection of all such texts— the Bible and the rabbis on sacrifice, blessings over the *mitzvah* of Torah study, and benedictions related to the daily miracle of waking up in the world—but he appended them to the beginning of his synagogue liturgy, thus transforming home devotion into preliminary synagogue meditation and study. There it remains to this day, as does a second sort of introductory material Amram included: songs of praise highlighted by a *Hallel* (Pss. 145-150).

We saw above the petition for salvation as defined in the *Tefillah* and as represented in the metaphor of the ultimate reign of God (from the *Kaddish*). But the arrival of God's promised realm presupposes the prior forgiveness of sin. The amoraim thus suggested a daily confession following the *Tefillah*. Amram went further, including not only the opportunity for private devotion there, but also an official supplication rubric (the *Tachanun*), composed of a collection of prayers acknowledging the lowliness of the human condition. These supplications later grew in importance among western European *Chasidei Ashkenaz* (see below), but were already present in Amram's *Seder*, as an apt continuation of the amoraic anthropology he inherited.

Thus with but one exception (the *Alenu*—see below) the major prayers of the daily morning service were in place by Amram's day. Beginning with 1) morning blessings and the study of sacrificial texts, the worshipper then recited 2) a *Hallel* and songs of praise. These introduced the two most important rubrics, namely: 3) the *Shema* and its blessings, and 4) the *Tefillah*. The *Tefillah*, technically a replacement for the Temple *Tamid* sacrifice, conjured up the cult's penitential function, and thus led to 5) private prayer, especially the supplicatory *Tachanun*. On appropriate days, 6) scripture and 7) a sermon followed, but in any case, 8) a concluding *Kaddish*, calling for God's promised reign on earth was the norm. The only important addition over the years has been the *Alenu*, composed originally as an introduction to Rosh Hashanah's blowing of the *Shofar*, but by the 14th century, added to the concluding prayers. It too calls for God's ultimate reign on earth.

With slight alteration, the above outline of daily morning prayer (*shacharit*) characterizes every other synagogue service. Mandated afternoon (*minchah*) and evening (*arvit* or *ma'ariv*) services featuring similar liturgies have by now coalesced into back-to-back services held at sunset. These daily occasions are suitably altered for Sabbaths, fasts and festivals, when, in addition, the home as worship setting usually looms larger than the daily norm. Thus, for example, Passover calls for additional synagogue poetry on the theme of the Exodus; but it also features the home *seder* ritual with family and friends. Home liturgy for Sabbaths and holy days includes, above all, 1) the kindling of lights, along with a prayer called *Kiddush*, an announcement

of the onset of sacred time; and 2) a *Havdalah* (or "separation") ceremony marking a "separation" between sacred and secular time, as the Sabbath or festival ends.

d. Medieval Developments in Europe— Structure and Theology

Seder Rav Amram was followed by a second comprehensive prayer book, *Siddur Saadiah*, a compendium by the renowned 10th-century philosopher, exegete, poet and polemicist: the gaon, Saadiah. Yet a third such book, no longer extant, is attributed to the last gaon of our period, Hai (d. 1038). But Amram, especially, made an impact on all Europeans who patterned their worship after his instructions and text. A broad division of rites into "Sefardic" as opposed to "Ashkenazic" differentiates later developments in the Iberian peninsula (*Sefarad*) from those in Northern Europe (France and Germany, known together as *Ashkenaz*). In both places, however, the texts grew in bulk as Spanish, French, German and other Jews composed poetic additions, especially for holy days. In 14th-century Ashkenaz, the expanding *siddur* (or "order" of prayer) was considered too bulky to be practical, and was split into: 1) a *siddur* for daily and Sabbath use; 2) a *Haggadah* for the Passover *seder*; and 3) a *machzor* for holy day prayers, often a separate volume for each of the three pilgrim festivals (*Pesach* = Passover; *Shavuot* = Pentecost; and *Sukkot* = "Booths") and for the High Holy Day occasions (*Rosh Hashanah* = New Year, and *Yom Kippur* = Day of Atonement). This prayer book taxonomy is common today.

The most important later medieval developments occurred in the mystical tradition that was in part continued, in part revived, and in part newly enriched, both in 12th-century Germany, and in 13th-14th century Spain. Under the influence of medieval piety, particularly that of the mendicant monastic orders of the time, the former movement, known as *Chasidei Ashkenaz* ("The pietists of northern Europe"), favored a severely penitential, even ascetic, attitude to prayer, and their influence was substantial in northern and eastern Europe for centuries. The Spanish school, the *Kabbalah*,—really a philosophy rooted in Provencal neo-platonism, and transferred south over the Pyrenees—spread throughout the Mediterranean, especially to the Land of Israel, with the expulsion of Jews from Spain in 1492.

In terms of creativity and daring, only the very founding Pharisees and tannaim even approach these 16th-century kabbalists, who not only composed an entirely novel service to introduce the Sabbath (*Kabbalat Shabbat*, which precedes Friday evening—or *arvit*—worship), but also redefined the very goal of worship, introducing ecstatic practices reminiscent of the trance-inducing customs of earlier times. These included rote recitation of divine names, and the use of music for self-hypnotic purposes. Implicit in their worship was a bold theology whereby 1) God and the universe are declared coterminous; 2) the human existential state is thus equivalent to God's; 3) as the dominant metaphor for the fractured state of being on earth (and in God!) we find the sexual image of an androgynous deity, whose male and female elements are divorced from each other and in anxious search for reunification. Worship is nothing less than the most important means to restore God's male and female parts to wholeness. Thus the normative rabbinic theology contained in the manifest content of the benedictions was suppressed in favor of a hidden mystical meaning assumed to underlie the prayers. Worshippers were instructed to pray with only the secret meaning in mind. To facilitate that end, introductory meditations called *kavvanot* (sing. *kavvanah*) were composed, some-times with a prayer's hidden purpose expressly stated, and sometimes with it only alluded to. In the 17th century—and especially in the 18th, under the influence of Polish/Russian Chasidism, a theological outgrowth of Kabbalah—kabbalistic thought spawned new prayer books replete with mystical *kavvanot*, as well as other more exotic innovations, such as diagrams pointing toward the divorced state of God; or to revived gnostic traditions regarding a dual world of light and darkness; and to a new anthropology as well, featuring human beings as a reflection of a divided God and a divided world, but yearning in prayer for the unity we call *shalom*— "peace" and "wholeness."

Theology Implicit in the Jewish Mode of Worship

The message of worship comes from more than its words. The way of worship prescribed by the rabbis has theological and ecclesiological presuppositions.

The primary expression of traditional worship is corporate. The Jew may pray privately any time, any place, and with any words, gestures or songs. But the Jew *must* pray with the community three times daily. The assembly must therefore include a quorum (or *minyan*) of at least ten men, the minimum necessary to represent the people Israel. (Traditional Judaism does not recognize women here. On modern-day attitudes to women in worship, see below.) The text is almost invariably first-person plural, "We," indicative of the corporate covenant being celebrated. The prayer leader is included with the people, for the leader functions technically only as a *sheliach tzibbur*, an "agent of the congregation," presenting the public's praise and petition to God. An implicit social contract underlies the relationship: concerned that they may not achieve the proper spiritual dimension, the people give up their right to pray as they wish and entrust this "public agent" with the power to represent them on high. If the agent proves inept or unfit in character, a new one is selected.

Thus the most important single person in traditional Jewish worship became the *chazzan*, who grew from humble origins as a general caretaker and prayer leader of the ancient synagogue to be the modern cantor, entrusted with the proper recitation of the liturgy. Without a monastic tradition, Jews did not develop unison singing as Christianity did, but it did specialize in the solo song, as the prayer leader chanted blessing after blessing, from the beginning to the end of the service. Ideally, anyway, the *chazzan* was held accountable for the highest musical, vocal, and textual competence, no small matter, given the growth of worship traditions over the years. Textual enrichment had gone hand-in-hand with increased musical sophistication. The Torah—unmarked as to vowels and musical signs—had to be read without error, according to the proper cantillation mode; and even the prayer texts required specific knowledge of *nusach*—the name given to the musical systems—that varied with the season of the year and the service of the day.

congregation to sing the service antiphonally, a custom still to be found in Orthodox congregations: first, the congregation reads quickly through a prayer, each worshipper at a somewhat different speed, and often, out loud as well—a custom called *davvening*; the *chazzan* faces the same way as the congregation of which he—all cantors are male, in this traditional milieu—is an integral part, but the noise dies down, indicating to him that everyone has finished the blessing in question. The *chazzan* then repeats it, all or in part, but with the correct *nusach*, and, especially in recent Ashkenazic tradition, occasionally in extended melismatic form also, something akin to a jazz musician's improvisation around the melodies and harmonies of

traditional tunes. This "dialogic" model, however, is ancient, going back to the very origin of rabbinic worship, the implicit theological model being the angelic "dialogue" in Isaiah's vision whereby two groups of angels face each other alternately praising God.

"Praise" thus emerges as the dominant stance of the Jew before God. Jews may be thankful—indeed, they must be—but they stand in covenantal partnership with God. The stance of receiving everything as a gift of pure grace for which one can respond with nothing but intense gratitude alone is somewhat alien to Jewish tradition. True, in his famous prayer *avinu malkenu*, now recited in the high holy day period, Rabbi Akiba pleaded, "Have mercy on us . . . for we have no works." But a theology of *mitzvah* could hardly hold that extreme notion; the *mitzvot* were nothing if not works. So despite human sin God owes Israel something under covenantal terms. And Israel turns to God in a characteristically affirmative stance, praising the One from whom blessings flow, and acknowledging God as their origin and source.

Turning to private prayer, we see again the communal focus so far described, as well as another aspect of the Jewish world view: its appreciation of the cosmos as something valuable in its own right, an object to be enjoyed. Private prayer, it will be recalled, was established primarily around the memorization of set blessing formulas appropriate to acts of enjoyment or as introductions to performing commandments. In the latter category, we find once again the dominant image of the Jew as a member of a covenanted people, intent on performing covenantal acts with intentional awareness that they are precisely that: *mitzvot*, divine commands that one is fortunate enough to do. In the former case, we cannot miss the positive stance toward the world which persists despite even the heightened penitential consciousness of the *Chasidei Ashkenaz*, who may have insisted on the sinfulness of humanity but never imputed such negativity to God's cosmos. Thus men and women are to enjoy the world—its fruit and its rainbows, its sages and its scholars—all of which, among others, are to be greeted with pertinent blessings. Not only the sense of sight, but hearing too and even smell, are positively codified in blessing forms that celebrate what they do: for there are blessings on hearing good news (or bad news); and on smelling fragrant flowers or herbs; and so on. The theology of Jewish worship insists that it is a sin to evade the world which God has prepared us to experience.

Modern Developments
a. Europe

By the 19th century, post-Napoleonic Jewry in northern Europe found itself increasingly released from medieval ghettoes. Especially in large commerical and cultural capitals, enlightened Jewish communities faced the fact that their worship seemed still to be reflective of their pre-modern consciousness. Beyond even the outmoded tenets of its troubling content, it was the manner of traditional worship that Jews found disturbing. Services were long, entirely in Hebrew, lacking a sermon in the vernacular, and often conducted by cantors who were less than what the ideal prescribed. The average service featured a noisy congregation of individualistic worshippers rocking back and forth and shouting prayers not at all in unison. This *davvening* hardly accorded with the dominant aesthetic of 19th-century Europe where worship was assumed to call for quietude, reverence and decorum. Beginning in Alsace, but quickly spreading to Berlin, Hamburg, Vienna, and elsewhere, Jews initiated rapid and sometimes thorough worship reform.

Musically, the old modes and sounds were notated according to modern standards, and recast so that "folk" music came out sounding like western classics. The *chazzan* was removed in favor of a singer and choir, who would render the tunes without the traditional cantorial embellishment. Rabbis learned to preach in German, and to direct truncated worship services out of translated prayer books, stripped down to a basic liturgy. German translations or paraphrases omitted difficult-to-hold doctrines like the belief in bodily resurrection or an ultimate return from "exile," and emphasized the universalist strains of Jewish thought at the expense of particularistic ones. Of the two loci for Jewish worship, the home shrunk in importance as Judaism shifted to the synagogue which modern Jews saw as their "church."

European reform was not as far-reaching as it would become on American shores. Men generally still wore the traditional garb of power—a headcovering and prayer shawl (*tallit*); and though women were granted theoretical equality and admitted into the main sanctuary, they still sat in a separate section reserved for them. But the Reform Movement had been born.

Three rabbinic conferences in mid-century featured deliberations of this religious "reformation" of Judaism, including such matters as the use of Hebrew in prayer. One rabbi—later claimed as the progenitor of the Conservative Movement (see below)—walked out of the proceedings when his liberal colleagues refused sufficiently to privilege Hebrew as a sacred tongue. In 1819 and again in 1841, a Hamburg congregation published a liberal prayer book, with resulting charges and counter-charges, condemnations and excommunications, between traditionalists and modernists. But 19th-century European politics was increasingly reactionary, so that the fight for change moved to America.

b. United States

American Jewish worship has gone

through three stages. The first is the period known as Classical Reform, which reached its zenith in 1894/95, with the publication of a *Union Prayer Book* for Reform congregations. Reforms begun in Europe were carried through here, generally in a sweeping fashion undreamed of across the ocean. Worship featured short services almost entirely in English. It was dominated by western music sung by a hidden choir and a sermon similar to what one would hear in an Episcopalian or Congregationalist church. Folk traditions like specialized worship garb, and old-world customs like carrying the Torah through the congregation were erased. The mood was one of awe, and the congregation was almost completely passive, expected to rise and sit in unison, sometimes to read some responses together, rarely ever to sing, and by and large, to recognize the presence of God as a transcendent being suggested by the staid architectural and cultural magnificence which enfolded them.

The second stage developed with the migration from 1881 to 1924 of eastern European Jews for whom classical Reform seemed cold and devoid of Jewish substance or feeling. The new immigrants developed their own Conservative Movement, which remained true to worship styles they had known as Europeans, albeit in a modernized format. By the 1930s eastern Europeans were joining Reform Temples as well, bringing with them a yearning for traditional melodies and the warmth of the folk culture that classical Reform had jettisoned. The depression and then World War II delayed rapid evolution for two decades, and the shock of the Holocaust as well as the need to build and then to support the State of Israel readjusted Jewish concern away from local spirituality and toward world politics. But movement to the suburbs brought with it a recognizably different form of Jewish worship, especially for Reform Jews, whose classical style had been dependent on huge sanctuaries and pipe organs that no one in suburbia could afford, or, for that matter, even wanted any more.

By the 1960s, the third stage, a veritable second reformation for Jews had begun. Unhappiness with suburban worship and the need to express theologically the loss of the 6,000,000, and the miracle of a modern Jewish state led to the publication of new liturgies. In 1972, the Reform Movement began ordaining women as rabbis and investing them as cantors, reforms that eventually were replicated by Conservative and Reconstructionist Jews as well. (Reconstructionism, American Judaism's fourth movement, broke away from Conservative Judaism following the philosophy of Mordecai Kaplan, who emphasized Judaism as a civilization, held a high regard for tradition, but denounced many traditional Jewish beliefs including a personal deity and chosen peoplehood.)

Present directions suggest increased affirmation of egalitarianism in worship, and thus, revised liturgies with inclusive language. Musically, the cantor (man or woman) has made a dramatic reappearance as have traditional melodies, and a new "American sound" is being created by a small but growing cadre of synagogue composers. Above all, we find an accent again on spirituality, not only in the synagogue, but in the home too, which is emerging again as a licit locus for the Jew's stance before God.

Joseph Heinemann, *Prayer in the Talmud: Forms and Patterns,* Richard Sarason, trans. (Berlin and London: Walter de Gruyter, 1977). Lawrence A. Hoffman, *The Canonization of the Synagogue Service* (Notre Dame and London: University of Notre Dame Press, 1979). Lawrence A. Hoffman, ed., *Land of Israel: Jewish Perspectives* (Notre Dame: University of Notre Dame Press, 1986). Louis Jacobs, *Hasidic Prayer* (New York: Schocken Books, 1973). Jakob J. Petuchowski, *Prayerbook Reform in Europe* (New York: World Union for Progressive Judaism, 1968). Lawrence A. Hoffman,

Beyond the Text: a Holistic Approach to Liturgy (Bloomington: Indiana University Press, 1987).

LAWRENCE A. HOFFMAN

JOHN THE BAPTIST, FEASTS OF

John the Baptist, great precursor of the Lord, is honored by two feasts in the Roman calendar: the Solemnity of the Birth of John the Baptist (June 24) and the memorial of the beheading of John the Baptist (August 29).

History

There was great devotion to the Baptist in both East and West from earliest times. Five sets of Mass texts are found in the Veronese (Leonine) Sacramentary (ca. 550; it is more of a compilation of texts than a sacramentary so called. Two of the sets are for a celebration of the eucharist at the baptismal font. Evidently it was a day in which more than one liturgy was celebrated: a vigil, at the altar and at the font.

In the East, the great day for the Baptist is January 7, connected with Epiphany, which is the commemoration of the Lord's baptism in the churches of the East. The West follows the gospel story and places John's conception six months before Christmas (Lk 1:36).

The memorial of the beheading was originally an Eastern celebration, probably marking the date of the dedication of a church of John the Baptist in Sebaste (4th century). It was celebrated in the Gallican and Mozarabic churches in the 7th century and only entered the Roman calendar later in the Middle Ages.

The Eastern churches celebrate a feast of the conception of the Baptist on September 24 (or 23: only the Lord is born exactly nine months after conception). This feast was found in several Western churches, but was not included in the Missal of 1570. There is also a feast of the discovery of the head of the Baptist on February 24. Again it found a place in some Western churches but was not included in the Tridentine reform.

Theology of the Celebrations

The celebration of the eucharist focuses on the story of John the Baptist. The readings proclaim him as the prophet known from before time began (Jer 1:4-10 [vigil]; 17-19 [beheading]; Is 49:1-6). His birth was surrounded by portents and he is revealed as one with a mission, growing to maturity in the desert (Lk 1:5-17 [vigil]; 57-66,80). He preached a message of baptism for the remission of sins and pointed to Christ as the one who was to come, greater than he (Acts 13, 22-26). He ultimately gives his life and leaves the scene to the Lamb of God (Mk 6:17-29 [beheading]).

The prayers develop some of these themes, though unfortunately the English translations do not capture the richness of the Latin. He is the precursor (vigil: opening prayer, preface; beheading: opening prayer; not in English), the great prophet who witnesses to the coming of the Savior (preface; beheading: opening prayer; birth: prayer after communion), greater than all those born of woman (preface). He points out to all the world the Lamb of God, who is now our sacrifice whom we receive (preface; prayer after communion for both vigil and birth). We can come to Christ because John has showed him to us and pointed out the way to follow him (vigil: opening prayer).

The celebration of the liturgy of the hours follows the same basic thought pattern. John is the prophet and herald of Christ. He is seen as the fulfillment of the prophecy that Elijah will return to herald the Messiah (birth: morning prayer; Mal 3:23-24). There is a bit more emphasis on John as found in the Prologue to John's gospel: the one sent to give testimony to the truth (birth: evening prayer II, Magnificat antiphon). There is the concern to keep John in proper context as the forerunner: he must increase and I must decrease (beheading: evening prayer, Magnificat antiphon).

John is still our herald, pointing out to us Christ from among those who claim our attention. He gave himself to the point of death for his message and challenges us to follow.

A. Adam, *The Liturgical Year* (Collegeville: Liturgical Press, 1981), pp. 232-235. A. Nocent, *The Liturgical Year* (Collegeville: Liturgical Press, 1977), Vol. 1:124-128, 143-151. P. Rado, *Enchiridion Liturgicum* (Rome, 1961), Vol 2:1381-84.

MICHAEL WITCZAK

JOSEPH, FEASTS OF

St. Joseph, husband of Mary, protector of the boy Jesus, carpenter of Nazareth, is honored by two feasts in the Roman calendar: the Solemnity of Joseph, husband of Mary (March 19) and the optional memorial of St. Joseph the Worker (May 1).

History

Devotion to St. Joseph is relatively late. The first traces can be found among the Copts in the 8th/9th centuries. In the West the first celebrations are found in the 12th century: the Crusaders had a special devotion to Joseph, building a church in his honor in Nazareth. The devotion was subsequently fostered especially by the Franciscans, in particular Bernardine of Siena. The feast of Joseph became universal in the church in the late 15th century (by Sixtus IV, a Franciscan) and was made a holy day of obligation by Gregory XV in 1621. Pius IX declared Joseph the Patron of the Universal Church in 1870.

A second feast of St. Joseph, the *Patrocinium*, began among the Carmelites in 1680. It was extended to the whole church by Pius IX in 1847 on the third Sunday after Easter. Pius X in reforming the rubrics wanted to reemphasize the importance of Sunday, and so (among other changes) moved this feast of Joseph to the Wednesday before

the third Sunday after Easter. Finally the feast was abolished in 1956 with the advent of the new feast of St. Joseph the Worker on May 1.

This new feast was promulgated by Pius XII in 1955 as a way of showing the church's relevance to the laboring person in a Europe which was threatened by communism and socialism and which celebrated Labor Day on May 1. The day was reduced to an optional memorial in 1969, noting that it might be used on any country's labor day.

Theology of the Celebrations

The celebration of the eucharist presents us with a brief catechesis on the meaning and role of Joseph. The readings for the solemnity situate Joseph within the plan of salvation history: he is the one who forms the connection with the Davidic promise (2 Sam 7:4-5; 12-14;16). He is seen as one whose life is founded, like Abraham, on faith. Abraham became the father of many nations; Joseph is the father of the one who saved all the nations in faith (Rom 4:13,16-18,22). The gospels give the choice of reflecting on Joseph the dreamer, called to play a role in God's plan of incarnation (Mt 1:16;18-21;24), or the worried parent seeking his child who is instructing the doctors (Lk 2:41-51). [Note that many of these readings are pastiches: there is not a great deal about Joseph in the gospels.] The readings for Joseph the Worker are about the value of labor (Gen 1:26-2:3; Col 3:14-15,17,23-24). The gospel presents the parentage of Jesus: the carpenter's son (Mt 13:54-58).

The prayers offer further reflection on Jesus. The preface offers a wonderful synthesis: Joseph is the faithful servant, entrusted to be husband of Mary and protector of Jesus. As the protector of our Savior (opening prayer, prayer over the gifts) he also is committed to the care of the family of the church (opening prayer). We pray that our service will be as pure as that of Joseph (prayer over the gifts). Joseph is a model of proper stewardship of the gifts of this earth (worker opening prayer) and a model of the way we should spend our lives in love (worker prayer after communion).

The celebration of the liturgy of the hours sees Joseph primarily in his role as the link between the two testaments: he is the faithful servant, the fulfillment of the prophecies, one who embodies wisdom and fear of the Lord. The prayer for Joseph the Worker highlights that this world must be cared for since it is the creation of God and the arena in which the incarnation took place and our salvation unfolded.

Celebrating Joseph today reminds us that the incarnation is a historical reality, unfolding in time and in the lives of individuals demanding faith and terrible choices to remain true to the call of God in our lives.

A. Adam, *The Liturgical Year* (Collegeville: Liturgical Press, 1981), pp. 230-232. A. Nocent, *The Liturgical Year* (Collegeville: Liturgical Press, 1977), Vol. 2:237-238. P. Rado, *Enchiridion Liturgicum* (Rome, 1961), Vol. 2:1378-79.

MICHAEL WITCZAK

JUNGMANN, JOSEF (1889-1956)

Jesuit professor of theology and liturgy at the Collegium Canisianum in Innsbruck, Jungmann devoted most of his professional life to unearthing and making available in published form the history and theology of the church's prayer. His legacy, in addition to his many students, is a massive bibliography. The list of those available in English includes: *The Eucharistic Prayer* (Fides, 1956); *The Early Liturgy* (Notre Dame, 1959); *Handing on the Faith* (1959); *Pastoral Liturgy* (Herder and Herder, 1962); and, *Christian Prayer Through the Centuries* (Paulist, 1978). Without doubt, his most influential works are: *The Place of Christ in Liturgical Prayer* (Alba House, 1965) and his monumental *Missarum Solemnia (The Mass of the Roman Rite)* (publ. 2 vol., Benziger, 1951-55; edited to a single vol., 1959; revised as *The Mass* [Liturgical Press, 1976]) which he prepared during World War II when the faculty at the Canisianum was disbanded.

See **Liturgical movement, the (1830-1969)**

L

LAITY, THEOLOGY OF THE

Historical Overview

Jesus preached to the laity of his day and picked his disciples from the laity, but he did not establish specific offices or structures of church or ministry such as we have today. In fact, our present terms laity, office, ministries, hierarchy, priesthood, diaconate, and religious have no immediate counterpart in Jesus' mission.

The Greek translations of the Bible generally used the word *laos* to mean the chosen people in contrast to the pagans around them. Early Christian writings refer to the community of the church as "the people of God" (*laos theou*), a term frequently complemented by references such as "the elect" (*kletus*), or "the holy ones" (*hagioi*), or "disciples" (*mathetai*), or "brothers and sisters" (*adelphoi*). These positive descriptions of the faithful are common in the first two centuries of the church, with only five or six possible exceptions in which the word *laos* describes the simple, inferior(?) people in contrast to their leadership. The term "laity" (*laikos*) derives from this rather negative use of *laos*. Clement of Rome (c. 96) in his letter to the Corinthians (40) is the first to use *laikos* in a way that suggests the incompetent masses of the people. This use is also found in Origen (*In Jerem., hom.* XI, 3), and especially in Clement of Alexandria ([d. 215] *Strom* III, 12, 90, 1; V, 6, 33,3; *Paed.* III, 10, 83,2). This consideration of laity as the "plebs" of the church is intensified due to three developments in the life of the early church: Neo-platonism's influence on several Church Fathers, the growth of monasticism, and the development of the clerical dimension of the church. All three movements gave laity the image of second-class citizens because of their involvement with the material world which was thought to make them profane. The equation of holiness with monasticism thus introduced a minimalist approach to lay spirituality, and the introduction of a grading or ranking of church membership left the laity subordinated and powerless. By the 4th century, church structures were similar to political ones, and the subordination of laity was already a firm part of church life; "lay" meant profane, and in the liturgy laity were separated from clergy by the construction of solid screens dividing the sanctuary from the people (Antioch as early as 390, and Hagia Sophia, Constantinople, in 570).

Paralleling these structural changes in the life of the church, with the resulting downgrading of laity, were significant developments in liturgy that, at times, evidenced a positive approach to laity, and, at other times, confirmed the move to passivity and exclusion. In early NT times, all the faithful shared in decision making, mission priorities, and ministry. The first negative development for laity occurred with the exclusion of women

636

from leadership roles in the church. Although Jesus had preached respect for the freedom of women, their roles in the new community were soon suppressed and their new found leadership stifled. Lay faithful chose from among their community those who would exercise leadership, and once chosen, the individual led the celebration without any thought of priesthood. Early Christian writings speak of teachers and prophets presiding at the eucharist (*Didache*, 9-10), or other eminent individuals with the consent of the people (Clement, *Letter to the Corinthians*, 44, 3), or those who confessed their faith under persecution (*Apost. Trad.* of Hippolytus, 9). The presumption of the Fathers is that the leader of the community presides at the eucharist. Moreover, with or without the use of terms such as bishop, there is no explicit reference to the priesthood of the presider at the eucharist before the beginning of the 3rd century. While writings rarely refer to the ministerial priesthood, they frequently speak of the priesthood of all believers (Origen, *In Lev. hom.* IX, 1; VI 2; Tertullian, *De orat.*, CXXVIII; Ambrose, *De myst.*, VI, 30). Even after the sacerdotalization of ministry, Tertullian, himself a layperson, told other laity to celebrate the eucharist in the absence of a priest (*De Exhort. Cast.*, 7,3; see also *De Praesc.*, 41:5-8). Other Fathers, including St. Augustine, rejected this possibility (*Litt.* 3,8). Theodoret informs us that laity celebrated the eucharist during the early 4th century evangelization of Ethiopia (*Hist. Eccles*, I, 23, 5). Even when lay presiding was no longer allowed, and lay people no longer viewed as extraordinary presiders of the eucharist, they gave communion to each other and to themselves, keeping communion in their homes for such purposes (St. Basil, *Letter*, 93). Laity, then, presided over the community and at the celebration of the eucharist, and even when the church institutionalized its ministries of overseer and deacon, these clerics were warned not to exalt themselves over the people (*Apost. Const.* VIII, 1, 20).

Documents of the early church also refer to the involvement of laity in the preparation and celebration of baptism. A layperson contributed both to the educational component of the catechumenate and to the rituals of prayer and imposition of hands (*Apost. Trad.*, 19). Tertullian did not restrict the layperson's role to catechist and sponsor, important though these were, but he also told the laity to baptize in the absence of a priest (*De Exhort. Cast.* 7, 3).

The history of the sacrament of penance is complicated. Laity always played a major community role in the ceremonies and in the spiritual counselling and direction that accompanied conversion. Clement of Alexandria considered saintly laity on a par with priest and bishop in the forgiveness of sins (*Strom.* VI, 13). Confession to a layperson was practiced during the Carolingian reform; first lesser sins and later even grave sins were confessed to a layperson. Albert the Great considered such confession a sacrament (*IV Sent. dist.* xvii, art, 59). Lay confession, at times a widespread practice, survived until the 14th century.

Innocent I (*Ep. ad Decentium*, [c.416] 8, 11) confirms the expressed views of other early writers that in the first centuries laity kept oils at home and anointed their sick. This practice continued in subsequent centuries when writers like Caesarius of Arles ([d. 543] *Sermon* 279, 5) and later the Venerable Bede ([d. 735] *Commentary on Ep. James*) still considered the layperson as the extraordinary minister of the anointing of the sick, even though admittedly there was no fixed ritual until priests became the ordinary ministers.

In addition to involvement in the liturgical rituals, laity preached and evangelized, often as official catechists, as Origen did in Caesarea while still a layperson. Others were traveling missionaries, as Paul had been.

In early centuries, Christian marriage was a family affair, validly established by the consent of the partners. While clerical interventions for pastoral reasons are traceable to the time of Ignatius of Antioch, it was generally considered superfluous. Marriage in the presence of the church's clergy was unknown in the early centuries, except in the cases of marriages of clergy and of catechumens. From the 4th century, clergy became ecclesiastical witnesses, guardians for the marriages of poor orphans, and gave marriage blessings when invited to the celebrations. Since baptism was understood to sanctify the marriage of Christians, liturgical ceremonies that accompanied marriage were not essential but pastorally helpful to show the church's support of the partners' decision. Mutual consent was enough even in the 9th century. Accompanying ceremonies were provided optionally by local churches, with individual ecclesiastics insisting on their necessity. By the 10th century, bishops who were also feudal overlords claimed not only pastoral and moral authority, but jurisdictional power too; never however diminishing the fact that the partners' consent was the only component for validity. Theologians and church leaders of the 11th to 13th centuries debated the sacramental nature of marriage, including it among the seven sacraments accepted in the early 12th century. It was not until the Council of Trent that a ceremony presided over by clergy was declared necessary for validity, and even then, it was primarily to prevent clandestine marriages.

The writings of Church Fathers firmly establish the laity's right to choose their leaders (Clement, Ignatius, Justin, Tertullian, Hippolytus, Cyprian). Moreover, the person who presided over the community presided at the eucharist in the name of the priestly people in the communal sharing of the action of Christ the priest. Even after the sacerdotalization of ministry, laity still elected their leaders, and the prohibition of absolute ordinations, i.e., without a community, forbidden by canon 6 of Chalcedon, was only changed in the 12th century.

The ecclesiasticalization and sacerdotalization of ministry gradually led to the exclusion of laity from functions they had performed, in some cases, for centuries. Sometimes exclusion resulted from a different understanding of a sacrament, as in the case of a juridical emphasis on the sacrament of penance, implying the power of the keys which it was thought only belonged to clerics. Sometimes the progressive restriction of laity was based on prudence not doctrine, as was the case with preaching; the prudence then being justified by theological arguments. Sometimes politics, education, and sociological developments led to the current clerical/non-clerical church. Liturgy is an excellent portrayal of ecclesiology, and of the history of ecclesiology, and it manifests the main lines in the historical development of the roles of laity in the church. Community and democracy characterize the apostolic church more than any hierarchical structure. Its many ministries are not stated to be sacerdotal and the primary celebrant of liturgy is the community. Even after the sacerdotalization of ministry, laity are still the extraordinary ministers of baptism, the eucharist, penance, and the anointing of the sick.

While it is easier to deal with the clear-cut canonical distinctions of today, such artificial distinctions are hardly faithful to the dynamic interrelationships between the community and its chosen hierarchy in the first three centuries. In a political community that esteemed rank, the church soon established ranks for those who served the community, and these extended their control to the laity's loss, eventually producing a two-tiered church, even minor ministries being brought under the power of the priesthood. Thus, we gradually pass from an ecclesiology of communion to an ecclesiology of power (Congar). The passivity of laity increased in feudal times, and medieval councils further consolidated it. Eventually, Trent legitimized the separation between clergy and people, seen so clearly in the people's passivity in the liturgy of the imposed Roman Canon. Laity are excluded from all active participation in the life of their church, clerical control reaching such proportions that in the minds of most people "the church" came to mean the hierarchy.

Vatican II and the Laity

Three developments of Vatican II reversed the downward trend in the life and role of laity that began at the end of the 3rd and beginning of the 4th century. The ecclesiology of Vatican II, reinforced by the extraordinary Synod of 1985, stressed the church as a communion (L.G., 31:1), in which "each individual part of the Church contributes through its special gifts to the good of the other parts of the whole Church" (L.G., 13:3). This ecclesiology of communion, "the central and fundamental idea of the council's documents" (1985 Synod, *Final Report*, C, 1), finds both its source and culminating expression in the liturgy, and must be manifested in a co-responsible and collaborative approach to the church (*Final Report*, C, 6). Second, linked to this vision of communion is the council's affirmation of the universal call to holiness: "It is evident to everyone that all the faithful of Christ of whatever rank or status are called to the fullness of the Christian life and to the perfection of charity" (L.G., 40:3). This vision of a common calling must direct the reading of conciliar texts, as the document on the church implies, when it reminds readers that "Everything which has been said so far concerning the People of God applies equally to the laity, religious, and clergy"

(L.G., 30:1). A third development of paramount importance is the council's declaration on the autonomy of earthly realities (G.S., 36), and the insistence that building a better world is part of God's plan (A.A., 7:1).

These three core convictions are united in the council's theological evaluation of lay life (L.G., 31). This paragraph changed through four schemas, from the rather negative and minimalistic view of lay life in the first schema, to a more positive appreciation of both the world and lay life in the second and third schema, to the ecclesial vision of the final draft, which characterizes laity by their active belonging to the church and co-responsible sharing both in internal church life and in ecclesial outreach to the world to build up the Kingdom. This evaluation avoids any split between clergy and laity, acknowledges that laity share in the responsibility for the entire church while not holding office in the organization, and affirms that the earthly ordering of temporal society is the specific way in which a layperson seeks the Kingdom of God. This synthesis is restated by the 1987 Synod on Laity when it claims that the vocation and mission of laity is to be the communion of the church and that their ministry is to serve primarily in secular situations.

This integration of laity into a positive vision of the church as communion is complemented by the teachings of the *Constitution on the Sacred Liturgy*. The document insists that liturgy is a celebration of the whole community, as a sacrament of unity (S.C., 26:1), in which each Christian participates according to the distinction of roles (S.C., 26:2; 28). While speaking of liturgy the document offers a vision of church when it states, "whenever rites ... make provision for communal celebration involving the presence and active participation of the faithful, this way of celebrating them is to be preferred" (S.C., 27:1).

640

In the years since the council, we have seen several different theologies of laity, often due to a separating of one of the three conciliar developments from the other two. One approach sees laity as totally dependent on clergy for the inner life of the church and as instruments in the hands of the hierarchy, who are presumed in this approach to have exclusively received mission and authority for ministry from Jesus. A second theology sees laity as an ecclesial presence to the world. Inserted into secular circumstances, the laity are called to influence the world with Christ's message and to be present to the world in the name of the church. The church's inner life of word and sacrament nourishes the laity for this task. A third theology of laity interprets their role as one of world transformation and clearly emphasizes their social responsibility, world transformation, and the fight against injustice. A fourth theology stresses collegiality, co-responsibility, and the priesthood of all the faithful. This approach implies a restructuring of the church, and is frequently experienced in basic ecclesial communities, team ministry, and intervocational work. A fifth theology is the open-ended exploratory approach of many laity today, who courageously launch into new approaches to church life, spirituality, and ministry. Each of these theological approaches is extensively promoted, but none of them has obtained exclusive support.

From Vatican II to the 1987 Synod on the Laity

From the close of the Second Vatican Council in 1965 to Pope John Paul's post-synodal *Apostolic Exhortation on the Laity* in 1988 there have been both struggle and clarification in the understanding of the vocation and mission of laity in the church and in the world.

The council still defines laity primarily in a negative way, sees their proper and special characteristic as secularity, and

understands their vocation as engaging in temporal affairs (L.G., 31). As Christians in the heart of the world, their mission includes: the work of evangelization (A.A., 6:1) by the quality of their lives (A.G., 36:3; L.G., 31:3-4; 35:3-5), by promoting the word (A.A., 6:3) and by transforming the environment in which they live (A.A., 13:1); personal responsibility for the charitable service of the needy (G.S., 21:6); the development of Christian dimensions of family life (A.A., 11:1) by making families into schools of holiness (L.G., 35:4; G.S., 48), of social virtues (G.E., 3), of ministry (L.G., 35:3-4), and of the social defense of family values (G.S., 52); and a social mission (A.A., 13:1) that includes working for justice (A.G., 12:3), defending human dignity (G.S., 26:2), educating at all levels of the community (G.S., 60:1), and serving the public in communications and politics (I.M., 14; G.S., 75:7; A.A., 14:1-2). The secular mission of laity is their "proper and indispensable role in the mission of the Church" (A.A., 1:1), their way of sharing the priestly, prophetic, and royal office of Christ (A.A., 2:2). For these tasks laity receive charisms, "so that all according to their proper roles may cooperate in this common mission of the Church with one heart" (L.G., 30:2). Laity have a right to use these gifts (A.A., 3:3), and conciliar documents urge pastors to recognize and use them (L.G., 30:2) as an essential complement to their own mission and ministry (A.A., 10:1).

In addition to a mission in the world, the council states that "every layman [and woman], by virtue of the very gifts bestowed upon him [or her], is at the same time a witness and a living instrument of the mission of the Church herself" (L.G., 33:2). While not developed as fully as their secular mission, the council recognizes laity's responsibility for the internal life of the church (A.A., 3:3; 16:3), seen in collaborative efforts with their pastors (A.A., 10:1), and including liturgical participation (S.C., 11), community building (G.S., 92:1; A.G., 19), and co-responsibility for the life of their church (A.A., 10).

In the years following the council, laity emerged with new roles and opportunities in the local and international church. This period of growth and new awareness was accompanied by years of doubt, frustration and dissatisfaction. In 1980 the U. S. bishops published their pastoral *Called and Gifted: Catholic Laity 1980* in which they urged the laity to rekindle their excitement in the vision of the council, calling them to adulthood, holiness, ministry and community. The decade of the 1980s has witnessed the growth of collaboration, with its accompanying need to clarify roles in the church. The new *Code of Canon Law*, published in 1983, gives an unprecedented list of rights for all the faithful, specifically for laity as members of the church and in their internal service of the church, for laity in their local parishes, and in the exercise of diocesan offices. Unfortunately the new code's ecclesiology, hardly that of the council, reinforces the hierarchical, centralized power of the church, more than any previous document of church history.

First announced in 1985, the Synod on Laity stimulated a worldwide reflection on the roles of laity. In 1985, the Vatican Synod Secretariate distributed its *Guidelines* ("Lineamenta") on *The Vocation and the Mission of the Laity*, calling for wide consultation with laity. The document, which suffered from unhealthy dualistic language, expressed concern over what it saw as role confusion between the vocations and as laity's over-accommodation to modern culture. It recommended a reaffirmation of the strong distinctions between clergy, religious, and laity, and a clearer tension between faith and secular culture. It offered no new vision or reinterpretation, but drew its solutions from a restatement of traditional responses. More basically, the *Lineamenta* failed to take account of the ecclesiological developments in and since the council, or to interpret the Vatican Council's theology of laity in light of its ecclesiology, but simply relied on the council's statements about laity without filtering these through its new understanding of church. Following an analysis of responses from around the world, a new *Working Paper* was presented in 1987, correcting some of the weaknesses of the *Guidelines*, and most notably introducing a distinction between the vocation of laity to participate fully in the communion of the church and their mission to be involved primarily in secular situations. This fine document formed the basis of the Synod's reflections, and most of the resulting 54 propositions can be paralleled with the document's developments. The 1987 Synod on Laity ended with a "Message to the People of God," and its recommendations were the basis for Pope John Paul II's *Apostolic Exhortation on the Laity* (*Christifideles Laici*), published on December 30, 1988, and distributed in February 1989.

Pope John Paul II's Apostolic Exhortation is a positive and affirming document in which he speaks respectfully throughout of the lay faithful, presenting a positive vision for them, based upon a common dignity in baptism (10) and a basic common call to holiness (11) while exercising functions distinct from clergy and religious. All vocations equally belong to the church and its mystery and share a common call to ministry. Lay faithful have the source of their life and call in baptism that regenerates, unites, and anoints them in the mystery of the church's communion, and grants them a share in the priestly, prophetic, and royal office of Jesus (14). Sharing a common dignity and responsibility for the church's mission, laity exercise their mission in secular circumstances, which is not only a sociological statement, but part of their theological and ecclesiological reality (15). Their call to holiness, which they share with all members of the church, is likewise distinguished and specified by their commitment and call to renew the temporal order (16). Lay faithful participate in the life of the church as communion (18), which is an organic life of diversity and complementarity (20). Lay faithful accept and realize this call to communion through their complementary capacity for participation in the life and mission of the church. The church's mission is achieved by all in solidarity, each carrying out the ministries, offices, and roles proper to the way they vocationally live their baptism (21), sustained by the charisms each have for the benefit of the ecclesial communion and the world that the church serves (24). Pope John Paul II calls lay faithful to foster a sense of the universal church (25), a dedication to the parish as the most visible expressions of ecclesial community (26), and the development of concrete forms of participation in local church life that are both individual and group (28). Turning to develop the co-responsibility of the lay faithful in the church's mission, the pope urges lay faithful to accept a mission to build up communion (32), to undertake a re-evangelization first of the ecclesial community (34) and then also of the world (35), to serve the dignity of individual persons (37), their rights and freedom, and of society, especially in the family (40), in solidarity with all, in public life, and in socio-economic and cultural life. The pope directs part IV of his letter to the varied vocations in the church (45-56), calling all to be stewards of God's varied graces. His final focus is on the formation of the lay faithful in their life (57), vocation, and mission (58), on building an integrated life through collaboration with the Lord (59), and on reciprocal openness to each other (63).

Components of a Theology of Laity Baptismal Vocation

The Vatican Council presented baptism as the common fundamental experience of Christianity, even interpreting priestly ordination and religious profession as intensifications of baptismal vocation. This common calling is the special dignity given equally to all Christians.

Sacramental Life. The church in this century moved away from any elitist approach to Christian life and holiness, rather presenting the sacramental system of the church as the basis for all growth. The liturgy and the sacraments become the central expression of the whole covenanted people's commitment to the Lord.

Church as Communion. A central idea of the council and major post-conciliar documents, this understanding sees the church as a community of disciples with equal dignity and rights, structured according to functions. This vision of church is visibly portrayed through participatory styles of government and collaboration in ministry. All the baptized share a common vocation to be the communion of the church.

Sharing Christ's Life. A result of baptism is the sharing in the life of Jesus, particularly in the three-fold office of the Lord. Jesus' priestly, prophetical, and royal offices are shared with all members of the church, even though each will live them according to his or her distinct baptismal vocations.

The Holy Spirit's Varied Charisms. Laity are living instruments of the mission of the church, endowed by the Holy Spirit with charisms for the common good of both the inner life of the church and its mission of outreach to the world. A community that mutually appreciates each member's gifts, the church is composed of varied vocations, each one realizing that it is incomplete without the others, since we are an intervocational community that finds life and enrichment in each other.

Christian Priesthood. The prime priestly reality in Christianity is the priesthood of all the baptized, and the ministerial priesthood, essentially different, and therefore not implying a difference of dignity, is established to support the priesthood of all the baptized. The latter is exercised by active participation in the liturgy and in the secular circumstances of daily life.

Condition is Mission. One experiences the call of the Lord in the concrete circumstances of one's life, partly the result of one's history and partly the result of choice—one's own and God's. The condition of the lay faithful is secularity. While not diminishing their vocation to be living members of the communion of the church and to equally share in the church's mission to spread the redemptive grace of the Lord, laity do this in the secular circumstances of life. This condition modifies their way of responding to the Lord, of developing their own holiness, and of collaborating with the church community.

Growth From the Foundations. The council complemented its teachings on the universal church with a strong emphasis on the local church, whether seen as diocese, parish, basic ecclesial group, or family. If ecclesial life is strong in these basic and primary groups of local church, then it can be strong at other levels. Emphasis on laity as fully contributing to the life, holiness, and mission of the church, appreciates that growth rises from the members as well as filters down from the leaders.

Viewing the laity as integrally church, active contributing members, is both respectful and theologically sound. However, there are a few potential problems that can weaken this vision. 1. Some recent documents, maintaining exaggerated distinctions between clergy and laity, could encourage the maintenance of a clergy-laity split in the church, and thwart authentic collaboration. While the clericalization of laity may be a potential danger in very restricted circumstances, the secularization of laity who are presumed to have no interest in the inner life of the church and the greater clericalization of clergy are far more serious problems. 2. The dangerous desire to control laity, individually or in groups, is as real as ever. The renewal of lay life by the hierarchy is potentially a paternalistic put-down of lay life in which laity become a renewed object of clerical apostolate rather than collaborators in mutual renewal. 3. A third danger for lay life is the lay mimicking of prior clerical autocratic styles of life and government. As we see hierarchies of laity surfacing around the nation and the world, whether in local churches, in spiritual movements, or in national lay organizations, the baptized have reason to worry and to challenge. 4. A fourth is a lack of an integrated renewal of lay life which values both the lay faithful's internal service to the church and their mission to renew the temporal order. Movements that stress either one of these to the exclusion of the other are hardly likely to have long-term effects. 5. A further danger is to leave things as they are, maintaining current distinctions which are not based on baptismal choices and functions, but history, economics, and laws. We have witnessed plenty of adaptations in lay life, but very little doctrinal renewal in the Church that effectively leads to a renewed understanding of the lay faithful's original roles in the community of the Lord.

Russell Barta, ed., *Challenge to the Laity* (Huntington, IN: Our Sunday Visitor, Inc., 1980. Yves M.-J. Congar, *Lay People in the Church* (Westminster, MD: Newman Press, 1957). Leonard Doohan, *The Lay-Centered Church: Theology and Spirituality* (San Francisco: Harper and Row, 1984); *The Laity: A Bibliography* (Wilmington, DE: Michael Glazier, Inc., 1987); *Laity's Mission in the Local Church: Setting a New Direction* (San Francisco: Harper and Row, 1986). Georgia M. Keightley, "Laity," *New Dictionary of Theology*

(Wilmington, DE: Michael Glazier, Inc., 1988), pp. 558-564. Robert L. Kinast, *Caring for Society: A Theological Interpretation of Lay Ministry* (Chicago: The Thomas More Press, 1985). Edward Schillebeeckx, "The Typological Definition of Christian Layman according to Vatican II," *The Mission of the Church* (New York: The Seabury Press, 1973), pp. 90-116.

LEONARD DOOHAN

LANGUAGE AND HUMAN EXPERIENCE

During the 20th century there has been a great surge of interest in language studies among philosophers. Though no single method or approach has emerged to embrace the whole field, one common concern that has come to the fore is the relationship between language and human experience. This article treats this relationship in four sections: (1) language, (2) human experience, (3) linguistic disclosure of human experience, and (4) liturgical implications and questions.

Language

At least three major currents can be identified within contemporary language studies. One includes both logical positivists and linguistic analysts, on the one hand (e.g., Moore, Russel, Ryle, Ayer), and those concerned with the functioning and composition of linguistic units, on the other (e.g., Levi-Strauss, Chomsky). These approach language study as *science*, with the same methodic rigor that is employed in the physical sciences. Largely empirical in their method, they seek an objectivity similar to that enjoyed by physical scientists. In this systematic and technical approach to language they neglect any reference that lies outside the scientific and methodic examination of language structure. Their contribution is to establish language study as an objective science with results that must be taken seriously.

A second current focuses on linguistic *usage*, either in the form of "language games" or as linguistic performativity (e.g., Wittgenstein, Austin, Searle, Evans). Since these are principally concerned with communication, their primary issue is the effect of language on, and the relationship of language to, interlocutors. They consider language as a subjective act which expresses the meaning which human experience has. The limit to their approach is that they offer no explanation as to how the language used is related to the experience which is expressed.

A third group, I'll call them simply "philosophers of language" (e.g., Husserl, Heidegger, Ricoeur), does address this relationship question. Going beyond language usage, these philosophers of language are not content to say simply that language *expresses* human experience. Rather, they wish to uncover the determinate relationship *between* language and human experience and its ontological significance. They seek to explain how language *discloses* being in *new ways*. For them, language not only expresses human experience, but in fact constitutes a creative redescription of reality.

Each of these currents has, of course, many variations and fine points that distinguish thinkers within their own specific grouping. For our purpose here, however, it is the positive contribution of each group taken as a whole that provides an advance to the question at hand, namely the relationship between language and human experience. Language study (a) is a methodic science, (b) involves a subject and a subjective act, and (c) potentially redescribes reality.

What is common ... [continue para. 2, p. 3].

What is common to each group is a concern for the question of meaning. The linguistic analysts consider meaning to be uncovered within the structure of the text itself. The performativity theorists see meaning as having much to do with the relationship of language to, and its affect on, the subjects involved in communication. Philosophers of language locate meaning at the level of the experience which is disclosed by language.

Language philosophers assume that the source of meaning is anterior to its expression in language. "Anterior" is used here in a logical sense, that is, experience comes to expression in language, but not necessarily in the chronological sense that one is aware of experience before its expression in language. In actuality, awareness usually first focuses on language which provides an at-hand cipher of experience. Then *through reflection* there is a cognizance of experience itself. One of the challenges of interpretation is to say just *what it is* that comes to language, what is the experience being expressed and what is the meaning attached to that human act.

When the interlocutors are present to each other, communication of meaning is a fairly straightforward process because there can be a "checking up" between them to ensure common understanding. For the most part, however, the meanings which shape the world in which people live do not come from situations where the interlocutors are physically present to each other. More usually meaning is determined by various tracers left in society or in various communities by human action. The most common of these traces are written texts (but not limited to them). In these acts of communication the determination of meaning is not so straightforward. It requires tools of interpretation. One heuristic approach which was put forth first by Frege and later adapted and used extensively by Ricoeur is the distinction between *sense* and *reference*.

Sense is one level of meanwhich can be uncovered in the structure of the discourse itself. The linguistic analysts address their task at this level of meaning. Sense is an ideal meaning which can be uncovered

by application of any number of scientific linguistic approaches. If this were all there were to meaning, univocity and clarity would be the standard fare in communication. Usually, however, this is not the case. Language is most often equivocal and strains at these structural limitations.

For Ricoeur, meaning is a dialectic between sense *and* reference. Reference insures that language relates to what is. When one speaks, one speaks *about* something. It is at this deeper level of meaning that the philosophers of language make their ontological claims. Reference is that logically prior source of meaning (experience) which is brought to language and is uncovered in the interpretive act as an extralinguistic dimension of discourse.

The reference brought to language is not a predetermined "givenness" that merely must be enunciated. More is at stake than this. The reference of a text is the world of possibilities that lies before the text. Here, one's ownmost possibilities are projected and, through the interaction of the world of the text and one's own world, new possibilities for human living emerge which are none other than the redescription of reality referred to above. The logical sequence is experience-articulation-new experience. Thus the interpretation of a text enlarges the horizon of the hermeneut in such a way that there is a new self-understanding. Interpretation, then, means more than determining the sense of a text. More importantly, interpretation of discourse is a process whereby meaning emerges as new possibilities to be lived, with and through its potential redescription of reality. This process delivers an extralinguistic import that effects an ontological claim on language-use and its relationship to human experience.

Human Experience
Rather than sense data or feelings of

"good" or "bad," human experience is a subject's reflective engagement with reality. Thus, experience is dialectical: it has both a reference to reality as well as a self-reference (subject). In other words, experience is more concerned with a subject's *response* to reality than with taking it in.

The concept of experience as a "response" to reality supports experience understood as an event which, in turn, evokes the notion of temporality. Human experience occurs in history. In its very broadest extension, history can be thought simply in terms of that which occurs between two points in the human reckoning of time; for example, between birth and death, between now and when the guests arrive, or between one celebration and the next. Or, history can be understood in a more specific and rich meaning: as unlocking the sources, a sequence of human events and meaning that fills human temporality. In this sense, history is not a structure imposed on time but a reflection on and interpretation of human events that reveal the structure of those events. To interpret is to engage in the work of history. What is interpreted? Human action as given in the traces of its structure.

Various linguistic concretizations of the *traces* of human action—to borrow from Aristotle's *Poetics*—are a *mimesis*, an *imitation* of human action. Here "imitation" does not mean "artificial reproduction" or a "mere duplication" of human action. Rather, *mimesis* is a structuring of human action by the construction of its traces in concrete works, a creative event which makes human action available within timeness and enables both the possibility of recovering human action and of redescribing reality. It is this redescription which requires interpretation and empowers a new self-understanding. *Mimesis* brings together the linguistic and temporal dimensions of

human activity. Linguistic concretizations which are mimetic of human events are indicative of the way people or societies order human experience. The infinity of human events becomes somewhat manageable in mediation by a finiteness of structure available for examination and interpretation. What takes place in time, between two points in time, is viably structured by human creativity which then renders human activity recoverable at another point in time. There are two events: the first is a point in time which is a fleeting event—here follows the second event—that nevertheless remains accessible when, through reflection, history is created and experience is deciphered.

Besides temporality, the concept of human experience as response suggests sociality. There is a certain "connectedness" about human living which breaks down isolation barriers between persons and between times. This connectedness constitutes tradition, a more or less definite sequence for doing things proportionate to the depth of connectedness of the community. In a well-defined community such as Christianity, tradition begins in what can be called an "originary" experience. More than just a handing down or repeating of experience, communication through tradition is, first of all, an appropriation of experience to oneself in light of the originary event. Additionally, communication pertains to the redescribing of that experience in light of ongoing experiences. Communication, then, is a wholly engaging activity whereby one's own experiences interact with a tradition of redescriptions of the "originary" experience.

Human experience is communicated by means of language, and different experiences require different expressions. Therefore, one task is to identify the different modes of expressions through which the common experience of a community comes to language.

Linguistic Disclosure of Human Experience

Not all modes of linguistic expressions promise to deliver the same richness with respect to the possibility of redescribing reality. Certain linguistic forms are privileged in addressing this special ontological task and, similar to the gains evidenced by the different currents of language studies, different linguistic expressions make certain gains in their capacity to redescribe reality. Basically, three classes of linguistic forms have been at center front of language studies: word (or symbol), propositions (or discourse), and text. The pursuit has been to indicate what experience is uncovered by each of these linguistic forms.

(a) *Word*

The *word* (or symbol) has long held an esteemed position in language studies. Its primary access to experience has been through its unique multivalent capacity. There would arise no problems with interpretation and no problems with meaning if natural languages were univocal. This is not the case. Natural languages are inherently equivocal: in any dictionary most words have more than one "definition." By means of one meaning, evident and available in the linguistic code itself, a second (hidden) meaning revelatory of human experience becomes accessible. However, to progress in uncovering the dynamic relationship of language and human experience one must realize that multivalence in itself has no potential to redescribe reality. This, because the word (or symbol) lacks the predicative thrust of other linguistic forms.

(b) *Performance*

Language has come to be viewed not so much as an ideal code composed of words in a dictionary (in French, *langue*), multivalent though they may be, but in a much broader, *propositional* sense. The human sciences have made a significant contribution towards shaping this broad notion of language as speech (French: *parole*) as having something to do with the human subject *predicating* something about human experience. In this, the noteworthy contribution of language-use philosophers has been that certain utterances are even more than propositional statements of fact. Indeed, the very speaking implicates the interlocutors in a certain kind of human activity. Every utterance is a *performance*, that is, in the very speaking one involves oneself or another in a certain human activity. For example, the liturgical formula "I confess" is not so much concerned with a propositional statement as it is with the public declaration of faith of the speaker(s) *apart from* or *in addition to* any propositional value. When the import of the utterance redounds to the speaker(s), it is an "illocutionary" speech act; when it redounds to the one(s) spoken to, it is a "perlocutionary" act. An example of the latter speech act would be "I command you to do such-and-such," where the command is given in the very saying and bids the hearer to do such-and-such an action. Distinguishing self-involving utterances is one way to account for the truism that discourse is always language with a subject. Discourse is grounded in the human experience that gives rise to it on the one hand, and, on the other hand, it is the subject's self-involvement which is constitutive of the act of communication itself. The very act of discourse is a response to reality that discloses meaning. But this still does not address the question about language's capacity to *redescribe* reality. Discourse itself remains limited in its relationship to human experience. A third use of language, the textual moment, brings this relationship to its fullest articulation.

(c) *Text*

Words can be purposely combined in creative, genre-governed, and stylistic ways to yield a certain use of language called *text* (not necessarily written, but any concretization of human activity). A special case of text that uniquely illustrates interpretation's capacity to redescribe reality is that of text as metaphor. These linguistic constructions necessitate attention at two levels, namely, from the vantage points of two different semantic fields. A metaphor says one thing that makes no literal sense but means another thing that makes eminent poetic sense. For example, "This [bread] is my body" makes no literal sense; at the literal level the language defies sense data. Bread is not body. Nonetheless, as sacramental theology has always insisted, a metaphor expresses what is real and true. The nature of metaphor is to juxtapose two fields of meaning, the poetic and the conceptual. The poetic field of meaning has a certain literal linguistic sense that is "non-sense," that grates, and that has a semantic "twist." This is precisely what pushes one beyond a literal meaning toward an innovative meaning learned by reflection from within the conceptual field. The dialectic of these two semantic fields generates something new.

Ricoeur speaks of a "split" sense (literal, poetic non-sense and reflective, conceptual, innovative sense) that results in a "split" reference. The split reference is both the literal reference which belies an experience of the "really real" (and in that sense is untrue) and the conceptual reference which opens up a world of possibilities (hence, makes the metaphor "true" and, indeed, an apt disclosure of experience). Within the conceptual field believing Christians can truly and with meaning assert, "This is my Body." And with that statement of metaphor there opens a reference, a world of possibilities, that enlarges the horizon of understanding Christians have of themselves. In this way metaphor not only has a reference to reality, but also a self-reference. Metaphor *discloses* reality *and* it enlarges self-

understanding. Metaphor is a way of speaking experience. With metaphor one sees clearly the ontological import of language.

(d) *Narrative Text*

There is another, longer kind of text which also shows the ontological underpinnings of language and at the same time adds a temporal dimension to the discussion, namely, the narrative. The theory of narrativity has its various identifiable currents and representative thinkers as does the theory of language (e.g., Scholes and Kellogg, Genette, and Auerbach; liturgically, Stevick). Two aspects particularly advance these reflections on language and human experience. First, narrative is a larger unit of poetic discourse having its own rules of composition that employ human action. Second, narrative allows one to speak experience in time (that is, within a particular temporal frame of reference).

Inherent to narrative is a concreteness realized in its "story-telling" characteristic. Necessary for narrative is a storyteller and a certain sequence of actions (Aristotle: plot) that keep the story moving, draw it to a conclusion, and render it plausible. When the audience/readers can easily identify with the characters and events, they can be drawn into the story such that there is an extension of the story beyond the temporal framework of the story itself into the temporal framework of the immediate circumstances of the audience. The experience that the language of the story makes available to the audience is appropriated by the audience as new possibilities for their own living. Thus the story does not remain an element of literature but opens up a world of possibilities to be appropriated by the audience or the readers.

Though stories may be repeated, each "reading" of a story is a new event offering new possibilities. Repetition of a narrative is always a new event. There is, then, both a literary temporality and an existential temporality about narrative. Its literary temporality is the (historical or fictional) frame of temporal reference particular to the story. Its existential temporality is the projection beyond the literary work into the real experience of the audience or readers and here, again, one approaches an ontology of language. While the ontological as such is never directly accessible, it is recoverable in narrative through the relationship of the world given in the literary language and in the redescription of the world of the readers by means of their having entered into the story and having thus appropriated new possibilities to their experience. The more significant meaning of narrative as speaking experience in time is this appropriate act. In a sense, the reading/hearing of a story is none other than a reshaping of human action.

Language studies have taught that there can be no *direct* recovery of self or experience or knowing; these are always mediated by language and therefore demand an attentiveness to language. Nonetheless, though the link between language and human experience can only be demonstrated as an indirect one, this link does assure that various uses of language carry traces of the fleeting efforts of human activity. And, from the other side, critical examination of language-use, expecially poetic texts, is a window into the meaning, never entirely lost, of human activity.

Liturgical Implications and Questions

The relationship between language and human experience is more than just an interesting philosophical concern. It has ramifications cutting across many disciplines, not the least of which is the study of sacraments and liturgy. A number of points are pertinent: liturgical texts as "originary" expressions of Christian experience, liturgical participation as self-involving, liturgy as dynamic event, and the relationship of liturgy and culture.

Originary experiences are communicated through originary expressions. For Christians, this is primarily by means of scripture and liturgical formulae. One approach to this inscription of tradition is to treat scriptural and liturgical texts as objects for scientific investigation. Much information has been gained from historical and comparative approaches to these texts, but this is not enough because there is a residue of meaning which cannot be uncovered by rigorous, structural methods alone. Attentiveness to the surplus of meaning in language-use requires other hermeneutical methods, but those liturgists who have turned their hermeneutical attention to this problem have done so primarily by focusing on liturgical symbols. However, liturgical expressions of sacramental reality are more than assortments of symbols. Liturgical language, in addition to the verbal, also takes into account the poetic, visual, aural, gustatory, tactile, olfactory, gestural: in effect, a whole linguistic gamut which cries out for interpretation especially in its textuality. As such, these liturgical texts require an interpretation that employs language-use and textual methods, areas just beginning to open up among liturgists which promise rich reward for the advancement of the meaning of liturgy particularly with respect to a liturgical text's relationship to experience.

Another concern of contemporary liturgists is that liturgy cannot be isolated from the lives of those who celebrate. Contemporary sacramental theology—a hermeneutics of liturgy—does not begin with the divine and deduce principles therefrom, but begins with *human experience* and therein discovers the divine. No wonder a clarion call for "participation" by S.C. brought about immediate and recognizable changes. By means of the revision of all the liturgical rites, a certain level of participation was achieved, certainly aided by celebrations in the vernacular. Further, while the revision of the rites struggled with verbal, textual aspects and promoted "active participation" within this context, other approaches seeking to understand language in its broader extension and as relating to human experience suggest a deeper level on which to evaluate the meaning of participation. New concerns emerged from these renewal efforts, concerns to which liturgists have been attentive. One quickly discovered that "involving the people" in liturgy did not necessarily in itself effect the desired fruits of those celebrations. What was initially dealt with, by means of a *de facto* reductionist approach to participation, is now looked at in a new light. The self-involving implications of performative language suggest a whole new meaning to the notion of "participation." Christian worship is chiefly a celebration of the paschal mystery. In the context of the relationship between language and human experience, this says that the Jesus event cannot be relegated to time past. The meaning of Christian celebration is to interpret that originary event within time now. The self-involving language of liturgy—I confess, profess, pray, praise, ask, promise, proclaim, etc.—says that liturgy's interpretive activity is ultimately a redescription of present Christian experience in light of the tradition of interpretations of the paschal mystery. This is the deepest significance of the meaning of "participation," so much so that participation does not occur until there is an appropriation of the redescription of reality made possible by entering into the celebration. In other words, physically "being there" and singing and standing and kneeling simply is insufficient for the meaning and dynamic of worship to emerge. Participation really means that the very act of worship is a kind of interpretive activity engaged in by all the worshippers.

A third concern opened up by studying liturgy as a textual moment is the *event* character of liturgy. Liturgy is dynamic because the Jesus events being celebrated become *my* events in the interpretive redescription of reality. The dynamic of Christian worship unfolds as a past event taking on new shape and meaning when it is appropriated and lived as an event *for me*. This dynamic event restructures the individual's/community's human experience. Liturgy's re-enactment is really a redescription, such that the event always has new meaning.

Granting the relationship between language and human experience, another implication is that human experience is always *cultural* experience. It is the experience of a people at a given time and in a particular set of cultural circumstances. As such, liturgy must incorporate the familiar, the everyday, the traditional for a specific people. Its poetic language is universal only in that the ultimate reference is the paschal mystery, the traces of which are captured in the deep structure constitutive of every liturgical celebration. However, this structure can be—must be—expressed in very localized poetic language respective of the cultural variations and genius of the many peoples and nations who now call themselves "Christian."

These remarks certainly do not address all the difficulties encountered today with respect to celebrating meaningful liturgies. They do, however, begin to point both professional liturgist and ordinary worshipper alike in a common direction where certain questions emerge with timely importance.

The question of the relationship between liturgy and life parallels the relationship between language and experience. Far more than disseminating ethical injunctions on how to be a good Christian, liturgy's essential relationship to life lies in its power to redescribe reality.

Rather than fulfilling obligation, whether it be canonical or societal or culturally dictated, choosing to worship is an articulation of one's orientation in life, of the way one desires to live.

Another area of investigation just opening is that of liturgical genre. If the deep structure of liturgy is mimetic of human Christian activity, then explicit identification of the literary genre that produces liturgical texts would be helpful for critically reflecting on what it means to be Christian. It would also be an aid for better cultural expressions of worship in that each cultural community would have the functional tools to produce a meaningful liturgical expression for their particular community.

Another problematic area that follows from the presupposition about, and understanding of, the relationship of language and human experience is that liturgy is the affair and privilege of the *whole* Christian community, and not just one involving those ordained or elected to preside. Additionally, liturgy must reflect a range of human experience, not just that of a select few. Meaningful worship speaks out of the experience of every member of the Christian community. The differing authoritative structures of the various Christian communities have little as such to do with the intrinsic power of liturgy to redescribe reality. Yet frequently such diverse issues as those of authority and the liturgical redescription of reality tend to be confused.

The importance of the relationship between language and human experience for the worship life of the church can hardly be underscored enough. An appreciation of the character and import of that relationship will help assure that worship is expressive of what Christian living is all about: living the paschal mystery. Liturgy as language of faith is a privileged expression of the paschal mystery. Liturgy as related to the human subject is an expression of the lived faith of the church, a celebration of one's appropriation of the Jesus event. Ultimately, what is at stake in a consideration of the relationship between liturgical language and human experience is speaking, doing and living the paschal mystery of Christ.

Alexandre Ganoczy, *An Introduction to Catholic Sacramental Theology*, Trans. William Thomas and Anthony Sherman (New York: Paulist Press, 1984). Walter Kasper, *The God of Jesus Christ*, Trans. Matthew J. O'Connell (New York: Crossroad, 1986), esp. pp. 79-99. Jean Ladriere, "The Performativity of Liturgical Language," *Concilium* 9-1 (1973): 50-62. Dermot A. Lane, *The Experience of God: An Invitation To Do Theology* (New York: Paulist Press, 1981). Charles E. Reagan and David Stewart, eds., *The Philosophy of Paul Ricoeur: An Anthology of His Work* (Boston: Beacon Press, 1978). Paul Ricoeur, "Philosophy and Religious Language," in *The Journal of Religion* 54 (1974): 71-85. Joyce Ann Zimmerman, *Liturgy As Language of Faith: A Liturgical Methodology in the Mode of Paul Ricoeur's Textual Hermeneutics* (Lanham, MD: University Press of America, 1988).

JOYCE ANN ZIMMERMAN, C.PP.S.

LANGUAGE, LITURGICAL

Liturgical language will be considered at two levels, the socio-historical and the theoretical. The first concerns the actual diversity of languages used for public worship in the history of the church. The second concerns contemporary reflection on how language functions in the liturgical event.

Vatican II: Development in the Historical Tradition

The Vatican II Constitution on the Sacred Liturgy, *Sacrosanctum Concilium* (S.C.), 4 December 1963, contains six articles that speak directly to the matter of liturgical language as socio-historical: nos. 36, 39, 54, 63, 101, and 113. The first of these, art. 36, provides basic norms, which are then applied to specific liturgical rites in subsequent articles. Art. 36 itself has four parts. The first states that the Latin language is to be preserved in the Latin rite. The second acknowledges that the use of their mother tongue in public worship may have advantages for the gathered worshippers and so authorizes in principle more extensive use of the mother tongue, especially for liturgical readings, instructions, and some prayers and chants. The third section specifies that "competent territorial ecclesiastical authority," as identified in S.C. 22.2, is to determine the actual extent of the use of the mother tongue, with the confirmation of its judgment by the Roman See. The fourth specifies that all translations of liturgical texts from Latin into the mother tongue must be approved for use by the competent, territorial, ecclesiastical authority.

Art. 54 applies art. 36 to the Mass, specifying that the readings and "the universal prayer," also called the prayer of the faithful, may be in the mother tongue, and also, without further identification of them, "those parts belonging to the people." Then it delineates procedures for extending these limits to the use of the mother tongue, while advising that the Catholic people should nevertheless continue to learn the Latin ordinary or fixed texts of the eucharistic liturgy.

Art. 63 applies art. 36 to the sacraments and sacramentals, setting no limits on the use of vernacular languages in these worship settings and in fact promoting the use of particular local languages for all non-eucharistic liturgical rites. Art. 101 takes up the question of the language of the divine office, first specifying that clerics are to retain the Latin language for their daily prayer and then authorizing bishops to give permission in particular cases for use of approved vernacular translations of this liturgy. Religious superiors of non-clerical institutes of both men and women may authorize the use of approved vernacular translations for either choral or private praying of the hours. Art. 113 specifies that these norms apply also for the translation of sacred Latin song into vernacular languages.

By the very procedure of enunciating a permissive attitude toward the use of vernacular translations in public worship, these five articles effectively confirm the normative and privileged status of Latin as the language of the Roman liturgy. However, art. 39 provides for competent, territorial ecclesiastical authority to make "legitimate variations and adaptations" in the Roman liturgical books, and specifies liturgical language as one likely area for such adaptation. Art. 40 provides for "even more radical adaptation of the liturgy" where this seems pastorally necessary, without specifying the possible nature of such radical adaptations. Each of these articles anticipates the composition of original liturgical texts in vernacular languages to supplement what is found in the *editio typica* of the Roman liturgical books and their authorized translations.

Several matters raised in *S.C.* invite further comment, among them the history of Latin as the preferred liturgical language for the West, the translation process, and operative assumptions about the nature and purpose of liturgical language. The first of these matters will be addressed through a brief survey of the history of liturgical language, the second through an account of the development of the post-conciliar English language liturgical books, the third through a consideration of theoretical issues that have arisen as liturgiologists have begun to explore the nature and purpose of liturgical language.

Liturgical Languages

S.C. states that Latin retains its privileged character as the official language of the Roman liturgy. The Latin language acquired that role in the public worship of the city of Rome as late as the 4th century. The original language of all Christian public worship, as of the Christian scriptures, was *koine* Greek, the spoken language of the people of the Hellenistic world. However, wherever the Christian gospel was preached beyond the administrative centers of the ancient Hellenistic empire, public worship in the mother tongues of local peoples was most often its normal accompaniment. Thus, while Alexandria on the Mediterranean coast of Egypt developed a Greek liturgy, the Egyptian people living along the upper Nile worshipped in Coptic. In the Mesopotamiam city of Edessa, on the borders between two empires, the Hellenistic and the Persian, a Syriac-language liturgy developed. Ethiopian and Armenian Christians, too, who lived in regions removed from the centers of imperial culture, developed liturgies in their mother tongues. In the early Christian East, seven local languages in addition to Greek were used for public worship (Korolevsky, 1957).

As long as liturgical prayer remained primarily an oral form, that is, for the first three Christian centuries, an interplay between the public language of the empire and mother tongues was characteristic of the developing rites of public worship. This situation persisted in the East, with the resulting development there of "bilingual" traditions of public prayer. No concept of sacral language was operative in this formative period.

By the 3rd century, written liturgical texts, most commonly the eucharistic anaphoras of local bishops, began to circulate among churches of various regions; most of those which survived did so in Greek versions, a testimony to the prevalence of Greek as the earliest language of public worship because it was the dominant language of public life. However, shifting political circumstances, beginning in the 3rd century, gave new prominence to Latin over Greek as the public language of the western Roman empire. The conservative nature of liturgy in the city of Rome and the sacralizing tendencies of Roman culture delayed the full acceptance of a Latin, that is, vernacular, liturgy in the city of Rome until the next century.

Christian churches that were established in the other urban centers and western provinces of the Christian Roman empire were perhaps more readily disposed to Latin as the language of public worship than the city of Rome, since Latin had long been the official public language of government, commerce and high culture in these provinces. The value of having a uniform and unifying language for government, commerce, and public worship went virtually unchallenged in western Europe until the rise of modern European languages was accompanied by new shifts in political power. With the 16th century Protestant Reformation, new vernacular language liturgies developed in the West, notably in German, French, English, Swedish, and Dutch. In response to the challenge of the Protestant reformers who were calling for vernacular liturgy, the Council of Trent (Session XXII, 1562) judged that it was not advisable to celebrate the Mass in the vernacular. S.C. 36 reflects a re-evaluation of the pastoral situation.

Twenty-five years after S.C. the National Conference of Catholic Bishops of the United States, taking full advantage of the conciliar norms authorizing the use of mother tongues, has prepared liturgical books in English, Spanish, Choctaw, Navaho, Pima-Papago, and Lakota, the latter four the languages of native American peoples. This contemporary provision for balancing the use of English, the language of the dominant U.S. culture, with the mother tongues of peoples marginal to that dominant culture reflects in a new form the ancient ecclesial valuing of local liturgies—e.g., the Coptic and Syriac or Chaldean—as vehicles of resistance to the encroachment of the imperial Greek-speaking culture. *Notitiae*, the publication of the Roman

Congregation for Worship and the Sacraments, provides a record of the post-conciliar decisions of each national episcopal conference on the use of local languages for public worship.

The English Translation Process

S.C. 36.4 directs that the translation of the Latin liturgical books into vernacular languages would be the responsibility of "various kinds of competent territorial bodies of bishops lawfully established" (S.C. 22.2). In 1963, in order to facilitate the work of translation, eleven episcopal conferences with responsibility for producing English language translations of Latin liturgical texts formed the International Committee (subsequently, Commission) on English in the Liturgy (I.C.E.L.) in order to collaborate in the project. Member conferences include Australia, Canada, England and Wales, India, Ireland, New Zealand, Pakistan, the Philippines, Scotland, South Africa, and the United States; thirteen other conferences using English as a public language have associated themselves with I.C.E.L.. An episcopal board made up of eleven bishops, each named by and accountable to his own conference, directs the work of I.C.E.L.; a secretariat in Washington, D.C. administers the policy and programs of the episcopal board. Action to receive the I.C.E.L. translations is the responsibility of the member episcopal conferences who, in turn, request Roman confirmation of their action. The formation of I.C.E.L. in 1963 anticipated the 16 October 1964 letter of Cardinal Lercaro calling for such collaboration among episcopal conferences which shared a common language.

In 1969, when national episcopal conferences were six years into the work of preparing vernacular translations of Latin liturgical texts, the Consilium, the international body charged with the implementation of S.C. issued its instruction, *Comme le prévoit*, on the translation of liturgical texts. The instruction reflected some of the issues already faced, and it also anticipated emerging questions about translation. Among the principles it enunciated to guide translators were the following: 1) liturgical texts are intended as oral communication and require an oral rhetorical style; 2) every translation involves the interpretation of meaning, not a simple rendering of equivalent words, so that adequate translation may require a change of metaphor to retain meaning; 3) translators must use scientific methods of textual studies to understand the full meaning available in Latin of the texts to be translated; 4) translators must take into account the intended speakers and hearers in choosing a suitable manner of expression. The 1969 instruction also expressed the judgment that the earliest efforts of translators would need to be reviewed after a period of use. Development of a vernacular liturgical vocabulary, appropriate idiom, and effective rhetorical style for public proclamation of Christian faith were expected to require the efforts of more than a single generation of believers. A parallel with the gradual development of liturgical Latin in the ancient church can be drawn here.

Liturgical Language: Emerging Theoretical Considerations

The 1969 mandate that translators employ scientific methods of textual study has pressed liturgical scholars to develop competence in contemporary theories of language. The complexity of developing an adequate theory of liturgical language is grounded in the complexity of the phenomenon itself. The liturgical books to be translated are repositories for essentially oral prayers recorded not to be read but to be spoken in the context of public ritual events. The texts are written, but for the purpose of oral delivery. A multiplicity of distinct oral genres is employed in each liturgical event.

Further, because the meaning to be communicated orally is publicly shared religious meaning, the verbal symbols of the Christian tradition control the contents of both compositions and translations. Many of these symbols are biblical in their origins, and contemporary Bible translations provide translators with a vernacular resource for Christian religious language. But equally as many of the linguistic symbols of the Roman liturgy are expressions of ecclesiastical Latin, the Christian idiom that developed as Christian orators and writers appropriated and reinterpreted the everyday language of their societies for public proclamation and celebration of the mystery of salvation in Christ. Thus, many of the originating metaphors for the Latin liturgical language are tied to the cultural experiences of other epochs and can be broken open to contemporary insight only with great skill on the part of translators. In addition, the context for adequate interpretation of the meaning of liturgical texts is public ritual action, in which multiple non-verbal codes of meaning are interacting simultaneously; so a theory adequate to account for the relationship of verbal to non-verbal meaning in liturgical events needs to be worked out.

Scholars concerned to develop a theory adequate to the task of understanding the complex phenomenon of liturgical language have been dependent upon the relative adequacy of contemporary theories of ordinary language, theories of the nature of religious language, and also upon theories of the distinctive nature of ritual utterance. At an even more fundamental level, scholars have had to determine whether "liturgical language" was properly understood to refer comprehensively or only analogously to both verbal and non-verbal elements in a liturgical rite. All such explorations into language theories have been directed toward developing appropriate theories about the nature, purpose, and correct interpretation of liturgical language. Some small measure of consensus is emerging; many areas need further investigation.

Areas of Consensus

Four areas of agreement can be identified at the level of theory. First, liturgy is an act of communication. Second, liturgy is ritual communication. Third, liturgy is a text, i.e., a humanly crafted work. Fourth, liturgy is a text needing interpretation. Each of these can be explored here only briefly.

1. Liturgy is an act of communication. This viewpoint is already reflected in S.C.; but the conciliar document itself and many of its subsequent interpreters have often assumed a univocal, pre-critical, common sense notion of the nature of this communication. This unexamined viewpoint has fostered the idea that the fundamental issue in the development of liturgical language is the achievement of unambiguous clarity in expressing the content of Christian faith (S.C. 21; 33;34). Such an approach takes as its premise the notion that liturgy's primary purpose is didactic. The approach assumes that effective liturgical language will impart to worshippers knowledge of the Christian message with little or no basis for misperception.

At a critical level, however, liturgical scholars agree that what liturgical language aims to disclose is something more profound than information about doctrines. Its purpose is to reveal the essentially unfathomable mystery of salvation at work in the world of human history. Liturgical speech and non-verbal ritual elements cumulate and coalesce in liturgical action to serve divine mystery. Every adequate understanding of liturgical language will embrace this viewpoint.

Nevertheless, it should be noted that this theoretical affirmation is not a concealed revival of a claim for the necessity of an esoteric sacral language in public worship. Contemporary language theory supports the use of vernacular languages in liturgy because of its judgment that it is within the power of ordinary human language used in particular ways to disclose ultimate mystery. The key to understanding this aspect of language is found in contemporary theories of metaphor.

Metaphoric language typically engages two domains of experience to trigger cognitive and emotional interaction, thereby generating insight into reality. Thus in baptism, Christians are "washed by the Blood of the Lamb" through entry into a bath of flowing water. They are "reborn in the womb of mother church"; they are "buried with Christ for three days and rise glorified with him." They "pass through the waters of death and arrive at the promised land." They "pass from this present age to become a new creation."

The believing church has given historical shape to its baptismal liturgy and even its initiatory space by drawing upon not one but a whole collection of metaphors. Multiple referents to human and religious experience have been available simultaneously within the gathered assembly as it has interacted with rivers, pools, and fonts of water, the cross, oils, even milk and honey and an abundance of allusive language. The verbal components of the baptismal liturgy from early on have alluded to the shared memory of the foundational Exodus-Sinai event of biblical religion, itself reinterpreted to point to the new covenant in Christ. Yet baptismal words and ritual actions have just as often pointed to more immediate domains of the experience of believers: birth, death, bathing, safe passage from danger, identity within a people. Through this profusion of language and ritual action, the church has sought to celebrate its faith in the mystery of salvation in Christ. The mystery is unfathomable and unutterable; yet it has also been revealed and believed.

Because first generation Christian homilists tagged the mystery "paschal," this biblical allusion has served as an anchor for subsequent developments in the historical, liturgical tradition. Yet the mystery of salvation is greater than what the believing community has ever been able to know or say. Accordingly, the liturgical composition, by intentionally mixing and heaping up metaphors, invites worshippers to venture into the realm of mystery through the stuff of ordinary experience, shared memory, and the power of language. The terse formula of scholastic theology was that sacramental liturgy graced its participants by signifying the mystery: *significando causant.*

The renewal of liturgical language is jeopardized by recurrent impulses for greater clarity than is possible in expressing mystery, impulses to simplify liturgy by reducing a rite to one controlling metaphor and then further reducing that metaphor by providing a univocal statement of what it all means. Such tendencies run counter to the fundamental dynamic of liturgical language. If liturgy is an act of communication, it is the communication of poetry rather than that of the information booth. Liturgy is ritual metaphor disclosing salvation.

2. Liturgy is ritual communication, which involves "an inseparable combination of articulate speech and purposeful action" (Wheelock, 50). Philosophers of language and ritual theorists concur that it is the combination of words and acts that characterizes ritual language and distinguishes it from other, wholly verbal forms of religious language such as the language of theology. A comprehensive theory of liturgical language will have to take account of spoken language used in an action context where gesture, posture, movement or location in space, and transactions and interactions with ritual objects are presumed to have cognitive

content. In liturgical events, words interact with multiple parallel symbol systems, and the orchestrated whole effects the disclosure.

Each of the operative symbol systems within a ritual event—verbal and non-verbal—also has its own syntax and grammar, its set of operations and rules for effective communication of meaning, the violation of which yields incoherence or meaninglessness. These are subject to investigation according to the postulates of structuralist theory. Momentary reflection on the arrangement and use of ritual space within a liturgical event illustrates the analogous structure of non-verbal and verbal language. Within the gathered assembly, spaces are assigned according to liturgical roles, and movement in and out of assigned spaces is controlled according to a transcendent sense of cosmic divine order given symbolic expression in the spatial code. The rules for moving within liturgical space during liturgical action constitute a discreet "language," with distinct cognitive content known to the participants, all of whom routinely take their place without explicit direction. Yet no one presumes that this particular language considered in isolation expresses the full meaning being set out in the liturgical event. Spatial language participates in the religious disclosure of the mystery of salvation. It is the liturgy itself as an instance of complex ritual communication, and not only one of its several languages, for which sound theoretical foundations must be established.

3. In any attempt to establish theoretical foundations, liturgy is best understood as a "text," in the broad sense in which "text" is understood among contemporary language theorists. What characterizes text in this realm of discourse is not primarily that it is written, but that it involves human composition, the structuring of a whole which bears its meaning in its wholeness.

The act of composition involves human composers in decisions about genres. Selecting from among literary and ritual forms available in a cultural tradition is a generative act in the formation of the full liturgical text. Further, the actual production of the work in the form and genres chosen inevitably will carry with it the distinctive stamp or style of the composers. Thus, there are Eastern and Western liturgies, and Roman terseness and Syriac exuberance are not likely to be confused. There are compositions credited to Pope St. Leo, to St. John Chrysostom, and to St. Ambrose; and these are distinguishable. Original liturgical prayers being composed in local languages within contemporary African cultures will be notably different from Native American liturgical prayers, even when liturgical authors in each community emulate classical Christian liturgical forms.

It should be noted that in oral cultures, where the production of meaning through crafted language is accomplished without recourse to writing, the crafted language of oral liturgical traditions will have the characteristics typical of any "work" or language. Historical evidence documents the oral nature of early Christian liturgical texts. While it is true that most recent liturgical composition, like that involved in the production of the reformed Roman liturgical books of Vatican II, has been a literary process, committing texts to written form was a secondary act in the earliest composition of Christian liturgy.

The genre "liturgical text" is a distinct form of religious composition. When a liturgical composition is given its full written form and presented in a liturgical book, the text oscillates between two constitutive elements: utterances (themselves in many distinctive liturgical subgenres, e.g., prayers, acclamations) to be enunciated by the ritual participants and directions for the ritual actions to be performed. A full liturgical text is not straightforward, as would be characteristic of narrative or expository discourse. The presentation of words to be uttered is designedly interrupted by contextual considerations. Yet just how the word-related ritual actions are to be performed is more often suggested than explained in detail in a liturgical text.

Thus, a tradition of ritual performance regularly supplements the brief directions for action which are recorded as part of the written text of the liturgical book. Efforts have been made periodically to consign the tradition of performance to writing in the form of a "ceremonial." Nevertheless, full access to the living tradition of performance is actually available only within the liturgical events as they are regularly celebrated. Some things go without saying.

It is this complex liturgical text which demands a foundational theory of language adequate to give liturgical language intelligibility as an act of religious meaning.

4. The meaning of a liturgical text is complex, however simple its intention. Appropriate and adequate methods of interpretation are required to set out its cognitive content. From the perspective of contemporary language theory, the interpretation of a liturgical text can be grasped as a semiotic issue with three possible and related foci.

The interpreter can focus on the relationships between and among the many ritual symbols, verbal and non-verbal, that constitute the whole. This is a study in the syntax of the rite. A second focus for the interpreter is the meanings of the symbols. Here the interpreter will examine the relationship between the ritual symbols and the realities to which they refer, establishing criteria for making judgments about the adequacy and the truth of the ritual symbols. This is a study in the semantics of the liturgical rite. Finally, the interpreter can focus on the relationships between and among the symbols, the users of the symbols, and the environment of the users. This area concerns the pragmatics of the liturgical rite.

Recent work in liturgical syntactics has been approached through methods of structural analysis associated with French anthropologist Claude Lévi-Strauss and subsequently modified by later structuralists and post-structuralists like J. van Velsen and Victor W. Turner. Such studies as these contribute to an understanding of the normative "grammar of ritual behavior"; and they also serve to identify ritual deviance and the locus of emergent ritual change within a liturgical community.

For example, the normative grammar of Christian liturgy has had traditional gender inflection, expressed in its systems of male and female liturgical roles, masculine and feminine images and symbols, and sex-linked access to ritual space. The liturgical reforms of Vatican II disrupted that normative grammar when it promulgated new norms governed by the principle that "full and active participation by all the people is the aim to be considered before all else" (S.C., 14). Women were subsequently authorized to take on the roles of lector and communion minister. This authorized breakdown of the once-normative gender inflection of Christian ritual grammar has found further spontaneous expression in forms of ritual deviance. These range from the emergence of girl altar servers to the use of feminine images and metaphors to refer to God. Liturgical syntactics helps to uncover the structural intelligibility of such deviance.

Liturgical semantics concerns itself with the meaning available in the liturgical text considered as a whole and in its several parts. The problem is essentially hermeneutical: how to interpret a text? In recent years liturgiologists have begun to explore both performative language or speech-action theory and narrative analysis for methodological models adequate to the task of interpreting the liturgical text. These investigations are still in their early stages. Few fully elaborated models have been devised; fewer have been adequately tested.

Speech-act theory has received a widely favorable reception in the area of liturgical semantics because of its understanding of all speaking as intentional action carrying force and affecting the relationships among the parties to the speech-event. The first formulation of speech-act theory is found in the work of Anglo-American philosopher J.L. Austin. Further theoretical developments by J. Searle and R. Jakobson are being taken into account in most contemporary explorations of speech-act theory as a hermeneutical resource for the interpretation of liturgical texts.

At an early stage of the investigation of the relevance of speech-act theory for understanding liturgical action, efforts to superimpose this theory on classical scholastic sacramental theology proved too narrow. For example, the mid-1970s debate carried on by B. Brinkman and A. Martinich in *The Heythrop Journal* presumed two parties in the liturgical speech act. One was the "recipient" of the sacrament, but the theologians grappled with the identity of the second. Was it the priest or Christ whose speaking had direct efficacy? The investigation lacked an ecclesiological theology. It also assumed a scholastic theory of instrumental causality for sacramental efficacy. This has given way in more recent discussion to a fuller understanding of symbolic metaphorical disclosure of the graced situation.

Jean Ladriere took a broader approach to the matter, identifying a three-pronged performativity in liturgical language: existential induction, institution, and presentation. The first mode operates to bring about the self-engagement of all parties with the ritual text and its intentions. The second mode constitutes the parties as an existential communion in which they intend together the reality to which their liturgical speaking refers. The third mode of performativity for liturgical speech is its making present to the participants the reality, i.e., the "mystery of salvation," which has gathered them. Subsequently, Wade Wheelock has offered a comparable analysis of the performative efficacy of a liturgical text, pointing to its power to create a religious situation capable of involving its participants. It is the extravagant metaphorical composition of the liturgical text which generates this creative power. Performative language or speech-act theory thus provides a contemporary philosophical foundation for the scholastic *significando causant*.

The theory that the liturgical text "creates the religious situation" finds further support in the textual hermeneutics of Paul Ricoeur. Ricoeur talks about the "world" of a text, i.e., the way of understanding reality that the text makes available to all those who let themselves be engaged by its language, however distant later readers may be from the original world of its composition. Thus, a tradition of relatively stable liturgical texts operates as a living tradition precisely because each generation engages itself regularly with the world of meaning available in its quasi-fixed liturgical language.

The believing church is always being drawn to explain the cognitive content of the experience of salvation in Christ it apprehends and celebrates. Yet the work of textual analysis of its liturgical language to establish the meaning of faith is also a work of constituting meaning. The relationships among verbal liturgical constants like "covenant," "priest," "sacrifice," "body" and "blood," "Christ crucified and glorified," "the holy Spirit" and the non-verbal constants like water, bread and wine, altar-table, cross, hands extended, presider and people have been arranged and rearranged in liturgical compositions and configured and reconfigured in homilies and catechesis to disclose to the Christian people of different cultures and epochs successively different religious worlds in which to live their life in Christ and anticipate their salvation. Speech-action theory has proved helpful in understanding *how* liturgical texts mean as well as *what* they mean.

Narrative analysis provides another potentially fruitful foundational theory for the interpretation of the liturgical text. Employing the semiotic analysis of A.-J. Greimas, some liturgiologists have focused upon the narrative structure of the liturgical text as a linguistic fact and as the key to the interpretation of its deep meaning. Greimas' own theory has evolved during this era and his principal interpreters have continued to refine its implications. As is the case with performative language or speech-action theory, the hermeneutical usefulness of the method for the interpretation of liturgical texts is in the early stages of exploration.

Whatever hermeneutic methods are developed for the work of interpretation, liturgical semantics has both an analytical and a critical moment. Uncovering the world of meaning in the liturgical text is the first moment; judging the adequacy and appropriateness of the text to accomplish its work of disclosure of the mystery of Christ is a second moment. This second moment requires that the interpreter differentiate both the cultural and the religious horizons of the liturgical text and the liturgical participants and correlate them dialectically. In authorizing the reform of the sacred liturgy to insure that "the texts and rites express more clearly the holy things which they signify" (S.C., 21), and in acknowledging that the liturgy had suffered the intrusion of elements out of harmony with or no longer suited to its religious meaning, the Vatican II liturgy constitution underscored the challenge of developing adequate foundational theory for the work of liturgical semantics.

Liturgical pragmatics has only recently been identified as a distinct area for interpretation, and it remains the least developed theoretically and methodologically. As a third focus in the work of textual interpretation, pragmatics studies "the behavioral effect of symbol." It considers not what meaning is available in the world of the text but rather what behaviors express a reader's appropriation of that meaning, i.e., what ways of being and acting show that readers have come to dwell in the world of the text. The issue is not simply one of ease and familiarity with ritual language, roles and rules in the cultic setting. What is of greater importance is whether persons shown "the mystery of salvation" through liturgical performance move with insight from the ritual celebration of the mystery to mysteriously redemptive historical existence.

New-found awareness of the issue of the social dimension of the liturgy and its ethical demands is a by-product of the circumstance of cultural pluralism and cultural secularity. If they ever did, people no longer live and act as though "by second nature" in a world of faith. Critics of the liturgical reform have charged that liturgy remains disconnected with ordinary human existence despite the intuition, the hope, and even the claim that liturgical reform would foster social regeneration. At the present neither pastoral liturgists nor their critics have adequate theoretical foundations to probe the potential or actual ecclesial, social, political and personal behavioral consequences of engagement with the world constituted through liturgical language. Cultural anthropologists, systems theorists, and critical theorists, among them feminist theorists, may provide as-yet-inadequately-explored resources for establishing the relation between the meaning of liturgical language and social existence.

See **Hermeneutics and worship; Human sciences, sacraments and the; Inclusive language; Language and human experience; Aesthetics, liturgical; Liturgical texts in English; Word and sacrament**

J. Calloud, "Semio-linguistique et texte liturgique,"*La Maison Dieu* 114 (1973): 36-58. J. Danielou, *The Bible and the Liturgy* (Notre Dame, Ind: Univ. of ND Press, 1956). C. Duquoc et al., *Politique et vocabulaire liturgique* (Paris: Cerf, 1975). C. Geertz, "Religion as a Cultural System," in *The Interpretation of Cultures* (New York: Basic Books, 1973). P. Guiraud, *Semiology* (London: Routledge and Kegan Paul, 1975). F. Isambert, *Rite et Efficacite Symbolique* (Paris: Les Editions du Cerf, 1979). C. Korolevsky, *Living Languages in Catholic Worship: An Historical Inquiry* (London: Longmans, Green, and Co., 1957). J.P. Ladriere, "The Performativity of Liturgical Language," in *Liturgical Experience of Faith* (Concilium 82). Ed. H. Schmidt and D. Power (New York: Herder and Herder, 1973): 50-62. G. Lardner, "Communication Theory and Liturgical Research," in *Worship* 51 (1977): 299-307. E.T. Lawson, "Ritual as Language," in *Religion* 6 (1976) 2, 123-39. D. Pellauer, "The Significance of the Text in Paul Ricoeur's Hermeneutical Theory," in C.E. Reagan, ed., *Studies in the Philosophy of Paul Ricoeur* (Athens, Ohio: Ohio University Press, 1976): 98-114. M. Searle, "Liturgy as Metaphor," *Worship* 55 (1981) 2, 98-120. W.T. Wheelock, "The Problem of Ritual Language: From Information to Situation," in *Journal of the American Academy of Religion*, 50 (1982) 1, 49-71. J.A. Zimmerman, *Liturgy As Language of Faith* (Lanham, Md: University Press of America, 1988).

MARY COLLINS, O.S.B.

LAW, LITURGICAL

Canon Law, in the broad sense, includes not only the laws that appear in the form of canons in the Code of Canon Law, but all manner of church law, including liturgical law. Liturgical law is the Canon Law that orders the liturgy of the Roman Catholic Church. The term "liturgy" is understood as worship "carried out in the name of the church by persons lawfully deputed and through acts approved by the authority of the church" (can. 834, sec. 2). Such deputed persons are all the baptized faithful (L.G., 11; S.C., 14; can. 836) as well as those who exercise the several liturgical ministries, both lay and ordained. The "acts approved by the authority of the church" which make up the liturgy include all the rites published in the official liturgical books approved by competent ecclesiastical authority. Not included in the canonical notion of liturgy are other prayers and devotions even though they may be approved by the local ordinary or other competent ecclesiastical authority (can. 839, sec. 2).

The discussion that follows is limited to the liturgy of the Latin rite; the Eastern ritual churches have their own canonical discipline and liturgical traditions, and they are not affected by the laws in the Latin rite code and liturgical books (can. 1). The topics treated are: the purpose of liturgical law, its sources, regulation of the liturgy, liturgical customs, dispensation of law, and revocation of law. This essay considers some foundational canonical principles and institutes and their application to liturgical law; the reader who desires greater treatment of current pastoral issues, or further discussion on the interpretation of liturgical law, should consult the works in the bibliography.

Purpose

Canon Law is intended to serve a pastoral purpose by providing harmony and unity in the external life of the Christian community as a reflection of its Spirit-guided inner unity. Liturgical law also has this pastoral function. Liturgical law aims to ensure the unity and authenticity of Catholic worship within and among the local churches that make up the universal church. Unity of worship does not mean total uniformity or rubricism, the kind of slavish adherence to ceremonial minutiae that characterized fidelity to liturgical law before Vatican II. It pertains rather to the ordering and maintenance of the essential structures, spirit, and character of the sacraments and other liturgical rites. The deepest purpose of liturgical law is that of the liturgy itself: to build up the body of Christ through Spirit-filled celebrations of the saving mysteries. In order to fulfill this purpose, liturgical law is best observed not by mere rubrical exactitude but by ministers and assemblies who enflesh the law through meaningful liturgical celebrations that effectively signify and build up the local church in communion with the church universal. This requires that those responsible for preparing for and ministering at the liturgy receive a sound formation which includes knowledge of liturgical norms and principles of canonical interpretation.

Sources

Universal liturgical law is found chiefly in the official liturgical books published in Latin by the Apostolic See and in the various approved vernacular translations published under the authority of the episcopal conferences. The principal liturgical books include: the Roman Missal (Lectionary and Sacramentary); the Roman Ritual (the rites, published separately, at which a priest, or in some cases a deacon or lay minister, presides); the Roman Pontifical (the rites at which a bishop presides); the Liturgy of the Hours; and the Ceremonial of Bishops. All of these are service books for use at worship except for the Ceremonial which is a compilation of norms intended as a guide for bishops, masters of ceremonies, and others entrusted with the conduct of episcopal ceremonies.

A major part of the liturgical law contained in the liturgical books is that found at the beginning of the books or rites. The Sacramentary and Liturgy of the Hours begin with a general instruction (*institutio generalis*). Most of the service books or rites begin with introductions (*praenotanda*), although a few have general introductions (*praenotanda gen-*

eralia) and subsequent *praenotanda* which introduce the several parts of the rites. Often these precise distinctions are not made by authors who refer to all of them generically as *praenotanda*. This is not unfitting, since the nature and purpose of these laws are much the same. They provide a theological and pastoral orientation to the rites and establish much of the major canonical discipline for them. They consist of doctrinal, catechetical, historical and other information followed by dispositive norms, many of which are hortatory and broadly stated.

Another category of liturgical law found in the liturgical books are the rubrics. Rubrics take their name from the red color in which they are printed which sets them apart on the page from the actual texts used in worship that are printed in black. Most rubrics are precise directions that guide the ministers in the performance of the rite, or they may be other kinds of law related to that part of the rite where they are located in the liturgical book. All the norms in the liturgical books, whether *praenotanda* or rubrics, have the force of law and are subject to the same rules for interpretation, dispensation, and revocation as are the canons of the code.

Another major source of laws for the liturgy is the Code of Canon Law which was promulgated by Pope John Paul II on January 25, 1983, and which became effective on November 27 of that year. The code "for the most part does not define the rites which are to be observed in celebrating liturgical actions" (can. 2). This principle implies, on the one hand, that most liturgical laws are found outside the code in the liturgical books and elsewhere and, on the other hand, that some liturgical laws are to be found in the code. Indeed, extensive legislation governing the liturgy and the discipline of the sacraments is contained in Book IV of the code, although it should be noted that many canons in Book IV are only remotely related to liturgy as it is defined above in the introduction.

Book IV of the Code of Canon Law, entitled "The Sanctifying Office (*Munus*) of the Church," consists of 420 canons and is divided into three parts. Part I, "The Sacraments" (cans. 840-1165), begins with nine introductory canons on general aspects of sacramental theology and discipline followed by the remaining canons organized into seven "titles" for each of the sacraments. Each title typically is divided into chapters on: the celebration of the sacrament, the minister, those receiving or participating in the sacrament, and other matters that may be unique to that sacrament, for example, godparents, record and proof of celebration, the reservation and veneration of the eucharist, Mass offerings, indulgences. Part II of Book IV, "Other Acts of Divine Worship" (can. 1166-1204), consists of five titles treating: sacramentals (blessings, dedications, consecrations, exorcisms); the liturgy of the hours; ecclesiastical funeral rites; the veneration of the saints, sacred images, relics; and vows and oaths. Part III, "Sacred Times and Places" (cans. 1205-1253), establishes regulations for churches, oratories, private chapels, shrines, altars, cemeteries, feast days, and days of penance. There are, additionally, six canons (834-839) introducing Book IV which treat basic liturgical-theological principles and general rules for the regulation of the liturgy. Canon 767 in Book III of the code, on the homily, also can be classified as a liturgical law.

Liturgical laws not found in the code or liturgical books can be enacted by the legislator in the form of general decrees. General decrees are true laws that have the same force as the laws of the code and the liturgical books (can. 29). Authentic interpretations of laws are also a source of law. An authentic interpretation is one given by the legislator or the person or group who has been delegated by the legislator to give authentic interpretations (can. 16, sec. 1). An authentic interpretation of a law has the force of law and can even change the law by extending or restricting its meaning (can. 16, sec. 2). The Pontifical Council for the Interpretation of Legal Texts has the competence to give authentic interpretations of papal laws, including liturgical laws.

Regulation of the Liturgy

The regulation of the liturgy refers here to its moderation, promotion, and custody. This regulation is chiefly exercised by church authorities who possess legislative or executive power of governance, whether for the universal church, the particular church, or groupings of particular churches. The regulation of the liturgy occurs through various means, such as the promulgation of laws, the issuance of executory documents, the granting of dispensations. In addition to such functions of the power of governance, the liturgy is also regulated by the teaching office (*munus*) of the church through various means, such as magisterial documents, preaching, catechesis. Although the teaching *munus* of the church is not a concern here, it must be noted that the moderation, promotion, and custody of the liturgy is significantly and effectively accomplished by the church's teachers and preachers at all levels. Finally, the role of custom is important in regulating the liturgy of local communities.

The Universal Church. The pope and the college of bishops enjoy supreme power in the church, both for the Latin church and the Eastern churches (cans. 331, 336). The pope acting alone, or the bishops of the world acting collegially in union with the pope, each constitute the highest legislative, executive, and judicial authority in the universal church. The major liturgical reforms following Vatican II were promulgated by the authority of the pope. The college of bishops historically has exercised its supreme power only in an ecumenical council, although theoretically it could do so even by some other kind of collegial act (can. 337, sec. 2). The *Constitution on the Sacred Liturgy* of the Second Vatican Council established the major principles and directions for the liturgical reforms accomplished primarily during the papacy of Pope Paul VI (1963-1978). The liturgy constitution remains the fundamental source for the proper interpretation and implementation of postconciliar liturgical law.

Only the supreme ecclesiastical magisterium can authentically determine what constitutes divine law (cf. cans. 750; 1075, sec. 1.). Divine laws are those recognized by the church as having been established by God. The divine positive law has its source in revelation, either in scripture or tradition; the divine natural law is based on the order of creation and can be known by human reason. Purely ecclesiastical laws are human laws established by legislation or by custom. Unlike divine laws, merely ecclesiastical laws can be changed, abolished, or dispensed. Most liturgical laws are purely ecclesiastical laws, but they serve to regulate what are at root more fundamental divine laws, such as: the divine command to celebrate the eucharist in memory of Christ; to preach the gospel; to baptize with water in the names of the Father, Son and Holy Spirit; to keep holy the Lord's day; to do penance.

Also restricted to the supreme authority is the determination of what constitutes the essential requirements necessary for the validity of the sacraments (can. 841). The concepts of validity and liceity are basic to understanding the laws governing the sacraments. If a legal requirement for the validity of a sacrament is not met, the sacrament is juridically inefficacious, null and void. The valid celebration of the seven sacraments variously depends upon the essential matter and form, the capability and intention of the recipient, and the person and intention of the minister. In baptism, for example, the matter is water; the form is the trinitarian formula; the minister who baptizes is anyone with the intention of doing what the church does when it baptizes; the recipient must be someone not yet baptized who, if possessing the use of reason, freely intends to be baptized. If any of these essential requirements is absent or deficient the rite and its effects are juridically null and void.

All laws not affecting validity are for liceity only. Liceity means licitness, or lawfulness. The transgression of a law affecting only liceity would not invalidate the sacrament or other act, and its juridical consequences would be recognized. For example, can. 861, sec. 1, which states that the ordinary minister of baptism is a bishop, presbyter or deacon, is a law affecting only liceity. For validity, anyone can baptize who intends to do what the church does when it baptizes. Unless lay persons are authorized to be ministers of baptism (cf. can. 230, sec. 3), their conferral of baptism outside a case of necessity would be an illicit act, but the baptism would nonetheless be valid.

The moderation of the liturgy in the universal church is the competence of the Apostolic See, or Holy See, a term which includes the pope, the secretary of state, and the Roman curia (can. 838, sec. 1; 361). The Apostolic See publishes the original edition (*editio typica*) of each of the Roman liturgical books in Latin. It also exercises in various ways a role of vigilance over the liturgy to ensure that liturgical laws and directives are faithfully observed everywhere (can. 838, sec. 2).

The congregation of the Roman curia entrusted with the moderation, promotion, and custody of the liturgy of the Latin rite is the Congregation for Divine Worship and the Discipline of the Sacraments. The Congregation for Oriental Churches has competence over the Eastern rites. Liturgical matters of a doctrinal nature are the competence of the Congregation for the Doctrine of the Faith. In the decades after Vatican II, several restructurings of the Roman curia affected the congregation or congregations entrusted with the regulation of the liturgy and the discipline of the sacraments. In 1969 the Congregation of Sacred Rites was divided into two congregations, the Congregation for Divine Worship and the Congregation for Causes of Saints. At this time there also existed a separate Congregation for the Discipline of the Sacraments. In 1975 the latter congregation was joined to the Congregation for Divine Worship to become the Congregation for the Sacraments and Divine Worship. In 1984 they were divided into separate congregations, only to be reunited once again in 1989 to form the Congregation for Divine Worship and the Discipline of the Sacraments.

The congregations of the Roman curia constitute a principal executive arm of the papacy; they do not have legislative power in their own right. They can issue laws only if they are expressly delegated this power by the pope (can. 135, § 2). Most of the documents issued by curial congregations are therefore not legislative but are administrative, or executory, in nature. The Apostolic See has published various kinds of executory documents on liturgical matters, including declarations, circular letters, directories, letters, norms, notes, guidelines, and instructions (*instructiones*). Executory documents typically deal with the administration or execution of the law, treating matters which are less important or too detailed to be in the law itself. Similar to laws, executory documents have binding force, but they are always subservient to the law. Executory documents cannot revoke or change laws, and if any provisions in them are contrary to the law, those provisions would lack all force. Also, if the law on which they are based ceases to have force, then they too cease to bind.

The Particular Churches. The code uses the term "particular churches" to refer to dioceses and their canonical equivalents, namely, territorial prelatures, territorial abbacies, apostolic vicariates, apostolic prefectures, and apostolic administrations erected on a stable basis (can. 368). The canonical authority of those who head these other particular churches is generally equivalent in the law to that of the diocesan bishop (can. 381, § 2).

Bishops are "high priests, principal dispensers of the mysteries of God and moderators, promoters, and custodians of the whole liturgical life of the church entrusted to them" (can. 835, § 1). The custody of the liturgy is an important canonical duty of the diocesan bishop. "He is to be watchful lest abuses creep into ecclesiastical discipline, especially concerning the ministry of the word, the celebration of the sacraments and sacramentals, the worship of God and devotion to the saints ... " (can. 392, § 2). Other officials who have the duty of vigilance over the liturgy include vicar foranes (deans), pastors, and rectors of churches (cans. 555, § 1, 3°; 528, § 2; 562).

The bishop is moderator of the liturgy of the particular church in a way parallel to that of the Apostolic See for the universal church (can. 838, § 1). In many instances the universal law gives the bishop the competence to make liturgical adaptations or adopt optional practices at his discretion. As sole legislator within the diocese, the diocesan bishop can promulgate particular liturgical laws provided they are not contrary to universal law (cans. 838, § 4; 391; 135; § 2). Particular laws are those enacted for a particular territory such as a diocese, province, or region, or they may be personal laws passed for a particular group such as an institute of consecrated life or a society of apostolic life. While universal and personal laws bind everywhere, particular laws that are established for a certain territory bind those resident in the territory, while they are actually in the territory, in accord with the rules of cans. 12 and 13. Diocesan liturgical laws pertaining to the public exercise of divine worship are also binding on members of religious institutes of pontifical right (can. 678, § 1).

The bishop can also issue binding executory documents on liturgical matters. The other local ordinaries in the diocese (the vicar general and episcopal vicar who have executive power) can make administrative decisions and issue executory decrees affecting the liturgy within the limits of their competence (cans. 31, 479, 480). For example, any local ordinary is competent to grant the imprimatur required for the reprinting in whole or in part of liturgical books whether in the original Latin or in the approved vernacular translations (can. 826, § 2).

The diocesan bishop is obliged to have a liturgical commission to assist him in the promotion of the liturgy (S.C., 45). Commissions on sacred music and sacred art should also be part of the diocesan curia insofar as possible (S.C., 46). Such commissions are advisory to the bishop and cannot on their own authority establish diocesan policies or make binding decisions, although the local ordinary is free to delegate executive power to them for specific kinds of functions, for example, issuing administrative guidelines, giving permissions, granting approvals.

Groupings of Particular Churches. The regulation of the liturgy for groupings of particular churches, namely, ecclesiastical provinces and regions, may take place through several canonical structures. Plenary and provincial councils may promulgate liturgical laws (cans. 439-446), but such particular councils occur rarely. The bishops of a province may jointly issue particular legislation or common policies on liturgical matters, but each bishop must promulgate them for his own diocese since the provincial meeting of bishops is not a legislative body.

The most effective structure today for the regulation of the liturgy for groupings of particular churches is the episcopal conference. The conference of bishops of a nation or other territory is a permanent institution that meets on a regular basis (cans. 447-459). In accord with the provisions of can. 455, episcopal conferences can enact general decrees, whether legislative or executory. For a decree to be binding, it must be adopted by a two-thirds majority of the members who have deliberative vote, and it must pertain to a matter on which the conference has the authority to act. This authority to enact binding decrees must be expressly granted to the conference either by the universal law or by special mandate of the Apostolic See. The liturgical books, the Code of Canon Law, and other liturgical documents give legislative competence to the episcopal conference on many liturgical matters, especially those which allow for some options or variations in the universal discipline.

A major responsibility of the episcopal conference is to prepare translations of the liturgical books into the vernacular languages and make the appropriate adaptations of them within the limits defined in the liturgical books themselves (can. 838, § 3). All translations and adaptations of the liturgical books as well as all other decrees of the episcopal conference must be submitted to the Apostolic See for review (*recognitio*) before they can be promulgated and become binding. The requirement of the *recognitio* may be seen in part as a way of protecting the rights of individual diocesan bishops who are bound to such decisions. It also may be seen as an act of communion between bishops of a nation or other territory and the Apostolic See.

The episcopal conference may be assisted by a liturgical commission entrusted with regulating pastoral liturgical action throughout the nation or other territory and with promoting studies and necessary experiments leading to the adoption of liturgical adaptations (S.C., 44). Such commissions are only advisory and cannot issue binding norms on their own authority. However, documents issued by a national episcopal liturgical commission may contain binding content derived from other legislative or executory texts. The commission's documents may also possess a significant moral authority because they are authored under the auspices of a nation's bishops who can draw on the advice of noted experts in fields related to the liturgy.

Custom and Dispensation

The liturgy is regulated not only by laws but also by customs. Customs are the living practices of the Christian community. They are introduced not by the legislator but by the community itself. Historically, liturgical practices originated more often by custom than by law, but the role of custom was significantly reduced as the church became more centralized and a uniform Roman liturgy became normative. However, even in the centuries of greatest centralization after Trent, the role of custom in ordering the life of the church, including its liturgy, has continued to be acknowledged in the canonical system.

Any community capable of receiving a law is capable of introducing a custom, including a diocese, a parish, or a religious community, but not a family or a small group of individuals. Customs that are contrary to or apart from the law can obtain the force of law only when they have been legitimately observed for 30 continuous and complete years in accord with cans. 23-26. Such legal customs enjoy a status equal to the law and cannot be abolished except by the legislator himself. Customs that are centenary (at least 100 years old) or immemorial (older than the memory of the oldest living person in the community) are highly esteemed by Canon Law. Even if such well established customs are contrary to the Code of Canon Law they can continue to be practiced if the ordinary judges that they should be tolerated due to local circumstances (can. 5, § 2).

Factual custom, as opposed to legal custom, does not have the force of law. Factual customs are the many actual, non-obligatory practices of the community often expressed colloquially as "the way things are done here." Factual customs can play an important role in the way the liturgy is celebrated in local communities. As can. 27 states, "Custom is the best interpreter of the law." This traditional canonical maxim means that the living practices of the local Christian community best indicate how laws are to be observed. It shows the great respect in the canonical tradition for the role of custom.

On the other hand, some customs can be abuses contrary to sound principles of liturgy and theology that result from ignorance or negligence on the part of ministers or assembly. In such cases liturgical law can serve as a corrective for unsound practices that have become a routine part of the local liturgy. Law and custom ideally should exist in creative and dynamic tension. The role of liturgical law is to establish the general principles and the more important disciplinary norms; the role of custom is to enflesh these basic norms with practices and styles of worship that best express the unique character of the people of God in the local churches. When both law and custom operate in proper balance, the indigenization or inculturation of the liturgy can proceed harmoniously in fidelity to the Roman tradition.

Local control of the liturgy can also be exercised in a lesser, though not insignificant, way through the dispensation of liturgical law. A dispensation is the relaxation of a merely ecclesiastical law in a particular case. It is an administrative act and can be granted by someone who has executive power. The diocesan bishop may validly dispense from universal liturgical laws and from particular laws established for his territory or for his subjects by the supreme authority of the church (can. 87, § 1). The local ordinary (diocesan bishop, vicar general, episcopal vicar) can dispense from diocesan laws and particular laws passed by particular councils or the episcopal conference (can. 88). Presbyters and deacons cannot dispense from laws unless this power is expressly granted to them by law or delegation (can. 89). For example, the code permits the pastor and the superior of a clerical religious institute or clerical society of apostolic life of pontifical right to dispense from Sunday and holy day obligations, from the obligations of fast and abstinence on days of penance, and from private vows (cans. 1245, 1196).

Dispensations can be validly granted only if there is just and reasonable cause for the dispensation and provided the person dispensing takes into consideration the circumstances of the case and the gravity of the law from which the dispensation is given (can. 90). Only disciplinary laws are subject to dispensation, not divine laws, constitutive laws, penal laws, procedural laws, or constitutive laws. Many liturgical laws are constitutive, that is, they define matters that essentially constitute juridical institutes or acts (can. 86). Most of the liturgical laws that affect the validity of sacraments are constitutive. For example, the law requiring water and the trinitarian formula for valid baptism could not be dispensed to permit some other matter or form. On the other hand, the canonical form of marriage is required for validity but it is a disciplinary law that may be dispensed by the local ordinary in mixed marriages (can. 1127, § 2). (The law of the canonical form obliges Catholics, for validity, to celebrate their marriage in the presence of a priest or deacon who has the faculty to assist at the marrige.) Many other constitutive laws, moreover, affect only liceity. Such constitutive laws may pertain to the authentic structure of the sacramental rites even though they are not essential for validity, for example, the requirements for the imposition of hands in confirmation, or the anointing(s) in baptism, or the liturgy of the word in the eucharist.

Universal disciplinary laws can be dispensed by the diocesan bishop provided they are not reserved to the Apostolic See (can. 87, § 1). Most liturgical laws are disciplinary laws that do not regulate matters affecting the basic structure or nature of the rites. They may therefore be dispensed provided that the dispensing authority bears in mind the gravity of the law in question together with the importance of the reason for the dispensation. It is sometimes difficult, however, to determine whether a law is constitutive or disciplinary. For example, the law of the Roman Missal regarding the time for the Easter vigil states that it must not begin before nightfall and it must end before daybreak on Sunday. One could argue that this is a constitutive law, that the vigil is by nature a night service and cannot be celebrated in daylight under any circumstances. On the other hand, one could argue that this law is merely disciplinary because, prior to the Holy Week reform in 1955, the Easter vigil had been celebrated in the morning of Holy Saturday.

Revocation of Law

Abrogation is the total revocation of a law; derogation is a change in the law that revokes part of it. Abrogation or derogation occurs in three ways: when a later law expressly states that it is abrogating an earlier law or derogating from it; when a later law is directly contrary to an earlier law; or when a later law integrally reorders the subject matter of the former law (can. 20). When the 1983 Code of Canon Law went into effect, the following were expressly abrogated by can. 6: (1) the Code of Canon Law promulgated in 1917; (2) other universal or particular laws contrary to the prescriptions of the code, unless particular laws are otherwise expressly provided for; (3) any universal or particular penal laws whatsoever issued by the Apostolic See, unless they are contained in the code; (4) other universal disciplinary laws dealing with a matter which is integrally reordered by the code.

The revised code revoked a number of liturgical laws which were contrary to it or which had been integrally reordered by it. In 1983 the Congregation for Sacraments and Divine Worship issued a lengthy list of changes that had to be made in the liturgical books as a result of the revised code (*Notitiae* 20:540-555). There is no official list of changes in the many executory documents that were issued by the Apostolic See in the decades following Vatican II. Some of the content in these documents has been revoked or made obsolete by later revisions of the liturgical books and the Code of Canon Law. In some cases even experts find it difficult to determine whether a certain provision in these earlier documents has been revoked or whether it remains in force. According to can. 21, "in a case of doubt the revocation of a pre-existent law is not presumed, but later laws are to be related to earlier ones and, insofar as it is possible, harmonized with them." This principle presumes the stability and continuity of the law, but it can be difficult to apply in practice.

The Code of Canon Law: A Text and Commentary

Commissioned by the Canon Law Society of America, Ed. by James A. Coriden, Thomas J. Green, and Donald E. Heintschel (New York/Mahwah: Paulist Press, 1985). R. Kevin Seasoltz, *New Liturgy, New Laws* (Collegeville: The Liturgical Press, 1980). Thomas Richstatter, *Liturgical Law: New Style, New Spirit* (Chicago: Franciscan Herald Press, 1977). Frederick R. McManus, ed., *Thirty Years of Liturgical Renewal: Statements of the Bishops' Committee on the Liturgy* (Washington: United States Catholic Conference, 1987). John Huels, *Liturgical Law: An Introduction.* American Essays in Liturgy 4. Series ed. Edward Foley (Washington: The Pastoral Press, 1987). John Huels, *One Table, Many Laws: Essays on Catholic Eucharistic Practice*, especially chap. 1: "The Interpretation of Liturgical Law" (Collegeville: The Liturgical Press, 1986). John Huels, *Disputed Questions in the Liturgy Today* (Chicago: Liturgy Training Publications, 1988).

JOHN M. HUELS, O.S.M.

LAY LEADERSHIP IN LITURGY

Where two or three or more gather in prayer, there is need for a leader. Lay animation and leadership often arise out of exigency. There is no ordained leader available. It may also arise out of circumstance. One is asked to lead prayer with a specific group on a particular occasion. The layperson called forth to lead prayer does so because she/he is baptized and demonstrates the charism of leadership, the skill and training to do so, and, when necessary, the authorized delegation to serve in this ministry.

Lay leadership may occur in domestic settings. This might include the blessing of food or children or elders in a household. It may take place in an ecumenical or interreligious setting. For example, one may be involved in prayer to begin or conclude a Jewish-Christian study day. Or one may be asked to lead prayer and offer prayer in a setting accompanying public protest or witness. Often lay leaders serve in official, pastoral situations. Increasingly more often lay leaders preside at the liturgy of the hours because they are pastoral ministers in a parish. Sometimes they lead a liturgy of the word in a reconciliation service during a retreat or they distribute ashes at the beginning of Lent. More and more, lay leaders visit the sick and lead those who are ill (and sometimes the rest of the family) in the reception of communion. Lay animation finds laypersons called upon to conduct a Sunday celebration at a prison where laypersons are part of a ministry team. This service might also include base ecclesial communities, wakes, and the praying over catechumens who have gathered to break open the word on a weekday night.

To lead liturgical prayer requires not only charism, but also training in the skills of public prayer and presidency. This lay leadership is a task and a function. One who animates an assembly needs to develop in a variety of ways.

First, she or he needs knowledge about the structures of public prayer. This includes knowing something of the tradition as well as the ability to make text come off the printed page into an aural/oral experience. The animator will need to be able to collaborate with other ministers who serve the same assembly (e.g., readers, communion ministers, cantors, musicians, etc.). She/he will also want to develop familiarity with symbolic language and life as she/he learns to be at home with ritual activity, i.e., the use of the body as a prayerful conveyer of reverence, joy, lament, consolation and festivity.

Secondly, she/he learns by doing public prayer. This includes practical training, critique and the openness to develop skills into the art of lay leadership.

Thirdly, she/he not only functions in a liturgical role, but also begins to put on Christ whose leadership did not oppress or overpower others. Christ served others. One's style of leading prayer eventually develops into a spirituality based on the paschal mystery, i.e., by dying and rising unto Christ. This means that the lay leader puts on Jesus' way of life. Leadership entails simplicity, transparency and a willingness to be vulnerable.

Since the eucharist is at the heart of public prayer, especially on Sunday, the Lord's Day, lay leadership emerges due to the worldwide shortage of ordained presbyters. Lay leaders, in the absence of presbyters, are called upon to lead a Sunday celebration of the hours (morning or evening) and a liturgy of the word with or without reception of communion. This ministry calls for some kind of delegation and commissioning as well as a connection with the local parish and the pastoral guidance of the diocese and its bishop. The shape of the Sunday celebration in the absence of a priest includes an introductory rite, the liturgy of the word, a thanksgiving prayer (not to be confused with the eucharistic prayer), communion rites and a conclusion. While reception of the reserved eucharist is never a felicitous substitution for the celebration of the full eucharist, it is nonetheless one way of meeting pastoral need. This requires that the lay leader continue to develop skills in presidency, preaching and public prayer. In many instances this will be the principal means a particular assembly has for celebrating Sunday.

See **Formation, liturgical**

Kathleen Hughes, *Lay Presiding: The Art of Leading Prayer* (Washington, D.C.: The Pastoral Press, 1988). J. Frank Henderson, "When Lay People Preside at Sunday Worship" *Worship* 58 (1984): 108-117. Congregation for Divine Worship, *Directory for Sunday Celebrations in the Absence of a Priest* (Washington, D.C.: United States Catholic Conference, 1988).

JOHN J. O'BRIEN, C.P.

LAY MINISTRIES, LITURGICAL

The exercise of liturgical ministries by lay women and men (which here is understood to include religious sisters and brothers) after Vatican Council II is based in part on the principle of active participation: "Mother Church earnestly desires that all the faithful should be led to that full, conscious, and active participation in liturgical celebrations which is demanded by the very nature of the liturgy, and to which the Christian people ... have a right and obligation by reason of their baptism" (S.C., 14). The Constitution on the Church spells out in more ecclesiological terms the belief that the church as a whole, and lay persons as well as the ordained, participate in the priestly, prophetic and kingly ministry of Jesus Christ.

Another principle is that of "division of labor": "In liturgical celebrations each person, minister, or layman who has an office to perform, should carry out all and only those parts which pertain to his office by the nature of the rite and the norms of the liturgy" (S.C., 28).

Finally, lay roles known at the time of the Council are considered to be real ministries: "Servers, readers, commentators, and members of the choir also exercise a genuine liturgical function. They ought, therefore, to discharge their offices with the sincere piety and decorum demanded by so exalted a ministry ... " (S.C., 29).

At a general level, the first liturgical ministry to be considered is that of the assembly as a whole, including both lay and ordained members. The primary minister of every liturgy, after Jesus Christ in the Holy Spirit, is the entire local church assembled; at this level, every baptized person participates in the liturgical ministry of this church.

Second, it needs to be remembered that the apostle Paul describes the entire Christian life in liturgical terms, and hence the daily life of every lay Christian is a liturgical ministry in this sense.

In a more specific sense, a large number of individual lay liturgical ministries have been named or have been recognized in recent years with the gradual publication and implementation of a full range of revised liturgical rites.

Certain kinds of liturgical ministries

exercised by laity are part of most liturgical celebrations. Often forgotten, but of great importance, are lay persons who participate in the planning of liturgies, as well as those who minister through art and environment. Ministers of hospitality play an important role in receiving parish members and guests at the door, seating guests and seeing that they have participation aids and hymnals, taking up the collection, being alert to any emergency, and greeting people again as they leave.

The importance of the ministry of reader reflects the centrality of the word of God at almost every liturgical celebration. Readers need skills in public speaking, some knowledge of scripture, and a spirituality that allows them to proclaim the word of God, and not just read from the lectionary.

Musicians also play a role at almost every celebration. They may include the cantor, the leader of song, the choir, and various instrumentalists. As almost all liturgies are supposed to be musical in nature, their role is almost essential.

Servers, acolytes and cross bearers constitute another group. The term "server" is sometimes used to refer to children and youth, while "acolyte" is used for adults carrying out virtually the same ministry. In other cases "acolyte" is used for adults who are also special ministers of communion.

The eucharist, especially the Sunday eucharist, requires several additional lay ministers. In some places lay persons meet ahead of time with the presbyter who will preach to plan the homily; they may also evaluate the preaching afterward. Again, in some places (largely in Africa and Latin America) lay persons, following the homily, "witness" to the impact of the word of God in their daily lives. In addition, lay persons may plan and lead special liturgies of the word for the small children of the community.

Local lay persons should prepare the

general intercessions of the Sunday eucharist (and may contribute to litanies used in other liturgies as well). These prayers should be based both on the scripture readings of the day and the needs of the world as evidenced, for example, in the daily newspaper; they need to be forceful, concrete, and moving. Other lay persons may give the announcements, which are expressions of the weekday life of the Christian community and its members.

Other lay persons will participate in the procession of the gifts at the preparation of the altar and the gifts, and, as already mentioned, in taking up and carrying forward the collection for the poor and the needs of the church.

Special ministers of communion may participate in the Sunday eucharistic liturgy, especially if there is—as there should be—communion from the cup.

If no presbyter is available on Sunday, lay persons may be asked to preside and preach at a liturgy of the word, a liturgy of the word and communion, or other suitable service for the Lord's day. Circumstances may call for such lay presiders also to minister at the distribution of ashes on Ash Wednesday, at the Easter triduum, and on other occasions.

The rites of Christian initiation call for still other liturgical ministers in addition to those already named. In the Rite of Christian Initiation of Adults, sponsors play an important role in giving example to the catechumens, but they are succeeded by godparents during the period of purification and enlightenment and afterwards. Catechists and other teachers, those who lead catechumens into the prayer life and the ministerial life of the church, those who preside at the exorcisms and blessings and those who lead the litanies of intercession at many liturgies all have important roles to play.

In the rite of baptism for children parents and godparents respond to the questions of the presbyter as representatives of the church. In proclaiming the renunciations and professing the faith they speak not for the child, and not just for themselves as individuals, but also for the entire church. The parents, especially, continue their ministry in the raising of the children as maturing Christians. The rite names yet another ministry in the person (presumed to be a woman) who cares for the child during the liturgy of the word. This allows the parents to listen clearly to the word without distraction. The child is returned to the mother by the "liturgical babysitter" following the homily.

Lay persons may baptize persons in danger of death, and the liturgical books provide rites for such occasions that are fuller than simply the pouring of water with the recitation of the baptismal formula.

At weddings, the bride and groom are considered to be the official ministers of matrimony, and as well they exercise a significant ministry to the congregation and guests in the way of hospitality and example. The witnesses also have a ministerial role, as may the parents of the couple.

In the liturgical rites for the sick and the dying there are significant liturgical roles for lay women and men. Visiting and praying with sick persons is named as a ministry of the church, whether carried out by laity or ordained persons. Lay persons may take communion from the church to the sick and preside at a brief liturgy of communion; they may pass on the essence of the liturgical homily. Lay persons may, if required, celebrate the sacrament of the dying— viaticum—and lead or say the commendation of the dying and prayers for the dead.

At communal celebrations of the sacrament of penance the lay persons present are called upon to pray for penitents who will be reconciled, as well as for sinners. On other occasions they may preside and preach at penitential celebrations that do not include the sacrament.

Increasingly, lay persons are taking the leadership of wakes or funeral vigil celebrations. They may also preside and preach at funeral services both in the church and at the cemetery when no presbyter is present.

The liturgy of the hours also may be presided over by lay persons, and they may preach if this is appropriate.

A number of blessings may also be celebrated by lay persons.

Finally, lay persons may plan and exercise all the required ministries, including presiding and preaching, at liturgies for small groups and other "unofficial" liturgies that seem called for.

Lay liturgical ministry is based on baptism and the appropriate gifts, but also requires education, training in the necessary skills, an appropriate spirituality, proper attitudes, diligence, acceptance of responsibility, and accountability. At all times the lay minister should strive to do his or her best, seek to improve, and derive strength and inspiration from a serious life of prayer. The lay minister always needs to consider that he or she is serving the greater ministry of the assembly and church as a whole.

In a parish setting the ministry of a particular individual may be for a limited period. Appropriately gifted elderly persons and persons with disabilities should be allowed to participate in liturgical ministries.

It is important to initiate neophytes into liturgical ministries, as seems opportune after their initiation, and to bring up the children of the parish to act as liturgical ministers as well. Even small children can participate in the ministry of hospitality and of bringing up the gifts, and older children can act as servers and musicians. In addition, some children can read quite well.

Lay liturgical ministers need to work together as a team, and usually will be working together with an ordained minister as well. His role, in part, is to coordinate the ministries of the lay persons, and this needs to be respected by the lay ministers.

The Liturgical Press (Collegeville, MN) has an extensive series of booklets describing individual lay liturgical ministries. A similar series is published by Novalis (Ottawa, ON) under the general title, *New Parish Ministries*, Virginia Sloyan, ed., *Touchstones for Liturgical Ministers* (Washington: The Liturgical Conference and The Federation of Diocesan Liturgical Commissions, 1978).

J. FRANK HENDERSON

LAY MINISTRY

See **Ministry, lay**

LAY SPIRITUALITY

The concept of lay spirituality is not new in the Christian church, but in the last half century the Roman Catholic tradition has benefited by greatly expanded expressions of spirituality for lay Christians. The phenomenon of lay spirituality and a theology of the lay vocation were topics of the 1987 World Synod of Bishops and of several papal documents in recent years. Understanding the radical nature of this aspect of *aggiornamento* requires an understanding of the terms "lay" (or "laity") and "spirituality" in the church, and a cursory glance at the history of Christian spirituality.

The term "laity" technically means non-ordained (i.e., everyone who is not a deacon, priest or bishop) but in popular church usage it identifies those baptized Christians who are neither ordained nor under the discipline of religious vows. When speaking of "lay spirituality" then, most people are referring to emerging expressions of life in Christ that are rooted in sources other than the vocations of holy orders or vows of poverty, chastity and obedience.

Religious and secular literature has given many definitions for the phenomenon of spirituality. In Christian terms, it is a relationship between a believer and God, mediated by the life, death and resurrection of Jesus Christ, and brought forth by the power of God's Spirit within the personality of the believer and according to the believer's cooperation.

For the first three hundred years of the church's history the community of believers was always confronted with the possibility—even the probability—that members would have to die in public forums for the sake of the gospel. To profess faith in Jesus Christ was treasonous in the Roman Empire and frequent persecutions reminded those who accepted this faith that they were entering a very dangerous course. This experience had a tremendous impact on the quality of faith life (i.e., spirituality) of the early Christians. Surely there were "lazy" Christians, and some who questioned their faith and the power of Jesus in their lives, but they were, by all reports, the minority.

Legalization of Christianity changed all that and within a short time after Constantine allowed Christians free practice of the faith, there were numerous members of the baptized who were not living the faith as fully as they had been invited by the gospel. This (and a number of other factors) created the ground out of which the phenomenon of monasticism arose in the 5th and 6th centuries. By the 9th century, there was a general sense in the church that if one wanted to be truly "holy," that is close to Christ and filled with God's Spirit, then one left behind the ordinary world of commerce and family with all its temptations and entered a cloister where one prayed, practiced various penances, and studied holy writings (scripture, the letters and ser-

mons of the Fathers of the church, etc.).

This lifestyle, with its vows of poverty, chastity and obedience, became the norm for authentic Christian living from the 6th until the 20th centuries in the Catholic tradition. A caste system by vocation developed within the church whereby "real" Christians were priests, deacons or religious who could devote their lives to prayers and works of charity. Lay Christians were those weaker ones whose salvation depended upon Sunday Mass attendance, reception of annual communion, and providing financial support for the "real" Christians. The architects of the Reformation in the 16th century fought against this increasingly clerical/religious mindset, but with only minor success in terms of developing a strong lay spirituality.

Seven realities of human experience, both secular and religious, have converged in the 20th century to establish the ground for a new call to holiness to the men and women in the world. These factors are not all of equal weight, nor are they all positive in themselves. Nonetheless, they have all been used by the Spirit of God to bring forth a new fire upon the earth, not unlike that experienced by the early Christians. This phenomenon, which for want of a better term is simply called lay spirituality, is slowly reshaping the self-identity of the institutional church.

After exploring these seven factors, I will briefly describe three primary milieux where the Spirit of God appears to have combined the impact of these factors and brought forth something new and rich for the church, and then outline twelve characteristics to identify this new lay spirituality.

Factors Shaping Lay Spirituality
1) Education. For the first time in human history as we know it, the majority of peoples worldwide are literate in some language. Even in Third World countries

the corner has been turned in the last decade and the majority of the populations of all seven continents can read and write as the 20th century comes to a close.

This phenomenon enormously affects the Christian churches of the First World. No longer are sacred books and theological studies the province of only the educated clergy, as they were barely a century ago. Lay men and women can read the scriptures, history and church documents of past and present. They can and do read scientific studies, and they are educated to think and to question, to evaluate, to probe and even to distrust. Perhaps no other single factor has created such a crisis and opportunity for the church as an educated laity. Leonard Doohan, in the preface to his book, *The Lay Centered Church*, states, "In fact, for the first time in history there are in the Church today more theologically trained laity than priests or religious" (p.i).

2) Scripture Research. Great strides were made in scripture scholarship and Bible translations during the century from 1850-1950, but with the establishment of the Jewish state in Israel (and the subsequent opening up of archaeological digs there) and the critically important discovery of hundreds of scrolls and scroll fragments from the Qumran caves, the explosion of scriptural research, scholarship, and discovery has completely revolutionized Christian theological studies.

One simple effect of this scholarship is the growing awareness of the essentially lay leadership of the life in the early Christian churches. This gives impetus to a broadened appreciation of the vocation of all members of the faith community.

In the Catholic popular experience a more important effect of this scripture knowledge explosion has been the re-establishment of the newly understood scriptures as a primary base for authority in the spiritual life. Meeting the real presence of Christ in the word, newly explained and understood, has had the dramatic effect of re-evangelizing millions of "cradle Catholics."

3) Ecumenism. Since the Holy Synod of the Orthodox Church of Constantinople in 1919 issued a worldwide invitation to Christian churches to form a League of Churches, the Ecumenical Movement has been one of the dominant religious forces of this century. It is remarkably important in shaping the growth of lay spirituality because it provides a broad arena for sharing among clergy and laity of all Christian traditions our rich heritage of belief in Christ Jesus.

Many Christian denominations, furthermore, have had a more highly developed sense of lay leadership and participation than the Roman church, because they were founded, at least in part, in opposition to the excessive clericalism of the Roman church of the 16th-19th centuries.

More importantly, however, the Ecumenical Movement has contributed greatly in reshaping the self-image of the whole Christian church, which is foundational to an authentic expression of spirituality. The common baptism that all Christians share is the basis for all spirituality, for it is through baptism that we are first inspired and transformed "into Christ." Recognizing that we share this essential unity with brothers and sisters of all Christian denominations causes lay persons to recognize the dignity of each vocation and of all vocations.

Finally, the Ecumenical Movement has reopened the eyes of Christians of all traditions to the inescapable truth that each one must work to undo the scandal of the divided body of Christ. Ecumenism stresses that this is not the work of bishops, synods and councils alone. It is inherent in the mission of each Christian to effect unity in the body to the best of his or her ability, so that in Christ all may be one.

4) World Crises. Two world wars; more than 100 smaller, but nevertheless deadly, conflicts; the great depression; concerned efforts by nations or leaders to wipe out entire races or groups of people culminating in, but not ending with, the terrible holocaust in Europe of the 1930s and 1940s; the vast hoards of refugees following wars, plagues, and continental droughts; the division of the world into those who live in plenitude and those who exist in absolute want; whole nations, even continents destroyed by environmental pollutants; and the division of the world into camps armed with nuclear weapons capable of destroying the earth 13 or 15 or 20 times over—the litany of world crises that mark the passage of the 20th century is yet another critical factor that has shaped and is shaping a lay spirituality for our day.

How does a baptized Christian respond to the horror of war, the destruction of human dignity through racism or sexism, and the appalling inequities that confront him or her daily on the news? If such a person takes the gospel of Jesus Christ seriously, the crises of the wounded world demand an investment of time, resources and personal ingenuity to bring about peace and healing. The profound sense that the church must respond justly and compassionately to a broken world is perhaps the strongest ground for desiring to cooperate in the ongoing incarnation of Christ in the church.

The knowledge that so-called Christians could perpetrate and support the evils of this century gives all religious persons reason to pause and question what equally powerful forces for good might well be in the Sunday church pew if appropriately encouraged and enabled.

5) The Renewal of Vatican II. The dramatic call for a springtime of faith unleashed by the Spirit through the Second Vatican Council and the implementation of its documents, is the fifth factor to consider.

The theology of church described in *Lumen Gentium* whereby all the baptized are identified as the people of God; the definition of the church as celebrant of the sacramental mysteries in the *Constitution on the Sacred Liturgy*; the restoration of the meal aspect of the eucharist and the location of the eucharist squarely at the heart of the Christian faith life; the search for the energy of founding spiritual charisms in traditional spirituality movements of the church; the compelling call of *Divino Afflante Spiritu* to more fully mine the treasures of the scriptures; the restoration of the richness of the sacramental signs, especially the restoration of the catechumenate—which presupposes a process of spiritual growth at the heart of conversion; above all, the clarion call to the church to be servant to the world, not to be divided from the world, issued in the *Constitution on the Church in the Modern World*—all these and many more changes effected a groundswell of commitment among many already educated lay men and women to seek a true holiness in the context of living in the world.

6) The Influence of the Social Science. A sixth factor that has greatly contributed to a renewed Christian spirituality is the marked influence of the social sciences upon Western culture. Most notably the field of psychology exerts a tremendous influence on the average lay person (in this case *lay* means non-doctor, non-therapist and non-ordained) who has laid claim to the insights of Freud, Jung, Adler, Maslow and hundreds of other healers and researchers of the human psyche through the publications of the scholars themselves and through the works of numerous popularizers. For many people this psychological movement has been a tremendous source of division from traditional religions. Many have turned to psychology to answer questions about the inner life that religion formerly answered. So much has the language and concept of psychology taken over that an American psychiatrist, Karl Menninger, raised the question "Whatever became of sin?" in a book of that title in 1971, revealing that no one spoke of sin anymore, even from the pulpits of the Christian churches.

With the passing of the 1970s however, the traditions of religion and psychology began to seek out each other more frequently. The proliferation of the 12-step support groups provides a traditional Christian formula for spiritual growth apart from the name of and belief in Jesus Christ. Alcoholics Anonymous and its numerous off-shoot groups create spiritual havens of healing and strength for many who find no such support in the pews of traditional Christian churches.

For large numbers of believers, however, reclaiming the 12-step spirituality and/or a long roster of other insights from modern psychology in the context of the broader Christian spiritual traditions has been the source of a profoundly enriched interior life. The marriage of psychology and religion (through spirituality) is increasingly evident in academic programs, hospital and hospice care, clinics and other long term therapeutic approaches.

7) Cultural Malaise. A seventh contributing factor to the emergence of a compelling lay spirituality is the widespread cultural malaise that is often described as a profound sense of meaninglessness or alienation from life itself.

This malaise is identifiable in all the cultural landmarks of the radically secularized first world. Music, art, theater, television, cinema, and literature all celebrate alienation and meaninglessness. The drug culture among young and old effects a virtual paralysis wherever it takes hold. Rising incidents of crime and violence in every community leave citizens riddled with fear. Proof that disrespect for human life and for human relationships is increasing is demonstrated equally in the statistics of abortion clinics, divorce courts, and nuclear weapons factories. In every city hall where the effort to keep the poor from having a home or a decent meal is successful the resulting hopelessness deepens the malaise.

The sources of the cultural blight are many and difficult to specify. Highly developed technology that puts barriers between people and which appears to remove immediate consequences for behaviors has been blamed, as has rapidly developing scientific information that undermines traditional religious myths. The constant threat of nuclear annihilation has been cited as another significant cause. Whatever the cause, one unpredictable effect is the enlarged pursuit of the meaningful. The resurgence of the Catholic and Oriental mystical traditions, the development of new methods of meditation and the return to the wisdom of past generations to observe how humans have dealt with change and life threatening issues, and the development of small intentional communities to provide encouragement, energy and experiences of faith, are all evidences that the malaise is driving men and women to seek relief and to find hope, to work against the gathering darkness by proclaiming and unveiling the light.

While these seven forces differ in scope and implications, all are the ground out of which the Holy Spirit has forged a new spirituality of the laity. Three milieux have fostered this emerging vitality and we turn next to explore these briefly.

A. Parishes

The parish or local church is the first arena where these seven factors have converged in people's lives. In many parishes throughout the world the efforts at implementing the reforms of Vatican II have been sporadic and ineffective. In many more, however, the pastors and communities have worked hard to grasp the full implications of the documents and to put them into practice. It is in such places where the renewal of the liturgy, the implementation of the catechumenate process, the awakening of consciousness toward the oppressed, the need for lay ministry formation, and the ongoing adult formation and education programs spur the development of lay spirituality.

In each of these parishes, urban, suburban or rural, large or small, a Christian community of support and challenge is at the center of its life. Here the cycle of evangelization, conversion, and commitment to discipleship which is the hallmark of the Christian spiritual life weave a binding circle of love around male and female—married, never married, divorced, or widowed, children, adult and aged—far from any seminary, monastery or convent.

B. Universities

One ground of renewal in the church for 800 years or more has been the university, college and secondary school. Academic institutions sponsored by religious communities have been particularly noted for carrying on the renewal work of the church past and present. It is no accident therefore that a second milieu for emerging lay spirituality is this classic arena of formation.

Seminary programs, spirituality studies, degree and certificate tracks that wed science and religion or social science and theology have all formed a new generation of Christians among the young. Mature men and women who long for more than they were given in the past have returned for more education. Laity and clergy exploring the spiritual traditions together have brought new energy to all the vocational groups in the Christian body.

C. Renewal Movements

The third arena of this newly energized lay spirituality is intentional groups or communities of people who band together for prayer, dialog, scripture study, therapy, faith sharing, adult education, support in overcoming addiction, to accomplish a common goal, to fight a common enemy, to change unjust structures, or any combination of these.

A whole catalog of renewal movements, groups and experiences have been established or radically revised in the last 25 years. Some of these have emerged from within the church and are blessed by the church, and some without any initiation or blessing of the church have nonetheless contributed greatly to the spiritual growth of the members.

Whether founded by members of the church or not, such groups are rarely limited by traditional parish boundaries, and most are not limited denominationally or even religiously. Some, notably the 12-step groups and various other therapy or support groups, do not immediately cast themselves as spiritual-growth groups at all (and are careful to separate themselves from any institutional religion), but provide the kind of companionship, challenge, and inner journeying that characterize the development of Christian spirituality.

Renewal movements and basic community groups rarely identify a structural hierarchy with holy orders or religious vows, but count each member as equal simply because of membership, or create a hierarchy based on the quality of service rendered.

Some of these movements actually have historic roots in church tradition specifically as lay movements, but until Vatican II were governed by clergy or vowed religious leadership. Now such groups are generally directed by and for lay members even if clergy or religious continue to participate.

Many groups call forth lay members to provide counsel, spiritual direction, prayer leadership and other forms of ministry to the membership that were often reserved to ordained or religiously vowed chaplains in the past. The phenomenon of highly trained lay spiritual directors, catechists or theologians educating, guiding and forming deacon and priest candidates, novices and seminarians, as well as other lay persons, once virtually unknown in the Catholic tradition, is now, if not exactly universal, at least not uncommon. Much of the experience and training for the laity in this kind of leadership has come through the initiative of renewal movements and small basic communities.

Characteristics

Having thus explored seven factors that have shaped the phenomenon of lay spirituality and the milieux of its rebirth, it is now appropriate to complete this study by briefly identifying certain characteristics which describe lay spirituality as it has flowered in the last three decades in the Roman Catholic tradition.

1) The vocation to life in Christ through God's Spirit, i.e. holiness, is rooted in the priesthood of the baptized. Baptism is the act of initiation into the body of Christ and through baptism one dies to self and rises with Christ through the power of the Holy Spirit.

2) Participation of the body of Christ in his mission of salvation is incumbent upon the baptized and therefore Christian faith is always corporate or communal rather than private or individual.

3) The mission of Christ (and therefore the church) is to reconcile all humanity with God and with each other. Lay spirituality is always characterized by the work of peace-making, division-healing and unifying.

4) The eucharist, celebrated together by all the baptized, identifies and effects the church into the one body of Christ. It is therefore, the "source and the summit" (S.C., 7) of spirituality for laity, clergy and religious. Furthermore, this eucharistic center presents an appropriate christological focus for believers rather than excessive devotion to Mary and the saints as has sometimes characterized lay spiritualities of past eras.

5) The mission of the body of Christ is to and within the broken world. Lay spirituality finds its fruitfulness not from moving the believer out of contact with the world, but rather into contact with the heart of world affairs in order to transform the world by bringing life, hope, peace and justice.

6) Lay spirituality finds nourishment in prayer that is rooted in sound scriptural knowledge and contemplation. The work of reading, studying, pondering scripture is central to the believer's prayer time whether that time be brief or extended.

7) Lay spirituality is rooted in a scriptural value-base that demands emphasis on a lifestyle that is characterized by simplicity and human dignity in a world sharply divided between the powerful rich and the oppressed poor. Lay spirituality calls not for radical impoverishment or non-ownership of property as much as for responsible and respectful stewardship of the world's resources. Real holiness often emerges in the struggle to live and support a family in the world and not be swallowed up or possessed by a worldly value system.

8) Lay spirituality is rooted in a healthy knowledge of self as a loved sinner before God. Today's holiness is identified in respect for one's own dignity and appreciation of one's talents while possessing true knowledge of one's weakness and sinfulness. This provides a solid basis for love and respect for one's neighbors in a way that is non-possessive and non-controlling.

9) Lay spirituality celebrates God's presence and loving mercy in a balance between the sacramental life of the church and the familial rituals of the domestic church.

10) Lay spirituality is both affective and intellective. A healthy human response to love is with the whole self. All dimensions of the human psyche are shaped by and

shape one's relationship to God which in turn shapes the relationship with all persons. Characteristically lay spirituality among married couples is enriched by a healthy appreciation of God's gift of sexual expression as a means for growing in love.

11) Contemporary lay spirituality is not threatened by scientific advances, but is rather enriched by the search for truth on all frontiers.

12) Lay spirituality is not confined or defined by denominational boundaries. Truly spiritual men and women see the call to unity among Christians at the heart of the mission of reconciliation, and see the division and self-righteousness of denominationalism as destructive of the gospel message. Ecumenical and interfaith relationships are as rich and life-giving in faith as those within one's own tradition.

The growth of lay spirituality is one of the great gifts of the Spirit of God at a time in history when being Christian is so much more than wearing a denominational label and attending the church of one's choice on Sunday. The demands of the so-called post-Christian era of the waning years of the 20th century upon all believing Christians are no less than those placed by Christ upon the first apostles. For any Christian to respond with less courage, less spirit of conviction, or less generosity, is to deprive our broken world of the healing message that could be the only force between us and total self-annihilation. For the institutional churches to be anything less than utterly committed to the re-awakening of the fervor of the church described in the Acts of the Apostles, is to be untrue to the command of the gospel.

Leonard Doohan, *The Lay Centered Church: Theology and Spirituality* (Minneapolis: Winston Press, 1984). Pope John Paul II, *The Vocation and the Mission of the Lay Faithful in the Church and in the World* (Christifideles Laici), Post Synodal Apostolic Exhortation, December 30, 1988 (Washington, D.C.: United States Catholic Conference, Office of Publishing and Promotion Services, Publication #274-8).

EILEEN C. BURKE-SULLIVAN

LECTIONARY, PREACHING THE

See **Preaching the lectionary**

LENT

Lent is the most common name for what is chronologically the first part of the paschal cycle, a cycle which in its entirety extends from Ash Wednesday to the Sunday of Pentecost. Lent, or the time of preparation for the paschal celebration, runs from "Ash Wednesday until the Mass of the Lord's Supper exclusive" (GNLYC, 28), ending with the beginning of the Easter triduum on Holy Thursday evening. The three days of the Easter triduum include this celebration of the Mass of the Lord's Supper and continue through evening prayer on Easter Sunday. The Easter triduum in turn is followed by the Easter season of fifty days, concluding on Pentecost Sunday. In addition to these official calendar divisions within the paschal cycle, the last part of Lent and the first part of the Easter triduum are also traditionally referred to as Holy Week, which "has as its purpose the remembrance of Christ's passion, beginning with his Messianic entrance into Jerusalem" (GNLYC, 31).

Included in the actual season of Lent are Ash Wednesday, a "universal day of fast" (GNLYC, 29) which begins the season, and six Sundays, known since 1969 only by their numerical designation except for the sixth Sunday of Lent, officially called Passion (Palm) Sunday. In addition, Lent includes the Chrism Mass on Holy Thursday morning and, as a primary focus of the season, the final stages of catechumenal preparation for initiation, expressed liturgically in the Rite of

Election on the first Sunday of Lent, and the three Rites of the Scrutinies on the third, fourth, and fifth Sundays in Lent. The integrity of Lent as a focused season is maintained in the weekday liturgies which also provide the suggested time for the Rites of Presentations in the R.C.I.A. Two of the ten fixed solemnities in the universal calendar generally fall during the Lenten season: Joseph, husband of Mary, March 19; and the Annunciation, March 25.

Historical Development

The origins of Lent are subsequent to and dependent on the annual celebration of the Pascha. The preparatory fast of Holy Saturday prior to the vigil was joined to the traditional Friday fast of early Christians, creating a foundation which evolves into the eventual fast of forty days. But this development extending chronologically backwards from the Easter vigil and based primarily on baptismal preparation has been joined through recent research to a parallel pattern of a forty-day fast immediately following the celebration of Epiphany and finding its basis in the imitation of Jesus' life (see Talley, 1986). This second pattern exerts an influence on both the focus and duration of Lent and consequently both patterns are integral to the study of the historical development of Lent.

The earliest document which actually describes the process of baptismal preparation is the *Apostolic Tradition*, commonly ascribed to Hippolytus and dating from c. 215. Although Hippolytus relates the ritual moments of the conversion process in detail, he never identifies the celebration of initiation with Easter itself nor does he clarify the length of the intense preparation prior to the rites of initiation. By at least the 5th century, however, there is evidence in Rome of a backwards extension of the Easter triduum to the preceding Sunday, based on the readings of the passion accounts during that time. This week-long paschal fast, known by the 3rd century in other geographical centers, has no discernible connection to baptismal preparation in Rome. A clearer picture of a nascent Lent in Rome is provided by the 5th century historian Socrates who describes a fast of three consecutive weeks before Easter, apparently an earlier practice no longer observed in his time. These three weeks of preparation mentioned by Socrates are supported by additional information from the Gelasian Sacramentary, an 8th-century collection which still contained Masses for baptismal scrutinies on the third, fourth, and fifth Sundays of Lent. Although the actual scrutinies had been moved to weekday liturgies due to the predominance of infant baptism by the time of the Gelasian Sacramentary, the presence of the Mass titles undoubtedly points to an earlier custom. In addition, the fifth Sunday of Lent was called *Dominica mediana*, a designation which makes sense only if indeed the fifth Sunday were the middle Sunday of three. The sequence of Johannine gospel readings beginning on the fourth Sunday and continuing through the passion on Good Friday also points to these three weeks as a unit in continuity with Easter. These three weeks of Lent, directly linked to the catechumenate in Rome, develop into a fast of forty days by the 4th century, an expansion perhaps given impetus by the Council of Nicea in 325 which mentioned an undefined forty-day period in its fifth canon. Athanasius of Alexandria, exiled to Rome in 340, writes back to his own church about a fast of forty days kept in Rome, and evidence of a pattern of forty fast days multiplies quickly within the second half of the 4th century.

Concurrent with this development in Rome, the Christian center of Alexandria gave rise to a different type of fast. In addition to a six-day fast prior to the celebration of Easter, which may have been commemorated as early as the 3rd century, several sources of the 4th century reveal a penitential fast for the purposes of reconciling penitents or for spiritual health. The fast is not associated with paschal baptism like that of Rome, but instead is an ascetical exercise in imitation of Jesus' fast. The chronology of this fast follows the gospel of Mark used in Egypt, which places the forty-day period immediately after the celebration of Epiphany, paralleling Jesus' sojourn in the desert following his own baptism. This forty-day ascetical fast was not continuous with the paschal fast of six days; the forty-day fast ended on the Friday prior to the feast of Palms, a celebration which preceded Easter by several weeks in the earlier Egyptian calendars. Adding to the differences is the apparent absence of Egyptian paschal baptism until 385. In developing a hypothesis for the timing of baptism prior to the adoption of a paschal celebration, Talley speculates that, based on later references to baptism and on the 2nd century expanded text of the gospel of Mark (the so-called secret gospel of Mark), the pre-4th-century baptismal celebration in Egypt took place at the end of this forty-day fast in imitation of the day when Jesus baptized Lazarus. This ingenious theory also allows for an explanation of the baptismal allusions connected with Lazarus on Saturday which appear in later Byzantine and in Mozarabic sources.

The post-Epiphany fast of the Egyptian tradition not only contributes to the historical development of Lent as a representation of an alternative pattern, but directly affects the expansion of Lent in other areas. The exportation of monastic elements from Egypt is reflected in the adoption of this fast in the closely related Celtic monastic tradition and its influence is probably reflected in the foundational monastic rule titled *Regula Magistri* which has an extended fast of one hundred days between Epiphany and Easter. This ascetical and monastic extension of Lent may originally have been a reconciling of two different traditions—the pre-paschal fast and the post-Epiphany fast—but its establishment in the West prior to the waning of adult baptisms provides a seasonal focus for the rise of penitential aspects of Lent. During the 5th and particularly the 6th centuries, the practice of adult baptism declined for several reasons, most notably because of the rise of infant baptisms for the offspring of Christian parents, itself encouraged by growing adherence to a doctrine of original sin. The result is a diminishing of the ritual process of conversion, specifically the latter part of the catechumenate simultaneous with the season of Lent, which found its logic in the personal commitment and response of adult converts. In the theological space created by the diminishing of the baptismal dimensions of Lent, the penitential aspects, which were also present from the earliest references to Lent, blossom into full growth. Part of this development is manifested in the ritualization of reconciliation, specifically the rise of canonical penance and the order of penitents. Public penance is witnessed to as early as Origen, the *Didascalia*, and in the practice of the 3rd century North African church, but the growth of the church in the 4th century sees more the institutionalization of the ritual process and an identification of that process with the season of Lent which can properly be called canonical penance. In Rome, the first extant reference to public penance occurs in a letter of Innocent I (416) with an explanation of the reconciliation of penitents on Holy Thursday, but the beginning of the process which ended on Holy Thursday is not clarified until later.

In the East, the structure and duration of Lent varied from area to area but with one consistent difference from the West, namely a sharp differentiation between Lent and Great Week (Holy Week). The *Apostolic Constitution* (c.375) records a practice of six weeks of Lent, a festal break of Lazarus Saturday and Palm Sunday, and then the six-day paschal fast immediately preceding the celebration of Easter. This same pattern can eventually be seen throughout the Eastern churches, exemplified in the rich tradition of Jerusalem. Although the primary sources on Lent and the catechumenate from Jerusalem in the 4th century offer somewhat conflicting evidence on the length of Lent (Cyril of Jerusalem in his *Baptismal Catecheses* seems to reflect a six-week Lent; Egeria in her diary of travel speaks of an eight-week Lent), by the 5th century the Armenian lectionary has conformed to the Eastern pattern of six weeks of Lent with an additional six days of Great Week following that. The important writings of Cyril and Egeria reveal in Jerusalem a Lent focused on the preparation of baptismal candidates for paschal initiation, the same focus seen in the catechetical writings of John Chrysostom in Antioch and Theodore of Mopsuestia. All of these sources reflect an elaborate process of ritual and catechesis occurring during the season of Lent, augmented especially in Jerusalem by the system of stational liturgies which used the holy places to enrich and reinforce the readings of Lent and Great Week.

In the Byzantine capital of Constantinople, the early sources on Lent are scanty, but reconstruction from later liturgical books shows a similar pattern to the Eastern practice of a six-week Lent, a two-day festal interlude, and a six-day Great Week prior to Pascha. In the 6th century an additional week of fasting was added to the beginning of Lent by the monophysite churches, perhaps influenced by the Coptic practice of retaining a post-Epiphany fast. As an ecumenical gesture aimed at reuniting the churches, the emperor Heraclius also added an extra week of light fasting to the Chalcedonian churches' Lent in the 7th century, extending the celebration by another week.

This same expansion of the season can be seen in the medieval West by tracing the development of Lent in Rome. The liturgical sources and calendars reveal a double extension in the season of Lent: an interior development reflected in the growth of weekday stations and liturgies, and a lengthening of the season of Lent by the addition of an anticipatory period prior to the First Sunday of Lent. From the homilies of Pope Leo I in the 5th century we learn that Wednesdays and Fridays were the only official assemblies during the week and that the eucharist was not celebrated on those days. The fasting of Lent was observed Monday through Saturday. By the 6th century, however, the days of assembly (stational liturgies) had been extended to Mondays, Tuesdays, Wednesdays, Fridays, and Saturdays during Lent and they included the celebration of eucharist. The 6th century also saw the official extension of Lent to include the Wednesday and Friday before the First Sunday of Lent. By the 7th century, this Wednesday preceding Lent I becomes the beginning of the fast, the *caput ieiunii*, which will later become known as Ash Wednesday, and which allowed for a precise number of forty fasting days. In the 8th century, the remaining aliturgical day, Thursday, received its liturgical formularies, creating a system of daily Lenten liturgies. The anticipatory season of a mini-Lent is seen by the 6th century addition of the seventh Sunday before Easter, *Quinquagesima*, followed shortly by the addition of *Sexagesima*, and finally *Septuagesima* in the early 7th century. Gregory I suppressed the singing of the Alleluia during this three-week period, extending additional ties with Lent chronologically back into this period. Both of these Roman developments were spread throughout the Western Christian realm by the liturgical renewal of Charlemagne which adopted Roman liturgical customs as universal.

The custom of distributing ashes on Ash Wednesday did not originate with Roman tradition but came from the Mozarabic and Gallican liturgical traditions where it was connected with entrance into the order of penitents. Although not at first related to the season of Lent, the custom gained popularity as many of the penitential practices once reserved for serious public sinners became standard for all the faithful. It was not until 1091, when Pope Urban II ordered the imposition of ashes on the heads of all the faithful, that the reception of ashes became mandatory and the Wednesday preceding the First Sunday of Lent became known as Ash Wednesday. This reception of ashes by all the faithful was in keeping with the primary stress of Lent which had become penance, and conversely, the demise of baptismal theology within the season.

The popularity of Ash Wednesday and of the ritual of ashes for the faithful was paralleled by a change in emphasis on the last Sunday of Lent, Palm Sunday. This Sunday was maintained as Passion Sunday in Rome well into the medieval age, but elsewhere the second focus of celebration on the sixth Sunday of Lent, namely the commemoration of Jesus' entrance into Jerusalem, began to overshadow the passion emphasis. The first reference to an actual procession with palms comes from 4th century Jerusalem. Although Jerusalem may not represent the origins of this particular celebration, the presence of holy places made the procession all the more popular and contributed to the growth in palm processions in Gaul and Spain throughout the medieval period. The participatory nature of the processions led to the full scale urban processions of the 8th century, characterized by the composition of the Palm Sunday hymn known in English as *All Glory, Laud, and Honor* by Theodulph of Orleans, and eventually to the liturgical dramas of the Middle Ages.

In the Roman tradition, the remaining days of Lent, following Palm Sunday and leading to the culmination of Lent in the Easter triduum, focused on the passion of Christ as recounted in the remaining synoptic gospels of Mark and Luke (Matthew having been read exclusively on Palm Sunday). On Holy Thursday the last two rituals of Lent were celebrated: the consecration of the chrism, and the reconciling of those penitents who had undergone the last stages of public penance during Lent. The consecration of chrism, and originally the blessing of both the oil of the sick and of catechumens, was the prerogative of the bishop. In 400, the Council of Toledo had restated not only that this was the privilege of bishops but that they could consecrate chrism at any time. Shortly after that, however, the consecration of chrism came to be identified with Holy Thursday, undoubtedly because of the necessity of preparing chrism for use at the Easter sacraments. In Rome, the pope consecrated chrism during the one Mass at which he presided on Holy Thursday, namely the Mass of the Lord's Supper. But in the morning of Holy Thursday, the priests attached to the titular churches of Rome blessed the oil of catechumens and of the sick at the liturgies over which they presided. This Roman city pattern was adapted in the Frankish sacramentaries by adding the text for the consecration of chrism to the presbyteral Mass, creating a single liturgy focused on the consecration and blessing of all oils. This Gallican adaptation became the norm for the medieval Western church outside of Rome. The reconciliation of penitents took place in the presence of the bishop prior to the celebration of eucharist on the evening of Holy Thursday, and this first communion to which the reconciled Christians were welcomed was the completion of their term of excommunication. The details of the liturgy of reconciliation are first found in the Gelasian Sacramentary, and the rite endured in liturgical books and memory beyond the actual practice of public penitents. The medieval liturgies of reconciliation represented an unparalleled sense of hospitality and ecclesiology in an age where those elements were often diminished in liturgy.

Contemporary Practice

The double focus of baptism and penance in the season of Lent was restored with the reforms of Vatican II, particularly with the *Constitution on the Sacred Liturgy* (1963) and the *Rite of Christian Initiation of Adults* (1972). From the primary (and often solitary) focus on penance, the conciliar document reminds the church of the original baptismal character of Lent: "The two elements which are especially characteristic of Lent—the recalling of baptism or the preparation for it, and penance—should be given greater emphasis in the liturgy and in liturgical catechesis. It is by means of them that the Church prepares the faithful for the celebration of Easter ... " (S.C., 109). The constitution's charge to make more use of the baptismal features of Lent, including those "of an earlier tradition" (S.C., 109a), was brought to fruition with the promulgation of the final draft of the R.C.I.A. in 1988. "The sacraments of initiation are celebrated during the Easter Solemnities, and preparation for these sacraments is part of the distinctive character of Lent. Accordingly, the Rite of Election should normally take place on the first Sunday of Lent and the period of final preparation of the elect should coincide with the Lenten season. The plan arranged for the Lenten season will benefit the elect by

reason of both its liturgical structure and the participation of the community" (R.C.I.A., 126).

This twofold emphasis is reflected in the structure, readings, and prayers of the reformed Lenten liturgies. The revised structure of Lent has restored the integrity of the season by eliminating the anticipatory period of *septuagesima*, *sexagesima*, and *quinquagesima* prior to the first Sunday of Lent, and by eliminating the anticipation of Passion Sunday on the fifth Sunday of Lent (itself called Passion Sunday prior to the reforms of 1969) which had created a two week period of Passiontide. Ash Wednesday is retained as the beginning of Lent, and it continues the call to reform and to acts of charity while emphasizing the movement towards Easter. The prayer preceding the blessing of ashes expresses this by saying: "May they keep this Lenten season in preparation for the joy of Easter" (1969 Sacramentary, Ash Wednesday).

While Ash Wednesday recalls the penitential aspects of Lent, the structure and focus of the R.C.I.A. has had a profound effect on recalling the baptismal nature of Lent. The readings for the Sundays of Lent, like those of the entire liturgical year, are on a three year cycle, and the first of the three, Cycle A, restores the catechumenal readings associated with adult initiation in the early church. This cycle can be used every year in parishes which have an R.C.I.A., and the accompanying scrutinies and prayers on the third, fourth, and fifth Sundays of Lent, together with the Rite of Election on the first Sunday of Lent, ritually support the theology that Lent finds its ultimate purpose in the celebration of Easter.

The first Sunday of Lent in all three cycles uses the story of Jesus' temptation in the desert from either Matthew, Mark, or Luke, to focus on the beginning of the journey to the resurrection. The accompanying Preface for Lent I strengthens this movement: "Each year you give us this joyful season when we prepare to celebrate the paschal mystery with mind and heart renewed." The second Sunday also has the same gospel story in all three cycles, the transfiguration of Jesus, which points again to the glory of a life in Christ beyond the cross and death. The second Sunday of Lent also has its own Preface related to the gospel reading.

Beginning with the third Sunday in Cycle A, the ancient baptismal pericopes from John dominate the liturgies for three weeks. On the third Sunday, the story of the meeting of Jesus with the Samaritan woman is centered on the "living water" which Jesus gives for eternal life. The story of the man born blind and healed by Jesus is the focus of the fourth Sunday, Cycle A, a baptismal story dependent on the early church understanding of baptism as enlightenment. The fifth Sunday uses the gospel of the raising of Lazarus, a reading with a rich historical background of its own and one that holds out to all Christians the ultimate goal of life with Christ after death.

All three of these Sundays in Cycle A have their own proper Prefaces, the other two cycles continue to use the Preface of Lent I or II. Both Cycles B and C in these three Sundays present readings selected to speak to those already baptized and continuing to grow in their faith. Cycle B, particularly in the OT readings, retraces the covenant of God and God's people through the new covenant in Christ Jesus. The gospel readings culminate on the fifth Sunday in the dying and rising of all Christians on the journey through life with the use of the gospel of John pericope on the grain of wheat which dies to bear fruit, reflecting both Christ's passage from death to life and that of all Christians. Cycle C has a stronger focus on transforming faith and uses gospel stories in these three weeks which recount cycles of failure and ultimate victory

through faith. The gospel reading for the fifth Sunday in Cycle C is the only one in this cycle taken from John; here the story of the adulterous woman who receives the mercy of God and begins again reflects the theme of victorious faith begun on the first Sunday of Lent with the story of Jesus' victory over Satan.

All three cycles move to the passion account on the sixth Sunday of Lent (properly called Passion Sunday) which begins Holy Week. The first part of the liturgy commemorates Jesus' entrance into Jerusalem, a commemoration retained in the liturgical reforms in three options: an actual procession with palms, a solemn entrance, or a simple entrance. The gospel of Jesus' entrance into Jerusalem is read from one of three synoptic accounts prior to the procession or entrance. The focus changes from the entry of Jesus to the passion of Jesus, however, with the prayers and readings of the eucharistic liturgy itself, moving toward the proclamation of the passion from one of the three synoptic accounts (the gospel of John being reserved for Good Friday). This last Sunday of Lent also has its own Preface for use in all three cycles which speaks of the efficacious dying and rising of Christ, tying this Sunday's liturgy to the Easter triduum at the conclusion of Lent.

The weekdays of Lent also continue the theme of movement towards Easter. The importance of the season is seen in the fact that each weekday has its own proper of the Mass. Beginning with the fourth week of Lent, the gospel of John is read in a semi-continuous manner which creates a coherent whole with the Sunday readings of Cycle A.

The one historical aspect of Lent which was not addressed in the reforms of the rites and of the calendar since Vatican II is the identification of Lent with an order of penitents and a formal reconciliation of those in a temporary period of being outside the full communion of the church.

Experience has taught liturgical scholars and pastoral practitioners that the ritualization of re-entry is very important to many people and a process of conversion like that of the final stages of the R.C.I.A. would allow for a time period of sufficient duration in order to facilitate such a ritualization. The future of Lenten reforms may be enriched by the addition of just such a process and group of people, restoring in a more profound way the richness of Lent as a time of preparation for initiation for some, a time of preparation for reconciliation for others, and a time of renewal in both areas for the faithful in the church.

See **Calendar, liturgical; Holy week, liturgies of; Easter season; Initiation, Christian; Catechumenate; Penitents, order of**

Adolf Adam, *The Liturgical Year* (New York: Pueblo Publishing Company, 1981). Adrian Nocent, *The Liturgical Year: Lent and Holy Week*, Vol. 2 (Collegeville: The Liturgical Press, 1977). Thomas J. Talley, *The Origins of the Liturgical Year* (New York: Pueblo Publishing Company, 1986).

LIZETTE LARSON-MILLER

LITURGICAL BOOKS

"Liturgical books" may refer to any collection of texts (readings, prayers, songs) employed in the course of liturgical celebrations, with or without descriptions or directions for ritual celebration. More commonly, it is used for the actual books, official in character, prepared for the ministers, readers, and others who have special roles in the liturgical assembly, and specifically sung and spoken parts.

It is evident that the first such collections were the canonical scriptures themselves, at whatever stage or in whatever form. In this sense an antecedent of later liturgical books is seen in the scroll from which Jesus read in the synagogue (Lk 4:16-30) and in the psalms, canticles, and euchological texts of both OT and NT. The arrangement of the gospels themselves, for example, has even been seen as influenced by their reading in the church assembly—a pattern that has now influenced modern Roman liturgical reform: the semi-continuous reading of biblical passages in the eucharist and the introduction of a three-year Sunday cycle of readings following the synoptic gospels.

More precisely, however, liturgical books are the collections designed and compiled directly for such use, and these have gradually developed from the lists of readings or the booklets (*libelli*) of prayers in ancient times into the officially sanctioned volumes of the modern period. The most highly developed books are found in the Eastern churches, the Roman and other Western Catholic rites, and in the Protestant and Anglican churches with strong liturgical traditions. This article is concerned with the books of the Roman rite, which in many respects are paralleled by other usages.

The traditional categories of such collections, variously named, represent first of all the several services of Christian worship, especially the eucharist and the other sacraments, lesser rites, and ecclesial prayer. Thus a collection for the sacraments of initiation or for the offices of prayer differs from the book or books for the eucharistic liturgy. More important, especially in the case of the eucharist and the office of prayer, books were originally distinguished according to their use and user: books for the presiding bishop or priest (largely prayer texts), books for deacons and other readers of the scriptures (or other non-biblical writings, particularly in the ecclesial prayer), books for the cantors and other singers, including the whole assembly.

The names attached to these books at different periods vary greatly but are generally indicative of their content and use. A lectionary is a book of lections or readings—with the evident possibility of a further division such as an evangelary or book of gospels; alternatively, an order or list of pericopes has sufficed, to be used with a full Bible. A sacramentary is a book for the presiding minister of the sacrament (of the eucharist and of other sacraments). An antiphonal or a *cantatorium* or a gradual is a book of chants: for the intervenient chants of the liturgy of the word or for the processional rites of the eucharist. The daily prayer offices or hours had their corresponding collections with, for example, distinct books or hymns, homilaries of readings, and the martyrology from which the solemn listing of saints' names was proclaimed.

Rituals for the sacraments other than the eucharist and for lesser services have had a variety of names: manuals, sacerdotals, pastorals, etc. Here a distinction has been made from medieval times between such general manuals and the "pontifical," the term employed for the liturgical celebrations (the sacraments of orders and, in the West, confirmation, but also major consecrations and blessings) reserved to the presidency of the bishop. An *ordo*, later called a ceremonial, generally differs from other liturgical books: it consists of descriptions or directives, without liturgical texts. (The generic term *ordo* has recently come to be used not only for the rite and ritual of a given celebration such as the order of Mass or the order of reconciliation, but for the several parts of the revised liturgical books themselves, for example, the Order for the Christian Initiation of Adults.)

Of all the developments in the liturgical books, none was more significant in the West than the compilation of a unified book for the eucharistic celebration. In the High Middle Ages missals were compiled to combine the sacramentary of the presiding celebrant, the book or books of readings for the deacon and other readers, and the antiphonal, gradual, or similar books for the singers. The convenience of this kind of book for private celebration, in which the priest took the roles of all but a server, is evident. Nevertheless it represented a serious deterioration of the public eucharistic celebration—to the extent that, in the medieval and modern period, the presiding bishop or priest was expected to read quietly all the readings and all the sung parts either before or while these were proclaimed or chanted by others. This distortion, which was not corrected until the 1950s with the reform of the Holy Week services, was canonized by the medieval missal—and, for the offices of prayer, by the breviary which similarly combined the several books needed for the communal celebration into a volume for private reading of those bound to pray the ecclesial office.

The ancient and medieval norm, once the early period of improvised prayer texts and freer choice of readings had passed, was that each church or province or region had its own liturgical books, with much in common—at least in the liturgies dependent upon the Roman rite and within other Western rites—but still with great diversity. The exchange of manuscripts of such collections, especially the great sacramentaries, was a means of diffusing a given rite and a step toward greater unity and even uniformity. The printing of liturgical books in the 15th and 16th centuries facilitated diffusion of texts, but the principle of divergency according to established local or regional tradition remained intact.

It was only in the 16th and 17th centuries, in the aftermath of the Council of Trent, that an almost uniform pattern of Roman liturgical books emerged. In its concluding session (December 4, 1563), the council entrusted the revision of the Roman breviary and missal (along with the catechism and index of prohibited books) to Pius IV. The commission of revision completed the breviary in 1568 and the missal in 1570, and both were promulgated by Pius V; although the volumes were the result of intensive research into older sources, they made rather slight ritual or structural changes. The most striking development was a radical reduction in saints' days, but still more important was the canonical norm: that these Roman books were to be used throughout the West, except in those local churches (and religious orders) which had their own rite or use of some two hundred years' standing. This was the beginning of greater and greater uniformity; it demonstrates the effectiveness of liturgical books not only as the tools of worship but also as instruments of reform and relative rigidity.

In 1588 Sixtus V established the Congregation of Sacred Rites which was to undertake, among other things, the still incomplete work of revising the Roman books. The third major book was the Roman Pontifical, issued in 1596; the fourth was the Roman Ritual of 1614. By exception the latter was not imposed throughout the Latin church, and local rituals continued until, by the 20th century, most of them took the form of mere supplements or appendices to the Roman book—just as the formularies for local feasts were supplementary to the missal and breviary of the Roman rite. During these five decades after Trent, the Roman Martyrology also appeared (1584), and the tradition of the *Ordines Romani* and later Roman ceremonies was continued in the Ceremonial of Bishops (1600); the latter was a descriptive volume rather than a liturgical book of texts.

From the early 17th through the 19th centuries the four principal books were only slightly revised. The missal was supplemented by the *Memoriale Rituum* of 1725 for less solemn services in Holy Week and on other occasions. The many additions to the missal and breviary were by way of added saints' days, devotional feasts, votive offices and Masses, etc., partly seen also in a supplementary volume, the *Octavarium Romanum*, with readings for the ever-increasing octaves celebrated in local churches and religious orders. In the mid-20th century the eight post-Tridentine books just enumerated were officially counted as the Roman "liturgical books" along with a ninth, the collection of decrees (*Decreta Authentica*) of the Congregation of Rites, which had been issued by authority of Leo XIII in 1898-1901. Like the Ceremonial of Bishops, this was not a liturgical book in the usual sense, since it consisted of a large selection of decrees and responses rather than liturgical texts as such.

The (limited) liturgical reform of the Pius X, largely a simplification of excesses in the breviary and missal, with a radical suppression of saints' days and votive observances that had again come to overshadow the celebration of Sundays and the central mysteries, required a new missal (1914) and breviary (1920). At the same time the critical correction of Gregorian chant permitted the issuance of the Roman Gradual for the missal (1907) and the Roman Antiphonal for the daytime offices of the breviary (1912). Again, in 1925 a revised Roman Ritual appeared, to incorporate in its introductory *praenotanda* the new sacramental law of the 1917 *Code of Canon Law*.

For the most part, the initial and piecemeal liturgical reforms of Pius XII, some of them completed only after John XXIII became pope in 1959, could be issued in separate volumes such as the *ordines* for the Easter vigil (1951), for the restored Holy Week (1955), and for the baptism of adults in several stages of the catechumenate (1962), as well as the second part of the Roman Pontifical for the dedication of churches and for consecrations and blessings of places and objects (1961). The partial simplification of the rubrics in 1962 (the "code of rubrics") required interim revisions of missal and breviary, in an effort to return to the simpler calendar of Pius X and even that of Pius V, but without alteration of the rites themselves.

Vatican II's constitution, *Sacrosanctum concilium*, provided not only general principles and some specifics for liturgical reform but an explicit mandate that the entirety of the Roman liturgical books be revised "as soon as possible; experts are to be employed in this task and bishops from various parts of the world are to be consulted" (S.C., 25). At the level of the Roman rite as a whole, the books were to be a principal instrument of reform; at the same time the door was opened, particularly by the introduction of the vernacular, to "particular" liturgical books truly proper to various countries or regions. Consistent with the revised Roman books, these would go beyond the latter and offer the possibility of a recovery of the tradition of diverse uses.

The content of the new Roman books, revised by the Consilium for the Implementation of the Constitution on the Liturgy established by Paul VI (January 1964) and related to the older Congregation of Rites, belongs to an account of the liturgical reforms of Vatican II (q.v.). Their pattern and style can be described briefly.

1. Beginning with the first section of the Roman Pontifical "restored by decree of the Second Vatican Ecumenical Council and promulgated by authority of Pope Paul VI" (1968), the official books in Latin were gradually introduced until by 1973 the principal ones were complete (the ritual for blessings and the Ceremonial of Bishops appeared only in 1984). The pattern of four major "books" was retained: missal, office or liturgy of the hours, ritual, and pontifical. But the ritual of sacraments, still called the Roman Ritual, is now in various sections corresponding to the *tituli* of the old single-volume book; the same is true of the Roman Pontifical.

The massive work of post-conciliar revision of Roman books can be seen in tabular form: (a) missal: Order of Mass (1969), lectionary (1969), presidential prayers or sacramentary (1970)—along with provision for the corresponding book of Gregorian chants (*Ordo cantus Missae*, 1971); (b) ritual: marriage (1969), baptism of children (1969), funerals (1969), religious profession (1970), adult initiation (1971), anointing and care of the sick (1972), communion and eucharistic cult (1973), penance (1973), blessings (1984); (c) pontifical: ordinations (1968), consecration to a life of virginity (1970), blessing of abbots and abbesses (1970), blessing of oils (1970), confirmation (1971), institution of readers and acolytes (1972), dedication of a church (1977); (d) liturgy of the hours (1971).

The Roman calendar (1969), related to both missal and liturgy of the hours, and the Ceremonial of Bishops (1984), describing the bishop's presidential role in the liturgical celebrations, should be added to this listing of the chief liturgical books of the contemporary rite. All of the revised books have been translated—and, in varying degrees, rearranged, augmented, and adapted—in the vernacular editions.

2. The number and enlarged scope of the new Roman liturgical books and even the sequence in which they appeared may be attributed to practical considerations: the larger quantity of liturgical texts, the complex processes of achieving the noble simplicity sought by Vatican II in the basic Roman rite, and the like. In one case, however, the pattern of the medieval missal was deliberately broken to express and to enforce the principle of the differentiation of roles in the celebration (S.C., 28). Thus the *Ordo lectionum Missae* appeared first as the basis for the Roman Lectionary, the presidential prayers for the eucharist appeared in a distinct volume, and both are considered parts of the Latin *Missale Romanum*—along with the *Graduale* of chants published later. Some English

editions of the volume of presidential prayers have correctly restored the term "sacramentary" to that book, thus clarifying the distinction of prayers, readings, and song—and helping to separate the roles of those who take the several parts in the one celebration.

3. The revised books are marked by extensive introductory material, in the form of *praenotanda* or general instructions, of a doctrinal, liturgical, and pastoral nature over and above the pragmatic directions or rubrics and descriptions of the services. Among the 15th/16th century Roman liturgical books, only the Roman Ritual had pastoral and canonical notes, and these were very limited. The new pattern was introduced at the insistance of Vatican II. While respecting the right and indeed duty of the national or regional churches to create their own rituals, the council nonetheless insisted that the full Roman prefatory material be included "whether the instructions are pastoral or rubrical or have some special social bearing" (S.C., 63b).

4. One characteristic of the new books may be taken for granted, namely, their inclusion of constant directions for full participation of the whole assembly; Vatican II drew special attention to this need (S.C., 31). Another specific mandate, related to the creation of particular liturgical books by the respective conferences of bishops, was that the Roman books themselves should provide potential areas for "legitimate variations and adaptations to different groups, regions, and peoples . . . " (S.C., 38).

The degree to which national or regional liturgical books go beyond the Roman revision, with which they are to be in harmony, is not completely resolved and is in part a canonical question. The 1983 C.I.C. retains the norm that the Roman See alone gives official approbation to the basic Latin books (cc. 826, 1; 838, 2); the conferences of bishops give the same approbation to the vernacular (and adapted) versions (c. 838, 3). The term *editio typica* is used of such original, official editions. In turn, the permission to reprint belongs to the diocesan bishop or other local ordinary of the place of publication (c. 826, 2).

Although the conferences of bishops regularly act jointly in preparing liturgical books in the respective languages through their joint or "mixed" commissions, each conference must act separately and formally in approving texts and books for the churches of its own territory. This approbation requires, in accord with the decree of Vatican II (S.C., 36.3; 63b), review by the Roman See—a review, technically called confirmation or recognition (*recognitio*), that is intended to support and strengthen the original decision. This can create tension and conflict if the Roman review demands changes that radically alter the decision of the territorial authority.

Liturgical books are only an instrument, only a means to an end. Misused they can create an artificial rigidity and excessive uniformity. Well prepared, and appropriately adapted to regional and local needs, they can support the communion of the churches in the liturgy and enrich its forms and words.

P. Batiffol, *History of the Roman Breviary* (London, 1912). A. Nocent, "I libri liturgici," In *Anàmnesis 2: La Liturgia, panorama storico generale*, ed. S. Marsili *et al.*, pp. 131-183 (Casale Monferrato, 1978). P. de Puniet, *The Roman Pontifical: A History and Commentary* (London, 1932). H.A.P. Schmidt, *Introductio in Liturgiam Occidentalem.* (Rome, 1960). "Libri liturgici," pp. 148-158. L.C. Sheppard, *The Liturgical Books* (New York, 1962). H.A.J. Wegman, *Christian Worship in East and West: A Study Guide to Liturgical History* (New York, 1985).

FREDERICK R. McMANUS

LITURGICAL COMMITTEES

One of the distinctive characteristics of the liturgical revisions following the Second Vatican Council is the need to prepare the liturgy before it is celebrated. This preparation is necessary because of the numerous options that are now provided depending on the pastoral circumstances that surround a particular liturgy and the need for pastoral adaptation. The options may require selecting a particular text among several provided. There may be an option as to where a rite is celebrated, such as the blessing and procession of palms on Passion Sunday. The selection and appropriate integration of music also requires advance preparation for the liturgy.

In many cases only a general rubric is provided in the ritual book which requires forethought and creative planning. For example, in the Rite of Acceptance into the Order of Catechumens, the rubrics state that the celebrant greets the candidates in a friendly manner. "He speaks to them, their sponsors, and all present, pointing out the joy and happiness of the Church" (R.C.I.A., 49). Need for preparation here should be obvious since a specific text is not provided.

At times the rubrics may simply state that the celebrant addresses the assembly "in these or similar words." While there is room for extemporaneous remarks, the need for advance preparation in the rites is always necessary.

One of the positive signs of the growing involvement of the faithful in the liturgy is the expansion of liturgical ministries to include deacons, lectors, cantors, extraordinary ministers of communion, etc. The effective involvement of these ministries in the liturgy requires training and formation and a careful coordination of their roles in the liturgy.

Although there is no explicit mention of them in the *Constitution on the Sacred Liturgy*, the need for preparing the liturgy has naturally led to the formation of parish liturgy committees. Because the liturgy is the community's prayer, it is presumed that the faithful would assume some responsibility for its preparation. The *General Instruction on the Roman Missal* states: "All concerned should work together in preparing the ceremonies, pastoral arrangements, and music for each celebration. They should work under the direction of the rector and should consult the people about the parts which belong to them" (G.I.R.M. 73).

The *Constitution on the Sacred Liturgy* called for each diocesan bishop to establish a liturgy committee as well as committees for music and art (S.C., 45-46). The parish liturgy committee seems to parallel what is a need on a diocesan level for carefully attending to the care of the liturgy and the pastoral implementation of the rites of the church.

The structure of a parish liturgy committee will vary from place to place but would ordinarily consist of a representative group of parishioners willing to work in collaboration with the pastor in the preparation of the liturgy and the ongoing formation of the assembly in the spirituality engendered by the church's worship. Depending on the size and needs of a parish, the committee may consist of a number of teams working together under the leadership of a central committee. It may be composed of the parish priests and the heads of each liturgical ministry (lectors, extraordinary ministers of communion, musicians, etc.) or it may be composed of individuals specifically chosen for their competence or particular perspective they would bring to liturgical planning. In all cases the members of the committee ought to exhibit a genuine love for the liturgy and regard it as a high priority in parish life. *Music in Catholic Worship* 12 states: "The planning group should include those with the knowledge and artistic skills needed in celebration: men and women trained in music, poetry, and art, and familiar with the current resources in these areas; men and women sensitive also to the present day thirst of so many for the riches of scripture, theology, and prayer. It is always good to include some members of the congregation who have not taken special roles in the celebrations so that honest evaluations can be made."

An effective liturgy committee will not only commit itself to the work of preparing the liturgy, but to making the prayer of the liturgy the foundation of their own spiritual lives. The committee should allow for ample time together for prayer and reflection that is rooted in the liturgy.

Every liturgy committee needs to outline a plan for its own ongoing formation in the liturgy. Members need to be thoroughly acquainted with the rites of the church and acquire an understanding and appreciation for the church's liturgical tradition, including the current official liturgical documents. They need a respect for liturgical law and need to understand its meaning and purpose.

Liturgy committees can take advantage of the resources of the diocesan liturgy office or liturgical commission and any local or national conferences on the liturgy which may be available. The parish budget should allow for continuing education to take place and funds should be available to build a resource library to include basic liturgy documents and other published materials that can be useful in understanding and preparing the liturgy.

In order for a parish liturgy committee to function effectively it must first of all perceive its service as a ministry to the assembly. It cannot pretend to function in a vacuum, choosing ritual expressions that are suitable only to itself. The liturgy committee must strive to be inclusive of the full assembly, sensitive to the presence of the elderly, the handicapped, small children, single adults, the hearing impaired, cultural diversity, etc.

A parish liturgy committee oversees the liturgical life of the parish. It oversees the training, scheduling and exercise of the various liturgical ministries. It sets long range goals by reviewing the full liturgical year and planning for the proper observance of the major feasts and seasons. The committee works to establish a rhythm for the year into which special events in the parish's life, such as anniversaries, first communion celebrations, etc., can be appropriately integrated. Long range goals such as the ongoing liturgical formation of the assembly, establishing standards for good worship, the ongoing evaluation of liturgical celebrations, and the possible redesign of the worship space would also be part of the liturgy committee's responsibilities.

The Sunday eucharist takes priority among the liturgy committee's responsibilities. Selecting texts from the legitimate options, preparing the worship space, coordinating the ministries, choosing appropriate music, preparing the assembly and preparing whatever special needs may be called for in a particular liturgy are all part of making the Sunday assembly's worship a worthy and dignified celebration. Consistent attention to the details of the Sunday eucharist establishes a quality and regularity to the liturgy that should be expected week after week.

Although the work of the parish liturgy committee needs to place a priority on the Sunday eucharist, it ought to be concerned as well about the celebration of all the sacraments, the rites of Christian initiation, the celebration of the liturgy of the hours, funerals, devotional practices, encouraging prayer at home, etc. There is always a danger of becoming so interested and invested in the small details of the liturgy that the broader concerns are overlooked. For example, the much broader issue of integrating liturgy into the parish's life and mission and leading the community to full and conscious participation needs to be an overarching goal of the liturgy committee.

The liturgy committee needs to engage

in a regular process of evaluation. At times this evaluation may require the assistance of an outside professional, perhaps the diocesan liturgy office or liturgical commission. Even on a week-to-week basis the liturgy committee needs to review how its plans and preparations were received and judge its effectiveness. Good records will be helpful when the calendar returns the committee to plan the same events again.

Frequently overlooked in liturgy committees is the need for good communication. Good communication between committee members and pastoral staff is essential. The committee needs to work closely with presiders and homilists to ensure that they are comfortable with what is planned and that their roles are carefully coordinated with the other ministries.

The musicians need to be well integrated into the liturgical organization of the parish and included in the planning process. The religious education ministry of the parish also needs to be integrally connected with the work of the liturgy committee so that the link between liturgy and catechesis is not lost. Through the parish council communication with the assembly can be maintained, as the council serves not only in a consultative role but also in an advisory capacity.

Whether setting long range goals or establishing short range goals such as preparing Sunday's Mass, a penance service, evening prayer, or decorating the church for a particular feast, goal setting will require careful consideration at liturgy committee meetings. Part of a committee's education and organization will include establishing a clear and definite system to facilitate the development of long range and short range goals.

Thomas Baker and Frank Ferrone, *Liturgy Committee Basics* (Washington, D.C.: The Pastoral Press, c.1988). Secretariat, Bishops' Committee on the Liturgy, NCCB, *Promoting Liturgical Renewal Guidelines for Diocesan Liturgical Commissions*

and Offices of Worship (Washington, D.C.: U.S. C.C., Inc., c. 1988).

RONALD J. LEWINSKI

LITURGICAL DIRECTOR

A parish liturgical director is responsible for the overall liturgical life of the community and ordinarily assumes leadership of the parish liturgy committee. The parish liturgy director may be a competent and well-trained volunteer or a salaried professional on the parish staff.

While a degree in liturgy or theology is not a requirement, a thorough understanding of the liturgy is to be expected on the part of the parish liturgy director. The parish liturgy director is not expected to be an expert on all liturgical issues but needs to be aware of where to find help and resources needed in the community.

The parish liturgy director does not exercise his/her leadership independently. The nature and dynamic of the liturgy require the parish liturgy director to work very closely with the priest presiders, the liturgy committee, the parish council, musicians and other liturgical ministers, as well as the parish school and religious education program. The parish liturgy director assumes responsibility for maintaining good communication among all who are involved in the preparation and celebration of the liturgy. The parish liturgy director may also be expected to prepare and manage the worship budget in collaboration with the pastor.

The leadership of the liturgy director is not simply administrative. The parish liturgy director ought to be gifted with a love and understanding of the liturgy that enables him/her to create a workable vision for effective worship in the parish. He/she must be able to effectively communicate the basic principles of worship and the liturgical tradition of the church.

The parish liturgy director needs to be a capable leader, able not only to chair a meeting, but to provide firm direction and to motivate others to work diligently and harmoniously. The parish liturgy director must be prepared to deal with conflict situations and the inevitable complaints that arise especially associated with change.

Whether volunteer or salaried the parish liturgy director ought to have a well-defined job description so that the important responsibilities and expectations associated with this position will not be left to chance or be the subject of confusion or misunderstanding.

In many parishes it is not uncommon to find the director of liturgy position combined with the director of liturgical music. When it is necessary that these two offices be exercised by the same individual, especially in a small parish, a well defined job description will be all the more important.

Diocesan Director of Liturgy

The diocesan director of liturgy is appointed by the diocesan bishop whose responsibility it is to be the promoter and guardian of the liturgical life of the diocese (*The Church at Prayer: A Holy Temple of the Lord*, N.C.C.B., no. 51, p. 26). "Each director should enjoy due freedom in his (her) own ministry, in as much as he (she) has shown himself (herself) worthy of trust by his (her) competence and virtue" (*Promoting Liturgical Renewal*, Bishops' Committee on the Liturgy, N.C.C.B., 1988, p. 8).

The diocesan director of liturgy may or may not be the chairperson of the diocesan liturgical commission. In some dioceses it may be necessary to combine these two roles and appoint one individual to either a part-time or full-time position.

The diocesan director of liturgy oversees the proper implementation of the rites of the church by organizing the necessary catechesis and training for parochial ministers. In most dioceses the director of liturgy will be responsible for coordinating the preparation of diocesan liturgies, especially for those occasions when the bishop presides. The diocesan director of liturgy works closely with the bishop in establishing liturgical and sacramental guidelines and norms for the diocese.

Even in those dioceses where a full time office of worship is not feasible, the director of liturgy ought to be sufficiently trained to assume responsibility for liturgy in the diocese. A thorough understanding of the liturgical tradition and the laws and norms pertaining to the liturgy is necessary, if the diocesan director of liturgy is to competently assist the bishop and provide guidance and education for parochial ministers. In addition to the liturgical competencies required for this position a pastoral sensitivity and effective management skills are highly desirable.

Thomas Baker and Frank Ferrone, *Liturgy Committee Basics* (Washington, DC: The Pastoral Press, c. 1988. Department of Personnel Services, *Coordinating Parish Ministries* (Chicago: Archdiocese of Chicago, 1987).

RONALD J. LEWINSKI

LITURGICAL MOVEMENT, THE (1830-1969)

In its broadest meaning, the liturgical movement was the century-long effort made to enrich the appreciation and experience of worship. The liturgical movement requires a broad definition since it lasted from 1830 to 1969, encompassing several countries and passing through various phases that changed its orientation, purpose, and even its participants' perception of its central element.

This broad effort on behalf of worship qualifies as a "movement" in purely social terms, for a movement is a gathering of people focused around a cause, often oriented toward change in the existing pattern of behavior in an organization, an institution, or society at large. This cause generates leaders with a commitment and, often, with charisma, and its sole criterion for its members is a general willingness to embrace the cause. A movement is distinguished from a formal organization, which is characterized by stated goals, an elaborate system of explicit rules and regulations, and a formal status structure with clearly marked lines of communication and authority. Movements follow a cycle beginning with issues, widening into a cause, coming to a climax or confrontation, and being absorbed into a new or existing organization.

It can easily be argued that the liturgical movement that began with Dom Lambert Beauduin met all of these criteria. The liturgical movement is wider than the liturgical reform, which formed only part of the wider movement. The reform of the liturgical rites was carried on in Rome, first by the existing central authorities, then by the bishops of the Second Vatican Council, followed by the newly established committees to implement the conciliar decisions. The liturgical movement, on the other hand, grew from a beginning in Benedictine monasteries, was conducted in countries throughout the world by pastorally oriented persons, and was supported by a specific group of scholars and legislators.

So the liturgical movement and the liturgical reform were deeply affected by one another, but they are quite separate. The history of the liturgical reform can be chronicled in the specific changes that occurred in the rites, e.g., a new approach to music for the liturgy with *Tra le sollecitudini* in 1903, the revision of the Holy Week ceremonies in 1956 (*Maxima Redemptionis*), and the reform of the Mass in 1970. The story of the liturgical movement, on the other hand, is told country by country, in the development of its ideas, its leaders, and its meetings.

History

There were four major phases or segments to the movement: the Benedictine or monastic movement, research and scholarship, the pastoral element, and legislation (i.e., liturgical reform). The Benedictine or monastic liturgical movement began with the re-establishment of St. Peter's Monastery at Solesmes, France, by Dom Prosper Guéranger in 1833. It flourished in the foundations influenced by Guéranger's approach, especially the German community at Beuron. Maredsous, a Belgian foundation (1872) from Beuron, Maria Laach, and Mont César (a foundation from Beuron) all contributed, as did St. John's Monastery in Collegeville, Minnesota.

The research or academic aspect of the movement began quietly, first in the study of chant manuscripts at Solesmes and Regensburg for chant book projects (1870). Simultaneously, biblical research and patristic scholarship were developing interest in early periods of Christianity, and several discoveries of early liturgical manuscripts spurred specific writings on the liturgical year and the history of the ritual books. Research centers grew up in France, Germany, and England; and the "jewel" of the academic liturgical movement was Josef Jungmann's *Missarum Sollemnia* (1948; translated into English as *Mass of the Roman Rite* 1950, 51).

The pastoral liturgical movement, which had the highest visibility of the four elements, began in Belgium (1909) with Lambert Beauduin, a monk of Maredsous. He directed his efforts to nearby parishes, suggesting educational programs and new ideas about the role of the laity, popularizing some of the academic discoveries, sharing the spiritual enrichment found in monastic liturgical experiences, and eventually even suggesting legislative changes. The pastoral liturgical movement gathered a number of new ideas about the church under its broad umbrella, and almost every country in the world had a taste, at least, of this pastoral movement by the beginning of the Second Vatican Council—some in the form of a beautiful liturgy celebrated at national conferences, others in the form of suggested changes argued before skeptical friends. "Pastoral" meant "popular," and this widespread aspect of the liturgical movement was carried primarily through word of mouth, experience by experience, by those committed to the effort made to enrich the appreciation and experience of worship.

The legislative elements connected with the liturgical movement are a study in contrast, sometimes supporting the development of liturgical renewal, often resisting it. In 1903, in *Tra le sollecitudini*, for instance, Pius X called for the active participation of the people: "from the Church's most important and indispensable source, active participation in the sacred mysteries and in the public and solemn prayer of the Church." This statement was quoted by Beauduin in 1909 to launch the pastoral side of the movement. Numerous legislative reforms followed slowly, building to an avalanche at Vatican II and giving a specific focus to the liturgical movement. By 1955, legislators were still insecure about widespread participation in the popular liturgical movement, and they were surprised by the call of Pope John XXIII for an ecumenical council, which in its documents and its legislation eventually endorsed the efforts of the monastic, scholarly, and pastoral arms of the liturgical movement.

Stage One: The Beginnings

The Benedictine or Monastic Liturgical Movement. In a conservative reaction to neo-Gallican developments in religion, music, and art, P. Guéranger, O.S.B., reestablished the ancient monastery of St. Peter at Solesmes in 1833 and dedicated himself to reinstating the Benedictine monastic tradition. Central to Guéranger's project were his views that (1) monastic liturgy should center on the

Mass, not reflecting current trends in neo-Gallican liturgies, but following the Roman liturgy as he understood it; (2) monastic life should center on the major feasts of the church year, as reflected in his work, *L'année liturgique*; (3) monastic life should use chant rather than contemporary music, a decision that led the monks of Solesmes to become a central resource for chant research in the 1870s.

While Guéranger's ideas are at the root of many elements in the liturgical movement, our present vantage point shows us that his positions were frequently undocumented, highly conservative, and often incorrect. Numerous members of the modern liturgical movement wrestled to correct his positions, which had become firmly entrenched in popular understanding.

It was the suppression of the monasteries during the French Revolution (1792) that provided a fertile field in which the new foundation at Solesmes could flourish and spread. From 1833 to 1900, Benedictine foundations, many founded or influenced by Solesmes, carried a version of Guéranger's vision. Most notable are Beuron, a German parallel to Solesmes founded by Maurus and Placidus Wolter (1863), famous for its art in a pseudo-Romanesque style. Dom Anselm Schott, following a French idea, published the first German-Latin Missal in 1884, the *Messbuch der hl. Kirche*. The *Vesperbuch* quickly followed (1893), and each contained numerous explanations taken from Guéranger's *L'année liturgique*.

Maredsous was a Belgian foundation (1872) of Beuron financed by the Desclée family. Dom Gerard van Caloen, rector of the abbey school, published the first French-Latin Missal, *Missel des fidéles* (1882). At the Eucharistic Congress in 1883, he suggested lay participation in the Mass and communion during Mass (radical ideas for which he was removed as school rector). He founded *Messager des fidéles* (later to become the *Revue Bénédictine*), the first publication founded to promote the liturgical movement. Its main contributor, Dom Germain Morin, took on the conservatism of Guéranger. A later abbot of Maredsous (from 1909), the Irish monk, Dom Columba Marmion, proclaimed through various writings a spirituality that was firmly based on the liturgical texts.

Maria Laach, a German foundation in the Rhineland, was taken over from the Jesuits in 1893 by monks from Beuron, who developed the art style they carried from their home abbey. Dom Odo Casel, a monk of Maria Laach, wrote *The Mystery of Christian Worship,* which was to influence the thinking of the liturgical movement in the first forty years of the 20th century. In theological circles of the day, the sacraments were seen as ceremonial, chiefly rubrical, and mainly the responsibility of canon lawyers, masters of ceremonies, and ritualists. Casel presented the sacraments (Gk: *mysterion*) as mysteries, internal actions of Christ. While based incorrectly on the hypothesis that sacraments were rooted in Greek mystery cults, this thinking led to theories about the action of Christ in the sacraments offering praise to the Father and, also to the new language that described the church as the mystical body of Christ that acts in the sacraments. Like Guéranger's publications, Casel's work was hotly contested throughout the liturgical movement, being discredited by those opposed to the popular reforms offered by the advocates of the liturgy, and expanded, corrected, and sometimes adamantly defended with a blind faith by members of the liturgical movement.

Mont César, another foundation in Belgium (1899), but this time by monks of Maredsous, was the monastery of L. Beauduin. Members of this monastery included Abbot Bernard Capelle, the cantor Dom Ildephonse Dirkx, and Dom Bernard Botte, who was to found the Institut Supérieur de Liturgie in Paris in 1945.

The Scholarly Liturgical Movement. The cultural backdrop for Beauduin's call for active participation in 1909 reached far beyond the Benedictine phase of the liturgical revival. A characteristic of the liturgical movement in Europe was its foundation in the research of diverse, international scholars which provided deeper views into the history of texts, rites, attitudes, and practices and which eventually served as a scathing critique of contemporary practice, which was often defended blindly by its guardians.

The roots of this scholarly research are in the middle of the 19th century. Between 1860 and 1903, Europe experienced tremendous intellectual activity. In the political arena the freeing of governments from ecclesiastical dominance had two consequences for church thinkers. First, they became subject to challenge by their contemporaries, such as Darwin in evolution, Hume and Hegel in philosophy, the pietists in religion, Marx and Engels in political social thought, and the application of historical criticism (Wellhausen) and the methods of *Religionsgeschichte* to the Bible, which led to a new understanding of the Bible and the foundation of the biblical movement. Secondly, they were unsure how far they could go in proclaiming their new insights in the face of ecclesiastical reaction to change. Such uncertainty came from new but untested discoveries and from repression and retaliation from ecclesiastical leadership, which ultimately led to the condemnation of a series of propositions incorrectly classed as a unified "Modernist" position.

In this exciting and challenging climate, major historical work on the liturgical documents was done by Louis Duchesne (1843-1922), especially his critical edition of and commentary on the *Liber Pontificalis* (1877) and *Christian Worship, Its Origin and Evolution*, and Pierre Battifol (1861-1929), whose *History of the Roman*

Breviary appeared in 1893 and his *Leçons sur la Messe* in 1913.

The scholarly publications coming from the Abbey of St. Michael, Farnborough, England (founded in 1895), reflected the work of its Prior/ Abbot Dom Fernand Cabrol (1855-1937). This is especially true of his study of the liturgy of Jerusalem in the 4th century based on the *Peregrinatio Silviae* (discovered by Gamurrini some ten years before), his *Introduction aux études liturgiques*, and a little popular work, *Le Livre de la Prière Antique*. On a more comprehensive level are his *Monumenta ecclesiae liturgica* and the *Dictionnaire d'archéologie chrétienne et de liturgie*, begun in 1903 with Dom Henri Leclercq (1913-45) and finally completed by H. Marrou in 1953. These works reflected the recent rediscovery and publication of the Greek text of the *Didache* (full title: *The Lord's Instruction to the Gentiles through the Twelve Apostles*) by Metropolitan Philotheus Bryennios of Constantinople in 1883, as well as the publication of other important early documents: the canons of Hippolytus, the anaphora of Serapion, Bishop of Thmuis, the *Testamentum Domini*, the Apostolic Constitutions and the *Peregrinatio ad Locas Sanctas*. In 1905 Dom Cabrol gave a series of lectures at the Institut Catholique in Paris that outlined his method of historical research.

When scholars approached liturgy with the developing tools of strict historical criticism, some big problems arose. First of all there was the question of making these tools acceptable in ecclesiastical circles. Since rationalists and unbelievers not only had made use of them but had developed them, they were immediately suspect. Critical methods were sure to offend cherished beliefs and overthrow legends of long standing. Above all, they might bring about a dangerously critical attitude in young seminarians and even the entire clergy. And as a matter of fact, this did happen.

The Legislators and the Liturgical Movement. In addition to the work of the Benedictines and the scholars, there was a third element in the cultural backdrop to Beauduin's call for a popular liturgical movement, and that was Roman legislation. Woven through the liturgical movement is an undocumented relationship among reformers, promoters, scholars, and legislators. The reformers, promoters, and scholars were Belgian, French, Austrian, and German, while the legislators were Italian (or at least were headquartered at the Vatican). Only now are studies documenting the exchanges among them before 1943; in fact, the legislative reforms seem remarkably random compared to the ideas developed within the rest of the liturgical movement.

The most significant legislation at the end of the 19th century concerned music for the liturgy, while two "sleepers"— pieces of legislation with much larger later consequences—appeared at the beginning of the 20th century. In 1872 Frederick Pustet of Germany obtained from Pope Pius IX permission to publish a comprehensive book of chants, together with a thirty-year exclusive contract forbidding other publishers from producing "official" chant books. The monks of Solesmes reacted with a series of studies indicating the inadequacies of the chant manuscript used as the basis for the Pustet chant book and promoting the "Solesmes Chant" based on more ancient manuscripts. Controversy raged in Europe for the next thirty years over what was "authentic" chant.

Six months after the thirty-year privilege ended, Giuseppe Sarto (Pius X), formerly a seminary choir director, issued a *motu proprio* (22 November 1903), *Tra le sollecitudini*. While it did not resolve the chant question, it contained this statement: "As it is indeed our most fervent wish that the true Christian spirit should flourish again in every field and be upheld by all the faithful, we should above all be mindful of the sanctity and dignity of the Church building; for it is there that the faithful meet to draw that same spirit from its most important and indispensable source, active participation in the sacred mysteries and in the public and solemn prayer of the Church" (28).

The "sleeper" legislation concerned the practice of communion, restricted at that time in several ways, especially by frequency and the age of first communicants. Daily communion by the faithful was permitted in *Sacra Tridentina Synodus* (22 December 1905), and the age for first communion for children was lowered to the "age of reason" (i.e., about seven) in *Quam singulari* (10 August 1910).

The Popular Liturgical Movement

The European Popular Movement Begins (1909-1917). At the National Congress of Catholic Action held at Malines, Belgium, in 1909, Dom Lambert Beauduin presented an address, "The Full Prayer of the Church," in which he issued a call for the active participation of the people in the work of the church, especially in the liturgy, using a quote from Pius X's *motu proprio* of 1903 to encourage a lay involvement rooted in the "Church's most important and indispensable source, active participation in the sacred mysteries and in the public and solemn prayer of the Church." Some saw it as a call for democratization of the church's worship.

The unique characteristics of Beauduin's activity were that (1) it called for the active participation of the people; (2) it was popular, based in parochial ministry; (3) it took theoretical ideas and translated them into popular language; (4) it used mass media elements, publications and conferences to gather people and disseminate ideas.

Beauduin was ordained in 1897, and two years later he joined the Aumôniers du Travail, a priests' society for the care of workers. He served as a parish priest for seven years before he became a Benedictine (1906). Now, in addition to his own interests, he had the resources of his abbey at his disposal. He founded *La vie liturgique* (1909) with the support of Père Joseph Wyns, who collected two hundred subscriptions at the high school in Charleroi, and he was assisted in production by two Benedictine brothers, Antoine Pierard and Landaold de Waeghe. Beauduin published what came to be considered the "manifesto" of the popular liturgical movement, *La piété de l'église*, in 1914.

To promote his work, Beauduin relied on Louis Duchesne, Fernand Cabrol, Pierre Batiffol, and Pierre de Puniet in France and on Edmund Bishop and Henry Albert Wilson in England.

Public meetings devoted to liturgy began in Holland, with the First Netherlands Congress on Liturgy at Breda (16-17 August 1911), which drew fewer than fifty people. But the next year, the Propaganda Commission of Breda was given episcopal approval to promote the liturgical life in the diocese. A Liturgical Society was formed in the Diocese of Haarlem (1912) and Utrecht (10 February 1913); they formed the Dutch Federation in 1915.

Beauduin's call for the democratization of the liturgy was heard by Abbé (later Canon, then Cardinal) Joseph Cardijn of Laeken, Belgium, who was developing the Young Christian Worker's movement (the Jeunesse Ouvriére Chrétienne or Jocist movement), as a conscious response to strong Marxist activity and appeal among Christian workers in Europe. Active participation in governing (democratization), Cardijn believed, would flow over to active participation in liturgy. The JOC (YCW in English-speaking countries) developed retreat methods that used the sacraments to interrelate with its social goals of involving the working class in the liturgy which was too often seen as a bourgeois activity, with its pomp, courtly dress, and ceremony. Cardijn's involvement showed that the liturgical movement was a social movement, too.

The legislation during this period appears unrelated to the popular movement, but it was clearly influenced by the scholars' discoveries. For instance, Rome published a new arrangement of breviary psalms in 1911 (*Divino afflatu*) and then reformed it again (1914).

Later, Rome established a *Sectio Historica* in the Congregation of Rites, whose first purpose was to deal with the canonization of saints, although it was also to "be consulted in connection with reforms, amendments, and new editions of liturgical texts and books."

The growing movement for popular participation in the liturgy gradually began to have an influence in official circles, however. The apostolic constitution on sacred music, *Divini cultus* (20 December 1928), stated this: "But in order that the faithful shall take a more active part in worship, Gregorian chant (in so far as it is intended for the people) is to be taken back into use by them. And it is absolutely necessary that the faithful should attend the sacred actions, not as outsiders or silent spectators, but thoroughly imbued with the beauty of the liturgy ... so that they may join their voices to those of priest and choir in accordance with antiphonal rules" (IX).

The beginning date of the popular movement in Germany is often given as 1918, the publication date for the first number of *Ecclesia Orans*, the well-known collection directed by Dom Ildefons Herwegen, Abbot of Maria Laach, (who was influenced by the scholarly Flemish journal, *Liturgisch Tijdschrift*, begun by the Benedictines of Affligem, Brabant, in November 1910).

Whatever one makes of the birth date, German activity after 1909 was a mixture of scholarly research and popular questions, both circulated in bold ways through popular journals. At the center of the popular liturgical movement in the German-speaking world were the canons of Klosterneuberg, Austria, especially Pius Parsch and his popular work on the church year. The work of Romano Guardini, *The Spirit of the Liturgy* and *Liturgical Education*, written while he was still a university student (1908-10), contained the influences of the liturgy celebrated at Beuron and during his Tübingen studies.

Scholarship and the popular movement continued to have repercussions in the legislative realm. On 4 August 1922 Rome issued a decree on the value of the dialogue Mass, and on 9 December 1925, one on the form of vestments.

The American Popular Movement Begins: The Era of Virgil Michel (1926-1939). The event that began the popular liturgical movement in the United States is clear: Dom Virgil Michel, a thirty-three-year-old monk of St. John's Abbey in Collegeville, Minnesota, spent nineteen months (February 1924—August 1925) in Europe, visiting the Benedictine monasteries and L. Beauduin, who was then professor of fundamental theology (1921-1925) at the Benedictine College in Rome. From Solesmes he learned about the chant revival; from Maredsous, publishing; from Mont César, the popular movement. And most especially from Beauduin, his fellow Benedictine, he learned method and content. Beauduin had mastered a style of writing, teaching, and publishing that emphasized clarity and mass communication.

This nine-month visit changed Dom Virgil Michel and, quite literally, the face of American Catholicism. On Michel's return to St. John's, Abbot Alcuin Deutsch supported the beginnings of an American liturgical movement by authorizing the foundation of the magazine *Orate Fratres* (later *Worship*) and the Liturgical Press, which began publishing

The Popular Liturgical Library, a series of pamphlets and short treatments of elements connected with the liturgy. Its first major work was the English version of Beauduin's only book, *La piété de l'église*. From 1926 to 1930 the Press was directly under the control of Dom Virgil Michel. Between 1930 and his death in 1938, a number of events occurred that gave a particular shape to the early stages of the liturgical movement in the United States.

First, Michel experienced a breakdown and was sent to recuperate in northern Minnesota, serving the Native Americans there from 1930 to 1933. The stock market crash of 1929 and the subsequent Great Depression left more than ten million workers unemployed in the United States. When Michel returned to reassume the leadership of the liturgical apostolate in 1933, he was deeply committed to wrestling with the results of the Depression. As in Europe with Beauduin, whose movement took root as part of the Catholic reaction to Marx through the Catholic Worker Movement, so in the United States, Michel recognized that the liturgical movement could not be separated from the social issues created by industrialized society, and especially that the concerns of the worker could not be separated from the celebration of liturgy in the modern world.

Michel's work was shared by many collaborators, but perhaps his strongest influence outside the circles of the liturgical movement was in the burgeoning catechetical revival. One of those catechetical collaborators was Sr. Jane Marie Murray, O.P., who first met Michel in a visit to Collegeville in 1929. With other members of her order at that Liturgical Summer School, she wrote five laboratory manuals for grades three through twelve, *With Mother Church*. Combining her interest in liturgy with the available results of the biblical, theological, and social action movements, she became the sole author or a major collaborator in *The Christ Life Series*, *The Christian Religion Series*, and *The Christian Life Series*, all major ways that the popular liturgical movement was introduced into Catholic schools and other education programs.

The editorials in *Orate Fratres* and the publications coming from the Liturgical Press in the years between 1933 and 1938 were dominated by Michel's twin focus on liturgy and social reform and by the drive to popularize these twin ideas. Virgil Michel died rather suddenly in 1938, and he was replaced by Dom Godfrey Diekmann as the editor of the magazine, which was soon retitled *Worship*, and as director of the Liturgical Press.

In 1927, a small group of Roman Catholic laymen, fledgling artists, architects, and draftsmen from the Boston and New York areas gathered for a retreat. From this meeting was born the Liturgical Arts Society (1928-1972) and its publication, *Liturgical Arts* magazine. The two became indistinguishable under the remarkable leadership of Maurice Lavanoux. He proposed the best of the old—honesty in materials and simplicity in design—as well as a call for the new—that the modern church must find its religious expression in contemporary art forms.

Stage Two: The Movement Widens (1934-1945)

Liturgical Conflicts in Germany (1934-1942). Even though the Great Depression spread from the U.S. to Europe, sometimes with an impact even greater than in the United States, interest in the liturgy remained high. Perhaps because of a heightened intensity of thought in reaction to the rise of the Nazis in Germany and German rearmament, popular journals such as *Liturgisches Leben*, begun in 1934 under the editorship of J. Pinsk, the Berlin students' chaplain, began asking more provocative questions about the role of liturgy and popular participation. Throughout the course of the liturgical movement there were a number of conflicts, battles, and disagreements between supporters of the movement and those representing the contemporary practice of the institutional church. Not every one of these battles can be narrated, but it is important for any student of the liturgical movement to understand that almost every change in the liturgy, no matter how small or insignificant, occurred in the midst of controversy, risk taking, and sometimes loss of position and prestige in the very institution that those persons served.

One of the earliest examples of such conflict occurred in Germany between 1939 and 1943, at the height of Germany's military power in Europe. In reaction to the articles appearing in *Liturgisches Leben*, M. Kassiepe, O.M.I., published the sensational book *Irrwege und Umwege im Frömmigkeitsleben der Gegenwart,* strongly attacking the liturgical movement. In reaction, the bishop of Passau established a Liturgical Working Party, whose members included J. Jungmann, R. Guardini, H. V. Meurens, and H. Kahlefeld. The controversy escalated to the entire German hierarchy, and two bishops, Landesdorfer and Stohr of Mainz, were asked to take a referendum of the bishops at their upcoming meeting in Fulda (1942). The two bishops established a Liturgical Commission composed of the Liturgical Working Party members together with representatives from Maria Laach, Beuron, and the oratories of Leipzig and Klosterneuburg. This Liturgical Commission provided a vehicle for communication among the leading members of the German liturgical movement and a common front against attacks on the movement.

Those opposed to the movement continued to react to representatives of the movement, however. J. Doerner's book *Sentire cum Ecclesia* led Archbishop C. Gröber of Freiburg im Breisgau to write an open letter to the German hierarchy on the study of theology, the ecumenical movement, biblical interpretation, and the liturgical movement, reproaching the latter for taking matters into its own hands. At the 1942 bishops' meeting in Fulda, guidelines on the liturgical form of parochial worship were approved and published, based on the results of the liturgical referendum among the bishops.

The next year (1943) was quite significant for developments in the liturgical movement. In Germany, Cardinal Bertram, Archbishop of Breslau, sent a report to Rome about the German liturgical movement that asked for several privileges for German Catholics, including the reform of the ritual, the breviary, and other liturgical books (10 April 1943). Cardinal Maglione, Vatican Secretary of State, approved the form of the *Gemeinschaftsmesse* (community Mass) and announced that the Holy See "sympathetically tolerates" the *Deutsches Hochamt* (sung Mass) which included the singing of hymns in the vernacular contrary to the rubrics (24 December 1943).

Despite the devastation of war, other events continued to support the developing liturgical movement. In 1943 the *Centre de Pastorale Liturgique* (CPL) was established in occupied Paris under A.-M. Roguet, O.P., and Pie Duploye, O.P. This center, which became a hive of activity, was an independent foundation, i.e., not subject to the bishops, though entertaining close relations with the hierarchy. Two years later, after the liberation, *La Maison-Dieu* began publication.

In that same year in Rome, the encyclicals *Mystici Corporis* (29 June 1943), on the church and liturgy, and *Divino Afflante Spiritu* (30 September 1943), on the study of Scripture, were issued. During this same time (1939-45), Jungmann was in Vienna, writing what was to be a major instrument of the liturgical movement, the massive *Missarum Sollemnia*, published in 1948 (and quickly translated into English by Francis X. Brunner as the *Mass of the Roman Rite*, later to be condensed by Jungmann's student, C. Riepe, from two volumes to one).

Liturgical Weeks in the United States. Following the death of Virgil Michel (1938), a series of annual gatherings was held every year from 1940 to 1969. Known as "Liturgical Weeks," they were sponsored first by the Benedictine Liturgical Conference and after 1943 by The Liturgical Conference. The history of the liturgical movement in the United States is certainly dominated by the activity surrounding these National Liturgical Weeks. They served (1) to gather and support the leadership of the U.S. liturgical movement (which from 1940 to 1957 consisted of about three hundred persons); (2) to provide a forum for exchanging ideas and information with those who had contact with activities in Europe, challenging the leadership to become progressively bolder in its vision of what the liturgical movement could become; (3) to provide a support base for change, especially encouraging those who were meeting strong opposition from ecclesiastical leadership by allowing them an opportunity to gather with others who "thought the way they did"; (4) to educate those in attendance from the local diocese in which the conference was held (between eight hundred and fifteen hundred people from the local area participated in one way or another in each Liturgical Week); (5) to provide concrete experiences and models of how the liturgy could be celebrated within the existing rubrics; and (6) to bring together current thinking about a specific topic or theme.

From its beginning the leaders of the U.S. liturgical movement were characterized by their desire to apply the liturgy to a pastoral setting. Most of them were pastors seeking ways for their parishioners to pray. They thus stood in contrast to the leaders of the European movement, who were more scholarly in their approach and who used their meetings to exchange new directions for research, insight, and comparative study. Few Americans contributed original research in liturgy; but the eventual reform of the liturgy suffered from not including more information that the Americans had learned from their practical experience.

A group of pioneers met in Chicago under the patronage of Archbishop (later Cardinal) Samuel Stritch in the Holy Name Cathedral School for the first Liturgical Week (21-25 October 1940). The topics of the addresses were the parish, parish worship, the Mass, the Divine Office, devotions, and artistic expression. In attendance were 1,260 persons (863 of them from Illinois). News coverage of the event was light: the word "liturgy" was not too familiar in American Catholic circles. The idea of a Liturgical Week in the United States germinated in the previous autumn (1939) at the Catechetical Congress in Cincinnati, when the section on liturgy quite spontaneously and unexpectedly outgrew the space allotted to it. Pioneer planners Revs. Ducey, Diekmann, Laukemper, and Huelsmann, with Msgrs. Morrison, Hellriegel, Busch, and Hillenbrand responded to this interest by forming a conference and planning a special week devoted to liturgy.

After the success of that first week, Liturgical Weeks were held even though the nation was at war (1941-1945). The next two weeks kept to "generic" themes, covering various aspects of liturgy. In St. Paul, Minnesota (6-10 October 1941), 1,345 people attended (918 of them from Minnesota), with similar numbers in attendance at St. Meinrad, Indiana (12-16 October 1942). It was not until the 1943 Week at St. Procopius Abbey in Lisle, Illinois, that a central topic or theme for each week began to emerge. That year the topic reflected the shortages of the wartime economy: the meaning of sacrifice, sacrifice and the individual, sacrifice and society. In New York in 1944 the topic "Liturgy and Catholic Life" attracted 1,212 attendees (997 from New York and New Jersey), while "Catholic Liturgy in Peace and Reconstruction" drew 1,344 people (1,232 "locals") to New Orleans (11-13 December 1945). Although the coming of peace made national conventions easier, subsequent Liturgical Weeks did not draw large national crowds; the majority in attendance were from the city in which the meeting was held.

Stage Three: Postwar Activity (1945-1950)

Postwar Europe (1945-1950). Because of World War II (1939-1945), liturgical congresses in Europe had ceased, with the exception of a small congress in Varnes (January 1944) to study the liturgy. But immediately after the war, the First French National Liturgical Congress was held at Saint Flour with the theme "La Messe paroissiale du Dimanche" ("The Sunday Parish Mass"). Those involved in the liturgical movement were keenly aware that great strides had been made in the scholarly world, and they wanted to get in touch with one another. Due to wartime limitations on communication and the uncertain ecclesiastical climate about liturgical reform, insights and discoveries that were being made were not being communicated in writing, but by more or less "back room" meetings. This atmosphere added tremendously to the intensity of such meetings, their importance, and the trust level built among the leaders.

In August 1946 a Liturgical Congress at Maastricht, Holland, brought Dutch- and French-speaking participants together around the topic, "What is the problem of the popular liturgy?" Among the participants were Pères Duploye, Roguet, and Doncoeur, S.J.

Soon after this, the first permanent national "hub" of liturgical activity was founded in Germany, with the establishment of a chair of liturgy in the theology faculty of the University of Trier, with B. Fischer as its first occupant. Soon afterward (14 May 1947) the Liturgical Institute of Trier was founded with J. Wagner, Secretary of the Liturgical Commission, as Director. The Herwegen Institute for the Promotion of Liturgical Studies at Maria Laach soon followed, and on 31 January 1948 it commenced publication of the *Archiv für Liturgiewissenschaft.* Three years later, the Liturgical Institute in Trier began publishing *Liturgisches Jahrbuch.*

In the area of liturgical architecture, the Liturgical Committee in Germany issued instructions on the building of churches (January 1949), reflecting the fact that postwar Germany provided many opportunities for creative renovation, not only in the use of modern design, but also in a more fundamental rethinking of the basic arrangement of liturgical space. This rethinking progressed from locating the altar in the center of worship space, to removing the reserved Blessed Sacrament first from the main altar and then from the worship space, to relocating the baptismal font, and finally to a refocusing of the liturgical action from the altar to the assembled worshippers. Many experimental steps in this process were taken early in the restored and rebuilt churches of Germany.

Legislation after the War. Beginning in 1947, Rome began to take charge of the liturgical movement's direction. On 18 September 1947, Pius XII gave an introductory talk on the liturgical movement, the first time that a "movement" was officially recognized by the legislators. Shortly thereafter the encyclical letter *Mediator Dei* was issued (20 November 1947), called by those in the movement the "Magna Carta" of the liturgical movement. Between 1909 and 1947, the leadership of the liturgical movement had their own sense of the rightness of their cause, but they had no official recognition that the desire to improve liturgical celebration was acceptable. While Pius XII's encyclical had sharp directives about abuses and excesses in liturgical change as well as praise for the positive elements of the liturgical movement as they were perceived by the legislators (a truly political document), it was the first encyclical letter devoted entirely to the liturgy. More importantly, *Mediator Dei* inaugurated the period of actual changes in the liturgy. No longer was the liturgical movement simply about education; it was now refocusing on change.

The Belgian, and to a lesser extent the French, bishops began petitioning Rome for liturgical changes. Remarkably, the American bishops remained aloof from the liturgical movement's activity in the United States and seemed totally unaware of the presence of a movement now influencing the hierarchies of France, Belgium, the Netherlands, and Germany.

Belgium was given permission to have evening Mass on Sundays and holydays for those unable to attend in the morning, originally for one year (28 January 1947). The Diocese of Bayonne (France) was given permission to recite the complete psalm at the introit (29 January 1947), and a translation of the *Rituale Romanum* was approved for a Latin-French edition of the ritual (28 November 1947). Meanwhile, the Diocese of Liège (Belgium) was authorized to use a bilingual ritual (22 October 1948).

With the news of a new openness in Rome, requests for liturgical changes began to come from other parts of the world. The bishops of Japan were given permission to authorize evening Masses under certain conditions (11 March 1948), and in Poland some priests were given permission to celebrate daily evening Masses (15 August 1948). The Holy Office authorized the translation of the *Missale Romanum* into Mandarin Chinese, except for the canon of the Mass, but no practical use could be made of this faculty (12 April 1949). India was given permission for evening Masses and a reduction in the eucharistic fast (17 June 1949), while the church in Holland was granted permission to use the Little Breviary, an abbreviated form of the Divine Office (21 February 1950). The Italian legislators (the Curia) were led by G. Lercaro, who served as secretary of state, A. Bugnini, G. Montini (later, Paul VI), and assisted by the Italian liturgist, C. Vagaggini.

Postwar Liturgical Weeks (1946-1956). For ten years, the themes and structure of the National Liturgical Weeks in the United States fell into a pattern: topics were selected based on the events in Rome or the current needs of the planners. Total attendance ebbed and flowed, largely depending on the local area's support (attendance ranged from a low of 1,244 in Denver in 1946 and 1,247 in London, Ontario, in 1956 to a high of 4,399 at St. Louis in 1949, with 3,688 of those people coming from Missouri). Those committed few who traveled to the Liturgical Week each year from outside the area ranged from 114 to 425. The picture is clear: there was a small core group learning from each other and sharing what they knew and believed with those who came from the local church. Each year, the ideas of the liturgical leadership spread, but almost by one diocese at a time.

A list of the themes of these Liturgical Weeks and the cities in which they were held is a helpful reminder of the topics of liturgical interest and the places such interest was being generated. (Some of those cities remain centers of liturgical development today.) "The Family in Christ" was the focus in Denver, Colorado (14-17 October 1946); while the

Week in Portland, Oregon, (18-21 August 1947) concentrated on "Christ's Sacrifice and Ours" (this was the first Week in which an art exhibit was held; it was under the direction of Mrs. R.W. Prentis of Portland). In 1948 (2-6 August) the participants at Boston, Massachusetts, focused on "The New Man in Christ," while the Week in St. Louis (22-26 August 1949) looked at the "Sanctification of Sunday." The 1950 Week (21-24 August) was "For Pastors and People" at Conception Abbey, Missouri; and "The Priesthood of Christ" was the focus in Dubuque, Iowa (20-23 August 1951). (The line art that became identified with the liturgical renewal first appeared in the Proceedings for this week, drawn by Carl William Merschel of Chicago.) Popular education continued under the direction of Gerald Ellard, H. A. Reinhold, Mary Perkins Ryan, Anselm Scholz, and Michael Mathis.

In the summer of 1947, on the campus of the University of Notre Dame, South Bend, Indiana, Michael Mathis began "The Liturgy Program," a summer program for undergraduate students, with three courses: "The History of the Liturgy," "Some Aspects of the Liturgy," and "Gregorian Chant." The "Aspects" course was pastoral and practical, taught by the leaders of the liturgical movement. G. Diekmann presented "The Christian Way of Life: The Sacramental Way"; W. Nutting talked about how "A Layman Looks at the Liturgy"; H.A. Reinhold described "Ecclesiastical Places: Churches and Cemeteries"; R. Hillenbrand discussed "The Place of the Liturgy in Catholic Action;" while B. Laukemper described "Stational Church and Latin Masses." Bede Scholz presented "The Ecclesiastical Year"; Damasus Winzen, "The Scriptural Background of the Ecclesiastical Year"; and Gerald Ellard, "Aims and Objects of the Liturgical Movement."

By 1951 the Notre Dame Program had expanded to include the European liturgical leaders: Donald Attwater, Cornelius Bouman, Louis Bouyer, Patrick Cummins, Jean Daniélou, Balthasar Fischer, Joseph Goldbrunner, Pierre-Marie Gy, Martin Hellriegel, Johannes Hofinger, Josef Jungmann, Boniface Luykx, Christine Mohrmann, Herman Schmidt, and Ermin Vitry. Books derived from this summer school influenced American thought; among them were Louis Bouyer's *Liturgical Piety* and *Rite and Man*, Josef Jungmann's *The Early Liturgy*, and Jean Daniélou's *The Bible and the Liturgy*.

Bolstered by the activity in Rome, the 1947 Liturgical Week petitioned Rome for an English translation of the *Collectio Rituum*. While this resolution was brought before the American bishops and discussed briefly at their annual meeting in 1950, it was not until 1951 (after a German-language ritual had been approved by Rome) that the bishops approved the formation of a committee to study the feasibility of such a request on behalf of the American church. A first committee headed by Gerald Ellard was replaced by a committee headed by Michael Mathis, with committee members Joseph Garvin, Chester A. Soleta, Dr. John Julian Ryan, and Mary Perkins Ryan. By June 1953 the committee had completed the translation, except for the marriage exhortation (later done by Louis Bouyer), and the musical notation (later composed by Ermin Vitry but never used). The new ritual was approved for use in the United States on 2 June 1954.

Stage Four: The Liturgical Movement in Action (1950-1959)

At the First German National Liturgical Congress (June 1950) the topic was *Die Eucharistiefeier am Sonntag* (The Sunday Celebration of the Eucharist). This Congress was organized by the Trier Liturgical Institute, Fischer and Wagner. Particularly important was R. Guardini's talk on the Easter vigil, for it resulted in the Congress's adoption of the resolution:

"That the bishops be asked to petition Rome for the transfer of the Holy Saturday celebration to the evening or night." On 2 November 1950 the bishops of Germany, France, and Austria formally petitioned the Holy Father to move the celebration of Holy Saturday to the evening.

Rome responded with much more than they had asked. The *Ordo Sabbati Sancti*, issued 9 February 1951, provided a restored Easter vigil (ad experimentum), and the liturgical movement was now fully engaged in liturgical reform.

As a result of their success with the initial Easter vigil revision, European liturgists now saw liturgical study weeks as essential to get the best thinking together internationally. So in 1951 (12-15 July), the First International Liturgical Study Week was held at Maria Laach, this time jointly sponsored by the Liturgical Institute at Trier and the French C.P.L. with the theme "Problems of the Roman Missal." About thirty persons attended from Germany, France, Belgium, Austria, Holland, and Switzerland.

The Second International Study Meeting (20-24 October 1952) was held at Mont Saint Odile with the theme "Modern Man and the Liturgy." The discussions centered around the progress taking place in society's understanding of itself and the changes needed to bring the liturgy in line with those developments. Many ideas discussed here were to reappear in the Vatican Council's Constitution *Gaudium et Spes* (The Church in the Modern World).

In the midst of these weeks, the legislators were at work responding, at times, to earlier points raised by the scholars. In 1952, for instance, the Roman legislators produced *Christus Dominus*, an apostolic constitution that extended permission for evening Masses and revised the eucharistic fast for the whole church. And on 30 June 1952 the Holy Office published a directive on sacred art.

In 1953 the Third International Study Week (13-18 September) was held in northern Italy (Lugano), in an attempt to include the Italians as well as the French, German, Dutch, and Austrian scholars. Two months before the meeting, Bishop A. Bernareggi of Bergamo, head of the liturgical movement in Italy, died, to be succeeded by Bishop Rossi of Biella. The Lugano Week was attended by two cardinals and sixteen European bishops, as well as by Pére Antonelli, O.F.M., relator generalis of the Historical Section of the Congregation of Rites. Johannes Hofinger, S.J., a missionary from the Philippines, presented a major address on "Mission and Liturgy," and proposals sent to Rome included (1) the extension of the reform of the Holy Saturday liturgy to the whole of Holy Week, (2) permission for the general introduction of the *Deutsches Hochamt* (with congregational singing in the local vernacular), (3) readings in the vernacular, and (4) further stimulation of active participation.

On 12-14 September 1954 the Fourth International Study Week met at Mont César (Louvain) with the theme: "Pericope System and Concelebration." No resolutions were made, as some of the points appeared to have been insufficiently studied. Speakers on the pericope question included B. Botte, Chavasse, H. Kahlefeld, and J. Hofinger; on the topic of concelebration: Raes, Franquesa, O.S.B. (Montserrat), Jungmann, Martimort, K. Rahner, S.J., and C. Davis.

As a result of the unsatisfactory scholarly work at this meeting and especially because of opening the "hot" topic of concelebration, planners felt that the annual meetings were forcing topics too quickly. A decision was made to hold national congresses on the odd year, and when the members reconvened the power and impact of their meeting was a surprise even to them. The liturgical movement as a reformer was in full swing.

Pius XII's encyclical on sacred music,

Musicae sacrae disciplina was issued on 25 December 1955. While it followed the pattern set by Pius X and XI, it reflected the presence of a little more "give" among the legislators, at least in its relaxation of restrictions on the use of orchestral instruments and the performance of some religious compositions at non-liturgical services and its approval of the use of vernacular hymns during the eucharistic liturgy, where such has been the practice "according to old or immemorial custom" (47).

Meanwhile, the National Liturgical Weeks continued in the United States. While the European Study Weeks were restricted in attendance and provided a scholarly exchange, the liturgical weeks in the United States were open to all interested parties and were popular in their presentations. Still, the American leaders were anxious to keep in touch with the latest developments in Europe, as was shown dramatically in 1952, when the theme of the liturgical week in Cleveland, Ohio, was "The Easter Vigil." The presentations explained the new rites, and this began a new approach to the liturgical weeks. While the American leaders did not directly influence the changes themselves, they were quick to popularize the ideas and put them into practice. This difference between the Americans as practitioners and the French and Germans as theoreticians characterized their different approaches to the liturgy.

Additional American weeks during this period treated "St. Pius X and Social Worship" (Grand Rapids, Michigan, 1953) and "Mary in the Liturgy" (16-19 August 1954, Milwaukee, Wisconsin). The National Liturgical Weeks in 1955 and 1956 focused on the ritual changes being requested by the European scholars and approved by the Roman legislators: "The New Ritual: Liturgy and Social Order," 22-25 August 1955 in Worcester, Massachusetts, and "People's Participa-

tion and Holy Week" at London, Ontario, 20-23 August 1956. The hard work of organizing these weeks was shouldered by a team of priests: Revs. Carroll, Wilmes, O'Connell, S. Sheehan, Randolph, W. Leonard, and E. Walsh, to name the central organizers.

By 1956 it was clear to the leaders of the European liturgical movement that a bolder move was needed. At the Fifth International Study Week in September of that year, the topic was "The Breviary," and the list of speakers included J. Pascher, Augustine Bea, and Jungmann. But more important was the decision to go international and popular and move the event closer to Rome, in Assisi. So held in conjunction with this study week was the First International Congress for Pastoral-Liturgical Guidance, to survey the achievements during the pontificate of Pius XII. Speakers included Bea and van Bekkum. Among those present were six cardinals, eighty bishops, and 1,200 participants from all over the world. The President of the Congress was the Prefect of the Congregation of Rites, Gaetano Cardinal Cicognani. The event became known as "the Assisi Congress."

Without question this was a turning point for the liturgical movement. Now politics was in full swing, the issues of reform were crystallized, and those involved in renewal sensed the sweet taste of reform. They wanted deeper changes.

Even before the Germans held their Third National Congress at Strasbourg on the theme "Bible and Liturgy" (July 1957), with massive popular participation, Rome began to react to the pressure by issuing a series of *monita* (warnings) against any highhanded introduction of new practices in the liturgy (14 February 1957), on delaying baptism (18 February), and against omitting the words *mysterium fidei* at the consecration of the elements (24 July). At the same time, some concessions were appearing, e.g., permission for the readings and hymns to be in the vernacular during Holy Week in India and a definition of "active participation" in the Instruction from the Congregation of Rites on Sacred Music and the Sacred Liturgy (3 September 1958). But the restrictive attitude was also present. The view that liturgy is celebrated only by the clergy and liturgy is only that which is written in the Roman Books, together with the detailed control of liturgical innovation, indicated that tensions between the legislators and the leaders of the liturgical movement were clear and open, and almost everyone in the church felt the tension. Church people were being forced to take sides, "for" the liturgy or "against" it. Change was afoot; but change had not yet been authorized.

In 1958 the Sixth International Study Week (8-13 September) was held at Montserrat, Catalonia, Spain, with the theme "Baptism and Confirmation." Shortly after this study week events outside the movement began to affect it. Pius XII died on 9 October 1958, and Pope John XXIII, his successor and a long-time friend of L. Beauduin, announced his intent to summon the Second Vatican Council just over three months later (25 January 1959).

The *monita* ceased, and Japan was given approval for a bilingual ritual (December 1958). Other relaxations of tensions and promulgation of new permissions quickly followed. The Sacred Congregation of Rites settled what had become a controverted question: whether it was, in fact, permissible to sing hymns in German at the *Deutsches Hochamt*, and it issued a decree that, in certain cases, the "prayers after Mass" might be omitted (9 March 1960). Further, the Congregation agreed that communion in the afternoon outside of Mass was permissible in certain cases, and published a reordering of the rubrics and a revision of the second part of the *Pontificale Romanum* (13 April 1960). No doubt this flurry of activity by the Congregation of Rites was an attempt to assert control, for simultaneously with these actions the members of the preparatory liturgical commission for the Second Vatican Council were being appointed (5 June 1960).

Interest in the liturgical movement continued to spread and grow. In Holland, for instance, an interdiocesan Liturgical Secretariat was opened in Nijmegen (17 February 1959), while the fiftieth anniversary of the Belgian Liturgical Movement was celebrated (23 July 1959), and a great International Congress was assembled in Nijmegen-Uden with the theme "Mission and Liturgy." Just months after these events, the man who began the popular liturgical movement, Dom Lambert Beauduin, died (11 January 1960). In that same year, the Seventh International Liturgical Study Week added a new focus to liturgical study with a concentration on the Eastern as well as the Western churches. The theme of this week, held in Germany, was "The Eucharistic Celebration in the East and West."

The Impact of the Liturgical Movement on the Second Vatican Council

Like several other movements of the time—the biblical revival, renewal of patristic studies, growth of the "social gospel" movement—the liturgical movement began and grew because (1) there was a need in the church to re-examine the liturgy, (2) there was a climate in the secular community for change, (3) new discoveries from historical studies revealed the inadequacies of existing understanding and practices, and (4) there were leaders willing to take on the project of exploring the new ideas and exposing them to a wider public. Some of the ideas were explosive, not because the leaders chose them to be, but because when the new idea discovered from history was compared with present practice, it became apparent that present practice was "out of sync" with the tradition. There were only two options: ignore the historical data or call for change in the present practice.

The early leaders of the liturgical movement certainly were not interested in change or confrontation. It is clear that their intentions were simply to explore, in a rather scientific, scholarly, or even abstract manner, the liturgy of the Roman Catholic church. There is no way to date precisely when the change-over from scholarly reflection to political action occurred, for it was a gradual awakening, developing differently in different leaders. Some leaders, when they recognized the need for change, either ignored it or left the movement. Others downplayed the need for change and continued on with what they believed was the central activity of the liturgical movement, namely, developing and communicating a deeper understanding and appreciation of the liturgy as it then existed. But to some, it became obvious that change was needed. The same thing was happening in other areas of scholarly research and in other aspects of church life. And that converging awareness among various leaders was not lost on the new pope. So John XXIII called for a new ecumenical council.

Many, but not all, of the contemporary leaders of the liturgical movement were connected in one way or another to the various committees and advisory groups preparing for and assisting the decision makers of the council. But certainly the reform mandated by the Council Fathers in the Constitution on the Liturgy and overseen by the more important implementation committees was deeply influenced by the work and words of the leaders of the liturgical movement. The Catholic church has been changed radically because of the ideas and intellectual effort of about four hundred persons working over about a century, many of them active at the time of the council and the post-conciliar reform.

A partial list of the key players in the liturgical renewal mandated by Vatican II would include Godfrey Diekmann, O.S.B. (St. John's Abbey, Collegeville, Minnesota); Balthasar Fischer (Trier, West Germany); Adalberto Franquesa, O.S.B. (Montserrat, Spain); Joseph Gelineau, S.J. (Paris, France); Anton Hänggi (Fribourg, Switzerland); Bishop Denis Hurley (Durban, Union of South Africa); Josef A. Jungmann, S.J. (Innsbruck, Austria); Thierry Maertens, O.S.B. (St. Andrieu, Belgium); Juan Mateos, S.J. (Rome, Italy); Fredrick McManus (Washington, D.C.); Cipriano Vagaggini, O.S.B. (Bologna, Italy); Cyrille Vogel (Strasbourg, France); Johannes Wagner (Trier, West Germany); and Helmut Hucke (Neu Isenburg, West Germany).

The Final American Liturgical Weeks (1957-1969)

A Growing Phenomenon (1957-1964). Several of the most important American leaders had attended the Assisi Congress in 1956. They returned to the United States certain that a popular liturgical movement was no longer merely a speculative possibility, but a burgeoning reality tied to the leadership in Europe and even in Rome. This certainty was a morale booster after the low attendance at the National Liturgical Week in London, Ontario, in 1956 (1,247 people). The next year the Liturgical Week returned to St John's Abbey, Collegeville, Minnesota, home of the American liturgical movement. Its theme was "Education and Liturgy," and something dramatic happened in attendance. 2,241 people were present—not the largest Week by any means, but for the first time, more than half of them (1,142) were from out of state (in the previous year, only 425 were from out of state). From this Week on, large numbers from all across the United States began gathering on a regular basis in the last weeks of August for an annual liturgical meeting.

Great news keeps coming from Rome: an Easter vigil restored, a new order for Holy Week, a ritual in English. The Liturgical Conference incorporated as a nonprofit organization, with John B. Mannion as executive director and Frederick McManus as president. A national campaign of writing and speaking sponsored by the Liturgical Conference to explain and enlist interest in the changes in the liturgy began.

The influence of the liturgical movement was felt in other areas of church life. For instance, Gerard Sloyan, one of the key leaders of the Liturgical Conference, revised the Department of Religious Education at The Catholic University of America to train catechists. His own involvement in liturgy as well as his interest in the biblical renewal was shared with students eager to learn theology in English. Frequently, seminarians who were using manuals in Latin reflecting dogmatic statements gravitated to the more dynamic "new" methods. An entire generation of catechists and clergy was trained in the best theology available before the council.

A climate of change began to influence even the most conservative aspect of the liturgical movement—the musicians. From the time of *Tra le sollecitudini* in 1903 through the 1950s the musical aspect of the movement focused mainly on a recovery of Gregorian chant and polyphony. But under the influence of two key people—Joseph Gelineau, S.J., in France and Rembert Weakland, O.S.B., in the United States—that focus began to shift. It was their influence, primarily, that shifted musicians to a consideration of contemporary culture and music as sources for liturgical music. Rather than a recovery of one period from the past, they maintained, a renewal of church music should be concerned about a recovery of the present, rooted in the whole history of sacred music. Few formally trained composers took up the challenge; a notable exception was C. Alexander Peloquin.

Events began to cluster around the National Liturgical Weeks. At the National Week in 1958 (18-21 August), in the midst of talks about "The Church Year," the new Cathedral of St. Peter in Chains was inaugurated in Cincinnati, Ohio. The next year (23-26 August 1959), on the campus of the University of Notre Dame, Andrew Greeley chose to address the main topic, "Participation in the Mass," without wearing a Roman collar and caused a sensation. In Pittsburgh (22-25 August 1960), on the theme "The Liturgy and Unity in Christ," Bishop Wright gave a stirring talk entitled *"Sperabamur,* We Used to Hope."

The Liturgical Week had become a national event, a gathering point particularly for the liberal hopes of those interested in church matters. The Conference took the bold step of opening a central office in Washington, where F. McManus, G. Sloyan, and J. Mannion directed a huge service of information, publication, and organization.

Other movements began to have an impact on the liturgical movement, as reflected in the topics of the next few Weeks. 1961 (Oklahoma City) saw a focus on the biblical renewal: "Bible, Life, and Worship," while the 1962 Week in Seattle, Washington, reflected an interest in eschatology, hope, modernity, and the future: "Thy Kingdom Come: Christian Hope in the Modern World." 1963 brought together the catechetical and liturgical revivals in the topic, "The Renewal of Christian Education" (Philadelphia).

The years between 1963 and 1965 saw all focus shift to events in Rome and to the impact of Vatican II on the American church. In 1964 the Liturgical Week was titled "The Challenge of the Council: Person, Parish, World." More than 20,000 persons gathered in St. Louis, Missouri, and heard Clarence Jos. Rivers sing a "catholic" song derived from the African-American gospel tradition: "God is Love." In that year, it can be said, the liturgical renewal was born, but the liturgical movement began to die. In the full tide of renewal after the promulgation of the *Constitution on the Sacred Liturgy* (4 December 1963), the Weeks grew almost unbelievably large and became an expression of many hopes and expectations. One could see assembled scripture scholars, professors of theology, parish priests, dedicated lay people, seminarians, urban planners, teachers, military chaplains, and always the eager and loyal religious sisters and brothers.

The Largest Liturgical Week (1965) and the Time of Confrontation (1966-69). During the period immediately after the Vatican Council, the Liturgical Weeks continued; indeed they had become so large that the leadership decided to split the one Week into three in 1965. Under the topic "Jesus Christ Reforms His Church," three sites were chosen: Baltimore, Maryland (2,717 in attendance), Portland, Oregon (3,054 attending), and the largest of the three in Chicago, Illinois (attendance of 5,637).

But now the board of directors of The Liturgical Conference faced a major dilemma. For the past twenty years, the leadership of the Conference had been "on the cutting edge," confronting the system, struggling against hope that change might come; such is the nature of a "movement." But when the bishops of the Second Vatican Council endorsed about 95 percent of everything the leadership had sought, then the leadership had to choose between two directions— either serve as an educational force to promote the renewal that it had been part of, or continue to search for the "cutting edge" issues of change. A major disagreement occurred among The Liturgical Conference's directors, and half of the board (led by David McManus, William Baroody, Stephen McNierney)

resigned. The remaining leadership chose to address the volatile issues of the late 1960s as the liturgical movement's new agenda: the secular city, the Vietnam War, and anti-institutionalism. These were the main topics of the next few Liturgical Weeks: "Worship in the City of Man" in Houston, Texas (22-25 August 1966); "Experiments in Community," 22-24 August 1967, in Kansas City, Missouri; and in 1968, in Washington, DC, "Damn Everything but the Circus."

The plans for the 1968 Week led to a direct confrontation between Cardinal O'Boyle of Washington and the board of directors over some of the speakers and the issue of liturgical experimentation at the Week's eucharist. O'Boyle withdrew his endorsement of the National Week; the board proceeded without it. The next year the National Conference of Catholic Bishops withdrew The Liturgical Conference's episcopal moderator, a symbolic gesture that was to push the Conference to become an ecumenical organization, independent of the Catholic hierarchy. Simultaneously, the Federation of Diocesan Liturgical Commissions (F.D.L.C.), which represented the official liturgical commissions or worship offices of dioceses, assumed the responsibility of providing education and policy leadership, and the staff of the Bishop's Committee on the Liturgy (B.C.L.) was expanded.

Until this time, Frederick McManus had served as president of The Liturgical Conference and executive director of the Bishops' Committee on the Liturgy, insuring that the best of the liturgical movement's leadership had direct access to the policy-making decisions of the bishops. Creative policy documents, such as *Music in Catholic Worship*, published in 1972, were the direct result of McManus's connective and integrative influence.

But after the split between the "official" and "unofficial" leadership, there was also a split between the post-conciliar liturgical renewal and the liturgical movement. Liturgical education now became centered, for the most part, on understanding and implementing the renewed rites as they appeared from Rome and, in some instances, were adapted for use in various countries. (Such education took diverse approaches, of course, and there were "liberal," "mainline," and "conservative" approaches to the documents and their implementation.) But the liturgical movement as a "cutting edge" popular movement was "marginalized" in official disrepute. It had largely returned, by the end of the 1970s, to its quiet pursuit of scholarship and popular, if less dramatic, forms of education and often, to a large extent, without a focus on changing liturgical legislation. In a sense, it was back where it had begun a century before.

The Renewal Continues (1969)

The shift from advocacy and promoting interest in liturgical reform to implementation of the liturgical renewal conceived in the documents of Vatican II created different organizations, types of leadership and meetings.

In 1976, The National Association of Pastoral Musicians was formed by Virgil C. Funk, with assistance from Sr. Jane Marie Perrot, D.C., former director of the National Catholic Music Educators Association. In 1978, in Scranton, Pennsylvania, the first of a series of national conferences began to be held by N.P.M., gathering parish musicians and clergy for education and celebration. While similar to National Liturgical Weeks, N.P.M. conferences focused on issues dealing with the implementation of the liturgical renewal.

In 1973, John Gallen, S.J., director of the Notre Dame Center for Pastoral Liturgy and successor to Aidan Kavanagh, O.S.B., gathered a group of teachers and students of liturgy in Scottsdale, Arizona, who formed the North American Academy of Liturgy. The Academy uniquely serves the ecumenical community as an exchange among liturgical leaders.

On an international level, the Societas Liturgica held its first international congress in 1969 in Glenstal Abbey, Ireland, on the topic "Liturgical Language." An ecumenical organization for scholars, it was begun two years earlier by Placid Murray, O.S.B.. Congresses have been held every two years: in 1971 in Strasbourg, France, on "Contemporary Worship"; in 1973 at Montserrat, Spain, on "Contemporary Common Prayer"; at Trier, Germany, in 1975 on "Current Eucharistic Prayers"; in 1977, in Canterbury, England, the topic was "Christian Initiation"; the 1979 meeting in Washington, DC, focused on "Ordination"; in 1981 in Paris, France, the members discussed "Liturgical Time"; the 1983 meeting (Vienna, Austria) was about "Liturgy and Spirituality"; and the focus in Boston, Massachusetts, (1985) was "The LIMA Document"; in 1987 at Brixen, Italy, "Penance and Reconciliation"; and in 1989 the meeting was in York, England, on the topic, "Liturgy and Inculturation."

Universa Laus was founded in 1965 by Joseph Gelineau for the study of music and liturgy. Serving as a study group, in 1980 Universa Laus published a consensus document on music called a "Manifesto," containing principles of liturgical music.

Conclusion

In 1909 the interest in liturgy which had existed in academic circles and within Benedictine monasteries broke the surface of placid scholarship with the declaration of Dom Lambert Beauduin at the Malines Congress. In fewer than fifty-five years, the seeds which had been watered and fertilized in parish rectories, in seminaries, and around family kitchen tables blossomed forth in the liturgical renewal proposed by the leaders of the Vatican Council.

On almost every issue there was debate and often open resistance. Persons took sides, for and against the liturgical movement, and often religious houses were deeply divided among the advocates of both positions. The energy and enthusiasm of both leaders and followers in the face of this resistance stirred the "sense of movement." The most dramatic and visible element of the liturgical renewal of Vatican II, the use of the vernacular in the liturgy, was not a central element in the discussions of the liturgical movement. The structure of the Mass, concelebration, the role of the laity, and music were the major concerns.

What was central to the liturgical movement was a desire to make the liturgical prayer of the church more meaningful to the participants. Full, conscious, active participation led to a realization that the rite itself needed to be revised and to a call for a new understanding of education, evangelization, ecclesiology and Christology, which in turn led to a rethinking of theology, religion, ecumenism, and the way Christians relate to the world.

In fifty-five years, through the unswerving efforts of dedicated men and women, the liturgical movement spread throughout Europe and North America. Simultaneously, there was an ecumenical liturgical movement and renewal interacting with the desire to reform the Roman rite. This ecumenical liturgical movement contained its own leaders and eventually brought about a renewal of liturgical books in all major liturgical denominations.

In the future, the agenda of liturgical issues includes (1) the implementation of the liturgical renewal within the parish, especially in music and art; (2) discovering a way of celebrating liturgy in a multicultural setting; and (3) the inculturation of the liturgy within the unique culture of each country where the liturgy is celebrated.

While the sense of "a movement" passed with the liturgical reform and renewal embodied in Vatican II, the challenge of enriching the appreciation and experience of worship still remains.

See **Reform, liturgical, of Vatican II; Documents, Roman liturgical, since Vatican II; Reform, liturgical, in Eastern churches; Reform, liturgical, in Reformation churches; Reform, liturgical, history of**

Joseph A. Jungmann, S.J., *The Mass of the Roman Rite*, trans. by Francis A. Brunner, rev. by Charles K Riepe, 1959. Jeremy Hall, "The American Liturgical Movement: The Early Years" in *Worship 1987*. Oliver Rousseau, O.S.B., *The Progress of the Liturgy, An Historical Sketch* (Newman Press, 1951). H. Ellsworth Chandlee, "The Liturgical Movement" in *The New Westminster Dictionary of Liturgy and Worship*, ed. by J. G. Davies, 1986. Bernard Botte, *From Silence to Participation, An Insider's View of Liturgical Renewal* (The Pastoral Press, 1988). Pierre Jounel, "The History of the Liturgy" in *The Church at Prayer*, Vol. 1, *Principles of the Liturgy* (The Liturgical Press, 1987). L. Brinkhof, O.F.M., "Chronicle of the Liturgical Movement" in *Liturgy in Development*, ed. by Alting Von Geusau, (Sheed and Ward, 1965). R.W. Franklin, Robert L. Spaeth, *Virgil Michel, American Catholic* (Liturgical Press, 1988). Patrick Regan, "How Did Liturgical Change Get Started ... and Why? in *Pastoral Music* 8:2 (1984).

VIRGIL C. FUNK

LITURGICAL REFORM
See **Reform, liturgical, ...**

LITURGICAL SOURCES
See **Sources, ...**

LITURGICAL TEXTS IN ENGLISH

The Constitution on the Liturgy dramatically changed the Roman Catholic church's approach to the language of the liturgy (S.C., 36). While it did not give the vernacular pride of place in the church's liturgical rites, it opened up significant possibilities for the use of the vernacular in the Mass and other sacramental rites.

For the first time in sixteen centuries, apart from some minor exceptions, the place of the vernacular was established in the Roman church's worship. Art. 36 begins by stating, "Particular law remaining in force, the use of the Latin language is to be preserved in the Latin rites." Its focus, however, shifts immediately as it goes on to declare: "But since the use of the mother tongue, whether in the Mass, the administration of the sacraments, or other parts of the liturgy, frequently may be of great advantage to the people, the limits of its use may be extended. This will apply in the first place to the readings and instructions and to some prayers and chants, according to the regulations on this matter to be laid down for each case in subsequent chapters."

Art. 36 then goes on to spell out the competence of bishops' conferences and the role of the Holy See for decisions concerning the use of the vernacular in the liturgy: "Respecting such norms and also, where applicable, consulting the bishops of nearby territories of the same language, the competent, territorial, ecclesiastical authority mentioned in art. 22, 2 (territorial bodies of bishops lawfully established) is empowered to decide whether and to what extent the vernacular is to be used. The enactments of the competent authority are to be approved, that is, confirmed by the Holy See."

The article concludes by speaking specifically of the authority of bishops' conferences over translations from Latin into the vernacular: "Translations from the Latin text into the mother tongue intended for use in the liturgy must be approved by the competent, territorial ecclesiastical authority already mentioned."

Art. 54 of the Constitution opened the possibility of the vernacular in the Mass even wider by stating: "Wherever a more extended use of the mother tongue within the Mass appears desirable, the regulation laid down in art. 40 [concerning more profound or radical adaptations] of this Constitution must be observed."

The third major reference to the vernacular in the Constitution comes in art. 63 which deals with the vernacular in the sacraments and sacramentals: "Because the use of the mother tongue in the administration of the sacraments and sacramentals can often be of considerable help for the people, this use is to be extended according to the following norms:

a. With art. 36 as the norm, the vernacular may be used in administering the sacraments and sacramentals.

b. Particular rituals in harmony with the new edition of the Roman Ritual shall be prepared without delay by the competent, territorial ecclesiastical authority mentioned in art. 22, 2 of the Constitution. These rituals are to be adapted, even in regard to the language employed, to the needs of the different regions. Once they have been reviewed by the Apostolic See, they are to be used in the regions for which they have been prepared."

Two further references to the vernacular are found in articles 101 and 113. Art. 101 sanctions the use of the vernacular for clerics obligated to the recitation of the liturgy of the hours if "the use of Latin constitutes a grave obstacle to their praying the office properly." The same concession is given to nuns and nonclerics who recite the office in choir. Art. 113 specifies that texts for singing in the various rites should be in the vernacular according to the norms laid down in articles 36, 54, 63, and 101.

In summary, the Constitution takes the following approach to the use of the vernacular: recognition of the vernacular in a limited form in the Mass but the possibility of wider use; recognition of the use of the vernacular in the sacraments and sacramentals without restriction; recognition of the authority of the conferences of bishops to decide on the extent of the vernacular for their territories; recognition of the authority of the conferences to prepare and approve the vernacular translations, submitting their decrees of approval to the Holy See for confirmation; encouragement for neighboring bishops' conferences sharing the same language to consult together on translations; allowance for the possibility of adapting texts to make them more suited to a particular country or region.

The bishops of the conciliar commission on the liturgy probably did not foresee the extent to which the vernacular, especially in the Mass, would become the norm in the church's liturgy. At most they expected various countries, and perhaps chiefly in parts of Europe and in North America, to approve the vernacular on a restricted basis.

As a result of petitions from conferences of bishops, the Holy See gradually widened the conciliar permission to employ the vernacular liturgy until the point in 1967 when authorization for an entirely vernacular liturgy had been granted, including the canon of the Mass or eucharistic prayer and the texts for the ordination rites, including the sacramental forms [see *Tres abhinc annos,* 4 May 1967 (*Documents on the Liturgy* [D.O.L.] 39, no. 474)]. Authorization was also given in 1971 for the celebration of the liturgy of the hours in the vernacular without the restrictions stated in the Constitution on the Liturgy (See D.O.L., 216, no. 1773). Pope Paul VI on 19 April 1967 emphasized the pastoral reasons that underlay this shift from limited concessions to a fully vernacular liturgy when he said in an address to the members and *periti* of the Consilium for the Implementation of the Constitution on the Liturgy: "Latin is an issue certainly deserving serious attention, but the issue cannot be solved in a way that is opposed to the great principle confirmed by the Council, namely, that liturgical prayer, accommodated to the understanding of

the people, is to be intelligible. Nor can it be solved in opposition to another principle called for by the collectivity of human culture, namely, that the peoples' deepest and sincerest sentiments can best be expressed through the vernacular as it is in actual usage" (D.O.L. 86, no. 639).

During the first session of the council, several bishops from various English-speaking countries, already anticipating a limited use of the vernacular in the liturgy, had informal discussions about the possibility of English-speaking countries pooling their resources to provide a common English text. These informal discussions led in the following year to the establishment by ten conferences of bishops on 17 October 1963 of what would become known as the International Commission on English in the Liturgy (I.C.E.L.). The bishops of these English-speaking hierarchies thus anticipated the Constitution on the Liturgy by several weeks and by exactly one year the explicit encouragement given by Cardinal Giacomo Lercaro, president of the Consilium, for conferences of bishops sharing the same languge to form "mixed commissions" to prepare uniform vernacular texts [See *Consilium ad exsequendam*, 16 October 1964 (D.O.L., 108)].

The founding conferences of I.C.E.L. gave it a mandate, the principal charge of which was "to work out a plan for the translation of liturgical texts and the provision of original texts where required in language which would be correct, dignified, intelligible, and suitable for public recitation and singing."

Among other specifications in the mandate were the following: "to propose the engagement of experts in various fields as translators, composers, and critics and to provide for the exchange of information with the sponsoring Hierarchies and with other interested Hierarchies ... ; to give special attention, within the scope of this plan, to the question of a single English version of the

Bible for liturgical use or at least of common translations of biblical texts used in the liturgy."

From the first then I.C.E.L.'s task involved not simply translations of liturgical and biblical texts but also the creation of new texts. From the beginning the sponsoring conferences also directed I.C.E.L. to cooperate wherever possible with other Christian churches in the preparation of common liturgical texts.

I.C.E.L.'s work began in earnest in 1964. Its overall direction had been entrusted by the conferences to a board of bishops, each conference designating a bishop as its representative. The Episcopal Committee (later Board) established a group of specialists in liturgy, theology, classics, scripture studies, English studies, and music known as the Advisory Committee to oversee the preparation of the texts. In 1965 the day-to-day work was committed to a permanent Secretariat, established in Washington, D.C.

The first English text prepared by I.C.E.L. for the sponsoring conferences of bishops was the Roman Canon (Eucharistic Prayer I), issued in 1967. The style of the text was the result of a number of discussions and consultations and was in many ways characteristic of the approach that I.C.E.L. would take to vernacular liturgical texts. It was somewhat spare and direct in wording and syntax. Simplicity, dignity, and attentiveness to the needs of proclamation were its primary characteristics. There was a conscious effort to provide language that was at once worthy of Christian worship and at the same time suited to the needs of the late 20th century. The style of this first text was carried forward into all of the work of I.C.E.L. over the next decade. While some critics contended that reverence and sacrality had been sacrificed for contemporaneity and pastoral aims, others praised the texts for boldly attempting to find a language that owed its primary inspiration to the spirit of the Second Vatican Council and to a modern literary culture rather than to earlier centuries of English liturgical and popular prayer.

In January 1969, the Holy See issued an Instruction on the Translation of Liturgical Texts (D.O.L. 123), an important theoretical and practical document, which in its main lines took an approach to liturgical translation similar to the course followed in the first I.C.E.L. translations. Since 1969 the Instruction has been the principal guide followed by I.C.E.L. in its translation work. It is worth noting just a few of the guidelines found in that document.

1. " . . . it is not sufficient that a liturgical translation merely reproduce the expressions and ideas of the original text. Rather it must faithfully communicate to a given people, and in their own language, that which the Church by means of this given text originally intended to communicate to another people in another time. A faithful translation, therefore, cannot be judged on the basis of individual words: the total context of this specific act of communication must be kept in mind, as well as the literary form proper to the respective language."

2. "The translator must always keep in mind that the 'unit of meaning' is not the individual word but the whole passage. The translator must therefore be careful that the translation is not so analytical that it exaggerates the importance of particular phrases while it obscures or weakens the meaning of the whole."

3. "The prayer of the Church is always the prayer of some actual community, assembled here and now. It is not sufficient that a formula handed down from some other time or region be translated verbatim, even if accurately, for liturgical use. The formula translated must become the genuine prayer of the congregation and in it each of its members should be able to find and express himself or herself."

4. "It is to be noted that if any particular kind of quality is regarded as essential to a literary genre (for example, intelligibility of prayers when said aloud), this may take precedence over another quality less significant for communication (for example, verbal fidelity)."

The Instruction on Translation also gave encouragement to the provision of original texts in its concluding paragraph by stating: "Texts translated from another language are clearly not sufficient for the celebration of a fully renewed liturgy. The creation of new texts will be necessary. But translation of texts transmitted through the tradition of the Church is the best school and discipline for the creation of new texts so "that any new forms adopted should in some way grow organically from forms already in existence" (S.C., 23).

The Roman reform also gave explicit encouragement to new texts in the *praenotanda* of several of the revised liturgical books. See, for example, *Ordo exsequiarum*, no. 22,3 (D.O.L. 416, no. 3394).

In *The Roman Missal* or *Sacramentary* (1973) I.C.E.L. provided original opening prayers for Sundays and solemnities as alternatives to the translated opening prayers. Additional examples of original prayers as alternatives to the translated prayers or to provide for pastoral situations not covered in the Latin *editiones typicae* can be found in *Pastoral Care of the Sick: Rites of Anointing and Viaticum* (1982) and in the *Order of Christian Funerals* (1985).

The authority for the provision of liturgical texts, their preparation and publication, rests with the conferences of bishops. Ten English-speaking conferences—Australia, Canada, England and Wales, India, Ireland, New Zealand, Pakistan, Scotland, South Africa, and the United States of America—established I.C.E.L. to prepare texts for their consideration and possible decision. (The Philippines joined as a member conference in 1967.) Fifteen associate member conferences of bishops that use English as a secondary language also participated in the work. The Episcopal Board of I.C.E.L., made up of a bishop representing each of the eleven member conferences, must approve every final text prepared within I.C.E.L. by a two-thirds majority vote before a text can be submitted to the conferences of bishops. Each conference of bishops must also approve a text by a two-thirds majority and request from the Apostolic See a confirmation of its decision. Once that confirmation is given, the conference formally promulgates the text for use in its territory.

I.C.E.L. follows a process that involves wide consultation of the English-speaking bishops and their consultants. Most texts are first issued in consultation form and, after the results of the consultation have been studied and the text revised accordingly, they are issued in final form. Since 1967 I.C.E.L. has issued some one hundred texts and other supplementary and informational publications. Major texts issued include the *Rite of Baptism for Children* (1969); the *Rite of Marriage* (1969); the *Rite of Funerals* (1970); *The Roman Missal* (1973); the *Rite of Penance* (1974); the *Rite of Religious Profession* (1974); *Holy Communion and Worship of the Eucharist outside Mass* (1974); *The Liturgy of the Hours (1974-76); the Rite of Confirmation* (1975); *Ordination of Deacons, Priests, and Bishops* (1975); *Eucharistic Prayers for Masses of Reconciliation* and *Eucharistic Prayers for Masses with Children* (1975); the rite of *Dedication of a Church and an Altar* (1978); *The Roman Pontifical* (1978); *Pastoral Care of the Sick: Rites of Anointing and Viaticum* (1982); *Order of Christian Funerals* (1985); *Rite of Christian Initiation of Adults* (1986); *Book of Blessings* (1987); *Ceremonial of Bishops* (1989). These texts have been accepted with virtual unanimity by the churches of the English-speaking world, the only notable exception being *The Divine Office* (1974-75), the translation of the *Liturgia Horarum* sponsored by the hierarchies of Australia, England and Wales, and Ireland.

The sponsoring conferences of bishops directed I.C.E.L. to be attentive insofar as possible to the ecumenical dimensions of its work. I.C.E.L. has carried this on through its role as a founder and participant in the North American Consultation on Common Texts (C.C.T.), established in 1967, and through its role as a founder and participant in the International Consultation on Common Texts (I.C.C.T.), which carried out its work from 1969 to 1975, and its successor, the English Language Liturgical Consultation (E.L.L.C.), established in 1985. Through these organizations some common texts for the Christian churches in the English-speaking world have been achieved, especially for use in the celebration of the eucharist. These associations have also allowed for a sharing of information and occasionally of additional liturgical texts between the churches. In the same period in which I.C.E.L. began the work of preparing English liturgical texts for Roman Catholic use, a number of the other English-speaking Christian churches were preparing new service books incorporating new or revised rituals and a revised, more contemporary language of liturgical prayer. Some examples of these are Presbyterian church, U.S., *Worshipbook* (1970); the Evangelical Lutheran Church in America, *Lutheran Book of Worship* (1978); Episcopal Church, U.S., *The Book of Common Prayer* (1979); Church of Scotland, *The Book of Common Order* (1979); Church of England, *The Alternative Service Book* (1980); Anglican Church of Canada, *The Book of Alternative Services* (1985); United Methodist Church, U.S., *Book of Services* (1985);

Uniting Church in Australia, *Uniting in Worship* (1988).

In its opening paragraph the Instruction on Translation of Liturgical Texts stated that "after sufficient experiment and passage of time, all translations will need review." The founding conferences of I.C.E.L. understood that a vernacular liturgy would need to undergo periodic review and revision. In 1981 I.C.E.L. began such a process looking towards the systematic and careful revision of the nearly thirty liturgical books issued in final form up till that time. For some years a careful evaluation of the first group of I.C.E.L. texts had been carried on within I.C.E.L.. Comments on the style and diction of the I.C.E.L. texts, both laudatory and critical, were thoroughly discussed and analyzed. From the late 1970s a slight shift to a somewhat fuller, richer language began to take place. As the work of revision began in earnest in the early 1980s, I.C.E.L. reaffirmed its adherence to the 1969 Instruction on Translation and to contemporary texts suited to proclamation and singing in the liturgical assembly. At the same time, in light of the experience of the past fifteen to twenty years, I.C.E.L. also recognized that in some instances, for example, in the collects of *The Roman Missal*, a somewhat more elaborate, poetic style might be appropriate without in any sense violating the sound principles of the Instruction and concern for public proclamation.

The experience of the past two decades has been especially instructive in two respects.

First, far more study of the Latin texts of the post-conciliar reform has gradually been possible. A number of these Latin texts are new compositions; others were created through editing and rearranging existing Latin texts taken from a variety of historical sources. When the texts were issued, very little information was provided (beyond the work of A. Dumas, which appeared in the 1971 issues of *Notitiae* under the title "Les Sources du Missel Romain") on their provenance and on the methods used when texts were edited. This defect has over time been remedied, especially in the case of the *Missale Romanum*. In 1982, J. Deshusses and B. Darragon, *Concordances et tableaux pour l'etude des grand sacramentaires* (3 vols., Fribourg) appeared. And in the following year another valuable research tool, T. Schnitker and W. Slaby, eds., *Concordantia verbalia Missalis Romani: Partes euchologicae* (Munster) was published. In its revision of *The Roman Missal* texts, I.C.E.L. has spent considerable effort in studying the sources and background of the Latin texts and their vocabulary. The latter effort has led to the compilation of *A Lexicon of Terms in the Missale Romanum*, a 415-page resource instrument containing 647 entries dealing with the varied uses in the liturgical texts of such words as *communio, munus, mysterium, sacramentum, votum*

Second, the first English texts prepared by I.C.E.L. were done with considerations of public proclamation uppermost, but this was necessarily derived from a somewhat theoretical approach. There had been no tradition of Roman Catholic liturgical prayer in English. Experience gained over time with the first generation of texts exposed certain strengths and weaknesses. Valuable lessons were learned through experience with the first texts in such important areas as cadence, balance, register, phrasing, vocabulary, subordination, suitable lengths for spoken grammatical units—phrases, clauses, and sentences.

The work of revision has also allowed for the addition of a far greater number of original prayers in all the liturgical books, including the preparation of opening prayers related to the scripture readings for the revised Roman Missal. The work of providing a body of original

prayers opens the way to a deeply enriched tradition of contemporary English liturgical prayer, composed by gifted English writers for use by English-speaking people. The period of revision has made possible in addition a greater attention to the presentation and format of each book to ensure its pastoral application and effectiveness. Although such matters were dealt with in official statements implementing the reform (see, for example, *Liturgicae instaurationes*, no. 11 [D.O.L., 52, 529], *Ordo unctionis infirmorum eorumque pastoralis curae*, no. 38f [D.O.L., 410, no. 3358] and *Ordo exsequiarum*, no. 21 6 [D.O.L., 416, no. 3393]), it was not possible to put them fully into effect when there was a necessity to have the vernacular texts fairly rapidly. *Pastoral Care of the Sick: Rites of Anointing and Viaticum* (1982) and the *Order of Christian Funerals* (1985) are examples of the second phase of I.C.E.L.'s preparation of the liturgical books for the English-speaking churches.

Frederick R. McManus, "I.C.E.L. The First Years" (Washington, DC: I.C.E.L., 1981). Frederick R. McManus, *Thirty Years of Liturgical Renewal: Statements of the Bishops' Committee on the Liturgy* (Washington, DC: Secretariat, Bishops' Committee on the Liturgy, National Conference of Catholic Bishops, 1987).

JOHN R. PAGE

LITURGICAL THEOLOGY

Contemporary interest in liturgical theology is due to a number of factors, among which is the statement in the *Constitution on the Sacred Liturgy* of Vatican II that "the study of liturgy is to be ranked among the compulsory and major courses in seminaries and religious houses of studies; in theological faculties it is to rank among the principal subjects. It is to be taught under its theological, historical, pastoral, and juridical aspects" (S.C., 16). This statement endorsed the contemporary shift in liturgical methodology away from a study of rubrics to a study of the historical evolution of rites and their meaning (Anton Baumstark). Thus the liturgy constitution ratified and endorsed the important work of Alexander Schmemann, Cipriano Vagaggini, Irénée H. Dalmais, Salvatore Marsili and others whose work gives emphasis to the theological aspects of liturgical celebration.

While there was at that time, or even since, no agreed-upon meaning for "liturgical theology," at least two meanings were operative in the writings of these authors. First, liturgical theology was a reflection on the church's act of worship, seeking to draw out and explore for both catechesis and systematic theology, and in particular sacramental theology, the theological meaning of the liturgy as the actualization of the paschal mystery through an act of proclaiming and hearing the word and/or celebrating sacramental rituals. Second, liturgical theology meant using the liturgy as a source for systematic theology in the sense that the theological meaning of terms and concepts operative in liturgy were explored, for example, God, Christ, Spirit, redemption, salvation and sanctification. The uniqueness of liturgy as fundamentally a *ritual action* is understood here. The texts of the liturgy alone are not regarded as equivalent to other sources of positive theology (e.g., scripture, magisterium). Liturgical texts accompany ritual and symbolic gestures, and it is through this ritual whole that theological and spiritual meanings are disclosed. The fact that the church celebrates liturgy in order to experience the paschal mystery in a ritual *event*, suggests both the importance of liturgy as a source for theology and also the difficulty in delineating an acceptable method for engaging in liturgical theology.

Historical Overview

The phrase *legem credendi lex statuat supplicandi* (sometimes shortened in the literature to *lex orandi, lex credendi*) is generally ascribed to Prosper of Aquitaine. In its original setting the statement refers to the solemn intercessions of the Good Friday liturgy when the church prays for a variety of people who need the grace of God. The liturgical theology derived from this practice was understood to mean that this act of praying is proof against the semi-Pelagians about the absolute necessity of God's grace for salvation. Methodologically the point made is that the church's "law of belief" in the necessity of grace for salvation is evident in its "law of prayer."

That the church's *lex orandi* influenced patristic explanations of sacraments and theological terms is demonstrated in the pre-baptismal catecheses and the post-baptismal mystagogic catecheses of Cyril of Jerusalem, John Chrysostom, and Theodore of Mopsuestia where the meaning of liturgical gestures and texts finds an important role in such instructions. Both the flexibility of the church's rites at this point of its history as well as the variety in their explanation in these instructions, attests to the fact that variety marked both the church's *lex orandi* and its *lex credendi.* That the liturgy continued to function in the medieval period as a theological source, especially in how the rites were carried out (e.g., confirmation separated from baptism and anointing of the sick as the last anointing), is clear in the writings of Peter Lombard and Thomas Aquinas. At the same time, however, the actual celebration of liturgy in the sense of exploring the meaning of euchology, gesture and symbolic action grew less important as a source for theology in this period.

This separation was solidified after Trent when the Roman Catholic church sought to defend itself against the Reformers in both manuals of theology and the Tridentine catechism. Debated issues in liturgy and sacramental theology were emphasized in post-Tridentine treatises of sacramental theology, often to the point of eclipsing other, more traditional, aspects of theology. For example, establishing the fact of the real presence in the eucharist and that the eucharist was a real sacrifice took a prominent place in conventional treatises on the eucharist, as opposed to delineating the theology of the eucharist from the rite itself. As a result the anamnetic character of eucharist and the role of the Spirit in the act of eucharist was all but eclipsed. What enabled the Western church to reorient its theology and catechesis on liturgy and the sacraments away from these polemical preoccupations was the historical and comparative study of the church's rites and commentaries upon them, largely from the patristic era. This historical recovery, from the end of the 19th century and continuing through to the present, led to the restoration of *lex orandi, lex credendi* to a position of prominence in liturgical method. In addition to the work of liturgists and church historians there are papal statements which endorsed the importance of liturgy as a primary source for theology. Among these is the often cited statement of Pius XI that "the liturgy ... is the most important organ of the ordinary magisterium of the Church.... The liturgy is not the *didascalia* of this or that individual, but the *didascalia* of the Church" (*Quas primas*, Dec. 11, 1925, in *Acta Apostolicae Sedis 17* [1925] p. 603).

Contemporary Liturgical Theology

That liturgy needs to be understood as the enactment of an *event* (S. Marsili et al.) of the *church* (Lambert Beauduin, A. Schmemann, et al.) is central to a number of contemporary investigations of liturgical theology. In such explorations the component parts of liturgy in terms of symbol, language, gesture, and euchology, as well as the participation of the assembly in relation to a variety of liturgical ministers, are discussed with all their ambiguity. Since none of these components of liturgy can be reduced to a single meaning, it is not surprising to find variety and pluriformity in the liturgical theologies gleaned from such investigations.

While the study of liturgical theology cannot be reduced to a study of euchological texts, the important work of establishing critical editions of liturgical books (e.g., sacramentaries, antiphonaries, pontificals, etc.) has enabled contemporary liturgists to establish the antiquity, use and theological meaning of a wealth of liturgical texts. Textual studies of the eucharistic prayer such as that of Louis Bouyer (*Eucharist: The Theology and Spirituality of the Eucharistic Prayer*, Notre Dame, Univ. Press, 1968) have helped to recontextualize the notions of eucharistic presence and sacrifice so that the meaning of eucharistic *memorial* can be seen to be a primary element of the liturgical theology of the eucharist. Textual studies of the present sacramentary (e.g., by Pierre Jounel) help to establish the theological and anthropological foundation for what is contained in the present church's *lex orandi.*

With regard to the present liturgical reform, the theological meaning of liturgical rites is partially disclosed in the *General Instructions* for each reformed rite. Thus these instructions help shed light on the theological meaning of the contemporary liturgical rituals they accompany. In addition, the fact that the present reform of the liturgy has variety and option built into its very structure (as opposed to the rather fixed Tridentine rite) requires that the method employed in liturgical theology today seek to be comprehensive in terms of what is actually experienced in worship, as opposed to developing a liturgical theology that would be based on the euchology and rubrics of a fixed rite. At present most contemporary proposals for developing an appropriate method for liturgical theology respect the inherent variety of post-conciliar liturgical rituals.

Among the more important ground-breaking proposals from Europe for post-conciliar liturgical theology are those of Gerard Lukken and Albert Houssiau. For both authors, the primary source for liturgical theology is what is actually experienced in liturgy, not merely what the reformed rites say or describe. The particular contribution of North American liturgists to this discussion is the importance given to contemporary hermeneutics as well as the social sciences for developing a liturgical theology from actual liturgical celebrations.

While liturgists will commonly agree on the importance of the *lex orandi* to ground *lex credendi*, it should be pointed out that some authors understand a reciprocal relationship between these two terms, at least to some degree (Yngve Brilioth, Geoffrey Wainwright). Theology is seen to serve as a corrective to the church's rule of prayer where the forms of prayer are judged to be deficient and in need of correction. Therefore, some authors cite the important role which theology, based on scripture, played in the Reformers' concern to purify the medieval liturgy from unnecessary accretions that were far removed from a gospel purity. Here the church's theological tradition is seen to contribute to the adjustment of its liturgical tradition.

This insight has led other more recent authors to emphasize the critical function of liturgical theology in the sense that developments in contemporary theology can contribute to a critical assessment of the present liturgical reforms so that the ongoing agenda of liturgical indigenization and continued ritual reform can be based on a solid contemporary theology which would influence the ongoing development of liturgical rites (Angelus Haussling, Mary Collins, David Power).

Meanings of Liturgical Theology

At present one can establish at least three meanings of *lex orandi, lex credendi*: (1) A Theology of Liturgy, (2) A Theology Drawn from the Liturgy, and (3) Doxological Theology.

(1) *A Theology of Liturgy.* This describes what the liturgy is and what it does in terms of enacting in the present the reality of Christ's paschal mystery. One way to concretize this is to see the liturgy as a ritual enactment of the transhistorical event of Christ's dying and rising. As an act of memory it includes the manifestation of this unique saving act in word and gesture, myth and symbol, narrative and ritual. Understandings of the liturgy of the word as well as the central liturgical term *anamnesis* would be operative in this meaning of liturgical theology. In such an approach the historical study of rites can help establish what is constitutive and what is peripheral to the act of liturgy.

(2) *Theology Drawn from the Liturgy.* This concerns how the words and symbols of liturgy can be utilized as a generative source for developing systematic theology. This would mean that concepts in systematic theology can be fruitfully explored and described by data found in liturgical rites. Clear examples of this include how the rites, including general instructions, image the very being of God, how they describe the work of Christ, how they image the Church and how they reflect our need for grace as experienced through liturgy. One of the desired results of the kind of liturgical study called for in S.C. 16 would be met if the liturgy is thus mined for the way it deals with these central aspects of Christian faith and theology.

For example, if one were to reflect on the way Christ is imaged in the liturgy one would come up with a variety and pluriformity of usages. Such a study would necessarily refer to our need for Christ and for liturgy since most usually the rites both image Christ and, at the same time, describe our need for Christ's salvation (e.g., redemption, sanctification, forgiveness, reconciliation). Here the disciplines of Christian anthropology and Christology would converge in the act of liturgy. In addition, the various images for the church found in liturgical rites would deepen our appreciation of how the church is actualized in the liturgy and how local churches are united with each other through the act of worship. The point here would be to utilize liturgy as a source for more than sacramental theology. All systematic theology is intrinsically connected to the act of worship.

This understanding relates to the distinction between symbolic and technical language in theology. If the languages of liturgy (speech, symbol, gesture, etc.) are essentially symbolic, one needs to be aware that these modes of expression will be found wanting when one attempts to delineate the meaning of rites in the more technical language of dogmatic assertions or contemporary systematics. However this itself may well be an important contribution to the ways in which contemporary liturgical and systematic theologians approach their work.

(3) *Doxological Theology*. This understanding of liturgical theology has been more hinted at than delineated in full (Harvey Guthrie, L. Bouyer). In such an understanding, systematic theology would have a doxological cast to it, in the sense of thanks, praise and acknowledgment. It would also reflect the belief of the theologian. This is to suggest that the very nature of theology ought to be oriented to praise and the acknowledgment of God in prayer and reflection as opposed to a theology which tries to define, or even describe, sacred realities. What is operative in this approach to theology is the important notion of *mystery*, that through both theology and liturgy the mystery of God is acknowledged and experienced.

One application of this approach to the theological enterprise in general would be to require theology to be both reflective of the act of faith experienced in the liturgy as well as rigorously scientific, since this experience leads to second order reflection in theological discourse. Related to this is the understanding that in doing theology one expresses what one experiences and believes and in delineating this as theology one hands on what one believes is for the good of others, particularly in developing their own faith. Such an approach involves the whole person in the act of theologizing. It relates to self-appropriation in theology of what is described in theological terms. This kind of theology would emphasize notions of conversion and growth in the faith as well as growth in understanding.

The Law of Prayer and Belief Enacted

The present agenda of some liturgical theologians (A. Houssiau, G. Lukken, M. Collins) has also influenced the way contemporary liturgical theologians want to expand the *lex orandi, lex credendi* equation to include a third, viz., *lex agendi*. At this stage of liturgical study (often termed the critical function of liturgiology) we can note at least two meanings of this *lex agendi*.

Actual Celebrations As a Theological Source. Since liturgical rituals are *enacted* rites, a contemporary method for studying them needs to be developed that takes seriously what is experienced in actual celebrations rather than merely what is written in liturgical texts and rubrical directions. Here the use of methods from the social sciences is crucial in delineating a successful method of liturgical observation and reflection on the act of worship. In this framework, in addition to asking the question "what is experienced in actual liturgical rites," those involved in preparing, enacting and critiquing the liturgy ask a second question as well: whether what is offered and experienced in liturgy reflects the faith vision which is enunciated in the general instructions as well as in the rites themselves.

For example, by its nature liturgical ritual calls for restraint in the doing of worship. Individual pieties and idiosyncrasies recede in order to allow the communal faith vision and experience of God inherent in the liturgy to come forth. Thus the corollary of using actual celebrations as a theological source is to evaluate the adequacy of the liturgical celebrations in what is said, done, experienced and enacted liturgically.

Liturgy and Spirituality. A second meaning of *lex agendi* concerns the living out in life of the implications of liturgy. This influence of liturgy on life is an aspect of liturgical participation traditionally understood to be constitutive of the act of worship. This may be called a *liturgical spirituality* where the act of engaging in liturgical prayer is seen to have implications for the living of the Christian life (i.e., the life of virtue).

This relation of life to liturgy has been given added stimulus in contemporary discussion by liberation theologians who examine the ethical demands of the Christian faith. How shall one live the Christian life as set forth in the teachings of Jesus and as intended to be experienced in liturgy, especially in situations that are either indifferent to such a life or actually inhibitive of it? The challenge to live what is celebrated can mean critiquing and then revitalizing social structures of oppression. It can also mean emphasizing individual commitments to reform oneself as well as structures of society.

This understanding of the *lex agendi* emphasizes how liturgy influences life lived outside the ritual itself in terms of the commitments in life which liturgical participation necessarily implies. Where formerly the notion of *ex opere operato* and *operantis* stressed the correct enactment of the liturgical ritual in order to ensure the effective manifestation and appropriation of the mystery celebrated, here *lex agendi* would emphasize the *operato* and *operantis* of liturgy to insure the appropriation of the mystery of liturgy outside the liturgy as well. Hence, the *lex agendi* aspect of liturgical theology puts emphasis on the implications of doing liturgy.

A Method for Liturgical Theology

It has been established that to have an adequate liturgical theology one must examine the component parts of the liturgical rites in terms of texts, symbols, actions and gestures in light of the times and places of the communities which engaged in them in the past or engage in them in the present. This is because liturgical rites are adequately understood and interpreted only in relation to their experienced context. Hence one could say that liturgical context is "text," in the sense that context provides the source (or "text") for developing liturgical theology. Here *context* can mean at least three things.

First, it is the historical evolution of a given liturgical rite studied to determine its origin, component parts, and historical variations. The purpose of this study is to uncover the theological meanings which the rite has traditionally conveyed and to distinguish between essential and peripheral aspects of the rite. Second, it is an examination of the present reformed rites undertaken to determine whether the contemporary celebration of these rites in specific contexts expresses what is actually envisioned in the rites. This means examining liturgical acts as a whole so that words, symbols and gestures are interpreted in relation to each other. It also means trying to determine the extent to which the setting for liturgy, e.g., assembly itself or environment, and the conducting of liturgy, e.g., types of music and forms of participation, facilitates and enhances the assembly's appropriation and understanding of the prayers, symbols and gestures of the liturgy. The third notion of context shifts attention to the critical function of liturgical theology. Here the contemporary cultural and theological context of liturgical celebration is noted in order to determine the adequacy of the present liturgical rites and to explore ways of adapting them to a variety of changing ecclesial and cultural contexts. These three meanings of "context" need to be expounded.

(1) Historical Evolution of Rites

Part of the context of every liturgical rite is provided by a study of the historical evolution of liturgical forms and, at least implicitly, by the evolution of liturgical theologies which have accompanied or accompany their use. The kind of historical investigation envisioned here differentiates those aspects of ritual worship that are essential from those that are peripheral so that this investigation can underscore the importance of the evolution of liturgical forms and the theologies which comprise liturgical tradition. The Church's actual liturgical tradition cannot be determined without such historical study and reflection.

The historical study of liturgical rites and forms requires that the investigator review how liturgical forms and rites changed and developed in relation to the prevailing sociocultural ambience. Apart from this, rites cannot be fully understood. This approach to liturgical method draws on the pioneering work of the editors of critical editions of liturgical sources who have compiled and edited a wealth of liturgical texts. It also draws upon the work of liturgical theologians such as L. Bouyer (*op. cit.*) who compiled a wealth of eucharistic texts and commented on their theological meaning. However, it takes these approaches a step further to interpret this data in light of their lived religious and cultural contexts. In this connection the work of Herman Wegman (*Christian Worship in East and West*, New York: Pueblo, 1985) is a move in this direction. Wegman introduces most chapters by describing the liturgical evolution of a period in light of its contemporary "historical" and "cultural data."

This approach demands that a number of issues be raised about the data derived from historical research. First, what texts, symbols and gestures were used in the liturgy and who spoke or participated in them? To what extent did the assembly participate in liturgy through movement, symbolic action, singing and speaking? Second, what kinds of sources were used to compose the liturgy? Was the biblical foundation the essential source for the imagery and metaphors used in ritual language or were the evolving rites influenced or even controlled by contemporary theological controversies or prevailing currents in contemporary spirituality? Third, how do the various components of liturgical rites relate to one another and how is each component interpreted in relation to the others? This question acknowledges the various genres of communication which comprise the act of worship: proclamation of texts, gestural use of symbols, participation in song, etc. Fourth, one must ask how accurately the descriptions of liturgical rites, e.g., in patristic sources or *ordos*, reflect what was actually celebrated, lest more weight be given to how a rite *was supposed to be celebrated* as opposed to how it was actually carried out and experienced.

In addition to studying liturgical history and liturgical tradition in light of the contemporary cultural and sociopolitical situation, such an investigation needs to study the relationship between liturgy and contemporary theology on the one hand, and between liturgy and contemporary spirituality on the other. This shift from an exclusive concern with ritual evolution enhances liturgical study because it is a move in the direction of recontextualization, and therefore toward being faithful to the way actual liturgical sources functioned. This approach is also necessary in order to make appropriate judgments about liturgical theology since judgments need grounding in the empirical data of the liturgical event.

Related to this consideration is the notion of the normativity of liturgical tradition. Contemporary liturgical rites have histories that need to be considered when interpreting or critiquing them. Liturgical tradition ought to ground contemporary reform and guide future adaptation in order that what is presently experienced be truly part of an organic development. It should be made clear, however, that "normative" does not mean determinative so that liturgical tradition alone, including historical study, assesses the adequacy of the present rites or the ongoing evolution of rites. Normativity means that a core of elements such as texts, gestures and symbols, especially in sacraments, have perdured in the church's liturgical tradition and that this composite of elements may be said to constitute the church's normative celebration of a given sacrament or liturgy. However, in the present or future evolution of a given rite the exact texts or gestures discovered from history need not be imitated word for word or rubric for rubric. Liturgical tradition supplies a "genetic vision of the present" (R. Taft), and it is this genetic vision of the liturgy which is normative. Tradition does not determine *a priori* what should comprise contemporary ritual.

For example, we can note the perdurance in liturgical tradition of certain symbolic actions such as washing in water for baptism and the importance attached to the blessing prayer over the baptismal water. This evidence can be used to correct those rites in which the ample use of symbol or blessing text has been neglected. Thus liturgical tradition may be said to have provided the means

whereby the preconciliar liturgy, which had minimalized sacramental liturgy to "matter" and "form," was changed in the light of liturgical tradition to maximize symbols and to expand on the use of blessing prayers. In baptism this means the preference of immersion over infusion, and blessing the water at every baptism with an extensive blessing prayer instead of using water blessed once yearly at the Easter vigil. This normative tradition alone, however, cannot provide an adequate contemporary ritual. Other factors must contribute to the development as well.

An essential component of the present liturgical context is determined by liturgical tradition, part of which is discoverable by reviewing liturgical history. At the same time, however, it is important to emphasize that tradition is not merely something from the past. Tradition is the present shaped by past experience. The present is integral to tradition. Thus the conserving function of ritual in terms of Christian identity is preserved: liturgy and liturgical theology are not created *ab ovo* in each age. They are products of historical evolution. At the same time, the creative function of ritual is preserved as well. Evolution involves ongoing theological and pastoral reform and renewal.

(2) Postconciliar Liturgical Reforms

One of the chief aims of the present liturgical reform enunciated in the liturgy constitution is to provide easily comprehended rites that facilitate full and active participation (S.C., 14, 21). A key issue is to determine to what extent the present rites as implemented and practiced facilitate popular participation and comprehension. A second key issue is to determine to what extent contemporary celebrations of liturgy conform to the revised rites themselves. The method proposed here that context is "text" can help this investigation because appropriate participation cannot be measured merely by determining that a correct rite has been published. It requires investigation into actual celebrations of liturgy.

While the word "performance" has the negative connotation of leaving liturgical communities passive during a rite, nevertheless it does point out that how a rite is conducted has an important bearing on how the liturgy engages the assembly's participation. It is certainly an anomaly that for centuries the text proposed as the church's norm for eucharistic worship and understanding, the Roman Canon, was not audible to the assembly and was not proclaimed in the vernacular. Performance clearly mitigated the kind of comprehension and full, active participation which the liturgy demands. Thus the distinction between reformed rite and context is important since contemporary liturgical contexts may well mitigate comprehension and participation, the very things which the Vatican II reform sought to achieve. Factors in the liturgical context which influence performance, and thus participation in and comprehension of the liturgy, include the physical setting in which the liturgy takes place, the arrangement of the assembly and the worship environment, the use of music, participation in ministries and symbolic actions.

Some examples. (a) With regard to environment, while the Roman Canon and new eucharistic prayers use the pronoun "we" to articulate the prayer of the whole assembly, the arrangement of the assembly can speak more about individuals separated from each other in private prayer than about communal worship. (b) If the texts for the music sung at the communion rite refer to individual reception or to adoration, then the music in which the people participate will reflect messages at variance with those proper to the eucharistic rite at this point which emphasizes the communal sharing in the eucharist to build up the church as the body of Christ. (c) The performance of the ritual by a single priest celebrant instead of by different people assuming the varied liturgical roles envisioned and demanded by the present rites speaks a message at variance with the notion of the church at prayer clearly articulated in the texts and the general instructions of the revised rites. (d) Hearing this text proclaimed from the sanctuary of a mammoth cathedral provides an experience far different from that of hearing the same text in a parish church, in a small chapel or at a domestic liturgy. Related to this is whether the assembly assumes a kneeling or standing posture while the anaphora is proclaimed. While the recitation of the canon in Latin was an obvious barrier to comprehending the meaning of the gathering of the church around the altar, one could argue that today some contemporary liturgical contexts make full comprehension of these same texts impossible precisely because of the way in which contexts, e.g., physical arrangements, so influence how texts are heard.

Another aspect of how context functions to help interpret liturgical texts is found in the postconciliar use of the scriptures in the liturgy. Liturgists have rightly pointed out the theological and liturgical value of the word as that which reveals the mystery of salvation and makes it operative for contemporary communities to hear it. For the word to be interpreted properly the context of the liturgical action must be part of the hermeneutic that is applied to the texts proclaimed. This builds on the premise that to choose texts for a lectionary means displacing them by taking them out of their native context in a particular book of the Bible, which has its own context among other biblical books, and assigning them as appropriate readings for a given liturgical gathering. Scripture readings proclaimed at liturgy have a life independent of the canon of scripture.

This is not to suggest that the original setting of a scripture reading is not important or that historical, redactional, source, and literary criticism are unimportant for interpretation. But the additional factor needed for proper interpretation is the liturgical context in which a given text is heard. Thus a key issue here is the hearing and appropriation of a scriptural text as experienced at liturgy.

Context is an essential factor in understanding texts but it also follows that the present liturgical rites, including the introductory instructions, lectionary readings, prayer texts, gestures and symbols function as norms and critique the inadequate *contexts* of contemporary liturgical celebration. An example of the normative value of the reformed rites concerns the primacy of the assembly as the primary symbol for all liturgy and locus for all liturgical celebrations. The very fact that the assembly is continually referred to in the General Instruction and throughout the present eucharistic rite signals a shift from the Tridentine missal which was rubrically self-conscious and oriented toward the actions of sanctuary ministers only, especially the priest. Therefore the emphasis on actualizing the assembly's role in the contemporary liturgy and understanding liturgical ministers as functioning in communion with and on behalf of the assembly, signals a shift in how the liturgy is to be experienced and understood. This same evidence also signals a shift in the liturgical theology of the eucharist away from objective presence in the elements to communal transformation through the eucharistic action.

As another example, the fact that every revised ritual states where and how the roles of reader and deacon are to function liturgically is itself a theological statement about how the church is to be imaged in liturgy—through a variety of roles serving the assembled community. Liturgical theologians rightly capitalize on such directives as indications of a paradigm shift in ministry away from the medieval absorption of liturgical roles into that of the priest. When these ministers do not function in the liturgy and their roles are again assumed by one, or even by a few, the texts of the reformed liturgy function as appropriate critiques of these contexts. The reformed liturgy is normative inasmuch as it shows that inadequate contexts need to be corrected in the light of what the rituals disclose about the ecclesiology of liturgy. One reason why some texts are simply not "heard" is that some liturgical contexts (environment, music, ministries, performance) are simply not congruent with the reformed rites.

The normative value of the reformed rites also indicates that one's interpretation of texts used liturgically is not relative. Interpretation and meaning are grounded in revised rites which are bearers of a rich liturgical and theological tradition. Hence liturgical rites must be interpreted in a way that respects their nature as bearers of theological meanings disclosed in liturgical celebration. In addition, the employment of a research method which attempts to determine what actually occurs at liturgy and how what occurs is appropriated by the gathered community, can help assess the extent to which the revised rites are truly normative in the sense outlined above. It can tell us whether or not the envisioned liturgical reform has taken place.

Poignant examples of facets of liturgical tradition that have been restored in the present sacramental rites and which need evaluation are the proclamation of the word and the act of preaching. If one of the purposes of the lectionary reform is to provide a greater variety in the texts heard and preached, one could ask how much variety is experienced in the texts proclaimed, for example at sacramental celebrations of baptism. Further, one needs to ask at sacramental liturgies how well homilies relate the scripture readings to the enactment to follow in sacrament. One could also ask to what extent preaching is biblically based now as opposed to before the reform and whether its content is primarily didactic or moralistic.

Inquiry about the implementation of the post-conciliar liturgy in general should include determination of the extent to which variety and option mark actual celebrations. In the eucharist this means inquiry about the introduction to the liturgy, the formula for the penitential rite, texts for preface and eucharistic prayers, and texts for the dismissal rite including solemn blessings and prayers over the people. Are some options never used? Is there sufficient variety in comments, introductions and intercessions? Are these freely composed texts liturgically appropriate and theologically accurate? With regard to the liturgical reform in general one could ask about the people's positive and negative reaction to the rites they experience, whether there is resistance to further change, and if so, why, and how people view the relationship between liturgy and devotion.

The investigation into context is advanced here in two ways. First, it requires that liturgical units be interpreted in relation to each other and that the whole liturgical event be regarded as an essential component in interpreting liturgical texts, symbols and gestures. Crucial in this first stage is the actual liturgical performance. Second, the postconciliar rites set a standard and measure against which to evaluate present liturgical practice. This suggests that the rites as revised present a minimum standard for the celebration of liturgy which is marked by option, flexibility and direct relationship to the given liturgical assembly. In addition, the current reform presents a contemporary theological vision that is to be understood and imaged both in liturgical celebration and in liturgical theology.

(3) Critical Liturgical Theology and Indigenization

As noted above, the orientation of the contemporary liturgical reform toward adaptation and indigenization (S.C., 37-40) must be kept in mind when considering the normative value of the revised rites because they present a basis from which to work toward indigenization of the liturgy. They represent a necessary first step in an ongoing task. It is important that liturgical theology be developed in light of a liturgical reform that is to be regarded as ongoing. This is also important because ritual changes usually reflect shifts in theology and spirituality.

There is a reciprocity between liturgy and theology in ritual evolution inasmuch as changed liturgical rites most often reflect developments in theology. This means that it may be a liturgical anachronism to reintroduce an ancient liturgical practice or rite simply because it is well attested in the tradition. Critical liturgiology must assess the adequacy of the present reformed rites in relation to tradition, contemporary theology, church teaching and present pastoral needs. This assessment implicitly acknowledges that the provisional nature of liturgical forms, despite their importance, invites a critical consideration of them.

Recent advances in ecclesiology, Christology, Trinity, eschatology and anthropology need to be incorporated into this study and revision. For example, implicit in the theological and liturgical agenda of indigenization is the importance given to the local church in post-conciliar ecclesiology. Some of the growing pains of liturgical indigenization correspond to the tensions also being experienced in ecclesiology in general. Another example is the crucial issue of theological language and names for God which needs to be dealt with squarely in the ongoing revision, especially because of the formative nature of liturgical prayer.

A clear example of how knowledge of

liturgical tradition, linked with contemporary theology, helps cast a critical eye on the liturgical reforms, concerns the way the Holy Spirit is imaged in the reformed liturgy. One can legitimately criticize the present liturgical rites of the West for an absence of an adequate pneumatology in its euchology and theology of liturgy. Advances in scripture study and in the theology of the person and work of the Holy Spirit could help revise Western euchology which is primarily christocentric. Thus theology would influence the liturgy and help liturgical theology to progress.

An example of how liturgists use liturgical tradition to critique the present liturgy is their criticism that all the new eucharistic prayers of the Roman rite use the same structure, lack an adequate theology of creation, and make limited use of acclamations during the anaphoras, especially in comparison to many Eastern formulas. Recent research, some of which was undertaken in an ecumenical framework, indicates that variety in anaphoral structures is possible. Furthermore, present biblical and liturgical research reveals the need to re-evaluate and to make more precise the commonly held assumption that there is a direct relationship between Jewish blessing prayers and Christian anaphoras.

Liturgical pluriformity and variety from country to country and continent to continent would help meet the needs of worshippers who differ in terms of self-expression, patterns of bodily involvement and habits of singing because of their differing cultural backgrounds. The advantage of the eucharistic rite developed in Zaïre, for example, is that it is not concerned simply with texts. Rather it takes into consideration the readiness of the participants to participate in many verbal and nonverbal ways, particularly through bodily movement.

This aspect of critical liturgiology and ongoing indigenization is necessarily open-ended because of the nature of the criteria for liturgical indigenization which includes contemporary theology, liturgical tradition and pastoral practice. Because research in all three fields is ongoing, liturgical indigenization must be regarded as an ongoing task. In addition, indigenization to meet specific liturgical needs can be achieved only in specific ecclesial groups. This makes the determination of specific cultural contexts crucial in the process of establishing new liturgical rites. The agenda of indigenization also requires that liturgical theology be attentive to acculturation in theology and liturgy, because the variety found there is largely dependent on variations in the cultural or societal context.

To state that liturgical context is "text" involves shifting attention from the components of liturgical rites alone, i.e., euchology, rubrics, selection of readings, etc., to a consideration of how they are experienced and understood in the actual context of liturgical celebration. The method outlined here is intended to recontextualize liturgical sources and thus provide a more adequate approach to liturgical theology.

Mary Collins, "Liturgical Methodology and the Cultural Evolution of Worship in the United States," *Worship* 49 (February 1975) 85-102. Karl Federer, *Liturgie und Glaube. Eine theologiegeschichtliche Untersuchung, (Paradosis 4)* Legem credendi lex statuat supplicandi (Freiburg: Paulusverlag, 1950). Angelus Haussling, "Die kritische Funktion der Liturgiewissenschaft," in H.B. Meyer, ed., *Liturgie und Gesellschaft* (Innsbruck, 1970): 103-130. Albert Houssiau, "The Rediscovery of the Liturgy by Sacramental Theology," *Studia Liturgica* 15 (1982-83) 158-177. Aidan Kavanagh, *On Liturgical Theology* (New York: Pueblo, 1984). Gerard Lukken, "La liturgie comme lieu théologique irremplacable," *Questions Liturgiques* 56 (1975): 97-112. Salvatore Marsili, "Teologia Liturgica," in *Nuovo Dizionario di Liturgia*, eds., D. Sartore and A.M. Triacca (Rome: Edizioni Paoline, 1984): 1508-1525. David N. Power, "Cult to Culture: The Liturgical Foundation of Theology," *Worship* 54 (November 1980): 482-495. Klemens Richter, ed. *Liturgie—Ein vergessenes*

Thema der Theologie? (Freiburg: Basel, 1987). Alexander Schmemann, *Introduction to Liturgical Theology*, trans., Ashleigh Moorhouse (London: The Faith Press, 1966). Geoffrey Wainwright, *Doxology, The Praise of God in Worship, Doctrine and Life. A Systematic Theology* (New York: Oxford University Press, 1980).

KEVIN W. IRWIN

LITURGICAL TIME, THEOLOGY OF

Introduction: Time in Religion and Science

Speculations about time have occupied thinkers for centuries. Scientists and mathematicians, social scientists, philosophers and theologians have reasoned about time, considering categories such as measure of change, motion, duration, infinity, space-time continuum, direction of time, consciousness of time, absolute and relational time, creation, free will, and eschatology. Yet time remains essentially a mystery: "What is time then? If nobody asks me, I know: but if I were desirous to explain it to one that should ask me, plainly I know not" (Augustine, *Confessions* XI, 14).

Scientific and religious approaches to time differ both in scope and in the attempt to join the eternal with the ever-changing expression of being.

Religion, like philosophy, seeks to comprehend all of reality, but is not content with expressing ideas about reality. Religious life aims not at thinking about reality, but at apprehending it through worship, prayer, revelation, etc., activities that transcend the subject-object dualism.

Religious experience shifts people from isolated onlookers to united participants. Worship is more a "looking with understanding"—a contemplative union—rather than a knowledge through observation. Thus, the experience of liturgical time is a certain disengagement from measured time, a focus on eternity present in time.

Scientific theories of time—absolute or relative—are intrinsically linked to space. Even Newtonian physics which posits an absolute time, measured independently of space, links time with distance. Science, as well as philosophies rooted therein, treat time as extrinsic.

While the liturgy takes place in a measured and extended time-space manifold, it is not bounded by either extrinsic time or space.

Abraham Heschel in his essay, "The Sabbath," sharply separates time from space. Space, he asserts, can be divided and dominated; territory can be acquired. Space belongs to the earthly kingdom. Time, however, remains indivisible and undominated; it cannot be amassed.

Human physicality makes us rivals *vis a vis* space: we cannot occupy the same exact space. Time, however, can be shared; living in the same time makes us contemporaries, not rivals. While our bodies occupy space, our spirits live in time. Time concerns God's kingdom; the reign of God is a matter of time—an inscape of eternity in time.

Vatican II's ecclesiology raised the image of God's pilgrim people to consciousness—an image related more to time than space. Spatial notions, e.g., parish and diocese as geographic divisions, were subordinated and contextualized by this dominating image. Even the Pauline notion of the body of Christ bespeaks more a temporal notion than a spatial one. This spiritual reality implies growth and change; becoming is an intrinsic movement. Recent church architectural studies demonstrate a shift from a holy place as a tabernacle for God's localized presence to a place for congregational worship, an experience of God in temporal action.

Time and History in Society

The apprehension and measurement of time in ancient cultures depended on events occurring in time. What happened in time qualified humanity's inescapable involvement with and consciousness of time; time considered abstractly mattered less than meaning articulated in time. Children experience time in this way and this approach holds for adults in certain circumstances.

If moderns image time as an imaginary line, it is the self which locates the past behind and the future ahead. In contrast, ancient Jews viewed sacred events, e.g., creation, exodus, giving of the covenant, etc., as fixed points with history as a pilgrimage movement of a people. The event, not the self, determines time. Ancestors, having passed these markers, were ahead on the journey. People of the future would be coming up behind on the pilgrimage.

Since modern societies hold that history is irreversible, people have freedom and responsibility to shape both time and history. For the Christian believer, time and history belong to God whose love is revealed in the unfolding plan of salvation and whose promise is assured in Christ. God completes time and history in a movement of love.

In contrast to the Christian belief system, viewing eternity as the ripening fruit of time, secular approaches conceive of time as a relentless succession of moments. Aware of freedom, but lacking a faith that sees time as meaningful and redemptive, the secularized modern must achieve salvation alone. Not bonded in a society of shared beliefs, empty time can be filled by stoic resignation, flight through instant gratification, authoritarianism, etc.

In a society dominated by rational, enlightened ideas where autonomous action in history is the rule, worship will be pushed off into a private sphere, becoming a monument to a past age. Worship may be rejuvenated through rational principles, bathed in ethical sensitivity or political action. Worship becomes an event of control, rather than a response to God's revelation in time.

Sacred and Symbolic Time

A. Sacred Time

Beginning and ending with the eternal, religion tries to grasp the momentary, every-changing mode of existence in eternity's light. Attitudes towards time reflect attitudes about the meaning of life. If, for example, time is viewed as timeless instants expressing the eternal, then history itself is meaningless.

The Judeo-Christian tradition views time linearly as a sequence of moments related to God's plan, while other traditional religions view time as cyclical. If time's course is cyclic, then re-presentation of the original cosmogony periodically regenerates time: the past is wiped out and a new beginning ensues. In all religions, however, temporal moments (time as timely) are related in varied and complex ways to the timeless (time as eternity).

The Jewish scriptures speak powerfully of temporal time, i.e., history is progressive, guided by God from the moment of creation to its culmination. At the end of finite time, God's purpose will be fulfilled. Jewish faith, characterized by expectant messianism, also holds that within each moment of time, even in mundane history, there is the presence of eternity. Hence fulfillment resides in kernel within moments of time.

Christianity also relates time to eternity; timely time is rooted in eternity. Christian tradition structures history around the manifestations of the eternal in the temporal, primordially the Christ-event. In the gospel of John absolute eternal reality is present in the temporal for those who believe. Timely significance is transcended.

History for Jews and Christians alike is the locus of God's action. Time is bracketed by its beginning at creation and its end, the parousia; in between stretches the line of God's redemptive activity. In the Christian tradition the focal center is the life and work of Jesus Christ, historical and eternal, giving Christianity the tension between the already and the not-yet. With Christ the new age to come has begun (Eph 1:21; 2:7).

B. Symbolic Time

Time serves an organizing function for the symbols in a religious system. Time is intimately tied to the development of some religious symbols and ritual performance, e.g., spring festivals. Time relates dynamically to the religious social bond, e.g., in celebration social relations are articulated. Time relates also to the intentional life of the individual, e.g., subjective symbols announce public meaning.

While time does organize chronology (calendar), symbolic time is perceived differently from the succession of mere chronological units of regular periodicity. The uneven distribution of religious festivals throughout a calendar year, e.g., shows that something different from "clock time" is at work.

In their complex temporal features, religious symbols organize and articulate relationships within history. The public symbol of time—time as a mode of human becoming—defines transformation systems. A new intentional social reality is generated within time and what is created is a processional social reality that has transformative power.

Liturgical Time

A. Biblical Time

Words for time, biblically understood, make time distinctive for the believer. Two basic views of time appear in the scriptures. Quantifying measurement of time (related to scientific speculation) stands in contrast to qualifying time (related to history of religions).

Quantifying time. Quantifying measurement correlates one time with others on the basis of passage of moving objects (sun, moon, etc.) or a recurring routine.

Temporal experience is handled analogically. One understands a unique moment in terms of something universal.

For example, cult was interested in time as quantum—cyclic repetition of special days. Legislation for an historicized Passover festival (Exod 13:3-10) calibrated to natural phenomena commands remembrance of historical significance, but moves to the continuance through time of this event "year after year." The unique event is managed and regularized. Quantification moves from time as history to the discovery of meaning above or beyond history.

Quantification can take place by comparing human experience with an exemplary standard; time is objectivized. If this is a "day of wrath," certain consequences follow for this quantified time. Behavior, appropriate to the time period, is aided by a set of rules.

Qualified time. Qualified time views each day and moment as unique. Purposiveness and distinctiveness are hallmarks of this experience. If quantified time relates one day to another through cultic cycles or regulated appropriate behavior, qualified time sees each moment as a possible decisive confrontation with God.

Past and future are related analogically, being measured by the now; the *instant* becomes the viewpoint. Biblical prophecy, the appropriate response of an imminent future, awakens God's people in a moment of crisis. Sacred history, a living memory of God's saving plan, stirs up trust and hope. In either movement, the present is unique, relating to a past and future.

B. The Liturgy's Use of Time

Liturgy's time-specific texts show a preference for the present. While liturgical celebration makes remembrance of the past a present unfolding of the future, the NT concentrates on the fullness of time; in Christ Jesus the eternal word is present in time. Church seasons and feasts and daily prayer situate the Christian through time-oriented texts.

The invitatory psalm verse, "If today you hear God's voice, harden not your hearts," begins the cycle of daily prayer. Easter's "This is the day the Lord has made" resonates with the Christmas antiphon "Today Christ is born." Paul's admonition "You know what hour it is, how it is full time now for you to wake from sleep" (Rom 13:11) begins the Advent cycle and "Even now, says the Lord, return to me with all your heart" (Joel 2:21) is the opening proclamation on Ash Wednesday.

The liturgy is thus time-centered rather than space-centered. It expresses not only time as timeless, intimations of an unfolding eternity, but also time as timely, a mediation of God's presence in the moment. Time is intrinsic to the mode of becoming; in liturgy time is the mode of sanctification.

The liturgy's understanding of time, grounded in incarnational theology, takes seriously God's communication of the definitive word in Jesus become flesh. Jesus remains present to God's people in all time through the Spirit outpoured.

"Christ yesterday and today, the beginning and the end, Alpha and Omega, all time belongs to him and all the ages; to him be glory and power through every age for ever" runs the proclamation at the Easter vigil. God's word to humanity does not change; it remains forever the same, yet is experienced as a timely reality.

Some conclusions can be drawn at this point.

1. Time, understood philosophically or scientifically, names events as before or after. Thus, temporal structures insert human beings into narrativity. For Christians who believe that God is manifest in human events, God is present in humanity's time. Christian life is an insertion into sacred narrativity, both for the individual and the collectivity. The liturgy rehearses that sacred story, not as a pious memory, but as a living reality.

2. The Christian attends to the present moment as revelatory (time as timeless), but within the context of sacred narrativity (time as timely). The present becomes meaningful in relationship to a past and future. Not only is the individual's experience important, but also the social body's experience. The liturgy announces God as humanity's future, already experienced mysteriously in the present.

3. The liturgy also deals with quantified time, but not *per se*. The cyclic repetition of festivals, quantitatively determined, provides an understanding of and perspective on present reality—time as qualified. This symbolic time generates a future and calls for appropriate behavior. Liturgy shapes the Christian stance in the world.

4. Within liturgical celebration itself memory and hope become critical. The commemoration of the historic Christ-event leading to the parousia provides symbolic images in timely time. Memory becomes active so that commemoration is not only of a past, but a past present. Hope becomes enlivened to the point of shaping a future present. The present reality of life in Christ—the fullness of time—is celebrated and renewed.

5. In the liturgical celebration, the psychological arrow of time points in two directions. Like several Eastern eucharistic prayers, that of Basil of Caesarea prays: " ... remembering his holy sufferings, and his resurrection from the dead and his return to heaven ... and his glorious and fearful coming again...." Liturgical *anamnesis* in this context defies the scientific arrow of time—we remember the future.

While scientists and philosophers would bristle at the assertion, it provides a way of viewing liturgical time. The active remembering of the fullness of the present encompasses both past and future. Those who have gone before us are ahead of us; liturgy remembers the future present.

In liturgy the punctiform present is not what exists, but the presence of eternity in time, the communication and regeneration of the Christ-life in timely time.

C. Feasts and Rituals

Despite some NT passages' ambivalence toward feasts and seasons (cf. Col 2:1), the Christian scriptures attest to the fact that Christian faith was articulated in temporal terms. Christ, however, has fulfilled the meaning of all time-bound ritual observances. The historical manifestations of God-incarnate provided a framework for the elaboration of celebration within calendric structure.

1. Sunday is the place to begin. The scriptures are careful to note that it was the morning of the first day that the empty tomb was discovered. Belief in the Resurrection meant the dawning of a new age in Christ and the fullness of time.

Christians celebrated this newness of life on the first day of the week, the "Lord's day" (1 Cor 16:2; Rev 1:10; Acts 7:11). Sunday for the Christians was not a day of rest, but a day of the Lord; it was the day for gathering as people of new creation to celebrate the eucharist. Not only did Christians name it the Lord's Day, but also the eighth day, a day which stood outside of the calendar, a day that pre-figured eternity in time. Sunday commemorated not what had happened in time to Jesus raised from the dead, but celebrated what Christians had become in light of the timely and timeless Christ-event. It was a feast of identity. So the day itself manifested symbolic time; end-time revealed and celebrated the new social identity of Jesus' followers.

If Christians do not regenerate time through repetitions of cosmogony, Sun-

day does renew time, not by a return to first creation, but by being a festival of fulfilled creation. The primacy of Sunday makes it iconic; as a ritual symbol it gives character to the rest of the week.

2. Feasts and Seasons. By the 2nd century, the feast of Easter had developed as an annual commemoration. While the focus was on the passion, death and resurrection of the Lord, the language of interpretation was analogous to the language of Jewish passover. Just as Passover, on which the messiah's coming was awaited, celebrated deliverance from slavery, Easter celebrated deliverance from sin and death through Christ, in expectation of his parousia. Both were feasts of redemption and hope.

While the Resurrection became a dominant motif, Easter was a unitive celebration of charter historical Christic events: passion, death and resurrection. What gives significance and constitutive character to the feast is not the chronological aspect of the sequence, but rather its relation to the transformative power within a social group.

The feast of Easter prepared for by fasting was a special time for initiation of Christians through the sacraments of baptism, chrismation and eucharist. Gradually there developed a prolongation of the period through fifty days of rejoicing, Eastertide, and a protracted period of ascetical preparation for initiates, Lent.

The entire cycle was the cycle of life, celebrated under ritual time with symbols of darkness and light, fast and feast, desert and mountain, flood and water, milk and honey, bread and wine. For the initiates the ritual time of the season is structured as a sequence passing from creative intentional crisis to transformation, a passage from a condition of death to one of life, i.e., entrance into a fullness of time.

The date of Easter was determined by historical calculations. The December 25

Nativity date may have arisen in similar fashion from an identification of March 25 with 14 Nisan, the date of Jesus' death in the Jewish lunar calendar according to Johannine chronology. In Rome the 4th-century feast of Christmas was also associated with the celebrations of the mythic *Sol Invictus*, the invincible sun. This temporal motif was reinterpreted through Christian images. The birth of the sun is now the commemoration of the birth in time of the timeless Son of God, the one who brings light to the darkness of sin.

If the Easter cycle was a cycle of life, the Christmas season, gradually prepared for by Advent, and prolonged through Christmastide, was the cycle of light.

The particular significance of annual feasts stems from the widespread notion of the year as a full completed unit of time. While some religions' annual celebrations herald an entirely new beginning through a return to origins, Christian annual festivals do not admit of a totally new creation, but an on-going transformation of Christian life in time and history. Time is primarily a mode of becoming.

3. While the celebration of Sunday framed the week and Easter and Christmas framed the year, there was another experience of time, that of the day. That ancient peoples lived by the natural rhythms of the day is not surprising, nor is it unusual that humankind's religious spirit would find sunrise and sunset, beginning and end of the day, apt times for prayer.

What is noteworthy is that the day itself was interpreted symbolically by Christians. Clement of Rome, writing toward the end of the 1st century C.E., speaks of how day and night make visible a resurrection. "Night goes to sleep, the day rises; the day departs, the night follows" (1 Clem 24:3). Time itself becomes a sacrament, a visible sign of an invisible reality.

While some NT texts emphasize the imperative of "pray always," other writings make note of specific times for prayer. In the early church a tension between praying always and praying at specific times existed—a tension that is perennial.

Gradually systems or patterns for prayer throughout the day developed, differing according to geographic locale and the lifestyle of the participants. Despite differences many of the recommended prayer times were interpreted christologically. Prayer at day's end took the setting sun as an antitype of Christ, the sun that never sets; prayer at the beginning of the day saw Christ the Sun of Righteousness; prayer at the third, sixth and ninth hours were variously interpreted in light of Christ's passion or the descent of the Spirit. In other words, the day itself was seen as sacrament, revelatory of the Christian message.

While the *General Instruction on the Liturgy of the Hours* uses the phrase "sanctification of time" in reference to daily prayer, the phrase is not apt; liturgical prayer is for the glorification of God and the sanctification of people. For Christians the rhythms of the day become lenses for seeing the reality of the Christ-life; prayer becomes an experience of union with God. If these ritual times differ from, e.g., the transformative power of Easter sacraments, they are similar insofar as they rearticulate an existing convenantal bond.

Pastoral Considerations

While the *Roman Calendar: Text and Commentary* presents a lofty vision of how the church keeps festival, often the actual celebration of Sunday, feasts and seasons, and day falls short of the ideal.

A. Erosion of Sunday

Culture competes with liturgical celebration. Three factors contribute to the erosion of Sunday. First, the spirit of individualism, while helpful in many areas of life, militates against Sunday as *the* day for assembly. The pressure of individualism affects not only the family unit, but also the church at prayer. Can we actually engage in a truly corporate act of prayer and praise? The tide of individualism can lead to Sunday shipwreck.

Second, culture presents a skewed vision of work and leisure. Research has shown that ancient Greek and Roman slaves and medieval European laborers worked no longer than an employee in the 1970s. Leisure time in bygone days was genuine leisure, but today many tasks that resemble work encroach on leisure. Free time becomes a respite to recoup energies for work. Further, people today are caught up in the work of creating happiness, fulfillment and self-realization. Can the Sunday once again be a time for communitarian liberating activity? If the cycle of production and self-fulfillment yields to a true feast, a useless time, then worship can celebrate what God is accomplishing in our time.

Third, corresponding to secular causes (e.g., ecology day) and economic trends (e.g., Labor Day sale), the church has adopted similar approaches with "theme" Sundays. Various church lobby groups—ational and international—supporting their cause, usurp the calendar. Vocation Sunday, Catechetical Sunday, Mission Sunday, etc., become a round of church "sales," promoting what are surely worthwhile causes. Nonetheless the trajectory of the church year and lectionary is interrupted. Life is presented as fragmented, a sequence of unrelated events; information is overlaid on the day's character and the local church is left responding to decisions *ad extra*.

B. Erosion of the Season

Liturgical seasons seem to be taken more seriously today, especially Advent and Lent. The growth of the R.C.I.A., for example, has rightly shaped the Lenten season. There are, however, some difficulties which persist.

1. Anticipation takes precedence over prolongation. Advent and Lent may be strong seasons, but their prolongation often suffers. Churches would benefit if the rhythm of the Advent season extended through the Baptism of the Lord, and Lent became a gateway not only to Easter, but to Eastertide.

2. Intellectualization overrides experience. Often the seasons are intellectualized with parish themes and slogans. Far more spiritually enriching is the concentration on the ritual image. The image gives rise to thought. Those parishes which allow the liturgy to break open the dominant images of the seasons better facilitate deeper experiences of faith.

3. Historicism infects celebrations. Good Friday illustrates the point. The appropriate question for Good Friday is not "Were you there when they crucified my Lord?" but how is the passion, death and resurrection of Jesus as present reality a faith reality experienced among God's people today. Historicized celebrations distance congregations from the mystery, whereas genuine liturgy draws people into the mystery present.

C. Erosion of the Day

1. If ancient peoples lived by cosmic rhythms of light and darkness and saw in them icons of grace, today's Christians live by other rhythms, especially because we can control darkness with artificial lighting. Is it still possible to celebrate morning, evening and night as God's?

2. Culture views time pragmatically. Time is money. As the national treadmill speeds up, exhaustion and collapse become more prevalent, but time is for productivity. Daily prayer, however, offers non-pragmatic praise and intercession, celebrating time as God's gift. Entering into this contemplative vision of the world is a challenge that remains.

History moves according to God's plan; seasons and days move similarly. For the Christian, history, seasons and days can be interpreted as part of God's unfolding plan. The Christian is to cooperate with the movement of God's spirit that the risen Christ may be incarnated in all times.

See **Calendar, liturgical**

United States Catholic Conference, *The Roman Calendar. Text and Commentary* (Washington, D.C.: 1976). A-M. Roguet, *The General Instruction on the Liturgy of the Hours with Commentary* (Collegeville: Liturgical Press, 1972). James Barr, *Biblical Words for Time*, Studies in Biblical Theology, First Series 33 (Naperville, IL: Allenson, 1969). Irenee Henri Dalmais, Pierre Jounel and Aime Georges Martimort, *The Liturgy and Time*, Vol. IV, The Church at Prayer: An Introduction to the Liturgy, New Edition (Collegeville: The Liturgical Press, 1986). Abraham Joshua Heschel, *The Earth Is the Lord's and The Sabbath* (N.Y.: Harper and Row, 1966). David Power, ed., *The Times of Celebration*, Concilium Vol. 142 (N.Y.: Seabury, 1981). *Studia Liturgica* 14 (1982) Liturgical Time. Thomas J. Talley, *The Origins of the Liturgical Year* (N.Y.: Pueblo, 1986). Stephen W. Hawking., *A Brief History of Time. From the Big Bang to Black Holes* (N.Y.: Bantam, 1988).

JOHN ALLYN MELLOH, S.M.

LITURGY

Liturgy is the word currently used among Roman Catholics and among some Episcopal and Protestant scholars to describe the public worship of the church. In classical Greek, liturgy (*leitourgía*) had a secular meaning; it denoted a work (*érgon*) undertaken on behalf of the people (*laós*). Public projects undertaken by an individual for the good of the community in such areas as education, entertainment or defense would be called *leitourgía*.

The Greek OT, however, uses the word to refer to divine worship and to the ministry of the Levites. Similarly in Heb 8:2 it is used to refer to the priestly work of Christ. Christ is called "a minister (*leitourgós*) of the sanctuary." In Rom 15:16 Paul speaks of himself as "a minister (*leitourgòn*) of Christ Jesus among the Gentiles.

Among Greek-speaking Christians in the first centuries of the Christian era, the word indicated both the ministry of church officials and any act of divine worship. But by the 4th century in the Eastern church the word was used to refer only to the celebration of the eucharist.

In the Western church the word fell out of use for many centuries. Other words such as "divine office," "ecclesiastical office," or "sacred rites" were used to denote worship services. When the word liturgy returned into use in the 18th century it referred to the entire cultic activity of the church. It is that usage which has been confirmed in the documents of the Second Vatican Council and in the 1983 Code of Canon Law.

Vatican II's *Constitution on the Sacred Liturgy* does not present a strict definition of liturgy but rather it offers several descriptions of liturgy, each of which illuminates a different aspect of this most important activity of the church. The liturgy is "the outstanding means whereby the faithful may express in their lives and manifest to others the mystery of Christ and the real nature of the true Church" (S.C., 2). The liturgy is considered "an exercise of the priestly office of Jesus Christ, that is, by the head and his members" (S.C., 7). From the liturgy "grace is poured forth upon us; and the sanctification of men in Christ and the glorification of God ... is achieved in the most efficacious possible way" (S.C., 10). The liturgy is "the summit towards which the activity of the Church is directed; at the same time it is the fount from which all her power flows" (S.C., 10).

The liturgy "does not exhaust the entire activity of the Church" (S.C., 9) nor is it the only time when Christians offer worship to God. The church engages in many other activities essential to its mission which are acts of worship: evangelization, catechesis, social action and various other forms of Christian service. But it is full and active participation in the liturgical celebrations of the church which is "the primary and indispensable source from which the faithful are to derive the true Christian spirit" (S.C., 14).

The liturgy comprises public, communal, ritual activities in which "the sanctification of man is signified by signs perceptible to the senses, and is effected in a way which corresponds with each of these signs" (S.C., 7). The council undertook to reform the individual rites of the church in order that their authentic form would appear. Thereafter when enacted by the faithful assembled they would speak with their own power to the present generation of Christians. This work called for careful historical reconstructions, theological understanding and pastoral sensitivity. It continues to require of the church careful adaptation of these inherited rites to various cultures in the contemporary world.

The proper enactment of liturgical rites requires attention to various symbolic language employed in ritual activity. The most obvious of these is the text of the rite. But other elements are also of great importance: music, gesture, vesture, various ritual objects and environment. The Bishops' Committee on the Liturgy has addressed these aspects of the liturgy in *Environment and Art in Catholic Worship* (1978) and *Music in Catholic Worship*, (1972, revised 1983).

Over the centuries various aspects of the paschal mystery began to be celebrated at different times of the year. In addition to Sunday, the original Christian feast, and Easter, the principal yearly celebration of the paschal mystery, other feasts celebrating different aspects of the mystery and life of Christ, as well as feasts honoring the Virgin Mary and the saints were gradually introduced in different parts of the Christian world. A yearly cycle of seasons and feasts known as the liturgical year was the result.

The amount and kind of Christian prayer that has been referred to by the term liturgy has varied over time. Today the term is understood to refer to the rites contained in officially promulgated liturgical books. This includes all seven sacraments: baptism, confirmation, eucharist, reconciliation, ordination, marriage and anointing of the sick. Also included would be the newly created rites of installation to the liturgical ministries of acolyte and reader, along with two rites for the dying: viaticum, the final eucharistic communion, and the commendation of the dying. The rites of Christian burial are included as well as the rites for the dedication of a church, for religious profession and the consecration of virgins. The church's official morning and evening prayer, the divine office, is included in the term liturgy as are the contents of the revised Roman liturgical Book of Blessings.

Liturgy is to be distinguished from private prayer and from other pious exercises. The celebration of liturgical prayer requires an assembly of the church. This means that at least two Christians must be present. Liturgical prayer must be related to the paschal mystery and it must be under the official regulation of the church (C.I.C., 834, 2). While many celebrations of liturgical prayer require leadership by an ordained person, some, such as the liturgy of the hours, the commendation of the dying, certain burial rites and many blessings do not.

Liturgical prayer is usually characterized by a spirit of praise and thanksgiving stemming from the assembly's recollection of God's saving deeds on behalf of God's people. It is also characterized by a lively hope in the final establishment of the Kingdom of God. Prayers of supplication as well as songs of lament are also regular features of liturgical prayer.

See **Reform, liturgical, of Vatican II; Worship; Prayer, types of, in the liturgy; Aesthetics, liturgical**

Documents on the Liturgy 1963-1979: Conciliar, Papal, and Curial Texts, Trans. Thomas O'Brien, International Commission on English in the Liturgy (Collegeville, MN: The Liturgical Press, 1982). *Music in Catholic Worship*, Bishops' Committee on the Liturgy, 1972. *Environment and Art in Catholic Worship*, Bishops' Committee on the Liturgy, 1978. *The Rites of the Catholic Church*, Two volumes (New York: Pueblo Publishing Co., 1976).

LAWRENCE J. MADDEN, S.J.

LITURGY AND CHRISTIAN LIFE

I. Introduction

(1) Meaning and Purpose

In the important sense that liturgy is an essential constituent of Christian life, the duality supposed by the title of this article is misleading. As involving formal, communal and explicit activities of Christian worship, liturgy may be distinguished from the rest of Christian life. Distinction without separation is central to the Christian and Jewish traditions. The further complexities of the relationship whereby Christian life is a form of worship and Christian worship a concentration and manifestation of the life will gradually emerge. The purpose of this article is to expose and explore these complexities as they have developed in the Christian tradition and continue to challenge the Christian community.

(2) Liturgy and Moral Theology

As a central theological discipline the study of liturgy is relatively new. In the Catholic tradition moral theology has been a major, to many a dominant, part of theology since the Council of Trent. Although there was no adequate alternative for a time, it would be a mistake to call moral theology a theology of Christian life in that phase. It was too narrow in scope, too juridical in form and too preoccupied with the failures of sin. Its relationships with liturgy were extrinsic and legal. The obligation to attend Sunday Mass, etc., and the requirements for validity and licitness in the sacraments were typical.

The renewal of moral theology and its ambition to become a theology of Christian life coincided by and large with the renewed interest in the liturgy and in its theological significance. Since Vatican II this has led to a more self-conscious interest by both moral theologians and liturgists in the interaction between worship and Christian action in the world. Eucharist and justice, a theme frequently addressed in contemporary theology, would have been unintelligible to moral theologians of an earlier generation.

These welcome developments raise a number of problems for theologians. How does one study moral theology, as theology of Christian life, in separation from liturgy and also in separation from doctrinal or dogmatic theology and scripture? Who can command the expertise to range over these disciplines and their historical evolution? Is some new alignment of specialties required? Should there be specialists in (provisional) synthesizing as well as in analyzing theological issues? Is team theology now necessary? What form could it take? It is necessary to mention these questions here to alert readers to the inevitably partial treatment of the relationship of liturgy and Christian life which is all that is possible here, not for reasons of space but for reasons of method and expertise in current theology.

(3) Outline

The main sections of this article will involve systematic exposition of the Christian tradition and its current understanding of the relationship between liturgy and Christian life. The biblical and historical basis will be for the most part integrated into the systematic. This in turn will open up some new questions or rather new aspects of perennial questions. Theology shares the pilgrim condition of its people, God's people. In this area theology has still much exploring to do. As the people of God moves on, so do theological areas of exploration.

The emphasis will be on the interaction of formal Christian worship and general Christian living in the idiom of contemporary moral theology with all the attendant limitations. After a brief comment on the biblical and historical background (II), the systematic sections will deal with (III) Liturgy, Life and the Kingdom of God; (IV) Divine Word and Human Communications; (V) Sacraments, Society and Environment; (VI) Kingdom Values and Sacramental Engagement. More exploratory sections will consider (VII) the problem of evil, sin and redemption in terms of consumption and communion and (VIII) the triune God and a holistic view of liturgy and life.

II. *Biblical and Historical Background*

A few biblical points need to be recalled and underlined. The Mosaic Covenant, central to Hebrew religion, maintained a close connection between response to Yahweh and response to the neighbor. Its charter in the Decalogue is so structured. The great 8th-century prophets, their predecessors and successors, insisted that liturgical worship of God was futile, indeed offensive, from a people who neglected and exploited the poor and the stranger. Justice (*sedaqah*) in life was essential to authenticity in liturgy. Love of God and love of neighbor belonged together.

The relation between love of God and love of neighbor was re-emphasized and deepened by Jesus and the NT. Prayer without care was valueless. Indeed the NT reader might be forgiven for taking love of neighbor as the only test of the authentic follower of Jesus (Matthew 25; Romans 13; 1 Corinthians 13, et al.). Such a life of love does, however, depend on love for God and particularly love by God, who first of all loved us (1 John 4). This love by God was manifested above all in Jesus' death and resurrection, recalled and shared in the liturgies of eucharist and baptism (1 Corinthians 12; Roman 6).

This basic connection between liturgy and life shaped the early church. Christian life was that of a member of Christ's body into which Christians were integrated in baptism and by which they were nourished in eucharist. Serious life-failures (sins) cut people off from such sharing unless they repented and were forgiven in the liturgy of penance. Christian moralists, subtle and sophisticated like Clement of Alexandria, or harsh and prophetic like John Chrysostom, maintained the crucial connection between true worship and good living. Liturgy as summons to, judgment on and empowerment of Christian life remained a church constant through the centuries.

III. *Liturgy, Life and the Kingdom of God*

The early Christian linking of Christian liturgy and Christian life emphasized, without always developing, the intrinsic nature of these links. Yet the incorporation into Christ by baptism, the nourishment in eucharist, the reconciliation in penance shaped from within the new life of the Christian its liturgical actions and its life-tasks. The seven sacraments were themselves related to critical needs and moments in Christian living and dying. The word of scripture carried its saving power and significance as part of every complete liturgy. In seeking an integrating vision for the celebration of liturgy and the challenges and achievements of life, Christians are bound to look to the Kingdom of God preached and inaugurated by Jesus. Despite its linguistic awkwardness in many modern contexts, God's Kingdom remains the most comprehensive and fertile symbol for the new pattern of worship and living established by God for humanity through Jesus Christ.

This Kingdom in its "already" stage is to be discerned and celebrated. In its "not-yet" stage it is to be prayed for, striven for and received. Christian liturgy in its remembering for the future symbolizes, realizes in word and sign the divine achievement of the kingdom in Jesus and prays for, anticipates its complete human and cosmic reception. Humanity and cosmos are opened to the healing and transforming presence and power of God by the community of disciples, taking bread and wine as Jesus' body and blood until he comes again. What is announced in word and signified in sacrament liberates human beings and cosmic forces to seek the fullness which is to be theirs by the self-giving of God. Human and cosmic fulfillment by the transforming presence and power of God is the scope of the kingdom as symbolized in the liturgy and expressed in the Christian living of the explicit and implicit followers of Jesus Christ.

IV. *Word of God and Human Communications*

The conventional duo of word and sacrament, with their Reformed and Catholic/Orthodox associations, can be useful in more detailed relating of liturgy and Christian life. Their essential belonging together must not be ignored if artificial divisions are not to emerge in Christian community and life as well as liturgy. In undertaking in this section then to examine in detail the relation between the word of God and human communications, the word-sacrament unity as proclaiming and realizing God's Kingdom must be kept continuously in mind. Human communications in turn are not to be understood in a narrowly verbal way but as meaningful expressions between members of the human community which are in turn forming (or deforming) of that community.

Liturgy as word of God and human language/communications share many of the great dualities of the human condition. Both are received (as gift) and achieved by human effort. For the word of God, gift and reception may be the more obvious aspect. Yet the decline of any single dictation theory of inspiration and the increasing awareness of the human context and the human struggle which shaped the diverse documents of the Hebrew and Christian scriptures reveal the other dimension of the Bible as word of God, human achievement. The role of the word of God in liturgy requires further human effort from presenter and listener if the gift is to be effectively received.

Human communication is clearly a matter of some human effort and achievement. Yet each receives the language of parents and larger community as a gift. The struggle to speak, to communicate, is the struggle to learn a language which has been handed on as tradition and gift. Even the great refiners of language in literature are operating out of gift, of a language given, of talents received, of people encountered and not invented, of experiences undergone, often without any advance planning, and certainly without predetermined conclusions.

The word of God and of humanity as gift to be recognized and accepted, celebrated and enjoyed, marks a critical connection between liturgy and Christian life. An ethics of speech and communication for Christians will start from this divine and human gift to be celebrated, in part by celebrating the donors. Praising God in liturgy and honoring one's father and mother and community in the language received draw together the liturgical and ethical. So did the Decalogue in the range of its ethical demands and in the original liturgical setting of its recitation.

Such connections suggest another important human duality, the personal and the communal. Language is a communal heritage to be used personally. Liturgy is a communal religious celebration to be entered into personally. The word of God in its liturgical character operates communally and personally for humanity. It was given to a people to become a people, a community of persons with personal gifts and responsibilities to be exercised in forming community.

Word and communications require an ethics that is personal and communal. Traditionally this has been an ethics of truth-telling, of not bearing false witness. The Hebrew origins of truth (*emeth*, fidelity of God to his word) and the NT concept of saving and liberating truth require a larger vision of word and truth for person and community. What we celebrate as the word and truth of God in liturgy must exercise its liberating, Kingdom function in the community of disciples, the church and in the larger human community. Personal authenticity, witnessing in word first of all to the truth that is in one and witnessing before the others, telling the truth, is an inescapable demand of the gift of truth.

Truth-telling as personal charge is not the whole of it. Truth-seeking and truth-sharing as personal and communal tasks belong just as much to the divine gift and human capacity. The ethics of truth for Christians insists on the seeking (e.g., freedom of research) and the sharing (e.g., freedom of information) in church and society in ways that often will be disturbing for power-holders. Stirring up the people with his kingdom-truth was one of the more serious charges against Jesus. His disciples may do no less. Liturgical celebrations of the word of God by people who refuse these tasks of truth deserve the age-old condemnations of Amos on "such solemn assemblies" (Amos 5). To dare to proclaim the word of God in public is to take on a formidable task, which can be discharged only by somebody open to the grace of that word. "Lord be merciful to me a sinner."

Word and truth as community-building and person-developing take narrative-form. Narrative of origins and subsequent history provides identity for community and person. The Hebrew and Christian scriptures perform that task for Christian community in its liturgy. Political and ethnic communities have their own narratives of origin and development. The Christian community narratives touch on human origins at their deepest and on human destiny at its furthest. They are faith-narratives shaping identity, and hope-narratives for a destiny which finally transcends (hi)story. Their truth does not conflict with the truth of other human narratives of origin (e.g., evolution, discovery and development of the Americas by Europeans) but it provides at once critique and transcendence. Purely human narratives of origin and destiny must be continually tested against the ultimate in the stories of God if they are not to become imprisoning ideologies like some forms of racism, nationalism and marxism. The word in liturgy offers judgment as well as challenge and empowerment.

The truth of divine and human word is not only the truth of history. The stories on which communities are built may be larger than any modern concept of evidence warrants without declining into ideological packages. The creative story-tellers of the past and present are liberatingly truthful in ways not measurable by the contemporary canons of history. The authors of the books of Genesis and of Job, of the *Divine Comedy* and *Hamlet*, have a range of liberating truth for the sensitive reader or listener. Creative word of God moves close to creative human word in its fictional, dramatic and poetic forms. Liturgy and literature have more in common than an indifferent reading of the word of God and an equally indifferent homily may often suggest. The historic relationship of drama and liturgy is only one part of an association that has enriched Christian liturgy and human culture over centuries. Christian life and liturgy must take seriously this connection of prayer and poetry in church and home, in school,

746

theatre and concert hall, indeed wherever two or three gather together. This interconnection concerns not just "high culture" any more than it concerns just "high" liturgy. Both liturgy and culture are essentially people's work. And the word of God did not come to any elite. It was the poor who were to have the gospel preached to them. The tension between the popular and the sophisticated in liturgy as in literature can be critical and creative for both.

The inauthentically high and the trivializing popular threaten language, living and liturgy in multiple ways. Christians as carriers of the word of God have their own responsibility to oppose the inauthentic and the trivial. A community whose communications are dominated by the trivial and the purely commercial (and inauthentic) is readily exposed to the living lie and beyond the reach of life-giving truth. When the trivial and the commerical combine to operate a pseudo-liturgy, Jesus is doubly denied before men. The word of God as a two-edged sword remains a permanent challenge to all genuine human communication in life and in liturgy.

V. *Sacrament, Society and Environment*

Word and sacrament are distinguishable but inseparable in celebration of Christian liturgy and in proclamation and promotion of God's Kingdom. The distinction centers on the sacraments as symbolic actions by the community, as enacted and ritual remembering, realizing and anticipating the work of God in Jesus Christ rather than simply verbal remembering. The words come too. Such enactment carries its own verbal narratives, songs of praise and words of blessing. As signs of the Kingdom, sacraments are liturgical dramas in which the cast is the Christian community but the director and leading actor is Jesus Christ. Encountering Christ in the sacrament has been a form of theological

short-hand since Edward Schillebeeckx' work in the 1950s, a period of considerable renewal in sacramental theology involving people like Schillebeeckx, Rahner and Semmelroth.

The transforming presence and power of God in cosmos and history, which Jesus proclaimed and inaugurated as God's Kingdom, emerges in different forms in those actions of the Christian community called sacraments. The different forms relate to different stages and dimensions of Christian life and need. What is significant here is that they are directed to the in-breaking Kingdom of God and so to the transformation of person and community in history and cosmos, a transformation to be completed like the resurrection of Jesus in transcending history.

Sacraments are then gifts and tasks of the Kingdom. They are expressions of and resources for that transformation of humanity and cosmos which became available in the life, death and resurrection of Jesus Christ. They are personal and community activities with personal and community implications. In recent times they had become almost exclusively clerical in performance and individualist and passive in reception.

There was the clerical confessor and individual penitent in isolated confessional, or individual priest with isolated-in-public recipient of communion at the altar-rail. The essential community dimension of liturgy and sacraments had been obscured to the point of vanishing. The implications for life were equally serious. An individualist and sometimes trivializing morality prevailed: eating meat on Friday was on the same sinful level as adultery or murder. Person was diminished as well as community.

The thrust of the current liturgy of the sacraments is to promote personal participation and community celebration. The inherent tension of Christian and human living, personal differentiation in fuller community, is seen to cohere with the liturgical structures of encounter between God and humanity. The gifts and tasks of Kingdom and humanity are revealed at their deepest in the sacraments. Person and community are judged in their failures, as well as healed and empowered for new life. For Christians their ethical tasks in society and cosmos relate closely to their engagement with liturgical celebration of the sacraments.

Personal and community events, the sacraments have clear cosmic connection. Earthly elements, the matter of traditional theology, are integrated with the symbolic action and words into a unified mediating of the divine-human encounter. Water and oil, bread and wine, breath and fire, light and darkness, place and time, are recognized in their earthly reality and at the same time transformed into instruments of divine activity. Respect for the earth and its elements, required by the Christian stories of creation, acquires a deeper range and urgency with their sacramental role. Sacraments, as signs of the Kingdom and so of God's design for the ultimate human community, also proclaim the current value and ultimate significance of planet earth and of the whole cosmos. A sacramental ecology is basic for Christians to an ecological ethics.

VI. *Kingdom Values and Sacramental Engagement*

The fuller relationship of sacraments and Christian life in ethical terms may be best pursued by exploring the connections between individual sacraments and what are sometimes called Kingdom values and virtues. These Kingdom values and virtues derive from the biblical tradition of the Kingdom in Hebrew and Christian scriptures. The primary Kingdom values and virtues are faith-hope-love, taken as a dynamic, interconnecting triad in the Pauline fashion. They are both entrance values/virtues and continuance values/virtues. To enter the Kingdom and remain

in it, faith-hope-love are essential. Christian life then is first of all a life of faith-hope-love. Christian liturgy and sacraments require and confer faith-hope-love. Christian community lives by faith-hope-love. Christian faith-hope-love must themselves be expressed and developed in Christian life, in what have been traditionally called the moral virtues. No entirely satisfactory classification or ordering of these is available. A crucial value and virtue for Christians and one very akin to the primary virtue of faith is that of truth and truthfulness already discussed. For biblical, sacramental and contemporary social reasons three others are considered here: liberation and freedom; justice and equality; solidarity and peace. Their biblical and Christian background cannot be fully pursued here although it will emerge in discussing their connection with particular sacraments. Their contemporary social and political connections may be discerned by comparing them with the revolutionary political triad of the last two hundred years, *liberté, égalité, fraternité*.

(1) *Liberation and Freedom*

The coming of God's reign or Kingdom constituted a liberating event for the Hebrews released from captivity in Egypt (Exodus), for Jesus' disciples offered the truth that would set them free (John), for the early Christians set free indeed (Galatians 5 et al.). This liberation from poverty, privation and prison (Luke 4, Isaiah 61 et al.), from sin, death and the law (Paul), has once again become a central concern in Christian life and theology. As effective signs of this liberation, of this Kingdom both come and to come, the sacraments are to be celebrated by the Christian community as liberating events, liberating human beings to one another and to God. They form countersigns to oppression and enslavement, personal and communal. Baptism as the first sacrament of Christian life draws candidate(s) and community together in the liberating death and resurrection of Jesus, in the new exodus from slavery in Egypt. The liberating presence of God at baptism judges, challenges and empowers candidates and community to live together in freedom and to renounce the demons of oppression and exploitation. To celebrate baptism with Christ authentically, and to complete it in confirmation, community and candidate must be willing to go beyond the oppressions of race, class and sex. "For as many of you as were baptized into Christ have put on Christ. There is neither Jew nor Greek, there is neither slave nor free, there is neither male nor female; for you are all one in Christ Jesus" (Gal 3:27f).

Other sacraments such as penance and eucharist offer their own witness to the liberating power of Jesus' death and resurrection. So does the sacrament of anointing in face of the spiritual, mental, emotional and physical ills to which humanity is heir. Embodiment and sexuality, interpreted too often in human history as entrapment for human beings, enjoy their own Christian liberation in the sacrament of marriage, symbol of the free surrender of Jesus Christ out of love for his friends (Ephesians 5). Freedom to serve the community liturgically and otherwise and so the Kingdom is what is at issue in the sacrament of ordination. As that freedom cannot be restricted by race or class, one must question if it can be restricted by gender?

In sacramental theology today, the community-church is the primary sacrament, at once sacrament of Christ and of humanity transformed in Christ. It is as a liberated and liberating people that it is to be effective sign of the Kingdom of God and of the new humanity. In liturgy the community-church acts precisely as such a sacrament of liberation. The individual sacraments must bear their own witness to this liberated and liberating community and so set the standard and provide the capacity for the divine and human work of liberation. The community-church is in turn challenged to be its sacramental self by the liberation movements abroad in the world.

(2) Justice and Equality

Justice (*sedagah, dikaiosune*) is one of the central themes of the Hebrew and Christian scriptures, of the Mosaic Covenant and the New Covenant in Jesus Christ. The outcome of all that is described in another great Pauline word "justification," making just parallel to liberation and setting free. The community of disciples, the primary sacrament, becomes the community of the just. What is to be witnessed and realized is the breakthrough of divine justice in human person and community, the person and community which are Jesus Christ.

Without rehearsing the relations to all the sacraments as with liberation/freedom, it will be more useful to examine two aspects of the biblical tradition of justice, equality and preference for the poor. Created in the image of God, re-created in Jesus, the New Adam, all human beings enjoy basic equality. Paul's rejection of age-old division and discrimination in Gal 3:28 underlines the impact of Jesus' dismissal of power and privilege to be replaced by openness to the least. A certain paradox emerges here in Jesus' leveling mission. Nobody is to lord it over others ("and yet the last shall be first and the first last"—Mk 9:35). Jesus is picking up on the divine strategy of Yahweh in his call of Israel, a fragmented group of slaves lost in the imperial grandeur of Egypt. Indeed he is rehearsing the strategy of Abba in choosing a marginal person and place ("can anything good come out of Nazareth?"—Jn 1:46), and a person destined to be rejected as a criminal on a cross, as the "corner-stone" of the new temple, the Kingdom come.

To establish equality in glory for all through identification with the poor and deprived has been the strategy of Yahweh, Abba and Jesus. It must remain the strategy of the community of disciples. The community's liturgy and sacraments are intended as symbols of that strategy.

The interactions between liturgy/sacraments and equality/preferential option for the poor in Christian life must be mutual. Each dimension of liturgy and life is challenge and empowerment to the other. The liberating effect of liturgy and sacraments discussed earlier relates closely to equality and preference for the poor. In more political terms, human rights, which can be great protectors of the weak, are human freedoms due in justice to persons. The overlap between liberation, justice and preference for the poor has been critically developed in liberation theology. It may be less obvious in Christian liturgy where wealth and power may be displayed and indulged in counter-sacramental ways, at least where one is speaking of sacraments as effective signs of Christ. There is still much need for dialogue on liturgy and Christian living before their implementations of Jesus' strategy is manifest and effective.

(3) Solidarity and Peace

For all its revolutionary resonance *fraternité* has a certain hollow ring today. This partly because, of the 18th century triad, it is one which has had least evident effect. The wars and massacres of the 20th century alone make a mockery of that 18th-century aspiration. The gender block also suggests a change in terminology. Solidarity has attained in current usage a sense close to *fraternité* and the biblical fellowship (*koinonia*). Responsibility for and to others, interdependence, living community are all suggested by solidarity with its ecclesial and civil, national, international and even cosmic dimensions, all in the same ecological

boat. Only one earth for the only one human community.

The biblical *shalom* suffered some impoverishment in the translation process: through *eirene*, *pax* and into *peace*. Originally it probably meant something like "flourishing in communion" for Israel first and then for all the nations as well. It was both Yahweh's gift and Israel's (humanity's) task. It became in turn Jesus' gift ("My peace I leave with you"— Jn 14:27) and the disciples' task ("Blessed are the peace-makers"—Mt 5:9).

The relation between solidarity and peace in the sense of *shalom* is obvious and close. The gift which the community-church has received is also its Kingdom task. The community of solidarity and shalom is to provide the pre-view, the first earnest (*arabon*, 2 Cor 1:22) of the final flourishing in communion. This shalom was promised to Israel and definitively offered in Jesus Christ. This community is called and empowered to be sacrament of solidarity and shalom. In its self-manifestation and self-realization in the liturgy and in the individual sacraments, its peace-giving and peace-making character is to be manifest and realized. It is to be sacramentalized.

Eucharist and penance have clear peace-giving and peace-making capacities. They are both in the traditional sense sacraments of reconciliation, even if their forms of celebration have not always made that clear. In the interchange between liturgy and Christian life this reconciliation dimension has been frequently over-individualized: "my sin, my confession, my God, my forgiveness." Social division, oppression and sinfulness have been obscured. More seriously the administration of the sacraments and the call for reconciliation have too often endorsed deeply divisive and oppressive conditions. Performing signs of reconciliation without any conversion of heart and structure renders these sacramental signs futile. God is mocked and humanity is more deeply injured. Christian life in genuine search of peace and solidarity will challenge with Amos such inauthentic liturgy.

VII. Communion in a Consuming Universe

Christian life and liturgy occur in the context of sin and evil. The great symbols of God's achievement in Israel and Jesus, liberation, salvation, redemption, justification, new creation, make clear this presence of evil to be overcome. Jesus' own suffering and death which are basic to Christian life and liturgy ("If anyone will come after me"—Mk 8:34; "Do this in remembrance of me"—Lk 22:19) confirm the reality of evil in the world and the need to overcome it. The book of Job wrestles with one of the most poignant and puzzling aspects of evil in the world: why do the innocent suffer? The power of that book rests eventually in its acceptance of the mystery of this suffering but set off against the transcendent power and goodness of God. The passion and resurrection narratives in the NT follow much the same pattern. Suffering is real and puzzling, in Jesus' case (and in many other cases) undeserved. But out of that goodness may come, as the loving and creative power of God prevails. And the final enemy, death, has been overcome in God's raising Jesus to life as first fruits for all.

Liturgy properly insists on the goodness of God and creation in psalm and hymn, prayer and creating, saving narrative. Praise and thanksgiving are primary liturgical functions. So are they primary functions of Christian life. Yet the tragic dimension of life continues to assert itself and to demand liturgical response. In the liturgies of forgiveness and of entrusting the dead to their merciful God, this tragic dimension finds some response. Yet the pervasiveness and depth of evil in the world, its connection with the very dynamism of life itself, has not

been fully addressed so far in this examination of liturgy and life.

"God looked on the world and saw that it was good." After the creation of humankind "that it was very good." Yet this becomes rapidly the world of evil and sin, of human division ("she did it"), alienation from nature, fratricide (Cain and Abel), breakdown of all communications (Babel) (Genesis 1-11.) The fertile myths of Genesis and other Hebrew works were struggling to reconcile the good work of a good creator with the undoubted presence of destruction and evil. Job undertook the most searching examination of this puzzle in life and thought and, while he banished the easy answers, he too had to bow before the mystery.

In a different world with its own fertile, truth-bearing myths, such as evolution, and its own potent, destructive myth of consumerism, a rather different symbolic and imaginative effort may be needed to relate evil to Christian life and liturgy. Something analogous was attempted by Pierre Teilhard de Chardin (*The Hymn of the Universe*). His emphasis was on the predominantly good creative and evolving world with less attention to the interweaving evil. One of his great liturgical images was his "Mass on the world," a eucharist of the universe, a fitting anticipatory sign for his vision of the coming Kingdom in the emerging Christogenesis. The richness of his vision remains to be developed in various ways by the Christian community in its life and liturgy.

A less simply hopeful, less optimistic vision than that of Teilhard de Chardin would undoubtedly look with awe and respond with praise to the created masterpiece of our physical and human world. It would also look more closely and less uncritically at the consuming, destroying, nature of that world.

In what Teilhard called the biosphere, the sphere of living things or the chain of life as it is called in ecological terms, the dynamism of survival and growth is that of consumption. All living beings live off other living beings. To survive is to consume the others. Such consumption extends, as certain environment crises indicate, from that of the ozone layer to that of fossil fuels, from the living to non-living. We live in a self-consuming universe. And it is no decisive mark of human difference that we as humans may consume non-human or sub-human reality and avoid consumption ourselves. In the end we too are consumed. From dust to dust. Earth-consumers, we are finally consumed by earth. And in the interim we humans are frequently busy consuming one another. The necessary and natural consuming of the baby at its mother's breast has its own beauty and value. The malice or weakness which issues in adults or even children consuming one another, from the most intimate relations of marriage and family to the more distant but no less potent relationships of politics and commerce, provides so many modern parables of sin. Natural consumption with its inevitable killings and dying for plants, animals and humans, reaches the new human sphere of tragedy and sin in human hatred and war, power-seeking and oppression, self-indulgence and other-destruction. What we may lightly call a consumerist world is deeply pervasive of us all in continuity with structures of the universe. The culling of seals has its parallels in the periodic culling of humans we call war or massacre. The dignity, freedom, equality and solidarity for which humans are created in the Jewish and Christian vision reveals their own tragic role in self-destruction.

The history of Yahweh's relation with Israel marks a struggle to overcome human self-destructiveness within what remained a consuming universe. Israel's consumption of the prophets, God's messengers, drew Yahweh further into the self-giving task of forming this people as God's own people, from there to all people as God's. Last of all God sent God's son (Hebrews 1). The entry to God in Jesus into this destructive and consuming universe was the final challenge. As human, Jesus was a consumer from his mother's breast, through childhood and adolescent needs to table-fellowship with publicans and sinners.

His person and ministry were directed beyond the inevitable and necessary biological consumption: with "living water" by which one will never thirst, for the Samaritan woman (John 4); for the disciples "fruit for eternal life" (John 4) and "the bread which comes down from heaven" (John 6). In the more mundane synoptic accounts he confronts consuming and consumed humanity by feeding the hungry, healing the sick, raising the widow's son, forgiving sinners. All these are signs of the Kingdom, of the new presence and power of God which could overcome the trap of simply consuming and being consumed. Not yet though. Not until he himself was drawn into the circle of malicious human consumption, betrayed and deserted by his closest friends, mocked and tortured, given a show trial, had a notorious criminal preferred to him, unjustly sentenced and cruelly executed. The savage consumerism of the powers and the powerless, the political and religious leaders and the mob, could indulge their consuming lust in his passion and death.

God had died, had been consumed by human destructiveness. *Consummatum est.* It was all over. Yet the night before he died "as they were eating, Jesus took bread, and blessed, and broke it, and gave it to the disciples and said: 'Take, eat: this is my body.' And he took a cup, and when he had given thanks he gave it to them saying, 'Drink of it; for this is my blood of the covenant, which is poured out for many for the forgiveness of sins'" (Matthew 26).

"And after the sabbath, toward the dawn of the first day of the week, Mary Magdalene and the other Mary went to see the sepulchre . . . the angel said to the women: 'Do not be afraid: for I know that you seek Jesus who was crucified. He is not here; for he has risen, as he said '" (Matthew 28).

Jesus' passion narrative is framed by the last supper and the resurrection. His gift of himself to his disciples in bread and wine, his body and blood, in memory of him, until he comes again, is the critical acceptance and transcendence of our human consumption of one another. Consumption must yield to communion at least in symbol. The ultimate reality of that symbol, of communion beyond all consumption, only emerges with the resurrection of Jesus. When consumption had done its worst in death, indeed in killing unto death, the life-giving power of God raised Jesus to communion with God and with all in ways which human destructiveness could never again touch. The age of natural and sinful consumption had been conquered in the dying and rising of Jesus. The symbol, the sacrament of that conquest had already been given in eucharist. The central liturgical act of the community of disciples became a gift of communion to enable communion to overcome consumption. The final overcoming must wait until he comes again. Doing this in memory of him establishes communion now in and through the very consumption of the elements, of the body and blood of Christ. By taking consumption on at its most destructive Jesus has shown how symbolically or sacramentally, in a life nourished by liturgy, communion may be sustained in a world still dependent on controlled consumption, but exposed to the temptations of uncontrolled, self-indulgent and exploitative consumption.

VIII. *In the End God: The Danse Macabre and Perichoresis*

Liturgy and Christian life belong to history but are not confined by it. The irruption of God into human history has opened it up to the transhuman, the transcendent and the eschatological. The coming of the Kingdom now eschatologically shapes Christian life and liturgy in many significant ways. Both are expressions of hope for final liberation to one another and to God, for ultimate flourishing in communion, a communion that completely transcends consumption. Liturgy and life look to resurrection and to eternal life, life with God and with one another in eternal fulfillment. In the end, God. Of course in the beginning God also. And in the interim God who became human, who took on the conditions of history and surrendered to the consuming universe to establish true communion.

God thus proved to be a communion God for creation but also for the creator. The community of God which was gradually revealed/discerned was the mystery of triune God. Yahweh, the God of Israel and of Christians, emerged for Christians as triune, one God in three persons: Abba/Father; Word/Son/Redeemer; Spirit/Sanctifier.

In liturgy and in life it is possible to worship the one God, saying *abba* in Christ by the Spirit's gift of daughterhood and sonship. In concept and language the triune God is less easy to deal with. Further connecting points with the mystery may be developed in liturgical celebration and Christian living by attesting to the character of communion within God and its exemplary and empowering force for those created in God's image.

The traditional doctrine of the Trinity as it developed in the early centuries stressed the differentiation, the equality and the unity. Many theologians see in this a model for human community with differentiation, equality and unity keeping close to freedom, equality and fraternity in both their recent political and more ancient biblical senses. A trinitarian shaped liturgy addressed to Abba through Christ by the Spirit provides in turn a model and power for human society. Developments in freedom, equality and solidarity in human society make the divine image in humanity more evident and challenge liturgy to do likewise.

In the idiom of consumption and communion, the triune God forms dynamic communion without consumption. This is the eschatological operating in history. What Jesus did, what we recall in liturgy, what we attempt in living is to realize the communion that breaks through the destructive circle of consumption that the divine communion may be shared with all, that God may be "all in all."

The Eastern tradition had a term for the dynamic triunity of God, which may take us a little further. *Perichoresis* referred to God's dynamic community in terms of the dance, the moving, harmonious and loving interchange of the three persons. Dance sometimes figures significantly in liturgy. As image for liturgy and life it is rich in possibilities. Connecting the divine perichoresis with the dance or the loving musical movements of liturgy and with the harmonious, loving movement of life at its best, can illuminate the gifts and tasks of Christians. The invitation to the dance, finally to the eternal and divine perichoresis, is offered in history. But the offer is never closed. The historical dance may not be self-enclosing. The range of partners is all humankind. The poor, the sick, the racially or sexually excluded, all these must be sought out by Christians to be genuine partners in the dance of life. Only thus will the *danse macabre* be replaced by perichoresis. Liturgy and Christian life are enabled and called to be exhibitions and expressions of that dance of life. Together, in mutual confirmation, challenge and empowerment, they create a widening ciricle of human involvement in the dance of God.

See **Initiation, Christian; Imagination and worship; Politics, liturgy and; Social issues, liturgy and**

T. Bala Suriya, *The Eucharist and Human Liberation,* 1972. Bernard Cooke, *Sacraments and Sacramentality,* 1983. D.W. Hardy and David F. Ford, *Jubilate, Theology in Praise,* 1984. Bernard Haring, *The New Covenant,* 1965. Herbert McCabe, o.p., *The New Creation,* 1963. E. McDonagh, "Liturgy and Christian Living" in *Invitation and Response,* 1972; "Liturgy" in *The Making of Disciples,* 1982; "Prayer, Poetry and Politics" in *The Gracing of Society,* 1989. Joseph Martos, *Doors to the Sacred,* 1982. Juan Luis Segundo, s.j., *The Sacraments Today,* 1971. G. Wainwright, E. Yarnold, C. Jones, (eds.), *The Study of Liturgy,* 1978. Teilhard de Chardin, *Hymn of the Universe,* Fontana, 1970. G. Wainwright, *Doxology,* 1979.

ENDA McDONAGH

LITURGY AS PROPHETIC

It might seem strange to speak of liturgy as "prophetic." Prophets seldom praised and often lamented priests, false worship and ritualism.

Your piety is like a morning cloud,
    like the dew that early passes away.
For this reason I smote them through
    the prophets,
I slew them by the words of my
    mouth;
For it is love that I desire, not sacrifice,
    and the knowledge of God rather
    than holocausts (Hos 5:4-6).

Jesus distanced himself from the role and title of the priesthood and its association with empty sacrifices. Is it possible to hold liturgy and prophecy together? And in spite of the history of abuses in all religions and churches, is it possible for liturgy be prophetic?

We shall explore three common denominators of liturgy and prophecy: 1. both proclaim God's word; 2. both read the signs of the times and either judge or console; 3. both look to present and future.

Proclaiming God's Word

In Hebrew the prophet (*nabi*) is one called *to speak on behalf of another*, in this case to speak with passion on behalf of God. Of course, God's message of covenant and grace and justice is in turn speech on behalf of us. Prophets speak God's message especially on behalf of the poor and victims of oppression. In speaking on God's behalf they inveigh against all idols, all principalities and powers, all personal and social systems of oppression and sin which are not divine. For prophets only God is divine. Every system is subject to prophetic judgment.

Prophets include more voices than the authors of the canonical books of the prophets. The Jews see Moses as the greatest of Hebrew prophets. Although Jesus may not have seen himself as a prophet since he spoke *on his own authority*, his disciples saw him as a prophet (cf. Lk 24:19). Prophecy continues in those who see God's presence (or absence) in our wounded world and speak boldly on behalf of God for a new world where God reigns and only God reigns.

Prophets speak not just in word but in deeds. The Hebrew word for "word" (*dabar*) means *word/deed*. The prophets' most powerful preaching is often in symbolic action. These actions function as sacraments, e.g., Jeremiah buys a field (Jeremiah 32); Ezekiel turns to mime (Ezek 4:1-5:4, 12:1-7, 21:23f, 37:15f); Jesus eats with sinners (Lk 15:1-3). Their entire lives are prophetic, e.g., Hosea's tragic marriage. No chasm lies between word and deed. Like sacraments, they effect what they signify. Jesus *is* the Word made flesh. His life enfleshes God's message of self-giving love and life through death. Jesus' life is his great parable. We think we know how stories will end, but great storytellers and parable makers throw a curve at the end— workers overpaid, prodigals embraced, Samaritans who heal. We know that Jesus' cross and death are the end, but God throws us a curve—life out of death, power out of powerlessness, fullness out

of emptiness. That is what the parable of Jesus' life proclaims for him and for us.

In that sense, liturgy and sacramental actions also speak of covenant, grace, and justice on behalf of God. "...the liturgical (sacramental) event is best understood as a communications event. It rests upon the conviction that a liturgical service as a whole, together with its constitutive elements, says something" (Searle, "Liturgy as Metaphor," p. 98).

We noted that the great lament of prophets is the gulf between what rituals say and who the people are and what they do.

I hate and despise your feasts,
I take no pleasure in your solemn festivals,
When you offer me holocausts,
I reject your oblations....
But let justice flow like water,
Integrity like an unfailing stream
(Amos 5:21-22, 26).

The actual *dabar* of the people meant worshipping idols and victimizing the poor. The "din of their chanting" and "strumming on harps" (Amos 5:22) failed to drown out their treachery and infidelity. Empty ritualism. Liturgy as lie— worship without witness, celebration without service, liturgy cut off from life, supper without the washing of feet, and Jesus-and-me divided from Jew-Gentile, male-female, slave-free, black-white, Wall Street-Skid Row, cleric-lay, Anglo-Hispanic, East-West, North-South.

The challenge is to stop lying and to become and do what we say at liturgy. That lie persists until we cease seeing sacraments as magic moments (words of institution) done in sacred spaces (sanctuaries) performed only by sacred persons (ordained) and consisting only of sacred things (bread and wine). The great sacraments are not things but persons— Jesus, sacrament of God, and church, sacrament of the risen Christ (L.G., 1; S.C., 5). These *persons* are "visible signs of invisible grace" who enflesh God's message of covenant love and justice. No lies. No gulf between worship and justice, liturgy and life. Dying/rising in church buildings is our *dabar* outside those buildings. Just as Jesus most powerfully proclaims that message at meals, so the church acts as prophet at eucharist where bread broken and grapes crushed witness that we wash feet and share the brokenness of sisters and brothers crushed and crucified.

The bishops of the United States published a pastoral letter entitled *To Teach As Jesus Did* which called the church to preach his message of good news. The church most boldly proclaims that message not in word but in word/deed, in action, when the community welcomes to table those welcomed by Jesus—*to eat as Jesus did.*

The seven derivative sacraments, therefore, are best seen as actions of a people (initiating, eating/drinking, reconciling, healing, marrying, leading, dying/rising) and not as static objects (water, oil, bread and wine). The theology of transubstantiation too often reified sacraments into objects. Only the priest was "in on the action," and his action was often limited to changing those objects. The community was passive. Even the verbs spoke passivity—we "received" sacraments, we "attended" or "saw" Mass. If the community is the basic sacrament, we transform the seven sacraments from objects to actions of that community, from nouns to active verbs.

Vatican II in the *Constitution on the Sacred Liturgy* insists, therefore, that communal celebrations with every sacrament take preference to individual and quasi-private rites (S.C., 27) so that the community can act. That constitution called for "active participation" (S.C., 14). That means far more than words and song. It means being and acting as sacrament of the body of Christ broken for the life of the world. It means prophecy.

When the church gathers to celebrate and proclaim that message in ritual, the community remembers and resounds that message from its privileged source—the scriptures, the word of God broken open by homily for human life today. Homilies do not exegete texts; they exegete our lives in light of scriptural texts. Vatican II restored the "paramount importance" of God's word and called for a "warm and living love" of scripture (S.C., 24). All liturgies are to proclaim God's word. If the scriptures are full of prophecy, liturgies are full of prophecy. We hear again and again prophetic voices decrying liturgies as lies.

We not only have scripture as our privileged text. Although church is the basic sacrament, among the other sacraments the church sees the sacraments of initiation (baptism/confirmation/eucharist) and the eucharist (the repeatable sacrament of initiation) as privileged. The eucharist, seen not as things but as the body of Christ continuing to break body and shed blood for our sisters and brothers, is the "summit" and "fountain" of the Christian life (S.C., 10). Many insist that the *Rite of Christian Initiation of Adults* (R.C.I.A.) is the most prophetic document since Vatican II. Ralph Keifer claims it calls us from a penitential spirituality centered on the sacrament of penance, which held sway for centuries, to a spirituality of paschal mystery and baptismal vocation rooted in adult initiation (*Mass in a Time of Doubt*). The R.C.I.A. calls the entire community as sacrament to be about its prophetic mission of proclaiming good news (R.C.I.A., 4;9). It calls the community to a galaxy of rites and prophetic, symbolic acts—to welcome, sign senses, proclaim the word, bless, present our life of faith and prayer, elect, scrutinize exorcize, bathe, anoint, eat and drink. At the heart of prophecy is our experience of paschal mystery, the dying/rising of Jesus. All sacraments celebrate that, but their source is baptism/eucharist. In paragraphs that follow when I speak of liturgies as prophetic, I assume that this is especially true of initiation and eucharist. When the church as sacrament truly proclaims the dying/rising begun in initiation and renewed in eucharist and extends that to our wounded world, we shall be akin to prophets who speak God's message of covenant and grace and justice.

Signs and Seasons for Judgment or Consolation

Both prophets and liturgies deal with human life. They read the signs of the times. Those times are full of both agony and ecstacy. Viktor Frankl says humans are so evil that they built the gas chambers of Auschwitz but so magnificent that they entered the chambers proudly with the "Lord's Prayer" or the *Shema Israel* on their lips. John Shea claims humans stand tall but never so tall we aren't brought to our rear by a banana peel. Ernst Becker complains that we are torn apart as body/spirits; we are "angels who crap."

Since prophets know both the horror and the glory, their message changes with the times. Especially in pre-exilic times they are prophets of judgment, doom, threat and punishment (Amos, First Isaiah). During the exile they are often prophets of hope and consolation (Second Isaiah). After the exile the message is restoration and pardon (Haggai, Zechariah). Jeremiah both judges and consoles; he is sent to "tear up and to knock down, ... to build and to plant" (Jer 1:10).

Therefore, if judgment and consolation/restoration mark the polarities of prophets responding to signs of their times, they will mark our liturgies. Liturgies will name the dark and the light side of human life.

First, concerning judgment, Bruggeman insists that prophets do not scold. They complain and grieve. They are not nags ranting from outside the people. They stand in compassion with the deathliness gnawing at the people and "bring to public expression the dread of endings, the collapse of our self-madeness, the barriers and pecking orders that secure us at each other's expense, the fearful practice of eating off the table of a hungry brother or sister," and the ultimate consumerism of consuming each other (*The Prophetic Imagination*, p. 50).

Bruggeman states that Moses as prophet first assaulted this deathliness by his radical break from the imperial reality of Egypt sustained by gods which were immovable lords of order. He frees Israel both from the *religion* of static triumphalism and the *politics* of exploitation. "In place of the gods of Egypt, creatures of the imperial consciousness, Moses discloses Yahweh the sovereign one who acts in his lordly freedom ... and is captive to no social perception.... Religiously, the gods were declared no-gods. Politically, the oppressiveness of the brickyard was shown to be ineffective .... Moses introduced not just the new free God and not just a message of social liberation. Rather, his work came precisely at the engagement of the *religion of God's freedom* with the *politics of human justice*" (*The Prophetic Imagination*, pp. 16, 17).

Bruggeman claims Israel soon lost that engagement with the development of a "royal consciousness" that saw the Davidic king as necessary agent of God's purposes. The primary vision became the well-being of the king and not the role of advocate for the marginal.

He sees that imperial model in our culture present in a civil religion where we identify national purpose with God's purpose. It is in an *economics* of affluence with some so well off they can eat their way around pain; in a *politics* of oppression which hears cries of the marginal as noises of kooks and traitors; in a *religion* of immanence and accessibility with God so present that we don't notice God's hard message, absence, banishment; and we reduce the problem to psychology (cf. *The Prophetic Imagination*, p.41). During the period of the kings, that is the economics, politics, and religion condemned by prophets. Jesus condemns it in Roman empire and Jewish church. Liturgy as prophecy will echo that rebuke today for both churches and states.

That is hardly what happens in practice. Liturgies still lie. Church becomes cozy with state and wary of prophetic critique. The church of martyrs was clearly counter-cultural and rebuked the idols. Ralph Keifer says: "Again and again it was the problem of idolatry as a fact of virtually all spheres of public life which forced the church to remain a separate enclave within the culture of the ancient world. It is clear, both from the refusal to compromise with the idolatrous state and the immense concern for such things as the concrete care for the poor, that the church's evangelization of individuals had nothing in common with modern approaches to a gospel of personal salvation which elicits no concern for justice, and which gladly joins in contemporary versions of emperor worship" (Ralph Keifer, "Christian Initiation: the State of the Question," p. 144).

Our emperor worship means: "We are as American as the pollution of Lake Erie, as beaches littered with flip tops, as houses not forty years old and in shambles, as health care that sucks away the lifeblood of the destitute. We are as American as the quick solution, the throwaway art, the despising of all that is not obvious, instantly perceptible, and of immediate pragmatic relevance. We are as American as the tolerance of all ugliness except human misery, which can be hidden away in nursing homes and ghettos and buried under rhetoric" (Keifer, "Christian Initiation...," p. 143).

To confront that America, prophetic liturgy proclaims and creates a different world. When we celebrate the Judaeo/Christian world of Moses and Jesus, we again engage the religion of God's freedom with the politics of human justice. When we tell and renew the stories of exodus from slavery to freedom and of paschal mystery through death to life, we name and create a world which shatters idols and empires. That is the power of story, myth, and ritual language. We shape the nature of things by naming and calling it so. That was God's great gift to Adam—to create by naming. In liturgy we name our world as the place of God's freedom and human justice. We proclaim, "This God and no other! This world of the beatitudes and no other!"

"Lord have mercy" is a weak rendering of *Kyrie eleison*. It also bears the meaning of "the Lord reigns." In times when the emperor (the *kyrios*) was god, *Kyrie eleison* was a Christian protest. "No, Jesus is *Kyrios*. God is King. In this space, in this world, God reigns."

In empires of American consumerism and Marxist materialism, with imperial armies bearing arms of nuclear holocaust, divided by racism, sexism, nationalism and every other "ism," with resources diverted from wars on poverty and homelessness to wars on drugs, liturgy proclaims that God reigns in this people. That God judges nations and people on what we do for the hungry, thirsty, naked, prisoner and stranger (cf. Mt 25). That is why pioneer liturgists, such as Virgil Michel and H.A. Reinhold, could not conceive of liturgy divorced from justice. Some liturgical concoctions today seem aimed primarily at producing feelings and fellowship. These trailblazers saw liturgy's purpose as changing worlds, creating worlds, judging all imperial worlds of tyranny and oppression and celebrating God's world of freedom and justice. *Kyrie eleison*!

Is the contemporary church capable of such liturgical prophecy? Would Amos and Isaiah judge our church and rituals with their usual outrage? In practice, does liturgy lie?

For example, Keifer claims we are in danger of baptismal lying, because the R.C.I.A., that supposedly prophetic document, is so far from present pastoral practice that it is either "suicide or prophecy of a very high order." "The clear intent of the reform is that initiation should be experiential, not only for those who are initiated, but also, and equally important, for the local church which does the initiating. Here is the pastoral difficulty. The conception of church as local communion in faith, as vehicle of the experience of the risen Lord, as eschatological sign, exists only in official text and clerical rhetoric, not something perceived by the great majority of churchgoers." (Keifer, "Christian Initiation...," pp. 141-142).

What Keifer says about baptismal lying Tom Conry says about eucharistic lying. We spew forth theologies about all the baptized called to their dignity as people of God, yet eucharistic liturgy often treats them as serfs back in Egypt and the empire: "There is an announcement that everyone should stand and greet our celebrant" and he walks solemnly to the front of the room . . . in a procession that is clearly the remnant of court royalism. He turns to the assembly from his point in front of everyone where only he has access to the important ritual furniture and his first substantial ritual action is to forgive the assembly for being in its own space; 'for all the times we have gotten out of line, Lord have mercy.' ...A mere two minutes and thirty seconds into the liturgy we have already said everything about that parish's theology of the importance of baptism that there is to say" (Conry, "How Can We Keep from Singing?" p. 33).

In light of this and other less than stunning stabs at renewal Mark Searle asks: "Is the concept (and practice) of 'active participation' a genuine step towards the redistribution of responsibility in the church, or is it a means to heading off more radical forms of participatory democracy?... Is the revised liturgy serving the pedagogical role of fostering a genuinely new consciousness, or is it a way of perpetuating the old imperialist theology in more attractive packaging?" (Searle, "The Pedagogical Function of the Liturgy," p. 347).

Therefore, before rhapsodizing about liturgy as prophetic we need to submit liturgy itself to critique and the prophecy of judgment. Prophets lament a royal consciousness and imperial power wherever it appears.

Second, when times call not for judgment but consolation/restoration, liturgies welcome, reconcile, and heal with prophetic compassion and mercy. As Hosea lures his unfaithful wife back, so will the church lure those who are alienated or in sin: "When that day comes ... I will betroth you to myself forever, betroth you with integrity and justice, with tenderness and love; I will betroth you to myself with faithfulness, and you will come to know Yahweh" (Hos 19, 21-22).

In a homily echoing that propetic word Bishop Untener calls the church to be a sacrament of God's faithful love and mercy: "There has been a prevailing wind in the Church moving us away from softness and toward severity. But John XXIII brought a fresh emphasis on mercy and love. But we're not sure how to handle this new breeze.... Our tendency will surely be to stifle it.... You will pass on the tradition of a Church remarkable for its tenderness and mercy" (Kenneth Untener, "A Church Remarkable for Tenderness and Mercy," *Origins*, 16:47, p. 826).

The church doing eucharist is *the* sacrament of reconciliation. If our church moves toward severity, at prophetic liturgies of consolation/restoration we need to eat as Jesus did, with the most rejected and alien, e.g., the woman "who had a bad name in the town" (Lk 7:36-50), prodigal children (Lk 15:11-32), Zachaeus the hated tax collector (Lk 10:1-10), motley crowds at wedding feasts (Mt 22:1-10), entiles finally sharing loaves with Jews (Mk 8:1-10), all brought to a climax by broken disciples who recognize the Lord in shared brokenness when they break bread (Lk 24:13-35). That church as prophet will hear the self-righteous grumbling heard by Jesus: "This man welcomes sinners and eats with them" (Lk 15:3). It is even more scandalous if we recall that then and now at meals in the Middle East both host and guest begin with rituals of heaping praise on each other. Jesus is sacrament of God's love at those ritualized meals. At our meals he calls us to set no condition for restoration than the one which he set—accept the Father's mercy.

Robert Hovda describes the prophetic witness of such meals in a society riddled with cutthroat competition and upward mobility. "Where else in our society are we all addressed and sprinkled, bowed to, incensed, touched and kissed and treated like *somebody*—all in the very same way? Where else do economic czars and beggars get the same treatment? Where else are food and drink blessed in a common prayer of thanksgiving, broken and poured out, so that everybody, everybody shares and shares alike?" (*Liturgy 80,* June/July 1982, p. 6).

Much of Christian liturgical life proclaims reconciliation in the broadest sense—within our body/spirits, with all creation, each other, the community of faith, all races, nations and males/females, with God. When everybody is somebody at font and table, all liturgy consoles/restores with that wonderful prophetic vision of St. Paul: "There are no more distinctions between Jew and Greek, slave and free, male and female, but all of you are one in Christ Jesus" (Gal 4:28).

Bruggeman also makes helpful distinctions regarding the psalms which also speak on behalf of both God and us. Psalms are the cult of Israel, the liturgical response to varied times and seasons. They resound in Christian liturgy. He names poems of *orientation*—sung in *seasons of well-being* and evoking gratitude for the constancy of blessing, e.g., Psalm 145. Second, there are *seasons of hurt, alienation and darkness* evoking rage, resentment, self-pity which appear in *psalms of disorientation,* e.g., Psalm 13. The Faithful One and the Judge promises to be in the darkness with us, and we find it transformed by the power of relentless solidarity. Bruggeman quotes Elie Wiesel: "Poets exist so that the dead may vote." They do vote in the Psalms. They vote for faith. But in voting for faith they vote for candor, for pain, for passion—and finally for joy" (*The Message of the Psalms,* p. 12). Bruggeman adds that the church continues to sing songs of orientation in a world disoriented, "a frightened, numb denial and deception that does not want to acknowledge or experience the disorientation of life" (p. 51). Third, there are *seasons of surprise* which overwhelm us with new gifts of God, when joy breaks through despair. We sing *psalms of new orientation,* e.g., Psalm 30.

If Israel in her cult sings of orientation, disorientation, and new orientation, a prophetic Christian liturgy also attends to all these seasons. As Bruggeman notes, the church is better at psalms and liturgies of orientation praising God for the way things are than at entering the death side of paschal mystery in disorientation or the surprise/resurrection side of paschal mystery in new orientation. Cultic songs of orientation are often creation psalms praising God's creative fidelity found in the present as generosity, continuity, and regularity. Chaos is not present and is not permitted a hearing. At times this might not be a high and noble faith. It may celebrate the status quo, the unfair way that the powerful arrange life. It can be social control. Bruggeman proposes that if we praise God in doxology as always good and in charge, never acting, we become worshippers who are docile, passive, a satiated, conformist community without energy nor vocation nor hope, who only treasure and defend "the way things are" (cf. Bruggeman, *Message*..., pp. 25-28).

Tom Conry complains that much contemporary church music is only about praise in a world well oriented and devoid of death and terror. He finds: "lots of songs about the comfort of Jesus, about good-old-faithful-God, lots of music consisting of melodic and textual appeals to 'come and worship, come and praise, honor the Lord, sing a joyful song, praise, honor, wisdom, praise, alleluia, alleluia, alleluia and more praise.' It puts one in mind of Goethe's declaration that 'those who cannot love must cultivate flattery.'... C. Alexander Peloquin says that all of this music can be reduced to the lyrics: 'I like Jesus, you like Jesus, why the hell don't we get together?'" (Conry, p.33).

Prophetic liturgy which prays and sings and names a world on behalf of the God of the oppressed believes not just in civil religion which goes "from strength to strength" but in a God present in the darkness, weakness, emptiness, in times of disorientation. In those deathly places when it is clear that we cannot save ourselves, God gives new life.

How much longer will you forget me, Yahweh? Forever?

How much longer will you hide your face from me?

How much longer must I endure grief in my soul?...

But I for my part rely on your love Yahweh...(Ps 13:1-2, 5).

In a culture often closed to change and surprise, in which self-made messiahs don't need grace, prophetic liturgy also prays and sings and names a new world of unearned grace, a new orientation.

"Yahweh, my God, I cried to you for help, and you have healed me.... You have turned my mourning into dancing, you have stripped off my sackcloth and wrapped me in gladness and now my heart, silent no longer, will play you music; Yahweh, my God, I will praise you forever" (Ps 30:2, 11-12).

In celebrating times demanding judgment or crying for consolation/restoration and seasons of well-being, chaos, or surprise, prophetic liturgy makes the absolutely critical connection between liturgy and life, worship and justice. It bridges any gap between the *Constitution on the Sacred Liturgy* and the *Constitution on the Church in the Modern World* by linking liturgy with life in our world. In liturgy we proclaim that: "The joys and the hopes, the griefs and the anxieties of the people of the age, especially those who are poor or in any way afflicted, these too are the joys and hopes, the griefs and anxieties of the followers of Christ. Indeed, nothing genuinely human fails to raise an echo in their hearts" (G.S., 1).

Present and Future

Here again, tensions between judgment and consolation/restoration emerge. From the perspective of time and history the tension is between immanence (restoration) and transcendence (judgment), the "already" and the "not yet," the horizontal and the vertical, realized eschatology and proleptic eschatology, liturgy as present "pledge of future glory" (S.C., 47) and liturgy as sustenance of a pilgrim people on the way to the future.

Concerning immanence, prophetic consciousness sees that God is already present in the signs of the times. Prophets see the future and what it will bring because they see so clearly the present. They summon us to hope and consolation because they not only see the evils of the present time (calling for judgment by a God who summons us to a better future); they see the movements of God in Christ Jesus through the Spirit acting in our times to create a world marked by poverty of spirit, thirst for righteousness, fullness of mercy, and the making of peace (Mt 5:1-10). Jesus is risen now. The Spirit gifts us now. We are Christ's body now. The reign of God is happening now. The future is present now.

That brings us back to a vision of church and liturgy as sacraments which enflesh the life of God now. Prophetic liturgy speaks in behalf of God in the present and acts symbolically in the present to inaugurate the future now. Eucharist is the eternal banquet now. Initiation makes us one now and anticipates St. Augustine's vision of heaven— "one Christ loving himself." Reconciliation and anointing heal divisions and wounds now. Marriage of two in one flesh enfleshes Christ's eternal love and union with the church now. Most important, the church is sacrament of Christ and his presence in the world now.

That is why *the* Catholic difference (shared by other sacramental churches) is the experience of incarnation and sacramentality—the discovery of God in Christ through the Spirit already enfleshed in creation and human life which are sacraments of God's life and love. That experience leads to seven, not just two sacraments. It means celebration of God's presence in all kinds of "smells and bells," in Mary and the saints, in ministries of the baptized, the ordained, popes and peasants. Ultimately, it means that human life is the place of God's presence and revelation. Prophets see the mystery of God in all human moments of dying and rising. They see what the poet Gerard Manley Hopkins calls "the dearest freshness deep-down things." John Shea says: "There are moments which, although they occur within the everyday confines of human living, take on larger meaning.

They have a lasting impact; they cut through to something deeper; they demand a hearing. It may be the death of a parent, the touch of a friend, falling in love, a betrayal, the recognition of what has really been happening over the last two years, the unexpected arrival of blessing, the sudden advent of curse. But whatever it is, we sense we have undergone something that has touched upon the normally dormant but always present relationship to God" (*An Experience Named Spirit*, Chicago: Thomas More Press, 1983, p. 98).

Prophets call us to remember God's promise and God's covenant to be with and in God's people in such moments. "I will adopt you as my own people, and I will be your God" (Exod 5:7). "I am in my Father and you in me and I in you" (Jn 14:19). "You are a chosen race, a royal priesthood, a consecrated nation, a people set apart" (1 Pet 2:9). Liturgies of consolation/restoration and psalms and prayers of orientation and new orientation celebrate that prophetic memory and vision of the covenant with an immanent and faithful God always present to our lives now.

If immanence and sacramentality, however, constitute the Catholic difference, they also bear the Catholic peril— idolatry. The Reformation was in essence a protest and a prophetic judgment against equating the human with the divine—church with reign of God, popes with Christ, sacraments with God's actions which worked magically without the need for faith, the present with the future. Reckless talk about an immanent God who is already present in a realized eschatology can shatter hope in a more just future for all God's people. It can identify human structures of both church and state with divine presence and yield new forms of imperialist social control. In that world, "the present ordering, and by derivation the present regime, claims to be the full and final ordering. That claim means there can be no future that either calls the present into question or promises a way out of it. Thus the fulsome claim of the present arrangement is premised on hopelessness. This insidious form of realized eschatology requires persons to live without hope" (Bruggeman, *The Prophetic Imagination*, p. 63).

It can radically rend asunder the constant prophetic commitment to monotheism; for prophets there is only one God, and only God is God. Prophets forever remind us that the future is God's future, and only God can make us one at the eternal banquet which we hope for and anticipate at eucharist. In that regard the *Constitution on the Sacred Liturgy* is strong on language of anticipation but woefully weak in naming ethical imperatives implied in the chasm experienced in liturgy and life between "the already" and the "not yet."

Prophetic liturgy will name those gaps, call to conversion, challenge the status quo, and proclaim God's promise and God's future. It will proclaim a transcendent God who is always more than and beyond our rites of church and state. It will proclaim God's word, with judgment or consolation/restoration according to the signs of the times, and interpret the present while stretching us into the future.

See **Liturgy and Christian life**

Walter Bruggeman, *The Message of the Psalms* (Minneapolis: Augsburg Publishing House, 1984); *The Prophetic Imagination* (Philadelphia: Fortress Press, 1978). Thomas Conry, "How Can We Keep from Singing?" *Pastoral Music* (Oct/Nov 1988): 33-36. Ralph Keifer, "Christian Initiation: the State of the Question," in *Made Not Born* (Notre Dame: University of Notre Dame Press, 1978): 138-151. Ralph Keifer, *Mass in a Time of Doubt* (Washington, D.C.: National Association of Pastoral Musicians, 1983). Mark Searle, "Liturgy As Metaphor," *Worship* (March 1981): 98ff; "The Pedagogical Function of the Liturgy," *Worship* (July 1981): p. 343ff.

JAMES B. DUNNING

LITURGY IN A TECHNOLOGICAL AGE

Introduction

Before the liturgical reforms of Vatican II, the American Catholic community expressed itself primarily along paraliturgical lines, its most meaningful religious symbols appearing in a host of popular devotions. The Sorrowful Mother, the Infant of Prague, the Nine First Fridays, the Miraculous Medal, Benediction and the Forty Hours: these and many others flourished. Alongside these devotions, four unquestioned characteristics symbolized a good Roman Catholic: meatless Fridays, attendance at Sunday Mass, no birth control except for the rhythm method, and no divorce. The Latin Mass expressed the mystery of the bond with God by providing a required weekly event wherein one could pray in quiet while the priest conducted the sacred ritual.

Vatican II called this individualistic model into serious question, arguing for and eventually legislating reforms aimed at a much more radically communal form of worship. Now, a quarter century later, the success of the reforms remains spotty. Some extraordinary parishes, helped by the Rite of Christian Initiation of Adults (R.C.I.A.) and other programs for renewal, exhibit a vibrant liturgical life. Others appear to have lost touch with the vital core of their faith life. The old popular devotions have died but the symbolic expression of the new liturgy has failed to engage their hearts. Significant numbers of younger adults have opted for the "silent schism" of nominal church membership, often with the complaint that the Mass seems insipid and offers little help in coping with the challenges of their lives. For the Vatican II liturgical reforms to succeed in renewing Catholic life, it would seem necessary to address this question: "how can the church integrate its commitment to a communal liturgy with contemporary symbolic experience?

In the years since Vatican II it has become commonplace to observe that liturgy depends, for its vitality, on a meaningful intersection of symbol and community. Catholic tradition is rooted in the fleshy, sacramental relationship between God and human beings. The church flourishes only when it lives as a community of shared symbolic meaning. This essay begins by asking how Catholic communites of shared symbolic meaning operated in the pre-Vatican II era and how the council's liturgical reforms have interacted with contemporary technological and societal changes to influence present liturgical experience. With the help of this broad cultural perspective, I will conclude with several observations about trends that may point the way toward a deepening of popular liturgical renewal.

Popular Devotion Before the Council

The devotions depended on symbols that were *publicly* shared within a culture. Symbols such as the Sacred Heart, the Infant of Prague, the Lady of Lourdes, created frames of reference in which people could relate their ordinary lives to God, where daily life—success and failure, birth and death, violence and tranquility— had a meaningful place. They were "popular" because they were local, rooted deeply in the fabric of a people's history. Like many good wines, they did not travel easily. In contrast to Latin sacramental worship, with its monolingual embodiment of church universality, devotions called to us from the depths of our unique traditions. They reminded us that while we were one human family, the people of God, we were also beautiful in our diversity.

Catholicism has always provided a home for both experiences. It is not surprising, nor is it theologically unsound, that Mary appears in the cultural clothing of many lands, nor that many saints reside in particular home towns. "God," so this tradition seems to say, "loves the flesh and blood of our local existence." Jesus, the Galilean, emerges as the universal Christ precisely from his fleshly embrace of a historically unique starting point. Seen from this perspective, local popular devotions participate in the core tension of Christianity: Christ, human and divine, culture-bound and Lord of all. Our centuries-long experience wherein the hierarchical church responds to and evaluates popular devotions, sometimes approving them and sometimes not—one thinks of the "appearances" at Guadalupe and at Necedah, Wisconsin, as contrasting examples—continally renews the mystery of the incarnation.

The conditions that rendered this division of church experience into sacramental life (Latin and global) and paraliturgical devotional life (local and fleshy) have, however, been transformed in the decades since World War II. In the process the balance between sacrament and popular devotion has been disturbed so that a new understanding of the tension between locality and universality has become necessary.

Popular devotions require, as a necessary precondition, the existence of a local culture which I shall call a "community of shared symbolic meaning." Before any saint or any vision of Jesus or Mary can spring forth as a focus for daily faith life there must first exist a people who perceive reality within the same frame of reference. Human beings, as Karl Rahner reminds us, are symbolic at the core and our experience of God and of the meaning of life itself withers when reduced to fleshless abstraction. The popularity of devotions such as the Sacred Heart depended therefore on the existence of a cultural frame of reference in which holy symbols, such as the Heart of Jesus, carried deep religious meaning.

In the United States we have often

called that common culture "ghetto Catholicism." U.S. parishes typically reflected specific European imigrant traditions. Thus, in the 1950s my small mill town in northern Wisconsin supported four parishes—French, German, Irish, and Polish—even though the presence of the Staudenmaiers in the Irish parish presaged the breakdown of those tight ethnic communities. Popular devotions "worked" because the Catholic ghetto "worked." That is to say, Catholics experienced themselves as a distinct people within the larger civil order that was the United States of America. We knew who "we" were. Our insularity provided the cultural frame of reference in which mid-century American Catholic practices—devotions, parish life, the place of priests and sisters—made sense. Of course this oversimplifies the matter considerably. Ethnic American Catholics felt powerful ambivalence about their relationship with the larger social order. We longed to prove ourselves good Americans even as we held on to our Catholic identities.

A Crisis of Community and of Symbol

A host of developments, which gained significant momentum during World War II, began to revolutionize ghetto life. This extraordinarily popular war galvanized most citizens and provided a common goal that challenged old prejudices. The pressure of national emergency broke open the nation's subcultures as previously disparate men and women mixed on an almost equal basis in the armed services and the factories of the land. The same forces that began to erode black-white racial barriers served a similar purpose among Catholics, other Christians, Jews and people of other faiths, or none. Indeed only a decade and a half later, our ethnic search for American legitimacy reached its apogee in the election of an Irishman and a Catholic to the presidency.

One could say that Catholic devotional life began to decline as American Catholics began to settle into the mainstream of the nation's cultural life. As far as it goes, this is a valid and helpful interpretation. Taken alone, however, it overlooks two related technological developments which complicate devotional life still further. The first has to do with an extraordinary change in the way people today experience "community" and the second with the pervasive assault of contemporary advertising on symbolic meaning.

The Changing Sense of Community

In the United States, as in Western Europe, the 19th and 20th centuries saw a gradual shift from a village life-style toward an urban, national, and global frame of reference. The change followed in the wake of the new rail, air, and auto transport networks, on the one hand, and electronic media (telegraphic wire services, telephone, radio, television, computer networks) on the other. Village and neighborhood culture prevailed as long as the transportation of information was limited to the speed of physical bodies traveling only a few miles per hour. Because information moved so slowly, most social interaction took place within walking distance of where one slept at night. Thus, whether one lived one's entire life within the same neighborhood or migrated to distant places, one's primary frame of reference was necessarily local. One depended for friendship, for livelihood, and for cultural meaning, on the handful of people close by. Letters to loved ones, given the uncertain and painfully slow transportation systems of the time, were no substitute for the daily interactions that constitute the stuff of ordinary life.

In the past few decades, however, community has become increasingly individualized and fragmented. Who, one might ask, belongs to "my community"?

As sociologist Claude Fischer has observed, once-local communities have begun to be replaced by "support networks," an array of individuals with whom we communicate via telephone or transport systems. Support networks differ most radically from village and neighborhood communities in that the members of one's support network often do not know one another. They constitute a meaningful social entity only in their relationship with "me." How readily do such social groupings share a common symbolic life? Friends and colleagues represent not only many ethnic traditions and work experiences, they are religiously pluralistic as well. What forms of popular devotion can emerge from affiliations that are polyglot in the most basic sense of the term?

Twentieth-Century Advertising

Historians of advertising commonly agree that, in the U.S., World War I marked the rise to dominance of consumerist advertising. The new style grew in part from an obsession with social control as the nation's traditional elites reacted to the eastern and southern European immigrants who surged across the U.S. border at the century's beginning. Social psychologists, progressive-era politicians, and proponents of scientific management sought to Americanize the newcomers by such "melting pot" processes as the Ford Motor Company's English language schools and by the study of human motivation to control what appeared to be chaotic cultural pluralism. At the same time, the maturation of mass production in the automotive and electrical appliance industries demanded a revolution in the selling of goods. U.S. citizens, it was felt, had to be taught to consume the flood of new products.

In response, advertising agencies gradually shifted from a rational style that focused on product *qualities* to emotional appeals that called attention to product *benefits*. The advertiser's task, in the new dispensation, was to forge a powerful affective bond between consumer and product.

Semiotics, a recent theory of the process of symbol making, provides a helpful model for explaining one of the most common agency procedures. Advertisers faced the task of taking a product which has an already-accepted symbolic meaning and attaching some other cultural symbol to that meaning in order to enhance its marketing appeal. Before 1920, for example, the wildly popular Model T carried the symbolic meaning of a tool for transportation: durable, economical, and easy to repair. The symbol worked well for Ford because the vast majority of buyers were purchasing their first car. But the saturation of this virgin car market in the next decade led General Motors and the advertisers it employed to search out other American symbols that might enhance the car's affective appeal. They chose four: individual freedom, independent mobility, sexual prowess, and rising social status. Their advertising success created a new symbolic entity in the nation. The car began to be seen less as a transportation tool and more as what ad specialists call an "ego-enhancer," a commodity that dispensed freedom, mobility, sexuality, and status.

Advertising historian Roland Marchand (*Advertising the American Dream*) has identified a host of such symbolic transfers that emerged during the 1920s and 1930s. One type, of particular importance when considering popular devotions, was the application of sacred symbols to secular products. Thus the 1925 Oldsmobile was shown surrounded by radiant beams streaming from heaven. Listerine ads adopted the ritual of family night prayers ("now I lay me down to sleep"). Marchand offered this observation of the cumulative effect of such symbolic transference on public discourse: "To the extent that they attained the numinosity of "sacred symbols," the visual cliches of advertising acquired what cultural anthropologist Clifford Geertz describes as the "peculiar power ... to identify fact with value at the most fundamental level." In so doing, they pushed forward the process ... of appropriating traditional symbols for modern ends" (p. 284).

Today however, after seven decades of the process, we find ourselves living in a society whose capacity for symbolic meaning has become jaded. "The cultural impact was reciprocal. Products gained temporary enhancement, but traditional symbols were 'trivialized.' And the process has continued, so that now, in our own time, *it seems inconceivable that traditional and sacred symbols can be further impoverished*" (*ibid.*, emphasis added).

This sketch necessarily oversimplifies these patterns. Much more could be said about the complex interrelationships between the technological, social, political, and business factors involved in advertising's new consumerist style. Still, even this brief overview raises troubling issues. How might the church retrieve the basis for a community rooted in sacred symbols in a culture whose technological infrastructure fragments community even as its best funded form of public discourse, advertising, demeans the symbols themselves?

Recent Substitutes: Cults and TV Entertainments

Given the cumulative effect of World War II and these several technologically-based developments, it should come as no surprise that Catholics have begun to lose their taste for the old popular devotions. In their place a number of popular practices, embodying widely divergent ideological perspectives, appear to be responding to our malnourished symbolic condition. Consider the role of cults and TV evangelists, on the one hand, and soap operas and music videos, on the other.

Cults such as the Moonies or, more tragically, James Jones' fatal Jonestown movement, share central characteristics with television preaching. Both forms of prayer life offer the security of a symbolic ghetto at a very high price: namely, surrendering adult judgment and creative interaction with nonmembers. Jonestown's fatal flaw was its jungle isolation. Cult members lacked the balancing perspective of outsiders who, if taken seriously and listened to reverently, might have warned the group of its suicidal tendencies. Television evangelists, though much less extreme in their articulation and necessarily less effective in enforcement, often call adherents to cultic uniformity by savage attacks on outsiders who do not share the group's beliefs. Their appeal to Catholics is suggested by a startling recent statistic claiming that Catholics make up almost forty percent of the audiences for the television church.

The hunger for meaningful symbols may well explain the enormous popularity of two of the most popular current offspring of 20th-century advertising techniques, television soap operas and music videos. Many young people are mesmerized by the always compelling, sometimes savage, high pressure symbolic rituals of the videos. The soap operas' formulaic dramatizations of "ordinary life," routinely punctuated by episodes of sexual turmoil or violent conflict, attract an audience from across the age spectrum.

These trends, fundamentalist faith and intensely secular drama, mark the existence of a serious crisis of community and symbol for the contemporary world as a whole and for the church in particular. Insofar as it is cut off from ideological diversity and ancient tradition, cultic community tends toward fanaticism. The marketing of high-intensity televised symbols, for its part, erodes viewer capacity to find meaning in the ordinary fare of non-televised life. Neither form, in its present state, offers much hope for a renewal of Catholic faith life.

Indeed, they threaten the core of Vatican II's achievement. By convening the council, John XXIII reaffirmed the essential incarnational character of Jesus' call to "read the signs of the times" (Mt 16:2). The human reality of the Jesus of history cannot be replaced by an abstract and a-historical faith that ignores the culturally specific graces and temptations of subsequent eras. Recognizing this central faith requirement, the council inaugurated what Karl Rahner has called "the third major epoch" in Christian history: the "world church" (the first being the Jewish-Christian era and the second, the many centuries of a Europeanized church).

From this perspective, the shift from a universal Latin liturgy to a host of local vernacular forms, together with a correlative de-emphasis on popular devotions, can be seen as the incarnational response to a world rendered radically interactive by the world-shrinking transport and media technologies noted above. For citizens of the 20th century, the cultural isolation of earlier village life can no longer serve as a valid form of local context within a universal and monolingual church. Thus the attempt of cults and TV evangelists to reconstitute an essentially village form of communal life is in fact a rejection of the church's essential vocation to read and respond to the signs of the times. Christians must learn to be polylingual, must learn the radically new art of translating faith from one vernacular to another. Symbolic uniformity has, in short, lost its innocence and no longer offers Christians a faith-centered alternative.

Just as important and perhaps even more challenging, the church must learn how to bond contemporary polycultural experience with the ancient traditions of sacred symbols and articulated theolog-

ical wisdom. This task is rendered more challenging still by the complicating factor of consumerist advertising and its omnivorous appetite for fresh symbolic meat.

A final factor is perhaps most ominous. There is today in the U.S. a hitherto unprecedented division of Catholics along the lines of economic class as earlier immigrant groups enter the middle and upper middle classes and recent immigrants, Hispanics in particular, are relegated to a Catholic underclass. Middle class Catholics appear to have bought into the fragmented individualism so aptly described in *Habits of the Heart* (Robert Bellah, et.al., 1985) at about the same rate as their non-Catholic peers. Thus, to reconstitute the Catholic church into one community of shared symbolic meaning calls for a conversion at once affective and economic.

How then might the church, in countries especially where consumerist advertising and new technologies dominate, integrate Vatican II's call for communal worship with the chaotic symbolic experience of contemporary believers?

Conclusion

A number of post-World War II movements, such as Cursillo, Charismatic Renewal, and Marriage Encounter, indicate a widespread desire for a more communal manner of faith life. It is possible, given the cultural climate in which they exist, that such movements could drift into cult-like group individualism. Thus, participants in these movements are faced with the same challenge that confronts the church as a whole, namely, to create forms of communal life which are characteristically Catholic, forms that foster local, daily and physically-interactive symbolic life while remaining open to the holy pluralism of the diverse cultural perspectives found in the universal church community.

Three recent trends offer considerable

hope for the success of such a venture. First, our centuries-long commitment to theater, music, and the arts generally continually drew from and contributed to popular media. In keeping with that tradition we find a movement toward increasing attention, at once critical, contemplative and creative, to current media of all forms. Given the council's mandate to reincarnate the church in the modern world, it is not surprising to see Catholic media research centers and diocesan sponsored media specialists. No less surprising, John Paul II represents our first media-conscious pope. Still in an early stage of maturity, these developments respond directly to one of the major areas in which a healthy faith life must engage.

Attention to the media finds its necessary complement in the remarkable renewal of interest in the tradition of spiritual direction which has, for centuries, taught the art of discernment. Thus, the R.C.I.A. and similar adult renewal programs foster *individual* responsibility for following the journey of one's faith life as an essential requirement of communal faith life. In a world of overworked and polyvalent media symbols it is hard to imagine how faith life could do without spiritual direction's habits of discernment.

Perhaps even more to the point, spiritual direction provides a striking example of the recent renewal of theological and ecclesial commitment to narrative. Spiritual direction involves the integration of two modes of narrative, telling the story of one's inner journey to the director and situating that personal inner journey in scriptural narrative. More than almost any other human activity, storytelling calls forth fresh and vital symbols which offer access to the self-transcendent dimensions of human life. As such, the very process of spiritual direction promises to renew jaded imaginations.

The liturgical renewal begun by the Vatican II emerged as a necessary faith response to the radically changed cultural context in which 20th century believers must learn to live an incarnate faith life. It may well be that the related post-conciliar developments noted here: struggles with multi-cultural church governance, a faith-centered interpretation of media, and renewed emphasis on spiritual direction and narrative theology, will prove to be key areas in which the church is finding its way to integrate the passion and turbulence of culture-specific affective life into the faith life of the universal church.

Robert Bellah, Richard Madsen, William M. Sullivan, Ann Swidler, and Steven M. Tipton, *Habits of the Heart: Individualism and Commitment in American Life* (Berkeley: University of California Press, 1985). Donald Gelpi, ed., *Beyond Individualism* (Notre Dame: University of Notre Dame Press, 1989). Roland Marchand, *Advertising the American Dream: Making Way for Modernity, 1920-1940*, (Berkeley: University of California Press, 1985). Joshua Meyrowitz, *No Sense of Place: The Impact of Electronic Media on Social Behavior*, (New York: Oxford University Press, 1985). Karl Rahner, S.J., "Towards a Fundamental Theological Interpretation of Vatican II," *Theological Studies* 49 (December 1979).

JOHN M. STAUDENMAIER, S.J.

LORD'S PRAYER, THE

It is now more commonly recognized that the evangelists relied upon pre-Christian Jewish prayer forms in fashioning what has come to be called the Lord's Prayer or the Our Father. The Lord's Prayer has been handed down at two places in the NT. It is found in Matthew as part of the Sermon on the Mount (Mt 6:9-13), and in Lk 11:2-4. As the gospels of Matthew and Luke were being composed (c. A.D. 75-85), the Lord's Prayer was being transmitted in two forms which are in essential agreement, though one is longer than the other. The longer form is found in Matthew and also, with minor variations, in the *Didache* (8:2), while the shorter form is found in Luke.

The structure of the Lord's Prayer is made up of: (1) the address; (2) two "thou-petitions" in parallel (in Matthew there are three); (3) two "we-petitions" in parallel, both forming an antithesis; (4) the concluding request. The doxology is not found in Luke's account, and in Matthew it is not present in the oldest manuscripts. It is first found in the *Didache*. It would be incorrect, however, to conclude from this that the Lord's Prayer was used without some concluding words of praise to God.

In the course of Christian history, the Lord's Prayer has come to be used universally and regularly in personal and liturgical prayer. Hippolytus advocates its use as part of the daily prayer of the Christian. It was not a part of the eucharistic liturgy, however, prior to the middle of the 4th century at the earliest, its use being first clearly indicated in Cyril of Jerusalem's *Mystagogical Catecheses*. Since the practice in Jerusalem at this time is probably representative of the ancient church as a whole, it is likely that the Lord's Prayer was a part of the Lord's Supper and, together with the creed, is one of the elements of instruction to which catechumens were introduced just prior to, or immediately following their baptism.

Beginning with John Chrysostom, liturgical commentators in the East refer to praying the Lord's Prayer as a preparation for communion. In the West, both Ambrose and Augustine assume its use for the same purpose. From about 400 on, the Lord's Prayer has occupied a place in the communion rites in eucharistic worship. Though its place in the communion rites has not always been uniform, the Byzantine liturgy and, since Gregory the Great, the Roman liturgy, put it immediately after the *anaphora*.

Early interpreters emphasize that it is appropriate to pray the Lord's Prayer as a preparation for communion in the body and blood of the Lord, highlighting the petition for forgiveness of sins and for daily bread. The connection between daily bread and the heavenly bread, or eucharist, is often made in the early liturgical tradition, thus providing Christian writers, such as Ambrose, with occasion to advocate more frequent reception of communion.

Not surprisingly, the Lord's Prayer came to be viewed as the paradigm for all Christian prayer, as exemplified in the treatises on prayer in the writings of Cyprian in the West and Origen in the East.

The contemporary usage of the Lord's Prayer in liturgy includes, but is not limited to, the following: (1) as the creed is presented or "handed on" to the candidates for baptism during the week after the Sunday of the first scrutiny, so the Lord's Prayer is represented to them during the week after the third scrutiny; (2) it is recited regularly as part of the liturgy of the hours; (3) it concludes the general confession of sins, done in the form of a litany, in the use of the second and third forms of the revised Rite of Penance (1973); (4) the Lord's Prayer opens the communion rite in both the Roman and Byzantine liturgies, but in the Byzantine liturgy, it is integrated in that place into a prayer for unity in faith.

The revised Roman rite stands in continuity with the ancient custom of praying this prayer as a preparation for communion, affirming the association between daily bread and the eucharistic bread received in holiness through the forgiveness of sin which is petitioned in the Lord's Prayer. The presiding minister offers the invitation to pray. The assembly says the prayer with him. He alone adds the embolism, *Deliver us . . .*, which the assembly concludes with the doxology. The embolism, developing the final request of the Lord's Prayer petitions, in the name of the entire community, deliverance from the power of evil. The invitation, the Lord's Prayer itself, the embolism, and the doxology are sung or recited aloud.

As an expression of personal or liturgical prayer, the Lord's Prayer is an affirmation of the sovereignty of God and of human dependence upon the divine initiative. Praying the Lord's Prayer entails a recognition of human interdependence as well as the interdependence of all creation. It is an acknowledgement of human failure and sin, and of the need for forgiveness, both human and divine. It is a bold statement of confidence in God's graciousness in the face of evil, and a proclamation of belief in the power of love which prevails over all evil.

The Lord's Prayer expresses confidence that the age of salvation is not being realized. It expresses the conviction that the consummation of God's reign is bestowed in advance, and that the divine presence breaks into human life in the present. Praying in the name of Jesus with childlike confidence, trusting that God's presence will be revealed, and that the heavenly "Abba" will provide daily bread and grant forgiveness from sin, is itself a manifestation of the rule of God for which Christians pray.

———————

Raymond E. Brown, "The Pater Noster as an Eschatological Prayer," in *New Testament Essays* (NY: Paulist, 1965, 1982): 217-253. Joachim Jeremias, "The Lord's Prayer in the Light of Recent Research," in *The Prayers of Jesus* (London: S.C.M. Press, 1967): 82-107. C. Jones, G. Wainwright, E. Yarnold, eds., *The Study of Liturgy* (NY: Oxford University Press, 1978): using the index under "Lord's Prayer." *Documents on the Liturgy, 1963-1979: Conciliar, Papal, and Papal Texts* (Collegeville, MN: Liturgical Press, 1982): using the general index under "Lord's Prayer."

MICHAEL DOWNEY

M

MARGINALIZED, LITURGY AND THE

Referring to a person or group as *marginalized* is a practice of rather recent custom. To which person or group the designation applies is not always as clear as it may seem at first. The marginalized may be said to be those who are at the margins or edges of a social body which, from this perspective, may be viewed as the mainstream. The reasons for marginalization vary. Marginalization may result from the poverty which relegates one to a lower economic status or class than that of the mainstream. The mentally and physically handicapped are often viewed as marginalized because of their difference from "normal people," the healthy and robust in mind and body. Gender or sexual identity may also place one at the margins of a social body: women in a "man's world," and homosexuals in a world where heterosexual relationships are the norm, same-sex relationships being viewed as unnatural or abnormal. A person or group may be marginalized because of race or language.

In the Roman Catholic church those at the margins include, but are by no means limited to, single persons in parishes where the virtues of marriage and family life are extolled in sermonizing week after week, the divorced and remarried, laicized priests, and couples in interchurch marriages.

Common to all of these persons and groups is the element of difference from that which is identified as acceptable, regular, normal or *status quo*. Such differences more often than not place persons and groups in positions of powerlessness in the face of a predominant ideology, economic system or political structure. The marginalized are those who have little or no access to the power at the core of a dominant ideology, or at least their access to it is more restricted than that of the privileged. As a result, those at the margins have little or no determination over the systems of meaning and value, the predominant modes of perceiving and being, which, nonetheless, profoundly affect them. From this perspective, they may be said to be voiceless.

Related to the notion of the marginalized are the terms "the alienated" and "the oppressed." The first of these signifies much the same as what is designated by the term "marginalized," but from an economic or political perspective, while the latter bears the connotation of persons as victims of a more active form of violence.

Another related term, "scapegoat," signifies the worst form of marginalization. With origins in the Mosaic ritual of the Day of Atonement (Leviticus 16), the scapegoat was one of the two goats chosen to be sent out alive into the wilderness to die, the sins of the people having been symbolically laid upon it, while the other was appointed to be sacrificed. The scapegoat is the person or group who is blamed for the failure or wrongdoing of others, and cast out or expelled from the social body. Such a person or group is often already distinct from the main body by reason of national identity, social status or religious practice. In the history of Christian countries, the way in which Jews have been used as scapegoats is particularly significant.

The NT is particularly instructive on the subject of liturgy and the marginalized, if the various accounts of the meal, and of Jesus partaking of food and drink, are integrated into an understanding of the eucharist and, by extension, all Christian liturgy. Jesus eats with sinners (Lk 5:29-32; Mk 2:15-17; Mt 9:10-13), and feeds the crowds (Mt 15:32-39; Mk 6:30-44; 8:1-10), thereby indicating his willingness to be in a relationship of communion with them. The sharing of a meal with them indicates sharing of life and the strengthening of a bond with outcasts: those at the margins of society and religious institutions. It is more than likely that an early understanding of the eucharist is presented in these meal stories, and in the way Jesus is depicted partaking of food and drink.

The manner in which Paul dealt with divisions and factions in the Christian community is also instructive. The social world of the apostle Paul was marked by rigid stratification. Such stratification was judged incompatible with the *communio* in Christ, which had particular appeal to those who occupied an ambiguous or marginal place in society, especially because of the co-equal discipleship in which all were called to share through their baptism into the one body of Christ (Gal 3:27-28). There were no outsiders in the *communio* in Christ. But layers of the rigid social stratification carried over into the life and practice of the church, so that Paul was pressed to chide the church at Corinth for liturgical practices which hindered the participation of some members of the body because of their economic or social status (1 Cor 11:17-34).

One of the functions of liturgy in the Christian *communio* of the early church was to provide a sense of belonging and shared identity, particularly for those who occupied an ambiguous place in society. Those who were baptized into Christ's body and shared at the eucharistic table were invited to live in the promise of a world in which the rich and powerful will be cast down from their thrones, and the poor and wounded will hold pride of place (Lk 1:46-55). This stands in marked contrast to the social world in which their place was uncertain and tenuous, and provided a vision of unity, a sense of purpose, cohesion and hope. Further, the alternative vision projected and enacted in the liturgy of the early *communio* stood in marked contrast to the dominant ideology of the "world" and functioned as a critique of it.

Alongside others, then, liturgy may be said to have two important functions which are brought to the fore by a consideration of liturgy and the marginalized. First, liturgy is to facilitate building the *communio* in Christ by projecting and enacting a vision of God's reign in which those who occupy an ambiguous or marginal place in social and religious bodies will hold pride of place. Second, liturgy is to serve as a critique of those political, social, economic and religious systems and ideologies which keep persons and groups at the margins, thus preventing the *communio* from being realized, and obfuscating the reign of God to which Christians look in hope and confidence.

History has gone to show that these two functions have not always been operative in Christian liturgy. Perhaps due to an emphasis on matters of doctrine and discipline, liturgical practice has often excluded, rather than included, those who occupy an uncertain or marginal place in the social and religious body. And, more sadly still, rather than serve as a critique of the dominant ideological assumptions of economic systems, political structures, and religious institutions, liturgical practice has often uncritically endorsed these as divinely ordained, thus clouding the non-identity between them and the coming reign of God.

The recovery of these two functions of liturgy more often than not occurs through alternative liturgical practices of marginalized communities of self and mutual help which gather in the name of Jesus in memory and in hope. The liturgical life of the base Christian communities in Central and South America and of groups of Christian feminists, and the liturgical services of communities of handicapped persons and their families and friends, may serve as examples of practices rooted in an ethic of inclusion more in keeping with the *communitas* in Christ and the call to co-equal discipleship at the heart of the gospel. Further, such liturgical practices raise critical questions about dominant modes of perceiving and being in the human and Christian communities.

The identity of the Christian community is found precisely in difference (1 Corinthians 12). It remains an unfinished task to bring about liturgical forms which are inclusive of a wide array of persons who are pressed to the margins of social and religious bodies. This calls for much more than welcoming the marginalized into the mainstream, or incorporating the alternative practices of these communities into the larger tradition.

Matthew L. Lamb, *Solidarity with Victims* (NY: Crossroad, 1982). Wayne A. Meeks, "Ritual," in *The First Urban Christians* (New Haven, CT: Yale University Press, 1983), 140-163. Sharon D. Welch, *Communities of Resistance and Solidarity* (Maryknoll, NY: Orbis, 1985). Michael Downey, "Status Inconsistency and the Politics of Worship," *Horizons* 15 (1988): 64-76.

MICHAEL DOWNEY

MARRIAGE RECORDS
See **Records, sacramental**

MARRIAGE TRIBUNAL

The judicial courts, or tribunals, of the Roman Catholic church handle almost exclusively cases of marriage nullity, hence, their common though non-technical designation as "marriage tribunals." According to church teaching, a sacramental marriage (between two baptized persons) that has been consummated is indissoluble; the bond of marriage cannot be broken by any human power, and it persists until the death of one of the parties. Since the church does not recognize civil divorce, in order to remarry in the church while one's first spouse is living it is necessary to obtain a declaration of nullity of the first marriage. This declaration, commonly called an "annulment," is a judicial sentence given by the tribunal judges who reach moral certainty that the marriage in question was from its inception invalid on some legal basis. Although the relationship may have had the semblance of a marriage, and may even have lasted many years, an annulment acknowledges it to have been juridically null and void from the beginning.

Annulment petitions are most frequently based on one or more grounds of defective consent. The consent of the parties, their free will decision to give and accept one another in matrimony, constitutes the juridical essence of marriage. In virtue of the natural law, the parties to marriage, whether Christian or non-Christian, must give free consent. If this consent is lacking or is juridically defective, the marriage is invalid and can be declared such by a church tribunal.

The various grounds for defective consent are found in canons 1095-1103 of the Code of Canon Law. The so-called "psychological grounds" are the most frequently alleged bases of defective consent. In these cases the petitioner attempts to establish that one party or both parties to the marriage either suffered from grave lack of discretion of judgment concerning essential matrimonial rights and duties, and/or were incapable of assuming the essential obligations of matrimony due to causes of a psychic nature (cans. 1095, 1°, 2°).

Another frequent basis for marriage nullity is lack or defect of canonical form. The law of the canonical form obliges a Catholic in ordinary circumstances to marry in the presence of an authorized priest or deacon and two witnesses (can. 1108). Those who are baptized in or received into full communion with the Catholic church are bound to the canonical form unless they have left the church by a formal act. If a Catholic who has not formally left the church marries without observing the canonical form, the marriage is invalid and can be annulled quite easily through a documentary process. A less frequent basis for marriage nullity is the presence of a diriment impediment that was not dispensed (cans. 1083-1094).

Every diocese is required to have a tribunal unless an indult has been given by the Holy See for a regional, interdiocesan tribunal. The diocesan bishop usually exercises judicial power vicariously through the judges he appoints. The principal judge who oversees the operation of the tribunal is called the judicial vicar, or officialis. The bishop also appoints other judges according to the needs and resources of the diocese, one or more of whom may be given the title of adjutant judicial vicar, or vice-officialis. In marriage cases the judges must weigh carefully the evidence in light of church law and come to moral certainty before declaring a marriage invalid.

An important officer of the court for marriage cases is the defender of the bond whose task it is to ensure that the procedural and substantive law is correctly observed and interpreted in the trial. Nullity proceedings are handled as contentious cases between the two parties, between the petitioner who requests the annulment and the defendant, called the respondent, who can respond to the allegations of the petitioner. In reality, marriage cases are seldom truly contentious, since both parties usually are civilly divorced and the respondent often desires the annulment also or is indifferent to the outcome of the case. The presence of the defender of the bond in the trial theoretically maintains the contentious nature of the process.

Both parties may also have their own advocate, an attorney who represents them in the case. The respondent may not require an advocate, unless he or she wishes to contend the petition. All officials of the tribunal, including advocates, must be approved by the diocesan bishop and meet all other qualifications required by law. Deacons and laypersons are eligible for all tribunal offices except officialis and vice-officialis, which can be held only by a priest.

Every marriage nullity case must receive an affirmative sentence from two separate tribunals before the annulment is granted. An affirmative decision in first instance must be appealed to the court of second instance, usually the metropolitan tribunal, a designated suffragan tribunal, or a regional appeals court. Marriage cases are decided by a collegiate tribunal of three judges, at least two of whom must be clerics. With permission of the episcopal conference, the diocesan bishop can constitute in first instance a tribunal consisting of a single judge who must be a cleric (can. 1425, §4). If a single judge decides a case in first instance, it must be reviewed by a collegiate tribunal of three judges in second instance.

Remarriage in the church is also possible after a dissolution of a non-consummated or a non-sacramental marriage, even if the first marriage is valid. Dissolution cases, though they often are initially processed by the marriage tribunal, are not properly judicial in nature.

Theodore Mackin, *Marriage in the Catholic Church: What is Marriage?* (New York: Paulist Press, 1982). John T. Noonan, Jr., *Power to Dissolve: Lawyers and Marriages in the Courts of the Roman Curia* (Cambridge: The Belknap Press of Harvard University Press, 1972). Ladislas Örsy, *Marriage in Canon Law: Texts and Comments, Reflections and Questions* (Wilmington: Michael Glazier, 1986).

JOHN M. HUELS, O.S.M.

MARRIAGE, VOWS, RENEWAL OF

Wedding anniversaries are being recognized more frequently as a time of celebration for the whole community. In times past, couples and their families did tend to celebrate their wedding anniversaries, especially the twenty-fifth, fiftieth, and sixtieth. Today, however, there is greater recognition of the specialness of enduring love, of faithful love, not only for the married couple and their immediate family, but also for the community and society at large.

The foundational concept of marriage as a covenant, which was enunciated in Vatican II, has led us to a deeper respect for the ongoing dynamics of the partnership of a husband and a wife, a communion which involves their whole lives (G.S., 47, 48). A covenant leads us to celebration again and again; a contract is often celebrated only at the time of its signing. Covenant touches the mutual and ongoing gifting and acceptance of each other. This gifting and acceptance can never cease; it is continuous and ever-sensitive.

The celebration of this reality on an ongoing basis is reflected in the development of prayers and blessings for wedding anniversaries. These celebrations may take the form of focusing on a twenty-fifth or fiftieth annivesary, cele-brated by a votive Mass of thanksgiving, or by a prayer service, or by a banquet at which not only the specific couple but other married couples are recognized and prayed for. It may take the form of having a eucharist each month for all couples whose anniversaries fall within the month.

There are not many times in a person's life where one's story can be shared with the community. Each couple has a unique story of their married life and has developed personal symbols of their happy and sad moments. The pastoral possibilities of storytelling and symbol sharing go beyond imagination. These times are too precious to be ignored or performed in a perfunctory manner. Various formulae are suggested for the renewal of vows or for the recollection of vows. However, the vows take on a much deeper meaning after these stories of married life.

The impact of reaffirming these vows is very profound and, often, quite moving. In an analogous way, it is similar to the renewal of our baptismal vows during the Easter vigil. Married lives, as our Christian lives, are lived on a daily basis. However, it is important to stop, to move from chronological time to kairotic time, to affirm and celebrate the mystery at hand, to remember the journey travelled and to enunciate and hope and promise for the future.

After the renewal of the vows, a prayer of thanksgiving is offered to God for the gift of married love which has been experienced and lived by the couple. This thanksgiving is offered by the whole community who recognize the symbolic quality of this covenantal love. Here again, others may be invited to share their experience of the love and life of this couple. God's blessing is then requested for the couple, for all couples, for the community, that it may live its covenantal calling to be one with Christ in a manner that touches every fibre of their being, and for the world, that it may recognize its hunger for love, its source, and its fulfillment in God.

To face one's spouse after many years of married life—of moments of happiness and sadness, success and failure—and once again to pledge love and commitment and fidelity, is a moment of sacredness, of wonder, of the presence of God. It is a time which grounds us in the mystery of love as lived in daily life. It is not a superfluous liturgy; it is a liturgy which is open to great depth and significance.

"The Celebration of Wedding Anniversaries," *National Bulletin on Liturgy*, 12 (1979): 175-179. "Wedding Anniversary," *National Bulletin on Liturgy*, 20 (1987): 236.

JAMES A. SCHMEISER

MARRIAGE, CANONICAL ISSUES CONCERNING

Canonical references are to *The Code of Canon Law*, promulgated by Pope John Paul II in January 1983. This Code came into legal effect on November 27, 1983, and abrogated the first Code, which with subsequent emendations, had been in effect since 1918.

I. *The Legal Dimensions of Marriage*

Marriage is generally understood to have private and public effects; it serves the good of the persons who marry and common, societal goods, such as the stability of family, boundaries of kinship, and nurture of offspring. Consequently, various jurisdictions, cultures and societies have recognized a number of legal dimensions of the marriage of a man and a woman, including:

A. rights and obligations in law, such as common life, domicile, economic sustenance, productivity and the use of income from productivity, protection from harm, and the nurture and supervision of offspring;

B. consequences in law, such as legitimacy of and liability for offspring, entitlement, beneficiary, use and ownership of property, succession to title or office;

C. juridical requirements governing how people marry, record keeping, who (if anyone) may or must officiate at a wedding ceremony, what words may or must be spoken;

D. legal determinations of how, when, and by whom a marriage may be terminated, either by separation ("from bed and board"), dissolution, annulment or divorce;

E. categories of persons who by law are capable or incapable of marrying, or of marrying one another; the status of persons who marry; requisite conditions, knowledge, intention; even certain criminal effects of fraud, deception, or bigamy.

Whether social or cultural, civil or religious in origin, there are any number of regulations, rules and requirements, permissions and prohibitions, rights and obligations attached by law to the action of marrying and the status of being married persons, and to the consequences of a marriage contract or marriage bond. Different authorities claim the power to regulate marriage and/or divorce in accord with divine, canonical and civil law.

II. *The Church and Marriage*

Motivated by scripture and theological reflection, influenced by cultural and social environment, guided by or reacting to existing customs and practices, and shaped by historical contexts, various Christian churches and communions have regulated some or all of these dimensions of marrying, marriage and divorce. The rediscovery of Roman law in the 12th century, the systematization of sacramental theology in the 12th and 13th centuries, and the 16th-century reform canons and decrees of the Council of Trent (especially those establishing the requirement of canonical form for the validity of the marriage) are influences which continue to shape the norms of the Roman Catholic church governing the act of marrying, the state of marriage, the rights and duties of married persons, and the boundaries for dissolving certain marriages.

In some countries, and again for historical reasons, what was or is determined by ecclesiastical authority still serves also as civil law; in other instances, religious authority has instead adopted laws enacted by civil authorities. In the Western Christian world, this spectrum of legal approaches to marriage reflects the religious and political aftermath of the Anglican, Reform and Catholic Reformations of the 16th century. In the Eastern Christian world, the effects of civil and canon law on marriage reflects the fluctuating relationship of the Oriental churches (especially the Orthodox) to the political rule of the several empires: Eastern (Byzantine) Roman, Ottoman (Muslim), and Russian (now, Soviet Union), as well as the rule of other non-Christian political and religious entities.

III. *Documents on Marriage: Evolving Theology and Legislation*

Oftentimes, church documents on marriage employ different technical languages and intermingle a variety of statements: dogma, doctrine, theological opinion, liturgical practice, aids for pastoral ministry, as well as juridical elements strictly speaking, i.e., laws or rules of behavior to govern individuals and a community. Each genre of literature must be interpreted according to its own nature.

Foundational doctrinal texts on marriage are: *The Pastoral Constitution on the Church in the Modern World* (G.S., 1965), nos. 48-53, of the Second Vatican Council, and the papal text, "Exhortation on the Family" (1981) by Pope John Paul II, prepared after the deliberations of "The Synod on the Family" (1980). The primary liturgical and ritual text is the revised *Rites of Marriage* of the Roman Ritual (1969). The legal text which currently regulates marriage in the Catholic church is the *Code of Canon Law* (1983). This revised Code, the work of a papal commission, is intended to reflect conciliar texts and post-conciliar documents issued by Pope Paul VI, particularly those that dealt with "mixed marriage" (*Matrimonii sacramentum*, 1966, and *Matrimonia mixta*, 1970) and the marriage of Latin (Roman) Catholics and Oriental non-Catholics (*Crescens matrimonium*, 1967).

Six canons (cans. 834-839) introduce "Book IV: The Office of Sanctifying in the Church"; eight canons (cans. 840-847) introduce "Part 1: The Sacraments." Several of these are foundational canons, and are broad in scope; all of these govern the interpretation and application of the marriage canons. They deserve careful reading for their notes on the faith dimensions of worship and sacraments, the public activity of liturgy, the valid celebration of sacraments, the duties and rights of both ministers and all the faithful regarding access to and preparation for sacraments.

Under Title 7, "De matrimonio," are found the 111 canons on marriage (cans. 1055-1165). Thirty-seven canons, under the title, "Certain Special Procedures," (cans. 1671-1707), regulate the procedures to be observed in various marriage cases.

IV. *"De Matrimonio": The Content of the Revised Code*

A. *An issue: rewriting the laws*

A number of the disciplinary laws governing the formalities of marrying, marriage tribunals, personnel and procedures, and norms to be used in cases of nullity and dissolution, as established in the 1917 Code, had undergone significant development both prior and subsequent to Vatican II. With the revision of the Code we have not only an updated compendium of these modified canons, but also changes in the canons on marriage itself.

778

Table 1: *Canons on Marriage in the 1917 Code which have no corresponding canon in the 1983 Code.*

The following lists those canons on marriage in the 1917 Code for which there is no existing corresponding canon (in whole or in part) in the 1983 Code of Canon Law. These deleted canons no longer have legal effect:

Cans. 1021, §1; 1022; 1030; 1031; 1036, §§1 & 3; 1042; 1048; 1049; 1050; 1051; 1052; 1053; 1054; 1055; 1056; 1057; 1058; 1059; 1063, §§2 & 3; 1064; 1075, 1°; 1077, §2; 1079; 1089, §4; 1092, 1° & 2°; 1095, §1, 3°; 1097, §1, 2° & 3°; 1099, §2; 1101; 1102; 1108; 1112; 1120, §2; 1124; 1126; 1142; 1143.

Comments on Table 1: When the 1983 Code took legal effect, 37 of the 132 canons on marriage in the prior Code, or 28%, no longer had legal effect, i.e., more than 1/4 of the previous canons.

Table 2: *Canons on Marriage that are new to the Code.*

The following lists the canons on marriage that are entirely or in part (subparagraph or number) new to the Code; i.e., these have no corresponding or equivalent canon in the prior Code. Many of these embody previously enacted legislation and administrative directives:

Cans. 1063, 2°, 3° & 4°; 1064; 1071, §1, 2° & 3°; 1079, §4; 1083, §2; 1095; 1098; 1102, §3; 1108, §2; 1112; 1120; 1121, §3; 1123; 1126; 1127, §2; 1128; 1143; 1147; 1161, §3; 1165,§2.

Comments on Table 2: Twenty of the 111 canons on marriage, i.e., 18% or nearly 1 in 5, are new to the Code.

Table 3: *Canons on Marriage in the 1983 Code that have been substantially revised.*

The following lists marriage canons in the 1983 Code corresponding to canons in the 1917 Code, but which have been significantly revised, i.e., the canon:

(a) contains a reversal of previous rule

or principle; namely, cans. 1055; 1078; 1111, §1; 1117; 1118, §3; 1163, §2.

(b) amends, deletes, or adds to a canon, and as a result alters the sense of the canon considerably; e.g., cans. 1057, §2; 1059; 1067; 1084, §2; 1108, etc.

(c) contains an exceptive clause not stated in prior canon, which radically alters the prior rule; namely, cans. 1099 and 1100. Listed in order they are:

Cans. 1055; 1057, §2; 1059; 1063, 1°; 1067; 1071, §1, 4° & 5°; 1078; 1079, §1; 1084, §2; 1099; 1100; 1101; 1102, §§1 & 2; 1108; 1111, §§1 & 2; 1115; 1117; 1118, §3; 1124; 1125; 1127; 1130; 1142; 1148, §§1 & 2; 1153; 1163, §2; 1165, §1.

Comments on Table 3: Some 27 of the 111 canons on marriage in the revised Code which correspond to canons in the 1917 Code have been substantially changed, i.e., 24.3%, or nearly 1 in 4 of the canons on marriage.

Summary: Nearly 1/3 of all the canons on sacraments deal with the sacrament of marriage (111 of 326); that high number reflects the manifold aspects of marriage as a human and sacred reality, as a legal and sacramental entity, and as an event, an ongoing state, and an interpersonal relationship.

An assessment of the legislative activity that culminated in the revised Code, therefore, must note something more than the reduction in the number of canons on marriage (from 132 to 111). It must also account for the extensive revision of the content of the canons. Noting that 20 canons on marriage that are entirely new, that 27 have been substantially revised (these two groups alone constitute some 47 of the 111 canons on marriage; i.e., 42.3% of the existing canons) and that 37 out of 132 canons of the prior Code have been abrogated, we have a better measure of the extensive revision in the content of the canons.

B. The Scope of the Canons
Underlying all the canons on marriage

is a fundamental legal and theological distinction: the sacramental marriage of two baptized persons, and the non-sacramental marriage of two non-baptized persons, or a baptized person and a non-baptized person (cans. 1055, §§1 & 2; 1056; 1061, §1; and 1134). The distinction has broad canonical, liturgical, pastoral and juridical consequences, e.g., in the way these marriages are (are not) celebrated (cans. 1059; 1086, §1; 1117; 1124-1129), and in their legal effects (e.g., in the procedures that govern their (in) dissolubility, cans. 1141; 1142; 1143ff).

Seven introductory canons head the chapter; two of these contain a theological and canonical description of marriage:

Can. 1055: §1: "The matrimonial covenant, by which a man and a woman establish between themselves a partnership of the whole of life, is by its nature ordered toward the good of the spouses and the procreation and education of offspring; this covenant between baptized persons has been raised by Christ our Lord to the dignity of a sacrament."

§2: "For this reason a matrimonial contract cannot validly exist between baptized persons unless it is also a sacrament by that fact."

Can. 1056: "The essential properties of marriage are unity and indissolubility, which in Christian marriage obtain a special firmness in virtue of the sacrament."

Can. 1057 serves as a "table of contents" of the canonical issues concerning marriage: that marriage is brought about through the consent of the parties (cans. 1095-1103, 1107); legitimately manifested (canonical form: cans. 1058; 1108-1123); between persons who are capable according to law of giving consent (cans. 1073-1094).

Several canons give legal principles and definitions. Can. 1058 is a statement of a fundamental human right: "All persons who are not prohibited by law can contract marriage."

This right, however, is not unrestricted. Divine, canon and civil laws regulate marriage, and especially the marriage wherein at least one of the parties is a Catholic (can. 1059). Another legal rule is stated: "Marriage enjoys the favor of the law," and consequently its validity is upheld until the contrary (invalidity; lack of legal effect) is proven (can. 1060). Can. 1061 defines several legal terms describing different kinds of marriage according to: the baptismal status of the persons who marry; whether or not the marriage is consummated after it has been contracted; and whether or not the marriage is valid. A single canon treats the much-restricted legal implications of betrothal (can. 1062).

V. Canonical Issues and Method: "First Rule, Second Rule"

The canonical system of the church rests upon the interaction of general and particular norms: the general (universal) rule operates as a "first rule," the particular (specific) rule, which may appear as a sub-paragraph or number, a dependent clause, or an exception or "unless" clause, operates as a "second rule."

A. Consent: the indispensable personal act which brings marriage into being; nature and notions; how intention and knowledge interact; the invalidating effect when consent is lacking or inadequate.

(1) The "first rule." Can. 1057, §1, contains the basic legal principle: marriage comes into existence through the consent of the two parties who marry; no other human power can replace this consent; §2 offers a definition of that consent and a description of the intended object of that consent: it is an act of the will by which a man and a woman, through an irrevocable covenant, mutually give and accept each other in order to establish marriage.

(2) Consent is a complex notion; hence, the canons include an extensive series of

"second rules." The law recognizes that not all persons are capable of giving the requisite consent (can. 1095) due to the insufficient use of reason (1°); or because a person suffers from a "grave lack of discretion of judgment" concerning the essential rights and duties of marriage which are to be mutually given and accepted (2°); or because a person is "incapable of assuming the essential obligations of matrimony due to causes of a psychic nature" (3°). The latter two numbers of the canon are new to the Code, and derive from the jurisprudence of the Roman Rota developed in the last half century. They also are the ground of nullity cited in the greatest number of nullity cases adjudicated by tribunals.

(3) Several other "second rule" canons deal with the legal implications of the interaction and operations of the will (the locus of intention) and the intellect (the locus of knowledge), namely, the automatic or potentially nullifying effects of: ignorance (can. 1096); error (cans. 1098; 1099); deception by fraud (can. 1098); knowledge or opinion about nullity (can. 1110); the positive act of the will to exclude (a kind of "negative intention") either the marriage itself (see cans. 1055 and 1135), some essential element of marriage (see can. 1096, §1: that marriage is a permanent consortium of a man and a woman which is ordered toward the procreation of children by means of some sexual cooperation), or an essential property of marriage (see cans. 1056, 1099 and 1134: perpetuity, exclusivity, and in a Christian marriage, sacramentality); conditions placed at the time of the marriage (can. 1102); and force or grave fear inflicted upon a person (can. 1103).

(4) Notable evolution in the Code's understanding of the relationship of the will and intellect is traceable in two canons. Whereas the former Code (can. 1084) practically ruled out any interaction in its expression "simple error," implying that error might remain simply in the mind without passing over into the will, the revised can. 1009 reads: "Error concerning the unity, indissolubility or sacramental dignity of marriage does not vitiate matrimonial consent *so long as it does not determine the will*" (emphasis added).

The final clause of the revised canon is new, and creates another instance of the "first rule, second rule" method of the Code. The first rule is: certain kinds of error do not vitiate consent; the second rule is: that certain kinds of erroneous knowledge could determine the will, and so vitiate consent. Similarly, in can. 1110: "The knowledge or opinion of the nullity of a marriage *does not necessarily* exclude matrimonial consent" (emphasis added).

Here also the revised canon, in its expression "not necessarily," creates a "first rule" presumption: a person's sure knowledge or belief does not preclude that person from validly marrying; but the "second rule" admits the possibility that knowledge or opinion could vitiate consent.

B. The Formalities of Marrying: the meaning of "legitimate manifestation" of consent; "canonical form"; provisions for flexibility: permissions and dispensations; jurisdiction and its delegation.

The act of marrying consists of the expression of consent in words or equivalent signs (can. 1104, §2), and personally (can. 1104, §1), through proxy (can. 1105), or through an interpreter (can. 1106).

(1) Can. 1059 initiates the series of canons which establish the "first rules" for the marriage of a Catholic; later canons will provide "second rule" exceptions: "Even if only one party is Catholic, the marriage of Catholics is regulated not only by divine law but also by canon law, with due regard for the competence of civil authority concerning the merely civil effects of such a marriage" (see also can. 1127, §1).

Under the title of "form of the celebration of marriage," several canons regulate the legal and liturgical formalities of marrying which bind a baptized Catholic or a person who has been received into the Catholic church and who has not "left the Catholic church by a formal act" (can. 1117). That latter clause is new legislation; as a result, those who have left the Catholic church in some formal, external and provable manner are no longer bound by the Catholic form for marrying.

(2) The "canonical form" for marrying is a complex legal institute which regulates whether or not the marriage will enjoy legal standing. Enacted originally as a remedy for clandestine marriage, the institute guarantees the public celebration of marriage. Failure to observe canonical form may result in the invalidity of the marriage.

Canonical form for marriage consists of this: the ceremony must be conducted by a person to whom jurisdiction has been given, i.e., who has been delegated according to the norms of law to officiate at a marriage ceremony (cans. 1108, §1; 1109; 1110; 1111). The actual contracting of marriage must occur in the presence of a bishop, a priest-pastor, or another authorized priest or deacon, as well as two other witnesses (can. 1108, §2). The liturgical rites approved by church authority (cans. 1119; 1120) are to be used. New legislation (can. 1112) provides that in situations where clergy are lacking, a qualified lay person may be delegated by ecclesiastical authority to officiate at the wedding ceremony.

(3) Before the ceremony occurs, and before delegation to officiate is given, the law requires that the freedom of the persons to marry must be established (cans. 1113; 1114). After a marriage has been celebrated, the marriage is to be recorded properly (cans. 1121-1123).

(4) Whereas the former Code required that the marriage be celebrated in the parish church of the bride-to-be, the revised canon (can. 1115) designates the parish where either party has legal permanent or part-time residence; the same canon provides that the ceremony could take place "elsewhere" (generally understood as another church or chapel) with the permission of the local bishop or the pastor. Can. 1116 provides special rules for validly contracting marriage in the presence of two witnesses only in situations such as danger of death, or the prolonged absence of an officiant, when it is "impossible without serious inconvenience" to observe canonical form.

(5) Dispensations from canonical form. Can. 1127, §1, contains special provisions for the form required, or the grant of dispensation from form, for the marriage of a Catholic to a non-Catholic of an oriental rite (e.g., Orthodox); §2 provides for the possibility of dispensation from form in other mixed marriage cases, requiring for validity, however, that a public celebration occur; and §3 forbids either repeated or divided religious ceremonies in mixed marriages.

A ruling handed down in May 1985 by the Pontifical Commission for the Authentic Interpretation of the Code decreed that the local ordinary may not dispense from the requirement of canonical form in a marriage of two Catholics. *C. "Second Rules"*: special provisions for "mixed marriage" and the pastoral care of couples and family.

These revised canons largely derive from post-conciliar legislation. Cans. 1117 and 1127, §1 restate the general rule of canonical form in "mixed marriage."

(1) Can. 1118 contains a new rule in the case of "mixed marriage": reversing the prohibition in the earlier Code, the revised Code permits the celebration of a mixed marriage in a parish or other church (§1), or, when the local bishop permits, in "some other suitable place" (§2); if it is the case that the Catholic is marrying a non-baptized person (see can. 1086 on

"disparity of cult") that marriage can take place "in a church or in some other suitable place" (§3). A new chapter entitled "Mixed marriages" contains six canons (1124-1129) regulating the marriage of a Catholic and a baptized non-Catholic (can. 1124), and the marriage of a Catholic and non-baptized person (can. 1129).

(2) The present Code distinguishes more consistently the "permission" required for a "mixed marriage" (cans. 1124; 1125) from the "dispensation" required for a disparity of cult marriage (cans. 1129; 1086, §1), both of which may be granted by proper ecclesiastical authority "when there is just and reasonable cause" and provided that certain requirements are met (can. 1125). In some dioceses, it is the practice that pastors have been delegated the faculty to grant permission for mixed marriage; granting the dispensation from disparity of cult, however, remains restricted to the diocesan bishop or his delegate.

(3) Whereas the prior Code obliged both the Catholic and the non-Catholic party, the current law requires only the Catholic party to affirm his or her faith and make "a sincere promise to do all in his or her power to have all the children baptized and brought up in the Catholic church" (1°); the non-Catholic is "to be informed at the appropriate time" of the promise and obligation of the Catholic (2°); and both parties are to be instructed on the essential ends and properties of marriage that are not to be excluded by either party (3°).

Can. 1128 obliges bishops and pastors to provide spiritual assistance to the Catholic spouse and children of mixed marriage. This new canon is a positive change from the "deter" and "danger" attitudes of the former Code; but one wonders why the canon does not extend spiritual care to both spouses.

(4) Can. 1071, §1, 4° and §2 treat of the permission required in the special case of a Catholic seeking to contract marriage with a person who has "notoriously" left the Catholic church.

D. *The Capacity in Law of a Person to Marry*: invalidating (nullifying) impediments; dispensations (relaxation of the requirements of law).

Can. 1058 establishes the general rule: "All persons who are not prohibited by law can contract marriage." Some persons, however, are legally prohibited from marrying.

(1) "Licit" celebration of marriage: "permissions." Several canons of the former Code regulated the so-called "impedient impediments," which affected only the licit celebration of the marriage but not its validity. That title has been suppressed; in its stead one canon (can. 1071) treats several situations in which a certain caution is to be exercised. The canonical concept of permission does not, however, touch the validity of the marriage.

Can. 1071 lists the seven cases when the permission of the local ordinary is required for the licit celebration of the marriage: (1°) of transients; (2°) which cannot be recognized or celebrated according to the norm of civil law; (3°) of a person who, because of a prior union, is bound by natural obligations toward another party or children; (4°) of a person who has "notoriously" rejected the Catholic faith (see also §2); (5°) of a person under ecclesiastical censure; (6°) of a minor child (someone under the age of 18) when the parents are unaware of it or are reasonably opposed to it (see also can. 1072: Pastors are to prevent youths from marrying before the age at which marriage is usually begun in accord with practices of the region; and can. 1083, §2, on the power of the conference of bishops to establish a minimum age for the licit celebration of marriage.) and (7°) when entered into by proxy (see also can. 1105).

Can. 1118 refers to "permissions" for

the celebration of a mixed marriage in a place other than the parish church.

(2) "Valid" celebration of marriage: legal standing. The general rule of can. 1058 is limited also by a series of canons which establish that, because of a "diriment impediment" (a legal obstacle to marrying; see cans. 1073-1082) a person is incapable in law of validly contracting a marriage. The institute of invalidating impediments is complex, and is regulated as to who may establish such an impediment (cans. 1075; 1076); the extent of the power of the local ordinary either to prohibit a marriage for a time (can. 1077), or to grant a dispensation from the impediment (can. 1078); certain special cases when dispensation can be otherwise granted (cans. 1079: in danger of death; 1080: when, at the last minute, it is learned that an impediment exists; and 1081); and certain prerogatives of the Apostolic See (cans. 1075, §1; 1078).

The prior Code distinguished so-called major and minor invalidating impediments, according to their origin, and whether or not they could be dispensed from. That distinction has been eliminated. The impediment of "spiritual affinity" deriving from baptism has been suppressed.

The twelve specific impediments with invalidating effect are: lack of minimum age, which is 16 years for the male, 14 for the female (can. 1083, §1); antecedent, perpetual, and certain impotence to have sexual intercourse, whether on the part of the male or female (can. 1084, §1; §2 states that in cases where there is a doubt concerning the impotence, the marriage is not to be impeded nor declared null; §3 makes it clear that sterility neither prohibits nor invalidates a marriage); prior bond of marriage (can. 1085); disparity of cult: a Catholic seeking to marry a non-baptized person (can. 1086; dispensation from this impediment is commonly granted); persons who are in holy orders (can. 1087; see also can. 1009:

the orders are episcopacy, presbyterate, diaconate); persons who are bound by a public perpetual vow of chastity in a religious institute (can. 1088; see also cans. 654 and 658, on such vows); abduction or detention of a woman for the purpose of marriage with her (can. 1089); persons who physically or morally cause the death of either one's spouse for the purpose of being freed from an existing bond of marriage (can. 1090); persons within a certain degree of consanguineous (blood) relationship (can. 1091; see also cans. 108; 1078, §3) or affinity (relationship through marriage); (can. 1092; see also can. 1093: affinity arises only through a valid marriage); "public propriety," that is, a kind of affinity relationship arising from an invalid marriage or cohabitation; and certain degrees of legal relationship arising from adoption, as determined by civil law (can. 1094).

(3) Convalidation of marriage (cans. 1156-1165). Two legal procedures exist for validating an invalid marriage. The general rule (can. 1157) recalls the indispensable requirement of consent: "The renewal of consent must be a new act of the will concerning a marriage which the person who is renewing consent knows or thinks was null from the beginning."

The first procedure, "simple convalidation" requires a new act of consent, and can be applied in three types of cases:

(a) when a marriage is invalid due to an impediment: when the impediment has ceased, or has been dispensed, renewed consent is required at least by the one who knew of the impediment (can. 1156).

(b) when a marriage is invalid due to a defect of consent: the party who had not consented must give consent (can. 1159).

(c) when a marriage is invalid due to a defect of form: then the marriage must be contracted anew according to canonical form (can. 1160).

The second procedure, "radical sanation," is a more subtle canonical entity.

It presupposes that the consent of both parties continues. Sanation is validation of a marriage without the renewal of consent "with retroactivity into the past of the canonical effects" (can. 1161, §1).

(a) Provided that the consent of both parties continues, sanation can be applied in cases where the marriage was invalid because there was an impediment, and/or canonical form was not observed (cans. 1161, 1163); dispensations can be granted retroactively in both latter instances (can. 1163). Convalidation is understood to have occurred "at the moment the favor is granted" (can. 1161, §2).

(b) A marriage cannot be sanated if consent was lacking in the beginning or was revoked; it may be sanated if, although originally lacking, consent was afterwards given (can. 1162).

(c) The sanation can be granted by the Apostolic See (can. 1165, §1) and, in a new canon, by the diocesan bishop, certain restrictions applying (§2).

The two sets of procedures operate differently: convalidation requires the renewal of consent (usually, in a simple liturgical ceremony, popularly spoken of as "having the marriage blessed"); sanation, presupposing consent continues, is a documentary process. The mere existence of both institutes acknowledges the reality of the non-observance of marriage laws. Both procedures have a single canonical (and pastoral) focus: validating an otherwise invalid marriage.

E. Pastoral Preparation for Marriage. A new chapter heading, and ten canons, treat "pastoral care and what must precede the celebration of marriage." New canons expand the notion and importance of "pastoral preparation" beyond the canonical obligations of the pre-marital investigation.

(1) Can. 1063 is one of the lengthiest canons of the revised Code. It is a foundational and comprehensive canon, describing the obligation both of pastors and members of the ecclesial community to provide assistance to the Christian faithful "so that the matrimonial state is maintained in a Christian spirit and makes progress toward perfection." Four extensive sub-paragraphs outline: the remote, early preparation that occurs in preaching, catechesis, and media; the proximate, personal preparation of couples; the fruitful liturgical celebration of marriage; and assistance for those who are married. The canon requires pastoral care of the persons and the sacrament; something more is called for than merely making wedding arrangements.

Can. 1064 obliges the local ordinary to provide such assistance; it seems overly cautious in adding: "even after consulting men and women of proven experience and skill, if it seems opportune."

Can. 1065 urges the reception of the sacrament of confirmation before marrying, and penance and eucharist, as aids in the fruitful celebration of marriage.

(2) Cans. 1066-1070 shift the focus to more juridical aspects: before the marriage is celebrated, it must be determined that nothing stands in the way of its valid and licit celebration; the episcopal conference is to enact norms concerning the publication of banns, the examination of the parties, and the necessary inquiries regarding impediments, dispensations or permissions. A wise canon urges caution in the marriage of youths who are minors (can. 1072).

F. "In Order to Establish Marriage": the purposes of the marriage covenant; the "ends" and "goods" and effects of marriage.

(1) The prior Code, in can. 1013, §1, stated that the "primary end of marriage was the procreation and education of children; its secondary end is mutual help and allaying of concupiscence." Consistent with this view, the "object" of matrimonial consent was described in can. 1081, §2: "Matrimonial consent is an

act of the will by which each party gives and accepts a perpetual and exclusive right over the body, for acts which are of themselves suitable for the generation of children" (see also can. 1082, §1).

Can. 1111 reads: "From the beginning of the marriage both parties have the same right and duty as regards the acts peculiar to the conjugal life." This canon was commonly understood to refer first of all to the primary end of marriage.

(2) Can. 1055, §1, in accord with the doctrine of marriage of Vatican II (see G.S., 48), restates the ends of marriage: "The matrimonial covenant, by which a man and a woman establish between themselves a partnership of the whole of life, is by its nature ordered toward the good of the spouses and the procreation and education of children...."

Consistent with this doctrine, the revised can. 1057, §2 states the purpose of marriage (which is the object of matrimonial consent): "Matrimonial consent is an act of the will by which a man and a woman, through an irrevocable covenant, mutually give and accept each other *in order to establish marriage*" (emphasis added).

In like manner, the scope of can. 1135 has been expanded: Each of the spouses has equal obligations and rights to those things which pertain to the partnership of conjugal life."

The net effect of these changes is the incorporation of the doctrine of Vatican II into the church's law: that the ends of marriage are so interrelated that although distinguishable, they cannot be separated nor ranked, and that persons who marry do so "to establish married life." In this way, the description of marriage as a "partnership of the whole of life" takes on a richer, more personal and more integrated sense: nothing of the mutual rights and duties, "goods" and effects of marriage is to be excluded.

Also, the phrase "as a remedy for concupiscence," derived from an Augustinian justification for sexual intercourse even within marriage, has been deleted from the revised canon.

G. *"Covenant" As Framework; "Contract" As Content.* Whereas the prior Code described the act of marrying and the marriage bond in contractual language, in three instances the revised Code substitutes the conciliar expression "matrimonial covenant" (*matrimoniale foedus;* cans. 1055, §1; 1057, §2, and 1063, 4°). The language of covenant evokes a richer biblical and theological appreciation of marriage; notwithstanding, there are forty-five references to the language of contrast in the revised Code. In its laws, then, the church continues to use and largely regulates marriage primarily according to the legal concept of marriage as a contract.

H. *Contract and Sacramentality.* The doctrinal identification of the valid contract of marriage of two baptized persons and the sacramentality of marriage has not been changed:

Can. 1055, §1: "... this covenant between baptized persons has been raised by Christ the Lord to the dignity of a sacrament."

§2: "For this reason a matrimonial contract cannot validly exist between baptized persons unless it is also a sacrament by that fact."

Can. 1056: "The essential properties of marriage are unity and indissolubility, which in a Christian marriage obtain a special firmness in virtue of the sacrament."

Can. 1134: "From a valid marriage arises a bond between the spouses which is by its very nature perpetual and exclusive; furthermore, in a Christian marriage the spouses are strengthened and, as it were, consecrated for the duties and the dignity of their state by a special sacrament."

(1) Despite some early theological opinions (e.g., that all marriages are sacraments "in the order of creation," or, that a marriage is sacramental even if

only one of the parties was baptized), it is generally held, as affirmed by the Council of Trent, that a marriage is sacramental when both parties are baptized. Nonetheless, contemporary questions are raised concerning the *ipso facto* identity of a valid contract of marriage between baptized persons and its sacramentality, when, e.g., faith is lacking altogether, as in the case of those baptized non-Catholics who neither know nor intend a sacrament, or as in the case of the baptized Catholic whose inadequate faith does not include a sacramental marriage (some of these latter approach the church merely as the socially acceptable manner and place to marry). While recognizing that these present acute pastoral problems, the church continues to insist that the valid contract of marriage of two baptized persons cannot be separated from its sacramental dimension.

I. The Doctrine of Indissolubility: the practice of dissolution cases. The "essential properties" of all marriage are unity and indissolubility (can. 1056); from a valid marriage arises a bond between the spouses which by its very nature is perpetual and exclusive (can. 1134). However, the actual practice of the church admits the relative dissolubility of certain kinds of marriages, not by the parties themselves but by a power invested in the church.

(1) Can. 1141 states the general, "first rule": A ratified and consummated marriage cannot be dissolved by any human power or for any reason other than death. By definition (see can. 1061), a ratified marriage is the valid marriage of two Christians. Thus, the canon ascribes absolute indissolubility only to the valid contract of marriage of two baptized persons (a sacrament) which subsequently is consummated. This canon implies, then, that other kinds of marriage are only relatively indissoluble. In fact, the "second rule" canons which follow describe those marriages which can be dissolved.

(2) Can. 1142 gives the first of these "second rules": "A non-consummated marriage between baptized persons or between a baptized party and non-baptized party can be dissolved by the Roman Pontiff for a just cause, at the request of both parties or of one of the parties, even if the other party is unwilling."

A non-consummated marriage of two baptized persons, although a sacrament, can be dissolved; likewise, a non-consummated, non-sacramental marriage. In both instances, it is by means of a dispensation from the pontiff that the marriage is said to be dissolved. Formerly, can. 1119 of the 1917 Code provided also that solemn profession of religious vows *ipso facto* dissolved a non-consummated marriage. Although a practice of the church that lasted for nearly eight centuries, that clause has been deleted from the current Code.

(3) The "Pauline privilege." Cans. 1143-1147 apply in the case of a marriage of two non-baptized persons, when one of these two persons receives baptism. Portions of this practice can be traced to the early church, although it is uncertain at what point the church went beyond merely permitting the separation of the spouses, to allowing a new marriage. The legal elements of the institute have evolved considerably during the centuries, but still require the verification through interrogatories (or, dispensation from these) of at least the baptism of one of the spouses and the non-baptism of the other, with his or her departure, refusal to cohabit, or refusal to cohabit in peace.

In this case, the baptized person has the right to contract a new marriage (can. 1143, §1) with a Catholic party (can. 1146) or, with the permission of the local ordinary, with a non-Catholic, whether baptized or not (can. 1147). The latter provision recognizes a series of developments which considerably expanded the use of the Pauline privilege.

(4) Can. 1148, §1, is a distillation of

two 16th century papal constitutions on the dissolution of marriage (see 1917 Code, can. 1125), with still-evolving elements. This "second rule" canon permits a polygamous man or woman, after receiving baptism, to contract marriage (§2) with any one of his or her non-baptized spouses, while dismissing the others, "if it is difficult for him [her] to remain with the first"; §3 is new, and rightly urges that the local ordinary, "after considering the moral, social and economic situation of the area and the persons ... take care that sufficient provision is made in accord with the norms of justice, Christian charity and natural equity for the needs of the first and of the other wives that are dismissed."

(5) Can. 1149 similarly abstracts from another 16th century papal constitution on the dissolution of marriage of non-baptized persons in cases of slavery and deportation. The new canon, however, reflects a continuing evolution, with its references to situations wherein cohabitation cannot be restored "due to captivity or persecution." Either of the spouses, after receiving baptism, can contract another marriage.

In the latter two instances, as with the Pauline instance (but unlike the dispensation from a non-consummated marriage), it is understood that the consent by which the new marriage is contracted dissolves the bond of the former valid but non-sacramental marriage (the former Code termed these "natural" or "legitimate" marriages). Also unlike the instance of non-consummation, these cases are adjudicated by the local ordinary.

Can. 1150 provides the underlying motive for such dissolutions: the privilege of the faith, i.e., that the church favors the reception of baptism of the person(s). A non-sacramental marriage is not to be an obstacle to one's being baptized (see cans. 842, §1 and 849 on the salvific significance accorded to baptism). Since it is not required that the newly contracted

marriage be a sacramental marriage, it is clearly baptism that is favored.

(6) Beyond the boundaries of the Code: "favor of the faith" cases. During the process of revision, a newly formulated canon was drafted, underwent several revisions, and was included in the 1980 schema of the proposed Code, can. 1104, §1: "Marriage entered into by parties, one of whom at least was not baptized, may be dissolved by the Roman pontiff in favor of the faith, as long as the marriage was not consummated after both were baptized." The schema also proposed several procedural canons regulating such cases.

The proposed canon was an attempt to formulate a legal principle for a practice begun already in the 1930s, whereby the church allowed the dissolution of a marriage of a baptized person and a non-baptized person. For several decades, that practice was the subject of sometimes intense debate, even as it simultaneously underwent considerable development (e.g., its boundaries were eventually extended to include the dissolution of a disparity of cult marriage contracted with the church's permission). Inappropriately labelled the "Petrine privilege," the still-evolving practice, the theoretical discussions, and the proposed canon seemed destined to assert that the non-sacramental marriage of a baptized person and a non-baptized person was dissolved by power of the pontiff.

That proposed canon was not promulgated in the revised Code; the practice, however, continues. Norms for such cases, issued in 1973 by the Congregation for the Doctrine of the Faith, and affirmed in 1983, remain in effect. Jurisdiction belongs solely to the Apostolic See. An instruction accompanying a recent decision clarifies that the "favor" is granted in view of the new marriage (*Canon Law Digest* 9, 678). The conclusion to be drawn is that the actual dissolution is effected not by the power of the pontiff but by the consent to the new marriage. If that is the case, then "favor of the faith" privilege cases are akin to the Pauline privilege. The valid but non-sacramental marriage is dissolved, where there is evident good and serious cause, in favor of the baptism of one of the parties, and the dissolution results from the new consent.

J. "Separation While the Bond Endures" (cans. 1151-1155). Can. 1151 states the first and second rules: "Spouses have the duty and the right to preserve conjugal living unless serious causes excuse them." Specific examples of the exceptive clause are the case of adultery, wherein the innocent spouse "does have the right to sever conjugal living" (can. 1152, §1) and the case of "serious danger of spirit or body to the other spouse or children" which creates a "legitimate cause" for separating (can. 1153, §1). Woven into these canons are a "recommendation" that pardon not be refused, that the innocent spouse "be induced" to forgive the misdeed or to readmit the guilty spouse to conjugal life (can. 1155), as well as the qualification that the adultery not have been expressly or tacitly condoned. Additionally, after the separation, provision is to be made for the adequate support and education of the children (can. 1154).

K. Procedures: tribunals and marriage nullity cases. Three canons establish the general rules: the first two operate as presumptions of law (see cans. 1584-1586); the third states the church's jurisdiction over marriage cases of the baptized.

Can. 1060: "Marriage enjoys the favor of the law; consequently, when a doubt exists the validity of a marriage is to be upheld until the contrary is proven."

Can. 1101, §1: "The internal consent of the mind is presumed to be in agreement with the words or signs employed in celebrating marriage."

Can. 1671: "Marriage cases of the baptized belong to the ecclesiastical judge by proper right."

Different cases follow different procedures:

(1) *Documentary procedures* apply not only in the above-mentioned dissolution cases (see, e.g., on non-consummation, cans. 1697-1706) but also in the cases of presumed death of spouse (can. 1707), separation of spouses (cans. 1692-1696), and impediment or lack of canonical form (cans. 1686-1688).

(2) Formal cases of marriage nullity, however, involve *judicial procedures*, and are subject to the rules governing tribunals (cans. 1400-1500), contentious causes (cans. 1501-1670), and special norms for matrimonial cases (cans. 1671-1685).

It is generally held that the specific object of a marriage nullity case is the contract of marriage; it must, however, be remembered that doctrine inseparably identifies the valid contract of marriage of two baptized persons with its sacramental nature. Particularly sensitive canonical and pastoral situations arise when the case to be adjudicated involves a marriage and divorce of two baptized non-Catholics, neither of whom recognize the authority of the Catholic church to rule over them or their former marriage. Such cases arise when, e.g., one of those persons seeks to marry a Catholic, or, being already in another marriage, seeks to be received into the Catholic church.

VI. *Conclusions*

The canonical issues surrounding marriage are many: baptismal status, consent, consummation, canonical form, permissions and dispensations, jurisdiction and delegation, impediments (and dispensations from them), preparation for marriage, the properties attributed to different kinds of marriage, and various procedures of convalidation, separation, dissolution and nullity.

It has been criticized that marriage in

the church has been overly juridicized, that the numerous canons have overwhelmed its theological, liturgical, pastoral and personal aspects. Perhaps, however, the law is elaborate because marrying and marriage are complex human and sacred realities, and the persons who marry are complex beings with varying capacities to will and to know, to initiate and to fulfill the rights and obligations of marriage which is described as "a partnership of life and love."

It is the task of pastoral and liturgical ministers, as well as those who prepare couples for marriage, to ensure that the legal considerations are neither the sole nor primary metaphor of a person's experience of marriage and the church.

See **Allied issues under marriage...; Divorced, ministry to the**

The Code of Canon Law: Latin-English Edition, translation prepared under the auspices of the Canon Law Society of America (Washington, DC: Canon Law Society of America, 1983). Thomas P. Doyle, in James A. Coriden, Thomas J. Green and Donald E. Heintschel, gen. eds., *The Code of Canon Law: A Text and Commentary*, commissioned by the Canon Law Society of America (Mahwah, NJ: Paulist Press, 1985). Ladislas Örsy, *The Canons on Marriage* (Wilmington, DE: Michael Glazier, 1987). Geoffrey Robinson, "Unresolved Questions in the Theology of Marriage," *Jurist* 43 (1983): 69-102. T. Lincoln Bouscaren, Adam Ellis and Francis Korth, *Canon Law: A Test and Commentary*, 4th rev. ed., with minor revisions (Milwaukee: Bruce, 1966). *Canon Law Digest*, vols. 1-10, eds., T. Lincoln Bouscaren and James I. O'Connor, *The Guide to American Law: Everyone's Legal Encyclopedia,* (St. Paul, MN: West Publishing Co., 1985).

JOSEPH J. KOURY, S.J.

MARRIAGE, CIVIL, CHURCH AND

The attitude of the church toward civil marriage manifests one of the more convoluted areas of Catholic theology, Canon Law and practice. Vatican II states very clearly that all sacraments "not only presuppose faith, but by words and objects they also nourish, strengthen, and express it; that is why they are called 'sacraments of faith!'" (S.C., 59). *The Rite of Marriage* (1969), again stipulates that "Priests should first of all strengthen the faith of those about to be married for the sacrament of matrimony presupposes and demands faith" (7).

Both of these references seem simple enough. However, they do not take into account the situation today where a number of baptized Catholics no longer exercise any form of faith. Some may wish to have their marriages recognized as valid by the Christian community because of family and community connections or for other personal reasons. In order for that to happen they would have to pretend that they have faith and then celebrate their marriage in the church as a so-called sacramental marriage. There is no other alternative. Officially, the civil marriage, which in many ways would respond to their situation, is not recognized as valid. The paradox is obvious. As will become apparent, there are other paradoxes around this issue.

It was within this context that a number of dioceses in France developed a program of a ritual welcome or acknowledgement of the mandatory (in France) civil marriage for those couples who are not able to profess the faith which is the basis of a sacramental marriage (Schmeiser, "Marriage: New Alternatives"). Although this program has not been followed in the English-speaking world, the knowledge and concerns underlying its development were very present during the 1980 Synod of Bishops on the role of the Christian family in the modern world. Canadian Archbishop Henri Légaré, stated in regard to baptized non-believers: "We would like to refer to a final question, the marriage of baptized nonbelievers, or rather the refusal by incapacity—the sacrament being an affirmation of faith—of sacramental marriage to baptized non-believers, dismissing them by this fact to the state of public sinner as well as denying them the right to a natural or civil marriage. On one side, how do we establish the relationship of the human institution of marriage in its anteriority as a place of God's gift with the sacrament; on the other side, how do we establish the relationship between baptism, faith, intention and marriage as sacrament? In other words, would it not be opportune to support further the actual questioning of the teaching which joins the matrimonial contract of baptized persons who no longer believe and the sacrament?" (*Pastorale et Famille*, 76 [1980], p. 61 [author's translation]).

Other submissions were equally forceful.

One of the underlying concerns of these bishops is the importance of faith in all sacramental celebrations. Marriage has been designated as a covenantal relationship, a relationship which is symbolic of the relationship of Christ and the church. This covenantal relationship is rooted in the faith of the ministers and the receivers of the sacrament (i.e., the couple). Faith, as we know, is not a static reality. Levels of faith are certainly possible and the absence of active faith, even among the baptized, is also in the realm of possibility. To state, as has the present Code of Canon Law, that "a valid marriage cannot exist between baptized persons without its being by that very fact a sacrament" (C.I.C., 1055), places baptized nonbelievers in an untenable situation. They are unable, according to the law, to be validly married.

This certainly raises the issue of religious freedom and respect for the basic marriage relationship, in which the sacrament of marriage finds its home for those who share in Christian faith. The Declaration on Religious Freedom clearly states that "...in matters religious every manner of coercion on the part of men should be excluded" (D.H., 10). As well, the *Pastoral Constitution on the Church in the Modern World* stipulates that the church should be ready to renounce any practice that raises doubts about the sincerity of its witness or when new conditions of life demand different arrangements (G.S., 76). It is serious to state that those who marry in a form other than that approved by the church are not really married, thus living in concubinage and in sin. On the other hand, great respect for sacramental marriage is not demonstrated when a person, breaking a previous civil marriage by divorce, is permitted to celebrate a new marriage in the church with little or no regard paid to the reality of the previous marriage.

Historically, we know that the position taken by the Code of Canon Law in can. 1055, par. 2, is significantly different from the statement of the Council of Trent and it is certainly debatable whether all marriages between baptized persons are sacraments. The International Theological Commission, sponsored by the Sacred Congregation for the Doctrine of Faith, studied the issue and were unable to come up with a definite answer (*Origins*, 8 [1978-79]: 237). Many scholars have not had the same difficulty in affirming the impossibility of celebrating the sacrament of matrimony against one's will.

The propositions of the 1980 Synod of Bishops, although recognizing that no person is a believer if he or she formally rejects the faith (and thus cannot marry within the church), does not indicate whether these same people have the right to marry and whether this marriage is to be recognized by the church (*The Tablet*, 31 January [1982], p. 117, no. 12).

The Apostolic Exhortation on the Family, issued by John Paul II (Nov. 22, 1981) does not deal with the right to marry. Faith is required (*ibid.*, p. 459-460, no. 68) and a civil marriage is not acceptable (but not forbidden) (*ibid.*, p. 464, no. 82). This document does recognize the difference between a civil marriage and concubinage because of the commitment present in a civil marriage (*ibid.*, p. 464, no. 82).

Research on the attitudes of the American and Canadian hierarchy toward civil marriage was carried out and published after the synod (Schmeiser, "Faith and the Right to Marry," Larson). Canadian pastors are frequently encouraged to recommend a civil marriage to couples when they are unable to celebrate a sacramental marriage. The authentic human value of this marriage is recognized and others are encouraged to respect the decision of the couple to marry in a civil ceremony. There is no reference to "concubinage" or "living in sin."

The American documentation is much more cautious. Almost nothing is said about civil marriage apart from condemning it as an evil. On the other hand, there are the usual statements about the necessity of faith for a sacramental marriage.

Other research on the good faith solution (internal forum) for Catholics living in a second marriage without the blessing of the church also indicates that there is implicit recognition of some kind of authentic validity to a marriage that is technically invalid (Schmeiser, "Internal Forum..."). A marriage is considered valid, in the internal forum, even though it is beyond legal or technical validity.

One other aspect of this issue is the historical recognition for sixteen centuries of a civil marriage as the sacramental marriage for Christians. These marriages were recognized as valid and sacramental even when a priest was not present and no blessing was given. This is still the situation where death is imminent or when a priest is unable to be present for a month (C.I.C., 1116). Possibly, a similar recognition of a civil marriage lies in the dispensation from the canonical form of marriage which can be given by an ordinary when a Catholic and baptized non-Catholic marry in a ceremony apart from the Catholic community (C.I.C., 1127).

Many scholars, in addition to many members of the hierarchy, are examining the possibility for two baptized persons to enter into a civil marriage. There is a pastoral need for some way to celebrate the marriage of a couple who have inadequate faith for a sacrament, but who are otherwise prepared. Chapter III of the *Rite of Marriage* offers a rite for celebrating a marriage between a Catholic and an unbaptized person. Possibly this rite could be broadened to include couples who may be baptized but who really have inadequate faith for a full sacramental celebration.

_____

Jan R. Larson, James A. Schmeiser, "Marriage and Non-Believing Catholics," *Eglise et Théologie*, 16 (1985): 207-213. James A. Schmeiser, Jan R. Larson, "Faith and the Right to Marry," *Liturgy*, 4 (1984): 51-55. James A. Schmeiser, "Internal Forum (Good Conscience) Solution and the Canadian Church," *Eglise et Théologie*, 18 (1987): 221-236. James A. Schmeiser, "Marriage: New Alternatives," *Worship*, 55 (1981): 23-34.

JAMES A. SCHMEISER

MARRIAGE, ECUMENICAL

Within the Roman Catholic church the source of new approaches to ecumenical or mixed marriages can be traced to the Second Vatican Council's *Constitution on the Church* (esp. L.G., 15), where it is acknowledged that the Catholic church is "joined in many ways" to all the baptized who are rightly honored by the name of Christian. From this perspective Catholics see that there is a real, even if yet imperfect communion which unites all baptized Christians. That is to say that as Christians we are linked through our churches and ecclesial communities to one another in various degrees of communion, even when we are not yet in full communion.

This understanding of degrees of communion is not found in earlier official

Catholic documents, such as the 1917 *Code of Canon Law*. In the view of the earlier document, either one was in full communion with the Catholic church or one was not. No further distinctions were made as far as other Christians were concerned. It was when the council highlighted the truth that even when not in full communion, Catholics remained linked by various bonds to other Christians, that Catholics began to speak of their "separated brethren." Perhaps because of its quaintness, that expression has begun to fade from official Catholic documents, being replaced simply by "other Christians" or "members of other churches and ecclesial communities."

From this shift in perspective, we can see developing many other shifts in pastoral outlook and practice. Some of the most notable can be seen with respect to mixed marriages uniting Catholics with other Christians. In years gone by, such marriages were seen to constitute a danger to the faith of the Catholic spouse and the children of the family. An impediment to such marriages was established in church law and no Catholic could validly enter such a marriage unless first dispensed from the impediment by the Catholic bishop for certain specific "canonical reasons." In 1967, Pope Paul VI removed this impediment from the law in his apostolic letter *Matrimonia Mixta*. Thereafter, with the permission of their bishop, Catholics could enter such mixed marriages for any just and reasonable cause. At the same time the pope waived the prior requirement of Canon Law that other Christians sign promises that children be baptized and brought up as Catholics. Now, only the Catholic party entering a mixed marriage is asked to promise to do what he or she could to share the Catholic faith with future children. The other Christian party is to be informed of the Catholic partner's promise. Pope Paul VI at the same time modified what had previously been the

Catholic church's nearly universal insistence that all mixed marriages involving a Catholic partner be entered into according to "canonical form," i.e., in the presence of a Catholic priest and two witnesses. This requirement was originally introduced into church law to obviate the danger of clandestine marriages. In the 1983 Code of Canon Law, following the direction of Paul VI, Catholic bishops may dispense from the required canonical form "if serious difficulties pose an obstacle to its observance" and as long as there is "some public form of celebration of the marriage" (can. 1127).

As the provisions of Catholic law changed, one can also perceive a gradual shift in Catholic attitudes as revealed in successive statements of the popes. While inter-Christian marriages involving Catholics could be more readily provided for, the emphasis at first remained on the undoubted difficulties couples in such marriages must face, rather than on the positive ecumenical contribution they might make. This was not unexpected given the higher incidence of marital break up in exogamous marriages. Thus in the 1967 apostolic letter, Paul VI wrote that "The Church is indeed aware that mixed marriages, precisely because they admit differences of religion and are a consequence of the divisions among Christians, do not, except in some cases, help in re-establishing unity among Christians." Later in 1975 in his apostolic exhortation on Evangelization in the Modern World, he advanced a somewhat more positive view of the ecumenical role of mixed marriages. There he wrote that "families resulting from a mixed marriage also have the duty of proclaiming Christ to the children in the fullness of the consequences of a common baptism; they have, moreover, the difficult task of becoming builders of unity." In 1980 a synod of bishops met in Rome to discuss the situation of the family in contemporary society. The following year, Pope

John Paul II issued another apostolic exhortation, *On the Family,* which speaks still more positively about the ecumenical role of mixed marriages. He wrote: "Marriages between Catholics and other baptized persons have their particular nature, but they contain numerous elements that could well be made good use of and developed, both for their intrinsic value and for the contribution that they can make to the ecumenical movement. This is particularly true when both parties are faithful to their religious duties. Their common baptism and the dynamism of grace provide the spouses in these marriages with the basis and motivation for expressing their unity in the sphere of moral and spiritual values. For this purpose and also in order to highlight the ecumenical importance of mixed marriages which are fully lived in the faith of the two Christian spouses an effort should be made to establish cordial cooperation between the Catholic and the non-Catholic ministers from the time that preparations begin for the marriage and the wedding ceremony even though this does not always prove easy."

Though not always easy, pastoral practice in recent years has evidenced great strides forward in this area. Catholic deacons and priests as they prepare couples for mixed marriages will show the respect due to the conscience and religious liberty of the partner who is not a Catholic just as they hope to ascertain the same respect for the religious rights and duties of the Catholic partner. Often these matters come into clear focus in the counseling sessions when the religious upbringing of future children is discussed by the couple. Experience in this field has led pastoral counselors to certain practical conclusions.

If it is at all possible to do so, it is far better for the couple, acting jointly, to come to a clear determination concerning the religious formation of children prior to their marriage and then to hold to it unless serious new factors in the future demand a reconsideration. As a married couple they shall have to make many serious decisions jointly. Their capacity to reach this decision together would be one clear indication of their preparation as persons to enter married life together. When the couples' decision is known beforehand, they are also somewhat protected from an ensuing tension between their families which may seek to exert claims on the religious upbringing of children once they are born and eliciting strong bonds of affection from their grandparents, uncles, aunts and others. If, on the other hand, the couple find themselves truly unable, even with the help of counselors, to come to an agreement about the religious upbringing of future children, they have *prima facie* reason to pause and reconsider their situation. They may be facing incompatibilities of a serious nature which they shall no more be able to resolve in married life than before it.

Pastoral experience has also convinced many counselors that it is not a solution to defer the question with the proposal that when the children are old enough they may choose their church allegiances for themselves. Such an approach does not readily provide a secure religious orientation for young children, a sense of truly belonging, since they are being prompted to defer and avoid a childhood identification with one church community. As they grow older and are asked to come to a decision, the psychological factors of having to choose for the father or the mother's side can be very stressful for a child approaching adolescence.

Thus there is a real advantage in taking up such matters prior to the marriage and dealing with them in a sensitive, respectful and realistic manner. There is clearly an additional advantage when it is possible for the ministers of both churches of the couple to offer such counseling jointly or collaboratively. In such a setting further confidence is gained that the religious rights and obligations in conscience of both parties are being respected and that neither is subjected to one-sided pressure.

In the course of such preparation, the couple will have to explore the ways in which they will develop a life of shared prayer, devotion and service in their households while still being members of distinct religious communities. The possibilities will vary, depending on how divergent their religious backgrounds and communities are. Again, an approach that matches respect with realism is called for. Yet a family which cannot discover a common life of prayer in which all members can share equally is missing an important life sustaining element. Here, too, expert pastoral counseling can serve to point out possibilities the couple themselves may not have been aware of. Also, since personal religious discussion may not have been a prominent feature of their conversations while dating, they need to be alerted to the fact that many people sense their religious interests, commitment and fervor rising in the early years of marriage. Otherwise, when this phenomenon occurs, it may be misinterpreted as a distancing factor in the marriage, the attempt of each partner to assert a distinct identity over against the other in a competitive way.

The actual celebration of the marriage offers possibilities for Catholic ministers to join with or be joined by other ministers in ways that were not open before Vatican II. There can be little doubt that when the churches and religious communities through their representative ministers show themselves united in prayer and support for a couple entering a mixed marriage, that a strong and hope-filled message is conveyed to all, especially to the couple, their family and friends. It is an important teaching moment. The Catholic church in the United States stresses that there should be only one celebration of the marriage following an established public form, not double or successive wedding ceremonies. When the marriage is celebrated according to the canonical form of the Catholic church, the Catholic minister (deacon or priest) is the one who will witness the exchange of marital consent by the couple. If the marriage, with the requisite dispensation from the canonical form, is celebrated according to another religious rite, the Catholic minister may take an active part, but not the leading ministerial role or one on a par with the minister of the church whose marriage service is being followed. The ministers themselves arrange in advance for the proper distribution of their roles in keeping with the guidelines set down in 1968 by the National Conference of Catholic Bishops.

Many concur that since Vatican II the Catholic church in collaboration with other churches has made genuine progress in developing new and more supportive ways to assist couples in their preparation for and celebration of mixed marriages. A number of Catholic dioceses have, in fact, issued joint guidelines to this end with other church judicatories. Where a need remains to be met is in offering support for ongoing married life. In spite of all that is done in preparation for their marriage, mixed couples can still feel themselves marginalized by the church communities after marriage. Their families can tend to fall in the gaps between the churches. When attending each other's churches, the one who is not a member of that church can subtly (sometimes not so subtly) be made to feel an outsider. The difficulties for the couple to remain active and in regular attendance at two different churches is undeniable. Here much more must be done to extend further and more effective pastoral care to the special needs of these couples. That is something few experienced observers would deny. While the field needs to be addressed, it is not entirely free of controversy among

Catholics. As an example, one may witness the Catholic Marriage Encounter movement divided into two wings. One welcomes non-Catholic Christians. The other restricts itself exclusively to Catholics, suggesting that other Christians should maintain their own distinct counterpart movements.

Since Vatican II the Catholic church has not made any special provisions for mixed marriage couples in terms of joint worship or sacramental sharing. It has, however, adopted new policies in this field which it offers for all. It encourages Christians to participate to the extent possible in one another's worship. But it places some clear restrictions on sacramental sharing, for it regards such sharing as a sign of full communion or a very high degree of communion within the church. It provides for exceptions, but these are in response to individual need and not as a matter of regular practice. Catholic ministry may permit other Christians to share in the eucharist, in penance and reconciliation, and in the anointing of the sick as these sacraments are celebrated in the Catholic church. The conditions upon which such permissions may be extended are summarized in can. 844 of the 1983 *Code of Canon Law*. In brief there are three: another Christian in need may be admitted a) if they spontaneously request these sacraments, b) are unable under the circumstances to receive them from their own minister, and c) are properly disposed, approaching these sacraments as Christians should, in faith and with repentance for personal sins. Catholics in need may similarly request the sacraments from ministers in other churches whose sacraments the Catholic church regards as valid.

The first two conditions reveal the concern of the Catholic church that the sacraments not be used as inducements to draw a Christian from one church community into another. A counterpart

sensitivity is shown in the matter of funeral services. Can. 1183 of the 1983 Code allows Catholic ministers to officiate at the funeral of other Christians under two provisions: a) that this would not be evidently against the will of the deceased, and b) that the proper minister of the deceased is unavailable to conduct the funeral.

Each of these measured steps by the Catholic church reflects the impact of Vatican II. That council remains a living force within the Catholic community. As experience is gained, pastoral practice may reveal the advisability of still further steps to be taken.

In the particular cases of Catholic-Orthodox mixed marriages such further steps have in fact already been taken by the Catholic church. In its Decree on Eastern Catholic Churches, n. 18, Vatican II established that when Eastern Catholics and Orthodox Christians marry, the canonical form would be required only for liceity. Should the couple marry without the requisite dispensation from the form, the marriage would still be considered valid by the Catholic church. A subsequent decree, *Crescens Matrimonium*, was issued by the Congregation for the Eastern church in 1967 stating that by the decision of Paul VI this same provision was extended to marriages between Latin rite Catholics and the Orthodox.

The Catholic church also provides for greater common worship, including sacramental sharing, between Catholics and Orthodox due to the close communion that exists between these churches. This applies to all Catholics and Orthodox, but naturally has particular relevance to Catholic-Orthodox couples. No restrictions are placed on the Orthodox who of their own accord and with proper dispositions wish to receive the sacraments of penance, the eucharist and anointing of the sick in the Catholic church. And no objection is made to

Catholics receiving these sacraments from Orthodox priests when it is physically or morally impossible to receive them from a Catholic priest.

In opening up these possibilities the Catholic church has stressed the importance of consultation with Orthodox bishops. Since the Orthodox churches hold to the principle of restricting admission to the sacraments in their churches to the Orthodox faithful, one can see that the situation in fact is not as open as it would seem simply from the point of view of Catholic policy. Other questions are engendered by the fact that the Orthodox hold that any Orthodox who wishes to enter a sacramental marriage must do so before an Orthodox priest who is considered to be the minister of the sacrament. The Orthodox point out that Latin rite priests do not administer the sacrament since they have no intention of doing so, because they regard the couple themselves to be the ministers of it. In effect this has meant that should an Orthodox and Catholic marry in the presence of a Catholic priest, the status of the Orthodox partner becomes irregular in the eyes of the Orthodox church and there can be no further participation in the sacramental life of that church until the marriage is regularized through the sacramental blessing of an Orthodox priest. The search for an equitable solution to such difficulties continues to be sought by Catholic and Orthodox authorities.

Pope Paul VI, Apostolic Letter, *Matrimonia Mixta* (Washington, D.C.: USCC Publications, 31 March 1970). National Conference of Catholic Bishops, "Statement on the Implementation of the Apostolic Letter on Mixed Marriages" (Washington, D.C.: USCC Publications, 1 January 1972). Pope John Paul II, Apostolic Exhortation, *Familiaris Consortio* (Washington, D.C.: USCC Publications, 15 December 1981). Committee for Pastoral Research and Practices, National Conference of Catholic Bishops, "Faithful to Each Other Forever: A Catholic Handbook of Pastoral Help for Marriage Preparation" (Washington, D.C.: USCC Publications, forthcoming). Secretariat for Promoting Christian Unity, "Ecumenical Directory" (Rome and Washington, D.C., U.S.C.C. Publications, forthcoming).

JOHN F. HOTCHKIN

MARRIAGE, LITURGY OF

Christ neither established the state of marriage nor provided us with a liturgy for matrimony. However, Jesus did display a sensitive regard for the joining of husband and wife, spoke several significant words about that union and elevated this natural relationship to the divine level of a sacrament.

The fact that his initial miracle took place at a wedding in Cana of Galilee and eliminated a potentially embarrassing situation for the bridal couple has been cited by many as a sign of Christ's special concern for marriage and his particular blessing upon this state.

Jesus likewise uttered apodictic, unqualified and straightforward comments about the unbreakability of the marital bond which quite sharply challenged the prevailing view of his time. His very words as he repudiated divorce recalled the original Genesis ideal of two becoming one and remaining faithful forever.

According to Roman Catholic belief, Christ finally lifted the natural union of spouses to the status of a supernatural sacrament. Nevertheless, it took the church many centuries, a millennium or more, to articulate a somewhat complete understanding of marriage's sacramental nature and an equally long or longer period to develop a standard rite of marriage.

Historical Development

For a thousand years after the Cana event, the secular state tended to handle most marriage and divorce details. The church was always present with prayer and blessing, but not until the civil society started to break down did it enter more fully into the legal and ceremonial aspects of marital relationships.

Church leaders began to view marriage as one of the seven official sacraments during the 12th and 13th centuries. The Second Council of Lyons (1274) listed marriage among the seven church sacraments; the Council of Florence (1439) formally proclaimed matrimony as a sacrament; the Council of Trent (1563) more explicitly defined this teaching; the Second Vatican Council reiterated these concepts (G.S., 47-52).

In the 11th century an obligatory church ceremony emerged and by the 12th century there was an established wedding ritual in different parts of Europe. However, numerous local variations prohibited the development of a standard nuptial rite.

The Council of Trent in the 16th century, reacting against the harmful effects of secret or clandestine marriages, declared: no Christian marriage would be valid or a sacrament unless contracted in the presence of a priest and two witnesses. Those who did not follow this step would be judged guilty of grave sin and treated as adulterers; moreover, the forthcoming marriage had to be announced publicly three weeks in advance and registered in the parish records immediately afterwards.

That teaching remained in effect for subsequent centuries and continues today with the adaptations and exceptions which will be touched upon below. The wedding liturgy in the Catholic church prior to Vatican II reflected those Tridentine directives. Nuptial celebrations had a fixed and clerical character. They were fixed in that the ritual, the readings, and other texts never varied. For example, the rite always included St. Paul's admonitions to the Ephesians in chap. 5 and Matthew's account of the exchange between Jesus and the Pharisees. They were clerical in that the priest did almost everything during the ceremony itself.

All of this changed radically in 1969 with the publication of the revised *Rite of Marriage* according to the dictates of the Second Vatican Council. The new ritual contains a rich variety of biblical readings, prayers, and blessings from which to choose and encourages the bride and groom to select those texts which best correspond to their hopes for the future. It provides other options for the celebration and urges the involvement of lay persons as leaders in the rite, such as lectors or readers. Finally, it stresses full congregational participation in the liturgy by word, song, and deed.

Framework of the Liturgy

The renewed format understandably follows the standard pattern or framework employed for all the restored sacramental liturgies. It includes an entrance or gathering rite, a liturgy of the word, a rite of marriage, a liturgy of the eucharist or a prayer-blessing section, and a conclusion or dismissal rite. The ritual provides a "Rite for Celebrating Marriage During Mass," a "Rite for Celebrating Marriage Outside Mass," a "Rite for Celebrating Marriage Between a Catholic and an Unbaptized Person," and "Texts for Use in the Marriage Rite and in the Wedding Mass." Both the framework and the content will become clearer as one examines each part of the ritual in detail.

The *entrance rite* is intended to gather together the people present—clergy, wedding party, relatives and guests—and mold them swiftly, but gently into a community of believing worshippers. The ritual, in a typically general, flexible way, describes the rite with several possibilities, but urges the priest (or deacon or delegated presider) to meet the "bride and bridegroom in a friendly manner, showing that the Church shares their joy" (n. 19).

That permissible adaptability for the procession has been played out in the United States generally in one of these ways: a procession led by the presiding clergy and ministers; one including ushers, bridesmaids, maid or matron of honor, bride and father; another in similar order but with both parents accompanying the bride; still another arrangement with both bride and groom flanked by parents and preceded by ushers and bridesmaids.

This gathering rite concludes by an opening prayer with four alternatives provided in the ritual.

The *liturgy of the word* has been designed to stir up the faith of the participants, to communicate a biblical message about marriage to them, and to help them recognize the presence of Christ in the sacramental rite soon to follow.

The ritual cites many suitable OT/NT texts and the engaged couple is encouraged to select those which they find most appropriate for them. The rite lists eight OT passages, ten from the NT, specifically from the various letters or the book of Revelation, ten gospel excerpts and seven responsorial psalms. Moreover, the couple may choose other scriptural texts provided that they appear in an approved lectionary and may select as many as three readings in addition to the psalm.

The homily should be drawn from these sacred texts and speak about the "mystery of Christian marriage, the dignity of wedded love, the grace of the sacrament and the responsibilities of married people, keeping in mind the circumstances of this particular marriage" (n. 22).

A rubric in the "Introduction" to the *Rite of Marriage* contains this very pastoral advice: "Priests should show special consideration to those who take part in liturgical celebrations or hear the gospel only on the occasion of a wedding, either because they are not Catholics, or because they are Catholics who rarely, if ever, take part in the eucharist or seem to have abandoned the practice of their faith. Priests are ministers of Christ's gospel to everyone" (n. 9).

The *Rite of Marriage* begins with an introduction or invitation to the bride and groom and the posing of three questions about their freedom of choice, faithfulness to each other, and acceptance and upbringing of children. There follows the declaration of consent (two formulas are provided), the blessing of rings (three options are given) and the exchange of bands accompanied by "Take this ring as a sign of my love and fidelity. In the name of the Father, and of. . . ."

What occurs after this section depends upon whether the celebration will take place during or outside of Mass. When marriage occurs during Mass, the blessing and exchange of rings is followed by the general intercessions and the liturgy of the eucharist which includes the nuptial blessing. When marriage occurs outside of Mass, the blessing and exchange of rings is followed by a combination of general interecessions with the nuptial blessing and the Our Father. As in other similar situations, several alternative formulas are given in the rite for the prayer over the gifts, the preface, nuptial blessing and the prayer after communion.

The *conclusion* or dismissal rite contains a blessing either with the simple trinitarian benediction or with a more solemn form of which four are provided, including one unique to the United States.

The "Rite for Celebrating Marriage Between a Catholic and an Unbaptized Person" observes the pattern outlined and described above with some obvious and necessary, but minor adaptations.

There are a number of other issues or concerns connected with the liturgy of marriage besides the official rite itself which should be touched on here.

Engagement
In the United States couples in the past often have requested a simple blessing upon the recently given or received engagement ring. Very few, however, ask for a formal betrothal or engagement ceremony. Nevertheless, couples from a

Hispanic tradition frequently observe a series of ritualized customs connected with the prospective bride and groom's request for engagement.

While there are good reasons for encouraging an integration of the couple's religious practices and their nuptial engagement, the American bishops have emphasized that the freedom and even responsibility of either person or both to terminate the engagement and not proceed with the marriage must always be taught and fostered.

The *Catholic Household Blessings and Prayers* published in 1988 by the U.S. Bishops' Committee on the Liturgy contains a rite for the "Blessing of an Engaged Couple." The rubrics suggest that ordinarily this ritual is celebrated by both families, perhaps at a meal together. One of the parents serves as the prayer leader and both sets of parents place their hands on their children's heads in blessing.

Music

In 1972 the American Bishops' Committee on the Liturgy issued a pivotal document, *Music in Catholic Worship*, which was subsequently revised in 1983. It addressed the sometimes thorny question of wedding music with these words: "Great care should be taken, especially at marriages, that all the people are involved at the important moments of the celebration, that the same general principles of planning worship and judging music are employed as at other liturgies, and, above all, that the liturgy is a prayer for all present, not a theatrical production."

In 1982 the same group published a second document, *Liturgical Music Today*, which expanded upon its earlier recommendations for music at nuptial liturgies. Among other things, they said: "Weddings present particular challenges and opportunities to planners. It is helpful for a diocese or a parish to have a definite (but flexible) policy regarding wedding music. This policy should be communi-

cated early to couples as a normal part of their preparation in order to avoid last minute crises and misunderstandings. Both musician and pastor should make every effort to assist couples to understand and share in the planning of their marriage liturgy. Sometimes the only music familiar to the couple is a song heard at a friend's ceremony and one not necessarily suitable to the sacrament. The pastoral musician will make an effort to demonstrate a wider range of possibilities to the couple, particularly in the choice of music to be sung by the entire assembly present for the liturgy."

Since publication of those documents, two developments have occurred in the United States. First, some dioceses have introduced the kind of flexible policies on wedding music urged by the Bishops' Committee on the Liturgy in its directives. Secondly, more and more parish music directors personally meet with the engaged couple to demonstrate and discuss appropriate musical selections for their approaching wedding. These sessions both expand the artistic horizons of the bride and groom and at the same time reduce potential tensions caused by their insistence upon songs or styles which may be personal favorites, but would be liturgical liabilities.

Rehearsals

A confluence of factors makes the wedding rehearsal a great challenge for those in pastoral ministry. There is a gathering of strangers, a complexity of attitudes or feelings and a high level of nervous anxiety within the bride and groom. Those who conduct the rehearsal, either the person who will preside over the liturgy or, with greater frequency today, trained wedding coordinators, clearly in this situation need to possess patience, tact and a sense of humor.

Some have found that after assembling and settling down the groups, a brief informal period of prayer can quickly help create a relaxed, but serious and reverent atmosphere. This prayerful interlude includes a passage from scripture, some silence, the Our Father and a spontaneous prayer petition seeking God's blessing upon the rehearsal, the wedding and the marriage.

While couples are still urged to receive reconciliation or penance prior to their marriage, the custom of hearing confessions after the rehearsal has declined.

Place of Marriage

The 1983 *Code of Canon Law* indicates that marriage involving a Catholic should take place in the parish church. However, it also makes provision for the legitimate celebration of the nuptial liturgy in other churches and in other places.

Many dioceses in the United States have now issued norms that marriages normally should take place in a church to emphasize the spiritual and sacramental nature of the event. Nevertheless, there are several occasions when the greater good of the couple and of the families involved will warrant the celebration of marriage in a place other than a church. The wedding of a Catholic person to a Jewish partner is a clear case in point.

Within or Outside of Mass

Various official church documents urge the celebration of matrimony within the context of a nuptial Mass. However, this ideal has in many instances become a pastoral difficulty in contemporary times. There are several reasons which have created that situation:

(1) The decline in the number of available priests has compelled many to offer multiple Masses each weekend. The need to celebrate additional nuptial eucharists compounds that burden for them.

(2) Deacons, with increasing frequency, are celebrating marriages.

(3) Engaged couples of a marginal religious nature may have sufficient faith for the reception of matrimony, but seemingly inadequate faith for the reception of the eucharist.

(4) It is often more pastorally suitable to celebrate an interreligious, interfaith, ecumenical or mixed marriage outside of, rather than within Mass.

(5) Delegated lay persons can today assist at marriages where priests or deacons are lacking.

Interreligious Weddings

The celebration of interreligious or mixed marriages, i.e., the wedding of a Catholic and one who is not a Catholic, has undergone significant modifications within the past half century. For example, in the 1940s, the exchange of vows took place in the rectory or outside the church; in the 1950s, such weddings might be celebrated in the church, but outside the sanctuary; in the 1960s, these moved inside the sanctuary; in the 1970s, they might include a previously prohibited nuptial Mass and blessing.

This gradual change represents the church's attempt to balance two pastoral concerns: the church wishes to encourage marital unions in which both share the same faith and religious practice, but it also wishes to show great solicitude for the many couples who will enter interfaith marriages.

On January 1, 1971, the U.S. Catholic bishops, following norms issued by Pope Paul VI, issued directives covering the celebration of interfaith or interreligious marriages. These guidelines contained the following practical points:

(a) The couple may have the banns or announcements of the forthcoming marriage published in advance.

(b) As noted above, they may celebrate their vows in the context of a nuptial Mass.

(c) The non-Catholic's minister is welcomed to participate in the ceremony.

(d) The person who is not Catholic signs no statement and makes no promises about the Catholic upbringing of the children.

(e) The Catholic signs or gives orally this promise: "I reaffirm my faith in Jesus Christ and, with God's help, intend to continue living that faith in the Catholic church. I promise to do all in my power to share the faith I have received with our children by having them baptized and reared as Catholics." The non-Catholic spouse needs to be aware of this promise.

(f) With the bishop's permission the marriage may take place in the church of the person who is not a Catholic and be witnessed by the clergy of that tradition.

The current *Code of Canon Law* in effect confirms these developments in the celebration of such interreligious marriages within the Catholic church.

Adaptations

There have been many informal adaptations of the official rite to individual celebrations of the Roman Catholic nuptial liturgy. These include, for example, use of a wedding or unity candle, comments from relatives or guests made to the couple as part of the homily or just before dismissal, blessing of the bride and groom by the parents, a symbolic gift for the poor, the exchange of vows made facing the assembly and other regional or ethnic variations.

However, in this country no substantive adaptations have traveled the full journey required for formal incorporation as part of the ritual. That path would involve study and proposal by the U.S. Bishops' Committee on the Liturgy, endorsement by the National Conference of Catholic Bishops and approbation or confirmation by the Holy See. Such possibilities are mentioned in church legislation and may occur in the future, but presently we do not possess these types of innovations.

What we do witness, nevertheless, is the active participation of the engaged couple in the preparation and celebration of the liturgy for marriage. A comparision of statistics on the sale of booklets needed for preparing the nuptial service and on the number of Catholic weddings, annually indicates that almost every bride and groom is at least offered the option of selecting their texts and planning a personal ceremony. In addition, there are signs of an accelerating trend for full congregational participation in song.

This growing active involvement of all in preparing and celebrating the liturgy of marriage is indeed welcome news, especially in the face of a 1989 report by sociological researchers which projects that two-thirds of contemporary first marriages will end in separation or divorce. Good nuptial liturgies may in fact help curb those bad cultural patterns.

National Conference of Catholic Bishops, *Faithful to Each Other Forever: A Catholic Handbook of Pastoral Help for Marriage Preparation* (Washington, D.C.: United States Catholic Conference Publications Office, 1989). Joseph Martos, *Doors to the Sacred* (New York: Doubleday and Company, Inc., 1981). Joseph M. Champlin, *Special Signs of Grace* (Collegeville, Minnesota: Liturgical Press, 1986).

JOSEPH M. CHAMPLIN

MARRIAGE, MINISTERS OF

In the tradition of the Latin church, the bride and groom are understood to be both the ministers and the recipients of the sacrament of marriage. As important as his role may be, the priest, deacon, or even designated lay person, is considered to be the assistant or principal and official witness of the Christian community, as well as the minister of the nuptial blessing.

The theological development during the past century has accentuated the ecclesial dimension of all sacraments. The community, gathered in faith, is the primary minister of the liturgy, and as such cannot give up its role or delegate its role to either the couple or to the priest. An overemphasis on the couple as ministers of the sacrament could lead to a diminution of this ecclesial dimension.

This understanding is reflected within

the statements of Vatican II as well as in other documents. Christian marriages and all sacraments are celebrations of Christian faith and celebrations of the entire believing community. As such, the normal place for a marriage celebration is the parish church. It is recommended by some that since the wedding Mass is not a private or family affair, the entire parish be invited to come and participate fully in the liturgical celebration. In Canada, all are encouraged to receive the eucharist under both species. The families or members of the community may provide the bread and the wine for the eucharistic celebration. The choice of music should facilitate the active participation of the community.

What is important is that all are celebrants, no one is a spectator. The congregation, as well as the bride and groom, are invited to respond "Amen" to the reception of the vows by the priest and to the priest's prayer of blessing over the rings. During the nuptial blessing all are invited to pray for the couple and, again, all conclude the prayer by "Amen." In the general intercessions the community prays for the couple and for the needs of the church and the world.

Part of the basis for the position that spouses are the ministers of marriage was the understanding of marriage as a contract, a concept which dates back to Roman times. However, Vatican II did change the vocabulary of marriage as contract to a "community of love" (G.S., 47), an "intimate partnership of conjugal life and love" (G.S., 48), a "conjugal covenant of irrevocable personal consent" (G.S., 48). The understanding of marriage as covenant has significance, not only for the couple, but for the whole community, which has a vested interest in the symbolism of this covenant. When a marriage is celebrated and lived as a community of love, the relationship of Christ with the community is signified, realized, and deepened. As such, the community is a vital part of this reality, an involvement that is to be manifested in the celebration as well as in support for the married couple.

There is a long tradition in the Western church that valid and sacramental marriages may be celebrated without a priest being present. This tradition is reflected in current documents. Deacons may now assist at a marriage (C.I.C., 1108). In addition to the ancient norm that, in danger of death or even when a priest is absent for a month, a valid and lawful marriage may be contracted before witnesses alone (C.I.C., 1116), the new code goes on to state that the "diocesan bishop can delegate lay persons to assist at marriages where priests or deacons are lacking" (C.I.C., 1112, par. 1). It is also the opinion of some that a lay person could give the nuptial blessing or say the other presidential prayers (McManus, p. 101). To extend this position even further, with permission, an interfaith marriage between a Catholic and another Christian may be celebrated in the absence of an ordained minister (C.I.C., 1127). It has been argued by some that the shift from the active form as enunciated by the priest ("I join you in marriage, in the name of the Father, and of the Son, and of the Holy Spirit"), which seemed to specify a joining power, to the more nuanced form ("You have declared your consent before the Church. May the Lord in his goodness strengthen your consent and fill you both with his blessings. What God has joined, men must not divide") is also indicative of the central ministerial role of the couple.

The couple are invited to express their ministerial role in many ways: in the gathering of the community; in the choice of the opening prayers; in the preparation of the presidential introduction to the liturgy of the word; in the choice of the number and the selection of the readings; in the choice of the responsorial psalm and antiphon; in the choice between the statement or question format of consent (the statement form is more active without the formal interrogation by the priest); in the choice of different blessings of the rings or the possibility of composing another suitable formula; in the composition of the prayers of the faithful; in the choice of the preface; in the choice of the eucharistic prayer; in the choice of the nuptial blessing; in the choice of the solemn blessing; in the kiss of peace.

As well, the couple may bring the gifts—bread, wine and water—to the priest. Finally, the couple, as well as others present, may also receive communion from the cup.

Vatican II did balance the emphasis on the role of the couple with the new stipulation that the nuptial blessing was never to be omitted, and that the priest is to ask for and receive the consent of the couple (S.C., 77 and 78). The presidential prayers of the priest emphasize his liturgical ministry. He receives the couple's consent to a Christian marriage in the name of the church; he commissions them in the name of the church; he blesses them in the name of the church; he preaches the word of God; and he promises them the support of the community. As such, he represents the local church as well as the universal church. To that extent, he functions as a co-minister of this sacrament.

In conclusion, whatever the historical reasons in the West for the designation of the couple as the ministers of the sacrament of marriage, it is important to stress their active participation in this celebration of faith. Within the current atmosphere of divorce and anonymous relationships, it is crucial that the couple recognize their role in developing a covenantal relationship which will touch their entire lives. Passivity, whether in the liturgical celebration or in their societal lives, will lead to a deadening of their spirit and of their relationship. They are to be ministers of committed love to each other, they are to be ministers of embodied love within the community, on the day of their wedding and during their married lives.

However, it is also recognized that we do not live in isolation from each other. The community must minister to the couple, affirming its love, its support, its faith, its history, and its hope. The experience of isolation by many of our married couples may be symptomatic of a community that no longer experiences itself as a ministering community.

The role of the priest is situated within the facilitating function for both the couple and the larger community. As the liturgical presider, he functions as he does in all sacramental celebrations. One main area of concern is how the exceptions to the role of the priest will influence ecumenical discussions with the Orthodox church which emphasizes the essential role of the priest as the minister of this sacrament. These exceptions also leave the door open to the recognition of a civil marriage as the public form of celebration of a Christian and sacramental marriage.

When considered liturgically, as distinct from canonically, the ministers of marriage are the couple, as well as the larger community and the priest. All exercise an essential role.

Michael G. Lawler, *Secular Marriage, Christian Sacrament* (Mystic, Twenty-Third, 1985). Rev. Msgr. Frederick McManus, "The Ministers of the Sacrament of Marriage in Western Tradition," in *Studia Canonica,* 20 (1986): 85-104. Kenneth W. Stevenson, *To Join Together: The Rite of Marriage* (N.Y.: Pueblo, 1987).

JAMES A. SCHMEISER

MARRIAGE, PREPARATION FOR

This article begins with a description of marriage preparation as I remember it during my initial years as a priest in the mid-1950s just prior to the Second Vatican Council. It is essentially a comparison between two moments in

Roman Catholic pastoral practice. The processes described will hopefully be of interest to other Christians as well.

The clergy in those days first met with the engaged couple, established the time and date for the wedding and explained the required church and civil documentation. He then either exhorted the pair to participate in one of the diocesan-sponsored pre-Cana programs or perhaps planned a few evenings for the three of them to discuss the sacrament of matrimony and other marital matters. Later, the priest would complete the necessary forms, conduct the rehearsal and carry out the ceremony.

The pre-Cana programs at that time usually emphasized the priest as the speaker-teacher, although there was a developing movement to include married couples for presentations on topics that were considered to be within their competence such as budgeting finances or purchasing furniture. The sessions might have included an audio-visual and a question box, but the uses of multiple media and process education were only in their infancy stages.

Vatican II and the subsequent renewal naturally changed marriage preparation in radical ways, just as its reforms brought about enormous transformations in almost every aspect of Catholic life and practice. Specifically, the church officially called lay persons to be involved in marriage preparation efforts. The *Decree on the Apostolate of Lay People* spoke about a "like to like" ministry and explicitly cited "assisting engaged couples to make a better preparation for marriage" as an example of works of the family apostolate (A.A. , 13, 11).

Almost two decades later the 1983 *Code of Canon Law* stated that the total "ecclesial community," not merely the clergy, provide assistance for, among other things, the engaged couple's "personal preparation for marriage." It also suggested that the local ordinary consult

"men and women of proven experience and skill" to help organize marriage preparation and enrichment programs (cans. 1063-1064).

Couples, through official church encouragement and their individual inclination, began to prepare much more personal wedding liturgies. Pre-Vatican II nuptial services, on the other hand, were almost identically alike and mainly the work of the presiding priest.

The renewed marriage ritual followed the model of all revised rites and included a resource of many prayers, biblical readings and blessings from which to choose. Moreover, the church, directly with its general liturgical directives and indirectly with its introduction to the *Rite of Marriage*, urged active participation by the wedding party and the assembled community in the preparation and celebration of the wedding liturgy itself.

The explosion of creative religious education materials and processes understandably flowed over into marriage preparation efforts.

A 1982 study revealed that 88 U.S. dioceses, even then, used some form of instrument or inventory to facilitate pre-marriage dialogue between the couple and those guiding them in their preparatory steps. The most common ones employed today are *F.O.C.C.U.S.* (Facilitating Open Couple Communication, Understanding and Study), *P.M.I.* (Pre-Marital Inventory) and *P.R.E.P.A.R.E.* (Premarital Personal and Relationship Enrichment).

Films, filmstrips and videotapes are now an expected part of every marriage preparation program, as are various group processes based on the discoveries of adult education experts.

Engaged couples generally can select from a variety of preparation programs the type with which they are most comfortable. These include: an Engaged Encounter weekend; an all day or several evening diocesan or regional event; a similar activity offered instead on the parish level; a somewhat structured *Evenings for the Engaged* conducted in four or more sessions by local faith community of married couples; an informal one-to-one, couple-to-couple or sponsor-couple exchange ordinarily hosted in the home of the married persons.

A very delicate and frequently difficult issue facing church leaders at the present is the request for a nuptial liturgy by couples whose adherence to Catholic faith practices is minimal or seemingly non-existent and/or whose natural readiness for marriage appears highly questionable.

In his 1982 apostolic exhortation, *Familiaris Consortio (On the Family)*, Pope John Paul II dealt with that particular challenge. His guidelines recognize the natural right of the couple to marry, but establish flexible norms to determine the existence of the minimal faith demanded for the sacrament of matrimony. These directives also express the hope that pastors will use the preparation and celebration of the nuptial liturgy as vehicles for the rediscovery, sustaining and deepening of the couple's religious belief and practice (par. 68).

His teaching echoes the words of the *Constitution on the Sacred Liturgy* which state that the sacraments are acts of faith and presuppose faith, but they also nourish, strengthen and express faith (S.C., 59).

Pope John Paul II in that apostolic exhortation likewise widens our understanding of marriage preparation. We customarily identify it with those activities which begin when the engaged couple approaches the clergy to arrange the wedding and conclude when the bridal pair march down the aisle and out of the church. The Holy Father, however, maintains that marriage preparation in truth starts at the womb and ends in the tomb. Children from their very first moments are, for better or for worse, being prepared to marry by the very life lived at home. Similarly, the later marriage is helped or hindered by the many environmental forces surrounding the husband and wife as they fulfill their marital vows over the years.

The pope, consequently, divides marriage preparation into remote (from birth until puberty), proximate (from puberty to the engagement), immediate (from the engagement through the wedding celebration) and aftercare (from the nuptial celebration onward).

How successful are contemporary marriage preparation efforts? For many reasons we do not possess solidly scientific statistics which prove that couples who complete marriage preparation programs are happier, enjoy more successful marital lives and experience a lower divorce rate. There are, nevertheless, surveys which indicate that such programs do make a constructive difference and promote growth in a couple's relationship.

Pope John Paul II provided this wise, even if simple, observation about marriage preparation: "Experience teaches that young people who have been well prepared for family life generally succeed better than others" (F.C., 66).

National Conference of Catholic Bishops, *Faithful to Each Other Forever: A Catholic Handbook of Pastoral Help for Marriage Preparation* (Washington, D.C.: United States Catholic Conference Publications Office, 1989). Joseph M. Champlin, *Together for Life* (Notre Dame, Indiana: Ave Maria Press, 1970, Fourth revised edition, 34th printing, 1988). Paul Covino, ed., *Celebrating Marriage: Preparing the Wedding Liturgy* (Washington, D.C.: The Pastoral Press, 1987).

JOSEPH M. CHAMPLIN

MARRIAGE, SACRAMENT OF

This article will deal with marriage as *covenant*, marriage as *sacrament*, and the special case of *divorce and remarriage*.

I. *Christian Marriage As Covenant*

Vatican II provides a contemporary Roman Catholic description of Christian marriage: "The intimate partnership of married life and love has been established by the Creator and qualified by his laws. It is rooted in the conjugal covenant of irrevocable personal consent. Hence, by that human act whereby spouses mutually bestow and accept each other, a relationship arises which by divine will and in the eyes of society, too is a lasting one. For the good of the spouses and their offspring as well as of society, the existence of this sacred bond no longer depends on human decisions alone" (G.S., 48).

Marriage is a community of life and love, founded in a mutual and irrevocable covenant, by which a Christian man and a Christian woman give and accept one another for the purpose of establishing an intimate partnership of their whole life. Reflection on this description will clarify our subject, the sacrament of marriage.

The word *covenant* is not idly chosen. It is an ancient theological word, conjuring up for Christian spouses biblical images of both the great covenant between God and God's people and the extension of that covenant in the new covenant between Jesus and his people. It is also a new canonical word, replacing in the 1983 *Code of Canon Law* the long-established legal word *contract*. Reflection on the distinctive nuances of contract and covenant will highlight crucial changes which have taken place in the Roman Catholic approach to the sacrament of marriage in the latter half of the 20th century.

Covenant is clearly a more biblical word than contract; it is also a more personal word. Contract bespeaks obligations; covenant, interpersonal gift. Paul Palmer has attempted to clarify the meanings of covenant by contrasting it with contract: "Contracts deal with things, covenants with people. Contracts engage the services of people; covenants engage persons. Contracts are made for a stipulated period of time; covenants are forever. Contracts can be broken, with material loss to the contracting parties; covenants cannot be broken, but if violated, they result in personal loss and broken hearts. Contracts are secular affairs and belong to the market place; covenants are sacral affairs and belong to the hearth, the temple or the church. Contracts are best understood by lawyers, civil and ecclesiastical; covenants are appreciated better by poets and theologians. Contracts are witnessed by people with the state as guarantor; covenants are witnessed by God with God as guarantor. Contracts can be made by children who know the value of a penny; covenants can be made only by adults who are mentally, emotionally and spiritually mature" (*Theol. Studies* 33 [1972]: 639).

These acute distinctions, which need not just to be read but also to be pondered, enable us to distinguish covenant from contract and also to name a significant change in the Roman Catholic approach to Christian marriage. It has become thoroughly personalist.

The description of marriage as covenant links it to the two model covenants in the Christian tradition, the Great Covenant between Yahweh and Yahweh's holy people and the New Covenant between Christ and his holy people called the church. There is, first, the Great Covenant; then there is the extension of this Great Covenant in the New Covenant; and, finally, there is the covenant of Christian marriage which is not only an extension of, but also a participation in, both. That final assertion needs some reflection.

The imaging of marriage as covenant has been traditionally a Protestant approach; the Catholic tradition has imaged it more as sacrament. The covenant approach emphasizes abiding interpersonal relationship founded in the abiding consent of the spouses. The sacramental approach emphasizes abiding and sacred bond which, though initiated by the consent of the spouses to be married, continues to exist even if that consent be withdrawn. That abiding bond continues to be a block to another marriage after a civil divorce. I hope to demonstrate that the two approaches are not as different as they might seem or as they have been made out to be. We must first ask, however, about the implications, both theoretical and practical, of saying that Christian marriage is a covenantal relationship?

To covenant is to commit oneself radically and solemnly. When a man and a woman covenant in Christian marriage, they commit themselves mutually to create a life of equal and intimate partnership in abiding love. They commit themselves mutually to create and sustain a climate of personal openness, acceptance, trust and honesty that will nurture such intimate community and abiding love. They commit themselves mutually to create rules of behavior which will respect, nurture and sustain intimate community and abiding love. They commit themselves mutually to explore together the religious depth of human existence, and therefore of marital existence, and to respond to that depth in the light of their Christian faith. They commit themselves mutually to abide in love and in covenant, and to withdraw from them only if the life of intimacy has ceased to exist and if all available means to restore it have been tried and have failed (See Yates, "The Protestant View of Marriage," *Jour. of Ecumenical Studies* 22 [1985]: 41-54). A brief commentary on these assertions will lead us from the Protestant image of marriage as covenant to the Catholic image of it as sacrament.

In Christian marriage, a man and a woman commit themselves to create a life of equal and intimate partnership in abiding love. When the Lord Yahweh made the heavens and the earth, when no plant had yet sprung up from the earth because the Lord Yahweh had not yet caused it to rain upon the earth, a mist went up from the earth and watered the ground. The mist, of course, turned the dry earth to mud, in Hebrew 'adamah, and from that 'adamah the Lord Yahweh formed 'adam and breathed into her and his nostrils the breath of life. And 'adam became a living being (Gen 2:4-7). "When the Lord Yahweh created 'adam, he made him in the likeness of Yahweh. Male and female he created them, and he blessed them and he named them 'adam" (Gen 5:1-2).

This myth, for it is a myth, provides those who accept it with an answer to a perennial question. Where did we come from? We, in English *humankind*, in Hebrew 'adam, came from God. Male and female as we are, we are from the Lord Yahweh, and together we make up humankind or 'adam. This fact alone, that Yahweh names man and woman together 'adam, founds the equality of man and woman as human beings. The further myth, which speaks of the creation of woman from the man's rib, intends in the original Hebrew to emphasize their equality, not their separate creation.

In their recent pastoral response to the concerns of women in the church, the Catholic bishops of the United States insist on this fact. Since "in the divine image ... male and female (Yahweh) created them" (Gen 1:27), man and woman are equal in human dignity and favor in Yahweh's eyes. They are equal in everything that is human; they are "bone of bone and flesh of flesh" (Gen 2:23). It is because they are equal, says the myth, that woman and man may marry and "become one body" (Gen 2:24).

Western Christians have seriously misunderstood the Eastern myth about equal man and woman, 'adam. They have also misunderstood the Eastern myth about becoming one body. They have linked it too exclusively to a single facet of becoming one in marriage, namely the sexual. That facet is part of what is involved in becoming one body, but it is far from all that is involved. In the original biblical myth, *body* does not refer to the external, physical part of the human being, as it does in English. It refers rather to the whole person. In marriage, therefore, a man and a woman enter into not just a physical union, in which their physical bodies are made one, but into a personal union, in which their whole persons are made one. The union of their bodies in sexual intercourse is, at root, but the symbol of the union of their entire selves.

The covenant of marriage is a mutual commitment not only to create a life of equal partnership, but also to nurture and sustain it. When a man and a woman covenant in Christian marriage, therefore, they commit themselves mutually to create rules of behavior which will nurture and sustain the marriage resulting from their covenant. For committed Christians, those rules are found by paying careful attention to their tradition.

The letter to the Ephesians provides scriptural rules for the living out of the marriage covenant. Its writer, too late to be the apostle Paul, inherits a list of household duties traditional at the time and the place. He critiques the cultural assumption of inequality in this list, and instructs all Christians to "give way to one another because you stand in awe of Christ" (5:21). This critique challenges the absolute authority of any one Christian group over another, of husbands over wives for instance. It establishes as the basic attitude required of all Christians, even in marriage, an awe of Christ and a giving way to one another because of this.

As all Christians are to give way one another, it is hardly surprising that a wife is to give way to her husband, "as to the Lord" (5:22). There is a surprise, however, in the instruction given to husbands, at least for those husbands who see themselves as lord and master of their wives and who appeal to the letter to the Ephesians to support this perspective. The instruction is not that the husband is the head of the wife, which is the preferred male reading, but that "the husband is the head of the wife *as* (that is, in the same way as) Christ is head of the church" (5:23). An obvious question arises: how does Christ act as head of the church? The writer gives the equally obvious answer: "He gave himself up for her" (5:25). It is an echo of a self-description that Jesus offers in Mark's gospel: "The Son of Man came not to be served but to serve" (10:45).

The Christ-way to exercise authority is to serve. Jesus constantly pointed out to his power-hungry disciples that in his kingdom a leader is one who serves (Lk 22:26). A husband who wishes to be head over his wife, or a wife who wishes to be head over her husband, in the way that Christ is head over the church will be head by serving, by giving himself or herself up for the other.

Christlike headship is not absolute control of another human being. It is not making decisions and passing them on to another to carry out. It is not reducing another human being to the status of chattel. To be head as Christ is head is to serve. The Christian head is called always to be the servant of others. As Markus Barth puts it so beautifully, the Christian husband-head becomes "the first servant of his wife" (Barth, 618), and she becomes his first servant. One rule of behavior for the nurturing and sustaining of the covenant of Christian marriage is the rule of mutual service.

The letter to the Ephesians embraces another rule for behavior in Christian marriage, a great Jewish and Christian commandment: "You shall love your neighbor as yourself" (Lev 19:18; Mk 12:31). Husbands are instructed that they "should love their wives as (that is, for they are) their own bodies" (5:28a), and that the husband "who loves his wife loves himself" (5:28b). We can assume the same instruction is intended also for a wife. The Torah and gospel injunction to love one's neighbor as oneself applies in Christian marriage. As all Christians are to give way to one another and to love one another, so also are the spouses in a Christian marriage. The rules of Christian behavior that will respect, nurture and sustain the covenant and the community of marriage are easy to articulate: love of one's neighbor-spouse as oneself, love which is giving way, love which is mutual service, love which is abiding.

A Christian marriage is not just a wedding ceremony to be celebrated. It is also a loving and equal partnership of life to be lived. When they covenant in marriage, Christian spouses commit themselves to explore together in their married life the religious depth of their existence, and to respond to that depth in the light of Christian faith.

One of the most central affirmations of Christian faith is the affirmation of discipleship. *Disciple* is an ever-present NT word, occurring some two hundred and fifty times throughout the gospels and the Acts, and always implying response to a call from the Lord. By definition disciples are learners, and the disciples of Christ are learners of mystery. They gather to explore together a triple mystery: the mystery of the one God who loves them and seeks to be loved by them; the mystery of the Christ in whom this God is revealed and whom God raised from the dead (1 Cor 15:4; Acts 2:24); the mystery of the church in which they gather and which is the body of Christ (Eph 1:22-23; Col 1:18, 24). Spouses in a covenant marriage are called to be disciples of these mysteries and of their implications for their married life together.

Christian marriage does not separate spouses from life. It immerses them in life and confronts them with the ultimate questions of life and of death that are the stuff of religion. There are questions of joy in love and loving and the birth of new life; of pain in illness and suffering and alienation; of grief and fear in loneliness and isolation and death; of happiness in friends and beauty and success. Marriage demands that sense be made out of these competing questions and a thousand others like them. Christian marriage demands that sense be made out of them in the light of the shared Christian faith of the spouses.

As they find together adequate responses to the demands their married life imposes on them, Christian spouses mutually nurture one another into Christian discipleship. They learn together and they grow together in Christian maturity. The more they mature, the more they come to realize the ongoing nature of becoming married and of becoming a covenant sign. They come to realize that, though their marriage is already a sign of the covenant between Christ and his church, it is not yet the best sign it can be and is called to be. In Christian marriage, which is a life of ongoing Christian discipleship, even more than in secular marriage, the answer to the question of when two people are married is simple: thirty, forty, even fifty years later.

II. *Christian Marriage As Sacrament*

Religions are always on the lookout for the images of God and of God's relationship to the human world. In the Jewish prophets, we find an action image, known as the prophetic symbol. Jeremiah, for instance, buys an earthen pot, dashes it to the ground before a puzzled crowd and explains to them what it is he is doing. "Thus says the Lord of Hosts: so will I break this people and this city, as one breaks a potter's vessel" (19:11). Ezekiel takes a sharp knife, shaves his hair with it and divides the hair into three bundles. He burns one bundle, scatters another to the wind and carries the third around the city and shreds it further with his knife. In prophetic explanation of his actions, he proclaims: "This is Jerusalem" (5:5).

Each prophet clarifies the radical meaning of his actions, which clarifies for us the radical meaning of a prophetic symbol. As Jeremiah shattered his pot, as Ezekiel cut and burned and scattered his hair, so God shatters and scatters and burns Jerusalem. The depth meaning and reality symbolized by Jeremiah is not the shattering of a cheap pot, but the shattering of Jerusalem and of the covenant relationship between Yahweh and Yahweh's people. The prophetic symbol is a representative action, that is, an action which proclaims, makes explicit and celebrates in representation some other, more fundamentally meaningful reality.

Since the idea of their special relationship to Yahweh arising out of their mutual covenant was so central to the self-understanding of the Israelites, it is easy to predict that they would search out a human reality to symbolize the covenant relationship. It is equally easy, perhaps, to predict that the reality they would choose is the mutual covenant that is marriage. The prophet Hosea was the first to act in and speak of marriage as the prophetic symbol of the covenant.

On the superficial level, the marriage of Hosea and Gomer is like many other marriages. But, on the depth level, Hosea interpreted it as a prophetic symbol, proclaiming, making humanly explicit and celebrating in representation the covenant union between Yahweh and Israel. As Gomer left Hosea for other lovers, it was proclaimed in representation, so also did Israel leave Yahweh for other gods. As Hosea waits for Gomer to return to him, and as he takes her back without recrimination when she

does return, so also does Yahweh with Israel. Hosea's human action is prophetic symbol, representative image, of God's divine action, an abiding love in spite of every provocation. In both covenants, the human and the divine, the covenant relationship had been violated. But Hosea's action both mirrors and reveals Yahweh's abiding love. It proclaims, makes explicit and celebrates not only Hosea's faithfulness to his marriage covenant, but also Yahweh's faithfulness to Israel.

One basic meaning about Hosea and Yahweh is clear: each is steadfastly faithful. There is also a clear, if mysterious, meaning about marriage. Besides being a universal human institution, it is also a religious and prophetic symbol proclaiming, making explicit and celebrating in the human world the abiding union of Yahweh and Yahweh's people. Lived into from this perspective, lived into a faith as we might say today, marriage becomes a two-tiered reality. On one level, it bespeaks the mutual covenant love of this man and this woman; on another, it represents and symbolizes the covenant love of Yahweh and Yahweh's people. First articulated by the prophet Hosea, this two-tiered view of marriage becomes the Christian view of marriage that we have found in the letter to the Ephesians. Jewish prophetic symbol becomes ultimately Christian sacrament.

We noted in the preceding section that, while the classical Catholic teaching presents Christian marriage as a sacrament, the classical Protestant teaching presents it as a sign of the covenant but not as a sacrament. These different perspectives depend on different definitions. John Calvin defined sacrament as a sign instituted by Christ for the whole of the faithful. The Lutheran church defines it as an action of the church enjoined by Christ to be enjoyed by all Christians. Since only baptism and eucharist were so instituted and enjoined, the Reformation churches believe they are the only rituals acknowledged as sacraments.

The classical Roman Catholic definition of sacrament, an outward sign instituted by Christ to give grace, took a thousand years to become established, with all sorts of realities, including marriage, floating in and out of the sacramental picture until the definition became universally acceptable (See Lawler, *Symbol and Sacrament*, 29-34). We can now offer a more fully explicated version of that definition. A sacrament is a prophetic symbol in and through which the church, the body of Christ, proclaims, makes explicit and celebrates in representation that presence and action of God which is called grace.

To say that Christian marriage is a sacrament is to say that it is a prophetic symbol, a reality that has two tiers. On one tier, it proclaims and makes explicit and celebrates the intimate community of life and love between a Christian man and a Christian woman. On another, deeper tier, the religious and symbolic tier, it proclaims and makes explicit and celebrates the intimate community of life and love between Yahweh and Yahweh's people and between Christ and Christ's people, the church.

A couple entering into any marriage say to one another before the society in which they live: "I love you and I give myself to and for you." A Christian couple entering into a Christian marriage say that too, and more. They say also: "I love you as Christ loves his church."

From the first, therefore, a Christian marriage is more than just the union of this man and this woman; it is more than just human covenant. It is also religious covenant. God and God's Christ are present in it, gracing it, from the beginning. The presence of grace in its most ancient Christian sense, namely, the presence of the gracious God, is not something extrinsic to the covenant of Christian marriage. It is something essential to it, something without which it would not be *Christian* marriage at all. Of course, Christian marriage proclaims, makes explicit and celebrates the mutual and abiding love of this man and this woman. It also proclaims, makes explicit and celebrates their abiding love for their God and for the Christ they confess as Lord. It is in this sense that it is a sacrament, both a sign and an instrument, of the presence of Christ and of the God he reveals.

In every symbol there are two levels of meaning. There is a foundational level and, built on this foundation, a symbolic one. On the foundational level, for instance, water produces both death and life, which makes it wonderfully apt to express on the symbolic level meanings of death and resurrection to new life, as it does in the sacrament of baptism. Christian marriage has the same two levels of meaning.

The foundational level of Christian marriage is the community of life and love between a man and a woman who are disciples of Jesus. The symbolic or sacramental level is the reflection and representation in this community of the community of life and love between Christ and the church. On the one level, Christian marriage proclaims, makes explicit and celebrates the mutual love of the spouses; on another, symbolic level, it proclaims, makes explicit and celebrates the mutual love of Christ and the church. This two-tiered meaningfulness is what the Catholic church means when it says that Christian marriage is sacramental.

In Christian marriage, the symbolic meaning takes precedence over the foundational meaning, in the sense that the abiding love of Christ and the church is the model for the mutual love of the spouses. Christian spouses are not merely this wife and this husband covenanted to one another. They are the church in microcosm covenanted to their Lord; they are, in Vatican II's words, the "domestic church" (L.G., 11). Since a Christian family is a little domestic church, Christian marriage which founds that family participates in the covenant between Christ and Christ's universal church. Christian marriage, that is, is essentially graced from its beginning. God and God's Christ are present in it, gracing the spouses with their presence, offering them models of steadfast and abiding love.

To say that it is a sign of grace, even an effective sign of grace, is never to be equated with saying that Christian marriage automatically effects grace. That is a complaint that has been made against Roman Catholic sacramental teaching since the Reformation. But the Catholic church has never taught that any sacrament automatically effects grace. It has taught only that sacraments, including Christian marriage, are signs and instruments of grace, signs and instruments, that is, of the presence of God and of the Christ confessed as God's son.

Even the superficial reader of the NT has to be struck by the insistence on the necessity of personal faith for salvation. Jesus complained sorrowfully about the absence of personal faith; Paul passionately defended its necessity against the Judaizers. At the Reformation, both the Reformers and the Council of Trent agreed on the primacy of faith, a "comprehensive 'yes' to God revealing himself as savior in Christ" (Alfaro, *Sacramentum Mundi*, 2: 315). Luther made "faith alone" one of the foundations of his theological system. The council taught that "we may be said to be justified through faith," citing in its support the saying in the letter to the Hebrews "without faith it is impossible to please God" (D.S., 1532; cp. 1529). There can be no doubt that, despite the post-Reformation polemics which tended to obscure this common agreement, the primacy of personal faith is as much a Catholic as it is a Reformed doctrine.

The Council of Trent also taught that sacraments confer the grace they signify on those who present no obstacle (D.S., 1606). It opted for this minimalistic formula to cover in one umbrella statement the cases of both infants in baptism and adults in all sacraments, but it applies positively only to infants. In the prior Council of Florence, the Catholic tradition had already carefully specified that, for an adult, placing no obstacle meant having a positive intent. The sacraments, it taught, give grace only to those who receive them worthily (D.S., 1310). This doctrine demands a personal, positive, active disposition of self-surrendering faith on the part of one who wishes to be graced in sacrament. Such a teaching highlights the fact that a sacrament is a true sign of faith. It is a sign, that is, not only of the faith of the church which seeks to make explicit and to celebrate in sacrament the presence of God and of Christ, but also of the faith of Christians who seek to confess and to concelebrate that presence with the church.

The Second Vatican Council reaffirms the necessity of faith as the Catholic position. It teaches that sacraments "not only presuppose faith" but also "nourish, strengthen and express it," which is why "they are called 'sacraments of faith'" (S.C., 59). Catholic teaching is, and always has been, clear. Grace, the loving presence of God and God's Christ, is never automatic, not even in sacrament, not even in the sacrament of marriage. Grace is never effected by some external action alone without the matching internal disposition of believers, their faith, their love, their comprehensive "yes" to the presence of God and of God's Christ. It is only when the external action and the internal disposition come together that there is effective sacrament.

The most Catholic of theologians,

Thomas Aquinas, never doubted this. The saving action of God and Christ, he taught, "achieves its effect in those to whom it is applied through faith and love and the sacraments of faith"(S.Th., 3, 49, 3 ad 1). Personal faith, the internal disposition of a believer that he called *opus operantis*, is as essential to the reception of grace in and through sacrament as the most carefully crafted external action that he called *opus operatum*. Speaking of eucharist, Aquinas argues that it has effect "only in those who are united to the passion of Christ in faith." Even for them, "it is of more or less value according to their devotion"(S.Th., 3, 79, 7 ad 2). The same is true of Christian marriage.

The sacramental, marital intercourse between spouses takes place, Aquinas explains, on three levels, the animal level, the human level and the religious level (S. Th., 3 suppl, 65, 1 corp.). To become one body, prophetic symbol and sacrament of the one-body union between Christ and the church, Christian spouses must come to terms with their needs, feelings and desires on all three levels. Becoming one personal body includes not only union of spirits, not only union of minds but also union of bodies. Only because the physical and sexual level of marital intercourse has been much maligned in Christian history, and not because of some exalted significance of its own, we need to say a special word about the place of sexuality and sexual intercourse in the sacrament of marriage.

There are three kinds of love, in real life as well as in Greek language. There is *agape*, the love of the spouse for the spouse's sake; there is *philia*, the love of the spouse as a friend; there is *eros*, the love of the spouse for one's own sake. Married love is certainly *agape*, but also more than *agape*. It is certainly *philia*, but also more than *philia*. It is certainly also *eros*, but also more than *eros*. Lest there be any confusion about that last statement, let me hasten to put it another way. Marital love is loving your neighbor *as yourself* (Mt 22:39).

Since Augustine, the Christian commandment to love one's neighbor as oneself has been recognized in the wisdom of the Catholic tradition as the foundation for a wholly justifiable self-love. Such self-love is much in evidence when two people are well along the way to becoming one body, for in such a marriage both spouses have become mutually full and fully esteemed personal partners. In such a marriage, "I love you" matures into "I love me and you," and ultimately into "we love us," as Millhaven puts it so beautifully (*Theol. Studies*, 35 [1974]: 705). One of the most common reasons that many men and women have difficulty truly loving another human being is that they have difficulty ever truly loving themselves.

So back to *eros*, that rambunctious, non-rational, selfish component of human sexuality and human love. The spiritualizers always want to transform it into *agape*, though there is no alchemy to effect such a transformation. *Eros* is an essential, and therefore inescapable, quality of human and marital love. It participates in the sacramental nature of Christian marriage on the basis of the simple theological fact that it is from God. It is God's creation gift to 'adam; it is, so to speak, God's wedding gift, to a man and a woman. When used as a good gift in the process of becoming one in Christian marriage, it is used in a way that points to its origin in God. That is already to use it mysteriously and sacramentally, in a way that is not only physical and human and spiritual but also religious and grace-full.

Physical union is not all there is to a sacramental marriage, but it is an essential part of it. If such a marriage is, as it is said to be, a prophetic symbol and sacrament of the covenant between Christ and the church, then the physical and personal and spiritual union achieved in sexual intercourse is an integral part of that symbol. That means that sexual intercourse proclaims, makes explicit and celebrates the love and mutual presence not only of this man and this woman but also of the God who is Grace. It honors the Giver and the gift, as well as the man and the woman who use the gift to make not only human but also "divine" love.

III. *Divorce and Remarriage*

The liturgies of all the Christian churches witness to their common conviction that a man and a woman marry for as long as life lasts. I share this Christian conviction. I take it to be self-evident that the covenant of Christian marriage creates a moral obligation to be faithful to both the covenant and the commitment it implies. For that is what both covenant and love *mean*. Covenant creates a relationship in which I am bound morally to keep my word; love by its very nature tends to be life-long.

Some marriages, however, do not last as long as life; they cease to be; they die. The Christian churches are as divided about the proper pastoral approach to such failed marriages, and to the second marriages which frequently follow them, as they are united in their common theological conviction about the life-long nature of marriage. These divisions are serious for the lives of the churches; they are also an important corollary to all we have discussed. We need, therefore, to say a brief word here about how marriages end in the Roman Catholic church.

The Catholic church has long agreed with the vast majority of moralists that the obligation deriving from commitment is limited, not absolute, and can be withdrawn for a reason "higher" than the marriage obligation. This is what I intended to insinuate when I asserted earlier that, in the covenant that is Christian marriage, a man and a woman commit mutually to abide in love and in covenant, and to withdraw from them only if the life of intimacy has ceased to exist and if all available means to restore it have been tried and have failed. A consideration of Roman Catholic practice, will clarify this statement.

Though the Roman Catholic church's reading of Jesus' saying on divorce and remarriage leads it to consider all valid marriages as indissoluble, it does dissolve valid marriages. Or, in plainer language, it does grant divorces. The most ancient of these divorce procedures is one derived from Paul's letter to the Corinthians and called, therefore, the Pauline privilege. It applies to the question of divorce in the marriage in which one spouse has become Christian and the other remains non-Christian. Paul has two pieces of advice for the spouse in such a marriage, each of them hinging on the behavior of the unbaptized spouse.

If the unbaptized spouse is willing to continue to live peacefully with the now-baptized spouse, then the traditional Torah instruction holds: what God has joined together, let no man put asunder. But if the unbaptized spouse is unwilling to continue to live in peace, then she or he is to be allowed to withdraw from the marriage. There is no suggestion that Jesus' command does not apply in this case. There is only the suggestion that, in this specific case, Paul is making an exception to Jesus' command ("I say, not the Lord" [7:12]).

The reason given for the exception is interesting. "In such a case, the brother or sister is not bound. For God has called us to peace" (7:15). Peace, it would appear, is one of those higher reasons that make possible release from the marriage commitment. The Roman Catholic church sanctioned this approach to dissolving a valid marriage in the 12th century, still sanctions it today (cf. can. 1143), and names it the Pauline privilege. In the centuries that have elapsed since Paul, it has also extended the Pauline privilege into the so-called Petrine privilege, by which valid marriages are dissolved on the authority of the pope in favor of the higher good called faith (cf. cans. 1148-1150).

There is yet a third way to dissolve a valid marriage in the Roman Catholic church. The ancient Roman answer to the question as to when a marriage actually took place was that it took place when a couple freely consented to marry. The northern European answer was that it took place when the couple engaged in their first marital sexual intercourse. Unable, or unwilling, to discriminate between these two points of view, the medieval church combined them and taught that marriage was *initiated* by consent and *consummated* by sexual intercourse. If after the giving of consent, which initiates a valid marriage, there is no sexual intercourse, then the valid marriage may be dissolved (cf. can. 1142), or, in plainer English, a divorce may be granted.

These Roman Catholic divorce procedures have never caused any problems for Christians, because only the specialists ever knew about them. The case is quite different with the famous, perhaps now infamous, procedure known as annulment. Annulment is an entirely different procedure from the dissolution procedures. The latter dissolve marriages held to be valid, while annulment declares that, because of some deficiency in the beginning, there never was a valid marriage bond between these two people.

Ordinary people, of course, usually cannot comprehend the technical niceties of difference between annulment and the divorce procedures, and they lump them all together. They know that annulment is granted today in the United States more commonly than ever before, and they conclude that the Catholic church is talking out of one side of its mouth about being opposed to divorce and acting out of the other side by granting divorces

called annulment. They need to know two things to understand the Catholic practice: first, despite its firm belief that marriage is intended to be life-long, the Catholic church does grant divorces; secondly, annulment is not one of those divorces but merely a declaration that, in a specific case, there never was a valid marriage.

The breakdown of marriage is always a human tragedy, causing hurt and harm to the spouses, their children, their families, their friends. When a marriage fails, and a brief glance at the concrete reality of human life shows that some marriages do fail, concrete people experience turmoil, anger and hatred in the very context in which they expected to experience security, peace and love. It is for this reason, for the hurt and the harm it causes, that divorce is an evil in the human community and, therefore, forbidden by God. Those who believe that divorce is evil because it is forbidden by God, and they are legion, miss this point entirely, putting the cart before the horse. Kevin Kelly points out, invoking the support of Aquinas, that "God is not offended by us except in so far as we harm ourselves and other people. Marriage breakdown and divorce is evil because of the human hurt and suffering caused by it. It offends God because people precious to him are being harmed and are hurting each other" (Kelly, 39).

Each time the Roman Catholic church dissolves a marriage, it is for a good judged to be greater than the good that is indissolubility. For Paul in 1st-century Corinth, it was the good called peace. For Pope Pius XII in 20th-century Rome it was the good called "the salvation of souls, in which both the common good of the religious society ... and the good of individuals find due and proportionate consideration" (*Acta Apost. Sedis*, 33 [1941]: 425-6). Some contemporary Roman Catholic theologians are asking today if the good of concrete Catholic individuals can find due and proportionate consideration in the situation of divorce and remarriage. They are even suggesting some possibilities.

First there is the ancient practice of the Eastern church, going back to its most revered bishops, Basil and John Chrysostom. While holding as firmly as the Roman church to the belief that the gospel message presents a demand for indissoluble marriage, it acknowledges also that concrete men and women sometimes do not measure up to the gospel. It acknowledges that some marriages, even specifically Christian marriages, do end, and that when they end, it makes no sense to insist that spouses are still bound together by an indissoluble bond. It seeks to deal in a pastorally compassionate way with the former spouses, even to the extent of permitting and blessing the remarriage of an *innocent* spouse.

The practice of the Reformation churches is akin to this Orthodox practice. While holding firm to the belief that marriage is life-long, and while never resigning themselves to the inevitability of divorce, they acknowledge also that some marriages do cease to exist, a fact which is easily ascertainable. When a marriage does die, they feel free to bless a second marriage and to hope that it will achieve what was not achieved in the first marriage, namely, a greater conformity to the mutual servant love of Christ and the church and, therefore, a greater sign of the covenant union between them. The Final Report of the Roman Catholic-Lutheran-Reformed Study Commission on the theology of marriage calls attention to three gospel bases for such as approach: "1) the doctrine of the justification of the sinner; 2) a view of the gospel which, over and above all its requirements, sees the need for a spirit of mercy and forgiveness; 3) an interpretation of the passage in Matthew as indicating a Christian tolerance of divorce." It goes on to point out

what we already know, namely, that "there is some support for this doctrine in certain facts in the history of the Catholic Church" (*Growth in Agreement*, ed. H. Meyer and L. Vischer, [New York: Paulist, 1984]: 288-9).

The Roman Catholic church, which remember has its own array of canonical processes to dissolve valid marriages, has never condemned the Orthodox practice. Even the hard-pressed Council of Trent, which had before it a proposal to condemn the Eastern practice as contrary to the gospel, explicitly refused to make such a statement. In 1980, among the propositions presented to the pope from the Synod of Bishops was one asking that the Eastern practice be considered carefully for the light that it might shed on Roman pastoral practice. Fidelity to Jesus' prohibition of remarriage does not exclude pastoral provision for the spiritual welfare of those who have entered second marriages which have become so stable that they cannot be broken without grave economic, emotional and spiritual harm to the parties involved.

All external forum solutions to the problem of divorce and remarriage in the Catholic church are offered on the basis of the lack of some reality canonically judged to be indispensable for a valid marriage. In the case of the Pauline privilege, that lack is the lack of baptism in one of the parties, along with the lack of will to live in peace. In non-consummation cases, the lack is of the physical consummation of the marital oneness. In annulment cases, the lack is of some reality canonically required for the marriage to be valid. All these lacks are of some reality required for the validity of *marriage*. Since it is clear that, in Roman Catholic history, only that marriage is absolutely indissoluble which is both sacramental and consummated, Catholic theologians are asking today about the effect of the lack of some reality integral to the nature of *sacrament*?

The present *Code of Canon Law* declares that "a valid marriage contract cannot exist between baptized persons without its being by that very fact a sacrament" (can. 1055, 2). It states that because it assumes that what is called in the theological tradition the gift of faith is given in baptism. That assumption appears to be quite false in our day, which has brought to our attention that anomalous group of so-called Christians known as *baptized non-believers*. These are Christians who, though having undergone a baptism rite (usually in infancy), have grown up non-believers. Their lack of faith raises serious questions about the sacramentality of any marriage into which they might enter.

The primacy of personal faith in the process of salvation was affirmed as the Catholic tradition by the Council of Trent. "We may be said to be justified through faith," it taught, "in the sense that 'faith is the beginning of man's salvation' ... 'without which it is impossible to please God' (Heb 11:6) and to be counted as his children" (D.S., 1532). The equally-ecumenical Council of Florence had already taught that sacraments give grace only to those who receive them worthily (D.S., 1310). This doctrine demands an active, positive disposition of self-surrendering faith on the part of one entering into a sacramental action. As Aquinas said: the saving action of God and Christ "achieves its effect in those to whom it is applied through faith and love and the sacraments of faith," and even for them "it is of more or less value according to their devotion" (S.Th. 3, 49, 3 ad 1, and 3, 79, 7 ad 2). Vatican II stood squarely in this same tradition, teaching that the sacraments of faith are so called because they "not only presuppose faith" but "also nourish, strengthen and express it" (S.C., 59).

The Catholic tradition is clear: personal sacramental fruitfulness presupposes active faith. A believer comes to sacrament personally sharing in the faith of the church, and with that personal faith transforms ordinary actions and words into prophetic symbols and sacraments. That personal faith, what the medievals called *opus operantis*, is as essential to sacramental fruitfulness as the most carefully crafted sacramental action, what they called *opus operatum* (See Lawler, *Symbol and Sacrament*, 36-45).

There is a serious doctrinal flaw, therefore, in the *Code*. To claim that consent makes marriage is true; there is no marriage, sacramental or otherwise, without it. To claim that marriage, created by mutual consent, is transformed into prophetic symbol is true as a statement of the faith of the church. The claim, however, that marriage is transformed into prophetic symbol by each and every person who has undergone a baptismal rite requires a major distinction: by those who have grown to share the faith of the church, "yes"; by those who have not grown to share the faith of the church, "no". No one is graced or justified or saved without faith, not even in sacraments, not even in the sacrament of Christian marriage.

A marriage entered into with free consent but no faith is still a marriage, for consent makes marriage (can. 1057). But it is not a sacrament, for it is personal faith, not consent that makes concrete sacrament. The universal tradition of the Catholic church teaches that, since it is not a sacrament, neither is it indissoluble. Personal faith is, of course, difficult to assess. But it is no more difficult to assess than free consent, which canonical procedures have claimed to assess for centuries.

As there are putative marriages which are clearly not valid marriages because the consent which was thought to initiate them was not adequately free, so also are there putative sacramental marriages which are not sacraments because those who entered them were not adequately faith-full. As marriages are annulled for lack of consent, so also can they be annulled for lack of faith. Since such is the case, the church requires that the pre-marriage preparation of those seeking sacramental marriages ascertain the status and the quality of their faith. For "without faith it is impossible to please God" (Heb 11:6), even in marriage.

Markus Barth, *Ephesians: Translation and Commentary on Chapters 4-6* (New York: Doubleday, 1974). Walter Kasper, *Theology of Christian Marriage* (New York: Crossroad, 1981). Kevin T. Kelly, *Divorce and Second Marriage: Facing the Challenge* (New York: Seabury, 1983). Eugene Kennedy, *What a Modern Catholic Believes about Marriage* (Chicago: Thomas More, 1972). Michael G. Lawler, *Secular Marriage, Christian Sacrament* (Mystic: Twenty-Third Publications, 1985). Michael G. Lawler, *Symbol and Sacrament: A Contemporary Sacramental Theology* (New York: Paulist Press, 1987). Theodore Mackin, *What Is Marriage?* (New York: Paulist Press, 1982). Edward Schillebeeckx, *Marriage: Secular Reality and Saving Mystery* (New York: Sheed and Ward, 1965). Elisabeth M. Tetlow and Louis M. Tetlow, *Partners in Service: Towards a Biblical Theology of Christian Marriage* (Lanham: University Press of America, 1983).

MICHAEL G. LAWLER

MARY, FEASTS OF

In the liturgical traditions of both the Eastern and the Western churches, feasts in honor of Mary have a distinctive importance, midway between celebrations of the great events of the life of Jesus and commemorations of other saints and anniversaries. All Christian worship is christocentric, in that it unites the church, as Christ's body, with his eternal, incarnate worship of the Father, and so allows it to share, through the Spirit, in his risen life. The celebrations of the Christian week and the Christian year have always been centered on the paschal mystery, and on the human history of Jesus in which that mystery is imbedded. Yet, as Pope Paul VI remarked, "every authentic development of Christian worship is necessarily followed by a fitting increase of veneration for the Mother of the Lord" (*Marialis Cultus* [1974], introduction). The reason is Mary's unique place in the Christian story of salvation: as the one in whose humanity, and through whose graced but free consent, the incarnation of God the Word took place, she is singularly involved in the paschal mystery. Her closeness both to Jesus and to us, the concentration on Christ of her wholly human life, has led the church, throughout the centuries, to see in her both the chief guarantor of the Word's full humanity and the first instance of our full redemption. The fifteen feasts of Mary in the reformed calendar of the Roman church celebrate either her involvement in the birth and life of Jesus, the remarkable working of grace in her own history, or the importance she has had in the life of the Christian faithful as model and instrument of the grace we share.

History. Liturgical celebration of the birth and infancy of Jesus on Jan. 6 seems to have begun in Egypt in the 2nd century and to have spread throughout the Eastern churches during the next two hundred years. The pilgrim Egeria reports a further celebration of the presentation of Jesus in the Temple, forty days later, in late 4th-century Jerusalem, and the Roman commemoration of the birth of Christ on Dec. 25 was also celebrated in the Eastern churches outside Palestine before 400. Clearly there is a strong Marian dimension to all these feasts, and to the whole Advent and Christmas cycle as it developed. It is understandable that when the Syrian and Byzantine churches began, probably in the 6th century, to commemorate the Mother of God on a day of her own, they should choose Dec. 26 as the appropriate date. The Roman church celebrated a special feast in her honor (*Natale S. Mariae*) on Jan. 1, the octave-day of Christmas, from shortly before 600, and the churches of Spain observed a "solemnity of the Mother of the Lord" on Dec. 18, a week before

Christmas from about the same time. The Gallic churches, too, celebrated a *festivitas sanctae Mariae* on Jan. 18, from the early 7th century—again, it seems, because of the closeness of this date to Christmas.

The first commemoration of Mary fully independent of the Christmas cycle was an institution of the Jerusalem church, probably begun in the 430s: a feast in honor of "Mary, Mother of God" on August 15, at the site three miles outside of Bethlehem where Mary and Joseph were said to have rested on their journey to the stable (*Protevangelium of James* 17). After Juvenal (bishop of Jerusalem 422-458) built a church on the Mount of Olives, near the place where Mary was thought to have lived and died, the feast was transferred there, and its theme came to be focussed on her death or "dormition"; the accounts of her "assumption" or resurrection, first attested in Syria and Palestine in the late 5th century, probably grew out of this Jerusalem celebration. In the 6th century, commemorations of Mary's birth (on Sept. 8) and presentation in the Temple (Nov. 21)—two incidents likewise drawn from the apocryphal *Protevangelium*— were also instituted in Jerusalem, probably on the dedication days of two other churches built in her honor. Although the evidence is scanty, the celebration of the Annunication on Mar. 25 seems to have had its origin in Jerusalem as well about the year 550.

By the early 7th century, the four main Jerusalem feasts of Mary—Feb. 2, Mar. 25, Aug. 15 and Sept. 8—were celebrated not only throughout the Byzantine Empire, but had been adopted in Rome as well. Pope Sergius I (687-701), a Sicilian of Syrian ancestry, ordered that each of these four feasts be marked with a solemn procession from the Forum to the basilica that had been dedicated in her honor by Sixtus III two and a half centuries earlier (St. Mary Major).

Carolingian liturgical reforms in the late 8th century, spurred on by Alcuin, not only canonized these Roman feasts for the Frankish Empire, but introduced— as part of the new genre of "votive" or devotional Mass texts—the custom of commemorating Mary liturgically, in eucharist and office, on Saturdays not otherwise specified as feasts.

In the Middle Ages, the Western church continued to adopt Eastern celebrations of Mary, sometimes altering their themes to express Western theological interests. The commemoration of the miraculous conception of Mary by an aged, childless couple (*Protevangelium* 4), observed in Jerusalem since the 7th century at the Church of St. Anne near the Sheepgate on Dec. 8, was introduced in 12th-century England and France under the influence of Anselm of Canterbury and his pupil Eadmer, as a celebration of her conception without original sin. Strongly promoted by the Franciscans, it was introduced into the Roman missal in 1476 by the Franciscan Pope Sixtus IV. The ancient Jerusalem commemoration of Mary's presentation in the temple on Nov. 21, found in various Latin sacramentaries from the 12th century, was adopted by the Franciscan order and the papal curia at Avignon in 1371. The Byzantine custom of commemorating the deposition of Mary's robe at the Church of the Blachernae in Constantinople on July 2, for which the account of Mary's visit to Elizabeth (Lk 1:39-56) was the assigned gospel, became the Western feast of the Visitation, prescribed for the Latin church— also under Franciscan influence—by Urban VI in 1389.

Following the mandate given the Holy See by the last session of the Council of Trent (1563), Pope Pius V published a reformed breviary (1568) and missal (1570), intended to be normative for the entire Latin church. Taking as its model the Roman liturgy of the time of Gregory

VII (1073-85), this new liturgical order included only seven prescribed Marian feasts: six of the ancient Eastern feasts (Feb. 2, Mar. 25, July 2, Aug. 15, Sept. 8, Dec. 8) plus the Roman commemoration of the dedication of the basilica of Mary Major, on Aug. 5. The Presentation of Mary (Nov. 21) was omitted, presumably because of its apocryphal roots, but was restored by the Franciscan Pope Sixtus V (1585-90).

A century later, however, new Marian feasts began to join the calendar, usually either in commemoration of some Catholic victory (e.g., the Holy Name of Mary, on the Sunday after Sept. 8 [from 1683]; Our Lady of the Rosary, on the first Sunday of October [1716]) or as a way of universalizing the celebration of a particular religious order (e.g., Our Lady of Ransom, on Sept. 24 [from 1696; a Mercedarian feast], Our Lady of Mt. Carmel, on July 16 [from 1726; a Carmelite feast], the Seven Sorrows of Mary, on the Friday before Palm Sunday [from 1727; a medieval German feast promoted by the Servites] and on the third Sunday of September [in 1814; also a Servite feast, promulgated to celebrate the return of Pope Pius VII from captivity]). The 20th century saw the addition of four new Marian feasts to the Western church's calendar: Our Lady of Lourdes, on Feb. 11 (1907, to commemorate the 50th anniversary of Mary's first apparition there); the Maternity of Mary, on Oct. 11 (1931, to commemorate the 15th centenary of the Council of Ephesus, at which her title "Mother of God" was affirmed); the Immaculate Heart of Mary, on Aug. 22 (1942, originally a feast of the Eudist congregation) and the Queenship of Mary, on May 31 (1954, to commemorate the centenary of the proclamation of the dogma of her immaculate conception). By 1960, the seven Latin Marian feasts of the missal of Pius V had grown to eighteen.

The Second Vatican Council, in its Constitution on the Liturgy, directed that the annual liturgical cycle be centered on the paschal mystery (S.C., 107) and give main emphasis to feasts of the Lord (*ibid.*, 108). Feasts of Mary were to be seen as subordinate ways of celebrating the mysteries of Christ and of recognizing "the excellent fruit of the redemption" (*ibid.*, 103). As a result, some post-Tridentine Marian feasts were dropped from the universal calendar in the reformed missal of 1969, while others were changed in rank or moved to more appropriate dates. The last week of Advent (Dec. 18-25), a time traditionally linked with Mary in most Western rites, again received a strong Marian emphasis in its prayers and its scriptural readings. The celebrations of the Presentation (Feb. 2) and the Annunciation (Mar. 25), both strongly Marian in theme, were listed now as feasts of the Lord; the ancient Roman celebration of Mary on Jan. 1, the octave of Christmas, was restored in place of the feast of the circumcision of Jesus. Despite the general trend towards simplification, however, 15 Marian celebrations (including Feb. 2 and Mar. 25) remain in the universal Roman calendar, and other local commemorations, such as the feast of Our Lady of Guadalupe (Dec. 12) in North and South America, have been retained or added by the appropriate episcopal conferences.

Feasts and Their Themes

The particular characters and themes of the 16 feasts of Mary in the present liturgical calendar in the United States may be summarized as follows:

1) *Mary, Mother of God* (Jan. 1; solemnity). As both the octave of Christmas and the start of the new civil year, this day's prayer is appropriately focused on Mary as mother of the newly born Savior and as the graced one who has become a bearer of blessing for all humanity. So the OT reading (Num 6:22-27) is simply

the formula by which the Aaronic priests were to bless the people, and the reading from Paul (Gal 4:4-7) reflects on the new blessings of maturity and freedom brought to humanity in "the fulness of time" by God's Son, "born of a woman." The gospel (Lk 2:16-21) tells the story of the circumcision and naming of Jesus eight days after his birth, but also shows Mary as "keeping in her heart" all the astonishing events surrounding her Son's birth and so as inviting the believer, at the start of a new year, to join in her grateful contemplation.

2) *Presentation of the Lord* (Feb. 2; feast). This ancient feast, called "the feast of meeting (*Hypapante*)" in the Greek church, commemorates the events recounted in the gospel (Lk 2:22-40): Jesus' being presented to God in the temple at Jerusalem by his parents, in accordance with the law, and the meeting of parents and child with the aged Simeon and Anna, who speak with the faith of Israel. Elements of the early Roman rite of purgation (perhaps pagan in origin) formerly performed on this day remain, both in the procession with candles and in the opening prayer. The main focus of the liturgy, however, is now on the encounter of Jesus, the compassionate high priest (NT reading: Heb 2:14-18), with the worshipping community, and the enlightenment and purification his presence brings to the people's expectant prayer (OT reading: Mal 3:1-4; gospel: Lk 2:22-40).

3) *Our Lady of Lourdes* (Feb. 11; optional memorial). This day commemorates the first of Mary's 18 apparitions to Bernadette Soubirous at Lourdes, on Feb. 11, 1858. It is the only celebration of a Marian apparition in the universal Roman calendar, and remains because of the continuing importance of Lourdes to the whole church as a place of pilgrimage and grace. Readings may be selected from the Common for Feasts of Mary; the suggested first reading is Isa 66:10-14,

which speaks in maternal terms of a transformed Jerusalem—often linked with Mary, as the "place" of God's presence, in Christian liturgy and art—and promises peace and prosperity to Israel "like an overflowing stream," an image which suggests the healing springs at Lourdes.

4) *Annunciation of the Lord* (Mar. 25; solemnity). This celebration of the incarnation of the Word in Mary's womb, nine months before the celebration of Jesus' birth, is rightly described by Paul VI as "a joint feast of Christ and the Blessed Virgin" (*Mar. Cult.*, 6). Following rabbinic tradition, many early Christian writers identified the dates of the creation and end of the world, and of the conception and crucifixion of the Savior, with the date of Passover (14 Nisan). Since this was often interpreted as Mar. 25 in the Julian calendar, the Roman dating of the birth of Christ may originally depend on the date of this feast, and not *vice versa*. The main scripture passage for the feast is of course the narrative of the annunciation (Lk 1:26-38), emphasizing both the overshadowing grace and power of God in the coming of Christ and Mary's free consent. The OT reading (Isa 7:10-14) underlines Christian belief that the child born to Mary is not only a "sign" of God's power, but is named "God-with-us"; the NT reading (Heb 10:4-10) reminds us that it is through his body, taken from Mary's flesh, that the Son fulfills his Father's will and offers God the sacrifice that makes us holy.

5) *Visitation of the Blessed Virgin Mary* (May 31; feast). Celebrated previously on July 2, this feast was transferred in the new missal to May 31 (replacing the Queenship of Mary), probably in order to place it between the celebrations of the Annunciation and the birth of John the Baptist. Commemorating the story of Mary's visit to the Baptist's mother Elizabeth, which follows the annunciation account in Luke's gospel (1:39-56), the

liturgy emphasizes two aspects of that narrative: the exultation of both Israel (represented by Elizabeth and the unborn John) and the community of disciples (represented by Mary) at the coming of Christ, and the mutual, loving concern of these two kinswomen for each other. The OT reading (Zeph 3:14-18) echoes the first of these themes, the alternative NT reading from (Rom 12:9-16) calls us to imitate the second. Luke's narrative also seems to contain parallels to the story of the coming of the ark of God to Jerusalem in 2 Samuel 6, reminding us again of Mary's privileged role in the history of salvation.

6) *Immaculate Heart of Mary* (Saturday after the Second Sunday after Pentecost; optional memorial). Established by Pope Pius XII for the octave of the Assumption (Aug. 22) in 1942, when he consecrated the world, then at war, to the heart of Mary, this celebration directly follows the feast of the Sacred Heart of Jesus in the reformed missal. The heart, traditionally thought of as the physical and affective center of the person, suggests life, remembrance, love and freedom. St. John Eudes, who first promoted devotion to the heart of Mary, saw in her heart "the exemplar and model of our hearts"; as people of faith, open to God's will and so fruitful in the works of love, we, like Mary, can "hear the word of God and keep it." The first reading may be chosen from the Common; the gospel is Lk 2:41-51, reflecting both the pain and the trust motherhood brought to Mary's heart.

7) *Our Lady of Mt. Carmel* (July 16; optional memorial). Since their origins in the 12th century, the Carmelite friars have cherished a special devotion to Mary, as protectress and as a model of the contemplative life; their promotion of the brown scapular has been an important influence on the spread of popular dedication to Mary. This feast, originally celebrated by the Carmelites to mark the end of the Second Council of Lyons (1272), which allowed the young

order to continue, was extended to the whole Western church in 1726 and retained in the 1969 missal. Central to the celebration is the recognition of our sister Mary's total dedication to the love of God, and the call—symbolized in the scapular—to clothe ourselves in her attitude of quiet, receptive faith. Readings may be selected from the Common of the Blessed Virgin; particularly appropriate would be Sir 24:1-21 (OT no. 6: Mary as the Wisdom of God) or Zach 2:14-17 (OT no. 11: a call to silence at the coming of the Lord) and Lk 11:27-28 (gospel no. 9): "Blessed are they who hear the word of God and keep it").

8) *Dedication of the Basilica of St. Mary Major* (Aug. 5; optional memorial). This great Christian monument, on the Esquiline Hill in Rome, was built by Pope Liberius (352-66) and refurbished and dedicated to Mary by Pope Sixtus III (432-40), in the aftermath of the controversy over her title "Mother of God." Formerly called "Our Lady of the Snow" because of a 14th-century legend that the site of the basilica was originally marked out by a miraculous August snowfall, this feast commemorates the dedication of what is probably the first church directly associated with Mary in the West, and thus acknowledges both the unity of the Roman communion and its tradition of devotion to the Mother of God. Readings may be taken from the Common; Rev 21:1-5 (Easter reading no. 3: the new Jerusalem, where God dwells among his people) would be an appropriate first reading.

9) *Assumption of the Blessed Virgin Mary* (Aug. 15; solemnity). This feast, the oldest exclusively Marian celebration, remains her most important day in the year—her "Easter." In the Western church, it is the only remaining feast of Mary with a liturgical vigil, and in the Eastern churches it is preceded by a two-week period of fasting similar to Lent. The content of the celebration, since the

late 5th century, is the belief—proclaimed as a dogma by Pius XII in 1950—that Mary, as the human person uniquely "full of grace," already shares with her risen Son the eschatological fulness of the new creation, the transformation of both body and spirit that her brothers and sisters await at the end of history. Thus while the feast focuses on her "assumption into heaven" or resurrection as a special privilege of the Mother of God, it also celebrates, as grounds for hope, the Christian conviction that the divinization of the human is no longer simply reserved to the Lord, but is now also fully shared by a member of the believing church. The readings for the vigil underline Mary's privilege, suggesting her entry into the presence of God (1 Chronicles 15-16: entry of the Ark of God into the tabernacle) and her share in Christ's victory over death (1 Cor 15:54-57), both rooted in her readiness to "hear the word of God and keep it" (Lk 11:27-28). The readings for the day celebration, reflect the feast's message of joyful hope for all Christians, pointing to the salvation of the woman in Revelation 11-12, the symbolic mother of the eschatological Israel, as a "great sign," and repeating Paul's promise of resurrection for all who "belong" to Christ (1 Cor 15:20-26), then inviting us to listen to the triumphant, humble *Magnificat* of her who is "blessed among women."

10) *Queenship of Mary* (Aug. 22; memorial). Celebrated since 1954 on May 31, this feast marks the octave of the Assumption in the reformed missal, and reflects the theme of Mary's share in the glory of the Lord, which is the main focus of that solemnity. Christian poetry has called Mary "queen" since the 4th century (Ephraem), and Christian art has portrayed her in royal attire, enthroned with her child, since shortly after that: presumably because of the conviction that the Kingdom of God has fully "come" in her, the believing woman, and

that she enjoys the fulfilment of Jesus' promise that his disciples will share in his reign (Mt 19:28 par; cf. 1 Tm 2:11f). Readings may be taken from the Common; Isa 9:1-6 (OT no. 8; the promise of a child-king) and Lk 1:26-38 (gospel no. 3: Mary's royal child) or Lk 1:39-47 (gospel no. 4: Mary's blessedness) seem particularly apt.

11) *Birth of Mary* (Sept. 8; feast). Originally a Jerusalem feast celebrating the miraculous birth of Mary as narrated in the apocryphal *Protevangelium*, this day reflected the early church's conviction that the holiness and the very life of Mary are completely God's gifts to his people. The only births liturgically celebrated by the church are those of the three great figures of Luke's infancy-narrative, whose persons mark the start of the New Covenant: John the Baptist, Mary and Jesus. The readings prescribed for this feast focus attention on God's providential involvement in leading human history towards Christ: Mic 5:1-4 (naming Bethlehem as the birthplace of the future king) or Rom 8:28-30 (pointing to God's plan to save his chosen ones through his Son), and Mt 1:1-23 (contrasting the human genealogy of Jesus with the God-given circumstances of his conception). It is Mary, born by God's plan but simply one of us, who is the point where this hidden working of grace becomes historical, human reality.

12) *Our Lady of Sorrows* (Sept. 15; memorial). An outgrowth of medieval devotion to Mary at the foot of the Cross, this feast was originally peculiar to the Servite order, and was extended to the Latin church in 1814; another feast in honor of the Sorrows of Mary, German in origin, was celebrated on the Friday before Palm Sunday, from 1727 until it was suppressed in the reformed missal of 1969. Following directly the feast of the Triumph of the Cross, this day invites the church to enter contemplatively into Mary's compassion, as she witnesses the

faithful suffering of her son, and so to experience the mystery of communion between God and a vulnerable humanity that lies at the heart of salvation. The first reading, Heb 5:7-9, points to Jesus' share in our sufferings as our "source of eternal salvation"; the gospel may be either Lk 2:33-35 (Simeon's prediction that Mary's "soul will be pierced") or Jn 19:25-27 (Mary being named by the dying Jesus as mother of his disciples). The great medieval sequence, *Stabat Mater*, may be said or sung before the gospel.

13) *Our Lady of the Rosary* (Oct. 7; memorial). Although the practice of praying the rosary in the Western church is at least as old as the 12th century, this feast commemorates the defeat of the Turkish fleet at Lepanto on Oct. 7, 1571, which the Dominican Pope Pius V attributed to Mary's intercession; it was made a feast of the whole Latin church after another defeat of the Turks in Hungary in 1716. As a prayer to Mary which is attached to simple meditation on the "mysteries" of Christ, the rosary presents Mary as the model of both contemplative and intercessory prayer in the life of the church. Readings may be chosen from the Common; Lk 1:26-38 (gospel no. 3), from which much of the "Hail Mary" is taken, would be appropriate.

14) *Presentation of Mary* (Nov. 21; memorial). Originally commemorating the dedication to Mary of the "New Church" in Jerusalem, on the temple mount, by the Emperor Justinian on Nov. 21, 543, this feast soon became associated with the story of Mary's being brought to live in the temple at the age of three, recounted in *Protevangelium of James* 7:2-8:1—an incident closely modelled on the story of the child Samuel in 1 Sam 1:21-28. Although the apocryphal source of the narrative made the acceptance of this feast slow in the West, it has been celebrated by the whole Greek church since the 8th century, and is regarded as one of the twelve great feasts

of the Eastern liturgical calendar. The main point is clearly Mary's lifelong holiness and purity, rooted in her total dedication to the service of God. It is rightly considered to be the Eastern church's equivalent to the Western celebration of Mary's immaculate conception. Readings may be chosen from the Common; appropriate would be 1 Chronicles 15-16 (OT no. 4: the ark comes to the tabernacle) or Zech 2:14-17 (OT no. 11: God dwelling on Zion), and Lk 11:27-28 (gospel no. 9: "blest are they who hear the word of God and keep it").

15) *The Immaculate Conception of Mary* (Dec. 8; solemnity). Originally a Jerusalem celebration of the miraculous conception of Mary by her childless parents, Joachim and Anna (*Protevangelium* 4), this feast was transformed by the medieval Latin church into a celebration of her being conceived *without sin*. This belief about Mary was explained by the Franciscan theologian Duns Scotus (c. 1265-1308) as based on her unparalleled closeness to Christ: since God's redeeming grace could be expected to be uniquely effective in her, and since the highest form of redemption is undoubtedly not forgiveness but the preservation from all sin, Mary must have been kept sinless by the grace of Christ from the first instant of her human existence—from her conception in the womb. Proclaimed a dogma of the church by Pope Pius IX in 1854, the doctrine of this feast is really that of Mary's election, her providentially secured holiness as Mother of God. Yet like the dogma of her assumption, it also expresses the Christian conviction that all of us are called by God to sinlessness, and can look forward in faith to the healing of our wounded humanity by the unmerited grace of Christ, since that grace has already triumphed in her utterly sinless life. The readings are Gen 3:9-20 (recounting the origin of our "history of sin"), Eph 1:3-12 (proclaiming God's

eternal choice of those who would be his children by grace), and Lk 1:26-38 (in which Mary, "full of grace," freely assents to her vocation as mother of Christ).

16) *Our Lady of Guadalupe* (Dec. 12; in the United States, feast). This feast, peculiar to the Americas, commemorates the apparition of Mary to Juan Diego, an elderly Mexican native, on the hill of Tepeyac near Mexico City in 1531; the picture of Mary now venerated at Guadalupe, in which Mary is represented with Aztec features, is said to have miraculously appeared on the inside of Juan Diego's cloak when he went before the bishop of report what he had seen. The object of great devotion in Mexico since the earliest years of Spanish and Christian presence there, Our Lady of Guadalupe was proclaimed patroness of New Spain in 1746, and patroness of Latin America in 1910. In 1979, the Latin American bishops, assembled at Puebla in Mexico, referred to her apparition at Guadalupe as "the great sign of the nearness of the Father and Christ" to the poor and faithful people of Latin America. For all Christians of the Americas, this feast is a reminder that Mary's importance as type and mother of the church crosses all cultural boundaries; she stands as a promise to every people that our God "puts down the mightly from their thrones, and raises the lowly." Readings may be chosen from the Common; particularly appropriate are Isa 61:9-11 (OT no. 9: "God will make justice and praise spring up before all the nations") and Lk 1:39-55 (gospel of Aug. 15, including full *Magnificat*).

B. Capelle, "La liturgie mariale en Occident," in H. Du Manoir, *Maria* (Paris, 1949): 217-45. P. Jounel, "The Year: the Veneration of Mary," in A.G. Martimort, I.-H. Dalmais and P. Jounel (eds.), *The Church at Prayer*, trans. M.J. O'Connell (Collegeville: The Liturgical Press, 1985): 4:130-150. B. Kleinheyer, "Maria in der Liturgie," in W. Beinert and H. Petri (eds.), *Handbuch der Marienkunde* (Regensburg, 1984): 404-39. Pope Paul VI, *To Honor Mary* =Apostolic Exhortation *Marialis cultus* (London, 1974). C. O'Donnel, O. Carm., *At Worship with Mary. A Pastoral and Theological Study* (Wilmington: Glazier, 1988).

BRIAN E. DALEY, S.J.

MEDIA, USE OF, IN THE LITURGY

Electronic media (film, filmstrips, slide presentations, video and sound recordings) are part of everyday life—communicating information, selling products, and providing entertainment. In general, these media are polysensual, appealing to all the senses of the whole person and can be more engaging than the more traditional print medium. Audio visual media can enhance the "irrational" dimensions of the liturgy and underscore the sacramental and spiritual power within worship.

Media in worship can be a help, highlighting the participation of the assembly with non-verbal and symbolic elements; or a nemesis, encouraging passivity and overpowering the congregation. For the liturgist, the proper use of audio-visual material in worship, like other art forms, is linked to the nature of the worshipping community. The governing concern is that the audio visual elements enable the assembly to worship together and not be intrusions into the prayer life of the community.

The U.S. bishops examined the liturgical use of electronic media in their statement "Environment and Art in Catholic Worship." Even though the document's mention of audio-visuals is limited to three paragraphs, the content is clear and open for future development.

With such varied media usage in the American church, it is difficult to assess the present use made of media in parish churches. Some dioceses prepare audio cassettes or videotapes of the ordinary's homily or address on a certain topic for playback in parishes of the diocese, often in conjunction with diocesan appeals. In the past, these requests were read at the Sunday Mass by the presider, often in letter form. Some parishes use projections of song and prayer texts as an alternative to songbooks and missalettes. Sound recordings have been used effectively, especially in rural areas where access to trained musicians and instruments is often a problem.

There are four liturgical moments in which audio visual media might best be employed in worship: (1) the opening rites: to introduce the theme of the liturgy, bringing the sights, sounds, colors, smells and textures of the world into the worshipping community; (2) liturgy of word: to reflect on the scripture theme, as a response to the readings or as part of the homily; (3) the prayer of the faithful: to connect the needs of the world with the petitions of the community; (4) after communion: to meditate on the liturgical or scriptural theme as part of the communion reflection.

There can be technical and liturgical problems with using media in existing church spaces. Some older churches are inadequate for liturgical media because of poor sightlines and acoustics and the inability to darken the space. For new church buildings or renovation projects, the bishops wisely make provision for audio-visual projections, recommending good sightlines and the use of acoustical material for better sound reproduction.

The concerns around the use of electronic media in worship highlight the very experiential nature of the liturgy. The liturgy should be audible in all parts of the church and visible with the celebration space open and free of clutter so that the congregation can see the celebrant, the altar, the bread and wine; and the microphone should not visually overpower the altar.

Technical problems can abound in using liturgical media. Ill-produced images, an inaudible soundtrack or the improper placement of material within the liturgy can draw attention to the medium rather than the message. The result is that the audio visuals interrupt rather than heighten the liturgy. Images that fall away from the text, losing the integration of sight and sound, can create discomfort or distraction to the congregation.

The bishops mention two kinds of skills that are required in using audio-visuals in the liturgy: (1) the liturgical and pastoral skill of understanding the dynamics and rhythms of the liturgy, coupled with a sensitivity to the parish community; and (2) the artistic skill in putting an audio-visual presentation together or in selecting a "packaged" presentation, done by a media center or publishing house.

The following guidelines are suggested for creating or using audio visual materials in the liturgy.

The making of audio-visuals requires discipline. In everyday life, electronic media are the tools of the professional communicator. To put together an effective, coherent audio-visual presentation takes time and presupposes critical discipline. It entails developing a religious or gospel theme, selecting the media form, experimenting with various ways the message can be expressed, creating the flow and continuity of sight and sound, and rehearsing the final version until it has the proper sense of flow.

Audio-visuals require an understanding of aesthetic principles. Electronic media are art forms that follow certain design principles (unity, variety, balance and harmony) that can enhance or heighten the material. These principles are not always consciously applied, but are part of the artists' soul or intuition.

In designing a visual presentation, variety suggests using different kinds of images: close-ups, medium shots, and long shots. Unity might be the way this variety is held together: unity of theme, content or color. Each image has the potential of telling a story or eliciting a mood or feeling. The artistic skill is in the arrangement and continuity of the material.

Audio-visuals require clarity of expression and access to the content. Unlike art in a gallery or a film in a movie theater, a visual presentation in church is rarely seen more than once. The congregation often cannot go back for a second look and carefully examine the brush strokes. In liturgy, especially, visual presentations need to be direct and clear. This does not mean the presentation cannot work on several levels of meaning, nor does it reduce the communication to a puerile level.

Audio-visuals require professional production values. Because congregations have been exposed to professional productions (television, business meetings, and mass media), these same standards must be adopted in the liturgical use of media. This does not mean slickness or a show-business attitude. Rather, the visuals should be of highest quality, sharp and clear; the equipment should be in good running order; the projectionist should have a workable knowledge of the equipment; the screen should be visible to the congregation, be integrated into the worship space and have good light-reflective qualities. To use media in church means to use the best. Second-rate visuals or ill-timed sight and sound presentations detract from the liturgy and can interfere in the prayer of the community. Practice, discipline, and careful planning are crucial elements in using media-visual material.

Audio-visuals require a sensitive selection of images. Beware of the stereotyped or literal image. Image selection implies an understanding of how to read, interpret and use images for content, form and design. A common error in selecting images is to be completely literal: the word peace evokes a bird in flight; loneliness, an old person sitting on a bench; creation, an autumnal forest scene. Peace may be an image of someone exhibiting interior peace; not all old people are lonely; and creation needs people, not only pretty landscapes. Good art challenges us to see, to look beyond, to see in the familiar, new possibilities, and to see in the unfamiliar what we never suspected was there. This is the strength which audio-visuals can bring to our church worship.

Electronic media is still in the infant or adolescent stage of development in most churches. As video and laser technology develops and expands, there will be new possibilities for media-enhanced worship and for the envisioning of new technological ministries. The use of media in worship, when used effectively and in the proper liturgical spirit, offers the church community a powerful tool to communicate the gospel message, to evoke a meditative response within the assembly and to re-create the wonder and awe of God's creation, by refreshing our imaginations to love and serve.

U.S. Bishops, *Environment and Art in Catholic Worship*, 1978. Pierre Babin, *Audio-Visual Man* (Dayton, Ohio: Pflaum, 1970). Marshall McLuhan, *Understanding Media* (New York: Signet, 1964).

THOMAS A. KANE, C.S.P.

MICHEL, VIRGIL (1890-1938)

Benedictine of St. John's Abbey in Collegeville, Minn., Dom Virgil was introduced to the Liturgical Movement in Europe during his studies in Rome and Louvain. Upon his return to the United States, he brought the movement to Collegeville where he established the two great organs of liturgical education, which continue their noble service to this day: The Liturgical Press and *Orate Fratres* (later renamed *Worship*). His own primary interests and contributions were in the relationship between liturgy and social issues, a legacy which continues to challenge liturgical theologians today. This relationship remains the unfinished business of the contemporary liturgical reform.

See **Liturgical movement, the (1830-1969); Benedictines and liturgical renewal**

MINISTRY

Ministry in the life and experience of the church is a larger reality than the "ordained ministry" of the clergy. It consists of a broad spectrum of services in the church which have come into existence over the centuries. This article will survey the different kinds of ministries which have emerged in the historical experience of the church. It is written with the conviction that as the church continues to live in the world, new forms of service for nourishment and leadership in the church will continue to emerge under the guidance of the Spirit of Christ.

The New Testament Church

The traditions concerning ministries in the church contained in the NT are traditions formed in the context of the *sacramental worship* of the church. The Pauline and other epistolary traditions as well as the gospels and Acts of the Apostles are in a real sense *liturgical* traditions, developed for and handed on within the praying assemblies which were gathered for the preaching of the word and the "breaking of the bread."

The first uses of the expression "ministry" (Gk. *diakonia*) in the NT are Paul's uses of it to name his own service of the "saints," viz., the preaching of the "good news" of righteousness by faith and reconciliation through the cross of Christ. But the idea behind Paul's ministry, his service of the gospel of God (Rom 1:1) and of the church, includes a wider sense of the whole of Christian life as service. Paul's description of the life of faith is cast in a spiritualized cultic and civic language in which the community itself is called the "temple of the living God" (1 Cor 3:16,17; 6:19; 2 Cor 6:16) in which the life of faith is lived as "sacrifice and service" (2 Cor 9:12, *thusia, leitourgeia*) offered to God and to each other.

Throughout the Pauline corpus, Paul gives a variety of names to his own ministry and that of those who work with him establishing and maintaining the churches which he founded. Paul's own vocation is above all that of *apostolos* (apostle), one who has "seen the Lord" (1 Cor 9:1) and who has therefore received the ministry of preaching the gospel of God (Rom 1:1-6). Paul describes his calling as *leitourgeia* (public service) and speaks of his fellow-workers, co-apostles,— men and women who labor with him to establish and to maintain the churches.

In 1 Corinthians, Paul specifies other shapes in which the ministry of the life of faith is lived in the service of the community (chap. 12). The community is endowed with a variety of gifts, services and operations by the Spirit, by the Lord and by God (12:4-6). In all their diversity their common function is the building up (*oikodome*) of the whole community (14:26). One listing includes ministries of the word: word of wisdom and word of knowledge, prophecy, speaking in and interpreting tongues, and the distinguishing of spirits. Others involve charismatic powers: faith, the gift of cures and the operations of power. In the context of disputes over gifts in the community, he states a divine origin and order of leadership functions in the community: God has placed: first, apostles; second, prophets; third, teachers (12:38). After this, Paul lists other services placed by God in the community: "then powers; then gifts of healing, helps, administration and tongues."

In 1 Corinthians 14, in the context of a discussion of the meaning and value of glossalalia (speaking in tongues), Paul mentions a number of other gifts which are exercised in the service of the community which comes together for prayer, instruction and the Lord's Supper (cf. 11:17,33). *Each member* of the community contributes: a hymn, a teaching, a revelation, a tongue, the interpretation of tongues. The function of all these manifestations of the Spirit, however, is the building up (*oikodome*) of the whole gathering (*ekklesia*).

Through this variety of gifts and manifestations Paul shows that God is present in Christ's body (the living, praying, teaching community) through the gifts given by the Spirit of God as the Spirit wishes and distributes in works of leadership, power and edification.

In the greetings opening the letter to the Philippians, Paul makes use of names for community leadership taken over from the religious associations of the Roman world in which the church came into existence and operation: *episcopoi* (overseers) and *diakonoi* (public servants, ministers). *Diakonos* is a secular term designating a servant or functionary in public service as well as table servants. The NT uses the term to designate Christ, secular rulers, Paul's associates and so on. *Episcopos* is likewise an available secular term designating someone who holds the care or oversight (*episkopé*) of some organization or project (Acts 1:20; 20:28).

In the later "pastoral letters" (1 and 2 Timothy), written after Paul's lifetime, the author treats of several *fixed statuses* in the community. Widows, elders, older men (*presbuteroi*), overseers or super-intendents (*episcopoi*) and servants or ministers (*diakonoi*). Widows must meet a set of criteria in order to be enrolled (1 Tim 5:9ff.) into the body of widows whose function in the community is portrayed as one of good deeds (5:10), care of the sick, hospitality, care of children and the saints. Older men (*presbuteroi*) are mentioned as those who rule (well) and labor in "the word and teaching," men whose functions are

administration, preaching and teaching. *Diakonos* is mentioned as a status in the community with requirements for selection as in the case of the widows, requirements which correspond to those demanded of the *episkopos* (overseer, super-intendent): they must be sober, trustworthy, with a well-managed household, a dignified wife and obedient children. Timothy himself is called a "good *diakonos*" (4:6). *Episkopé* (overseeing) is mentioned as a "good work" and the requirements for the *episkopos* likewise indicate one who is a trustworthy teacher, a man of good sense, dignity and hospitality and father of a well-ordered household.

The Acts of the Apostles presents a Lucan perspective on the origins of the church and her ministries, especially in its portrayal of Paul's missionary travels and the communities which he is credited with establishing. Paul, Barnabas, as well as the churches established in their ministry, are portrayed as the ministers of the Spirit, the same Spirit which identifies Jesus and gives origin and shape to his ministry. The Jerusalem community to which Paul travels is described as "the apostles and the brethren in Judea" (11:1), the "apostles and elders" (15:22) and "the brethren and elders" (21:18). Outside Jerusalem, Acts tells how Paul and Barnabas were commissioned and sent by the "laying on of the hands" of the "prophets and teachers" of the "church of Antioch" (13:1-3). In his travels with Barnabas Paul is shown appointing and laying hands on elders in the churches of Asia. On his journey to Rome, he gives a final exhortation to the elders of the church of Ephesus whom he reminds that the Holy Spirit has made them the overseers (*episcopoi*) of the flock, the church (20:28).

The brief mention of "the seven" in chap. 6 describes men who are chosen by the community to care for the daily management of the community. Their service, however, goes beyond the care for material needs. Stephen is presented as a healer (6:8) who gives a powerful prophetic witness (6:8-7:53); and Philip is seen as an evangelist in Samaria (8:5-8), in Gaza with the Ethiopian eunuch and in Ashdod and the coast cities (8:26-40). Acts *does not call* these men *diakonoi* (deacons).

The *gospels*, narrative witnesses to the identity of Jesus and, in and through Jesus, to the identity of the church, came into being and were handed on from generation to generation of believers in the worshipping sacramental community. One focus for the image of Jesus (and of the church) is that of *service, ministry*. The life and especially the death of Jesus are interpreted as acts of service. In Mk 10:45, Jesus interprets his life and death as his service ministry: "The Son of Man came not to be served, but to serve (*diakonesai*) and to give his life as a ransom in the place of many" (10:45). This service of Jesus is given as the basis for the serving mission of the community: "...whoever would be great among you will be your servant, and whoever would be first among you will be the slave of all" (10:43,44). There is no mention in the gospels of the later forms for structured ministry in the church: *episkopos* (bishop), *presbuteros* (presbyter) or *diakonos* (deacon).

The manner in which this ministry is presented varies according to the agenda of each of the evangelists. For Mark, Jesus is the son of God whose sonship takes the form of being rejected by his people, misunderstood by his disciples in spite of all his teaching and healing and executed by the religious authorities of his people. His is to the end a *ministry of faithful witness* to the "good news" which he preaches. The strongest affirmations of his identity are voiced by demons (1:24, 3:11, 5:7) and by the pagan soldier "seeing how he died" (15:39). Jesus' service

is the model for true service in the church; he warns his community of false Christs and false prophets (13:22) whose claims to power will lead them astray and insists that the greatest among the disciples are those who serve all the rest like slaves (10:43,44). On the eve of Jesus' death, Mark uses the liturgical tradition to present Jesus as one who offers his life as "blood of the covenant" (14:24), a liturgical service of reconciliation and covenant with God.

Although he uses much of Mark's tradition, Matthew expresses Jesus' ministry more as a *ministry of teaching*. Into Mark's framework, Matthew inserts five "books of teaching" (cc. 5-7, 10, 13, 18, 24-25), the sermons found only in Matthew's "book" (1:1). In Matthew's account, the disciples of Jesus are learners who, in their turn, are sent into the whole world as teachers (28:20) to "make disciples" of all the nations. Luke's narrative of Jesus' ministry is the story of Jesus as the minister of God's Spirit. Everyone connected with Jesus' origin is "filled with the Spirit" (Mary, Elizabeth, Zechariah, John the Baptist, etc.) and Jesus, returning from the desert "filled with the Spirit" begins his ministry as the one on whom the Spirit of the Lord rests (4:1,14,18). The disciples are charged to wait for the power from on high at whose coming they are sent to the ends of the earth as ministers of the Spirit to preach the forgiveness of sins (24:47-50). Acts narrates the church's ministry of the Spirit to the ends of the earth, especially in the missionary journeys of Paul.

In the fourth gospel, the narrative of Jesus' life culminates in the solemn meal in which Jesus gives his disciples (now friends rather than servants) a model for their behavior as friends in the community by washing their feet and instructing them to wash each other's feet. John describes Jesus' own ministry as the manifestation through the "signs" which he works (20:30) of the presence of God in all that he, the living image of God, says and does. His commission to his disciples is the same mission that he has from the Father: the ministry of the forgiveness of sins in the power of the Holy Spirit (20:21-23).

Chapters 4-10 of the letter to Hebrews interpret the life and death of Jesus as a "priestly" event, contrasting the "once-and-for-all" effectiveness of Jesus' self-offering to God to the annually repeated rituals of atonement in which the blood of the covenant was sprinkled in the mercy seat in the Holy of Holies. The priest-king Melchisedech serves as an illustration of the superiority of Jesus' priestly service of God to that of the hereditary priesthood in Israel. Whatever its origins and whoever its original addressees, the letter was known and used in the primitive church as early as Clement of Rome's letter to the Corinthians (c. 95 C.E.). Its extensive use of priestly imagery to interpret the meaning of Jesus has had pervasive effects both in Christology and in the theology of the priesthood and of ministry.

Two noteworthy conclusions emerge from the images of church life presented in the letters and narrative accounts of the NT. The first is that the church manifests diverse, flexible and evolving forms of organization together with a rich multiplicity of services animating the local communities and a fluid nomenclature for the structure and the variety of services in the Christian communities. In their organization and organizational nomenclature, the local churches show influences of their Jewish origins as well as the creative ways in which these origins were adapted to the forms, structures and nomenclature of religious associations in the Roman religious world of the 1st century.

In the Pauline communities the ministries originate in the "manifestation" of the Spirit of God. They are the ministry of Christ and the operation of God at work "building up" the community. In later traditions the prophetic prayer and the laying on of hands serve as rituals of blessing and election to the missionary and leadership services described in the pastorals and in Acts. The gospel narratives root the service of the community in the direct call of Jesus to be followers and imitators of his own life and death.

A second conclusion worthy of note is that the ministries mentioned in these sources of Christian experience are functional realities which serve the church in leadership, the preaching and teaching of "the word" and physical and spiritual "works of power." There is no mention of a permanent sacral power, later to be called "sacramental power," which is held and exercised by one stable group within the church, viz., the ordained. Paul himself states emphatically that his own ministry is rooted in his "vision of the Lord" (1 Cor 9:1), and that he has not baptized anyone (1 Cor 1:14). In his one treatment of the eucharist (1 Cor 11:17-34) there is no mention of a presider (although someone obviously served as leader at the church's gathering); the community eats the bread and drinks the cup and the community must understand what they do when they eat and drink. In the later account of Acts, Luke has the twelve clearly state their own function: prayer and the preaching of the word (Acts 6:2,4).

The Early Church (A.D. 100-1000)

The movement of the church into the world of the Roman Empire in the first centuries of its history is a complex reality geographically, culturally, politically and religiously. The church came to live in a number of different geographical settings, each with its own set of socio-political and religious patterns of thought, expression and practice: Greece, Italy, Egypt, Spain, Gaul (France),

Africa, and so on. The rich variety of these experiences found expression in a large body of literature: sermons, letters, biblical commentaries, philosophical and theological treatises, dogmatic and canonical legislation. Modern interpretation of this vast field of literature (its dating, content and interpretation) is filled with conflict and contradiction. However, some broad general developments in the practice and understanding of ministries in the life of the church can be indicated.

Administrative functions. The ministry of leadership of the community evolved in diverse ways in different parts of the growing church. The letters of Ignatius of Antioch (d. 125) stress vigorously the importance of the single *episcopos* (overseer) surrounded by his *presbuteroi* (elders) and *diakonoi* (ministers) as the guarantee of unity and solidity of church life: baptism, eucharist, marriage, doctrine, etc. The church in Egypt also seems to have been organized around the leadership of a single *episcopos* for the whole of Egypt. Other churches, such as that of Rome and Corinth, mention a plurality of *presbuteroi* who are *episcopoi* charged with the leadership of the community. One 3rd-century document mentions the existence of teachers and prophets still functioning in the church in Rome along with the elders and overseers. By the mid-3rd century, the tri-partite pattern of church leadership, bishop-presbyter-deacon, is attested to in the *Apostolic Tradition* of Hippolytus of Rome. By the 4th century, the role of the bishop as the leader of the community and also the "college" of bishops had become an established pattern. This is attested to by the practice of the *koinonia* (communion between churches) and of the councils which were convened by the emperors to deal with issues of church doctrine and order as these issues impacted on the public civil order.

Selection of church leaders. Just as the shape of church leadership evolved over the first four centuries, the manner of selecting church leaders evolved into an increasingly centralized procedure. The *Didache* (c. 90-100) simply states that the communities are to "select for yourselves overseers and ministers." Gradually the selection and installation of candidates for the episcopate became the function of the clergy and the participation of the people became increasingly formalized into a *pro forma* acclamation of the one chosen by the clergy. In the 4th and 5th centuries the emperor appointed the patriarchs of Constantinople and the bishops of the Eastern church looked more and more to the civil power as the guarantee of their status in the church.

The official ritual for the installation (*ordinatio*) of the chosen bishop was the *imposition of hands* by episcopal colleagues from other churches as a sign of their "communion" with the new bishop. Presbyters and deacons were chosen, assigned and installed by their bishop with the imposition of hands, by the bishop and other presbyters in the case of presbyters, by the bishop alone in the case of deacons.

By the 3rd century the application of Jewish biblical categories to the church and her ministries resulted in characterizing the eucharist as a "sacrifice" and those who presided at it as "priests." With the establishment of the church in the 4th century, the ordained priests constituted a legal social class in Roman society with the traditional civic rights and privileges of the "order" of priests in Roman social structure. With the application of the concept of the *character* to the "sacrament of order" in the 3rd-and 4th-century Donatist controversies, ordained ministry came to be understood as a *permanent state* in the church, an idea which was expanded and ontologized in the Gregorian reform of the 12th and 13th centuries.

However, the service of leadership and

administration did not exhaust the ministries available to and functioning in the church. The *charismatic offices* of apostle, prophet and teacher continue to be found in Rome in the 3rd century. "Apostles" were still missioned by the church in the 4th century as, e.g., Wulfilas, who was ordained and missioned to the Gothic tribes by the Council of Ephesus in 341. The fluidity of the language dealing with ministerial functions (presbyters, overseers, ministers) as well as the evolving shape of ecclesiatical authority and administration showed considerable elasticity both in the understanding and the shape of ministries for the life of the church.

During the persecutions, the functions and ministry of confessors/martyrs came to be recognized. Their witness to the faith made them not only examples of courage and fidelity but also spiritual leaders whose intercession for sinners functioned as a kind of "indulgence" for reconciliation. In some churches, those who had been imprisoned for their faith needed no "ordination" to serve as leaders and presiders in the communities. Widows and deaconesses performed a number of ministries of instruction, care of the sick and poor, and assistance of women in baptism and interviews with male clergy.

The monastic communities (largely lay communities) functioned as a rich resource of men and women who ministered to the churches' spiritual needs by example, exhortation and spiritual direction.

A variety of forms of service within the church emerged during the formative years of the church as it adapted itself to the culture within which it lived and served the needs which arose within it for nourishment, encouragement and leadership. The function of leadership gradually coalesced into the form of a specific class within the church and secular society: the *kleros* or "clergy."

However these functions did not exhaust the forms in which the life of the church was built up and furthered.

The Medieval Western Church (1000-1500)

By the year 1000 the church had been thoroughly feudalized. After the collapse of Roman culture in the 5th-8th centuries, the lay lords of northern Europe subjugated and united the disparate tribal cultures of the area into what came to be called "feudal culture." The life of the church was a part of this process. The "secular" and "religious" spheres were not seen as separate. Royalty itself was considered a "sacrament" and sacred ministry was conferred by God in the sacred anointing of the king. The appointment of bishops and the management of church affairs was controlled by the lay lords and the religious leaders who functioned in their courts. Liturgy, architecture and art all functioned within the relatively unified experience of church and society. What came to be called "Roman liturgy" was a blend of Roman traditions and Franco-Germanic usages incorporating the spirit of this culture into the unified religious and secular world of the Early Middle Ages: the "Romanesque." Clergy, like other functionaries in the social-cum-religious culture, were inducted into their offices by means of "investiture" with the symbols of their position (keys, books, chalices, patens, etc.). This ritual was considered to be of the "essence of sacramental orders" until its change by Pius XII in 1947.

During the 8th and 9th centuries monks from the British Isles who were brought into Europe by kings to christianize the local populations exercised the apostolic ministry in a new guise. Ministry took the shape of missionary preaching and the foundation of monastic/missionary centers with their rich variety of ministries: preaching and evangelization; the ministries of liturgical prayer (Mass and canonical hours); education, libraries, scholarship; pastoral care in the mode of the "familial" monastic community, i.e., spiritual direction and exhortation. The ministry of the monastic church existed along with and sometimes in tension with the episcopal church. The ministry of reconciliation as well as the ordination of monks to sacred orders (subdeacon, deacon and priest) was a source of tension between the abbots and the local bishops well into the Gregorian reform (1045-1215).

With the development of *urban society* in the 11th and 12th centuries, a new stratum of social and ecclesiastical life emerged: the *bourgeoisie* who formed a new social reality situated between the secular nobility and religious establishments (monasticism and the local church). A variety of ministries emerged out of this new culture. The merchants, artists, and other guilds organized forms for works of mercy: nursing the sick, burying the dead (especially during the plagues which occurred soon after emergence of urban life) and a more systematic care for the now unavoidable urban poor. Pious lay associations also organized "spiritual treasuries," the fruits of prayers, indulgences and other good works, which treasure was placed at the disposal of the members, their families and other beneficiaries.

The experiences of the Crusades as well as the growing religious reaction among clergy and laity to the "capitalism" of medieval urban culture form part of the background for the emergence, especially in the 12th and 13th centuries, of the evangelical ministry of mendicant preachers: laity and clergy, men and women, devoted to the reading of scripture, the imitation of the poor Christ, the service of the poor and the proclamation of evangelical reform in the head and members of the church. These movements formed a matrix for a new flowering of

the ministry of the word whose demise was the topic of frequent complaint in the medieval calls for reform. The popes of the Gregorian reform considered the mendicants a valuable tool for their own visions of reform, granting them papal approval and privileges and clericalizing many of the lay movements. The independence (exemption) of these groups from the local bishops occasioned intense discussions of the proper locus for the preaching ministry within the church.

The first formal theological treatises on the church appeared in the beginning of the 14th century mirroring the concerns of the Gregorian reform and the struggles over control of the life of the church. The church was depicted in terms of competences to function officially and sacramentally as a divinely instituted structure in which the power to function "officially" was conferred by sacramental ordination. Thus an ontological and essential distinction between the ordained and the non-ordained came to be seen as the basis for the restriction of the power of official sacramental ministry to the ordained, usually understood as the priest or bishop. The ministry of the word eventually came to be seen as the exercise of this sacramental power by delegation of the power to preach by the bishop. These and other factors created an ecclesiastical, liturgical/sacramental and theological tension between the traditional clerical ministry of the sacraments and the evangelical ministry of the word, a tension which reached a climax in the Protestant Reformation of the 16th century.

Reformation and the Council of Trent

Medieval evangelical reform movements appealed to a number of biblical images to express their visions of a renewal of life and ministry in the church: the unique priesthood of Christ alone, the priesthood of all believers through baptism into Christ, the word of scripture as the warrant for the life and ministry of the church, the preaching and hearing of the word as the heart of the eucharistic assembly. The radical Protestant reformers built an understanding of the church on these images and used them to open the reality of ministry in the church to the whole Christian people. The Reformers insisted on the radical evangelical equality of all believers. This involved the elimination of a specific ordained class in the church who alone was empowered for sacramental ministry and preaching. Martin Luther (1483-1546) insisted on an office of ministry in the church in opposition to the radical Reformers, but maintained with them that ministry in the church consists essentially in the proclamation of the word of God. Priests were seen as men chosen by the faithful to proclaim the word. It is this ministry which constitutes the community in faith and mediates the true invisible mystery of the church to the visible historical communities gathered in faith around the gospel.

The Council of Trent (1545-1563) responded to the Reformation views of ministry by insisting on the essential necessity of the ministry of the word for bishops and pastors (Sess. V, 1546). It also defended the traditions of the seven sacraments instituted by Christ (Sess. VII, 1547), including the sacrament of order, and of the proper ministers for the sacraments. It specifically condemned the claim that "all Christians have the power to administer the word and the sacraments" maintaining the Gregorian image of the church as structured by sacramental and jurisdictional power conferred in valid ordination. The teaching of the manuals of dogmatic theology which formed the core curriculum of the seminaries established by the council (Sess. XXIII, 1563) focused the theology of ministry and sacraments on these issues. The result is that the vision of the ministry of the church taught and learned in the seminaries and preached to the faithful since the 17th century has centered almost exclusively on the sacramental ministry of those ordained to "sacred orders." But in spite of this clerical focus for the understanding of ministry, the care of the sick and of the poor, the care and education of children, religious and secular secondary and university education, the works of spiritual direction, counselling and other physical, mental and spiritual works of mercy, the missionary work of the church—all these continued to flourish in the many religious orders and lay organizations which had come into existence during the Middle Ages, the Renaissance, and post-Reformation periods.

The 19th Century and Vatican I

The 18th and 19th centuries witnessed the emergence of the critical spirit of the "enlightenment," with its intellectual and political rejection of traditions and dogma in the name of human maturity and liberation. The official church responded to the new democratic and economic liberalisms with condemnation. One effect of the liberal movements was a desire on the part of some segments of the church for the assertion of papal independence from the secular power and papal primacy and infallibility in the church (ultramontanism). The First Vatican Council (1869-1870) decreed the dogmas of papal primacy and infallibility leading to an increasing centralization of authority in the church and a renewed "Gregorian" view of the separation of the church from the world. The first *Code of Canon Law* (1917) mirrored these views and the ecclesiology of the Roman schools which prevailed throughout the world in the early 20th century imaged a highly centralized church along the lines envisioned in the Gregorian reform. The view of ministry is basically clerical, with the ministries of the religious orders under clerical control.

Beyond the "official" ministries recognized in the *Code of Canon Law*, however, forms of ministry continued to emerge as Christians living in the world confronted the concerns of their own times. In the 20th century, the Young Christian Workers and Young Christian Students, the Catholic Interracial Council, the Catholic Worker Movement in the U.S. and Catholic labor unions; Scout organizations and press, radio and television in the U.S. and Europe arose to serve the needs of Catholics in an increasingly secularized society. Catholic education, largely under the care of religious orders of women and men, has since flourished all over the world.

Vatican II

The *Second Vatican Council* (1962-1965) attempted to formulate and implement an image of the life of the church in terms which incorporated many aspects of the spirit, the problems and concerns of the 20th century. The council treated issues concerned with ministries in a number of its decrees. Its *Constitution on the Sacred Liturgy* (1963) emphasized that the whole congregation is the agent of the liturgical life of the church in its gathering, prayer and song. It decreed that all members of the worshipping congregation take an active part in liturgical celebrations and outlined the proper roles for all members of the congregation in the proper performance of the prayer-life of the church. The result of this insistence has been expansion of the forms of ministry exercised in the celebration of the eucharist. Functions formerly restricted to the seminary preparation for priesthood or exercised by the ordained priest in the ordinary parish Masses, have been opened to laity: the roles of acolyte, lector, minister of communion in the liturgy of the eucharist and the bringing of communion to those unable to attend the parish eucharist.

The *Dogmatic Constitution on the Church* (1964) balanced the image of the church as a hierarchy of sacred power with other images of the church. The entire church is the sacrament or mystery of Christ in which all the members are endowed by the Spirit with functions for the service of the church (n. 7). The entire church as the "people of God" shares in Christ's prophetic, priestly and royal ministry. The constitution stresses that these gifts and their exercise are the function of the local church, clergy, religious and laity gathered around their bishop, a life and energy expressed in their eucharist.

Thus, along with decrees on the pastoral office of bishops in the church (1965) and on the life and ministry of priests (1965) reiterating much of the traditional understandings of the functions of bishops and priests, the council devoted a decree to the apostolate of the laity (1965) in which the laity's function in the ministry of the church is called their "apostolate." This apostolic ministry is exercised in the lives of the laity as they fulfill their own prophetic calling to bring the message of salvation to the whole world (n. 3). Because of their baptism, the laity have been gifted with the prophetic, priestly and royal dignity of Christ and have the right and the duty to exercise the gifts of the Spirit, which each has received, in the church and the world. This decree explicitates quite clearly the vision of the *whole* church as a "servant church" a church created for ministry and enlivened by its ministries both in the world and in the church.

The years since Vatican II have witnessed a significant decrease in the numbers of men and women entering the priesthood and religious life in the church. This has entailed a crisis in many of the traditional forms of ministry which have been carried out by the religious and the clergy: parishes, schools, hospitals and nursing facilities. In some cases this decrease has been matched by an increase in lay involvement in some of these ministries. Laity have assumed larger roles in the administration of parishes, taking full charge of parish administration in an increasing number of cases. Hospitals and schools have been forced to open themselves to lay cooperation, and some laity have adopted the visions of religious orders which continue to sponsor these ministries. Of course, this is an ambiguous phenomenon. Some parishes have effectively ceased being able to celebrate the eucharist regularly, relying on communion services instead or on the occasional, sometimes annual, presence of an ordained priest for eucharist, reconciliation and marriages. As yet the official church refuses to ordain women or married men to assume full pastoral sacramental leadership in the churches. The situation will apparently intensify as the years go on and the remaining clergy and religious become older and fewer in number.

However, the lived experience of the ministries which believers have performed for each other throughout the history of the church shows a continuous spontaneity and a rich variety in forms of service. Faith in the church (we believe in one, holy, catholic, apostolic church) involves a continued trust that the Spirit will continue to raise up and energize people in the church to meet the needs which arise as the church lives out its faith from one generation to the next. Our faith also implies that we believe that the church will always grow to be a credible witness to the power of the mystery of Christ within her in her service of those who continually need to hear "good news" in the world. As Paul said to his church in Corinth in the 1st century, "There are varieties of gifts but the same Spirit, and there are varieties of service (ministries) but the same Lord, and there are varieties of working, but it is the same God who inspires them all in every one" (1 Cor 12:4-6). The same Spirit, the same Lord, the same God are still at work serving the church through the abundant gifts with which its members are gifted for the building up of the body of Christ and the Kingdom of God.

B. Cooke, *Ministry to Word and Sacraments. History and Theology* (Philadelphia, 1976). P. Gilmour, *The Emerging Pastor. Non-ordained Catholic Pastors* (Kansas City, Mo., 1986). J.T. McNiell, *A History of the Cure of Souls* (New York, 1951). N. Mitchell, *Mission and Ministry. History and Theology in the Sacrament of Order* (Wilmington, DE: Glazier, 1982). T. O'Meara, *Theology of Ministry* (New York, 1983). E. Schillebeeckx, *The Church with a Human Face. A New and Expanded Theology of Ministry* (New York, 1985). G. Tavard, *A Theology for Ministry* (Wilmington, DE: Glazier, 1983). James and Evelyn Whitehead, *Method in Ministry. Theological Reflection and Christian Ministry* (New York, 1980).

JOSEPH M. POWERS, S.J.

MINISTRY SCHOOL, LITURGY IN

Good liturgical celebrations in a ministry school are both more important, and more difficult to achieve than we thought them to be in the recent past.

Importance

Today nearly everyone realizes the importance of the creative integration of the teaching of worship in a ministry school and the actual prayer life of the seminary community: the integration of the theoretical and the practical, the pedagogical and the mystagogical, the classroom and the chapel. The directives for ministry schools of the various churches stress this integration and recent studies of liturgy in seminaries try to determine if this integration is being achieved.

For example, in the Roman Catholic church, the Sacred Congregation for Catholic Education issued an *Instruction on Liturgical Formation in Seminaries* (1979) which treats not only how liturgy is to be *taught* in Catholic seminaries, but how the liturgy is to be *lived* and *celebrated*. The instruction states (art. 2):

"All genuine liturgical formation involves not only doctrine but also practice. This practice, as a *mystical* formation, is obtained first and mainly through the very liturgical life of the students into which they are daily more deeply initiated though liturgical actions celebrated in common."

Those who research the teaching of worship in seminaries (e.g., the studies of CARA and James White) are concerned not only with the teaching of worship but also its celebration in the ministry school. The studies show that while nearly everyone realizes the importance of quality worship in the seminary community, there is now a painful awareness of how very difficult this is to achieve. Some of these difficulties are obvious, others are more subtle.

Difficulties

(1) *Liturgy Makes the Church Visible.* A basic liturgical principle states that liturgy makes the church visible. At worship we "draw a picture" of the church. The *Constitution on the Sacred Liturgy* (art. 2) puts it in these words: the liturgy "is the outstanding means whereby the faithful may express in their lives and manifest to others the mystery of Christ and the real nature of the true Church." The same constitution (art. 41) states that the "best" picture is achieved when the bishop of the local church presides in the cathedral, assisted by presbyters and deacons, and surrounded by the entire community of the local church. As this is not always possible, the Sunday parish liturgy provides the usual liturgical context for making the church visible.

No matter how "good" liturgy in the seminary might be, the seminary community is too limited to provide an adequate picture of church. The group is too homogeneous to adequately image the body of Christ. In proportion to the church at large, the seminary community is too clerical, too male, too young, too educated, too rich, too healthy. In most seminary communities black Christians and Hispanic Christians are under-represented.

In those seminaries in which women cannot exercise certain ministries, their very presence at the community worship provides a picture of a church under strain. For example, in a Roman Catholic seminary which might employ women as professors of scripture, liturgy, homiletics, or pastoral ministry, and not allow these same professors to "take their turn" with the male professors and administrators preaching or presiding at liturgy, the liturgy can become the very place where discrimination is made painfully evident. Frustration never makes for good liturgy.

It is difficult to provide "model liturgy" in a seminary for those denominations and churches which are experiencing a diminishing number of available ministers, when the seminary community itself has an high proportion of ordained clergy. An "ideal" liturgy for a minister who has already presided at eucharist twelve to eighteen times during a given week is different from that of a minister who presides only two or three times a month, alternating with the other professors and students in the ministry school.

The practice of "concelebration" of the eucharist, in those denominations with this custom, brings its own problems. Concelebration, as indeed any liturgical symbol, is polyvalent: what it might symbolize in a parish on Holy Thursday, or on the occasion of the pastor's jubilee, it might not symbolize when it is employed daily in a context in which it highlights the differences between students and faculty and between the ordained faculty and the non-ordained faculty.

While we want every worship service of the seminary community to be "good liturgy" there are many considerations which influence the liturgical planning and celebration. The best presider or best preacher is not always selected; nor do we always use the best vestment or sing the best song. There is an important value exercised when various members of the faculty and staff preside and preach at community worship.

Scholarship, teaching ability, administrative skills, presiding at worship, the ability to preach—these are distinct skills which are not necessarily found in the same individual. A professor may be a genius when it comes to parish administration and an inspiring teacher of that subject; this does not necessarily mean that this same professor has a facility for symbolic expression and poetic speech. It is important that students exercise various ministries in the seminary worship services; the preaching of the students can serve an important spiritual value in the community. This is real ministry, not just "practice" or "student preaching." At the same time it is not expected that the student homily be delivered with the same professional skill or confidence as would be exercised by the professor of homiletics. Quality liturgy in a seminary always involves the creative integration of a number of positive values.

(2) *Sunday and the Church Year.* Quality liturgy cannot be achieved independently of the rhythms and seasons of the church year. While Sunday is the ordinary focus of Christian worship, in many seminaries and ministry schools Sunday finds the chapel dark because the professors and student ministers have returned to their primary prayer communities to preside over and participate in the liturgies in their parishes. Even in Roman Catholic seminaries, where students are not allowed to preside at Sunday worship until after they are ordained, many students are "doing ministry" in parishes on the Lord's Day. In these schools the principle liturgy for the seminary community is of necessity on a day of lesser liturgical importance.

In seminaries where eucharist is celebrated seven days a week, a different problem emerges: how to keep every day from becoming Sunday. Some believe that until a special eucharistic rite for weekdays is developed, this problem cannot be solved.

The seasons of the church calendar present their own special difficulties for the seminary community. Many seminaries are closed for the principal feasts of the year. Students often want some sort of "Christmas" liturgy before leaving their classmates for Christmas vacation and ministry. While the rest of the church shouts the Advent "Come, Lord Jesus," the seminarians sing "Silent Night." When the liturgy in the ministerial school is more influenced by the school year than by the church year, quality liturgy becomes difficult.

In those churches in which Christian initiation takes place during the Easter vigil, the awareness is growing that it is Christian initiation which is at the very heart of that holy night's liturgy, and a vigil without baptisms is lacking something essential. Yet, the vigil in a ministry school is ordinarily celebrated without the active presence of catechumens—not a "model" situation.

This does not mean that it cannot be prayerful or fruitful. Most Roman Catholic priests over fifty years of age were formed in a seminary context where each Sunday began with a silent communion Mass and then, later Sunday morning, they celebrated the climax of the liturgical week with the solemn Sunday liturgy at which none of the seminarians received holy communion. If Mass without communion can nourish a church, so can the vigil without baptisms.

(3) *The Needs of the Praying Community.* While everyone would recognize that the needs of a community gathered for a funeral are different from the needs of a community gathered for a wedding, and that at a "good" liturgy, pastoral

sensitivity would be exercised to adapt the liturgy to the needs of the participants, it is more difficult to see the difference between the needs of a parish community and those of a ministerial school. In a parish, Christians may come to the Sunday service hungry for the word of God, eager to hear a sermon which will put their lives in a Christian perspective and help them with their daily living. Indeed, this may be the only time of the week when they have such an opportunity. In a ministry school, on the other hand, the participants may come to a service fresh from several hours of scripture study and reflection on the word of God and they may want a "quiet" liturgy, without homily and without much interaction with their teachers and peers. Without commenting on whether these "needs" and "wants" are good or bad, the fact is that a liturgy that "fits" a community in a ministry school and is "good liturgy" for them is probably not good liturgy in a parish. The seminary chapel is not a classroom where one learns "neat things" which can be imitated in a parish. The "teaching" that goes on in the seminary chapel concerns the formation of liturgical spirituality and the general liturgical principles which constitute good worship. The difficulty is that these are the very things which are the most difficult to teach. Imitation is easier to learn than common sense or pastoral sensitivity.

(4) *Collective Responsibility*. Perhaps the greatest difficulty in assuring quality liturgical celebrations in a ministerial school is determining who is responsible for this judgment. Who is "in charge" of the seminary liturgy? An assignment which was a coveted position in the 1960s (chapel director, worship coordinator, etc.) has become a terrible responsibility and often a burden in the 1990s.

No matter who is placed "in charge" of the worship of the school, the entire faculty and administration have a vested interest in its celebration. The seminary liturgy is not merely the concern of the professors of worship. The homiletics professors are concerned that the preaching reflects the quality of their classrooms. The professors of scripture are concerned with the way the word of God is proclaimed and interpreted. Professors of systematic and sacramental theology know that what they teach in the classroom can be undone in the chapel. Administrators are concerned when chapel services alarm the sensitivities of the sponsoring denominations or the bishops who send students to the school. The one responsible for the seminary liturgy has a lot of people to please!

The *Constitution on the Sacred Liturgy* (art. 16) states that liturgy is to be taught "under its theological, historical, spiritual, pastoral, and canonical aspects. Moreover, the other professors, while striving to expound the mystery of Christ and the history of salvation from the angle proper to each of their own subjects, must nevertheless do so in a way that will clearly bring out the connection between their subjects and the liturgy, as also the underlying unity of all priestly training. This consideration is especially important for professors of dogmatic, spiritual, and pastoral theology and for professors of holy Scripture."

The institutional structures and the personal cooperation and expertise necessary for this type of cooperation and integration in the classroom are often lacking, and even when the structures are present the integration is very difficult to achieve. And if this is true of the classroom, it is even more true of the chapel. The chapel is not a classroom, yet the teaching that goes on in the chapel is often more powerful than that of the classroom. *Legem credendi lex statuat supplicandi.*

As the liturgy forms the future ministers of the churches, those responsible for these liturgies are forming not only the future ministers but the future churches—an awesome responsibility and a most difficult task. The following lines from the study of James White indicate an example of this dimension of seminary worship: "Of great potential significance is the move to a weekly Eucharist in Protestant seminaries of liturgically central denominations.... Moves to a weekly eucharist are important when a strong eucharistic piety is not present in the churches of the denomination. It may mean a generation of frustrated graduates or a generation of active change agents. The personal development of eucharistic piety among students over their three or four years in seminary may be far more important than what is taught about worship in the classroom. At the same time, exposure to well-prepared and skillfully delivered homilies may spark a change for future Roman Catholic priests from the parish life they have known. Seminary worship formation is a crucial part of the seminary experience. Unfortunately, this is rarely recognized by many students until long after they graduate and never perceived by some faculty.... One of the most frequent frustrations expressed was the integration of the teaching of worship into the curriculum as a whole" (White, 310-311).

(5) *Creativity and Legislation.* If the entire faculty and staff is to be responsible for the quality of the liturgy in the ministerial school, another difficulty is encountered: "too many cooks spoil the broth." The creative action of any artist can be stifled when the artist is required to please too many different critics. While "the absence of limitation is the enemy of art" often presiders in a seminary context feel so limited by the expectations of the seminary worshipping community, faculty, students, administration, and by the larger concerns of their denominations/bishops, that the artistic and the beautiful is stifled and we are left with a mere observance of the rubrics and the denominational laws. This can result in liturgies that have been compared to a "paint by numbers" landscape. It takes a truly great artist to produce a work of beauty with a "paint by numbers" kit.

Not everyone realizes the amount of compromise and human understanding necessary to preside at a worship service, whether as a faculty or as a student minister, while trying to engage in prayer the professor of sacramental theology, the director of the liturgical practicum, the professor of homiletics and the scripture professors, all of whom have criteria for what makes "good worship."

"Spontaneity" and "creativity" are not leftovers from the 1960s but, rightly understood, are essential elements of every worship service. Every liturgical tradition must be creatively adapted to the here-and-now worshipping community. There must always be a creative balance between preserving the liturgical tradition and adapting it to the present liturgical needs. To quote again James White: "There is always danger in making seminary worship too clinical, too self-conscious in looking over one's shoulder to see what one is doing. On the other hand, many possibilities will never be encountered unless students experience them first in seminary worship" (White, 309-310).

(6) *High Expectations.* The very fact that everyone realizes that the prayer life of the seminary community is so important places a certain strain on the worshipping community. Everyone—students, administrators, and faculty—comes to the service with the expectation that it will be "good" and indeed exemplary. Funds are budgeted for quality liturgical furnishings; experts in scripture, music and homiletics are all present. However, a basic liturgical principle reminds us that quality worship is not achieved merely by the quality of the symbols and metaphors employed but by the quality of the realities to which

they point. A wedding ring may be simple or elaborate in itself but its function as a symbol is directly related to the quality of the love in the relationship it signifies. A beautiful ring does not make a beautiful marriage. Good liturgy is a free gift of God, most often bestowed on holy (those who know in the Spirit that they are poor) participants.

It is easy to expect that the liturgy in a ministry school can be "perfect" simply because it is possible to provide quality materials: exquisite vestments, a congregation both versed in scripture and capable of singing in parts, the absence of crying infants and non-communicants who leave before the service is over—all those things a pastor might wish for and dream of during a parish Sunday worship service! However, it is by the bread of our daily lives being broken that we can recognize the divine presence in the breaking of the eucharistic bread. Holy participants make quality worship. The unfounded presumption of some members of the worshipping seminary community is that ministry students are, by the very fact of being ministry students, somehow automatically holy. Those experienced in seminary life and formation know that is not always the case. Christ often chooses the less than holy, the less than brilliant, the weaker voice, to be his minister.

Those concerned with liturgy in a ministry school agree on the importance of the quality of the community worship. At the same time, they are becoming more aware of the difficulties involved in achieving quality worship and hopefully more tolerant and appreciative of those whose task it is to assure this quality.

National Conference of Catholic Bishops, *Liturgical Formation in Seminaries: A Commentary*, (Washington, DC: Office of Publishing Services, USCC, 1984). National Conference of Catholic Bishops, *The Program of Priestly Formation*, 3rd ed. (Washington DC: Office of Publishing Services, USCC, 1981). Thomas Krosnicki, "A Survey Report

on the Teaching and Celebration of Liturgy," *CARA Seminary Forum*, 3:4 (September 1974): 1-8. Nathan Mitchell, "Liturgical Education in Roman Catholic Seminaries: A Report and an Appraisal," *Worship* 54:2 (March 1980): 129-157. James F. White, "The Teaching of Worship in Seminaries in Canada and the United States," *Worship* 55:4 (July 1981): 304-318.

THOMAS RICHSTATTER, O.F.M.

MINISTRY, LAY

This article addresses three questions. How did the lay ministries that emerged in many local church settings following Vatican II affect the subsequent "explosion of lay ministeries" cited by Thomas O'Meara, O.P. (*Theology of Ministry*, 1983)? What impact on liturgy did lay participation engender? What connections between lay ministry and liturgy await further attention?

Emergent Liturgical Lay Ministries. In the minds of countless lay adults following Vatican II, leadership in a liturgical role, e.g., as lector or as eucharistic distributor, was first and foremost *official*. The origination came from the institutional church, from hierarchical figures, official documents and the local pastor. This movement did not originate in the impulse of the laity. Liturgical involvement was often designated by ordained leaders as *ministry*, including the somewhat cumbersome early title "extraordinary minister of the eucharist."

For decades lay adults had participated in church work—teaching in Catholic colleges and schools and in leadership roles within associations such as the Knights of Columbus and the Daughters of Isabella. But as Bishop John Cummins pointed out at the N.C.C.B.—sponsored *Learning to Share Ministry Responsibly Conference* in February 1980, these roles were not considered *ministry* until Vatican II. The movement into ministerializing church work accomplished by lay adults had its origin in the invitation from the church to the laity regarding liturgical functions identified as ministries.

For many lay women and lay men, who are today engaged in a professional ministerial leadership position (as a pastoral associate or hospital chaplain or diocesan director or campus minister), the initial step in that faith journey started when the lay minister held the cup or proclaimed the word as a liturgical minister in a local church setting and perceived self in a new ecclesial role, that of *minister*.

Liturgical Impact of Lay Participation

The use of Latin and the singular role of the priest and his "back-to-the-people" placement prior to the council encouraged a focus on a transcendent remote God. After the council, the use of the vernacular and the participatory role (individual and corporate) of lay adults, as well as the new placement of the priest, pointed to the assembly, and was, for the most part affirmed by the assembly (See: Notre Dame Study of Catholic Parish Life). Two outcomes of this more inclusive approach were the experience of the *community* during liturgy and the emergence of *collaboration* between laity and priests. The assembled people, some of them at least, began to perceive themselves as a participative people rather than a regulated people. Within the worship experience God became immanent within a community that was collaborative.

This communal, liturgical participation eventually unfolded into outreach in two directions. One was a liturgical outreach to those not present. Parishioners who were sick and hospitalized, or elderly and too feeble to attend Mass, began to be perceived as the responsibility of the parish and not only of its priestly leadership. Gradually the needs of those no longer present, including their liturgical needs, were served by lay ministers who were trained and prepared for this new ministerial role within the parish.

Lay participation within eucharistic leadership also became in time outreach toward other sacramental functions. Today it is not uncommon to find significant leadership in baptismal, first eucharist, and confirmation preparatory programs within any inventory of lay ministries. Eulogies at funerals are given by family members. Weddings are planned by the engaged couple. Peer ministry within R.C.I.A. programs is lay. The initial and modest steps taken to include lay adults *from* the assembly in the leadership *of* the assembly, gathered for the Sunday eucharistic celebration, has permeated the entire life of the parish including its sacramental life.

In some settings this intertwining of community and collaboration has culminated in lay and clerical collaboration in planning as well as facilitating the central eucharistic celebrations of the week.

The above movements influenced the symbolic meaning of liturgy in a way analogous to the description of spiritual direction cited by Janet Ruffing, S.M., in *Uncovering Stories of Faith* (N.Y.: Paulist, 1989, p. 50): "The influence of this tradition (spiritual direction) is even more profound than simply a continuity of pastoral praxis. The Christian tradition itself is characteristically narrative in its scriptures, worship, and catechesis. The story-telling that takes place within the spiritual direction conversation is already contextualized within a 'storied' tradition which forms the consciousness of the contemporary storyteller through the shared story of Jesus and salvation history which reaches back into the narratives of the Hebrew scriptures and strains forward through the age of the church to the end times themselves."

The Mass, no longer perceived only as a transcendent opportunity for grace, has rooted many lay believers in their "storied" tradition. The particular story of this particular people gathered *to participate* in worship in this place has become one with the story embodied in the story of tradition ... from the believing people who far into the past first gathered to worship their one God to the believing people who will in the future witness the apocalypse.

Areas Needing Further Attention

Spirituality. Surprisingly little consideration on local levels has been directed to the relationship between needs of a personal spiritual nature and the communal experience of liturgy. Prior to Vatican II distinctions between popular piety, exercised through devotionals, and the sacramental life of the parish, were understood and acknowledged. Since the council there appears to be a tendency to collapse all lay spiritual needs into the liturgical experience. However, as the 1984 and 1989 National Association for Lay Ministry studies of the spiritual experiences of lay believers reveal, for many lay adults, active in liturgical lay ministries, the spiritual experiences remembered and cited take place beyond the sacramental life of the parish.

One reason for this may be that despite the enormity of liturgical change opportunities are few and far between for lay adults to articulate what is happening to them interiorly during the liturgical experience. In addition, the initial instruction given to lay liturgical ministers has tended to focus on functions (a "how-to-do-it" approach). Without a like focus on meaning and spirituality, an integration of function with the faith life of the lay minister has been neglected.

Lay Preaching. Excluding the issue of the ordination of women and married men, which is beyond the limits of this article, two conflictual issues regarding the laity and liturgy pertain to private confession and lay preaching. The shunning of private confessional practice by the laity continues in a now-regularized fashion.

The issue of lay preaching had champions on both sides within the American hierarchy at the 1989 N.C.C.B. November meeting. Availability of priest personnel determined somewhat the parameters of the argument. By a close vote the American bishops decided against all practice of lay preaching within liturgical celebrations for adults, adhering to distinctions based on gender and ecclesial status rather than on preparation and qualifications.

Interestingly, the shunning of private confession by lay believers and the shunning of lay preaching during liturgy by the American hierarchy represent the only two areas regarding liturgy and lay ministry which have eluded the development of community and limited the collaboration which has increasingly characterized the church in the United States. In all other areas, twenty years of engagement in gradual process has integrated lay believers within the liturgical life and leadership of the local church community.

See **Ministry; Lay leadership in the liturgy; Lay ministry, liturgical; Lay spirituality**

VIRGINIA S. FINN

MINISTRY, TEAM

Team ministry uses the circular, rather than the pyramid model for the sharing of people and their gifts in the service of the church and community. The goal of such a model is the healing and reconciliation of persons and institutions working for change through a process of honest relationships, theological and pastoral training, and openness to being changed by that very process, therefore conversion. It is a mirror of Jesus' own ministry with his apostles.

As Paul looks at Jesus' ministry, he proposes that all Christian serving be grounded in the gifts (charisms) given in baptism for the building up of the body of Christ (1 Cor 3:16; Rom 12:4). Some of these gifts would lead to public ministries gradually producing the bishop-presbyter-deacon model, and the full membership of women in these churches was a cultural breakthrough, both in their positions and their prestige.

The source of ministry, then, was God's living Spirit, but that Spirit as given to *all*, to the entire church as ambassadors for Christ (2 Corinthians 5). This tradition of ministry as a function of the *whole* church meeting human need waxed and waned across the centuries, e.g., the 19th century, where the church hid from politico-cultural involvement, and the 20th, when for the first time since Paul we seem ready for a laity-centered church made up of more theologically trained laity than priests or religious. Yet much of the credit for this lay explosion of competence is due to the work of said priests and religious.

Vatican II did the formal spadework for this development in turning away from the scholastic approach to the meaning of priesthood, forging a new definition based on Christ's own ministry as teacher, sanctifier, and leader. So, the priest's presiding at the eucharist, then, becomes not the most important of a priest's activities, but just the chief act of his role as sanctifier. Here the council moved to a theology of ordained ministry basing all ministries on that of Jesus' three-fold role. We are *all* sent; some hold office, but, yet to be fully developed theologically, is the question of what "holding office" or being ordained means today. Nor was the connection of Jesus as the primordial sacrament and the church as basic sacrament developed fully so that we could see clearly that the fundamental priesthood in the church is that of the church itself. Ordained priesthood, then, is a *part* of this total priesthood of God's people, a theology of ministry now developing through praxis (as the number of priests diminishes),

though incomplete and only partially accepted.

Vatican II's *Lumen Gentium* (34-36) had stated that the laity "share in the mission of the whole Christian People with respect to the Church and the world." Baptism and confirmation provide the basis for an apostolate of all Christians ordained or not, sharing in Christ's three-fold ministry, with the source of this ministry God/Jesus, and not delegation by pastor, bishop, or pope. But Vatican II named an "essential difference" between ordained and lay ministries; again, however, they gave no theological definition of what this difference consisted in. Again, work for an evolving pastoral practice and theological reflection.

The uneven nature of the theological accomplishment of Vatican II appears, also, in its three-fold approach to Jesus' ministry as "teacher, sanctifier, and leader." It is not scriptural, nor from the early church, nor even the Scholastic period; it is a piece of contemporary theology in its application to present pastoral questions, and like all theologies, culturally conditioned and somewhat adequate for now.

In regard to the present developing models of team ministry, this cultural approach to theologies permits us to ask, as we must (if we adopt the three-fold ministry theory), should we not (to be consistent) ask why the voices of priest, deacon, or lay are not *collegially* consulted in the exercise of the "teaching" (magisterium) functions of the people of God, a task assigned them by said church?

What, too, does "ordination" or the lack of it actually mean in today's crisis of massive transition in church and society, let alone in theology? If 10% of the parishes in the U.S. today have no resident ordained priest (43% worldwide) how theological, let alone rational, is it to continue a denial game of "substituting," of holding "services" instead of Masses, of consecrating thousands of hosts for distribution to unknown masses in a semi-magical use of the sacrament? Certainly the needs of today's parishes for healing and reconciliation, for ministry, should not be denied them because of an inadequate theology of eucharist or ordination or ministry. God is hardly impotent because we cling to outmoded theories of what God is about.

Facing the facts of a predominantly lay church membership may push us to consider the principles we find operative in team ministry when it is grounded in a theology of the gifts, because it fits the present need to evoke, train, and call out these gifts for the needs of the world.

Looking at one model (Donnelly, 79) we see the recent developments in theology sketched above coming to bear on a theory and practice of said team ministry. The starting point for such a model is that of sharing (*koinonia*) which implies the community of believers engaged in giving and receiving both their God-given gifts and their human services. This common theology of the gifts calls for a process of building a common understanding or meaning of what such shared serving means: Christians with gifts and limitations pledged to give and receive their presence and gifts for the common good. This theological-spiritual approach to team as the place of conversion is quite different from line and staff organization job descriptions. It implies committing self to learning the art of communication, the life-blood of the team, so that assumptions are exposed and prayerfully dealt with so that all can agree that the Spirit is "chair" of the team; then living out this common theology in practice, supported by weekly team meetings and daily prayer for and with team members for the solidarity that promotes whatever conversion is called for in each life.

Team also implies a shared sociology, learning the dynamics of the entity they

strive to be, a group, motivated at this crucial moment of Christian history to be the small base community trying to live out the values of Jesus, empowered by his love. Such an endeavour implies a growing spirituality, empowered by prayerful listening to the Spirit in their own hearts and in the lives of others. This individual spiritual growth then fuels the team spirituality when the group comes together for liturgy, meetings, social life, modeling the apostolic life of Jesus' own team.

For such a team to operate efficiently, some six factors are operative: 1. *Consultation*: people learn to ASK for advice, help, opinions both within and without the team; 2. *Coalition*: they ally themselves with like-goaled groups in their pastoral ministry, especially in ecumenical and inter-religious issues; 3. *Organization*: they study and practice sound structural group techniques; 4. *Referral*: they learn to limit their scope according to their gifts and goals, avoiding over-extension and Messiah complexes; 5. *Representation*: of the team, by and for the team (and of those they serve) on the team; 6. *Participation*: sharing in responsibility for roles and resources; in decision-making on decided levels; in rewards and sufferings.

These six marks of team spell out the meaning of a theology of sharing; the shape of service is circular because it disperses power and concentrates on human development; it demands daily listening to the Spirit. Certain elements are needed for such sharing to happen, some measuring rods for membership: a shared *sense of belonging*; all are taken seriously, even women members! Shared *achievement* as contributing to the ministry of all, along with deep respect for human difference as God's way to break through the isolation and the *sharing of ideas and feelings* openly fueled by theological reflection and prayer. Lastly, what ensures the circular, equal functioning of the team and prevents it from becoming a patriarchal pyramid: the element of *accountability*. Members feel committed to the team and freely accept responsibilities for the team. No one is unaccountable; chairpersons are elected *by* the team for a fixed period of time; no one has life-tenure in any office or position. Conflict-resolution and consensus are constantly employed. The team works at the fulfillment of *Lumen Gentium's* two aspects of ministry here: *teaching* and *sanctifying*.

The third area the council highlighted for priestly (and Christian) spirituality and ministry was that of *leadership*. The team can act as corporate pastor, a role seemingly dictated by the present crisis in priestly vocations, but its leadership is also corporate; no individual is encouraged to shape the team into a pyramid of sole control, decision-making, or unaccountability. The movement is from a purely sociological definition of leadership: "exercising influence in a group in a given situation through communication"— to: leadership (as sharing) is "exercising influence multiplied incredibly by the Spirit in the community through presence and ministry." This is mutual leadership; it takes turns moving around the group through corporate listening and the individual listening of members through prayer.

Contemporary team ministry is often labeled "collaborative ministry," stressing both the lay-clergy and the man-woman aspects of such sharing. If this means re-emphasizing "laity" as some distinct theological or canonical entity, it may reverse the achievement of the corporate leadership team demands as does the gospel model we find in Jesus' values of justice and love. As we have seen above, if the church has *one* ministry with people functioning in various ways and times, then the distinction between clergy and laity needs careful re-examination; it is not scriptural nor is it viable theological

theory for today's historical moment. The role called "priest" is moving to the periphery of both church and society; historically, the Spirit, faithful to the church, helps us supply and develop persons and means to replace whatever functions that role fulfilled in the body of Christ. So, also, the term/role "laity." It no longer carries a valid theological charge, and throws no light on the contemporary situation of Christian community. All baptized Christians are the church and as church need to fulfill its mission. Collegiality and subsidiarity fostered by the council can help today's ordained and unordained to work together to shape an appropriate theology and pastoral practice to fit contemporary needs. Team ministry is one such suggested form.

Another distinction that needs addressing for collaborative/team ministry is that of sexual difference. The team model of equality in access to the use and sharing of one's gifts, to offices, decision-making and accountability is a fine example to society of how men and women could function in corporate endeavors where the gifts are the criterion of operation and position, not one's sex, as Paul so heartily wished: . . . "neither male nor female for you are all one in Christ Jesus (Gal 3:28). The team model might be a way of stopping the great draining away of female church members, especially the younger women, who find themselves accepted and valued more adequately in the culture than in their Christian churches.

Even more delightful is the modeling the team unit can do for the total church, for the Vatican itself. As the team strives to carry out teaching, sanctifying, and leading in the light of Vatican II, it provides what sound theological theory always demands: working pastoral models that exemplify and incorporate gospel principles in meaningful ways. Whether teams work as social change agents or as targets of their own need for conversion, they supply a social form in which the gospel can be lived, spirituality can be nourished, and the neighbor served in a theology-praxis of sharing.

Dody H. Donnelly, *Team: Theory and Practice of Team Ministry* (New Jersey, 1977). K. Osborne, O.F.M., *Priesthood: A History of the Ordained Ministry* (New Jersey, 1988). B. Cooke, *Ministry To Word and Sacrament* (Philadelphia, 1976).

DODY H. DONNELLY

MINISTRY, WOMEN IN

Preliminary Observations

It is appropriate that an essay on women in ministry begin with a reflection on its inclusion in a dictionary of sacramental worship. In earlier decades, the strict definitional boundaries of both "sacrament" and "ministry" would have precluded even the consideration of such a topic. Therefore, its inclusion here speaks to the distance journeyed in the understandings of women, of ministry, and of worship.

The specificity of its inclusion at the same time identifies the distance yet to be travelled, insofar as it reveals fundamental attitudes toward and the status and acceptance of women at this point in history.

"Women in ministry," offered as a special topic implies that the concept is somehow novel or atypical. "Men in ministry," a topic not included in this volume, is, by implication, normative. Other categories for ministry in this volume (lay ministries and team ministries) also point to evolution as regards the notion of ministry in the church. Rather than be taken as a criticism, these observations are meant to move the reader in the direction of understanding some of the complexities that mark a contemporary consideration of this issue.

Recognizing that other scholars have devoted volumes to tracing the impact of women in a variety of ministerial positions over the centuries and to considering their place in history (see Hellwig, 1985), it is the intent of this essay to address the issues that underlie our contemporary understandings and struggles with the concept of "women in ministry."

Historical Considerations

From the time of Jesus, the participation of women in the public life of Jesus and his church has been documented. The gospel accounts are replete with references to those women who ministered to Jesus, who were delegated to announce the "good news," and who gave silent witness to his agonies.

Paul in his letters and Luke in the Acts also note the activity of the women in the early Christian community. Both the influence they exerted and the respect they received attest to the unquestioned role accorded to the women who ministered to the early community.

Since that time, and up to the present, the role of women in public ministry has waxed and waned. Little has appeared in our traditional histories and accounts, and this may be seen as mirroring the larger culture where the activities, contributions and accomplishments of women have tended to be ignored or, at the very least, downplayed. The focus of religious histories has commonly been upon affairs of the institutional churches precisely as institutions. The systematic exclusion of women from ordination and from positions of institutional authority guarantees that in these histories we read little or nothing about women.

The Face of Women in Ministry: Structural Implications

While neither ignoring the pain women have experienced as a result of their exclusion from many church structures nor affirming nor condoning the blatant sexism and sometimes subtle misogyny that have marked our church practices and structures, reflection on the conseuences of that reality leads to some interesting observations. Having experienced exclusion from ministry in a hierarchical structure, gifted women have shaped alternative means to minister to the body of Christ and once again to be Christ on this earth. Horizontal leadership based on mutual support, inspiration, and the convening of community marked the public ministry of many. Given their exclusion from institutional politics, other women were free to opt for a more prophetic style of public ministry than is usually possible for those who must accept the limits of conventional roles and institutional approbation. Finally, for reasons already mentioned and often precisely because of their position, women were often better able to notice and to attend to that which was left undone and to those who were overlooked, omitted, or excluded in the pastoral practice of the institutional church. Monika Hellwig observed that, in such instances, the impact of women in public ministry has tended to be prophetic, radical in its implications for the social structures of society in the long run, and, in terms of the social dynamics, a movement from below.

The Face of Women in Ministry: Psychological Issues

A key factor influencing the concept of women in ministry is to be found in the reality that the authentic involvement of women in ministry brings to ministry a potentially counter-cultural aspect. To better understand this, Anne Wilson-Schaef's identification of two operative "systems" in our culture is helpful. The first of these is the "dominant" system, typically characterized by current male-oriented values. The second is an "emerging" system, marked by what has been traditionally characterized as a feminine style. The shift that is currently occurring is in the increased identification and acceptance of the emerging system. In

this process, women and men are experiencing an enhancement of many previously non-valued styles of thinking and interacting and are exploring the implications of these shifts in both their personal and professional lives.

This transformation has major implications for an understanding of ministry. To begin, it affects how the notion of ministry itself is defined and integrated into the life of the minister. Traditionally reflective of the dominant system, ministry and work were seen as fairly synonymous. John Futrell, for example, in writing on *The Challenge of Ministry*, describes ministries as "human services performed in response to the human needs of people." In the emerging system, relationships rather than work are seen as core or focal, and everything must go through, relate to, and be defined by relationships. Hence, ministry is construed in terms of relationship. It becomes that which one does with one's life in order to make sense of other aspects of one's life. Neither profit- nor power-oriented, ministry takes its meaning from creativity, from bonding, from its inherent humanness touched by the reality of the incarnation, and from a keen sense of service. Ministry is, in the emerging system, an expression of one's relationship with God, with others, and with oneself.

Other aspects to be considered in light of this shift in world view and in terms of their impact on the notion of ministry include structure, power, healing and various understandings of God and spirituality.

The structure of the dominant system is hierarchical, with no ambiguity as regards accountability or control. God is superior to man is superior to woman is superior to child is superior to animal is superior to plant is superior to things inanimate. Boundaries are clear, and dichotomous (either/or) thinking abounds. Ministry is something "done to" others, with the minister clearly in a superior stance as the one who imparts (grace, benefits, etc.).

The emerging system has a less clearly defined structure. Boundaries are fairly permeable, categories are less clear, and structures are more easily flexed to address the needs of all. "Neatness" is not a hallmark of such a system. Ministry in this context is a shared experience, which reverences varied needs of individuals. While roles are defined, there is a giving/receiving dynamic that is consonant with the emphasis on relationship mentioned above.

Power is another critical concept. Jean Baker Miller defines power as "the capacity to implement." As such, power has two components: power *for* oneself, and power *over* others. With this in mind, the dominant system has traditionally seen the power of another person or group of persons to be dangerous: you control them, or they control you. This is based, in part, on the assumption that power is a "zero-sum" entity; there is just so much power available. (If, for example, the amount of available power is 20 units, one's having 12 leaves only 8 units available to others.) The dominant system, therefore, jealously guards power and sets deliberate limits as regards its use.

The emerging system provides another consideration of power. Here, power, like love, is assumed to be limitless. When shared, it regenerates and expands. Women and men need power to grow and develop, but the greater the development of each individual, the more able, more effective, and less in need of limiting or restricting others she or he will be.

Because of their place in the structure of the dominant system, many women have marked difficulty in coping with and appropriating power. Given their limited understandings, many have used power in the style of the dominant system.

Others, fearful of such an outcome or distrustful of their own giftedness, have abrogated any power that is even rightfully theirs. Distortions of spirituality, where humility has become equated with actively avoiding the recognition of one's or others' gifts and talents, also has discouraged individuals from appropriating that which is their God-given heritage. Interestingly, references to the Spirit of God often reflect a gender difference that may be an indication of this even deeper power issue as women refer to the "Spirit of love" and men invoke the "power of the Spirit."

There is another aspect to be considered in terms of power and the role of women in ministry. It comes in terms of weakness, or powerlessness. For women, weaknesses are typically seen in terms of vulnerability, helplessness, and neediness. The dominant system encourages men to abhor these feelings in themselves while it has encouraged women to cultivate this state of being. In reality, however, these feelings are common to all. Those who are typically better able consciously to admit to and tolerate these feelings have a ministerial "edge" in this regard as this ability puts them more closely in touch with basic life experiences. Having to defend less and deny less, they are in a position to understand and minister to weakness. As persons more comfortable with their own weakness, they are more readily able to illumine the path to wholeness for others.

As might be expected, "healing" in the dominant system is something done by the healer, who is "certified" by the system. Failure in the treatment is most typically construed in terms of some deficit of the patient. Linear logic marks the thought construction of this system. In contrast, the emerging system views "healing" as a process that occurs within a person with the facilitation and help from the healer. The relationship between healer and patient is a key factor. Transating this understanding to the terms of ministry, it is easy to understand the existence of tensions in the church as regards the determination of who, for example, is "legitimately" minister to a community and how that role/relationship is expressed.

In the dominant system, understandings of God and spirituality parallel the schema already outlined. The structure of most theological assumptions is a dominance-submission scheme. With the perpetuation of the belief that the suffering servant is the holiest of all, women and others found "lower" in the order of things have been encouraged to be suffering servants, thus achieving absolution for their status. God, the "prototype" of perfection of this system, is perfect, all-knowing, and unchanging. The role of the minister is to mediate between God and those lower in the hierarchy so that salvation might be accomplished.

The emerging system's view of God also parallels that system. Here, God is viewed primarily in terms of relationship and, therefore, as is true with relationship, subject to growth and change. Coming to know God is imaged as a deepening and broadening process rather than one of climbing a ladder. Boundaries between the "sacred" and the "secular," between what is "holy" and what is "profane," are less rigid and apt to be informed by the lived experience of those who come to worship. The role of minister, here, is to facilitate that identification process and to enable the community to encounter the holy in this way.

New/Old Directions

What is it that marks the movement that is publicly acknowledging and incorporating women in ministry? While some might describe it as "tokenism," or a long overdue acknowledgement of the real contribution made by women, there also seems to be a subtle yet discernible shift in the understanding of what

ministry involves. The affirmation of the emerging (female) system described in the previous section attests to this. The shift might also be interpreted as the acknowledgement that the "works" or activities of women in public ministry, different as they have been from traditional or formally "sanctioned" works, are not only true expressions of ministry, but by the accompanying acceptance of this reality, are activities that are to be embraced by all in the church.

The image that best expresses one of the greatest contributions that women have to offer to the emerging understanding of what it means to be a public minister in the church may be found in that of pregnancy. For centuries, the male model of potency, impact, and discharge has dominated the cultural image of ministry. Filling empty churches, establishing flourishing programs, and erecting tangible structures were frequently the measures of effective ministry. The emergence of the "women's movement," particularly in the United States, has brought with it some alternative approaches to these familiar activities of ministry. In contrast to the male style, the image of pregnancy depicts attitudes of trust, surrender, and receptivity. The pregnant one is intimately connected to the new life within, yet is not in total control of either the ultimate outcome or many aspects of the process. She does not, for example, determine that on this day "we will work on the nervous system" and that at another time "we will develop fingers and toes." Yet, the one who is pregnant cannot help but be mindful of the new life within and must direct a significant portion of consciousness toward its nurturance. She continues in the faith that development is proceeding as it should and is in keeping with a thrust toward health and wholeness. While often finding herself in a stance of reverent reflection, she is an active participant in the process of forming this new life. At no point is the pregnant one a passive observer.

The shift in the culture's attitude toward pregnancy also provides a fitting metaphor for the new understandings of the role and influence of women in ministry. It is not long ago that pregnancy and all it entails was marked by embarrassment, seclusion, and disfavor. Euphemistically referred to as being "in seclusion," women were typically excluded from the public eye. Only in recent years have pregnant women been "allowed" to continue and experience acceptance in "public" roles. The condition of pregnancy no longer needs to be hidden. Hence, there appears an increasing readiness to acknowledge the value of the lessons of pregnancy: that experience of actively waiting, in hope and in faith, with participation in the process, surrender to the mystery, and commitment to its product. Such might be wholesome attitudes to inform those who are committed to ministry in this age of transformation.

Monika K. Hellwig, *Christian Woman in a Troubled World* (New York: Paulist Press, 1985). Anne Wilson Schaef, *Women's Reality* (Minneapolis, MN: Winston Press, 1985).

MIRIAM D. UKERITIS, C.S.J.

MUSIC MINISTRIES

Musicians play an essential role in the work of God within the assembled people that is the liturgy. Many great composers like Franz Josef Haydn and Franz Schubert received their primary musical training as members of a church choir or ensemble. The creations of musicians within worship situations have stirred the human psyche to prayer since the dawn of history. Music, evanescent as wind, touches the heart like few other arts. The church since Vatican II has viewed music as so much a part of the fabric of worship that if it is bad or inappropriate, it tears at the very soul of the rite, interrupts prayerful communication, and diverts attention from the mysteries being celebrated. Bad music distracts from worship as much as a torn, garish chasuble might.

Thus the term *music ministry* has validity in that it denotes a service publicly designated by the church to assist in the fulfillment of the active participation of the people and presider within the ritual act. The ministry of music, even in its general understanding as a ministry of the non-ordained, proclaims the gospel, celebrates the sacraments, stirs the faithful to witness and serve Christ within his people (see *Catholicism*, by Richard P. McBrien, [Winston Press, Minneapolis, 1981], p. 808).

Liturgical scholars have declared that "musical liturgy is normative" (John Gallen, S.J., National Association of Pastoral Musicians, Spring, 1978). A Mass without music, indeed any liturgy of the word without sung psalms and acclamations, lacks something intrinsic to the very idea of ritual celebration. Music is a cultural expression of a given community, with all its identifiable characteristics. It goes to the heart of what liturgy accomplishes—that the worshippers express their own style of singing praise to God.

Musical ministry began with the psalm-singing in the synagogues of the first Christians. Much later, after the conversion of western Europe, largely through the efforts of traveling Irish monks like St. Columban and his disciple, St. Gall (A.D. 900), music appeared in the form we now call "Gregorian chant." After the invention of the musical staff and notation, the newly built cathedrals of France echoed with the splendid variation of melody over the chant bass, that we now term "polyphony." By the time Netherlander masters came to compose their brilliant and complex Masses in the late 15th century for presentation in Italian Renaissance court chapels, liturgical singing became the realm of clerical experts. The unlettered people were left to roam in silence through the sacred spaces. The vernacular languages they spoke removed them further from the increasingly mysterious world of ritual music (ever in pure Latin).

This gave way to insistent demands of the Protestant Reformers like Luther, and later Wesley in England, to re-incorporate popular styles of singing and vernacular hymns into liturgy. It remained for Pope St. Pius X to make the breakthrough for Roman Catholics in his *motu proprio* on the feast of St. Cecilia (1903). He called for singing within liturgy to be restored to the use of the worshipping people "so that they may take a more active part in the offices, as they did in former times." Sixty years later, almost to the day, the Second Vatican Council restored vernacular song to the liturgy (S.C., 112-121).

The common thread in the history of service to worship by musicians is to support the people in prayer. The primary role of all those involved, from composers and publishers to the parish music director, choir member, cantors and celebrant centers on getting the assembly to respond with one voice in proclaiming God's word and work.

The roles of the music ministry vary as widely as the talents of the musicians called to pray with song and music within the assembly. Thus one could list: *composers*, without whom there could be no sung prayer; performing musicians would include the *choir* of men, women, and young people, whose voices are united by the parish *music director, organist and instrumentalists*; closer to the altar one finds the *cantor* and the *celebrant*; but the greatest performing music ministry is found right within the *congregation* itself!

The *parish music director* usually is a paid professional who has the experience as well as the knowledge of the reformed Catholic rites. Usually this person conducts the *choir* of parishioners of dif-

fering abilities, perhaps supplemented with professional singers. The task of the director is to instill in the choir a knowledge of the repertory of church music—some classical, even Latin chant and polyphony. Certainly newer material that befits the vernacularized liturgy is selected as well. This person of competence will exercise good judgment in selecting music and hymns that are good artistically, suited to the rite being celebrated, and fitting in with the pastoral needs of the assembly that gathers to worship.

The *cantor* with the *choir* play the most important role in animating the music for liturgy. The French word used for the ministry of cantor is *animateur*. The role is filled by a trained solo voice of any range who will lead the singing of responsorial psalms and acclamations. The cantor may also guide the congregation in the singing of hymns, though many places prefer to have a "leader of song" do this. The primary role of *choir* in aiding and encouraging people to sing cannot be emphasized enough. A trained organist, with an adequate choir, can produce vibrant hymn singing within worship.

Likewise, the *organist* and other *instrumentalists* also play an important, though subordinate role in music ministry. With the reformed Order of Mass there is simply less time for instrumental interludes and solo pieces within the liturgy. Virtuoso playing may be done before and after the liturgy, but generally speaking, talented instrumentalists are called on to be humble servants of choral and congregation singing.

The liturgical decrees of Vatican II make it clear that both the *celebrant* (presider) and the *congregation* have roles to fill in the ministry of music. Some priests conveniently forget that they are not freed of the duty of singing "ministerial chants," such as the prayers, prefaces, lead-ins to eucharistic acclamations, as well as the occasional singing of the eucharistic prayer itself. People who come to worship understand today that their song is an inherent right of baptized members that enables them to enter into the paschal mystery. "You are a royal priesthood," the first letter of Peter tells God's people, and therefore their united voice is a vital part of all worship. Thus the only way to get a real feeling of joy into the Sunday assembly is through the linking up of the various solo, choral and congregational voices, supported in full-throated singing by gloriously played musical instruments. This is music ministry in its fullness.

To insure that every parish has musical liturgy, it is important to see that the music director have a hand in all groups and persons that sing at the Mass, whether the repertory is folk-oriented, popular or more traditional music. The pastor and his council ought to insure that they have the right person as music director for their parish. But while they are to consult him or her in a pastoral way regarding the direction of the individual season liturgies, there must be an element of trust given to the ministers of music by the pastoral council. Choirs of any type can become too independent, providing music that is more listened to than joined in with. The parish music minister ought to have a degree in music from a college or conservatory, so that the requisite esthetic judgment will prevail in the matter of repertory and quality of performance. Music ought to be beautiful in the rites.

There should be a balance of music within the reformed rite. With the differentiation of roles within the liturgical action, a kind of symphonic movement is achieved between and among the various soloists, the choir, the assembly and the instrumentalists. "Symphonic" here is used in its root meaning of "consonance of sound," or a gathering of varying voices and sounds into a unified whole. Liturgical aptness is an important judg-

ment to be made by the parish music director. Music that ties one part of the Mass to the other, with proclamations, acclamations, psalms, hymns and prayers, has to be carefully chosen by the competent music minister.

The pastoral judgment of what kind or quality of music works best in a particular congregation falls to the music minister. Obviously this will have a consultative function among all the music ministers. It falls to the professional music minister, however, to see that preference is not generally given to what is popular over what is good art in the unfortunate least-common-denominator approach that all too often infects liturgical music in our times.

In the 1982 statement of the American Bishops' Committee on Liturgy, "Music in Catholic Worship," it is stated: "Each Christian must keep in mind that to live and worship in community often demands a personal sacrifice. Everyone must be willing to share likes and dislikes with those whose ideas and experiences may be quite unlike his or her own" (M.C.W., 17). As long as each minister of music keeps that desire to attain a beautiful and moving experience of liturgy, all can work together to make "a joyful noise unto the Lord!" This is after all the fundamental motive for being involved with music ministry. That achievement of creating beautiful sounds within the communal celebration is at the heart of what it means to "make music" within celebration.

EDWARD J. McKENNA

MUSIC, LITURGICAL
Clarification of Terms

Various terms have emerged over the centuries for designating the music employed in the church's worship. The most common of these are: church music, liturgical music, religious music and sacred music. Though often used interchangeably these terms are not synonymous. The ancient designation church music (*musica ecclesiastica*) has come to denote virtually any music employed within worship during the history of the Christian churches. Thus it is a phrase which frequently appears in titles of general introductions to the topic or historical works such as K. Fellerer's *The History of Catholic Church Music* (Baltimore, 1961). Liturgical music (*musica liturgica*) is a more recent formulation, infrequently employed in the literature before this century, which came to prominence in the 1960s as a specific term for music integral to the reformed liturgy of the Roman Catholic church after the Second Vatican Council. As the preferred term in the United States today it was incorporated into the title of the most recent episcopal document on the topic, *Liturgical Music Today* (1982). Religious music (*musica religiosa*) currently serves as a popular label for any music that is perceived to have an explicit or implicit religious theme, be that Christian rock, Hindu chants or Afro-American spirituals. Sacred music (*musica sacra*) is at once the preferred term in universal documents of the Roman Catholic church for music composed for "the celebration of divine worship" (*Musicam sacram* [1967], n. 4a) yet in common usage is a generic term for religious music, especially that which is considered art music such as J.S. Bach's *St. John Passion* (1724).

Gelineau (1964) attempted to develop a taxonomy of definitions largely based upon distinctions found in existing ecclesiastical legislation, especially in the instruction *De musica sacra* (1958). He considered religious music the broadest term, denoting "all music which expresses religious sentiment but which is not designated for use in the liturgy." More narrowly defined is sacred music which "by its inspiration, purpose and destination, or manner of use has a connection with faith." Liturgical music is more specifically that "which the Church admits, both in law and in practice, to the celebration of her official and public worship." It is Gelineau's emphasis on liturgical music as music *of* the liturgy and not merely occurring *in* the liturgy which is pivotal for an adequate understanding of this term today. In view of this emphasis liturgical music can be defined as that music which weds itself to the liturgical action, serves to reveal the full significance of the rite and, in turn, derives its full meaning from the liturgy. The ability of this term to emphasize the fundamental link between music and the liturgy recommends its usage and highlights the ambiguity of the more generic term, sacred music.

Historical Perspective

Though a significant number of historical works have been published they are for the most part histories of church music, i.e., chronologies of the music itself. The history of liturgical music, however, is the story of the interplay of the music with the rites. It requires not only an accurate chronology of musical composition but also attentiveness to: 1) the shape and implied theology of the worship which was the context for such music; 2) the physical setting for this worship; and 3) the role of the specialized musicians, ministers and assembly who enacted this worship. Corbin's work (1960) continues to be one of the best examples of such writing.

Ancient Jewish Worship. Since Judaism, like many ancient civilizations, did not make a clear distinction between singing and speaking, it is not possible to discuss music as an isolated element in their worship. The proclamatory nature of public reading, praying and preaching presumed rhythmic and melodic features which migrated toward song. Though clearly designated musicians existed in the worship of the temple, it would be misleading to limit a consideration of ancient Jewish liturgical music to a discussion of their performance. To the extent that there was audible ritual in Judaism so did that ritual possess a distinguishable lyricism.

Jewish cult was enacted in three important centers at the time of Jesus: the temple in Jerusalem, the various synagogues which arose in virtually every place that there was a Jewish community and the homes of the believers. The temple had a large staff of professional musicians drawn from the tribe of Levi. It was the musician-king David who is remembered as having appointed some of the Levites as temple musicians (1 Chr 25:1). A Levitical choir of at least twelve adult male singers and an orchestra composed of a similar number of instrumentalists served in the temple built by Herod. The psalms as well as various other poetic texts from the Bible were sung during the sacrifices which characterized this worship. The official musicians were the dominant musical force in temple worship and the people's musical participation was normally limited to the repetition of refrains. In this hierarchical institution there was a marked degree of professionalism in the worship music which tended toward art music (Werner, p. 149).

The great difference between the rituals of the temple and those of the synagogue made for similar differences in their ritual music. As a lay organization without sacrifice, the synagogue was a place where the word was studied and proclaimed and prayers were offered. The performance of this word-centered worship continuously migrated back and forth between what we would call heightened speech and song. Central in this worship at the time of Jesus was the proclamation of the *Shema*, probably by the whole assembly, and the chanting of the *Amidah* or Eighteen Benedictions by a prayer leader with responses by the assembly. Readings from the law and the prophets were also cantillated as part of this worship. There was no preappointed presider for this worship and the music-prayer leadership was taken up by various members of the congregation at the invitation of the president(s) (*archisynagogos/oi*) of the synagogue as in Acts 13:15. After the destruction of the temple professional's assumed a larger leadership role in synagogue worship. It was through their influence that the art music of Jewish cantors eventually developed. Initially, however, the musical elements of this worship were word-centered, *a cappella*, tending toward folk-song (Werner, p. 150). A similar musical style marked the various home rituals that were a central part of the Jewish worship life.

Emerging Christianity. Although early followers of Jesus continued to frequent the temple (Acts 3:1) and synagogues (Acts 13:14), it was especially in the homes of believers that a distinctive Christian cult emerged. Despite the pluralism of worship forms in emerging Christianity some elements were common. These included meal rituals, public narrations of the Jesus story, preaching, readings from letters, prayers and songs. The idealized image of an early community in Acts 2:42 presumes some of these elements. As with Jewish worship of the period it is both difficult and anachronistic to attempt hard and fast distinctions between musical and non-musical elements in early Christian worship. To the extent that any worship element included public vocalization so to the same extent did it presume what we would consider a certain degree of musicality.

Aside from the general lyricism of this emerging cult, there are some specific elements in which a marked degree of musicality is identifiable. The NT, for example, contains many remnants of what Deichgräber (1967) calls short praise-passages (Rom 16:27), God-hymns 1 Pet 1:3-5), and christological hymns Phil 2:6-11). Futhermore, a variety of lyric fragments ("Marana tha"), ejaculations ("Hosanna") and other musical allusions (e.g., Revelation 4) punctuate the NT.

It is clear that the music-prayer style of the synagogue more than that of the temple influenced emerging Christian worship. Given what we know about music-prayer leadership in the synagogue at the time of Jesus (see. J. Heinemann, *Prayer in the Talmud* [Berlin, 1977], 104-111), as well as Paul's instruction on public prayer for the Gentile community (e.g., 1 Cor 14:13-19), it is possible to suggest that early Christian "music" was prone to support and serve the word in its proclamation or elaboration and engage the community in what we might consider a relatively democratic form of lyric worship. Musical elements were vocal not instrumental, amateur not professional, and integrated not separate parts of the worship. Though some solo and even professional musical contributions occurred within the worship, they did not dominate the musical language of primitive Christian prayer. Lyricism like the other aspects of the Christian life was shaped for the common good. The integration of music and liturgy is similar to the integration of liturgy and life in this era (see F. Hahn, *The Worship of the Early Church* [Philadelphia, 1973], 32-39).

2nd-3rd Centuries. There was unmistakable continuity between these centuries and the previous period and it is not possible to distinguish music as a separate liturgical component in the Christian worship of this time. The influence of synagogal worship persisted with an emphasis on unaccompanied vocalization. This vocal lyricism pervaded the proclamation of readings, the articulation of improvised prayers and the communal responses which marked the relatively intimate worship of Christians in the house churches of this period. Parallel to this vocal emphasis was a growing objection to the employment of instruments in any part of the Christian life including worship. The virtually unanimous objection to instrumental music seems to have been more a matter of morality than liturgy (McKinnon, p. 260). The writers of this period considered instruments to be associated with sexual immorality, evil in themselves and, therefore, inappropriate for any use by Christians.

Besides continuity with the sounds and spirit of synagogue worship, Christians in this period also began to develop distinctive and distinguishable musical texts and forms. As there is general agreement that the Pauline admonition to sing psalms (Col 3:16) cannot be accepted as proof that biblical psalms were an ordinary part of Christian prayer, it is not until the late 2nd and early 3rd centuries that we have the first clear evidence that such were actually employed in Christian worship (*Acta Pauli* 7.10; Tertullian, *De Anima* 9.4). Some suggest that the psalter became a book of liturgical song in the Christian community only when the church returned to the Bible at the end of the 2nd century as a way of rejecting freely composed, heterodox hymns (B. Fischer, "Le Christ dans les psaumes," *La Maison-Dieu* 27 [1951]:88). Besides biblical psalms, newly composed non-biblical psalms or *psalmi idiotici* began to appear, such as the *Odes of Solomon*. Christian hymns in the more narrowly defined sense of newly composed works of poetry not in imitation of biblical prose, shaped into symmetrical stanzas of two or more lines, also arose at this time (e.g., Clement of Alexandria, *Ante-Nicene Fathers* 2.296). The earliest Christian hymn with music, Oxyrhynchus papyrus 1786, dates from this period (c. A.D. 300).

Despite evidence for the existence of many ministries there is no specific mention of a cantor, psalmist or singer in the Christian literature of this period. Although solo singing did exist in early Christian worship (Tertullian, *Apologeticum* 39.18), it does not appear to have yet been institutionalized and was certainly not the norm. Musical-liturgical leadership was more probably focused on engaging the community in sung prayer. Generally speaking, the whole of worship seems to have been lyrical and to the extent that this worship belonged to the entire assembly so did the music belong to them.

4th-7th Centuries. With the political triumph of Constantine in A.D. 312, the subsequent legalization and imperial adoption of Christianity, its worship and music underwent a significant transformation. Because of Constantine's conversion, Christianity rapidly changed from a church of the martyrs to an imperial church. Christian worship dramatically changed as well. No longer the prayer of an illegal, extended family gathered in house churches, Christian liturgy became the public prayer of Roman society, enacted in large basilicas, richly appointed, and performed by a growing class of professional clerics. The music underwent comparable changes.

It is from the 4th century that we have the first evidence of specially designated and commissioned cantors (Canons of Laodicea, c. A.D., 343/381 n. 15). In the following centuries the forerunner of a special school for liturgical singers (*schola cantorum*), traditionally associated with Gregory the Great (d. 604), seems to have developed in Rome, though the origins of this school are very obscure and Gregory's role in the same is dubious. This period also offers the first clear evidence of choirs of boys (*Itinerarium Egeriae*, c. A.D. 383, n. 24.5) and women (Quasten, pp. 75-87) in orthodox worship. Originally such musical specialists engaged the community in sung praise and embellished the liturgy with their art. With the decline in adult baptism and baptismal fervor which marked the worship of an earlier age, the physical and spiritual distancing of the people from the center of the cult, and the spread of Latin worship in the West to people who no longer understood the language, the specialists who led the music eventually became the specialists who performed all of the music. As specialists took over the music, women were excluded from it (e.g., Council of Auxerre, A.D. 561/605 can. 9) and by the early Middle Ages women singers disappeared from public worship in the West, while the singing of boys continued to be cultivated in the monasteries. Throughout these developments the music continued to be a vocal, word-centered art.

The growth of distinctive Christian music which began in the 2nd and 3rd centuries flourished along with Christianity in the 4th century. Christian hymnody as a specific musical genre received new impetus especially through the work of Hilary (d. 367) and Ambrose (d. 397) in the West and Ephraim (d. 373) in the East. Despite various prohibitions against employing non-biblical texts in worship (e.g. First Council of Braga, A.D. 563, can. 12), hymnody grew in popularity and found a special place in the liturgy of the hours.

The establishment of important ecclesiastical centers during this period such as Benevento, Constantinople, Milan, Metz, Rome, and Toledo influenced the shaping of new families of liturgical plainsong. From these there developed Ambrosian, Beneventan, Gallican, Greco-Byzantine, Gregorian, Mozarabic, and Old Roman chant. Though the sources for studying such plainsong date from a latter era and a consensus on the origins and relationship of these various families of chant does not exist (see the overview in G. Cattin, *Music of the Middle Ages I* [Cambridge, 1984], 21-47), this chant does testify to an expanding body of identifiable Christian music throughout the East and the West. The development of such music points to the growing complexity of Christian worship, the developing alliance between Christian liturgy and what a later age will call the fine arts, and the increased demand for professional performance. Liturgical chant, performed by liturgical specialists, is virtually the only Western music to survive from this era.

Although the beginning of this period shared the same auditory environment as the ancient world in which there was no clear distinction between music and speech, such had changed by the end of this period. Not only was there a new body of professional liturgical music, but there was a clear distinction between sung and spoken worship. The ability to make this distinction allowed for the eventual development of music-less worship in which prayer and song texts were inaudibly recited by the presider. The silent recitation of the canon appeared in the 8th century and became a fixed practice in the North by the 9th century (*Ordo Romanus* 5.58). Hereafter music could clearly be considered a separate element of the rite.

8th-11th Centuries. Constantine's establishment of a new capital at Constantinople in A.D. 330 and the subsequent shift of power to the East foreshadowed the political decline of Rome in the Early Middle Ages. Weakened by internal corruption and the barbarian invasions, Roman civil government collapsed at the end of the 5th century. Though the ecclesiastical government remained strong, its influential ties with the emperor dissolved. The dissolution of this union which had produced the Roman liturgy prepared the way for a new political and liturgical partnership with the Frankish kingdoms. Under the leadership of Pepin III (d. 768) and his son Charlemagne (d. 814), the Roman liturgy and its chants were mandated

throughout the Frankish kingdoms (*Admonitio Generalis*, A.D. 789, n. 80). This necessitated both the importation of liturgical books as well as cantors from Rome who could teach the chants in this pre-notation period. As a result both the Roman liturgy and its chants underwent significant transformation. Musically this meant the fusion of imported Roman plainsong with local Gallican chants. According to one well-accepted theory, Gregorian chant is the result of this encounter (H. Hucke, "Toward a new historical view of Gregorian Chant," JAMS 33 [1980]: 437-467.

Though important cathedral centers existed in the Frankish regions, this musical-liturgical transformation was especially centered in the monasteries. These were likewise instrumental in the development of a new architecture (Romanesque) whose tunnel vaulting was ideal for plainchant (K. Conant, *Carolingian and Romanesque Architecture*, 2nd ed. [Middlesex, 1978], p. 148). It was also in these monastic centers of professional liturgists and musicians that means for recording and notating music developed. Until this time memorization was the only way to learn a chant, for "Unless sounds are remembered by man they perish because they cannot be written down" (Isidore of Seville, *Etymologiae* effective system of signs (neumes) was developed to aid the singer in recalling a chant and by the mid-11th century the system was so accurate that music could be learned from a page and not from another person. In some respects this development was antithetical to the auditory environment of primitive Christianity, for now this singular act of orality (music) became wedded to a visual symbol system.

With the codification and gradual standardization of the chant repertoire in the West the professionals who dominated the liturgy and its music sought new outlets for their creativity. Novel forms such as the sequence and the trope developed in the 9th and 10th centuries as textual and/or musical elaborations of existing chants. The flowering of these two forms epitomized the growing tendency of worship music to develop independently from the worship and to take on a life of its own. Rather than integrating themselves into the liturgical action these innovations served as poetic commentaries and accretions to the rites, contributing to the tendency to elaborate secondary elements of the liturgy.

Parallel to this need for creative outlets among the professionals was the need for new religious songs among the people. These had been a part of Christian worship since its inception. Previously, however, the people's religious songs, performed in the same language as the liturgy, easily found a place in the church's worship which itself was more fluidly defined. With the increasing standardization of the Roman liturgy and its chants, however, especially in countries where Latin was a foreign language, there developed for the first time in Christianity what can be considered non-liturgical, religious song. Such vernacular songs were sometimes employed during Mass (e.g., after the sermon), but were not integral to the rites as were the official chants or recent accretions such as the sequence. More commonly they accompanied pilgrimages and other popular devotions and were sometimes used for religious instruction. Bede (d. 735) reported the existence of vernacular "devotional and religious songs" (*Historia Ecclesiastica* 4.24) in England where missionaries had established the Roman liturgy (H.E. 1.27) and introduced Roman chant (H.E. 2.20, 4.2). After the imposition of the Roman liturgy and chants under Charlemagne, vernacular religious song developed in the Frankish kingdoms. The *Ruf* (Germ. "call") and *Leise* (from "Kyrie eleison") are two early forms of such song dating from at least the 9th

century. It is noteworthy that evidence for such vernacular, non-liturgical, religious song comes from those times and places in which the Roman liturgy was imposed on a non-Roman culture.

Finally this era witnessed the birth of polyphony in which two lines of music sound simultaneously. In its earliest form, known as *organum*, a second line was matched note against note to an original chant line. Though the earliest forms of polyphony presumed simultaneous singing of the same text on parallel pitches, this innovation which dominated Western music in the next period eventually led to a dramatic obscuring of the text. It thus contributed to an ever widening gap between music and the ritual texts. It further reinforced the tendency to surrender Christian worship music to the professionals who were keen to explore musical possibilities that obscured the true nature of the liturgy.

The musical elaboration of some worship during this period was matched by the total disappearance of music from other worship of the time. Mass books which included chant texts as an appendix began to appear. Such books, which developed into the full missal by the 13th century, attested to the growing practice of private Mass during which the priest assumed all the ministries, reducing the chants to silent recitation, (e.g. *Udalrici Consuet. Clun.*, c. A.D. 1083, 2:30). There is evidence that Masses for the dead in the 9th century had no chant texts and apparently originated without music. It is from this period, therefore, that one can first distinguish between a sung Mass (*missa cantata*) and a read Mass (*missa lecta*).

12th-15th Centuries. T. Klauser refers to this era as the period of "Dissolution, Elaboration, Reinterpretation, Misinterpretation" (*Short History of the Western Liturgy* [New York, 1979], p. 94). This unflattering assessment underscores the basic liturgical tendencies of this period and the growing estrangement between the liturgy and its music. From the end of the 11th century, Rome did enact a series of reforms aimed at reasserting its control over the "Romano-Frankish Mass" and imposing its liturgical practice on all of Latin Christianity. During this period, as well, John XXII (d. 1334) issued one of the first authentic papal documents specifically dealing with music, *Docta sanctorum patrum* (A.D., 1324/5), which challenged the introduction of many contemporary compositional practices into the liturgical music of the day.

Despite any such reforming efforts the new musical directions announced in the previous period developed unimpeded. Most dramatic were the advances in polyphony. Two-part works (*organum duplum*) gave way to three-part (*organum triplum*) and four-part (*organum quadruplum*) works at great centers like Notre Dame. Besides the addition of further musical lines the *organa* became more florid with the chant performed very slowly in the lower voice while ornate passages were sung in the upper voice(s). What had begun as a simple ornamentation of the plainsong thus came to supercede and obscure the chant which was often reduced to an underlying drone performed on the primitive organs of the period. These melodic developments were matched by rhythmic advances such as the introduction of a repeated rhythmic pattern or mode which served as an important organizing element in 13th-century music. Such composition, marked by a new verticality and rhythmic coherence, found an architectural parallel in the Gothic buildings of the day whose characteristic luminosity was achieved by higher vaulting and undulating buttressing in rhythmic precision. Though much sacred chant was written after 1200, it faded from the musical forefront as did the monasteries which produced it. The musical leadership in polyphonic composition was taken over by the urban

cathedrals (R. Crocker, *A History of Musical Style* [New York, 1986], p. 73) where Gothic architecture also developed and flourished (see. O. Von Simson, *The Gothic Cathedral*, 3rd ed. [Princeton, 1988]).

Besides *organum* other musical advancements attested to the growing independence of music from its liturgical origins. The *clausula* was a polyphonic work based on a chant fragment whose text was usually a single, drawn out word sustained in the lower voice, such as DO-MI-NE from a setting of "Benedicamus Domine." The *conductus*, a note against note polyphonic work largely based on newly invented melodies with an original text, was the first polyphonic work employed in worship without a melodic or textual link to chant. The motet originated in the 13th century through the addition of a Latin text to the upper voice(s) of the *clausula*. Eventually a second text (Latin or French) was added. The resulting polytextuality dramatically obscured the text. Originally motet writing was used for the gradual and alleluia in the Mass and in the office responsories. The growing preference for Marian texts soon led to the motet's strong association with vespers. Like the hymns of the past, this new compositional form found a place in the more fluid liturgy of the hours rather than in the Mass.

Early polyphonic composition was confined to the changeable or proper parts of the Mass. Renewed interest in liturgical compositions in the 14th century shifted polyphonic attention to the ordinary (*Kyrie, Gloria, Credo, Sanctus* and *Agnus Dei*). One reason for this new focus on the ordinary was the awareness that a setting of the ordinary could be more useful than a proper which occurred only once a year. It is also possible that the textually stable ordinary appeared to be a more venerable part of the ritual and less open to musical manipulation or

862

expansion. It was only with the growing independence of music from the rite and the need for newer compositional territories that composers felt bold enough to tamper with these most central of chants. This is especially true of the *Sanctus* which was considered a chant of the people even as late as the 12th century (Hildebert of Lavardin, d. 1133, P.L. 171.1182). The first complete Mass setting by a single composer was *La Messe de Notre Dame* by Machaut (d. 1377). Machaut and his musical contemporaries became the first composers to achieve fame for their individual achievements: a further indication that music and its creators were assuming a life of their own independent of worship.

Ordinary people continued to develop their own devotional songs and hymns. Vernacular forms such as *cantigas* in Spain and Portugal, *cantiques* in France, carols in England, *Gleisslerlieder* in Germany and *laude* in Italy flourished. They also moved farther and farther away from the heart of the church's worship. Dwarfed by the Gothic cathedrals, separated by enormous distances from the sanctuary, excluded by worship in a foreign language, relegated to a second class position by the professionals who dominated the liturgy, ordinary people were essentially spectators to the sights and sounds of medieval worship. Their popular musical efforts often found a place in the flourishing devotions of the period and not in official worship.

16th-19th Centuries. Though the various reforms which erupted in the 16th century were not liturgical-musical at their root, the liturgy and music of the period effectively reflected the state of the church and became focal in the ensuing reforms. Convinced of the priesthood of all believers, for example, Martin Luther (d. 1546) shifted musical emphasis away from professional musicians to the congregation by using vernacular hymns and chants. Through his reforms, Luther transformed non-liturgical, religious song into liturgical music, integrating vernacular hymnody once more into the worship. Convinced that "next to the word of God ... music is the greatest gift" (Preface to Rhau's *Symphoniae iucundae* [Wittenberg, 1538]), Luther believed that returning the music to the people was a way of returning the word of God to the people. In contrast, the Swiss reformer Ulrich Zwingli (d. 1531) considered music to be an essentially secular reality with no place in worship. Though he was the most gifted musically of the Reformers, Zwingli eliminated all music from the churches in Zurich during his lifetime. John Calvin (d. 1564) held the middle ground between Luther and Zwingli. He believed that music could serve the word of God and encourage one to prayer. Though he banned polyphony from worship because it obscured the word and disliked instrumental music because it distracted one from God, Calvin did allow for monophonic singing, especially of the psalms.

Aware of the musical-liturgical abuses which to a large extent had spawned the reform (*Concilium Tridentinum* [Freiburg, 1901ff] 8:916-924), the Council of Trent emphasized the need for intelligibility and restraint in music (discussion of 10 Sept. 1562). In language reminiscent of John XXII, the 22nd session of the Council (17 Sept. 1562) issued a supplemental decree which banished from church all vocal or instrumental music which contained things "lascivious or impure." This insistence on intelligibility, however, was framed in view of the clergy who understood Latin and not the assembly. A major musical consequence of Trent was an implicit affirmation of a style of composition embodied in the work of Palestrina (d. 1594) who believed that music was to serve the text.

Though Trent did not offer support for vernacular singing during worship, the ancient tradition of popular devotional song fueled by the example of various Reformers contributed to the development of such music within the Catholic church. The first vernacular Catholic hymnal was Michael Vehe's *Ein new Gesangbuechlin geystlicher Lieder* (1537). Numerous others appeared in various German dioceses of the 16th century. Though these were largely devotional or catechetical hymns, some were integrated into the worship of the day (e.g., after the sermon). The Cantual of Mainz (1605) allowed the substitution of German hymns in place of the proper of the Mass and by the 18th century such hymns were permitted in place of the ordinary of the Mass. This phenomenon, known as the *Singmesse*, gave the people a new sense of participation though such participation was never fully integrated into the worship and was more music *in* worship than music *of* the worship. This musical mixed message was similar to the architectural emergence of the baroque church (e.g., Il Gesù in Rome) which eliminated the choir as an obstacle to the congregation's worship by moving it from the front to the back of the church. Though these buildings were very effective places for preaching and brought the community closer to the altar the people remained spectators and peripheral to the worship. So in the *Singmesse* did the community come closer to the worship while remaining musically dispensable.

Though the Reformers had emphasized vernacular, monophonic singing, they did not rule out polyphonic or Latin works which flourished in some segments of the reform. Under the influence of baroque secular composition, especially the opera, sacred music of the various traditions underwent a distinctive process of elaboration. Calvinists turned to part settings for the psalter, composers of the English reform wrote polyphonic anthems and settings of the "Service" (i.e., morning prayer, evening prayer and Holy Communion), and Lutherans composed chorale motets, chorale concerti and chorale or church cantatas culminating in the compositions of J.S. Bach (d. 1750). In the Catholic church the compositional restraint of Palestrina was abandoned. Massive choral works such as the 53 part *Missa salisburgensis* by O. Benevoli (d. 1672), instrumental church music such as the *sonata da chiesa* of A. Corelli (d. 1713), and the composition of operatic vocal works such as the *Stabat Mater* by G. Pergolesi (d. 1736) so overwhelmed the worship that "the liturgy was not only submerged under this ever-growing art but actually suppressed" (Jungmann, *Mass of the Roman Rite*, 1:149).

By the mid-18th century the churches were losing their role as musical centers in western society. Aside from the composition of organ works, music for the church declined. Though a few great religious works were written for the church (e.g., the Masses of Mozart, d. 1796), most were written for the concert hall like Beethoven's (d. 1827) *Missa Solemnis* or Brahms' (d. 1897) *Ein deutsches Requiem*. Parallel to this development of non-liturgical, sacred art-music was a new reform in the Catholic church. The Catholic "restoration" sought a return to Gregorian chant and polyphony in the style of Palestrina. One of the most celebrated proponents of this reform was the Society of St. Cecilia, whose work was sanctioned by Pius IX (*Multum ad commovendos animos*, A.D. 1870). Though effective in rejecting the elaborating effects of the Baroque and Romantic periods, this reform virtually eliminated all vernacular music from worship.

20th Century. Although there is much in the early part of this century to suggest that the musical-liturgical spirit of the 20th century was in continuity with the previous era, such continuity was challenged by new thinking early on. Shortly after the turn of the century, Pius X (d. 1914) issued a series of documents which helped to promote the active participation of the assembly and contribute to the popularity of the liturgical movement begun in the previous century. The first of these, *Tra le sollicitudini* (1903), called for the participation of the people in the worship and song of the church. Though such participation was considered only in terms of Gregorian chant, Pius X was nonetheless determinative for reaffirming the centrality of the community in worship and recognizing music as the hand aid of the liturgy. He further asserted that music was "an integral part of the solemn liturgy" (n. 1). Believing that music's principal role is to serve the liturgical text (n. 1), Pius X delineated three criteria for "sacred music": it must be holy, it must be true art, and it must be univeral (n. 2). The musical result of his work was not only a revival in Gregorian chant but the first step toward reintegrating the song of the assembly into the liturgy. In 1928 Pius XI reaffirmed the intentions of his predecessor in the apostolic constitution *Divini cultus* and emphasized that the faithful should not appear "as outsiders or as silent spectators."

Though these papal declarations forbade the use of vernacular music in worship, the long tradition for the same eventually led to Rome's reinstatement of this permission. During this century there existed in Germany, France and other countries various liturgical forms which called for sung participation in the vernacular and which, contrary to *Tra le sollicitudini*, Rome allowed. The dialogue Mass (*missa recitata*), for example, was a form of low Mass in which the people recited some of those parts taken over by the choir, first in Latin and then in the vernacular. In Germany the *Betsingmesse* was another kind of low Mass at which the people assisted with prayers and songs in the vernacular. In various places the high Mass (*missa cantata*) was also sung by the congregation both in Latin and in the vernacular. Germany received

permission for a vernacular setting of the high Mass (*deutches Hochamt*) in 1943.

In 1955 Pius XII issued *Musicae sacrae disciplina* which, in many respects, reiterated the principles of Pius X. More so than any previous document, however, this work began to distinguish between sacred music which is part of the liturgy and religious music which does not properly belong to the liturgy (n. 36). While this instruction also affirmed the traditional belief that sacred music was to serve the text, it also made great strides in emphasizing music's overall contribution to the liturgical action. During the pontificate of Pius XII the Sacred Congregation of Rites issued an additional instruction in 1958, *De musica sacra*. This work further clarified the nature of sacred music (n. 4), popular religious song (n. 9) and religious music (n. 10), a clarification which eventually shaped the taxonomy developed by Gelineau. It also offered distinctions between the read Mass (*Missa lecta*) and the sung Mass (*Massa in cantu*), the latter being divisible into the solemn Mass (*Missa solemnis*) and the sung Mass (*Missa cantata*) (n. 3). Directions about the inclusion of vernacular hymns in the read Mass led to the popular four-hymn pattern of entrance, offertory, communion and dismissal hymns.

In 1963 the Fathers of the Second Vatican Council approved *Sacrosanctum concilium*. Chapter 6 of S.C., entitled "Musica sacra," outlined the basic principles for music in the liturgy whose reform this same constitution mandated. S.C. reiterated Pius X's position that music was to serve the liturgy and form a necessary or integral part of the liturgy (n. 112). The basic reason for music's integral role in worship is the oft cited ability of music to unite with and serve the liturgical text. S.C. further recognized music's power to serve not only the word but also the ritual action (n. 112). While affirming the priority of Latin in the liturgy, S.C. allowed the use of vernacular in worship and its music.

In 1967 the Sacred Congregation of Rites issued the instruction *Musicam sacram*. Though maintaining the distinctions between the solemn, high and low Mass of *De musica sacra*, this instruction did not treat all elements of the ordinary or proper as equal and distinguished between three degrees of solemnity for the sung Mass. The first degree included singing such elements as the opening prayer, gospel acclamations and the preface (n. 29); to the second degree belonged the *Kyrie, Gloria* and *Agnus Dei* (n. 30); the third degree included the chants after the epistle, alleluia, and songs for the presentation of the gifts (n. 31). This instruction further forbade entrusting to the choir alone the entire singing of the whole ordinary and proper of the Mass to the complete exclusion of the people's participation (n. 16c). Although S.C. had noted that it was desirable that religious of both sexes be schooled in the church's music (n. 115) it was not until *De musica sacra* that women were explicitly allowed to sing in the choir. When they did so, the choir had to be located outside of the sanctuary (n. 23c).

The distinction between solemn, high and low Mass finally disappeared in the first edition of the G.I.R.M. (General Instruction on the Roman Missal, 1969) and the 1972 document of the United States bishops, *Music in Catholic Worship*, noted the outdated nature of this formulation (n. 54). M.C.W. further eliminated the distinction between the ordinary and the proper parts of the Mass (n. 51) and outlined a new priority for singing the various elements at Mass: first acclamations (nn. 53-59), processional songs (nn. 60-62), responsorial psalms (n. 63), ordinary chants (nn. 64-69), and supplementary songs (nn. 71-74). This document also moved away from the criteria articulated by Pius X (holy, good art, universal), stressing that evaluation of liturgical music required a threefold judgement: musical, liturgical and pastoral (nn. 25-41). In the process of explaining the nature of the musical judgement, M.C.W. broke with past documents by not asserting the musical priority of chant and polyphony. Rather M.C.W. noted that style and value are two distinct judgements and one must judge value within each style (n. 28). Since M.C.W. was largely focused on music in the eucharist, the United State's bishops issued a companion document, *Liturgical Music Today* (1982), which more specifically addressed the place of music within sacramental rites and the liturgy of the hours.

The Role of Music in Worship

The developments in liturgical music throughout this century, especially since the Second Vatican Council, are more than contemporary adaptations of traditional views about music in worship. Rather, they indicate a fundamental shift in understanding the meaning and purpose of music in worship. This shift is well symbolized in the growing preference for the term "liturgical" rather than "sacred" music.

From the time of the ancient Greeks there has persisted the belief that music embodies a significance or meaning apart from its usage and is capable of having a moral effect on the listener. This belief, called the doctrine of *ethos*, was shared among many ancient civilizations but found its most influential articulation in Greek philosophy. Pythagoras (d. c. 479 B.C.) is said to have discovered the numerical basis of the musical scale and thought that this numerical structure was a key to the universe which also had an arithmetic basis. In this view music was not only a means to interpret the universe but a way to affect it as well. Plato (d. 347 B.C.) elaborated this belief, teaching that music could permanently affect an individual's character. Each musical system or mode produced a specific and consistent result in the listener. The Mixolydian mode could move people to lament, the Ionian mode made one soft and lax and only the Dorian and Phrygian modes were to be employed since they were temperate and brave (*Republic* 3:398c-399d).

Although many specifics of this doctrine were rejected, even by other Greek philosophers of the day, the residue of this viewpoint persisted in the Hellenistic world. Strongly influenced by the continuation of Plato's thought in Middle and Neoplatonism, early Christian writers perpetuated the belief that music was an image of a higher order, that it had an objective and definable significance apart from its usage and that this significance had moral consequences. Thus musical forms and sounds were accepted or rejected, at least in part, because of what was perceived to be their ontological and moral significance (see R. Skeris, *Chroma Theou* [Altötting, 1976], 157-160). This is certainly part of the reason why early Christian writers rejected all instrumental music. It was not the use of the instrument but the instrument itself which was considered immoral and incapable of uniting with the harmony of all creation redeemed by Christ.

An explicit affirmation of this perspective is found in the work of the Roman philosopher Boethius (d. 524) who became the most influential authority on music in the Christian West during the Middle Ages. His *De institutione musica libri quinque* was a compilation of selections from various ancient Greek writers, many of whom held to the doctrine of *ethos*. Heavily influenced by the writing of Pythagoras and Plato, Boethius noted in the introduction to the first book of this work, "music is related not only to speculation but to morality as well." Through the work of Boethius, and to a lesser extent the monk Cassiodorus (d.

583), the belief that music embodied the essence of virtue or vice was perpetuated in the church. John XXII quoted Boethius in his *Docta sanctorum patrum* and in the spirit of Boethius condemned those musicians who did not promote devotion with their art but instead created "a sensuous atmosphere."

One effect of this implicit acceptance of the doctrine of *ethos* by the church was a tendency to legislate music as though it were an objective reality which in itself could be virtuous or immoral. For John XXII this meant banning certain dissonant intervals which were thought to be capable of weakening the soul. More recently Pius X required that music must be holy and "exclude all profanity not only in itself but also in the manner in which it is presented" (T.L.S. n. 2). Though this norm recognized the possibility of a profane performance, it also admits that music, apart from any usage, had the potential for profanity in and of itself. From this view-point the most appropriate music for worship was considered to be "sacred" (=holy) music.

A significant departure from this approach, foreshadowed in *Musicae sacrae disciplina* (nn. 34-35), was made explicit in S.C. which did not rely heavily upon abstract philosophical or theological criteria for evaluating worship music but emphasized the *function* of such music. Thus S.C. notes that it is in the wedding of music to words that music forms an integral part of the liturgy (n. 112). Even more significant is the statement that sacred music will be the more holy the more closely it is joined to the liturgical rite (n. 112). While employing the language of holiness reminiscent of Pius X, S.C. clearly moved towards a functional definition of sacred music, stressing that its holiness is not only or essentially a matter of ontology or ethics but, instead, is related to music's ability to wed itself to text and rite. This shift is akin to a change which has taken place in sacramental and liturgical theology in this century which attempts to understand sacraments not only from a philosophy of nature but also from anthropology (E. Schillebeeckx, *Eucharist* [New York, 1968], 97-101).

This tendency to balance the philosophical/aesthetical approach with an anthropological/functional approach is partly the result of recent interactions between music and the behavioral sciences. In the early part of this century a series of empirical studies on the effect of music on the human body demonstrated that most messages about music's meaning (e.g., major=happy, minor=sad) are learned (C. Heinlein, "The affective characters of the major and minor modes in music," *Journal of Comparative Psychology* 8 [1928]: 101-142). Such studies did much to challenge the belief that certain effects were inseparably wedded to certain kinds of music. Next came sociological and anthropological studies which attempted to discover how music operated in the thought and social life of a community. These studies demonstrated that music is not valued for its own sake but serves a variety of functions in human society (A. Merriam, *Anthropology of Music* [Evanston, 1964], 209-277). The encounter between anthropology and music gave rise to a new science called ethnomusicology which is concerned with the relationship between living music and culture. This science rehabilitated the concept of "folk music" and to a certain extent demonstrated that "all music is structurally as well as functionally folk music" (J. Blacking, *How Musical is Man?* [Seattle, 1973], p. xi).

This interaction between music and the behavioral sciences, like the parallel interaction between sacramental/liturgical theology and the behavioral sciences, has dramatically shifted our understanding of the nature and purpose of liturgical music. Worship music is not an independent reality only to be evaluated according to objective musical and aesthetic standards apart from particular usage. Rather, the significance of worship music is directly tied to its ministerial function (S.C., 112). M.C.W. acknowledges this reality by suggesting that liturgical music needs to be evaluated not only according to musical but also liturgical and pastoral standards (nn. 25-41).

This reintegration of the functional with the aesthetical perspective is not a repudiation of the Hellenistic influences which shaped emerging Christianity but is, instead, a recovery of our Jewish heritage. It was Judaism's influence on emerging Christian worship which stressed music's service to the word. *Logogenic* or "word-born" music (K. Sachs, *The Rise of Music in the Ancient World* [New York, 1943], p. 52) was an essential part of the Judaeo-Christian tradition, perpetuated through the centuries by the continued insistence on intelligibility in music and music's need to serve the word. One of the reasons Gregorian chant has been so highly prized by the church is precisely its ability to support and nuance the text. This reintegration of the functional (Jewish) with the aesthetical (Greek) results in the double requirement that liturgical music must be quality composition that effectively serves the rite.

Emphasis on music's function in ritual has led some to suggest that the most accurate term for such music is "Christian ritual music" ("The Music of Christian Ritual: Universa Laus Guidelines 1980, *Bulletin of Universa Laus* 30 [1980]: 5). Huijbers defines ritual music as "music whose quality is determined by, and subordinated to its integration into the liturgical action" (p. 113). While in some ways "ritual music" and "liturgical music" can be considered synonymous, the former more clearly accents the total subordination of music to the rite. It also underscores the relationship of the music to the whole of the rite and not merely to

868

the liturgical texts. One result of this emphasis is the search for new ways to categorize and prioritize musical elements in worship. Rather than simply emphasizing sung texts and prioritizing them according to the liturgical importance of the text, a ritual-music approach suggests that there are four types of ritual music: 1) music alone, 2) music wedded to a ritual action, 3) music united to a text, and 4) music wedded to a text accompanying a ritual action (E. Foley and M. McGann, *Music and the Eucharistic Prayer* [Washington, D.C., 1988], 7-15). Selecting appropriate music for worship from this perspective requires more than an understanding of what texts are considered primary and worthy of song. Instead it requires an understanding of the macro- and micro-structures of the rite in order to discern what is at the heart of the rite and, therefore, to discover how music can contribute to the fulfillment of this ritual center.

The Theological Significance of Music in Worship

As one of the "languages" of the rite, liturgical music is considered integral or necessary to worship according to the official teaching of the church. As the Universa Laus guidelines explain this teaching, "In Christian liturgy music is not indispensable but its contribution is irreplaceable." The irreplaceable nature of music's contribution to worship is a function of its special acoustic properties. These enable music to engage the assembly, reveal the divine and enable the communion between the assembly and God in ways unique to this art form. Four acoustic properties which allow music to accomplish these things are as follows.

Music Is Time Bound. Music is a temporal art which "makes time audible" (S. Langer, *Feeling and Form* [New York, 1953], p. 110). Whereas a painting or building can exist throughout the

centuries and appear almost impervious to the passage of time, music requires performance in historical time in order to exist. W. Ong contends that sound as one of the basic building blocks of music is more real or existential than any other sense object and situates us in the midst of actuality and simultaneity (*The Presence of the Word* [New Haven, 1967], pp. 111, 128). Because of this existential quality, music is able to image a God who in the Judaeo-Christian tradition intervened in time and reveals Self in human history. Furthermore, this time bound art has the ability to engage the community in the present reality of worship and signal that union with God in Christ is an existential possibility.

Music Is an Indicator of Personal Presence. Though we sometimes speak as though various animals are capable of song, music properly speaking is a human achievement and is one of the universal symbols of human civilization. Since it is a human creation, music is itself a symbol of human presence. As W. Ong asserts, an experience of "acoustic space" is an experience of inhabited space (p. 164). God in the Judaeo-Christian tradition is not only believed to be an abstract power intervening in history but a personal God who intervenes on behalf of a beloved. More often than not, this intervention in the OT took an auditory form and a preeminent image of God's presence was the Word (*dabar*). Though there are many visual images in the NT, even here there continues to be a strong emphasis on the auditory. Thus Jesus as the definitive revelation of this personal God is proclaimed to be the Word (Jn 1:1). In view of this auditory bias in God's self revelation as recorded in OT and NT, music as the most sophisticated form of sound has the capacity to symbolize the personal nature of God's self revelation (J. Wilkey, "Prolegomena to a Theology of Music," *Review and Expositor* 69

[1972]: n. 513) especially as it unites to the word.

Music Is Dynamic. Sound in general and music in specific have the ability not only to announce presence but to engage another in dialogue and communion. Because of sound's ability to resonate inside two individuals at the same time it has the capacity to strike a common chord and elicit sympathetic vibrations from those who hear. It, therefore, is dynamic in its ability to enter the world of the other and elicit a response. Thus music effectively reflects the dialogic impulse of God in the Judaeo-Christian tradition who continuously initiates dialogue with believers. This characteristic emphasizes not only God's historical intervention or personal nature but further embodies the belief that God has been and continues to be engaged in the individual and corporate life of humankind.

Music Is Intangible. The paradox of all sound phenomena including music is that sound/music is perceivable but elusive, recognizable but uncontainable. The apparently insubstantial nature of music is one of the reasons why it has symbolized the mysterious and wholly other since the dawn of creation. Music as a nondiscursive symbol is not only perceived as an insubstantial but itself seems to have an "ambivalence of content" (S. Langer, *Philosophy in a New Key*, 3rd ed. [Cambridge, 1976], p. 243). This elusiveness in form and content is part of the reason why music is so often used for communicating with the spirit world. In the Judaeo-Christian tradition music is an effective means for communicating with a God who is both present and hidden (S. Terrien, *The Elusive Presence* [San Francisco, 1978], p. 470). Furthermore, music offers itself as a powerful symbol for the Divine Self who is recognizable while remaining the unnameable "I am who I am" (Ex 3:14). Music thus enables us to encounter and know God without presuming to capture or contain the divine Self.

Summarily, music as the most refined of all sound events, reflects the characteristics of all sound phenomena to the highest degree. Music's temporality, human genesis, dynamism and apparent insubstantial nature enable it to serve as a unique symbol of God, suggesting presence without confinement, eliciting wonder without distance and enabling union which is both personal and corporate. More critical than any other characteristic for liturgy is music's capacity to wed itself to word (*dabar*) and share in its power, for music like word is both event and utterance. Music can, therefore, be understood as necessary or integral to liturgy because it has the capacity to reveal images of God and the community as well as to realize the implications of those images in a unique and irreplaceable way. Thus music has rightly been called "a sounding image of the Wisdom of God" (O. Söhngen, "Music and Theology," *Sacred Sound*, ed. J. Irwin [Chico, 1983], p. 14).

Solange Corbin, *L'Eglise á la conquête de sa musique*, Pour la musique, eds. Roland-Manuel (Paris: Gallimard, 1960). Reinhard Deichgräber, *Gotteshymnus und Christushymnus in der frühen Christenheit* (Göttingen: Vandenhoeck & Ruprecht, 1967). Karl Gustav Fellerer, ed., *Geschichte der katholischen Kirchenmusik*, 2 vols. (Kassel: Bärenreiter, 1972). Joseph Gelineau, *Voices and Instruments in Christian Worship: Principles, Laws, Applications*, trans. Clifford Howell (Collegeville: The Liturgical Press, 1964). Bernard Huijbers, *The Performing Audience: Six and a Half Essays on Music and Song in Liturgy*, 2nd rev. ed. (Phoenix: North American Liturgy Resources, 1974). James McKinnon, *The Church Fathers and Musical Instruments* (Ph. D. Dissertation, Columbia University, 1965); *Music in Early Christian Literature* (Cambridge: Cambridge University Press, 1987). Johannes Quasten, *Music and Worship in Pagan and Christian Antiquity*, trans. Boniface Ramsey (Washington, D.C.: National Association of Pastoral Musicians, 1983). Fiorenzo Romita, *Ius Musicae Liturgicae: Dissertatio Historico-Iuridica* (Rome: Edizioni Liturgiche, 1947). Erik Routley, *The Music of Christian Hymns* (Chicago: GIA Publications, 1981). Eric Werner, *The Sacred Bridge II: The Interdependence of*

Liturgy and Music in Synagogue and Church during the First Millennium (New York: Ktav Publishing House, Inc., 1984).

EDWARD FOLEY, O.F.M. Cap.

MUSIC, STYLES OF LITURGICAL

There probably has been more disagreement about the appropriateness of various styles of music for worship than any other aspect of the musical life of Christianity. Paul appears to have criticized the charismatic improvisation of songs in Corinth (1 Cor 14:13-19). Augustine vacillated on the question of music in worship before grudgingly giving his approval. Charlemagne suppressed the liturgical music of his time, replacing it with what is now called Gregorian chant. Luther made music central to worship, Zwingli forbade it, and Trent seriously debated banning all music but the chant.

With the reform of the Roman Catholic liturgy mandated by Vatican II, there has been a tremendous incease in the types and styles of music employed in worship. *Musicam sacram* (1967) addressed the question of musical style: "No kind of sacred music is prohibited from liturgical actions by the Church as long as it corresponds to the spirit of the liturgical celebration itself and the nature of its individual parts, and does not hinder the active participation of the people" (M.S., 9). This seemingly simple statement, however, raises a number of questions: 1) what is sacred music? 2) how does music correspond to the spirit of a liturgical celebration? 3) how should music respect the individual parts of worship? 4) what is the appropriate active musical participation of the people?

Liturgical Music

The term sacred music has generally been replaced in contemporary discussion by the term liturgical music. This shift in terminology helps to focus attention on the function of a musical piece rather than simply on its content. Just because a song text mentions God or a Christian event, that does not mean it is proper liturgical music. Liturgical music is functional music; through it the liturgical action is advanced. It is not a break in the action or a filler of dead space. It is integral to the very nature of the liturgy and must be rooted in the nature of the ritual itself. It finds its inspiration in the experience of liturgical prayer. It is always communal in nature, although not always in performance. The image of the believing community as a choir united in song stems from the earliest of the Church Fathers.

Often the form of liturgical music is dictated by the context in which it is to be employed. Yet it is often of a style that unites it with human cultures outside of the church, styles that have been molded and shaped into liturgical prayer. Many of the early Lutheran hymns were based on Renaissance dance tunes. The well-known American hymn, "Mother Dear, O Pray for Me," was originally a popular, secular song of the same title. Liturgical music does not exist in a cultural vacuum, but within specific times and cultures. Just as the early Christians gradually christianized the music of the ancient world, so too should each generation add to the treasury of liturgical music the best of its own time and place.

The history of musical style in the Christian churches records a fluctuation between the cultivation of diversity and the cultivation of universality. While early medieval times saw the coexistence of various styles of chant (e.g., Ambrosian, Roman, Gallic, Mozarabique), a slightly later period emphasized the symbolic unity of all churches employing Gregorian chant. In a time of great missionary expansion for the Roman church, Alexander VII instructed missionaries not to bring European styles and customs to a foreign land, but to respect the traditions of these cultures. Two hundred years later the Gregorian revival sparked by the Benedictines of Solesmes sought to introduce both uniform repertoire and uniform performance style to the Catholic church. Contemporary times emphasize the diversity of musical styles and national idioms.

Spirit of the Liturgy

The "spirit of the liturgical celebration itself" might be too easily interpreted as referring to suitability or good taste, but quite often such judgments are based on extra-liturgical considerations such as polite social or aesthetic conventions. Taste in church music is all too often a reflection of childhood familiarity or a Hollywood-inspired idea of what is spiritually evocative. But a music that is rooted in the spirit of the liturgical act does not attempt to create a religious atmosphere by manipulating emotions. Rather, it reflects, sustains and articulates on a different level the dynamics of our ritual prayer.

The spirit of Christian worship calls us to thanksgiving and unity, the joining of our hearts and minds in Christ. This is not some romantic ideal, but a real and challenging goal that can indeed be fostered through our use of music. As D. Saliers has pointed out, good church music can "bring our beliefs and emotions into a deeper harmony with Jesus Christ active and present in the world" (Saliers, p. 296). Thus our music should not be merely an expression of how we feel or think, but a way of shaping our emotions and thoughts in the way of Christ.

We come to an understanding of the spirit of our worship only through a study of the rites themselves and even more importantly through an ongoing experience of prayerful worship. It can be difficult for musicians to maintain this experience. Employed with a host of details throughout a service, their attention is easily focused more on the performance of music than on the leading of musical prayer. This is perhaps the fundamental violation of the spirit of worship for a musician. Whatever the musical style employed, it must be in keeping with the abilities and training of both the musicians and the congregation. Otherwise musical prayer is almost impossible. It must always be remembered that Christ "is present when the Church prays and sings" (S.C., 7).

Ritual Integrity

Music must also respect the "nature of the individual parts" of the liturgy. Each element of the ritual has specific functions which relate it to the whole. These functions must be respected and reinforced by the choice of music; music that obscures or works against them must be avoided. If the call for the congregation to "join with the angels and saints in our triumphant hymn of praise" is followed by a musical setting of the Sanctus that leaves the congregation standing in silence, the nature of that moment of the rite has been violated.

Liturgical planning often tends to look at the scriptural readings for the day, making musical choices based on a string of key words or phrases common to the readings. It is tempting to look at that which is different rather than that which is familiar. But in doing so, we run the very real risk of obscuring the nature of our worship. Our first concern must be those structural elements of musical worship that are fundamental to the rite itself, items such as the acclamations and the dialogue between the celebrant and congregation. The style of music employed at these moments must be one a congregation can sing repeatedly, a style that will hold up over many repetitions, a style that the people can sink their teeth into.

The absurdity of a soloist singing the Our Father within a eucharistic celebration is obvious. The more one begins to understand the nature of the individual moments of the liturgy, the more other stylistic requirements become obvious as well. If one regards the communion song as a processional song of the people, one would not ask them to read long, unfamiliar lyrics at that point. The deeper one's understanding of the prayer "alleluia" is, the less inclined one is not to sing it.

Active Participation

The "active participation of the people" must also be served by the choice of musical style. The styles employed for those parts of worship, which by nature and right belong to the people, must be styles that are singable by the congregation. This often has less to do with the style of music than it has to do with the musical training and experience of the congregation. Whole congregations have successfully learned music of a style and complexity that would be impossible for a less well-trained group. The key to the active participation of the people is a systematic and patient building up of a repertory suitable for both the congregation and the liturgy. Not only must a musical director look for music in keeping with worship; a director must also look for music that can stand the test of time, that can hold up with repeated use not just over a span of weeks but over years.

In order to guarantee the active participation of the people in song, there must be a sense of ownership of the repertoire that is fostered. A congregation must have a sense that the music employed is *their* music. Although the repertoire was somewhat limited, many American Catholics of the first half of the 20th century had this sense of ownership: Gregorian chant, "Holy God We Praise Thy Name" and "Tantum Ergo" belonged to them. With the sudden introduction of so much "new" music, some of it associated with other churches or styles considered secular or even profane by some,

there was a loss of ownership. Ownership need not be exclusive; many different groups can feel such ownership over the same music.

Another important factor in fostering the active participation of the people in song is "significance." People sing when they have a reason to sing, not just because they are told to sing. Many people who insist they never sing actually do; it is a rare person who will not join in singing "Happy Birthday," a national anthem or "Silent Night." These are songs that have meaning and significance for vast groups of people. For some people the act of singing itself is sufficient significance; for others there must be a felt need in their present situation. The act of singing must be seen as important and meaningful.

The tremendous diversity of musical styles in contemporary culture, often stratified by age and/or social class, makes the acceptance of a particular musical style by such a diverse group of people as a typical congregation somewhat difficult. The simple fact is that musical styles do represent things, such as ideas, movements or ethnic groups. Attempts in the 1960s to employ folk music in the liturgy were sometimes labeled "leftist" by those who associated it with the politics of the 1950s. Those who have attempted to retain Gregorian chant have sometimes been labeled reactionary. The question of musical style can become a divisive one, a sad irony for a church whose primary image of song is unity.

It would be a mistake, however, to assume that the symbolic nature of musical style is a negative factor. A clear example of the positive role of such symbolism can be found among American black Catholics. The development of a "black Catholic gospel" style of music has been very successful. The adoption and adaptation of a living religious musical tradition has provided a basis for both the unity of the diverse members and identification with their heritage. The adaptation of this style for use in the Catholic liturgy has often been done with great sensitivity to the dynamics of the ritual itself.

It should also be noted that the active participation of the people refers to participation in the entire liturgy, not just the musical aspects. The music employed should not hinder this participation at any level; it is not limited to the voice, but includes all aspects of emotional, mental and physical concentration on the action taking place within the assembly. The style and selection of music employed must allow for this non-vocal participation of the people. It can be fostered by the development of a repertoire that respects not only the integrity of the individual celebration, but the rhythm of the yearly cycle of the liturgical year.

The strains of "O Come, O Come Emmanuel" bring us far deeper into the Advent spirit than a lector's announcement that we are celebrating the first Sunday of Advent. Those who were steeped in the chant found many of those seasonal associations with individual chants. They can stir up the emotions of the season, the things we have learned and experienced in years past.

Any effective repertoire of church music must build on these intelligently and patiently. There is no reason that even the parts of the ordinary of the Mass and the various acclamations cannot develop these seasonal associations. But once again, the music must be of sufficient quality and depth to endure through the cycles of many years. It must be the return of a well-loved friend, not of a boring acquaintance.

Textual Consideration

Having looked at each of the criteria for kinds of church music as set forth in *Musicam sacram*, at least a brief mention must be made of the style of the song texts which are employed.

If a text is taken directly from a lectionary or sacramentary there is obviously little difficulty. Paraphrased or freely composed texts can, however, be problematic. Dropping a stanza or two of a hymn because of time considerations can distort the meaning of the text. Omitting the third verse of a trinitarian hymn often results in removing the Holy Spirit from the Trinity. If one sings only the first verse of the traditional version of "A Mighty Fortress," one is left with a somewhat strange affirmation of Satan, "on earth is not his equal."

The military imagery of some older hymns is found offensive by some; the lack of inclusive language can be offensive to others. But the two fundamental considerations in judging a song text are theological soundness and the style of the text. One must be concerned not only with what is conveyed but also how it is conveyed. A straightforward didactic style is easily ignored; a too heavily poetic text style can be obscure. The primary way that the church teaches the mysteries of the Christian faith is through images. Many of these images are conveyed through our songs and have a very real impact on people's understanding of their faith. It should always be remembered that textual considerations are as important as musical ones in the selection of church music.

Styles of Music

Bearing these considerations in mind, we can turn our attention to the vast array of styles of music that presently exist in the treasury of church music. Any group would be foolish to turn its back on almost 1500 years of tradition and art. At the same time, this treasury also includes masterpieces of art that are now museum pieces. Although no one would doubt their aesthetic value, they are no longer of real service to the contemporary worshipping community. Yet it is the task of the trained church musician to continually survey the vast resources of the past as well as the present with an eye and ear to their service to the contemporary church. What follows does not intend to be a complete history of Christian church music, but simply a survey of those areas most likely to be fruitful in the search for a contemporary repertoire of music for the Christian church.

Chant. Perhaps the greatest loss in the musical life of the church in recent years is the on-going tradition of Gregorian chant. This is music deeply rooted in Christian worship. Scholars dispute the exact age and origin of the chant; some see the bulk of the repertoire being a mere thousand years old, while others trace its roots to the music of ancient Israel. Regardless of its exact age and origin, it is a rich, fruitful tradition. It is not music of instant appeal or showmanship; it is music deeply rooted in prayer, not unlike the chant of many Eastern religions. It is music that must be slowly and carefully cultivated within a community, but that yields great fruit. The more simple chants are easily learned by an entire congregation. Perhaps the greatest perceived difficulty with the chant is the Latin language so essential to it. Yet this should cause little difficulty with the ordinary of the Mass. Through familiarity and repetition most congregations know these texts by memory. The occasional use of Latin in our worship, the language of no particular country, may also serve to remind us that the church is not bound by national or linguisitic boarders.

It should also be pointed out that a great deal of research into the chant has gone on in this century, research that has changed the way the chant had been performed. The refined and ethereal performance style of Solesmes with which most musicians are familiar has yielded to styles which are perhaps closer to the true medieval style. It is an area well worth investigation by both liturgists and musicians.

Hymnody. The question of Latin hymnody is somewhat more difficult. Simply stated, we need poets to translate these great works into new great works. Some translations already made are serviceable; a few, such as Gerard Manley Hopkins' translation of the "Adoro Te Devote," are masterpieces. The strength and beauty of these texts must not, however, be lost to us.

There is no doubt that the great polyphonic tradition of the West, from Machaut to Palestrina, is a tremendous cultural heritage. The use of this heritage in contemporary worship is nonetheless problematic. Motets and other set forms can certainly be an asset to any church musician, properly placed within the liturgy and with printed translations available for the congregation when appropriate. The greater difficulty is in the use of the great tradition of settings of the ordinary of the Mass which by necessity completely exclude the congregation's active participation. This is not to say that performance of this music is never possible within worship, but that in general it is best left to extra-liturgical events.

The Reformation saw a great increase in both the use and production of vernacular hymnody. This tradition goes back two hundred or more years before the Reformation, however; some of the earliest, extant examples of such hymnody are German translations of medieval sequences. Martin Luther, recognizing the importance of church music, authored many hymn texts himself, often translations of Latin hymnody. The melodies were often those of secular songs. The German chorale tradition, as well as the later English and American hymn tradition, were for many years the mainstay of Protestant church music. In recent years much of this tradition has been adopted by Catholic churches as well.

There are good reasons for the popularity of this tradition of song. The strophic form of the hymn does not put unreasonable musical demands on the congregation; it can be easily learned and remembered. The metrical nature of both the text and tune allows for the interchange of texts among a number of melodies of similar meter. The relative simplicity of the congregational part can be augmented by descants and harmonizations by a choir and creative accompaniment by a skilled organist. There is also a wealth of material available in the English language.

As valuable as this tradition is for all Christian churches, a few words of caution are necessary when discussing its use within Roman Catholic worship. The chorale and hymn tradition grew up within the dynamics of Protestant worship, dynamics quite different from those of the Catholic worship. Indeed, hymnody was never a significant part of Catholic eucharistic worship; hymnody belonged to the liturgy of the hours. Anyone who is familiar with the so-called "four-hymn-Mass" phenomenon has experienced the violence that hymnody can do to the proper dynamics of Catholic worship. The restriction of congregational music to the entrance, offertory, communion and recessional hymns focuses attention away from the most important dynamics of Catholic worship. This is certainly not implying that metrical hymnody has no place in Catholic eucharistic worship, but rather that the placement of such hymns within the liturgy must be done with sensitivity to the structure of the rite. According to the directives of *Musicam sacram* (29-31) these musical elements are of the lowest priority; they are certainly desirable, but only after more important structural elements of the eucharistic liturgy have been sung.

Psalmody. The tradition of chanting the psalms has a long history in Christian worship. Two main styles have come down to us, the Gregorian psalm tones and Anglican chant. Both of these styles can be useful musical forms for English prose texts. The Gregorian psalm tone is a single monophonic line which may be supported by organ accompaniment. Anglican chant is a harmonized version of the psalm tones, most often in four parts, and includes very useful and effective settings by a number of great composers including Thomas Tallis and William Byrd. Once the basic principle of applying these tones to a pointed text is understood, they can serve numerous functions within worship. One should not fall into the trap of learning a single psalm tone and forcing it to suffice in all cases.

Ethnic Music. In recent years there has been a great increase in interest in spirituals and various ethnic religious musics. There is certainly a great wealth of musical materials in these various traditions that can enrich the repertoire of any congregation. They should of course be judged by the same standards any liturgical music is judged by. Many standard hymnals contain fine examples of such music. This music can also connect us with our heritage, our history and our identity, although it should never do so in an exclusionary fashion. A number of the major Protestant hymnals publish companion volumes giving short histories of each of the hymns. These can be helpful in understanding the nature and significance of these songs. Musicians performing music of traditions other than their own should, however, take the time and effort to learn the proper performance styles of such music.

Classical Music. The mainstream tradition of Western art music has over the last four hundred years produced many musical masterpieces that are settings of liturgical texts; far fewer of them can be considered liturgical music. It is highly doubtful that anyone ever considered the

Bach *B minor Mass* or Beethoven's *Missa Solemnis* suitable for use within the eucharist. Nevertheless, one can find music from this period which is highly suited for use in worship. The orchestral Masses of this period involve the same difficulties mentioned in regard to polyphonic Masses of an earlier period. But from Bach's chorale harmonizations and Mozart's *Ave Verum Corpus* to Bruckner's motets and Stravinsky's *Ave Maria* there are many treasures that can enrich the worship of all Christians.

The Contemporary Task

Our own time has witnessed an explosion in the publication and dissemination of religious music of all types and styles. The sheer volume of music that is produced makes it difficult for the church musician to stay abreast of it all. The mass marketing of much religious music has produced a phenomenon similar to that found in the field of popular music; a song is produced, becomes a hit and fades away in a relatively short period of time. Much of the so-called folk music published for worship tends to sentimentality. Yet there is also music of lasting quality to be found both in this "folk" style and dozens of various styles. Thus, a major task of the church musician today is that of a music critic, judging and discerning both the quality of the music and its suitability for a particular worshipping community.

A sad irony of recent years is the dissolution of many church choirs with the renewed emphasis on congregational singing and the more recent increase in the use of prerecorded music in worship. The use of records or tapes for personal devotion is fine; such use should never even attempt to replace the union of individual voices joined together in praise and thanks to God.

There is a wealth of musical styles appropriate to Christian worship and available to us today. There are certainly challenges to be met but perhaps even more opportunities to take advantage of. Our song *is* our prayer. It unites our breath, our minds, our hearts and our bodies in the worship of our God.

Edward Foley, "Let us Pray. In God We Trust....," *Pastoral Music* 10, 1 (1985): 22-29. Virgil C. Funk, (ed.), *Music in Catholic Worship: The NPM Commentary* (Washington, D.C.: The Pastoral Press, 1983). Erwin Esser Nemmers, *Twenty Centuries of Catholic Church Music* (Westport, CT.: Greenwood Press, 1978). Don Saliers, "The Integrity of Sung Prayer," *Worship* 55 (1981): 290-303. Marius Schneider, "On Gregorian Chant and the Human Voice," *The World of Music* 24,3 (1982):3-21. Miriam Therese Winter, *Why Sing? Toward a Theology of Catholic Church Music* (Washington, D.C.: The Pastoral Press, 1984).

ROBERT R. GRIMES, S.J.

MUSIC, TYPES OF LITURGICAL

Liturgical music, being a type of sacred music, has been called by all the popes of the 20th century, from Pius X to John Paul II, the finest of all the arts employed in service to worship. Sacred music is the term preferred by the hierarchy in reference to musical arts applied to the liturgical rites. It implies artistic worthiness, holiness in style, and a general acceptability, or universality. These elements were not appreciably changed in the aftermath of changes that affected music after the Second Vatican Council. But the nature of liturgical music began to be more defined, as that branch of sacred music that has immediate applicability to the collective song (vernacular or Latin) of the whole assembly within the reformed rites and ceremonies.

It is clear from the *Constitution on the Sacred Liturgy* that Gregorian (Latin) chant and 16th-century polyphony of the Roman school continue to be the ideals whereby all liturgical music is judged worthy and acceptable (S.C., 112ff). However, the specialized nature of interpreting this music as found in the *Graduale Romanum* or in the highly polished polyphonic works of Palestrina has led liturgists in many countries where vernacular missals are in use to question the liturgical usefulness of much of this "treasury of sacred music." It is certain that the Gregorian Masses VIII and XVI have a popular style that lends them to singing by even large assemblies. Furthermore the Latin language as found in commonly known hymns like "Salve Regina" or "Adoro te devote" cannot be seen as impeding the song of the people. Rather it gives a true universality to worship. Nevertheless the Latin tradition has in many places barely survived as an actual method of common liturgical song. Thus the American bishops have written, "singing and playing the music of the past is a way for Catholics to stay in touch with and preserve their rich heritage" (Liturgical Music Today [L.M.T.], U.S.C.C., 1982, n. 52).

The types of liturgical music found in today's worship are quite varied. Some are very ancient, several are revivals of lost traditions, and a few are of modern invention. Music used in worship passed from the Middle Ages through the period of Renaissance and Counter-Reformation in a gradual evolution to 20th century practice. The "Order of Mass" in the Roman rite has remained relatively stable in its musical dimension. The ancient usage of litanies in the *Kyrie* of the entrance rite and in the *Agnus Dei* of the communion has been fortified in post-conciliar worship. The *Gloria* remains from its medieval foundation as an opening hymn, largely choral in its conception and execution. The *Sanctus* has been linked to eucharistic acclamations and final doxology, and has been stipulated as belonging to the congregation's role in singing.

The gospel acclamation ("Alleluia" in all seasons but Lent) and the doxology after the Lord's Prayer have been heightened in importance as songs of the assembly. The gospel acclamation, along with the entrance song (usually a psalm, litany or hymn) and the communion hymn, have a processional aspect to their performance. They are tunes wedded to text, accompanying a visible motion, usually done by the people, with cantor and choir in vigorous alliance. The re-introduction of cantor or solo singer into the Roman rite has precedent in both ancient and medieval practice. In ancient churches in Rome even today one can see the elegant *ambos* of marble and Cosmati inlay where the solo singers proclaimed the *Graduale* a millennium ago, for instance, in San Clemente or Santa Maria in Cosmedin. This in turn was a reflection of the even more venerable traditions inherited from Hebrew cantillation in the formative Christian communities of the city. In the new order of Mass (promulgated by Pope Paul VI in 1969) it is quite clear that a new type of psalm-singing is to be practiced, namely responsorial psalmody. Although not mandatory, it is quite clear that a cantor is needed for the most effective usage of this psalmody. The alternation between the solo introduction of the antiphon or refrain and the congregational repetition, together with the solo singing of the psalm verses, require a cantor. While principally featured as a response to the first reading at Sunday Masses, responsorial psalmody has found its way also into the communion rite as an effective way to utilize the communion antiphon with a corresponding psalm. As the refrain consists of a complete sentence from scripture, it is easily remembered by the congregation during the reception of communion with or without printed copy.

Metrical hymns have been adopted into common practice of reformed liturgy. The final liturgical Instruction of the pontificate of Pope Pius XII in 1958 dealt with the introduction of vernacular hymns within the traditional structure of "high Mass." It was seen in post-war Europe as a growing practice to have the people sing hymns in their own language even during the all-Latin solemn celebration. Thus "Englishing" the Mass began a couple of years before the convocation of Vatican II. Hymnals in English, such as Liturgical Press' *Our Parish Prays and Sings*, appeared at the end of the 1950s to encourage active participation of the Sunday assembly. In today's liturgy the hymn serves often as an entrance or "gathering" song. As many hymns, some from the Genevan psalter or Wesleyan provenance, others newly composed in folk-style, are actually direct paraphrases of psalms, they can function in place of responsorial psalms between scripture readings. But there is a conscious discouragement by liturgists regarding the accompaniment of the preparation of the gifts at eucharist (formerly called offertory) with hymnody. Hymns are increasingly sung with at least four verses. Thus the length of hymn-singing is considerable, and ought to be reserved for times of reflection (such as after communion) or during processions and recessions. The multitude of tunes as well as poetic texts borrowed from Protestant resources has tripled the quality and quantity of hymns in use in the American Roman rite. Just after the council the accessibility of good hymns was very limited, and in the confusion, hastily written texts and poorly composed music crept in abundance throughout the new liturgy. There arose a mistaken "four-hymn syndrome" (entrance-offertory-communion-dismissal) that dealt a blow to smoothly functioning liturgical practice. In other words, the singing of four hymns sufficed at solemn celebrations of the eucharist. With the correct understanding of the relationship of song to all the parts of the Mass, this practice is happily subsiding, and music and song are becoming part of the fabric of ritual.

Choral music has been for centuries a major element in Catholic worship. Nothing in the post-conciliar reform discourages the formation and implementation of choral song. The Roman Consilium that dealt with liturgical music issued a strong encouragement of choral practice in its well-known Instruction, *Musicam sacram* (M.S.) in 1967. Calling for "full, conscious and active" participation of the people in the celebration, the instruction notes that the role of the choir is "to ensure the proper performance of the parts which belong to it, according to the different kinds of music sung, and to encourage the active participation of the faithful in the singing." It further emphasizes that large choirs already existing in basilicas, cathedrals, monasteries and major churches, are to continue to preserve and develop "a musical heritage of inestimable value . . . retained for sacred celebrations of a more elaborate kind" (M.S., 19-20). Therefore, Latin *motets* and Mass sections from the classical masters may still be considered as having valid liturgical function. The document earlier speaks of the need to have internal participation of the laity as well as external songful responses. To hear a masterwork of sacred music performed by a refined choir in no way interrupts the flow of contemporary worship, for it calls the people to reflect on their religious heritage and to be moved by the beauty of sound during the whole celebration. The American bishops have stated that now is the time "to make realistic assessments of what place the music of (our) past can still have in the liturgies of today (L.M.T., 50).

Ministerial singing or *proclamations* have always been a type of liturgical song. The opening and closing dialogs, the preface proclamation and exhortations to respond, such as the deacon's introduction to the eucharistic acclamation, "Let us proclaim the mystery of faith," ought to be sung. Prayers of the celebrant, also known as orations, may be intoned in plainsong formulas that adapt well to the vernacular. The reintroduction of the sung eucharistic prayer is officially encouraged with "tonus simplex" editions of the four prayers appearing in the appendix of the Roman Missal. Liturgists, together with contemporary composers, have seen this relatively new type of liturgical song as enhancing the solemn prayer and giving greater musical balance to the two great liturgies (word and eucharist). Alongside the priest's chanting, the lectors and deacon may chant the scriptural pericope. Surely the concluding versicles of the chosen readings are best chanted. Where once such ministerial singing was normative, it remains an option that enhances the solemnity of the rites. The most important Easter proclamation ("Exsultet") continues to be sung in most places. In such similar services as blessings of water and oils, proclamations of praise at the end of the reconciliation rite, or prayers over the people, ministerial chants are not mere decoration, but rather are an integral mode of proclaiming the mystery.

This is especially true in the rites of Christian initiation and other sacraments. The rite of baptizing children calls for sung dialogs, litanies and hymns. Hymns that befit the rite of election and scrutinies during the adult initiation (R.C.I.A.) become "an essential element throughout the entire prayer experience" (L.M.T., 25). Communal celebrations of reconciliation in their various forms require song in praise of God's mercy. A special effort to find suitable hymns and acclamations for weddings is the job of every pastor and church musician.

Scholars of the history of church music such as Johannes Quasten have studied all types of music used in worship. From pre-Christian times, flutes, harps and drums have accompanied the chanting of priests and vestal virgins. Music even accompanied the human sacrifices of antiquity: Plutarch stated that loud instrumental music was used to cover the screams of children offered to Saturn at Carthage (Quasten: *Music and Worship in Pagan and Christian Antiquity*). Thus there has been in Christian worship a certain historical hesitancy regarding the use of musical instruments in worship. The medieval pope, John XXII, railed against "dissonant" part-singing in church, and the early Cistercians forbade organ playing in the monastery. Yet the Roman rite has preferred the moderate path: never forbidding instrumental music as such, but preferring certain instrumental types, such as stringed instruments and organs, over percussion and brass. The admission of the guitar and piano as liturgical instruments is very recent, only post-conciliar. While brass and timpani are used in church for solemn occasions, their usage is at the periphery of liturgy. Liturgical use of instruments ought to be in a reverent context.

Joseph Gelineau wrote some years ago that music can be considered liturgical when the church recognizes in it a prayerful spirit. (Gelineau: *Chant et musique dans le culte chretien*). When people are comfortable enough to pray in and through the music that music is deemed liturgical. For years, the official liturgical music was coextensive with what today we term "sacred music," Latin chant or settings of the Latin Ordinary for polyphonic choir. Certain types of religious music were always seen as concert pieces. These would be oratorios or lengthy Mass-settings for chorus and orchestra (such as Beethoven's *Missa Solemnis*). In the last century much music was written for the organ intended as accompanying the priest's softly read "low Mass." Length, size and forces required to perform the music were more determinant of the liturgical appropriateness than any given style.

Pope St. Pius X rectified much by insisting that liturgical music be inclined toward encouraging people to participate actively in the liturgy, rather than giving a feeling of being in the concert hall or opera house. He called on composers to respect the specialness of worship, even in the manner of their composing. "Holiness" has become the norm for judging the appropriateness of music within worship for most of this century. The conciliar reform did nothing to replace that norm, but rather heightened and expanded it to include music from the vernacular traditions or national vogues. Still the liturgical text, whether proper to the feast or part of the ordinary of the rite, remains the central point in wedding the melody to worship, in becoming the people's prayer. Conversely, music that is truly secular can never be thought liturgical. Musical instruments are accessories to the vocal praise of God by his people.

From the time of the earliest Christian Jews, liturgical music has been heard in the gentle cantillation of psalms and scriptural songs (such as in Phil 2:6-11), inspired prayers, and melismatic "Hallels." It developed into the "jubilus" of Alleluias and other acclamations in the Gallican churches, and longer poetical "sequences" in medieval England. Before the notation of music made Gregorian chant possible, there were orally preserved chant traditions in the earliest Celtic liturgies, as preserved in the 7th-century Bangor antiphony and Stowe missal that show a rich variety in its unique distribution of psalmody, with a marvelous vein of hymnody (such as "Sancti venite," the oldest known eucharistic hymn). These monks from Scotland and Ireland were "great travelers and ardent lovers of liturgy, indefatigable in collecting every book on the subject, copying, retouching and sometimes adding a formula here and a rite there" (New Grove Dictionary of Music and Musicians, Vol. 11, Macmillan, London, 1980). With their patchwork collection of liturgical songs and harps strung on their backs, from Luxeuil (France), St. Gall (Switzerland) and Bobbio (Italy), the Celtic pilgrims enriched the Roman rite with a lilting treasury of sacred music in its darkest hours. There is no doubt some of it survived in our recorded notes of plainchant.

With the purifications that church music has undergone in the Council of Trent and recently in Vatican II, liturgical music in our times is both sacred and relevant to contemporary people at prayer. Its forms and formulae have varied greatly over the ages, yet there remains a consistency of purpose that can be traced from the earliest canticles to the latest creations in modern harmony. Through it all, however, runs the prevailing type of ecclesiastical *modality*. The ancient scales that marked the first notations of church singing have prevailed, through Palestrina and Tallis, to be heard today in the sacred compositions of Hindemith, Vaughan Williams and Britten, of the Canadian Willan and the American Woollen, or in the Appalachian folk carol, "I Wonder As I Wander." North America has a fine tradition of ecclesiastical song-writing reflected in the unprecedented outpouring of new songs and scriptural paraphrases since the post-conciliar era began in 1964. Whether it be in a tune that has taken universal roots in English, such as "Gift of Finest Wheat" (Omer Westendorf and Robert Kreutz), or the continuation of "Roman school" polyphony in the works of Domenico Bartolucci (Sistine Choir director), Catholic liturgical music finds its truest voice in the flow of the modes of plainsong. This "musica perennis" is no mythical music of the spheres, but the perfect melody of Christ praising his Father in the voice of his singing people.

Instruction of the Congregation of Rites on Music in the Liturgy *Musicam Sacram* (Washington, DC: United States Catholic Conference, March 5, 1967). Bishops' Committee on the Liturgy, "Liturgical Music Today" (Washington, DC: U.S.C.C., 1982). Johannes Quasten, "Music and Worship in Pagan and Christian Antiquity" (Washington, D.C.: National Association of Pastoral Musicians, 1983). Joseph Gelineau, S.J., "Chant et musique dans le culte chrétien," (Paris: Editions Fleurus, 1962). *Encyclopedia della Musica.* Vol. 4, (Milano: Rizzoli Editore 1972). *New Grove Dictionary of Music and Musicians,* Vols., 4, 11, Edited by Stanley Sadie (London: Macmillan Co., 1980).

EDWARD J. McKENNA

MYSTAGOGY

The term mystagogy means the interpretation of mystery. The earliest allusion to be found in early Greek refers to someone, a mystagogue, who initiates neophytes into the Elusinian mysteries. It later becomes associated with the teaching of mysteries found in secret religions. In the early Christian tradition (circa late 2nd century), the *Katecheseis Mystagogikai* refers to the post-baptismal catechesis delivered to the neophytes during the "week of white robes." This period of instruction lasted five to seven days, depending on local custom, during Easter week. The purpose of the mystagogical catechesis was to explain to the newly baptized the spiritual and theological significance of the various signs, symbols and gestures of the initiation rites that they had experienced on Holy Saturday night.

There are few intact or complete mystagogical instructions before the 3rd century. The reason for this can only be surmised. What is clear, however, is that by the time of the early Church Fathers there was an established pattern, which was more or less universal, for initiation into the Christian community. The final movement of this structure was a period of post-baptismal catechesis. While sacramental initiation was celebrated during the Easter vigil, catechetical initiation continued for at least another week.

It is perhaps owing to the growing political tolerance toward the early Christian community, coupled with an ever-increasing number of converts, that we have complete and intact procatecheses and catecheses from the 3rd to the 5th centuries. The primary sources are: Cyril of Jerusalem (though there is some debate as to the authenticity of his mystagogies, with some scholars attributing them to Cyril's successor, John), Theodore of Mopsuestia, Ambrose, John Chrysostom, and Augustine. The baptismal sermons of these Fathers reflect some of the richest sources of sacramental theology during the patristic period. The style is most often extemporaneous, with a scribe taking dictation, combining a commentary upon the various symbols of the rite itself with scriptural exegesis. Most often the tone of the mystagogies are poetic and lyrical, though at times they can be logically inconsistent, soporific (for example, Cyril chides his listeners to remain awake) and long-winded (Ambrose complains of losing his voice).

Since the nascent Christian community was essentially a secret sect religion, some period of post-baptismal instruction was necessary. Consequently, the catechumens were allowed to attend only the Mass of the catechumens (today, the liturgy of the word), being dismissed after the homily. They would, therefore, not have participated in the full sacramental life of the community before their baptism. A practical function of the *mystagogia* was to articulate the meaning of these sacraments so that the newly baptized could enter more fully in spirit and understanding into the worship-life of their community.

For the most part, the patristic mystagogues reserved any discourse on the sacraments until after the catechumens had experienced the initiation ceremony first-hand (exceptions to this are Theodore of Mopsuestia and John Chrysostom who explain to the elect the meaning of baptism). Yet, to ascribe this practice simply to the discipline of secrecy would miss a crucial understanding of mystagogy. The Church Fathers were not so much concerned with the initiation sacraments as mysterious; rather with the mystery that the initiated experienced in the sacraments. As Cyril of Jerusalem points out in the preamble to his first mystagogical discourse, "It has long been my wish, true-born and long-desired children of the church, to discourse to you upon these spiritual mysteries. On the principle, however, that seeing is believing, I delayed until the present occasion..." (Riley, 171). When the catechumens gather on the paschal night, they were unprepared for what they were about to experience. While they knew the purpose of their assembly, they knew not the form it would take. It was the general belief that in the baptismal experience the neophyte had participated in the paschal mystery of Jesus Christ, the significance of which lies beyond the understanding of the newly baptized, but which needs none the less to be articulated.

The structure of the mystagogical preachings is a step-by-step analysis and explanation of each symbol and gesture of the baptismal rite intertwined with scriptural commentary. In his explanation of the water font, for example, Cyril of Jerusalem will speak of the waters of creation, the exodus and passage through the Red Sea, allusions to Second Kings and the Song of Songs, culminating in the Lord's baptism as a harbinger of his resurrection from the dead, his descent into the "nether world" and ascension into heaven. It is clear, however, that this is not an artificial ordering, i.e., the Easter vigil will be explained in the pattern that it was experienced. Rather, the events of Holy Saturday night are calculated to engage the initiand in a dynamic process that leads from death to life. The mystagogue asks the neophytes to call upon the memory of their sacra-

mental initiation and to "attend to the invisible as if it were visible" (Yarnold, 161). The rite of initiation is a representation of a much broader struggle, one of spiritual, or cosmic, proportions. From the initial confrontation of the evil one in the darkness of the night to the immersion in the water to the sharing of the eucharistic table, a foreshadowing of the heavenly banquet, the initiand is thrust into a struggle of a primordial tension: darkness and light, chaos and creation, evil and good, death and life. The patristic mystagogues perceive in the complex of baptismal symbols the watershed of salvation history, recapitulated and unfolded *in hoc tempore*. It is from this notion of participation that the Fathers draw forth an ontology of the baptismal symbols. As Theodore of Mopsuestia attests, "We are not concerned with empty symbols but reality," and he adds, "By dying and rising with Christ and being born to a new life, you come to share in the reality of the signs that attracted you" (Yarnold, 193). In continuity with Pauline death/resurrection theology, the mystagogues ascribed to the initiation ceremony a "stripping of the old man" and a "putting on of Christ." In baptism, the initiand was buried with Christ, with whom he also emerges, new, in the victory of the resurrection. The initiation ceremony is the external drama that signifies the interior transformation, *vita ex morte*, after the pattern of Christ's death and resurrection. The Fathers do not engage in a polemic that defends this substantial change, but are intent to interpret that it *is* so. The Eastern Fathers name this transformation "divinization" and the Western Fathers name it as "restoration." Both in their own traditions point to the ontological efficaciousness of the initiation sacraments.

Unlike the pedagogical catechesis during the preceding periods of inquiry, catechumenate and election, *mystagogia* cannot be described at all in terms of creedal formulas to be understood or doctrines to arm the neophytes against heresy. The pre-baptismal catecheses are concerned with communicating the central truths of the early Christian faith, creation, sin, and redemption, grounded in the understanding that the events of the OT prefigure those of the NT, and characterized by a strong emphasis on ethical teaching. By contrast, the post-baptismal catecheses are rarely so didactic. Their content, tenor and style is marked by a rhetorical ornamentation and theological splendor that is unparalleled by contemporary standards. The patristic mystagogues are given to images, metaphors and stories that reveal the significance and deeper meaning of the baptismal symbols. It is owing to the theological incisiveness of the Fathers that they are able to discern in the external complex of baptismal symbols, gestures, and signs the economy of salvation that is offered to the neophyte. It was at the culmination of this period of post-baptismal catechesis that the neophyte was incorporated as a full member into the Christian community.

For all practical purposes the formal period of mystagogy, including the term itself, disappeared from the liturgical argot, along with the early Christian pattern of initiation, during the Middle Ages. It was re-introduced into the liturgical vernacular in 1972 in *The Rite of Christian Initiation of Adults*. The modern day application of this period of catechesis does not differ, at least in understanding, from its ancient forebearer delineated above. This document intends that the mystagogical instructions should take place during the Mass on Sundays of the Easter season, culminating in the celebration of Pentecost. This final period of initiation is valued not only for the pedagogical significance it holds for the neophytes but also for the ongoing sacramental and theological education of the entire local community. Some scholars have argued that the restoration of this particular period of initiation is artificial, given that modern day Catholicism no longer bears the traits of a secret sect religion. Such an understanding, however, fails to grasp the key insight of the patristic mystagogues, an insight that is as binding today as it was in the 4th century: *mystagogia* seeks to uncover the Mystery that is encountered in the signs, symbols and gestures of the initiation rite. No matter the historical context, the condition of the neophyte is the same. The deepest significance of the baptismal event is not immediately ascertainable and requires some time of mystagogical reflection and catechesis. In a broader context, this period of catechesis is essential, not only for the newly baptized, but also for the continuing initiation of all Christians, a process which is, in fact, life-long.

Hugh Riley, *Christian Initiation: A Comparative Study* (Washington, D.C.: Catholic University of America Press, 1974). Edward Yarnold, *The Awe-Inspiring Rites of Initiation* (London: St. Paul Publications, 1981). Anne Field, O.S.B., *From Darkness to Light* (Ann Arbor: Servant Books, 1978).

JEFFREY P. BAERWALD, S.J.

MYSTERY THEOLOGY

In more than one hundred articles, letters and books from 1918-1941, Dom Odo Casel, O.S.B., clarified and defended a doctrine known as mystery theology. His purpose was to set out an explanation of the relationship between Christians and the saving activity of Christ in the sacraments, especially in the eucharistic celebration of the church. He based that doctrine on the notion of mystery (*mysterium*) and asserted that this theology, while avoiding the myriad abstractions and distinctions of Scholastic theology, was nevertheless true to the tradition of the chuch as found in the scriptures, patristic writings, and the most ancient Christian liturgies. Although serious controversy ensued, and even though today certain points are best set aside, the basic intention and effort of mystery theology, especially regarding the meaning of initiation and its relationship to the meaning of the eucharist, are recognized as significant contributions to the shift in theological method, as well as to the Liturgical Movement, in the 20th century.

Historical Context

The life of Odo (John) Casel (born Sept. 27, 1886, died March 28, 1948) extends through one of the most embattled periods in the history of the church and theology. The contributions of mystery theology, as well as its controversial nature, can be understood only by recognizing their roots in the ambience of Roman Catholic theology in general at the turn of the 20th century, as well as from within the historical and intellectual situation in Germany in particular.

With the loss of World War I and the subsequent political and economic upheaval, the mood in Germany was marked by profound disillusionment. The optimism engendered by the industrial revolution and by a philosophy which had glorified autonomous subjectivity had collapsed. Further, the theological situation, governed as it was by the web of 19th century neo-Scholastic objective categories and distinctions, was not able to respond to the anguished questions revealed in the human situation. In other words, neither official church theology, characterized by the extreme objectivity of neo-Scholastic categories nor the extreme concentration on subjectivity and individuality had proven adequate sources for addressing the human search for meaning.

The tremendous theological renewal initiated by the Catholic Tübingen School (J.S. Drey, J.A. Moehler, J.B. Hirscher,

J.E. Kuhn, F.A. Staudenmeier) was rejected and condemned, because it was wrongly associated with the name of Modernism (A. Loisy, G. Tyrrell). The rigid, hair-splitting categories of neo-Scholasticism were joined to an analogy of the church as a civil monarchy (R. Bellarmine). Consequently, ecclesiology was articulated in juridical-organizational categories, and was expressed by the notion of a *societas perfecta*. Accordingly, liturgy was understood as the manifestation or "action of the state." On the one hand, the faithful were expected to be present for the celebration of the liturgy, but on the other hand, their presence was characterized by private devotional forms of prayer. In the end, the sacraments were understood as means of grace, whose objective power was understood as an a-personal, instrumental cause which guaranteed the communication of divine grace as the "effect" in the soul. The intrinsic relation between the activity of Christ and the faith of the participants was not articulated.

The entire controversy over mystery theology arose over what Casel believed was an answer to an individualistic piety which he saw flourishing at the beginning of the 20th century. He decried this isolationist piety which, influenced by Rationalism, had led persons to imagine that the Mystery could somehow be possessed by one's own effort and without relationship to the public, social worship of the church. Casel developed the doctrine of the mysteries (*Mysterienlehre*) to address that individual-centered piety. The doctrine appears most clearly in his book, *The Mysteries of Christian Worship*, and in an extensive article, "*Mysteriengegenwart*" (Presence of the Mysteries).

According to Casel, the Mystery means "three things and one." First, the Mystery is God, as the infinitely Other and Holy One, to whom no person may draw near and live. Second, the union of the Word of God and human nature in the person of Jesus of Nazareth has given the notion mystery a new and deepened meaning. The incarnation, passion, death and resurrection have manifested the glory of God in Jesus the Christ; therefore, this saving pattern is not merely a teaching, but Christ's saving acts. Third, Christians meet the person of Christ, his saving deeds, the working of his grace, in the sacraments, first in the sacrament of initiation and especially thereafter in the celebration of the eucharist. Casel supported this mystery theology (a) by his reading of Rom 6, 1-11, (b) by constant citations from patristic writings, and (c) by a linguistic analogy to the Hellenistic mystery cults.

Casel might well be termed a mystical theologian whom we now recognize to have been a pioneer both in moving beyond the Scholastic method in theology, as well as by participating in the "return to the sources" of the early church and patristic writings. However, in articulating the three-fold content of mystery, Casel moved beyond the formal doctrine of the church regarding the relation of Christians to the saving activity of Christ as contained in Scholastic theology, and especially as expressed at the Council of Trent, Session XXII, Sept. 17, 1562: "For the Victim [Christ] is one and the same, the same [Victim] now offering by the ministry of the priests, who then offered himself on the Cross, the manner alone of the offering being different. The *fruits* indeed of which oblation, of the bloody one ... *are received.*"

However, from Casel's reading of the tradition, the Christian not only receives the *fruits* or effects of the saving activity of Christ, which is certainly true, according to the teaching of Trent; the Christian, Casel maintained, really encounters Christ in his saving activity in and through the liturgical activity of the church. To substantiate this claim, he repeatedly referred to St. Leo the Great: "What was visible in the Lord has passed over into the mysteries" (Sermon 74,2), and to St. Ambrose: "I find you [Christ] in your mysteries" (*Apologia prophetae David*, 58). In any case, it was to this assertion, beyond the teaching of Trent, to which he and his confreres at the abbey of Maria Laach addressed themselves, and to which others reacted negatively.

Fundamentally, mystery theology was the locus of several points of controversy. What is the relationship between what Christians do in the celebration of the sacraments and Hellenistic mystery cults? What is really present in the liturgy? Is the saving activity of Christ simply historically in the past, or is it suprahistorical? Is the person of the Lord present alone, or the Lord with his saving acts? Is the saving activity of the cross present, or the saving activity of the Lord's entire life? How is the saving activity of the Lord rendered present?

Casel argued that it is not simply grace as the fruit or effect of the redemption which is present in the liturgy (*Kultmysterium*), but the redeeming acts themselves; the effect of grace flows from these saving acts. He justified his claim by saying that the real presence of Christ's redeeming acts must not be limited to a short period in Palestine; persons must share in them. That is, the person and saving acts of the Lord must be made contemporaneous in some way with all generations of Christians, since salvation can be effected only according to the economy (pattern) established by Christ as known in the scriptures and tradition. Therefore, this implies that the death and resurrection of the Savior must be made present in the action of the liturgy itself. Otherwise, no real participation by Christians can take place.

This position, according to Casel, was not simply a retrieval of the tradition, a value in itself; it provided for a response to alienation by positing the co-activity of the members of the body of Christ in the offering of the sacrifice of praise.

Casel found his strongest support for the logic of his mystery theology in Rom 6: 1-11. Here Paul asserts that in baptism, the Christian dies to sin with Christ and rises with him *now* to new life. Casel claimed that in baptism we have a sacrament, a liturgical-mystery (*Kultmysterium*) in which the death and resurrection of Christ are re-actualized in order that the Christian may realize justification (being set in right-relation to God) by union with the Savior. So, unless that saving act of the Lord is somehow re-presented, how can anyone die together with Christ?

Casel's use of words is crucial. He uses verbs like *gegenwärtigsetzen* and *vergegenwärtigen* which mean to re-present or make present, and not *darstellen* which means to exhibit, as if the object is outside of the situation.

Method

Casel invoked the NT far more frequently than the OT to support his doctrine of the mysteries, and cited the letters of Paul, especially Romans, Ephesians, and Colossians. For Casel, Romans 6 makes Paul a major exponent of mystery theology. Casel's use of Romans 6 reveals his three-pronged method: (1) the manner of interpreting scripture, (2) the use of the patristic writings, and (3) the use of the Hellenistic mystery cults as a framework within which to articulate the meaning of Christian liturgical activity.

Use of Scripture

Casel's scriptural method consisted generally in the use of Dom Simon Striker's exegesis of Romans 6, where Paul speaks of a death and resurrection. A synthesis of Striker's exegesis follows: (1) The destiny of Christians unfolds in a manner parallel to the destiny of Christ. Christ is dead and risen and lives for God. Likewise, Christians are dead to sin and risen to that new life, and must, therefore, walk in the newness of that life. (2) The destiny of the baptized does not unfold exactly in a parallel manner to that of Christ. The baptized do not die as Christ died, but with Christ. Therefore, the baptized die neither along side Christ nor after him. (3) The baptized die with Christ because they die *in* Christ, that is, in the death of Christ. The death and resurrection of the baptized is a participation in the death and resurrection of Christ. (4) The death of the baptized is realized in the *homoioma* (*Gleichbild*, reproduction) of the death of Christ. (5) Since the resurrection is inseparably bound to the death of Christ, the baptized participate infallibly in the resurrection of Christ as well. Nevertheless, Christ does not at first make the baptized participate indirectly in his life as well as his death. The baptized are inserted first into the death of Christ in order to be thereby inserted into his life. (6) It is only by faith that we have the certitude of the reality of the new life which is received in baptism.

Obviously, the meaning of v. 5 is crucial: "For if we have been united with him in a death *like* his, we shall certainly be united with him in a resurrection *like* his." Therein lies the word *homoioma*. Casel, following Striker, gave that verse the following meaning: in fact, we have become one with Christ by the *reproduction* of his death, then we will also participate in the resurrection. The word *homoioma* is translated in several ways. According to Theodore Filthaut, German exegetes most often used the word *Ähnlichkeit* or resemblance. Dom Striker rejected that as too abstract. For him, *homoioma* has a concrete meaning which the word *resemblance* does not render satisfactorily. *Homoios* really means "essentially identical under another form." Striker cites Mt 22:39 as a supporting example: "The second (obligation) is *homoia* as the first."

Philologically, the word *homoioma* itself mean "a copy which is filled with the same reality as its model." Hence, Striker's translation with the word *Gleichbild* or reproduction. Baptism is, therefore, the complete copy of the death of Jesus; the death of Jesus is present in the baptismal action.

It followed for Casel that if the one death of Christ is not present in the baptismal action, Christ cannot die in the baptized and the baptized cannot die the death of Christ, but rather, Christ would have to suffer another death than the death on the cross. But, the death on the cross is present; and that death is brought so close to the baptized that they can there "die with" Christ. The baptized are crucified "with," die "with" and are buried "with" Christ. The most important act of Christ, his saving death, becomes present in baptism in such a way that the baptized acquire a participation in that act.

It seems that Casel was not interested in presenting a detailed exegetical study, but a simple explication of that text which proposed to be nothing but a direct presentation. He stated that his method was: "Let us read what is written (scripture itself) and let us understand what we have read . . . then we shall have fulfilled the duty of perfect faith." From this perspective, the true job of the theologian is to discard the weakness and foolish manner of earthly thinking, and to widen all the impasses of this imperfect form of insight in devoted expectation of true learning. The path of learning is faith, although the *pneuma* precedes the capacity to believe; this leads to *gnosis* (knowledge of God) and beyond *sophia* (God-like wisdom) to the point where one gives up the rational and falls into the delightful state of *agape* and surrender to divine revelation.

Consequently, Casel maintained that the method of scriptural interpretation must be *pneumatic*. It is not human writing, but is written out of the inspi-ration (breathing-upon) of the Holy Spirit by the will of the Father through Jesus Christ. It contains and conveys mystical plans in a symbolic manner.

Use of the Fathers

In addition to this approach to scripture, Casel marshalled a formidable host of the Fathers of the church. He believed they had used the vocabulary of the Hellenistic mystery cults, and saw in their writings an articulation of his thesis on the objective presence of the saving activity of Christ in the liturgy. To mention a few: Origen, Justin, Tertullian, Cyprian, Athanasius, Gregory of Nazianzus, Ephrem of Syria, John Chrysostom, Theodore of Mopsuestia, Augustine, Ambrose, Maximus the Confessor, Leo the Great, Bede, and Paschasius Radbertus. Casel returned to these sources because he believed that from the 9th century on, the corporate ecclesiology manifested in the NT and patristic writings had been lost. With this loss, theology concentrated on articulating the real presence of the body and blood of Christ to such an extent that the real presence of the sacrifice of Christ, as articulated by the Fathers, became buried in the rubble of the controversy over the manner of the real presence of the body and blood under the forms of bread and wine. In the Fathers, Casel saw the doctrine that salvation is obtained not by a simple application of Christ, but by a mystical and real participation in the life, death and resurrection of Christ here and now, in the time of the church. By initiation and thereafter in the celebration of the eucharist, Casel argued that the total identification of the Christian with the person of Christ comes about, and in this way, the Christian lives the life of Christ.

By joining his perceived insights from the Fathers with his use of Romans 6, Casel argued that, if for Christ death was real, that is, soul was really separated from body, then, in initiation, the Christian is inserted into the likeness, the pattern of Christ's death and suffering, and in this way truly experiences the reality of salvation. The saving activity of Christ is, therefore, objectively beyond human control, yet made available for salvation.

Understanding of Pagan Mystery Religions

Casel's constant stress on the objective presence of the saving activity of Christ was a response to the excessively anthropocentric, subjective, rationalistic concept of religion against which he was struggling. In opposition to that attitude, he insisted that Christianity was not a "religion" in that sense, but a *Mystery*.

From his study of the history of religions, Casel believed that he had found in the pagan mystery cults a *ritual type* which could lend support for his argument that the saving activity of Christ was objectively present in Christian liturgy. According to Casel's understanding, the lord of a mystery cult is a god who has entered into human misery and struggle, and made his appearance on earth and fought here, suffered, even been defeated; the whole sorrow of humanity in pain is brought together in mourning for the god who must die. But then, in some way, the god returns to life, and the god's companions and the whole of nature revive and live on. Yet, since the world is always in need of life, the manifestation of the god goes on and on in cult-worship, that is, the saving act of the god is performed over and over. Worship is, therefore, the way of making the saving act real once more.

Even though this understanding of the mystery cults has been proven inaccurate, it is understandable that Casel would have seen this language and ritual type as supportive of his thesis on the objective presence of Christ in the liturgical activity of the church.

Evaluation of Mystery Theology

(1) The mystery theology of Odo Casel is part of the over-all effort of Catholic theologians during the first decades of the 20th century to break out of a theological method which found it difficult to relate divine activity and human response. Along with such figures as R. Guardini, P. Parsch, J.A. Jungmann, K. Adam, and many others, Casel saw a return to the sources of the early church and patristic writings, not simply as the way to escape the confines of neo-Scholasticism, but as a way to address the individualism inherent in that system and the alienation which flowed from it. Hence, Casel insisted that mystery theology was not just any theological system, but rather the expression of the primordial belief of the church. From his perspective, medieval Scholasticism, as well as its expression in neo-Scholasticism, had damaged the core of the faith and had deviated from it by alleging to be the norm for theological discourse. His own and others' return to the sources was motivated by a desire for radical reform, indeed by the desire to return to language which could bear the weight of the core of Christianity.

(2) Since the appearance of mystery theology, biblical scholarship has determined that the concept of mystery used by both Paul and the Fathers of the church is rooted in the Jewish tradition, rather than in the Hellenistic mystery cults.

(3) Granting that Casel's use of the pagan mystery cults was misunderstood, and indeed that his understanding of them was itself inadequate, his purpose in drawing an analogy between them and Christian liturgy was not. He intended to move from a common understanding of pagan worship to an understanding of the content and significance of the liturgical-sacramental actions of the church. He did not intend to argue for a genetic dependency upon or derivation

of the sacraments from pagan religions. Rather, given the renewed interest in the history of religions at that time, he argued that the use of the same terminology by Paul and the Fathers indicated a fundamental analogy, not at the level of content, but in the manner of expression.

Casel found in pagan practices what he thought was an apt structure and language by which he could explain the relationship of the Christian to the "once-for-all" saving activity of Christ. Rather than the current form of mysticism which emphasized individual piety to the point of "auto-soteriology," the ancient structure seemed to be able to express the sovereign activity of God in Christ in the Christian sacraments. Needless to say, Casel knew that the moment one affirms that that dependence is at the level of content, the originality and uniqueness of the Christian revelation is compromised.

(4) Casel's primary purpose in returning to the sources, however, was to elucidate the unique mode of spiritual knowledge inherent in corporate, liturgical activity. From this starting point, the *gnosis* (knowledge of God) bestowed in the sacramental activity of the gathered church is not knowledge which leads to an escape from the world. For, given the incarnation of the Word of God in Jesus the Christ and the union of Christians with Christ, the sacraments of the church are not "mere symbols" but *real* symbols; they reveal and make present the saving activity of Christ in human history through the church.

(5) Mystery theology did not want to say that the liturgy is a mere instrument of the mediation of grace, whereby grace is understood simply as an "effect" of the once-and-for-all saving activity of Christ. Rather, Casel wanted somehow to articulate the "simultaneousness" of the liturgical-sacramental activities of the church with the "charter event" which brought the church into existence: the saving activity of Christ, which extends beyond space and time to all generations of Christians. By articulating the union of Christians with the Savior, he believed he had been able to set forth the faith of the church that the sacraments effect what they signify, that is, accomplish what they mean: salvation through union with the Savior by "imitation of his mysteries" in the liturgy of the church.

Enduring Challenge

While it is true that the perceived authority of the mystery religions has been definitively questioned, as has the thesis that Paul and the Fathers freely used Hellenistic mystery languge to posit the objective presence of the saving activity of Christ in the sacraments, the fundamental contribution of mystery theology remains a major impulse for the on-going spiritual and theological renewal of the church. In the intervening years, mystery theology could well be understood not only as an example of what David Tracy has named the "analogical imagination" in theological method, but also, and for that reason be recognized to be a major source for liturgical theology.

The contribution of mystery theology to the retrieval of the notion of the church as a living organism is certainly present in the 1945 encyclical of Pius XII, *Mystici Corporis*, and Casel himself believed that the 1947 encyclical of Pius XII, *Mediator Dei*, had vindicated the basic insights of mystery theology. Its impact is obvious in the 1963 *Constitution on the Sacred Liturgy*, promulgated by the Second Vatican Council. Further, ecumenical theology has directly considered its contents, especially with regard to the articulation of the sacramental representation of the saving act of Christ. This specific contribution addressed the incorrect notion, in Protestant circles, that Catholic theology asserts the "repe-

890

tition" of the sacrifice of the cross in the celebration of the eucharist. The regard for this corrective is evidenced by the direct reference to mystery theology in the 1952 report of the Faith and Order Commission of the World Council of Churches. Its influence is also found in the 1982 report, *Baptism, Eucharist and Ministry*.

The longing for mystery, which Casel observed during the early decades of this century, continues today. The challenge of Vatican II to address the relation and confrontation between faith and culture, that is, "of scrutinizing the signs of the times and interpreting them in the light of the Gospel" (G.S., 4), was issued by Casel and many others. The idea of considering the Mystery, the Totally Other, as manifested in Christ in and through the church, remains an enduring challenge, especially in technological cultures which devalue persons, and in which persons themselves experience alienation from self, others and God.

Casel's passion for mystagogy, that is, for the explanation of the mystery made flesh in Christ and now present in his members at worship, is richly fruitful for the contemporary effort to speak of the various modes of Christ's presence in human life. His notion of *gnosis*, Spirit-given knowledge of God in the sacramental celebrations of the church, gives support to the efforts of religious anthropologists, that is, to the articulation of the *mode of knowledge* available only in corporate, ritual activities. The *Constitution on the Sacred Liturgy* simply asserts these insights: "The liturgy does not exhaust the entire activity of the Church (9).... Nevertheless, the liturgy is the summit toward which the activity of the Church is directed; at the same time it is the fountain from which all her power flows" (10). Further, in comparing private or personal spirituality with liturgical spirituality, the constitution reads: "Popular devotions ... should be so

drawn up that they harmonize with the liturgical seasons, accord with the sacred liturgy, are in some fashion derived from it, and lead the people to it, since the liturgy by its very nature far surpasses any of them" (13).

Christo-Ecclesial Theocentrism

Casel's anthropological approach to mystagogy was grounded on the conviction that all events of grace are rooted in nature which is embraced and transformed by grace. Any other explanation of the relation of grace to the world and human existence would be a denial of the incarnation, that is, a rejection of the radical union of the Word of God and human nature in Christ.

From this perspective, Casel fixed the core and very being of Christianity in the phenomena of the liturgical-sacramental activity of the church in which the Christ-mystery is made present, and in which Christians are joined together in Christ by the power of God. This concentration on liturgical-event resisted the approach of neo-Scholasticism, with its stress upon objective divine power to the point of understanding the faithful as passive recipients of grace, an effect in the soul; further, it confronted anthropological individualism, with its stress on subjective piety to the point of denying the corporate nature of the church. In as much as the liturgical-sacramental activities are not carried out in individualistic isolation, but essentially in the context of the assembled church, Christians are drawn into a posture before God *in Christ* which cannot ignore the radically social nature of the experience of salvation.

As Arno Schilson has shown, this Christo-ecclesial theocentrism remains a challenge today. For Casel's theocentrism was not one which imagined the Totally Other God in a disjunctive relationship to human history, but one which saw humanity as oriented to God in its innermost being through the merciful gift of the incarnation. Hence, humanity finds its true salvation in a posture of adoration.

This God-language at first glance may appear similar to the dialectical theology of K. Barth, E. Brunner, and others. However, precisely because of its anthropological consideration of humanity as grounded in and oriented to God, it is best associated with the dialogical personalism of R. Guardini or the transcendental theology of K. Rahner.

By concentrating the whole reality of Christian faith on the living celebration of the liturgy and sacraments, Casel powerfully counter-acted the neo-Scholastic conceptual fragmentation of the faith into a collection of isolated truths and norms: Christian existence is oriented to God, in Christ, through the church, and therefore through the experience of Christ himself and his saving activity in the liturgy and the sacraments. Such a summary demands no specialized theological training, since it transcends all time-bound formulations of the faith, and is preserved from the burden of philosophical abstractions. In the liturgy, both learned theologian and any other Christian stand before the Mystery, intimately united to the perfect act of faith, obedience and worship of Christ, the Mystery made flesh. The dynamic kernel of Christianity is known, as in no other way, in the liturgical praxis of the church.

While it is true that mystery theology never pretended to be a complete, systematically organized account of the faith, its anthropologically grounded Christo-ecclesial theocentrism is increasingly recognized as a source for a systematic theology. Its concentrated attention to praxis is a rich source for liturgical theology, especially in the on-going effort to reform the rites as concrete expressions of the reality of faith: Christ at prayer in his members. Therein rests the ability to overcome the sometimes perceived dichotomy between word and sacrament, as well as a powerful source for recognizing the public worship of the church as a primary source for Christian moral knowledge, and the demanding ethics which bind worship and social justice.

See **Theologians, modern, and liturgical renewal**

Odo Casel, *The Mystery of Christian Worship* (Westminister, MD, 1982, German, 1932). Odo Casel, "*Glaube, Gnosis und Mysterium,"Jahrbuch für Liturgiewissenschaft* 15 (1941): 155-305. Odo Casel, "*Mysteriengegenwart,"* JLW 8 (1929): 10-224. Simon Striker, "*Der Mysteriengedanke des hl. Paulus nach Römerbrief 6. 2-11,"* *Liturgisches Leben* 1 (1943): 285-96. Theodore Filthaut, *Die Kontroverse über die Mysterienlehre* (Warendorf, 1947). B. Neunheuser, "Odo Casel in Retrospect and Prospect," Worship 50 (1976): 489-503. Arno Schilson, ausgewaelt und eingeleitet von. *Odo Casel: Mysterientheologie: Ansatz und Gestalt.* Herausgegeben vom Abt-Herwegen-Institut der Abtei Maria Laach (Regensburg: Verlag Friedrich Pustet, 1986).

THERESA F. KOERNKE, I.H.M.

N

NATIVE AMERICAN RITUAL

Vatican II opened the door for indigenous liturgy. "Even in the liturgy the Church does not wish to impose a rigid uniformity in matters which do not involve the faith or the good of the whole community. Rather does she respect and foster the various races and nations" (S.C., 37).

The council also invited all peoples to be at home in the liturgical forms that are theirs. "Mother Church earnestly desires that all the faithful should be led to that full, conscious, and active participation in liturgical celebrations which is demanded by the very nature of the liturgy..." (S.C., 14). "In the restoration and promotion of the sacred liturgy the full and active participation by all the people is the aim to be considered before all else" (*ibid*). In speaking about liturgical rites and symbols, the constitution goes on to say: "The Christian people, as far as it is possible, should be able to understand them with ease and take part in them fully, actively and as a community" (S.C., 21). These words of the council are particularly relevant to Native American peoples.

Knowing the mandate of Vatican II, and speaking in simple words, I would define ritual, as it applies to Native American peoples, as an external expression of an internal reality. Ritual, which is more clearly expressed in our Native culture as ceremony, is intimately related with the land. Our "traditional" ceremonies are founded in our myths which narrate the way we view the creation. Our ceremonies and stories show us how we are a part of the whole family of creation and of how and why people act as they do.

The spirituality of our people, which is based on and drawn from all that is mentioned above, has to deal, first of all, with the "world view" of our people, on which all ritual must be based.

World View: the Basis of Ritual

Charles Kraft (*Christianity in Culture*, 55-57) names the significance of "world view." The world view of a person, or a society, is one's basic view of reality around one's self. It touches the how and why things got to be as they are and how and why they change. It is the "theology" of the individual and society. The world view of the person judges and evaluates the values and goals of society. It is the ground for the supernatural.

World view encourages the person or society to continue or to take over situations in their experience: birth, death, illness, puberty, marriage, planting and harvest, uncertainty and elation. This is often done through ritual or ceremony, in which many people participate: some by prayer, some by trance. The person or community is provided security and support for their behavior. World view integrates, systematizes and orders a person's or society's perception of reality. It shows what reality should be like. It understands and interprets the many events of life. In all this it establishes and validates basic premises about the world and men and women's place in it. World view also relates the striving and emotions of each person to his/her perceptions of reality.

How we look at reality determines how we approach God and how we see God. It also determines how we are going to celebrate this relationship to God in our daily lives as a person or as a community or society.

In the western culture, which brought the truth about Jesus and Christianity, we see a world view of creation and the land as that of a relationship of dominance and subservience. The world view of the Native American person and society, in contrast, is that of relationship of equals. The world and all of creation is family together. Creation is not to be controlled but is and does empower us in our daily life and relationships. The sacred history of our peoples contains all the creation stories, legends of who we are as a people, where we came from, and who we are today. There are about 450 different traditions of peoples with whose sacred stories Christian spirituality and ritual has to deal. There are many teachings, in all the tribes, that are similar. How each tribe celebrates these teachings differs.

Native Ritual: Native Ceremony

For the Native person ceremonies are not occasions for display, they are a necessity. The prime reason for having a ceremony is to restore or ensure the health of an individual. The mystical spillovers from the ritual benefits the health of everyone who attends. The ritual heals the spirit as well as the body. It heals the community, drawing those in attendance together into the mystical body of the people" (Hurdy, p. 152). Hurdy's description of ceremony brings out a world view of a people who have a close relationship with the land.

Liturgy (ritual and ceremony) has to do with the expression of our selves and our way of being religious. It draws us to become who we really are in relationship to God and to each other as community. It is the external expression of our internal relationship to God and neighbor. This external expression of our internal relationship should both assist us and empower us to become who we are to be in the family of creation. In our Native ceremonies, therefore, we allow our relatives of the world to assist us. We do not use the "things" we use in our ceremonies as objects to be used. We pray in thanksgiving as with a relative who shares of self and life to empower us to become who we should be in relationship to God, to self, to community. Even when we go to gather the medicines (our prayer objects) of the people we give thanks for the life of what we have picked. We pray for the continuance of the life of the family of the sweet-grass, the tobacco, the sage and the cedar. I mention these because these are four of the medicines that I use when I pray. Every tribe has medicines that are proper to their ceremonies.

Ceremonies in our tribes are owned by certain people. The person who has the right to conduct a certain ceremony is gifted with this or that ceremony by the people because of a certain respect they have in the community. Among the Navajo, as in many of our tribes, it takes a lifetime of prayer and learning to own even one ceremony. It requires "an incredible feat of memory to hold clearly in mind to the last detail the symbols and their position, the colors and materials of the dry paintings, the equipment, the elaborate rituals, the dances, the hour long chants" (Hurdy, p. 153).

Certain people are given the right to conduct a sweat, to carry a pipe, to perform the many ceremonies of our Native American life. In all the ceremonies there are different people who have the right to do certain ceremonies that make up the total ritual. Take for example, my medicine lodge. There are certain peoples to drum and sing, certain songs to be sung. There is the *oshkabawis*, who is the helper in the ceremonies. There is the *botaweinini*, who is the fire tender. There are the teachers, the elders. Each person has special ceremonies which are proper to each thing they do.

Ritual: Our Way of Being Christian

Richard McBrien says that Christian spirituality is "the cultivation of a style of life consistent with the presence of the Spirit of the Risen Christ within us and with our status as members of the Body of Christ. Christian spirituality has to do with *our way of being Christian*, in response to the call of God issued through Jesus Christ in the power of the Holy Spirit" (*Catholicism*, vol. II, 1057f).

Western Christianity has been brought to the Native American in the western world view, and has done violence to the spirituality of the Native peoples of the Americas. The rituals that have been given to us are foreign to how we experience our view of the world. Perhaps this is why we see the great dichotomy of 80 percent of some tribes being baptized Catholics and only 5 percent living the sacramental life of the church. How can the Native peoples respond to "this call of God issued through Jesus Christ. . .?"

In the document on liturgy the council fathers clearly state that the liturgy "is made up of unchangeable elements divinely instituted, and elements subject to change. These latter not only may be changed but ought to be changed with the passage of time, if they have suffered from the intrusion of anything out of harmony with the inner nature of the liturgy or have become less suitable . . . . Christian people, as far as is possible should be able to understand them with ease and take part in them fully, actively, and as a community" (S.C., 21). The elements of Christian liturgy that can be changed need to be translated into the world view of the Native American people.

I have explained some aspects of ritual, ceremony, as it exists among our Native American peoples. This is not an exhaustive treatment of the subject. There are many different ways of existing and many possible rituals that can be drawn from the many tribes of Indian people. One example of a Christian use of Native American ceremony can be found in the Native ceremony of purification which can easily be used as the reconciliation rite in the eucharist (See, Hascall, "Native American Liturgy," in *Liturgy*, 7, 1, 1988, pp. 35-39).

Native American Ritual

Spirituality is the heart of the struggle of our Native people to be strong and proud as individuals and as a people. This spirituality is closely tied to the land and to all of creation. The land gives us strong religious experiences, which nurture and renew our experience of God and our relationships with each other. In the past we have been forced to separate from our reality what spirituality is. What was sacred to us was seen as pagan. The loss of a strong spirituality among the Native peoples can be attributed to our being alienated from the land and being put on reservations. Many have rejected their spirit ways and are now lost in the rapidly changing world. Instead of full, conscious and active participation in the rituals of the church, which the council fathers envisioned, we see alienation. Those people who try to adapt their world view to this new world view struggle in faith.

If we are to come to this "understanding with ease and taking part fully, actively, and as a community" among the Native peoples of this country, there has to be the sincere dialogue between the two world views of reality. We must search the rituals, ceremonies, myths and legends of the Native peoples and find Jesus, who is the Truth, find Christ who is already present in the ceremonies and teachings of our peoples. We must look at the sacred history of all the tribes of our peoples to see how our reality of God has taught us and led us to worship, which is the purpose of all religious ritual. We must search the ceremonial celebrations of life that are already present in the Native people's lives and draw forth the Christ who is already there.

I cannot tell what these rituals will be or who will perform these ceremonies. That is the future. What can we do today to allow the people to grow into that which the Father wants us to be?

See **Culture, liturgy and**

Charles H. Kraft, *Christianity in Culture, A Study in Dynamic Biblical Theologizing in Cross-Cultural Perspectives* (Maryknoll, New York: Orbis Books, 1979). John Major Hurdy, *American Indian Religions*. For the Millions Series (Los Angeles, CA: Sherbourne Press, Inc., 1970). John S. Hascall, O.F.M. Cap., "Native American Symbols: The Sacred Circle," *Liturgy*, Journal of the Liturgical Conference 7, 1 (1988).

JOHN S. HASCALL, O.F.M. Cap.

O

OILS, SACRED, HOUSING FOR

The housing for the sacred oils is called an "ambry"; the word comes from the Latin word for "armory." The Christian needs protection on natural levels beyond the graces asked in the seven sacraments. The oils, in the tradition of the church, symbolize the graces asked over and above the supernatural graces asked in the sacrament.

There are three oils brought to the parochial churches from the diocesan center at Eastertime. Blessed by the bishop these oils signify the universal charisms of the church for healing, consecration (chrism), and faith building (oil of the catechumens). The first is for blessing the sick and asking the healing of mind, body, spirit from God through the ministry of the church. The second is used in the consecration of priests, bishops, and the church building itself — consecration for the service of the church. The third oil is for asking at baptism for the blessing of God in the natural gifts of the neophyte so that they might be shared with the body of Christ. The three oils obviously have connection with baptism, the sacrament of the sick (the reserved eucharist), and the ambo, altar, and presidential seat (the places from which the priest and deacon are ordained to preside). So an ambry has an appropriate place of reservation near baptistry, tabernacle, or sanctuary. Since it is, however, in baptism itself that all other ministries are implied for all Christians, the ambry's most appropriate place in the church building is at the baptism entry because all Christians, nourished by Christ's sacraments, are baptized into his death, and called to share in his priesthood through ministry.

See **Architecture, liturgical**

DENNIS McNALLY, S.J.

ORDER, CHURCH

See **Church order**

ORDERS, SACRAMENT OF

This article will treat of the sacrament of orders in the Western church from a Roman Catholic perspective, and in the main the approach will be historical. It does not attempt to identify a series of periods through which to trace the history of orders. It indicates elements, questions, processes and changes that are historically important and so contribute to the understanding of the issue today. Since the ordination of women belongs to a separate article, this is not considered here even in its historical aspects.

The New Testament

The present state of scholarship demands great caution in our speaking about ordination, its meaning or its rites in the NT. The words "ordain" and "ordination" are not found there, and there is considerable disagreement about the extent to which this later Christian use may coincide with the categories of the NT and with its pattern, or varied patterns, of understanding, vocabulary and practice.

The evidence suggests that the church had both unity and differentiation from the beginning. There is equality based on baptism: equality nevertheless that requires authority, leadership; that is structured and maintained as a unity through special ministers. Ministry rather than order or status is the predominant emphasis: a mission to be accomplished, a task to be done, rather than a class to be entered or a status to be attained. These differences should not be exaggerated: ministry may well involve position, and a mission may carry with it or may require a certain personal status, and ministers may be grouped together because of the nature of their function.

Ministry does not arise merely out of sociological pressure; its necessity is found at a deeper level in the person and mission of Jesus Christ. The entire ministry is ultimately the work of God (1 Cor 12:6), the gift of Christ (Eph 4:7-12) and of the Holy Spirit (1 Cor 12:4-11; cf. Acts 20:28) in and through and for the church, the body of Christ. The most important forms of ministry can be characterized as those of leadership: preaching the gospel and founding new churches, supervising and nurturing the growth of the young churches, leading the communities as they become established. This ministry of leadership manifests itself in a variety of activities: instruction, encouragement, reproof, visitation, appointment and supervision of some ministries, and so on—all that is demanded by the task of building up the body of Christ.

Scholars are not agreed about the manner in which such Christian leaders came into being in the early church. The recent trend has been towards the view that leaders emerged or were appointed in different ways in different communities with different church orders. Is there any evidence of a rite associated with this? Rather than discuss the question simply as a NT issue, it seems best to look at it with an eye to subsequent developments.

The NT mentions the laying-on of hands on four main occasions that could be important for our consideration of the sacrament of orders (Acts 6:6; 13:3; 1 Tm 4:14; 2 Tm 1:6; and cf. 1 Tm 5:22). Scholars do not agree on the background to this Christian action, whether it was borrowed from a supposed Jewish rite of ordination or was derived from more general OT influences or was primarily a Christian introduction. Nor is there agreement that in these instances the function and the meaning of the gesture are the same.

In Acts 6:6 the seven are chosen in Jerusalem by the whole body of disciples for appointment by the apostles, who pray and lay their hands upon them. In Acts 13:1-3 Barnabas and Saul are set apart in the church at Antioch for a mission in obedience to a command of the Holy Spirit. After fasting and prayer they (the prophets and teachers? others?) lay hands on Barnabas and Saul and send them on their mission. They are understood to be sent out by the Holy Spirit (13:4). In neither of these cases do scholars agree about the function or the meaning of this imposition of hands. The second especially may have been no more than a blessing or the acknowledgment of a mandate (cf. Acts 14:26, which may interpret this rite in saying that they were commended to the grace of God for this work). One other text from Acts makes an interesting parallel. According to 14:23, Paul and Barnabas appointed elders in every church with prayer and fasting. The mention of prayer and fasting and the absence of reference to the laying-on of hands are worth noting, though it could well be that the latter is presupposed.

Although there is also disagreement as to the meaning of the imposition of hands in the two instances from the pastoral epistles (1 Tm 4:14; 2 Tm 1:6), perhaps there is a firmer consensus that it is part of what may be called with greater confidence an ordination rite. The choice of Timothy may have been made by prophetic utterance (1 Tm 1:18; 4:14; cf. Acts 13:2) and the core of the rite by which he was commissioned is presented as the laying-on of hands done by the body of presbyters and by Paul (1 Tm 4:14; 2 Tm 1:6). Probably this was done in public (cf. 2 Tm 2:2 "before many witnesses"). In or through this rite a spiritual gift, a gift of God, has been conferred. This gift is at the service of the word, strengthening Timothy to bear public witness to the gospel (2 Tm 1:8-14). He is warned "not to neglect"; he is to "rekindle" this gift of God that he has received and in fact the last two chapters of 1 Timothy envisage a broad range of responsibility for the apostolate and the community. It is a power that enables him to carry out his ministry, a charism for the office that he has received. Here we have the makings of a later explicitly "sacramental" understanding of such a rite.

No doubt these texts, partial as they are, represent different situations of time and place. They may not simply be collated in the expectation that the ensemble will provide the ordination rite of the early church or of St Paul. Scholars maintain that the pattern of ministry, its understanding and its mode of appointment or recognition, may be more varied than has been acknowledged in the past. In addition, as has been pointed out, the precise influences that led to the Christian use of the laying-on of hands are unclear and so the meaning of this action, and in some cases its role, are also unclear. It is not evident that some such form was always and everywhere used during the NT period or indeed for some time after it, nor is there any probability that all these elements were present on all occasions. But neither can it be proved from the evidence of the NT that such a form was exceptional. Elements do undoubtedly emerge from the church of the NT that will influence all later generations and that will in fact endure.

Subject to all the qualifications that have been made, the following may serve as a summary of some of the points from the NT that will be prominent also in the subsequent tradition. In the appointment of ministers to positions of leadership the whole local body of the church and yet also particular ministers or groups of ministers have an important role. The context of worship, of prayer and fasting is mentioned, suggesting a liturgical setting and referring the ministry and appointment to it to God. Hands are laid on the candidate by a group within the church and/or by such individuals as Paul and Timothy. What the church does through its corporate action or through its leaders is regarded as inspired by the Holy Spirit, and through the church's choice and the liturgical action, God provides for the church and gives a spiritual gift that in some way endures. This inter-working of God-whole church-special ministers in the appointment of ministers is to be noted, as is the religious form of prayer-fasting-liturgical rite that is part of it.

Early Developments

During the 2nd century, episcopacy, presbyterate and diaconate emerge almost everywhere as the most important ministries and form what will be the universal pattern. From the letter of Clement onwards, correspondences are noted between the Jewish structure of authority and the Christian. Ignatius of Antioch already presents the bishop as an image of the Father, and here and elsewhere bishop, presbyter and deacon are related in a variety of ways to God and to Jesus Christ. These comparisons manifest the conviction that the existence and the pattern of this ministry in the church are willed by God and mediate the authority and the power of God. Between God and the church is Jesus Christ, who came from God and from whom the power and the authority of the church originated historically. In the 2nd and 3rd centuries a consensus may not yet have emerged as to the way in which the church commissions these ministers.

Order, Ordain, Ordination. Clement of Rome and Irenaeus had employed the language of structure and function with regard to the church, but Tertullian is the first that we know to use the Latin words *ordo-ordinare-ordinatio* as part of the Christian terminology. The meaning the words have in his writings is that of the common usage of the time, but he extends this to certain Christian realities and actions, giving them a new application. He is followed closely by his fellow North African, Cyprian, and some of Cyprian's contemporaries. The terminology is still fluid at this stage and the words are not yet the technical terms that they will become later. *Ordo* for Tertullian generally denotes a certain group or class in the church and, with the adjectives *ecclesiasticus* or *sacerdotalis*, denotes at least the combined episcopacy, presbyterate and diaconate, which are thus distinguished from the *plebs* or *laici*. This *ordo* is marked by authority and function in the church. The word is thus strongly institutional. The verb *ordinare* and its noun *ordinatio* are used in a similar way. To ordain is to designate someone to some function, to install in a charge, to give a mandate. It is a juridical word, suggesting a legal act carried out by authority, and it fits well into an understanding of the church as structured in different groups distinguished by different responsibilities and powers. It conveys a markedly functional understanding of the act and its effects.

In broader usage the ordination could include the preparatory stages but in a more formal sense it was distinguished from the election of the candidate by the community. By ordination the minister is invested with his charge and with all the powers that it requires. There is strong and widespread evidence for the laying-on of hands, at least in the ordination of bishops, but it cannot be proved that this took place in every instance. However, it seems more plausible to hold that it was used also for the presbyterate and the diaconate. It may have been regarded as a sign, but not an essential one, of the intention to ordain the candidate to the particular charge. In some places the ordination of a bishop required the approval of neighboring bishops or provincial synods, thus showing concern for such ecclesial realities as the apostolic succession, the unity and communion of the churches in the universal church, and the personal and ecclesial standing of the new bishop.

Though this cluster of words conveys a primarily juridical understanding of the reality they refer to, there is also a spiritual side that is important. There is emphasis on the qualities of holiness demanded in the person to be ordained, on the acts of sanctification for which ordination grants authority and power and on the priestly nature of the order to which it gives access. The church's act of ordination is grounded on the will of God and the authority of Christ. God ordains and the church ordains, and these are in direct relation. The sanctifying mission of the church that has its origin in God and is derived through Christ is engaged, and through the act of the qualified leaders of the church the candidate is divinely empowered to sanctify. Thus while the early terminology of order and ordination is primarily juridical, from the beginning it is also spiritual and has clearly sacramental elements.

Ordination Rites. A picture that is different in some respects emerges from the *Apostolic Tradition* (written in Greek at Rome about 215 by Hippolytus). There bishop, presbyter and deacon are ordained (Hippolytus uses the word) by the bishop in a liturgical rite which has as its core the imposition of hand(s) accompanied by prayer. The bishop certainly (and probably the other ministers) was chosen by the whole community. The prayers provide a context of understanding for the ordination by referring to deeds of God in the OT or in the event of Christ and all pray for the gift of the Holy Spirit upon the candidate, indicating the tasks that the ministry involves.

Thus, by imposition of hand(s) and prayer the bishop—the qualified minister of ordination—accompanied by other bishops or other ministers and by the people, gives the church's commission. Through this ordination a gift of the Holy Spirit is communicated, a gift that is the ground of the ministry in question and that empowers the candidate for its exercise. This represents an understanding of ministry and commissioning for it for which there is evidence in the NT and which had been growing in confidence during the 2nd century.

The pattern of ordination so plainly given in Hippolytus will be followed in the later Roman rituals. The prayers will have the same general character; they will be strong in OT typology; they will continue to be addressed to the Father and to have a clearly trinitarian structure; they will have a petition for the gift of the Spirit and will set it in some relation to the tasks of the ministry and requisite qualities in the minister.

From all this there emerges the conviction that the ministry of leadership in its threefold form is a gift of God for the church, a gift foretold and prefigured in the OT, a gift that had its historical origin and was supremely manifest in Jesus Christ, a gift that God continues to make to the church through the Holy Spirit in each ordination. This is a gift to be acknowledged and proclaimed in a prayer that has a certain eucharistic quality, a gift to be prayed for humbly over the candidates. When the community of the church chooses its candidates, this is understood to be the expression or announcement of God's choice, as the rite of ordination is the act of the church through which God operates. In other words, no opposition is thought to exist between God and the church in the process and the rite of ordination. God announces and accomplishes the divine will through the church's election and its ordination; the church's action makes known and realizes God's provident gift. Through the church's act of ordination, then, the gift of the Holy Spirit is communicated to the candidate, conveying the ministry or function together with the spiritual empowerment required for its fulfilment. These are elements that later theologians will bring together in speaking of the sacrament of ordination.

Ordination rites will grow in importance and be acknowledged as the ground of these ministries. Whereas in the first two to three centuries it seems that one presided at the liturgy because of one's position as leader of the community, subsequently one is understood to preside and so to lead the community because one has been ordained.

Qualities. Five important qualities of ordination and of the ordained ministry should be noted from this period.

(a) *Christological.* Jesus, coming from God, is the *historical origin* of this authoritative ministry in the church, which therefore must always be related back to him. In his life he gave the supreme example of authentic ministry, and so he remains always the *model.* What he taught and preached must be passed on faithfully, so that the church's ministers must at all times be *faithful to Christ's gospel*. As the risen Lord he is active in the church through *his Spirit and the Spirit's gifts*. In carrying out his responsibility the minister is serving Jesus Christ, who is thus in a sense the *goal* of the ministry. This characteristic of ministers and ministry can be summed up in the phrases, "servants of Jesus Christ," "the service of Jesus Christ," understood in all their virtualities. It is much of this that is implied in the word increasingly used from the second century, "apostolic." The apostolic character of the ministry declared its authentic relationship to its historical origin in Jesus Christ, and so grounded its fidelity to him.

(b) *Pneumatological*. There is recurring reference to the role of the Holy Spirit in the provision of ministry and regular petition for the appropriate gift of the Spirit in the various rites of ordination.

(c) *Ecclesial*. The ecclesial character of ministry and ordination is particularly evident in these early centuries. Ministers are of the church and represent it, public figures of leadership in and for the community (recall the prohibition of absolute ordinations by the Council of Chalcedon), in many cases chosen by the whole people, ordained by the qualified minister of the church, the bishop, in the presence of all, and perhaps confirmed by neighboring churches. Public service in the church is the summary of the ministry.

(d) *Priestly*. As is well known, while the NT uses priestly terms both of Jesus and of the whole church, it does not do so of any Christian minister. It is only about the turn of the 2nd century that such an extension of sacerdotal vocabulary begins to be common: first of all and primarily with reference to the bishop and then more slowly and in a subordinate way of the presbyter (notably so in the Roman tradition). By the Carolingian era in the West there will be a change, and it will become more and more the practice to speak of the presbyter primarily as *sacerdos*. Involved in this change of usage there can be detected a practical and theological shift in the relationship between bishop and presbyter, to which we shall return. Priestly vocabulary was not generally extended to the deacon, and Hippolytus had said of him explicitly that he was not ordained to the priesthood. The introduction of priestly terminology and its increasingly widespread acceptance had enormous theological and practical consequences for the understanding and the exercise of the sacrament of orders.

(e) *Personal*. The one ordained is not merely a functionary but a minister of Christ and of the church, so that his call requires a full personal response: commitment to this ministry and holiness of life in imitation of Christ.

Bishops, Presbyters, Deacons. The triple pattern of episcopacy-presbyterate-diaconate takes some time to emerge and to establish itself, but it then becomes universal in the church (though the Reformation will bring some break in the West). However, the functions of these orders and the relationships between them do not remain unchanged. The bishop becomes the focus of ministry, the center of leadership; the office mediates divine authority, involving supervision or leadership by the individual bishop and on the part of the whole episcopal college (a reality of which the patristic church was strongly conscious). But the exercise of this changes considerably as the territory of the bishops' *episkope* grows. The presbyterate, for some time primarily a council to advise the bishop, becomes more diversified: individual presbyters, regularly and no longer only in the absence of the bishop, carry out many formerly episcopal functions, emerging as leaders of areas and groups of Christians, preaching, presiding over the eucharist and other liturgical functions, so that the presbyterate becomes more markedly pastoral and liturgical in character. Throughout the patristic period deacons have important pastoral and administrative tasks in addition to their liturgical functions, and it will be some time before the deacon loses his strong and distinctive role in the church to become almost exclusively a liturgical minister overshadowed by the presbyter. It is important to note of all these that the ministry has a broad scope that is not exclusively or predominantly liturgical either in its exercise or in the way it is understood.

The Middle Ages

The theological contribution of the Scholastics in the 12th and 13th centuries was influenced by changes in the practical exercise of orders that had been taking place for several centuries previously, changes that reflected a sharpening of the distinction between laity and clergy and were part of an older and broader process of clericalization. With the spread of the church and the social organization of the time, the presbyter continued to establish himself and the functions of his ministry in a more defined and more independent way vis-a-vis the bishop (and also at the expense of the deacon). In practice he became *the* priest, the minister *par excellence* of the eucharist and of other sacraments too. Decline in the popular understanding of Latin and generally in the level of popular participation in the liturgy changed the relationship between him and the people and increased the emphasis on his sacramental power. Mass celebrated by the priest alone or with a single minister began to be common. There were changes too in the Roman ritual of ordination, which now came to incorporate investiture, anointing and the *traditio instrumentorum*. The last two would become important for the Scholastic discussion of the matter of the sacrament, while all three would enhance the perception of the ordained minister

as a figure of sacred status and power. A more general change of great consequence was the gradual loss of communication and mutual influence between the churches of West and East.

The Sacrament of Orders. In the course of the 12th century "sacrament" came to be defined narrowly; orders was recognized as one of the seven sacraments, and "the sacrament of orders" became a technical term. In addition to the issues common to all the sacraments, this raised a number of particular questions. There had long been discussion about the number of orders, and this continued to be debated. The more common view emerged that there were seven orders, though there was less agreement that subdiaconate and the minor orders, recognized to be of ecclesiastical institution, were sacramental in the strict sense. The question was posed most acutely of the episcopacy, as we shall see. Theologians agreed that order was a single sacrament and not several, but they disagreed about the precise relationship between this unique sacrament and its several parts. For some, no one order had the fullness of the sacrament, which was constituted rather by all the orders taken together. However, the more common opinion was that the priesthood contained the fullness of the sacrament as being the fullness of order and that the other orders participated in this plenitude, being ordered to this single end. This view fit well into the widespread medieval way of understanding reality in terms of hierarchy, order and participation.

The Status of Episcopacy. The status of episcopacy and the relationship between it and the presbyterate were not new issues. Although in the patristic church episcopacy was commonly presented as the supreme order and the high priesthood, with the presbyterate, especially in the Roman rite of ordination, explicitly and emphatically designated as subordinate, from at least the time of St. Jerome and Ambrosiaster there had been another view. The proponents of this argued that *presbyteroi* and *episkopoi* were synonymous in the NT and maintained that bishop and presbyter were equal as priests, the difference between them being a matter of ecclesiastical institution related to authority. We have seen already the change in the way in which the term "priest" came to be applied to bishops and presbyters. Now the Scholastics posed the question: is episcopacy an order? Among theologians there developed a strong tendency to define orders with reference to the eucharist and to locate the essence of priesthood in the power over the body and blood of Christ exercised in the eucharist. Since in this precise respect the powers of bishop and of presbyter (now increasingly called "priest," *sacerdos*) are the same, the majority of theologians held that episcopacy in itself is not an order but an ecclesiastical honour, an office of jurisdictional power only, and so they denied it sacramental status. The contrast with the earlier tradition is obvious: the high priest of the liturgy, the pastor and teacher *par excellence* was in danger of becoming an administrator. Nevertheless, the memory of the past had not disappeared, and some theologians, together with canonists generally, tried to provide for the episcopal office within the scheme of orders. Others, too, recognized the special dignity of the episcopacy on the grounds that its power of jurisdiction is also a power over the body of Christ, the mystical body that is the church.

Character. A number of factors contributed to the development of the concept of character among the Scholastics, notably the earlier and continuing debate about the status of those ordained by a heretical or schismatic minister. The question had arisen in a corresponding way earlier for baptism, and the Scholastic theologians took up the words *signaculum* (seal) and *character* to provide the basis of an answer to the controverted question. The words were used by the Scholastics both of the external sacramental rite and of its interior effect, the inner reality that was the necessary effect of the celebration of the sacrament and that remained in the recipient in a permanent manner. In general theologians maintained that the character was a spiritual power or capacity, divinely given, enabling the recipient to carry out the proper ministerial functions. Because of the close link established between order and the eucharist, a number of theologians gave the character a christological interpretation, and it was St. Thomas more than anyone who developed and deepened this.

St. Thomas was strongly conscious that all Christian cult, with the eucharist at its center, is derived from the unique priesthood of Christ. Christ is the source of this and its true celebrant, and others can join in it only to the extent that he gives them this capacity, through the participation in his priesthood that they receive from him. This is precisely what the character is and does. It is "the character of Christ," a configuration to him, a sharing in his priesthood that empowers the Christian to have part in the whole Christian economy. This general presentation of the character applies analogously to baptism, confirmation and orders. St. Thomas' understanding of it in respect of orders can be dealt with appropriately through consideration of the phrase "in persona Christi."

In Persona Christi. In general this traditional phrase was originally used of biblical words, to attribute or refer to someone the words spoken by another, as if the one were represented in and spoke through the other. Hence *in persona Christi* meant that the words spoken should be referred or attributed to Christ.

During the Scholastic period, however, the use of the phrase underwent considerable development, particularly in respect to the eucharist, in a desire to determine the status of the biblical eucharistic words of Christ as spoken by the priest at the consecration. St. Thomas gave the phrase a technical sense, to mean that the consecratory words were spoken by the priest in the name of Christ, who so engages himself in the priest's speaking of the words that the deed is in fact his and not the priest's. The phrase is used almost exclusively of the eucharist by St. Thomas, but it is worth noting that on occasion he refers to the whole ministerial priestly action as action *in persona Christi*. He expresses a similar understanding in different terms in his teaching that the priest as minister is an instrument of Christ's own action. This power to act *in persona Christi* is conferred through the sacrament of priestly ordination, because there the priest is configured to Christ by the sacramental character, being made to share in Christ's priesthood. The character is permanent, which means that the minister's participation in Christ's priesthood, his priestly ompowerment, cannot be lost.

St. Thomas' technical use of the phrase *in persona Christi* together with the somewhat broader expressions *gerere personam, gerere vicem Christi* sum up for his time and later in respect to the priesthood and the eucharist the earlier universal tradition that in the sacraments as celebrated by the ministers of the church Christ is present and active.

There was a similar traditional phrase, *in persona ecclesiae*, which resembled *in persona Christi* in that it indicated that words were spoken by someone in the name of the church. With the Scholastics, St. Thomas especially, it too was developed, so that in celebrating the eucharist the priest was said to offer the sacrifice, to proclaim faith, to utter the prayers *in persona ecclesiae*, though the use of the phrase was not confined to the eucharist or to the church's ministers. For the great Scholastics it acquired the sense that the church engages itself and its faith in the official cultic actions of its ministers so that they represent it and act with its authority and its sanctifying power. However, *in persona Christi* and *in persona ecclesiae* are not exactly parallel expressions, since the latter had a somewhat broader usage (for example, the server at Mass or even the unbaptized person who baptizes in emergency act *in persona ecclesiae*). Moreover, for St. Thomas while the validly ordained priest who has been rejected by the church does indeed act *in persona Christi* in celebrating the eucharist, he does not act *in persona ecclesiae*. Later this expression will largely lose its strong Scholastic sense and will come to be interpreted in a more juridical way, as if it were merely a matter of delegation to act in the name of the church.

The two phrases and the relationship between them are important for understanding the nature and function of the ordained ministry. Overwhelmingly but not exclusively cultic in their reference, they sum up the traditional datum that the Christian liturgy is an act both of Christ and of the church, and in their different ways they aim to state more exactly the role of the minister particularly in the celebration of the eucharist. They have entered into the Catholic theological tradition and express theological positions acquired and confirmed by later tradition. But they are still phrases of their time, from their own background of theology and practice. That theology lacked a developed ecclesiology, and neither theology nor liturgical practice was strong in attending to the role of the lay faithful in the celebration of the sacraments.

Thus in the Middle Ages the understanding of orders became more narrowly cultic. Theologians commonly defined order by its reference to the eucharist, and they characterized it in terms of spiritual power. The majority of the great Scholastics, including St. Thomas, held as the matter and form of the sacrament of priestly ordination the handing over of the chalice with wine and the paten with bread to the candidate together with the accompanying formulary, seeing in this the act that confers the essential priestly power.

Through all of this another change may be detected: the predominant image of the ordained person, formerly that of a minister, now became more sacral or hieratic. The central work of the ordained person was related to the eucharist, and a more sacral understanding was found to correspond well with this. In the ritual for ordaining priest and bishop a rite of anointing was introduced, and slowly the interpretation of the central prayer and of the rite as a whole changed. The earlier sense of the prayer has been referred to above, and in that sense it had also been spoken of as a "blessing" or "consecration" (which seem to have been equivalent). The blessing in early times might still have been understood in the Jewish sense as a prayer in which God is blessed. Later it was thought of as a prayer which sought the blessing of God on the candidate. Now it came to be interpreted as a prayer that blessed, or through which God blessed, the candidate, a prayer of consecration. And so, the ordained minister became a consecrated person, and in the case of bishop and priest the anointing served to confirm this. The investiture in appropriate apparel likewise can be interpreted in such a way as to reinforce the predominantly hieratic image that emerged. This new image of a sacral figure with sacred, spiritual power remained the dominant one until the changes set in motion by Vatican II.

It is easy to see how this sacral model of the priesthood can be linked to the strongly christological understanding involved in the phrase *in persona Christi* and the configuration to Christ on which this is based, to produce eventually the common conception of the priest as *alter Christus.* The connection is made directly and immediately between the individual and Christ. But the christological point of reference is almost exclusively liturgical, and in this respect is much narrower than what we have seen in the patristic period. And the ecclesiological reference too is inadequate, although order is presented as order in and for the church.

The 16th Century

The questions raised by the Reformation about the sacrament of orders arose chiefly from the more basic issues of justification, grace and good works, the nature and the application to us of Christ's redemption, etc. that were the ground of the 16th-century controversy. But there were also some more particular questions: is there a sacrament of orders in the church by the institution of Christ? Is the rite of ordination as practiced by the Catholic church a sacrament? What are the essential functions of such special ministry? How is this special ministry related to the priesthood of all believers? Issues such as these challenged both the current theology and the practical exercise of orders in the Catholic church.

The Council of Trent did not purport to give a full, worked-out theology of orders or priesthood. What it did was to defend on the basis of the church's long tradition the theology and practice of orders that it had received: in the face of attack it affirmed what it regarded as essential positions and legitimate practice, and it did so largely in the categories and the terms of the Scholastic theologians. In addition, it issued a set of reform decrees and attacked abuses, thus initiating a change in the context that had given rise to some more theological criticisms.

Thus Trent upheld a visible, external priesthood with its center in the eucharist and the remission of sin; this is not a priesthood belonging to all believers nor is it a simple ministry of preaching. Orders-ordination is a true and proper sacrament instituted by Christ; it is not simply the act of the people or of the candidate or of any secular power; by it the Holy Spirit is given and a permanent character is imprinted (the nature of this character is not determined). There is a hierarchy in the church that is divinely instituted, comprising several ranks; of these, bishops are superior to priests (but the precise ground of the superiority is not stated, so that Trent left open the question whether or not episcopacy as such belongs to the sacrament of order); the hierarchy also contains "ministers" (who are likewise unspecified). Thus Trent reaffirmed the traditional datum that the special ministry is not a human invention but the provision of God, and it reinforced this by its insistence on the true sacramentality of orders and ordination.

The strength of Trent was the long earlier tradition and particularly the great Scholastic synthesis on which it rested. Its weakness was its failure to come to grips with some of the issues raised by the Reformers together with the narrowness of the eucharistic base of the medieval theology of orders and priesthood. The teaching of Trent and the long anti-Reformation polemic that ensued combined to prolong the life and influence of this theology in the Catholic church down into the present century. It is only in the past few decades that new and broader theological thinking has made its impact.

The Second Vatican Council

The following summarizes some of the salient points of Vatican II on orders and priesthood.

(1) While the Scholastic framework of orders took the eucharist as its base, Vatican II represented an important change in two respects: it preferred to start from the person and mission of Jesus Christ, and it broadened the scope beyond the liturgical to include teaching and pastoral leadership. The church's ministry is essentially related to that of Jesus. As he was prophet/teacher, priest and king/pastor, so the church shares in his work of teaching, sanctifying and shepherding/ruling.

(2) Vatican II explicitly and deliberately affirmed that episcopacy is the fullness of orders. As we have seen, medieval theologians commonly had identified the presbyterate as the highest degree of orders, seeing in the episcopacy a dignity or office superior in its authority or power of jurisdiction but not in its power of orders. From the post-Reformation period onwards there had been a change of theological opinion, but it was not until Vatican II that this was given such authoritative corroboration. This teaching rejoins the common tradition of the patristic church; it enhances the episcopal office by giving it a sacramental rather than a jurisdictional foundation. This means that the episcopal functions of teaching, sanctifying and pastoral leadership are grounded on the sacrament itself—and hence on Christ—and not on papal delegation. It also strengthens the basis of episcopal collegiality, since membership of the college of bishops too derives from the sacrament and not from any other authority.

(3) The result of this is to make the episcopacy rather than the presbyterate the primary theological reference point of orders and priesthood. This was accompanied by restoration of the ancient idea of the *presbyterium*, the single priestly body formed by the presbyters together in communion with their bishop. It also rejoins another element from the early centuries, the understanding that the presbyters formed a sort of council of advisers to the bishop. Thus the inter-

relationship of episcopacy and presbyterate is stressed. This does not make the individual priest the delegate of the bishop any more than the bishop is the delegate of the pope, since the sacrament of ordination—and therefore the call of the Lord—rather than episcopal empowerment is the source of the presbyteral ministry.

(4) The council had little to say about the diaconate, but subsequent developments opened the possibility that it might emerge in time as a full and permanent ministry once again.

(5) Thus not only did the council modify considerably the Catholic church's theological presentation of orders but it also aimed to strengthen the different orders and the network of relationships between them.

(6) Vatican II also recognized unambiguously the apostolate of all the baptized, the participation that all Christians have in the triple function of Christ through the sacraments of initiation. At the same time, it asserted an essential difference between the common priesthood of the faithful and the ministerial priesthood while acknowledging that they are ordered one to the other.

(7) All of this opened up new possibilities, but Vatican II could not work out fully either theologically or practically all the relationships that are involved (between the mission and ministry derived from the sacraments of initiation and that derived from ordination, for example, or between episcopal collegiality and papal power). Much was incomplete, as the succeeding years have shown. Nevertheless, a different model of ministry began to emerge, more dynamic, multi-dimensional, ecclesiological, and a strong impetus was given to renewal and innovation.

Conclusion

What does it mean to speak of the sacramentality of orders? It is to recognize the mystery of the church, that it is the fundamental sacrament of salvation. Ultimately it is the economy of God revealed and realized in Jesus Christ by the Holy Spirit that justifies and requires this ministry in the church; it is this trinitarian mystery of salvation that grounds it. The experience of history has shown that this ministry is referred in a double way to Christ: to his historical mission and ministry, which is the origin, exemplar and reference point of the church's mission and ministry; to his abiding presence in the church, as head of his body, in his Holy Spirit. And it is referred to the Holy Spirit, who accomplishes in the church the mystery first achieved in Christ.

The sacramentality of orders proclaims that the church does not exist of itself or for itself or by its own resources. What it preaches is the gospel of Christ entrusted to it. Its work of sanctifying can begin and end only in God through Jesus Christ in the Holy Spirit. What it is to build up is the body of Christ—and ultimately the aim for which it organizes itself is the Kingdom of God. Sacramentality also proclaims that the ministerial activity of these orders is a genuine and efficacious preaching of Christ's gospel, sanctifying his church and building up his body to the glory of God. This ministry represents Christ to the church. Contemporary Roman Catholic theology speaks of different ways in which Christ is present to his church. This ministry and its work is a primordial mode of the dynamic presence of Christ, through word, sacrament and pastoral leadership.

The sacramentality of orders also proclaims that the church is the fruit of Christ's work, the communion of life achieved among Christ's members by the Holy Spirit; the ordained ministry gives witness to and expresses the church, its faith, its unity, its life of grace in the Holy Spirit in its return to the Father through

Christ. Thus this ministry represents the church to itself, to God, to the world.

Ministry or representation of Christ, ministry or representation of the church: together these two express the essential unity and the essential differentiation of the church, and finally they are identified in the one complex reality that is the church.

To number orders among the sacraments then is to acknowledge that this ministry belongs to the essential structure of the church, expressing and engaging the mystery of salvation in all its dimensions: trinitarian, christological, pneumatological, ecclesiological.

This mystery, however, is working itself out in the flux of history, a fact that touches the theology of orders in two related ways: historical issues have been posing questions for some time to the theology accepted since the Middle Ages; the great practical and theological changes that have been occurring inside and outside the church affect theological reflection on the sacrament of orders. The Roman Catholic church has begun to face the first of these seriously. This effort coupled with the work initiated by Vatican II bears closely on the second.

Four influences may be noted briefly.

(a) The general renewal of ecclesiology and of pneumatology together with the broadening of the concept of sacrament to embrace the church have provided a better ecclesiological context and basis for the theology of orders, and they suggest a fuller theological integration of the traditional data that the ordained minister represents Christ and represents the church.

(b) Revived appreciation of the dignity and the role of all the baptized has brought not only a shift in theology but also significant changes in liturgical and pastoral practice. This has been leading both in theory and in practice to some reassessment of the relationship between clergy and laity.

(c) Since 1972 ministry is no longer exclusively clerical, and there has been a remarkable expansion of interest in and diversification of ministry and ministries. This is an important change in the context in which theologians reflect on ordination and the ordained ministry. It also raises questions about the terminology to be used that may be theological issues at base.

(d) History shows that the present triple form of the ordained ministry, while very ancient, does not seem to have existed everywhere from the beginning, and that the functions of each order together with the relationships between them have undergone considerable change. And despite the debates of history and the declarations of Vatican II, both the meaning of "fullness of order" and the nature of the theological relationship between episcopacy and presbyterate still require clarification.

All of this suggests that the nature of order or orders has still much to offer to the attention of theologians.

See **Priesthood; Ordination rites; Ministry; Church order**

David N. Power, *Ministers of Christ and His Church. The theology of the priesthood* (London-Dublin-Melbourne: Geoffrey Chapman, 1969). Bernard Cooke, *Ministry to Word and Sacraments. History and Theology* (Philadelphia: Fortress Press, 1976). Thomas Franklin O'Meara, O.P., *Theology of Ministry* (New York/Ramsey: Paulist Press, 1983). Edward Schillebeeckx, *The Church with a Human Face. A New and Expanded Theology of Ministry* (New York: Crossroad, 1985). Kenan B. Osborne, O.F.M., *Priesthood. A History of Ordained Ministry in the Roman Catholic Church* (New York/Mahwah: Paulist Press, 1988). Gisbert Greshake, *The Meaning of Christian Priesthood* (Blackrock, Ireland: Four Courts Press, 1988).

PATRICK McGOLDRICK

ORDERS, SYMBOLS OF

The primary symbols of ordination or of the ordained ministry are found in the rites of ordination to the orders of bishop, presbyter, and deacon. These symbols consist of actions or gestures, vestments or ornaments given to the newly ordained minister, and objects presented as a sign of office or of the duties connected with the particular order.

Primary Symbol of Orders: Imposition of Hands

The most basic symbol of ordination is an action common to the rites of ordination to all three orders of ministry: the imposition of hands. The action of the bishop laying or imposing hands on the head of the one to be ordained is mentioned in the NT and is found in the subsequent liturgical books of the Latin church, the Eastern churches, and the Reformation churches. In his *Apostolic Tradition*, written in the early part of the 3rd century, Hippolytus of Rome notes that the bishop lays hands on the head of the one being ordained during the ordination prayer of consecration. The bishop alone lays hands on the deacon, since the deacon is to assist the bishop; the bishop and presbyters lay hands on the presbyter, since the presbyter will share in the council of the presbyterate; the bishop and the other bishops present lay hands on the one chosen for the office of bishop. These directions as articulated by Hippolytus eventually found their way into the later ordination rites and continue to be found in the church's present ordination rites. The act of imposing hands on the one to be ordained is a multi-valent symbol. It is a sign of blessing, and an epicletic gesture, whereby the Holy Spirit is invoked upon the person being ordained. In the Latin church, the imposition of hands is now done in silence, immediately before the prayer of consecration. In the Eastern churches and in most Anglican, Lutheran, and Protestant churches the imposition of hands occurs during the ordination prayer or formula of ordination. Pope Pius XII declared in *Sacramentum Ordinis* (1947) that the imposition of hands was

the sacramental matter of ordination and that the epicletic section of each prayer of consecration was the sacramental form of ordination.

Secondary Symbols of Orders

In addition to this primary level of symbolic action, the ordination rites contain a series of symbolic presentations of vestments and other objects and anointings which help to explain the meaning of the imposition of hands and prayer of consecration.

Vestments and Ornaments. The vestments given to new presbyters and deacons and the pontifical ornaments given to a new bishop are visual symbols of the order which has just been conferred. In the earliest Roman ordination rites the candidates were presented to the bishop in the vestments of the order they were about to receive. Eventually the practice was changed and the vesting was postponed until after the prayer of consecration. In the present ordination rites the candidates are presented to the bishop wearing the vestments of their previous order. The candidates for the diaconate are dressed as acolytes in alb (amice and cincture), and the candidates for the presbyterate wear the vestments of the deacon: alb (amice and cincture) and diaconal stole. The bishop elect wears all the eucharistic vestments of the presbyter, namely, alb (amice and cincture), stole, and chasuble, with the addition of the dalmatic which is worn under the chasuble. The new deacon is given the diaconal stole (worn over the left shoulder and fastened under the right arm) and the dalmatic. The new presbyter has the stole ehanged to the presbyteral manner of wearing it, i.e., around the neck with the ends hanging straight down before him, and he is given the chasuble. The new bishop receives the pontifical ornaments of office: mitre, ring, and pastoral staff (crozier).

Anointing. The rites for the ordination

of presbyters and bishops contain an ancient symbolic action that probably came from the Celtic church: the hands of a presbyter are anointed with chrism, as is the head of a bishop. The more ancient practice seems to have been that the hands of the deacon were anointed and the hands and head of the presbyter were also anointed. The practice of anointing the deacon's hands was quickly abandoned and the anointing of the presbyter's head was transferred to the ordination of a bishop. These anointings are explanatory in nature and attempt to underline the significance of the consecration of the person effected by the imposition of hands and prayer of ordination. During the Middle Ages many theologians thought the anointing of the presbyter's hands to be an essential rite, but a careful examination of the ordination rites as they developed and of the texts used for the anointing clearly shows their secondary and explanatory nature.

Presentations. The presentation of a symbol (*porrectio instrumentorum*) of the order which has been given concludes the ordination rite. The bishop is presented with the *Book of Gospels* which was placed on his head immediately after the imposition of hands and was then held over his head during the prayer of consecration. The words said during the presentation of the gospels remind the the new bishop that he is to "preach the word of God with unfailing patience and sound teaching." The new presbyter is given the chalice of wine and the paten with the bread for the eucharist which were presented to the bishop by the faithful. In the Middle Ages many theologians thought this rite to be the matter and form of ordination. The medieval text associated with the presentation gave the impression that the power to celebrate the eucharist was being conferred by this rite. The present text is a welcome theological correction to previous misunderstandings of this rite. As he presents the offerings to the new presbyter, the bishop says: "Accept from the holy people of God the gifts to be offered to him. Know what you are doing, and imitate the mystery you celebrate: model your life on the mystery of the Lord's cross." The deacon is given the *Book of Gospels* as a reminder that he is to be a "herald" of the gospel. He is told: "Believe what you read, teach what you believe, and practice what you teach."

G.J. Cuming, *Hippolytus: A Text for Students,* Grove Liturgical Study, No. 8 (Bramcote, Notts.: Grove Books, 1976). C. Jones, et al., ed., *The Study of Liturgy,* Part IV: Ordination. (London: S.P.C.K., 1978). A.G. Martimort, et al., ed., *The Church at Prayer,* Vol. III: *The Sacraments,* trans. by Matthew O'Connell (Collegeville, MN: The Liturgical Press, 1988). *Ordination of Deacons, Priests and Bishops.* Study Edition (Washington, D.C.: United States Catholic Conference, 1979).

ALAN F. DETSCHER

ORDINATION OF WOMEN

The ordination of women was not a practical question in any Christian church before September 15, 1853, when Antoinette Brown was ordained in the Congregational church in the U.S. Since that date most Protestant churches have come to admit women to ordination. The exceptions are the fundamentalist churches and, among Lutherans, the Missouri and the Wisconsin Synods. In 1976, the Episcopal church decided to ordain women. In September 1988, the Lambeth Conference approved the ordination of women for the generality of the Anglican Communion, the practical adoption of it being left to each ecclesiastical province. In the Anglican bishops' intention, this canonical authorization of an untraditional practice "implies no departure from the traditional doctrine of the ordained ministry" (Final Report of Anglican-Roman Catholic International Commission, p. 44).

The Contemporary Problem

However appropriate it may have

seemed in its time, the Scholastic argumentation does not provide a solid basis for the permanent canonical affirmation that *"solus vir baptizatus* validly receives sacred ordination" (can. 1024). For contemporary exegesis and theology do not admit that Jesus instituted the sacraments in all their details and applications. It is therefore thought that the church must have more extensive power and initiative over their form and their use than was believed in the Middle Ages. In fact, the study of the NT and post-apostolic writings shows that several women (such as Prisca) actively shared Paul's ministry, and that one of them, Junia, was called an apostle in Rom 16:7. In establishing the orders of widows and virgins, in organizing the religious orders of women, in giving a number of medieval abbesses quasi-episcopal jurisdiction over their subjects, who often included laymen and priests, the church adapted the ministry to varying circumstances and cultures. In addition, contemporary philosophy and political experience deny the belief that women are interior to men in essence, as citizens, or in the professions. When Paul VI solemnly proclaimed Teresa of Avila and Catherine of Siena "doctors of the Church" (September 27 and October 4, 1970), he seriously undermined the Scholastic objections to ordaining women. Given the contemporary emancipation of woman and the spread of the feminist liberation movement, the question of the ordination of women needed to be reviewed in the aftermath of Vatican II. Yet when he reformed the minor orders (motu proprio *Ministeria quaedam* August 15, 1972), Paul VI decided to maintain the principle of the non-ordination of women even to minor orders: reception of these orders, "in keeping with the Church's venerable tradition, is reserved to men."

The Declaration of 1976

On July 9, 1975, Donald Coggan, Archbishop of Canterbury, wrote to Pope Paul on the question of the ordination of women. Paul VI answered (November 30, 1975): the Catholic Church "holds that it is not admissible to ordain women to the priesthood, for very fundamental reasons. These reasons include, the example recorded in the Sacred Scriptures of Christ choosing his apostles only from among men; the constant practice of the church, which has imitated Christ in choosing only men; and her living teaching authority, which has consistently held that the exclusion of women from the priesthood is in accordance with God's plan for his church." In another letter to the archbishop (March 23, 1976), Paul VI expressed his sorrow that the ordination of women in the Anglican Communion would be a "new obstacle and a new threat" on the way to reconciliation. From this point of view, it is regrettable that the Anglican Communion decided to act unilaterally in admitting women to the priesthood and (as was decided in principle) to the episcopate.

The Scholastic Reflection

The theoretical question of the possibility of ordaining women to the priesthood becomes classic in Scholastic theology. It takes the form of a reflection on Gratian's *Decretum.* The Decree forbids women "to handle sacred vessels and vestments and to act as thurifers around the altar" (part I, d 23, chap. 25). Nor may women "teach men in the assembly" (chap. 29). In other sections, the decree asserts that women are not "in the image of God," and that sin began through Eve. This spiritual inferiority makes women inapt to teach in the church and to dominate men. But the decree does not establish a connection between this inferiority and the non-ordination of women.

It is with St. Thomas that woman's essential unordainability is clearly affirmed: woman has an inner incapacity to receive the sacrament of orders (Commentary on the Sentences, bk 4, d 25, a 2, q 1). For the sacrament requires a "natural likeness" between *signum* and *res*, the sign and the reality shown by the sign. The priesthood must include a sign of "eminence and authority," whereas women are by the law of nature "in a state of subjection." There would therefore be a contradiction between being a priest (signifying authority) and being a woman (signifying inferiority). As understood by Aquinas, woman's state of subjection is not only natural and social (enforced by society), but also scriptural (taught by St. Paul). While they generally espouse the same basic position, the other great Scholastics are not so assertive as St. Thomas. St. Bonaventure deems it only "saner and more prudent" to hold that women cannot been ordained. It is for him a question of congruity. The sacrament of orders is not "congruous with the female sex," because, being subordinate to man, woman cannot be a sign of mediation between God and man (C.S., bk 4, d 25, a 2, q 1). Here the chief concern is not authority, but mediation.

John Duns Scotus, however, is embarrassed by the traditional practice and the canonical legislation. Unlike his predecessors, he cites Gal 3:28: "In Christ Jesus there is . . . neither male nor female. . . ." He understands this statement to apply to the state of grace and glory, not to that of nature, and still less to that of fallen nature. Scotus believes that Mary Magdalen was chosen by Christ as a true Apostle (*Reportata Parisiensia*, bk 4, d 25, q 2). Moreover, he judges that, had the church refused ordination to women on its own authority, it would be guilty of a deep injustice toward the entire female sex. If women cannot be ordained, it must be because Christ does not allow it. Proof of this is that the Virgin Mary was not a priest. Christ, however, has not explained his reasons and cannot be accused of injustice. If one wishes to speculate, one may find that it would be against nature for women to be in "a position of superiority," and that women lack the "quick intellect" and the "stable will" that are needed to know and to maintain the truth as teachers (*doctores*).

The Deaconesses

That women functioned as prophetesses in early Christianity is attested by the NT and is commonly admitted. Prophets and prophetesses took an active part in the communal prayer of the synaxis. What role, if any, they played in the eucharistic prayer is itself debated. Prophets, however, were never identified with priests, even if some of them, according to the *Didache*, may have presided over the eucharist. In any case, the Montanist crisis in the 2nd century inspired a distrust of prophets and especially, several women being closely associated with Montanus, of prophetesses. Nonetheless, the patristic tradition in the East did admit the ordination of women to the diaconate. The practice is attested in the 3rd century *Didascalia Apostolorum*. The ritual of ordination is the same as for deacons. It includes *cheirotonia* (laying on of hands), vesting with a deacon's robes, and porrection of the chalice. The women deacons work in the pastoral care of women and children, teaching the faith, anointing women during baptism, attending those who are sick; they supervise women's participation in worship; in some places they distribute communion to women. The age of ordination varies; in 451 the council of Chalcedon (can. 15) fixes it at 40 years of age. For reasons that are not clear, women deacons, or deaconesses, disappeared in the Byzantine church in the 12th century, and in the Syriac church in the 15th.

From the East, the institution of deaconesses spread to the West, though with a difference: in 441 the 4th council of Orange forbade their ordination with the laying on of hands. In other words, they do not constitute, as in the East, an order in the strict sense. The Latin deaconesses are not women deacons. Their group is assimilated to the early order of widows and to the later order of virgins. These institutions do not raise the matter of ordination: a blessing only accompanies the veiling of women as widows or virgins.

The question of ordaining women to the priesthood is mentioned for the first time by St. Epiphanius, shortly after 376. In his book against heresies, the *Panarion*, Epiphanius denounces the "Collyridians," women who worship the Virgin Mary, offering her cakes that they eat in communion, and performing "priestly acts" in her name. There is no suggestion that these women are ordained. On the contrary, Epiphanius' condemnation of this "sect" gives him the occasion to assert that women have never been ordained to the priesthood. It also includes a diatribe against women, who are said to be "a feeble race, untrustworthy, and of mediocre intelligence." The later Fathers of the church, whether in the East or in the West, do not seem to have been concerned with the question.

It was in keeping with the guidance given by Paul VI that, on October 15, 1976, the Congregation for the Doctrine of the Faith issued the declaration *Inter insigniores*, on the question of the admission of women to the ministerial priesthood. This is a delicately balanced document, that is in part quite progressive. All arguments that assume the inferiority of women in any domain are rejected. The question of women deacons being left aside, the problem is carefully circumscribed. It is limited to one basic point: is the church authorized to ordain women? The modern liberation of woman is considered irrelevant, for a theological question cannot be solved according to standards borrowed from secular society. Yet the negative conclusion is maintained: the church is not authorized to ordain women. This belief is based: (1) on the continuity of the traditional practice, where the congregation sees an apostolic tradition; (2) on the biblical testimony that Jesus did not include women among the twelve apostles, which is taken to be normative for ordination, the priesthood being considered a participation in the apostolate of the twelve; (3) on the sacramental requirement that the priest, as *signum*, have a "natural likeness" to the *res*, which is Christ, the Word of God incarnate as a man; (4) on the nature of the vocation to the priesthood, that is neither a right to ordination nor a purely inner and subjective call, but results from the "authentication by the church" of an inner call.

A basic methodological flaw, however, considerably weakens the persuasiveness of this case: the position adopted by the Pontifical Biblical Commission, after two meetings held in April 1975 and April 1976, is disregarded. In answer to specific questions, the commission warned that "difficulties" result from "a study of the biblical data from the perspective of a later conception of the eucharistic priesthood." Its conclusion was that the NT does not settle the question whether women can be ordained to the priesthood. One may infer from these two points: (1) that reading the NT in light of the fact that women have never been ordained to the priesthood is likely to lead to a misinterpretation of the intent of the biblical texts; and, (2) that the opinion that a clear apostolic tradition excludes women from the priesthood is not supported by the NT. Admittedly, the Biblical Commission is no more than advisory to the congregation, which is not bound by its conclusions or recommendations. Furthermore, the answers given by the commission were never officially released to the public. Yet this does not detract from the weight of these findings regarding the biblical witness.

Two points of the declaration remain

untouched by this methodological flaw: the sacramental requirement of "a natural likeness" between *signum* and *res*, and the nature of the priestly vocation. The first is universally recognized in sacramental theology. But it is compatible with the principle that the likeness between the ordained priest and the heavenly High Priest resides in their common humanity rather than in their sex. The second is unimpeachable. Yet it need not exclude that the church may some day authenticate a call that is not at this time acknowledged.

An Underlying Problem

The exclusion of women from the Catholic priesthood is tied to certain assumptions in anthropology. This does not clearly appear in most of the recent discussion. Yet it is patent in Scholastic theology. The problem of Thomas Aquinas is not only sacramental. It is primarily anthropological, in that he assigns to women a position in humanity and in society that is incompatible with the duties and responsibilities of priests. This position he calls "subjection" to men, and "weakness" of body and mind. Such is not, however, the understanding of womanhood in contemporary Catholic thought. One may then ask if the exclusion of women from the sacrament of orders is founded in a normative theological anthropology. The medieval conception being, for many reasons, obsolete, Catholic thought needs a new theological anthropology. The nearest one comes to this is found in the many documents of the ordinary magisterium, in which modern popes and bishops have spoken about the tasks of women. These documents generally describe men and women as standing in a relation of "complementarity." Yet, as is pointed out in feminist writings, the model of complementarity, that has its fundamental source in sexual roles and customs, has been universally oppressive of women, for it has always assigned to men general and glorious tasks (defense of the country, hunting, wage earning) and to women repetitive and menial tasks (cooking, gardening, keeping house, cleaning). As applied in the church, the complementarity model has given men the primary power of magisterial and priestly leadership, while women have been left with secondary roles of discipleship. Of course, Christian dignity does not reside in a function, but in the holiness to which all are called. Yet this is not to the point. For the call to holiness does not answer the question of the proper structure of the church and of its priesthood.

The Anglican-Roman Catholic dialogue in the U.S. has examined some of these questions, the only ecumenical dialogue to do so. The resulting document is entitled, *Images of God: Reflections on Christian Anthropology* (December 22, 1983). While generally accepting the complementarity model, it saw it as "open," underlining the universal "call to communion," and imaging the disciples' "identity-in-difference." It also noted that another model may be proposed: "The mutual relationship of male and female is not one of complementarity...; it is rather a supplementarity. Each, being already fully human, receives from the other a supplement of humanity."

A modern Christian anthropology needs to be more fully elaborated along these lines. Further theological reflection and ecumenical consultation will be required before all legitimate questions can be properly answered. Yet the incidence of these questions on the matter of the ordination of women is unavoidable. It was on the basis of a certain conception of the role of men and women that the decisions of the early church were made; and this conception was itself informed by the experience of men and women in Judaism, in Greek civilization, and in Roman society. The contemporary experience inspires a legitimate doubt concerning the present validity of a conclusion drawn in other contexts, and dominated by the social and intellectual conditions of another period.

Conclusion

It would be utopian to expect from the near future a change in the Catholic practice of not ordaining women to the priesthood. Agitation in favor of the ordination of women may well be a useful consciousness-raising exercise. But it cannot be the instrument of a radical change in the discipline of the sacrament of orders. For a change, if it is to come, has to be based on more serious theological reflection than is compatible with a polemical intent. Such reflection can take the form only of a development in Christian anthropology, supported by a converging reflection on the symbolism of the sacraments, and specifically of the sacrament of orders. In the meantime, no basic obstacle would seem to stand in the way of ordaining women to the diaconate, where this may be useful, on the model of the ancient Greek church.

The question of ordaining women to the episcopate is not basically different from that of ordination to the priesthood. For episcopacy and priesthood are one sacrament in two degrees (or, counting the diaconate, in three degrees). Nonetheless, it is to be expected that the ordination of women to the episcopate in the Anglican Communion will make the Catholic hierarchy still more hesitant to consider the ordination of women to the priesthood. In this, the Catholic bishops will find support in the Orthodox church and the Old Catholic church, that are just as reluctant drastically to alter the traditional structure of the church. In the long run, however, the *episcope* of women bishops in the Anglican Communion, like the already impressive performance of many of its women priests, will have to be taken into account, whenever the Spirit brings the still separated churches to the point of reconciliation.

Haye van der Meer, *Women Priests in the Catholic Church? A Theological-historical Investigation* (Philadelphia: Temple University, 1973). George H. Tavard, *Woman in Christian Tradition* (South Bend: University of Notre Dame, 1973). Ida Raming, *The Exclusion of Women from the Priesthood, An Investigation of can. 968 sec. 1* (Metuchen, N.J.: Scarecrow Press, 1976). Leonard and Arlene Swidler, eds., *Women Priests, A Catholic Commentary on the Vatican Declaration* (New York: Paulist Press, 1977). Fran Ferder, *Called to Break Bread? A Psychological Investigation of 100 Women Who Feel Called to the Priesthood in the Catholic Church* (Mt. Ranier, MD: Quixote Center, 1978).

GEORGE H. TAVARD

ORDINATION RITES

Comparatively little is said in the NT about the rites by which the leaders of the church were commissioned for their ministry. This is not surprising, since ministry in the NT period was still undergoing development and change. We find references to the twelve and to the apostles (Mt 10:1-5; Mk 3:14-19; Lk 6:13) in the gospels and to apostles, prophets, and teachers in 1 Cor 12:28. Acts and the epistles speak of leaders (Heb 13:7), presbyters or elders (*presbuteroi*, 1 Pet 5:1; Jas 5:14; Acts 11:30), teachers (Gal 6:6), overseers, i.e., bishops (*episkopoi*, Acts 20:17,28; Phil 1:1; Tit 1:5ff), and ministers (*diakonoi*, Phil 1:1; 1 Tm 3:1ff). These various titles represent charismatic ministries and offices common in the Pauline communities, as well as more institutionalized forms of office which seem to have existed in the Jerusalem community. A common characteristic of these offices or ministries is that appointment to them is by the apostles and their successors (see Tit 1:5) and that they originated from the apostles or were associated with them (see Acts 6:1ff; 11:30; 14:23). In Acts, appointment to an office or ministry is by the imposition of hands (*epithesis ton cheiron*) and through an associated confirmation by the Holy Spirit (Acts 13:2; 20:28). In the pastoral epistles, imposition of hands is also mentioned as a means of recognizing a ministry exercised prophetically (1 Tim 4:14) or of appointing a person to a ministry or office (2 Tm 1:6). The actual rites described in Acts and the epistles of Paul contain no liturgical texts and the barest of descriptions. In Acts 6:1-6 we are told of the selection of seven men to serve the needs of the widows of the Hellenists in Jerusalem. They are selected by the community and presented to the apostles who prayed and laid hands on them. Acts 13:2-3 describes how Paul and Barnabas are set apart for their ministry: "Then, completing their fasting and prayer, they laid hands on them and sent them off." Paul and Barnabas, during their first missionary journey, appointed presbyters in each church and "with prayer and fasting, commended them to the Lord in whom they had put their faith" (Acts 14:23). This practice of praying over and laying hands on those appointed as ministers is also alluded to in the two letters to Timothy (1 Tm 4: 14; 5:22; 2 Tm 1:6; 4:1-8). It is this pattern which formed the core of the ordination rites of the church as they were developed and elaborated over the centuries.

Ordination in the Early Church

The most ancient ordination rite of the church is that of Hippolytus of Rome (c. 225), and is contained in his *Apostolic Tradition.* Hippolytus provides us not only with a description of the ordination of a bishop, but also with the ordination prayers for presbyters, and deacons. The rubrics contained in the *Apost. Trad.*, and the prayers, especially that for the ordination of a bishop, have had a great influence on ordination rites in both the Eastern and the Western churches. The ordination rite takes place on a Sunday in the context of the celebration of the eucharist. The bishop is chosen by the people and the bishops who are present give their consent. The bishops silently lay hands on the candidate while the members of the presbyterate stand by in silence. One of the bishops, in the name of all, says the prayer of ordination while continuing to lay hands on the one being ordained bishop. The prayer is addressed to the "God and Father of our Lord Jesus Christ" and recalls that God has established ministers for the church. A brief *epiclesis* follows which asks God to "Pour forth now that power which is from you, of the princely Spirit which you granted through your beloved Son Jesus Christ to your holy apostles who established the church in every place as your sanctuary, to the unceasing glory and praise of your name." The prayer continues with intercessions for the new bishop. He is to feed the flock and exercise a blameless high priesthood by unceasing prayer and offering the holy gifts of the church. The bishop is to forgive sins and every other bond. All this is done through the Servant/Child Jesus Christ. After the prayer all exchange the kiss of peace with the new bishop and he proceeds to receive the offerings of the people from the deacons and then proclaim the eucharistic prayer.

Similar prayers are provided for the ordination of a presbyter or deacon. The prayer for presbyters indicates that the role of the presbyter is to assist the bishop in the governance of the church. Hippolytus notes that "When, moreover, a presbyter is ordained, let the bishop lay his hand on his head, while the presbyters also touch him...." He goes on to say that when a deacon is ordained only the bishop lays hands on him. "For he is not ordained for the priesthood, but for serving the bishop.... For he is not a member of the council of the clergy, but attends to responsibilities and makes known what is necessary to the bishop; not receiving the common spirit of the presbyter.... Wherefore, let the bishop alone make him a deacon; on a presbyter, however, the presbyters as well should also lay on their hands because of the common and like spirit of the clergy. For the presbyter has only this power to receive; he does not on the other hand have power to give. Because of this he does not ordain clergy; he rather is to put his seal on the ordination of a presbyter while the bishop ordains."

The 5th century *Statuta ecclesiae antiqua*, which was probably written in Gaul, substantially reproduces the directions of Hippolytus in cans. 2, 3, and 4. All three texts speak of the imposition of hands as the central act. All bishops present impose hands on a new bishop; the bishop and presbyters present lay hands on the new presbyter; and the bishop alone lays hands on the deacon. Eventually these texts become rubrics which are prefixed to the ordination rites of the medieval pontificals.

The actual terminology used for ordination in the early church changes over a period of time. The pagan term for election by a show of hands, *cheirotonein*, is seen in the NT and in early Christian writings. It is eventually replaced by the term *cheirepithesia* which refers to the imposition of hands. By the 4th century a distinction is made between the imposition of hands performed by a priest, *cheirothetei*, and ordination, *cheirotonei*, which is done by the bishop. Thus the emphasis changes from raising the hand to elect the candidate to that of imposing or laying hands on the one elected to the office of ministry. This distinction between election and ordination is manifested in the later ordination rites which either presume a previous election of the candidate, or have a brief rite of election by the bishop with the consent of the people at the beginning of the rite.

Ordination Rites of the Roman Sacramentaries and Ordines

In the 6th, 7th, and 8th centuries the ordination rites are found in the ancient sacramentaries of the Roman church and in Gaul as well as in the collections of rubrics known as the *Ordines Romani*. The *Sacramentary of Verona* (Sacramentarium Veronense), also known as the *Leonine Sacramentary* (5th to 6th centuries), contains the texts of the ordination prayers for bishops, priests, and deacons (nn. 952-954 in the Mohlberg edition). As is common in the early liturgical books, no rubrics are provided and it is necessary to go to the *Ordines Romani* XXXIV-XL for rubrics. The ordination of the bishop of Rome took place before the *Gloria*, while the ordination of presbyters and deacons occurred between the epistle and gospel. The ordination of the bishop begins with two collects, whereas the rites for presbyters and deacons have an invitatory and collect which originally probably introduced and concluded the litany of the saints. By the 7th to 8th centuries, the collect and invitatory followed the litany. The ordination prayer follows the collect. In the case of the bishop and presbyter, the prayer is given the title, *consecratio*, and that of the deacon, *benedictio*. These titles vary in the liturgical books and the difference in terminology has no major significance during this period.

The ordination prayers, which are totally unrelated to those of Hippolytus, are filled with allusions to the ministry of the high priests, priests, and levites of the OT. In a characteristic Roman fashion, they are preoccupied with the *cursus honorum* or progression of honor from a lesser dignity to a greater one. There is no reference to the laying on of hands in the *Verona Sacramentary* itself, and, in fact, the *Ordines Romani* are not always clear about the matter. They do mention that the *Book of Gospels* was held over the head of the one being ordained bishop of Rome, but nothing is said about the bishops present imposing hands on his head. When the pope ordained bishops he alone laid hands on them. Nevertheless it is probably safe to assume that the imposition of hands took place at Rome during the ordination prayer for deacons and presbyters.

In this early period of the Roman ordination rites, the candidates were clothed in the vestments of their order before they were presented for ordination. After their ordination, deacons and presbyters took their places with their fellow presbyters and deacons for the remainder of the liturgy.

As the Roman liturgy spread north into Gaul, it began to be intermixed with rites and prayers taken from this region. The resulting hybrid rite eventually returned to Rome and effected the subsequent Roman liturgical books. The *Gelasian Sacramentary* and the *Missale Francorum* reflect this mixed form of the Roman ordination rites. In addition to the Roman prayers, these books contain prayers of Gallican origin. The Gallican ordination rite of the 5th or 6th century probably consisted of an admonition to the faithful and the clergy, a bidding or invitatory (*praefatio*), and the prayer of consecration (*consecratio*). These consecration prayers are more centered on Christ and the notions of ministry in the NT than those of the Roman tradition. In the case of the presbyter, an anointing of the hands followed the ordination prayer. In the *Missale Francorum* and the *Gelasian Sacramentary*, the Roman prayers are followed by the Gallican texts so that there is a doubling of ordination rites. At first a choice was probably made between the Roman texts and the Gallican texts, but eventually both were recited, one set after the other. The anointing of the hands of the priest seems to have come from the Celtic church and then passed on to the church in Gaul. It was not until after the 9th century that this practice was accepted by the Roman church. The 8th to 10th century English ordinations have an anointing of the deacon's hands and an anointing of both the hands and head of the presbyter.

Medieval Ordination Rites

By the end of the 9th century the rubrical texts from the *Statuta ecclesiae antiqua* referring to the imposition of hands are inserted before the invitatory of the Roman ordination prayers, with the result that the imposition of hands now occurs in silence before the prayer of ordination, rather than during it. In some manuscripts, e.g., the English *Pontifical of Egbert*, the rubrics infer that the imposition of hands also continued throughout the ordination prayers.

A basic structure has evolved by the 10th century in which the Roman and Gallican prayers are separated from each other by the vesting of the newly ordained minister, and the presentation of symbols or instruments of office. Accordingly, the crozier and ring were given to the bishop, the chalice and paten were given to the presbyter, and the gospels were given to the deacon. This presentation of the symbols of office was a common feature of the rites for the ordination of ministers to the minor orders. The incorporation of the presentations into the ordination rites for bishops, presbyters, and deacons began a change that would eventually lead theologians and bishops to regard them as the essential act of ordination, rather than the imposition of hands before or during the ordination prayer. The 10th century *Roman-German Pontifical* of Mainz is the primary example of these new developments in the ordination rites. It contains, in addition to the usual material, an inquiry into the worthiness of the candidate, an anointing of the head, hands, and thumb of a bishop and the hands of a presbyter, the presentation of a symbol or instrument of the order being conferred, a final blessing and the kiss of peace.

The Pontifical of William Durand(us), the 13th-century bishop of Mende, elaborates rites in a more theatrical manner. The ordination rites for a bishop begin with a formal presentation of the candidate, examination, and profession of faith. After the gradual there is an invitatory followed by the litany of the saints, the imposition of the gospels on the head of the candidate and the imposition of hands by the consecrator and co-consecrators with the words: *Accipe spiritum sanctum*. The ordination prayer is interrupted by the singing of the *Veni Creator* while the head of the bishop-elect is anointed; the ordination prayer then continues. After the prayer, the hands of the new bishop are anointed, and he is presented with the crozier, ring, and gospels. The ordination rite proper concludes with the kiss of peace. In the rite for the ordination of a presbyter a whole new series of rites is added. As in the rite for the ordination of a bishop, there is a presentation which is followed by the election of the candidate at the beginning of the rite. The ordination prayer is preceded by the imposition of hands and followed by the vesting of the new priest. His hands are anointed and he is then presented with the chalice and paten. A second imposition of hands takes place after communion and the recitation of the creed. This imposition of hands is accompanied by an imperative formula, *Accipe Spiritum Sanctum...*, which had previously been used in various places in connection with the first imposition of hands. The use of such a formula is a reflection of the medieval concept that the forms for the sacraments should be declarations rather than prayers. Following the imposition of hands the back of the chasuble is lowered (which hitherto had been pinned up). The new presbyter then makes a promise of obedience, receives the kiss of peace, and is admonished concerning the manner of celebrating Mass. The bishop concludes the rite by giving the newly ordained priest a penance and a final blessing. In a sense, this all forms a second ordination rite at the end of Mass. The most significant change in the rite for the ordination of a deacon is the division of the ordination prayer into two parts by the imposition of hands and a formula beginning, *Accipe....* After the new deacon is vested in stole and dalmatic, he is presented with the gospels. The Gallican ordination prayer is used to conclude the rite. The ordination rites of Durand are the foundation of the rites contained in the post-Tridentine *Pontificale Romanum*, and, in reality, they are nearly identical.

In the 13th century, the practice of the newly ordained bishop concelebrating with the consecrator becomes common. The newly ordained priests are told to come near the altar and from the offertory on they read all the prayers of the Mass in a low voice, as if they were celebrating individually. Both newly ordained bishops and priests receive the body of Christ from the presiding bishop.

At the time of the Reformation, the continental Reformers stripped away all that they considered to be unbiblical in the ordination rites. As a result, the rites consisted, with local variations, of reading from scripture, a long admonition, the laying on of hands with an imperative formula, and a prayer for the ministry of the church. Unfortunately, the *epicletic* and eucharistic nature of the ordination prayers of consecration were lost and replaced by a questionable medieval concept of ordination using a formula rather than a prayer. Vesting, anointing, and the presentation of symbols of office generally disappeared, with the exception of the giving of a Bible to the one being ordained.

Contemporary Ordination Rites

The rites for the ordination of bishops, priests, and deacons were revised in 1968 under the title, *De Ordinatione diaconi, presbyteri et episcopi*. The revised rites follow the principle established by Pius XII in his constitution *Sacramentum ordinis* (1947) that the matter of ordination is the imposition of hands and the sacramental form is contained in the prayer of consecration of each rite. The imposition of hands by the bishop and the ordination prayer of consecration are clearly made the central features of the revised rites. All three ordination rites begin with the celebration of the liturgy of the word of the Mass. The ordination rites proper take place after the gospel. The candidates for the diaconate and presbyterate are presented to the bishop, elected by him, and the people give their consent. The rite for the ordination of a bishop begins with the *Veni Creator*, the presentation of the bishop-elect, and the reading of the apostolic mandate. All three rites then follow with the homily and the examination of the candidate. When deacons are ordained, the examination is preceded by a commitment to celibacy for those who will later be ordained presbyters. The examination is followed in the rites for deacons and presbyters by a promise of obedience to the bishop and his successors.

All three rites continue with an invitation to prayer, the litany, and a concluding prayer. The laying on of hands then takes place in silence. The presbyters join the bishop in imposing hands on candidates for the presbyterate, and all bishops present lay hands on the bishop-elect. The gospels are then placed on the head of the bishop-elect. In each rite the ordination prayer of consecration is then sung or recited. After the prayer, the new bishop's head is anointed with chrism. Deacons and presbyters are vested by members of their new order with the dalmatic and stole (for deacons) or the chasuble and stole (for presbyters). A new bishop is then presented with the gospels, ring, mitre, and pastoral staff. A new presbyter has his hands anointed with chrism and is presented with the offerings (bread on the paten and wine and water in the chalice), which have been brought to the bishop by the faithful.

A deacon is given the gospels by the bishop. The new bishop is seated in his episcopal chair if he is ordained in his cathedral. The ordination rites proper end with the kiss of peace given to the new minister by the bishop and other members of the diaconate, presbyterate, or episcopate. At the ordination of a bishop, he is led through the congregation after the prayer after communion, while the *Te Deum* or another similar hymn is sung, in order to bless the people. A new bishop who is ordained in his cathedral takes over the presidency of the eucharist, otherwise he takes the first place among the concelebrants. New presbyters concelebrate with the bishop, and new deacons carry out their diaconal functions during the liturgy of the eucharist.

These new rites attempt to express the theology of ordination and holy orders as articulated by the Second Vatican Ecumenical Council. In one case, namely the prayer of consecration for a bishop, the ancient prayer of Hippolytus has replaced the traditional prayer of the Roman rite. This prayer is also being used in the Episcopal church for the ordination of bishops. It is unfortunate that the ordination prayers for presbyters and deacons were not replaced with texts that are more focused on the imagery of the NT, perhaps the Gallican ordination prayers. The rites themselves follow the common pattern that emerged after the Second Vatican Council of being placed after the liturgy of the word and before the liturgy of the eucharist. The laying on of hands and the prayer of consecration take their rightful place as the center of these rites. And the rites of vesting, anointing, and presentation of symbols of office take a secondary place.

Comparable revisions have taken place in the Anglican, Lutheran, and many of the Protestant churches in the United States and Europe.

B. Botte, ed., *La Tradition apostolique de saint*

Hippolyte. LQF, No. 39 (Muenster: Aschendorffsche Verlagsbuchhandlung, 1963; reprinted, 1972). Paul F. Bradshaw, *Ordination Rites of the Ancient Churches of East and West* (New York: Pueblo, 1990). G.J. Cuming, *Hippolytus: A Text for Students*, Grove Liturgical Study, No. 8 (Bramcote, Notts.: Grove Books, 1976). C. Jones., et al., ed., *The Study of Liturgy*, Part IV: Ordination (London: S.P.C.K., 1978). B. Kleinheyer, *Die Priesterweihe im Romanischen Ritus: Ein Liturgiehistorische Studie*, Trierer Theologische Studien, No. 12 (Trier: Paulinus Verlag, 1962). A.G. Martimort, et al., ed., *The Church at Prayer*, Vol. III: *The Sacraments*, trans. by Matthew O'Connell (Collegeville, MN: The Liturgical Press, 1988). *Ordination of Deacons, Priests and Bishops*, Study Edition (Washington: United States Catholic Conference, 1979). H.B. Porter, *The Ordination Prayers of the Western Church*, Alcuin Club Collections, No. 49 (London: S.P.C.K., 1967). D.N.Power, *Ministers of Christ and His Church* (London: Geoffrey Chapman, 1969).

ALAN F. DETSCHER

P

PALM SUNDAY

Also called Sunday of the Passion or Passion Sunday, this day inaugurates the week that is called Holy. The movement that begins today culminates in the paschal triduum of Holy Thursday, Good Friday and the vigil of Easter. On the liturgical tone of this week the words of Pius Parsch remain to the point: "We must not separate the passion from the resurrection, but rather regard the Cross as the way to Easter victory. The liturgy does not make this week one of sorrowful lamentation or tearful sympathizing with our suffering Lord. That was the medieval approach. No, through the whole week there runs a note of victory and joy, a realization that Christ's sacred passion was a prerequisite to Easter glory" (*The Church's Year of Grace*, Vol. 2, p. 290).

An irony presents itself in today's liturgy. The first part enacts the joyous entrance of Jesus into Jerusalem amidst loud cries of "hosanna." The naive bravado of disciples unaware of their own sinfulness and of the extent of Jesus' own journey is plainly set out. In the passion proclamation that follows, the same people who cried "hosanna" now cry "crucify," and the disciples, so boldly ready to "follow him anywhere" are seen to abandon him. Together, however, they proclaim a more important fidelity: the fidelity of Jesus to his mission, and the fidelity of *Abba* to his Son.

See **Holy Week, liturgies of; Calendar, liturgical**

PAPACY, MODERN, AND LITURGICAL RENEWAL

Although some claim that the liturgical movement began with the publication of Dom Prosper Gueranger's monumental *L'année liturgique* (1840), his work remained on the scholarly, academic level and never really affected the grass roots. If one considers the movement as an advance toward an intelligent participation in the liturgy of the church, then one has to look to the Catholic congress in Malines, Belgium (1909), under the leadership of Lambert Beauduin or the first liturgical week held for lay people at Maria Laach, Germany, during Holy Week of 1914 for its origin (cf. Koenker, 11-12; Jungmann, 11-12; Kolbe, 6).

Be that as it may, this article limits itself to developments in the 20th century and the impact of the papacy upon them. Gueranger in France, Dom Gerard van Caloen in Belgium and J.A. Moehler in Germany had laid the groundwork for liturgical reform and people like Ildefons Herwegen, Romano Guardini, Lambert Beaudiun, Pius Parsch and Virgil Michel, to mention but a few, stand as pioneering giants in its development. Yet without the influence of the popes of our century, their efforts may never have had such widespread and relatively rapid effects (cf. Koenker, 13-17).

Pope Pius X is a case in point. On November 22, 1903, he issued a motu proprio *On Sacred Music* in which he sounded the rallying cry for the liturgical movement: "Our people assemble for the purpose of acquiring the Christian spirit from its *first and indispensable source, namely active participation in the most sacred mysteries and in the public prayer of the Church*" (St. Meinrad translation, St. Meinrad Abbey, 1951, p. 4. Emphasis added). Pius XI was to return to this statement in his apostolic constitution *Divini cultus* (1928) as was Pius XII in his encyclical *Mediator Dei* (1947): "It should be clear to all ... that the worship rendered to God by the Church in union with her divine Head is the most efficacious means of achieving sanctity" (art. 26). Fittingly, the decisive vote during Vatican II on the *Constitution on the Sacred Liturgy* took place fifty years to the day that Pius X had issued his statement. The Constitution again echoed his cry: "In the restoration and promotion of the sacred liturgy, the full and active participation by all the people is the aim to be considered before all else; for it is the primary and indispensable source from which the faithful are to derive the true Christian spirit" (S.C., 14).

Not only did Pius X provide a rallying cry. His decree *On frequent and even daily communion* (1905), coupled with his earlier urging that the faithful participate in the singing, had paved the way for a new sense of community in and through the liturgy. Although it would take time for the reception of communion to resume its rightful place within the eucharistic celebration, this pope—known for his strong reaction to Modernism and other currents—had begun the movement to which catchwords, inaccurately attributed to him, gave voice: "Do not pray at Mass, pray the Mass" or "Do not sing at Mass, sing the Mass" (Koenker, 12-13, 235 n. 10; Jungmann, 20-21; Kolbe, 31, 57, 86).

Pius X was also known for his efforts to reform the breviary and to reduce the number of saints' feasts in the Roman calendar. Pius XI immediately "cluttered"

the calendar again but he also reenforced the exhortation that the people learn Gregorian chant as a means of involving them in the liturgy (Koenker, 58, 154-55).

It was Pius XII, however, who would be the next dominant, papal figure in the liturgical movement. His encyclical *Divino afflante spiritu* (1943), which recognized developments in biblical studies, was of great value to the movement. The same was true of the encyclical *Mystici corporis* (1943) which gave official sanction to the notion of the church as the body of Christ. The liturgical movement was to stress this doctrine as integral to liturgical life. It did not, however, emphasize the hierarchical structure as much as *Mystici corporis* did and it stressed the spiritual life of the body rather than its visible, institutional character (Koenker, 37, 89).

Pius XII also gave the liturgical movement a more direct impetus. This is all the more surprising since he was not always known for his great liturgical sense. He cautioned Benedictine abbots against those who extol liturgical forms of "bygone days" and who belittle popular devotions. In *Mediator Dei* (1947), rather than criticize certain characteristics of non-liturgical practices, he warmly recommended them. It was clear at times that he wanted to tighten the reins on the liturgical movement. But the progress and toleration granted the movement was even more surprising than the warning and repression. His emphasis, in *Mediator Dei*, on the liturgy as not only exterior but, especially, interior worship and as " ...the most efficacious means of achieving sanctity" (art. 26) is a case in point. His address to conclude the Pastoral Congress of Assisi (1956), in which he referred to the liturgical movement as a sign of God's care for the present times and a movement of the Holy Spirit in the church, offered encouragement along with caution

(Koenker, 20, 64-65; Kolbe, 70-71, 84-85, 110-111).

Pius XII also echoed Pius X's concern that church music be pastoral. In his encyclical *Musicae sacrae disciplina* (1955), he pointed out that church music was never to be art for art's sake but was to be the handmaid of liturgical celebration. While some of the changes made under Pius XII might at first glance seem minor in themselves, they underlined the link between liturgy and pastoral concern. Some examples of this were: the decree on the simplification of rubrics (1955); the reform of the Easter vigil and then of Holy Week (1951-55) and permission for evening Mass and new laws for the communion fast (1957) (cf. Kolbe, 90, 97, 102; Jungmann, 25). These changes and the attitudes behind them also set the stage for the momentous changes that were to follow.

And onto the stage walked Angelo Giuseppe Roncalli or Pope John XXIII, as he was to be called. The biblical, liturgical and ecumenical movements seemed ripe. Theological trends were more or less developed. But by announcing (January 25, 1959) and then officially convoking Vatican II in the apostolic constitution *Humanae salutis* (December 25, 1961), John XXIII triggered changes that would profoundly affect the universal grass roots level. As early as 1919, Roncalli had admitted to an *idée fixe*: "The need to popularize study of the liturgy and encourage living participation in it" (P. Hebblethwaite, *Pope John XXIII*, Doubleday, 1985, p. 91). Dom Lambert Beauduin, one of the pioneers of the liturgical movement as well as of social action and ecumenism, was a good friend of Roncalli and had left a lasting imprint on him. Beauduin had to suffer much until John XXIII vindicated both him and his ideas by placing great emphasis on liturgy and ecumenism during Vatican II (Hebblethwaite, 116; Kolbe, 36, 148-49). It was John XXIII who

determined that liturgy would be the first topic dealt with at the council, since this most directly affected the people. He also signaled an easing of the opposition to the mother tongue in the liturgy (Kolbe, 112-113). Although he died on June 3, 1963, six months before the promulgation of the *Constitution on the Sacred Liturgy* (December 3, 1963), there could be little doubt that John XXIII had had an enormous impact on the liturgy he loved and saw as a key to the church unity for which he longed (Kolbe, 148-50).

The man who did promulgate the constitution was Giovanni Battista Montini, Pope Paul VI. It was he who in 1925 had comforted Roncalli with the ecumenical possibilities of the latter's apparent exile to Bulgaria and who in 1958 called *Mediator Dei* the "Magna Charta" of liturgical renewal (Hebblethwaite, 116; Kolbe, 85). It was to him that the carrying out of the post-conciliar reform fell.

The liturgical documents which appeared during the time of Paul VI varied in emphasis, tenor, style, terminology and even their underlying theology. They reveal the complexity of the task that was at hand and while some may see in them a sign of harmful vacillation, others would hail Paul VI as a reconciling genius. A few examples should suffice. The liturgy constitution, for all its compromises, remains positive and pastoral in tone. The resurrection, or more precisely the paschal mystery, receives frequent mention, as it does throughout the conciliar documents. The constitution opens new avenues of adaptation and decentralization, at least in principle. It is basically an optimistic document. The encyclical *Mysterium fidei* (September 3, 1965), on the other hand, reveals a different tone as well as different emphases. Surprisingly for a document on the eucharist, the resurrection or paschal mystery is mentioned only twice and in both cases the passages are quotes from elsewhere. The document is basically restrictive, cautionary and negative in tone. The *Instruction on eucharistic worship* (May 25, 1967) is more positive than *Mysterium fidei* both in content and tone. The resurrection and paschal mystery receive frequent mention. The instruction speaks in turn of important principles for the catechesis of the eucharistic mystery (here used in the biblical sense), of the celebration of the memorial of the Lord and the worship of the eucharist. This document clearly seeks an overall view which sees the various facets of the eucharist in their relationship to one another. It also indicates certain priorities among these facets.

The document which best illustrates the tension produced by the various approaches to liturgical renewal is the *General Instruction of the Roman Missal* (April 6, 1969). The basic draft was finished in October 1965. In 1967 a number of changes were made and the document was submitted to the Bishops' Synod for consultation. In 1968, after further changes reflecting the suggestions of the synod and of the pope himself, Paul VI approved it orally and in writing. Following its promulgation in 1969, however, a storm of protest in certain circles led to a new Foreword or Introduction (March 1970) to the General Instruction. This checkered history accounts for the different style, terminology and theology within the same basic document (McKenna, 162-64).

Paul VI guided the liturgical renewal through those complex times and may very well have earned the title of reconciling genius which has been attributed to him. Whatever the tenor of the document, his papal addresses, especially to the clergy, left no doubt that he was committed to liturgical reform and its implementation (cf. J. Megivern, ed., *Worship and Liturgy*, Wilmington, N.C.: McGrath Publ., 1978, p. xix).

The history of Pope John Paul II's contribution to the liturgical movement

remains to be written. Following his encyclical *Dominicae cenae* (February 24, 1980) on the mystery and worship of the Holy Eucharist (cf. D. Power, *The Sacrifice We Offer*, New York: Crossroad, 1987, pp. 21-26, 132, 134), the Sacred Congregation issued an instruction *Inaestimabile donum* (April 3, 1980) on certain norms concerning worship of the eucharistic mystery. In October 1984, the same congregation granted permission to use the Tridentine Mass under certain circumstances. Most recently John Paul II issued an apostolic letter on the 25th anniversary of Vatican II's *Constitution on the Sacred Liturgy* dated December 4, 1988, and released May 13, 1989. To date the overall impression of the pope's influence is reminiscent of that of Pius XII—encouraging yet cautionary.

The journey of the liturgical movement has been complex and varied. While the impetus came from the people of God (Jungmann, 26-27), there can be no doubt that the papacy played a crucial role in shaping its path. One can expect the future to be no different. The papacy will play a crucial role—and so will the people of God.

Joseph Jungmann, *Liturgische Erneuerung Ruckblick Und Ausblick* (Cologne: Butzon & Becker, Kevelaer, 1962). Ernest B. Koenker, *The Liturgical Renaissance in the Roman Catholic Church* (St. Louis: Concordia Publishing House, 1966). Ferdinand Kolbe, *Die Liturgische Bewegung* (Aschaffenburg: Paul Pattloch Publishers, 1964). John H. McKenna, "Liturgy after Vatican II: Harmful Vacillation or Reconciling Genius?" *The Furrow* 30 (March 1979): 155-167.

JOHN H. McKENNA, C.M.

PARISH RENEWAL

This investigation of parish renewal begins with three related introductory considerations.

First, the experience of parish life in the United States can be mapped in three stages. The first style of parish existed from c. 1760 to 1860. Catholics were a minority. Their church buildings were often purchased from Protestant neighbors and redone. Clergy were few. Laity exercised significant roles in policy-making and participation. These parishes can be described as congregational and democratic. The second style of parish, rooted in European ethnic heritage, flourished from 1860 to 1950. Catholics swelled in number, built their own buildings for worship and education, and developed a devotional style under ample clerical leadership. The last and present style of parish is no longer based on one's georgraphical location, ethnicity (save for newer immigrants), or sense of obligation. From 1950 Catholics in this country belong to a parish through voluntary association. They choose to remain because their needs are met and they have some say in parish life and direction.

Second, due to the shift from parish as building to parish as voluntary association, parish is people. A parish "is a definite community of the faithful established on a stable basis in a particular church; the pastoral care of the parish is entrusted to a pastor as its own shepherd under the authority of the diocesan bishop" (C.I.C., can. 515). This legal statement faithfully reflects the imagery and ecclesiology of Vatican II which described the church as "the people of God." It also expresses the lived reality. Parish is church, and church is people.

Third, parish is about people-in-relationship. Church is about being a group. A parish shares characteristics common to any group in its dynamics and interpersonal workings. But what distinguishes parish from other groups is that the basis for its being, its assembling, and its voluntary belonging is God's ability to be donative. God freely invites this group of people into covenant and faith relationship so that the group might respond with faith, with a vital inner life and external mission. The Spirit, reminding this group about the life of Jesus, is entrusted to the parish as people-in-relationship. This modifies the mentality that parish exists for privatized salvation or sectarian exclusion from the affairs of humankind.

While the above considerations affirm both the transcendent origin of the church and the divine gift of grace that the Spirit is for a parish, they also remind us that the parish is a historical, empirical and concrete reality. The parish that is renewing is a local church, a group of people in this here-and-now place. They are shaped by their culture, geography, language and historicity. Each local church, in communion with its other ecclesial groups, has to renew according to the ways God involves "Godself" with this people, a group changing, developing, living and being a historical, empirical and concrete church. This suggests that parish renewal may present one challenge to a particular parish that can be distinctively different from the challenge faced by another.

A renewing parish will be helped by norms and guidance from credal confessions and codes of ethics and law. But its vitality will need to be illuminated by a historical, empirical and concrete ecclesiology-from-below. Thus the undergirding ecclesiology for parish renewal is an historical-theological one that directs people in their relationship with God and with their world.

Renewal and Liturgy

Numerous attempts have been made, in the United States and elsewhere, to foster parish renewal during the last two decades. Cursillo weekends, Marriage Encounter, Christ Renews His Parish, Renew, have all been a boon for parish renewal. Many have come away with an experience of conversion, dedication and enthusiasm. What all of these movements have in common is a strong sense of bonding, affective appeal and a missioning of members back into their social settings. What is unfortunate among all these "good news" renewal movements is that liturgical renewal has not captured the same vitality. Or is it that we have failed to unearth the treasures and potential of the liturgy itself to renew?

Liturgy is the public work of this particular local church. It is hard work; it calls for energy expended in public celebration. It demands careful preparation, full and active participation, and follow-up evaluation. Liturgy is often thought of, particularly by clergy and well-educated planners, as primarily textual. This means that liturgy is viewed as rites residing in ritual books. But liturgy is communal, public, ritual activity; its stylized action is a prayerful doing of the mighty deeds of God in the here-and-now.

When liturgy is performed well, it is the source of personal prayer because its biblical and ecclesial images invade the assembly's mentality and inner life and eventually convert the heart by pushing out images of darkness. When liturgy is effective, it is the basis for people-to-people relationship in parishes because the Spirit gives various charisms to build up the assembly. When liturgy uses symbols authentically, it enables the assembly to be energized in order to be sent forth to connect the symbolic life with the doing of the works of justice and compassion, mercy and peace. When liturgy attends to this praying group, it begins to engage the assembly with its surrounding culture and the culture with the church.

Perhaps parish renewal has not happened as we might like because we have not believed that the liturgy has the power to effect renewal! What might occur if we took the liturgical renewal seriously! How might it renew the parish?

Renewal Through the Liturgy of the Word

One source of renewal through liturgy is the liturgy of the word. The specific church we call parish is a people who hears the word of God. This word invites people to faith by revealing the person of Jesus. It presents him to a people who can be converted to loyalty, friendship and allegiance with him. The word of God proclaimed in assembly puts this group back in touch with the authentic origins of this people: with Jesus and his movement.

On one hand, the church is always servant of the word of God. A parish is renewed by obedience to the word. On the other hand, the NT churches created and authored the word (and later determined which texts were canonical) in order to keep the memory of Jesus and his prophetic movement alive. The biblical texts are thus heuristic. They trigger a skein of images in order to unroll the scroll of salvation history. The original compositions were intended to meet the ecclesial needs of NT communites and to form their members in relationship to one another and to their social setting.

The reforms of Vatican II introduced a three-year Sunday lectionary so that a richer fare of scripture would be heard. This has been a boon for Catholics who indicate that, twenty years later, they have a better and deeper appreciation of Sacred Scripture because of the lectionary. This has been an ecumenical blessing as well because all the major churches have reshaped their Sunday lectionaries in like manner. The new lectionary was also designed to meet the need of catechumens whose journey might last up to three years. R.C.I.A. directors, catechists and pastors base their instruction on the lectionary. Still, much of the promise in this reform is still to come.

What might enable the Word of God to reform parishes? Four proposals are offered here.

First, each cycle focuses on one of the synoptic pictures of Jesus. Each year an assembly hears the word about Jesus through the eyes of Matthew, Mark or Luke (with selections from John inserted at various places). What still calls for development is the ecclesial, prophetic and mission significance of each gospel tradition, not only for its original hearers, but also for contemporary hearers. What this concretely means is this: obviously each parish does not redo its ministries and activities each year. But what if these ministries and activities were shaped by, focused on, and colored through the christological lens of the gospel heritage being proclaimed and presented that year. Even more concretely, as each gospel presents its own rendition of the passion, death and resurrection of Jesus, each one does so from its own perspective. Could not the perspective of that particular gospel begin to be directed practically to the life and ministries of this here-and-now assembly. The implications of this hold out important challenges to parish staffs and members.

Second, we have seen a recent desire of people to grow in their spiritual life and to deepen their personal bonds with God through spiritual direction. This is often done in one-to-one reflection or by small groups meeting with a spiritual director or guide. Whatever the setting, the process is one of listening, disclosure of the innermost heart, an evaluation of how God is working there, challenge, direction and encouragement. These same elements are also found corporately when the Sunday assembly hears the liturgy of the word. The assembly listens to God who is disclosing divine relationship with this assembly. The assembly evaluates its life in obedience to the word. It is challenged, directed and encouraged by the preached word, especially when that word is given by one who has intimate experience of the assembly. The consequence is that hearers of the word are able to offer prayer of petition and the great prayer of thanks and are sent forth to do the mission of Jesus.

Third, the blessing of literacy is at times a bane to those hearing the word.

Since the printing press and the ability of many to read easily accessible printed material, the church has risked losing its ability to be at home in an oral-aural world. Liturgical proclamation of the word demands that proclaimers and listeners reclaim an ancient orality if the word is to resonate in their hearts. Proclamation, like all good story telling, commands attention because it is sound heard in the here-and-now. It is actual and present. The voicing of sound enables the inner meaning, the interior, to be heard and known by the listeners because sound echoes and reveals the interior through the instrumentality of the proclaimer. Sound differs from print; the former allows listeners to hear simultaneously, the latter allows for assimilation of inner meaning at each reader's pace. A skillful proclaimer engages the listener totally by the sound of his or her voice, by posture and pace, by bodily expression, and by facial communication. When a group hears, sounds are united and the group moves towards harmony.

A modern assembly is often bombarded by multiple sounds every day. Even the best of proclaimers faces a difficult task with an assembly. In addition, modern people are so used to the privacy of printed text, that it is easy to assume that the oral-aural is endemic to a more ancient culture. Finally, so pervasive is the influence of print that our church space is often arranged like print type on a page (simply look down on an assembly seated neatly in pew after pew). Nonetheless, albeit a difficult task, a reclaiming of oral proclamation is crucial to parish renewal.

Fourth, the word of God is never confined to the proclamation of biblical text. The word is fleshed out for this assembly by homiletic preaching. The task of the homilist is to speak a word that rekindles faith and that enables the assembly to know God's loving presence. The skillful homilist is first a student and pray-er of the word. The homilist is also one who can draw on the texts to help people interpret their lives and to offer eucharist.

The homily can often be the word that facilitates conversion, reconciliation, consolation and peace for people in their real life situations. This requires that the preacher know the life situation of the parish members. It also means that the homilist is one who has become imbued in biblical and ecclesial images and has become a disciplined wordsmith at home with the picture-language of metaphor and parable.

The homily does not exhaust the preaching ministry. People still hunger for conversion-preaching presented by artful preachers and for catechesis given by catechists who can use beautiful language to instruct and motivate the heart. We thus turn to a second source of renewal, R.C.I.A.

Renewal Through R.C.I.A.

The specific church we call parish is a people who are responsible for new birthing in their midst. Thus a second source of parish renewal is the assembly's role in inviting new members and in assisting their conversion. The R.C.I.A. has become a significant means of parish renewal, not only for catechumens, but also for those who have been Christian for many years. Parishes are still learning that this is not a program but a formative process done in the midst of the assembly. It is easier, especially for parish staffs, to administer a program. It is more difficult to make a group commitment to all the ambiguities and vicissitudes entailed in a process.

For the R.C.I.A. to be a vital means of parish renewal, assemblies must estimate their spirit of welcome and hospitality. The R.C.I.A. demands that people use their gifts to minister to one another because these people have shared in the hospitality of the Lord, have eaten and drunk with him. It forces people already

baptized to examine their values, interests and lifestyles. In short, parish members are asked to plumb their praxis and the quality of service exercised in this assembly. In turn, "the catechumens are now part of the household of Christ, since the church nourishes them with the word of God and sustains them by means of liturgical celebrations" (47).

Evangelization. A ministry to catechumens is also a means of evangelization for the already baptized. The period of catechumenate is "an extended period during which the candidates are given suitable pastoral formation and guidance, aimed at training them in the Christian life. In this way, the dispositions manifested at their acceptance into the catechumenate are brought to maturity" (75).

Pastoral formation, guidance and training are spelled out in n. 75, 1-4. First, catechumens receive catechesis, gradual and complete, accommodated to the liturgical year and solidly supported by celebrations of the word. Second, their conversion journey is aided by the example and support of parish members who act in collaboration, e.g., sponsors, godparents, pastors, catechists, fellow catechumens and the entire Christian community. The quality of their presence can support or hinder Christian conversion. The hopes of this period are attitudinal and spiritual: that catechumens turn to God in prayer; that they bear witness to faith; that they keep their hopes set on Christ; that they follow supernatural inspiration in their deeds; that they practice love of neighbor, even if that entails self-renunciation. What this local community hopes for is that the process will foster for all a change in outlook and conduct, "made manifest by its social consequence." Third, n. 75 indicates that the assembly, a mothering church, helps the journey by liturgical rites that both purify and strengthen the candidates with God's blessing. It also witnesses to its life and commitment by having the catechumens join them for the Sunday celebration of the liturgy of the word, after which the catechumens are kindly dismissed in order to break open the word they have heard. Fourth, since the Christian life is apostolic, catechumens learn to work actively with others to spread the gospel and build up the church by the witness of their lives and by professing their faith.

These four points seem to be *ad rem* not only for catechumens but also for the entire assembly. In short, they indicate what parish renewal is. It is, first, a learning from the word of God lived out in the seasons of the liturgical year. Second, it is fostered by collaborative, not competitive ministries which help people cultivate a Christian way of life, including self-renunciation and praxis for social justice. Third, it requires that the entire assembly, patterned on the self-emptying of Jesus, be purified of toxins that destroy Christian life in order that the Spirit will fill the church with strength. Last, it is not intramural; it calls for apostolic service done with others as constitutive of the Christian life.

Any parish which is serious about its continued life will find ample basis for renewal in n. 75, 1-4. This will invite internal renewal based on the word of God, prayer, sharing, collaborative ministry, communal discernment, and mutual nurture and edification. It will also invite external vitality by a praxis of social justice, apostolic service rendered others for the sake of the reign of God, and a style of working with others.

Mystagogy. The second area of initiation ministry is the period of mystagogy, the post-baptismal period of fifty days. Part of the difficulty with this period is cultural. Many parishes do a fine job preparing people for sacramental moments and do celebrate the moments well. But they do not always know what to do with follow-up and with enthusiastic levels of rejoicing.

Parish groups are only now learning what it means to reflect back on the paschal mystery. This requires a method of theological reflection and faith sharing, an ability to spend time in being glad (without anyone's input), and the willingness to cherish mystery through contemplation, celebration and conversation. Perhaps the baptized will learn how to savor their paschal life only when they have learned how to minister this with the newly baptized.

The implications of this are significant for a sense of belonging to the diocesan church, for perseverance in faith by annual reunions, and for establishing bonds that sustain old and new-born when struggle, suffering and discouragement set in. There are no instant cures for an underdeveloped mystagogy. Perhaps parish renewal will entail a commitment to the entire process and a willingness to confront the product-oriented culture that the local church may have to oppose.

Renewal Through Sunday Eucharist

The specific church we call parish is a people who celebrate the Lord's Day. Parish renewal, if it be authentic to the heritage of faith, finds its highpoint in the Lord's Supper shared on the Lord's Day. Western Catholics, often accustomed to achieving results, may seek to get something out of Sunday eucharist. The experience of the Eastern tradition is a corrective. Eastern Christians celebrate because of the inestimable privilege of glorifying God. Sunday is not just a leisure time component which makes up the weekend. Sunday is the first day, the symbolic day, a sign of the privileged and graced time of the church between the ascension and the final coming of the Lord, the time we now live.

Parish renewal means reclaiming Sunday in its entirety—by keeping vigil as a people await the dawn to push aside and invade darkness so that the church discovers the risen Christ, by celebrating the

Lord's Supper, by a spirit of leisure and communion with one another. It means that each historical, empirical, concrete assembly take seriously its primary ministry of assembling because a people is most clearly church when it assembles on Sunday (S.C., 7-10). Sunday liturgy is the *lex orandi* that is the norm and locus for *lex credendi*.

A number of concerns, when addressed by a parish, will indicate how its renewal is going. First, each parish might wish to measure how well it incorporates those who are liminars, the outcast and pariahs in society. This includes many women, some of whom are divorced, separated, single, widowed and often highly significant contributors to a local parish's life. It includes children who are sometimes abused, neglected, ignored or excluded from taking any significant role in liturgy. It includes elders, members of minorities, the disabled, those who are absent due to their being ill or in prison, and those who experience societal prejudice because of sexual orientation or who are angry because they perceive church discrimination—all these seek a place of welcome at the Lord's table.

Second, each parish might examine the language it uses. The old dictum, *nomen est omen*, still obtains. Liturgical language can no longer be exclusively male. This is not an issue because a parish needs to placate women or avoid conflict. What is at stake here is how we name God, how an assembly uses language to open up people's affective appreciation of the mystery of God, church, humankind and world. When texts are crafted (e.g., in penitential rites, in the prayer of the faithful, in introducing the Lord's Prayer and in inviting to table sharing), they need to be fashioned to expand meaning, to avoid idolatry, and to enable the entire assembly to express both lament and doxology in public prayer. Those who shape prayer texts need to be attentive to the cultural context of its

people and to how words both shape and express meaning.

Third, each parish might critique its worship space to ensure that it creates a setting congenial to reverence and warm hospitality. This is not simply to make people feel at home. It is for the sake of being what liturgical prayer claims an assembly is, i.e., sisters and brothers who offer praise to a God who is lavish in love, generous in mercy, and abundant in forgiveness. Either we shape space or it will shape us. If liturgical space is ill suited, our celebrations may result in a faith that is hindered or at risk of being destroyed. If space is fashioned according to how a parish wants to be church, if it even allows for some flexibility and possible rearrangement, then it is space that serves the assembly. In turn, an assembly that is thoughtful about its worship space may begin to work for hospitable and beautiful housing for its members and others in a neighborhood.

A parish can renew through its Sunday liturgy by calling forth an assembly that acknowledges and uses its people's gifts. Those who are proclaimers, cantors, musicians, artists, environmental ministers, greeters, servers, deacons, presiders and preachers serve the primary group, the assembly, in its prayerful dialogue with God. This assembly gathers around the font as it initiates new members in the awe-inspiring, death-defying waters. It gathers around the Lord's table as an assembly that voices the prayer of thanksgiving. Further liturgical renewal will require texts that manifest the eucharistic prayer as a dialogue between presider and assembly and that show that this prayer is an ecclesial doxology offered to God for the gifts of redemption and creation.

Renewal Through Pastoral Care
Parish renewal at its finest is never focused on liturgy alone. It looks for ways to connect public prayer with

pastoral service. If the public work of prayer is effective, then its challenge makes a parish attentive to wholesome pastoral care. Liturgy often addresses critical turning points in the life of people and by doing so through ritualized prayer, points to and nourishes pastoral ministry at these turning points. If the liturgy models how we want to be church, i.e., different gifts used in service of the assembly, then pastoral care will create ways for gifted people to care for others.

Pastoral care includes those who are absent from the assembly due to illness or disability. Pastoral visitation of the sick, communion for the sick and their families, anointing of the sick in hospitals and homes and care for the dying require those gifted and trained to minister both personally and liturgically. Pastoral care will be exercised by both ordained and non-ordained, professional and volunteer ministers, and more informally by friends, neighbors and family members.

Pastoral care will create ways for people to serve those who are alienated or cut off from ecclesial communion. A ministry of reconciliation requires an ability to listen and a variety of ministers to facilitate groups of penitents seeking reconciliation. Liturgies of reconciliation presume a process of conversion and ritualize what has been developing due to God's grace working in those ministering and those being served.

Pastoral care will create ways for parish renewal by creative engagement of Catholics and other Christians to gather for conversation, liturgical prayer (e.g., a liturgy of the word or the liturgy of the hours), and for planning out social ministry (e.g., advocacy for others or assembling for public witness and prayer on behalf of justice and peace).

Renewal and Mission

Parish renewal, through liturgical celebration and pastoral care, does not exist solely for itself or its own members'

personal salvation. A historical, empirical, concrete church is not only a community which celebrates liturgy, but also a people sent forth in mission. Liturgical and parish renewal are for the sake of the world, a world where Christians live the gospel. When an assembly uses elements authentically (e.g., bread, wine, oil, water), when it attends to their symbolic meaning, then it will call attention to the waters of the seas and streams, the soil which grows wheat, the welfare of vineyards that give grapes. How terrible that water used in baptism as a symbol of life, could become a symbol of death because it became so irrevocably polluted! How sinful a church would be if, in using the elements of the earth authentically, it did not care for those who picked grain or grape in sometimes inhuman or unjust situations. A local parish is never an isolated sect. As a church, it is most vital when it expresses its communion with other churches, when it looks beyond its own horizons and celebrates its communion with churches of other nations and concerns itself with being part of a global connection.

The United States bishops, in their pastoral letter *Economic Justice for All*, linked worship with justice. "Challenging U.S. economic life with the Christian vision calls for a deeper awareness of the integral connection between worship and the world of work. Worship and communal prayer are the wellsprings that continually call the participants to greater fidelity to discipleship. To worship and pray to the God of the universe is to acknowledge that the healing love of God extends to all persons and to every part of existence, including work, leisure, money, economic and political power and their use, and to all those practical policies that either lead to justice or impede it. Therefore, when Christians come together in prayer, they make a commitment to carry God's love into all these areas of life (329).... The liturgy teaches us to have grateful hearts.... We are encouraged to use the goods of the earth for the benefit of all" (331).

Bishops' Committee on Priestly Life and Ministry, *Fulfilled in Your Hearing, The Homily in the Sunday Assembly* (Washington, D.C.: U.S.C.C., 1982). Regis A. Duffy, *On Becoming a Catholic, The Challenge of Christian Initiation* (San Francisco: Harper and Row, 1984). Roger Haight, "Historical Ecclesiology: An Essay on Method in the Study of the Church," *Science et Esprit* 39 (1987): 27-46 and 345-374. Thomas P. Ivory, *Conversion and Community, A Catechumenal Model for Total Parish Formation* (New York: Paulist Press, 1988). Joseph A. Komonchak, "Ecclesiology and Social Theory: A Methodological Essay," *The Thomist* 45 (1981): 262-283. Mark Searle, ed., *Sunday Morning: A Time for Worship* (Collegeville, Minnesota: The Liturgical Press, 1982).

JOHN J. O'BRIEN, C.P.

PASTORAL ADMINISTRATOR

Because of the increasing shortage of Roman Catholic presbyters, more and more parishes lack full time, resident presbyters as pastors. In such cases, lay women and men, religious sisters and brothers, and deacons are being appointed as leaders and principal pastoral ministers. This ministry is often referred to as that of pastoral administrator.

Other terms that are also used in North America include pastoral coordinator, parish life coordinator, parish director, resident pastoral minister, pastoral leader, parochial minister, and lay pastor.

The term "administrator" may be inadequate on two grounds. In Catholic canonical terminology, it is a temporary position, yet the end of the present shortage of presbyters does not seem very close. More importantly, "administrator" does not convey the spiritual dimensions of this minister's role and function.

Canon 517.2 requires that a presbyter be appointed to supervise and support the ministry of one or more pastoral administrators. He may be known as the presbyteral moderator, canonical pastor, priest supervisor or regional pastor. In addition, the ministry of the pastoral administrator may be supplemented by that of one or more presbyters who preside at the eucharist and other liturgical celebrations on a regular or occasional basis. This presbyter may be known as the sacramental priest or supply priest.

Pastoral administrators provide pastoral leadership to parishes on a full time basis, and should have appropriate qualifications. They minister as a presbyter-pastor would in administration, in ministering to people in crisis, in enabling individuals and groups to take leadership in ministry, in education and preparation for sacramental celebrations, in preparing and promoting good worship, and in generally building up the community of faith. They relate both to the presbyteral moderator and sacramental priests.

The liturgical ministry of the pastoral administrator will vary according to the availability of the sacramental priest and local needs and customs. However, he or she may be called upon to preside and preach at the following liturgies at least on an occasional basis: weekday celebrations of the liturgy of the hours, liturgy of the word, or other communal prayer; Sunday celebrations of the liturgy of the word or liturgy of the word and holy communion; penitential services; visits and communion to the sick; viaticum and prayers for the dying; marriages; funerals, including the wake, church service and burial; various blessings; baptism of persons in danger of death; acceptance into the catechumenate and the rites of the catechumenate of the Rite of Christian Initiation of Adults; distribution of ashes on Ash Wednesday; the Easter triduum (omitting the eucharist). When a sacramental priest is available only infrequently, the pastoral administrator may also preside and preach at baptisms for children and at other liturgies.

Resources for Sunday liturgies include:

Other resources are being prepared by the Bishops' Committee on the Liturgy in the United States, and by the National Liturgical Office in Canada.

J. FRANK HENDERSON

PENANCE

The term *penance* names both a religious practice and a sacrament of the church. The practice, which may arise from the desire to undo the damage of one's own sinfulness, or which may be undertaken as a prayer-action on behalf of someone else, or even the more inclusive "sins of the world," is primarily an act of worship, a turning to God who alone can overcome the reality of sin. It is not a spiritual payment that somehow buys forgiveness and mercy; it is the opening of the human heart to ask for, trust in and receive the mercy which God freely gives. The sacrament of the church goes under many names: confession, forgiveness, reconciliation, penance. In that sacrament the full religious practice of penance is set in motion; one surrenders even one's sinfulness to the mystery of God, in which mystery sin (alienation from God, from others and from oneself) is transformed into praise, forgiveness, communion and reconciliation. See entries below; also, Reconciliation; Forgiveness, theology of; Conversion from sin.

PENANCE AND CHILDREN

See **Children, first penance and**

PENANCE AND RECONCILIATION

The terms "reconciliation" and "penance" (*metanoia*) in their NT origins had a comprehensive reference to the impact of the saving work of Christ upon a fallen world and upon those who came to believe in Christ. The principal ritual focus of these terms was on baptism, the sacrament by which the saving work of Christ became effective and the eucharistic communion of believers was established.

This essay is concerned with a second usage of the terms "penance" and "reconciliation": their reference to the modern post-baptismal rites of the Roman Catholic church. The use of the terms in this context is characterized by considerable terminological instability. In an examination of the 1974 Roman Rite of Penance, Paul de Clerck has identified five meanings for the word "reconciliation" and six meanings for the word "penance" (de Clerck, 313-314). De Clerck found little logic in the manner of employment of these terms and concluded that the rite as a result betrays an overall lack of coherence. A further problem is that the terms "penance" and "reconciliation" are often used interchangeably in official documents, as well as in general ecclesiastical parlance. This is often the case even in instances where some distinction is being suggested. For example, the 1984 Apostolic Exhortation on Reconciliation suggests a distinction between penance and reconciliation, yet generally follows interchangeable usage.

In order to establish some terminological stability, we shall suggest a distinction between reconciliation and penance in post-baptismal context. By post-baptismal reconciliation is meant the formal restoration of baptized believers to the communion of the church after virtual excommunication through serious sin. By post-baptismal penance is meant the comprehensive ongoing process, involving every feature and practice of Christian life, by which believers are more fully converted to Christ. The use of the term "reconciliation" in the way suggested here is quite traditional and reflects the understanding of early Christianity. The term was habitually used to refer to the formal conclusion of the process by which those who had entered the order of penitents were restored to the communion of the church by the bishop and allowed to return to the eucharist.

This usage is reflected in the later-developed tradition. For instance, the prayers for the public restoration of a sinner found in the 8th-century Gelasian sacramentary (itself a compilation of earlier materials) manifest a strong reconciliation motif. These prayers are profoundly ecclesial in character and indicate a definite conception of the church as the community of reconciliation. At least up to the beginning of the Middle Ages, the rites of reconciliation were markedly public, processual in character, and clearly restricted to cases of serious sin. Typically they involved some form of excommunication, a period of intense ascetical reparation, and a liturgical act of reconciliation by the bishop. When this tradition eventually was replaced with the private form of penance developed in the Celtic church, the critical reconciliation motif remained intact and survived in all subsequent developments of the rite. Thus there is clear precedent for speaking of "the sacrament of reconciliation" in reference to the ritual act that performs the task of restoring sinners to the church.

This concept and practice of reconciliation is underlined in the decree prefacing the 1974 Roman Rite of Penance in which we read: "Because of human weakness, Christians 'turn aside from (their) early love' (see Rev 2:4) and even break off their friendship with God by sinning. The Lord, therefore, instituted a special sacrament of penance for the pardon of sins committed after baptism

(see Jn 20:21-23), and the Church has faithfully celebrated the sacrament through the centuries—in various ways, but retaining its essential elements" (*The Rites of the Catholic Church*, English translation prepared by The International Commission on English in the Liturgy, New York: Pueblo Publishing Co., 1976, 339). The Introduction to the rite declares that in this sacrament "the faithful 'obtain from the mercy of God pardon for their sins against him; at the same time they are reconciled with the Church which they wounded by their sins and which works for their conversion by charity, example, and prayer'" (n. 4; *The Rites*, 344). By the church's reconciling ministry in the sacrament, "those who by grave sin have withdrawn from the communion of love of God are called back" to the life they have lost (n. 7; *The Rites*, 346). The choreography of return and reconciliation is dramatized in a set of biblical images: "the Father receives the repentant son who comes back to him"; "Christ places the lost sheep on his shoulders and brings it back to the sheepfold"; "there is great joy at the banquet of God's Church over the sinner who has returned from afar" (n. 6; *The Rites*, 346).

If the term "reconciliation" in post-baptismal ritual context refers to the specific process by which those in serious sin are reconciled to the church, "penance" has a much wider and more inclusive reference and incorporates all those actions and processes that facilitate the sanctification, moral transformation and ongoing conversion of the church and its members at every level of corporate and individual Christian life. The closest biblical equivalent to penance is *metanoia*, which has to do with the profound interior conversion of life that accompanies the drama by which men and women become disciples of Christ. Latin Christianity translated *metanoia* as *paenitentia*, a word suggesting conversion of life or moral transformation. If baptism was *paenitentia prima*, the whole complex of prayer, ascetical practices and forms of life that advance baptismal commitment had the character of *paenitentia secunda* (Tertullian, *De paenitentia*, 6, 14). St. Augustine devised a scheme in which he identified three kinds of penance which together represent the whole ecclesial process of sanctification. There was pre-baptismal penance associated with the process of conversion; everyday penance which extends through the whole of life and achieves forgiveness from daily sins; and major penance for grave sins (cf. Sermons 351, 352).

While the term "reconciliation" traditionally had limited reference to the restoration of sinners to ecclesial communion, "penance" was used to refer to the comprehensive range of ascetical and sanctifying activities to which every faithful Christian is obliged. The 1974 Roman Rite of Penance, despite some conceptual instability, seems to conceive of penance in this comprehensive sense. On the question of the name of the revised rite, the U.S. Bishops' Commission on the Liturgy had this explanation: "The rite does not contain only the sacramental rites of reconciliation but also presents a variety of non-sacramental celebrations which, while penitential in character, are not sacramental celebrations. The broader title of Rite of Penance also embraces these celebrations" (*Commentary on the Rite of Penance*. Study Text 4 [Washington, D.C.: U.S.C.C., 1975], 10).

This comprehensive and progressive sense of penance is underlined by the 1984 Apostolic Exhortation on Reconciliation and Penance: "If we link penance with the *metanoia* which the synoptics refer to, it means the inmost change of heart under the influence of the word of God and in the perspective of the kingdom" (No. 4; Apostolic Exhortation on Reconciliation and Penance, published in *Origins* 14 [1984], 435). Accordingly, "it is one's whole existence that becomes

penitential, that is to say, directed toward a continuous striving for what is better" (*ibid.*). Penance means, "in the Christian theological and spiritual vocabulary, asceticism, that is to say, the concrete daily effort of a person, supported by God's grace, to lose his or her own life for Christ as the only means of gaining it" (*ibid.*). It refers to the "effort to put off the old man and put on the new; an effort to overcome in oneself what is of the flesh in order that what is spiritual may prevail; a continual effort to rise from the things of here below to the things of above, where Christ is" (*ibid.*). Penance is "a conversion that passes from the heart to deeds and then to the Christian's whole life" (*ibid.*).

The terms "reconciliation" and "penance" and the theological concepts they enshrine resist complete compartmentalization. There is considerable overlap and their somewhat interchangeable character yields up insights that are integral to biblical and liturgical theology. However, within the more limited realm of modern Roman Catholic ritual theory and practice, there are good grounds for more stable and restricted usage.

See **Forgiveness, theology of; Reconciliation, sacrament of**

Paul de Clerck, "Celebrating Penance or Reconciliation," *The Clergy Review* 68 (1983): 310-321. M. Francis Mannion, "Penance and Reconciliation: A Systemic Analysis," *Worship* 60 (1986): 98-118.

M. FRANCIS MANNION

PENANCE SERVICES, NON-SACRAMENTAL

In the revised Rite of Penance (1973) for the Roman Catholic church, in addition to three forms for the sacrament of reconciliation, liturgical services without sacramental absolution are likewise recommended for use. In structure these are essentially services of the word. Proclamation from scripture calls the assembly to conversion of heart. There is an examination of conscience led by a lector. People may come forward to speak publicly those things for which they feel the community needs to ask God's forgiveness: healing and liberation. All pray the *confiteor*, and the service is brought to completion with the Lord's Prayer and some form of blessing (e.g., laying on of hands by the presider).

The intent of such services is clearly stated: "to foster the spirit of penance within the Christian community; to help the faithful to prepare for confession which can be made individually later at a convenient time; to help children gradually to form their conscience about sin in human life and about freedom from sin through Christ; to help catechumens during their conversion" (R.P., 37). How successful these services are in achieving this intent, however, is another matter.

Experience with these non-sacramental penance services seems to show that they are not as satisfying to the faithful as are the sacramental forms. This is perhaps due to patterns of habit; perhaps to the Catholic instinct that requires some sacramental action to respond to and complete the word. The contrast is particularly evident in places where communal sacramental forms (Form II or III) were first experienced, and where non-sacramental services are forced to take their place due to shortage of priest-confessors and/or to increased restrictions on the use of general absolution. In a large American suburban parish, for example, where general absolution was given to assemblies of five to seven hundred people at a time during Advent and Lent, there are but seventy to eighty who attend the non-sacramental service of the word.

Non-sacramental penance services can be both successful and quite helpful if a proper context is provided for them. In parishes, for example, where an order of penitents is established, Lent can provide such a context. All members of the parish may be invited to become liturgical penitents and to confess their sins on Ash Wednesday and carry out a penance of prayer, fasting and almsgiving toward eventual reconciliation with God and the church on Holy Thursday. The Mass of the Lord's Supper is then seen as the goal of the reconciliation process and the completion of its celebration. In such a context, non-sacramental services may provide faithful, formal penitents, as well as catechumens and candidates for entry into the church at Easter, with opportunities for conversion at an increasingly deeper level.

Such celebrations may also be appreciated by groups of engaged couples as part of their preparation for marriage. Since both parties of the marriage are not always from the same Christian community, and since these services can welcome other Christians as well, from the Roman Catholic perspective, non-sacramental services can be very appropriate celebrations of God's reconciling love. They can also help alleviate some of the stress and tension that may arise between the engaged couple and their families as marriage preparation unfolds.

Children can be led to a better experience of sacramental reconciliation by simple celebrations of the non-sacramental rites. In an American culture, teenagers find the non-sacramental rites much less threatening than the auricular confession which they have almost universally abandoned.

Other seasons and feasts can also provide a helpful context for non-sacramental penance services. Advent can offer a welcome ground for them as preparation for Christmas. Pentecost can be a good time to proclaim the victory of Christ over sin and the power of the Holy Spirit coming among us for the forgiveness of sins.

See **Reconciliation, liturgies of; Absolution, general; Penitents, order of**

ROBERT H. BLONDELL

PENANCE, CANONICAL

In its first perception of how the victory of Christ over sin may be offered to men and women, the early church adopted and adapted the water bath; baptism for the forgiveness of sin (see Acts 2:38). In its second perception, it pointed to the "breaking of bread," the Lord's Supper enacted in his memory (see Mt 26:28). In its third perception, the church had to deal with those who, by public acts such as murder, apostasy and adultery, had severed themselves, after baptism, from the communion of the eucharist. Sinners had to be restored to eucharistic communion.

Canonical penance refers to an elaborate form of restoration to communion that developed in the early centuries in tandem with the elaborate form of Christian initiation. It addressed serious public sinners and therefore involved them in public acts of penitence on their path to reconciliation with God and with the church. An order of penitents was established. The whole community, by its own prayer of intercession, was involved in the process of reconciliation. Penitents were publicly reconciled on Holy Thursday (in the West) and Good Friday (in the East). It had one severe drawback which eventually led to its demise as a practical sacramental response to human sinfulness: it was allowed but once. It was therefore put off by many until their death bed.

See **Reconciliation, sacrament of; Forgiveness, theology of**

PENANCE, CELTIC

The church order of the Celtic church differed from the church on the continent in that it was arranged around monastic spiritual centers rather than according to territorial dioceses. In these spiritual centers, beginning in about the 5th century, a different response to human sin-

fulness took shape. The context was spiritual direction and guidance; private rather than public. The process was confession or acknowledgement of sin, some penitential acts for the reform of life, and forgiveness or "absolution" pronounced in private once the penitential acts had been completed. Its advantage over the earlier form of the sacrament, namely canonical penance, was its frequency. Its disadvantage was its separation of the reconciliation process from the liturgical assembly.

The rise of Celtic penance signified a changed understanding of sin as well as a changed understanding of God's forgiveness. No longer a public act with its own public consequences, sin was regarded as "code violation" and its consequence was the incurring of debt. The "model" was of serf and Lord; it was also called "tariff penance." Debt had to be paid before the debt could be "absolved."

In the earlier form of penance, canonical penance, the prayer of intercession allowed the people of the church a part in one's reconciliation process. This instinct of community support continued in Celtic penance, though in somewhat bizarre fashion. The debt of one could be paid by many (substitutions); the debt of the dead could be paid by the living (remissions); the debt of both the living and the dead could be paid by "tapping" the unused merit of those "holy ones" called "saints" (indulgences); most of all the debt could be completely dissolved by applying to the sinner, living and dead, the fruits of Christ's own sacrifice. The eucharist became once again the sacrament of reconciliation, but in the *quid pro quo* mindset of economic exchange, rather than the ecclesial mindset of the church gathered for prayer.

The current practice of "private confession" derives from the Celtic form of penance. Where once it was the unwelcome intruder on the normative pattern of canonical penance, it is regarded now as the norm. Contemporary desires for more communal forms of the sacrament seem to reverse the earlier pattern of evolution where Celtic penance wrested priority of place from canonical penance.

See **Reconciliation, sacrament of; Order of penitents; Forgiveness, theology of; Reconciliation, liturgies of**

PENITENTIAL DAYS

Penitential days refer to those periods in the liturgical calendar when special attention is given to the discipline of ascetical practices such as prayer, fasting and almsgiving. The *General Norms for the Liturgical Year and the Calendar* (1969) and the revised Code of Canon Law (1983) both absorbed the reforms made by Paul VI in the apostolic constitution *Paenitemini* (1966). This reorganization of penitential discipline includes the observance of penitential days formerly known in the church's calendar as ember days. However, they are not numbered among the days on which fast or abstinence is required.

By the 8th century in Rome, penitential acts observed on particular days of the week came to be known as the *quattuor tempora*, the four seasons, and hence *ember days* by way of the German *Quatember*. Twelve liturgical days arranged in four triads, i.e., the Wednesday, Friday and Saturday of four weeks of the year, were located approximately at the beginning of the four seasons. Although origins remain unclear, it seems certain that their observance began in the church in Rome and became part of western practice only when the Roman liturgy made its way into other western countries.

The *Didache* (8:1), an early Christian document dating from the end of the apostolic period, testifies to the observance of Wednesdays and Fridays as fast days. Wednesday marked the day anticipating the Lord's arrest thus beginning

the passion, and Friday commemorated the day of his death on the cross. The origin of the penitential character of Saturdays remains obscure. It may have developed because it was the day the disciples fasted while their Lord rested in the tomb. It also followed Friday, the day of pain and sorrow, and preceded Sunday, the day of joy and glory.

The earliest testimony to ember fasts came from the 4th-century author, Pontius Maximus, who affirmed their observance with an appeal to Zech 8:19: "The fasts of the fourth month and of the fifth, the seventh, and the tenth, shall become festivals of joy and gladness." By the 5th century the ember fasts were established and familiar practice as witnessed in the ember week sermons of Pope Leo I (d. 461) who considered them binding moral precepts of the new covenant that originated in OT regulations and in apostolic tradition. He was the first to associate the practice with the four seasons of the year: in the spring a fast during the forty days before Easter, in summer a fast at Pentecost, in the fall during September and in winter during December. The purpose of the cycle of fasting was to learn from the constant and recurring rhythm of the year's cycle that all the baptized were in constant need of purification. At least since Pope Gelasius I at the end of the 5th century, candidates were presented and scrutinized for ordination on Wednesday, presented for public approbation on Friday and ordained at the vigil liturgy on Saturday. The *Liber pontificalis* which dates from the early 6th century testifies that Pope Callistus I (217-222) ordered a fast on three Saturdays of the year, in summer, autumn and winter, in keeping with the prophecy of Joel 2:15-19, at the season of new grain, wine and oil.

Each ember week ended between Saturday night and Sunday morning with a long vigil mentioned several times by Pope Leo I in his sermons. The Mass of this night vigil counted for the Sunday. However, by the 7th century a special Mass was formulated for this Sunday while the nocturnal liturgy was regularly moved to an earlier hour until it was finally celebrated on Saturday morning. As a result Saturdays in ember weeks also took on a penitential character such as Wednesdays and Fridays.

The custom of seasonal fasting as observed on particular penitential days spread throughout northern Europe with the acceptance of the Roman liturgy. The sending of Augustine and his monks to England by Pope Gregory I (d. 604), the missionary work of Boniface (d. 754) from England to Germany and the efforts of Pepin (d. 768) and Charlemagne (d. 814) extended these penitential practices.

By the middle of the 9th century the observance of the four groups of ember days was widespread in the West. At the Roman synod of 1078, Pope Gregory VII resolved confusion about the exact weeks within which the ember days were to be observed. His decision marked the first time that the exact dates for the church's observance of ember days were determined authoritatively. They were to begin on the Wednesday after the first Sunday of Lent (spring), in the octave of Pentecost (summer), after the feast of the Exaltation of the Cross on September 14 (autumn) and the week after the third Sunday of Advent (winter). These days represented an intense ascetical effort at the beginning of each of the four seasons. The liturgical observance of each ember day included its own proper office. The priest or bishop who presided at Mass wore violet vestments with the exception of red during the octave of Pentecost. The traditional penitential exercises of prayer, fasting and almsgiving were complemented and balanced by days of thanksgiving and gratitude for the seasonal harvests.

The revision of the liturgical year and calendar which followed Vatican II retained the ember days in principle while leaving their date and form to the discretion of episcopal conferences so that observances could be adapted to the needs of the local churches. Paul VI reformed the section of the 1917 Code of Canon Law on penitential days with the apostolic constitution *Paenitemini* (1966). That same year the National Conference of Catholic Bishops in the United States instructed Catholics to abstain from eating meat on Ash Wednesday and on all Fridays during Lent and to fast on Ash Wednesday and Good Friday. A recommendation was also made to the entire Catholic community to abstain from meat on all Fridays of the year; individuals were encouraged to impose a fast on themselves on all weekdays of Lent. The penitential nature of the Lenten season was thus highlighted and reinforced while the Advent season was characterized less by penance and more by expectation and vigilance.

The *General Norms for the Liturgical Year and the Calendar* (nn. 45-47) acknowledge the traditional observance of ember days and affirm their value. The revised Code of Canon Law contains five canons (1249-1253) which deal with the purpose and particulars of days of penance. They largely echo *Paenitemini*. The purpose of penitential days, especially all Fridays of the year and the season of Lent, is to unify all Christians in a common observance of penance by way of fidelity to prayer and works of charity, to self-denial and the observance of fast and abstinence. Such practices no longer seek self-abnegation as their goal; rather, they constitute a discipline that enables a faithful and effective response to the gospel mandate of love. The particulars of penitential observances, such as their time, number and purpose, are entrusted to the discretion of the episcopal conferences.

Adolf Adam, *The Liturgical Year*, trans. Matthew J. O'Connell (New York, Pueblo Publishing Co., 1981), 91-119, 186-197. *Documents on the Liturgy*,

1963-1979: Conciliar, Papal, and Curial Texts, trans. Thomas C. O'Brien, International Committee on English in the Liturgy (Collegeville, Minn.: Liturgical Press, 1982), 942-943, 1161, 1253.

DANIEL P. GRIGASSY, O.F.M.

PENITENTIAL PRACTICES

"Repent and believe the gospel" is a call to conversion, but it involves more than just a change of heart. To repent is not merely to be sorry for sin, but to undo the damage caused by sin, to reform one's life, to make the crooked ways straight and the rough paths smooth for the coming of the Lord. In Christian tradition, penitential exercises were absolutely essential for the forgiveness of sins. The link between forgiveness and doing penance was weakened by reducing the "penance" of the sacrament of reconciliation to the recitation of prescribed prayers after absolution had already been given.

Church teaching and practice distinguished four parts in the sacrament of forgiveness: contrition, confession, satisfaction and absolution. The first three are acts of the penitent, and belong together as parts of a single process of repentance. The "satisfaction" was a program of prayer, fasting and almsgiving which gave concrete expression to the inner conversion, strengthened and developed it, and helped to undo the damage caused by sin. During the first eight centuries this was the normal pattern. In the smaller communities of early Christianity the sinner was easily recognized by his sinful behavior and was "excommunicated" from the community, both to teach him a lesson and to protect the community from the contagion of his sin. He was re-admitted only after he had proved the sincerity of his repentance by carrying out the "penance" prescribed by the community. In the case of secret grave sins, the sinner would confess these to a spiritual counsellor who would decide whether they were grave enough to warrant public penance. But absolution came only after the penance had been completed, and it was a solemn reconciliation, usually on Holy Thursday.

In the early centuries the penances were mostly public, and re-admission to the community was allowed only once in a lifetime. By the 8th century frequent confession had become common, but because many penitents did not return for absolution after doing the prescribed penance, the practice developed of doing the penance afterwards. This inversion of the order in the acts of the penitent was meant to be pastorally helpful, but in fact it introduced an artificial break in the natural process of repentance. A more serious consequence of the change was that a new outlook developed in the understanding of penance. It came to be seen as a punishment for sin, and the model for the sacrament of forgiveness came to be the criminal one, the court of law with judge, sentence, punishment. More and more, penance was seen simply as a penalty to be paid for wrongdoing. The system of tariff penances helped this process with its detailed lists of graded penances for different kinds of sins. Prayer, fasting, abstinence from marital relations, pilgrimage or exile were all imposed. Some were for life, others for years, from thirty down to one year. Seven days fasting was the penance for drunkenness, one day on bread and water for immoderate eating. The severity needs to be judged against the general harshness of life in those centuries, and it must be admitted that the penitential books did stress the need for conversion and strove to emphasize the ecclesial and sacramental aspect of penance. Good intentions, however, were not enough. The judicial model is still largely dominant. In spite of the new rites of reconciliation, there is still a crisis about the sacrament. The judicial model needs to give way to more biblical and more caring models, of healing (medicine), of pastoring (the shepherd looking for the lost sheep), of the weak, immature person needing help to grow.

Of the papal documents since the council, Pope Paul VI's exhortation *Paenitemini* (1966) is the one most in line with Vatican II thinking and contemporary theology. It emphasizes the social dimension of sin, conversion and penance, and makes clear that penance and social responsibility cannot be separated. It takes up the traditional penitential activities of prayer, fasting and almsgiving, but stresses that they need to be developed in line with the needs of today's world. The penitential dimension of all Christian life is underlined as part of ongoing conversion, with a strong emphasis on social responsibility.

Any rehabilitation of penitential practices needs to relate them intrinsically to the nature and effects of sin. They are not punishments imposed for wrongdoing, but medicinal practices to heal the harm done by sin. When seen in this light, the traditional ones make a lot of sense. Augustine listed them as: prayer, fasting, almsgiving, endurance of the sufferings of daily life, forgiveness of insults, works of service, but most of all praying the Our Father in the liturgical assembly.

In religious terms, sin brings about a break in the relationship with God, alienates one from one's better self, from one's fellow human beings and in a certain sense from the environment. The penitential practices work in all of these areas. Prayer can heal the break with God and rebuild the love relationship he offers. But for this to happen, more is needed than the recitation of a few formal prayers. It is not a question of placating an angry God to make up for the offense. God does not need our prayer, but we need it in order to allow God's love to come back into our lives. Sin is basically self-assertion, putting self before all else, deciding for oneself what

is right and wrong. To change this attitude we need first to recognize and accept that we have done wrong: "I have sinned against you, you only, O God" (Ps 51:4). We need to admit our need for God: "Create a pure heart in me, O God" (Ps 51:10). But most of all we need to become prayer-full people so that God *can* put a new spirit in us without forcing our freedom.

Augustine saw the Our Father as most efficacious for repentance and forgiveness. He says: "God has established in his church ... a remedy which we need to take each day by saying: 'Forgive us our trespasses'" (Sermon 352.8). To pray the words Jesus gave us is not merely to recite a prayer, but to want to take on the basic attitude of mind and heart expressed in the words: that we truly want God's name (his person, his will) to be blessed, respected, honored; that we really want his kingdom to come, a kingdom of justice and peace, of harmony, of mutual love and service; that we recognize God's goodness in the gifts of the earth, our daily bread, that we recognize our dependence on him in meeting our needs. When we pray: "Forgive us our trespasses" we truly want to be healed of our sinfulness, even if it costs, and especially we ask God's help in forgiving others. To the extent that we forgive others, we become more like our heavenly Father who forgives all with equal love. As a penitential practice to enable us to relate to God as we should, the Our Father needs to be more than a formula. It needs to become a basic attitude and outlook, a whole pattern of life. Augustine points to its strategic position in the eucharist, where it is an expression of reconciliation with God and with the community, so that it is both a means for becoming the body of Christ and a preparation for receiving the body of Christ.

Fasting is closely allied to prayer. Jesus speaks of certain demons that can be cast out only through prayer and fasting. From earliest times fasting has been a common religious practice: as atonement for sins, as an expression of sorrow and conversion of heart, as a purification, as a discipline to control the body and facilitate prayer, and as a means of getting God's ear. The church no longer imposes the rigid fasting periods of former times, but devout Christians are rediscovering the benefits of fasting for improving the quality of spiritual life. Although the traditional fast meant only one full meal a day, it is not uncommon now to find committed people who observe a total fast from solid food for a full day each week. The mortification involved (death to the unbridled self) helps to heal the selfishness and internal alienation involved in sin, bringing a new wholeness to one's life. Fasting can be understood in the broad sense also to include restriction or abstinence in all one's appetites.

When sin directly hurts one's neighbor there is need to undo the damage caused to his person, property or reputation, to make restitution if something has been stolen. This is a matter of strict justice. But every sin has a social dimension in so far as the sinner's selfishness lessens the holiness of the body of Christ and also leaves him less capable of reaching out in love to his neighbors. Almsgiving and the other corporal works of mercy have always been the means of overcoming this aspect of sin. But the spirit of almsgiving can be broadened to include all giving of oneself to help others in need. In today's world of refugees, famine and natural disasters there is no shortage of worthy causes needing help. But a special form of almsgiving aimed at overcoming the social effects of sin is work for justice and peace. In his closing address to the 1983 Roman Synod of Bishops, John Paul II spoke of the social dimension of sin and penance, and he stressed that working for peace is an integral part of conversion. It is difficult

to trace individual responsibility for sinful, unjust structures of discrimination and exploitation, but we are all involved, however unwittingly. Communal celebrations of penance can heighten awareness of our solidarity in sin, and we can pray for God's healing forgiveness, but to avoid the accusation of "cheap grace" our penitential practice should include some action for social justice.

Alienation from the environment is another effect of sin. The earth God gave us as our home and garden can become a hostile environment, so that we earn our bread in sweat and toil (Genesis 3). But a new form of alienation is taking place at present in so far as we exploit the resources of our planet with no thought for the delicate balance of nature so essential for the common well-being of all God's creatures. Our concern for comfort, luxury, efficiency and profit has raped the earth and poisoned the sea and air so that we have no gift to leave to future generations. Pope Paul VI's call to the church to find new forms of penance to meet the social dimension of sin is a special challenge in this area. The size of the problem should not be an excuse for inaction. Penitential exercises can reach from personal discipline in the purchase and use of certain goods, to involvement in tree-planting, political lobbying, consciousness-raising.

To discuss penitential practices simply in terms of the penance to be done as part of the sacrament of reconciliation fails to do justice to Paul VI's statement: "By divine law all the faithful are required to do penance." It is an integral part of Christian life. Although Jesus had no need of personal repentance, he fasted for forty days. Following the Master, every Christian must take up his/her cross and share in the sufferings of Christ. There are many sins for which the sacrament is not necessary, but none can be forgiven without conversion, contrition; and these need to be externally expressed in penitential exercises. Whether used as remedies for venial sins or accepted as satisfaction for sins confessed in the sacrament, penitential exercises are directed towards a new way of life. Their purpose is to express and develop the ongoing conversion to which all Christians are called.

J. Dallen, *The Reconciling Community* (New York, Pueblo, 1986). R.J. Kennedy, *Reconciliation: The Continuing Agenda* (Collegeville: Liturgical Press, 1987).

SEÁN FAGAN, S.M.

PENITENTIAL RITE AT MASS

Part of the introductory rites of the revised order of Mass, the penitential rite follows the entrance song and greeting and precedes the *Gloria* and collect or gathering prayer. It is given as an alternative to the rite of blessing and sprinkling which is not itself penitential in character; its purpose is to express the paschal nature of Sunday and to be a memorial of baptism. In pastoral practice the penitential rite is more often used than the sprinkling rite.

Three versions of an invitation to repentance followed by a pause for silent prayer lead into three forms of penitential prayers. The first option is the Confiteor which all pray in unison. The second is a two-fold exchange between the presider and assembly which acknowledges corporate sinfulness and asks for the Lord's mercy. The third alternative lists eight possible invocations, each one structured around a three-fold litany of praise to the Lord which the presider or deacon invokes and to which the assembly responds after each entry, ". . . Lord, have mercy, . . . Christ, have mercy, . . . Lord, have mercy." The eight models offer a pattern for presiders and planners in composing original versions. The invocations are to be addressed to Christ; they are to be brief, direct and adapted to the season of the year, the day's feast or the images and metaphors of the day's scripture readings. They should never be turned into an examination of conscience. (A number of publishers of leaflet missals as well as enthusiastic presiders have unfortunately promoted invitations to the "Lord, have mercy" litany which begin, "For the times we have . . . , Lord, have mercy.")

The third invitation to the penitential prayers, "let us call to mind our sins," is more exactly rendered: "let us acknowledge our sins," a translation that yields a subtle though significant difference for a proper understanding of the penitential rite. An acknowledgement of sinfulness and a call for mercy avoid slipping into an examination of conscience or a listing of particular sinful acts. Thus the purpose of the penitential rite at Mass in its various forms is not to replace or be the occasion for the sacrament of reconciliation. Nor is it to drive the assembly inward into a review of sins. Rather, it is to move the assembly outward into an acknowledgement that the community at worship stands before a merciful God.

The presider concludes each of the three forms of penitential prayers with a formula of absolution during which no sign of the cross is required. The *Kyrie, eleison* or *Lord, have mercy* has been retained in the first form of the rite, after the Confiteor, but it tends to be disconnected from what precedes and follows.

The inclusion of a penitential rite as a public and communal act at the beginning of Mass is an innovation in the 1969 missal of Paul VI, its one single feature that is without precedent in the Roman rite. Formerly the presider's vesting prayers in the sacristy and the prayers at the foot of the altar were his private penitential devotion. The processional usage of the *Kyrie, eleison* chant rooted in the movement of the bishop from the altar to his throne in the apse of a church has faded in the missal of Paul VI. The penitential rite has been experienced in its various forms as a disturbance in the tual flow of the liturgy, an afterthought etween the greeting and gathering rayer.

Many pastors, liturgists and litur-iologists note the misplacement of the enitential rite. If the purpose of the ntroductory rites is "to make the as-embled people a unified community and) prepare them properly to listen to iod's word and celebrate the eucharist" *General Instruction of the Roman Missal*, 24), why run the risk of individ-alizing members of the assembly in a enitential mode after they have gathered recisely as a worshipping community? Vhile this unevenness is adjusted in aptismal, wedding and funeral Masses where there is no call for the use of the enitential rite and where the intro-uctory rites proper to those liturgies uffice, it remains in other eucharistic elebrations.

In its current position after the entrance ong and greeting, the penitential rite arries a semi-Pelagian thrust and seems o imply that people inaugurate their own conversion. The recommendation las been made that the rite be placed at he end of the liturgy of the word prior to he prayer of the faithful since it is the proclamation of the word of God that nakes penitence possible. A penitential leart is open and receptive to the word .nd life of Christ; however, the initiative or such conversion always comes first rom the Lord.

Simply because the communal peni-ential rite at Mass is unprecedented does lot imply that penitential forms find no .lace in the Mass. The use of a Kyrie itany as an acclamation or as an ac-:ompaniment to processional movement s a valuable form of supplication when .uch litanies are called for. Thus, some iturgical theologians find no need for a)enitential rite in every eucharistic cele-)ration. Their proposal encourages future 'evisions of the introductory rites to .djust to the spirit of the liturgical season.

In the season of Lent or on other peni-tential days that call for more attention to supplication and penitence, a peni-tential entrance psalm or Kyrie litany would enhance the spirit of the event. Any proposal to revise the introductory rites ought to come, not from a desire to simplify and clarify the rite for the sake of expedience, but as an effort to highlight the most important aspect of the rites which is the gathering of the assembly for worship.

See **Gathering rites**

___

John F. Baldovin, "Kyrie Eleison and the Entrance Rite of the Roman Eucharist," *Worship* 60 (1986): 334-347. Johannes H. Emminghaus, *The Eucharist: Essence, Form, Celebration*, trans. Matthew J. O'Connell (Collegeville, Minn.: Liturgical Press, 1978), 104-133. Josef A. Jungmann, *The Mass: An Historical, Theological, and Pastoral Survey*, trans. Julian Fernandes, ed. Mary Ellen Evans (Collegeville, Minn.: Liturgical Press, 1976), 160-174. Ralph A Keifer, *To Give Thanks and Praise: General Instruction of the Roman Missal* (Washington, D.C.: National Association of Pastoral Musicians, 1980), 105-115.

DANIEL P. GRIGASSY, O.F.M.

PENITENTS, ORDER OF

The order of penitents is a process of intensive pastoral care for Roman Catho-lics who have been suffering estrangement or alienation from the institutional church and who feel called by the Holy Spirit to return to practice through reconciliation. It strives to respect the person's own story of constant conversion and the challenges of the gospel as proclaimed by the Roman church.

It is a contemporary pastoral move-ment that originated in the United States in the early 1980s, in a few parishes, out of a concern for the alienated. It has grown significantly in the United States and Canada, principally, through the efforts of the North American Forum for the Catechumenate's Office of Remem-bering Church. The Forum has become a network for parishes and pastoral min-isters reaching out with gestures of reconciliation and offering a process that ministers healing, liberation, and forgiveness.

The contemporary ministry of the order is solidly based in the patristic church of the 2nd through the 4th centuries, when it was parallel to the ancient catechumenal journey for those coming into the church. Fathers in the age of Tertullian, Cyprian, and Leo welcomed serious sinners into a process of healing called exomologesis. It was considered the heart of the ancient order and brought the penitent, by stages of penitential process, back to full communion with the church. It respected and thrived on the liturgical year with entrance into the order on Ash Wednesday and the joyful celebration of solemn sacramental reconciliation on Holy Thursday. It was a ministry of the whole church with much emphasis on the strength of the praying community. Small groups of faithful would meet periodically with individual penitents, at their request, to pray with them. Similar groups surrounded each penitent to fast for them as well as give alms for the forgiveness of their sins. Bishops, presbyters, and deacons met frequently with the penitents and faithful for simple forms of exorcism, much like those found in the contemporary experience of the R.C.I.A.. These exorcisms were always accompanied by the rite of imposition of hands, as a parting gesture, and the continuing ministry of the church toward reconciliation of the penitents.

While the contemporary version of the order of penitents is a natural parallel to the restored catechumenate, it lacks the severity of the old acts of public penance. It was those acts of penance which eventually brought the ancient order to a close, and the imposition on the church of private, auricular confession at the Fourth Lateran Council. Pastoral creativity has served the tradition well by laying plans for a restored order of penitents that is fashioned on our patristic tradition. It respects the latest research on con-

version and aims to cooperate with the movement of the Spirit in the community as well as in the individual penitent.

The process of formal reconciliation is marked by stages of catechesis and moments of inner healing. It begins with a parish effort of evangelization to call back to faith and practice those who are alienated from the community. Each penitent is given a companion with whom to walk the journey of reconciliation. A team of ministers is formed and penitents and companions meet weekly for catechesis, prayer, and Sunday liturgy. The lectionary becomes the basis of the catechesis each week while the formation focuses on the liturgy. As Lent approaches, the penitents, in the midst of the community, are signed with the ashes and begin to journey through the liturgical season serving the community as a witness to everyone's call to repent and reform.

In the parish community, the penitent is a fellow journeyer with the others. As penitents are called to the confession of sins and God's mercy on Ash Wednesday so are all parishioners. A penance is negotiated with each penitent by the priest and absolution is postponed until after the homily in the Mass of the Lord's Supper on Holy Thursday. Following the absolution the mandatum is celebrated with the penitents and the peace rite anticipated from the communion ritual. Newly reconciled penitents are invited into the action of the eucharistic prayer. At the communion time they are invited to the table for the Lord's Prayer and are the first to participate in the communion.

Like the catechumens, the penitents spend time in reflection on their experience of being forgiven, restored to the table and reconciled with the church at Easter. As the penitents anticipate the Feast of Pentecost and prepare for it, they are called to a commitment of ministry in the parish. This is not to be interpreted as a "reinstatement." Penitents come to the table on Holy Thursday with a new set of relationships with the community of the faithful. Now they are present with the faithful as apostles and witnesses. They share more deeply in the mission of the whole church to preach the word, to care for the poor, to give praise and thanks to the Father. They are a new people in the risen Christ.

I have pastored this process of a restored order of penitents for eight years at St. Ephrem, Sterling Heights, Michigan. The parish now has a team of three couples who are the principal care givers in the order. It is a permanent part of the structure of this large suburban parish and welcomes, for pastoral care, alienated Catholics. In this experience the most crucial issue has been the connectedness of the order with the ongoing liturgical life of the parish at large. Because the order is built around the liturgical calendar, as is the R.C.I.A., penitents are in full view of the praying community and often the object of that powerful prayer.

The community understands well that the small wooden cross given penitents on the first Sunday of Advent is a request for prayer and an invitation for the faithful to express some form of welcome home to penitents upon meeting them. Penitents are part of the entrance procession at every eucharist and enjoy the approving nods and smiles of parishioners as they process behind catechumens on the way to the altar. As penitents gather around the processional cross in the sanctuary, the faithful chant the penitential rite over them, praising God for his wonderful mercy and generous forgiving love. The opening prayer is prayed and all are seated to hear the word. Catechumens and penitents alike are dismissed at the appropriate time after the homily.

On Ash Wednesday penitents and faithful are encouraged to come for auricular confession of sins and negotiate a penance for Lent, of prayer, fasting, and almsgiving. Having agreed upon a penance, all leave without absolution to practice the penance and deeply embrace the Lenten spirit. Holy Thursday, then, becomes the day for celebrating reconciliation with absolution available to parishioners all day beginning at six in the morning until the beginning of the Mass of the Lord's Supper in the evening during which penitents are absolved after the homily. This effort of separating the confession from the absolution provides all with an opportunity toward some form of process in the sacrament. People begin to see the healing and liberating effects of penance. It is more clearly perceived as medicinal rather than punitive.

The liturgical thrust of our Lenten observance is always done in the framework of a universal call to penance. Members of the order are reminded over and over that they are witnesses to all the faithful, that all are called to be penitents. Parishioners are reminded in a Lenten booklet, the Sunday homily, the parish paper, that all are walking the journey of repentance with this small group of formal penitents in their midst, to be a sacrament of God's mercy for all. Holy water fonts at church entrances are drained the day before Ash Wednesday and filled with the ashes. Parishioners are encouraged to use these ashes all during Lent until the sacred triduum.

Evaluation of this ministry is very important. About eighty-five people have been part of the order during the past eight years. Recidivism is a factor but it is very low. It occurs principally in those who have not taken on a ministry in the parish following their reconciliation.

Joseph Cardinal Bernardin, "New Rite of Penance Suggested" *Origins* (October 1983): 324. James Dallen, *The Reconciling Community* (New York: Pueblo, 1986). Joseph A. Favazza, *The Order of Penitents* (Collegeville, Minnesota: The Liturgical

Press, 1988). James Lopresti, *Penance: A Reform Proposal for the Rite* (Washington, D.C.: The Pastoral Press, 1987).

ROBERT H. BLONDELL

PENTECOST

The term "Pentecost" in the Christian liturgial calendar refers both to the fifty-day celebration of Easter and to the culminating day of the celebration, Pentecost Sunday. The calendar pattern before the Vatican II reform had for all practical purposes lost the sense of "the fifty days of Easter," and Pentecost was considered an isolated feast, celebrating the birth of the church, provided with its own vigil and quite oddly, its own octave. In the post-conciliar reform, priority is restored to the more original sense of Pentecost as a celebration of fifty days; Pentecost Sunday concludes the celebration of Easter, and does not stand on its own as an independent feast. Some ambiguities, however, remain. The octave has been removed, but the vigil remains; and while the Easter vigil is clearly given as *the* time for the initiation sacraments—baptism, confirmation and eucharist—some provision is made for the delayed celebration of confirmation on Pentecost.

For those in charismatic movements, Pentecost is *the* day: the day of the Spirit. For those more liturgically inclined, Easter is *the* day: the day of resurrection *and* the Spirit. The tension or dispute between the two is not unlike that between those who prefer the unity of initiation sacraments (baptism, confirmation, eucharist *in that order*) and those who urge confirmation as a sacrament of adulthood, thereby celebrated long after baptism and first eucharist. Both are biblically grounded. Johannine and Pauline theology hold resurrection and Spirit-sending together as one act; Luke-Acts separates them in time. The theological task seems to be first to recapture the unity of the mystery of Christ (a unity ruptured in the West, though preserved in the East) and in the context of that unity to understand the difference. Resurrection and Spirit-sending are indeed two movements. How best to "express the mystery of Christ" (S.C., 2) in this regard remains to be discovered.

See **Calendar, liturgical; Easter season; Holy Spirit in Christian worship; Confirmation**

PIETY, LITURGICAL

See **Prayer, liturgical; Spirituality, liturgical; Devotions, popular; Eucharistic devotions**

POLITICS, LITURGY AND

At its most general level, this issue concerns the relationship between the public worship of a faith community and the organization and regulation of life in a society. Because both are essentially public activities, liturgy and politics, whether of the faith community or the civil society, can influence each other in many ways.

The polity of a faith community will be reflected in its worship. The attitudes and values, norms and structures, goals and concerns of the wider community can also affect public worship, especially the prayers, preaching, and modes of participation in it. When found congruent, elements from political life can be reflected in the form or substance of public worship; when they are seen to be alien or incompatible, the liturgy can take shape in opposition to them. In either case political realities can be significant for liturgical life.

For its part, public worship always makes a statement about human life and the relationship of persons to God and the community. It readily influences participants' activities and judgments in the ecclesiastical and civil communities, particularly when faith, morality, or mission are involved. These effects can originate from the faith or mysteries of faith at the heart of worship. Worship can also be deliberately designed or used to advance particular causes in the community.

In the Roman Catholic church, the liturgy is the full public worship of God by the church as mystical body of Christ (S.C., 7), principally the celebration of the sacraments. In the liturgy, by means of word and sign, the church encounters the Lord who died and rose in human history and will one day return in glory. The liturgy is therefore a powerful source of transformation and understanding for persons and communities (S.C., 5-10, 47-48, 59). Especially when they celebrate the eucharist, the faithful are enriched with divine life and transformed for worship and service as God's holy people (S.C., 2, 7, 10). The church is reminded of its mandate to teach, preach forgiveness, and witness reconciliation to all nations until the end of time (Mt 28:18-20; Lk 24:47). The liturgy thus has decidedly temporal and political effects and implications. The church is part of the human community and must proclaim the gospel, defend the God-given dignity of each person and promote justice and peace in the human community. This religious mission sometimes requires it to criticize objectionable conditions and give provisional support to worthy projects in the earthly city (G.S., 40-43, 76).

To assure that it serves the mysteries of faith and the human community in light of faith, the liturgy is regulated by ecclesiastical authorities. Since Vatican II the church has permitted the liturgy to be celebrated in vernacular languages. Within stated limits and to promote full and fruitful participation (S.C., 11, 14), the liturgy has been opened to adaptation by episcopal conferences, diocesan bishops, and individual presiders. These steps have made the liturgy more responsive to local conditions and influences. Local church leaders must now shoulder a greater share of responsibility for the liturgical life of their communities, including its political aspects. In this regard, liturgical education, planning, and preaching call for particular attention.

For the Roman Catholic community, the relationship between liturgy and politics involves certain other considerations. Among these are the autonomy proper to civil political life; the balance between the transcendent and historical dimensions of the liturgy; the adequacy of the language and signs actually employed in it; and the control, planning, and evaluation of liturgical worship in light of the purpose and integrity proper to it. In the background is the fundamental issue of the church and its relationship with the world (G.S., 33-36, 53-59, 73-76).

See **Liturgy and Christian life; Liturgy as prophetic**

Jean Daniélou, *Prayer As a Political Problem* (London: Burns & Oates, 1967). Herman Schmidt and David Power, eds., *Politics and Liturgy, Concilium*, Vol. 92 (New York: Herder & Herder, 1974). Vatican Council II, *Pastoral Constitution on the Church in the Modern World.*

WALTER J. WOODS

PRAYER, LITURGICAL

Within the common purpose of all prayer to be the expression of communion with God, liturgical prayer is that distinct type of prayer which may be characterized as ecclesial. It is the shared activity of the whole people of God which articulates the faith in which they are united. As a consequence of this ecclesial character, liturgical prayer is usually marked by an official dimension. It involves the authorization through some competent means of established forms or rites which, during the period of their authorization, have a normative status in the common, public prayer of the faith community. Although those forms may also be used as a basis for private or informal prayer, their normative status is most evident when they serve the common prayer of the people assembled for public, liturgical worship.

Prayer is a deeply human activity in which the unconditional authority of God is acknowledged or at least implied. It is thus an activity which grows out of the creature's experience of dependence, and which through disposition and word and gesture ascribes to the Creator the ultimacy which is God's alone. All prayer expresses that relation of creature to Creator, but it is through the multifaceted experience of public worship that the remembrance of that relation is renewed with special power and scope. Public worship may be ascribed that particular importance because of its ecclesial character as the response of a community of believers to their shared experience of God's presence and power in their lives.

The authorization of specific forms to serve such ecclesial acts must always be carried out with an awareness of the primacy of the corporate liturgical act within the faith experience. The use of authorized texts for prayer is not an end in itself, nor is it the essential characteristic of liturgical prayer. This must be said because the historical evolution of the liturgy carried it into a sidetrack of canonical and clerical priorities which lost sight of the ecclesial nature of liturgical prayer, a mutation which will be considered later in this article.

The positive value of such authorized forms for the common prayer of the faith community, however, remains. They foster the prayer of the people when they assemble for public worship, and they strengthen a sense of the unity of faith between the local community and other communities of faith throughout the world. Authorized liturgical forms are an external expression of that unity in which all share through the one baptism. They promote the experience of that unity in common prayer. Yet conformity to a fixed text is not the first priority in liturgical prayer. The forms serve to point the community to the divine reality which infinitely transcends all forms or rites or symbols. The forms used in prayer can direct the mind and heart to that numinous mystery before whom all our words, even our most splendid liturgical phrases, are but the stammerings of infants. The goal of liturgical prayer is to bring us to the threshold of an encounter with the Holy One about whom our words are only hints.

If liturgical prayer has so high a purpose, why is that purpose so often obscured by the familiar models in our liturgical experience? At least in part the answer may be found in the mutation referred to above, namely in the evolution of liturgical models which have eroded the ecclesial nature of liturgical prayer. One of the results of that erosion has been the loss of an understanding of the counterpoint between corporate and individual prayer in the life of faith. Many Christians have been formed to carry the expectations of private prayer into the experience of liturgical prayer. Lack of formation in the life of prayer, both corporate and individual, has obscured for many worshippers the distinctions between liturgical and private prayer. If Christians attend the liturgy with the expectation, conscious or not, that the needs of their individual piety will there be fulfilled, then the experience of the liturgy as a corporate act of prayer will, in the end, be found at odds with their purpose in being there. In positive terms, a new perception of corporate prayer may emerge, but there may also be a resulting disorientation of personal piety with the loss of the familiar model.

This type of liturgical disorientation has been a serious pastoral dilemma during the recent decades of liturgical change not least because, for many of the clergy as well as for the laity, public worship had been the occasion of an intense act of private piety. The gradual ecovery of a corporate model of liturgical celebration has disrupted the former pattern in ways which leave the question of the relation of individual prayer to liturgical prayer unresolved. Although liturgical prayer is different from prayer in private or in a small group, it does not negate the importance of these other forms of prayer. There is a deep complementarity between different types of prayer which becomes evident when each is experienced in its integrity; yet they are not alike.

The liturgical prayer which the Christian community celebrates when it assembles is the essential act of its common memory, in which the baptized are reminded through the proclamation of scripture and the homily, and through the sacramental action, of the plan of redemption which God has accomplished in Christ. Through the liturgical signs, the story of salvation is lifted up within the experience of the gathered assembly, and there becomes the focus of a shared offering of praise and thanksgiving. Liturgical prayer is thus the dynamic remembrance of God's act of redemption into which each member of the assembly has been grafted through baptism.

In this perspective, we can assert that our private prayer as Christians is a type of prayer which is derived from our membership in the Christian family of faith and our participation in the common prayer of that community. Our primary experience of prayer is found in the liturgical prayer which is characteristic of the life of the church and is expressive of the common faith professed by all the baptized members of that society.

To speak of private or family prayer as derived from the church's common prayer implies a complementarity which has not generally been explored. It is striking how often manuals of private prayer show little connection to the familiar forms of the liturgical tradition. This may be a carry-over from the time when official liturgical texts were seen as the private domain of the clergy, but it fails to draw upon the natural complementarity which would seem to characterize all types of prayer. If we may take the Lord's Prayer as an example, it is a prayer which Christians have used extensively both in liturgical and in private prayer. This familiar double use offers a model of the interplay between the church's liturgical prayer and more private acts of devotion.

Yet if the Lord's Prayer, because of its preeminence among Christian forms of prayer, finds a natural home both within the liturgical context as well as in private prayer, Christians have, on the whole, failed to apply that double usage to the other great common forms of our liturgical rites. The complementarity between liturgical prayer and private devotion echoes powerfully as we recognize in familiar liturgical texts a splendid resource for private prayer. To take, for example, such a text as "Holy, holy, holy Lord, God of power and might, Heaven and earth are full of your glory...," and to interweave it into the framework of private prayer offers a tangible opportunity to experience the union of our personal prayer with that of the church in heaven and on earth. Such a bridge between liturgical and private prayer fosters an integration of the intensity of private devotion with the experience of corporate liturgical prayer.

The German liturgist Balthasar Fischer has commented on this relation between corporate and private prayer in the experience of the faithful during the early centuries of Christianity. "The most important characteristic of common prayer in the ancient Christian family seems to me to lie in the extension, into the home, of public worship.... (The Church had not come) to the painful dichotomy that is the hall-mark of mediaeval domestic piety, which is obliged to set up a second universe of prayer—easily understood, and so more primitive, more subjective—side by side with the liturgy, since the latter was now incomprehensible and dominated by the clergy" (Fischer, p. 118). With these words, Fischer raises the specter of clericalization as the fundamental cause of the alienation of the church in general from the true spirit of corporate liturgical prayer. The history of the liturgy reveals that the gradual domination of public worship by the clergy is paralleled by the emergence of a private world of lay piety cut off from the normative and unifying influence of the church's corporate prayer. All in the church, laity and clergy alike, were victims of this development as the life of the ordained came to be seen as radically set apart from the ordinary lives of the people as a whole.

Impact of Clericalization

The emergence of a clericalized understanding of the celebration of the official rites of the church led to a fundamental separation of those rites from the common experience, not to mention common celebration, of Christians. The recitation, for example, of the eucharistic prayer in a low voice, inaudible to the assembly, became a prelude to a changed understanding of the eucharistic action to be essentially the work of the ordained rather than of the whole people of God. What may have begun as a somewhat innocent style of priestly devotion, or a misguided sense of eucharistic mystery, led eventually to a generalized piety of passive participation in which the people lost any sense of their integral role in the celebration of the rites of Christian faith.

Another important expression of the clericalization of the corporate prayer of the church is found in the imposition of a monastic model for the divine office as an expectation for secular clergy. This had the effect of linking the liturgical piety of parish clergy to monastic prayer rather than to the daily prayer of the local church. Since many of the parish clergy did not reside in communities in which the monastic cycle might be celebrated in common, a further result was the eventual privatization of what had once been a significant pattern of ecclesial liturgical prayer.

From the 4th century, a document called *The Diary of a Journey* by a Spanish nun named Egeria offers us a description of daily meetings for prayer by the local community at Jerusalem. These services of prayer were clearly ecclesial in character, involving both laity and clergy in their celebration. The growth of the monastic movement led to the expectation that the whole pattern of daily prayer would be shared by all the members of the community, and that absent brethren would say in private any hour of prayer which they had missed. This obligation was, however, an aspect of the monastic discipline and not an obligation for ordained clergy. For the latter, daily prayer seems to have been linked to pastoral responsibilities, and it was the prayer of the church community rather than a specifically clerical obligation. Each local community might do only some modest part of the whole cycle of daily prayer; but in large urban churches, with numerous clergy in residence, the complete cycle was introduced, probably under the influence of the monastic mode.

Beginning with the 6th century, the church grew dramatically outside the great urban centers. By this time, however, the monastic model had reshaped the church's concept of the daily office, and the hours of prayer came to be understood as an expectation imposed upon the clergy. By the late 8th century, legislation on these matters made clear that the recitation of the daily office was required of all clergy. If it could not be said formally, in the church to which they were assigned, then it was to be said in private.

The evolution toward private recitation of the office received added strength in the 13th century under the impact of two factors, the lifestyle of the itinerant Franciscans and the situation of student clergy at the universities. The fact that Franciscans were often on the road in order to fulfil their special ministry, and the absence of clergy from the churches or communities to which student clergy were related while they pursued their studies, encouraged the private recitation of the hours of prayer. Although the choir office continued to be upheld by bishops and councils, private recitation gained ground in what had become by now a narrowly clerical concern. Eventually the obligation of the divine office was linked to ordination to the subdiaconate and higher orders, and theologians, including St. Thomas Aquinas, justified its recitation in private. This movement away from the ecclesial understanding of the office reached a brief official status in 1535, with the publication of the breviary of Cardinal Francisco Quiñones which was designed for private recitation. Although its authorization was eventually withdrawn, the practice of private recitation had found a firm place in the private prayer of secular clergy.

The gradual clericalization of both the eucharist and the divine office which we have observed here, mark a major defection, albeit well intentioned, from the ecclesial understanding of liturgical prayer discussed above. What had been the two primary expressions of corporate prayer—eucharist and office—had been progressively claimed as a separate domain of prayer by the ordained clergy and become the constitutive elements of their own private piety. In regard to the eucharist, the church's insistence upon lay attendance under normal circumstances assured that the Mass continued to be a public act, but one at which lay participation was limited to a passive piety of vision. With the exception of cathedral churches and monastic communities, the divine office became generally an act of private priestly piety. We see here the situation in which liturgical prayer and private prayer lost their distinctive character: the authorized liturgical rites became the nucleus of the private piety of the ordained, and the laity, even while attending public liturgical celebrations, were left with only private devotions or para-liturgical rites.

This historical development shows the importance of our earlier insistence on the ecclesial nature of liturgical prayer as the normative understanding of such prayer. The gradual identification of liturgical prayer with the action of the clergy which is outlined above indicates a shift in which that prayer became more readily defined as "official prayer according to authorized rites," with little concern whether the rites were celebrated by an assembly or by one ordained person. The corporate celebration of liturgical prayer and the church's authorization of prescribed forms for such corporate acts are not mutually exclusive priorities, but when liturgical prayer most fully realizes its intentions, they ought to be but two aspects of a single reality. Such mutuality, however, has been undermined in the history of the church when an overemphasis upon textual and canonical priorities has led to the clerical domination of the rites.

The latter part of the 20th century has seen a gradual reversal of this clericalized model under the impact of the renewed ecclesial understanding which emanated from Vatican II and similarly within the wider ecumenical context. This renewal has fostered a recovery of an ecclesial understanding of liturgical prayer in which the weekly assembly of all the baptized under the pastoral leadership of the ordained offers a common ground for a shared experience of the community's corporate identity in Christ.

The local assembly thus becomes a kind of icon of the church, the gathering of all the baptized people of God being represented in each of the local assemblies of the faithful, (see, S.C., 2).

As was suggested earlier, the great texts of the liturgical tradition should appropriately flow over into the family and private devotions of Christians as they live their daily lives during the week, and thus form a bridge leading back to the common assembly the next Sunday. This mutuality between corporate and private prayer was, as Balthasar Fischer has suggested, characteristic of the common prayer of the early church, and it offers a model for the renewal of liturgical worship in our own time.

At the heart of such a model of common liturgical prayer is the active remembrance of the shared faith into which all have been initiated and which is the underlying energy of ecclesial prayer. It is essentially corporate prayer precisely because it is expressive of the unity within the body of Christ shared by those who profess a common faith. Through baptism into the paschal mystery of Christ, Christians are committed to a life characterized by prayer in common. That prayer has its source in the trinitarian faith which is the mark of Christian identity, and thus expresses that faith in thanksgiving to God the Father who is the Creator of all that exists; in remembrance of Christ, who in the incarnation united divinity with humanity and thus enabled the members of his body to become Christ to others; and in calling upon the Holy Spirit to unite the church through his power and grace to be God's instrument in the world. This trinitarian foundation of the Christian life is renewed and nourished in the corporate worship of the church. Liturgical prayer is thus the outward manifestation of the common faith into which all in the assembly have been baptized.

Liturgical Prayer and Faith

A traditional way of expressing the relation between the prayer of the church and its faith is found in the adage, "the law of prayer establishes the law of faith." The question which arises at once, however, is how the phrase is to be interpreted with regard to the shaping of the liturgical prayer of Christians. Does public prayer have, in the light of the adage, a didactic purpose? Certainly the liturgy has been exploited at times for this purpose, as though the assembly of Christians for worship must be claimed as a primary opportunity for the teaching of the faith. We observe this phenomenon, for example, in the Reformation of the 16th century when pastoral concern for the ignorance of the laity led to the reshaping of public worship as an occasion for teaching about the faith. Although the state of lay formation during the preceding centuries encourages us to look with sympathy at the situation and attempts to address it, nevertheless, the effect of the imposition of a didactic character upon the rites had far-reaching consequences. The rites came to reflect the polemical debates which separated Christians and thus to be a sign of division rather than unity in faith. Recent decades have seen a recovery of the understanding of liturgical prayer as expressive of the church's *common* faith. In this perspective, the adage, "the law of prayer establishes the law of faith," has taken on dramatic importance for an ecumenical understanding of liturgical prayer.

The liturgy manifests the faith in a common celebration by God's people assembled for liturgical prayer. The trinitarian faith which is the foundation of this common prayer is celebrated in a corporate act of praise which proclaims that faith as the basis of the common identity which all the baptized share. It is in the eucharistic rite that the proclamation of trinitarian faith has its clearest focus, in the eucharistic prayer. The various forms of the eucharistic prayer in the traditions of both the East and the West offer a rich array of images through which that faith has been articulated down the centuries. We see here a primary expression of the role of liturgical prayer as an act of faith. The eucharistic prayer is not merely a formula of consecration or a definition of eucharistic doctrine. It emerges out of the ground of the Christian experience of God.

The classical forms of liturgical prayer follow a consistent theological pattern shaped by the trinitarian debates which preoccupied the church during the 4th century. At the Synod of Hippo in 393, for example, it was decreed that "at the altar, prayer shall always be addressed to the Father" (Vagaggini, p. 210). This rule was evident in the pattern of address in the collects of the eucharist and in the eucharistic prayer. The address is then followed by a reference to one or more of the divine attributes, e.g., Almighty, Creator. Liturgical prayer thus begins with the naming of the God in whom the assembly places its faith, the One whom Jesus called Abba, Father. It is this name which has taken the primary place in Christian liturgical prayer, and it always echoes with Jesus' personal experience of intimacy with God. It is this term of intimacy, translated as the name of the male parent, which in turn became part of the Christian sacred vocabulary.

The source for the addressing of God as "Father" is found in the Hebrew Scriptures. When God adopts the Israelites, they become, by way of metaphor, the children of God, and God, their Father. It is a title reserved to the chosen people. It is an expression of the covenant relationship. In the NT, as we have observed, it is Jesus who claims this metaphor to express his own intimate relation to God, and who then makes that relation available to those who believe and are baptized. There is a lack of congruence which must be acknowledged: God is neither male nor parent, and yet as a metaphor the term "Father" is a powerful expression of our unity with Jesus in his own relation to God.

As the church confronted the Arian heresy, which denied the full divinity of the Son, the practice grew of addressing prayer to Christ not only in private prayer but also in liturgical prayer. This was a way of expressing the church's belief in the divinity of Christ since, if he were not divine, such prayer would have been idolatrous: prayer might be addressed only to God. By addressing prayer to Christ in liturgical worship, a heresy was denied but a serious consequence resulted. The classical model of liturgical prayer which was affirmed at the Synod of Hippo lost its theological balance. Eventually forms were introduced into the liturgy in which it is often unclear as to whether the prayer is addressed to the Father or the Son. Thus blurring of the Father and the Son led to the loss of a clear sense of Christ's role in salvation history as mediator, a role which was clearly expressed in the classical model of liturgical prayer "through Jesus Christ our Lord."

How is this mediatorial role of Christ in the liturgy to be understood? Liturgical prayer is ecclesial prayer, the prayer of the church, but it is at the same instance the prayer of Christ. It is Christ's body, the baptized community, which assembles for public prayer and thus becomes, according to Mt 18:20, a special mode of Christ's presence: "Where two or three are gathered in my name, there am I in the midst of them." This presence of Christ in the liturgical prayer of the church is one of the foundational principles of the renewal of the church's worship in this century.

In *The Constitution on the Sacred Liturgy* of Vatican II, this principle was clearly stated. "Christ is always present in his Church, especially in her liturgical celebrations. He is present in the sacrifice of the Mass, not only in the person of his minister 'the same one now offering, through the ministry of priests, who formerly offered himself on the cross' but especially under the eucharistic species. By his power he is present in the sacraments, so that when a man baptizes it is really Christ himself who baptizes. He is present in his word, since it is he himself who speaks when the holy scriptures are read in the church. He is present as well when the church prays and sings" (S.C., 7). The Church is united with Christ through the waters of baptism and thus acts with him and in him in the whole range of its liturgical actions, sharing in an intimate bond of union which is the work of the Holy Spirit. It is thus appropriate to speak of Christ's real presence in the assembly as the means by which the church prays in Christ and through Christ.

The presence of Christ in the assembly is a transformative presence which is signified to the church in every eucharistic celebration as the ordinary material realities of bread and wine are transformed to be the body of Christ for the assembled body of Christ. It is a dynamic personal encounter in which the believing community is challenged to see and claim once again what it is called by God to be. St. Augustine preached this to his people assembled at the eucharist. "If you are the body and members of Christ, then what is laid on the Lord's table is the sacrament of what you yourselves are, and it is the sacrament of what you are that you receive. It is to what you yourselves are that you answer 'Amen,' and this is your affidavit. Be a member of Christ's body, so that your 'Amen' may be authentic" (Sermon no. 272).

This transformation of the community of believers is not automatic or magical, as much as we might wish it were that easy. It is, rather, a gradual process which is begotten in us through baptism. Our incorporation into Christ, our participation in the paschal mystery of his death and resurrection, is the basis of our belief that Christ is truly present in the liturgical assembly and that all our common prayer is offered to God as an outward, ritual sign of the unity of the whole body, head and members. This unity of the church with Christ is an awesome dignity since by it we become "a chosen race, a royal priesthood, a holy nation, God's own people, that you may declare the wonderful deeds of him who called you out of darkness into his marvelous light" (1 Pet 2:9). Liturgical prayer holds before us the constant reminder of who it is we are called to be.

The role of the Holy Spirit in liturgical prayer has, on the whole, received inadequate attention during the recent decades of liturgical renewal. In the traditional texts of the liturgy, especially in the *epiclesis* or invocation of the Spirit within the eucharistic prayer, the church prays for the action of the Holy Spirit upon the community and for the transformation of the gifts, although even in this significant context Western Christianity has, in general, given far more attention to the action of Christ than to the activity of the Holy Spirit. This theological focus, namely, the two-fold activity of the Holy Spirit traditionally associated with the eucharistic *epiclesis*, is a clue to the more general role of the Spirit within the life of the church and within the framework of liturgical prayer. The Spirit is the agent of sanctification and unity. The work of the Spirit is thus, in the deepest sense, complementary to the work of Christ. The two are inseparable.

The liturgical prayer of the church, whatever the focus of the particular celebration or of the feast or season of the year, is always rooted in the celebration of the paschal mystery. As the gathered community of faith, we celebrate not merely the commemoration of the past event, the death and resurrection of Jesus, but the present and dynamic reality of God's saving action. The event which we commemorate is made present so that we may enter into it and share in its power. Through baptism the believer has entered into a lifelong pattern of death and resurrection as the fundamental symbol of religious meaning. Each occasion of liturgical prayer, and with special intensity the eucharist, becomes a re-entry into that basic symbol of Christian identity as the paschal mystery is actualized in the faith-action of the assembly.

Through word and sign, the liturgical rites make explicit the church's experience of the grace of God. The effect of grace is union with God, participation in the life of God. Through faith we become conscious of this gift of God's presence to us, the gift of intimacy with God which is characteristic of the relation of Jesus to his Abba. That intimate relation has now become God's gift to us. God's saving action is an abiding gift, not limited to specific moments in time.

Liturgical celebrations are grace-events within that continuum, specific occasions in which that gift is manifested through the means of a rich complex of expressive signs, offering to the assembled community of faith the opportunity consciously to accept the gift of God's grace. The gathering of Christians for liturgical prayer is thus an event of supreme importance in the life of faith; for in these regular occasions, especially those associated with Sunday as the day of the Lord's resurrection, the church is constituted and manifested as a visible icon of the baptized community which shares a common faith in the Holy One.

New Images in Liturgical Prayer

The church has lived for many centuries with a high degree of liturgical stability. Even allowing for periodic adjustments to new vernacular forms, the basic patterns of Christian liturgical prayer remain closely related to those trinitarian formulas which were worked out especially within the context of the christological debates of the 4th century. The church is understandably conservative in this sensitive area since all of our language for the Trinity is fragile, reflecting the delicate balance which was achieved as the church found a vocabulary to articulate its faith. In the realm of academic theology in particular there is a tendency to require precision of meaning for all technical terms, especially those which are used in reference to the divinity.

Liturgical prayer, as we have observed, is nurtured in the soil of Christian faith, but its language is not that of academic theology and its purpose is not didactic. Liturgical language is that of metaphor and image, as, for example, in our calling God our Father. This language of prayer and sacrament ultimately has more impact upon the common theological understanding of the church than lectures in theology. The only problem with this is an apparent tendency, at least in our culture, to literalize the metaphors and images. With this there results a loss of the awareness that all of our language about God is drawn from words which offer the closest human analogies available to us to express our intuitions about God's nature. We need these words if we are to speak about God at all, and yet they are always inadequate. They always fall far short of the divine reality to whom they point. Our mental pictures may place a crown upon God's grandfatherly head. Such anthropomorphic images have often been nourished by depictions of God which we see in medieval art. Yet, we forget that such images can be claimed only by way of analogy, not as literal depictions of the divine being. When the metaphor is drawn from nature rather than from a human image, as when Jesus says, "I am the vine," we recognize that it is not to be taken literally. When we speak of God or Christ as King, on the other hand, it is evident that the image has been literalized not only in art but in liturgical ceremonial as well.

We considered earlier the tradition of calling God "Father" as an inheritance to the church from Jesus' own intimate relation with God. In an essay like this, it is possible to explain how this name came to be applied to God and to acknowledge that the term does not suggest an association of maleness with God. Yet recent decades have seen a growth in the church of impatience on the part of many Christians with the excessive dominance of male images for God both in our liturgical prayer as well as in the vocabulary of ordinary speech. Historical studies have demonstrated the enormous influence which social norms have had in the shaping of this situation. At the same time, there has developed an awareness of the richness and diversity of biblical images for God which, it would seem, offer an unassailable source for an expansion of our own vocabulary.

The use of masculine images for God developed in the context of Jewish patriarchal society. The models for authority in the Roman world of early Christianity confirmed this cultural bias. Yet in the NT we find the evidence of a radical restructuring of the accepted views of male domination, as when Paul writes to the Galatians that "there is neither male nor female; for you are all one in Christ Jesus" (3:28). The question is not that of the removal of masculine images for God, since many of these are deeply rooted both in scripture and the liturgical tradition. Initial experiments with more inclusive language have shown that the effect of replacing such images with gender-free abstractions results in an impersonal and impoverished language of prayer. What is needed is a recovery of the breadth and richness of images to be found in the full biblical and liturgical tradition.

If the ancient adage is correct, that is, if "the law of prayer establishes the law of faith," then the narrowing of our liturgical language for God to predominantly male images has shaped the way the church thinks about God. We suggested earlier that the metaphors and images which we use in prayer shape our understanding of the faith and that all such metaphors must be approached with caution. It would seem that a rich vocabulary of images would offer a ground for mutual correction for the inadequacy of any one.

The naming of the God of Christian faith as Holy Trinity—Father, Son, and Spirit—stands at the center of the Christian tradition in both its liturgical prayer and its theological reflection. The challenge before the church today in regard to its liturgical language is to find ways in which faith in the Trinity can be professed and articulated in prayer which is consonant with the insights of the church in the early centuries—the patristic era—and which yet embrace an inclusivity of the whole of humanity which faith in the incarnation demands.

New alternatives are being tested in the liturgical prayer of the church, sometimes with authorized texts and sometimes with forms which have emerged within a very specific local situation. If we remember how painfully the church arrived at the classical formulations of trinitarian faith in the 4th century, it will not surprise us that the present search for an expanded vocabulary will be often painful and will require energy and time. As new images are proposed, they will be tested against those which have been found most adequate in the church's tradition of faith. The goal is to find images, either neglected ones from the tradition or new ones which may emerge, which challenge the church to expand its understanding of the Holy One who is beyond what language can describe and yet who lovingly accepts the stammerings of our praise.

See Spirituality, liturgical; Language, liturgical; Inclusive language

Balthasar Fischer, "The Common Prayer of Congregation and Family in the Ancient Church," *Studia Liturgica*, Vol. 10 (1974): 106-124. John Gallen, (ed.) *Christians at Prayer* (Notre Dame, IN: Notre Dame University Press, 1977). Gabe Huck, "Family and Individual Prayer," *Liturgy 80* (Special issue, July 1980). Joseph Jungmann, *The Place of Christ in Liturgical Prayer* (London: Geoffrey Chapman, 1965). David Nicholls, "Images of God and State: Political Analogy and Religious Discourse," in *Theological Studies*, Vol. 42, No. 2 (1981): 195-215. Gail Ramshaw-Schmidt, *Christ in Sacred Speech* (Philadelphia, PA: Fortress Press, 1986). Pierre Salmon, *The Breviary Through the Centuries* (Collegeville, MN: Liturgical Press, 1962). Daniel B. Stevick, *Language in Worship — Reflection on a Crisis* (New York, Seabury Press, 1970). Cyprian Vagaggini, *Theological Dimensions of the Liturgy* (Collegeville, MN: Liturgical Press, 1976). Louis Weil, *Gathered to Pray. Understanding Liturgical Prayer* (Boston, MA: Cowley Publications, 1986).

LOUIS WEIL

PRAYER, TYPES OF, IN THE LITURGY
Introduction

Taxonomies of types of prayer tend to appear arbitrary. Authors, both ancient and modern, who attempt euchological classification use various principles of inclusion and arrive at different lists, sometimes even within the span of a single piece of writing. Origen, for example, in his treatise *On Prayer*, divides prayer into four distinct categories, that of supplication, prayer, intercession and thanksgiving. He then reorganizes his classifications according to a developmental pattern: supplication for spiritual goods, prayer as self-abandonment to God, doxology in praise of God's glory, and intercession for others. In the conclusion of the same treatise he proposes that the essential parts of prayer are doxology, thanksgiving, and petition. Origen is not being inconsistent; he is approaching prayer in each instance from a different optic (Origen, *On Prayer*, passim). Others provide a more expansive understanding of types of prayer by the inclusion of physical postures and even prayer's locale as significant in differentiating human response to the God of mystery. St. Dominic, for example, names nine ways of prayer: inclinations, genuflections, prostrations, penance, contemplation, earnest intercession, supplication, thoughtful reading, and praying on a journey ("The Nine Ways of Prayer of St. Dominic," trans. S. Tugwell, *Canadian Catholic Review* [March 1983], 22/93).

A second reason why a comprehensive taxonomy of prayer may be difficult to achieve is that often particular fixed patterns of prayer participate in several categories at the same time. The words "The Lord be with you," for example, might be classified as a greeting, an invitation to prayer, or a blessing of the community. A collect appears to be both a confession of praise and a petition. The Our Father is essentially a prayer of petition yet also contains praise and confession. And a eucharistic prayer, while obviously a prayer of thanksgiving since that is the meaning of its name, is actually composed of eight different movements: thanksgiving, acclamation, invocation, narration, remembrance, offering, intercessions, and doxology (G.I.R.M., 55).

The following article will attempt to classify and describe types of liturgical prayer from yet another point of view, that of communication patterns within the liturgical event. It will first treat some characteristics of liturgical language as a mode of human communication distinct from that of solitary prayer. Second, it will specify seven different patterns of communication which may be identified within the liturgy, namely: 1) non-verbal communications including silence, gestures, and bodily attitudes; 2) the presider's formal address to the community; 3) the presider's informal address to the community; 4) the presider's personal address to God; 5) the presider's address to God in the name of the community; 6) the prayers of presider and community in dialogue; and 7) the prayers of presider and community in unison. Under each heading, certain fixed patterns of liturgical prayer will be considered.

Liturgical Prayer As a Mode of Communication

Liturgical and solitary prayer are both necessary for the Christian life, each acting as a corrective and enrichment of the other. These two types of prayer may be distinguished from each other in a number of ways. Solitary prayer tends to be informal—sometimes even totally formless. It may be characterized as subjective, intimate, specific, free-flowing, flexible, and spontaneous. The language of solitary prayer is that of first person communication. It employs the singular voice since solitary prayer generally focuses on the individual's relationships with God, self, others and the environment within which prayer takes place.

On the other hand, liturgical prayer as the public worship of the church accomplished in the name of the whole church is communication common to each participant, expressing the worship of all, affecting all who are gathered. Liturgical prayer is, by its very nature, a corporate act which manifests and expresses the church in a highly condensed fashion. Since liturgical prayer is the language of a community its content must be about its shared life in Christ; its structure must include certain devices and the ordering of elements to facilitate communication. For communication to happen, hearers and speaker need to use the same language categories; certain models need to be employed to ensure that communication takes place; certain structured patterns of dialogue, language conventions, and even the cadence of one's voice will invite corporate response. In short, liturgical prayer will tend to be formal, stylized, comprehensive, inclusive, universal, ordered, repetitive and familiar in order to facilitate communication within an assembly gathered for prayer.

Types of Liturgical Communication

Non-verbal Communications Including Silence, Gestures, and Bodily Attitudes. Because of the nature of the liturgical act, silence is a primary and essential form of communication within the liturgy. All worship is response to the presence and invitation of God. This truth is expressed simply in Preface IV for weekdays: "You have no need of our praise, yet our desire to thank you is itself your gift." In liturgical prayer all is gift; all is response. Silence enables a waiting upon and resting in God, a listening posture under the consolation and the challenge of the word, an awesome silence in face of the Mystery who is God. Out of silence worship is born.

The function of silence in the celebration varies according to its location in the rite: it may be a preparatory silence, a silence of recollection, meditation, praise, or silent prayer (G.I.R.M., 23). The Foreword to the G.I.R.M. notes that "the proper use of periods of silent prayer and reflection will help to render the celebration less mechanical and impersonal and lend a more prayerful spirit to the liturgical rite." In addition, this document underscores the necessity of liturgical silence by stating emphatically: "Just as there should be no celebration without song, so too there should be no celebration without periods of silent prayer and reflection."

Similarly, bodily attitudes communicate attentiveness, respect, reverence, wonder, and awe in God's presence. These forms of communication, for such they are, are largely culturally determined. Adoration, for example, might be expressed by a bow in one culture, a genuflection in another, prostration in yet a third. For that reason it is left to national conferences of bishops to determine appropriate liturgical postures within their locales. Bodily postures of standing, sitting, kneeling, and prostration will have different meanings in different cultures—but each posture will be a profound means of communication. As stated in *Environment and Art in Catholic Worship* (E.A.W.): "The liturgy of the Church has been rich in a tradition of ritual movement and gestures. These actions, subtly, yet really, contribute to an environment which can foster prayer or which can distract from prayer. When the gestures are done in common, they contribute to the unity of the worshipping assembly. Gestures which are broad and full in both a visual and tactile sense, support the entire symbolic ritual. When the gestures are done by the presiding minister, they can either engage the entire assembly and bring them into an even greater unity or if done poorly, they isolate" (E.A.W., 56). The non-verbal modes of communication within the liturgy, reverent silence, actions, gestures, and bearing, are among the means of promoting the community's full, conscious, and active participation in the liturgy (S.C., 30).

The Presider's Formal Address to the Community. A second mode of communication within the liturgy is a presider's formal address to the community, a category which includes greetings, invitations, ritual dialogue, and dismissals.

The presider speaks formally in *greeting* the assembly. At the beginning of a celebration, a presider may use a Pauline greeting, for example, "The grace of our Lord Jesus Christ and the love of God and the fellowship of the Holy Spirit be with you all," or, may greet more simply, "The Lord be with you." Greetings may introduce certain actions: "The peace of the Lord be always with you" precedes the exchange of peace. New forms of greeting have been incorporated into revised ritual books such as *The Order of Christian Funerals*: "May the Father of

mercies, the God of all consolation, be always with you."

Formal communication includes a presider's ritual *invitations*: "Let us pray"; "To prepare ourselves to celebrate the sacred mysteries, let us call to mind our sins"; "Let us proclaim the mystery of faith"; "Let us offer each other the sign of Christ's peace." Other forms of invitation include the traditional diaconal commands preceding the solemn prayers on Good Friday: "Let us kneel; let us stand."

Certain forms of *ritual dialogue* are instances of formal communication between presider and assembly: "Lift up your hearts." "We lift them up to the Lord." "Let us give thanks to the Lord our God." "It is right to give God thanks and praise." The liturgy of the hours contains a variety of such exchanges, for example: "O God, come to my assistance," "O Lord, make haste to help me" or "O Lord, open my lips." "And my mouth shall declare your praise."

Dismissals are also instances of formal communication addressed to the community, for example, "Go in peace to love and serve the Lord." Dismissals may also be addressed to a particular group within the assembly. The dismissal of the elect during Lent is an example: "Dear elect, go in peace, and join us again at the next scrutiny. May the Lord remain with you always."

Through communication patterns of salutation, invitation, dialogic exchange, and dismissal, the community is invited to active participation through response or ritual action.

The Presider's Informal Address to the Community. In a variety of situations, after an opening formal greeting, for example, liturgical rubrics provide an opportunity for an informal word, a very brief introduction to the Mass of the day, or a word of greeting and welcome to candidates preparing to receive a particular sacramental rite. Introductory words may precede the liturgy of the word and the eucharistic prayer; informal comments may conclude the liturgical rite before a dismissal. Every liturgical rubric which notes, "In these or similar words," invites a presider's informal communication with the assembly. This rubric provides the opportunity to contextualize the celebration. The Congregation for Divine Worship, in a circular letter of April 27, 1973, offered the following caveat regarding informal introductions and admonitions: "By their very nature such introductions do not require that they be given verbatim in the form they have in the Missal; consequently it may be helpful, at least in certain cases, to adapt them to the actual situation of a community. But the way any of these introductions is presented must respect the character proper to each and not turn into a sermon or homily. There must be a concern for brevity and the avoidance of wordiness that would bore the participants" (14).

The homily may also be regarded as an informal mode of communication with the assembly since the etymology of the word *homileo* suggests communication which is familiar, personal, and conversational rather than that of a speech or a structured lecture. *Fulfilled in Your Hearing*, a document of the United States Bishops' Committee on the Liturgy, describes the appropriate manner of homiletic communication in this way: "What we should strive for is a style that is purposeful and personal, avoiding whatever sounds casual and chatty on the one extreme or impersonal and detached on the other" (24).

The Presider's Personal Address to God. Occasionally, in the course of liturgical celebrations, a presider addresses God personally. In such instances, the substance of the prayer is a petition that the ministry of the presider may be exercised with attention and devotion (G.I.R.M., 13). Before the reading of the gospel, for example, the priest bows

before the altar and says: "Almighty God, cleanse my heart and my lips that I may worthily proclaim your gospel." The washing of the hands is accompanied by the words: "Lord, wash away my iniquity, cleanse me from my sin." The private prayer of the presider before communion is yet another example: "Lord, may I receive these gifts in purity of heart. May they bring me healing and strength, now and forever."

These prayers, in light of the distinction made above between solitary and liturgical prayer, are essentially a-liturgical. They are prayers of private devotion, spoken in the first person singular, and are meant to be inaudible as their rubrics indicate.

The Presider's Address to God in the Name of the Community. The fifth type of communication within the liturgy, and that which predominates, is the presider's address to God in the name of the whole community and with the assent of their "Amen." Within this category, a further distinction is possible, namely, the classification of fixed patterns of prayer according to their essential elements of praise and thanksgiving, petition, or penitence. These elements combine in many instances but one element will generally predominate.

The presider gives voice to praise and thanksgiving, above all, in the *eucharistic prayer* through which "the entire congregation joins itself to Christ in acknowledging the great things God has done and in offering sacrifice" (G.I.R.M., 54). Particularly in the *preface*, the presider gives praise and thanksgiving "for the whole work of salvation or for some special aspect of it that corresponds to the day, feast or season" (G.I.R.M., 55a). The prefaces of the Roman Missal, though varying greatly in length, have a uniform pattern. Following upon the *Sursum corda*, the preface praises the Father, through Christ, by recalling God's fidelity in Christ, in the mystery being celebrated, in the lives of holy men and women throughout the ages, or in the lives of those assembled. This latter emphasis is found particularly in prefaces for ritual Masses. Such narration leads the community "with hearts full of love to join the angels and saints in a hymn of endless praise."

This pattern typifies a dialogic relationship in the liturgy in which the praise and thanksgiving expressed in the name of the community draws forth a community response of praise whether in the "Holy, holy," the acclamations throughout the eucharistic prayer, or before and after the readings.

Doxology generally terminates prayer, whether a particular prayer is one of thanksgiving, petition or reparation, in recognition that the one before whom we stand is worthy of all praise. Particular forms of doxology include the solemn close of the eucharistic prayer, the great doxology, "through him, with him, in him, in the unity of the Holy Spirit, all glory and honor is yours almighty Father, for ever and ever"; the doxology of the Lord's Prayer, "for the kingdom, the power and the glory are yours, now and for ever"; and the conclusion of the collect which functions as a doxology, "We ask this through our Lord Jesus Christ, your son, who lives and reigns with you and the Holy Spirit, one God, for ever and ever" (G.I.R.M., 32). This last doxology expresses, in highly compressed and simple fashion, the theology of Christian liturgical prayer, namely, that it is directed to the first person of the Trinity, through the mediation of Christ, in the power of his abundant and life-giving Spirit.

Praise is that impulse of the human spirit which often precedes (or prefaces) other modes of prayer, particularly prayers of petition. The *collect*, for example, is essentially a prayer of petition and yet it begins by addressing God and expressing some aspect of God's goodness before begging, yet again, for God's gracious gifts. The structure of a collect, most simply expressed, is a twofold structure: Because you . . ., please do. . . . The petition thus is a request rooted in confident hope.

Collects, those prayers which gather and express the silent prayer of the community, are ubiquitous in the rites. They occur in four locations in the celebration of the eucharist: the opening prayer concludes the introductory rites; the prayer over the gifts concludes the preparation of the table and the gifts; the prayer after communion concludes the liturgy of the eucharist and reception of communion (G.I.R.M. 32, 53, 56k). In addition, the prayer voiced by the presider at the conclusion of the general intercessions (G.I.R.M., 47) follows a collect structure, namely, address of God, amplification of address, petition, and concluding doxology. In some instances, the petition is followed by a clause which expresses why the community is asking for this particular grace or what they hope to do once they receive it. In every instance the collect will be more effective if it is preceded by adequate silence so that its function as *summing up* the silent prayer of the community might be realized.

The content of a collect prayer is fairly well determined by its location in the rite. The opening prayer in most general terms expresses the theme of the celebration. The collect concluding the intercessions asks that our needs be heard and answered in God's wisdom and love. The prayer over the gifts is a preparation for the eucharistic prayer and in it we express the hope that our gifts and we ourselves will be transformed. The prayer after communion is a petition for the effects of the mystery just celebrated.

The collect pattern of prayer is also found in other sacramental rites, particularly in their opening and closing prayers, and, just as with their analogues in the eucharistic rite, such collects in a general fashion express the theme of the celebration or ask that what has just been given ritual expression will now be lived out by the community. The psalm prayers of the liturgy of the hours are other examples of collect prayers. As will be seen below, it is the collect pattern which is imitated in some blessings and in prayers of exorcism.

Blessings are another form of petitionary prayer rooted in praise. In the action of blessing, the community acknowledges that all of creation is gift of God and thus that "there is hardly any proper use of material things that cannot be directed toward human sanctification and the praise of God" (S.C., 61). Blessings are also used to mark various occasions in human life since almost every event "may be made holy by divine grace that flows from the paschal mystery of Christ's passion, death, and resurrection, the fount from which all sacraments and sacramentals draw their power" (S.C., 61).

Blessings are of two distinct types: constitutive and invocative. A constitutive blessing begins with the praise of God and then petitions that God impart a new state of consecration, a new setting aside of a person or a thing wholly for God's service. Included in constitutive blessings would be the blessings of an abbess or abbot, religious profession, the blessing of a church, an altar, a bell, a paten, or chalice or other sacred vessel. Typical blessing language includes praise and thanksgiving for the way God has been source of grace and life through such persons or objects throughout salvation history followed by a petition that *this* person or object now be set aside for God's service. More solemn constitutive blessings, sometimes accompanied by the use of oil, are called consecrations.

An invocative blessing asks God's gracious favor on those persons who make use of certain objects such as water, oil, or palms. An example of an invocative blessing is the blessing of ashes on Ash Wednesday: "Lord, bless these ashes by which we show that we are dust. Pardon our sins and keep us faithful to the discipline of Lent, for you do not want the sinner to die but to live with the risen Christ, who reigns with you for ever and ever."

Often the petition of a blessing will take the form of an *epiclesis*, an element of prayer found in every eucharistic prayer in East and West. An epiclesis includes an invocation of God and a petition that God send the Spirit to transform that which is being blessed. The blessing of the oil of the sick, an extended collect-style prayer, contains an example of a Spirit-focused epiclesis: "God of all consolation, you chose and sent your Son to heal the world. Graciously listen to our prayer of faith: send the power of your Holy Spirit, the Consoler, into this precious oil, this soothing ointment, this rich gift, this fruit of the earth. Bless this oil and sanctify it for our use. Make this oil a remedy for all who are anointed with it; heal them in body, in soul, and in spirit, and deliver them from every affliction." The simple and solemn blessings of the concluding rite of the eucharist are examples of invocative blessings of persons.

A particular species of blessing of persons is that of the *scrutinies*, the rites belonging to the period of purification and enlightenment in the Rite of Christian Initiation of Adults. Scrutinies are patterns of ritual prayer for the third, fourth and fifth Sundays of Lent which invoke God to assist candidates for baptism "to uncover, then heal all that is weak, defective, or sinful in the hearts of the elect; to bring out, then strengthen all that is upright, strong, and good" (R.C.I.A., 141). Within the scrutinies, a collect-style prayer called an *exorcism* asks God to deliver the elect from the power of sin, to heal them, to strengthen them against temptation, and to fill their spirit with Christ the Redeemer. One such exorcism reads in part: "Free (the elect) from the slavery of Satan, the source of sin and death, who seeks to corrupt the world you created and saw to be good. Place them under the reign of your beloved Son, that they may share in the power of his resurrection and give witness to your glory before all" (5th Sunday of Lent).

A final example of a prayer addressed by the presider to God in the name of the community is an *absolution*. In the eucharist, the absolution is a very brief formula which follows the community's confession of sins. In it the presider asks God's pardon on the assembly in these words: "May Almighty God have mercy upon you, forgive you your sins, and bring you to life everlasting."

Prayers of Presider and Community in Dialogue. The *Prayer of the Faithful* constitutes a ritual unit of prayer in which presider and community each participate. The prayer of the faithful, also called general intercessions or bidding prayers, provides an opportunity for the whole community to exercise its priestly function, interceding before God on behalf of humanity. The scope of intercessions includes the needs of the church, public authorities, those suffering oppression, and the concerns of the local community (G.I.R.M., 45).

It is the role of the presider, by means of a brief introduction, to invite the community to make known its needs, and, at the conclusion of the intercessions, to offer a prayer summing up the intercessions and asking God's gracious response. The intercessions proper are expressed by the deacon, a lector, commentator, or by individuals within the assembly. The whole assembly participates in the act of supplication through a brief response. The intercessions are one of several forms of litanic prayer in the liturgy.

The *litanic prayer* is a simple and popular responsorial style of prayer made up of a series of invocations together with an invariable congregational response, for example, "pray for us" or "Amen." Litanies are often, though not always, a form of petitionary prayer. Such is clear from typical litanic responses: "Lord, hear our prayer"; "Lord, save your people"; "pray for us." Psalm 136, an ancient litanic pattern of verse and response in a thanksgiving mode is a notable exception to this general rule: "Give thanks to the Lord, for God is good. God's mercy endures forever."

Chief among liturgical litanies are the Lord, have mercy (*Kyrie*), the Lamb of God (*Agnus Dei*), and the litany of the saints. The Kyrie litany is a tiny vestige of a much longer intercessory prayer which can be traced back to the Jerusalem church of the 4th century. Once the diaconal litany of intercession was moved from the end of the Mass of the Catechumens to near its beginning and the petitions had been suppressed there remained only the invocation, Kyrie eleison, and its echoed response. Form C of the penitential rite of the eucharist elaborates this particular litanic pattern and clarifies its true nature as a song of praise focused on the redeeming action of Christ—"You were sent to heal the contrite; You came to call sinners; You plead for us at the right hand of the Father"—rather than on the sinfulness of the community.

The Lamb of God (*Agnus Dei*) is another traditional litany in the Mass whose petitions each begin with the address: Lamb of God. Gradually reduced to only three repetitions, the earlier use of this litany to cover the action of the breaking of the bread has been restored in the revised rite, with the possibility that other titles for the Lamb of God might supplement the text: Bearer of our sins, Redeemer of the world, Prince of peace, etc.

A more elaborate litanic prayer is that of the litany of the saints, a prayer used on special occasions such as the Easter vigil, and in the rites of ordination and religious profession. The litany of the saints has a five-part structure which includes: introductory verses, "Lord have mercy"; invocation of the saints, "Saint Mary Magdalene, pray for us"; invocation of Christ, "Lord, be merciful, Lord, save your people"; prayer for particular needs, "Give new life to these chosen ones by the grace of baptism, Lord, hear our prayer"; and a conclusion, "Lord Jesus, hear our prayer." A community is encouraged to adapt the litany for its use by adding other saints, invocations appropriate to the occasion, and various needs of the local community.

Prayers of the Presider and Community in Unison. Through the prayer of the faithful and other litanic models, presider and community are in dialogue. There are also a number of prayers which the presider and the community express as one voice. The community prays with one voice: in praise of God in the *Gloria*; in confession of God's saving acts in the creed; and in response to the teaching of Jesus, in the Our Father.

Known also as the greater doxology, the Gloria "is an ancient hymn, in which the church, assembled in the Holy Spirit, praises and entreats the Father and the Lamb" (G.I.R.M., 31). The Gloria is one of the few extant liturgical prayers addressed, in part, to Christ since a Synod in 393 dictated that at the altar all prayer shall be addressed to the Father. First found in Eastern sources as a hymn of praise at dawn and used as a concluding hymn at morning prayer, the Gloria only gradually entered the celebration of the eucharist, and became a fixed element by the 11th century. Known as the angelic hymn because of the first verses which pick up Lk 2:13, the hymn of the angels at the birth of Christ, the text continues in praise of God and of Christ in a series of acclamations. It is a hymn for the whole community, a festive hymn of praise and thanksgiving.

The community's creed, in the beginning, was principally associated with the preparation of candidates for incorporation into the community and with their baptismal celebration. Immediate preparation for baptism included the "giving over" of the creed to one about to be baptized who learned it by heart and "gave it back" by reciting it before the bishop. At their baptism, members of the elect went down into the baptismal waters and were there interrogated in a triple series of questions modeled on the creed and referring, in turn, to each member of the Trinity. After each of the candidate's responses, the candidate was immersed in the waters.

The origin of the profession of faith known as the Nicene Creed is conciliar rather than liturgical. The Nicene Creed is a summary of beliefs formulated at the Councils of Nicaea 325 and Constantinople 381, a brief synthesis of the fundamental truths of the community in face of particular heresies. This credal statement became a fixed part of the Mass by the beginning of the second millennium in the West. It serves as an announcement of God's saving acts in Jesus and as the community's confession of that which draws us together and unites us. A litanic form of creed is proclaimed by presider and community at the Easter vigil; otherwise, except in Masses with children, the Nicene Creed is used in dioceses of the United States on Sundays and Solemnities.

The G.I.R.M. assigns the creed an important structural role: "The symbol or profession of faith in the celebration of Mass serves as a way for the people to respond and to give their assent to the word of God heard in the readings and through the homily and for them to call to mind the truths of faith before they begin to celebrate the eucharist" (43). The G.I.R.M. suggests that the creed acts as a kind of fulcrum: as response to the word and in anticipating the great mysteries of faith which will be reiterated in the eucharistic prayer.

Another prayer said in unison by presider and community is the Lord's Prayer, whose use in Christian liturgy is very ancient. This perfect prayer was taught to those preparing for baptism and was "given back" by candidates who had learned it "by heart" along with the Apostles' Creed. From very early times, the Our Father entered the celebration of eucharist immediately after the eucharistic prayer and as a preparation for the reception of communion. This prayer is "a petition both for daily food, which for Christians means also the eucharistic bread, and for the forgiveness of sins, so that what is holy may be given to those who are holy (G.I.R.M., 56a). It also finds a place in the celebration of the liturgy of the hours.

The Our Father is a perfect summary of various types of Christian prayer, nearly all of which seem to be patterned on praise, petition and confession. It begins with an address of God hallowed by Jesus: Father. In a series of petitions it asks that God's name be praised, God's kingdom be established, God's will be accomplished throughout heaven and earth. The focus is on God and the work of redemption in all the universe. Then, as confident children rooted in God, the community petitions for its own needs: daily nourishment in anticipation of the end-time banquet; forgiveness of sins; preparation through daily triumph for the great end-time testing. In an embolism on this final petition, the presider begs in the name of community deliverance from the power of all evil, and then presider and community conclude in a final burst of praise.

Conclusion

An examination of types of ritual communication within the liturgy reveals a variety of prayer patterns, a variety of ways the community gives voice to its praise and thanksgiving, its needs, its desire for reconciliation, its faith. In some instances, through silence and gestures, through dialogue, responsorial participation, through prayers proclaimed in common, the community and its presider give voice together to the prayer of the church. In other instances the presider prays in the name of the community. In all instances, the assent of the community is expressed through its "Amen," a word sometimes rendered as the community's assent to that which is said—but it is more. "Amen," interspersed throughout every liturgical gathering, "Amen" at the conclusion of every type of prayer, is the community's proclamation of faith. "Amen" assures that it is the whole community participating in the priesthood of the one and only high priest, Jesus Christ, who alone stands before the throne of grace, interceding on our behalf.

See **Eucharistic prayers; Psalms as liturgical prayer; Silence, liturgical role of; Gestures, liturgical**

Allan Bouley, *From Freedom to Formula* (Washington: Catholic University of America Press, 1981). Louis Weil, *Gathered to Pray: Understanding Liturgical Prayer* (Cambridge, MA: Cowley Publications, 1986). Gail Ramshaw-Schmidt, *Christ in Sacred Speech* (Philadelphia: Fortress Press, 1986). Agnes Cunningham, *Prayer, Personal and Liturgical* (Wilmington: Michael Glazier, 1985).

KATHLEEN HUGHES, R.S.C.J.

PREACHING AS ART AND CRAFT

This article has for limited scope a basic practical aspect of homiletics: effective communication. Even such a limitation, however, raises a prior question: What is the Catholic preacher attempting to communicate? On broad lines, two replies are proposed in our time.

One approach contends that we should scrap the Vatican II homily and return to instructional sermons. In this view today's critical Catholic problem is abysmal ignorance. Our people do not know "the faith." A trinitarian God and an incarnate Son, original sin and actual sin, one true church and seven saving sacraments, created grace and Uncreated Grace, the Mass as sacrifice and the pope as successor to Peter, the Ten Commandments and six precepts of the church, the immorality of birth control and abortion—this is what our faithful must be taught. Vatican II? Why, Catholics do not know Baltimore Catechism One. Especially these days, when elementary Catholic education is vanishing, there is only one viable way to teach: via the Sunday sermon. Deliver the dogma, the doctrine, and deliver it with consummate clarity, with unquestioning certitude.

The approach I espouse disagrees. It concedes that many a Catholic is distressingly ignorant of God's revelation, does not know what the Son of God took flesh to tell us. Somehow, somewhere the faithful should learn this. But not *ex professo* in the liturgical sermon. The homily, like the liturgy of which it is part and parcel, should proclaim, re-present, make effectively present "God's wonderful works in the history of salvation"; "the mystery of Christ" should be "made present and active within us" (S.C., 35). But this is not done by instructions on dogmas to be believed, doctrines to be accepted. It is done by an art and a craft.

Concretely, three affirmations. (1) For a preacher, words are all-important. (2) The homiletic word comes alive as a work of art principally through imagination. (3) Imagination demands a contemporary idiom, living symbols. The remainder of this article is an effort to argue those affirmations and to draw conclusions therefrom.

Words

For a preacher, words are all-important. Not only are words a Christian preacher's primary medium of communication; words are the way the Judeo-Christian revelation reaches us. In the Prior Testament the word is wondrously alive. For the Israelites the spoken word was a distinct reality charged with power: it posited the reality it signified and in so doing posited the reality that spoke the word; it conferred intelligibility upon the thing and disclosed the character of the person who uttered the word. In the NT the word as a distinct reality charged with power is fulfilled to perfection. For in Jesus Christ is fulfilled the word as a distinct, dynamic being; as that which gives form and intelligibility to what it signifies; as God's self-disclosure; as a point of personal contact between heaven and earth.

The word, the Letter of James declares, is a perilous thing. "We use it to bless the Lord and Father, but we also use it to curse men and women fashioned in God's likeness" (Jas 3:9). And still, in Paul's eyes, the word is indispensable: without it, belief is impossible (Rom 10:14).

Words, we learn from experience, can be weapons, and words can be healing. Words can unite in friendship or sever in enmity, unlock who I am or mask me from others. Two words, *"Sieg Heil,"* bloodied the face of Europe; three words, "Here I stand," divided the body of Christendom. Words have made slaves and freed slaves, have declared war and imposed peace. Words sentence to death ("You shall be hanged by the neck") and words restore to life ("Your sins are forgiven you"). Words covenant a life together in love, and words declare a marriage dead. Words charm and repel, amuse and anger, reveal and conceal, chill and warm. A word from Washington rained down atomic hell on Hiroshima; words from an altar change bread and wine into the body and blood of Christ.

A word is real; a word is sacred; a word is powerful; a word is ... I.

In our context, however, word is not just any word, it is a liturgical word. In mid-century the "liturgy of the word" meant relatively little. A Catholic could miss *Gloria* and creed, epistle and gospel and homily, and still "hear Mass." For the sole stress was on sacrifice. One word held sway: the consecratory word. Here was *the* real presence, the efficacious word, objectively infallible, utterly trustworthy, limpidly clear. No need for lips to be touched by live coals; enough that they murmured distinctly, "This is my body." Today's liturgical attitude is refreshingly more balanced. In Vatican II's wake, there is fresh stress on the *whole* word as a locus where God transpires. Music, readings, homily, dance—God is or can be there, a real presence.

From official declarations two concerns should dominate the homiletic word: this liturgy and this people. This liturgy, because the lectionary and missal reveal the substance of what is to be preached: "the proclamation of God's wonderful works in the history of salvation." This people, because in the liturgy "God's wonderful works" are not just read or remembered; "the mystery of Christ ... is made present and active within us" (S.C., 35).

The crucial issue: How can words take flesh today? Homilists will not link worship to life unless, as Karl Rahner phrased it, they become translators. The Judeo-Christian revelation, for all its divine authorship, comes to us through human words that carried meanings and overtones from the surrounding world. "Lamb of God" made a strong impression on the earliest Christians not only because the paschal lamb was a venerable religious symbol, but because that symbol struck them where they lived. Jesus was born and bred among people for whom the lamb was a primary source of food and clothing, a fundamental factor in their economy. Transfer that symbol to Papua, where the sacred animal is a pig, where women may nurse piglets at their breast if no sow is around, and the preacher confronts a problem.

Moreover, when revelation is translated into dogma or interpreted by theology, it is not yet the preacher's word: it is jargon-infested and culture-conditioned. The homilist's constant question must be: What do these words say to this people? John Courtney Murray's warning is still valid: "I do not know what I have said until I understand what you have heard." What does this congregation hear when I say "holy mother church"? Institution? Community? Sacrament? Herald? Servant? Disciple? Does its experience of the church conjure up the love and tenderness I associate with my physical mother? Is "holy" too trimphalistic for Christians aware of a community ceaselessly in need of reform?

The homiletic movement from scripture through dogma and theology to the present liturgical moment is a dismaying task. The homilist must (1) grasp the genuine meaning of a word as it emerged from the mouth of Jeremiah or the pen of Paul or the contemplation of a Johannine community, (2) touch it to the paschal mystery celebrated by the church, and (3) transform it so that the word takes on the personal and cultural clothes of this moment, of these believers. Here is the agony of preparation, here its occasional ecstasy. A word is not simply an entry in Webster; it is colored by living experience. The eucharist is indeed a bread that gives life. But when *I* hear the word "life," I hear something quite different from the 200,000 skin-and-bones starving who "live" in the streets of Calcutta, build tiny fires to cook scraps of food, defecate at curbstones, curl up against a wall to sleep—perhaps to die.

But clarity is not enough. A homily is not a catechism or a manual of dogma or a textbook in theology. The word flings forth a challenge; it is a summons to decision; God wants a reply. Living men and women are addressed in preaching, moved to fashion their lives in accordance with what is said. But are they? God's grace, admittedly all-powerful, dashes against two potent Catholic adversaries: a homilist dead below the larynx, and a minimal vocabulary dominated by abstract nouns ending in -tion. If I am to persuade, my whole person should be aflame with what I proclaim. If I am to move, the words I utter must be chosen with care and love, with sweat and fire.

Words can be made flesh today. But only on condition that we take words seriously, handle them sacredly. Every word: the scriptural word, the sacramental word, the secular word, the homiletic word.

Imagination

The homiletic word comes alive as a work of art principally through imagination. What is imagination? The capacity we humans have to make the material an image of the immaterial, of the spiritual. It is a creative power, a fresh way of seeing. It is a breaking through the obvious, the surface, the superficial, to the reality beneath and beyond. It is the world of wonder and intuition, of amazement and delight, of festivity and play.

How does imagination—specifically, religious imagination—come to expression? I mention five primary ways. (1) A vision: e.g., Ezekiel's "four living creatures," St. Margaret Mary Alacoque's vision of the Sacred Heart. (2) Ritual: a group enacts the presence of the sacred and participates in that presence, usually through some combination of dance, chant, sacrifice, or sacrament. (3) Story, especially three types: parable (parables of Jesus), allegory (C.S. Lewis' *Chronicles of Narnia*), and myth, which, whether fact or fancy, intends to narrate the fundamental structure of human being in the world (the creation myth). (4) Symbol: an externally perceived sign that works mysteriously on the human consciousness so as to suggest more than it can clearly describe or define (a totem, a crucifix, the brazen serpent). (5) The fine arts: painting (da Vinci, Picasso); poetry (John Donne, e.e. cummings); sculpture (the Pietà, Rodin); architecture (Chartres, Frank Lloyd Wright); music (Beethoven's *Missa solemnis*, George Winston); dancing (David whirling and skipping before the Ark of the Covenant, Suzanne Farrell); and dramatic art (the mystery dramas of the Middle Ages, movies).

From this, two significant conclusions emerge. First, imagination is not at odds with knowledge; it is a form of cognition, a way of illuminating the facts. Not indeed a process of reasoning. Still, a work of our intellectual nature; through it our spirit reaches the true, the beautiful, and the good.

Second, the imagination does not so much teach as evoke; it calls something forth from the person who sees, hears, touches, tastes, smells. And so it is often ambiguous; the image can be understood in different ways. Recall the reporters asking Martha Graham, "What does your dance mean?" Her reply: "Darlings, if I could tell you, I would not have danced it!" Something is lost when we move from imagining to reasoning, from art to conceptual clarity. Not that imagination is arbitrary, that *Swan Lake* or the Infancy Narrative or *Hamlet* or the Transfiguration is whatever anyone wants to make of it, my gut feeling. Hostile to imagination is creativity run wild, without roots, tradition, or discipline. Still it is true, the image is more open-ended than the concept, less confining, less imprisoning. The image evokes our own imagining.

What has imagination to do with preaching? Just about everything. Return to the two conflicting approaches to preaching, to my contention that, for communication, imagination is more effective than indoctrination. Why? Because indoctrination plays upon one faculty of the human person: the intellect's ability to grasp ideas, concepts, propositions. It pays little heed to an old scholastic axiom, "Nothing is present in the intellect that was not previously present in the senses." Our ideas are triggered by sense experience. On the whole, then, the more powerful the sense experience, the more powerfully will an idea take hold. If I want to sell you on Veal Marsala or Oysters Rockefeller, I don't hand you a recipe; I let you smell it, taste it, savor it. If I want you to "see" the Holocaust, I won't just say "six million were exterminated"; I'll let you see the gas ovens, the mountains of human bones. It's not enough to show you the score of Handel's *Messiah*; you must drink it in with your ears. It is one thing to hear "I love you," quite another to experience love's touch.

In short, the homily is a fascinating wedding of the varied ways in which imagination comes to expression: vision and ritual, symbol and story, the fine arts. This is the homily at its best, the homily that makes God's wonderful works come alive, immerses in the mystery, evokes a religious response.

A response—there's the magic word. The sermon might be different if the task of the liturgy were simply to *recall* God's saving works, simply to *remember* the mystery that is Christ. Then I might merely explain lucidly what it all means. But if the liturgy must make the mystery "present and active within us," a homily should be evocative. It should help the believer open up to God speaking now. Not a cold assent to a proposition: "Yes, there are three persons in one God." Rather, "What do you want from me, Lord?" And the most effective approach to such a reaction is not ratiocination, not demonstration; it is imagination.

The evidence for imagination's incomparable power surrounds us. We keep saying, "A picture is worth a thousand words." Americans spend billions each year on movies, theatre, concerts. Students study to stereo, skip lectures readily when Bruce Springsteen comes to town. Jesuits too read the comics before the front page, go wild over sports—poetry in motion. Our children's supreme educator, for good or ill, is TV. Its commercials sell us with the greatest array of imaginative talent since the creation story in Genesis and John's vision on Patmos.

The homily is an instrument; God uses it to speak to the soul; *God* speaks. The external word is indeed the preacher's; but if God is to speak, the homiletic word has to open the way, not close off all avenues save the homilist's. Not, therefore, "When you go back to your kitchen, this is what you must do." Rather, so artistic a presentation of a message that different people hear from God what they need to hear. Like a remarkable piece of music—Bach's church cantatas, full of symbolism, allusion, and word painting in the context of the Lutheran service—the homily will have different meanings for different listeners, will touch them not where the preacher lives but where they live, where God wants them to live.

Here imagination is indispensable. The image is more open-ended than the concept; the image evokes imagining. This is not indifferentism. From a Catholic homily the faithful should not emerge with a Unitarian God, an Arian Christ, abortion on demand. The preacher presumes, or insinuates, or proclaims the tradition. Still, the preacher is not so much exposing as evoking, not so much imposing on the ignorant a revealed truth with specific applications as drawing the already faithful into the mystery of Christ in such a way that *they* can apply it, can say "yes" to a living God speaking now. The priest, Urban Holmes insists, is "one who incites people to imagine."

How, concretely, is the preacher to achieve this? Specific counsel might include: read storytelling theologian John Shea; immerse yourself in Lewis and Tolkien; tune in on the apocalyptic vision of the TV preachers; shift your language from abstract to concrete; remember that the verb carries the action; listen to the flowers. But there is a more basic need: Catholic homilists require a conversion, fresh insight into their priesthood. Here I wed three elements: the "I," the revelation and the people.

First, I who communicate. Most older priests have been educated to objectivity—by scholastic philosophy, by a theology that lived off magisterial affirmations, by spiritual masters who stressed reason and will, suspected emotion and experience. The subjective had illegitimate parents: Protestantism and Modernism. At the altar, then, and behind the confessional screen, in teaching and preaching, in lecturing and counseling, the "I" was submerged, that Christ alone might appear, that only the truth might transpire. The conversion? I am not an ecclesiastical computer, spewing forth force-fed data. I too am a symbol, a sign that says more than my words can express. In the pulpit I may well be the most powerful image of all.

Second, the revelation we communicate. How was it initially communicated? In earlier days we had no problem: divine revelation consists of truths set forth in the Bible and in authoritative church pronouncements; God has embodied divine self-disclosure in propositional language so that it can claim our unswerving assent. No doubt, revelation can be and has been mediated through true propositions. Still, as Avery Dulles has shown, a richer vision permeates our century: revelation is symbolic disclosure. Revelation is always mediated through an experience in the world—specifically, through symbol. The kingdom of God in the preaching of Jesus is not a clear concept with univocal meaning. It is a symbol that can represent or evoke a whole range of ideas. The point is, our biblical symbols, from the theophanies of Sinai through the cross of Christ to the descent of the Spirit, are too rich to be imprisoned in any single conception. Moreover, the knowledge that symbols give is not cold, abstract information; it is participatory knowledge. A symbol is an environment I inhabit, live in, the way I live in my body; I recognize myself within the universe of meaning and value it opens up to me. And because revelation is this sort of truth, it can transform us, initiate us into a saving relationship with God; it can radically influence our commitments and our behavior; it can give us insight into mysteries reason cannot fathom.

Third, the people with whom the preacher communicates. The faithful do not come to the liturgy primarily to learn—sheep needing to be led. Catholic homilists must grasp why some Protestant pulpits confront the preacher graphically with the request of the Greeks to Philip: "Sir, we would like to see Jesus" (Jn 12:21). How simple a request, and how stunning! Here is the homilist's burden and joy: to help believing Christians to see Jesus—not with his eyes but with their own.

Given conversion on these three levels, the homilist will inevitably prepare and preach imaginatively: (1) be part and parcel of the homily, strike sparks because aflame with the word; (2) be overwhelmed by the many-splendored possibilities within the biblical symbols, their refusal to be imprisoned in a formula, their openness to fresh imaginings; (3) learn to dream dreams and see visions, retell the parables of Jesus in a modern idiom.

Modern Idiom

Scholars tell us that in the middle of the 19th century not only novelists and poets but preachers as well were often exciting and creative. Two linked reasons: discourse in the antebellum period was rooted in a religious tradition and it was built upon popular language. Here I assume a religious tradition: the content of a Catholic sermon is always and everywhere the gospel, god-spell, the good news of Jesus Christ, as understood within the church. The present question is: how to present the living tradition in a style appropriate to history's most remarkable record of God's dealings with humankind—a style of speech that captures an audience, keeps people pleading for more. My basic response, for the United States, is: American words and American symbols, words and symbols that speak to the heart of our age, to the experience of our people.

Symbols come and symbols go. The Sacred Heart was a symbol of love that pervaded American Catholicism before Vatican II; now it is scarcely alive in Catholic devotion. The Beatles are far from dead, but Beatlemania is not the idolatry it once was. I am not suggesting that we empty our rhetoric of all the classical Hebrew and early Christian symbols: abandon "kingdom (or reign) of God" because kings are anchronisms, dictators or figureheads; forsake "suffering servant" because this wedding of words does not appeal to the American psyche. Deep within many ancient images and symbols are powerful forces that need only be intelligently grasped by the preacher and imaginatively presented for hearts to be set aflame.

I do submit that effective preaching, while refusing to sacrifice symbols long and deeply identified with Christ and Christianity, must take place in the context of contemporary symbols. Not only patriotic symbols: the Statue of Liberty, the Stars and Stripes, "America the Beautiful," the Vietnam Memorial with more than 58,000 names etched into black granite. Broader cultural symbols are riding an unprecedented wave. Some fit well together, others are contradictory. Most are secular; some are explicitly or potentially religious.

We have heavy metal and MTV; the computer, car phones, and crack; stretch limos or a Volvo with a baby seat; country, pop, and rock; "We shall overcome" and "Power to the people"; Michael Jackson and Jesse Jackson; Madonna or Mother Teresa; Rambo and Dirty Harry's "Make my day"; a comic-strip Peanuts and a former President's jelly beans; yuppie or Alzheimer; Walkman and the boob tube; *Ms.* or *Playgirl*; Sushi or Mexican beer; Super Bowl or Big Mac; pro-choice or pro-life; Kareem and Steffi Graf; a wasted *Challenger* or a Mars-bound *Discovery*; Wall Street and Häagen Dazs; the "Army: Be All You Can Be" or the Community for Creative Non-Violence; the recreational hobo or the homeless on Washington's winter grates; black power and ERA; Star Wars and strawberry daiquiris; Marcel Lefebvre or John Paul II; Bill Cosby or "The Young and the Restless"; God as mother, God as lover, God as friend of the earth; AIDS and the compassionate Christ.... Fifty-five and still counting. There is ever so much more—symbols my shortsightedness stops me from seeing, images the younger and more restless than I can surely spy.

Precisely how a given preacher shapes a sermon within this welter of symbols is not within the ambit of this article. But unless U.S. preaching is molded in large measure by our cultural context, homilists will be whistling down the wind—Shakespeare's "sound and fury" perhaps, but "signifying nothing." Preach as part and parcel of this concrete world, aware of its paradoxes and contradictions, attuned to its limitless potential for good, saddened or enraged by so much folly and insensitivity, alive to the grace of God with whom nothing on earth is impossible, start with the real-life symbols that surround and all but suffocate us—and the "American words" will come.

Several specific suggestions. First, focus on film. We Catholics who live with symbols (word, sacrament, church), who play with mystery (spirit and matter, divine and human, nature and grace), should thank the silver screen for tackling more powerfully and profoundly than we the common task that is ours: human experience and its meaning. What makes the movies so unparalleled an expression of experience is that film is now consciously all the arts in one art: sculpture and architecture, painting and poetry, music and the dance, dramatic art. Sermons can be crafted from *Chariots of Fire*—three succinct sentences of 1924 Olympic runner Eric Liddell: "God made me fast." "The power is within." "When I run, I feel His pleasure." From *Amadeus*—two men with diverse fatal flaws: the genius Mozart, obscene child who never grows up, self-centered adolescent aware of naught save his music and his pleasure; the moderately talented Salieri, eaten by envy, unable to understand how God can make him mute and gift with genius that foul-mouthed boor with the social graces of Caligula. From *The Gods Must Be Crazy*—the empty Coke bottle that falls from a plane among Bushmen in South Africa's Kalahari desert, the single bottle through which Eden becomes Babel, primitive innocence discovers the ways of civilization. From Woody Allen, Steven Spielberg, George Burns.

Second, for American symbols search through songs. The decibels may drive to distraction, but even the decibels are a contemporary symbol. There is a powerful message—heavy or haunting, loving or lustful, tender or raw—all the way from Amy Grant's "Love of Another Kind" to soft-spoken Randy Travis with his contention that country music "covers everything."

Third, look to everyday experience for American words and symbols, images, metaphors. They surround us, invade our privacy, circulate in our bloodstream: on our streets and in our schools, in *Newsweek* and *Rolling Stone*, in "M*A*S*H" and radio's top 40 tunes, in *The Yellow Christ* of Gauguin and Whoopi Goldberg's sizzling social commentary, in the scores of men and women we touch each day. All day we hear language that burns or soothes, wounds or heals, frightens or amuses, delights or challenges, murmurs in rapture or cries out in pain. By what sleight of hand do they disappear from our pulpits, become classified information, top secret, or sacred to sacerdotal socials?

Fourth, struggle to recapture in captivating language the rich humor in scripture. Basil the Great's conclusion from the gospel text that Jesus never laughed despite his "merriment of soul" must yield to a more human interpretation of him who was like us in simply everything save sin. How could he have wept for sorrow and not laughed for joy? How could he fail to smile when a child cuddled comfortably in his arms, or when he saw little Zacchaeus up a tree, or when Peter put his foot in his mouth once again? I refuse to believe that he did not laugh when he saw something funny, or when he experienced in the depths of his manhood the presence of his Father.

Religous writers and scholars have studied scripture specifically for its humor: not only Jesus' irony, dazzling paradoxes, deliberately hyperbolic statements, but the "comic eschatology" of the Prior Testament itself, notably in Isaac, "the child of laughter." Perhaps no storyteller has recaptured the gospel as comedy with such insight and felicity as has the Presbyterian preacher and novelist Frederick Buechner. Regrettably, Catholic preachers on the whole have not led the faithful to expect humor as part and parcel of a sermon's structure, have not themselves recognized what Buechner calls the "preposterous meeting" of sin and grace, of God's absence and presence, "as the high, unbidden, hilarious thing it is." A grim gospel, excessive seriousness, is not only soporific; it keeps the gospel from coming through as good news, the best of news, a preposterous God preposterously saving God's preposterous image.

A final word. The wine of the gospel is always and everywhere new. But "new wine must be put into fresh wineskins" (Lk 5:38). A homilist's risk and joy is the effort to do for God's people in our time what preachers like Jeremiah and Joel, Peter and Paul, did for God's people in their time: express God's inexpressible word in syllables that wed felicity to fidelity, that flare and flame, that capture minds and rapture hearts, syllables charged with the power of God.

Such an art falls under Bonhoeffer's "costly grace." If Catholic preaching remains at a low ebb, an overriding reason is that homilists either see the sermon as a product that comes cheap or, conceding its high cost, are reluctant to pay the price. Effective preaching is not an option, not primarily a privilege; it is a vocation that may not be refused.

Frederick Buechner, *Telling the Truth: The Gospel as Tragedy, Comedy, and Fairy Tale* (San Francisco: Harper & Row, 1977). Walter J. Burghardt, S.J., *Preaching: The Art and the Craft* (New York/Mahwah: Paulist Press, 1987). James W. Cox, *Preaching* (San Francisco: Harper & Row, 1985). Reginald H. Fuller, *Preaching the Lectionary: The Word of God for the Church Today*, rev. ed. (Collegeville: The Liturgical Press, 1984). Andrew M. Greeley, *God in Popular Culture* (Chicago: Thomas More Press, 1989). Robert P. Waznak, S.S., *Sunday after Sunday: Preaching the Homily As Story* (New York/Ramsey: Paulist Press, 1983).

WALTER J. BURGHARDT, S.J.

PREACHING AT FUNERALS

See **Funerals, preaching at**

PREACHING BY LAY PERSONS

When one remembers that the Council of Trent anathematized anyone who would say that all Christians have the power for the ministry of the word, it is easy to understand how slowly any subsequent change would come about. What was needed was a shift in the dominant image of the church, from hierarchical institution to the pilgrim people of God. Only as the implications of this self-understanding gradually became clear did the basis for preaching come to be recognized as residing in baptism. As the people of God, all are called to share in the priestly, prophetic, and kingly roles of the risen Lord, ever made present in today's world.

The theology of the Second Vatican Council is a given succinct expression in the revised 1983 Code of Canon Law which states that "all the Christian faithful have the duty and the right to work so that the divine message of salvation may increasingly reach the whole of humankind in every age and in every land" (can. 211). Furthermore, "in virtue of baptism and confirmation, lay members of the Christian faithful are witnesses to the gospel by word and by example of a Christian life; they can also be called upon to cooperate with the bishop and presbyters in the exercise of their ministry of the word" (can. 759). More recently, in November 1988, the U.S. bishops approved "Guidelines for Lay Preaching" (G.L.P.), further delineating how lay preaching would be advantageous to the faith community. We have obviously moved a distance from the mind of Trent.

The Tradition and Lay Preaching

Sandra Schneiders persuasively presents NT evidence which indicates that not only were women called to the ministry of the word in the first communities but that preaching was not restricted to any office or group (see Foley, 60-90). The stories of the Samaritan woman (John 4) and of the commissioning of Magdalene on Easter Sunday

(John 20) point to the understanding that Jesus himself entrusted this ministry to them. Furthermore, in both the letters of Paul and Acts a number of instances are presented in which women are seen to function as prophets and teachers. Such figures as the daughters of Philip, Prisca, and possibly Junias are some of those named. The prohibition against women preaching found in 1 Cor 14:33b-35 is thought to be an interpolation from the later 1 Tim 2:11, a document more interested in protecting the community from controversy than in protecting its members' freedom. Indeed, in 1 Cor 11:5, Paul insists on women wearing head covering when they pray and prophesy, which could refer to praying the eucharistic prayer and prophetically preaching the sermon.

At the heart of Paul's message is a tremendous affirmation of the power of the Spirit, of the gifts of the Spirit that need to be discerned and used for the good of all, and of the gift of the word generously given to all Christians. "Let the word of Christ dwell in you richly, as you teach and admonish one another in all wisdom..." (Col 3:16).

While preaching shortly became linked to the local offices of bishop, priest, and deacon, still there were isolated instances recorded during the times of the Church Fathers in which bishops themselves noted they had called on laity to preach. In the Later Middle Ages, especially the 12th and 13th centuries, theologians speculated on the basis for proclaiming the gospel. Edward Schillebeeckx notes four: (1) the *vita apostolica*, founding the right to bear witness in a life given over to the evangelical imitation of Jesus; (2) the *missio*, the fact that one was "sent" by an appropriate authority; (3) the *ordo clericorum*, the clerical rank, or at least the reception of tonsure; and (4) priestly ordination (in Foley, 16-17). The controversies waged over preaching during these times centered mostly on the tension

between the monks and the canons regular in the 12th century, and then between the mendicants and the diocesan clergy in the 13th. The issue was resolved by Gregory who forbade non-ordained monks and laymen to preach, no matter how educated they might be. The end result was the clericalization of preaching until today.

By the present theological shift which grounds preaching in *missio*, the call to mission given to every Christian at baptism, new possibilities arise. Schillebeeckx eloquently speaks of this: "The real norm and justification for competent proclamation of the gospel message is the praxis of Jesus himself embodied in the life of the preacher. The Christian who is really competent to preach today is one who, in his or her faith, is able to enter into the *sequela Jesu* fully. The competent preacher is one who can be totally concerned with human situations, one who can set in motion the processes of admiration, joy and liberation that Jesus himself set in motion and continues to initiate today" (Foley, 37).

The U.S. Bishops' Guidelines on Lay Preaching

The introduction to G.L.P. begins by providing a rationale for restricting the homily to those in orders, a point which shall be taken up later. It then proceeds to name some of the other forms of preaching in which the laity may take part in the ministry of the word: retreats, revivals, spiritual exercises, missions, gatherings of the faithful for public reflections and public assemblies.

The guidelines themselves are noteworthy for several aspects:

(1) They provide general and specific criteria which offer reasonable safeguard of the quality of preaching. Thus, the preachers should be persons of good standing, who live good Christian lives, are active members of the church, familiar with the needs of their community, and

faithful to the leadership and teaching of the magisterium. More specifically, they should have solid grounding in scripture, theology, tradition, and liturgy, in addition to suitable communication and language skills. In a society often caught up in frenzied behavior, lay preachers are to have the time, ability, and intention to prepare properly; in this way they might serve as models for many clerical preachers.

(2) They acknowledge that on the local level the work of the Spirit is evidenced by the increased participation of lay men and women in various apostolates and in a deepened knowledge of scripture and theology. Furthermore, circumstances can arise when persons can be called on to "supplement" the preaching of the ordained for the common good. Might one even say "complement"?

(3) They recognize that some may have the gift of preaching on a continuing basis, others on a frequent basis, and still others for a specific occasion. This allows greater latitude in discerning those through whom the Spirit has elected to speak.

(4) There is a sensitivity not only to the competence of the preacher but also to assuring that the community is prepared to welcome the preacher.

The Lay Preacher and the Homily

While these guidelines are proposed only as a means "to assist the individual diocesan bishop" and "not intended to serve either as a pastoral exhortation or as a comprehensive theological treatment of lay preaching or of the ministry of the word," still in light of the overwhelming support they received by the bishops, being approved by a vote of 195-42, attention is deservedly given to them. Most likely they will play some role in establishing diocesan policy regarding lay preaching. Particularly unfortunate, however, is the decision in the guidelines to restrict the liturgical homily to those in holy orders.

Liturgically, it is argued that the one who presides is the one who preaches. But if the eucharist is the act of the entire people of God, the one presiding might see the responsibility of this office to assure whatever collaboration is necessary so that a worthy, life-giving celebration will come about. Certainly, a major area of concern is who can best preach the homily on this occasion. This seems to have been the approach taken in drawing up the "Directory for Masses for Children," in which it states that there is no reason for one of the adults not to give the homily in these instances if the priest has difficulty communicating with children. Oddly, the guidelines refer to preaching in Masses for children as being a preaching form other than a homily. That's one way to handle an uncomfortable precedent.

Historically, when one looks back to those earliest preachers, one finds listed apostles, prophets, and teachers. It seems that the present liturgical homily continues to be perceived primarily as a form of teaching. The *Constitution on the Sacred Liturgy* said that "by means of the homily the mysteries of the faith and the guiding principles of the Christian life are expounded from the sacred text during the course of the year" (S.C., 52). Furthermore, *Inter Oecumenici*, which implemented the constitution, saw the homily as the exposition of some point in either the readings from Sacred Scripture or in another text from the ordinary or proper of the day's Mass, keeping in mind the mystery being celebrated and the needs of the listeners (I.O., 54). Both of these understandings of the homily are quoted in *G.L.P.* Both see the homily as a teaching moment. And the traditional teacher has been those called to that office as bishops, priests, and teachers.

Still, the question arises, granted that the homily is approached as an instructional moment, is there no opening for a lay person to preach in light of the reality which *G.L.P.* itself notes, namely, "the deepened knowledge of scripture and theology which many lay persons possess" today? Certainly, authorization would be required in order to assure that the people will be appropriately nourished. With that precaution, however, an opening does exist.

The U.S. Bishops' Committee on Priestly Life and Ministry offered a different paradigm for the liturgical homily. "Fulfilled in Your Hearing: The Homily in the Sunday Assembly" (1982) proposed an understanding of the homily as "a scriptural interpretation of human existence which enables a community to recognize God's active presence, to respond to that presence in faith through liturgical word and gesture, and beyond the liturgical assembly, through a life lived in conformity with the Gospel" (29). Rather than seeing the homily as an exposition of the scripture text or an expounding of mysteries and principles, the key words here are "to provide a scriptural interpretation of life." Scripture is employed to interpret life today, to name God's presence now, to name grace, to point to how God is challenging, calling us. One does not preach *on* scriptures but *from* and *through* them. We find this approach resonant with an early statement in the Constitution on the Liturgy which speaks of the homily as "the proclamation of God's wonderful works in the history of salvation, which is the mystery of Christ ever made present and active in us, especially in the celebration of the Eucharist" (S.C., 35.2). This emphasis on pointing to what is happening *now* is one of the earliest forms of preaching.

This type of preaching is quite in line with what was called prophecy in the early tradition, the charism given to those men and women who brought the gospel into immediate contact with the present life of the community. Certainly those in orders are not the only ones who can see how the scripture speaks to the life of a particular community. Is it possible to carefully discern if others in a particular community might be called to address the community and offer the homily out of their *vita apostolica*?

Conclusion

In the first days of the Christian community, Paul asked, "how can they believe unless they have heard of him? And how can they hear unless there is someone to preach?" (Rom 10:14). More recently, can. 225.1 acknowledges the obligation of laity to work for the spread of the gospel, especially "in those circumstances in which people can hear the Gospel and know Christ only through lay persons." It seems clear that the ministry of the word, in all its forms, is the primary arena to which the Spirit is calling all of God's people. It is a work requiring humility, trust, and courage, and an abiding in the Spirit who is given for the building up of the church.

See **Lay leadership in the liturgy; Lay ministries, liturgical; Ministry, lay**

Bishops' Committee on Priestly Life and Ministry/ N.C.C.B., *Fulfilled in Your Hearing: The Homily in the Sunday Assembly* (Washington: U.S.C.C., 1982). "U.S. Bishops' Guidelines for Lay Preaching," *Origins,* (Dec 1, 1988): 402-404. Nadine Foley, O.P., (ed.) *Preaching and the Non-Ordained* (Collegeville: The Liturgical Press, 1983).

JAMES A. WALLACE, C.SS.R.

PREACHING THE LECTIONARY

The church, throughout its history, has produced a variety of systems for the choice of scripture to be read and expounded in its worship and for use in private devotions. These are known as lectionaries. There are two basic varieties of lectionaries: *lectio selecta*, a system in which readings from scripture are selected from all the biblical books according to theme or calendar concerns, and *lectio continua* in which readings follow one another Sunday by Sunday in a continuous sequence through a book or books of the Bible. This second system was the one used in the earliest centuries as indicated by the writings of Justin Martyr and others. But a different method finally came to prevail in the Roman rite of the West, and this is the one we call *lectio selecta*. During the Reformation these two methods came to divide the various churches, Reformed and Roman Catholic. The Reformed churches adopted the continuous reading from scripture early on in the Reformation. However, Reformed churches today have generally abandoned anything like the "in course readings" and its ministers often choose a particular scripture reading for each or follow the Common Lectionary.

The word "lectionary" refers to a book or list of readings of scripture for the church year. It is derived from the Latin, *lectio*, meaning an act of reading. An individual reading is called a lection or more commonly a pericope. A pericope is a selection from a book and in liturgical language it refers to a specific reading from a book of the Bible. The word is derived from Greek and literally means "an act of cutting." A pericope is a passage "cut out" of a book of the Bible for use in worship. The function of the lectionary readings selected for each Sunday is to relate the time of the church as it lives "between the times" of resurrection and the return of Christ (narrated in the cycles of Christmas and Easter) to the time of salvation which is spelled out in the reading and preaching of scripture.

The Common Lectionary of Protestant churches and the Roman Catholic Lectionary produced by the Second Vatican Council are very similar and provide three readings for every Sunday over a three-year period. There are other lectionaries which follow a two-year cycle or other time frame. But the three-year cycle known as Year A, Year B and Year C, respectively, is the one this article will deal with in regard to preaching.

Following the lectionary can give both a focus and discipline to preaching and to the church's life. When Sunday church school curriculum follows the lectionary this prepares the hearers for the sermon. Announcing the lectionary readings a week in advance and requesting members of the congregation to read and reflect on them during the week also prepares the hearers' hearts for the homily based on the lectionary readings. However, the preacher should reserve the freedom to respond to world and local crises and to pressing congregational needs as led by the Holy Spirit, and to depart from the lectionary if needed.

One of the chief benefits of preaching the lectionary is that this systematic proclamation of scripture enables both preacher and congregation to follow through the seasons of the church year, preparing for and celebrating the central events of the Christian faith. Thus, preaching from the lectionary channels the energy and study of the church, enabling members to relate their faith to the world in which they live.

In preaching from the lectionary one should be aware of the two cycles which make up the Christian calendar: the weekly cycle of Sunday to Sunday, and the annual cycle which deals with two major festivals of the church: Christmas and Easter. The weekly cycle is the older and is the foundation and kernel of the church year. For instance, Easter is a "big Sunday" since Sunday is the day on which the early church celebrated Christ's resurrection and for this reason it is called "the Lord's Day."

One advantage in preaching on the lectionary is that preaching by necessity takes on a christological center. The two foci of the church year are Christ-celebrations: Christmas which celebrates the incarnation, and Easter which celebrates redemption. Examining these two foci more closely we see that the church year begins with Advent which prepares for the Christmas celebration (including Christ's return) and Epiphany which reflects the Christmas celebration. In a similar fashion, Lent serves to prepare for Easter and the fifty days following Easter are a reflection of that celebration. The fifty days climax in Pentecost. Thus we see that preaching from the lectionary leads the preacher and congregation in an annual rehearsal of the history of our salvation accomplished in the life, death, resurrection/ascension and return of Jesus Christ. The time after Epiphany, and after Pentecost and before Advent is really not a season but is made up of ordinary Sundays. Thus the Christian year is, strictly speaking, only half a year, extending from Advent through Pentecost.

The time from Pentecost to Advent offers the preacher an extended period of time to structure preaching on passages or books of the Bible other than those of the lectionary if one desires. A happy compromise might be found in reading OT and gospel lessons from the lectionary and preaching on the epistle for a period of time, preaching on some gospel passages omitted from the lectionary, or preaching on the minor prophets or other portions of the OT which are given little or no place in the lectionary.

Slavish following of the lectionary can, after a period of years of preaching, create for preacher and congregation a new canon of scripture. This can be avoided by seeking to balance the lectionary readings with other passages not included in the lectionary. One of the chief criticisms of the lectionary is that it too carefully avoids many of the abrasive and hard texts of the Bible. The preacher should read and reflect not only on the pericope chosen but on the larger section of scripture in which it is found, especially on verses omitted or occurring immediately before or following the pericope. Unfortunately the lament and complaint psalms are not at the center of the lectionary readings. While a reading from a psalm is specified for each Sunday, these are seldom laments. The result of omitting most of the hard sayings dealing with judgment, hell, etc., the minor prophet material and the lament psalms, is that the lectionary creates a romantic view of life over against the reality of the culture in which we live and over against the abrasion which is an integral part of the biblical faith. The preacher should be aware of this serious fault of the lectionary and work to remedy it with substitutions during the non-festival six months of the church year and also by including before, in and after the pericope, key verses which were omitted by the shapers of the lectionary.

One of the main advantages for both preacher and congregation of preaching from the lectionary is that over a period of three years the preacher will have either read, or read and preached on, many of the central themes and key passages of scripture. For example, Year A usually takes the gospel lessons from Matthew; Year B uses passages from both Mark and John since Mark is the shortest gospel. Year C takes gospel passages from Luke. The gospel of John is used also in Cycles A and C on occasion. During the fifty days from Easter to Pentecost, readings from the book of Acts are used in the place of OT lessons to stress the ongoing ministry of the church in the world by the power of the risen and living Christ.

Preaching which does not follow the lectionary or some other plan of systematic preaching through scripture can easily fall prey to the preacher's own whims and favorite themes and texts. One prominent preacher was well known for attacking his favorite targets of psychology, education, nationalism and Marxism. Following the lectionary in preaching can help avoid focusing either on a pietistic, invidualistic form of Christianity, or stressing, on the other hand, only the social and political aspects of the Christian faith. Following the lectionary in preaching can help avoid riding theological hobbyhorses found in a selected few passages of scripture. These are themes to which the preacher keeps returning rather than covering the full sweep of scripture.

Another strong argument for following the lectionary in preaching during this period of growing biblical illiteracy is to better acquaint congregations with the books of the Bible and their message. Also, as the same passages recur every three years, following the lectionary can offer an opportunity for the preacher to study these passages in greater depth and then develop sermons on the same passages but from a fresh perspective. Because of the growing use of the lectionary in preaching there is a vast volume of exegetical, liturgical and homiletical literature available to the preacher.

The lectionary provides an integrative role for worship in three particular aspects of the church's life: liturgical, educational and ecumenical. Preaching from the lectionary allows the preacher and church musicians to plan the theme of each worship service some months in advance. Congregations appreciate the fact that other churches are dealing with the same lections. The lectionary enables church-school and church-worship to become integrated through the use of the same lections. Thus, the lectionary is playing an increasingly important and visible role in the ecumenical movement, bringing Roman Catholic and other Christian churches closer to one another as they read and hear scripture from the same passages each Sunday. This has enabled preachers to gather for small group study of the lectionary passages early in the week as they share exegetical and homiletical work. Some church musicians are playing the same anthems and hymns, sometimes going to different churches on the same Sunday to do so. Thus, the preaching of the lectionary can enhance the whole worship service and give visible evidence of the unity which exists around the scriptures, even if churches are not yet united at the holy table.

Underlying the lectionary is a basic principle which asserts that the New Covenant and the Old Covenant are related. This is sometimes indicated in the maxim that the NT is latent in the OT, and that the OT lies open in the NT. A word of caution should be given in preaching the lectionary texts, however, and seeking to relate OT and NT lessons. The preacher should not deprive the Hebrew Bible of its true and original meaning in an effort to force lections into a Christian mold. Nor should the Hebrew Scriptures be used only as a quarry for prophecies of Jesus Christ and the time of salvation. The lectionary texts from the OT and NT sometimes relate to each other by a common theme or allusions to themes. Sometimes they do not. During ordinary time the Lutheran version of the lectionary chooses OT lessons to relate to the gospel lessons. But the Common Lectionary does not. It provides a continuous reading, for example, of the life of David in Year B. Sometimes the NT passage reinforces the message of the OT and carries it further. On other Sundays the OT and NT lessons may contrast with each other. Or the OT event or miracle or teaching may foreshadow a similar one in the NT. Whenever these ways of relating the passages occur the preacher should make use of them to enrich the reading and preaching of the pericopes.

No one knows how or when lectionaries came into use in the Christian church. There is little evidence of lectionaries before the 4th century. However, in Judaism after Jesus' time there was a fixed lectionary in which there were two lessons for each Sabbath. One was from the Torah and the other from the prophets. Some Jewish scholars claim this system was in use even as early as the time of Jesus. The earliest Western lectionaries date from the 5th century. The Greek Orthodox adopted a semi-continuous reading of scripture in the 9th century. It was only natural that certain books and texts would come to be associated with the Christmas and Easter cycles and with the seasons of the year. In the early spring when fields and vineyards were being cultivated appropriate passages such as the parables of the Laborers in the Vineyard, and the Sower were read. Certain pericopes came to be associated with saints' days. While two lessons, one always from the gospels, were standard practice in the West, sometimes there were more lessons.

It may be that Luke assumed Jesus was using such a lectionary reading when he preached in the synagogue of Nazareth (Lk 4:18f). After reading from the prophet Isaiah, chap. 61, Jesus sat down and spoke to the congregation. He said, "Today this scripture is fulfilled in your hearing." This is one of the purposes of preaching the lectionary passages: to let a selection from an ancient book speak directly to the hearers.

One of the surprises reported by preachers who follow the lectionary is the amazing way in which the prescribed texts speak to the particular needs and events of the congregation.

Preaching from the lectionary has several benefits for the preacher such as eliminating the nagging question which recurs each week: "What shall I preach about this Sunday?" It gives direction to the preacher's study of the scripture if the preacher follows the gospel or OT or epistle pericope for a period of time. The preacher is more likely to study the gospel of Mark, for example, in greater depth if the preacher plans a number of sermons from that book than if the preacher merely "dips" into Mark for a text for one Sunday alone. This also benefits the congregation who can gain a sense of continuity in the sermons based on a particular book of the Bible.

A number of objections have been raised to preaching from the lectionary. They can be summed up briefly: 1) The freedom of the pulpit and of the preacher is hampered; 2) Scripture orders time, rather than time ordering scripture as in the lectionary; 3) The world sets the agenda for selecting scripture if the preacher is to speak to the world and its needs; and, 4) The needs of people should set the agenda for text selection, rather than an impersonal system of text selection. Space does not permit the refutation of each of these objections, but the preacher who considers following the lectionary should be aware of these objections.

Some other objections are the lack of sufficient OT passages illustrating the role of women in sacred history, the simplistic use of prophecy-fulfillment themes in the selection of OT passages, an insufficient number of OT passages and the breaking up of OT books into short snippets. Other problems arise in a close examination of the lectionary. The Common Lectionary is not a fixed entity but is subject to change by the Consultation on Common Texts. As the Roman Catholic lectionary was revised by the Second Vatican Council, so it is likely that future councils will make further revisions.

Never before in the history of the church, Catholic and Reforming, has there been such a potent instrument and symbol as the lectionary to enable preachers to work toward expressing unity in the word and the calling to mission. Perhaps this is the greatest strength of the lectionary and the chief motive for preaching it.

See **Liturgical calendar**

Perry H. Biddle, Jr., *Preaching the Lectionary: Workbooks for Year A* (Philadelphia: Westminster Press, 1989). Peter C. Bower, *Handbook for the*

Common Lectionary (Philadelphia: The Geneva Press, 1987). Reginald H. Fuller, Preaching the Lectionary, rev. ed. (Collegeville, MN: The Liturgical Press, 1984). Sherman E. Johnson, The Year of the Lord's Favor: Preaching the Three-Year Lectionary (New York: The Seabury Press, 1983).

PERRY H. BIDDLE, JR.

PREACHING THE SCRIPTURES

The practice of preaching on scripture is deeply rooted in the Christian tradition. The OT was the Bible of the early church, and one of the first exercises in Christian theology was to make manifest the relation between the biblical texts (usually in the Greek Septuagint version) and Jesus Christ. The units that make up the synoptic gospels and the long discourses in the fourth gospel are sometimes traced back to early Christian preaching ("In the beginnng was the sermon," according to M. Dibelius). Paul used the rhetorical devices and logical patterns developed by Jewish midrashists as well as the techniques of Greek and Latin rhetoricians. Among the NT documents it is customary to classify the letter to the Hebrews as a sermon (see Heb 11:22, "my word of exhortation").

In the patristic period and indeed throughout Christian history the biblical homily or sermon has been a principal vehicle for expressing the truths of Christian faith and showing their relevance for the lives of believers. The line of great biblical preachers runs from John Chrysostom and Augustine through Martin Luther to Karl Barth and Martin Luther King.

Why the Bible should be the starting point for Christian preaching follows from what the church believes the Bible to be: "the words of God expressed in the words of men" (D.V., 13). The Bible is divine revelation because in it God "chose to show forth and communicate the eternal decisions of his will" (D.V., 6). The Bible is inspired in that God made use of the human authors to teach "firmly, faithfully, and without error that truth which God wanted to put into the sacred writings for the sake of our salvation" (D.V., 12). As the authoritative collection of sacred writings the scriptures function as the "canon," that is, as the measure by which the church's faith and life can be assessed. These traditional theological affirmations about the Bible (revelation, inspiration, inerrancy, canonicity) indicate the great authority of the Bible within the church and help to explain why it is the starting point for Christian preaching.

The documents of Vatican II affirm the pre-eminent position of scripture in Christian preaching. The Constitution on Divine Revelation insists that "all the preaching of the church must be nourished and ruled by Sacred Scripture" (D.V., 21). The Constitution on the Sacred Liturgy instructs that "by means of the homily the mysteries of the faith and the guiding principles of the Christian life are expounded from the sacred text during the course of the liturgical year" (S.C., 52). The General Instruction of the Roman Missal directs that the homily should develop "some point of the readings" or of the other prayers connected with the eucharistic liturgy (G.I.R.M., 41). The table at which the bread of life is offered to the faithful is constituted by both the word of God and the body of Christ (D.V., 21).

In the revised lectionary of the Roman Catholic church (which has been accepted and adapted by major Protestant denominations) the preacher finds an array of biblical texts and faces the task of showing how these texts may illumine the lives of God's people today. The arrangement of texts in the liturgical cycle leads the church each year through the dynamic of Christian life from Advent to Christ the King who reigns forever. On Sundays the OT, psalm, and gospel readings are usually correlated around a common theme, with the selection from the epistles or Revelation running on a separate cycle. On weekdays the OT epistle and gospel readings proceed on separate, continuous tracks, and the psalm often ties in with the first reading. There is a three-year cycle for Sundays and a two-year cycle for weekdays. Thus the lectionary is a kind of anthology from which the preacher may choose what speaks best to the experience and situation of the particular congregation.

Biblical Criticism and Preaching

The modern approach to scripture study is a combination of literary and historical methods that is often referred to as "biblical criticism" or the "historical-critical" method. The goal of biblical criticism is to learn as much as possible about the meaning of a text in its original historical setting; that is, what the human author sought to communicate to the original audience in the 5th century B.C. or the 1st century A.D. Biblical critics try to establish as much as possible the original Hebrew and Greek texts, and then base their modern translations on them. They apply literary methods to biblical texts in order to understand their style and content, and historical methods in order to learn about their origin and setting.

Though historical criticism presents the preacher with some challenges, it also performs important services. An appreciation of what the biblical text may have meant in its original setting protects the preacher from fanciful interpretations and applications today, from using the biblical text as the mere occasion or pretext for putting forward prejudices or pet theories. On the other hand, application of the various critical methods can help the preacher to generate themes and strategies for preaching. Without the serious work of textual critics and translators the preacher would not have a reliable text on which to preach. The Bible is literature, and the preacher reads and interprets biblical texts on behalf of the congregation. By attending to the concerns of general literary criticism (word study, context, literary genres, characterization, plot development, structure, etc.) the preacher finds clues toward an imaginative application of the text for today.

Even the more recondite procedures of biblical criticism can help the preacher. Form criticism seeks to determine the literary genre of a text (narrative, legal statement, parable, proverb, hymnic fragment, etc.) and what the genre says about the history of the community. Without a clear idea of the nature of the text that one is preaching, the preacher risks mistaking parable for historical narrative, or admonition for law. Moreover, through form criticism the preacher comes to recognize that many biblical texts arose out of the experience of a faith-community (setting in life) and met its needs—precisely what the preacher today does. Likewise, redaction criticism, which gives special attention to the unique views or unusual emphases that the biblical writers placed on their sources, enables the preacher to identify the distinctive perspective from which the ancient author viewed an event or person in response to a problem facing the community.

The material culture and spiritual atmosphere of the biblical world have been greatly illumined by archaeological excavations and textual discoveries. These enable us to know far more about the setting in which the biblical writers worked than our ancestors ever knew. These findings allow the preacher today to understand the cultural assumptions and modes of expression current among people in antiquity. Thus the preacher can discern where a biblical text is merely repeating "what everyone knows" and where it may be challenging the commonly received wisdom in the light of the perspective of faith.

Thus the historical-critical method need not be viewed as inimical to faithful preaching within the church. The methods themselves are ideologically neutral. The Christian preacher can profit greatly from applying them in the context of faith.

For many preachers the OT presents a special challenge. They sometime find its content and manner of expression strange and difficult. In the Sunday lectionary the OT selection usually supplies the "background" to the gospel text and has been chosen in light of a promise-fulfillment theology. The OT is seldom taken on its own terms.

Vatican II insisted on the importance of the OT for Christians. The OT according to D.V. 14-16 is not only the complement to the NT and the preparation for Christ's coming but also the witness to God's plan of salvation and treasury of divine pedagogy. Though the OT is said to contain some things that are "incomplete and temporary" (D.V., 15), the Christian story reaches back to Adam and Abraham, and would be incoherent apart from the Hebrew Bible. When the preacher's focus is the OT text, it is often possible to view the gospel in a fresh way. The psalms, with their open and metaphorical language, are particularly helpful in promoting an identification between the ancient text and the modern reader, thus accounting for their perennial popularity.

Hermeneutical Challenges

The term "hermeneutics" (interpretation) is applied sometimes to the whole process of determining what a biblical text meant in the past and means now, sometimes primarily to express what it means now. The chief hermeneutical challenges that have arisen from biblical criticism concern the differences between the biblical world and today's world, and the variety of theological perspectives and ways of expression in the Bible. How does the preacher move from the world of the Bible (there) to a congregation today (here)? How does the preacher find meaning in biblical texts and make them meaningful for a congregation today?

Fundamentalist preachers operate on the assumption that there is no real difference from the biblical world and that scripture's divine origin guarantees uniformity of teaching within the Bible. The Fathers of the church frequently resorted to the allegorical methods developed in pagan circles to make the Greek epics (*Iliad* and *Odyssey*) more meaningful and serious for a later age. The Fathers interpreted biblical narratives (especially in the OT) and parables in terms of the Christ-event, and discovered in each detail an element in the central story of salvation.

Most biblical preachers today seek out parallels between the biblical situation and their own. For example, they may find symmetries between the community divisions in 1st-century Corinth that Paul addressed and the factions within their own church. In drawing parallels between the biblical text and the life of the congregation today the preacher may urge people to identify with biblical characters such as the man who was robbed and left for dead in the parable of the Good Samaritan (Lk 10:30-35), or with those who stood at the foot of Jesus' cross ("Were you there when they crucified my Lord?"). Or the preacher may provide an imaginative recreation of the biblical scene and bid the congregation to see and feel what Peter or some other character experienced. Many preachers "spiritualize" a text by substituting a spiritual reality (spiritual obtuseness or obduracy) for a material one (physical blindness). Or they may draw a universal lesson out of a particular text, as some have derived a doctrine of church and state from Rom 13:1-7 (often with unfortunate consequences). One rather extreme example of this kind of substitution was Rudolf Bultmann's program of demythologization in which he interpreted scripture in light of Martin Heidegger's existentialist philosophy and turned mythical or theological terms into statements about the human condition (anthropology).

The chief problem with drawing parallels between scripture and today's situation is the risk of turning the texts into allegories and ignoring the real difference between the world of the Bible and the present situation. Moreover, there are important issues not covered directly by the biblical writers such as the morality of nuclear warfare, birth control, abortion, the ethical problems connected with "test tube" babies, and so forth. In these cases the preacher can draw general principles and guidelines from the Bible, but not direct and explicit advice on the matters at hand.

The preacher's task is to listen to the biblical texts and to bring them to bear on the life of a specific community today. The preacher must try to remain faithful to the biblical tradition and to the community's situation. The act of preaching is personal (depending on the gifts and limitations of the preacher) and concrete (depending on the particular situation of those who are addressed—their problems, educational level, etc.). An effective homily might range from seven minutes to an hour, according to local custom. It may be largely an exposition of the biblical text with applications along the way. Or it may simply develop a point in the text in a wholly new imaginative framework.

Biblical preaching cannot be reduced to abstract principles or even practical guidelines. Nor is it merely the performance of an articulate or highly educated person. Rather it must flow from the Christian theology of the word. So Paul described his ministry: "When you received the word of God which you heard from us, you accepted it not as the word of men but what it really is, the word of God, which is at work in you believers"

(1 Thess 2:12-13). Likewise, Heb 4:12 calls the word of God "living and active, sharper than any two-edged sword." And it is surely not accidental that the prologue to John's Gospel celebrates Jesus the revealer and revelation of the Father as the Word of God (Jn 1:1-18). The power of God's word makes biblical preaching possible.

See **Scripture in the liturgy; Word, liturgy of the; Hermeneutics and worship**

Elizabeth Achtemeier, *Preaching from the Old Testament* (Louisville: Westminster/John Knox, 1989). Ernest Best, *From Text to Sermon*, rev. ed. (Edinburgh: T. & T. Clark, 1988). Reginald H. Fuller, *The Use of the Bible in Preaching* (Philadelphia: Fortress, 1981). *Preaching the Lectionary*, rev. ed. (Collegeville: Liturgical Press, 1984).

DANIEL J. HARRINGTON, S.J.

PREACHING, CATHOLIC, IN THE UNITED STATES

While historians from many ecclesiastical disciplines have frequently relied upon the evidence of sermons to supplement their research, little scholarly attention has been given to historical homiletics. For this reason, few definitive conclusions can be offered about nearly five hundred years of Catholic preaching in the Americas, particularly in those territories and among people of the United States. From the arrival of Spanish friars to the New World in 1493, the gospel has been continuously proclaimed and preached among us, yet the character of that preaching and its effect upon the Catholic body remains relatively unknown. This condition need not persist. In fact, the U.S. Catholic bishops gave special impetus to the search for our preaching heritage in their 1982 document, *Fulfilled in Your Hearing: The Homily in the Sunday Assembly*. In the absence of a body of critical literature on the subject, we can begin to construct our homiletic history out of a myriad of sources, especially out of sermons themselves.

The surviving remnants of U.S. Catholic pastoral preaching, when pieced together, reveal the multiple patterns of worshipping communities at prayer. In their variety of design and expression, homiletic artifacts contribute to the portrait of our faith communities in all their catholicity. As historical documents, sermon manuscripts, outlines, and notes chronicle the formation of the church in North America. As rhetorical texts, homiletic literature captures collective concerns and attitudes of local assemblies that have helped shape the national and global character of Catholicism. From the perspective of history and rhetoric, sermons tell us more than about the faith or preoccupations of an individual preacher; they reflect the ethos of the entire community.

For every regional, social, or theological expression of the *ecclesia*, there is a corresponding homiletic. This is most evident when sermons are considered as the voices of a religious community's self-understanding about such things as faith and culture. In this way, the corpus of this country's Catholic sermons reflect the predominant stance of the church toward the socio-political context in which it finds itself. In another way, our preaching is remarkable only for the peculiar ways in which it imitates ancient patterns of proclamation. Humanist preachers of the past like Bernard of Clairvaux or Charles Borromeo find their counterparts in U.S. homiletic history. More commonly, our preachers have adopted the formal, didactic tradition first explicated by Augustine and later canonized by scholastic theologians at Trent. Epochs in our national and religious history have been shaped by or have given shape to a homiletics that has attempted to explain or interpret life's ambiguities in light of the gospel. This essay provides only a faint sketch of our preaching profile, highlighting some distinctive features of parochial, liturgical homiletics from the birth of the Republic to the present.

Maryland's small and homogeneous band of English Catholic colonists began to think of themselves as Americans well before the outset of our national period. Their preachers, too, revealed a fermenting republicanism and an effort to integrate into their sermons expressions so important to the Enlightenment: "civil and religious liberty," "rights of conscience," and "freedom of determination." At its best, this Catholicism and its preaching, personified by Bishop John Carroll (1735-1815), was Enlightened and self-consciously "American." This relatively short-lived period of Enlightened Catholic preaching had a two-fold agenda. First, it aimed to build up the community of faithful through an eloquence of adaptation, one that accommodated a predominantly French cultivated rhetoric and spirituality to the needs of the infant republic. Since it was not until 1791 that the United States had its own seminary, Catholic clergy relied upon Europe, especially France, for their education. Seminary students bound for America discovered no national idiom in the sermons of their baroque French models, Massillon and Bossuet; they had to discover this on their own. Second, Enlightened Catholic preaching became a vehicle for social acceptance by the more powerful forces of Protestant America. Catholic preachers like Carroll, understanding themselves as a minority, used eloquence to enhance the church's reputation among the majority and to persuade both Catholics and Protestants of their mutual concerns as Christians and as neighbors. Thus, for example, did Carroll's preaching reflect ecumenical sensibilities, since Protestants often attended Catholic services. That Carroll frequently addressed his congregation as "Catholic Christians" or "citizens" is typical of an irenic strategy intended to underscore the reality of America's religious pluralism.

Enlightened Catholic preaching fostered Christian humanism by stressing the harmony of nature and grace, the church and state, the person and society. But even among those small communities of prosperous colonists, such preaching was also frequently apologetical, voicing the Anglo-American Catholic gentry's lingering sense of its own political and religious disenfranchisement. These concerns only intensifed and resounded from the pulpits of burgeoning immigrant communities in the 19th century.

The humanist, liberal character of Enlightened Catholic preaching found muted expression among Americans during the "brick and mortar" age of the church. Preachers like Paulist founder Isaac Hecker (1819-1888), Bishop John Lancaster Spalding (1840-1916), and Bishop John J. Keane (1838-1918), were atypical promoters of a manifest destiny Catholicism, emphasizing the church and nation's mutual contributions to civilization and progress. More widespread were religious, social, and political currents that formed a steady stream of preaching that is best described as "formalist." A formalist homiletic offered order and stability by emphasizing the role of preacher as teacher and by promoting the continuity of the church's devotional life. Inhospitable forces from within and without the predominantly immigrant Catholic community moved preachers to explicate, preserve, or defend the constants and universals of Catholic identity.

Aside from their regional or ethnic distinctions, Catholics experienced in common varying degrees of persecution, alienation, and isolation during the first sixty years of the last century. Preachers contended more or less successfully with the outside challenges posed by ethnic discrimination, political nativism, and cultural estrangement. They preached a message of assurance and comfort to people who had escaped European conflicts and famine only to find abject poverty and civil war. Their sermons provided the community a momentary refuge from a bewildering and threatening society. By content and design, the Sunday sermon rarely commented on contemporary events but lifted the listeners up or away from their social or personal turmoil. This explains, in part, why so few references to the Civil War exist among the homiletic artifacts of the 1860s.

The proliferation of ethnic parishes throughout the 19th century made it possible for a mostly immigrant clergy to formalize, and thus preserve, both the cultural and religious identity of their communities. At the same time, such preaching often advanced a view of humanity and society that favored pessimism and acceptance of this "vale of tears." New York's first archbishop, John Hughes (1797-1864), warned his congregation: "There is reason to fear, that when God permits men or nations to prosper to the extent of their desires, it is a mark of his disfavor...." Preachers like Hughes used the pulpit as a medium for assuaging the suffering of impoverished immigrants and for maintaining their Catholic ethos throughout the slow process of Americanization. In a less polemical way did the first archbishop of Santa Fe, Jean B. Lamy (1814-1888), preach a gospel of assimilation. For example, he began his episcopacy in Santa Fe with a series of sermons in Spanish that sought to move his Hispanic congregation away from their native spirituality. In its place, he presented to them Anglo-European religious art and devotions to encourage their more rapid religious and social acculturation.

We know more about the preaching of the American hierarchy because their sermons have been preserved. But we also know that, in many cases, bishops set the standard and the tone for local churches. Hughes insisted that his priests preach regularly, even if the sermons were not of their own composition, and threatened deportation for those who refused. The sermon collections of several priests of Hughes' diocese vary little from the archbishop's except in the inferiority of their eloquence. To compound the problem of sheer resistance to the pulpit, preachers were themselves mostly ill-prepared for their task.

Those few pulpit orators who gained prominence among American Catholics did so in spite of their severely limited access to homiletic resources and education. The 1829 emancipation of Catholics in England signalled the first real opportunity to create or translate manuals of preaching in English. It was not until the 1866 Plenary Council in Baltimore that the bishops actually required the teaching of homiletics in the nation's seminaries. Needless to say, homiletic education did not arise as an immediate priority. Instead, seminary professors and their students continued to rely on the fine, but not always pertinent, French Sulpician-Vincentian methods. Immigrant clergy in America, if they preached at all, often continued the practice of reading the sermon texts of continental masters. Most pastoral preaching, regardless of the language in which it was delivered, focused primarily on catechetical topics. Since preachers feared great "leakage" from the church brought on by ignorance, their sermons stressed the knowledge of doctrine and the necessity of proper religious practice to insure one's Catholicity.

Untrained preachers, uncatechized congregations, pervasive anti-Catholicism, and a hierarchy made defensive by papal edicts like the 1864 Syllabus of Errors took their toll on the nation's preaching. Such conditions produced a curious blend of preaching and teaching that rarely considered the liturgical context during which the sermon occurred. A random sampling of some sermon titles preached in New York in the later 19th century is fairly representative: "On the Temporal Power of the Pope," "Sanctifying Grace," "The Uncanonized Saints of Ireland," and "Freemasonry." The gap between preaching and worship simply widened as the century progressed. In 1884, during the Third Plenary Council, the bishops endorsed Irish Vincentian Thomas Mac-Namara's *Sacred Rhetoric* (1882) as an official preaching textbook. While not widely used in seminaries, this text reveals the collective mentality of those responsible for the country's preaching. Mac-Namara's book simply collates and promotes for preachers tenets of the popular elocutionary movement that had been recently imported from France. The textbook features a fold-out series of posed figures dressed in cassock, surplice, and biretta modelling the orator's proper stance and gesture for emotions like horror, pity, and shame.

MacNamara's text was eclipsed by another Irish cleric's works, Thomas Potter's *Sacred Eloquence* (1866) and *The Spoken Word* (1869). Potter's works, while highly derivative, put forth a stunning collection of instruction and example from Cicero to Newman that influenced homiletic instruction well into the 20th century. The popularity of these excellent books indicates that, by and large, seminary professors provided their students with the best resources available.

Living memory continues to inform, if not prejudice, our characterization of 20th-century preaching. The periodical literature on preaching from the early 1900s to the 1950s in *Ecclesiastical Review* (later *The American Ecclesiastical Review*), *The Homiletic and Pastoral Review*, and *Orate Fratres* (later *Worship*) corrects the temptation to dismiss the efforts of preachers caught between

Modernism and Vatican II. The impressive attention given to preaching and the recurring themes covered by these journals provide some insights into American Catholic homiletic theory. First of all, throughout an era known for its neo-Thomist biases, many homiletic contributors had a strong affinity for Potter's use of Ciceronian rhetoric. These authors rarely advanced new theories or techniques; rather, they adapted for preachers the enduring prescriptions of classical rhetoric. For example, where the ancients would select the matter for their discourses from a list of *topoi*, the American priest found in his journals topical outlines for an entire year's worth of Sunday sermons. Secondly, in spite of the plethora of sermon suggestions and rhetorical instruction that experts provided, the evidence of actual pastoral sermons contributes to the homogeneous and predictable reputation of American Catholic homiletics. That is to say, for the most part, preachers delivered for their assemblies Sunday after Sunday short courses in doctrinal or moral instruction. This focus on the perennial questions and universal concerns of Catholic life extended the formalist, didactic character of U.S. Catholic preaching into the 1960s.

The impulse to explain, teach, or defend the Catholic faith inspired many forms of preaching that, to date, have received minuscule scholarly attention. Even less accessible than the history of our parochial preaching, then, is that of special preaching outside of the eucharistic liturgy. It is beyond the scope of this article to comment on the effects of sermons heard from farm fields, street corners, or televisions. But noting this rich variety of preaching acknowledges how colorful is the fabric of our homiletic history.

Before the national period, Maryland Jesuits, along with Dominican and Franciscan friars, had spent themselves evangelizing the indigenous people of America. From the early 19th century, mission bands of Redemptorists and other congregations made the circuit from coast to coast reviving the faith of thousands in urban parishes and rural communities. By the 20th century, clerical and lay street preachers brought religious apologetic into greater prominence. Lay members of movements like the Catholic Truth and Evidence Guilds criss-crossed the country with their revival repertoire between 1917 and the 1940s. Simultaneously, Catholic clergy and laity cooperated in developing a flourishing retreat movement that generated special forms of conference preaching. The electronic media enticed Catholic preachers from the start. The 1940s and 1950s featured several nationally broadcast radio and television preachers, most notably Bishop Fulton J. Sheen. Throughout the waxing and waning of these preaching movements reside the same tendencies and tensions as in liturgical preaching, namely, the effort of these preachers to interpret or explain how one can be both Catholic and American.

The explicit connections between liturgy and preaching are themselves too recently emphasized to be taken for granted by most U.S. Catholics. The birth of the liturgical movement in the United States, starting with the 1926 publication of *Orate Fratres*, initiated a limited series of articles on liturgy and preaching. But it was the 1943 encyclical *Divino Afflante Spiritu* that opened the doors to Catholic biblical scholarship and, subsequently, to that form of biblical preaching we call the "homily." The conciliar reforms initiated by the *Constituion on the Sacred Liturgy* (1963) and the adoption of the Lectionary of the Roman Missal (1971) encouraged liturgical, biblical preaching. More than this, it signalled a renewed pulpit humanism reminiscent of Bishop John Carroll's era in which Catholics and Protestants preach today, not from common pulpits but from a common lectionary.

The homily, by taking its life both from a particular liturgical moment and from the special concerns of the assembly, fosters the integration of the gospel into every aspect of Christian life. This implies more than advocating from the pulpit the lived expression of Christian values; for Americans, in particular, this integration promotes the shared *expression* of the gospel. Not surprisingly, the emphasis on the communal nature of the homily raises the issue of "equal access" to the pulpit. So, while U.S. bishops wrestle with the question about who might properly preach the homily, liberation theologians teach from the homilies of our Third World poor, uneducated and unordained brothers and sisters. These perspectives are metaphoric for that persistent tension in American Catholic preaching between the humanist and formalist, the interpreter and teacher. Such tension mirrors the social, cultural, and religious diversity that has always described our preaching. In no small way does it also describe the very character of American Catholicism.

See **Preaching . . . ; Homily; Word, theology of the**

Joseph Michael Connors, S.V.D., "Catholic Homiletic Theory in Historical Perspective," (Diss. Northwestern University, 1962). Mary E. Lyons, "A Rhetoric for American Catholicism: The Transcendental Voice of Isaac T. Hecker," (Diss. University of California, Berkeley, 1983).

MARY E. LYONS

PREACHING, LITURGICAL MINISTRY OF

Vatican II set as one of its principal goals "to impart an ever-increasing vigor to the Christian life of the faithful" (S.C., 1). Having sounded the call to renewal, the constitution continues: "the liturgy daily builds up those who are in the Church, making of them a holy temple of the Lord, a dwelling place for God in the Spirit, to the mature measure of fullness of Christ" (S.C., 2). The liturgy concomitantly increases the power of the members of the church "to preach Christ and thus show forth the Church" (S.C., 2).

Since the liturgy is an action of Christ and his body the church it surpasses all others (S.C., 7); worship is both the summit of Christian life and the source of Christian living (S.C., 11).

Critical to the insight of the conciliar framers is the notion that it is the assembly which is the subject of the liturgical act. No body of mere spectators, the assembly itself joins with Christ in offering a sacrifice of praise and thanksgiving (cf. S.C., 7, 14, 26; G.I.R.M., 54.2).

The liturgical homily is an integral part of the worship celebration (S.C., 52). To open up the mysteries of redemption in such a way that God's power and mercy is present to the body of believers is central to the liturgy itself and therefore central to liturgical preaching (S.C. 2, 102). Like the liturgy itself, preaching is a necessary source of nourishment of the Christ-life (G.I.R.M., 41).

The presentation of the mystery of Christ, dead and risen, within the preaching event is to be articulated for the building up of the particular community (G.I.R.M., 41). Liturgical preaching, like worship itself, glorifies God and sanctifies people, renewing baptismal commitment to service of God, neighbor and world. Preaching is thus a genuine liturgical ministry to be carried out with utmost care and fidelity (S.C., 35).

This ministry of preaching continues the earthly mission of Jesus "to gather into one the children of God who are scattered abroad" (Jn 11:52). In the preaching event God's active word renews and empowers God's people for mission.

Preaching and Faith

If liturgy builds up the community for its mission to the world, it does so by articulating and embodying the believers' faith in Christ. Through word and song, gesture and action, the liturgy incarnates faith, expressing the mystery of an ever-present God, revealed in Christ Jesus and shared in his Spirit.

Preaching witnesses to faith in Christ Jesus. "We cannot but speak of what we have seen and heard" (Acts 4:40; cf. Acts 2:32; 3:15; 10:39). If Jesus preached the reign of God and the church preaches Jesus, then Christ as the advent of God's reign—the *autobasileia* as Origen phrased it (in Mt 18:23)—is what the church preaches. The historical Jesus preached God's reign in existential terms, e.g., the blind see, the lame walk, etc. The modern preacher needs to preach this Jesus, the incarnation of God's reign, in similarly existential terms.

In worship, then, preaching is directed toward an embodiment of the mystery of faith. Liturgical preaching makes present the mystery celebrated rendering faith palpable for the hearers. "Today this scripture has been fulfilled in your hearing" (Lk 4:22). Standing at one with the assembly, the preacher proclaims the good news of Christ, dead and risen, not as an abstraction, but as experiential. This proclamation is not of a past reality, but of an ever-present and continuing reality. "Today, when you hear his voice, do not harden your hearts" (Heb 3:7). In other words, the paschal mystery of Christ is the continual experience and constant life pattern of faithful Christians. Preaching contextualizes this mystery and unfolds it as a way of living the Christ-life.

Preaching As Prayer

If worship is a corporate expression of praise and intercession shared by the assembly, its heart is prayer. So too must preaching itself be prayer-in-word. As part of a ritual event, preaching operates in a ritual mode. Expressing and incarnating through the symbols of word and gesture, preaching gives voice to cor-porate yearnings for the graced life. As the preaching event rehearses the great deeds of God on behalf of God's people—not as past, but as present paradigmatic realities—it elicits response, just as the other ritual moments in worship elicit response.

In a eucharistic setting, the homily also serves a ritual function of bridging the gap between the liturgy of the word and the liturgy of the table. Leaving the hearers with a renewed faith and a desire to render thanks, the homily calls for completing the word-service in eucharistic table fellowship. Effective preaching, eliciting wonder at God's goodness, moves to the great thanksgiving prayer of God's people.

Preacher As Presider; Presider As Preacher

"The homily should ordinarily be given by the celebrant" (G.I.R.M., 42). Thomas Aquinas identified preaching as the *officium principalissimum sacerdotis*, the chiefest sacerdotal duty. Vatican II echoed the same idea: " ... the first task of priests as co-workers of the bishops [is] to preach the Gospel of God to all" (P.O., 4).

One of the earliest descriptions of the Sunday eucharist, given by Justin, relates how the presider preaches: "When the lector has finished, the president addresses us and exhorts us to imitate the splendid things we have heard" (*1 Apol.*, 67). After the presentation of bread and wine, Justin continues, "the president then prays and gives thanks according to his ability," a succinct description of the eucharistic prayer.

This early account shows the unity of word and table. The presider, having broken open God's word in preaching, now proclaims the eucharistic prayer, "leading the people in offering sacrifice" (G.I.R.M., 60). This blessing prayer, while not in homiletic form, is also Christian preaching. The public rehearsal of the charter events of Christ within a context of praise and thanksgiving is truly an act of homiletic: a faith-embodying ritual proclamation. Breaking open the word leads to the ritualized thanksgiving prayer, culminating in a communion shared in the bread broken and cup outpoured.

If the eucharistic prayer is a kind of preaching, it is not the same as the homily, for in the eucharistic prayer the presider leads the assembly in a corporate proclamation of ecclesial faith. An epitome of the gospel, the thanksgiving prayer enunciates not a personal witness of the presider's faith, but the "mystery of faith" to which all respond "Amen."

Deacons and Others

If there is a certain unifying of the celebration when the presider both preaches and proclaims the eucharistic prayer, it does not follow that *only* the presider should preach. The presider, also a member of the gathered assembly, is charged with the responsibility for ensuring the faithful proclamation of God's word in reading, in preaching, and in the table prayer.

"The deacon . . . sometimes preaches God's word" (G.I.R.M., 61). While the bishop's address to the candidate for diaconal ordination admonishes: "Never turn away from the hope which the gospel offers; now you must not only listen to God's word but also preach it," the prayer of consecration refers to the appointment of deacons for table service (cf. Acts 6:1-6), works of charity and holiness of life; it relegates the preaching task to the apostles. Controversy over whether historically deacons' ministry specifically included preaching seems to be reflected in the ordination rite. Nonetheless what is clear is that diaconal service in any form is modelled after Jesus' own ministry: "I am among you as one who serves" (Lk 22:27). If charitable works are a chief element of diaconal ministry, history does attest to deacon's service at the liturgy.

It is consonant with the diaconal charism of charitable service for deacons to preach on those occasions when God's word calls the church to work on behalf of others, especially the poor. Additionally, of course, the deacon preaches at those rites in which he leads the community in prayer, e.g., baptism, marriage, etc.

The Directory for Masses with Children asserts that "one of the adults may speak to the children after the gospel, especially if the priest finds it difficult to adapt himself to the mentality of the children" (D.M.C., 24). This sound principle focuses on the necessity of being able to hear the word proclaimed and preached. What is critical for faith-building is a proclamation that is adequate to the hearers.

Thus, while the presider has a genuine responsibility for leading the assembly in their corporate prayer, the responsibility for preaching is not necessarily a presbyteral function.

Conclusion

If in the present dispensation preaching is generally reserved to priests and deacons, perhaps because preaching is seen as part of the church's teaching office, the changing physiognomy of parochial life and the publication of *Guidelines for Lay Preaching* signal a new opportunity for other Christians to be actively involved in this ministry. "So we are ambassadors for Christ, God making his appeal through us" (2 Cor 5:20).

The *Decree on the Laity* noted particularly the Holy Spirit's action of moving the laity to greater responsibility to service to Christ (see A.A., 1). Prophetic may be the words of that document: "in the hearts of all should the apostle's word find echo: 'Woe to me if I do not preach the Gospel' (1 Cor 9:1)" (A.A., 6).

See **Preaching . . .; Homily; Word, theology of the**

JOHN ALLYN MELLOH, S.M.

PREACHING, SPECIAL OCCASION

To preach on special occasions is to utter a word which illuminates an event and transforms it into an experience. It is to weave a tapestry of words that bids the eye to focus and rejoice in what it beholds. Preaching on special occasions enables a gathered group to become a community which can proceed into the heart of the mystery being celebrated, whether that mystery is a celebration of ritual feast, or festive event.

The special occasion preaching considered here takes into account: (1) preaching which occurs within liturgical settings other than Sunday and weekday eucharists in ordinary time (e.g., baptisms, weddings, funerals, penance and anointing services); (2) preaching which takes place on feasts, whether christological, Marian, or sanctoral; (3) preaching which occurs at the celebration of special events such as religious professions, anniversaries of weddings and ordinations, gatherings for special groups with a particular focus. Some comments will now be offered on each of these three areas.

Preaching During the Rites

Each of the rites calls for a homily, offering some direction as to its purpose. The rite of baptism asks that the homily explain to those present the significance of the readings, trying to lead the gathered community to a deeper understanding of the mystery of baptism and encouraging both parents and sponsors to accept their responsibilities stemming from this sacrament. The rite of marriage calls the preacher to draw from the texts to speak about the mystery of Christian marriage, the dignity of married love, the grace of the sacrament, and the responsibilities of married people. The rite of anointing asks the preacher to speak to the meaning of illness within the plan of salvation and of the grace this sacrament provides. The rite of penance calls for motivating penitents to examine their consciences and renew their lives. Finally, the rite of funerals notes that the homily should include an expression of gratitude to God for his gifts, especially the gift of a Christian life to the deceased. The homily should link this death to the paschal mystery. All of these descriptions can be found in *The Rites of the Roman Catholic Church* (Pueblo, 1976). Since these rites were promulgated between 1969 and 1973, the common understanding of the homily points to an instructional moment. In light of the N.C.C.B. document, *Fulfilled in Your Hearing* (1982), one might revision this approach and see the homily as an interpretive moment, one which biblically interprets the action of God in the life of the community celebrating a particular rite.

What must be kept in mind is that on all these occasions the preacher is tryng to touch the hearts of the congregation so they can enter prayerfully into the subsequent ritual and go on to live in a way that supports this event in their daily lives. The goal is to transform observers into active participants.

The homily must always be addressed to the gathered community, directly or indirectly. It is not only for the parents and sponsors of those to be baptized or for the bride and groom or for the immediate family of the deceased. Rather, it is addressed to all those assembled so that their lives are more fully understood as being the arena in which God is graciously present, calling us all more deeply into communion with the Trinity and with one another.

In ritual moments, it is appropriate to allow the scriptural texts to interpret these events for the life of the entire community. The homily is meant to be both an interpretive and an enabling event. The question is: how does this text bring meaning to the event that is being celebrated by this community today? How does the pericope of Jesus with the children (Mk 10:13-16) help the community understand what is happening in his baptismal event in which all are participating? How does it metaphorically mediate its meaning to those present and enable them to take part in this event and assume their responsibility in relation to those baptized? How does the Pauline hymn to agape (1 Cor 12:31-13:8) provide a perspective to interpret what is happening here and now for this community when two of their members vow their love? How does the meeting of Jesus and Martha (Jn 11:21-27) allow the preacher to interpret a particular death so that the community in faith and hope can give thanks and praise to God for this particular person and his/her participation in the paschal mystery? How do healing and forgiveness texts interpret communal anointing and penance services, revealing God's presence now in the lives of this group with its need for such graced moments? In other words, the homily preached on these special occasions must go beyond an instructional exercise and interpret this particular and unique event in the life of this particular community. It must be a poetic act that shapes understanding, elicits response, and calls the gathered community to go hopefully into a future in which God will increasingly become all in all.

Preaching on the Feasts

In a similar fashion, preaching on the great feasts like Christmas, Pentecost, Trinity Sunday, or the Immaculate Conception is not to be an occasion to lecture on the theology of the feast, or even to apply the theology of this feast to our lives. Instead, one must ask this question: how do the readings provide access to this feast in such a way that the feast can interpret the lived experience of this community of faith? How does the mystery of incarnation speak to what is happening in our lives by way of these readings? How does the poem that images the light shining in a darkness that cannot be overcome reveal how God is being enfleshed in our world today? How on Easter is the present community to understand its life in the risen Lord through the story of those who go to the tomb? How does the Immaculate Conception speak to our existence, shedding light on it through the story of the annunciation to Mary, a tale that images freedom, grace, and abiding love?

Unfortunately, the most boring preaching often happens on the feasts with the greatest theological importance. Sometimes it is due to this felt imperative to provide instructional material from the tradition that rarely rises above the bewildering terrain of theological jargon. Or the preacher works with all three texts as discrete units, providing a series of mini-homilies. As with the preaching that takes place during the liturgical rites, this homily must remain integral to the eucharist. It should function to move people to praise and thanks.

The preaching task is to bring an assembly to such an affective state that when the preacher says, "Lift up your hearts," the assembly can truly respond, "We have lifted them up to the Lord." Its role to stir up the faith of the people is achieved by bringing them to see how this feast, by means of these readings, helps them to understand their own lives as the arena in which God is working.

Then, too, there are the feasts of the saints honored during the church year, those men and women who are our family, our ancestors in the faith. One of the great needs for many believers is contact with people who have struggled to live the Christian life, who have sought to know and serve God in the ordinary settings of life. While there are few lay men and women who have achieved this status, still those saints whose lives have been documented often reveal common areas of identification in their attempts to love God and neighbor. Great saints like

Teresa, Francis, Ignatius, to name but a few, continue to motivate and speak to contemporary lives.

One mistake in preaching on the feasts of the saints is to see it as an opportunity to provide a brief history lesson, thereby leaving the saints in the past, removed and often elevated above us. But, as with the feasts, the readings assigned to a particular saint can allow access to an incident or saying or aspect of the saint's life that functions as a link for identifying God's call, challenge, action in our lives. Here, too, the end of the sanctoral homily is not knowledge of the saint, but insight into the dealings of God with this community. The saint can be a means of achieving this, serving in some way as a metaphor for God's dealings with us. That aspect of the saint used to function metaphorically is determined by its connection with the assigned or suggested biblical text. In this way, sanctoral preaching remains biblically grounded.

Preaching at Special Events

Special occasions like anniversaries of marriage, religious profession, and ordination can become opportunities for sharing humorous anecdotes about those involved or premature eulogies. Such events can more fittingly be occasions to celebrate how the divine has interpenetrated the human in the course of a long period. Time is recognized as sacred time. Such moments provide an invitation to contemplate how such periods of fidelity help the community to know itself and what it is called to. To be a homily, the preaching must use the biblical text(s) to provide a lens through which such occasions are interpreted.

Finally, preaching at gatherings for special groups with a particular focus is also an occasion to allow the work of the group to be biblically grounded and celebrated in the act of eucharistic thanksgiving. The preacher can take advantage of the occasion to select those biblical passages that call the group to rededicate themselves in a spirit of confidence and hope, trusting in the God who has called them to this work.

See **Catechesis, liturgical; Christ, feasts of; Funerals, preaching at; Mary, feasts of; Preaching the lectionary**

Bishops' Committee on Priestly Life and Ministry/ N.C.C.B., *Fulfilled in Your Hearing: The Homily in the Sunday Assembly* (Washington: U.S.C.C., 1982). James M. Schmitmeyer, *The Words of Worship: Presiding and Preaching at the Rites* (New York: Alba, 1988). James A. Wallace, C.SS.R., *Preaching Through the Saints* (Collegeville: Liturgical Press, 1982).

JAMES A. WALLACE, C.SS.R.

PREACHING, THEOLOGY OF

The need for a contemporary theology of preaching from a Catholic perspective has been reaffirmed repeatedly since the time of the Second Vatican Council. In 1962 Charles Davis commented that even the phrase "theology of preaching" was new to the Catholic community and in the same decade Karl Rahner remarked that the crisis in preaching required "a theology of the annunciation of the Word of God" that went beyond the psychological and pedagogical insights of rhetoric and homiletics. Since the time of the catechism of the Council of Trent, a systematic presentation of Catholic doctrine had been presumed to provide the best guide to preaching. In the post-Reformation era the NT understanding of preaching as announcing the good news of salvation and the patristic and medieval practice of preaching as exploring the "spiritual sense" of the scriptures had given way to a view of preaching as doctrinal instruction. At its best, this neo-scholastic approach that reflected an underlying propositional model of revelation, preserved the Thomistic insight that "faith ends not in propositions, but in the reality" [of union with God] (S. Th. II-II, q. 1, a. 2, ad 2). Priests (the presumed preachers) were encouraged to explain the church's doctrines in a pastoral way that would draw believers more deeply into the whole mystery of faith. As early as 1936, however, Josef Jungmann noted that preaching had become "the vulgarization of theological tracts" and called for a return to the biblical understanding of preaching as the proclamation of the good news of salvation.

Return to the Sources

A return to the scriptures and to the liturgical preaching of the early church highlights key dimensions that need to be retrieved in any contemporary reformulation of a theology of preaching. The preaching of Jesus as pictured in the gospels stands within the prophetic tradition of announcing the saving power of God active in human history here and now. Especially in Luke's gospel Jesus is portrayed as proclaiming "good news" in contrast to John the Baptist's call for repentance in the face of the coming disaster of the end of time. The salvation of God is already at hand in the person of Jesus—as the "signs of the kingdom" reveal: the blind see, captives are set free, prisoners are released, and the poor hear good news proclaimed (cf. Luke 4). In the parables he preached in word and deed as well as in the parable he was, Jesus reinterpreted the living tradition of faith handed on to him in his Jewish tradition and in the scriptures, and announced the unlimited compassion and forgiveness of the God he knew as Abba. The proclamation and manifestation of that mystery of salvation called forth a response of gratitude and conversion to a life of discipleship on the part of those who heard and believed.

Recent studies have linked the Matthean and particularly the Johannine Jesus with the figure of Wisdom, the prophetic street preacher from the book of Proverbs who proclaims God's message of reproach and promise in the market place, who reaches out her hand to the needy, who clings to truth, decides for justice, and orders all things rightly. Jesus enfleshed the word (*dabar*) of God that brings about what it signifies as well as the wisdom (*sophia*) of God who gathers her children around bread and wine at the eschatological banquet.

During the time of his ministry, Jesus gathered a band of disciples whom he sent to proclaim the good news of salvation trusting in the power of the Holy Spirit and the fidelity of the God of their ancestors. After the experience of the death and resurrection of Jesus, the apostolic proclamation of God's fidelity and promise centered on what God had done in Jesus. Jesus, the messenger of salvation, became the message. Early Christian preaching as described in the Acts of the Apostles drew on both the story of Israel and the story of Jesus to testify to God's fidelity in the past, God's power in the present, and God's promise for the future. The apostolic preaching events also included healings, exorcisms, and other manifestations of the power of the name of Jesus and the presence of his Spirit. The proclamation of the gospel identified by Paul as "the power of God for salvation" was in itself a call to conversion (*metanoia*)—radical turning away from sin towards the God of Jesus; hence the call to baptism as incorporation into the community of the church, the body of Christ. Paul, who describes his life's vocation as "a compulsion to preach" summarizes the impact of the preaching of the word of God on both preachers and hearers: "Our preaching of the gospel proved not a mere matter of words for you but one of power; it was carried on in the Holy Spirit and out of complete conviction ... while still among you we acted on your behalf. You, in turn, became imitators of us and of the Lord, receiving the word despite great trials, with the joy that comes from the Holy Spirit" (1 Thess 1:5-6).

In the early church a variety of ministries of the word were exercised by male and female prophets, teachers, and apostles within diverse local communities. By mid-2nd century there is evidence (in the *First Apology* of Justin Martyr) of liturgical preaching (the homily) as an integral part of the Christian eucharist. While the ministries of preaching and teaching were not sharply distinguished since both were directed toward drawing others more deeply into the mystery of faith in Christ Jesus, eventually the issue of false prophecy/teaching emerged. Concern that the authentic tradition and not "some other gospel" be handed on resulted in a growing emphasis on bishops as the official preachers/teachers of the faith, although gifted and educated lay preachers such as Origen, head of the catechetical school at Alexandria, were known to preach even in the liturgical assembly.

Since the theologians of the early church were both preachers and pastors, their sermons and writings on preaching provide a rich source for a theology of preaching. The sermon was integrally linked to both scripture and sacrament reflecting a profound theology of the word of God as revealed pre-eminently in Christ (hence the predominance of christological interpretations of even the Hebrew Scriptures); but also in the Sacred Scriptures and in the community of faith and worship. Mystagogical preaching emphasized that the sacraments continue in the present the great works of God recorded in the scriptures, or as Leo the Great expressed it: those things which were conspicuous in the life of our Redeemer here pass over into the worship of the church (*Sermon* 74, 2).

Preaching in the early church was rooted in a pastoral approach to theology that involved an integration of the study of scripture, prayer and spirituality, and the use of human reason in the kind of search for wisdom that led ultimately to a contemplative union with God. Since wisdom was viewed as both practical and theoretical, the link between pastoral care and preaching was also clearly evident. Gregory the Great, for example, in his *Pastoral Care*, gives advice on how to preach to 36 different types of people and Augustine in *On Christian Doctrine* proposes as the hermeneutical key for the interpretation of any scripture passage the core of the gospel: love of God and love of neighbor.

Seeing themselves as essentially interpreters of the word of God in diverse human and ecclesial situations, the early Christian preachers plumbed the literal meaning of the scriptures in search of a deeper "spiritual sense" (the *sensus plenior* intended by the Holy Spirit). Convinced that the same Holy Spirit who inspired the authors of scripture continued to inspire the church in their day, they probed for patterns of promise and fulfillment in typological and allegorical interpretations of the scriptures that opened up hope in God's continued fidelity in the struggles of their own time.

Emphasizing that it is the word of God who speaks through the mouths of preachers, Augustine spoke of Christ as the primary preacher/teacher of the mystical body: "It is Christ who teaches; his pulpit is in heaven ... and his school is on earth, and the school is his (mystical) body" (*Sermo de disciplina christiana*, ML 40, col. 678). Augustine further provides the basis for later sacramental theologies of preaching in writing of the sacrament as the *verbum visibile* (visible word) and preaching as the *sacramentum audibile* (audible sacrament). The role of the preacher or catechist was to interpret the "signs" or footprints of the Trinity that are to be found throughout creation and history and in particular in salvation history culminating in Christ. For such a task rhetoric is helpful (hence the guide to homiletics in Book IV of *On Christian Doctrine*), but wisdom is essential.

While early medieval preaching (e.g., Bernard of Clairvaux) remained pastoral and mystical in tone, the eventual shift of theology to the university context during the medieval period resulted in more formal commentaries complete with definitions, divisions, and arguments aimed at teaching university students to penetrate the literal meaning of the text in such a way as to discover the deeper meaning of the biblical symbols. Preachers were to comment on the spiritual senses of scripture in a way that exhorted their hearers to live a more faithful Christian life, or as Alan of Lille suggested "to offer instruction in matters of faith and behavior" (*The Art of Preaching*, ch. 1). Lay preaching bands committed to intense living of the apostolic life (*vita apostolica*) were officially permitted to preach words of exhortation, but not doctrine concerning faith and sacraments since the latter presumed knowledge of scripture and theology.

The medieval understanding of preaching remained grounded in the early Christian theology of the word as sacrament and ultimately in the mystery of the incarnation: in the divine economy all of creation and in a unique way every word of scripture speaks of Christ (cf. Hugh of St. Victor's *De verbo Dei* and the sermons of Bonaventure). The trinitarian foundation of Aquinas' understanding of preaching is evident in his explanation that conversion requires a twofold action of God: the inner word of grace (the anointing of the Holy Spirit) and the outer word of the preacher (S. Th. II-II, q. 1, a. 4., ad 4; q. 6, a. 1; q. 2, a. 9, ad 3). Within the context of his discussion of prophecy, Aquinas describes a "grace of speech" that enables one not only to instruct the intellect, but also to move the affection so that others willingly hear the word of God, and may love what is signified by the words and want to fulfill what is urged (S. Th. II-II, q. 177, a. 1, reply).

The continued emphasis that in preaching it is the word of God—and not some human word—that is communicated was expressed in images of preachers as the channels through which the voice of God passes, tongues in which God speaks, cases that contain the seed of the sower God, or interpreters and instruments of God, culminating in Aquinas's scholastic terminology: God is the principal cause of preaching, while the apostles and all preachers are the instrumental cause through which God preaches (In Ep. I ad. Thess., c. 2, lect. 2). In the polemical context of the Reformation, however, in order to defend the validity and necessity of the sacraments against adversaries who emphasized the power of the preached word, most scholastic theologians began to make a new distinction: the principal cause in preaching is a human cause, while the principal cause in the sacraments is God; therefore, only the sacraments can be said to "confer grace." Disputes about the efficacy of preaching (preaching brings about faith, but not sanctifying grace) and the relationship between the sacraments and preaching (preaching is not an eighth sacrament) dominated theological writings about preaching well into the 20th century. Creative resolution of the impasse required broader understandings of sacramentality, grace, faith, symbolic causality, word as symbol, and sacraments as "words of the church" to be developed later by Karl Rahner and others.

Vatican II Shifts: Implications for Preaching

The liturgical reforms of the Second Vatican Council combined with fundamental shifts in ecclesiology and theology of revelation provided new foundations on which to build a theology of preaching. The *Constitution on the Sacred Liturgy* emphasized the active role of the gathered assembly in the entire liturgical celebration, described preaching as a call to faith and conversion (S.C., 9; cf. Rom 10:14-15), and highlighted the intimate connection of word and sacrament speaking of the "real presence" of Christ not only in the consecrated bread and wine, but in the gathered community and the proclaimed word as well (S.C., 7). Now explicitly claimed as an act of worship—"part of the liturgy itself" (S.C., 35, 52)—the homily is described in terms of ancient liturgical homilies: "the proclamation of God's wonderful words in the history of salvation, that is, the mystery of Christ, which is ever made present and active within us, especially in the celebration of the liturgy" (S.C., 35). Since faith is born of the word and nourished by it, the preached word is an essential part of the celebration of the sacraments (P.O., 4). While the *Constitution on the Sacred Liturgy* emphasized that the homily was to be drawn from scriptural and liturgical texts of the day (S.C., 35), the *Decree on the Life and Ministry of Priests* highlighted a second essential dimension of the homily—the necessity that it "apply to concrete circumstances of life and particular needs of hearers" (P.O.,4).

The *Dogmatic Constitution on the Church* underscored that the priestly people of God form the church—the body of Christ is made up of all the baptized. Emphasizing the primacy of preaching in the mission of the church (L.G., 17; cf. A.G., 3) it both restored the primary importance of preaching in the ministries of bishop and priest (L.G., 25, 28; C.D., 12; P.O., 4) and provided the ecclesiological foundations for the active role of all the baptized in the preaching mission of the entire body of Christ as called for in other documents of the council (A.A., 2; G.S., 41).

The *Dogmatic Constitution on Divine Revelation's* move away from the pro-positional notion of revelation that had predominated in Roman Catholic theology since Vatican I toward a sacramental and trinitarian approach to a theology of revelation centered on the word of God demanded rethinking of earlier approaches to a theology of preaching as doctrinal explanation of the mysteries of faith. The mystery of revelation is ultimately the mystery of God's self-communication to humanity in the interrelationship of word and deed through all of creation and human history, climaxing in salvation history and culminating in Christ who is the Word made flesh. That one mystery of the Word of God has been entrusted to the "entire church in union with its shepherds" (D.V., 10) and is to be handed on in every age and culture. The return to the early Christian understanding of tradition as the transmission of the one mystery of faith, the word of God, provides a context for understanding preaching as a fundamental mode of the transmission of the gospel. The opening quotation of the *Dogmatic Constitution on Divine Revelation* suggests the pattern of the entire revelatory process which continues in the mystery of preaching. "What we have seen and have heard we announce to you..." (1 Jn 1:2-3).

Taking a new stance in terms of the post-Reformation separation of word and sacrament, the *Constitution on Divine Revelation* insisted that "The Church has always venerated the divine Scriptures just as she venerates the body of the Lord ...; all preaching of the Church must be nourished and ruled by sacred scripture" (D.V., 21). While the concern has been raised in recent years about the role of doctrinal preaching in the Catholic tradition, as Gerard Sloyan has noted, true biblical and liturgical preaching does communicate the doctrinal tradition of the church, but in the mystagogical mode appropriate to liturgical celebrating ("Is Church Teaching

Neglected When the Lectionary is Preached?" *Worship* 61 [1987]: 126-40).

Contemporary Theological Resources

Vatican II's recognition and encouragement of biblical scholarship bore fruit in a number of biblical resources on the power of the proclaimed word along with studies of the prophets and apostles as preachers. The recovery of the liturgical context of preaching further contributed to a renewed theology of word and sacrament. Still a specifically theological understanding of the preaching event in light of post-Vatican II theological perspectives has not yet been fully developed. From an ecumenical perspective, Karl Barth and the new hermeneutic (word-event) theologians (notably E. Fuchs, G. Ebeling) have made major contributions toward a fuller understanding of the power of the proclaimed word, yet the underlying understanding of theological anthropology in both cases remains decidedly negative: the image of God has been destroyed or fundamentally distorted in human beings as a result of sin; neither can grace be viewed as a radical transformation of the human person. Hence the theology of preaching that emerges from the Reformation traditions remains a law-gospel approach to sinful human beings who are nevertheless redeemed in Jesus Christ (cf. Richard Lischer, *A Theology of Preaching* (Nashville: Abingdon, 1981).

Drawing on the resources of the later Heidegger as did the new hermeneutic theologians, but with a typically Catholic emphasis on creation and human existence as graced, Karl Rahner wrote powerfully of the word as symbol and of the event character of "grace come to Word." While he did not develop a systematic theology of preaching, numerous essays in his *Theological Investigations* (notably "Priest and Poet," Vol. III, and "Word and Eucharist," Vol. IV) suggest an approach to the proclaimed word as sacrament in which grace (i.e., God's offer of self-communication) is embodied in the explicitness of word. The preacher names the depth dimension of the mystery of human existence as God's self-offer and thus draws the hearers of the word into a deeper relationship with God. Like all free personal self-communication, grace requires the word to re-veal (un-veil) definitively the offer of relationship. This explicit, social, historical mediation of grace is necessary precisely because human beings are constituted as body-spirit (spirit-in-the-world) and the spiritual (or transcendental/depth) dimension of human existence can be experienced only insofar as it is mediated. God's self-offer which has remained anonymous/ambiguous throughout creation and human history became definitive and irrevocable in the incarnation when the word became flesh in Jesus Christ. The trinitarian foundations of a theology of preaching according to Rahner are evident here: the one God who freely chooses to go out of self in relationship with humanity is made known in the depths of the human heart (in/through the Spirit) and in the concreteness of human history (in the incarnation of the word in Jesus).

Just as the church is called to be the abiding presence in the world of the primal sacramental word of definitive grace which is Christ, preaching and the sacraments function as the self-expression of the church, naming, proclaiming, and celebrating the deepest truth at the heart of reality: God's self-offer in love. In this incarnational/sacramental view of reality, the interdependence of, rather than the distinctions between, word and sacrament are emphasized. Basically Rahner develops Augustine's insight that a sacrament is a "visible word" and the proclaimed word is an "audible sacrament." All the words of the church, and preaching in a particular way, are oriented toward the sacraments and specifically toward the eucharist, "the highest word of the church" in which the church locates its deepest identity in the death and resurrection of Jesus Christ.

Reflecting further on preaching as a means of mediating God's word to human beings and a distinct form of address, William J. Hill has emphasized that the purpose of preaching is to arouse the response of faith and conversion of life ("surrender to the unconditional claims of God"). As God's offer of salvation/reconciliation, the proclaimed word is itself a saving word since the proclamatory act achieves symbolically (through the mediation of meaning) the actual encounter with the living word of God. In the preaching event, it is not the preacher, but the word of God that confronts the hearers and makes an unconditional summons to conversion. Taking the NT preachers as models, Hill suggests that the task of the preacher is to render salvation history present and operative in the world today. Yet this process of "kerygmatic reinterpretation" of texts and events from the past history of our faith tradition is not possible except from the perspective of our contemporary cultural milieu. New questions and experiences on the part of the preacher and the community of faith will elicit dimensions of the text not previously recognized—a genuinely new word.

This kerygmatic reinterpretation requires both personal conversion and serious theological reflection on the part of the preacher. Drawing on the resources of Bernard Lonergan, Hill observes that preaching can be viewed as "a moment" in the theological process in which the preacher attempts to discern the meaning God intends and the human response required in this new 20th-century context based on the normative expression of God's word located in the NT read in the church. Thus meaning "incarnates itself" in the words and deeds of the preacher. The word inaugurates conversion in both preacher and community. The preacher mediates God's meaning in a way that constitutes the preacher as one enabled to announce the message of Christ and through this shared meaning the community is constituted as "the place where the word takes root."

Edward Schillebeeckx' recent contributions toward a theology of revelation made yet a further contribution towards a contemporary theology of preaching. Moving beyond his earlier distinction of revelation-in-reality from revelation-in-word, Schillebeeckx now emphasizes that there is no uninterpreted experience and that revelation occurs only within human experience, although the two cannot be identified. Arguing that all experience has a narrative structure (occurs in the context of a tradition that provides a framework for interpretation), Schillebeeckx claims that the question of whether faith comes from hearing (Rom 10:17) or faith begins with experience is a false dilemna. The Christian story originated as an experience of salvation in Jesus. Now as an explicit message the Christian story offers a new possibility of life experience to all who hear and follow.

The new insight that comes to the fore here is that the "good news of salvation" which the preacher is called to announce is not only the past history of God's fidelity as recorded in the scriptures but also the present workings of God's Spirit in ordinary human life. The preacher's task is to interpret the human story in light of the story of Jesus or conversely, to tell the Christian story in such a way that people can recognize the experience of grace—God's presence—in their everyday lives.

Further, Schillebeeckx along with contemporary liberation theologians emphasizes that the "good news" to be announced in the proclamation of the gospel is for most people of the world today in the context of radical suffering, a "liberating grace" (L. Boff) that is discovered only "on the underside" of their experience and in eschatological hope. If the Christian community is to announce that hope they can do so only after listening to people's concrete experience until it "yields an echo of the gospel" and then retelling the story of Jesus in deed as well as word. The narrative that the Christian community proclaims is a "dangerous memory" (Metz) that calls for conversion at the level of political action as well as inner heart. While the preacher speaks in the name of the community, the whole community is involved in "retelling the story of Jesus" that requires ultimately the "writing of a fifth gospel with our lives." Preaching remains the announcing of the good news of salvation proclaimed in the scriptures in a way that draws people more deeply into the living of the Christian life, but Schillebeeckx and other contemporary theologians expand our understanding of what salvation is, where it is to be discovered, how and by whom this good news is to be proclaimed, and what conversion will require.

See **Word, theology of the; Homily**

William J. Hill, "Preaching As a 'Moment' in Theology," *Homiletic and Pastoral Review* 77 (1976): 10-19, and "Towards a Theology of Preaching: One Model and One Question," in *Preaching and the Non-Ordained*, ed. Nadine Foley (Collegeville: Liturgical Press, 1983), 91-110. Mary Catherine Hilkert, "Naming Grace: A Theology of Proclamation," *Worship* 60 (1986): 434-449. Domenico Grasso, *Proclaiming God's Message* (Notre Dame, Ind.: University of Notre Dame Press, 1965). Thomas K. Carroll, *Preaching the Word* (Wilmington: M. Glazier, 1984).

MARY CATHERINE HILKERT, O.P.

PRESBYTER

In Roman Catholic church order (L.G., 28), and in many other Christian churches, the presbyter is co-worker with the bishop in ministry to the local church, and the presbyteral ministry is in fact an extension of the episcopal ministry.

Presbyters, therefore, likewise embody the threefold ministry of Christ: to teach, to lead in prayer, and pastorally to govern the church. Presbyters who are local pastors in fact present and represent the *episcope* to their local assembly, and serve as such in communion with both the bishop and all other pastors in the diocese. Presbyters, in this communion, form with the bishop a "unique sacerdotal college" (*ibid.*) and provide in the many faces of their ministry the many faces of the priesthood of Christ. The Roman Catholic ordination rite reminds the presbyter that the ministry assigned is to "teach in the name of Christ," to "sanctify in the power of Christ," and to share "in the work of Christ"; presbyters should "seek to bring the faithful together in a unified family and to lead them effectively, through Christ and in the Holy Spirit, to God the Father" (Homily-instruction).

See **Church order; Priesthood; Ordination rites; Orders, sacrament of; Orders, symbols of**

PRESENCE, PASTORAL

This article treats first the prerequisites of pastoral presence, and then a variety of forms or types this presence may take.
Prerequisites

In the Christian tradition pastoral presence has always been seen as a continuation of the ministry of Jesus through the inspiration of the Spirit. For one person, therefore, to be pastorally present to another presupposes a conscious faith in the risen Christ who is always actively available to those who believe in him. The desire to demonstrate the love of Christ by offering care and concern for an individual is the starting point of any type of pastoral presence. One's intention then is to act not just in his or her own name but in the name of Jesus Christ.

More specifically, the ongoing ministry of Jesus through pastoral presence is based on the gift of compassion, the same attitude that allowed Jesus' heart to be touched by the joys and sorrows of everyone he encountered. Compassion is the ability to enter somewhat into the experience of another and to respond with actions or words that communicate authentic concern. To be compassionate toward another person means that, like the Good Samaritan, a disciple of Christ opens his heart to the plight of a sister or brother and reaches out positively to offer assistance. Without compassion there is no truly Christian pastoral presence.

In most circumstances, however, compassion needs to be supplemented by skills and training in order to enhance the quality of pastoral presence. Some of these skills and training include the capacity for listening attentively, intellectual understanding of the dynamics of faith, a practical knowledge of the psychology of the human person, a flexibility in communicating effectively and a facility for reflecting productively on one's experience. Depending on the type of pastoral presence, the necessary skills and training can be acquired through informal or formal pastoral education. Usually Christians who wish to be as effective as possible in their pastoral presence require some professional guidance by those who are more experienced. Learning to respond pastorally often involves the art of compassion that is honed by both practical skills and competent direction.

Recognition by the community of faith is also needed to validate an individual's pastoral presence to others. Whether through ordination, religious profession or lay missioning, the personal identity of Christians who offer pastoral presence must be confirmed by some form of public acknowledgement and acceptance. Acting as representatives of the community of believers and not just as individuals allows pastoral ministers to situate their presence in the context of the church's mission and speaks to the recipients of the whole community's pastoral care for them. Finding creative rituals for commissioning pastoral ministers, especially the non-ordained, and providing for their support and encouragement represents an important challenge for local churches today.

In addition to the desire to participate in the pastoral ministry of Christ, to the gift of compassion, to acquired skills and training, and to validation by the faith community, Christians who offer pastoral presence benefit greatly from regular supervision. Either with one other person or in a group setting, pastoral ministers need opportunities to reflect aloud about their experience, to clarify their feelings and insights, and to become revitalized to continue their involvements. Many people who receive such supervision also value the chance to pray with other pastoral care-givers, invoking the Spirit's help and blessing on their efforts. Without some sort of regular supervision it is easy for pastoral ministers to become overburdened and isolated, resulting eventually in withdrawing emotionally from those who need their pastoring and sometimes from the ministry itself. The quality of pastoral presence often depends on good supervision.

Types of Pastoral Presence

Liturgical forms of pastoral presence are very varied. Celebrations of the sacraments, particularly when they are tailored to the needs of the participants, individual or communal prayers with or for those receiving pastoral care, selective readings from scripture, the use of music and dance to communicate one's deeper feelings to God, symbols, such as candles, incense, and water, which help create an atmosphere for prayer and reflection— all of these liturgical expressions are attempts to render the presence and love of God more palpable. Every liturgical celebration can be an opportunity to highlight the pastoral ministry of Jesus if it calls attention to and evokes in the participants a personal encounter with God and with one another. In leading or facilitating liturgies that are truly pastoral, therefore, a ministering person has to be aware of the specific struggles and hopes of all those who participate and try to use the words, symbols, and gestures to help people experience God's loving care.

Counseling is another valuable type of pastoral presence, especially when it includes exploring one's relationship with God, as well as intrapersonal and interpersonal dynamics. Individual psychotherapy, marriage counseling and group therapy are examples of methods that seek deeper self-knowledge and adaptive behavior; they become forms of pastoral presence when the counselor is identified as a person in ministry and when the counselor encourages the discussion of the dimension of faith. Spiritual direction, one specific mode of pastoral counseling, focuses on that faith relationship with God as it affects all the aspects of a person's life and *vice versa*. Whether counseling involves one session or many, the goal usually is to help an individual achieve a more satisfying sense of self in relationship with others. A pastoral counselor operates from the premise that a person's relationships with self, with others and with God are interconnected.

Education can likewise be a form of pastoral presence when its aim is to assist people to discover how God wants them to live. Sometimes education encompasses direct study of God and God's revelation; at other times the subject relates more to humanity itself with implicit attention to one's relationship with God. Frequently education becomes pastoral when the teacher is viewed as engaging in ministry; the contours of the teacher/student relationship are attempts to mirror the love of God and to guide the students toward understanding and

choosing a way of living that is pleasing to God. Education becomes most pastoral when it provides students, whether children or adults, with the knowledge and skills to discern God's Spirit at work in their lives.

Companionship frequently represents a form of pastoral presence when the expectation centers not so much on accomplishing a task but on being with another person(s). In hospitals and nursing homes, with prisoners and addicted individuals, at parties and dinners, in silence or in conversation, pastoral companionship looks toward the nature of the presence of one person to another. A recognition that someone offers presence in the name of Christ and of the church is often sufficient to make the companionship pastoral. While this companionship is neither formal counseling nor task-oriented, it remains open-ended enough to include moments of socializing, listening, and discussing dilemmas of faith. More often than not it is the *way* in which a ministering person is present that makes this companionship truly pastoral.

Recently another form of pastoral presence has been emerging: a *structural* approach to ministry that seeks to change unjust procedures and systems and laws. Anyone who participates in pastoral ministry even for a short time becomes keenly aware of the structures in society that oppress people, particularly the most powerless. Some ministering people chose to devote much of their time and energy trying to change these unjust structures in order to assure greater fairness and compassion for those who are most in need, economically, socially and emotionally. It may be in courtrooms, state houses or city halls, with advocacy groups or lobbying personnel, by peaceful demonstration or civil disobedience, through letter-writing campaigns or speaking out to the media that pastoral ministers are found boldly defending the rights of those victims of inhuman and unjust policy and attitudes. Their courageous voices summon all pastoral ministers to make *working for justice* a part of their presence to God's people.

Conclusion

In a very real sense all Christians are invited and even commanded by Jesus to be pastorally present to one another. Any and every interpersonal encounter holds possibilities for revealing the love of Christ alive and active in our relationships and in our world. Learning how to respond pastorally to others depends primarily on our ability to appreciate how we have received valued and valuable pastoral presence ourselves.

Joseph Dolan. *Give Comfort to My People* (New York: Paulist, 1977).

GERALD J. CALHOUN, S.J.

PRESIDENTIAL STYLE

Presidential style refers very simply to the way in which the presiders of worship pray in the midst of the liturgical assembly. Because liturgy is ritual, that is, patterned symbolic activity, it requires leadership. To lead the liturgy, which is to lead the community in prayer, is a task assigned to public ministers, both lay and ordained. What is said of the style of prayer leadership refers to all liturgical ministers such as lectors, cantors, and communion ministers. In an ecclesial climate where liturgy no longer equals rubric more is demanded of the liturgical minister than fidelity to the required gestures and sequence of prayers. Such competence now is but the basic point of departure for adequate style in presiding, much in the same way as technical proficiency at the keyboard is but the starting point for the musicianship of the pianist.

The change in the practice of presiding is primarily one of quality of style. What at one time was considered a virtue, namely, an impersonal manner of relating to the congregation, is now a serious deficiency to be eschewed. Because liturgy is now understood to intersect with ordinary human experience and is not to be divorced from daily life, the expectation is that the presider will promote that connection by a more personal manner of leadership. Rather than adopting an overly objective stance before the congregation, presiders are expected to be transparent in what they believe about the actions they are performing.

The desired more personal style of the presider is not reducible to just a friendly way of celebrating. Such friendliness, especially when it suggests artificiality, can place the leader of worship outside of the ritual context in isolation from the praying community. The most fundamental meaning of this more personal style is that it must be obvious to the worshippers that their leader is really praying, not in front of them, but in their midst. For only when the presider is part of the primary symbol of the liturgy, that is, the gathered assembly, can full participation of all be fostered by creating a sense of community and an experience of genuine prayer. But because this more prayerful and personal style of leading worship is not easily delineated in terms of strict rules such as the liturgical legislation of former times, only general observations can be proposed which would be true in most cases. These more open ended guidelines might well be summarized under the phrase, "celebrational presence."

The presider manifests a committed and transparent faith. Unless personal commitment to the belief system and symbolic structure of Christianity is evident in the way the leader of worship functions in the liturgy, all else is pointless. The most fundamental experience upon which any summoning of the assembly to prayer is based is the personal commitment that the gospel and the liturgy are indispensable for the life of the

Christian. This commitment will be most clearly manifested in the prayerful attitude of the presider. It means that the leader must manifest a faith in God at all times in the liturgy, even when humanly speaking the assembly does not seem to be responsive.

In order to radiate a faith appropriate to good liturgy, the presider needs to communicate: 1) that the God being worshipped cares for humankind, 2) that the paschal mystery, the coming, dying, rising, and returning of Jesus Christ is real and able to be experienced, 3) that salvation history is being accomplished now in the concrete present moment, and 4) that what God did once and for all in Jesus Christ is now continued through the sacramental life of the church. Such a presider is able through genuine and manifest prayer to teach the worshippers how their love of God must move into the areas of social concern, how the Kingdom of God can and is being accomplished in their own time, and how the bringing about this Kingdom should be characterized by a thrust into the future as well as an attitude of openness to the present. Many of the techniques of good prayer leadership are simply ways of letting one's faith show through unambiguously.

One way in which the presider's own faith comes through clearly in a liturgical celebration is the acknowledgement that s/he experiences doubt and ambiguity in the area of belief, whether it be central affirmations of the biblical tradition or specific teachings of the church. It would be a mistake for the presider to engage in agonizing soul-searching in front of the congregation, but on the other hand presiders should not attempt to establish an objective atmosphere of faith which is not grounded in their own commitment. In preaching it is important that the presider deal with the doubts and questions of the congregation honestly.

It is unfortunate but true that at times presiders and preachers continue to func-tion liturgically after their own faith commitment has vanished. It is imperative that such a situation be remedied by church leadership as soon as possible.

The presider places a high value on personal communication, respect for others, and the principle of subsidiarity. This guideline begins with the basics of human communication. Can the priest, the lector, the cantor be heard? Audibility is a necessity, not a luxury. Audibility relates intimately to effective proclamation. The latter presumes proper preparation and adequate understanding of what is to be proclaimed. The congregation has the right to hear. It is the responsibility of the presiders to transform texts and sounds into living prayer that become the transforming expression of the community. This cannot be done without practice beforehand.

Communication in liturgical presidency takes on the forms of reading, preaching, and proclaiming. All readers need to be acquainted with the many liturgical aids for lectors that are available. There are some general practical suggestions to be followed: read the text several times beforehand; act as if the congregation does not have the texts in printed form before them; clearly pronounce obscure names and words; never read while the congregation is moving; create the climate for the reading; make affective use of the pause; be aware of the acoustics of the building; and maintain poise. Readers are called upon to be good storytellers in the liturgy.

Preachers are advised to take to heart the following suggestions: do not use "canned" homilies; do not read from a text; be concise; maintain poise; be direct and clear; avoid religious jargon or a "preacher's tone"; and do not speak in a complicated fashion. Storytelling in the homily is not for the purpose of illustrating a point, but it is an integral part of the way a homily preaches. In proclaiming specific parts of the liturgy, presiders should be aware of the different styles of liturgical language, e.g., greetings, prayers, invitations, the eucharistic prayer, and prayers which are to be silent. In proclaiming it is especially important that attention carefully be paid to how words and gestures go together. Presiders must become fully human in word and in action.

Respect for others can be shown in many ways. There are the obvious attributes of the respectful presider: warm and friendly, modest about self, positive in dealing with others, dignified in bearing, and confident in the ministry. All these will put the worshipper at ease. These qualities are especially demanded of priests because they can assist them in their role of bringing the other liturgical ministries together in a unified way. A less obvious characteristic of presiders who respect others is their good taste. Sensitivity to what is liturgically appropriate will prevent a trivialization of the liturgy and so of the worshipper. Presiders who are familiar with poetry or other art forms have an opportunity to open up the symbols for the assembly. This is a high form of respect for others. Presiders who train their aesthetic sensitivity will be less tempted to explain the symbols of the liturgy. Finally, presidential style of any minister will be only as good as the attention of the minister. Attention to the liturgical deed and to the assembly itself is one of the chief ways of attaining that presence upon which good liturgical leadership is based.

The principle of subsidiarity here means that while the presider has responsibility for the overall rhythm and dynamic of the liturgy, s/he achieves this end through the proper facilitation of the other liturgical ministers in their respective roles. The requirements of subsidiarity are not fulfilled through the careful observation of the rubrics alone. Whatever will promote the full awareness and active engagement of the assembly falls within the domain of the subsidiarity. Subsidiarity is the concrete effect of responsibility to the community rather than only to the law. It means in the area of liturgical planning that the priest will be an equal participant in the process of preparation, will not pre-empt the judgment of others, especially those with special competence, will manifest an abiding attitude of flexibility, will be noted for a care for the quality of worship, and will be at home with the symbols.

The presider is a person of the church, a bearer of the Christian tradition, and a leader of prayer. Presiders, of whatever kind, perform a public office in the church. This has certain implications for the manner in which they lead the congregation in prayer. On the one hand they are called to embody the faith of the local congregation so that it will be enlivened and enhanced. On the other hand, they represent the local leader of liturgy in the diocese, the bishop, as well as the larger church. They are not free to conduct themselves as private individuals in the course of worship. That means that they demonstrate a respect for liturgical procedure and etiquette, but even more it demands that they do not pray merely as individuals. It would be inappropriate for presiders to give the impression that they are praying *in front of* the congregation rather than *in the midst of* the congregation. For instance, the manner in which the person presides at the eucharistic liturgy is not simply a matter between him/her and God. The purpose of presiding at the eucharist is to help create an *ecclesial* experience of union with God through the ritual. Since the liturgy is the expression of the church, establishing its identity in Christ through the ritual experience, the priest must also act in dialogue with the congregation and the other liturgical ministers so that it is the faith of the church and not one's own individual faith which is being brought to symbolic articulation. Leading people in prayer is creating a space where people can enter into the presence of their God as community, and recall the depths of that relationship.

Presiders, as bearers of tradition, do not unthinkingly accept the past. Nor do they presume that all ancient symbols are meaningless. To communicate the tradition of the church is to search for the depth of the Christian life and inspire others in that same dimension. One cannot preside well if one "presides" over the destruction of one's symbol system. One brings the tradition to the assembly in one's preaching of the word of God by interpreting what has been handed down in the liturgical texts and structures and by imaginatively recreating in any particular liturgy the experience of the church at prayer throughout its history. One does not bear the tradition by becoming authoritarian or bureaucratic. The president of the assembly is truly traditional when s/he bears self in a Christ-like way through posture, walk, dignity, personal humility, and freeing gestures. One is not traditional if one is embarrassed by the wearing of vestments or if one pays more attention to the physical elements (e.g., book, bread, wine) than to the members of the congregation.

The role and style of liturgical presiding is rooted in the personal experience of God of the one presiding. In good ritual there is a two-fold structure which requires presiders to assume the role of the person of faith at the same time that they are aware of their limitations in believing. However, the leader of worship cannot be play-acting in the sense that what is done in the rite is only loosely connected to the personal life. As a person of prayer, the presider must be one who is pervaded, if not overwhelmed, by the presence of God. Authenticity here does not imply that one forces one's spiritual life to fit the texts of the liturgy, but it does demand that in the action of presiding the congregation senses here, not a person self-conscious about role, but one who lets God shine through in all actions, words, and bodily movements.

The presider ritualizes and symbolizes in an embodied way. The spirituality of the church is enfleshed in the liturgy. By means of patterned symbolic activity, that ritual called Christian liturgy becomes the place where the visible and invisible meet. The celebration of the imperceptible reality of Jesus Christ takes place through perceptible liturgical symbols. The way these symbols are handled, dealt with, and performed matters immensely to the quality of the celebration and makes a difference regarding the manifestation of that imperceptible paschal mystery. The presider is the one most called upon to coordinate those symbols into a unified experience of ritual. Moreover, the presider is a liturgical symbol also. Therefore, how s/he performs symbolically and conducts others through the symbol system of Christian worship is of primary importance. Liturgy does not work on its own. The phrase *ex opere operato* implies that the embodiment of worship is of tremendous concern. Good liturgy depends upon good presidential style.

The most difficult of the many challenges that confront presiders today is that of befriending the body. While the notion that the body is the manifestation of the spirit flows logically from the incarnational character of Christianity, in fact the mind/body dualism has been more characteristic. But listening to bodily experience need not be in competition with rationality and discursive thinking. Rather the body through its language of movement and gesture can make our lives fuller epiphanies of God and so more sacramental. However, if we consider the body a foe, as many presiders seem to do, we experience a separation from our body which automatically separates us from others. For the presider whose vocation is to bring symbols together in the formation of community, such separation can render him/her dysfunctional.

Befriending the body is not to be confused with the cultural pursuit of the body beautiful. While the contemporary practices for obtaining health and fitness can be appropriate for the presider to gain a more holistic sense of self, the purpose would not be to conform to fashion trends, but to rediscover the body sacramental.

The experience of the body sacramental is the antithesis of the kind of dualism which has found its way into Christian spirituality. In achieving wholeness through awareness of one's body, presiders can experience their whole self as the place of God's presence. In their bodiliness and sensuality these leaders of worship celebrate the glory of ongoing creation and the unity which all have in Christ. Presiders are those who tell the story of the paschal mystery in the liturgy. By attending to themselves as bodies, and getting to know themselves as bodies, they are able to let the story of Jesus Christ come to light by means of their own story which may have remained hidden had they maintained the body/mind division in themselves. When one does exercises aimed at getting in touch with one's body and when they are done in the context of one's relationship with God, they become examples of what can be called body praise. The presider who has been healed in this way and on this level will be qualified to lead the Christian community in praise of its God, which is what liturgy is.

Lucien Deiss, *Persons in Liturgical Celebrations* (Chicago: World Library Publications, Inc., 1978). Mary Ann Finch, "Befriending the Body," *The Way* 29:1 (January 1989): 60-67. Lawrence A. Hoffman, *The Art of Public Prayer* (Washington, D.C.: The Pastoral Press, 1988). Robert W. Hovda, *Strong, Loving and Wise: Presiding in Liturgy* (Washington, D.C.: The Liturgical Conference, 1976).

JAMES L. EMPEREUR, S.J.

PRESIDING, MINISTRY OF

The title of this article is not "the ministry of celebrant." Many of our liturgical books (e.g., Sacramentary, R.C.I.A.) continue to use the term. It is both infelicitous and poor because it restricts the ministry of the presider to the cultic and it sets the presider over against, and in isolation from, the entire assembly which is the true celebrant in liturgical action.

The presider is a baptized person ordained to a pastoral office of service. The ministry of presiding is one of mediating the high priesthood of Jesus Christ in the midst of a priestly people. Thus the presider is charged with the task of animating, overseeing and ordering the gifts of the priestly people in order that the church might be built up in its life of holiness, in its ministries, and in its mission to herald the reign of God. Because of this leadership ministry in the midst of God's people, he presides at the eucharistic table where the church is most clearly visible as church (S.C., 7-10) and where the assembled body of Christ manifests its various gifts in offering the eucharist.

The ministry of presiding is not one of quasi-divinity, nor is it one of power personally residing in the person of the presider. It is one of service; its model is that of Jesus, shepherd and martyr. The origins of this ministry are not easy to trace in NT texts. The term "priest" is used to describe Christ and his church. While various gifts flourish, such as prophet and teacher, there is Pauline evidence that some kind of unifying ministry was needed in moments of conflict. The pastoral letters indicate overseeing ministries, but one would be chary to translate them into the current ministries of bishop, presbyter and deacon.

What does emerge as definable presidential ministry from the 2nd century onwards is due, in large measure, to the church's situation in the late ancient

Roman Empire. P. Brown (*The Making of Late Antiquity*) points out that both Christian and Roman religious systems vied for allegiance. In the end, the question became: who is friend of God, who has access to the divine? For the Christian system, the martyr became imitator of Christ in the most graphic way possible. But also the bishop emerged as another heroic symbol of Christ, especially when local churches were beset with Roman persecution. Ignatius of Antioch not only articulated ecclesial unity, he also incarnated that by his martyrdom, a martyrdom expressed in eucharistic imagery (*Ad Rom* 4:1-2). Ignatius presided over the sacrifice of unity and he provided one of the most beautiful images for this role. "Consequently it is right for you to run together with the purpose of the bishop, which you indeed do; for your worthily reputed presbytery, worthy of God, is attuned to the bishop like strings to a cithara; therefore, in your concord and harmonious love, Jesus Christ is sung" (*Ad Eph* 4:1). H-M Legrand points out that presidency was not left to happenstance. The presider pastored the entire life of the church, was a symbol of and articulate spokesperson for its unity, and shepherded the church as it entered into mystery through its celebrations of initiation and eucharist. Justin indicated that the presider functioned by being present in the midst of the community and with its consent.

Cultic presidency required that the presider oversee the reading of the memoirs of the apostles and that the presider might offer the prayer of thanksgiving with skill, some spontaneity and according to a pattern that had assumed an oral shape. Irenaeus and Anicetus indicated that the bishop presided at the table. Tertullian indicated that the bishop presides at the table because he has care for the life of the community, not because of a sacerdotal quality. It is only with Hippolytus and Cyprian that presidency is expressed in terms of priesthood. The former noted that the bishop, presiding over the church by an ordination conferring apostolic charism, presides at the eucharist as high priest. The latter saw the bishop as both the bond of unity as he presided at the table and, as president, functioning as *sacerdos* symbolizing Christ, the high priest (*summus sacerdos*).

The presider was a type of Christ and functioned in imitation of Christ. The ministry shaped the presider so that he began to act with the inner intention of Christ, the holiness of Christ. As presider he also taught as Jesus did. If the bishop delegated this presidential role, the presbyter was also to be shaped in the spirit and style of Christ, the high priest. As J.D. Laurance has stated: "The power or authority of the *sacerdos* is based upon the same foundation as the authority found in the *gloria* of the martyr: the *passio* of Christ.... To the degree that the *sacerdos* individually (*auctoritas*) and as an office holder in the church (*potestas*) has power in the church, he has that power only by virtue of his imaging and therefore making present Christ in his saving deeds...." There is for Cyprian no division among these titles regarding their ultimate significance. "One is *episcopus*, *presbyter*, or *sacerdos* only by virtue of representing the holiness of the church through representing the holiness of Christ's *passio* (*gloria*). This alone is the basis both for his holding office and for his authority" (Laurance, pp. 214-215).

Presidency might be extended to a vision as a mark of affection, respect and admiration for the visitor's charism. Presidency shared was a manifestation of ecclesial unity and hospitality. It eventually is a pastoral office that is delegated as the church moves beyond urban centers into the country regions of the empire.

In short, the picture of presidency is one of pastoral office which oversees the life of the local church, fosters its unity internally and with other ecclesial communities, functions sometimes to represent Christ (*summus sacerdos*), and acts to extend or deny eucharistic hospitality and charity. Later historical developments will sacerdotalize and clericalize the office, thereby swallowing up other cultic, charitable and diaconal ministries of service. The picture of the 2nd to 4th centuries is more germane and in harmony with contemporary readings of presidential ministry than its later developments.

Presiding Today

The ministry of presiding today requires that office holders in the church look to four areas for direction: theology, style based on praxis, ecumenicity, and lay leadership.

Theology. Those called forth to preside are called forth from an assembly, presented by the assembly to the bishops, and prayed for by the assembly. Ordination is "an act of Christ who is present *in* and *as* the assembled church, and who acts *when* and *as* the church itself acts" (Fink, p. 485). The presider serves among sisters and brothers called church. This is clear from the words of the bishop: "accept from the holy people of God the gifts to be offered to him." The presider acts in such a way that the assembled church invokes the Spirit, already present in the church, to act now in Bible proclamation and preaching, eucharist, initiation, reconciliation, anointing the sick, etc. The presider, as one who animates, oversees and orders the gifts of this priestly people in its life of holiness, its ministries and its mission, leads this assembly and calls it to prayer.

Both the priesthood of the ordained and the priesthood of the faithful manifest the one priesthood of Jesus Christ. The sacrament of Christ is embodied in the liturgical assembly and its activity. The ordained summon the faithful to go beyond what it is, to become more fully the church. Fink identifies this becoming as largeness. "It is because of this largeness of both gospel and eucharistic prayer that the ministers who proclaim them have come to be appointed by the college of bishops.... To serve the largeness of Christ and church the ministers themselves must manifest and be rooted in that largeness. The ordained ... embody and manifest this largeness of Christ *so that* the assembly may see in someone living among them what they themselves are summoned to become. No one takes on this ministry by virtue of baptism which, by incorporating one into Christ, entitles one to be *a member* of the assembled church. Because such an embodiment involves a transformation and a mission this church once again in its prayer invokes the Spirit of God. The transformation is to be a sacrament of the ecclesial Christ; the mission is to exhibit in life, in action, and in the specific ministries which the church assigns, the identity and destiny of the church itself" (Fink, p. 491).

Therefore there is established a mutual relationship between the ordained presider and the assembly. Fink describes the relationship beautifully as mutual iconography. "The ordained person is commissioned to be an icon of the church in its identity as the sacrament of Christ. In the life and ministry of the ordained the church asks and expects to see a manifestation of its own identity and vocation.... The assembled church is itself the icon of the priest's identity and vocation" (Fink, p. 491). The ordained presider is called to listen and to call forth, to summon the church to be itself more fully. "The ordained embody in sacrament the as yet unfulfilled destiny of the entire church. The principal ministry of the ordained ... is to activate and thus call forth the priesthood of the church" (Fink, p. 492). Both the priesthood of the ordained and the priesthood of the faithful rise and fall together.

Style Based on Praxis. The ministry of presiding will make great demands upon those ordained to serve in this way. It requires energy expended. In turn, the presider is energized by the assembled church in cult and its witness of holiness. What keeps one energized? One avenue, little explored to date, is to learn images that can energize. The following images are rooted in presidential action. The presider is mother. Anyone who takes a person out of the womb like waters of the font or who consoles those in grief knows what it means to be a mother in the *mater ecclesia.* The presider is mediator of story because he listens to others' stories of salvation, he is attentive to prayer text and biblical text, and is asked to be a wordsmith crafting homiletic and prayer word. The presider is medicine man because he is asked to console the sinner, comfort the afflicted, heal the wounded. The medicine man of the tribe attends to the power of ritual form and movement. He puts on and internalizes the affective sentiments and qualities of the rites. The presider is martyr because he is called to stretch if he is to embody what the assembled church is to become and because he witnesses how Christ touches the hearts of a people. Finally, the presider is a melodist because he sings, as voice of the assembly, the great deeds of God done in history and in this assembly.

Ecumenicity. Because other churches have admitted both men and women to this ministry at their tables, male presiders in Roman Catholic and Orthodox tradition will find themselves learning what women do in this ministry, how they preside and how they reflect on its meaning. An ordained female presider is going to function according to her rhythms and sensitivities as a woman. She is going to embody Christ and his priestly praying according to her charisms, her experience and even her vulnerability. What images energize her ministry might be a blessing in an all male presidential ministry.

Lay Leadership. Not only is the presider to animate and encourage the gifts and ministries of the assembly, but, more and more, the ordained presider will be called upon to share presidential ministry with lay leaders who likewise preside at public worship. This development will demand a cooperative and collaborative style, a sharing of prayer and insight, and a respect and reverence for lay presiders. In turn, the entire church, the priestly people, will be enriched and faithful to its life of holiness, its ministries and its mission to proclaim the reign of God.

See **Formation, liturgical; Presidential style**

Peter Brown, *The Making of Late Antiquity* (Cambridge: Harvard U.P., 1978). Peter E. Fink, "The Sacrament of Orders: Some Liturgical Reflections," *Worship* 56 (1982): 482-502. John D. Laurance, *'Priest' as Type of Christ: The Leader of the Eucharist in Salvation History according to Cyprian of Carthage* (New York: Peter Lang, 1984). Herve-Marie Legrand, "The Presidency of the Eucharist According to the Ancient Tradition," *Worship* 53 (1979): 413-438.

JOHN J. O'BRIEN, C.P.

PRIESTHOOD

In English the term *priest* connotes two distinct religious functions: (1) a cultic, or hieratic priesthood, which mediates the presence of God through ritual, especially through sacrifice, and (2) the oversight of the Christian community exercised by the presbyter/bishops in the NT and by their successors. As the structures of Christian ordained ministry evolved these two senses of the term blended theologically.

Among the pagan nations in the ancient Middle East, the hieratic priesthood played an important political function. In Mesopotamia and in Egypt, for example, the king secured the religious function of the cultic priest but in the expectation that the priestly caste would endow royal authority with religious sanction.

Among the Jewish patriarchs we find

no evidence of a politicized hieratic priesthood. The Hebrew patriarchs who built altars and offered sacrifice (Gen 12:7 ff; 13:18; 22:31, 54; 26:25; 46:1) exercised instead a familial priesthood also common among the peoples of the ancient Middle East, a kind of priestly ministry which continued to shape Hebrew worship even after the emergence of the levitical cult (Judg 6:18-29; 13:19; 17:5; 1 Sam 7:1).

We do not know for certain whether the tribe of Levi exercised a hieratic function within Israel from the beginning or whether it acquired that function over time. Moses, called a priest only once in the OT (Ps 99:6), consecrated Aaron and his sons high priest (Exod 29:20-21; Lev 8:23-24). After the conquest of Canaan, however, levitical priests certainly presided over cult in sanctuaries throughout Israel in a way that parallelled and sought to replace Canaanite sanctuaries of pagan worship (Judg 17-18; 1 Sam 1-4; 22:9-23).

A number of historical events during the period of the Hebrew monarchy tied the levitical priesthood to the throne of David: David's transportation of the ark of the covenant to Jerusalem; his appointment of Abiathar and Zadok to preside over worship in the capital city (2 Sam 6:1-23; 8:17); Solomon's construction of the temple in Jerusalem in the 11th century B.C. (1 Kgs 6:1-14); and King Josiah's abolition of local shrines in 621 B.C. and centralization of all cult in Jerusalem.

In 587 B.C. the Babylonians deported the priestly class into exile along with the other inhabitants of Jerusalem, razed the temple and put a temporary end to its cult. In the post-exilic period, however, the Zadokite priestly aristocracy reasserted its control of temple worship. As a result of the political machinations of the Zadokite priesthood, the Hasmonean rulers of Israel ended its domination of temple cult by appointing their own priests. By the time of Jesus the high priesthood had degenerated into a political appointment with no claim of genealogical legitimacy.

Levitical priests functioned above all as men of the sanctuary. They offered sacrifices to God (Exod 29:38-42). Once a year the high priest functioned as supreme mediator between God and Israel by offering a sacrifice of atonement for the sins of the people (Lev 16:1-34). Priests also presided over rites of consecration and purification (1 Kgs 1:39; 2 Kgs 12:1-8; Lev 14:1-33). Until David's time priests delivered oracles through the use of the Urim and Thummim (1 Sam 14:36-42; 30:7-8; Deut 33:8). Finally, on feast days and at covenant renewals priests proclaimed and interpreted the Torah (Exodus 1-15; Joshua 2-6; Exodus 24:7; Deuteronomy 27; Nehemiah 8). The priestly caste supervised the final redaction of the Pentateuch, which after its proclamation by Ezra in 445 B.C. commanded obedience as sacred scripture and as law (Neh 8:1-18). Thereafter priests functioned as ordinary interpreters of the law until rabbinic teachers largely replaced them. By the time of Jesus the levitical priesthood functioned primarily as hieratic cult leaders.

Jesus did not belong to the tribe of Levi. Instead he exercised a ministry of teaching that combined rabbinic and prophetic elements. He gave rudimentary institutional shape to the religious movement he headed by choosing the twelve to function as judges of the New Israel he hoped to found (Mk 3:13-19; 10:28-31; Mt 10:1-4; 19:27-29; Lk 6:12-16; 18:24-27). Jesus also demanded of the twelve that they renounce the arrogance of pagan rulers and embrace the way of powerlessness in the image of a servant messiah (Mk 9:33-37; 10:17-20; 35-45; Mt 20:20-28; Lk 22:24-27; Jn 13:1-20). The twelve participated in Jesus' own charismatic authority to proclaim the kingdom by healing and casting out demons (Mk 6:7-13; 11:27-33; Mt 10:5, 8, 9-14; 21:23-27; Lk 9:1-6; 20:1-8).

Jesus called for the purification of temple worship (Mk 11:15-19; Mt 21:12-17; Lk 19:45-48; Jn 2:14-16) and prophesied the destruction of Jerusalem and its temple (Lk 19:41-44; 21:5-7; Jn 2:19; Mk 13:1-4; 14-20; Mt 24:1-3). In instituting the eucharist Jesus described his own impending death as a covenant sacrifice (Mk 14:22-25; Mt 26:26-29; Lk 22:15-20; 1 Cor 11:23-25).

The NT consistently portrayed the death of Jesus as either a covenant sacrifice or a sacrifice of atonement (1 Cor 5:7; 1 Pet 1:18; Rom 3:25; Gal 2:20; Eph 5:2). The letter to the Hebrews, however, transformed these cryptic allusions by proclaiming Jesus the supreme high priest of the new covenant. Unlike the levitical high priest who belonged to a religious power elite, the eternal Son of God became high priest first by the self-humiliation of becoming human and then, in his passion and obedient death, by identifying totally with humanity in its suffering and need. Jesus' glorification reveals the divine scope of his high-priestly authority (Heb 4:12-15; 5:1-6:20). A priest forever of the order of Melchizedek, Jesus through the single, eternally efficacious sacrifice of his death, through his eternal and efficacious intercession for us at the throne of God, and through the new eschatological future which his death and glorification began has ended once and for all any need for a hieratic levitical priesthood (Heb 7:11-28; 8:1-10:18).

Nowhere did the NT portray either the apostles or the presbyter/bishops who succeeded them as hieratic, sacrificing priests, although both 1 Peter and Revelation portray the Christian community as a whole as the priestly people of God (1 Pet 2:4-10; Rev 4:1-5:14; 14:1-5; 19:1-10). Indeed, in contrast to the levitical priest who belonged by ancestry to a religious power elite, the first leaders of the Christian community exercised a charismatic ministry of service and of oversight. Indeed, we discover in the apostolic church a variety of leadership ministries. In the post-apostolic church, however, with the emergence in the 2nd century of the *monepiscopos*, or single bishop presiding over a local Christian church, episcopal supervision of Christian cult evolved into episcopal control. By the 3rd century we find increasing references to the ordained as clergy: i.e., as "specially chosen" or "set apart." One also finds with increasing regularity references to bishops (and occasionally to presbyters) as the high priests of the new covenant. These tendencies culminated in the 4th century in the theological movement known as *sacerdotalism*.

Sacerdotalist theology reflected the changed political status of Christianity as it became, first, one of the official religions, then, the only official religion of the Roman empire. Sacerdotalist theologians sought to protect the authority of the bishop from imperial encroachment. Basil of Caesarea laid the foundations for the new theology of Christian priesthood by teaching that bishops participate directly in the priestly authority of Christ in church matters in a manner analogous to the emperor's direct participation in divine authority in secular matters. Such an interpretation of episcopal priesthood endowed bishops with a priestly function different in kind from the priesthood of all believers. Moreover, the sacerdotalist portrayal of bishops as the levitical priests of the new covenant cast them, in what concerned their relationship to the emperor, in a role analogous to the relationship of the levitical high priesthood to the throne of David.

Sacerdotalist theology re-enforced elitist perceptions of the episcopacy in other ways as well. After Constantine's appointment of the episcopacy in A.D. 318 to the post of imperial judges, sacerdotalist theologians sought to protect bishops from the corruption traditionally associated with that office by holding up to them the highest moral ideals. In the dualistic world of Christian Platonism, the imposition of episcopal celibacy endowed the office with quasi-angelic pretentions and vindicated its superiority to the first levitical priests, who incurred ritual impurity through sexual activity (Lev 15:16-18). Christian bishops, who exercised a more spiritual kind of hieratic priesthood, renounced marriage altogether.

The 2nd and 3rd centuries witnessed the temporary eclipse of the Christian presbyterate, as deacons, who functioned as administrative assistants to the bishops, played a more prominent role in the community than its presbyteral elders. In the 4th century, however, presbyters began to preside at eucharists especially in rural areas where the bishop could not. As the presbyterate gained in ecclesial prominence the diaconate declined. By the end of the 4th century, the presbyter, or priest, ranked second only to the bishop in clerical authority.

In the 6th century, a Syrian writer with the pseudonym of Dionysius the Areopagite, an Athenian whom Paul the apostle converted in the 1st century (Acts 17:34), proposed a hierarchical interpretation of the structures of church government. By a "hierarchy" Pseudo-Dionysius meant "a holy ordinance," an eternal, divinely established principle of order which gives intelligible structure to the universe (*The Celestial Hierarchy*, III, 1). A Christian Platonist, Pseudo-Dionysius believed that the church on earth participated in the order of the three angelic hierarchies. The first angelic hierarchy included seraphim, cherubim, and thrones; the second, dominations, powers, and authorities; the third, principalities, archangels, and angels. Moreover, Pseudo-Dionysius believed that the angelic capacity for grace and enlight-

enment decreased as one descended the hierarchical ladder (*Ibid.*, V, 1-IX, 2). He divided the church on earth into two similarly structured hierarchies. Bishops, priests, and deacons comprised the clerical hierarchy. Religious, laity, and catechumens comprised the lay hierarchy. Pseudo-Dionysius described the bishop as "a deified and divine person, instructed in all-holy knowledge, in whom the entire hierarchy which depends on him finds the pure means of perfecting and expressing itself" (*The Ecclesiastical Hierarchy*, I, 3).

This quaint understanding of church order made the clergy into the laity's only channel of divine grace, and with the disappearance of the catechumenate left the laity in a position of pure passivity on the bottom rung of the hierarchical ladder. This peculiar ecclesiology exerted little influence at first; but it strongly informed both church reform and theological reflection on the priesthood in the Late Middle Ages, when it was mistaken as a description of 1st-century church order.

By the Late Middle Ages, scholastic theologians were moving to a broad consensus about the meaning of priesthood, a consensus informed not only by sacerdotalist and hierarchical thinking but also by medieval church order and sacramental controversies. The schoolmen saw priests as the principal agents of the Christian eucharistic sacrifice endowed by ordination with the power to change bread and wine into the body and blood of Christ. Ordination also empowered priests to baptize, absolve, and anoint the sick and dying. The character of priestly ordination, a mysterious spiritual mark on the soul, conformed the ordained to Christ the great high priest of the new covenant and enabled them to function as sacramental channels of grace for the laity. The Scholastics saw episcopal ordination as conferring jurisdictional authority and the right to confirm and ordain (Albert the Great, *On the Sacraments*, Tr. VIII q. iv, a. 3; Bonaventure, *Commentary on the Book of Sentences* IV, d. xiv, p. 2, a. 1, qq. 1-3; Thomas Aquinas, *Summa Contra Gentiles*, IV lxxiv-lxxvi, *Summa Theologiae*, III [Supple.], xxxiv-xl).

The Reformation witnessed the collapse of this medieval consensus as the Protestant Reformers, who took Sacred Scripture as the only norm of faith, correctly realized that the NT offered no sanction for either a sacerdotalist or a hierarchicalist interpretation of priestly ministry. Both Luther and Calvin placed the proclamation of the gospel rather than cultic leadership at the heart of ordained ministry (Luther, *Works*, 36:113; Calvin, *Institutes*, IV xix, 22-23), although the *Augsberg Confession* (16) acknowledged that the ordained do lead worship, as did Calvin (*Institutes*, IV, xiv, 22-23). Luther also rediscovered the NT doctrine of the priesthood of all believers, but interpreted it as denying any difference in kind between the priesthood of clergy and laity (*Works*, 36:116). Zwingli recognized no priesthood save that of Christ (*Commentary on True and False Religion*, 21).

The Council of Trent responded to the Protestant challenge by both defending and reforming the medieval sacramental synthesis. Trent defended both the hierarchical structure of the church and a qualitative difference between the priesthood of the ordained and that of the laity. It insisted that ordination gives the power not only to consecrate and offer the eucharist but also to forgive sins. Trent denied that ordination merely commissions one to preach the gospel. Trent extended sacerdotalist thinking to include the presbyterate but left the sacramental status of the episcopacy vague (D.S., 1767-1769, 1771, 1774).

Both the liturgical and ecumenical movements softened the contrast between Catholic and Protestant interpretations of the character of ordained ministry, as the teachings of Vatican II illustrate. In contrast to Trent, Vatican II made a ministry of proclamation rather than cultic leadership the primary responsibility of the ordained, treating sacramental worship as a special and particularly efficacious mode of proclaiming the gospel. Although Vatican II asserted with Luther the priesthood of all the faithful, it continued to defend a difference in kind between ordained and lay priesthood (L.G., 10; P.O., 4-5). Although the council still employed the term "hierarchical," it refused to portray the clergy as the laity's only channel of grace, as Pseudo-Dionysius had. It also portrayed the clergy as standing within the church rather than over it and as orienting the laity through word and sacrament to receptive openness to the Holy Spirit. While the ordained have the responsibility of evoking, coordinating, and discerning the gifts of the Spirit, they never have the right to suppress the Spirit (L.G., 10; A.A., 3, 30). In retrieving a NT interpretation of the responsibilities of presbyteral ministry, Vatican II also acknowledged its charismatic basis (*Optatam totius*, 13-14; P.O., 5-6). In the end, however, Vatican II juxtaposed a sacerdotalist and a NT theology of priesthood without attempting to resolve the theological tensions between the two (L.G., 21).

In other words, while Vatican II closed the theological gap between a Catholic and Protestant interpretation of ordained ministry, it left unresolved many of the dialectical tensions in the development of a Christian theology of priesthood. For example, the letter to the Hebrews asserted that Jesus the great high priest of the new covenant has put an end forever to the need for a levitical priesthood; but sacerdotalism portrayed first bishops and then presbyters as the levitical high priests of the new covenant. Similarly, if with Trent and Vatican II one defends a difference in kind between the priesthood of the laity and ordained priesthood, one may nevertheless question whether assimilating Christian ordained leadership to the levitical priesthood offers the best theological explanation of that difference. Finally, both sacerdotalism and hierarchicalism helped rationalize the rise of clericalism, which, when it prevailed, transformed ordained church leadership from a service into a power elite. Clericalism, however, for its part, would seem to contradict the mandate of Jesus to the apostles that leaders in the new Israel must imitate a servant messiah by acting as the least of all and as the servants of all.

Vatican II may, however, have pointed to paths that lead beyond these dialectical impasses. While official leadership of a community of worship necessarily entails not only the responsibility to oversee worship but even the right to lead worship in accord with the accepted discipline of that community, if one distinguishes a hieratic understanding of priesthood from the presbyteral oversight exercised in the apostolic church, one can assert with Vatican II that bishops enjoy the fullness of presbyteral oversight while still maintaining with Hebrews that Jesus enjoys the fullness of hieratic priesthood. Similarly, if with the NT and with Vatican II one asserts the charismatic basis of Christian priestly ministry, then one can explain the difference in kind between the priesthood of the faithful and ordained priesthood without endorsing a sacerdotalist interpretation of that difference. The charisms of the Holy Spirit differ in kind from one another and specify the way in which individual Christians participate in the priestly ministry of the church as a whole. Because the ordained exercise a different kind of charism of service, their priestly ministry differs in kind from the ministry of those who exercise other charisms in the church. Such a charismatic interpretation of the difference between ordained and lay priesthood would not, in the manner of sacerdotalism, portray the ordained as participating directly in the priesthood of Christ in a way that sets them apart from and over the laity. Instead the priesthood of the church, the responsibility of God's priestly people as a whole to mediate Christ to the world, would also mediate between the priesthood of both clergy and laity whose diverse charisms empower them to share in the church's priestly ministry in different ways. Such an interpretation of priestly ministry would also require that the ordained model their ministry on Jesus rather than on the levitical priesthood. By purifying the theological understanding of ordained leadership of the clericalistic connotations of sacerdotalism and hierarchicalism such a theology could better reconcile priestly service with the demands of discipleship.

Raymond Brown, *Priest and Bishop: Biblical Reflections* (Paramus, N.J.: Paulist, 1970). Kenan Osborne, O.F.M., *Priesthood: A History of the Ordained Ministry in the Roman Catholic Church* (New York: Paulist, 1988). Albert Vanhoye, *Pretres anciens, pretre nouveau selon le Nouveau Testament* (Paris: Editions du Seuil, 1980).

DONALD L. GELPI, S.J.

PRIESTHOOD, RECONCILIATION AND

See **Reconciliation and priesthood**

PRIESTLY SPIRITUALITY

All Christian spirituality flows from incorporation into the body of Christ through faith and baptism. The priest's spirituality is no exception. Basically, then, priestly spirituality is Christian spirituality. However, since the priest has a special role in the body of Christ, it is appropriate to discuss how this role specifies the practice of Christian spirituality. But an integral examination of priestly spirituality must first situate the priest within the body and only then discuss the aspects of spirituality proper to the priest *as priest*. This article is concerned with priesthood in the Roman Catholic church, hence the terms *body of Christ* and *church* have primary reference to this community. By extension, however, it has application *mutatis mutandis* to the pastoral office in all Christian churches.

Body of Christ: Priest As Member

Priests are members of the body of Christ. Their dignity as members of the body has frequently been obscured by treatment of their special role within the body. The *Decree on the Ministry and Life of Priests* from Vatican II clearly situates the priest's leadership role through ordination within the priest's membership in the body through the sacraments of initiation: "Therefore, while it indeed presupposes the sacraments of Christian initiation, the sacerdotal office of priests is conferred by that special sacrament through which priests, by the anointing of the Holy Spirit, are marked by a special character and are so configured to Christ the priest that they can act in the person of Christ the head" (P.O., 2). Membership and leadership must be seen together for comprehensive understanding of priestly identity and spirituality.

It is significant that Vatican II chose the image of the body of Christ to discuss priestly identity. This image highlights both the equality of all in the body as well as the difference of roles in the body. The equality of all members within the body is clear: "There is but one body and one Spirit, just as there is but one hope given all of you by your call. There is one Lord, one faith, one baptism; one God and Father of all, who is over all, and works through all, and is in all" (Eph 4:4-6). Equally clear is the difference of roles within the body: "There are different gifts but the same Spirit; there are different ministries but the same Lord; there are different works but the same God who accomplishes all of them in everyone. To each person the manifestation of the Spirit is given for the common good" (1 Cor 12:4-7). Furthermore, Paul's image of the body of Christ highlights the Spirit as the source of all life within the body. Membership in the body flows from the Spirit received through faith and baptism. Specific roles (charisms) within the body flow from the special gifts given by the Spirit to different members of the body for the sake of the entire body.

Finally, the church as the body of Christ shares Christ's mission. This mission so clearly presented in all the gospels is serving the Kingdom of God. Each member is called by baptism to assume a share of responsibility by accepting ministry according to his or her specific charisms. This ministry is oriented to serving the Kingdom of God within the body of Christ itself as well as beyond the body in the world. The example is, of course, Jesus himself. Jesus ministered to his disciples; the washing of the feet in John's gospel is the most dramatic example of his role of service to his disciples. Still this concern for his own in no way lessened his ministry toward those outside his community of followers; his preaching, healing and love extended to everyone he encountered.

Body of Christ: Priest As Leader

As members of the body of Christ priests have received the Spirit incorporating them into the body and giving them charisms for the service of the Kingdom. What, then, differentiates the priest's ministry from that of other members of the body? Most agree that ministerial priesthood in the church implies a permanent office flowing from charism and formally recognized by the church: "In summary, the holder of an office in the Church would be (1) a person endowed by the Spirit, (2) with personal gifts (charisms), (3) called to a public and permanent ministry and this call is formally recognized by the Church" (*As One Who Serves*, 20). The fact that this office implies a role of leadership in the community is also agreed upon by the magisterium and by most theologians. Yet there remain theological disagreements on the relationship between the priest's role as head of the body (always with the bishop) to the body itself. The discussion is focused on a passage from *The Dogmatic Constitution on the Church* from Vatican II: "Though they differ from one another in essence and not only in degree, the common priesthood of the faithful and the ministerial or hierarchical priesthood are nonetheless interrelated. Each of them in its own special way is a participation in the one priesthood of Christ" (L.G., 10). Since this article is concerned primarily with the spirituality of priests as leaders of the body—an identity that is acknowledged by most—it does not seem necessary to treat the doctrinal disputes.

Christian spirituality flows from response to the Holy Spirit, the sanctifier. Priestly spirituality is simply the priest's effort to respond faithfully to the Spirit in living the priestly identity as defined by the church. The church teaches that ordination establishes the priest in three new, distinctive and permanent relationships: with Christ, with the church and with the world beyond the church. This identity today includes—for both diocesan as well as religious order priests—a call to observe the evangelical counsels. Since observing these counsels affects the living out of the three basic relationships, they must be discussed with them. It should be recalled again that this discussion focuses on those aspects of priestly spirituality that distinguish the priest as priest; it does not focus on aspects of spirituality common to all Christians through baptism.

Priest and Christ: Person-Symbol of Christ the Head of Body

Through ordination the priest is established in a new, distinctive and permanent relationship to Christ. The priest becomes the person-symbol of Christ in the church: priests receive an anointing of the Spirit that enable them to act in the name of Christ the head (P.O., 2). Thus priests are empowered to act *in persona Christi*. A document prepared for the American bishops makes the crucial observation that priests can be the person-symbol of Christ only because of their membership in the body of Christ: "It is only because of the Church that the priest can be said to act *in persona Christi*. He is called to be an effective sign and witness of the Church's faith in the reconciling Christ, who works through the Church and through the one whom the Church has sent to be the steward of its gifts and services" (*As One Who Serves*, 22). It is the body of Christ that is holy through the presence of the Spirit. Priests as head of this body are given the gift of the Spirit to act *in persona ecclesiae* and so also *in persona Christi*.

Through ordination the priest is established in a special relationship to Christ. As head of the body the priest becomes an "effective sign" or sacrament of Christ's authoritative presence in the church. All aspects of priestly spirituality flow from this relationship. Since it is the role of a symbol to make present what it represents, the priest is called by the church through ordination to make Christ present in all actions for the church. Consequently priestly ministry to the church must be done in a way that awakens faith within the community. This awakening of faith in others is possible only if the priest has a deep relationship personally with Christ. The biggest challenge of priestly spirituality is to become internally one with the Christ who is symbolized externally. To a great extent the effectiveness of priestly ministry flows from a heart transformed by the Spirit that ministers to others.

All Christians desiring to follow Christ fully are called to observe the evangelical counsels of poverty, chastity and obedience within their own state of life. The priest is no exception. However the priest's observance of the evangelical counsels is oriented toward conforming the priest more closely to Christ and so increasing effectiveness as the person-symbol of Christ. In the Latin rite of the Catholic church, the priest is called to celibacy and so to meet personal affective needs in ways consonant with the celibate state. Christ is the model of priestly celibacy in his relationships with the Father, his community and his apostolate. Above all the celibacy of Christ was founded on his relationship to his most dear Father, Abba. From within this intimate and often solitary presence before his Father, Christ's entire life flowed. Christ's relationship to the Father is the model for the priest's relationship to Christ. As Christ's heart flowed instinctively to the Father, so does the priest's heart flow to Christ and the Father. Love unites without obliterating personal distinctiveness. As Christ was able to say "The Father and I are one," and as Paul could say, "I live, now not I, but Christ lives in me," so the priest prays to become equally one with the Father and Jesus. By embracing celibacy the priest imitates Jesus in allowing sufferings of failure, loneliness and isolation to foster even deeper intimacy with God and with Jesus himself.

Christ is the model of priestly celibacy in his relationship to his community. He looked to certain of his apostles and disciples for the personal support he needed to sustain the failures and loneliness of his ministry. So Christ is the model for priests in developing deep human relationships, especially with fellow priests. Finally Christ's affectivity was also directed toward those he served.

We recall how Jesus wept over Jerusalem because he was not able to draw the chosen people of God to himself as a mother hen draws her chicks to herself. In embracing the vow of celibacy the priest strives to imitate Christ in each of these three dimensions of affectivity and so to become a more effective person-symbol of Christ as head of the body.

Priest and Church: Servant-Leader of Body

Through the anointing of the Spirit at ordination the priest is also established in a new, distinctive and permanent relationship to the church; the priest becomes the servant-leader of the church, the "effective sign" of Christ the head of the body. As the preeminent leader of the community the priest also acts *in persona ecclesiae*. This leadership of the body is marked by four functions essential for the community. The priest is called to serve the church by proclaiming the word of God, by presiding at worship, by pastoral care of the people of God and by facilitating the different charisms within the church. But the priest's leadership will take many differing forms depending on the talents of the priest and the needs of the community. The American bishops highlighted the importance of sensitivity to varying forms of priestly leadership with which the Spirit endows priests: "All priests are endowed by the Spirit in various ways to serve the People of God. These are forms of leadership.... The gifts differ and each must discern in the Spirit how he has been gifted. No one has all the gifts. Some seem to disappear in the history of the Church; some are transient even in the lives of priests" (*As One Who Serves*, 32).

Christ is the model for the priest's leadership of the church. Just as Jesus' love of the Father impelled him to live for the Father's Kingdom, so does the priest's love of Christ impel the priest to live for the body of Christ. The priest will, furthermore, exercise leadership in the same way Jesus exercised leadership—through service: "The Son of Man has not come to be served but to serve—to give his life in ransom for the many" (Mk 10:45). And through the special anointing of the Spirit in ordination Christ now stands with the priest empowering the priest to be an "effective sign" of Christ in all ministry to the church. Thus the priest can fulfill the vocation to be the sacramental symbol-person of Christ actually making Christ more present through his daily service to the church.

In a new way since Vatican II priests are being called to facilitate service and leadership of others within the church. The role has been compared to that of a conductor of an orchestra: "The conductor succeeds when he stimulates the best performance from each player and combines their individual efforts into a pattern of sound, achieving the vision of the composer. The best leader is one who can develop the talents of each staff person and coordinate all their efforts, so that they best complement each other and produce a superior collective effort" (*As One Who Serves*, 46). In facilitating ministry of others the priest is not unlike Christ who prepared the disciples and then sent them off on their own. The priest recognizes that the Spirit in baptism both incorporates members into the body and simultaneously gives them differing gifts of ministry for the body. Yet according to the above document the priest remains the one "in whom the mission of the Church, and therefore its ministry, finds focus and visibility" (34); thus the priest acts within the community preeminently *in persona ecclesiae*.

To enhance the priest's effectiveness as a person-symbol of Christ, the church calls the priest to evangelical obedience through the promise or vow of obedience to their bishops or religious superiors. This promise or vow of obedience places the priest in special union with the uni-versal church and so enhances the ability to act *in persona ecclesiae*. The priest symbolizes the unity of the entire church in Christ: the local parish, the diocese, the national church, the universal church. In addition the priest symbolizes the continuity of the church through the ages from the apostles and Peter to the present-day Roman Catholic church and the bishops and pope. It follows from this that the priest must fully own the position in the church given through ordination. And the priest must love the church and protect and defend it at every level. And while acknowledging the church's faults and foibles past and present, the priest still believes it is the privileged place of the Spirit's activity in this world for the Kingdom of God: "I for my part declare to you, you are "Rock," and on this rock I will build my church, and the jaws of death shall not prevail against it" (Mt 16:18).

The model for the priest's obedience is again Christ. Nothing stood between Christ and doing his Father's will. The priest's obedience is to God. The priest is convinced that the will of God is now revealed through the authoritative structures of the church. In obeying these structures the priest is obeying the Father. The priest's obedience to the bishop or religious superiors gives eloquent testimony to the belief that Christ continues to work through the ages within the authoritative structures of the church. By embracing the promise or vow of obedience the priest refuses to allow any personal desire not in accord with God's will as expressed through church superiors to determine actions. The sufferings of obedience to God's will are accepted and offered to the Father in the same manner as Christ's.

Priest and Society: Promoter of Justice in the World

Through ordination the priest is established in a new, distinctive and permanent relationship to Christ and to his church. Contained in this identity is a new relationship to the world beyond the church. Because the priest now acts *in persona ecclesiae* and *in persona Christi*, the priest becomes the preeminent witness of the church's and Christ's concern for the world. Recent church documents have put increasing emphasis on this aspect of the church's mission. The statement of the World Synod of Bishops in 1971 entitled *Justice in the World* is apt: " . . . action on behalf of justice and participation in the transformation of the world fully appear to us as a constitutive dimension of the preaching of the Gospel, or in other words, of the Church's mission."

The American bishops echo this thrust by presenting their description of priestly ministry under four co-equal divisions: to proclaim the word of God, to preside at worship, to serve the Christian community, to serve humankind. The last-named section begins as follows: "The Church is called to serve all of society: that is its mission and the hope of its ministry. While the priest may have a certain primary responsibility to the Catholic community which he serves, nonetheless he has been sent by Christ and the Church to all people who the larger community in which the parish community exists. The concern for all people gives reality to the presence of the risen Lord" (*As One Who Serves*, 50).

The priest has a double role in this ministry to humankind. As head of the body the priest is called to be personally engaged in actions on behalf of justice to witness to the church's concern. In addition the priest is called to facilitate action and leadership within the church for the transformation of society. Church teachings acknowledge that time constraints may limit the priest's personal involvement but also point out that the apostolate within society is also most appropriate for the laity: "The apostolate of the social milieu, that is, the effort to infuse a Christian spirit into the mentality, customs, laws and structures of the community in which a person lives is so much the duty and responsibility of the laity that it can never be properly performed by others. In this area the laity can exercise an apostolate of like towards like" (*Decree on the Apostolate of the Laity*, 33). In addition to working for justice throughout society, the priest is called to have special concern for the poor: "Although the presbyter has obligations towards all persons, he has the poor and the lowly entrusted to him in a special way. The Lord himself showed that he was united to them, and the fact that the Gospel was preached to them is mentioned as a sign of his messianic activity" (P.O., 6).

Again Christ is the model of the priest in this dimension of ministry. Jesus' concern for others was not limited to his immediate community of disciples. He continually extended himself beyond his followers to others. His entire ministry is marked with personal compassion for any person who came to him in need. In addition to his one-on-one concern for others Jesus also spoke out against society's injustices. At times the condemnation was marked by actual disobedience to laws when he viewed them as contradictory to the revelation he received from his Father. Indeed his criticism was so threatening to the establishment that it eventually precipitated his death. And finally the gospel reflects that Jesus had special care and concern for the poorest of the poor, the outcasts of society. The parable of the Last Judgment testifies to the centrality in Jesus' eyes of service to the hungry, thirsty, shelterless, imprisoned.

To enhance the priest's effectiveness as a witness of Christ, the church asks all priests to have special concern for evangelical poverty within their own priestly vocation, diocesan or religious. And again the model is Christ himself. Christ was poor. He let no material desire or possession come between himself and doing the Father's will. He was detached from possessions in order to be more free to serve. And Christ chose to live a simple lifestyle, perhaps to be more approachable by the poor or to witness to the sufficiency of the Father's providence for his material needs, taking his cue from the birds of the air and the lilies of the field. Through embracing evangelical poverty the priest refuses to allow any inordinate attachment to food, clothing, shelter, possessions to affect service of the Kingdom either within or outside the body of Christ. With this inner quality of heart the priest thus becomes an even more effective witness of Christ to the church and the world.

Conclusion

Through ordination priests receive an anointing of the Spirit that enables them to be so configured to Christ that they can act in the person of Christ the head. The priest then exists in a new, distinctive and permanent relationship to Christ, to the church and to society. The Holy Spirit stands behind priests enabling them to live this identity. In their relationship to Christ, the Spirit enables priests to be poor, celibate and obedient. In their relationship to the church, the Spirit enables priests to be effective servant-leaders in proclaiming the word of God, presiding at worship, caring for the pastoral needs of community and facilitating charisms of the community. In their relationship to society, the Spirit enables priests to be effective witnesses of Christ in promoting justice in the world and most especially in serving the poor both personally and in their leadership of the body of Christ. The challenge of priestly spirituality is to develop rhythms of living in tune with the Spirit so that the Spirit can indeed animate each aspect of priestly identity and transform the priest

into a truly effective person-symbol of Christ.

See **Body of Christ; Character, sacramental; Holy Spirit, gifts of the; Ministry; Orders, sacrament of; Presbyter; Priesthood; Sacraments; Lay spirituality; Symbol**

F. Moloney, *A Life of Promise* (Wilmington, 1984). N. Mitchell, *Mission and Ministry* (Wilmington, 1982). T. O'Meara, *Theology of Ministry* (New York, 1983). D. Power, *Gifts That Differ* (New York, 1980). P. Rosato, "Priesthood of the Baptized and Priesthood of the Ordained," *The Gregorianum* 68 (1987): 215-265. E. Schillebeeckx, *Ministry* (New York, 1981).

RICHARD J. HAUSER, S.J.

PSALMS AS LITURGICAL PRAYER

This article will consider the psalms under three headings: (a) the OT: the psalms in Israel's worship; (b) the psalms in the NT; and (c) the psalms in contemporary liturgy.

The OT: The Psalms in Israel's Worship
Yahweh the God of the Psalms. The OT psalms, outwardly like the liturgical poetry of Israel's neighbors, take their distinctiveness from the unique God they confess, "Yahweh alone." Unlike comparable religions, divine activity was not attributed to many deities. Yahweh shaped all and hence is at the center of every psalm.

Monotheism made Israel's worship distinctive. Yahweh, omnipotent and omniscient, did not need human beings' labor. Mesopotamian creation accounts, in contrast, uniformly depict human beings as slaves created to build palaces for the gods and to provide them with food, drink, and honor. OT texts emphasize the dignity and responsibility of human beings. Even in the Mesopotamian-influenced Genesis 2-3, the man is a dignified gardener, not a slave; God asks the man and the woman for their obedience, not their labor. Clearer still is Genesis 1 in which the human couple as the apex of creation encounter God. To the priestly source of Genesis 1 human beings are *animae naturaliter liturgicae*, i.e., part of the world and hearers of the divine word. "Humans are created in such a way that their very existence is intended to be their relationship to God" (C. Westermann, *Genesis 1-11*, Minneapolis, p. 158). Genesis 1 aptly prefaces the psalter as well as the pentateuch.

Monotheism also forbids images; no single being adequately represents the creator of all. In Israel's imageless worship the word is privileged: "You heard the sound of words, but saw no form; there was only a voice" (Deut 4:12). The words of the psalms thus bring Israel before the Lord in a special way.

The Temple and the King. The psalms are the "hymnbook of the second temple," and cannot be understood apart from the temple or palace of Yahweh. King David brought the venerable ark of the covenant to Jerusalem, making the city the central sanctuary of all the tribes (Psalm 132). The temple was actually built by David's son Solomon in the mid-10th century B.C.. Destroyed in the 6th-century exile and rebuilt later in the century (afterwards enlarged), it was the place of official worship until the Romans leveled it in A.D. 70.

The temple building was of modest size (90' x 30' and ca. 45' high) but of the finest materials and workmanship. It had three rooms, a porch (30' x 10'), a nave or main room (60' x 30'), and the holy of holies (a perfect cube of 30') where Yahweh was invisibly enthroned upon the ark. The people did not gather inside the temple as in a modern church or synagogue; it was exclusively the house of God. There God was fed and honored by his priests in ceremonies designed for a potentate. Some of the ceremonial was private, performed within God's house by the priests, e.g., the setting out of food and incense before God. The public ceremonies took place in the surrounding open-air court, which was considered part of the temple. The psalms were part of the public ceremonial.

Zion (the favorite psalm name for the temple site) is important because divine presence was conceived in spatial terms. Yahweh is in other places but preeminently present in Zion; only there is Israel "before Yahweh." In Zion Yahweh sits enthroned upon the cherubim to judge or rule, and meets Israel. Zion is the goal of the exodus-conquest and of the three annual feasts of pilgrimage. In a threatening universe it is the one secure place (Pss 46:2-3; 48:3; 76:3). The "Songs of Zion" (Psalms 46, 48, 76, 84, 87, 121, 122 and cf. 137) celebrate the city as the site of the victory over primordial enemies, as the residence of Yahweh and the Davidic king, and the place of divine decrees. In early Judaism Jews began the practice of turning toward Jerusalem in prayer (Dan 6:10; 9:21).

The king played a major role in the psalms since church and state were one; religion pervaded what is considered "secular" in contemporary society. The king was the instrument of God's governance. As son of God he ensured that his patron received due honor; he sponsored the liturgy and, in the early period, celebrated major feasts. Though in Israel royal power was tempered by an egalitarian tradition and the prophetic word, the king plays a major role in the psalms. Psalms 2 and 110 hymned his installation as king; Psalm 45 celebrated his marriage, and Psalm 72, his exemplary fertility. When the king led the army into battle, prayers were offered for him (Psalms 18, 21, and 144). When he returned victorious, the congregation was jubilant (Psalm 118). When he was defeated in battle, the congregation wept, reminding God that the Davidic king was as much a part of the universe as the heavens; his defeat called into question Yahweh's power and fidelity. The embellishments and hyperbolic language of the royal psalms ("court style") also characterize the royal poetry of neighboring cultures. When kings ceased in Israel after the 6th century B.C., people prayed the royal psalms for a future Davidic king. The process illustrates liturgical poetry becoming "text," i.e., lifted up from its immediate liturgical context to a new use. Since God is the author of the psalms, they are valid for new situations.

The Psalms in the Temple Liturgy. The OT gives almost no information on how the psalms functioned in the temple liturgy. Psalm superscriptions contain tantalizing allusions to liturgy, e.g., "for remembrance," "for the dedication of the temple," "according to Lilies (a melody?)," but scholars are nowhere near consensus on their meaning. Rituals concerning sacrifice such as those in Exodus 35-39 and Leviticus 1-16 do not mention accompanying psalms. Some scholars conclude that all sacrificial worship was in silence, with "no sound but the bleating of the sheep," but one cannot conclude absence from non-mention. The rituals direct the correct performance of sacrifice; they are not descriptions of the liturgy. In fact many psalms refer to liturgical action: feasts (Pss 65:1-4; 81:3; 118:26); visits to the temple (Pss 5:7; 23:6; 27:6; 53:9; 63:2; 65:4; 73:17; 84:2, 4; 95:2, 6; 100:4; 118:19-20; 132:7; 134; 135:2); processions (Pss 24:7-10; 42:4; 48:12-14; 68:24-27; 118:26-27; 122:1-2; 132:8); sacrifices (Pss 4:5; 5:3; 27:6; 50:14; 54:6; 66:13-15; 107:22; 116:17-18); oracles (Pss 2:6, 7-9; 12:5; 21:8-12; 60:6-8; 62:11-12; 81:5-16; 82:2-7; 91:14-16; 95:8-11; 108:7-9; 110:4); and priestly benedictions (Pss 115:14-15; 118:26; 128:5; 134:3). Many psalms explicitly mention a congregation (Psalms 20, 21, 45, 91, 110) and some presume two choirs or a choir and cantor (Psalms 15, 24, 118, 120, 122, 123, 131, 132, 134). Psalm verbs of human response—those translated "rejoice," "give thanks," "meditate," etc.—describe not the interior attitude but the exterior expression. They mean "shout joyously," "lift up your voice in praise," etc. Musical instruments are mentioned often: the trumpet (ram's horn, 4x), the *kinnôr*, a lyre generally accompanying the voice (13x), and the *nebel*, an angular harp or another kind of lyre (12x). Sirach 50 portrays the beauty and liveliness of temple worship ca. 180 B.C. The evidence thus points to popular, even noisy, performance of psalms.

The high points of the liturgical year were the three festivals of pilgrimage to the Jerusalem temple: Passover and Unleavened Bread in early spring; Pentecost at wheat harvest seven weeks later, and Ingathering (also called simply the Feast, or Booths) in early fall (Exod 23:14-17, 34:18-26; Lev 23:1-44; Deut 16:1-17). The first, Passover, especially commemorated the exodus from Egypt (Exodus 12-13). Hence psalms of the exodus-conquest, e.g., Psalms 23, 105, 114, 135, 136, and 147, were probably sung then. Psalms 113-118, called in early Judaism "the Great Hallel (praise)," were sung at Passover. The second feast, Pentecost (also called Firstfruits and the Feast of Weeks) had become for some Jewish groups a feast of the Law by the 2nd century B.C. and for mainstream Judaism by the 2nd century A.D. The connection to law-giving may be much earlier, however, since Exod 19:1 begins Israel's stay at the foot of Mount Sinai on "the third new moon" [= Pentecost]. Association with the Law would have made Pentecost an appropriate moment for the covenant renewal ceremonies of Psalms 50 and 81; they indict the people for violating the Sinai covenant and prepare them for repentance and re-commitment. The third and most important feast was Ingathering, a time of giving thanks for summer fruits and nuts. It was the feast of the New Year in the early period before Israel transferred the beginning of the year to the spring. At the New Year festival comparable religions enthroned their god as king after his creation victory over the forces of chaos. Whether Israel had a New Year enthronement for Yahweh is disputed. Some scholars believe it would have been contradictory for Yahweh, unique and omnipotent, to *become* king each year. Annual enthronement would have been possible, however, if Israel took Yahweh's becoming king through creation victory as renewal of kingship, with no implication he ever ceased being king. Enthronement, at any rate, provides a good context for psalms of kingship such as Psalms 47, 93, 95-100, and for psalms of Yahweh's cosmogonic victory such as Psalms 29, 46-48, 76, 93,95-99, 104.

Though many psalms celebrate public institutions and national events, most seem designed for individual or small group rites. The largest formal category (nearly one third of the psalms) is the individual lament, which strictly requires the presence of only the individual and the priest. "Songs of trust" such as Psalms 23, 27:1-6, and 91 are highly personal. "Meditations" like Psalms 49 and 73, which respond to troubling faith problems, do not demand a congregation. Evidently the temple offered worshippers a variety of rituals. Some were for the great public festivals involving the king and the national traditions. Others were for the individual or family: to complain of suffering or disorientation; to give thanks for a rescue; to receive counsel about a vexing problem.

The psalter, like a modern hymnal, embraced widely different types of liturgical poetry—old and new, national and private, formulaic and original. Small collections grew into larger ones until the Psalter of 150 psalms was formed, a process completed at the latest by the late 3rd century B.C., as the Septuagint psalter shows. The collections must have been preserved by the Jerusalem temple.

The rituals of the temple gradually shaped the religious practice of the common people. Temple activity became democratized. Daniel, the pious hero of the Book of Daniel (composed in the 3rd-2nd century B.C.), prays toward Jerusalem three times a day, in synchronization with the oblations in the temple (Dan 6:10; 9:21). The rabbis later declared that every Jew must pray twice daily (morning and afternoon), since prayer corresponded to the Tamid sacrifices and was no less obligatory than the Tamid itself. Passages in the psalms declaring that prayer is superior (Pss 40:6-9; 69:30-33; 51:16-17) or equal (Pss 119:108; 141:2) to the sacrificial cult are probably petitions to God to accept prayers that do not include sacrifice. Sirach (ca. 180 B.C.) equated right living with sacrificial worship: "The one who keeps the law makes many offerings; he who heeds the commandments sacrifices a peace offering" (Sir 35:1 and cf. vv. 2-11 and Rom 12:1). Most important, the psalms became a prayer book for the people.

Literary Analysis of Psalms as Liturgical Prayer. Even within the biblical period the psalms shifted from liturgical scripts to sacred texts, which can be analyzed literarily. Form-criticism particularly has been a successful method for studying the psalms. It is sensitive to the conventions of the poetry and to the dynamics of the main genres, especially laments, thanksgivings, and hymns. Since almost two-thirds of the psalms fall into these three categories, the method has proven to be efficient.

About twenty-five psalms are *hymns*: Psalms 8; 29; 33; 47; 92; 95-100; 104; 105; 107; 111; 113; 114; 117; 135; 136; 145; 146; 147; 148; 149. The hymn structure is simple: a call to worship, often with the addressees named, e.g., "Praise Yahweh, all you nations," and sometimes even the musical instruments ("praise him with trumpet voice"). The invitatory is often reprised in the last section.

The main section of the hymn, usually introduced by the preposition "for (*kî*)," gives the basis for praise; it is always what

Yahweh has done. Divine activity is distinguished by many commentators into "creation" and "history" (or "redemption") but the distinction is not a biblical one. Hymns describe the acts of God either from a heavenly (suprahistoric or mythic) perspective or from an earthly (historic) perspective; the perspectives actually shade into one another. In OT hymns God's action brings into being or protects a human community, which is often depicted with its own land, tradition (legal and narrative), king, and God (Psalms 33, 66, 100, 111, 113, 114, 117, 135, 136, 145, 146, 147, 149). Hymns invite human worshippers to praise God's act of creating or governing and hence enhance God's glory on earth.

The verbs frequent in the hymns merit discussion—"to praise" and "to bless." The Hebrew verb commonly translated "to praise" is *hallēl* (Greek *ainô*); it occurs in the English word "hallelujah," lit., "Praise Yah[weh]!" Its non-religious usage clarifies its psalmic use; the princes of Pharaoh praise Sarah for her beauty (Gen 12:15); Tyre is a city praised for its wealth (Ezek 26:17); one should not praise oneself but leave that to others (Prov 27:2). To praise therefore means to acknowledge and make public the worth or virtue of someone or something. Usually a group rather than an individual is the subject of the verb. In the psalms God is the object of praise and the temple is where praise is given. "To praise" is sometimes paralleled by "to sing," "to make melody," "to tell," "to thank," and sometimes modified by "with dancing" and "with music"; the verb describes a forceful public act.

Hebrew *bĕrak* "to bless" (Greek *eulogein*) is occasionally a synonym for "to praise" (when paired with it as in Pss 34:2 and 145:2) but has its own nuance. God's blessing brings humans increase (typically children, sometimes wealth and land) and general enhancement of life. Humans' blessing God does not of course increase or enhance the divine splendor. Rather humans acknowledge before others benefits received, thus widening the circle of God's admirers. The phrase "Blessed be Yahweh" is regularly followed by a complementary relative clause describing the benefit ("who did thus and so," e.g., Gen 14:20; cf. Ps 103:1-5). The whole is a statement about God rather than a speech made to him, and is intended for others to hear. God has done a good deed for the speaker, who now returns the favor by making God's glory known on earth.

The *individual lament* is the most frequent psalm genre (Psalms 3, 4, 5, 6, 7, 9-10, 13, 14, 17, 22, 25, 26, 27: 7-14, 28, 31, 35, 36, 38, 39, 41, 42-43, 51, 52, 53, 54, 55, 56, 57, 59, 61, 63, 64, 69, 70, 71, 77, 86, 88, 102, 109, 120, 130, 139, 140, 141, 142, 143). Scholars generally assume its situation in life (*sitz im leben*) is a transaction between an individual sufferer and a priest of the temple staff, something like that recorded between the priest Eli and Hannah at Shiloh, the predecessor of the Jerusalem sanctuary, in 1 Sam 1:9-18. Hannah goes to the Shiloh to lament a private grief (she is barren and despised by the second wife), speaks with the priest Eli who tells her, "Go in peace, and the God of Israel grant your petition which you have made to him" (1 Sam 1:17). It is now generally recognized that individual laments are deliberately non-specific and stereotyped so that they can serve as prayers for any sufferer.

The genre of individual lament has fixed parts in a flexible sequence. The person lamenting typically begins with a direct and unadorned *cry* to Yahweh, "Yahweh, help!" The *complaint* is a vivid description of the affliction, e.g., sickness, unfair legal process, treachery of former friends, or the consequences of sin such as ostracism or the ridicule by one's enemies. Nearly always there is a *statement of trust*, which the psalmist manages to utter in spite of the troubles, "The promises of Yahweh are promises that are pure" (Ps 12:6). The *petition* prays for rescue and sometimes for the downfall of the enemy. Scholars generally assume that a priest spoke a *word of assurance* to the lamenter; it was not transmitted with the psalm (Pss 12:5 and 60:6-8 are the exceptions) because it was apparently considered the priest's part. Finally there was a *statement of praise* in striking contrast to the turmoil of the rest; the psalmist states the intention to live according to the word of assurance just delivered by the priest.

The lament dramatizes the sufferer's plight in order to persuade God to intervene. There are three actors—God, the psalmist and "the wicked." The appeal is to God's *noblesse oblige*: Will you, just God, allow me, innocent and poor, to be vanquished by the wicked? God's word of assurance functions like a judicial verdict; it affirms that Yahweh does not allow evil to triumph ultimately and will vindicate the poor person. In the vow of praise the psalmist promises to live in the hope that God will act. The rite of individual lament enables the sufferer to make a devastating experience into a healing encounter with the just and merciful God. The details of the ritual are not known, but it presumably took place in the temple precincts.

The *communal lament* (Psalms 44, 60, 74, 77, 79, 80, 83, 85, 89, 90, 94, 123, 126) is a complaint by the community that Yahweh has abandoned them to destruction. In some (Psalms 44, 60, 74, 77, 80, 89), the people "remember" the event that brought them into existence (e.g., transplanting a vine from Egypt to Canaan; defeating sea and installing leaders in the new land). They thus pose the question to Yahweh: will you allow another power to destroy what you once created? The Hebrew word "remember" (*zākar*, Greek [*ana*]*mimnēskesthai*), important in these psalms, does not mean suddenly to bring to mind something

forgotten, but to recite publicly, to make the event verbally present before God and the community. Psalm 77 illustrates the psalmist's recital of the originating event in the face of threat: "Has [God's] steadfast love forever ceased? Are his promises at an end for all time?. . . I will remember the deeds of Yahweh, I will remember your ancient deed. I will recite all your works, I will speak of your actions" (vv. 8, 11-12).

The *individual thanksgiving* (Psalms 18, 21, 30, 32, 34, 40:1-11, 92, 108, 116, 118, 138) is closely allied to the individual lament; the psalmist reports the rescue from the hands of the wicked. The speaker acknowledges before the community what God has done for me. Like the hymn and lament, it is modeled on a social transaction: you have done me a good turn by your rescue and now I return the favor by enlarging the circle of your admirers and worshippers. The chief Hebrew word for "to give thanks" is *hôdû* (Greek *exomologein*). In a few specialized contexts it means "to confess (sin)" but ordinarily is translated "to give thanks." The translation "to give thanks" is misleading since there is no exact Hebrew equivalent to the modern idiom "to say thank you." Biblical thanksgiving is illustrated by Jacob's wife, Leah: scorned by her sister and neglected by her husband, her prayer is finally answered by a fourth son. She "says thank you" by giving praise: "This time I will praise (*'ôdeh*) Yahweh" (Gen 29:35). What evokes the vow of praise in both communal and individual laments is the same—a threat to life. As verbs paired with it show, praise involves intense emotion—exultation, singing and playing, "glorifying." The one giving thanks/ praising involves others in the act, which always has God as its exclusive object. Praise is also associated with life; only the living can praise God (Isa 38:19; Pss 30:10, 88:11).

The Psalms in the NT

In the post-exilic period, at least by the 4th century B.C., the psalms had become sacred texts and part of the Bible. Psalm parts could be rearranged into new wholes by the Chronicler (1 Chron 16:8-36; 2 Chron 7:41-42). This "anthological style" (A. Robert) reflects a silver-age mentality. Conscious of the Spirit's absence, early Judaism used or reworked writings of the earlier Spirit-filled golden age. The NT church took from Judaism the anthological style of psalm composition but differed in believing the new age of the Spirit had come.

Jewish Christians of the NT period accepted the Hebrew psalms for worship, discovering in traditional words like "messiah," "salvation," and "son of God" new meanings appropriate to the age of the Messiah (Lk 24:44). Jesus himself most probably prayed the psalms in Hebrew, though his everyday language was Aramaic. Early Christian worship developed from Jewish liturgy, which made use of psalms: "Now Peter and John were going up to the temple at the hour of prayer, the ninth hour" (Acts 3:1). 1 Cor 14:26 suggests that psalms in Christian liturgies had a teaching function, natural enough in a new religion: "When you come together, each one has a psalm, a lesson, a revelation, a tongue, or an interpretation. Let all things be done for edification." Eph 5:19-20 and Col 3:16 emphasize the traditional celebrative function of psalms in worship. "Psalms" in these passages may mean a free and highly personal composition like the lengthy thanksgiving hymns from Qumran, an anthological composition like the hymns in Luke or Revelation, or a catena of traditional psalm verses. Early apologists made use of psalms in controversies to demonstrate that Jesus was the messiah and king and that his sufferings were divinely intended; Psalms 2, 22, 69, 110, and 118 were special favorites. Ps 2:6-11 is an example of an early Christian hymn of Christ's death and resurrection.

Original psalm compositions in the NT are largely confined to two books—Luke and Revelation. Luke 1-2 with its Magnificat (1:46-55), Benedictus (1:68-79), and Nunc Dimittis (2:29-32), takes phrases and verses from the Septuagint, reassembling them for their associations and references. Classic parallelism is softened.

The largest collection of NT psalms comes from the book with a keen sense of a new prophetic age—Revelation (Apocalypse). "Blessed is he who reads aloud the words of the prophecy" (1:3); "He who has an ear, let him hear what the Spirit says to the churches" (2:7). The hymns are sung to the Lord who has done *the* great deed of liberation and salvation: the defeat of evil through the victory of the cross (4:11; 5:9-10; 7:15-17; 11:17-18; 15:3-4; 16:5-6; 19:6-8).

The Psalms in Contemporary Liturgy

The Authority of the Psalms. Jews and Christians value the psalms as the privileged human response to God's mighty acts and employ them in worship today. Because Christians differ from Jews in believing that the God of the psalter is the God of Jesus Christ, and that the psalter celebrates Christ's work, its authority for them is distinctive. That authority is three-fold.

(a) The authority of the psalms comes from their being the word of God, scripture. They thus transcend their original situation and become texts for new environments. The NT depicts Christ doing what Yahweh did in the OT. Psalms praising Yahweh therefore praise Christ; the NT gives him the title "the Lord" (*ho kyrios*) from the Septuagint. "Salvation," "victory," "righteousness"—words frequent in the psalter—refer to what Christ has done.

The psalter, part of "the scriptures," was especially authoritative for the new church; of OT texts only Isaiah is cited more frequently by the NT. As scripture the psalms validated Jesus as the messiah foreordained to suffer (Pss 22; 69; 41:9) and as the universal king.

(b) The psalms impose themselves upon readers like any classic text. Divine inspiration has taken away nothing from their human authors' spontaneity, depth of feeling, and artistry. They explore and record the full range of human responses to God and express them with memorable artistry. Every emotion, positive or negative—exultation, grief, rage—is turned into prayer. The psalms liberate those who pray them, bringing people before God as they are. Images and phrases of the psalter have entered the language to shape people's images of themselves before God: "Out of the depths I cry to thee, O Lord, Lord, hear my voice"; "The Lord is my shepherd, I shall not want: he makes me lie down in green pastures"; "Even the sparrow finds a home, the swallow, a nest for herself, . . . at thy altars, O Lord of hosts." Like the Our Father in the NT, the psalms pray and teach how to pray.

(c) The psalms are venerable and universal. They have been the prayer of Israel for 3,000 years and Christians joined in that prayer from the earliest period. The psalms are recited worldwide by Christians of all denominations; the divine office is a practice of the universal church. The Christian thus prays the psalms with countless others and feels united with the church in prayer.

Recent Liturgical Reforms. In recent years, especially since the Second Vatican Council, the Roman Catholic church has reformed the use of the psalms in its liturgy. Mass propers now have a wide variety of psalms: the entrance hymn (usually only a single verse), the response to the first reading, and the communion verse (again a single verse). The responsorial psalms are generally chosen for a few key verses rather than for the internal logic of the whole psalm. The one-verse entrance and communion "hymns" do little more than mention a theme.

The divine office has been reformed so that all 150 psalms are recited each month. A brief title and quotation (biblical or patristic) has been prefaced to each psalm to help the reader understand the often difficult logic of the psalm. A satisfactory English translation of the psalms is an urgent *desideratum.* A good translation must be accurate, retain as far as possible biblical imagery and even idioms, and respect the strophic structure of each psalm.

Difficulties in Praying the Psalms. Hallowed as the psalms are, many Christians find it difficult to pray them in the liturgy. Catechesis on the psalms as Christian prayer was recommended by the Apostolic Constitution and General Instruction on the Divine Office of Paul VI in 1970. Christian catechesis might deal with the following difficulties.

(a) The chief difficulty is theological, arising from the psalms as OT texts. How can texts originally performed before Yahweh in the Jerusalem temple liturgy be performed by the church of Christ? The question is part of a larger question—the relation of Christianity and Judaism. Christian theology is only beginning to work out a satisfactory answer to this fundamental relationship.

The church does not replace Judaism but is graciously brought within its sphere: "you, a wild olive shoot, were grafted in their place to share the richness of the olive tree" (Rom 11:17). "New" in NT does not mean new as if nothing existed before but new as divinely rebuilt and renewed. The covenant humans broke is the covenant God remade. The scriptures of the first covenant retain their meaning precisely because God is their author. The OT is thus not simply cast aside. New depths can be found in old words. God's victory that brings a world and people into being, God's king who rules that people, God's salvation that rescues that people—these psalmic themes can be sung today but with a clearer awareness of who God is and who the people are.

(b) A second difficulty is that the psalms are oriental poetry. To the English apologist C.S. Lewis, divine providence insured that the most distinctive feature of Hebrew poetry—synonymity of verses ("parallelism")—translates perfectly into any language: "Yahweh reigns; let the peoples tremble! Yahweh sits enthroned upon the cherubim; let the earth quake!" (Ps 99:1). Every line is repeated with slight variation, making a statement by dramatic interplay of verses, providing the redundancy necessary for aural comprehension. Westerners, literate and precise, need to appreciate what parallelism and other poetic techniques (e.g., chiasm, reprise, word-play) add to biblical prayer.

Psalmic poetry has its own logic, which is often difficult to discover in the course of recital. Sometimes the logic is discovered through refrains (Psalms 42-43; 67:3, 5; 99:5, 9), sometimes through parallelism of scenes (Ps 78:12-39; 40-72), sometimes through extrinsic acrostic structure, i.e., beginning successive verses with the letters of the Hebrew alphabet. The quickest route to the logic of a psalm is through form criticism (cf. above). Most psalms fall into three genres— lament, hymn, or thanksgiving—and are ruled by the genre conventions. If one correctly identifies the genre, one will know what to expect of the psalm. The logic is often in the interplay between reader expectation and this psalm's statement.

(c) Vindictive psalms are difficult especially for Christians who view Christianity as utterly gentle and concerned primarily with the individual soul. "May the Lord cut off all flattering lips!" (Ps 12:3) is invoked against God's (and the psalmist's) enemies. Another psalm has no less than fourteen curses against

enemies, among them, "May his children be fatherless, and his wife a widow!" (Ps 109:8-9). Most notorious is the curse against Babylon: "Happy shall be the one who takes your little ones and dashes them against the rock!" (Ps 137:9). The modern reader needs to recall that such psalms pray the just God to redress a here-and-now wrong; God's power and glory would otherwise remain invisible. The psalms glow with zeal against every injustice disfiguring God's world. That zeal is expressed by the psalmists, who think in a non-abstractive manner, as the elimination of unjust people, including their potential for living on in their children (cf. "their little ones" of Psalm 137). The Christian "hungering and thirsting for divine justice" (Mt 5:6) can pray these psalms (at least in private) by leaving everything—execution and time-table—in God's hands.

(d) Another difficulty for modern readers is the frequent recitals of Israel's history in the psalms. Some are largely detailed retellings of Israel's history, e.g., 78, 105, 106, 135, 136. Others allude constantly to individual historical events. The psalms presuppose the reader knows the history well and finds it fascinating.

Moderns must recognize that Israel encountered God not only in "nature" but also in the events of their history. Decisive moments of that history—the journey from Egypt to Canaan, the law giving at Sinai, key battles, the words of leaders—were intensely revelatory for the people. They delighted in their active God and treasured the memory of his interventions, which they handed on in a variety of versions. Like other ancient Near Eastern peoples, they accepted multiple versions of the same event; meaning was conveyed through narrative details and narratives were not seen as "historical" in a modern objective sense. Events of their history are thus sacramental in that they reveal God within the world. Christians are heirs to that history and should learn its main details. Much of the history is essentially the exodus and conquest and can be learned quickly.

See **Jewish worship; Jewish roots of Christian worship; Prayer, types of, in the liturgy**

B.W. Anderson, *Out of the Depths: The Psalms Speak to Us Today* rev. ed. (Philadelphia: Westminster, 1983). E. Beaucamp, "Psaumes, II, Le Psautier: Origine cultuelle," *Dictionnarie de la Bible, Supplément* (Paris: Letouzey, 1979), cols. 132-157. H.-J. Kraus, *Worship in Israel: A Cultic History of the Old Testament* (Richmond: Knox, 1966; German original 1962). R.F. Taft, *The Liturgy of the Hours in East and West: the Origins of the Divine Office and Its Meaning for Today* (Collegeville: Liturgical Press, 1985). N.M. Sarna, "The Psalm Superscription and the Guilds," *Studies in Jewish Religious and Intellectual History* (Altman Volume) (Univ. of Alabama, 1979): 281-300. S. Mowinckel, *The Psalms in Israel's Worship*, 2 vols. (New York, Abingdon: 1967). M. Shepherd, *The Psalms in Christian Worship: A Practical Guide* (Minneapolis: Augsburg, 1976).

RICHARD J. CLIFFORD, S.J.

R

RECONCILIATION

Reconciliation is one of the key words used by Christians to name the life and mission of Jesus Christ: "... and I, when I am lifted up from the earth, will draw all men to myself" (Jn 12:32); "God was in Christ reconciling the world to himself..."(2 Cor 5:19). It names as well the mission given to the church: "...entrusting to us the message of reconciliation..." (2 Cor 5:19). In an early eucharistic prayer text it appears as the primary request: "... so gather your church..." (*Didache*). And it is used to name that special sacrament of the church which is also entitled: of forgiveness, of confession, of penance. See entries below; also, Eucharist; Penance; Forgiveness, theology of.

RECONCILIATION AND CHILDREN

See **Children, first penance and**

RECONCILIATION AND PRIESTHOOD

Reconciliation is an achievement, a process, and a goal in the life of the human community. It suggests the divisions and hostilities found among nations and peoples, within societies and families, between people and their environment, and even within each person.

Priesthood, on the other hand, is a term that has meaning only within a religious frame of reference. Usually concerned with mediation or sacrifice, the term priesthood can assume a variety of meanings and is sometimes used in analogous or extended senses. To associate reconciliation with priesthood is to suggest that alienation and reconciliation pertain to humanity's relationship with God and that priesthood concerns some of the most decisive events in human life.

For the Roman Catholic tradition, reconciliation and priesthood are to be understood only in light of Jesus Christ and God's work in him. In Christ, God created the human family with one purpose in view: that each person should freely accept a share in eternal life and communion with the triune God (L.G., 2-3). This creative purpose established unity and peace as a perfection proper to human life (Eph 1:3-10; G.S., 24-32).

Rather than accept God's dominion in their lives, human beings have chosen to live in ways that declare their independence from God and his life-giving purpose. This causes alienation from God and accounts for the evil and hostility found in human life (Genesis 3; John Paul II, 14-15). These effects lead to new rejections of God in an ongoing process that enmeshes all people (Rom 3:9, 5:12; G.S., 13, 37). The term "sin" can refer to the cause, state, or results of this complex condition of evil and alienation.

Given this state of affairs, reconciliation necessarily requires the overcoming of sin by means of repentance and forgiveness, and ultimately by an inner transformation that eliminates the tendency to sin and alienation (Jer 31:33; Ezek 36: 25-28; Ps 51:10). This could be accomplished only by God's special intervention, which took place through the incarnation of Jesus Christ. Because he was fully divine and fully human, Jesus was uniquely able to mediate between and draw together God and the human family. By his suffering, death, and resurrection, Jesus reconciled us to God and made possible the forgiveness of our sins and the hope of a human life marked by justice, peace, and unity (Rom 5:1-11; Col 1:19-22; 2 Cor 5:18-19; G.S., 22, 38-39).

Although there is no question as to who Jesus was or the reconciliation he accomplished, the NT seldom uses the terms mediator or priest in speaking of him. The principal exception is the epistle to the Hebrews which seeks to understand Jesus and his work in light of the Israelite priesthood and especially that of Melchizedek. This epistle and the background it assumes made it inevitable that later generations would also view Jesus Christ as priest of the new dispensation and consider his work as uniquely priestly.

Jesus Christ and his work of reconciliation were unique and effective for all people and all times (1 Tm 2:5). Even so he required the service of others to extend the fruits of his reconciliation to people in every age and place (Mt 28:18-20; Mk 16:15-16; Lk 24:47-49; Jn 20:21-23). Until the work of Christ is brought to its final perfection, sin and alienation remain urgent problems in human life. Christ relies on apostles and others to call people to repentance, forgiveness, and reconciliation. Required by Christ's explicit mandate, this missionary apostolate is an essential part of the life and ministry of the church (L.G., 17; Paul VI, *On Evangelization in the Modern World*,

esp. 14-16). Members of the church must confront all forms of alienation and work to remedy them by preaching forgiveness and witnessing reconciliation (A.G., 1-4). A preferential option for the poor, peacemaking between adversaries, teaching and interpreting the signs of the times, care for the sick and dying, giving hospitality to the homeless, and especially work on behalf of justice and peace are important aspects of the missionary apostolate.

These activities are important and called for on their own terms. They must also interpret the meaning of human alienation and evil and point toward the reconciliation with God in Christ that all people need and are called to share. This witness will be credible only to the degree the church shows forth a convincing example of reconciliation in its own life (A.G., 5-6, 11-12; Paul VI, *On Evangelization*, 77).

As the reconciliation with God Jesus Christ won for us is progressively shared with more and more people through the ministries of word and forgiveness, a visible community of reconciled people is assembled, the church (Eph 2:11-22; L.G., 9, 19). The church has an intimate relationship to Christ, whose life and power it shares (Acts 1:8, 2:1-4; 1 Cor 3:16, 12:27; L.G., 7-8). The church increases as the preaching of the gospel prompts its hearers to repentance, faith, and a request for baptism. In baptism their past sins are forgiven and they begin to share in the church's reconciled life (Acts 2:22-41; Rom 6:3-11). In this context, baptism counts as the primary sacrament of reconciliation.

The church's supreme act of worship is the eucharist. Nourished by the word, the ecclesial assembly celebrates in sacrament the mystery of Christ's passion, death, and resurrection. From this mystery the church draws its life and unity. At the eucharist, the church most intensely realizes itself as a reconciled community, a priestly people who offers God the sacrifice of a holy life (1 Pet 2:5,9). From the perspective of the church's life, the eucharist is the sacrament of its reconciliation, its communion with God in Christ (L.G., 11; S.C., 6).

The eucharist sets the standard for the church's life. The church must always hold itself accountable to the demands associated with its reconciliation. This requires that serious failures and divisions in the church must be prevented and promptly addressed when they occur. Every effort must be made to assure that justice and peace characterize relationships within the church. Its own integrity and the credibility of its witness and preaching are at stake (John Paul II, 9).

The church's eucharistic life is decisive in its response to the various ways its members fail to live up to the demands of ecclesial reconciliation. A crisis occurs when a member of the church insists on living in a way that means abandonment of the commitments undertaken in baptism and inherent in the eucharistic life of the church. This kind of failure simultaneously involves the offender's personal responsibility, alienation from the church and its eucharistic life, and a turning away from God. Since it brings spiritual death to the offender, such a posture constitutes the act and condition of mortal sin. Though it is sometimes hard to judge when spiritual death has actually occurred, this event involves crisis for the church as well as the offender (John Paul II, 17).

Because this case involves alienation or re-alienation from God and the church, the offender's position is analogous to that of one as yet unconverted and unbaptized. Reconciliation is urgently needed. The process required to bring this about takes account of many factors, notably the nature of the offense, the disposition of the offender and the adequacy of the repentance shown, and the requirements of the ecclesial community. Reconciliation normally involves a cooperative effort by the repentant offender and an authorized minister of the church; it is another evidence of the faithful love of Christ and the church (International Theological Commission [ITC], III.4-5; John Paul II, 31).

Because of practical need and the essentially ecclesial and public nature of reconciliation, the church soon developed liturgical rites and legal norms for the reconciliation of its alienated members. This process, which has taken different forms in the history of the church, is sacramental in nature. Reconciliation reaches its perfection when the forgiven brother or sister reassumes full participation in the eucharist.

Very different is the case of one who is responsible only for those minor failures that are inevitable in the course of daily life. With contrition, these faults can be overcome by means of prayer, sincere acts of repentance and charity, and the support of the community. Tradition refers to such faults as forgivable or venial sins. They are negative factors in the lives of individuals and the community. But since they do not constitute a posture of turning away from Christ and the church, the believer's participation in the eucharistic life of the church continues uninterrupted and is a powerful means of inspiring and strengthening repentance (ITC, IV.b.1; John Paul II, 17, 31).

People aware of only venial failings may also avail themselves of sacramental penance as part of their effort to live the church's life of grace, repentance, and reconciliation more fully. Their use of this sacrament is devotional and not obligatory. In these cases the sacrament does not effect reconciliation since the penitent was not alienated by mortal sin.

The mandate of Christ and the life and integrity of the church require many ministries and services. Certain of these are so important that they were quickly assimilated to specific offices, especially those of bishop, presbyter, and deacon (1 Tm 3:1,8, 5:17). The exact nature of these offices and their relationship to other services and ministries in the early church are not always clear. During the 2nd century, however, the bishop emerged as the authoritative figure in the local church. He was responsible for the church's overall well-being and especially its fidelity to the apostolic tradition. The bishop alone presided by right at the eucharist and in the process by which alienated members were reconciled to the church. Particularly when increased numbers made this necessary, the bishop confided these responsibilities to presbyters who acted with the bishop's authority.

The bishop's pre-eminent position in the local church, and especially his presidency at the eucharist, set the stage for a new development. During the 2nd century the concept of priesthood began to be applied to the bishop and his ministry. This usage was analogous and developed in light of the levitical priesthood, the sacrificial aspects of Christ's passion and death, and the epistle to the Hebrews. Only several centuries later was the term priest generally applied to presbyters as well, and with due recognition of their subordinate position (Congar, 136-43).

During the scholastic period the notion of a priesthood common to bishops and presbyters began to overshadow the distinctions rooted in their respective positions in the church. The ordination of a presbyter came to be seen as a priestly ordination, one that conferred sacred powers, particularly with respect to the sacraments of eucharist and penance. The identification of bishops and presbyters as priests became a settled point in the Catholic tradition (Congar, 138-39; L.G., 21, 28).

The priestly nature of the ministries of bishops and presbyters has been a significant factor in the discussion of the priestly nature of the church as a whole, especially the common priesthood of the laity. That the church is priestly is clear from the NT (1 Pet 2:5,9; Rev 1:6, 5:10). Vatican II however taught that the common priesthood of the faithful and the hierarchical priesthood "differ from one another in essence and not only in degree" (L.G., 10). Whether the general priesthood properly relates to specific liturgical and apostolic activities or simply to the living of a holy life by the community of the baptized is a point on which there is disagreement.

How Christ's one priesthood is shared by the church and by persons in the church and what this means in practice are important questions. While these issues are pursued, Christ and his paschal mystery must be kept central to both theology and praxis. The eucharist and its normative function in the life of the church will also need to be given due priority. This is essential for the church's domestic life and its mission to evangelize those not yet reconciled to God in Christ.

See **Reconciliation, liturgies of**

Yves M.-J. Congar, *Lay People in the Church: A Study for a Theology of the Laity* (Westminster, MD: Newman Press, 1957). International Theological Commission, "Penance and Reconciliation," *Origins* 13 (1983-84): 513, 515-24. John Paul II, "Apostolic Exhortation on Penance and Reconciliation," *Origins* 14 (1984-85): 432, 434-57. J.M.R. Tillard, "The Ordained 'Ministry' and the 'Priesthood' of Christ," *One in Christ* 14 (1978): 231-46.

WALTER J. WOODS

RECONCILIATION AND SPIRITUAL DIRECTION

When the Second Vatican Council refocused the sacrament dealing specifically with the forgiveness of sin, the emphasis moved from the official name *penance* (and from the popular name, emphasizing *confession*) to the more ancient and biblical tradition of *reconciliation*. Reconciliation stresses the initiative of God and our human response to a call of conversion within the community of faith.

Reconciliation and the Sacrament

Following the tradition of both the OT and NT scriptures, the early church used the terminology of *reconciliation* for both the renewed relationship of the newly baptized with God and the one-time-only forgiveness of the Christian who had seriously ruptured the baptismal relationship with God and with the community. The strength of this understanding lies in its viewing one's relationship with God in the context of the ecclesial community. By the end of the 6th century this public penance form was slowly replaced by the "tariff" penitential form made popular by the Irish monks evangelizing Europe. The strength of this penitential form was in its emphasis on ongoing conversion through more frequent confession of one's sins as well as through the directives for a penance (the analogous "tariff" or "tax" idea from a secular judicial system) which embodied the first corrective steps away from a person's particular sinful behavior.

In the theological development of the sacrament of penance, particularly through the Scholasticism of the 13th century and its subsequent pastoral implementation, we see a greater emphasis on the *absolving* power of the priest-minister of the sacrament, with less acknowledgement of the community or ecclesial context. The Council of Trent in the 16th century, reacting to the proposals of the Reformers, even more tightly defined the sacrament of penance within a judicial forum, with the priest as judge, speaking out God's forgiveness and assigning an appropriate sentence for wrong committed by an individual penitent. It was this practice which needed to be updated as decreed by the Fathers of the Second Vatican Council so that "both the nature and the effect of the sacrament" (S.C., 72) might become more luminous for all Christians.

Reconciliation and Direction

In emphasizing more reconciliation as the foundational understanding and practice of this sacrament of Christ's forgiveness, the church once again stressed certain aspects which relate this sacrament to a Christian ministry called *spiritual direction*. Although spiritual direction can take on various forms, we need to consider only the personal spiritual direction form in order to make comparison with the one-to-one nature of the sacrament. Personal spiritual direction can be described as the help one Christian gives to another in the ongoing development of one's relationship with God in Christ and in one's continuing involvement in Jesus' mission.

The emphasis in our understanding of spiritual direction focuses on our Christian growth and development. Yet overcoming what have been our failings and what holds us back is obviously a necessary part of human spiritual growth. The spiritual direction process, then, touches into areas of our human lives requiring reconciliation, although this aspect would not be its primary focus. Within the spiritual direction process, true reconciliation with God may be effected by the grace of God abundantly bestowed upon the person in direction. But wonderful as this moment of reconciliation is, the context of the spiritual direction session is ordinarily limited to the individual's relationship with God. By contrast, the renewed understanding of the sacrament of reconciliation allows us to grasp more fully the necessity for a Christian to enter into the sacramental action of Christ and his church not only to effect but also to celebrate a reconciliation which is at the same time with God and with the ecclesial community.

The ministry of spiritual direction ordinarily involves two people over some period of time. Spiritual direction, then, looks to a process of spiritual growth, with all the usual human patterns of setbacks and accelerated growth times, consolations and desolations, and often apparently long periods of aridity or a "walking in the darkness of faith." In celebrating the sacrament of reconciliation, the church once again calls our attention to the ongoing nature of Christian conversion. There is no one magic moment in a sacramental celebration which effects a total change in one's behavior patterns. The priest-minister of the sacrament needs to enter into a kind of spiritual direction relationship in order to dialogue with the penitent about pursuing effective means for personal spiritual growth. The sacramental forum, even in a face-to-face situation, often suffers from time constraints for more in-depth dialogue sessions as well as from the relational rapport presumed in the personal spiritual direction context. As a result, the current rite of reconciliation more clearly highlights the continuing need for spiritual direction as a distinct ministry, alongside of and in cooperation with the sacrament.

The way in which the priest-minister in the sacrament of reconciliation is meant to interact with the penitent invites comparison with the role of the spiritual director and the one being directed. In the present-day ritual of the sacrament the priest is not a functionary dispensing absolution, but rather shares in the penitential healing moment with the scripture readings, dialogue, and prayers spoken in conjunction with the penitent. There is a similarity here with the traditional role of the spiritual director who is always a participant in the spiritual life-journey of the one being directed. The role of the priest-minister of the sacrament and the minister (lay, religious, or priest) of spiritual direction appears more significantly parallel in terms of mutual participation and sharing.

Just as the early church was beginning to lose the central focus of reconciliation in its penitential practice, pseudo-Dionysius in a famous letter to Demophile described two sorts of confessions: 1) accusations of sin so as to obtain forgiveness; and 2) manifestation of thoughts so as to receive direction.

Since the Second Vatican Council, reconciliation as a sacrament is once again the direct focus for the first kind of human "confession." In its wider sense reconciliation, a healing and developmental grace of the sacrament, and reconciliation, one aspect of spiritual growth fostered in direction, together look to the second kind of "confession" named by pseudo-Dionysius.

See **Reconciliation, liturgies of; Spiritual direction and liturgy**

David L. Fleming, s.j., ed., *The Christian Ministry of Spiritual Direction* (St. Louis: Review for Religious, 1988). Richard M. Gula, s.s., *To Walk Together Again. The Sacrament of Reconciliation* (New York: Paulist, 1984). Robert J. Kennedy (ed.), *Reconciliation: The Continuing Agenda* (Collegeville, MN: The Liturgical Press, 1987).

DAVID L. FLEMING, S.J.

RECONCILIATION AND THERAPY

In their history of pastoral care originally published in 1964 Clebsch and Jaeckle make this startling statement: "There is no place in the structure and rhythm of the life of modern congregations where a serious discussion concerning the state of one's soul is expected." They then go on to speak of the anxiety of many clergy who feel like amateur psychiatrists. "Part of the reason for this anxiety may be the feeling that usual pastoral routines provide no contact with alienated people face to face in situations that define the minister as one who is alerted to and talented in a certain kind of spiritual conversation that can knit together broken bonds between God and man. This extemporizing virtually deprives the church of its ministry of pastoral reconciling at a time when alienation is at the root of much human woe and anxiety" (*Pastoral Care*, p. 66).

When they made this judgment, the confessional in Roman Catholic churches was still a well-used place where people could discuss the state of their souls and experience the healing power of the sacrament of reconciliation. With the reforms initiated by the Second Vatican Council the sacrament of reconciliation has become even more the place where a serious discussion of the state of one's soul is expected. It is ironic, then, that just when the sacrament could be of immense help to people, it has fallen into practical disuse. One can only hope that more and more priests will develop the kinds of pastoral skills needed to make the sacrament of reconciliation once again popular. A pastorally well handled rite of reconciliation can bring immense relief and peace to a person. If the person is in psychotherapy, such a rite can also be therapeutically advantageous.

Psychotherapy and the sacrament of reconciliation have a number of affinities. The model for both is the one-on-one encounter. Both therapists and priests listen with sympathy and empathy while clients or penitents reveal intimate details of their lives. Both settings invite confidences. And in both settings a person can experience deep healing and peace in telling the whole truth to someone who listens without condemnation. In the therapies which rely on the working alliance between therapist and client as the means of therapeutic growth, the person of the therapist, his or her integrity and warmth and tough love, becomes the vehicle for the change. In the sacrament of reconciliation the person of the priest, his integrity, compassion and tough love, is the sacramental sign of God's love. Indeed, a therapist can be a sacramental sign of God's compassion in a fashion analogous to the sacramental role of the priest in the reconciliation rite even if the therapist is not aware of such a possibility.

There are, of course, great differences in the two roles. Therapists are not interested in sin as such. Their task is to help their clients to develop more mature and self-fulfilling ways of behaving by means of the relationship to themselves. They search for psychological meaning in the thoughts, feelings, and behavior of their clients; the psychological dimension of experience is their field of interest. The religious dimensions of experience would only interest them if it had relevance to the psychological difficulties of their clients. They would never take it upon themselves to assure their clients of God's acceptance and forgiveness, for example, nor as psychotherapists would they let their own faith or lack thereof enter into the therapeutic process.

The priest in the sacrament of reconciliation is interested in sin as such, in the need for forgiveness their penitents have. The religious dimension of experience is the priest's main focus. He is interested in the penitent's relationship with God and the penitent's conscious lapses in living in harmony with that relationship. Quite explicitly, therefore, the priest focuses on the relationship with God and the penitent's sense of alienation from God and from God's people. The priest is interested in the psychological dimensions of the penitent's experience only insofar as this dimension illuminates the state of the penitent's soul, the penitent's relationship to God and to God's people. Finally, quite explicitly the priest makes a judgment that God has forgiven the penitent and conveys that judgment by word and action in the act of absolution. The sacramental sign of God's compassion and forgiveness is explicitly expressed. The priest wants the penitent to experience that compassion and forgiveness through his sacramental action.

The priest in the sacrament of reconciliation can be a help to a penitent in therapy precisely by being clear about his role in the sacrament. He tries to convey the forgiveness and compassion of God to the penitent. People seek therapy because they have learned unhealthy patterns of relating to others. Often enough these unhealthy patterns of relating also affect their relationship with God. They have unreal attitudes toward God. God, for example, is a demanding parent ready to pounce on every flaw and failure. Such people can be helped in the sacrament of reconciliation to experience God sacramentally as compassionate and forgiving.

The scrupulous person, for example, can be particularly difficult to deal with in the sacrament of reconciliation. Such a person has an image of God as an "ogre" ready to pounce on the slightest infraction. Such a person is bedeviled by a compulsion that cannot be overcome by reasoning within the compulsive system itself. The scrupulous dynamic itself must be seen as the illness of uncontrollable compulsion. It is like a paranoid delusional system. The scrupulous person has already thought through all the rational arguments that could be adduced to counter the scruples. If the confessor enters into the system to try to dislodge the person from it, he is doomed to failure.

Ignatius of Loyola gives an example in his autobiography. He was so bothered by scruples that he came close to suicide. At one point his confessor "ordered him not to confess anything from the past, unless it should be something very clear. But inasmuch as he thought all those things were very clear, this order was of no benefit to him, and so he continued with his difficulty" (*Autobiography*, p. 35).

Somehow or other the confessor has to get across to the scrupulous penitent that the scrupulous dynamic itself is the problem and that the confessor will not deal with this dynamic directly. In one instance I asked whether the person loved the God who made such demands. The question led to an outburst of anger against this God which I could affirm and

which gradually led to the discernment that this God was an idol to be hated. Scrupulous people can drain a confessor's compassion and draw him into angry arguments. It helps to remember that scrupulous people are harder on themselves than on anyone else and that they can only help themselves if they experience a love that is genuine but also tough, a love that is compassionate, but which will not make any concessions to the compulsion.

It might also be well to remember that people resist therapy, resist developing more mature patterns of behavior. Sometimes a penitent in therapy may try to use the confessor to abet the resistance. "My therapist told me that I needed to get some sexual gratification. What do you think of that?" It must be admitted that some therapists could make such a statement, but I would be very chary of accepting the penitent's account as absolute truth. One can be drawn into taking sides with the penitent against an absent therapist. If the penitent asks me my opinion, I would wonder why he or she is asking me. The penitent has a conscience and can decide what is right. Moreover, if the penitent has doubts about the propriety of the therapist's remarks, the therapy will only move forward if he or she speaks openly to the therapist about his/her reactions to the therapist's interventions. If the client cannot be open with the therapist, the therapy is doomed.

A confessor who knows God experientially as a God of love and freedom and who knows the strengths and limitations of his role as confessor can be a great help to people who come to the sacrament of reconciliation. Such a confessor will meet penitents with a compassionate heart because he, too, has needed and experienced the compassionate heart of Jesus. Such a confessor will also know that compassion does not mean creating an unhealthy dependency in penitents. He knows that he is not the one who saves, and so he will continually try to help penitents to meet the only one who can save. The priest who becomes known as a good confessor probably needs to have some adequate supervision just as much as a good spiritual director does (See, Barry and Connelly, 175-91). Alienation is still at the root of the problems of modern men and women, as Clebsch and Jaeckle said in 1964. The sacrament of reconciliation can be one of the best places where people can be healed of their alienation from the Mystery at the center of their beings and from one another.

William A. Clebsch and Charles R. Jaeckle, *Pastoral Care in Historical Perspective: An Essay With Exhibits* (New York: Harper Torchbooks, 1967). Ignatius of Loyola, *The Autobiography of St. Ignatius of Loyola with Related Documents,* trans. Joseph F. O'Callaghan, ed. John C. Olin (New York: Harper Torchbooks, 1974). William A. Barry and William J. Connolly, *The Practice of Spiritual Direction* (San Francisco: Harper & Row, 1982).

WILLIAM A. BARRY, S.J.

RECONCILIATION ROOM

In Christian worship parlance this term in the Roman Catholic tradition refers to a room specially designated for the celebration of the sacrament of penance/reconciliation. Care must be taken in the design of this room to provide several alternatives for celebrating the sacrament. If the individual penitent prefers to celebrate the sacrament in an anonymous fashion, the priest presider should be unable to recognize the penitent. Usually this provision is handled by some kind of screen. In addition to the possibility of celebrating the sacrament with visual anonymity, however, care must also be taken to provide another alternative. If the penitent prefers, s/he can choose a part of the room which enables the priest and the penitent to see each other face-to-face so that they can discuss and pray together

openly. Ecclesial encouragement of this latter provision is recent. Since the Second Vatican Council, each of the sacramental rites was reformed in such a way that the nature and purpose of the sacrament was clarified. Providing for the possibility of a face-to-face encounter clarifies several dimensions in this sacramental celebration. All people stand together as sinners called to conversion. Allowing for the penitent to be out in the open clarifies that there is no need to hide from others, whether that be human beings or God. People acknowledging their sinfulness are accepted by the presider in the name of the church and God with an unconditional love. God's forgiving love is emphasized and proclaimed as more powerful than the individual's sinfulness. There is no need to stay in the dark closet (confessional) unless, for some reason, this environment helps in reconciling with God and the church.

Unfortunately the culture of the United States tends to cultivate a way of understanding experience which equates the personal and the private, and too often assumes that communal events are impersonal. As a sacrament, this celebration of reconciliation is common prayer; it is a liturgy. Whatever facilitates audibility, visibility, a sense of contemplation and hospitality ought to be fostered. In worship each of the senses are to be engaged easily, although historically this culture tends to encourage a minimalist approach in this regard. Without a screen separating the presider and the penitent, for example, it is possible to touch the penitent in a gesture of blessing.

The post-conciliar reform helped to recover some awareness of the social dimension of every sinful act as well as every good one. The evil or goodness of one has an effect on others, for their edification or destruction. This sacramental ritual of penance entails reconciliation with sisters and brothers (church) as well as God. This is more clearly embodied in allowing a face-to-face encounter.

The furnishings of the reconciliation room are simple: chairs for the presider and penitent, a table with a cross and a Bible. Since the purpose of a reconciliation room is the celebration of the sacrament and not counseling or therapy or casual conversation, the American bishops recommend calling the reconciliation room a chapel. Any other ornamentation ought to be simple and certainly ought not to detract from the primary action, praying together the Sacrament of Reconciliation.

National Conference of Catholic Bishops, *Environment and Art in Catholic Worship* (Washington: United States Catholic Conference Publications, 1978). M.Hellwig, *Sign of Reconciliation and Conversion: The Sacrament of Penance for Our Times* (Wilmington: Michael Glazier, 1982). J. Dallen, "Reconciliatio et Paenitentia: the Postsynodal Apostolic Exhortation," *Worship* 59:2 (1985): 98-116. E. Siedlecki, "Reconciliation Rooms," *Modern Liturgy* 12:5 (1985): 44-45.

T. JEROME OVERBECK, S.J.

RECONCILIATION, EUCHARIST AND

See **Eucharist and reconciliation**

RECONCILIATION, LITURGIES OF

In its broad sense, reconciliation is the process of restoring an original harmony after that harmony has in some way been disrupted. It can be personal, where the disharmony resides within oneself. It can be interpersonal, where disruption has occurred between persons. It can be among groups (e.g., families, churches, nations). It can be cosmic, addressing a fundamental disharmony in "the way things are."

Christian theology recognizes the need for reconciliation in all of these areas, naming the source of disruption and disharmony *sin*, be it personal sin, interpersonal sin, social sin, or original sin. In Judaeo-Christian revelation creation itself, once in harmony with the creator God (Gen 1:31), suffered a "fall" (Genesis 3), and the story that follows in both Hebrew and Christian Scriptures traces the restoration of creation, brought about by God, to its original harmony. That final restoration is an eschatological hope; it is presented as God's fulfillment of God's creative act.

For Christian theology, however, the full reconciliation for which creation yearns is not simply a future to be patiently awaited. In the life, death and resurrection of Jesus Christ, that "eschaton" has already begun, and in Christ it is revealed that the process of reconciliation is already under way, and has been since the dawn of creation itself.

Christian liturgy enacts in ritual form the truth of God's creation as it is revealed in Jesus Christ. It is itself a privileged mode of speaking that revelation. Christian liturgy is, however, more than simple announcement. It is "effective proclamation," that is, as a human event in human history Christian liturgy effects the revelation of God in Christ and makes it historically actual. It is both promise and fulfillment. It is a future destiny announced and a brief moment in which that future is in fact present. Christian liturgy is thus *sacramentum* of God's creation.

Liturgies of reconciliation present the *sacramentum* of both original and final harmony of all in God. The sin that disrupts is acknowledged, but it is acknowledged as defeated, not defeating. Thus, in whatever form they take, liturgies of reconciliation both announce the final truth of creation *as reconciled to God* and, for a brief moment in history at least, express that final truth. In so doing, liturgies of reconciliation serve to overcome disharmony of all kinds, and make incarnate in those who enact them the actual reconciliation brought about by Christ.

This essay will focus on (a) the original Christian liturgies of reconciliation, namely, baptism and eucharist, (b) the subsequent liturgies of reconciliation, especially as they are currently presented in the revised Roman Catholic *Rite of Penance*, and (c) some future liturgies of reconciliation as they may yet be devised and employed by the Christian assembly at prayer.

Baptism and Eucharist

The original disruption is described in Genesis 3 as *disobedience*. This same disruption under different names (e.g., "hardness of heart") continues to be portrayed as Israel's prime sin. It is towards the day when this will be reversed that the prophets (esp. Jeremiah and Ezekiel) set their gaze. It is in Christ, so Paul proclaims, that this disruption has been undone (esp. Romans 5 and 1 Corinthians 15).

The first ritual response to the announcement of what God has done in Jesus Christ is clearly set forth in Acts: "Repent and be baptized every one of you in the name of Jesus Christ for the forgiveness of your sins; and you shall receive the gift of the Holy Spirit" (2:38). In Paul the ritual of water unites us to the dying and rising of Christ, a union which brings us into the reconciled state of the New Creation. In John the ritual of water gives us part in Christ and in the victory over sin which his death and resurrection accomplished. It is new birth. In the many forms which this ritual of water has taken in the history of the church its prime intent has been constant: to place human life into the mystery of Christ, to anoint that life with the Spirit of God and to unite that life to the people of God. In baptism men and women are reconciled to God and set in harmony with one another.

The post-conciliar rituals for baptism, both for infants and for adults, signal this reconciliation in a variety of ways. In the prayer of exorcism before the baptism itself the church prays: "set them free from original sin, make them temples of your glory, and send your Holy Spirit to dwell with them." The *berakah* (blessing prayer) over the font announces: "You created humanity in your own likeness: cleanse them from sin in a new birth to innocence by water and the Spirit," and it goes on to ask: "May all who are buried with Christ in the death of baptism rise also with him to newness of life." The baptism itself is *into* the faith of the community and the community of faith, and it is followed (unless confirmation is to be conferred) by the post-baptismal anointing: "God the Father of our Lord Jesus Christ has freed you from sin, given you a new birth by water and the Holy Spirit, and welcomed you into his holy people. He now anoints you with the chrism of salvation. As Christ was anointed Priest, Prophet and King, so may you live always as a member of his body, sharing everlasting life."

The second ritual enactment of the reconciliation won by Christ is the eucharist. It exposes and condemns disruption in the community of believers (see, I Cor 11:27); even more important, it brings about union and harmony in the body (I Cor 10:17). It is clear from the earliest eucharistic prayers that the dominant thrust of the prayer itself was fulfilment of the Lord's own prophetic word: "...and I, when I am lifted up from the earth, will draw all men to myself" (Jn 12:32). The prayer of the *Didache* (ca. A.D., 110), for example, asks God to gather the church from the ends of the earth into the unity of God's own kingdom. The anaphora of Hippolytus (ca. 215) likewise prays that God will gather into one all who share in the mysteries. The eucharist was from its earliest times the ordinary sacrament of reconciliation in which Christians would find and grow in the reconciliation brought about by Christ.

Unfortunately, this concern for unity and reconciliation disappeared from later eucharistic prayers, replaced first by concern for personal strength and, later, by a focus on the transformation of the elements. In the post-conciliar liturgy, however, the concern for unity *as primary* has been restored: "May all of us who share in the body and blood of Christ be brought together in unity by the Holy Spirit" (E.P., II); "Grant that we, who are nourished by his body and blood, may be filled with his Holy Spirit, and become one body, one spirit in Christ" (E.P., III); ". . . and by your Holy Spirit, gather all who share this bread and wine into the one body of Christ, a living sacrifice of praise" (E.P., IV); not to mention the two prayers specifically devoted to the theme of reconciliation.

The Rite of Penance

In its origin the sacrament of penance (also, confession, reconciliation, forgiveness) was a deliberate act of reconciliation with God and with the church. Need for such an act arose when the commission of specific sins (e.g., adultery, murder, apostasy) separated the sinner (ex-communication) from the ordinary sacrament of reconciliation, the eucharist. A third ritual pattern was enacted to restore the sinner to the eucharistic communion. The shape of this third liturgy of reconciliation has varied in the history of the church from a solemn public process followed by a solemn public reconciliation (canonical penance) to a private encounter between penitent and presbyter-confessor (Celtic penance and its derived forms). Its prime intent has likewise varied from restoration to eucharistic communion to forgiveness of sins as a necessary pre-requisite for partaking of the eucharist. As a sacramental response to the reality of sin, its forms have been shaped by the various ways in which sin has been understood and experienced. The relationship between the experience of sin and the form of the sacrament is crucial both for an understanding of the revised Roman Rite of Penance and for any ritual projections that may be made. Where sin is experienced exclusively as a personal reality, personal forms of the sacrament are all that are required. When the experience of sin begins to have other faces as well, e.g., interpersonal sin, social sin, and even global or cosmic sin (evil over which no one seems to have control), the sacrament needs to address these as well.

The revised Rite of Penance (1973) emerges in the church not only in the context of the more general liturgical renewal of Vatican II; it emerges at a time when the consciousness and experience of sin is radically shifting. On the personal level sin is more likely to be named in terms of attitudinal stance than in a long list of nameable specific acts. Beyond the personal, however, the evil involved in broken or dysfunctional relationships, in forms of injustice and forces of oppression, in wars that seem interminable and in such unspeakable atrocities as the holocaust, cries out from the human heart for the healing and forgiving word of Jesus Christ. The new Rite of Penance does not effectively address all these forms of evil and sin; it does, however, make a significant first step in addressing the new experience and consciousness of sin.

The revised Rite of Penance offers three liturgical forms for the sacrament of reconciliation as well as some suggestions for non-sacramental penance services. Our concern here is with the three sacramental forms: the rite of reconciliation of individual penitents (Rite I); the rite of reconciliation of several penitents with individual confession and absolution (Rite II); and, the rite for reconciliation of several penitents with general confession and absolution (Rite III). Reflections on the non-sacramental penance services are given elsewhere in this volume.

All three sacramental rites follow the same ritual structure: greeting, word, interchange between penitent and confessor, absolution and thanksgiving. It is a liturgical structure, and this structure itself marks a significant departure from the more juridical model of private confession which was the norm before the conciliar reform. The opening greeting between penitent and confessor places both under the word of God; the confessor is fellow sinner with the penitent; it is not a judge-penitent relationship. The sacramental exchange takes place under the word of God. Penitent and confessor both listen to the word of God; the sacramental exchange is made in response to that word. The penitent is asked to open himself/herself in integrity to the Lord whose mercy is proclaimed; the confessor is asked to speak that mercy and forgiveness faithfully and effectively. The atmosphere is one of prayer where God is worshipped and human healing is sought. The formula of forgiveness (absolution) retains its declarative structure ("I absolve you"); it is coupled, however, with both narrative thanksgiving ("God the Father of mercies, through the death and resurrection of his Son, has reconciled the world to himself; and has sent the Holy Spirit among us for the forgiveness of sins") and prayerful invocation ("through the ministry of the church may God grant you pardon and peace"). Finally the *telos* of the sacramental act (both "end" and "goal") is praise and thanksgiving. It is thus linked to the act of eucharist even if it is ritually separate from it.

The first form (Rite I) is the most personal form, and most apt to address personal sin at its most intense. It is in no way "time bound," and can therefore be tailored to the needs of the penitent. The interchange can be long or short, and can contain pastoral advice, exhortation, guidance, a time of prayer. The scripture, which is given as "optional," can be brought in or not as the needs dictate, can be formal proclamation or informal paraphrase. The sacrament itself can unfold in the course of one meeting, or spread out over several, all with the single design that the penitent be open to and effectively receive the proclamation of God's forgiveness.

The third form (Rite III) is the most communal form, and most apt to address less focused experiences of sin. It is a fully communal rite designed to welcome and encourage "full and active participation by all the people" (S.C., 14, 27). As a public liturgical act it is "time bound": it is scheduled, and it needs to unfold within an acceptable liturgical time frame. Scripture is publicly proclaimed, and pastoral advice, exhortation and guidance are offered by the presiding priest in the form of homily. There follows a public and communal confession of sin ("I confess...") and some prayers of intercession, capturing an ancient sense of mutual support of all in the assembly in the church's common task of reconciliation and forgiveness. The sinfulness of each participant is acknowledged in a general way, by means of a sign or a gesture, and the proclamation and prayer of absolution is likewise done in general, for all together. The rite concludes with a common thanksgiving and blessing.

The second form (Rite II) is a hybrid form, combining both the communal and the personal. It begins and ends as a communal liturgical rite; private confession with individual absolution is offered during its course. Its structure is identical to Rite III up to and including the confession and prayers of intercession. Penitents then go to priests designated for individual confession. It is not stated where these priests are located (in the confessional, in another room, at designated places in the sanctuary or around the assembly). The confession is to be made simply. Each one receives and accepts a fitting act of satisfaction and is absolved. After hearing the confession and offering suitable counsel the priest gives absolution. All gather again in assembly for the concluding prayer of thanksgiving.

While these three rites are presented in the ritual book as three variant but equal forms for the enactment of this sacrament, they are not received as such in current Roman Catholic discipline. "Individual, integral confession and absolution remain the only ordinary way for the faithful to reconcile themselves with God and the Church, unless physical or moral impossibility excuses from this kind of confession" (R.P., 31). Use of Rite III is severely restricted; it continues to be viewed as applicable only to emergency situations. This is somewhat of an anomaly in light of the norm set forth in the *Constitution on the Sacred Liturgy* drawn from the communal nature of the liturgy: "Whenever rites, according to their specific nature, make provision for communal celebration involving the presence and active participation of the faithful, it is to be stressed that this way of celebrating them is to be preferred, as far as possible, to a celebration that is individual and, so to speak, private. This applies with special force to the celebration of Mass and the administration of the sacraments..." (S.C., 27). A further anomaly is the requirement that those who do receive absolution for grave sins according to Rite III "should go to individual confession before they receive this kind of absolution again" (R.P., 34).

Rite I does remain the most apt ritual form when personal sin and personal conversion are experienced in a forceful and significant way. The difficulties that arise in its regard are not so much difficulties with the rite as with reception of the rite. Even before the revision of the ritual, patterns of participation in this sacrament in its individual form had

radically changed. Frequency of reception had fallen off drastically. Neither the new ritual nor the conversion of the confessional to the more friendly reconciliation room has reversed this shift. This form of the sacrament continues to enjoy popularity in the context of spiritual direction (where, in fact, it began in the Celtic church), at times of retreat and at significant personal moments. It seems unlikely, however, that it will regain its status as it is envisioned by church discipline as the only ordinary way for the faithful to reconcile themselves with God and the church.

Rite II presents its own difficulties, both pastoral and liturgical. The most poignant pastoral difficulty rests in the availability of priests for the individual confessions. In large urban centers, where neighboring parishes are in close proximity to each other, this is usually not problematic. In rural areas, however, and in areas where there are few priests, Rite II is impractical, if not impossible. The liturgical difficulties cluster around the fact that, while it intends to combine the communal and the personal, Rite II fails, or at least may fail, in both. The communal experience is aborted at its sacramental peak, particularly if the individual confessions take place elsewhere than visibly in the assembly. The personal experience is restricted by the pressures of time, and the need for all to gather again for the rite's conclusion. This can be avoided if the concluding thanksgiving is scheduled for another liturgical act (e.g., the eucharist on the following day), but no provision is made for this in the ritual as presented.

Where there are sufficient priests available, Rite II begins to enjoy popularity as a seasonal, and thus ordinary, celebration of the sacrament. Lent and Advent surface as the most apt times for its use. Other times, such as graduation in a school community or the anniversary of a parish community, also surface as appropriate. Where priests are not available, however, desire continues to be expressed for a more expanded use of Rite III.

There is no doubt that the Rite of Penance seeks to address both the communal and the personal experience of sin. The discipline of the church gives priority to the personal and thus relativizes the communal in favor of the personal. One must go from the communal form to the personal form. On the other hand, the desires expressed for a more expanded use of Rite III, as well as the popularity of Rite II where it is practical and possible, express a reverse priority: to relativize the personal in favor of the communal. In such reversal, one might be expected to go from the personal form to the communal form. Both views can be grounded in the introduction to the Rite of Penance which speaks of the sacrament in one moment as an act in which a sinner "by the grace of a merciful God embraces the way of penance" (R.P., 5), and in the next as an act "in which the Church proclaims its faith, gives thanks to God ... and offers its life as a spiritual sacrifice in praise of God's glory" (R.P., 7b). Personal forms are clearly appropriate to the first; communal forms are clearly appropriate to the second.

There is a limitation in all three forms in regard to the range of sin they are capable of addressing. The ritual forms, and especially the introduction, envision sin primarily as personal, with some possible address, in the communal forms, to interpersonal sin. To reach beyond this restricted experience of sin and evil to the social and the global, other ritual forms for this sacrament need yet to be imagined.

Future Liturgies of Reconciliation

There is some boldness in an article of this type to project future liturgies for the sacrament of reconciliation. Such boldness, however, is less whimsical than first might appear. Efforts at imagining the future of sacramental worship have already entered the literature, and have been presented as well at Roman synods (e.g., the 1983 Synod of Bishops). The faith conviction beneath these efforts remains the victory of Christ over all sin, and the desire of Christ effectively to address sin in all of its forms. The pastoral conviction rests on the human need for healing wherever disruption and alienation might show themselves.

For any ritual of reconciliation to be a liturgy of reconciliation it must be guided by, and take place under, the word of God proclaimed. It must involve confrontation of evil with God's word in full human integrity. And it must issue forth in confidence of forgiveness and healing, and come to some ritual conclusion in an act of praise and thanksgiving. It must be, in other words, an act "in which the Church proclaims its faith, gives thanks to God ... and offers its life as a spiritual sacrifice in praise of God's glory" (R.P., 7b). Ritual forms will vary in accordance with the human experience of evil and sin which is addressed.

One such effort at imagining the future is the suggestion to re-establish an *order of penitents* which was presented by Cardinal J. Bernardin at the 1983 Synod of Bishops (see, *Origins*, v. 13, n. 9, Oct. 20, 1983). This suggestion involved a four-stage process of conversion modelled on, and celebrated in parallel with, the Rite of Christian Initiation of Adults. The first stage would be the confession of sin which would open out on the second, a time of penance and conversion. The third would be the celebration of the sacrament itself, to take place at a time when conversion has begun to manifest itself in a profound change in the person's life and manner. The fourth stage would be a "prolongation of the sacramental experience," a post-sacramental mystagogy. There the penitent would continue to enjoy the support of the community and the community would continue to be served by the penitent's witness to conversion and forgiveness.

Four additional efforts at imagining the future of this sacrament were explored in *Alternative Futures for Worship* (1987), in the volume devoted to reconciliation. The first is an extension of Rite II to be in effect a more tangible communal form. The sacramental interchange is in the form of a dialogue (Are you sorry for all your sins? I am, and especially for...), and only the declarative part of the absolution formula is used (the other part is prayed in common before the confessions begin). The sacramental interchange takes place in full visibility in the midst of the assembly. A second involves a two-stage liturgical act and addresses the pastoral situation where sufficient priests are not available, or more positively, where nonordained ministers (such as spiritual directors, retreat guides, etc.) actively serve in the ministry of reconciliation. Appointed ministers, even though not ordained, receive the confession of sinfulness, speak a word of forgiveness and pardon, and then, together with the penitents involved, bring this to public liturgical assembly for its full sacramental completion in formal absolution by the presider. A third addresses the experience of cosmic evil, of "evil too large." Drawn in parallel with the Jewish day of Atonement, it suggests a liturgy for a Christian day of Atonement. In a spirit of surrender to the goodness of God, this ritual addresses the sins of the local community, the sins of the church and the sins of the world. A final set of liturgical rituals focuses on the reconciliation of groups.

Other liturgies of reconciliation can also be imagined. Liturgies for healing and forgiveness after the disruption of a family by divorce would bring some insight from the Eastern churches to ritual expression in the West. Liturgies of reconciliation between individuals and groups, addressing that form of sin popularly known as "falling through the cracks," as well as the common situation in which institutions damage individuals, would bring Christ's healing word to a human reality that is keenly felt by those affected yet seldom noticed either by the institution or by others. Liturgies drawn from the tradition of the "Church Unity Octave" to address the scandal of a divided Christianity would shape the desire of the churches according to the desire of Christ "that all be made one," and may well provide a healthy and holy impetus to bring that unity about.

In approaching the sacrament of reconciliation the church needs to stamp out that undercurrent of sacramental stinginess that first showed itself in the early church's restriction on canonical penance, namely, that it be offered only once, and which may still be operative in the restrictions currently imposed on Rite III. The gospel mandate for reconciliation remains the generous "seven times seventy" of the Lord. And the words of Paul to the church at Corinth, "All this is from God, who through Christ reconciled us to himself and gave us the ministry of reconciliation" (2 Cor 5:18), remain a prime identification of the mission which has been entrusted to the church.

See **Reconciliation, sacrament of; Penitents, order of; Penance services, non-sacramental; Reconciliation, ministers of**

Archdiocese of Detroit, *The Sacrament of Penance: the Detroit Experience* (Detroit: Diocesan Offices, 1987). James Dallen, *The Reconciling Community: The Rite of Penance* (New York: Pueblo, 1986). Peter E. Fink, S.J., ed., *Alternative Futures for Worship*, Vol. 4: Reconciliation (Collegeville: Liturgical Press, 1987). Ladislas Örsy, *The Evolving Church and the Sacrament of Penance* (Denville, New Jersey: Dimension, 1978). John Paul II, *Reconciliatio et paenitentia* (Post-Synodal Apostolic Exhortation on Reconciliation and Penance in the Mission of the Church Today) (Washington, D.C.: USCC, 1984).

PETER E. FINK, S.J.

RECONCILIATION, MINISTERS OF

The ministry of reconciliation was clearly articulated for the Christian community by the apostle Paul. "So whoever is in Christ is a new creation: the old things have passed away; behold, new things have come. And all this is from God, who has reconciled us to himself through Christ and given us the ministry of reconciliation.... So we are ambassadors for Christ, as if God were appealing through us. We implore you on behalf of Christ, be reconciled to God" (2 Cor 5:17-20).

There are two basic ways the ministry of reconciliation may be understood. The first is the more generic, in line with the ambassadorial frame of reference of St. Paul. Accordingly, we are *all* called to carry on the ministry of reconciliation. A second more specific understanding of the term "ministers of reconciliation" focuses on the role of the ordained minister with regard to reconciliation within the sacrament of penance. We will consider both of these. The reader interested in the pastoral problematic of non-ordained persons who are called to be ministers of reconciliation in situations approximating that of sacramental confession would do well to consult the work of Peter Fink cited in the bibliography.

Ambassadors of Reconciliation.

The vocabulary of foreign service and the diplomatic corps is used by the apostle Paul to suggest the importance of the work of reconciliation and our participation in it. Ambassadors hold a privileged place with the leader they represent; they are carriers of the most sensitive and urgent missions on his/her behalf. The rank of ambassador is an honor; the service, a privilege.

The scope and weight of the ambassador's responsibility is assumed in Paul's commissioning statement: "You are ambassadors for Christ" called to "the ministry of reconciliation" (2 Cor 5:18).

When Paul passes the mantle of ambassadorial rank to each of us, we may surmise two things: first, that God's intention for the world is unity; and second, that the mission to gather the world as one, begun by Jesus but left incomplete by him, has been delegated to the community of believers Jesus left behind.

Ambassadors of reconciliation live, act, and breathe out of the basic insight that the human race is interconnected. We may entertain the illusion that we are separate and that we do not need each other, but Paul sets the record straight over and over again. We interexist. So our responsibility as ministers of reconciliation is riveted in an unalterable conviction of interdependence: "You are members of one body" (Eph 5:30). "There is no such thing as Jew and Greek, slave and freeperson, male and female: for you are all one person in Christ Jesus" (Gal 3:28).

Ambassadors of reconciliation begin their ministry by facing the splits and divisions that exist, especially those connected with relationships, or with positions that polarize or systems that oppress. In such situations, ministers of reconciliation mediate for families who are not speaking with each other, governments at war with each other, and individuals who harbor resentments towards each other. When principles of justice are in jeopardy, reconcilers take on a direct service role protecting the victim while at the same time working for ways to change the system.

In brief, the ministry of reconciliation is accomplished through the following commitments:

1. Ministers of reconciliation work against the popular trend: they identify divisions, grieve over them and treat them with the seriousness they deserve. They challenge a culture that values indifference and individualism.

2. Ministers of reconciliation bring

ruptures and divisions to public attention, often annoying the power brokers who have the most to lose when their unilateral power base is brought into question.

3. Ministers of reconciliation urge a sense of responsibility among all parties and encourage broad-based involvement towards reconciliation. Even when it appears that positions are so polarized that harmony is impossible, ministers of reconciliation believe *glasnost* is always possible and that it often occurs in the least likely places mediated by the most unlikely ambassadors.

4. Ministers of reconciliation are themselves a sign of "church." They remind us of our corporate mission to reconcile the whole world with the lifegiving news of the gospel and not to rest until it happens in its glorious fulness.

Ministers of Sacramental Reconciliation.

Official ministers of the sacrament of penance are ordained clerics who receive the confession of sins from penitents, accept a sign of their contrition and life amendment, and declare the forgiveness of God and absolution.

The *Rite of Penance* (1973) reflected the concern of the *Constitution on the Sacred Liturgy* (1963) that the sign-value of the sacrament of penance was not communicating its own substantive theology. The juridicism and individualism manifested in the sacrament since the Council of Trent did not adequately signify the relational, communal and ecclesial theology that was part of the reform of the Second Vatican Council.

The R.P. sought to refocus the identity of the minister by situating him as a member of the Christian community, proclaimer of the word, healer, and shepherd.

As a member of the community, the minister of the sacrament of reconciliation is a person whose priesthood is marked by service (*diakonia*), prayer, the gifts of the Holy Spirit (especially spiritual discernment). The restoration of the integrity of the word of God in the sacrament of penance pervades the use of scripture in the examination of consciences, the penitent's prayers, the prayers of the minister, the dismissal and blessing.

A metaphor that is pervasive throughout the R.P. and that situates itself unambiguously in the section on ministry is that of healing. A long if frequently submerged history of penance as "medicine for sin" and of priest as "wise and compassionate physician" supports this understanding. The *Didascalia Apostolorum* advised bishops continually to grant the medicine that heals.

Like Jesus who ate with sinners and partied with them, the minister of the sacrament of penance is asked to lead the penitent as a shepherd in the process of unfolding and accepting the truth of who she/he is in the freedom and love of Christ.

Last of all, the R.P. also affirms the model of priest as judge. Within the total pastoral perspective of the R.P., however, the positive and more biblical way of looking at judgment suggests that the judgment made is that sin is dead and that grace lives, or as one commentator phrased it, reconciliation affirms the positive in face of the negative. The judgment is the judgment of Christ. It is an authoritative proclamation of reconciliation and forgiveness of God, exercised in a provisional manner in the present Christian community while looking forward to the final judgment as the complete victory over sin and death.

The R.P. calls the minister to authenticity and transparency. In particular, he is asked to live fully the life of the Spirit and to be sensitive to the stirrings of the Spirit with whom Christ connected the forgiveness of sins.

James Dallen, *The Reconciling Community: The Rite of Penance* (New York: Pueblo Publishing Company, 1986). Peter E. Fink, s.j., "Liturgy of Reconciliation Where Unordained Ministers Receive the Confession of Sin, Pray for Forgiveness and Reconciliation, and Together Present This for

Confirmation and Completion in the Liturgical Assembly," in *Alternative Futures for Worship*, Vol. 4: *Reconciliation* (Collegeville, MN: The Liturgical Press, 1984): 109-126. Richard S. Gula, S.S., *To Walk Together Again: The Sacrament of Reconciliation* (New York: Paulist Press, 1984). Denis J. Woods, "Reconciliation of Groups," in *Alternative Futures for Worship*, Vol. 4: Reconciliation (Collegeville, MN: The Liturgical Press, 1984): 33-42.

DORIS DONNELLY

RECONCILIATION, SACRAMENT OF

"Reconciliation" has been the most often used name of this sacrament since Vatican II, although both "penance" and "confession" are also still used. In this sacrament the redemptive force of Christ's Easter mystery renews the church by restoring to its communion those alienated from it by grave sin and making them once more full members of the eucharistic assembly. That redemptive force also deepens the sharing of ecclesial communion by those not conscious of such sin and thus not excluded from the eucharist. In that way it offers support for the continuing conversion or transformation into Christ that is the Christian life.

The reformed ritual of 1973 is titled *Rite of Penance* (R.P.). Prior to the council, "penance," with the meaning of "conversion," was the preferred theological term. This derived from the patristic use of *paenitentia secunda* ("second" conversion, to distinguish it from the conversion which preceded baptism). Penance, including both conversion from grave sin leading to reconciliation and conversion from lesser sins, accents human effort to change but can, in our culture, be understood as the effort of isolated individuals.

Popular understanding since the Early Middle Ages has focused on the forgiveness of sins and used the term "confession," a metonomy derived from the familiar liturgical format which gave prominence to the individual penitent's narration of sins to the priest so as to receive absolution. This term, still popularly used for the reconciliation of an individual penitent, risks giving the sacramental ritual priority over the reality and making the individual's acts (both sins and the repentance expressed through the ritual acts of contrition, confession, and satisfaction) more the focus than God's grace experienced in the community of salvation.

Both penance and forgiveness are personal, but neither is simply individual. Reconciliation, the broader term, gives priority to God's gracious love which, in Christ, draws sinner-disciples into a life-giving communion which transforms them into the likeness of Christ and frees them from sin. It thus includes penance or conversion, the human struggle to be transformed, and the forgiveness of sins, liberation from the obstacles to such transformation. Current theological understanding, evident in the introduction to the *R.P.* regards both God's reconciling work and the church's ministry of reconciliation as deeper and more extensive than the liturgical celebration. Yet the liturgies of the *R.P.* also show that communion or community—reconciliation in Christ—is the goal of the conversion whereby individuals are set free from the alienation or isolation entailed by sin.

The key to understanding and appreciation of the sacrament is its history. This article explores that history, outlines the contemporary theological consensus as presented in the *R.P.*, and notes major questions currently discussed.

History

The confusing history of this sacrament is often over-simplified by speaking of "public" penance in ancient times and "private" penance in medieval and modern times. This terminology grew out of post-Reformation polemics as scholars tried to prove or disprove the early existence of the private confession which the Protestant Reformers had, for the most part, rejected. The disjunction is misleading as it ignores the variety of forms in which the sacrament existed prior to the Late Middle Ages. Period divisions are more helpful: ancient (1st through 6th centuries), medieval (7th through 15th centuries), modern (16th century to the present).

Ancient History

The sacrament's origins lie in the early need to deal with the reality of sinful members in a community called to be holy as sign of God's saving power in Christ (e.g., Acts 5). Though healing could come through others' prayer (Jas 5:16), some communities considered prayer inappropriate for certain sinners (1 Jn 5:14-17). In some cases, disciplinary action was called for, sometimes even shunning the serious sinner in the hope that the sinner would return to the Christian way of life or at least not obscure the community's holiness (1 Corinthians 5). This was the community's responsibility (Mt 18:15-18; Jn 20:23), although community officials sometimes continued the synagogue's discipline of excluding sinners and re-admitting the repentant (binding and loosing, Mt 16:19).

Though most NT communities welcomed back the repentant, some refused to do so in certain cases (Heb 6:4-8; Mk 3:29). Other early documents also show the call to repentance and the welcome of the repentant (1 Clement; *Didache*), as well as controversy over whom to reconcile and under what conditions. The apocalyptic 2nd-century Shepherd of Hermas, for example, allowed a "second chance" which, in the course of controversy, came to be understood as "once only."

Tensions accompanied Christianity's movement into the mainstream of Greco-Roman culture: how much accommodation could there be without compromising principles? Struggles with Montanism and Novatianism, both of which denied reconciliation to some grave sinners, intensified already-existing disagreements. Such tension and controversy influenced the development of an institution supervising the postbaptismal conversion of those whose sinfulness particularly endangered the community's holiness. That of Carthage is the best known because of the writings of Tertullian (*De paenitentia* and *De pudicitia*; d. 225) and Cyprian (d. 258).

This penitential institution developed in most urban centers in the late 2nd and early 3rd centuries. It was an "order of penitents" paralleling the catechumenate and providing for the reformation of those whose pre-baptismal formation had been insufficient to prevent serious sin after baptism. The community received penitents in a liturgy praising God's mercy (*exomologesis*). The community supported and encouraged them throughout the period of conversion.

As the 2nd and 3rd-century controversies were resolved, this institution was open to all repentant sinners. After the penitents evidenced sufficient maturation in conversion, they were reconciled with the faithful in a liturgy at which the bishop presided. This showed that the penitents were officially restored to the status of faithful Christians.

The laying on of hands, both as a prayer of exorcism and as a gesture of solidarity, was a prominent symbol in the liturgies before and at reconciliation. However, repentance and reformation—conversion—were the chief concern and were symbolized by weeping, sackcloth and ashes, and prayer, fasting, and almsgiving. Only in the case of penance and reconciliation for the dying (the only instance of "private" penance in the ancient period) did the ritual substitute for the supervised process of conversion.

Cyprian's writings, in the context of the confusion and controversy that accompanied the Decian persecution, describe the intended operation of the order of penitents and explain how sinners come to experience divine forgiveness. The repentant seek conversion, showing repentance and making satisfaction (a legal term earlier used by Tertullian) by external acts. They join in the community's worship of the merciful God ("exomologesis," also used for the entire process). They are reconciled to the church as the precondition for God's forgiveness. For Cyprian, penitents do not gain forgiveness simply through penitential acts, nor does the bishop directly forgive sins. Because he does not make the later distinction between personal and ecclesiastical factors, Cyprian sees the whole process as both personal and ecclesial, manifesting reconciliation with God achieved in solidarity with the church, in which the Spirit is active.

The struggle with Montanism and Novatianism helped clarify the church's consciousness of its ability to mediate divine forgiveness. Fourth-century bishop-theologians such as Ambrose of Milan and Pacian of Barcelona further explained the church's authority. The struggle also affected the understanding and practice of the institution, making it more rigorous and punitive. Moreover, the controversies had a long-lasting effect in that reconciliation, like baptism, was allowed only once in a lifetime. This disciplinary restriction now seems at odds with the doctrinal affirmation of complete authority over sin.

However, only serious sinners were required or able to take advantage of this unrepeatable process of rehabilitation. Others continued their conversion in the church in a variety of more informal ways: they sought change through prayer, fasting, and almsgiving; they turned to holy men and women for individual guidance and support; they experienced God's transforming power and community support in the eucharist. Though these were less formal and public than the order of penitents, they were still ecclesial means of experiencing conversion and reconciliation.

In general, similar procedures and liturgies developed in both West and East. However, Eastern practice was usually less rigorous and legalistic than the Western (e.g., Clement of Alexandria, d. 215; Origen, d. 254; the early 3rd-century *Didaskalia*). It also gave somewhat greater place to the practice of spiritual direction as an aid to those not subject to the requirements of the order of penitents and sometimes allowed it as an alternative for those reluctant to be publicly recognized as penitents. The East also maintained a stronger communal sense by having penitential rites in the liturgy. In this way it also balanced its occasional willingness to overlook the usual ecclesiastical requirements of supervised conversion and eventual reconciliation (e.g., John Chrysostom, d. 407, who permitted confession directly to God).

The legal and liturgical determination of the status of sinners and penitents intensified in the 4th and 5th centuries in the West as a consequence of Christianity's becoming legal and public. Laws required ecclesiastical supervision of conversion in a growing number of cases. Liturgy became more elaborate and dramatic. Lifelong consequences (e.g., celibacy, prohibition of certain offices and occupations) followed entrance into penance.

The formal ecclesiastical process in the 4th century and after is generally called "canonical penance." Legal regulation through synodal canons led to regional consistency of practice and understanding. However, canonical enforcement was only partially successful. Without a clear sense of the Christian life as a call to continuing growth in holiness and a sense of solidarity in community, fewer Christians, other than the most pious, saw the point of the official penitential institution and entered it. Thus penance often came to be regarded more as coercive penalty and punishment than as a voluntary means of healing and rehabilitation.

By the 6th century, few individuals entered the order of penitents voluntarily. However, many people did choose to become penitents on their deathbeds. Thus, penance for the dying, an emergency adaptation of an exceptional institution, became the most common form of penance liturgy near the end of the ancient period. Even clerics and religious, otherwise not eligible to enter the order of penitents, were able to share in this devotional practice. Those who did voluntarily enter the order of penitents, the *conversi*, generally did so as an expression of commitment akin to that of those who today enter communities of vowed religious.

The close correlation of initiation and penance is also evident in the changing focus of the Lenten season. In 5th-century Rome many people not subject to canonical penance became ceremonial penitents for the duration of Lent, which had earlier centered on catechumens' final preparation for baptism. As the order of penitents declined, the numbers of ceremonial penitents in Rome and elsewhere grew, and by the 10th century all Christians were expected to be Lenten penitents.

Medieval History

Unsettled conditions during the barbarian invasions and the inadequate evangelization and catechesis of converts also contributed to the demise of the order of penitents. Irish monk-missionaries in Gaul during the 6th to 9th centuries compensated for the failure of bishops to meet new pastoral needs by developing "tariff penance."

A practice borrowed from the East was prominent in Celtic monasticism: monks, not subject to canonical penance or not guilty of sins requiring canonical penance, sought advice from spiritual experts on how to resume or continue conversion. Eastern monastic liturgy included communal prayers for forgiveness and declarations of reconciliation, but these—the latter in particular—never became so highly regarded in Celtic monasticism. However, the practice of private counseling with a spiritual director was extended to laity associated with a monastery.

Irish monk-missionaries in Gaul spread this practice of confessing sins as they evangelized and catechized. They also popularized (or at least reinforced) an understanding of sin as a contaminating stain which put the sinner in debt to God. Conversion too underwent something of a transformation as it was understood less as ecclesial rehabilitation than as private reparation or payment of an individual debt. Each sin was compensated for by certain penitential practices. The satisfaction that needed to be made for each type of sin was listed in books called penitentials (derived from synodal regulations and the recommendations of respected authors) and was assigned according to the individual's confession of sins.

Where the order of penitents had been a one-time repetition of the catechumenate, private confession and satisfaction provided a repeatable post-baptismal formational procedure. Since the practice was not canonical, there was no official reconciliation—this was reserved to the bishop—after satisfaction had been made. The prominence of the confession of sins (which enabled the confessor to assign appropriate satisfaction) led to the procedure being called "confession" from the 8th and 9th centuries on.

Yet to most people the monastic practice seemed much like the official canonical process where, it seemed, harsh mortification obtained God's forgiveness of sin. What the monks (who were not necessarily priests) offered was more practical: no public knowledge, no social stigma, no lifelong consequences—and it could be repeated whenever necessary. Such private penitents were not excluded from the community but only from receiving communion (by now infrequent). The absence of the liturgical ritual of reconciliation through the bishop's imposition of hands apparently went unnoticed because the canonical process was nonexistent (in Ireland and England) or rarely used (in Gaul). Most importantly, the new practice offered the individual a greater sense of security.

Superficially, the monastic innovation did resemble the already-familiar practice of spiritual direction for those not subject to canonical penance. It also resembled the growing practice in Gaul of priests supervising penitents' conversion and then presenting them to the bishop for reconciliation.

In fact, its spirit was very different, due to a changed understanding of both sin and conversion. Sin put a person in debt to God and under threat of punishment. Conversion meant repentance and expiation, making satisfaction by self-punishment (fasting and other forms of mortification). The confessor, a spiritual expert (not necessarily a priest), advised the individual on appropriate means of satisfaction. The accumulation of penitential debt was alleviated by the practices of commutation and redemption (lesser, substitute penalties) which developed eventually into indulgences as a means of ecclesial assistance to the debt-ridden sinner.

Tariff penance and the confession of sins provided reassurance in an age of individual fear and anxiety. However, as the monastic practice grew more popular during the 8th and 9th centuries, the bishops often reacted against it. They did so less because of the sense of sin and penance that it was teaching—one that further diminished the experience of liturgical community—and more because the monk-confessors were offering a novelty that went contrary to the canons and bypassed the bishop.

Carolingian reform councils tried, without success, to outlaw or regulate the penitentials and to revive canonical penance. A series of compromises, all ultimately not accepted by the laity, prepared the way for a new official form of penance. The compromises generally had the common feature of requiring that the confession be to a priest. (From the 8th century on, a steadily increasing number of monks were ordained.) Among the attempts to save canonical penance by compromise were: confession either to God or to priests of sins not subject to the canonical discipline; canonical penance for canonical crimes publicly known and private confession for canonical crimes not publicly known; private confession and private satisfaction followed by the bishop's formal reconciliation during Holy Week or the priest's absolution.

Clericalization during the Carolingian era increasingly emphasized "absolution" as an exercise of the power of the keys paralleling the bishop's reconciliation. Absolution, originally a blessing concluding a liturgy, became a ritual declaration that the penitent was under no further obligation to make satisfaction.

However, many people, accustomed to the monastic practice, did not return for the reconciliation or absolution. Near the end of the 9th century, canons provided for the immediate absolution of those unlikely to return (*Statuta quaedam*, can. 31). The tariff ritual of the Romano-Germanic Pontifical (c. 950) apparently regards immediate absolution as normal practice. The reason for the confession (assigning satisfaction) remained unchanged, but the satisfaction gradually declined in both amount and importance, with the confession and absolution given greater theological emphasis since they preceded satisfaction.

Though the new procedure highlighted the significance of priestly absolution, it did not immediately eliminate lay confession. This remained relatively common into the 14th century for less serious sins or in emergencies and still existed in the 16th century (e.g., Ignatius of Loyola, before the battle of Pamplona).

Though private confession was a distinctive medieval adaptation to pastoral needs, other forms of conversion and reconciliation were also prominent and frequently communal in nature. From the 10th century ashes were imposed on all at the beginning of the Lenten penance. Lenten fasting became a significant means of purification and expiation; confession was often expected at the beginning of Lent or during it. Canonical penance was infrequently used, but the Carolingian efforts at revival developed elaborate liturgies; from the 12th century this is called "solemn penance." Pilgrimage, often called "public penance," was also an important medieval means of expiation. From the 9th to the 14th century, absolution was often given communally at Mass, especially at times when people were expected to receive communion.

As the patristic period had regarded conversion as the requirement for re-entering the community of salvation, the early medieval period saw satisfaction as the cause of divine forgiveness. As the amount of satisfaction declined with absolution given immediately, confession (once the praise of the merciful God), as the expression of contrition, became humiliation and self-punishment and absorbed the function of satisfaction. In the 12th century the ritual combination of confession and absolution came to replace confession and satisfaction as the central factor in obtaining divine forgiveness.

Scholastic theologians labored to fit this within their new category of sacrament. The individual focus of medieval penance had broken the earlier unity of the personal and ecclesial dimensions of penance. What, then, was the relationship of the penitent's contrition and confession to the priest's absolution? Some theologians emphasized the personal contrition (Abelard, Lombard), others the ecclesial power of the keys (the Victorines).

Aquinas' synthesis, on the model of Aristotelian hylemorphism, argued for an intrinsic causal relationship: the acts of the penitent (contrition, confession, satisfaction) are the matter of the sacrament (conversion) and the priest's absolution is the ecclesial form. The experience of grace in the sacramental ritual enables contrition to mature. Aquinas thus unites the personal and ecclesial elements in a manner reminiscent of Cyprian, giving priority to divine grace and regarding faith and love as necessary for forgiveness in every case. However, by this time the ecclesial ministry of confrontation (binding) was almost exclusively legal discipline and the ecclesial ministry of assistance (loosing) was priestly absolution.

Later Scholastics (e.g., Duns Scotus, d. 1308) saw the relationship as extrinsic and emphasized absolution as the grant of forgiveness. Consequently, from the 14th century on, ritual elements other than confession and absolution tended to be abbreviated and the acts of the penitent regarded as conditions for absolution's efficacy. As in the ancient penance for the dying, the ecclesial ritual substituted for full personal conversion; i.e., forgiveness outside the sacrament required perfect contrition, but imperfect contrition was sufficient in the sacrament.

Modern History

The transition from medieval to modern penance began with Lateran Council IV (1215) which focused on confession and absolution as the means of ecclesiastical forgiveness and required it annually before Easter communion. The obligation bound all who had reached the age of discretion. (The council probably had in mind fourteen, the age for marriage.) Sanctions ensured reluctant compliance, although theologians emphasized that this was compulsory only for those conscious of grave sin (now stated in the 1983 C.I.C., can. 989).

Other means of experiencing divine forgiveness thus declined in importance. After the 15th century the modern system of penance was complete: confession and absolution were the dominant symbol of post-baptismal conversion and the only normal form of the sacrament. It operated as the church's means of disciplining sinners and supporting the repentant, although it was often used in a rather mechanical fashion.

The Protestant reformers generally rejected this confession-and-absolution format, often claiming Lateran IV had invented it. However, Luther was rather ambivalent and was often willing to regard confession as a third dominical or evangelical sacrament.

In defending the late medieval system and the church's right and responsibility to be involved in its members' conversion, Trent insisted on integral confession (all mortal sins of which the penitent was conscious, according to number and kind, together with circumstances changing their nature) to the priest (D.S., 1701) as an earlier age had required penitents to manifest conversion to the community. As the ancient period had required that conversion be authenticated and the penitent then reconciled with the faithful in the community of salvation, so Trent saw the priest acting like a judge (D.S., 1709) and his absolution as effecting forgiveness (D.S., 1709-1710). Unaware of the sacrament's historical development, Trent spoke as if the familiar practice of private confession had existed from the beginning and regarded it as *iure divino*: consistent with Christ's will for the church and required by God for the forgiveness of serious sins.

The *Rituale Romanum* of 1614 provided a simple ritual that minimized prayer and ecclesial elements, highlighted the penitent's confession of sins and expression of contrition, and climaxed in the priest's absolution. Private confession thus grew in importance throughout the era of the Counter-Reformation as a mark of loyalty to the church and the means of forgiveness. Only when death threatened and confession was impossible was absolution permitted without previous individual confession.

It was also increasingly used by sinners not conscious of mortal sin, since it seemed to have advantages over other means, notably the *ex opere operato* efficacy of absolution which made only imperfect contrition necessary for receiving forgiveness and grace. As communion became more frequent, so did confession, regarded not only as means of purification from sin and liberation from guilt but also as a means of sanctification (gaining grace). Even when there were no specific sins to be forgiven, devotional confession was a significant act of piety.

Though polemics between Protestants and Catholics motivated historical research, historical data was rarely interpreted on its own terms. The dominant motive was to prove or disprove that private confession had existed in the early church. Efforts to reform the discipline or ritual (e.g., Jansenism and, during the Enlightenment, communal celebrations) were condemned, as were attempts at the time of the modernist controversy to understand the history more precisely.

The focus on individual forgiveness and sanctification remained constant until the 20th century. Rediscovered patristic liturgies were regarded as simply ceremonial enhancements or canonical penalties. However, the publication of Xiberta's

Clavis Ecclesiae (1922) marked the beginning of a new development: the recognition that ancient penance had been social and communal in character, oriented to reconciling sinners with the church and thereby with God. Significant 20th-century figures in applying the historical-critical method to penance include Paulus Galtier, Bernard Poschmann, Joseph Grotz, and Karl Rahner.

Theological controversy over the nature of ancient penance spilled over into a questioning of devotional confession in the 1930s and 1940s. Pius XII defended the ascetic practice in *Mediator Dei* (1943) and elsewhere, but his encouragement of the Liturgical Movement intensified studies that led to further reflection, calls for reform, and changing practice. Perhaps the most significant change in practice was, in the context of the World Wars, the broadened opportunity for using general absolution (see especially the 1944 Instruction of the Sacred Penitentiary), though mortal sins were to be confessed subsequently if possible. In the early 1960s general absolution was also permitted in mission territories, sometimes without the requirement of subsequent confession.

In the 1950s, in response to perceived pastoral needs, communal celebrations of the sacrament began to develop in France and Belgium and then in The Netherlands and were subsequently approved by bishops in several countries. This grassroots reform was the emergence of the first new forms of penance in a millennium: confession services (private confessions within a communal liturgy), fully communal liturgies (a general confession of sinfulness by the community and absolution by the priest without specific individual confession of sins), and penitential celebrations (a general confession of sinfulness but no absolution). Theological criticism was minimal, since by then most theologians had come to regard the social and communal

nature and effect of the sacrament as primary. However, official reaction, in some cases by bishops but more often by Rome, was generally negative when absolution was not preceded by confession or when, in the case of children, the practice led to delaying first confession until after first communion.

In 1963 Vatican II called for a reform that would clearly show the social and ecclesial nature and effects of the sacrament (*Sacrosanctum concilium*, 72, and declaration accompanying the final draft; see also *Lumen gentium*, II, and *Presbyterorum ordinis*, 5). Related reforms came first: the discipline of fasting, abstinence, and personal penance (*Paenitemini*, 1966); indulgences (*Indulgentiarum doctrina*, 1967).

Despite the mandate and clear principles for liturgical reform, behind-the-scenes controversy impeded the preparation of the new ritual; e.g., in 1966 the Congregation of the Doctrine of the Faith criticized theological and pastoral emphasis on the social function of reconciliation with the church. Such disagreement prevented publication of the draft, completed in 1969, which allowed extensive use of general absolution. Then the June 1972 *Pastoral Norms* of the Congregation for the Doctrine of the Faith grudgingly permitted communal celebrations, though restricting absolution without previous confession. A new draft was quickly prepared which corresponded to the 1972 Norms and took advantage of the experience of other liturgical reforms. After extensive study and revision by Roman congregations, the *Ordo Paenitentiae* was promulgated on December 2, 1973, and published in February 1974. The English translation (R.P.) was completed and approved in 1975 and went into effect in the United States in 1977.

This portion of the reformed Roman Ritual begins with an introduction describing the church's understanding of penance and its ministry (R.P., 1-11) and giving norms for celebration (R.P., 12-40). (This introduction is especially important as it outlines the doctrinal and theological understanding on which the ritual is based.) Chapter I (R.P., 41-47) is the rite for reconciling individual penitents, a much-enhanced liturgy for the familiar private confession. Chapter II (R.P., 48-59) is a rite for reconciling several penitents with individual confession and absolution; it is a communal celebration much like the French confession service. Chapter III (R.P., 60-66) is the rite for reconciling several penitents with general confession and absolution; like the Dutch communal celebration, it lacks the specific confession of sins and does not absolve penitents individually. Chapter IV (R.P., 67-216) provides additional texts and options for use in celebration. Appendix I gives formulas for absolving from censures and irregularities. Appendix II provides regulations and nine models for penitential celebrations (communal celebrations without absolution). Appendix III is a model examination of conscience. Overall, the *R.P.* reflects current theological consensus, although compromises with the Counter-Reformation outlook are also evident.

By the time the new rite was promulgated, many commentators, especially in the hierarchy, considered the sacrament to be in a state of crisis. The primary concern was that confession, which had steadily increased in frequency from the time of Trent until the 1950s, was becoming increasingly infrequent. A U.S. study by the National Opinion Research Center in 1964 showed 38 percent of American Catholics confessed monthly; in 1974 this had declined to 17 percent. Explanations included: the loss of the sense of sin (already mentioned by Pius XII), spiritual lukewarmness and carelessness (although in the same period those receiving communion weekly increased from less than 20 percent to more

than 80 percent), inadequate understanding and appreciation of the sacrament, inadequate celebrations.

During the pontificate of John Paul II, efforts have been made to revitalize the sacrament, primarily by emphasizing individual confession. John Paul stresses that both Christ and the penitent have the right to the personal encounter that individual confession makes possible (e.g., *Redemptor hominis*, 20). He has been critical of communal celebrations where there is no individual confession and has downplayed the significance of community celebrations. He has also prohibited postponing first confession until after first communion (C.I.C., can. 914).

The negative evaluation of communal celebrations influenced the 1983 *C.I.C.* which speaks of confession rather than reconciliation. Many participants in the 1983 Synod of Bishops (on "Reconciliation and Penance in the Mission of the Church") apparently took issue with what appeared to be regression from Vatican II reforms. However, John Paul's post-synodal apostolic exhortation, *Reconciliatio et paenitentia* (1984), reiterates his emphasis on the "profoundly personal character" of the sacrament and Trent's requirement of individual confession. The social and ecclesial dimension, expressed especially in communal celebrations, receives little attention.

Contemporary Theology, Ministry, and Celebration

The rationale for the customary treatment of the history of the sacrament in terms of public and private penance lies in the fact that theology and ministry in the ancient period saw individual conversion and forgiveness in relation to the community of the church, while theology and ministry in the medieval and modern periods has centered on the forgiveness of the individual's sins. As a consequence of the rediscovery in history of "forgotten truths" (Rahner, Th. Inv., 2), contemporary theology seeks to bring individualistic theology and ministry to a more deeply personal character and to resituate it within a broader ecclesial context.

Three trends characteristic of the 20th-century theology and ministry of the sacrament have been incorporated into documents of Vatican II and the 1973 R.P.; the nature and effects of the sacrament as social and ecclesial; the sacrament as an act of ecclesial worship; sacramental celebration in relation to a life of personal conversion which includes responsibility for the church's mission of reconciliation. Each contrasts sharply with the late-medieval and Counter-Reformation forms of the sacrament. This is the source of tension in a time of transition and indicates areas for future work. The teaching of Vatican II and the R.P. are thus both the official acceptance of previous theological development and the base for further exploration.

Social and Ecclesial Character

Once it was rediscovered that reconciliation with the church is an effect of the sacrament, a theological consensus developed within a few decades which was expressed pastorally in celebration and ministry (communal celebrations), and was officially accepted at Vatican II. Many theologians concluded that penitents experience God's reconciling love more through experiencing reconciliation with the church than through experiencing interior repentance—in scholastic terms, reconciliation with the church is the *res et sacramentum* of penance and reconciliation. Though the council correlated reconciliation with the church and reconciliation with God (L.G., 11; P.O., 3), it took no position on priority, since there was no theological consensus on that point. It did, however, stress the social and ecclesial character of both sin and conversion.

In preferring reconciliation as the name for the sacrament, the R.P. highlights both divine initiative and human response—both in the context of church community—and incorporates the new theological orientations. The introduction to the R.P. 1-7 shows that the mystery of reconciliation is the key to understanding God's work, redemption in Christ, sacramental conversion, the church and its life and worship, and ministry to repentant sinners. The R.P. 8-11 emphasizes the communal and ecclesial character of the sacrament, its celebrants (ministers and penitents), and liturgy. The same outlook is evident in remarks on sacramental celebration (12-35), related liturgies (penitential celebrations) (36-37), and adaptation (38-40).

Thus the church, a reconciling community (1-5, 18), is where God and humanity are reconciled (4, 8), as the sacraments indicate (2, 4, 5). Salvation history shows that the purpose of penance is reconciliation with God and church (5); this is clearly expressed in the absolution formulas (6d, 46, 62). The penitent's role is ecclesial (6, 11). The church itself is penitent (3), as is evident in communal celebrations, although the church is renewed even when an individual is reconciled (3, 7, 11). Laity participate in planning and preparing celebrations (40b) and are agents of reconciliation (5, 8).

In the celebration, the imposition of hands symbolizes reconciliation with the church and the restoration of the penitent sinner to the community where the Spirit of Jesus is active (5, 6d, 9a, 19, 24). By this renewal of grace sinners are reconciled with God (2). Penitents are again part of the Easter mystery by being restored to the church (1, 2, 7, 19): the broken covenant is remade (5, 6d). These points suggest that the R.P. favors the position that reconciliation with God is through reconciliation with the church.

The R.P. also stresses that the Christian goal is likeness to Christ (6a, 15), not conformity to law, and that there is both social sin and social dimensions to all sin (4, 5, 7, 18, 25c). It encourages communal celebrations because they more clearly manifest penance's ecclesial nature (22) and show the church's involvement in conversion (4). Through this ministry, in which the whole church acts (8), God grants remission of sins (6). The ecclesial ministry is not only judgment but leadership in prayer, discernment of spirits, pastoral dedication, and human warmth (10). The church exercises the ministry through bishops and priests (9), ministers of God (6, 10d) and church (6) who act in the person of Christ (6, 9), though all the faithful share the work of reconciliation (8).

Contemporary theological emphasis on the social and ecclesial nature and effects of the sacrament establishes the need to express this in both celebration and ministry. It is complementary to an emphasis on personal conversion (also evident in contemporary theology) but contrasts sharply with the individualistic theology, ritual, and ministry of recent centuries. This is currently the source of tension and controversy, particularly surrounding the fully communal celebration where penitents are reconciled with general confession and absolution. ("General absolution" is not the best term here: as it has been used, it connotes an emergency situation where a full liturgy is not possible.) Further work on interpreting the sacrament's historical development and the teaching of Trent in this regard should enrich theological hermeneutics as well.

A sustained effort to implement the R.P. fully is necessary. The variety of forms for the sacrament provided in the R.P. also needs to be strengthened and expanded. Particularly important theologically is a clarification of how the church and the local community are involved and affected in every celebration. A key theme here is that of the penitent church and a promising area for investigation that of the penitential celebration. How, for example, does the non-sacramental penitential celebration differ from the sacramental celebration, so far as the nature and effects are concerned? Efforts to develop a modern order of penitents for reconciling the alienated should also prove fruitful in expanding the understanding and expression of ministry in this sacrament, as the R.C.I.A. has done in the case of initiation.

Ecclesial Worship

Twentieth-century sacramental theology views sacraments more liturgically than canonically or ascetically, seeing them in relation to the mystery of Christ and church. Pastorally, communal celebrations and individual celebrations based on a shared-prayer model have helped restore the sense of community worship in the sacrament. Vatican II gave preference to communal sacramental celebrations (S.C., 26-27), affirmed the place of scripture (S.C., 24, 35), and called for adaptation to pastoral needs in different cultures (S.C., 27-40, 62).

In the R.P., the sacramental celebration is an act of community worship and its atmosphere is one of shared prayer (4, 7, 11, 15, 16, 19, 20, 22, 23, 27, 29, 36, 37). This is clearest in the communal celebrations, especially that with general confession and absolution, but that the individual rite is also ecclesial worship (11) is evident; e.g., emphasis on dialogue (6d, 16, 18), prayer and the word, and seeing the priest's ministry as liturgical presidency. In every case, the focus is on God's action (6) and on praise (20, 29) and joy (6d) in response to it. Scripture is the foundation for this and has a place in every celebration; the word reveals sin, calls to conversion, encourages trust in God's mercy, and shows the nature of conversion and penance (17, 22, 24, 36-37). A compromise is evident in the optional character of scripture in the individual rite (17, 43).

Divine initiative and human response meet in liturgical celebration, but the sacramental expression of both extends beyond the role of the presider. Although the *R.P.* puts somewhat more emphasis on priestly power than does contemporary sacramental theology, it does not restrict the work of reconciliation to priests nor restrict the priestly ministry to absolution. Yet it is rather vague on both points. While theological work has been done on the role of the assembly and the variety of ministries in celebrating initiation and eucharist, almost nothing has been done on these points in the sacrament of reconciliation. These are important areas for future investigation and will become more crucial as the number of priests continues to decline. Again, the so-called non-sacramental penitential celebration and the modern order of penitents are likely to be key elements in future development.

Although the *R.P.* takes no explicit position on the disputed question of the sacramental priority of reconciliation with the church to reconciliation with God, it does seem to favor it. This has liturgical implications, particularly the significance of a warm climate of human acceptance and full participation in every celebration. How to further this in a sacrament which, in recent centuries, has centered on integral confession and priestly absolution is a major area for future work.

In any case, the life of conversion and reconciliation must precede and follow the sacramental ritual if the ritual is to be authentic worship. Thus the traditional acts of the penitent (contrition, confession, and satisfaction) are the ritual expression of the phases of conversion leading to reconciliation.

Personal Conversion and Mission

Contemporary theology and Vatican II regard sacraments as acts of worship whose effects extend into people's lives and are part of the church's overall mission and community life (S.C., 9, 59). Conversion is therefore broader than ritual, and reconciliation is more than forgiveness. Because sacraments are priestly acts of Christ (S.C., 6-7; P.O., 5) expressing the Easter mystery (S.C., 61), sacraments nurture spirituality and growth in faith (S.C., 61). Growth in likeness to Christ, which begins in baptism, is the goal of Christian life (L.G., 7, 11, 32-36, 40, 42). Continual conversion is the constant dynamic of Christian holiness. It is achieved by living in the church community and sharing its mission. It is renewed in the sacrament of reconciliation.

In the *R.P.*, baptism is the paradigmatic experience of reconciliation (1, 2, 7, 19). The purpose of penance is deeper love and friendship, reconciliation with God and church (5). Lent is a special time of community conversion and sacramental celebration (13, 40b), but conversion characterizes the whole of the Christian life (4, 6a, 7, 20).

Though the *R.P.* encourages frequent sacramental celebration, it also calls for caution and care (7b) and affirms other means of expressing repentance and achieving reconciliation (4, 7, 37). Living gospel repentance is a dimension of the mission of bringing salvation to the world by proclaiming the gospel and working for justice and peace (5, 7). Thus, neither life nor liturgy is viewed individualistically. The sacrament helps in attaining baptism's goal of full freedom and likeness to Christ (2, 4, 6a, 7b), but penitent sinners "should help each other in doing penance so that freed from sin by the grace of Christ they may work with all of good will for justice and peace in the world" (5). This first correlation of sacrament, everyday penance, and social justice in an official document is strengthened in R.P. 7.

The revitalization of the sacrament of reconciliation depends not only —not even primarily—on further theological development but also, and especially, on the development of liturgy and ministry. Most importantly, the church must be, and be experienced as, a reconciling community. This requires sustained commitment to the effort to reconcile its alienated members while, at the same time, reaching out as a reconciling force in society and the world. To be the "voice of the voiceless," the church must acknowledge its own sin and alienation and speak out for the poor and oppressed. While liberation theologians have not focused their attention on this sacrament, their work offers significant hints for future work.

Similarly, theological reflection on the relationship between the sacrament and spiritual direction or pastoral counseling will be important, as will the emerging ministry of the laity in these and other areas. What, for example, does the sacramental celebration add to counseling or direction if the individual has not been excluded from the eucharistic assembly by grave sin? In what circumstances may a lay presider reconcile, as in past instances of lay confession?

As in other sacraments, so here: the rituals of penance and reconciliation cannot substitute for the reality of conversion and reconciliation. Insofar as sacramental liturgy is the human response to God, the life of conversion and reconciliation must precede and follow the celebration. The human sciences have much to offer the theologian in this regard, but the socio-eschatological character of the church's life and mission also requires investigation because what is at issue is far more than individual growth and development. The sacrament is an intimate expression of community worship as part of the church's mission in service to God, humanity, and the reign of God.

Conclusion

The rediscovery of the historical development of the sacrament has provided the foundation for revitalizing theology, ministry, and celebration. The major orientations of the contemporary theology of the sacrament were accepted at Vatican II and incorporated into the *R.P.* Current tensions are the consequence of an incomplete assimilation of these orientations, an inadequate implementation of the *R.P.*, or a partial rejection of either or both. Sacramental theology has the task of deepening the understanding of the historical development and clarifying how to adapt the sacrament to respond to pastoral needs. Efforts to implement the *R.P.* will provide a faith-experience upon which to reflect in further developing the sacrament.

James Dallen, *The Reconciling Community* (New York: Pueblo, 1986). Joseph A. Favazza, *The Order of Penitents* (Collegeville: Liturgical Press, 1988). Richard Gula, *To Walk Together Again* (New York: Paulist Press, 1984). Monika K. Hellwig, *Sign of Reconciliation and Conversion* (Wilmington: Michael Glazier, 1982). Robert J. Kennedy, ed., *Reconciliation: The Continuing Agenda* (Collegeville: Liturgical Press, 1987). Ladislas Örsy, *The Evolving Church and the Sacrament of Penance* (Denville, NJ: Dimension Books, 1978). Bernhard Poschmann, *Penance and the Anointing of the Sick* (New York: Herder and Herder, 1964). Karl Rahner, *Penance in the Early Church*, Th. Inv., 15 (NY: Crossroad, 1982). *The Rite of Penance: Commentaries*, 3 vols. (Washington, D.C.: Liturgical Conference, 1975-1978). Herbert Vorgrimler, *Busse und Krankensalbung* (Freiburg: Herder, 1978).

JAMES DALLEN

RECORDS, SACRAMENTAL

Parish Records

The *parish* has the primary responsibility for maintaining sacramental records. The pastor or administrator of the parish oversees the proper recording of all information in the sacramental record books. The following individual sacramental registers should be carefully maintained in every parish (C.I.C., 535).

Baptismal Register (C.I.C., 877). This is

the most important source of information about every person baptized into the Catholic church. Before a person dies, it contains all necessary sacramental information because records about sacramental reception are always sent to the church of baptism.

The primary information is entered on the occasion of baptism: name, father, mother's maiden name, date and place of birth, date of baptism, person baptizing, sponsors, and witnesses. Whether the person remains in the same parish or moves anywhere in the world, when other sacraments are received or things that affect sacraments occur, notice of the following are sent to the church of baptism to be entered into the baptismal register:

-confirmation, date, place
-marriage, date, spouse, place
-orders (diaconate, priesthood, episcopacy), date, place
-perpetual profession in a religious institute, date, name of institute, place
-change of rite, name, date, place
-convalidation of marriage, date, spouse, place
-declaration of nullity of marriage, date, place, protocol number (includes: Pauline privilege; privilege of the faith and ratified but non-consummated marriages).

It should be noted that the church takes great care to assure the accuracy of these records and until recently notice was sent not only to the church of baptism but notice of reception was returned to the sender. All notations placed in the baptismal register are required to be recorded on every certificate issued. This is why a new (within six months) certificate of baptism is required for marriage preparation, orders, etc.

Register of Catechumens. This is required by the *Rite of Christian Initiation of Adults* (46) and includes: names of catechumens, their sponsors, minister, date and place of acceptance into the order of catechumens. Because these persons have the right to Catholic marriage and funeral celebrations, their names must be recorded in an official register of the parish.

Book of the Elect. This is a register of names of those who receive the rite of election according to the *Rite of Christian Initiation of Adults* (123, 132). The names of the elect are enrolled and the names of the godparents may also be included. It would seem that this book could be incorporated into the register of catechumens as a further step in the initiation process.

Marriage Register (C.I.C., 1121). Names of the spouses, their parents, witnesses, official witness (usually priest or deacon), place and date of marriage, are recorded in the marriage register maintained by the parish. One also includes any other information which may be helpful in the future: civil license number and place of issue, dispensations and their protocol numbers, other pertinent records attesting to the freedom of the parties to marry.

It should be noted that extenuating circumstances in marriage situations necessitate the recording of some marriages in the diocesan office. One such case is where a dispensation from the form of marriage is granted; but the wedding is also recorded in the marriage register of the parish of the Catholic party. When a marriage takes place in extraordinary form (C.I.C., 1116), it should be reported to the pastor of the place and duly recorded.

Death Register (C.I.C., 1182). After interment the person's name, date of death and funeral are recorded in a separate register.

Diocesan Records

The Diocesan Office of the Ordinary also has responsibility to maintain some sacramental records which are of diocesan concern or require special handling. They are the following.

Confirmation Register (C.I.C., 895). Record of the persons confirmed, including the minister, parents, sponsors, place and date of confirmation, (usually the name chosen), is to be kept in the diocesan office. The diocesan bishop or the conference of bishops could require that the record of the confirmation also be maintained in the parish. Record of confirmation is always sent to the church of baptism.

Register of Ordinations (C.I.C., 1053. 1). After ordinations to diaconate, priesthood and episcopacy, the names of the ordained, the ordaining minister, date, place of ordination are recorded. All documents of ordination are preserved. Those who are ordained outside of the diocese must present a certificate of ordination for the diocese to register this fact in its archives.

Secret Archives (C.I.C., 489). Because of situations which the church respects, not everything about people must be a matter of public record; yet sacramental celebration must be recorded somewhere. The diocesan office carefully maintains such records, for example secret marriages (C.I.C., 1133), dispensations from impediments for orders (C.I.C., 1047-1048).

The church keeps sacramental records for the sake of the people and for the common good. To date most records are in bound registers with a backup copy in some dioceses on microfilm. Parish records date back many years especially in older countries. People interested in their lineage are searching baptismal and marriage registers to know more about their ancestors. The registers tell a great deal. In this age of computers, we must use current technology to store information and make it more readily available. Parishes today utilize computers for census information; in fact some dioceses place the whole Catholic population on computer disks for review and mailings.

Every year the bishop or his delegate must visit every parish to see the sacramental records (C.I.C., 535.4) and make sure they are in order. Record keeping is a serious responsibility and requires responsible people. At one time the priest alone took care of the sacramental registers; today it is usually done by secretarial help, but the pastor must take vigilant care to oversee this responsibility.

Frederick R. McManus, *The Code of Canon Law: A Text and Commentary*, "The Sacrament of Penance (CC 959-997)" (New York: Paulist Press, 1983).

JOSEPH L. CUNNINGHAM

REFORM, LITURGICAL, HISTORY OF

The aim of this essay is to set the liturgical reform of Vatican II in a two-fold historical perspective. The first part presents a brief sketch of earlier liturgical reforms in the West. Thus we will survey the following periods and movements: the ancient church; the Franco-Germanic adaptation of the liturgy of Rome; the Gregorian reform; the post-Tridentine reform; and the Reformation reforms. The second part will focus on three aspects of the Vatican II reform: (a) the *Constitution on the Sacred Liturgy*; (b) implementation of the constitution at the official and local levels; and, (c) an assessment from an historical perspective of the achievement and possible future directions of the current reform.

Earlier Liturgical Reforms

In the early and patristic church, which was characterized by creativity and to a great extent freedom of improvisation, the concept of reform does not apply, at least beyond the limits of the local church. A worship of authentic signs, signs of the love of God and of resurrection, celebrated the new life in Christ. An eschatological, prophetic and spiritual Christian worship was dispossessed of elaborate and external ritual. *The Traditio*

Apostolica of the 3rd century still spoke of improvisation "according to the abilities of the presider" who must nevertheless safeguard the rule of faith.

This spirit of creativity led to an authentic "liturgical revolution," especially from the 4th century on, during which Christian worship was creatively adapted to the Greco-Roman cultural and religious elements. A long process of sacralization continued from the 4th through to the 7th centuries. This sweeping reform changed the language from Greek to Latin; the place of worship from the home to the basilica; as well as the cultic elements and ways of participation. During this period, the liturgical year was expanded, the models of texts and rituals were codified, and bishops started a direct supervision of the liturgy, resulting in the most creative renewal in the history of Christian worship.

During the 7th century, the liturgical work of Gregory I represented the first "official" reform which affected the church of Rome. Gregory the Great brought about a broad liturgical reorganization in the line of the Roman tradition. The new uneducated crowds and dramatic circumstances of a besieged Rome favored a new trend of compilation of texts and a more passive participation by the people who were now separated from the presbyters by the choir. The pastoral concerns prevailed in a more popular, simple and practical structure of liturgy. This liturgy of the church of Rome was still open to some creativity and receptive to the practices of other churches. At the same time, its influence radiated throughout Europe through the missionary activity of the Benedictine monks.

The Franco-Germanic adaptation of the Roman liturgy is the best example of the greater liturgical role which the bishop of Rome began to play after Gregory the Great. This period from the 7th century on, provides one of the best models for the post-Vatican II work of adaptation of the Roman liturgy "to the genius and traditions of peoples" (S.C., 37-41). In fact, the adoption of the Roman sacramentary under the political rule of Pepin (754) and his son, Charlemagne (783), who received a "pure" Roman sacramentary from Pope Hadrian I, did not happen without a process of integration. The sacramentary was first supplemented with local liturgical practices and, later on, adapted to the more sentimental and moralizing Franco-Germanic spirit. This Franco-Germanic reform resulted in a type of hybrid and, to a certain extent, anarchic liturgy. As a result, it brought about a revitalizing and creative movement in the Franco-Germanic churches of the 8th through 10th centuries. The pastoral rationale still prevailed, although within the limited possibilities of theological and ritual creativity, and the new trend towards liturgical institutionalization and creativity. The cultural and ecclesiastical vacuum of the impoverished leadership of Rome made possible a reversed movement of reform under the Ottonian influence (10th century), in which the Roman Franco-Germanic liturgy was officially introduced in Rome.

The Gregorian reform consummated the process of unification of the Latin liturgy under the centralizing supervision of the greater ecclesiastical power of the bishop of Rome. The different local churches of medieval Europe had to adopt the Roman *ordo*. The most renowned case of Romanization is the decision to abolish the Hispanic liturgy, at the time of Gregory VII (11th century), an ancient, rich, and unique liturgical order. This liturgical reform, promoted by Pope Gregory VII and later by Innocent III (1198-1216), was not a formal reform by decree as much as a factual reform initiated by Rome as means of unification of European Christendom and the renewal of ecclesiastical and religious life. The key of this new liturgical reorganization was pastoral, but was within the limits of a new ecclesiology of Christendom and hierarchical structure centered in Rome. The rationale of the Gregorian reform meant a paradigmatic shift similar to the work of Vatican II: a return to "the ancient Fathers," a religious renewal, and the implementation of a unified order of worship (*Ordo Romanus*). Nevertheless, neither the ecclesiology of the time nor the cultural factors allowed an actual return to the biblical-patristic sources and spirit in the liturgy. The liturgical reform of the 12th and 13th centuries, especially under Pope Innocent III, still remained the quasi-official codification of Roman rituals (the Roman Pontifical and Missal) and was promoted mainly by the Friars Minor. In addition to a new legalistic spirit, allegorism and devotional piety prevailed.

The Tridentine reform ended a period of liturgical misinterpretation and, to a certain extent, cultural materialism of the High Middle Ages (14th and 15th centuries). On the one hand, this reform invigorated spiritual piety, stated the dogmatic foundations of the eucharist and sacraments. On the other hand it also inaugurated a period of four centuries of rubricism and liturgical stagnation. Liturgical reform was not *per se* the goal of the Council of Trent (1545-1563), but its institutional ecclesiological model and dogmatic focus supported a new trend of tight liturgical supervision under the newly created Sacred Congregation of Rites (Pope Sixtus V, 1588). Trent's reform followed, to a great extent, the same lines of Gregorian reform in returning "to the primitive norm and rite," without actually reaching it in the new centralized Roman Catholic missal and rituals.

The different movements of the Reformation initiated diversified liturgical families from a more conservative to a freer and more radical attitude in regard to liturgical reformation: Lutheran, Anglican, Reformed and Free Churches, with still others following after the 17th century. Their common strengths rested in pastoral zeal, theological and didactic rationale (especially in the adoption of the vernacular), and their theology of the active presence of Christ in the word. In general, their weakness stemmed from their underestimation of the value of sign and image, and the authentic return to the biblical-patristic tradition of the total liturgical mystery.

Vatican II Reform

The liturgical reform of Vatican II constituted the single most concrete and dynamic change within modern Roman Catholicism. The Magna Carta of this reform is the Constitution on the Liturgy, *Sacrosanctum concilium*, issued on December 4, 1963. This document was not only the first fruit of Vatican II, but also was one of its major contributions to the internal renewal of Christianity. Such importance, at least for the Catholic church, was stressed by Pope Paul VI when he promulgated the constitution: "Treated before others, in a sense it has priority over all others for its intrinsic dignity and importance to the life of the Church" (Address, December 4, 1963).

The Liturgical Constitution. This document constituted the official and universal approval of a new synthesis between the doctrinal and pastoral agenda of the liturgy. Also it helped develop a new ecclesial vision, founded on biblical and patristic theology. This liturgical-pastoral movement, intensified at the beginning of the century with Pius X (especially from 1903 to 1914), gave rise to different centers of study in France, Germany, and elsewhere, and became progressively a European and American movement after the encyclical *Mediator Dei* of Pius XII (1947) and the international pastoral congress of Assisi (1956). This historical movement made possible the relatively simple preparation of the conciliar schema by an international commission of bishops and liturgical consultants. Under the direction of A. Bugnini, the preparatory liturgical commission approved the schema after four drafts and presented it to the president, Cardinal Cicognani. This was in January of 1962. Despite the many amendments made during the first fifteen general meetings of the council (fall of 1962), the original schema was accepted without substantial change. The biblical-patristic basis and the liturgical-pastoral vision of the movement had inaugurated a new ecclesiological horizon radically different from the defensive and juridical framework of the Council of Trent. The inherent value of the liturgical reform, which provided the theological tone and the pastoral horizon of the council, was seen as a sign of God and as a movement of the Spirit in the church (S.C., 43).

The goal of the constitution was the revival of Christian spirituality and pastoral life in bringing the faithful to the source of Christian life in the Christ mystery of the liturgy. The constitution was rooted in biblical theology and consequently provided the fundamental elements of a liturgical celebration in the framework of a new ecclesiology. Its development went hand in hand with the Constitution on the Church. This theological vision of the nature of worship was characterized by the criteria of reform and development, adaptation and creativity with concrete directives in regard to the sacraments and all liturgical exercises. The profound and ecclesiological vision centered around the priestly ministry of Christ in the mystery of the church and opened up new pespectives particularly regarding the role of the people of God in the local church.

From this paramount ecclesial perspective important liturgical understandings evolved: the baptismal priesthood of the faithful, the full participation of the people at both tables, word and eucharist,

the importance of the sign of the assembly, the need for flexible ritual norms, relevant symbolism, and catholicity of worship rooted in tradition (unity and stability). All of these are open to the dialogue of inculturation in a church open to the world—to its creativity and its pluralism. In the light of the constitution this new order of worship restored a more Roman and patristic structure, and it opened the way for the transcendent universality inherent in ecumenical pastoral praxis and theological thinking.

Implementation of the Reform. A month after the approval of the constitution, Paul VI created the main organ of its implementation, the Consilium (January 25, 1964), headed by the renowned Cardinal G. Lecaro, with A. Bugnini as his secretary. The fundamental purpose of this official council under the direct supervision of the pope was both to direct the correct and concrete application of the constitution in the reform of the liturgical books, and also to promote the conciliar magisterium through doctrinal and practical liturgical instructions. The international nature of the Consilium formed by bishops and a body of internationally renowned experts with a few non-Catholic observers, made the liturgical reform a collegial enterprise. Following the spirit and directives of the council, this reform had to be rooted in the tradition, to open the way to legitimate progress, and to respond pastorally to the needs of the people of our time and cultures. From 1965 on an informative organ of the Consilium, the journal entitled *Notitiae*, was issued. A parallel Vatican office, the Congregation of Rites, officially issued the instructions of the Consilium until they both merged into the Congregation of Divine Worship (May 8, 1969). After a lengthy preparation of many interim directives and many theological-pastoral instructions, the main work of the reform was promulgated, the Roman Missal of Paul VI

(June 1970). Following not only the specific guidelines of the constitution, but also the primary criteria and ecumenical scope of the whole body of conciliar doctrine, a thorough revision of all the rites and liturgical books was undertaken, and new *ordines* were issued from 1968 to 1978.

Although the liturgical restoration of the rituals was substantially accomplished by 1975, the suppression of the Congregation for Divine Worship that year and the dismissal of A. Bugnini as its secretary, signalled a more direct institutionalization of the liturgical-pastoral movement by the Roman Curia.

At the level of the local church, the reform was thoroughly planned in Rome and mostly enthusiastically implemented as its ancient texts were faithfully translated into more than 350 languages or dialects. However, the liturgy in general was only minimally adapted "to the genius and traditions of peoples" (S.C., 37-40). If, in one instance, the episcopal conferences seemed to prevail in adapting the vernacular, trying to make the preservation of Latin a mandate of the council—at least in regard to the divine office—the role of the bishops, for the most part, was limited to establishing the structures of the new *ordines* and enforcing the liturgical norms issued by the Holy See. The trend toward uniformity and centralization seemed apparent since the creation of the Congregation for the Sacraments and Divine Worship in 1975, Congregation of Divine Worship and the Discipline for the Sacraments, (1988), and in the new Code of Canon Law (can. 1257) of 1983. This was so despite the mandate of the council to enter into communion with cultures and talents of peoples (S.C., 37; G.S., 58).

The historical restoration was only partially achieved. A great challenge remained in regard to inculturation, especially in the non-Western world of cultures. Examples like the officially approved Roman rite for the church in Zaire, and other experiments in the Third World countries, were only the first attempts at symbolic and linguistic creativity, maintaining, however, the substantial unity of the Roman rite (S.C., 38).

The reform certainly constituted a strong movement of pastoral awareness and missionary concern in opening the spiritual treasure of liturgy to the people and making it the center of the life of the local church. By and large the new order of worship was well received. Two factors seemed to be underlying causes of dissatisfaction: the lack of adequate liturgical catechesis needed to invigorate the renewal of both worship and the community; and, the impoverishment of the contemplative, religious and symbolic action of worship which calls for a continuous revival. Planned from above, the reform was then handed to the people. It was not sufficiently animated from below and made relevant to the spiritual needs of the people.

In regard to the possible celebration of the old Latin Tridentine Mass (1984) under very restricted circumstances and with the permission of the ordinary, the decision in Rome was seen as a sign of compromise. While revealing the crisis brought about by a sweeping reform in the most sensitive area of religious life, this perplexing situation revealed the need for a new phase of the liturgical movement of renewal from below.

Outcome and Future Directions. For Catholics, and even for many Protestants, the liturgical constitution has remained the undisputed charter yet to be discovered in its broad vision and goals. Despite the remarkable progress made through a mainly historical restoration from across a thousand years of evolving Christian worship, the primary goal of the pioneers of the liturgical movement and the conciliar fathers is yet to be realized in a credible and profound way. A reform of a more flexible and essential nature has been established, not without some polarizations, and even contradictions; but from now on perennial renewal in the celebration lies ahead.

The work of a generation should not be considered the point of arrival, but rather the point of departure. Much lies ahead, and this demands new attitudes and a new reception on the part of the hierarchy and of the people. In biblical terms, "new wine asks for new skins." This means more than "mere observance of laws," a passive and rubrical reception of the changes. It means rather a creative assimilation of the fundamental dimensions of the liturgical renewal: on the one hand, biblical symbolism, ecclesiology of communion, mystagogy; on the other hand, the understanding of the anthropological grounding and the "mental grammar" of the religious experience of today's people. If liturgy builds community, community makes liturgy.

Though an assessment of the reform is needed, it is difficult because the reality of worship in the lives of people is a complex phenomenon which goes beyond the limits of the context of worship itself. Critics usually refer to three major areas of concern in the present crisis of worship: leadership, catechetics and the emergence of new problems.

Despite the many compromises and the dilemmas of the reform (the most apparent being the rite of penance, 1974), the new rituals and the hundreds of documents issued in Rome provided both a flexible ritual which was normative and a theological-pastoral direction for the future. The constitution demanded not only a translation into the vernacular and structural changes, but also adaptation, reception of the letter and the spirit of the reform, liturgical sensibility and a new mind in promoting its ideals. A step further demanded in the longer term is the creativity of inculturation and indigenization. In this sense, the council opened the door to new opportunities for liturgical growth, foreseeing a new balance between the universal oversight of the primacy and the promotion of the liturgical action of the episcopacy.

This collegial balance can foster decentralization and pluralism, safeguarding "the substantial unity of the Roman rite" (S.C., 37-47). However, because of the tight control from above, some bishops made it the practice to show more interest in juridical approval of the changes than to face the compelling spiritual needs of the people. The problems of the promotion of the renewal of liturgical praxis were certainly compounded by profound cultural transition and the new secular trends of the post-Vatican II years. In fact, as the World Council of Churches acknowledged, "behind the crisis of worship there is a general crisis of faith" (Upsala, 1968).

The underestimation of long-term liturgical catechetics has been a perennial problem reflected in the poor reception of the reform. The quality of participation in engaging liturgies depended on preparation and renewal of the community. The crisis of meaning could stem not only from the irrelevant spirituality of ritual and textual mystification, and inadequate symbolic expression of the mystery, but also from the lack of an experiential initiation into that mystery. In this respect, the new Rite of Christian Initiation of Adults (1972) is a serious effort to cultivate the great potential of liturgical catechetics, but only if this most authentic and far-reaching reform is taken seriously.

Finally, new problems emerge from several areas. The restoration itself seems too pragmatic, with the consequent impoverishment of contemplative and festive sense of the mystery, and the translation of the old texts inadequate to a renewed spirituality. In addition, the new liturgy demands a faithful expression in the role of the presider, a renewed liturgical music, and good preaching. Moreover, the new liturgical vision projects unforeseen demands, especially from the new self-discovery of the local church and the priesthood. Other unexpected developments could be added, such as the crisis of the oral confession, the priestless liturgies (Directory of the Congregation for Divine Worship, 1988), and the emergence of non-ordained ministries, especially the ministry of women and the global phenomenon of grassroots communities.

All these point to an unfinished agenda of the liturgical renewal and the need for ecclesiastical leadership which would further the dynamic spirit of the council. In fact, after a quarter century of the promulgation of the liturgical constitution, "the work of liturgical reform and renewal remains at the heart of the Church's life and mission" (*Promoting Liturgical Renewal; Guidelines for Diocesan Liturgical Commissions and Offices of Worship*. Secretariat, Bishops' Committee on the Liturgy, N.C.C.B., Washington, D.C.: 1988). This renewal and reform will chiefly be along the two poles of the current liturgical dialogue: the anthropological-cultural pole, which in dialogue between human sciences and liturgical theology and praxis will help us understand the concrete religious story and experience; and the ecclesiological pole, which through serious consideration of the common priesthood of the community-celebrant will renew a liturgy that builds community within and is expressed in active mission and ministry.

The liturgical reform of the council was highly positive, especially in its theological and pastoral dimensions. The ecclesiological dimension, developed in the *Dogmatic Constitution on the Church,* is still in need of theological clarification and pastoral affirmation, especially from the perspective of the local and ministerial community. The anthropological and cultural dimensions, the least explicitly developed in the Vatican documents, will be an important part of the unfinished agenda of liturgical creativity and inculturation. Pastoral liturgical studies have been ever since in search of a deeper understanding of a phenomenology of worship which embodies the essential fullness of Christian belief and the living religious traditions.

See **Reform, liturgical, . . . ; Adaptation, liturgical; Liturgical movement, the (1830-1969); Inculturation of the liturgy**

Documents on the Liturgy 1963-1979, Conciliar, Papal, and Curial Texts, trans. Thomas O'Brien, International Commission on English in the Liturgy (Collegeville, MN: The Liturgical Press, 1982). Carl Last, ed., Remembering the Future: Vatican II and Tomorrow's Liturgical Agenda (New York: Paulist Press, 1983). German Martinez, "Catholic Liturgical Reform," Theology Today 43 (1986): 52-62.

GERMAN MARTINEZ

REFORM, LITURGICAL, IN EASTERN CHURCHES

The Second Vatican Council in its *Decree on Eastern Catholic Churches* expressed its high esteem for the rich traditions of these churches and urged the latter to preserve and honor their liturgical rites and restore them where they had been altered or abandoned. Changes within Eastern Catholic liturgical rites since that time have come about in a slow pace through local desire to return to authentic traditions as well as through the urging of the Oriental Congregation in Rome. Many of these changes have appeared in the form of the return to traditional vesture and the reintroduction of ancient liturgical anaphoras and prayers. Alongside these in many places the vernacular has replaced the ancient languages in liturgical celebrations and many of the Latin Catholic liturgical insertions have been dropped.

Not all of these Latin influences (Latinizations) however have been forsaken everywhere since some of these practices (such as prayers before the statues of saints, the rosary, stations of the cross, and daily Mass) have become identified in the minds of uninformed faithful with tradition itself. Nor has the return to traditional ways been complete where it had begun. The return to ancient architectural settings and liturgical forms still remains a challenge for many Syriac churches that await the reintroduction and use of the *Bema* (a central platform for the liturgy of the word), the lack of which leaves many of the prayers and liturgical actions out of tune with their proper liturgical context. Along with these, some juridical restrictions are still in effect and are in need of reform, e.g., married priesthood is still restricted outside the immediate jurisdiction of these churches.

The carrying forward of this process of returning to tradition has become even more of a challenge in recent times since many of these churches have considerable immigrant populations in the West creating new pastoral situations and the need for liturgical recontextualization and readaptation. Thus, not all practices within a church's liturgical tradition would be appropriate for modern needs and prudent adaptations by liturgical commissions would be necessary. Many of these adaptations have taken the form of liturgical abbreviations and simplifications where the reform efforts are unorganized and without clear directions. Alongside these efforts lie the urgent need for the religious education of the faithful to enlighten them about the riches of their traditions, along with the arts and means of appropriating these traditions for modern needs. Much in this regard depends on the leadership and direction of the persons in authority in these churches—especially on their discernment a clearer sense of future directions for their people—together with the liturgical and catechetical commissions in their diocese and the cooperation of the Latin church.

In the following paragraphs I have sketched some of the efforts in liturgical reform made by the various Eastern Catholic churches in their attempts to return to tradition, and to keep in step with the times. In many cases these reforms are small and uncoordinated. They reveal the complexity of carrying forward such a challenging task and how much more effort and organization need to be undertaken.

The Maronites

The liturgical reforms in the Maronite church worldwide began in the early 1970s and continue today. The renewal, or better said, restoration of the Maronite Sunday liturgy began in both Lebanon and the U.S. (which has more than 50 parishes) through the guidance of the Vatican's Sacred Congregation for Eastern Churches in Rome and the activities of the Patriarchal Synod and Liturgical Committee in Lebanon to restore the Maronite liturgy to its original framework. These reforms have led to the restoration of the cycle of prayers and hymnals of the Sunday liturgy of the word as well as the uncovering of a very rich tradition of liturgical prayers and hymnals. While the yearly cycle for this Sunday liturgy has been restored— replacing the single form which had become common up to the end of the 1960s—the architectural aspect including the use of the *Bema* still remains to be restored. Many of the prayers and sacramental forms in this tradition, originally in Syriac, have been translated into Arabic and English for modern-day use.

Among the restorations of the Sunday liturgy have been the separate preparation of gifts at a side altar, and the dropping of the penitential rites and offertory prayers which were Roman additions. Thus the Mass begins with the liturgy of the word, with its own proper that is separate from the rites around the altar. The offertory procession has been restored with its prayers and incensing. The *Bema* however has not been reintroduced as yet and thus the first part of the Mass is held in front of the altar with the priest and deacon facing the people. Some of the litanies for this part have been abbreviated. The veil in front of the altar has not been restored. Among the new innovations, the priest faces the people during the liturgy of the eucharist, and some of the prayers from the Anaphora of Sharar and priestly prayers have been dropped or abbreviated. The traditional formula for the words of the institution has been restored with its variant forms according to the different anaphoras. The *epiclesis* has been brought to its proper position as an integral part of the consecration. Attempts at restoring early Maronite musical and hymnal forms have been made at the Holy Cross University and Maronite Seminary in Lebanon. In the U.S. the office, along with texts for all the sacraments, have been translated (and also revised) into English. Some experimentation at integrating the matrimonial rite or the office with the Mass have also been attempted. With the exception of a memorial Sunday liturgy, however, only few Maronites attend their own parishes on a regular basis.

The Chaldeans

Among the Chaldeans since the Second Vatican Council some changes in Iraq and in the U.S. have begun to take place based on mostly local initiatives and without formal organization. Among these have been the use of modern Syriac as well as Arabic languages in place of the classical Syriac. This latter however still remains in use in some parishes. Aside from the dropping of the feasts of Western saints and the restoration of the feast days of the Syriac saints in the liturgical calendar and some abbreviations of liturgical prayers, very little has been done in terms of organized liturgical reform. In many of the parishes in Iraq the priest faces the people for the liturgy of the word but his back is turned on them for the eucharistic liturgy. By contrast in the U.S. and in Western countries the Chaldean priest faces the people during the whole liturgy. In this rite too the *Bema* awaits to be restored for proper liturgical celebration in its authentic tradition.

In Iraq, in the cities, eucharistic celebrations are held mostly in Arabic with some Syriac included, while in most villages they are held in modern or in classical Syriac (still understood by some) with an Arabic scripture sometimes included. The Sunday Mass is usually sung at least in part. Variant hymns (some ancient and some modern) are also sung in all three linguistic forms: Arabic, modern Syriac, and classical Syriac. There is generally a good level of participation in the Mass, and in some parishes when the deacon is not present the laity are assigned to the ministry of reading from scripture. The other sacraments as well, such as baptism and matrimony, are often celebrated in Arabic or in modern Syriac with responsorial participation from the laity. In some parishes these Sunday activities are supplemented with a basic local catechetical program for children. Bible prayer groups for adults are also emerging now in the cities.

The Malabar Churches of India

Liturgical reform in the Malabar rites in Kerala was becoming evident after the Vatican Council, as the main liturgical language was changed from Syriac to Malayalam, the native tongue. An experimental version of the Chaldeo-Malabar rite in Malayalam was implemented and approved by the Oriental Congregation in Rome in 1968. This text of the Mass—Qurbana—with some adjustments was fixed in 1981. The latter move however has been criticized by scholars who consider the fixing of the present text as obstructing the process of return to authentic traditions which is not yet liturgically completed and which still has a good residue of the old Roman rite practices. In this rite too the *Bema* needs to be restored. A similar case can be made for the Syro-Malabar churches who have also translated their liturgical forms into the native tongue Malayalam. A few variations of the Sunday celebration according to diocese have emerged. The first part of the Mass—the liturgy of the word—is often celebrated with the priest facing the people. For the eucharistic liturgy, depending on local piety, the priest either faces the people or turns his back to face the altar. In the last few years there has been a preference in some dioceses to have the priest turn towards the altar with his back to the people. A very few churches still use the original Syriac for consecration. Participation in the liturgy is adequate due to the original participatory nature of the liturgy and because of the present use of the vernacular along with hymns and songs in Malayalam.

As with the other Eastern rites, office prayers seem to have fallen from use. In place of the office in many homes family prayer is common where the rosary is often recited. Vocations are high and many are from the middle-class and from among those families that pray together. Parish priests often live together in basic support groups. All these elements: the use of the vernacular in liturgical prayer with participation, prayer at home, and community life for the clergy seem to enhance the spiritual life of the community. The need to continue the process of reform and renewal, however, is evident. There are still old customs, especially towards women, that are in effect and that need to be changed (e.g., the purification of the mother before the baptism of her child). Some reforms also appear to be taking place in the Syrian Orthodox church (rite of Malankara). A recent Synod in Kotayam has enacted

reforms to enhance the role of women in the church. Among these: young girls, and not just boys, are taken around the altar at their baptism. No longer does the first child to be baptized in the newly consecrated font have to be the male. In addition, the bishops are encouraging women to read to the congregation from the Bible during the liturgy, and to take part in the general meetings of local parishes.

The Melkites

The Melkites have adapted their liturgy to local languages wherever they have immigrated; thus, English has been in liturgical use in the U.S. and Canada three decades before the Vatican II reforms. Other liturgical reforms, however, have taken place mainly in the form of dropping some of the Roman liturgical insertions and devotions. The original Greek usage is very limited and in the West either English or Arabic (in case of newcomers from the Mideast) dominates. Priests tend to improvise and select their own prayers based on the three anaphoras and the litanies combined. An abbreviated version of the Mass has been provided for priests where parishioners have complained about the length of the Sunday liturgy. Attendance, especially of youth, tends to be low.

The biggest immigrant Melkite population is in South America (followed by the U.S.), especially in Brazil, which also has the lowest church attendance. In the U.S., where there are Melkite parishes (of about forty in number), regular Sunday church attendance is low and on average the American-born Melkites attend more often than the Mideastern ones. Shortages in the number of priests constitute a major problem for this immigrant community spread over vast areas. The Sunday eucharistic celebrations have been supplemented with a religious education program for youth prepared in the early 1970s that is common among all the

Byzantine rites, with adaptations made by each rite.

The Ruthenians and the Ukrainians

There has been limited change within the Catholic Byzantine rites of the Russian traditions. Liturgical reforms and renewal have taken the form of dropping many of the old Roman rite insertions along with reductions of litanies and of some priestly private prayers. In some parishes in the U.S. daily Mass has become an accepted tradition. Frequent Sunday communion is now encouraged. Most Sunday liturgies among the Ruthenians are sung in English while among the Ukrainians a few are found still celebrated in the native language. New translations of liturgical prayers have appeared depending on the efforts of each diocese, along with pastoral applications suited for local needs. Most eucharistic liturgies are conducted from behind the iconostasis, including the liturgy of the word in some dioceses. In most dioceses, however, the priest comes out to read the gospel to the people and to preach from in front of the iconostasis. Other developments within the Byzantine Catholic communities are appearing very slowly in the form of local adaptations mostly arranged by liturgical commissions in each diocese.

Differences in Sunday eucharistic celebrations between the Orthodox Byzantine churches and the Catholic ones in the U.S. show that the Orthodox tend to use choirs while the Byzantine Catholics have relied mostly on cantors who would lead the people in singing the liturgical prayers. The strong presence of Russian Orthodox churches in the U.S., along with a major seminary and publishing press (St. Vladimir's) as well as other Orthodox seminaries, have helped further establish this Byzantine tradition and make it known and better understood. Some considerations towards further church renewal have been suggested by a limited few on both the Orthodox and the Catholic sides. Among these have been the creative use of the iconostasis in liturgical celebrations, the readmitting of children's communion after baptism for Catholic Byzantine churches, and a greater liturgical participation by all. However there are no major changes planned or expected on either side.

The Armenian Catholics

There is a strong national and ecumenical affiliation between Catholic and Orthodox Armenians (as well as the few Protestant ones) with a common sense of being united as one ethnic and Christian people. The co-suffering of the Armenians under persecutions in this century has strengthened their sense of affiliation and communion. On the Catholic side this sense of unity is expressed in terms of liturgical conformity with the Orthodox. Other ways in which Armenians have shown their sense of unity is through their social clubs and schools which welcome all Armenians and even share in a common religious education. Memories of persecution as well as recent suffering and the earthquake tragedy of the Armenians in Russia have brought the parties into even greater national and spiritual communion. The Mass, as in the Orthodox liturgy, is still celebrated in classical Armenian. However some adaptations and abbreviations have been made, e.g., at the liturgy of the word the scriptures may be read in modern Armenian and so are the sermons in the vernacular to facilitate understanding. In the U.S. preaching is done sometimes in English along with modern Armenian. Most Roman introductory prayers and insertions were dropped after the Second Vatican Council. Thus the present form of the Catholic Armenian Sunday liturgy is in conformity with the Orthodox with the only differences being of brevity in some places.

The Copts

The Copts of Egypt constitute a sizable majority among the Christians in the Middle East. Most of these are Orthodox with a small minority of Catholic Copts. There is also a sizable number of immigrant Copts in the West (in the U.S. the Orthodox have thirty five churches). It would be best to describe liturgical developments in this rite primarily in terms of lingual adaptations for the benefit of the new multi-lingual congregations emerging today. In Egypt the Sunday eucharist is celebrated in Coptic and Arabic while in the U.S. it is a tri-lingual celebration in Coptic, Arabic, and English. The celebration lasts more than three hours. The fewer in number Catholic Copts celebrate the same liturgy but in a more abbreviated form.

Summary Observations

It would be reasonable to conclude from the above observations that long-term planning is necessary and even essential for a worthy process of liturgical reform and renewal for the Eastern churches. When a clear outlook to the future is lacking, the liturgical process becomes lost in its direction and many "band-aid" solutions to keep up with the times begin to emerge. These temporary solutions, often in the form of improvisations, do not draw properly on the riches of that church's tradition nor do they adequately meet the spiritual needs of the faithful. It would be of great importance that Eastern Catholic bishops work collaboratively to insure that this process continues to perform adequately over the years with frequent consultations with the laity. Since many of the Eastern churches today experience themselves as over-extended minority communities around the world, the interest, support, and cooperation of local Latin rite churches would be valuable in helping these Eastern Christian communities to value and share their heritage.

The Maronite Liturgical Year, Vols. 1-3 (Diocese of St. Maron, U.S.A., 1983). J. Madey, "The Reform of the Liturgy of the Syro-Malabar Church and the Holy See of Rome," *Ostkirchliche Studien*, 30, (1981): 130-168. R. Taft, "The Question of Infant Baptism in the Byzantine Catholic Churches of the U.S.A." *Diakonia* 3:3, (1982): 201-214.

STEPHEN BONIAN, S.J.

REFORM, LITURGICAL, IN REFORMATION CHURCHES

To describe the diverse worship practices of the many and varied Reformation churches is almost beyond possibility. Lutherans, Presbyterians, Methodists, Anglicans, Congregationalists, Pentecostals, the Society of Friends, and Baptists are only some of the multiplicity of denominations and sects that were spawned by the Reformation and various revivals and splits since. An acknowledgement of diversity, then, is perhaps the first thing that has to be said about these churches before proceeding to talk about liturgical reform. The possibility of such diversity appears to have been a fundamental characteristic of the Reformation challenge to the authority of the Roman Catholic church in the 16th century.

A preliminary look at liturgical reform in the 20th century, however, reveals a movement, not toward greater diversity, but rather toward ecumenical convergence in liturgy. This is seen in such achievements as the World Council of Churches' document on *Baptism, Eucharist and Ministry*, with its accompanying consensus eucharistic service, the Lima liturgy. The convergence extends to almost all areas of liturgy, including the eucharist, Christian initiation, calendar and lectionary, daily prayer and other services such as ordination, marriage, funeral and a wide range of pastoral liturgies. A new generation of services has been emerging among the churches in the decades of the 1970s and 1980s that have in common a reform of worship in all these areas.

This convergence is far from being only a Protestant phenomenon. Much of its impetus has come from the liturgical movement in the Roman Catholic church earlier in this century that bore remarkable fruit in the Second Vatican Council. The reform also reaches out to embrace with new appreciation the worship of the Orthodox churches. And now new sources of challenge and renewal beyond the traditions of the West are emerging globally from newer churches in Asia and Africa. There is also an increasing knowledge and appreciation of worship in other religions which were at one time dismissed as heathen. Furthermore, new voices calling for reform are emerging nearer at hand from the poor, the oppressed and the generally disregarded ones in our midst, including women, native peoples, disabled persons, homosexuals, and so on.

The picture is exceedingly vast and difficult to comprehend. But we have still been looking only at the movement of ecumenical convergence that is happening primarily among those churches which are usually characterized as being more "liturgical" or "mainstream." Other churches, which have identified themselves as "evangelical," "fundamentalist," or "charismatic," have not participated as yet to any great extent in the ecumenical convergence. They indeed would probably regard their freedom for diversity to be truer to the Protestant ethos than is the movement of convergence.

The convergence in the mainstream churches, however, is not simply a recovery of a pre-Reformation uniformity. It is rather toward a unity that can embrace difference and indeed encourages new and creative responses in liturgy through the charismatic and artistic gifts of the people. This openness is clearly indicated in the rubrics of many of the new service books. They ask their users, not merely to follow a prescribed liturgy, but to use the contents of the books—the prayers, responses, symbolic actions—as resources and samples to assist and guide the people's own work and initiatives in liturgy.

This recovery of the people's participation in the liturgy is profoundly in keeping with the Reformation insistence on the priesthood of all believers. The Reformers sought to render the liturgy accessible to all the people through such means as translation of the liturgical texts into the vernacular and the encouragement of congregational singing of psalms, hymns and canticles. The recovery of the notion of the whole people of God as celebrants in liturgy may indeed be one of the greatest contributions of the Reformation to the modern climate of liturgical renewal. This remains a goal even if history has shown it to unleash factions that disrupt the unity of Christ's body.

I have identified convergence as a primary characteristic of the current movements of liturgical reform among the churches, Reformed, Orthodox and Catholic. We need to consider what is at the root of this convergence and whether there is anything in the legacy of the Reformation, despite the diversity it unleashed, that has contributed to it. The modern liturgical convergence, I would maintain, has its source in a recovery of the biblical basis for Christian prayer and praise. The biblical witness to the saving acts of God in covenant with the people of Israel and culminating in the life, death and resurrection of Jesus Christ is the source *non pareil* of the Christian enactment of faith in the liturgy. Christians see all the events of their lives in the light of God's illuminating word, proclaimed and enacted in the liturgy. Our own stories, as is commonly said, belong in the larger context of the biblical story, and, together, these are celebrated week-by-week in the liturgy.

A unique place was given to the scriptures as the primary authority for faith and worship in the Reformation principle of *sola scriptura*. The scripture principle was enunciated by the Reformers in their conflict with the teaching authority of the Roman church with its claim of equality with the authority of scripture. Whether that is a correct reading of the Catholic understanding of authority does not need to concern us here. Of continuing importance is the Reformers' efforts to restore the Bible to the people and to reaffirm its authority for all matters of faith and life. But the scripture principle did not ensure unity among the Reformation churches. Many of the churches differed in how they understood *sola scriptura*. Some, like the Puritans, maintained that worship ought to consist only of that which is directly authorized by the scriptures. The consequence of the strict application of this criterion to worship was a drastic reduction of ceremonial practices and a focusing almost exclusively on the scriptures read and preached, and on prayer. Other churches of the Reformation, including those that followed Luther and Calvin most closely, regarded *sola scriptura* not as eliminating all other sources for liturgy, but rather placing scripture in the position of being *without equal* beside all other sources. Both Luther and Calvin appealed often, for example, to the authority of the primitive churches and the church fathers. Their study of both the scriptures and the early church led them to advocate a weekly celebration of the eucharist with both bread and wine distributed among the people.

Whereas the Reformers are noted for their efforts to restore the scriptures to the people, it is less known that they sought, albeit unsuccessfully, to do the same for the sacraments. Calvin's efforts to establish the eucharist every Sunday in Geneva, for example, were stymied by a ruling of the city magistrates, who favored the practice of four times a year that was already the rule in Zwingli's church in Zurich. This rule has been, with some exceptions, the practice in most Reformation churches until the recent liturgical reform. Perhaps the failure of the Reformation to restore fully the sacraments has to be understood in relation to their application of the scripture principle. Whether *sola scriptura* was applied strictly or more broadly, it served to cleanse the liturgy of what the Reformers regarded as human inventions and accretions. Only baptism and the Lord's Supper, for example, of the seven sacraments designated by the church of the Middle Ages, had the required dominical institution for acceptance as sacraments in the Reformation churches.

In the eucharist Luther also almost totally eliminated the Roman canon because of its unbiblical emphasis on sacrifice. His objections to the sacrifice of the Mass were not, it has to be said, against the notion of sacrifice itself. According to his understanding, to make the Mass into a sacrifice that could be repeated was a denial of what God had done once-for-all in the sacrifice of Christ. The biblical notion of justification by faith in this once-for-all sacrifice of Christ became a criterion for rejecting any worship that became a pious work rather than a response in thanksgiving to God's work of grace. The Reformers regarded much of the ceremonial practices and private acts of devotion in the Roman church as pious works designed to win God's favor rather than to express joyful thanksgiving for that favor already bestowed. This Reformation insight into the biblical doctrine of grace has had immense significance for the modern understanding of true motivation for prayer and worship.

The Reformers, however, did not recover, as the modern churches in their eucharistic renewal have, the biblical understanding of *berakah*, or blessing God, as an act of praise for God's saving acts. The worship of the Reformation churches tended to retain the penitential note of medieval piety. To that they added a strong note of moral exhortation and didacticism, partly because of the emphasis on word as opposed to symbol and ritual. The Hebrew understanding of *berakah* was missed by the Reformers largely because the scriptures were not fully accessible to them in their attempts to reform the liturgy. Greater accessibility has come only with the development of the modern discipline of historical-critical study of the scriptures. This study arose in large measure out of the empiricism and historicity of the 18th-century Enlightenment period with its rejection of metaphysics and faith as giving access to truth that is beyond ordinary human sense experience. Because the churches for long regarded the atheistic tendencies of the philosophy of the Enlightenment as antagonistic to religion and worship they tended also to reject historical-critical study of the scriptures. The acceptance of the value of this study for greater discernment of the truth of the scriptures in many modern churches, both Reformation and Catholic, is a prime factor, I believe, in the present liturgical convergence.

Because Protestant scholars generally have been, until recently, in the vanguard of scriptural study, Catholics have regarded their work as one of the greatest contributions of the Reformation churches to liturgical reform. At the same time the Reformation churches have been able to see more clearly the value of the great liturgical heritage of the Roman Catholic and Orthodox churches, particularly as those churches have been rediscovering through critical study their roots in the churches of the first few centuries. Inquiring behind the circumstances of the beginning of Christendom in the establishment of Christianity as the favored religion of the Roman Empire is being seen by many Christians today as uncovering an important source for renewal. The Reformation churches have been quick to appropriate such historical discoveries as the tradition of Hippolytus, among other early sources, for the structure and content of the eucharistic prayer. Early baptismal practices that were the sole rite of membership in the church, following an extensive catechumenate, and combining ample use of water, anointing with oil, and the laying on of hands with prayer for the Holy Spirit, are seen as essential in this era of recovery of the ministry of the whole people of God. Discoveries pertaining to the liturgy of time, including the calendar and lectionary and the liturgy of the hours or daily prayer, are being acknowledged also as critical to living in a secular realm by the rhythm of the gospel.

This appropriation of liturgical practices by the Reformation churches, in my opinion, has been made both possible and necessary because of a new appreciation of the nature and function of symbol and ritual. Modern study of language is revealing the dynamic nature of both words and symbols. Liturgy comprises both word-events and sign-acts. And both are means by which God can communicate and be present with human beings and human beings with God and one another. Liturgy that seeks to embrace the whole of reality, as revealed by a God who acts in incarnational ways, must be an embodied liturgy, appealing to all the senses of the body. Symbolic liturgy that includes sights as well as sounds, actions and gestures, the movements of procession and dance, and a renewed appreciation of the sacraments, opens up new possibilities for all to participate as they are able. For many Protestants, with their suspicion of ritual and symbol, the discovery by anthropologists that human beings are, by nature, ritual-making creatures has been an important one. It is through their rituals that human beings can come together in community around the apprehension of a deeper reality. Symbols and rituals are means by which reality is communicated and people are enabled to participate.

Many of the earlier debates between Protestants and Roman Catholics concerning the mode of God's presence in the sacraments are being superseded by a new language that speaks of God's presence in the symbolic action of the liturgy. The discovery of the biblical notion of the eschatological nature of the gospel has provided a new understanding of God's presence both within and beyond history. The words and symbols of the liturgy express both the "now" and the "not yet" of the reign of God that was proclaimed by Jesus and inaugurated in his ministry. Liturgy can be experienced as a foretaste of the future God has in store for the world. To participate in this anticipatory event is to commit oneself to working toward the justice, peace and love to which God is beckoning the whole world.

The renewal of liturgy in the Reformation churches finds its genuine motivation, in unity with other churches, in praise of a Creator who summons all earthly creatures to respond in faith, and in commitment to the renewal of a creation that is still "groaning in travail." "For in this hope we were saved" (Rom 8:22).

Baptism, Eucharist and Ministry, Faith and Order paper No. 111 (Geneva: World Council of Churches, 1982). Ferdinand Hahn, *The Worship of the Early Church*, trans. by David E. Green (Philadelphia: Fortress Press, 1973). David R. Newman, *Worship As Praise and Empowerment* (New York: Pilgrim Press, 1988). Hughes Oliphant Old, *Worship That is Reformed According to Scripture* (Atlanta: John Knox Press, 1984).

DAVID R. NEWMAN

REFORM, LITURGICAL, OF VATICAN II

Liturgical reform, sometimes euphemistically called restoration or renewal, can generally be distinguished from liturgical promotion, catechesis, and efforts for better participation. These latter do not necessarily involve altering or revising the received liturgical forms, elements, and words. Vatican II devoted a very small but important part of its constitution on the liturgy, *Sacrosanctum concilium* of December 4, 1963, to promotion and instruction (articles 14-20; 43-46—the articles of the constitution will simply be referred to below by number); the rest of the document deals with reform of the Roman liturgy. To say this is not to minimize the substantial doctrinal section on the nature of the liturgy at the beginning of chap. I (5-13) or the doctrinal paragraphs at the head of each of the six other chapters. But these doctrinal statements are to explain or support the reform, and the constitution is basically disciplinary, a reform decree. And the church as a human and earthly institution always stands in need of "perennial reformation" (U.R., 6).

Given the predominance of the Roman rite in the worldwide church, the direct concern in 1962-1963 was not with the other rites of the Latin church, much less with the rites of the Eastern churches, although the council invited a parallel revision of other rites where needed (4) or their organic development (O.E., 6), and even allowed for the possible creation of new rites in the future (4). Similarly, the non-liturgical or extra-liturgical life of the church was not ignored, but its reform is mentioned only once and then in strong terms: devotions "should be so fashioned that they harmonize with the liturgical seasons, accord with the sacred liturgy, are in some way derived from it, and lead the people to it, since, in fact, the liturgy by its very nature far surpasses any of them" (13).

The Context of Vatican II's Reform

The broader context of liturgical reform decreed by Vatican II and carried out in the years after the council is the modern liturgical movement. In the 19th century this was a matter of fresh scholarship, monastic and Gregorian chant revival, and the particular phenomenon of the suppression of the neo-Gallican rites in favor of the Roman liturgy. In the early 20th century these forces took a different turn in the direction of the broadest liturgical participation of the whole ecclesial community and a deeper theological appreciation of the social and spiritual implications of Christian public worship. For the most part, however, the movement or apostolate in Europe and elsewhere was directed toward better understanding and participation in the existing liturgical forms rather than in revision or reform.

The only substantive reform in the Roman liturgy since the 16th century was initiated but not completed by Pius X at the beginning of the 20th century. It involved a radical purging of the Roman liturgical calendar and other simplifications, affecting the eucharistic celebration and the daily offices, with the purpose of strengthening the primacy of the Lord's Day and the temporal cycle, especially the Lenten season. Concomitant with that pope's exhortations concerning Gregorian chant and the sense of liturgical participation as the source of Christian life was the even more important disciplinary revolution of early and frequent communion. None of this, however, touched upon the change of structures, rites, or even the prayer elements of the liturgy. Although the 16th-century Congregation of Rites had followed its mandate of revising the Roman liturgical books, the corrections in new editions were always minor. Even in 1930 when Pius XI added a historical section to the old congregation, its principal work by far was in the cases of beatification and canonization that involved historical research rather than the reform of the liturgical books, much less real revision of the rites themselves.

The 1947 encyclical of Pius XII on Christian worship, *Mediator Dei et hominum*, was welcomed as the first thorough exposition of contemporary doctrine on the liturgy and a strong support for popular participation. It contained no indication of plans—under consideration since 1946—to take up the reform of Pius X, but on May 28, 1948, the pope established a special commission for general liturgical reform. The work of this commission, slight only by comparison with the later conciliar reform, continued through the remaining years of Pius XII and even into the first years of John XXIII. It formed the immediate context of what would be undertaken by the council itself, and Pope John made the point explicitly in promulgating the new "code of rubrics" in 1962: "that the more basic principles (*altiora principia*) affecting the general liturgical restoration should be proposed" to the conciliar fathers for their determination.

The several accomplishments of the commission of Pius XII were significant enough in themselves, more significant as a forecast of what was becoming more evident: the encouragement of full participation by the whole people in the liturgy—and even the use of the vernacular, insinuated by Pius XII in the encyclical *Mediator Dei* and begun on a limited scale in the regional bilingual rituals of the sacraments in the 1950s—would be inadequate. In addition to the simplification of the calendar and rubrics and a private survey of the episcopate concerning the breviary (1956-1957), a few rites were actually revised by the commission: the Easter vigil (1951), the other services of Holy Week (1955), the pontifical rites for dedicating churches and for other occasions—but not ordinations (1961), and the baptism of adults (1962). In each case, however, the principles at work were the very ones which would later become commonplace: directions that "all" respond, listen to the readings, etc.; concentration on Christian initiation (both in the revised Easter vigil and in the baptismal rites for the stages of the catechumenate); suppression of duplications in which the priest had to recite the readings and chants properly belonging to others; occasional omission of the medieval accretions at the beginning and end of Mass; simpler and clearer structural elements in the revised section of the Roman Pontifical of 1961.

As in other historical instances of reform, the participation of particular individuals in the commission of Pius XII is significant, for example, that of Cardinal Agostino Bea, Redemptorist Josef Loew (who had initiated the project within the Congregation of Rites after the prefect and secretary had been directed by the pope to pursue the study

of reform in 1946), and Vincentian Annibale Rugnini, the commission's secretary, who effectively guided the Roman reform from 1948 to 1975. From outside the Roman Curia came the influence of the post-World War II liturgical centers in Paris and Trier, both pastoral and scholarly in character, and the regular, informal gatherings of liturgical scholars—now concerned with reform as well as with promotion—during the 1950s.

The Role of Vatican II

In 1959 John XXIII invited proposals for the work of the general council he had announced. Among the responses received from the Catholic episcopate, universities and faculties and from the Roman Curia were very many concerning liturgical reform; they are included among the ante-preparatory *acta* of the council. These recommendations were subjected to study by the Preparatory Commission on the Liturgy, which worked from November 1960 to January 1962 to produce a draft of a disciplinary constitution for debate, amendment, and possible adoption by the conciliar fathers. Chaired by Cardinal Gaetano Cicognani, with Bugnini as secretary and principal organizer of the project, the bishops and priests of the commission made use of the worldwide proposals but also contributed a wealth of pastoral experience, scholarship, and above all their own positive commitment to liturgical reform.

The draft approved unanimously by the commission in early 1962 resembles the final document of the council closely enough. Before the opening of the council, however, the draft had first to be presented for review to the Central Preparatory Commission in the early spring of 1962. This was done by the liturgical commission's new president, Cardinal Arcadio Larraona, who had succeeded Cicognani upon the latter's death and who was clearly out of sympathy with the draft and with liturgical reform in general. In this he reflected judgments or attitudes within the Roman Curia which continued throughout the council and in the period after the council.

Although the review by the Central Preparatory Commission revealed substantial dissatisfaction with the draft, the number of emendations was relatively small. A few were serious, in particular a radical lessening of the proposed role of the national and other conferences of bishops in liturgical development—a role which was reduced to that of petitioning change rather than legislating it. A simple note was prefixed to the draft, attributing the program of potential liturgical reform exclusively to the existing Congregation of Rites. And explanatory "declarations" attached to the draft were suppressed, with the effect that the conciliar fathers later engaged in some needless debate because they lacked this information.

During the first weeks of Vatican II, in the fall of 1962, the draft of the constitution was debated exhaustively at fifteen meetings or general congregations, with as many negative arguments as positive. At the end, however, the text was almost unanimously accepted in principle, that is, as the basis of amendments to be prepared by the new Conciliar Commission on the Liturgy—a commission elected in larger part by the council but chaired by Larraona, with the Franciscan Ferdinando Antonelli, a major official of the Congregation of Rites, as secretary. Because it was the first document to be considered by the council, the procedural rules of amendments, extensive reports, review of specific objections or *modi* from those who were otherwise favorable, successive votes on sections and on the full text were scrupulously followed: the conciliar fathers voted 114 times in the two-year period before enacting the amended document by a vote of 2,147 to 4.

The opening chapter of the con-stitution—including the introductory doctrine and norms for liturgical promotion and education as well as the principles of reform—had been successfully completed and agreed upon in the first period of the council, leaving to the second period in 1963 the remaining chapters which deal with the more specific basics of reform. A detailed study of the variations, from draft to final decree, that is, the legislative history, has its own importance; these may be followed in the *Acta Synodalia* of Vatican II. The principal developments are especially revealing.

In chap. I, two restorations of the Preparatory Commission's original plan were achieved. All reference to the Congregation of Rites was suppressed; it was taken for granted (and explicitly mentioned in reports from the Conciliar Commission to the council) that a distinct reform commission would be created by the pope (see 25). More broadly, the implementation and enlargement of the reform—over and above the initial revision of the Roman rite as a whole—was attributed not only to the individual bishops of the local churches but also to their conferences or assemblies (22, 36, 39-40, 63, etc.).

During the amendment process, the heart of chap. I and indeed of the whole document, on the norms or principles of liturgical reform (21-40), was refined, strengthened, and given a more logical arrangement, with a guarantee of a limited but still open-ended concession of the vernacular. The most important reworking was perhaps that of the "norms for adapting the liturgy to the cultures and traditions of peoples" (37-40). As noted below, this section alone had and has the potential to recover the original style and polity of liturgical development arising out of the diverse customs and usages of worship within the Spirit-filled ecclesial community—a value far greater than the immediacies of Roman liturgical reform, successful as these have been as the fruit of Vatican II.

During the fall of 1963, revisions were approved in each of the succeeding chapters of the constitution, generally strengthening the force of the reform provisions in view of the initial and largely unexpected success of chap. I in 1962. Because the pastoral-liturgical scholarship on the eucharistic celebration was further advanced than in the other rites, chap. II on the eucharist could be sharply defined, clarifying especially the need for thorough reform of the Order of Mass (50); in the case of controverted matters like concelebration and communion from the cup, concessions were redrawn by way of examples without closing the door to any future expansion of the practices (55, 57).

In chap. III—on "the other sacraments and the sacramentals"—again the limited achievements in the preconciliar reform of the liturgical catechumenate were solidified (65-71) along with the ritual reform of other sacraments and services, and the draft was amended substantially to allow the use of the vernacular without even the nominal limitations agreed upon in 1962 (63).

The amendment of chap. IV on the divine office was done carefully enough but without resolving the problem of the daily prayer of the whole Christian community as compared or contrasted to the traditions of an ecclesial prayer celebrated usually by the ordained and by religious. Without major questions, chap. V on the church year was improved in the light of debate, retaining among other things the purpose of subordinating the sanctoral observances to the celebration of the mysteries of the Lord, as had the reforming popes of the past (Pius V, Pius X, and John XXIII himself). In the treatment of liturgical music in chap. VI, a considerable abbreviation of the draft was achieved, partly in the hope of avoiding controversies over musical theory, while insisting upon popular participation in liturgical song and supporting the sung as well as the recited vernacular. A separate chapter of the draft on church appurtenances was suppressed in favor of a single article (128) within the final chapter of the document, concerned with liturgical art, architecture and furnishings.

By all counts the completed constitution, amended at the recommendation of a Conciliar Commission as sympathetic to reform as the Preparatory Commission had been, was stronger than the draft. As the first decree of Vatican II, it foreshadowed and influenced what was to come in the other 15 documents. The constitution begins with a summary of the conciliar purposes as a whole (renewal of Christian life, accommodation to contemporary life, ecumenism, and evangelization (1) and a seminal description of the church which celebrates the liturgy (2); this description would be taken up in the *Dogmatic Constitution on the Church* (see L.G. 1-17, esp. 8). The constitution's project for the ritual reform of Christian initiation (65-71) is respected in the other conciliar documents, e.g., whenever the interrelated sacraments of baptism, confirmation, and eucharist (and their sequence) are mentioned (see L.G., 11). Its project for the reform of the lectionaries and of homilizing is likewise reflected in treating the scriptures (D.V. 21, 24-25) and the ordained ministry (P.O., 4). Sometimes more obviously, sometimes in passing, the other documents incorporate a heightened sense of the place of a restored liturgy in the total life of the church community (see C.D., 30; P.O., 4-6; P.C. 6, 15; and O.T. 8, 16—although with much less concern for academic liturgical studies in presbyteral formation than decreed in 15-17). The importance of the liturgy in ecumenical relationships is heightened in the decree on that topic (see U.R. 15, 22).

In some instances the discipline of the

liturgical constitution is directly augmented in other decrees, for example, in the restoration of the diaconate (L.G., 29). Canonically, the embryonic and indeterminate responsibilities attributed to conferences of bishops and their traditional antecedents, particular or regional councils (called "various kinds of competent territorial bodies of bishops lawfully established" in 22 § 1) are given a fixed procedure in the decree on the pastoral office of bishops in the church (C.D., 36-38). Here the principle of ecclesial subsidiarity, first explicitly applied to the church by Pius XII, is at work—as it affects both individual local churches and groups of local churches (compare also 22 § 1 and C.D., 8).

Another matter, in which the liturgical constitution could deal directly only with the ritual celebrations of Christian initiation, was taken up from a broader ecclesial viewpoint in the *Decree on the Missionary Activity of the Church* (A.G., 13-14; see also L.G., 14). In this case the total process of catechumenal formation is described in terms integrating it with (and sanctifying it by) the liturgical celebrations.

Conciliar Norms for Liturgical Reform

Despite the experience, scholarship, and basic agreement among the original authors and the conciliar revisers of the document, the statement of reform principles (given in 21-40) had inevitably to be abstract and general. This was all the likelier because a consensus had to be reached among at least two-thirds of the conciliar fathers. This makes the strong articulation of general principles, designed to govern the disciplinary reform after the council had acted, still more remarkable.

The formal norms or principles are enumerated under four headings after a rather euphemistic reference to the need for reform, namely, to change elements "if they have suffered from the intrusion of anything out of harmony with the inner nature of liturgy or have become pointless" (21) and the altogether fundamental (and explanatory) statement of purpose: "In this reform both text and rites should be so drawn up that they express more clearly the holy things that they signify and so that the Christian people, as far as possible, are able to understand them with ease and to take part in the rites fully, actively, and as befits a community" (21). This language explains in part what is sometimes called the rather cerebral or intellectual nature of the reform. In fact it aims at intelligibility as an essential prerequisite to participation that is total—of the whole person, mind and body, will and intellect, interior and exterior, rather than accidental or partial; active rather than passive; and communal rather than individualistic. None of this goal need be, nor was intended to be, at the expense of inner piety, the aesthetic dimension of the liturgy, or the full psychological and indeed emotional commitment of each member of the assembly—quite the opposite.

(1) *General Norms* (22-25). Under this heading, the locus of power and liturgical authority is first determined in the bishop of Rome, the chief bishop, and in each of the diocesan bishops at the head of the respective local churches and, at the intermediary level, in assemblies of bishops from a group of churches (22). The determination is made by the council itself, by the supreme authority of the college of bishops—and then the means to reform the Roman liturgy as a whole is mandated: by revising the traditional liturgical books "as soon as possible" (25). The first decree, on the holders of authority, governs whether there is reform or not; the second, on revision, is directed toward the immediate future, but may be taken also as a reminder that the reform at the universal level, or at least throughout the Latin church, is something that

must not be done and then neglected for three or four centuries as had happened once the post-Tridentine revisions were complete.

Two central matters are touched on as "general," and both are critical. The first is that reform should be an organic development, preceded by exhaustive study and introduced only if "the good of the Church genuinely and certainly requires... " (23). Here a balance is proposed between sound tradition (always in contrast to the weaknesses and defects long evident in the "traditional" Roman liturgy) and legitimate progress. It has particular application also to the fourth set of norms, on liturgical adaptation. On the one hand, the most radical development is not ruled out, even to the extent of a new and entirely non-Roman or non-Latin rite in different cultures (see 4, 40); on the other hand, the hope and expectation are clear: it should be possible to reform the Roman rite and, still within its substantial unity (38), adapt and accommodate it. The balance between innovation and precedent—if the precedent or tradition is itself sound—corresponds to the constitution's initial statement of the total conciliar purpose, in particular, the strengthening of the Christian life and accommodation of any and all changeable institutions to the needs of the times (1).

The second central question treated among these general norms is the grave deficiency of the preconciliar Roman liturgy in the use of the Hebrew and Christian Scriptures. The weakness is not mentioned but only understood in the positive exposition of the place of scripture in the liturgy: readings, psalms, prayers, songs, the source of religious meaning for actions and signs. At this point the terms of the reform of the use of scripture are not stated, only that the promotion of the role of the written word of God as proclaimed in the assembly is "essential to achieve the reform, progress, and adaptation of the liturgy" (24).

Unspoken but underlying this statement—and the more specific norms that appear in the third section of the rules for reform—is the fact that in the 16th century other Christian churches of the West restored the place of the word of God in the assembly of worship, sometimes disproportionately at the expense of the eucharistic sacrament, sometimes in the balanced style now planned by Vatican II. It is a good example also of something preserved outwardly in the Roman liturgy (that is, an actual liturgy of the word within every eucharistic celebration) but clearly subordinate as well as unintelligible because of the Latin language employed, with the homily in practice an interruption when indeed it was included.

(2) *Hierarchic and Communal Nature of the Liturgy* (26-32). Despite its title, the principles set down in this section are almost entirely concerned with non-hierarchic participation in the celebration—since this had to be the basic reform: to return to the whole Christian assembly its full share in the services of worship and to accord individual members of the community, including lay as well as ordained, their special and appropriate roles. This dimension of reform is a kind of declericalization of the Roman liturgy. By no means does it deny or minimize the hierarchic role of bishops and presbyters as the presidents of the liturgical assembly or of deacons assisting and guiding the assembly. Rather it corrects the medieval assumption of all the parts—prayers, readings, and song—by the presiding celebrant, especially in the commonest liturgical rite, the non-sung eucharist.

Two of the norms, on the public and communal nature of all liturgical services and on communal participation, are very broadly stated. The first puts into more concrete terms the constitution's own definition of the Christian liturgy (7); it insists on the differentiation of liturgical roles "of the individual members of the Church in different ways, according to their different [sacramental] orders, offices, and actual participation" (26). The principle is made normative for the reform—and for the future—by stating once for all that "each one, [ordained] minister or layperson, who has an office to perform, should do all of, but only, those parts which pertain to that office by the nature of the rite and the principles of liturgy" (28).

The other rule gives preference to communal celebration over "a celebration that is individual and, so to speak, private" (27). An application is made in the first place to the eucharist, but with a proviso that "every Mass has of itself a public and social character." This is one of the more cautious or hesitant elements of the document: the *Missa privata* of priest and server, though not necessarily the solitary Mass, must not appear to be condemned out of hand. The same point might have been made of auricular confession, where the minister and penitent constitute the ecclesial community at worship and where again the council, for all its preference for truly communal celebration, could hardly condemn the medieval and modern tradition.

Direct guidance for the Roman reform is offered in another paragraph, one that enumerates the parts to be assigned to the people in the revised liturgical books: "acclamations, responses, psalmody, antiphons, and songs, as well as by actions, gestures, and bearing" (30). To this was added an element overlooked in the original draft: "And at the proper times all should observe a reverent silence." The reference to "all" means the assembly as a whole and also the presiding celebrant, the ministers, singers, and others. This directive proposed to correct a severe defect in the old Roman rite: there were no formally prescribed periods of liturgical silence, and what silence there was existed because people were silent when they should have been speaking or singing, because the priest said the central eucharistic prayer quietly, or because there were practical gaps in the service. The reform, proposed in a brief clause, was to introduce religious and communal silence at certain points.

(3) *Teaching and Pastoral Character of the Liturgy* (33-36). At least one-third of the 131 articles of the constitution are concerned with communal celebration in terms of the active participation of the congregation, externalized in word or act or gesture, or in common silence as just mentioned. The preconciliar rite did not formally prohibit such participation, but the restrictions on the recited or dialogue Mass did not disappear until 1958. Even the Roman instruction of that year did not stimulate anything like universal acceptance, and the form of the rites themselves, whether of the eucharist or of other sacraments and services, inhibited such participation.

The concern for comprehensible rites, in which the doctrine of the liturgy as the act of the Christian community might become evident, stands at the head of the entire treatment of reform mentioned already (21), and the explicit concern for simplicity is found in this third section. A balance is struck between the cultic dimension of the liturgy, the community's union with Christ in the worship of God (and God's action in the liturgy, as defined in 7) and what is described as the teaching, formative, and didactic element.

The constitution does not show great anxiety on this point, but it cannot be read properly to permit the liturgy to become a catechetical lesson or a largely didactic, indoctrinating exercise. Instead the theory is enunciated that, even prescinding from the intangible working of divine power, all the liturgical elements as compiled or created—and now to be reformed—have an instructive side and effect. This is obvious in the case of the explicit proclamation of the word in readings and preaching, but also in prayers, songs, action, whether these are done by the assembly as a whole or assimilated by it and affirmed by it. The doing is the more important, whether it is the celebration of the word or the singing of a psalm or the assent of an "Amen," but the learning by that doing is demanded in the reform. The liturgy is thus declared to have a teaching and a pastoral nature, and it is the purpose of third set of norms to guide the reform in this direction.

If the mention of the didactic side includes a certain peril—that the rites might become classroom lectures—the same is true of the specific directive that "the rites should be marked by a noble simplicity; they should be short, clear, and unencumbered by useless repetitions; they should be within the people's powers of comprehension and as a rule not require much explanation" (34).

The background of this norm of the decree involves the historical development of the Roman liturgy, which is understood to have been characterized in the beginning by great austerity and simplicity, for example, in the ancient presidential prayers. In some measure Vatican II intended to canonize this simplicity in view of the complex excesses of medieval or earlier ecclecticism in the rite, while allowing (in the fourth set of norms) room for adaptability and augmentation. Instances of complexity (and incomprehensibility) had been canonized after the Council of Trent, despite the pruning of the calendar: excessive verbalization, repetitiousness of gestures, court ceremonial carried to an extreme, minutiae of rubrical directions, preservation of the obsolete—all remained as characteristic of the modern preconciliar rite.

The danger in reform was recognized in the qualification that the desired and required simplicity be noble. This is stated to counter the possibility that the simplification might itself be extreme, inelegant, or unaesthetic, although none of such defects is a necessary mark of simplicity in human creations. The weight, moreover, is placed upon clarity, brevity, avoidance of clumsy and meaningless (and wearying) repetition, and a degree of comprehensibility that needs little explanation to the assembly. While recognizing the dangers of what has been called over-verbalization, the constitution had to leave unresolved the general level of understanding at which the rites should be comprehensible. Elsewhere it is clear that the ordinary Sunday assembly is meant (see 42, 49) and certainly not a gathering of a sophisticated and highly cultivated elite. The use of the loosely definable term "pastoral" at the head of the section is thus explained and justified.

Noble simplicity, brevity, and clarity apply equally to rites and to words. In the case of words, however, the reform of the Roman rite in the Latin language, although necessary and here decreed by Vatican II, could not achieve these purposes without transferring these goals to the genius of the respective vernacular language. Before touching this matter of the vernacular, however, the section on teaching and pastoral nature of the liturgy deals directly with the relation of words and rites, stating broadly but significantly that more of scripture should be read in the worshipping assembly, with selections or pericopes more varied and apposite (34, 1); that preaching is integral to the liturgical celebration and should have a content consistent with its context in the celebration—as the proclamation of God's wonderful works (35, 2; see 52, 92); and that the needed liturgical catechesis may be supplemented even during the liturgy by brief and discreet explanations (35, 3).

A final norm (35, 4), not in the draft, was added to encourage (non-eucharistic) celebrations of the word of God in general and also in place of the eucharist when no ordained priest is present to preside. Underlying this is dissatisfaction with the style of existing popular non-sacramental services (see 13), a recognition that the canonical office of daily hours is inadequate for the purpose, and awareness of the paucity of ordained ministers in some regions, to grow graver in succeeding years.

As a matter of reform, the cautious concession of the vernacular is of vast impact but rather simple in terms of the Roman revision, since the matter of determining the extent of such use was simply left to the discretion of the conferences of bishops, subject to Roman review, and the translation into the vernaculars might be of either a revised or an unrevised Roman rite. The constitution at this point treats the matter as one of discipline (36) and subsequently as a lesser kind of regional adaptation (39)—almost distinct from the formal liturgical reform of the Roman rite being decreed.

(4) *Adaptation to Cultures and Traditions* (37-40). Just as the doctrinal and promotional parts of chap. I of the constitution might have been decreed without reform taking place, so the first three sections concerned with reform could have been agreed upon and carried out with a radically changed but still rigidly uniform Roman liturgy celebrated by most of the hundreds of millions of Christians in full communion with the See of Rome—but in the respective vernaculars. This makes the final section on reform all the more significant, if necessarily embryonic.

These paragraphs recognize that a reform of the Roman liturgy, however thorough and sound in its implementation, will be inadequate for the diversity of cultures and traditions in the local churches. This is evident in the case of cultures far removed from the relatively common and shared European culture, such as those in the younger churches of missionary lands now known as the Third World, but the text of the constitution is carefully crafted to extend the potential adaptability or diversity to regions no longer considered missionary, perhaps especially those where there are major differences among cultures and subcultures.

Since this development was almost unknown terrain in 1963 and the conciliar fathers could deal directly only with the perceived needs of reforming the basic, nuclear, and exemplary Roman rite, the principles are broadly stated and the norms are canonical.

The principle of adaptation—using the term in its broadest sense of any development arising out of the Roman liturgical reform already mandated—is stated both negatively and positively: to avoid "rigid uniformity in matters that do not affect the faith or the good of the whole community"; to "preserve intact" and even "admit such elements [of indigenous cultures and traditions] into the liturgy itself, provided they are in keeping with the true and authentic spirit of the liturgy" (37). No elaboration into questions of acculturation or inculturation was made, nor was it then possible. The openness to incremental (or abbreviating) variants of the rite, once revised, was established in principle, and it remained only to set up a pattern for regional reform.

In turn this was done by distinguishing between, first, the variants or adaptations which would be judged ordinary and usual and, second, those of a more profound or radical kind. For the first, the "substantial unity of the Roman rite" was to be respected (38), the conferences of bishops would be competent to make the decisions, and the Roman revision itself should anticipate these adaptations and enumerate them in the rubrics of the Roman liturgical books "especially in the case of the sacraments, the sacramentals, processions, liturgical language, sacred music, and the arts" (39). By saying that the revised Roman liturgical books should make provision for anticipated variants, thus determining *a priori* the more evident or likely ways in which conferences of bishops would feel it desirable to act, a category of lesser adaptations was defined and the potential development made a part of the basic Roman reform. What was not done, and could not have been done *a priori*, was to give an adequate rationale for distinguishing such adaptations from the more profound developments also envisioned; in fact this is a matter of degree and almost an invitation to subjectivity, ordinarily by judging small variants major.

For the second category of truly major and profound adaptations, more than the usual Roman review of national or regional liturgical books was demanded by the conciliar constitution: after study the conferences may "propose" such radical changes—even outside the (undefined) "substantial unity of the Roman rite"— to the Roman See, the consent of which is required for the actual introduction of radical adaptations. In this connection the conciliar decree raises the expectation that the Roman See will empower the conferences "to permit and direct, as the case requires, the necessary preliminary experiments within certain groups suited for the purpose and for a fixed time" (40). Not every case need require trial use, but the Roman See undertook to permit experiment even prior to giving its definitive assent to the serious adaptations of this nature.

In this fashion a total plan of reform was designed: the revision of the Roman liturgy, together with its use in the vernacular; the incorporation of potential adaptations into the revised rites, with their adoption left to the judgment of the respective assemblies of bishops; and more radical changes introduced, possibly after trial use, but only with Roman prior assent. Thus, too, the liturgical reform of Vatican II was not only defined and decreed with norms, guidelines, and principles, but its potential further reform on a regional basis was vastly enlarged in a few brief sentences.

It is arguable that the norms for revision decreed in this fashion had omissions, and certainly they could not foresee all the needed liturgical reforms—not even in the details which filled chaps. II-VII of the document. In a sense they are inward-looking, oriented toward the church community in itself and almost exclusively when the church is at worship (see 41). The references to the relationship of the liturgy to the whole of Christian life are few (see 1, 9-12); the references to the liturgy as a function of the church's relation to "those outside" (see 1-2) are relatively slight. Much of this was simply left to the *Dogmatic Constitution on the Church* (L.G.)—undergoing thorough reworking while the liturgical document was being put in final form—and the *Pastoral Constitution on the Church in the Modern World* (G.S.), plans for which were being discussed just as chap. I of the document was being completed in 1962.

There is no explicit mention, moreover, of the phenomenological or anthropological dimensions of the "theological, historical, and pastoral [including empirical] investigation" that should, along with contemporary experience, precede the project or projects of reform (23), whether of the Roman rite or of its adaptation (see 40). All this is left under the broad heading of "cultural." Nonetheless a substantive charter was drawn up, far beyond anything done by any council or pope before, for pastoral and practical implementation.

The Process of Reform

When it was certain that the constitution on the liturgy would be ready for final vote at the end of the second period of Vatican II, Paul VI began preparations for its implementation. He directed one of the papal delegates or moderators of the council, Cardinal Giacomo Lercaro, Archbishop of Bologna and also an elected member of the Conciliar Commission on the Liturgy, to assemble a few *periti* in order to prepare an executory or implementing document. Lercaro chaired the group of nine, with Annibale Bugnini as secretary, and the first meeting was held on October 12, 1963. Although the instruction on implementation itself was not to appear until ten months after the promulgation of the constitution, the planning was underway and only a few weeks after the promulgation, in January 1964, Paul VI established a formal post-conciliar commission, called the Consilium for the Implementation of the Constitution on the Liturgy. This was in full harmony with the thinking of the council's own commission, which had repeatedly left matters to a future commission, yet to be named, distinct from the existing Congregation of Rites.

Although the details of the procedure and the persons involved are less important than the results of the massive project—the reform of all the liturgical books of the Roman rite—the body was somewhat out of the tradition of the curial congregations. Its membership ultimately included almost sixty bishops, only a small fraction of whom were cardinals. There were about 150 consultors in all and an additional 75 counselors, the latter being consulted on occasion and on particular points. Half a dozen observers from other churches also participated in the work, and were regularly present during the Consilium's plenary meetings, of which there were 13 from 1964 to 1970.

The consultors directly engaged in the work were formed into study bodies called *coetus studiorum* corresponding to the liturgical books to be revised, with various subgroups. Over the period from 1964 to 1969, when the Consilium was in effect succeeded by the new Congregation for Divine Worship, again with Bugnini as secretary, the groups or committees developed an immense volume of schemata of documents, texts, and sections of liturgical books. These in turn were repeatedly revised and then reviewed by a small central group of consultors for submission to the Consilium members themselves and, upon approval, to Paul VI. Other avenues of consultation were undertaken, especially within the Roman Curia, either by the Consilium or by the pope himself, until final promulgation of the several parts of the revised Roman books.

Although the initial creation of the Consilium was not in terms of an adjunct body of the Congregation of Rites, in mid-1964 the other body acquired the right to review the definitive work of the Consilium. Beginning with the first instruction of implementation issued in September 1964 and continuing through the publication of the Roman missal in 1969, the decrees of publication were regularly issued in the congregation's name and signed by its prefect and secretary as well as by the Consilium's president. This was at best an uncomfortable procedure, since the congregation did not have staff or consultors competent in the field of liturgical revision; the relationship continued through the curial reform of 1967, in which the Consilium was acknowledged to retain its responsibility, its experts considered experts of the congregation, but its decisions subject to review by the congregation's section on worship. In 1969 distinct Congregations, for Divine Worship and for the Causes of Saints, replaced the old congregation and the anomalous situation ceased.

The Congregation for Divine Worship succeeded the Consilium, but its constituent membership was principally cardinals and its body of consultors reduced to a minimum. Nonetheless it continued the Consilium's work in much the same style until it was combined, in 1975, with the Congregation for the [Discipline of the] Sacraments, and Bugnini, who had provided almost uninterrupted continuity in Roman liturgical reform since 1948, was transferred to the papal diplomatic service. By that time all the major work of immediate implementation had been completed; later documents and books depended largely on the study during the decade after the council. The potential for regional adaptation, well underway in some countries by 1975, remained in doubt thereafter.

The task facing the Consilium from the beginning was complicated by the need to distinguish between the reforms which could be put into effect almost immediately (including the introduction of the vernacular, although this was the primary responsibility of the conferences of bishops) while using the existing liturgical books or slight supplements to them and those reforms which would require several years of study, experiment, and preparation. A policy of gradualism was adopted, and until 1968 a series of instructions and minor liturgical publications was employed to introduce the changes mandated by Vatican II. Then, with the issuance of the rites for the celebration of the sacrament of holy orders, the series of reformed liturgical books (q.v.) began to appear, generally as soon as the work was completed to the satisfaction of the Consilium itself, the interested bodies of the Roman Curia, and Paul VI, who diligently examined each document or volume to be issued.

During this period, the revised rites were subjected to experiment—not the experiment mentioned in the liturgical constitution as the responsibility of conferences of bishops when needed to make major adaptations (40), but for the direct purpose of reforming the Roman rite as a whole. The most important experiments were with the Order of Mass, first with smaller groups and then with the whole Consilium, later with the Synod of Bishops (1967), and finally with the participation of Paul VI on several occasions. Concelebration (which, together with the rite for communion under both kinds, went into effect universally in early 1965), the funeral rites, Christian initiation (both the rites related to the catechumenate and the order for the baptism of children), and other rites were tried out in many places throughout the world, generally in restricted circumstances or limited groups.

The total, if initial and basic, reform of the Roman liturgy can be seen only in the fully developed liturgical books, but the series of intervening steps in the process, both the study and the published documents, are revealing, since no such legislative history has ever been available in cases of earlier liturgical reform. The published instructions of the Roman See constitute only part of this record but, next to the definitive liturgical books themselves, are the most important.

The initial instruction of implementation (September 1964) introduced simplifications into the Order of Mass and, to a lesser degree, the other sacramental celebrations. A second and similar instruction appeared in 1967, again following the plan of gradual introduction of reforms, especially in the eucharist, and still limited by the need to complete the fully revised books. A third instruction of implementation, issued in 1970, had a different character, enjoining observance of liturgical discipline and appearing to inhibit regional adaptations, especially adaptations of the Roman missal, which had just been completed.

Other reform instructions included one on music in 1967, which attempted, among other things, to reconcile the chant and the sung liturgy in general with use of the vernacular. A second instruction of the same year dealt with questions of eucharistic cult, especially outside Mass—an issue carefully avoided in the conciliar treatment of the reform; the instruction attempted to strengthen the relationship betwen the eucharistic celebration and secondary devotions, while demonstrating, for example, how and why the eucharist should be reserved and worshipped in a chapel or area distinct from the church sanctuary. Another influential instruction prepared by the Consilium treated liturgical translation (1969), both freeing it from any kind of slavish literalism and acknowledging, in its final paragraph, the greater need for the new composition of liturgical prayers in accord with the genius of each language.

Reform "by Decree of Vatican II"

The Roman books for liturgical celebration, especially from 1968 onward, may be studied directly for their fidelity to the conciliar norms. They never exceed the mandate given by Vatican II and reveal all the pastoral, liturgical, and doctrinal study that went into their careful preparation. The rites as a whole are marked by the noble simplicity but also by a degree of flexibility—especially the inclusion of options and alternatives— and a richness of texts that was hardly anticipated before the work got under way in 1964. On the other hand, although done promptly enough (25), as each year passed the pressures grew to publish quickly and to accept compromises that seemed to weaken the conciliar resolve. These may be attributed to forces within and outside the Roman Curia, still greatly disaffected by conciliar reform, and the desire of Paul VI and indeed of the Consilium itself to achieve greater consensus.

The best means to follow the history of the development of the liturgical reform, in addition to the unpublished documents of the Consilium and later of the Congregation for Divine Worship that are pre-

served in archives, is the collection, in English translation, *Documents on the Liturgy 1963-1979: Conciliar, Papal, and Curial Documents*, prepared by the International Commission on English in the Liturgy; the basic documents in the original texts are collected in Reiner Kaczynski's *Enchiridion Documentorum Instaurationis Liturgicae* covering the period 1963-1983. Bugnini's *La riforma liturgica (1948-1975)* gives an exhaustive and accurate account of the work. Only the briefest mention of the principal rites can be given here.

For the eucharistic celebration, the critical task was the restoration of the Order of Mass itself, designed to be an exemplar for both simpler and more solemn eucharistic celebrations (1969). Despite the objections raised to it—one curial group considered it heretical—it is a traditional rite, one in which the more radical plan anticipated by the conciliar fathers has become somewhat more complex. Of equal weight were the critical improvement and generous enlargement of the corpus of euchological texts— from the simple presidential prayers to the anaphoras with their prefaces (1970); the new calendar, applicable to the daily liturgy of the hours as well as the eucharist (1969); and the vastly enlarged order of biblical readings, both in the three-year Sunday cycle based largely on the semi-continuous reading of the synoptic gospels and in the weekday lectionary (1969).

The lectionary deserves special mention in itself. While the quality of proclamatory preaching within the eucharist could not be reformed by simple decree, the passages of the written word of God could be appointed for announcement in the assembly more generously and with clearer design. It also deserves mention because of its impact and acceptance, more direct than any other element of the Roman reform, in many other churches in the English-speaking world which now follow the Roman pattern of Sunday readings. The calendar, on the other hand, achieved the chief purposes of chap. V of the constitution but only with a major compromise. Instead of leaving those saints' days which lack universal cult or significance to regional or local calendars, two new principles were introduced which overburdened the sanctoral: a large number of lesser saints' days remained in the Roman calendar as options but with almost as much prominence as ever, to the detriment of the temporal cycle of the church year, and—with similar effect—observances were added to reflect universality, by including representative feasts of saints from each region or continent.

In the rites of the other sacraments, a better celebration of the word of God was uniformly introduced, even in cases in which the sacrament is not celebrated within a eucharistic liturgy. The primary concern was Christian initiation, to which the constitution had directed major attention. The work of the Consilium was complicated by the need to produce a rite of baptism of children promptly (1969)—for pastoral reasons and because the existing rite was so unsuitable for infants and young children—so that the integral nature of sacramental initiation through baptism, confirmation, and eucharist was not immediately apparent. Similarly, the pastoral reality of postponing confirmation in many parts of the Latin church and even inverting the sequence of confirmation and eucharist required a separate book for confirmation (1971). Nevertheless the total rite, the order of Christian initiation of adults corresponding to the catechumenate of those who are no longer infants, respected the tradition of both East and West—the older tradition of the West—and the liturgical and theological doctrine embraced by Vatican II (1971).

The rite of marriage was completed early on (1969), enhanced by texts from non-Roman usage and new wedding blessings—and with greater allowance than in other cases for regional differences, a diversity which had been protected even by the Council of Trent. The order for the care and for the sacrament of anointing of the sick, with its primary purposes recovered (see 73-75) and the language of its form (like that of confirmation) revised, was published along with the rite for the eucharist as viaticum for the distinct case of the dying—all enriched with readings and prayers (1972).

The sacrament of penance was issued only after some delay (1973)—partly because the plan to employ a deprecatory form or forms as alternative expressions of sacramental absolution was defeated and partly because the rites of communal celebration, whether with or without individual auricular confession of sins, had first to be restricted by more rigid canonical controls than the revisers sought. In particular, the second or communal rite of reconciliation with individual confession of sins, expected by Paul VI to become frequent or usual, demanded individual absolution instead of a more traditional absolution by the presiding minister; the third rite prepared by the Consilium, fully developed for sacramental reconciliation without individual confession, was more and more hemmed in by canonical norms. But the new rites were richer in their prayer texts, open to wide accommodation by the minister of the sacrament, and supplemented by suggested patterns for non-sacramental penitential services.

In the case of the sacrament of orders, the revision (1968) achieved a major shortening and simplification for the ordination of bishops, presbyters, and deacons, including the substitution of an ancient form for the ordination of bishops. The completion of the rites associated with other ministries had to await the decision, already clear enough from the sense of Vatican II (L.G., Chap.,

III), to suppress tonsure and minor orders; even here the carefully constructed rites of institution of lay ministers (1971) were frustrated in practice by the canonical rule that they be employed also for those who would later seek to be admitted to the sacramental orders—and by the restriction of liturgical institution to men.

The other major services, whether called sacramentals, lesser sacraments, or blessings and dedications, were prepared with careful study by the Consilium, one of the most successful being the order of funerals (1969)—although it demanded and allowed considerable regional or cultural adaptation. As in the case of ordinations, the Gallican rites for the dedication of churches and the like were radically reformed and reduced in length (1977). Only the collection of diverse blessings was greatly delayed, largely because of an initial policy to keep to a minimum of such rites—they had increased notably in the modern Roman Ritual—and to leave the rest to the conferences of bishops according to national or regional need. The policy changed, and it was only a decade after the final sacramental rite (penance) was issued that a large and diffuse book of blessings appeared (1984). It respected, however, the conciliar decree to give a greater place to the reading of the scriptures (35, 1) and to permit qualified lay persons to celebrate certain of the blessings (79).

Parallel to the reform of the Roman eucharistic and other sacramental liturgies was the complex matter of a new office of daily ecclesial prayer, renamed the liturgy of the hours (1971). The result was a compromise: on the one hand, a greatly enriched and improved collection of prayers and readings, new intercessory prayers, and structures better suited to either communal or individual praying; on the other hand, so much attention to the so-called monastic office and to the individual praying of the office by or-dained ministers that the chief hours of morning and evening prayer could not be said to satisfy, as the Order of Mass had satisfied, the pastoral situation in parochial life. Plans to add to the structure a restored form of psalm prayers were not followed (although they appear in English versions of the liturgy of the hours), nor were alternative volumes of biblical, patristic, and other readings published.

Inevitably, judgments will differ about the quality of the reform, done by the Roman See "by decree of the Second Vatican Ecumenical Council and promulgated by authority of Pope Paul VI" and, in a couple of later instances, by Pope John Paul II. Looked at as a whole and most certainly in comparison with any earlier reworkings or refurbishing of the Roman liturgy, the work was an extraordinary success. It was achieved under pastoral pressure from the Catholic episcopate in their conferences and by the Catholic people of the Latin church at large; it was done also in the realization that minimizing and anti-conciliar forces, though a minority during the celebration of Vatican II, were so influential as to require a rapid if gradual reform lest greater compromises or retrenchment be demanded. If the liturgical books are looked upon as collections of texts, as euchologies or lectionaries, they are in every way superior to earlier books, certainly to those of the post-Tridentine period; if they are looked at as revisions of ritual structures and elements, they fall short in some ways—some remain less clear and simple than Vatican II had decreed—but again they come vastly closer to the perceived needs of the worshipping assemblies of the church.

Two unresolved questions remain. The first, less important, is the continuing evolution of the basic Roman rite through further revision—lest the experience of the centuries from 1568 (the Roman breviary of Pius V) to the 1960s and 1970s be lost and another rigidity and uniformity become the norm or a false ideal. The second, both more challenging and more promising, is the recapture of the openness of Vatican II to liturgical adaptation, that is, to move beyond the achieved reforms to the cultural suitability of the rites—further altered, supplemented creatively but in accord with the best traditions, and even carefully pruned—to the particular churches of individual nations and areas.

Thus the immediate liturgical reform of Vatican II has been achieved at the quasi-universal level and in the printed texts of service books, first in Latin and then in the various vernaculars. The degree of its success in the living communities of faith that follow the Roman rite can be known only through the most elaborate accumulation of empirical evidence—and then largely in terms of external celebration. What is clear and certain is that the excellence of what was done in compliance with the conciliar decision should not be an obstacle to the cultural and other adaptability then envisioned.

See Liturgical movement, the (1830-1969); Liturgical books; Documents, Roman liturgical, since Vatican II

W. Baraúna, ed. The Liturgy of Vatican II, 2 vols. (Chicago, 1966). C.J. Barry, Worship and Work (Collegeville, MN, 1956). C. Braga, et al., eds., Liturgia opera divina e umana. Studi sulla riforma liturgica offerti a S.E. Mons. Annibale Bugnini (Rome, 1982). A. Bugnini, La riforma liturgica (1948-1975) (Rome, 1983). C. Braga and A. Bugnini, eds. The Commentary on the Constitution and on the Instruction on the Sacred Liturgy (New York, 1964). A.J. Chupungco, Cultural Adaptation of the Liturgy (New York, 1982). M. Collins, Worship and Renewal (Washington, 1987). Congregazione per il Culto Divino, Atti dei Convegno dei Presidenti e Segretari delle Commissioni Nazionali di Liturgia 23-28 Ottobre 1984 (Padua, 1986). J.D. Crichton, The Church's Worship (New York, 1964). International Commission on English in the Liturgy, ed. Documents on the Liturgy 1963-1979: Conciliar, Papal, and Curial Texts (Collegeville, MN, 1982). J.A. Jungmann, "Constitution on the Sacred Liturgy," In Commentary on the Documents of Vatican II, ed. H. Vorgrimler, I: 1-88 (New York, 1967). R. Kaczynski, ed., Enchiridion Documentorum Instaurationis Liturgicae, I (1963-1973),

Turin, 1976; II (1973-1983), Rome, 1988. B. Koenker, The Liturgical Renaissance in the Roman Catholic Church (Chicago, 1954). C. Last, ed., Remembering the Future: Vatican II and Tomorrow's Liturgical Agenda (New York, 1983). B.J. Lee, ed., Alternative Futures for Worship, 7 vols. (Collegeville, MN, 1987). A.G. Martimort, ed., The Church at Prayer, 4 vols. (Collegeville, MN, 1986-1988). F.R. McManus, "Liturgical Reform," In New Catholic Encyclopedia, 8: 908-910. F.R. McManus, Sacramental Worship (New York, 1967). A. Nocent, The Future of the Liturgy (New York, 1963). O. Rousseau, Progress of the Liturgy (Westminster, MD, 1951). H. Schmidt, La constituzione sulla sacra Liturgia (Rome, 1966).

FREDERICK R. McMANUS

REFORMATION CHURCHES

See Traditions, liturgical, in the West: post-Reformation; Sacraments in the Reformation churches; Reform, liturgical, in Reformation churches

REFORMATION OF LIFE

As a result of forgiveness of sins one is expected to change one's life. Metanoia is the technical word for "change of heart" which embraces sorrow for sin and the intention of leading a new life. One expresses this by confession made to the church, by making due satisfaction for the sins committed and by amending one's life (Rite of Penance, 6).

When one sins, one turns away from God as the younger son turned from the father to dissipate his inheritance (Lk 11:13). Forgiveness entails turning back to God with a change of heart as the prodigal son made up his mind to return home and ask forgiveness of his father (Lk 11:18). By accepting and performing the penance or satisfaction for sins committed; by changing the conduct of one's life; by repairing the injury and damages caused by one's former ways, the sinner demonstrates true conversion. Life can no longer be conducted as it was in the past, metanoia must be lived out in daily existence.

True conversion is completed by acts of penance, satisfaction for the sins committed, amendment of conduct and also by the reparation of injury (R.P., 6C). Satisfaction is meant to be a remedy for the sin committed and can take the form of good works, fasting, service or prayers. Thus the sinner is required to do something that will directly remedy the evil of the sinful act which will give a powerful reminder of past sin and the loving forgiveness of God. Amendment of conduct means to change habits, actions, style of life; it means avoiding persons and places connected with sin. Reparation of injury means restitution which is necessarily connected with reformation of life. One cannot restore the disorder of sin without giving back what was taken, be this reputation, goods, property, etc. The confessor has the obligation to advise the penitent on proper restitution.

See **Contrition; Conversion from sin; Satisfaction**

James Dallen, *The Reconciling Community, The Rite of Penance* (New York: Pueblo Publishing Company, Inc., 1986).

JOSEPH L. CUNNINGHAM

RESERVATION OF THE EUCHARIST

See **Eucharist, reservation of the; Eucharistic chapel**

REVERENCE

Reverence (Lat. RE + *vereri*, to feel awe of, fear) is both a noun and a verb indicating a relational stance of deep respect before a person, or by extension, any reality that is held to be sacred or worthy of honor. In matters liturgical, we treat here (a) reverence to God, (b) reverence to the people assembled, and (c) reverence for the liturgical materials: rites, prayers, symbolic acts and holy objects.

(a) *Reverence to God.* In both the OT and NT God is acknowledged to be the Holy One (e.g., Isa 43:3; Rev 16:5), worthy of love, honor and praise, before whom heaven and earth bow low in humble adoration. In almost all eucharistic anaphoras God is proclaimed "thrice holy" for filling the heavens and the earth with God's own glory. In all liturgical action, the *ecclesia*, the gathered assembly, takes its stance before the mystery of God, to listen to God's word, to raise their voices to God in prayer, and to welcome God's own gracious approach and even more gracious action into their lives. Liturgy is the "work of the people" in the presence of the Holy One *and* the work of the Holy One in the midst of the people.

If the "work of the people" is to be at the same time the "prayer of the people," reverence before God must be a prime attitudinal stance of the assembly, and of all who minister within it. The presider especially, who is commissioned to lead the church's prayer, needs both to have and exhibit this sense of reverence as essential to his or her assigned ministry. Without this sense of profound reverence, liturgical action will appear empty, or at least hollow, and become a mere celebration of the human, not the human as ennobled and transformed by the holiness of God.

Christian worship names God as Father, Son and Spirit. Reverence for each name of God calls for a different stance. To name God "Father" is to name the "otherness" of God from whom all that is has its being. It is likewise to name the "creaturehood" of women and men, which, more than a statement of simple dependence, names as well the noble origin and noble destiny of humanity. To name God "Son" is to name the "historicity" of God, the fact of incarnation. In spite of this "otherness," God nonetheless has entered human history on its own terms: God has become a human person. All that is human has been, and is therefore capable of being, a history of God. To name God "Spirit," is to name the "indwelling" of God, the on-going incarnation that is the deepest truth of all human life, of all human history and indeed of all creation.

Reverence for the "otherness" of God invites excitement and wonder that the One who is beyond is not unknown, but rather One who speaks, relates and covenants in love. It also invites a humility that forbids enclosing the mystery in images, categories or doctrines that would limit and control rather than unveil God's gracious presence. Reverence for the "historicity" of God puts one beyond the never-ending categorical clash—human and divine—and invites men and women to pursue and be pursued by the human in God and the divine in themselves. Reverence for the "indwelling" of God invites everyone to see human life, and indeed all that is, as sacred, worthy of honor and respect, holy with the holiness of God. Christian worship to the Father with the Son in the Spirit is itself an act of wonder and awe that, more than the moon and the stars, invites and even urges the human cry: who are we that you be mindful of us; who are we that you care for us (Ps 8:4)?

(b) *Reverence to the People Assembled.* In both the OT and NT the people God chooses are called the holy ones of God (e.g., Num 16:7; 1 Pet 2:9). Holiness is both gift and vocation. "The Church, whose mystery is set forth by this sacred Council, is held, as a matter of faith, to be unfailingly holy. This is because Christ, the Son of God, who with the Father and the Spirit is hailed as 'alone holy,' loved the Church as his Bride, giving himself up for her so as to sanctify her; he joined her to himself as his body and endowed her with the gift of the Holy Spirit for the glory of God. Therefore all in the Church, whether they belong to the hierarchy or are cared for by it, are called to holiness" (G.S., 39).

The liturgy of the church gathers the church together. It is the visible mani-festation and actual living out of the mystery of Christ (S.C., 2). Whatever the liturgical action, the people assembled are God's chosen people (G.S., chap. 2), visibly assembled as "the Mystical Body of Jesus Christ, that is, by the Head and his members" (S.C., 7), to carry out to-gether "an action of Christ the Priest and of his Body, which is the Church" (*ibid.*).

Every liturgical action opens with some form of welcome and greeting by the presider. It is a human action, and there-fore requires that the welcome and greet-ing be humanly true. Even more, however, it is a sacramental act: the human action is at the same time an action of Christ. It is Christ who gives both welcome and greeting in and through the human mini-stry of the presider. As a sacramental act, the greeting and welcome must be true to Christian faith as well. The presider cannot assume so elevated and detached a stance as to render Christ alien to his members, nor so casual a stance as to make Christ trivial, nor so insignificant a stance as to render him invisible. Presiders must have reverence for the ministry they carry out and for the mystery they em-body in that ministry. At the same time they must so conduct their ministry as to invite reverence from the assembly for themselves, the ministry, and Christ.

There is another dimension of reve-rence to the welcome and greeting which ought to hold throughout the liturgical act. The people the presider calls to assembly are themselves the mystery of Christ. Vatican II named the assembly as one of four modes of Christ's presence in all liturgical prayer (S.C., 7). To call a people to assembly is, as it were, to "consecrate" them, to establish them in that unique relationship with Christ where they are so intimately one with him as to be his presence, his body. The assembled church is not a group, nor a crowd, nor even the most splendid of human gatherings. It is *sacramentum*, the visible embodiment of Jesus Christ. Presiders must likewise have profound reverence for the mystery they assemble by their welcome and greeting, and invite reverence of all for all.

The same may be said for those who proclaim the word, in reading, in homily, or in whatever form. Proclamation is a human ministry, and must therefore be humanly true. It is not to the deacon alone that the mandate is given: "believe what you read, preach (proclaim) what you believe, and put into practice what you preach" (said while entrusting the gospel to the deacon in the diaconate ordination rite). Those words belong as mandate to anyone who would proclaim the word. Yet the proclamation of the word is a sacramental act as well: "He (Christ) is present in his word since it is he himself who speaks when the holy scriptures are read in the Church" (S.C., 7). Both those who proclaim and those who hear need to be alive with wonder and awe that this human word so humanly spoken gives voice to Jesus Christ. As they walk to the place of proclamation, or carry the book of scripture in procession, and especially as they read or speak, proclaimers of the word will serve their ministry well who hold in profound reverence the scripture, their ministry of proclamation, and the people whose very lives give body to the word proclaimed.

(c) *Reverence for the Liturgical Materials: Rites, Prayers, Symbolic Acts, Holy Objects.* Liturgical action is made up of words and objects and symbolic human interactions whose purpose is to express, nourish and strengthen faith (S.C., 59). Each prayer, each ritual, each symbolic act and each object has as its purpose to embody and to unveil some dimension of God's saving presence and activity in and among God's people. Nothing is trivial. And nothing is at the free disposal of bishop, presider, liturgical minister, or liturgical assembly. Liturgical materials, be they the water or oil or food of Christian sacraments or the words of prayer, the incense to be burned, the candle to be carried or the vessel to be handled, are human realities that must be humanly true (e.g., "that the bread may effectively signify the meaning it is intended to convey, it must really look like food" (G.I.R.M., 283). They are likewise *sacramentum*, unveiling and serving to carry out the saving actions of Jesus Christ. They must therefore be true to Christian faith as well.

Reverence for liturgical materials acknowledges that they are human realities that are placed at the disposal of Jesus Christ, his prayer, his work and his presence among his people. Their meaning and purpose are guided both by their own human truth and by the truth of faith they serve. They are not used by people to express and give meaning to whatever people determine. They draw their meaning from the mystery of Christ proclaimed in scripture and enacted in the church's liturgy, and are used by people to express and be captured by this same mystery of Christ.

Liturgical materials are sacred, not in the sense of belonging to another world, but precisely because they belong to this one. They are sacred carriers of the mystery of God, who is Father ("otherness"), Son ("incarnate"), and Spirit ("indwelling"). Reverence is due to them because of the mystery they serve, and because of the awe and wonder that must arise when simple things, water, oil, food, sweet smells and not-always-eloquent words, are embraced by the Holy One, employed by the Holy One, able to allow the Holy One to be and work among us.

See Doxology; Assembly; Presidential style; Art, liturgical

Robert W. Hovda, *Strong, Loving and Wise: Presiding in Liturgy* (Washington: The Liturgical Conference, 1976). David Power, "Sacramental Celebration and Liturgical Ministry," in *Liturgy: Self-expression of the Church*, New Concilium, 72, ed. H. Schmidt (New York: Herder and Herder,

1972), 26-42. Peter E. Fink, "Perceiving the Presence of Christ," in *Worship*, 58, 1 (Jan.84): 17-28.

PETER E. FINK, S.J.

RITUAL

The 20th century has witnessed a gradual, yet dramatic, shift in the understanding and appreciation of human ritual behavior. Ritual has increasingly become highlighted as an essential element in the development, integration and sustenance of the human person and the human social community. While once designated as a peripheral topic of scientific inquiry, ritual now commands significant attention in a wide range of scholarly disciplines, especially psychology, sociology and anthropology. Recent theological investigations in areas of sacramental and liturgical theology have likewise been keenly attentive to ritual studies and have been greatly enhanced and enriched by them.

Human ritual possesses four distinguishing characteristics. It is a *behavior*, which is *repetitive, interpersonal*, and *value oriented*. Ritual is a performance or activity. This behavior is not random but displays observable repetition both in its structural organization and its chronological framework. Every ritual develops a pulse or rhythm which is part of the larger life rhythm of a people.

Ritual is never individualistic or private. Ritual is the behavior of and within a community. Ritual always bears an indelible interpersonal and social stamp. As a repeated interpersonal behavior, ritual is purposeful. It seeks to attain a particular end or goal. Ritual allows contact with an event or person which called the ritual community into existence. Within this field of contact, the ritual participants are offered the possibility of once again encountering this event or person and embracing the meaning and values which are offered. Ritual should not be confused with either rubrics or routine. Rubrics are mere stage directions. While they may be important to the proper execution of ritual celebrations, they are only a surface feature of the whole ritual ensemble. Routine, on the other hand, while it is likewise repetitive interpersonal behavior, either does not address significant human goals or values or has become impotent to do so.

Psychology and Ritual

Recent psychological research has underscored the centrality of ritual in the development, integration and maintenance of a stable human personality. Erik Erikson's ground-breaking research into the *Ontogeny of Ritualization* clearly demonstrated that the integration and stability of human personality requires the transmission, appropriation and integration of crucial social values and norms. The distinct chronological stages of development, identified as *infancy, early childhood, play age, school age, adolescence*, witness the corollary values of *intimacy, discrimination of good/bad, dramatic elaboration, rules of performance* and *solidarity of convictions*. In the earlier stages of development, biological needs call forth the appropriate values. In the later stages of development, the demands of social life require the intrusion of particular social values.

Each segment of personality development and integration is related to the others as an organic whole. While a "new" stage introduces a "new" value, it also re-enforces the values of earlier stages. Similarly, the balanced, mature and integrated personality of *adult life* is enriched and sustained by the continual encounter with these fundamental values.

How does a person experience the values which are crucial to personality development and integration? Where do adults continue to encounter these essential values throughout their lifetime? In both instances, psychology has identified ritual as the normal locale and medium. Through the interpersonal, repetitive and adaptive behavior of ritualization, individuals attain and preserve an integrated and healthy psycho-social existence. From a psychological viewpoint, ritual is a normal and necessary human behavior. The absence or severe truncation of ritual in the process of personality development can result in psycho-social personality disorders. Without ritual participation or appropriation of the values mediated by ritual activity, the human person faces potentially serious psychological conflicts, personality impairment and estrangement from inner self and outer society.

Ritual is well equipped to function as an appropriate means for the mediation of values. It possesses instructional, interpretive and indoctrinating elements which support this task. Ritual instructs by creating specific experiences for the developing person. Through the particular structure of ritual, the range of possible interpretations of the experience is narrowed. Gradually, ritual imposes the horizon or worldview of the community on those who participate in its rituals and fashions or indoctrinates them into one of its own.

Sociology and Ritual

Sociology has detected three essential elements in communities or social groups. They share a common language. They embrace appropriate common patterns of behavior. They construct social institutions or structures as a means of ordering and sustaining a common life. Ritual assumes an important role in each of these areas.

On first glance, language is a way to describe the world and our experiences. It is a faculty of communication, a power which enables us to build a common world. Deeper analysis shows, however, that language is more complex.

Language is a living human construct. As such, it always includes within it the social community's fundamental presuppositions and prejudices. Furthermore, language always communicates information or content with a particular *force*. This force can exhort, demand, question or simply declare. Any analysis of language, therefore, requires concurrent attentiveness to both what was said (content) and to how it was said (force). When the linguistic dimensions of social prejudice, content and force are attended to, it becomes clear that the importance of language transcends its logical structure or correct usage. Language reaches deep down into the mystery of life. It not only endeavors to describe reality. It also attempts to express the *meaning* of reality.

Language's ability to disclose meaning is relative. At times, language appears adequate for the task. On other occasions, all our words seem to fall short. Ian Ramsey's analysis of religious language has helpfully addressed this linguistic ambivalence.

Ramsey identified two different categories of language or discourse: ordinary and odd. Ordinary discourse is the type of language we encounter in the normal course of our experience. It is the language of sharing information, transacting business or attending educational lectures. Ordinary discourse is successful at expressing the meaning present in ordinary events and experiences. There are, however, events and experiences which "stand out," "touch the depths of our hearts," "shake us from our usual manner of life." In relation to the "normal" unfolding of our lives, these "odd" events or experiences are super-charged with meaning that is extraordinarily real, yet mysterious. Every attempt to express the depth of meaning experienced in these "odd situations" in ordinary discourse falls short, is judged inadequate. Yet, the undeniable reality of our experiences demands that we try to explain, communicate and understand. Ramsey insightfully noted that we abandon "ordinary discourse" and utilize "odd language" to express the meaning of our "odd situation."

What makes "odd" language "odd"? The answer is not the content specified by the particular words of a sentence. Rather, "odd language" is characterized by how the content is modified or qualified. Usually, the content is qualified by concepts of infinity, uniqueness or absoluteness. In the sentence, "God is all knowing," the content "knowledge" ascribed to God is qualified by the absolute "all." Human beings understand knowing. Analogously, human beings can comprehend what it means to ascribe knowledge to God. Yet, the modifier "all" places God's knowledge beyond any exact literal definition.

In using "odd" language to describe "odd" situations or "odd experiences," the speaker is seeking to *disclose* a depth of meaning which resists ordinary explanation and comprehension. "Odd" language pushes human understanding to its "brink" or limit. In the "limit situation," human beings face experiences and their questions which evade complete answers from within our usual range of understanding. Yet, answers, even if partial, are demanded. Human beings construct "odd language" as a statement that a meaning and answer does exist, is really experienced. This meaning or answer, however, defies literal description or definition. Its proper linguistic expression is the arena of *metaphor* or "odd language."

Religious ritual language is odd language, the language of metaphor. It possesses five key characteristics: descriptive, heuristic, prescriptive, promissory and performative. Ritual language functions as a *narrative* or *myth* which offers an explanation or exegesis of ritual actions. This exegesis limits the range of interpretation applicable to ritual gestures/behavior by supplying a linguistic context within which the ritual performance should be understood.

Ritual language possesses a *heuristic* power. It arouses interest and evokes discovery of meaning and reality not immediately evident in ritual action. It invites the ritual community to turn to a transmitted chain of symbols. For example, during the celebration of the eucharistic liturgy one can detect the following transmission of symbols: priest-Christ-bread-Last Supper-crucifixion-resurrection-grace-life. The interaction of symbols and ritual language activates and intensifies the human potential for transcendence and its consequent discovery of meaning.

Ritual language is *prescriptive*. The meaning disclosed in the language/action of ritual is normative for the life of the ritual community. This meaning becomes a "rule" or "law" of social life. The normative force of ritual language/action is not the result of an external imposition by authority. On the contrary, it arises from the experience of meaning and truth experienced within ritual activity accompanied by its heuristic narrative.

Ritual language is *promissory* and *performative*. The meaning expressed and experienced in ritual elicits a commitment from the participants. This promise is to be incarnated in a life style which expresses the meaning embraced in the ritual experience. The promissory and performative dimensions of ritual language enhance community coherence and stability.

Ritual, by its very nature, structures human behavior. In achieving this goal, ritual fosters intra-group communication, social bonding, solidarity and common performance. By structuring behavior, ritual effects intimacy, social direction, interiorization and presence. Through social interaction, cultural symbols and the power of the human imagination, ritual enables a community to achieve contact with their origins, meaning and one another. The appeal to imagination is not a flight into fantasy. The human imagination is not merely one of the capacities of human beings. Imagination defines the human as human. It is an empowering and incorporating power of all other human powers. Imagination is the pervasive movement of the human person in life, confronted by experience and struggling to discover and create meaning. Imagination is the driving power of the human spirit seeking truth and reality. Imagination is concerned with the whole of life which continually evades partial answers. The world of symbols and ritual is the home of the human imagination.

In effecting intimacy, ritual must shrink spacial and temporal distances. In religious situations both a vertical and horizontal distance must be traversed. The human imagination projects a "God" who is *above* in a position of power and transcendence. It also projects a time continuum of past, present and future. Through the specific use of symbols and symbolic gestures, language and environment, ritual stimulates and focuses the imagination so that the distant God is experienced as present and the ritual community is "thrown back" to their origin or "charter event."

Proximity with God and the charter event allows the ritual participants to interpret their life-experiences within the fundamental meaning systems of their community. It also identifies "unfinished business." The community can discern where they have not lived up to or expressed the meaning which they claim as the basis for their life and actions. Having returned to their origins and been nourished by its deep meaning, the task of finishing unfinished business can be taken up with new enthusiasm and fortitude.

The intimacy attained through ritual is thoroughly social. In ritual, it is the social community which organizes social symbols and symbolic behaviors. This social character enters into the very efficacy of ritual. An individual is invited to surrender the control of their individuality and participate in a common experience of the community. In this process, there emerges a common imaginative insight which underpins a community experience and discernment of meaning which expresses itself in a shared community life and behavior system.

Ritual challenges the individual and community to interiorize or appropriate the foundational meaning of the community. The stimulation of the imagination through symbols and symbolic behaviors empowers it to critically grasp where individuals or the community at large have failed to make their own and live out the meaning which makes them who they are. At the same time, the imagination proposes new schemes through which this meaning can be more fully embraced and lived. Ritual does not allow its participants merely to play act. Ritual demands that role become autobiography.

The final component of ritual's patterning of behavior is presence. The performance of ritual activates a "directionality" in the human imagination. Symbols and symbolic actions can have an infinite variety of interpretations. The structuring of ritual, however, limits these interpretations by focusing the human imagination. There is one ultimate purpose to directionality: the attainment of presence. The presence attained through ritual is not imaginary or fanciful. It is the product of intimacy, social coherence and interiorization. Intimacy creates a feeling of closeness and reassurance which neutralizes noxious threats. Interiorization demands conformity to the fundamental meaning which called the community into existence and sustains its life. Together, within the ritual context of the living community, they render present the powerful "charter event" of the ritual community.

Anthropology and Ritual

Contemporary anthropology has persuasively argued that every culture possesses a root metaphor. A culture's root metaphor is the corporate ground and basis for a common interpretation of experience and from this, corporate life and action. Root metaphors are events, ideas or persons which a culture employs as an analogical tool to discover meaning in a world of ambiguity and conflict.

Root metaphors articulate the worldview or horizon of a particular culture. They are powerful presuppositions which permeate the multiple layers of cultural thought and life. The key medium for the expression and mediation of a culture's root metaphor is ritual. By examining a culture's ritual, one finds an entryway to the unconscious presuppositions upon which the very existence of the culture rests.

Cultures are not static entities. They are in a continual process of alteration and change which can be called the social drama. Root metaphors exercise several crucial functions in the process of cultural transformation.

First, root metaphors are born in the context of cultural transformation. The social drama commences with an action-event-person which is a breach of the established social order. The breach may intensify into a crisis. Two alternatives emerge. The culture will successfully answer the challenge of the "revolutionary" group or it will be forced to expel them from the community. In the former case, the expelled group will establish its own cultural world with its distinctive metaphor and central ritual.

Second, root metaphors set the interpretive parameters of culture. They constitute a hermeneutical horizon for articulating the meaning of life as experienced and lived within a particular culture.

Root metaphors function as positive norms of meaning. They continue to survive as long as they continue to "make sense" of life as lived within the boundaries of a culture.

Third, root metaphors are the basis for corporate coherence and group bonding. Root metaphors enhance "communitas," the interpersonal relationship of group members grounded in shared identity and experience. In its institutionalized form, communitas is dependent upon the ability of ritual to clearly express and make present a culture's root metaphor. A symbiotic relationship exists between communitas and ritual. In providing access to the community's charter event or root metaphor, ritual preserves and intensifies the experience of communitas and group solidarity by re-enforcing origin, meaning and purpose. The experience of communitas triggers ritual celebration.

Finally, root metaphors exercise a social corrective. The clear expression of a root metaphor in ritual challenges the ritual community to evaluate how successfully the community's behavior and institutions conform to and adequately express the meaning of their foundational metaphor. The ritual experience always issues a call to renewal, reform and correction. By answering this call, a culture will be equipped to undertake the growth, transformation and adaptations necessary for survival without losing its fundamental identity.

Conclusion

Ritual is endemic to individual and corporate life. It is a powerful medium for expressing the deepest meanings and values which make a people who they are. The strength, clarity and adequacy of ritual life are criteria by which the health and continued existence of a community can be assessed. Ritual is to be cherished as a life-sustaining system for individuals and their communities.

See **Human sciences, sacraments and the**

William Doty, *Mythography: the Study of Myths and Rituals* (University, Ala.: Univ. of Alabama Press, 1986). Roger Grainger, *The Language of the Rite* (London: Darton, Longman and Todd, 1974). Ronald Grimes, *Beginnings in Ritul Studies* (Washington, D.C.: Univ. of America Press, 1982). Leonel Mitchell, *The Meaning of Ritual* (Wilton, Conn.: Morehouse-Barlow, 1977). Elaine Ramshaw, Don Browning, eds., *Ritual and Pastoral Care* (Philadelphia: Fortress, 1987). Don Saliers, *The Soul in Paraphrase* (New York: Seabury, 1980). James Shaughnessy, ed., *The Roots of Ritual* (Grand Rapids: Eerdmans, 1973). Victor Turner, *The Ritual Process* (Chicago: Aldine Pub. Co., 1969). Victor Turner, ed., *Celebration: Studies in Festivity and Ritual* (Washington, D.C.: Smithsonian Institute Press, 1982). George S. Worgul, Jr., *From Magic to Metaphor* (New York: Paulist, 1980).

GEORGE S. WORGUL, JR.

S

SACRAMENTAL THEOLOGY AFTER VATICAN II

The most obvious thing to have issued forth from the Second Vatican Council in regard to the church's sacraments is the liturgical revision of the sacramental rites and the new directives that are given for their celebration. Perhaps less obvious, though no less significant, is the radical restructuring of the rhetoric employed both to name and to explore the meaning of sacraments. Pre-conciliar reflection in the West gave shape to the theology of sacraments according to the diptych "sacraments in general" and "sacraments in particular," where the former identified what the seven sacraments held in common, and the latter then applied these common notes to each individual sacrament. The language was structural and quasi-scientific. Post-conciliar theology departs from this tradition in several significant ways. The language now employed to explore what is common to the church's sacraments is liturgical rather than structural. Emphasis is on their relationship to the mystery of Christ and to the church as a whole, both of which are expressed in each liturgical act. The concept of *sacramenta in genere* has receded somewhat, and, if it is to be developed at all, it would be arrived at after consideration of individual sacraments in their uniqueness; it would not be the point of departure. Priority focus is given to the richness of each sacrament as

a unique liturgical act, and to the relationship that exists among them in the sacramental life of the church. Symptomatic of this radical shift in rhetoric is the contrast between the way sacraments are identified in the 1917 Code of Canon Law and in the revised code of 1983. In the former they are listed under the heading *de rebus* (on things); in the latter, under the title "the office of sanctifying in the church."

This article presents a brief survey of the evolution in sacramental theology from its pre-conciliar scholastic garb to its contemporary theological "shape," where its language is liturgical, its methodologies are garnered as much from the human sciences as from philosophy, and where it has taken its place firmly in the arena of Christian spirituality. We will consider (a) the gains and limitations of scholastic sacramental theology, (b) the first level move from the scholastic mode to a more personal and phenomenological mode of discourse, and (c) a second level move into a more properly liturgical mode of discourse. Finally (d), we will suggest some tentative directions for the future.

Scholastic Theology

The scholastic methodology which dominated Catholic theology in the West from the 13th to the 20th centuries can rightly boast of a number of achievements in regard to the theology of sacraments.

It advanced the distinction between sacrament and sacramental, thus securing special significance for the (then) seven distinct liturgical actions that displayed and continued the saving mission of Christ. It struggled to preserve the effectiveness of these actions, and rooted this effectiveness firmly in the action of Christ. In an articulation that was not always correctly understood, it identified Christ's gracious presence and action as the "within" (*gratia continetur*) of the sacrament actions, and insisted that only two things were required for Christ to touch people effectively through them. Those responsible for enacting the sacraments had to do so according to the mind and intent of the church (*ex opere operato*), while those participating in sacraments as "recipients" (people ministered to) needed to do so with no obstacle placed in the way (*ex opere operantis*). In other words, fidelity to the church's actions and an openness to the ways of those actions allowed the saving grace of Christ to be appropriated by believers through the medium of Christian sacraments.

Scholastic theology employed a specific model in its reflection on and in its examination of the sacraments. It looked on them as "objective realities," quasi-scientific objects, which could be observed and analyzed from without. Appropriately it asked questions of sacraments that were fitting to scientific objects: who made it? where did it come from? what constitutes it to be what it is? when does it cease to be itself? who may use it? when? and for what purpose? This question set allowed theologians to weave together a well-wrought network of understanding which rooted the institution of sacraments directly, or at least indirectly, in the life of Christ, which insisted that these actions were indeed the actions of Christ, and which examined the conditions for and the effects of sacraments in relation to people. The heart of scholastic reflection

was to see the church's sacraments as sacred objects (holy signs) given by Christ to be received by all through the ministry of some, usually ordained priests.

In spite of its achievements, however, scholastic sacramental theology labored under some severe limitations. It lacked a sound ecclesiological base, for it had replaced the Augustinian image of the *totus Christus* (Christ in the midst of the church, together with the church which is gathered to himself) by an image of *Christus solus* (Christ alone, present in the ministry of the priest, and acting on behalf of the people). The sacramental theology of the Scholastics also lacked a proper sense of the relation between word and sacrament, a deficiency that became particularly poignant during the 16th-century Reformation. A third burden was the conflation of the trinitarian structure of sacramental worship into a purely christological framework, with serious neglect of the role of the Spirit as the agent of transformation of all that is placed with Christ. Western theology paid a heavy price for having replaced the *epiclesis* of Eastern prayer with the *verba Jesu* of Ambrose. Finally, and with added force at the time of the post-Tridentine liturgical reform, scholastic theology lacked the sense of the liturgy itself as a theological locus. Liturgical forms were frozen to protect doctrine; they were neither seen as, nor given free reign to be, living expressions of the church's living faith.

It is this set of limitations, and the growing awareness by the mid-20th century that they were in fact limitations, that gradually exposed the scholastic mode of reflection as no longer adequate to the task of understanding the church's sacramental life. The awakening owed itself to a number of converging factors: the liturgical movement of the 19th and 20th centuries, the advance in biblical scholarship in both Protestant and Catholic circles, the non-scholastic theological ventures of M. de la Taille and O. Casel, and such official pronouncements from Rome as *Mystici corporis* (1943), which re-captured the church as Christ's Body, and *Mediator dei* (1947) which brought new focus to Christ himself as sole mediator between God and humankind.

Beyond Scholastic Theology

The first major step away from scholastic methodology was made by E. Schillebeeckx (*Christ, the Sacrament of the Encounter with God,* Eng., 1963). Drawing on patristic and biblical richness, Schillebeeckx re-established the proper sacramental relationship between Christ and the church, and identified this relationship as foundational to any theology of sacraments. Christ was present *as one to be encountered* in his primary sacramental manifestation, the church, and specifically in the church as it gathers for prayer and its sacramental acts. Schillebeeckx introduced a paradigm shift, a new hermeneutical lens through which to view sacramental faith and the sacramental tradition of the church. Moreover, in replacing the "object model" of scholastic reflection with the more phenomenological and experiential model of "human encounter," he turned sacramental theology away from the extrinsic *quid pro quo* language of economic exchange (do this and receive grace) to the interpersonal language of relational human experience. As a result, theology could no longer be content simply to be explanation of the church's faith (the *fides quaerens intellectum* of Anselm); it had to be seen in addition as "promise" (*intellectus quaerens fidem*), pointing to and unveiling a meeting with Christ that continues to unfold in the church.

Schillebeeckx set several things in motion which continue to influence theological reflection on sacraments. He broadened the resource base of sacramental theology by re-discovering, as it were, the biblical and patristic roots of the sacramental tradition. He introduced a distinction that had been seriously neglected in earlier sacramental reflection between the unique manner of existence that is peculiar to human persons and the objective mode of "being there" that is proper to things of nature. He insisted that religion is a saving dialogue between human persons and the living God, and that, according to the Christian confession of the incarnation, the God who addresses us does so *as human among humans.* By employing a personalist model for his theology, in contrast to the objective model of the Scholastics, he unveiled the fact that all sacramental theology employs models in its investigation of Christian worship. He thus opened the door for the employment of other models as well.

The rhetorical shift which Schillebeeckx effected in sacramental theology found a complement in the language employed at Vatican II, especially in the Constitution on the Church (*Lumen gentium*) and the Constitution on the Sacred Liturgy (*Sacrosanctum concilium*). Both documents reflect the fruit of the liturgical and biblical scholarship that had been under way since before the turn of the century. Both secure the language of sacrament for the church in its relation to Christ, and both name the mystery of Christ as a mystery of personal presence in and to the church.

The *Constitution on the Sacred Liturgy* did not offer a new definition of sacraments. Rather, it began to speak of sacraments in a radically new way. It reinstated the primitive concept of liturgy as *the work of the people,* and it unequivocally included all of the sacraments firmly within its scope. The image of sacrament as "vehicle of grace administered by some to others" was quietly replaced by one more active and inclusive. Sacraments are not things at all, but lively expressions by the whole church assembled of its faith and its mission to embody and make accessible the saving work of Christ. The liturgy is "the outstanding means whereby the faithful may express in their lives and manifest to others the mystery of Christ and the real nature of the true Church" (S.C., 2). In addition, the constitution stated in a way that is both appropriate to and directed to human experience the time-honored tradition of sacramental effectiveness: "In the liturgy, by means of signs perceptible to the senses, human sanctification is signified and brought about in ways proper to each of these signs" (S.C., 7). If scholastic theology had labored to root sacramental effectiveness in the action of Christ, to the neglect of the way in which this effectiveness was achieved (i.e., *significando*, by signifying), Vatican II brought forward with remarkable force this complementary truth. The scholastic tradition insisted that sacraments effect what they signify; Vatican II demanded that sacraments signify all that they effect, because it is by signifying that sacraments are effective for those who enact them.

The initial impact of *Sacrosanctum concilium* on the church was to guide and direct the liturgical reform which it called for. Its primary first contribution to sacramental theology was to bolster the major insights advanced by Schillebeeckx and others (e.g., K. Rahner): the centrality of Christ and the church in sacramental reflection; the dynamic notion of sacrament as action; and the call for experiential language both to name the reality of sacraments and to describe the effects which sacraments have on people. Only later, when its initial pragmatic task was accomplished in the issuance of reformed liturgical rites, would the *Constitution on the Sacred Liturgy* have an even more radical effect on the procedures of sacramental theology.

The decade or so that followed Schillebeeckx's introduction of a new model for sacraments can well be called the decade of models in sacramental theology. B. Cooke (*Christian Sacraments and Christian Personality*, 1968) and J. Powers (*Spirit and Sacrament: The Humanizing Experience*, 1973) drew insights from psychology and personality development to explore the question of meaning in sacraments and to name the process through which the sacramental experience might lead one. Cooke aimed to "explain the function of sacraments in the actual living of Christianity and in the development of the Christian person" (p. 10). The goal of all sacramental activity is the development of a mature Christian person; sacraments are *formative*. Powers, on the other hand, focused on the human experience that lies behind all sacraments. It is, in a first instance, the experience of "no-thingness" in the face of the Transcendent, and in the second instance, the experience of being drawn along the path of self-transcendence. The purpose of sacraments is to provide a new quality of consciousness and a new quality of living marked by an ever increasing freedom, hope, and possibility for love. If Cooke sees sacraments as formative of the mature Christian person, Powers sees them as *transformative* of human consciousness. For both, sacraments advance the quality of human life.

G. McCauley (*Sacraments for Secular Man*, 1969) employed a sociological model to unearth the human meaning which sacraments held. Sacraments are "secular gestures; they deal with secular reality; they promote a greater secularity than we are accustomed to associate with human existence; in themselves they embody secular experience" (p. 15). An enriched human life on the secular level is the fruit of sacramental worship. McCauley's model drew sharp attention to the human reality which underlies the church's sacraments.

A further insight of Schillebeeckx (*God, the Future of Man*, 1968) that the church is to be sacrament of dialogue with the world, coupled with his and Rahner's earlier perception of the church as sacramental embodiment of Christ present and active in the world, gained new force in the political model employed in the liberation theology of J. Segundo (*The Sacraments Today*, Eng., 1974) and others in Latin America. If the mission of Christ in the church is to thwart and overcome all forms of oppression among people, the church as sacrament of Christ must be about that saving business. In function of that mission, Segundo sees sacraments primarily as signs to the church of what it must be about, and they will be effective "to the extent that they are a consciousness-raising and motivating celebration of man's liberative action in history" (p. 55). If there is no raising of consciousness toward the liberative force of human action in the world, then, however perfect the ritual enactment of sacraments might be, there is no Christian sacrament to speak of. Liberation theology calls forth the ethical dimension of Christian sacraments.

Still other models were employed. The categories of process thought, for example, shaped B. Lee's investigation of church, sacrament and the structure of Christian experience (*The Becoming of the Church*, 1974), and raised to sacramental theology the need to speak of God, the church and Christian sacraments in the language of *becoming* rather than the language of *being*. In Great Britain, structural analysis, as well as considerations of the symbolic imagination, guided B. Brinkman (in *The Heythrop Journal*, 1972-1973) through his exploration of "sacramental man," and called attention to the experience of intimacy, interiorization, and social relationship as integral to sacramental prayer. Later, G. Worgul (*From Magic to Metaphor*, 1980) examined the ritual experience through the combined eyes of sociology and anthropology to draw out the relationship between sacraments, human life and social interaction.

In some ways the "model" approach continues to be employed in more recent theological works: e.g., D. Power (*Unsearchable Riches*, 1984) draws heavily on the "symbol" structure of P. Ricoeur and M. Lawler (*Symbol and Sacrament*, 1987) develops an understanding of sacrament as "prophetic symbol," but these show as well the influence of the second shift in sacramental theology since Vatican II, the movement from sacrament as theological concept to sacrament as liturgical act. They can therefore be considered both continuous and discontinuous with the first level shift which Schillebeeckx set in motion.

Beyond Sacramental Theology

The first movement away from scholastic sacramental theology raised the issue of meaning in experiential categories. It sought to relate Christian life and Christian worship within sacramental theology itself. This second movement continues that project, yet adds an additional dimension. The focus of attention is on the liturgical enactment of the sacraments, rather than on sacrament as an abstract theological concept. At this second stage, the term "sacramento-liturgical theology," or simply "liturgical theology" arises to name the theological venture.

One of the primary gains in this move from sacramental to liturgical theology is the recovery of the liturgical act itself as a *theological locus*. It has been classically known and accepted that faith gives rise to theology. In the first move from scholastic modes of reflection, it became equally known and accepted that theology must feed back into, and in some sense be verified in, the experience of faith. In this second move from sacramental to liturgical theology the liturgical act arises as the necessary intermediary between faith and theology. Paul Ricoeur's noted phrase, "the symbol gives rise to thought," is very much to the point. Faith gives rise to theology only after it finds its first articulation in the form of myth and symbol, i.e., the stuff of liturgical ritual. Conversely, theology does indeed return to faith by way of promise, but it is in the engagement with symbol and in the enactment of liturgical ritual that the promise is made, received and actualized. Liturgy expresses and manifests the mystery of Christ (S.C., 2); it is itself a primary statement of both theology and faith.

Liturgical theology is still very much in the process of being formed. It moves in a variety of directions. The shape of this dictionary itself bears witness to the many faces of liturgical theology, weaving together as it does the doctrinal, the biblical, the historical, the liturgical, the aesthetic, and the pastoral. Liturgical theology studies liturgical texts as privileged expressions of the church's faith. It examines as well the inner movements of faith which ritual action calls forth. It examines the correspondence between what is portrayed in ritual and what is lived by individuals and by the community. It calls on the arts, the human sciences, and pastoral experience as well as the more traditional sources of doctrine, philosophy and liturgical history. The liturgy of the church cannot be studied in isolation from the life realities and the faith realities which it both brings to expression and fosters. It is open to any source and any method which serves to link worship, faith and human life.

By holding the liturgy itself as a central theological locus, a new understanding of sacraments can emerge on the basis of what the church in fact does. There is an understanding of sacrament embedded within the ritual actions themselves. This realization led D. Power to advance fresh insight first into the theology of orders (*Ministers of Christ and His Church*,

1969) and, later, into the wider spread of ministers and ministries that are evolving in the contemporary church (*Gifts that Differ*, 1980). It guided J.B. Ryan to explore the eucharist from the texts of eucharistic prayers (*The Eucharistic Prayer*, 1974), a venture which was taken further for the ecumenical church by F. Senn (*New Eucharistic Prayers*, 1987). And it has guided a number of theologians to examine the various sacraments from the revised liturgical texts which present them to the church: e.g., A. Kavanagh (*The Shape of Baptism*, 1978) on the initiation rites; G. Austin (*Anointing with the Spirit*, 1985) on confirmation; J. Dallen (*The Reconciling Community*, 1986) on penance; C. Gusmer (*And You Visited Me*, rev. 1989) on pastoral care of the sick; and R. Rutherford (*The Death of a Christian*, 1980) on rites of Christian burial.

Liturgical theology is concerned, however, not only with ritual text, but also with the dynamics of ritual action which constitute the inner workings of the text. Exploring this terrain E. Kilmartin (in Eigo, 59-110) examined the word dimension of Christian sacraments and its intrinsic relation to the action that is both called forth from and empowered by its proclamation. R. Duffy (*Real Presence*, 1982) has studied the sacramental fare in terms of the human commitment which sacraments call forth and engender. Similar studies appear in the volumes of *Alternative Futures for Worship* (1987), esp. by J. Glen on the experience embedded in sickness and healing and by P. Fink on the process of conversion in reconciliation. Concern for dynamics also gave rise to new studies on the rhythms of liturgical time, e.g., M. Hatchett (*Sanctifying Life, Time and Space*, 1976) and T. Talley (*The Origins of the Liturgical Year*, 1986), and essays into liturgical spirituality, e.g., K. Irwin (*Liturgy, Prayer and Spirituality*, 1984).

Liturgical theology also seeks to intersect with issues and concerns in the broader field of systematic theology. Three works in particular deserve note. G. Wainwright (*Doxology*, 1980) offered a full systematic theology with specific and illustrative links drawn to corresponding liturgical texts. A. Kavanagh (*On Liturgical Theology*, 1984) presents a more finely focused systematic slice where the liturgical enactment of Christian faith is considered, not simply as one theological locus among many, but as the premier expression of Christian faith. Finally, E. Kilmartin (*Christian Liturgy*, 1988) delivers what may be seen as either a foundational theology for Christian worship or a liturgically based fundamental theology. His work stands in the tradition of *sacramenta in genere*, but unfolds on a much more profound level. In addition, voices from outside the traditional arena of systematics or liturgics contribute to the task: e.g., social moralist D. Hollenbach (in Haughey, 1977) who urges liturgical theology to recover its ethical dimension, and to include within its scope questions of faith, justice, and the community's social responsibilities.

There is a multi-faceted ferment within contemporary liturgical theology that only can be suggested in this essay. As the living church continues to experience its renewed liturgical forms, new issues and new areas of investigation will continue to shape its on-going task. The impact, for example, of liberation movements, of feminist theology and of liturgical evolution in non-Western, non-European parts of the globe is only beginning to make itself felt. These must be addressed by liturgical theology as well.

A Forward Look

It is safe to say that the future of liturgical theology will be both continuous and dis-continuous with its present contours. Lines of continuity can more easily be drawn. Certainly liturgical theology will continue to be "liturgical," i.e., it will continue to learn from the liturgy as it is enacted by the living church. It will continue to explore the interface between sacramental rituals and the human life realities which those rituals presuppose and embody. It will continue to engage fundamental theological realities such as the trinitarian God, church, salvation and grace, and locate itself more firmly at the center of those investigations. It will continue to be enlightened by new modes of discourse, new paradigms and new methodologies. Points of discontinuity are harder to name.

One point of potential discontinuity lies in the introduction of local languages and customs into the liturgy and the encouragement given in S.C. 37-40 that the tradition be adapted to the various peoples of the world. It remains to be seen just how radical that adaptation will be, and what impact such adaptation will have. It could be that the process will simply issue forth in rituals that differ one from another only in nuance. It is equally possible, however, that adaptation will lead to ritual forms as different from the current praxis in the church as Gentile ritual differed from Jewish-Christian ritual, or as Byzantine ritual differs from Coptic, and both from the liturgies of the West. K. Rahner once named the contemporary moment in the church as the "emergence of the world church." If such be the case, it is reasonable to expect that emerging ritual forms at least could be unlike anything the church to date has known. If this were to happen, liturgical ritual *as theological locus* would present a radically new face to the church's faith and therefore present a radically new challenge to the liturgical theologian who seeks to understand that faith.

A second point of potential discontinuity depends on how seriously the church takes the symbolic nature of its liturgy, and how deeply theology takes

A. Kavanagh's assertion that liturgy is the "premier" statement of the church's faith. The place where this will impact the most is on the ecumenical reality of the church, and ultimately on the issue of church unity. To date, the ecumenical task seems to be the pursuit of church unity by reaching some level of agreement forged in bi-lateral and multi-lateral discussions. Agreement is sought on the level of doctrine, which is essentially the level of interpretation, and the task rests on the assumption that agreement can be reached. Yet, what if it were the case that agreement can and should never be reached; that unity should be sought on a level different from that of doctrinal agreement? If it is true that the nature of symbol demands a plurality of interpretations, it might well be discovered that the disunity which the churches are trying to overcome does not really exist, and, on the deepest level of the church's life and prayer, never did. Deep appreciation of the symbolic nature of ritual may force the church to confront the fact that, while different communities of Christians disagree as to what they *think* they are doing sacramentally, nonetheless, within a reasonable range of deviation based on culture, language, and perception, all Christian communities continue to *do* the same thing. The impact of such a realization on the theology of Christian worship, and indeed on Christian life and theology in general, would be enormous.

The future of liturgical theology remains essentially a task to be pursued: to explore the human events that are Christian sacraments both as human and as liturgical (i.e., as works of the entire assembled church); to penetrate ever more deeply the truth which faith names as the "within" of those events; and to draw lines of connection between sacraments and those realities of every day life which sacraments both draw on and point to. It must be done in many directions and on many levels at once.

Christian worship proclaims and enacts the transformation by God of human life, of human history, and of creation itself. The ways of liturgical theology can be no less than the ways in which humans seek to understand their life, their history and their world.

See **Liturgical theology; Adaptation, liturgical; Aesthetics, liturgical; Culture, liturgy and; Doctrine, liturgy and; Feminism and the liturgy; Human sciences, sacraments and the; Imagination and worship; Inculturation of the liturgy; Liturgy and Christian life; Reform, liturgical, of Vatican II; Theologians, modern, and liturgical renewal**

David Hollenbach, "A Prophetic Church and the Sacramental Imagination," in J. Haughey, *The Faith That Does Justice* (New York: Paulist, 1977), 234-263. Aidan Kavanagh, *On Liturgical Theology* (New York: Pueblo, 1984). Edward Kilmartin, *Christian Liturgy* (Kansas City: Sheed and Ward, 1988); also, "A Modern Approach to the Word of God and Sacraments of Christ," in F. Eigo, ed., *The Sacraments: God's Love and Mercy Actualized* (Villanova: University Press, 1979), 59-110. E. Schillebeeckx, *Christ the Sacrament of the Encounter with God* (New York: Sheed and Ward, 1963 [orig. 1960]). R. Vaillancourt, *Toward a Renewal of Sacramental Theology*, trans. M. O'Connell (Collegeville: Liturgical Press, 1979 [Fr. orig. 1977]).

PETER E. FINK, S.J.

SACRAMENTALS

The term *sacramentals* can change its precise meaning according to the starting point one adopts for building a theology of sacraments. We begin here with the present canonical definition of sacramentals in the Western church: "Sacred signs by which spiritual effects are signified and are obtained by the intercession of the Church" (C.I.C., 1166).

In this context, the word *sacramental* refers primarily to a "sign," i.e., an object or prayer that provides the occasion for a personal and "gracing encounter" with Christ. The sacramental relates to a sacrament. It is not itself a sacrament but it does bring with it the possibility of our being graced as a consequence either of the church's prayers or of private prayers approved by the church. Thus understood, some examples of sacramentals would be the use of holy water, rings that are blessed at a wedding, parents invoking God's blessing on their children, and so on. According to the rules laid down in church law (C.I.C., 1167-1172), the administering of sacramentals would normally be done by clerics but there are several cases where, rightly, they would be administered by lay people.

Historically, the concept of sacramentals understood as objects or actions "resembling" the sacraments was not firmly established until the 13th century; it was the Second Council of Lyons (1274) that named seven specific "sacraments" which then were considered to be instituted by Christ and to bring about, i.e., effect, what they signified. Other things such as the sign of the cross, blessed ashes, religious vows, had sometimes been called sacraments. From later medieval times, they were more clearly described as signs "pointing to" a reality rather than as actually "effecting" that reality. They were sacramentals.

The spiritual effect following from the use of a sacramental depends upon the intercession of the church. Underlying this assertion is, ultimately, the notion that the church, as the body of Christ (1 Cor 12:12-28) is so united with him that her actions and formally approved prayers have their own peculiar efficacy. The church, both "institutes" sacramentals and can nominate new ones (S.C., 79). The central Roman authority has held the right of granting approval to new sacramentals since the time of the Council of Trent; previously, the approval would more usually have come from a local bishop in response to a devotion or usage that had grown up in his diocese.

Quite often, under the influence of an older theology of sacraments, sacramentals were spoken of as "imitating" sacraments. It would be more common today to view them as "occasions" for the gracing process of the sacraments to take hold of us and for the Christ-life to deepen in us.

It is clear that, while the sacraments are richly symbolic, they cannot carry explicitly every nuance of Christian life and experience—a cogent reason, then, for using various sacramentals to assist in expressing particular dimensions of that life: for example, while the sacrament of the sick is a major event in the process of our becoming reconciled with our mortality, prayer and reflection before a crucifix, a sacramental relevant to that process, is a powerful aid for achieving that reconciliation. The church has relied very heavily in recent years on the sacraments and liturgical rites to carry by themselves the full meaning of encounter with Christ; this has often been at the expense of the warmth and richness of Christian daily life; a more general care for and use of sacramentals would go a long way towards integrating the sacraments with our overall growth in humane Christianity. Sacramentals, based on and relating to the church's sacraments, both prepare for and flow from the celebration of those sacraments. They are mutually enriching.

As signs, then, we would consider today that sacramentals can have a wider reference, namely to any object or prayer or action that can put us in touch with God's grace in Christ. Underlying this understanding of sacramental is the notion that Christ, the primary sacrament of encounter with God, renders the whole of creation new and redeemed. In this sense, while the church has nominated only certain actions as sacraments, there is "hardly any proper use of material things which cannot be ... directed toward the sanctification of men and the praise of God" (S.C., 61).

Bernard Cooke, *Sacraments and Sacramentality* (Mystic, CT: Twenty-Third Publ., 1983). Thomas Marsh, "The Sacramentals Revisited" *Furrow* 33

1116

(1982): 272-281. Karl Rahner, *The Church and the Sacraments* (NY: Herder and Herder, 1963).

PATRICK BISHOP, S.J.

SACRAMENTS

Though this essay deals with *Christian* sacraments, it is good to recall at the beginning that sacramentality is not monopolized by Christianity; it extends to all human experience. Basically, sacramentality involves three elements: (1) the ultimate meaning of human experience, (2) divine saving presence, and (3) some transformation of humans individually and communally.

(1) Whether in the context of Christian sacraments or in the broader context of world religions, sacramentality points to the fact that human life is distinctive because men and women exist self-consciously, that existence for humans is a sequence of experiences and that each of these experiences is what it is because of the particular meaning it has. To change that meaning is to change the experience. Religious sacramentality touches on the *ultimate* meaning of people's experience, that which confirms or challenges all other meaning.

(2) However, this ultimate meaning does not come originally from some abstract intellectual understanding, even though in some religions it may be expressed in formulated doctrines. Rather, the meaning comes from the *presence* of God, a presence that is the result of divine communication with humans through God's word of revelation and the human response in faith to that word. Because of God's being with and for humans, present to them in this mystery of divine self-revelation, there is a basic change in what it means to be a human person.

(3) Not only is the meaning of people's lives changed, but they as persons are radically transformed by this divine-human relationship. They are changed precisely through the altered worldview they now possess, through the new values and goals which that worldview provides and through the deeper motivation that flows from the relationship. This transformation which is effected by the religious sacramentality of human experience can be referred to as "sacramental grace."

Within that wider picture of sacramentality, Christian sacraments have a distinctive meaning and effectiveness because of Jesus' life, death, and resurrection. So, the very succinct description of Christian sacraments: "sacred signs, instituted by Christ, to give grace."

The Emergence of Christian Sacraments

Even during Jesus' public ministry his disciples were becoming aware that Jesus was bringing into being some new order of things, a new breaking into human history of "the Kingdom of God." He was providing a new perspective on God, his Father, and pointing to a new way of relating to God. However, it was only with the "Easter experience" after Jesus' crucifixion, i.e., with their awareness that Jesus was still humanly alive and mysteriously present to them in his Spirit, that these disciples slowly grasped the profound transformation of life's meaning that had occurred.

Gathering together, especially for communal meals, these first Christians shared with one another their awareness of this enduring Christ-mystery which changed the whole meaning of their lives and shared their recollections of Jesus' life and death. Slowly, too, they developed certain rituals to celebrate the new divine-human covenant that Jesus' death and resurrection had brought into existence. In particular they gave a special form to the practice of baptizing people and used it to initiate into the community those who accepted the gospel message, and they celebrated some special meals which quickly developed into "the breaking of the bread," the Christian eucharist. Though Jesus himself did not leave these rituals as such to his followers, it was his life and particularly his death and resurrection that "instituted these sacramental rituals" by being the mystery the rituals celebrate.

Early Christians, then, lived and prayed with the awareness of sharing in "the great mystery revealed in Christ," the mystery of God's saving presence to the lives of people. This was, in the full sense of the term, a "new life"; actually, it was the beginning of that unending life which Jesus had promised to those who would receive him as sent from his Father. Through the ritual of Christian initiation one entered into this new Spirit-life that came from Jesus' own passage into Spirit-filled risen life. As Paul explained in his letter to the Christians at Rome, in baptism one enters somehow into the death and resurrection of Christ and possesses the Spirit as the creative source of unending life.

It was this "great mystery" that was celebrated in "the breaking of the bread." Without yet reflecting on the way in which the eucharist "gave grace," the early decades—indeed the early centuries—believed that sharing the bread and wine become body and blood of the risen Lord was a continuing "food" for the new life that had begun with baptism. At the same time, they were aware that in "proclaiming the death of the Lord until he comes in glory" they were professing together their Christian faith. They were stating their acceptance of the preached gospel, but more than that they were pledging themselves to faithful living out of their Christianity. So, it was that the Latin word *sacramentum* (which meant "an oath, a solemn promise"), along with the earlier Greek word *mysterion*, came to be applied to these rituals, as well as to other Christian rituals like "ordination" or "reconciliation" which emerged in the life of the church.

Fairly early, however, another way of looking at the sacramental rituals came into existence and slowly gained ground. This was the instrumental view which considered the liturgical acts as means used by God, acting through the mediation of the ordained minister, to give grace to people. In this perspective Christians came to liturgy to *receive* sacraments, to be freed from their sins, to be blessed. This receptive approach to the role of the faithful coincided with their increasing exclusion from active participation in sacramental liturgy.

Throughout much of the first millennium the people's sense of involvement in the Christ-mystery through sacramental ritual remained quite strong, though with diminishing understanding of the mystery. For a variety of reasons, many of them having to do with the unsettled social situation of those days, the bulk of Christians received rudimentary religious instruction at best. This, plus the fact that Latin remained the liturgical language, while it was gradually becoming foreign to most people, meant that the level of theological insight into the reality of sacramental liturgy was minimal. So, by the 9th century and thereafter we find explanations of the liturgy, very many of them allegorical, which reflect the community's loss of understanding.

As the faithful had less and less of a role in the liturgical actions, as the language became strange to them, as the celebrant was situated at the far end of a sanctuary where he did "the sacred act," the sacraments and particularly the Mass became a spectacle which people attended. Obviously, this meant that the intrinsic significance of the sacramental liturgies no longer interacted with the significance of people's lives, except for the general outlook that something was given people through sacraments that enabled them to persevere amidst conflict with "the world, the flesh, and the devil" and so to reach their heavenly destiny.

In the 12th century a key development in the understanding and the practice of sacraments took place. As part of the overall intellectual struggle to understand things more clearly, there was an effort to clarify the nature of sacraments, if possible to arrive at a definition of "sacrament" that would permit people to say what was or was not a sacrament. This proved very difficult for an intrinsic reason: because the Christian sacraments cannot really be fitted into a category—technically speaking they are *analogous realities*—no strict definition of "sacrament" is possible. However, there was one element common to all the areas of Christian sacrament: by that point in history all of them, including marriage, involved a liturgical ceremony. As a result, it was the ritual action, for example, the wedding ceremony, that by itself was identified as the sacrament, and the focus of understanding Christian sacramentality became more limited than it had been in earlier periods of the church.

Because of an increasing awareness of the decline of liturgy, the late Middle Ages witnessed movements for reform, but these were not sufficient to ward off the explosive reaction of the Protestant Reformation in the early 16th century. On the positive side, the Reformation drew attention to the role of personal faith and the active participation of the faithful in sacramental liturgy; on the negative side, many of the Reformation churches downgraded the role of ritual and tended to substitute reflection on the Bible for sacramental celebration.

The Roman Catholic reaction to these Protestant tenets came with the Council of Trent (1545-1563) which provided the first systematized official statement about Christian sacraments. The teaching of Trent is of special importance because it has provided the framework and basic doctrinal positions for Catholic teaching about sacraments up to the 20th century. While the decrees of the council regarding sacraments need to be carefully studied and explained in the light of their historical context, a few of the leading notions can be mentioned here.

In the section that provides the general statements about Christian sacraments, the council insisted that Christ himself is the one who instituted the sacraments, though no explanation was given about the manner in which this took place—a later section specifically on the Mass linked the institution of eucharist with the action of Jesus at the supper and with his death. Countering the Protestant contention that "sacrament" could be applied in the true sense only to baptism and the Lord's Supper, Trent insisted that five other instances of liturgical celebration (confirmation, reconciliation, ordination, anointing of the sick, and marriage) were truly sacraments.

The heart of the debate between Catholics and Protestants dealt, however, with the efficacy of sacramental actions, specifically of baptism and eucharist. Consistent with their basic teaching about justification, namely that sinners though forgiven become "just" only in the next life, the Reformers looked on sacramental liturgies as proclaiming Christ's promise of human salvation but not yet transforming the people by grace. What liturgy did was to announce the gospel message so that people's faith might be aroused and increased; sacraments did not give grace, they only promised it.

Opposing this view, the Council of Trent insisted on the intrinsic grace-giving power of sacraments. "Sacraments contain and give grace." While its decrees took explicit account of the need for proper dispositions, including faith, in those who receive sacraments, the council viewed the sacramental liturgies as possessing *in themselves* a saving power that derives from the death of Christ. When properly performed by a celebrant who has the basic intention of accomplishing what the church intends in its sacramental acts, a sacrament has *ex opere operato* the power of conferring grace.

The term *ex opere operato* has been a key element in Roman Catholic sacramental teaching and in much Protestant disagreement with that teaching. If understood accurately, it refers to the belief that whenever the essential elements of the rite are carried out by a minister with a serious intention, the action, because it involves the agency of the risen Christ and his Spirit, possesses intrinsically the power of transforming people by grace. Unfortunately, the term has often been misunderstood to imply that sacramental effectiveness is automatic and independent of the care or understanding with which it is enacted or of the faith or devotion of those involved. Clearly, such was not the intention of the Council of Trent, nor do its decrees suggest such an interpretation.

Little changed in either official teaching or in popular attitudes regarding sacramental liturgies between the Council of Trent and the mid-20th century. However, the experience of the two great world wars and the convoking of the Second Vatican Council have opened up a new epoch in the life of Christianity and have led to a deepened interest in the role of liturgy in Christian life and to a creative development of sacramental theology.

The Nature of Christian Sacraments

What is becoming increasingly recognized is that "sacrament," even "Christian sacrament," refers to much more than religiously identifiable practices such as baptizing people. Vatican II pointed to this when it spoke of the church, i.e., Christians in the entirety of their lives and activity, as the fundamental sacrament. All the basic experiences that comprise the fabric of people's lives— birth, growth into adulthood, sickness and suffering, love and friendship, success and failure, caring for one another, sin and reconciliation, and in a special way death—are meant to be transformed by what has happened in the life and death and resurrection of Jesus. In all these areas, ritual has an important, indeed an indispensable, role to play; but effective rituals do not function apart from that which they ritualize. It is the entire experience with a particular focus on the ritual moment that deserves the name "sacrament."

Central to the effect caused by sacramental liturgies is the transformation of the *meaning* of people's experience. While a key area of human living, e.g., marriage or sin and reconciliation, is changed in its entirety by the meaning coming from the life and death and resurrection of Jesus, it is the ritual that formally states this meaning and relates human life to the significance of Jesus' saving action. As modern social and psychological study has given us a clearer and deeper understanding of the role that meaning plays in human experience, we begin to see how basic to the process of "grace" is the meaning given to life by any Christian individual or community.

Traditionally we have seen baptism as the first exposure of *an individual* to this new Christian meaning. Now we are regaining more awareness of the *community* dimension: we are more aware that the liturgy of Christian initiation, begun in baptism and complemented in confirmation, is entry into a community that is constituted by faith in the saving power of Jesus' death and resurrection. Christian initiation involves a process of communication and sharing that is meant to continue throughout people's lives: the community shares with the baptized its faith vision of human life, its belief that life finds an ultimate explanation through the significance of Jesus' Passover; and the newly baptized shares publicly in the ritual his or her commitment to Christian faith, life and discipleship.

Because it is not an abstract understanding of life that has been radically changed by Jesus' Passover, but rather the entire psychological response of imagination and motivation and free choice along with intellectual insight, the baptismal commitment embraces the whole of a person's future life. The ritual of initiation is intended to be a revelation, a revelation of what it means to be human, a revelation of the role of Christ and of Christianity in history, and most basically a revelation of the God revealed in Jesus. In the ritual the neophyte professes acceptance of that revelation and begins a life-long process of interiorizing more deeply the truth of that revelation and of living out its implications amid the changing circumstances of life.

Instead of being simply actions done to a person by an ordained minister, baptism and confirmation are meant to be joint actions of the individual who is entering the community by professing faith and of the community that is receiving this new member. And since the Christian community into which the newly baptized is being received exists as "body of Christ," the person is joined to the risen Lord in the mystery of "the whole Christ"—he or she becomes Christian. This is a human social reality; but it is more than that, for "body of Christ" expresses the mystery of the church existing as a living unity whose animating principle is the Spirit breathed out in history by the risen Christ. In the initiation liturgy the baptized shares that Spirit by which the church lives and ministers to the world.

However, for those baptized in infancy, which today is the more common practice, involvement in the sacramentality of the Christian community begins even earlier than the ritual of baptism. The child born of a Christian couple who are truly living out their faith is from its earliest moments exposed to the faith of its parents. The love experienced by the infant, the love of each parent in the critical process of bonding, is essential to the child's healthy psychological development. But the environment of the home, the love or lack of it between the parents, the harmony or strife among the siblings— all of which share in the sacramentality of Christian marriage, also have a deep effect on the infant for good or ill. Though it will be years before the child's own awareness of self and world will be developed enough to share explicitly the parents' faith, that faith is already being instilled into the child's consciousness at the level of implicit impression.

Realizing this makes us aware of the very basic role of marriage in Christian sacramentality. In a true sense, marriage is the most basic area of human and Christian sacramentality, for its significance deals precisely with relationships among humans, and above all with the saving and humanly enriching relationship of love and friendship. Christian marriage does not contain the whole of this sacramentality; it is not a sacrament in isolation. Within the broader saving sacramentality of human love it is a special paradigmatic instance of transforming love between two Christians who in a unique way share their faith, their daily routine of life, their goals, their concern for others, their selves.

The wedding ceremony plays a distinctive role within the sacrament of marriage; it is the public commitment to the relationship. The essence of the sacrament is, however, the two persons wedded to one another. Marriage is a process, an unfolding relationship between two persons that gives expression to the saving self-gift of Jesus in his death and resurrection. The life-long love and care for one another expressed by a Christian woman and man is meant to find a deeper meaning by the couple's insight into the way in which Jesus' death as passage into new life throws light on the sacrificial self-giving their married life requires. Conversely, the experience each has and the experience they share of striving to be for one another in mature fashion and the experience of personal growth that emerges over the years as they work out a shared destiny provide a realistic understanding of what Jesus has done in his self-giving redemptive action.

Though Christian marriage has long been acknowledged as a sacrament, it is only recently that some theologians have drawn attention to the sacramentality attached to the broader experience of friendship into which marriage fits. In many instances, the love and concern between friends functions as a genuine, even if not religiously formulated, revelation of what the saving love of God is all about. Among a group of people who are believing Christians, the transforming experience of human love finds deepened expression because of their sharing faith in the risen Lord. Their Christianity is a lived-out deepening of their humanly rewarding and enriching experience of true friendship. Marriage, then, does not enjoy a monopoly on the sacramentality it shares in distinctive fashion; rather, its role within Christian life is to provide insight into the way in which love among humans is meant to mirror the God revealed in Jesus as the Christ, a God who so loved the world that he sent that Christ to give humans unending life.

Desirable as is this picture of humans bonded together in friendship, it is somewhat idealistic. The reality of life, even Christian life, is that humans are incapable of constant and unqualified fidelity to such relationships. We exploit one another, we betray one another, we use others for our own earthly benefit, we hurt one another, and we often end up alienated from one another as individuals and as groups. Quite simply, we *sin* against one another.

Sin, though, is not meant to triumph; it is not meant to have the last word. Jesus' saving work was directed precisely to the overcoming of sin, and that means to the reconciliation of humans to one another and to God. Christian life should be, then, the experience of loving relationships maintained despite wounds to the friendship, wounds that have healed through honest recognition of one's own need for forgiveness and through genuine willingness to forgive the other. Reconciliation is meant to be a hallmark of Christian community existence; it is practically equivalent to peace.

Just as the broader reality of human friendship is sacrament, so is the fundamental experience of Christians living reconciled with one another. It is what speaks of the divine forgiveness that led to Jesus' reconciling death and resurrection. As in other major areas of experience, there is a place—indeed a need—for ritual expression of individual and social reconciliation, and so sacramental liturgies of reconciliation have been prominent in the church's life. Today's revision of the liturgy of reconciliation is but the latest stage in the enduring Christian task of injecting the healing significance of Jesus' death and resurrection into the constant need of reconciliation in human life.

While Jesus' healing ministry and the healing ministry of the church in history deals primarily with the spiritual aspects of human existence—with overcoming error and ignorance, instilling trust and hope instead of fear and suspicion and prejudice, leading humans to love rather than to hate, overcoming the power of sin—it does not neglect human bodiliness. So, among the sacramental liturgies of the church there is the anointing of the sick. Linked with other healing ministries practiced by physicians and nurses and psychologists and all those who care for the infirm, the Christian sacrament of anointing is meant to put human suffering into context, to give it a meaning it could not have apart from the life, death and resurrection of Christ, and to make it more bearable through the Christian community's personal support to which the liturgy points.

All Christians are meant to share in the task of ministering to those in need, whether that need be economic or social or physical or psychological or religious. Discipleship is a responsibility intrinsic to identity as a baptized Christian. Christians are to care for one another as well as for other sister and brother humans; and this care is a key manifestation, or sacrament, of the divine care. Historically, there was a tendency to limit this sacramentality to the ordained, the holy orders; today there is a growing recognition that while the ordained do have a distinctive ministerial role, the sacrament of Christian ministry is not limited to them.

The eucharistic celebration, the Mass, has always been recognized as the high point and focus of Christian sacramentality. It is in this ritual, whose enactment clearly goes back to the earliest generation of Christians, that the significance of the other areas with which sacraments deal—initiation, death, reconciliation, family, friendship, healing, ministry—are most sharply and explicitly related to the continuing mystery of Christ. It is in the eucharist that Christians are challenged by the proclamation of the gospel to assess the meaning of their lives and their implementation of that meaning. It is in the covenant commitment intrinsic to the eucharistic action that people face an ongoing invitation to deeper faith and more active discipleship. It is in the eucharistic ritual that, other things being equal, Christians are meant to become most aware of the saving presence of the risen Lord and the transforming, i.e., grace-giving, activity of his Spirit.

Because Roman Catholics for so long had thought in very limited fashion about Christ's presence in eucharist, fixing their attention almost wholly on "the real presence" connected with the consecrated elements of bread and wine, there is need today to broaden the understanding of God's saving presence through sacraments and specifically through the eucharistic celebration. Modern behavioral and social sciences have helped a great deal to make clearer the nature of personal presence, its connection with processes of communication, its dependence upon people being consciously *for one another*, its fundamental independence from spatial location; and all this has found application in recent theological attempts to explain the presence of the risen Christ in eucharist.

Basically, presence is a matter of one person being aware of another as a result of some form of communication between them. When someone speaks to me, that person is present in my *awareness*, even though quite obviously their spatial location is somewhere outside my consciousness. And how that person is present to me is determined by what they say or do—or to put it another way, the communication from which the presence results comes from use of some symbol such as language or gesture. The deepest level of presence exists when, through whatever symbols are most appropriate, persons truly share themselves *as the persons they are* with those they love. This is the kind of presence that is involved in Christian sacraments when the symbolic actions of Christians as they express their relationship to the risen Christ and to one another function also as the symbols through which God becomes present to people through self-sharing in word and Spirit.

Personal presence is not a static reality; as we suggested, it is not "being somewhere." Instead, because it is people being for one another, most specially in friendship, it is a creative force in human life. People become what and who they are through their relationships, through being for others and having others be for them. Christians believe that the ultimate and most creative instance of this occurs in the divine saving presence to humans. Because of God's saving presence in the risen Christ and their Spirit, people are transformed as people beyond what would otherwise be possible; divine friendship realizes a potential for existing personally that would not otherwise be even known.

This transformation of persons under the impact of divine presence, of God being for them, is what traditionally has been called "sanctifying grace"; and because this occurs through the changed sacramentality of human experience, the term "sacramental grace" points to the effect of sacraments on people's lives. So, as the Council of Trent insisted, the sacraments through which God is made present to believing Christians do "contain and give" grace; for the entirety of human life is—if its meaning is deepened by the meaning revealed in Jesus' death and resurrection—filled with the transforming presence of God.

W. Bausch, *A New Look at the Sacraments* (Mystic, CT: Twenty-Third Publ., 1983). B. Cooke, *Sacraments and Sacramentality* (Mystic, CT: Twenty-Third Publ., 1983). M. Downey, *Clothed in Christ* (New York: Crossroad, 1987). M. Hellwig, *The Meaning of the Sacraments* (Dayton: Pflaum,, 1972). A. Kavanagh, *On Liturgical Theology* (New York: Pueblo Publ., 1985). D. Power, *Unsearchable Riches* (New York: Pueblo Publ., 1984). *Message of the Sacraments*, series ed. by M. Hellwig, (Wilmington: Michael Glazier).

BERNARD COOKE

SACRAMENTS IN THE EASTERN CHURCHES

Introduction

Vatican II's decree on ecumenism (*Unitatis redintegratio*) acknowledged the distinctive role of Eastern churches not in full communion with Rome (13-19). It asserted that: " ... from their very origins the churches of the East have had a treasury from which the church of the West has drawn largely for its liturgy, spiritual tradition, and jurisprudence. Nor must we underestimate the fact that the basic dogmas of the Christian faith concerning the Trinity and the Word of God made flesh from the Virgin Mary were defined in ecumenical councils held in the East" (14). It also commended the East's stress on worship, noting that "these churches, although separated from us, yet possess true sacraments, above all—by apostolic succession—the priesthood and the Eucharist, whereby they are still joined to us in closest intimacy" (15).

In regard to Eastern churches already in full communion with Rome, the council devoted an entire decree, *Orientalium ecclesiarum*, which commends their sacramental life and practices. Vatican II " ...confirms and approves the ancient discipline concerning the sacraments which exist in the Eastern [Catholic] churches, and also the ritual observed in their celebration and administration, and wishes this to be restored where such a case arises" (12).

A major result of recent improvement in ecumenical contacts between Roman Catholics and Eastern Orthodox has been the establishment of a Joint International Commission for Theological Dialogue. Since its first session in Patmos and Rhodes in 1980, the commission has already met five times (as of 1989) and published three consensus statements on the sacraments: the Munich (1982), Bari (1987), and New Valamo (1988) agreements.

Who are "Eastern" Christians?

The designation "Eastern" (or "Oriental") churches has become a customary way of identifying that large number of Christian churches whose distant origins are rooted in Eastern regions of the ancient Roman Empire, as opposed to the Western or Latin-speaking regions that included Italy, Spain, Gaul and Africa. These Eastern churches emerged from the ancient sees of Antioch, Alexandria, Jerusalem and the "New Rome," namely Byzantium or Constantinople. Today many members of these Eastern churches live in the Western "diaspora." In contemporary usage Eastern churches are classified in four groups: (a) the Oriental Orthodox churches, (b) the Eastern Orthodox churches, (c) the Assyrian church of the East, and (d) the Eastern Catholic churches in full communion with the church of Rome.

(a) The Oriental Orthodox churches have also been known in the past as the Ancient Oriental, the pre-Chalcedonian, the non-Chalcedonian churches, or even the Lesser Eastern churches. Their members have been incorrectly labeled as "Monophysites." The Oriental Orthodox churches are a communion of five distinct ancient churches of the East: Armenian, Coptic (Egyptian), Ethiopian, Syrian ("Jacobite"), and Malankar (Indian).

(b) A very small group of Eastern Christians is called the Assyrian church of the East, an East Syrian church which originated in Palestine, grew in Antioch and Edessa with only minimal Greek influence, and which flourished in the Persian Empire. At a synod held in A.D. 484 this church adopted the Christology of Nestorius.

(c) The third and most extensive group of Eastern Christians belongs to the Orthodox church made up of churches associated with the four ancient patriarchates of Constantinople, Alexandria, Antioch and Jerusalem and to which in modern times has been added Moscow. They comprise the largest part of Eastern Christianity. What unifies the Orthodox church besides its adherence to scripture and the ancient Christian creeds is acceptance of the teachings of the first seven ecumenical councils.

The various churches among the Eastern Orthodox are commonly subdivided according to the following designations: the autocephalous (or autonomous) churches, associated with the patriarchates or churches of Constantinople, Alexandria, Antioch, Jerusalem, Russia, Romania, Greece, Serbia, Bulgaria, Georgia, Cyprus, Poland, Albania and Czechoslovakia as well as several independent canonical and irregular non-canonical churches. Because the Orthodox, especially those following the Byzantine liturgy, make up the majority of Eastern Christians and are the most influential theologically, this article often cites their sacramental practices.

(d) The fourth grouping of Eastern churches are the Eastern Catholic churches in full communion with the church of Rome. These have also been known by the perjorative term "Uniate" churches, a designation nowadays usually avoided. These churches have tried to maintain their original traditions and practices, but have sometimes undergone various degrees of Latinization. These Eastern Catholic churches usually have either a counterpart in the Oriental Orthodox, Eastern Orthodox, or the Assyrian church of the East. Among those related to the Oriental Orthodox are: the Armenian Catholic, the Coptic Catholic, the Ethiopian Catholic, the Syrian Catholic and the Malankar Catholic churches; those related to the Orthodox churches of Byzantine traditions: the Melkite Catholic, the Ukrainian Catholic, the Ruthenian Catholic, the Romanian Catholic, the Greek Catholic, the Bulgarian Catholic, the Slovak Catholic, the Hungarian Catholic. Corresponding to the Assyrian church of the East are the Chaldean Catholic church and the Malabar Catholic church. The Maronites and Italo-Albanian Catholics have no counterparts among the Orthodox.

General Remarks

It is not possible in this article both to explain in detail the basic similarities of sacramental practices and to enumerate the rich diversity of Eastern sacramental theology and practices. For specific treatment of a particular Eastern church, a scholar would need to consult specialized research.

Bishops and theologians of the Orthodox church and the Roman Catholic church have been involved in the last decade in explaining how the two churches express the faith in continuity with the apostles. Both churches understand themselves as a communion of faith and sacraments, preeminently manifested in eucharistic celebrations presided over by an ordained bishop or priest. Catholics and Orthodox in the 1988 New Valamo consensus statement agreed that " ...on all essential points concerning ordination, our churches have a common doctrine and practice, even if on certain canonical and disciplinary requirements, such as celibacy, customs can be different because of pastoral and spiritual reasons" (30).

The two churches now wish to present their sacramental beliefs in theological language that avoids Western Scholastic or Eastern Palamite categories. The new sacramental theology being formulated together draws upon scriptural, liturgical and patristic language. Since the Eastern churches did not undergo a Renaissance, a Reformation or an Enlightenment, they have preserved some ancient traditions forgotten in the West but have not elaborated a systematic sacramental theology. The church of Rome and the Eastern Orthodox church recognize their basic credal affirmations on the sacraments as the same, despite the fact that the Orthodox are often puzzled, troubled, and unwilling to imitate some practices of Rome.

To refer to the sacraments, Eastern Christians use the word derived from the Greek word *mysterion*, the holy "mysteries." Eastern Christians speak of participating in the sacramental life of the church rather than "receiving" sacraments. What are seen as making present and partially accessible, in sensible form, the invisible reality of God's love expressed in trinitarian life through encounter with the Incarnate Word are the holy mysteries or sacraments. Christian sacramental life is a salvific union with the glorified Christ by participation in the mystery of the heavenly liturgy.

Roman Catholics note that Eastern Christians often do not use their distinction between sacraments and sacramentals. For Eastern Christians sacramental living means participating in the mystery of the incarnation through gestures and activities which, even if practiced in the home, are linked with the church's liturgy. Numerous blessings connected with foods, water, and holy places are seen as possessing a kind of sacramental function that fosters ecclesial communion and turns the believers' minds to the heavenly liturgy where Christ intercedes without end.

Two religious practices of Eastern Christianity strongly color their sacramental life and should be noted even if, in the West, these practices are not considered directly sacramental. These practices are fasting and veneration of icons.

Through fasting Eastern Christians blend daily living with the liturgical calendar. Four major fasts are celebrated each year: Lent (seven weeks before Easter); the apostles' fast (the second Monday after Pentecost to June 28); the fast of the falling asleep of the Theotokos (August 1-14), and the forty days' Christmas fast (November 15 to December 24). Fasting in the Eastern tradition is measured more by what is not eaten rather than by amounts. On most days in Great Lent and Holy Week not only is meat not allowed but neither fish nor animal products (milk, cheese, eggs, etc.), and wine and oil are also excluded. Eastern Christians do not use the distinction found in the West between fasting and abstinence. Observing fasting regulations in the modern living conditions of the diaspora is not always feasible. One of the preparatory commissions planning position papers for the forthcoming Great and Holy Synod of the Orthodox Church proposes to adjust fasting requirements. Fasting is not seen as punishment of the flesh but as a gesture used to open oneself more fully to the presence of the Holy Spirit.

Secondly, through veneration of icons Eastern Christians are to enter into the spiritual realities signified by the sacraments. Eastern Christians venerate a spiritual presence in these religious paintings which Westerners would never associate with statues, stained-glass windows, or holy cards. In the West there is neither an equivalent of icon veneration (*proskynesis*) nor iconic incorporation into the liturgy as in the East. By the incarnation of the word, the image of the Father (2 Cor 4:4), God's image is seen as being restored in every human being. The material world is viewed as sanctified and again capable of mediating divine beauty. Icons express, as far as can be, the glory of God seen in the face of Christ. And so icons are judged to be sacred words in painting or the "visible gospel." An icon is not a random decoration but an integral part of the church's life and worship. Production and use of icons are always controlled by theological criteria. The location of the iconostasis (the screen that displays the principal icons), the screen's doors, the shape of the sacred vessels, and even of the church building contribute to the liturgical interplay between the visible and the invisible reality.

The Number of Sacraments

The doctrine of the "seven sacraments," to the extent that it exists in the East, has been influenced more by the West than by Eastern theology. As is well known the seven-fold listing of the the sacraments emerged in the West during the 12th century and became official only in the 13th. In the East it appears for the first time in the Profession of Faith which Pope Clement IV required of Byzantine Emperor Michael Paleologus in 1267. The East has never committed itself to any specific list of sacraments such as the Roman church did at the Council of Trent. For pedagogical reasons and to facilitate dialogue with the West, Eastern churches make use of the teaching that there are seven sacraments. At the same time some consider other rituals as sacraments such as monastic profession, anointing of monarchs, burial of Christians, consecration of church buildings, etc.

Baptism/Chrismation

Among Eastern Christians infant baptism and chrismation are celebrated together and are seen, with the reception of eucharistic communion (received from a golden spoon containing consecrated wine), as the sacrament or sacraments of initiation. Baptism and chrismation are deemed to belong together as the Resurrection and Pentecost. Important for the Eastern churches is the sequence of sacramental initiation: baptism, chrismation, eucharist. Eastern Christians are puzzled, even shocked, at practices now common in Roman Catholicism: (a) of not observing the ancient sequence by allowing children to receive the eucharist before chrismation, and (b) of "depriving" baptized infants of eucharistic communion until the "age of reason." All the parts of Christian initiation in the East are administered by a priest. The liturgy begins with the blessing of the water which symbolizes the whole realm of matter. The Byzantine formula of baptism is pronounced not in the name of the minister as in the West ("I baptize you..."), but rather by declaration on

behalf of the baptizand ("The servant of God/handmaid of God is baptized...").
The East retains triple immersion although the infant is not usually totally submerged. In Greece the infant is baptized between the ages of one and two years and remains unnamed until baptism. The role of the sponsors still has strong religious and social functions.

Catechetical material explaining the Eastern liturgy of baptism does not stress a relationship between the sacramental baptism and the remission of original sin. The predominant emphasis is on entry into the body of Christ. The Orthodox do not accept baptism administered by an unbeliever who acts on behalf of the church. The minister of the sacrament must be a believer; there is even reluctance to consider a baptism as performed properly when done by a lay person.

Chrismation is seen as sign of the seal of the Holy Spirit (Acts 2:38). Unlike the normal practice in the Roman church, chrismation is not reserved to the bishop although the *myron* (chrism) used to anoint the person has been blessed by the bishop who thereby maintains a link with the liturgy.

The Eastern Orthodox do not use the terminology of Roman Catholic theology regarding an "indelible character" for confirmation or chrismation. They commonly confirm/reconfirm those entering the Orthodox church, even from Catholicism, as a sign that a baptism performed under irregular circumstances, outside the canonical boundaries of the church, is now regularized through this sealing. As have Roman Catholics, the Orthodox have sometimes practiced "rebaptism" of those previously baptized in another church. But by the principle of "economy" (*oikonomia*) an Orthodox bishop may declare as objectively administered something administered outside the boundaries of Orthodoxy.

Eucharist or Synaxis

This essay can not give an account of all the eucharistic liturgies or families of eucharistic anaphoras within the Eastern churches nor can it provide a summary of the specific theological explanations used to explain the structure and significance of eucharistic prayers.

Both Catholics and Orthodox agree on the meaning of the eucharistic celebration. The eucharistic celebration is the memorial (*anamnesis*) of Christ's work as Savior. The eucharistic sacrifice is seen as involving the active presence of Christ the High Priest, acting through the Christian community presided over by the bishop or persons delegated by the bishop to celebrate the eucharistic mysteries. In the eucharistic celebration believers not only commend themselves and one another to Christ but also accept the diaconal mandate of the gospel to mediate Christ's salvation to the world. God the Father is seen as sending the Holy Spirit to consecrate the elements of bread and wine so as to become the body and blood of Jesus Christ for the sanctification of the faithful. The Holy Spirit transforms the sacred gifts into the body and blood of Christ in order to bring about the growth of the body which is the church. In this way the entire celebration is an epiclesis which at certain moments becomes more explicit. The church may be said to be continually in a state of *epiclesis* (see Munich document, 12-16).

In the Byzantine liturgy and in most Eastern liturgies the bread used in the eucharist is leavened bread (i.e., bread made with yeast). In the Roman rite unleavened bread (*azyme*) is used. A specially prepared loaf of bread is cut into cubes in the preparatory rites of an Eastern liturgy. Communion under the double form of bread and wine is distributed from the chalice in which the eucharistic bread, soaked in eucharistic wine, is administered by the priest to the communicant from a golden spoon.

Today there is a notable difference between the Eastern Orthodox and the

Roman Catholics regarding the frequency of reception of the eucharist. Orthodox believers out of reverence observe certain practices before approaching the table of the Lord: receiving the sacrament of reconciliation, fasting for several days before reception, neither eating nor drinking from midnight. Communicants are expected to abstain from conjugal relations prior to receiving communion. Women during their menstrual period are counseled not to receive communion. Some pious Eastern Christians communicate only four times a year: Easter, Christmas, Dormition of the Virgin, and on their own feast day. They find the practice of weekly or daily communion, as now practiced in the Roman church, fraught with the dangerous possibility of its becoming casual or irreverent.

Intercommunion, that is, offering eucharistic hospitality to Christians who are not Orthodox, is strictly forbidden by the Orthodox and sedulously avoided. Whereas at Vatican II and in subsequent guidelines the Roman Catholic church expressed its willingness to permit Orthodox who approach Catholic priests to receive communion under specific circumstances, the Orthodox did not reciprocate. Orthodoxy requires that a communicant share in the entire range of essential Orthodox beliefs before being eligible for communion. Thus the exceptional decision by the Moscow Patriarchate (December 16, 1969) to allow some measure of intercommunion for Roman Catholics who approach the sacrament was regarded as very unusual. The Orthodox church of Greece, for example, expressed its "surprise, wonderment, and sorrow" at this decision.

Although lay participation in the Divine Liturgy is often regarded as active, even Orthodox observers are now complaining about the isolation and passivity of the laity at liturgies. This is another concern that will be addressed at the forthcoming Great Council.

The Eastern churches do not practice eucharistic devotions outside of the Divine Liturgy. Hence, Catholic devotions such as Benediction of the Blessed Sacrament are unknown.

Sacramental Reconciliation with the Church

The Eastern churches practice private confession of post-baptismal sins to a priest. Such a confession takes place in front of the iconostasis. On a nearby stand have been placed a cross as well as an icon of the Savior or the book of the gospels. After the penitent's confession of sins, the priest places his liturgical stole and his hands upon the penitent's head. Such a laying on of hands is seen as an important sign attesting to the power of the Holy Spirit to forgive sins.

Originally in East and West confession of sin or *exhomologesis* was a public act consisting of enrollment on a list of sinners and public penance over a lengthy period of time for serious sins. By the 4th century private confession was practiced and even associated with spiritual direction from monks or other holy persons. Sacramental confession or reconciliation in the East is not practiced as frequently as it was in modern Catholicism especially up to the 1960s. The formulas of absolution in the Byzantine *euchologia* and penitentials use a prayer that is declaratory and avoids the first person, as in the case of baptism. The priest was rarely ever described as judge as in Western theological writings.

Marriage

In the teaching of the East sacramental marriage requires the mutual consent of the believing Christian partners and God's blessing imparted through a priest of the Church. The discipline of the Orthodox church accepts as sacramental only those marriages sanctified through blessing by an Orthodox priest.

The wedding service in the Byzantine

tradition consists of two parts. The first part, the betrothal, takes place in the church's vestibule and includes the blessing of rings and their exchange. After a procession into the church this is followed by the crowning, a term sometimes used for the marriage service. The bridal couple then follows the officiating priest in a circular procession to symbolize their spiritual journey to eternity.

Basing their teaching on Ephesians 5, Eastern Christians regard marriage as a *mysterion* symbolizing the union between Christ and the church. As such there can only be one, eternal bond. Unlike the view of the West which sees marriage also as a legal contract that ceases with the death of one of the partners, for the East the bond perdures. Up to the 10th century no second marriage, not even one performed after widowhood, was ever formally blessed liturgically in Eastern churches. A distinction was drawn between first and second marriages and a special service was introduced for the latter, dissociated from the eucharist and penitential in character. A second marriage was not the norm and hence somewhat deficient sacramentally.

By the principle of "synergy," that is humankind's cooperation with grace, marriage as a sacrament is seen as bestowing of God's grace but requiring human cooperation. The East combines a lofty ideal of indissolubility with realistic legislation that admits exceptions. Eastern teaching interprets the exception clause about divorce in Mt 19:9 regarding *porneia* to apply to adultery. Adultery is seen as so incompatible with the nature of marriage that Jesus allowed a person to regard a matrimonial bond as nonexistent after adultery. The church therefore simply testifies to a cessation when it grants a divorce. The church allows a decree of divorce and remarriage out of mercy in order to avoid greater evil and suffering.

The Roman Catholic church prefers rather to declare if possible an annulment stating that a marriage bond in fact never existed. To the Orthodox this seems a legal fiction contrary to the intuition of those many Christians in this situation who argue that a real marriage did in fact exist but has died. Eastern churches do not have marriage tribunals or ecclesiastical courts as such.

The Orthodox are particularly concerned about the pastoral problems connected with mixed marriages in the diaspora, and how to provide religious education to the children of such marriages.

Laying on of Hands: Sacrament of Order

The sacramental life of the church also includes sharing in the ordained priesthood which is conferred through the laying on of hands by a bishop. Ordination designates one permanently for service of the church's life and continued existence by the Holy Spirit. Priesthood is conferred to assure the continued celebration of the eucharistic liturgy.

The Eastern Orthodox church allows the ordination of married men but does not allow them to remarry even after the death of a spouse once they have been ordained. Since the Synod of Trullo (691-692) only the unmarried are ordained or consecrated to the office of bishop.

The liturgy of ordination to the priesthood contains four parts: the approval of the people asserting the person's worthiness (*axios*); the invocation or epiclesis of the Holy Spirit, praying for bestowal of grace; the laying on of hands by the bishop; the clothing in liturgical vestments.

Consecration to the episcopate is seen as entry into the fullness of priesthood. A bishop must be consecrated by at least three bishops concelebrating together.

Official Eastern Orthodox teaching corresponds to Roman Catholic teaching in affirming the traditional exclusion of women from ordination to the priesthood based on the selection of men only as apostles by Jesus Christ and on what is seen as the necessity of the priest to serve as an iconic representation of Christ.

Anointing with Oil for Healing

In its teaching on the role of anointing of the sick with holy oil, the Eastern tradition preserves a double tradition, one which associates this anointing with the forgiveness of sins, and a second, drawing upon James 5:14 ff., stressing the healing of the sick. Hence there are really two separate liturgical anointings, one of which is the anointing for the forgiveness of sin even of the healthy at the liturgy of High Thursday, and another which is anointing of the sick. These anointings are both associated with the sacrament of reconciliation.

The practice of anointing the sick which is not frequently administered today in many Orthodox communities, has all the necessary elements of a *mysterion*: invocation of the Holy Spirit at the blessing of the oil making it a material vehicle for the Spirit's power.

The rite of Christian burial is sometimes listed among the sacramental liturgies belonging to the Eastern church.

The three consensus statements of the Joint International Commission for Theological Dialogue between the Roman Catholic church and the Orthodox church: Munich document (July 6, 1982). "The Mystery of the Church and of the Eucharist in the Light of the Mystery of the Holy Trinity," Text in: *Origins* 12 (August 12, 1982): 157-160; Bari document (August 1, 1987), "Faith, Sacraments and the Unity of the Church," Text in: *Origins* 17 (April 14, 1988): 743-749; New Valamo document (June 26, 1988), "The Sacrament of Order in the Sacramental Structure of the Church with Particular Reference to the Importance of Apostolic Succession for the Sanctification and Unity of the People of God," Text in: *Origins* 18 (October 13, 1988): 297-300. See also: Robert Hotz, *Sakramente im Wechselspiel zwischen Ost und West* (Zurich: Benziger, 1979). Januarius Izzo, "A Comparison of Some Sacramental Doctrines and Practices of the Roman Catholic and Eastern Orthodox Churches," *Diakonia* 10 (1975): 233-243; 11 (1976): 42-51. C. Konstantinidis, and E.C. Suttner, *Fragen der*

Sakramentenpastoral in orthodox-katholisch gemischten Gemeinden (Regensburg: Pustet, 1979). Gennadios Limouris, and N.M. Vaporis, eds. *Orthodox Perpectives on Baptism, Eucharist, and Ministry* (Brookline: Holy Cross, 1985). John Meyendorff, *Byzantine Theology* (New York: Fordham, 1974). Hans-Joachim Schulz, *The Byzantine Liturgy* (New York: Pueblo, 1986; original German ed., 1980). Alexander Schmemann, *For the Life of the World: Sacraments and Orthodoxy* (New York: St. Vladimir, 1973). Robert Taft, *Beyond East and West: Problems in Liturgical Understanding* (Washington: Pastoral Press, 1984).

MICHAEL J. FAHEY, S.J.

SACRAMENTS IN THE REFORMATION CHURCHES

The traditional role of the sacraments in the Christian life came under intense scrutiny during the period of theological ferment in the early years of the 16th century. Although the various ecclesial bodies which were born out of this ferment (called collectively the "Reformation churches") have developed their own distinctive ways of interpreting the sacraments, their common theological roots allow us to speak with some accuracy of a Protestant sacramental tradition. The modern descendants of the Reformation churches—Lutherans, Presbyterians, Anabaptists, Anglicans, Methodists, and the Free Churches—continue to debate matters of sacramental practice, but always with an eye to their own specific theological and historical origins.

Origins of a Sacramental Revolution

The early 16th century was a period of intense piety and popular demand for theological understanding in Northern Europe. Vernacular hymnody, preaching services, pious confraternities, and lay devotional manuals and prayerbooks proliferated as Renaissance humanism took hold of the religious imagination. At the same time, however, papal prestige had increasingly eroded since the Babylonian Captivity (1378-1417), and political and financial crises in the Vatican had precipitated the rise in influence of

At the flashpoint of sacramental reformation is Martin Luther (1453-1546), Augustinian monk and professor of scripture at the University of Wittenberg. Luther combined the textbook theology of the day with medieval penitential piety and his own Augustinian insistence on total dependence on a just God into a sacramental system in which divine generosity was a central theme. The sale of indulgences, in which Mass stipends were sold to those who wished to accumulate dispensations of various sorts, flew in the face of Luther's sacramental vision, and precipitated publication of his famous "95 theses" in 1517. Disputations on the dogmatic status of indulgences followed, but at the center was the larger question of the relationship between faith and divine grace in the sacraments.

A fuller explication of Luther's sacramental theology is found in the *Babylonian Captivity of the Church* (1520), in which transubstantiation, the sacrifice of the Mass, and the denial of the chalice to the laity are condemned. Because of total human dependence on God, the sacraments can never be looked upon as a "good work," and can certainly never be bought and sold as mere commodities. In addition, Luther insists that since explicit institution by Christ is necessary for an authentic sacrament, only baptism and the Lord's Supper qualify.

Within a remarkably short time, Luther's theological ideas spread throughout Germany and were eagerly received by those hungry for reform. Two eucharistic rites, the *Formula Missae* in Latin (1523) and the vernacular *Deutsche Messe* (1525-6), translated Luther's sacramental theology into reformed practice, and he insisted that at each Mass the word of God be preached, and that the whole congregation, and not merely the priest alone, partake of the elements. But soon those who had responded to Luther's call for reform began to disagree about the direction in which reformation of the sacraments should proceed.

For many of those who followed, the sacraments were not so much active vehicles of the grace of God (as in Luther's thought), but rather signs that the promises God made in the past continue to be valid and operative in the present. At the Marburg Colloquy (1529), the Swiss reformers Ulrich Zwingli (1484-1531), John Oecolampadius (1482-1531), and Martin Bucer (1491-1551) met face to face with Luther and his compatriot Philipp Melanchthon (1497-1560). Their failure to agree on the matter of the carnal presence of Christ in the elements of bread and wine marks the first substantial fracture in the Reformation. Having taken the conservative view, Martin Luther carried his ecclesiastical descendants away from a purely symbolic or memorialistic understanding of the eucharist, while the Zwinglian position resulted in a far more radical sacramental theology among many of the second generation of Reformers.

One of these, John Calvin (1509-1564), who took up the reformation of the church at Geneva, attempted a compromise position between the Lutheran and Zwinglian view of sacramental grace. In his remarkable theological treatise *The Institutes of the Christian Religion* (1536), Calvin insisted on the absolute authority of God in all matters, including the sacraments. Baptism and the Lord's Supper were viewed as testimonies of the grace of God, with the water of baptism and the eucharistic bread and wine the external sign that we are subjects of that grace, but he was always clear that the presence of Christ in the sacraments was truly, if spiritually, received. Like Luther, Calvin hoped for weekly communion. But since he insisted that the Lord's Supper not be celebrated without communicants, and since most people were used to receiving communion only once a year, he was able to manage only quarterly communion at Geneva.

Although among most of the early Reformers baptism was less the subject of debate than the eucharist, one group sought a more thoroughgoing purification of the church and saw the baptism of mature believers as a crucial element in their reform agenda. Because of their refusal to accept the validity of infant baptism, these so-called "Anabaptists" began rebaptizing those adults who made a profession of faith. Many Anabaptist groups also emphasized pacificism, the restriction of the Lord's Supper to those demonstrating purity of life, and the communal ownership of property, seeking to achieve an undefiled community of faith. As a result, Anabaptists were denounced by Luther, Zwingli, and Calvin, as well as by Roman Catholics, and under severe persecution many believers were martyred.

Despite these major differences, there was agreement among the early Reformers on several points related to sacramental theology and practice. First, the sacraments are activities of the church which are specifically instituted by Jesus in scripture. Second, only two ecclesiastical activities have this kind of scriptural warrant, namely: baptism and the Lord's Supper (e.g., Mt 28:19 and 1 Cor 11:23-26). Third, the human person brings nothing to the sacraments except faith in the promises of God, by which faith alone can one be confident of salvation. Although relative emphasis on these points differed among the ecclesiastical descendants of the early Reformers, all are common to Protestant sacramental theology today.

The Second Generation of Reformers

As the Reformation spread west to the British Isles, its sacramental theology and practice continued to be profoundly influenced by political realities. At the same time, it became more eclectic in character, choosing and combining previously isolated strands of theological thinking. Although Thomas Cranmer (1489-1556) gave a lasting shape to the worship of the reformed church in England in two editions of the *Book of Common Prayer* (1549 and 1552), his eucharistic theology continues to be the subject of scholarly debate. Both Cranmer's eucharistic and baptismal rites suggest strong Zwinglian and Calvinist influences on his sacramental theology, and his reliance on the work of Martin Bucer also allows a more conservative interpretation. At the same time, changes in the religious affiliation of the reigning monarch further complicated the situation, and sacramental theology came to be a test of loyalty for courtiers and clergy alike. Those with both reformed and Catholic understandings of such matters as the presence of Christ in the eucharist were martyred during the turbulent century between 1550 and 1650.

Cranmer's counterpart in Scotland, John Knox (c. 1505-1572), is less ambiguous in his theological leanings. Persecution of Protestants in Scotland during the reign of the Catholic Queen Mary (1553-1558) forced Knox to Geneva where he came under the direct influence of John Calvin. Upon his return to Scotland, Knox preached Calvin's sacramental doctrine, and framed the services in the *Book of Common Order* (1556-1564) to reflect these views. As in Switzerland, communion was celebrated four times per year, and each occasion was preceded by a time of penitential reflection so that the unworthy might not participate. Knox, like Calvin, affirmed the presence of Christ in the sacraments, spiritually received by the faithful believer.

The Rise of Puritanism

During the 17th century, those desiring a more thorough reformation of the church began to gain influence, and the sacraments again came under intense scrutiny. Fear of idolatry led to the demand for the abandonment of many rites and ceremonies, including the sign of the cross at baptism, kneeling at communion, and the positioning of the altar so that it more clearly suggested a common table. Scripture was the ultimate authority in all matters regarding the sacraments, and the desire to create a pure commonwealth with congregational autonomy in matters of church government precipitated both an ecclesiastical and constitutional crisis in England. Under the common term Puritanism, these ideas about the sacraments spread with the colonization of the New World and have had profound influence on the shaping of the American religious imagination.

An extreme example of this puritanizing effort is found in the sacramental theology of what came to be called the Society of Friends (Quakers). Under the theological leadership of George Fox (1624-1691), the Quakers believed that reliance on the Inner Light of the living Christ was all-sufficient and available to every individual Christian who waited for it in silence. For this reason, baptism and the Lord's Supper came to be wholly spiritualized, with the physical elements bread, wine, and water abandoned in favor of inward feeding on Christ and cleansing from sin. This is the sacramental reformation at its most radical, and continues today with little change.

The Impact of the Enlightenment

The Enlightenment of the 18th century made a significant impact on the sacramental practice and piety of all of the reformation churches, from Lutherans on the one hand to Puritans on the other. Because of its exaltation of human reason, Enlightenment rationalism put any form of the supernatural under suspicion, and preaching and the informed study of scripture came to be seen as normative Christian worship. The theology of baptism and the Lord's Supper during this period stressed their impact on the human mind, their usefulness as a method of recalling the virtues of Christ. This emphasis on the memorial aspect of the sacraments led to the further decline of sacramental piety in much of Protestantism, with both the eucharist and baptism forced to the margins of Christian experience.

There is one major exception to this trend toward a rationalist approach to the sacraments. John Wesley (1703-1791), a devout and scholarly Anglican priest, sought a practical religion to serve the increasing masses of the urban poor. His return to patristic sources of Christian practice led him to reevaluate the prevailing apathy in the matter of the sacraments, and also to restore theological elements lost since the Reformation. An ardent and successful preacher, Wesley encouraged weekly celebration of the Lord's Supper, the revival of pneumatology and eschatology in the sacraments, the idea of baptismal regeneration, and the sacrificial aspect of the eucharist. "Classes" and "bands," small groups which met weekly for prayer and examination of conscience, were designed to nurture sacramental piety. Although Wesley hoped that his movement would lead to a revival of sacramental life within the Church of England, a break was inevitable, and Wesleyan Methodism spread independently to all parts of the globe. After his death, however, Methodist interest in the sacraments was never as strong as he had intended it to be.

Romanticism and Revivalism

Protestant sacramental life in the 19th century was shaped by two seemingly opposing forces. The first of these was Romanticism, which had its beginnings in Germany at the end of the previous century. In part a reaction to the excesses of Enlightenment rationalism and to the fragmentation of experience resulting from the industrial revolution, Romanticism sought to recapture an idealized past in which work and religion and society were thought to have been a cohesive whole. The Oxford Movement in the Church of England, Mercersberg theology in the American Calvinist churches, the work of Johann Loehe (1808-1872) in Lutheranism each sought in its own way to restore the sacraments to the center of Protestant religious life. In those segments of the church affected by the Romantic movement, eucharistic devotion and frequency of communion increased dramatically (although baptismal theology was less profoundly influenced.) Concomitant with this, however, was a rise in sentimentality and privatization of sacramental piety, with some groups moving close to the idolatry so greatly feared by the 16th-century reformers.

The second major influence on sacramental practice in the 19th century, particularly in American Protestantism, was the rise of frontier revivalism. With a vast land area being settled rapidly, practical measures were necessary to serve the religious needs of an increasingly unchurched populace. Charles Grandison Finney (1792-1875), a Presbyterian lawyer and church leader, began conducting revivals in the mid-1820s after a profound conversion experience during which he received, as he put it, "a mighty baptism of the Holy Ghost." During these open-air gatherings, fiery preaching for conversion, sentimental hymns, and emotional prayer and responses all led to the celebration of the Lord's Supper and the baptism of those who had repented of their sin. This pragmatic use of the sacraments for the making of converts has left its mark on most of the mainline Protestant churches in the United States, and was carried with missionaries as new territory was evangelized.

The Sacraments in 20th-Century Protestantism

The opening of the 20th century saw a new expression of reformed faith and piety which had important consequences for Protestant sacramental life. Pentecostalism, which sees itself as the restoration of authentic apostolic faith, emphasized the necessity of "baptism of the Spirit," as distinct from water baptism. Marked by spontaneous ecstatic utterances, speaking in tongues, and revivalist-style preaching, Pentecostal worship presupposes the constant possibility that God may break into human experience, which separates it decisively from the Enlightenment suspicion of the supernatural. Although most closely associated with such denominations as the Churches of God, Assemblies of God, and Foursquare Gospel churches, charismatic sub-groups have begun to influence mainline Protestants and Roman Catholics as well.

By the middle of the 20th century, the Roman Catholic liturgical movement began to affect the sacramental life of the mainline Reformation churches. Emphasis on the centrality of the eucharist, the recognition of the importance of baptism, the restoration of ancient signs and symbols, and the importance of what the Second Vatican Council referred to as "full, conscious, and active participation" became part of the ordinary theological discourse of many American Protestants during this period. Beginning in the late 1960s, Episcopalians, Methodists, Lutherans and Presbyterians each underwent their own versions of a sacramental revival, resulting in a whole generation of revised rites and texts. Many of the ecclesiastical descendants of the reformers remain untouched by these changes, however, and revivalist, romanticist, and Enlightenment sacramental pieties are still strong among large numbers of Protestant Christians.

In the theologically turbulent 1960s, a

great deal of experimentation with the sacraments took place in the Reformation churches, at times taking extreme forms. (The substitution of such things as soda pop and potato chips for the eucharistic elements was not unusual, for example.) This period seems to have passed and although Protestant sacramental theology has reached no widely accepted consensus, there is a growing common interest in the return to early sources and to the Reformation for insight into the nature of baptism and the Lord's Supper. Among many if not most Protestant Christians, however, the sacraments remain on the margins of religious experience, with such elements as exhortation, prayer, and the reading and preaching of scripture continuing to be central.

The future of sacramental piety and practice in the Reformation churches will be shaped by a number of forces at work in the modern world. Since the birth of the World Council of Churches in 1948, concern with ecumenical convergence among separated Christian bodies took on a more formal aspect. Important bilateral dialogues resulted in the 1982 consensus statement entitled *Baptism, Eucharist, and Ministry*, which highlights many points of agreement on sacramental matters. In the years to come, lines of influence among the various Protestant denominations should grow even more complex as ecumenical bonds continue to solidify.

Besides ecumenism, the adaptation of baptismal and eucharistic practice to diverse cultural circumstances should also have major impact on the sacramental future of the Reformation churches. The idealistic missionary zeal of the 19th and early 20th centuries which sought to eradicate local customs and styles of celebration has largely been replaced in recent decades by an acceptance of the variety of religious experiences. The churches in the non-industrial world are growing at an astonishing rate and the balance of power is rapidly shifting away from the West. At some point, quite certainly, American Protestants will have to begin listening carefully to the sacramental experience of Third World Christians, and perhaps adjust their own sacramental practice in response to what they hear.

Finally, the impact of what has been termed the "religious Right," and its communications vehicle "televangelism," cannot be underestimated. With 1 billion television sets in operation throughout the world, evangelical services of worship come into almost every home, subtly shaping the sacramental expectations of large numbers of people. The ultimate impact of the largely neo-Enlightenment and individualist understanding of the sacraments which is presented to viewers has yet to be thoroughly analyzed. It is quite possible, however, that to the extent that this form of televised worship replaces local parish churches, it may tend to work against the recovery of the sacraments as central moments in Protestant worship and piety.

_____

Horton Davies, *Worship and Theology in England*, 5 vols. (Princeton: Princeton University Press, 1970). Irmgard Pahl, *Coena Domini I* (Freiburg: Universitatsverlag, 1983). Max Thurian, ed., *Ecumenical Convergence on Baptism, Eucharist and Ministry*, WCC Faith and Order Paper 116 (Geneva: World Council of Churches, 1983). James F. White, *Protestant Worship* (Louisville: Westminster, 1989).

SUSAN J. WHITE

SACRIFICE

Sacrifice (offering), even if only by way of spiritualization or rejection, figures prominently in most cultures and religions. But its plurality of manifestations and meanings resists general definition. Further, predominantly negative connotations of popular contemporary profane usage, as opposed to the more positive connotations often associated with ancient religious practice, makes unambiguous theological use of the term extremely difficult. Nevertheless, of the five most common suggestions from the history of religions for the *primary element* of sacrifice (gift, homage, expiation, communion, life), the one most relevant for the Judaeo-Christian tradition is the *gift* idea. At times, however, the expiation idea obviously dominates.

The OT sacrificial code (Leviticus 1-7; Numbers 28-29) probably represents an idealized post-exilic priestly theology more than a codification of actual practice. Not to be forgotten is that the fierce criticism of both pre- and post-exilic prophets (Isa 1:11-17; Jer 6:20, 7:21-26; Amos 5:21-25; Hos 6:16, 9:4; Mic 6:6-8; Mal 1:10-14, 2:13) does not radically reject but presumes the validity of the sacrificial cult. The most frequent type of OT sacrifice was the holocaust or *whole burnt offering* (cf. Leviticus 1; Gen 8:20-21, 22:1-14; 1 Kgs 18:20-38), but by NT times, the *sin offering* (cf. Leviticus 4 and 16) with its attendant theology of atonement had become the dominant type (cf. Heb 9:22; Mt 26:28). One can find in the OT not only the primitive idea of a God-directed human action which assuages or buys off the divinity, but also the more purified idea of atonement, whether positive or negative, as a creature-directed gracious action *of God*. This development is associated with the process of *spiritualization* of sacrifice which in Judaism never excluded the material or external, and in Christianity, became a christologization leading to the sacramentalization of Christian life.

For NT Christianity, offering sacrifice was seen as a pagan or Jewish, not a Christian activity. Yet the NT, especially the Pauline and deutero-Pauline writings, is rich in spiritualized (i.e., christologized) sacrificial language and imagery. Some of these texts speak of or refer to *Christ's sacrifice* (cf. 1 Cor 5:7; 2 Cor 5:21; Gal 3:13; 2 Cor 5:14-15; Rom 5:6-11; 8:23;

Gal 2:20; Eph 5:2; 25; Col 1:24; 1 Tm 2:5-6; Tit 2:13-14; 1 Jn 3:16; Hebrews *passim*; the eucharist institution narratives). Others speak of *Christians as the new temple* (1 Cor 3:6-17; 6:15, 19; 2 Cor 6:16; cf. Rom 5:5; 8:9, 11, 15-16; 1 Thess 4:8; 1 Cor 2:10-16; 12:12-31; 2 Cor 1:22; 1 Tm 3:15; 2 Tm 2:20-22; Tit 2:14; Eph 1:22; 2:16, 19-22; 3:6; 4:4, 11-16; 5:23-24; 1 Pet 2:4-10). Still others speak implicitly or directly of the *sacrifice of the Christian* (cf. Rom 8:36; 2 Cor 4:10-11; Gal 2:20; Phil 2:17, 25 and 4:18 in connection with Rom 12:1; 15:15-16; 1 Pet 2:4-10; Heb 10:19-25 and 12:18-13:16). It is most significant that whenever the NT speaks of or alludes to Christian sacrificial activity, it is never liturgical or cultic but always an ethical activity.

Culminating in the NT, three phases of spiritualization can be seen: (1) the relatively early (beginning with the Yahwist) awareness of the necessity of proper dispositions; (2) the (post-exilic) shift of the dynamic center of sacrifice away from the external ceremony to the dispositions of the worshipper; (3) a "christologization" of sacrifice which sees Christian life and works as the material of sacrifice and identifies the dispositions of the sacrificer with Christ's self-giving love.

This explains the meaning of the two apparently contradictory statements: "Christianity has no sacrifice," and "Christian life is profoundly sacrificial."

Sacrifice and Sacramental Worship

Only from this background can one come to understand the history and theology of the role of sacrifice in Christian sacramental worship. Until the 3rd century, Christians apparently did not offer sacrifice except the radically spiritualized sacrifice of prayer, thanksgiving, and good works (see Heb 3:16, " . . . such sacrifices are pleasing to God"). The sacrificial references to the eucharist as in Did. 14:1, "That your sacrifice may be pure" are not exceptions; their primary reference is to the eucharistic *prayer* rather than to a performed ritual.

As the epistle to the Hebrews shows, this highly spiritualized attitude was not easy to maintain. With Hippolytus in the early 3rd century one finds language which suggests that Christians are beginning to look on their bishops not just as leading the spiritualized worship of the eucharistic prayer, but also as presiding over or performing a ritual sacrificial action (*Apost. Trad.*, 4). Presbyters begin to be called "priests"; the eucharistic elements begin to be called "offerings." As the centuries passed, many of the institutional, cultic phenomena associated with OT and even pagan priesthood and sacrifice find their way into Christian practice. For good and for ill, "Christian sacrifice" has remained fraught with the ambiguities of this checkered history.

On the good side, Origen's clear insight into Christ as both the priest and the offering of his perfect sacrifice to the Father, and the universal calling to all the baptized to be, in and with Christ, the priest and offering of their own sacrifice to God (*Hom. Lev.*, 9.9), is taken up by Augustine (*City of God*, 10.6), and becomes part of the common spiritual heritage of Christianity. But where Origen's connotation is primarily the ethical one of practical Christian life, in Augustine the specifically eucharistic connotation has begun to dominate. We are not far from the aberration, against which the Reformers so vigorously protested, of the priest seeming to have quasi-absolute personal power, even apart from the church, to offer the sacrifice of the Mass as a (in popular misconception) "repetition" of the once-for-all atoning sacrifice of Christ. What was for the Fathers the absolutely central reality that Christ is the principal agent in the eucharistic sacrifice which is not a repetition but a representation (*Vergegenwärtigung*) of his all-sufficient offering at the Last Supper and on Calvary became increasingly obscured by the horrendous misconception that the priest is the principal agent offering this sacrifice *in persona Christi*. This misconception wreaks its havoc even to this day, with many priests unable to resist acting out (as if they were Christ) the words of institution instead of properly proclaiming them as an integral part of the eucharistic prayer.

On the popular level, "sacrifice" still suffers under the negative and, at times, deeply aberrational notions which have been associated with it in Judaism and Christianity for three millennia. Despite this, the spiritualization and, with Christianity, the christologization of sacrifice has become a central feature of Christian spirituality and asceticism. In addition, the liturgical and ecumenical developments of the 20th century have allowed the Christian churches with sacramental traditions to achieve a remarkable theological rapprochement in their understanding of the "offering of the church" and of the eucharist as sacrifice. The greatest single contribution to this development seems to have been the historical research and theological reflection stimulated by the "mystery theology" of Odo Casel. Nevertheless, on the popular level, "sacrifice" is still laden with the negative misconceptions which have burdened it in the Jewish-Christian tradition for some three millennia. Until these are purified, what theology has achieved will remain fragile.

For a fuller treatment of the background of the Christian use of *sacrifice*, see *The New Dictionary of Theology* (ed. Komonchak, et al. [Glazier, 1987]).

See **Eucharist, theology of**

ROBERT J. DALY, S.J.

SAINTS, CULT OF THE

The veneration of the saints is related to the cult of the dead. It initially took the from of praise and imitation of the deceased holy ones (Greek *hagioi*, Latin *sancti*), and involved as well, gatherings of celebration and prayer at the place of burial. In its origin, the Christian practice is not unlike the funerary practices among the Romans, the Egyptians and the Hebrews. The major difference is to be found in the Christian attitude toward death, rooted in the resurrection of Jesus Christ (as attested to by funerary inscriptions). In Israel the dead were buried either in the ground or in the floor of a sepulchre. The Egyptians and Romans both practiced inhumation, while the latter admitted cremation as well. The early Christians employed both forms, though they favored inhumation due to their belief in the resurrection of the dead.

In the ancient world, in which Christianity began, tombs were places of contact between humans and the gods. The tomb represented a home for the dead, a place to be visited by survivors. Libations were poured out upon the tomb, and funerary feasts (*refrigerium*) were celebrated near it, especially on the birthday of the deceased (*dies natalis*). Among the Jews it was customary to give special honor to the tombs of the patriarchs; among the pagans, to the tombs of dead heroes. In like manner, the early Christians held the tomb to be the privileged place of the saint. And like the Greek hero, the saint was considered to be an intercessor (*daemon*) who functioned as an intermediary between this world and the next.

Origins and Historical Development

The cult of the saints began in the early church with the commemoration (*memoria*) of the victims of persecution. The term martyr (Greek *martyrion*) simply means "witness," but in Christian usage, very early on, it came to mean, more precisely, those who had witnessed to the faith by dying for it. Christ is called the first of the martyrs (Rev 1:5), and this title was extended immediately to Antipas, who died for his faith at Pergamum (Rev 2:13). From the beginning of the 2nd century, references are made to martyrdom as the preferred form of Christian perfection (Ignatius of Antioch). From the middle of the 2nd century until the 4th, the martyr represents the ideal of holiness. At first the interest was limited only to the martyr's death, and by the second half of the 2nd century, documentation in the form of letters gives us authentic and reliable accounts of their deaths.

One of the oldest non-biblical references is found in a letter, the *Martyrdom of Polycarp*, from the church of Smyrna to the church of Philomelium in Phrygia. Polycarp, the bishop of Smyrna, was brought to the stake, stabbed, and his body burned in the year A.D. 155. According to the account, "We did gather up his bones—more precious to us than jewels, and finer than pure gold—and we laid them to rest in a spot suitable for the purpose. There we shall assemble, as occasion allows, with glad rejoicing, and with the Lord's permission we shall celebrate the birthday of his martyrdom. It will serve both as a commemoration of all who have triumphed before, and as training and preparation for any whose crown may still be to come" (*Mart. Poly.*, 18). Another is a letter from the churches of Vienne and Lyons to the churches of Asia and Phrygia, telling of the persecutions in Lyons (A.D. 177-78). In confessing their faith, the martyrs are one with the risen Christ. A third account is the *Passion of Perpetua and Felicity* (A.D. 202-03), presenting a first-hand description of their visions in prison. By the mid-2nd century, the term "martyr" designates almost exclusively those who witnessed with their blood.

The cult of martyrs is the beginning of the cult of saints and the veneration given to martyrs is not unlike that given to the dead in general, in that it is localized near the tomb. One great difference, however, is its communitarian dimension by which the believers who celebrate all become brothers and sisters of the martyr in faith. Instead of celebrating the memory of the martyr on the birthday, the early Christians chose to remember the day of death or of rebirth. This gave rise to saints' days and the origin of the calendar for the sanctoral cycle. The first attempts at a sanctoral calendar date to the mid-3rd century, when each local church composed a list of names of martyrs and confessors (those who confessed their faith) including the date of death and the place of burial (see Cyprian, *Ed.*, 12, 2).

Often the eucharist was celebrated at the place of burial. A link was thus established between the eucharist and martyrdom: celebrating the eucharist for those called upon to shed their blood or remembering in the eucharist those who have already undergone martyrdom. In addition, the eucharist served as a support for martyrdom and even a source leading to fulfillment in martyrdom. The eucharistic sacrifice linked to the sacrifice of Calvary gave meaning to the self-sacrifice of the martyr. The death and resurrection of Jesus Christ constituted the paschal mystery which began for each Christian at baptism and was fulfilled and completed in death. By the 3rd century Christians would pray to the martyrs to intercede to God on their behalf. Belief in the resurrection of Christ and its effects on all who fall asleep in Christ prompted the early Christians to ask the saints to intercede for those still living. Some of the most ancient graffiti of the *Memoria Apostolorum* dating to about 260 attest to this form of intercession. By the end of the 4th century we find expression of this in the commentary on the eucharist of Cyril of Jerusalem: "Then we commemorate also those who have fallen asleep before us, first, patriarchs, prophets, apostles, martyrs, that at their prayers

and intervention God would receive our petition" (*Catech. Mystag.*, v. 9).

The early Christians focused on the place of burial. By the 4th century in the East, and the 8th century in the West, this veneration expanded to include objects (relics) as well. This shift came about where the transfer of bodily remains to new locations (*translatio reliquiarium*) became necessary. Inevitably, attention shifted from the place of burial to the remains themselves. Between the 4th and 8th centuries in the West, because the translation and dismembering of bodies was contrary to Roman law, the primary focus remained on the place of burial; the only relics of martyrs and confessors that were tolerated were objects that had been in physical proximity to their tombs. In the mid-8th century, however, largely due to the Lombard invasions, many bodies of saints and martyrs had to be moved from the extra-urban catacombs into the city of Rome in order to defend them from the invaders. Urban monuments (churches) were built to house their remains. The veneration of saints took yet another turn.

Some scholars have attributed this shift to include relics among the objects of veneration to "popular" religion, as opposed to an "enlightened" religion (Brown, pp. 16-22). This opposition of "popular" to "enlightened" is, however, a false opposition. Brown goes on to assert that "the cult of the saints involved imaginative changes that seem, at least, congruent to changing patterns of human relations in late-Roman society at large. It designated dead human beings as the recipients of unalloyed reverence, and it linked these dead and invisible figures in no uncertain manner to precise visible places and, in many areas, to precise living representatives. Such congruence hints at no small change. But in order to understand such a change, in all its ramifications, we must set aside the 'two-tiered' model" (*ibid.*, p. 21).

As a complement to this sociological explanation of the change in attitudes toward the bodies of the dead, a religious explanation might be offered as well. The value given to the body through Christ's incarnation and resurrection is equally able, and possibly more apt, to explain how human remains can serve as an object of veneration translated into words and ritual acts (Fontaine, p. 21). In a world dominated by Gnostic overtones which looked with suspicion on anything material, Christian faith proclaims a contrary view. The value of creation as manifested in human form is underscored. The veneration of saints, including the later development of relics, points out the fundamental sacramentality of the human body. A church which gives high value to sacraments would place veneration of the saints, including their bodily remains, in this sacramental context.

From the mid-4th and early 5th centuries, the cult of the saints, began to blossom, e.g., Martin of Tours, Ambrose and Augustine. The early 4th century saw the end of Christian persecution. Consequently a new concept of sanctity, marked by a sense of constant self-martyrdom worthy of venerating, began to develop. As a result, ascetics were also regarded as holy ones capable of mediating people's prayers and intercessions. "Mortify and crucify your body and you too will receive the crown of the martyr" (John Chrysostom, *Ep. ad Hebr. Homil* II, 3). Reputed for their hidden supernatural powers manifested in miracles, these ascetics were sought out as regional patrons. Upon their death their tombs were honored and their bodies preserved and venerated as much as those of the martyrs. When Hilarion went to celebrate the first anniversary of the death of St. Anthony with his sons, he notes that they tried to hide the tomb of their father out of fear that a rich neighbor might take the body away to his villa where he would erect a shrine to him (St. Jerome, *Vita Hilarionis*).

Consecrated virginity also came to figure in the cult of the saints as well as the veneration of bishops. Before the end of the 3rd century, virginity consecrated to the Lord was accorded the same honor as martyrdom and considered superior to asceticism. In this same category, widows in service to the church were counted among the saints and their state was likewise considered a form of Christian asceticism. And finally bishops. In the first centuries many of the great bishops were martyrs (e.g., Ignatius of Antioch, Pontian, Fabian, Cornelius and Sixtus of Rome and Polycarp of Smyrna). When bishops began to play a role in the ideal of holiness, other bishops who were not martyrs were included as models of holiness as well.

The Middle Ages saw the rise of great pilgrimages with many devotional practices centered around penitence. Churches built especially to house relics of the saint to whom it was dedicated dotted the pilgrimage routes through Europe and the Holy Land. The dedication of the churches came to be included as another aspect of the veneration of the saints. Frequent visits to shrines often culminated with devotions to the relics. Many of the popular practices (*devotio moderna*) surrounding the cult of the saints provoked responses from various councils which attempted to clarify the role of the saints and to avoid abuses, e.g., the Council of Avignon in 1209, and Lateran IV in 1215. By the 13th century the Cathari and Waldenses reacted violently to the notion of intercession by the saints. This set the stage for the Reformation.

Beginning in the 16th century, reformers questioned the practice of veneration of the saints. In the Augsburg Confessions of 1530, which were approved by Luther, the role of intercession by the saints was denied in favor of Christ's mediation. The Reformers acknowledged the example of the saints for the Christian life but reacted to the far-fetched legends of the saints which abounded in Christendom.

The Council of Trent in the twenty-fifth session approved of the invocation of the saints with the clarification that "it is good and beneficial suppliantly to invoke them and to have recourse to their prayers, assistance and support in order to obtain favors from God through his Son, Jesus Christ our Lord, who alone is our redeemer and savior" (D.S., 1821). In emphasizing the christological nature of the cult of the saints, this council reaffirmed Catholic doctrine against wrong interpretation. The Council of Trent provided a firm footing for the theology of the veneration and invocation of the saints. This underwent a subsequent development at Vatican II.

The Second Vatican Council in the *Dogmatic Constitution on the Church* summarized the current position of the church on the veneration of the saints: " ...from the earliest days of the Christian religion, (the church) has honored with great respect the memory of the dead.... The Church has always believed that the apostles and Christ's martyrs, who gave the supreme witness of faith and charity by the shedding of their blood, are closely united with us in Christ; she has always venerated them, together with the Blessed Virgin Mary and the holy angels, with a special love, and has asked piously for the help of their intercession. Let us teach the faithful, therefore, that the authentic cult of the saints does not consist so much in a multiplicity of external acts, but rather in a more intense practice of our love, whereby, for our own greater good and that of the Church, we seek from the saints 'example in their way of life, fellowship in their communion, and the help of their intercession.' On the other hand, let the faithful be taught that our communion with these in heaven, provided that it is understood in the full light of faith, in no way diminishes the worship of adoration given to God the Father, through Christ, in the Spirit; on the contrary, it greatly enriches it" (L.G., 50-51).

The *Constitution on the Sacred Liturgy* proposes that the veneration of the saints be realized in the following manner: "The Church has also included in the annual cycle memorial days of the martyrs and other saints. Raised up to perfection by the manifold grace of God and already in possession of eternal salvation, they sing God's perfect praise in heaven and pray for us. By celebrating their anniversaries the Church proclaims achievement of the paschal mystery in the saints who have suffered and have been glorified with Christ. She proposes them to the faithful as examples who draw all men to the Father through Christ, and through their merits she begs for God's favor" (S.C., 104).

Hagiographical Literature

Several forms of literature worthy of note in the development of the cult of the saints are the Acts of the Martyrs (*acta martyrum*), Lives of the Saints (*vitae sanctorum*) and accounts of martyrdom (*passiones*). Two other written forms which served to anchor the veneration of saints in Christian culture are the *libri miraculorum* (miracles of martyrs and confessors) and *translationes* (accounts of transferral of relics).

The Acts of the Martyrs are the most precious documents for hagiography, but they are very few in number. Justin Martyr and Cyprian of Carthage provide some of the few fragments which have survived to our day. The accounts of martyrdom are a much later source that has a lesser historical value. They played a central role in providing the cult of the saints with annual feasts. The genre is a series of stereotyped questions posed by judges with the martyrs' response. Within a liturgical context, the reading of these accounts functioned to actualize the presence of the salvation of God in the assembled body of hearers.

The *vitae* are the next most notable. Many survive from the late 4th and early 5th centuries and were rewritten during the Carolingian period. They bear a literary style which is legendary. In the East, St. Athanasius composed a life of St. Anthony, which became a prototype for many *vitae*, and which served as well as an ideal for monastic life. In the West, the accounts of St. Ambrose by Paulinus and St. Augustine by Possidius served as important models of episcopal sanctity, although they contain many legendary embellishments. These *vitae* were highly dependent upon the life of St. Martin of Tours, composed in 397 by Sulpicius Severus in Gaul, which circulated as a model for Western monasticism. Gregory the Great (d. 604) gathered the miracles of the Fathers of Italy in his *Dialogues* and Gregory of Tours (d. 594) wrote in great detail of the Gallo-Roman and Merovingian saints in his *History of the Franks*. Also attributed to Gregory of Tours and of capital importance are the *Glory of the Martyrs, Glory of the Confessors*, and *Lives of the Fathers*. In North Africa, Victor of Vita recounts the history of the African persecutions and St. Fulgentius Ferrundus wrote of the life of Fulgentius of Ruspe.

As the term "legend" indicates, these literary pieces were intended to be read for the spiritual edification of the hearer with little regard for historical accuracy. In the 8th century, the *vitae* were read as part of the nightly office. By the 9th century, they were even more stereotyped. In 10th-century France, this hagiographic activity expanded further through the writings of Hucbald of Saint-Amand, Adso of Montier-en-der, Odo of Cluny and Flodoard of Rheims. These literary sources, although historically dubious, are a valuable source in understanding the various ideals of holiness during this

time as well as some of the sacramental and religious practices of the day.

Two other rich hagiographical sources, liturgical in nature, are lists of martyrs (*martyrologium*) and calendars (*calendario*). The list of martyrs has a highly local value because it lists the various martyrs attached to a local church. The oldest list is that of the Chronographer of 354, which includes a list of martyrs (*depositio martyrum*). These lists contain ostensibly three elements: *nomen, locus, die* (Gregory the Great, *Registrum* lib. 8, ep. 28) and have an almost juridical value for the transmission of the cult of the martyrs. They indicate the authentic name of the martyr, the place and date of burial or the date and place where the assembly should meet to commemorate the feast, known as the stations. Often the notice of death of a martyr comes from the Passions or other legendary sources. Calendars are a development of the martyrologies and include a wider variety of saints. For example, in the list of the Chronographer of 354 there is a list of bishops (*depositio episcoporum*).

Modern hagiography began with the work of J. Bolland, s.j. (1595-1665) and the Maurists (J. Mabillon, T. Ruinart) whose task was to sift through all the existing hagiographical material for the revision of the *vitae* according to a critical method. Since the refounding of the Bollandists in Brussels in 1837, they have been responsible for the development of hagiography through their publications of *Acta Sanctorum, Analecta Bollandiana* and the *Subsidia Hagiographica*, for both the Latin and the Greek traditions.

Theology of Cult

Regarding worship (*cultus*), St. Augustine in the City of God (*Civ.* 10, 1) spoke about the absolute worship given to God alone (Latin *latria*). Confusion still remained at the Second Council of Nicaea in 787 (D.S., 601) which dealt with the question of the veneration of icons. This council also made recourse to the term *latria*, reiterating that it is worship rendered only to God.

Medieval theology, classically distinguished between the supreme worship offered to the Trinity (Greek *latreia*; Latin *adoratio*) and veneration of the angels and saints (Greek *douleia*; Latin *veneratio*). Due to the religious excellence of the saints, service is rendered to them as beings less than God. Regarding the veneration of Mary, who has a most privileged place among all the servants of God, the term of *hyperdulia* was coined to indicate her superiority among the saints.

There exists a bond of confident intimacy (*communio*) between the saints and those on earth which enriches and deepens the relationship with Christ and with God. The theology of the veneration of saints does not attempt to supplant the saving power of God by the saints. Imitation and invocation does not detract from the prerogatives of Christ, but serves to glorify his redemption. By extension of the theology of incarnation and redemption, invocation of the saints implies no essential addition to Christ's mediation but rather a realization of its potentialities and a subordinate cooperation of his members applying the fruits of his redemption (see Aquinas, *s. Th.* 3a, 25, 6; 26, 1). Through participation in the life of the Godhead, the saints continue to live some degree of divine life and as sharers in this divine life, they beseech God on our behalf.

Belief in the resurrection ensures that all who have died in Christ live on, and that they constitute, with the living, the church as the mystical body of Christ. Thus the living members who have not yet reached the end of their journey invoke the saints as mediators and intercessors through, with and in Christ. The saints therefore are worthy of religious veneration (*doulia*), as a sign of God's providential action in the church. The church declares them to be the norm and example of a truly Christian life. The theology of veneration of the saints is christologically based, and indicates clearly that the greatness of the saints is derived from and is founded wholly on Christ, who elevates them to share in divine life because of their practice of Christian virtue.

Peter Brown, *The Cult of the Saints: Its Rise and Function in Latin Christianity* (Chicago: University of Chicago, 1981). Jacques Fontaine, "Le culte des saints et ses implications sociologiques: réflexions sur un récent essai de Peter Brown," *Analecta Bollandiana* 100 (1982): 17-41. William M. Thompson, *Fire and Light: The Saints and Theology* (New York: Paulist Press, 1987). Stephen Wilson, ed., *Saints and Their Cult: Studies in Religious Sociology, Folklore and History* (Cambridge: University Press, 1983).

MICHAEL S. DRISCOLL

SATISFACTION

In sacramental theology, satisfaction is a term used to describe the good works assigned by the confessor and carried out by the penitent as a way of restoring the order disturbed by sin and as a remedy for sin. It is also called "act of penance" or simply "penance." The sinner accepts the satisfaction during the sacramental celebration of penance after the confession of sin.

In the recent past satisfaction was often reduced to recitation of prayers but the Rite of Penance (6c) directs that it really be a remedy for sin and a help to renewal of life. Thus satisfaction can take the form of good works, service, donation of time or money and fasting, as well as prayers. It should be related to the sins confessed and help restore the good order lost by sin. The personal condition of the penitent should be taken into consideration.

Satisfaction is not a price one pays for the forgiveness obtained since one cannot repay or buy the gratuitous forgiveness of God. Acts of satisfaction are signs of personal commitment that Christians make to God in the sacrament, to begin a new life.

Through the whole history of the celebration of the sacrament of penance, the church has been concerned about the satisfaction element of the rite. In the time of public or canonical penance, and during the tariff penances which date from the Celtic and Anglo-Saxon regions of the 6th century, satisfaction or penance was completed before sins were forgiven. Satisfaction was administered to fit the sin. Suitable penances were listed in penitential books available to confessors for both serious and light sins. Obviously some penances were quite severe, which led to commuting penances and the abuse of paying others to do the penance. By the year 1000 absolution of sin preceded satisfaction in one single rite. This, however, changed the purpose of satisfaction from good works to deal with the sin itself to good works to deal with the effects or punishment due for sin. It became clear to the Scholastics that eternal punishment for sin was forgiven through the sacrament but that satisfaction served as a means of eliminating temporal punishment and was a remedy against sin. This led to an emphasis on indulgence, which is a remission before God of the temporal punishment for sin the guilt of which is already forgiven (C.I.C., 992).

With Trent and in the 1614 ritual, satisfaction was still linked to punishment for sin, but it became increasingly symbolic and for the most part was reduced to prayers. Satisfaction during the course of history changed from severity to mildness. The present Rite of Penance does not speak of satisfaction as related to temporal punishment due to sin but relates it to Christ's work of reparation, requiring works of penance as well as charity toward God and neighbor (25d). It specifically restores the purpose of satisfaction as remedy for sin and the renewal of life.

See **Reformation of life**

James Dallen, *The Reconciling Community, The Rite of Penance* (New York: Pueblo Publishing Co., Inc. 1986). Monika Hellwig, *Signs of Reconciliation and Conversion* (Wilmington: Michael Glazier, Inc., 1984). Bernard Poschmann, *Penance and the Anointing of the Sick* (New York: Herder and Herder, 1968).

JOSEPH L. CUNNINGHAM

SCRIPTURE IN THE LITURGY

Christian theological enterprise of the last century has been marked by the mutually illuminating study of its sources: the Bible, the liturgy, patristics and church history. Each of these disciplines helps to interpret the others and has had a strong impact on the self-understanding of the churches, their ecumenical commitment and their pastoral practice. Perhaps this is nowhere so evident as in the renaissance of biblical studies among Roman Catholics, the opening up of the scriptures within the reformed liturgical rites and in the consequent interest in biblical studies flowing from the increased use of the Bible in the liturgy. On the other hand, contemporary biblical scholars frequently offer challenging criticisms regarding the church's use of the scriptures within the liturgy.

That the post-Vatican II rites of the Roman Catholic church have been reformed in the light of the church's renewed appreciation of and return to the scriptures is without doubt. *S.C.* states: that liturgical acts derive their meaning from the scriptures (24); that one of the norms of liturgical revision is to be the increased use of the scriptures (35,1); that Bible services are to be encouraged (35,4); and that pastors are to strive to catechize the people to understand and appreciate the liturgy of the word as an integral element of one act of eucharistic worship (56).

What are presented by the liturgy document as some practical norms of liturgical reform rooted in a renewed awareness of the Scriptures finds its broader theological base in *Dei Verbum*, The Dogmatic Constitution on Divine Revelation. Both of these conciliar documents are grounded in more than a century of biblical, patristic and liturgical scholarship. In the *Lectionary for Mass* (1969), and more especially in the second edition (1981) of the Introduction to that liturgical book, we discover the pastoral synthesis and fruit of the dialogue between biblical scholars, liturgists and other theologians.

Biblical Formation of the Assembly

The proclamation of the word of God is essential to the liturgical act because the liturgy itself is the church's most profound moment of self-actualization. Because the church is called into being by God's inviting word, that word must be proclaimed day after day. God's call in history is a word calling us now. One might justifiably maintain that "today" or its equivalents (now, this day) is the most critical word in liturgical celebration. Thus the word of God must be enacted in celebration wherein the story of God's enduring love for creation (the mystery) is recounted and experienced again as God's call to us now. Thus we see that a renewed vision of the importance of the scriptures in the liturgy is not primarily a matter of information but more of communal identity and, most importantly, a matter of spirituality. The proclamation of the word of God within the liturgy is constitutive of the church precisely because it is an act calling forth our response in faith. What is proclaimed in words (the readings or lessons) is responded to in chants (the psalms) and prayers which themselves are biblical texts or are directly inspired by them (the eucharistic prayer, other presidential prayers, solemn prayers of blessing). The hearing of the word and the assembly's response are themselves acts of commitment which have moral implications,

and these, in their turn, lead us back to worship.

The Lectionary

Because the liturgical proclamation of the scriptures is so formative an element of Christian spirituality, the very fact that a church arranges sections (pericopes) of biblical books to be read in particular liturgical services and how the church goes about shaping that arrangement is of vital importance. Any systematic arrangement of pericopes based upon a liturgical calendar is called a lectionary. The concept goes back to at least the synagogue and may have exerted some influence on the very shaping of the gospels. More specifically, "lectionary" is the generic title applied to the liturgical book which contains these ordered pericopes. More specific titles are applied to liturgical books containing only one class of readings, e.g., the evangeliary or gospel book.

Since at least the Reformation period the pericopes to be proclaimed in the Roman Catholic celebration of the eucharist were contained within the missal which also held all the ordinary and proper texts needed by the priest. For all practical purposes, eucharistic ministry had been reduced to the person of the presiding priest. The postconciliar *ordo missae*, however, bears witness to a broader restoration of ministries. Among these is that of lector or proclaimer of the word of God. Thus with the 1969 publication of the *Lectionary* we see not only a remarkable opening of the Bible for all the faithful but also an indication of a renewed sense of ministry centered on the scriptures.

The order of readings in the Roman *Lectionary* is described in chap. V of the revised introduction. This order is itself the fruit of ecumenical scholarship for it was drawn up in cooperation with experts in exegesis, pastoral studies, catechetics and liturgy (58). These scholars studied, however, not only former arrangements · of readings in the Roman liturgical tradition but also in other liturgical families and churches (59). In turn the Roman Lectionary has had a tremendous ecumenical impact in the liturgical revisions of the Anglican Communion, Lutherans, Methodists, Presbyterians and others.

Though the intention of those who arranged the *Lectionary* was to provide the faithful "with a knowledge of the whole of God's word" (60), not every chapter of every book of the Bible nor every verse within a particular pericope is assigned a place in the *Lectionary for Mass* or in the other rites. Thus it is clear that the liturgy shapes a liturgical canon of scripture within the broader canon of the Bible itself. The ordering of pericopes employed in the celebration of the church year is itself an interpretive element— even before the act of preaching. Moreover, the assignment of particular pericopes, their use in relationship to others, the chapters and verses chosen or omitted and their employment in conjunction with various liturgical actions or objects is rooted in the hermeneutical stances of the arrangers of the lectionary and the redactors of the liturgical rites. At the local level this holds true for liturgical planners who have a wide range of choices, especially in regard to the chants of the eucharist.

Principles of Arrangement and Selection: Sundays

The introduction to the lectionary gives the general plan and description of the readings to be used in the celebration of the eucharist in addition to presenting the principles employed in drawing up this order (chaps. IV and V). Proper to the celebration of Sundays and solemnities is the provision for three readings. The first of these is almost always from the OT and is chosen because of its "harmony" (66-67) with the gospel pericope. The third reading or gospel, at least in ordinary

time, is a semi-continuous reading from Matthew (cycle A), Mark (cycle B) or Luke (cycle C). During the major liturgical seasons the second reading (always taken from a NT letter or Revelation) has also been chosen in harmony with the gospel and the OT text of the first reading. This "harmony" principle of selection is intended to show forth the unity of the OT and NT and to illustrate the centrality of Christ in salvation history.

Some would maintain that the juxtaposition of OT texts chosen to provide a "type" for what will be heard in the gospel sets up a prediction-fulfillment claim which is not true to contemporary understanding of prophecy. Thus the "harmony" suggested could, they maintain, foster anti-Semitism in that it suggests that anyone who knew the Hebrew Scriptures should have been able to recognize Jesus as the Messiah. Defenders of the present lectionary arrangement argue that prediction-fulfillment was at work already in the formation of the OT and certainly in the NT, and that the "harmony" principle therefore respects a process still operative in Judaism (Jensen).

Principles of Arrangement and Selection: Weekdays and Celebrations of the Saints

Weekday celebrations are provided with two readings: the first from the OT or a non-gospel NT reading and the second which is always from one of the four gospels. During the major liturgical seasons both of these are chosen on the basis of themes proper to the season, e.g., baptism and penance during the season of Lent.

In the commemoration of the saints, celebrations of higher rank have three (solemnities), or two (feasts) proper readings. Some memorials also have proper texts assigned but more frequently texts for these celebrations are from the commons of saints or, more preferably, the weekday readings are used so that the priority of the temporal cycle may be maintained, especially during the liturgical seasons.

Chants

Though biblical readings present the most preponderant and obvious use of the Bible in the liturgy, the chants which comprise the full celebration of the eucharist in the Roman rite are normatively biblical texts most often taken from the psalms. These are the entrance antiphon, the responsorial psalm and the communion antiphon. The responsorial psalm is of particular importance as it is an integral part of the liturgy of the word (IL 81,19). It is a unique liturgical moment in that it is at one and the same time an act of proclamation, response and meditation. This is most clearly experienced when the psalm is sung.

The psalm or other biblical text given in the missal as the entrance and/or communion antiphon is most appropriately used when it is sung as the response to the psalm which is assigned for these liturgical actions in the eucharist.

Prayers

The formative influence of the Bible in the composition of the prayers employed in the liturgy may not be immediately evident. Yet in the liturgy the assembly employs texts taken directly from the scriptures, e.g., the Lord's Prayer, and continues to compose others whose logic and shape (the eucharistic prayer and the orations of the Roman rite) are in direct line with that of biblical prayer, especially as seen in prayers of blessing and in the praise psalms. The biblical nature of liturgical prayer may become clearer as the increased opening of the scriptures within the liturgy and the impact of biblical studies exerts a greater influence on homiletics and sacramental catechesis. The ongoing revision of liturgical texts also plays and will continue to play a critical role in this regard. This is already

evident in the revision of first editions of vernacular translations of the Roman Missal, e.g., in Italy, Spain and Poland, where new presidential prayers have been composed for each of the three Sunday cycles so that these orations may better prepare the assembly for and resonate with the biblical readings of the day.

The Homily and General Intercessions

In addition to readings, chants and prayers taken directly from the Bible and biblically shaped prayers composed by the church, the reformed liturgy also envisions texts which are prepared by local ministers for each particular celebration. Among these the homily and general intercessions are critical. The homily is normatively based upon the scriptures proclaimed or upon the biblically inspired liturgical texts. The general intercessions are "enlightened by God's word and (are) in a sense responding to it" (IL 81,30).

The Liturgy of the Hours

Though the L.O.H. is more properly considered a celebration of the paschal mystery in and through the symbolism of dawn and dusk, it is in the hours that we see the most exhaustive liturgical use of the psalms in Christian prayer. Biblical readings, OT and NT canticles and prayers are also regularly employed. The use of the psalms in the L.O.H. is governed by the dynamics of two traditions operative in the reform of the present books for the hours: the "cathedral" which tends to choose principally those psalms which seem most appropriate to the praise of God in the morning and the liturgical confession of the assembly's sin in the evening; the "monastic" which is more committed to integral use of the psalter generally in serial arrangement, except for morning and evening prayer where the "cathedral" dynamic is more operative.

It is in the L.O.H.'s use of the psalms

that we see the most explicit evidence of the church's christological appropriation of the psalter. By means of antiphons, psalm titles, NT or patristic phrases and psalm collects, the psalms are christocentrically interpreted and celebrated.

The Sacraments

Christian liturgy is ultimately unintelligible without an initiation into the biblical narratives, metaphors and images which generate, shape and interpret the rites and symbols of worship. In the reformed rites of the Roman church no sacramental celebration is without at least a brief proclamation of the word. As in the eucharist, chants, formulae of sacramental ministration and other prayers are direct biblical quotations or texts inspired by the scriptures. The choice of texts for the various celebrations of the sacraments, though often traditional, is sometimes out of harmony with contemporary exegetical understanding of these texts. This is especially the case where texts traditionally employed to prove Christ's institution of various sacraments are, in the present context of biblical, sacramental and ecumenical theology, understood in a different way. This is perhaps seen most clearly in the readings, chants and prayers employed in the celebration of confirmation and ordination to the episcopacy, presbyterate and diaconate.

The R.C.I.A. both presumes a catechetical component which introduces the catechumen to the community's biblical language system and celebrates the word in that setting which is the Christian's most critical place of encounter with the word, the liturgy. This initiatory process has had a tremendous influence on the shape of the lectionary, especially in the Lenten and Easter cycles.

The Word of God in Human Words

The flowering of biblical study and liturgical revival since the last century have borne fruit in reformed rites wherein the tables of word and sacrament are experienced as indissolubly joined and mutually interpretative. It is paradoxical that biblically informed liturgical revision should also give rise to often bitter debate about the role and use of the scriptures in the liturgy. Questions such as the prediction-fulfillment inspired principle of "harmony" in the arrangement of many pericopes, the appropriateness of texts chosen for the celebration of the sacraments, disagreement over where to begin and/or end a pericope or what verses, if any to omit, debate over the benefit or disadvantage of not employing the entire psalm text for the responsorial psalm of the eucharist, the elimination of cursing psalms from the revised L.O.H.— these are but some of the questions raised by rigorous biblical scholarship in a church very much in the process of liturgical renewal.

Perhaps no question has such an immediate contemporary impact on the relation of Bible to liturgy, however, as that of the very language in which the scriptures are proclaimed, sung and prayed. The publication of *An Inclusive Language Lectionary* (National Council of Churches) and the less radical *Lectionary for the Christian People* (Pueblo Publishing Co.) bear witness to this.

Not that the contemporary challenge of translations of the scriptures or the translation and composition of liturgical texts is restricted to the question of inclusive language alone. Biblical criticism, for example, has given us a new sensitivity to the genius of Hebrew poetry. This has inspired new psalter translations such as the *I.C.E.L. Psalter Project* (still in process) which brings together biblical scholars, liturgists, poets and musicians committed to addressing collaboratively the challenges of translation which confront any church desirous of praying the psalms today.

In displaying a willingness to address

these challenges the church bears witness to the fact that the church is, in fact, born of the word-in-worship. Yet the church gives shape to the sacramental form of the word both in the biblical text and in its primary form of proclamation, the liturgy. Much of the Bible is rooted in or has taken its final textual shape from an explicitly liturgical context. The assembly's primary and ordinary encounter with the word is in the liturgy, whose celebration presumes a community formed by the biblical story and intelligibly employing its language in proclamation, song and prayer.

See **Psalms as liturgical prayer; Word and sacraments, relation between; Word, liturgy of the**

Jean Daniélou, *The Bible and the Liturgy* (Notre Dame, IN: Univ. of Notre Dame Press, 1956). *General Instruction of the Liturgy of the Hours* (Washington, D.C.: N.C.C.B., 1971). *Introduction to the Lectionary for Mass* (Washington, D.C., U.S.C.C., 1982). Joseph Jensen, "Prediction-Fulfillment in Bible and Liturgy," CBQ 50 (1988), 646-662. Centre de Pastorale Liturgique, *The Liturgy and the Word of God* (Collegeville: The Liturgical Press, 1959).

ANDREW D. CIFERNI, O.PRAEM.

SCRUTINIES

Services, held generally during Lent, to prepare adult converts for baptism. Evidence as to how these services were celebrated in the early church is found in the sermons and mystagogical catecheses (Augustine, Ambrose, Cyril of Jerusalem) which explain both the ceremonies and the truths of the faith in detail.

Adults who chose to become Christians were first enrolled as catechumens (learners) or hearers (*audientes*). At the enrollment ceremony they were signed with the cross, and in the West they were given salt—a valuable medicine and preservative in the ancient world, and thus an apt sign of the spiritual health and stability the catechumen sought from God. Hands were laid on the catechumens in blessing, prayers were said for them,

and they were exorcised. After a long period, often lasting three years or more, catechumens could move to the next stage by enrolling as applicants (*competentes*), chosen ones (*electi*), or persons to be enlightened (*illuminandi*). They enrolled by giving in their names near the beginning of Lent, and they would be baptized at Easter the same year. At the time they submitted their names, the applicants were questioned (i.e., "scrutinized") about the moral character of their life. Their sponsors and other acquaintances were also questioned. At a series of ceremonies throughout Lent they were repeatedly exorcised (i.e., they were "scrutinized" for any areas of their life that still needed to be freed of evil influences), read to from the scriptures, and instructed on the meaning of the readings and the basic Christian teachings. At Rome there was a ceremony of opening the ears (*apertio aurium*) at which they were introduced to the four gospels. Eventually they were taught the creed and (at least in some places) the Lord's Prayer, in a type of ceremony called a *traditio* (handing over). Before being baptized they had to publicly recite these texts to show they had learned them; this was called *redditio* (handing back). In southern Italy, Psalm 23 was also handed over to the catechumens. At Milan, this psalm was sung while the newly baptized received their first communion.

The number of scrutinies varied from place to place, but in Rome there were originally three, held on the 3rd, 4th, and 5th Sundays in Lent. The gospels read on these days, from John 4, 9, and 11, recounted the stories of the Samaritan woman who asked Jesus for living water, the blind man healed by bathing in a pool at Jesus' direction, and the resurrection of Lazarus. Psalm 34 was sung with the response: "Come, children, ..." (34:11). Three scrutinies were still celebrated in the early 6th century, according to a letter from a certain John the Deacon, possibly the man who would become Pope John I (523-6) (Whitaker, 154-8). By the late 7th century, however, the number of scrutinies had expanded to seven, and they had come to be held on Lenten weekdays rather than on Sundays. This is the arrangement of Ordo Romanus XI (Whitaker 196-204). Chants and readings from two of these scrutinies (on Wednesday and Saturday after the 4th Sunday of Lent) survived in the Roman Missal until the reforms following Vatican II. The Gelasian Sacramentary preserves traces of both the Sunday and weekday arrangements (Whitaker, 166-96).

The practice of celebrating scrutinies began to die out with the conversion of the empire, as adult baptism became more rare and infant baptism more usual. The entire series of services, from enrollment to baptism, was collapsed into a single baptismal service, but somewhat differently in each of the Eastern and Western churches. Thus the traditional baptismal service of every rite begins with a selection of ceremonies derived from the old scrutiny services, but the particular selection varies from one rite to another. In the Roman rite, such abridged services already existed in the early 9th century, when one of them was included in the supplement to the Gregorian sacramentary of Hadrian; a similar one formed part of the Roman Ritual down to modern times. After Vatican II, the new Rite of Christian Initiation of Adults (1972) authorized a return to the older practice of three scrutinies on Lenten Sundays. The original gospel readings were restored in Year A of the new lectionary.

See Initiation, Christian; Baptism

St. Augustine, *The First Catechetical Instruction,* trans. by Joseph P. Christopher, Ancient Christian Writers 2 (New York: Paulist Press, 1946). E.C. Whitaker, *Documents of the Baptismal Liturgy,* 2nd ed. (London: S.P.C.K, 1970). Edward Yarnold, S.J., *The Awe-Inspiring Rites of Initiation: Baptismal Homilies of the Fourth Century* (Middlegreen: St. Paul Publications, 1972). William Telfer, ed., *Cyril of Jerusalem and Nemesius of Emesa,* The Library of Christian Classics 4 (Philadelphia: Westminster Press, 1955).

PETER JEFFERY

SEAL OF CONFESSION

On the part of a confessor, or minister of the sacrament of reconciliation, the seal of confession is the absolute requirement of strict confidentiality in regard to information presented by the penitent for forgiveness; on the part of the penitent the seal of confession is the guarantee that such confidentiality will be observed. Under the "seal" the confessor may neither reveal nor use in any way material which the penitent names unless the confessor receives from the penitent explicit permission to do so. The primary reason for such a requirement, in addition to the obvious ones of privacy and protection, is that the material is presented to the confessor *as a mediator* of God; the material is presented directly to God. It in no way becomes the property of the confessor since the confessor receives it in the name of God.

See Confidentiality; Confession of sins

SECULAR RITUALS

Since ritual activity is an important component of religious faith and practice, the term "secular rituals" may seem inherently contradictory. Yet in a modern, secularized society there are many communal events which can best be understood by making analogies to traditional religious ritual. In this article we shall consider, first, certain formal and psychological congruities between secular and sacred rites and ceremonies. We shall then try to determine where analogy falters and speculate on how civic rituals may help us better understand the nature and function of traditional liturgies.

Formal Correspondence

Persons taking part in religious rituals gather at particular places to enact ceremonies that unfold within a certain time frame. Locations for ritual activity have ranged in complexity and architectural form—from simple outdoor sites or caves to magnificent cathedrals. Some interior spaces have been austere, without ornament or image. In others, walls are lavishly adorned with painting and sculptures. Although they may be diverse in construction and ornamentation, ritual spaces share a common function, to establish a spatial boundary within which liturgy occurs. However complex or simple, liturgical space differs from that of the mundane environment; in a revered setting a pattern of rites or worship takes place. The bounded space is enlivened by ordered actions which have a beginning, middle, and end. These demarcations and rhythms, like those of space, may be simple or ornate, but in all instances ritual time is different from everyday, clock-measured reality.

Secular rituals are associated with a variety of special times and places, but in American culture they are particularly prevalent in politics and sports. In both spheres formalized spaces and carefully ordered events are comparable to those of traditional religion. Civic rituals related to the democratic processes became increasingly elaborate in the later 20th century as television brought pictures of important political events into millions of homes.

The Republican and Democratic conventions, once occasions for the selection of candidates, became increasingly ritualized media extravaganzas to reinforce belief in a previously chosen candidate. To assure the best use of television coverage, political leaders have hired public relations firms to design and oversee an ordered flow of events through four evenings of prime-time TV viewing. Ornamented, balloon-filled convention halls now become "sacred" spaces through which stream carefully orchestrated speeches, representative heroes, minidramas, and processions. Finally on the last evening there is a triumphant, happy ending in which all the major players take part.

Every four years these presidential conventions signal the beginning of a series of civic rituals which culminate in the inauguration of the president of the United States. Shortly after the conventions come the debates between candidates—both presidential and vice-presidential. These have been squeezed into a ritualized structure that almost seems to undercut their original purpose. The detailed calculation of time, place, and subject matter has tended to stifle a more open, unpredictable confrontation between candidates. Like traditional mythological heroes and heroines, the debaters now seem programmed to follow certain themes and actions.

Election night brings with it additional hallowed spaces and times. Each network creates a special booth, usually with an illuminated map of the United States as background. In their special locations the major anchorpersons officiate like priests. In constant communication with commentators and observers throughout the nation, they lead viewers through the final moments of the campaign. Immediately following the election, the president elect and his staff begin to prepare for the climactic ritual of politics; the inauguration of the president of the United States. Since for millions there is no possibility to attend this momentous event, the inauguration has become a major telecast ritual. At the time of his inauguration Ronald Reagan advised Americans that the best place to take part in the occasion was in one's living room before the TV screen. There, as the camera lens zooms in on a tight shot of the president, one is "closer" to the action than diplomats, dignitaries, relatives, friends, or even the chief justice who administers the oath of office.

Like politics and religion, sports evoke some of our most passionate beliefs and loyalties. Devoted followers long to be present at the most important sites, for example, the Super Bowl or the World Series. At such times a stadium is transformed into a "holy" place where throngs of devotees are present in the competitive drama of winning first place. Yet in sports as in politics ritualistic circles have widened across national and cultural boundaries to encompass millions. Throughout the world faithful fans, through the mandala of the TV tube, enter vicariously the sacred time and space of the Super Bowl, World Series, or the Olympics.

Secular rituals, like traditional religious rituals, have primary and secondary actors or participants. Politicians, sports heroes, and anchorpersons, like a clerical hierarchy, are the major players. At the same time, ardent supporters in the stadium or on the convention floor—or even those watching in their living rooms or the local pub—play parts unlike their roles in ordinary life. Cheerleaders and band members who wear special costumes and occupy select spaces like church choirs lead the crowd in litanies and victory songs. Even the ordinary participant may dress up especially for this liturgical event. Secular rituals have become an opportunity for people to transform themselves into fantastic creatures. Sports fans dress in the team's colors and many wear T-shirts or sweaters with the teams symbol or logo. Some with masks impersonate the team's mascot.

Political conventions also liberate ordinary people and encourage them to wear appropriate ritual costumes. Now that television coverage includes camera sweeps and close-up details of those on the convention floor, many people come especially prepared for the pageantry. At the Republican and Democratic conventions loyal followers adorn themselves with hats and masks—mostly variations on the themes of elephants and donkeys. Any kind of dress is acceptable so long as it carries a message or slogan. Hand-held banners—of any color, but generally red, white, and blue—are commonplace, and people carry noisemakers and horns that blast forth their approval of leaders. Garbed in such ritualistic attire, enthusiastic delegates readily rush out into aisles for parades and demonstrations of support for their candidates.

Ancient and medieval pilgrims to holy places liked to bring home trinkets and charms—symbols of gods, goddesses, saints, or other reminders of their experience. Similarly, today's faithful who take part in civic rituals may bring back souvenirs. Those fortunate enough to get to conventions or playoffs have a choice among many different kinds of mementos: pennants, miniature and plastic footballs and baseballs, pictures of heroes, audio-visual tapes of the event to replay later. Viewers at home who feel left out may order memorabilia in advance to share with friends and neighbors as they watch the telecast event.

Thus far the analogies between secular and religious rituals have been based on similarities of form—closed, extraordinary space, bounded segments of time, and the dramatic action and interaction of primary and secondary participants. Yet traditional liturgies are not valued primarily for their formal qualities, and undue emphasis upon them does not do justice to their substance and function in human experience. Proponents of secular rituals, too, would insist that there are other corresponding features which are life-enhancing and fulfill certain basic human needs.

Psychological Affinities

The sacred time and space of traditional religious ritual are communal; participants, however, may experience a wide range of emotions. Even though changes in human hearts and minds are ultimately unknowable, theologians, anthropologists, psychologists, and poets have written about the states of mind that accompany ritual action. Such discussions are speculative and cannot penetrate the mystery of a single, private moment; still, one can investigate some of the basic dynamics of religious rituals and then ask whether similar emotions are experienced in secular rituals.

It is commonly observed that religious ritual provides an opportunity to step outside the flux of time and space. In the ritually constructed closure one can escape the ceaseless linear motion of every day life and enter a different realm of being—a divine enclave which humans occupy only briefly before they return to daily life.

Religious liturgy enables one through withdrawal to experience a radically different orientation to reality. At such time a faithful participant may live in a state of self-forgetfulness, released from the boundaries of individual consciousness. Here in effect, one may momentarily counter the suffering and uncertainty that are part of life. This is the essentially saving dimension of religion which enables women and men to rise above the pain and futility, and sense of impermanence of life. During these moments a person "understands" things that are beyond understanding. Such self-transcendence, accompanied by feelings of awe, wonder, and humility, transforms the outlook of believers. It enables them to return to the tedium of existence with reassurance and hope and to live a fresh vision in an old world.

Anthropologists, such as Victor Turner, have commented on the transformative dimension of ritual. The spectrum of transformations is vast, and individual members of religious groups may be touched by ritual in different,

unpredictable ways. The common denominator is a feeling of belonging, of being a part of a larger whole. In liturgy repeated rhythms, gestures, sounds, and shared sacraments nurture a sense of community. Even in informal rites of worship, members of congregations join in responsive readings, reciting the creed and singing hymns. Common worship creates among persons of different social or political views at least a tacit sense of accord and a shared vocabulary of faith.

Turner and others have suggested that in a complex, secular society the power and dynamics of traditional religious ritual have migrated into other domains such as politics, aesthetics, sports, and popular culture. Indeed artists—musicians, dancers, painters—and athletes have experienced a self-transcendence at the height of a performance. Persons who attend rock concerts feel the sense of community there and the revivification of emotions associated with the events. Do these secular activities contain residual elements of religious ritual? Or do religious and secular rituals derive their transformative and integrative power from a common source?

For scholars such as Johan Huizinga and Hugo Rahner, the concept of *homo ludens* becomes a symbolic bridge between secular and religious rituals. The human drive to play is the primeval source from which issue both secular and sacred games of life. The game—characterized by particular rules, space, and time—is the prime metaphor that allows us to understand better the regenerative escape from life and the loyalties evoked by the serious ritual play. Thus to Rahner, for example, liturgy is a reflection or counterplay that celebrates the cosmic game of grace. Yet even without such a theological vision of redemption, the dynamics of serious play may generate transforming and community-creating energies.

Persons who reject traditional religious

beliefs and church affiliation may find emotional reassurance and a sense of community in the ritualistic dimensions of secular culture. There they can be enthusiastically caught up in the serious play of the arts, sports, or politics where particular rules give a sense of order and where closures of time and space offer opportunities for self-transcendence.

The close relationship between professional football and television in American society has created ritualistic sanctuaries every Monday evening. In their armchairs before TV, millions of viewers find a momentary way out of unresolved, day-to-day confusion. For over an hour every week there is an opportunity to get outside of reality and to lose oneself enthusiastically in the dramatic action of game time. Here one can "live" for a while in a world that has rules and order. And, like the liturgical calendar, the football season develops in complexity and the drama intensifies, coming to a climax in the Great Liturgy, the Super Bowl.

The fans before TV sets and those in the stadium experience a sense of community. One can converse with strangers at the ballpark or discuss the playoffs with the check-out clerk at the local grocery. Persons who understand little and care less about catholicity in religion, nevertheless appreciate and live within an extensive belief system of loyal supporters of say, the Boston Celtics, Washington Redskins, or New York Mets. Bolstering that sense of community is the mythology of sports. TV commentators and newspapers fill believers in on the games they missed, as well as major events in the lives of the players. Fans are conscious of records and heroes who may eventually be tapped for the Hall of Fame. Legends comparable to those of religious heroes and heroines help to nurture the sense of belonging to a community, one that reaches back into time and looks ahead to the future.

Because play is believed to be central to human culture, it is not accidental that political activity is described with words like "race" or "runoff." Moreover, TV coverage has accelerated its game-like characteristics. While there is probably more cynicism about politicians than sports heroes, campaign managers confident in the democratic processes and its players use political rituals to reinforce and legitimate belief. Persons who attend the political conventions, as well as those who view them on TV, are expected to be transformed, to experience a loyalty and reassurance that will prepare them for the campaigns to be fought later in the everyday world.

In the late 20th century special events in American society became ritual opportunities for all Americans regardless of political affiliation. On July 4, 1976, ceremonies and happenings throughout the nation were orchestrated by networks and telecast during the entire day. Anchorpersons wove together a continuous fabric of sights and sounds from various cultural spheres—high and popular arts, sports, and politics—designed to reinforce a sense of community and confidence in the American way. Similarly on July 4, 1986, when Ronald Reagan officiated in the relighting of the torch of the Statue of Liberty, it was a rite of renewal of faith in an open, democratic society peopled by immigrants from throughout the world. On less joyous occasions television has enabled the nation to join in rituals of mourning. Americans first experienced an encompassing nationwide lamentation when millions "shared" their grief during the telecast funeral of John F. Kennedy. Years later, President Reagan became priest and pastor, leader and comforter of the nation during the telecast memorial service for the Challenger astronauts.

We may recognize that secular rituals inspire a sense of community and even evoke moments of self-forgetfulness; still, there are lingering questions. Are concepts of transcendence and belonging that are attributed to religious and secular rituals really comparable? Are there limits to formal and psychological correspondences?

Theological Distinctions

To demonstrate distinct, ineluctable differences between religious and secular ritual one must center on the symbolic content of the action or event, rather than on its formal or psychological dimensions. In addition, the distinctions need to be reinforced by a definition of religion which presupposes a metaphysical reality that is not humanly constructed, one that is the ultimate source of meaning and being. Differences in symbolism become clear when we use these theological presuppositions to speak about the nature of transcendence associated with religious ritual. In the course of liturgy faithful participants counter the suffering and death experienced in life, anticipating a "something more." Although theologians and ritual participants may disagree about the nature of this saving realm of being, they share the conviction that there is an unknowable "Other" which is the object of human desire and which may be "known" tentatively, obliquely and momentarily in ritual experience. The physical gestures, prayers, biblical readings, and sacraments of the eucharist, for example, draw us (in Rahner's terms) into the playing of God, the everlasting game. Thus ritual time, space, and action encompass a very special, incomparable game because its rules, measures, and Chief Player are beyond human imagination and creation.

The sense of belonging inspired by many secular rituals seems parochial in contrast to the cosmic sense of salvation present in many world religions. Moreover, in Christian theology, the doctrine of the Holy Spirit assures believers of an abiding presence in all aspects of individual and corporate life. In addition, for many religious groups the consciousness of community brings with it not only an identification with others but also certain ethical obligations to them. The eucharist, for example, ends with an admonition to go in peace and serve with gladness and singleness of heart.

Theological distinctions held by faithful communicants do not preclude participation in civic or secular ritual. They do, however, point to the uniqueness of religious ritual as an encounter with grace, an attunement to Being beyond the humanly constructed games of art, politics, and sports. Yet we must wonder why our secular play seems to have more vitality than that of religion. Is it because the values and dogmas of our civic belief system consume our creative energies? Or have the symbols of religious groups become so identified with those of the secular, materialist society that the theological distinctions which set them apart become obscured? Have traditional religious symbols become so encrusted and inadequate for our time, that persons looking for serious play and a cosmic view go elsewhere?

Religious ritualists may learn from secular liturgists. From sports, politics, and even commercials, they can learn how important the arts—dance, music, drama, images—are to human communication. In the playoff—in the stadium or before TV—they may observe how passion and loyalty enliven ritual. Environmentalists and peace groups may challenge them to give new meanings to old symbols and to enlarge their vision of community. Secular rituals dramatize the human need for serious play that transforms the ordinariness of life. The vitality of these humanly constructed worlds, their symbolism and celebrations challenge the church to re-examine and revitalize its sacramental forms.

Gregor T. Goethals, *The TV Ritual: Worship at the Video Altar* (Boston: Beacon Press, 1981). Johan Huizinga, *Homo Ludens: A Study of the Play Element in Culture* (Boston: Beacon Press, 1962). Hugo Rahner, *Man at Play* (New York: Herder and Herder, 1972). Victor Turner, "Variations on a Theme of Liminality," *Secular Ritual*, eds. Sally F. Moore and Barbara G. Myerhoff (Assen/Amsterdam: Van Gorcum and Company, 1977).

GREGOR T. GOETHALS

SECULARIZATION AND WORSHIP

An understanding of the phenomenon of secularization is important because it is a major underlying sociocultural, and to a great extent, religio-theological process which influences worship for the modern person. We will discuss the relationship between secularization and worship under the following topics: 1) the cultural and theological context; 2) its challenge to worship; 3) NT perspective; 4) persons, times and places; and, 5) towards a new integration.

The Cultural and Theological Context

The meaning and implications of the historical process of secularization are ambiguous, complex and sometimes contradictory. The concept has been used not only by ancient philosophers, like Anaxagoras, Xenophanes and Socrates in their critique of the popular gods and myths, but also by modern theologians, especially Protestants, like K. Barth, D. Bonhoeffer, and the "death-of-God" theologians in the United States. Although departing from different perspectives in their interpretation of a "religionless Christianity," the common denominator of the theologians has been in general a positive view of the phenomenon of secularization in a world which has come "of age." From the perspective of the science of religions, secularization is interpreted within the theoretical parameters of the dialectic presence of the two opposing poles of the sacred and the profane, and the religious and the secular. The sacred means something separated,

different and extraordinary, a mysterious, transnatural and impersonal power. At the other extreme, the experience of the profane in secularist ideology is an horizontal conception which underlies "secular religion" and proclaims the autonomy of universal human values. In political terms, secularism denies the social and public value of religion because it is seen as substituting the irrational for the rational. Social sciences, especially the sociology of religion, offer a major contribution to the modern debate concerning secularization. They emphasize the ambiguity of its terminology, which is more ideological than scientific. Examples of this critique against reductionist and mystifying terminology especially in the 1960s, are T. Rendtorff in Germany and D. Martin in England.

Etymologically speaking, "secularization," which comes from the Latin *saecularis*, means "becoming worldly." It refers to a social, cultural and political process of emancipation of organized society from the hegemony of religious institutions and symbols. While secularization, an ambivalent term, does not imply *per se* the diminution of religious symbolism and the experience of faith, it has contributed to the decreasing influence of institutional religion in the modern world. Historically, secularization has meant the usurpation of church property by the state, especially in the transfer of educational religious institutions. This new shift in the relationship between church and state which began after the Reformation in England, became a widespread phenomenon during the 19th-century liberal movement in Europe.

The above approaches speak of the many meanings of the complex phenomenon of secularization and the possible ideological ambiguities in our modern world. It is a world in transition. There is no doubt that a paradigmatic shift from a sacred conception of nature and society to a secular vision of the universe and humankind took place in Western culture. This shift undoubtedly brought about the crisis of the traditional role of religion in a post-agrarian, technological and science-based society. Approaching the third millennium, Christianity lives in a critical age of cultural crisis and unresolved tensions. It can approach the crisis of secularization in a more positive fashion, and in that very crisis find an opportunity to renew itself.

In general, secularization is not only a pervasive reality, it is also—in its extreme version—the myth of modernity, especially the latter. The end of religion and ritual did not take place as predicted in the 1960s by secularism. The same anthropocentric and rationalistic cultural presuppositions on which those predictions were based are now changing. Today there is not only a renewed vitality within religion but also a real interest in the restoration of sacramental and symbolic religiosity. The new constellation of ideas presents the opportunity for an integration of the vision of the true secular and the authentic religious spheres, the cosmos and the person, God and humankind.

The challenge presented by secularization to worship, which is the cradle of religion, calls for a wider approach from the theological perspective. Much seminal research was done by K. Barth, P. Tillich and D. Bonhoeffer, among others. In their attempt to understand positively the process of secularization in the light of biblical revelation, a more realistic approach in Christian thinking was made possible. The defensive Catholic ecclesiology could not come to terms with a positive evaluation of the values of secularization until the Vatican II period. At any rate, both theologies of secularization followed different perspectives: the Protestant, which departed from the theology of justification, and the Catholic, which in valuing the secular order and its consecration in Christ, viewed a theo-logical criterion in the incarnation in Christ who assumed the human condition. Vatican II's *Constitution on the Church in the Modern World* (cf. especially G.S., 36), represented a realistic evaluation of the phenomenon of secularism as one of the signs of modern times to be interpreted critically in the light of the gospel. Three major points of progress were made: the value of human activity in the rebuilding of the secular order, the unity of the secular and the religious realities in the mystery of Christ; and the dignity of the universal values of the human person (moral conscience, freedom) within the rightful autonomy of the modern world and within the design of God.

Its Challenge to Worship

Overcoming a false dichotomy of two spheres in the world, this critical but optimistic evaluation of secularity paved the way for a new integration of the secular and religious, the sacred and the profane. This integration leads to two important questions: is the person of the scientific-technological civilization, because of that very civilization, capable of the liturgical act? Is our worship realistic, or is there a profound gap between faith and culture? The first question has been asked since the beginning of the liturgical movement. There is no doubt that "behind the crisis of worship there is a general crisis of faith" (Upsala, 1968). Nevertheless, despite the fact that modern, non-religious culture is divorced from a vision of faith, the individual person is still in need of providing an adequate answer to existential questions and especially to the ultimate meaning of his/her existence. The change from a sacral to a secular consciousness made those questions even more acute and can be answered only with a critical acceptance of the values of present culture lived and celebrated in the transcendence of the mystery of the incarnation. Consequently, the meaning and role of religion has changed, and so has the perceived meaning and the actual role of worship. A "free world" points to a worship freed of alienating, ultra-sacralizing elements; that is, worship is to be a liberating and salvific experience of faith, not separated from daily life, but at the heart of it.

In fact, if there is a liturgical crisis, it is not only because a change of cultural presuppositions took place, but also because the correspondence between the meaning of worship and the living reality of the Christian as a "being in the world" is missing. A clear example of this gap is seen in Roman euchology, in the absence of a theology of creation, and of temporal realities, and an emphasis, instead, on an idiom which corresponds to an archaic social order. The significance of a ritual for the modern person's spiritual needs is mediated by a concrete cultural climate because culture is never accidental in people's lives, but serves as an essential condition for human realization. On one hand, worship must always be an uncompromised prophetic sign of the biblical-evangelical message to an anthropocentric and materialistic culture. Yet, on the other hand, worship cannot remain aloof or isolated from the secular universe of values and ideas, struggles and hopes of the secular order. Corporate worship is the real matrix of social configuration through which a culture is endowed with Christian meaning. The integration of the positive values of secularity and the religious experience is crucial. Symbolic ritual actions and language that are in contact with the social life, and thus capable of transfiguring it become meaningful when they inspire a personal response and illustrate present conditions.

Both dialectic bipolarities of the secular and religious, sacred and profane have an intrinsic relationship with worship. Worship is a person's response to the transcendent and the divine. How do we conceive this transcendent and divine

presence in the nature of worship? How can we have a secular liturgy which celebrates the transcendent sacredness of God? The answer to the above bipolarities and to these questions should stem from an authentic interpretation of a biblical theology of worship.

NT Perspective

Christian worship is the actualization of the priestly ministry of Christ through the signs of the ecclesial community. Realizing a spiritual and prophetic sacrifice, Christ restored the whole of creation and life and, thus, opened up all dimensions of the created world to the effects of God's redemptive mystery (cf. Col 1:20). Christ became the priest, the temple and the altar, radically transforming all created things. This christological impact of the Easter victory altered the vision of the sacred, nullifying its false separation from the profane. The whole of life came to be sacred, experienced in the presence of the transcendent reality. Christ became present in the heart of the human and secular realities celebrated in worship. Consequently, there is nothing sacred or profane in itself, but only that which is made holy by reason of divine grace present whenever human life is lived and celebrated in faith. This pervasiveness of the sacred was already prepared in the OT and especially in prophetic revelation. God is seen not only as the Creator of all, whose image marks every person, but also the Lord of a cult of obedience and service to the totality of life (Hos 6:6). The NT accomplished this covenantal idea of worship with a passion for existential meaning in the divine initiative and commitment. This meant the rejection of cultism as the denial of God's design, and the realization of a worship "in spirit and in truth," as an offering of the totality of the person and his/her life (1 Cor 16:15; 1 Pet 2:5). The christological event constituted the end of the dualistic opposition between the sacred and the secular, and consequently the beginning of an eschatological worship centered in Christ.

This concept of worship is fundamentally linked to a pneumatic reality. Christ is the fullness of this pneumatic reality which breaks the boundaries of any created cult and abolishes any magico-sacral attitude toward worship. The rebirth of a Christian in that pneumatic reality through baptism allows the possibility of true liberating worship: "The world, life and death, the present and the future, are all your servants; but you belong to Christ and Christ belongs to God" (1 Cor 3:22-23).

The radicalizing Christian attitude of worship does not abolish the sacramental expressions rooted existentially in the core of life. On the contrary, it acknowledges the deeper and wider sacramental dimension of human life. Sacramental and liturgical celebrations spring from key human experiences which are transformed by God's sanctifying presence. Those celebrations draw their power from the paschal mystery which consecrated the authentically human. Thus, the sacramental significance subsumes the created and natural significance. From this line of thought we can conclude that Christianity accomplished a shift from the cosmos to the person, to a person conceived as an embodied spirit and as a unified being. A person is not just part of nature, but the center of it. This biblical anthropocentric shift meant a secularization of the naturalistic views of cosmic religions, and furthermore a purification of any utilitarian or ambiguous sacralization in regard to the meaning of persons, times, and places in liturgical context.

Persons, Times and Places

Since the whole of life is holy, the total person is holy. In NT terms, Christian identity goes beyond the creative order. It shares the corporate priestly identity of a consecrated community (cf. 1 Pet 2:9). As a chosen and priestly people, this community's worship is a worship of the whole of life, not different from it, and it cannot be understood as an extension of a cultic priesthood of a sacral office. Priest and priesthood are applied only to Christ and his redemptive work; from him the universal priesthood of the people of God derives. This concept was not applied to the office-holders in the church until the 3rd century. From then on an artificial distinction between clergy and laity prevailed until the new theology of Vatican II. The council presented the whole community as the integral subject of the liturgical celebration (see, especially, L.G., 10, 11).

In the eschatological event of Christ, secular time is a special opportunity of grace because of the abiding presence of God (*kairos*). It goes beyond the sacrality of the succession of ordinary time (*kronos*) in the natural cycle of life and death celebrated by the cosmic religions. Christianity is an historical religion which conceives time as the arena in which God's action of creative and liberating fidelity is revealed.

From this perspective the totality of time has a focus "in the word who came to dwell among us," and moves toward a divine goal from the center of Christ, the beginning and end of secular time. The Lord's day is an instrument and a means, not an end in itself, because the whole life of a Christian, not a particular day or feast, is new time and an opportunity for receiving the salvific gift from the paschal event. As Paul says to the Colossians, "Never let anyone else decide what you should eat or drink, or whether you are to observe annual festivals, new moons or sabbaths. These were only pale reflections of what was coming: the reality of Christ" (Col 2:16-17).

Sacred places do not exist in the economy of the spiritual worship of the fulfilled Kingdom of God. Here we can distinguish on one hand a primary theology of the body of Christ as a reality of the presence of God, and the body of the church, a sign of the presence of Christ. On the other hand, we should value the theological reality of the place of worship in which the joyous manifestation of the church-assembly takes place and allows the gathering of thanksgiving, the action of the mystery, an atmosphere of contemplation, a sense of transcendence and a milieu of prayer.

The early Christian writers vigorously affirmed that they did not have temples or altars. In fact, from the very beginning, Christians celebrated their eucharist in a family-like setting in the home. Even when their numbers and social standing required a larger and more public place during the Constantinian historical shift, they rejected the religious temples and chose the secular basilica of civic and social life. The patristic theology of the presence of God rejected the idea of emphasizing the materiality of the temple and its mode of worship to comprehend the temple of the new humanity through the incarnate epiphany of Christ. By his incarnation Jesus became the final priest of the new temple of his body (cf. Jn 2:19, 21), and the living stone on which the living stones of the people of God make their spiritual temple (cf. 1 Pet 2:5; Heb 8:1). Consequently, this primary theology of the *domus ecclesiae* should not only prevail but be served by the secondary and functional theology of the *domus Dei*. Transferring the vision of holiness from the assembly to a sacral place has negative effects on the orthopraxis of the ministerial community. A living temple is the only metaphor of a worship anchored in the heart of daily living, not apart from it. That living temple becomes the only meaningful sign-symbol of the worship of God's presence in the world.

Towards a New Integration
The movement of secularization, not

only of the false sacred in persons, times and places, but also in objects, language and rites calls for a critical balance which demands a relative sacralization of the totality of the liturgical action. If secularism denies the relation to the divine, the access to its transcendent mystery, or simply the reverent acceptance and awe of its salvific presence, the oversacralization overburdens liturgy with mysterious ritualism, magical and supernaturalistic attitudes. Secularism, as the denial of the transcendent sense, could reduce the celebration of the mystery of God in us through Christ to a partial psychological or pedagogical exercise. Christian worship can only happen through the binomial sacrament-word in which the corporeal and the cosmic are symbolically related to the transcendent and the spiritual. Furthermore, the theocentric and christological character of liturgy demands a sacredness of the sacramental mediation in the encounter of the divine irradiation of grace with the human need for transformation. However, this mediation does not happen automatically, but depends on the quality of the faith community, and on the relevance of the symbol and the prophetic word. Vatican II states that "every liturgical celebration is a sacred action" (S.C., 7), precisely because it is the action of the paschal mystery of Christ and of his body, the church. The post-Vatican II reform purified liturgy of the historical accumulations of the late medieval over-sacralization and called for a renewed sense of the sacred (cf. Synod of 1985; Apostolic Letter of John Paul II, 1989).

In reviewing the phenomenon of secularization and the action of worship, one must try to clarify the complexity of the issue and its implications for a Christian community which is immersed in present history and fully actualized in the liturgy of the incarnation. Secularization has been a challenge to, not the end of worship, especially in the presently developing climate of a post-enlightenment culture which is more sensitive to sacramental and transcendent reality. A shift from the sacred to the inclusive secular understanding of persons has made possible a new synthesis between the mystery of worship and the person of present-day urban-scientific culture. Different theological trends (secular, political, liberationist) which followed the affirmation of Vatican II of modern humanistic values, allowed different interpretations of the function and meaning of worship. The never-ending process of the cult and culture interchange calls today for a renewed liturgical movement in which other liturgical dimensions (popular-religious, contemplative, festive, ministerial) could bring the dialectic between secularization and worship to a higher level of an integral and transcendent vision of the person in the unity of the mystery of Christ.

See **Liturgy in a technological age**

Langdon Gilkey, *Society and the Sacred* (Crossroad: New York, 1981). Luis Maldonado, *Secularización de la Liturgia* (Madrid: Ediciones Marova, 1970). Raimundo Panikkar, *Worship and Secular Man* (New York: Orbis Books, 1973).

GERMAN MARTINEZ

SICK, ANOINTING OF, FREQUENCY OF

Until the recent reforms of the Second Vatican Council, the repetition of the sacrament of the anointing of the sick was a rare occurrence. This was the consequence of developments concerning this sacrament during the Middle Ages. At that time anointing came to replace viaticum as the last sacrament of the Christian. As such, anointing became associated with the practice of deathbed penance and came to have attached to it the same sense of unrepeatability that once-in-a-lifetime penance had. And although the Council of Trent maintained in its teaching the larger tradition that anointing was for the sick, including ("especially") the dying, the medieval understanding and practice concerning the sacrament continued to dominate pastoral practice in the Latin church until Vatican II. Anointing continued to be delayed until the point of death with the understanding that in this way the dying Christian was ushered into eternal life having been forgiven any remaining vestiges of sin. Under these circumstances, the possibility of a later repetition of the sacrament (for which some provision had been made by Trent and, later, the 1917 Code of Canon Law) was rarely even a question.

The reforms of Vatican II replaced anointing with viaticum as the sacrament proper to the dying Christian. Anointing was recovered as the sacrament which the church associates particularly with the sick, some of whom may be preparing for death. The criterion for deciding the proper time for anointing is now "serious illness" rather than "danger of death"— "Great care and concern should be taken to see that those of the faithful whose health is seriously impaired by sickness or old age receive the sacrament" (*Pastoral Care of the Sick*, 8). In catechesis the community should come to understand that the sacrament of anointing is to be requested at the right time, that is, the beginning of serious illness. This will help to avoid "the wrongful practice of delaying the reception of the sacrament" (P.C., 13). Thus, the celebration can take place "while the sick person is capable of active participation" (P.C., 99).

Under these conditions, the possibility of repeating the anointing of the sick can arise. This is addressed directly. "The sacrament of anointing may be repeated: (a) when the sick person recovers after being anointed and, at a later time, becomes sick again; (b) when during the same illness the condition of the sick person becomes more serious" (P.C., 102). In the first instance, that is, serious illness followed by recovery and subsequent illness, it is presumed that the subsequent illness is also "serious." The second condition makes it possible for the sacrament to be celebrated again when the progress of an illness presents the sick person with a deeper and further challenge to perseverance and belief. The sacrament may also be celebrated again, if warranted, in the case of those who are "chronically ill or elderly and in a weakened condition" (P.C., 102).

In these instances, as in all decisions about anointing, the priest is to make a careful, pastoral judgment, "without scruple," about whether the sick person's condition warrants the care represented by anointing; if necessary, a doctor may be consulted before deciding (see P.C., 8). Some form of serious impairment due to sickness or old age is the criterion for judgment. The simple fact of illness or advanced age is not sufficient reason (P.C., 108). Pastoral care and responsibility require that in each case the priest know the sick person's condition in order to ensure that this sacramental ministry of the community of faith is brought to bear at the proper time and with those persons who are in true need and able to benefit from it.

JAMES M. SCHELLMAN

SICK, COMMUNAL ANOINTING OF THE

Anointing of the sick has been one of the most universally well-received revisions of the post-Vatican II liturgical renewal, especially in its communal format now sanctioned *de jure* by the new Code of Canon Law (1002). This widesweeping reform has meant a transformation of what had earlier been the most misunderstood (fatalism associated with "last rites"), most unliturgical (mini-malism in celebration), and most uncommunal (one-on-one encounter with priest) of all the seven sacraments of the church. Ecumenically, communal anointings have always been practiced by the Eastern Orthodox churches in an elaborate service (*euchelaion*) whenever possible involving seven concelebrating priests, and more recently are now celebrated by the member churches of the Anglican Communion and the Lutheran church.

The Tradition

Communal anointings find a precedent in the oldest full ritual for the application of the oil of the sick dating from the early 9th century. Prior to this time the only extant sources have to do with the blessing of the oil by the bishop. The rite, a Carolingian composition from Roman, Gallican, and Mozarabic sources, was concelebrated by the presbyters (Jas 5:14-15) and included sung chants. The service begins with introductory prayers "for visiting the sick" and presumes the sick Christian is still able to "bend the knee or knees" and participate in the liturgy. The priests are enjoined to anoint with signs of the cross on the neck and on the throat, and between the shoulders and on the breast, or to anoint further "the place where the pain is more pronounced" while an accompanying prayer of supplication is said. The rite concludes with holy communion, which, together with the anointing, is to be repeated for seven days. The later association of anointing with death bed reconciliation led to a privatization of the sacrament (*extreme unction*) whose effects were often improperly confused with penance and viaticum.

The *Constitution on the Sacred Liturgy* declared a preference for the name "anointing of the sick" over "extreme unction" and suggested the earliest possible time for the anointing (*Sacrosanction concilium* [S.C.], 73). The same document also restated that sacraments are celebrations of the church and their communal celebration is to be preferred (S.C., 26, 27). Perhaps the most significant teaching of the Second Vatican Council on this sacrament is found in the Constitution on the Church: "By the sacred anointing of the sick and the prayer of the priests the whole Church commends those who are ill to the suffering and glorified Lord, that he may raise them up and save them. And indeed she exhorts them to contribute to the good of the People of God by freely uniting themselves to the passion and death of Christ" (*Lumen gentium*, 11). This statement both contextualizes the anointing squarely within the life and ministry of the church and recognizes the church itself as a fundamental sacrament which brings the healing strength and grace of Jesus Christ to its afflicted members. This communal context is conveyed in the very title of the typical edition *Ordo Unctionis infirmorum eorumque pastoralis curae* (1972), first translated as *Rite of anointing and Pastoral Care of the Sick* (1974), and in the subsequent I.C.E.L. revision as *Pastoral Care of the Sick: Rites of Anointing and Viaticum* (1983).

Liturgical Celebration

What was once the most misunderstood of sacraments is now restored to its original meaning as an anointing of sick Christians who are "seriously impaired by sickness or old age" (8). What was once the least communal of sacraments is now a liturgical celebration wherever possible involving a representative gathering of the faithful, from family members and medical personnel who care for the sick to a large scale celebration in a parish or cathedral church. What was once the least liturgical of sacraments now has two attractive settings (chap. 4): "anointing outside Mass" and "anointing within Mass." The structure for both rites is similar: introductory rites (greeting, optional sprinkling with holy water,

instruction/reception of the sick, penitential rite, opening prayer, liturgy of the word, liturgy of the anointing—which may be followed by holy communion outside Mass, and concluding blessing. The liturgy of the anointing consists of: a litany, the laying on of hands, the prayer over the oil, the anointing, and the prayer after anointing.

In the litany the interceding church prays for all the sick and for those who care for them. The last petition serves as a transition to the laying on of hands by the priests. This biblical gesture of healing and basic sacramental sign should be a deliberate action done in prayerful silence. The oil used for the anointing should be blessed by the bishop at the annual Chrism Mass, in which case the priest prays a prayer of thanksgiving over the oil. When pastoral need arises, the priest himself is empowered to bless the oil. In either case it is advisable that vessels with oil, preferably crystal or glass, replace the tiny oil stocks stuffed with cotton. Even better, a single larger container could be placed on a table (not the altar) in the sanctuary and the oil later transferred to smaller vessels to be applied by the concelebrating priests. The prayer of anointing reflects the church's theology of the sacrament and is drawn from Jas 5:14-15, the teaching of the Council of Trent, and from the earlier anointing prayer. Anointing the forehead the priest prays: "Through this holy anointing may the Lord in his love and mercy help you with the grace of the Holy Spirit. Amen."

Anointing the hands he continues: "May the Lord who frees you from sin save you and raise you up. Amen." After this, an appropriate prayer after anointing is said.

Pastoral Provisions

Communal anointings have deservedly become a regular feature in the life of many parishes. Usually the anointing takes place within Mass, a unique opportunity to provide an inspiring and reverent eucharistic celebration for those unable to participate regularly at Mass. Provision for anointing at a Sunday eucharistic assembly also has much to commend itself in terms of participation and the priority the parish assigns to its ministry to the sick. Preparation for the service is important. Essential is a prior catechesis on the meaning of illness in salvation history, the grace of anointing, and the parish's ministry to the sick and afflicted. As far as possible, those to be anointed should be known to the pastoral ministers and prepared in advance. The list of communion calls in the parish is a good place to begin to extend an invitation; transportation to and from the church may also need to be provided. Indiscriminate anointing of everyone in the church regardless of their condition is an abuse which will serve only to trivialize the sacrament; the family and participating parishioners are there to support the sick with their prayers and faith. Environmental considerations presume a church building completely accessible to handicapped persons and a seating arrangement which allows access to the sick during the laying on of hands and the anointing. The ministers for the celebration will hopefully include a full complement of ordained and non-ordained (choir/leader of song, servers, readers, eucharistic ministers). Sung acclamations enhance the participation of the congregation. A program or booklet in large print easily legible which incorporates devotional prayers and readings for use afterwards can serve as a remembrance and ongoing support for those anointed. A reception or meal provided by parish groups can prolong the spirit of communal concern and love which reflects the healing the risen Christ extends to the suffering members of his body.

See **Sick, pastoral care of the**

Pastoral Care of the Sick: Rites of Anointing and Viaticum (Washington, DC: I.C.E.L., 1982). Charles W. Gusmer, *And You Visited Me: Sacramental Ministry to the Sick and the Dying,* rev. ed., New York: Pueblo, 1989).

CHARLES W. GUSMER

SICK, COMMUNION TO THE

In the earliest full account of a Sunday eucharistic assembly at Rome, St. Justin Martyr concludes with an injunction that deacons are to bring holy communion to those Christians unable to be present (*Apologia* 1, 67). Today not only priests and deacons, but also lay eucharistic ministers may be entrusted to bring the bread of life and cup of salvation to the sick. Indeed, as the church has consistently restated, the primary and original reason for eucharistic reservation outside Mass is to provide for communion for the dying (viaticum); secondary reasons are the distribution of communion and adoration of the blessed sacrament (*Holy Communion and Worship of the Eucharist Outside Mass*, 35). Especially appropriate is the public dismissal of the eucharistic minister from Sunday Mass in order to bring communion to those confined at home: in this way communion to the sick is seen as an extension of the parish's eucharistic assembly.

For those instances when Mass is not able to be celebrated in the presence of the sick, chap. 3 of *Pastoral Care of the Sick* provides two liturgical formats: "Communion in Ordinary Circumstances" and "Communion in a Hospital or Institution." "Communion in Ordinary Circumstances" would regularly be used for visits to the homes of the sick, where family and friends may also communicate. The introductory rites include a greeting, optional sprinkling with holy water, penitential rite (or sacrament of penance). The liturgy of the word is an important new feature. In addition to one of the five options from John's gospel, virtually any passage of scripture may be proclaimed. Part III of the ritual provides a rich selection of readings. The response to the reading may be silence or a brief explanation of scripture. The general intercessions, which may be created spontaneously, give the sick person the opportunity to unite his/her sufferings with the crucified and risen Lord for the work of the church and the salvation of the world. The liturgy of holy communion follows the revised order of Mass beginning with the Lord's Prayer. In addition to the traditional words of showing the eucharistic bread ("This is the Lamb of God... "), a new option is provided: "This is the bread of life. Taste and see that the Lord is good."

Communion may be offered under both forms of bread and wine; sick persons unable to communicate under the form of bread may receive communion under the form of wine alone. The rite concludes with a blessing: ordained ministers may further make a sign of the cross with whatever remains of the blessed sacrament.

"Communion in a Hospital or Institution" is an abbreviation of the normative fuller rite for situations when there are many communicants. Ideally, the residents or patients could be gathered in groups with several assisting ministers of communion. Even when the full rite is not used, elements such as the scripture reading may be added to the simplified format. Beginning in the church, hospital chapel, or first room, the minister prays one of a choice of three antiphons: the traditional *Sacrum convivium* or two scriptural alternates. The Liturgy of Holy Communion consists of a greeting, the Lord's Prayer, and holy communion. The rite concludes with a prayer.

In both manners of communicating the sick an attitude of joyful reverence should prevail. At home a table covered with a linen cloth and candles can serve to promote this reverence. In hospitals and institutions every effort should be made to find an appropriate time to create a proper environment of worship so that holy communion can be received as an act of faith. *Pastoral Care* highlights why the most important visits to the sick are those in which sacramental communion is received: "In receiving the body and blood of Christ, the sick are united sacramentally to the Lord and are reunited with the eucharistic community from which illness has separated them" (51).

Pastoral Care of the Sick: Rites of Anointing and Viaticum (Washington, DC: I.C.E.L., 1982). Charles W. Gusmer, *And You Visited Me: Sacramental Ministry to the Sick and the Dying,* rev. ed. (New York: Pueblo, 1989).

CHARLES W. GUSMER

SICK, MINISTRY OF THE

Human life is permeated with paradox. The joy and pleasure of the act of conception result in the risk and pain of childbirth. The rich process of physical, mental, and spiritual development is pervaded by the anxiety that accompanies all human growth. And the grand promise of youth and health must eventually come to terms with the experience of limitation, illness, debilitation, and, ultimately, death. Promise and pain bracket human life at every turn.

The creation story of Genesis reveals that God did not intend the great gift of human life to be experienced in this way. In Genesis, suffering and death are shown to be intruders in the creator's original design. They reveal humanity's separation from God, the result of our fallen state. By human choice, sin entered the created order, and with it, death.

Jesus Christ, the Word incarnate, was sent by God into this ruptured creation to reclaim it and humanity for God. Jesus suffered. Jesus entered into the very heart of the paradox of human life by willingly embracing death on the cross. By raising him to life, God overcame death and restored humanity within the original, creative design revealed in Genesis. This does not mean that suffering and death have been removed from human experience, but that they have been conquered and made salvific, the very means of eternal life.

It is within the context of the mystery of Christ's dying and rising that Christians who are sick are seen to have a ministry to the community of faith and to the world as a whole. With Christ, they stand in the center of the paradox of life, the grandeur of its promise and the inclination to hopelessness with which it is rife because of suffering and the certainity of death. On the one hand, by their active struggle against illness, the sick members of the community of faith witness to the fact that sickness and suffering are evil and alien to God's plan for creation. In this they proclaim the goodness and gift of life and the greatness of humanity's place within the created order. As the introduction to *Pastoral Care of the Sick* (P.C.) states: "Part of the plan laid out by God's providence is that we should fight strenuously against all sickness and carefully seek the blessings of good health, so that we may fulfill our role in human society and in the Church" (3).

On the other hand, by their willing acceptance of the suffering that they cannot avoid, Christians who are sick experience and witness to the reality and mystery of suffering: "...their faith helps them to grasp more deeply the mystery of suffering and to bear their pain with greater courage" (P.C., 1). In the heart of this mystery they discover that the experience of suffering need not be one of futility and despair. In union with Christ's own suffering and death, these old enemies of the human race, these strangers to God's creative intent have been transformed into the means of grace and salvation: "From Christ's own words they know that sickness has meaning and

value for their own salvation and for the salvation of the world" (P.C., 1). By embracing the suffering that is theirs as members of a flawed yet beloved race, the sick unite themselves with the sufferings of Christ and help witness to and achieve the restoration of all in Christ: "...we should always be prepared to fill up what is lacking in Christ's sufferings for the salvation of the world as we look forward to creation's being set free in the glory of the children of God—see Colossians 1:24; Romans 8:19-21" (P.C., 3).

Christians who are sick minister to the well first and foremost by being witnesses to and embodiments of these fundamental truths of Christian revelation. It is in this sense that *Pastoral Care of the Sick* says "...the role of the sick in the Church is to be a reminder to others of the essential or higher things. By their witness the sick show that our mortal life must be redeemed through the mystery of Christ's death and resurrection" (P.C., 3). By their struggle with illness they recall the community of faith to its belief in the fundamental good of created life as a gift of God. And by associating themselves "willingly with the passion and death of Christ" (P.C., 5), they share with him the cost of redeeming that mortal life.

By facing the reality of sickness, the weakness, dependency, and fear that it entails, the sick Christian can help the Christian community and society as a whole acknowledge and accept the fundamental frailty of human nature that all people experience, whether or not they are sick. The denial of this reality can succeed only temporarily and is not without cost both for the individual and for society. In the individual who attempts it, this denial can result in an incapacity to deal with the changes and chances of life and one's own weaknesses. It can also mean an unwillingness to see change in others and can result in anger at the sight of one's own unacknowledged weaknesses reflected in others. These characteristics can also be evident on a larger stage in societies where frailty and the nonproductivity associated with it are viewed as having no value. In such a society the infirm and aged are relegated to the margins of the normal life of the group and even may be viewed with disdain. They are potentially painful reminders of a fundamental frailty that no one wants to admit, and within a social structure where measurable productivity is the gauge of personal worth.

The tendency in each of us and in the society we inhabit to deny human weakness and dependency is the outcome of fear, a fear which has its roots in an abiding sense of our mortality. Sickness puts us in touch with mortality, our own and others', in a direct and inescapable way. And those who are sick can minister to the well by showing them first of all that this fear is not to be denied, that it has positive value and rests on a true intuition that things were not meant to be like this. Second, the sick can help the rest learn that this fear can be faced and thereby become the way to hope and healing, the occasion for coming to an acceptance of our full humanity.

The sick are not, then, in a marginal relationship with the rest of human society. Even less so are they on the periphery of the Christian community. They have an essential role at the very heart of the mystery of Jesus, dead and risen. The gospels portray Jesus as having a constant concern for the sick and infirm, whom he sought out, consoled, healed. Jesus recognized that in their weakened or impaired condition the sick were allowed only a marginal existence in society. Some were considered outcasts. Jesus' ministry to them was at one and the same time an affirmation that such suffering was the result of an evil completely opposed to his Father's design and a proclamation of the kingdom that he came to inaugurate, a kingdom heralded by Jesus' own divine compassion

and healing. And in his utter self-giving on the cross Jesus suffered fully the effects of the evil loose in the world. In Jesus we see the face of a God who is for ever at one with the abandoned, the destitute, the victim, all who experience hopelessness. The whole of Jesus' life, death, and resurrection show us a God passionately attached to us, to our restoration and the restoration of all creation.

The community of faith needs those who are sick to teach it about the vulnerability of God in Christ, who "is still pained and tormented in his members, made like him" (P.C., 2). The sick teach the community about Christian hope found paradoxically in human vulnerability when united to Christ, the suffering servant. In the face of a society which can view the sick only as those who are in need and for whom so much must be done, the Christian community proclaims the place and dignity of the sick by the very way in which it loves, cares for, and depends upon them. And even as the community encourages them to offer their sufferings in union with Christ, it relies upon them to pray, in the privileged way that is theirs by virtue of this union, for the whole church and for the entire world: for peace in the world, for the many needs of the church, for individuals and families in crisis, for all those caught up in the mystery of human sufferings, whether in body, mind, or spirit (see P.C., 56).

JAMES M. SCHELLMAN

SICK, PASTORAL CARE OF THE

Following the commandment implicit in the last judgment parable recorded in Mt 25:34-40, the church has long included visiting the sick among the corporal works of mercy urged upon all the faithful. The tradition of assisting, encouraging and praying with the sick and their families and friends is the bedrock upon which is based all of the church's pastoral care of the sick. That tradition has taken ritual form in a variety of ways as the Christian assembly and its ministers have gathered over the centuries to pray and to share communion with the sick as well as to anoint them with oil in the name of the Lord. Although the term "pastoral care" has sometimes been preempted in our day to name the work of professionally accredited chaplains in health care institutions, this article will focus upon the older and enduring tradition of ritual pastoral care of the sick which frames their efforts. Moreover, it will focus upon that tradition largely as it has come to be actualized in the current Roman Catholic book of rites for the sick entitled *Pastoral Care of the Sick* (P.C.).

Sickness and Healing

Experience. Sickness and healing are terms defined by human experience interpreted through the double lens of personality and culture. Sickness is a process; it may begin in a disorder of the body, but it reaches out to encompass the human spirit in both its individual and its social dimensions. In time of illness, whether acute, chronic, or terminal, the human person confronts the limit imposed by bodiliness on the limitless desire of the spirit for life, meaning, and love. The ultimate expression of that limit is death. In some sense, therefore, every illness conceals within it a taste of one's own mortality, whether consciously recognized or not.

Death is the boundary of human hope. Sickness deprives us of the future we had imagined. The deprivation may be temporary, if the illness interferes only briefly with our plans for this day or this week or this month; or it may be permanent, if the illness threatens to end in death. Hope may be understood as that act of the imagination whereby we project the future as both possible and desirable. Sickness, then, may cast us into a crisis of hope. To the extent that we order our lives within the future as we imagine it, loss of that future may provoke the concomitant loss of our sense of purpose in life. Bereft of our usual goals, we may feel that our life has no meaning or value. In this sense, sickness induces a crisis of faith defined not as religious belief but as trust in life as ultimately meaningful. Finally, sickness may disrupt the ordinary relationships of which our lives are made: our relationship with ourselves as integrated body-persons perceived to be free and responsible; our relationship with other people; and, if we are religious people, our relationship with God. When our survival is threatened, we tend to concentrate our energies upon ourselves and our own needs. In this sense, sickness provokes a crisis of love. Potentially, then, sickness, as a confrontation with mortality, whether hidden or overt, creates for the sick a threefold crisis of hope, faith and love.

Nor is this crisis confined to the sick alone. It may extend to any whose lives are touched and affected by the sickness of a family member, friend, co-worker, fellow parishioner. Sickness calls into question the hopes, the goals, the relationships of the whole community within which it occurs. Sickness, then, is not a mere bodily reality but a total human experience shared, to some extent, by the social world to which the sick person belongs.

The ways in which both the sick person and the surrounding society interpret and respond to this experience are largely determined both by personality and by culture. Contemporary technological cultures tend to respond with medical structures and tools ordered to the cure of the physiological component of the illness, without regard for its spiritual or social dimensions. The movement toward a more holistic approach to medical care is based upon a larger vision of both sickness and healing as human and social processes. The experience of sickness described above generates a corresponding description of healing as a social process directed toward the transformation of the threefold crisis of hope, faith and love as it is rooted in bodily disorder.

Theological Interpretation. The church's interpretation of sickness and healing is rooted in the mission of Jesus Christ. Biblical imagery captures the goal of that mission in terms of wholeness: persons are healed and forgiven, society becomes a city ruled by the law of love of God and neighbor, the cosmos is made one in Christ. Borrowing upon considerable OT precedent, the gospel especially gathers this vision of salvific transformation into the evocative image of the reign of God, where all reality is brought into harmony. Sickness disrupts this harmony. It fragments the personal integrity of the individual; it disturbs relationships within society; it is ordered toward the utlimate disruption of death. Sickness therefore stands in contradiction to the reign of God. It is a manifestation of the chaotic reign of evil from which creation is to be redeemed. The evangelists frequently depict Jesus healing the sick as a sign of the in-breaking of the reign of God upon the chaos of a world under the rule of sin and death. In the new Jerusalem, sickness and suffering, sin and death, will be no more. The work of healing is therefore an expression of the work of redemption.

Ministerial Response. The church's ministry to the sick is necessarily also rooted in the mission of Jesus Christ. Healing in the fullest sense addresses all the dimensions of sickness. It has both a medical and a pastoral component. As Jesus cured the sick, so Christians throughout the ages have undertaken medical work for the sake of the gospel. The church has a long history of sponsoring hospices and hospitals for the physical as well as the spiritual care of the sick. However, healing done in the name of Jesus Christ is essentially a soteriological action. Every aspect of Jesus' life and ministry serves the one purpose, summarized in Mk 1:14f., of calling all people to conversion and acceptance of the reign of God. That acceptance implies commitment to a way of life. To heal the sick in Jesus' name, therefore, is to invite them into the reign of God as their way of life. In this context, whatever physical cure may take place is a bodily taste of the deeper healing which embraces every dimension of the human person affected by sickness. While a total cure is always desirable, it is not always possible. Moreover, it is always temporary. Cured of one ailment, we will eventually sicken from another until, inevitably, death claims us in the end. True healing consists less in cure than in conversion. To recall the terms used above to describe the human experience of sickness, the Christian work of healing invokes the power of God made available in Jesus Christ to enable the sick and all who participate in their sickness to resolve whatever aspects of the crisis of hope, faith and love stand in the way of their wholehearted commitment to the life of the reign of God. Healing, then, is a corporal work of mercy which embraces the whole person both as individual and as social being.

Rites for the Sick
The full title of the 1982 English-language edition of the Roman church's rite for the sick is *Pastoral Care of the Sick: Rites of Anointing and Viaticum* (P.C.). This title reflects the growing recognition that ritual constitutes a core expression of the church's ministry of pastoral care. The ritual book itself reflects that same awareness. In 1963, the *Constitution on the Sacred Liturgy* of Vatican II mandated specific reforms with regard to the sacrament of anointing itself and the order of the sacraments

given to the dying (S.C., 73-75). In 1972, the Latin *Ordo unctionis infirmorum eorumque pastoralis curae*, drawn up in response, took significant steps toward situating the sacraments of anointing and viaticum in the context of a larger vision of pastoral care of the sick which includes both theological reflection on the experience of sickness and pastoral directives for the medical care and community support of the sick. The International Commission on English in the Liturgy (I.C.E.L.) published the provisional English translation of the text in 1973 under the literal title *Rite of Anointing and Pastoral Care of the Sick* (R.A.P.C.S.). After a lengthy period of consultation, I.C.E.L. published the definitive text in 1982 under the present title. This version, approved for use in the United States in 1983, represents an adaptation rather than a mere retranslation of the Latin text. *P.C.* furthers the movement toward situating the sacraments within the context of a vision of pastoral care through the addition of new pastoral notes, especially a theological reflection on communion for the sick, new texts for particular circumstances, and new rites for visiting and praying with both sick adults and sick children. It supplies the minister's need for access to other rites by reprinting relevant portions of the rites of Christian initiation, penance, and funerals.

General Principles

In the context of care for the sick, there is a risk of interpreting the church's rites primarily as a form of pastoral "medicine," administered by professionals with an eye to curing the sick. The theological manifestation of this image of the rites is a preoccupation with identifying their effects. While that is a legitimate theological enterprise to which this article will indeed attend below, it distorts the nature of the church's ritual care for the sick if it fails to recognize that the rites are primarily acts of public worship. It is in

the context of our corporate surrender to the abiding yet transcendent mystery of God in a characteristically eucharistic action of remembrance and thanksgiving that we invoke God's saving intervention for those caught up in the experience of sickness. In this context, the sick themselves, as well as all those who participate in their sickness as social process, are themselves invited by the very nature of the act to surrender in remembrance and thanksgiving. To return to the terms introduced earlier, they are challenged and supported by the worshipping community to entrust themselves to God in hope, in faith and in love. It is in this rehearsal of the Christian act of death that they are healed, whether or not any physical cure takes place.

For this reason, all of the rites for the sick must be interpreted and celebrated in light of the principles of liturgical worship established through the process of liturgical reform since Vatican II. The symbolic character of Christian liturgical worship must be fully respected: symbols must be permitted to speak in depth and in power (cf. P.C., 107). As is evident from the structure and texts provided in P.C., the central symbols common to all the rites are the Christian assembly and the proclamation of the word of God. A communal celebration of the rites is always to be preferred over the semiprivate forms long familiar in pastoral practice (cf. S.C., 27; P.C., 33). The dialogic structure of each rite clearly presupposes the presence and participation of a community, however minimal. The rubrics consistently provide for the ordinary distribution of liturgical ministries where circumstances permit. The pastoral notes urge a communal rather than a private form of celebration whenever possible. Moreover, every rite includes a liturgy of the word which may be as brief as a few sentences from the gospel or as long as that of the Sunday eucharist, depending upon the condition of the sick. Only a medical emergency or an insuperable shortage of ministers justifies the omission of the word (e.g., P.C., 78; cf. 149). (P.C.) Part III provides an extensive lectionary imaginatively addressed to the crisis of faith, hope and love as it might occur in almost every dimension of the experience of sickness. Like most of the reformed liturgical books of the Roman rite, (P.C.) offers little in the way of explicit directives concerning the environment and music for worship. However, precisely because the rites for the sick are ecclesial acts of public prayer, they are subject to the same norms for symbolic ritual action as all of the other rites in the Christian liturgical repertoire. Pastoral sensitivity to the reality of the human sufferer suggests the wisdom of an attentive concern for the nonverbal dimensions of worship in the midst of the emotional and physical disruptions engendered by sickness.

Prayer

Family members, friends, and members of the faith community encourage, support and challenge the sick by gathering to pray with and for them. Both the OT and NT contain stories of miraculous cures attributed to the power of the prayer of a recognized prophet or healer, including Jesus himself (e.g., Jn 11:41-44). The description of the rite of anointing found in Jas 5:14-16 emphasizes the power of the prayer of faith, rather than the act of anointing itself, to "save" and "raise up" the sick. No doubt the custom of praying with and for the sick continued unabated in Christian communities long before it was formalized in the prayers and Masses for the sick found in the medieval liturgical books and in subsequent church rituals down to the present day. P.C. repeatedly urges pastoral ministers and family members to pray with the sick on occasions other than those marked by sacramental celebrations (e.g., 34). Ordained ministers are en-

couraged to pray with the sick and dying as public representatives of the ecclesial community (e.g., 44). Visitors are urged to share with the sick the word of God, especially as it has been proclaimed in the gatherings of the assembly from which the sick person was absent (46). They are also encouraged to pray the psalms and other prayers (46). Unlike its 1973 predecessor, P.C., (Part I) provides sample rites for prayer with sick adults and sick children. Both rites are modeled on the pattern of the liturgy of the word, to which are added the Lord's Prayer, a closing prayer, and a concluding blessing. P.C. (Part II) includes biblical and other texts for the community's use in praying with the dying and for the dead. Several of the prayers given for the commendation of the dying are taken from the early medieval European liturgical books which contain the prayers used by the church to accompany its dying members on the journey from deathbed to grave. Through prayer, the church seeks to sustain the dying Christian in a union with the pasch of Christ "until it is brought to fulfillment after death" (P.C., 212). In addition to praying with the sick and dying, the community of worship is urged to remember and to pray at the regular Sunday assembly for those whom sickness has taken from their midst (e.g., P.C., 43). Prayer, then, is the essential thread which binds into one, every aspect of the church's multi-faceted pastoral care of the sick.

Communion of the Sick and Dying

Eucharistic communion is the sacramental means through which the sick participate in the paschal mystery of Jesus Christ. It is also the sacramental means through which the community of faith and worship, divided by the absence of its sick members, is restored to communion in the one body of Christ (cf. P.C. 73). When death is imminent, the dying Christian receives communion under the title of viaticum, "food for the passage through death to eternal life" (P.C., 75).

History. In his *First Apology* (ca. A.D. 150), Justin Martyr made the statement that the deacons distributed the bread and wine to those who are present at the eucharistic celebration and took them to those who are absent. In the 3rd and 4th centuries, authors as scattered geographically as Hippolytus in Rome, Tertullian and Cyprian in North Africa, and Basil the Great in Caesarea, took for granted the custom of lay Christians reserving and receiving at home bread brought from the community's eucharist, perhaps with a cup of wine which they themselves blessed as part of this domestic communion rite. This practice seems to have continued in some places until the 7th or 8th century, but it began to diminish after the 4th century. Although the texts cited did not single out the sick and dying for specific mention, such persons were no doubt numbered among those who took communion outside the community celebration.

Other sources do attest to the custom of communicating the sick and dying. Where reliable medical care was unavailable, every sickness could and frequently did result in death. Therefore, it is not possible to distinguish communion for the sick from viaticum for the dying through much of the church's history. The church of the martyrs especially placed great emphasis on the importance of the eucharist as the sacramental anticipation of the Christian's literal participation in the pasch of Christ through death. As the Christian community adopted and adapted the Greek and Latin customs of providing their dead with a coin as fare for their journey after death across the river Styx, they gradually narrowed their use of this imagery of viaticum to the eucharist received in immediate preparation for death, whether death by violence or death by disease.

Beginning with the Council of Nicaea in 325, church legislation has repeatedly insisted on the importance of providing communion for the dying. Similarly, hagiography is filled with stories indicating the value placed on eucharist as the one necessary food for those facing death. So well was this lesson taken to heart that church councils in West and East from the 4th through the 7th centuries found it necessary to reiterate their condemnation of placing the eucharist in the mouth of those already dead, a Christian echo of the older customs of Greece and Rome.

Prior to the medieval clericalization of all eucharistic ministries, communion was given either by ordained ministers, by laypeople, or, in some instances, even by the sick themselves. Formal rituals for the communion of the sick and dying began to emerge in the Western church in the 8th century. According to the oldest surviving texts, viaticum was to be given in the context of prayer and the proclamation of the passion according to St. John. Medieval sources later described three types of rituals: a church rite, sometimes quite elaborate in its ritual and sometimes inclusive of penance before and anointing after communion; a home eucharist, probably using special Mass formularies composed for such occasions, until such home Masses were forbidden by Rome; or, most commonly, a home communion service using the reserved sacrament in a format eventually patterned on the communion rite at Mass, at times preceded by a biblical reading. Until the 12th century, communion was given to the sick under both kinds, though for practical reasons intinction had commonly replaced the cup by the 9th century. The *Rituale Romanum* of 1614 made no distinction between communion for the sick and viaticum for the dying. The priest was the sole minister of both, which were given only under the form of the bread.

Today, the Roman church presently possesses two distinct but similar rituals for the communion of the sick and viaticum for the dying: *Holy Communion and Worship of the Eucharist Outside Mass* (1973) and *P.C.* (1982). Following the instruction *Immensae caritatis* (1973), authorizing the appointment of lay ministers of communion to the sick, *Holy Communion Outside Mass* provides a form for the administration of communion or viaticum to be used only by lay ministers, while P.C. offers forms to be used by priests, deacons, and lay ministers alike. Both rituals contain long and short forms for the communion of the sick, but P.C. discourages minimizing the full rite (78). This full rite includes: introductory rites (greeting; optional sprinkling with holy water, penitential rite), the liturgy of the word (reading/s, response, general intercessions), the liturgy of holy communion (Lord's Prayer, communion, silent prayer, prayer after communion) and a concluding blessing. In both rituals, viaticum is distinguished from communion not only by the use of texts referring specifically to the advent of death but also by the inclusion of the baptismal profession of faith renewed by the dying person and the optional apostolic pardon given to the dying person. P.C. also recommends a sign of peace shared with the dying person. In addition, P.C. provides rites for the celebration of viaticum both within and outside Mass. The rituals offer a great degree of flexibility to allow for the condition of the sick or dying person as a primary criterion for determining what is to be included in the celebration.

Symbols. The central symbols of the rite of communion for the sick or dying, apart from the assembly and the word of God common to all the rites found in P.C., are the bread and wine blessed, broken, and shared in grateful remembrance of Jesus Christ's dying and rising. It is not possible in this brief space to explore the full depths of the eucharistic images called into play in the rites of communion and viaticum. Let a few hints suffice to invite the pastoral imagination of presiders, homilists, and musicians to draw out in the celebration the multi-faceted invitation to hope, to faith, and to love offered to the sick and dying, as well as their co-sufferers, in these rites. The eucharistic meal recalls such human experiences as hunger and thirst felt and satisfied, especially in the context of a meal shared with others. Hunger and thirst are experiences of mortality: deprived of food and drink, our very bodies know that they face certain death. Moreover, hunger and thirst may carry hints of human isolation; without a wide web of social cooperation, we cannot eat or drink. In time of famine, we discover the truth of our commitment to the common enterprise of our humanity; we deprive ourselves to feed others' hunger or we fight one another for the few available resources. The sick and dying must face their mortality, with all its attendant isolation. To provide them with food and drink is therefore a significant action. To share food and drink with them from the community's common table, is equally so. Moreover, this food and drink assuage more than the body's hunger and thirst for life. It dispels more than the basic loneliness of the human person. The rite of communion draws upon the rich biblical tradition of manna given by a delivering God to the Israelites facing starvation in the desert (Exodus 16), of water flowing from the rock for those who thirst (Exod 17:1-7), of food and wine provided in abundance at the table of God's kingdom where all the nations are gathered in from their isolation (e.g., Isa 25:6-8). It calls upon such stories as those of the prophet Elijah, discouraged and calling for death, being given bread and water so he could journey on to the mountain where he was to meet God (1 Kgs 19:4-8). It invokes especially the central imagery of the body and blood of Christ, given over and shared on the cross and at the table so that all who receive it in the memorial meal may be gathered into one in the paschal body of Christ in the journey through death to life everlasting. In these rites, there is nourishment for the human spirit in its confrontation with a world potentially reduced to chaos by the prospect of our common death.

The two Roman communion rituals differ slightly in the way they incorporate the symbolic actions of sharing the bread and wine blessed and broken at the community's table. Both rites do emphasize that communion must always be perceived in relationship to the assembly's eucharistic celebration (Holy Communion, 13, 15; P.C., 73). P.C. provides a new theological introduction to the rite of communion for the sick which stresses that the purpose of that communion is not only to unite the sick person to the paschal Christ but also to reunite the eucharistic assembly divided by sickness (73). Representatives sent from the sick persons' ordinary community of worship rather than from a health care facility's chaplaincy department are clearly assumed to be the ordinary ministers of communion to the sick and dying. Moreover, they are encouraged to take communion "from the community's eucharistic celebration," especially from the Sunday eucharist (73). *Holy Communion Outside Mass* seems to imply that communion and viaticum are given either under the form of bread or under the form of wine, depending upon the condition of the communicant. The pastoral directives accompanying the rites of communion and viaticum in P.C. state that communion may be given under the form of wine alone if the communicant is unable to swallow the eucharistic bread (74), but they make no reference to communion under the form of bread alone. In fact, the pastoral notes affixed

to the rite of viaticum state specifically that "The minister should choose the manner of giving communion under both kinds which is suitable in the particular case" (181). This statement is followed by detailed instructions for the storage and transporting of the consecrated wine. Moreover, the actual rites for communion and viaticum seem to assume communion under both kinds as the norm.

Anointing of the Sick

The anointing of the sick is central to the church's ritual pastoral care of the sick. However, it gathers in and focuses the many manifestations of God's healing love provided by the Christian community through their neighborly concern, prayer, visits, and eucharistic ministry. It does not supplant them.

History. The biblical foundation for the sacrament of anointing lies in the healing work of Jesus Christ. The NT contains only two references to an actual anointing of the sick with oil. Mk 6:13, describing the mission of the twelve, simply notes that they cast out demons and healed the sick, anointing them with oil. The association of healing with exorcism appears to be of greater theological interest than this single gospel mention of anointing. Jas 5:14-16 presents a more formal ecclesial rite of anointing the sick. The leaders are the church elders. The recipient is a sick person who is evidently well enough to send for the elders but not well enough to go to the community's place of worship. The ritual consists of prayer and anointing in the name of the Lord. The effect, attributed more to the prayer of faith than to the act of anointing, is that the Lord will "save," "raise up," and if necessary, forgive the sins of the sick person. The meaning of the verbs "save" and "raise up" has been much disputed among scholars who have sought in them an answer to the question of whether the proper effect of the sacrament is a spiritual healing in preparation for death or a physical healing. Most scholars today prefer a more holistic interpretation consonant with biblical anthropology: it is the entire person who is healed through the church's prayer.

Prior to the Carolingian reform in the West, the practice of anointing did not actually follow the ritual pattern set out in the letter of James. Surviving texts of prayers of blessing over the oil, hagiographic writings, and patristic letters and sermons suggest that the faithful developed the custom of taking home the oil blessed by the bishop at the community's eucharist. When illness struck, the sick drank the oil, rubbed it on the afflicted part, rubbed it over the entire body, or others applied it for them. The sick may or may not have been dying, although, as noted above, illness could lead swiftly and unpredictably to death for those who had no access to reliable medical attention. The texts indicate that the blessed oil was used for healing. However, it is an oversimplification to say that the intended effect was simply a physical cure. Anointing with blessed oil was clearly seen to be a religious act invoking the healing power of God over whatever powers of evil or sin were at work in the sick person.

The 9th-century Carolingian reform confirmed the trend toward the clericalization and ritualization of the church's ministry to the sick. Priests were called to the bedside of dying Christians to administer the sacrament of penance, available only once and therefore often delayed until the moment of death. The ritual books that began to appear for their use provided additional prayers for the sick and dying, including rites of anointing and viaticum. The rite of penance preserved the vestiges of the older practice according to which one was admitted to the order of penitents, lived a penitential life for some time, and then was reconciled to the community through absolution. In the case of a deathbed visit, the sick person was admitted to the order of penitents, and then either anointed and reconciled or reconciled and anointed. Viaticum often followed, though it might sometimes be given at another time. The prayers accompanying the rite of anointing took on strongly penitential overtones from their context. When the two sacraments of penance and anointing were eventually separated, anointing retained its penitential character and even penitential consequences. Anointing was sometimes interpreted as a consecration of the dying. Once anointed, the sick person who recovered, as if one returned from the dead, was expected to live a spiritualized, even penitential life, until death. Moreover, like deathbed penance, the anointing came to be considered unrepeatable. Finally, the ritual became increasingly elaborate as anointings and other aspects of the rite were multiplied. These factors caused the faithful to delay the anointing whenever possible until the moment of death, if they received it at all. Thus anointing became in practice a penitential sacrament administered by priests, using oil blessed by the bishop, exclusively to the dying.

This was the practice for which the theologians of the schools fashioned their theological explanation. Although some early Scholastics continued to hold that the sacrament of anointing could effect a physical cure, the predominant opinion came to be that a sacrament, a means of supernatural grace infallibly effective in the recipient rightly disposed, could not be said to confer a bodily cure as its primary effect, especially as, in fact, few of its dying recipients recovered. Rather, its primary effect was considered to be the healing of the soul afflicted by sin as it prepared for death. However, sacraments do not duplicate one another in their effects. Therefore, the anointing could not be said to replicate the removal of original sin effected by baptism or the remission of personal sin accomplished by sacramental penance. Therefore, it was held to remove either the remnants of sin (Dominicans) or venial sin (Franciscans) in immediate preparation for entry into glory. This interpretation further endorsed the practice of delaying the sacrament until the moment of death. By the 14th century, in most of the Western church, the order of the sacraments of the dying had changed from penance, anointing, and viaticum to penance, viaticum, and anointing. "Extreme unction" had indeed become not only the last of the anointings received by the Christian, as the title had first implied, but also anointing in extremis.

The Council of Trent called for no decisive change of practice. In response to the issues perceived to have been raised by the Reformers, the council stated that the sacrament of anointing was instituted by Christ, though "promulgated by James"; that it confers the grace of the Holy Spirit to remove sin and its remnants, to support and strengthen the recipient through trust in God in the face of suffering and the temptations of the devil, and, if helpful for salvation, to effect a physical healing; and that its proper minister is the ordained priest. However, the council did not entirely endorse the theology of the schools. When presented with a proposed document which would have restricted the administration of the sacrament exclusively to the dying, the council required that the draft be reworded to say that the sacrament is to be given to the sick, "especially to those who are so dangerously ill that they seem near to death."

Although the council thus opened the door to the retrieval of the notion of a sacrament of the sick, both pastoral practice and theological discussion continued most commonly to treat "extreme unction" as the sacrament of the dying. In the late 17th and the 18th centuries, liturgical historians paved the way for Pope Benedict XIV to speak of the sacrament for the sick which ought to be available to be given more than once. However, it would appear that in practice, the sacrament continued to be administered largely to the dying or the recently dead, on the assumption that the soul might linger in the body even after all physical signs of life had ceased. The neoscholastic revival of the first part of the 20th century, however, employed a variety of images to reinforce the notion that the purpose of the anointing was to prepare the dying person for glory. Despite the efforts of 20th-century popes to halt the practice of delaying the administration of the sacrament until the person had reached or passed the moment of death, pastoral practice continued for the most part to reflect that theological understanding.

Vatican II, inspired by the historical studies of the scholars of the liturgical movement, endorsed a possible reinterpretation of "extreme unction" by noting that it "may also and more properly be called the anointing of the sick" and that "it is not a sacrament for those only who are at the point of death" (S.C., 73). The council also mandated an adaptation in the number of anointings and the revision of the rite of anointing to "correspond to the varying conditions of the sick who receive the sacrament" (S.C., 75). In response, R.A.P.C.S. provided three rites of anointing, which continue to appear in P.C.: anointing outside Mass, anointing within Mass, and anointing in a hospital or institution. Anointing outside Mass includes introductory rites (greeting, optional sprinkling with holy water, instruction, and penitential rite), a liturgy of the word (reading, response), the liturgy of anointing (litany, laying on of hands, prayer over the oil, anointing, prayer after anointing, the Lord's Prayer), an optional liturgy of holy communion (communion, silent prayer, prayer after communion) and a concluding rite.

Anointing within Mass adds to the structure of an ordinary eucharistic celebration a "reception of the sick" after the greeting, a liturgy of anointing (see above), and a blessing of the sick during the concluding rite. Anointing in a hospital or institution is an abbreviated rite to be used on "those occasions when only the priest and sick person are present and the complete rite cannot be celebrated" (P.C., 149). An even more abbreviated rite of anointing is provided for cases of acute emergency. *P.C.* not only retranslated these rites but also added new prayers for particular pastoral circumstances. Finally, the council decreed the restoration of the sacraments for the dying to their primitive order: penance, anointing, viaticum, to be given in a continuous rite (S.C., 74). Both *R.A.P.C.S.* and *P.C.* comply.

Symbols. The central symbolic actions of the rite of anointing, apart from the gathering of the assembly and the proclamation of the word of God, are the prayer of faith, the laying on of hands, and the anointing with oil (P.C., 104).

The letter of James, as previously noted, identifies the prayer of faith as the key to the effectiveness of the rite of anointing. Like all liturgical actions, the entire rite is structured as an act of prayer on the part of the church, made present in the assembly (P.C., 105) and led in this case by a presiding priest. Only one text appears to identify the "prayer of faith" with the litany prayed for the sick person and the caregivers immediately prior to the laying on of hands (P.C., 121).

The laying on of hands is a gesture widely employed in the sacramental rites of the Roman church. It evokes the human experience of touch as a medium of human relationship and of healing. The human body serves as a boundary which both identifies and separates individual human persons. Touch bridges the separation which, in the case of illness particularly, easily becomes isolation.

Ritualized touch, done with appropriate reverence, acknowledges and reclaims as valuable the embodied person (cf. P.C. 106) removed from the ordinary relational context precisely by a bodily condition defined by the societal environment as disordered and perhaps even dangerous. Moreover, a religious rite of touch summons and reinterprets within the community's faith horizon every experience of the healing power of the human hand as that power is communicated in the various rituals of the medical world. The laying on of hands evokes not only the human experience of touch but also the biblical stories of hands raised or laid on in a gesture invoking God's Spirit in blessing (e.g., Gen 48:14-17; cf. P.C., 106). Among the blessings of the messianic era, when God's Spirit is poured out in profusion (cf. Joel 3:1), is abundant life, untrammeled by disease or death (cf. Isa 25:7-8; Rev 21:1-4). Jesus touches the sick to heal them (e.g., Lk 4:40; cf. P.C. 106) as a sign of the coming reign of God, where life triumphs over every limit of sickness, suffering and mortality. The text of the rite itself interprets the laying on of hands, done in silence, as an invocation of the Spirit (P.C., 106) in petition for "life and health" (P.C., 121 and par.). The imposition of hands upon the sick in the sacrament of anointing bears ritual echoes of the same gesture as it appears in the sacraments of initiation and penance, with all their overtones of life-giving relationships within the community and with God. This gesture also evokes the biblical and liturgical traditions of conferring the Spirit of God on some members of the community to empower them for a role of responsibility. It is true that *P.C.* explicitly in its introductory notes (1, 3) and at least tacitly in its rites, acknowledges the responsibility of the sick to participate in Christ's paschal work of redemption for the sake of others as well as themselves. However, although the sick carry out this responsibility in a particular way through their suffering, or perhaps more profoundly, through their conversion in the midst of suffering, they share this mission with all the baptized. Sickness, and its attendant suffering, are interpreted by the rite as an undesirable condition to be overcome with every possible means (3f., 6) so that the sick can return to the more common ways of participating in the redemptive work of Christ incumbent upon every Christian in ordinary daily life. Initiation, then, seems a more appropriate tool than ordination for interpreting the significance of the laying on of hands in the rite of anointing by the light of the meanings acquired by this gesture through its occurrence in the repertoire of sacramental rites taken as a whole. The sick are called to reaffirm and live out their baptismal commitment in the midst of sickness rather than to assume a new, even permanent role in the community as members of some type of "order of the sick."

The anointing with oil is another symbolic action rich in significance. Although frequently disguised under other names, oil is applied to the human body today as a means of beautification, of refreshment, of healing. In the ancient Mediterranean and therefore biblical world, anointing with oil was also used to beautify, to refresh and to heal. In addition, it was used as a sign of festivity, as a mark of honor, as an agent of strength, as a preparation for burial, and, in religious rituals, as a sign of consecration both of persons and of objects. Moreover, the olive oil itself was a primary source of light and of nourishment. In biblical and in extra-biblical Jewish literature, olive oil becomes another sign of the abundance of life in the promised land (e.g., Deut 7:13), a promise to be fulfilled most completely with the coming of the messianic age. Indeed, olive oil flows in the rivers of paradise (2 En 8:5, Rec. A). Its source is the tree of life, seen as the olive tree, whose fruit is healing, even the healing of mortality itself (cf. 2 En 5, Rec. B; Apoc of Moses 9:3; Rev 22:1-2). In the world of Christian symbols, however, the meanings of anointing with oil are gathered together in the person of Jesus Christ, the Anointed One. The rite of anointing the sick calls upon many of these meanings, particularly those referring to healing, to strengthening, and to the invocation of God's Spirit (P.C., 107), the great symbol of life given in abundance (cf. Gen 1:2; 2:7). Ultimately, however, the anointing conforms the sick person to the paschal Christ whose suffering brings about the eschatological refreshment, health, and life of all peoples. Ritually, it echoes again the sacraments of initiation and ordination, but it preserves a certain distinction by making use of the oil blessed specifically for the sick rather than the oil of catechumens or the chrism used in those other rites. The oil is blessed either by the bishop at the Chrism Mass or by the presiding priest during the sacramental rite of anointing the sick, after the laying on of hands. When using oil blessed by the bishop, the priest offers a prayer of thanksgiving over the oil prior to the anointing itself. Obeying the call of Vatican II for an adaptation in the number of anointings (S.C., 75), the priest anoints only the forehead and hands of the sick person, rather than the five senses, while saying the new sacramental form approved by Pope Paul VI in the Apostolic Constitution "Sacrament of the Anointing of the Sick" (1972) and translated into English as: "Through this holy anointing may the Lord in his love and mercy help you with the grace of the Holy Spirit (R. Amen). May the Lord who frees you from sin save you and raise you up" (P.C., 124 and par.). The ritual adds this note: "Depending upon the culture and traditions of the place, as well as the condition of the sick person, the priest may also anoint additional parts of the body, for example, the area of pain or injury. He does not repeat the sacramental forms" (P.C., 124 and par.).

Pastoral Theological Issues. As the practice of anointing the sick continues to develop, at least two major issues remain unresolved. One concerns the subject of the sacrament, the other its minister.

The Subject of the Sacrament. Throughout the complex history of this rite, the theological interpretation of the sacrament's effect and the pastoral decision about who should be anointed have marched hand in hand. Sometimes pastoral practice has determined theology; sometimes theology has determined pastoral practice. With its cautious statement that "extreme unction . . . may also and more properly be called the anointing of the sick" and its exhortation that "it is not a sacrament for those only who are at the point of death" (S.C., 73), Vatican II gave official impetus to the pastoral question of whether the anointing serves primarily the sick or the dying and its theological corollary concerning the nature of the healing conferred by the sacrament. Both the 1973 *R.A.P.C.S.* and the 1982 *P.C.* define the effect of the sacrament along Tridentine lines: "This sacrament gives the grace of the Holy Spirit to those who are sick: by this grace the whole person is helped and saved, sustained by trust in God, and strengthened against the temptations of the Evil One and against anxiety over death. Thus the sick person is able not only to bear suffering bravely, but also to fight against it. A return to physical health may follow the reception of this sacrament if it will be beneficial to the sick person's salvation. If necessary, the sacrament also provides the sick person with the forgiveness of sins and the completion of Christian penance" (P.C., 6). The priorities are noteworthy: the foremost effect attributed to the sacrament is the salvation of the whole person in the midst of the challenge to faith and to hope posed by the experience of sickness. The focus of the sacrament appears to be on sustaining the person in the midst of illness, however brief that might be in an emergency situation, rather than on preparing the person for certain death. Both physical cure and the forgiveness of sins are secondary effects contingent upon the need of the recipient. Popular efforts to identify the sacrament's healing effect exclusively as bodily recovery or cure of the sinful soul in preparation for death founder upon the holistic vision of this text.

However, between 1973 and 1982, many pastoral decisions concerning the proper recipient of the sacrament seem to have been based upon one of these two popular theologies, as attested by experience, by the periodical literature of those years, and, finally, by the significant revisions made in the 1982 ritual. The 1973 text specified that the subject of the anointing is "those who are dangerously ill due to sickness or old age," but cautioned against scrupulosity in determining the seriousness of the illness (8). In fact, the general tenor of the rite's pastoral prescriptions was to make the sacrament more accessible than it had been previously. The rite recommended the anointing of dangerously ill candidates for surgery (R.A.P.C.S./P.C., 10), elderly persons "if they are in weak condition although no dangerous illness is present" (R.A.P.C.S./P.C., 11), and sick children "if they have sufficient use of reason to be comforted by this sacrament" (R.A.P.C.S./P.C., 12). Moreover, the sacrament could be repeated in case of a new need (R.A.P.C.S./P.C., 9). However, although retaining the notion of mortal illness as a condition for anointing, the text does take a fairly clear stance against using the sacrament as immediate preparation for death. In fidelity to the position taken by Vatican II, and, indeed, supported by the theology articulated in *R.A.P.C.S./P.C., 6,* quoted above in its

1982 translation, the rite not only discourages delaying the celebration of the sacrament until the moment of death (R.A.P.C.S./P.C., 13) but, in fact, forbids the anointing of even the recently dead unless there is sufficient doubt of death to permit a conditional anointing (R.A.P.C.S./ P.C., 15). It does permit the anointing of an unconscious or demented person "if, as Christian believers, they would have asked for it were they in control of their faculties" (R.A.P.C.S./P.C., 14). The ritual reiterated the traditional understanding of viaticum as the sacrament for the dying, an understanding enshrined among the so-called precepts of the church, one of which was that the dying Catholic must seek to receive holy communion (R.A.P.C.S., 27, 116; P.C., 26, 237). The precept does not mention anointing. Nevertheless, this stance is not unequivocal, perhaps because, even now, the path through illness to death follows no neat and predictable progression. Sickness may be long and slow, or short and swift to yield to death. In cases of emergency, the sick ideally receive the three sacraments, penance, anointing and viaticum. If time is short and choices must be made, anointing is to be omitted. However, if the dying person lingers after receiving viaticum, he or she is to be anointed. Moreover, if the nature of the illness prevents the person from receiving communion, he or she is to be anointed instead (R.A.P.C.S./P.C., 30).

Pastoral practice from 1973 to 1982 seems to have been equally ambivalent. On the one hand, priests continued to be called to the bedside of the dying and even of the recently dead to confer "the last rites," usually perceived popularly as the sacrament of anointing rather than of viaticum. Even eucharistic ministers now authorized to give viaticum will often say that they have never heard of or seen the rite in practice, though they are quite familiar with the anointing of the sick. On the other hand, the communal cele-

brations of anointing endorsed by the rite itself (R.A.P.C.S., 67; cf. P.C., 108) seem especially to have become occasions for issuing a general invitation to receive the sacrament if one felt the need for healing from any kind of physical ailment at all, however slight. Emphasis was frequently placed upon the curative properties of the sacrament, with little or no attention to its soteriological significance. The rising popularity of charismatic healing seems to have given added impetus to this trend. Moreover, it became commonplace in many communities to offer the anointing regularly, even monthly, to all of the aging, often defined as those over 65, whether or not they suffered from the "weakened condition" specified by the rite. Finally, the sacrament was frequently offered during retreats or on other occasions as a means of "healing" whatever form of suffering or loss one might be experiencing, whether or not physical illness was its cause.

Theological reflection kept pace with pastoral practice. Although some theologians continued to explore the meaning of the sacrament in relation to the dying, the majority seem to have concentrated their efforts on articulating its significance for the sick. They have employed the tools of historical research, biblical studies, sacramental theology, theological anthropology, and ritual hermeneutics largely to affirm and amplify the holistic vision of sickness and sacramental healing found in R.A.P.C.S./ P.C. itself. Despite disagreements on individual points, there seems to be some consensus that the healing offered in this sacrament, as a salvific action of Christ in the church, must be understood in terms of the soteriological needs specific to the person and community in the midst of the actual human experience of sickness. It cannot be interpreted exclusively in terms of either bodily or disembodied human reality.

P.C., both as it appeared originally in

1982 and as it was subsequently corrected in the light of later 1983 Code of Canon Law, reflects the major movements in both pastoral practice and theological reflection. In a significant departure from the 1973 text, *P.C.* identifies the proper subjects for anointing as "the faithful whose health is seriously impaired by sickness or old age." An accompanying footnote draws attention to the authors' explicit decision to remove the notion of danger of death from consideration with the intention of excluding two extremes in pastoral practice: the sacrament is not to be restricted to those who are dying; nor is it to be "given indiscriminately or to any person whose health is not seriously impaired." It is thus clearly identified as a sacrament for those who are wrestling with serious illness. This revision is fully consistent both with the definition of the sacrament's effects (R.A.P.C.S./P.C., 6) and with the breadth of the tradition revealed through historical studies. It is underlined by the structural decision to locate the sacrament of anointing, together with visits and communion, among the rites for the sick (Part I) and the sacrament of viaticum, together with prayers for the dying and rites for exceptional circumstances among the rites for the dying (Part II). However, as in *R.A.P.C.S.*, the distinction is not absolute: Part II does include the continuous rite of penance, anointing and viaticum for the dying and a short rite of anointing for emergency use. Several further emendations make the sacrament still more accessible: in case of doubt concerning the adequacy of their use of reason, sick children are to be anointed (12); in case of doubt, those who appear to be dead but may still be living are to be anointed not conditionally but in the usual way (15). Perhaps more significant, the rite incorporates the decision made earlier by the U.S. bishops that the sacrament may be given to those determined to be suffering from serious mental illness (53). Given the nebulous interaction between the bodily and the spiritual dimensions of the human person in every illness, this decision frees the minister from undue scruples concerning the degree of physical disorder present in some types of psychological dysfunction, including the complex cases of substance addiction. However, it does hold open to some extent the door the ritual attempts to close when it specifies that the sacrament may not be given to those whose need for "healing" is prompted by some form of distress other than serious physical illness. Although the rite does not say so, such needs might sometimes be more appropriately met through the sacraments of eucharist or penance. Two other emendations place restrictions on the administration of the sacrament. One is quite explicit: the sacrament may not be given to "anyone who remains obdurately in open and serious sin" (15). As early as 416, Pope Innocent made clear in a letter to Decentius, Bishop of Gubbio, that the sacrament was not to be given to penitents. Still less, then, should it be given to one who had not even begun the process of sacramental reconciliation. The second emendation is less apparent. The 1973 text (8) refers to the sacrament's subjects as "those who are dangerously ill ...," whereas the 1982 text refers to them as "those of the faithful whose health is seriously impaired ..." Particularly when taken together with the explicit exclusion of serious public sinners, the addition of the phrase "of the faithful," a technical term referring to the baptized, suggests a desire to clarify the fact that the sacrament is reserved to those who are in full eucharistic communion with the church. This clarification, perhaps slight, seems again to echo the tradition articulated by Pope Innocent, who said that catechumens as well as penitents were ineligible to receive the anointing. Both of these emendations have obvious implications for pastoral practice.

Publication of *P.C.* did not, of course, place closure upon the issue of the meaning and subject of anointing. Both pastoral practice and its accompanying theological reflection continue to raise and to explore the question of the sacrament's effect and therefore its appropriate recipients.

The Minister of the Sacrament. Both *R.A.P.C.S.* and *P.C.* follow the Council of Trent in stating that "[t]he priest is the only proper minister of the anointing of the sick" (R.A.P.C.S./P.C., 16). However, both the general ecclesial climate and pastoral need have raised the issue of restoring in some form the pre-Carolingian practice of lay anointing of the sick, using oil blessed by the bishop. The restoration of the permanent diaconate has led to the proposal that deacons be permitted to anoint the sick, although there seems to be no historical evidence to support a specifically diaconal rite of anointing. The employment of lay ministers to the sick, particularly as professional chaplains, has led to a similar concern that those who actually minister regularly to the sick be allowed to anoint those in their care. The creation of special ministers of communion who give the bread/wine consecrated by a priest to the sick has suggested the similar establishment of special ministers of anointing who would apply the oil blessed by the bishop to the sick. The growing shortage of priests has added considerable urgency to these proposals. However, the decision of the Council of Trent is held to be binding upon the present practice of the Roman church. Contemporary theologians continue to explore the issue of the historical relativity of the Tridentine position in order to assist in opening the way for a change in current discipline.

Pastoral Care of the Sick is the title both of a ritual book and of the multifaceted healing work through which the church continues to actualize the mission of Jesus Christ to establish the reign of God in a world still fragmented by sin, disease and death.

Jennifer Glen, "Rites of Healing: A Reflection in Pastoral Theology," In *Alternative Futures for Worship*, Vol. 7, *Anointing of the Sick*, ed. by Peter E. Fink, SJ (Collegeville MN: The Liturgical Press, 1987): 33-63. Jennifer Glen, "Sickness and Symbol: The Promise of the Future," *Worship* 54 (1980): 397-411. Gisbert Greshake, "Extreme Unction or Anointing of the Sick? A Plea for discrimination," trans. by Patrick J. Madden, *Review for Religious* 45 (1986): 435-451. Charles Gusmer, *And You Visited Me: Sacramental Ministry to the Sick and Dying* (New York: Pueblo,1984). Adolf Knauber, *Pastoral Theology of the Anointing of the Sick*, trans. by Matthew J. O'Connell (Collegeville MN: The Liturgical Press, 1975). William F. Lynch, *Images of Hope* (Notre Dame IN: The University of Notre Dame Press, 1974). Thomas Marsh, "A Theology of Anointing the Sick," *The Furrow* 29 (1980): 89-101. Nathan Mitchell, *Cult and Controversy: The Worship of the Eucharist Outside Mass* (New York: Pueblo, 1982). Claude Ortemann, *Le sacrement des malades: histoire et signification* (Paris: Editions du Chalet). David N. Power, "Let the Sick Man Call," *Heythrop Journal* 19 (1978): 256-270. Philippe Rouillard, "From Human Meal to Christian Eucharist," In *Living Bread, Saving Cup*, ed. by R. Kevin Seasoltz (Collegeville MN: The Liturgical Press): 126-157. Alfred C. Rush, "The Eucharist, the Sacrament of the Dying in Christian Antiquity," *The Jurist* 34 (1974): 10-35. Orlo Strunk, "The Human Sciences and the Experiences of Diminishment and Dissolution," In *Alternative Futures for Worship*, Vol. 7, *Anointing of the Sick*, ed. by Peter E. Fink (Collegeville MN: The Liturgical Press, 1987): 17-32. John J. Ziegler, *Let Them Anoint the Sick* (Collegeville MN: The Liturgical Press, 1987).

JENNIFER GLEN, C.C.V.I.

SICK, SACRAMENT OF, MINISTERS IN

In *Pastoral Care of the Sick: Rites of Anointing and Viaticum* (P.C.), the description of those who have a ministry to the sick is a broad and comprehensive one. Before it even mentions the ministry which belongs to members of the community in faith, *Pastoral Care* stresses the role of doctors and other medical personnel who work to heal or alleviate the suffering of the sick. Their efforts are a fulfillment of Christ's command to visit the sick (P.C., 4), and this is the case whether or not they themselves believe in

Christ: "Every scientific effort to prolong life and every act of care for the sick, on the part of any person, may be considered a preparation for the Gospel and a sharing in Christ's healing ministry" (P.C., 32). Sickness and the suffering that accompanies it are natural realities and not a form of punishment for personal sins. Such suffering is a sign of the condition of a world alienated from God's original plan for it (P.C., 2). The work of medical personnel to overcome the physical suffering that is a sign of this alienation is thus a part of God's redemptive plan, a sign of the kingdom already begun and still to be fully accomplished.

Within the community of faith, the body of Christ, whenever one member of the body suffers, all members have a share in that suffering. Such is the organic and intimate nature of membership in Christ's church (1 Cor 12:26). The disruption caused by illness and the challenge to personal and corporate faith that it can create become disruption and challenge for the community of faith. This changed situation is most deeply experienced by the members of the community whose lives are most closely bound to the sick through family ties and friendship. And it is felt by the community as a whole assembled for worship as the community realizes the absence of those separated from it by illness and prays for their healing.

Christ's own concern for the physical and spiritual good of the sick is carried on by the whole church. "This ministry is the common responsibility of all Christians, who should visit the sick, remember them in prayer, and celebrate the sacraments with them" (P.C., 43). Members of the faith community who have a particular role in this ministry of comfort are the family and friends of the sick, priests, deacons, and other ministers within the community, for example, special ministers of communion. The priest is re-

sponsible for the coordination of these various ministries and for himself visiting the sick and leading the celebration of the sacraments with them, particularly the sacrament of the anointing of the sick (P.C., 44). This vision of the ministry which the Christian community has to its sick members is significantly different from that found in the previous Roman ritual (1614). The 1614 ritual saw the care of the sick as almost exclusively the responsibility of the local pastor. Only if "legitimately impeded" from carrying out these duties could he associate other ministers with himself in this task (other priests and even lay people). *Pastoral Care* thus contains a broadened view of ministry and a renewed ecclesiology which find their fullest expression in the communal celebration of the new rites for the sick.

The concern of the community is first expressed in the care shown to the sick person and his or her family by neighbors and friends. They are usually the first to learn of illness and are often best placed to gauge the extent and effects on the sick and on family members. The uncertainty and fear brought about by illness are felt not only by the sick but also by the members of the family as they face the changes in family expectations and routine that sickness imposes. By their solicitude and readiness to help with the practical details of life (for example, food preparation and child care), neighbors and friends can be the first to minister on behalf of the community and can help to keep the community and its pastoral ministers informed of any changes in the family's situation.

The pastoral concern offered by the Christian community as a whole receives particular expression when it gathers as an assembly for worship. The community recalls those members who because of illness are physically unable to take part as well as family members and others who care for the sick. This intercession is particularly appropriate on the Lord's Day (P.C., 43). Through the general intercessions at Mass and the intercessions at morning prayer and evening prayer, the ministry of the whole community is brought to bear in a powerful way as it assumes its privileged role of intercession on behalf of a world replete with suffering and hungry for healing.

This pastoral solicitude receives concrete and full expression through an array of other sacramental activities suited to the circumstances of illness. This activity includes visits to the sick accompanied by prayer, communion of the sick, the sacrament of anointing, and, in the case of sick persons preparing for death, communion in the form of viaticum. Underlying these various forms of prayer and worship are several simple actions and gestures offered by the community's ministers, gestures laden with human and Christian meaning. They are the simple gestures of touching and embracing, the tracing of the sign of the cross on the forehead, the laying on of hands, and the anointing with blessed oil of the forehead and hands and, as circumstances suggest, other parts of the body, for example, the place of pain or injury (P.C., 124). Through these sacramental actions the ministers of the community express Christ's healing and strengthening presence and the solidarity of the community with those who because of illness are physically separated from full participation in its activities and worship.

In *Pastoral Care of the Sick*, the laying on of hands that is done in the rite of anointing, and may be done in the context of visits to the sick, as well as the anointing itself are reserved to the priest celebrant. All other sacramental gestures may appropriately be used by other pastoral ministers, who may lead the various rites for the sick with the exception of the anointing rite in its several forms, penance, and viaticum celebrated within Mass (P.C., 44).

Regardless of who the minister is, these physical and sacramental signs are offered and celebrated within a whole context of communal care and concern, and it is this lively reality that makes these moments full actions of the church by which the Lord conveys love and healing. A community that has surrounded the sick and their families with practical, pastoral solicitude, that is, the compassion of Christ, ensures that the rites which it celebrates with its sick, particularly the anointing of the sick, have their full sacramental force as moments of care and healing for those in need. The community's concern is then visibly expressed in the actual celebration of the rites through the presence and participation of members of the community. This presence helps to bring out the communal context more vividly (P.C., 33), a point given even stronger emphasis in connection with the anointing rite: "Because of its very nature as a sign, the sacrament of the anointing of the sick should be celebrated with members of the family and other representatives of the Christian community whenever possible. Then the sacrament is seen for what it is—a part of the prayer of the church and an encounter with the Lord (P.C., 99).

Among the ministers referred to in *Pastoral Care* in addition to priests, deacons and special ministers of communion receive consistent mention. Care of the sick has traditionally been associated with the role of the deacon, as part of the responsibility which the deacon has for the ministry of charity in the community. Special ministers of communion are given particular attention as those who can help to ensure that the sick are able to receive communion frequently, particularly on the Lord's Day, which is the community's special day to assemble for the eucharist (P.C., 73). This connection between the Sunday eucharistic assembly and its sick members is difficult to achieve regularly through the ministry of priest and deacon. Their responsibilities on the Lord's Day often prevent their giving the necessary time to visit and take communion to the sick. Special ministers of communion can become the way in which the community sustains this contact on Sunday and, if available in sufficient numbers, they can help to ensure that visits with the sick are not hurried because of the numbers to be seen. The importance of this ministry cannot be stressed too strongly: "The faithful who are ill are deprived of their rightful and accustomed place in the eucharistic community. In bringing communion to them the minister of communion represents Christ and manifests faith and charity on behalf of the whole community toward those who cannot be present at the eucharist. For the sick, the reception of communion is not only a privilege but also a sign of support and concern shown by the Christian community for its members who are ill" (P.C., 73).

The near monopoly of the priest (pastor) in ministry to the sick that is assumed in the ritual of 1614 was the result of an evolution in pastoral ministry over the course of the first millennium of Christianity. This can be illustrated by the anointing of the sick in particular. For the first 800 or so years the issue of who blessed the oil for use in anointing the sick was of greater concern than the question of who actually applied it to the sick. Historical sources indicated that the oil should be blessed by the bishop, as a sign of the unity and compassion of the whole local church in its care of the sick. The oil could then be taken home by families and applied either by a family member or by the sick themselves (see *Apostolic Tradition* of Hippolytus of Rome, c. 215). Anointing by various members of the community was not uncommon. The oil could also be used by the presbyters or elders of the community in ministry to the sick (Jas 5:14-16), but these ministers should not be confused

with the ordained clergy of today. Even at a later date when lay and presbyteral anointings were distinguished (for example, Pope Innocent I in the early 5th century and Bede in the late 7th and early 8th centuries), no particular weight was given to one over the other. The 9th century saw the beginnings of a more exclusive emphasis on priestly anointing. This coincided with a growing concern with the priestly ministry as such and with the increasing association of anointing with the practice of once-in-a-lifetime or deathbed penance. By the 12th century, sacramental anointing had come to be distingushed from other kinds of anointings of the sick as was anointing by ordained ministers from anointings by lay persons.

The historical evolution with regard to anointing of the sick is instructive of what happened to ministry to the sick as a whole. The 1614 ritual represents the eventual concentration of this once rich and active communal care of the sick in the ministry of the priest alone. *Pastoral Care of the Sick* opens up once again the possibility of making this ministry the active concern of the whole community. This new ritual book also can become the basis for the ongoing evolution of ministry to the sick. Because of the association of the diaconate with the church's work of charity, it would seem appropriate for the restored diaconate to have a greater role in the coordination of the various ministries to the sick. The laying on of hands, which even in visits to the sick is at present reserved to the priest, would seem a gesture that could accompany any care of the sick, whether this is done by a priest, deacon, or lay person. And the future evolution of the sacrament of anointing, now restored to its proper place as the sacrament of the sick, may well include a broader understanding of who may anoint. Historical precedent would seem to allow this to become a liturgical celebration led by a deacon, especially if that deacon has particular responsibility for the local community's ministry to the sick.

Regardless of its future, the present experience of ministry to the sick has great possibility. In *Pastoral Care of the Sick* the church has in its possession a worthy instrument for a full recovery of a lively and passionate care on behalf of the community of faith for those of its members who suffer from illness that prevents them taking full part in its life.

See **Sick, pastoral care of the**

JAMES M. SCHELLMAN

SICKNESS, CHRISTIAN VIEW OF

Most religious traditions have attempted to make sense of illness and disease. The interpretative frameworks they employ involve elements of medicine, religion and magic, and in some religions all three elements are totally interwined. The basic question frequently dealt with is the cause of illness, though this is scarcely adequate. A theological and pastoral approach to illness cannot be reduced to questions of origin and cause; it must answer the question of the significance of illness in the economy of creation and salvation. This significance is closely tied with the meaning of suffering in human existence.

Illness is a complex reality. It is a physical, spiritual, psychological state with deep social and cultural consequences. Emphasis in the recent past has been put on the physical causes of illness and on the necessary science and technology to eradicate illness. Today, however, there is a greater awareness of the social and cultural factors affecting health and illness and a deeper understanding of the interactions of the physical and emotional.

Given the concept of health as a structural and functional wholeness, disease can be defined as the breakdown of such wholeness and integration. Illness represents a disharmony of many forces and fronts. A common denominator of serious illness is the radical disruption of one's ordinary life. Sickness modifies the ordinary patterns of women/men's existence, sets them out of the ordinary sphere of their social activities and roles, and brings about a new personal world. Such an occurrence can be accompanied by melancholy, confusion, anger, outrage, depression and a variety of other confusing feelings. The collapse of one's ordinary world often leads to passivity and a sense of helplessness.

Because religion is a basic shaper of attitudes and dispositions, Christianity as a religious tradition can profoundly inform the way believers perceive and respond to illness, and can provide a significant resource for coping with it. The relationship between the experience of illness and faith is a two-way street. If Christian faith can help form interpretations of sickness, sickness itself can alter the shape of one's faith. Severe illness often leads to questions about God and involves a re-evaluation of one's whole faith-stance.

Illness in the Hebrew Scriptures

The Christian stance towards illness has been shaped by a long faith tradition with roots in the Hebrew Scriptures. Judaism is marked by its monotheism. God is creator of everything and the existence of everything including man and woman depends totally upon God. Everything is subordinated to God, even evil forces. Furthermore, God is characterized as a God of justice and compassion, attributes revealed in God's covenantal relationship with Israel. Within that theology illness cannot be attributed to a god of evil, such as the spirit of darkness in Zoroastrianism. In Israel a close relationship exists between sin and illness: illness being God's punishment for sinfulness. In Deut 32:39, God affirms:

"I kill and I make alive; I wound and I heal." Both health and sickness are under God's control. The acknowledgement of and repentance for sin is necessary for the restoration of health (Ps 32:3-5). Sickness is finally not simply vindictive punishment, but a corrective, a possibility for spiritual growth.

Illness in the NT

In its approach to illness, the NT reflects a greater influence by Persian thought than the earlier Jewish writing. We find in the NT a certain modified dualism. Within God's creation, which is basically good, there exist certain evil powers such as Satan who insinuate evil into the world. A real struggle between such forces and God is taking place in the world.

Jesus himself, whose ministry is characterized by healing, appears to break through the understanding of illness as a consequence of sinfulness and thus posits illness in a very different light (Jn 9:31, 11:4; Lk 13:1-11). Jesus does not declare that illness contributes to one's salvation. Nor does he interpret illness as divine punishment. God does not provoke illness, either as a reprisal or to put women/men to the test. Illness is seen as going against God's compassionate love and as a contradiction to God's plan for creation.

Illness in the Church's Tradition

The development of NT material in the early church took various directions. It seems that the Alexandrian and Cappadocian Fathers, especially Basil, were the first to develop a theological doctrine of illness. Their positions were influenced by their understanding of original justice and original sin. Women and men were created to image God, a God understood as impassible and unchangeable. So whence illness? Illness can only be seen as a consequence of original sin, the product of human sinfulness.

Basil offers various reasons why Christians are affected by illness. Illness can have a corrective effect. It can be seen as punishment for sin. It can test one's faith and provide a way to develop detachment and the acceptance of death. Discerning the cause or reason for illness was important since it determined whether one should seek a possible relief from a physician. Only when sickness is the result of natural causes or as a corrective should a physician be summoned. When sickness is discerned as punishment, it should simply be accepted. Some of this understanding could still be found much later in the church. In 1829, for example, Leo XII declared, "Whoever allows himself to be vaccinated ceases to be a child of God. Smallpox is a judgement of God, the vaccination is a challenge toward heaven."

Throughout the history of Christianity there has always been a degree of tension between theology and medicine. In certain positions recourse should be to God alone since God is the source and also the healer of ills for others. In other positions physicians can be understood as God's instrument in healing the sick. Because of these differing positions, the relationship between the cure of the soul and the care of the body has often been conflictual. A canon promulgated at the Fourth Lateran Council in 1215 (22 *Decretales* 5.38.13) affirmed the physician's obligation to call a confessor before taking care of the patient.

Following the practice recommended in Jas 5:14-16, the early church employed a ritual for physical healing which later came to be used almost exclusively as anointing for the terminally ill and as a preparation for death. Compassion for the sick found expression in other ways as well. Already in 372 we find the establishment of a charitable institution, the *Basileias*, which became the prototype of Christian hospitals. Gregory of Nazianzus in his panegyric on St. Basil refers to this institution as a place "where disease is regarded in a religious light . . . and sympathy put to a test" (*On St. Basil*, 63). St. Jerome also recounts the establishment of a hospital in Rome by a lady friend, Fabiola. He narrates how she gathered the abandoned sick and nursed them (*Epistle* 77.6.1-2).

Such institutions as anointing the sick and the establishment of hospitals follow Jesus' example of compassion, whose object was not only the soul but also the body. Moreover, the visitation and the care of the sick has always been encouraged and understood as a basic expression of one's love for God (Mt 25:35-40).

Christian Attitude Toward Illness

What meaning, what attitude should a Christian have towards illness? Contemporary existentialist thought has pointed out several important elements of sickness as a state of being. Sickness re-emphasizes the experience of contingency and the fragility of human existence. Sickness, with all the limitations it imposes on the body, can bring about a deeper grasp of human freedom. Recovery from sickness often entails a greater exercise of one's freedom. Every illness is a limitation upon freedom and an opportunity to transcend such limitation. While illness often tends to isolate, it also leads to a greater sense of dependence upon the "Other." The meaning of every illness is dying and in a real way every healing is resurrection. In a sense illness is always the passage point, the threshold between a dying and a living. Sickness is liminal. Sickness is the enemy of life.

The Christian response to illness is a stance of acceptance and of refusal. Acceptance is necessary since illness is the consequence of our finitude and the precariousness of our existence. Refusal is also necessary, for sickness, which is a negative element in life, is often an impediment to human development,

weakening one's capacity for spiritual development and self-understanding.

Pastoral Approaches

Conflicting views on the cause, nature and meaning of illness have made a pastoral approach to illness difficult. In the medical approach, there is more focus on the illness than on the ill person. In the religious approach, in contrast, there is more attention given to the afflicted person than to the affliction. A holistic pastoral approach would have to pay attention to both the illness and the person.

Many contemporary illnesses such as hypertension, cancer and AIDS do not easily lend themselves to one single pastoral approach. These illnesses are deeply related to stress, to lifestyles and to relationships. Illness itself affects a person's relationships, to God, to oneself, and to one's family and friends. In many cases sickness is correlative to sin, not in the sense that it is sent upon an individual as punishment, but as a result of personal decision or action. The etiology of many diseases can be directly related to the lifestyle individuals have created for themselves. There is clearly personal responsibility and possible guilt. A pastoral approach to illness must recognize the tendency of afflicted persons either to perceive their sickness as punishment or to excuse themselves completely from responsibility. Furthermore a pastoral approach must recognize the need to emphasize Jesus' attitude toward the sick. To exhort a sick person to offer her/his suffering to God would imply that there is some virtue in remaining unwell. Jesus never questions the afflicted person's desire for healing. He in fact encourages it. Illness is not meant of itself to "sanctify" us or to test our faith. It serves to invite us into the mystery of God's own suffering. What the paschal mystery reveals to us is not the necessity of suffering for salvation, but the great truth that, although sickness tends to isolate us and cause us to withdraw, God is our companion, a fellow-sufferer with us.

See **Suffering; Healing**

Jack Harold Kahn, *Job's Illness: Loss, Grief and Integration, a Psychological Interpretation* (New York: Pergamon Press, 1975). L. Bowman, *The Importance of Being Sick* (Wilmington: Consortium Books, 1976). Susan Sontag, *Illness As Metaphor* (New York: Farrar, Strauss and Giroux, 1978). Daniel Berrigan, *We Die Before We Live: Talking With the Very Ill* (New York: Seabury, 1980). Norman Cousins, *Anatomy of Illness As Perceived by the Patient* (Toronto: Bantam Books, 1981). Joseph H. Fichter, S.J., *Religion and Pain* (New York: Crossroad, 1981). B.M. Sourkes, *Psychological Aspects of Life-Threatening Illness* (Pittsburgh: University of Pittsburgh Press, 1982). J.L. Empereur, *Prophetic Anointing: God's Call to the Sick, the Elderly and the Dying* (Wilmington, Delaware: Glazier, 1982). Gerald May, *Addiction and Grace* (San Francisco: Harper and Row, 1988). David Power, "Let the Sick Man Call," *The Heythrop Journal* 9 (July 1978): 256-270. Jennifer M. Glen, "Sickness and Symbol: The Promise of the Future," *Worship* 54 (November 1980): 397-411.

LUCIEN J. RICHARD, O.M.I.

SILENCE, LITURGICAL ROLE OF

In addition to the symbols, words, gestures, and music which together constitute the liturgy, there is silence, a vital dimension of liturgical prayer. In the context of the liturgy, silence may be viewed as an activity of the gathered assembly. It is an expression of the assembly's corporate attentiveness to the word of God proclaimed in the scriptures, and of its receptivity to the Spirit present in the celebration of Christ's mysteries in memory and in hope. The role of silence in the liturgy is not properly understood as an occasion for members of the assembly to engage in private, mental prayer, or to practice meditation undistracted by the liturgical action. Rather, when liturgy is viewed as a community's response to the divine initiative in word and sacrament, silence is understood as that dimension which enables the person and community to be brought more fully into the mystery of Christ's presence celebrated in liturgy.

Silence is a necessary dimension of all liturgical activity. The Foreword to the American edition of the *Sacramentary* draws attention to the importance of silence for eucharistic worship, but what is said of silence has implications for all liturgical celebration. "The proper use of periods of silent prayer and reflection will help render the celebration less mechanical and impersonal and lend a more prayerful spirit to the liturgical rite. Just as there should be no celebration without song, so too there should be no celebration without periods for silent prayer and reflection" (p. 13).

Similarly, the significance of silence for all liturgical activity is brought to the fore in the *General Instruction of the Liturgy of the Hours*. Care should be taken in liturgical services to assure that "at the proper times all observe a reverent silence" (201). Silence is also suggested so that those at prayer might receive in their hearts "the full sound of the voice of the Holy Spirit" and unite their prayer to the word of God and to the prayer of the whole church (202). To this end, intervals of silence are placed after the recitation of the psalms and concluded with psalm prayers. Silence also follows the readings during the liturgy of the hours.

Historically, the role of silence in the eucharistic liturgy may be viewed from three perspectives. First, there are those periods of silence which are intrinsic to the liturgy itself. Second, there are the silent, or barely audible, prayers of private devotion said by the presiding minister. Finally, there is the silent recitation by the presiding minister of those prayers properly said aloud, or at least intended to be said aloud at their inception.

This last form of silent prayer is found in some of the historic liturgies in which major parts of the eucharistic prayer were recited in silence. This was linked to the notion that the priest alone entered and celebrated the awesome mystery of sacrifice.

As for the second form, during the later Middle Ages, priests were furnished with private prayers to be said silently at certain parts of the Mass, and some of the public prayers began to be said secretly. All of this was connected with the developing notion of the priest's role in offering the sacrifice and celebrating the mysteries. Very few of these silent prayers remain for the presiding minister in today's liturgy because it was recognized that the recitation of such prayers tended to separate his action from the action of the assembly.

As an integral dimension of the eucharistic liturgy, silence disposes an assembly to listen attentively in response to the divine initiative. *The General Instruction of the Roman Missal* (esp. 9, 12, 55) underscores the importance of listening in silent attention as a vital form of liturgical participation. Both the proclamation of the word and the recitation of the presidential prayers are expressive of the "dialogical" character of liturgy, calling for the undivided attention of the assembly and its wholehearted response at their conclusion.

The revised *Roman Missal* either prescribes or suggests the following among various times for silent prayer: before the blessing of water or the penitential rite during the introductory rites; after the invitation to pray (*oremus*), before continuing with the opening prayer; after the readings and homily; after communion; and again, unless silence has already been observed after communion, between the invitation to pray (*oremus*) and the postcommunion prayer

Silence need not be restricted to these regular and customary times. It may be useful to note briefly that the practice of silent prayer before and after the liturgy increased during those periods of history when times of silence integral to the liturgy waned. This would seem to warrant due attention to the role of silence as an intrinsic dimension of liturgy alongside symbol, word, gesture and music in appropriating the fullness of Christ's mysteries celebrated in liturgy.

Kevin W. Irwin, "Liturgy: An Experience of Prayer," *Liturgy, Prayer and Spirituality* (New York: Paulist, 1984): 249-276. Cyprian Vagaggini, *Theological Dimensions of the Liturgy* (Collegeville, MN: Liturgical Press, 1976), using the analytical index under "Silence." "Foreword," *Sacramentary* (New York: Catholic Book Publishing Company, 1974). "General Instruction of the Liturgy of the Hours," and "General Instruction of the Roman Missal," in *Documents on the Liturgy, 1963-1979: Conciliar, Papal, and Curial Texts* (Collegeville, MN: Liturgical Press, 1982).

MICHAEL DOWNEY

SIN, EXPERIENCE OF

The concept of sin is central to Christian faith. The gospels present the good news of Christ as victory over sin, and the freedom he brings as the forgiveness of sin. Christian liturgy uses symbols indicating faith in the forgiveness of sin, provides texts for the celebration of this belief, and frequently refers to the many and varied forms that sin takes in human life. Without a consciousness of sin, we cannot make sense of the penitential aspect of many liturgical celebrations. At the high point of the eucharist we are reminded that the blood of Christ is shed "so that sins may be forgiven." Sin is one of the basic words of Christian tradition, as fundamental as "grace" or God. In fact, what really distinguishes Christianity is its attitude to sin, and this has been an important element in the evangelizing force of the Christian message, which not only preaches repentance but promises forgiveness even of the greatest faults.

Sin is essentially the free and deliberate disobedience of a creature to the known will of God. It is primarily a religious and theological reality, a symbol which expresses our alienation from God. Though it involves moral fault and moral evil, it is much more. It is a mysterious phenomenon whose roots escape human understanding. As the total Christian vision gives meaning to the mystery of the world and human life, sin is the symbol which expresses the darker side of our relationship with God. As symbol it was subject to historical and cultural development, from biblical times to the present day, but theological reflection has added little of substance to what is implicit in the NT.

In the early centuries the understanding of sin was affected by the practice of public penance, then later by feudal notions, and from the 12th century onwards by the organization of confessional practice and the elaboration of a corpus of moral theology concerned with law and measurement. Freudian psychology in its earlier years was used to explain sin in non-moral terms, and the secularizing forces of recent decades made sin problematic, if not archaic, by removing it from its religious context and depriving it of its central meaning. For Catholics, the more positive approach to worldly realities espoused by the Second Vatican Council, and a reaction against the church's traditional "sin-grid" led to a marked decline in confessional practice and some confusion in the understanding of sin. But the recognition of demonic forces in contemporary civilization has led to a new emphasis on the reality of sin, and theologians are now trying to make the symbol come alive in ways that will make sense in today's world.

Biblical Background. Any new understanding of the concept, however, must be rooted in its biblical background, because sin is a religious dimension before being ethical. King David's sins of adultery and murder were certainly against a fellow human being and the order of society, but in the moment of conversion he acknowledged them as sins against God. The psalmist goes to the heart of the matter when he exclaims to God: "Against you, you only, have I sinned and done what is evil" (Ps 51:4).

There is no special word in Hebrew for the theological notion of sin, but the OT uses different words to describe what the Jewish people understood by sin. The most common is the verb meaning "to miss the mark," not simply a mistake in judgment, but a failure to reach a goal, and this could be a non-action, an omission. Other words used were iniquity, guilt, rebellion, disorder, abomination, lie, folly. From the contexts in which these words appear it is clear that sin was not simply the transgression of a law, but actually caused a break in the relationship between God and his people. Israel understood this relationship as a covenant, alliance or pact of love, initiated by God himself. Because of this special choice of God, they were his people and were expected to act as the people of God. The laws they devised for their conduct and for the ordering of their society, whether discovered by their own experience or borrowed from the surrounding peoples, were understood as the laws of God, coming from God himself. They were the path he meant them to follow if they were to become the holy people he wanted them to be. Failure to observe them meant to miss the mark of God's love. It meant iniquity, a deviation from how things ought to be, and this meant guilt, the distortion produced by sin, the state of being divided from one's better self, from one's environment and neighbors, and most of all from God. Guilt was thought of as a burden too heavy to bear, a rust that eats into a person's soul and remains engraved on the sinner's heart.

The description of sin as rebellion is not to be understood in terms of today's political relationships. In the ancient world the relationship between sovereign and servant was one of beneficence, so rebellion was ingratitude and personal insult, much like the rebellion of a child against the goodness of its parents. When sin is described as folly, this is not to imply diminished responsibility, but to indicate that the sinner becomes foolish by his sin.

But the basic notion of sin throughout the OT is that of a break in the relationship between God and human beings. This relationship is not primarily between creator and creature, but that between the divine and human partners in a personal union, a mutual relationship of belonging. Israel actually experienced the ever-present love of God through the long years of its history, and in that sense *knew* God, as a wife knows her husband and is known by him. God speaks through Jeremiah with all the heartbreak of a deserted husband: "My people, why do you turn away from me without ever turning back? I listened carefully, and you did not speak the truth. Not one of you has been sorry for his wickedness.... Everyone keeps on going his own way.... You do not know the laws by which I rule you" (Jer 8:5-7).

This background is taken for granted by the NT writers, but they added new elements: that sin is not only an individual act, but also a state or condition, that it is a power at work in the world, but it is finally overcome by Jesus. In the Synoptics Jesus does not speak directly about sin, but he was conscious of its reality and in his actions showed he could conquer sin and death. His mission was to be with sinners, to bring them forgiveness, and with them he accepted the closest fellowship known to the oriental world, i.e., table fellowship. He drew sinners into fellowship with himself and restored them to fellowship with God.

In the writings of John, sin is described as lawlessness, unrighteousness. The one who sins is from the devil and is the slave of sin. Sin is the lust of the flesh, the lust of the eyes, and the pride of life. The sinner loves darkness more than the light. More often than not, John uses the word sin to describe a state rather than a single act.

The fullest theology of sin is to be found in the Pauline letters, where the word occurs sixty times. For Paul, sin is universal, something in which every human being is involved. It is first and foremost a state or condition of human nature from which sinful acts come. It is a power which has us in its grip, so that we are "under sin" in the same way that a child is said to be under its parents. Sin "takes us captives" as prisoners are taken in war. It is not merely an external power, but gets right inside us, into our every fibre, so that we become the "slaves of sin." But Paul also affirms our freedom in the face of sin. We can resist and overcome it by Christ dwelling in our hearts, by his spirit taking possession of us (Rom 8:1-17).

Original Sin. The NT speaks of the consequence of sin. Sin results in a hardening of the heart, a dulling of the moral sense, so that there is less and less reluctance to sin, and thus sin begets sins. It also results in "death," because sin is the denial of life, and the sinner dies to his better, potential self each time he sins. Because of the relation between sin and death, Paul argues from the universality of death to the universality of sin (Rom 5:12-21). Because all must die, all are sinners, even though they have not sinned personally. He uses this condition of sin and death as a foil to emphasize the new life brought by Christ. In developing the parallel between Christ and Adam he traces our sinful condition to the sin of the first humans as its historical origin. Because of his belief in the universality of grace through Christ, Paul makes much of the sinful condition in which all of us find ourselves even before and apart from any personal sin. This is the basis for what later theology and church teaching came to describe as *original sin*. Traditionally this means the sinful condition brought about as a result of the "original" or first sin of the first humans, as portrayed in Genesis, chap. 3.

Fifteen centuries of tradition accepted

the Genesis story as an historical account of the primal sin which gave rise to the sinfulness passed on genetically to all of Adam's descendants. This tradition implies an historic "fall" of humans from an idyllic state at the dawn of history. It can also give the impression that the incarnation and redemption were a kind of back-up plan devised by God to overcome the "happy fault" (Adam's sin) which occasioned them. But the picture of an historical state of perfection in which the first humans were tested and found wanting, with catastrophic results for their descendants, has lost its credibility for us. Theologians who in recent decades have turned amateur scientists to harmonize scripture and science have been less than convincing. Science has little to say that would throw light on the theological understanding of the reality we refer to as original sin.

Almost all scholars admit that the third chapter of Genesis tells us nothing about what happened at the beginning of time, but that it is a story to explain what is happening all of the time. Instead of describing an historical first sin, it presents an ingeniously simple picture of what every sin really is: human self-assertion of those who want to be God, who want to go their own way in deciding what is right and wrong. It is more than a simple act of disobedience. Deep inner processes are involved, as indicated by the expression "being as God" and "knowledge of good and evil." The root of sinful action is to be found in the arrogance of human freedom. The paradise story describes God's plan for all people. He created us "in his own image and likeness," and we are most like him in our freedom. He shares with us his "dominion over all the creatures of the earth." He invites us to intimacy with him, wishes to treat us as friends who "walk with him in the garden." But we cannot be satisfied simply to accept his goodness. We want to be like him in

deciding for ourselves what is good or evil. The one thing we cannot have, to be gods, is the one thing we want. This is the essence of all sin, to put self before God, to want something which is not ours, to want it so much that we ignore the consequences to ourselves or others. This, of course, is deception. We are blinded by our selfishness, and it is only afterwards our eyes are opened, we discover that we are naked, and have to hide from God and from each other. Not only have we turned from God, but we are no longer at peace with ourselves; we are at odds with our neghbors and even the material world itself seems to turn sour on us; what was meant to be our garden becomes a hostile environment. We do not wish to be called to account by God, and when we cannot avoid it we resort to excuses and rationalizations. The story is not of a primeval event beyond normal experience, but a true-to-life description of the psychology of all sin. All humans would behave in the same way if placed in similar circumstances.

The Genesis account paints a telling picture of the psychological process we call sin, but in its context it is also a symbol of the existential situation of the human race in the totality of its sinfulness. While the scriptures identify individual sins of persons and groups, they also speak of sin in the singular as a state or condition of humankind as a whole, as an evil power at work in the world. John the Baptist pointed to Jesus as the Lamb who takes away the *sin* of the world, as the one who not only brings forgiveness of individual sins, but conquers sin in its very root. The sinful condition we recognize in the world must have had an historical beginning, but we have no details about what it was or when it occurred. What we do believe is that it grew and developed as a power so that it is now inexorably mingled with our culture and social structures; it even affects our physical and psychological prenatal existence. The drug addiction or depression of an expectant mother can affect the future of her unborn child, and a person born into a racialist society will have difficulty in recognizing and responding to values like equality and respect for all persons. Our joining the human race involves us in an environment of sin before we ever become capable of personally contributing to it. The situation is well described by Monika Hellwig: "Sin has become the condition of human life in history. The consequences of evil deeds haunt us down the centuries with their reverberating echoes. They become hardened into standard expectations and patterns of behavior, into the structures of society that are seen as the guarantees of the good. Sin incarnates itself in every kind of violence and compulsion and disguises itself under the masks of law and order in society—ways of stabilizing and maintaining oppressive power and privilege for those who already possess it. Sin expresses itself in fears and suspicion and hatred ill-disguised. It leaves its deposits in prejudices, rivalries, quest of security in the hoarding of goods and the claiming of privilege to the disadvantage of others. It emerges constantly in an irrational lust for power to compel other human beings and shape the world to one's own imaginings" (*Jesus, the Compassion of God*, Michael Glazier, 1983, p. 98).

This description, however, does not mean that original sin is nothing more than the sin of the world which affects us as environment. If we describe original sin simply in terms of exposure to the sin of the world, we are not faithful to the teaching of Trent, which speaks of our *intrinsic*, natural predisposition to sin even before we are exposed to any sinful social influences. It is true that the Council of Trent took a literal view of Genesis and was unaware of modern views on the origin of the human species, but we have to respect the essential teaching which

transcends the cultural background of Trent. The core of doctrine defined by the council may be expressed in three basic assertions: that Christ is central to the whole plan of creation, revelation and redemption; that every human being is in need of the redemption won by Christ; and that this need is antecedent to the commission of personal sin or exposure to sinful environment. Karl Rahner reminds us that such notions as "redemption," the "need for redemption," "salvation" and "deliverance from evil" are theological terms and should not be connected in a temporal sequence. He also stresses that the idea of the first sin of the first human person (or persons) being transmitted to us biologically has absolutely nothing to do with the Christian dogma of original sin (*Foundations of Christian Faith*, pp. 90, 110). The essential meaning of original sin is that every human being begins life in a state of alienation from God insofar as without grace we will be unable to rise to the level of existence God had planned for us. Even with grace we will continually fail, because we are free and grace will always respect our freedom. There is a deep mystery in the interplay between divine omnipotence and human freedom, and the further mystery that God creates us imperfect although his plan is that we, under grace, will freely grow into the fullness of the maturity of Christ. There is no personal guilt in being born into the state of "original sin," yet humankind brought it on itself by going against God's plan through deliberate wrong choices, and the whole human race is continually involved in sin.

The new rite of baptism no longer emphasizes liberation from original sin as the primary purpose and effect of the sacrament, but initiation into the Christian community, incorporation into the body of Christ. Being introduced into the mystery of Christ's death and resurrection involves forgiveness of sin, but the primary emphasis is on the new life of grace which, of course, empowers the baptized person to conquer evil and sin.

Actual Sin. The mystery of original sin transcends time and space, and in that context the passage from sin to grace is not a temporal, before-and-after one. Only the present continuous tense is adequate to express what is happening in this mystery of creation and redemption. But the sins we personally commit by our failure to respond to grace do take place in time and history, and tradition refers to them as *actual sins.* Original sin is original in the sense of being basic, fundamental, the root of all sin, but not necessarily in the sense of temporal priority. It is called sin only by analogy, because it does not involve personal guilt. But its effect is to leave us prone to personal sin. Because grace respects and does not block our freedom, we can still say "no" to God's plan in the details of our lives. Indeed, it may be said that, statistically, sin is normal.

The early Christians soon discovered that in spite of their new life in Christ, they were subject to temptation and sin, so there was need for repentance and continual conversion. They needed to be helped too by identifying the activities to be avoided as sinful. The OT has several catalogues of sins (Deut 27:15-26; Amos 2:4-8, 8:4-6; Hos 4:2; Ezek 18:5-20). Jesus himself gives an abbreviated version of the Decalogue (Mk 10:18-19) and gives further examples of sinful behavior in his description of the last judgment (Mt 25:41-46). There are several lists of sinful activities in the rest of the NT: 1 Cor 6:9-10; Gal 5:19-21; Rom 1:24-32; 1 Tm 1:4-11; 1 Pet 4:2-5; 2 Pet 2:12-22. The people of God have always been conscious of degrees of seriousness in sin, but the gradation was differently understood at different times.

Mortal and Venial Sin. The modern division of sins into mortal and venial is not to be found as such in scripture or in the early church, but was conditioned by the church's later legislation about confession. St. John distinguishes degrees of sin in his first letter: "If you see your brother commit a sin that does not lead to death, you should pray to God, who will give him life. This applies to those whose sins do not lead to death. But there is a sin which leads to death, and I do not say that you should pray to God about that. All wrongdoing is sin, but there is sin which does not lead to death" (1 Jn 5:16-17). It is not clear what precisely is the sin that leads to death, or the "deadly sin." In the context, it probably refers to the "sin against the Holy Spirit," final impenitence, the attitude of the person who simply refuses forgiveness and is impervious to the power of prayer (Mt 12:21-32; Mk 3:28-30; Lk 12:10).

This reference to "attitude" recalls an important element in the biblical notion of sin. Though OT and NT make clear that individual actions can be sinful, the emphasis is more on sin as a basic attitude, a state of sinfulness. In his various catalogues, Paul was not so much listing sins as describing the kind of people who exclude themselves from the kingdom of heaven by their way of life. The sinful attitude, of course, is built up by individual actions, as James writes: "A person is tempted when he is drawn away and trapped by his own evil desire. Then his evil desire conceives and gives birth to sin; and sin, when it is full-grown, gives birth to death" (1:14-15). John too speaks more of sin as a state than of individual sinful actions. To emphasize the seriousness of the sinful state he quotes Jesus at the Last Supper: "Whoever hates me hates my Father also" (Jn 15:23). This is the origin of our notion of mortal sin or sinfulness, namely a state of mind and will, a way of life amounting to a total rejection of God, a condition of total selfishness. Nowhere in the NT do we get a list of individual mortal sins meriting the punishment of hell or needing confession and special absolution, but the various sin-lists are warnings and indications as to the kind of behavior that can lead to the state of mortal sinfulness, spiritual death.

In the early church the more serious sins brought excommunication (1 Cor 5:3-11). The sinner was excluded from the community and shunned by fellow-believers, both to shock the sinner into repentance and to protect the community from the contagion of sinfulness. Such sins were called crimes, grave sins, capital sins, and the main ones were idolatry, apostasy, murder, abortion and publicly-known adulterous relationships. For centuries the excommunicated sinner could be re-admitted only once in a lifetime, but gradually re-admission became more frequent and the list of "grave sins" became more extensive, including even internal sins. The final phase of this development came when the Council of Trent decreed that penitents were to confess all mortal sins according to number and kind.

The decree did not specify what constituted mortal sin, but theologians had already begun to define mortal and venial sins. Mortal sin was a serious act of immorality carried out with full knowledge and full consent, whereas venial sin was present when the matter was light or there was not full knowledge or full consent. Mortal sin involved a total break in the relationship with God, a total loss of divine grace, hence spiritual death, whereas venial sin involved some moral disorder, but did not destroy the life of grace. To die in the state of mortal sinfulness meant the loss of God, eternal damnation.

Fundamental Option. This clearcut division was the common currency of the church's teaching and pastoral practice for centuries. But it has been seriously questioned in recent times and a number of theologians prefer a threefold division, namely: (1) mortal sinfulness, (2) serious or grave sin, and (3) less serious or venial sin, the daily faults of the normally good person. They use the term "mortal sinfulness" in the biblical sense explained above to describe the state of one whose basic stance is total selfishness, such that there is no room for any reference to God or consideration of others. Such a stance may come about as a result of a serious immoral action, but it involves something deeper than a single decision, action or omission. It involves a person's basic attitude to life, to others, to the world, and in and through all of this, to God. It involves a person's *moral identity* as a person, the kind of person he or she has become through free decisions and actions. Common human experience as well as the insights of modern psychology suggest that our moral identity (basic goodness or badness) at this deep level does not change back and forth quickly or frequently. A person's basic goodness may persist in spite of occasional actions that seem to conflict with it. Such actions could be considered "serious" sins, but without the malice and the serious consequences associated with mortal or lethal sin. Church discipline may well decree that they be submitted to sacramental confession for forgiveness, but they would not automatically destroy one's basic outlook, attitude and general moral goodness.

This newer approach rejects the simple notion of mortal sin being defined in terms of knowledge, freedom and serious matter. It is not the gravity of the matter that makes a particular sin mortal, but rather the degree to which the individual is personally involved, the degree to which the action flows from the core of the person. If the totality of the person is not involved, then even serious matter does not automatically change the person's basic moral stance. Contemporary theologians speak of *fundamental option* to describe this level of moral responsibility. Categorical or ordinary freedom is exercised in ordinary free decisions and actions, but fundamental freedom is involved when it is a question of the disposition of the whole person to God, when one's whole pattern of life is either in line with God's will and the true human good, or in opposition to this.

This fundamental option, basic choice, or general life-direction (for or against God) flows from the core of our personality and determines the overall pattern of our lives. But not all our decisions and actions come from the center of our person. Many of our actions are at the periphery. They come from instinctual drives, both positive and negative, such as the sexual urge, aggressiveness, fear, insecurity, all of which obscure our insight, or from routine, so that our full freedom is not involved. Such actions may be in line with our basic option, perhaps strengthening it, or they may be inconsistent with it and so weaken it, though not central enough to change it.

It is clear that mortal sinfulness in the biblical sense of spiritual death is not present except in the case of central acts coming from the core of our personality, acts which change our basic attitude away from God. The change need not be a dramatic one concentrated in a single act, but the end result of a continued pattern of selfish living until we arrive at a state where we discover that God has been excluded from our lives. Human life, however, is seldom a clearcut, black-and-white picture, so we cannot be certain where we stand in God's eyes. Only God himself knows: "I, the Lord, search the minds and test the hearts of men. I treat each one according to the way he lives, according to what he does" (Jer 17:10). Thomas Aquinas reminds us that we can never have more than a moral certainty that we are in the state of grace. Christian realism demands that we accept this uncertainty and learn to live creatively with it.

The uncertainty applies not only to our basic option, but at times even to individual sinful actions. Such is the basic imperfection of our human nature, the influence of subconscious factors, the weight of external pressures from the sinful world around us, and the gradual and groping development of our freedom and moral insight, that we can seldom be sure that a particular action is central, that it flows from the core of our person and the depth of our conscience. However, the sin-lists of scripture and church teaching are intended to indicate that certain actions are so serious in their consequences that a morally developed person performing them could normally presume that they came from the center of the person and not from the periphery. A person could well have a moral certainty that such is the case, but no one is ever justified in judging someone else is in mortal sin; only God knows. In fact, actions in themselves are not sins, no matter how serious; sin applies only to persons.

Other dimensions. Christian tradition has never seen sin as a purely private affair affecting only the sinner and God. Every sin has a *social dimension.* Even the most private sins affect the holiness of the body of Christ. In some sins forgiveness requires making restitution. In the sacrament of reconciliation the priest represents both God *and the community.* But the tradition paid little attention to *collective sin* and *collective guilt*; in this context we think of phenomena like Naziism. This is more than just the social repercussion of individual sin.

But there is a still further kind of sin. Personal and communal sins affect the area of primary relationships between people, but *social* or *societal* sins are in the more complex, impersonal, structural level of secondary relationships. The 1971 Roman Synod of Bishops spoke of "sin both of individuals and of society as a whole," without explaining the relationship between them. But the Latin

American bishops in their Puebla document emphasized social sin as "the objectification of sin in the economic, social, political and ideological-cultural field" (Puebla, 1113). They pointed out that sin affects entire systems, such as Marxism and liberal capitalism (P., 92) and can even affect culture (P., 405). The apostolic exhortation *Reconciliatio et Paenitentia* of John Paul II (1984) speaks very strongly of social sin.

Social sin has existed since humankind moved from the simple primary relationships of individuals and a few families to the more complex structure of organized society. But we are more aware of this kind of sin since the social sciences have shown us that hunger, poverty and misery do not "just happen," but are the result of socio-economic and political relationships. The root of this sin is selfishness and the arrogance of power, but it is also an evil which exists almost independently of individual conscience and which imposes itself on that conscience.

The Christian community can feel helpless in the face of such sinful structures, but it needs to acknowledge them. In 1969 the bishops of Peru acknowledged that "we as Christians through inadequate loyalty to the gospel have contributed to the present situation of injustice with our words, attitudes, omissions and silence." We need to repent of such sins, to ask forgiveness of God for them. The communal celebration of the liturgy of reconciliation can be most helpful here, allowing people to put this sinfulness before God, in repentance, whereas a private confession would feel unreal since it is so hard to measure our individual responsibility for social sin. Such celebrations help to create a community of conversion, in which individuals begin to realize that conversion of heart and improvement of social structures belong together. Salvation from sin means more than the acknowledgement of guilt; it includes the dismantling of the sinful

system and the removal of suffering and its causes. As the Pueblo document states: "the transformation of structures is an external expression of inward conversion" (P., 1221). To change sinful structures requires concerted effort on the part of Christians, but to discern the appropriate action calls for an understanding of how those structures function. A thorough knowledge of the social sciences is needed here. This is a new challenge to the church's penitential practice, going beyond, though not replacing, the traditional prayer, fasting and almsgiving.

The complexity and insidious pervasiveness of social sin remind us of the scriptural description of sin as an evil power at work in the world. It is a frightening reality, but Paul reminds us of our Christian belief that "where sin increased, grace increased much more" (Rom 5:20). In Christ Jesus we have the forgiveness of all sin. No matter how great or how powerful, evil does not have the last word.

G. Berkouwer, *Sin* (Grand Rapids: Eerdmans, 1971). S. Fagan, *Has Sin Changed?* (Wilmington: Glazier, 1988). J. Gaffney, *Sin Reconsidered* (Ramsey, NJ: Paulist, 1983). B. Häring, *Sin in the Secular Age* (Garden City: Doubleday, 1974). P. Schoonenberg, *Man and Sin* (London: Sheed and Ward, 1966).

SEÁN FAGAN, S.M.

SOCIAL ISSUES, LITURGY AND

The relationship between liturgy and social issues is ecclesiological in nature and has important theological and pastoral aspects. At issue is the liturgy's function in the church and the church's mission in the world. There will always be some relationship between liturgy and mission, but its nature and content will reflect what the liturgy does and is expected to do in the life of the church. It will also depend on how moral obligation is conceived, particularly with respect to interventions in political and social affairs. Because important developments in these areas are underway, the relationship between liturgy and social issues continues to evolve.

The church has certainly recognized human distress and the many serious problems in the human community. Its liturgical life has been shaped in part as a response to them. Baptism, for example, confronts sin and alienation in human life and reconciles people to God and the church. The sacramentary used at Mass provides prayers for such intentions as the unity of Christians, peace and justice, refugees and exiles, and relief from famine. The sacrament of penance testifies to the church's continuing struggle against sin in its own members and its commitment to forgive offenses and support personal conversion. On all occasions the liturgy calls people to holiness and reminds them of their obligation to practice justice and live in charity with all.

Another facet of the church's response is its official statements on social and political issues. These statements deal with a wide range of local, national, and international problems, considering them theoretically as well as concretely. Especially since Pope Leo XIII's encyclical *Rerum Novarum* issued in 1891, a large and significant body of literature has accumulated. These interventions manifest the seriousness with which Catholic leaders have taken contemporary social and political problems.

Although the popes and other church leaders invariably acknowledged faith in God the creator and fidelity to the gospel, they often de-emphasized religious arguments in addressing social issues. Because they were speaking to a wide secular audience, they tried instead to base their case on a human nature common to all and knowable by all. In light of a natural order linked to human nature, certain essential relationships among individuals and groups in society were discerned, and

a series of mutual rights and obligations elaborated (e.g., John XXIII, *Pacem in Terris*, 3-7). This approach, which reflects the moral theology of the time, shows that the church was trying to be specific and reasonable in promoting justice and peace in social life.

The liturgy's promotion of justice, charity, and peace through prayer and personal conversion is appropriate and helpful. When these mainly transcendent and private dynamics predominate, however, they can eclipse the historical and public dimensions that are also proper to liturgy. It then becomes more difficult for worshippers to see how the liturgy relates to the corporate life of the church or an active ministry in a world inherently social and political. A tendency to disassociate this kind of social engagement from the liturgy is reinforced by the natural law argumentation often found in official statements. Despite their merits, these abstract and deductive arguments usually fail to persuade those who are not sympathetic to begin with. Moreover, because this approach appears tangential to the church's faith and worship, some have felt justified in questioning the substance of official social teachings and the legitimacy of church involvement in social and political affairs (G.S., 43).

A different relationship emerges when liturgy and engagement with the world are renewed by contact with the sources proper to them. In this regard one of the most important developments has been the biblical renewal. Underway since the latter part of the 19th century, this renewal culminated in the *Dogmatic Constitution on Divine Revelation*. The church now appreciates better the primacy of God's word for its entire life (D.V., 21). The sacred scriptures proclaim God's mighty deeds in human history and testify that God spoke to the human family first through the prophets and finally through his son, Jesus Christ (Heb 1:1-2). God's word calls the church to a response that is personal, total, and unreserved (D.V., 5). The scriptures furthermore show the centrality of the New Covenant in the blood of Christ for the life of the church (Lk 22:20; 1 Cor 11:23-29; L.G., 9). The covenant is fundamental because it locates our relationship with God and gives it an inescapably ecclesial quality.

Building on the biblical renewal, the Second Vatican Council instituted a major reform of the Roman liturgy. God's word now has a position of paramount importance in all sacramental celebrations (S.C., 24). Not only is the word proclaimed more generously in the various liturgies, but the word makes the Lord present to the assembly and manifests the primacy of the Lord in the church, its life, and its worship (S.C., 7, 35).

The presence of the Lord by means of word and sign is essential to the liturgical event. The Lord engages the church and makes it present and active as well (S.C., 7). The liturgy is therefore an essentially ecclesial activity; individuals participate as members of the church (S.C., 26). The liturgy involves both transcendent and historical dimensions. The Lord once died and rose in human history, is now present in word and sign, and will come again at the end of time. Human history assumes transcendent meaning and forms the essential context for the church's life and mission to the nations (Mt 28:18-20; G.S., 40; S.C., 10). The Lord's presence in liturgy is a powerful source of renewal for the church and its members. The liturgy prompts the church to respond to Christ with the same whole-hearted, obedient, and kenotic love it finds in its Lord. This is the soul of worship and inspires repentance for sin and self-donation to neighbor.

The return to the scriptures has likewise promoted a renewed understanding of the moral life. The primacy of the word means that Christ and the new covenant must be central to a person's moral life. Because conversion and repentance, faith and right living are intimately related, morality can no longer be considered simply a matter of keeping specified commandments. On the contrary, being called to life in Christ involves a positive mission that knows no pre-determined limits. The council referred to it as an "obligation to bring forth fruit in charity for the life of the world" (O.T., 16; also G.S., 43).

Personal conscience occupies a pivotal position in the moral life. Conscience draws life and power first from an inner encounter with God and a related awareness of responsibility to live according to goodness, charity, and truth. It prompts the person to search for the specific and correct insights needed in moral judgments. It continues to direct and bind the person as the concrete decisions of daily life are made (G.S., 16-17; P.H., 3). The council's teaching on conscience and its mandate for the renewal of moral theology emphasize the essentially religious and apostolic qualities of moral life. This implies that liturgy and social engagement will be more integrally related as two aspects of one overall personal response to Christ's presence and call.

A closely related question is the influence of the revealed word on the living of daily life. The word can have important practical effects on the person since it calls to conversion, fuller ecclesial and missionary participation, and deeper living of the theological and moral virtues. Whether the word also specifies how one should decide issues of behavior depends on a number of related considerations. Any use of the scriptures first requires a competent exegesis of the relevant texts. Also needed is a carefully reasoned judgment whether and to what degree the text actually applies to a given contemporary problem (D.V., 12). The effort to determine morally correct conduct must furthermore take into account the meaning of the created order for the matter to be decided; this involves the attempt to specify what the dignity of the human person requires within the context of the common good (G.S., 26, 35).

These considerations rule out the direct and literal application of most scriptural passages and demand great care in the use of others. Reverence for the scriptural word goes hand in hand with the assembly of data from human experience and the working out of reasonable judgments. The task of forming good practical decisions for moral life is sometimes as difficult as it is necessary. It requires humility and cooperation with others, a tolerance for shortcomings and mistakes, and a readiness to accommodate honest differences of judgment in many areas (G.S., 16, 17, 43, 74, 75; D.H., 2-3).

Recent official statements on social issues reflect these developments. In these texts church authorities have tried to scrutinize the signs of the times and interpret them in the light of the gospel (G.S., 4). This has given Catholic social doctrine a more contemporary, concrete texture and brought the gospel itself into high relief. The need to address alienation and injustice in the world is explicitly described as an important part of the church's overall response to God's work in Christ. Work on behalf of justice is required by the gospel (G.S., 72, Paul VI, *Evangelii Nuntiandi*, 29-31; John Paul II, *Sollecitudo Rei Socialis* [S.R.S.], 13, 31).

The greater reliance on specifically Christian grounds and motives is a significant development. Rational arguments in support of specific conclusions tend to be de-emphasized in recent documents, but not eliminated from consideration. Church authors commonly disclaim the ability or the responsibility to work out concrete solutions to actual problems; they leave this task to others who are in a better position to carry it out (e.g., G.S., 33, 42-43; S.R.S., 41). This approach applies to the responsibility and consciences of people at all levels of church and civil societies. At the same time, there are more substantial references to the function of the liturgy with respect to social issues. Liturgy educates to justice, forms a Christian conscience, lends religious significance to human activity, and prompts action on behalf of justice and peace in the world. Social engagement in turn should inform one's participation in the liturgy (1974 Synod of Bishops, *Justice in the World*; S.R.S., 48).

The effort to read the signs of the times and interpret them in the light of the gospel reflects a greater historical consciousness and the imperative to subordinate all human activities to the word of God. This has led recent social teachings to highlight the affinities between faith and social issues and between liturgy and efforts on behalf of justice and peace. This more integral outlook can be expected to continue to mature. It should contribute to a positive reception of Catholic social doctrine and a better appreciation at the local level of the dynamic bonds among God's word, liturgy, and conscientious work for justice and peace in human society.

See **Liturgy and Christian life; Liturgy as prophetic**

John C. Haughey, ed., *The Faith That Does Justice* (New York: Paulist Press, 1977). Christopher Kiesling, "Liturgy and Social Justice" *Worship* 51 (1977): 351-61. Mark Searle, ed., *Liturgy and Social Justice* (Collegeville: Liturgical Press, 1980). R. Kevin Seasoltz, "Justice and the Eucharist" *Worship* 58 (1984): 507-25.

WALTER J. WOODS

SOURCES, EARLY LITURGICAL

Sources for the study of early Christian liturgy do not commonly take the form of liturgical texts (missals, prayer books, etc.) or systematic treatments of liturgical subjects. In consequence, it has often been concluded that early Christian liturgical practice and thought were "undeveloped" or "fluid."

In fact, even the earliest writings of our period, from the letters of Paul and the traditions underlying the gospels onward, come from communities which understood themselves to be constituted by baptism and eucharist. For their authors, the liturgical gatherings of the church are primary theological data, concrete evidence that God is bringing into being a new people through the death and resurrection of Christ and the outpouring of the Spirit as a witness to the inbreaking of the Kingdom of God. All the remains of the period, including its apologetic and theological no less than its more strictly liturgical—including catechetical and homiletic—writings, have to be studied with an eye to their liturgical allusions.

The Oral-Formal Tradition

The allusive character of this evidence is due in particular to the fact that early Christian liturgy, like its Jewish and pagan counterparts, was an oral-formal phenomenon. The early liturgical gatherings were not lacking in basic shape and structure, in the use of specific confessional formulas, and structures of prayer. While what was said allowed for improvisation and adaptation, it was not by any means "extemporaneous" in our modern sense. It followed rules, essentially unwritten, but important for that very reason to be observed by those responsible for their conduct if others were to take their appropriate parts. But it was, in principle and practice, not something to be written down for reading in the manner of later times. Those familiar with the classical tradition of poetry and oratory, and of public speaking or rhetoric more generally, will at once recognize here an assumption as natural to that time as it is foreign to ours.

The oral-formal character of early Christian liturgy helps to explain the general value placed on liturgical language as a means of appropriating and transmitting the Christian proclamation (tradition, *paradosis*), as in the famous dictum of Prosper of Aquitaine that the structure of prayer underlies the structure of belief ("*Lex orandi statuat legem credendi*"). But it has a specific significance for the study of the sources which provide us with descriptions of liturgical gatherings. These sources were written only in particular circumstances, with the specific purposes of preservation, explanation and—often most important—when there was dispute over what should be done and said. These sources are badly mishandled when studied, and even printed out, as if they were extracts of liturgical books of the sort with which we are familiar. They need to be studied in the light of the particular purposes which impelled their writing in the time before circumstances made continuation of the oral-formal tradition difficult.

The Physical Evidence

Early Christian liturgy, like that of any period, is physical as well as vocal. The physical evidence of places used for liturgical gatherings has at last begun to receive the attention it deserves. This evidence includes the badly called "house churches" ("Christian houses" or sometimes, by an obvious association, "temples of the Christians"), renovated domestic structures of which we have increasing evidence from the 2nd century onward. It also includes the baptistries and basilicas, and the complexes of buildings of which they were part, erected under the auspices of Constantine and his successors following the period of persecution. These all, whether still in use or in ruins, tell us much about the character and significance of the rites for which they made physical provision. So, too, do the pictorial evidence of the catacombs at Rome and elsewhere, the wall decorations of the later buildings, which show us the people who gathered for the Christian meetings and the vesture and furnishings with which they were familiar.

The NT and Contemporary Writings

Particular problems are posed by our earliest written sources. Many but by no means all of these writings were later collected into the NT. The rest were designated "Apostolic Fathers" by the Anglican patristic scholar, Archbishop James Ussher (d. A.D. 1656). For our purposes, all of these writings provide evidence of the liturgical practices of the communities of the first and early 2nd centuries. Those later regarded as "scriptures," however, must also be studied for their subsequent liturgical influence. A case in point is the command of Mt 28:19-20, to "baptize into the name of the Father, the Son, and the Holy Spirit," itself an interpretation of the significance of baptism rather than a liturgical formula, which had a wide influence on later catechetical and baptismal practice. Another, is the Last Supper "tradition" of 1 Cor 11:23-5 (cf. Mk 14:22-4; Mt 26:26-8; Lk 22:17-19), once again not itself a liturgical formula, which became the "institution narrative" incorporated into later eucharistic prayers.

Paul and the Gospels. Among the writings which later became part of the NT, the Pauline letters deserve special attention. 1 Corinthians contains our earliest references to baptismal practice, at least in the negative sense of insisting that it is baptism "into the name" of Christ rather than that of the baptizer (1:15). It also contains our earliest references to eucharistic practice, in the form of instructions for the observance of the blessings over the bread and wine mandated by the Last Supper "tradition" (11:17-43), with its own even earlier implication that the eucharist is a "memorial" of the new paschal sacrifice of Christ (cf. 1 Cor 5:7-8). In both cases, these rites are interpreted by Paul as

entrance into and sustenance in the life of the members of the body of Christ effected by the Holy Spirit (12:12-31).

Within the Pauline collection there are more allusions to baptism than to the eucharist. Indeed, the long discussion of the new life in Christ in Rom 6:3-8:17 (cf. Gal 3:27-4:7), with its reference to baptism into the death of Christ as establishing the identity of the baptized as members of his risen body through the Spirit, takes on something of the form of a post-baptismal catechesis. Moreover, the "Pauline" author of *Ephesians*, perhaps originally the covering letter of the collection, draws on this discussion, and on themes from *Colossians*, for his broadly baptismal interpretation of the new unity of Jews and Gentiles foreordained in the plan of God (Eph 1:13-18; 2:4-10; 13-19).

The synoptic gospels, however different in *genre* from the Pauline letters, must also be read as intended for communities constituted by baptism and eucharist. Here baptismal allusions include reference to Jesus' death as a baptism foreshadowing the martyrdoms of principal disciples (Mk 10:38-40; Lk 12:50). Moreover, in Matthew the account of the baptism of Jesus is so treated as to anticipate the new relationship to God, in Christ, through the Spirit in which the baptized stand, and into which others are to be brought. Indeed, the command of Mt 28:19-20 ("make disciples ... baptizing them 'in the name of the Father, the Son, and the Holy Spirit' ... and teaching them...") may well assume a pattern of practice, conversion, baptism, and catechesis, not unlike that assumed by Paul.

Synoptic eucharistic allusions abound. The accounts of the miraculous feedings (Mk 6:41-2; 8:6-8; Mt 14:19-20; 15:36-7; Lk 9:16-17), which employ the technical language of "taking, blessing over, breaking, and giving," had almost certainly been taken as foreshadowings of the eucharist before their incorporation into these narratives. Moreover, the inclusion of a form or forms of the Last Supper "tradition" (cf. 1 Cor 11:23-5) in the passion narrative, and its placing of the last meal on the day of the slaughter of the Passover lambs, is a crucial element in its view of Jesus' death as a new Passover sacrifice. Whatever the historical accuracy of this narrative, it incorporates an already established "tradition" conveying this interpretation of the death of Jesus through the use of eucharistic terminology familiar to its readers.

Of particular interest is Lk 24:13-35, where the appearance of the risen Christ to the disciples at Emmaus is recounted in language reminiscent of a eucharistic meal, perhaps even suggesting familiarity with an introductory interpretation of the scriptures but certainly employing the technical language of "taking, blessing over, breaking, and giving" at the supper of which the risen Christ is the host.

In the gospel of John, baptismal and eucharistic allusions are carefully disguised. Moreover, the subject of baptism is easily recognized in the discussion between Jesus and Nicodemus over being "born again" through the Spirit (Jn 3:1-15), while allusion is again made to the baptism with which the disciples must be baptized (18:1). Similarly, while the Last Supper "tradition" is replaced with the account of the washing of the disciples' feet and its accompanying command (13:3-11), eucharistic interpretation is given in connection with the miraculous feeding (6:25-65) and in the discussion of the vine and branches at the last meal (15:1-8). Baptism and eucharist are doubtless to be discerned in the references to water and wine (or blood) in the account of the marriage feast at Cana (2:1-11) and in the passion narrative (19:34).

Other NT Evidence. Among the other writings now collected in the NT, special interest centers on Hebrews, which exhorts those who have been baptized and have participated in the eucharist against apostasy in the face of persecution (6:1-8), and was later appealed to as grounds for rigorous refusal to restore apostates to the communion of the church (see below, Cyprian). I Peter, whether or not it is the baptismal instruction some have found it, assumes that its readers belong to the community of the baptized (1:3, 21-23; 2:2) and are eucharistic participants (2:5). Revelation, which describes its visions as received on the Lord's Day (1:9-10), has been thought to reflect a structure of scriptural interpretation and eucharistic action, and certainly promises the martyrs "heavenly manna and ... a new Name" at the final "marriage feast of the Lamb" (2:17; 19:7-9).

More specific references to baptismal and eucharistic practice are found in the Acts of the Apostles. While something like a paradigmatic sequence of repentance, baptism "into the name of Jesus Christ," and the gift of the Spirit, seems to be assumed (2:38), the accounts of baptisms (presumably drawn from diverse sources) do not exhibit this sequence in practice (8:9-16, 26-40; 10:44-8). The reference to a daily "breaking of bread" in the primitive Jerusalem community (2:46), if it is eucharistic, is unusual in view of the normal practice of meeting for the eucharist on the Lord's Day. But clearer, even graphic, is the account of Paul's healing of Eutychus during a meeting for the "breaking of bread" at Troas (27:7-12), presumably on the evening of the end of the Sabbath and the beginning of the Lord's Day on the Jewish reckoning of days from sunset.

The Apostolic Fathers

The works designated "Apostolic Fathers" also contain allusions to the significance of baptism and eucharist in the same period as that of the NT.

Of these, two are Italian in provenance.

"The first letter of Clement to the Corinthians" (1 Clement) is a formal letter from the Roman church, to be dated after the Domitian persecution at Rome in A.D. 96, supporting the authority of the leadership of the Corinthian church against certain detractors. The letter probably has the baptized in view when it speaks of the duties of those who bear "the name" of Christ (58:1-2). But it certainly has the eucharistic community in view when it elaborates the Pauline theme of the various functions of the members of the body of Christ (1 Cor 12:12-31) with a complicated analogy between the responsibilities of the high-priest, Levites, and people in offering the sacrifices of the old covenant and the functions of the apostolically appointed leaders and members of the church (1 Clem 42-44). Moreover, the lyric blessing prayer for the unity of the church, with which the letter draws to a close (59:3-64:1), is a free adaptation of the structure of Jewish blessing prayers with which we may assume Clement was familiar from eucharistic use.

Closely related to 1 Clement, both in time and place, are the apocalyptic visions of the *Shepherd of Hermas*, which exhort the leaders of the church to oversight of the baptized (*Vis.* IX, 7-10), and take baptism as the mandate for repentance and the cultivation of purity (*Man.* III, 1-7) in seeming qualification of Heb 6:1-8.

Of Asian provenance are the letters of Ignatius, bishop of Antioch, written to the churches he expected to visit on his way to martyrdom at Rome in the reign of the Emperor Trajan (d. A.D. 117). In warning against "docetic" teaching of a proto-Gnostic sort, which denies the incarnation of the Word, Ignatius asserts the importance of the eucharistic gathering of the baptized with the bishop, elaborating Johannine themes (cf. 1 Jn 1:18-25, 5:6-12) to show its importance as exhibiting the faith that "there is only one flesh of our Lord Jesus Christ and one cup to unite us in his blood" (Philadelphians 4; cf. ad Eph 13:1, Smyrna 7:1, etc.).

Also of Asian provenance is the *Martyrdom of Polycarp*, bishop of Smyrna (d. A.D. 156), himself numbered liturgically among the "Quartodecimans" who observed the Passover on the Jewish 14 Nisan (see below, Justin). This work, which contains evidence of later elaboration of various sorts, nonetheless preserves a blessing prayer attributed to Polycarp at the time of his death (chap. 14), which may well reflect his normal eucharistic blessing prayer but is here adapted to giving thanks for his being worthy of death and asking that he be accepted as a "pleasing sacrifice." Like the blessing prayer of 1 Clem. 59:3-64:1, it is evidence of the free Christian use of the form of Jewish blessing prayers.

Didache

Among other writings "The teaching of the twelve apostles" (*Didache*), was long unrecognized in an adapted version incorporated in the late 4th century *Apostolic Constitutions* (Apost. Const.), but is now known through the late 19th-century discovery of an independent MS. This is an unusual 2nd-century Greek compilation and editing of early Aramaic materials from Syria-Palestine (a minority view says Egypt) perhaps as early as the late 1st century. In its present 2nd-century form, *Did.* brings together moral instruction (the "two ways" document) (I-VI), directions "about baptism" (VII) fasting, and prayer (VIII), and "about the eucharist": blessings to be said over wine and bread before the meal and a connected set of blessings to be said afterwards (IX-X). There follows directions covering the right of visiting prophets to give thanks and the need to appoint bishops and deacons (XI-XV), together with an exhortation to observe the Sunday eucharist (XIV).

As a 2nd-century document, *Did.* follows an outline roughly similar to that found in Justin and Hippolytus (see below), in which a pre-baptismal catechesis precedes a description of paschal baptism and eucharist, and is followed by reference to the Sunday eucharist and other matters. It is, for this reason, sometimes called an early "Church Order," though the particular circumstances which impelled its effort to conform earlier materials to newly emerging norms of practice are not clear.

As to these early materials, interest perhaps naturally centers on the blessings to be said before and after meals, unquestionably Christian adaptations of the Jewish Sabbath and festival meal blessings. The order of wine and bread, and the lack of reference to the Last Supper "tradition," still causes some skepticism regarding them. But plain words of the text, as well as the paschal context in which they have been set in conjunction with baptism, makes it likely that they are eucharistic blessings, and even that the connected series after the meal, Christian adaptations of the Jewish blessings over the final "cup of blessing," supply us with the long-needed clue as to the structure of prayers into which the blessings over the eucharistic bread and wine were set together when it became normal to gather for the eucharist apart from an actual meal.

2nd and 3rd-Century Evidence

From the mid-2nd century to the end of the period of persecutions, we have an increasing body of liturgical evidence, in the form of actual descriptions of liturgical practices, as well as of other writings with liturgical implications. The former, Justin Martyr, "Apology" (I *Apol.*) and Hippolytus' *Apostolic Tradition* (Apost. Trad.), require special attention, though at least a selection of the latter must be noticed.

Justin. Justin, I *Apol*, the work of a teacher of the Greek-speaking Roman church (d. A.D. 167), is easily neglected where it is assumed that liturgical writings will be of the sort with which we are familiar. As a general explanation and defense of Christianity for a pagan readership, it concludes with a description of Christian meetings for baptism and eucharist (61-7) designed to allay suspicions to which their private character gave rise and consequently incomplete from our perspective. Despite its generality, however, this description precisely follows the pattern, not of Justin's making, whereby details of paschal baptism and eucharist ("how we dedicated ourselves to God when we were made new through Christ," 61) are followed by reference to the Sunday eucharist ("on the day called of the sun, there is a meeting in one place," 67). Indeed, this pattern, roughly that already encountered in the present *Did.*, doubtless reflects the practice of the Roman church once the Passover had come to be celebrated on a Lord's Day following the Jewish feast, as was the case by the time of the visit of Polycarp of Smyrna to Pope Anicetus in A.D. 155 (Eusebius, *HE*, IV, 14).

Moreover, Justin's description is by no means lacking in specific detail. The paschal description assumes pre-baptismal catechesis, fasting, and prayer before a three-fold washing "into the name of the Father, and the Son, and the Holy Spirit" (cf. Mt 26:18-19), after which the newly baptized join the eucharist for common prayers and the kiss of peace (61, 65). The elaborate interpretation of this new birth and remission of sins, with the use of the term "illumination" (cf. Heb 6:4) and exposition of the divine triad (62-4) is likely catechetical in origin.

Justin's appended description of the eucharist (65), repeated briefly in his treatment of its weekly use (67), exhibits the shape of taking, blessing over, breaking (here omitted), and distribution as it had evolved when detached from an actual meal, with a unified oral-formal blessing prayer and assenting *Amen*. His interpretation of the rite, as a "memorial" commanded by Jesus (cf. 1 Cor 11:23-6), participation in the body and blood of Christ, and the pure sacrifice of the New Covenant (66, cf. *Dial.*, 41, 70, 117), likely reflects the themes expected to inform the blessing prayer. But the treatment of the Sunday eucharist adds reference to preliminary readings from the Jewish Scriptures and the "memoirs of the apostles," followed by a homily, before the common prayers and kiss of peace, and thus provides our earliest evidence of such a Christian adaptation of the synagogue service in connection with the Sunday eucharist.

Irenaeus. Unavoidable among theological writers of liturgical significance is Irenaeus of Lyons (d. 190 ?), native of Asia Minor, correspondent of members of the Roman church, presbyter and bishop of the Greek-speaking community at Lyons. His "Detection and refutation of falsely so-called Knowledge"(*Adversus Haereses*) is at once a response to Valentinian, Marcionite, and Gnostic teachings and a compendious presentation of Christian belief of far-reaching influence. His brief "Demonstration of Apostolic Preaching" (*Dem.*) is a catechetical digest of its main themes.

Irenaeus' liturgical value is at once seen in his main contention that his opponents rely on a false interpretation (*hypothesis*) of the scriptures different from the apostolic tradition (*paradosis*) communicated by the bishops at baptism (*Adv. Haer.* I.8.1, 9.1, 4, cf. III.2.2, 3.3). This tradition is "what we believe" about the one God and Father, the one Word incarnate in the flesh, and the Spirit which communicates new life in Christ to believers (I.10.1, cf. I.3.6, 22.1, II.28.1-3). Not only does Irenaeus refer here to the baptismal catechetical instruction with which he is familiar and which would eventually take shape in baptismal confes-sions of faith (creeds), but his whole work is, in *genre*, an expanded form of such instruction.

Irenaeus' treatments of baptism and eucharist assemble and develop now traditional interpretations, particularly those of baptismal rebirth (I.21.1, II.22.4, III.17.1) for the remission of sins (III.12.7) and the gift of righteousness and incorruption (III.17.2), and of the eucharist as the prophecies' pure sacrifice of the last days (IV.17.5), the oblation commanded by the Lord (IV.18.1), in which the bread and wine become the body and blood of Christ after "the invocation of God" (IV.18.5). In his own view, the baptismal and eucharistic use of water, bread, and wine as means of participation in Christ show the goodness and usefulness of the physical creation (III.17.2, IV.18.2, 4-6, V.2.2-3) in contrast to the views of his opponents, who are inconsistent in continuing their use (IV.18.5).

The Apostolic Tradition. It is hard to overestimate the importance of the identification (E. Schwartz [1910] and R.H. Connolly [1916]) of a Coptic document, discovered in 1848 and called "An Egyptian Church Order," as the "*Apost. Trad.*" listed among the writings of Hippolytus of Rome (d. 236). Now pieced together, on this basis, from a hitherto unidentified Latin MS, from Greek excerpts included in the later 4th century *Apost. Const.*, and other sources, this work is now generally regarded as that of the aforesaid Irenaean theologian, presbyter of the Roman church, opponent of the bishops Zephyrinus (d. 217) and Callistus (d. 233), and schismatical bishop. As such, it purports to describe the proper conduct of the rites of the Roman church in Hippolytus' time. While still not a liturgical book it is an invaluable discussion of Roman liturgical practice.

Apost. Trad. follows the outline already familiar from Justin. Here, however, an extensive section on ordinations (2-15) precedes that on paschal baptism and eucharist, and includes a detailed description of the eucharist of the newly ordained bishop. In consequence, the paschal section (16-23) treats baptism in detail, but adds only brief notes on the eucharist which follows it, while the Sunday eucharist is omitted in the interest of a scattering of directions on other matters, including the continuation of communal meals whose non-eucharistic character is insisted on (25-26).

The Roman provenance of *Apost. Trad.* is evident from its broad structural similarities to Justin, and its use in the paschal baptism of interrogations accompanying the three washings ("Do you believe ...? I believe ... ") which employ much of the language of the Roman baptismal confession later attested by the letter of Marcellus of Ancyra to Pope Julius I in A.D. 340 (Epiphanius, *Panarion* 72) and Rufinus of Aquileia's early 5th-century *Commentary on the Apostles' Creed*.

But an uncertain number of features of *Apost. Trad.* may be Hippolytus' own adaptations or proposals. His rigorist position on the restoration of apostates in persecution is evident in the care with which he insists catechumens be selected (16), in his acceptance of the "baptism of blood" as an alternative baptism in water (19), and just possibly in the dramatic positioning of the baptismal interrogations. The careful descriptions of the functions of bishop, presbyters, and deacons in the ordination prayers (3, 8, 9) may also owe something to his own views, as may the unified language of his episcopal eucharistic prayer or *anaphora* (4), the theological stress on the independent existence of the word in its opening thanks for the work of God, and in the appearance of an oblation of the "memorial" and invocation of the Spirit following the "institution narrative." In this latter respect, its similarities with later Eastern eucharistic prayers rather than the later Roman

canon have often been noticed. But there is no reason why a Roman prayer should not have had parallels with contemporary Asian types (cf. *Martyrdom of Polycarp*, 14), and we are not clear as to the limits of improvisation acceptable at the time.

Some Other Evidence

Only a selection of other materials from the 3rd century can be noticed here, and then only for its correspondence with the types of evidence thus far encountered.

Didascalia. From Syria, perhaps quite early in the 3rd century, comes the "Catholic teaching of the twelve apostles and holy disciples of our Savior" (*Didascalia*), now reconstructed by conflating a Syrian translation with Greek excerpts incorporated in the later 4th-century *Apost. Const.* Though often described as a "church Order," this work does not follow the structure which we have in the present *Did.*, Justin, or *Apost. Trad.*, but is a "disorderly" collection of material on various matters of belief and morals. Its liturgical interest lies in its provision, in connection with comments on the pastoral responsibilities of the bishop, of prayer forms for the reconciliation of the excommunicate (6-7), its brief reference to the bishop's liturgical functions (9), and its assortment of graphic details concerning the physical arrangement and appropriate conduct of the sorts of people who might gather at the eucharistic meetings (15).

Tertullian and Cyprian. Other contemporary liturgical evidence is found in the two major Latin writers of the period. Of these, Tertullian (d. A.D. 220), is the earlier and more comprehensive, a presbyter (?) of the church of Carthage, appropriator of Irenaeus and contemporary of Hippolytus, who came to accept the claims of the Montanist martyrs to a special possession of the gifts of the Spirit. By contrast, Cyprian (d. A.D. 258), bishop of Carthage, though a devoted reader of Tertullian, supported the authority of bishops to restore apostates to communion, and opposed the claims of the "confessors," who had been prepared to die in persecution, to special powers of forgiveness.

Tertullian's treatise "On Baptism" (*De bapt.*), the only work on the subject in our period, might be the exception to our rule that liturgical matters are not subjects of treatment in themselves were it not essentially an anti-Gnostic tract, concerned to defend (cf. Irenaeus) the regenerative power of water, the primordial source of life, when the Spirit is invoked upon it, the triune name employed, and the Spirit given through anointing and laying on of hands (2-8). In pursuing this subject, Tertullian provides details of baptismal practice not otherwise found in Justin or even Hippolytus (e.g., baptism at Pentecost as well as at the paschal feast), as well as, with the challenge of persecution in view, endorsing (16) the "baptism of blood" (see Hippolytus) and discouraging (18) the apparently hitherto common practice of baptizing infants (i.e., "households").

Tertullian, "On prayer" (*De orat.*) is perhaps more topical, though it is in arguing the superiority of Christian to Jewish prayer that it provides the earliest commentary on the Lord's Prayer (2-9), incidentally taking "daily bread" to refer to the eucharist, "daily" referring to the "perpetuity" and "indivisibility" of our membership in the body of Christ (6). Once again, the treatise supplies details otherwise lacking, in this case of practices of corporate and private prayer, such as comments on kneeling and standing with hands extended (*orans*), the exchange of the kiss of peace and the reception of the communion, and the prohibition of kneeling at the paschal feast and Pentecost.

More at large, Tertullian develops themes of Irenaeus to the point that the body is washed and fed in baptism and eucharist so that both body and soul may be saved (cf. *De res. carnis* 8), and introduces his own subsequently influential interpretation of the eucharistic sacrifice as a service or duty assigned as a means of rendering satisfaction to God (*De orat.* 19).

Cyprian. Cyprian's extensive debt to Tertullian includes an underlying assumption regarding the purity of the church, which leads, in his case, to insistence on the importance of eucharistic communion with the bishop rather than of such extraordinary spiritual gifts as Tertullian had come to value in the Montanists (*De unit. eccl* 5-6, 8, 23). Thus he rejected (perhaps recalling Tertullian, *De bapt.* 15) the baptisms performed by the schismatical bishops who followed Novatian in condemning, in part on the basis of Heb 6:4-8, his willingness to allow the restoration of apostates to communion (*Epp.* 69-74).

In this badly so-called "rebaptism" controversy, Cyprian was opposed by the Roman bishop Stephen, who supported the reception of the schismatically baptized, and himself, in his stress on unity with the bishop as the guarantee of the purity of the church, inadvertently laid the foundation for the later Donatist schism, which originated in refusal of communion with any bishops who had committed apostasy in persecution. For our purposes, this controversy is further indication, here provided in characteristically Latin form, of the significance of baptism and eucharist as defining true Christian identity.

4th and 5th-Century Sources

With the end of the persecutions and the beginning of the period in which Christianity became the public cultus of the Roman imperial government, the number and variety of liturgical sources multiply, though they still reflect the oral-formal tradition continued in these new circumstances.

Families of Rites. It has been common to speak of this period as witnessing the emergence of "families of rites," results of the growing influence on local practices of the great sees of the time. It would perhaps be truer to say that our evidence, still scattered and incomplete, suggests a more specific process of consolidation, at least in the East.

The *Apost. Const.* already mentioned as coming from Antioch in the late 4th century, is the central body of evidence. Long available, it has been recognized only recently for the compilation of the diverse materials it is. It opens with directions for various aspects of Christian life (I-VI) containing excerpts of *Didascalia*, incorporates the blessing prayers of *Did.* partially reorganized into a contemporary eucharistic structure (VII 25-6), and includes (VIII 1-5) a version of the ordination section of *Apost. Trad.* If *Apost. Const.* is still a "church Order" based on the sort of structure of description found in *Did.*, Justin, and *Apost. Trad.*, it has been stretched out of shape by the diverse materials accommodated within it, perhaps in an effort to organize the variety of practices in use in the region of the Syrian capital.

Central to *Apost. Const.*, however, are elaborate directions and prayers for baptism (VII 39-45) and eucharist (VIII 6-15), generally thought to reflect the practices of the church of Antioch itself. Distinctive features of baptism include a unified taking of the confession of faith separate from the washing itself and a subsequent episcopal anointing with invocation of the Spirit. Those of the eucharist include the dismissal of catechumens and litanic prayers of the faithful led by deacons, and an elaborate *anaphora* similar in shape to that reflected in *Apost. Trad.* but including extended Preface and Sanctus and introducing diaconal prayers for the living and dead before the concluding doxology.

Other Eastern Evidence. Less well-known from this period is the recently discovered East Syrian evidence of the use in the church of Edessa of the *Anaphora of Addai and Mari*, notable for retaining early Jewish Christian blessing forms reminiscent of the type found in *Did.*, but set within a structure roughly similar to that elaborated in *Apost. Const.* From Egypt as well, light has been shed on the background of the Alexandrian Liturgy of St. Mark by the late 19th-century discovery of the "prayer book" (*euchologion*) of Serapion (d. 360 ?), bishop of Thmuis and correspondent of Athanasius. This collection may have been preserved because of the intrinsic interest of its prayers at the scripture readings, homily, dismissal of the catechumens, and common prayers before the eucharist (1-12), and at the baptismal (19-25) and ordination (26-8) rites. But it also preserves an *anaphora* different in shape from *Apost. Const.* and of undoubted Egyptian pedigree (cf. the *Der Balizeh* and *Strasbourg* frags.), in which Preface and Sanctus are followed by invocations over the oblation before and after the institution narrative.

For the East in general, however, similarities between *Apost. Const.* and the later rite of Constantinople suggest that its central sections contain a version of the rites eventually adopted in the new imperial capital. With additions of its own, notably its use of the *anaphora* attributed to John Chrysostom (d. 407), and occasionally replaced by those of Basil of Caesarea (d. 379) and the Jerusalem Liturgy of St. James, these latter rites eventually commended themselves widely where imperial influence extended in the East.

Egeria, *Diary of a Pilgrimage*, the account of a journey of a Gallo-Hispanic religious woman through Asia Minor, Palestine, and Egypt at the turn of the 5th century, offers graphic descriptions of liturgical life, including the paschal rites at Jerusalem and its environs.

The West. Comparable Western evidence is restricted to much later books, all showing effects of the promotion of the Roman rites under the Frankish auspices of Pepin IV and Charlemagne in the 8th and 9th centuries. The peculiar features of the north Italian *Ambrosian Missal*, the Gallo-Hispanic *Missale Gothicum* and *Bobbio Missal*, and the Gallo-Irish *Stowe Missal*, many of which may reflect the appropriation of Eastern practices through Italy, must be studied in the light of such writings as those of Ambrose of Milan (d. 396) and Isidore of Seville (d. 636). Evidence of the rites of Latin Africa, before the Vandal conquest of the 5th and the Justinian reconquest of the 6th century, is entirely in the form of allusions in such writings as those of Augustine (d. 421).

Of the Roman rites themselves, after the 4th century introduction of Latin as the liturgical language, such evidence as we have comes from similarly later books, though it is here possible to identify the oldest form of the Roman eucharistic prayer or *canon*, wrongly attributed to Gelasius I (d. 496), and early seasonal materials which may partly derive from the time of Leo I (d. 461), before encountering the work attributed to Gregory I (d. 604), whose name is traditionally attached to the rites adopted by the Frankish liturgical reformers. Apart from a certain restraint in the adoption of Eastern practices, and the formulation of a eucharistic *canon* different in structure from that of *Apost. Trad.* but perhaps not entirely without contemporary parallels (cf. Ambrose, *De sacramentis*), we may think of the earliest Latin rites of the Roman church as similar to those which preceded them.

Catecheses and Homilies. Of unique significance for this period are the bodies of catechetical and homiletic material, which are themselves liturgical in character as well as in contents, which reflect the newly public position of the church, and provide a wealth of detail about liturgical practice.

While we have references to catechetical instruction before baptism in Justin and *Apost. Trad.*, and in Tertullian, Origen (d. 254 ?), and other earlier writers, it is from the 4th century onward that we have evidence of two types of formal episcopal addresses, the first delivered at and after the formal acceptance of candidates for the paschal baptism, devoted to the exposition of the teachings of the baptismal confession of faith, and occasionally the Lord's Prayer, the second consisting of post-baptismal ("mystagogical") addresses devoted to the meaning of baptism and eucharist for those who had now participated in them.

Of such addresses, we have a series, not always complete or given in the same years, by Cyril, Bishop of Jerusalem (d. 386), Theodore of Mopsuestia (d. 428), and John Chrysostom (d. 407), the last as presbyter of Antioch. We also have two post-baptismal catecheses of Ambrose of Milan, *De mysteriis* and (now widely accepted) *De sacramentis*. Among other evidence, Augustine, *De catechizandis rudibus*, provides advice and a model *narratio* to a Carthaginian deacon charged with the initial address to those seeking admission as catechumens, while his *De fide et symbolo* purports to be based on his own catechetical instructions as presbyter of Hippo. Maximus the Confessor's (d. 662), *Mystagogia*, is a mystical interpretation of the Constantinopolitan eucharistic liturgy of his time, and an important source for its study, rather than a catechetical instruction.

Such earlier homilies as survive include that of Melito, bishop of Sardis (d. 190), *On the passover*, and the great collections of the scriptural homilies of Origen. From the 4th century onward, however, comes a profusion of homilies too great to be enumerated, including series of Gregory of Nazianzus (d. 390), Gregory of Nyssa (d. 395), John Chrysostom, and Cyril of Alexandria (d. 444), as well as of Ambrose, Augustine, Leo I, and Gregory I. With respect to all of these, it can only be noticed, in general, that the public liturgical assemblies of this period allowed and even required new forms of homiletic address, having in view non-Christians as well as Christians, and larger physical spaces than had before been the case. Several writings of the period, most notably Chrysostom, *On priesthood*, but also Gregory of Nazianzus, *On his flight*, and even Ambrose, *On the duties of ministers*, are of interest as addressing or reflecting the challenge of preaching in these circumstances.

Such catechetical lectures and homilies were, in this period as distinct from ours, regarded as integral parts of the liturgy itself rather than as attachments or additions to it. Initially taken down in shorthand in the course of delivery, they often reflect another stage in the appropriation of classical styles of public address, in this case oratory, for Christian purposes.

Later Theological Issues

Liturgical theology in this period turns, as might be expected from that before, on the theological significance of liturgical practice. Thus, both Athanasius (*Ad Serap.* I. 14, 30) and the "homoiousian" Basil of Ancyra (Epiphanius, *Panar* 73.3) argue for their different ways of stating the equality of the persons of the Godhead against the Arians on the ground that Father, Son, and Spirit are together at work in baptism, while the enhanced specificity of the invocation (*epiklesis*) of the Spirit on the oblation in the various forms of *anaphora* in the Constantinopolitan rite emphasizes what seemed the orthodox trinitarian implications of earlier liturgical prayers. While the Carolingian theologians, Ratramnus and

Radbertus, developed their several views of the relation of the body and blood of Christ to the eucharistic bread and wine with references to a variety of early Christian writers, it is doubtful if the latter would have understood the terms of the debate, prone as they were to proceed by reference to the theology inherent in liturgical language rather than to raise questions on the basis of it.

Conclusion

The erosion of the oral-formal tradition of liturgical practice is not easily traced in our sources themselves. The consolidation of rites in the East may well have impelled a new concern for precision in liturgical language, though the 9th-century Constantinopolitan *euchologion* (Barberini MS) is the first surviving document to appear to assume the actual use of liturgical books. For the West, it may be assumed that inroads upon the classical tradition required the use of such books at a much earlier date, perhaps particularly in Spain and Gaul, though the late date of our actual sources, which generally assume their use, makes it hard to say when this occurred. It is only in Carolingian ivory bookcovers that liturgical books appear on altars in tandem with books of the gospels, though these may reflect a practice long-familiar at the time.

The issue here is not a small one. Much that is central to the character of early liturgical practice hinged on the continuation of the oral-formal tradition, and was obscured when the cultural decline of the later centuries necessitated its abandonment. At that point, whenever and by what stages it occurred, different notions of the nature of Christian liturgical gatherings began to make their influence felt.

B. Altaner, *Patrology*, trans. H.C. Graef (Edinburgh-London: Nelson, 1960). L. Bouyer, *Eucharist* (Notre Dame and London: University of Notre Dame Press, 1968). A. Benoit, *Bapteme chretien au second siecle* (Paris: Presses Universitaires de France, 1953). R.F. Evans, *One and Holy: The Church in Latin Patristic Thought* (London: S.P.C.K., 1972). C. Jones, G. Wainwright, E. Yarnold, eds., *The Study of Liturgy* (Oxford: Oxford University Press, 1978). J. Jungmann, *Mass of the Roman Rite*, 2 vols., trans. F.A. Brunner (New York: Benziger, 1950). A. Kavanagh, *The Shape of Baptism* (New York: Pueblo, 1978). J.N.D. Kelly, *Early Christian Creeds*, 3rd ed. (New York: McKay, 1972). G.A. Kennedy, *Classical Rhetoric and Its Christian and Secular Tradition* (Chapel Hill: University of North Carolina Press, 1980). T. Klauser, *A Short History of the Western Liturgy* (Oxford: Oxford University Press, 1969). W. Rordorf, *et al.*, *The Eucharist of the Early Christians*, trans. M.J. O'Connell (New York: Pueblo, 1978). T.J. Talley, *The Origins of the Liturgical Year* (New York: Pueblo, 1986). E.C. Whitaker, *Documents of the Baptismal Liturgy*, 2nd ed. (London: S.P.C.K., 1970). F. Van der Meer, *Early Christian Art* (Chicago: University of Chicago Press, 1959).

LLOYD G. PATTERSON

SOURCES, LITURGICAL

The *Constitution on the Sacred Liturgy* of Vatican II stated that the liturgy "is the outstanding means whereby the faithful may express in their lives and manifest to others the mystery of Christ and the real nature of the true Church" (S.C., 2). Earlier in the century Pope Pius XI had written that "the liturgy is the most important organ of the ordinary magisterium of the Church" (*Quas primas*, A.A.S., 17 [1925], 603). Statements such as these continue the line of thinking of the famous 5th-century axiom of St. Prosper of Aquitaine, who declared that the law of worship constitutes the norm of belief: *legem credendi statuit lex orandi*. The liturgy has enjoyed a privileged place throughout history in the handing down of the tradition of the church, especially the belief tradition. A study of liturgical sources is thus part of the total theological task of uncovering the past in order to better understand the present and to shape the future.

According to a leading specialist in the area of liturgical sources, Cyrille Vogel, liturgical literature includes three kinds of documents: (a) liturgical books properly so-called, that is, the books actually utilized in the course of Christian worship; (b) works that treat of divine worship such as commentaries, sermons, and explanations or descriptions of liturgies; (c) liturgical monuments such as sacred buildings, inscriptions, mosaics, paintings, sculptures, liturgical furniture and vestments. (The work of Cyrille Vogel, *Medieval Liturgy: An Introduction to the Sources*, is absolutely unequaled as an aid to the study of liturgical sources.) This article will limit itself to key written sources of the West.

The very earliest Christian liturgical sources would be found in sacred scripture itself which included certain liturgical acclamations, doxologies, hymns and credal confessions. While NT data contain such elements, we do not find any actual order of service or any complete description of early worship. Nevertheless, the NT does reveal a great deal about the life of faith of the first Christians and the expression of that faith. An important aspect of this would be their prayer life.

Major liturgical sources would be the early church orders. Most important among them should be mentioned: *Didache* (Syria ca. 50 (?)-150); *Apostolic Tradition* (Rome/Alexandria, ca. 215); *Didascalia Apostolorum* (Syria, 220-250); *Apostolic Constitutions* (Syria, ca. 380); *Canons of Hippolytus* (Alexandria, 320-350); *Testament of the Lord* (Syria, 5th century). The *Apostolic Tradition* is a work of bishop Hippolytus of Rome (the majority opinion) and it stands out as a unique ante-Nicene liturgical source due to the outstanding influence it played on later liturgies both in the West and in the East. The document was written in Greek, but comes down only in Coptic, Arabic, Ethiopic and Latin versions. The recommended English translation is that of G.J. Cuming, *Hippolytus: A Text for Students* (Grove Liturgical Study 8), Bramcote Notts, 1976. Also high on the list of important sources among these church orders would be the *Didascalia Apostolorum* which makes use of the *Didache* and which in turn is used by the later *Apostolic Constitutions.*

The Fathers of the church and other ecclesiastical writers often allude to the liturgy, even though the information they provide is usually fragmentary and incomplete. Justin, Tertullian, Cyprian, Ambrose and Augustine would be good examples of writers who provide us with helpful descriptions of liturgical practices of the times. In a famous description of the liturgy of the Lord's Day Justin writes: "On the day which is called 'Sunday', all, whether they live in the town or in the country, gather in the same place. Then the memoirs of the apostles or the writings of the prophets are read for as long as time allows. When the reader has finished, the president speaks, exhorting us to live by those noble teachings. Then we rise all together and pray. Then, as we said earlier, when the prayer is finished, bread, wine and water are brought. The president then prays and gives thanks as well as he can. And all the people reply with the acclamation: Amen" (*First Apology*, chap. 67).

Another valuable source for the description of early worship (again, without providing the actual texts of the liturgies) is the diary of a female pilgrim, probably a nun, who traveled to Egypt, the Holy Land, Edessa, Asia Minor and Constantinople at the end of the 4th century: J. Wilkinson, trans., *Egeria's Travels*, London, 1971, and 2nd ed., Jerusalem, 1981. She describes in great detail the Jerusalem liturgy of the year 383. Since she seldom makes reference to the scripture readings, one should complement this particular source by using the parallel lectionary of the time: A. Renoux, *Le Codex Arménien Jérusalem 121*, Vol. 1, Turnhout, 1969; Vol. 2, Turnhout, 1971.

The ancient Christian era was a period when local churches created their own liturgical formulas. Improvisation was the task of the presider of the gathered community. Worship was a corporate action, and the leader spoke in the name of the entire community. He directed the service from tradition, the historical tradition that Jesus instituted the rite of the eucharist. Local churches were quite free, however, to develop the forms of this worship in diverse manners and styles. There was no set formula and the presiders certainly varied in personal talents. As Justin had put it: "The president then prays and gives thanks as well as he can."

In time some of the prayers began to be written down and we have the *libelli missarum*, oral improvisations put into written form. They certainly must have been a great help for less gifted celebrants. The earliest and most well known collection of *libelli missarum* would be the Verona collection: L.C. Mohlberg-L. Eizenhofer-P. Siffrin, eds., *Sacramentarium Veronense*, Rome, 1956. This collection is sometimes called the Leonine sacramentary, but in reality, is neither a work of Pope Leo nor does it seem that it was a book actually used at the altar. Vogel says of this collection: "It appears too haphazardly put together and too incomplete for that (being used at the altar), and it follows the unusual plan of distributing its formularies according to the months of the civil calendar rather than according to the plan of the liturgical year" (p. 39).

While the Verona collection does not contain a eucharistic prayer, it does contain some very important prayers for the study of liturgy, e.g., ordination of bishops, deacons and priests (nos. 942-954), and the oldest nuptial blessing (nos. 1105-1110). Of its 1,331 formulas (most coming from the 5th and 6th centuries), 175 made their way into the *Missal of Pius V* of 1570.

The next major liturgical source to be mentioned would be the so-called Old

Gelasian Sacramentary: L.C. Mohlberg-L. Eizenhofer-P. Siffrin, *Liber Sacramentorum Romanae Aecclesiae Ordinis Circuli*, Rome, 1960. This was truly a sacramentary, and played an important role as a liturgical source in the Western church. The Vatican manuscript (*Reginensis latinus 316*) of this sacramentary is the only one of its kind and is as important for the history of art as it is for the history of liturgy. It is considered a major work by those in the fields of pre-carolingian paleography and early medieval book art. It was used at Rome during much of the 7th (some would even say 6th) and the first part of the 8th century. It was carried into Gaul and widely used there, at least until around 750 when the book was copied at a monastery of northeastern France (probably Chelles), giving us the famous Vatican manuscript, *Reginensis latinus 316*. The sacramentary is a "mixed" book in that it represents an intermingling of Roman *libelli* of both papal and presbyteral usages, and in that it is a mixture of both Roman and Frankish liturgical elements. Vogel comments on the latter: "These Gallican additions should not be regarded as blocks of material mechanically juxtaposed to the older Roman elements but as fresh additions or combinations which were gradually amalgamated, to varying degrees, with the older Roman structures" (p. 67). Such an opinion represents the view of the majority of researchers, but some would disagree, and the matter is still far from settled. At any rate, the influence of the Old Gelasian Sacramentary can be shown by the fact that 344 of its prayer-texts are to be found in the *Missale Romanum* of 1975.

The Vatican manuscript of the Old Gelasian Sacramentary is in a particularly fine state of preservation. This is due to the fact that a few years after this copy was made the liturgy contained in it was replaced by a new type of liturgy which resulted from the Romanizing effort of King Pepin. This source is called the Frankish Gelasian or the Eighth-Century Gelasian Sacramentary. A number of manuscripts that survive of this type of liturgy postulate the existence of a single archetype called the Sacramentary of Flavigny, which is now lost. The Sacramentary of Flavigny was assembled by a team of Benedictine monks around 760-770. It represented a fusion of different types of Roman sacramentaries that had penetrated Gaul by the mid-8th century. Its goal was to provide a liturgy that was eminently usable by parishes and monasteries. The best extant source for this category of liturgy would be: A. Dumas-J. Deshusses, eds., *Liber Sacramentorum Gellonensis*, Turnhout, 1981.

Besides the Old Gelasian and the Eighth-Century Gelasian, another type of Roman Mass book circulated in northern Europe and exercised a major role as a liturgical source. This was the Gregorian: J. Deshusses, *Le Sacramentaire grégorien* (3 vols.), Fribourg, 1971, 1979, 1982. This work goes back to the 7th century when a sacramentary was drawn up from the *libelli* used for papal liturgy both at the Lateran and at stational liturgies. Vogel explains: "Although this distinctive book can no longer be attributed to Gregory the Great (590-604), it was probably redacted under Pope Honorius I (625-638) and was gradually augmented as new stational liturgies and fresh feasts emerged in the course of the VII and VIII centuries" (p. 79).

When Charlemagne sought a "pure" Gregorian sacramentary from Pope Hadrian I, the pope sent something in the realm of a gift rather than a usable sacramentary (called in history the *Hadrianum*). The book had to be supplemented for practical usage, and scholars now agree that the author of the supplement was St. Benedict of Aniane rather than Alcuin as was previously held.

Benedict used a wide range of liturgical sources in composing his additions. Vogel summarizes: "Thanks to all these additions, Benedict of Aniane contributed mightily to the resulting hybrid Romano-Frankish liturgy destined to become the liturgy of the entire Latin patriarchate" (p. 89). Of all the various types of Gregorian sacramentaries, it was this *Hadrianum* with the supplement of St. Benedict of Aniane that was the chief source for the *Missale Romanum* of 1570 and the *Missale Romanum* of 1975.

The Frankish or Gallican component of this hybrid liturgy was the product of the 5th to the 9th century (when Charlemagne introduced the *Hadrianum*). There was a great sense of liturgical freedom under the Merovingian kings of the 7th and 8th centuries, consonant with the very nature of the Franco-Gallic people itself. One striking characteristic of the Gallican rite was a type of variable eucharistic prayer. There is certainly no one "pure" Gallican liturgical source, but perhaps most fruitful for study would be the Vatican manuscript of the beginning of the 8th century representing liturgical usage in Gaul during the 7th century, the *Reginensis latinus 317*: L.C. Mohlberg, ed., *Missale Gothicum*, Rome, 1961.

The sacramentaries contained only the prayers needed by the celebrant and not the directives or descriptions of the rite, or at least not in any extended way. Thus the sacramentaries had to be supplemented by the *ordines*. The classical collection of these is: M. Andrieu, *Les Ordines romani du haut moyen âge* (5 vols.), Louvain, 1931, 1948, 1951, 1956, 1961. The *ordines* were absolutely necessary from the 8th century onward in the churches of Europe north of the Alps due to the changing forms of worship. At first the Roman *ordines* traveled northward in the form of independent entities, being gathered together as collections only in Gaul. The form in which we possess them

is a hybrid one, Romano-Frankish or Romano-Germanic. They vary in size from being a single page to the size of a book, and in date of origin from the 7th to the 8th century. Just as the sacramentaries contained things other than strictly the prayers of the presider, so the *ordines* contained things other than the descriptions of the rites, e.g., prayers, didactic material, etc.

The *ordines* played a key role in the history of Western liturgy at least until the appearance of the pontifical, the book that resulted from combining the non-eucharistic *ordines* with the corresponding prayers from the sacramentary. Without doubt, the most important was a collection compiled by a monk of St. Alban in Mainz in the middle of the 10th century. Andrieu recognized its unique importance and called it the "Romano-Germanic Pontifical" by which it has been known ever since. C. Vogel-R. Elze, *Le Pontifical romano-germanique du dixième siècle* (3 vols.), Vatican City, 1963-1972. Since this was the collection the Ottonian emperors took with them to Rome and imposed there, it became the major point of departure for all later episcopal books. This is important insofar as the collection contained many non-Roman elements, which when fused with the Roman, gave rise to a new hybrid liturgy. This liturgy was celebrated in Rome, and then passed on to the entire Latin West.

The first official edition, in the modern sense, of the pontifical was that of Pope Clement VIII in 1595. This was the first time in the history of the church that a pontifical was edited by a pope which was to be the unique model, abrogating all other previous pontificals in the Latin church.

Up until the end of the 13th century the pontifical contained not only the non-eucharistic texts for bishops but *de facto* also rites for priests as well. The book for priests (excluding the office) was the ritual. The history of the ritual shows that it developed proximately from the pontifical and remotely from the sacramentary. Interestingly, the oldest rituals are monastic. Before the 12th century rituals are most frequently found attached to the monastic collectary. One discovers the following general trend in the historical development of the ritual: a move from monastic to parochial to diocesan to national to international. One important ritual went through sixteen editions over a period of 75 years (20 years prior to Trent and 35 years after Trent): the *Liber Sacerdotalis* of Alberto Castellani, O.P., Venice, 1523. It influenced the Ritual of Santori (1612) and the first official Roman ritual (*Rituale Romanum Pauli V*) of 1614. Unlike the first official pontifical whose use had been strictly compulsory, the ritual of 1614 was only recommended for use.

After the Protestant Reformation the ritual took on an increasingly important teaching role with catechetical comments being inserted into the rites (*monitiones*). Another such didactic effort among liturgical sources would be the *expositiones missae*. Since the patristic period there had been the practice of "exposing" certain things (in the catechetical sense) as the texts of scripture, the Our Father and the Creed. In the 9th century this practice was extended to the Mass prayers. It was considered the job of the parish priest not only to be able to lead the prayers but also to understand the meaning of those prayers. The *expositiones missae* were thus written to instruct priests with the hope that their knowledge would filter down to the people to whom they preached and gave instructions. The weakness of the effort was that the *expositiones* tended to stress the allegorical aspects of the liturgy, often to the detriment of the essentials. Certainly the most well known writer of such treatises would be Amalarius of Metz of the 9th century: J.H. Hanssens,

ed., *Amalarii episcopi opera liturgica omnia* (3 vols.), Vatican City, 1948-50.

The same 9th century witnessed the beginning of a dramatic change: the change from the sacramentary (containing only the prayers that the priest recited) to the full missal (the *Missalis Plenarius*) which contained everything, even the readings. This change was more than a shift in the contents of liturgical books. It represented a new way of viewing the liturgical action. The liturgy of the eucharist was no longer a joint action of celebrant, singers, ministers and people; it was now seen as the action of the priest. By the 11th century the priest is obligated to recite by himself even the sung parts of the Mass.

Sacred Scripture has always been viewed as a unique liturgical source. The *Constitution on the Sacred Liturgy* of Vatican II reflected this long tradition: "Sacred Scripture is of the greatest importance in the celebration of the liturgy. For it is from Scripture that the readings are given and explained in the homily and that psalms are sung; the prayers, collects, and liturgical songs are scriptural in their inspiration; it is from the Scriptures that actions and signs derive their meanings" (S.C., 24). The historical development of the lectionary is a complicated terrain. The opinion that Gregory the Great fixed the readings at the end of the 6th century is no longer held. It seems that great freedom and variety existed in the area of scripture readings at Mass. It was pretty much the local bishop who regulated the choice and length of the readings. The gospel tradition has left more traces of evidence and is thus easier to study, yet the epistle tradition is more archaic and preserves older features all along the way ("epistle" in the wide sense to include all non-gospel readings, including the OT readings). The most important recent insight into the historical development of the lectionary reveals that the epistle tradition and gospel tradition grew up as independent entities, and were combined only much later on, and then in a rather haphazard way. For Gallican usage the most important lectionary is: P. Salmon, *Le Lectionnaire de Luxeuil* (2 vols.), Rome, 1944, 1953. For Roman usage, the readings that were fixed in the *Missale Romanum* of 1570 were basically those of the *Comes of Murbach* of the 8th century.

For the liturgy of the hours, no special liturgical book existed at the beginning. The Bible sufficed. The psalms were chanted from memory and the prayers were improvised. In time, just as was the case for the eucharist, the best of the prayers were collected in *libelli* and eventually they found their way into the sacramentary and then into the collectary. Eventually other books were used in the recitation of the office: the office-lectionary, the antiphonary for sung parts, the psalter, etc. By the 11th and 12th centuries, as many as ten different books were involved. When all of these were brought under one cover around the 12th century it was termed the breviary. Scholars today recognize that that did not involve a reduction or curtailment of texts, nor did it have to do with private recitation outside choir. It had more to do with the changing nature of monasticism. S.J.P. Van Dijk stated: "Once interest had been turned towards study, the intellectual level of monastic society as such rose. Every monk became a professional liturgist, able to take an active part. The ancient choir books were no longer a mystery to him nor a prerogative of the few leading authorities. Both his education and the elaborate ritual required that he should have access to the whole text of the whole office" (p. 35).

While the breviary contained the official prayer of the church, the prayer book of the laity escaped any such official control and was called *horae* (book of hours). In origin it grew out of the breviary in that it was comprised of the elements that grew up as accretions to the official office, as the seven penitential psalms, the office of the dead and the office of the Blessed Virgin. The *horae* are crucial for understanding the piety of the Middle Ages since they shaped to a great extent the spirituality of the laity. While it is true that no two manuscript *horae* are exactly alike, one major source in this area would be: V. Leroquais, *Les Livres d'Heures Manuscrits de la Bibliothèque Nationale* (3 vols.), Paris, 1927.

The liturgical sources involving musical notation present a unique case. We simply do not possess any such manuscripts until the 9th and 10th centuries. Most would argue that they simply did not exist, since the chant was handed down orally. A minority position would hold that there were earlier manuscripts with neumes, but they have been lost. One of the oldest Roman graduals dates from the mid-9th century (the *Cantatorium of Monza*), but it contains only texts without any musical notation. The terminology for the chant books is not always easy to determine. Some authors would argue that the parts of the Mass sung by the *schola cantorum* were gathered together in the antiphonary while those sung by a soloist were contained in the cantatorium (e.g., *Ordo Romanus Primus* used the term cantatorium for the book used by the cantor at the gradual and alleluia verse). At any rate, in time both these books were combined and from the 9th century were called the gradual. A very helpful source whose earliest manuscript is the 8th century (again, the texts only) would be R.J. Hesbert, ed., *Antiphonale missarum sextuplex*, Brussels, 1935. For the office, see: R.J. Hesbert, ed., *Corpus antiphonalium officii* (5 Vols.), Rome, 1963-1975. For an extremely helpful overview of musical manuscript sources, see: "Sources, MS," pp. 590-702 in Vol. 17 of *The New Grove Dictionary of Music and Musicians*, Washington, D.C., 1980.

During the first millennium or more of the church's life, liturgical books were compiled according to functions; a particular book contained only (more or less) what would be needed by its user. During those centuries no liturgical book contained everything needed for a liturgical service. Some historians list more than fifty different liturgical books when they study the domain of liturgical manuscripts. Approximately one out of ten manuscripts we possess today is a liturgical manuscript, and happily, certain scholarly organizations are attempting to preserve them for posterity. The most important organ in this regard is C.I.P.O.L.: Centre International de Publications Oecuméniques des Liturgies; 4, avenue Vavin: 75006 Paris, France. It comprises a group of liturgists from different churches from throughout the world whose goal is to put major liturgical sources on microfiche.

A perennial problem for researchers in the area of liturgical sources is the frequent confusion encountered in the cataloging of liturgical manuscripts. Liturgists and librarians do not always use the same nomenclature. The problem seems to be twofold: first, the difference between the modern and the medieval notion of just what constituted a liturgical book; and second, the diverse way that librarians and catalogers have solved the problem. Today we limit a liturgical book to one which contains the approved, official cult of the church. All others are books of private devotion. The medieval notion was not so stringent. Custom played a greater role: a liturgical book was one that contained the elements of the praying church, at all levels. As to cataloging, some have listed certain manuscripts as liturgical which others would have listed as biblical, patristic, or hagiographic.

Working in liturgical sources today is a far easier task than in the past. Not only has cataloging improved, but critical editions of texts are now often available and some are accompanied by concordances and tables that greatly simplify the task of working with these sources. A unique service has been provided by the *Subsidia* series of *Spicilegium Friburgense*: University of Freiburg Press; Freiburg, Switzerland. Two in the series deserve special mention: Klaus Gamber, *Codices liturgici latini antiquiores* (2 vols.), Freiburg, 2nd ed. 1968; A. Hänggi-I. Pahl, eds., *Prex eucharistica: Textus e variis liturgiis antiquioribus selecti*, Freiburg 2nd ed. 1978. The former is an absolutely indispensable bibliographical tool for working with early Western liturgical sources and the latter provides students with a collection of eucharistic prayers from ancient liturgies that they could never possibly have been able to gather themselves.

For work in recent liturgical sources a helpful service has been provided by R. Kaczynski, *Enchiridion documentorum instaurationis liturgicae I 1963-1973*, Rome, 1976. The documentary collection includes one hundred eighty separate items in 3,216 numbered sections. The arrangement is chronological rather than topical, but there is a large analytical index. Perhaps its greatest usefulness is the inclusion of certain thus far unpublished curial sources. For English-speaking students of liturgical sources a very helpful collection is: *Documents on the Liturgy 1963-1979: Conciliar, Papal, and Curial Texts*, Collegeville, 1982. Topically rather than chronologically arranged, this collection includes 554 official documents concerning the Vatican II liturgical renewal.

Unique to the Vatican II liturgical reform is the inclusion of introductions (*praenotanda*) within the new liturgical rites. These provide far more than mere rubrical background for the new rites; they provide the theological and pastoral context in which the rites are to be understood and interpreted. The same can be said for the general instruction (*institutio generalis*) provided for the new rites of eucharist and liturgy of the hours. Never before in the history of the church have liturgical rites been accompanied by such rich theological introductions. At times there can seem to be a tension or dichotomy between a particular rubric or text in a new rite, and the introduction accompanying that rite.

Likewise there can be conflict between an aspect of the Vatican II liturgical reform and the Code of Canon Law. The Code states: "For the most part the Code does not define the rites which are to be observed in celebrating liturgical actions. For this reason current liturgical norms retain their force unless a given liturgical norm is contrary to the canons of the Code" (C.I.C., 2). The changes that the new Code wrought on the Vatican II liturgical reform are listed in *Emendations in the Liturgical Books Following upon the New Code of Canon Law*, Washington, D.C., 1984.

Examining liturgical sources from the point of view of the written prayer-texts only can lead to an impoverished understanding of the liturgical event, or even, in the extreme, to a misunderstanding of it. The written prayers have to be contextualized by the wider surrounding or environment. The music, the architecture and bodily posture help create a certain mood. The mind-set of the participants, created by previous liturgical experience and by catechesis, all contribute to the way the prayer-texts are "heard." Alexander Schmemann refers to this as "liturgical piety" and comments that "it is important for the historian of worship to know that the 'liturgical piety' of an epoch can in various ways fail to correspond to the liturgy or cult of which the piety is nevertheless the psychological perception or experience.... Liturgical piety has the strange power of 'transposing' texts or ceremonies, of attaching a meaning to them which is not their

plain or original meaning" (p. 77). This makes the study of liturgical sources a very complex task. The prayer-text of a particular period must be studied in the light of a vast arena of other disciplines: social-political history, art history, various social sciences, etc. Thus, the prayer-texts found in sacramentaries and other liturgical books are but part of a puzzle that is being put together only in a gradual and collegial way.

This accounts for the fact that liturgical sources are of capital importance for the study of theology. The faith life of the church is not limited to the sphere of the conceptual; it is a total lived experience, and the liturgy is a unique expression of that experience.

See **Church order; Documents, Roman liturgical, since Vatican II; Liturgical texts in English; Reform, liturgical, of Vatican II**

Cheslyn Jones, Geoffrey Wainwright, Edward Yarnold, eds., *The Study of Liturgy* (New York: Oxford University Press, 1978). David Power, "Two Expressions of Faith: Worship and Theology," in *Liturgical Experience of Faith* (Concilium 82), Herman Schmidt and David Power, eds. (New York: Herder and Herder, 1973): 95-103. Alexander Schmemann, *Introduction to Liturgical Theology* (Portland, Maine: American Orthodox Press, 1966). S.J.P. Van Dijk and J. Hazelden Walker, *The Origins of the Modern Roman Liturgy* (Westminster, MD: Newman Press, 1960). Cyrille Vogel, *Medieval Liturgy: An Introduction to the Sources*, trans. and rev. William Storey and Niels Rasmussen (Washington, D.C.: Pastoral Press, 1986). Herman Wegman, *Christian Worship in East and West: A Study Guide to Liturgical History*, trans. Gordon Lathrop (New York: Pueblo Publishing Co., 1985).

GERARD AUSTIN, O.P.

SPIRITUAL DIRECTION AND LITURGY

The relationship between spiritual direction and liturgy has received little attention or study and, as a result, has seldom been explicated.

Liturgy, for our purposes here, can be understood in its common usage as "the public worship of God by the church." Spiritual direction can be described as the help a person seeks in order to grow in a loving relationship with God, thereby affecting all aspects of human life. In a specifically Christian context, spiritual direction has the focus of a person's growth-in-Christ. It looks to develop a relationship with God, who is addressed by Jesus' love-word *Abba*, and to enhance in one's life and activity the manifestation of God's reign which is brought about by Jesus' gift of the Spirit and human cooperation with grace. Although Christian spiritual direction is ordinarily thought of as a personal relationship between the one directing and the one being directed, even in this form of spiritual direction there is necessarily present a prior liturgical setting—the Christian community at worship—in which both parties are situated and formed.

How are spiritual direction and liturgy related in our Christian lives? Faith is the common foundation, and the lived expression of our faith comes in prayer and in action. This lived expression of faith is identified by the word *spirituality*. So a spirituality provides the necessary context for both the understanding and the practice of liturgy and spiritual direction. Prayer provides the atmosphere of the spiritual direction encounter just as it underlies every liturgical expression. Both liturgy and spiritual direction not only presume some sort of prayer stance, but they are also directed towards developing a richer prayer life in every participant as well as a more reflective and vibrant Christian action. In this way, liturgy is always in the context of a spirituality. Spiritual direction, for its part, is aimed at the personal integration of a spiritual life—developing one's own spirituality within a basic Christian spirituality and, at the same time perhaps, nuanced by a specific school of spirituality also present in and approved by the church.

Liturgy and Spirituality

A liturgical spirituality finds its foundation in public worship, that is, the worship of God by a community in the name of the church. But liturgical spirituality encompasses more than the moment of worship since it takes in all our life and activity insofar as we are affected by the liturgical celebration. Whether we consciously recognize it or not, as members of a worshipping Christian community we imbibe some sort of liturgical spirituality. A liturgical spirituality is one way of describing the foundational spirituality of the church, since it always puts us in contact with some aspect of celebrating the paschal mystery which identifies all Christians with Christ.

In addition to a liturgical spirituality, there has also developed a number of particular spiritualities called forth by the Spirit within the Christian community over the centuries. Quite often these spiritualities develop because Christians, moved by the Spirit, attempt to make a creative gospel response more focused to the needs of the culture or the times. Some spiritualities, such as *devotio moderna* associated with Thomas à Kempis (1379-1471) and his classical work, *The Imitation of Christ*, or the spirituality popularized by Francis de Sales (1567-1622) in his classical work, *Introduction to the Devout Life*, were meant for the whole church from their very beginnings. But there remains the more usual development of schools of spirituality rooted in a particular religious life tradition, such as Benedictine, Carmelite, Franciscan, Dominican, Ignatian or Jesuit, Sulpician, and so on. These spiritualities have eventually come to influence the wider church. How each of these spiritualities incorporates liturgical spirituality varies, but a liturgical spirituality remains essential to and compatible with every legitimately recognized spirituality within the church.

Spirituality and Spiritual Direction

Since Christian spirituality basically receives its focus within a liturgical spirituality, we can describe spiritual direction as the help which we receive from our participation in the liturgy of the eucharist and the liturgy of the hours to love and serve God and to live lives infused with Christian principles and values. This foundational spirituality, often called liturgical and particularly identified with a daily participation in the eucharist and office celebrations, has its own corresponding equivalent in a direction which we might signify by the term *general spiritual direction*. General spiritual direction in no way opposes or eliminates the need for other forms of direction in our personal assimilation of the Christian life. For example, we can also describe a direction which is so identified with the celebration of sacraments other than the eucharist that it can be distinguished by its own designation as *sacramental spiritual direction*. Finally we can explain direction in its most widely understood contemporary form as *personal spiritual direction*.

General Spiritual Direction. General spiritual direction considers the instruction, clarification, challenge, and motivating power which comes from the celebration of the eucharist, both in its liturgy of the word, particularly in the scripture readings and their explication in the homily, and in its liturgy of the sacramental action. In a similar way, general spiritual direction looks to the celebration of the liturgy of the hours to instruct, correct, lead on, and stir up the participant in the practice of the Christian faith. No one active in the Christian community, then, is devoid of receiving this kind of spiritual direction for growth and advancement in Christian living.

Sacramental Spiritual Direction. The sacraments which are less frequently celebrated than the eucharist have their own instructional, motivational, and empowering content. This content is distinctive enough to be identified as a kind of spiritual direction called specifically sacramental. The renewal of the sacrament celebrations called for in Vatican II has only served to highlight this spiritual direction aspect. For example, the R.C.I.A. (Rite for the Christian Initiation of Adults) program is recognized for its carefully designed developmental process in Christian growth, not only for the catechumen but also for the baptized—all in terms of the meaningful participation in the sacramental celebration. The preparation and instruction prior to celebrating the sacrament of matrimony is also a clear instance of direction for growth in a whole new stage of Christian living, which the actual sacramental celebration encapsulizes. The celebration of the sacrament of anointing, especially in its communal form, again presents a special occasion for directing people's growth in the central Christian paschal mystery of dying and rising. Finally the Vatican II renewal of the sacrament of penance and its re-designation as the sacrament of reconciliation brought to the fore the area where spiritual direction and liturgical or sacramental celebration have been most closely related throughout the centuries.

Traditionally the Celtic monasticism of the 6th and 7th centuries stressed the sacrament of penance beyond the confession of sins to the identifying and rooting out of one's evil tendencies and the personal directing for growth in the virtuous life. Because St. Columban is credited with bringing the Irish penitential system to the Continent, he remains a major figure in this Western Christianity movement. Because of the private nature of the sacramental encounter between priest and penitent, the direction in this instance is obviously within the context of a liturgical or sacramental rite, but at the same time is very personal in its application to a particular penitent. The Irish penitentials presented patterns of penances appropriate to certain sins confessed by the penitent; this was both an advance in personalizing the sacrament and a movement in adapting advice and counsel to the particular penitent.

Through the confession practices of the Middle Ages and through the clarifications made in the Council of Trent, the sacrament of penance grew in its importance for the personal spiritual direction of the Christian faithful. So frequent was the identification of a confessor with a spiritual director function that more and more spiritual direction was thought of in terms of priestly action. Often the occasion of spiritual direction in seminary training and in the consecrated religious life form was only to be found in the confessional.

Vatican II renewal of the sacrament emphasized anew the dialogic nature of the sacrament. More than just a simple accusation of sins and a pronouncement of absolution, the sacrament is now placed in the context of a dialogue between priest and penitent—with scripture, prayer, and counsel all having their appropriate moment. The sacrament of reconciliation stands out most clearly as a repeated instance of sacramental spiritual direction within the Christian life.

Personal Spiritual Direction. Besides the general spiritual direction which we receive in the celebration of the eucharist and potentially also in praying the liturgy of the hours, and the kind of instruction and empowerment received in sacramental celebrations, particularly in the sacrament of reconciliation, there is a long and constant tradition in the church for the role of the spiritual director, frequently called a spiritual father or spiritual mother, who helps to nurture in a one-to-one encounter the life-in-the-Spirit development of a fellow Christian.

The terminology of spiritual father or mother in the tradition of personal spiritual direction seems to be a parallel usage to the ministry of priests (called "Father") in their nurturing in the Spirit through the celebration of the eucharist and in all the other sacraments. There appears also a similarity in the understanding of the role of sponsors in baptism—sometimes called "godfathers" or "godmothers." The emphasis in the mother-father language is not on the unequal dependency relationship of parent-child since the basic reality is imaged as two adults in this relationship. Rather the reality of two adults coming together in a helping relationship serves to emphasize the consistent way that God works incarnately or sacramentally to bring forth or share divine life. God remains the only source of life (truly the only *Abba*), and yet Christians at various times merit the analogous use of the *abba* or *ammas* terminology as sacraments or instruments of God's dealings with a fellow Christian.

A Relationship of Balance

Spiritual direction and liturgy need to be related in providing a necessary balance in living and growing in the Christian faith. For example, liturgy continues to recall and celebrate God's great interventions in human history, particularly the ultimate intervention in the incarnation, passion, death, and resurrection of Jesus. Spiritual direction, with its emphasis on God's particular action within the personal history of *this* Christian, needs the largeness of vision provided by liturgy. But through personal spiritual direction, a Christian brings his or her own redemption moments of God's saving action into the community celebration so that each Christian truly fills in what is lacking in the sufferings of Christ. Both liturgy and spiritual direction, then, help form the Christian identity and call forth a personal transformation.

Liturgy provides a ritual—a combination of gestures and language expressions, of music and a total environmental setting for our contact with God. Spiritual direction encourages various means to enhance the growth in prayer—methods and techniques, bodily positions, environmental settings, and so on—and reflectively to integrate one's life activities into a putting on the mind of Christ. While spiritual direction intends to provide a necessary interior vitality to the ritual prayer form to keep it from being merely empty show, the ritual action calls the individual Christian out of a privatized relationship with God to the communal worship which is ours as the body of Christ and with Christ as our head and our one high priest. To enter into liturgical celebration always enters us as individual pray-ers into the prayer shared by all Christians.

Finally liturgy is the prime setting for the celebration of the gifts of the Spirit poured out upon the church. The celebrations of liturgy are made possible only by the Spirit's gifts of ministries accepted by individuals, recognized by the community, and exercised in the name of the Church and in a public manner—the worship of the community. Spiritual direction is also a ministry—a gifting of the Spirit to various members of the church. Spiritual direction, too, must be accepted as a gift by a particular Christian, who then receives in some way recognition from the church to exercise truly a ministry in the church—a public ministry. But in distinction to liturgical ministers, spiritual directors will ordinarily exercise their ministry—public as it may be in recognition—in a private or personal manner with individuals or with groups.

If the liturgy is celebrated in a strong and vibrant manner, there will always be present spiritual direction in some form in the community. If spiritual direction functions in all its various forms among members of the Christian community, then the liturgy itself will contine to be strong and vibrant. For "the liturgy is the summit toward which the activity of the Church is directed; at the same time it is the fountain from which all her power flows" (S.C., 10).

See **Spirituality, liturgical**

K.W. Irwin, *Liturgy, Prayer, and Spirituality* (New York: Paulist, 1984). K. Leech, *Soul Friend. The Practice of Christian Spirituality* (San Francisco: Harper and Row, 1980). D.E. Saliers, *Worship and Spirituality* (Philadelphia: The Westminster Press, 1984). "Liturgy as a Formative Experience," *Studies in Formative Spirituality* (November 1982): 3.

DAVID L. FLEMING, S.J.

SPIRITUAL DIRECTION, RECONCILIATION AND

See **Reconciliation and spiritual direction**

SPIRITUALITY, LAY

See **Lay spirituality**

SPIRITUALITY, LITURGICAL

Liturgical spirituality is the participation of a faith community in God's creative and transformative love for the world. Christian liturgical spirituality is the community's participation in the liberating embrace of the world in, with, and through Jesus Christ. "God has given us the wisdom to understand fully the mystery, the plan that was decreed in Christ, to be carried out in the fullness of time" (Eph 1:9-10).

Though the paschal mystery of Jesus Christ is at the heart of all Christian spirituality, liturgical spirituality is formed and informed through the ritual celebrations of the paschal mystery. Though all Christians celebrate the cultic liturgy of the church, Christians who live a liturgical spirituality experience the liturgical life of the church as their source of spiritual direction. For these Christians, the cultic liturgy of the church clearly is "the summit toward which the activity of the church is directed" and "the fountain from which all her power flows" (S.C., 10).

The history of Christian spirituality reflects many ways for growing in and mediating the power of the resurrection of Jesus Christ. The way of liturgical spirituality is one which is nourished and critiqued by the cultic liturgy of the church. The intimacy and infinity of the love of Christ that enlightens the varieties of forms of smallness of heart is particularly manifest in the ritual of the Lord's Supper or eucharist. This communal celebration clearly points to the reality that "The Son of God has united himself in some fashion with everyone. Christ died for all" (G.S., 22). Those who gather to do this authenticate the gathering and the doing by living a liturgical spirituality that embraces all of life.

Though the ritual life of the Christian community is one expression of liturgical spirituality, liturgical spirituality is broader than its cultic expression. While cultic liturgy provides meaning and direction, liturgical spirituality embraces all of life as the content of and context for living in Christ. Paul comes close to this description of liturgical spirituality as he reflects, "Let the word of Christ dwell in you richly, as in all wisdom you teach and admonish one another, singing psalms, hymns, and spiritual songs.... And whatever you do in word or in deed, do everything in the name of the Lord Jesus Christ, giving thanks to God the Father through him" (Col 3:16, 17).

Though there are a variety of approaches that could enhance the understanding of Christian liturgical spirituality, only three will be summarized here. First, some aspects of Jewish liturgical spirituality will be developed, for this spirituality provides foundational understandings for Christian liturgical spiritu-

ality. Second, the scriptural meaning of the New Covenant ritualized in the Lord's Supper will be summarized through focusing the transformed meanings of the Passover cups. Third, the manner in which spiritual discipline is inherent in liturgical spirituality will be described.

Jewish Liturgical Spirituality

Jewish liturgical spirituality is the lived awareness that all of life can be a means of becoming holy as God is holy. For a devout Jew, all of life can be liturgy. The prayer of blessing and praise (berakah) enables everything to be a source of remembering who one is in the presence of the All Holy One.

The living word of God, the Torah, and cultic liturgy are central to the living of a liturgical spirituality. Together, Torah and cultic liturgy encompass the life of the community in its ongoing journey into the heart of God. Both foster communion with God which is expressed through actions like those of God. To be holy as God is holy is the purpose both of Torah and of cultic liturgy (Lev 19:2). Though the two are intimately related, they can be considered separately.

Torah has varied meanings. Torah can refer to the first five books of the Jewish scriptures (Pentateuch), the entire Hebrew scriptures (Tenakh), the scholarly exposition of the scriptures as these apply to changing times, and the meditative study of God's living word by the people.

Torah, God's living word, is a creative dialogue of God with the chosen people. Because Torah is God's word, the community will never hear that word in its fullness. At the same time, Torah is addressed to the heart of the community who will hear and have their lives informed by it. The changing contours through which the word of God is heard means there must be ongoing interpretation of that Word (halakha). The ongoing interpretation is no less God's word than the written word.

God's word addresses the heart of the community in many ways. The community must discern the meaning of the address at its place and time in history. Because God's word is greater than human hearing and interpretation, there is no need for everyone to agree on the meaning, as the rabbinical schools attest. As long as the people are living the commandments of loving God and loving others, their interpretation is a valid one.

Commandments are an essential part of God's living word, for commandments unite the doer with the heart of God. Commandments are not fulfilled in merely doing what is specified as religious deeds. Commandments are only fulfilled if the doing somehow unites the doer with the heart of God and the neighbor. To have 613 commandments in Torah is a blessing, not a burden. What other people have so many ways to be united with God?

Commandments guide the covenant community in a way of life that helps them remember who they are as God's people. There are many commandments because all of life, whether eating, drinking, celebrating, journeying, searching, weeping or working, can reveal the living God. To remember is to know the living presence of God; to forget is to become lost in meaninglessness. Whom God remembers, looks upon, or hears has life. Whom God forgets descends into darkness. Commandments are a means of remembering, blessings that further communion.

Those who fulfill commandments will be known by the fruits of communion with God and with others. To be a blessing and not a curse, to be a means of life for all is a sign that the spirit of the commandments is being lived. Because the spirit is what gives and sustains life, not the literal living of the 613 commandments, the meaning of the command-

ments has been summarized throughout Jewish history. David reduced the meaning of the commandments to eleven (Psalm 15). Isaiah reduced the number to six (Isa 33: 25-26). Micah reduced the meaning to three (Mic 6:8). Amos reduced the number to one (Amos 5:14). The rabbi, Jesus Christ will also do this.

What this points to is that the purpose of Torah and its commandments is communion with the source of life that is known through how one lives. The living word of the living God is an ongoing dialogue with a living and historically conditioned people. Because the word of God is spoken to the heart of the community, there can be no authentic interpretation without the entire community discerning the meaning. The fullness of Torah lies ahead, not behind, so there is room for differences on the journey toward that fullness. The word will not return empty, but it may return with a fullness greater than human interpretation could hope or dream or imagine.

God's living word is known not only through Torah, but also through cultic liturgy that has Torah as a vital part. Cultic liturgy provides expression, identity, and life direction for the Jew. The daily, weekly, and seasonal celebrations of the covenant people are central to Jewish liturgical spirituality. Life's liturgy is given direction through cultic liturgy that provides the sacred space for the community to remember its call to become God's people.

In the morning and evening, the devout Jew remembers the history and mystery of creation, redemption, and covenant. This daily prayer recalls the past, reflects upon the present through the images of creation, redemption, and liberation, and expresses hope for ongoing liberation from all that is not holy. "Help me to be awake to this day . . . alive to beauty and love, aware that all being is precious, and that we walk on holy ground wherever we go" (*Gates of the House*, p. 3). In the morning and evening, the creed (*Shema*, Deut 6:4) is recited as well as a variety of blessings that enable the people to remember who they are and can yet be.

The Lord's Day (*Shabbat*) is a time to remember that rest is as sacred as work if it is the creative rest that God intends. Keeping the Sabbath is doing the work of God. The workers who refuse to do God's work, which is to be recreated on Sabbath, will remain unprofitable servants. Sabbath begins on the eve as God's compassion is recalled. "As we begin this day of holiness, we shall not forget the words of your prophet who called us to share our bread with the hungry, to clothe the naked, and never to hide ourselves from our own" (*Gates of the House*, p. 29). The ritual of candles, meal, and blessings begins sabbath time that shall not ritually end until the next day's evening service.

Seasonal festivals provide rhythms for liturgical life. In fall, the days of awe usher in the new year with an eight-day period extending from *Rosh Hashanah* to *Yom Kippur*. On this holiest day of the year, prayer, fasting, atonement, and forgiveness are the means of furthering the kingdom in this time and receiving blessings in the year ahead. Days of thanksgiving, Tabernacles, are celebrated for seven days in later fall. In winter, a feast of light, *Hanukkah,* celebrates a variety of accumulated meanings with gifts and joy.

A major festival, Passover, marks the spring season. This festival is kept as a night different from other nights. The ritualized meal provides a clear expression of the past, present, and future meanings of God's liberating the covenant people. Seven weeks after Passover, Pentecost celebrates the receiving of the law of God with new wine and leavened bread.

Jewish liturgical spirituality is guided by the ritualized meanings of that spirituality. Though the whole life of the devout Jew can be called liturgy, Torah and cultic liturgy are central to the formation and expression of liturgical spirituality. There is need to remember who the covenant people are called to be. Torah and cultic liturgy are means for remembering and for living a liturgical spirituality.

For Christians, Jesus Christ is Torah and the source of a new and eternal covenant. Cultic liturgy is a means for Christians to remember who they are as a new creation in Christ. Liturgical spirituality is formed by the ritualization of the memory of Jesus Christ who asks his people to remember by doing what he did and continues to do through the Spirit. The early church ritualized the memory at the Lord's Supper. Some early meanings of this memory can be located in the way Christian Scriptures describe this new and eternal covenant.

The New and Eternal Covenant of the Lord's Supper

Though the Last Supper was probably not a Passover meal, the scriptural accounts structure the meaning of the meal in a framework of Passover ritual. A summarized comparison of the meaning of the Passover cups is one way to illustrate the new meaning that early Christianity assigned to the Lord's Supper or eucharist.

The Passover ritual was opened by blessing this day as one of hope, by a washing, and then by offering and sharing a cup of joy and blessing. The NT accounts have Jesus being joyful for the celebration, and washings occur. The ritual dipping of foods in the dish served as an hors d'oeuvre, with the main meal to follow. The departure of Judas fits in well here (Jn 13:2-15, 21-30; Lk 22:24-27; Mt 26:20-25; Mk 14:17-21).

At the Passover ritual, a second wine cup was mixed, blessed and shared. The ritual meal was served. The youngest child asked the question, "Why is this night different from every other night?"

The story of Passover (*haggadah*) and its application to the present was then told by the leader. Two psalms of praise and a prayer over the bread were recited. The bread was broken and shared, as was a third cup of blessing at the end of the meal.

For the disciples gathered with Jesus Christ, the night of this Last Supper is a night "different from all other nights." On this night, bread and wine are symbols that have new meaning of a New Covenant. The covenant blood of Jesus Christ will be poured out for all so that sins can be forgiven (Mt 26:29). The radical nature of Jesus telling the disciples to drink his blood can escape contemporary hearers. For the Jews, blood symbolized life and life belonged only to God. Whoever drank blood was acting as God and would be cut off from the covenant people (Lev 2:12; 7:27; 17:10-14; Gen 9:3-5). Now whoever does not eat the flesh and drink the blood of Jesus Christ will not have life (Jn 6:53). The intimacy of this New Covenant with its sharing in the life of God is a dramatic change in religious imagination.

A fourth cup of Passover was a cup poured and drunk for the completion of the Hallel, Psalms 114-118. The participants could eat or drink no more after drinking this cup, for they must continue to taste only the mystery of Passover through the night. To fully taste the mystery of Passover, Jesus Christ will experience a cup of suffering. He prays that this cup be taken away (Jn 18:11; Mt 26:39-44; Mk 14:36-39; Lk 22:42-44). When the cup cannot be taken away, it will be accepted and those who poured it will be forgiven (Lk 23:24).

The fifth cup of Passover is a cup of the future. Some name it Elijah's cup, for Elijah was expected before the fullness of God's kingdom would come. As this cup was poured, the door was opened as a symbol of readiness for the kingdom to come. This cup would not be drunk until the kingdom came. The passion accounts make interesting references to this symbolic cup and to Elijah (Mt 27:47,49; Mk 14:36; Lk 23:37). In the two accounts of the death of Jesus that have been influenced by Psalms 22, the cup is not drunk (Mt 27:48; Mk 15:36). In a third account, the fifth cup is drunk as Jesus announces his life is over. He breathes forth the spirit of the kingdom (Jn 19:30). In a fourth account, the risen Christ gathers with disciples of Emmaus to eat and drink the meal of the kingdom, for the kingdom is here (Lk 24:32). All accounts point to the kingdom that has come in Christ, who now eats and drinks with his friends who are part of that new creation.

The apostles appear on Pentecost as those who knew of this new wine of the kingdom. For the Jews, Pentecost celebrated the receiving of the law of the covenant with new wine and leavened bread. Christian Scriptures point to the transformed meaning of Pentecost. Jesus Christ is the living Word of the living God. The apostles are ridiculed for being filled with new wine (Acts 1:2-13). The new creation of which Peter speaks has its first fruits in the life, death, and resurrection of Jesus Christ. All can be baptized into this new creation, for there shall be no further distinctions between slave and free, Jew and Gentile, male and female. The Spirit gives gifts to whomever the Spirit chooses.

The Lord's Day was a celebration of the new creation ushered into time through the life, death, and resurrection of Jesus Christ. The community who gathered to "do this in memory of me" were called to conversion and critiqued for areas of non-conversion. The hope of God for the world had been revealed in Jesus Christ, whose life was given for all. The Lord's Supper celebrated the infinite and intimate dimensions of reconciliation in Christ. It was formative of a liturgical spirituality whose embrace was to be as cosmic as that of the Lord Jesus.

The centrality of the paschal mystery was evident in the spirit of Vatican II. Also evident was the awareness that the paschal mystery of Jesus Christ is incarnated in diverse cultures in diverse ways. There is an awareness today that different cultures must be brought into the Christ-story in a manner respectful of the culture. The evocative, creative, and participative possibilities of Christian liturgical life have only begun to affect the reforms of liturgical life. The universality and inclusiveness of the paschal mystery is only beginning to be symbolized through careful use of liturgical symbols, rituals, language, and persons.

The eucharistic prayers that focus the meaning of Christian faith for many believers reflect one area of needed reform. As the Jewish thanksgiving prayer took on fullness only if it extended to all of the community's life, so the eucharistic prayer is authentically prayer only if it too affects all of the Christian life. Christian prayer is fully proclaimed when it becomes a religious deed. Liturgical prayer is prayer only when it enables the community to consecrate all of life to the glory of God in Christ through the power of the Spirit.

The content and language of the eucharistic prayers have become a concern for liturgists in the last decade because these prayers are among the most familiar expressions of the meaning of the Christian memory. The beginning of the eucharistic prayer (preface) has a variety of expressions of thanksgiving that harmonize with the liturgical cycle of seasons and festivals. An invocation of the Spirit (*epiclesis*) has been placed before the account of institution to avoid old controversies about a moment of consecration. The Spirit is invoked again after the commemoration of the Lord's death and resurrection (*anamnesis*). This latter invocation is an inclusive one. The gathered body of Christ prays for "all your (God's) children wherever they may be" (E.P. III); "those whose faith is known to you alone" (E.P. IV); "the entire people your Son has gained for you" (E.P. III) and "those who have died in the peace of Christ" (E.P. IV). The prayers do not forget the gathered community. "Make us worthy to share eternal life" (E.P. II). "Enable us to share in the inheritance of your saints" (E.P. III).

At the same time, there remain areas of necessary reform. The remembrance (*anamnesis*) still seems preoccupied with the consecratory nature of the institution narrative and with sacrificial language, both of which obscure the consecratory nature of the whole eucharistic prayer. The commemoration could serve the unity of the eucharistic prayer better if it remained a short, recapitulative acclamation of praise and blessing. This could then serve as a foundation for the invocation of the Spirit, who convenes, forms, renews, and inspires the new creation as one body in Christ.

The God-images used in the eucharistic prayers, and the people whose deeds are recalled, are still too selective. God-language and imaging remains impoverished by limited textual imagination. The proof-texting of Jewish history is an embarrassment to ecumenical dialogue. The non-participative structure, the non-poetic language, and the exclusion principle forgets that the community is the context for all prayer texts.

Is there a world escaping religiosity, a racial, religious, sexual, or power symbol distinction among those who claim to be the new creation? Prayers, scriptural readings, intercessions, hymns, aesthetic use of space, gender of prayer leaders, and the poetic expressions of the eucharistic prayer texts can aid or block the liberating power of liturgical worship in different cultural settings.

The unfolding renewal of liturgical

spirituality will take the implications of universality more seriously in the coming decades. Ecumenical prayer and dialogue, discernment of cultural diversities and values, and increased sensitivity to the community as primary symbol of liturgical spirituality will affect the renewal of liturgical rituals. These in turn will enhance the liturgy's possibilities for being a school of spirituality. As this occurs, the spiritual discipline inherent in that spirituality may become a more directive and integral part of the Christian life.

Spiritual Discipline and Liturgical Spirituality

Spiritual discipline for Christians flows from discipleship. No one can follow Jesus Christ without the participative discipline of dying and rising. Though there are varieties of private spiritual disciplines, there is also a communal spiritual discipline that is guided by the rhythm of the liturgical year. The liturgical year unfolds the mystery of Christ in festivity and in feriality. There is a time for everything, for fasting and feasting, for being alone and being together, for dying and rising.

Liturgical prayer gives direction to these life rhythms. It provides a framework for the prayer of solitude, which in turn flows back to liturgical prayer. For Christians, the prayer of solitude is not a prayer of isolation, for all prayer has its origin in being a member of the body of Christ. However, the prayer of solitude acknowledges the uniqueness of individual life that is placed before the Lord.

The discipline of solitude is not always a natural response to a busy life. Busy lives can become pre-occupied lives. The choice for solitude is a disciplinary choice to touch and stand in the mystery of God's hope for the world revealed in Christ. This hope leads the individual back to the prayer of the community, for the discipline of Christian solitude cannot stand apart from the body of Christ. To

pray in community is also a discipline, for communal prayer requires letting go of personal prayer preferences, ego boundaries, and privatized hearing of the Spirit. It enlarges the community of discernment so that one may be led where one might choose not to go.

Liturgical prayer that guides communal vision is grounded in a discipline of active listening. The prayer of the church, guided through the liturgical year, is not a soft communal mutuality that closes out the world. It is not a prayer that allows the community to cling in fear to each other in self-enclosure. It is rather a prayer of liberation that acknowledges solitary as well as communal responsibility for mediating the Kingdom of God.

The discipline of communal prayer, like that of solitary prayer, offers new possibilities for the discipline of obedience. Listening together to the Lord present in the breaking of bread can open a new and challenging vision of the demands of the kingdom at this point in time. The call to be a community of disciples who are made new in the Spirit can be dangerous if it is heard. To keep the eyes of the heart "fixed on Jesus who inspires and perfects our faith" may lead to a liberation that has not been predicted or hierarchically ordered (Heb 12:2).

The seasons of the liturgical year serve as guide to the traditional Christian discipline of fasting, though fasting is certainly not limited to special seasons. For Christians, as for their Jewish ancestors, fasting is meant to enhance remembering. To remember that the life of Christ has been given for all implies both fasting and feasting. Fasting fosters remembering that there are still many who hunger and thirst because those who have enough will not share their bounty. Fasting fosters the remembering that hungering for the Lord is authenticated by hungering and acting for justice. Fasting fosters remembering that the sacrilege of power and privilege, in the world and in the church, may be a demon cast out only by prayer and fasting.

While fasting is one sign of the kingdom, its sign value can be complemented by feasting. Christians proclaim a Lord whose presence is known at a banquet table. The bridegroom has come, and the wedding feast of the lamb has begun. To pretend it is otherwise is to negate the value of shared tables as a means for conversion to greater sharing of the fruits of the earth and the work of human hands. There is a time for everything, for fasting and for feasting, for solitude and for community, for death and resurrection.

The Christ images that unfold through the liturgical year provide a context for spiritual discipline. Liturgical spirituality is nourished and challenged by the imagination of God revealed through Jesus Christ, whose Spirit continues to make all things new. Christians who live a liturgical spirituality accept the awareness that God's hope for the world is greater than we can hope or dream or imagine. The invitation to enter the imagination of God revealed in Jesus Christ is also a call to experience death and resurrection.

The early church prayerfully accepted the challenge as it prayed "Come, Lord Jesus." The celebration of the Lord's Supper was a call to surrender to the power of resurrection. Liturgical spirituality is grounded in the ritual liberation and spiritual direction into the unfolding mystery. "I am the Alpha and the Omega, the first and the last, the beginning and the end.... Come, Lord Jesus" (Rev 22:13, 20).

Regis Duffy, O.F.M., ed., *Alternative Futures for Worship*, Vol. 1 (Collegeville: Liturgical Press, 1987). Shawn Madigan, *Liturgy, Source of Spirituality* (Washington, D.C.: Pastoral Press, 1989). *Gates of the House: The New Union Home Prayer Book* (New York: Central Conference of American Rabbis, 1977). Frank Senn, ed., *New Eucharistic Prayers: An Ecumenical Study of Their Development and Structure* (Mahwah: Paulist, 1987). Leo Trepp, *The Complete Book of Jewish Observance* (New York: Behrman House, 1980).

S. SHAWN MADIGAN, C.S.J.

SPIRITUALITY, PRIESTLY

See Priestly spirituality

SPONSORS FOR INITIATION

Canonical and liturgical reforms have recovered the specialized ministry of sponsor for adult initiation (R.C.I.A.), and amplified sponsorship for the baptism of children, and the confirmation of Catholics baptized as infants, and Christians entering into the full communion of the Roman Catholic church. In each instance, sponsorship entails pastoral and liturgical responsibilities.

The renewal of sponsorship is threefold: it is to be restored to an *authentic* ministry which provides *witness* to the faith of the church and *guidance* for the candidate. As an authentic ministry, sponsorship departs from widespread practice of a minimal ceremonial role. As a witness and guide, the sponsor exemplifies the Christian life and mission while accompanying the candidate through the initiation process and beyond. The manner in which a sponsor fulfills these duties is conditioned by the pastoral situation. For example, a sponsor, distinguished from the canonical godparent, is required for each catechumen at the rite of acceptance into the catechumenate (R.C.I.A., 10). Frequently the sponsor becomes the godparent (*patrinus*) at the rite of election, though another meeting canonical requirements may be chosen. At infant baptism the godparents (*patrini*) serve as sponsors in a unique and different manner from adult initiation (can. 872). A sponsor, ideally the candidate's godparent, is required "as far as possible" at confirmation celebrated apart from baptism (can. 892). Throughout this entry "sponsor" and "godparent" are interchangeable.

All Christians are potential sponsors when they exercise their baptismal commitment and apostolic vocation, "spreading the faith according to their abilities" (R.C.I.A., 9). The presiding minister at the rite of acceptance asks all present if they are "ready to help the candidates find and follow Christ." Indeed, throughout the first three centuries of the church we find no evidence of a delegated ministry of sponsor. Candidates were presented to the bishop by any Christian attesting to their readiness. Amid Christianity's rapid growth in the 4th and 5th centuries, the church designated exemplary persons to accompany the newcomers from the catechumenate through mystagogy and beyond. John Chrysostom called sponsors spiritual parents who instructed spiritual children in Christian living. When the catechumenate went into decline, some bishops reminded all Christians that the task of modeling the Christian life to the candidates was a duty of the whole church and not limited to sponsors.

By the middle of the 5th century, infant baptism was the normal practice, affecting both the catechetical and liturgical structures of formation. Candidates for initiation were assumed to be infants by the 6th and ensuing centuries, and the catechumenal rites were compressed into one Lenten season. Clearly, Christian parents serve as immediate witnesses and guides in the life of faith, but the rite did not recognize them. Sponsors presented the child on a Lenten Sunday, stood by at the scrutinies (which had become multiple prayers of exorcism), and recited the creed on the child's behalf at the baptism. Since the newly baptized would be raised by the parents, the sponsor's pastoral role became less ecclesial and more familial. Godparents were chosen for their ability to provide for a child's physical welfare should the parents become incapacitated or die. With today's improved health and longevity, the role of godparent often is reduced to an honorific bestowed on friends or relatives. Contemporary reforms press for a more supportive and informed ministry, accomplished in part by raising the standards.

The Code of Canon Law (C.I.C.) lists several qualifications for a godparent. Every person must have one godparent, two are allowed, but only one of each sex (cans. 872 and 873). The godparent must be designated by the one who is to be baptized, by the parents, by someone in their place or absence, or by the parish priest or minister. In addition, the godparent must intend to fulfill the role by engaging in a continuous spiritual relationship with the baptized person (can. 874, §1, 1°). Sixteen is the minimum age for godparents: the ordinary may establish another age in his diocese, or the local pastor or minister may grant an exception (can. 874, §1, 2°). Godparents must be fully initiated Catholics (can. 874, §1, 3°), although Orthodox Christians may be a godparent when a Catholic godparent is present (*Eucumenical Directory*, 48). A validly baptized Protestant may be admitted only as a *witness* to the baptism, provided a Catholic godparent is designated (can. 874, §2). Godparents must be free of any canonical penalty, and not be the father or mother of the baptized (can. 874, §1, 4° & 5°). Unlike its predecessor, this Code does not prohibit priests and religious from becoming godparents.

Infant Baptism

The reformed *Rite of Baptism for Children* (1969) recognizes that parents have a more important ministry and role than godparents, for "they will be the first teachers of their children in the ways of the faith" (R.B.C., 70). Since a child's formation begins in the "domestic" church, godparents are "added spiritually to the immediate family of the baptized" and represent the wider church (*General Introduction to Christian Initiation*, 8). Before the baptism, godparents are to be instructed in the meaning the sacrament and obligations attached to it (can. 851, 2°). During the celebration of baptism, godparents are present and join with the parents in the profession of faith. Thereafter, godparents help the baptized to meet their baptismal promises (can. 872). Both code and ritual expect godparents to assist parents in modeling the Christian life for the child. How godparents fulfill their duties is determined more by local custom and family tradition than legislation.

Adult Initiation

While parents and home constitute the primary experience of church for infants and small children, the adult candidate will benefit from a peer relationship with an exemplary Catholic. Just as the formation process of the catechumenate is directed towards adult needs and experience, the sponsor's duties are more extensive than those required for infant baptism. The R.C.I.A. requires that sponsors "have known and assisted the candidates, and stand as witnesses to the candidates' moral character, faith and intention" (R.C.I.A., 10). The ministry of godparents for adults, officially beginning at the rite of election, is more specific: accompanying the candidates at election, the sacraments of initiation and mystagogy; showing candidates how to live the gospel, sustaining them in hesitancy, bearing witness, and guiding their progress in the baptismal life (R.C.I.A., 11). At the rite of election, godparents testify that the catechumens have faithfully listened and begun to conform their lives to God's word, and shared the company and prayer of their fellow Christians. By accompanying the candidates through the initiation sequence, the sponsors-godparents serve as one-to-one evangelists, and links between the newcomers and broader church community.

In practice the sponsors may fulfill the most significant ministry of the catechumenate. Sponsors join the catechumens at the catechetical sessions, listen and share their faith, introduce and explain Catholic practices such as devotions, the cycles and customs of the church year, etc., assist them with private and public prayer, guide and encourage their participation in various social ministries. With catechists and clergy, they discern the catechumens' readiness for election to the Easter sacraments. Sponsors, therefore, should be instructed with catechists and other ministers. Programs of sponsor formation should include training in listening skills and spiritual direction.

Uncatechized, baptized Catholics preparing for confirmation and eucharist, as well as persons seeking reception into full communion, are assigned sponsors meeting the qualifications noted above. Sponsors, with catechists, clergy and parishioners, are cognizant of the candidates' baptism. Moreover, all ministers respect the experience and prior ecclesial formation which a candidate for full communion brings to the church.

Programs preparing adolescent and adult Catholics for confirmation celebrated apart from baptism increasingly enlist the aid of sponsors. When the candidate has chosen a canonical sponsor not involved in the process, an older teen or adult may accompany the person during formation. Most respond well to these "companions." Some parishes have experimented successfully with a peer ministry whereby fully initiated teens associate socially with the candidates and accompany them in some social ministry. The parents of the candidate may *present* their child at the celebration of confirmation, but cannot be recorded as the canonical sponsors. When godparents can be sponsors, provided they have fulfilled their initial obligations and meet canonical requirements, they help to demonstrate the link between baptism and confirmation.

The renewed ministry of sponsor, like the catechumenate itself, has challenged the church to realize its missionary character and the communal nature of faith and its formation. Following centuries of religious privatization, Catholics struggle with what it means to share the faith. It is not surprising, therefore, that sponsorship continues to evolve. To the extent the church responds to the dominical mandate, its own nature and the nature of its ministries become more clear.

Michel Dujarier, *Le Parrainage des adults aux trois premiers siècles de L'Eglise; recherche historique sur l'évolution des garanties des étapes catéchuménales avant 313* (Paris: Editions du Cerf, 1962).

A. BRANDT HENDERSON

SUFFERING

Christianity embraces the theme of suffering at the very heart of its belief system. Theologians, past and present and of all persuasions, are by necessity obliged to consider human suffering. Its history is as old as human history. It has limitless shades: death, physical illness, social inequalities, loneliness and alienation. The history of suffering is a continuing and apparently progressive history considering the events of this century such as the holocaust and the threat of nuclear war.

The common human address to suffering has been religious. Religion in its various traditions asks, "Does life have some central meaning despite suffering, and the meaninglessness and chaos it brings?" For suffering passes into the problem of evil and poses the God question: If God is omnipotent and all loving, why evil? Theodicy simply means that the whole question of suffering must be answered in the light of fundamental insights of faith. The theodicy question

originates in two felt needs: a sense that human affairs are far worse than any good reason can justify or that our powers alone can alter, and a yearning that refuses to settle for despair.

The classical answers to the problem of suffering paint a very questionable picture of God. They have their sources both in the OT and in the NT. Evils cause suffering and it is God, the creator who made the existence of evils possible in the world, although evil remains constantly under divine control, and ultimately God will abolish all evils. The Hebrew Scripture does not contrast physical and mental suffering since the human reality is not understood in a dualistic manner. Israel was not particularly interested in the origin of suffering, but in its reason and purpose. In an earlier stage suffering was understood as a punishment for sin. A later development brought about serious questions about the suffering of the righteous and the innocent. Suffering is also understood as a divine *paideia*, and ultimately as vicarious.

Suffering in the Hebrew Scripture

The Hebrew Scripture has much to say about suffering. A great deal of its wisdom concerning suffering can be found in the book of Job. The solution to suffering from a religious point of view is not fateful resignation or denial of God's existence, but belief in a personal God. Job subjects his own understanding, rebellion and pain to God's wisdom. Righteousness and wisdom are at work in human suffering.

Suffering in the New Testament

Jesus' suffering dominates the NT. The passion story is the longest section of the gospel message. The NT word for suffering is *paschein*, which has a passive meaning: to experience something that comes from outside. It is a question of "bearing" or of "enduring." Jesus "endures" death on the cross.

The gospel writers also describe Jesus'

attitude toward those who suffer. The first thing we notice about Jesus' behavior towards those who suffer is that he is never indifferent. The texts tell us that he is moved and upset and describe his compassion and even his tears (Mt 9:36; 14:14; 15:32). Jesus never asks that suffering be offered up to God either for the benefit of the sufferer or for someone else. Jesus' God does not require suffering. In fact through Christ's healing ministry God reveals his will for salvation and health. Nowhere does Jesus declare that suffering brings about one's salvation, or one's sanctification.

What the gospel writers wrote about Jesus' own suffering tends to be different from his behavior towards those who suffer. The NT writers have a great deal of difficulty in making sense of Jesus' suffering and death in light of the fact that they confess Jesus to be the Messiah. Why Jesus' suffering and death were necessary and what meaning they had is variously explained. The Synoptics emphasized the passion prediction and the fact that in his passion he fulfilled the promises of old. His death and suffering is according to the scriptures: it fulfills the Father's will; Jesus "must" suffer (Mk 8:31; Lk 9:22). In Paul the emphasis is on redemption. Jesus' suffering and death are the results of God's love for humankind (Phil 2:6-11).

The call to discipleship demands the acceptance of suffering. Whoever follows Jesus must bear his cross (Mk 13:10-13). According to Paul, the disciple is destined to suffer as Jesus did (1 Cor 4:9-13). Paul gloried in his suffering and saw such suffering as proof of his apostolic commission (1 Thess 2:2).

The suffering of Jesus is the suffering of the innocent. It is closely connected to God. The question is clearly posed whether God needs human suffering, whether God is incapable of saving woman/man without demanding suffering. The suffering of Jesus poses the question about God: "who is this God who demands such suffering?" It presses the whole issue of theodicy. It is not enough to say that one believes in God. What is important finally is the kind of God in whom one believes.

Classical Answers

While there is no unified theology of suffering, from the time of Tertullian, and especially in Augustine, suffering was considered God's punishment brought about by sin. The suffering of the innocent can be offered up for others.

In John Paul II's letter on "The Christian Meaning of Human Suffering" of February 1989, one finds a summary of the Catholic tradition on the nature of suffering. The basic thrust of the pope's message is that of the salvific meaning of suffering. Suffering seems to be particularly essential to the nature of woman/man. Suffering seems to belong to human transcendence. It is one of those points in which man/woman is in a certain sense destined to go beyond the self, and is called to this in a mysterious way. The emphasis is on the fact that redemption was accomplished through suffering. The church is born of the mystery of Christ's redemptive suffering, and must "meet humanity in a special way on the path of suffering" for "suffering is inseparable from humanity's earthly existence."

Each form of suffering poses the question why? A question about the cause is a question about meaning. In the context of faith in a loving God suffering becomes a question *about* God. The answer is Jesus Christ: suffering conquered by love. The pope's emphasis is on the intimate connection between suffering and redemption. "It is precisely through his suffering that he accomplished the redemption ...." "It seems to be part of the very essence of Christ's redemptive suffering that this suffering requires to be unceasingly completed."

This leads the pope to affirm that, "Suffering is something good before which the church bows down in reverence with all the depth of her faith in the redemption."

Toward a Theology of Suffering

Suffering in its widest sense means being acted upon. It means to bear, to undergo. There is a basic connotation of passivity as distinct from activity in suffering. "Receptivity" is essential to suffering. Yet, while there is an essential dimension of passivity in suffering, there is also a great deal of activity. Suffering is the price we have to pay for our limitations, our finitude.

By suffering we mean an anguish which we experience not only as pressure to change, but as a threat to our composure, our integrity and the fulfillment of our intentions. Suffering has the character of a threat to our self-direction and therefore implicitly to our being. It challenges our capacity to maintain ourselves and retain the poise of self-direction. In Heidegger's understanding suffering has the aspect of a threat of non-being. Suffering is disclosive of our own radical contingency, of the fact that ultimately our situation is neither one of our own making nor under our control. Suffering is therefore real anguish because of felt threat to our own integrity and to the real possibility of the disintegration of the self.

Suffering is always an interpersonal phenomenon. Even though we experience it as if it were totally within ourselves, both its locus and source are in relationship. While pain is primarily related to the body and can be inflicted by things, suffering is personal. It is related to one's personhood. We primarily suffer in our relation to others. Suffering is the result of the breakdown of interdependence. Because suffering is essentially interpersonal, it therefore has a social dimension, which has been called *affliction*. Affliction involves isolation and abandonment. The degradation shows itself in the isolation that accompanies affliction. The lack of solidarity with the afflicted is a common phenomenon. The dimension of affliction is more fully understood when one realizes the significance of the ongoing quest for the esteem of others.

As basically an interpersonal reality, suffering can be given a meaning. Meaning transforms the whole person and gives a definite directedness to existence. Two basic questions must be asked about suffering in order to give it meaning: what causes suffering and how can it be eliminated? Both questions need to be asked simultaneously in order to avoid any form of masochism. Suffering always remains an attack on human life. It can never be glorified nor sought masochistically. Taken by itself suffering is meaningless. There is also a sharp distinction between suffering before which we stand powerless and meaningful suffering. Suffering can be so acute and so long-lasting that the sufferer feels powerless to break away from it.

Only the suffering that can be changed and from which we can learn is potentially meaningful. Potentially meaningful suffering is one that is not completely passive. What a person does when she/he suffers is the active dimension of suffering. It is in the doing that meaning can be given to suffering, and the doing is in the interpersonal realm. The doing involves the opening of the sufferer's horizons and the transcending of self to the other.

Suffering can lead to a discerning of the vicariousness of interpersonal existence. Since suffering is basically caused by the breakdown of interdependence, that interdependence may be restored vicariously by someone not responsible for the original breakdown. And this is because vicariousness is a fundamental characteristic of interdependence. Personal life is vicarious in that it involves living from and for others. Vicariousness s not something esoteric but the fundamental principle of all personal life. When interdependence has been broken and affliction and alienation have resulted, the breakdown can be remedied by someone not involved in the original breakdown. Interdependence is broken by self-centering. Vicariousness involves self-giving.

Jesus' death on the cross was vicarious. "But God shows God's love for us in that while we were yet sinners Christ died for us" (Rom 5:8). The vicariousness of Jesus' suffering is not something necessitated by the condition of a sinful world, but is characteristic of the interdependence of human existence. Vicarious and representational suffering is not necessitated by God, but a dimension of Jesus' life of self-giving.

The salvific meaning of Jesus' death is rooted in the salvific meaning of his life, in the radical dimension of his love. There is no need to refer Jesus' death to an arbitrary decision on the part of the Godhead; it has its sufficient basis in the love with which and in which Jesus identified himself with us. Through Jesus' love the depth of interdependence in reality is revealed to us: "No human has ever seen God; if we love one another, God abides in us and God's love is perfected in us" (1 Jn 4:12). One cannot say that God required the death of Jesus as compensation for our sins. It is not possible to make God responsible for what human injustice has done to Jesus. Jesus' death comes as a reaction to his life and ministry, as the consequence of his love.

The paschal mystery is Christianity's final answer to Job's dilemma. God does not instigate our suffering, nor did God decree the sufferings of Jesus. Rather, God participated in them. Our God, Jesus' God, is not the executioner but the co-sufferer. During his life and his preaching Jesus proclaimed God as the God of outcasts, not as someone remote, but as someone close to human reality. Jesus' God is a God *for us*. The cross reveals God as a redeeming God and a compassionate God.

The cross cannot become the symbol of an evil that no longer needs to be taken seriously. If evil and suffering have already been so definitively overcome, then history is trivialized and human responsibility for the future set aside. The cross cannot function as a sanctuary against the harsh realities of evil in our world. Nor can it be set against the darkness of experience as an apparently thorough victory that easily explains away negation, evil, death. Suffering always remains an attack on human life. It can never be glorified nor sought. It can be given some meaning if *ultimately* it can be eliminated, and that is the basic meaning of the resurrection.

See **Sickness, a Christian view of; Healing**

George Arthur Buttrick, *God, Pain, and Evil* (Nashville: Abingdon Press, 1966). A. McGill, *Suffering: A Test of Theological Method* (Philadelphia: Geneva Press, 1968). John Bowker, *Problems of Suffering in the Religions of the World* (Cambridge: Cambridge University Press, 1970). Michael Taylor, ed., *The Mystery of Suffering and Death* (Staten Island: Alba House, 1973). Dorothy Soelle, *Suffering* (Philadelphia: Fortress Press, 1975). Andrew Elphinstone, *Freedom, Suffering, and Love* (London: SCM Press, 1976). E.S. Gerstenberger and W. Schrage, *Suffering* (Nashville: Abingdon, 1977). Elizabeth Moberly, *Suffering Innocent and Guilty* (London: S.P.C.K., 1978). Stanley Hauerwas, "Reflections on Suffering, Death, and Medicine," *Ethics in Science and Medicine* 6:4 (1979): 229-237.

LUCIEN J. RICHARD, O.M.I.

SYMBOL

This essay will focus upon the following issues: (1) the emergence of symbolic elements in worship from Judaism and Hellenistic cultures; (2) the development of symbolic styles; (3) a typology of symbolic styles in Western worship; and, (4) the use of symbols in a post-modern age. For the epistemological, philosophical, and general theological issues that govern the contemporary understanding of symbols, see *The New Dictionary of Theology*, ed. Komonchak, et al., Glazier, 1987, also s. v. *symbol*.

Introduction

A working definition for symbol would be a complex of gestures, sounds, images, and/or words that evoke, invite, and persuade participation in that to which they refer.

Symbols have multiple levels of meaning and value. Unlike signs or signals (such as a stop sign or mathematical symbols), symbols do not refer to one item or indicate a one-to-one correspondence between the sign and the signified. They disclose reality by making available to their participants meanings and values that involve them intellectually, emotionally and morally, while exceeding the physical components of the signifier. Part of their emotional power is due to this multiplicity of appeals.

As a result, the regions in which symbols operate are almost universal, as extensive as human life and history. They can be found in daydreams, the nightmares of sleep, the arts and literature as well as in social rituals like the common meal or ceremonies as distantly powerful as presidential inaugurations. Poets, lobbyists, preachers, advertisers, and televangelists use symbols to convince their audiences of the truth of the subject matter, the speakers' sincerity and their products' goals.

This ambiguity of symbols has made them suspect to modern science, linguistic philosophy, and ordinary common sense. Contemporaries find it difficult to trust themselves to symbols since they cannot discern whether the polysemantic character of symbols is deception or simple radical mystery.

This multidimensional character of symbols has made it imperative to limit the discussion of symbols here to the sacraments and the public worship of the churches. However, the ambiguity of symbols has also affected the experience of Christian worship, so the factors that affect the credibility and construction of contemporary Christian symbols for worship will be treated.

Early Christian Symbols Within Hellenistic Judaism. Christians forged their symbols within the molten tradition of Judaism. Hellenistic Judaism itself was not a uniform cultural phenomenon. It included not only the large population of Jews in the Diaspora, but many different groups within Palestine itself (for example, Pharisees, Sadducees, Zealots, and Essenes). Hellenistic Jews, for good or ill, had assimilated many economic, political, and cultural attitudes of the Graeco-Roman world. And since many early converts to Christianity were Jews and Jewish proselytes (Gentiles who partially followed the Torah), the overlap, even syncretism, of cultures was to be expected.

In the synagogue and in the Christian assembly hall at Dura-Europos, in the catacombs in Rome, in the desert libraries of Egypt, and in the emerging NT texts themselves, we can see communities vying for their interpretation of the founding stories, such as Adam and Eve, Noah and the flood, Moses and the journey to the promised land. The vine of David, the root of Jesse flower in Jesus the Christ the shepherd of Israel gives authority to Christ the Good Shepherd; the sacrifice of Isaac by Abraham illuminates the self sacrifice of Jesus.

Christian communities initiated their followers into the meaning of their life by surrounding them with words, gestures and images that interpreted their decisions. On the walls and in sermons, they painted images of rescue: Daniel in the lions' den, Moses striking the rock, Elijah reviving the widow's son, David conquering Goliath. Taking their cue from Jewish catechesis, they described the new way of light and distinguished it from the way of darkness, maintaining that they had the authentic teaching about those primal stories.

In effect, Jewish symbols and stories gained a new referent: the preaching, life, death, and resurrection of Jesus. The first exodus was an anticipation of another exodus. Symbols are always embedded in cultural stories. Christians re-examined the symbols by extending the story. In shifting the temporal significance of the symbols, they transformed the religion and found that the story in which they believed no longer had a home in Judaism itself.

The symbols of the shepherd, the teacher, even the chariot-driver or paradise as a garden overlapped with non-Jewish motifs. The teacher of the sermon on the mount could be painted as a philosopher with his pupils; the shepherd could be seen as the god Apollo, piping his flock; Elijah's fiery chariot was analogous to the golden chariot of the sun god. Images that could be extended temporally to include the past (as prologue) and the future (as anticipation) could be reshaped to include the underworld and the eternal spheres.

The process of developing symbols among the early communities of believers involved seeing the polysemy of Jewish symbols to include the crucial instance of Jesus. This changed the historical references of the symbols. Though Hellenistic Judaism included speculation about the cosmos, the increasing analogies with non-Jewish images shifted Christian symbolic structures to emphasize spatial dimensions. The Christian story understood itself as encompassing all of time, from the genesis of the cosmos and its first inhabitants to the final battles between good and evil and the arrival of a new heaven and a new earth—and as including all of space as well. These claims to universal interpretive competence would have seemed mere wishful thinking, had it not been for the appearance of the Christian emperors in the 4th century and their successors in the East and the West, who made Christian worship publicly legitimate and supported the order created by clergy and laity.

In this context of Jewish images and stories, symbolically reinterpreted through the primary Christian story of Jesus, early Christians participated in worship that broke and shared bread and wine, immersed in water, and anointed with oil, using words that invoked divine presence. Entrance into the community meant learning the stories and sharing in the worship. Symbols focused the identity of the believer. By being immersed in water, neophytes died and rose with Christ; they entered the Christian passover. Breaking bread together shared the Last Supper of Christ with the disciples and anticipated the future wedding feast. Jesus' symbolic actions, like those of prophets before him, announced the challenging reign of God; Christians reenacted those symbols and created a tradition.

Symbolic Styles. Traditions coalesce around certain symbols and their cultural articulation. Style may be described as that interlocking network of images, metaphors, and symbols that define a particular mode of action and thought. It is style that allows the participant to say "this" is a Graham ballet, a Hemingway novel, or a Brahms symphony. No one would mistake Brahms for Sun Ra or Hemingway for Trollope. Vocabulary, images, grammar and syntax characterize the rhetoric of their creators.

In any particular context, it is possible to describe the root metaphors and basic symbols. The apostolic witnesses that identified themselves with Alexandria (Mark), Jerusalem (James), Rome (Peter and Paul) or India (Thomas) generated styles of worship and attendant theologies. Ritual differences developed as ways of recovering the stories and symbols in specific contexts. Linguistic difference

(Greek, Syriac, Coptic, Latin, and eventually Slavonic) shaped the rites with their particular communicative competences. By the end of the 4th century, the main metaphoric expressions in the Eastern empire had been determined. The normative ritual usage seemed to be Jerusalem. Scholars have been able to note how doctrinal differences grew from symbolic expressions.

Even in the Western empire, where Latin was eventually dominant, styles of symbolic expression developed. The Ambrosian rite of the city of Milan and the Gallican rite north of the Alps had their own symbolic particularities. Rites developed around the cities of Toledo and Braga. But by the end of the 10th century, the major ritual metaphors had been determined in the West, where Rome's rituals became the norm.

What we now know as the Roman rite, particularly in comparison with the others in both Eastern and Western churches, is sober and somewhat severe. It made minor adaptations of Eastern ritual elements (the *Kyrie, Sanctus, Agnus Dei*). But there were primarily a simplicity of movement, austerity of language, and asceticism of gesture. The choreography of processions was dignified and measured.

The rites that developed to the north were more elaborate. The Gallican (French) and Mozarabic (Spanish) rites used more words, reflected the penitential piety of their communities, and stressed personal unworthiness. The sometimes apocalyptic tone of prayers reflected the precarious character of life at the edges of the decaying empire. They tended to be free in their adaptations of prayers for local feasts and particular saints.

Different genres of books appeared to codify these developments in worship. Lectionaries were collections of scriptural readings, rationalized on the basis of the developing church year and the feasts of saints. As a genre of symbolic expression, they too note the theology and sensiblity of particular churches. This replaced the continuous reading of the scriptures that Christians had in common with their Jewish ancestors. Sacramentaries appeared for the use of the person presiding; they collected the opening prayers, prayers over the gifts, eucharistic prayers, and conclusions, substituting for the earliest forms of spontaneous rhetoric (based no doubt on oral formulae). Songbooks (graduals) developed to provide singers with appropriate psalms for the seasons.

The coalescence of rites in the West with Rome as its norm owes as much to Charlemagne's (768-814) convictions about religious uniformity and public order as it does to the theology of the churchmen who served him. In 781, Charlemagne asked Pope Hadrian I (d. 795) for an authentic copy of the Roman liturgy to be used as a book to be copied in his realm. The volume arrived by 790. Alcuin revised the manuscript to fit usage north of the Alps with its more flowing rhetorical style. All other ritual usage was forbidden. Though it took some time, Alcuin's missal with some variations became the basis for Christian worship until the reformation in the 16th century.

The theology of the sacraments that Augustine (354-430) bequeathed to the Middle Ages included a strong emphasis upon the permanent effect of certain signs, the nourishing or assimilative dimension of the Eucharist, and the ways in which worship formed community in the present and anticipated the future reign of God. Consecratory prayers made a difference in the real world, whether in baptism (character) or in marriage or in the eucharist. His interpretation of signs (symbols), however, as indicating the past, and his realism about personal assimilation to Christ did not always cohere. Controversies in France during the 9th and 10th centuries asked exactly "what" was presented in the eucharist as distinct from baptism or anointing. What was the figure (signifier) and what the reality (signified)? The ecclesiastical tradition settled on the side of the realism of signs. The symbols effected redemption as a present reality, not simply as a reminder of a past event.

By the 10th century, the root metaphors that governed the amalgamated Roman rite were sacrificial, hieratic, hierarchical, and impersonal. Though the ritual of the eucharist began as table prayers over a meal, the memory of the sacrifice of Christ dominated Roman spirituality. The ritual of the eucharist was performed by a presider with his back to the congregants. His gestures and words were primarily directed to God and to the sacred instruments. If more than one minister was present, a carefully prescribed order of precedence was established. The often illiterate and under-catechized community were spectators at a sacred act. The sacral objects of consecrated bread and wine provided a permanent watchful presence for believers.

Thus, though we can speak of symbols inviting the baptized into the history of Christ and Christ's dominion over the universe, each rite in every age has established a rhetorical style that appeals to its own period and region. In a world in which rhetoric is determined by the norms of king and bishop, it is hardly surprising that Christian rituals should be established by and partake of the same hierarchical sensibilities.

Liturgical Styles in the West. The basic austerity of the Roman liturgy did not remain so. If we can speak of a "familial style" (with its house-churches and married church leaders) that marked the Apostolic Age and a "basilical style" after the official buildings donated by Constantine to the early church) that succeeded it upon the legitimation of Christianity, we can mark the medieval developments as "monastic." Ecclesial

architecture focused upon the development of an area for the community's daily recitation of the psalms. The hieratic character of sacrificial worship was distanced from a lay congregation by a lengthier nave and an elongated choir. Roodscreens distinguished the sanctuary of the clerics from the world of the lay people.

In the East, worship assumed a neo-Platonic cast. Taking a cue from the letter to the Hebrews about the way in which the high priest Christ has entered the Holy of Holies in eternity (Heb 4:14-9:28), theologians in the East described Christian worship as an icon of the heavenly liturgy where the angels are constantly praising their maker. Directions for the service itself (rubrics) began to be written to create this earthly mirror of a divine action.

In the West, worship took a peculiarly historical cast. In the 9th century, Amalarius of Metz (780-850) described the service catechetically as a mythic history of Jesus' life, death, and resurrection. The realism of the story shaped the symbolic gestures and objects. The profusion of liturgical directions that developed throughout the Middle Ages, though often local in their adaptation, obscured the straightforward apostolic structure of a service of readings, an offering of goods including bread and wine, a prayer of thanksgiving, and sharing of bread and wine.

Monastic, mendicant, and academic theologians tried during the Middle Ages to reform worship just as they tried to rethink theology. But little was accomplished until the crisis of the Protestant Reformers forced upon the Western churches a rethinking of their doctrines, theology, and symbols. In a very important sense, the two dimensions of Augustine's theory about signs (its realism of conveying meaning and its secondary signifying quality) divided into the two main branches of Christendom. Protestant Reformers, such as Luther, Calvin, or Zwingli, often miscalculated history and contemporary meaning as badly as the scholastic theologians they criticized. They focused upon the rememorative side of the Augustinian interpretation of signs. The Catholic revival settled on the other side: that of symbolic realism, participation, and the triumphal present.

While Protestant worshippers emphasized simplicity of dress, a minimum of gestures, images, and symbols in favor of the word as preached, 17th and 18th-century Catholic worship stressed elaborate ornament, decorative building, and polyphonous music. We might call it the development of an "operatic style" of symbolic expression. Worship was accomplished by professionals for spectators.

The church participated in 19th-century Romanticism by emphasizing its symbolic dimensions even more, turning worship into an evocation of mystery and uncanny silence through vestments, church bells, and incense. The rationalism of the 18th-century civic culture now past, the church shared in a sentimental cult of nature, an emphasis upon the affective in prayer, and the revival of things medieval. Idealized notions of the unity of architecture, worship, theology, and social concern won many Christians away from the harsh realities of industrializing economies in England, France, and the United States. The origins of the liturgical movement are in this romanticism of the medieval worship. Plainsong was revived; neo-gothic churches were built. A "romantic style" of symbolic worship was born.

Symbols in a Post-Modern Age. The world of modernity stressed subjective perspectives, historical origins, relativity of values, and the possibility, even probability, of cultural and political change. Contemporary industrialized bureaucracies and their socialist cognates have now moved from the sublime heights of

romantic frenzy and the fearful despairs that accompanied them through the delights of modernity into its difficulties and even self-destructive impulses. No longer seduced by easy progress or consumerized productivity, citizens and believers now espouse an eclectic pluralism about the role, history, and function of symbols (whether in culture as a whole or within Christianity).

Believers have dual loyalties: to their religious traditions and to the integrity of their civil culture which develops with its own goals often unrelated to faith. This radical pluralism of allegiance has often placed believers in a position of eclectically choosing from the styles of past symbolic expressions. Thus one may move from one parish church with high monastic worship, including flowing gothic vestments, elaborate plainsong, incense, and visual mystification to a congregation that aggressively insists upon a familial, demotic style of worship. Communities that prefer Renaissance polyphony and hierarchically ordered ministers face pastors who want symbols that are more democratically decided and executed by parish liturgical committees. Cathedral liturgies, because of the very structure of the building, regularly demand a formal basilical style of worship, though the bishop himself might prefer a style much less formal.

Contemporary Questions. The search for a common contemporary symbolic style eludes the Christian communities, whether Catholic or Protestant. The questions: "What does it mean to be faithful to our tradition?" and "What does it mean to be loyal to our world?" are no longer luxuries of the theologian's or liturgist's workshop. Every Christian community is forced to define its own symbolic style or styles of worship to remain authentic to its traditions.

What does it mean to be faithful to modernity and its post-modern successors?

(a) The emergence of the modern sciences in the 17th and 18th centuries demystified space by making it possible to quantify the relationships of cause and effect. God may have been a remote cause of physical events; but the immediate causes could be isolated and measured. This permitted a control over nature. It also made experimental knowledge the criterion for all knowing. Symbolic ambivalences became suspect, particularly if they extended their meanings beyond the empirical realm.

Post-modern sciences, however, pay just as much attention to the particular without necessarily agreeing with the limitations placed upon human knowing. They recognize the metaphoric quality of models in science, the uncertainty of measurement, and the negative consequences of simply trying to control nature without respecting it. Being faithful to the insights of modern and post-modern science requires attention to particulars, respect for the sheer materiality of symbols, serious concern for the inner-worldly connections between things, and the honesty of responding with ignorance to inquiring questions to which one does not have a ready answer.

(b) Romantic poetry and philosophy taught modernity that all knowledge was filtered through the affective and cognitive subjectivity of the inquirer. Without the intricate interiority of the subject, there would be no science, no poetry, no common sense. Post-modern literature has discovered the solipsism of the ego, the overweening pride of the genius, and the psychological fragmentation of the subject. Post-modern philosophy has shown just how the mental acts of the subject are shaped by the common linguistic tradition and the culture of a people or nation. The subject has its own shadowside, its own "other," an ever-unconscious that dogs any attempts to schematize the conscious self. It has become clear that the subject is actually a community of subjects speaking a conversation in which any given action is the product of mixed motives and multiple understandings.

To be responsible for such a subject requires a subtlety of approach and the recognition of ambiguity. On the one hand, there is an attention to the development of the interior life and a discussion of the appropriate symbols that may express and shape the inner life at any given stage from children to the elderly. On the other, there is the recognition that symbols must challenge the subject to change. But the invitation to shift one's horizons by participating in another symbol cannot be accomplished brutally without destroying the delicate conversation of the heart.

(c) For the modern world since the revolutions in the United States and France, change is a value. Hierarchical uniformity and stability are destructive. The 19th-century human sciences knew themselves as radically historical, shaped by the passage of time. They recognized that the meanings of history were humanly constructed. And if they could be understood as made by humans, they could be unmade. Such a shaping of time was progress, leading toward a free world economy in which all who were deserving would enjoy a consumerist utopia.

This optimism about history was destroyed in the trenches of World War I, the genocides and holocaust of World War II, and the nuclear destruction that ended that war and threatens the present. Few would assume without considerable presumption that history's story is progressing toward the greatest good for the many. Post-modern human sciences are more conscious of their limitations.

Yet being faithful to the values of history means to be sensitive to change in the lives of individuals and communities. It means to be honest about the community's historical past and to anticipate judiciously the future without triumphalism. History can be seen as a treasure-house of warnings or of self-congratulating confirmations. In a post-modern world, it is neither. It is a world where the heroes and heroines of the past have flaws, where the saints could be obnoxious, and where heretics were often noble—because they were human.

(d) Finally, being faithful to modernity means recognizing that knowledge leads to action. Art-for-art's sake, worship for its own sake, knowledge-in-itself are all luxuries; they can shape and must lead to action. As Samuel Taylor Coleridge once remarked: "The metaphysics of one age is the common sense of the next." Risking a plan of action for the present and the future, however limited, however pain-fully formed, is part of the loyalty one owes modernity.

(e) There are escapes from modernity. Identification with a religious or a cultural past can be one, whether in a funda-mentalism of the book or of doctrines. In effect, this option is a romanticism of the symbolic structures, hoping that repe-tition of the past will cure the pluralist ambiguities of the present. An alternate form of this problem is the apocalypticism that decries the present for the sake of the future. This can be a secular (nuclear winter; the greenhouse effect; the club of Rome) or a religious (Armageddon) apocalypse. The liberal option that tends to collapse all religious symbols into a creational optimism neglects the some-times fearsome otherness of nature itself. Hurricanes, tornadoes, and solar wind-storms are more uncontrollable than we pretend.

What does it means to be faithful to the Christian tradition?

(a) The primary symbol of Christian meaning is the life, death, and resurrection of Christ. Responsibility to that parabolic discourse requires the willingness to hear the dangerous memory that overturns cherished expectations, comforts the af-flicted and the poor, and commits the community toward building the con-ditions for a better future. This person is the touchstone by which all other symbols are interpreted.

(b) The Christian tradition has a wealth of symbols and stories that have nour-ished its present. Being faithful to that tradition means allowing all those voices, especially those that have not had their day, to speak. An antecedent willingness to listen to the tradition can permit contemporary communities to "try on" old symbols to see if they have continuing power for change.

(c) The same attention must be given to the deeply felt interiority of the heroes and heroines of the tradition. The sanc-toral cycle of the church year is not a luxury. It may require additions, sub-tractions, and contextualizations—but it can provide icons of identification for contemporary believers. Yet rather than emphasizing behavior (whether bizarre or ordinary), the community begins to see the interiority of religious ancestors.

(d) Emphasis upon the moral action that derives from symbolic expression makes it clear that Christian symbols are not for self-comforting, fragile psyches. Application is part of human under-standing; if application is not included, the *status quo* is maintained and history is repeated. More of the same occurs. Those faithful to the death and resur-rection of Jesus cannot claim to espouse a return to the way things were.

We may take David Tracy's notion of an analogical imagination as a guide in our attempts to develop a contemporary style of symbolic worship. It will be *pluralist* to recognize the many voices of the community; it will be *conversational* in the best sense, willing to listen, risking speech, and strengthening the interloc-utors; it will be both *affirming* of our post-modern world and *critical* of its confusions. If it is *pluralist*, it will accept difference as enriching and struggle to discern which differences are morally and intellectually compatible, but it will not pre-judge the conclusions. It will seek out the suppressed voices in the tradition. If it is *conversational*, it is unlikely to tolerate speakers who stand on ceremonial office rather than competence. It will encourage people to speak their piece. If it is *affirming*, it will rejoice at the "signals of transcendence" in our world; if it is *critical*, it will correct as the gospels require.

This dialogical mode of imagination will look for the overlapping commonalities between Christianity and contemporary cultures and notice the accompanying differences. Because it is dialogical, it will be willing to converse about the dissymmetries; because it is imaginative, it will risk sympathy with the other in a willingness to view the world from another's perspectives. This risk to see the similarities in the differing expressions and to view the differences as participating in one another and creating a unity is the movement toward faith. But this faith is a firm conviction that the Christian God never ceases to be incarnate in symbolic forms.

See **Traditions, liturgical ...; Liturgical time, theology of; Imagination and worship**

M. Eliade, *Images and Symbols* (New York, 1961). T. Fawcett, *The Symbolic Language of Religion* (London, 1970). E.S. Goodenough, *Jewish Symbols in the Graeco-Roman Period*, ed. J. Neusner (Princeton, 1988). S. Happel (and James Walter), *Conversion and Discipleship: A Christian Foundation for Ethics and Doctrine* (Philadelphia, 1986): 85-101. C. Jones, G. Wainwright, E. Yarnold, *et al., The Study of Liturgy* (New York, 1978). B.J.F. Lonergan, *Method in Theology* (London, 1972): 57-99. L. Maldonado and D. Power, *Symbol and Art in Worship* (Edinburgh, 1980). D. Power, *Unsearchable Riches: The Symbolic Nature of Liturgy* (New York, 1984). K. Rahner, "The Theology of Symbol," *Theological Investigations* IV (Baltimore, 1966): 221-252. P. Ricoeur, *Interpretation Theory: Discourse and the Surplus of Meaning* (Fort Worth, 1976). E. Schillebeeckx, *Christ the Sacrament of the Encounter with God* (New York, 1963). J.L. Segundo, *The Sacraments Today*, Vol. 4 (New York, 1974). J. Shaughnessy, *The Roots of Ritual* (Grand Rapids, 1973). D. Tracy, *The Analogical Imagination: Christian Theology and the Culture of Pluralism* (New York, 1981). D. Tracy, *Pluralism and Ambiguity: Hermeneutics, Religion, Hope* (San Francisco, 1987).

STEPHEN HAPPEL

T

TECHNOLOGY

See Liturgy in a technological age; Media, use of, in the liturgy; Television, liturgy via

TELEVISION, LITURGY VIA

Liturgy is often defined as the work of the people; worship as the gathering of a community who join together around bread, book and cup to remember the Lord's Supper. In communication terms, liturgy could be defined as direct and interpersonal.

Mass media often defines its differences with other forms of communication because media, by its nature, demands that gatekeepers enter into the communication process. Therefore, the communication is indirect. The communication process between the source of messages in mass media and the receivers of those messages is normally separated by time and distance. For example, television performers do not receive feedback from their audiences as immediately as a pulpit preacher does.

Liturgy in McLuhan terms is information-laden and, therefore, a hot medium. Television in those same terms does not carry much information and, therefore, is a cool medium. It would seem, therefore, that liturgy in the form that Catholics normally celebrate it is a hot medium and not suitable for television, a cool medium.

These communications theories lead to a practical reality. The Catholic church's access to television airwaves, particularly in the United States, has been increasingly limited over the years because of government deregulation. The audience for free over-the-air television remains filled with people of numerous faith commitments. Many ministers who are actively engaged in the Catholic church's communications apostolate believe that the best use of the church's limited access to the airwaves for evangelization can be made when programs are produced and distributed that meet the needs of the largest number of *people* watching television. The broadcast of the Mass on over-the-air television, does not meet the criteria, since the Mass is designed for *Catholic* participation. Nonetheless, the Mass is oftentimes the only outreach a local church has for evangelization through television, and it continues to meet the need of the sick and shut-ins of particular local communities.

In the *Constitution on Social Communications*, the Second Vatican Council announced that the church "considers it one of its duties to announce the Good News of salvation . . . with the help of the media of social communications." The Fathers of the Council seemed clearly aware that the use of the media should take into account the "nature of what is communicated, given the special character of each of these media." It would seem then that Vatican II reinforces the theory that over-the-air television and the liturgy of the eucharist do not easily co-exist.

The Council Fathers further stated that care must be taken that television and radio programs created by church agencies ". . . are outstanding for their standards of excellence and achievement." The demand for excellence is clear. That the eucharistic liturgy is presented on television is a fact. Therefore, liturgy presented on television should be both good liturgy, and good television.

Good liturgy binds a people together, gives them a shared sense of community, and reminds them of God's presence in their lives. Liturgy does that by bringing diverse elements into a single whole. God's word carefully spoken, music that inspires, vessels crafted artistically, vestments of substance and style, a celebrant who understands his role as presider, a preacher who grabs people's attention— each of these elements when brought together with God's grace and among a believing people produces liturgies, the work of the people.

Good television is intimate, and eucharistic liturgy offers television cameras the possibility of intimacy at many points in the action. Television offers liturgical actions in close up form that are difficult to see even in a well-built and well-lighted sacred space. When a homily is shot with an eye to intimacy, for example, television offers preachers the chance to use the power of their eyes and the expressions on their face that are often missed in a large church. The intimacy of liturgy as seen by television is, therefore, a plus. There are many minuses.

Television broadcasts are bound by time. The constraints of time must be observed, but the current common practice of allowing under thirty minutes for the celebration of the liturgy strains the ability of the celebrant and those assisting him to create meaningful liturgy.

Whenever possible, to save money, it seems that most television liturgies are shot in studios. However, television liturgies should be live. The setting should be in a church rather than a studio since it is almost impossible to create a fitting sacred space in a studio.

Television is usually watched by one or two people at a time. The ability of television to create a community—one of the key characteristics of good liturgy— is, therefore, not likely to occur. However, there is a sense in which those who watch the liturgy on television become a community bound by the common bond of television. Just as a nation can be bound together by television during a crisis such as John Kennedy's assassination, so also can a group of people watching television discretely be bound together by the liturgical events they witness on television.

The advent of television as a medium whose audiences are segmented, rather than a mass medium, will make it possible for larger numbers of Catholics to view liturgies on television whether watching their videotape players, cable free television, or direct broadcast satellites. Because the number of "windows" to audiences will increase in the future, those who wish to create eucharistic liturgies for television viewing will have an easier time finding an audience. But those increased number of "windows" to the audience may well prove to viewers that the elements that create successful worship, particularly participation in a community, are still beyond the reach of mass media, especially television.

See **Communication, ritual as; Imagination and worship; Media, use of, in the liturgy**

JOHN GEANEY, C.S.P.

THEOLOGIANS, MODERN, AND LITURGICAL RENEWAL

The modern liturgical renewal would not have been possible without the contributions of many prominent theologians such as A. Baumstark, J. Betz, L. Bouyer, Y. Congar, J. Danielou, M. de la Taille, B. Leeming, O. Semmelroth, P. Schoonenberg, and C. Vagaggini. Other theologians, such as J. Corbon, A. Kavanagh, E. Kilmartin, B. Lonergan, D. Power, J. L. Segundo, R. Vaillancourt, and G. Wainwright have opened up new possibilities for the liturgical theology of the future. But the theologians who have had the greatest impact on the renewal of liturgical thought and practice in the 20th century are unquestionably Odo Casel, Edward Schillebeeckx and Karl Rahner. These scholars completely reshaped our understanding of the liturgy through their insights into mystery theology, Christ as sacrament, the church as sacrament, the universality of grace, grace as self-communication of God, and the nature of symbols.

I. Odo Casel

No theologian had a more profound and indelible impact on the modern liturgical renewal than Odo Casel (1886-1948), a German Benedictine of the abbey at Maria Laach. Based on his studies in the patristic period, Casel developed a refreshing understanding of the liturgy as the mystery of Christ made present. Casel's work stimulated a flurry of scholarly activity as a wide variety of theologians returned to their sources to debate the merits and demerits of his approach. In the process, some of the details of his approach were rejected, particularly his interpretation of the relationship between Christian liturgy and the mystery cults of late antiquity. Some scholars found his exegesis of the scriptures and the Fathers somewhat nonchalant. His exposition of just how in fact the mystery of Christ was present in the mystery of worship left most theologians unsatisfied. He was also criticized for having an excessively romantic view of the church's liturgical practice. Nevertheless, his core insights won enthusiastic acceptance and are now largely taken for granted. Whereas Josef Jungmann led the liturgical movement to the historical perspective required to renew the liturgy, Odo Casel was the first to inspire it with the necessary theological vision.

Casel summarized his insights in a collection of writings which appeared in English in 1962 entitled *The Mystery of Christian Worship*. This book has since become a theological classic. Casel sees Christianity as a mystery and the liturgy as that mystery made present. "Mystery" for Casel is not what we normally mean by it, i.e., a truth inaccessible to human reason. It is originally and primarily God himself as the infinitely distant, holy, unapproachable one. This God reveals himself as mystery to those whom he has chosen. His revelation remains a mystery because it is not open to the profane world but hides itself and shows itself only to believers.

The incarnation gave the word "mystery" a second and deeper meaning. Christ is the mystery in person because he shows the invisible God in the flesh. But the mystery of Christ is not just his person. His life, death, resurrection and exaltation are mysteries because God reveals his glory through them in a unique and unsurpassable way. The paschal mystery, the passing of Christ from life in the flesh to a risen life with the Father in the Spirit, is the center of the mystery of Christ.

Salvation means that what was realized in Christ must be realized in us. Being a Christian does not mean just that we accept the teaching of Christ and receive the grace won by him. It means a real participation in the very saving acts that constitute the mystery of Christ. Therefore the past mystery of Christ must be made present so that we can enter into it and relive it in an openness to Christ.

This participation in the mystery of Christ takes place in the liturgy. For Casel the liturgy makes present the unique, unrepeatable mystery of Christ which was realized historically in the past and is sacramentally re-presented in the liturgical commemoration. The liturgy itself, therefore, is a mystery. Thus "mystery" has a third sense, intimately connected with the first two. As mystery, it is the revelation of God in the redeeming work of the risen Lord through the sacred actions which Christ appointed for the church. As liturgy, it is the action of the church in conjunction with the saving action of Christ. Christ and the church work together inseparably in the mystery of worship.

Although Christ is no longer visible among us, we encounter him and his saving deeds, and through him the mystery of God, in the mystery of the liturgy. The revelation of the mystery of God in Christ is carried on and made present in the mystery of worship. Here Christ performs his saving work, invisible but present in the Spirit and acting upon people of faith. Christ himself acts in this mystery; not alone as he did in the mystery of the cross, but with the church. When the church celebrates the liturgy, Christ is at work in it and so what the church does is truly mystery. The mystery of the liturgy is, therefore, the most central and most essential action of the church.

Consequently, Casel stressed the importance of the full and active participation of the entire assembly in the liturgy. The whole church, not merely the clergy, is to take an active part in the liturgy. All members are sacramentally joined to Christ through baptism and confirmation. The laity do not merely assist with private devotion and prayer at the clergy's liturgy. Rather, by their membership in the body of Christ they are necessary and real participants in the liturgy. All are meant to actually participate in the mystery of Christ.

II. Edward Schillebeeckx

Edward Schillebeeckx (b. 1914), a Dutch Dominican, has written extensively on sacramental questions. In the process he successfully translated the key insights of scholastic sacramental theology into contemporary philosophical terms. His most influential work in this regard appeared in English in 1963 as *Christ the Sacrament of the Encounter with God.*

Schillebeeckx thought that the traditional theology of the manuals did not adequately distinguish the unique manner of existence which is peculiar to human persons from the mere "being there" which is proper to impersonal things. Thus, this theology did not do justice to the personal communion with God which is the center of Christianity. The sacraments were studied with a purely impersonal, almost mechanical approach in which they were considered chiefly in terms of physical categories.

Schillebeeckx based his study of the sacraments on a highly nuanced concept of human, personal encounter. He understands Christianity as a saving dialogue between humanity and the living God. Christianity, therefore, is essentially a personal encounter with God. Because God lovingly takes the initiative and comes to meet us in grace, we live in a condition of active and immediate communication with God. Grace is this "indwelling" of God, the communion of God the Trinity and human persons. This act of encounter with God, which can take place only in faith, is what we call salvation.

Jesus Christ is the supreme realization of this encounter with God. He is himself a personal dialogue with God the Father and the whole human community. There are two movements to this dialogue. In Christ's love for human beings there is a movement down from above, a coming to us of God's love by way of Jesus's human heart. And there is a movement up from below, from the human heart of Jesus to the Father. The human actions of Jesus' life as they come from above bring redemption to his fellow human beings. As coming from below, they are expressions of his worship of the Father. Thus Jesus is not only the revelation of the redeeming God; he is also the supreme worshipper of the Father, the supreme realization of the encounter with God. The actions of Jesus' life, therefore, are manifestations both of the divine love for humanity and of human love for God. They are both bestowal of grace and worship.

Since the humanity of Jesus represents us all, it is clear that Jesus is not only the visible offer of divine love to humanity. He is also the supreme realization of the response of human love to this divine offer. Whatever Christ does as a free human being is not only a realization in human form of God's activity for our salvation. It is also at the same time the positive human acceptance, representative for all of us, of this redeeming offer from God.

For Schillebeeckx, therefore, Jesus as the personal, visible realization of the Father's redeeming grace is *the* sacrament, the primordial sacrament, of the encounter with God. Encounter with Jesus is therefore the sacrament of encounter with God. The foundation of all this is the incarnation, which in turn was completed by Jesus' death, resurrection and exaltation. This mystery of Christ is a mystery of saving worship: a mystery of praise (the upward movement) and of salvation (the downward movement). Christ is supreme worship of the Father. Christ lived this worship of God in a completely human way in the course of an ordinary human life.

The supreme moment in his life, the death to which he freely assents, is "liturgical." The death on the cross, as that in which Jesus' inward adoration of God becomes an external reality is an act of the community (i.e., a liturgy), not yet performed by the people itself but offered by the representative of the whole human family in the name of all and to the advantage of all. The cross itself is the great liturgical mystery of worship through which Christ pleads with the Father for the grace of redemption for the world. In and through the liturgical mystery of worship that is his sacrifice on the cross, against the background of the whole of his life in God's service, the being of the Son of God as "from the Father" and "to the Father" is fully revealed and given reality on the human plane.

Through this earthly mystery of worship, Christ "merited" or obtained for us from the Father the grace of redemption which now as risen Lord he can in fact give us to the full. The heavenly liturgy of Christ is still a filial intercession with and worship of the Father, but it is also a continual sending out of the Holy Spirit upon humanity. Hence the mystery of worship which is Christ is at the same time our salvation. It is a mystery of saving worship.

Christ's earthly and heavenly mystery of worship, then, is the foundation of the Lord's unfailing gift of redeeming grace. When we speak of Christ's mystery of saving worship or about his work of salvation-through-worship, we must not lose sight of the fact that Jesus' human adoration of the Father is itself the revelation of the divinity which he receives from the Father. This adoration arises therefore from God's own love. For Jesus this means that even his adoration itself is a pure gift and grace from the Father without whom he can do nothing. Our salvation through Jesus' adoration is thus intelligible only by virtue of the fact that Jesus as human was himself sanctified by the Spirit of God; the redeeming activity of Jesus' love is a personal worship-through-salvation, and so in our regard salvation-through-worship.

The personal encounter with God which is our salvation remains bound up with our personal encounter with Christ. We encounter that mystery of Christ in the church's sacramental liturgy. The sacraments are not things; they are personal encounters with the risen Lord, the primordial sacrament of encounter with God. Through the sacraments we are placed in living contact with the mystery of Christ's saving worship.

The sacraments are such a living encounter with the mystery of Christ because the church, which the sacraments express and make visible, is the sacrament of the risen Lord. The church is the historical manifestation of God's own love for humanity in Christ (bestowal of grace) and, at the same time, of humanity's own love and adoration of God in the same Lord (worship). In this way the church is a community of salvation and worship and the embodiment of the mystery of Christ. It is the primordial sacrament of Christ.

The sacraments are fundamentally and primarily visible, official acts of the church. Since the church is the primordial sacrament of encounter with Christ, each sacrament is a personal saving act of the risen Christ himself realized in the visible form of an act of the church. To participate in the sacraments of the church in faith is, therefore, the same thing as to encounter Christ. This is what Casel pointed to in his concept of "mystery presence." Schillebeeckx' contribution has been to show that the presence of Christ in mystery stems from the fact that the sacraments are personal acts of Christ in the church.

III. Karl Rahner

Karl Rahner (1904-84), a German Jesuit, had a more extensive influence on the renewal of Roman Catholic theology in general, and on the renewal of the liturgy in particular, than any other modern theologian. He criticized the conventional sacramental theology of his day for presenting the liturgy as the means through which grace is made available to a world which is otherwise normally deprived of it. He proposed a different view, in which the liturgy of the church is seen as the symbolic manifestation of the "liturgy of the world," i.e, the dynamic process of God's continual self-communication to the world and our response. Rahner built this idea of worship on his key insights into theological anthropology, the theology of grace, salvation history, Christology and ecclesiology.

Worship presupposes that we finite creatures are able to enter into a dialogical relationship with the infinite mystery of God. Rahner claims that a fundamental openness to such a relationship with God is the essence of what it means to be human.

It is precisely because we have a transcendental openness to the absolute mystery of God that we know anything, that we are free and responsible, and that we are persons and subjects. To be human is to be fundamentally and completely open to unfathomable mystery. Our transcendental orientation can be suppressed or ignored but it is always present as a condition of possibility of our subjectivity.

Thus our experience of ordinary daily life presupposes a relationship with God. And our relationship with the absolutely transcendent God is mediated by daily human life. When we direct ourselves to the explicit worship of God, we are not entering into a relationship with God as though none had existed previously. On the contrary, when we worship, the relationship with that unfathomable mystery which is a secret ingredient of every moment of our daily lives is expressed and manifested. Furthermore, it should not be surprising that our relationship with the transcendent God in worship is mediated by the particular and the historical: by material objects like water, oil, bread and wine, by word and song, by symbol and ritual. Our experience of anything historical is always also an experience of God, and our experience of God is always mediated by the historical. We are transcendent beings precisely as historical beings, a fact which receives special expression in worship.

The liturgy presupposes that we do not merely relate to God as a distant and aloof horizon of mystery, but that in fact when we worship we experience a God who is near to us and transforms us in grace. The fundamental tenet of Rahner's theology of grace is that grace is properly understood not as the communication of a finite created gift separate from God, but as the *self*-communication of God. God does not merely give us some indirect share of himself in grace by creating and giving us finite realities through efficient causality. Rather, in something which approaches formal causality, God really and in the strictest sense of the word gives himself.

In grace, therefore, the absolute, holy mystery which is experienced as the horizon of our transcendence is communicated to us while remaining absolute mystery. Through this self-communication we participate in the life of God; we are transformed and become like God without, however, becoming God. Such a transformation is the fulfillment of our deepest human potential and our salvation.

The world is always encompassed and permeated with this grace of the divine self-communication at least as an offer made to our freedom. The world as it actually exists is never simply a secular and profane reality to which grace is subsequently added by God. It is always graciously endowed with God's self-communication and oriented to God. The objective situation in which we live is one in which God wills the salvation of everyone. God continually offers himself to us, but that offer can become effective and fruitful for salvation when it is freely accepted in faith.

All of this means that liturgy is not fundamentally about an exchange of gifts between ourselves and God. It is not a matter of God giving us some-*thing* called grace. Worship is an experience of grace and so it is an experience of the immediate presence of the absolute mystery of God mediated by the historical. But God is not present to us in worship as though he were otherwise absent from our lives; we are always and everywhere in the gracious presence of God. The ways in which the unfathomable mystery is present in worship are different from the ways God is present in daily life, but God is graciously present in both. And this gracious self-communication of God never becomes fruitful and effective inside or outside of worship unless it is actively accepted in faith.

The historical mediations of the offer of God's saving self-revelation and our response to it take place not only in specifically religious events but in a hidden and ambiguous way in every event of our lives. Perfectly common and ostensibly "profane" experiences mediate the gracious self-revelation of the unfathomable mystery of God. The entire range of human endeavors can mediate our response to God. For Rahner, life cannot be divided into mutually exclusive secular and sacred spheres. There is no such thing as a purely secular realm lying alongside or below a purely sacred realm which is made up of religious and sacramental events. The realm of events and realities which are explicitly sacred lies *within* a secular realm which is itself permeated by the effective grace of God. The history of salvation and revelation, therefore, is co-extensive with the ordinary history of the world.

The dynamic process of God's gracious self-communication and our response, which takes place throughout the routine course of human life, is usually hidden and ambiguous. The official history of salvation is nothing more or less than the way in which that history of salvation and grace which pervades our lives and extends throughout our history becomes explicit and historically tangible. In Jesus Christ, this special history of salvation reached its final, irrevocable highpoint and fulfillment.

Jesus Christ, in whom God's absolute self-communication to the whole human race is present both as offer and acceptance, is the unsurpassable and definitive offer and acceptance of God because he is not only established by God but is God himself. The very meaning of human nature is to be realized and fulfilled by being filled with the mystery of God. When our indefinable nature was assumed by God as his self-expression it reached its fulfillment. The incarnate Word of God fulfills the essential transcendental openness which always orients us to God. He completely realizes our potential to receive the absolute self-communication of God.

The death and resurrection of the incarnate Word is the ultimate manifestation of his fulfillment of salvation history. The life of Jesus Christ was summed up and finalized in his death on the cross and then ratified in his resurrection from the dead. In Christ, God has communicated himself in such a unique way that Christ became the definitive and irreversible self-gift of God to the world. Christ freely accepted the divine self-gift in such a manner that this acceptance too became irreversible, i.e., through his death and resurrection as the definitive culmination of his free actions in history. The cross and resurrection, therefore, are the primary sacramental sign of the universal availability of saving grace. Thus Jesus Christ is the original sacrament of the salvation of the world.

For Rahner, then, the ordinary and "profane" history of the world is the stage on which takes place the continual drama of the self-communication of God and our response to it, a drama which reached its highpoint and fulfillment in the incarnation, death, and resurrection of Jesus Christ. This is what he meant by "the liturgy of the world." Worship manifests the holiness of our lives and our world for we worship from within a graced and redeemed world. It is precisely because our worship takes place in such a world, because it is the symbolic manifestation of this liturgy of the world, that it is an event of grace for us. Worship expresses the limitless grace of God and thus makes that grace available to us. The liturgy of the church is best understood as the symbolic expression of the liturgy of the world.

The necessity of worship does not depend upon the supposition that it alone provides us with a grace that is otherwise unavailable in a fallen world, for that is patently not the case. It derives, on the one hand, from our need to express our hidden, implicit relationship with God and, on the other, from our responsibility to take advantage of those explicit ways in which the eschatologically triumphant fulfillment of this relationship in Christ have been made available to us in the liturgy of the church. Worship is important and significant not because something happens in it that does not happen elsewhere but because there is present and explicit in it that which makes the world important: that it is everywhere blessed by gracious and triumphant self-communication of God.

The liturgy of the world, and therefore all true worship, is first and foremost something that God celebrates. God freely chose to communicate himself and so God created a world and listeners within it who could receive and hear his word. This liturgy takes place at the initiative of God; it is all grace. Even our response is made possible and effected by God, for it is precisely in the freedom of which God is the source that we are empowered to respond to God. But while worship is at heart something that God brings about in us, it nonetheless takes place in and through our free history. The self-communication of God is directed toward our freedom, a real freedom which is made possible by God. God sustains our freedom in such a way that we really do have the possibility of accepting or rejecting God's self-gift. We shape this free response in all the concrete, ordinary events of our lives. It is impossible for us to be passive spectators in the liturgy of the world; the gracious initiatives of God demand our response. Active response and participation is something that is required of us at all levels of worship.

For Rahner, the church's worship is not merely *a* manifestation of the liturgy of the world. Rather, it is *the* expression of the liturgy which is co-extensive with the history of the world and which has been fulfilled in Christ Jesus. The liturgy of the church is the clearest and most effective symbolic expression of the liturgy of the world.

The liturgy of the world is necessarily directed toward the kind of social and public expression that it finds in the liturgy of the church. We participate in the liturgy of the world as social beings and if the symbolic expression of that liturgy is to be complete it must take a social form. Communal worship is necessary and essential because only it can express the fact that the liturgy of the world embraces our lives as social beings.

The church's communal worship is a unique expression of the liturgy of the world due to the church's distinctive relationship to Christ. The church is what Rahner calls a "real symbol" of the risen Christ: it remains distinct from what it symbolizes, but is the way in which Christ expresses himself and renders himself present in the world. The church is the basic sacrament of Christ, the highpoint and fulfillment of the liturgy of the world. As this sacrament the church is brought to manifestation on the historical and social levels and thereby "effects" that grace which is already present in the innermost heart of the world and of the whole of human life. It is the historical realization of the fundamental liturgical drama which lies at the center of the world and its history.

The church, then, is the permanent presence in the world of the fulfillment of the liturgy of the world. This relationship to Christ distinguishes the church's liturgy from every other kind of worship. When the church celebrates its liturgy, it celebrates it as the community of faith through which the highpoint of the liturgy of the world is permanently present. This is why Rahner calls the church the basic sacrament. The church symbolically expresses the liturgy of the world in an absolutely unique fashion. The individual sacramental worship activities of the church are the occasions in which the church concretely expresses its nature as the basic, ongoing manifestation of the liturgy of the world. The abiding, indestructible union of the church with Christ is manifested whenever the church celebrates its sacraments. And so the sacramental liturgy of the church is the clearest and most effective symbolic manifestation of the liturgy of the world.

Conclusion

Casel, Schillebeeckx, and Rahner were not the only modern theologians to make significant contributions to the liturgical renewal. Nor have all of their ideas stood the test of time equally well. But by giving new life to some ancient theological insights they completely reshaped the way we understand worship. By the beginning of this century, it was clear to many that the liturgical practice of the church was badly in need of renewal. Historians showed the movement how and why the liturgy should be renewed by investigating its historical development. Theologians like Casel, Schillebeeckx, and Rahner made an enormous impact on the movement by providing it with bold new visions of the place of the liturgy within the mystery of our life in God. One measure of their impact is that today so many of their insights are taken for granted. But perhaps their most enduring accomplishment is that they have inspired a whole new generation of theologians to develop other, fresh perspectives on the liturgy.

See **Mystery theology**

Odo Casel, *The Mystery of Christian Worship* (Westminster: The Newman Press, 1962). Edward Schillebeeckx, *Christ the Sacrament of the Encounter with God* (New York: Sheed and Ward, 1963). Karl Rahner, *The Church and the Sacraments* (New York: Herder and Herder, 1963); "Considerations on the Active Role of the Person in the Sacramental Event," *Theological Investigations* Vol. 14 (New York: Seabury, 1976): 161-84; "On the Theology of Worship," *Theological Investigations* Vol. 19 (New York: Crossroad, 1983): 141-49; and, "The Theology of the Symbol," *Theological Investigations* Vol. 4 (Baltimore : Helicon, 1966): 221-52.

MICHAEL SKELLEY, S.J.

THERAPY, RECONCILIATION AND

See **Reconciliation and therapy**

TIME, LITURGICAL

See **Calendar, liturgical; Liturgical time, theology of**

TRADITIONS, LITURGICAL, IN THE EAST

The distinction within the ecumenical church between the churches of the East and the churches of the West is rooted in patterns of evangelization and evolution in the first six centuries of the Christian Era. As Christianity spread beyond Jerusalem to the whole Mediterranean world, four regions, in addition to Jerusalem, became major centers of Christian life: North Africa (Carthage), Rome, Antioch and Alexandria, each developing its own distinctive forms of faith and prayer.

These initial centers had varying fates. Jerusalem was destroyed in A.D. 70. The church of North Africa, where Latin Christianity was born and developed [Tertullian (d. ca. A.D. 240), Cyprian (d. A.D. 258)], was destroyed by the Moors in the 7th century, but not before exerting a major influence on the church of Rome. This latter (Rome) evolved in three stages: a primitive apostolic stage (Clement of Rome (fl. ca. A.D. 80); a developed Greek stage (Hippolytus of Rome (d. A.D. 235), and, in the fourth century, Latin Rome (usually taken to be the Roman tradition) which adopted as its own, and further evolved, the Latin Christianity of North Africa. The church of Alexandria developed for a time as the major intellectual center [Clement (d. A.D. 215), Origen (d. A.D. 253/254), Athanasius (d. A.D. 373) and Cyril (d. A.D. 444)] until the Council of Chalcedon (A.D. 451), which Alexandria rejected. Alexandria is also known for its monastic movement, which likewise had an effect on its evolving liturgical forms. The Antiochene influence was felt throughout Asia Minor with the churches of Cappadocia [Basil of Caesarea (d. A.D. 379), Gregory of Nazianz (d. A.D. 389) and Gregory of Nyssa (d. A.D. 394)] helping further to shape both theological and liturgical evolution. Finally, from the late 4th century onward, the new imperial capital at Constantinople began to emerge as yet another major Christian center, under whose influence the later Byzantine church, still Antiochene in root, would develop its own distinctive liturgical forms.

The term *liturgical tradition*, as it is

employed here, refers to these five centers (Jerusalem, Rome, Carthage, Antioch and Alexandria), the forms of faith and prayer characteristic of each, and the forward evolution of these forms in the many churches that constitute the one church of Jesus Christ. Though there are countless instances of mutual influence, one tradition on another, it can generally be said that the Latin tradition (Carthage and, especially, Latin Rome) is the *root* tradition of the churches of the West, while the Syriac and Greek traditions (Jerusalem, Antioch and Alexandria) form the *root* traditions of the churches of the East.

Because of the early disappearance of the Jerusalem church, the churches to be considered here as *liturgical traditions of the East* are derived from either Antioch or Alexandria. The Jerusalem tradition was absorbed into certain strains of Antioch Christianity and no longer exists as an independent living liturgical tradition. Antioch gave rise to an *East Syrian* strain manifest in the Nestorian and Chaldean churches of Iran and Iraq and in the Malabar church in India, and a *West Syrian* strain which appears in several layers of evolution. In its most primitive form it shows itself in the Syrian (monophysite and Catholic) and Maronite churches of the Middle East, and in the Orthodox and Malankara churches of India. In more complex and developed form it appears in the Byzantine churches and also in the Armenian church, which has been significantly influenced by other traditions (e.g., Cappadocia and Rome) as well. The two primary manifestations of the Alexandrian tradition are the Coptic church in Egypt and, though again with a variety of secondary influences (esp. West Syrian), the national church of Ethiopia.

The primary focus here will be on these traditions as they exist in living churches today. Since sacraments in the East are treated elsewhere, the focus is further restricted to the eucharistic liturgy. The aim is to examine each of these ritual forms and uncover the distinctive theology and spirituality which they contain.

All of the churches follow the standard ritual pattern where proclamation of the word precedes and leads into the sacramental offering. It is the general Eastern custom to prepare the bread and wine for offering at the beginning of the liturgy, and it is a common understanding in the East that these gifts somehow already represent Christ even before the consecratory *anaphora* or eucharistic prayer. In many of the churches the ancient custom of conducting the first part of the liturgy from the *bema* (raised platform for the celebration of the word) and away from the altar is being restored. Except in cases where Western influence imposed otherwise, these churches generally use leavened bread and distribute the eucharistic wine by intinction, by spoon, or directly from the chalice. Some of the liturgies, notably the Byzantine and the Armenian, and to some extent the Coptic, are space dependent; others less so, or not at all.

East Syrian Churches: Nestorian, Chaldean and Malabar

The Churches

Antioch was the original center of Syrian Christianity, with a second center developing by the end of the 2nd century in Edessa. Edessa itself became divided by early christological disputes between Monophysites (one person, one nature in Christ) and Nestorians (two persons, two natures in Christ), and soon political pressure drove the Nestorians further east into the Persian Empire.

The Nestorian church was centered at Nisibis and organized as a distinct church in the 4th century by the bishop of Seleucia-Ctesiphon. Because it developed outside of the Roman Empire, it did so with a large measure of independence from what it called "the churches of the

West" (i.e., everything to the west of itself). The Nestorian church preserves a very primitive layer of liturgical evolution.

These East Syrian Christians adhered to the decrees of Nicea, but not to those of Ephesus or Chalcedon, and eventually they adopted Theodore of Mopsuestia (d. A.D. 428), who was condemned by the Chalcedonian churches, as their champion theologian. From the 4th to the 7th centuries they engaged in great missionary activity throughout the East. The rise of Islam, however, put a stop to their missionary expansion, cut the mission territories (see Malabar church below) off from the mother church, and left the Nestorian church but a remnant community living peaceably, if under severe restrictions, among the Moslems. Since the 16th century some have been united to the church of Rome, these being the Catholic Chaldeans, while others remain non-Chalcedonian Nestorians.

The Malabar church, also called St. Thomas Christians because they claim Thomas the apostle as their link to the apostolic church, came under the missionary influence of the Persian Nestorians until they were cut off from them by the advance of Islam. The St. Thomas Christians were re-discovered in the 16th century by Portugese missionaries who tried unsuccessfully to impose the Latin liturgy upon them. These missionaries did succeed, however, in heavily Latinizing the Malabar liturgy, a deed which has only recently been undone. Liturgical revisions begun in 1962 have restored the Malabar eucharist to its Syro-Chaldean form, and translated it from Syriac into modern Malayalam.

The liturgy of the Nestorian, Chaldean and Malabar churches is essentially the same. The primary *anaphora* (eucharistic prayer) is that of Sts. Addai and Mari, which is unique in that no words of institution are to be found in it. These words are inserted in the text by the Catholic Chaldeans and Malabarese. Two other prayers are also found in the tradition, one attributed to Nestorius and one to Theodore of Mopsuestia, though these are used only occasionally by the Nestorians and Chaldeans, and not at all by the Malabar church. These prayers do contain the institution narrative in its proper place, which makes its absence from the Addai-Mari text, in spite of great efforts to prove otherwise, most probably a simple absence rather than a reasoned omission.

The text cited to examine the East Syrian liturgical tradition as it lives today is the revised text of the Syro-Malabar church (see, *Celebration of the Eucharist according to the Syro-Malabar Rite*, Bangalore: Biblical, Catechetical and Liturgical Centre, 1973). Differences between this and the Chaldean liturgy are noted. The major differences between the Chaldean and Nestorian liturgies are the saints who are called upon in the prayers and, of course, the insertion of the institution narrative in the Addai-Mari text.

The Liturgy

(a) Introductory Rites. The *introductory rites* of the liturgy are remnants of a monastic office. They consist of an abbreviated *doxology* ("Glory to God in the highest and to all on earth, peace and hope forever"), the Lord's Prayer, a variable psalm and a prayer of incense, which concludes with the *lakhoumara*, a 4th century prayer of praise to Christ the Lord. The gifts are prepared in the Chaldean rite simply, and before the liturgy begins; in the Malabar rite the offerings are prepared during the pre-anaphora, after the celebrants have come to the altar. In an earlier version of both rites, the gifts were prepared more formally between the *lakhoumara* and the *trisagion*.

(b) Liturgy of the Word. The *liturgy of the word* begins with the *trisagion* ("Holy God, holy strong one, holy and immortal, have mercy on us") and consists of two

(Malabar) or four (Chaldean) readings. A homily, prayer of the faithful (Malabar), and creed conclude this part of the liturgy. An earlier version of both rites concluded with an imposition of hands and blessing of the people, and probably the dismissal of catechumens as well.

(c) Pre-anaphora. The *pre-anaphora* includes the "access to the altar" by the celebrant(s), transfer of the gifts (if prepared elsewhere) or their presentation and preparation.

(d) Anaphora. The *anaphora* or *Qurbana* of the Apostles (Addai and Mari) follows. The *anaphora* includes more than the eucharistic prayer alone. It begins with a prayer of gratitude on the part of the ministers ("...through the multitude of your mercies, you have made us worthy to be ministers of the sacred mysteries of the body and blood of your Christ..."), the greeting of peace, the unveiling of the gifts (the veil is folded and placed around the gifts to represent the sepulchre of Christ), and the incensing of the gifts. After the customary dialogue, the eucharistic prayer gives thanks to God for creation, leads into the "Holy, Holy, Holy," and continues in thanksgiving for the incarnation and redemption. At this point the narrative of institution is inserted.

There follows the prayer of remembrance (*anamnesis*), prayers of intercession (it is characteristic of the East-Syrian tradition to locate the intercessions here), the invocation of the Spirit (*epiclesis*) and the concluding doxology.

(e) Post-anaphora. At the conclusion of the *anaphora*, priest and people proclaim faith in the living and life-giving bread of heaven. The bread is broken and signed with the precious blood. The people are invited to "approach the mysteries of the precious body and blood of our savior" with an invitation as well to "turn away from our faults." A litany prayer for forgiveness and the Lord's prayer (a second time) lead into the

distribution of communion to all. This is followed by a brief thanksgiving prayer, blessing and dismissal.

Theology and Spirit

The over-all tone of the Syro-Chaldean liturgy is one of glory and praise to God. This doxological note is set at the very beginning with the "Glory to God" and the Lord's Prayer. It continues in the prayer that concludes the psalm ("For all the helps and graces you have given us, for which we cannot thank you enough, we will praise and glorify you unceasingly in your triumphant church forever") and in the *lakhoumara* ("You, Jesus Christ, we glorify; you are the one who raises our bodies and you are the savior of our souls"). After the *trisagion*, and before the first reading, the presiding priest prays "that love and hope may grow in us, that we may find salvation, and praise you forever." Before the gospel: "O Christ, Light of the world and Life of all, glory forever to the eternal Mercy that sent you to us." In coming to the altar, the priests pray: "We give you thanks, our Father, Lord of heaven and earth, Father, Son and Holy Spirit, for though we are sinners, you have made us worthy by your grace to offer you these holy, glorious, life-giving and divine mysteries...." A prayer of praise introduces the greeting of peace ("We offer you praise and honor, worship and thanksgiving now and always and forever"), and again the fraction rite ("Glory be to your name, O Lord Jesus Christ, and worship to your Majesty forever"). Finally, the concluding prayers and blessing continue this theme to the end: "It is our duty, O Lord, Father, Son and Holy Spirit, to offer always to your most Blessed Trinity praise and honor, worship and perpetual thanksgiving...," and "Let us sing the praises of Christ who has nourished us with his body and blood."

The liturgy is heavily christocentric. While many of the prayers are addressed to the triune God or simply to the Father, many more are addressed directly to Christ himself. Even within the *anaphora*, a prayer most often addressed exclusively to the Father, the section on redemption is addressed to Christ.

The East Syrian liturgy is a remembrance that looks forward to the eschaton rather than to the past (the Lord's Supper) or present (*this* eucharistic offering or the heavenly mysteries as they are *now* being enacted). This is captured most forcefully in the *epiclesis* of the Addai-Mari *anaphora*: "let your Holy Spirit come and rest upon this oblation of your servants; may he bless it and sanctify it that it may be unto the pardon of our offenses and forgiveness of our sins, and for the hope of resurrection and for the new life with the just in the kingdom of heaven."

Finally, the East Syrian liturgy exhibits a theological note derived from Theodore of Mopsuestia who considered the bread and wine, once placed upon the altar and before the invocation of the Spirit, to represent Christ in the tomb, with the *epiclesis* itself signifying the resurrection. Once the gifts are prepared, the veil is folded around them "as a sepulchre" and is not removed until after the *epiclesis*.

The Addai-Mari anaphora has several distinctive marks. In addition to being in part addressed to Christ, the intercessions are placed between the *anamnesis* and *epiclesis*, and therefore form part of the offering itself. The *anamnesis* is untypical in that, while it does commemorate the "passion, death, burial and resurrection" (no mention is made in the *anamnesis* of the future coming of Christ), it does not lead into the offering of the gifts, but only to the more general offering of "praise and honor, worship and thanksgiving." Finally, the institution narrative, where it is inserted by the Catholic Chaldeans and Malabarese, is in fact a somewhat awkward fit; most probably the original text served as a perfectly adequate eucharistic prayer without it. If so, it bears witness to a primitive strain of eucharistic understanding that was lost to other liturgical traditions.

West Syrian Churches: Syrian, Maronite, Syro-Indian
The Churches

The churches which follow the primitive West Syrian tradition are the primary heirs to the tradition of Jerusalem. Though these churches employ many anaphoral texts, the oldest and most treasured among them is that attributed to St. James, "the brother of the Lord." The three churches, Syrian, Maronite and Syro-Indian, need to be identified separately.

In the wake of the Council of Chalcedon, the West Syrian church of Antioch was divided between those who accepted the council's decrees and those who tended toward Monophysitism. The former, considered not only orthodox Catholics but also loyal subjects of the emperor, came to be called *Melchites* (also, *Melkites*; Heb. *melek*, king, monarch, emperor); the latter, organized by the monk Jacob Baradai, came to be called *Jacobites*. In the centuries that followed, the Melchites came "more and more under the ecclesiastical domination of Constantinople, and by the end of the 13th century they had abandoned their own liturgies to the Monophysites and adopted that of imperial Byzantium" (see, *The Christian Churches of the East*, Vol. 1, Donald Attwater, p. 55). The Syrian church was in effect the Syro-Jacobite church. In the 17th century, some of these sought union with Rome, and since that time there have been Syrian Catholics as well as Syrian Jacobites. It is questionable just how strongly monophysite these Jacobites are; the preferred term for them is non-Chalcedonian Syrians.

The Syro-Jacobite tradition came to the Malabar region of India as a result of resistance to the Portuguese missionaries who, as noted above, tried first to Latinize the St. Thomas Christians, but succeeded only in Latinizing their East Syrian liturgy. Some who resisted sought support from the West Syrian Jacobites, and these West Syrian Orthodox Christians continue to flourish today. In 1934, some of these sought union with Rome, thus forming the Syro-Malankara Catholic church.

The history of the Maronites is transmitted more by legend than by established fact. Legend has it that a 5th century monk, Maron, founded a monastery in Syria and supported the positions taken at Chalcedon. Threat of persecution drove these "Catholic" monks to the mountains of Lebanon where, in the 7th century, under their first patriarch John Maron, the monastery of Maron became the Maronite church. Legend further has it that these Maronites were from their beginning loyal to the see of Rome and in communion with it. Available facts paint a much less precise picture, and suggest a probable Jacobite origin to this corporate entity that emerged only in the 8th century as a distinct Maronite church (Moosa).

Over the centuries, the Maronite liturgy was heavily Latinized. In a post-Vatican II revision, it has been restored to its primitive West Syrian form. The text cited to examine the West Syrian liturgical tradition as it lives today is this revised Maronite text (see, *The Maronite Liturgical Year*, Diocese of St. Maron, USA, 1982).

The Liturgy

(a) Introductory rites. The liturgy begins with a hymn sung during the entrance of the ministers and the preparation of the gifts. This latter is done simply at a side table. The introductory rites and service of the word are conducted at the *bema*. The opening doxology and prayer are followed by a general greeting of peace ("Peace be with the church and her children"), which is followed in turn by a seasonal psalm. The rites conclude with the *Hoosoyo*, a penitential prayer of incense, which is unique to the West Syrian tradition. It consists of a *proemium* or introduction, which invites the assembly to "praise, glorify and honor the Lord," the *sedro*, which is a rich, seasonal instruction as well as a prayer, a psalm to be sung or recited by the assembly, and the *etro*, or conclusion, asking the Lord to "be pleased with our service of incense."

(b) Liturgy of the Word. The service of the Word begins with the *trisagion*, chanted in Aramaic, and the *mazmooro*, a psalm chanted by the assembly and priest. One or two readings precede the gospel, which is introduced by the characteristic "Let us be attentive to the gospel of life and salvation of our Lord Jesus Christ as recorded by...." A brief seasonal response of the assembly, the *korozooto*, the homily and the creed conclude the service of the word.

(c) Pre-anaphora. The service of the Mysteries begins with the pre-anaphora, which consists of the prayer of access to the altar ("I have entered your house, O God, and I have worshipped in your temple. O King of glory forgive all my sins"), the transfer of the offerings to the altar, the prayer of offering, and an incensation of offerings, altar, cross and assembly.

(d) Anaphora. As in the East Syrian liturgy, the *anaphora* includes more than the eucharistic prayer itself. Strictly speaking, the term refers to the whole second part of the liturgy, right through its concluding prayer and blessing. It begins with the rite of peace, in which the "peace" is sent from the altar (which represents Christ) to the whole congregation. The eucharistic prayer follows the typical West Syrian structure: dialogue; thanksgiving narrative which includes the "Holy, Holy, Holy," and the narrative of institution; *anamnesis*;

epiclesis; intercessions and final doxology. Even where the liturgy as a whole is celebrated in a local vernacular, it is customary, at least among the Maronites, to chant the institution words in Aramaic: not only the "words of Jesus" but the language of Jesus as well. The bread is broken and signed with the precious blood. The Lord's prayer follows. A brief penitential rite (priest touching the consecrated offerings with one hand, extending the other over the congregation and praying for forgiveness) leads into the invitation to communion ("Holy things for the holy, with perfection, purity and sanctity"). Communion is distributed by intinction.

(e) Concluding prayers. The conclusion of the rite is simple: a prayer of thanksgiving and final blessing. The last prayer is a "farewell" to the altar: "Remain in peace, O altar of God, and I hope to return to you in peace...."

Theology and Spirit

The dominant theme running through the West Syrian liturgy is that of anticipation. The eucharist is celebrated in expectation of the Lord's second coming. While the liturgical texts are generous in singing the glory of the Lord, it is a glory that is yearned for rather than already present in its fullness. The eucharist is at one and the same time *rabouno*, a pledge of the glory to come, and *zouodo*, a viaticum which transforms us into citizens of the heavenly kingdom.

The typical prayer ending is both forward-looking and optimistic. Three examples: (a) "Then we will praise you, your only Son, and your living Holy Spirit, now and forever" (*rite of peace, Anaphora of the Twelve Apostles*); (b) "Make us worthy to live by your Spirit, leading a pure life, and we shall praise you, now and forever" (*epiclesis, Anaphora of the Twelve Apostles*); (c) "We will glorify your Father who sent you for our salvation and your Holy Spirit, now and forever" (*rite of incense, First Sunday of Epiphany*). This ending reveals a subtle nuance, namely, a sense of confident hope in the future that is anticipated.

The *anamnesis* in the eucharistic prayers is also typically a prayer that "looks forward." Even where the note of "offering" is included as well, it remains secondary to the expectation and anticipation. This prayer combines both the pledge of glory to come and the purification that transformation into God's kingdom requires. "We remember, O Lover of all, your plan of salvation, and we ask you to have compassion on your faithful. Save us, your inheritance, when you shall come again to reward justly everyone according to his or her deeds" (*Anaphora of the Twelve Apostles*).

The *Hoosoyo*, the offering of incense for purification, always begins, in some form or other, "May we be worthy to praise, confess, and glorify the Lord who...," where a seasonal reference follows the word "who." It is a prayer for purification, but it is not a self-conscious prayer that focuses on the sinfulness of those who pray. The emphasis is rather on the deeds of God recounted in narrative form and on the *confidence* with which we approach, even while the sense of *unworthiness* is strongly stated. Again, the conclusion anticipates the requested action of God which allows us (will allow us) to give God praise and glory.

As with the East Syrian liturgy, the West Syrian eucharist is strongly christocentric. Christ is addressed in prayer. After the institution narrative in the eucharistic prayers, Christ is first prayed to ("We commemorate *your* death, O Lord. We confess *your* resurrection. We await *your* coming") and then asked in turn to pray with the church to the Father ("Your people beseech you, and through you and with you, the Father, saying..." —the prayer returns to direct address of the Father). The greeting of peace is given to all present from the altar which represents Christ. At the prayer of forgiveness before communion the priest places one hand on the consecrated bread and wine while praying blessing on the assembly: "Bestow your blessings upon your people who love you and await your mercy" (*Anaphora of St. James*); "O Lord, with the strength of your powerful right hand, come now to bless your servants who bow before you" (*Anaphora of St. John the Evangelist*).

The liturgy moves comfortably between the awesome language of mystery and the harsh realities of everyday life. This is nicely illustrated in the *peace* prayer of the *Anaphora of St. James*: "O Lover of all people, through your redemption, free us from personal bias and hypocrisy, that we may greet each other in peace. Then, united in a unique bond of love and harmony by our Lord Jesus Christ we will glorify and praise you and your living Spirit, now and forever."

The West Syrian liturgy captures the full scope of eschatological prayer. It is optimistic, prayed in hope against the horizon of a victory already achieved. Yet it is realistic, prayed in the face of ample evidence that the victory has not yet unfolded in its fullness in human life and human history. Finally, though it is indeed forward-looking in anticipation and yearning, it is nonetheless a prayer that recognizes the importance of the present. The eschaton is even now unfolding in the lives of those who pray. The announcement of the victory at one and the same time (a) proclaims a victory achieved, (b) unveils the historical incompleteness of that achievement, and (c) purifies those who yearn for the victory proclaimed.

The Byzantine Churches
The Churches

The family of churches that follow the Byzantine rite is comprised of three groups: those directly linked to the see of Constantinople, those historically evangelized from the church of Constantinople, particularly Russia and the slavic countries, and the contemporary national churches (e.g., Orthodox Church in America, with links to the church of Moscow) which likewise claim the title Orthodox. Catholic Byzantine churches (in union with Rome) include Melkites (see above), Ukrainians, Russian Catholics and Ruthenians. Apart from very slight differences, both Orthodox and Catholics follow essentially the same liturgical rites. For the eucharist three ritual forms are used: most commonly, that attributed to St. John Chrysostom; occasionally, that attributed to St. Basil of Caesarea (Cappadocia), and on some days during Lent a liturgy of the presanctified attributed to Gregory the Great. The liturgical texts cited here are from *The Byzantine Liturgy of St. John Chrysostom* (New York: Fordham University Russian Center, 1955).

The Liturgy

The Byzantine liturgy is a complex ritual form that evolved in several stages from the 6th to the 14th centuries. Structurally it has the form of two interwoven liturgies, that which is prayed in the sanctuary (Holy of Holies) by the bishop and priest concelebrants, with the assistance of the deacon, and that conducted by deacon with assembly in front of the icon screen. A third layer of prayers consists of private prayers of the priest who prays in support of the action of the deacon and the assembly. The icon screen, and indeed the iconic display throughout the church, are integral to the liturgical act. They provide a visual focus for contemplative prayer which itself is aided by the abundant mantra-style litanies which form the heart of the deacon-assembly liturgical act. There are some churches where a deacon is not regularly employed, though this obscures the structure and flow of the liturgy itself.

The liturgy is an evolution of the West Syrian Antiochene tradition.

(a) Introductory Rites. Two elaborate rites introduce the Byzantine liturgy: the *proskomidia* (preparation of gifts) and a collection of litanies, hymns and prayers that are remnants of a liturgical office. The *proskomidia* is conducted by the priest and his assistants at a small table in the sanctuary; the three litanies are introduced and concluded by the priest and led by the deacon with the assembly or the choir providing the antiphons and hymns.

The primary focus of the *proskomidia* is the round loaf of leavened bread bearing the letters IC XC NI KA ("Jesus Christ conquers"). The center square is cut and placed on the paten to represent Christ. From the rest, particles are cut and arranged in rows to honor Mary, the angels, the apostles and the saints, and to commemorate the living and the dead. A particle is added for the priest himself. This whole represents the church: Christ, the Lamb, at the center gathering the church in heaven and the church on earth into one. The gifts are covered (the bread covered with the asterisk or "star of Bethlehem"), offered, and reverenced with incense. The sanctuary, the icon screen, the church and the assembly are honored with incense as well.

The second introductory rite begins the public prayer. It is introduced by the priest ("Blessed is the kingdom of the Father, and of the Son, and of the Holy Spirit, now and always and for ever and ever") and consists of a long litany, with a prayer and antiphon, and two shorter litanies, also with prayer and antiphon. The hymn of the incarnation ("O only-begotten Son and Word of God...") is sung after the second antiphon.

(b) The Liturgy of the Word. The liturgy of the Word once began with the entrance of the bishop. This is now the Little Entrance, with the gospel book representing Christ carried in solemn procession ("O come, let us worship and bow down to Christ. Save us, O Son of God, risen from the dead, save us who sing to You. Alleluia"). Two seasonal hymns, the *troparion* and *kontakion*, and the *trisagion* precede the scripture readings. After the epistle and gospel, the prayer of intercession (the insistent litany) and prayer for, and dismissal of, the catechumens bring the liturgy of the word to a close.

(c) Pre-anaphora. The pre-anaphora begins with a prayer of access to the altar ("We thank You, O Lord, Almighty God, for having allowed us to stand here now before Your holy altar ..."). This leads into the litany prayer of the faithful and the transfer of the gifts. Known as "the Great Entrance," the transfer of the gifts is made in solemn procession while the choir sings the Cherubic Hymn ("Let us who here mystically represent the Cherubim in singing the thrice-holy hymn to the life-giving Trinity, now lay aside every earthly care so that we may welcome the King of the universe who comes escorted by invisible armies of angels"). The hymn is stopped halfway through so that the commemorations of the day may be announced. The gifts are placed on the altar and incensed, the priest prays the offering while the deacon and assembly sing the litany of offering.

(d) Anaphora. The greeting of peace and the creed precede the eucharistic prayer proper. This latter, though more elaborate, follows the standard West Syrian structure: narrative of thanksgiving, including the "Holy, Holy, Holy," and narrative of institution; *anamnesis* ("Remembering ... we offer"); *epiclesis* for consecration ("...and make this bread the precious Body of Your Christ, and that which is in this chalice the precious Blood of Your Christ, having changed them by the Holy Spirit"); the commemorations and the final doxology.

The preparation for communion consists of: a litany of supplication, the

Lord's Prayer, a blessing of the assembly, the presentation of the eucharist to the people ("Holy things for the Holy"), and a prayer of personal faith ("I believe, Lord, and profess that You are in truth the Christ..."). Communion is distributed with a spoon or, in some churches where wafers are used, by intinction.

(e) Concluding Prayers. The liturgy concludes with a thanksgiving, dismissal and blessing. There are additional prayers as well, and frequently the eucharist is immediately followed by one of the liturgical hours or other prayers. The liturgy thus concludes slowly and in stages.

Theology and Spirit

The theology and spirit of the Byzantine liturgy is as complex as its ritual form. Indeed the two evolved together, with perhaps a greater influence on each other than in any other liturgical tradition. It does have a single, strong theme: the *presence of Christ*. This presence, however, has many forms and many manifestations. It is at one and the same time the presence of Christ *in* the liturgical action and the presence of the liturgical assembly with Christ *to* the heavenly liturgy which is eternally enacted. The liturgical forms reveal this presence; so too does the iconic design of the liturgical space in which the liturgy unfolds.

Some sense of the evolution of this liturgy is required to understand its complex theology and spirit. Hans-Joachim Schulz (*The Byzantine Liturgy*) traces its successive stages from the time of John Chrysostom (A.D. 344-407) and Theodore of Mopsuestia to its 14th-century codification.

Chrysostom spoke of the liturgy as mystery, whereby heavenly realities are made manifest in human form. Theodore focused on the individual rites as imaging different aspects of the saving work of Christ (e.g., gifts on altar representing Christ in the tomb; *epiclesis* as the resur-

rection). Special attention was given to Christ as "high priest," understood less in terms of "interceding" and more as "seated at the right hand of the Majesty in heaven."

This theological (mystagogical) reading of the liturgical actions took a turn to the spiritual in Dionysius the Areopagite (6th cent.), who "became *the* model for later Byzantine explicators" (Schulz, p. 25). Liturgical forms do indeed mediate salvation, but they do so by unveiling a spiritual process which unfolds in a higher sphere. It is the reverse of Theodore's stress on the actual liturgical forms making "present" Christ's saving work.

Under Maximus the Confessor (d. A.D. 662) the church structure itself became "liturgical." With the Hagia Sophia set as *norm*, the church building was envisioned as an image of the cosmos: two spheres, the earthly (the nave) and the heavenly (the sanctuary), not separated by, but bridged by the iconostasis. After the iconoclast controversy (8th cent.), and the vindication of reverence to icons (Nicea II, A.D. 787), decoration of the icon screen and the church itself became part of the liturgical act. Schulz says of this middle Byzantine development: "In this decorative use of images the Byzantine church structure shows itself to be what it had to be according to Dionysius' vision of the world and what Maximus actually saw it as being: a copy of the cosmos that comprises heaven and earth, a cosmos ordered to Christ and filled with a cosmic liturgy. By reason of the images that adorn it the church itself henceforth becomes a liturgy, as it were, because it depicts the liturgico-sacramental presence of Christ, the angels, and the saints, and by depicting it shares in bringing it about. The iconography of the church also shows it to be the place in which the mysteries of the life of Christ are made present" (p. 51).

The Byzantine liturgy exhibits this dual focus. The life-of-Jesus symbolism gives shape to the *proskomidia* which is interpreted as the birth, infancy and hidden life of Christ. It shows itself as the gifts are placed on the altar ("The venerable Joseph took down from the cross Your immaculate Body, and wrapping it in a clean shroud with sweet spices, he carefully laid it in a new grave") and at the *epiclesis* ("O Lord, who sent Your most Holy Spirit upon Your Apostles at the third hour, do not, O gracious One, take him away from us, but renew us who pray to You"). The heavenly liturgy symbolism is expressed in the Great Entrance, with its Cherubic hymn, and the prayer at the Little Entrance ("O holy God, who rests among the saints, whose praises are sung by the Seraphim with the hymn of the Trisagion, who are glorified by the Cherubim and adored by all the powers of heaven..."). Both are integral to the iconic design of the liturgical space where, on the one hand, the *Christos Pantokrator,* set majestically in the dome, looks down over all, and, on the other hand, the biblical events of Jesus' life are set out in rich, visual display.

In several places, the Byzantine liturgy reveals itself as a public statement of Christian doctrine. The *Hymn of the Incarnation* ("O only-begotten Son and Word of God, though You are immortal, You condescended for our salvation to take flesh from the holy Mother of God and ever-virgin Mary") was introduced in the 6th century as a proclamation of orthodox faith against the Nestorians (see above). The wording of the *epiclesis* ("...having changed them by Your Holy Spirit") is a clear affirmation of the role of the Spirit as consecrator of the bread and wine, in contrast to the Western belief that it is Jesus' own words, rather than the *epiclesis*, that effect the consecration.

The liturgy conducted, mostly in silent prayer, by the bishop and priest concelebrants in the sanctuary is, by and large, the West Syrian liturgy as described above. This liturgy is hidden from the assembly in silence, and occasionally by a drawn veil. The priest and his actions are part of the visual, iconic display. The deacon is the primary link between these actions and the assembly, assisting the priest, announcing what is taking place, and leading the assembly in an appropriate litany prayer (e.g., during the offering: "For the precious gifts that are offered, let us pray to the Lord"; after the eucharistic prayer: "For the precious gifts that are offered and consecrated, let us pray to the Lord"). The experience of the assembly is not shaped by the intrinsic meaning of the various liturgical actions, but rather, as an aesthetico-religious contemplative experience, by the sensual environment composed of music, iconography, incense, and the various bodily movements (bows, signing oneself with the cross, kissing of icons, etc.) that are assigned to them. By entering into the assembly, they enter into a cosmos ruled by God and filled with mystery, and are transported to that realm where the heavenly liturgy is eternally unfolding.

The Armenian Church
The Church

The church of Armenia was evangelized from Edessa, and later by missionaries from Cappadocia. Its early liturgy was thus both Syrian and Greek. Its evolution as the Armenian church, with its own distinctive liturgy, is due to Gregory the Illuminator, a late 3rd/early 4th century aristocrat who was converted to Christianity in Caesarea (Cappadocia), and who returned to Armenia to convert the king (Trdat II) who had been, up to then, persecuting the Christians. As a result, Christianity became the state religion in A.D. 301, and Gregory became the leader (*Catholicos*) of the Armenian Church.

Gregory is not acclaimed as the "apostle of Armenia." The legends which recount the origin of Christianity in Armenia attribute this to Jude Thaddaeus and Bartholomew. The Armenians thus claim apostolic roots. Gregory's accomplishment was the conversion of the whole country and the establishment of the Armenian church.

Under Gregory, the church was more aristocratic than popular; the people had no access to the liturgy which was in Syriac and in Greek—revisions came only in the 5th century. These involved the creation of an Armenian alphabet and the translation of both scripture and the liturgy into Armenian. The Armenian liturgy is certainly Antiochene in its roots, but, apparently for political reasons, the Armenian church sided with Alexandria after the Council of Chalcedon. Hence it only recognizes the first three councils. Today there are Armenian Catholics in union with Rome, and Armenians who remain an independent church. The preferred title for these latter is the Armenian Apostolic church.

The liturgy of the Armenian church, called "The Liturgy of our Blessed Father Saint Gregory the Illuminator, revised and augmented by the Holy Patriarchs and Doctors, Sahag, Mesrob, Kud and John Mandakuni," is, as noted, rooted in the Antiochene tradition. Its evolution, however, reveals the influence of many sources: Coptic, Byzantine, and later (12th cent.) Latin. There is a sub-stratum of the Syrian liturgy of James, which may have come via the liturgy of Basil (in use in Cappadocia). It was later embellished with texts from the Chrysostom (Byzantine) and Latin liturgies. It is not therefore *simply* an evolution of the Syrian/Antiochene tradition. Nonetheless it remains Syrian at its deepest level. The texts cited here are from *The Armenian Liturgy* (tr. into English, Venice: Monastery of St. Lazarus, 1862).

The Liturgy

(a) Introductory Rites. The intro-
ductory rites consist of the vesting of the ministers in the sacristy, the entrance and absolution of the officiating priest, and the preparation of the gifts. The first two are carried out in rich ceremonial; the last is done without the elaborate ritual of the Byzantine *proskomidia*. When prepared and veiled, the gifts are honored with incense. Most significant in these rites is the focus on the priest.

(b) Liturgy of the Word. The liturgy of the Word originally began with the chanting of the *trisagion*. It was later embellished with texts from the Byzantine liturgy. It begins now with the blessing ("Blessed be the reign of the Father, the Son, and the Holy Ghost..."), the *Monogenes* of the Byzantine liturgy ("O only-begotten Son and Word of God..."), which may be replaced with a seasonal hymn, a blessing, and four prayers recited by the priest while the choir sings the psalm and hymn of the day. These four prayers are the three antiphon prayers from the Byzantine introductory rites and the prayer of the Byzantine Little Entrance.

The *trisagion* is then sung, while the priest prays the Byzantine prayer of the *trisagion*. This is followed by a litany, the epistle and gospel reading, the creed (to which is appended an anti-Arian *anathema*), another litany and blessing, and the dismissal of the catechumens.

(c) Pre-anaphora. The pre-anaphora begins with a proclamation ("The Body of our Lord, and the Blood of our Redeemer are about to be here present..."). There follows the *hagiology* of the day (a seasonal catechesis), while the celebrant, if a bishop, removes the vestments of honor; or, if a priest, removes his cap. The gifts are transferred to the altar while the choir sings the Cherubic hymn and the priest prays the corresponding Byzantine prayer "humbled before the altar." The gifts are incensed, the deacon exhorts the assembly ("With faith and holiness, let us pray before the holy altar of God, filled with profound dread..."), and the priest prays the prayer of oblation.

(d) Anaphora. The *anaphora* proper begins with a benediction and peace greeting. The deacon kisses the altar and the arms (sic) of the priest, and then brings the greeting to the others. The eucharistic prayer, after the customary dialogue, again follows the classic West Syrian structure: thanksgiving narrative for creation and redemption, including the "Holy, holy," and leading into the institution account, *anamnesis, epiclesis,* intercessions and doxology. This prayer is interspersed with other prayers, blessings, greetings and gestures (incense, signing with cross, etc.), and it includes seasonal commemorations as well.

(e) Post-anaphora. The Lord's Prayer and incensing of the people begins the communion or post-anaphora. This is followed by a prayer of penitence addressed to the Holy Spirit. The gifts are presented to the people in rather elaborate fashion: a trinitarian benediction oft repeated by deacon, choir and people. The priest then invites all to communion: "Let us partake holily of the holy, holy and precious Body and Blood of our Lord and Redeemer Jesus Christ, who, descended from Heaven, is distributed among us. He is life, the hope of the resurrection, the expiation and pardon of sins. Sing to the Lord our God...." This last part is echoed by the deacon. Then, with curtain drawn, the priest prepares to take communion with a series of prayers and gestures, the longest prayer being that of John Chrysostom ("I give Thee thanks, I exalt Thee, I glorify Thee, O Lord my God, Thou hast rendered me worthy on this day to partake of Thy Divine and fearful Sacrament...").

After communion of the faithful, the priest blesses all ("Lord, save Thy people, and bless Thine inheritance..."). The bishop, if presiding, puts on his episcopal robes. There are prayers of thanksgiving,

a prayer for a blessing, the prologue of John read as the "last gospel," a prayer for peace, and the final blessing. As is customary among the Byzantines, the Armenians too distribute blessed bread as the people leave.

Theology and Spirit

The tone of the Armenian liturgy is that of a "temple" liturgy, and throughout the text it stresses the notion of sacrifice more than any other Eastern liturgy.

References to the temple are clear and abundant. The hymn sung during the vesting proclaims that "holiness becomes Thy dwelling, since Thou alone art enveloped in splendor." After the confession and absolution of the priest, he prays: "Within the precincts of this temple ... we adore with trembling." And again: "In the Tabernacle of holiness, and in the place of praise ... we adore with trembling." During the preparation of the offerings, the priest incenses and prays: "In the Lord's temple, open to our offerings and our vows, united as we are to accomplish in obedience and in prayer the mystery of this approaching and august sacrifice, let us together march in triumph round the tribune of the holy temple...." And he is clearly a temple priest who prays: "Thou hast confided to us the Priesthood for this holy ministry and for Thine unbloody Sacrifice."

References to the sacrifice are likewise clear and abundant. A prayer during the vesting reads: "Full of fear and awe we approach Thee, to offer the Sacrifice due to Thine Omnipotence." The deacon proclaims just before the eucharistic prayer: "Christ, the Immaculate Lamb of God, offers Himself as victim." The intercessions of the same prayer are introduced by: "Grant by virtue of this Sacrifice..."; and a thanksgiving prayer chanted by the deacon mentions *sacrifice* no less than four times.

The way the liturgy views the priest is consistent with both temple and sacrifice.

In contrast to the Byzantine *proskomidia*, with its elaborate focus on the bread and wine as Christ, the Armenian introductory rites come to focus much more strongly on the priest. He confesses his sins ("I confess in the presence of God ... all the sins I have committed") and receives absolution ("May the all-powerful God have mercy on you, and grant you the pardon of all your sins...") before going ahead with his service. Prayers of purification are numerous.

In addition, the texts of the liturgy put a strong accent on the majesty of God. They are more than generous in speaking of God as profound, incomprehensible, boundless, infinite, inscrutable, etc., and thus worthy of glory, power, worship, honor, praise.

Finally, note should be made of the place of the Holy Spirit in the Armenian liturgy. While it is common in both East and West to address the Spirit in the mode of invocation (*epiclesis*, *Veni Sancte Spiritus*), the Armenian text addresses the Spirit in other forms of prayer as well. To give but one example, the blessing after the Lord's prayer: "O Holy Spirit! Thou who art the source of life and of mercy, have pity on this people who, kneeling, adores Thy Divinity...," with its adjoining doxology: "Through Jesus Christ our Lord, to whom, as to Thee, O Holy Spirit, and to the Almighty Father, belong glory...."

The Alexandrian Churches: Coptic and Ethiopian
The Churches

Legend has it that Christianity spread to Egypt at the hands of St. Mark, and to Ethiopia via the eunuch of Candace (Acts 8:26-40). The legends concerning Mark attribute to him the complete shaping of the church in Alexandria: he was bishop and first patriarch, ordained deacons, presbyters and other bishops, and in general was responsible for establishing the church order that was in fact a much later development (see, Atiya, *A History of Eastern Christianity*). With regard to Egypt it is more likely that, because of the commerce between Jerusalem and Alexandria, the path of Christianity's spread was much less precise. As for Ethiopia, it is not until the 4th century, under Frumentius and Aedesius of Tyre, that any authentic evangelization is recorded (see, Attwater, *The Christian Churches of the East*, Vol. 1, p. 138), with more serious evangelization coming still later at the hands of Monophysite monks from Syria.

In the 6th century, however, the Coptic church was given missionary responsibility for Ethiopia, and the church there came under the jurisdiction of the Coptic patriarch of Alexandria, a dependency that has begun to dissolve only in the 20th century. As a result of this dependency, and although the Ethiopian church had other influences as well, and indeed does have its own particular liturgical "flavor," the two can be taken to constitute a single liturgical tradition. This tradition is Alexandrian in its theological outlook, dominantly Monophysite in its Christology, and in many ways it is the polar opposite of the traditions rooted in Antioch.

The Coptic liturgy is austere, and quite evidently the product of monastic origins. Among the Ethiopians the liturgy is far more colorful, with dance, elaborate costume and a far more vibrant musical setting. Textually, however, the two liturgies are similar. The Coptic text cited here is from *The Coptic Morning Service for the Lord's Day* (trans. John Patrick Crichton Stuart, London: Cope and Fenwick, 1908); the Ethiopian text, which has been modified and somewhat simplified, is taken from *The Ordinary and the Anaphora of the Apostles* (ed. T. Baraki, Washington, DC, 1984).

The Liturgy—Coptic

The Coptic liturgy employs three

anaphoras: that of St. Basil, used on all occasions save four; that of St. Gregory, used at midnight at Christmas, Epiphany and Easter, and addressed directly to Christ; and the oldest Egyptian prayer, attributed to St. Cyril of Alexandria (d. A.D. 444) (also called the *anaphora* of St. Mark), used on the Friday before Palm Sunday. In the sanctuary of Coptic churches one finds three altars to allow multiple celebrations of the eucharist (Coptic custom allows only one eucharist on an altar per day). The Sunday liturgy is frequently preceded by the morning prayer of incense, parts of which are prefixed to the eucharist when the full morning prayer is omitted.

(a) Introductory Rites. The introductory rites consist of the morning office (whole or in part, as noted above), the preparation of the altar and the preparation of the offerings. The preparation of the altar consists of two prayers, both of which are prayers for the priest in his ministry. The preparation of the offerings is quite elaborate, involving the selection of the bread and wine for the eucharist, multiple blessings of the triune God, frequent processions around the altar, blessing the four corners of the earth with the hand cross, a prayer of thanksgiving, which leads into a prayer of oblation (an *anaphora* style prayer) addressed to Christ who is asked to "cause Thy face to shine upon this bread and upon this cup, which we have set upon this Thine holy table, bless them, sanctify them, hallow and change them, that this bread may become indeed Thine own holy Body and the mingled wine and water which is in this cup may become indeed Thine own Honourable Blood, that they may be unto us all help and healing and health for our souls, and our bodies, and our spirits."

There follows a prayer of absolution (addressed to Christ) in which Christ is asked to "bless us, purify us, absolve us, and absolve all Thy people." Incense is prepared ("The censer of gold is the Virgin; her sweet cloud is our Saviour; she hath borne him; he saved us; may he forgive our sins") and offered. The altar is reverenced, with multiple processions around it, the priest stopping to kiss the four corners of the altar during each, and the "first *anaphora*" concludes with petitions and doxology ("Through whom (Christ) are due unto Thee (Father), with himself, and the Holy Ghost, the Lifegiver, who is of one substance with Thee, glory, and honor, and power, and worship, now and ever, and to the ages of all ages. Amen"). This doxology concludes the introductory rites as well.

(b) Liturgy of the Word. There is in fact no clear transition to the liturgy of the word. After the doxology, the priest incenses the altar three times, each time with an appropriate prayer (1. "We adore Thee, O Christ, and Thy good Father, and the Holy Ghost"; 2. "Before the angels will I sing praise unto Thee, and will worship toward Thine holy temple"; 3. "As for me, I will enter into Thine house, in the multitude of Thy mercies, and will worship toward Thine holy temple"). The picture of Mary is likewise incensed ("Hail to thee, Mary, the fair dove, which hath borne for us God the Word . . ."); so too are the other images. The service of readings then begins.

The Coptic liturgy employs three readings before the gospel itself: from the letters of Paul, from the catholic epistles, and from the Acts of the Apostles. Attached to each is a lengthy prayer. Between these readings and the gospel there are a series of petitions, accompanied by additional reverences to (processions around) the altar, an offering of incense on behalf of the people and the *trisagion*. After the gospel, which is greeted in a solemn and elaborate procession, the priest prays the gospel prayer (". . . may we be made worthy to hear Thine holy gospels, and may we keep Thy precepts and commandments . . .").

Catechumens may have been dismissed at this point.

(c) Pre-anaphora. A prayer is prayed privately by the priest as he approaches the altar (Prayer of the Veil). The priest then introduces the intercessions which are each led by the deacon (response of the people: "Lord, have mercy") and augmented by the priest. The ministers, the people and the altar are incensed and all proclaim the Nicene Creed.

(d) Anaphora. As in the other Eastern liturgies we have seen, the greeting of peace precedes the eucharistic prayer. The eucharistic prayer of Basil is West Syrian in its structure: thanksgiving narrative, which includes the "Holy, holy" and the Supper narrative, *anamnesis, epiclesis*, intercessions and doxology. The institution narrative is interspersed with frequent acclamations of the people ("Amen"), as is the *epiclesis* ("Amen" and "I believe"). The intercessions, which include a reading of the diptychs of the dead, are quite lengthy.

(e) Post-anaphora. The prayer of fraction, which precedes the Lord's Prayer, includes acclamations of faith in the presence of Christ and acts of adoration. The Lord's prayer is followed by several prayers of remembrance and one of absolution (addressed to the Father). The gifts are presented ("The Holy to the Holy"), and after a further series of preparation prayers, including an additional proclamation of faith ("I believe, I believe, I believe and confess till the last breath that this is the life-giving Flesh which Thine only begotten Son, our Lord and God and Savior Jesus Christ took from our Lady, the Lady of us all, the holy Mother of God, the holy Mary ... "), communion is distributed. The liturgy concludes with a prayer, blessing and dismissal.

The Liturgy—Ethiopian

The Ethiopian tradition knows of at least 22 eucharistic prayers, unique among which is one addressed in part to the Virgin Mary. The most commonly used, however, is the *anaphora* "of the Apostles," which is in fact an Alexandrian derivation from the prayer of Hippolytus (3rd-cent. Rome), and a variant on the Coptic anaphora of St. Cyril. The liturgical language is Ge'ez, though it is usually celebrated in the contemporary vernacular, Amharic.

Noticeably absent from the Ethiopian liturgy, when compared with the Coptic, are the frequent processions around the altar with reverence (kissing) given to the altar's four corners.

(a) Introductory Rites. After the opening sign of the cross (remnant of the Coptic office of incense), the priest announces: "How wondrous this day and how marvelous this hour in which the Holy Spirit will come down from the high heaven and overshadow this offering and sanctify it." This same text is employed in the West Syrian liturgy as a diaconal announcement prior to the *epiclesis*.

Attention is then turned to the offerings, with the same lengthy ritual form we saw in the Coptic liturgy. The bread is blessed ("Christ, our true God, sign with your right hand + and bless this bread, + hallow it with Your power and strengthen it with your Spirit"). The offering is made (again, a West Syrian text), the chalice is blessed, and then the bread and wine both are given the trinitarian blessing. A doxology introduces a prayer of thanksgiving and another of absolution, and the first *anaphora* (addressed to Christ) is begun. Reminiscent of Theodore of Mopsuestia, whose theology is evident in both the East Syrian and West Syrian traditions, the prayer of the veil, as the celebrant covers the bread and wine, recalls: "What we have placed upon this blessed paten is in the likeness of the sepulchre in which you stayed three days and three nights...." Long prayers of general intercession conclude the introductory rites.

(b) Liturgy of the Word. The liturgy of the word begins with an invitation to stand, a greeting of peace, and invitation to adore "the Father, the Son and Holy Spirit, three persons, one God," and the prayer to Mary, recited by all ("You are the golden censer, that bore the glowing charcoal..."). The traditional four readings are reduced to two though the "reading prayers" have been retained. Between the epistle and the gospel praises of Mary and the *trisagion* are prayed and the blessing of the four "cardinal points" is given.

(c) Pre-anaphora. The rites before the eucharistic prayer include: a prayer of blessing and intercession, the creed, a prayer of purification (washing of hands), a doxology ("Glory to God in the heavens, and peace on earth to men of good will"), and kiss of peace.

(d) Anaphora. The *anaphora* of the apostles is essentially the Hippolytus text, with the "Holy, Holy, Holy," and other acclamations of the people included. There are, as in the original, no intercessions within the eucharistic prayer proper.

(e) Post-anaphora. A complex fraction rite follows the eucharistic prayer, and, together with a prayer of thanksgiving, introduces the Lord's prayer. This is followed by a series of prayers (of blessing, for forgiveness, of remembrance—including the commemoration of the dead). When the gifts are presented to the people ("Holy things to the holy"), a prayer over penitents and a profession of faith in the eucharist is made ("I believe, I believe, I believe and profess..."). Final prayers of preparation for communion follow.

After communion there are prayers of thanksgiving, an imposition of hands in blessing of the people, a final blessing and dismissal.

Theology and Spirit

The Alexandrian theological tradition stands in contrast to the Antiochene on several counts. Its emphasis on the majesty and otherness of God is stronger, its ability to deal with the fullness of the incarnation weaker. In trinitarian theology it tends towards subordinationism, of Son to Father, of Spirit to both. In Christology it tends to emphasize the divine over the human. In liturgical theology it tends to stress the spiritual meaning of the symbols and the eternal realm in which that meaning resides. The sanctuary screen in the Coptic churches separates heaven from earth rather than uniting the two and bridging the gap.

Probably the most notable piece in both the Coptic and Ethiopian liturgies is the attention given to the bread and wine in the introductory rites and the seemingly consecratory "first *anaphora*" to Christ. There is a parallel in the Coptic baptismal liturgy which may illuminate this prayer. Before the baptism, ordinary water is solemnly "consecrated" for the baptism; afterwards, with a prayer equally as solemn, it is "returned to ordinary use." It is as though materials of the earth, in this case the bread and wine, require a preliminary "consecration" to render them fit for the subsequent consecratory action of God.

Equally of note, at least in the Coptic version of this liturgical tradition, is the attention paid to the altar. The altar is the altar of sacrifice which the priest approaches unworthily. Many of the processions around the altar, including kissing the altar's four corners, accompany prayers of intercession offered in worship to God. The altar is likewise a symbol of the one who is offered ("We adore Thee, O Christ, and Thy good Father, and the Holy Ghost. Behold, Thou hast come, Thou has saved us"—said while incensing the altar). Placing the gifts upon the altar places them as well on the altar above ("Receive them upon Thine holy reasonable Altar in heaven for a sweet savour of incense"—said while incensing the gifts placed upon the altar).

Finally, the place of Mary is unique. She is called the "censer of gold" whose "sweet cloud is our saviour" (Coptic) and the "golden censer that bore the glowing charcoal whom the blessed One ... accepted from the Sanctuary" (Ethiopian). She is also the one who makes strong supplication for us before God.

Conclusion

The liturgical traditions of the East contain a vast richness of Christian faith and prayer, a richness that only can be hinted at in these brief descriptions and reflections. Their perceptions of God range from the distant Other to the One "made flesh" who "dwelt among us." Their perceptions of the people who worship range from those free to participate in the heavenly mysteries to those unworthy to approach, from those who rejoice in the victory of Christ to those who must wait for the day of its fullness, from those who stand tall before the majesty of God to those who bow low in humble and awe-filled adoration. Together they reveal the many faces of the Mystery, of God creator, of Christ redeemer, of Spirit sanctifier. Together they reveal the many ways in which God approaches us and summons us to approach God in return.

See Eucharist, history of, in the East; Reform, liturgical, in Eastern churches; Sacraments in Eastern churches

A.S. Atiya, *A History of Eastern Christianity* (London: Methuen and Co., 1968). I. Dalmais, *Eastern Liturgies*, trans. D. Attwater (New York: Hawthorn, 1960). A. Schmemann, *Historical Road of Eastern Orthodoxy*, trans. L. Kesich (Crestwood: St. Vladimir's Seminary Press, 1977; orig. 1963). A. Butler, *The Ancient Coptic Churches of Egypt*, 2 vols. (Oxford: Clarenden, 1884, rev. 1970). J. Meyendorff, *The Byzantine Legacy in the Orthodox Church* (Crestwood: St. Vladimir's Press, 1982). H.-J. Schulz, *The Byzantine Liturgy*, trans. M. O'Connell (New York: Pueblo, 1986; orig. *Die byzantische Liturgie*, Trier: Paulinus-Verlag, 1980).

D. Attwater, *The Christian Churches of the East*, Vol. I: "Churches in Communion with Rome"; Vol. II: "Churches not in Communion with Rome" (Milwaukee: Bruce, 1961 [Vol. I], 1962 [Vol. II]). T. Nersoyan, trans., *The Divine Liturgy of the Armenian Apostolic Orthodox Church* (London: St. Sarkis, 1984). S. Mercier, *The Ethiopic Liturgy: its sources, development and present form* (Milwaukee: Young Churchmen, 1915). Diocese of St. Maron, U.S., *The Maronite Liturgical Year*, 3 vols. (1982). M. Moosa, *The Maronites in History* (Syracuse: University Press, 1986). G. Every, *Understanding Eastern Christianity* (London: S.C.M., 1980).

PETER E. FINK, S.J.

TRADITIONS, LITURGICAL, IN THE WEST: POST-REFORMATION

Since 1500, Western Christianity has been blessed with the development of no fewer than ten different liturgical traditions. But before we describe each of these in turn, we need to begin with some basic definitions. By the "West" we mean the Christianity of western Europe and the areas colonized by it including the Americas, Australia, New Zealand, and segments of Africa and Asia. "Traditions" are inherited liturgical practices and the understanding of those practices which can be transmitted relatively intact from generation to generation. We shall define our period as roughly the last five centuries, beginning with the start of the Reformation in 1517.

The process of developing new Christian liturgical traditions is a natural process of inculturation as worship patterns are adjusted to reflect, and sometimes create, changes in peoples. Even within traditions there normally are cultural and ethnic styles: black Lutheran congregations, for example, where gospel song seems more natural than chorales but where the liturgical tradition is definitely Lutheran. Thus it is easier to define the center of a liturgical tradition than it is to be precise about its edges since most can accommodate a wide variety of styles. In addition, no tradition is static. All change from generation to generation so that they must always be seen as in transition even when service books are frozen. The prayerbook of the Church of England did not change for more than three hundred years but everything else in its worship did. We are not examining unchanging essences but living objects.

All ten traditions ultimately derive from the worship life of late medieval western Europe. This was loosely centralized in Rome but consisted in considerable variety according to diocesan uses and religious communities. Our method will be to treat the ten traditions emanating from this background in order of conservatism, i.e., the degree to which they continued to reflect the late medieval synthesis. Some elements persisted longer among Protestants than Catholics, some Catholic changes were more radical than some changes among Protestants, so we must deal with a mixed bag. But the total degree of conservatism can give us an organizing principle. Everyone thought in the 16th century that they were restoring the worship life of the early church even more than we fancy we are doing so today. The political metaphor of conservative, moderate, and radical in degree of change will serve us well. Thus we have three basically conservative traditions: Roman Catholic, Lutheran, and Anglican; two moderate ones: Reformed and Methodist; and five radical groups: Puritan, Anabaptist, Frontier, Pentecostal, and Quaker. In each instance, we move from right to left.

Roman Catholic

The Council of Trent (1545-1563) sought to bring about a conservative reform by radical means. The Fathers of Trent were concerned to end avarice, corruptions, and superstitions in worship but their minds were directed to defending the status quo whenever possible, partly because the lack of liturgical scholarship allowed them to believe, for example, that St. Peter had composed the Roman canon and that to change existing practices was to abolish that which was apostolic. Futhermore, changes would be seen as conceding that the Protestant Reformers were right after all.

The method of reform chosen was that of liturgical standardization, a possibility with the advent of the printed book. The revision of the liturgical books was entrusted to the curia and proceeded with the breviary (1568), the missal (1570), the martyrology (1584), pontifical (1596), bishops' ceremonies (1600), and the ritual (1614). The means of enforcing global uniformity was entrusted to the new Congregation of Rites, established in 1588. So began almost four centuries of liturgical uniformity, reaching even to China (and thus devastating evangelization of that country). The "era of rubricism" that ensued found theological safety in rigid liturgical uniformity.

At the same time, much of worship did change because books and bureaucrats could control only so much. A brilliant period of Baroque architecture spread around the world, inspired by the work of Gian Lorenzo Bernini (1598-1680) and the example of the Jesuit church in Rome, Il Gesu. Jungmann speaks of the Baroque spirit and the traditional liturgy as "two vastly different worlds." New devotions came to the forefront, especially benediction and exposition of the Blessed Sacrament; the cult of the saints came to focus largely on the Virgin Mary. Devotions to the Sacred Heart of Jesus and visits to the Blessed Sacrament became popular. In France, the new standardized books were resisted for three centuries, coming into consistent use only in the late 19th century after experimentation with much local variety and vernacular uses.

The Enlightenment of the 18th century failed to make much of a mark despite the efforts of the Synod of Pistoia (1786) to make reforms that were two centuries too early. The 19th century saw the beginnings of the first liturgical movement, led by Prosper Guéranger (1805-1875) and a series of monastic leaders notably Lambert Beauduin (1873-1960), Virgil Michel (1890-1938), and Odo Casel (1886-1948). This lasted until after World War II and was acknowledged in the conservative encyclical *Mediator Dei* (1947). A later liturgical movement began after the war, deriving its agenda largely from Protestant worship (vernacular, cultural pluralism, active participation, preaching at Mass, popular hymnody) and centered largely in countries with Protestant majorities.

More recently, Vatican II in its *Constitution on the Sacred Liturgy* (1963) moved Roman Catholicism to embrace these newer reforms. The result has been revision of the Tridentine liturgical books in less than twenty-five years and translation of them all. The introduction of the vernacular has been accompanied by much more flexibility and a variety of options in the rites. While these reforms have been widely welcomed by the laity, Rome seems presently concerned with preventing adaptation or inculturation from going too far. Even so, the distance traveled since Trent has been enormous.

Lutheran

There are a number of reasons for considering the Lutheran tradition as the most conservative of the Protestant traditions of worship. Martin Luther (1483-1546) had a high respect for the existing Christian cultus; his inclination was to purge those aspects that could not be reconciled to his theology and to retain the rest. He could be quite radical on occasion (as with the canon of the Mass) but on the whole retained more than he rejected. He tended to move carefully; others anticipated him on vernacular liturgies.

After statements in *The Babylonian Captivity* (1520) that were to be determinative for almost all subsequent Protestant sacramental theology, Luther moved to litugical reform with vernacular baptismal rites in 1523 and 1526. The same years also saw new eucharistic rites, the *Formula Missae* (in Latin) and *Deutsche Messe* (in German). Later years saw forms for marriage, ordination, and penance. In general, existing practices endured but rites were in the vernacular and popular participation was promoted whenever possible.

Three emphases stand out: music, preaching, and frequent communion in both kinds. Luther considered music one of God's greatest gifts and cultivated its use in worship through service music and hymnody. He led the way in writing hymns himself and vigorous hymn singing has always been a hallmark of this tradition. Luther's insistence that preaching be a part of all congregational worship contributed to a rebirth of preaching. He also encouraged all the laity who were properly prepared to receive the bread and wine at each eucharist.

As for vestments, images, and much of the medieval cultus that was theologically neutral, Luther allowed their continuance; they came to be known as "adiaphora" or things indifferent. Thus much more survived in Lutheran countries, especially in Sweden and Finland where Lutheran worship remained its most conservative, than in other Protestant countries. Yet even this is relative. Recent studies have shown just how much survived during the long period of Lutheran Orthodoxy. In Bach's Leipzig there were daily public prayers, a weekly eucharist with a great many communicants, and a rich observance of the church year. Although the services were in German, one gets the feeling that not all that much had changed from the Middle Ages in two hundred years of Lutheranism.

The real change came not with the Reformation but with the Enlightenment.

Daily services in Leipzig ended in the 1790s and much of the continuing medieval cultus vanished in the face of rationalism, even in the church of Sweden. Much of this has been blamed on the influence of the Reformed tradition but more is probably due to the *Weltgeist*. The 19th century, saw a gradual reaction to the Enlightenment with an attempt to recover early Lutheran worship. In Germany, Wilhelm Loehe (1810-1895), in Denmark, Nikolai Grundtvig (1783-1872) and various other leaders elsewhere sought a return to Lutheran orthodoxy and orthopraxis. The indication of their success is successive revisions of various service books and hymns. More recent versions, especially the American *Lutheran Book of Worship* (1978), have moved into the ecumenical mainstream while retaining a Lutheran character, especially in the emphasis on music.

Anglican

The Anglican tradition is ambiguous: what started off as a fairly moderate reformation and remained so for three centuries reversed itself in the 19th century and moved to reappropriate a great deal of the medieval cultus. To modern observers, Anglican worship seems more conservative than Lutheran but the theological origins are far more liberal. Anglican liturgy began with Archbishop Thomas Cranmer's (1489-1556) two editions of the *Book of Common Prayer*, that of 1549 and the much more radical 1552 book. Using the latest technology, Cranmer sought to put all the services in the hands of everyone by translating, condensing, and revising them before publishing them in popular versions under a price ceiling.

Cranmer succeeded in recovering daily services of public prayer, which became a staple of Anglican worship. Many of the ceremonies associated with the sacraments and other rites disappeared from the 1552 edition and the theology became much more unambiguously Zwinglian. Martin Bucer (1491-1551) provided much of the structure for the ordination rite but Cranmer was not prepared to accept as high a view of the eucharist as Bucer and Calvin. A great ornament of the book was Cranmer's linguistic ability to cast traditional Latin prayers in the language of his contemporaries.

After the brief regression of the Marian years, Anglican worship tended to stabilize during the long reign of Elizabeth I. As a political settlement, episcopal forms of church government were retained as well as something of the appearances of public worship, although there had been much iconoclasm even before the rise of Puritanism. Weekly communion proved to be too radical a step for most people and canon law eventually settled for a minimum of three celebrations a year. The normal Sunday service came to be morning prayer, litany, ante-communion, and sermon. Popular hymnody was lacking but magnificent choral daily services characterized worship in the cathedrals. The poet-priest George Herbert (1593-1633) offered an example of Anglican parish ministry at its best.

The Puritan takeover of the Church of England from 1644 to 1660 moved things leftward in a radical direction but only temporarily. The restoration period afterwards attempted to return to the status quo of 1604, as the prayer book of 1662 showed. Despite the survival of a high church tradition (without much ceremonial) most Anglicans were comfortable in a tradition that avoided the excesses of either Catholicism or Puritanism. In the 18th century, this meant worship that was edifying and moralistic but with little concern for the sacraments or anything overtly supernatural.

In the 19th century, reactions came in the form of a recovery of patristic theology (the Oxford Movement, Tractarianism, Puseyism) and to a full scale recovery of late medieval ceremonial (the Cambridge Movement, Ritualism). These brought back weekly celebrations of the eucharist at just the same time this was occurring among Disciples of Christ, Mormons, Plymouth Brethren, and the Catholic Apostolic church. A new emphasis was placed on baptism, penance, and the revival of medieval architecture, liturgical arts, and choral music. Congregational hymnody also made its advent.

The 20th century has seen an indigenous liturgical movement in the Church of England, manifesting itself as the parish communion movement in the 1930s. Recent years have seen wholesale revision of Anglican prayerbooks around the world, usually either following the patterns of Cranmer or trading in such late medieval forms for the 3rd century model of Hippolytus.

The Reformed

We now move further left to the central or moderate traditions: Reformed and Methodist. The Reformed Tradition has several roots: Zurich, Basel, Strassburg, and Geneva. In some ways, it preserved more than its share of the penitential strain of late medieval piety. In other respects, however, it moved beyond the forms which Lutheranism and Anglicanism were content to continue. In time it was largely seduced by the Puritan tradition (in Great Britain) and the Frontier Tradition (in America).

Ulrich Zwingli (1484-1531) began his reformation of Zurich heavily influenced by humanistic studies and a thorough biblicism. He was anxious to return worship to its biblical roots and eager to make it more spiritual, reflecting the gap he saw between the physical and the spiritual. Although a fine musician, he rejected music in worship as distracting one from spiritual worship. Iconoclasm in Zurich purified or devastated the churches, according to one's viewpoint.

Zwingli retained the four Sundays or festivals when his people were accustomed to receive communion or the eucharist, a preaching service being held on the other Sundays. These four occasions saw a drastically simplified rite which focused on transubstantiation of the people, not the elements.

Martin Bucer in Strassburg and John Oecolampadius (1482-1531) in Basel began experimenting with vernacular services. At Strassburg this included daily prayer services and a Sunday service derived from the Mass. Bucer's influence was spread further by a visiting preacher out of a job, John Calvin (1509-1564). While serving temporarily a French-speaking congregation in Strassburg, Calvin adapted the German rite Bucer was using. Calvin brought this rite to Geneva and from 1542 on it became the model for much of the Reformed tradition. Although deriving its structure from the Mass via Bucer, it had moved to highlight the penitential aspects of worship and was highly didactic and moralistic. Relief from this somber mood was wrought by encouraging the congregation to sing metrical paraphrases of the psalms which they did with fervor. Such devotion to psalmody (and the exclusion of hymnody) marked Reformed worship for several centuries and still does in some churches.

Calvin's low esteem for human nature was balanced by a high view of God's word and the sacraments. (Although almost all Protestants considered baptism and the eucharist as sacraments, Luther was willing to include penance, Calvin possibly ordination, and Zinzendorf marriage.) Calvin's doctrine of eucharistic feeding on Christ through the operation of the Holy Spirit, although certainly not without problems, was the most sophisticated Reformation eucharistic doctrine but largely lost by his heirs.

John Knox (ca. 1505-1572) transmitted this tradition to Scotland as others brought it to France, the Netherlands, and the Germanic countries. Knox's liturgy, renamed the *Book of Common Order*, flourished in Scotland for eighty years after 1564. Only then did the Scots yield to the Puritan effort to achieve national unity in worship through the *Westminster Directory* of 1645. This moved away from set forms to more permissive patterns yet the *Directory* remained vaguely normative in later editions in America. On the American frontier, the newly emerging frontier patterns of worship tended to engulf the Reformed tradition.

A pattern of recovery, similar to the one we have seen already slowly eventuated in America. Charles W Baird (1828-1887) led the way in 1855 with a title many thought oxymoronic, *Presbyterian Liturgies*. German Reformed Christians experienced a recovery of both theology and liturgy in the so-called Mercersburg Movement. Eventually an American service book, the *Book of Common Worship*, followed in 1906 as did service books in the Kirk of Scotland. In recent years, Presbyterians have followed closely in the same post-Vatican II ecumenical mainstream as other traditions of the right and center, signified by publication of their Supplemental Liturgical Resources.

Methodism

We move to a later period, the 18th century, to observe the origins of Methodism. Basically it can be seen as a countercultural movement in the midst of the Enlightenment. When the sacraments were on the margin of church life, early Methodism put them at the center; when religious zeal was in disrepute, Methodism made enthusiasm essential; where religion was confined to the churches, Methodism took it to the fields and streets. John Wesley (1703-1791), the founder of Methodism, was a faithful son of the Church of England and never

ceased in his love for its worship. The Methodists under Wesley functioned virtually as a religious order under a General Rule within the established church.

Distinctive features of early Methodist worship were "constant communion," i.e., frequent eucharist, fervent preaching for salvation, vigorous hymn singing (then a novelty), care of souls in small groups, and a mixture of extempore and fixed prayers. Charles Wesley (1707-1788) wrote hymns by the thousands; he and John created a great treasury of 166 eucharistic hymns. John Wesley practiced pragmatic traditionalism, preferring ancient forms for modern needs when possible: vigils became the Methodist watchnight, the agape surfaced as the love feast, and the covenant service was adapted from Presbyterianism. In 1784, John Wesley published his service book for America, the *Sunday Service*, advocating, among other things, a weekly eucharist.

Much of this did not survive the transit of the Atlantic, and American Methodism soon discarded Wesley's service book but not his hymn book. Much of the sacramental life was dissipated although the texts for the rites remained largely intact. Instead, Methodism tended to adapt many of the techniques of the frontier. Camp meetings abounded for a time and eventually resulted in a distinctive revival type service. Fanny Crosby (1820-1915) wrote many hymns of personal devotion to the blessed Saviour while Charles A. Tindley (1856-1933) was a prolific black hymn writer.

Despite the prevalence of revival style worship, there persisted in America a number of areas where more formal worship was preferred, such as in Birmingham and Nashville. Thomas O. Summers (1812-1882) was the leader of a 19th-century liturgical movement in the south which effected the reprinting of Wesley's service book and produced a standard order of worship. Wesley's prayer book long remained in use in England, or even the *Book of Common Prayer*. In general, Methodists in the 19th century reacted against the new ritualism of the established church in England, only to adopt some aspects of it several generations later.

Revivalism gave way to a period of aestheticism with much discussion of "enriching worship." This, in turn, gave way to a neo-orthodox period of recovering historic liturgies, especially Wesley's. Recent decades have seen more attention to assimilating the post-Vatican II Roman Catholic reforms, especially the lectionary. The new (1989) *United Methodist Hymnal* shows how far this has gone and may mark the beginning of a neo-Protestant emphasis on keeping the identity of one's own tradition.

Puritans

We move beyond the central traditions in our steady progression to the left to look at the five remaining traditions. It is not always easy to say which is the most radical but we shall place Puritanism closer to the center than the Anabaptists because the Puritans insisted on national reformation through a state church and the Anabaptists did not. The exception to this rule is small groups of Separatists who believe in reformation without tarrying for anyone and went ahead and did in private what the Puritans did openly when they controlled the national church. Since some Separatists picked up antipedobaptist ideas in the Netherlands, there are also close links between them and the Anabaptists.

Puritanism began in the ranks of Anglican exiles fleeing the persecutions of Queen Mary, although Edwardian Bishop John Hooper (?-1555) was a proto-Puritan. Puritans could favor various forms of church government— Episcopal, Presbyterian, and Congregational—as in accord with God's word,

but they had one common theme in worship: it must be according to God's word. Even the blessed John Calvin had been so blinded by the brightness of the new light that he had not gone far enough. Calvin had been content with general prescriptions for worship drawn from scripture; the Puritans wanted specifics. If it was wicked to disobey God's ethical injunctions, liturgical disobedience was no less reprehensible. Papistical ceremonies which survived in Anglican worship such as the sign of the cross in baptism, the wedding ring, confirmation, and holy days were all of human invention and therefore unscriptural. In this sense, no issue was minor for all were clear questions of obedience.

The Puritans' opportunity came when they controlled Parliament in the 1640s and 1650s and were able to enact a series of reforms. The *Book of Common Prayer* was abrogated from 1645 to 1660 and the *Westminster Directory* substituted. In Scotland, a *Directory for Family-Worship* was instituted in 1647 and became the basis for a long continuing practice of daily prayers in families. But it was in America that the Puritans first were able to institute a state church reformed according to God's word. In Salem (1629) and Boston (1630) the Reformation was finally completed according to their lights. Holy communion was celebrated monthly, worship was heavily dominated by preaching, but the congregation could respond and question the minister's exegesis and application, and psalmody provided another form of participation.

In the 18th century much of this was superseded by the emotional fervor of the Great Awakening which brought a variety of other churches to New England villages. In England and America, a considerable segment, usually those preferring a more dignified style of worship, moved into Unitarianism. Unlike other traditions, little effort was spent in recovering past patterns. Much of the Puritan tradition passed into liberal Congregationalism or Unitarianism without much concern for recovering a 17th century golden era.

In recent years much of the same post-Vatican II time of assimilation has occurred, especially in accepting the lectionary, church year, and other common themes. The newest United Church of Christ service book, *Book of Worship* (1986), is the most liberal denominational service book, especially in inclusive language, and is probably not widely used except for special services.

Anabaptists

We must return to the 16th century to pick up our last tradition originating in that period of liturgical ferment. It is not easy to generalize about the Anabaptist elements of the Radical Reformation known largely today as Mennonites, Amish, and Hutterites but we can trace some common features. Surprisingly, the more radical traditions tend also to be most conservative when it comes to stabilizing and continuing the same worship forms across the centuries.

The earliest Anabaptists, the Swiss Brethren, began in contact with Zwingli in Zurich. But they took his biblicism a step further than he was willing to and argued vehemently against the baptism of any but believers. Their basic premise came to be the need for a pure church of believers who led holy lives. This was impossible to reconcile with the magisterial reformation which relied upon state support. Both Protestants and Catholics vied with each other to persecute Anabaptists or "rebaptizers" as they became known because of their refusal to accept their own baptisms as infants. Immersion was not an issue and most of these groups baptized by pouring or sprinkling.

A variety of leaders arose with small groups of followers. The typical congregation met in a secluded spot under a leader called and ordained by the congregation. Because persecution was so constant, martyrdom was frequent and a rich hymnody of martyrdom developed, some of it still in use. For the church to be kept pure, not only must the entrance be narrow in the form of baptism for believers only, but members not living a holy life were expelled by the ban and shunned in accordance with biblical precept (1 Cor 5:13).

Despite their radical origins, several Anabaptist groups have kept faithful with genuine conservatism. The Old Order (Amish) worship in private homes much as their ancestors did, the Hutterite communities even retain the use of 16th century sermons, and even the larger Mennonite groups resisted most 19th century American influences by remaining relatively isolated communities. Although their numbers remain relatively small, the disciplined lifestyle of these people make them much admired.

The American Frontier

We leap forward now to the very beginnings of the 19th century in America. A new social situation developed in America after the Revolution with the development of widely scattered pioneers on the frontier. No traditional parish system was adequate and large numbers of the population were as unchurched as they were illiterate. A means of reaching them soon developed, strangely enough out of the sacramental seasons which Presbyterians of Scotch-Irish origins observed several times a year. These periods of intense preparation before celebration of the eucharist developed soon into the camp meeting in which thousands of people assembled from miles around for a period usually of four days of preaching, singing, spiritual direction, baptism of converts, all culminating in the Lord's Supper. More than any other individual, Charles G. Finney (1792-1875) brought the frontier techniques or "new measures" back to the east coast despite stubborn resistance from his fellow Presbyterian ministers. Domesticated into east coast gentility, these included protracted meetings lasting over several days, the mourner's bench, prayer for individuals by name, and frequently midweek prayer meetings at which even women were allowed to speak.

The great attraction of this new frontier tradition was that it worked. It had completely substituted pragmatism for traditionalism (unlike Wesley) and Finney had a great scorn for previous forms of worship. Frontier style worship worked in the sense that it made converts, snatching them from darkness into the blinding light of conversion and could rekindle that fire again and again. The normal patterns of worship came to be tripartite: prayer and praise, preaching for salvation, and harvest of converts. Music played a great part in the first portion, often caricatured as "preliminaries." So attractive did this style of worship become that like a black hole it pulled many a Lutheran, Reformed, Methodist, Puritan, and even Quaker congregation into it.

As such it is the dominant worship tradition in the United States. Great denominations such as the Southern Baptist, Disciples of Christ, and Churches of Christ feel at home within this tradition although the latter two insisted on a weekly eucharist led by lay people. In recent years, this tradition has felt little temptation to borrow from the recent Roman Catholic reforms, although the lectionary has made some inroads. As worship for the unchurched, this tradition is a natural for modern television evangelism. Millions participate in this kind of worship via television each Sunday. By its standards it still works and works very well, so why change? Hence radical as it was, it has conserved many of its forms, only adapting them to new media.

Pentecostal

The advent of the 20th century brought an even more radical tradition, the Pentecostal. Whereas all the traditions we have examined thus far proceeded on the basis of structured worship, usually led if not dominated by a single leader, the Pentecostals turned the doors wide open to the Spirit which might blow anywhere or use anyone in the congregation. Here was a tradition in which blacks and women played major roles from the very beginning.

The beginnings were inauspicious, a broken down faith healer, Charles Parham (1873-1929), playing John the Baptist to a one-eyed black holiness preacher, William J. Seymour (1870-1922). From Topeka to Houston, the fire smoldered and suddenly in 1905 burst into flame at the Azusa Street Mission in Los Angeles. Crowds attended from America and the fire spread to Portland, to Chicago, to Norway, and to England, soon touched Chile and Brazil, and eventually reached out to Africa.

Pentecostal worship centered in the unexpected possibilities of the Holy Spirit reaching out by showering gifts on individuals for the benefit of all. Speaking in tongues came to be the best known gift, revealing an individual's baptism of the Spirit. But it was by no means the only gift: healing, interpretation, and prophecy blossomed where least expected. It was true liturgical democracy. Women leaders were prominent and often more colorful than the men. Every black neighborhood has a Pentecostal chapel or two, yet in recent years highly affluent communities have also seen the advent of this worship tradition.

Beginning in 1960, Pentecostal or charismatic worship made its advent among Roman Catholics. After initial resistance, it has been welcomed in Roman Catholic and Protestant communities alike. Meanwhile, classical Pentecostalism has reached millions of people in Latin America and become one of the largest forces shaping Christianity in Africa. Sober historians have predicted that the majority of Christians one day will be in the southern hemisphere and that most of them will be Pentecostals.

Quakers

It is easy to identify the Quakers or Society of Friends as the most radical tradition of all in its break from late medieval forms of worship. All the groups we have mentioned thus far have clergy, the preaching of sermons, and outward and visible sacraments. The classical forms of Quaker worship have none of the above although we may detect some indirect links with medieval mysticism. Paradoxically, most Quakers have tempered their radicalism by being the most conservative in fidelity to their original forms. Roman Catholic worship has changed far more than has Quaker worship in England or the east coast of America.

The origins of Quaker worship lie in the soul-searching of George Fox (1624-1691) and his discovery of the inner light in every human. This brought one closer to God than scripture or sacraments for it was direct access to the Spirit itself with no need for the mediation of clergy or set forms. Furthermore, such direct access was available to all, male or female, slave or free. It was as radical as Paul's concept of baptism. Thus any study of liturgy and justice must begin with the Quakers, for what they practiced in worship was what they felt compelled to practice in all of life. What F.D. Maurice (1805-1872) and Percy Dearmer (1867-1936) or Virgil Michel (1890-1938) and H.A. Reinhold (1897-1968) later advocated had been common practice among Quakers for several centuries. Since all were equal before the Spirit, women had as much right to speak in worship as men and anyone who could see the Spirit in a black person had no right to keep him or her in slavery. Since no one was marginalized in worship, it also meant no one

should be honored by clothing or titles in society. Decisions were to be made by the "sense of the meeting" since a vote always means defeat for a minority. Whatever else it is, the Spirit seems to be fair and consistent.

But though it could dispense with sermons and sacraments, the one thing Quaker worship could not surrender was the Christian community itself, the "meeting." Hence as all Christians have discovered, the most important act in worship is coming together in Christ's name. Quaker worship is a form of corporate mysticism in which the Spirit uses individuals to speak to the group. Greatly to be feared is putting oneself forward by rushing into words. Only after a time of centering down can one feel ready to speak under the compulsion of the Spirit. It was felt that Christ had not intended outward baptism and communion to continue any more than footwashing. So these sacraments occur in inward and visible ways only.

Quaker worship involves a great sense of personal restraint and even great Quaker saints such as John Woolman (1720-1772) worried after first-day meeting (Sunday) that they might have spoken from the self rather than the Spirit. A high degree of biblical literacy is also presupposed. The Spirit, after all, is the author of scripture too and will not contradict itself whether in the Bible or in reason.

On the American frontier, as had so many other traditions, some Quakers adopted frontier forms of worship, especially in Indiana. Thus evolved services with structured worship, paid clergy, and even outward sacraments. Sometimes unstructured or unprogrammed worship could be integrated into services which were basically structured. But many east coast and English Quakers worship still in ways that would not astonish George Fox, so stable has Quaker worship been.

This has been a quick journey through

five centuries of worship in the West. Worship forms have continued to develop as people have changed. The Puritans were the pious yuppies of their times and they demanded worship forms that reflected who they were. The evolution of new traditions is as natural as the change in peoples. Modern attempts to conflate liturgical traditions, to obtain any form of consensus in the ways a variety of Christian peoples worship their God, are highly dubious efforts. Just as social change sneaks up on us when we least expect it, so new liturgical traditions will evolve in the West where unexpected. They may be feminist, or incorporate insights of eastern cultures, or reflect the effects of new technologies on people (as did book publishing), but they most likely will occur in ways no one yet can anticipate. They may be already in our midst.

Horton Davies, *Worship and Theology in England* (Oxford and Princeton: Oxford University Press and Princeton University Press, 1961-1975). Hughes Oliphant Old, *Patristic Roots of Reformed Worship* (Zurich: Theologischer Verlag, 1975). Bard Thompson, *Liturgies of the Western Church* (Cleveland: Meridian, 1961). James F. White, *Protestant Worship: Traditions in Transition* (Louisville: Westminster John Knox Press, 1989).

JAMES F. WHITE

TRADITIONS, LITURGICAL, IN THE WEST: PRE-REFORMATION

In origin, evolution, and spirit, the liturgical tradition of the Western church is complex and diverse. What is known as the Roman rite was only one of several Western rites which existed between the 4th and 16th centuries; the others are known as the North African, Ambrosian, Spanish, Gallican, and Celtic rites.

Liturgical Diversity and Roman Influence

In matters of worship, local churches were free to develop their own forms, and often did so in conjunction with the churches of the same region under the authority of the metropolitan bishop who served as primate of the region or "diocese" as it was termed in the Roman Empire. The bishop of Rome, as primate of the part of Italy extending south of the city of Rome (*i.e., Italia suburbicaria*), had the right to insist that churches in that region conform to Roman usages (See letter of Innocent I to Decentius of Gubbio; 19 March 416). In like manner, the bishop of Milan as primate of *Italia annonaria*, the bishop of Carthage as primate of Africa, the bishop of Carthago Nova (until 531) or of Toledo (after 531) as primate of *Hispania*, the bishop of Arles as primate of Septimania, and the bishop of Lyons as primate of Gaul, could convoke synods and insist upon adherence to liturgical canons.

Until 1080, the Roman see never attempted to control the liturgical observances of churches outside of *Italia suburbicaria*. Indeed, because of the Lombard invasions, it's sphere of liturgical influence was limited to the narrow corridor which joined Rome and Ravenna. As a matter of fact, the bishop of Rome was well aware of the need for diversity of forms to suit the temperament of different peoples. In 597, when Augustine of Canterbury wrote to ask Gregory I why the churches of Gaul and of Rome had different usages and which rite to use for the newly converted Angles, the pope replied: ". . . you should carefully select for the English church whatever is most able to please almighty God, whether it come from the Roman, Gallican or whatever church you may find it. . . . Things ought not be loved because of the place from which they come, but because they are good in themselves. Therefore choose elements that are reverent (*pia*), awe-inspiring (*religiosa*), and orthodox (*recta*) from each and every church and arrange them as in a little book in accord with the mind of the English and so establish them as custom"

(Monumenta Germaniae Historica, *Epistolae* 2, 334).

Emergence of the Traditions

Although most of what we know about the individual rites can be discerned only from the evidence of extant liturgical texts and artifacts, the various Latin rites emerged when improvisation was still predominant, and long before the date of the oldest surviving manuscripts. The practice of improvisation, however, presupposed the faithful observance of certain canons, guidelines or principles which were transmitted in the local church from one generation to the next. At the core of his liturgical patrimony was the structure of the service, the framework for improvisation. In all the traditions, the first composition of written texts was nothing more than a new type of improvisation. A set of texts was prepared for a specific celebration and afterwards placed in the local archives as a record of the celebration. Fifth-century Rome witnessed the production of a great number of variable texts for the eucharist, the composition or editing of euchological texts for the administration of the sacraments and for use at the liturgy of the hours. By the end of the same century, examples of this written improvisation had found their way to northern Italy, southeastern Gaul, and northeastern Spain, inspiring a veritable explosion of euchological creativity throughout the West, giving additional impetus to the emergence of the local rites, and leading eventually to the compilation of the numerous liturgical books of each tradition (6th-9th centuries).

. Liturgy of North Africa

It is certain that North Africa, the cradle of Latin Christianity, was likewise the first place to use Latin in the liturgy. Without discouraging the ancient practice of improvisation, councils and synods (e.g., Hippo [393] can. 25) provided guidelines for formulating liturgical prayers and insisted that prayers composed elsewhere be approved by the teachers (*fratres instructiores*). The composition of prayers by heretics prompted a later synod to direct that "*preces, prefationes, commendationes* and *impositiones manuum*" be composed under supervision of the hierarchy and used by all (Carthage [407], can. 10).

African collections of *libelli missarum* and even sacramentaries are referred to in writings from the 5th century; but, apart from a few Arian fragments, no actual liturgical texts have survived. Nevertheless, details of the rite have been gleaned from non-liturgical sources, e.g., conciliar decrees like those already mentioned and especially the writings and sermons of Augustine of Hippo. The following order of the Mass is based on a reconstruction by F. Van Der Meer (*Augustine the Bishop*, [Sheed & Ward, 1961], pp. 388-402).

(In this and all subsequent outlines, the asterisk marks a chant by the people or choir; the readings are marked in SMALL CAPITALS.)

Entrance of the Clergy
Greeting

EPISTLE
*PSALM (Aug. considered this a reading)
GOSPEL
Homily
[announcements]
Dismissal of the Catechumens

Solemn Intercessions
Offering with *Psalm singing
Preface dialogue
Improvised Preface without Sanctus
Approved Eucharistic prayer
"Amen"
Fractio
Lord's Prayer
Communion with *Psalm 33

Final prayer
Dismissal

The year after Augustine's death (430) the African church saw the beginning of more than a century of bitter persecution by the Arian Vandals. In 698, Carthage was taken by the Moors and the church that had given birth to Latin Christianity ceased to exist altogether.

2. The Gallican Liturgy

Properly speaking, the *Gallican rite* refers exclusively to the liturgical tradition which emerged in the southern part of Gaul at the beginning of the 6th century and remained in use throughout the province until it was replaced (fused) with the Roman rite under the Carolingians (late 8th-9th centuries).

The study of the Gallican rite is hampered by the sparsity of its liturgical books and some major elements of the liturgy remain completely deprived of any documentation. There are euchological texts for the celebration of the eucharist and for the administration of the sacraments (*Missale Gothicum, Missale Bobbiense, Missale Francorum*, and several Mass-fragments; benedictionals=collections of episcopal blessings given before communion; diptychs=tables of names for the commemoration of the living and dead; and *ordines scrutiniorum*=formulas for the celebration of the scrutinies) and the system of readings has left fragmentary evidence in lectionaries, *capitularia* =lists of first and last words of the pericopes and *passionaria* =lives of the saints read both at Mass and the office on their feasts. No Gallican antiphonary for the Mass or hours has been preserved though the hymns of the Gallican hours and a few genuine Gallican chants may have survived in the Gregorian chant tradition (Huglo, 114-122). To complicate matters further, most of the sources already mentioned include Roman material; for example, the Bobbio missal preserves the structure of the Gallican Mass only as far as the preface where it abandons the variable Gallican prayer for the Roman canon.

In contrast with the Spanish, Milanese, and Roman rites, the Gallican sources indicate an enormous diversity, even between neighboring dioceses; for example, the church at Auxerre—as evidenced in the collection of Masses published by Mone in 1850—used very different formularies but followed basically the same order of service as the church of Autun where the *Missale Gothicum* was compiled. At the time other rites were being codified and standardized to some extent, the churches of Gaul and Septimania suffered the successive invasions and ensuing political divisions of the Visigoths, Ostrogoths and Franks— all in the first half of the 6th century. Codification was far from systematic or uniform in spite of the attempts of local councils to regulate church life and worship.

The following outline of the Gallican order of the Mass has been re-constructed from letters of Pseudo-Germanus of Paris (ed. Ratcliff, 1971) and the sacramentaries mentioned above:

[Preparation of Offerings
at side altar or in sacristy]
*Antiphona ad praelegendum with Psalm
Call for silence and Greeting
*Trisagion and *Kyrie
Prophetia (=*Benedictus*; or a hymn in Lent)
Collectio post Prophetiam

LECTIO PROPHETICA
*Responsorium (?)
LECTIO EX APOSTOLO
*Canticle from Daniel (=*Benedictiones* on feasts; or (?)
*Trisagion ante evangelium
EVANGELIUM
*Sanctus post evangelium
Homilia
Preces
Collectio post precem
Dismissal of catchumens
Solemn presentation of the Gifts with *Sonus
Praefatio missa and *collectio*
Names and *collectio post nomina*
Collectio ad pacem and Pax

Contestatio (Immolatio missae) and *Sanctus
Vere sanctus-institution narrative-*post   mysterium*
Confractionem

Lord's prayer

Episcopal Benediction
Communion and* *Trecanum*
Post Eucharisticam and *Collectio post communionem*
Dismissal

A distinguishing characteristic of the Gallican rite lies in its use of variable texts in the eucharistic prayer before and after the institution narrative (*post sanctus* and *post mysterium*). In this it contrasted with the fixed canon in the Roman and Milanese rites but also to some degree with the Spanish rite which also used variable pieces in the eucharistic prayer. The Gallican provides no system but simply a repertoire of texts for the three pieces—*contestatio* (preface), *post sanctus, post mysterium*—without coordination or connection among them. This is all the more noteworthy given the fact that there was an attempt to match "proper" orations for the other parts of the Mass to the feast or season.

With regard to the euchology for other ritual and sacramental celebrations, the typically Gallican approach included an introductory invitation directed to the faithful (bidding) which anticipated and sometimes contained the blessing which followed. In the case of ordinations, the unit included three elements: the instruction of the candidates, the invitation to prayer and the blessing/ordination prayer. This form was an expansion of the ancient and universal liturgical prayer unit (which is best known in the Solemn Intercessions on Good Friday in the Roman rite): invitation to prayer-silent prayer-concluding oration. The practice is so characteristic of the Gallican rite that a number of the variable texts for each Mass originally assumed this form of instructive invitation to prayer (*Praefatio missa, Post Eucharisticam*). The combination of instruction, invitation, and prayer in the compilation of texts for other ritual and sacramental celebrations was amply employed by the liturgical compilers of the Carolingian

period and served as one of several ways in which the ancient Roman liturgy was "Gallicanized" (Vogel, 150-155).

Given the heterogeneity of the Gallican repertoire, it is almost impossible to make an evaluation of style and content which is universally applicable. However, those texts which actually originate with the Gallican rite betray a conservative tendency in using the traditional vocabulary, phrasing, and syntax that are found in the oldest Gallican sources. Although the same phenomenon has been noted in a few Ambrosian and Spanish prayers, it is a veritable characteristic of Gallican euchology. An important indication of the adherence to the tradition appears in the Gallican equivalent to the *anàmnesis* in the *post mysterium*: only the *death* of the Lord is recalled as in the Pauline gloss of 1 Cor 11: 26 and as seems to have been the case in North Africa at the time of Cyprian. In this, the Gallican rite stands alone; even the Spanish include at least the death and the resurrection in the *post pridie*.

It has often been suggested that the Gallican style is one of exuberance and prolixity, elaborate ceremonial and splendor. Such an evaluation is not justified and neither does it take into account the varied origin of the Gallican repertoire of prayers and practices. In reality, at least among the texts which are genuinely Gallican, one finds extreme conciseness and density of content, reflecting the prose style of the time and region. The fact that so much was so readily borrowed and adapted from Eastern and Spanish sources—another Gallican characteristic in itself—contributes to the impression that Gallican means long-winded.

On the other hand the later Gallican compilers did add extra prayers to the rites. The so-called *apologiae* and "accompanying prayers" first make their appearance in Gallican sources, though it is difficult to say whether or not they were inspired by the Irish. The apologies were private prayers in which the priest acknowledged his sinfulness and unworthiness; the others include private prayers for vesting, for the offertory and for before and after communion. Many of these made their way into the Gallicanized-Roman books of the 8th and 9th centuries but the famous *Missa Illyrica* (=sacramentary of Sigebert of Minden [10th century]) includes nearly 200 of them newly composed or compiled from several sources.

3. The Spanish Liturgy

The Spanish liturgy, also known rather inaccurately as "Mozarabic" or "Visigothic," is the autonomous liturgy which was in constant use in Spain from the beginning of the 6th century until it was suppressed by the Council of Braga (1080) at the insistence of Pope Gregory VII (1073-1085). At the time of its codification, when Visigothic rule reached its greatest extension (7th cent.), the Spanish rite was celebrated throughout the Iberian peninsula and in the region of southwestern France known as *Gallia Narbonese*. After its suppression, it continued to be celebrated in a few parish churches for a time, and with intermittent periods of complete abandonment, in a single chapel at the cathedral of Toledo into the 20th century.

Among the surviving manuscripts of the Spanish liturgy there are *dittici* (=variable texts for the eucharist) that may have been copied from 3rd century sources and constitute the major evidence of a native liturgical patrimony. In the *dittici* contained in the *missale mixtum* of Cisneros (16th century), there is resonance with both the letters of Cyprian of Carthage (d. 258) and the *Acta* of the martyrdom of S. Fructuoso of Tarragona (d. 258) who, like Cyprian, suffered under the persecution of Valerian.

Although inspired by the Roman *libelli* of variable texts, neither the Spanish nor the Gallican authors renounced the order of the Mass they had received as part of their ancient liturgical patrimony. The Spanish left the prayer of the faithful and the kiss of peace where they had been after the liturgy of the word and composed a series of variable texts for them (*ad orationem; ad pacem*) in addition to the variable *inlatio, post sanctus* and *post pridie* which formed their eucharistic prayer. Thus, in contrast to the Roman system which spread variable texts throughout the Mass but maintained a fixed canon, the Spanish concentrated their variable texts at the center of the celebration.

In spite of the relative independence of individual pieces, the Spanish used brief formulas, (remnants of the old improvisational structure?) to make a transition from one piece to the next. With this system it was possible to achieve innumerable variations on the same theme, and at the same time give a sense of unity and cohesion to the whole euchological complex. The aim for unity and cohesion with great variety is a distinguishing trait of the Spanish authors and one that was maintained throughout the evolution of the rite.

This characteristic is apparent as well in the richness, harmony and refinement of the chants and orations of the office books and in the *Liber Ordinum* (=ritual/pontifical for other sacramental celebrations). The coordination of the Mass and hours with the other sacramental celebrations is also worthy of note; for example there was not only a votive Mass for marriage, for the sick, for the dead, but a votive office in each case as well. The ritual/pastoral care extended beyond the actual exchange of rings, anointing, or burial to include the entire liturgical life of the community and the role of the individual in that life. The introduction to the Lord's Prayer in the votive Mass for the sick illustrates the strong ecclesial sense in the Spanish rite; it ends: "so that when the sickness of body and soul has been driven out, these who are ill may pray *with us*, saying 'Our Father...'" (Férotin, *Liber Ordinum*, col. 377).

Several historical factors contributed to the systematic codification of the Spanish rite. From the time of its invasion by the Arian Visigoths in 414 until the invasion of the Moors in 711, the Iberian peninsula was politically united. With the conversion to Catholicism of the entire kingdom in 589, the political unity was reinforced by religious unity. The resulting climate favored the collection, codification, and eventual standardization of liturgical texts and practices.

In addition, because their greatest liturgical creativity postdated that of other Western rites, the Spanish could incorporate the "teaching" of liturgical texts from other rites, the canons of the christological councils, and the liturgical theology in the patristic sermons of such as Augustine and Leo. As in Milan, the liturgy in Spain was considered the most efficient means for planting the truths of the faith in the minds and hearts of the Christian people and was purposely formulated with orthodox precision. In part this explains why the Spanish authors of this era applied themselves to the composition of liturgical texts instead of the production of ascetical or dogmatic treatises, exegetical commentaries on the scriptures, or long homiletic sermons.

A clear example of their high esteem for the liturgy is the *De ecclesiasticis officiis* of Isidore of Seville (d. 636), the first treatise on the liturgy which not only describes the local rite, but contains much useful information about Milanese and African uses as well. Complementing Isidore's treatise are the invaluable liturgical canons of the synods and councils, especially the "national" Councils of Toledo IV-X (633-656). Knowing their own rite to be in a state of flux, the council fathers enumerated and illustrated the ancient liturgical uses which they felt

should be maintained by all but simultaneously provided a forum for exchanging the innovations of the liturgical creativity which flourished in the various provinces. As a result, the Spanish rite represented euchological schools from several provinces: Tarragona —S. Eugenius (d. 657); Seville —Ss. Leander (d. ca. 600) and Isidore (d. 636); Braga — Profuturus (fl. ca. 538) and S. Martin (d. 580); Toledo —Ss. Eugenio II (d. 657), Ildefonso (d. 667), and Juliano (d. 690). The saintly bishops of Toledo were responsible for the definitive form of the liturgical books that survived the subsequent onslaughts of the Moslem invasion, Carolingian expansion, and theological controversies that would reach a climax in the Gregorian suppression of 1080.

With regard to the office, the Spanish and Gallican churches maintained a strict distinction between "cathedral" and "monastic" hours. Iberian councils directed that monastic and ecclesiastical customs should not be mixed (Braga 563, can 1); and that monks were not permitted to use the public churches for anything but cathedral services: matins, vespers and Mass (11 Toledo 675, can 3). One of the earliest books produced in the Spanish rite is the *Liber psalmographus*, an office book filled with several series of psalm prayers which constitute a veritable commentary on the psalms, most of which have been given a christological and ecclesiological interpretation.

The Spanish order of the Mass is outlined as follows:

* *Prelegendum* with psalm
 Trisagion
 Greeting

 LESSON (PROPHETIC)
* *Psallendum* / *Psallmo (Trenos* in Lent)
 [* *Clamor* on certain days]
 EPISTLE
 GOSPEL
* *Laudes*
 Dismissal of catechumens

* *Sacrificium* with verses for offertory procession
 Missa (= bidding)

Alia oratio
Nomina Offerentium
Diptychs
Post Nomina
Ad Pacem
Pax
Preface Dialogue ("Aures ad dominum"
...."Sursum corda" ...Deo ac Domino
nostro, Patri, et Filio, et Spiritui Sancto, dignas
laudes et gratias referamus...)
Inlatio and *Sanctus
Post Sanctus
Missa Secreta (=Institution Narrative)
Post Pridie

*Laudes ad Confractionem
[Creed on Sundays and Feasts]
Ad orationem Dominicam
Lord's Prayer and variable embolism
Commixtio and Trisagion
Benedictio (Three-fold Blessing of the people)

Invitation to communion
*Ad Accedentes (variable, often beginning with
Ps. 33/34)
Communion of all with both species

Completuria = post-communion prayer (after
10th century)
Dismissal

4. The Ambrosian Liturgy

Though usually associated with the metropolitan see once occupied by Saint Ambrose (d. 397), the Ambrosian rite includes in addition to the liturgy celebrated in the city of Milan (i.e., the *Milanese* liturgy), the liturgy of several other dioceses of Northern Italy (Bergamo, Ticino, Novara, Vercelli, etc.), and to a certain extent, the liturgy of Aquileia

Unlike the other non-Roman Western rites, the Ambrosian liturgy was never *officially* suppressed by emperor or pope. In spite of Carolingian and later attempts to "Romanize" everywhere, the Ambrosian liturgy survived with numerous medieval accretions (Roman and non-Roman), but underwent major restorations first under Carlo Borromeo (d. 1584) and then at the beginning of the 20th century under Cardinals A. Ratti (later Pius XI) and I. Schuster. It was completely revised and translated into Italian in the 1970s.

The liturgical patrimony of the Ambrosian liturgy was largely the result of strong Roman and Eastern influences. After its emergence as a distinct rite it came to share many of its features with all the Western rites, often serving as the bridge between East and West. What distinguishes it from all the other liturgical traditions, however, can be understood only in the context of the theological and political anti-Arianism in which it arose and evolved. With the exception of the Roman liturgy, the Arian controversy had a major effect on the euchology of all the Western traditions, though in no case did this struggle perdure as at Milan. In fact in its emergence (4th-5th centuries), its development (6th-7th centuries) and in the period of its stabilization (8th-9th centuries) the Ambrosian liturgy had to fight constantly against this heresy in one form or another. The most obvious result is the strong christocentricism of the Ambrosian prayers, in both original texts and in the the editing of texts borrowed from Roman and Carolingian sources.

The centrality of Christ is manifest not only in the careful consideration of the incarnation and the virginal birth but also in the veneration of the Virgin Mary. In Ambrosian iconography it is possible to trace a progression from the *Kyrios-Pantocrator* to *Deus-Homo, Homo-Deus,* and *Nobiscum-Deus,* which corresponds to the various stages in the development of Ambrosian euchology. It is here that the Ambrosian influence on the other Western liturgies was most strongly felt.

In the early Middle Ages, the Ambrosian eucharist had the following order:

*Ingressa no psalm
*Kyrie
Oratio super populum = collect

PROPHETIC LESSON
*Psalmellus
EPISTLE
*Alleluia with verse (Cantus during Lent)
GOSPEL
Homily

Dismissal of Catechumens
*Kyrie and *Antiphona post Evangelium
Pax

Oratio super sindonem
Offertory procession; *Offerenda with verses

Proper Preface and Sanctus
Invariable Canon
Fraction and Commixtio; *Confractorium

Lord's Prayer and embolism
Communion; *Transitorium no psalm
Oratio post communionem
*Kyrie and Dismissal

The Ambrosian office was unique in the West in spreading the psalter over two weeks. Like the Roman and Benedictine cursus, however, the Ambrosian assigned psalms 109/110-147 to vespers. As in the cathedral office of 4th-century Jerusalem and the "Chaldean" rite, the morning office at Milan consisted of three canticles, the Laudate psalms (148-150), gospel reading and a procession to the cross or baptistery, while vespers began with the lucernarium.

The Ambrosian chant tradition is preserved in some 300 north Italian manuscripts, most from the late 12th century and later. Though sharing many features and texts with Gregorian chant, the Ambrosian has a closer affinity to the Old Roman and Beneventan traditions.

5. The Celtic Liturgy

The term "Celtic rite" has been used for the ancient liturgy celebrated in Ireland, Scotland, Britain, Gallicia and Brittany before these churches gradually adopted the calendar and liturgy of Rome (as early as 633 in Gallicia and as late as the 11th century in Scotland). In a more restricted sense, the "Celtic rite" refers to the liturgy celebrated in the churches and monasteries of Ireland and regions heavily influenced by Irish missionary-monks from the late 6th to early 9th century.

With regard to the Mass, the liturgy represented by the few books and fragments that are of Irish provenance do not possess a sufficient cohesion nor do they reflect a work sufficiently autonomous and original to constitute a separate rite. While all rites borrowed elements from other traditions, the Irish seem to have done very little in the way of composing original prayers or codifying texts and arranging ceremonies. Some evidence indicates the adoption of an expanded Roman ordinary with few variable texts (exemplified in the Stowe Missal) while other sources follow a Gallican or Spanish order (as in the sacramentary fragments of Fulda and St. Gall). When the work of an Irish hand does appear, it betrays a remarkable familiarity with obscure patristic writings and liturgical formularies from all over the Christian world — Egypt, Rome, Gaul, but especially Spain and Milan —genuine "souvenirs" of the missionary activity of Irish monks.

In outline, the structure of the Mass in the Stowe missal follows:

Confession of sins and litany of saints
(Roman and Irish)
[preparation of gifts at the altar]
several collects
*Gloria
collects
EPISTLE and collect
*Psalm and collect
diaconal litany
collects post precem
GOSPEL
*Alloir=Alleluia
oratio super evangelium

partial uncovering of the gifts
Creed
full uncovering of gifts
collect
[names or litany]
oratio post nomina
additional collects
[pax]

Preface Dialogue
Celtic preface and *Sanctus
  Roman canon (with names for both mementos)
  or post sanctus leading to qui pridie
Elevation of Chalice and Host

Fraction with *Antiphon and collect
Lord's Prayer with embolism
Pax
Commixtio

Communion; *Processional hymn
Collects
Dismissal

According to the "tract" which follows the Masses in the Stowe missal, the Mass was sung in its entirety. Although no written melodies survive from the Celtic chants, the Irish are known to have taught them to the monks of Northumbria (northern England) who abandoned them when John the Archcantor from St. Peter's was "borrowed" to teach the Roman chants (ca. 675).

Dependence on continental sources is also discernible in the Celtic celebration of the hours, though similarities to other Western rites are not as pronounced as in the Mass. What survived of the early cathedral office in Irish monastic rules relates closely to the cathedral tradition in the rest of the West; lauds in the Antiphonary of Bangor (late 7th century) is almost identical to the office at Milan. The purely monastic hours, on the other hand, show remarkable creativity. None of the Gallican monastic rules followed Cassian's description of Egyptian monastic practice as closely as the Irish who arranged the psalms for the *horae diurnae* (secunda (sic)=prime, terce, sext, none, vespers), assigning three thematically appropriate psalms to each. For the night office, the Irish monastic rules are unique: Columban assigned 12 psalms to the first two night hours (*initium noctis* = Gallican *duodecima?*, *medium noctis*) but during the third hour (*matutinum* or *vigilia*) his monks prayed anywhere from 24 (summer weeknights) to 75 psalms (Saturdays and Sundays from Nov 1 - Jan 31). The division of the night office into three hours is itself unique to the Irish.

Unlike the liturgists of the Mediterranean rites, the Irish authors had neither an ancient liturgical patrimony nor a tradition of Christian-Latin literature of their own as a basis for formulating Celtic euchology. The fact that they used a language that was not their own may explain, at least in part, the extent of their eclecticism. But the Irish monks were avid scholars, collectors and copyists of everything they could obtain —Greek and Latin. Their particular choice of elements from so many liturgical traditions betrays, if anything, a fascination with the unusual and the obscure.

The Irish proved themselves most original in illumination of manuscripts and the composition of hymns and collects for the office. They used the idioms, language, ideas, and forms that had grown out of the various traditions of the Church and transformed them into artistic and poetic forms that clearly reflect their native genius. The Eastern influence can be discerned in their illuminations which are nevertheless filled with Gaelic serpents and dragons. Though in Latin, many of the hymns and collects in the Antiphonary of Bangor are composed in meter that do not reflect either classical or accentual rhythmic patterns but instead follow the ancient meters of their native poetry, replete with rhyme and alliteration.

The devotional practices and original texts of the Celtic authors reflect a lifestyle that is centered more on a personal than on an ecclesial relationship with Christ and the ever-present Trinity. The most obvious and influential example is the practice of private penitence which followed the missionary monks on all their journeys. This typically Irish individualism was absorbed into the "renaissance" of the Carolingian era and reflected in its reshaping of the Western liturgy. The piety which produced long lists of *apologiae* (prayers of unworthiness) and influenced the Romano-Frankish or Romano-Germanic liturgy for the rest of the Middle Ages was manifest quite early in the liturgical texts of Ireland.

6. *The Roman Liturgy*

As mentioned at the beginning, the

Roman rite was originally confined to the city of Rome and its suburbicarian dioceses. But even within the city itself there were differences in ceremonies, prayers, chants and melodies for the Mass and office.

(a) *Ordo romanus I* describes a stational Mass when the pope presides. The stational liturgy was celebrated only on certain days and was intended as the main liturgical celebration of the day or hour. As such, it was attended by "everyone" in the city or at least by the clergy.

(b) *Ordo romanus II* prescribes a different order if one of the seven "suburban" (as opposed to nearly 100 "suburbicarian") bishops, or one of the Roman presbyters as the pope's representative presides at the stational liturgy.

(c) A simpler order was used by the presbyters when they presided in the *tituli* on stational days (no basilica was large enough for the whole city) or on ordinary Sundays when there were no stational celebrations.

(d) The presbyters—and later the monks—who had the task of supplying the daily liturgical needs of pilgrims at the cemeterial shrines combined elements of both the stational and titular celebrations.

The differences in celebration were first recorded in different collections of *libelli missarum* and *ordines* that were later shaped into the so-called Gregorian (=stational) and Gelasian (=presbyteral or titular) sacramentaries and in *ordines romani* (=collections of rubrics for nearly every kind of celebration). In the meantime records were being kept of the cycle of feasts, the readings, and the chants of the stational celebrations that would eventually be compiled into lectionaries and antiphonaries. Once the major basilicas were staffed with their own full-time clergy and monastic communities (5th-10th centuries) records were kept of particular customs, chants, and reading lists for Mass and office that differed

considerably from one side of the city to the other.

The order of the Mass in all these different circumstances was eventually, if not always, identical to that described in *Ordo romanus I*:

Entrance of ministers; **Introit* with psalm
*Kyrie
[Gloria; at first at presbyteral masses on Easter only]
Collecta

APOSTULUS
*Gradual (Alleluia in Easter)
*Alleluia (Tractus in Lent)
EVANGELIUM

Offertory procession; **Offertorium* with psalm
Super oblata (Secreta)

Preface Dialogue
Praefatio and **Sanctus*
Canon missae

Lord's Prayer and embolism
Pax
[Announcements/ Dismissals]
Fractio; **Agnus Dei*
Communion with both kinds; **Communio* with psalm
Ad completa (post communionem)
Dismissal

This was the Roman liturgy that impressed the Germans and Franks long before the Carolingian era. Beginning in the 7th century, bishops or monks returning from pilgrimage or diplomatic mission to Rome were anxious to adopt Roman customs—especially those of St. Peter's or the Lateran—in their churches and monasteries. They were the first to bring copies of *libelli*, sacramentaries, *ordines*, lectionaries, antiphonals, even relics of the Roman martyrs and choir directors to teach the *cantilena romana* so they could truly replicate the "rite of the Apostolic See."

The decision by Pepin (d. 768) and Charlemagne (d. 814) to replace the chaos of the Gallican rite with what they perceived to be a fully organized and standardized liturgy from Rome simply continued the process of Romanization. It was only partially successful, however, for two reasons: (a) the reform extended only as far as real authority was able to enforce it; and (b) the papal (=stational) texts sent from Rome were incomplete and had to be supplemented with additional material drawn from the local, previously Romanized sources (i.e., the Gallicanized Gelasians of the 8th century; see Vogel, 64-105; 144-155). Even where a Roman text was complete the Frankish copyists tended to insert Gallican elements they simply refused to do without (e.g., the paschal candle and its *Exsultet*). The next two centuries saw the continued creation of a hybrid, Romano-Frankish or Romano-Germanic liturgy that, under the influence of the German emperors (962-1073), became the Roman rite in the city itself.

The hybridization of the rite did not mean the *deletion* of Roman material; it meant the addition of new material. Both the hours and the Mass became so overburdened with accretions (such as the votive offices of the dead, of all saints, and of the Blessed Virgin and the numerous *apologiae* already mentioned) that the public worship of the church became an unbearable burden. "Medieval monastic life suffered from sheer exhaustion, from overnutrition and consequent spiritual indigestion" (S.J.P. Van Dijk and J.H. Walker, *Origins of the Modern Roman Liturgy*, [Westminster, MD: Newman, 1960] pp. 16-17). In order to get its work done, the papal court had to prune back the overgrowth and practically abandon the ancient stational system of the city, producing shorter offices and less elaborate ceremonial for celebrations *in cappella* (in the papal chapel).

There is an undeniable difference in the theology of the eucharist, holy orders, and church between late antiquity when the Roman rite developed as an expression of the church of Rome gathered around its bishop and the Middle Ages with its piling up of Masses and its ordaining of priests to "offer the sacrifice

for" a multitude of intentions. The liturgical forms and *formulae*, however, though suffocated by accretions, were maintained throughout the Middle Ages "as a treasured inheritance of the liturgy, guarded as the "tradition of the Apostles from the City of the Apostles" (Vogel, p. 158).

With so many accretions to choose from, ancient local traditions to preserve, the lack of efficient means for standardization, liturgical uniformity could hardly be attempted if even conceived. For the remainder of the Middle Ages and beyond, there were enough divergences in calendars, texts, chants, and ceremonial from one diocese to the next or from one religious congregation to the next to constitute separate "rites" though technically there were countless variants or "uses" of the Roman rite; to list a few: the "Uses" of Sarum, York, Hereford, Aberdeen; the "liturgies" of Nidaros, Lyons, Rouen, Braga, Benevento, Hungary, and Jerusalem (sic); and the "rites" of the Cluniacs, Carthusians, Cistercians, Praemonstratensians, Dominicans and Franciscans. This last usage (Franciscan) is nearly identical to the abbreviated form used regularly in the papal chapel. Carrying this "papal" Mass and office on their journeys across the Alps, the friars couldn't have realized history was repeating itself. The liturgy in this form was the direct ancestor of the *Breviarium Romanum* (1568) and the *Missale Romanum* (1570) "restored by the sacred council of Trent; published by order of the supreme pontiff Pius V," and, for the first time made binding — with some reservations —on the whole Western church.

Cyrille Vogel, *Medieval Liturgy: An Introduction to the Sources*, trans. and rev. by W. G. Storey and N.K. Rasmussen, O.P. (Washington, D.C.: Pastoral Press, 1986). Richard W. Pfaff, *Medieval Latin Liturgy: A Select Bibliography* (Toronto: University of Toronto Press, 1982). Salvatore Marsili, ed., *Anamnesis 2: la Liturgia panorama storico generale* (Casale Monferrato: Casa Editrice

Marietti, 1978). Klaus Gamber, *Codices liturgici Latini antiquiores*, Spicilegii Friburgensis subsidia 1, 2 vols. (Freiburg: Universitätsverlag, 1968). Maurice Férotin, *Le Liber Ordinum en usage dans l'église wisigothique et mozarabe d'Espagne du cinquiéme au onziéme siécle*, Monumenta Ecclesiae Liturgica, 5 (Paris: Librairie de Firmin-Didot, 1904). Maurice Férotin, *Le Liber Mozarabicus Sacramentorum et les manuscrits mozarabes*, Monumenta Ecclesiae Liturgica, 6 (Paris: Librairie de Firmin-Didot, 1912). Michael Curran, M.S.C., *The Antiphonary of Bangor* (Blackrock, Ireland: Irish Academic Press, 1984). Robert Taft, S.J., *The Liturgy of the Hours in East and West: The Origins of the Divine Office and Its Meaning for Today* (Collegeville: Liturgical Press, 1986). Joseph A. Jungmann, S.J., *The Mass of the Roman Rite: Its Origin and Development*, trans. by F.A. Brunner, C.Ss.R. 2 vols. (Westminster, MD: Christian Classics, 1986). Juan Francisco Rivera, *Estudios sobre la Liturgia Mozarabe* (Toledo: Diputación Provincial, 1965). Michel Huglo, *Les Livres de chant liturgique* (Brepols: Turnhout, 1988).

JOHN K. BROOKS-LEONARD

TRINITY AND LITURGY

The doctrine of the Trinity is the specifically Christian doctrine of God. It expresses what it means to believe in the God who saves through Jesus Christ, by the power of the Holy Spirit. The purpose of trinitarian doctrine is not so much a speculative theory about the nature of God, but the explication of the meaning of God's presence in the economy of salvation as it stands in relationship to what God is from all eternity (the being of God).

The economy of salvation is God's plan for creation (*oikonomia* = plan or administration), brought about through Christ and the Spirit. Jesus Christ is the revelation of God, the visible icon of the invisible God. The Holy Spirit restores the image of God in us by conforming us to the person of Christ, thereby making each person a partaker in the divine nature ("deification" or *theosis*). According to the doctrine of the Trinity, the mystery of grace and redemption and the mystery of the triune God are to be thought of as two dimensions of one reality. Put another way, the mystery of

Christ and the Spirit and the mystery of God are one and the same mystery of love: God gives to us God's very *self*. Further, the goal of the economy of salvation, as well as the fulfillment of the human person, is nothing other than the eschatological glorification of God (cf. Eph 1:12; 2 Cor 3:18; John 17).

The primary purpose of the trinitarian confession of faith is doxology (praise of God). The doctrine of the Trinity is therefore a prime instance in which worship and doctrine are inherently bound up with each other. Since theology and liturgy are related to each other as types of doxology, we should be able to determine something about what we believe on the basis of how we pray (*lex supplicandi legem statuat credendi*; the law of prayer founds the law of belief). Consequently, the doctrine of the Trinity should function as the central doctrinal explication of what we practice daily in public prayer: the praise and glorification of God (Father) through Christ in the power of the Holy Spirit. Just as liturgy should function as a source and context for trinitarian theology, so liturgical theology and theological reflection on the liturgy should proceed within the context of the specifically Christian doctrine of God, namely, the doctrine of the Trinity.

Even if trinitarian doctrine and theology have not always played a vital role in shaping Christian thought patterns and religious consciousness, the format of Christian prayer and worship is a continual reminder that Christian faith is indeed trinitarian faith. Christian liturgy has sometimes been called "the cult of the Trinity" (*la culte de la Trinité*), not for dogmatic reasons but because its symbols, structures, and rhythms disclose the basic pattern of Christian faith: everything comes from God (Father), through Christ, in the Spirit, and everything returns to God (Father), through Christ, in the Spirit (Eph 1:3-14).

The trinitarian dimension of Christian faith is reflected both in individual sacraments and in other liturgical practices (e.g., liturgy of the hours). In one sense, *every* aspect of Christian liturgy is trinitarian —not because of the number "three" nor even because God is always named Father, Son and Spirit –but because the purpose of liturgy is to glorify the God of the *oikonomia*, the very God who is revealed through Christ and the Spirit. The trinitarian character of Christian liturgy is to be sought and located in the fact that liturgy, by definition, is the ritual celebration of the events of the economy of redemption and as such is the celebration of the mystery of God.

Four aspects of Christian liturgy deserve particular mention here: the structure of the liturgical year; the sacraments of initiation; doxologies; creeds.

Liturgical Year. The liturgical year constitutes the basic framework for the church's public prayer. Each year the Christian community re-lives the principal events of the one divine economy centered around Christ and the Spirit. The Christmas season begins with Advent and ends with the baptism of the Lord. Easter begins at Ash Wednesday and culminates with Pentecost. The remainder of the year is called ordinary time. Sunday liturgy is the principal occasion to commemorate the paschal mystery of Christ. The three-year lectionary cycle presents the important narratives of the Christian story and nourishes the memory of the Christian community. Special feastdays commemorate the lives of holy women and men, saints and martyrs, who exemplify one or another aspect of the Christian life. Other solemnities and feasts (e.g., Corpus Christi) highlight a revered theme within Christianity or a particular aspect of the life of Christ or of Mary. The liturgical year is "trinitarian" precisely in its concreteness, in the way that it binds Christian memory and ritual gesture to the events by which God comes to us in word and Spirit.

Sacraments of Initiation. Through sacraments of initiation, believers are united to the very life of God. Baptism into the threefold name of God, Father, Son and Spirit (Mt 28:19) is the primary symbol of trinitarian faith. To be baptized into the name of God means to identify with the history and presence and activity of that name, past, present and future. By "putting on Christ" we are made into a "new creation"; persons are brought into right relationship with themselves, with each other, with creation, and with God. Old patterns of alienating and unjust relationships (Jew-Greek, slave-free, male-female) are abolished; Christ is the model for the right relationships of the kingdom of God.

Baptism inaugurates the deifying work of the Spirit who perfects the image of God in us. Even though the fullness of the Spirit is bestowed at baptism, many churches administer confirmation as a separate sacrament of initiation. What is important to remember is that Christian baptism is always into Christ *and* the Spirit. A more adequate trinitarian theology and pneumatology, in which Christ and the Spirit are always seen as two essential poles in the economy of salvation, is the key to an adequate sacramental theology and pastoral practice for both baptism and confirmation.

The eucharist is a central means of participation in the trinitarian life of God. The very act of "eucharist" which means "thanksgiving" indicates the proper attitude of the Christian who acknowledges the redeeming power of God in Christ.

Many eucharistic rites open with the benediction of 2 Cor 13:13: "May the grace (and peace) of our Lord Jesus Christ, and the love of God, and the communion of the Holy Spirit, be with you all." The invocation signals that what is about to take place in the eucharist is possible only if we dwell in God and God in us. This encounter with a personal God brings about both our union with God and our communion with each other.

In the eucharistic prayer we give thanks for what God has done in salvation history, especially in Christ. Following the words of institution and the memorial acclamation, the Holy Spirit is "called down upon these gifts to make them holy" (*epiclesis*) and, in some rites, the Spirit is also called down upon the community. The eucharistic prayer ends with the *Per Ipsum*: "Through him, with him, in him, in the unity of the Holy Spirit, all glory and honor is yours, Almighty Father, both now and forever." Finally, the eucharistic celebration ends with the missionary charge to "go in peace to love and serve God." The Spirit-constituted community of the baptized, who no longer distinguish themselves from each other on the basis of race, gender or position, is charged with the mission of living out in the world its new relational life of intimacy with the God of Jesus Christ. This sending forth of each Christian reflects the eternal missions of Word and Spirit who also are sent by God to reveal God's face to the world.

Doxologies. Trinitarian doctrine developed in part in the 4th century as a solution to various theological controversies which were generated by different interpretations of Christian worship. Early doxologies directed praise to God *through* Christ the mediator (cf. Eph 5:20; 1 Cor 15:57; Col 3:17; Rom 1:8, 16:27, 7:25; 2 Cor 1:20; Heb 13:15; 1 Pet 4:11). The mediatory pattern of prayer is also found in the anaphoral portions of virtually all extant liturgical texts of the pre-Nicene church. The emphasis on the mediatory role of Christ was used by Arian theologians to support their view that Christ is inferior to God. Reciting the doxologies soon became an occasion to express doctrinal convictions. Basil (d. 374) formulated a new doxology: "to God the Father *with (meta)* the Son, *together with (sun)* the Holy Spirit." In defense of his innovation he wrote a treatise, *On the Holy Spirit.* To avoid any suggestion of Arianism, doxologies eventually followed the non-mediatory form in which Christ and the Spirit are praised together with God the Father.

Today's liturgy retains both forms of the doxology; the mediatory form is found in the *Per Ipsum*; the coordinated form is also recited: "Glory be to the Father, and to the Son, and to the Holy Spirit...." Both forms of the doxology are appropriate, provided that they enable us to direct our praise to God from whom all things come and for whom all things are destined.

Creeds. The original setting of early Christian creeds was the administration of baptism. The form of the creeds was interrogatory; the candidate for baptism was asked three questions: Do you believe in God, the Father Almighty? Do you believe in Christ Jesus, Son of God...? Do you believe in the Holy Spirit...? The triple interrogation was followed by a triple affirmation, and a triple immersion in water, all to reflect the trinitarian pattern of Christian faith. Declaratory creeds (which typically begin, "I believe in...") also display a trinitarian ground-plan, since each article of the creed focuses on one of the divine persons.

Creeds are living statements of faith whose purpose is primarily doxological and only secondarily didactic. The two creeds most commonly used in connection with baptism, the Apostles' Creed and the Nicene-Constantinopolitan Creed, are largely narratives of salvation history. The Creed was in fact called a "symbol" (*symbolum*), a sign or token reminder of the God into whose name Christians were baptized. The Nicene-Constantinopolitan Creed is now recited at the eucharist, reminding us of our trinitarian faith: in God who is source of all that is; in Jesus Christ who was born, suffered, died, was raised for our salvation and who will stand as judge over all at the end-time, in the Spirit who spoke through the prophets and whose ongoing presence is associated with the life of the church, who is now leading us through Christ back to God.

In sum, the connection between "Trinity and liturgy" is rooted above all in the economy of salvation. The God we praise is God who comes to us in Christ and the Spirit. The purpose of the doctrine is to articulate the meaning and nature of the God who comes to us in Christ and the Spirit.

See **Baptism; Doxology; Creed, praying the**

CATHERINE MOWRY LaCUGNA

TRINITY SUNDAY

The Feast of Trinity Sunday is celebrated on the first Sunday after Pentecost (in the Byzantine rite the Feast of the Trinity is Pentecost Sunday). Although the Feast of Trinity Sunday was initially resisted by Rome, several elements of the feast predate its formal institution in 1334.

History of the Feast. In the Gelasian Sacramentay (8th cent.) are found the preface and collect which later became part of the Mass for that day (A. Chavasse, *Le Sacramentaire Gélasien* [Tournai, 1958] 254-262). This preface was probably drawn up in the 5th century, in a Roman milieu, under the influence of Leo the Great. There are three versions of the preface, one Roman and two Mozarabic; the Roman version is the original. The preface is primarily doctrinal and abstract, focusing on the inner relations among Father, Son and Spirit.

At the end of the 8th century Alcuin composed a votive Mass for the Trinity (*Liber Sacramentorum*, P.L. 150,445).

Stephen, Bishop of Liege (903-920), wrote a complete office for the Sunday after Pentecost. This Sunday had been a *Dominica vacat* (no special office existed), since the preceding Saturday was ordination day. Stephen's move was resisted by Rome. Pope Alexander II (d. 1073) refused the petition for a special feast and remarked that the Roman church daily honored the Trinity in psalmody and in the *Gloria Patri*. The feast was rejected also by Bernhold of Constance (d. 1100) in the *Micrologies* (*Micrologus*). Subsequent popes were also opposed to the feast, but in 1251 Pope Innocent IV visited Trinity church in Krahan and authorized an indulgence of 400 days for observing the feast. The Synod of Arles adopted the feast in 1260; the Order of Citeaux also adopted it in 1271, as Cluny had earlier. A new office had been composed by John Peckam, Canon of Lyons and later Archbishop of Canterbury (d. 1292). In 1334, during his exile in Avignon, Pope John XXII approved the feast and extended it to the whole church.

Trinity Sunday had been a double of the second class but was raised to a primary of the first class by Pius X in 1911. Trinity Sunday is known as an "idea feast," since it commemorates not an event in salvation history but a particular aspect of doctrine. The reform of the liturgy reduced the number of idea feasts, showing a preference for more event-centered feastdays. Trinity Sunday remains one of the nine solemnities of the church calendar, along with Corpus Christi (estab. in 1264), Sacred Heart of Jesus (1856), Holy Family (1921), Christ the King (1925), Motherhood of Mary (1931), Immaculate Conception (1863), Assumption (1950), Joseph, Husband of Mary (14th cent.).

Cycle of Readings. From the 10th century until the introduction of the three-year lectionary cycle, the readings for Trinity Sunday in the *Missale Romanum* were Rom 11:33-36 and Mt

28:18-20. Today, the readings for Cycle A are Exod 34:4-6, 8-9; 2 Cor 13:11-13; Jn 3:16-18; for Cycle B, Deut 4:32-34, 39-40; Rom 8:14-17; Mt 28:16-20; for Cycle C, Prov 8:22-31; Rom 5:15; Jn 16:12-15.

Preaching on Trinity Sunday. The new cycle of readings provides a rich source for homilies on Trinity Sunday. The focus should be the mystery of redemption by God through Christ in the power of the Holy Spirit, as well as its consequences for Christian life. Preachers need not use the technical language of dogma (e.g., *hypostasis*) nor is it necessarily desirable to explain particular trinitarian theories, even those of Augustine and the church councils. Since liturgy is the ritual celebration of the events of the economy of salvation, preaching on Trinity Sunday should concentrate on the concrete reality of grace and divine love in the economy of salvation.

_____

A. Adam, *The Liturgical Year* (New York: Pueblo, 1981). F. Cabrol, "Le Culte de la Trinité dans la liturgie de la fête de la Trinité," *Ephemerides Liturgicae* 45 (1931): 270-278. L.-A. Gignac, "Etude liturgique. La préface de la Trinité," *Fête de la Sainte Trinité*, in *Assemblées du Seigneur* 53 (1970): 7-12. C.M. LaCugna, "Making the Most of Trinity Sunday," *Worship* 60 (1986): 210-224.

CATHERINE MOWRY LACUGNA

V

VALIDITY, SACRAMENTAL

The term *valid*, when applied to a sacrament, names both its truth, authenticity and effectiveness in itself and its recognition as true, authentic and effective by the church. Sacramental validity is therefore both a theological reality and a canonical judgment.

The theological reality is determined by the mystery of Jesus Christ. As such, it is not historically conditioned, except insofar as Jesus Christ is himself, by the incarnation, an element in human history. True sacraments continue the incarnation of Christ. The canonical judgment, on the other hand, is made by the church in light of its understanding of the mystery of Christ, an understanding that can shift and grow over time. Because the canonical judgment is determined by human understanding of the mystery of Christ, it is subject to historical variation.

Since the *Constitution on the Sacred Liturgy* maintains that all liturgy "expresses the mystery of Christ" (S.C., 2), the church must determine the validity of sacraments to the extent that they truly express, or fail to express, this mystery. Yet, since the mystery itself can be variously understood at different periods of the church's life, its judgment of validity will always be subject to change. Witness, for just two examples, the redefinition of essentials in the current reform in regard to ordination (the laying on of hands rather than the assignment of instruments of office) and confirmation (the adoption of the Eastern form of prayer, "N., be sealed with the gift of the Holy Spirit," in preference to the classic Western form, "I sign you with the sign of the cross and anoint you with the chrism of salvation..."). Such changes are not arbitrary; they reflect a deeper understanding of the Christ mystery itself. As Paul VI announced in his *Apostolic Constitution on the Sacrament of Confirmation* (1971): "As regards the words which are pronounced in confirmation, we have examined with due consideration the dignity of the venerable formula used in the Latin Church, but we judge preferable the very ancient formula belonging to the Byzantine rite, by which the Gift of the Holy Spirit himself is expressed and the outpouring of the Spirit which took place on the day of Pentecost is recalled (see Acts 2:1-4, 38). We therefore adopt this formula, rendering it almost word for word."

A.-G. Martimort advises that "an act is valid that has been truly carried out, that does not have to be repeated, and that is in itself capable of producing its proper effects" (*The Signs of the New Covenant*, Collegeville: Liturgical Press, 1963, p. 42, n. 14). He goes on to say that the sign must be "effectively constituted" in such a way that the sacramental grace is *offered* (*res et sacramentum*) even if it is not, due to some defect on the part of the recipient, freely received (*res*). The determining factor for validity on the part of the church is the presentation through sacramental signs of the saving grace of Christ to one who is capable of receiving that grace.

Vatican II noted that "it (the liturgy) involves the presentation of man's sanctification under the guise of signs perceptible to the senses and its accomplishment in ways appropriate to each of these signs" (S.C., 7). The liturgical reform which the council set in motion was determined that "both texts and rites should be drawn up so as to express more clearly the holy things which they signify" (S.C., 21). "The rites should be distinguished by a noble simplicity. They should be short, clear, and free from useless repetitions. They should be within the people's powers of comprehension, and normally should not require much explanation" (S.C., 34). This concern for clear signification was the practical outcome of the theological concern that the mystery of Christ be honestly expressed and his saving grace be truly and effectively presented.

It is probably the case that the sharp line drawn between *valid* and *invalid* is no longer the most helpful way to assess the truth or untruth of sacraments. Both are minimalist judgments: either the essentials are there or not. They are also judgments which presume we can have a clear understanding of what the essentials are. That is in fact not as easy as might ordinarily be assumed. Nonetheless, even where the essentials are judged to be present, there is a large spectrum of sacramental truth that stretches between the "bare necessities," and the full liturgical action envisioned by Vatican II. Minimalist judgments are not adequate to the Vatican II liturgical reform.

On the other hand, even where the essentials are judged not to be present, it is difficult to dismiss the act as empty and without sacramental value; defective, perhaps, but not without value. The judgment of invalidity implicit in marriage annulment, for example, is proving pastorally problematic to many who find it far more truthful to their experience to say that their marriage died or fell apart than that it never existed in the first place. Similarly, especially in this ecumenical era, the Roman Catholic judgment that Anglican orders are "null and void" (Leo XIII), or the Orthodox judgment that Catholic confirmation is ineffective, rings more untrue than true. It may be proper for Roman Catholics to re-ordain priests who come to the Roman church from Anglicanism, and it may be proper for Orthodox to chrismate (confirm) Roman Catholics who enter Orthodoxy, but this could be done for reasons other than that the original ordination or confirmation was null and void. Repetition does not necessarily indicate original invalidity.

Vatican II did in fact retreat from the clear and harsh judgments of earlier days. With regard to realities within other churches, and in its desire to promote Christian unity, rather than stall or hinder it, the council advised that every effort be taken "to avoid expressions, judgments and actions which do not represent the condition of our separated brethren with truth and fairness" (U.R., 4). And with regard to its own sacramental life, it set down norms for adaptation, versatility and development that potentially, at least, could give the "essentials" so many ritual faces that it will be discovered that the "essentials" are not linked to any specific ritual form (see, Amaladoss).

Nonetheless, the church does have both the right and the responsibility to make judgments, however historically conditioned they might be, that "this act" is in conformity with the truth of Christ and "that act" is not. Such judgment is important for people; it is important for a proper unfolding of a healthy liturgical life. What is required, however, for this judgment to be made with gospel integrity, is that the church stand humbly before Christ's truth, especially as that truth may manifest itself in the lives of those whose actions are called into question, and pass such judgment softly and tentatively, and only with the deep desire that the mystery of Christ be truly expressed and the mission of Christ be sacramentally set forth and effectively accomplished.

See **Law, liturgical; Sacraments**

Michael Amaladoss, *Do Sacraments Change?* (Bangalore: Theological Publications in India, 1979). Karl Rahner, "The Abiding Significance of Vatican II," in *Theological Investigations* (II)XX (New York: Crossroad, 1981): 90-102. Karl Rahner, "What is a Sacrament?", in II XIV (New York: Seabury, 1976): 135-148.

PETER E. FINK, S.J.

VATICAN II, LITURGICAL REFORM OF

See **Reform, liturgical of Vatican II; Documents, Roman liturgical, since Vatican II**

VESSELS, SACRED

Receptacles which contain elements used in Christian worship can be called sacred vessels. They are considered sacred because they are set aside for the worship of God. Some Christian denominations require particular blessing prayers by an ordained minister as part of a ritual signification of these vessels as sacred.

Some of the many vessels used in Christian worship are: the chalice, paten, ciborium, pyx, monstrance, censer, cruets, aspergillum, ambry, tabernacle, reliquary, etc.

Chalice

The word *chalice* is derived from the Latin term *calix* which means cup. This sacred vessel is the only one explicitly mentioned in each of the four scriptural accounts of the Lord's Supper. Evidence suggests that the form of the chalice probably developed from the cup of Aegean culture. One could reasonably suppose that the cup which Jesus used at the Supper was the ordinary two-handled cup in use at the time in that part of the world. In which case it would have been derived from the Roman drinking bowl and the two-handled cup of the Greeks. This style of chalice can be seen today in the mosaics at San Vitale in Ravenna, dating from at least the 6th century, as well as at St. Mark's in Venice.

From the early days of Christianity chalices were fashioned from various materials: wood, glass, horn, gold, copper, silver. During the first Christian millennium, persistent efforts were made to retain the use of common substances in the design of chalices. Not only was there a need to respect the limits of poorer worshipping communities, but also a recurring desire to avoid the appearance of luxury. For example, St. Clement of Alexandria (3rd century) vigorously opposed the use of precious stones, gold and silver. Sts. Chrysostom and Ambrose (4th century) and Boniface (8th century) also spoke out in this regard. There were numerous stories of saints who melted their chalices and gave the proceeds to the poor, for instance, Sts. Lawrence, Augustine, Gregory, Hilary of Arles, Exupere.

While poorer materials were frequently used in chalices, there was a tendency from the beginning to use precious substances for vessels designed for the most significant act of worship in the Christian life. This tendency was especially evident with the legal and consequent popular recognition of Christianity by Emperor Constantine, who furthered the impetus toward the use of precious metals such as gold and silver and the use of precious gems and other substances for ornamentation. From at least the 8th and 9th centuries the church prohibited substances other than the precious metals of gold or at least silver. For example, the Council of Calchyth (787) forbade the use of horn and Leo IV (847) and later the Council of Tribur (897) forbade the use of wood and glass.

Sometimes chalices were designed of such size and weight that they were intended to be positioned near the altar for decoration and not for use during a eucharist. The gold chalices given by Charlemagne at his coronation exemplify this custom.

Two additional kinds of chalices were used in the early medieval period in the Western church: the ministerial chalice (*calix ministerialis*) and the offering chalice (*calix offertorialis*). The former was a cup usually with two handles for distribution of eucharistic wine to the entire assembly; the latter was a larger cup into which the assembly poured their contributions of wine. The chalice used for consecration was smaller since it was used for communion of the presider. Since by the 9th century communion of the laity was no longer the customary practice, only the chalice of the priest remained.

Emphasis upon ornamentation of the chalice continued through the High Middle Ages, Renaissance and Baroque periods. Distinctive styles developed in various regions of the world, while almost always maintaining the common shape (base, knob and bowl). With the Reformation, the recovered emphasis upon participation of the laity in the eucharist modified the chalice to provide once again for the communion of all who worshipped in the reformed Christian traditions. Due to the English Reformation, even the name of *chalice* was modified to the *communion cup* for denominations who followed this Christian tradition.

In the reform of liturgy in the Roman Catholic church since the Second Vatican Council, the design of the chalice deserves special care. It should be made of high quality material and capable of bearing mystery so as to communicate the central significance of this symbol. While precious metals are often used in chalices, they are not required for them (not even gold-plated lining for the cup). Reception of both the eucharistic bread and wine at Mass is recommended as the fuller expression and cultivation of the primary symbolic actions of eating and drinking at the table of the Lord. Therefore a chalice large enough for the entire assembly or a flagon of wine which is poured into additional cups/chalices during the fraction rite is preferable at each eucharist. The number and the design of these cups depends on the size and the cultural sensibilities of the assembly. Duplication of symbols is discouraged as well as any design or decoration which impedes the renewed emphasis upon the action of the assembly.

Paten

The word *paten* comes from the Greek word *patane* meaning dish or plate. This vessel used in Christian worship is the container for the bread at the celebration of the eucharist. It is likely that Jesus used the ordinary domestic vessel of the time for the bread at the Lord's Supper. The early centuries of Christians used patens of various sizes and shapes, but many were large and deep so that they could contain the loaves of bread brought by those who arrived for worship. Like the chalice, it is probable that there were two types of patens —one for the presider and one for distribution to the assembly at communion. Blue molten glass seems to have been a customary material for many early patens. For instance St. Zephyrinus (3rd century) prescribed a glass paten with handles. Also St. Caesarius (6th century) justifies his selling of some sacred vessels made of precious metal by saying that Jesus was content to use a dish of glass.

Following the conversion of Constantine, there was a growing emphasis upon the use of precious metals and other valued materials. For example, in the *Liber Pontificalis* (a collection of early papal biographies) some patens are described as being made of silver and gold and bordered with precious stones and pearls. Medieval patens varied in design and decoration from one region to another. By the 9th century, the reception of communion by the entire assembly became infrequent. In addition, the Western church required the use of wafer bread rather than leavened bread by the end of the 9th century. These factors affected the consequent size of the paten. The circular shape with a wide rim and a depression in the center was customary and eventually regulated.

The Reformation restored regular reception of the eucharistic bread by all, including the laity. In England the use of leavened bread was reintroduced. These developments required the redesign of a communion plate (paten) which could contain enough eucharistic bread for all the assembly to receive.

Early in the 20th century Roman Catholics were also encouraged to receive communion frequently. The Roman Catholic liturgical reformation since the Second Vatican Council recommended that Catholics use bread that looks and tastes more like food. Since this could well involve larger quantities of bread than hosts, the size of patens/dishes/baskets has varied depending upon the size of the assembly. In all cases, high quality materials and artistic expression capable of bearing mystery are the norm.

Ciborium

This Christian worship vessel contains bread to be consecrated at eucharist or bread already consecrated from a previous eucharist. The origin of the word is debated. Some say the etymology of this Latin term refers to a Byzantine canopy over an altar; some say it emanates from the Latin *cibus* meaning food. The ciborium developed from the pyx in the 13th century. It would be used in addition to a paten if the amount of communion bread needed for a service was more than the paten could hold. This is the way ciboria are used today.

In addition to its original purpose, the ciborium was used to reserve some of the eucharistic bread for use outside the eucharistic celebration. At first this reserved consecrated bread was used to bring communion to those who could not worship with the gathered assembly, for example, the dying and seriously ill. Later the reserved sacrament in the ciborium was also used as an object of veneration. By at least the 12th century, ciboria were sometimes suspended in accord with the custom of protecting food.

As mentioned earlier, reception of communion became infrequent. Eucharistic bread previously consecrated and reserved in a ciborium was used for distribution of communion to the assembly at Mass. The size of many ciboria was large and the shape often resembled a cup with a lid. Often this cup and lid were decorated with lavish ornamentation. This size and shape of ciboria perdured until the Reformers eliminated this practice of distributing communion from a previous eucharist. Likewise the Roman Catholic church has discouraged this practice since her contemporary liturgical renewal, with the result that the size and shape of ciboria vary depending primarily upon the needs of the worshipping assembly.

Pyx

The word *pyx* comes from the Greek *puxis* meaning wooden box and the Latin *pyxis* meaning a small box. The pyx is a Christian worship vessel which contains some of the consecrated bread from a eucharist. The original purpose for the vessel was to contain communion to be brought to those who could not gather for eucharist due to sickness, bitter persecution, imprisonment, etc. This custom is described as early as the middle of the 2nd century by Justin Martyr in his Apology I. 65. By the later Middles Ages the term *pyx* also began to designate a receptacle for a large host which was placed in a monstrance for veneration.

Originally the pyx was made of wood, glass, enamel, ivory, metals, parchment or linen. Today the pyx (for carrying the eucharistic bread) is frequently made of metal, but various other materials are used as well. The pyx for a monstrance contains at least a facade of glass in order to view the host easily.

Monstrance

This Christian worship vessel was designed in response to the devotion to the Blessed Sacrament which spread in the later Middle Ages. The veneration of the eucharist in the closed ciborium gave way to a monstrance so that the host could be seen. Another name for the monstrance is ostensorium, from the Latin *ostentare* meaning to display. The development of the personal devotion to the consecrated host came to calendrical expression in the 14th-century Feast of Corpus Christi. The monstrance with the host was carried in procession as well as prominently positioned in the church for veneration in special services. These services developed into benediction or exposition of the Blessed Sacrament, as this liturgy is also called.

Censer

This Christian worship vessel which is used to incense people, places and things is sometimes called a thurible, from the Latin *thus*, meaning incense. The use of incense in worship antedates Christianity. When it was introduced into Christian worship in the 4th century, Christians used the same kind of vessel, usually clay pots or metal pots with perforated lids (by the Middle Ages), and sometimes with a chain for swinging. Since the 12th

century an accompanying vessel shaped something like a boat was called by the Latin terms *navis* or *navicula*, meaning ship or skiff.

Cruets

These two vessels used in Christian worship contain the wine and water to be used in the celebration of a eucharist. The term comes from the medieval French term *cruette* meaning a little jug. They are made of many materials, e.g., glass, metal, clay, ceramic, etc. During the High Middle Ages and well into the 17th and 18th centuries the design of some cruets was richly ornamented, yet with the intent of not competing in importance with the chalice and paten. Some of the Reformers wanted cruets eliminated from the celebration of Mass; some wanted their design simplified. In the recent Roman Catholic liturgical reformation, little is expressed other than that their quality and appropriate design convey the importance of the ritual action being celebrated.

Aspergillum

Derived from the Latin word *aspergere* which means to spray or to sprinkle, this vessel is used in Christian worship to sprinkle the assembly with water to remind all of their baptism. This container is either filled from the baptismal font or filled before a ceremony and then blessed during it.

The origins of an *asperges* rite are clouded. Psalm 50 and Ezekiel 47 seem to indicate a pre-Christian ritual sprinkling. The early Christian writings about the celebration of the paschal vigil contain a blessing of the baptismal waters and consequent contact with the water. It is probable that the custom of a Sunday *asperges* rite developed from the medieval practice of blessing the monastery on that day. Currently in the reformed Roman Catholic liturgy, the sprinkling of the assembly, reminiscent of baptism, is the first option presented for the introductory rites in order to help the assembly gather and to prepare them to hear the word of God and celebrate eucharist.

Ambry

The term for this Christian worship object is derived from the Latin *armarium* meaning a cupboard or chest. This is a special place to hold materials used in Christian worship, such as oils, consecrated bread from a eucharist, etc. The ambry could be a niche in a wall or a cupboard or, as early as the 6th century, we find evidence that ambries were placed in the base of altars. Sometimes the ambry had a door or doors, sometimes not. By the early 13th century, Innocent III decreed that eucharistic ambries must be locked. With the increase of devotion to the eucharist, these ambries were eventually placed in more prominent locations in the church. The eucharistic ambry developed into the tabernacle by the 16th century. Currently an ambry is sometimes used as a special cupboard for the oils used in the celebration of sacraments.

Tabernacle

Derived from the Latin *tabernaculum* meaning tent, this Christian vessel recalls the Jewish "meeting tent" which housed the Ark and was believed to embody the presence of God among people. The Christian tabernacle contains the consecrated bread from a eucharist. This term was introduced by Bishop Matthew Giberti of Verona in 1525 and ratified by the Council of Trent. Reserving some of the eucharist for those who could not attend the actual celebration of eucharist, for example, for the sick and the imprisoned, was a custom since the early church. Between the 2nd and 4th centuries Justin, Tertullian, Cyprian and Basil have frequent references. Sometimes the eucharist was kept in the sacristy; sometimes in the church in a fixed ambry or in a pyx shaped as a casket, tower, or dove, which could be taken to those who could not attend.

Even though reception of communion became infrequent during the Middle Ages, devotion to the eucharist grew. A reverence for the eucharist culminated in the establishment of the feast of Corpus Christi in the 14th century. By the 16th century, reserving some previously consecrated eucharist on the main altar in a fixed tabernacle became customary. The general prescription appeared in the 1614 Roman Ritual.

Today the normative guideline of the Roman Catholic church is that the tabernacle rest upon a pillar or in a niche, but not upon the altar where the eucharistic action takes place. The tabernacle should be dignified and properly ornamented, but no specific materials are required for its construction. As has been the custom for centuries, a lamp should burn continuously near the tabernacle to indicate the presence of the consecrated eucharist.

Reliquary

This Christian worship object contains relics. The earliest reliquaries contained fragments of Jesus' cross, which reportedly was found in the 4th century. These receptacles took a variety of shapes: caskets, crosses, rings, boxes, buildings, ampullae, shapes of parts of the body, encolpia, etc., and they were made of precious materials of every kind, especially metals. During the Middle Ages a popular devotion to revere a piece of the body of a saint (sometimes the entire body) or the saint's clothing became customary. During the later Middle Ages the monstrance also carried relics to embellish the ritual exposition of the Blessed Sacrament. The design and ornamentation of reliquaries vary considerably depending upon the period and country.

The Reformers found the emphasis upon devotion to the saints intolerable. In the recent liturgical reform of the

Roman Catholic church, reliquaries continue to afford a respected place among objects used in Christian worship, but they are never to be placed upon the altar or even set into the table of the altar.

National Conference of Catholic Bishops, *Environment and Art in Catholic Worship* (Washington: United States Catholic Conference Publications, 1978). F.L. Cross and E.A. Livingston, *The Oxford Dictionary of the Christian Church* (Oxford: Oxford University Press, 1978). A.A. King and C.E. Pocknee, *Eucharistic Reservation in the Western Church* (London: Mowbray 1965). H. Kaufmann et al., *Eucharistic Vessels of the Middle Ages* (Cambridge: Busch-Reisinger Museum, 1975). J. Hazelden-Walker, "Reflections on the Earliest Vessels Used for Transportation of the Reserved Sacrament," *Studia Liturgica* 16:3-4 (1986-1987): 93-103. J. Hazelden-Walker, "Reservation Vessels in the Earliest Roman Liturgy," *Studia Patristica* 15:1 (1984): 568-572. J. Huels, "Trent and the Chalice: Forerunner of Vatican II?" *Worship* 56:5 (1982): 386-400.

T. JEROME OVERBECK, S.J.

VESTMENTS, LITURGICAL

Just as any clothing manifests the person who wears it, so likewise does the church in the liturgy disclose its inner mystery through the wearing of special, liturgical vestments. An understanding of the liturgy therefore necessarily includes some knowledge of the history and meaning of liturgical clothing. The purpose of this article, then, is to outline the (1) historical origins and development, (2) use of colors, and (3) theological meaning of the major vestments of the Roman rite.

I. Origins and Development

Scholars agree that in the first centuries of Christianity liturgical clothing in no way differed in form from that worn by people in ordinary life. When it did differ, it did so only in quality of material and/or in cleanliness. Thus Clement of Alexandria (d. ca. 215) calls for clothes that are both clean and bright. And Jerome (d. 420) states, "We ought not to enter into the holy of holies in our everyday garments, just as we please,

when they have become defiled from the use of ordinary life, but with a clean conscience and in clean garments hold in our hands the sacraments of the Lord" (In Ezek 44:17ff.).

If every Christian in the early church was expected to celebrate in clean, bright garments, even more so did bishops, presbyters and deacons "dress up" for the liturgy. Origen (d. 253) states that the bishop wears one set of clothes in "the ministry of the sacrifices" and another when he moves out among his people (*In Lev. hom.* 4.6). Jerome adds that it does not dishonor God—rather, just the opposite—if clerics at the liturgy wear white tunics more handsome than normal (*Adv. Pelag.*, 1.4). The Canons of Hippolytus prescribe that the ordained and the lectors "be dressed in white vestments more beautiful than the rest of the people" (Can. 37). Such garments were normally made of whitened linen, the fabric the OT prescribes for high priestly vestments (Lev 16:4). On the other hand, since the Bible links death to sin, writers such as Jerome and Augustine argued that furs or hides, taken from dead animals, ought not be used in the liturgy. In fact, even wool, because it comes from a mortal animal, was sometimes avoided.

Although church leaders in the early church were repeatedly encouraged to place more importance on adorning their souls with noble virtues than their bodies with precious clothing, two factors especially led to the establishment of a special kind of liturgical garb. The first factor was the Roman legalization of Christianity in the 4th century when the Emperor Constantine honored bishops on the level of civil magistrates. Senatorial sandals, the dalmatic and the ceremonial pallium all became signs of their office. The second factor was a dramatic shift in the style of men's secular clothing during the 5th and 6th centuries. When Germanic tribes invaded Rome, they brought their custom of wearing trousers, a type of clothing dictated by harsher northern climates. Although the clergy adapted to the times, yet, as normally happens in festive situations across all cultures, at the celebration of the liturgy church leaders continued to wear their traditional clothes. Later there developed the additional practice, as recorded by the synod of Narbonne in 589, of wearing liturgical vestments *over* one's ordinary clothes. Consequently, most of today's liturgical vestments can still trace a direct lineage back to the everyday clothing of imperial Rome.

A. *Alb*. Ancient Mediterranean clothing could be categorized into two basic types: (1) clothes that one "puts on" (*indumenta*), and (2) clothes that one "wraps around" (*amictus*) the body. For the Greeks the first type—vertical, form-fitting clothing—expressed the bodily, material part of the human being. The second type, circling the body around the head as its focal point, symbolized the human being's spiritual transcendence to a merely physical world.

An example of the first type of clothing, the alb ("white") derives from the old Roman *tunica*. Itself a descendent of the classical Greek *chitôn*, the tunic originated as a rectangular piece of woolen fabric wrapping horizontally around the body and reaching to the knees. It was girded at the waist and held by clasps from each shoulder. In time, first the open side and then the shoulder-joints were either woven or sewn together, leaving openings for the head and arms. The Roman *tunica talaris* was the longer version of the same garment reaching down to the feet.

As is evidenced in Christian catacomb frescoes and mosaic art, the Romans overcame the visual monotony of the tunic's solid light color with two vertically parallel reddish or purple stripes called *clavi*, i.e., "spikes." These stripes, whether woven into or sewn onto the tunic, ran top to bottom, front and back, over each shoulder. Some scholars conjecture that the liturgical stole developed as an extension of this ancient ornamentation.

In general the Romans disdained sleeves, a characteristic to them of barbarian clothing, but in 270 the Emperor Aurelian broke down this resistance by presenting the sleeved tunic (*tunica manicata*) to his friends. This modification completed the basic form of today's liturgical alb (*tunica alba*).

With the renewed practice of concelebration and a greater differentiation of ministries in the liturgy since Vatican II, the alb has developed toward two separate styles: (1) the wider, traditional *undergarment*, gathered at the waist with a cincture, to be worn beneath the dalmatic, chasuble or cope; and (2) the heavier, more elegant *outer-garment*, without cincture but hanging in straight vertical folds, with full sleeves and a close-fitting collar, to be worn as *the* external garment.

B. *Dalmatic*. In the late 2nd century another version of the tunic, the dalmatic (*tunica dalmatica*), was introduced from Dalmatia. Originally a calf-length fine woolen tunic, worn without cincture and with wide, generous sleeves, the dalmatic was despised at first because of its sleeves. But when the emperor Heliogabulus (218-222) entered Rome in triumph dressed in a dalmatic, it became popular among the senatorial class. Eusebius (d. 340) states that bishop Cyprian of Carthage (d. 258) before his martyrdom removed both an outer mantle and the dalmatic he wore over an underlying linen tunic (*linea*) (*Eccl. Hist.*, IV, 2). By the 4th century, as signs of their office, civil magistrates were arrayed in fine quality dalmatics of silk, wool or a mixture of the two (*subserica*). Constantine also granted this honor to major Christian bishops. The *Liber Pontificalis* states that Pope Sylvester (314-335) began the practice of conferring dalmatics on papal deacons as well. Three centuries later, in the time of Gregory the Great (590-604), the dalmatic, worn under the chasuble, remained a privilege of the pope, which he bestowed sometimes on other archbishops, but which normally he reserved to himself and to his deacons at Rome (see *Ep. ex Reg.* 3.2). Only in the 11th century was it definitively prescribed as a liturgical garment for all bishops and deacons. In later times, made heavy and thick with rich ornamentation, the dalmatic sometimes exchanged its sleeves for shoulder pieces, and left open slits on the sides for easier vesting and movement. The dalmatic today is the characteristic outer vestment for deacons alone and ought to be worn at all Sunday and feast day liturgical celebrations.

C. Pallium. From at least the 6th century B.C. onwards the *himation* was worn by Greek men. This was an oblong piece of clothing, approximately 6 by 18 feet, draped from front to back over the left shoulder, around and under the right arm, across the front and then over the left arm, leaving the right arm free. Whereas most men wore the *himation* over a *chitôn*, philosophers and thinkers marked the divine simplicity of their lives by wearing it as their only outer garment. In the Roman world the *himation* was called the *pallium* (= "a cut of cloth"?). Because of its association with humility and holiness, Tertullian (d. ca. 220) argued that the pallium signified Christ, and therefore was more befitting for Christians than the pretentious Roman toga (*De Pallio*, 6; C.C. 2:750).

Early catacomb art attests to its popularity among Christians. In fact, throughout history Christ himself has regularly been pictured wearing the ancient pallium. In ordinary life, however, by the 4th and 5th centuries the pallium was replaced by the even more practical *tunica dalmatica* and *paenula*. It survived briefly in Roman society no longer as functional clothing, but only as an ornamental insignia, shrunken to a narrow woolen band draped from left front to back and looped once again around the neck. This ceremonial pallium was used to indicate high civil office, and so Constantine granted it to bishops of major sees as well. The *Liber Pontificalis* records that Pope Mark (d. 336) signified his pre-eminence among church authorities in the West by conferring the pallium on his suffragan, the bishop of Ostia.

Early on, the pope bestowed the pallium only on especially notable bishops of major sees (e.g., Arles, Ravenna), but by the 9th century all Latin rite archbishops and metropolitans were allowed to wear it within their own domains as a sign of their pastoral office. Explaining the wool pallium on the shoulders of the bishop as the lost sheep carried by "a type of Christ," Isidore of Pelusium (ca. 412) introduced a liturgical mystagogy which has survived to this day (*Epp.* 1.136). From this symbolism arose the tradition that pallia be woven by the nuns of St. Cecilia's convent in Rome from pure white wool taken from blessed lambs. A series of six purple crosses were later added, making more explicit the symbolic connection between the pallium on the shoulders of the church's pastor and the "sweet yoke" of Christ's cross. By the 10th century the pallium was given the double front and back Y-shape it has today, having the tips of its pendants weighted down with lead and covered in black silk.

In the past some confusion about the history of the pallium resulted from the fact that during the 5th and 6th centuries this same name was also used to denote the ascetical rough garment worn by Christian monks in imitation of John the Baptist. Thus when certain bishops in southern France began wearing the *pallium*, it was to this episcopal affectation of monastic virtue that Pope Celestine (d. 432) so strongly objected: "Why should the customary clothing worn by great bishops over many years be discarded for this garb? What ought to distinguish us from the laity and everyone else is right teaching, not garments; probity of life, not what we wear; purity of mind, not status symbols" (P.L. 67:274). Consequently, instead of objecting to the ceremonial pallium, Pope Celestine actually intends that his fellow bishops continue to wear such traditional clothing of good quality when celebrating the liturgy.

D. *Chasuble, Cope.* The chasuble, the outer liturgical vestment worn today by both bishops and priests, originated from the ancient Greco-Roman *paenula* (etym. unkn.). Popular among the lower classes, the paenula was an enveloping, poncho-like outdoor garment that reached down around the calves. It was normally made of skins or of rough, dark wool. For protection against the cold, the paenula might also include a cap (*cucullus*), either sewn on in the form of a cowl or completely detachable with long tabs to be wrapped around the neck for warmth. Constructed from more or less a semi-circle of material, the paenula gathered around the body in a funnel-like, conical shape, and was either sewn together or left open in the front. The narrower, sewn paenula was known also as the *casula* (= chasuble), that is, "little house." When left open, it formed a cape-like garment, sometimes called the *pluviale* ("rain cape"), the probable origin of today's liturgical cope (*cappa* = "hooded mantle"). A larger paenula, the *amphibalus*, was made from up to a full circle of material (thus explaining how St. Martin of Tours could divide his cloak, give half [*capella*] to a beggar and still have enough to keep himself warm).

The paenula normally had no sleeves or arm-openings. Consequently, in order to handle anything the wearer of the closed paenula had to reach down on both sides until the hands became free. This action resulted in having extra material falling in beautiful, but heavy folds from each arm. To allow easier, less-encumbered use of the arms, the material used in later liturgical chasubles was sometimes cut back on the right side, often on both sides, or even in the front (e.g., the Eastern rite *phelōnion*). With these variations the once circular hemline now rose up and down around the person, inspiring Greek Christians, and later Latins as well, to call the chasuble "*planeta*," i.e., "wanderer" (See Isidore, *De Orig.*, 19.21). By the 4th century the chasuble became one's normal outer clothing both within and outside of the liturgy. The earliest evidence that it was required for bishops and priests comes from the 4th Council of Toledo (633). When in the Middle Ages the laity no longer understood liturgical Latin and the presider through most of the liturgy faced away from the people, the back of the chasuble was often decorated with symbols and images to provide a visual explanation of the sacred rites. From the 13th century onward, therefore, owing to its rich brocades and encrustations, sometimes the stiffness of the material so impeded the wearer's arm movements, especially at the elevation of the host, that both sides of the garment had to be reduced back to the shoulders. What resulted throughout Europe, along with the continued use of lighter, fuller chasubles, were national varieties of the sandwich-board vestment known today as the "Roman" chasuble.

In the 19th century a hybrid of the two styles was created by extending material down the arms from the shoulders of a "Roman" type, forming a chasuble mistakenly called "Gothic." It was so named in the belief that this style stemmed from what was considered to be that most authentic of all periods in church history (Sutfin, 86). With the return by Vatican II to early liturgical sources, chasubles in recent times have been fashioned as real clothing once again, reclaiming the shape of the ancient *planeta*.

Today the chasuble remains the vestment proper to the bishop and priest celebrant at the Mass and at other rites immediately connected with the Mass. However, concelebrating priests are allowed for sufficient reason to wear only an alb and a stole (G.I.R.M., 161). The chasuble may replace the cope (1) during the sprinkling with holy water before Sunday Mass, (2) for the distribution of ashes at the beginning of Lent and (3) while performing the funeral absolution. Furthermore, the chasuble is to be worn *over* the alb and the stole (G.I.R.M., 299). The contrary practice of draping a large stole (sometimes even imitating the archbishop's yoked pallium) over the chasuble is not only a redundant sign of presbyteral office, but it obscures the noble simplicity and focusing function of the chasuble itself.

Recent attempts to simplify liturgical clothing have resulted in combinations of alb and chasuble forms in a single vestment. Thus, the "chasuble alb" has become popular. This extra wide alb is made normally of heavier material and has extended sleeves that droop in imitation of the falling lines of a chasuble. The "alb chasuble," on the other hand, begins with the chasuble form but is fashioned from the white, light material of the traditional alb. To be worn beneath properly colored stoles, these combinations are permitted for (1) concelebrating priests and (2) presiders at "Masses for particular groups" or when some other pastoral situation might warrant it (*Notitiae* 9:96-98). Because they reduce two traditional vestments into one, their regular use by the presider weakens the liturgy's symbol system, fostering a liturgical minimalism. Therefore they are not to be worn by the main celebrant under normal parish conditions, especially on Sundays or at other large celebrations.

E. Stole. The origin of the liturgical stole is uncertain. When first used in connection with the liturgy, the Greek word *stole* signified either "vestment" in general or that particular shawl-like garment shaped like the wrap which older Roman women typically wore around their shoulders (*stola*). Thus when Theodoret (d. 457) called the golden raiment for performing baptisms which Constantine gave Macarios of Jerusalem (d. 333) a "sacred stole" (*hieran stolēn*), he intended something more substantial than the narrow strip of cloth used in the liturgy today.

The "stole" worn today by deacons most probably derives from the ancient Roman *orarium*, a long towel for the hands and mouth (*os, oris*), carried or draped over the left shoulder, which in colder weather could also be used to keep the head or neck warm. Liturgical use in the East of the "*orarion*" is witnessed to as early as the council of Laodicea (372). And the Council of Braga (Spain) in 563 associates it with deacons who wore it like a waiter's towel in preparing gifts for the liturgy. Recalling an ancient symbolism, Germanus of Constantinople (d. 730) states that the oraria on the shoulders of deacons, waiters at the earthly liturgy, are like the wings of angels, those who serve the heavenly liturgy (*Mustikē Theoria*, 16). At the 4th council of Toledo (633), probably in imitation of the archbishop's wearing the pallium, the orarium, worn like the ancient stola or Jewish prayer shawl around one's neck, became required vesture for ordinary bishops and priests as well. Later, the Council of Mainz (813) insists that priests wear it at all times, even when travelling, as a sign of their office. Possibly because in the Middle Ages pastoral office in the church was often compared to OT priesthood, as early as Germanus of Paris (d. 576) the orarium became known as the "*stola*," the name given by the Septuagint to a high priestly garment. Traditionally worn by deacons over the left shoulder and crossing at the right hip, by priests and bishops looping around the back of the neck and falling from both shoulders straight down or crossing in the front, the stole has remained throughout the centuries a major, indispensable sign of ordained office in the church.

F. Maniple. The maniple (*mappa*, dim. = *mappula*) originated as a napkin and/or hand towel. Servants at table typically draped it over their left forearms. During the Roman empire it was also used decoratively and as a sign of authority. Emperors and consuls reportedly waved or dropped the maniple to start public games in the circus. In the 4th century Christian deacons covered their hands with this cloth when handling the sacred offerings at the liturgy. And in later centuries subdeacons as well were given the maniple as a sign of their office. Since the High Middle Ages it has been worn by all the major orders, attached to the left wrist and only during the celebration of the eucharist. With the reforms of Vatican II the maniple is no longer a required liturgical vestment.

G. Amice. The liturgical amice (*amictus* = "wrapped around") is an oblong linen cloth with long strings that is worn under the alb, wrapped about the neck and secured by its strings at the waist. Derived from a similar cut of cloth (*superhumerale*), which in Roman times was worn on top of the tunic to protect outer garments from perspiration, the amice became part of papal vesture in the 8th century. By the 12th century it was a common vestment for all liturgical ministers. Placed first on the head to protect the hair from dishevelment during subsequent vesting, then slid back, it formed a cowl-like collar around the neck. Today the amice is required only when the alb does not completely cover the street clothes underneath.

H. Mitre. In earlier centuries the clergy wore the common headgear of the day in outdoor liturgical activities such as processions. The first mention of any special head covering occurs in the 8th century when popes wore a cloth hat referred to as a "*camelaucum*," i.e., imperial crown. In "The Donation of Constantine," written between 757 and 767 and claiming to be a 4th-century document, Pope Sylvester refuses the crown which Constantine offers him as the "vicar of Christ." He accepts instead the simple white phrygian cap, called the "mitre," as a sign of his office. Inspired by this document and the passage in Exodus 39 granting the "*mitra*" to OT high priests, by the 12th century most other bishops and abbots as well had adopted the phrygium as part of their own insignia. In ancient Greek "*mitra*" referred to any kind of band, such as that which circled the crown of the head to make a cap fit snugly. Securing the bishop's hat, this band was tied in the back, with its two ends (fanons) falling loose from behind. A second band across the top of the head from front to back created two horn-like protrusions of cloth on both sides. During the 13th and 14th centuries this cloth was stiffened and the hat was rotated 90 degrees, effecting the front and back beaks of the liturgical mitre. Today special rules govern the wearing of the mitre during the liturgy. In general, it is removed whenever the bishop leads common prayer or any enactment of the sacraments.

I. Surplice. The Latin name of the surplice, *superpelliceus* ("over fur pelts"), belies its origin in the 11th century as a choir vestment that was worn over a fur-lined cassock. This white linen garment originally had the shape of a conical chasuble fashioned with short, wide sleeves. Gradually the surplice was shortened, squared at the shoulders and sometimes highly decorated with lace. Today, worn over a cassock, it is allowed to substitute for the alb, except when a chasuble or dalmatic is called for, or when one wears the stole to replace the chasuble or dalmatic.

J. Cassock. The cassock derives from a

garment of barbarian origin called the *caracalla*. The emperor who introduced its use into Roman society was also given its name, "Caracalla" (211-217). Originally a sleeved tunic that opened in front and reached to the knees, the emperor donned a longer version, one that covered the ankles. From the 5th century onward the *caracalla* in both lengths became popular among monks and clerics, producing a great variety of religious habits and cassocks. The English name "cassock" is thought possibly to result through medieval Italian (*casacca*) and French (*casaque*) from a corruption of "*caracalla*." Itself not properly a part of the liturgy, the cassock is often worn under (*subtanea*=soutaine) true liturgical vestments. Normally black, its color can vary. The papal cassock is white; those of cardinals, scarlet; while archbishops, bishops and other prelates wear purple.

II. Liturgical Colors

A. *Original White*. From ancient times, originating from Egyptian and Mesopotamian sun worship, the wearing of white has traditionally been associated with light and divine life. Thus, priestly Israel wore white, along with other bright colors, to symbolize the "glory" of God (Leviticus 16). The Romans, especially on birthdays (*dies candidatus*), also wore white garments to express their aspirations to moral purity and their desire for unending life with the gods.

The NT as well associates white with divinity, linking it to Christ's work of redemption: e.g., in the accounts of the transfiguration, the apparitions of angels, and the redeemed whose clothes are washed white in the blood of the Lamb (Rev 7:14). Probably as early as the 2nd century (Farrell, 90-93), and certainly by the 4th century, baptism included a vesting in white clothing to signify the baptized's share in the glory of Christ. The white robe signaled a return in baptism through Christ's resurrection to the original body-soul integrity of paradise, a passage from sinful nakedness to that nudity which existed before the fall in which the whole person was completely ordered to God and "clothed" in his grace. For early Christians such unsoiled, white garments also signified high virtue and doctrinal purity.

B. *Other Colors*. In Tertullian's time (ca. 150-220) popular culture ascribed various colors to each of the seasons: white to the snows of winter, red to the summer's sun, green to the fertility of spring, and blue to darker autumn skies. In addition, just as light colors signified happiness, dark clothes connoted sadness and mourning. Black was identified with death probably because in the ancient near-East showing proper grief at funerals included rolling on the ground, so that one's clothes became soiled and dark. In fact, early church writers severely criticized Christians for their lack of faith if, during periods of mourning, they wore the traditional black instead of the white of Christ's resurrection. Furthermore, since red is the color of blood, in the ancient world it too was associated with death.

Until the 9th century clothing dyes were rare and expensive in the Roman world. The colorfast purple procured from the rare *murex* shellfish signified wealth and importance, so that the darker the color and the more extensive its use, the more noble the person (e.g., Lk 16:19). When a broader spectrum of colors became available, individual churches assigned different colors to each of the feasts and seasons. Blue, yellow, silver and gold were among those included. Pope Innocent III (1198-1216) was the first to set down a canon of liturgical colors for the local church at Rome (P.L. 217:799-802). He used only four colors: white for feasts of the Lord and the saints; red for Pentecost, for feasts of the cross, the apostles and martyrs; black for mourning and seasons of repentance

(Advent and Lent); and green for days without special feasts. Purple was allowed to substitute for black on Holy Innocents and Laetare Sunday.

When Trent renovated the liturgy and standardized it for the whole Latin church, Innocent's canon was adopted with some modifications. It is this canon that is still used by the Roman rite today: white for feasts of the Lord, the Blessed Virgin, non-martyr saints, John the Baptist (June 24), John the Evangelist (Dec. 27), Chair of St. Peter (Feb. 22), Conversion of St. Paul (Jan. 25) [in the U.S. also as an option for offices and Masses for the dead]; red for Passion (Palm) Sunday, Good Friday, Pentecost, feasts of Apostles, Evangelists and martyrs; green for ordinary time; purple for Lent and Advent, an option for Masses for the dead; black an option for Masses for the dead; and rose for the 3rd Sunday of Advent ("*Gaudete*") and the 4th Sunday of Lent ("*Laetare*"). "On solemn occasions more precious vestments may be used, even if not of the color of the day" (G.I.R.M., 309).

Since 1864 blue vestments have been permitted in Spain and in its former dominions on the feast of the Immaculate Conception. Likewise, Vatican II's reforms allow local episcopal conferences in principle to adapt liturgical colors to the traditions of their national cultures. Thus, in the United States white is now an option for offices and Masses for the dead. However, after review in 1988 by the N.C.C.B., simple blue, whether light or dark, remains outside the sequence of liturgical colors in the United States. Rather, in order to differentiate the seasons and their meanings, the bluer *violet* tone of purple is suggested for Advent and the redder, more authentically *purple* for "the specifically penitential season of Lent."

C. *Symbolism.* "Variety in the color of the vestments is meant to give effective, outward expression to the specific character of the mysteries of the faith being celebrated and, in the course of the year, to a sense of progress in the Christian life" (G.I.R.M., 307). Just as white symbolizes the presence of the resurrected Lord in the church and his saints, the other colors radiate the various modes of his presence throughout the year. Thus red reflects the burning intensity of Christ's love in his death on the cross, in the blood shed by his martyrs, and in the fire of the Spirit poured out on the whole body of Christ. The darker, more somber color of purple connotes both the church's share in the kingship of Christ (Jn 19:1) and how it was realized through the suffering and death caused by our sins. Finally, green recalls how the same Christ through whom the outer green world was created (Col 1:16) is also the source of the church's inner life and growth throughout the year.

The wearing of colors, shades or combinations other than those in the liturgical canon solely on the basis of aesthetics, and without concern for traditional symbolism, makes the liturgy itself more ambiguous and lessens its power to communicate Christ in the saving events of his life, death and resurrection.

III. Theological Meaning

From ancient times the wearing of beautifully draped clothes has been a sign of civilization and of the human being's place in an ordered world. By their arrangement they evidence self-possession and self-mastery. Anthropologists isolate five possible reasons why humans began to wear clothing. In various cultures, besides the practical interests of protecting against weather and injury and covering nakedness, clothes can also signify a person's place or importance in society, enhance sexuality and augment personal mystery or magical powers. Simply put, clothing extends the natural symbolism of the body by bringing the person into a fuller, more articulated existence in the world.

According to the Bible, "the body, before the fall, existed in a wholly other way for the human being because the human being existed in a totally other way for God" (Peterson, 8). In rebelling against God's sovereignty, Adam and Eve rejected their true "clothing," their fundamental orientation to God and his love. God continued his care for them, fashioning temporary clothes out of skins to cover their shame (Gen 3:21). Indeed, the ancient wearing of sackcloth and ashes was no more than a recognition of this human insufficiency and need for God. For only in Christ does God truly clothe the human race, transforming by his grace, removing the shame of sinful human nature that is experienced in physical nakedness. In his taking on our humanity, the flesh of Adam, Christ is humiliated on the cross, stripped of his garments, so that creation itself is moved to cover him with darkness. With the resurrection on Easter morning he no longer needs mere human clothing. His bodily wrappings appear deliberately folded and laid aside in the tomb (Jn 20:7). In his glorified humanity, Christ, the "first-born of the dead" (Col 1:18), is fully transformed and clothed in the glory of God's love. Therefore, just as he put on and transformed our humanity, we humans, in order to be true to ourselves, must "put on Christ" (e.g., Rom 13:12-14), that is, live our lives "in Christ, ... a new creation" (2 Cor 5:17).

A. *Special Vestments.* For Christians, then, all clothing, especially liturgical clothing, is meant to express the church's life in Christ. In Revelation the church is depicted as the bride of Christ who "has been given a dress to wear made of finest linen, brilliant white" (19:7), a garment which symbolizes both redemption in the blood of the Lamb and the holy works that flow from this new life (2:2-5). Thus, the white worn by the newly baptized, by

brides in Christian weddings and by liturgical ministers, is all meant to signify the church's *common* life in Christ.

At the same time, the NT also speaks of the church as a "people of God" (Heb 4:9). This image recalls that each Christian has a unique calling and dignity in Christ's body, and that the Church itself is a communion of love among free individuals (1 Cor 12:4-11). Thus, at the liturgy not all are dressed in identical clothes. The calling of the ordained to be personal symbols of the one Christ who dwells in the hearts of all Christians is expressed in their individual liturgical vestments. The unique vestment of the single presider is thus both a reminder to the church of each Christian's uniqueness in Christ and of the one Lord who is common to all. The physically enveloping chasuble, especially in the colors of the season, allows the rest of the church to see in the presider, not primarily a single individual, but its own single voice in Christ, proclaiming the faith and praising the Father. Truly precious vestments worn by liturgical ministers announce that the liturgy is the summit of Christian life (S.C., 10) and remind all the baptized of their dignity as part of a royal priesthood, a holy nation, a people set apart (1 Pet 2:9).

"The beauty of the vestment should derive from its material and design rather than from lavish ornamentation" (G.I.R.M., 306). Indeed, this royal, festive dimension of liturgical vestments is achieved primarily by the use of natural, noble materials: e.g., linen, silk, wool. Although often dictated by cost, polyester vestments, no matter how beautifully designed, do not drape or flow with movement nearly as beautifully and therefore lack the festive ability to symbolize the excess of God's love for humanity demanded by a true Christian celebration.

Furthermore, the level of festivity of a celebration corresponds to the rank and the meaning of the occasion. Consequently, it is essential to the liturgy as stylized Christian life that on more festive occasions, such as Sundays and major feast days, *all* liturgical ministers, including acolytes, readers and eucharistic ministers, be fully vested in their proper liturgical attire.

B. Ordinary Clothes. Finally, the fact that other members of the assembly do not wear stylized vestments acts as an important complement within the liturgy's symbolism. For the liturgy as an action is not removed from the world, but is rather the high point of all human life *in this world.* Therefore, by their wearing contemporary clothes, indeed their "Sunday best," the laity witness to the historicity of the church, to its necessary incarnation in every age. Dressed like those at the Passover meal prepared for the journey (Exod 12:11), the congregation embodies and expresses the church itself, ready to be sent into the world to gather all into that heavenly banquet of which the liturgy is but a pledge and foretaste on earth.

E. Haulotte, *Symbolique du vêtement selon la bible* (Paris: Aubier, 1966). H. Norris, *Church Vestments: Their Origin and Development* (New York: E.P. Dutton, 1950). E. Peterson, *Pour une théologie du vêtement*, trans. by Y. Congar (Lyon: Éditions de l'Abeille, 1943 , [Orig.: "Theologie des Kleides," *Benediktinische Monatsschrift* 16 (1934), 347-356]). R. Berger, "Liturgische Gewänder und Insignien," 309-346 in: *Gottesdienst der Kirche: Handbuch der Liturgiewissenschaft: Teil 3*, eds. H.B. Meyer *et al.* (Regensburg: F. Pustet, 1987). J. Farrell, "The Garment of Immortality: A Concept and Symbol in Christian Baptism" (Dissertation: Catholic University of America, Washington, D.C., 1974). E. Sutfin, "The Chasuble in the Roman Rite," *Liturgical Arts* 24 (1956): 76-104.

JOHN D. LAURANCE, S.J.

VIATICUM

The post-Vatican II church has taken giant strides toward restoring the original tradition of anointing as a sacrament of the sick: no longer "extreme unction" or "last rites," but a sacrament for those seriously impaired by sickness or old age. At the same time, however, we need to be careful not to neglect another revered tradition of the church, namely, its sacramental ministry to the dying which finds its centerpiece in the eucharist received as viaticum. Indeed, the full title of the revised ritual is *Pastoral Care of the Sick: Rites of Anointing and Viaticum* (I.C.E.L., 1982): Part I has to do with "Pastoral Care of the Sick"; Part II is entitled "Pastoral Care of the Dying." Viaticum is described with these words: "The celebration of the eucharist as viaticum, food for the passage through death to eternal life, is the sacrament proper to the dying Christian. It is the completion and crown of the Christian life on this earth, signifying that the Christian follows the Lord to eternal glory and the banquet of the heavenly kingdom" (175).

The Tradition

"Viaticum" means quite literally "food for the journey." In Greek and Latin antiquity the custom prevailed of providing a meal for people undertaking a journey, as evidenced by the Latin *viaticus* (of or pertaining to a journey) or the Greek *ephodion* (provisions for a journey). Viaticum usually referred to the practice of providing the fare for the voyage after life: the *obolus* or coin placed in the mouth of the deceased to pay the ferryman Charon for passage across the river Styx.

In ecclesiastical language viaticum eventually came to have the specific meaning of the eucharist administered to a dying Christian. So great was the church's insistence that dying Christians be communicated that the first ecumenical Council of Nicaea in 325 condemned a rigorism which would exclude public penitents from the reception of viaticum. In canon 13 the council decreed that "the ancient and canonical ruling is to be observed" that a dying Christian "is not to be deprived of the last and necessary provision for the journey, viaticum." This canonical prescription about the importance of viaticum continues in the new *Code of Canon Law* of 1983 (can. 921, 922).

Viaticum is thus a striking instance of liturgical inculturation on the part of Christian antiquity. But there are also marked dissimilarities from the pagan rites. Pagans gave "viaticum" to those already dead, placing the coin in the mouth of the deceased; Christian viaticum like all sacraments is for the living. Pagans provided the dead with an inanimate coin as viaticum; Christians provided the living with life itself, the sacrament of the Lord's body and blood. And finally, Christian viaticum was not intended to pay for the journey of the soul to the place of eternal rest, but was rather a provision for passage to eternity, being itself a pledge of eternal life.

The oldest surviving Western liturgical sources for the ministry to the dying are found in Phillips 1667, a transcription of an 8th-century Gelasian sacramentary, and in *Ordo Romanus* 49. In the Phillips sacramentary communion by viaticum takes place after the reading of the passion according to John's gospel and other prayers, perhaps a witness to the primitive practice of dying with communion on the tongue. The dying Christian is accordingly prepared for death from both the table of the word and the table of the eucharist. On the other hand, *Ordo* 49 from 8th century Rome reverses the order and lists first the communion of the dying and then the reading of the passion as the Christian departs from this life. The striking rubric reads: "As soon as you see death approaching, he is to be communicated from the holy sacrifice, even if he communicated the same day, because communion will be his defender and helper. For it will raise him up."

Until the 12th century, communion was administered under both elements, often with the bread intincted with the wine. There were three manners of ministration: the dying person could be brought to church, Mass could be celebrated at home, or —the most common usage —the reserved sacrament could be brought from church for communion at home. In the *Rituale Romanum* of 1614 viaticum was considered under Title V on the eucharist as communion of the sick. Title IV devoted to the sick and the dying made no mention of viaticum except for an isolated rubrical suggestion for helping the dying: following viaticum and anointing was the commendation of the soul. Not only did the arrangement misrepresent the original sequence of the continuous rites with extreme unction following viaticum, it also confused the purpose of viaticum with communion for the sick by including it within the same service. This impropriety has been rectified by paragraph 74 of the *Constitution on the Sacred Liturgy*: "In addition to the separate rites for the anointing of the sick and for viaticum, a continuous rite shall be prepared in which a sick person is anointed after confession and before viaticum."

Liturgical Revision

The pastoral notes suggest that when anointing of the sick is celebrated at the beginning of a serious illness, viaticum celebrated when death is near will be more clearly perceived as the last sacrament of the Christian life. Priests and other ministers should do everything they can to ensure that those in proximate danger of death receive viaticum.

The revised ritual presents two formats: viaticum within Mass, considered the normative celebration, and viaticum outside of Mass, when particular circumstances render a full eucharistic celebration impossible. In either case, as far as possible, the celebration should be a communal one involving the participation of family and friends with appropriate readings, prayers, and even song. Some of the distinctive features of the rite of viaticum are the renewal of baptismal promises, the exchange of the sign of peace, the eucharist administered with special words proper to viaticum, and communion under both kinds.

The baptismal profession of faith takes place after the homily: the Christian preparing for the consummation of the paschal mystery uses the words of the original baptismal commitment which hopefully has been renewed many times at Easter. The sign of peace is shared with a genuine sense of leave-taking brightened by the joy of Christmas hope. The special words for reception capture the meaning of the eucharist received as a pledge of resurrection and nourishment for the passage through death: "May the Lord protect you and lead you to eternal life." Whenever possible, the dying Christian is to be communicated under both kinds; sometimes reception under the form of wine alone may be the only recourse. In addition to all of the above, special texts are provided for the general intercessions and final solemn blessing, and an opening instruction or address in the case of viaticum outside of Mass. The Apostolic Pardon is now part of the concluding rites of viaticum within Mass; for viaticum outside Mass the Apostolic Pardon follows the penitential rite.

All these provisions underscore the importance of administering viaticum at a time when the dying Christian can more consciously enter into the celebration. In order to avoid a sense of fatalism, the pastoral notes wisely suggest that when a Christian communicated with viaticum continues to linger on for some time, "he or she should be given the opportunity to receive the eucharist as viaticum on successive days, frequently if not daily" (par. 183). This prescription is reiterated in the new *Code of Canon Law* (can. 921.3).

See **Sick, pastoral care of the; Death, ministry at the time of**

Pastoral Care of the Sick: Rites of Anointing and Viaticum (Washington, D.C., I.C.E.L., 1982). Charles W. Gusmer, *And You Visited Me: Sacramental Ministry to the Sick and the Dying,* rev. ed. (New York: Pueblo, 1989).

CHARLES W. GUSMER

W

WEDDINGS, MUSIC AT

The role of music at weddings has changed considerably since Vatican II. In the past, music was performed mostly by the organist and the soloist/choir. It usually consisted of a processional, recessional, and several musical selections interspersed throughout the liturgy. Participation by the assembly was not practiced.

In light of the reform, music has a significant place in liturgy, including weddings. The goal of all liturgy is the full and active participation of the faithful, and music allows people to participate in a unique way.

The American bishops' statement on music, *Music in Catholic Worship*, notes the importance of music at liturgies: "Among the many signs and symbols used by the church to celebrate its faith, music is of pre-eminent importance. As sacred song united to the words it forms an integral part of the solemn liturgy. Yet the function of music is ministerial; it must serve and never dominate. Music should assist the assembled believers to express and share the gift of faith that is within them and to nourish and strengthen their interior commitment of faith. It should heighten the texts so that they speak more fully and more effectively. The quality of joy and enthusiasm which music adds to community worship cannot be gained in any other way. It imparts a sense of unity to the gathered assembly

and sets the appropriate tone for a particular celebration. Music, in addition to expressing texts, can also unveil a dimension of meaning and feeling, a communication of ideas and intuitions which words alone cannot yield. This dimension is integral to the human personality and to our growth in faith" (23-24).

This statement provides a foundation for the role of music for weddings. The entire assembly, that is, the invited guests as well as the bride, groom and other members of the wedding party, is the celebrator of the liturgy. Musical selections should assist the assembly in expressing and sharing its faith within the wedding liturgy.

Music that is familiar and uncomplicated will best implement the participation of those gathered. The hymnal in the pew is usually a good starting place for choosing accessible music. Appropriate texts are those which include praise and thanksgiving to God for the love bestowed upon the people, this occasion, and on this couple. Love songs which do not include God's love are more acceptable at the wedding reception than during the liturgy. Popular music of the day may be considered if it fulfills these requirements.

Primary areas of consideration for assembly singing are: gospel acclamation; "Holy, holy, holy"; memorial acclamation; great *Amen*; communion and the responsorial psalm. Secondary places for song are: gathering, preparation of gifts, Lord's Prayer, Lamb of God, and closing. The use of the psalms is always encouraged and the Rite of Marriage recommends verses from the following psalms for the responsorial: Psalms 33,34,103,-112,128, 145,148. A sung response is the most appropriate. These psalms may also be used at other times throughout the liturgy when music is called for.

Instrumental music may also effectively complement the sung music and help unveil a level of meaning and emotion that words cannot express. The choices of instrumental music will determine the tone of the particular moment of the celebration. Instrumental music can be effective: during the seating of the guests; as a processional; during the preparation of the gifts (instead of sung music); after the communion song; as a recessional. The parish musician is the best resource for instrumental music.

The primary purpose of the solo voice at weddings as with other liturgical celebrations is to serve the liturgy. The primary role of the soloist is to lead the assembly in song. Only soloists who are capable of leading an assembly should be asked to do so. When solo or choir "performances" must take place they are best relegated to the same places as instrumental music in the liturgy. The responsorial psalm, however, can provide ample opportunity for musical expression.

A wedding is an opportunity for an engaged couple either to begin a relationship with a parish community and/or certainly an occasion to deepen that relationship with a parish community.

Enforcement of wedding policy must take place within this context with sufficient catechesis and pastoral care.

The use of the "traditional" *Wedding March* from Wagner's opera, *Lohengrin* (more commonly known as "Here comes the Bride"), and the "traditional" wedding processional from Mendelssohn's *Midsummer Night's Dream* are rapidly declining in popularity. Apparent successors to this tradition are the processional used at the wedding of Prince Charles —the *Trumpet Voluntary* attributed to Jeremiah Clarke, and for recessional the *Trumpet Tune* of Henry Purcell.

The performance of the *Ave Maria* is best suited to the seating of the mothers of the bridal couple as a prelude or otherwise should be eliminated.

Mary Ann Simco, ed., *Handbook of Church Music for Weddings*, rev. ed. (Chicago: Liturgy Training Publications, 1985). Paul Covino, ed., *Celebrating Marriage*, Preparing the Wedding Liturgy: A Workbook for Engaged Couples (Washington, D.C.: The Pastoral Press, 1987). *Music in Catholic Worship* (U.S.C.C., 1972).

ELAINE J. RENDLER

WESTERN CHURCHES

See **Traditions, liturgical, in the West: pre-Reformation; Eucharist, history of, in the West; Reformation churches**

WOMEN IN MINISTRY

See **Ministry, women in**

WOMEN, ORDINATION OF

See **Ordination of women**

WORD AND SACRAMENT

Contemporary discussions regarding the relationship of word and sacrament are grounded in a biblical theology which considers God's word to be more than mere external utterance or intellectual discourse. It is, rather, the efficacious self-communication of God to creation. For God, to speak is to do. The word of

God is an event of encounter. In Jesus Christ the word is incarnate. This incarnation continues through history in the church where the word continues to be preached and "made flesh" in the celebration of the sacraments. The early church clearly experienced and understood the complementarity of word and symbol. For theologians such as Augustine it was precisely the mutually enlightening relationship of word and sign which comprised the reality of sacrament as a *visible word (In Johannem* 80, 3).

The fracturing of the church's understanding and experience of these realities was largely rooted in a loss of the Jewish sense of the word as event. When the proclamation of the word became focused upon the communication and maintenance of intellectual truth, preaching became more an act of polemical theology and less a revelation of how the scriptural narrative proclaimed in the liturgy is God's story happening today in the life of the worshipping community. In this context preaching declined and the proclamation of the word was reduced to a non-essential prelude to sacramental celebration, while the celebration of the word was for all practical purposes reduced to the minister's pronouncement of the sacramental form deemed necessary for the valid celebration of the sacrament. The 16th-century Reformers reacted to this imbalance and opened a debate extending from their time until the Second Vatican Council. This polemic tended to categorize Protestantism as "the church of the word" in a negative state of tension with Roman Catholicism as "the church of the sacrament." The 19th-century revival of biblical and patristic studies led, however, to a theological revival in which the new context of liturgical and ecumenical movements encouraged Protestants and Catholics alike to move beyond their polemical medieval and Reformation positions to a renewed understanding of the relationship between word and sacrament.

In this century various Roman Catholic theologians (Grasso, Rahner, Semmelroth) have attempted to deal with a renewed understanding of God's efficacious word in a way which would not seem to contradict Trent's insistence upon the *ex opere operato* efficacy of the sacraments. Some proposed that the word apart from the sacrament works *ex opere operantis* while the word within the sacramental celebration works *ex opere operato*. K. Rahner posed the question in terms of revived biblical studies which communicate the scriptural understanding of the word of God as a saving event rendering present the grace of God which it announces. How then does word differ from sacrament? Rahner posits the word of God as an analogous concept, a reality taking place in the church in varying degrees of concentration and intensity. The supreme and most intensive realization of the word of God is precisely the sacramental word.

Rahner develops his position from the nature of the church as the primary sacrament, the historically visible and audible proclamation of Christ's victory and the actual presentation of that victory in the world. The fullest actualization of this reality occurs in the sacraments, especially within the eucharist, when the church, depending upon the free decree of Christ, addresses God's word to human beings in decisive situations of human salvation. All other acts of the church are ordered to the sacraments and all the sacraments to the eucharist where Christ is present by the power of his own word. Here Rahner develops the idea that the word is not the form of the sacrament simply within the celebration of the eucharist, but the word is permanently constitutive of the sacrament. The elements (matter) always refer back to the word whose power brings about Christ's abiding presence.

The theological development of these concepts rooted in the renewed study of scripture and patristics, ecclesiology and sacraments, ecumenism and the liturgy bore fruit in and took a major step forward in the teachings of the Second Vatican Council. S.C.'s expressed desire for a more lavish opening up of the Bible (51) and a renewal of preaching (52) gave new impetus to attempts at restoring the mutuality of word and sacrament. This is echoed and fostered in D.V., chap. VI, and is seen most concretely in the *Lectionary for Mass* (1969) and in the fact that every liturgical revision issuing from the council includes the proclamation of the word of God as an integral element.

The pastoral application of this renewed vision of word and sacrament is evidenced not only in ongoing calls for a renaissance of liturgical preaching but also in consistent efforts to open up the sacramental symbols. This has been a thoroughly ecumenical enterprise in which both traditional Catholic and Protestant theology have been enriched by the insights of contemporary studies of human communication in language and symbol. There is hardly a single Christian church which would today admit to an opposition between word and sacrament. These are no longer considered independent and different manners of divine self-communication but complementary realities incapable of accomplishing their task without reciprocal penetration. Every sacrament communicates the divine life by means of the word which is a direct address to the human person. The totality of the human person is touched by the word incarnated in sacramental signs.

See **Word, theology of; Sacraments**

Domenico Grasso, *Proclaiming God's Message: A Study in the Theology of Preaching* (Notre Dame, IN: Univ. of Notre Dame Press, 1965). David Power, *Unsearchable Riches. The Symbolic Nature of Liturgy* (New York: Pueblo, 1984). Karl Rahner, "The Word and the Eucharist," *Theological*

Investigations, Vol. IV (Baltimore: Helicon, 1966): 253-286. Karl Rahner, "What is a Sacrament," *Worship* 47 (1973): 274-284.

ANDREW D. CIFERNI, O. PRAEM.

WORD, LITURGY OF THE

The liturgy of the word is that part of the eucharist beginning with the first reading and ending with the general intercessions. This same ritual action may be celebrated as a separate service (S.C., 35,4), in which case a blessing and dismissal usually follows the general intercessions.

The liturgy of the word is more than a bare recitation of the scriptures in the midst of the assembly. Christians do not simply recite God's word in a public setting. They proclaim and celebrate God's story and theirs in ritual gesture, song, silence and symbol. This tradition is an integral and constitutive part of our heritage from Israel. Early Christian liturgical sources bear witness to the importance of the proclamation of the word in the Christian assembly. In this proclamation the community's myth-mystery is experienced as a present reality. The present shape of the liturgy of the word within the reformed rites of Roman Catholicism is in radical continuity with the church's tradition (cf. Justin, *Apologia I*, 65. 67, 3-5), while exhibiting every sign of a renewed appreciation for the formative power of the scriptures, preaching and the active liturgical celebration of God's word (S.C., 24, 51-53).

The celebration of the liturgy of the word (within the eucharist or as an independent service) in the Roman rite is preceded by an introductory rite which, though not an essential or integral part of the liturgy of the word, is intended to prepare the assembly to hear God's word and respond to that proclamation both within the liturgy of the word itself and at the eucharistic table liturgy which may follow it.

Ministries

Christ is present to his people in the very act of their assembling. The same Christ is present to his people in the proclamation of God's word (S.C., 7). The entire assembly, of which every liturgical minister is a member, has the primary ministry of listening attentively to the word proclaimed and responding actively and consciously to what has been heard in word, silence, song and gesture. The interplay of proclamation and response symbolizes the divine economy in which God's initiative is always a call asking for the hearer's faith-filled response. The church's continually deepening sense of her call to hear and respond to God's word in the liturgical assembly is underlined in the second edition of the *Introduction to the Lectionary* (I.L., 81) which presents a more expanded exposition of this topic.

The lectors (readers) proclaim as the living word of God the scriptural texts other than the gospel. The deacon, presider or some other priest (a concelebrant and/or homilist other than the presiding priest) proclaims the gospel. The homilist interprets the word that it might be experienced as the ongoing story of God happening today in this assembly's life. Leaders of song, cantors, schola (choir) members and instrumentalists enable the assembly's response in psalmody, in the greeting of the gospel and in intercessory prayer.

Textual and Other Verbal Elements

Sundays, solemnities, feasts of the Lord which fall on Sundays in ordinary time and some special celebrations, e.g., Ash Wednesday, are marked by the normative proclamation of three readings: the first (from the OT or the NT other than one of the gospels) is always followed by the responsorial psalm; the second (from the NT other than one of the gospels) and the third (always from one of the four gospels) which is preceded by

the gospel acclamation and followed by the homily, profession of faith (on Sundays and solemnities) and general intercessions.

On other feasts, memorials and weekdays (whether in ordinary time or within the liturgical seasons) there are two readings: the first from the OT or NT but never from the gospels and the second which is always from one of the four gospels. Though the *Introduction to the Lectionary* (I.L., 81,78-88) and the *Directory for Masses with Children* (D.M.C., 42) give broad allowance for pastoral adaptation in the choice and omission of readings, the gospel reading may never be omitted in the celebration of the eucharist. The Roman rite makes no provision for the proclamation of nonscriptural readings within the eucharistic liturgy of the word.

Since the liturgical reforms of the Second Vatican Council, the homily is seen to be an integral part of the liturgy of the word. The *G.I.R.M.* 41 specifies that it may be based not only upon the scriptures proclaimed but also upon any of the liturgical texts and upon the mystery being celebrated. This distinguishes the homily from the sermon which is a religious but not a strictly liturgical form of oratory and which may have no relation to the readings or other liturgical elements of the celebration in which it is delivered.

The Nicene Creed is the text almost always employed for the profession of faith on Sundays and solemnities. The *D.M.C.* 49 allows for the use of the Apostles' Creed. At all Easter Masses the profession of faith is made within the renewal of baptismal vows. In that setting a more ancient primitive question-response form is employed.

General intercessions have been restored within the Roman liturgy of the word as part of the liturgical reform instituted by the Second Vatican Council. This liturgical prayer form is expressive of the logic of biblical prayer, i.e., the proclamation of God's story is an act of *anamnesis* which inspires renewed confidence from which the assembly brings its needs before God. These prayers are introduced by the presider's invitation. The petitions are sung or recited by the deacon, a lector or the leader of song. The entire assembly responds with a short sung or recited call upon God's mercy. The presider concludes with a prayer addressed to God. The order of the general intercessions within the liturgy of the word is modified by the celebration of some of the rites of the R.C.I.A.

In every art form voids are as integral as solids. Silence is as integral to the liturgy of the word as rests are to music for the word issues forth from silence and the prayer which rises to God in the silence is as much response as sung psalmody and acclamation. Brief periods of silence are most appropriate after the reading(s) and psalm which precede the gospel, after the homily and after the final petition of the general intercessions.

The Book(s)

The lectionary contains all the readings selected for the celebration of the eucharist according to the order of the calendar for the liturgical year. Readings for the celebration of some other rites are also contained in this liturgical book. The *I.L.M.* 81.17 and the *G.I.R.M.* 84 and 131 also make provision for a gospel book (*evangeliary*) which may be carried in the entrance procession and placed on the altar until the gospel acclamation when the deacon or the priest who will proclaim the gospel brings it to the ambo.

The lectionary (and, where employed, the evangeliary) are primary ritual objects within the celebration of the liturgy of the word. Every care and attention is to be devoted to their visual presentation and their ritual treatment. Missalettes or other printed forms of the readings detract from the dialogic nature of the liturgical act and weaken the symbolic role of the lectionary.

Musical Elements

Though all of the readings may be chanted, this is rarely done except for the gospel in very solemn celebrations. The *I.L.M.* 81.17-18 indicates that the concluding salutation of each reading may be sung even when the reading has been recited. The most essentially musical element in the liturgy of the word is the gospel acclamation which may be omitted if it is not sung (G.I.R.M., 39). This acclamation, though it follows the second reading (Sundays and solemnities), is the assembly's joyful song of praise to welcome Christ in the proclamation of the gospel narrative of the day. It is also the processional chant for the movement of the priest or deacon to the ambo.

The responsorial psalm is also a primary musical element in the rite. Its name derives from its normative mode of performance: an easily accessible sung response is first repeated by the assembly after it has been intoned by the leader of song and is sung again by all after every appointed verse of the psalm sung by the cantor and/or schola.

The profession of faith may be sung and this text is one of the chants recommended to be learned by all in Latin. Finally the general intercessions may be sung. This is entirely appropriate to the litanical nature of this text: the response to the petitions, sung or recited by the deacon, a lector or the leader of song, is made by the entire assembly.

Posture, Gesture and Movement

Posture is indicative and constitutive of prayer. The assembly is seated to hear the non-gospel readings and for the responsorial psalm and homily. All stand for the gospel acclamation, the proclamation of the gospel, the profession of faith and the general intercessions. The gospel procession holds the potential for the fullest bodily engagement. In this ritual element the gospel acclamation is sung, all stand and the one who will proclaim the gospel is led in procession to the ambo. This procession may include thurifer and acolytes carrying lit candles.

Environment

The normative arrangement of Roman Catholic worship spaces calls for one ambo (lectern, pulpit) whence the scriptures are proclaimed and the homily preached. From this privileged place of proclamation the Easter *Exsultet*, the responsorial psalm and the petitions of the general intercessions may also be sung. Other elements of liturgical leadership in the liturgy of the word, e.g., the gospel acclamation, and other liturgical elements requiring some sort of reading desk, such as concluding announcements, are done from a less significant and often portable lectern or stand. The homily is given from the ambo or the presidential chair. In the latter case the presider-homilist may sit or stand.

Sunday Worship in the Absence of a Priest

Celebrations of the liturgy of the word are most frequently experienced within the larger ritual action of the eucharist, the other sacraments, the *L.O.H.*, the rites of initiation into religious life and the rites of burial. *S.C.* 35's suggested celebration of Bible services would seem to be met by the provision for the celebration of the office of vigils in the revised *L.O.H.* The contemporary crisis of priestless parishes presents the church with a pastoral situation in which non-ordained ministers may frequently be called upon to lead the Sunday assembly in liturgical prayer. In these cases, morning prayer, evening prayer or a liturgy of the word may be celebrated with or without the distribution of communion.

A shortage of ordained ministers can not keep the local assembly from responding to God's call to gather for worship on the Lord's Day. Even where the full eucharistic form of Sunday celebration is not possible, the word of God proclaimed and celebrated in the liturgy —even without the distribution of communion—is a baptismally grounded imperative. For in every liturgical celebration of the word in which the assembly strives to hear the scriptures with united heart and mind and to respond in unity of voice and action Christ is present and the face of the church is made manifest in the world.

Congregation for Divine Worship, *Directory for Sunday Celebrations in the Absence of a Priest, Origins* 18 (1988): 301-307. *Lectionary for Mass: Introduction.* Eng. trans. of the 2nd *editio typica* (1981) (Washington, D.C.: USCC, 1982). R. Cabié, *The Eucharist,* vol. II of A.G. Martimort, ed., *The Church at Prayer* (Collegeville, MN: The Liturgical Press, 1986).

ANDREW D. CIFERNI, O.PRAEM.

WORD, THEOLOGY OF THE

"Word of God" is a broad theological term that embraces all of God's self-revealing activity. It refers to the communication in human history of what is hidden in God, and is ultimately, therefore, the communication of the very person of God. God has spoken in many and diverse ways (Heb 1:1-2; D.V., 4), but God's word has come to be associated primarily with the person of Jesus, the sacred scriptures, and the preaching or proclamation of the church.

"Word of God" is a phrase that has been in the Christian tradition from the beginning and is accepted by all Christian confessions. The Protestant churches understand it primarily as the scriptural word, while the Roman Catholic church identifies the term more with the reality (the person of Jesus Christ) itself. As a theological term, i.e., one developed by the science of theology, "word of God" means what those who use it wish it to mean. Since thought is culturally conditioned, terms take on nuances which they may not previously have had, and thus they work differently in different theological systems. There is not therefore one monolithic meaning of "word of

God"that has been handed on unchanged through the centuries.

The term is central to the whole theological endeavor. It has implications for all branches of theology. In fact, "word" is at the heart of Christian theology for it has to do with the offer of salvation which is addressed to human freedom, where men and women say "yes" or "no" in an act of faith that springs from the work of the Holy Spirit.

In spite of its centrality to the theological endeavor, however, "word of God" has only quite recently been given a notable place in Catholic theology. Some reasons for a more comprehensive understanding include: contemporary discussions of grace understood as the uncreated self-communication of God; renewed interest in the Greek Fathers with their emphasis on the incarnation as a moment of redemption; the felt need for a theology of preaching; the insights of biblical theology into the nature of the living, creative, penetrating word of God; and closer communication between Catholic and Protestant theologians which has resulted in a greater agreement that sacrament is as revelatory as is the word of God, and that the word itself achieves its highest point of fulfillment in the sacramental act.

These developments have not yet produced a coherent theology of the word. What follows here is an attempt to disclose some characteristics of the word which bring out its essence as word of God in and to the church. Two notions are particularly helpful in understanding the concept. One comes from a philosophical analysis of language and human speech and the other from the insights of biblical theology into the nature of the word.

Language and Human Speech

The concept of "word" raises questions about what words are in human life, and specifically for Christian theology, life lived in the image of God. It is out of our own human experience that we posit speech in God. If we look at human experience and the way human beings arrive at self-knowledge, we see that we express a word to ourselves about who we are. Indeed, we must speak to become who we are; to find out who and what we are and what we are not. Although word is not merely something *about* a person, i.e., pure information for a practical purpose, it is this first. Beneath that, however, is the intention of the one speaking to communicate himself or herself. The real power of language is in the donation of self, the offer of self. To say "Good morning," for example, is not just information that the sun is up but an opening up to the person listening. Word, then, is not merely something about a person; it is, even more, self-expression and self-gift. The one who speaks ultimately gives his or her self to those who listen and receive. Word is free, personal self-disclosure. It is the basis of all friendship, including friendship with God.

This relationship between word and human existence sheds light on the function of "word of God" as it carries both communication about God and communication of God's own self. Knowledge may be communicated to others by concept or by metaphor. When concept is employed, knowledge remains somewhat informational and objective; concept communicates by analogy. When metaphor is employed, however, the knowledge communicated is more than informational; the person of the speaker is communicated as well. The language itself becomes invitational and mutually involving of both speaker and listener; it becomes doxological, the language of worship. Thus "word of God" refers to the self-disclosing, self-unveiling act of God. When applied in Christian discourse to Jesus Christ, it names Christ as the very self-expression of God, Jesus revealed as God's Son. In parallel with human communication, where word speaks both about the person and the very selfhood of the person, God's word conveys both knowledge about God and God's very self. God speaks to women and men whom God's love is seeking out. The aim of such speech is to involve the hearer in what is heard, and to call forth surrender of the hearer's life into God's love.

Biblical Studies

The second area that sheds light on our use of the term is biblical theology with its insights into the nature of the word. The tendency of Western thought to concentrate on the objective content of the word caused a certain distortion in Catholic theology in which word was restricted to matters of doctrine or to the word that spoke *about* something. Biblical theology has retrieved for us what scripture has to say about the living, effective, creative word of God. The biblical authors describe word as a saving power or force let loose in the world; as an event of salvation. "For the word of God is living and active, sharper than any two-edged sword, piercing to the division of soul and spirit, of joints and marrow, and discerning the thoughts and intentions of the heart" (Heb 4:12). "Finally, pray for us, that the word of the Lord may speed on and triumph, as it did among you" (2 Thess 3:1). "Let us go over to Bethlehem and see this word that has come to pass" (Luke 2:15).

The background for this understanding can be found in the Hebrew *dabar* (word), which means, not simply speech in the ordinary sense of "word," but a kind of deed, happening or event. *Dabar* is dynamic; it has meaning and power. More than the expression of thought, word is something operative and efficient. It is not just the speaker, but the word itself, that is active. Word goes forth as a reality in its own right, achieving the end for which it was sent (see Isa 55:10-11).

The dynamic power of the *dabar Yahweh*=word of God, is never far from the Hebrew mind. As the word proceeds from the mouth of God, it both reveals God's will and carries God's power. God's word is primarily a powerful act which creates the world (Gen 1:3; Ps 33:6,9; Ps 147:4, 15-18; Wis 9:1; Isa 48:13); gives the Torah (Deut 5:5; 8:3; 32:47; Exod 34:1,27-28; Ps 147:19); and directs history (Deut 4:20; Sir 44:1-50:24).

But in the Hebrew Scriptures, it is the word of the prophet that is most particularly word of God. The prophet is claimed by God's word and compelled to declare that word to the people. The prophetic word, charged with the power of God "to root up and to tear down, to build and to plant" (Jer 1:9-10), was at once instructive and transformative. Jeremiah describes it as a fire burning in his bones (20:7-9), or a hammer that splits rock (23:29), or again as a fire that devours people like wood (5:14). For Hosea it was Yahweh's means of slaying the people (6:5), and for Isaiah, a force that explodes like a bomb (9:8). These descriptions suggest that the prophetic word has a dynamism to bring into existence the reality of which it speaks.

These qualities of the word are carried forward into the NT where the Greek *logos* is employed in this dynamic Hebrew sense. In the gospels, word first refers to Jesus' message, his preaching and his teaching (Mk 2:2; 4:33; 8:32). The crowds are amazed at the power of Jesus' words which expel demons (Mt 8:16; Mk 1:25), effect bodily healing (Mt 8:8; Mk 7:34), and control nature (Mk 4:39). But his words also make salvation real; they bring about the kingdom. His words have the same power and authority as Yahweh's word; Luke, the theologian of the word, even equates Jesus' word with the word of God (Lk 5:1; 4:32; 8:11).

There is a discernible shift in the understanding of word from the preaching *of* Jesus to the preaching *about* Jesus, i.e., preaching which has as its *content* the person of Jesus. This is an important distinction: between Jesus' own preaching about God and about the kingdom at hand, and the church's preaching about Jesus when word becomes not simply word of God but word of the church as well. In the Lucan writings, particularly the Acts of the Apostles, word of God is a technical term for the gospel message understood as the whole Christ event, an event full of power (Acts 1:1; 15:7; Lk 1:2). Paul, too, uses word as a synonym for the Good News about Jesus and he emphasizes the dynamic character of the message. It is the saving power of God at work in the world (Rom 1:16; 1 Thess 1:4,6; 1 Cor 1:18). The word is revealed through his preaching, but Paul wants to make sure there is no mistake about the source of his power (2 Cor 4:7; 1 Cor 3:5-7; 1 Thess 2:13). It is the very word of God; the word of life (Phil 2:16); of reconciliation (2 Cor 5:19); of faith (Rom 10:8); of truth (2 Cor 6:7; Eph 1:13; Col 1:5, 2 Tm 2:15).

Finally, in the Johannine writings, the word is personalized in Jesus. Wherever he is, the Word of God is (Jn 1:1-2, 14). Jesus, in his person, his message, the Spirit that he brings, is the saving Word of God. Sent to reveal the inner life of God (D.V. 4), he speaks of what he has heard and seen (Jn 3:34; 8:37). All that God wants to say to us is said in the flesh of this man Jesus. He is the Word that is heard and seen and touched and handed on (1 Jn 1:1). Jesus the Word is truth (Jn 1:14) and life (Jn 1:4, 13); he reveals the glory of the Father (Jn 1:14).

Word As Event

All of this prepares the way for an understanding of God's word as an event in which the loving intention of God for humanity is revealed. God's word is creative and so we have to say it is sacramental, i.e., it is mediated or revealed in matter. It is also historical, i.e., we cannot know the word except in and through matter and in the experience of human history. God's word means God's activity first and foremost revealing God's self in, through and by way of finite reality. As God speaks in history, grace inspires and enables one to see through the historical event to its revelatory character: that this man on the cross, for example, is God's own Son achieving through his death God's salvation. In the speaking, God's unveiling of God's own self to be known and loved has to be interpreted in an act of faith so that ordinary realities, specifically the life and mission of Jesus, mediate salvation. The word spoken eternally in the depths of the Trinity is spoken temporally in our history.

There is a strong anthropological element inherent in the concept. Only human beings use words. The human being is constituted by language; the main feature of being is language. Theological anthropologists point out that the human being is marked precisely by the capacity to speak. The only place where language originates and exists is in the human. Without human speech God cannot say who God is because the mystery of God transcends all human experience. God has to assume human words for humans to experience and receive God's self-communication.

This indirect reference or requisitioning of human language is described in an apt phrase of Vatican II: "God reveals himself by revealing man (sic) to himself" (G.S., 41). If God is to speak to the human person, then God must speak in a language that can be understood. The self-communication of God is mediated in, through and by way of concrete, finite things. God's word is always mediated. In our reaching to God it is always a question of mediation. But this should not conceal the truth that in God's approach to us there is an immediacy at the core of mediation. From God's side there is such a thing as mediated immediacy.

The second person of the Trinity, in assuming human self-consciousness, had to subject himself to the process of human language. God desired to offer salvation to humanity through Jesus Christ. It is through Christ's human life and human language, continued now in the language which the church employs to convey the experience of salvation, that the offer is made.

The word of God, then, is no longer a disembodied Logos: Jesus is the incarnate Word. Scripture is embodied, and the proclamation by the church must make do with human sounds, images and experiences. We cannot know God's self-revelation if we bypass human experience. The word links us to God's activity but God's activity is bound to our human truth. In order for God to achieve this self-communication, God created in us a desire for the word, a propensity to hear. But on our part there has to be openness to what God reveals if there is not to be rejection.

Word As Revelation

Since word has a revealing function, it is most closely linked with revelation. The two terms are more similar than dissimilar, and are often used interchangeably. They are not, however, synonymous. Their connotations are different. Revelation evokes images of *activity* with the emphasis on God who speaks. Word evokes images of *content*, with emphasis on what is being said. In the end, however, they point to the same reality. Word contains meaning which is ultimately much more than information or knowledge about God; the meaning of word is God's own self freely and powerfully given. Revelation is much more than the act of God speaking; it is God's action of self-communication.

Vatican II stressed this personal and dynamic nature of revelation: "It pleased God, in his (sic) goodness and wisdom, to reveal himself and to make known the mystery of his will (cf. Eph 1:9). . . . By this revelation, then, the invisible God (cf. Col 1:15; 1 Tm 1:17), from the fullness of his love, addresses men (sic) as his friends (Exod 33:11; Jn 15:14-15), and moves among them (cf. Bar 3:38), in order to invite and receive them into his own company" (D.V., 2). The person and mystery of God as offering salvation, and not simply as offering ideas and truths about God, is *the* great truth which is communicated. The most important revelation is the very self-gift of God which is made and accomplished through the word. The word of God is itself the content of God's self-revelatory activity.

A theology of the word must include proclamation as well as revelation. That which is heard must be spoken in turn to others. The initiative in speaking belongs to God; it remains always "God's word." That word, however, is addressed to women and men, and those who respond to and accept God's word and who are formed by the word into the church are by that very fact commissioned and enabled to speak what they have heard. Not everyone will accept the word; it is directed to human freedom, and there must always be the possibility of refusal. God's word is addressed to all humans, both those who accept it and those who refuse or repudiate it. Those who do accept, however, are constituted as the church (word forms and constitutes the church) and as the church are charged in turn with the proclamation of what is heard and believed. And as it continues its mission of proclamation, the church continues to realize itself.

The primary response of the church to the word that is heard is gratitude and eucharist. Gratitude and eucharist, however, contain in themselves a desire to speak that word further to those who have not yet heard. Yet as word continues to be spoken, Christ himself remains the one who is spoken and the one who speaks: "He is present in his word, since it is he himself who speaks when the holy Scriptures are read in the Church" (S.C., 7).

When God speaks, there has to be someone who listens, who hears and who understands. God speaks, but speaks *to* someone. It is this which constitutes the body of believers who form the church. The reason why the church can proclaim the word is that it has itself heard it in faith, accepted it and been formed by it. The church continues to put in human words what God has communicated to the church in God's revelatory, inspirational act. Yet God continues not only to speak, but also to interpret what God speaks. The agent of interpretation remains God's Spirit placed in the human heart. "But the Counselor, the Holy Spirit, whom the Father will send in my name, he will teach you all things, and bring to your remembrance all that I have said to you" (Jn 14:26). The full meaning of the word, not just its human meaning, is given by God who sends the Spirit to enable believers to hear the word, understand the word and speak the word, and thus be the church of Jesus Christ.

All this happens in the realm of grace, God's gracious self-communication, which includes within itself the power to hear and respond. "The obedience of faith (Rom 16:26; cf. Rom 1:5; 2 Cor 10:5-6) must be given to God as he reveals himself.... Before this faith can be exercised, man must have the grace of God to move and assist him; he must have the interior helps of the Holy Spirit, who moves the heart and converts it to God, who opens the eyes of the mind and makes it easy for all to accept and believe the truth" (D.V., 5). The grace to respond, moreover, involves more than simple hearing; hearing the word means a commitment to it. And the commitment, in the realm of faith, is to proclaim that

word further, and to continue to allow God to interpret that word so that God may "share with us divine benefits which entirely surpass the powers of the human mind to understand" (D.V., 6).

In other words, God's speaking, which includes God's acting, has to be interpreted for human life, but the act of interpretation itself remains God's work: interpretation by the human heart and mind is the work of the Holy Spirit. There is meaning in the word; the Holy Spirit enables the church to unearth it. It is thus grace that enables the church to grasp God's meaning. The Spirit who teaches all things (Jn 14:26) and who searches all things, even the depths of God (1 Cor 2:10), prompts us to lay hold of God's meaning.

Word In Contemporary Theology

In contemporary theology, dating from the work of Karl Barth, "word of God" has been used in three foundational senses: it is primarily the Incarnate Word; it is secondarily the articulation of that word in sacred scripture; and, it is thirdly the preaching or proclamation of the church. While these three forms of the word owe a great deal to Barth, they have been taken over by others including Karl Rahner.

The word of God in its primary sense refers to the Incarnate Word. Jesus of Nazareth, Logos incarnate, is the Word of God. The second Person in God is therefore God's Word. It is that word which becomes incarnate; not the Father who speaks the word nor the Holy Spirit who disperses the word and takes it to humanity forming the church. The second person of the Trinity precisely in his hypostatical, personal character as word is the one who becomes incarnate. Only the second person is word and revelatory in that sense. All that God means to say to us is said through him. He bears God's life and meaning for us. He is God's Word. "For he sent his Son, the eternal word who enlightens all men, to dwell among men and to tell them about the inner life of God.... He revealed that God was with us, to deliver us up to eternal life" (D.V., 4).

The word that happened in the incarnation determines all other words. When we say "Word of God," the primary reference is always to the second person of the Trinity.

A secondary meaning of "word of God" is the sacred scriptures themselves as bearing witness to that primary word. It is commonly accepted by Christians that the Bible is the locus of divine revelation and as such holds a unique position in the life and faith of the church (D.V., 21). Although the Bible itself takes for granted that scripture is the word of God and uses "God says" and "scripture says" interchangeably, scripture itself is not identical to God's word, i.e., it is not the word *per se* but the articulation of God's word in language. Nonetheless, the content of God's word has been brought to language in a normative way in the sacred scriptures, especially for Christians in the NT. It is done here in a normative way because the experience of those who wrote the NT is unique. What is experienced by the first followers of Jesus is his own preaching: "the time is fulfilled, and the kingdom of God is at hand; repent and believe in the gospel" (Mk 1:15). They share the conviction that God is now in Jesus offering salvation. Because it is normative, it is the point of reference for all other expressions of the "word of God."

Scripture has the character of human testimony and is marked with all the limitations of human utterance. This, however, is "without prejudice to God's truth and holiness" (D.V., 13). For the authority of scripture is the authority of God revealing; the writing is a continued incarnation. God's act here is a kenosis. "Hence, in sacred Scripture, without prejudice to God's truth and holiness, the

marvellous 'condescension' of eternal wisdom is plain to be seen 'that we may come to know the ineffable loving kindness of God and see for ourselves how far he has gone in adapting his language with thoughtful concern for our nature' (St. John Chrysostom). Indeed the words of God, expressed in the words of men, are in every way like human language, just as the Word of the eternal Father, when he took on himself the flesh of human weakness, became like men (D.V., 13). It is for this reason that scripture, according to the Catholic view, not only contains but *is* the word of God.

Scripture is the full and faithful reflection of God's action in history. But to understand it as word of God, we have to approach it not as a mere report, as information, but as an invitation into dialogue with God in God's saving activity. "Word," then goes beyond the text and occurs in the consciousness of believers who read it as God's free offer of salvation. Read in faith and in the church, scripture is the saving word of God (S.C., 7).

Since the mediation of God to us in sacred scripture takes the form of narrative that is passed on from one generation to the next, there can be distortions. For the Protestant, private reading with the illumination of the Holy Spirit can gain the true meaning. For the Catholic, however, the Holy Spirit's authority is in the community and proper meaning is conveyed and judged by the corporate church. This interpretive understanding and handing on of what is in the gospel is called tradition. Tradition does not add anything new but interprets in the act of handing on.

The act of proclaiming the word in community is the word of the Lord. The church takes the place of Christ now ascended to the right hand of the Father and continues in time and place what the first believers experienced in Jesus. The church is really the word of God whose whole being proclaims the presence of Christ. Preaching prolongs the sending from the Father; once again the second person of the Trinity is offered. It is a bestowal of the life which the second person has in the Trinity, and it gives us a participation in that life. The proclamation of the word, the proclamation of this living word, the living Christ, speaking in his body. Now the Father's word is uttered in and through the church. So God's word is now spoken in human words which the church can hear and speak. It is God's word still but God's word spoken and incarnate in the church.

The announcement of the word of God is the efficacious proclamation which brings about the reality of which it speaks, the grace announced. It is a way in which the reality being proclaimed discloses itself. The word being spoken and then embraced by those who hear explains the efficacy of the word. At the moment the word takes place there is the offer of salvation. The proclamation is directed to believing ears and hearing in faith is acceptance of the grace offered. While preaching has a content (the life, death, and resurrection of Christ), it also has the character of present address. And the grace of God or the forgiveness of God or the love of God are not merely spoken about but occur as an event. For what is ultimately spoken and accepted is God *as the one who confers* salvation. Thus preaching is not a mere occasion for encounter with the word (Barth) but is itself a saving word. It renders Christ present in his saving power.

The goal of the proclamation of the word of God is always the total self-bestowal of God and the total acceptance of God's offer on the part of believers. The goal, however, is an eschatological goal; human life and human history must always unfold where that goal is only partially realized. Human expressions of the word of God can never present the fullness of God; the presence of God in word is not always the same in each of its expressions. At the same time, human acceptance of the word will always be done in degrees. Short of the eschaton, the full reality of God's efficacious word can be made present only in sacrament, where the sacraments of the church hold forth both the fullness of the word and its ever-partial human realization. Word and sacrament are not only not mutually exclusive, they are in fact complementary. Augustine's adage still holds: *accedit verbum ad elementum et fit sacramentum* (the word is spoken upon the human reality and it becomes a sacrament) (*In Joann. Ev.* tr. 80,3).

It is certainly an over-simplification to distinguish Roman Catholic and Protestant piety on the basis of a division between sacrament and word. But clearly the emphasis in Roman Catholic theology has fallen more markedly on sacrament while primary emphasis in Protestant theology has been given to word. Since the time of Vatican II, however, both have come to recover and treasure the richness of what each had neglected, and to recover as well the necessary link that exists between sacrament and word. Word that is spoken unveils and clarifies the meaning of the human sacramental act; the act itself gives living voice to the word that is spoken.

See **Preaching...; Homily; Word, liturgy of the; Word and sacrament; Language, liturgical; Language and human experience; Evangelization; Catechumenate; Communication, ritual as; Hermeneutics and worship; Inclusive language**

Bernard Cooke, *Ministry to Word and Sacrament: History and Theology* (Phila: Fortress, 1976). Frederick Crowe, *Theology of the Christian Word* (New York: Paulist, 1978). Jerome Murphy-O'Connor, *Paul on Preaching* (New York: Sheed and Ward, 1964). Karl Rahner, "The Word and the Eucharist" in *Theological Investigations* IV (1966): 253-86. Otto Semmelworth, *The Preaching Word: On the Theology of Proclamation* (New York: Herder & Herder, 1965). *The Word: Readings in*

Theology, ed. by students at the Canisianum, Innsbruck (New York: P.J. Kenedy & Sons, 1964).

KATHLEEN CANNON, O.P.

WORSHIP

Worship is a universal phenomenon. It consists in a response of veneration in the face of the recognized presence of God.

God, as the object of worship is perceived as "Other"—transcendent, all-powerful, creator, benevolent Father. God is seen as "mysterious," i.e., partly-revealed to the worshipping subject and yet needing to be revealed further by some continuing or deepening encounter. The person who worships realizes that his/her response to God demands a total and whole-hearted commitment to faith in God and to a life in accord with God's "laws." The form that worship takes would, in the main, be words, music, bodily action, or silent contemplation. Its content would be expressed by means of adoration, reverence, sorrow for one's sinfulness, gratitude for past favors, petition for future gifts.

Worship may be private or even individualistic. However, and especially in a Christian context, it very often carries the overtone of an official and communally sanctioned activity: and in this sense, the Christian church's formal public worship of God in and through Christ is called 'liturgy" (S.C., 5). It not only responds to God's recognized presence but it also seeks to enter into a relationship of communion with him through Christ Rom 6:8-11).

Worship arises, generally, from remembering, *anamnesis*, that is, recounting of a specific intervention of God in human existence, or from an archetypal story of humankind in relation to God. The technical name for this basis of worship is *myth*, a profoundly true story which has validity independent of any particular historical circumstances.

For the Christian, the myth of salvation history, i.e., God's continuing presence in events prior to and within the life of Jesus, spills over and continues into our lives. It becomes for us both an exemplar to recognize his active presence now and a spur to respond ethically to that loving presence. Specific events in that history/myth provide occasions for our worship of God. The factual sequence of events that is the life, death, resurrection and glorification of Jesus the Christ lies at the heart of our worship of God. The "paschal mystery," which is the revelation and glorification of Jesus, is the culminating point of salvation history. *Par excellence* for Christians, worship of whatever nature is through, with and in Jesus Christ (see, doxology of eucharistic prayer).

Worship uses words or things that are seen as *symbols*, i.e., "presence-carriers," in that they either put us in touch with God through the meaning that is given to them, or they actually indicate for us the presence of God's love. For example, water used in baptism is symbolic and worthy of veneration because we believe that it puts us in touch with the dying and rising of Jesus Christ. We die to sin and we rise to a new and transformed life by association with him. Bread and wine used in eucharistic worship are carriers of the presence of Christ as the personal embodiment of God's love. Jesus Christ, the final and full expression of that love, is truly present for us in the symbols of bread and wine. Furthermore, Jesus' offering of his life to God the Father and to us was itself an act of worship. We become, through the symbol, participants in his act of worship.

An important dimension of worship is that it is repetitive or celebratory. It considers and reviews again and again God's love and goodness. Not only may a particular ritual be repeated but the worshippers may repeat the myth/story under various titles (e.g., baptism as *giving life* in Christ, eucharist as *nourishing life* in Christ, penance as *restoring life* in Christ, etc). Along with words, individual rites and bodily actions in worship will indicate the particular grounds on which we worship or celebrate God's love for us in Christ.

Another facet of worship as celebratory is that it remembers the past, while it considers the present, and looks toward the future. While we worship, we recall God's past favors, recognize his presence now, and reflect on how that presence and goodness speak to our current experience of life and to the way in which we will conduct our personal and communal lives in the future. By way of model and goal for their worship, Christians are encouraged to look to the scriptural picture painted for us of the worship offered at God's throne in heaven (Rev 4, 5, 7:9ff).

Celebratory worship tends to center around major events in human life: birth, membership in a community, nourishment, restoration of broken relationships, the recognition of our mortality, and so on. Most Christians would see their sacraments of baptism and eucharist as celebrations of coming to life in Christ and the nourishing or deepening of that life. These official actions of the church are, through Christ, actions of worship of the Father and of his love as it is found in the inception and growth of Christ's life in us. Catholic and Orthodox Christians go further to say that some key moments of an individual's life within the Christian community are also formal worship moments that call for official actions of the church. Thus all of the sacraments are part of our liturgical worship. We can recognize and encounter God's love in Christ in each of them, and we worship him as we perform them.

Christians envisage the life and worship of the church now as being under the guidance and direction of God's Spirit (Gal 5:25; Eph 2:18). When the church gathers to worship God the Father through Jesus Christ the Son, it does so "in the Spirit" (Rom 8:26-27). It calls upon (*epiclesis*), the Holy Spirit of God to unify and empower it to worship God in a worthy manner, i.e., in union with the worship of Jesus Christ (L.G., 7; S.C., 6).

Christian worship has a twofold thrust or direction: at once it is oriented towards communion with God, and it works to sanctify the individual worshipper as well as the whole community that worships. It should have the effect, then, of developing union with others, *koinonia,* for the glory of God from whom it begins and towards whom it moves (S.C., 8, 48).

Worship, by its very nature, imposes an ethic upon us: if we are to be at all sincere, we must live in accordance with the demand that our lives be motivated by love as God's life is (2 Cor 5:14). Christian worship has practical repercussions far beyond any place or time in which we engage in it. It constrains us also to work for the spread of God's kingdom in such ways as will be just and fair to all, bringing harmony and integrity not only in relation to ourselves and to others but also to our environment and to all creation.

See **Liturgy and Christian life; Adoration, theology of**

J.D. Crichton, "A Theology of Worship" in Jones, Wainwright and Yarnold, *The Study of Liturgy* (London: S.P.C.K., 1978). L. Bouyer, *Rite and Man* (Burns & Oates, 1963). C. Vagaggini, *Theological Dimensions of the Liturgy* (Collegeville, 1959).

PATRICK BISHOP, S.J.

YOUNG ADULTS, LITURGY FOR

The following article is not based on theory, but rather on years of experience with young adults, principally of high school age. It offers ten principles or words of pastoral advice for any who would do ministry in general, and liturgical ministry in particular, for this specific age group.

(1) *Presume Disinterest*, if not outright hostility. That way, you will be reaching the receptivities of everyone in your youth congregation —from those who would rather feed their parents to piranhas than be at your Mass, to those who yearn for martyrdom. The former will outnumber the latter by a million to one. Remember that you are offering worship to young people who have been baptized without having gone through any real inner conversion. You are offering Mass for people whose career choices (in all but a few cases) will be in no way affected by their being Christians; their motives are no different from those of a well-intentioned atheist or pagan. They are by no means bad kids; they are just not yet genuinely, internally Christian.

To test out that last, seemingly cynical remark, ask a group of young people to respond to the following: if someone reliable were to offer you a full college scholarship and a $75,000 job for which you had only to go on TV with the other recipients and deny your belief in Jesus Christ, what would you do? The results are sobering, but if we deal with our young where we would like to think they are, rather than where they really are, we are fools shouting gibberish into the maelstrom.

Psychologist Jerome Bruner said you can teach anything, to anyone, anyplace in his or her development, in a meaningful way, *provided* you can adapt the message to *their* receptivities.

(2) *Adol-escence*. The word is inchoative; it means a process has begun but is still continuing, as in "convalescence." They are physically capable of producing children, and yet they are not yet adult enough to be parents. Contrary to the facts, parents think adulthood (and the time to treat their young as more than children) clicks on like a thermostat at midnight of the twenty-first birthday, while the youngsters think adulthood clicked on the moment puberty occurred. Neither "side" realizes the difference between being "grown-up" and being "adult." The one happens without either the cooperation or permission of the victim; the other happens only through a long, active process of learning, suffering, and deciding. Of all the natures in the universe we know of, only human adulthood is an invitation and not an ineluctable command. Unlike any other species, we are free *not* to be human —to vegetate, to act like beasts. This is the invitation we have to offer our young: to become truly human, *before* they can even comprehend our invitation to Christianity. Grace builds on nature, not the other way around.

The personally validated adult self is one's character. And the Greek word for "character" is *ethos*: ethic. Until one painfully evolves a personal ethic, there is no character, only an entity with a certain personality. The individual's soul is merely a hodge-podge of "do's" and "don't's" taped on his or her superego from hundreds of contradictory sources: parents, media, teachers, peers, music. Sorting out all those voices and determining which are true and which are corrosive takes a great deal of effort — which is something teenagers by nature are loath to do, fed up as they are with a soul-less, efficient, left-brain education which seems to them to have no relevance whatever to the dog-eat-dog world they're preparing themselves for. What's more, they get little help from us. Those who go to public schools get no training in ethics —in character —but rather some vague sense of "values," lest the school be accused of teaching religion. Even those who go to Catholic schools get little training in psychology —which is an adolescent's principal problem —but instead a list of rules which, to them, seem sheerly arbitrary, from a church which seems, again to them, interested almost exclusively in keeping people from enjoying sex. "Be honest, be chaste, be committed; it's good for you" is about as real a motivation as "the spinach is good for you." Sez who?

We are all human, and so we are all alike. But each of us is a self, and so no two of us are alike. First, we have to show the teenage audience at our liturgies that being ethical (that is, acting humanly) is in fact good for them—in ways *they* acknowledge are in fact good. The human species has all the qualities of the lower species, and yet only we can know and love and grow in our ability to know and love. Just as Labrador retrievers wag their tails, even when they're exhausted from chasing sticks, so we are fulfilled when we know and love and grow. Easy enough to prove: do you really feel peachy-terrific when you yield to the blahs, to senioritis, to feeling sorry for yourself? Why not? Because it's unnatural. You weren't born to be a vegetable or a beaten cur.

A step further: we share being human, and the more we lower our self-defensive barriers, the more humanly enriched we become. We all fear the same things, yearn for the same things, suffer the same inertia, the same temptation to yield principle in return for acceptance. "Ice-breakers," methods for breaking down barriers are legion; we should use them more, even in place of a homily. *Feeling* that human sense of belonging beneath the surface defensive cocoons is far more important than hearing about it.

Still further, we must then help each youngster to focus in a bit closer on who he or she is as a *unique* individual. One hopes that the process of self-discovery goes on for a lifetime, but many go to their graves never having had anything but the slightest notion of who they were, no sense of a coherent storyline, only a

list of unrelated problems endured. Again, there are many instruments available to help teenagers discover at least what type of persons they are *not* (the Enneagram, the Myers-Briggs Type Indicator)—and therefore the goals they can set aside as unrealistic. They can then direct their energies to making a difference with the unique combination of talents each one is.

Until each youngster can get at least a temporary, tenuous grasp on who-I-am, how can we ever expect them to make anything out of who they are? Far more important, how can we tell them, "unless you lose yourself, you will never find yourself"? How can they lose what they've never really grasped? How can they forget a self which is so incessantly confusing? Grace builds on nature.

(3) *Don't Be Taken in By the Surface "Cool."* Whether the mask is macho, or Gidget-sweet, or bland to the point of anonymity, until the teenager has some realistic sense of self, there's a lot of tension and turmoil going on behind the mask. Each of them is, on the one hand, cocksure they will live as well as their parents within ten years of college graduation (egotism), and yet at the same time deadly sure that everybody's out to get them (paranoia), both of which contraries add up to the classical definition of narcissism. It is impossible to sell either genuine love or genuine faith to an egotist or a paranoid or a narcissist. Cool and defensive masks are the precise opposite of the vulnerability requisite for both.

Many religious educators believe youngsters' main concern is with sex. More likely, sexual expression is merely an ersatz way to find a self-value mirrored back from seeming total acceptance by someone else. They struggle against the genuinely felt pull of principle and commitment from the one side, and the pull of adaptability, acceptance by others, and "keeping an open mind" from the other side. Again, as with sex, without a personally accepted sense of self, "belonging" looks like a good substitute until a sense of self "happens along."

There are many corollary obstacles springing up within the teenager from that inadequate sense of self and the fear of risk which that lack of self-trust engenders.

They at least seem impervious to symbols. Years ago, faith fed on and was fed by an unlimited menagerie of symbols: medals, rosaries, summer schools of Catholic action, benedictions, knights of the Blessed Sacrament, May crownings. No kid today would be caught dead with a scapular! For the moment, even varsity letter sweaters seem to be "out." I have asked young men if they were ever brought to tears by a film; one or two say "Elephant Man" or the end of "Ordinary People." But the rest had either never had that bittersweet fellow-feeling or, if they had, were too embarrassed to admit it. Pose yourself a problem then, perhaps for a homily-substitute: what symbols still genuinely have meaning *to them*? Which ones are adaptable to liturgy?

They seem impervious to tradition. Nothing truly meaningful happened before they came on the scene. Show them "Fiddler on the Roof," and ask them if they have any sense whatever what was going on inside Tevye when his daughter married a Gentile and he refused ever to speak to her again. Show them the film of John Kennedy's funeral and ask what the traditions and symbols were trying to "say," how they were trying to purge grief. Pose a problem to them and to yourself, then: what traditions are still meaningful? Which ones can we use?

In the same vein, they seem impervious to honest hero-worship, which is another act of vulnerability and awe in an age where such things seem very uncool and naive. Several boys have said to me that their true heroes were *both* Mother Teresa *and* Donald Trump —and they really

meant it! They want, at one and the same time, to be unassailably rich and unassailably virtuous. A difficult goal. Pose the problem to them and to yourself: if a hero *were* possible in a world where *The National Enquirer* delights in debunking heroes, what would he or she be like? Are there people like that still around — perhaps unsung? Are there people like that in history or literature? Do we want to be heroes, somebodies, or to be nobodies, who tread water for a lifetime —and then die? They *do* want to be somebodies. They're just afraid of the risk.

They also seem —although they definitely are not —impervious to altruism. They will admit that TV and music have had far more of an influence on their values than religion, their teachers, or even their own parents. There, too, their parents are often indifferent to religion, far more interested in their children's material success than in their fulfillment as human beings. There is no way we can uproot those influences which are dyed into our youngsters' psyches. But we can counter-challenge it. Rather than merely telling them about the world's poor, give them something they can *do* about it: a nursing home, retarded children, soup-kitchens, tutoring —liberate them into responsibility instead of shackling them to sterile and corrosive guilt-trips.

(4) *Don't Underestimate Their Capacity for Challenge.* Since Vatican II, we have overcompensated for the triumphalism and the severe Great Accountant God. Our hymns are now pastel paeans to the Good Shepherd who strokes and cherishes and never challenges. Banish them from your choir lofts like the Arian heresies they are! There are at least two or three dozen kids in any parish who have bands (of varying quality.) Set them the problem of writing songs that will appeal to the young —spirited and enspiriting but reverent, voicing their problems: loneliness, fear, yearning to be

somebody who makes a difference. Precisely the subjects (other than sex) that the rock bands hymn from a pagan point of view. They know where the kids are coming from, and the kids can't get enough of them. We've surely borrowed songs from pagans before and baptized them!

Whatever you do, don't let them think being Christian is easy. It isn't. Don't soft-pedal the gospel where Jesus noted it should be played with all the stops full-out. If there is a single way in which religion classes and homilies have subverted the appeal of Jesus, it is in making him a pushover.

(5) *Clarify the Goal.* Surely, the goal is not merely to get teenagers to endure Mass. We are trying to bring them to a personal and communal relationship with God. All the religion courses and homilies and liturgies in the world will remain as cold as calculus unless one has a personal commitment to the Person religion is all about. Whipping a boy or girl to church —either with the threat of hell or the threat of being grounded—is like forcing a boy to go to a prom with a homely neighbor. He'll go, all right. But there won't be much communication and very little likelihood of a personal relationship. And he's not likely to ask her out again.

Unless we teach young people to pray —in schools and in retreats —all our other efforts are in vain. And not merely "saying prayers." No, teaching how to short-circuit the calculating intelligence and be at peace, centered, vulnerable — opening up and letting God enter the soul. If we could *only* effect that, all the rest would take care of itself. Till then, all we're doing is stumbling over our good intentions, turning our best efforts into obstacles instead of inducements.

(6) *Be Vulnerable to Them.* In 57 years, I can't remember a priest from a pulpit or a lectern every saying, "When I pray . . . ." Only on rare occasions have I heard a priest tell of times when he felt touched by God or furious at God. When I ask young men to ask their parents how they see God, 90 percent of them prefer to guess: "It'd be too much of a hassle; stuff like that's too personal." Are we trying to foist on them a God we seem to have no time for ourselves? As one student said, "I treat God the way I treat my parents' other friends."

Priests and parents talk of honesty, chastity, "getting to" Mass, thrift. All pretty much head-trip stuff. When do they open their souls? When do they make the pain they have suffered wrestling with God bear fruit in lives other than their own? If teenagers are allowed the erroneous idea that their parents and pastors have certitude or that doubt is some kind of sin, we have lost them, because certitude is impossible to fallible human beings and because doubt is the prerequisite of learning.

(7) *The Motivation Is Not Fear.* Fear of punishment will secure conformity, not faith. Like every teacher, parents and priests ought to be trying to render themselves unnecessary, sure that their young will do freely and knowingly what for a long while they did merely to please or avoid punishment. As becoming-adults, they ought not to be motivated by what would motivate children. When their parents are in nursing homes, they ought not to visit them sheerly because the fourth commandment insists on it. Nor should they visit their Father on Sunday merely because the third commandment enjoins it. For an adult, "salvation" has to mean something more than merely a guarantee against hell.

Until the young have *owned* the fact of their own inevitable and unpredictable deaths, they will never value the gift of Christianity. Until they realize that, without the reality of an afterlife, we are Beckett's futile clowns, hungering for an answer which will never show up, the core of Christianity is meaningless to them. All their efforts —all their medals and raises and triumphs —are ultimately Monopoly money. As one student put it, "If there is no God, life is an Easter-egg hunt. And there are no Easter eggs." But Jesus is our invitation into forever! Surely, that's something to celebrate.

Gratitude is another motive the young begin to value. If a zillionaire stopped you on the street and said, "You look like a nice kid. Here's a million bucks. No strings. But maybe, if you don't mind, drop around occasionally and we could talk." If you made no attempt to find out who the man was, if you never took time to say thanks, if you only rarely and grudgingly dropped around to see him, you'd be a pretty mean-spirited S.O.B.. But God opened the door to . . . everything.

(8) *Small Groups, Not Large.* Especially in schools, we get the idea that full-school liturgies are great for giving ourselves a false sense of community. All one has to do is look around and see the hundreds of unmoving lips during the Christmas hymns all the students know and even during the Our Father. The same is true of large parish youth Masses: they're all there; they're all young; but there is no more sense of community than in an airport waiting room. It's merely a congregation of strangers gathered together for their own self-interests. We hunker in our cocoons, certain that everybody in the place is staring at *me*, when, of course, each of them thinks everybody's staring at him or her.

(9) *Community Makes the Liturgy, Not Vice-Versa.* All the kids know that. It's a commonplace: "I like the Masses at school but not the ones in my parish." Not that school Masses are better done, nor that the priests are nicer, but that the students know at least some of the people in the school congregation with them; there's at least an inchoate sense of community.

The more pastors and parents can get youngsters to know one another —not merely by playing basketball or dancing but by serving together —the better their (small) youth Masses will be. Again, not yet having a sense of self, a teenager simply can't have a truly meaningful liturgy surrounded by a gaggle of intimidating strangers. And which adult has not told youngsters again and again to beware of strangers?

(10) *Finally, Remember It's a Celebration!* An alien who attended a great many of our Sunday liturgies would hardly report back to home base that he/she had witnessed a celebration. Study what youngsters would honestly call "celebrations": Christmas dinner, birthday parties, parties in general, rock concerts. Granted, many of them might seem a slight too . . . rowdy for worship. And yet didn't Paul face precisely the same problem with his Corinthian enthusiasts? But Paul did not shut down his rowdy charismatics; he subjected them to discernment to see if they were the result of the Holy Spirit or the self-deceptive Evil Spirit. Was this a genuine experience of God, or was it mere self-excitation? Did their enthusiasm bear fruit in the form of people more open-hearted, open-minded, open-handed? Or did it result in gnostic snobbery, exclusivity, and self-righteousness? The rock Masses which our parish bands bring forth will have to face the same impartial discernment.

If it is true that our young are baptized but not yet truly converted, then we must find them where they are and deal with them where they are: good-hearted pagans. We have to use means and motives that are meaningful to them, not those which were meaningful to us when we were young or are meaningful to us now as adults. They are not adults, and they became who they are in a world light-years distant from the 1960s, the 1950s and 1940s.

There is a beautiful Jewish parable, much like the one about the prodigal son. The father shouts to his boy, "At least meet me halfway!" And the boy shouts, "I *can't* meet you halfway." And the father replies, "Then come as far as you can. And I'll come the rest of the way."

William J. O'Malley, "Mass and Teenagers," *America*, October 8, 1988. William J. O'Malley, "P.T. Barnum and the Catechetical Quest," *America*, October 10, 1987. William J. O'Malley, "Selling Faith to Skeptics," *America*, September 3-10, 1988. William J. O'Malley, "Teenagers and . . . You-Know-What," *America*, April 15, 1989. William J. O'Malley, "Teenage Spirituality," *America*, April 29, 1989.

WILLIAM J. O'MALLEY, S.J.

Topical Index

(d) Order and orders

(e) Marriage

(f) Reconciliation

4. The Church at Prayer

(a) General liturgical acts

(b) Forms of prayer

(c) Proclaiming the word

Contributors

Gerard Austin, O.P., The Catholic University of America, Washington, D.C.

Jeffrey P. Baerwald, S.J., LeMoyne College, Syracuse, New York

John F. Baldovin, S.J., Jesuit School of Theology, Berkeley, California

William A. Barry, S.J., Boston College, Chestnut Hill, Massachusetts

Teresa Berger, The Divinity School, Duke University, Durham, North Carolina

Perry H. Biddle, Jr., Presbyterian Minister and Author, Old Hickory, Tennessee

Patrick Bishop, S.J., St. Thomas More College (University of Western Australia), Crawley, Western Australia

Robert H. Blondell, St. Ephrem Parish, Archdiocese of Detroit, Michigan

Stephen J. Bonian, S.J., Pontifical Mission for Palestine, Amman, Jordan

Paul F. Bradshaw, University of Notre Dame, Indiana

John K. Brooks-Leonard, University of Notre Dame, Indiana

Walter J. Burghardt, S.J., Editor-in-chief, *Theological Studies,* Baltimore, Maryland

Eileen C. Burke-Sullivan, All Saints' Parish, Dallas, Texas

Richard J. Butler, Sacred Heart Parish, Lexington, Massachusetts

Gerald J. Calhoun, S.J., Jesuit Novitiate, Jamaica Plain, Massachusetts

Stanislaus Campbell, F.S.C., St. Mary's College High School, Berkeley, California

Kathleen Cannon, O.P., Catholic Theological Union, Chicago, Illinois

Joseph M. Champlin, St. Joseph's Church, Camillus, New York

Andrew D. Ciferni, O.Praem., The Catholic University of America, Washington, D.C.

Richard J. Clifford, S.J., Weston School of Theology, Cambridge, Massachusetts

Mary Collins, O.S.B., The Catholic University of America, Washington, D.C.

Bernard Cooke, College of the Holy Cross, Worcester, Massachusetts

Paul F.X. Covino, Georgetown Center for Liturgy, Spirituality and the Arts, Washington, D.C.

Joseph L. Cunningham, St. Vincent de Paul Regional Seminary, Boynton Beach, Florida

Emmanuel Cutrone, Spring Hill College, Mobile, Alabama

Brian E. Daley, S.J., Weston School of Theology, Cambridge, Massachusetts

James Dallen, Gonzaga University, Spokane, Washington

Robert J. Daly, S.J., Boston College, Chestnut Hill, Massachusetts

Carl Dehne, S.J., Loyola University, Chicago, Illinois

Frank P. DeSiano, C.S.P., Director, Parish Based Evangelization, Washington, D.C.

Carla DeSola, Director, Omega Liturgical Dance Company, New York, New York

Alan F. Detscher, Associate Director, Secretariat for the Liturgy (N.C.C.B.), Washington, D.C.

Everett A. Diederich, S.J., Diocese of Fort Wayne-South Bend, Indiana

Doris Donnelly, John Carroll University, University Heights, Ohio

Dorothy (Dody) H. Donnelly, S.F. Theol. Sem., Graduate Theological Union, Berkeley, California

Leonard Doohan, Gonzaga University, Spokane, Washington

Catherine Dooley, O.P., The Catholic University of America, Washington, D.C.

Michael Downey, Loyola Marymount University, Los Angeles, California

Michael S. Driscoll, Carroll College, Helena, Montana

Arlo D. Duba, University of Dubuque Theological Seminary, Dubuque, Iowa

Ruth C. Duck, Garrett-Evangelical Theological Seminary, Evanston, Illinois

James B. Dunning, North American Forum on the Catechumenate, Arlington, Virginia

James L. Empereur, S.J., Jesuit School of Theology, Berkeley, California

Seán Fagan, S.M., Secretary General of the Society of Mary, Rome, Italy

Michael A. Fahey, S.J., University of St. Michael's College, Toronto, Ontario

Barbara Finan, Ohio Dominican College, Columbus, Ohio

Peter E. Fink, S.J., Weston School of Theology, Cambridge, Massachusetts

Virginia Sullivan Finn, Weston School of Theology, Cambridge, Massachusetts

Austin Flannery, O.P., President, Dominican Publications, Dublin, Ireland

David L. Fleming, S.J., *Review for Religious*, St. Louis, Missouri

Edward Foley, O.F.M., Cap., Catholic Theological Union, Chicago, Illinois

Richard N. Fragomeni, The Catholic University of America, Washington, D.C.

Mark R. Francis, C.S.V., Catholic Theological Union, Chicago, Illinois

Virgil C. Funk, National Association of Pastoral Musicians, Washington, D.C.

John Gallen, S.J., Corpus Christi Center, Phoenix, Arizona

John Geaney, C.S.P., Director, Intercommunity Telecommunications Project, Silver Spring, Maryland

Donald L. Gelpi, S.J., Jesuit School of Theology, Berkeley, California

Jennifer Glen, C.C.V.I., University of St. Thomas School of Theology, Houston, Texas

Gregor T. Goethals, Rhode Island School of Design, Providence, Rhode Island

Daniel P. Grigassy, O.F.M., Christ the King Seminary, East Aurora, New York

Robert R. Grimes, S.J., University of Pittsburgh, Pennsylvania

Charles W. Gusmer, Immaculate Conception Seminary, Seton Hall University, South Orange, New Jersey

Kenneth Hannon, O.M.I., Oblate School of Theology, San Antonio, Texas

Stephen Happel, The Catholic University of America, Washington, D.C.

Daniel J. Harrington, S.J., Weston School of Theology, Cambridge, Massachusetts

John S. Hascall O.F.M., Cap., St. Charles Mission, Pryor, Montana

Richard J. Hauser, S.J., Creighton University, Omaha, Nebraska

A. Brandt Henderson, The Church of Our Lady of Sorrows, Sharon, Massachusetts

J. Frank Henderson, University of Alberta, Edmonton, Alberta

Mary Catherine Hilkert, O.P., Aquinas Institute of Theology, St. Louis, Missouri

Lawrence A. Hoffman, The Hebrew Union College—Jewish Institute of Religion, New York

John F. Hotchkin, Executive Director, Secretariat for Ecumenical and Inter-religious Affairs (N.C.C.B.), Washington, D.C.

John M. Huels, O.S.M., Catholic Theological Union, Chicago, Illinois

Kathleen Hughes, R.S.C.J., Catholic Theological Union, Chicago, Illinois

Kevin W. Irwin, The Catholic University of America, Washington, D.C.

Pamela Jackson, Boston College, Chestnut Hill, Massachusetts

Peter Jeffery, University of Delaware, Wilmington, Delaware

Thomas A. Kane, C.S.P., Weston School of Theology, Cambridge, Massachusetts

Aidan Kavanagh, O.S.B., The Divinity School, Yale University, New Haven, Connecticut

Margaret Mary Kelleher, O.S.U., The Catholic University of America, Washington, D.C.

Martha Ann Kirk, C.C.V.I., Incarnate Word College, San Antonio, Texas

Theresa Koernke, University of Notre Dame, Indiana

Joseph J. Koury, S.J., Weston School of Theology and Boston College: Institute of Pastoral Ministry, Massachusetts

Thomas A. Krosnicki, S.V.D., Washington Theological Union, Silver Spring, Maryland

Michael Kwatera, O.S.B., St. John's Abbey, Collegeville, Minnesota

Catherine Mowry LaCugna, University of Notre Dame, Indiana

Lizette Larson-Miller, Jesuit School of Theology, Berkeley, California

John D. Laurance, S.J., Creighton University, Omaha, Nebraska

Michael G. Lawler, Creighton University, Omaha, Nebraska

Ronald J. Lewinski, Director, Office for Divine Worship, Archdiocese of Chicago, Illinois

Mary E. Lyons, Franciscan School of Theology, Graduate Theological Union, Berkeley, California

Lawrence J. Madden, S.J., Georgetown University, Washington, D.C.

S. Shawn Madigan, C.S.J., College of St. Catherine, St. Paul, Minnesota

Willy Malarcher, (Deacon), Liturgical Design Consultant, Englewood, New Jersey

M. Francis Mannion, The Cathedral of the Madeleine, Salt Lake City, Utah

Stanley B. Marrow, S.J., Weston School of Theology, Cambridge, Massachusetts

Thomas Marsh, St. Patrick's College, Maynooth, Ireland

German M. Martinez, Fordham University, Bronx, New York

Joseph Martos, Allentown College of St. Francis de Sales, Center Valley, Pennsylvania

Marchita B. Mauck, Louisiana State University, Baton Rouge, Louisiana

Brian O. McDermott, S.J., Weston School of Theology, Cambridge, Massachusetts

Enda McDonagh, St. Patrick's College, Maynooth, Ireland

Patrick McGoldrick, St. Patrick's College, Maynooth, Ireland

Edward J. McKenna, Editor, *The Collegeville Hymnal*, Collegeville, Minnesota

John H. McKenna, C.M., St. John's University, Jamaica, New York

Frederick R. McManus, The Catholic University of America, Washington, D.C.

Dennis McNally, S.J., St. Joseph's University, Philadelphia, Pennsylvania

John Allyn Melloh, S.M., University of Notre Dame, Indiana

Andrew L. Nelson, Saint Francis Seminary, Milwaukee, Wisconsin

David R. Newman, Emmanuel College, Toronto, Ontario

John J. O'Brien, C.P., Catholic Theological Union, Chicago, Illinois

Hughes Oliphant Old, Center for Theological Inquiry, Princeton, New Jersey

William J. O'Malley, S.J., Fordham Preparatory School, Bronx, New York

Ladislas Örsy, S.J., The Catholic University of America, Washington, D.C.

Gilbert Ostdiek, O.F.M., Catholic Theological Union, Chicago, Illinois

T. Jerome Overbeck, S.J., Loyola University, Chicago, Illinois

John R. Page, International Commission on English in the Liturgy, Washington, D.C.

Sharon Daloz Parks, Weston School of Theology, Cambridge, Massachusetts

Lloyd G. Patterson, Episcopal Divinity School, Cambridge, Massachusetts

Kathryn Ann Piccard, priest of the Episcopal Diocese of Massachusetts, Dorchester, Massachusetts

Mary Alice Piil, C.S.J., Seminary of the Immaculate Conception, Huntington, New York

David N. Power, O.M.I., The Catholic University of America, Washington, D.C.

Joseph M. Powers, S.J., Jesuit School of Theology, Berkeley, California

Madeleine B. Provost, Bureau for Exceptional Children and Adults, Diocese of Springfield, Massachusetts

Frank Currier Quinn, O.P., Aquinas Institute of Theology, St. Louis, Missouri

Elaine J. Rendler, Georgetown University, Washington D.C.

Lucien Richard, O.M.I., Weston School of Theology, Cambridge, Massachusetts

Thomas Richstatter, O.F.M., St. Meinrad School of Theology, Indiana

Theodore Runyon, Candler School of Theology, (Emory University), Atlanta, Georgia

John Barry Ryan, Manhattan College, Riverdale, New York

John R. Sachs, S.J., Weston School of Theology, Cambridge, Massachusetts

Don E. Saliers, Candler School of Theology, (Emory University), Atlanta, Georgia

Mary M. Schaefer, Atlantic School of Theology, Halifax, Nova Scotia

James M. Schellman, International Commission on English in the Liturgy, Washington, D.C.

J. Peter Schineller, S.J., Nigeria-Ghana Mission, Surulere, Logos State, Nigeria

James A. Schmeiser, King's College, University of Western Ontario, London, Ontario, Canada

Frank C. Senn, Lutheran Church of the Holy Spirit, Lincolnshire, Illinois

Michael F. Skelley, S.J., Marquette University, Milwaukee, Wisconsin

Walter J. Smith, S.J., Weston School of Theology, Cambridge, Massachusetts

Grant Sperry-White, Doctoral Candidate, University of Notre Dame, Indiana

John M. Staudenmaier, S.J., The University of Detroit, Michigan

Daniel Stevick, Episcopal Divinity School, Cambridge, Massachusetts

Thomas J. Talley, The General Theological Seminary, New York, New York

George H. Tavard, Methodist Theological School, Ohio

Paul Turner, St. John Francis Regis Church, Kansas City, Missouri

Miriam D. Ukeritis, C.S.J., Boston University, Boston, Massachusetts

Julia Upton, R.S.M., St. John's University, Jamaica, New York

Edward Collins Vacek, S.J., Weston School of Theology, Cambridge, Massachusetts

Robert Ver Eecke, S.J., Boston College, Chestnut Hill, Massachusetts

Geoffrey Wainwright, Duke University, Durham, North Carolina

James A. Wallace, C.SS.R., Washington Theological Union, Silver Spring, Maryland

Janet R. Walton, Union Theological Seminary, New York, New York

Robert P. Waznak, S.S., Washington Theological Union, Silver Spring, Maryland

Louis Weil, Church Divinity School of the Pacific, Berkeley, California

James F. White, University of Notre Dame, Indiana

Susan J. White, Westcott House, Cambridge, England

James A. Wilde, Editor, Liturgy Training Publications, Archdiocese of Chicago, Illinois

Michael G. Witczak, St. Francis Seminary, Milwaukee, Wisconsin

Christopher Witt, C.S.P., North American Conference of Separated and Divorced Catholics

Walter J. Woods, St. John's Seminary, Brighton, Massachusetts

George S. Worgul, Jr., Duquesne University, Pittsburgh, Pennsylvania

Edward J. Yarnold, S.J., Campion Hall, Oxford, United Kingdom

Jean C. Zeidler, Pastor in the Evangelical Lutheran Church in America, Luthersburg, Pennsylvania

Joyce Ann Zimmerman, C.PP.S., St. Paul University, Ottawa, Ontario

The Editor

Peter E. Fink, S.J. teaches sacramental theology at Weston School of Theology in Cambridge, Massachusetts. He is a graduate of Fordham University in physics; Rensselaer Polytechnic Institute in natural science; he studied theology at Woodstock College; and he holds a doctorate in systematic theology from Emory University. He has concentrated his research in sacramental and liturgical studies, and is widely respected for his learning, clarity and innovative thinking in his chosen fields.